S0-BLM-708

Moving & Relocation

Sourcebook and Directory

2001

Third Edition

Edited by

Nancy V. Kniskern and Dawn Bokenkamp Toth

A Reference Guide for Moving and Relocation, With Profiles for 121 U.S. Cities, Featuring Mailing Addresses, Local and Toll-Free Telephone Numbers, Fax Numbers, Web Site Addresses, and E-Mail Addresses for:

- Chambers of Commerce, Government Offices, Libraries, and Other Local Information Resources (including Online Resources)
- Suburban and Other Area Communities
- Major Employers
- Educational Institutions and Hospitals
- Transportation Services
- Utility and Local Telecommunications Companies
- Banks and Shopping Malls
- Newspapers, Magazines, and Radio & TV Stations
- Attractions, Sports Teams, and Facilities
- Annual Events

and also Including Statistical, Demographic, and Other Data on Location, Climate and Weather, History, Economy, Education, Population, and Quality and Cost of Living

615 Griswold Street • Detroit, MI 48226

Editorial Staff
Darren L. Smith, *Managing Editor*
Jennifer C. Perkins, *Senior Editor*

Nancy V. Kniskern and Dawn Bokenkamp Toth, *Editors*

Contributing Editors and Staff
Pam Gaulin and Penny Hoffman, *Senior Associate Editors*
Patricia H. Cook, *Associate Editor*
Joy Freeman, Sharlene C. Glassman, Jacqueline M. Lewis,
Melissa Salus, and Bethany N. Turcotte, *Assistant Editors*
Sue Lynch, *Senior Editorial Assistant*
Lori Alvarez and Judy Black, *Editorial Assistants*
Alicia Elkiss, *Administrative Associate*

Jocelyn R. Perreault, *Verification Manager*
Debbie Cerny, Bettie M. Farnham, Kimberly Hagee, Elizabeth K. Kelly,
Pamela A. Layton, Lionel Lokos, Dorothy M. Murphy, Cheryl Small,
and J. Amanda Wilson, *Verification Assistants*

Production
Jamezy Cesar, *Database Administrator*
Nigel A. Simms, *Network Administrator*

Kevin Hayes, *Production Coordinator*

* * * * *

Peter E. Ruffner, *Senior Vice President*
Matthew P. Barbour, *Vice President—Operations*
Kay Gill, *Vice President—Directories*
Laurie Lanzen Harris, *Vice President—Editorial*
Mark A. Lizardi, *Vice President – Information Systems*
Thomas J. Murphy—*Vice President—Finance*
Jane J. Steele — *Marketing Coordinator*

Frederick G. Ruffner, Jr., *Publisher*

ISBN 0-7808-0431-7

Printed in the United States of America

OMNIGRAPHICS, INC.
615 Griswold Street · Detroit, MI 48226
Toll Free Phone: 800-234-1340 · Toll-Free Fax: 800-875-1340
www.omnigraphics.com · E-mail: mr-editorial@omnigraphics.com

Contents

Cities in State Sequence

Cities in State Sequence (Cont'd)

Introduction

Moving & Relocation Sourcebook and Directory provides important contact information, demographics, and other details for 121 U.S. cities, including major population centers as well as smaller cities that are popular relocation destinations. While this work is designed specifically to assist people planning to relocate and to help familiarize them with their destination cities and the surrounding areas, it is also a useful tool for librarians, students, and other researchers seeking local information.

Information contained in *Moving & Relocation Sourcebook and Directory* is obtained through original research, including direct contact with chambers of commerce, government offices, and independent real estate firms. All of the contact information obtained from these organizations, or from printed or other resources, is independently verified to assure the highest level of accuracy.

21 New Cities in This Edition

This third edition of *Moving & Relocation Sourcebook and Directory* adds profiles for 21 new cities:

- Amarillo, TX
- Anchorage, AK
- Brownsville, TX
- Eugene, OR
- Fort Collins, CO
- Honolulu, HI
- Lafayette, LA
- Las Cruces, NM
- Lexington, KY
- Lincoln, NE
- Modesto, CA
- Montgomery, AL
- Naples, FL
- Olympia, WA
- Provo, UT
- Reno, NV
- Salem, OR
- Savannah, GA
- Springfield, IL
- Springfield, MO
- Tallahassee, FL

New also in this edition are listings for local Internet Service Providers (ISPs), which are included under the Telecommunications heading in each profile. The ISPs listed for each city are based either in that city or one of its surrounding communities.

Content and Arrangement of Listings

Individual listings for each of the 121 cities in *Moving & Relocation Sourcebook and Directory* provide important contact data for local resources as well as descriptive information and useful demographic and statistical figures. For listings that provide contact information, complete addresses and telephone numbers are given, and most include fax numbers as well. Toll-free telephone numbers, World Wide Web addresses, and e-mail addresses also are included as available. ***(The number of web sites provided has increased significantly in this edition, both in the Online Resources section of each profile and as part of the contact information given for individual listings.)***

The overall arrangement of *Moving & Relocation Sourcebook and Directory* is alphabetical by city name, with the name of the county in which a city is located given as part of the general heading for that city. Information provided for each of the 121 cities listed is then grouped according to the following categories:

1. **LOCATION.** A brief description of the city's location is given first, followed by a list of "city facts" denoting its land and water area, elevation, latitude and longitude, time zone, and area code(s).

2. **CLIMATE.** A general description of the city's climate is followed by a table of average monthly high and low temperatures and average monthly precipitation.

3. **HISTORY.** This section provides details about the city's history, from its early days to the present.

4. **POPULATION.** The figures given here include growth indicators as well as breakdowns by race/ethnic group, age, and gender. Population figures are based on the most current estimate available, which, in most cases, was the 1990 census.

5. **GOVERNMENT.** The city's government type is noted here, followed by detailed contact information for principal city government departments.

6. **IMPORTANT PHONE NUMBERS.** Included here are local or toll-free telephone numbers for AAA, American Express Travel, Emergency, HotelDocs, Poison Control, Time/Temp, Weather, local realtors' association, as well as numbers for driver's license and vehicle registration, voter registration, and state and local tax information. Medical and/or Dental Referral, Road Conditions, and Events hotlines are also listed, as available.

7. **INFORMATION SOURCES.** Listed here are the city's Freenet program (if applicable); Better Business Bureau; convention and visitor bureau, visitor center, or similar organization; convention center; chamber of commerce; county seat; and similar information resources. In instances where one or more other communities in the area are especially large or

closely associated with the city profiled, information resources also are listed for these cities. (For example, relevant information for the city of Long Beach, California is included with the listings for Los Angeles; listings for Tempe, Arizona, are included with those for Phoenix, etc.) A subcategory for **Online Resources** appears at the end of the contact listings for Information Sources.

8. **AREA COMMUNITIES.** Detailed contact information is provided for selected suburbs and/or other area communities. Selection is usually based on population, and the specific criterion employed is noted at the beginning of the list.

9. **ECONOMY.** A general description of the city's economy is followed by various economic indicators such as unemployment rate, per capita income, median family income, and principal industries and number of wage earners. The data given apply only to the profiled city unless otherwise indicated. This section also includes contact information for major employers in the area, including employers representing both public and private sectors, as available. (In most cases where federal or state government are among an area's largest employers, this is indicated in the description of the economy rather than in the contact list.)

10. **QUALITY OF LIVING INDICATORS.** Crime statistics from the FBI's Preliminary Annual Uniform Crime Reports 1999 are listed for each city, as available. Cost of living and median home price are also listed here. The median home prices for most cities were obtained from the National Association of Realtors and reflect 1999 annual averages; however, if the city was not included on the association's list, the information was obtained from the 1990 census or from local resources.

11. **EDUCATION.** This section includes extensive listings, with full contact information, for area colleges and universities, as well as contact information for the local public school board(s). Other data provided here include: the number of public elementary, middle, high schools, and in some cases, special schools; student/teacher ratio for public schools; and the number of private schools in the area. In cities where there is no single school board that governs all city schools and/or districts at both the elementary and secondary levels, contact information for the largest and/or most centralized district(s) (elementary, secondary, or unified) is listed. For example, a number of elementary and high school districts serve the city of Bakersfield, California; contact information and student/teacher ratio data are given for both the largest elementary district and the largest secondary district serving the area.

12. **HOSPITALS.** Contact information is provided for major general hospitals, children's hospitals, and VA hospitals located within the city and in its surrounding area.

13. **TRANSPORTATION.** Telephone numbers are given for major airports, mass transit, and rail and bus transportation serving the city and surrounding area. (Listings for the principal rail and bus stations also include other contact information.) Other useful details provided here include the distance and cab fare from the airport to the city's downtown area and the base fare for mass transit services.

14. **UTILITIES.** Telephone numbers and, as available, web site addresses are listed here for electric, gas, water, and garbage collection/recycling. (The phone numbers listed here are primarily for use within the profiled city and its immediate area. For information regarding utilities serving outlying communities, local city halls should be contacted.)

15. **TELECOMMUNICATIONS.** Telephone numbers and, as available, web site addresses are listed here for residential telephone, cable television, and Internet services (local providers only).

16. **BANKS.** Contact information is listed here for the main branches of banks located within the profiled city.

17. **SHOPPING.** Addresses and telephone numbers are given for major shopping centers and malls as well as independent department stores (not located within a mall) in the profiled city and surrounding area.

18. **MEDIA.** Full contact information is provided for local newspapers (daily and weekly), magazines, and business journals; television stations; and radio stations. Television station listings note the network affiliation; and radio station listings include the format. (A chart explaining the codes used to describe radio formats is presented at the back of the book. The chart also includes television network abbreviations.)

19. **ATTRACTIONS.** A brief description highlighting prominent attractions located in or near the city is given here, followed by contact information for local cultural, historical, and recreational attractions.

20. **SPORTS TEAMS & FACILITIES.** Contact information is provided for local sports teams as well as similar facilities such as racetracks.

21. **ANNUAL EVENTS.** Listings in this section include the name of the event, telephone number for information, the time of year in which the event is scheduled to take place, as well as online resources, as available.

Other Features

In addition to the city listings that make up the main body of this publication, a number of useful quick-lookup features also are included:

- A table of **abbreviations** that are commonly used in this book.
- Detailed **area code tables** organized both numerically, by area code, and alphabetically by state name (or, in some cases, by particular regions within a state). Accompanying these tables is information concerning upcoming area code changes, including the dates such changes are scheduled to take effect and the permissive dialing period that will precede the changes.

- A **mileage table** illustrating the distance (by air and by car) between major U.S. cities.
- A **radio formats and television network abbreviations** chart that explains the format abbreviations appearing in individual radio station listings and the network abbreviations appearing in individual television station listings for the cities profiled.
- A **United States time zone map.**

Included also at the front of the book is a special section on **Where to Get Help for Moving.** A number of important resources for information and assistance with moving are noted here, with contact information for leading organizations representing the industry as well as listings for online resources. This is followed by detailed listings, with full contact data (as available), for:

- **city and state chambers of commerce**
- **national moving companies**
- **State Realtors Associations**

The **Index of Cities & Counties**, located at the back of the book, provides page references for the 121 cities profiled as well as for the associated cities and towns listed under the heading "Area Communities" within each profile. The index also includes citations for the principal counties in which the 121 cities, as well as selected other communities, are located, with references given for the page on which contact information is given for each county.

Comments Welcome

Comments concerning this publication, including suggestions for additions or improvements, are welcome. Please send to:

Editor, *Moving & Relocation Sourcebook and Directory*
Omnigraphics, Inc.
901 E. Las Olas Blvd., Suite 201
Fort Lauderdale, FL 33301
Phone: 954-524-3511
Fax: 954-524-7041
E-mail: mr-editorial@omnigraphics.com

1:00
Pacific Time Zone
2:00
Mountain Time Zone
3:00
Central Time Zone
Seattle
Tacoma
Olympia
Spokane
WASHINGTON
Portland
Salem
Eugene
OREGON
MONTANA
NORTH DAKOTA
SOUTH DAKOTA
Boise
IDAHO
WYOMING
Sioux Falls
CALIFORNIA
NEVADA
Reno
Sacramento
Salt Lake City
Provo
NEBRASKA
Omaha
Lincoln
Fort Collins
Denver
Stockton
San Francisco
Modesto
San Jose
UTAH
Colorado Springs
Fresno
Topeka
KANSAS
COLORADO
Las Vegas
Bakersfield
Wichita
Los Angeles
Tulsa
OKLAHOMA
ARIZONA
Albuquerque
Amarillo
Oklahoma City
San Diego
Phoenix
NEW MEXICO
Tucson
Fort Worth
Dallas
Las Cruces
El Paso
TEXAS
ALASKA
Austin
Houston
San Antonio
Anchorage
Corpus Christi
Honolulu
HAWAII
Alaska...12:00
Hawaii...10:00
Brownsville

United States Time Zones Map

This map provides the locations of all the cities listed in this directory. State capitals are indicated by a ★.

Information about time zones is also provided here.

Area Code Changes (Recent and Upcoming)

- Area code 369 was scheduled to take effect in **California** on December 2, 2000, as a result of the split of the 707 area code.*
- Area code 442 was scheduled to take effect in **California** on October 21, 2000, as a result of the split of the 760 area code.*
- Area code 657 was scheduled to take effect in **California** on October 7, 2000, as a general purpose overlay, within the same geographic area where the 714 area code is in effect.*
- Area code 669 was scheduled to take effect in **California** on January 1, 2000, as a general purpose overlay, within the same geographic area where the 408 area code is in effect.*
- Area code 752 was scheduled to take effect in **California** on February 12, 2000, as a general purpose overlay, within the same geographic area where the 909 area code is in effect.*
- Area code 935 was scheduled to take effect in **California** on June 10, 2000, as a result of the split of the 619 area code.*
- Area code 951 was scheduled to take effect in **California** on February 12, 2000, as a result of the split of the 909 area code.*
- Area code 647 is scheduled to take effect in **Canada (Ontario)** on January 8, 2001, as a general purpose overlay, within the same geographic area where the 416 area code is in effect.
- Area code 475 was introduced in **Connecticut** on July 1, 2000, as a general purpose overlay, within the same geographic area where the 203 area code is in effect.
- Area code 959 was introduced in **Connecticut** on July 1, 2000, as a general purpose overlay, within the same geographic area where the 860 area code is in effect.
- Area code 321 was introduced in **Florida** on April 1, 1999. In the first phase, the new area code was used as a general purpose overlay within five counties where the 407 area code was in effect. In the second phase, which began on November 1, 1999, the 321 area code was introduced as a result of the split of the 407 area code along the Atlantic coast. Permissive dialing will allow callers to continue using 407 in this area until October 1, 2000.
- Area codes 229 and 478 were introduced in **Georgia** on August 1, 2000, as a result of the split of the 912 area code. Permissive dialing will allow callers to continue using 912 until August 1, 2001.
- Area code 641 was introduced in **Iowa** on July 9, 2000, as a result of the split of the 515 area code. Permissive dialing will allow callers to continue using 515 until December 3, 2000.
- Area code 859 was introduced in **Kentucky** on April 1, 2000, as a result of the split of the 606 area code.
- Area code 278 was scheduled to take effect in **Michigan** on November 4, 2000, as a result of the split of the 734 area code.*
- Area code 586 was scheduled to take effect in **Michigan** on May 6, 2000, as a general purpose overlay, within the same geographic area where the 810 area code is in effect.*
- Area code 679 was scheduled to take effect in **Michigan** on February 3, 2001, as a general purpose overlay, within the same geographic area where the 313 area code is in effect.*
- Area code 989 was scheduled to take effect in **Michigan** on August 19, 2000, as a result of the split of the 517 area code.*
- Area codes 763 and 952 were introduced in **Minnesota** on February 27, 2000, as a result of the split of the 612 area code. Permissive dialing will allow callers to continue using 612 until January 14, 2001.
- Area code 845 was introduced in **New York** on June 5, 2000, as a result of the split of the 914 area code. Permissive dialing will allow callers to continue using 914 until December 4, 2000.
- Area code 980 was introduced in **North Carolina** on May 1, 2000, as a general purpose overlay, within the same geographic area where the 704 area code is in effect.
- Area code 234 is scheduled to take effect in **Ohio** on October 30, 2000, as a general purpose overlay, within the same geographic area where the 330 area code is in effect.
- Area code 971 is scheduled to take effect in **Oregon** on October 1, 2000, as a general purpose overlay, within the same geographic area where the 503 area code is in effect.
- Area code 878 was introduced in **Pennsylvania** on July 17, 2000, as a general purpose overlay, within the same geographic area where the 412 and 724 area codes are in effect.
- Area code 682 was introduced in **Texas** on April 8, 2000, as a general purpose overlay, within the same geographic area where the 817 area code is in effect.
- Area codes 936 and 979 were introduced in **Texas** on February 19, 2000, as a result of the split of the 409 area code.
- Area code 385 is scheduled to take effect in **Utah** on December 31, 2000, as a result of the split of the 801 area code. Permissive dialing will allow callers to continue using 801 until June 30, 2001.
- Area code 571 was introduced in **Virginia** on April 1, 2000, as a general purpose overlay, within the same geographic area where the 703 area code is in effect.
- Area code 564 was introduced in **Washington** on February 5, 2000, as a general purpose overlay, within the same geographic area where the 360 area code is in effect.

*As of the date of this publication, code assignments have been suspended pending further review.

Area Codes in Numerical Order

201 ... New Jersey
202 ... District of Columbia
203*... Connecticut
204 ... Manitoba
205 ... Alabama
206 ... Washington
207 ... Maine
208 ... Idaho
209 ... California
210 ... Texas
212 ... New York
213 ... California
214 ... Texas
215 ... Pennsylvania
216 ... Ohio
217 ... Illinois
218 ... Minnesota
219 ... Indiana
224 ... Illinois
225 ... Louisiana
228 ... Mississippi
229 ... Georgia
231 ... Michigan
234 ... Ohio
240 ... Maryland
242 ... Bahamas
246 ... Barbados
248 ... Michigan
250 ... British Columbia
252 ... North Carolina
253 ... Washington
254 ... Texas
256 ... Alabama
262 ... Wisconsin
264 ... Anguilla
267 ... Pennsylvania
268 ... Antigua and Barbuda
270 ... Kentucky
281 ... Texas
284 ... British Virgin Islands
301 ... Maryland
302 ... Delaware
303 ... Colorado
304 ... West Virginia
305 ... Florida
306 ... Saskatchewan
307 ... Wyoming
308 ... Nebraska
309 ... Illinois
310 ... California
312 ... Illinois
313 ... Michigan
314 ... Missouri
315 ... New York
316 ... Kansas
317 ... Indiana
318 ... Louisiana
319 ... Iowa
320 ... Minnesota
321 ... Florida
323 ... California
330*... Ohio
334 ... Alabama
336 ... North Carolina
337 ... Louisiana
341 ... California
345 ... Cayman Islands
347 ... New York
352 ... Florida
360*... Washington
361 ... Texas
385 ... Utah
401 ... Rhode Island
402 ... Nebraska
403 ... Alberta
404 ... Georgia
405 ... Oklahoma
406 ... Montana
407 ... Florida
408 ... California
409*... Texas
410 ... Maryland
412*... Pennsylvania
413 ... Massachusetts
414 ... Wisconsin
415 ... California
416*... Ontario
417 ... Missouri
418 ... Quebec
419 ... Ohio
423 ... Tennessee
424 ... California
425 ... Washington
435 ... Utah
440 ... Ohio
441 ... Bermuda
443 ... Maryland
450 ... Quebec
469 ... Texas
473 ... Grenada
475 ... Connecticut
478 ... Georgia
480 ... Arizona
484 ... Pennyslvania
501 ... Arkansas
502 ... Kentucky
503*... Oregon
504 ... Louisiana
505 ... New Mexico
506 ... New Brunswick
507 ... Minnesota
508 ... Massachusetts
509 ... Washington
510 ... California
512 ... Texas
513 ... Ohio
514 ... Quebec
515*... Iowa
516 ... New York
517 ... Michigan
518 ... New York
519 ... Ontario
520 ... Arizona
530 ... California
540 ... Virginia
541 ... Oregon
559 ... California
561 ... Florida
562 ... California
564 ... Washington
570 ... Pennsylvania
571 ... Virginia
573 ... Missouri
580 ... Oklahoma
601 ... Mississippi
602 ... Arizona
603 ... New Hampshire
604 ... British Columbia
605 ... South Dakota
606*... Kentucky
607 ... New York
608 ... Wisconsin
609 ... New Jersey
610 ... Pennsylvania
612*... Minnesota
613 ... Ontario
614 ... Ohio
615 ... Tennessee
616 ... Michigan
617 ... Massachusetts
618 ... Illinois
619 ... California
623 ... Arizona
626 ... California
628 ... California
630 ... Illinois
631 ... New York
636 ... Missouri
641 ... Iowa
646 ... New York
647 ... Ontario
649 ... Turks and Caicos
650 ... California
651 ... Minnesota
660 ... Missouri
661 ... California
662 ... Mississippi
664 ... Montserrat
671 ... Guam
678 ... Georgia
682 ... Texas
701 ... North Dakota
702 ... Nevada
703*... Virginia
704*... North Carolina
705 ... Ontario
706 ... Georgia
707 ... California
708 ... Illinois
709 ... Newfoundland
712 ... Iowa
713 ... Texas
714 ... California
715 ... Wisconsin
716 ... New York
717 ... Pennsylvania
718 ... New York
719 ... Colorado
720 ... Colorado
724*... Pennsylvania
727 ... Florida
732 ... New Jersey
734 ... Michigan
740 ... Ohio
757 ... Virginia
758 ... Saint Lucia
760 ... California
763 ... Minnesota
764 ... California
765 ... Indiana
767 ... Dominica
770 ... Georgia
773 ... Illinois
775 ... Nevada
780 ... Alberta
781 ... Massachusetts
784 ... Saint Vincent & the Grenadines
785 ... Kansas
786 ... Florida
787 ... Puerto Rico
800 ... Toll-free; all states
801*... Utah
802 ... Vermont
803 ... South Carolina
804 ... Virginia
805 ... California
806 ... Texas
807 ... Ontario
808 ... Hawaii
809 ... Caribbean
810 ... Michigan
812 ... Indiana
813 ... Florida
814 ... Pennsylvania
815 ... Illinois
816 ... Missouri
817*... Texas
818 ... California
819 ... Quebec
828 ... North Carolina
830 ... Texas
831 ... California
832 ... Texas
843 ... South Carolina
845 ... New York
847 ... Illinois
850 ... Florida
856 ... New Jersey
858 ... California
859 ... Kentucky
860*... Connecticut
863 ... Florida
864 ... South Carolina
865 ... Tennessee
867 ... Northwest Territories
868 ... Trinidad and Tobago
869 ... Saint Kitts and Nevis
870 ... Arkansas
876 ... Jamaica
877 ... Toll-free; all states
878 ... Pennsylvania
888 ... Toll-free; all states
901 ... Tennessee
902 ... Nova Scotia
903 ... Texas
904 ... Florida
905 ... Ontario
906 ... Michigan
907 ... Alaska
908 ... New Jersey
909 ... California
910 ... North Carolina
912*... Georgia
913 ... Kansas
914*... New York
915 ... Texas
916 ... California
917 ... New York
918 ... Oklahoma
919 ... North Carolina
920 ... Wisconsin
925 ... California
931 ... Tennessee
936 ... Texas
937 ... Ohio
940 ... Texas
941 ... Florida
949 ... California
952 ... Minnesota
954 ... Florida
956 ... Texas
959 ... Connecticut
970 ... Colorado
971 ... Oregon
972 ... Texas
973 ... New Jersey
978 ... Massachusetts
979 ... Texas
980 ... North Carolina

*Area codes affected by upcoming changes. Please refer to the table on page 12, Area Code Changes (Recent and Upcoming). Information there is organized by state name, with the state name presented in bold.

Area Codes in State Order

Alabama
205 Birmingham and Tuscaloosa
256 north and east central
334 south

Alaska
907 all locations

Arizona
480 east of Phoenix including Tempe and Scottsdale
520 outside Phoenix
602 Phoenix
623 west of Phoenix including Glendale

Arkansas
501 Little Rock and northwest
870 east and south

California
209 central
213 Los Angeles
310 Long Beach/west
323 Los Angeles
341 Oakland
408 west central
415 San Francisco
424 Long Beach/west
510 Oakland
530 north
559 central
562 Long Beach/east
619 San Diego and surrounding area (except north)
626 Pasadena/east
650 south of San Francisco
661 Bakersfield and northern LA county
707 northwest
714 northern Orange County
760 southeast except San Diego area
764 south of San Francisco
805 south
818 Burbank and Glendale area
831 west central
858 San Diego/north
909 San Bernardino
916 Sacramento and surrounding area
925 east of Oakland
949 southern Orange County

Canada
204 all locations in Manitoba
250 outside Vancouver area including Vancouver Island
306 all locations in Saskatchewan
403 southern Alberta
416* Toronto
418 eastern Quebec
450 outside Montreal metro area
506 all locations in New Brunswick
514 Montreal metro area
519 southern Ontario
604 Vancouver area
613 northeast of Toronto
647 Toronto
705 eastern Ontario
709 all locations in Newfoundland
780 central and northern Alberta
807 western Ontario
819 western Quebec
867 all locations in Yukon & Northwest Territories
902 all locations in Nova Scotia & Prince Edward Island
905 north of Toronto

Caribbean, Bahamas & Bermuda
242 Bahamas
246 Barbados
264 Anguilla
268 Antigua & Barbuda
284 British Virgin Islands
345 Cayman Islands
441 Bermuda
473 Grenada
649 Turks and Caicos
664 Montserrat
758 Saint Lucia
767 Dominica
784 Saint Vincent & Grenadines
787 Puerto Rico
809 Caribbean
868 Trinidad and Tobago
869 Saint Kitts and Nevis
876 Jamaica

Colorado
303 Denver
719 south and east
720 Denver
970 west and north

Connecticut
203* southwest
475 southwest
860* except southwest
959 except southwest

Delaware
302 all locations

District of Columbia
202 all locations

Florida
305 southeast
321 central and east central
352 Gainesville area
407 central
561 east
727 Saint Petersburg/ Clearwater
786 southeast
813 Tampa
850 northwest
904 northeast
941 central and southwest
954 Fort Lauderdale and surrounding area

Georgia
229 southwest
404 Atlanta
478 central
678 Atlanta area
706 north except Atlanta area
770 Atlanta suburbs
912* southeast

Guam
671 all locations

Hawaii
808 all locations

Idaho
208 all locations

Illinois
217 central
224 suburban Chicago
309 west
312 Chicago
331 northeast
464 northeast
618 south
630 northeast
708 northeast
773 Chicago (outside central commercial area)
815 north
847 suburban Chicago
872 Chicago

Indiana
219 north
317 Indianapolis metro area
765 central except Indianapolis metro area
812 south

Iowa
319 east
515* central including Des Moines and Ames
641 south central and east central
712 west

Kansas
316 south
785 north except Kansas City
913 Kansas City

Kentucky
270 west
502 north including Louisville
606* east
859 north central

Louisiana
225 east central
318 north and west
504 southeast

Maine
207 all locations

Maryland
240 west
301 west
410 east
443 east

Massachusetts
413 west
508 southeast
617 Boston metro area
781 outside metro Boston
978 northeast except Boston

Michigan
231 northwest
248 east (Oakland County)
313 Detroit and inner suburbs
517 south central
616 southwest
734 west of Detroit
810 east (except Oakland County)
906 north

*Area codes affected by upcoming changes. Please refer to the table beginning on page 12, Area Code Changes (Recent and Upcoming). Information there is organized by state name, with the state name presented in bold.

Area Codes in State Order (Cont'd)

Minnesota
218 north
320 central except Minneapolis/Saint Paul metro area
507 south
612* Minneapolis
651 Saint Paul and east central
763 suburbs north and northwest of Minneapolis
952 suburbs south and southwest of Minneapolis

Mississippi
228 Gulfport/Biloxi and surrounding area
601 south except Gulfport/Biloxi and surrounding area
662 north

Missouri
314 Saint Louis
417 southwest
573 east except Saint Louis metro area
636 east (outside Saint Louis)
660 north except Kansas City and Saint Joseph
816 Kansas City and Saint Joseph

Montana
406 all locations

Nebraska
308 west
402 east

Nevada
702 Las Vegas area
775 all locations except Las Vegas

New Hampshire
603 all locations

New Jersey
201 northeast
609 southeast
732 east central
856 southwest
908 west central
973 northwest

New Mexico
505 all locations

New York
212 New York City
315 north central
347 New York City
516 Long Island
518 northeast
607 south central
646 New York City
716 west
718 New York City
845 north and west of Westchester County
914* Westchester County
917 New York City
945 north and west of Westchester County

North Carolina
252 east
336 Greensboro and Winston-Salem areas
704* southwest
828 west
910 south central
919 north central
980 southwest

North Dakota
701 all locations

Ohio
216 Cleveland metro area
234 northeast except Cleveland
330* northeast except Cleveland
419 northwest
440 north central except Cleveland metro area
513 southwest
614 Columbus area
740 east and central except Columbus area
937 southwest except Cincinnati area

Oklahoma
405 central
580 south and west
918 northeast

Oregon
503* Portland area
541 outside Portland area
971 Portland area

Pennsylvania
215 Philadelphia
267 Philadelphia
412* Pittsburgh metro area
484 southeast
570 northeast
610 southeast
717 southeast
724* outside Pittsburgh metro area
814 west
878 Pittsburgh and surrounding area

Rhode Island
401 all locations

South Carolina
803 central
843 east
864 northwest

South Dakota
605 all locations

Tennessee
423 east
615 north central
901 west
931 Nashville and north central

Texas
210 San Antonio metro area
214 Dallas
254 north central
281 Houston
361 Corpus Christi and surrounding area
409* east of Houston area
469 Dallas
512 Austin and surrounding area
682 Fort Worth metro area and Arlington
713 Houston
806 northwest
817* Fort Worth metro area and Arlington
830 south central
832 Houston
903 northeast
915 west
936 north of Houston area
940 north
956 south
972 Dallas
979 west of Houston area

Toll calls: from Canada and the Caribbean
880
881

Toll-free; all states
800
877
888

Utah
385 areas north and south of Salt Lake County
435 all locations except Salt Lake City/Ogden/Provo metro areas
801* Salt Lake County

Vermont
802 all locations

Virginia
540 west and north
571 northeast
703* northeast
757 Norfolk and surrounding area
804 east

Washington
206 Seattle area
253 Tacoma area
360* west except Seattle, Tacoma and Everett areas
425 east of Seattle between Everett and Kent
509 east
564 west except Seattle, Tacoma and Everett areas

West Virginia
304 all locations

Wisconsin
262 southeast except Milwaukee
414 Milwaukee
608 southwest
715 north
920 southeast except Milwaukee and surrounding area (south)

Wyoming
307 all locations

*Area codes affected by upcoming changes. Please refer to the table beginning on page 12, Area Code Changes (Recent and Upcoming). Information there is organized by state name, with the state name presented in bold.

Mileage Between Major United States Cities

	Atlanta	Baltimore	Boston	Charlotte	Chicago	Cleveland	Dallas	Denver	Detroit	Houston	Indianapolis	Jacksonville	Kansas City	Los Angeles	Memphis	Miami	Milwaukee	Minneapolis	New Orleans	New York	Philadelphia	Phoenix	Pittsburgh	Portland	Saint Louis	San Antonio	San Diego	San Francisco	Seattle	Washington DC
Atlanta		654	1110	240	710	728	820	1430	732	790	527	313	822	2190	382	665	799	1121	480	855	748	1827	683	2664	565	995	2146	2485	2625	620
Baltimore	577		427	418	717	358	1357	1643	514	1404	569	751	1070	2647	911	1094	790	1113	1135	199	102	2312	245	2797	828	1632	2681	2823	2708	45
Boston	945	360		848	1005	657	1755	2000	799	1830	929	1162	1435	3015	1341	1520	1091	1390	1507	210	315	2670	574	3144	1207	2018	2984	3130	3016	450
Charlotte	227	365	721		737	516	1058	1580	630	1029	551	390	974	2412	630	740	827	1151	722	618	512	2034	495	2779	731	1239	2407	2721	2739	382
Chicago	590	606	855	587		348	920	1020	279	1090	185	1007	542	2050	537	1395	90	410	919	810	785	1742	476	2117	289	1209	2093	2173	2052	710
Cleveland	554	308	551	435	308		1189	1362	172	1306	318	909	819	2382	732	1252	435	758	1055	471	428	2032	129	2432	579	1453	2385	2483	2391	360
Dallas	730	1212	1550	930	800	1025		785	1156	245	892	1039	505	1400	454	1345	1015	949	517	1560	1443	1002	1208	2043	655	270	1348	1750	2131	1305
Denver	1210	1510	1765	1358	900	1227	655		1283	1035	1063	1743	606	1030	1043	2105	1038	920	1277	1795	1739	813	1427	1261	863	946	1095	1255	1341	1615
Detroit	596	397	613	504	238	90	999	1156		1276	284	1045	769	2288	719	1385	360	685	1070	649	609	2008	296	2384	534	1445	2368	2399	2327	516
Houston	695	1251	1595	927	940	1114	215	865	1105		995	887	743	1540	574	1190	1179	1183	352	1610	1511	1164	1365	2243	839	199	1490	1910	2369	1365
Indianapolis	426	511	807	428	165	263	763	1000	240	865		840	501	2063	474	1186	270	593	802	731	659	1725	364	2237	246	1191	2078	2289	2245	575
Jacksonville	285	681	1017	341	863	770	908	1467	831	821	699		1135	2353	694	348	1112	1456	557	951	845	2002	829	2961	882	1082	2355	2747	2972	715
Kansas City	676	963	1251	803	414	700	451	558	645	644	453	950		1577	482	1481	564	443	839	1233	1170	1235	870	1820	256	784	1588	1861	1858	1042
Los Angeles	1935	2320	2595	2119	1745	2049	1240	850	1983	1375	1809	2147	1356		1807	2715	2069	1857	1858	2795	2703	376	2430	962	1836	1387	124	385	1134	2645
Memphis	337	793	1137	521	482	630	420	879	623	484	384	590	369	1603		997	622	914	414	1102	1007	1465	759	2308	283	725	1805	2116	2317	854
Miami	605	954	1255	652	1190	1087	1110	1715	1152	970	1024	326	1241	2340	872		1458	1769	860	1334	1230	2348	1180	3257	1226	1385	2678	3093	3303	1055
Milwaukee	668	642	857	658	81	335	857	914	252	1005	243	942	443	1744	556	1267		337	1033	894	872	1771	564	2023	376	1287	2132	2172	1979	811
Minneapolis	907	939	1123	939	355	630	862	700	543	1056	511	1191	413	1524	699	1511	299		1346	1217	1195	1677	887	1724	630	1245	2001	1979	1653	1090
New Orleans	424	999	1359	649	833	924	443	1082	939	318	712	504	680	1673	358	669	910	1051		1335	1229	1496	1138	2536	698	547	1840	2278	2590	1099
New York	760	172	190	533	740	405	1375	1640	482	1420	646	838	1097	2465	957	1090	733	1018	1171		101	2445	379	2914	976	1820	2803	2930	2841	235
Philadelphia	666	90	271	451	666	360	1299	1579	443	1341	585	758	1038	2394	881	1019	694	985	1089	83		2374	308	2859	904	1737	2773	2902	2816	143
Phoenix	1592	2005	2300	1783	1453	1749	887	586	1690	1017	1499	1794	1049	357	1263	1982	1464	1280	1316	2145	2083		2087	1268	1481	1002	353	762	1465	2300
Pittsburgh	521	197	483	362	410	115	1070	1320	205	1137	330	703	781	2136	660	1010	446	743	919	317	259	1828		2549	609	1476	2440	2609	2521	259
Portland	2172	2361	2540	2290	1758	2055	1633	982	1969	1836	1885	2439	1497	825	1849	2708	1719	1427	2063	2445	2412	1005	2165		2057	2095	1086	637	174	2784
Saint Louis	467	733	1038	568	262	492	547	796	455	679	231	751	238	1589	240	1061	327	466	598	875	811	1272	559	1723		952	1833	2118	2135	862
San Antonio	882	1418	1766	1105	1051	1256	252	802	1238	189	999	1011	702	1204	631	1148	1107	1110	507	1584	1507	849	1291	1720	792		1297	1740	2180	1587
San Diego	1891	2296	2584	2081	1734	2034	1184	834	1971	1304	1788	2092	1336	112	1561	2272	1738	1532	1609	2433	2373	299	2117	931	1564	1129		514	1258	2602
San Francisco	2135	2457	2699	2301	1860	2166	1470	955	2091	1645	1949	2374	1506	345	1802	2595	1842	1584	1926	2570	2523	653	2264	534	1744	1490	458		810	2845
Seattle	2182	2334	2493	2285	1737	2026	1681	1021	1938	1891	1872	2455	1506	959	1867	2734	1692	1395	2101	2408	2380	1114	2138	145	1724	1787	1063	678		2721
Washington DC	545	35	395	330	595	306	1185	1465	396	1220	494	647	945	2280	765	925	637	934	966	215	123	1983	192	2354	712	1388	2276	2435	2329	

Road mileage: bold
Air mileage: light

Where To Get Help For Moving

Each year, millions of Americans face the sometimes arduous task of moving. Although some people are fortunate enough to have their relocations handled by their employers, many others are responsible for making their own arrangements. Careful planning, organization, and research are essential to minimize complications and ensure a successful relocation. Fortunately, many excellent resources are available that provide a variety of information for persons planning to relocate from one place to another.

One such resource is the local **chamber of commerce**. Most chambers offer relocation guides and maps, often free of charge or for a nominal fee, that provide useful information about the city and surrounding area. These guides often include details on topics ranging from the local economy to education to recreation, and some include sections that focus specifically on moving and relocation, complete with checklists and tips. (Detailed contact information for city and state chambers of commerce is provided at the end of this section.)

Many chambers of commerce pass on the names and addresses of prospective residents to member insurance and **real estate companies**, which in turn offer their services and (often) additional relocation information. Some communities also have newcomers groups that provide information and bring together people new to the area. (Contact information for local realtor associations is included for each of the cities profiled in this directory; state realtor associations are listed at the end of this section.)

The **American Moving and Storage Association (AMSA)** (formerly the American Movers Conference), a national organization of 3,400 professional moving companies, is another excellent source of relocation information. The association's web site contains an abundance of useful information for people planning a move, including a directory of professional moving companies, details about liability, relocation assistance, worksheets for evaluating the cost of moving, and dozens of valuable tips to help ensure a successful move. The web site also contains a list of AMSA Certified Movers and Van Lines, which are companies that "have voluntarily agreed to abide by a Code of Conduct that requires complete disclosure of moving information to consumers, written estimates of charges, timely service, and prompt response to claims and complaints. They have also agreed to arbitrate disputes of up to $5,000 arising from loss or damage to the articles in your shipment." Free brochures are available online on the AMSA web site, or they may be ordered by telephone or by mail. Contact the association at:

American Moving & Storage Assn
1611 Duke St. — Phone: 703-683-7410
Alexandria, VA 22314 — Fax: 703-683-7527
Web: www.amconf.org
E-mail: amconf@amconf.org

Contact information for top national moving companies is provided at the end of this section. The regulatory agency that governs the practices of interstate movers in the U.S. is the **Federal Motor Carrier Safety Administration (FMCSA)**. (FMCSA was formerly the Office of Motor Carriers in theFederal Highway Administration). Moving companies are required to comply with FMCSA rules regarding estimates and receipts and, most importantly, they are required to give customers a copy of a Federal Highway Administration publication entitled "Your Rights and Responsibilities When You Move." To verify that a particular moving company has a valid license, consumers may consult FMCSA's Licensing and Insurance System, available online at the web address listed below or by calling the Administration's Insurance Compliance Division. The organization cannot furnish information on amoving company's past performance, however. The Administration is in the process of setting up a task force to investigate carriers of household goods who have established a "substantial pattern of consumer abuse," but as an extra precaution the FMCSA recommends that consumers contact their local Better Business Bureaus or Chambers of Commerce to find out if any complaints have been filed against the moving company or companies that are being considered. They also recommend that consumers read "Your Rights and Responsibilities When You Move" carefully before choosing a moving company. The publication is available online at www.fmcsa.dot.gov/factsfigs/moving.htm or by calling the FMCSA at (202) 358-7063. For other matters, consumers can contact the Administration at:

Federal Motor Carrier Safety Administration (FMCSA)
Insurance Compliance Division — Phone: 202-358-7027
400 Virginia Ave SW, Suite 600 — Fax: 202-358-7100
Washington, DC 20024
WWW: fhwa-li.volpe.dot.gov

A wealth of information for prospective movers is also available on the **Internet**, ranging from lists of moving companies to tips for moving plants and pets to links to real estate listings for the destination city. Many national and worldwide moving companies also have their own web sites. Sites that offer information specifically for moving and relocation, community profiles, links to local resources, demographic data, and/or other information helpful to those planning a move, include:

AAA Move
www.aaamove.com

American Relocation Network
www.relo-usa.com

AMS Homefinder Relocation Resource System
www.amshomefinder.com

Avatar Consumer's Guide to Moving & Storage
www.avatar-moving.com

Clickandmove.com
www.clickandmove.com

Employee Relocation Council
www.erc.org

Excite Travel Destinations: United States
www.excite.com/travel/countries/united_states

Homebuyer's Fair
www.homefair.com

Homes.wsj.com
homes.wsj.com

Homestore.com: Moving
www.homestore.com/Moving

HouseLocators.com Relocation Network
www.houselocators.com

Insiders' Guide to Relocation Online
www.insiders.com/relocation

InternetRelo.com
www.internetrelo.com

Location Guides
www.ditell.com/tmackowi/LocGuide.html

***Money*.com: Best Places to Live 2000**
www.pathfinder.com/money/depts/real_estate/bestplaces/

Move Links
www.movelinks.com

MoveCentral
www.movecentral.com

Mover Directory
www.moverdirectory.com

Movers Network
www.movernet.com

MoversNet
www.usps.gov/moversnet

Moving Basics at theWhiz.com
thewhiz.snap.com/1998/05/980522i.asp

Moving-Guide: A Directory of Movers & Moving Services Worldwide
www.moving-guide.com

MovingResource.net
www.movingresource.net

National Moving Network
www.nationalmoving.net

Relocate-america.com
www.relocateamerica.com

Relocation Central
www.relocationcentral.com

Relocation Mall
www.relomall.com

ReloLinks.com
www.relolinks.com

Rent Net Moving & Relocation Resources
www.movingresources.com/cgi-bin/chome/RentNet/scripts/OTHERS/resHome.jsp

RPS Relocation
www.rpsrelocation.com

U.S. Census Bureau State & County Demographic & Economic Profiles
www.census.gov/datamap/www

Vanlines.com
www.vanlines.com

Virtual Relocation
www.virtualrelocation.com

Welcomewagon.com
www.welcomewagon.com

Yahoo! Get Local
local.yahoo.com

Yahoo! Real Estate
realestate.yahoo.com

Chambers of Commerce—City

	City	State	ZIP	*Phone*	*Fax*
Akron Regional Development Board					
1 Cascade Plaza Suite 800	Akron	OH	44308	330-376-5550	330-379-3164
TF: 800-621-8001					
www.ardb.org					
Greater Albuquerque Chamber of Commerce					
PO Box 25100	Albuquerque	NM	87125	505-764-3700	505-764-3714
asutten@gacc.org					
www.gacc.org					
Alexandria Chamber of Commerce					
801 N Fairfax St Suite 402	Alexandria	VA	22314	703-549-1000	703-739-3805
www.alexchamber.com					
Lehigh County Chamber of Commerce					
462 Walnut St	Allentown	PA	18102	610-437-9661	610-437-4907
www.lehighcountychamber.org					
Amarillo Chamber of Commerce					
1000 S Polk St	Amarillo	TX	79101	806-373-7800	806-373-3909
www.amarillo-cvb.org					
Anaheim Chamber of Commerce					
100 S Anaheim Blvd Suite 300	Anaheim	CA	92805	714-758-0222	714-758-0468
anaheimchamber.org					
Anchorage Chamber of Commerce					
441 W 5th Ave Suite 300	Anchorage	AK	99501	907-272-2401	907-272-4117
www.anchoragechamber.org					
Ann Arbor Area Chamber of Commerce					
425 S Main St Suite 103	Ann Arbor	MI	48104	734-665-4433	734-665-4191
gen@annarborchamber.org					
www.annarborchamber.org/					
Annapolis & Anne Arundel County Chamber of Commerce					
PO Box 346	Annapolis	MD	21404	410-268-7676	410-268-2317
www.annapolischamber.com					
Arlington Chamber of Commerce					
316 W Main St	Arlington	TX	76010	817-275-2613	817-261-7535
TF: 800-834-3928					
www.chamber.arlingtontx.com					
Arlington Chamber of Commerce					
2009 N 14th St Suite 111	Arlington	VA	22201	703-525-2400	703-522-5273
www.arlingtonchamber.com					
Atlanta Chamber of Commerce					
PO Box 1740	Atlanta	GA	30301	404-880-9000	404-586-8464
metroatlantachamber.com					
Metro Augusta Chamber of Commerce					
600 Broad Street Plaza	Augusta	GA	30903	706-821-1300	706-821-1330
augustausa@aol.com					
www.metroaugusta.com					
Aurora Chamber of Commerce					
562 Sable Blvd Suite 200	Aurora	CO	80011	303-344-1500	303-344-1564
auroracham@aol.com					
www.aurorachamber.org					
Greater Austin Chamber of Commerce					
PO Box 1967	Austin	TX	78767	512-478-9383	512-478-6389
www.austin-chamber.org					
Greater Bakersfield Chamber of Commerce					
1033 Truxtun Ave	Bakersfield	CA	93301	661-327-4421	661-327-8751
chamber@bakersfield.org					
www.bakersfield.org/chamber					
Baltimore City Chamber of Commerce					
3 W Baltimore St	Baltimore	MD	21201	410-837-7101	410-837-7104
www.baltocitychamber.com					
Greater Baton Rouge Chamber of Commerce					
PO Box 3217	Baton Rouge	LA	70821	225-381-7125	225-336-4306
info@brchamber.org					
www.brchamber.org					
Birmingham Area Chamber of Commerce					
2027 1st Ave N	Birmingham	AL	35203	205-323-5461	205-250-7669
www.birminghamchamber.com					
Boise Metro Chamber of Commerce					
PO Box 2368	Boise	ID	83701	208-472-5205	208-472-5201
www.boise.org					
Bossier Chamber of Commerce					
710 Benton Rd	Bossier City	LA	71111	318-746-0252	318-746-0357
bcchamber@aol.com					
www.bossierchamber.com					
Greater Boston Chamber of Commerce					
1 Beacon St 4th Fl	Boston	MA	02108	617-227-4500	617-227-7505
chamber@gbcc.org					
www.gbcc.org					
Boulder Chamber of Commerce					
2440 Pearl St	Boulder	CO	80302	303-442-1044	303-938-8837
chamber.boulder.net					
Brownsville Chamber of Commerce					
1600 E Elizabeth St	Brownsville	TX	78520	956-542-4341	956-504-3348
info@brownsvillechamber.com					
www.brownsvillechamber.com					
Buffalo Niagara Partnership					
300 Main Pl Tower	Buffalo	NY	14202	716-852-7100	716-852-2761
www.thepartnership.org					
Carson City Area Chamber of Commerce					
1900 S Carson St Suite 100	Carson City	NV	89701	775-882-1565	775-882-4179
www.carsoncitychamber.com					
Charleston Metro Chamber of Commerce					
81 Mary St	Charleston	SC	29403	843-577-2510	843-723-4853
chambercomm@charleston.net					
www.charlestonchamber.net					
Charlotte Chamber of Commerce					
PO Box 32785	Charlotte	NC	28232	704-378-1300	704-374-1903
www.charlottechamber.org					
Chattanooga Area Chamber of Commerce					
1001 Market St	Chattanooga	TN	37402	423-756-2121	423-267-7242
info@chamber.chattanooga.net					
www.chattanooga-chamber.com					
Chicagoland Chamber of Commerce					
330 N Wabash Ave 1 IBM Plaza Suite 2800	Chicago	IL	60611	312-494-6700	312-494-0196
www.chicagolandchamber.org					
Chula Vista Chamber of Commerce					
233 4th Ave	Chula Vista	CA	91910	619-420-6602	619-420-1269
cvcc@pacbell.net					
www.chulavistachamber.org					
Greater Cincinnati Chamber of Commerce					
441 Vine St Carew Tower Suite 300	Cincinnati	OH	45202	513-579-3100	513-579-3102
info@gccc.com					
www.gccc.com					
Greater Cleveland Growth Assn					
200 Tower City Ctr	Cleveland	OH	44113	216-621-3300	216-621-6013
TF: 800-562-7121					
www.clevelandgrowth.com					
Colorado Springs Chamber of Commerce					
PO Box B	Colorado Springs	CO	80901	719-635-1551	719-635-1571
www.cscc.org					
Greater Columbia Chamber of Commerce					
930 Richland St	Columbia	SC	29201	803-733-1110	803-733-1149
www.gcbn.com					
Greater Columbus Chamber of Commerce					
37 N High St	Columbus	OH	43215	614-221-1321	614-221-9360
TF: 800-950-1321					
www.columbus-chamber.org					
Greater Corpus Christi Business Alliance					
1201 N Shoreline Blvd	Corpus Christi	TX	78401	361-881-1888	361-883-5027
TF: 800-678-6232					
Greater Dallas Chamber of Commerce					
1201 Elm St Suite 2000	Dallas	TX	75270	214-746-6600	214-746-6799
www.gdc.org					
Dayton Area Chamber of Commerce					
1 Chamber Plaza Suite 200	Dayton	OH	45402	937-226-1444	937-226-8254
www.daytonchamber.org					
Greater Denver Chamber of Commerce					
1445 Market St	Denver	CO	80202	303-534-8500	303-534-3200
www.den-chamber.org					
Greater Des Moines Partnership					
700 Locust St Suite 100	Des Moines	IA	50309	515-286-4950	515-286-4974
TF: 800-376-9059					
www.dmchamber.com					
Greater Detroit Chamber of Commerce					
1 Woodward Ave	Detroit	MI	48232	313-964-4000	313-964-0531
www.detroitchamber.com					
Greater Durham Chamber of Commerce					
300 W Morgan St Suite 1400	Durham	NC	27701	919-682-2133	919-688-8351
www@herald-sun.com					
www.herald-sun.com/dcc/					
Greater El Paso Chamber of Commerce					
10 Civic Ctr Plaza	El Paso	TX	79901	915-534-0500	915-534-0513
www.elpaso.org					
Eugene Chamber of Commerce					
PO Box 1107	Eugene	OR	97440	541-484-1314	541-484-4942
www.eugene-commerce.com					
Flint Area Chamber of Commerce					
519 S Saginaw St Suite 200	Flint	MI	48502	810-232-7101	810-233-7437
flintchamber@flint.org					
www.flintchamber.org					
Fort Collins Area Chamber of Commerce					
225 S Meldrum St	Fort Collins	CO	80521	970-482-3746	970-482-3774
www.fcchamber.org					
Greater Fort Lauderdale Chamber of Commerce					
512 NE 3rd Ave	Fort Lauderdale	FL	33301	954-462-6000	954-527-8766
www.ftlchamber.com					
Greater Fort Wayne Chamber of Commerce					
826 Ewing St	Fort Wayne	IN	46802	219-424-1435	219-426-7232
www.fwchamber.org					

	City	State	Zip	Phone	Fax
Fort Worth Chamber of Commerce 777 Taylor St Suite 900 www.fortworthcoc.org	Fort Worth	TX	76102	817-336-2491	817-877-4034
Fremont Chamber of Commerce 39488 Stevenson Pl Suite 100 fmtcc@infolane.com www.fremontbusiness.com	Fremont	CA	94539	510-795-2244	510-795-2240
Fresno Chamber of Commerce 1649 Van Ness Ave Suite 103 www.fresnochamber.com	Fresno	CA	93721	559-495-4800	559-495-4811
Garden Grove Chamber of Commerce 12866 Main St Suite 102 www.gardengrovechamber.org	Garden Grove	CA	92840	714-638-7950	714-636-6672
Garland Chamber of Commerce 914 S Garland Ave information@garlandchamber.com www.garlandchamber.org	Garland	TX	75040	972-272-7551	972-276-9261
Glendale Chamber of Commerce PO Box 249 *TF:* 800-437-8669 info@glendaleazchamber.org www.glendaleazchamber.org	Glendale	AZ	85311	623-937-4754	623-937-3333
Glendale Chamber of Commerce 200 S Louise St info@glendalechamber.com www.glendalechamber.com	Glendale	CA	91205	818-240-7870	818-240-2872
Grand Rapids Area Chamber of Commerce 111 Pearl St NW *TF:* 800-376-6437 www.grandrapids.org	Grand Rapids	MI	49503	616-771-0300	616-771-0318
Greensboro Area Chamber of Commerce 342 N Elm St Suite 100 www.greensboro.org	Greensboro	NC	27401	336-275-8675	336-230-1867
Greater Greenville Chamber of Commerce 24 Cleveland St	Greenville	SC	29601	864-242-1050	864-282-8509
Virginia Peninsula Chamber of Commerce 1919 Commerce Dr Suite 320 *TF:* 800-556-1822 www.vpcc.org	Hampton	VA	23666	757-262-2000	757-262-2009
Metro Hartford Chamber of Commerce 250 Constitution Plaza info@metrohartford.com www.metrohartford.com	Hartford	CT	06103	860-525-4451	860-293-2592
Hialeah Chamber of Commerce & Industries 1840 W 49th St Suite 410 www.hialeahchamber.com	Hialeah	FL	33012	305-828-9898	305-828-9777
Hialeah-Miami Springs-Northwest Dade Area Chamber of Commerce 59 W 5th St hiamscc@bellsouth.net www.hialeahnwdade.com	Hialeah	FL	33010	305-887-1515	305-887-2453
Greater Houston Partnership 1200 Smith St Suite 700 www.houston.org	Houston	TX	77002	713-844-3600	713-844-0200
Huntington Beach Chamber of Commerce 2100 Main St Suite 200 www.hbchamber.org	Huntington Beach	CA	92648	714-536-8888	714-960-7654
Chamber of Commerce of Huntsville/Madison County PO Box 408 hcc@hsvchamber.org www.hsvchamber.org	Huntsville	AL	35804	256-535-2000	256-535-2015
Independence Chamber of Commerce PO Box 1077 rchamber@independencechamber.com www.independencechamber.com	Independence	MO	64051	816-252-4745	816-252-4917
Indianapolis Chamber of Commerce 320 N Meridian St Suite 200 *TF:* 800-333-4492 chamber@indylink.com www.indychamber.com	Indianapolis	IN	46204	317-464-2200	317-464-2217
Greater Irving Chamber of Commerce 3333 N MacArthur Blvd Suite 100 www.irving.net/chamber	Irving	TX	75062	972-252-8484	972-252-6710
MetroJackson Chamber of Commerce PO Box 22548 www.metrochamber.com	Jackson	MS	39225	601-948-7575	601-352-5539
Jacksonville Chamber of Commerce 3 Independent Dr memberservices@jacksonvillechamber.org www.jacksonvillechamber.org	Jacksonville	FL	32202	904-366-6600	904-632-0617
Hudson County Chamber of Commerce 574 Summit Ave Suite 404	Jersey City	NJ	07306	201-653-7400	201-798-3886
Kansas City Kansas Area Chamber of Commerce PO Box 171337 kckacc@enterway.net www.kckacc.com	Kansas City	KS	66117	913-371-3070	913-371-3732
Greater Kansas City Chamber of Commerce 911 Main St Suite 2600 www.kcity.com	Kansas City	MO	64105	816-221-2424	816-221-7440
Knoxville Area Chamber Partnership 601 W Summit Hill Suite 300 www.knoxville.org	Knoxville	TN	37902	865-637-4550	865-523-2071
Greater Lafayette Chamber of Commerce 804 E St Mary Blvd www.lafchamber.org	Lafayette	LA	70503	337-233-2705	337-234-8671
Lansing Regional Chamber of Commerce 300 E Michigan Ave Suite 300 www.lansingchamber.org/	Lansing	MI	48933	517-487-6340	517-484-6910
Las Cruces Chamber of Commerce 760 W Picacho Ave lascruces.org/chamber	Las Cruces	NM	88005	505-524-1968	505-527-5546
Las Vegas Chamber of Commerce 3720 Howard Hughes Pkwy info@lvchamber.com www.lvchamber.com	Las Vegas	NV	89109	702-735-1616	702-735-2011
Greater Lexington Chamber of Commerce 330 E Main St Suite 100 www.lexchamber.com	Lexington	KY	40507	859-254-4447	859-233-3304
Lincoln Chamber of Commerce PO Box 83006 www.lcoc.com	Lincoln	NE	68501	402-436-2350	402-436-2360
Greater Little Rock Chamber of Commerce 101 S Spring St Suite 200 www.littlerockchamber.com	Little Rock	AR	72201	501-374-4871	501-374-6018
Los Angeles Area Chamber of Commerce 350 S Bixel St www.lachamber.org	Los Angeles	CA	90017	213-580-7500	213-580-7511
Greater Louisville Inc 600 W Main St www.greaterlouisville.com	Louisville	KY	40202	502-625-0000	502-625-0211
Greater Madison Chamber of Commerce 615 E Washington Ave www.greatermadisonchamber.com	Madison	WI	53703	608-256-8348	608-256-0333
Memphis Area Chamber of Commerce PO Box 224 www.memphischamber.com	Memphis	TN	38101	901-543-3500	901-543-3510
Mesa Chamber of Commerce 120 N Center St www.arizonaguide.com/cities/mesa/index.html	Mesa	AZ	85201	480-969-1307	480-827-0727
Greater Miami Chamber of Commerce 1601 Biscayne Blvd *TF:* 888-660-5955 www.greatermiami.com	Miami	FL	33132	305-350-7700	305-374-6902
Miami Beach Chamber of Commerce 420 Lincoln Rd Ste 2D www.sobe.com/miamibeachchamber	Miami Beach	FL	33139	305-672-1270	305-538-4336
Newport County Chamber of Commerce 45 Valley Rd www.newportchamber.com	Middletown	RI	02842	401-847-1600	401-849-5848
Metropolitan Milwaukee Assn of Commerce 756 N Milwaukee St www.mmac.org	Milwaukee	WI	53202	414-287-4100	414-271-7753
Greater Minneapolis Chamber of Commerce 81 S 9th St Suite 200 info@tc-chamber.org www.tc-chamber.org	Minneapolis	MN	55402	612-370-9132	612-370-9195
Mobile Area Chamber of Commerce 451 Government St info@mobcham.org www.mobcham.org	Mobile	AL	36602	334-433-6951	334-432-1143
Modesto Chamber of Commerce 1114 J St www.modchamber.org	Modesto	CA	95353	209-577-5757	209-577-2673
Montgomery Area Chamber of Commerce 41 Commerce St www.montgomerychamber.org	Montgomery	AL	36104	334-834-5200	334-265-4745
Naples Area Chamber of Commerce 895 5th Ave S chamber@naples-online.com www.naples-online.com	Naples	FL	34102	941-263-1858	941-435-9910
Nashville Chamber of Commerce 161 4th Ave N *TF:* 800-657-6910 musiccity@nashville.com www.nashvillechamber.com	Nashville	TN	37219	615-259-4755	615-256-3074
Greater New Haven Chamber of Commerce 900 Chapel St 10th Fl www.newhavenchamber.com	New Haven	CT	06510	203-787-6735	203-782-4329
New Orleans & River Region Chamber of Commerce 601 Poydras St Suite 1700 chamber@gnofn.org chamber.gnofn.org	New Orleans	LA	70130	504-527-6900	504-527-6950
New York City Partnership & Chamber of Commerce 1 Battery Park Plaza info@chamber.com www.nycp.org	New York	NY	10004	212-493-7500	212-344-3344
Hampton Roads Chamber of Commerce 420 Bank St info@hrccva.com www.hrccva.com	Norfolk	VA	23501	757-622-2312	757-622-5563

					Phone	Fax
Oakland Metropolitan Chamber of Commerce						
475 14th St	Oakland	CA	94612		510-874-4800	510-839-8817
www.oaklandchamber.com						
Chamber Ogden/Weber						
2393 Washington Blvd	Ogden	UT	84401		801-621-8300	801-392-7609
TF: 888-621-8306						
www.chamberogdenweber.org						
Greater Oklahoma City Chamber of Commerce						
123 Park Ave	Oklahoma City	OK	73102		405-297-8900	405-297-8916
TF: 800-616-1114						
ccadmin@soonernet.com						
www.okcchamber.com						
Olympia/Thurston County Chamber of Commerce						
PO Box 1427	Olympia	WA	98507		360-357-3362	360-357-3376
info@olympiachamber.com						
www.olympiachamber.com						
Greater Omaha Chamber of Commerce						
1301 Harney St	Omaha	NE	68102		402-346-5000	402-346-7050
gocc@accessomaha.com						
www.accessomaha.com						
Orlando Regional Chamber of Commerce						
PO Box 1234	Orlando	FL	32802		407-425-1234	407-839-5020
www.orlando.org						
Oxnard Chamber of Commerce						
400 S 'A' St	Oxnard	CA	93030		805-385-8860	805-487-1763
info@oxnardchamber.org						
www.oxnardchamber.org						
Greater Philadelphia Chamber of Commerce						
200 S Broad St Suite 700	Philadelphia	PA	19102		215-545-1234	215-790-3600
www.gpcc.com						
Greater Phoenix Chamber of Commerce						
201 N Central Ave Suite 2700	Phoenix	AZ	85073		602-254-5521	602-495-8913
www.phoenixchamber.com						
Greater Pittsburgh Chamber of Commerce						
425 6th Ave	Pittsburgh	PA	15219		412-392-4500	412-392-4520
TF: 800-843-8772						
info@pittsburghchamber.com						
www.pittsburghchamber.com						
Portland Metropolitan Chamber of Commerce						
221 NW 2nd Ave	Portland	OR	97209		503-228-9411	503-228-5126
pdxchamber.org						
Greater Providence Chamber of Commerce						
30 Exchange Terr	Providence	RI	02903		401-521-5000	401-751-2434
www.provchamber.com						
Provo/Orem Chamber of Commerce						
51 S University Ave Suite 215	Provo	UT	84601		801-379-2555	801-379-2557
www.thechamber.org						
Greater Raleigh Chamber of Commerce						
800 S Salisbury St	Raleigh	NC	27601		919-664-7000	919-664-7099
www.raleighchamber.org						
Greater Richmond Chamber of Commerce						
201 E Franklin St	Richmond	VA	23219		804-648-1234	804-780-0344
chamber@grcc.com						
www.grcc.com						
Greater Riverside Chamber of Commerce						
3685 Main St Suite 350	Riverside	CA	92501		909-683-7100	909-683-2670
www.riverside-chamber.com						
International Business Council of Rochester						
55 Saint Paul St	Rochester	NY	14604		716-454-2220	716-263-3679
www.rnychamber.com						
Sacramento Metro Chamber of Commerce						
917 7th St	Sacramento	CA	95814		916-552-6800	916-443-2672
chamber@metrochamber.org						
www.metrochamber.org						
Saint Augustine & Saint Johns County Chamber of Commerce						
1 Riberia St	Saint Augustine	FL	32084		904-829-5681	904-829-6477
chamber@aug.com						
www.staugustinechamber.com						
Regional Commerce & Growth Assn						
1 Metropolitan Sq Suite 1300	Saint Louis	MO	63102		314-231-5555	314-444-1122
TF: 800-444-7653						
rcginfo@stlrcga.org						
www.stlrcga.org						
Saint Paul Area Chamber of Commerce						
332 Minnesota St Suite N-205	Saint Paul	MN	55101		651-223-5000	651-223-5119
www.saintpaulchamber.com						
Saint Petersburg Area Chamber of Commerce						
100 2nd Ave N Suite 150	Saint Petersburg	FL	33701		727-821-4069	727-895-6326
www.stpete.com						
Salem Area Chamber of Commerce						
1110 Commercial St NE	Salem	OR	97301		503-581-1466	503-581-0972
www.salemchamber.org						
Salt Lake City Area Chamber of Commerce						
175 E 400 South Suite 600	Salt Lake City	UT	84111		801-364-3631	801-328-5098
www.slachamber.com						
Greater San Antonio Chamber of Commerce						
602 E Commerce St	San Antonio	TX	78205		210-229-2100	210-229-1600
www.sachamber.org						
San Bernardino Area Chamber of Commerce						
PO Box 658	San Bernardino	CA	92402		909-885-7515	909-384-9979
sbacc@eee.org						
www.sbachamber.org						
San Diego Regional Chamber of Commerce						
402 W Broadway Suite 1000	San Diego	CA	92101		619-232-0124	619-234-0571
info@sdchamber.org						
sdchamber.org						
San Francisco Chamber of Commerce						
465 California St Suite 900	San Francisco	CA	94104		415-392-4520	415-392-0485
www.sfchamber.com						
San Jose Silicon Valley Chamber of Commerce						
310 S 1st St	San Jose	CA	95113		408-291-5250	408-286-5019
info@sjchamber.com						
www.sjchamber.com						
Santa Ana Chamber of Commerce						
PO Box 205	Santa Ana	CA	92702		714-541-5353	714-541-2238
saccinfo@santaanacc.com						
www.santaanacc.com						
Savannah Area Chamber of Commerce						
101 E Bay St	Savannah	GA	31401		912-644-6400	912-644-6499
TF: 800-444-2427						
cvb@smvga.com						
Scottsdale Chamber of Commerce						
7343 Scottsdale Mall	Scottsdale	AZ	85251		480-945-8481	480-947-4523
TF: 800-877-1117						
www.scottsdalechamber.com						
Greater Scranton Chamber of Commerce						
222 Mulberry St	Scranton	PA	18503		570-342-7711	570-347-6262
www.scrantonchamber.com						
Greater Seattle Chamber of Commerce						
1301 5th Ave Suite 2400	Seattle	WA	98101		206-389-7200	206-389-7288
www.seattlechamber.com						
Greater Shreveport Chamber of Commerce						
400 Edwards St	Shreveport	LA	71101		318-677-2500	318-677-2541
www.shreveportchamber.org						
Sioux Falls Area Chamber of Commerce						
200 N Phillips Ave Suite 102	Sioux Falls	SD	57104		605-336-1620	605-336-6499
www.siouxfalls.org						
Spokane Area Chamber of Commerce						
PO Box 2147	Spokane	WA	99210		509-624-1393	509-747-0077
chamber@spokane.org						
www.spokane.org/chamber/						
Greater Springfield Chamber of Commerce						
3 S Old State Capitol Plaza	Springfield	IL	62701		217-525-1173	217-525-8768
www.gscc.org						
Greater Springfield Chamber of Commerce						
1441 Main St	Springfield	MA	01103		413-787-1555	413-731-8530
www.gschamber.org						
Springfield Area Chamber of Commerce						
202 S John Q Hammons Pkwy	Springfield	MO	65801		417-862-5567	417-862-1611
spfdcham@spfld-mo-chamber.com						
www.spfld-mo-chamber.com						
Greater Stockton Chamber of Commerce						
445 W Weber Ave Suite 220	Stockton	CA	95203		209-547-2770	209-466-5271
www.stocktonchamber.org						
Greater Syracuse Chamber of Commerce						
572 S Salina St	Syracuse	NY	13202		315-470-1800	315-471-8545
chamber.cny.com						
Tacoma-Pierce County Chamber of Commerce						
950 Pacific Ave Suite 300	Tacoma	WA	98402		253-627-2175	253-597-7305
www.tpchamber.org						
Tallahassee Chamber of Commerce						
100 N Duval St	Tallahassee	FL	32301		850-224-8116	850-561-3860
www.talchamber.com/						
Greater Tampa Chamber of Commerce						
401 E Jackson St Suite 2100	Tampa	FL	33602		813-228-7777	813-223-7899
TF: 800-298-2672						
www.tampachamber.com						
Tempe Chamber of Commerce						
PO Box 28500	Tempe	AZ	85285		480-967-7891	480-966-5365
info@TempeChamber.org						
www.tempechamber.org						
Toledo Area Chamber of Commerce						
300 Madison Ave Suite 200	Toledo	OH	43604		419-243-8191	419-241-8302
joinus@toledochamber.com						
www.toledochamber.com						
Greater Topeka Chamber of Commerce						
120 SE 6th St Suite 110	Topeka	KS	66603		785-234-2644	785-234-8656
topekainfo@topekachamber.org						
www.topekachamber.org						
Mercer County Chamber of Commerce						
214 W State St	Trenton	NJ	08608		609-393-4143	609-393-1032
www.mercerchamber.org						

				Phone	Fax
Tucson Metropolitan Chamber of Commerce					
465 W St Mary's Rd	Tucson	AZ	85701	520-792-2250	520-882-5704
www.tucsonchamber.org					
Metropolitan Tulsa Chamber of Commerce					
616 S Boston Ave Suite 100	Tulsa	OK	74119	918-585-1201	918-585-8016
mtcc@webzone.net					
www.tulsachamber.com					
Greater Vancouver Chamber of Commerce					
404 E 15th St Suite 11	Vancouver	WA	98663	360-694-2588	360-693-8279
www.vancouverusa.com					
Chamber of Commerce of the Palm Beaches					
401 N Flagler Dr	West Palm Beach	FL	33401	561-833-3711	561-833-5582
palmbeaches.com					
Wichita Area Chamber of Commerce					
350 W Douglas Ave	Wichita	KS	67202	316-265-7771	316-265-7502
www.wichitakansas.org					
Greater Winston-Salem Chamber of Commerce					
601 W 4th St	Winston-Salem	NC	27101	336-725-2361	336-721-2209
www.winstonsalem.com					
Worcester Area Chamber of Commerce					
33 Waldo St	Worcester	MA	01608	508-753-2924	508-754-8560
chamber.worcester.ma.us					
Yonkers Chamber of Commerce					
20 S Broadway Suite 1207	Yonkers	NY	10701	914-963-0332	914-963-0455
info@yonkerschamber.com					
www.yonkerschamber.com					

Chambers of Commerce—State

				Phone	Fax
US Chamber of Commerce					
1615 H St NW	Washington	DC	20062	202-659-6000	202-887-3437
TF: 800-638-6582					
www.uschamber.org					
Alabama Business Council					
PO Box 76	Montgomery	AL	36101	334-834-6000	334-262-7371
www.bcatoday.org					
Alaska State Chamber of Commerce					
217 2nd St Suite 201	Juneau	AK	99801	907-586-2323	907-463-5515
asccjuno@ptialaska.net					
www.alaskachamber.com/					
Arizona Chamber of Commerce					
1221 E Osborn Rd Suite 100	Phoenix	AZ	85014	602-248-9172	602-265-1262
www.azchamber.com					
Arkansas State Chamber of Commerce					
PO Box 3645	Little Rock	AR	72203	501-374-9225	501-372-2722
www.aiea.ualr.edu/dina/statcham					
California Chamber of Commerce					
PO Box 1736	Sacramento	CA	95812	916-444-6670	916-444-6685
www.calchamber.com					
Colorado Assn of Commerce & Industry					
1776 Lincoln St Suite 1200	Denver	CO	80203	303-831-7411	303-860-1439
caci@capcon.com					
Connecticut Business & Industry Assn					
350 Church St	Hartford	CT	06103	860-244-1900	860-278-8562
www.cbia.com					
Delaware State Chamber of Commerce					
PO Box 671	Wilmington	DE	19899	302-655-7221	302-654-0691
dscc@inet.net					
www.dscc.com					
District of Columbia Chamber of Commerce					
1301 Pennsylvania Ave NW					
Suite 309	Washington	DC	20004	202-347-7201	202-638-6764
www.dcchamber.org					
Florida Chamber of Commerce					
PO Box 11309	Tallahassee	FL	32302	850-425-1200	850-521-1219
TF: 877-521-1200					
www.flchamb.com					
Georgia Chamber of Commerce					
235 Peachtree St NE Suite 900	Atlanta	GA	30303	404-223-2264	404-223-2290
staff@gachamber.org					
www.gachamber.org					
Hawaii Chamber of Commerce					
1132 Bishop St Suite 402	Honolulu	HI	96813	808-545-4300	808-545-4369
info@cochawaii.org					
www.cochawaii.com					
Idaho Assn of Commerce & Industry					
PO Box 389	Boise	ID	83701	208-343-1849	208-338-5623
iaci@iaci.org					
www.iaci.org					
Illinois State Chamber of Commerce					
311 S Wacker Dr Suite 1500	Chicago	IL	60606	312-983-7100	312-983-7101
www.ilchamber.org					
Indiana State Chamber of Commerce					
115 W Washington St Suite					
850 S	Indianapolis	IN	46204	317-264-3110	317-264-6855
www.indianachamber.com/					
Iowa Assn of Business & Industry					
904 Walnut St Suite 100	Des Moines	IA	50309	515-280-8000	515-244-8907
TF: 800-383-4224					
www.iowaabi.org					
Kansas Chamber of Commerce & Industry					
835 SW Topeka Blvd	Topeka	KS	66612	785-357-6321	785-357-4732
kcci@kansaschamber.org					
www.kansaschamber.org					
Kentucky Chamber of Commerce					
464 Chenault Rd	Frankfort	KY	40602	502-695-4700	502-695-6824
www.kychamber.com					
Louisiana Assn of Business & Industry					
3113 Valley Creek Dr	Baton Rouge	LA	70808	225-928-5388	225-929-6054
www.labi.org					
Maine Chamber of Commerce & Business Alliance					
7 University Dr	Augusta	ME	04330	207-623-4568	207-622-7723
Maryland Chamber of Commerce					
60 West St Suite 100	Annapolis	MD	21401	410-269-0642	410-269-5247
mcc@mdchamber.org					
www.mdchamber.org					
Michigan Chamber of Commerce					
600 S Walnut St	Lansing	MI	48933	517-371-2100	517-371-7224
TF: 800-748-0266					
www.michamber.com					
Minnesota Chamber of Commerce					
30 E 7th St Suite 1700	Saint Paul	MN	55101	651-292-4650	651-292-4656
TF: 800-821-2230					
www.mnchamber.com					
Mississippi Economic Council					
PO Box 23276	Jackson	MS	39225	601-969-0022	601-353-0247
TF: 800-748-7626					
www.msmec.com					
Missouri Chamber of Commerce					
PO Box 149	Jefferson City	MO	65102	573-634-3511	573-634-8855
mchamber@computerland.net					
www.computerland.net/~mchamber/					
Montana Chamber of Commerce					
PO Box 1730	Helena	MT	59624	406-442-2405	406-442-2409
Nebraska Chamber of Commerce & Industry					
PO Box 95128	Lincoln	NE	68509	402-474-4422	402-474-5681
nechamber@sescor.com					
Nevada State Chamber of Commerce					
1 E 1st St 16th Fl	Reno	NV	89501	775-686-3030	775-686-3038
www.reno-sparkschamber.org					
New England Council Inc					
250 Boylston St	Boston	MA	02116	617-437-0304	617-437-6279
newenglandcouncil@msn.com					
www.newenglandcouncil.com					
New Hampshire Business & Industry Assn					
122 N Main St 3rd Fl	Concord	NH	03301	603-224-5388	603-224-2872
ngrbia@aol.com					
www.nhbia.org					
New Jersey State Chamber of Commerce					
216 W State St	Trenton	NJ	08608	609-989-7888	609-989-9696
www.njchamber.com					
New Mexico Assn of Commerce & Industry					
PO Box 9706	Albuquerque	NM	87119	505-842-0644	505-842-0734
aci@nm.net					
www.aci.nm.org					
New York State Business Council					
152 Washington Ave	Albany	NY	12210	518-465-7511	518-465-4389
TF: 800-358-1202					
mattison@emi.com					
www.bcnys.org					
North Carolina Citizens for Business & Industry					
PO Box 2508	Raleigh	NC	27602	919-836-1400	919-836-1425
www.nccbi.org					
North Dakota (Greater) Assn					
PO Box 2639	Bismarck	ND	58502	701-222-0929	701-222-1611
www.gnda.com					
Ohio Chamber of Commerce					
PO Box 15159	Columbus	OH	43215	614-228-4201	614-228-6403
TF: 800-622-1893					
www.ohiochamber.com					
Oklahoma State Chamber					
330 NE 10th St	Oklahoma City	OK	73104	405-235-3669	405-235-3670
info@okstatechamber.com					
www.okstatechamber.com					

	City	State	ZIP	Phone	Fax
Pennsylvania Chamber of Business & Industry					
417 Walnut St	Harrisburg	PA	17101	717-255-3252	717-255-3298
TF: 800-225-7224					
www.pachamber.org					
Puerto Rico Chamber of Commerce					
PO Box 9023789	San Juan	PR	00902	787-721-6060	787-723-1891
camarapr@coqui.net					
camarapr.coqui.net/e_h1.htm					
Rhode Island Economic Development Corp					
1 W Exchange St	Providence	RI	02903	401-222-2601	401-222-2102
riedc@riedc.com					
www.riedc.com					
South Carolina Chamber of Commerce					
1201 Main St AT & T Bldg Suite 1810	Columbia	SC	29201	803-799-4601	803-779-6043
www.sccc.org					
South Dakota Chamber of Commerce & Industry					
PO Box 190	Pierre	SD	57501	605-224-6161	605-224-7198
icasdghd@iw.net					
Tennessee Assn of Business					
611 Commerce St Suite 3030	Nashville	TN	37203	615-256-5141	615-256-6726
www.tennbiz.org					
Texas Assn of Business & Chamber of Commerce					
1209 Nueces St	Austin	TX	78701	512-477-6721	512-477-0836
www.tabcc.org					
Vermont Chamber of Commerce					
PO Box 37	Montpelier	VT	05601	802-223-3443	802-229-4581
www.vtchamber.com					
Virginia Chamber of Commerce					
9 S 5th St	Richmond	VA	23219	804-644-1607	804-783-0903
TF: 800-477-7682					
www.vachamber.com					
Association of Washington Business					
PO Box 658	Olympia	WA	98507	360-943-1600	360-943-5811
TF: 800-521-9325					
members@awb.org					
www.awb.org					
West Virginia Chamber of Commerce					
PO Box 2789	Charleston	WV	25330	304-342-1115	304-342-1130
www.wvchamber.com					
Wisconsin Manufacturers & Commerce					
PO Box 352	Madison	WI	53701	608-258-3400	608-258-3413
wmc@wmc.org					
www.wmc.org					

National Moving Companies

	City	State	ZIP	Phone	Fax
Ace World Wide Moving					
1900 E College Ave	Cudahy	WI	53110	414-764-1000	414-764-1650
TF: 800-223-6683					
www.aceworldwide.com					
Air Van Lines Inc					
1280 116th Ave NE	Bellevue	WA	98004	425-453-5560	425-453-0892
TF: 800-877-1442					
Allied International					
215 W Diehl Rd	Naperville	IL	60563	630-717-3500	630-717-3496
TF: 800-393-1909					
www.alliedintl.com					
Allied Van Lines Inc					
215 W Diehl Rd	Naperville	IL	60563	630-717-3000	630-717-3396
TF: 800-470-2851					
marketing@alliedvan.net					
www.alliedvan.net					
American Red Ball Transit Co Inc					
1335 Sadlier Circle E Dr	Indianapolis	IN	46239	317-353-8331	317-351-0650
TF: 800-733-8077					
rball@redball.com					
www.americanredball.com					
Amodio Moving & Storage Inc					
1 Hartford Sq	New Britain	CT	06052	860-223-2725	860-223-0370
TF: 800-326-6346					
www.amodio.com					
Andrews Van Lines Inc					
310 S 7th St	Norfolk	NE	68701	402-371-5440	402-371-1349
TF: 800-228-8146					
sales@andrewsvanlines.com					
www.andrewsvanlines.com					
Arnoff Moving & Storage Inc					
1282 Dutchess Tpke	Poughkeepsie	NY	12603	845-471-1504	845-452-3606
TF: 800-633-6683					
www.arnoff.com					
Arpin Paul Van Lines					
99 James T Murphy Hwy	West Warwick	RI	02893	401-828-8111	401-823-8451
TF: 800-343-3500					
Atlantic Relocation Systems Inc					
1314 Chattahoochee Ave NW	Atlanta	GA	30318	404-351-5311	404-350-6530
TF: 800-241-1140					
www.atlanticrelocation.com					
Atlas Van Lines Inc					
1212 St George Rd	Evansville	IN	47711	812-424-2222	812-421-7125
TF: 800-638-9797					
www.atlasvanlines.com					
Barrett Moving & Storage Co					
7100 Washington Ave S	Eden Prairie	MN	55344	952-944-6550	952-828-7110
TF: 800-879-1283					
service@barrettms.com					
www.barrettmoving.com					
Barrieau Moving & Storage					
301 Murphy Rd	Hartford	CT	06114	860-249-9373	860-247-0870
TF: 800-488-9370					
barrieau@compsol.net					
Bekins Van Lines Co Inc					
330 S Mannheim Rd	Hillside	IL	60162	708-547-2000	708-547-2107
TF: 800-723-5467					
info@bekins.com					
www.bekins.com					
Bernd Moving System Inc					
660 N 18th Ave	Yakima	WA	98902	509-453-5621	509-453-5623
TF: 800-332-6683					
Bohrens United Van Lines					
3 Applegate Dr	Robbinsville	NJ	08691	609-208-1470	609-208-1471
TF: 800-326-4736					
Bolliger Inc					
88 Viaduct Rd	Stamford	CT	06907	203-324-5999	203-324-2672
TF: 800-243-9517					
www.bolliger.net					
Buehler/Mayflower Moving & Storage Co					
3899 Jackson St	Denver	CO	80205	303-388-4000	303-388-0296
TF: 800-234-6683					
Capital City/Bekins Moving & Storage					
1465 Johnson St NE	Salem	OR	97303	503-581-6683	503-581-6924
TF: 800-828-1641					
Cartwright Van Lines Inc					
11901 Cartwright Ln	Grandview	MO	64030	816-763-2700	816-763-7863
Coast to Coast Moving & Storage Co					
470 Pulaski St	Brooklyn	NY	11221	718-443-5800	718-445-6435
www.ctcvanlines.com					
Colonial North America Inc					
17 Mercer St	Hackensack	NJ	07601	201-343-5777	201-343-1934
acolna@aol.com					
www.colonialmoving.com					
Continental World Wide Movers					
PO Box 200	Farmingdale	NY	11735	631-420-9287	631-420-9287
TF: 800-253-6481					
www.hometown.aol.com/cwwmovers					
Cook Moving Systems Inc					
1845 Dale Rd	Buffalo	NY	14225	716-897-0700	716-893-0500
TF: 800-828-7144					
cookbflo@pce-net					
Corrigan Moving Systems					
23923 Research Dr	Farmington Hills	MI	48335	248-471-4000	248-471-0939
TF: 800-446-1996					
www.corriganmoving.com					
Dearborn's Moving & Storage					
29 Garfield St	Exeter	NH	03833	603-772-2666	
DeVries Moving Packing & Storage					
3808 N Sullivan Rd Spokane Industrial Pk Bldg 22	Spokane	WA	99216	509-924-6000	509-924-0041
TF: 800-333-6352					
East Side Mayflower					
PO Box 86216	Portland	OR	97286	503-777-4181	503-775-8443
TF: 800-547-4600					
info@move-northwest.com					
www.move-northwest.com					
Fogarty Van Lines					
1103 E Cumberland Ave	Tampa	FL	33602	813-228-7481	813-228-9100
TF: 800-237-7529					
www.fogartyvl.com					
Global Van Lines Inc					
810 W Taft St	Orange	CA	92865	714-921-1200	714-921-4945
TF: 800-854-3007					
moveme@globalvanlines.com					
globalvanlines.com					

National Moving Companies (Cont'd)

Company / Address	City	State	ZIP	Phone	Fax
Graebel Van Lines Inc PO Box 8002 *TF:* 800-568-0031	Wausau	WI	54402	715-848-3399	715-848-6599
Haviland-Callan/Allied Van Lines 900 Hwy 212 *TF:* 800-348-2235	Michigan City	IN	46360	219-874-3274	219-872-0776
Heil Windermere/National Van Lines 8649 Freeway Dr *TF:* 800-821-7166 heilwin@aol.com	Macedonia	OH	44056	330-467-1111	330-468-3029
Hilford Moving & Storage 1595 S Arundell Ave *TF:* 800-739-6683 www.hilford.com	Ventura	CA	93003	805-642-0221	805-654-8402
Hoffman/Allied Van Lines PO Box 325 *TF:* 800-226-2224	Ramsey	NJ	07446	201-825-7297	201-825-2442
Hollister Moving & Storage 1650 Lana Way	Hollister	CA	95023	831-637-6250	831-636-5029
I-Go/United Van & Storage 9820 S 142nd St *TF:* 800-228-9276	Omaha	NE	68138	402-891-1222	402-891-6762
Interstate Van Lines 5801 Rolling Rd *TF:* 800-336-4533 interstate@invan.com www.invan.com	Springfield	VA	22152	703-569-2121	703-569-3006
Jackson/Joyce/Allied Van Lines 31W 330 N Aurora Rd *TF:* 800-323-7800	Naperville	IL	60563	630-820-1191	630-820-0803
Johnson Storage & Moving Co 221 Broadway *TF:* 800-289-6683 www.johnsonstorage.com	Denver	CO	80203	303-778-6683	303-698-0512
Jones Storage & Moving 803 S Wichita St *TF:* 800-475-6637	Wichita	KS	67213	316-267-6267	316-262-4425
King Relocation Services 13535 Larwin Cir *TF:* 800-854-3679 kingds1@aol.com www.amconf.org/k/king.htm	Santa Fe Springs	CA	90670	562-921-0555	562-802-3060
Larmore Moving Systems Inc PO Box 3043 *TF:* 800-527-6673 www.xonex.com	Wilmington	DE	19804	302-323-9000	302-328-3518
Leppla Moving & Storage Co 303 W Southern Ave *TF:* 800-922-6344	Mesa	AZ	85210	480-946-6230	
Mayflower Transit Inc 1 Mayflower Dr www.mayflower.com	Fenton	MO	63026	636-305-4000	636-326-1106
McCollister's Transportation Systems Inc 1800 Rt 130 N *TF:* 800-257-9595 mcburl01@earthlink.net www.mccollisters.com	Burlington	NJ	08016	609-386-0600	609-386-5608
Nassau World Wide Movers Inc 57 Central Ave *TF:* 800-327-9343	Farmingdale	NY	11735	631-420-8340	631-420-8354
National Van Lines Inc 2800 W Roosevelt Rd *TF:* 800-323-1962 nvl@nationalvanlines.com www.nationalvanlines.com	Broadview	IL	60155	708-450-2900	708-450-0069
North American Van Lines Inc PO Box 988 www.northamerican-vanlines.com	Fort Wayne	IN	46801	219-429-2511	219-429-2374
North Shore Movers 600 Waukegan Rd *TF:* 800-244-6560	Northbrook	IL	60062	847-498-6560	847-498-6935
Palmer Moving & Storage Co 24660 Dequindre Rd *TF:* 800-521-3954 palmer@palmermoving.com www.palmermoving.com	Warren	MI	48091	810-834-3400	810-834-3414
Pan American Van Lines Inc 12231 Florence Ave *TF:* 800-537-2630	Santa Fe Springs	CA	90670	562-941-0044	562-941-3805
Paxton Van Lines Inc 5300 Port Royal Rd *TF:* 800-336-4536 cortiz@paxton.com www.paxton.com	Springfield	VA	22151	703-321-7600	703-321-7729
Pickens-Kane Moving Co 410 N Milwaukee Ave *TF:* 800-853-6462	Chicago	IL	60610	312-942-0330	312-942-0319
Scobey Moving Services 9625 N Broadway St *TF:* 800-403-9764 scobeymove@aol.com	San Antonio	TX	78217	210-828-8393	210-828-4873
Skaleski Moving & Storage Inc 2475 S Broadway	Green Bay	WI	54304	920-431-6666	920-431-6672
Starving Students Moving & Storage Co 1850 Sawtelle Blvd *TF:* 800-441-6683 ssmovers.com	Los Angeles	CA	90025	310-854-4464	310-289-1145
Sterling Corp 27 Sterling Rd *TF:* 800-257-0044	North Billerica	MA	01862	978-667-9666	978-671-0044
Stevens Worldwide Van Lines 527 Morley Dr *TF:* 800-678-3836 stevens@stevensworldwide.com www.stevensworldwide.com	Saginaw	MI	48601	517-755-3000	517-755-0570
Truckin Movers 1031 Harvest St *TF:* 800-334-1651	Durham	NC	27704	919-682-2300	919-688-2264
Two Guys Relocation Systems Inc 3571 Pacific Hwy	San Diego	CA	92101	619-296-7995	619-296-7704
UniGroup Worldwide 1 Worldwide Dr *TF:* 800-282-0636 ugiint1@inlink.com www.unigroupworldwide.com	Fenton	MO	63026	636-305-6025	636-305-6097
United Van Lines Inc 1 United Dr united@inlink.com www.unitedvanlines.com	Fenton	MO	63026	636-326-3100	636-326-1106
Walds Moving & Storage Services Inc 5205 S Rice Ave *TF:* 800-527-1408	Houston	TX	77081	713-512-4800	713-512-4881
Wheaton Van Lines Inc PO Box 50800 *TF:* 800-932-7799 info@wheatonworldwide.com www.wheatonworldwide.com	Indianapolis	IN	46250	317-849-7900	317-849-3718

State Realtors Associations

Association / Address	City	State	ZIP	Phone	Fax
Alabama Assn of Realtors PO Box 4070 *TF:* 800-446-3808 www.alabamarealtors.com	Montgomery	AL	36103	334-262-3808	334-263-9650
Alaska Assn of Realtors 741 Sesame St Suite 100 info@alaskarealtors.com www.alaskarealtors.com	Anchorage	AK	99503	907-563-7133	907-561-1779
Arizona Assn of Realtors 255 E Osborne Rd Suite 200 *TF:* 800-426-7274 www.aaronline.com	Phoenix	AZ	85012	602-248-7787	602-351-2474
Arkansas Realtors Assn 204 Executive Ct Suite 300 *TF:* 888-333-2206 ara@cei.net www.arkansasrealtors.com	Little Rock	AR	72205	501-225-2020	501-225-7131
California Assn of Realtors 525 S Virgil Ave www.car.org	Los Angeles	CA	90020	213-739-8200	213-480-7724
Colorado Assn of Realtors 309 Inverness Way S *TF:* 800-944-6550 administration@colorealtor.org www.colorealtor.org	Englewood	CO	80112	303-790-7099	303-790-7299

Association / Address	City	State	Zip	Phone	Fax
Connecticut Assn of Realtors 111 Founders Plaza 11th Fl *TF:* 800-335-4862 www.ctrealtor.com	East Hartford	CT	06108	860-290-6601	860-290-6615
Delaware Assn of Realtors 9 E Loockerman St Suite 315 *TF:* 800-305-4445 dar@dca.net www.delawarerealtor.com	Dover	DE	19901	302-734-4444	302-734-1341
Greater Capital Area Assn of Realtors 1818 'N' St Suite T50 gcaarstaff@gcaar.com www.gcaar.com	Washington	DC	20036	202-789-8889	202-789-4141
Florida Assn of Realtors PO Box 725025 far@fl.realtorusa.com fl.realtorplace.com	Orlando	FL	32872	407-438-1400	407-438-1411
Georgia Assn of Realtors 3200 Presidential Dr info@garealtor.com www.garealtor.com	Atlanta	GA	30340	770-451-1831	770-458-6992
Hawaii Assn of Realtors 1136 12th Ave Suite 220 www.hawaiirealtors.com	Honolulu	HI	96816	808-737-4000	808-737-4977
Idaho Assn of Realtors 1450 W Bannock St iar@idahorealtors.com www.idahorealtors.com	Boise	ID	83702	208-342-3585	208-336-7958
Illinois Assn of Realtors 3780 Adloff Ln Suite 400 iaraccess@iar.org www.illinoisrealtor.org	Springfield	IL	62703	217-529-2600	217-529-3904
Indiana Assn of Realtors PO Box 50736 www.indianarealtors.com	Indianapolis	IN	46250	317-842-0890	317-842-1076
Iowa Assn of Realtors 1370 NW 114th St Suite 100 *TF:* 800-532-1515 www.iowarealtors.com	Clive	IA	50325	515-244-2294	515-453-1070
Kansas Assn of Realtors 3644 SW Burlingame Rd *TF:* 800-366-0069 kar@midusa.net www.kansasrealtors.com	Topeka	KS	66611	785-267-3610	785-267-1867
Kentucky Assn of Realtors 161 Prosperous Pl kar@kar.com www.kar.com	Lexington	KY	40509	859-263-7377	859-263-7565
Louisiana Realtors Assn PO Box 14780 larealtors.org	Baton Rouge	LA	70898	225-923-2210	225-926-5922
Maine Assn of Realtors 19 Community Dr mar@mint.net www.mainerealtors.com	Augusta	ME	04330	207-622-7501	207-623-3590
Maryland Assn of Realtors 2594 Riva Rd *TF:* 800-638-6425 info@mdrealtor.org www.mdrealtor.org	Annapolis	MD	21401	410-841-6080	301-261-8369
Massachusetts Assn of Realtors 256 2nd Ave info@marealtors.com ma.living.net	Waltham	MA	02451	781-890-3700	781-890-4919
Michigan Assn of Realtors PO Box 40725 *TF:* 800-454-7842 mar@mirealtors.com www.mirealtors.com	Lansing	MI	48901	517-372-8890	517-334-5568
Minnesota Assn of Realtors 5750 Lincoln Dr *TF:* 800-862-6097 info@mnrealtor.com www.mnrealtor.com	Edina	MN	55436	952-935-8313	952-935-3815
Mississippi Assn of Realtors PO Box 5809 mar@stellar3.com ms.living.net	Brandon	MS	39047	601-932-9325	601-932-0382
Missouri Assn of Realtors 2601 Bernadette Pl *TF:* 800-403-0101 mo.realtorplace.com	Columbia	MO	65205	573-445-8400	573-445-7865
Montana Assn of Realtors 208 N Montana Ave Suite 105 *TF:* 800-477-1864 mtmar@mtmar.com www.mtmar.com	Helena	MT	59601	406-443-4032	406-443-4220
Nebraska Realtors Assn 145 S 56th St Suite 100 *TF:* 800-777-5231 info@nebraskarealtors.com www.nebraskarealtors.com	Lincoln	NE	68510	402-488-4304	402-488-4674
Nevada Assn of Realtors PO Box 7338 *TF:* 800-748-5526 info@nvar.org www.nvar.org	Reno	NV	89510	775-829-5911	775-829-5915
New Hampshire Assn of Realtors PO Box 550 www.nhar.com	Concord	NH	03302	603-225-5549	603-228-0385
New Jersey Assn of Realtors 295 Pierson Ave www.njar.com	Edison	NJ	08818	732-494-5616	732-494-4723
New Mexico Realtors Assn PO Box 4190 *TF:* 800-224-2282 www.nmrealtor.com	Santa Fe	NM	87502	505-982-2442	505-983-8809
New York State Assn of Realtors 130 Washington Ave *TF:* 800-422-2501 admin@nysar.com www.nysar.com	Albany	NY	12210	518-463-0300	518-462-5474
North Carolina Assn of Realtors 2901 Seawell Rd *TF:* 800-443-9956 ncar@ncrealtors.org www.realtor.org	Greensboro	NC	27407	336-294-1415	336-299-7872
North Dakota Assn of Realtors 1120 College Dr Suite 112 *TF:* 800-279-2361 realtors@btigate.com nd.living.net	Bismarck	ND	58501	701-258-2361	701-258-7211
Ohio Assn of Realtors 200 East Town St www.ohiorealtors.com	Columbus	OH	43215	614-228-6675	614-228-2601
Oklahoma Assn of Realtors 9807 N Broadway oar@oklahomarealtors.com www.oklahomarealtors.com	Oklahoma City	OK	73114	405-848-9944	405-848-9947
Oregon Assn of Realtors PO Box 351 *TF:* 800-252-9115 oar@oregonrealtors.org or.realtorplace.com	Salem	OR	97308	503-362-3645	503-362-9615
Pennsylvania Assn of Realtors 4501 Chambers Hill Rd www.parealtor.org	Harrisburg	PA	17111	717-561-1303	717-561-8796
Rhode Island Assn of Realtors 100 Bignall St www.riliving.com	Warwick	RI	02888	401-785-3650	401-941-5360
South Carolina Assn of Realtors PO Box 21827 *TF:* 800-233-6381 www.screaltors.com	Columbia	SC	29221	803-772-5206	803-798-6650
South Dakota Assn of Realtors 120 N Euclid Ave info@dakota2k.com www.sdrealtor.org	Pierre	SD	57501	605-224-0554	605-224-8975
Tennessee Assn of Realtors PO Box 121149 www.tarnet.com	Nashville	TN	37212	615-321-0515	615-320-0452
Texas Assn of Realtors PO Box 2246 *TF:* 800-873-9155 info@tar.org www.tar.org	Austin	TX	78768	512-480-8200	512-370-2390
Utah Assn of Realtors 5710 S Green St *TF:* 800-594-8933 www.utahrealtors.com	Murray	UT	84123	801-268-4747	801-268-4778
Vermont Assn of Realtors 148 State St www.vtrealtor.com	Montpelier	VT	05602	802-229-0513	802-229-0995
Virginia Assn of Realtors 10231 Telegraph Rd *TF:* 800-755-8291 members@varealtor.com www.varealtor.com	Glen Allen	VA	23059	804-264-5033	804-262-0497
Washington Assn of Realtors PO Box 719 *TF:* 800-562-6024 www.warealtor.com	Olympia	WA	98507	360-943-3100	360-357-6627
West Virginia Assn of Realtors 2110 Kanawha Blvd E wvar@wvrealtors.com www.wvrealtors.com	Charleston	WV	25311	304-342-7600	304-343-5811

				Phone	*Fax*
Wisconsin Realtors Assn					
4801 Forest Run Rd Suite 201	Madison	WI	53704	608-241-2047	608-241-2901
TF: 800-279-1972					
wra@wra.org					
www.wra.org					

				Phone	*Fax*
Wyoming Assn of Realtors					
PO Box 2312	Casper	WY	82602	307-237-4085	307-237-7929
TF: 800-676-4085					
war@trib.com					
wy.living.net					

Akron, Ohio

***County:* Summit**

AKRON is located along the Cuyahoga River in northeastern Ohio. Cities located within 125 miles of Akron include Cleveland and Columbus, Ohio; and Pittsburgh, Pennsylvania.

Area (Land)	62.2 sq mi
Area (Water)	0.4 sq mi
Elevation	1,027 ft
Latitude	41-08-14 N
Longitude	81-51-92 W
Time Zone	EST
Area Code	330

Climate

Akron's climate has cold, snowy winters and mild summers. Winter high temperatures average only in the mid-30s and average lows range from the mid-teens to the low 20s. Snowfall totals in Akron average 48 inches a year, more than double the national average. Summer days are warm, with average high temperatures near 80 degrees, while evenings cool down to around 60 degrees. July is the wettest month in Akron; January is the driest.

Average Temperatures & Precipitation

Temperatures

	Jan	Feb	Mar	Apr	May	Jun	Jul	Aug	Sep	Oct	Nov	Dec
High	33	36	47	59	70	79	82	80	74	62	50	38
Low	17	19	29	38	48	57	62	60	54	43	34	24

Precipitation

	Jan	Feb	Mar	Apr	May	Jun	Jul	Aug	Sep	Oct	Nov	Dec
Inches	2.1	2.2	3.3	3.2	3.7	3.2	4.1	3.3	3.3	2.4	3.0	3.0

History

Founded in 1825, Akron is a city that owes its growth and prosperity to manufacturing. Many settlers began moving into the area after the Ohio Canal opened in 1927, drawing a number of manufacturers to the city. At the time, the primary products were farm machinery and various clay products. Rubber, the product that Akron is best known for, was introduced to the city in 1870 with the opening of Doctor Benjamin Franklin Goodrich's rubber factory. The invention of the automobile some 30 years later greatly increased the demand for rubber, and Akron's reputation grew as the "Rubber Capital of the World." In the early 1900s, the city also became the primary center for airship and dirigible construction in the world. The U.S. Navy's dirigible that bears the city's name was constructed there. The rubber industry has attracted many newcomers to the Akron area from the early part of the 20th Century to the present. Today, Akron is a major center for polymer research and development and remains the home of the top U.S. rubber companies.

The Tri-County area surrounding Akron, which includes Summit, Medina, and Portage counties, is now home to more than three-quarters of a million people, over 200,000 of whom live in the city of Akron.

Population

1990 Census	223,019
1998 Estimate	215,712
% Change	-3.3
2005 Projection	542,000*

Racial/Ethnic Breakdown

White	73.8%
Black	24.5%
Other	1.7%
Hispanic Origin (may be of any race)	0.7%

Age Breakdown

Under 5 years	7.6%
5 to 17	16.9%
18 to 20	5.4%
21 to 24	6.9%
25 to 34	17.4%
35 to 44	13.9%
45 to 54	8.5%
55 to 64	8.6%
65 to 74	8.6%
75+ years	6.2%
Median Age	32.5

Gender Breakdown

Male	47.2%
Female	52.8%

* *Information given is for Summit County.*

Government

Type of Government: Mayor-Council

Akron City Council
166 S High St 3rd Fl
Akron, OH 44308
Phone: 330-375-2256
Fax: 330-375-2298

Akron City Hall
166 S High St
Akron, OH 44308
Phone: 330-375-2121
Fax: 330-375-2524

Akron Finance Dept
166 S High St Rm 205
Akron, OH 44308
Phone: 330-375-2316
Fax: 330-375-2291

Akron Fire Div
146 S High St 10th Fl
Akron, OH 44308
Phone: 330-375-2410
Fax: 330-375-2146

Akron Health Dept
177 S Broadway
Akron, OH 44308
Phone: 330-375-2960
Fax: 330-375-2154

Akron Income Tax Div
1 Cascade Plaza 11th Fl
Akron, OH 44308
Phone: 330-375-2290
Fax: 330-375-2112

Akron Law Dept
161 S High St Suite 202
Akron, OH 44308
Phone: 330-375-2030
Fax: 330-375-2041

Akron Mayor
166 S High St Suite 200
Akron, OH 44308
Phone: 330-375-2345
Fax: 330-375-2468

Akron Personnel Dept
146 S High St Suite 130
Akron, OH 44308
Phone: 330-375-2720
Fax: 330-375-2239

Akron Planning & Urban Development Dept
166 S High St
Akron, OH 44308
Phone: 330-375-2770
Fax: 330-375-2387

Akron Police Div
217 S High St
Akron, OH 44308
Phone: 330-375-2244
Fax: 330-375-2127

Akron Public Utilities Bureau
146 S High St Suite 900
Akron, OH 44308
Phone: 330-375-2627
Fax: 330-375-2072

Akron Public Works Bureau
1436 Triplett Blvd
Akron, OH 44306
Phone: 330-375-2834
Fax: 330-375-2822

Akron Recreation Bureau
220 S Balch St
Akron, OH 44302
Phone: 330-375-2804
Fax: 330-375-2818

Akron-Summit County Public Library
55 S Main St
Akron, OH 44326
Phone: 330-643-9000
Fax: 330-643-9033

Important Phone Numbers

AAA....330-762-0631
Akron Area Board of Realtors....330-434-6677
Akron Info Line....330-376-6660
American Express Travel....330-836-9577
Crime Victim Assistance....330-376-0040
Driver's License/Vehicle Registration Information....330-867-1101
Emergency....911
Medical Referral....330-384-2462
Ohio Dept of Taxation....513-852-3300
Poison Control Center....330-379-8562
Summit County Auditor....330-643-2625
Time/Temp....330-673-9811
Voter Registration Information....330-762-5200
Weather....330-869-8686

Information Sources

Akron Regional Development Board
1 Cascade Plaza Suite 800
Akron, OH 44308
www.ardb.org
Phone: 330-376-5550
Fax: 330-379-3164
TF: 800-621-8001

Akron/Summit County Convention & Visitors Bureau
77 E Mill St
Akron, OH 44308
www.visitakron-summit.org
Phone: 330-374-7560
Fax: 330-374-7626
TF: 800-245-4254

Better Business Bureau Serving the Akron Area
222 W Market St
Akron, OH 44303
www.akronbbb.org
Phone: 330-253-4590
Fax: 330-253-6249

John S Knight Convention Center
77 E Mill St
Akron, OH 44308
Phone: 330-374-8900
Fax: 330-374-7626
TF: 800-245-4254

Summit County
175 S Main St
Akron, OH 44308
www.co.summit.oh.us
Phone: 330-643-2500
Fax: 330-643-2507

Online Resources

Akron Community Online Resource Network
www.acorn.net

Akron Index
www.akr.net

Area Guide Akron
akron.areaguides.net

Excite.com Akron City Guide
www.excite.com/travel/countries/united_states/ohio/akron

Lodging.com Akron Ohio
www.lodging.com/auto/guides/akron-oh.html

Online City Guide to Akron
www.olcg.com/oh/akron/main.html

Area Communities

Communities in Summit and Portage counties (Medina County communities are listed in the profile on Cleveland) with populations greater than 15,000 include:

Barberton
576 W Park Ave
Barberton, OH 44203
Phone: 330-753-6611
Fax: 330-848-6663

Cuyahoga Falls
2310 2nd St
Cuyahoga Falls, OH 44221
Phone: 330-971-8000
Fax: 330-971-8168

Franklin Township
5611 Manchester Rd
Akron, OH 44319
Phone: 330-882-4324
Fax: 330-882-7052

Green
PO Box 278
Green, OH 44232
Phone: 330-896-6602
Fax: 330-896-6612

Hudson
27 E Main St
Hudson, OH 44236
Phone: 330-650-1799
Fax: 330-656-1585

Kent
319 S Water St
Kent, OH 44240
Phone: 330-678-8100
Fax: 330-678-8033

Stow
3760 Darrow Rd
Stow, OH 44224
Phone: 330-688-8206
Fax: 330-688-8532

Tallmadge
181 Strecker Dr
Tallmadge, OH 44278
Phone: 330-633-0145
Fax: 330-633-1359

Twinsburg
10075 Ravenna Rd
Twinsburg, OH 44087
Phone: 330-425-7161
Fax: 330-963-6251

Economy

The Akron area is home to several Fortune 500 companies, including the BF Goodrich Company, the Goodyear Tire and Rubber Company, GenCorp, and A. Schulman. The area is a leader in the rubber and plastics industries and also in the field of polymer research and development. Total job growth in the Akron metropolitan area has increased during the past 30 years. Akron's workforce includes some of the nation's most qualified workers in high technology, production, and technical occupations.

Unemployment Rate 5.9%
Per Capita Income $27,940*
Median Family Income $27,543

** Information given is for Summit County.*

Principal Industries & Number of Wage Earners

Summit County - 1998

Industry	Wage Earners
Agriculture	1,720
Construction	10,977
Finance, Insurance, & Real Estate	11,994
Government	27,671
Manufacturing	65,500
Mining	255
Services	72,839
Trade	67,887
Transportation & Public Utilities	13,448

Major Employers

Acme Stores
PO Box 1910
Akron, OH 44309
www.ohio.com/acme/
Phone: 330-733-2861
Fax: 330-733-8782

Akron City Hall
166 S High St
Akron, OH 44308
www.ci.akron.oh.us
Phone: 330-375-2121
Fax: 330-375-2524

Akron General Medical Center
400 Wabash Ave
Akron, OH 44307
www.agmc.org
Phone: 330-384-6000
Fax: 330-996-2300
TF: 800-221-4601

Akron Public Schools
70 N Broadway
Akron, OH 44308
E-mail: kingraha@akron.k12.oh.us
www.akronschools.com
Phone: 330-761-1661
Fax: 330-761-3225

Children's Hospital Medical Center of Akron
1 Perkins Sq
Akron, OH 44308
www.akronchildrens.org
Phone: 330-543-1000
Fax: 330-543-3008

DaimlerChrysler Corp Twinsburg Stamping Plant
2000 E Aurora Rd
Twinsburg, OH 44087
Phone: 330-425-1777
Fax: 330-487-2622

FirstEnergy Corp
76 S Main St
Akron, OH 44308
www.firstenergycorp.com
Phone: 330-384-5100
Fax: 330-384-3866
TF: 800-633-4766

FirstMerit Corp
106 S Main St
Akron, OH 44308
www.firstmerit.com
Phone: 330-384-8000
Fax: 330-384-7008

Goodyear Tire & Rubber Co
1144 E Market St
Akron, OH 44316
E-mail: consumer_relations@goodyear.com
www.goodyear.com
Phone: 330-796-2121
Fax: 330-796-3753
TF: 800-321-2136

Kent State University
500 E Main St
Kent, OH 44242
www.kent.edu
Phone: 330-672-2121
Fax: 330-672-2499

Roadway Express Inc
PO Box 471
Akron, OH 44309
E-mail: rexmail@roadway.com
www.roadway.com
Phone: 330-384-1717
Fax: 330-258-6087
TF: 800-762-3929

Saint Thomas Hospital
444 N Main St
Akron, OH 44310
Phone: 330-375-3000
Fax: 330-375-3445

Sterling Inc
375 Ghent Rd
Akron, OH 44333
Phone: 330-668-5000
Fax: 330-668-5184

Summit County
175 S Main St
Akron, OH 44308
www.co.summit.oh.us
Phone: 330-643-2500
Fax: 330-643-2507

University of Akron
302 Buchtel Common
Akron, OH 44325
www.uakron.edu
Phone: 330-972-7111
Fax: 330-972-7022
TF: 800-655-4884

Quality of Living Indicators

Total Crime Index 10,907
(rates per 100,000 inhabitants)

Violent Crime
Murder/manslaughter 6
Forcible rape 112
Robbery 400
Aggravated assault 260

Property Crime
Burglary 2,329
Larceny theft 7,031
Motor vehicle theft 769

Cost of Living Index 96.7
(national average = 100)

Median Home Price $104,900

Education

Public Schools

Akron Public Schools
70 N Broadway
Akron, OH 44308
E-mail: kingraha@akron.k12.oh.us
www.akronschools.com
Phone: 330-761-1661
Fax: 330-761-3225

Number of Schools
Elementary 41
Middle 9
High 8

Student/Teacher Ratio
All Grades 18.3:1

Private Schools

Number of Schools (all grades) .... 25+

Colleges & Universities

Kent State University
500 E Main St
Kent, OH 44242
www.kent.edu
Phone: 330-672-2121
Fax: 330-672-2499

Southern Ohio College Northeast Campus
2791 Mogadore Rd
Akron, OH 44312
www.socaec.com
Phone: 330-733-8766
Fax: 330-733-5853

University of Akron
302 Buchtel Common
Akron, OH 44325
www.uakron.edu
Phone: 330-972-7111
Fax: 330-972-7022
TF: 800-655-4884

Hospitals

Akron City Hospital
525 E Market St
Akron, OH 44309
Phone: 330-375-3000
Fax: 330-375-3050

Akron General Medical Center
400 Wabash Ave
Akron, OH 44307
www.agmc.org
Phone: 330-384-6000
Fax: 330-996-2300
TF: 800-221-4601

Barberton Citizens Hospital
155 5th St NE
Barberton, OH 44203
www.barbhosp.com
Phone: 330-745-1611
Fax: 330-848-7824

Children's Hospital Medical Center of Akron
1 Perkins Sq
Akron, OH 44308
www.akronchildrens.org
Phone: 330-543-1000
Fax: 330-543-3008

Cuyahoga Falls General Hospital
1900 23rd St
Cuyahoga Falls, OH 44223
www.cfgh.org
Phone: 330-971-7000
Fax: 330-971-7155

Medina General Hospital
1000 E Washington St
Medina, OH 44256
Phone: 330-725-1000
Fax: 330-722-5812

Robinson Memorial Hospital
6847 N Chestnut St
Ravenna, OH 44266
Phone: 330-297-0811
Fax: 330-297-8671

Saint Thomas Hospital
444 N Main St
Akron, OH 44310
Phone: 330-375-3000
Fax: 330-375-3445

Transportation

Airport(s)

Akron-Canton Regional Airport (CAK)
13 miles S of downtown Akron
(approx 20 minutes) 330-896-2385

Mass Transit

Metro Regional Transit Authority
$1 Base fare 330-762-0341

Rail/Bus

Greyhound/Trailways Bus Station
781 Grant St
Akron, OH 44311
Phone: 330-434-5171

Utilities

Electricity
Ohio Edison 330-384-5100
www.firstenergycorp.com

Gas
East Ohio Gas Co 330-794-0790
www.cng.com/eog/

Water
Akron Public Utilities Dept 330-375-2554

Garbage Collection/Recycling
Akron Public Utilities Dept 330-375-2554
Akron Recycle Dept 330-375-2129

Telecommunications

Telephone
Ameritech 800-660-1000
www.ameritech.com

Cable Television
Time Warner Cable 330-633-9203
www.twcneo.com

Internet Service Providers (ISPs)
Gateway to Internet Services 330-656-5511
www.gwis.com

Banks

Bank One Akron NA
50 S Main St
Akron, OH 44308
Phone: 330-972-1984
Fax: 330-972-1122
TF: 800-999-5585

Charter One Bank FSB
333 S Broadway
Akron, OH 44308
Phone: 330-762-8491
Fax: 330-762-8732

Fifth Third Bank
3750 W Market St Suite Q
Akron, OH 44333
Phone: 330-665-4710
Fax: 330-665-1566
TF: 800-589-5355

Firstar Bank
156 S Main St
Akron, OH 44308
Phone: 330-535-2240
Fax: 330-535-2470

FirstMerit Bank NA
106 S Main St
Akron, OH 44308
Phone: 330-384-8000
Fax: 330-253-4476

KeyBank NA Akron District
157 S Main St
Akron, OH 44308
Phone: 330-379-1446

National City Bank Northeast
1 Cascade Plaza
Akron, OH 44308
Phone: 330-375-8714
Fax: 330-375-8108

North Akron Savings Bank
158 E Cuyahoga Falls Ave
Akron, OH 44310
E-mail: nasbhq@aol.com
www.banknasb.com
Phone: 330-434-9137
Fax: 330-434-4726

Ohio Savings Bank
1835 Brittain Rd
Akron, OH 44310
Phone: 330-630-9666
Fax: 330-630-0161

Second National Bank of Warren
76 S Main St
Akron, OH 44308
Phone: 330-376-1444
Fax: 330-376-1286

Shopping

Aurora Premium Outlets
549 S Chillicothe Rd
Aurora, OH 44202
www.premiumoutlets.com/location/aurora/auro.html
Phone: 330-562-2000
TF: 800-837-2001

Chapel Hill Mall
2000 Brittain Rd
Akron, OH 44310
Phone: 330-633-7100
Fax: 330-633-1503

Fairlawn Town Centre
2855 W Market St
Akron, OH 44333
Phone: 330-836-9174
Fax: 330-836-5139

Orangerie Mall at Akron Centre
76 S Main St
Akron, OH 44308
Phone: 330-384-9306
Fax: 330-384-9134

Plaza at Chapel Hill
Howe & Main Sts
Akron, OH 44307
Phone: 216-464-5550

Quaker Square
135 S Broadway
Akron, OH 44308
Phone: 330-253-5970
Fax: 330-253-2574

Quaker Square Mall
120 E Mill St
Akron, OH 44308
Phone: 330-253-5970

Rolling Acres Mall
2400 Romig Rd
Akron, OH 44322
Phone: 330-753-5045
Fax: 330-753-7625

Silver Valley Plaza
299 N Main St
Monroe Falls, OH 44262
Phone: 330-867-4836

Summit Mall
3265 W Market St
Akron, OH 44333
Phone: 330-867-1555
Fax: 330-867-5852

West Point Market
1711 W Market St
Akron, OH 44313
www.westpoint-market.com
Phone: 330-864-2151
Fax: 330-869-8666
TF: 800-838-2156

Media

Newspapers and Magazines

Akron Beacon Journal*
44 E Exchange St
Akron, OH 44328
www.ohio.com/bj
Phone: 330-996-3000
Fax: 330-376-9235
TF: 800-777-2442

Cuyahoga Falls News-Press
PO Box 1549
Stow, OH 44224
Phone: 330-688-0088
Fax: 330-688-1588
TF: 800-966-6565

Gateway Press
1675 SR 303
Streetsboro, OH 44241
E-mail: add119~ald.net.
Phone: 330-626-5558
Fax: 330-626-5550

**Indicates major daily newspapers*

Television

WEAO-TV Ch 45 (PBS)
1750 Campus Center Dr
Kent, OH 44240
E-mail: programs@wneo.pbs.org
www.ch4549.org
Phone: 330-677-4549
Fax: 330-672-7995

WEWS-TV Ch 5 (ABC)
3001 Euclid Ave
Cleveland, OH 44115
E-mail: news@newsnet5.com
www.newsnet5.com
Phone: 216-431-5555
Fax: 216-431-3666

WJW-TV Ch 8 (Fox)
5800 S Marginal Rd
Cleveland, OH 44103
E-mail: wjwfox8@en.com
Phone: 216-431-8888
Fax: 216-432-4239

WKYC-TV Ch 3 (NBC)
1403 E 6th St
Cleveland, OH 44114
E-mail: wkyc@aol.com
Phone: 216-344-3333
Fax: 216-344-3326

WOIO-TV Ch 19 (CBS)
1717 E 12th St
Cleveland, OH 44114
www.woio.com
Phone: 216-771-1943
Fax: 216-436-5460

WUAB-TV Ch 43 (UPN)
1717 E 12th St
Cleveland, OH 44114
Phone: 216-771-1943
Fax: 216-515-7152
TF: 800-929-0132

WVPX-TV Ch 23 (PAX)
26650 Renaissance Pkwy Suite E-4
Cleveland, OH 44128
www.pax.net/WVPX
Phone: 216-831-2367
Fax: 216-831-2676

Radio

WAKR-AM 1590 kHz (Sports)
9 W Market St
Akron, OH 44313
E-mail: wakrradio@aol.com
www.wakr.net
Phone: 800-543-1495
Fax: 330-864-6799

WAPS-FM 91.3 MHz (Jazz/Alt)
65 Steiner Ave
Akron, OH 44301
www.wapsfm.com
Phone: 330-761-3098
Fax: 330-761-3240

WCUE-AM 1150 kHz (Rel)
4075 Bellaire Ln
Peninsula, OH 44264
Phone: 330-920-1150
TF: 800-543-1495

WHLO-AM 640 kHz (Rel)
4 Summit Park Dr Suite 150
Independence, OH 44131
Phone: 216-901-0921

WKDD-FM 96.5 MHz (Urban)
1867 W Market St
Akron, OH 44313
www.wkdd.com
Phone: 330-836-4700
Fax: 330-836-5321

WKSU-FM 89.7 MHz (NPR)
1613 E Summit St
Kent, OH 44242
www.wksu.org
Phone: 330-672-3114
Fax: 330-672-4107

WNIR-FM 100.1 MHz (N/T)
PO Box 2170
Akron, OH 44309
E-mail: newstips@wnir.com
www.wnir.com
Phone: 330-673-2323
Fax: 330-673-0301

WONE-FM 97.5 MHz (Rock)
1795 W Market St
Akron, OH 44313
E-mail: woneradio@aol.com
www.wone.net
Phone: 330-869-9800
Fax: 330-864-6799

WQMX-FM 94.9 MHz (Ctry)
1795 W Market St
Akron, OH 44313
E-mail: wqmxmail@aol.com
www.wqmx.com
Phone: 330-869-9800
Fax: 330-865-7889

WTOU-AM 1350 kHz (Sports)
1867 W Market St
Akron, OH 44313
Phone: 330-836-4700
Fax: 330-836-5321

WZAK-FM 93.1 MHz (Urban)
2510 St Clair Ave
Cleveland, OH 44114
www.wzak.com
Phone: 216-621-9300
Fax: 216-566-8238

WZIP-FM 88.1 MHz (Urban)
302 E Buchtel Ave
Akron, OH 44325
www.wzip.fm
Phone: 330-972-7105
Fax: 330-972-5521

Attractions

Attractions in Akron include the Goodyear World of Rubber, which traces the discovery and growth of rubber-making and the history of the rubber industry in Akron, as well as the homes of several of Akron's most notable residents. These include Stan Hywet Hall, former home of Frank A. Seiberling, co-founder of Goodyear and Seiberling Rubber companies; and Dr. Bob's Home, which belonged to the co-founder of Alcoholics Anonymous, Dr. Bob Smith. Akron also hosts two major sporting events each year, the All-American Soap Box Derby and NEC's World Series of Golf.

Akron Art Museum
70 E Market St
Akron, OH 44308
E-mail: mail@akronartmuseum.org
www.akronartmuseum.org
Phone: 330-376-9185
Fax: 330-376-1180

Akron Civic Theatre
182 S Main St
Akron, OH 44308
www.akroncivic.com
Phone: 330-535-3179
Fax: 330-535-9828

Akron Symphony Orchestra
17 N Broadway
Akron, OH 44308
www.akronsymphony.org
Phone: 330-535-8131
Fax: 330-535-7302

Akron Zoological Park
500 Edgewood Ave
Akron, OH 44307
E-mail: azoologi@neo.lrun.com
www.akronzoo.com
Phone: 330-375-2525

Blossom Music Center
1145 W Steels Corners Rd
Cuyahoga Falls, OH 44223
www.blossommusic.com
Phone: 330-920-8040
Fax: 330-920-0968

Boston Mills/Brandywine Ski Resort
7100 Riverview Rd
Peninsula, OH 44264
E-mail: bmbuski241@aol.com
www.bmbw.com
Phone: 330-657-2334
Fax: 330-657-2660

Brown John Home
714 Diagonal Rd
Akron, OH 44320
Phone: 330-535-1120
Fax: 330-376-6868

Carousel Dinner Theatre
1275 E Waterloo Rd
Akron, OH 44306
E-mail: carouseldt@earthlink.net
www.carouseldinnertheatre.com
Phone: 330-724-9855
Fax: 330-724-2232
TF: 800-362-4100

Carriage Trade
8050 Brandywine Rd
Northfield, OH 44067
Phone: 330-467-9000
Fax: 330-468-2845

Children's Magical Theatre Co
565 W Tuscarawas Ave
Barberton, OH 44203
Phone: 330-848-3708
Fax: 330-848-5768

Cleveland Play House
8500 Euclid Ave
Cleveland, OH 44106
E-mail: cphbox@en.com
www.cleveplayhouse.org
Phone: 216-795-7000
Fax: 216-795-7005

Coach House Theatre
732 W Exchange St
Akron, OH 44302
Phone: 330-434-7741

Cuyahoga Valley National Recreation Area
15610 Vaughn Rd
Brecksville, OH 44141
www.nps.gov/cuva/
Phone: 440-526-5256

Cuyahoga Valley Scenic Railroad
1630 W Mill St
Peninsula, OH 44624
www.cvsr.com
Phone: 330-657-2000
Fax: 330-657-2080
TF: 800-468-4070

Dover Lake Water Park
1150 Highland Rd
Sagamore Hills, OH 44067
www.doverlake.com
Phone: 330-467-7946
Fax: 330-467-1422
TF: 800-372-7946

Dr Bob's Home
855 Ardmore Ave
Akron, OH 44302
www.drbobs.com
Phone: 330-864-1935
TF: 800-992-2354

Durbin Adell Arboretum
760 Darrow Rd
Stow, OH 44224
Phone: 330-688-8238
Fax: 330-688-8532

FA Seiberling Naturealm
1828 Smith Rd
Akron, OH 44313
Phone: 330-865-8065
Fax: 330-865-8070

Goodyear Community Theatre
1144 E Market St
Akron, OH 44316
Phone: 330-796-3159
Fax: 330-796-2222

Goodyear World of Rubber Museum
1144 E Market St
Akron, OH 44316
Phone: 330-796-2121
Fax: 330-796-5045

Hale Farm & Village
PO Box 296
Bath, OH 44210
www.wrhs.org/sites/hale.htm
Phone: 330-666-3711
Fax: 330-666-9497

Hower House
60 Fir Hill University of Akron
Akron, OH 44325
Phone: 330-972-6909

Hywet Stan Hall & Gardens
714 N Portage Path
Akron, OH 44303
www.stanhywet.org/
Phone: 330-836-5533
Fax: 330-836-2680

Inventure Place
221 S Broadway
Akron, OH 44308
www.invent.org
Phone: 330-762-4463
Fax: 330-762-6313
TF: 800-968-4332

Kent State University Museum
E Main & S Lincoln Sts Rockwell Hall
Kent, OH 44242
www.kent.edu/museum/
Phone: 330-672-3450
Fax: 330-672-3218

National Inventors Hall of Fame
221 S Broadway Inventure Place
Akron, OH 44308
E-mail: index@invent.org
www.invent.org
Phone: 330-762-4463
Fax: 330-762-6313

Ohio Ballet
354 E Market St
Akron, OH 44325
www.ohioballet.com/
Phone: 330-972-7900
Fax: 330-972-7902

Perkins Stone Mansion
550 Copley Rd
Akron, OH 44320
Phone: 330-535-1120
Fax: 330-376-6868

Police Museum
217 S High St
Akron, OH 44308
Phone: 330-375-2390
Fax: 330-375-2412

Portage Hills Vineyards
1420 Martin Rd
Suffield, OH 44260
E-mail: portage@portagehills.com
www.portagehills.com
Phone: 330-628-2668
Fax: 330-628-1311
TF: 800-418-6493

Portage Lake State Park
5031 Manchester Rd
Akron, OH 44319
Phone: 330-644-2220
Fax: 330-644-7550

Porthouse Theatre Co
Kent Rd Kent State University
Kent, OH 44242
E-mail: porthouse@kent.edu
www.kent.edu/theatre/porthouse/
Phone: 330-672-3884

Pro Football Hall of Fame
2121 George Halas Dr NW
Canton, OH 44708
www.profootballhof.com
Phone: 330-456-8207
Fax: 330-456-8175

Riverfront Centre
2100-2200 Front St
Cuyahoga Falls, OH 44221
Phone: 330-929-2068

Sea World of Ohio
1100 Sea World Dr
Aurora, OH 44202
www.seaworld.com/seaworld/sw_ohio/swoframe.html
Phone: 330-995-2121
Fax: 330-995-2115

Six Flags Ohio
1060 N Aurora Rd
Aurora, OH 44202
www.sixflags.com/ohio
Phone: 330-562-7131
Fax: 330-562-7020

Summit County Historical Society
550 Copley Rd
Akron, OH 44320
Phone: 330-535-1120
Fax: 330-376-6868

Thomas EJ Performing Arts Hall
198 Hill St University of Akron
Akron, OH 44325
Phone: 330-972-7570
Fax: 330-972-6571

Weathervane Community Playhouse
1301 Weathervane Ln
Akron, OH 44313
Phone: 330-836-2626
Fax: 330-873-2150

Winery at Wolf Creek
2637 S Cleveland-Massillon Rd
Norton, OH 44203
Phone: 330-666-9285
Fax: 330-665-1445

Sports Teams & Facilities

Akron Aeros (baseball)
300 S Main St Canal Pk Stadium
Akron, OH 44308
www.akronaeros.com
Phone: 330-253-5151
Fax: 330-253-3300
TF: 800-972-3767

Akron Racers (softball)
1575 Firestone Pkwy Firestone Stadium
Akron, OH 44301
E-mail: tickets@akronracers.com
www.akronracers.com
Phone: 330-376-4487
Fax: 330-376-1165

Barberton Speedway
3363 Clarks Mill Rd
Barberton, OH 44203
Phone: 330-753-8668

Canal Park Stadium
300 S Main St
Akron, OH 44308
Phone: 330-253-5151
Fax: 330-253-3300

Northfield Park
10705 Northfield Rd
Northfield, OH 44067
www.northfieldpark.com
Phone: 330-467-4101
Fax: 330-468-2628

Annual Events

Akron Arts Expo (late July) 330-375-2804
Akron Rib & Music Festival (early July) 330-995-0812
All-American Soap Box Derby (late July) 330-733-8723
Antique & Classic Car Show (mid-June) 330-836-5533
Boo at the Zoo (late October) 330-375-2550
Boston Mills Art Festival (late June-early July) 330-657-2334
Cherry Blossom Festival (mid-May) 330-745-3733
Chickenfest (early September) 330-753-8471
Christmas Craft Show (early-mid-December) 330-972-7570
Civil War Reenactment (mid-August) 330-666-3711
Crooked River Fine Arts Festival
(late July-early August) 330-971-8137
First Night Akron (December 31) 330-762-9550
Harvest Festival (early October) 330-666-3711
Holiday Lights Celebration (December) 330-375-2550
Holiday Tree Festival (late November) 330-379-8424
Home for the Holidays (December) 330-836-5533
Jazz Festival (early April & early October) 330-657-2291
Labor of Love Run (early September) 330-688-9078
Maple Sugaring Days (late February-mid-March) 330-666-3711
May Garden Mart (mid-May) 330-836-5533
Mum Festival (late September) 330-745-3141
NEC Invitational (late August) 330-644-2299
Peninsula Jazz Festival (early April) 330-657-2665
Pro Football Hall of Fame Week (early July) 330-456-8207
Shakespeare at Stan Hywet Hall (mid-July) 330-836-5533
Stitchery Showcase (mid-April) 330-836-5533
Summit County Fair (late July) 330-633-6200
Twinsburg Twins Days Festival (early August) 330-425-3652
Victorian Holiday Tour (December) 330-972-6909
Witan's Annual French Market (late February) 330-928-7179
Wonderful World of Ohio Mart (early October) 330-836-5533
Yankee Peddler Festival (mid-late September) 800-535-5634

Albuquerque, New Mexico

County: **Bernalillo**

ALBUQUERQUE is located in central New Mexico, bisected by the Rio Grande River. Major cities within 100 miles include Santa Fe, Gallup, Los Alamos, and Taos, New Mexico.

Area (Land) .... 132.2 sq mi
Area (Water)................................ 0.6 sq mi
Elevation.....................................5,311 ft
Latitude ....35-08-44 N
Longitude............................... 106-65-06 W
Time Zone .... MST
Area Code.. 505

Climate

Albuquerque has a dry climate (humidity averages 43 percent) that features four distinct seasons. Winter days are fairly mild, with average high temperatures in the high 40s to low 50s, while evening temperatures drop into the low to mid-20s. The average annual snowfall is 10 inches. Summer days are hot, with high temperatures around 90 degrees, while evenings cool down dramatically into the high 50s to low 60s. Rainfall is rare in Albuquerque—August, with an average precipitation of just over an inch and a half, is the wettest month.

Average Temperatures & Precipitation

Temperatures

	Jan	Feb	Mar	Apr	May	Jun	Jul	Aug	Sep	Oct	Nov	Dec
High	47	54	61	71	80	90	93	89	82	71	57	48
Low	22	26	32	40	49	58	64	63	55	43	31	23

Precipitation

	Jan	Feb	Mar	Apr	May	Jun	Jul	Aug	Sep	Oct	Nov	Dec
Inches	0.4	0.5	0.5	0.5	0.5	0.6	1.4	1.6	1.0	0.9	0.4	0.5

History

Although fossil evidence proves that the Albuquerque area was inhabited as early as the Ice Age, some 10,000 years ago, the first recorded settlers were the Anasazi Indians, who inhabited northwestern New Mexico from around 1100 until 1300 A.D. The first European settlers, led by Spaniard Francisco Vasquez de Coronado, explored the area in 1540 on a quest for the treasures of the Seven Cities of Cibola. Over the course of the next two years, Coronado's conquistadors used a pueblo outside the present-day city of Bernalillo as their expedition headquarters. The remains of that pueblo stand today as the Coronado National Monument. Unsuccessful in his search for gold, Coronado eventually returned to Mexico in disgrace.

At the turn of the 17th Century, conquistador Don Juan de Onate visited the area and claimed the entire region for Spain, establishing El Camino Real, the main thoroughfare between Mexico City and Taos, New Mexico. Santa Fe was declared the capital of the new colony in 1610. The new Spanish settlers coexisted with the native tribes until the Pueblo Revolt of 1680, which resulted in the death of more than 400 Spaniards. Many of the remaining settlers eventually fled to El Paso, and the Indians took control of the area until 1692, when Don Diego de Vargas reclaimed the land for Spain. Once again, Spanish settlers began establishing villages, farms, ranches, and churches in the area.

In 1706, New Mexico's provisional governor Don Francisco Cuervo y Valdez petitioned Spain for permission to establish a villa in the area. Spanish law dictated that 30 families were necessary to establish a villa—Cuervo, who only had a total of 18 families, falsely claimed that he had 35. To ensure that his petition was granted, he declared that the new settlement would be named Alburquerque (the extra "r" in the name was eventually dropped), in honor of the Duke of Alburquerque, Viceroy Francisco Fernandez de la Cueva (who happened to be responsible for preliminary approval of Cuervo's petition). The petition was granted, and the new settlement of Albuquerque was founded. (Cuervo was eventually tried for lying on his application.) Throughout the 1700s and into the 1800s, the Territory of New Mexico remained under Spanish Rule.

During the 19th Century, New Mexico was under Mexican rule for 25 years, from the time Mexico gained independence from Spain in 1821 until the Mexican-American War, when New Mexico became a United States Territory. An American military outpost was established at Albuquerque and new residents began moving to the area from other parts of the country. Albuquerque was occupied briefly by Confederate troops during the Civil War, and eight cannons remain in the plaza today as a reminder of this event. Albuquerque grew rapidly during the remainder of the 19th Century. Thousands of new residents were drawn by the city's economic opportunities, which were created primarily by the arrival of the railroad in 1880. By the mid-1880s, Albuquerque's population was predominantly Anglo for the first time in the city's history. Another factor that affected Albuquerque's growth was the city's dry climate. Many Americans who suffered from respiratory diseases were encouraged to relocate to Albuquerque, as the climate was conducive to relieving their symptoms.

In the years following World War II, the Albuquerque area began its legacy as a major high-tech research and development site with the establishment of Kirtland Air Force Base and Sandia National Laboratories. Nearby Los Alamos was also a site of the Manhatten Project, the birthplace of the world's first atomic bomb. Home to more than 419,000 people, Albuquerque today continues to grow steadily as a center for high-tech research and development that is also rich in history and cultural diversity.

Population

1990 Census 384,619
1998 Estimate..............................419,311

% Change 8.9
2005 Projection 469,300

Racial/Ethnic Breakdown
White 78.3%
Black 3.0%
Other 18.7%
Hispanic Origin (may be of any race) 34.5%

Age Breakdown
Under 5 years 7.4%
5 to 17 .... 17.6%
18 to 20 .... 4.5%
21 to 24 .... 6.3%
25 to 34 .... 18.9%
35 to 44 .... 16.2%
45 to 54 .... 9.9%
55 to 64 .... 7.9%
65 to 74 .... 6.7%
75+ years 4.4%
Median Age 32.5

Gender Breakdown
Male 48.5%
Female 51.5%

Government

Type of Government: Mayor-Council

Albuquerque City Clerk
1 Civic Plaza
Albuquerque, NM 87103
Phone: 505-768-3030
Fax: 505-768-2845

Albuquerque City Council
PO Box 1293
Albuquerque, NM 87103
Phone: 505-768-3100
Fax: 505-768-3227

Albuquerque City Hall
400 Marquette Ave 1 Civic Plaza
Albuquerque, NM 87102
Phone: 505-768-2000
Fax: 505-768-3019

Albuquerque Cultural & Recreation Services Dept
PO Box 1293
Albuquerque, NM 87103
Phone: 505-768-3566
Fax: 505-768-2846

Albuquerque Finance & Administrative Services Dept
PO Box 1293
Albuquerque, NM 87103
Phone: 505-768-3500
Fax: 505-768-3581

Albuquerque Fire Dept
724 Silver SW
Albuquerque, NM 87102
Phone: 505-764-6300
Fax: 505-764-6323

Albuquerque Human Resources Dept
1 Civic Plaza Rm 703
Albuquerque, NM 87103
Phone: 505-768-3700
Fax: 505-768-3777

Albuquerque Mayor
PO Box 1293
Albuquerque, NM 87103
Phone: 505-768-3000
Fax: 505-768-3019

Albuquerque Planning Dept
PO Box 1293
Albuquerque, NM 87103
Phone: 505-924-3860
Fax: 505-924-3339

Albuquerque Police Dept
400 Roma NW
Albuquerque, NM 87102
Phone: 505-768-2200
Fax: 505-768-2331

Albuquerque Public Works Dept
PO Box 1293
Albuquerque, NM 87103
Phone: 505-768-3627
Fax: 505-768-3629

Albuquerque Transit Dept
601 Yale Blvd SE
Albuquerque, NM 87106
Phone: 505-764-6100
Fax: 505-764-6146

Albuquerque Water Utility Div
PO Box 1313
Albuquerque, NM 87103
Phone: 505-768-2800
Fax: 505-768-2882

Rio Grande Valley Library System
501 Copper Ave NW
Albuquerque, NM 87102
Phone: 505-768-5140
Fax: 505-768-5191

Important Phone Numbers

AAA 505-291-6611
Albuquerque Board of Realtors 505-842-1433
American Express Travel 505-291-6575
Bernalillo County Assessor 505-768-4050
Bernalillo County Treasurer 505-768-4031
Dental Referral 800-917-6453
Driver's License/Vehicle Registration Information ... 888-683-4636
Emergency 911
Event Information 800-284-2282
HotelDocs 800-468-3537
New Mexico State Taxation & Revenue Dept 505-827-0948
Non-emergency Police 505-242-2677
Poison Control Center 505-272-2222
Road Conditions 800-432-4269
Time/Temp 505-247-1611
Voter Registration Information 505-768-4085
Weather 505-821-1111

Information Sources

Albuquerque Convention & Visitors Bureau
20 First Plaza Suite 601
Albuquerque, NM 87102
www.abqcvb.org
Phone: 505-842-9918
Fax: 505-247-9101
TF: 800-284-2282

Albuquerque Convention Center
PO Box 1293
Albuquerque, NM 87103
Phone: 505-768-4575
Fax: 505-768-3239

Albuquerque Economic Development Board
851 University Blvd SE Suite 203
Albuquerque, NM 87106
www.abq.org
Phone: 505-246-6200
Fax: 505-246-6219
TF: 800-451-2933

Bernalillo County
1 Civic Plaza NW 10th Fl
Albuquerque, NM 87102
www.bernco.gov
Phone: 505-768-4000
Fax: 505-768-4329

Better Business Bureau Serving New Mexico
2625 Pennsylvania NE Suite 2050
Albuquerque, NM 87110
www.bbbnm.com
Phone: 505-346-0110
Fax: 505-346-0696
TF: 800-873-2224

Greater Albuquerque Chamber of Commerce
PO Box 25100
Albuquerque, NM 87125
www.gacc.org
Phone: 505-764-3700
Fax: 505-764-3714

New Mexico Indian Tourism Assn
2401 12th St NW Rm 211
Albuquerque, NM 87104
Phone: 505-246-1668
Fax: 505-246-0344

Online Resources

4Albuquerque.com
www.4albuquerque.com

About.com Guide to Albuquerque/Santa Fe
albuquerque.about.com/local/southwestus/albuquerque

Albuquerque CityLink
usacitylink.com/albuquer/

Albuquerque New Mexico
albuquerque-new-mexico.com

Albuquerque Online
www.albq-online.com

Albuquerque Santa Fe Web
www.abq-sfe.com

AlbuquerqueNM.com
www.albuquerquenm.com

Anthill City Guide Albuquerque
www.anthill.com/city.asp?city=albuquerque

Area Guide Albuquerque
albuquerque.areaguides.net

Boulevards Albuquerque
www.albuquerque.com

City Knowledge Albuquerque
www.cityknowledge.com/nm_albuquerque.htm

Collector's Guide to Albuquerque
www.collectorsguide.com/ab/abtr.shtml

Desert USAGuide to Albuquerque
www.desertusa.com/Cities/nm/albuque.html

DigitalCity Albuquerque
home.digitalcity.com/albuquerque

Excite.com Albuquerque City Guide
www.excite.com/travel/countries/united_states/new_mexico/albuquerque

Great Locations Guidebook Albuquerque
www.nmgl.com

InAlbuquerque.com
www.inalbuquerque.com

Link Jewish Newspaper
www.swcp.com/~thelink/

Lodging.com Albuquerque New Mexico
www.lodging.com/auto/guides/albuquerque-area-nm.html

Online City Guide to Albuquerque
www.olcg.com/nm/albuquerque/main.html

Area Communities

Communities in the Albuquerque metropolitan area (Bernalillo, Sandoval, and Valencia counties) with populations greater than 5,000 include:

Belen
100 S Main St
Belen, NM 87002
Phone: 505-864-8221
Fax: 505-864-8408

Bernalillo
333 Becker Ave
Bernalillo, NM 87004
Phone: 505-867-3311
Fax: 505-867-0481

Los Lunas
660 Main St NW
Los Lunas, NM 87031
Phone: 505-865-9689
Fax: 505-865-6063

Rio Rancho
4330 Meadowlark Ln SE
Rio Rancho, NM 87124
Phone: 505-891-5000
Fax: 505-891-7274

Economy

High-technology continues to play a leading role in Albuquerque's ever-diversifying economy. Sandia National Laboratories, a major U.S. nuclear research, development, and testing facility, is the area's fifth largest employer. High-tech manufacturers that have operations in the area include Intel, Motorola, Honeywell, and Philips Semiconductors. Many of Albuquerque's residents are employed in the government sector—in addition to the government-related agencies listed below, the State of New Mexico is among the area's top 10 employers. The services sector is currently the fastest-growing in Albuquerque, with health care an integral part of this employment sector—four of the top 15 area employers are health care-related.

Unemployment Rate	4.6%*
Per Capita Income	$24,478**
Median Family Income	$42,000*

** Information given is for the Albuquerque Metropolitan Statistical Area (MSA), which includes Bernalillo, Sandoval, and Valencia counties.*
*** Information given is for Bernalillo County.*

Principal Industries & Number of Wage Earners

Albuquerque MSA* - 1998

Construction/Mining	21,100
Finance, Insurance & Real Estate	16,800
Government	64,200
Manufacturing	29,300
Retail Trade	64,400
Services & Miscellaneous	104,800
Transportation & Public Utilities	15,500
Wholesale Trade	16,400

** Information given is for the Albuquerque Metropolitan Statistical Area (MSA), which includes Bernalillo, Sandoval, and Valencia counties.*

Major Employers

Albuquerque City Hall
400 Marquette Ave 1 Civic Plaza
Albuquerque, NM 87102
www.cabq.gov
Phone: 505-768-2000
Fax: 505-768-3019

Albuquerque Public Schools Phone: 505-842-8211
725 University Blvd Fax: 505-842-3629
Albuquerque, NM 87125
www.aps.edu/aps/

Intel Corp Phone: 505-893-7000
4100 Sara Rd SE
Rio Rancho, NM 87124
www.intel.com

Kirtland Air Force Base Phone: 505-846-0011
Kirtland, NM 87117 Fax: 505-846-4275
E-mail: mooresb@knt2.kirtland.af.mil
www.kirtland.af.mil

Lovelace Medical Center Phone: 505-262-7000
5400 Gibson Blvd SE Fax: 505-262-7729
Albuquerque, NM 87108
www.lovelace.com/lhs/lmc.shtml

Presbyterian Healthcare Services Phone: 505-823-8750
5901 Harper Dr NE Fax: 505-823-8749
Albuquerque, NM 87109
www.phs.org

Saint Joseph Healthcare Phone: 505-727-8000
7850 Jefferson St
Albuquerque, NM 87109
www.sjhs.org

Sandia National Laboratories Phone: 505-844-5678
PO Box 5800 Fax: 505-844-6636
Albuquerque, NM 87185 TF: 800-417-2634
www.sandia.gov

Smith's Food & Drug Centers Inc Phone: 505-271-4000
200 Tramway Blvd SE Fax: 505-271-4014
Albuquerque, NM 87123
www.smithsfoodanddrug.com

University Hospital Phone: 505-843-2111
2211 Lomas Blvd NE Fax: 505-272-1827
Albuquerque, NM 87106
uhwww.unm.edu

University of New Mexico Phone: 505-277-0111
University Hill NE Fax: 505-277-6686
Albuquerque, NM 87131 TF: 800-225-5866
E-mail: unmlobos@unm.edu
www.unm.edu

US Postal Service Phone: 505-245-9750
1135 Broadway Blvd NE
Albuquerque, NM 87101
new.usps.com

Wal-Mart Phone: 505-856-5274
8000 Academy Rd NE Fax: 505-856-5978
Albuquerque, NM 87114
www.walmartstores.com

Quality of Living Indicators

Total Crime Index 41,034
(rates per 100,000 inhabitants)

Violent Crime
Murder/manslaughter 48
Forcible rape 220
Robbery 1,667

Property Crime
Burglary 6,809
Larceny theft 24,277
Motor vehicle theft 4,963

Cost of Living Index 103.6
(national average = 100)

Median Home Price $130,300

Education

Public Schools

Albuquerque Public Schools Phone: 505-842-8211
725 University Blvd Fax: 505-842-3629
Albuquerque, NM 87125
www.aps.edu/aps/

Number of Schools
Elementary 79
Middle 24
High 11

Student/Teacher Ratio
All Grades 23.2:1

Private Schools

Number of Schools (all grades) .... 50+

Colleges & Universities

Albuquerque Technical Vocational Institute Phone: 505-224-3000
525 Buena Vista SE Fax: 505-224-3237
Albuquerque, NM 87106
E-mail: melissa@tvi.cc.nm.us
www.tvi.cc.nm.us

National American University Albuquerque Campus Phone: 505-265-7517
1202 Pennsylvania St NE Fax: 505-265-7542
Albuquerque, NM 87110
www.nationalcollege.edu/campusalb.html

Nazarene Indian Bible College Phone: 505-877-0240
2315 Markham Rd SW Fax: 505-877-6214
Albuquerque, NM 87105 TF: 888-877-6422

Southwestern Indian Polytechnic Institute Phone: 505-346-2346
PO Box 10146 Fax: 505-346-2343
Albuquerque, NM 87184 TF: 800-586-7474
E-mail: jjohnson@kafka.sipi.tec.nm.us
kafka.sipi.tec.nm.us

University of New Mexico Phone: 505-277-0111
University Hill NE Fax: 505-277-6686
Albuquerque, NM 87131 TF: 800-225-5866
E-mail: unmlobos@unm.edu
www.unm.edu

Hospitals

Lovelace Medical Center
5400 Gibson Blvd SE
Albuquerque, NM 87108
www.lovelace.com/lhs/lmc.shtml
Phone: 505-262-7000
Fax: 505-262-7729

Presbyterian Hospital
1100 Central Ave SE
Albuquerque, NM 87106
Phone: 505-841-1234
Fax: 505-841-1153

Presbyterian Kaseman Hospital
8300 Constitution Ave NE
Albuquerque, NM 87110
Phone: 505-291-2000
Fax: 505-291-2983

Saint Joseph West Mesa Hospital
10501 Golf Course Rd
Albuquerque, NM 87114
Phone: 505-727-2000
Fax: 505-727-2121

University Hospital
2211 Lomas Blvd NE
Albuquerque, NM 87106
uhwww.unm.edu
Phone: 505-843-2111
Fax: 505-272-1827

Veterans Affairs Medical Center
1501 San Pedro SE
Albuquerque, NM 87108
Phone: 505-265-1711
Fax: 505-256-2882

Transportation

Airport(s)

Albuquerque International Airport (ABQ)
5 miles SE of downtown (approx 10 minutes) 505-842-4366

Mass Transit

Sun Tran Bus Service
$.75 Base fare 505-843-9200
Sun Trolley Transit
$.75 Base fare 505-843-9200

Rail/Bus

Albuquerque Amtrak Station
214 1st St SW
Albuquerque, NM 87102
Phone: 505-842-9650

Greyhound/Trailways Bus Station
300 2nd St SW
Albuquerque, NM 87102
Phone: 505-243-4435

Utilities

Electricity
Public Service Co of New Mexico 505-246-5700
www.pnm.com

Gas
Gas Co of New Mexico 505-246-7460

Water
Albuquerque Water Dept 505-768-2800

Garbage Collection/Recycling
Albuquerque Refuse & Recycling Service 505-857-8060

Telecommunications

Telephone
Qwest 505-245-6800
www.qwest.com

Cable Television
Comcast Cable 505-344-0690

Internet Service Providers (ISPs)
Engineering International Inc 505-343-1060
www.rt66.com
New Mexico Internet Access Inc 505-247-0888
www.nmia.com
New Mexico Technet 505-345-6555
www.nm.org
Southwest Cyberport 505-232-7992
www.swcp.com
Verio New Mexico 505-872-2927
home.verio.net/local/frontpage.cfm?AirportCode=ABQ

Banks

Bank First
2900 Louisiana Blvd NE Suite 101
Albuquerque, NM 87110
Phone: 505-872-1536

Bank of Albuquerque NA
201 3rd St NW Suite 1400
Albuquerque, NM 87102
www.bankofalbuquerque.com
Phone: 505-855-0855
Fax: 505-222-8481

Bank of America
303 Roma Ave NW
Albuquerque, NM 87102
Phone: 505-282-4353
Fax: 505-243-9606
TF: 888-279-3264

Capital Bank
4700 Montgomery Blvd NE
Albuquerque, NM 87109
Phone: 505-830-8040
Fax: 505-872-2510

Charter Bank
4400 Olsen Rd NE
Albuquerque, NM 81709
Phone: 505-237-4136

Compass Bank
505 Marquette NW
Albuquerque, NM 87102
Phone: 505-888-9000
Fax: 505-888-9021

First Federal Bank
6700 Jefferson St NE
Albuquerque, NM 87109
Phone: 505-341-3240
Fax: 505-344-3991

First Security Bank of New Mexico NA
PO Box 1305
Albuquerque, NM 87103
Phone: 505-765-4000

First State Bank
5620 Wyoming Blvd NE
Albuquerque, NM 87109
Phone: 505-241-7631
Fax: 505-241-7637

High Desert State Bank
12700 San Rafael NE Suite 2
Albuquerque, NM 87122
Phone: 505-821-9854
Fax: 505-821-9855

Interamerica Bank
2400 Louisiana Blvd NE American Financial Ctr Bldg 1
Albuquerque, NM 87110
Phone: 505-880-1700
Fax: 505-880-1777

New Mexico Bank & Trust
320 Gold St SW
Albuquerque, NM 87103
Phone: 505-830-8100
Fax: 505-830-8140

Peoples Bank
2155 Louisiana Blvd Suite 1000
Albuquerque, NM 87110
Phone: 505-888-3300
Fax: 505-888-3200

Union Savings Bank
1500 Mercantile Ave NE
Albuquerque, NM 87107
Phone: 505-343-0900
Fax: 505-343-1083

Wells Fargo Bank
200 Lomas Blvd NW
Albuquerque, NM 87102
Phone: 505-765-5000
Fax: 505-766-6095

Western Commerce Bank
1910 Wyoming Blvd NE
Albuquerque, NM 87112
Phone: 505-271-9964
Fax: 505-271-9879

Shopping

Albuquerque's Indoor Mercado
2035 12th St NW
Albuquerque, NM 87104
Phone: 505-243-8111
Fax: 505-243-8419

Classic Century Square Antique Shops
4616 Central Ave SE
Albuquerque, NM 87108
Phone: 505-265-3161
Fax: 505-342-1108

Coronado Center
6600 Menaul St NE
Albuquerque, NM 87110
Phone: 505-881-4600
Fax: 505-881-0145

Cottonwood Mall
10000 Coors Bypass
Albuquerque, NM 87114
Phone: 505-899-7467
Fax: 505-897-6576

First Plaza Galeria
20 First Plaza Suite 510
Albuquerque, NM 87102
Phone: 505-242-3446

New Mexico State Fair Open Air Market
300 San Pedro Dr NE
Albuquerque, NM 87108
E-mail: info@nmstatefair.com
www.nmstatefair.com
Phone: 505-265-1791
Fax: 505-266-7784

Old Town
323 Romero St NW
Albuquerque, NM 87104
Phone: 505-243-6393

San Felipe Plaza
Mountain Rd & San Felipe NW Old Town
Albuquerque, NM 87104
Phone: 505-843-8297

Western Warehouse
11205 Montgomery Blvd NE
Albuquerque, NM 87111
www.westernwarehouse.com
Phone: 505-296-8344
Fax: 505-296-0278

Winrock Shopping Center
2100 Louisiana Blvd NE
Albuquerque, NM 87110
Phone: 505-888-3038
Fax: 505-881-6122

Yesterday's Favorites Antique Mall
2551 Coors Blvd NW
Albuquerque, NM 87120
Phone: 505-831-9384
Fax: 505-877-2214

Media

Newspapers and Magazines

Albuquerque Journal*
PO Drawer J
Albuquerque, NM 87103
E-mail: journal@abqjournal.com
www.abqjournal.com
Phone: 505-823-7777
Fax: 505-823-3994
TF: 800-990-5765

Albuquerque Monthly
625 Silver Ave SW Suite 355
Albuquerque, NM 87102
Phone: 505-768-7008

New Mexico Business Journal
420 Central Ave SW Suite 104
Albuquerque, NM 87102
E-mail: sierrapg@ix.netcom.com
www.nmbiz.com
Phone: 505-243-3444
Fax: 505-243-4118

Weekly Alibi
2118 Central Ave Suite 151
Albuquerque, NM 87106
E-mail: alibi@alibi.com
desert.net/alibi
Phone: 505-346-0660
Fax: 505-256-9651

**Indicates major daily newspapers*

Television

KASA-TV Ch 2 (Fox)
1377 University Blvd NE
Albuquerque, NM 87102
www.kasa.com
Phone: 505-246-2222
Fax: 505-242-1355

KASY-TV Ch 50 (UPN)
50 Broadcast Plaza
Albuquerque, NM 87104
Phone: 505-764-5279
Fax: 505-767-9421

KBIM-TV Ch 10 (CBS)
214 N Main St
Roswell, NM 88201
Phone: 505-622-2120
Fax: 505-623-6606

KCHF-TV Ch 11 (Ind)
216 TV E Frontage Rd
Santa Fe, NM 87505
Phone: 505-473-1111
Fax: 505-474-4998
TF: 800-831-9673

KHFT-TV Ch 29 (UPN)
50 Broadcast Plaza SW
Albuquerque, NM 87104
Phone: 505-764-5279
Fax: 505-767-9421

KLUZ-TV Ch 41 (Uni)
2725 F Broadbent Pkwy NE
Albuquerque, NM 87107
Phone: 505-344-5589
Fax: 505-344-0891

KNME-TV Ch 5 (PBS)
1130 University Blvd NE
Albuquerque, NM 87102
E-mail: viewer@knme1.unm.edu
www.pbs.org/knme
Phone: 505-277-2121
Fax: 505-277-2191
TF: 800-328-5663

KOAT-TV Ch 7 (ABC)
3801 Carlisle Blvd NE
Albuquerque, NM 87107
E-mail: news@koat7.com
Phone: 505-884-7777
Fax: 505-884-6354

KOB-TV Ch 4 (NBC)
4 Broadcast Plaza SW
Albuquerque, NM 87104
E-mail: opinion@kobtv.com
www.kobtv.com
Phone: 505-243-4411
Fax: 505-764-2522

KOBF-TV Ch 12 (NBC)
825 W Broadway
Farmington, NM 87401
Phone: 505-326-1141
Fax: 505-327-5196

KOBR-TV Ch 8 (NBC)
124 E 4th St
Roswell, NM 88201
Phone: 505-625-8888
Fax: 505-624-7693

KREZ-TV Ch 6 (CBS)
158 Bodo Dr
Durango, CO 81301
Phone: 970-259-6666
Fax: 970-247-8472

KRQE-TV Ch 13 (CBS)
PO Box 1294
Albuquerque, NM 87103
Phone: 505-243-2285
Fax: 505-842-8483
TF: 800-283-4227

Radio

KANW-FM 89.1 MHz (NPR)
2020 Coal Ave
Albuquerque, NM 87106
www.kanw.com
Phone: 505-242-7848

KHTL-AM 920 kHz (N/T)
500 4th St NW 5th Fl
Albuquerque, NM 87102
Phone: 505-767-6700
Fax: 505-767-6767

KKOB-AM 770 kHz (N/T)
500 4th St NW Suite 500
Albuquerque, NM 87102
www.kobam.nmsource.com
Phone: 505-767-6700
Fax: 505-767-6767

KKOB-FM 93.3 MHz (AC)
500 4th St NW
Albuquerque, NM 87102
www.kobfm.nmsource.com
Phone: 505-767-6700
Fax: 505-767-6767

KKSS-FM 97.3 MHz (CHR)
8009 Marble Ave NE
Albuquerque, NM 87110
E-mail: requests@973.com
www.973.com
Phone: 505-262-1142
Fax: 505-262-9211

KLSK-FM 104.1 MHz (CR)
2700 San Pedro NE
Albuquerque, NM 87110
Phone: 505-830-6400
Fax: 505-830-6543

KMGA-FM 99.5 MHz (AC)
500 4th St NW 5th Fl
Albuquerque, NM 87102
www.99.5magicfm.com
Phone: 505-767-6700
Fax: 505-767-6767

KNML-AM 1050 kHz (Sports)
500 4th St NW 5th Fl
Albuquerque, NM 87102
E-mail: 1050@sportsanimal.com
www.sportsanimal.nmsource.com
Phone: 505-767-6700
Fax: 505-767-6767

KRST-FM 92.3 MHz (Ctry)
500 4th St NW 5th Fl
Albuquerque, NM 87102
www.krst.nmsource.com
Phone: 505-767-6700
Fax: 505-767-6767

KTBL-FM 103.3 MHz (Ctry)
500 4th St NW
Albuquerque, NM 87102
www.kbull.nmsource.com
Phone: 505-767-6700
Fax: 505-767-6767

KUNM-FM 89.9 MHz (NPR)
Onate Hall University of New Mexico
Albuquerque, NM 87131
kunm.unm.edu
Phone: 505-277-4806
Fax: 505-277-8004

KZRR-FM 94.1 MHz (Rock)
2700 San Pedro NE
Albuquerque, NM 87110
E-mail: kzrr@94rock.com
www.swcp.com/kzrr
Phone: 505-830-6400
Fax: 505-830-6543

Attractions

Albuquerque originated in the part of the present-day city known as Old Town, which features more than 150 shops, galleries, and restaurants housed in historic adobe buildings. Just north of the Old Town area is the Indian Pueblo Cultural Center, which features arts and crafts from all 19 of New Mexico's pueblos. The Center also houses a restaurant that specializes in Native American-style cooking. On the west side of the city is Petroglyph National Monument, with more than 17,000 ancient images representing the world's largest accessible collection of prehistoric rock art. From downtown Albuquerque one can board the Sandia Peak Aerial Tramway, rising 2.7 miles above deep canyons to the Sandia Peak observation deck, with a panoramic view spanning some 11,000 square miles. Annual events in Albuquerque include the International Balloon Fiesta, which draws 650 hot-air balloons and 1.6 million spectators each October; and the Gathering of Nations Pow Wow, featuring 5,000 Native American singers and dancers representing more than 300 tribes.

Adobe Theater
9813 4th St NW
Albuquerque, NM 87107
Phone: 505-898-9222

Albuquerque Aquarium
903 10th St
Albuquerque, NM 87102
www.cabq.gov/biopark/aquarium
Phone: 505-764-6200
Fax: 505-848-7192

Albuquerque Biological Park Rio Grande Zoo
903 10th St SW
Albuquerque, NM 87102
www.cabq.gov/biopark/zoo
Phone: 505-764-6200
Fax: 505-764-6281

Albuquerque Little Theatre
224 San Pasquale SW
Albuquerque, NM 87104
E-mail: alt@swcp.com
www.swcp.com/~alt
Phone: 505-242-4750
Fax: 505-843-9489

Albuquerque Museum
2000 Mountain Rd NW
Albuquerque, NM 87104
E-mail: musjcm@museum.cabq.gov
www.collectorsguide.com/ab/m005.html
Phone: 505-243-7255
Fax: 505-764-6546

American International Rattlesnake Museum
202 San Felipe NW Suite A
Albuquerque, NM 87104
E-mail: zoomuseum@aol.com
www.rattlesnakes.com
Phone: 505-242-6569
Fax: 505-242-6569

Archaeology & Material Culture Museum
22 Calvary Rd
Cedar Crest, NM 87008
Phone: 505-281-2005

Beach Waterpark
1600 Desert Surf Loop NE
Albuquerque, NM 87107
www.beachwaterpark.com
Phone: 505-345-6066
Fax: 505-344-6759

Casa Rondena Winery
733 Chavez Rd NW
Albuquerque, NM 87107
E-mail: info@casarondena.com
www.casarondena.com
Phone: 505-344-5911
Fax: 505-343-1823

Chamber Orchestra of Albuquerque
2730 San Pedro NE Suite H
Albuquerque, NM 87110
www.aosys.com/coa/
Phone: 505-881-2078
Fax: 505-881-2078

Cibola National Forest
2113 Osuna Rd NE Suite A
Albuquerque, NM 87113
Phone: 505-346-2650
Fax: 505-346-2663

Cliff's Amusement Park
4800 Osuna Rd NE
Albuquerque, NM 87109
E-mail: info@cliffs.net
www.cliffs.net
Phone: 505-881-9373
Fax: 505-881-7807

Coronado State Monument
485 Koala Rd
Bernalillo, NM 87004
Phone: 505-867-5351
Fax: 505-867-1733

Doll Museum & Shoppe
5201 Constitution Ave NE
Albuquerque, NM 87110
Phone: 505-255-8555
Fax: 505-255-1259
TF: 877-280-3805

El Malpais National Monument
PO Box 939
Grants, NM 87020
www.nps.gov/elma/
Phone: 505-285-4641
Fax: 505-285-5661

El Morro National Monument
Rt 2 Box 43
Ramah, NM 87321
www.nps.gov/elmo/
Phone: 505-783-4226
Fax: 505-783-4689

Ernie Pyle Memorial Library
900 Girard Blvd SE
Albuquerque, NM 87106
www.cabq.gov/rgvls/branch.html
Phone: 505-256-2065
Fax: 505-256-2069

Explora! Science Center & Children's Museum
2100 Louisiana Blvd NE
Albuquerque, NM 87110
E-mail: explorainfo@esccma.org
www.explora.mus.nm.us
Phone: 505-842-1537
Fax: 505-842-5915

Fine Arts Center
University of New Mexico
Albuquerque, NM 87131
www.unm.edu/~finearts/
Phone: 505-277-2111
Fax: 505-277-0708

Gruet Winery
8400 Pan American Frwy NE
Albuquerque, NM 87113
Phone: 505-821-0055
Fax: 505-857-0066

Hinkle Family Fun Center
12931 Indian School Rd NE
Albuquerque, NM 87112
E-mail: hfamfun@aol.com
www.hinklefamilyfuncenter.com
Phone: 505-299-3100
Fax: 505-299-3777

Indian Pueblo Cultural Center
2401 12th St NW
Albuquerque, NM 87102
www.indianpueblo.org
Phone: 505-843-7270
Fax: 505-842-6959

Isleta Gaming Palace
11000 Broadway
Albuquerque, NM 87105
www.isletagamingpalace.com
Phone: 505-869-2614
Fax: 505-869-0152
TF: 800-460-5686

KiMo Theater
423 Central Ave NW
Albuquerque, NM 87102
www.cabq.gov/kimo/
Phone: 505-848-1370
Fax: 505-764-1572

Maxwell Museum of Anthropology
University of New Mexico
Albuquerque, NM 87131
www.unm.edu/~maxwell
Phone: 505-277-4405
Fax: 505-277-1547

Musical Theatre Southwest
4804 Central Ave SE
Albuquerque, NM 87108
E-mail: acloa@aol.com
www.musicaltheatresw.com
Phone: 505-262-9301
Fax: 505-262-9319

National Atomic Museum
Kirtland Air Force Base E Wyoming Ave
Albuquerque, NM 87185
www.atomicmuseum.com
Phone: 505-284-3243
Fax: 505-284-3244

New Mexico Ballet Co
PO Box 21518
Albuquerque, NM 87154
E-mail: dwestbrk@unm.edu
www.mandala.net/nmballet
Phone: 505-292-4245

New Mexico Jazz Workshop
3205 Central Ave NE
Albuquerque, NM 87106
www.flash.net/~nmjw/
Phone: 505-255-9798
Fax: 505-232-8420

New Mexico Museum of Natural History & Science
1801 Mountain Rd NW
Albuquerque, NM 87104
www.nmmnh-abq.mus.nm.us
Phone: 505-841-2800
Fax: 505-841-2866

New Mexico Symphony Orchestra
PO Box 30208
Albuquerque, NM 87190
www.nmso.org
Phone: 505-881-9590
Fax: 505-881-9456
TF: 800-251-6676

Old Town
323 Romero St NW
Albuquerque, NM 87104
Phone: 505-243-6393

Opera Southwest
515 15th St NW
Albuquerque, NM 87105
Phone: 505-242-5837
Fax: 505-242-5837

Petroglyph National Monument
6001 Unser Blvd NW
Albuquerque, NM 87120
www.nps.gov/petr/
Phone: 505-899-0205
Fax: 505-899-0207

Popejoy Hall
University of New Mexico
Albuquerque, NM 87131
www.popejoyhall.com
Phone: 505-277-3824
Fax: 505-277-7353

Rio Grande Botanic Garden
2601 Central Ave NW
Albuquerque, NM 87104
www.cabq.gov/biopark/garden
Phone: 505-764-6200
Fax: 505-848-7192

Rio Grande Nature Center State Park
2901 Candelaria Rd NW
Albuquerque, NM 87107
www.unm.edu/~natrcent/
Phone: 505-344-7240
Fax: 505-344-4505

Salinas Pueblo Missions National Monument
PO Box 517
Mountainair, NM 87036
www.nps.gov/sapu/
Phone: 505-847-2585
Fax: 505-847-2441

San Felipe Plaza
Mountain Rd & San Felipe NW Old Town
Albuquerque, NM 87104
Phone: 505-843-8297

Sandia Peak Ski & Tramway
10 Tramway Loop NE
Albuquerque, NM 87122
www.sandiapeak.com
Phone: 505-856-7325
Fax: 505-856-6490

South Broadway Cultural Center
1025 Broadway SE
Albuquerque, NM 87102
Phone: 505-848-1320
Fax: 505-848-1329

Southwest Repertory Theater Co
516 Central Ave SW
Albuquerque, NM 87102
E-mail: zolister@aol.com
Phone: 505-244-3634
Fax: 505-242-0174

Telephone Pioneer Museum of New Mexico
110 4th St NW
Albuquerque, NM 87102
E-mail: lxturne@eni.net
www.nmculture.org/cgi-bin/showInst.pl?InstID=TPM
Phone: 505-842-2937

Tinkertown Museum
121 Sandia Crest Rd
Sandia Park, NM 87047
E-mail: tinker4u@tinkertown.com
www.tinkertown.com
Phone: 505-281-5233
Fax: 505-286-9335

Turquoise Museum
2107 Central Ave NW
Albuquerque, NM 87104
Phone: 505-247-8650
Fax: 505-247-8765
TF: 800-821-7443

Turquoise Trail
Hwys 536 & 14
Sandia Park, NM 87047
E-mail: trail@turquoisetrail.org
www.turquoisetrail.org
Phone: 505-281-5233
TF: 888-263-0003

YesterDave's Auto Museum
10601 Montgomery Blvd NE
Albuquerque, NM 87111
Phone: 505-293-0033
Fax: 505-298-5549

Sports Teams & Facilities

Albuquerque Dukes (baseball)
1601 Avenida Cesar Chavez SE Dukes Stadium
Albuquerque, NM 87106
www.albuquerquedukes.com
Phone: 505-243-1791
Fax: 505-842-0561
TF: 800-905-3315

Albuquerque National Dragway
5700 Bobby Foster
Albuquerque, NM 87105
Phone: 505-873-2684

Albuquerque Sports Stadium
1601 Avenida Cesar Chavez
Albuquerque, NM 87106
E-mail: kggr90a@prodigy.com
Phone: 505-243-1791
Fax: 505-842-0561

Downs at Albuquerque
Copper & San Pedro NE New Mexico State Fairgrounds
Albuquerque, NM 87108
E-mail: thedowns@aol.com
www.nmracing.com
Phone: 505-266-5555
Fax: 505-268-1970

New Mexico Scorpions (hockey)
300 San Pedro Dr NE Tingley Coliseum
Albuquerque, NM 87109
E-mail: scorpion@scorpionshockey.com
www.scorpionshockey.com
Phone: 505-881-7825
Fax: 505-883-7829
TF: 888-472-6777

New Mexico Slam (basketball)
300 San Pedro Dr NE Tingley Coliseum
Albuquerque, NM 87108
www.nmslam.com
Phone: 505-830-2255

New Mexico State Fair Racetrack
300 San Pedro Dr NE
Albuquerque, NM 87108
E-mail: info@nmstatefair.com
www.nmstatefair.com
Phone: 505-265-1791
Fax: 505-266-7784

Tingley Coliseum
300 San Pedro Dr NE
Albuquerque, NM 87108
Phone: 505-265-1791
Fax: 505-266-7784

Annual Events

Albuquerque International Balloon Fiesta (early-mid-October) 800-284-2282
American Indian Week (late April) 505-843-7270
Arts in the Park Sundays (June-August) 505-768-3483
Bernalillo Wine Festival (early September) 505-867-3311
Brown Bag Noontime Concert Series (July-August) 505-242-8244
Children's Fair (late March-early April) 505-767-6700
Duke City Marathon (late September) 505-768-3483
Fall Arts Fiesta (early December) 505-834-7235
Father's Day Multi-Cultural Festival (mid-June) 505-843-7270
Festival Flamenco Internacional (early-mid-June) 505-277-1855
Fiery Food Show (early March) 505-873-8680
Gallup Inter-Tribal Indian Ceremonial (mid-August) 800-233-4528
Gathering of Nations Powwow (late April) 505-836-2810
Grecian Festival (early October) 505-247-9411
Herb & Wildflower Festival (mid-May) 505-344-7240
Holiday Olé (mid-November) 505-260-0199

Holiday Parade (early December) 505-768-3555
Holiday Stroll (early December) 505-842-8102
Indian Festival of Living Arts (mid-March) 505-843-7270
Indian Pueblo Christmas Celebrations
(late December) 505-843-7270
Inter-Tribal Indian Ceremonial Powwow
(late May) 800-233-4528
International Arabian Horse Show (late October). . . .800-733-9918
Jemez Red Rocks Arts & Crafts Show (late May) . . .505-834-7235
Las Fiestas de San Lorenzo (early August) 505-867-3311
Luminaria Tours (late December) 505-842-9918
Magnifico! Albuquerque Festival of the Arts
(mid-May) 505-242-8244
New Mexico Arts & Crafts Fair (late June) 505-884-9043
New Mexico State Fair (early-late September). 505-265-1791
Rio Grande Arts & Crafts Festival (early March) 505-292-7457
Run for the Zoo (early May) 505-764-6200
San Felipe Pueblo Arts & Crafts Show
(early October) 505-867-3381
Santa Fe Furniture Expo (mid-June) 800-299-9886
Southwest Arts Festival (early November) 505-875-1748
Summer Festival & Frontier Market
(early August) 505-471-2261
Summerfest Saturdays (June-August) 505-768-3483
Weems Artfest (mid-November) 505-293-6133
Ye Merry Olde Christmas Faire (late November) 505-856-1970
Zia Arts & Crafts Festival (late November) 505-842-9918

Allentown, Pennsylvania

***County:* Lehigh**

ALLENTOWN is located in the Lehigh Valley in east central Pennsylvania. Major cities within 100 miles include Scranton, Philadelphia, and Harrisburg, Pennsylvania.

Area (Land) .... 17.7 sq mi
Area (Water)............................... 0.2 sq mi
Elevation...................................... 387 ft
Latitude ....40-35-46 N
Longitude................................ 75-28-39 W
Time Zone ....EST
Area Code....................................... 610

Climate

Allentown has a variable climate that may feature periods of bitterly cold weather during the winter and warm, humid summers. Winter high temperatures average in the mid- to upper 30s and lows average in the high teens to low 20s. An average of 31.3 inches of snow falls in Allentown each year. Summer daytime high temperatures average in the low to mid-80s, while evenings cool down to near 60 degrees. August the wettest month in Allentown; October is the driest.

Average Temperatures & Precipitation

Temperatures

	Jan	Feb	Mar	Apr	May	Jun	Jul	Aug	Sep	Oct	Nov	Dec
High	34	38	49	60	71	80	85	82	75	64	52	39
Low	19	21	30	39	49	59	64	62	54	43	34	24

Precipitation

	Jan	Feb	Mar	Apr	May	Jun	Jul	Aug	Sep	Oct	Nov	Dec
Inches	3.2	3.0	3.3	3.5	4.2	3.8	4.1	4.3	3.9	2.9	3.9	3.5

History

Originally inhabited by Native Americans of the Lenni-Lenape tribe, Allentown was founded by chief justice William Allen in 1762 as a community called Northamptontown. Even in its early days, many people referred to the settlement as "Allen's Town," although the city's name was not officially changed to Allentown until the 1830s. Most of the Lehigh Valley's early European inhabitants were Germans, whom the English referred to as Pennsylvania Dutch (derived from the German word "Deutsch"). In 1777, during the American Revolution, the Liberty Bell was hidden in the basement of Zion's Reformed United Church of Christ in Allentown when the British occupied Philadelphia. The Liberty Bell Shrine, a popular historical attraction in Allentown, stands today as a reminder of this event.

In 1811, Allentown was incorporated as a borough and was chosen as the county seat of the newly formed Lehigh County the following year. During the 1820s the completion of the Lehigh Canal sparked development in the area by opening up distribution routes for various industries. The Lehigh Valley's first commercially successful iron furnace was built in 1840, and the iron industry fueled the area's economy for the next three decades. In 1867, Allentown was incorporated as a city.

By the 1870s, many towns in the Lehigh Valley were forced to develop alternative industries as the demand for iron declined as steel became more popular. Allentown turned its efforts to silk manufacturing and by the early 1900s became known as "Silk City." One iron company that continued operations was Bethlehem Iron, which produced armor plate for battleships through the late 1800s. Bethlehem Iron became Bethlehem Steel at the turn of the century, and quickly became one of the nation's largest steel manufacturers. The company is presently the fourth largest employer in the Lehigh Valley.

Allentown today is home to more than 100,000 people and remains an important industrial and commercial center in the Lehigh Valley Region.

Population

1990 Census 105,301
1998 Estimate.............................100,757
% Change .... -4.3
2010 Projection 318,860*

Racial/Ethnic Breakdown
White.................................... 86.0%
Black 5.0%
Other..................................... 9.0%
Hispanic Origin (may be of any race) 11.7%

Age Breakdown
Under 5 years.............................. 7.3%
5 to 17.................................. 14.7%
18 to 20.................................. 4.7%
21 to 24.................................. 6.7%
25 to 34................................. 18.8%
35 to 44................................. 13.2%
45 to 54.................................. 8.7%
55 to 64.................................. 9.1%
65 to 74.................................. 9.2%
75+ years 7.7%
Median Age................................33.8

Gender Breakdown
Male..................................... 47.2%
Female................................... 52.8%

* *Information given is for Lehigh County.*

Government

Type of Government: Mayor-Council

Allentown City Clerk
435 Hamilton St
Allentown, PA 18101
Phone: 610-437-7539
Fax: 610-437-7554

Allentown City Council
435 Hamilton St
Allentown, PA 18101
Phone: 610-437-7556
Fax: 610-437-7554

Allentown City Hall
435 Hamilton St
Allentown, PA 18101
Phone: 610-437-7511
Fax: 610-437-8730

Allentown Community Development Dept
435 Hamilton St Suite 325
Allentown, PA 18101
Phone: 610-437-7761
Fax: 610-437-8781

Allentown Downtown Improvement District Authority
822 Hamilton St
Allentown, PA 18101
Phone: 610-776-7117
Fax: 610-776-4117

Allentown Fire Dept
425 Hamilton St
Allentown, PA 18101
Phone: 610-437-7765

Allentown Human Resources Dept
435 Hamilton St Rm 233
Allentown, PA 18101
Phone: 610-437-7521
Fax: 610-437-7675

Allentown Mayor
435 Hamilton St
Allentown, PA 18101
Phone: 610-437-7546
Fax: 610-437-8730

Allentown Parks Bureau
2700 Parkway Blvd
Allentown, PA 18104
Phone: 610-437-7628
Fax: 610-437-7685

Allentown Planning & Zoning Dept
435 Hamilton St
Allentown, PA 18101
Phone: 610-437-7611
Fax: 610-437-8781

Allentown Police Dept
425 Hamilton St
Allentown, PA 18101
Phone: 610-437-7751
Fax: 610-437-8721

Allentown Public Library
1210 W Hamilton St
Allentown, PA 18102
Phone: 610-820-2400
Fax: 610-820-0640

Allentown Public Works Dept
435 Hamilton St
Allentown, PA 18101
Phone: 610-437-7587
Fax: 610-437-7614

Allentown Solicitor
435 Hamilton St Rm 519
Allentown, PA 18101
Phone: 610-437-7545

Allentown Treasurer
435 Hamilton St Rm 110
Allentown, PA 18101
Phone: 610-437-7558
Fax: 610-437-7675

Allentown Water Resources Dept
112 Union St
Allentown, PA 18102
Phone: 610-437-7641
Fax: 610-437-8790

Important Phone Numbers

AAA 610-434-5141
Allentown Tax Office 610-437-7516
Allentown-Lehigh County Board of Realtors 610-882-4100
American Express Travel 610-265-7450
Driver's License/Vehicle Registration Information 610-264-4060
Emergency 911
Lehigh County Assessment Dept. 610-782-3038
Medical Referral 610-402-2273
Pennsylvania State Revenue Dept 610-861-2000
Poison Control Center 800-722-7112
Time/Temp/Weather 610-797-5900
Voter Registration Information 610-782-3194

Information Sources

Allentown Downtown Improvement District Authority
822 Hamilton St
Allentown, PA 18101
Phone: 610-776-7117
Fax: 610-776-4117

Allentown Fairgrounds' Agricultural Hall
302 N 17th St
Allentown, PA 18104
www.allentownfairpa.org
Phone: 610-437-6020
Fax: 610-433-4005

Lehigh County
455 W Hamilton St
Allentown, PA 18101
www.pavisnet.com/lehigh
Phone: 610-782-3000
Fax: 610-820-3093

Lehigh County Chamber of Commerce
462 Walnut St
Allentown, PA 18102
www.lehighcountychamber.org
Phone: 610-437-9661
Fax: 610-437-4907

Lehigh Valley Convention & Visitors Bureau
2200 Ave A
Bethlehem, PA 18017
lehighvalleypa.org
Phone: 610-882-9200
Fax: 610-882-0343
TF: 800-747-0561

Online Resources

4Allentown.com
www.4allentown.com

City Knowledge Allentown
www.cityknowledge.com/pa_allentown.htm

Excite.com Allentown City Guide
www.excite.com/travel/countries/united_states/pennsylvania/allentown

Lehigh Valley Town Square
townsquare.ot.com

LehighvalleyNOW.com
www.lehighvalleynow.com

Area Communities

Lehigh Valley communities with populations greater than 10,000 include:

Bethlehem
10 E Church St
Bethlehem, PA 18018
Phone: 610-865-7100
Fax: 610-865-7019

Easton
1 S 3rd St
Easton, PA 18042
Phone: 610-250-6600
Fax: 610-250-6607

Emmaus
28 S 4th St
Emmaus, PA 18049
Phone: 610-965-9292
Fax: 610-965-0705

Lower Macungie Township
3400 Brookside Rd
Macungie, PA 18062
Phone: 610-966-4343
Fax: 610-965-3654

North Whitehall
3256 Levans Rd
Coplay, PA 18037
Phone: 610-799-3411
Fax: 610-799-9629

Salisbury
2900 S Pike Ave
Allentown, PA 18103
Phone: 610-797-4000
Fax: 610-797-5516

South Whitehall
4444 Walbert Ave
Allentown, PA 18104
Phone: 610-398-0337
Fax: 610-391-9471

Whitehall
3219 MacArthur Rd
Whitehall, PA 18052
Phone: 610-437-5524
Fax: 610-437-6963

Economy

Major corporations that have their headquarters or divisions in the Allentown area include Air Products and Chemicals, Bethlehem Steel, Lucent Technologies, and the Guardian Life Insurance Company of America. Although manufacturing remains vital to the economy of the Lehigh Valley, the region's economic base has diversified significantly in recent years. The services sector is currently the region's largest employment sector, and the greatest job growth in coming years is expected to occur in service, professional, paraprofessional, and technical positions.

Unemployment Rate 3.7%
Per Capita Income.......................... $27,599*
Median Family Income...................... $49,400*

** Information given is for the Allentown-Bethlehem-Easton Metropolitan Statistical Area (MSA), which includes the City of Allentown, the City of Bethlehem, the City of Easton, as well as Carbon, Lehigh, and Northampton counties.*

Principal Industries & Number of Wage Earners

Lehigh County - 1999

Industry	Wage Earners
Construction	8,685
Finance, Insurance, & Real Estate	14,878
Government	16,864
Manufacturing	34,037
Mining	323
Retail Trade	30,637
Services	61,493
Transportation & Public Utilities	10,802
Wholesale Trade	8,340

Major Employers

Air Products & Chemicals Inc
7201 Hamilton Blvd
Allentown, PA 18195
E-mail: info@apci.com
www.apci.com
Phone: 610-481-4911
Fax: 610-481-3855
TF: 800-345-3148

Allentown City Hall
435 Hamilton St
Allentown, PA 18101
www.allentownpa.org
Phone: 610-437-7511
Fax: 610-437-8730

Allentown School District
31 S Penn St
Allentown, PA 18105
www.allentownsd.org
Phone: 610-820-2211
Fax: 610-821-2618

Dun & Bradstreet Information Services
899 Eaton Ave
Bethlehem, PA 18025
www.dnbcorp.com
Phone: 610-882-7000
Fax: 610-882-7700

Easton Hospital
250 S 21st St
Easton, PA 18042
www.eastonhospital.org
Phone: 610-250-4000
Fax: 610-250-4877
TF: 800-532-1313

Kids Peace
1650 Broadway
Bethlehem, PA 18015
E-mail: admissions@kidspeace.org
www.kidspeace.org
Phone: 610-867-5051
Fax: 610-867-5447

Lehigh County
455 W Hamilton St
Allentown, PA 18101
www.pavisnet.com/lehigh
Phone: 610-782-3000
Fax: 610-820-3093

Lehigh University
27 Memorial Dr W
Bethlehem, PA 18015
www.lehigh.edu
Phone: 610-758-3000
Fax: 610-758-4361

Lehigh Valley Hospital
17th & Chew PO Box 7017
Allentown, PA 18102
E-mail: 402care@lvhhn.org
www.lvh.com
Phone: 610-402-8000
Fax: 610-402-9696

Lucent Technologies
555 Union Blvd
Allentown, PA 18103
www.lucent.com
Phone: 610-712-6011
Fax: 610-712-6451
TF: 800-372-2447

Mack Trucks Inc
2100 Mack Blvd
Allentown, PA 18103
www.macktrucks.com
Phone: 610-709-3011
Fax: 610-709-2405

PPL Utilities
827 Hausman Rd
Allentown, PA 10104
www.pplweb.com
Phone: 610-774-5151
Fax: 610-774-5408
TF: 800-342-5775

Rodale Press Inc
33 E Minor St
Emmaus, PA 18098
www.rodalepress.com
Phone: 610-967-8154
Fax: 800-813-6627
TF: 800-848-4735

Saint Luke's Hospital
801 Ostrum St
Bethlehem, PA 18015
www.slhn-lehighvalley.org
Phone: 610-954-4000
Fax: 610-954-3706

Victaulic Co of America
4901 Kesslersville Rd
Easton, PA 18040
E-mail: victaulic@victaulic.com
www.victaulic.com
Phone: 610-559-3300
Fax: 610-250-8817

Wood Co
6081 Hamilton Blvd
Allentown, PA 18106
E-mail: jsjolly@sprynet.com
www.woodco.com
Phone: 610-395-3800
Fax: 610-398-1599
TF: 800-545-7710

Quality of Living Indicators

Total Crime Index....................................5,561
(rates per 100,000 inhabitants)

Violent Crime
Murder/manslaughter........................... 11
Forcible rape 39
Robbery..................................... 350
Aggravated assault............................ 260

Property Crime
Burglary 1,113
Larceny theft 9,326
Motor vehicle theft............................ 726

Cost of Living Index...................................103.4
(national average = 100)

Median Home Price.................................$127,400

Education

Public Schools

Allentown School District
31 S Penn St
Allentown, PA 18105
www.allentownsd.org
Phone: 610-820-2211
Fax: 610-821-2618

Number of Schools
Elementary................................. 17
Middle 4
High.. 2

Student/Teacher Ratio
All Grades 20.1:1

Private Schools

Number of Schools (all grades).................... 35

Colleges & Universities

Allentown Business School
1501 Lehigh St
Allentown, PA 18103
E-mail: absinfo@allentownbusinesssch.com
www.chooseabs.com
Phone: 610-791-5100
Fax: 610-791-7810

Allentown College of Saint Francis DeSales
2755 Station Ave
Center Valley, PA 18034
E-mail: finley@www.allencol.edu
www.allencol.edu
Phone: 610-282-1100
Fax: 610-282-2254
TF: 800-228-5114

Cedar Crest College
100 College Dr
Allentown, PA 18104
E-mail: cccadmis@cedarcrest.edu
www.cedarcrest.edu
Phone: 610-437-4471
Fax: 610-606-4647
TF: 800-360-1222

Lafayette College
118 Markle Hall
Easton, PA 18042
E-mail: faccipop@lafayette.edu
www.lafayette.edu
Phone: 610-330-5000
Fax: 610-330-5355

Lehigh Carbon Community College
4525 Education Pk Dr
Schnecksville, PA 18078
www.lccc.edu
Phone: 610-799-2121
Fax: 610-799-1159

Lehigh University
27 Memorial Dr W
Bethlehem, PA 18015
www.lehigh.edu
Phone: 610-758-3000
Fax: 610-758-4361

Lincoln Technical Institute
5151 Tilghman St
Allentown, PA 18104
www.lincolntech.com
Phone: 610-398-5301
Fax: 610-395-2706

Moravian College
1200 Main St
Bethlehem, PA 18018
www.moravian.edu
Phone: 610-861-1300
Fax: 610-861-1577

Muhlenberg College
2400 W Chew St
Allentown, PA 18104
E-mail: admissions@hal.muhlberg.edu
www.muhlberg.edu
Phone: 484-664-3100
Fax: 484-664-3234

Northampton Community College
3835 Green Pond Rd
Bethlehem, PA 18020
www.nrhm.cc.pa.us
Phone: 610-861-5500
Fax: 610-861-4560

Pennsylvania State University Lehigh Valley Campus
8380 Mohr Ln
Fogelsville, PA 18051
www.lv.psu.edu
Phone: 610-285-5000
Fax: 610-285-5220

Welder Training & Testing Institute
1144 N Graham St
Allentown, PA 18109
Phone: 610-820-9551
Fax: 610-820-0271
TF: 800-223-9884

Hospitals

Easton Hospital
250 S 21st St
Easton, PA 18042
www.eastonhospital.org
Phone: 610-250-4000
Fax: 610-250-4877
TF: 800-532-1313

Lehigh Valley Hospital
17th & Chew PO Box 7017
Allentown, PA 18102
www.lvh.com
Phone: 610-402-8000
Fax: 610-402-9696

Muhlenberg Hospital Center
2545 Schoenersville Rd
Bethlehem, PA 18017
Phone: 484-884-2200
Fax: 484-884-7747

Sacred Heart Hospital
421 Chew St
Allentown, PA 18102
Phone: 610-776-4500
Fax: 610-776-4559

Saint Luke's Hospital
801 Ostrum St
Bethlehem, PA 18015
www.slhn-lehighvalley.org
Phone: 610-954-4000
Fax: 610-954-3706

Transportation

Airport(s)

Lehigh Valley International Airport (ABE)
4 miles NE of downtown(approx 10 minutes) 610-266-6000

Mass Transit

LANTA Bus
$1.35 Base fare.................................610-776-7433

Utilities

Electricity
PPL Utilities..................................800-342-5775
www.pplweb.com

Gas
UGI Utilities..................................610-435-8080
www.ugicorp.com

Water
Allentown Water Resources Dept................610-437-7641

Garbage Collection/Recycling
Allentown Garbage & Trash....................610-437-7770
Allentown Recycling...........................610-437-8729

Telecommunications

Telephone
Verizon Communications.......................215-571-7050
www.verizon.com

Cable Television
Service Electric Cable Television...............610-865-9100

Internet Service Providers (ISPs)
Enter.Net 610-437-2221
www.enter.net
FASTNET Corp...............................610-954-5910
www.fast.net
NuNet Inc......................................610-882-5600
www.nni.com
Oasis Telecommunications Inc 610-439-8560
www.ot.com

Banks

First Union National Bank
702 Hamilton Mall
Allentown, PA 18101
Phone: 610-821-7452
Fax: 610-821-7484
TF: 800-225-5332

Firstrust Bank
701 Hamilton Mall
Allentown, PA 18101
Phone: 610-437-3701
Fax: 610-434-4030
TF: 800-220-2265

PNC Bank NA
730 W Emmaus Ave
Allentown, PA 18103
Phone: 610-797-2860
Fax: 610-797-4566
TF: 888-762-2265

Summit Bank
15th & Allen Sts
Allentown, PA 18102
Phone: 610-776-6788
Fax: 610-776-6712
TF: 888-878-6648

Shopping

Barns The
4186 Easton Ave
Bethlehem, PA 18020
www.christmasbarn.com
Phone: 610-861-0477
Fax: 610-861-5986

Hamilton Mall Shopping District
822 Hamilton St
Allentown, PA 18101
Phone: 610-776-7117
Fax: 610-776-4117

Lehigh Valley Mall
250 Lehigh Valley Mall
Whitehall, PA 18052
Phone: 610-264-5511
Fax: 610-264-5957

Media

Newspapers and Magazines

Bethlehem Star
531 Main St
Bethlehem, PA 18018
Phone: 610-867-5000
Fax: 610-866-1771

Eastern Pennsylvania Business Journal
65 E Elizabeth Ave Suite 700
Bethlehem, PA 18018
Phone: 610-807-9619
Fax: 610-807-9612
TF: 800-328-1026

Express-Times*
30 N 4th St
Easton, PA 18044
E-mail: staff@express-times.com
www.express-times.com
Phone: 610-258-7171
Fax: 610-258-7130
TF: 800-360-3601

Lehigh Valley Magazine
910 13th Ave
Bethlehem, PA 18018
E-mail: lvmcirc@fast.net
www.lvmag.com
Phone: 610-691-8833
Fax: 610-861-9924

Morning Call*
PO Box 1260
Allentown, PA 18105
www.mcall.com
Phone: 610-820-6500
Fax: 610-820-6693
TF: 800-666-5492

**Indicates major daily newspapers*

Television

KYW-TV Ch 3 (CBS)
101 S Independence Mall E
Philadelphia, PA 19106
www.kyw.com
Phone: 215-238-4700
Fax: 215-238-4783
TF: 800-238-4700

WCAU-TV Ch 10 (NBC)
10 Monument Rd
Bala Cynwyd, PA 19004
www.nbc10.com
Phone: 610-668-5510
Fax: 610-668-3700

WFMZ-TV Ch 69 (Ind)
300 E Rock Rd
Allentown, PA 18103
www.wfmz.com/
Phone: 610-797-4530
Fax: 610-791-3000

WLVT-TV Ch 39 (PBS)
123 Sesame St
Bethlehem, PA 18015
www.lehighvalleypbs.org
Phone: 610-867-4677
Fax: 610-867-3544

WNYW-TV Ch 5 (Fox)
205 E 67th St
New York, NY 10021
Phone: 212-452-5555
Fax: 212-249-1182

WPVI-TV Ch 6 (ABC)
4100 City Line Ave
Philadelphia, PA 19131
abcnews.go.com/local/wpvi
Phone: 215-878-9700
Fax: 215-581-4530

Radio

WAEB-AM 790 kHz (N/T)
1541 Alta Dr Suite 400
Whitehall, PA 18052
Phone: 610-434-1742
Fax: 610-434-3808

WAEB-FM 104.1 MHz (AC)
1541 Alta Dr 4th Fl
Whitehall, PA 18052
www.b104.com
Phone: 610-434-1742
Fax: 610-434-6288

WCTO-FM 96.1 MHz (Ctry)
2158 Ave C Suite 100
Bethlehem, PA 18017
Phone: 610-266-7600
Fax: 610-231-0400

WDIY-FM 88.1 MHz (NPR)
301 Broadway
Bethlehem, PA 18015
E-mail: fm881@wdiyfm.org
www.wdiyfm.org
Phone: 610-694-8100
Fax: 610-954-9474

WEST-AM 1400 kHz (Nost)
436 Northampton St
Easton, PA 18042
E-mail: comments@am1400west.net
www.am1400west.net
Phone: 610-250-9557
Fax: 610-250-9675

WGPA-AM 1100 kHz (Oldies)
528 N New St
Bethlehem, PA 18018
Phone: 610-866-8074
Fax: 610-866-9381

WHOL-AM 1600 kHz (Misc)
1125 Colorado St
Allentown, PA 18103
Phone: 610-434-4801

WKAP-AM 1470 kHz (Nost)
1541 Alta Dr 4th Fl
Whitehall, PA 18052
www.1470wkap.com
Phone: 610-434-1742
Fax: 610-434-6288

WLEV-FM 100.7 MHz (AC)
2158 Ave C
Bethlehem, PA 18017
Phone: 610-266-7600
Fax: 610-231-0400

WODE-FM 99.9 MHz (Oldies)
107 W Paxinosa Rd
Easton, PA 18040
www.oldies99.com
Phone: 610-258-6155
Fax: 610-253-3384

WTKZ-AM 1320 kHz (Span)
961 Marcon Blvd Suite 400
Allentown, PA 18103
E-mail: info@wtkz.com
www.wtkz.com
Phone: 610-465-1320
Fax: 610-465-1321

WZZO-FM 95.1 MHz (Rock)
1541 Alta Dr Suite 400
Whitehall, PA 18052
www.wzzo.com
Phone: 610-434-1742
Fax: 610-434-6288

Attractions

Allentown's Liberty Bell Shrine, located on Hamilton Mall, is one the city's most famous attractions. Other cultural and historical attractions in the area include the Allentown Art Museum; Lehigh County Museum, which features exhibits of the area's original Indian inhabitants, the Lennni-Lenape; Haines Mill Museum, an operating grist mill built in 1760 and restored in 1909; and Trout Hall, Allentown's oldest home. Mayfair Festival of the Arts, a week-long celebration of theater, dance, music, and visual arts, is held each May in Allentown's Cedar Beach Park; and the Great Allentown Fair, one of the nation's top 50 fairs, is held each August.

Allentown Art Museum
5th & Court Sts
Allentown, PA 18105
www.lvartspage.org/artmseum.htm
Phone: 610-432-4333
Fax: 610-434-7409

Allentown Symphony Orchestra
23 N 6th St
Allentown, PA 18101
E-mail: info@allentownsymphony.org
www.allentownsymphony.org
Phone: 610-432-7961
Fax: 610-432-6009

Ballet Guild of the Lehigh Valley
556 Main St
Bethlehem, PA 18018
E-mail: ythballet@aol.com
www.bglv.org
Phone: 610-865-0353
Fax: 610-865-2698

Bear Creek Ski & Recreation Area
101 Doe Mountain Ln
Macungie, PA 18062
www.skibearcreek.com
Phone: 610-682-7100
Fax: 610-682-7110
TF: 800-475-4363

Blue Mountain Ski Area
1660 Blue Mountain Dr
Palmerton, PA 18071
E-mail: information@skibluemt.com
www.skibluemt.com
Phone: 610-826-7700
Fax: 610-826-7723

Buchman Frank House
117 N 11th St
Allentown, PA 18105
Phone: 610-435-4664
Fax: 610-435-9812

Burnside Plantation
1461 Schoenersville Rd
Bethlehem, PA 18016
Phone: 610-868-5044
Fax: 610-868-5044

Bushkill Park
2100 Bushkill Park Dr
Easton, PA 18040
E-mail: party@bushkillpark.com
www.bushkillpark.com
Phone: 610-258-6941
Fax: 610-258-6004

Cedar Crest Stage Co
100 College Dr
Allentown, PA 18104
Phone: 610-606-4608
Fax: 610-606-4654

Civic Theatre Phone: 610-432-8943
527 N 19th St Fax: 610-432-7381
Allentown, PA 18104
www.civictheatre.com

Colonial Industrial Quarter Phone: 610-882-0450
459 Old York Rd Fax: 610-882-0460
Bethlehem, PA 18018

Crayola Factory Phone: 610-515-8000
30 Centre Sq Two Rivers Landing Fax: 610-559-6690
Easton, PA 18042
www.crayola.com/factory

Crystal Cave Park Phone: 610-683-6765
963 Crystal Cave Rd
Kutztown, PA 19530
www.crystalcavepa.com

Delaware National Scenic River Phone: 570-588-2435
Delaware Water Gap National Recreation Area Fax: 570-588-2780
Bushkill, PA 18324
www.nps.gov/dela/

Delaware Water Gap National Recreation Area Phone: 570-588-2435
Bushkill, PA 18324 Fax: 570-588-2780
www.nps.gov/dewa/

Discovery Center of Science & Technology Phone: 610-865-5010
511 E 3rd St Fax: 610-865-5010
Bethlehem, PA 18015
www.discovery-center.org/

Dorney Park & Wildwater Kingdom Phone: 610-395-3724
3830 Dorney Park Rd Fax: 610-391-7685
Allentown, PA 18104 TF: 800-551-5656
E-mail: info@dorneypark.com
www.dorneypark.com

Dutch Springs Phone: 610-759-2270
4733 Hanoverville Rd Fax: 610-759-9441
Bethlehem, PA 18017
E-mail: dutchspr@epix.net
www.dutchsprings.com

Fairgrounds Farmers Market Phone: 610-432-8425
17th & Chew Sts Fax: 610-427-0891
Allentown, PA 18104

Gross Malcolm W Memorial Rose Garden Phone: 610-437-7628
2700 Parkway Blvd Fax: 610-437-7685
Allentown, PA 18104

Haines Mill Museum Phone: 610-435-4664
3600 Haines Mill Rd
Allentown, PA 18104

Hugh Moore Historical Park & National Canal Museum Phone: 610-515-8000
30 Centre Sq Fax: 610-559-6691
Easton, PA 18042
E-mail: ncm@canals.org
canals.org

Kemerer Museum of Decorative Arts Phone: 610-868-6868
427 N New St Fax: 610-882-0460
Bethlehem, PA 18016
www.historicbethlehem.org/decor.htm

Lehigh County Historical Society Phone: 610-435-4664
Hamilton & 5th St Fax: 610-435-9812
Allentown, PA 18101

Lehigh County Museum Phone: 610-435-4664
501 Hamilton St Old Courthouse Fax: 610-435-9812
Allentown, PA 18101
www.voicenet.com/~lchs

Lehigh Valley Chamber Orchestra Phone: 610-266-8555
PO Box 20641 Fax: 610-266-8525
Lehigh Valley, PA 18002
E-mail: lvco@fast.net
www.lvco.org

Lenni Lenape Historical Society Phone: 610-797-2121
2825 Fish Hatchery Rd Fax: 610-797-2801
Allentown, PA 18103
E-mail: lenape@comcat.com
www.lenape.org

Liberty Bell Shrine Phone: 610-435-4232
622 Hamilton Mall Fax: 610-435-5667
Allentown, PA 18101

Lost River Caverns Phone: 610-838-8767
726 Durham St Fax: 610-838-2961
Hellertown, PA 18055
E-mail: info@lostcave.com
www.lostcave.com

Museum of Indian Culture Phone: 610-797-2121
2825 Fish Hatchery Rd Fax: 610-797-2801
Allentown, PA 18103
www.lenape.org/aboutmuseum.html

Pennsylvania Sinfonia Orchestra Phone: 610-434-7811
1524 W Linden St Fax: 610-434-6508
Allentown, PA 18102
www.pasinfonia.org

Queen City Nursery Phone: 610-437-7656
2901 Fish Hatchery Rd
Allentown, PA 18103

Repertory Dance Theatre Phone: 610-433-1680
1402 Linden St Fax: 610-967-2826
Allentown, PA 18102

Trout Hall Phone: 610-435-4664
414 Walnut St Fax: 610-435-9812
Allentown, PA 18101

Sports Teams & Facilities

Allentown Ambassadors (baseball) Phone: 610-437-6800
1511-25 Hamilton St Fax: 610-437-6804
Allentown, PA 18102
www.ambassadorbaseball.com

Nazareth Speedway Phone: 610-759-8800
Hwy 191 Fax: 610-759-9055
Nazareth, PA 18064 TF: 888-629-7223

Parkette National Gymnastic Team
401 ML King Jr Dr
Allentown, PA 18102
www.parkettes.com
Phone: 610-433-0011
Fax: 610-433-8948

Annual Events

Allentown Tree Lighting Ceremony
(late November) 610-776-7117
Antique Show (late October) 610-433-7541
Apparitions of Allentown: A Walk of Historic Haunts
(late October) 610-435-4664
Bach Choir of Bethlehem Christmas Concert
(early December) 610-866-4382
Boo at the Zoo (late October) 610-799-4171
Celtic Classic Highland Games & Festival
(late September) 610-868-9599
Cement Belt Free Fair (mid-June) 610-262-9750
Christkindlmarkt (late November-mid-December) . . .610-861-0678
Das Awkscht Fescht (early August) 610-967-2317
Elvis Birthday Bash (mid-January) 610-252-3132
Fall Foliage Festival (October) .610-799-4171
German Festival (late June-early July) 800-963-8824
Great Allentown Fair
(late August-early September) 610-433-7541
Lights in the Parkway
(late November-mid-January) 610-437-7616
Mayfair Festival of the Arts (late May) 610-437-6900
Musikfest (mid-August) 610-861-0678
Open Gate Farm Tours (mid-October) 610-868-5044
Pennsylvania Shakespeare Festival
(late May-early August) 610-282-3192
Riverside Art Festival (mid-September) 610-250-6710
Spring Corn Festival (early March) 610-797-2121
Time of Thanksgiving (mid-November) 610-797-2121
Wheels of Time Rod & Custom Jamboree
(mid-August) 610-865-4114

Amarillo, Texas

County: Potter, Randall

MARILLO is located in the "panhandle" of northern Texas. Major cities within 300 miles include Lubbock and Abilene, Texas; Santa Fe, New Mexico; and Oklahoma City, Oklahoma.

Area (Land)	88.0 sq mi
Area (Water)	0.4 sq mi
Elevation	3,676 ft
Latitude	35-13-13 N
Longitude	101-47-57 W
Time Zone	CST
Area Code	806

Climate

Amarillo has a moderate climate that features four distinct seasons and 351 days of sunshine each year. Winter days are cool, with average high temperatures near 50 degrees, while lows dip into the 20s. The annual mean snowfall Amarillo is just over 15 inches. Summer days are hot, with average highs around 90 degrees and evening lows cooling down into the 60s. Summer is also the wettest time of the year in Amarillo, with nearly half of the annual rainfall occurring from June through August.

Average Temperatures & Precipitation

Temperatures

	Jan	Feb	Mar	Apr	May	Jun	Jul	Aug	Sep	Oct	Nov	Dec
High	49	53	62	72	79	88	92	89	82	73	60	50
Low	21	26	33	42	52	61	66	64	56	45	32	24

Precipitation

	Jan	Feb	Mar	Apr	May	Jun	Jul	Aug	Sep	Oct	Nov	Dec
Inches	0.5	0.6	1.0	1.0	2.5	3.7	2.6	3.2	2.0	1.4	0.7	0.4

History

The area of northern Texas known today as Amarillo was first explored by Europeans in 1541, when Spanish conquistador Francisco Coronado passed through the area in search of the Seven Golden Cities of Cibola. Spanish exploration continued in the area through the 1700s, when a portion of El Camino Real was built through the area. Sheep and cattle herders from around the world were also drawn to the grazing grounds of the northern Texas plains.

In 1876, Potter County was established by the Texas Legislature, and one of the county's earliest settlers was Colonel Charles Goodnight, inventor of the chuckwagon. Goodnight is also credited with starting the area's cattle industry. In 1887, a new community had formed in the Texas Panhandle near a railway construction camp. Originally called "Ragtown" because of the buffalo hide huts that comprised the settlement, the community was soon renamed "Amarillo" (the Spanish word for "yellow") after the color of the clay deposits in a nearby creek. Amarillo became the seat of Potter County and was incorporated as a city several years later, in 1892. The arrival of various railroads helped to fuel the area's early economy and Amarillo grew quickly as a major cattle ranching and shipping center. At the turn of the century, Amarillo was home to approximately 1,400 people; by 1910, the population had grown to nearly 10,000.

Although agriculture was the mainstay of Amarillo's early economy, the discovery of natural gas in the Texas Panhandle in 1918 and the discovery of oil in 1921 helped to fuel Amarillo's growth and prosperity. Today, Amarillo has the largest natural gas development in the entire world, providing pipelines to many major American cities. The oil and gas industry has spawned new petrochemical industries that have helped to diversify the area's economy. However, despite the modern industries that have helped to propel Amarillo into the 21st century, the city remains a major center for cattle feeding and ranching, as it has been since the 1800s. Many of the area's cattle ranches have remained virtually unchanged since they were established in the 19th Century.

Home to more than 171,000 people, Amarillo today features a unique blend of modern cityscapes and Old West charm. Located in two counties (Potter and Randall), Amarillo is the leading center for agriculture, transportation, and industry in the Texas Panhandle.

Population

1990 Census	157,571
1998 Estimate	171,207
% Change	8.7

Racial/Ethnic Breakdown

White	82.7%
Black	6.0%
Other	11.3%
Hispanic Origin (may be of any race)	14.7%

Age Breakdown

Under 5 years	8.4%
5 to 17	19.8%
18 to 20	4.3%
21 to 24	5.5%
25 to 34	17.5%
35 to 44	14.5%
45 to 54	9.4%
55 to 64	8.7%
65 to 74	6.9%
75+ years	5.1%
Median Age	32.0

Gender Breakdown

Male	47.9%
Female	52.1%

Government

Type of Government: Commission-Manager

Amarillo City Commission
PO Box 1971
Amarillo, TX 79105
Phone: 806-378-3010
Fax: 806-378-9394

Amarillo City Hall
509 E 7th St
Amarillo, TX 79101
Phone: 806-378-3014
Fax: 806-378-9394

Amarillo City Manager
PO Box 1971
Amarillo, TX 79105
Phone: 806-378-3014
Fax: 806-378-9394

Amarillo City Secretary
PO Box 1971
Amarillo, TX 79105
Phone: 806-378-3013
Fax: 806-378-9394

Amarillo City Transit System
800 E 23rd Ave
Amarillo, TX 79103
Phone: 806-342-9142
Fax: 806-342-9146

Amarillo Community Development Dept
PO Box 1971
Amarillo, TX 79105
Phone: 806-378-3023
Fax: 806-378-9389

Amarillo Economic Development Corp
600 S Tyler St Suite1503
Amarillo, TX 79101
Phone: 806-379-6411
Fax: 806-371-0112

Amarillo Emergency Management Dept
PO Box 1971
Amarillo, TX 79105
Phone: 806-378-3022
Fax: 806-378-9366

Amarillo Finance Dept
509 E 7th Ave Rm 303
Amarillo, TX 79101
Phone: 806-378-3040
Fax: 806-378-3018

Amarillo Fire Dept
400 S Van Buren St
Amarillo, TX 79101
Phone: 806-378-3060
Fax: 806-378-9476

Amarillo Legal Dept
PO Box 1971
Amarillo, TX 79105
Phone: 806-378-4208
Fax: 806-378-3018

Amarillo Mayor
509 E 7th St
Amarillo, TX 79101
Phone: 806-378-3010
Fax: 806-378-9394

Amarillo Parks & Recreation Div
PO Box 1971
Amarillo, TX 79105
Phone: 806-378-4290
Fax: 806-378-3021

Amarillo Personnel Dept
509 E 7th Ave Rm 207
Amarillo, TX 79105
Phone: 806-378-9300
Fax: 806-378-9478

Amarillo Planning Dept
PO Box 1971
Amarillo, TX 79105
Phone: 806-378-3020
Fax: 806-378-9388

Amarillo Police Dept
200 SE 3rd Ave
Amarillo, TX 79101
Phone: 806-378-3038
Fax: 806-378-9469

Amarillo Public Health Dept
PO Box 1971
Amarillo, TX 79105
Phone: 806-351-7220
Fax: 806-351-7275

Amarillo Public Library
413 E 4th Ave
Amarillo, TX 79101
Phone: 806-378-3054
Fax: 806-378-9327

Amarillo Public Works Div
PO Box 1971
Amarillo, TX 79105
Phone: 806-378-3024
Fax: 806-378-9388

Amarillo Utilities Div
PO Box 1971
Amarillo, TX 79105
Phone: 806-378-3035
Fax: 806-378-3027

Important Phone Numbers

AAA.......806-354-8288
Amarillo Assn of Realtors.......806-358-7736
Driver's License Information.......806-351-1127
Emergency.......911
Highway Conditions.......800-452-9292
HotelDocs.......800-468-3537
Poison Control Center.......800-764-7661
Potter County Tax Assessor-Collector.......806-342-2600
Randall County Tax Assessor-Collector.......806-655-6287
Texas Comptroller of Public Accounts.......800-252-5555
Time/Temp.......806-372-2611
Vehicle Registration Information (Potter County).......806-342-2600
Vehicle Registration Information (Randall County).......806-655-6287
Voter Registration Information (Potter County).......806-379-2299
Voter Registration Information (Randall County).......806-655-6285
Weather.......806-358-7755

Information Sources

Amarillo Chamber of Commerce
1000 S Polk St
Amarillo, TX 79101
www.amarillo-cvb.org
Phone: 806-373-7800
Fax: 806-373-3909

Amarillo Civic Center
401 S Buchanan St
Amarillo, TX 79101
www.civicamarillo.com
Phone: 806-378-4297
Fax: 806-378-4234

Amarillo Convention & Visitor Council
PO Box 9480
Amarillo, TX 79105
www.amarillo-cvb.org
Phone: 806-374-1497
Fax: 806-373-3909
TF: 800-692-1338

Amarillo Economic Development Corp
600 S Tyler St Suite1503
Amarillo, TX 79101
www.amarillo-tx.com
Phone: 806-379-6411
Fax: 806-371-0112
TF: 800-333-7892

Better Business Bureau Serving the Texas Panhandle
PO Box 1905
Amarillo, TX 79105
www.amarillo.bbb.org
Phone: 806-379-6222
Fax: 806-379-8206

Potter County
PO Box 9638
Amarillo, TX 79105
www.co.potter.tx.us
Phone: 806-379-2275
Fax: 806-379-2296

Randall County
PO Box 660
Canyon, TX 79015
Phone: 806-655-6330
Fax: 806-656-6430

Online Resources

About.com Guide to Amarillo
amarillo.about.com/citiestowns/southwestus/amarillo

AmarilloPages.com
www.amarillopages.com

City Knowledge Amarillo
www.cityknowledge.com/tx_amarilo.htm

Excite.com Amarillo City Guide
www.excite.com/travel/countries/united_states/texas/amarillo

Internet Amarillo
www.amarillo.searchtexas.com/

Area Communities

Incorporated communities in the Amarillo MSA (which includes Potter and Randall counties) with populations greater than 10,000 include:

Canyon
301 16th St
Canyon, TX 79015
Phone: 806-655-5000
Fax: 806-655-5025

Economy

Amarillo's diverse economic base ranges from wheat farming to ordnance assembly. Cattle ranching, natural gas and oil exploration and production, and related industries remain important players in the area's economy, as they have throughout the 20th Century. Health care also has become a vital industry in Amarillo - four of the metro area's 15 largest employers are health care-related. Services, retail trade, and government are the metro area's largest employment sectors.

Unemployment Rate 4.0%
Per Capita Income $22,051*
Median Family Income $40,400

** Information given is for the Amarillo Metropolitan Statistical Area (MSA), which includes Potter and Randall counties.*

Principal Industries & Number of Wage Earners

Amarillo MSA* - 1999

Industry	Wage Earners
Construction	5,300
Finance, Insurance, & Real Estate	5,500
Government	16,900
Manufacturing	9,100
Mining	600
Retail Trade	20,800
Services	28,000
Transportation & Public Utilities	5,300
Wholesale Trade	6,300

** Information given is for the Amarillo Metropolitan Statistical Area (MSA), which includes Potter and Randall counties.*

Major Employers

Affiliated Foods Inc
PO Box 30300
Amarillo, TX 79120
Phone: 806-372-3851
Fax: 806-345-7837
TF: 800-690-7476

Amarillo City Hall
509 E 7th St
Amarillo, TX 79101
www.ci.amarillo.tx.us
Phone: 806-378-3014
Fax: 806-378-9394

Amarillo Independent School District
7200 I-40 W
Amarillo, TX 79106
www.amarillo.isd.tenet.edu
Phone: 806-354-4200
Fax: 806-354-4741

Baptist-Saint Anthony's Hospital
1600 Wallace Blvd
Amarillo, TX 79106
www.bsahs.com
Phone: 806-212-2000
Fax: 806-212-2932

IBP Inc
PO Box 30500
Amarillo, TX 79187
www.ibpinc.com
Phone: 806-335-1531
Fax: 806-335-7291

Mason & Hanger Corp-Pantex
PO Box 30020
Amarillo, TX 79120
Phone: 806-477-3000
Fax: 806-477-5568

Northwest Texas Hospital
PO Box 1110
Amarillo, TX 79175
www.nwths.com
Phone: 806-354-1000
Fax: 806-354-1122

Owens Corning Fiberglas
PO Box 8000
Amarillo, TX 79114
www.owenscorning.com
Phone: 806-622-1582
Fax: 806-622-4593

Southwestern Public Service Co
600 S Tyler St
Amarillo, TX 79101
Phone: 806-378-2121
Fax: 806-378-2995
TF: 800-750-2520

Texas Dept of Criminal Justice Bill Clements Unit
9601 Spur 591
Amarillo, TX 79107
Phone: 806-381-7080
Fax: 806-383-7126

Texas Dept of Criminal Justice Neal Unit
9055 Spur 591
Amarillo, TX 79107
Phone: 806-383-1175
Fax: 806-383-4487

Texas Tech Health Sciences Center
1400 Wallace Blvd
Amarillo, TX 79106
www.ttuhsc.edu
Phone: 806-354-5411
Fax: 806-351-3788

Veterans Affairs Medical Center
6010 Amarillo Blvd W
Amarillo, TX 79106
Phone: 806-355-9703
Fax: 806-354-7869

West Texas A & M University
2501 4th Ave
Canyon, TX 79016
E-mail: dana.olmstead@wtamu.edu
www.wtamu.edu
Phone: 806-651-0000
Fax: 806-651-2017
TF: 800-999-8268

Westgate Mall
7701 W I-40 Suite 140
Amarillo, TX 79160
westgatemalltx.com
Phone: 806-358-7221
Fax: 806-353-5424

Quality of Living Indicators

Total Crime Index 13,526
(rates per 100,000 inhabitants)

Violent Crime
Murder/manslaughter 10
Forcible rape 54
Robbery 234
Aggravated assault 921

Property Crime
Burglary 1,772
Larceny theft 9,832
Motor vehicle theft 703

Cost of Living Index 91.2
(national average = 100)

Median Home Price $81,400

Education

Public Schools

Amarillo Independent School District
7200 I-40 W
Amarillo, TX 79106
www.amarillo.isd.tenet.edu
Phone: 806-354-4200
Fax: 806-354-4741

Number of Schools
Elementary 44
Middle 14
High 8

Student/Teacher Ratio
All Grades 15.6:1

Private Schools

Number of Schools (all grades) .... 16+

Colleges & Universities

Amarillo College
PO Box 447
Amarillo, TX 79178
www.actx.edu
Phone: 806-371-5000
Fax: 806-371-5066
TF: 800-996-6707

West Texas A & M University
2501 4th Ave
Canyon, TX 79016
E-mail: dana.olmstead@wtamu.edu
www.wtamu.edu
Phone: 806-651-0000
Fax: 806-651-2017
TF: 800-999-8268

Hospitals

Baptist-Saint Anthony's Hospital
1600 Wallace Blvd
Amarillo, TX 79106
www.bsahs.com
Phone: 806-212-2000
Fax: 806-212-2932

Northwest Texas Hospital
PO Box 1110
Amarillo, TX 79175
www.nwths.com
Phone: 806-354-1000
Fax: 806-354-1122

Saint Anthony's Baptist Health System
1600 Wallace Blvd
Amarillo, TX 79106
Phone: 806-212-2000
Fax: 806-212-2919

Veterans Affairs Medical Center
6010 Amarillo Blvd W
Amarillo, TX 79106
Phone: 806-355-9703
Fax: 806-354-7869

Transportation

Airport(s)

Amarillo International Airport (AMA)
10 miles E of downtown (approx 20 minutes) 806-335-1671

Mass Transit

City Transit
$.75 Base fare 806-378-3094

Rail/Bus

Greyhound/Trailways Bus Station
700 S Tyler St
Amarillo, TX 79101
Phone: 806-374-5371
TF: 800-231-2222

Utilities

Electricity
Southwestern Public Service Co 806-356-4300

Gas
Energas 888-363-7427
www.energas.com

Water
City of Amarillo Utilities 806-378-4241

Garbage Collection/Recycling
City of Amarillo Utilities 806-378-4241

Telecommunications

Telephone
Southwestern Bell Telephone Co 800-464-7928
www.swbell.com

Cable Television
Cox Communications 806-358-4801
www.cox.com

Internet Service Providers (ISPs)
1Source Technologies 806-467-1515
www.1s.net
Amarillo Online 806-353-7638
www.amaonline.com
ARNet Inc 806-355-3539
www.arn.net

Banks

Amarillo National Bank
410 S Taylor St Plaza One
Amarillo, TX 79101
www.anb.com
Phone: 806-378-8000
Fax: 806-373-7505
TF: 800-262-3733

Bank of America
701 S Taylor St
Amarillo, TX 79101
Phone: 806-378-1400
Fax: 806-378-1514
TF: 800-247-6262

Bank One
600 S Tyler St
Amarillo, TX 79101
Phone: 806-378-3100
Fax: 806-378-3221
TF: 800-695-1111

First State Bank
3501 Soncy Rd Suite 1
Amarillo, TX 79121
Phone: 806-354-2265
Fax: 806-354-2407

Western National Bank
4241 W 45th St
Amarillo, TX 79109
Phone: 806-355-9641
Fax: 806-353-3269

Shopping

Route 66 District
6th St betw Georgia & Western Sts
Amarillo, TX 79106
Phone: 806-372-1060
Fax: 806-342-4770

Western Plaza Shopping Center
2201 S Western St
Amarillo, TX 79109
Phone: 806-355-8216
Fax: 806-352-8158

Westgate Mall
7701 W I-40 Suite 140
Amarillo, TX 79160
westgatemalltx.com
Phone: 806-358-7221
Fax: 806-353-5424

Wolflin Square & Village
1901 S Georgia St
Amarillo, TX 79109
Phone: 806-355-6131

Media

Newspapers and Magazines

Amarillo Daily News*
PO Box 2091
Amarillo, TX 79166
www.amarillonet.com
Phone: 806-376-4488
Fax: 806-373-0810

Amarillo Globe Times*
PO Box 2091
Amarillo, TX 79166
www.amarillonet.com
Phone: 806-376-4488
Fax: 806-373-0810

**Indicates major daily newspapers*

Television

KACV-TV Ch 2 (PBS)
PO Box 447
Amarillo, TX 79178
kacvtv.org
Phone: 806-371-5230
Fax: 806-371-5258

KAMR-TV Ch 4 (NBC)
1015 S Fillmore St
Amarillo, TX 79101
E-mail: kamr@arn.net
www.kamr.com
Phone: 806-383-3321
Fax: 806-381-2943

KCIT-TV Ch 14 (Fox)
1015 S Fillmore St
Amarillo, TX 79101
Phone: 806-374-1414
Fax: 806-371-0408

KCPN-TV Ch 65 (UPN)
1015 S Filmore St
Amarillo, TX 79101
Phone: 806-374-1414
Fax: 806-371-0408

KFDA-TV Ch 10 (CBS)
7900 Broadway
Amarillo, TX 79108
E-mail: 10assign@arn.net
www.newschannel10.com
Phone: 806-383-1010
Fax: 806-381-9859

KVII-TV Ch 7 (ABC)
1 Broadcast Ctr
Amarillo, TX 79101
www.kvii.com
Phone: 806-373-1787
Fax: 806-371-7329

Radio

KACV-FM 89.9 MHz (Misc)
PO Box 447
Amarillo, TX 79178
E-mail: kacvfm90@actx.edu
kacvfm.org
Phone: 806-371-5222
Fax: 806-345-5576

KARX-FM 95.7 MHz (CR)
301 S Polk St Suite 100
Amarillo, TX 79101
Phone: 806-342-5200
Fax: 806-342-5202

KATP-FM 101.9 MHz (Ctry)
5406 Winners Cir
Amarillo, TX 79110
Phone: 806-359-5999
Fax: 806-359-0136

KBZD-FM 99.7 MHz (Urban)
5200 Amarillo Blvd E
Amarillo, TX 79107
Phone: 806-372-6543
Fax: 806-379-7339

KGNC-AM 710 kHz (N/T)
PO Box 710
Amarillo, TX 79189
www.kgnc.com
Phone: 806-355-9801
Fax: 806-354-9450
TF: 800-285-0710

KGNC-FM 97.9 Mhz (Ctry)
PO Box 710
Amarillo, TX 79189
E-mail: kgnc@kgnc.com
www.kgnc.com/FM/fm_main.htm
Phone: 806-355-9801
Fax: 806-354-9450
TF: 877-765-9790

KNSY-FM 98.7 MHz (CR)
1703 Avondale St
Amarillo, TX 79106
Phone: 806-355-9777
Fax: 806-355-5832

KPUR-FM 107.1 MHz (Oldies)
301 S Polk St Suite 100
Amarillo, TX 79106
Phone: 806-342-5200
Fax: 806-342-5202

KQFX-FM 104.3 MHz (Span)
3639 B Wolflin Ave
Amarillo, TX 79102
Phone: 806-355-1044
Fax: 806-352-6525

KQIZ-FM 93.1 MHz (CHR)
301 S Polk St Suite 100
Amarillo, TX 79101
Phone: 806-342-5200
Fax: 806-342-5200

KZRK-FM 107.9 MHz (Rock)
301 S Polk St Suite 100
Amarillo, TX 79101
Phone: 806-342-5200
Fax: 806-342-5200

Attractions

A longtime agricultural center, Amarillo draws thousands of Old West enthusiasts each year who come to visit the area's numerous cattle ranches, many of which still function as they did when they were established more than a century ago, and to see the outdoor musical drama, "Texas." The Amarillo Civic Center also hosts the annual Farm and Ranch Show, which has been named one of the top five agricultural trade shows in the United States. Other attractions in the city include the Amarillo Zoo and Amarillo Museum of Art. In addition, Palo Duro Canyon State Park, the country's second largest canyon, is just a few miles from the city. Nearby also is Cadillac Ranch, where visitors can see ten Cadillacs buried nose-down in a field.

Alibates Flint Quarries National Monument
PO Box 1460
Fritch, TX 79036
www.nps.gov/alfl/
Phone: 806-857-3151
Fax: 806-857-2319

Amarillo Botanical Gardens
1400 Streit Dr
Amarillo, TX 79106
Phone: 806-352-6513
Fax: 806-352-6227

Amarillo Livestock Auction
100 S Manhattan
Amarillo, TX 79104
www.amarillo-cvb.org/cattle.html
Phone: 806-373-7464
Fax: 806-376-1765

Amarillo Museum of Art
2200 S Van Buren St
Amarillo, TX 79109
E-mail: amoa@arn.net
www.amarilloart.org
Phone: 806-371-5050
Fax: 806-373-9235

Amarillo Opera
PO Box 447
Amarillo, TX 79178
www.amarilloopera.org
Phone: 806-372-7464
Fax: 806-372-7465

Amarillo Symphony
1000 S Polk St
Amarillo, TX 79101
E-mail: symphony@dns.genesis.net
www.actx.edu/~symphony
Phone: 806-376-8782
Fax: 806-376-7127

Amarillo Zoo
Hwy 287 N Thompson Pk
Amarillo, TX 79107
Phone: 806-381-7911

American Quarter Horse Heritage Center & Museum
2601 I-40 E
Amarillo, TX 79104
Phone: 806-376-5181
Fax: 806-376-1005

Cadillac Ranch
I-40 W to Arnot Exit
Amarillo, TX

Cal Farley's Boys Ranch
PO Box 1890
Amarillo, TX 79174
www.calfarleysboysranch.org
Phone: 806-372-2341
Fax: 806-372-6638
TF: 800-687-3722

English Field Air & Space Museum
2014 English Rd
Amarillo, TX 79108
Phone: 806-335-1812
Fax: 806-335-1993

Harrington Don Discovery Center
1200 Streit Dr
Amarillo, TX 79106
www.searchtexas.com/discovery/
Phone: 806-355-9547
Fax: 806-355-5703
TF: 800-784-9548

Lake Meredith National Recreation Area
PO Box 1460
Fritch, TX 79036
www.nps.gov/lamr/
Phone: 806-857-3151
Fax: 806-857-2319

Lone Star Ballet
1000 S Polk St
Amarillo, TX 79101
Phone: 806-372-2463
Fax: 806-372-3131

Palo Duro Canyon State Park
Rt 2
Canyon, TX 79015
E-mail: pdc@amaonline.com
www.amintech.com/amarillo/paloduro/
Phone: 806-488-2227

Panhandle-Plains Historical Museum
2401 4th Ave
Canyon, TX 79015
E-mail: museum@wtamu.edu
www.wtamu.edu/museum
Phone: 806-651-2244
Fax: 806-651-2250

Route 66 District
6th St betw Georgia & Western Sts
Amarillo, TX 79106
Phone: 806-372-1060
Fax: 806-342-4770

Wonderland Amusement Park
2601 Dumas Dr
Amarillo, TX 79107
www.wonderlandpark.com
Phone: 806-383-4712
Fax: 806-383-8737

Sports Teams & Facilities

Amarillo Dillas (baseball)
3rd & Grand Sts Potter County Memorial Stadium
Amarillo, TX 79105
www.dillas.com
Phone: 806-342-3455
Fax: 806-374-2269

Amarillo Rattlers (hockey)
1422 S Tyler St Suite 100
Amarillo, TX 79101
E-mail: rattlers@arn.net
www.amarillorattlers.com
Phone: 806-374-7825
Fax: 806-374-7835

Annual Events

Amarillo Farm & Ranch Show (early December) 806-378-4297
Best of Texas Festival (late March) 806-374-0802
Boys Ranch Rodeo (Labor Day weekend) 806-372-2341
Circus Gatti (late February) 806-378-4297
Coors Ranch Rodeo (early-mid June) 806-376-7767
FunFest (late May) 806-374-0802
High Plains Book Festival (early October) 806-651-2231
Mel Phillips' Outdoor World Sportsman's Show (late January) 806-378-4297
Octoberfest (early September) 806-373-7800
Panhandle Boat Sport & Travel Show (early February) 806-383-4408

Range Riders Rodeo (early July) 806-355-2212
Super Bull Tour (late January). 806-378-3096
Texas Musical Drama (early June-late August) 806-655-2181
Tri-State Fair (mid-September) 806-376-7767
WRCA World Championship Ranch Rodeo
(mid-November). 806-374-9722

Anchorage, Alaska

***County:* Anchorage Borough**

NCHORAGE is located in southeastern Alaska on the shores of Cook Inlet. Major cities within 500 miles of Anchorage include Seward, Homer, and Valdez, Alaska.

Area (Land) .... 1697.6 sq mi
Area (Water).............................. 263.9 sq mi
Elevation.................................... 101 ft
Latitude ....61-21-81 N
Longitude.............................. 149-90-03 W
Time Zone .... Alaska
Area Code....................................... 907

Climate

Anchorage's proximity to the Pacific Ocean, via Cook Inlet and the Gulf of Alaska, helps to moderate its climate from temperature extremes. Although temperatures occasionally dip below freezing during the winter months, average temperatures range from highs in the low to mid-20s to lows around 10 degrees. An average of 70 inches of snow falls each year in Anchorage. Summer days are mild, with average highs in the mid-60s and lows near 50 degrees. Late summer and early autumn are the wettest times of the year in Anchorage.

Average Temperatures & Precipitation

Temperatures

	Jan	Feb	Mar	Apr	May	Jun	Jul	Aug	Sep	Oct	Nov	Dec
High	21	26	33	43	54	62	65	63	55	41	27	23
Low	8	12	18	29	39	47	52	50	42	29	15	10

Precipitation

	Jan	Feb	Mar	Apr	May	Jun	Jul	Aug	Sep	Oct	Nov	Dec
Inches	0.8	0.8	0.7	0.7	0.7	1.1	1.7	2.4	2.7	2.0	1.1	1.1

History

Originally occupied by the Eskimo people as early as 3,000 B.C., settlement did not begin in southern Alaska until the late 1700s when Russian explorers established trade routes in the area. Captain James Cook was the first European to explore the region, in 1778. In 1867, Alaska, then known as "Russian America," was sold to the United States for $7.2 million. During the late 1800s and early 1900s, area gold mines drew settlers to southeastern Alaska in search of fortune.

In 1915, construction of the Alaska Railroad began at Ship Creek Landing. A tent city was established at the anchorage of Ship Creek, and later that year the Anchorage Townsite Auction was held and a new community was formed. Anchorage was incorporated as a city in 1920. Early development of the city was fueled primarily by the railroad, which was completed in 1923. Initial growth was slow, but the 1940s marked a turning point in Anchorage's history. Before the war, Anchorage was home to 3,000 people. A military construction boom, which included the creation of Elmendorf Air Force Base and Fort Richardson, began in the area during the World War II. The influx of military personnel and others drawn by opportunity led to a population explosion. By 1951, Anchorage's population had risen to 47,000, surpassing Fairbanks to become the state's largest city.

The discovery of oil on the Kenai Peninsula in 1957 marked another pivotal event in Anchorage's development. Less than a decade later, in 1968, oil was discovered on the Arctic Slope of the Brooks Mountain Range. As a result, many oil companies established headquarters in Anchorage and spent millions of dollars on exploration. In 1972, construction began on the Trans-Alaska pipeline (TAP). Five years later the pipeline was completed and began transporting oil from the North Slope to the port of Valdez. The creation of the TAP also helped fuel the city's economy and sparked phenomenal growth - by the end of the 1970s Anchorage's population had skyrocketed to more than 184,000. At that time, more than half of the people in the entire state of Alaska lived in Anchorage.

Anchorage continued to grow and prosper throughout the remainder of the 20th Century. Today, with a population exceeding 254,000, Anchorage remains Alaska's largest city. The city is also a major center for trade, communications, transportation, healthcare, education, and finance.

Population

1990 Census 226,338
1998 Estimate..............................254,982
% Change 12.7

Racial/Ethnic Breakdown

White.....................................77.9%
Black 7.2%
Other.....................................14.9%
Hispanic Origin (may be of any race) 6.5%

Age Breakdown

Under 5 years...............................8.5%
5 to 19...................................24.7%
20 to 24....................................6.0%
25 to 34..................................15.8%
35 to 44..................................19.5%
45 to 54..................................14.3%
55 to 64....................................6.4%
65 to 74....................................3.2%
75+ years 1.7%
Median Age.................................32.1

Gender Breakdown

Male......................................51.3%
Female....................................48.7%

Government

Type of Government: Strong Mayor

Anchorage Assembly
PO Box 196650
Anchorage, AK 99519
Phone: 907-343-4311
Fax: 907-343-4499

Anchorage City Hall
632 W th Ave
Anchorage, AK 99501
Phone: 907-343-4311

Anchorage Community Planning & Development Dept
PO Box 196650
Anchorage, AK 99519
Phone: 907-343-4309
Fax: 907-343-4220

Anchorage Cultural & Recreational Services Dept
PO Box 196650
Anchorage, AK 99519
Phone: 907-343-4365
Fax: 907-343-4318

Anchorage Employee Relations Dept
PO Box 196650
Anchorage, AK 99519
Phone: 907-343-4453
Fax: 907-343-4511

Anchorage Finance Dept
PO Box 196650
Anchorage, AK 99519
Phone: 907-343-6610
Fax: 907-343-6616

Anchorage Fire Dept
1301 E 80th Ave
Anchorage, AK 99518
Phone: 907-267-4934
Fax: 907-267-4920

Anchorage Health & Human Services Dept
825 L St
Anchorage, AK 99501
Phone: 907-343-6718
Fax: 907-343-6740

Anchorage Mayor
PO Box 196650
Anchorage, AK 99519
Phone: 907-343-4431
Fax: 907-343-4499

Anchorage Municipal Clerk
PO Box 196650
Anchorage, AK 99519
Phone: 907-343-4311
Fax: 907-343-4313

Anchorage Municipal Manager
PO Box 196650
Anchorage, AK 99519
Phone: 907-343-4433
Fax: 907-343-4110

Anchorage Police Dept
4501 S Bragaw St
Anchorage, AK 99507
Phone: 907-786-8590
Fax: 907-786-8638

Anchorage Public Transportation Dept
3650-A E Tudor Rd
Anchorage, AK 99507
Phone: 907-786-8402
Fax: 907-563-2206

Anchorage Public Works Dept
PO Box 196650
Anchorage, AK 99519
Phone: 907-786-8161
Fax: 907-343-8125

Loussac ZJ Library
3600 Denali St
Anchorage, AK 99503
Phone: 907-343-2975
Fax: 907-562-1244

Important Phone Numbers

AAA....907-344-4310
American Express Travel....907-266-6600
Anchorage Board of Realtors....907-561-2338
Anchorage Finance Dept Tax Office....907-343-6650
Dental Referral....907-279-9144
Driver's License/Vehicle Registration Information....907-269-5551
Emergency....911
Events Line....907-276-3200
HotelDocs....800-468-3537
Medical Referral....907-562-1567
Poison Control Center....907-261-3193
Road Conditions....907-273-6037
Time/Temp....844
Voter Registration Information....907-522-8683
Weather....907-936-2525

Information Sources

Anchorage Chamber of Commerce
441 W 5th Ave Suite 300
Anchorage, AK 99501
www.anchoragechamber.org
Phone: 907-272-2401
Fax: 907-272-4117

Anchorage Convention & Visitors Bureau
524 W 4th Ave
Anchorage, AK 99501
www.anchorage.net
Phone: 907-276-4118
Fax: 907-278-5559
TF: 800-478-1255

Anchorage Municipality
PO Box 196650
Anchorage, AK 99519
www.ci.anchorage.ak.us/Services
Phone: 907-343-4311
Fax: 907-343-4313

Better Business Bureau Serving Alaska
2805 Bering St Suite 5
Anchorage, AK 99503
www.alaska.bbb.org
Phone: 907-562-0704
Fax: 907-562-4061

William A Egan Civic & Convention Center
555 W 5th Ave
Anchorage, AK 99501
www.egancenter.com
Phone: 907-263-2800
Fax: 907-263-2858

Online Resources

4Anchorage.com
www.4anchorage.com

About.com Guide to Anchorage
anchorage.about.com/local/alaskahawaii/anchorage

Alaska Scenes Guide to Anchorage & Southcentral Alaska
www.alaska.net/~design/scenes

Alaska's Best
alaskasbest.com

Anchorage CityLink
www.usacitylink.com/anchor

Anchorage Home Page
www.alaskaone.com/anchorage

Anchorage Online
www.alaskanet.com/Anchorage

Anchorage Points of Interest
www.alaska-online.com

Anchorage Restaurant Guide
www.akdining.com

Area Guide Anchorage
anchorage.areaguides.net

Bell's Alaska Travel Guide Anchorage
www.alaskan.com/bells/anchorage.html

City Knowledge Anchorage
www.cityknowledge.com/ak_anchorage.htm

Excite.com Anchorage City Guide
www.excite.com/travel/countries/united_states/alaska/anchorage

Lodging.com Anchorage Alaska
www.lodging.com/auto/guides/anchorage-ak.html

Online City Guide to Anchorage
www.olcg.com/ak/anchorage/main.html

Onroute Destinations Anchorage
www.onroute.com/destinations/alaska/anchorage.html

Rough Guide Travel Anchorage
travel.roughguides.com/content/1600/index.htm

Area Communities

Incorporated communities in the Anchorage area with populations greater than 1,000 include:

Palmer
231 W Evergreen Ave
Palmer, AK 99645
Phone: 907-745-9871
Fax: 907-745-0930

Wasilla
290 E Herning Ave
Wasilla, AK 99654
Phone: 907-373-9050
Fax: 907-373-9092

Economy

Anchorage has a diverse economic base that ranges from fishing to air transportation to retail trade. The oil industry continues to play a major role in the area's economy, with four of Anchorage's 10 largest private employers representing this industry. Services is Anchorage's largest employment sector, with health care being the largest service industry. Government is the second largest sector, providing jobs for more than 28,000 residents at the federal, state, and local levels.

Unemployment Rate	4.1%
Per Capita Income	$29,765
Median Family Income	$50,098

Principal Industries & Number of Wage Earners

City of Anchorage - 1998

Construction	7,000
Finance, Insurance, & Real Estate	7,500
Government	28,600
Manufacturing	2,000
Mining	2,700
Retail Trade	24,800
Services & Miscellaneous	36,600
Transportation	13,200
Wholesale Trade	6,500

Major Employers

Alaska Airlines Inc
4750 W International Airport Rd
Anchorage, AK 99502
www.alaska-air.com
Phone: 907-266-7200
Fax: 907-266-7229

Alaska Regional Hospital
2801 DeBarr Rd
Anchorage, AK 99508
www.akreg.com
Phone: 907-276-1131
Fax: 907-264-1143

Alyeska Pipeline Svc Co
1835 S Bragaw St
Anchorage, AK 99512
E-mail: alyeskamail@alyeska-pipeline.com
alyeska-pipe.com
Phone: 907-278-1611
Fax: 907-787-8611

Anchorage City Hall
632 W th Ave
Anchorage, AK 99501
www.ci.anchorage.ak.us
Phone: 907-343-4311

Anchorage School District
PO Box 196614
Anchorage, AK 99519
www.asd.k12.ak.us
Phone: 907-333-9561
Fax: 907-269-2296

BP Exploration (Alaska) Inc
900 E Benson Blvd
Anchorage, AK 99508
www.bpamoco.com/alaska/index_alaska.htm
Phone: 907-561-5111
Fax: 907-564-5441

Elmendorf Air Force Base
Elmendorf AFB, AK 99506
www.elmendorf.af.mil
Phone: 907-552-8151
Fax: 907-552-5111

Fred Meyer
2000 W Diamond Blvd
Anchorage, AK 99515
www.fredmeyer.com/fms/fms.shtml
Phone: 907-267-6700
Fax: 907-349-6672

National Bank of Alaska
301 W Northern Lights Blvd
Anchorage, AK 99503
www.nationalbankofalaska.com
Phone: 907-276-1132
Fax: 907-265-2068

Providence Alaska Medical Center
PO Box 196604
Anchorage, AK 99519
www.providence.org
Phone: 907-562-2211
Fax: 907-261-3048

Safeway Inc
6401 A St
Anchorage, AK 99518
www.safeway.com
Phone: 907-561-1944
Fax: 907-565-6093

Sam's Club
3651 Penland Pkwy
Anchorage, AK 99508
www.samsclub.com
Phone: 907-276-2996
Fax: 907-258-5691

Trident Seafoods Corp
5011 Spenard Rd Suite 203
Anchorage, AK 99502
www.tridentseafoods.com
Phone: 907-243-3166
Fax: 907-248-8933

US Public Health Service Alaska Native Medical Center
4315 Diplomacy Dr
Anchorage, AK 99508
Phone: 907-563-2662
Fax: 907-729-1984

Veco Corp
813 W Northern Lights Blvd
Anchorage, AK 99503
www.veco.com
Phone: 907-277-5309
Fax: 907-264-8142

Wal-Mart
3101 A St
Anchorage, AK 99503
www.walmartstores.com
Phone: 907-563-5900
Fax: 907-561-3807

Quality of Living Indicators

Total Crime Index....................................12,949
(rates per 100,000 inhabitants)

Violent Crime
Murder/manslaughter........................... 19
Forcible rape 161
Robbery.................................... 398
Aggravated assault...........................1,106

Property Crime
Burglary 1,543
Larceny theft 8,417
Motor vehicle theft 1,251

Cost of Living Index...................................122.9
(national average = 100)

Median Home Price.................................$109,800

Education

Public Schools

Anchorage School District
PO Box 196614
Anchorage, AK 99519
www.asd.k12.ak.us
Phone: 907-333-9561
Fax: 907-269-2296

Number of Schools
Elementary................................. 61
Middle 9
High....................................... 6
Alternative K-12, Middle, & High Schools 8
Charter Schools.............................. 4

Student/Teacher Ratio
All Grades................................ 17.6:1

Private Schools

Number of Schools (all grades).................... 10+

Colleges & Universities

Alaska Pacific University
4101 University Dr
Anchorage, AK 99508
E-mail: apu@corcom.com
www.alaskapacific.edu
Phone: 907-561-1266
Fax: 907-564-8317
TF: 800-252-7528

University of Alaska Anchorage
3211 Providence Dr
Anchorage, AK 99508
E-mail: ayenrol@uaa.alaska.edu
www.uaa.alaska.edu
Phone: 907-786-1800
Fax: 907-786-4888

Wayland Baptist University Anchorage
5530 E Northern Lights Blvd Suite 24
Anchorage, AK 99504
E-mail: wbualctr@alaska.net
www.wbu.edu/ak/index.html
Phone: 907-333-2277
Fax: 907-337-8122

Hospitals

Alaska Regional Hospital
2801 DeBarr Rd
Anchorage, AK 99508
www.akreg.com
Phone: 907-276-1131
Fax: 907-264-1143

Providence Alaska Medical Center
PO Box 196604
Anchorage, AK 99519
www.providence.org
Phone: 907-562-2211
Fax: 907-261-3048

Transportation

Airport(s)

Anchorage International Airport (ANC)
3 miles SW of downtown (approx 15 minutes) 907-266-2525

Mass Transit

People Mover
$1 Base fare 907-343-6543

Rail/Bus

Alaska Railroad Station
411 W 1st Ave
Anchorage, AK 99501
Phone: 907-265-2494

Utilities

Electricity
Chugach Electric Service.......................907-563-7366
www.chugachelectric.com
Municipal Light & Power 907-263-5340

Gas
ENSTAR Natural Gas Co.......................907-277-5551
www.semcoenergy.com/enstar.html

Water
Anchorage Water & Wastewater Utility 907-564-2700

Garbage Collection/Recycling
Anchorage Municpal Solid Waste Services 907-343-6262
Anchorage Refuse Inc 907-563-3717

Telecommunications

Telephone
Alaska Communication Systems 907-561-1221
AT & T Alascom 907-264-7000

Cable Television
GCI Cable 907-786-9200

Internet Service Providers (ISPs)
ACS Internet 907-565-2200
www.acsalaska.net
Core Communications 907-563-1191
www.corecom.net
Internet Alaska 907-562-4638
www.alaska.net
Matnet Inc 907-373-3580
www.matnet.com
Unicom Inc. 907-561-1674
unicom-alaska.com

Banks

First Interstate Bank of Alaska NA Phone: 907-277-2166
716 W 4th Ave Suite 102 Fax: 907-274-7343
Anchorage, AK 99501 TF: 800-688-2660
www.fibank.com

First National Bank of Anchorage Phone: 907-276-6300
PO Box 100720 Fax: 907-777-3528
Anchorage, AK 99510

KeyBank NA Alaska District Phone: 907-562-6100
101 W Benson Blvd Fax: 907-564-0387
Anchorage, AK 99510 TF: 800-478-6363

National Bank of Alaska Phone: 907-276-1132
301 W Northern Lights Blvd Fax: 907-265-2068
Anchorage, AK 99503
www.nationalbankofalaska.com

Northrim Bank Phone: 907-263-3226
311 C St Fax: 907-263-3205
Anchorage, AK 99503
www.northrim.com

Shopping

Anchorage 5th Avenue Mall Phone: 907-258-5535
320 W 5th Ave Fax: 907-279-3765
Anchorage, AK 99501

Antique Gallery The Phone: 907-276-8986
1001 W 4th Ave Suite B Fax: 907-276-8986
Anchorage, AK 99501
E-mail: antique@theantiquegallery.com
www.theantiquegallery.com

Dimond Center Phone: 907-344-2581
800 E Dimond Blvd Fax: 907-349-2411
Anchorage, AK 99515

Mall at Sears Phone: 907-264-6600
600 E Northern Lights Blvd Fax: 907-264-6600
Anchorage, AK 99508

Nordstrom Phone: 907-279-7622
603 D St Fax: 907-279-7622
Anchorage, AK 99501 TF: 800-478-3900

Northway Mall Phone: 907-276-5520
3101 Penland Pkwy Fax: 907-279-7192
Anchorage, AK 99508

Pia's Scandinavian Woolens Factory Outlet Phone: 907-277-7964
445 W 4th Ave
Anchorage, AK 99501

University Center Phone: 907-562-0347
3901 Old Seward Hwy Suite 9E Fax: 907-561-1963
Anchorage, AK 99503
E-mail: ucmarketing@alaskalife.net
www.shopuniversitycenter.com

Media

Newspapers and Magazines

Alaska Business Monthly Phone: 907-276-4373
PO Box 241288 Fax: 907-279-2900
Anchorage, AK 99524 TF: 800-770-4373
E-mail: info@akbizmag.com
www.akbizmag.com

Alaska Journal of Commerce Phone: 907-561-4772
4220 B St Suite 210 Fax: 907-563-4744
Anchorage, AK 99503
E-mail: journal@alaska.net
www.alaska.net/~journal/

Alaska Magazine Phone: 907-272-6070
619 E Ship Creek Ave Suite 329 Fax: 907-258-5360
Anchorage, AK 99501
E-mail: lac@groupz.net
www.alaskamagazine.com

Anchorage Daily News* Phone: 907-257-4200
PO Box 149001 Fax: 907-258-2157
Anchorage, AK 99514
www.adn.com

Anchorage Press Phone: 907-561-7737
702 W 32nd Ave Suite 203 Fax: 907-561-7777
Anchorage, AK 99503
E-mail: info@anchoragepress.com
www.anchoragepress.com

**Indicates major daily newspapers*

Television

KAKM-TV Ch 7 (PBS) Phone: 907-563-7070
3877 University Dr Fax: 907-273-9192
Anchorage, AK 99508
E-mail: kakm-tv@kakm.pbs.org

KIMO-TV Ch 13 (ABC) Phone: 907-561-1313
2700 E Tudor Rd Fax: 907-561-8934
Anchorage, AK 99507
www.aksupersite.com

KTBY-TV Ch 4 (Fox) Phone: 907-274-0404
1840 S Bragaw St Fax: 907-264-5180
Anchorage, AK 99508
www.fox4ktby.com

KTUU-TV Ch 2 (NBC)
701 E Tudor Rd Suite 220
Anchorage, AK 99503
E-mail: ktuu@ktuu.com
www.ktuu.com
Phone: 907-762-9202
Fax: 907-561-0882

KTVA-TV Ch 11 (CBS)
1007 W 32nd Ave
Anchorage, AK 99503
Phone: 907-562-3456
Fax: 907-273-3189

KYES-TV Ch 5 (UPN)
3700 Woodland Dr Suite 800
Anchorage, AK 99517
Phone: 907-248-5937
Fax: 907-243-0709

Radio

KASH-AM 1080 kHz (Ctry)
800 E Dimond Blvd Suite 3-370
Anchorage, AK 99515
Phone: 907-522-1515
Fax: 907-522-0694

KASH-FM 107.5 MHz (Ctry)
800 E Dimond Blvd Suite 3-370
Anchorage, AK 99515
Phone: 907-522-1515
Fax: 907-522-0672

KATB-FM 89.3 MHz (Rel)
6401 E Northern Lights Blvd
Anchorage, AK 99504
www.katb.org/katb/public_html/index.htm
Phone: 907-333-5282
Fax: 907-333-9851

KBFX-FM 100.5 MHz (CR)
800 E Dimond Blvd Suite 3-370
Anchorage, AK 99515
Phone: 907-522-1515
Fax: 907-522-0672

KBRJ-FM 104.1 MHz (Ctry)
9200 Lake Otis Pkwy
Anchorage, AK 99507
Phone: 907-344-2200
Fax: 907-349-3299

KBYR-AM 700 kHz (N/T)
1007 W 32nd Ave
Anchorage, AK 99503
Phone: 907-273-3170
Fax: 907-273-3189

KEAG-FM 97.3 MHz (Oldies)
9200 Lake Otis Pkwy
Anchorage, AK 99507
Phone: 907-344-2200
Fax: 907-349-3299

KENI-AM 650 kHz (N/T)
800 E Dimond Blvd Suite 3-320
Anchorage, AK 99515
Phone: 907-522-1515
Fax: 907-522-0694

KFAT-FM 92.9 MHz (Urban)
11259 Tower Rd
Anchorage, AK 99515
Phone: 907-344-4045
Fax: 907-868-2511

KFQD-AM 750 kHz (N/T)
9200 Lake Otis Pkwy
Anchorage, AK 99507
Phone: 907-522-5103
Fax: 907-349-7326

KGOT-FM 101.3 MHz (CHR)
800 E Dimond Blvd Suite 3-370
Anchorage, AK 99515
E-mail: kgot@alaskanet.com
www.kgot.com
Phone: 907-272-5945
Fax: 907-522-0672

KHAR-AM 590 kHz (Nost)
9200 Lake Otis Pkwy
Anchorage, AK 99507
Phone: 907-344-9622
Fax: 907-349-3299
TF: 800-896-1669

KKRO-FM 102.1 MHz (Rock)
11259 Tower Rd
Anchorage, AK 99515
Phone: 907-344-4045
Fax: 907-522-5576

KLEF-FM 98.1 MHz (Clas)
3601 C St Suite 290
Anchorage, AK 99503
E-mail: klef@klef.com
www.klef.com
Phone: 907-561-5556
Fax: 907-562-4219

KMXS-FM 103.1 MHz (AC)
9200 Lake Otis Pkwy
Anchorage, AK 99507
E-mail: mixed@kmxs.com
www.kmxs.com
Phone: 907-522-5103
Fax: 907-349-7326

KNBA-FM 90.3 MHz (NPR)
818 E 9th Ave
Anchorage, AK 99501
E-mail: knba@alaska.net
www.alaska.net/knba/
Phone: 907-279-5622
Fax: 907-258-8803

KNIK-FM 105.3 MHz (NAC)
907 E Dowling Rd Suite 24
Anchorage, AK 99518
Phone: 907-562-8119
Fax: 907-562-8117

KQEZ-FM 92.1 MHz (AC)
11259 Tower Rd
Anchorage, AK 99515
Phone: 907-344-4045
Fax: 907-868-2511

KSKA-FM 91.1 MHz (NPR)
3877 University Dr
Anchorage, AK 99508
Phone: 907-563-7070
Fax: 907-273-9192

KWHL-FM 106.5 MHz (Rock)
9200 Lake Otis Pkwy
Anchorage, AK 99507
E-mail: info@kwhl.com
www.kwhl.com
Phone: 907-522-5103
Fax: 907-349-7326

KYMG-FM 98.9 MHz (AC)
800 E Dimond Blvd Suite 3-370
Anchorage, AK 99515
Phone: 907-522-1515
Fax: 907-522-0694

Attractions

Anchorage's moderate climate allows for year-round outdoor activities. The area's national parks and forests are home to bears, moose, wolves, lynx, Dall sheep, mountain goats, and bald eagles. Mount McKinley, America's highest peak, is in Denali National Park, 122 miles north of Anchorage. Alaska's official sport, dog mushing, is showcased every spring in the 1,049-mile Iditarod Sled Dog Race from Anchorage to Nome. The Alaska State Fair is held each August in Palmer, 40 miles north of Anchorage.

4th Avenue Theatre
630 W 4th Ave Suite 300
Anchorage, AK 99501
Phone: 907-257-5600
Fax: 907-257-5620

Alagnak Wild River
PO Box 7
King Salmon, AK 99613
www.nps.gov/alag/
Phone: 907-246-3305
Fax: 907-246-4286

Alaska Aviation Heritage Museum
4721 Aircraft Dr
Anchorage, AK 99502
E-mail: museum@airmodels.com
www.airmodels.com
Phone: 907-248-5325
Fax: 907-248-6391

Alaska Botanical Gardens
Campbell Airstrip Rd
Anchorage, AK 99501
E-mail: garden@alaska.net
www.alaska.net/~garden
Phone: 907-770-3692
Fax: 907-265-3180

Alaska Center for the Performing Arts
621 W 6th Ave
Anchorage, AK 99501
E-mail: acpa@customcpu.com
www.alaskapac.org
Phone: 907-263-2900
Fax: 907-263-2927

Alaska Experience Theatre
705 W 6th Ave
Anchorage, AK 99501
Phone: 907-272-9076
Fax: 907-272-5716

Alaska Museum of Natural History
11723 Old Glenn Hwy
Eagle River, AK 99577
E-mail: info@alaskamuseum.org
www.alaskamuseum.org
Phone: 907-694-0819
Fax: 907-694-0919

Alaska Native Heritage Center
8800 Heritage Center Dr
Anchorage, AK 99506
E-mail: info@alaskanative.net
www.alaskanative.net
Phone: 907-330-8000
Fax: 907-330-8030
TF: 800-315-6608

Alaska Zoo
4731 O'Malley Rd
Anchorage, AK 99516
www.alaskazoo.com
Phone: 907-346-3242
Fax: 907-346-2673

Anchorage Concert Assn
430 W 7th Ave Suite 200
Anchorage, AK 99501
E-mail: info@anchorageconcerts.org
www.anchorageconcerts.org
Phone: 907-272-1471
Fax: 907-272-2519

Anchorage Museum of History & Art
121 W 7th Ave
Anchorage, AK 99501
E-mail: museum@ci.anchorage.ak.us
www.ci.anchorage.ak.us/Services/Departments/Culture/Museum/index.html
Phone: 907-343-4326
Fax: 907-343-6149

Anchorage Opera
1507 Spar Ave
Anchorage, AK 99501
www.anchorage.com/opera/
Phone: 907-279-2557
Fax: 907-279-7798

Anchorage Symphony Orchestra
400 D St Suite 230
Anchorage, AK 99501
E-mail: aso@corecom.net
Phone: 907-274-8668
Fax: 907-272-7916

Aniakchak National Monument & Preserve
PO Box 7
King Salmon, AK 99613
www.nps.gov/ania/
Phone: 907-246-3305
Fax: 907-246-4286

Artique Ltd
314 G St
Anchorage, AK 99501
E-mail: artique@artiqueltd.com
www.artiqueltd.com
Phone: 907-277-1663
Fax: 907-272-2024

Big Game Alaska Wildlife Park
Milepost 79 Seward Hwy
Portage Glacier, AK 99587
E-mail: biggame@alaska.net
www.biggamealaska.com
Phone: 907-783-2025
Fax: 907-783-2370

Chugach State Park
Milepost 115.3 Seward Hwy
Indian, AK 99540
Phone: 907-345-5014
Fax: 907-345-6982

Dance Spectrum
1300 E 68th Ave
Anchorage, AK 99518
Phone: 907-344-9545
Fax: 907-349-1804

Denali National Park & Preserve
PO Box 9
Denali Park, AK 99755
www.nps.gov/dena/
Phone: 907-683-2294
Fax: 907-683-9617

Denali Winery
1301 E Dowling Rd Suite 107
Anchorage, AK 99518
Phone: 907-563-9434
Fax: 907-563-9501

Eagle River Nature Center
32750 Eagle River Rd
Eagle River, AK 99577
Phone: 907-694-2108

Eklutna Historical Park
16515 Centerfield Dr
Eagle River, AK 99577
E-mail: ehp@alaska.net
www.eklutna.com
Phone: 907-696-2828
Fax: 907-696-2845

Elmendorf Air Force Base Wildlife Museum
8481 19th St
Elmendorf AFB, AK 99506
Phone: 907-552-2282

Elmendorf State Hatchery
941 N Reeves Blvd
Anchorage, AK 99501
Phone: 907-274-0065

Fraternal Order of Alaska State Troopers Museum
320 W 5th Ave
Anchorage, AK 99501
www.alaska.net/~foast/
Phone: 907-279-5050
Fax: 907-279-5054

Heritage Library Museum
301 W Northern Lights Blvd
Anchorage, AK 99503
Phone: 907-265-2834
Fax: 907-265-2002

Hilltop Ski Area
7015 Abbott Rd
Anchorage, AK 99516
www.hilltopskiarea.org
Phone: 907-346-1446
Fax: 907-346-3391

Imaginarium Science Discovery Center
737 W 5th Ave Suite T
Anchorage, AK 99501
E-mail: imagine@alaska.net
www.imaginarium.org
Phone: 907-276-3179
Fax: 907-258-4306

Katmai National Park & Preserve
PO Box 7
King Salmon, AK 99613
www.nps.gov/katm/
Phone: 907-246-3305
Fax: 907-246-4286

Kenai Fjords National Park
PO Box 1727
Seward, AK 99664
www.nps.gov/kefj/
Phone: 907-224-3874
Fax: 907-224-2144

Kincaid Park
Raspberry Rd
Anchorage, AK 99518
Phone: 907-343-6397

Lake Clark National Park & Preserve
4230 University Dr Suite 311
Anchorage, AK 99508
www.nps.gov/lacl/
Phone: 907-271-3751
Fax: 907-271-3707

Leiser Mann Memorial Greenhouses
5200 DeBarr Rd Russian Jack Springs Pk
Anchorage, AK 99508
Phone: 907-343-4717
Fax: 907-333-0344

Midnight Sons Barbershop Chorus
PO Box 100495
Anchorage, AK 99510
www.evg.org/~mnsons
Phone: 907-345-7708
TF: 800-406-7664

Mush a Dog Team Gold Rush Park
17620 S Birchwood Loop Rd
Chugiak, AK 99567
Phone: 907-688-1391
Fax: 907-688-7731

Oscar Anderson House Museum
420 M St Elderberry Pk
Anchorage, AK 99501
Phone: 907-274-2336
Fax: 907-274-3600

Port of Anchorage
2000 Anchorage Port Rd
Anchorage, AK 99501
E-mail: wwport@ci.anchorage.ak.us
www.ci.anchorage.ak.us/Services/Departments/Port
Phone: 907-343-6200
Fax: 907-277-5636

Russian Jack Springs Park
DeBarr & Boniface Rds
Anchorage, AK 99504
Phone: 907-333-8338

Wolf Song of Alaska
6th Ave & C St
Anchorage, AK 99511
E-mail: wolfsong@wolfsongalaska.org
www.wolfsongalaska.org
Phone: 907-346-3073
Fax: 907-346-1221

Wrangell-Saint Elias National Park & Preserve
Mile 105.5 Old Richardson Hwy
Copper Center, AK 99573
www.nps.gov/wrst/
Phone: 907-822-5235
Fax: 907-822-7216

Sports Teams & Facilities

Alaska Arctic Ice (hockey)
PO Box 212366
Anchorage, AK 99521
E-mail: jkknuejr@alaska.net
Phone: 907-333-8353
Fax: 907-249-6836

Alaska Sinbad Sailors (hockey)
3101 Penland Pkwy Suite K26
Anchorage, AK 99503
E-mail: kelsey@sinbad.net
Phone: 907-274-6223
Fax: 907-274-9444

Anchorage Aces (hockey)
1600 Gambell St Sullivan Arena
Anchorage, AK 99501
E-mail: office@anchorageaces.com
www.anchorageaces.com
Phone: 907-258-2237
Fax: 907-278-4297

Anchorage Bucs (baseball)
16th St Mulcahy Stadium
Anchorage, AK 99501
E-mail: admin@anchoragebucs.com
www.anchoragebucs.com
Phone: 907-561-2827
Fax: 907-561-2920

Anchorage Glacier Pilots (baseball)
16th Ave & Cordova St Mulcahy Stadium
Anchorage, AK 99503
Phone: 907-274-3627
Fax: 907-274-3628

George M Sullivan Sports Arena
1600 Gambell St
Anchorage, AK 99501
Phone: 907-279-0618
Fax: 907-274-0676

Annual Events

Alaska State Fair (late August-early September).....907-276-4118
Alyeska Ski Resort Winter Fest (early January).....907-754-1111
Anchorage Festival of Music (mid-June) 907-276-2465
Anchorage Folk Festival (mid-January) 907-566-2334
Bear Paw Festival (early July).....................907-694-4702
Carrs Great Alaska Shootout (late November).......907-786-1230
Freedom Days Festival (July 4) 907-276-4118
Fur Rendezvous Winter Carnival (mid-February)....907-277-8615
Girdwood Forest Fair (early July) 907-783-2931
Great Alaska Shootout (late November) 907-786-1230
Holiday Food & Gift Show (early November) 907-277-7469
Iditarod Trail Sled Dog Race (early March).........907-376-5155
Iditasport (mid-late February).....................907-345-4505
International Ice Carving Competition (late February-early March).....................907-279-5650
Irish Music & Cultural Festival of Alaska (mid-May) 907-566-2028
Juneteenth Festival (mid-June) 907-278-1778
Mayor's Midnight Sun Marathon (mid-June)........907-343-4474
Mount Marathon Race (July 4) 907-224-8051
Native Youth Olympics (late April-early May) 907-265-5900
Northern Lights (September-April) 907-276-4118
Polar Bear Jump Off Festival (mid-January)........907-224-5230
Quyana Alaska (mid-October).....................907-274-3611
Saturday Market (mid-May-mid-September).........907-272-5634
Seward Silver Salmon Derby (mid-late August) 907-224-3046
Ship Creek King Salmon Derby (early-mid-June).....907-276-6472
Sitka Summer Music Festival in Anchorage (September & February)........................907-747-6774
Sled Dog Races (January-February)................907-562-2235
Spring Carnival (mid-April).......................907-754-2219
Summer Solstice Festival (mid-June)..............907-279-9581
Swedish Christmas Celebration (early December) 907-274-2336
Taste of Anchorage (early June)...................907-562-9911
Three Barons Fair (early-mid-June) 907-272-2873
Torchlight Ski Parade (December 31 & mid-February) 907-754-1111
Tour of Anchorage Cross-Country Ski Race (early March) 907-276-4118
Tree Lighting Ceremony (late November) 907-279-5650

Atlanta, Georgia

***County:* Fulton**

ATLANTA is located in northwestern Georgia. Major cities within 100 miles include Macon and Athens, Georgia.

Area (Land) .... 124.9 sq mi
Area (Water)................................ 0.7 sq mi
Elevation....................................1,050 ft
Latitude ....33-74-89 N
Longitude................................ 84-38-81 W
Time Zone ....EST
Area Code....................................... 404

Climate

Atlanta's location in the foothills of the Appalachian Mountains helps to protect it from extreme heat and cold. Winters are fairly mild with highs in the low to mid-50s and lows in the low to mid-30s. Summer days are very warm, with average high temperatures in the upper 80s, but evening temperatures cool down into the upper 60s. March is the wettest month of the year in Atlanta; October is the driest.

Average Temperatures & Precipitation

Temperatures

	Jan	Feb	Mar	Apr	May	Jun	Jul	Aug	Sep	Oct	Nov	Dec
High	50	55	64	73	80	86	89	87	82	73	64	54
Low	32	35	43	50	59	66	70	69	64	52	43	35

Precipitation

	Jan	Feb	Mar	Apr	May	Jun	Jul	Aug	Sep	Oct	Nov	Dec
Inches	4.8	4.8	5.8	4.3	4.3	3.6	5.0	3.7	3.4	3.1	3.9	4.3

History

Originally the site of a Creek settlement called Standing Peachtree, Atlanta was founded in 1837 as the terminus of the Western & Atlantic Railroad. The village was actually called Terminus until 1843, when it was renamed Marthaville after the daughter of a former governor of Georgia. The city became known as Atlanta in 1845 and was incorporated two years later. Atlanta's location at the hub of four railroad lines enabled it to develop quickly as a manufacturing and distribution center. During the Civil War, Atlanta was one of the leading distribution centers for the Confederacy, making it a prime target for the Union Army. The Battle of Atlanta resulted in a major victory for the Union, and the city was burned to the ground in 1864 by General William Tecumseh Sherman. Atlanta was rebuilt quickly in the years following the war, and the city became the temporary state capital in 1868 and the permanent capital of Georgia nine years later. By the turn of the century, Atlanta had become the largest city in the state.

Over the course of the past century, the city has become the center of one of the leading metropolitan areas in the nation. Appropriately, the City of Atlanta's official symbol is the Phoenix, the bird of Egyptian myth that rose from the ashes with renewed strength. Home to more than 110,000 business establishments, including the corporate headquarters of more than 20 Fortune 500 companies, Atlanta today is considered the "Business Capital of the Southeast" and one of the top ranking business centers in the United States.

Atlanta's plentiful economic opportunities and relatively low cost of living result in an estimated 100,000 people relocating to the metro area each year. More than 3.7 million people currently reside in the Atlanta metro area, more than 400,000 of whom live in the city of Atlanta. By the year 2020 the population of the metro area is expected to exceed 5.2 million.

Population

1990 Census 393,929
1998 Estimate..............................403,819
% Change 2.5
2020 Projection 5,215,731*

Racial/Ethnic Breakdown

White...................................31.1%
Black 67.1%
Other.................................... 1.8%
Hispanic Origin (may be of any race) 1.9%

Age Breakdown

Under 5 years.............................. 7.6%
5 to 17..................................16.5%
18 to 20..................................5.9%
21 to 24..................................7.3%
25 to 34.................................19.3%
35 to 44.................................15.4%
45 to 54.................................. 9.4%
55 to 64.................................. 7.2%
65 to 74.................................. 6.0%
75+ years 5.3%
Median Age.................................31.5

Gender Breakdown

Male.....................................47.7%
Female...................................52.3%

** Information given is for the Atlanta Metropolitan Statistical Area (MSA), which includes the City of Atlanta, the City of Marietta, Barrow County, Butts County, Cherokee County, Clayton County, Cobb County, Coweta County, DeKalb County, Douglas County, Fayette County, Forsyth County, Fulton County, Gwinnett County, Henry County, Newton County, Paulding County, Rockdale County, Spalding County, and Walton County.*

Government

Type of Government: Mayor-City Council

Atlanta City Clerk
55 Trinity Ave SW Suite 2700
Atlanta, GA 30335
Phone: 404-330-6030
Fax: 404-658-6474

Atlanta City Council
55 Trinity Ave SW Suite 2900
Atlanta, GA 30335
Phone: 404-330-6030
Fax: 404-658-6474

Atlanta City Hall
55 Trinity Ave SW
Atlanta, GA 30335
Phone: 404-330-6000
Fax: 404-658-6454

Atlanta Emergency Management Agency
130 Peachtree St SW Suite G-157
Atlanta, GA 30303
Phone: 404-730-5600
Fax: 404-730-5625

Atlanta Finance Dept
68 Mitchell St SW
Atlanta, GA 30335
Phone: 404-330-6430
Fax: 404-658-6667

Atlanta Fire Dept
675 Ponce de Leon Ave NE Suite 2001
Atlanta, GA 30308
Phone: 404-853-7000
Fax: 404-853-7095

Atlanta Law Dept
68 Mtichell St Suite 4100
Atlanta, GA 30335
Phone: 404-330-6400
Fax: 404-658-6894

Atlanta Mayor
55 Trinity Ave SW Suite 2400
Atlanta, GA 30335
Phone: 404-330-6100
Fax: 404-658-7361

Atlanta Parks Recreation & Cultural Affairs Dept
675 Ponce de Leon Ave 8th Fl
Atlanta, GA 30388
Phone: 404-817-6785
Fax: 404-853-7643

Atlanta Personnel Administration Bureau
68 Mitchell St Suite 3200
Atlanta, GA 30335
Phone: 404-330-6370
Fax: 404-658-6892

Atlanta Planning Development & Neighborhood Conservation Dept
55 Trinity Ave SW Suite 1450
Atlanta, GA 30335
Phone: 404-330-6070
Fax: 404-658-7638

Atlanta Police Dept
675 Ponce de Leon Ave NE
Atlanta, GA 30308
Phone: 404-817-6900
Fax: 404-817-6887

Atlanta Public Works Dept
55 Trinity Ave SW Suite 4700
Atlanta, GA 30335
Phone: 404-330-6240
Fax: 404-658-7552

Atlanta Water Dept
55 Trinity Ave SW Suite 5700
Atlanta, GA 30335
Phone: 404-330-6075
Fax: 404-658-7189

Atlanta-Fulton Public Library
1 Margaret Mitchell Sq NW
Atlanta, GA 30303
Phone: 404-730-1700
Fax: 404-730-1990

Important Phone Numbers

AAA............404-843-4500
American Express Travel............404-262-7561
Atlanta Board of Realtors............404-250-0051
Atlanta Tax Assessors Board............404-730-6400
Dental Referral............404-636-7553
Driver's License Information............404-657-9300
Emergency............911
Fulton County Tax Commissioners............404-730-6131
Georgia Dept of Revenue Taxpayer Assistance............404-656-4071
HotelDocs............800-468-3537
Medical Referral............404-881-1714
Poison Control Center............404-616-9000
Time............770-455-7141
Travelers Aid............404-817-7070
Vehicle Registration Information............404-730-6100
Voter Registration Information............404-656-2871
Weather............770-455-7141

Information Sources

Atlanta Chamber of Commerce
PO Box 1740
Atlanta, GA 30301
metroatlantachamber.com
Phone: 404-880-9000
Fax: 404-586-8464

Atlanta Civic Center
395 Piedmont Ave NE
Atlanta, GA 30308
www.atlantaciviccenter.com
Phone: 404-523-6275
Fax: 404-525-4634

Atlanta Convention & Visitors Bureau
233 Peachtree St NE Suite 100
Atlanta, GA 30303
www.acvb.com
Phone: 404-521-6600
Fax: 404-584-6331
TF: 800-285-2682

Atlanta Planning Development & Neighborhood Conservation Dept
55 Trinity Ave SW Suite 1450
Atlanta, GA 30335
www.ci.atlanta.ga.us/dept/pdnc/all%20about%20the%20dpdnc-web_files/frame.htm
Phone: 404-330-6070
Fax: 404-658-7638

Better Business Bureau Serving Metropolitan Atlanta
PO Box 2707
Atlanta, GA 30301
www.atlanta.bbb.org
Phone: 404-688-4910
Fax: 404-688-8901

Fulton County
141 Pryor St SW
Atlanta, GA 30303
www.co.fulton.ga.us
Phone: 404-730-4000
Fax: 404-730-4237

Georgia International Convention Center
1902 Sullivan Rd
College Park, GA 30337
www.gicc.com
Phone: 770-997-3566
Fax: 770-994-8559

Online Resources

4Atlanta.com
www.4atlanta.com

About.com Guide to Atlanta
atlanta.about.com/local/southeastus/atlanta

Access Atlanta
www.accessatlanta.com

ACME Atlanta
www.acme-atlanta.com

Area Guide Atlanta
atlanta.areaguides.net

Atlanta by Moonlight
www.suspensionofdisbelief.com/atlanta/

Atlanta CityLink
www.usacitylink.com/citylink/atlanta/

Atlanta CityWomen
www.citywomen.com/atlwomen.htm

Atlanta Graphic City Guide
www.futurecast.com/gcg/atlanta.htm

Atlanta Guidebook
clever.net/qms/atl-page.htm

Atlanta Information Systems
www.atlnta.com/

Atlanta Web Guide
www.webguide.com

Atlanta.TheLinks.com
atlanta.thelinks.com

AtlantaEntertainment.com
www.atlantaentertainment.com/ATLANTA/index.htm

BestAtlanta.com
www.bestatlanta.com

Boulevards Atlanta
www.boulevards.com/cities/atlanta.html

Bradmans.com Atlanta
www.bradmans.com/scripts/display_city.cgi?city=231

Buckhead
www.buckhead.org/

City Knowledge Atlanta
www.cityknowledge.com/ga_atlanta.htm

CitySearch Atlanta
atlanta.citysearch.com

CityTravelGuide.com Atlanta
www.citytravelguide.com/atlanta.htm

Creative Loafing Atlanta
web.cln.com

CuisineNet Atlanta
www.cuisinenet.com/restaurant/atlanta/

DigitalCity Atlanta
home.digitalcity.com/atlanta

E2Atlanta
www.e2atlanta.com/

Excite.com Atlanta City Guide
www.excite.com/travel/countries/united_states/georgia/atlanta

Gay Atlanta
www.gayatlanta.org

Golf Atlanta
www.golfatlanta.com

Hot Atlanta
zaphod.cc.ttu.ee/vrainn/Atlanta/ahome.html

HotelGuide Atlanta
atlanta.hotelguide.net

Info Atlanta
travel.to/atlanta

Insiders' Guide to Atlanta
www.insiders.com/atlanta/

Lodging.com Atlanta Georgia
www.lodging.com/auto/guides/atlanta-area-ga.html

Metroscope Atlanta
metroscope.com/atlanta.html

Net Atlanta
www.netatlanta.com

Online City Guide to Atlanta
www.olcg.com/ga/atlanta/main.html

Online Menus Atlanta
menus.atlanta.com

Open World City Guides Atlanta
www.worldexecutive.com/cityguides/atlanta/

Restaurant Row Atlanta
www.restaurantrow.com/atlanta.htm

Rough Guide Travel Atlanta
travel.roughguides.com/content/703/

Savvy Diner Guide to Atlanta Restaurants
www.savvydiner.com/atlanta/

Surf Atlanta
surfatlanta.com

Traveler Information Showcase
www.atlanta-traveler.com

Virtual Voyages Atlanta
www.virtualvoyages.com/usa/ga/atlanta/atlanta.sht

WeekendEvents.com Atlanta
www.weekendevents.com/Atlanta/atlanta.html

Yahoo! Atlanta
atlanta.yahoo.com

Area Communities

Communities with populations greater than 10,000 in the 20-county (Barrow, Bartow, Carroll, Cherokee, Clayton, Cobb, Coweta, DeKalb, Douglas, Fayette, Forsyth, Fulton, Gwinnett, Henry, Newton, Paulding, Pickens, Rockdale, Spalding, and Walton) Atlanta metropolitan area include:

Alpharetta
2 S Main St
Alpharetta, GA 30201
Phone: 678-297-6000
Fax: 678-297-6001

Buford
95 Scott St
Buford, GA 30518
Phone: 770-945-6761
Fax: 770-932-7976

College Park
3667 Main St
College Park, GA 30337
Phone: 404-767-1537
Fax: 404-669-3799

Covington
PO Box 1527
Covington, GA 30210
Phone: 770-385-2000
Fax: 770-385-2060

Decatur
509 N McDonough St
Decatur, GA 30030
Phone: 404-370-4100
Fax: 404-378-2678

Douglasville
PO Box 219
Douglasville, GA 30133
Phone: 770-920-3001
Fax: 770-920-0499

Duluth
3578 W Lawrenceville St
Duluth, GA 30096
Phone: 770-476-3434
Fax: 770-623-2780

East Point
2777 East Point St
East Point, GA 30344
Phone: 404-765-1133
Fax: 404-765-1067

Forest Park
745 Forest Pkwy
Forest Park, GA 30297
Phone: 404-366-4720
Fax: 404-608-2344

Kennesaw
2539 JO Stephenson Ave
Kennesaw, GA 30144
Phone: 770-424-8274
Fax: 770-429-4559

Lawrenceville
PO Box 2200
Lawrenceville, GA 30046
Phone: 770-963-2414

Lilburn
76 Main St NW
Lilburn, GA 30047
Phone: 770-921-2210
Fax: 770-921-8942

Marietta
205 Lawrence St
Marietta, GA 30060
Phone: 770-794-5526
Fax: 770-794-5523

Monroe
227 S Broad St
Monroe, GA 30655
Phone: 770-267-7536
Fax: 770-267-2319

Newnan
25 Lagrange St
Newnan, GA 30263
Phone: 770-253-2682
Fax: 770-254-2353

Peachtree City
151 Willow Bend Rd
Peachtree City, GA 30269
Phone: 770-487-7657
Fax: 770-631-2505

Powder Springs
4488 Pineview Dr
Powder Springs, GA 30127
Phone: 770-943-1666
Fax: 770-943-8003

Riverdale
6690 Church St
Riverdale, GA 30274
Phone: 770-997-8989
Fax: 770-997-8992

Roswell
38 Hill St
Roswell, GA 30075
Phone: 770-641-3727
Fax: 770-594-6250

Smyrna
2800 King St
Smyrna, GA 30080
Phone: 770-434-6600
Fax: 770-319-5316

Economy

Atlanta recently ranked number one on DRI/McGraw Hill's list of the "Top 10 Metropolitan Areas for Job Creation 1995-2000" and number two on Fortune's 1995 annual list of the "Best Cities for Business." In 1999, more than 106,000 new jobs became available in the Atlanta area. Major corporations headquartered in Atlanta include Coca-Cola, BellSouth, United Parcel Service, Delta Air Lines, and Home Depot. The services sector accounts for the greatest number of jobs in Fulton County and in the metro area as a whole. Government (at the federal, state, and local levels) is also a leading employer—more than half of metropolitan Atlanta's top 20 employers are government-related. The United States Department of Defense is among Atlanta's largest employers, providing more than 10,000 jobs in various branches of the Armed Forces.

Unemployment Rate 2.8%*
Per Capita Income.......................... $28,252*
Median Family Income...................... $59,900*

** Information given is for the Atlanta Metropolitan Statistical Area (MSA), which includes the City of Atlanta, the City of Marietta, Barrow County, Butts County, Cherokee County, Clayton County, Cobb County, Coweta County, DeKalb County, Douglas County, Fayette County, Forsyth County, Fulton County, Gwinnett County, Henry County, Newton County, Paulding County, Rockdale County, Spalding County, and Walton County.*

Principal Industries & Number of Wage Earners

Fulton County - 1998

Industry	Wage Earners
Agricultural Services, Forestry, & Fishing	2,415
Construction	19,234
Finance, Insurance, & Real Estate	67,793
Manufacturing	54,603
Mining	126
Public Administration	50,110
Retail Trade	100,151
Services	284,480
Transportation & Public Utilities	85,607
Wholesale Trade	55,676

Major Employers

AT & T
1200 Peachtree St NE
Atlanta, GA 30309
www.att.com/hr/employment/
Phone: 800-562-7288

Atlanta Board of Education
210 Pryor St SW
Atlanta, GA 30303
www.atlanta.k12.ga.us
Phone: 404-827-8000
Fax: 404-827-8128

Atlanta City Hall
55 Trinity Ave SW
Atlanta, GA 30335
www.ci.atlanta.ga.us
Phone: 404-330-6000
Fax: 404-658-6454

BellSouth Corp
1155 Peachtree St NE
Atlanta, GA 30309
www.bellsouthcorp.com
Phone: 404-249-2000
TF: 800-295-2355

Cobb County Board of Education
514 Glover St
Marietta, GA 30060
Phone: 770-426-3300
Fax: 770-426-3329

Coca-Cola Co
PO Drawer 1734
Atlanta, GA 30301
www.thecoca-colacompany.com
Phone: 404-676-2121
Fax: 404-676-6792
TF: 800-438-2653

Cox Enterprises Inc
1400 Lake Hearn Dr
Atlanta, GA 30319
www.coxenterprises.com
Phone: 404-843-5000
Fax: 404-843-5775

DeKalb County
556 N McDonough St
Decatur, GA 30030
www.co.dekalb.ga.us
Phone: 404-371-2000
Fax: 404-371-2635

DeKalb County Board of Education
3770 N Decatur Rd Bldg B
Decatur, GA 30032
Phone: 404-297-1200
Fax: 404-297-1254

Delta Air Lines Inc
PO Box 20706 Hartsfield Atlanta International Airport
Atlanta, GA 30320
www.delta-air.com
Phone: 404-715-2600
Fax: 404-715-5494
TF: 800-221-1212

Emory University
200 Jones Ctr
Atlanta, GA 30322
www.emory.edu
Phone: 404-727-6036
Fax: 404-727-4303
TF: 800-727-6036

Fulton County Board of Education
786 Cleveland Ave SW
Atlanta, GA 30315
Phone: 404-763-4581
Fax: 404-669-4931

Georgia Institute of Technology
225 North Ave NW
Atlanta, GA 30332
E-mail: admissions@success.gatech.edu
www.gatech.edu
Phone: 404-894-2000
Fax: 404-894-1235

Georgia-Pacific Corp
133 Peachtree St NE
Atlanta, GA 30303
www.gp.com
Phone: 404-652-4000
Fax: 404-230-5774

Gwinnett County School System
PO Box 343
Lawrenceville, GA 30046
www.gwinnett.k12.ga.us
Phone: 770-963-8651
Fax: 770-513-6663

Home Depot Inc
2455 Paces Ferry Rd
Atlanta, GA 30339
E-mail: consumer-affairs@homedepot.com
www.homedepot.com
Phone: 770-433-8211
Fax: 770-384-2685
TF: 800-553-3199

Kroger Co
2175 Parklake Dr NE
Atlanta, GA 30345
www.kroger.com
Phone: 770-496-7400
Fax: 770-496-5376

Lockheed Martin Aeronautics Co Marietta Operations
86 S Cobb Dr
Marietta, GA 30063
www.lmasc.com
Phone: 770-494-4411
Fax: 770-494-6963

Turner Broadcasting System
PO Box 105366
Atlanta, GA 30348
www.tbssuperstation.com
Phone: 404-827-1700
Fax: 404-885-4326

United Parcel Service
55 Glenlake Pkwy NE
Atlanta, GA 30328
www.upsjobs.com
Phone: 800-742-5877

US Postal Service
3900 Crown Rd
Atlanta, GA 30304
new.usps.com
Phone: 404-765-7200

Wal-Mart Stores Inc
1025 Bullsboro Dr
Newnan, GA 30263
Phone: 770-502-0677
Fax: 770-502-8306

Quality of Living Indicators

Total Crime Index....................................55,478
(rates per 100,000 inhabitants)

Violent Crime
Murder/manslaughter.......................... 143
Forcible rape 321
Robbery......................................4,072
Aggravated assault...........................6,691

Property Crime
Burglary 8,571
Larceny theft 28,352
Motor vehicle theft 7,328

Cost of Living Index....................................99.2
(national average = 100)

Median Home Price.................................$123,700

Education

Public Schools

Atlanta Board of Education
210 Pryor St SW
Atlanta, GA 30303
www.atlanta.k12.ga.us
Phone: 404-827-8000
Fax: 404-827-8128

Number of Schools
Elementary 38

Middle 13
High.. 12

Student/Teacher Ratio
All Grades 16.6:1

Private Schools

Number of Schools (all grades) .... 150+

Colleges & Universities

Agnes Scott College
141 E College Ave
Decatur, GA 30030
E-mail: admission@agnesscott.edu
www.agnesscott.edu
Phone: 404-471-6000
Fax: 404-471-6414
TF: 800-868-8602

American InterContinental University Atlanta
3330 Peachtree Rd NE
Atlanta, GA 30326
www.aiuniv.edu
Phone: 404-965-5700
Fax: 404-965-5701
TF: 800-255-6839

Art Institute of Atlanta
6600 Peachtree Dunwoody Rd 100 Embassy Row
Atlanta, GA 30328
www.aii.edu
Phone: 770-394-8300
Fax: 770-394-0008
TF: 800-275-4242

Atlanta Christian College
2605 Ben Hill Rd
East Point, GA 30344
E-mail: chargers777@juno.com
www.acc.edu
Phone: 404-761-8861
Fax: 404-669-2024

Atlanta College of Art
1280 Peachtree St NE
Atlanta, GA 30309
E-mail: acainfo@woodruff-arts.org
Phone: 404-733-5001
Fax: 404-733-5107
TF: 800-832-2104

Atlanta Metropolitan College
1630 Metropolitan Pkwy SW
Atlanta, GA 30310
www.atlm.peachnet.edu/
Phone: 404-756-4004
Fax: 404-756-4407

Bauder College
3500 Peachtree Rd NE
Atlanta, GA 30326
www.bauder.edu
Phone: 404-237-7573
Fax: 404-237-1642
TF: 800-241-3797

Carver Bible Institute & College
437 Nelson St SW
Atlanta, GA 30313
Phone: 404-527-4520
Fax: 404-527-4526

Clark Atlanta University
223 James P Brawley Dr SW
Atlanta, GA 30314
www.cau.edu
Phone: 404-880-8000
Fax: 404-880-6174
TF: 800-688-3228

DeVRY Institute of Technology
250 N Arcadia Ave
Decatur, GA 30030
Phone: 404-292-7900
Fax: 404-292-7011
TF: 800-221-4771

Emory University
200 Jones Ctr
Atlanta, GA 30322
www.emory.edu
Phone: 404-727-6036
Fax: 404-727-4303
TF: 800-727-6036

Georgia Baptist Bible College
PO Box 429
Senoia, GA 30276
Phone: 770-252-4004

Georgia Institute of Technology
225 North Ave NW
Atlanta, GA 30332
E-mail: admissions@success.gatech.edu
www.gatech.edu
Phone: 404-894-2000
Fax: 404-894-1235

Georgia State University
University Plaza
Atlanta, GA 30303
E-mail: Admissions@GSU.edu
www.gsu.edu
Phone: 404-651-2000
Fax: 404-651-4811

Gupton-Jones College of Funeral Service
5141 Snapfinger Woods Dr
Decatur, GA 30035
www.gupton-jones.edu
Phone: 770-593-2257
Fax: 770-593-1891
TF: 800-848-5352

Herzing College
3355 Lenox Rd Suite 100
Atlanta, GA 30326
www.herzing.com
Phone: 404-816-4533
Fax: 404-816-5576
TF: 800-573-4533

Kennesaw State University
1000 Chastain Rd
Kennesaw, GA 30144
www.kennesaw.edu
Phone: 770-423-6000
Fax: 770-423-6541

Mercer University Cecil B Day Campus
3001 Mercer University Dr
Atlanta, GA 30341
E-mail: postmaster@mercer.edu
www.mercer.edu/cbd
Phone: 770-986-3000
Fax: 770-986-3135

Morehouse College
830 Westview Dr SW
Atlanta, GA 30314
www.morehouse.edu
Phone: 404-681-2800
Fax: 404-659-6536
TF: 800-851-1254

Morris Brown College
643 ML King Jr Dr NW
Atlanta, GA 30314
www.morrisbrown.edu
Phone: 404-220-0270
Fax: 404-220-0371

Oglethorpe University
4484 Peachtree Rd NE
Atlanta, GA 30319
www.oglethorpe.edu
Phone: 404-261-1441
Fax: 404-364-8491
TF: 800-428-4484

Southern Polytechnic State University
1100 S Marietta Pkwy
Marietta, GA 30060
www.sct.edu
Phone: 770-528-7281
Fax: 770-528-7292
TF: 800-635-3204

Spelman College
350 Spelman Ln SW
Atlanta, GA 30314
E-mail: admiss@spelman.edu
www.spelman.edu
Phone: 404-681-3643
Fax: 404-215-7788
TF: 800-982-2411

State University of West Georgia
1600 Maple St
Carrollton, GA 30118
www.westga.edu
Phone: 770-836-6500
Fax: 770-836-4637

Hospitals

Atlanta Medical Center
303 Parkway Dr NE
Atlanta, GA 30312
www.tenethealth.com/GeorgiaBaptist
Phone: 404-265-4000
Fax: 404-265-4595

Baptist Medical Center
1200 Medical Center Dr
Cumming, GA 30041
Phone: 770-887-2355
Fax: 770-844-4327

Crawford Long Hospital of Emory University
550 Peachtree St NE
Atlanta, GA 30365
www.ect.enron.com/products/assets/louisiana.fset.html
Phone: 404-686-4411
Fax: 404-686-2848

DeKalb Medical Center
2701 N Decatur Rd
Decatur, GA 30033
www.drhs.org
Phone: 404-501-1000
Fax: 404-501-5147

Dunwoody Medical Center
4575 N Shallowford Rd
Atlanta, GA 30338
Phone: 770-454-2000
Fax: 770-454-4279

Eastside Medical Center
1700 Medical Way
Snellville, GA 30078
Phone: 770-979-0200
Fax: 770-736-2395

Egleston Children's Hospital at Emory University
1405 Clifton Rd NE
Atlanta, GA 30322
Phone: 404-325-6000
Fax: 404-325-6166

Emory Northlake Regional Medical Center
1455 Montreal Rd
Tucker, GA 30084
Phone: 770-270-3000
Fax: 770-270-3446

Emory University Hospital
1364 Clifton Rd NE
Atlanta, GA 30322
www.emory.edu/WHSC/EUH/euh.html
Phone: 404-712-7021
Fax: 404-712-7801

Grady Memorial Hospital
80 Butler St
Atlanta, GA 30335
Phone: 404-616-4307
Fax: 404-616-9204

Henry Medical Center
1133 Eagle's Landing Pkwy
Stockbridge, GA 30281
www.henrymedical.com
Phone: 770-389-2200
Fax: 770-389-2083

Hughes Spalding Children's Hospital
35 Butler St
Atlanta, GA 30335
Phone: 404-616-6600
Fax: 404-616-5006

Mountainside Medical Center
1266 E Church St
Jasper, GA 30143
Phone: 706-692-2441
Fax: 706-692-6754

Newnan Hospital
80 Jackson St
Newnan, GA 30263
www.newnanhospital.com
Phone: 770-253-2330
Fax: 770-254-0566

Newton General Hospital
5126 Hospital Dr NE
Covington, GA 30014
Phone: 770-786-7053
Fax: 770-787-9059

North Fulton Regional Hospital
3000 Hospital Blvd
Roswell, GA 30076
www.tenethealth.com/NorthFulton
Phone: 770-751-2545
Fax: 770-751-2767

Northside Hospital
1000 Johnson Ferry Rd NE
Atlanta, GA 30342
www.northside.com
Phone: 404-851-8000
Fax: 404-303-3333

Parkway Medical Center
1000 Thornton Rd
Lithia Springs, GA 30122
Phone: 770-732-7777
Fax: 770-732-7896

Peachtree Regional Hospital
60 Hospital Rd
Newnan, GA 30263
Phone: 770-253-1912
Fax: 770-304-4244

Piedmont Hospital
1968 Peachtree Rd NW
Atlanta, GA 30309
Phone: 404-605-5000
Fax: 404-609-6832

Promina Gwinnett Medical Center
1000 Medical Center Blvd
Lawrenceville, GA 30045
www.gwinnetthealth.org
Phone: 770-995-4321
Fax: 770-682-2257

Rockdale Hospital
1412 Milstead Ave NE
Conyers, GA 30012
Phone: 770-918-3000
Fax: 770-918-3043

Saint Joseph's Hospital of Atlanta
5665 Peachtree Dunwoody Rd NE
Atlanta, GA 30342
Phone: 404-851-7001
Fax: 404-851-7339
TF: 800-678-5637

Scottish Rite Children's Medical Center
1001 Johnson Ferry Rd NE
Atlanta, GA 30342
www.scottishritechildrens.org
Phone: 404-256-5252
Fax: 404-250-2799
TF: 800-250-5437

South Fulton Medical Center
1170 Cleveland Ave
East Point, GA 30344
Phone: 404-305-3500
Fax: 404-305-4418

Southern Regional Medical Center
11 Upper Riverdale Rd SW
Riverdale, GA 30274
Phone: 770-991-8000
Fax: 770-997-3304

Southwest Hospital & Medical Center
501 Fairburn Rd SW
Atlanta, GA 30331
Phone: 404-699-1111
Fax: 404-505-5379

Spalding Regional Hospital
601 S 8th St
Griffin, GA 30224
Phone: 770-228-2721
Fax: 770-229-6489

Tanner Medical Center
705 Dixie St
Carrollton, GA 30117
Phone: 770-836-9666
Fax: 770-836-9897

Veterans Affairs Medical Center
1670 Clairmont Rd
Decatur, GA 30033
Phone: 404-321-6111
Fax: 404-327-4004

Walton Medical Center Phone: 770-267-8461
330 Alcovy St Fax: 770-267-1888
Monroe, GA 30655

Wellstar Cobb Hospital Phone: 770-732-4000
3950 Austell Rd Fax: 770-792-4976
Austell, GA 30106

Wellstar Douglas Hospital Phone: 770-949-1500
8954 Hospital Dr Fax: 770-920-6413
Douglasville, GA 30134

Wellstar Kennestone Hospital Phone: 770-793-5000
677 Church St Fax: 770-792-1450
Marietta, GA 30060

Wellstar Paulding Hospital Phone: 770-445-4411
600 W Memorial Dr Fax: 770-443-7049
Dallas, GA 30132

Transportation

Airport(s)

Hartsfield Atlanta International Airport (ATL)
10 miles S of downtown (approx 20 minutes).....404-530-6600

Mass Transit

MARTA
$1.50 Base fare................................404-848-4711

Rail/Bus

Amtrak Station Phone: 800-872-7245
1688 Peachtree St NW
Atlanta, GA 30309

Greyhound/Trailways Bus Station Phone: 404-584-1728
232 Forsyth St TF: 800-231-2222
Atlanta, GA 30303

Utilities

Electricity
Georgia Power Co............................888-660-5890
www.southernco.com/site/gapower/home.asp

Gas
Atlanta Gas Light Co..........................770-994-1946
www.aglc.com

Water
Atlanta Water Dept............................404-658-6500

Garbage Collection/Recycling
Atlanta Solid Waste Services...................404-330-6250

Telecommunications

Telephone
BellSouth....................................800-356-3094
www.bellsouth.com

Cable Television
AT & T Cable Services........................770-559-2000
www.cable.att.com
Comcast Cable...............................770-451-4785

Internet Service Providers (ISPs)
BellSouth.net................................770-522-4000
www.bellsouth.net
comstar.net Inc..............................770-485-6000
www.comstar.net
Lyceum Internet Services......................404-248-1733
www.lyceum.com
Net Depot Inc...............................770-434-5595
www.netdepot.com
Verio Atlanta................................770-389-7200
home.verio.net/local/frontpage.cfm?AirportCode=ATL

Banks

AmTrade International Bank of Georgia Phone: 404-898-1100
1360 Peachtree St NE Suite 1105 Fax: 404-898-1110
Atlanta, GA 30309

Atlantic States Bank Phone: 404-239-9138
3384 Peachtree Rd Suite 100 Fax: 404-365-9490
Atlanta, GA 30326

Bank of America NA Phone: 404-870-3040
1088 Peachtree St NE Fax: 404-870-3041
Atlanta, GA 30309

Bank One NA Phone: 404-898-8400
1200 Peachtree St NE Fax: 404-577-1155
Atlanta, GA 30361

Bankers Bank Phone: 770-805-2000
2410 Paces Ferry Rd Fax: 770-805-2121
Atlanta, GA 30339

Buckhead Community Bank NA Phone: 404-231-2265
415 E Paces Ferry Rd Fax: 404-237-2265
Atlanta, GA 30305
www.buckheadcommunitybank.com

Capitol City Bank & Trust Co Phone: 404-755-4254
562 Lee St SW Fax: 404-752-5862
Atlanta, GA 30310

Charter Bank & Trust Co Phone: 404-233-7177
4401 Northside Pkwy Suite 150 Fax: 404-233-2174
Atlanta, GA 30327

Citizens Trust Bank Phone: 404-659-5959
75 Piedmont Ave NE Fax: 404-653-2877
Atlanta, GA 30303
www.ctbatlanta.com

Colonial Bank Phone: 404-261-2612
3379 Peachtree Rd NE Fax: 404-240-2988
Atlanta, GA 30326

Embry National Bank Phone: 770-621-9797
3310 Henderson Mill Rd Fax: 770-491-8098
Atlanta, GA 30341

Fidelity National Bank Phone: 404-814-8114
3490 Piedmont Rd NE Fax: 404-814-8118
Atlanta, GA 30305
www.fidelitynational.com

First Security National Bank Phone: 404-252-8650
4241 Roswell Rd Fax: 404-252-8539
Atlanta, GA 30342

First Union National Bank
999 Peachtree St Suite 100
Atlanta, GA 30309
Phone: 404-865-3010
Fax: 404-865-3012

InfiBank
3490 Piedmont Rd Suite 900
Atlanta, GA 30305
Phone: 404-965-6061
Fax: 404-965-6073

Mutual Federal Savings Bank of Atlanta
205 Auburn Ave NE
Atlanta, GA 30305
Phone: 404-659-0701
Fax: 404-659-3916
TF: 888-476-2568

Premier Bank
950 E Paces Ferry Rd Suite 100
Atlanta, GA 30326
Phone: 404-261-7203
Fax: 404-261-5784

Prudential Savings Bank FSB
1 Ravinia Dr Suite 1000
Atlanta, GA 30346
Phone: 770-551-6700
Fax: 770-604-7999

Regions Bank
6637 Roswell Rd
Atlanta, GA 30328
Phone: 404-255-8550

Riverside Bank
300 Galleria Pkwy Suite 100
Atlanta, GA 30339
Phone: 770-303-8686
Fax: 770-303-8688

Scotiabank
600 Peachtree St NE Suite 2700
Atlanta, GA 30308
Phone: 404-877-1500
Fax: 404-888-8998

SouthTrust Bank NA
2000 Riveredge Pkwy NW
Atlanta, GA 30328
Phone: 770-951-4000
Fax: 770-951-4496
TF: 800-606-0634

Summit National Bank
4360 Chamblee-Dunwoody Rd
Atlanta, GA 30341
www.summitbk.com
Phone: 770-454-0400
Fax: 770-457-5531
TF: 877-226-5868

SunTrust Bank Atlanta
1 Park Pl NE
Atlanta, GA 30303
Phone: 404-588-7711
Fax: 404-724-3330

United Americas Bank NA
3789 Roswell Rd
Atlanta, GA 30342
Phone: 404-240-0101

Wachovia Bank NA
191 Peachtree St NE
Atlanta, GA 30303
Phone: 404-332-4116
Fax: 404-332-4139

Shopping

Atlanta State Farmers' Market
16 Forest Pkwy
Forest Park, GA 30297
Phone: 404-675-1782
Fax: 404-362-4564

Buckhead Village
Peachtree & E Paces Ferry Rds
Atlanta, GA 30305
Phone: 404-233-2228
Fax: 404-812-8222

Cumberland Mall
1000 Cumberland Mall
Atlanta, GA 30339
Phone: 770-435-2206
Fax: 770-438-0432

Galleria Specialty Mall
1 Galleria Pkwy
Atlanta, GA 30339
E-mail: info@galleriaspecialtymall.com
www.galleriaspecialtymall.com
Phone: 770-955-9100
Fax: 770-955-0792

Greenbriar Mall
2841 Greenbriar Pkwy SW
Atlanta, GA 30331
Phone: 404-344-6611
Fax: 404-344-6631

Gwinnett Place Mall
2100 Pleasant Hill Rd
Duluth, GA 30109
Phone: 770-476-5160
Fax: 770-476-9355

Lenox Square Mall
3393 Peachtree Rd NE
Atlanta, GA 30326
Phone: 404-233-6767
Fax: 404-233-7868

North DeKalb Mall
2050 Lawrenceville Hwy
Decatur, GA 30033
Phone: 404-320-7960
Fax: 404-728-1942

Northlake Mall
1000 Northlake Mall
Atlanta, GA 30345
Phone: 770-938-3564
Fax: 770-938-5850

Northpoint Mall
1000 Northpoint Cir
Alpharetta, GA 30022
Phone: 770-740-9273
Fax: 770-442-8295

Peachtree Center
225 Peachtree St NE Suite 300
Atlanta, GA 30303
Phone: 404-524-3787
Fax: 404-654-1200

Perimeter Mall
4400 Ashford-Dunwoody Rd Suite 1360
Atlanta, GA 30346
E-mail: management@perimetermall.com
www.atlantas-perimetermall.com
Phone: 770-394-4270
Fax: 770-396-4732

Phipps Plaza
3500 Peachtree Rd NE
Atlanta, GA 30326
www.phippsplaza.com
Phone: 404-261-7910
Fax: 404-264-9528

Rich's/Goldsmith's/Lazarus Co
223 Perimeter Ctr Pkwy
Atlanta, GA 30346
Phone: 770-396-2611
Fax: 770-913-5114

Shannon Mall
1000 Shannon Mall
Union City, GA 30291
Phone: 770-964-2200
Fax: 770-969-1273

South DeKalb Mall
2801 Candler Rd
Decatur, GA 30034
Phone: 404-241-2431
Fax: 404-241-1831

Southlake Mall
1000 Southlake Mall
Morrow, GA 30260
www.mallibu.com
Phone: 770-961-1050
Fax: 770-961-1113

Stone Mountain Village
891 Main St
Stone Mountain, GA 30083
Phone: 770-879-4971
Fax: 770-879-4972

Town Center at Cobb
400 Ernest Barrett Pkwy NW
Kennesaw, GA 30144
Phone: 770-424-0915
Fax: 770-424-7917

Underground Atlanta
50 Upper Alabama St Suite 007
Atlanta, GA 30303
www.underatl.com/
Phone: 404-523-2311
Fax: 404-523-0507

Vinings Jubilee
4300 Paces Ferry Rd NW
Atlanta, GA 30339
Phone: 770-438-8080
Fax: 770-438-8181

Media

Newspapers and Magazines

Alpharetta-Roswell Neighbor
10479 Alpharetta St Suite 10
Roswell, GA 30075
Phone: 770-993-7400
Fax: 770-518-6062

Atlanta Business Chronicle
1801 Peachtree St NE Suite 150
Atlanta, GA 30309
www.amcity.com/atlanta
Phone: 404-249-1000
Fax: 404-249-1048

Atlanta Journal-Constitution*
PO Box 4689
Atlanta, GA 30302
E-mail: info@cim.accessatlanta.com
www.accessatlanta.com/ajc
Phone: 404-526-5151
Fax: 404-526-5746

Atlanta Magazine
1330 W Peachtree St NW Suite 450
Atlanta, GA 30309
E-mail: atlmag@atlanta.com
atlantamagazine.com
Phone: 404-872-3100
Fax: 404-870-6230

Atlanta Tribune
875 Old Roswell Rd Suite C-100
Roswell, GA 30076
E-mail: sales@atlantatribune.com
www.atlantatribune.com
Phone: 770-587-0501
Fax: 770-642-6501

Austell-Mableton-Powder Springs Neighbor
PO Box 449
Marietta, GA 30061
Phone: 770-428-9411
Fax: 770-422-9533

Clayton Neighbor
5300 Frontage Rd Suite B
Forest Park, GA 30297
Phone: 404-363-8484
Fax: 404-363-0212

Creative Loafing Atlanta
750 Willoughby Way NE
Atlanta, GA 30312
web.cln.com
Phone: 404-688-5623
Fax: 404-420-3293
TF: 800-950-5623

Decatur/Tucker/Stone Mountain-DeKalb Neighbor
3060 Mercer University Dr Suite 210
Atlanta, GA 30341
Phone: 770-454-9388
Fax: 770-454-9131

DeKalb Neighbor
3060 Mercer University Dr Suite 210
Atlanta, GA 30341
Phone: 770-454-9388
Fax: 770-454-9131

Douglas Neighbor
7193 Douglas Blvd Suite 104
Douglasville, GA 30135
Phone: 770-942-1611
Fax: 770-942-4348

East Cobb Neighbor
PO Box 449
Marietta, GA 30061
Phone: 770-428-9411
Fax: 770-422-9533

Henry Neighbor
5300 Frontage Rd Suite B
Forest Park, GA 30297
Phone: 404-363-8484
Fax: 404-363-0212

Kennesaw-Acworth Neighbor
PO Box 449
Marietta, GA 30061
Phone: 770-428-9411
Fax: 770-422-9533

Northside-Sandy Springs Neighbor
5290 Roswell Rd NW Suite M
Atlanta, GA 30342
Phone: 404-256-3100
Fax: 404-256-3292

Revue The
319 N Main St
Alpharetta, GA 30004
E-mail: revue@appnews.com
Phone: 770-442-3278
Fax: 770-475-1216

South De Kalb Neighbor
3060 Mercer University Dr Suite 210
Atlanta, GA 30341
Phone: 770-454-9388
Fax: 770-454-9131

South Fulton Neighbor
5300 Frontage Rd Suite B
Forest Park, GA 30297
Phone: 404-363-8484
Fax: 404-363-0212

Tri-County News
PO Box 1586
Douglasville, GA 30133
Phone: 770-942-6571
Fax: 770-949-7556

**Indicates major daily newspapers*

Television

WAGA-TV Ch 5 (Fox)
1551 Briarcliff Rd NE
Atlanta, GA 30306
E-mail: feedback@wagatv.com
wagatv.com
Phone: 404-875-5555
Fax: 404-898-0169

WATL-TV Ch 36 (WB)
1 Monroe Pl
Atlanta, GA 30324
www.wb36.com
Phone: 404-881-3600
Fax: 404-881-3635

WGNX-TV Ch 46 (CBS)
1810 Briarcliff Rd NE
Atlanta, GA 30329
www.wgnx.com
Phone: 404-325-4646
Fax: 404-327-3003

WGTV-TV Ch 8 (PBS)
260 14th St NW
Atlanta, GA 30318
E-mail: viewerservices@gpb.org
www.gpb.org/gptv/gptv.htm
Phone: 404-685-2400
Fax: 404-685-2417

WPBA-TV Ch 30 (PBS)
740 Bismark Rd NE
Atlanta, GA 30324
www.wpba.org
Phone: 678-686-0321
Fax: 678-686-0356

WPXA-TV Ch 14 (PAX)
200 N Cobb Pkwy Suite 114
Marietta, GA 30062
www.pax.net/WPXA
Phone: 770-528-1400
Fax: 770-528-1403

WSB-TV Ch 2 (ABC)
1601 W Peachtree St NE
Atlanta, GA 30309
www.wsbtv.com
Phone: 404-897-7000
Fax: 404-897-7370

WTBS-TV Ch 17 (Ind)
1050 Techwood Dr NW
Atlanta, GA 30348
E-mail: tbssuperstation@turner.com
tbssuperstation.com
Phone: 404-827-1717
Fax: 404-827-1947

WUPA-TV Ch 69 (UPN)
2700 Northeast Expy Bldg A
Atlanta, GA 30345
E-mail: upn69@paramount.com
www.paramountstations.com/WUPA
Phone: 404-325-6929
Fax: 404-633-4567

WXIA-TV Ch 11 (NBC)
1611 W Peachtree St NE
Atlanta, GA 30309
www.11alive.com
Phone: 404-892-1611
Fax: 404-881-0675

Radio

WABE-FM 90.1 MHz (NPR)
740 Bismark Rd NE
Atlanta, GA 30324
www.wabe.org/wabe.html
Phone: 678-686-0321
Fax: 678-686-0356

WAEC-AM 860 kHz (Rel)
1465 Northside Dr Suite 218
Atlanta, GA 30318
Phone: 404-355-8600
Fax: 404-355-4156

WAFS-AM 920 kHz (Rel)
1827 Powers Ferry Rd Bldg 15 Suite 200
Atlanta, GA 30339
E-mail: wafs@moody.edu
wafs.mbn.org
Phone: 770-226-0920
Fax: 770-226-0927

WALR-AM 1340 kHz (Urban)
2970 Peachtree Rd Suite 700
Atlanta, GA 30305
Phone: 404-688-0068
Fax: 404-688-4262

WALR-FM 104.7 MHz (Urban)
2970 Peachtree Rd Suite 700
Atlanta, GA 30305
www.kiss1047.com
Phone: 404-688-0068
Fax: 404-688-4262

WAMJ-FM 107.5 MHz (Oldies)
75 Piedmont Ave 10th Fl
Atlanta, GA 30303
Phone: 404-765-9750
Fax: 404-688-7686

WAOK-AM 1380 kHz (Rel)
1201 Peachtree St NE Suite 800
Atlanta, GA 30361
Phone: 404-898-8900
Fax: 404-898-8916

WCLK-FM 91.9 MHz (NPR)
111 James P Brawley Dr SW
Atlanta, GA 30314
E-mail: gnsales@globolnet.com
www.cau-wclk.com
Phone: 404-880-8273
Fax: 404-880-8869

WCNN-AM 680 kHz (N/T)
1601 W Peachtree St
Atlanta, GA 30309
Phone: 404-897-7500
Fax: 404-897-7363

WFOX-FM 97.1 MHz (Oldies)
2000 Riveredge Pkwy Suite 797
Atlanta, GA 30328
www.fox97.com
Phone: 770-953-9369
Fax: 770-955-5483

WGKA-AM 1190 kHz (Misc)
2999 Piedmont Rd
Atlanta, GA 30305
E-mail: wgka@mindspring.com
www.wgka.com
Phone: 404-231-2395
Fax: 404-231-1200

WGST-AM 640 kHz (N/T)
1819 Peachtree Rd Suite 700
Atlanta, GA 30309
www.wgst.com
Phone: 404-367-0640
Fax: 404-367-1057
TF: 800-776-4638

WGST-FM 105.7 MHz (N/T)
1819 Peachtree Rd Suite 700
Atlanta, GA 30309
E-mail: wgst.feedback@sid.net
www.wgst.com
Phone: 404-367-0640
Fax: 404-367-1057
TF: 800-776-4638

WGUN-AM 1010 kHz (Rel)
2901 Mountain Industrial Blvd
Tucker, GA 30084
Phone: 770-491-1010
Fax: 770-491-3019

WHTA-FM 97.5 MHz (Urban)
75 Piedmont Ave 10th Fl
Atlanta, GA 30303
Phone: 404-765-9750
Fax: 404-688-7686

WJSP-FM 88.1 MHz (NPR)
260 14th St NW
Atlanta, GA 30318
www.gpb.org/pspr
Phone: 404-685-2400
Fax: 404-685-2684

WJZF-FM 104.1 MHz (NAC)
5520 Old National Hwy Suite B
College Park, GA 30349
www.accessatlanta.com/partners/wjzf
Phone: 404-761-2823
Fax: 404-761-2839

WKHX-AM 590 kHz (Misc)
210 I-North Pkwy 6th Fl
Atlanta, GA 30339
www.wkhx.com
Phone: 770-955-0101
Fax: 770-953-4612

WKHX-FM 101.5 MHz (Ctry)
210 I-North Pkwy 6th Fl
Atlanta, GA 30339
www.wkhx.com
Phone: 770-955-0101
Fax: 770-953-4612

WKLS-FM 96.1 MHz (Rock)
1800 Century Blvd Suite 1200
Atlanta, GA 30345
www.96rock.com
Phone: 404-325-0960
Fax: 404-325-8715

WNIV-AM 970 kHz (Rel)
2970 Peachtree Rd NW Suite 800
Atlanta, GA 30305
E-mail: wniv@wniv.com
www.wniv.com
Phone: 404-365-0970
Fax: 404-816-0748

WNNX-FM 99.7 MHz (Alt)
3405 Piedmont Rd Suite 500
Atlanta, GA 30305
www.99x.com
Phone: 404-266-0997
Fax: 404-364-5855

WPCH-FM 94.9 MHz (AC)
1819 Peachtree Rd NE Suite 700
Atlanta, GA 30309
www.peach949.com
Phone: 404-367-0949
Fax: 404-367-9490

WQXI-AM 790 kHz (N/T)
3350 Peachtree Rd NE Suite 1800
Atlanta, GA 30326
www.wqxi.com
Phone: 404-261-2970
Fax: 404-365-9026

WRAS-FM 88.5 MHz (Misc)
95 Piedmont Ave Suite 226
Atlanta, GA 30303
E-mail: deadair@mindspring.com
www.wras.org
Phone: 404-651-2240
Fax: 404-651-1705

WRFG-FM 89.3 MHz (Misc)
1083 Austin Ave NE
Atlanta, GA 30307
E-mail: wrfg@mindspring.com
www.wrfg.org
Phone: 404-523-3471
Fax: 404-523-8990

WSB-AM 750 kHz (N/T)
1601 W Peachtree St NE
Atlanta, GA 30309
www.accessatlanta.com/partners/wsbradio/
Phone: 404-897-7500
Fax: 404-897-7363

WSB-FM 98.5 MHz (AC)
1601 W Peachtree St NE
Atlanta, GA 30309
www.accessatlanta.com/partners/b98
Phone: 404-897-7500
Fax: 404-897-7363

WSTR-FM 94.1 MHz (CHR)
3350 Peachtree Rd NE Suite 1800
Atlanta, GA 30326
www.star94.com
Phone: 404-261-2970
Fax: 404-365-9026

WVEE-FM 103.3 MHz (Urban)
1201 Peachtree St NE Suite 800
Atlanta, GA 30361
www.v-103.com
Phone: 404-898-8900
Fax: 404-898-8916

WWWE-AM 1110 kHz (Span)
1465 Northside Dr
Atlanta, GA 30318
Phone: 404-603-8770

WYAY-FM 106.7 MHz (Ctry)
210 I-North Pkwy 6th Fl
Atlanta, GA 30339
www.wyay.com
Phone: 770-955-0106
Fax: 770-952-7461

WYZE-AM 1480 kHz (Rel)
1111 Boulevard SE
Atlanta, GA 30312
E-mail: wyze@mindspring.com
www.wyze1480.com
Phone: 404-622-7802
Fax: 404-622-6767

WZGC-FM 92.9 MHz (CR)
1100 Johnson Ferry Rd Suite 593
Atlanta, GA 30342
E-mail: feedback@z93.com
www.z93.com
Phone: 404-851-9393
Fax: 404-843-3541

Attractions

The City of Atlanta is home to the trendy neighborhood of Buckhead; CNN Center, which is also the world headquarters for Turner Broadcasting System; Underground Atlanta, a restored below-street-level marketplace, and the adjacent World of Coca-Cola; the shops and galleries of Antebellum Roswell; and Zoo Atlanta. Atlanta's Martin Luther King, Jr. Center for Nonviolent Social Change includes the Center itself, the home where Dr. King was born, his grave site, and the Ebenezer Baptist Church where he preached. The area south of downtown Atlanta, in Clayton County, was the setting for the novel "Gone With the Wind." Other notable attractions in Atlanta's metro area include Kennesaw Mountain National Battlefield Park and the Confederate Cemetery; and the 3,200-acre Stone Mountain Park, featuring the world's largest bas relief sculpture. In 1996, Atlanta hosted the Summer Olympic Games.

14th Street Playhouse
173 14th St
Atlanta, GA 30309
Phone: 404-733-4750
Fax: 404-733-4756

Academy Theatre
501 Means St
Atlanta, GA 30307
Phone: 404-525-4111
Fax: 404-525-5659

African-American Panoramic Experience Museum
135 Auburn Ave NE
Atlanta, GA 30303
E-mail: blackhis@bellsouth.net
www.apexmuseum.org
Phone: 404-521-2739
Fax: 404-523-3248

Alliance Theatre Co
1280 Peachtree St NE Woodruff Arts Ctr
Atlanta, GA 30309
www.alliancetheatre.org
Phone: 404-733-5000
Fax: 404-733-4625

Antebellum Roswell Historic District
617 Atlanta St
Roswell, GA 30075
www.cvb.roswell.ga.us/places.htm
Phone: 770-640-3253
Fax: 770-640-3252

Asian Square
5150 Buford Hwy NE
Doraville, GA 30340
Phone: 770-458-8899

Atlanta Ballet
1400 W Peachtree St NW
Atlanta, GA 30309
www.atlantaballet.com/
Phone: 404-873-5811
Fax: 404-874-7905

Atlanta Botanical Garden
1345 Piedmont Ave
Atlanta, GA 30309
www.atlgarden.com
Phone: 404-876-5859
Fax: 404-876-7472

Atlanta Brewing Co
1219 Williams St NW
Atlanta, GA 30309
Phone: 404-892-4436
Fax: 404-347-9356

Atlanta Contemporary Art Center
535 Means St
Atlanta, GA 30318
www.thecontemporary.org
Phone: 404-688-1970
Fax: 404-577-5856

Atlanta Cyclorama
800-C Cherokee Ave SE
Atlanta, GA 30315
E-mail: atlcyclorama@mindspring.com
www.webguide.com/cyclorama.html
Phone: 404-658-7625
Fax: 404-658-7045

Atlanta History Center
130 W Paces Ferry Rd
Atlanta, GA 30305
www.atlhist.org
Phone: 404-814-4000
Fax: 404-814-4186

Atlanta International Museum of Art & Design
285 Peachtree Center Ave
Atlanta, GA 30303
www.atlinternationalmuseum.org
Phone: 404-688-2467
Fax: 404-521-9311

Atlanta Opera
728 West Peachtree St NW
Atlanta, GA 30308
www.atlantaopera.org
Phone: 404-881-8801
Fax: 404-881-1711
TF: 800-356-7372

Atlanta Preservation Center Phone: 404-876-2040
537 Peachtree St Fax: 404-876-2618
Atlanta, GA 30308
E-mail: apcofcmgr@mindspring.com
www.preserveatlanta.com

Atlanta Symphony Orchestra Phone: 404-733-4900
1293 Peachtree St NE Suite 300 Fax: 404-733-4901
Atlanta, GA 30309
www.atlantasymphony.org

Buckhead Village Phone: 404-233-2228
Peachtree & E Paces Ferry Rds Fax: 404-812-8222
Atlanta, GA 30305

Callanwolde Fine Arts Center Phone: 404-872-5338
980 Briarcliff Rd NE Fax: 404-872-5175
Atlanta, GA 30306
E-mail: callanwolde@mindspring.com
www.mindspring.com/~callanwolde/

Centennial Olympic Park Phone: 404-222-7275
International Blvd & Techwood Dr Fax: 404-223-4499
Atlanta, GA 30313
www.gwcc.com

Center for Puppetry Arts Phone: 404-873-3089
1404 Spring St NW Fax: 404-873-9907
Atlanta, GA 30309
E-mail: puppet@mindspring.com
www.puppet.org/

Chastain Memorial Park Phone: 404-851-1273
135 W Wieuca Rd
Atlanta, GA 30342

Chateau Elan Winery Phone: 770-932-0900
100 Tour de France Fax: 770-271-6005
Braselton, GA 30517 TF: 800-233-9463
E-mail: chateau@chateaelan.com
www.chateauelan.com

Chattahoochee Nature Center Phone: 770-992-2055
9135 Willeo Rd Fax: 770-552-0926
Roswell, GA 30075

Chattahoochee River National Recreation Area Phone: 770-399-8070
1978 Island Ford Pkwy Fax: 770-392-7045
Atlanta, GA 30350
www.nps.gov/chat/

Children's Museum of Atlanta Phone: 404-659-5437
1 Park Tower Suite 2055 Fax: 404-223-3675
Atlanta, GA 30303

Clayton County International Park Phone: 770-478-1932
2300 Hwy 138 SE Fax: 770-477-1696
Jonesboro, GA 30236
www.thebeachccip.com

CNN Center/CNN Studio Tours Phone: 404-827-2400
1 CNN Ctr Box 105366 Fax: 404-827-3384
Atlanta, GA 30348
E-mail: cnn.studio.tour@cnn.com
www.cnn.com/StudioTour/

Concord Covered Bridge & Historic District Phone: 404-843-0018
Concord Rd Fax: 404-843-2510
Smyrna, GA 30080

Dad's Garage Theatre Co Phone: 404-523-3141
280 Elizabeth St Fax: 404-688-6644
Atlanta, GA 30307
E-mail: info@dadsgarage.com
www.dadsgarage.com

Ebenezer Baptist Church Phone: 404-688-7263
407 Auburn Ave NE Fax: 404-521-1129
Atlanta, GA 30312
www.ebenezer.org

ESPN Zone Atlanta Phone: 404-682-3776
3030 Peachtree Rd Fax: 404-682-3795
Atlanta, GA 30305
espn.go.com/espninc/zone/atlantainfo.html

Federal Reserve Bank Monetary Museum Phone: 404-521-8784
104 Marietta St NW Fax: 404-521-8050
Atlanta, GA 30303

Fernbank Museum of Natural History Phone: 404-378-0127
767 Clifton Rd NE Fax: 404-370-8087
Atlanta, GA 30307
www.fernbank.edu/museum/index.html

Fernbank Science Center Phone: 404-378-4311
156 Heaton Park Dr NE Fax: 404-370-1336
Atlanta, GA 30307
E-mail: fernbank@fernbank.edu
www.fernbank.edu/fsc/fsc.html

Fox Theatre Phone: 404-881-2100
660 Peachtree St NE Fax: 404-872-2972
Atlanta, GA 30365
E-mail: foxmanagement@mindspring.com
www.thefoxtheater.com

Frabel Studio & Galleries Phone: 404-351-9794
695 Antone St NW Fax: 404-351-1491
Atlanta, GA 30318 TF: 800-843-1450
E-mail: studio@frabel.com
www.frabel.com

Georgia State Capitol Phone: 404-656-2844
Atlanta, GA 30334

Goethe Institut Atlanta/German Cultural Center Phone: 404-892-2388
1197 Peachtree St NE Fax: 404-892-3832
Atlanta, GA 30361
E-mail: goetheatlanta@mindspring.com
www.goethe.de/uk/atl/

Governor's Mansion Phone: 404-261-1776
391 W Paces Ferry Rd Fax: 404-231-8621
Atlanta, GA 30305

Grant Park Phone: 404-624-0697
840 Cherokee Ave SE Fax: 404-624-0823
Atlanta, GA 30312

Hammonds House Phone: 404-752-8730
503 Peeples St SW Fax: 404-752-8733
Atlanta, GA 30310

Herndon House
587 University Pl NW
Atlanta, GA 30314
Phone: 404-581-9813

High Museum of Art
1280 Peachtree St NE
Atlanta, GA 30309
www.high.org
Phone: 404-733-4200
Fax: 404-733-4502

High Museum of Art Folk Art & Photography Galleries
30 John Wesley Dobbs Ave NE
Atlanta, GA 30303
www.high.org
Phone: 404-577-6940
Fax: 404-653-0916

Historic Marietta Square
4 Depot St
Marietta, GA 30060
E-mail: dbma@mariettasquare.com
www.mariettasquare.com
Phone: 770-429-1115
Fax: 770-428-3443
TF: 800-835-0445

Historic Oakland Cemetery
248 Oakland Ave SE
Atlanta, GA 30312
Phone: 404-688-2107
Fax: 404-658-6092

IMAX Theater
767 Clifton Rd NE Fernbank Museum of Natural History
Atlanta, GA 30307
Phone: 404-378-0127
Fax: 404-378-8140

Ivan Allen Jr Braves Museum & Hall of Fame
755 Hank Aaron Dr
Atlanta, GA 30315
E-mail: bravesmuseum@mindspring.com
www.atlantabraves.com/braves_tf_museum/0,1644,17,00.html
Phone: 404-614-2310
Fax: 404-614-1423

Jimmy Carter Library & Museum
441 Freedom Pkwy
Atlanta, GA 30307
E-mail: library@carter.nara.gov
carterlibrary.galileo.peachnet.edu
Phone: 404-331-3942
Fax: 404-730-2215

Kennesaw Mountain National Battlefield Park
900 Kennesaw Mountain Dr
Kennesaw, GA 30152
www.nps.gov/kemo/
Phone: 770-427-4686
Fax: 770-528-8398

Lillie Glassblowers
3431 Lake Dr SE
Smyrna, GA 30082
E-mail: sales@lillieglass.com
www.lillieglass.com
Phone: 770-436-8959
Fax: 770-435-0695

Main Street Gallery
93 Main St
Buford, GA 30518
Phone: 770-945-9718

Margaret Mitchell House & Museum
990 Peachtree St NE
Atlanta, GA 30309
www.gwtw.org
Phone: 404-249-7012
Fax: 404-249-9388

Martin Luther King Jr Center for Nonviolent Social Change Inc
449 Auburn Ave NE
Atlanta, GA 30312
E-mail: mlkctr@aol.com
www.thekingcenter.com
Phone: 404-524-1956
Fax: 404-526-8969

Martin Luther King Jr National Historic Site
450 Auburn Ave NE
Atlanta, GA 30312
www.nps.gov/malu/
Phone: 404-331-3920
Fax: 404-331-7620

Michael C Carlos Museum
571 S Kilgo St
Atlanta, GA 30322
www.cc.emory.edu/CARLOS
Phone: 404-727-4282
Fax: 404-727-4292

Oglethorpe University Museum
4484 Peachtree Rd NE
Atlanta, GA 30319
museum.oglethorpe.edu
Phone: 404-364-8555
Fax: 404-364-8556

Piedmont Park
400 Park Dr NE
Atlanta, GA 30306
Phone: 404-817-6788

Rhodes Hall
1516 Peachtree St NW
Atlanta, GA 30309
www.georgiatrust.org/rhodes.html
Phone: 404-881-9980
Fax: 404-875-2205

Rialto Center for the Performing Arts
80 Forsyth St
Atlanta, GA 30303
www.rialtocenter.org
Phone: 404-651-1234
Fax: 404-651-1332

Robert C Williams American Museum of Papermaking
500 10th St NW
Atlanta, GA 30318
www.ipst.edu/amp/
Phone: 404-894-7840
Fax: 404-894-4778
TF: 800-558-6611

Robert W Woodruff Arts Center
1280 Peachtree St NE
Atlanta, GA 30309
www.woodruff-arts.org
Phone: 404-733-4200
Fax: 404-733-4281

SciTrek Science & Technology Museum
395 Piedmont Ave NE
Atlanta, GA 30308
scitrek.org
Phone: 404-522-5500
Fax: 404-525-9606

Shakespeare Tavern
499 Peachtree Street NE
Atlanta, GA 30308
www.shakespearetavern.com
Phone: 404-874-5299

Six Flags Over Georgia
7561 Six Flags Pkwy
Austell, GA 30168
www.sixflags.com/georgia
Phone: 770-948-9290
Fax: 770-948-4378

Smith Plantation Home
935 Alpharetta St
Roswell, GA 30075
Phone: 770-641-3978
Fax: 770-641-3974
TF: 800-776-7935

Southeastern Railway Museum
3595 S Old Peachtree Rd
Duluth, GA 30096
www.srmduluth.org
Phone: 770-476-2013
Fax: 770-908-8322

Southface Energy & Environmental Resource Center
241 Pine St
Atlanta, GA 30308
www.southface.org
Phone: 404-872-3549
Fax: 404-872-5009

Stately Oaks Plantation
100 Carriage Ln
Jonesboro, GA 30236
Phone: 770-473-0197
Fax: 770-473-9855

Stone Mountain Park
6867 Memorial Dr
Stone Mountain, GA 30087
E-mail: mail@stonemountainpark.org
www.stonemountainpark.org
Phone: 770-498-5690
Fax: 770-498-5607

Stone Mountain Village
891 Main St
Stone Mountain, GA 30083
Phone: 770-879-4971
Fax: 770-879-4972

Swan House & Tullie Smith Farm
130 W Paces Ferry Rd
Atlanta, GA 30305
Phone: 404-814-4000

Telephone Museum
675 W Peachtree St NE Southern Bell Ctr
Atlanta, GA 30375
Phone: 404-223-3661

Theater of the Stars
660 Peachtree St NE Fox Theatre
Atlanta, GA 30365
www.theaterofthestars.com
Phone: 404-252-8960
Fax: 404-252-1460

Underground Atlanta
50 Upper Alabama St Suite 007
Atlanta, GA 30303
www.underatl.com/
Phone: 404-523-2311
Fax: 404-523-0507

Vines Botanical Gardens
3500 Oak Grove Rd
Loganville, GA 30052
Phone: 770-466-7532
Fax: 770-466-7854

White Water Park
250 N Cobb Pkwy
Marietta, GA 30062
E-mail: divein@whitewaterpark.com
www.whitewaterpark.com
Phone: 770-424-9283
Fax: 770-424-7565

William Breman Jewish Heritage Museum
1440 Spring St NW
Atlanta, GA 30309
E-mail: njc@jewishculture.org
jewishculture.org/jewishmuseums/breman.htm
Phone: 404-873-1661
Fax: 404-881-4009

World of Coca-Cola Pavilion
55 ML King Jr Dr
Atlanta, GA 30303
Phone: 404-676-5151
Fax: 404-676-5432

Wren's Nest House Museum
1050 Ralph David Abernathy Blvd SW
Atlanta, GA 30310
E-mail: wrensnest@mindspring.com
Phone: 404-753-7735
Fax: 404-753-8535

Yellow River Game Ranch
4525 Hwy 78
Lilburn, GA 30047
E-mail: gameranch@mindspring.com
www.yellowrivergameranch.com
Phone: 770-972-6643
Fax: 770-985-0150

Zoo Atlanta
800 Cherokee Ave
Atlanta, GA 30315
www.zooatlanta.org
Phone: 404-624-5600
Fax: 404-627-7514

Sports Teams & Facilities

Alexander Memorial Coliseum
965 Fowler St NW
Atlanta, GA 30332
Phone: 404-894-2000

Atlanta Braves
755 Hank Aaron Dr Turner Field
Atlanta, GA 30315
E-mail: braves@atlantabraves.com
www.atlantabraves.com/
Phone: 404-522-7630
Fax: 404-614-1329

Atlanta Classics
N Druid Hills Rd Adams Stadium
Atlanta, GA 30319
E-mail: news@atlantaclassics.com
www.atlantaclassics.com
Phone: 770-879-3668
Fax: 770-879-7110

Atlanta Falcons
1 Falcon Pl
Suwanee, GA 30024
www.atlantafalcons.com
Phone: 770-945-1111
Fax: 770-271-1221
TF: 800-241-3489

Atlanta Hawks
1 CNN Ctr Philips Arena
Atlanta, GA 30303
www.nba.com/hawks
Phone: 404-827-3865
Fax: 404-827-3806

Atlanta Motor Speedway
1500 Hwys 19 & 41 S
Hampton, GA 30228
www.atlantamotorspeedway.com
Phone: 770-946-3920
Fax: 770-946-3928

Atlanta Silverbacks (soccer)
116 E Howard Ave
Decatur, GA 30030
E-mail: tickets@atlantasilverbacks.com
www.atlantasilverbacks.com/home.html
Phone: 404-377-5575
Fax: 404-377-5558

Atlanta Thrashers
1 CNN Ctr Philips Arena
Atlanta, GA 30303
www.atlantathrashers.com
Phone: 404-878-3005
Fax: 404-878-3055

Atlanta Trojans (basketball)
3640 Burnette Rd
Suwanee, GA 30024
www.usbl.com/atlanta.html
Phone: 770-614-6686
Fax: 770-614-6993

Colorado Silver Bullets (baseball)
1575 Sheridan Rd NE Suite 200
Atlanta, GA 30324
E-mail: sbulletsi@aol.com
Phone: 404-636-8200
Fax: 404-636-0530
TF: 800-278-2772

Georgia Dome
1 Georgia Dome Dr NW
Atlanta, GA 30313
www.gwcc.com/domeinfo.htm
Phone: 404-223-9200
Fax: 404-223-8011

Philips Arena
1 CNN Center 13 South
Atlanta, GA 30303
www.philipsarena.com
Phone: 404-878-3005
Fax: 404-878-3055
TF: 800-326-4000

Road Atlanta Raceway
5300 Winder Hwy
Braselton, GA 30517
www.roadatlanta.com
Phone: 770-967-6143
Fax: 770-967-2668

Turner Field
755 Hank Aaron Dr
Atlanta, GA 30315
www.atlantabraves.com/turnerfield
Phone: 404-522-7630
Fax: 404-614-1329

Annual Events

Art of the Season
(late November-early December) 404-220-2659
Atlanta Boat Show (early January) 770-951-2500
Atlanta Caribbean Folk Festival (late May) 404-753-3497
Atlanta Dogwood Festival (early April) 404-329-0501
Atlanta Film & Video Festival (mid-May) 404-352-4254
Atlanta Garden & Patio Show (early February) 770-998-9800
Atlanta Greek Festival (late September) 404-633-5870
Atlanta Home Show (late March) 770-998-9800
Atlanta Jazz Festival (late May) 404-817-6851
Atlanta Marathon (late November) 404-231-9064
Atlanta Steeplechase (early April) 404-222-6688
CNN Center Tuba Christmas (mid-December) 770-887-5856
Down to Earth Day Celebration (April 22) 404-873-3173
Festival of Lights (late November-late December) ... 404-222-7275
Festival of Trees (early December) 404-325-6635
First Night Atlanta (December 31) 404-881-0400
Fright Fest (early October) 770-948-9290
Georgia Renaissance Festival
(late April-mid-June) 770-964-8575
Georgia Shakespeare Festival
(early June-late December) 404-264-0020
Holiday Celebration
(late November-late December) 770-498-5600
Holiday Express (December) 404-522-5500
Inman Park Spring Festival & Tour of Homes
(late April) 770-242-4895
Labor Day Weekend Festival (early September) 404-523-2311
Martin Luther King Jr Holiday (late January) 404-524-1956
Montreux Atlanta International Jazz Festival
(early September) 404-521-6600
Music Midtown Festival (early May) 770-643-8696
National Black Arts Festival
(late July-early August) 404-730-7315
New Year's Eve Peach Drop (December 31) 404-523-2311
Peach Bowl (late December) 404-586-8500
Peachtree International Film Festival
(early-mid-November) 770-729-8487
PGA BellSouth Classic (late March-early April) 770-951-8777
Roswell Arts Festival (late September) 770-640-3253
Saint Patrick's Day Celebration (mid-March) 404-523-2311
Salute 2 America Parade (July 4) 404-521-6600
Scottish Festival & Highland Games
(mid-October) 770-498-5702
Southeastern Flower Show (late February) 404-888-5638
Spring Moon Stroll (mid-May) 404-876-5859
Springfest Festival (early May) 770-498-5702
Stone Mountain Village Arts & Crafts Festival
(mid-June) 770-498-2097
Thunder over Atlanta Fireworks (July 4) 404-523-2311
Tour of Southern Ghosts (mid-late October) 770-469-1105
Vinings Fall Festival (early October) 770-438-8080
Virginia Highland Summerfest (early June) 404-222-8244
Yellow Daisy Festival (early September) 770-498-5702

Augusta, Georgia

County: Augusta-Richmond

AUGUSTA is located along the banks of the Savannah River in east central Georgia, 151 miles due east of Atlanta. The only major city within 100 miles is Columbia, South Carolina.

Area (Land) .... 19.7 sq mi
Area (Water)............................... 1.3 sq mi
Elevation.................................... 414 ft
Latitude ....33-46-67 N
Longitude.............................. 82-01-67 W
Time Zone ....EST
Area Code...................................... 706

Climate

Augusta's climate features short, mild winters and long, hot summers. The average annual temperature is 63 degrees. Winter temperatures generally average between 40 and 50 degrees, but occasionally drop below freezing. Snow is rare. Summer daytime high temperatures often reach the upper 90s and afternoon thunderstorms are common. March is the wettest month in Augusta; November is the driest.

Average Temperatures & Precipitation

Temperatures

	Jan	Feb	Mar	Apr	May	Jun	Jul	Aug	Sep	Oct	Nov	Dec
High	56	61	69	77	84	89	92	90	86	77	68	60
Low	32	35	42	49	58	66	70	70	63	50	42	35

Precipitation

	Jan	Feb	Mar	Apr	May	Jun	Jul	Aug	Sep	Oct	Nov	Dec
Inches	4.1	4.3	4.7	3.3	3.8	4.1	4.2	4.5	3.0	2.8	2.5	3.4

History

Georgia's second oldest city, Augusta was originally established as a trading post in 1736 by British General James Oglethorpe. The city was named in honor of Princess Augusta, the wife of Frederick Louis, Prince of Wales.

Augusta was a colonial military outpost during the Revolutionary War and served as the capital of Georgia between 1785 and 1795. The United States Constitution was also ratified in the city. During the Civil War, Augusta was home to the Confederate Powder Works, one of the world's largest munitions manufacturers.

The late 19th century was a period of rapid growth for Augusta, due to the city's thriving tobacco and cotton industries. Augusta's access to the Atlantic Ocean via the Savannah River helped make the city the second largest inland cotton producer in the nation.

Camp Gordon was established in Augusta during World War II. The military installation drew large numbers of people to the city and surrounding area during the war, and many of the soldiers that trained at Camp Gordon returned to settle in the area once the war was over. Fort Gordon remains one of the area's top employers. Today, Augusta is Georgia's second largest city.

Population

1990 Census 189,719*
1998 Estimate..............................187,689*
% Change 0.6
2001 Projection 214,900*

Racial/Ethnic Breakdown
White....................................53.0%*
Black 44.6%*
Other 2.4%*
Hispanic Origin (may be of any race) 2.0%*

Age Breakdown
Under 18 years............................27.7%*
18 to 24.................................11.6%*
25 to 34.................................16.8%*
35 to 44.................................15.3%*
45 to 54.................................10.9%*
55 to 64..................................7.6%*
65 to 74..................................6.1%*
75+ years 4.0%*
Median Age.................................31.4*

Gender Breakdown
Male.....................................48.6%*
Female...................................51.4%*

* *Information given is for Augusta-Richmond County.*

Government

Type of Government: County Commission/Council-Mayor (consolidated)

Augusta Administrator
530 Greene St Rm 801
Augusta, GA 30911
Phone: 706-821-2400
Fax: 706-821-2819

Augusta Attorney for Augusta-Richmond County
454 Greene St
Augusta, GA 30901
Phone: 706-821-2488
Fax: 706-722-5984

Augusta Board of Commissioners
530 Greene St
Augusta, GA 30911
Phone: 706-821-1821
Fax: 706-821-1838

Augusta City Hall
530 Greene St
Augusta, GA 30911
Phone: 706-821-2300
Fax: 706-821-2819

Augusta Clerk of the Commission
530 Greene St
Augusta, GA 30911
Phone: 706-821-1820
Fax: 706-821-1838

Augusta Finance Dept
530 Greene St Rm 209
Augusta, GA 30911
Phone: 706-821-2429
Fax: 706-821-2520

Augusta Human Resources Dept
530 Greene St Rm 601
Augusta, GA 30911
Phone: 706-821-2303
Fax: 706-821-2867

Augusta Mayor
530 Greene St Rm 801
Augusta, GA 30911
Phone: 706-821-1831
Fax: 706-821-1835

Augusta Planning Commission
525 Telfair St
Augusta, GA 30901
Phone: 706-821-1798
Fax: 706-821-1806

Augusta Public Transit Div
1535 Fenwick St
Augusta, GA 30904
Phone: 706-821-1721
Fax: 706-821-1752

Augusta Public Works Dept
1815 Marvin Griffin Rd
Augusta, GA 30906
Phone: 706-796-5040
Fax: 706-796-5045

Augusta Recreation & Parks Dept
2027 Lumpkin Rd
Augusta, GA 30916
Phone: 706-796-5025
Fax: 706-796-4099

Augusta Richmond County Fire Dept
1 10th St Suite 420
Augusta, GA 30901
Phone: 706-821-2909
Fax: 706-821-2907

Augusta Richmond County Sheriff's Dept
401 Walton Way
Augusta, GA 30911
Phone: 706-821-1000
Fax: 706-821-1064

Important Phone Numbers

AAA 706-738-6611
Augusta-Richmond County Tax Commissioner's Office 706-821-2391
Driver's License Information 706-771-7814
Emergency 911
Georgia Department of Revenue 706-737-1870
Greater Augusta Assn of Realtors 706-736-0429
Poison Control Center 800-282-5846
Riverwalk Special Events 706-821-1754
Vehicle Registration Information 706-821-2476
Voter Registration Information 706-821-2340
Weather 706-724-0056

Information Sources

Augusta Metropolitan Convention & Visitors Bureau
1450 Greene St Suite 110
Augusta, GA 30901
www.augustaga.org
Phone: 706-823-6600
Fax: 706-823-6609
TF: 800-726-0243

Augusta-Richmond County
530 Greene St
Augusta, GA 30911
www.co.richmond.ga.us
Phone: 706-821-2300
Fax: 706-821-2819

Augusta-Richmond County Civic Center
601 7th St
Augusta, GA 30901
www.augustaciviccenter.com
Phone: 706-722-3521
Fax: 706-724-7545

Better Business Bureau Serving Northeast Georgia & Southwest South Carolina
PO Box 2085
Augusta, GA 30903
www.augusta-ga.bbb.org
Phone: 706-722-1574
Fax: 706-724-0969

Historic Augusta Inc
111 10th St
Augusta, GA 30901
Phone: 706-724-0436
Fax: 706-724-3083

Metro Augusta Chamber of Commerce
600 Broad Street Plaza
Augusta, GA 30903
www.metroaugusta.com
Phone: 706-821-1300
Fax: 706-821-1330

Online Resources

4Augusta.com
www.4augusta.com

Anthill City Guide Augusta
www.anthill.com/city.asp?city=augusta

Area Guide Augusta
augustaga.areaguides.net

Augusta Georgia
augusta-georgia.com

Best Read Guide Augusta
bestreadguide.com/augusta

City Knowledge Augusta
www.cityknowledge.com/ga_augusta.htm

Excite.com Augusta City Guide
www.excite.com/travel/countries/united_states/georgia/augusta/

Area Communities

Other communities in the Augusta area with populations greater than 2,000 include:

Blythe
PO Box 60
Blythe, GA 30805
Phone: 706-592-6255
Fax: 706-592-0511

Grovetown
PO Box 120
Grovetown, GA 30813
Phone: 706-863-4576
Fax: 706-868-9312

Harlem
PO Box 99
Harlem, GA 30814
Phone: 706-556-3448
Fax: 706-556-3293

Hephzibah
2530 State Hwy 88
Hephzibah, GA 30815
Phone: 706-592-4423
Fax: 706-733-7712

Economy

The Augusta metropolitan area has a civilian workforce of more than 239,000 people, the majority of whom are employed in services, government, retail trade, and manufacturing. Health care is a major industry in Augusta—nearly half of the metro area's top 15 employers are health care-related. The Military also plays an important role in the city's economy, with Fort Gordon employing more than 4,500 civilians. Several Fortune 500 companies have divisions in the Augusta area, including Allied Signal, Archer Daniels Midland Company, PepsiCo, and Procter and Gamble.

Unemployment Rate 5.5%*
Per Capita Income.......................... $22,861*
Median Family Income...................... $20,973

** Information given is for Richmond County.*

Principal Industries & Number of Wage Earners

Richmond County - 1998

Agricultural Services, Forestry, & Fishing 363
Construction.. 5,444
Finance, Insurance, & Real Estate 3,304
Manufacturing 12,680
Public Administration.................................. 6,201
Retail Trade.. 21,172
Services 49,005
Transportation & Public Utilities 4,177
Wholesale Trade....................................... 3,217

Major Employers

Augusta-Richmond County
530 Greene St
Augusta, GA 30911
www.co.richmond.ga.us
Phone: 706-821-2300
Fax: 706-821-2819

Club Car Inc
PO Box 204658
Augusta, GA 30917
www.clubcar.com
Phone: 706-863-3000
Fax: 706-860-7231
TF: 800-227-0739

Columbia County School System
PO Box 10
Appling, GA 30802
Phone: 706-541-0650
Fax: 706-855-2503

Doctors Hospital
3651 Wheeler Rd
Augusta, GA 30909
www.doctors-hospital.net
Phone: 706-651-3232
Fax: 706-651-2041

Dwight David Eisenhower Army Medical Center
Hospital Rd Bldg 300
Fort Gordon, GA 30905
www.ddeamc.amedd.army.mil/
Phone: 706-787-5811
Fax: 706-787-7211

E-Z-GO Textron
PO Box 388
Augusta, GA 30903
www.ezgo.textron.com
Phone: 706-798-4311
Fax: 706-796-4540
TF: 800-241-5855

Fort Gordon
US Army Signal Center
Fort Gordon, GA 30905
www.gordon.army.mil
Phone: 706-791-0110
Fax: 706-791-2061

Gracewood State School & Hospital
100 Myrtle Blvd
Gracewood, GA 30812
Phone: 706-790-2011
Fax: 706-790-2025

Medical College of Georgia
1120 15th St
Augusta, GA 30912
E-mail: hbuchana@mail.mcg.edu
www.mcg.edu
Phone: 706-721-0211
Fax: 706-721-7028

Morris Communications Corp
725 Broad St
Augusta, GA 30901
www.morriscomm.com
Phone: 706-724-0851
Fax: 706-823-3440

Richmond County School System
2083 Heckle St
Augusta, GA 30910
Phone: 706-737-7174
Fax: 706-731-8794

Saint Joseph Hospital
2260 Wrightsboro Rd
Augusta, GA 30904
Phone: 706-481-7000
Fax: 706-481-7599

Thermal Ceramics Inc
2101 Old Savannah Rd
Augusta, GA 30906
E-mail: tceramics@thermalceramics.com
www.thermalceramics.com
Phone: 706-796-4279
Fax: 706-560-4055

University Health Care System
1350 Walton Way
Augusta, GA 30901
E-mail: info@medseek.com
universityhealth.org
Phone: 706-722-9011
Fax: 706-774-8699

Veterans Affairs Medical Center
1 Freedom Way
Augusta, GA 30904
Phone: 706-733-0188
Fax: 706-481-6726

Vogtle Electric Generating Plant
PO Box 1600
Waynesboro, GA 30830
Phone: 706-554-9961
Fax: 706-826-3102

Quality of Living Indicators

Total Crime Index.................................. 14,665
(rates per 100,000 inhabitants)

Violent Crime
Murder/manslaughter........................... 23
Forcible rape 141
Robbery...................................... 552
Aggravated assault............................ 226

Property Crime
Burglary 2,581
Larceny theft 9,580
Motor vehicle theft 1,562

Cost of Living Index....93.7
(national average = 100)

Median Home Price....$102,900

Education

Public Schools

Richmond County School System
2083 Heckle St
Augusta, GA 30910
Phone: 706-737-7174
Fax: 706-731-8794

Number of Schools
Elementary.... 38
Middle.... 9
High.... 9

Student/Teacher Ratio
All Grades.... 17.0:1

Private Schools

Number of Schools (all grades).... 22

Colleges & Universities

Augusta State University
2500 Walton Way
Augusta, GA 30904
www.aug.edu
Phone: 706-737-1400
Fax: 706-667-4355
TF: 800-341-4373

Medical College of Georgia
1120 15th St
Augusta, GA 30912
E-mail: hbuchana@mail.mcg.edu
www.mcg.edu
Phone: 706-721-0211
Fax: 706-721-7028

Paine College
1235 15th St
Augusta, GA 30901
www.paine.edu
Phone: 706-821-8200
Fax: 706-821-8293

Hospitals

Dwight David Eisenhower Army Medical Center
Hospital Rd Bldg 300
Fort Gordon, GA 30905
www.ddeamc.amedd.army.mil/
Phone: 706-787-5811
Fax: 706-787-7211

Medical College of Georgia Hospital & Clinics
1120 15th St
Augusta, GA 30912
Phone: 706-721-0211
Fax: 706-721-6126

Saint Joseph Hospital
2260 Wrightsboro Rd
Augusta, GA 30904
Phone: 706-481-7000
Fax: 706-481-7599

University Health Care System
1350 Walton Way
Augusta, GA 30901
universityhealth.org
Phone: 706-722-9011
Fax: 706-774-8699

Veterans Affairs Medical Center
1 Freedom Way
Augusta, GA 30904
Phone: 706-733-0188
Fax: 706-481-6726

Transportation

Airport(s)

Bush Field (AGS)
8 miles S of downtown (approx 20 minutes)....706-798-2656

Mass Transit

Augusta Public Transit
$.75 Base fare....706-821-1719

Rail/Bus

Greyhound Bus Station
1128 Greene St
Augusta, GA 30901
Phone: 706-722-6411
TF: 800-231-2222

Utilities

Electricity
Georgia Power Co....706-724-0892
www.southernco.com/site/gapower/home.asp

Gas
Atlanta Gas Light Co....800-427-5463
www.aglc.com

Water
Augusta Utilities Dept....706-821-1851

Garbage Collection/Recycling
Augusta Recycling Div....706-592-9634
Augusta Sanitation Dept....706-722-6090

Telecommunications

Telephone
BellSouth....800-356-3094
www.bellsouth.com

Cable Television
Comcast Cable....706-733-7712

Internet Service Providers (ISPs)
Georgia Business Net Inc....706-823-2115
www.gabn.net
ServDirect Services....706-860-4558
www.sdirect.com

Banks

Bank of America
1450 Walton Way
Augusta, GA 30901
Phone: 706-849-0660
TF: 800-299-2265

First Union Direct Bank NA
699 Broad St
Augusta, GA 30901
Phone: 706-823-2500
Fax: 706-823-2505
TF: 800-413-7898

Georgia Bank & Trust Company of Augusta
3530 Wheeler Rd
Augusta, GA 30909
www.georgiabankandtrust.com
Phone: 706-738-6990
Fax: 706-737-3106

Regions Bank
700 Broad St
Augusta, GA 30901
Phone: 706-821-3905
Fax: 706-821-3906

Southtrust Bank of Georgia
1 10th St
Augusta, GA 30901
Phone: 706-849-3200
Fax: 706-821-8816

SunTrust Bank of Augusta
801 Broad St
Augusta, GA 30901
Phone: 706-821-2000
Fax: 706-821-2071
TF: 800-688-7878

Wachovia Bank NA
1268 Broad St
Augusta, GA 30901
Phone: 706-821-6710
Fax: 706-821-6696

Shopping

Augusta Mall
3450 Wrightsboro Rd
Augusta, GA 30909
www.augustamall.com
Phone: 706-733-1001
Fax: 706-733-7980

Downtown Antique Mall
1243 Broad St
Augusta, GA 30901
Phone: 706-722-3571

Downtown Augusta
Main St
Augusta, GA 30901
Phone: 706-722-8000

Fairway Square Shopping Center
2825 Washington Rd
Augusta, GA 30909
Phone: 706-737-3381

Regency Mall
1700 Gordon Hwy
Augusta, GA 30904
Phone: 706-790-6535
Fax: 706-790-0437

Southgate Plaza Shopping Center
1631 Gordon Hwy
Augusta, GA 30906
Phone: 706-793-2094

Westtown Market
3830 Washington Rd
Martinez, GA 30907
Phone: 706-860-3966
Fax: 706-855-5359

Media

Newspapers and Magazines

Augusta Chronicle*
PO Box 1928
Augusta, GA 30903
www.augustachronicle.com
Phone: 706-724-0851
Fax: 706-722-7403

Augusta Focus
1143 Laney Walker Blvd
Augusta, GA 30901
Phone: 706-722-4222
Fax: 706-724-6969

Metropolitan Spirit
PO Box 3809
Augusta, GA 30914
www.metspirit.com
Phone: 706-738-1142
Fax: 706-733-6663

**Indicates major daily newspapers*

Television

WAGT-TV Ch 26 (NBC)
PO Box 1526
Augusta, GA 30903
www.wagt.com
Phone: 706-826-0026
Fax: 706-724-4028

WCES-TV Ch 20 (PBS)
PO Box 525
Wrens, GA 30833
Phone: 706-547-2107

WFXG-TV Ch 54 (Fox)
3933 Washington Rd
Augusta, GA 30907
www.wfxg.com
Phone: 706-650-5400
Fax: 706-650-8411

WJBF-TV Ch 6 (ABC)
PO Box 1404
Augusta, GA 30903
www.wjbf.com
Phone: 706-722-6664
Fax: 706-722-0022

WRDW-TV Ch 12 (CBS)
PO Box 1212
Augusta, GA 30903
www.wrdw.com
Phone: 803-278-1212
Fax: 803-279-8316

Radio

WAKB-FM 96.9 MHz (Urban)
104 Bennett Ln
North Augusta, SC 29841
Phone: 803-279-2330
Fax: 803-819-3781

WBBQ-FM 104.3 MHz (AC)
500 Carolina Springs Rd
North Augusta, SC 29841
E-mail: wbbq@csra.net
www.wbbq.com
Phone: 803-279-6610
Fax: 803-279-1175

WFAM-AM 1050 kHz (Rel)
552 Laney Walker Ext
Augusta, GA 30901
Phone: 706-722-6077
Fax: 706-722-7066

WGOR-FM 93.9 MHz (AC)
432 S Belair Rd
Martinez, GA 30907
E-mail: coolfm@gabn.net
www.gabn.net/coolfm/
Phone: 706-855-9494
Fax: 706-860-9343

WKSP-FM 96.3 MHz (Urban)
500 Carolina Springs Rd
North Augusta, SC 29841
Phone: 803-279-1977
Fax: 803-279-1175

WZNY-FM 105.7 MHz (CHR)
500 Carolina Springs Rd
North Augusta, SC 29841
www.y105augusta.com
Phone: 803-279-6610
Fax: 803-279-1175

Attractions

During the 1980s, the levee built along the Savannah River to protect Augusta from possible flooding was transformed into Riverwalk, the entertainment center of the city. Riverwalk features a brick-lined esplanade along the river, gardens, playgrounds, restaurants, shops, special events, and a variety of historical, educational, and recreational attractions. A recent addition to Riverwalk is the Fort Discovery/National Science Center, which offers more than 250 hands-on activities, including opportunities to experience walking on the moon and flying a high-performance jet. Augusta also plays host to the world-famous Masters Golf Tournament each April, and the Georgia Golf Hall of Fame and Gardens, which opened in 1998 and features a museum and interactive exhibits honoring the game's finest players.

Augusta Ballet
1301 Greene St
Augusta, GA 30901
Phone: 706-261-0555
Fax: 706-826-4716

Augusta Choral Society
1301 Greene St
Augusta, GA 30901
Phone: 706-826-4713

Augusta Opera
1301 Greene St Suite 100
Augusta, GA 30901
Phone: 706-826-4710
Fax: 706-826-4732

Augusta Players
1301 Greene St Suite 304
Augusta, GA 30901
E-mail: players@sdirect.com
www.sdirect.com/theatre/
Phone: 706-826-4707
Fax: 706-826-4708

Augusta Richmond County Museum
560 Reynolds St
Augusta, GA 30901
Phone: 706-722-8454
Fax: 706-724-5192

Augusta Symphony Orchestra
1301 Greene St Suite 200
Augusta, GA 30903
Phone: 706-826-4705
Fax: 706-826-4735

Confederate Powerworks
Downtown on Goodrich St
Augusta, GA 30904
Phone: 706-724-0436

Cotton Exchange Museum
32 8th St
Augusta, GA 30901
E-mail: amcvb@augustaga.org
www.augustaga.org/frames-tour.htm
Phone: 706-724-4067
Fax: 706-262-0287
TF: 800-726-0243

Enterprise Mill
1450 Greene St Suite 170
Augusta, GA 30901
www.enterprisemill.com
Phone: 706-774-6424
Fax: 706-774-6426

Fort Discovery/National Science Center
Riverwalk & 7th St
Augusta, GA 30901
www.nscdiscovery.org/
Phone: 706-821-0200
Fax: 706-821-0269
TF: 800-325-5445

Georgia Golf Hall of Fame
1 10th St Suite 745
Augusta, GA 30901
Phone: 706-724-4443
Fax: 706-724-4428

Gertrude Herbert Institute of Art
506 Telfair St
Augusta, GA 30901
Phone: 706-722-5495
Fax: 706-722-3670

Greater Augusta Arts Council
PO Box 1776
Augusta, GA 30903
www.augustaarts.com
Phone: 706-826-4702
Fax: 706-826-4723

Harris Ezekiel House
1822 Broad St
Augusta, GA 30904
Phone: 706-724-0436
Fax: 706-724-3083

Imperial Theatre
745 Broad St
Augusta, GA 30901
Phone: 706-722-8293
Fax: 706-722-8293

Krystal River Water Park
799 Industrial Park Dr
Evans, GA 30809
Phone: 706-855-0061
Fax: 706-855-0667

Lucy Craft Laney Museum
116 Phillips St
Augusta, GA 30901
E-mail: lclmuseum@therise.net
www.lucycraftlaneymuseum.com
Phone: 706-724-3576
Fax: 706-724-2866

Meadow Garden
1320 Independence Dr
Augusta, GA 30901
Phone: 706-724-4174

Morris Museum of Art
1 10th St
Augusta, GA 30901
E-mail: mormuse@themorris.org
www.themorris.org
Phone: 706-724-7501
Fax: 706-724-7612

Old Government House
432 Telfair St
Augusta, GA 30901
Phone: 706-821-1812

Riverwalk
15 8th St
Augusta, GA 30901
Phone: 706-821-1754
Fax: 706-821-1756

Riverwalk Marina
1 5th St
Augusta, GA 30901
Phone: 706-722-1388
Fax: 706-724-4787

Sacred Heart Cultural Center
1301 Greene St
Augusta, GA 30901
Phone: 706-826-4700
Fax: 706-722-2222

Saint Paul's Episcopal Church
605 Reynolds St
Augusta, GA 30901
www.saintpauls.org
Phone: 706-724-2485
Fax: 706-724-0904

Savannah Rapids Park
3300 Evans to Locks Rd
Martinez, GA 30907
Phone: 706-868-3349
Fax: 706-868-3484

Springfield Baptist Church
114 12th St
Augusta, GA 30901
Phone: 706-724-1056

Woodrow Wilson Boyhood Home
419 7th St
Augusta, GA 30901
Phone: 706-724-0436

Sports Teams & Facilities

Augusta Greenjackets (baseball)
78 Milledge Rd
Augusta, GA 30904
www.greenjackets.net
Phone: 706-736-7889
Fax: 706-736-1122

Augusta Lynx (hockey)
Telfair St Augusta-Richmond County Civic Ctr
Augusta, GA 30901
E-mail: hockey@augustalynx.com
www.augustalynx.com
Phone: 706-724-4423
Fax: 706-724-2423
TF: 877-284-5969

Annual Events

A Day in the Country (early May) 803-278-5404
Arts in the Heart of Augusta (mid-September) 706-826-4702

Augusta Cutting Horse Futurity & Festival (late January) 706-823-3417
Augusta Southern National Drag Boat Races (mid-July) 706-724-2452
Boshears' Memorial Fly In (late September). 706-733-1647
Christmas Made in The South (mid-November) 706-722-3521
Festival of Lights (late November). 706-821-1754
Garden City Folk Festival (early May). 706-826-4702
Gem & Mineral Show (mid-March) 706-796-5025
Grecian Festival (early October). 706-821-1755
Head of the South Regatta (HOTS) (late November) 706-722-4114
Hispanic Festival (mid-October). 706-821-1754
Historic Augusta Antique Show & Sale (early November) 706-724-0436
June Jazz Candlelight Concert Series (May) 706-821-1754
Masters Tournament (April) 706-667-6000
Oktoberfest (mid-October). 706-860-0935
Riverwalk Fourth Celebration (July 4) 706-821-1754
Sacred Heart Garden & Flower Show (late March) 706-826-4700
Saint Patrick's Day Celebration (mid-March) 706-821-1754
Springtime Made in The South (early March). 706-722-3521
Taste of Augusta (late September). 706-868-7683
West Paint Party (early June & mid-October) 706-826-4702

Austin, Texas

***County:* Travis**

USTIN is located in Travis County in central Texas along the banks of the Colorado River. Cities within 100 miles of Austin include San Antonio and Waco, Texas.

Area (Land) .... 213.7 sq mi
Area (Water)................................ 6.9 sq mi
Elevation...................................... 501 ft
Latitude ....30-26-69 N
Longitude................................ 97-74-28 W
Time Zone ....CST
Area Code.. 512

Climate

Austin has a temperate climate with an average annual temperature of 68 degrees. Winters are generally mild; however, the temperature occasionally drops below freezing, and the average annual snowfall is one inch. Summer days are hot, with average high temperatures in the low to mid-90s, but temperatures fall into the lower 70s in the evenings. Austin has an average of 300 days of sunshine annually. May is the wettest month in Austin; January is the driest.

Average Temperatures & Precipitation

Temperatures

	Jan	Feb	Mar	Apr	May	Jun	Jul	Aug	Sep	Oct	Nov	Dec
High	59	63	72	79	85	91	95	96	91	82	72	62
Low	39	42	51	60	67	72	74	74	70	60	50	41

Precipitation

	Jan	Feb	Mar	Apr	May	Jun	Jul	Aug	Sep	Oct	Nov	Dec
Inches	1.7	2.2	1.9	2.6	4.8	3.7	2.0	2.1	3.3	3.4	2.4	1.9

History

Originally a small community called Waterloo along the banks of the Colorado River, the city of Austin was settled in 1838. In December 1839, the city was incorporated as the capital of the Republic of Texas and renamed for Texas Revolution hero Stephen F. Austin, who is sometimes referred to as the "Father of Texas." The original State Capitol Building was destroyed by fire in 1881, and the building erected in its place is Austin's most important historic landmark. Considered by Texans a tribute to Texas pride, the State Capitol Building is not only the tallest of its 49 counterparts, but it is also seven feet taller than the U.S. Capitol in Washington, DC.

Until the 1960s, Austin's economy revolved around the state government and the University of Texas, which remain two of the area's major employers today. In 1967, IBM opened a plant in Austin, and many high technology companies followed. With new job opportunities came new residents, more than doubling Austin's population in the 25 years between 1970 and 1995. With a population of more than 552,000 people, Austin today is the 21st largest city in the United States.

Population

1990 Census 465,648
1998 Estimate..............................552,434
% Change 17.0
2005 Projection 1,168,000*

Racial/Ethnic Breakdown
White.................................... 70.6%
Black 12.4%
Other.................................... 17.0%
Hispanic Origin (may be of any race) 23.0%

Age Breakdown
Under 5 years.............................. 7.6%
5 to 17.................................. 15.5%
18 to 20.................................. 7.5%
21 to 24................................. 10.1%
25 to 34................................. 22.7%
35 to 44................................. 15.6%
45 to 54.................................. 7.9%
55 to 64.................................. 5.6%
65 to 74.................................. 4.3%
75+ years 3.2%
Median Age................................28.9

Gender Breakdown
Male..................................... 49.9%
Female................................... 50.1%

** Information given is for the Austin-San Marcos Metropolitan Statistical Area (MSA), which includes the City of Austin, Bastrop County, Caldwell County, Hays County, Travis County, and Williamson County.*

Government

Type of Government: Council-Manager

Austin City Clerk
PO Box 1088
Austin, TX 78767
Phone: 512-499-2210
Fax: 512-499-2374

Austin City Hall
PO Box 1088
Austin, TX 78767
Phone: 512-499-2000
Fax: 512-499-2374

Austin City Manager
PO Box 1088
Austin, TX 78767
Phone: 512-499-2200
Fax: 512-499-2832

Austin Financial & Administrative Services
124 W 8th St Rm 301
Austin, TX 78701
Phone: 512-499-2450
Fax: 512-499-2573

Austin Fire Dept
1621 Festival Beach Rd
Austin, TX 78702
Phone: 512-477-5784
Fax: 512-469-3601

Austin Human Resources Dept
206 E 9th St
Austin, TX 78701
Phone: 512-499-3210
Fax: 512-499-3321

Austin Law Dept
114 W 7th St
Austin, TX 78701
Phone: 512-499-2268
Fax: 512-499-2894

Austin Mayor
PO Box 1088
Austin, TX 78767
Phone: 512-499-2250
Fax: 512-499-2337

Austin Parks & Recreation Dept
200 S Lamar Blvd
Austin, TX 78701
Phone: 512-499-6700
Fax: 512-499-6774

Austin Planning Environmental & Conservation Dept
206 E 9th St
Austin, TX 78701
Phone: 512-499-3500
Fax: 512-499-6525

Austin Police Dept
715 E 8th St
Austin, TX 78701
Phone: 512-974-5000
Fax: 512-974-6611

Austin Public Library
PO Box 2287
Austin, TX 78768
Phone: 512-499-7300
Fax: 512-499-7403

Austin Public Works & Transportation Dept
505 Barton Springs Rd Suite 1300
Austin, TX 78704
Phone: 512-499-7037
Fax: 512-499-7084

Austin Solid Waste Services Dept
PO Box 1088
Austin, TX 78767
Phone: 512-499-2111
Fax: 512-499-1999

Austin Water & Wastewater Utility Dept
625 E 10th St
Austin, TX 78701
Phone: 512-322-0101
Fax: 512-322-2842

Important Phone Numbers

AAA 512-335-5222
American Express Travel 512-452-8166
Austin Board of Realtors 512-454-7636
Driver's License Information 512-424-2600
Emergency 911
Highway Conditions 800-452-9292
HotelDocs 800-468-3537
Poison Control Center 800-764-7661
Texas Comptroller of Public Accounts 512-463-4600
Time/Temp 512-973-3555
Travis County Tax Office 512-473-9473
Vehicle Registration Information 512-473-9473
Voter Registration Information 512-473-9188
Weather 512-451-2424

Information Sources

Austin Convention & Visitors Bureau
201 E 2nd St
Austin, TX 78701
www.austin360.com/acvb
Phone: 512-474-5171
Fax: 512-583-7282
TF: 800-926-2282

Austin Convention Center
500 E Cesar Chavez St
Austin, TX 78701
www.convention.ci.austin.tx.us
Phone: 512-476-5461
Fax: 512-404-4416

Better Business Bureau Serving Central Texas
2101 S IH 35 Suite 302
Austin, TX 78741
www.centraltx.bbb.org
Phone: 512-445-2911
Fax: 512-445-2096

Greater Austin Chamber of Commerce
PO Box 1967
Austin, TX 78767
www.austin-chamber.org
Phone: 512-478-9383
Fax: 512-478-6389

Travis County
PO Box 1748
Austin, TX 78767
www.co.travis.tx.us
Phone: 512-473-9188
Fax: 512-473-9075

Online Resources

4Austin.com
www.4austin.com

About.com Guide to Austin
austin.about.com/local/southwestus/austin

Anthill City Guide Austin
www.anthill.com/city.asp?city=austin

Area Guide Austin
austin.areaguides.net

Arrive @ Austin
www.arrive-at.com/austin/

Austin Axis
www.awpi.com/AustinAxis

Austin City Limits
www.pbs.org/klru/austin

Austin CityGuide
www.austincityguide.com

Austin Metro Entertainment
www.austinmetro.com

Austin Music Web
www.ddg.com/AMW/

Austin Relocation Center
www.io.com/house/tour.html

Austin Virtual Restaurant Mall
www.virtual-restaurants.com

Austin Web Page
www.austinwebpage.com

Austin.Data.Net
austin.data.net

Boulevards Austin
www.boulevards.com/austin/

Capitol City Arts & Entertainment Magazine
www.capitol-city.com/

City Knowledge Austin
www.cityknowledge.com/tx_austin.htm

CitySearch Austin
austin.citysearch.com

DigitalCity Austin
home.digitalcity.com/austin

Excite.com Austin City Guide
www.excite.com/travel/countries/united_states/texas/austin

HotelGuide Austin
hotelguide.net/austin

Insiders' Guide to Austin
www.insiders.com/austin/

Lodging.com Austin Texas
www.lodging.com/auto/guides/austin-area-tx.html

Metropolitan Austin Interactive Network
www.main.org

Online City Guide to Austin
www.olcg.com/tx/austin/main.html

Onroute Destinations Austin
www.onroute.com/destinations/texas/austin.html

Virtual Voyages Austin
www.virtualvoyages.com/usa/tx/austin/austin.sht

Yahoo! Austin
austin.yahoo.com

Area Communities

Communities with populations greater than 10,000 in the Austin metro area (Hays, Travis, and Williamson counties) include:

Georgetown
PO Box 409
Georgetown, TX 78627
Phone: 512-930-3636
Fax: 512-930-3659

Round Rock
221 E Main Ave
Round Rock, TX 78664
Phone: 512-218-5400
Fax: 512-218-7097

San Marcos
630 E Hopkins St
San Marcos, TX 78666
Phone: 512-353-4444
Fax: 512-396-4656

Taylor
PO Box 810
Taylor, TX 76574
Phone: 512-352-3675
Fax: 512-352-8483

Economy

In 2000, Forbes Magazine named Austin the best city for business in North America. Major high technology companies with divisions in Austin include Motorola, IBM, and Dell Computer Corporation. Manufacturing leads the area's economic growth, with a steady increase in employment over the past decade. The government and services sectors are the largest industries in the Austin area based on number of people employed. In addition to the major employers listed below, the Internal Revenue Service Austin Service Center also ranks among the top 10, providing jobs for 5,800 area residents.

Unemployment Rate	2.1%*
Per Capita Income	$29,087*
Median Family Income	$55,400*

** Information given is for the Austin-San Marcos Metropolitan Statistical Area (MSA), which includes the City of Austin, Bastrop County, Caldwell County, Hays County, Travis County, and Williamson County.*

Principal Industries & Number of Wage Earners

Austin-San Marcos MSA* - June 2000

Construction	40,400
Finance, Insurance, & Real Estate	35,100
Government	134,200
Manufacturing	84,200
Mining	1,300
Retail Trade	112,900
Services	194,300
Transporation & Public Utilities	22,900
Wholesale Trade	35,700

** Information given is for the Austin-San Marcos Metropolitan Statistical Area (MSA), which includes the City of Austin, Bastrop County, Caldwell County, Hays County, Travis County, and Williamson County.*

Major Employers

3M Electronic Products Div
6801 River Place Blvd
Austin, TX 78726
www.3m.com/US/electronics_mfg/index.html
Phone: 512-984-1800
Fax: 512-984-6972
TF: 800-225-5373

Advanced Micro Devices Inc
5204 E Ben White Blvd
Austin, TX 78741
E-mail: hw.support@amd.com
www.amd.com
Phone: 512-385-8542
Fax: 512-602-6369

Applied Materials Inc
9700 US Hwy 290 E
Austin, TX 78724
www.appliedmaterials.com
Phone: 512-272-1000
Fax: 512-272-3000
TF: 800-468-8888

Austin City Hall
PO Box 1088
Austin, TX 78767
www.ci.austin.tx.us
Phone: 512-499-2000
Fax: 512-499-2374

Austin Independent School District
1111 W 6th St
Austin, TX 78703
www.austin.isd.tenet.edu
Phone: 512-414-1700
Fax: 512-499-0270

Dell Computer Corp
1 Dell Way
Round Rock, TX 78682
www.dell.com
Phone: 512-338-4400
Fax: 512-283-1111
TF: 800-624-9897

IBM Corp
11400 Burnet Rd
Austin, TX 78758
E-mail: call-ibm@austin.ibm.com
www.austin.ibm.com
Phone: 512-823-0000
Fax: 512-823-8449

Motorola
6501 W William Cannon Dr
Austin, TX 78735
motorolacareers.com
Phone: 512-895-2000

Randall's Food Markets Inc
PO Box 4506
Houston, TX 77210
www.randalls.com
Phone: 713-268-3500
Fax: 713-268-3684
TF: 800-420-5385

Sematech Inc
2706 Montopolis Dr
Austin, TX 78741
www.sematech.org
Phone: 512-356-3500
Fax: 512-356-3086

Seton Medical Center
1201 W 38th St
Austin, TX 78705
www.goodhealth.com
Phone: 512-324-1000
Fax: 512-324-1672

Texas Attorney General
PO Box 12548
Austin, TX 78711
www.oag.state.tx.us
Phone: 512-463-2191
Fax: 512-463-2063

Texas Comptroller of Public Accounts
PO Box 13528 Capitol Stn
Austin, TX 78701
www.cpa.state.tx.us
Phone: 512-463-4600
Fax: 512-475-0352
TF: 800-531-5441

Texas Health Dept
1100 W 49th St
Austin, TX 78756
www.tdh.texas.gov
Phone: 512-458-7111
Fax: 512-458-7750

Texas Transportation Dept
125 E 11th St
Austin, TX 78701
www.dot.state.tx.us
Phone: 512-463-8585
Fax: 512-305-9567

Trilogy Software Inc
6034 W Courtyard Dr Suite 130
Austin, TX 78730
E-mail: info@trilogy.com
www.trilogy.com
Phone: 512-794-5900
Fax: 512-794-8900
TF: 877-292-3266

University of Texas Austin
Main Bldg Rm 1
Austin, TX 78712
E-mail: admit@utxdp.dp.utexas.edu
www.utexas.edu
Phone: 512-471-3434
Fax: 512-475-7515

US Postal Service
8225 Cross Park Dr
Austin, TX 78710
new.usps.com
Phone: 512-342-1283
TF: 800-725-2161

Quality of Living Indicators

Total Crime Index....................................40,023
(rates per 100,000 inhabitants)

Violent Crime
Murder/manslaughter........................... 27
Forcible rape 239
Robbery.....................................1,022
Aggravated assault............................1,671

Property Crime
Burglary 7,007
Larceny theft 27,265
Motor vehicle theft 2,792

Cost of Living Index..................................105.0
(national average = 100)

Median Home Price................................$130,300

Education

Public Schools

Austin Independent School District
1111 W 6th St
Austin, TX 78703
www.austin.isd.tenet.edu
Phone: 512-414-1700
Fax: 512-499-0270

Number of Schools
Elementary.................................. 67
Middle 15
High.. 11

Student/Teacher Ratio
All Grades 16.6:1

Private Schools

Number of Schools (all grades).................... 71+

Colleges & Universities

Austin Community College
5930 Middle Fiskville Rd
Austin, TX 78752
www.austin.cc.tx.us
Phone: 512-223-7000
Fax: 512-483-7665

Concordia University at Austin
3400 N IH-35
Austin, TX 78705
www.concordia.edu
Phone: 512-452-7661
Fax: 512-459-8517
TF: 800-865-4282

Huston-Tillotson College
900 Chicon St
Austin, TX 78702
Phone: 512-505-3000
Fax: 512-505-3190

Institute for Christian Studies
1909 University Ave
Austin, TX 78705
www.io.com/~ics/
Phone: 512-476-2772
Fax: 512-476-3919

ITT Technical Institute
6330 Hwy 290 E Suite 150
Austin, TX 78723
www.itt-tech.edu
Phone: 512-467-6800
Fax: 512-467-6677
TF: 800-431-0677

Saint Edward's University
3001 S Congress Ave
Austin, TX 78704
E-mail: sheryls@admin.stedwards.edu
www.stedwards.edu
Phone: 512-448-8500
Fax: 512-464-8877

Southwest Texas State University
601 University Dr
San Marcos, TX 78666
E-mail: fy01@swt.edu
www.swt.edu
Phone: 512-245-2111
Fax: 512-245-8044
TF: 800-782-7653

Southwestern University
PO Box 770
Georgetown, TX 78627
www.southwestern.edu
Phone: 512-863-6511
Fax: 512-863-9601
TF: 800-252-3166

University of Texas Austin
Main Bldg Rm 1
Austin, TX 78712
E-mail: admit@utxdp.dp.utexas.edu
www.utexas.edu
Phone: 512-471-3434
Fax: 512-475-7515

Hospitals

Brackenridge Hospital
601 E 15th St
Austin, TX 78701
Phone: 512-324-7000
Fax: 512-324-7051

Central Texas Medical Center
1301 Wonder World Dr
San Marcos, TX 78666
www.ctmc.org
Phone: 512-353-8979
Fax: 512-753-3598

North Austin Medical Center
12221 N Mopac Expy
Austin, TX 78758
www.adclinic.com
Phone: 512-901-1000
Fax: 512-901-1995
TF: 888-356-5315

Saint David's Medical Center
919 E 32nd St
Austin, TX 78705
www.stdavids.com/content_frame.html?id=10.00+top_lvl=FACILITIES
Phone: 512-476-7111
Fax: 512-370-4432

Saint David's Round Rock Medical Center
2400 Round Rock Ave
Round Rock, TX 78681
Phone: 512-341-1000
Fax: 512-238-1799

Seton Medical Center
1201 W 38th St
Austin, TX 78705
www.goodhealth.com
Phone: 512-324-1000
Fax: 512-324-1672

South Austin Hospital
901 W Ben White Blvd
Austin, TX 78704
Phone: 512-447-2211
Fax: 512-416-6222

Transportation

Airport(s)

Austin-Bergstrom International Airport (AUS)
5 miles SE of downtown (approx 10 minutes).....512-530-2242

Mass Transit

Capital Metropolitan Transit Authority
$.50 Base fare.................................512-474-1200

Rail/Bus

Austin Amtrak Station
250 N Lamar Blvd
Austin, TX 78703
Phone: 512-476-5684

Greyhound/Trailways Bus Station
916 E Koenig Ln
Austin, TX 78701
Phone: 800-231-2222

Utilities

Electricity
Austin Energy 512-494-9400
www.austinenergy.com

Gas
Southern Union Gas Co. 800-700-2443
www.southernunionco.com

Water
Austin Water & Wastewater Utility 512-494-9400
www.ci.austin.tx.us/water

Garbage Collection/Recycling
Austin Solid Waste Services Dept 512-499-2111
www.ci.austin.tx.us/sws

Telecommunications

Telephone
Southwestern Bell 512-609-3333
www.swbell.com

Cable Television
CableVision of Lake Travis 512-263-9194
Time Warner Cable 512-485-5050
www.timewarneraustin.com

Internet Service Providers (ISPs)
Austin Free-Net 512-326-9084
www.austinfree.net
Commuter Communication Systems Inc (CCSI) ...512-257-2274
www.ccsi.com
Freeside Communications Inc 512-458-9810
www.fc.net
Illuminati Online 512-462-0999
www.io.com
Internet Port Inc. 512-349-2791
www.inetport.com
MoonTower Inc 512-206-0106
www.moontower.com
Onramp Access Inc. 512-322-9200
www.onr.com
Real/Time Communications 512-451-0046
www.realtime.net

Banks

American Bank of Commerce
522 Congress Ave
Austin, TX 78701
www.theabcbank.com
Phone: 512-391-5500
Fax: 512-391-5599

Bank of America NA
501 Congress Ave Suite G260
Austin, TX 78701
www.bankamerica.com
Phone: 800-247-6262
Fax: 512-397-3164

Bank of Texas
1005 Congress Ave Suite 100
Austin, TX 78701
Phone: 512-485-7600
Fax: 512-485-7697

Bank One Texas NA
221 W 6th St
Austin, TX 78701
Phone: 512-479-5400
Fax: 512-479-5820
TF: 800-695-1111

Bank United
10135 Lake Creek Pkwy
Austin, TX 78729
Phone: 512-918-3808
Fax: 512-918-3833

Chase Bank of Texas NA
700 Lavaca
Austin, TX 78701
www.chase.com
Phone: 512-479-2444
Fax: 512-479-2601

City National Bank
401 Congress Ave
Austin, TX 78701
Phone: 512-494-8000
Fax: 512-494-8111

Comerica Bank
804 Congress Ave Suite 100
Austin, TX 78701
Phone: 512-427-7100
Fax: 512-427-7104
TF: 800-925-2160

Commerce National Bank
5300 Bee Cave Rd Bldg 2
Austin, TX 78746
Phone: 512-347-1959
Fax: 512-347-7559

Community State Bank
13945 Research Blvd Suite D-170
Austin, TX 78717
Phone: 512-335-4226
Fax: 512-335-1748

Compass Bank
321 W 6th St
Austin, TX 78701
www.compassweb.com
Phone: 512-476-2836
Fax: 512-421-5762
TF: 800-239-4357

First American Bank Texas
2110 Boca Raton Dr
Austin, TX 78747
Phone: 512-280-0001
Fax: 512-280-0005

First Commercial Bank NA
1110 Ranch Rd
Austin, TX 78734
Phone: 512-263-5253
Fax: 512-263-2065

First Texas Bank
7509 O'Connor Dr
Austin, TX 78717
Phone: 512-246-6010
Fax: 512-246-1008

Franklin Bank SSB
3720 Jefferson St
Austin, TX 78731
Phone: 512-374-1600
Fax: 512-374-1199

Frost National Bank
816 Congress Ave
Austin, TX 78701
Phone: 512-473-4343
Fax: 512-473-4750
TF: 800-562-6732

Guaranty Federal Bank FSB
301 Congress Ave
Austin, TX 78701
Phone: 512-434-1000
Fax: 512-320-1262

Norwest Bank Texas NA
111 Congress Ave
Austin, TX 78701
www.norwest.com
Phone: 512-344-7000
Fax: 512-756-6755
TF: 800-224-7334

Texas Heritage Bank
1721 Wells Branch Pkwy
Austin, TX 78728
Phone: 512-252-1152
Fax: 512-252-0743

Wells Fargo Bank NA
100 Congress Ave Suite 150
Austin, TX 78701
Phone: 512-794-2200

World Savings Bank of Texas SSB
9777 Great Hills Trail
Austin, TX 78759
Phone: 512-343-7585
Fax: 512-346-2551

Shopping

23rd Street Renaissance Market
23rd & Guadaloupe Sts
Austin, TX 78705
Phone: 512-474-5171

Arboretum The
10000 Research Blvd
Austin, TX 78759
Phone: 512-257-8500
Fax: 512-257-0522

Barton Creek Square Mall
2901 S Capital of Texas Hwy
Austin, TX 78746
Phone: 512-327-7040
Fax: 512-328-0923

Beall's
2415 S Congress Ave
Austin, TX 78704
Phone: 512-444-4711

Dillard's
2901 Capital of Texas Hwy
Austin, TX 78746
Phone: 512-327-6100
Fax: 512-347-3462

Drag The
Guadaloupe St-betw 21st & 25th Sts
Austin, TX 78705
Phone: 512-474-5171

Highland Mall
6001 Airport Blvd
Austin, TX 78752
Phone: 512-451-2920

Lakeline Mall
11200 Lakeline Mall Dr
Cedar Park, TX 78613
Phone: 512-257-7467
Fax: 512-257-0522

Northcross Mall
2525 W Anderson Ln
Austin, TX 78757
Phone: 512-451-7466
Fax: 512-451-2330

Scarbroughs
4001 N Lamar Blvd
Austin, TX 78756
Phone: 512-452-4220
Fax: 512-452-6608

West End
1100-1200 W 6th St
Austin, TX 78703
Phone: 512-474-8334

Media

Newspapers and Magazines

Austin American-Statesman*
PO Box 670
Austin, TX 78767
E-mail: help360@cimedia.com
www.austin360.com
Phone: 512-445-3500
Fax: 512-445-3679

Austin Business Journal
111 Congress Ave Suite 750
Austin, TX 78701
www.amcity.com/austin
Phone: 512-494-2500
Fax: 512-494-2525

Austin Chronicle
PO Box 49066
Austin, TX 78765
E-mail: mail@auschron.com
www.auschron.com
Phone: 512-454-5766
Fax: 512-458-6910

Texas Monthly
PO Box 1569
Austin, TX 78767
www.texasmonthly.com
Phone: 512-320-6900
Fax: 512-476-9007
TF: 800-759-2000

**Indicates major daily newspapers*

Television

KEYE-TV Ch 42 (CBS)
10700 Metric Blvd
Austin, TX 78758
E-mail: upah@k-eyetv.com
www.k-eyetv.com
Phone: 512-835-0042
Fax: 512-837-6753

KLRU-TV Ch 18 (PBS)
2504-B Whitis Ave
Austin, TX 78713
E-mail: info@www.klru.org
www.klru.org
Phone: 512-471-4811
Fax: 512-475-9090

KNVA-TV Ch 54 (WB)
908 W ML King Blvd
Austin, TX 78701
E-mail: prog54@knva.com
www.knva.com
Phone: 512-478-5400
Fax: 512-476-1520

KTBC-TV Ch 7 (Fox)
119 E 10th St
Austin, TX 78701
E-mail: news@fox7.com
www.fox7.com
Phone: 512-476-7777
Fax: 512-495-7060

KVUE-TV Ch 24 (ABC)
PO Box 9927
Austin, TX 78766
www.kvue.com
Phone: 512-459-6521
Fax: 512-459-6538

KXAN-TV Ch 36 (NBC)
908 W ML King Jr Blvd
Austin, TX 78701
E-mail: news36@kxan.com
www.kxan.com
Phone: 512-476-3636
Fax: 512-469-0630

Radio

KAMX-FM 94.7 MHz (Alt)
4301 Westbank Dr Bldg B 3rd Fl
Austin, TX 78746
E-mail: mornings@mix947.com
www.mix947.com
Phone: 512-327-9595
Fax: 512-329-6257

KASE-FM 100.7 MHz (Ctry)
PO Box 380
Austin, TX 78767
www.kase101.com
Phone: 512-390-5273
Fax: 512-495-1329
TF: 800-950-5273

KAZI-FM 88.7 MHz (Misc)
8906 Wall St Suite 203
Austin, TX 78754
E-mail: kazijams@aol.com
kazi.citysearch.com
Phone: 512-836-9544
Fax: 512-836-1146

KELG-AM 1440 kHz (Span)
7524 N Lamar Ave Suite 200
Austin, TX 78752
www.kelg.com/page1.htm
Phone: 512-453-1491
Fax: 512-458-0700

KEYI-FM 103.5 MHz (Oldies)
811 Barton Springs Rd Suite 100
Austin, TX 78704
www.oldies103austin.com
Phone: 512-474-9233
Fax: 512-397-1400

KFIT-AM 1060 kHz (Rel)
110 Wild Basin Rd Suite 375
Austin, TX 78746
E-mail: kfit1060@texas.net
www.kfitam.com
Phone: 512-328-8400
Fax: 512-328-8437

KFMK-FM 105.9 MHz (Oldies)
705 N Lamar Blvd
Austin, TX 78703
www.jamminoldies1059.com
Phone: 512-495-1300
Fax: 512-495-9423

KFON-AM 1490 kHz (Sports)
811 Barton Springs Rd Suite 100
Austin, TX 78704
Phone: 512-474-9233
Fax: 512-397-1400

KGSR-FM 107.1 MHz (AAA)
8309 N IH 35
Austin, TX 78753
www.kgsr.com
Phone: 512-832-4000
Fax: 512-832-1579

KHFI-FM 96.7 MHz (CHR)
811 Barton Springs Rd Suite 100
Austin, TX 78704
www.khfi.com
Phone: 512-474-9233
Fax: 512-397-1410
TF: 800-750-5434

KIXL-AM 970 kHz (N/T)
11615 Angus Rd Suite 120B
Austin, TX 78759
Phone: 512-372-9700
Fax: 512-372-9088

KJCE-AM 1370 kHz (Urban)
4301 Westbank Dr Bldg B Suite 350
Austin, TX 78746
www.kjuice.com
Phone: 512-327-9595
Fax: 512-329-6257

KJFK-FM 98.9 MHz (N/T)
12710 Research Blvd Suite 390
Austin, TX 78759
989kjfk.com
Phone: 512-331-9191
Fax: 512-331-9933

KKMJ-FM 95.5 MHz (AC)
4301 Westbank Dr Bldg B Suite 350
Austin, TX 78746
www.majic.com
Phone: 512-327-9595
Fax: 512-329-6257

KLBJ-AM 590 kHz (N/T)
8309 N IH-35
Austin, TX 78753
E-mail: klbj590@lbj.com
www.lbj.com/am/news.html
Phone: 512-832-4000
Fax: 512-832-1579

KLBJ-FM 93.7 MHz (Rock)
8309 N IH-35
Austin, TX 78753
www.lbj.com/fm
Phone: 512-832-4059
Fax: 512-832-1579

KLNC-FM 93.3 MHz (Ctry)
8309 N IH-35
Austin, TX 78753
E-mail: info@klnc.com
www.klnc.com
Phone: 512-832-4000
Fax: 512-832-1579

KMFA-FM 89.5 MHz (Clas)
3001 N Lamar Blvd Suite 100
Austin, TX 78705
E-mail: classical@kmfa.org
www.kmfa.org
Phone: 512-476-5632
Fax: 512-474-7463

KNLE-FM 88.1 MHz (AC)
12703 Research Blvd Suite 222
Austin, TX 78759
www.candle88.com
Phone: 512-257-8881
Fax: 512-257-8880

KOOP-FM 91.7 MHz (Misc)
PO Box 2116
Austin, TX 78768
E-mail: koopradio@bigfoot.com
www.koop.org
Phone: 512-472-1369
Fax: 512-472-6149

KPEZ-FM 102.3 MHz (CR)
811 Barton Springs Rd Suite 967
Austin, TX 78704
www.z102austin.com
Phone: 512-474-9233
Fax: 512-397-1410

KQQA-AM 1530 kHz (Span)
1707 N Mays St
Round Rock, TX 78664
Phone: 512-218-0111
Fax: 512-218-0111

KROX-FM 101.5 MHz (Rock)
8309 N IH-35
Austin, TX 78753
www.krox.com
Phone: 512-832-4000
Fax: 512-832-1579

KTXZ-AM 1560 kHz (Span)
7524 N Lamar Blvd Suite 200
Austin, TX 78752
www.ktxz.com/page3.htm
Phone: 512-453-1491
Fax: 512-458-0700

KUT-FM 90.5 MHz (NPR)
University of Texas Communications
Communications Bldg B
Austin, TX 78712
www.kut.org
Phone: 512-471-1631
Fax: 512-471-3700

KVET-AM 1300 kHz (Sports)
PO Box 380
Austin, TX 78767
E-mail: pressbox@amfm.com
www.sportsradio1300.com
Phone: 512-495-1300
Fax: 512-495-9423

KVET-FM 98.1 MHz (Ctry)
PO Box 380
Austin, TX 78767
Phone: 512-495-1300
Fax: 512-495-9423

Attractions

Nicknamed the "Live Music Capital of the World," Austin is home to nearly 200 live music venues and numerous annual music events. Music of every style, from blues to rock, country to jazz, can be heard in the city. Austin's musical heritage includes such performers as Stevie Ray Vaughn, Janis Joplin, Willie Nelson, Jerry Jeff Walker, and The Fabulous Thunderbirds. The center of the music district is Old Pecan Street (Sixth Street), a nine-block historic area with music and comedy venues, trendy restaurants, and shops.

Austin Chamber Music Center
4930 Burnet Rd Suite 203
Austin, TX 78756
E-mail: info@austinchambermusic.org
www.austinchambermusic.org
Phone: 512-454-7562
Fax: 512-454-0029

Austin Children's Museum
201 Colorado St
Austin, TX 78701
www.austinkids.org
Phone: 512-472-2494
Fax: 512-472-2795

Austin Civic Orchestra
PO Box 27132
Austin, TX 78755
Phone: 512-990-8226
Fax: 512-990-8226

Austin History Center
810 Guadalupe St
Austin, TX 78701
www.ci.austin.tx.us/library/lbahc.htm
Phone: 512-499-7480
Fax: 512-499-7483

Austin Lyric Opera
PO Box 984
Austin, TX 78767
www.austinlyricopera.org
Phone: 512-472-5927
Fax: 512-472-4143
TF: 800-316-7372

Austin Museum of Art Downtown
823 Congress Ave
Austin, TX 78701
www.amoa.org
Phone: 512-495-9224
Fax: 512-495-9029

Austin Museum of Art Laguna Gloria
3809 W 35th St
Austin, TX 78763
E-mail: info@amoa.org
www.amoa.org
Phone: 512-458-8191
Fax: 512-454-9408

Austin Music Hall
208 Nueces St
Austin, TX 78701
www.austinmusichall.com
Phone: 512-495-9962
Fax: 512-263-4194

Austin Nature & Science Center
301 Nature Ctr Dr
Austin, TX 78746
www.ci.austin.tx.us/nature-science
Phone: 512-327-8181
Fax: 512-327-8745

Austin Symphony Orchestra
1101 Red River
Austin, TX 78701
www.austinsymphony.org
Phone: 512-476-6064
Fax: 512-476-6242

Austin Theatre for Youth
PO Box 26794
Austin, TX 78755
E-mail: aty@aol.com
www.onr.com/user/aty
Phone: 512-459-7144
Fax: 512-459-7451

Austin Zoo
10807 Rawhide Trail
Austin, TX 78736
E-mail: austinzu@aol.com
www.austinzoo.com
Phone: 512-288-1490
Fax: 512-288-3972
TF: 800-291-1490

Ballet Austin
3002 Guadalupe St
Austin, TX 78705
www.balletaustin.org
Phone: 512-476-9051
Fax: 512-472-3073

Barton Springs Pool
2201 Barton Springs Rd Zilker Pk
Austin, TX 78746
Phone: 512-476-9044

Celis Brewery
PO Box 141636
Austin, TX 78714
E-mail: celis@celis.com
www.celis.com
Phone: 512-835-0884
Fax: 512-835-0130

Center for Women & Their Work
1710 Lavaca St
Austin, TX 78701
E-mail: wtw@eden.com
www.womenandtheirwork.org
Phone: 512-477-1064
Fax: 512-477-1090

Congress Avenue Bats
Congress Ave
Austin, TX 78716
Phone: 512-478-0098

Crowe's Nest Farm Animal Life Center
10300 Taylor Ln
Manor, TX 78653
E-mail: crowes@io.com
www.crowesnestfarm.org
Phone: 512-272-4418
Fax: 512-272-8313

Dougherty Arts Center
1110 Barton Springs Rd
Austin, TX 78704
Phone: 512-397-1468
Fax: 512-397-1475

Elisabet Ney Museum
304 E 44th St
Austin, TX 78751
Phone: 512-458-2255
Fax: 512-453-0638

Emma Long Metropolitan Park
1706 City Park Rd
Austin, TX 78767
Phone: 512-346-1831

Fall Creek Vineyards
1111 Guadalupe St
Tow, TX 78701
Phone: 512-476-4477
Fax: 512-476-6116

French Legation Museum
802 San Marcos St
Austin, TX 78702
E-mail: dubois@french-ligation.mus.tx.us
www.french-legation.mus.tx.us
Phone: 512-472-8180
Fax: 512-472-9457

George Washington Carver Museum & Cultural Art Center
1165 Angelina St
Austin, TX 78702
Phone: 512-472-4809
Fax: 512-708-1639

Governor's Mansion
1010 Colorado St
Austin, TX 78701
Phone: 512-463-5518

Hill Country Flyer Steam Train
PO Box 1632
Austin, TX 78767
www.main.org/flyer
Phone: 512-477-8468
Fax: 512-477-8633

Inner Space Caverns
4200 S IH-35
Georgetown, TX 78627
www.innerspace.com
Phone: 512-863-5545
Fax: 512-863-4276

Jack S Blanton Museum of Art
23rd & San Jacinto Sts University of Texas at Austin
Austin, TX 78712
E-mail: hag@www.utexas.edu
www.utexas.edu/cofa/hag
Phone: 512-471-7324
Fax: 512-471-7023

Jourdan-Bachman Pioneer Farm
11418 Sprinkle Cut Off
Austin, TX 78754
E-mail: jbfarmer@eden.com
Phone: 512-837-1215
Fax: 512-837-4503

Lady Bird Johnson Wildflower Center
4801 LaCrosse Ave
Austin, TX 78739
E-mail: wildflower@wildflower.org
www.wildflower.org
Phone: 512-292-4200
Fax: 512-292-4627

Lake Walter E Long Metropolitan Park
6614 Blue Bluff Rd
Austin, TX 78768
Phone: 512-926-5230

Lone Star Riverboat
PO Box 160608
Austin, TX 78716
Phone: 512-327-1388
Fax: 512-329-0677

Lyndon B Johnson Library & Museum
2313 Red River St
Austin, TX 78705
E-mail: library@johnson.nara.gov
www.lbjlib.utexas.edu
Phone: 512-916-5137
Fax: 512-916-5171

Lyndon B Johnson National Historical Park
PO Box 329
Johnson City, TX 78636
www.nps.gov/lyjo/
Phone: 830-868-7128
Fax: 830-868-7863

McKinney Falls State Park
5808 McKinney Falls Pkwy
Austin, TX 78744
Phone: 512-243-1643
Fax: 512-243-0536

Mexic-Arte Museum
419 Congress Ave
Austin, TX 78701
E-mail: mexicart@onr.org
www.main.org/mexic-arte
Phone: 512-480-9373
Fax: 512-480-8626

Mount Bonnell
3800 Mt Bonnell Dr
Austin, TX 78731
Phone: 512-499-6700

Neill-Cochran House
2310 San Gabriel St
Austin, TX 78705
Phone: 512-478-2335
Fax: 512-478-1865

O Henry Home & Museum
409 E 5th St
Austin, TX 78701
www.ci.austin.tx.us/parks/ohenry.htm
Phone: 512-472-1903
Fax: 512-472-7102

Old German Free School Building
507 E 10th St
Austin, TX 78701
www.main.org/germantxn
Phone: 512-482-0927
Fax: 512-482-0636

Old Pecan Street Historical District
E 6th St & Congress Ave
Austin, TX 78701
Phone: 512-583-7226

Paramount Theatre
713 Congress Ave
Austin, TX 78701
camalott.com/~paramnt/index.html
Phone: 512-472-5411
Fax: 512-472-5824

Republic of Texas Museum
510 E Anderson Ln
Austin, TX 78752
Phone: 512-339-1997
Fax: 512-339-1998
TF: 877-339-1997

Slaughter Leftwich Vineyards
4209 Eck Ln
Austin, TX 78734
Phone: 512-266-3331
Fax: 512-266-3180

Symphony Square
1101 Red River
Austin, TX 78701
www.austinsymphony.org/sym.html
Phone: 512-476-6064
Fax: 512-476-6242
TF: 888-462-3787

Texas Memorial Museum
2400 Trinity St
Austin, TX 78705
www.utexas.edu/depts/tmm/
Phone: 512-471-1604
Fax: 512-471-4794

Texas Military Forces Museum
2200 W 35th St Camp Mabry
Austin, TX 78703
www.kwanah.com/txmilmus/
Phone: 512-465-5659
Fax: 512-706-6750

Texas State Capitol Building
1100 Congress Ave
Austin, TX 78701
Phone: 512-463-0063
Fax: 512-305-8401

Texas State Cemetery
909 Navasota St
Austin, TX 78702
E-mail: statecemetery@gsc.state.tx.us
www.cemetery.state.tx.us
Phone: 512-463-0605
Fax: 512-463-8811

Texas State Library
PO Box 12927
Austin, TX 78711
www.tsl.state.tx.us
Phone: 512-463-5460
Fax: 512-463-5436

Town Lake Metropolitan Park
betw Tom Miller Dam & Longhorn Dam
Austin, TX 78767
Phone: 512-499-6700

Umlauf Museum & Sculpture Garden
605 Robert E Lee Rd
Austin, TX 78704
www.io.com/~tam/umlauf/
Phone: 512-445-5582
Fax: 512-445-5583

University of Texas Performing Arts Center
E 23rd St & E Campus Dr
Austin, TX 78705
www.utpac.org
Phone: 512-471-1444
Fax: 512-471-3636
TF: 800-687-6010

Vortex Theatre
2307 Manor Rd
Austin, TX 78722
E-mail: vortexrep@vortexrep.org
members.tripod.com/vortextheatre
Phone: 512-478-5282

Wild Basin Wilderness Preserve
805 N Capital of Texas Hwy
Austin, TX 78746
E-mail: hike@wildbasin.org
www.wildbasin.org
Phone: 512-327-7622
Fax: 512-328-5632

Wonder World
1000 Prospect
San Marcos, TX 78666
www.wonderworldpark.com
Phone: 512-392-3760
Fax: 512-754-0373
TF: 800-782-7653

Zachary Scott Theatre Center
1510 Toomey Rd
Austin, TX 78704
www.zachscott.com/
Phone: 512-476-0594
Fax: 512-476-0314

Zilker Botanical Gardens
2220 Barton Springs Rd
Austin, TX 78746
www.zilker-garden.org
Phone: 512-477-8672
Fax: 512-481-8253

Zilker Hillside Theatre
2201 Barton Springs Rd Zilker Pk
Austin, TX 78704
Phone: 512-479-9491

Zilker Metropolitan Park
2105 Andrew Zilker Dr
Austin, TX 78746
Phone: 512-472-4914

Zilker Park
2200 Barton Springs Rd
Austin, TX 78746
Phone: 512-476-9044

Sports Teams & Facilities

Austin Ice Bats (hockey)
7311 Decker Ln
Austin, TX 78724
E-mail: icebats@texas.net
www.icebats.com
Phone: 512-927-7825
Fax: 512-927-7828

Austin Lady Lone Stars (soccer)
5446 Hwy 290 W Suite 105
Austin, TX 78735
Phone: 512-892-7477
Fax: 512-892-7402

Austin Lone Stars (soccer)
5446 Hwy 290 W Suite 105
Austin, TX 78735
E-mail: lonestars@jump.net
www.austinlonestars.com/
Phone: 512-892-7477
Fax: 512-892-7402

Manor Downs
101 Hill Ln
Manor, TX 78653
Phone: 512-272-5581
Fax: 512-272-4403

Travis County Exposition & Heritage Center
7311 Decker Ln
Austin, TX 78724
Phone: 512-473-9200
Fax: 512-928-9953

Annual Events

Armadillo Christmas Bazaar (mid-late December) . . .512-447-1605
Austin Artists' Harvest (late October). 512-473-3866
Austin Boat & Fishing Show (mid-January) 512-494-1128
Austin Chronicle Hot Sauce Festival (late August). 512-454-5766
Austin Collectors Exposition (mid-December & early July) 512-454-9882
Austin Film Festival (October). 512-478-4795
Austin Fine Arts Festival (early April) 512-495-9224
Austin Founders Trail Ride (early April) 512-477-4711
Austin Herbfest (early October) 512-502-1974
Austin Home & Garden Show (mid-January) 512-476-5461
Austin International Poetry Festival (early April). . . .512-346-8717
Austin Jazz & Arts Festival (early September) 512-477-9438
Austin Powwow & American Indian Heritage Festival (early November) 512-338-9860

Austin Rugby Tournament (early April) 512-926-9017
Austin Salsa Music Festival (mid-September) 512-899-8585
Austin Shakespeare Festival
(late September-mid-October) 512-454-2273
Austin Theatre Week (mid-April) 512-454-9700
Ben Hur Shrine Circus (early October) 512-327-3810
Big Stinkin' International Improv & Sketch Comedy Festival (early-mid-April) 512-912-7837
Bob Marley Festival (mid-April) 512-312-0435
Canterbury Faire (late September) 512-327-7622
Carnaval Brasileiro (mid-February) 512-452-6832
Christmas Affair A (mid-November) 512-467-8942
Cinco de Mayo Celebration (May 5) 512-867-1999
Diez y Seis de Septiembre (mid-September) 512-385-8025
Freedom Festival & Fireworks (July 4) 800-926-2282
FronteraFest (late January) 512-499-8497
Frontier Days (mid-July) 512-255-5805
Gay & Lesbian International Film Festival
(early September) 512-302-9889
Halloween on Sixth Street (October 31) 512-476-8876
Heritage Homes Tour (early May) 512-474-5198
Heritage Oak Park Holiday Tree Lighting
(late November-early January) 512-258-4121
Holiday Tour of Lights (December) 512-477-8468
International Children's Festival (late September) . . .512-472-2499
Jerry Jeff Walker's Birthday Celebration
(late March) 512-477-0036
Juneteenth Freedom Festival (mid-June) 512-472-6838
Louisiana Swamp Romp (early April) 512-441-9015
Moon Festival (late October) 512-477-8672
New Texas Festival (early June) 512-476-5775
Oktoberfest (mid-October) 512-479-0598
Old Pecan Street Festival
(early May & late September) 512-441-9015
South By Southwest Music Festival (mid-March) . . .512-467-7979
Spamarama (early April) 512-834-1960
Star of Texas Fair & Rodeo (mid-March) 512-467-9811
Texas Bach Festival (mid-late March) 512-719-3300
Texas Hill Country Wine & Food Festival
(mid-April) 512-329-0770
Texas Independence Day Celebration
(early March) 512-477-1836
Texas Wildlife Exposition (early October) 512-389-4472
Trail of Lights Festival (mid-late December) 512-499-6700
Travis County Livestock Show & PRCA Rodeo
(mid-March) 512-467-9811
Victorian Christmas on Sixth Street
(late November) 512-441-9015
Volunteer Firemen's BBQ Extravaganza
(mid-September) 512-282-3600
Western Days (late July) 512-285-4515
Wildflower Days Festivals (early March-late May) 512-292-4200
Women in Jazz Concert Series (early June) 512-258-6947
Wooden Boat Show (early June) 512-288-5359
Zilker Fall Jazz Festival (early September) 512-440-1414
Zilker Garden Festival (early May) 512-477-8672
Zilker Kite Festival (early March) 512-478-0098
Zilker Park Bluegrass Festival (mid-May) 512-218-1567
Zilker Tree Lighting (early December) 512-397-1463

Bakersfield, California

***County:* Kern**

BAKERSFIELD is located in the southern San Joaquin Valley in central California. It is surrounded by three mountain ranges, the Sierra Nevadas, the Tehachapis, and the Temblor Range. Cities within 150 miles include Los Angeles, Santa Barbara, and Fresno, California.

Area (Land) . . . . 91.8 sq mi
Area (Water) . . . . 1.3 sq mi
Elevation . . . . 408 ft
Latitude . . . . 35-21-27 N
Longitude . . . . 119-00-16 W
Time Zone . . . . PST
Area Code 661

Climate

Bakersfield winters are typically mild, with average temperatures in the 40s and 50s and rarely (approximately 12 days each year) dips below freezing. Summer days are very hot, with temperatures averaging in the mid- to upper 90s and frequently climbing above the 100 degree mark. Summer evenings, however, cool down into the 60s. Bakersfield's climate is very dry, with an average annual rainfall of only six inches.

Average Temperatures & Precipitation

Temperatures

	Jan	Feb	Mar	Apr	May	Jun	Jul	Aug	Sep	Oct	Nov	Dec
High	57	64	69	76	85	92	99	97	90	81	67	57
Low	39	43	46	50	57	64	70	69	64	55	45	38

Precipitation

	Jan	Feb	Mar	Apr	May	Jun	Jul	Aug	Sep	Oct	Nov	Dec
Inches	0.9	1.1	1.0	0.6	0.2	0.1	0.0	0.1	0.1	0.3	0.7	0.6

History

Bakersfield was incorporated as a city in 1898, but its history dates back to the mid-1800's when the city's founder, Colonel Thomas Baker, planted alfalfa on a parcel of his land for weary travelers to rest and let their animals graze. The discovery of gold in 1851 and oil in 1865 sparked the development of Bakersfield. These discoveries attracted settlers from many different cultures, including French, Basques, Chinese, Italians, Greeks, and Portuguese, all of whom contributed to the development of the city. Agriculture and oil remain the area's largest industries today. In fact, in 1995, Kern County was named the leading oil producing county in the continental United States and the fourth most productive U.S. county in agriculture. The county seat of Kern County, Bakersfield is the 13th largest city in California.

Population

1990 Census 174,978
1998 Estimate 210,284
% Change 19.3
2010 Projection 958,300*

Racial/Ethnic Breakdown
White 72.7%
Black 9.4%
Other 17.9%
Hispanic Origin (may be of any race) 20.5%

Age Breakdown
Under 5 years 9.9%
5 to 17 . . . . 20.9%
18 to 20 . . . . 4.5%
21 to 24 . . . . 6.0%
25 to 34 . . . . 19.2%
35 to 44 . . . . 15.3%
45 to 54 . . . . 8.8%
55 to 64 . . . . 6.3%
65 to 74 . . . . 5.3%
75+ years 3.8%
Median Age 29.6

Gender Breakdown
Male 48.6%
Female 51.4%

* *Information given is for Kern County.*

Government

Type of Government: City Council-Manager

Bakersfield Building Div
1715 Chester Ave
Bakersfield, CA 93301
Phone: 661-326-3727
Fax: 661-325-0266

Bakersfield City Attorney
1501 Truxtun Ave
Bakersfield, CA 93301
Phone: 661-326-3721
Fax: 661-852-2020

Bakersfield City Clerk
1501 Truxtun Ave
Bakersfield, CA 93301
Phone: 661-326-3767
Fax: 661-323-3780

Bakersfield City Council
1501 Truxtun Ave
Bakersfield, CA 93301
Phone: 661-326-3767
Fax: 661-323-3780

Bakersfield City Hall
1501 Truxtun Ave
Bakersfield, CA 93301
Phone: 661-326-3751
Fax: 661-324-1850

Bakersfield City Manager
1501 Truxtun Ave
Bakersfield, CA 93301
Phone: 661-326-3751
Fax: 661-324-1850

Bakersfield Community & Economic Development Dept
515 Truxtun Ave
Bakersfield, CA 93301
Phone: 661-326-3765
Fax: 661-328-1548

Bakersfield Finance Dept
1501 Truxtun Ave
Bakersfield, CA 93301
Phone: 661-326-3742
Fax: 661-326-3760

Bakersfield Fire Dept
2101 H St
Bakersfield, CA 93301
Phone: 661-326-3911
Fax: 661-395-1349

Bakersfield Human Resources Office
1501 Truxton Ave
Bakersfield, CA 93301
Phone: 661-326-3773
Fax: 661-326-3078

Bakersfield Mayor
1501 Truxtun Ave
Bakersfield, CA 93301
Phone: 661-326-3770
Fax: 661-326-3779

Bakersfield Planning Div
1715 Chester Ave
Bakersfield, CA 93301
Phone: 661-326-3733
Fax: 661-327-0646

Bakersfield Police Dept
PO Box 59
Bakersfield, CA 93302
Phone: 661-327-7111
Fax: 661-326-3070

Bakersfield Public Works Dept
1501 Truxtun Ave
Bakersfield, CA 93301
Phone: 661-326-3724
Fax: 661-328-1027

Bakersfield Recreation & Parks Dept
4101 Truxtun Ave
Bakersfield, CA 93301
Phone: 661-326-3117
Fax: 661-861-0864

Bakersfield Water Resources Dept
1000 Buena Vista Rd
Bakersfield, CA 93311
Phone: 661-326-3715
Fax: 661-326-3098

Beale Memorial Library
701 Truxtun Ave
Bakersfield, CA 93301
Phone: 661-868-0701
Fax: 661-868-0799

Important Phone Numbers

AAA.......661-327-4661
American Express Travel.......800-528-4800
Bakersfield Board of Realtors.......661-635-2300
California State Franchise Tax Board.......916-845-4300
Dental Referral.......800-336-8478
Driver's License/Vehicle Registration Information...661-395-2825
Emergency.......911
HotelDocs.......800-468-3537
Kern County Auditor/Controller's Office.......661-868-3599
Medical Referral.......661-325-9025
Poison Control Center.......800-876-4766
Voter Registration Information.......661-868-3590
Weather.......661-833-8888

Information Sources

Bakersfield Convention Center
1001 Truxtun Ave
Bakersfield, CA 93301
www.centennialgarden.com
Phone: 661-852-7300
Fax: 661-861-9904

Better Business Bureau Serving the Bakersfield Area
705 18th St
Bakersfield, CA 93301
www.bakersfield.bbb.org
Phone: 661-322-2074
Fax: 661-322-8318

Greater Bakersfield Chamber of Commerce
1033 Truxtun Ave
Bakersfield, CA 93301
www.bakersfield.org/chamber
Phone: 661-327-4421
Fax: 661-327-8751

Greater Bakersfield Convention & Visitors Bureau
1325 P St
Bakersfield, CA 93301
www.visitbfield.com
Phone: 661-325-5051
Fax: 661-325-7074
TF: 800-325-6001

Kern County
1115 Truxtun Ave 5th Fl
Bakersfield, CA 93301
co.kern.ca.us/
Phone: 661-868-3198
Fax: 661-868-3190

Online Resources

4Bakersfield.com
www.4bakersfield.com

About.com Guide to Bakersfield
bakersfield.about.com/citiestowns/caus/bakersfield/mbody.htm

Anthill City Guide Bakersfield
www.anthill.com/city.asp?city=bakersfield

Area Guide Bakersfield
bakersfield.areaguides.net

Bakersfield Arts & Entertainment Guide
www.aeguide.com

Bakersfield Gateway.com
www.bakersfieldgateway.com

City Knowledge Bakersfield
www.cityknowledge.com/ca_bakersfield.htm

Excite.com Bakersfield City Guide
www.excite.com/travel/countries/united_states/california/bakersfield/

Kern Online
www.kernonline.com

Area Communities

Incorporated communities in Kern County with populations greater than 10,000 include:

Delano
PO Box 939
Delano, CA 93216
Phone: 661-721-3303
Fax: 661-721-3312

Ridgecrest
100 W California Ave
Ridgecrest, CA 93555
Phone: 760-371-3700
Fax: 760-371-1654

Shafter
336 Pacific Ave
Shafter, CA 93263
Phone: 661-746-6361
Fax: 661-746-0607

Tehachapi
115 S Robinson St
Tehachapi, CA 93561
Phone: 661-822-2200
Fax: 661-822-8559

Wasco
PO Box 190
Wasco, CA 93280
Phone: 661-758-7200
Fax: 661-758-5411

Economy

Agriculture has long played a role in Bakersfield's economy, and the area is still one of the country's largest agricultural producers, with grapes, cotton, citrus, and almonds as the primary crops. Agriculture and government are the top two employment sectors in Kern County. In addition to the major employers listed below, the U.S. Government and the State of California are among the top 15, employing more than 8,000 residents.

Unemployment Rate 10.7%*
Per Capita Income $28,710**
Median Family Income $38,700**

** Information given is for Kern County.*
*** Information given is for the Bakersfield Metropolitan Statistical Area (MSA), which includes the City of Bakersfield and Kern County.*

Principal Industries & Number of Wage Earners

Kern County - 1998

Agriculture 44,000
Construction..10,100
Finance, Insurance, & Real Estate 7,200
Government 48,900
Manufacturing 9,800
Services 45,600
Trade 42,800

Major Employers

ARB Inc
26000 Commercentre Dr
Lake Forest, CA 92630
www.arbinc.com
Phone: 949-598-9242
Fax: 949-454-7190
TF: 800-622-2699

Bakersfield City Hall
1501 Truxtun Ave
Bakersfield, CA 93301
www.ci.bakersfield.ca.us
Phone: 661-326-3751
Fax: 661-324-1850

Bakersfield Memorial Hospital
420 34th St
Bakersfield, CA 93301
www.chw.edu/bakersfield/default.asp
Phone: 661-327-1792
Fax: 661-326-0706

Bolthouse William Farms Inc
7200 E Brundage Ln
Bakersfield, CA 93307
E-mail: info@bolthouse.com
www.bolthouse.com
Phone: 661-366-7207
Fax: 661-366-2834

California Correctional Institution
PO Box 1031
Tehachapi, CA 93581
tehachapi.com/cci/
Phone: 661-822-4402
Fax: 661-823-5020

Dryden Flight Research Center
PO Box 273
Edwards, CA 93523
trc.dfrc.nasa.gov
Phone: 661-258-3311
Fax: 661-258-3567

Edwards Air Force Base
Edwards AFB, CA 93523
www.edwards.af.mil
Phone: 661-277-1110
Fax: 661-277-4392

Giumarra Vineyards Corp
PO Box 1969
Bakersfield, CA 93303
Phone: 661-395-7000
Fax: 661-395-7195

Kern County
1115 Truxtun Ave 5th Fl
Bakersfield, CA 93301
co.kern.ca.us/
Phone: 661-868-3198
Fax: 661-868-3190

Kern County Public Schools
1300 17th St
Bakersfield, CA 93301
Phone: 661-636-4000
Fax: 661-636-4134

Kern Medical Center
1830 Flower St
Bakersfield, CA 93305
www.kmcemed.edu
Phone: 661-326-2000
Fax: 661-326-2969

Mercy Hospital
2215 Truxtun Ave
Bakersfield, CA 93301
Phone: 661-632-5000
Fax: 661-327-2592

Naval Air Weapons Station
Administration Cir
China Lake, CA 93555
Phone: 760-939-9011
Fax: 760-939-2056

Paramount Farming Co
33141 E Lerdo Hwy
Bakersfield, CA 93308
Phone: 661-399-4456
Fax: 661-399-1735

State Farm Insurance Co
900 Old River Rd
Bakersfield, CA 93311
www.statefarm.com
Phone: 661-663-2771
Fax: 661-663-2609

Quality of Living Indicators

Total Crime Index....................................12,348
(rates per 100,000 inhabitants)

Violent Crime
Murder/manslaughter........................... 20
Forcible rape 31
Robbery....................................... 461
Aggravated assault............................ 506

Property Crime
Burglary 2,879
Larceny theft 7,143
Motor vehicle theft 1,308

Cost of Living Index.................................102.8
(national average = 100)

Median Home Price................................$118,200

Education

Public Schools

Bakersfield City School District
1300 Baker St
Bakersfield, CA 93305
www.bcsd.k12.ca.us
Phone: 661-631-4600
Fax: 661-326-1485

Kern County High School District
5801 Sundale Ave
Bakersfield, CA 93309
www.khsd.k12.ca.us
Phone: 661-827-3100
Fax: 661-827-3300

Number of Schools
Elementary 35
Middle 7
High.. 19

Student/Teacher Ratio
Grades K-8 ..... 24.8:1 (Bakersfield City School District)
Grades 9-12. . . 27.2:1 (Kern County High School District)

Private Schools

Number of Schools (all grades) .... 35+

Colleges & Universities

Bakersfield College
1801 Panorama Dr
Bakersfield, CA 93305
www.bc.cc.ca.us
Phone: 661-395-4011
Fax: 661-395-4241

California State University Bakersfield
9001 Stockdale Hwy
Bakersfield, CA 93311
www.csubak.edu
Phone: 661-664-2011
Fax: 661-664-3389
TF: 800-788-2782

Hospitals

Bakersfield Memorial Hospital
420 34th St
Bakersfield, CA 93301
www.chw.edu/bakersfield/default.asp
Phone: 661-327-1792
Fax: 661-326-0706

Good Samaritan Hospital
901 Olive Dr
Bakersfield, CA 93308
Phone: 661-399-4461
Fax: 661-399-4224

Kern Medical Center
1830 Flower St
Bakersfield, CA 93305
www.kmcemed.edu
Phone: 661-326-2000
Fax: 661-326-2969

Mercy Hospital
2215 Truxtun Ave
Bakersfield, CA 93301
Phone: 661-632-5000
Fax: 661-327-2592

Mercy Southwest Hospital
400 Old River Rd
Bakersfield, CA 93311
Phone: 661-663-6000
Fax: 661-327-2592

San Joaquin Community Hospital
2615 Eye St
Bakersfield, CA 93301
Phone: 661-395-3000
Fax: 661-324-5162

Transportation

Airport(s)

Meadows Field Airport (BFL)
3 miles NW of downtown (approx 12 minutes) 661-393-7990

Mass Transit

GET Bus
$.75 Base fare.................................661-324-9874

Rail/Bus

Amtrak Station
1501 F St
Bakersfield, CA 93301
Phone: 661-395-3175
TF: 800-872-7245

Greyhound Bus Station
1820 18th St
Bakersfield, CA 93301
Phone: 661-327-5617
TF: 800-231-2222

Utilities

Electricity
Pacific Gas & Electric Co 800-743-5000
www.pge.com
Southern California Edison 800-655-4555
www.sce.com

Gas
Pacific Gas & Electric Co 800-743-5000
www.pge.com

Water
California Water Service 661-396-2400

Garbage Collection/Recycling
Bakersfield Solid Waste Div 661-326-3114

Telecommunications

Telephone
Pacific Bell..................................800-310-2355
www.pacbell.com

Cable Television
Cox Communications.........................661-327-3372
www.cox.com
Popvision 661-638-2222
Time Warner Cable...........................661-327-9935
www.twcbak.com

Internet Service Providers (ISPs)
RidgeNET...................................760-371-3501
www.ridgenet.net

Banks

Bank of America
1440 Truxtun Ave
Bakersfield, CA 93301
Phone: 661-395-2313
Fax: 661-395-2301
TF: 800-338-5202

Bank of Stockdale
5151 Stockdale Hwy
Bakersfield, CA 93309
Phone: 661-833-9292
Fax: 661-833-9469

California Federal Bank
5554 California Ave Suite 110
Bakersfield, CA 93309
Phone: 800-843-2265
Fax: 661-323-3513

San Joaquin Bank
1301 17th St
Bakersfield, CA 93301
www.sjbank.com
Phone: 661-395-1610
Fax: 661-281-0301
TF: 800-281-0315

Sanwa Bank California
5201 California Ave Suite 100
Bakersfield, CA 93309
Phone: 661-327-5345
Fax: 661-322-3696
TF: 800-237-2692

Union Bank of California
5400 Stockdale Hwy
Bakersfield, CA 93309
Phone: 661-322-5035
Fax: 661-322-2624
TF: 800-238-4486

Washington Mutual Bank
4040 California Ave
Bakersfield, CA 93309
Phone: 661-322-4053
Fax: 661-633-1392

Wells Fargo Bank
1300 22nd St
Bakersfield, CA 93301
Phone: 661-861-9971
Fax: 661-322-0634
TF: 800-869-3557

Westamerica Bank
1810 Chester Ave
Bakersfield, CA 93301
Phone: 661-864-4900
Fax: 661-633-0451
TF: 800-848-1088

Shopping

Antique District
H St betw Brundage Ln & California Ave
Bakersfield, CA 93304

East Hills Mall
3000 Mall View Rd Suite 1178
Bakersfield, CA 93306
Phone: 661-872-7990
Fax: 661-872-4046

Valley Plaza Mall
2701 Ming Ave
Bakersfield, CA 93304
Phone: 661-832-2436
Fax: 661-832-4312

Media

Newspapers and Magazines

Bakersfield Business Journal
1612 19th St Suite 121
Bakersfield, CA 93301
Phone: 661-861-8512
Fax: 661-861-1631

Bakersfield Californian*
PO Box 440
Bakersfield, CA 93302
www.bakersfield.com
Phone: 661-395-7500
Fax: 661-395-7519

Bakersfield News Observer
1219 20th St
Bakersfield, CA 93301
Phone: 661-324-9466

**Indicates major daily newspapers*

Television

KABE-TV Ch 39 (Uni)
3223 Sillect Ave
Bakersfield, CA 93308
www.univision.net/stations/kabe-lp.htm
Phone: 661-325-3939
Fax: 661-325-3971

KBAK-TV Ch 29 (CBS)
1901 Westwind Dr
Bakersfield, CA 93301
Phone: 661-327-7955
Fax: 661-327-5603

KERO-TV Ch 23 (ABC)
321 21st St
Bakersfield, CA 93301
Phone: 661-637-2323
Fax: 661-323-5538

KGET-TV Ch 17 (NBC)
2120 L St
Bakersfield, CA 93301
www.kget.com
Phone: 661-283-1700
Fax: 661-327-1994

KPXF-TV Ch 61 (PAX)
4910 E Clinton Ave Suite 107
Fresno, CA 93727
www.pax.net/KPXF
Phone: 559-255-1161
Fax: 559-255-1061

KUVI-TV Ch 45 (UPN)
3223 Sillect Ave
Bakersfield, CA 93308
www.univision.net/stations/kuvi.htm
Phone: 661-326-1011
Fax: 661-328-7576

Radio

KBID-AM 1350 kHz (AC)
1400 Easton Dr Suite 144
Bakersfield, CA 93309
Phone: 661-861-1350
Fax: 661-861-0334

KCOO-FM 104.3 MHz (Oldies)
1400 Easton Dr Suite 144
Bakersfield, CA 93309
Phone: 661-328-1410
Fax: 661-328-0873

KCWR-FM 107.1 MHz (Ctry)
3223 N Sillect Ave
Bakersfield, CA 93308
Phone: 661-326-1011
Fax: 661-328-7503

KDFO-FM 96.5 MHz (CR)
1100 Mohawk St Suite 280
Bakersfield, CA 93309
Phone: 661-322-9929
Fax: 661-322-9239

KERI-AM 1180 kHz (N/T)
110 S Montclair St Suite 205
Bakersfield, CA 93309
www.keri.com
Phone: 661-832-3100
Fax: 661-832-3164

KERN-AM 1410 kHz (N/T)
1400 Easton Dr Suite 144
Bakersfield, CA 93309
www.kernradio.com
Phone: 661-328-1410
Fax: 661-328-0873
TF: 800-840-5376

KGEO-AM 1230 kHz (N/T)
1400 Easton Dr Suite 144
Bakersfield, CA 93309
Phone: 661-328-1410
Fax: 661-328-0873

KGFM-FM 101.5 MHz (AC)
1400 Easton Dr Suite 144
Bakersfield, CA 93309
Phone: 661-328-1410
Fax: 661-328-0873

KISS-FM 94.1 MHz (Urban)
1400 Easton Dr Suite 144
Bakersfield, CA 93309
Phone: 661-328-1410
Fax: 661-328-0873

KISV-FM 94.1 MHz (CHR)
1400 Easton Dr Suite 144
Bakersfield, CA 93309
Phone: 661-328-1410
Fax: 661-328-0873

KIWI-FM 92.1 MHz (Span)
5200 Standard St
Bakersfield, CA 93308
Phone: 661-325-5494
Fax: 661-327-0797

KKBB-FM 99.3 MHz (CR)
3651 Pegasus Dr Suite 107
Bakersfield, CA 93308
Phone: 661-393-1900
Fax: 661-393-1915

KKDJ-FM 105.3 MHz (Oldies)
1100 Mohawk St Suite 280
Bakersfield, CA 93309
www.kkdj.com
Phone: 661-322-9929
Fax: 661-322-9239

KKXX-FM 96.5 MHz (CHR)
1100 Mohawk St Suite 280
Bakersfield, CA 93309
E-mail: kkxx@lightspeed.net
www.kkxx.com
Phone: 661-322-9929
Fax: 661-322-9239

KLLY-FM 95.3 MHz (AC)
3651 Pegasus Dr Suite 107
Bakersfield, CA 93308
www.klly.com
Phone: 661-393-1900
Fax: 661-393-1915

KMYX-AM 1310 kHz (Span)
4600 Ashe Rd Suite 313
Bakersfield, CA 93313
Phone: 661-837-0745
Fax: 661-837-1612

KMYX-FM 103.9 MHz (Span)
4600 Ashe Rd Suite 313
Bakersfield, CA 93313
Phone: 661-837-0745
Fax: 661-837-1612

KNZR-AM 1560 kHz (N/T)
3651 Pegasus Dr Suite 107
Bakersfield, CA 93308
E-mail: knzr@knzr.com
www.knzr.com
Phone: 661-393-1900
Fax: 661-393-1915

KRAB-FM 1061 MHz (Rock)
1100 Mohawk St Suite 280
Bakersfield, CA 93309
E-mail: krab@lightspeed.net
www.krab.com
Phone: 661-322-9929
Fax: 661-322-9239

KRME-FM 97.7 MHz (Span)
3701 Pegasus Dr Suite 102
Bakersfield, CA 93308
Phone: 661-393-0103
Fax: 661-393-0286

KSUV-FM 102.9 MHz (Span)
3701 Pegasus Dr Suite 102
Bakersfield, CA 93308
Phone: 661-393-0103
Fax: 661-393-0286

KUZZ-FM 107.9 MHz (Ctry)
3223 Sillect Ave
Bakersfield, CA 93308
Phone: 661-326-1011
Fax: 661-328-7503

Attractions

Bakersfield's California Living Museum (CALM) has been described as a combination zoo-botanical garden-natural history museum, offering visitors the opportunity to learn about plants and animals native to California through its exhibits, which include an aviary and a coyote grotto, and its educational programs. Visitors can explore the area's history at the Kern County Museum, which includes more than 50 restored Victorian structures built between the 1860s and the 1940s, including a one-room schoolhouse and an 1899 general store, that have been moved from their original locations to the museum's 14-acre grounds.

Adobe Krow Archives
430 18th St
Bakersfield, CA 93301
Phone: 661-633-2736
Fax: 661-833-9074

Bakersfield Community Theater
2400 S Chester Ave
Bakersfield, CA 93304
Phone: 661-831-8114

Bakersfield Museum of Art
1930 R St
Bakersfield, CA 93301
www.csub.edu/bma
Phone: 661-323-7219
Fax: 661-323-7266

Bakersfield Music Theatre
1931 Chester Ave
Bakersfield, CA 93301
www.bmtshowtiks.com
Phone: 661-325-6100
Fax: 661-325-6354

Bakersfield Symphony Orchestra
1328 34th St Suite A
Bakersfield, CA 93301
Phone: 661-323-7928
Fax: 661-323-7331

Brock Lori Children's Museum
3801 Chester Ave
Bakersfield, CA 93301
www.kcmuseum.org
Phone: 661-852-5000
Fax: 661-322-6415

Buck Owens Production Co Inc
3223 Sillect Ave
Bakersfield, CA 93308
www.buckowens.com
Phone: 661-326-1011
Fax: 661-328-7503

Buena Vista Museum of Natural History
1201 20th St
Bakersfield, CA 93301
E-mail: bvmnh@datacourse.com
www.sharktoothhill.com
Phone: 661-324-6350
Fax: 661-324-7522

California Living Museum
10500 Alfred Harrell Hwy
Bakersfield, CA 93306
E-mail: calm@lightspeed.net
www.calmzoo.org/
Phone: 661-872-2256
Fax: 661-872-2205

Camelot Park Family Entertainment Center
1251 Oak St
Bakersfield, CA 93304
Phone: 661-325-5453
Fax: 661-325-4158

Fort Tejon State Historic Park
I-5 & 4201 Fort Tejon Rd
Lebec, CA 93243
Phone: 661-248-6692

Fox Theater
2001 H St
Bakersfield, CA 93301
Phone: 661-324-1369
Fax: 661-324-1854

Golden West Casino
1001 S Union Ave
Bakersfield, CA 93307
Phone: 661-324-6936
Fax: 661-324-6977

Kern County Museum
3801 Chester Ave
Bakersfield, CA 93301
E-mail: kcmuseum@lightspeed.net
www.kruznet.com/kcmuseum
Phone: 661-861-2132
Fax: 661-322-6415

Kern National Wildlife Refuge
10811 Corcoran Rd
Delano, CA 93215
Phone: 661-725-2767
Fax: 661-725-6041

Kern Valley Museum
49 Big Blue Rd
Kernville, CA 93238
Phone: 760-376-6683

Melodrama Music Theater
206 China Grade Loop
Bakersfield, CA 93308
www.melodrama.com
Phone: 661-393-7886
Fax: 661-393-8717

Minter Field Air Museum
Lerdo Hwy & Fwy 99 Shafter Airport
Shafter, CA 93263
Phone: 661-393-0291
Fax: 661-393-3296

Shafter Depot Museum
150 Central Valley Hwy
Shafter, CA 93263
Phone: 661-746-1557

Slikker Farms
10854 Redbank Rd
Bakersfield, CA 93307
Phone: 661-366-4200
Fax: 661-366-0288

Sports Teams & Facilities

Bakersfield Blaze (basketball)
4009 Chester Ave
Bakersfield, CA 93301
E-mail: blaze1@lightspeed.net
www.bakersfieldblaze.com
Phone: 661-322-1363
Fax: 661-322-6199

Bakersfield Condors (hockey)
1001 Truxton Ave
Bakersfield, CA 93301
E-mail: fog@lightspeed.net
www.bakersfieldcondors.com
Phone: 661-324-7825
Fax: 661-324-6929

Bakersfield Speedway
5001 N Chester Ave Ext
Bakersfield, CA 93308
www.bakersfieldspeedway.com
Phone: 661-393-3373
Fax: 661-393-7085

Mesa Marin Raceway
11000 Kern Canyon Rd
Bakersfield, CA 93306
www.mesamarin.com
Phone: 661-366-5711
Fax: 661-366-5123

Annual Events

5th of May Festivity (May 5) 661-323-9334
Appaloosa Horse Show (early June). 661-366-5110
Bakersfield Christmas Parade (early December) 661-325-3410
Bakersfield Jazz Festival (mid-May) 661-664-3093
Country Faire (early July) 661-245-1212
Downtown Street Faires (late May-late August) 661-325-5892
Fall Festival (mid-September). .661-822-4180
Fall Harvest Faire (late September). 661-822-6062
Great Kern County Fair
(mid-September-early October). 661-833-4900
Horseless Carriage Auto Expo (mid-April). 661-833-4917
Lilac Festival (late May) 661-242-4663
McFarland Christmas Festival (mid-December) 661-792-5531
Mountain Festival Art Show (early August). 661-245-3468
October Fest (early September) 661-245-1212
Oktoberfest (late October) 661-327-2424
One Act Festival (mid-June) 661-831-8114
Pacific Coast Junior National Livestock Show
(late March) 661-833-4934
Quarter Horse Show (mid-April) 661-833-4917
Saint Patrick's Day Parade (mid-March) 661-325-5892
Springtyme Faire (mid-June) 661-822-6062
Stampede Day's Rodeo (early May) 661-325-8476
Village Artisans Spring Fair (late April) 661-328-1943
Vintage Sailplane Regatta (late May) 661-822-5267
Western Street Rod Nationals (late April) 661-833-4917

Baltimore, Maryland

***County:* Independent City**

BALTIMORE is located in northern Maryland at the head of navigation of the Patapsco River, which empties into the western portion of the Chesapeake Bay. Major cities within 100 miles include Washington, DC; Wilmington, Delaware; and Philadelphia, Pennsylvania.

Area (Land) .... 80.8 sq mi
Area (Water)............................... 11.3 sq mi
Elevation....................................... 32 ft
Latitude ....39-29-51 N
Longitude............................... 76-62-31 W
Time Zone ....EST
Area Code....................................... 410

Climate

Baltimore has a changeable climate that is modified by the city's proximity to the Chesapeake Bay and Atlantic Ocean to the east and the Appalachian Mountains to the west. Winters are generally cold, with average high temperatures in the low to mid-40s and average lows in the mid-20s. The average annual snowfall for Baltimore is 22 inches. Summer days are very warm, with high temperatures in the mid-80s, while evenings cool down into the mid-60s. Precipitation in Baltimore is fairly evenly distributed throughout the year.

Average Temperatures & Precipitation

Temperatures

	Jan	Feb	Mar	Apr	May	Jun	Jul	Aug	Sep	Oct	Nov	Dec
High	40	44	54	64	74	83	87	85	79	67	57	45
Low	23	26	34	43	53	62	67	66	58	46	37	28

Precipitation

	Jan	Feb	Mar	Apr	May	Jun	Jul	Aug	Sep	Oct	Nov	Dec
Inches	3.1	3.1	3.4	3.1	3.7	3.7	3.7	3.9	3.4	3.0	3.3	3.4

History

Originally inhabited by Native Americans of the Susquehannock tribe, the Baltimore area was first settled by Europeans in 1661. The town of Baltimore was founded in 1729 and named for the founder of the Colony of Maryland, Lord Baltimore. The town grew quickly as a center for international trade (with tobacco as the primary export) and industry, including flour milling and shipbuilding. During the American Revolution, Baltimore served as a major supply center, and the Continental Congress met in the town after fleeing the British. The town's population tripled between 1760 and 1780. In 1797, Baltimore was incorporated as a city.

Shortly after the turn of the 19th Century, a fire destroyed a large portion of Baltimore. In the years that followed, the city was rebuilt and hosted several Whig presidential conventions. In 1814, Baltimore's Fort McHenry became the site of the Battle of Baltimore, during which Francis Scott Key was inspired to compose "The Star Spangled Banner." Over the course of the next 14 years, Baltimore became a city of firsts—the first museum building in the country, the Peale Museum, was built there in 1814; the first gaslights in the world were installed in the city in 1817; the nation's first umbrella factory was established there; and the nation's first railroad, the Baltimore & Ohio (B&O) was founded in Baltimore in 1828.

During the Civil War, the city's sympathies were divided between the Union and the Confederacy, but it was Pro-Confederate sentiment that led Baltimore to become the site of the first bloodshed of the war in April 1861, when the Sixth Massachusetts Regiment attacked and killed 16 residents as the troops passed through the city en route to Washington. After the war ended, Baltimore prospered during the remainder of the 19th Century. During that time several major educational and cultural institutions were established in the city, including the Peabody Institute, the Walters Art Gallery, and Johns Hopkins University, which is one of the nation's leading centers for medical research.

In 1904, the Great Fire, much like the one that occurred a century earlier, destroyed much of Baltimore's downtown area. With the financial support of Andrew Carnegie and the State of Maryland, the city once again rebuilt itself. Over the course of the 20th Century, Baltimore has remained an important port city and has become one of the nation's leading centers for research and development, primarily in the fields of aquaculture, pharmaceuticals, and medicine. Today, with a population of more than 645,000, Baltimore is the 16th largest city in the U.S.

Population

1990 Census 736,014
1998 Estimate..............................645,593
% Change .... -12.3

Racial/Ethnic Breakdown

White.................................... 39.1%
Black 59.2%
Other..................................... 1.7%
Hispanic Origin (may be of any race) 1.0%

Age Breakdown

Under 5 years.............................. 7.7%
5 to 17.................................. 16.7%
18 to 20.................................. 4.7%
21 to 24.................................. 6.6%
25 to 34................................. 18.7%
35 to 44................................. 14.3%
45 to 54.................................. 9.1%
55 to 64.................................. 8.5%
65 to 74.................................. 7.9%

75+ years 5.8%
Median Age 32.6

Gender Breakdown
Male 46.7%
Female 53.3%

Government

Type of Government: Mayor-Council

Baltimore City Council
100 N Holliday St Rm 400
Baltimore, MD 21202
Phone: 410-396-8019
Fax: 410-539-0647

Baltimore City Hall
100 N Holliday St
Baltimore, MD 21202
Phone: 410-396-3100
Fax: 410-396-9568

Baltimore Finance Dept
100 N Holliday St Rm 469
Baltimore, MD 21202
Phone: 410-396-4940
Fax: 410-396-4236

Baltimore Fire Dept
414 N Calvert St
Baltimore, MD 21202
Phone: 410-396-3083
Fax: 410-625-2699

Baltimore Housing & Community Development Dept
417 E Fayette St Suite 1346
Baltimore, MD 21202
Phone: 410-396-3232
Fax: 410-396-4943

Baltimore Law Dept
100 N Holliday St Rm 101
Baltimore, MD 21202
Phone: 410-396-8393
Fax: 410-659-4077

Baltimore Mayor
100 N Holliday St Rm 250
Baltimore, MD 21202
Phone: 410-396-4892
Fax: 410-576-9425

Baltimore Personnel Dept
201 E Baltimore St Suite 300
Baltimore, MD 21202
Phone: 410-396-1563
Fax: 410-396-1523

Baltimore Planning Dept
417 E Fayette St 8th Fl
Baltimore, MD 21202
Phone: 410-396-4329
Fax: 410-244-7358

Baltimore Police Dept
601 E Fayette St
Baltimore, MD 21202
Phone: 410-396-2525
Fax: 410-396-2110

Baltimore Public Works Dept
200 N Holliday St Rm 600
Baltimore, MD 21210
Phone: 410-396-5198
Fax: 410-396-3314

Baltimore Recreation & Parks Dept
3001 East Dr Druid Hill Pk
Baltimore, MD 21217
Phone: 410-396-7900
Fax: 410-889-3856

Baltimore Transportation Bureau
417 E Fayette St Rm 527
Baltimore, MD 21202
Phone: 410-396-6802
Fax: 410-547-1036

Baltimore Water & Wastewater Bureau
200 N Holliday St Suite 300
Baltimore, MD 21202
Phone: 410-396-3500
Fax: 410-539-0955

Enoch Pratt Free Library
400 Cathedral St
Baltimore, MD 21201
Phone: 410-396-5430
Fax: 410-396-1351

Important Phone Numbers

AAA 410-821-1458
American Express Travel 410-837-3100
Baltimore County Office of Budget & Finance 410-887-2400
Baltimore Finance Dept Billing Section 410-396-3987
Dental Referral 410-964-2880
Driver's License/Vehicle Registration Information 410-768-7000
Emergency 911
Greater Baltimore Board of Realtors 410-462-2500
HotelDocs 800-468-3537
Maryland State Assessment & Taxation 410-512-4900
Medical Referral 410-625-0022
Poison Control Center 410-528-7701
Time 410-844-1212
Voter Registration Information 410-396-5550
Weather 410-936-1212

Information Sources

Annapolis & Anne Arundel County Chamber of Commerce
PO Box 346
Annapolis, MD 21404
www.annapolischamber.com
Phone: 410-268-7676
Fax: 410-268-2317

Annapolis & Anne Arundel County Conference & Visitors Bureau
26 West St
Annapolis, MD 21401
www.visit-annapolis.org
Phone: 410-268-8687
Fax: 410-263-9591

Annapolis City Hall
160 Duke of Gloucester St
Annapolis, MD 21401
www.ci.annapolis.md.us
Phone: 410-263-7942
Fax: 410-280-1853

Annapolis Economic Development Office
160 Duke of Gloucester St
Annapolis, MD 21401
www.ci.annapolis.md.us/citizens/depts/econdev.htm
Phone: 410-263-7940
Fax: 410-216-9284

Annapolis Mayor
160 Duke of Gloucester St
Annapolis, MD 21401
www.ci.annapolis.md.us/citizens/depts/mayoff.htm
Phone: 410-263-7997
Fax: 410-216-9284

Anne Arundel County
PO Box 71
Annapolis, MD 21404
www.co.anne-arundel.md.us
Phone: 410-222-7000

Anne Arundel County Public Library
5 Harry S Truman Pkwy
Annapolis, MD 21401
web.aacpl.lib.md.us
Phone: 410-222-7371
Fax: 410-222-7188

Baltimore Area Convention & Visitors Assn
100 Light St 12th Fl
Baltimore, MD 21202
www.baltconvstr.com
Phone: 410-659-7300
Fax: 410-727-2308
TF: 800-343-3468

Baltimore City Chamber of Commerce
3 W Baltimore St
Baltimore, MD 21201
www.baltocitychamber.com
Phone: 410-837-7101
Fax: 410-837-7104

Baltimore Convention Center
1 W Pratt St
Baltimore, MD 21201
www.bccenter.org
Phone: 410-649-7000
Fax: 410-649-7008
TF: 800-207-1175

Baltimore Visitors Center
301 E Pratt St
Baltimore, MD 21202
Phone: 410-837-4636
Fax: 410-727-6769
TF: 800-282-6632

Better Business Bureau Serving Greater Maryland
2100 Huntingdon Ave
Baltimore, MD 21211
www.baltimore.bbb.org
Phone: 410-347-3990
Fax: 410-347-3936

Online Resources

4Baltimore.com
www.4baltimore.com

About.com Guide to Annapolis
annapolis.about.com/citiestowns/midlanticus/annapolis/

About.com Guide to Baltimore
baltimore.about.com/local/midlanticus/baltimore

Annapolis Maryland Area Information
www.azinet.com/annaarea.html

Anthill City Guide Annapolis
www.anthill.com/city.asp?city=annapolis

Anthill City Guide Baltimore
www.anthill.com/city.asp?city=baltimore

Area Guide Annapolis
annapolis.areaguides.net

Area Guide Baltimore
baltimore.areaguides.net

Baltimore CityLink
www.usacitylink.com/citylink/baltimor/

Baltimore Collegetown Network
www.colltown.org

Baltimore Marketplace
www.markpoint.com/index.htm

Baltimore on the WWW
www.baltimore.com

Baltimore What2Do Entertainment Guide
www.hyperstuff.com/md/balt/

BaltimoreMD.com
www.baltimoremd.com

BaltoLink.org
www.baltolink.org

Best of Baltimore.com
www.bestofbaltimore.com

Boulevards Baltimore
www.boulevards.com/cities/baltimore.html

City Knowledge Annapolis
www.cityknowledge.com/md_annapolis.htm

City Knowledge Baltimore
www.cityknowledge.com/md_baltimore.htm

Cityhits Baltimore
www.cityhits.com/baltimore/

CityTravelGuide.com Baltimore
www.citytravelguide.com/baltimore.htm

DigitalCity Baltimore
home.digitalcity.com/baltimore

East Baltimore Guide
www.ebguide.com

Encore Baltimore
encorebaltimore.org

Excite.com Annapolis City Guide
www.excite.com/travel/countries/united_states/maryland/annapolis

Excite.com Baltimore City Guide
www.excite.com/travel/countries/united_states/maryland/baltimore

InBaltimore.com
www.inbaltimore.com

Insiders' Guide to Baltimore
www.insiders.com/baltimore/

Lodging.com Baltimore Maryland
www.lodging.com/auto/guides/baltimore-area-md.html

My Baltimore.net
www.mybaltimore.net

Online City Guide to Baltimore
www.olcg.com/md/baltimore/main.html

Rough Guide Travel Baltimore
travel.roughguides.com/content/627/

VisitBaltimore.com
www.visitbaltimore.com

Area Communities

Incorporated cities and towns in the Baltimore metropolitan area with populations greater than 1,000 include:

Annapolis
160 Duke of Gloucester St
Annapolis, MD 21401
Phone: 410-263-7942
Fax: 410-280-1853

Bel Air
39 N Hickory Ave
Bel Air, MD 21014
Phone: 410-638-4550
Fax: 410-879-9225

Hampstead
1034 S Carroll St
Hampstead, MD 21074
Phone: 410-374-2761
Fax: 410-239-6143

Manchester
3208 York St
Manchester, MD 21102
Phone: 410-239-3200
Fax: 410-239-6430

Mount Airy
110 S Main St
Mount Airy, MD 21771
Phone: 301-829-1424
Fax: 301-829-1259

Taneytown
17 E Baltimore St
Taneytown, MD 21787
Phone: 410-756-2677
Fax: 410-751-1608

Westminster
PO Box 710
Westminster, MD 21158
Phone: 410-876-1313
Fax: 410-876-0299

Economy

Baltimore has a diverse economic base that ranges from international trade to medical research. Home to more than 60 federal research laboratories and numerous private labs, the Baltimore area is one of the nation's leading centers for research and development. Services is the largest employment sector in Baltimore, and government is the second largest, providing jobs for more than 86,000 Baltimore residents at the federal, state, and local levels. The State of Maryland is, in fact, the largest employer in the Baltimore metropolitan area, employing more than more than 69,000 people.

Unemployment Rate	3.9%*
Per Capita Income	$29,548*
Median Family Income	$60,600*

** Information given is for the Baltimore Metropolitan Statistical Area (MSA), which includes the City of Annapolis, the City of Baltimore, Anne Arundel County, Baltimore County, Carroll County, Hartford County, Howard County, and Queen Anne's County.*

Principal Industries & Number of Wage Earners

City of Baltimore - 1999

Construction & Mining	14,000
Finance, Insurance, & Real Estate	33,900
Government	86,000
Manufacturing	29,200
Retail Trade	43,500
Services	159,700
Transportation & Public Utilities	18,600
Wholesale Trade	18,600

Major Employers

Allfirst Financial Inc
25 S Charles St
Baltimore, MD 21201
E-mail: allfirst@allfirst.com
www.allfirst.com
Phone: 410-244-4377
Fax: 410-244-4222
TF: 800-441-8455

Anne Arundel County
PO Box 71
Annapolis, MD 21404
www.co.anne-arundel.md.us
Phone: 410-222-7000

Baltimore City Hall
100 N Holliday St
Baltimore, MD 21202
www.ci.baltimore.md.us
Phone: 410-396-3100
Fax: 410-396-9568

Baltimore County
401 Bosley Ave
Towson, MD 21204
www.co.ba.md.us
Phone: 410-887-2601
Fax: 410-887-3062

Baltimore Gas & Electric Co
PO Box 1475
Baltimore, MD 21203
E-mail: corpcom@bge.com
www.bge.com
Phone: 410-234-5000
Fax: 410-234-7406
TF: 800-685-0123

Baltimore Sun
501 N Calvert St
Baltimore, MD 21278
E-mail: baltsun@clark.net
www.sunspot.net
Phone: 410-332-6000
Fax: 410-332-6455
TF: 800-829-8000

Johns Hopkins Hospital
600 N Wolfe St
Baltimore, MD 21287
E-mail: www@www.med.jhu.edu
www.med.jhu.edu
Phone: 410-955-5000
Fax: 410-955-0890

Johns Hopkins University
3400 N Charles St
Baltimore, MD 21218
www.jhu.edu
Phone: 410-516-8000
Fax: 410-516-6025

Loyola College
4501 N Charles St
Baltimore, MD 21210
www.loyola.edu
Phone: 410-617-2000
Fax: 410-617-5097
TF: 800-221-9107

Sinai Hospital of Baltimore
2401 W Belvedere Ave
Baltimore, MD 21215
www.sinai-balt.com
Phone: 410-601-5678
Fax: 410-601-8356
TF: 800-444-8233

Social Security Administration
6401 Security Blvd
Baltimore, MD 21235
www.ssa.gov
Phone: 410-965-3120
Fax: 410-966-1463
TF: 800-772-1213

University of Maryland Baltimore County
1000 Hilltop Cir
Baltimore, MD 21250
www.umbc.edu
Phone: 410-455-2902
Fax: 410-455-1096
TF: 800-862-2482

University of Maryland Medical System
22 S Greene St
Baltimore, MD 21201
www.umm.edu
Phone: 410-328-8667
Fax: 410-328-0505

US Army Test & Evaluation Command Headquarters
Aberdeen Proving Ground
Aberdeen, MD 21005
www.dtc.army.mil/
Phone: 410-278-5201
Fax: 410-278-8754

US Postal Service Baltimore District
900 E Fayette St
Baltimore, MD 21233
new.usps.com
Phone: 410-347-4260
Fax: 410-234-8507

Verizon Communications
1 E Pratt St
Baltimore, MD 21202
www.verizon.com
Phone: 410-539-9900

Quality of Living Indicators

Total Crime Index....72,497
(rates per 100,000 inhabitants)

Violent Crime
Murder/manslaughter.... 312
Forcible rape.... 469
Robbery....7,687
Aggravated assault....7,556

Property Crime
Burglary....13,177
Larceny theft....35,938
Motor vehicle theft....7,358

Cost of Living Index....99.4
(national average = 100)

Median Home Price....$127,400

Education

Public Schools

Baltimore Public Schools
200 E North Ave
Baltimore, MD 21202
www.bcps.k12.md.us
Phone: 410-396-8700
Fax: 410-396-8474

Number of Schools
Elementary.... 116
Middle.... 24
High.... 16

Student/Teacher Ratio
All Grades.... 18.7:1

Private Schools

Number of Schools (all grades).... 100+

Colleges & Universities

Anne Arundel Community College
101 College Pkwy
Arnold, MD 21012
www.aacc.cc.md.us
Phone: 410-647-7100
Fax: 410-541-2827

Baltimore City Community College
2901 Liberty Heights Ave
Baltimore, MD 21215
Phone: 410-462-8000
Fax: 410-462-7677

Baltimore Hebrew University
5800 Park Heights Ave
Baltimore, MD 21215
E-mail: bhu@bhu.edu
www.bhu.edu
Phone: 410-578-6900
Fax: 410-578-6940
TF: 888-248-7420

Baltimore International College
17 Commerce St
Baltimore, MD 21202
E-mail: publicaffairs@bic.edu
www.bic.edu
Phone: 410-752-4710
Fax: 410-752-3730
TF: 800-624-9926

Capitol College
11301 Springfield Rd
Laurel, MD 20708
E-mail: ccinfo@capitol-college.edu
www.capitol-college.edu
Phone: 301-369-2800
Fax: 301-953-3876
TF: 800-950-1992

Catonsville Community College
800 S Rolling Rd
Catonsville, MD 21228
www.cat.cc.md.us
Phone: 410-455-6050
Fax: 410-719-6546

College of Notre Dame of Maryland
4701 N Charles St
Baltimore, MD 21210
www.ndm.edu
Phone: 410-435-0100
Fax: 410-532-6287
TF: 800-435-0300

Coppin State College
2500 W North Ave
Baltimore, MD 21216
E-mail: rkannan@coe.coppin.umd.edu
www.coppin.edu
Phone: 410-383-5400
Fax: 410-523-7238
TF: 800-635-3674

Dundalk Community College
7200 Sollers Point Rd
Baltimore, MD 21222
www.dundalk.cc.md.us
Phone: 410-282-6700
Fax: 410-285-9903

Essex Community College
7201 Rossville Blvd
Baltimore, MD 21237
www.essex.cc.md.us
Phone: 410-682-6000
Fax: 410-780-6211

Goucher College
1021 Dulaney Valley Rd
Baltimore, MD 21204
www.goucher.edu
Phone: 410-337-6000
Fax: 410-337-6354
TF: 800-468-2437

Howard Community College
10901 Little Patuxent Pkwy
Columbia, MD 21044
www.howardcc.edu
Phone: 410-772-4800
Fax: 410-772-4589

Johns Hopkins University
3400 N Charles St
Baltimore, MD 21218
www.jhu.edu
Phone: 410-516-8000
Fax: 410-516-6025

Loyola College
4501 N Charles St
Baltimore, MD 21210
www.loyola.edu
Phone: 410-617-2000
Fax: 410-617-5097
TF: 800-221-9107

Maryland Institute College of Art
1300 W Mt Royal Ave
Baltimore, MD 21217
www.mica.edu
Phone: 410-669-9200
Fax: 410-669-9206
TF: 800-293-5757

Morgan State University
1700 E Cold Spring Ln
Baltimore, MD 21251
www.morgan.edu
Phone: 443-885-3333
Fax: 443-885-3000
TF: 800-332-6674

Peabody Conservatory of Music
1 E Mt Vernon Pl
Baltimore, MD 21202
www.peabody.jhu.edu
Phone: 410-659-8110
Fax: 410-659-8102
TF: 800-368-2521

Saint John's College
PO Box 2800
Annapolis, MD 21404
www.sjca.edu
Phone: 410-263-2371
Fax: 410-263-4828
TF: 800-727-9238

Sojourner-Douglass College
500 N Caroline St
Baltimore, MD 21205
host.sdc.edu
Phone: 410-276-0306
Fax: 410-675-1810
TF: 800-732-2630

University of Baltimore
1420 N Charles St
Baltimore, MD 21201
www.ubalt.edu
Phone: 410-837-4200
Fax: 410-837-4793
TF: 877-277-5982

University of Maryland Baltimore County
1000 Hilltop Cir
Baltimore, MD 21250
www.umbc.edu
Phone: 410-455-2902
Fax: 410-455-1096
TF: 800-862-2482

US Naval Academy
117 Decatur Rd
Annapolis, MD 21402
E-mail: pao@nadn.navy.mil
www.usna.edu
Phone: 410-293-1000
Fax: 410-293-4348
TF: 888-249-7707

Hospitals

Anne Arundel Medical Center
64 Franklin St
Annapolis, MD 21401
www.aa-healthsystem.org
Phone: 410-267-1000
Fax: 410-267-1624

Bon Secours Liberty Medical Center
2000 W Baltimore St
Baltimore, MD 21223
Phone: 410-362-3000
Fax: 410-362-3450

Franklin Square Hospital Center
9000 Franklin Sq Dr
Baltimore, MD 21237
www.medstarhealth.org/hospitals/franklin.cfm
Phone: 410-682-7000
Fax: 410-682-7904

Good Samaritan Hospital of Maryland
5601 Loch Raven Blvd
Baltimore, MD 21239
www.medstarhealth.org/hospitals/goodsamaritan.cfm
Phone: 410-532-8000
Fax: 410-532-4599

Greater Baltimore Medical Center
6701 N Charles St
Baltimore, MD 21204
www.gbmc.org/
Phone: 410-828-2000
Fax: 410-825-1272

Harbor Hospital Center
3001 S Hanover St
Baltimore, MD 21225
www.medstarhealth.org/hospitals/harbor.cfm
Phone: 410-350-3200
Fax: 410-355-2853

Johns Hopkins Bayview Medical Center
4940 Eastern Ave
Baltimore, MD 21224
www.jhbmc.jhu.edu
Phone: 410-550-0100
Fax: 410-550-2700

Johns Hopkins Hospital
600 N Wolfe St
Baltimore, MD 21287
www.med.jhu.edu
Phone: 410-955-5000
Fax: 410-955-0890

Kennedy Krieger Institute
707 N Broadway
Baltimore, MD 21205
Phone: 410-502-9000
Fax: 410-550-9524

Maryland General Hospital
827 Linden Ave
Baltimore, MD 21201
Phone: 410-225-8000
Fax: 410-462-5834

Mercy Medical Center
301 St Paul Pl
Baltimore, MD 21202
www.mercymed.com
Phone: 410-332-9000
Fax: 410-962-8392

Mount Washington Pediatric Hospital
1708 W Rogers Ave
Baltimore, MD 21209
www.mwph.org
Phone: 410-578-8600
Fax: 410-466-1715

Sinai Hospital of Baltimore
2401 W Belvedere Ave
Baltimore, MD 21215
www.sinai-balt.com
Phone: 410-601-5678
Fax: 410-601-8356
TF: 800-444-8233

Union Memorial Hospital
201 E University Pkwy
Baltimore, MD 21218
www.medstarhealth.org/hospitals/union.cfm
Phone: 410-554-2000
Fax: 410-554-2652
TF: 800-647-7864

University of Maryland Medical System
22 S Greene St
Baltimore, MD 21201
www.umm.edu/system/hospital/univ-hosp-1.html
Phone: 410-328-8667
Fax: 410-328-0117

Veterans Affairs Medical Center
10 N Greene St
Baltimore, MD 21201
Phone: 410-605-7000
Fax: 410-605-7997
TF: 800-463-6295

Transportation

Airport(s)

Baltimore-Washington International Airport (BWI)
9 miles SW of downtown (approx 20 minutes) 410-859-7111

Mass Transit

Harbor Shuttle
$3 Base fare 410-675-2900
Metrorail
$1.35 Base fare. 410-539-5000
MTA Bus
$1.35 Base fare. 410-539-5000
Water Taxi
$3.50 Base fare. 410-563-3901

Rail/Bus

Amtrak Station
1500 N Charles St
Baltimore, MD 21240
Phone: 410-291-4260
TF: 800-872-7245

Greyhound Bus Station
210 W Fayette St
Baltimore, MD 21201
Phone: 410-752-1393
TF: 800-231-2222

Pennsylvania Station
1500 N Charles St
Baltimore, MD 21201
Phone: 410-291-4261

Utilities

Electricity
Baltimore Gas & Electric 410-685-0123
www.bge.com

Gas
Baltimore Gas & Electric 410-685-0123
www.bge.com

Water
Baltimore Bureau of Water & Wastewater. 410-396-5398

Garbage Collection/Recycling
Baltimore Solid Waste Collections 410-396-9950

Telecommunications

Telephone
Verizon Communications........................410-954-6260
www.verizon.com

Cable Television
Comcast Cablevision...........................410-427-9600

Internet Service Providers (ISPs)
ABSnet..410-361-8160
www.abs.net
Charm Net Inc.................................410-558-3900
www.charm.net
Magnus Computing Inc..........................410-893-4643
www.magnus1.com
NetGSI.com....................................410-638-1608
www.netgsi.com
Quantum Internet Services Inc..................410-239-6920
www.qis.net

Banks

Advance Bank
1405 E Coldspring Ln
Baltimore, MD 21239
Phone: 410-323-9570
Fax: 410-323-6867

Allfirst Bank
PO Box 1596
Baltimore, MD 21203
E-mail: allfirst@allfirst.com
www.allfirst.com
Phone: 410-244-4000
Fax: 410-347-6989
TF: 800-842-2265

AmericasBank
3621 E Lombard St
Baltimore, MD 21224
Phone: 410-342-8303
Fax: 410-276-0154

Arundel FSB
333 E Patapsco Ave
Baltimore, MD 21225
Phone: 410-355-9300
Fax: 410-355-0335

Baltimore American Savings Bank FSB
4023 Annapolis Rd
Baltimore, MD 21227
Phone: 410-789-6882
Fax: 410-789-0056

Baltimore County Savings Bank FSB
4111 E Joppa Rd Suite 300
Baltimore, MD 21236
E-mail: baltosav@clark.net
www.baltcosavings.com
Phone: 410-256-5000
Fax: 410-529-0147

Bank of America NA
7912 Belair Rd
Baltimore, MD 21236
Phone: 888-279-3457

BB & T
2 N Charles St Suite 100
Baltimore, MD 21201
Phone: 410-727-7511

Bradford FSB
6900 York Rd
Baltimore, MD 21212
E-mail: info@bradfordfsb.com
www.bradfordfsb.com
Phone: 410-377-9600
Fax: 410-377-0517

Carrollton Bank
344 N Charles St Suite 300
Baltimore, MD 21201
Phone: 410-536-4600
Fax: 410-625-0355

Chesapeake Bank of Maryland
2001 E Joppa Rd
Baltimore, MD 21234
Phone: 410-665-7600
Fax: 410-665-8604

Chevy Chase Bank FSB
2401 Cleanleigh Dr
Baltimore, MD 21234
Phone: 410-663-1561
Fax: 410-663-1563

Citibank FSB
6 Saint Paul St
Baltimore, MD 21202
Phone: 410-637-2140

Columbia Bank
830 W 40th St
Baltimore, MD 21211
Phone: 410-366-1314
Fax: 410-366-1328

Fairmount FSB
8201 Philadelphia Rd
Baltimore, MD 21237
Phone: 410-866-4500

First Mariner Bank
1801 S Clinton St
Baltimore, MD 21224
www.1stmarinerbank.com
Phone: 410-342-2600
Fax: 410-563-1594

First Union National Bank
7 Saint Paul St
Baltimore, MD 21201
Phone: 410-468-1600
Fax: 410-752-2769

First United National Bank & Trust Co
PO Box 9
Oakland, MD 21550
Phone: 301-334-9471
Fax: 301-334-8351

Hamilton Federal Bank
5600 Hartford Rd
Baltimore, MD 21214
Phone: 410-254-9700
Fax: 410-254-9059

Harbor Bank of Maryland
25 W Fayette St
Baltimore, MD 21201
Phone: 410-528-1800
Fax: 410-528-1420
TF: 800-423-7503

Harbor FSB
705 York Rd
Baltimore, MD 21204
Phone: 410-321-7041
Fax: 410-296-7713

Heritage Savings Bank FSB
4228 Hartford Rd
Baltimore, MD 21214
Phone: 410-254-6800

Homewood FSB
3228-30 Eastern Ave
Baltimore, MD 21224
Phone: 410-327-5220
Fax: 410-558-1719

Hopkins FSB
134 S Eaton St
Baltimore, MD 21224
Phone: 410-675-2828
Fax: 410-675-6354

Hull FSB
1248 Hull St
Baltimore, MD 21230
Phone: 410-625-5822
Fax: 410-625-8791

Leeds FSB
1101 Maiden Choice Ln
Baltimore, MD 21229
Phone: 410-242-1234
Fax: 410-247-7605

Madison Square FSB
5401 Belair Rd
Baltimore, MD 21206
Phone: 410-488-4800
Fax: 410-488-7055

Northfield FSB
1844 Joppa Rd
Baltimore, MD 21234
E-mail: info@nfsb.com
www.nfsb.com
Phone: 410-665-5190
Fax: 410-665-4510

Parkville Federal Savings Bank
7802 Hartford Rd
Baltimore, MD 21234
Phone: 410-882-4040
Fax: 410-882-4051

Provident Bank of Maryland
114 E Lexington St
Baltimore, MD 21202
www.provbank.com
Phone: 410-281-7000
Fax: 410-277-2664

SunTrust Bank
1300 N Charles St
Baltimore, MD 21201
Phone: 410-986-1540
Fax: 410-986-1505

Susquehanna Bank
100 West Rd
Baltimore, MD 21204
Phone: 410-938-8610
Fax: 410-938-2253
TF: 800-619-0334

Westview Savings Bank
1000 Ingleside Ave
Baltimore, MD 21228
Phone: 410-747-6200
Fax: 410-747-7202

Shopping

Annapolis Antique Gallery
2009 West St
Annapolis, MD 21401
Phone: 410-266-0635

Annapolis Harbour Shopping Center
2512A Solomon's Island Rd
Annapolis, MD 21401
Phone: 410-266-5857
Fax: 301-970-2508

Antique Warehouse @ 1300
1300 Jackson St
Baltimore, MD 21230
Phone: 410-659-0663
Fax: 410-685-7934

Brokerage The
34 Market Pl Suite 329
Baltimore, MD 21202
Phone: 410-659-9755
Fax: 410-685-8204

Golden Ring Mall
6400 Rossville Blvd
Baltimore, MD 21237
Phone: 410-391-8400
Fax: 410-687-2389

Harborplace & The Gallery
200 E Pratt St
Baltimore, MD 21202
E-mail: comments@harborplace.com
www.harborplace.com
Phone: 410-332-4191
Fax: 410-547-7317

Harbour Square Mall
110 Dock St
Annapolis, MD 21401
Phone: 410-268-8687

Hunt Valley Mall
118 Shawan Rd
Cockeysville, MD 21030
Phone: 410-785-3770
Fax: 410-785-0812

Lexington Market
400 W Lexington St
Baltimore, MD 21201
Phone: 410-685-6169
Fax: 410-547-1864

Maryland Avenue & State Circle Assn
80 Maryland Ave
Annapolis, MD 21401
Phone: 410-280-0202
Fax: 410-280-0202

Owings Mills Mall
10300 Mill Run Cir
Owings Mills, MD 21117
Phone: 410-363-7000
Fax: 410-363-7999

Security Square Mall
6901 Security Blvd
Baltimore, MD 21244
www.securitysquare.com
Phone: 410-265-6000
Fax: 410-281-1473

Towson Marketplace
1238 Putty Hill Ave
Baltimore, MD 21286
Phone: 410-337-0505
Fax: 410-321-7348

Village of Cross Keys
5100 Falls Rd The Gatehouse
Baltimore, MD 21210
Phone: 410-323-1000
Fax: 410-377-0876

Westfield Shopping Town Annapolis
2002 Annapolis Mall
Annapolis, MD 21401
E-mail: info@shoppingtown.com
annapolis.shoppingtown.com
Phone: 410-266-5432
Fax: 410-266-3572

Westview Mall
5748 Baltimore National Pike Suite 104
Baltimore, MD 21228
Phone: 410-744-5650
Fax: 410-747-1631

White Marsh Mall
8200 Perry Hall Blvd
Baltimore, MD 21236
www.whitemarshmall.com
Phone: 410-931-7100
Fax: 410-931-7120

Media

Newspapers and Magazines

Aegis The
PO Box 189
Bel Air, MD 21014
www.theaegis.com
Phone: 410-838-4400
Fax: 410-838-7867

Baltimore Alternative The
PO Box 2351
Baltimore, MD 21203
E-mail: alternative@baltalt.com
www.baltalt.com
Phone: 410-235-3401

Baltimore Business Journal
111 Market Pl Suite 720
Baltimore, MD 21202
www.amcity.com/baltimore
Phone: 410-576-1161
Fax: 410-752-3112

Baltimore Chronicle The
30 W 25th St
Baltimore, MD 21218
E-mail: baltcron@charm.net
www.charm.net/~marc/chronicle
Phone: 410-243-4141
Fax: 410-243-4780

Baltimore City Paper
812 Park Ave
Baltimore, MD 21201
E-mail: letters@citypaper.com
www.citypaper.com
Phone: 410-523-2300
Fax: 410-523-2222

Baltimore Gay Paper Phone: 410-837-7748
241 W Chase St Fax: 410-837-8889
Baltimore, MD 21201
E-mail: advertise@bgp.org
www.bgp.org

Baltimore Magazine Phone: 410-752-4200
1000 Lancaster St Suite 400 Fax: 410-625-0280
Baltimore, MD 21202 TF: 800-935-0838
E-mail: bmag@abs.net
www.baltimoremag.com/

Baltimore Press Phone: 410-342-7737
PO Box 2076 Fax: 410-342-5707
Baltimore, MD 21203
E-mail: comments@baltimorepress.com
www.baltimorepress.com

Baltimore Sun* Phone: 410-332-6000
501 N Calvert St Fax: 410-332-6455
Baltimore, MD 21278 TF: 800-829-8000
E-mail: baltsun@clark.net
www.sunspot.net

Baltimore Times Phone: 410-366-3900
2513 N Charles St Fax: 410-243-1627
Baltimore, MD 21218
E-mail: info@btimes.com
www.btimes.com

Capital The* Phone: 410-268-5000
2000 Capital Dr Fax: 410-268-4643
Annapolis, MD 21401
E-mail: capletts@annap.infi.net
www.capitalonline.com

Inside Annapolis Magazine Phone: 410-263-6300
519 Burnside St Fax: 410-263-8518
Annapolis, MD 21403
www.annapolismag.com

Weekender The Phone: 410-838-4400
PO Box 189 Fax: 410-838-7867
Bel Air, MD 21014

Where Baltimore Magazine Phone: 410-539-4373
516 N Charles St Suite 300 Fax: 410-539-4381
Baltimore, MD 21201

**Indicates major daily newspapers*

Television

WBAL-TV Ch 11 (NBC) Phone: 410-467-3000
3800 Hooper Ave Fax: 410-338-6460
Baltimore, MD 21211
wbaltv.com

WBFF-TV Ch 45 (Fox) Phone: 410-467-4545
2000 W 41st St Fax: 410-467-5090
Baltimore, MD 21211
E-mail: wbff45@aol.com
www.wbff45.com

WJLA-TV Ch 7 (ABC) Phone: 202-364-7777
3007 Tilden St NW Fax: 202-364-7734
Washington, DC 20008
www.abc7dc.com

WJZ-TV Ch 13 (CBS) Phone: 410-466-0013
3725 Malden Ave TV Hill Fax: 410-578-7502
Baltimore, MD 21211
E-mail: ridalld@wjz.groupw.wec.com
www.wjz.com/

WMAR-TV Ch 2 (ABC) Phone: 410-377-2222
6400 York Rd Fax: 410-377-0493
Baltimore, MD 21212
E-mail: wmartv2@aol.com
www.insidebaltimore.com/wmar/

WMPB-TV Ch 67 (PBS) Phone: 410-356-5600
11767 Owings Mills Blvd Fax: 410-581-4338
Owings Mills, MD 21117 TF: 800-223-3678
E-mail: comments@mpt.org
www.mpt.org

WMPT-TV Ch 22 (PBS) Phone: 410-356-5600
11767 Owings Mills Blvd Fax: 410-581-4338
Owings Mills, MD 21117 TF: 800-223-3678
www.mpt.org

WNUV-TV Ch 54 (WB) Phone: 410-662-9688
711 W 40th St Suite 330 Fax: 410-662-0816
Baltimore, MD 21211
www.wnuv54.com

WRC-TV Ch 4 (NBC) Phone: 202-885-4000
4001 Nebraska Ave NW Fax: 202-885-4104
Washington, DC 20016
www.nbc4dc.com

WTTG-TV Ch 5 (Fox) Phone: 202-244-5151
5151 Wisconsin Ave NW Fax: 202-244-1745
Washington, DC 20016 TF: 800-988-4885

WUSA-TV Ch 9 (CBS) Phone: 202-895-5999
4100 Wisconsin Ave NW Fax: 202-966-7948
Washington, DC 20016
E-mail: 9news@wusatv.com
www.wusatv9.com

Radio

WBAL-AM 1090 kHz (N/T) Phone: 410-889-0098
3800 Hooper Ave Fax: 410-338-6675
Baltimore, MD 21211
wbal.com

WBGR-AM 860 kHz (Rel) Phone: 410-825-7700
305 Washington Ave Fax: 410-583-2314
Towson, MD 21204

WBIS-AM 1190 kHz (N/T) Phone: 410-269-0700
1081 Bay Ridge Rd Fax: 410-269-0692
Annapolis, MD 21403
www.wbis1190.com

WBJC-FM 91.5 MHz (Clas) Phone: 410-462-8444
2901 Liberty Heights Ave
Baltimore, MD 21215
E-mail: info@wbjc.com
www.wbjc.com

WBMD-AM 750 kHz (Rel) Phone: 410-821-9000
305 Washington Ave Fax: 410-583-2314
Towson, MD 21204

WCAO-AM 600 kHz (Rel)
1829 Reisterstown Rd Suite 420
Baltimore, MD 21208
Phone: 410-653-2200
Fax: 410-486-8057

WCBM-AM 680 kHz (N/T)
1726 Reiserstown Rd Suite 117
Baltimore, MD 21208
E-mail: hottalk@wcbm.com
www.wcbm.com
Phone: 410-580-6800
Fax: 410-580-6810

WEAA-FM 88.9 MHz (Urban)
1700 E Cold Spring Ln
Baltimore, MD 21251
www.morgan.edu/geninfo/Weaa.htm
Phone: 443-885-3564
Fax: 410-319-3798

WERQ-FM 92.3 MHz (CHR)
100 Saint Paul St
Baltimore, MD 21202
Phone: 410-332-8200
Fax: 410-783-4791

WFSI-FM 107.9 MHz (Rel)
918 Chesapeake Ave
Annapolis, MD 21403
www.wfsiradio.com
Phone: 410-268-6200

WITH-AM 1230 kHz (Rel)
3700 Koppers St Suite 124
Baltimore, MD 21227
Phone: 410-644-9282
Fax: 410-644-3527

WIYY-FM 97.9 MHz (Rock)
3800 Hooper Ave
Baltimore, MD 21211
98online.com
Phone: 410-889-0098
Fax: 410-467-3291

WJFK-AM 1300 kHz (N/T)
1 W Pennsylvania Ave Suite 850
Baltimore, MD 21204
www.1300wjfk.com
Phone: 410-823-1570
Fax: 410-821-5482

WJHU-FM 88.1 MHz (NPR)
2216 N Charles St
Baltimore, MD 21218
E-mail: mail@wjhu.org
www.wjhu.org/
Phone: 410-516-9548
Fax: 410-516-1976

WJRO-AM 1590 kHz (Rel)
159 8th Ave
Glen Burnie, MD 21061
Phone: 410-761-1590

WLIF-FM 101.9 MHz (AC)
1 W Pennsylvania Ave Suite 850
Baltimore, MD 21204
Phone: 410-823-1570
Fax: 410-821-5482

WNAV-AM 1430 kHz (AC)
PO Box 829
Annapolis, MD 21404
www.wnav.com
Phone: 410-263-1430
Fax: 410-268-5360

WNST-AM 1570 kHz (Rel)
1550 Hart Rd
Towson, MD 21286
E-mail: nasty@pcbank.net
www.nastyone.com
Phone: 410-821-9678
Fax: 410-828-4698

WOCT-FM 104.3 MHz (Oldies)
1829 Reisterstown Rd Suite 420
Baltimore, MD 21208
www.thecolt.com
Phone: 410-825-1043
Fax: 410-602-8104

WOLB-AM 1010 kHz (N/T)
100 Saint Paul St
Baltimore, MD 21202
wolnewstalk.com
Phone: 410-332-8200
Fax: 410-732-1400

WPOC-FM 93.1 MHz (Ctry)
711 W 40th St
Baltimore, MD 21211
E-mail: wpoc93fm@prodigy.com
www.wpoc.com
Phone: 410-366-3693
Fax: 410-235-3899

WQSR-FM 105.7 MHz (Oldies)
600 Washington Ave
Baltimore, MD 21204
www.wqsr.com
Phone: 410-825-1000
Fax: 410-337-2772

WRBS-FM 95.1 MHz (Rel)
3600 Georgetown Rd
Baltimore, MD 21227
E-mail: info@wrbs.com
www.wrbs.com
Phone: 410-247-4100
Fax: 410-247-4533
TF: 800-899-0951

WRNR-FM 103.1 MHz (AAA)
112 Main St 3rd Fl
Annapolis, MD 21401
www.wrnr.com
Phone: 410-626-0103
Fax: 410-267-7634

WTMD-FM 89.7 MHz (AC)
8000 York Rd Towson University
Towson, MD 21252
E-mail: wtmd@netscape.net
www.towson.edu/wtmd
Phone: 410-830-8938
Fax: 410-830-2609

WWDC-FM 101.1 MHz (Rock)
8750 Brookville Rd
Silver Spring, MD 20910
www.dc101.com
Phone: 301-587-7100
Fax: 301-565-3329

WWIN-AM 1400 kHz (Rel)
100 Saint Paul St
Baltimore, MD 21202
Phone: 410-332-8200
Fax: 410-547-8783

WWIN-FM 95.9 MHz (Urban)
100 Saint Paul St
Baltimore, MD 21202
Phone: 410-332-8200
Fax: 410-783-4791

WWLG-AM 1360 kHz (B/EZ)
1726 Reistertown Rd Hilton Plaza
Suite 117
Baltimore, MD 21208
Phone: 410-580-6800
Fax: 410-580-6810

WWMX-FM 106.5 MHz (CHR)
600 Washington Ave Suite 201
Towson, MD 21204
www.wwmxfm.com
Phone: 410-825-5400
Fax: 410-583-1065

WXYV-FM 102.7 MHz (Urban)
600 Washington Ave Suite 201
Towson, MD 21204
Phone: 410-828-7722
Fax: 410-821-8256

WYRE-AM 810 kHz (Ctry)
112 Main St 3rd Fl
Annapolis, MD 21401
www.wyreradio.com
Phone: 410-268-5676
Fax: 410-268-9263

WZBA-FM 100.7 MHz (CR)
11350 McCormick Rd Executive Plaza 3
Suite 701
Hunt Valley, MD 21031
Phone: 410-771-8484
Fax: 410-771-1616

Attractions

The heart of the seaport city of Baltimore is the Inner Harbor area, which features shops, restaurants, and festivals, as well as cultural attractions such as the Baltimore Maritime Museum, National Aquarium, and the Maryland Science Center. Baltimore also has six public markets, including Lexington City Market, the nation's oldest continuously operating market. The Fort McHenry National Monument and Historic Shrine is a lasting reminder of the fort's significance during the War of 1812 as the site of the battle that inspired Francis Scott Key to write "The Star Spangled Banner." Other attractions in the city include the former homes of two of Baltimore's most famous residents, macabre storyteller Edgar Allen Poe and baseball legend Babe Ruth.

Nearby Annapolis is the capital of Maryland and the home of the U.S. Naval Academy. The city's National Historic Landmark District reflects its colonial beginnings, with many of its historic homes and other landmarks now used as shops and stores. Annapolis is situated at the confluence of Chesapeake Bay and the Severn River, and its City Dock is a popular site for visitors. Historic homes and other landmarks, food, and entertainment all are within convenient walking distance.

American Visionary Art Museum Phone: 410-244-1900
800 Key Hwy Fax: 410-244-5858
Baltimore, MD 21230
www.avam.org

Annapolis Chamber Orchestra Phone: 410-263-1906
801 Chase St Maryland Hall for the Creative Arts
Annapolis, MD 21401

Annapolis Opera Inc Phone: 410-267-8135
801 Chase St Maryland Hall for the Creative Arts Suite 304 Fax: 410-647-6440
Annapolis, MD 21401

Annapolis Summer Garden Theatre Phone: 410-268-9212
143 Compromise St
Annapolis, MD 21401
E-mail: summergarden@summergarden.com
www.summergarden.com

Annapolis Symphony Orchestra Phone: 410-269-1132
801 Chase St Maryland Hall Fax: 410-263-0616
Annapolis, MD 21401

Antietam National Battlefield Phone: 301-432-5124
5831 Dunker Church Rd Fax: 301-432-4590
Sharpsburg, MD 21782
www.nps.gov/anti/

Antique Row Phone: 410-383-2881
807 N Howard St Fax: 410-728-4677
Baltimore, MD 21201

B & O Railroad Museum Phone: 410-752-2490
901 W Pratt St Fax: 410-752-2499
Baltimore, MD 21223
E-mail: webinfo@borail.org
www.borail.org

B Olive Cole Pharmacy Museum Phone: 410-727-0746
650 W Lombard St Fax: 410-727-2253
Baltimore, MD 21201

Babe Ruth Birthplace Museum Phone: 410-727-1539
216 Emory St Fax: 410-727-1652
Baltimore, MD 21230
www.baberuthmuseum.com

Ballet Theatre of Annapolis Phone: 410-263-8289
801 Chase St Maryland Hall
Annapolis, MD 21401

Baltimore Center for the Performing Arts Phone: 410-625-4230
1 N Charles St Fax: 410-625-4250
Baltimore, MD 21201

Baltimore Civil War Museum & President Street Station Phone: 410-385-5188
601 President St Fax: 410-385-5189
Baltimore, MD 21202

Baltimore Maritime Museum Phone: 410-396-3453
Pratt St Pier 3 Fax: 410-396-3393
Baltimore, MD 21202
E-mail: nationalhistoricseaport@erols.com
www.baltomaritimemuseum.org

Baltimore Museum of Art Phone: 410-396-7100
10 Art Museum Dr Fax: 410-396-6562
Baltimore, MD 21218
www.artbma.org

Baltimore Museum of Industry Phone: 410-727-4808
1415 Key Hwy Fax: 410-727-4869
Baltimore, MD 21230
E-mail: bmi@mailhost.charm.net
www.charm.net/~bmi/

Baltimore Opera Co Phone: 410-625-1600
110 W Mt Royal Ave Suite 306 Fax: 410-625-6474
Baltimore, MD 21201
www.baltimoreopera.com

Baltimore Public Works Museum Phone: 410-396-5565
751 Eastern Ave Fax: 410-545-6781
Baltimore, MD 21202

Baltimore Streetcar Museum Phone: 410-547-0264
1901 Falls Rd Fax: 410-547-0264
Baltimore, MD 21211
www.baltimoremd.com/streetcar

Baltimore Symphony Orchestra Phone: 410-783-8033
1212 Cathedral St Fax: 410-783-8077
Baltimore, MD 21201 TF: 800-422-1198
www.baltimoresymphony.org

Baltimore Waterfront Promenade Phone: 410-396-3453
Baltimore, MD 21230 Fax: 410-396-3393

Baltimore Zoo Phone: 410-396-7102
Druid Hill Pk Fax: 410-396-6464
Baltimore, MD 21217
www.baltimorezoo.org

Banneker-Douglas Museum Phone: 410-216-6180
84 Franklin St Fax: 410-974-2553
Annapolis, MD 21401

Barge House Museum Phone: 410-268-1802
2nd St & Bay Shore Dr
Eastport, MD 21403

Barracks The
18 Pinkney St
Annapolis, MD 21401
www.annapolis.org/barracks.htm
Phone: 410-267-7619

Basilica of the Assumption
Cathedral & Mulberry Sts
Baltimore, MD 21201
Phone: 410-727-3565
Fax: 410-539-0407

Brice House
42 East St
Annapolis, MD 21401
Phone: 410-263-5596

Catoctin Mountain Park
6602 Foxville Rd
Thurmont, MD 21788
www.nps.gov/cato/
Phone: 301-663-9343
Fax: 301-271-2764

Center Stage
700 N Calvert St
Baltimore, MD 21202
www.erols.com/cntrstage/index.html
Phone: 410-685-3200
Fax: 410-539-3912

Charles Carroll House
107 Duke of Gloucester St
Annapolis, MD 21401
Phone: 410-269-1737
Fax: 410-269-1746

Chase-Lloyd House
22 Maryland Ave
Annapolis, MD 21401
Phone: 410-263-2723

Chesapeake & Ohio Canal National Historical Park
PO Box 4
Sharpsburg, MD 21782
E-mail: choh_chief_ranger@nps.gov
www.nps.gov/choh/
Phone: 301-739-4200
Fax: 301-739-5275

Chesapeake Music Hall
339 Busch's Frontage Rd
Annapolis, MD 21401
Phone: 410-626-7515
Fax: 410-626-7215
TF: 800-406-0306

Colonial Players of Annapolis
108 East St
Annapolis, MD 21401
E-mail: cplayers@toad.net
www.geocities.com/Broadway/9057/
Phone: 410-268-7373

Contemporary Museum The
100 W Centre St
Baltimore, MD 21201
www.contemporary.org
Phone: 410-783-5720
Fax: 410-783-5722

Cylburn Arboretum
4915 Greenspring Ave
Baltimore, MD 21209
Phone: 410-396-0180
Fax: 410-367-8039

Druid Hill Park
I-83 & Exit 7
Baltimore, MD 21217
Phone: 410-396-6106

Edgar Allan Poe House
203 N Amity St
Baltimore, MD 21223
www.comnet.ca/~forrest/museum1.html
Phone: 410-396-7932

ESPN Zone
601 E Pratt St
Baltimore, MD 21202
espn.go.com/espninc/zone/baltimore.html
Phone: 410-685-3776
Fax: 410-244-8222

Evergreen House
4545 N Charles St
Baltimore, MD 21210
www.jhu.edu/news_info/to_do/evergreen
Phone: 410-516-0341
Fax: 410-516-0864

Everyman Theatre
1727 N Charles St
Baltimore, MD 21201
E-mail: everymantheatre@erols.com
Phone: 410-752-6537
Fax: 410-752-5891

Fire Museum of Maryland
1301 York Rd
Lutherville, MD 21093
E-mail: info@firemuseummd.org
www.firemuseummd.org
Phone: 410-321-7500
Fax: 410-769-8433

Fort McHenry National Monument & Historic Shrine
2400 E Fort Ave
Baltimore, MD 21230
www.nps.gov/fomc/
Phone: 410-962-4290
Fax: 410-962-2500

George Peabody Library
17 E Mount Vernon Pl
Baltimore, MD 21202
archives.mse.jhu.edu:8000/peabody.html
Phone: 410-659-8179
Fax: 410-659-8137

Gordon Center for Performing Arts
3506 Gwynnbrook Ave
Owings Mills, MD 21117
E-mail: gordon-center@kohnet.com
www.gordoncenter.com/
Phone: 410-356-5200
Fax: 410-581-0561

Governor's Mansion
State Cir & School St
Annapolis, MD 21401
Phone: 410-974-3531
Fax: 410-974-5155

Great Blacks in Wax Museum
1601-03 E North Ave
Baltimore, MD 21213
Phone: 410-563-3404
Fax: 410-675-5040

Gwynn's Falls/Leakin Park
4921 Windsor Mill Rd
Baltimore, MD 21207
Phone: 410-396-0440
Fax: 410-396-0435

Hammond-Harwood House
19 Maryland Ave
Annapolis, MD 21401
Phone: 410-269-1714
Fax: 410-267-6891

Hampton National Historic Site
535 Hampton Ln
Towson, MD 21286
www.nps.gov/hamp/
Phone: 410-823-1309
Fax: 410-823-8394

Harborplace & The Gallery
200 E Pratt St
Baltimore, MD 21202
E-mail: comments@harborplace.com
www.harborplace.com
Phone: 410-332-4191
Fax: 410-547-7317

Historic Annapolis Foundation Museum Store & Welcome Center
77 Main St
Annapolis, MD 21401
www.annapolis.org
Phone: 410-268-5576
Fax: 410-267-6189

Homewood House Museum Phone: 410-516-5589
3400 N Charles St Johns Hopkins University Fax: 410-516-7859
Baltimore, MD 21218
E-mail: homewood@jhunix.hcf.jhu.edu

IMAX Theater Phone: 410-685-5225
601 Light St Maryland Science Ctr Fax: 410-545-5974
Baltimore, MD 21230

Inner Harbor Ice Rink Phone: 410-385-0673
200 W Key Hwy Fax: 410-385-0361
Baltimore, MD 21201
www.bop.org

James E Lewis Museum of Art Phone: 443-885-3030
1700 E Coldspring Ln Morgan State University Fax: 443-319-4024
Baltimore, MD 21251
www.morgan.edu/ACADEMIC/SCHOOLS/FineArts/gallery.htm

Jewish Museum of Maryland Phone: 410-732-6400
15 Lloyd St Fax: 410-732-6451
Baltimore, MD 21202
E-mail: jhsm@charm.net
www.jhsm.org

Lacrosse Hall of Fame Museum Phone: 410-235-6882
113 W University Pkwy Fax: 410-366-6735
Baltimore, MD 21210
lacrosse.org/museum/hall.cfm

Lovely Lane United Methodist Church & Museum Phone: 410-889-1512
2200 Saint Paul St Fax: 410-889-1501
Baltimore, MD 21218

Lyric Opera House Phone: 410-685-5086
110 W Mt Royal Ave Suite 101 Fax: 410-332-8234
Baltimore, MD 21201

Main Street Gallery Phone: 410-280-2787
109 Main St
Annapolis, MD 21401

Maryland Art Place Phone: 410-962-8565
218 W Saratoga St Fax: 410-244-8017
Baltimore, MD 21201
E-mail: map@charm.net
www.mdartplace.org

Maryland Hall for the Creative Arts Phone: 410-263-5544
801 Chase St Fax: 410-263-5114
Annapolis, MD 21401
www.mdhallarts.org

Maryland Historical Society Museum & Library Phone: 410-685-3750
201 W Monument St Fax: 410-385-2105
Baltimore, MD 21201
mdhs.org

Maryland Science Center Phone: 410-685-2370
601 Light St Fax: 410-545-5974
Baltimore, MD 21230
E-mail: info@mdsci.org
www.mdsci.org

Maryland Stage Co Phone: 410-455-2892
1000 Hilltop Cir Fax: 410-455-1046
Baltimore, MD 21218

Maryland State Archives Phone: 410-260-6400
350 Rowe Blvd Fax: 410-974-3895
Annapolis, MD 21401
E-mail: archives@mdarchives.state.md.us
www.mdarchives.state.md.us

Maryland State House Phone: 410-974-3400
91 State Cir Fax: 410-974-5598
Annapolis, MD 21401

Meyerhoff Joseph Symphony Hall Phone: 410-783-8100
1212 Cathedral St Fax: 410-783-8077
Baltimore, MD 21201 TF: 800-442-1198

Monocacy National Battlefield Phone: 301-662-3515
4801 Urbana Pike Fax: 301-662-3420
Frederick, MD 21704
www.nps.gov/mono/

Morris A Mechanic Theatre Phone: 410-752-1200
25 Hopkins Plaza Fax: 410-625-4224
Baltimore, MD 21201
E-mail: subs@themechanic.org
www.themechanic.org

Mother Seton House Phone: 410-523-3443
600 N Paca St
Baltimore, MD 21201

Mount Clare Museum House Phone: 410-837-3262
1500 Washington Blvd Carroll Pk Fax: 410-837-0251
Baltimore, MD 21230
E-mail: mountclaremuseumhouse@erols.com

Mount Vernon Cultural District Phone: 410-244-1030
217 N Charles St Fax: 410-234-2733
Baltimore, MD 21201

Myers Elizabeth Mitchell Art Gallery Phone: 410-626-2556
60 College Ave
Annapolis, MD 21404

National Aquarium Phone: 410-576-3800
501 E Pratt St Pier 3 Fax: 410-576-8238
Baltimore, MD 21202
www.aqua.org

National Juneteenth Museum Phone: 410-467-2724
2682 N Charles St Fax: 410-235-9112
Baltimore, MD 21218
E-mail: june19@smart.net
www.xchange.com/juneteenth

National Museum of Dentistry Phone: 410-706-8314
31 S Greene St Fax: 410-706-8313
Baltimore, MD 21201
www.dentalmuseum.umaryland.edu

Naval Station Annapolis Phone: 410-293-2385
58 Bennion Rd Fax: 410-293-9021
Annapolis, MD 21402
www.usna.edu/NavalStation

Oriole Park
333 W Camden St
Baltimore, MD 21201
Phone: 410-547-6234
Fax: 410-547-6279

Peabody Institute Friedheim Library
1 E Mount Vernon Pl
Baltimore, MD 21202
www.peabody.jhu.edu/lib/
Phone: 410-659-8255
Fax: 410-685-0657

Pennsylvania Dutch Farmers Market
2472 Harbor Ctr
Annapolis, MD 21401
Phone: 410-573-0770

Port Discovery Kid-Powered Museum
35 Market Pl
Baltimore, MD 21202
www.portdiscovery.org
Phone: 410-727-8120
Fax: 410-727-3042

Potters Guild of Baltimore
3600 Clipper Mill Rd
Baltimore, MD 21211
Phone: 410-235-4884

Power Plant Entertainment Complex
601 E Pratt St
Baltimore, MD 21202
Phone: 410-752-5444
Fax: 410-659-9491

Pumpkin Theatre
8415 Bellona Lane Ruxton Towers
Suite 115
Baltimore, MD 21204
Phone: 410-828-1645
Fax: 410-828-1954

Quiet Waters Park
Forest & Hillsmere Dr
Annapolis, MD 21403
Phone: 410-222-1777
Fax: 410-222-1545

Robert Long House
812 S Ann St
Baltimore, MD 21231
Phone: 410-675-6750
Fax: 410-675-6769

Rosenberg Gallery
Kraushaar Auditorium & Merrick Hall
Goucher College
Baltimore, MD 21204
www.goucher.edu/rosenberg/Welcome.htm
Phone: 410-337-6333

Saint Anne's Parish
Duke of Gloucester St
Annapolis, MD 21401
Phone: 410-267-9333
Fax: 410-280-3181

Saint Mary's Church
109 Duke of Gloucester St
Annapolis, MD 21403
Phone: 410-263-2396

Sandy Point State Park
1100 E College Pkwy
Annapolis, MD 21401
Phone: 410-974-2149
Fax: 410-974-2647

Schooner Woodwind
PO Box 3254
Annapolis, MD 21403
Phone: 410-267-6333
TF: 800-638-5139

Shiplap House Museum
18 Pinkney St
Annapolis, MD 21401
www.annapolis.org/shiplap.htm
Phone: 410-267-7619
Fax: 410-267-6189

Six Flags America
PO Box 4210
Largo, MD 20775
www.sixflags.com/america
Phone: 301-249-1500
Fax: 301-249-8853

SS John W Brown
Clinton St Pier 1
Baltimore, MD 21224
Phone: 410-558-0646
Fax: 410-558-1737

Star-Spangled Banner Flag House & 1812 Museum
844 E Pratt St
Baltimore, MD 21202
E-mail: info@flaghouse.org
www.flaghouse.org
Phone: 410-837-1793
Fax: 410-837-1812

Tawes Helen Avalynne Garden
Taylor Ave & Rowe Blvd
Annapolis, MD 21401
www.dnr.state.md.us/programs/tawesgarden.html
Phone: 410-260-8189
Fax: 410-260-8191

Three Centuries Tours of Annapolis
48 Maryland Ave
Annapolis, MD 21401
www.annapolis-tours.com
Phone: 410-263-5401
Fax: 410-263-1901

Timonium Dinner Theatre
9603 Deereco Rd
Timonium, MD 21093
E-mail: tdt@erols.com
Phone: 410-560-1113
Fax: 410-560-6861

Tobacco Prise House
4 Pinkney St
Annapolis, MD 21401
www.annapolis.org/prise.htm
Phone: 410-267-7619

Toby's Dinner Theatre
5900 Symphony Woods Rd
Columbia, MD 21044
E-mail: info@tobysdinnertheatre.com
www.tobysdinnertheatre.com
Phone: 410-730-8311
Fax: 410-730-8313

Top of the World Observation Level & Museum
401 E Pratt St World Trade Ctr 27th Fl
Baltimore, MD 21202
www.bop.org/totw/index.html
Phone: 410-837-8439
Fax: 410-837-0845

US Naval Academy Museum
118 Maryland Ave
Annapolis, MD 21402
Phone: 410-293-2108
Fax: 410-293-5220

Walters Art Gallery
600 N Charles St
Baltimore, MD 21201
www.thewalters.org
Phone: 410-547-9000
Fax: 410-783-7969

War Memorial Building
101 N Gay St
Baltimore, MD 21202
Phone: 410-752-6474
Fax: 410-783-2939

Washington Monument & Museum at Mount Vernon Place
Charles & Monument Sts
Baltimore, MD 21202
Phone: 410-396-7837
Fax: 410-396-7945

Westminster Hall & Burying Ground
500 W Baltimore St
Baltimore, MD 21201
Phone: 410-706-2072
Fax: 410-706-0596

William Paca House & Garden
186 Prince George St
Annapolis, MD 21401
www.annapolis.org/paca.htm
Phone: 410-263-5553
Fax: 410-626-1031
TF: 800-603-4020

Sports Teams & Facilities

Baltimore Arena
201 W Baltimore St
Baltimore, MD 21201
Phone: 410-347-2020
Fax: 410-347-2042

Baltimore Bay Runners (basketball)
201 W Baltimore St Baltimore Arena
Baltimore, MD 21201
www.iblhoops.com/teams/bayrunners
Phone: 410-332-4667
Fax: 410-625-8160

Baltimore Blast (soccer)
1801 S Clinton St
Baltimore, MD 21224
E-mail: questions@baltimorespirit.com
www.baltimoreblast.com
Phone: 410-732-5278
Fax: 410-732-1737

Baltimore Orioles
333 W Camden St Oriole Pk at Camden Yards
Baltimore, MD 21201
www.theorioles.com
Phone: 410-685-9800
Fax: 410-547-6272

Baltimore Ravens
1101 Russell St PSINet Stadium
Baltimore, MD 21230
www.baltimoreravens.com
Phone: 410-654-6200
Fax: 410-654-6212

Maryland Jockey Club of Baltimore City Inc
5201 Park Heights Ave
Baltimore, MD 21215
E-mail: mjc@smart.net
www.marylandracing.com
Phone: 410-542-9400
Fax: 410-466-2521
TF: 800-638-3811

Maryland Pride (soccer)
303 Najoles Rd Suite 112
Millersville, MD 21108
E-mail: info@mdpride.com
mdpride.com
Phone: 410-729-1100
Fax: 410-729-1604
TF: 888-592-5425

Oriole Park at Camden Yards
555 Russell St Suite A
Baltimore, MD 21230
Phone: 410-576-0300
Fax: 410-539-7640

Pimlico Race Course
5201 Park Heights Ave
Baltimore, MD 21215
Phone: 410-542-9400
Fax: 410-542-1221

PSINet Stadium at Camden Yards
1101 Russell St
Baltimore, MD 21230
www.baltimoreravens.com/stadium
Phone: 410-230-8000

Annual Events

ACC Craft Fair (late February) .800-836-3470
Annapolis Heritage Antique Show (late January) .410-222-1919
Annapolis Rotary Crab Feast (early August) .410-841-2841
Annapolis Waterfront Festival (mid-June) .410-268-8828
Anne Arundel County Fair (mid-September) .410-923-3400
Anne Arundel Scottish Highland Games (early October) .410-849-2849
Artscape (late July) .410-396-4575
Baltimore Holiday Tree Lighting (early December) .410-837-4636
Baltimore on Ice (January-March) .800-282-6632
Baltimore's New Year's Eve Extravaganza (December 31) .410-837-4636
Candlelight Pub Crawl (early-mid-December) .410-263-5401
Christmas at Harborplace (December) .410-332-4191
Christmas Holiday Stroll (late November-early January) .410-268-8687
Christmas Music at Lexington Marketplace (December) .410-685-6169
Fall Craft Show (early October) .410-923-3400
First Night Annapolis (December 31) .410-268-8553
Fourth of July Celebration (July 4) .410-263-1183
Kennedy Krieger Institute Festival of Trees (late November) .410-502-9460
Kunta Kinte Heritage Festival (mid-August) .410-349-0338
Lighted Boat Parade (early December) .410-837-4636
Martin Luther King Jr Memorial Concert (early January) .410-783-8100
Maryland Million Day (mid-October) .410-252-2100
Maryland Renaissance Festival (August-October) .410-266-7304
Maryland Seafood Festival (early September) .410-268-7682
Maryland State Fair (late August-early September) .410-252-0200
Mid-Atlantic Wine Festival (mid-June) .410-280-3306
Orioles Winter Carnival (mid-January) .410-685-9800
PJI National ArenaCross (late January) .410-347-2010
Portfest (early October) .410-752-8632
Preakness Celebration Week (early May) .410-837-3030
Rhythm Festival (mid-September) .410-664-6322
US Powerboat Show (mid-October) .410-268-8828
US Sailboat Show (early October) .410-268-8828
Zoo Lights (late November-early January) .410-396-7102

Baton Rouge, Louisiana

County: East Baton Rouge Parish

BATON ROUGE is located along the banks of the Mississippi River in southeastern Louisiana. Cities within 100 miles include New Orleans, Lake Charles, and Alexandria, Louisiana; and Natchez and Biloxi, Mississippi.

Area (Land) .... 73.9 sq mi
Area (Water)............................... 2.2 sq mi
Elevation...................................... 58 ft
Latitude ....30-45-06 N
Longitude.............................. 91-15-44 W
Time Zone ....CST
Area Code....................................... 225

Climate

Baton Rouge has a generally warm, humid climate. Summers are long and hot, with average high temperatures in the low 90s. July and August are the wettest months in Baton Rouge. Winters are typically short and mild, with average temperatures in the 50s. Snowfall is rare, averaging less than an inch a year.

Average Temperatures & Precipitation

Temperatures

	Jan	Feb	Mar	Apr	May	Jun	Jul	Aug	Sep	Oct	Nov	Dec
High	60	64	72	80	86	91	91	91	87	80	71	63
Low	40	43	50	58	65	70	73	73	69	57	49	43

Precipitation

	Jan	Feb	Mar	Apr	May	Jun	Jul	Aug	Sep	Oct	Nov	Dec
Inches	4.9	5.5	4.8	5.4	4.9	4.5	6.7	6.0	4.9	3.5	4.3	5.5

History

The Baton Rouge area was originally inhabited by Native Americans as early as 8000 B.C., but the first permanent European settlement there was not established until 1699. At that time, a colony was established by the French-Canadian explorer Pierre Le Moyne (Sieur d'Iberville). Le Moyne named the area "Baton Rouge," a French phrase meaning "red stick," after discovering a blood-stained cypress tree that marked the boundary between the hunting territories of two Native American tribes. Baton Rouge was incorporated as a city in 1817, with a population of 4,000 people, and became the capital of Louisiana in 1849.

Baton Rouge's location along the banks of the Mississippi River made the city an ideal spot for industry, with steamboat and railroad lines providing numerous distribution routes. The city really began to flourish during the World War II era as many shipbuilders, aluminum companies, and petrochemical companies opened operations in the area. The Baton Rouge metropolitan area today is home to more than a half-million people.

Population

1990 Census 219,531
1998 Estimate.............................211,551
% Change .... -3.6

Racial/Ethnic Breakdown
White.................................... 63.3%**
Black 34.8%**
Other 1.9%**
Hispanic Origin (may be of any race) 1.5%**

Age Breakdown
Under 18 years........................... 29.3%*
18 to 24.................................. 11.5%*
25 to 34.................................. 15.8%*
35 to 49.................................. 22.8%*
50+ years 20.6%*
Median Age................................30.8**

Gender Breakdown
Male...................................... 47.3%
Female.................................... 52.7%

** Information given is for the Baton Rouge Metropolitan Statistical Area (MSA), which includes Ascension, East Baton Rouge, Livingston, and West Baton Rouge parishes.*
*** Information given is for East Baton Rouge Parish.*

Government

Type of Government: Council-Mayor

Baton Rouge City Hall
222 Saint Louis St
Baton Rouge, LA 70801
Phone: 225-389-3100
Fax: 225-389-5203

Baton Rouge Community Development Office
300 Louisiana Ave 2nd Fl
Baton Rouge, LA 70821
Phone: 225-389-3039
Fax: 225-389-3939

Baton Rouge Council Administrator/ Treasurer
222 Saint Louis St
Baton Rouge, LA 70802
Phone: 225-389-3123
Fax: 225-389-3127

Baton Rouge Emergency Preparedness Office
222 Saint Louis St Rm B230
Baton Rouge, LA 70802
Phone: 225-389-3035
Fax: 225-346-0281

Baton Rouge Finance Dept
PO Box 1471
Baton Rouge, LA 70821
Phone: 225-389-3061
Fax: 225-389-5673

Baton Rouge Fire Dept
8011 Merle Gustafson Dr
Baton Rouge, LA 70807
Phone: 225-354-1400
Fax: 225-354-1440

Baton Rouge Human Resources Dept
1755 Florida St
Baton Rouge, LA 70802
Phone: 225-389-3141
Fax: 225-389-4962

Baton Rouge Mayor-President
222 Saint Louis St
Baton Rouge, LA 70801
Phone: 225-389-3100
Fax: 225-389-5203

Baton Rouge Metropolitan Council
222 Saint Louis St
Baton Rouge, LA 70802
Phone: 225-389-3123
Fax: 225-389-3127

Baton Rouge Parish Attorney
222 Saint Louis St
Baton Rouge, LA 70802
Phone: 225-389-3114
Fax: 225-389-5554

Baton Rouge Planning Commission
1755 Florida St 3rd Fl
Baton Rouge, LA 70802
Phone: 225-389-3144
Fax: 225-389-5342

Baton Rouge Police Dept
704 Mayflower St
Baton Rouge, LA 70802
Phone: 225-389-3800
Fax: 225-389-7630

Baton Rouge Public Works Dept
300 North Blvd Rm 208
Baton Rouge, LA 70802
Phone: 225-389-3158
Fax: 225-389-5391

East Baton Rouge Parish Library
7711 Goodwood Blvd
Baton Rouge, LA 70806
Phone: 225-231-3700
Fax: 225-231-3759

Important Phone Numbers

AAA.....225-293-1200
American Express Travel.....225-927-6002
Baton Rouge Board of Realtors.....225-761-2000
Driver's License/Vehicle Registration Information.....225-925-6146
East Baton Rouge Parish Tax Assessor.....225-389-3920
Emergency.....911
Greater Baton Rouge Assn of Realtors.....225-761-2000
HotelDocs.....800-468-3537
Louisiana Dept of Revenue & Taxation.....504-568-5233
Poison Control Center.....800-256-9822
Time/Temp.....225-387-5411
Voter Registration Information.....225-389-3940

Information Sources

Baton Rouge Community Development Office
300 Louisiana Ave 2nd Fl
Baton Rouge, LA 70821
www.ci.baton-rouge.la.us/dept/ocd
Phone: 225-389-3039
Fax: 225-389-3939

Baton Rouge Convention & Visitors Bureau
730 North Blvd
Baton Rouge, LA 70802
www.bracvb.com
Phone: 225-383-1825
Fax: 225-346-1253
TF: 800-527-6843

Better Business Bureau Serving South Central Louisiana
748 Main St
Baton Rouge, LA 70802
www.batonrouge.bbb.org
Phone: 225-346-5222
Fax: 225-346-1029

East Baton Rouge Parish
1755 Florida St
Baton Rouge, LA 70821
Phone: 225-389-3000
Fax: 225-389-4962

Greater Baton Rouge Chamber of Commerce
PO Box 3217
Baton Rouge, LA 70821
www.brchamber.org
Phone: 225-381-7125
Fax: 225-336-4306

Riverside Centroplex
275 S River Rd
Baton Rouge, LA 70802
www.brcentroplex.com
Phone: 225-389-3030
Fax: 225-389-4954

Online Resources

2BatonRouge.com
www.2batonrouge.com

About.com Guide to Baton Rouge
batonrouge.about.com/citiestowns/southeastus/batonrouge/mbody.htm

Area Guide Baton Rouge
batonrouge.areaguides.net

Baton Rouge Net
www.brnet.com

Baton Rouge On-line
www.br-online.com

Baton Rouge Town Planner
www.townplannerbr.com

City Knowledge Baton Rouge
www.cityknowledge.com/la_batonrouge.htm

Excite.com Baton Rouge City Guide
www.excite.com/travel/countries/united_states/louisiana/baton_rouge

Greater Baton Rouge Internet Rest Area
www.baton-rouge.com/BatonRouge

LDS iAmerica Baton Rouge
baton-rouge.iamerica.net

Online City Guide to Baton Rouge
www.olcg.com/la/batonrouge/main.html

Rhythm City Magazine Online
www.rhythmcitymag.com/

Area Communities

Communities in the Greater Baton Rouge area with a population greater than 9,000 include:

Baker
3325 Groom Rd
Baker, LA 70714
Phone: 225-775-9952
Fax: 225-775-9615

Denham Springs Phone: 225-665-8121
941 Government St Fax: 225-667-1584
Denham Springs, LA 70726

Zachary Phone: 225-654-6871
4650 Main St Fax: 225-654-1916
Zachary, LA 70791

Economy

The Baton Rouge metro area has a diverse economic base that ranges from aquaculture to high technology. The area is home to more than 100 chemical plants representing some of the largest chemical manufacturers in the U.S., including Dow Chemical, Ethyl Corporation, and BASF. Services is the largest employment sector in the Baton Rouge MSA. Government is the area's second largest employment sector—the Louisiana State Capital, four parishes, and Louisiana State University combined provide jobs for more than 60,000 area residents.

Unemployment Rate 4.1%*
Per Capita Income..........................$24,403*
Median Family Income......................$46,000*

** Information given is for the Baton Rouge Metropolitan Statistical Area (MSA), which includes Ascension, East Baton Rouge, Livingston, and West Baton Rouge parishes.*

Principal Industries & Number of Wage Earners

Baton Rouge MSA* - 1999

Construction..35,800
Finance, Insurance, & Real Estate.......................16,900
Government..60,800
Manufacturing..24,300
Mining..1,000
Retail Trade..54,100
Services..77,700
Transportation, Communications, & Public Utilities.......14,000
Wholesale Trade......................................16,300

** Information given is for the Baton Rouge Metropolitan Statistical Area (MSA), which includes Ascension, East Baton Rouge, Livingston, and West Baton Rouge parishes.*

Major Employers

Bank One Louisiana NA Phone: 225-332-4022
451 Florida St Fax: 225-332-3336
Baton Rouge, LA 70801 TF: 800-777-0142

Baton Rouge City Hall Phone: 225-389-3100
222 Saint Louis St Fax: 225-389-5203
Baton Rouge, LA 70801
www.ci.baton-rouge.la.us

Baton Rouge General Medical Center Phone: 225-387-7000
3600 Florida Blvd Fax: 225-387-7661
Baton Rouge, LA 70806
www.generalhealth.org/brgmc.html

Dow Chemical Co Phone: 225-353-8000
21255 Louisiana Hwy 1 N Fax: 225-353-6852
Plaquemine, LA 70764
www.dow.com

East Baton Rouge Parish School Board Phone: 225-922-5400
1050 S Foster Dr Fax: 225-922-5411
Baton Rouge, LA 70806
www.ebrpss.k12.la.us

Harmony Corp Phone: 225-922-5050
PO Box 2750 8687 United Plaza Blvd Fax: 225-922-5055
Suite 500
Baton Rouge, LA 70809
www.turner-industries.com/companies/hc.html

International Maintenance Phone: 225-922-5050
8687 United Plaza Blvd Suite 500 Fax: 225-922-5055
Baton Rouge, LA 70809

Louisiana State University Phone: 225-388-3202
3810 W Lake Shore Dr Fax: 225-388-4433
Baton Rouge, LA 70808
www.lsu.edu

Our Lady of the Lake Regional Medical Center Phone: 225-765-6565
5000 Hennessy Blvd Fax: 225-765-8759
Baton Rouge, LA 70808
E-mail: mail@ololrmc.com
www.ololrmc.com

Southern University & A & M College Phone: 225-771-4500
Main Branch Post Office Fax: 225-771-2500
Baton Rouge, LA 70813 TF: 800-256-1531
www.subr.edu

Turner Industries Ltd Phone: 225-922-5050
PO Box 2750 Fax: 225-922-5055
Baton Rouge, LA 70821
www.turner-industries.com

Quality of Living Indicators

Total Crime Index...................................24,291
(rates per 100,000 inhabitants)

Violent Crime
Murder/manslaughter........................... 64
Forcible rape................................ 110
Robbery....................................1,289
Aggravated assault..........................1,030

Property Crime
Burglary....................................5,165
Larceny theft..............................14,061
Motor vehicle theft.........................2,572

Cost of Living Index....................................97.3
(national average = 100)

Median Home Price.................................$103,600

Education

Public Schools

East Baton Rouge Parish School Board Phone: 225-922-5400
1050 S Foster Dr Fax: 225-922-5411
Baton Rouge, LA 70806
www.ebrpss.k12.la.us

Number of Schools
Elementary................................. 64

Middle 17
High....................................... 16

Student/Teacher Ratio
All Grades 15.5:1

Private Schools

Number of Schools (all grades) .... 45+

Colleges & Universities

Louisiana State University
3810 W Lake Shore Dr
Baton Rouge, LA 70808
www.lsu.edu
Phone: 225-388-3202
Fax: 225-388-4433

Louisiana State University A & M College
Baton Rouge, LA 70803
E-mail: help@unix1.sncc.lsu.edu
Phone: 225-388-3202
Fax: 225-388-4433

Louisiana State University Baton Rouge Campus
Tower Dr
Baton Rouge, LA 70803
unix1.sncc.lsu.edu
Phone: 225-388-3202
Fax: 225-388-5991

Southern University & A & M College
Main Branch Post Office
Baton Rouge, LA 70813
www.subr.edu
Phone: 225-771-4500
Fax: 225-771-2500
TF: 800-256-1531

Hospitals

Baton Rouge General Medical Center
3600 Florida Blvd
Baton Rouge, LA 70806
www.generalhealth.org/brgmc.html
Phone: 225-387-7000
Fax: 225-387-7661

Earl K Long Medical Center
5825 Airline Hwy
Baton Rouge, LA 70805
Phone: 225-358-1000
Fax: 225-358-1003

Lane Memorial Hospital
6300 Main St
Zachary, LA 70791
Phone: 225-658-4000
Fax: 225-658-4287
TF: 800-737-5263

Our Lady of the Lake Regional Medical Center
5000 Hennessy Blvd
Baton Rouge, LA 70808
www.ololrmc.com
Phone: 225-765-6565
Fax: 225-765-8759

Summit Hospital
17000 Medical Center Dr
Baton Rouge, LA 70816
Phone: 225-752-2470
Fax: 225-755-4883

Woman's Hospital
9050 Airlines Hwy
Baton Rouge, LA 70815
www.womans.com
Phone: 225-927-1300
Fax: 225-924-8777

Transportation

Airport(s)

Baton Rouge Metropolitan Airport (BTR)
8 miles N of downtown (approx 20 minutes)......225-355-0333

Mass Transit

Capitol Transportation
$1.25 Base fare................................225-389-8920

Rail/Bus

Amtrak Station
Railroad Ave
Hammond, LA 70401
Phone: 800-872-7245

Greyhound/Trailways Bus Station
1253 Florida St
Baton Rouge, LA 70802
Phone: 225-383-3124

Utilities

Electricity
Entergy/GSU 800-368-3749
www.entergy.com

Gas
Entergy/GSU 800-368-3749
www.entergy.com

Water
Baton Rouge Water Co.........................225-928-1000

Garbage Collection/Recycling
Baton Rouge Waste Management Dept...........225-664-8863

Telecommunications

Telephone
BellSouth 800-832-0679
www.bellsouth.com

Cable Television
Cox Communications..........................800-794-2635
www.cox.com
Skywire Cable...............................225-926-0555

Internet Service Providers (ISPs)
Eclipse Telecommunications Inc................225-343-3125
www.eclipsetel.com
InterSurf Online Inc 225-612-2950
www.intersurf.com

Banks

Alliance Bank of Baton Rouge
3700 Essen Ln
Baton Rouge, LA 70809
Phone: 225-926-1114

Bank of West Baton Rouge
4944 Florida Blvd
Baton Rouge, LA 70806
Phone: 225-924-4700
Fax: 225-924-0411

Bank One Louisiana NA
451 Florida St
Baton Rouge, LA 70801
Phone: 225-332-4022
Fax: 225-332-3336
TF: 800-777-0142

Citizens Bank & Trust Co
7646 Jefferson Hwy
Baton Rouge, LA 70809
Phone: 225-926-5037
Fax: 225-925-0569

Deposit Guaranty National Bank
7777 Jefferson Hwy
Baton Rouge, LA 70809
Phone: 225-234-7777

Dillard National Bank
1450 Main St
Baton Rouge, LA 70826
Phone: 225-389-7085
Fax: 225-389-7067

Fidelity Bank & Trust
9400 Old Hammond Hwy
Baton Rouge, LA 70809
Phone: 225-923-0232
Fax: 225-924-9667

First National Banker's Bank
PO Box 80579
Baton Rouge, LA 70898
Phone: 225-924-8015
Fax: 225-952-0899

Hancock Bank of Louisiana
301 Main St
Baton Rouge, LA 70801
Phone: 225-346-6380
Fax: 225-346-6326

Hibernia National Bank
440 3rd St
Baton Rouge, LA 70801
Phone: 225-381-2201
Fax: 225-381-2006

Liberty Bank & Trust Co
7990 Scenic Hwy
Baton Rouge, LA 70807
Phone: 225-775-6133
Fax: 225-775-0233

Louisiana Bank & Trust Co
7142 Florida Blvd
Baton Rouge, LA 70806
Phone: 225-924-0984
Fax: 225-925-8766

Regions Bank
5353 Essen Ln Suite 150
Baton Rouge, LA 70809
Phone: 225-767-0000
Fax: 225-767-0187

Union Planters Bank NA
8440 Jefferson Hwy
Baton Rouge, LA 70809
Phone: 225-924-9400
Fax: 225-924-9367

Whitney National Bank
445 North Blvd
Baton Rouge, LA 70802
Phone: 800-326-3503
Fax: 225-381-0458

Shopping

Bon Marche Mall
7359 Florida Blvd
Baton Rouge, LA 70806
Phone: 225-926-4546
Fax: 225-926-3457

Cortana Mall
9401 Cortana Pl
Baton Rouge, LA 70815
www.cortanamall.com
Phone: 225-923-1412
Fax: 225-928-7920

Landmark Antique Mall
832 St Phillip St
Baton Rouge, LA 70802
Phone: 225-383-4867
Fax: 225-383-9325

Mall of Louisiana
6401 Bluebonnet Blvd
Baton Rouge, LA 70836
Phone: 225-761-7228
Fax: 225-761-7225

Tanger Factory Outlet Center
2200 Tanger Blvd
Gonzales, LA 70737
Phone: 225-647-9383

Media

Newspapers and Magazines

Advocate The*
PO Box 588
Baton Rouge, LA 70821
E-mail: comments@theadvocate.com
www.theadvocate.com
Phone: 225-383-1111
Fax: 225-388-0371

Greater Baton Rouge Business Report
5757 Corporate Blvd Suite 402
Baton Rouge, LA 70808
E-mail: editors@businessreport.com
www.businessreport.com
Phone: 225-928-1700
Fax: 225-926-1329

**Indicates major daily newspapers*

Television

WAFB-TV Ch 9 (CBS)
844 Government St
Baton Rouge, LA 70802
E-mail: wafb@aol.com
Phone: 225-383-9999
Fax: 225-379-7880
TF: 800-324-7875

WBRZ-TV Ch 2 (ABC)
PO Box 2906
Baton Rouge, LA 70821
E-mail: mis@wbrz.com
www.wbrz.com
Phone: 225-387-2222
Fax: 225-336-2347

WBTR-TV Ch 19 (Ind)
914 N Foster Dr
Baton Rouge, LA 70806
Phone: 225-928-3146
Fax: 225-923-2822

WGMB-TV Ch 44 (Fox)
5220-B Essen Ln
Baton Rouge, LA 70809
E-mail: feedback@fox44.com
Phone: 225-769-0044
Fax: 225-769-9462

WLPB-TV Ch 27 (PBS)
7733 Perkins Rd
Baton Rouge, LA 70810
www.lpb.org
Phone: 225-767-5660
Fax: 225-767-4277

WTNC-TV Ch 21 (Ind)
914 N Foster Dr
Baton Rouge, LA 70806
Phone: 225-928-2121
Fax: 225-928-5097

WVLA-TV Ch 33 (NBC)
5220 Essen Ln
Baton Rouge, LA 70809
Phone: 225-766-3233
Fax: 225-768-9191

Radio

KBRH-AM 1260 kHz (Oldies)
2825 Government St
Baton Rouge, LA 70806
Phone: 225-383-3243
Fax: 225-379-7685

KLSU-FM 91.1 MHz (Alt)
B-39 Hodges Hall Louisiana State University
Baton Rouge, LA 70803
E-mail: reqshow@klsu.stumedia.lsu.edu
klsu.stumedia.lsu.edu
Phone: 225-388-6398
Fax: 225-388-1698

KOOJ-FM 93.7 MHz (Oldies)
650 Wooddale Blvd
Baton Rouge, LA 70806
Phone: 225-499-0937
Fax: 225-922-7019

KQXL-FM 106.5 MHz (Urban)
650 Woodale Blvd
Baton Rouge, LA 70806
Phone: 225-926-1106
Fax: 225-928-1606

KRVE-FM 96.1 MHz (AC)
5555 Hilton Ave Suite 500
Baton Rouge, LA 70808
Phone: 225-231-1860
Fax: 225-231-1873

WBRH-FM 90.3 MHz (Nost)
2825 Government St
Baton Rouge, LA 70806
Phone: 225-383-3243
Fax: 225-379-7685

WCAC-FM 103.3 MHz (Ctry)
650 Wooddale Blvd
Baton Rouge, LA 70806
Phone: 225-926-1106
Fax: 225-928-1606

WDGL-FM 98.1 MHz (CR)
PO Box 2231
Baton Rouge, LA 70821
www.eagle981.com
Phone: 225-388-9898
Fax: 225-499-9800

WEMX-FM 94.1 MHz (Urban)
650 Wooddale Blvd
Baton Rouge, LA 70806
Phone: 225-926-1106
Fax: 225-928-1606

WFMF-FM 102.5 MHz (CHR)
5555 Hilton Ave Suite 500
Baton Rouge, LA 70808
Phone: 225-231-1860
Fax: 225-231-1873
TF: 888-235-6673

WIBR-AM 1300 kHz (Sports)
650 Wooddale Blvd
Baton Rouge, LA 70806
Phone: 225-499-1300
Fax: 225-928-1606

WJBO-AM 1150 kHz (N/T)
5555 Hilton Ave Suite 500
Baton Rouge, LA 70808
www.wjbo.com
Phone: 225-231-1860
Fax: 225-231-1873

WNDC-AM 910 kHz (Rel)
3000 Tecumseh St
Baton Rouge, LA 70805
Phone: 225-357-4574
Fax: 225-355-6380

WPFC-AM 1550 kHz (Rel)
6943 Titian Dr
Baton Rouge, LA 70806
Phone: 225-926-1506
Fax: 225-926-4974

WRKF-FM 89.3 MHz (NPR)
3050 Valley Creek Dr
Baton Rouge, LA 70808
E-mail: wrkf@aol.com
www.wrkf.org
Phone: 225-926-3050
Fax: 225-926-3105
TF: 888-926-3050

WSKR-AM 1210 kHz (Sports)
5555 Hilton Ave Suite 500
Baton Rouge, LA 70808
Phone: 225-231-1860
Fax: 225-231-1869

WTGE-FM 107.3 MHz (Oldies)
929 Government St Suite B
Baton Rouge, LA 70802
Phone: 225-388-9898
Fax: 225-499-9800

WXCT-FM 100.7 MHz (Oldies)
929-B Government St
Baton Rouge, LA 70802
E-mail: emailus@tigercountry1007.com
www.tigercountry1007.com
Phone: 225-388-9898
Fax: 225-499-9800

WXOK-AM 1460 kHz (Misc)
650 Woodale Blvd
Baton Rouge, LA 70806
Phone: 225-926-1106
Fax: 225-928-1606

WYNK-AM 1380 kHz (Misc)
5555 Hilton Ave Suite 500
Baton Rouge, LA 70808
Phone: 225-231-1860
Fax: 225-231-1873

WYNK-FM 101.5 MHz (Ctry)
5555 Hilton Ave Suite 500
Baton Rouge, LA 70808
Phone: 225-231-1860
Fax: 225-231-1869

Attractions

Historical attractions in the Baton Rouge area include a number of 19th Century plantations such as the Oakley Plantation, former home of Audubon Society founder John Audubon, and the Houmas House Plantation and Gardens where the movie "Hush Hush Sweet Charlotte" was filmed. Baton Rouge is also home to the Louisiana Arts and Science Center, featuring the Challenger Learning Center, which offers simulated spaceflights on the first Saturday afternoon of each month.

Afton Villa Gardens
9247 Hwy 61
Saint Francisville, LA 70775
Phone: 225-635-6773
Fax: 225-861-7365

Argosy Casino
103 France St
Baton Rouge, LA 70802
www.argosycasinos.com
Phone: 225-378-5825
Fax: 225-344-8056
TF: 800-378-5825

Audubon State Commemorative Area & Oakley Plantation
11788 Louisiana Hwy 965
Saint Francisville, LA 70775
www.crt.state.la.us/crt/parks/audubon/audubon.htm
Phone: 225-635-3739
Fax: 225-784-0578
TF: 888-677-2838

Baton Rouge Ballet Theatre
275 S River Rd Centroplex Theatre
Baton Rouge, LA 70884
E-mail: ballet@aol.com
Phone: 225-766-8379
Fax: 225-766-8230

Baton Rouge Little Theater
7155 Florida Blvd
Baton Rouge, LA 70806
www.brlt.org
Phone: 225-924-6496
Fax: 225-924-9972

Baton Rouge Symphony Orchestra
275 S River Rd Centroplex Theatre
Baton Rouge, LA 70809
www.brso.org
Phone: 225-927-2776
Fax: 225-923-2772

Blue Bayou Water Park
18142 Perkins Rd
Baton Rouge, LA 70810
www.bluebayou.com
Phone: 225-753-3333
Fax: 225-751-4228

Bluebonnet Swamp Nature Center
10503 N Oak Hills Pkwy
Baton Rouge, LA 70810
Phone: 225-757-8905
Fax: 225-757-9390

Blythewood Plantation
400 Daniel St
Amite, LA 70422
Phone: 504-345-6419
Fax: 504-748-6246

Brec's Baton Rouge Zoo
PO Box 60
Baker, LA 70704
Phone: 225-775-3877
Fax: 225-775-3931

Casino Rouge
1717 River Rd N
Baton Rouge, LA 70802
E-mail: mail@casinorouge.com
www.casinorouge.com/
Phone: 225-709-7777
Fax: 225-709-7770
TF: 800-447-6843

Catalpa Plantation
9508 US Hwy 61
Saint Francisville, LA 70775
Phone: 225-635-3372

Celebration Station Entertainment Complex
10111 Gwenadele Ave
Baton Rouge, LA 70816
www.celebrationstation.com
Phone: 225-924-7888
Fax: 225-928-1952

Cohn Laurens Sr Memorial Plant Arboretum
12206 Foster Rd
Baton Rouge, LA 70811
Phone: 225-775-1006
Fax: 225-273-6404

Cottage Plantation
10528 Cottage Ln
Saint Francisville, LA 70775
Phone: 225-635-3674

Enchanted Mansion Doll Museum
190 Lee Dr
Baton Rouge, LA 70808
Phone: 225-769-0005
Fax: 225-766-6822

Firefighters Museum
427 Laurel St
Baton Rouge, LA 70801
Phone: 225-344-8558
Fax: 225-344-7777

Global Wildlife Center
26389 Hwy 40
Folsom, LA 70437
www.globalwildlife.com
Phone: 504-796-3585
Fax: 504-796-9487

Grandmother's Buttons Museum
9814 Royal St
Saint Francisville, LA 70775
Phone: 225-635-4107
Fax: 225-635-6067

Greenwood Plantation
6838 Highland Rd
Saint Francisville, LA 70775
Phone: 225-655-4475
Fax: 225-655-3292
TF: 800-259-4475

Heritage Museum & Cultural Center
1606 Main St
Baker, LA 70714
Phone: 225-774-1776

Hilltop Arboretum Louisiana State University
11855 Highland Rd
Baton Rouge, LA 70810
Phone: 225-767-6916
Fax: 225-768-7710

Historic Magnolia Cemetery
422 N 19th St
Baton Rouge, LA 70802
Phone: 225-387-2464

Houmas House Plantation & Gardens
40136 Hwy 942
Darrow, LA 70725
E-mail: henneman@gs.verio.com
www.houmashouse.com
Phone: 225-473-7841
Fax: 225-474-0480
TF: 888-323-8314

Independence Park Botanic Garden
7500 Independence Blvd
Baton Rouge, LA 70806
Phone: 225-928-2270

Louisiana Arts & Science Center
100 S River Rd
Baton Rouge, LA 70802
Phone: 225-344-5272
Fax: 225-344-9477

Louisiana Governor's Mansion
1001 Capitol Access Rd
Baton Rouge, LA 70802
Phone: 225-342-5855
Fax: 225-379-2043

Louisiana Naval War Memorial
305 S River Rd
Baton Rouge, LA 70802
E-mail: kidd661@aol.com
www.premier.net/~uss_kidd/home.html
Phone: 225-342-1942
Fax: 225-342-2039

Louisiana State Archives
3851 Essen Ln
Baton Rouge, LA 70809
www.sec.state.la.us/arch-1.htm
Phone: 225-922-1206
Fax: 225-922-0433

Louisiana State Capitol Building
State Capitol Dr
Baton Rouge, LA 70804
Phone: 225-342-7317

Louisiana State University Museum of Art
Memorial Tower Louisiana State University
Baton Rouge, LA 70803
Phone: 225-388-4003
Fax: 225-334-4016

Louisiana State University Rural Life Museum
4560 Essen Ln
Baton Rouge, LA 70808
E-mail: lhin@unix1.sncc.lsu.edu
rurallife.lsu.edu
Phone: 225-765-2437
Fax: 225-765-2639

Louisiana State University Theater
Dalrymple Dr 217 Music and Dramatic Arts Bldg
Baton Rouge, LA 70803
Phone: 225-388-4174
Fax: 225-388-4135

Magnolia Mound Plantation
2161 Nicholson Dr
Baton Rouge, LA 70802
Phone: 225-343-4955
Fax: 225-343-6739

Mount Hope Plantation
8151 Highland Rd
Baton Rouge, LA 70808
Phone: 225-761-7000

Nottoway Plantation
30970 Hwy 405
White Castle, LA 70788
www.nottoway.com
Phone: 225-346-8263
Fax: 225-545-8632

Old Arsenal Museum
PO Box 94125
Baton Rouge, LA 70804
www.sec.state.la.us/museums/arsenal/arsenal-index.htm
Phone: 225-342-0401

Old Capitol Gallery
303 North Blvd
Baton Rouge, LA 70801
Phone: 225-343-7333
Fax: 225-343-7334

Old Governor's Mansion
502 North Blvd
Baton Rouge, LA 70802
Phone: 225-387-2464
Fax: 225-343-3989

Old State Capitol
100 North Blvd
Baton Rouge, LA 70801
www.sec.state.la.us/osc-1.htm
Phone: 225-342-0500
Fax: 225-342-0316
TF: 800-488-5968

Plaquemine Lock Museum
57730 Main St
Plaquemine, LA 70764
www.crt.state.la.us/crt/parks/plaquemine_lock/plaqlock.htm
Phone: 225-687-7158
Fax: 225-687-8933

Port Hudson State Historic Site
756 W Plains-Port Hudson Rd
Zachary, LA 70791
www.crt.state.la.us/crt/parks/porthud/pthudson.htm
Phone: 225-654-3775
Fax: 225-654-1048
TF: 888-677-3400

River Bend Energy Center
5485 US Hwy 61
Saint Francisville, LA 70775
Phone: 225-635-6094
Fax: 225-381-4870

Rosedown Plantation & Historic Gardens
12501 Hwy 10
Saint Francisville, LA 70775
Phone: 225-635-3332

Saint James Episcopal Church
208 N 4th St
Baton Rouge, LA 70801
Phone: 225-387-5141
Fax: 225-387-1443

Saint Joseph's Cathedral
412 North St
Baton Rouge, LA 70802
Phone: 225-387-5928
Fax: 225-387-5929

Swine Palace Theater
Tower Dr Louisiana State University
Baton Rouge, LA 70803
E-mail: info@swinepalace.com
www.swinepalace.com
Phone: 225-388-3527
Fax: 225-388-4135

Tezcuco Plantation
3138 Hwy 44
Darrow, LA 70725
www.tezcuco.com
Phone: 225-562-3929
Fax: 225-562-3923

USS Kidd & Nautical Center
305 S River Rd
Baton Rouge, LA 70802
E-mail: rvnwolf@aol.com
Phone: 225-342-1942
Fax: 225-342-2039

West Baton Rouge Museum
845 N Jefferson Ave
Port Allen, LA 70767
www.lapage.com/wbrm
Phone: 225-336-2422
Fax: 225-336-2448

West Feliciana Historical Society Museum
11757 Ferdinand
Saint Francisville, LA 70775
Phone: 225-635-6330
Fax: 225-635-4626
TF: 800-789-4221

White Oak Plantation
17660 George O'Neal Rd
Baton Rouge, LA 70817
Phone: 225-751-1882
Fax: 225-751-0767

Sports Teams & Facilities

Baton Rouge Kingfish (hockey)
275 S River Rd Riverside Centroplex
Baton Rouge, LA 70802
E-mail: brkingfish@i-55.com
www.kingfish-hockey.com
Phone: 225-336-4625
Fax: 225-336-4011

Baton Rouge Raceway
Plank Rd
Baker, LA 70714
Phone: 225-275-5040

Evangeline Downs Race Track
3620 NW Evangeline Thruway
Carencro, LA 70520
E-mail: info@evangelinedowns.com
www.evangelinedowns.com
Phone: 337-896-7223
Fax: 337-896-5445

State Capitol Dragway
PO Box 159
Erwinville, LA 70729
Phone: 225-627-4574
Fax: 225-627-4408

Annual Events

Angola Prison Rodeo (early-late October) 225-655-2592
Audubon Pilgrimage (mid-March) 225-383-1825
Baton Rouge Blues Week (late October)............ 225-383-0464
Baton Rouge Earth Day Festival (mid-April)........ 225-383-1825
Battle of Baton Rouge Commemorative Ceremony (late August)................................. 225-387-2464
Big Easy Charity Horse Show (mid-March)......... 225-388-2255
Bon Fête (late March)........................... 225-383-1825
Bonfest (late December).......................... 225-344-2920
Boo at the Zoo (late October)..................... 225-775-3877
Breaux Bridge Crawfish Festival (early May)........ 225-383-1825
Cajun Day Celebration (late April) 225-774-1940
Cajun Oktoberfest (early October) 225-675-6815
Christmas on the River (December) 225-383-1825
Creole Christmas at Magnolia Mound (mid-December-early January) 225-343-4955
Dixie Jubilee Horse Show (early November) 225-388-2255
Festival of the Bonfires (mid-December)........... 800-367-7852
Greater Baton Rouge State Fair (late October)...... 225-383-1825
Jackson Assembly Antique Festival (late March) 225-383-1825
Jambalaya Festival (late May) 225-647-2009
July 4th Celebration (July 4)...................... 225-383-1825
July 4th False River Boat Parade (July 4) 225-627-6161
June Quarter Horse Show (mid-June) 225-388-2255
Junior Livestock Show (mid-February)............ 225-388-2255
Krewe Mystic Mardi Gras Parade (late February) 225-383-1825
Old Governor's Mansion Gala (late October)........ 225-387-2464
PRCA Rodeo (mid-February)..................... 225-388-2255
Spring Arts & Crafts Festival (late March) 800-442-5539
State Horse Show (mid-July) 225-388-2255
Zippity Zoo Day (early April)...................... 225-775-3877

Birmingham, Alabama

***County:* Jefferson**

BIRMINGHAM is located in the Appalachian Ridge and Valley Region in north central Alabama. Major cities within 100 miles of Birmingham include Montgomery, Huntsville, and Tuscaloosa, Alabama.

Area (Land) .... 144.4 sq mi
Area (Water)............................... 1.2 sq mi
Elevation.................................... 600 ft
Latitude ....33-52-06 N
Longitude............................... 86-80-25 W
Time Zone ....CST
Area Code...................................... 205

Climate

Birmingham's climate is generally mild, with an average annual temperature of 62 degrees. Summers tend to be hot and humid, with high temperatures in the upper 80s. Winters can be cold, with temperatures occasionally dropping below freezing, but the average annual snowfall amount is only 1-2 inches. March is the wettest month of the year in Birmingham; October is the driest.

Average Temperatures & Precipitation

Temperatures

	Jan	**Feb**	**Mar**	**Apr**	**May**	**Jun**	**Jul**	**Aug**	**Sep**	**Oct**	**Nov**	**Dec**
High	52	57	66	75	81	87	90	89	84	75	65	56
Low	31	35	42	49	58	65	70	69	63	50	42	35

Precipitation

	Jan	**Feb**	**Mar**	**Apr**	**May**	**Jun**	**Jul**	**Aug**	**Sep**	**Oct**	**Nov**	**Dec**
Inches	5.1	4.7	6.2	5.0	4.9	3.7	5.3	3.6	3.9	2.8	4.3	5.1

History

Birmingham was founded at the intersection of two railroad lines in Jones Valley by the Elyton Land Company (now Birmingham Realty). It was officially incorporated as a city in 1871 with 1,200 residents. The city was named for the steel center of England. At the turn of the century, Tennessee Coal and Iron began producing steel in Birmingham, and the industry began drawing large numbers of people to the area. Steel and iron manufacturing continued to play a major role in Birmingham's economy during the the 20th Century, with the city acting as one of the United States' rearmament centers during World War II.

The city of Birmingham also played a key role in the Civil Rights Movement of the 1960's as Dr. Martin Luther King, Jr. and other civil rights leaders fought to bring an end to segregation by organizing peaceful demonstrations at lunch counters and other public places. In mid-1963, Dr. King wrote his historic "Letter From Birmingham Jail." Later that same year, the Sixteenth Street Baptist Church was bombed during Sunday morning services, killing four young girls. National media coverage of this event and of Birmingham police attacks on the peaceful demonstrators saddened and outraged the country. The Birmingham Civil Rights Institute, the Sixteenth Street Baptist Church, and other Birmingham landmarks are lasting reminders to the efforts of Dr. King and his fellow civil rights leaders.

Now home to more than 250,000 people, Birmingham is Alabama's largest city.

Population

1990 Census 265,347
1998 Estimate..............................252,997
% Change .... -4.7

Racial/Ethnic Breakdown

White.................................... 36.0%
Black 63.3%
Other 0.7%
Hispanic Origin (may be of any race) 0.4%

Age Breakdown

Under 5 years.............................. 7.4%
5 to 17.................................. 17.9%
18 to 20................................... 4.5%
21 to 24................................... 6.3%
25 to 34................................. 17.7%
35 to 44................................. 14.2%
45 to 54................................... 8.5%
55 to 64................................... 8.7%
65 to 74................................... 8.1%
75+ years 6.8%
Median Age.................................32.9

Gender Breakdown

Male..................................... 45.7%
Female................................... 54.3%

Government

Type of Government: Mayor-Council

Birmingham City Attorney
710 N 20th St 600 City Hall Bldg
Birmingham, AL 35203
Phone: 205-254-2369
Fax: 205-254-2502

Birmingham City Clerk
710 N 20th St 3rd Fl
Birmingham, AL 35203
Phone: 205-254-2290
Fax: 205-254-2115

Birmingham City Council
710 N 20th St
Birmingham, AL 35203
Phone: 205-254-2294
Fax: 205-254-2603

Birmingham City Hall
710 N 20th St
Birmingham, AL 35203
Phone: 205-254-2000
Fax: 205-254-2115

Birmingham Community Development Dept
710 N 20th St Rm 1000
Birmingham, AL 35203
Phone: 205-254-2309
Fax: 205-254-2010

Birmingham Economic Development Office
710 N 20th St 3rd Fl
Birmingham, AL 35203
Phone: 205-254-2799
Fax: 205-254-7741

Birmingham Finance Dept
710 N 20th St Rm A100
Birmingham, AL 35203
Phone: 205-254-2205
Fax: 205-254-2937

Birmingham Fire & Rescue Service Dept
1808 N 7th Ave
Birmingham, AL 35203
Phone: 205-254-2052
Fax: 205-254-2440

Birmingham Mayor
710 N 20th St
Birmingham, AL 35203
Phone: 205-254-2277
Fax: 205-254-2926

Birmingham Parks & Recreation Board
400 Graymont Ave
Birmingham, AL 35204
Phone: 205-254-2391
Fax: 205-254-2515

Birmingham Personnel Dept
701 N 20th St 8th Fl
Birmingham, AL 35203
Phone: 205-254-2829
Fax: 205-254-2415

Birmingham Planning Div
710 N 20th St 2nd Fl
Birmingham, AL 35203
Phone: 205-254-2478
Fax: 205-254-2111

Birmingham Police Dept
1710 1st Ave N
Birmingham, AL 35203
Phone: 205-254-1701
Fax: 205-254-1703

Birmingham Public Library
2100 Park Pl
Birmingham, AL 35203
Phone: 205-226-3600
Fax: 205-226-3743

Important Phone Numbers

AAA 205-978-7000
Alabama State Taxpayer Service Center 205-323-6387
American Express Travel 800-528-4800
Birmingham Assn of Realtors 205-871-1911
Driver's License Information 205-252-7445
Emergency 911
HotelDocs 800-468-3537
Jefferson County Tax Assessor 205-325-5505
Medical Referral 205-581-9800
Poison Control Center 205-933-4050
Time/Temp 205-979-8463
Travelers Aid 205-322-5426
Vehicle Registration Information 205-325-5171
Voter Registration Information 205-325-5550
Weather 205-945-7000

Information Sources

Better Business Bureau Serving Central Alabama & the Wiregrass Area
1210 20th St S
Birmingham, AL 35205
www.birmingham-al.bbb.org
Phone: 205-558-2238
Fax: 205-558-2239

Birmingham Area Chamber of Commerce
2027 1st Ave N
Birmingham, AL 35203
www.birminghamchamber.com
Phone: 205-323-5461
Fax: 205-250-7669

Birmingham Metropolitan Development Board
500 Beacon Pkwy W
Birmingham, AL 35209
www.alpha2000.tech-comm/customer/mbd/
Phone: 205-942-7284
Fax: 205-942-7319

Birmingham-Jefferson Convention Complex
2100 Richard Arrington Jr Blvd
Birmingham, AL 35203
www.bjcc.org
Phone: 205-458-8400
Fax: 205-458-8437

Greater Birmingham Convention & Visitors Bureau
2200 9th Ave N
Birmingham, AL 35203
www.bcvb.org
Phone: 205-458-8000
Fax: 205-458-8086
TF: 800-458-8085

Jefferson County
716 N 21st St Rm A690
Birmingham, AL 35263
Phone: 205-325-5555
Fax: 205-325-4860

Online Resources

4Birmingham.com
www.4birmingham.com

About.com Guide to Birmingham
birminghamal.about.com/citiestowns/southeastus/birminghamal

Area Guide Birmingham
birmingham.areaguides.net

Birmingham Information Connection
www.bhaminfo.com

Birmingham Net
www.bham.net

City Knowledge Birmingham
www.cityknowledge.com/al_birmingham.htm

Excite.com Birmingham City Guide
www.excite.com/travel/countries/united_states/alabama/birmingham

Lodging.com Birmingham Alabama
www.lodging.com/auto/guides/birmingham-area-al.html

Online City Guide to Birmingham
www.onlinecityguide.com/al/birmingham

Area Communities

Communities with populations greater than 5,000 in the five-county Greater Birmingham Region (Blount, Jefferson, Saint Clair, Shelby, and Walker counties) include:

Alabaster
201 1st St N
Alabaster, AL 35007
Phone: 205-664-6800
Fax: 205-664-6841

Bessemer
1800 3rd Ave N
Bessemer, AL 35020
Phone: 205-424-4060
Fax: 205-428-3517

Fairfield
4701 Gary Ave
Fairfield, AL 35064
Phone: 205-788-2492
Fax: 205-783-6005

Fultondale
1210 Walker Chapel Rd
Fultondale, AL 35068
Phone: 205-841-4481
Fax: 205-841-2124

Gardendale
970 Main St
Gardendale, AL 35071
Phone: 205-631-8789
Fax: 205-631-1700

Homewood
1903 29th Ave S
Homewood, AL 35209
Phone: 205-877-8600
Fax: 205-877-8603

Hoover
100 Municipal Dr
Hoover, AL 35216
Phone: 205-444-7500
Fax: 205-444-7572

Hueytown
1318 Hueytown Rd
Hueytown, AL 35023
Phone: 205-491-7010
Fax: 205-491-8573

Irondale
101 S 20th St
Irondale, AL 35210
Phone: 205-956-9200
Fax: 205-956-0950

Leeds
629 1st Ave SE
Leeds, AL 35094
Phone: 205-699-2585
Fax: 205-699-6558

Midfield
725 Bessemer Super Hwy
Midfield, AL 35228
Phone: 205-923-7578
Fax: 205-923-7570

Mountain Brook
56 Church St
Mountain Brook, AL 35213
Phone: 205-870-3532
Fax: 205-879-6913

Pelham
3162 Pelham Pkwy
Pelham, AL 35124
Phone: 205-620-6400
Fax: 205-663-0050

Pell City
1905 1st Ave N
Pell City, AL 35125
Phone: 205-338-2244
Fax: 205-338-2320

Pleasant Grove
501 Park Rd
Pleasant Grove, AL 35127
Phone: 205-744-7221
Fax: 205-744-9556

Tarrant
1604 Penson Valley Pkwy
Tarrant, AL 35217
Phone: 205-849-2800
Fax: 205-849-2805

Trussville
131 Main St
Trussville, AL 35173
Phone: 205-655-7478
Fax: 205-655-7487

Vestavia Hills
513 Montgomery Hwy
Vestavia Hills, AL 35216
Phone: 205-978-0100
Fax: 205-978-0132

Economy

The city of Birmingham was built around manufacturing and the area is still home to 1,300 manufacturers, but service industries have taken over as the primary industry sector in the city's economy. Five Fortune Service 500 companies are headquartered in Birmingham, including AmSouth Bancorporation, Bruno's, and SouthTrust Corporation. Health care is a major service industry in Birmingham, employing nine percent of the city's workforce. Other important industries include finance, education, research, engineering, transportation, and distribution.

Unemployment Rate 2.8%*
Per Capita Income.......................... $26,582*
Median Family Income...................... $47,900*

** Information given is for the Birmingham Metropolitan Statistical Area (MSA), which includes the City of Birmingham, Blount County, Jefferson County, Saint Clair County, and Shelby County.*

Principal Industries & Number of Wage Earners

Jefferson County - 1997

Industry	Wage Earners
Construction	27,550
Finance, Insurance, & Real Estate	34,142
Manufacturing	51,483
Mining	3,275
Retail Trade	77,775
Services	130,458
Transportation & Public Utilities	29,750
Wholesale Trade	32,958

Major Employers

Alabama Power Co
PO Box 2641
Birmingham, AL 35291
E-mail: alapower@apc.com
www.southernco.com/site/alapower
Phone: 205-257-1000
Fax: 205-226-1988
TF: 800-245-2244

Alabama State Government
11 S Union St
Montgomery, AL 36104
www.state.al.us
Phone: 334-242-8000
Fax: 334-242-1110

American Cast Iron Pipe Co
1501 31st Ave N
Birmingham, AL 35207
www.acipco.com
Phone: 205-325-7701
Fax: 205-325-8092

AmSouth Bank
1900 5th Ave N
Birmingham, AL 35203
www.amsouth.com
Phone: 205-326-5164
Fax: 205-320-5185
TF: 800-284-4100

Baptist Health Systems
3201 4th Ave S
Birmingham, AL 35283
www.bhsala.com
Phone: 205-715-5000
Fax: 205-715-5333

BE & K Inc
PO Box 2332
Birmingham, AL 35201
www.bek.com
Phone: 205-969-3600
Fax: 205-972-6300

BellSouth Directory Sales Center
2200 Riverchase Ctr Suite 600
Birmingham, AL 35244
www.bapco.bellsouth.com
Phone: 205-987-6556
Fax: 205-733-4194
TF: 800-432-7143

Birmingham Board of Education
PO Box 10007
Birmingham, AL 35202
www.bhm.k12.al.us
Phone: 205-583-4600
Fax: 205-581-5089

Birmingham City Hall
710 N 20th St
Birmingham, AL 35203
www.ci.bham.al.us
Phone: 205-254-2000
Fax: 205-254-2115

Blue Cross & Blue Shield of Alabama
450 Riverchase Pkwy E
Birmingham, AL 35298
www.bcbsal.org
Phone: 205-988-2200
Fax: 205-733-7357
TF: 800-292-8868

Brookwood Medical Center
2010 Brookwood Medical Center Dr
Birmingham, AL 35209
www.brookwood-medical.com
Phone: 205-877-1000
Fax: 205-877-2279

Bruno's Inc
PO Box 2486
Birmingham, AL 35201
www.al.com/brunos
Phone: 205-940-9400
Fax: 205-912-4628

Jefferson County
716 N 21st St Rm A690
Birmingham, AL 35263
Phone: 205-325-5555
Fax: 205-325-4860

Jefferson County School Board
2100 S 18th St
Homewood, AL 35209
Phone: 205-379-2000
Fax: 205-930-3906

SouthTrust Bank NA
420 20th St N
Birmingham, AL 35203
Phone: 205-254-5000
Fax: 205-254-3200
TF: 800-239-2300

University of Alabama Birmingham
1619 S 19th St
Birmingham, AL 35200
www.uab.edu
Phone: 205-934-4011
Fax: 205-934-4779
TF: 888-309-8435

US Postal Service
612 37th St N
Birmingham, AL 35203
new.usps.com
Phone: 205-521-0302
TF: 800-275-8777

Veterans Affairs Medical Center
700 S 19th St
Birmingham, AL 35233
Phone: 205-933-8101
Fax: 205-933-4498

Quality of Living Indicators

Total Crime Index 22,533
(rates per 100,000 inhabitants)

Violent Crime
Murder/manslaughter 85
Forcible rape 206
Robbery 969
Aggravated assault 1,887

Property Crime
Burglary 4,130
Larceny theft 12,613
Motor vehicle theft 2,643

Cost of Living Index 98.4
(national average = 100)

Median Home Price $127,100

Education

Public Schools

Birmingham Board of Education
PO Box 10007
Birmingham, AL 35202
www.bhm.k12.al.us
Phone: 205-583-4600
Fax: 205-581-5089

Number of Schools
Elementary 47
Middle 18
High 11

Student/Teacher Ratio
Grades K-5 .... 17.0:1
Grades 6-8 .... 19.0:1
Grades 9-12 .... 18.0:1

Private Schools

Number of Schools (all grades) 50

Colleges & Universities

Bessemer State Technical College
PO Box 308
Bessemer, AL 35021
Phone: 205-428-6391
Fax: 205-424-5119

Birmingham-Southern College
900 Arkadelphia Rd
Birmingham, AL 35254
www.bsc.edu
Phone: 205-226-4600
Fax: 205-226-3074
TF: 800-523-5793

Herzing Institute
280 W Valley Ave
Homewood, AL 35209
E-mail: herzing@scott.net
www.herzing.edu
Phone: 205-916-2800
Fax: 205-916-2807

Jefferson State Community College
2601 Carson Rd
Birmingham, AL 35215
www.jscc.cc.al.us
Phone: 205-853-1200
Fax: 205-815-8499
TF: 800-239-5900

Lawson State Community College
3060 Wilson Rd SW
Birmingham, AL 35221
www.ls.cc.al.us
Phone: 205-925-2515
Fax: 205-929-6316

Miles College
50500 Myron Massey Blvd
Fairfield, AL 35064
Phone: 205-929-1000
Fax: 205-929-1668
TF: 800-445-0708

Samford University
800 Lakeshore Dr
Birmingham, AL 35229
www.samford.edu
Phone: 205-870-2011
Fax: 205-870-2654

University of Alabama Birmingham
1619 S 19th St
Birmingham, AL 35200
www.uab.edu
Phone: 205-934-4011
Fax: 205-934-4779
TF: 888-309-8435

Virginia College
65 Bagby Dr Suite 100
Homewood, AL 35209
www.vc.edu
Phone: 205-802-1200
Fax: 205-802-7045

Hospitals

Bessemer Carraway Medical Center
PO Box 847
Bessemer, AL 35021
Phone: 205-481-7000
Fax: 205-481-7595

Birmingham Baptist Medical Center-Montclair Campus
800 Montclair Rd
Birmingham, AL 35213
Phone: 205-592-1000
Fax: 205-592-5653

Birmingham Baptist Medical Center-Princeton Campus
701 Princeton Ave SW
Birmingham, AL 35211
Phone: 205-783-3000
Fax: 205-783-3758

Brookwood Medical Center
2010 Brookwood Medical Center Dr
Birmingham, AL 35209
www.brookwood-medical.com
Phone: 205-877-1000
Fax: 205-877-2279

Carraway Methodist Medical Center
1600 Carraway Blvd
Birmingham, AL 35234
Phone: 205-502-6000
Fax: 205-226-5280

Children's Hospital of Alabama
1600 7th Ave S
Birmingham, AL 35233
Phone: 205-939-9100
Fax: 205-939-9929

Cooper Green Hospital of Alabama
1515 6th Ave S
Birmingham, AL 35233
Phone: 205-930-3200
Fax: 205-930-3497

HealthSouth Medical Center
1201 11th Ave S
Birmingham, AL 35205
Phone: 205-930-7000
Fax: 205-930-7606

HealthSouth Metro West
701 Richard M Scrushy
Fairfield, AL 35064
Phone: 205-783-5121
Fax: 205-783-5279

Medical Center East
50 Medical Park East Dr
Birmingham, AL 35235
Phone: 205-838-3000
Fax: 205-838-3227

Saint Vincent's Hospital
810 St Vincent's Dr
Birmingham, AL 35205
www.stv.org
Phone: 205-939-7000
Fax: 205-930-2168

University of Alabama Hospital
619 S 19th St
Birmingham, AL 35249
www.health.uab.edu
Phone: 205-934-4011
Fax: 205-934-6321

Veterans Affairs Medical Center
700 S 19th St
Birmingham, AL 35233
Phone: 205-933-8101
Fax: 205-933-4498

Transportation

Airport(s)

Birmingham International Airport (BHM)
5 miles NE of downtown (approx 10 minutes) 205-595-0533

Mass Transit

Metro Area Express
$1 Base fare 205-521-0101

Rail/Bus

Amtrak Station
1819 Morris Ave
Birmingham, AL 35203
Phone: 800-872-7245

Greyhound Bus Station
618 N 19th St
Birmingham, AL 35203
Phone: 205-251-3210
TF: 800-231-2222

Utilities

Electricity
Alabama Power Co 800-245-2244
www.southernco.com/site/alapower

Gas
Alabama Gas Corp. 205-326-8200
www.alagasco.com

Water
Birmingham Water Works & Sewer Board 205-251-3261

Garbage Collection/Recycling
Birmingham Street Sanitation Dept. 205-254-6314

Telecommunications

Telephone
BellSouth 800-753-3320
www.bellsouth.com

Cable Television
Time Warner Cable. 205-591-6880
www.timewarner.com

Internet Service Providers (ISPs)
Group 8760 205-250-8053
www.8760.com
World Web Internet Service Provider Inc 205-942-4700
www.wwisp.com

Banks

Aliant Bank
92 Euclid Ave
Birmingham, AL 35213
Phone: 205-414-2000
Fax: 205-871-8766

AmSouth Bank
1900 5th Ave N
Birmingham, AL 35203
www.amsouth.com
Phone: 205-326-5164
Fax: 205-320-5185
TF: 800-284-4100

BancorpSouth Bank
1910 3rd Ave N
Birmingham, AL 35203
Phone: 205-323-7181
Fax: 205-251-2320

Bank of Alabama
2340 Woodcrest Pl Suite 200
Birmingham, AL 35209
E-mail: support@bankofalabama.com
www.bankofalabama.com
Phone: 205-870-1939
Fax: 205-879-3885

Citizens FSB
1700 3rd Ave N
Birmingham, AL 35203
Phone: 205-328-2041
Fax: 205-226-8008

Colonial Bank
1928 1st Ave N
Birmingham, AL 35203
www.colonialbank.com
Phone: 205-325-1649
Fax: 205-325-1825
TF: 800-388-1477

Compass Bank
701 32nd St S
Birmingham, AL 35233
E-mail: feedback@compassbnk.com
www.compassweb.com
Phone: 205-933-3000
Fax: 205-558-5157
TF: 800-239-2265

First Commercial Bank
300 21st St N
Birmingham, AL 35202
Phone: 205-868-4850
Fax: 205-868-4854

National Bank of Commerce of Birmingham
1927 1st Ave N
Birmingham, AL 35203
Phone: 205-583-3600
Fax: 205-583-3292

New South FSB
215 N 21st St
Birmingham, AL 35203
Phone: 205-951-1000
Fax: 205-951-1037

Pinnacle Bank
2013 Canyon Rd
Birmingham, AL 35216
Phone: 205-822-2265
Fax: 205-978-7401

Regions Bank
417 20th St N
Birmingham, AL 35202
Phone: 205-326-7100
Fax: 205-326-7756

SouthTrust Bank NA
420 20th St N
Birmingham, AL 35203
Phone: 205-254-5000
Fax: 205-254-3200
TF: 800-239-2300

Shopping

Brookwood Village
623 Brookwood Village
Birmingham, AL 35209
Phone: 205-871-0406
Fax: 205-870-7990

Century Plaza
241 Century Plaza
Birmingham, AL 35210
Phone: 205-591-2451
Fax: 205-591-2462

Cobb Lane
20th St S & 13th Ave S
Birmingham, AL 35205

Eastwood Mall
7703 Crestwood Blvd
Birmingham, AL 35210
Phone: 205-591-8077
Fax: 205-591-8074

Riverchase Galleria
3000 Galleria Mall
Birmingham, AL 35244
E-mail: info@thegalleria.com
www.thegalleria.com
Phone: 205-985-3039
Fax: 205-985-3040

Summit The
225 Summit Blvd
Birmingham, AL 35243
Phone: 205-967-0111

Western Hills Mall
PO Box 28286
Birmingham, AL 35228
Phone: 205-923-2525
Fax: 205-923-7952

Ye Olde Antique & Collectible Market
2331 Bessemer Rd
Birmingham, AL 35208
Phone: 205-822-3348
TF: 800-362-7538

Media

Newspapers and Magazines

Birmingham Business Journal
2140 11th Ave S Suite 205
Birmingham, AL 35205
www.amcity.com/birmingham
Phone: 205-322-0000
Fax: 205-322-0040

Birmingham Magazine
PO Box 10127
Birmingham, AL 35202
Phone: 205-323-5461
Fax: 205-226-8850

Birmingham News*
2200 4th Ave N
Birmingham, AL 35203
E-mail: feedback@al.com
www.al.com/birmingham
Phone: 205-325-2222
Fax: 205-325-2283

Birmingham Post-Herald*
2200 4th Ave N
Birmingham, AL 35203
E-mail: postherald@aol.com
www.postherald.com
Phone: 205-325-2343
Fax: 205-325-2410

Birmingham Times
115 3rd Ave W
Birmingham, AL 35204
Phone: 205-251-5158
Fax: 205-323-2294

Over The Mountain Journal
2016 Columbiana Rd
Birmingham, AL 35216
Phone: 205-823-9646
Fax: 205-824-1246

Southern Accents
2100 Lakeshore Dr
Birmingham, AL 35209
E-mail: letters@southernaccents.com
www.southernaccents.com
Phone: 205-877-6000
Fax: 205-877-6990
TF: 800-366-4712

**Indicates major daily newspapers*

Television

WABM-TV Ch 68 (UPN)
651 Beacon Pkwy W Suite 105
Birmingham, AL 35209
Phone: 205-943-2168
Fax: 205-290-2115

WBIQ-TV Ch 10 (PBS)
2112 11th Ave S Suite 400
Birmingham, AL 35205
www.aptv.org/InsideAPT/WBIQ10.html
Phone: 205-328-8756
Fax: 205-251-2192
TF: 800-239-5233

WBRC-TV Ch 6 (Fox)
PO Box 6
Birmingham, AL 35201
E-mail: info@wbrc.com
www.wbrc.com
Phone: 205-322-6666
Fax: 205-583-4386

WCFT-TV Ch 33 (ABC)
800 Concourse Pkwy Suite 200
Birmingham, AL 35244
E-mail: info@www.abc3340.com
www.abc3340.com
Phone: 205-403-3340
Fax: 205-982-3942

WIAT-TV Ch 42 (CBS)
PO Box 59496
Birmingham, AL 35259
Phone: 205-322-4200
Fax: 205-320-2713

WPXH-TV Ch 44 (PAX)
2085 Golden Crust Dr
Birmingham, AL 35209
www.pax.net/WPXH
Phone: 205-870-4404
Fax: 205-870-0744

WTTO-TV Ch 21 (WB)
651 Beacon Pkwy W Suite 105
Birmingham, AL 35209
Phone: 205-943-2168
Fax: 205-290-2115

WVTM-TV Ch 13 (NBC)
1732 Valley View Dr
Birmingham, AL 35209
www.nbc13.com
Phone: 205-933-1313
Fax: 205-323-3314

Radio

WAGG-AM 610 kHz (Rel)
2301 1st Ave N Suite 102
Birmingham, AL 35203
Phone: 205-322-2987
Fax: 205-324-6329

WAPI-AM 1070 kHz (N/T)
244 Goodwin Crest Dr Suite 200
Birmingham, AL 35209
Phone: 205-945-4646
Fax: 205-942-8959

WATV-AM 900 kHz (Oldies)
3025 Ensley Ave
Birmingham, AL 35208
Phone: 205-741-9288
Fax: 205-780-4034

WAYE-AM 1220 kHz (Rel)
836 Lomb Ave SW
Birmingham, AL 35211
Phone: 205-786-9293
Fax: 205-786-9296

WBFR-FM 89.5 MHz (Rel)
244 Goodwin Crest Dr Suite 118
Birmingham, AL 35209
Phone: 800-543-1495
Fax: 510-633-7983

WBHJ-FM 95.7 MHz (Urban)
2301 1st Ave N Suite 102
Birmingham, AL 35203
Phone: 205-322-2987
Fax: 205-324-6329

WBHK-FM 98.7 MHz (Urban)
2301 1st Ave N Suite 102
Birmingham, AL 35203
Phone: 205-322-2987
Fax: 205-324-6329

WBHM-FM 90.3 MHz (NPR)
650 11th St S
Birmingham, AL 35294
E-mail: patrick@wbhm.uab.edu
www.wbhm.org
Phone: 205-934-2606
Fax: 205-934-5075
TF: 800-444-9246

WDJC-FM 93.7 MHz (Rel)
2727 19th Pl S
Birmingham, AL 35209
Phone: 205-879-3324
Fax: 800-802-4555

WDXB-FM 102.5 MHz (Ctry)
530 Beacon Pkwy W Suite 600
Birmingham, AL 35209
www.dixie1025.com
Phone: 205-439-9600
Fax: 205-439-8390

WENN-FM 105.9 MHz (Oldies)
530 Beacon Pkwy W Suite 600
Birmingham, AL 35209
Phone: 205-942-9600
Fax: 205-439-8390

WERC-AM 960 kHz (N/T)
530 Beacon Pkwy W Suite 600
Birmingham, AL 35209
www.werc960am.com
Phone: 205-439-9600
Fax: 205-439-8390

WJLD-AM 1400 kHz (Misc)
1449 Spaulding-Ishkooda Rd
Birmingham, AL 35211
E-mail: wjld@juno.com
Phone: 205-942-1776
Fax: 205-942-4814

WJOX-AM 690 kHz (Sports)
244 Goodwin Crest Dr
Birmingham, AL 35209
E-mail: wjox@quicklink.net
www.wjox690.com
Phone: 205-945-4646
Fax: 205-942-8959

WJSR-FM 91.1 MHz (AC)
2601 Carson Rd
Birmingham, AL 35215
Phone: 205-856-7702
Fax: 205-815-8499

WLJR-FM 88.5 MHz (Rel)
2200 Briarwood Way
Birmingham, AL 35243
Phone: 205-978-2232
Fax: 205-824-8419

WLPH-AM 1480 kHz (Rel)
5200 Atlanta Hwy
Birmingham, AL 35210
Phone: 205-956-5470
Fax: 205-956-5471

WMJJ-FM 96.5 MHz (AC)
530 Beacon Pkwy W Suite 600
Birmingham, AL 35209
www.magic96fm.com
Phone: 205-439-9600
Fax: 205-439-8390

WODL-FM 106.9 MHz (Oldies)
301 Beacon Pkwy W Suite 200
Birmingham, AL 35209
www.wodl.com
Phone: 205-916-1100
Fax: 205-916-1151

WQEN-FM 103.7 MHz (CHR)
530 Beacon Pkwy W Suite 600
Birmingham, AL 35209
E-mail: requests@1037.com
www.1037.com
Phone: 205-439-9600
Fax: 205-439-8390

WRAX-FM 107.7 MHz (Alt)
244 Goodwin Crest Dr Suite 300
Birmingham, AL 35209
E-mail: sales@wraxfm.com
www.wraxfm.com
Phone: 205-942-1106
Fax: 205-942-3175

WRLR-FM 97.3 MHz (Rock)
301 Beacon Pkwy W Suite 200
Birmingham, AL 35209
Phone: 205-916-1100
Fax: 205-916-1116

WRRS-FM 101.1 MHz (Rel)
615 Brookwood Village Mall
Birmingham, AL 35209
E-mail: contactus@reality101.com
reality101.com
Phone: 205-870-1011
Fax: 205-870-5519

WYDE-AM 850 kHz (Rel) Phone: 205-942-8585
244 Goodwin Crest Dr Suite G-126 Fax: 205-942-1087
Birmingham, AL 35209

WYSF-FM 94.5 MHz (AC) Phone: 205-942-1004
244 Goodwin Crest Dr Fax: 205-945-3999
Birmingham, AL 35209
E-mail: wysf@dbcradio.com
www.softrock945.com

WZRR-FM 99.5 MHz (CR) Phone: 205-945-4646
244 Goodwin Crest Dr Suite 300 Fax: 205-942-8959
Birmingham, AL 35209
E-mail: wzrr@dbcradio.com
www.wzrr.com

WZZK-FM 104.7 MHz (Ctry) Phone: 205-916-1100
301 Beacon Pkwy W Suite 200 Fax: 205-916-1150
Birmingham, AL 35209
E-mail: wzzk@bhm.tis.net
www.wzzk.com

Attractions

Birmingham's steel industry roots can be seen at Sloss Furnaces National Historic Landmark, an ironworks plant that utilized ore dug from the Birmingham area hills between 1882 and 1971. The memorabilia of such state greats as Paul "Bear" Bryant, Jesse Owens, and Joe Louis are on display at the Alabama Sports Hall of Fame in Birmingham; exhibits at the Alabama Jazz Hall of Fame include the memorabilia of city native Erskine Hawkins, who wrote "Tuxedo Junction." Five Points South is Birmingham's top entertainment district, featuring live music, shopping, and restaurants.

16th Street Baptist Church Phone: 205-251-9402
1530 6th Ave N Fax: 205-251-9811
Birmingham, AL 35203
E-mail: chamlin@16thstreet.org
www.16thstreet.org

Alabama Jazz Hall of Fame Phone: 205-254-2731
1631 4th Ave N Fax: 205-254-2785
Birmingham, AL 35203
www.jazzhall.com/jazz

Alabama Princess Riverboat Phone: 256-549-1111
300 Albert Rains Blvd S
Gadsden, AL 35901

Alabama Sports Hall of Fame Phone: 205-323-6665
2150 Civic Ctr Blvd Fax: 205-252-2212
Birmingham, AL 35203
www.tech-comm.com/ashof

Alabama Symphonic Assn Phone: 205-251-6929
3621 6th Ave S Fax: 205-251-6840
Birmingham, AL 35222
E-mail: orchestra@nbc13.com
www.nbc13.com/aso

Alabama Theatre Phone: 205-252-2262
1817 3rd Ave N Fax: 205-251-3155
Birmingham, AL 35203
www.alabamatheatre.com

Arlington Antebellum Home & Gardens Phone: 205-780-5656
331 Cotton Ave SW Fax: 205-788-0585
Birmingham, AL 35211
www.ci.bham.al.us/arlington

Ballet South Phone: 205-322-4300
2726 1st Ave S Fax: 205-322-4444
Birmingham, AL 35233
www.alabamaballet.org

Barber Vintage Motorsports Museum Phone: 205-252-8377
2721 5th Ave S Fax: 205-252-8079
Birmingham, AL 35233
www.barbermuseum.org

Bessemer Flea Market Phone: 205-425-8510
1013 8th Ave N Fax: 205-425-8585
Bessemer, AL 35020

Bessemer Hall of History Phone: 205-426-1633
1905 Alabama Ave
Bessemer, AL 35020
www.bham.net/bessemercc/exhibits.html

Birmingham Botanical Gardens Phone: 205-414-3900
2612 Lane Park Rd Fax: 205-879-3751
Birmingham, AL 35223
www.bbgardens.org

Birmingham Broadway Series Phone: 205-328-8222
2805 6th Ave S Fax: 205-254-6068
Birmingham, AL 35233 TF: 877-328-8222
E-mail: bhambroadway@mindspring.com
www.bhambroadway.com

Birmingham Chamber Music Society Phone: 205-879-4902
Samford University Reid Chapel Fax: 205-879-8421
Birmingham, AL 35229

Birmingham Children's Theater Phone: 205-458-8181
3 Civic Center Plaza Fax: 205-458-8895
Birmingham, AL 35201
www.bham.net/bct

Birmingham Civil Rights Institute Phone: 205-328-9696
520 16th St N Fax: 205-323-5219
Birmingham, AL 35203
www.bham.net/bcri

Birmingham Festival Theater Phone: 205-933-2383
1901 1/2 11th Ave S
Birmingham, AL 35205

Birmingham Museum of Art Phone: 205-254-2566
2000 8th Ave N Fax: 205-254-2714
Birmingham, AL 35203
www.artsbma.org

Birmingham Opera Theater Phone: 205-322-6737
1817 3rd Ave N
Birmingham, AL 35203

Birmingham Zoo Phone: 205-879-0409
2630 Cahaba Rd Fax: 205-879-9426
Birmingham, AL 35223
E-mail: wreeder@traveller.com
www.bhm.tis.net/zoo

Children's Dance Foundation Phone: 205-870-0073
2828 19th St S Fax: 205-870-1301
Birmingham, AL 35209
E-mail: cdf@mindspring.com
www.mindspring.com/~cdf/home.htm

Cobb Lane
20th St S & 13th Ave S
Birmingham, AL 35205

DeSoto Caverns Phone: 256-378-7252
5181 DeSoto Caverns Pkwy Fax: 256-378-3678
Childersburg, AL 35044
E-mail: desoto@cavern.com
www.cavern.com/desoto

Environmental Center Phone: 205-226-4934
900 Arkadelphia Rd Birmingham Fax: 205-226-3046
Southern College TF: 800-523-5793
Birmingham, AL 35254

Five Points Music Hall Phone: 205-322-2263
1016 20th St S
Birmingham, AL 35205

Five Points South Phone: 205-458-8000
20th St S & 11th Ave S
Birmingham, AL 35233

George Ward Park Phone: 205-254-2391
16th Ave & 14th St S
Birmingham, AL 35204

Hoover Library Theatre Phone: 205-444-7888
200 Municipal Dr Fax: 205-444-7894
Hoover, AL 35216
www.hoover.lib.al.us/theatre

International Motor Sports Hall of Fame & Museum Phone: 256-362-5002
3198 Speedway Blvd Fax: 256-362-5002
Talladega, AL 35160
www.bham.net/sports/sports.html

John H Woods Imax Dome Theater Phone: 205-714-8300
200 19th St N Fax: 205-714-8400
Birmingham, AL 35203
www.mcwane.org/IMAX_Theater.htm

McWane Center Science Museum Phone: 205-714-8300
200 19th St N Fax: 205-714-8400
Birmingham, AL 35203
www.mcwane.org

Oak Mountain State Park Phone: 205-620-2520
S I-65 & Exit 246 Fax: 205-620-2531
Birmingham, AL 35124
www.bham.net/oakmtn

Rickwood Caverns Phone: 205-647-9692
370 Rickwood Park Rd
Warrior, AL 35180

Rickwood Field Phone: 205-458-8161
2100 Morris Ave
Birmingham, AL 35203
www.rickwood.com

Robert R Meyer Planetarium Phone: 205-226-4770
900 Arkadelphia Rd Birmingham
Southern College
Birmingham, AL 35254

Ruffner Mountain Nature Center Phone: 205-833-8112
1214 81st St S Fax: 205-836-3960
Birmingham, AL 35206
www.bham.net/ruffner

Sloss Furnaces National Historic Landmark Phone: 205-324-1911
20 32nd St N Fax: 205-324-6758
Birmingham, AL 35222

Southern Danceworks Phone: 205-307-6222
PO Box 11983
Birmingham, AL 35202

Southern Museum of Flight Phone: 205-833-8226
4343 73rd St N Fax: 205-836-2439
Birmingham, AL 35206
E-mail: pamip01@aol.com
www.bham.net/flight/museum.html

Southern Research Institute Phone: 205-581-2000
2000 9th Ave S Fax: 205-581-2726
Birmingham, AL 35205 TF: 800-967-6774
E-mail: southern@sri.org
www.sri.org

Tannehill Ironworks Historical State Park Phone: 205-477-5711
12632 Confederate Pkwy Fax: 205-477-9400
McCalla, AL 35111
www.tannehill.org/

Terrific New Theatre Phone: 205-328-0868
2821 2nd Ave S
Birmingham, AL 35233

Treetop Nature Trail Phone: 205-663-7930
Alabama Wildlife Ctr Oak Mountain
State Pk
Birmingham, AL 35124

VisionLand Amusement Park Phone: 205-481-4750
5051 Prince St Fax: 205-481-4758
Bessemer, AL 35022
E-mail: administration@visionlandpark.com
www.visionlandpark.com

Vulcan Brewing Co Phone: 205-326-6677
3118 3rd Ave S
Birmingham, AL 35233

Sports Teams & Facilities

Alabama Angels (soccer) Phone: 205-967-5854
3408 Westbury Pl Fax: 205-822-6321
Birmingham, AL 35223

Alabama Saints (soccer) Phone: 205-967-5854
3408 Westbury Pl Fax: 205-967-6321
Birmingham, AL 35223
E-mail: ronbuff@bham.mindspring.com

Birmingham Barons (baseball) Phone: 205-988-3200
100 Ben Chapman Dr Fax: 205-988-9698
Birmingham, AL 35244
E-mail: barons@barons.com
www.barons.com

Birmingham Bulls (hockey)
2100 Richard Arrington Jr Blvd N BJCC
Birmingham, AL 35203
www.birminghambulls.com
Phone: 205-458-8833
Fax: 205-458-8489

Birmingham Race Course
PO Box 101748
Birmingham, AL 35210
www.bhamdogs.com
Phone: 205-838-7500
Fax: 205-838-7407
TF: 800-998-8238

Birmingham Steeldogs (football)
2100 Richard Arrington Jr Blvd N BJCC
Birmingham, AL 35203
www.steeldogs.com
Phone: 205-458-8833
Fax: 205-458-8489

Birmingham-Jefferson Convention Complex
2100 Richard Arrington Jr Blvd
Birmingham, AL 35203
E-mail: info@bjcc.org
www.bjcc.org
Phone: 205-458-8400
Fax: 205-458-8437

Talladega Super Speedway
3366 Speedway Blvd
Talladega, AL 35160
www.daytonausa.com/ts
Phone: 256-362-2261
Fax: 256-761-4777

Annual Events

Alabama Jubilee Rodeo (mid-March) 205-458-8400
Alabama State Fair (late October) 205-458-8001
American Indian Dance Festival & Powwow (early April). 256-378-7252
Birmingham Fall Home Show (mid-September). 205-680-0234
Birmingham Festival of Arts Salute (mid-April). 205-252-7652
Birmingham Heritage Festival (early August) 205-324-3333
Bluegrass at Horsepens 40 (late April-early May). . . .256-570-0002
Bluff Park Art Show (early October). 205-822-0078
Bruno's Memorial Golf Classic (late April) 205-967-4745
Cahaba Riverfest (early June) .205-322-5326
Christmas at Arlington (December). 205-780-5656
Christmas at the Alabama (late December) 205-252-2262
Christmas Heritage Tour (December) 205-426-1628
Christmas Light Show (November-December) 256-378-7252
Christmas Tree Lighting (late November) 205-620-6403
Christmas Village Festival Arts & Crafts Show (early November) 205-836-7178
City Stages-A Birmingham Festival (mid-June) 205-251-1272
Cottontail's Arts & Crafts Show (early March) 205-836-7178
Crape Myrtle Festival (late July). 205-254-2472
Dixie Classic & Heartland Cruisers Open Car Show (late September) 205-477-5711
Do Dah Day Festival (mid-May). 205-595-7281
Eddleman Pro Tennis Classic (early May) 205-980-1000
Festival of Trees (late November-late December) 205-939-9671
Function at Tuxedo Junction Jazz Festival (late July) 205-788-3672
Garden Fiesta Plant Sale (early April). 205-414-3900
Halloween Fairyland (late October) 205-477-5711
Home & Garden Show (early March) 205-680-0234
Imagination Festival (late May) 205-595-6306
Magic City Classic Parade & Football Game (late October). 205-254-2391
Mexican Festival (early May & early July) 800-421-8564
NASCAR Talladega DieHard 500 (mid-April) 256-362-9064
NASCAR Winston 500 (mid-October). 256-362-9064
Oktoberfest (mid-September) 205-923-6564
Old Time Folk & Dulcimer Festival (mid-May) 800-421-8564
Powerman Alabama Duathlon (late March) 205-939-8892
Septemberfest (late September) 256-378-7252
Sidewalk Moving Picture Festival (early October) . . .205-414-1984
Southern Appalachian Dulcimer Festival (early May) 205-477-5711
Southern Women's Show (early October) 800-849-0248
Spring Fiesta (early April) 205-414-3900
Spring Folklore Festival (late April) 205-477-5711
Summerfest (early July-early August) 205-324-2426
Tannehill Civil War Reenactment (late May) 205-477-5711
Tannehill Labor Day Celebration (early September) 205-477-5711
Tannehill Spring Craft Show (early May). 205-477-5711
Tannehill Trade Days (mid-March-November). 205-477-5711
Tannehill Trout Tournament (late April) 205-477-5711
Tannehill Village Christmas (early-mid-December) 205-477-5711
Viva Health Vulcan Run Weekend (early November) 205-879-5344
Whistle Stop Festival & 5K Run (mid-May) 205-956-5962
World of Wheels Custom Auto Show (mid-February). 205-655-4950
Zoolight Safari (late November-December) 205-879-0458

Boise, Idaho

County: Ada

BOISE is located along the banks of the Boise River in southwestern Idaho. Major cities within 100 miles include Nampa and Caldwell, Idaho.

Area (Land)	46.1 sq mi
Area (Water)	0.2 sq mi
Elevation	2,726 ft
Latitude	43-61-36 N
Longitude	116-20-25 W
Time Zone	MST
Area Code	208

Climate

Boise's climate features cold winters and fairly mild summers. Winter high temperatures average in the high 30s to low 40s, with lows in the 20s. The average annual snowfall in Boise is just under 21 inches. Summer days are very warm, with high temperatures averaging near 90 degrees, while evenings cool down dramatically into the 50s. November and January are the wettest months in Boise; July and August are the driest.

Average Temperatures & Precipitation

Temperatures

	Jan	Feb	Mar	Apr	May	Jun	Jul	Aug	Sep	Oct	Nov	Dec
High	36	44	53	61	71	81	90	88	77	65	49	38
Low	22	28	32	37	44	52	58	57	48	39	31	23

Precipitation

	Jan	Feb	Mar	Apr	May	Jun	Jul	Aug	Sep	Oct	Nov	Dec
Inches	1.5	1.1	1.3	1.2	1.1	0.8	0.4	0.4	0.8	0.8	1.5	1.4

History

Originally inhabited by the Shoshone people, the Boise area was first settled by Europeans in 1834 with the establishment of Fort Boise (originally located some 40 miles from the present day city of Boise). Frequent attacks by the Indians led to the abandonment of Fort Boise in 1854, but eight years later, gold was discovered in the Boise Basin and pioneers were drawn to the area by the possibility of fortune. In 1863, a new Fort Boise was established by the U.S. Military to protect the new settlers from the Indians, and the city of Boise was established adjacent to the fort. Boise was incorporated the following year and chosen as the capital of the Idaho Territory.

Boise grew quickly during its early years, both as a center for gold mining and as a center for commerce—the city was a major thoroughfare along the Oregon Trail, which ran from Missouri to Oregon. Other factors that prompted Boise's growth throughout the years include economic opportunities brought about by improved irrigation in the valley and the construction of the Arrowrock Dam during the early 20th Century; the coming of the Union Pacific Railroad in 1925; the massive influx of Basque immigrants from Europe during the 1930s; and the new military presence that came to the area during World War II with the development of Gowen Field Air Force Base.

With more than 157,000 residents, Boise today continues to grow steadily. Known as the "City of Trees" (the name "Boise" was derived from the French phrase meaning "wooded"), Boise is not only Idaho's largest metropolitan area, but the city is also the governmental, financial, and commercial center of the state. Boise is the corporate home of several major U.S. companies, including Boise Cascade and Albertson's, and others, such as Hewlett-Packard, have regional headquarters or divisions in the area.

Population

1990 Census	125,551
1998 Estimate	157,452
% Change	24.3

Racial/Ethnic Breakdown

White	94.4%
Black	0.4%
Other	5.2%
Hispanic Origin (may be of any race)	2.7%

Age Breakdown

Under 5 years	7.4%
5 to 17	18.2%
18 to 20	4.6%
21 to 24	6.5%
25 to 34	18.5%
35 to 44	16.5%
45 to 54	9.5%
55 to 64	7.0%
65 to 74	6.6%
75+ years	5.3%
Median Age	32.3

Gender Breakdown

Male	48.4%
Female	51.6%

Government

Type of Government: Mayor-Council

Boise City Clerk
PO Box 500
Boise, ID 83701
Phone: 208-384-3710
Fax: 208-384-3711

Boise City Council
PO Box 500
Boise, ID 83701
Phone: 208-384-4422
Fax: 208-384-4420

Boise City Hall
PO Box 500
Boise, ID 83701
Phone: 208-384-3700
Fax: 208-384-3750

Boise Financial Management Div
PO Box 500
Boise, ID 83701
Phone: 208-384-3715
Fax: 208-384-3995

Boise Fire Dept
101 S Capitol Blvd Suite 701
Boise, ID 83702
Phone: 208-384-3950
Fax: 208-384-4453

Boise Human Resources Div
601 W Idaho
Boise, ID 83701
Phone: 208-384-3850
Fax: 208-384-3868

Boise Legal Dept
PO Box 500
Boise, ID 83701
Phone: 208-384-3870
Fax: 208-384-4454

Boise Mayor
PO Box 500
Boise, ID 83701
Phone: 208-384-4422
Fax: 208-384-4420

Boise Parks & Recreation Dept
1104 Royal Blvd
Boise, ID 83706
Phone: 208-384-4240
Fax: 208-384-4127

Boise Planning & Development Services Dept
PO Box 500
Boise, ID 83701
Phone: 208-384-3830
Fax: 208-384-3753

Boise Police Dept
7200 Barrister Dr
Boise, ID 83704
Phone: 208-377-6670
Fax: 208-377-6668

Boise Public Library
715 S Capitol Blvd
Boise, ID 83702
Phone: 208-384-4238
Fax: 208-384-4025

Boise Public Works Dept
PO Box 500
Boise, ID 83701
Phone: 208-384-3900
Fax: 208-384-3905

Boise Treasurer
PO Box 500
Boise, ID 83701
Phone: 208-384-3780
Fax: 208-388-3995

Important Phone Numbers

AAA....208-342-9391
Ada County Assessor's Office....208-364-2400
Ada County Assn of Realtors....208-376-0363
American Express Travel....208-343-7915
Associated Taxpayers of Idaho....208-344-5581
Driver's License/Vehicle Registration Information....208-377-6520
Emergency....911
Poison Control Center....800-860-0620
Voter Registration Information....208-364-2323
Weather....208-342-8303

Information Sources

Ada County
650 Main St
Boise, ID 83702
Phone: 208-364-2333
Fax: 208-364-2331

Better Business Bureau Serving Southwest Idaho & Eastern Oregon
4619 Emerald St Suite A2
Boise, ID 83706
www.boise.bbb.org
Phone: 208-342-4649
Fax: 208-342-5116

Boise Centre on the Grove
850 W Front St
Boise, ID 83702
www.boise.org/cvb/bcg.html
Phone: 208-336-8900
Fax: 208-336-8803

Boise Convention & Visitors Bureau
168 N 9th St Suite 200
Boise, ID 83702
www.boise.org/bcvb/index.html
Phone: 208-344-7777
Fax: 208-344-6236
TF: 800-635-5240

Boise Metro Chamber of Commerce
PO Box 2368
Boise, ID 83701
www.boise.org
Phone: 208-472-5205
Fax: 208-472-5201

Online Resources

4Boise.com
www.4boise.com

About.com Guide to Boise
boise.about.com/citiestowns/mountainus/boise/mbody.htm

Anthill City Guide Boise
www.anthill.com/city.asp?city=boise

Area Guide Boise
boise.areaguides.net

Boise CityLink
www.usacitylink.com/citylink/boise

Boiseonline
www.boiseonline.com

City Knowledge Boise
www.cityknowledge.com/id_boise.htm

Destination Northwest-Boise
www.destinationnw.com/idaho/boise.htm

Excite.com Boise City Guide
www.excite.com/travel/countries/united_states/idaho/boise

Insiders' Guide to Boise
www.insiders.com/boise/

Lodging.com Boise Idaho
www.lodging.com/auto/guides/boise-id.html

Onroute Destinations-Boise
www.onroute.com/destinations/idaho/boise.html

Area Communities

Communities in the Boise metropolitan area (Ada and Canyon counties) with populations greater than 5,000 include:

Caldwell
PO Box 1177
Caldwell, ID 83606
Phone: 208-455-3000
Fax: 208-455-3003

Garden City
201 E 50th St
Garden City, ID 83714
Phone: 208-377-1831
Fax: 208-377-9656

Meridian
33 E Idaho Ave
Meridian, ID 83642
Phone: 208-888-4433
Fax: 208-887-4813

Nampa
411 3rd St S
Nampa, ID 83651
Phone: 208-465-2225
Fax: 208-465-2227

Economy

Boise has a diverse economic base that ranges from agriculture to electronics manufacturing. Major U.S. corporations representing various industries that are headquartered in Boise include Albertson's (grocery chain), Boise Cascade (paper manufacturer), Micron Technology (electronics manufacturer), Morrison-Knudson (general contractor), and J.R. Simplot (agribusiness). Services is the largest employment sector in the Boise MSA, followed by retail trade and manufacturing.

Unemployment Rate 3.6%**
Per Capita Income.......................... $26,017*
Median Family Income...................... $48,500**

** Information given is for Ada County.*
*** Information given is for the Boise Metropolitan Statistical Area (MSA), which includes Ada and Canyon counties.*

Principal Industries & Number of Wage Earners

Boise MSA* - 1999

Industry	Wage Earners
Construction	15,186
Finance, Insurance, & Real Estate	11,339
Government	32,158
Manufacturing	36,588
Retail Trade	38,341
Services	53,982
Transportation, Communications, & Public Utilities	10,949
Wholesale Trade	12,570

** Information given is for the Boise Metropolitan Statistical Area (MSA), which includes Ada and Canyon counties.*

Major Employers

Ada County
650 Main St
Boise, ID 83702
Phone: 208-364-2333
Fax: 208-364-2331

Albertson's Inc
250 E Parkcenter Blvd
Boise, ID 83706
E-mail: cs_online@albertsons.com
www.albertsons.com
Phone: 208-395-6200
Fax: 208-395-6110
TF: 888-746-7252

Boise Cascade Corp
PO Box 50
Boise, ID 83728
E-mail: bcweb@bc.com
www.bc.com
Phone: 208-384-6161
Fax: 208-384-7189

Boise City Hall
PO Box 500
Boise, ID 83701
www.ci.boise.id.us/city_of_boise
Phone: 208-384-3700
Fax: 208-384-3750

Boise Public Schools Administration
1207 Fort St
Boise, ID 83702
www.sd01.k12.id.us/
Phone: 208-338-3400
Fax: 208-338-3487

Boise State University
1910 University Dr
Boise, ID 83725
www.idbsu.edu
Phone: 208-426-1156
Fax: 208-426-3765
TF: 800-824-7017

First Security Bank of Idaho NA
119 N 9th St
Boise, ID 83702
Phone: 208-393-4000
Fax: 208-393-2466
TF: 800-574-4200

Hewlett-Packard Co
11311 Chinden Blvd
Boise, ID 83714
www.hp.com
Phone: 208-396-6000
Fax: 208-396-2896

Micron Electronics Inc
900 E Karcher Rd
Nampa, ID 83687
E-mail: direct.sales@micron.com
www.micronpc.com
Phone: 208-893-3434
Fax: 208-898-7375
TF: 800-438-3343

Micron Technology Inc
8000 S Federal Way
Boise, ID 83707
www.micron.com
Phone: 208-368-4000
Fax: 208-368-4431

Morrison Knudsen Corp
720 Park Blvd
Boise, ID 83729
E-mail: mkcorp@mk.com
www.mk.com
Phone: 208-386-5000
Fax: 208-386-7186
TF: 800-635-5000

Saint Alphonsus Regional Medical Center
1055 N Curtis Rd
Boise, ID 83706
www.sarmc.org
Phone: 208-367-2121
Fax: 208-367-3123
TF: 877-341-2121

Saint Luke's Regional Medical Center
190 E Bannock St
Boise, ID 83712
www.slrmc.org
Phone: 208-381-2222
Fax: 208-381-4649

Sears Credit Center
9324 W Emerald St
Boise, ID 83704
Phone: 208-327-6009
Fax: 208-327-6084

Simplot JR Co
PO Box 27
Boise, ID 83707
E-mail: jrs_info@simplot.com
www.simplot.com
Phone: 208-336-2110
Fax: 208-389-7515
TF: 800-635-5008

US Bank NA
101 S Capitol Blvd
Boise, ID 83702
Phone: 208-383-7000
Fax: 208-383-7274
TF: 800-872-2657

Quality of Living Indicators

Total Crime Index.................................... 7,649
(rates per 100,000 inhabitants)

Violent Crime
Murder/manslaughter........................... 2

Forcible rape 74
Robbery....................................... 67
Aggravated assault............................ 351

Property Crime
Burglary 1,279
Larceny theft 5,548
Motor vehicle theft 328

Cost of Living Index...................................101.6
(national average = 100)

Median Home Price.................................$123,900

Education

Public Schools

Boise Public Schools Administration
1207 Fort St
Boise, ID 83702
www.sd01.k12.id.us/
Phone: 208-338-3400
Fax: 208-338-3487

Number of Schools
Elementary.................................. 34
Middle 8
High... 5

Student/Teacher Ratio
All Grades 19.0:1

Private Schools

Number of Schools (all grades)..................... 28

Colleges & Universities

Albertson College of Idaho
2112 Cleveland Blvd
Caldwell, ID 83605
www.acofi.edu
Phone: 208-459-5011
Fax: 208-459-5757
TF: 800-224-3246

Boise Bible College
8695 Marigold St
Boise, ID 83714
E-mail: biobible@micron.net
netnow.micron.net/~boibible
Phone: 208-376-7731
Fax: 208-376-7743
TF: 800-893-7755

Boise State University
1910 University Dr
Boise, ID 83725
www.idbsu.edu
Phone: 208-426-1156
Fax: 208-426-3765
TF: 800-824-7017

ITT Technical Institute
12302 W Explorer Dr
Boise, ID 83713
www.itt-tech.edu
Phone: 208-322-8844
Fax: 208-322-0173
TF: 800-666-4888

Northwest Nazarene College
623 Holly St
Nampa, ID 83686
www.nnc.edu
Phone: 208-467-8011
Fax: 208-467-8645
TF: 800-584-9812

Hospitals

Saint Alphonsus Regional Medical Center
1055 N Curtis Rd
Boise, ID 83706
www.sarmc.org
Phone: 208-367-2121
Fax: 208-367-3123
TF: 877-341-2121

Saint Luke's Regional Medical Center
190 E Bannock St
Boise, ID 83712
www.slrmc.org
Phone: 208-381-2222
Fax: 208-381-4649

Veterans Affairs Medical Center
500 W Fort St
Boise, ID 83702
Phone: 208-422-1000
Fax: 208-422-1148

Transportation

Airport(s)

Boise Air Terminal (BOI)
4 miles SW of downtown (approx 10 minutes) 208-383-3110

Mass Transit

The BUS
$.75 Base fare................................208-336-1010

Rail/Bus

Greyhound/Trailways Bus Station
1212 W Bannock St
Boise, ID 83702
Phone: 208-343-3681
TF: 800-231-2222

Utilities

Electricity
Idaho Power Co..............................208-388-2323
www.idahopower.com

Gas
Intermountain Gas Co 208-377-6840
www.igfcu.org

Water
United Water Idaho............................208-362-1300
www.unitedwater.com/uwid

Garbage Collection/Recycling
Browning-Ferris Industries 208-338-9326

Telecommunications

Telephone
Qwest.....................................800-244-1111
www.qwest.com

Cable Television
AT & T Cable Services.........................208-375-8288
www.cable.att.com

Internet Service Providers (ISPs)
CyberHighway Internet Services 208-323-9214
www.cyberhighway.net
Micron Internet Services.......................208-368-5400
www.micron.net
RMC Internet Services.........................208-336-9200
www.rmci.net

Banks

Bank of America
421 N Cole Rd
Boise, ID 83704
Phone: 208-323-8700
Fax: 208-323-8757
TF: 800-442-5002

Farmers & Merchants State Bank
209 N 12th St
Boise, ID 83702
Phone: 208-343-7848
Fax: 208-343-7979

First Security Bank of Idaho NA
119 N 9th St
Boise, ID 83702
Phone: 208-393-4000
Fax: 208-393-2466
TF: 800-574-4200

KeyBank NA Boise District
702 W Idaho St
Boise, ID 83702
Phone: 208-334-7000
Fax: 208-364-8540
TF: 800-777-5391

Washington Federal Savings & Loan Assn
PO Box 1460
Boise, ID 83702
Phone: 208-343-1833
Fax: 208-338-7374

Wells Fargo Bank
877 W Main St
Boise, ID 83702
Phone: 208-389-4020
Fax: 208-389-4016
TF: 800-869-3557

Shopping

Boise Factory Outlets
6852 S Eisenman Rd
Boise, ID 83716
Phone: 208-331-5000
Fax: 208-331-5002

Boise Towne Square Mall
350 N Milwaukee St
West Boise, ID 83788
Phone: 208-378-4400
Fax: 208-378-4933

Media

Newspapers and Magazines

Boise Weekly
109 S 4th St
Boise, ID 83702
E-mail: info@boiseweekly.com
www.boiseweekly.com
Phone: 208-344-2055
Fax: 208-342-4733

Idaho Statesman*
PO Box 40
Boise, ID 83707
www.idahostatesman.com
Phone: 208-377-6200
Fax: 208-377-6449
TF: 800-635-8934

**Indicates major daily newspapers*

Television

KAID-TV Ch 4 (PBS)
1455 N Orchard St
Boise, ID 83706
E-mail: iptv@idptv.idbsu.edu
idptv.state.id.us
Phone: 208-373-7220
Fax: 208-373-7245
TF: 800-543-6868

KBCI-TV Ch 2 (CBS)
140 N 16th St
Boise, ID 83702
www.2online.com
Phone: 208-336-5222
Fax: 208-472-2212

KIVI-TV Ch 6 (ABC)
1866 E Chisholm Dr
Nampa, ID 83687
Phone: 208-336-0500
Fax: 208-381-6682

KNIN-TV Ch 9 (UPN)
816 W Bannock St Suite 402
Boise, ID 83702
www.knin.com
Phone: 208-331-0909
Fax: 208-344-0119

KTRV-TV Ch 12 (Fox)
679 6th St N Ext
Nampa, ID 83687
ktrv.com
Phone: 208-466-1200
Fax: 208-467-6958

KTVB-TV Ch 7 (NBC)
5407 Fairview Ave
Boise, ID 83707
www.ktvb.com
Phone: 208-375-7277
Fax: 208-375-7770
TF: 800-559-7277

Radio

KBXL-FM 94.1 MHz (Rel)
1477 S Five-Mile Rd
Boise, ID 83709
Phone: 208-377-3790
Fax: 208-377-3792

KCIX-FM 105.9 MHz (AC)
5257 Fairview Ave Suite 250
Boise, ID 83706
Phone: 208-376-6666
Fax: 208-323-7918

KGEM-AM 1140 kHz (Nost)
5601 Cassia St
Boise, ID 83705
Phone: 208-344-3511
Fax: 208-336-3264

KIZN-FM 92.3 MHz (Ctry)
1419 W Bannock St
Boise, ID 83702
www.kizn.com
Phone: 208-336-3670
Fax: 208-336-3734

KJHY-FM 101.9 MHz (Span)
PO Box 1600
Nampa, ID 83653
Phone: 208-463-2987
Fax: 208-466-8750

KJOT-FM 105.1 MHz (CR)
5601 Cassia St
Boise, ID 83705
Phone: 208-344-3511
Fax: 208-336-3264

KKGL-FM 96.9 MHz (Rock)
1419 W Bannock St
Boise, ID 83702
Phone: 208-336-3670
Fax: 208-336-3734

KLTB-FM 104.3 MHz (Oldies)
PO Box 63
Boise, ID 83707
www.oldies1043.com
Phone: 208-384-5483
Fax: 208-385-9064

KTIK-AM 1350 kHz (Sports)
251 S Capitol Blvd
Boise, ID 83702
ktik.com
Phone: 208-377-5845
Fax: 208-375-9248

KXLT-FM 107.9 MHz (AC)
5257 Fairview Ave Suite 250
Boise, ID 83706
Phone: 208-376-6666
Fax: 208-323-7918

Attractions

The Boise River flows through the heart of the City of Boise, and 14 miles of riverside have been developed into a Greenbelt with a network of parks and outdoor recreational areas. Less than an hour's drive from the city is Bogus Basin Ski Resort, with both alpine and cross-country skiing, as well as night-lighted runs. Near Boise also is the Snake River Birds of Prey Natural Area, which has an especially large concentration of eagles, falcons, hawks, and owls.

Ballet Idaho
501 S 8th St Esther Simplot Annex Suite A
Boise, ID 83702
www.balletidaho.org
Phone: 208-343-0556
Fax: 208-424-3129

Basque Museum & Cultural Center
611 Grove St
Boise, ID 83702
E-mail: basqmusm@micron.net
Phone: 208-343-2671
Fax: 208-336-4801

Bishop's House
2420 Old Penitentiary Rd
Boise, ID 83712
Phone: 208-342-3279

Bogus Basin Ski Area
2405 Bogus Basin Rd
Boise, ID 83702
E-mail: info@bogusbasin.com
www.bogusbasin.com
Phone: 208-332-5100
Fax: 208-332-5102
TF: 800-367-4397

Boise Art Museum
670 Julia Davis Dr
Boise, ID 83702
E-mail: boiseart@micron.net
www.boiseartmuseum.org
Phone: 208-345-8330
Fax: 208-345-2247

Boise Philharmonic
516 S 9th St
Boise, ID 83702
Phone: 208-344-7849
Fax: 208-336-9078

BSU Pavilion
1910 University Dr
Boise, ID 83725
www.bsupavilion.com
Phone: 208-426-1900
Fax: 208-426-1998

Discovery Center of Idaho
131 E Myrtle St
Boise, ID 83702
Phone: 208-343-9895
Fax: 208-343-0105

Hagerman Fossil Beds National Monument
221 N State St
Hagerman, ID 83332
www.nps.gov/hafo/
Phone: 208-837-4793
Fax: 208-837-4857

Idaho Botanical Garden
2355 N Penitentiary Rd
Boise, ID 83712
E-mail: idbotgrd@micron.net
www.idahobotanicalgarden.org
Phone: 208-343-8649
Fax: 208-343-3601

Idaho Dance Theatre
1700 University Dr Boise State University Special Events Ctr
Boise, ID 83725
E-mail: idt@micron.net
theatre.boisestate.edu/idahodance
Phone: 208-331-9592
Fax: 208-331-8205

Idaho State Capitol
700 W Jefferson St
Boise, ID 83720
Phone: 208-334-3468

Idaho State Historical Museum
610 Julia Davis Dr
Boise, ID 83702
Phone: 208-334-2120
Fax: 208-334-4059

Idaho Theatre for Youth
520 S 9th St
Boise, ID 83702
Phone: 208-345-0060
Fax: 208-345-6433

Morrison Center for the Performing Arts
2201 Campus Ln Boise State University
Boise, ID 83725
mc.idbsu.edu
Phone: 208-426-1609
Fax: 208-426-3021

Morrison-Knudsen Nature Center
600 S Walnut St
Boise, ID 83706
www.state.id.us/fishgame/mknc.htm
Phone: 208-334-2225
Fax: 208-334-2148

Mountain Home Air Force Base
366 Gunfighter Ave Suite 152
Mountain Home AFB, ID 83648
E-mail: bleleoj@cs366.mountainhome.af.mil
www.mountainhome.af.mil
Phone: 208-828-2111
Fax: 208-828-6387

National Interagency Fire Center
3833 S Development Ave
Boise, ID 83705
www.nifc.gov
Phone: 208-387-5512
Fax: 208-387-5730

Old Idaho Penitentiary
2445 Old Penitentiary Rd
Boise, ID 83712
E-mail: oldpen@rmci.net
Phone: 208-334-2844
Fax: 208-334-3225

Opera Idaho
501 S 8th St Suite B
Boise, ID 83702
Phone: 208-345-3531
Fax: 208-342-7566

Snake River Birds of Prey Area
Swan Falls Rd
Kuna, ID 83634
Phone: 208-384-3300

Stage Coach Theatre
Orchard St & Overland Rd
Boise, ID 83705
nssnet.com/stagecoach
Phone: 208-342-2000

Warhawk Air Museum
4917 Aviation Way
Caldwell, ID 83605
Phone: 208-454-2854

Western Idaho Fairgrounds
5610 Glenwood
Boise, ID 83714
www.idahofair.com
Phone: 208-376-3247
Fax: 208-375-9972

World Center for Birds of Prey
566 W Flying Hawk Ln
Boise, ID 83709
www.peregrinefund.org
Phone: 208-362-8687
Fax: 208-362-2376

Zoo Boise
355 N Julia Davis Dr
Boise, ID 83702
www.sunvalleyski.com/zooboise/
Phone: 208-384-4260
Fax: 208-384-4194

Sports Teams & Facilities

Boise Hawks (baseball)
5600 Glenwood St Memorial Stadium
Boise, ID 83714
www.diamondsportsworld.com/hawks
Phone: 208-322-5000
Fax: 208-322-7432

Les Bois Horse Racing Park
5610 Glenwood Rd
Boise, ID 83714
www.lesboisracing.com
Phone: 208-376-7223
Fax: 208-376-7227
TF: 800-376-3991

Annual Events

Art in the Park (early September) 208-345-8330
Boise River Festival (late June) 208-338-8887
Boise Tour Train & Trolley (June-October).........208-342-4796

Buy.com Boise Open (mid-September) 208-939-6028
Festival of Trees (late November-early December) . . .208-367-2797
Hewlett-Packard LaserJet Women's Challenge
(early June) 208-672-7223
Idaho Business Expo (late January) 208-323-4464
Idaho City Arts & Crafts Festival (early June) 208-392-4553
Idaho Great Potato Marathon (early May) 208-344-5501
Idaho Shakespeare Festival
(mid-May-September) 208-336-9221
National Oldtime Fiddlers' Contest (mid-June). 208-549-0452
Race to Robie Creek (mid-April). 208-368-9990
Snake River Stampede (mid-July) 208-466-8497
Western Idaho Fair (mid-August). 208-376-3247
Womens Fitness Celebration (late September) 208-331-2221

Boston, Massachusetts

County: **Suffolk**

BOSTON is located in eastern Massachusetts on the Atlantic Coast. Cities within 100 miles include Worcester and Springfield, Massachusetts; Providence, Rhode Island; and Hartford, Connecticut.

Area (Land) .... 48.4 sq mi
Area (Water)............................. 41.2 sq mi
Elevation..................................... 20 ft
Latitude ....42-35-83 N
Longitude............................... 71-06-03 W
Time Zone ....EST
Area Code................................617, 781

Climate

Boston's climate is moderated by the Atlantic Ocean. Winters are cold and damp, with average temperatures around 31 degrees and an average annual snowfall of over 40 inches. November and December are Boston's wettest months. Summers are generally mild, with an average temperature of 71 degrees. Daytime high temperatures occasionally climb into the 80s, but evenings are usually cool, with temperatures in the low to mid-60s.

Average Temperatures & Precipitation

Temperatures

	Jan	Feb	Mar	Apr	May	Jun	Jul	Aug	Sep	Oct	Nov	Dec
High	36	38	46	56	67	76	82	80	73	63	52	40
Low	22	23	31	40	50	59	65	64	57	47	38	27

Precipitation

	Jan	Feb	Mar	Apr	May	Jun	Jul	Aug	Sep	Oct	Nov	Dec
Inches	3.6	3.6	3.7	3.6	3.3	3.1	2.8	3.2	3.1	3.3	4.2	4.0

History

Boston was founded and incorporated as a city in 1630, three years after the Pilgrims landed in nearby Plymouth. In the decade that followed, the first general court and the first Board of Selectmen in America were established in Boston, Harvard University was founded in nearby Cambridge, and Boston's population grew to 16,000 people.

During the 1770s, Boston was the site of numerous historical events, beginning with the Boston Massacre in March 1770. The Boston Tea Party took place in Boston Harbor in 1773. The first shots signaling the beginning of the American Revolution were fired at nearby Lexington and Concord in April 1775, and the Battle of Bunker Hill was fought in Charlestown in July of that year. In March 1776, the British withdrew their troops from Boston, marking the end of the Revolution. Twelve years later, in 1788, Boston was chosen as the capital of Massachusetts.

Historical figures associated with Boston and the surrounding area include Paul Revere, John Hancock, John Adams, John Quincy Adams, and John F. Kennedy. Literary giants, including Louisa May Alcott, Nathanial Hawthorne, Ralph Waldo Emerson, Henry David Thoreau, and Henry Wadsworth Longfellow, were also among the community's famous residents. In fact, publishing is an important industry in Boston today, with many top publishing companies, including Random House, headquartered in the area.

Boston's access to the Atlantic Ocean and rich natural resources in the surrounding area helped the city grow as a major center of industry and commerce. Today, major industries in the city range from fishing to shipbuilding, finance to high technology. With several of the nation's top universities, including Harvard, Boston University and MIT, and more than 30 other institutions of higher education, the Boston area is also the education hub of the northeastern United States.

Boston today, with a more than a half-million residents, is the largest city in New England. It is estimated that by the year 2010 the city's population will exceed 680,000.

Population

1990 Census 574,283
1998 Estimate.............................555,447
% Change ....-3.3
2010 Projection 688,112

Racial/Ethnic Breakdown

White....................................59.0%
Black 23.8%
Other.....................................6.5%
Hispanic Origin (may be of any race)........ 10.8%

Age Breakdown

Under 5 years.............................. 6.4%
5 to 14.....................................9.9%
15 to 44..................................57.0%
45 to 64..................................15.2%
65+ years 11.5%
Median Age.................................30.3

Gender Breakdown

Male.....................................48.1%
Female...................................51.9%

Government

Type of Government: Mayor-Council

Boston City Clerk
City Hall Rm 601
Boston, MA 02201
Phone: 617-635-4600
Fax: 617-635-4658

Boston City Council
1 City Hall Plaza
Boston, MA 02201
Phone: 617-635-3040
Fax: 617-635-4203

Boston City Hall
1 City Hall Plaza
Boston, MA 02201
Phone: 617-635-4000

Boston Fire Dept
115 Southampton St
Boston, MA 02118
Phone: 617-343-3610
Fax: 617-343-2104

Boston Human Resources Office
1 City Hall Plaza Rm 612
Boston, MA 02201
Phone: 617-635-4689
Fax: 617-635-2950

Boston Human Services Office
1 City Hall Plaza Rm 603
Boston, MA 02118
Phone: 617-635-3446
Fax: 617-635-3496

Boston Mayor
1 City Hall Plaza 5th Fl
Boston, MA 02201
Phone: 617-635-4500
Fax: 617-635-4090

Boston Neighborhood Development Dept
26 Court St 11th Fl
Boston, MA 02108
Phone: 617-635-3880
Fax: 617-635-0561

Boston Parks & Recreation Dept
1010 Massachusetts Ave
Boston, MA 02118
Phone: 617-635-4505
Fax: 617-635-3173

Boston Police Dept
1 Schroeder Plaza
Boston, MA 02120
Phone: 617-343-4500
Fax: 617-343-4587

Boston Public Library
700 Boylston St Copley Sq
Boston, MA 02117
Phone: 617-536-5400
Fax: 617-236-4306

Boston Public Works Dept
1 City Hall Plaza Rm 714
Boston, MA 02201
Phone: 617-635-4900
Fax: 617-635-7499

Boston Redevelopment Authority
1 City Hall Sq
Boston, MA 02201
Phone: 617-722-4300
Fax: 617-367-5916

Boston Transportation Dept
City Hall Rm 721
Boston, MA 02201
Phone: 617-635-4680
Fax: 617-635-4295

Boston Treasury Dept
1 City Hall Plaza Rm M5
Boston, MA 02201
Phone: 617-635-4138
Fax: 617-635-4702

Boston Water & Sewer Commission
425 Summer St
Boston, MA 02210
Phone: 617-330-9400
Fax: 617-439-3028

Important Phone Numbers

AAA....781-871-5880
American Express Travel....617-723-8400
Boston Treasury Dept....617-635-4138
Boston By Phone....888-733-2678
Dental Referral....508-651-7511
Driver's License/Vehicle Registration Information....617-351-4500
Emergency....911
Greater Boston Real Estate Board....617-423-8700
HotelDocs....800-468-3537
Massachusetts Assn of Realtors....781-890-3700
Massachusetts Dept of Revenue....617-887-6367
Massachusetts Dept of Revenue Div of Local Services....617-626-2300
Medical Referral....800-488-5959
Poison Control Center....617-232-2120
Time/Temp....617-637-1234
Travelers Aid Society of Boston....617-542-7286
Voter Registration Information....617-635-4635
Weather....617-936-1234

Information Sources

Better Business Bureau Serving Eastern Massachusetts Maine & Vermont
20 Park Plaza Suite 820
Boston, MA 02116
www.bosbbb.org
Phone: 617-426-9000
Fax: 617-426-7813

Boston Redevelopment Authority
1 City Hall Sq
Boston, MA 02201
www.ci.boston.ma.us/bra
Phone: 617-722-4300
Fax: 617-367-5916

Greater Boston Chamber of Commerce
1 Beacon St 4th Fl
Boston, MA 02108
www.gbcc.org
Phone: 617-227-4500
Fax: 617-227-7505

Greater Boston Convention & Visitors Bureau
2 Copley Pl Suite 105
Boston, MA 02116
www.bostonusa.com
Phone: 617-536-4100
Fax: 617-424-7664
TF: 888-733-2678

John B Hynes Veterans Memorial Convention Center
900 Boylston St
Boston, MA 02115
www.mccahome.com
Phone: 617-954-2000
Fax: 617-954-2125
TF: 800-845-8800

Suffolk County
55 Pemberton Sq Government Ctr
Boston, MA 02108
Phone: 617-725-8000
Fax: 617-725-8137

Online Resources

4Boston.com
www.4boston.com

About.com Guide to Boston
boston.about.com/citiestowns/newenglandus/boston/mbody.htm

About.com Guide to Boston: Cambridge/West Suburbs
cambridgema.about.com/citiestowns/newenglandus/cambridgema/mbody.htm

About.com Guide to Boston: South Suburbs
bostonsouth.about.com/local/newenglandus/bostonsouth

Area Guide Boston
boston.areaguides.net

ArtsAround Boston
www.artsaroundboston.com/

Boston Alternative Life
lexicon.psy.tufts.edu/alternative

Boston Cambridge Best Guide
www.bostonbest.com

Boston City Central
www.enn2.com/ccbos.htm

Boston City Page
boston.thelinks.com

Boston CityWomen
www.citywomen.com/boswomen.htm

Boston Graphic City Guide
www.futurecast.com/gcg/boston.htm

Boston Historic Tours of America
www.historictours.com/boston/index.htm

Boston Insider
www.theinsider.com/boston

Boston Online
www.boston-online.com

Boston Phoenix
www.bostonphoenix.com

Boston Restaurant Guide
www.bostondine.com

Boston Web
www.bweb.com

Boston.com
www.boston.com

Boulevards Boston
www.boulevards.com/cities/boston.html

Bradmans.com Boston
www.bradmans.com/scripts/display_city.cgi?city=232

City Insights Boston
www.cityinsights.com/boston.htm

City Knowledge Boston
www.cityknowledge.com/ma_boston.htm

CityBuzz Boston
www.citybuzz.com/

CitySearch Boston
boston.citysearch.com

CityTravelGuide.com Boston
www.citytravelguide.com/boston.htm

CuisineNet Boston
www.cuisinenet.com/restaurant/boston/index.shtml

DigitalCity Boston
home.digitalcity.com/boston

Excite.com Boston City Guide
www.excite.com/travel/countries/united_states/massachusetts/boston

HotelGuide Boston
boston.hotelguide.net

Open World City Guides Boston
www.worldexecutive.com/cityguides/boston/

Rough Guide Travel Boston
travel.roughguides.com/content/4603/

Time Out Boston
www.timeout.com/boston/

Tonite in Boston
www.2nite.com

Town Online
www.townonline.com

Underground Guide to Boston
www.newbury.com/guide.htm

Virtual Voyages Boston
www.virtualvoyages.com/usa/ma/boston/boston.sht

Virtually Boston
www.vboston.com/

WeekendEvents.com Boston
www.weekendevents.com/BOSTON/boston.html

Yahoo! Boston
boston.yahoo.com

Area Communities

The Boston Metropolitan Area includes over 100 cities in five counties: Essex, Middlesex, Norfolk, Plymouth, and Suffolk. Communities with populations greater than 30,000 include:

Andover
36 Bartlet St
Andover, MA 01810
Phone: 978-623-8200
Fax: 978-623-8211

Arlington
730 Massachusetts Ave
Arlington, MA 02476
Phone: 781-316-3000
Fax: 781-316-3019

Beverly
191 Cabot St
Beverly, MA 01915
Phone: 978-921-6000
Fax: 978-921-6052

Billerica
365 Boston Rd
Billerica, MA 01821
Phone: 978-671-0942
Fax: 978-671-0947

Braintree
1 JFK Memorial Dr
Braintree, MA 02184
Phone: 781-794-8000
Fax: 781-794-8128

Brockton
45 School St
Brockton, MA 02301
Phone: 508-580-7123
Fax: 508-559-7960

Brookline
333 Washington St
Brookline, MA 02146
Phone: 617-730-2000
Fax: 617-730-2298

Cambridge
795 Massachusetts Ave
Cambridge, MA 02139
Phone: 617-349-4000
Fax: 617-349-4307

Chelmsford
50 Billerica Rd
Chelmsford, MA 01824
Phone: 978-250-5201
Fax: 978-250-5252

Everett
484 Broadway
Everett, MA 02149
Phone: 617-389-2100
Fax: 617-387-5770

Framingham
150 Concord St
Framingham, MA 01702
Phone: 508-620-4811
Fax: 508-620-5910

Haverhill
4 Summer St
Haverhill, MA 01830
Phone: 978-374-2300
Fax: 978-373-7544

Lawrence
200 Common St
Lawrence, MA 01840
Phone: 978-794-5803

Lowell
375 Merrimack St
Lowell, MA 01852
Phone: 978-970-4000
Fax: 978-970-4007

Lynn
3 City Hall Sq
Lynn, MA 01901
Phone: 781-598-4000
Fax: 781-477-7032

Malden
200 Pleasant St
Malden, MA 02148
Phone: 781-397-7116
Fax: 781-397-7193

Marlborough
140 Main St
Marlborough, MA 01752
Phone: 508-460-3770
Fax: 508-624-6504

Medford
85 George P Hassett Dr
Medford, MA 02155
Phone: 781-396-5500
Fax: 781-391-2158

Methuen
41 Pleasant St
Methuen, MA 01844
Phone: 978-794-3213
Fax: 978-794-3215

Natick
13 E Central St
Natick, MA 01760
Phone: 508-647-6400
Fax: 508-647-6401

Newton
1000 Commonwealth Ave
Newton, MA 02159
Phone: 617-552-7000
Fax: 617-964-2333

Peabody
24 Lowell St
Peabody, MA 01960
Phone: 978-532-3000
Fax: 978-531-0822

Pepperell
1 Main St
Pepperell, MA 01463
Phone: 978-433-0333
Fax: 978-433-0335

Plymouth
11 Lincoln St
Plymouth, MA 02360
Phone: 508-747-1620
Fax: 508-830-4062

Quincy
1305 Hancock St
Quincy, MA 02169
Phone: 617-376-1000
Fax: 617-376-1139

Randolph
41 S Main St
Randolph, MA 02368
Phone: 781-961-0900
Fax: 781-961-0919

Revere
281 Broadway
Revere, MA 02151
Phone: 781-286-8100
Fax: 781-286-8199

Salem
93 Washington St
Salem, MA 01970
Phone: 978-745-9595
Fax: 978-740-9209

Somerville
93 Highland Ave
Somerville, MA 02143
Phone: 617-625-6600
Fax: 617-625-3434

Waltham
610 Main St
Waltham, MA 02154
Phone: 781-893-4040
Fax: 781-899-6404

Watertown
149 Main St
Watertown, MA 02172
Phone: 617-972-6465
Fax: 617-972-6404

Weymouth
75 Middle St
Weymouth, MA 02189
Phone: 781-335-2000
Fax: 781-335-3283

Woburn
10 Common St
Woburn, MA 01801
Phone: 781-932-4400
Fax: 781-935-1381

Economy

Boston is among the nation's top commercial, industrial, and financial centers, with a diverse economic base ranging from agriculture to biotechnology. Greater Boston, in fact, ranks second in the nation in terms of the number of biotechnology companies located in the area. Major U.S. corporations headquartered in the Boston area include Digital Equipment Corp., Raytheon Co., Gillette Co., and Fidelity Investments. Services and finance, insurance, and real estate are currently Boston's largest employment sectors, with healthcare being the leading service industry. Government also plays an important role in Boston's economy, providing jobs for more than 84,000 area residents at the federal, state, and local levels.

Unemployment Rate	3.3%
Per Capita Income	$37,844*
Median Family Income	$34,377

** Information given is for Suffolk County.*

Principal Industries & Number of Wage Earners

City of Boston - 1998

Agriculture, Forestry, & Fishing	614
Construction	11,452
Finance, Insurance, & Real Estate	84,997
Government	84,918
Manufacturing	28,595
Services	235,976
Trade	74,549
Transportation, Communication, & Public Utilities	33,079

Major Employers

Beth Israel Co
21 Autumn St
Boston, MA 02215
Phone: 617-632-9400
Fax: 617-632-9430

Boston City Hall
1 City Hall Plaza
Boston, MA 02201
www.ci.boston.ma.us
Phone: 617-635-4000

Boston Medical Center
1 Boston Medical Ctr Pl
Boston, MA 02118
www.bmc.org
Phone: 617-638-8000
Fax: 617-638-6905

Boston University
881 Commonwealth Ave
Boston, MA 02215
web.bu.edu
Phone: 617-353-2000
Fax: 617-353-9695

Brigham & Women's Hospital
75 Francis St
Boston, MA 02115
www.partners.org/bwh
Phone: 617-732-5500
Fax: 617-732-7452

Children's Hospital
300 Longwood Ave
Boston, MA 02115
E-mail: famres@a1.tch.harvard.edu
www.childrenshospital.org
Phone: 617-355-6000
Fax: 617-355-6434

FleetBoston Financial Corp
100 Federal St
Boston, MA 02110
www.fleetbankbostonmerger.com
Phone: 617-434-2200
Fax: 617-434-1632

FMR Corp
82 Devonshire St
Boston, MA 02109
www.fidelity.com
Phone: 617-563-7000
TF: 800-522-7297

Gillette Co
Prudential Tower Bldg
Boston, MA 02199
E-mail: corporate_public_relations@gillette.com
www.gillette.com
Phone: 617-421-7000
Fax: 617-421-7617
TF: 800-445-5388

John Hancock Financial Services Inc
PO Box 111
Boston, MA 02117
www.johnhancock.com
Phone: 617-572-6000
Fax: 617-572-7767

Liberty Mutual Insurance Group
175 Berkeley St
Boston, MA 02117
www.libertymutual.com
Phone: 617-357-9500
Fax: 617-574-6689

Massachusetts General Hospital
55 Fruit St
Boston, MA 02114
www.mgh.harvard.edu
Phone: 617-726-2000
Fax: 617-726-2093

New England Medical Center
750 Washington St
Boston, MA 02111
www.nemc.org
Phone: 617-636-5000
Fax: 617-636-5353

Northeastern University
360 Huntington Ave
Boston, MA 02115
www.neu.edu
Phone: 617-373-2000
Fax: 617-373-8780

Verizon Communications
185 Franklin St Suite 1800
Boston, MA 02101
www.verizon.com
Phone: 617-743-9800

Quality of Living Indicators

Total Crime Index....................35,078
(rates per 100,000 inhabitants)

Violent Crime
Murder/manslaughter.......... 31
Forcible rape.......... 337
Robbery..........2,467
Aggravated assault..........4,428

Property Crime
Burglary..........3,414
Larceny theft..........17,637
Motor vehicle theft..........6,764

Cost of Living Index..........136.6
(national average = 100)

Median Home Price..........$233,400

Education

Public Schools

Boston Public Schools
26 Court St
Boston, MA 02108
www.boston.k12.ma.us
Phone: 617-635-9000
Fax: 617-635-9059

Number of Schools
Elementary.......... 82
Middle.......... 20
High.......... 21
Other.......... 4

Student/Teacher Ratio
All Grades.......... 27.0:1

Private Schools

Number of Schools (all grades).......... 60+

Colleges & Universities

Aquinas College at Milton
303 Adams St
Milton, MA 02186
Phone: 617-696-3100
Fax: 617-696-8706

Babson College
Babson Park, MA 02457
www.babson.edu
Phone: 781-235-1200
Fax: 781-239-4006

Bay State College
122 Commonwealth Ave
Boston, MA 02116
Phone: 617-236-8000
Fax: 617-536-1735
TF: 800-815-3276

Bentley College
175 Forest St
Waltham, MA 02452
E-mail: moreinfo@bentley.edu
www.bentley.edu
Phone: 781-891-2000
Fax: 781-891-3414
TF: 800-523-2354

Berklee College of Music
1140 Boylston St
Boston, MA 02215
www.berklee.edu
Phone: 617-266-1400
Fax: 617-536-2632
TF: 800-421-0084

Boston Architectural Center
320 Newbury St
Boston, MA 02115
www.the-bac.edu
Phone: 617-536-3170
Fax: 617-536-5829

Boston College
140 Commonwealth Ave
Chestnut Hill, MA 02467
E-mail: admissions@bcvms.bc.edu
www.bc.edu
Phone: 617-552-8000
Fax: 617-552-0798
TF: 800-860-2522

Boston Conservatory of Music Dance & Theater
8 Fenway
Boston, MA 02215
E-mail: admissions@bostonconservatory.edu
www.bostonconservatory.edu
Phone: 617-536-6340
Fax: 617-536-3176

Boston University
881 Commonwealth Ave
Boston, MA 02215
web.bu.edu
Phone: 617-353-2000
Fax: 617-353-9695

Brandeis University
PO Box 9110
Waltham, MA 02454
E-mail: admitme@brandeis.edu
www.brandeis.edu
Phone: 781-736-2000
Fax: 781-736-3536
TF: 800-622-0622

Bunker Hill Community College
250 New Rutherford Ave
Boston, MA 02129
www.bhcc.state.ma.us
Phone: 617-228-2000
Fax: 617-228-2082

Curry College
1071 Blue Hill Ave
Milton, MA 02186
www.curry.edu:8080
Phone: 617-333-0500
Fax: 617-333-2114
TF: 800-669-0686

Eastern Nazarene College
23 E Elm Ave
Quincy, MA 02170
www.enc.edu
Phone: 617-773-6350
Fax: 617-745-3907
TF: 800-883-6288

Emerson College
100 Beacon St
Boston, MA 02116
E-mail: admission@emerson.edu
www.emerson.edu
Phone: 617-824-8500
Fax: 617-824-8609

Emmanuel College
400 The Fenway
Boston, MA 02215
www.emmanuel.edu
Phone: 617-277-9340
Fax: 617-735-9801

Endicott College
376 Hale St
Beverly, MA 01915
www.endicott.edu
Phone: 978-927-0585
Fax: 978-927-0084
TF: 800-325-1114

Fisher College
118 Beacon St
Boston, MA 02116
www.fisher.edu
Phone: 617-236-8800
Fax: 617-236-8858
TF: 800-446-1226

Franklin Institute of Boston
41 Berkeley St
Boston, MA 02116
www.franklin-fib.edu
Phone: 617-423-4630
Fax: 617-482-3706

Harvard University
1350 Massachusetts Ave Holyoke Ctr
Cambridge, MA 02138
E-mail: www-admin@harvard.edu
www.harvard.edu
Phone: 617-495-1000
Fax: 617-495-8821

Hebrew College
43 Hawes St
Brookline, MA 02446
www.hebrewcollege.edu
Phone: 617-232-8710
Fax: 617-264-9264

Hellenic College-Holy Cross
50 Goddard Ave
Brookline, MA 02445
www.hchc.edu
Phone: 617-731-3500
Fax: 617-850-1460

Katharine Gibbs School
126 Newbury St
Boston, MA 02116
Phone: 617-578-7100
Fax: 617-262-2610
TF: 800-675-4557

Laboure College
2120 Dorchester Ave
Boston, MA 02124
Phone: 617-296-8300
Fax: 617-296-7947

Lasell College
1844 Commonwealth Ave
Newton, MA 02166
www.lasell.edu
Phone: 617-243-2000
Fax: 617-796-4343

Lesley College
29 Everett St
Cambridge, MA 02138
E-mail: communic@mail.lesley.edu
www.lesley.edu
Phone: 617-868-9600
Fax: 617-349-8150

Massachusetts Bay Community College
50 Oakland St
Wellesley Hills, MA 02481
E-mail: mbccinfo@mbcc.mass.edu
www.mbcc.mass.edu
Phone: 781-237-1100
Fax: 781-239-1047

Massachusetts College of Art
621 Huntington Ave
Boston, MA 02115
E-mail: admissions@massart.edu
www.massart.edu
Phone: 617-232-1555
Fax: 617-739-9744

Massachusetts College of Pharmacy & Allied Health Sciences
179 Longwood Ave
Boston, MA 02115
www.mcp.edu
Phone: 617-732-2800
Fax: 617-732-2801
TF: 800-225-5506

Massachusetts Institute of Technology
77 Massachusetts Ave
Cambridge, MA 02139
E-mail: admissions@mit.edu
web.mit.edu
Phone: 617-253-1000
Fax: 617-258-8304

Mount Ida College
777 Dedham St
Newton Center, MA 02459
www.mountida.edu
Phone: 617-928-4500
Fax: 617-928-4760
TF: 800-769-7001

New England College of Finance
89 South St 1 Lincoln Plaza
Boston, MA 02111
www.finance.edu
Phone: 617-951-2350
Fax: 617-951-2533
TF: 888-696-6323

New England Conservatory of Music
290 Huntington Ave
Boston, MA 02115
www.newenglandconservatory.edu
Phone: 617-585-1100
Fax: 617-262-0500

Newbury College
129 Fisher Ave
Brookline, MA 02445
E-mail: info@newbury.edu
www.newbury.edu
Phone: 617-730-7000
Fax: 617-731-9618
TF: 800-639-2879

Northeastern University
360 Huntington Ave
Boston, MA 02115
www.neu.edu
Phone: 617-373-2000
Fax: 617-373-8780

Pine Manor College
400 Heath St
Chestnut Hill, MA 02467
www.pmc.edu
Phone: 617-731-7000
Fax: 617-731-7199
TF: 800-762-1357

Quincy College
34 Coddington St
Quincy, MA 02169
www.quincycollege.com
Phone: 617-984-1600
Fax: 617-984-1669

Radcliffe College
10 Garden St
Cambridge, MA 02138
www.radcliffe.edu
Phone: 617-495-8601
Fax: 617-495-8821

Regis College
235 Wellesley St
Weston, MA 02493
www.regiscollege.edu
Phone: 781-768-7000
Fax: 781-768-7071
TF: 800-456-1820

Roxbury Community College
1234 Columbus Ave
Roxbury Crossing, MA 02120
Phone: 617-541-5310
Fax: 617-427-5316

Salem State College
352 Lafayette St
Salem, MA 01970
www.salem.mass.edu
Phone: 978-741-6000
Fax: 978-542-6893

School of the Museum of Fine Arts
230 Fenway
Boston, MA 02115
E-mail: smfa_info@flo.org
www.smfa.edu
Phone: 617-267-6100
Fax: 617-369-3679

Simmons College
300 Fenway
Boston, MA 02115
www.simmons.edu
Phone: 617-521-2000
Fax: 617-521-3190
TF: 800-345-8468

Suffolk University
8 Ashburton Pl
Boston, MA 02108
E-mail: admission@admin.suffolk.edu
www.suffolk.edu
Phone: 617-573-8000
Fax: 617-742-4291
TF: 800-678-3365

Tufts University
Medford, MA 02155
E-mail: uadmiss_inquiry@infonet.tufts.edu
www.tufts.edu
Phone: 617-628-5000
Fax: 617-627-3860

University of Massachusetts Boston
100 Morrissey Blvd Quinn Bldg
Boston, MA 02125
E-mail: adminfo@umbsky.cc.umb.edu
www.umb.edu
Phone: 617-287-5000
Fax: 617-287-5999

Wellesley College
106 Central St
Wellesley, MA 02481
www.wellesley.edu
Phone: 781-283-1000
Fax: 781-283-3678

Wentworth Institute of Technology
550 Huntington Ave
Boston, MA 02115
E-mail: info@everyware.edu
www.wit.edu
Phone: 617-442-9010
Fax: 617-989-4010
TF: 800-556-0610

Wheelock College
200 The Riverway
Boston, MA 02215
E-mail: undergrad@wheelock.edu
www.wheelock.edu
Phone: 617-734-5200
Fax: 617-566-4453
TF: 800-734-5212

Hospitals

Beth Israel Deaconess Medical Center
330 Brookline Ave
Boston, MA 02215
www.bih.harvard.edu
Phone: 617-667-8000
Fax: 617-632-9430
TF: 800-535-3556

Beverly Hospital
85 Herrick St
Beverly, MA 01915
Phone: 978-922-3000
Fax: 978-921-7070

Boston Medical Center
1 Boston Medical Ctr Pl
Boston, MA 02118
www.bmc.org
Phone: 617-638-8000
Fax: 617-638-6905

Brigham & Women's Hospital
75 Francis St
Boston, MA 02115
www.partners.org/bwh
Phone: 617-732-5500
Fax: 617-732-7452

Brockton Hospital
680 Centre St
Brockton, MA 02302
www.brocktonhospital.com
Phone: 508-941-7000
Fax: 508-941-6100

Carney Hospital
2100 Dorchester Ave
Boston, MA 02124
Phone: 617-296-4000
Fax: 617-296-9513

Children's Hospital
300 Longwood Ave
Boston, MA 02115
www.childrenshospital.org
Phone: 617-355-6000
Fax: 617-355-6434

Franciscan Children's Hospital & Rehabilitation Center
30 Warren St
Brighton, MA 02135
www.fch.com
Phone: 617-254-3800
Fax: 617-254-6842

Good Samaritan Medical Center
235 N Pearl St
Brockton, MA 02301
Phone: 508-427-3000
Fax: 508-427-3010

Lowell General Hospital
295 Varnum Ave
Lowell, MA 01854
www.lowellgeneral.org
Phone: 978-937-6000
Fax: 978-937-6895

Massachusetts General Hospital
55 Fruit St
Boston, MA 02114
www.mgh.harvard.edu
Phone: 617-726-2000
Fax: 617-726-2093

MetroWest Medical Center
115 Lincoln St
Framingham, MA 01702
www.mwmc.com
Phone: 508-383-1000
Fax: 508-383-1166

Mount Auburn Hospital
330 Mt Auburn St
Cambridge, MA 02238
www.mountauburn.caregroup.org
Phone: 617-492-3500
Fax: 617-499-5017

New England Baptist Hospital
125 Parker Hill Ave
Boston, MA 02120
www.nebh.org
Phone: 617-754-5800
Fax: 617-754-6397
TF: 800-340-6324

New England Medical Center
750 Washington St
Boston, MA 02111
www.nemc.org
Phone: 617-636-5000
Fax: 617-636-5353

Newton-Wellesley Hospital
2014 Washington St
Newton, MA 02462
www.nwh.org
Phone: 617-243-6000
Fax: 617-243-6630

Saint Elizabeth's Medical Center
736 Cambridge St
Brighton, MA 02135
www.semc.org
Phone: 617-789-3000
Fax: 617-789-2124

South Shore Hospital
55 Fogg Rd
South Weymouth, MA 02190
Phone: 781-340-8000
Fax: 781-331-8947

Transportation

Airport(s)

Logan International Airport (BOS)
3 miles NE of downtown (approx 10 minutes) 617-561-1818

Mass Transit

MBTA Bus
$.60 Base fare 617-722-3200
MBTA Train
$.85 Base fare 617-722-3200

Rail/Bus

Amtrak South Station
Atlantic Ave & Summer St
Boston, MA 02210
Phone: 617-345-7591
TF: 800-872-7245

Greyhound Bus Station
700 Atlantic Ave
Boston, MA 02110
Phone: 800-231-2222

Utilities

Electricity
Boston Edison Co 800-592-2000
www.bedison.com/index2.htm

Gas
Boston Gas Co 781-751-3000
www.bostongas.com

Water
Boston Water & Sewer Commission 617-330-9400
www.bwsc.org

Garbage Collection/Recycling
Boston Garbage & Refuse Collection 617-635-7555

Telecommunications

Telephone
Verizon Communications 617-956-8000
www.verizon.com

Cable Television
Cablevision of Boston 617-787-8888

Internet Service Providers (ISPs)
Bitwise Internet Technologies Inc 617-261-4700
www.bitwise.net
Channel 1 Communications 617-864-0100
www.channel1.com
Complete Internet Access 617-558-0980
www.thecia.net
Conversent Communications Inc 508-486-6300
www.conversent.com
Cyber Access Internet Communications Inc 617-876-5660
www.cybercom.net
Digital Broadband Communications Inc 781-290-4000
www.digitalbroadband.com
Galaxy Information Services 617-558-0909
www.gis.net
Network Plus Corp 617-786-4000
www.npl.com
North Shore Access 781-593-3110
www.shore.net
Software Tool & Die Inc (The World) 617-739-0202
world.std.com
StarNet 781-935-3544
www.star.net
UltraNet Communications Inc 508-229-8400
www.ultranet.com
Verio Boston 617-375-0200
home.verio.net/local/frontpage.cfm?AirportCode=BOS
Xensei Corp 617-376-6342
www.xensei.com

Banks

Bank of Boston
460 W Broadway
Boston, MA 02127
Phone: 617-434-5873
Fax: 617-268-0635
TF: 800-788-5000

Bay State FSB
184 Massachusetts Ave
Boston, MA 02115
Phone: 617-536-9090
Fax: 617-536-0544

Boston Bank of Commerce
133 Federal St
Boston, MA 02110
Phone: 617-457-4400
Fax: 617-457-4430

Boston Safe Deposit & Trust Co
1 Boston Pl
Boston, MA 02108
Phone: 617-722-7000
Fax: 617-248-3132

Capital Crossing Bank
101 Summer St
Boston, MA 02110
E-mail: contactus@capitalcrossing.com
www.capitalcrossing.com
Phone: 617-880-1000
Fax: 617-880-1010

Century Bank & Trust Co
275 Hanover St
Boston, MA 02113
Phone: 617-557-2950
Fax: 617-367-1088

Citizens Bank of Massachusetts
28 State St
Boston, MA 02109
Phone: 617-725-5900
Fax: 617-725-5921
TF: 800-922-9999

East Boston Savings Bank
10 Meridian St
Boston, MA 02128
E-mail: ebsb@shore.net
www.ebsb.com
Phone: 617-567-1500
Fax: 617-569-5681

Eastern Bank
101 Federal St
Boston, MA 02110
www.easternbank.com
Phone: 617-345-0441
Fax: 617-345-0441

First Federal Savings Bank of Boston
19 School St
Boston, MA 02108
Phone: 617-742-0570
Fax: 617-523-7112

Fleet National Bank
1 Federal St
Boston, MA 02211
Phone: 800-841-4000

Hyde Park Savings Bank
1196 River St
Boston, MA 02136
Phone: 617-361-6900
Fax: 617-361-2662

Liberty Bank & Trust Co
21 Milk St
Boston, MA 02109
Phone: 617-338-4700
Fax: 617-338-1674

Mercantile Bank & Trust Co
61 Brookline Ave
Boston, MA 02215
E-mail: mercanbk@aol.com
Phone: 617-247-2800
Fax: 617-247-6581

People's FSB
435 Market St
Boston, MA 02135
Phone: 617-254-0707
Fax: 617-254-0087

Scotiabank
28 State St 17th Fl
Boston, MA 02109
Phone: 617-624-7600
Fax: 617-624-7607

State Street Bank & Trust Co
225 Franklin St
Boston, MA 02110
E-mail: information@ssb.com
www.statestreet.com
Phone: 617-664-3576
Fax: 617-664-4357

Wainwright Bank & Trust Co
63 Franklin St
Boston, MA 02110
www.wainwrightbank.com
Phone: 617-478-4000
Fax: 617-478-4010
TF: 800-444-2265

Shopping

Atrium Mall
300 Boylston St
Chestnut Hill, MA 02167
Phone: 617-527-1400
Fax: 617-969-7438

Bloomingdale's
175 Boylston St
Chestnut Hill, MA 02167
Phone: 617-630-6000
Fax: 617-630-6028

CambridgeSide Galleria
100 CambridgeSide Pl
Cambridge, MA 02141
www.cambridgesidegalleria.com
Phone: 617-621-8666
Fax: 617-621-6078

Charles Street
Beacon Hill
Boston, MA 02116

Copley Place
100 Huntington Pl
Boston, MA 02116
E-mail: info@shopcopleyplace.com
www.shopcopleyplace.com
Phone: 617-262-6600
Fax: 617-369-5002

Dedham Mall
300 Providence Hwy
Dedham, MA 02026
Phone: 781-329-1210
Fax: 781-329-0513

Downtown Crossing
59 Temple Pl
Boston, MA 02111
Phone: 617-482-2139
Fax: 617-482-1932

Faneuil Hall Marketplace
4 S Market St
Boston, MA 02109
www.faneuilhallmarketplace.com
Phone: 617-523-1300
Fax: 617-523-1779

Filene's Co
426 Washington St
Boston, MA 02108
www.mayco.com/may/fi_home.html
Phone: 617-357-2978
Fax: 617-357-2996

Hanover Mall
1775 Washington St
Hanover, MA 02339
www.hanovermall.com
Phone: 781-826-4392
Fax: 781-826-1575

Harvard Co-op Society
1400 Massachusetts Ave
Cambridge, MA 02238
www.thecoop.com
Phone: 617-499-2000
Fax: 617-499-2016
TF: 800-242-1882

Liberty Tree Mall
100 Independence Way
Danvers, MA 01923
Phone: 978-777-0794
Fax: 978-777-9857

Macy's Phone: 617-357-3000
450 Washington St Fax: 617-357-3102
Boston, MA 02111

Mall at Chestnut Hill Phone: 617-965-3037
199 Boylston St
Chestnut Hill, MA 02167

North Shore Mall Phone: 978-531-3440
Rts 128 & 114 Fax: 978-532-9115
Peabody, MA 01960

Prudential Center Shops Phone: 800-746-7778
800 Boylston St Fax: 617-236-2496
Boston, MA 02199
www.prudentialcenter.com

Quincy Market Phone: 617-338-2323
betw Chatham & Clinton Sts
Boston, MA 02109

South Shore Plaza Phone: 781-843-8200
250 Granite St Fax: 781-843-4708
Braintree, MA 02184
www.shopsimon.com/smt/servlet/SMTMall?mid=147&pn=ENTRY&rs=0

Square One Mall Phone: 781-233-8787
1277 Broadway Fax: 781-231-9787
Saugus, MA 01906

Media

Newspapers and Magazines

Boston Business Journal Phone: 617-330-1000
200 High St Fax: 617-330-1016
Boston, MA 02110
www.amcity.com/boston/index.html

Boston Globe* Phone: 617-929-2000
PO Box 2378 Fax: 617-929-3192
Boston, MA 02107
www.boston.com/globe

Boston Herald* Phone: 617-426-3000
PO Box 2096 Fax: 617-542-1315
Boston, MA 02106
E-mail: letterstoeditor@bostonherald.com
www.bostonherald.com

Boston Irish Reporter Phone: 617-436-5275
150 Mt Vernon St Suite 120
Dorchester, MA 02125
www.bostonirishreporter.com

Boston Magazine Phone: 617-262-9700
300 Massachusetts Ave Fax: 617-262-4925
Boston, MA 02115
www.bostonmagazine.com

Boston Phoenix Phone: 617-536-5390
126 Brookline Ave Fax: 617-536-1463
Boston, MA 02215
E-mail: phx-feedback@bostonphoenix.com
www.bostonphoenix.com

Where Boston Magazine Phone: 617-482-6777
45 Newbury St Suite 406 Fax: 617-482-3337
Boston, MA 02116

**Indicates major daily newspapers*

Television

WBPX-TV Ch 68 (Pax) Phone: 617-787-6868
1660 Soldiers Field Rd Fax: 617-562-4280
Boston, MA 02135
www.wabu.com

WBZ-TV Ch 4 (CBS) Phone: 617-787-7000
1170 Soldiers Field Rd Fax: 617-254-6383
Boston, MA 02134
www.wbz.com

WCVB-TV Ch 5 (ABC) Phone: 781-449-0400
5 TV Pl Fax: 781-449-6681
Needham, MA 02492
E-mail: wcvb@aol.com
www.wcvb.com

WFXT-TV Ch 25 (Fox) Phone: 781-326-8825
25 Fox Dr Fax: 781-467-7213
Dedham, MA 02026

WGBH-TV Ch 2 (PBS) Phone: 617-492-2777
125 Western Ave Fax: 617-787-0714
Boston, MA 02134
www.wgbh.org

WHDH-TV Ch 7 (NBC) Phone: 617-725-0777
7 Bulfinch Pl Fax: 617-723-6117
Boston, MA 02114
E-mail: stationmanagement@whdh.com
www.whdh.com

WLVI-TV Ch 56 (WB) Phone: 617-265-5656
75 Morrissey Blvd Fax: 617-287-2872
Boston, MA 02125
E-mail: wlvitv@tribune.com
www.wb56.com

WNDS-TV Ch 50 (Ind) Phone: 603-434-8850
50 Television Pl Fax: 603-434-8627
Derry, NH 03038
www.wndsnews.com

WSBK-TV Ch 38 (UPN) Phone: 617-783-3838
83 Leo Birmingham Pkwy Fax: 617-783-1875
Boston, MA 02135
E-mail: upn38@paramount.com
www.paramountstations.com/WSBK

WUNI-TV Ch 27 (Uni) Phone: 781-433-2727
33 4th Ave Fax: 781-433-2750
Needham, MA 02494

Radio

WBCN-FM 104.1 MHz (Alt) Phone: 617-266-1111
1265 Boylston St Fax: 617-247-2266
Boston, MA 02215
www.wbcn.com

WBMX-FM 98.5 MHz (AC) Phone: 617-236-6898
116 Huntington Ave Fax: 617-236-6832
Boston, MA 02116

WBOS-FM 92.9 MHz (AAA)
55 Morrissey Blvd
Boston, MA 02125
www.wbos.com
Phone: 617-822-9600
Fax: 617-822-6759

WBOT-FM 97.7 MHz (Urban)
90 Warren St
Roxbury, MA 02119
Phone: 617-427-2222
Fax: 617-427-2677

WBUR-FM 90.9 MHz (NPR)
890 Commonwealth Ave
Boston, MA 02215
E-mail: info@wbur.bu.edu
www.wbur.org
Phone: 617-353-2790
Fax: 617-353-4747
TF: 800-909-9287

WBZ-AM 1030 kHz (N/T)
1170 Soldiers Field Rd
Boston, MA 02134
www.wbz.com
Phone: 617-787-7000
Fax: 617-787-7060

WCRB-FM 102.5 MHz (Clas)
750 South St
Waltham, MA 02453
E-mail: wcrb-feedback@utopia.com
www.wcrb.com
Phone: 781-893-7080
Fax: 781-893-0038

WEEI-AM 850 kHz (Sports)
116 Huntington Ave
Boston, MA 02116
www.weei.com
Phone: 617-375-8000
Fax: 617-375-8905

WFNX-FM 101.7 MHz (Alt)
25 Exchange St
Lynn, MA 01901
fnxradio.com
Phone: 781-595-6200
Fax: 781-595-3810

WGBH-FM 89.7 MHz (NPR)
125 Western Ave
Boston, MA 02134
E-mail: feedback@wgbh.org
www.wgbh.org
Phone: 617-300-2000
Fax: 617-300-1025

WHRB-FM 95.3 MHz (Misc)
389 Harvard St
Cambridge, MA 02138
E-mail: mail@whrb.org
www.whrb.org
Phone: 617-495-4818
Fax: 617-496-3990

WILD-AM 1090 kHz (Urban)
90 Warren St
Boston, MA 02119
E-mail: sales@wildam1090.com
www.wildam1090.com
Phone: 617-427-2222
Fax: 617-427-2677

WJDA-AM 1300 kHz (N/T)
PO Box 690626
Quincy, MA 02269
E-mail: info@wjda1300.com
www.wjda1300.com
Phone: 617-479-1300
Fax: 617-479-0622

WJIB-AM 740 kHz (B/EZ)
443 Concord Ave
Cambridge, MA 02138
E-mail: wjibam740@email.com
www.wjib.homepad.com
Phone: 617-868-7400

WJMN-FM 94.5 MHz (CHR)
235 Bear Hill Rd
Waltham, MA 02451
E-mail: jamn@jamn.com
www.jamn.com
Phone: 781-290-0009
Fax: 781-290-0722

WKLB-FM 99.5 MHz (Ctry)
55 Morrissey Blvd
Boston, MA 02125
www.wklb.com
Phone: 617-822-9600
Fax: 617-822-6659

WMBR-FM 88.1 kHz (Misc)
3 Ames St
Cambridge, MA 02142
E-mail: music@wmbr.mit.edu
www.wmbr.org
Phone: 617-253-4000
Fax: 617-232-1384

WMJX-FM 106.7 MHz (AC)
55 Morrissey Blvd
Boston, MA 02125
www.magic1067.com
Phone: 617-822-9600
Fax: 617-822-6559

WNFT-AM 1150 kHz (Span)
529 Main St Suite 200
Charlestown, MA 02129
Phone: 617-242-1800
Fax: 617-241-0017

WNRB-AM 1510 kHz (Sports)
500 W Cummings Pk Suite 2500
Woburn, MA 01801
Phone: 781-937-0070
Fax: 781-937-7733

WNTN-AM 1550 kHz (Misc)
143 Rumford Ave
Newton, MA 02466
www.wntn.com
Phone: 617-969-1550
Fax: 617-969-1283

WODS-FM 103.3 MHz (Oldies)
1170 Soldiers Field Rd
Boston, MA 02134
www.oldies1033.com
Phone: 617-787-7000
Fax: 617-787-7524

WPLM-FM 99.1 MHz (MOR)
17 Columbus Rd
Plymouth, MA 02360
Phone: 508-746-1390
Fax: 508-830-1128

WQSX-FM 93.7 MHz (CHR)
116 Huntington Ave
Boston, MA 02116
www.eagle937.com
Phone: 617-375-8900
Fax: 617-375-8921

WRBB-FM 104.9 MHz (Misc)
360 Huntington Ave Northeast University
Boston, MA 02115
E-mail: wrbb-help@lynx.neu.edu
www.dac.neu.edu/wrbb
Phone: 617-373-4338
Fax: 617-373-5095

WRKO-AM 680 kHz (N/T)
116 Huntington Ave
Boston, MA 02116
www.wrko.com
Phone: 617-236-6800
Fax: 617-236-6890

WROL-AM 950 kHz (Rel)
20 Park Plaza Suite 720
Boston, MA 02116
Phone: 617-423-0210
Fax: 617-482-9305

WROR-FM 105.7 MHz (Oldies)
55 Morrissey Blvd
Boston, MA 02125
www.wror.com
Phone: 617-822-9600
Fax: 617-822-6471

WTKK-FM 96.9 MHz (N/T)
55 Morrissey Blvd
Boston, MA 02125
E-mail: wsjz@aol.com
Phone: 617-822-9600
Fax: 617-822-6859

WUMB-FM 91.9 MHz (NPR)
100 Morrissey Blvd
Boston, MA 02125
E-mail: wumb@umbsky.cc.umb.edu
www.wumb.org
Phone: 617-287-6900
Fax: 617-287-6916
TF: 800-573-2100

WXKS-AM 1430 kHz (Nost)
99 Revere Beach Pkwy
Medford, MA 02155
kissfm.amfmi.com
Phone: 781-396-1430
Fax: 781-391-8345

WXKS-FM 107.9 MHz (CHR)
99 Revere Beach Pkwy
Medford, MA 02155
www.kissfm.com
Phone: 781-396-1430
Fax: 781-391-3064

WZBC-FM 90.3 MHz (AAA)
107 McElroy Commons Boston College
Chestnut Hill, MA 02467
www.wzbc.org
Phone: 617-552-3511
Fax: 617-552-0050

WZLX-FM 100.7 MHz (CR)
800 Boylston St Prudential Tower Suite 2450
Boston, MA 02199
www.wzlx.com
Phone: 617-267-0123
Fax: 617-421-9305

Attractions

Numerous historical attractions lie along Boston's Freedom Trail, which winds throughout the city, beginning at Boston Common and ending in Charlestown at the Bunker Hill Monument. Along the Trail are Paul Revere's home, Old North Church, King's Chapel (the nation's first public school), the USS Constitution ("Old Ironsides"), and the Old South Meeting House, where patriots gathered before launching the Boston Tea Party. Also on the Trail, at the Boston Waterfront, are the Faneuil Hall and Quincy Market areas. Other areas of interest in Boston include Beacon Hill and Copley Square with the John Hancock Tower/Observatory. Boston is also a travel gateway to Nantucket, Martha's Vineyard, and Cape Cod.

57 Theatre
200 Stuart St
Boston, MA 02116
Phone: 617-457-2618

Adams National Historic Site
135 Adams St
Quincy, MA 02169
www.nps.gov/adam
Phone: 617-773-1177
Fax: 617-471-9683

American Jewish Historical Society
2 Thornton Rd
Waltham, MA 02453
E-mail: ajhs@ajhs.org
www.ajhs.org
Phone: 781-891-8110
Fax: 781-899-9208

Black Heritage Trail
46 Joy St
Boston, MA 02114
www.nps.gov/boaf/home.htm
Phone: 617-742-5415
Fax: 617-720-0848

Boston African-American National Historic Site
14 Beacon St Rm 503
Boston, MA 02108
www.nps.gov/boaf/
Phone: 617-742-5415
Fax: 617-720-0848

Boston Athenaeum
10 1/2 Beacon St
Boston, MA 02108
www.bostonathenaeum.org
Phone: 617-227-0270
Fax: 617-227-5266

Boston Ballet
19 Clarendon St
Boston, MA 02116
www.bostonballet.org
Phone: 617-695-6950
Fax: 617-695-6954

Boston Beer Co
75 Arlington St
Boston, MA 02116
E-mail: info@samadams.com
www.samadams.com
Phone: 617-368-5000
Fax: 617-368-5500
TF: 800-372-1131

Boston Center for the Arts
539 Tremont St
Boston, MA 02116
www.bcaonline.org
Phone: 617-426-5000
Fax: 617-426-5336

Boston Chamber Ensemble
6 Summer St
Hyde Park, MA 02136
www.mit.edu:8001/people/jcb/BCE/
Phone: 617-361-5975
Fax: 617-364-1944

Boston Common
Beacon, Park, Tremont & Charles Sts
Boston, MA 02118
Phone: 617-635-4505

Boston Conservatory of Music Dance & Theater
8 Fenway
Boston, MA 02215
E-mail: admissions@bostonconservatory.edu
www.bostonconservatory.edu
Phone: 617-536-6340
Fax: 617-536-3176

Boston Harbor Cruises
1 Long Wharf
Boston, MA 02110
Phone: 617-227-4321
Fax: 617-723-2011

Boston Harbor Islands National Recreation Area
408 Atlantic Ave Suite 228
Boston, MA 02110
www.nps.gov/boha/
Phone: 617-223-8666
Fax: 617-223-8671

Boston Lyric Opera Co
45 Franklin St 4th Fl
Boston, MA 02110
www.blo.org
Phone: 617-542-4912
Fax: 617-542-4913

Boston Museum of Fine Arts
465 Huntington Ave
Boston, MA 02115
www.mfa.org
Phone: 617-267-9300
Fax: 617-247-6880

Boston National Historical Park
Charlestown Navy Yard
Boston, MA 02129
www.nps.gov/bost/
Phone: 617-242-5601
Fax: 617-241-5797

Boston Pops
301 Massachusetts Ave Symphony Hall
Boston, MA 02115
www.bso.org
Phone: 617-266-1492
Fax: 617-638-9367

Boston Symphony Hall
301 Massachusetts Ave
Boston, MA 02115
Phone: 617-266-1492
Fax: 617-638-9367

Boston Symphony Orchestra
301 Massachusetts Ave Symphony Hall
Boston, MA 02115
www.bso.org
Phone: 617-266-1492
Fax: 617-638-9367

Boston Tea Party Ship & Museum
Congress Street Bridge
Boston, MA 02210
E-mail: bosott@historictours.com
www.historictours.com/boston/teaparty.htm
Phone: 617-338-1773
Fax: 617-338-1974

Bunker Hill Monument
Monument Sq
Charlestown, MA 02129
www.nps.gov/bost/
Phone: 617-242-5641

Busch-Reisinger Museum
32 Quincy St Harvard University Art Museums
Cambridge, MA 02138
www.artmuseums.harvard.edu/Busch_Pages/BuschMain.html
Phone: 617-495-9400
Fax: 617-496-2359

Cape Cod National Seashore
99 Marconi Site Rd
Wellfleet, MA 02667
www.nps.gov/caco/
Phone: 508-349-3785
Fax: 508-349-9052

Charles Hayden Planetarium
Science Pk
Boston, MA 02114
www.mos.org
Phone: 617-723-2500
Fax: 617-589-0362

Charles Playhouse
74 Warrenton St
Boston, MA 02116
Phone: 617-426-5225
Fax: 617-695-1230
TF: 800-992-9035

Cheers/Bull & Finch Bar
84 Beacon St
Boston, MA 02108
Phone: 617-227-9600
Fax: 617-723-1898

Children's Museum
300 Congress St Museum Wharf
Boston, MA 02210
www.bostonkids.org
Phone: 617-426-6500
Fax: 617-426-1944

Colonial Theatre
106 Boylston St
Boston, MA 02116
www.broadwayinboston.com
Phone: 617-426-9366
Fax: 617-482-8899

Commonwealth Shakespeare Co
Boston Common
Boston, MA 02117
Phone: 617-423-7600

Copley Theatre
225 Clarendon St
Boston, MA 02116
Phone: 617-236-1199
Fax: 617-859-2826

Emerson Majestic Theatre
219 Tremont St
Boston, MA 02116
E-mail: majestic@emerson.edu
www.maj.org
Phone: 617-824-8000
Fax: 617-824-8725

Faneuil Hall Marketplace
4 S Market St
Boston, MA 02109
www.faneuilhallmarketplace.com
Phone: 617-523-1300
Fax: 617-523-1779

Fogg Art Museum
32 Quincy St Harvard University
Cambridge, MA 02138
www.artmuseums.harvard.edu/Fogg_Pages/FoggMain.html
Phone: 617-495-9400
Fax: 617-495-9936

Fort Warren
Boston Harbor
Boston, MA 02110
Phone: 617-727-5290
Fax: 617-727-7059

Franklin Park
Blue Hill Ave & Columbia Rd
Boston, MA 02118
www.ci.boston.ma.us/parks/main.asp?main=Franklin+Park
Phone: 617-635-4505
Fax: 617-635-3173

Franklin Park Zoo
1 Franklin Pk Rd
Boston, MA 02121
www.zoonewengland.com/fpz/index.html
Phone: 617-442-2002
Fax: 617-989-2025

Frederick Law Olmsted National Historic Site
99 Warren St
Brookline, MA 02245
www.nps.gov/frla/
Phone: 617-566-1689
Fax: 617-232-3964

Freedom Trail
2 1/2 Miles
Boston, MA 02124
Phone: 617-536-4100

Gibson House Museum
137 Beacon St
Boston, MA 02116
Phone: 617-267-6338

Handel & Haydn Society
300 Massachusetts Ave Horticultural Hall
Boston, MA 02115
E-mail: handlhaydn@aol.com
www.handelandhaydn.org
Phone: 617-262-1815
Fax: 617-266-4217

Harvard University Art Museums
32 Quincy St
Cambridge, MA 02138
www.artmuseums.harvard.edu
Phone: 617-495-9400
Fax: 617-496-2359

Huntington Theatre Co
264 Huntington Ave Boston University Theatre
Boston, MA 02115
www.bu.edu/huntington/reachus/mail.htm
Phone: 617-266-0800
Fax: 617-421-9674

Isabella Stewart Gardner Museum
280 The Fenway
Boston, MA 02115
www.boston.com/gardner/
Phone: 617-566-1401
Fax: 617-278-5175

John F Kennedy Library & Museum
Columbia Point
Boston, MA 02125
www.cs.umb.edu/jfklibrary/index.htm
Phone: 617-929-4500
Fax: 617-929-4538

John F Kennedy National Historic Site
83 Beals St
Brookline, MA 02146
Phone: 617-566-7937
Fax: 617-730-9884

John Hancock Observatory
200 Clarendon St 60th Fl
Boston, MA 02116
www.cityviewboston.com
Phone: 617-247-1977
Fax: 617-572-6497

King's Chapel
64 Beacon St
Boston, MA 02108
E-mail: kchapel@kings-chapel.org
Phone: 617-227-2155
Fax: 617-227-4101

Longfellow National Historic Site
105 Brattle St
Cambridge, MA 02138
www.nps.gov/long/
Phone: 617-876-4491
Fax: 617-876-6014

Longwood Symphony Orchestra
290 Huntington Ave Jordan Hall
Boston, MA 02146
www.longwoodsymphony.org
Phone: 617-332-7011

Lowell National Historical Park
67 Kirk St
Lowell, MA 01852
www.nps.gov/lowe/
Phone: 978-970-5000
Fax: 978-275-1762

Mass Bay Brewing Co
306 Northern Ave
Boston, MA 02210
Phone: 617-574-9551
Fax: 617-482-9361

Minute Man National Historical Park
174 Liberty St
Concord, MA 01742
www.nps.gov/mima/
Phone: 978-369-6993
Fax: 978-371-2483

MIT Museum
265 Massachusetts Ave
Cambridge, MA 02139
web.mit.edu/museum
Phone: 617-253-4444
Fax: 617-253-8994

Mugar OMNI Theater
Museum of Science Science Pk
Boston, MA 02114
E-mail: information@mos.org
www.mos.org
Phone: 617-723-2500

Museum of Afro-American Artists
300 Walnut Ave
Boston, MA 02119
Phone: 617-442-8614
Fax: 617-445-5525

Museum of Science
Science Pk
Boston, MA 02114
www.mos.org
Phone: 617-589-0100
Fax: 617-589-0454

New England Aquarium
Central Wharf
Boston, MA 02110
E-mail: bwyman@neaq.org
www.neaq.org
Phone: 617-973-5200
Fax: 617-720-5098

New England Conservatory of Music
290 Huntington Ave
Boston, MA 02115
www.newenglandconservatory.edu
Phone: 617-585-1100
Fax: 617-262-0500

New England Sports Museum
1 Fleet Ctr 5th & 6th Fls
Boston, MA 02114
Phone: 617-624-1234
Fax: 617-787-8152

Nichols House Museum
55 Mt Vernon St
Boston, MA 02108
Phone: 617-227-6993
Fax: 617-723-8026

Nostalgia Factory
51 N Margin St
Boston, MA 02113
www.nostalgia.com
Phone: 617-720-2211
Fax: 617-720-5587
TF: 800-479-8754

Old North Church
193 Salem St
Boston, MA 02113
www.oldnorth.com
Phone: 617-523-6676
Fax: 617-720-0559

Old South Meeting House
310 Washington St
Boston, MA 02108
Phone: 617-482-6439
Fax: 617-482-9621

Old Statehouse
206 Washington St
Boston, MA 02109
www.bostonhistory.org/osh.html
Phone: 617-720-1713
Fax: 617-720-3289

Old Town Trolley Tours
380 Dorchester Ave
Boston, MA 02127
E-mail: bosott@historictours.com
www.historictours.com/boston/bostrolley.htm
Phone: 617-269-7150

Paul Revere House
19 North Sq
Boston, MA 02113
www.paulreverehouse.org
Phone: 617-523-2338
Fax: 617-523-1775

Peabody Essex Museum
E India Sq
Salem, MA 01970
E-mail: pem@pem.org
www.pem.org/
Phone: 978-745-1876
Fax: 978-741-8951
TF: 800-745-4054

Peabody Museum of Archaeology & Ethnology
11 Divinity Ave
Cambridge, MA 02138
www.peabody.harvard.edu
Phone: 617-496-1027
Fax: 617-495-7535

Public Garden
Charles, Boylestown, Arlington & Beacon Sts
Boston, MA 02118
Phone: 617-635-4505

Quincy Market
betw Chatham & Clinton Sts
Boston, MA 02109
Phone: 617-338-2323

Robsham Theater
50 St Thomas Moore Dr Boston College
Chestnut Hill, MA 02167
Phone: 617-552-4800
Fax: 617-552-2740

Salem Maritime National Historic Site
193 Derby St
Salem, MA 01970
www.nps.gov/sama
Phone: 978-740-1660
Fax: 978-740-1665

Salem Witch Museum
19 1/2 Washington Sq N
Salem, MA 01970
www.salemwitchmuseum.com
Phone: 978-744-1692
Fax: 978-745-4414
TF: 800-544-1692

Samuel Adams Boston Beer Co
30 Germania St
Boston, MA 02130
www.samadams.com
Phone: 617-522-9080
Fax: 617-368-5564

Saugus Iron Works National Historic Site
244 Central St
Saugus, MA 01906
www.nps.gov/sair/
Phone: 781-233-0050
Fax: 781-231-9012

Shubert Theatre
265 Tremont St
Boston, MA 02116
www.boston.com/wangcenter/
Phone: 617-482-9393
Fax: 617-451-1436

Sports Museum of New England
25 Shattuck St
Lowell, MA 01852
www.lowellarea.com/lowellpage/museums.htm#sportsmuseum
Phone: 978-452-6775

USS Constitution Museum
Charlestown Navy Yard Bldg 22
Boston, MA 02129
E-mail: info@ussconstitutionmuseum.org
www.ussconstitutionmuseum.org
Phone: 617-426-1812
Fax: 617-242-0496

Wang Center for the Performing Arts
270 Tremont St
Boston, MA 02116
Phone: 617-482-9393
Fax: 617-451-1436

Wilburt Theatre
246 Tremont St
Boston, MA 02116
Phone: 617-423-4008
Fax: 617-423-3054

Sports Teams & Facilities

Boston Bruins
1 Fleet Ctr FleetCenter
Boston, MA 02114
www.bostonbruins.com
Phone: 617-624-1900
Fax: 617-523-7184

Boston Bulldogs (soccer)
475 Union Ave Bowditch Stadium
Framingham, MA 01702
www.bostonbulldogs.com
Phone: 508-872-8998
Fax: 508-872-8822

Boston Celtics
1 Fleet Ctr FleetCenter
Boston, MA 02114
www.nba.com/celtics
Phone: 617-523-3030
Fax: 617-367-4286

Boston Red Sox
4 Yawkey Way Fenway Pk
Boston, MA 02215
www.redsox.com
Phone: 617-267-9440
Fax: 617-236-6797

Boston Renegades (soccer)
175 Union Ave Bowditch Field
Framingham, MA 01702
Phone: 508-872-8998
Fax: 508-870-0884

Brewster Whitecaps (baseball)
1 Boston Pl Suite 3620
Boston, MA 02108
Phone: 617-720-7870
Fax: 617-720-7877

Cape Cod Crusaders (soccer)
35 Winter St Suite 101
Hyannis, MA 02601
E-mail: pgorham@capecodcrusaders.com
www.capecodcrusaders.com
Phone: 508-790-4782
Fax: 508-778-8446

Fenway Park
4 Yawkey Way
Boston, MA 02215
www.redsox.com/fenway/index.html
Phone: 617-267-9440
Fax: 617-236-6797

FleetCenter
1 Fleet Ctr
Boston, MA 02114
www.fleetcenter.com
Phone: 617-624-1050
Fax: 617-624-1818

New England Patriots
Rt 1 Foxboro Stadium
Foxboro, MA 02035
www.patriots.com
Phone: 508-543-1776

New England Revolution (soccer)
60 Washington St
Foxboro, MA 02035
www.nerevolution.com
Phone: 508-543-5001
Fax: 508-384-9128

Suffolk Downs
111 Waldemar Ave
East Boston, MA 02128
E-mail: sufflkdown@aol.com
www.suffolkdowns.com
Phone: 617-567-3900
Fax: 617-567-5140
TF: 800-225-3460

Annual Events

Art Festival Newbury Street (early-mid-September) 617-267-2224
August Moon Festival (mid-August) 617-635-3485
Auto Zone World of Wheels (early January) 617-367-3555
Boston Antique & Classic Boat Festival (early September) 617-666-8530
Boston Common Tree Lighting (early December) 617-635-4505
Boston Film Festival (early-mid-September) 781-925-1373
Boston Globe Jazz Festival (early-mid-July) 617-929-2649
Boston Harborfest (late June-early July) 617-227-1528
Boston International Festival (late October) 781-861-9729
Boston Irish Film Festival (late March-early April) 617-552-3938
Boston Marathon (mid-April) 617-236-1652
Boston Tea Party Reenactment (mid-December) 617-338-1773
Boston Tug Boat Muster (late July) 617-536-4100
Boston Wine Expo (early February) 877-946-3976
Boston Wine Festival (January-April) 617-330-9355
Cambridge River Festival (early September) 617-349-4380
Caribbean Carnival (late August) 781-380-7559
Celebrate Seaport (early August) 617-385-4000
Central Square World's Fair (early June) 617-876-1655
Christmas Craft Show (late November) 617-367-3555
Christmas Festival (early November) 617-742-3973
Concerts on the Hatch Shell (early May-late October) 617-727-9547
Crafts at the Castle (early December) 617-523-6400
Dragon Boat Festival (mid-June) 617-426-6500

Festival Noir (early December) 617-536-4100
First Night Boston (December 31) 617-542-1399
Fourth of July on the Esplanade (July 4) 617-267-2400
Halloween on the Harbor (late October) 617-727-7676
Halloween Prowl (late October) 781-784-5691
Harvard Square MayFair (early May) 617-491-3434
Harvard Square Oktoberfest (early October) 617-491-3434
Head of the Charles Regatta (mid-October) 617-868-6200
Honey Harvest (mid-October) 617-333-0690
Kite & Flight Festival (mid-May) 617-635-4505
New England Home Show (late February) 617-385-5000
New England International Auto Show
(early November) 617-474-6000
New England Spring Flower Show (early March) 617-536-9280
Newburyport Fall Harvest Festival (mid-October) ... 978-462-6680
Quincy Blues Festival (late June) 617-536-4100
Regattabar Jazz Festival (late January-late May) 617-536-4100
Saint Patrick's Day Celebration (mid-March) 617-268-7955
Skating on Frog Pond
(early Novermber-mid-March) 617-635-2197
Tree Lighting & Carol Festival (early December) 617-236-2366
World of Wheels (early January) 617-474-6000

Brownsville, Texas

***County:* Cameron**

TEXAS' southernmost city, Brownsville is located in the lower Rio Grande Valley along the U.S./Mexican border. Major cities within 100 miles include Harlingen and McAllen, Texas and Matamoros, Tamaulipas, Mexico.

Area (Land) .... 27.9 sq mi
Area (Water)............................... 0.9 sq mi
Elevation....................................... 19 ft
Latitude ....25-55-30 N
Longitude............................... 97-28-55 W
Time Zone ....CST
Area Code....................................... 956

Climate

Brownsville has a semi-tropical climate with an average annual temperature of 74 degrees. Winters are mild, with average high temperatures near 70 degrees and lows around 50. Although summers are very warm in Brownsville, with average high temperatures around 90 degrees and lows in the mid 70's, the city's proximity to the Gulf of Mexico helps protect Brownsville from extreme heat. Brownsville is considered Texas' sunniest city, with an average of 230 days of sunshine annually. September is the wettest month in Brownsville, while March is the driest.

Average Temperatures & Precipitation

Temperatures

	Jan	Feb	Mar	Apr	May	Jun	Jul	Aug	Sep	Oct	Nov	Dec
High	69	72	78	84	88	91	93	94	90	85	78	72
Low	50	53	59	67	72	75	76	75	73	66	59	52

Precipitation

	Jan	Feb	Mar	Apr	May	Jun	Jul	Aug	Sep	Oct	Nov	Dec
Inches	1.6	1.1	0.5	1.6	2.9	2.7	1.9	2.8	6.0	2.8	1.5	1.3

History

The Brownsville region was originally settled in the early 1800s as part of the Mexican community of San Juan de los Esteros (known today as Matamoros), which is located across the Rio Grande. In 1836, Texas declared its independence from Mexico. A decade later, the Brownsville area became the site of a temporary fort established by United States military troops led by General Zachary Taylor during the Mexican American War. Originally called Fort Texas, the post was later renamed Fort Brown after its post commander, Major Jacob Brown. After the war ended in 1848, the area became part of the State of Texas, and the city of Brownsville was established. The new city became the seat of Cameron County in 1849, and four years later Brownsville was incorporated as a city.

Located on the Rio Grande, Brownsville quickly became an important transportation and trade center. The area drew merchants from around the world, many of which took advantage of the city's proximity to Mexico, shipping goods to the south Texas city and then smuggling them across the river to avoid paying Mexican duties. Later, ranching and farming became important to the development of Brownsville. By the turn of the century, Brownsville was home to 6,000 people. The arrival of the railroad in the early 1900s prompted rapid growth for the city. During the 1920s, a land boom drew people from other parts of the United States, and by 1930 Brownsville's population exceeded 22,000.

During the 1930s a 17-mile ship channel was completed between the city and the Brazos Santiago Pass, and in 1936 the Port of Brownsville opened. In 1949 the ship channel was widened and the Gulf Intracoastal Waterway was extended to Brownsville. Another pivotal event in Brownsville's history was the implementation of the Twin Plant Program (also known as the Maquiladora Program) in 1965, which allowed companies from the U.S. and other countries to establish production facilities in Mexico. Goods involved in this program are not subject to duty until they re-enter the U.S. market, at which point they are subject only to the product's value-added content. Hundreds of industrial firms took advantage of the Twin Plant Program, creating thousands of jobs in the Brownsville area in the latter part of the 20th Century. As a result, the city's population exploded, nearly quadrupling from 1960 to the present day. The Brownsville/Matamoros area has become the third largest Maquiladora production center in the U.S.

Today, Brownsville continues to thrive as a major center for international trade. In 1998, with a population exceeding 137,000, Brownsville was among the fastest growing cities in the United States.

Population

1990 Census 107,027
1998 Estimate...............................137,883
% Change 28.8

Racial/Ethnic Breakdown

White.................................... 84.7%
Black ....<0.1%
Other.................................... 15.3%
Hispanic Origin (may be of any race) 90.1%

Age Breakdown

Under 5 years.............................. 9.1%
5 to 17..................................27.5%
18 to 20.................................. 6.0%
21 to 24.................................. 6.1%
25 to 34.................................14.9%
35 to 44.................................12.7%
45 to 54.................................. 8.2%
55 to 64.................................. 6.9%
65 to 74.................................. 5.1%

75+ years 3.6%
Median Age 25.9

Gender Breakdown
Male 47.2%
Female 52.8%

Government

Type of Government: Commission-City Manager

Brownsville City Commission
PO Box 911 Market Sq
Brownsville, TX 78520
Phone: 956-548-6000
Fax: 956-548-6010

Brownsville City Hall
PO Box 911 Market Sq
Brownsville, TX 78520
Phone: 956-548-6000
Fax: 956-548-6060

Brownsville City Manager
PO Box 911 Market Sq
Brownsville, TX 78520
Phone: 956-548-6008
Fax: 956-548-6010

Brownsville Emergency Medical Services
954 E Madison St
Brownsville, TX 78522
Phone: 956-541-9491
Fax: 956-544-3257

Brownsville Finance Dept
PO Box 911 Market Sq
Brownsville, TX 78520
Phone: 956-548-6015
Fax: 956-548-6086

Brownsville Fire Dept
1010 E Adams St
Brownsville, TX 78520
Phone: 956-546-6351
Fax: 956-546-8539

Brownsville Human Resources Dept
PO Box 911 Market Sq
Brownsville, TX 78520
Phone: 956-548-6037
Fax: 956-548-6060

Brownsville Mayor
PO Box 911 Market Sq
Brownsville, TX 78520
Phone: 956-548-6007
Fax: 956-548-6010

Brownsville Parks & Recreation Div
PO Box 911 Market Sq
Brownsville, TX 78520
Phone: 956-542-2064
Fax: 956-982-1049

Brownsville Planning & Community Development Dept
1150 E Adams St
Brownsville, TX 78520
Phone: 956-548-6142
Fax: 956-548-6144

Brownsville Police Dept
600 E Jackson St
Brownsville, TX 78520
Phone: 956-548-7000
Fax: 956-548-7009

Brownsville Public Library
2600 Central Blvd
Brownsville, TX 78520
Phone: 956-548-1055
Fax: 956-548-0684

Brownsville Public Works Dept
PO Box 911 Market Sq
Brownsville, TX 78520
Phone: 956-542-7511
Fax: 956-504-6160

Important Phone Numbers

AAA 800-222-4357
American Express Travel 956-546-6112
Brownsville/South Padre Island Board of Realtors 956-546-8920
Cameron County Tax Assessor/Collector 956-544-0800
Driver's License Information 956-542-5301
Emergency 911
Highway Conditions 800-452-9292
Medical Referral 956-542-5433
Poison Control Center 800-764-7661
Texas Comptroller of Public Accounts 956-542-8426
Time/Temp 956-546-2481
Vehicle Registration Information 956-544-0804
Voter Registration Information 956-544-0809
Weather 956-546-5378

Information Sources

Better Business Bureau Serving South Texas
PO Box 69
Weslaco, TX 78599
www.weslaco.bbb.org
Phone: 956-968-3678
Fax: 956-968-7638

Brownsville Chamber of Commerce
1600 E Elizabeth St
Brownsville, TX 78520
www.brownsvillechamber.com
Phone: 956-542-4341
Fax: 956-504-3348

Brownsville Convention & Visitors Bureau
PO Box 4697
Brownsville, TX 78523
www.brownsville.org
Phone: 956-546-3721
Fax: 956-546-3972
TF: 800-626-2639

Brownsville Economic Development Council
1205 North Expy
Brownsville, TX 78520
www.bedc.com
Phone: 956-541-1183
Fax: 956-546-3938
TF: 800-552-5352

Cameron County
964 E Harrison St
Brownsville, TX 78520
Phone: 956-544-0815
Fax: 956-550-7287

International Convention Center
4434 E 14th St
Brownsville, TX 78521
Phone: 956-546-8878

Jacob Brown Civic Center
600 International Blvd
Brownsville, TX 78520
Phone: 956-982-1820
Fax: 956-982-1358

South Padre Island Convention & Visitors Bureau
600 Padre Blvd
South Padre Island, TX 78597
www.sopadre.com
Phone: 956-761-6433
Fax: 956-761-9462
TF: 800-767-2373

South Padre Island Convention Centre
7355 Padre Blvd
South Padre Island, TX 78597
Phone: 956-761-3005
Fax: 956-761-3024
TF: 800-657-2373

Online Resources

4Brownsville.com
www.4brownsville.com

Excite.com Brownsville City Guide
www.excite.com/travel/countries/united_states/texas/brownsville

Lodging.com Brownsville Texas
www.lodging.com/auto/guides/brownsville-tx.html

Online City Guide to Brownsville
www.onlinecityguide.com/tx/brownsville

Area Communities

Communities with populations greater than 5,000 in Cameron County include:

Harlingen Phone: 956-427-8800
118 E Tyler Fax: 956-430-8526
Harlingen, TX 78550

Port Isabel Phone: 956-943-2682
305 E Maxan St Fax: 956-943-2029
Port Isabel, TX 78578

San Benito Phone: 956-361-3800
485 N Sam Houston St Fax: 956-361-3805
San Benito, TX 78586

Economy

The Brownsville/Matamoros area has long been a transportation hub and a major center for international trade. Today, the city boasts five modes for importing and exporting goods from the area: land, air, rail, deep sea, and river transport. Brownsville's strategic location and high-quality, loyal workforce has allowed it to become one of the fastest-growing manufacturing centers in the nation. Fortune 500 companies that have a presence in the area include General Motors, Lucent Technologies, and Levi Strauss. Despite Brownsville's popularity as the manufacturing hub of the Rio Grande Valley, the city in fact has a diverse economic base. Services, retail trade, and local government surpass manufacturing, based upon the number of employees, and agriculture, now a multi-million dollar industry, continues to play an important role in Brownsville's economy.

Unemployment Rate 9.8%
Per Capita Income $13,766*
Median Family Income $16,681

** Information given is for Cameron County.*

Principal Industries & Number of Wage Earners

Brownsville MSA (Cameron County) - 1998

Construction 3,833
Federal & State Government 5,683
Finance, Insurance, & Real Estate 3,617
Local Government 17,700
Manufacturing 12,125
Retail Trade 20,158
Services 27,783
Transportation/Utilities 4,775
Wholesale Trade 3,842

Major Employers

AMFELS Inc Phone: 956-831-8220
PO Box 3107 Fax: 956-831-6220
Brownsville, TX 78523
E-mail: amfelscf@aol.com
www.triplesoft.com/amfels

Brownsville City Hall Phone: 956-548-6000
PO Box 911 Market Sq Fax: 956-548-6060
Brownsville, TX 78520
www.ci.brownsville.tx.us

Brownsville Independent School District Phone: 956-548-8000
1900 Prince Rd Fax: 956-548-8010
Brownsville, TX 78521
www.brownsville.isd.tenet.edu

Brownsville Medical Center Phone: 956-544-1400
1040 W Jefferson St Fax: 956-541-0712
Brownsville, TX 78520
www.brownsvillemedical.com

Brownsville Public Utilities Board Phone: 956-982-6100
PO Box 3270 Fax: 956-983-6103
Brownsville, TX 78523

Cameron County Phone: 956-544-0815
964 E Harrison St Fax: 956-550-7287
Brownsville, TX 78520

Fort Brown Mfg Phone: 956-541-9771
325 Mexico St Fax: 956-504-6010
Brownsville, TX 78520

H-E-B Food Stores Phone: 956-425-6677
1213 S Commerce Fax: 956-425-0815
Harlingen, TX 78550
www.hebgrocery.com

Horace Small Apparel Phone: 956-542-9136
1705 Billy Mitchell Blvd Fax: 956-542-4080
Brownsville, TX 78521
www.horacesmallapparel.com

Levi Strauss & Co Phone: 956-541-9131
2500 Billy Mitchell Blvd Fax: 956-541-1173
Brownsville, TX 78521
www.levistrauss.com

Rich-SeaPak Corp Phone: 956-542-0001
3555 E 14th St Fax: 956-504-4401
Brownsville, TX 78521
www.seapak.com

TRICO Technologies Corp Phone: 956-544-2722
1995 Billy Mitchell Blvd Fax: 956-544-6969
Brownsville, TX 78521

University of Texas Brownsville Phone: 956-544-8200
80 Fort Brown St Fax: 956-544-8832
Brownsville, TX 78520 TF: 800-850-0160
www.utb.edu

Valley Regional Medical Center Phone: 956-350-7000
100-A Alton Gloor Blvd Fax: 956-350-7117
Brownsville, TX 78521

Wal-Mart Stores Inc Phone: 956-544-0394
2721 Boca Chica Blvd Fax: 956-546-8218
Brownsville, TX 78521

Quality of Living Indicators

Total Crime Index 8,650
(rates per 100,000 inhabitants)

Violent Crime
Murder/manslaughter 4

Forcible rape 26
Robbery....................................... 166
Aggravated assault............................. 587

Property Crime
Burglary 1,227
Larceny theft 6,289
Motor vehicle theft 351

Cost of Living Index....................................92.9
(national average = 100)

Median Home Price...................................$39,400

Education

Public Schools

Brownsville Independent School District
1900 Prince Rd
Brownsville, TX 78521
www.brownsville.isd.tenet.edu
Phone: 956-548-8000
Fax: 956-548-8010

Number of Schools
Elementary 27
Middle 9
High.. 5

Student/Teacher Ratio
All Grades 15.1:1

Private Schools

Number of Schools (all grades)..................... 8+

Colleges & Universities

South Texas Vocational Technical Institute
2255 N Coria St
Brownsville, TX 78520
E-mail: stvtw@hiline.net
www.hiline.net/~stvtm
Phone: 956-546-0353
Fax: 956-546-0914

Texas Southmost College
80 Fort Brown St
Brownsville, TX 78520
www.utb.edu
Phone: 956-544-8200
Fax: 956-544-8832
TF: 800-850-0160

University of Texas Brownsville
80 Fort Brown St
Brownsville, TX 78520
www.utb.edu
Phone: 956-544-8200
Fax: 956-544-8832
TF: 800-850-0160

Hospitals

Brownsville Medical Center
1040 W Jefferson St
Brownsville, TX 78520
www.brownsvillemedical.com
Phone: 956-544-1400
Fax: 956-541-0712

Valley Regional Medical Center
100-A Alton Gloor Blvd
Brownsville, TX 78521
Phone: 956-350-7000
Fax: 956-350-7117

Transportation

Airport(s)

Brownsville-South Padre Island International Airport (BRO)
4 miles E of downtown (approx 10 minutes)......956-542-4373

Mass Transit

Brownsville Urban System
$.75 Base fare.................................956-548-6050

Rail/Bus

Greyhound/Valley Transit Bus Station
1134 E St Charles Ave
Brownsville, TX 78520
Phone: 956-546-2264
TF: 800-231-2222

Utilities

Electricity
AEP/Central Power & Light Co 800-274-2611
www.aep.com
Brownsville Public Utilities Board...............956-982-6100
Magic Valley Electric Cooperative 956-574-7150

Gas
Southern Union Gas Co.........................800-700-2089
www.southernunionco.com

Water
Brownsville Public Utilities Board...............956-982-6100

Garbage Collection/Recycling
BFI Waste Systems 956-423-7316

Telecommunications

Telephone
Southwestern Bell Telephone Co................800-464-7928
www.swbell.com

Cable Television
Time Warner Communications..................800-222-5355
www.timewarner.com

Internet Service Providers (ISPs)
HiLINE Internet Services Inc 956-686-5580
www.hiline.net
SmartCom Internet...........................956-687-7070
www.sc2000.net
South Texas Internet..........................956-504-5252
www.ies.net

Banks

Chase Texas
1034 E Levee St
Brownsville, TX 78520
Phone: 956-548-6968
Fax: 956-548-6929

Coastal Banc
3302 Boca Chica Blvd
Brownsville, TX 78521
Phone: 956-546-4528
Fax: 956-541-0997
TF: 888-393-3434

First National Bank
701 E Levee St
Brownsville, TX 78520
Phone: 956-986-7000
Fax: 956-986-7045

International Bank of Commerce Phone: 956-542-8060
630 E Elizabeth St Fax: 956-547-1006
Brownsville, TX 78520

Texas State Bank Phone: 956-546-4503
629 E Elizabeth St Fax: 956-547-3808
Brownsville, TX 78520

Wells Fargo Bank Phone: 956-504-2265
3310 Boca Chica Blvd Fax: 956-504-2619
Brownsville, TX 78521

Shopping

Amigoland Mall Phone: 956-546-3788
301 Mexico Blvd Fax: 956-546-5942
Brownsville, TX 78520

Palm Village Shopping Center Phone: 956-542-7733
21 Palm Village
Brownsville, TX 78520

Sunrise Mall Phone: 956-541-5302
2370 North Exwy Fax: 956-546-0251
Brownsville, TX 78526

Media

Newspapers and Magazines

Brownsville Herald* Phone: 956-542-4301
PO Box 351 Fax: 956-542-0840
Brownsville, TX 78520
E-mail: tbhsubscription@link.freedom.com
www.brownsvilleherald.com

El Bravo* Phone: 956-542-5800
1144 Lincoln St Fax: 956-542-6023
Brownsville, TX 78520

Rio Grande Valley Business Journal Phone: 956-546-5113
1300 Wild Rose Ln Fax: 956-546-0903
Brownsville, TX 78520
E-mail: bsales@rgvbusiness.hiline.net

**Indicates major daily newspapers*

Television

KGBT-TV Ch 4 (CBS) Phone: 956-421-4444
9201 W Exwy 83 Fax: 956-421-3699
Harlingen, TX 78552
www.kgbttv.com

KNVO-TV Ch 48 (Uni) Phone: 956-687-4848
801 N Jackson Rd Fax: 956-687-7784
McAllen, TX 78501
E-mail: feedback@knvo.com
www.knvo.com

KRGV-TV Ch 5 (ABC) Phone: 956-968-5555
900 East Expy Fax: 956-973-5016
Weslaco, TX 78596
E-mail: sales@krgv.com
www.krgv.com

KVEO-TV Ch 23 (NBC) Phone: 956-544-2323
394 North Expy Fax: 956-544-4636
Brownsville, TX 78521
E-mail: kvesales@hiline.net
www.kveo.com

Radio

KBNR-FM 88.3 MHz (Rel) Phone: 956-542-6933
216 W Elizabeth Fax: 956-542-0523
Brownsville, TX 78520
E-mail: kbnr@hcjb.org
www.hcjb.org/wrn/

KBOR-AM 1600 kHz (Span) Phone: 956-544-1600
1050 McIntosh St Fax: 956-542-4109
Brownsville, TX 78521

KFRQ-FM 94.5 MHz (Rock) Phone: 956-968-1548
901 E Pike Blvd Fax: 956-968-1643
Weslaco, TX 78596

KGBT-FM 98.5 MHz (Span) Phone: 956-631-5499
200 S 10th St Suite 600 Fax: 956-631-0090
McAllen, TX 78501
E-mail: sales@kgbt.com
www.kgbt.com

KIWW-FM 96.1 MHz (Span) Phone: 956-631-5499
200 S 10th St Suite 600 Fax: 956-631-0090
McAllen, TX 78501
E-mail: info@kiww.com
www.kiww.com

KKPS-FM 99.5 MHz (Span) Phone: 956-968-1548
901 E Pike Blvd Fax: 956-968-1643
Weslaco, TX 78596

KRGE-AM 1290 kHz (Rel) Phone: 956-968-7777
PO Box 1290 Fax: 956-968-5143
Weslaco, TX 78599

KTEX-FM 100.3 MHz (Ctry) Phone: 956-423-5068
3301 S Expy 83
Harlingen, TX 78550
E-mail: ktexx@aol.com
www.ktex.net

KTJN-FM 106.3 MHz (Span) Phone: 956-544-1600
1050 McIntosh St Fax: 956-542-4109
Brownsville, TX 78521

KTJX-FM 105.5 MHz (Span) Phone: 956-544-1600
1050 McIntosh St Fax: 956-544-0311
Brownsville, TX 78523

Attractions

Each year in February Brownsville hosts Charro Days, the city's version of Mardi Gras, with carnivals, parades, dances, and cultural events. The city is also home to the Gladys Porter Zoo, a unique, cageless zoo that is one of the top 10 zoos in the U.S. The 1850 home of Charles Stillman, the founder of Brownsville, is on display as the Stillman House Museum; and the 3,400-acre Palo Alto Battlefield National Historic Site is the site of the first battle of the Mexican-American War. The Historic Fort Brown Area, the oldest permanent U.S. Army post on the Rio Grande, is also located in Brownsville. South Padre Island, which is noted for its beaches and watersports, is only 20 minutes away.

Antonio Gonzales Park Phone: 956-542-2064
34 Tony Gonzalez Dr
Brownsville, TX 78521

Bentsen-Rio Grande Valley State Park
PO Box 988
Mission, TX 78572
www.tpwd.state.tx.us/park/bentsen/bentsen.htm
Phone: 956-585-1107
Fax: 956-585-3448
TF: 800-792-1112

Bro-Mat "Old Mexico" Tours
300 E 6th St
Los Fresnos, TX 78566
Phone: 956-233-1900

Brownsville Art League & Museum
230 Neale Dr
Brownsville, TX 78520
Phone: 956-542-0941

Confederate Air Force Museum Rio Grande Valley Wing
955 S Minnesota Brownsville Airport
Brownsville, TX 78521
Phone: 956-541-8585

Dean Porter Park
501 E Ringgold St
Brownsville, TX 78520
Phone: 956-542-2064
Fax: 956-982-1049

Edelstein Park
E 12th & Polk Sts
Brownsville, TX 78520
Phone: 956-542-2064
Fax: 956-982-1049

Garfield Park
E 16th & Garfield Sts
Brownsville, TX 78520
Phone: 956-542-2064
Fax: 956-982-1049

Historic Brownsville Museum
641 E Madison St
Brownsville, TX 78520
Phone: 956-548-1313
Fax: 956-548-1391

Laguna Atascosa National Wildlife Refuge
Hwy 106 & Buena Vista Rd
Brownsville, TX 78520
Phone: 956-748-3608
Fax: 956-748-3609

Lightner Camille Playhouse
1 Dean Porter Park
Brownsville, TX 78520
www.camilleplayhouse.vt1.com
Phone: 956-542-8900
Fax: 956-986-0639

Palo Alto Battlefield National Historic Site
1623 Central Blvd
Brownsville, TX 78520
www.nps.gov/paal/
Phone: 956-541-2785
Fax: 956-541-6356

Port of Brownsville
1000 Foust Rd
Brownsville, TX 78521
E-mail: marketing@portofbrownsville.com
www.portofbrownsville.com
Phone: 956-831-4592
Fax: 956-831-5006

Porter Gladys Zoo
500 Ringgold St
Brownsville, TX 78520
www.gpz.org
Phone: 956-546-7187
Fax: 956-541-4940

Sabal Palm Grove Sanctuary
Sabal Palm Rd & FM-1419
Brownsville, TX 78523
www.audubon.org/local/sanctuary/sabal
Phone: 956-541-8034
Fax: 956-504-0543

Santa Ana National Wildlife Refuge
FM-907 & Hwy 281
Alamo, TX 78516
southwest.fws.gov/refuges/texas/santana.html
Phone: 956-787-3079
Fax: 956-787-8338

Smith Marion Hendrick Outdoor Ampitheater
South Bldg University of Texas at Brownsville Campus
Brownsville, TX 78520
Phone: 956-544-8200

Stillman House & Museum
1305 E Washington St
Brownsville, TX 78520
Phone: 956-542-3929
Fax: 956-541-5524

Super Splash Adventure Water Park
1616 S Raul Longonia Rd
Edinburg, TX 78539
www.supersplashadventure.com
Phone: 956-318-3286
Fax: 956-316-1877

Washington Plaza Park
E 7th & Madison Sts
Brownsville, TX 78520
Phone: 956-542-2064
Fax: 956-982-1049

Whaling Wall Mural
7355 Padre Blvd Convention Centre
South Padre Island, TX 78597
Phone: 956-761-3005

Annual Events

Beachcomber's Art Show (late July) 956-423-6707
Birdathon (mid-May) 956-541-8034
Boo at the Zoo (late October) 956-546-7187
Brownsville Appreciation Day at the Zoo (mid-September) 956-546-7187
Brownsville Art League International Art Show (early March) 956-542-0941
Brownsville Art League International Student Art Show (late April-early May) 956-542-0941
Charro Days Festival (late February) 956-542-4245
Christmas Parade (early December) 956-542-4341
Christmas Tree Lighting Ceremony (late November) 956-546-3721
CineSol Latino Film Festival (early June) 956-428-8983
Confederate Air Force Fiesta (early March) 956-541-8585
Feast with the Beast (mid-May) 956-546-7187
Fly-Ins (October-March) 956-748-2112
Friday Night Fireworks Over the Bay (late May-early September) 956-761-3000
Memorial Day Fireworks over the Bay (late May) 956-761-3000
Rio Grande Valley Arts & Crafts Expo (early November) 956-542-0941
Semana Santa (Holy Week) (late March-early April) 956-761-6433
Sombrero Festival (late February) 956-542-4341
South Padre Island Bikefest (mid-October) 956-761-3000
South Padre Island Easter Egg Hunt (early April) 956-761-6433
South Padre Island Fireworks Extravaganza (July 4) 956-761-3000
Spring Faculty Art Exhibition (mid-February-early March) 956-544-8247
Zoofari Fundraiser (early October) 956-546-7187

Buffalo, New York

***County:* Erie**

BUFFALO is located in western New York at the eastern end of Lake Erie. Major cities within 100 miles include Rochester, New York and Toronto, Ontario, Canada.

Area (Land) .... 40.6 sq mi
Area (Water).............................. 11.9 sq mi
Elevation.................................... 600 ft
Latitude ....42-79-72 N
Longitude.............................. 78-82-36 W
Time Zone ....EST
Area Code...................................... 716

Climate

Buffalo's climate features four distinct seasons. Winters are long and snowy, with average high temperatures in the low 30s and lows in the high teens and low 20s. An average of 93 inches of snow falls at the Buffalo Airport annually. Summers are mild and sunny, with average daytime highs in the mid- to upper 70s and evening lows averaging near 60 degrees. August is the wettest month in Buffalo; February is the driest.

Average Temperatures & Precipitation

Temperatures

	Jan	Feb	Mar	Apr	May	Jun	Jul	Aug	Sep	Oct	Nov	Dec
High	30	32	42	54	66	75	80	78	71	59	47	35
Low	17	17	26	36	47	57	62	60	53	43	34	23

Precipitation

	Jan	Feb	Mar	Apr	May	Jun	Jul	Aug	Sep	Oct	Nov	Dec
Inches	2.7	2.3	2.7	2.9	3.1	3.6	3.1	4.2	3.5	3.1	3.8	3.7

History

French explorers and missionaries traveled through the Buffalo area for years prior to settlement, referring to the body of water known today as Buffalo Creek as a "beau fleuve" (meaning "beautiful river"). Early settlers who did not speak French pronounced the phrase "beau fleuve" as "boof-loo," and from this pronunciation the name Buffalo was derived. In 1780, members of the Seneca tribe established the first village in the Buffalo area. The first European settlement was established there by the Holland Land Company in 1803.

Much of Buffalo was burned by the British during the War of 1812, but the community was quickly rebuilt and was incorporated as a village in 1816. Less than a decade later, in 1825, Buffalo became the western terminus of the newly opened Erie Canal, and this marked the beginning of a major era of growth.

Buffalo was incorporated as a city in 1832 and, with its access to the Midwest and to Canada, quickly became a major trade and distribution center. Buffalo's reputation as a leading flour milling center began in 1843 with the creation of the world's first steam-powered grain elevator in the city. Today Buffalo is among the world's leading flour producers. With the area's access to raw materials, along with the development of hydroelectric generators at nearby Niagara Falls during the late 1800s, industry flourished in Buffalo, creating economic opportunities that attracted settlers of various ethnic backgrounds, including Irish, Germans, and Poles.

Buffalo continued to thrive as an industrial center until well into the 20th Century, but industrial decline in the late 1970s and early 1980s influenced Buffalo to diversify its economic base. Although the city suffered hard economic times during those years, Buffalo has bounced back with a stronger, more diverse economy, and it remains one of the nation's leading inland ports. Buffalo currently has more than 300,000 residents, making it New York's second largest city.

Population

1990 Census 328,175
1998 Estimate.............................300,717
% Change .... -8.4
2004 Projection 917,351*

Racial/Ethnic Breakdown

White.................................... 64.7%
Black.................................... 30.6%
Other..................................... 4.7%
Hispanic Origin (may be of any race)......... 4.9%

Age Breakdown

Under 5 years.............................. 7.8%
5 to 17.................................. 16.5%
18 to 20.................................. 5.2%
21 to 24.................................. 7.5%
25 to 34................................. 18.4%
35 to 44................................. 13.0%
45 to 54.................................. 8.2%
55 to 64.................................. 8.6%
65 to 74.................................. 8.4%
75+ years 6.5%
Median Age.................................32.0

Gender Breakdown

Male..................................... 46.7%
Female................................... 53.3%

** Information given is for Erie County.*

Government

Type of Government: Mayor-Council

Buffalo & Erie County Public Library
1 Lafayette Sq
Buffalo, NY 14203
Phone: 716-858-8900
Fax: 716-858-6211

Buffalo Administration & Finance Dept
City Hall 65 Niagara Sq Rm 117
Buffalo, NY 14202
Phone: 716-851-5722
Fax: 716-851-4983

Buffalo City Clerk
City Hall 65 Niagara Sq Rm 1308
Buffalo, NY 14202
Phone: 716-851-5431
Fax: 716-851-4845

Buffalo City Hall
65 Niagara Sq
Buffalo, NY 14202
Phone: 716-851-4200
Fax: 716-851-4234

Buffalo Civil Service Office
City Hall 65 Niagara Sq Rm 1001
Buffalo, NY 14202
Phone: 716-851-4614
Fax: 716-851-5401

Buffalo Common Council
City Hall 65 Niagara Sq Rm 1315
Buffalo, NY 14202
Phone: 716-851-5120
Fax: 716-851-6537

Buffalo Community Development Dept
City Hall 65 Niagara Sq Rm 920
Buffalo, NY 14202
Phone: 716-851-5016
Fax: 716-854-0172

Buffalo Fire Dept
195 Court St
Buffalo, NY 14202
Phone: 716-851-5333
Fax: 716-851-4364

Buffalo Law Dept
City Hall 65 Niagara Sq Rm 1100
Buffalo, NY 14202
Phone: 716-851-4343
Fax: 716-851-4105

Buffalo Mayor
City Hall 65 Niagara Sq Rm 201
Buffalo, NY 14202
Phone: 716-851-4841
Fax: 716-851-4360

Buffalo Parks Div
17 Meadowview Pl
Buffalo, NY 14214
Phone: 716-851-5806
Fax: 716-884-9669

Buffalo Police Dept
74 Franklin St
Buffalo, NY 14202
Phone: 716-851-4444
Fax: 716-851-4108

Buffalo Public Works Dept
City Hall 65 Niagara Sq Rm 502
Buffalo, NY 14202
Phone: 716-851-5636
Fax: 716-851-4201

Buffalo Street Sanitation Dept
City Hall 65 Niagara Sq Rm 218
Buffalo, NY 14202
Phone: 716-851-5949
Fax: 716-851-5961

Buffalo Water Dept
281 Exchange St
Buffalo, NY 14204
Phone: 716-847-1065
Fax: 716-847-0150

Important Phone Numbers

AAA 716-634-7900
American Express Travel 716-856-7373
Buffalo Dept of Assessment 716-851-5733
Buffalo Events Information Line 716-855-5534
Buffalo Place Entertainment Hotline 716-854-4386
Buffalo Tax Collections 716-851-4310
Driver's License/Vehicle Registration Information 716-858-7450
Emergency 911
Erie County Dept of Budget Management & Finance 716-858-8333
Greater Buffalo Assn of Realtors 716-636-9000
HotelDocs 800-468-3537
New York State Dept of Taxation & Finance 800-225-5829
Poison Control Center 716-878-7654
Time/Temp 716-844-4444
Travelers Aid 716-854-8661
Voter Registration Information 716-858-8891
Weather 716-844-4444

Information Sources

Better Business Bureau Serving Western New York & the Capital District
741 Delaware Ave
Buffalo, NY 14209
www.buffalo.bbb.org
Phone: 716-881-5222
Fax: 716-883-5349

Buffalo Convention Center
Convention Center Plaza
Buffalo, NY 14202
www.bfloconvcenter.org
Phone: 716-855-5555
Fax: 716-855-3158
TF: 800-995-7570

Buffalo Free-Net/WNYLRC
4455 Genesee St
Buffalo, NY 14225
freenet.buffalo.edu
Phone: 716-515-2100

Buffalo Niagara Enterprise
300 Main Place Tower
Buffalo, NY 14202
www.buffaloniagara.org
Phone: 716-842-1330
Fax: 716-842-1724

Buffalo Niagara Partnership
300 Main Pl Tower
Buffalo, NY 14202
Phone: 716-852-7100
Fax: 716-852-2761

Erie County
25 Delaware Ave
Buffalo, NY 14202
www.erie.gov
Phone: 716-858-8785
Fax: 716-858-6550

Greater Buffalo Convention & Visitors Bureau
617 Main St Suite 400
Buffalo, NY 14203
www.buffalocvb.org
Phone: 716-852-0511
Fax: 716-852-0131
TF: 800-283-3256

Online Resources

4Buffalo.com
www.4buffalo.com

About.com Guide to Buffalo/Niagara
buffalo.about.com/local/midlanticus/buffalo

Anthill City Guide Buffalo
www.anthill.com/city.asp?city=buffalo

Area Guide Buffalo
buffalo.areaguides.net

Artvoice.com-Buffalo's Alternative Arts News
www.artvoice.com

Buffalo & Western New York Dining Guide
www.buffalo-dining.com

Buffalo New York
buffalo-new-york.com

Buffalo Place Inc's Downtown Buffalo
www.dwntwnbuffalo.com

Buffalo Pride Online
www.buffalopride.com/

Buffalo.com
www.buffalo.com

City Knowledge Buffalo
www.cityknowledge.com/ny_buffalo.htm

DigitalCity Buffalo
home.digitalcity.com/buffalo

E-Z Eats Dining Guide
www.ezeats.com

Excite.com Buffalo City Guide
www.excite.com/travel/countries/united_states/new_york/buffalo

Online Buffalo
www.onlinebuffalo.com

Online Western New York
www.onlinewny.com/

Virtual Buffalo
www.virtualbuffalo.com/

Area Communities

Communities in the Buffalo area (Erie and Niagara counties) with populations greater than 20,000 include:

Amherst
5583 Main St
Buffalo, NY 14221
Phone: 716-631-7000
Fax: 716-631-7012

Cheektowaga
3301 Broadway
Cheektowaga, NY 14227
Phone: 716-686-3400
Fax: 716-686-3515

Clarence
1 Town Pl
Clarence, NY 14031
Phone: 716-741-8938
Fax: 716-741-4715

Hamburg
100 Main St
Hamburg, NY 14075
Phone: 716-649-0200
Fax: 716-646-6558

Lancaster
21 Central Ave
Lancaster, NY 14086
Phone: 716-683-9028
Fax: 716-683-0512

Niagara Falls
745 Main St
Niagara Falls, NY 14302
Phone: 716-286-4393
Fax: 716-286-4398

North Tonawanda
216 Payne Ave
North Tonawanda, NY 14120
Phone: 716-695-8555
Fax: 716-695-8557

Orchard Park
4295 S Buffalo St
Orchard Park, NY 14127
Phone: 716-662-6410
Fax: 716-662-6479

Tonawanda
200 Niagara St
Tonawanda, NY 14150
Phone: 716-695-1800
Fax: 716-695-8315

West Seneca
1250 Union Rd
West Seneca, NY 14224
Phone: 716-674-5600
Fax: 716-677-4330

Economy

Although trade and manufacturing remain important components of Buffalo's economy, other industries, including finance and health care, have gained significance in recent years. Services is currently the largest employment sector in Erie County. Government is also vital to Buffalo's economy—one-third of the area's fifteen largest employers are government-related, including the top two, New York State Government and the U.S. Government.

Unemployment Rate	8.8%
Per Capita Income	$26,183*
Median Family Income	$23,887

** Information given is for Erie County.*

Principal Industries & Number of Wage Earners

Buffalo-Niagara Falls MSA* - March 2000

Construction & Mining	17,600
Finance, Insurance, & Real Estate	30,600
Government	90,200
Manufacturing	85,500
Retail Trade	98,300
Services	171,800
Transportation & Public Utilities	25,900
Wholesale Trade	28,800

** Information given is for the Buffalo-Niagara Falls Metropolitan Statistical Area (MSA), which includes Erie and Niagara counties.*

Major Employers

American Axle & Mfg Inc
100 E Delavan
Buffalo, NY 14215
Phone: 716-891-7100
Fax: 716-891-7112

Buffalo City Hall
65 Niagara Sq
Buffalo, NY 14202
www.ci.buffalo.ny.us
Phone: 716-851-4200
Fax: 716-851-4234

Buffalo School District
712 City Hall
Buffalo, NY 14202
www.buffaloschools.org
Phone: 716-851-3575
Fax: 716-851-3771

Catholic Health System
515 Abbott Rd Suite 508
Buffalo, NY 14220
Phone: 716-828-2750
Fax: 716-828-2703

CGF Health System
901 Washington St
Buffalo, NY 14203
Phone: 716-843-7500
Fax: 716-843-7529

Erie County
25 Delaware Ave
Buffalo, NY 14202
www.erie.gov
Phone: 716-858-8785
Fax: 716-858-6550

General Motors Corp Delphi Harrison Thermal Systems Div
200 Upper Mountain Rd
Lockport, NY 14094
Phone: 716-439-2011
Fax: 716-439-2066

General Motors Corp Powertrain Div
2995 River Rd
Tonawanda, NY 14150
www.gm.com/careers
Phone: 716-879-5000
Fax: 716-879-5260

HSBC Bank USA
1 HSBC Ctr
Buffalo, NY 14203
www.us.hsbc.com
Phone: 716-841-2424
Fax: 716-841-4746

M & T Bank Corp
1 M & T Plaza 5th Fl
Buffalo, NY 14203
Phone: 716-842-4200
Fax: 716-842-5177
TF: 800-724-2440

New York State Government
65 Court St
Buffalo, NY 14202
www.state.ny.us
Phone: 716-847-7110
Fax: 716-847-7969

Tops Markets Inc
6363 Main St
Williamsville, NY 14221
www.topsmarket.com
Phone: 716-635-5000
Fax: 716-635-5102
TF: 800-522-2522

US Government
111 W Huron St Rm 912
Buffalo, NY 14202
Phone: 716-551-4596

US Postal Service
1200 William St
Buffalo, NY 14240
new.usps.com
Phone: 716-846-2400
Fax: 716-846-2407

Quality of Living Indicators

Total Crime Index 20,678
(rates per 100,000 inhabitants)

Violent Crime
Murder/manslaughter 32
Forcible rape 175
Robbery 1,473
Aggravated assault 1,562

Property Crime
Burglary 4,428
Larceny theft 10,018
Motor vehicle theft 2,990

Cost of Living Index 99.8
(national average = 100)

Median Home Price $81,400

Education

Public Schools

Buffalo School District
712 City Hall
Buffalo, NY 14202
www.buffaloschools.org
Phone: 716-851-3575
Fax: 716-851-3771

Number of Schools
Early Childhood Centers 11
Elementary 42
Intermediate 3
High 14
Ungraded 4

Student/Teacher Ratio
All Grades 15.0:1

Private Schools

Number of Schools (all grades) .... 60+

Colleges & Universities

Bryant & Stratton Career College Buffalo
465 Main St
Buffalo, NY 14203
www.bryantstratton.edu/main/campusdesc/buffalo.htm
Phone: 716-884-9120
Fax: 716-884-0091

Bryant & Stratton Career College Eastern Hills Campus
200 Bryant & Stratton Way
Williamsville, NY 14221
www.bryantstratton.edu/main/campusdesc/ehc.htm
Phone: 716-631-0260
Fax: 716-631-0273

Bryant & Stratton Career College Lackawanna
1214 Abbott Rd
Lackawanna, NY 14218
Phone: 716-821-9331
Fax: 716-821-9343

Buffalo State College
1300 Elmwood Ave
Buffalo, NY 14222
www.buffalostate.edu
Phone: 716-878-4000
Fax: 716-878-6100

Canisius College
2001 Main St
Buffalo, NY 14208
gort.canisius.edu
Phone: 716-883-7000
Fax: 716-888-2525
TF: 800-843-1517

D'Youville College
320 Porter Ave
Buffalo, NY 14201
E-mail: admissions@dyc.edu
www.dyc.edu
Phone: 716-881-3200
Fax: 716-881-7790
TF: 800-777-3921

Daemen College
4380 Main St
Amherst, NY 14226
www.daemen.edu
Phone: 716-839-3600
Fax: 716-839-8516

Erie Community College City Campus
121 Ellicott St
Buffalo, NY 14203
www.sunyerie.edu
Phone: 716-842-2770
Fax: 716-851-1129

Erie Community College North Campus
6205 Main St
Williamsville, NY 14221
Phone: 716-634-0800
Fax: 716-851-1429

Hilbert College
5200 S Park Ave
Hamburg, NY 14075
www.hilbert.edu
Phone: 716-649-7900
Fax: 716-649-1152
TF: 800-649-8003

Houghton College Seneca Campus
910 Union Rd
West Seneca, NY 14224
www.houghton.edu/pace
Phone: 716-674-6363
Fax: 716-674-0250
TF: 800-247-6448

Medaille College
18 Agassiz Cir
Buffalo, NY 14214
Phone: 716-884-3281
Fax: 716-884-0291
TF: 800-292-1582

Niagara University
Niagara University, NY 14109
www.niagara.edu
Phone: 716-285-1212
Fax: 716-286-8710
TF: 800-462-2111

State University of New York Buffalo
3435 Main St
Buffalo, NY 14214
www.buffalo.edu
Phone: 716-645-2000
Fax: 716-645-6411
TF: 888-822-3648

Trocaire College
360 Choate Ave
Buffalo, NY 14220
www.trocaire.edu
Phone: 716-826-1200
Fax: 716-826-6107

Villa Maria College of Buffalo
240 Pine Ridge Rd
Buffalo, NY 14225
Phone: 716-896-0700
Fax: 716-896-0705

Hospitals

Buffalo General Hospital
100 High St
Buffalo, NY 14203
www.bgh.edu/facilities/hospitals/bgh/bgh.html
Phone: 716-859-5600
Fax: 716-859-1530

Children's Hospital
219 Bryant St
Buffalo, NY 14222
www.chob.edu
Phone: 716-878-7000
Fax: 716-888-3979

Erie County Medical Center
462 Grider St
Buffalo, NY 14215
Phone: 716-898-3000
Fax: 716-898-5178

Kaleida Health/Millard Fillmore Hospital
3 Gates Cir
Buffalo, NY 14209
www.mfhs.edu
Phone: 716-887-4600
Fax: 716-887-4339

Kenmore Mercy Hospital
2950 Elmwood Ave
Kenmore, NY 14217
Phone: 716-879-6100
Fax: 716-447-6576

Mercy Hospital
565 Abbott Rd
Buffalo, NY 14220
Phone: 716-826-7000
Fax: 716-828-2596

Our Lady of Victory Hospital
55 Melroy
Lackawanna, NY 14218
Phone: 716-825-8000
Fax: 716-827-8635

Saint Joseph Hospital
2605 Harlem Rd
Cheektowaga, NY 14225
Phone: 716-891-2400
Fax: 716-891-2409

Sisters of Charity Hospital of Buffalo
2157 Main St
Buffalo, NY 14214
Phone: 716-862-2000
Fax: 716-862-1019

Veterans Affairs Medical Center
3495 Bailey Ave
Buffalo, NY 14215
Phone: 716-834-9200
Fax: 716-862-8759

Transportation

Airport(s)

Buffalo Niagara International Airport (BUF)
9 miles E of downtown Buffalo
(approx 35 minutes) 716-630-6000

Mass Transit

NFTA Bus
$1.25 Base fare 716-855-7211

Rail/Bus

Amtrak Station
75 Exchange St
Buffalo, NY 14203
Phone: 716-856-2075
TF: 800-872-7245

Greyhound Bus Station
181 Ellicott St
Buffalo, NY 14203
Phone: 716-855-7533
TF: 800-231-2222

Utilities

Electricity
Niagara Mohawk Power Corp 800-932-0301
www.nimo.com

Gas
National Fuel Gas Co 716-857-7000
www.natfuel.com

Water
American Water Services 719-847-1065

Garbage Collection/Recycling
Buffalo Street Sanitation Dept 716-851-5949

Telecommunications

Telephone
Verizon Communications 716-890-5555
www.verizon.com

Cable Television
Adelphia Cable 716-827-9444

Internet Service Providers (ISPs)
Buffalo Free-Net/WNYLRC 716-515-2100
freenet.buffalo.edu
BuffNET Div Marketing & Advertising Services Center Inc 716-825-1300
www.buffnet.net
Franklin Communications Services 716-651-4570
www.fcs-net.com

Banks

Charter One Bank FSB
414 Main St
Buffalo, NY 14202
Phone: 716-855-2532
Fax: 716-855-2536
TF: 800-457-7272

Citibank
2310 Delaware Ave
Buffalo, NY 14216
Phone: 716-873-4233
Fax: 716-873-4184
TF: 800-934-1609

First Niagara Bank
2141 Elmwood Ave
Buffalo, NY 14207
Phone: 716-447-9048
Fax: 716-447-1983

Fleet Bank of New York
10 Fountain Plaza
Buffalo, NY 14202
Phone: 716-847-7200
Fax: 716-849-3602
TF: 800-841-4000

HSBC Bank USA
1 HSBC Ctr
Buffalo, NY 14203
www.us.hsbc.com
Phone: 716-841-2424
Fax: 716-841-4746

KeyBank NA Buffalo District
50 Fountain Plaza
Buffalo, NY 14202
Phone: 716-847-7743
Fax: 716-847-7890

M & T Bank
788 Tonawanda St
Buffalo, NY 14207
Phone: 716-873-6300
Fax: 716-873-8607
TF: 800-724-2440

Manufacturers & Traders Trust Co
1 M & T Plaza
Buffalo, NY 14203
www.mandtbank.com
Phone: 716-842-5789
Fax: 716-842-5020

National Bank of Canada
350 Main St Suite 2540
Buffalo, NY 14202
Phone: 716-852-6831
Fax: 716-852-6832

Shopping

Antique World
10995 Main St
Clarence, NY 14031
Phone: 716-759-8483
Fax: 716-759-6167
TF: 800-959-0714

Boulevard Mall
730 E Alberta Dr
Amherst, NY 14226
www.boulevard-mall.com
Phone: 716-834-8600
Fax: 716-836-6127

Eastern Hills Mall
4545 Transit Rd
Williamsville, NY 14221
Phone: 716-631-5191
Fax: 716-631-5127

Main Place Mall
390 Main St
Buffalo, NY 14202
Phone: 716-855-1900
Fax: 716-855-2487

McKinley Mall
Milestrip Rd & McKinley Pkwy
Blasdell, NY 14219
Phone: 716-824-0462
Fax: 716-824-2433

Prime Outlets of Niagara Falls USA
1900 Military Rd
Niagara Falls, NY 14304
www.primeoutlets.com/NiagaraFallsUSA/
Phone: 716-297-2022
Fax: 716-297-6460
TF: 800-414-0475

Rainbow Centre Factory Outlet
302 Rainbow Blvd N
Niagara Falls, NY 14303
Phone: 716-285-5525
Fax: 716-285-2404

Summit Park Mall
6329 Williams Rd
Niagara Falls, NY 14304
Phone: 716-773-7638
Fax: 716-297-3594

Walden Galleria
1 Walden Galleria
Buffalo, NY 14225
www.waldengalleria.com
Phone: 716-681-7600
Fax: 716-681-1773

Media

Newspapers and Magazines

ArtVoice
500 Franklin St
Buffalo, NY 14202
www.artvoice.com
Phone: 716-881-6604
Fax: 716-881-6682

Buffalo Beat
25 Boxwood Ln
Buffalo, NY 14225
E-mail: editorial@buffalobeat.com
www.buffalobeat.com
Phone: 716-656-5219
Fax: 716-668-2640

Buffalo News*
1 News Plaza PO Box 100
Buffalo, NY 14240
www.buffnews.com
Phone: 716-849-3434
Fax: 716-856-5150

Buffalo Spree Magazine
5678 Main St
Buffalo, NY 14221
E-mail: info@buffalospree.com
www.buffalospree.com
Phone: 716-634-0820
Fax: 716-810-0075

Business First
472 Delaware Ave
Buffalo, NY 14202
www.amcity.com/buffalo
Phone: 716-882-6200
Fax: 716-882-4269

**Indicates major daily newspapers*

Television

WGRZ-TV Ch 2 (NBC)
259 Delaware Ave
Buffalo, NY 14202
Phone: 716-849-2222
Fax: 716-849-7602

WIVB-TV Ch 4 (CBS)
2077 Elmwood Ave
Buffalo, NY 14207
www.wivb.com
Phone: 716-874-4410
Fax: 716-879-4896

WKBW-TV Ch 7 (ABC)
7 Broadcast Plaza
Buffalo, NY 14202
E-mail: wkbwtv@wkbw.com
www.wkbw.com
Phone: 716-845-6100
Fax: 716-856-8784

WNED-TV Ch 17 (PBS)
PO Box 1263
Buffalo, NY 14240
www.wned.org
Phone: 716-845-7000
Fax: 716-845-7036

WNGS-TV Ch 67 (UPN)
9279 Dutch Hill Rd
West Valley, NY 14171
E-mail: wngs@wngstv.com
www.wngstv.com
Phone: 716-942-3000
Fax: 716-942-3010

WNYO-TV Ch 49 (WB)
699 Hertel Ave Suite 100
Buffalo, NY 14207
www.wb49.com
Phone: 716-875-4949
Fax: 716-875-4919

WUTV-TV Ch 29 (Fox)
951 Whitehaven Rd
Grand Island, NY 14072
www.wutv.com
Phone: 716-773-7531
Fax: 716-773-5753

Radio

WBEN-AM 930 kHz (N/T)
500 Corporate Pkwy Suite 200
Buffalo, NY 14226
E-mail: wben@cidcorp.com
www.wben.com
Phone: 716-876-0930
Fax: 716-876-1344

WBFO-FM 88.7 MHz (NPR)
205 Allen Hall
Buffalo, NY 14214
www.wbfo.buffalo.edu
Phone: 716-829-2555
Fax: 716-829-2277
TF: 800-829-6000

WBLK-FM 93.7 MHz (Urban)
14 Lafayette Sq Suite 1300
Buffalo, NY 14203
E-mail: talk2us@wblk.com
www.wblk.com
Phone: 716-852-9393
Fax: 716-852-9390

WBNY-FM 91.3 MHz (Alt)
1300 Elmwood Ave
Buffalo, NY 14222
Phone: 716-878-5104
Fax: 716-878-6600

WBUF-FM 92.9 MHz (Oldies)
14 Lafayette Sq Suite 1300
Buffalo, NY 14203
Phone: 716-852-9292
Fax: 716-852-9290

WDCX-FM 99.5 MHz (Rel)
625 Delaware Ave Suite 308
Buffalo, NY 14202
Phone: 716-883-3010
Fax: 716-883-3606

WECK-AM 1230 kHz (Nost)
1200 Rand Bldg Suite 1200
Buffalo, NY 14203
Phone: 716-852-7444
Fax: 716-852-0537

WEDG-FM 103.3 MHz (Alt)
464 Franklin St
Buffalo, NY 14202
E-mail: edgestu@localnet.com
www.wedg.com
Phone: 716-881-4555
Fax: 716-884-2931

WFBF-FM 89.9 MHz (Rel)
910 Union Rd
West Seneca, NY 14224
Phone: 800-543-1495

WGR-AM 550 kHz (N/T)
695 Delaware Ave
Buffalo, NY 14209
E-mail: wgr55@wgr55.com
www.wgr55.com
Phone: 716-884-5101
Fax: 716-885-8255

WGRF-FM 96.9 MHz (CR)
464 Franklin St
Buffalo, NY 14202
E-mail: info@wgrf.com
www.wgrf.com
Phone: 716-881-4555
Fax: 716-884-2931

WHLD-AM 1270 kHz (Misc)
225 Delaware
Buffalo, NY 14202
www.wnybiz.com/whld
Phone: 716-855-1270
Fax: 716-848-9518

WHTT-AM 1120 kHz (Rel)
225 Delaware Ave
Buffalo, NY 14202
E-mail: whtt@whtt.com
www.whtt.com
Phone: 716-848-1120
Fax: 716-848-9518

WHTT-FM 104.1 MHz (Oldies)
464 Franklin St
Buffalo, NY 14202
www.whtt.com
Phone: 716-881-4555
Fax: 716-884-2931

WJYE-FM 96.1 MHz (AC)
1200 Rand Bldg
Buffalo, NY 14203
www.wjye.com
Phone: 716-852-7444
Fax: 716-852-0537

WKSE-FM 98.5 MHz (CHR)
695 Delaware Ave
Buffalo, NY 14209
www.kiss985.com
Phone: 716-884-5101
Fax: 716-644-9329

WMJQ-FM 102.5 MHz (AC)
2077 Elmwood Ave
Buffalo, NY 14207
Phone: 716-876-0930
Fax: 716-875-6201

WNED-AM 970 kHz (NPR)
PO Box 1263
Buffalo, NY 14240
www.wned.org/Radio/AM
Phone: 716-845-7000
Fax: 716-845-7043

WNUC-FM 107.7 MHz (Ctry)
5500 Main St
Williamsville, NY 14221
E-mail: station@wnuc.com
www.wnuc.com
Phone: 716-626-1077
Fax: 716-626-1395

WUFO-AM 1080 kHz (Rel)
89 LaSalle Ave
Buffalo, NY 14214
www.apollo3.com/wufo
Phone: 716-834-1080
Fax: 716-837-1438

WWKB-AM 1520 kHz (Sports)
695 Delaware Ave
Buffalo, NY 14209
Phone: 716-884-5101
Fax: 716-881-0143

WWWS-AM 1400 kHz (Urban)
2077 Elmwood Ave
Buffalo, NY 14207
Phone: 716-876-0930
Fax: 716-875-6201

WXRL-AM 1300 kHz (Ctry)
PO Box 170
Lancaster, NY 14086
E-mail: country@wxrl.com
www.wxrl.com
Phone: 716-681-1313
Fax: 716-681-7172

WYRK-FM 106.5 MHz (Ctry)
14 Lafayette Sq 1200 Rand Bldg
Buffalo, NY 14203
www.wyrk.com
Phone: 716-852-7444
Fax: 716-852-5683

Attractions

Located at the eastern end of Lake Erie, Buffalo is ringed with 3,000 acres of parks, including the Buffalo Zoological Gardens and the Buffalo and Erie County Naval and Servicemen's Park, the nation's only inland naval park. However, the best-known area attraction is spectacular Niagara Falls, including the view of Goat Island, which separates the American and Canadian falls. The neighboring Great

Lakes create a snow belt that provides top skiing conditions in the Greater Niagara area throughout the winter season. Ice fishing is also popular, and the Erie and Chataqua Lakes are known as some of the best spots for the sport.

African American Cultural Center
350 Masten Ave
Buffalo, NY 14209
Phone: 716-884-2013
Fax: 716-885-2590

Albright-Knox Art Gallery
1285 Elmwood Ave
Buffalo, NY 14222
www.albrightknox.org
Phone: 716-882-8700
Fax: 716-882-1958

Alleyway Theatre
1 Curtain Up Alley
Buffalo, NY 14202
E-mail: email@alleyway.com
www.alleyway.com
Phone: 716-852-2600
Fax: 716-852-2266

Amherst Museum
3755 Tonawanda Creek Rd
Amherst, NY 14228
Phone: 716-689-1440
Fax: 716-689-1409

Anderson Gallery
1 Martha Jackson Pl
Buffalo, NY 14214
E-mail: andgal@pce.net
Phone: 716-834-2579
Fax: 716-834-7789

Aurora Historical Museum
5 S Grove St
East Aurora, NY 14052
Phone: 716-652-3280

Broadway Market
999 Broadway
Buffalo, NY 14212
E-mail: manager@broadwaymarket.com
www.broadwaymarket.com
Phone: 716-893-0705
Fax: 716-893-2216

Buffalo & Erie County Botanical Gardens
2655 S Park Ave
Buffalo, NY 14218
intotem.buffnet.net/gardens/welcome.html
Phone: 716-827-1584
Fax: 716-828-0091

Buffalo & Erie County Historical Society
25 Nottingham Ct
Buffalo, NY 14216
E-mail: bechs@buffnet.net
intotem.buffnet.net/bechs
Phone: 716-873-9644
Fax: 716-873-8754

Buffalo & Erie County Naval & Military Park
1 Naval Park Cove
Buffalo, NY 14202
E-mail: npark@ci.buffalo.ny.us
www.buffalonavalpark.org
Phone: 716-847-1773
Fax: 716-847-6405

Buffalo Chamber Music Society
Symphony Cir Kleinhans Music Hall
Buffalo, NY 14201
Phone: 716-838-2383
Fax: 716-838-2383

Buffalo Ensemble Theatre
95 N Johnson Pk
Buffalo, NY 14201
freenet.buffalo.edu/arts/pac/bet
Phone: 716-855-2225

Buffalo Fire Historical Museum
1850 William St
Buffalo, NY 14206
E-mail: bfdsteamer@aol.com
Phone: 716-892-8400

Buffalo Inner-City Ballet Co
2495 Main St
Buffalo, NY 14214
Phone: 716-833-1243
Fax: 716-833-1243

Buffalo Museum of Science
1020 Humboldt Pkwy
Buffalo, NY 14211
www.sciencebuff.org
Phone: 716-896-5200
Fax: 716-897-6723

Buffalo Philharmonic Orchestra
71 Symphony Cir
Buffalo, NY 14201
www.bpo.org
Phone: 716-885-0331
Fax: 716-885-9372

Buffalo State College Performing Arts Center
1300 Elmwood Ave Rockwell Hall Room 210
Buffalo, NY 14222
www.buffalostate.edu/~rockwell/
Phone: 716-878-3005
Fax: 716-878-4234

Buffalo Zoological Gardens
300 Parkside Ave
Buffalo, NY 14214
www.buffalozoo.org
Phone: 716-837-3900
Fax: 716-837-0738

Burchfield-Penney Art Center
1300 Elmwood Ave Buffalo State College Rockwell Hall
Buffalo, NY 14222
E-mail: burchfld@buffalostate.edu
www.burchfield-penney.org
Phone: 716-878-6011
Fax: 716-878-6003

Center for the Arts
North Campus University at Buffalo
Buffalo, NY 14260
Phone: 716-645-2787
Fax: 716-645-6973

City Hall Observation Deck
65 Niagara Sq
Buffalo, NY 14202
Phone: 716-851-5874
Fax: 716-851-4791

Cofeld Benjamin & Dr Edgar R Judaic Museum of Temple Beth Zion
805 Delaware Ave
Buffalo, NY 14209
Phone: 716-886-7150
Fax: 716-886-7152

Connecticut Street Armory
184 Connecticut St
Buffalo, NY 14213
www.dmna.state.ny.us/map/buf-conn.html
Phone: 716-887-2101
Fax: 716-884-5557

Elbert Hubbard-Roycroft Museum
363 Oakwood Ave
East Aurora, NY 14052
www.roycrofter.com/museum.htm
Phone: 716-652-4735

Explore & More-A Children's Museum
300 Gleed St
East Aurora, NY 14052
Phone: 716-655-5131
Fax: 716-655-5131

Forest Lawn Cemetery & Garden Mausoleums
1411 Delaware Ave
Buffalo, NY 14209
E-mail: FLC@forest-lawn.com
www.forest-lawn.com
Phone: 716-885-1600
Fax: 716-881-6482

Frank Lloyd Wright's Darwin D Martin House
125 Jewett Pkwy
Buffalo, NY 14214
www.darwinmartinhouse.org
Phone: 716-856-3858
Fax: 716-856-4009

Hallwalls Contemporary Arts Center
2495 Main St
Buffalo, NY 14214
darius.pce.net/hallwall
Phone: 716-835-7362
Fax: 716-835-7364

Irish Classical Theatre
625 Main St
Buffalo, NY 14203
www.irishtheatre.com
Phone: 716-852-2356
Fax: 716-853-0592

Iron Island Museum
1330 Lovejoy St
Buffalo, NY 14206
Phone: 716-892-3084

Karpeles Manuscript Library
453 Porter Ave
Buffalo, NY 14201
E-mail: kmuseumbuf@aol.com
www.rain.org/~karpeles
Phone: 716-885-4139
Fax: 716-885-4139

Kavinoky Theatre
320 Porter Ave
Buffalo, NY 14201
www.dyc.edu/Kavinoky
Phone: 716-881-7668
Fax: 716-881-7790

Kleinhans Music Hall
Symphony Cir
Buffalo, NY 14201
Phone: 716-883-3560
Fax: 716-883-7430

Martin's Fantasy Island
2400 Grand Island Blvd
Grand Island, NY 14072
E-mail: martinsfantasyisland@juno.com
www.martinsfantasyisland.com
Phone: 716-773-7591
Fax: 716-773-7043

Millard Fillmore House
24 Shearer Ave
East Aurora, NY 14052
Phone: 716-652-8875

Miss Buffalo Boat Trip
79 Marine Dr
Buffalo, NY 14202
E-mail: bfloboat@localnet.com
www.missbuffalo.com
Phone: 716-856-6696
Fax: 716-856-8901

New Phoenix Theatre
95 N Johnson Pk
Buffalo, NY 14201
connection.buffnet.net/bet
Phone: 716-855-2225

Niagara Falls
Prospect Park
Niagara Falls, NY 14303
www.niagara-info.com
Phone: 716-278-1770
Fax: 716-278-1744

Original American Kazoo Co
8703 S Main St
Eden, NY 14057
www.streethockey.com/brimms/kazoo_mus.html
Phone: 716-992-3960
Fax: 716-992-2728
TF: 800-798-3444

Pedaling History Bicycle Museum
3943 N Buffalo Rd
Orchard Park, NY 14127
E-mail: bicyclemus@aol.com
members.aol.com/bicyclemus/bike_museum/PedHist.htm
Phone: 716-662-3853
Fax: 716-662-4594

Pfeifer Theatre
681 Main St
Buffalo, NY 14203
www.arts.buffalo.edu
Phone: 716-847-6461

QRS Music Rolls Inc
1026 Niagara St
Buffalo, NY 14213
E-mail: qrs@aol.com
www.qrsmusic.com
Phone: 716-885-4600
Fax: 716-885-7510
TF: 800-247-6557

Robeson Paul Theatre
350 Masten Ave
Buffalo, NY 14209
Phone: 716-884-2013
Fax: 716-885-2590

Shea's Performing Arts Center
646 Main St
Buffalo, NY 14202
E-mail: sheas@buffnet.net
www.sheas.org
Phone: 716-847-1410
Fax: 716-847-1644
TF: 800-217-4327

Steel Plant Museum
560 Ridge Rd Lackawanna Public Library
Lackawanna, NY 14218
Phone: 716-823-0630
Fax: 716-827-1997

Studio Arena Theatre
710 Main St
Buffalo, NY 14202
www.studioarena.org
Phone: 716-856-5650
Fax: 716-856-3415
TF: 800-777-8243

Theatre of Youth (TOY) Co
203 Allen St
Buffalo, NY 14201
Phone: 716-884-4400
Fax: 716-887-9761

Theodore Roosevelt Inaugural National Historical Site
641 Delaware Ave
Buffalo, NY 14202
www.nps.gov/thri
Phone: 716-884-0095
Fax: 716-884-0330

Tifft Nature Preserve
1200 Fuhrmann Blvd
Buffalo, NY 14203
bms.buffnet.net/Tifft_Nature_Preserve
Phone: 716-825-6397
Fax: 716-824-6718

Toy Town Museum
636 Girard Ave
East Aurora, NY 14052
www.toytownusa.com
Phone: 716-687-5151
Fax: 716-687-5098

Ujima Theatre Co
545 Elmwood Ave
Buffalo, NY 14222
Phone: 716-883-4232
Fax: 716-882-4960

Victor Reinstein Woods Nature Preserve
77 Honorine Dr
Depew, NY 14043
Phone: 716-683-5959

Sports Teams & Facilities

Buffalo Bandits (lacrosse)
1 Seymour H Knox III Plaza Marine Midland Arena
Buffalo, NY 14203
Phone: 716-855-4100
Fax: 716-855-4110

Buffalo Bills
1 Bills Dr Ralph Wilson Stadium
Orchard Park, NY 14127
E-mail: info@buffalobills.com
www.buffalobills.com
Phone: 716-649-0015
Fax: 716-648-4099

Buffalo Bisons (baseball)
275 Washington St Dunn Tire Pk
Buffalo, NY 14203
E-mail: info@bisons.com
www.bisons.com
Phone: 716-843-4373
Fax: 716-852-6530

Buffalo Blizzard (soccer)
1 Seymour H Knox III Plaza Marine Midland Arena
Buffalo, NY 14203
www.buffaloblizzard.com
Phone: 716-855-4100
Fax: 716-855-4151

Buffalo Destroyers (football)
1 Seymour H Knox III Plaza Marine Midland Arena
Buffalo, NY 14203
www.buffalodestroyers.com
Phone: 716-881-5676
Fax: 716-881-4516

Buffalo Raceway
5600 McKinley Pkwy
Hamburg, NY 14075
Phone: 716-649-1280
Fax: 716-649-0033

Buffalo Sabres
1 Seymour H Knox III Plaza Marine Midland Arena
Buffalo, NY 14203
www.sabres.com
Phone: 716-855-4100
Fax: 716-855-4110

Buffalo Wings (roller hockey)
1300 Elmwood Ave Buffalo State Sports Arena
Buffalo, NY 14203
E-mail: wings@buffnet.net
www.buffalowings.net
Phone: 716-856-0102
Fax: 716-856-0214

Holland International Speedway
2 N Main St
Holland, NY 14080
E-mail: tbennett@hollandspeedway.com
www.hollandspeedway.com
Phone: 716-537-2272
Fax: 716-537-9749

HSBC Arena
1 Seymour Knox Plaza
Buffalo, NY 14203
Phone: 716-855-4100
Fax: 716-855-4110

Annual Events

Allentown Art Festival (mid-June) 716-881-4269
Antique World Expo (late May & late August). 716-759-8483
Blues Festival (late July) 716-855-8800
Buffalo Irish Festival (late August) 716-839-0002
Buffalo Marathon (early May) 716-837-7223
Canal Fest of the Tonawandas (mid-late July) 716-692-3292
Caribbean Festival (mid-August) 716-881-3266
Dyngus Day (early-mid-April) 716-852-0511
Erie County Fair & Expo (mid-August) 716-649-3900
Festival of Lights (late November-early January) 800-421-5223
First Night Buffalo (December 31) 716-852-0511
Friendship Festival (late June-early July). 716-852-0511
Friendship Tree Lighting (late November). 716-852-0511
Greek Hellenic Festival (mid-late May). 716-882-9485
Hawk Creek Wildlife Weekend (early August) 716-652-8646
Hellenic Festival (mid-May). 800-283-3256
Holiday Tree Lighting Ceremony (late November) . . .716-856-3150
Ice Castle Extravaganza/Winter Festival (mid-February). 716-357-4569
Italian Festival (mid-July) 716-874-6133
Italian Heritage & Food Festival (mid-July) 716-851-4144
Juneteenth Festival (mid-June) 716-691-8106
Olmsted Winter Carnival (mid-late February) 716-851-5806
Polish American Arts Festival (mid-August) 716-686-3460
Quaker Days (late July) 716-662-3366
Saint Patrick's Day Parade (mid-March) 716-825-9535
Scottish Festival & Highland Games (mid-late August). 716-689-1440
Shakespeare in Delaware Park (late June-late August) 716-856-4533
Taste of Buffalo (early July) 716-831-9376
Traditional German-American Festival (early September) 716-684-4745
Victorian Christmas Festival (early December) 607-587-9441
Waterfront Festival Summer Concert Series (July-August) 716-884-8865
World Pumpkin Weigh-Off (early October) 716-759-2260

Charleston, South Carolina

***County:* Charleston**

CHARLESTON is located on a peninsula between the Ashley and Cooper Rivers along the Atlantic Coast of central South Carolina. Cities within 100 miles include Columbia, South Carolina and Savannah, Georgia.

Area (Land)	43.2 sq mi
Area (Water)	8.4 sq mi
Elevation	118 ft
Latitude	32-77-85 N
Longitude	79-93-55 W
Time Zone	EST
Area Code	843

Climate

Charleston has a temperate to subtropical climate. Winters are generally mild, with daytime high temperatures averaging near 60 degrees and nighttime lows near 40; snowfall is rare. Summers are hot and humid, with daytime highs averaging near 90 degrees. The average humidity for the area is 86% at 6 a.m. Summer is also the rainy season in Charleston, with July and August being the wettest months. November is the driest month of the year in Charleston.

Average Temperatures & Precipitation

Temperatures

	Jan	Feb	Mar	Apr	May	Jun	Jul	Aug	Sep	Oct	Nov	Dec
High	58	61	67	76	83	88	90	89	85	77	70	62
Low	38	40	48	54	63	69	73	72	68	56	47	41

Precipitation

	Jan	Feb	Mar	Apr	May	Jun	Jul	Aug	Sep	Oct	Nov	Dec
Inches	3.5	3.3	4.3	2.7	4.0	6.4	6.8	7.2	4.7	2.9	2.5	3.2

History

Charleston was founded and settled in the 1670s by English colonists, who originally named the city Charles Towne, after King Charles II. The seaport city grew quickly with its successful cotton and tobacco trade and religious tolerance laws, which guaranteed residents the freedom to choose any spiritual belief. In addition to trade, agriculture also helped fuel the city's early economy, with rice, cotton, and indigo as the primary crops. Charles Towne prospered during the 18th Century. The nation's oldest continually operating chamber of commerce was established in Charles Towne in 1773. Sometimes referred to as the "Holy City," Charleston features dozens of historic churches that stand as a testament to the large numbers of immigrants of various religious backgrounds, including French Huguenots, Irish, Germans, and Sephardic Jews, who came to the city seeking religious freedom. Other historic buildings in Charleston have served as a backdrop for scenes in such famous films as "Gone With the Wind" and "North and South." Charles Towne was renamed Charleston and incorporated as a city in 1783.

In 1787, Charleston resident Charles Pickney was the first to propose the addition of a "Bill of Rights" to the U.S. Constitution. He was also among three Charlestonians who signed the famous document. In 1861 Fort Sumter, located in Charleston Harbor, was fired upon, marking the beginning of the Civil War. The war devastated Charleston, as have numerous hurricanes (including Hurricane Hugo in 1989), earthquakes, fires, floods, and tornadoes over the years. Through it all, the city has managed to maintain its historic Southern charm that draws an estimated five million visitors to the area each year.

Population

1990 Census	88,256
1998 Estimate	87,044
% Change	-1.4
2010 Projection	597,200*

Racial/Ethnic Breakdown

White	57.2%
Black	41.6%
Other	1.2%
Hispanic Origin (may be of any race)	0.8%

Age Breakdown

Under 5 years	7.2%
5 to 17	15.1%
18 to 20	8.3%
21 to 24	9.1%
25 to 34	17.8%
35 to 44	13.7%
45 to 54	8.5%
55 to 64	7.6%
65 to 74	7.7%
75+ years	5.2%
Median Age	30.5

Gender Breakdown

Male	47.2%
Female	52.8%

** Information given is for the Charleston Metropolitan Area, which includes the City of Charleston, Berkeley County, Charleston County, and Dorchester County.*

Government

Type of Government: Mayor-Council

Charleston Budget Finance & Revenue Collections Dept
116 Meeting St
Charleston, SC 29401

Phone: 843-579-7529
Fax: 843-720-3901

Charleston City Council Phone: 843-577-6970
80 Broad St Fax: 843-720-3959
Charleston, SC 29401

Charleston City Hall Phone: 843-577-6970
80 Broad St Fax: 843-720-3959
Charleston, SC 29401

Charleston Clerk of Council Phone: 843-577-6970
80 Broad St Fax: 843-720-3959
Charleston, SC 29401

Charleston Economic Development Dept Phone: 843-724-3796
75 Calhoun St 3rd Fl Fax: 843-724-7354
Charleston, SC 29401

Charleston Fire Dept Phone: 843-724-7386
46 1/2 Wentworth St Fax: 843-720-3991
Charleston, SC 29401

Charleston Housing & Community Development Dept Phone: 843-724-7347
75 Calhoun St Fax: 843-720-3836
Charleston, SC 29401

Charleston Human Resources Dept Phone: 843-724-7388
32 Ann St Fax: 843-724-7358
Charleston, SC 29403

Charleston Mayor Phone: 843-577-6970
80 Broad St Fax: 843-720-3827
Charleston, SC 29401

Charleston Parks Dept Phone: 843-724-7321
823 Meeting St Fax: 843-724-7300
Charleston, SC 29403

Charleston Planning & Urban Development Dept Phone: 843-724-3765
75 Calhoun St 3rd Fl Fax: 843-724-3772
Charleston, SC 29401

Charleston Police Dept Phone: 843-720-2495
180 Lockwood Blvd Fax: 843-722-4085
Charleston, SC 29403

Charleston Public Service Dept Phone: 843-724-3754
75 Calhoun St Fax: 843-973-7261
Charleston, SC 29401

Charleston Recreation Dept Phone: 843-724-7327
30 Mary Murray Dr Fax: 843-720-3943
Charleston, SC 29403

Important Phone Numbers

AAA.......843-766-2394
Charleston County Auditor's Office.......843-958-4200
Charleston County Treasurer's Office.......843-958-4360
Charleston Trident Assn of Realtors.......843-760-9400
Dental Referral.......800-327-2598
Driver's License/Vehicle Registration Information.......800-442-1368
Emergency.......911
HotelDocs.......800-468-3537
Medical Referral.......843-577-3613
Poison Control Center.......803-777-1117
South Carolina Dept of Revenue & Taxation.......843-852-3600
Time.......843-572-8463
Voter Registration Information.......843-744-8683
Weather.......843-744-3207

Information Sources

Better Business Bureau Serving Central South Carolina & the Charleston Area Phone: 803-254-2525
PO Box 8326 Fax: 803-779-3117
Columbia, SC 29202
www.columbia.bbb.org

Charleston Area Convention & Visitors Bureau Phone: 843-853-8000
PO Box 975 Fax: 843-853-0444
Charleston, SC 29402 TF: 800-868-8118
www.charlestoncvb.com

Charleston County Phone: 843-958-4030
2 Courthouse Sq Fax: 843-958-4035
Charleston, SC 29401
www.charlestoncounty.org

Charleston Metro Chamber of Commerce Phone: 843-577-2510
81 Mary St Fax: 843-723-4853
Charleston, SC 29403
www.charlestonchamber.net

Online Resources

4Charleston.com
www.4charleston.com

About.com Guide to Charleston
charleston.about.com/citiestowns/southeastus/charleston

Area Guide Charleston
charlestonsc.areaguides.net

Best Read Guide Charleston
bestreadguide.com/charleston

Charleston City Net
www.excite.com/travel/countries/united_states/south_carolina/charleston

Charleston Connections
www.aesir.com/Charleston

Charleston Navi-Gator
www.navi-gator.com/charleston

Charleston Net
www.charleston.net

Charleston Online
www.charleston-online.com

Charleston Traveler Online
www.charlestontraveler.com

City Knowledge Charleston
www.cityknowledge.com/sc_charleston.htm

Cityofcharleston.com
www.cityofcharleston.com

CityTravelers.com Guide to Charleston
www.citytravelers.com/charleston.htm

Destination Charleston
www.charlestonsfinest.com

Essential Guide to Charleston
www.ego.net/us/sc/chs/

InCharleston.com
www.incharleston.com/

Insiders' Guide to Charleston
www.insiders.com/charleston-sc/index.htm

Lodging.com Charleston South Carolina
www.lodging.com/auto/guides/charleston-area-sc.html

Open World City Guides Charleston
www.worldexecutive.com/cityguides/charleston/

Streets of Charleston
www.streetsofcharleston.com

Surf & Sun Beach Vacation Guide to Charleston
www.surf-sun.com/sc-charleston-main.htm

Tour Charleston
tourcharleston.com/

Area Communities

Communities with populations greater than 20,000 in the Charleston metropolitan area, which includes Berkeley, Charleston, and Dorchester counties, include:

Goose Creek
PO Box 1768
Goose Creek, SC 29445
Phone: 843-797-6220
Fax: 843-863-5208

Hanahan
1255 Yeamans Hall Rd
Hanahan, SC 29406
Phone: 843-554-4221
Fax: 843-747-3220

Mount Pleasant
100 Ann Edwards Ln
Mount Pleasant, SC 29464
Phone: 843-884-8517
Fax: 843-849-2060

North Charleston
4900 LaCross Rd
North Charleston, SC 29406
Phone: 843-554-5700
Fax: 843-745-1085

Summerville
104 Civic Ctr
Summerville, SC 29483
Phone: 843-871-6000
Fax: 843-871-6954

Economy

The three largest employment sectors in Metro Charleston—services, government, and trade—employ more than 70 percent of the total workforce. Charleston is the home of numerous military installations, and the U.S. Navy is the area's top employer, providing jobs for more than 7,800 area residents at the Charleston Naval Weapons Station, Naval Hospital and Naval Command, and the Control and Ocean Surveillance Center In Service Engineering, East Coast Division. Trade continues to be a major economic force in Charleston, as it has since the city's early days. The Port of Charleston today is the largest containerized port on the South Atlantic and Gulf Coasts.

Unemployment Rate	3.1%
Per Capita Income	$21,529*
Median Family Income	$43,200*

** Information given is for the Charleston Metropolitan Statistical Area (MSA), which includes the City of Charleston, Berkeley County, Charleston County, and Dorchester County.*

Principal Industries & Number of Wage Earners

Charleston-North Charleston MA* - 1999

Construction & Mining	18,800
Finance, Insurance, & Real Estate	8,900
Government	49,400
Manufacturing	22,200
Retail Trade	51,200
Services	69,700
Transportation & Public Utilities	13,100
Wholesale Trade	9,800

** Information given is for the Charleston-North Charleston Metropolitan Area (MA), which includes Charleston, Berkeley, and Dorchester counties.*

Major Employers

Berkeley County School District
PO Box 608
Moncks Corner, SC 29461
Phone: 843-899-8600
Fax: 843-899-8791

Bosch Robert Corp
8101 Dorchester Rd
Charleston, SC 29418
Phone: 843-760-7000
Fax: 843-760-7379

Charleston Air Force Base
Charleston AFB, SC 29404
www.charleston.af.mil
Phone: 843-963-6000
Fax: 843-963-5604

Charleston City Hall
80 Broad St
Charleston, SC 29401
www.charleston.net/charlestoncity
Phone: 843-577-6970
Fax: 843-720-3959

Charleston County
2 Courthouse Sq
Charleston, SC 29401
E-mail: publicinfo@charlestoncounty.org
www.charlestoncounty.org
Phone: 843-958-4030
Fax: 843-958-4035

Charleston County School District
75 Calhoun St
Charleston, SC 29401
www.charleston.k12.sc.us
Phone: 843-937-6300
Fax: 843-937-6351

Dorchester County School District II
102 Greenwave Blvd
Summerville, SC 29483
Phone: 843-873-2901
Fax: 843-832-7014

Medical University of South Carolina
171 Ashley Ave
Charleston, SC 29425
www.musc.edu
Phone: 843-792-2300
Fax: 843-792-0853

Piggly Wiggly Carolina Co Inc
4401 Piggly Wiggly Dr
Charleston, SC 29405
E-mail: pigsmail@thepig.net
www.thepig.net
Phone: 843-554-9880
Fax: 843-745-2730
TF: 800-243-9880

Roper Hospital
316 Calhoun St
Charleston, SC 29401
Phone: 843-724-2000
Fax: 843-724-2844

Trident Medical Center
9330 Medical Plaza Dr
Charleston, SC 29406
Phone: 843-797-7000
Fax: 843-797-4958

US Postal Service
7075 Cross County Rd
Charleston, SC 29423
new.usps.com
Phone: 843-760-5421
Fax: 843-760-5399

Wal-Mart
1481 US Hwy 17 N
Mount Pleasant, SC 29464
www.walmartstores.com
Phone: 843-881-6100
Fax: 843-971-7412

Westvaco Corp Chemical Div
PO Box 70848
Charleston Heights, SC 29415
www.westvaco.com/products/chemicals/chemicals.htm
Phone: 843-745-3000
Fax: 843-745-3641

Quality of Living Indicators

Total Crime Index.....................................7,617
(rates per 100,000 inhabitants)

Violent Crime
Murder/manslaughter............................ 6
Forcible rape 62
Robbery....................................... 244
Aggravated assault............................ 632

Property Crime
Burglary 1,003
Larceny theft 4,822
Motor vehicle theft 848

Cost of Living Index..................................103.0
(national average = 100)

Median Home Price.................................$131,700

Education

Public Schools

Charleston County School District
75 Calhoun St
Charleston, SC 29401
www.charleston.k12.sc.us
Phone: 843-937-6300
Fax: 843-937-6351

Number of Schools
Elementary.................................. 46
Middle 19
High... 16

Student/Teacher Ratio
All Grades 15.2:1

Private Schools

Number of Schools (all grades)................... 23+

Colleges & Universities

Charleston Southern University
PO Box 118087
Charleston, SC 29423
www.csuniv.edu
Phone: 843-863-7000
Fax: 843-863-7070
TF: 800-947-7474

Citadel The
171 Moultrie Ave
Charleston, SC 29409
www.citadel.edu
Phone: 843-953-5000
Fax: 843-953-7036

College of Charleston
66 George St
Charleston, SC 29424
E-mail: admissions@cofc.edu
www.cofc.edu
Phone: 843-953-5507
Fax: 843-953-6322

Medical University of South Carolina
171 Ashley Ave
Charleston, SC 29425
www.musc.edu
Phone: 843-792-2300
Fax: 843-792-0853

Trident Technical College
PO Box 118067
Charleston, SC 29423
www.trident.tec.sc.us
Phone: 843-574-6111
Fax: 843-574-6483

Hospitals

Bon Secours Saint Francis Xavier Hospital
2095 Henry Tecklenburg Dr
Charleston, SC 29414
Phone: 843-402-1000
Fax: 843-402-1808

Charleston Memorial Hospital
326 Calhoun St
Charleston, SC 29401
Phone: 843-577-0600
Fax: 843-577-2926

Charleston Naval Hospital
3600 Rivers Ave
North Charleston, SC 29405
Phone: 843-743-7000
Fax: 843-743-7256

Columbia Summerville Medical Center
295 Midland Pkwy
Summerville, SC 29485
Phone: 843-875-3993
Fax: 843-832-5037

East Cooper Regional Medical Center
1200 Johnnie Dodds Blvd
Mount Pleasant, SC 29464
www.tenethealth.com/EastCooper
Phone: 843-881-0100
Fax: 843-881-4396

Medical University of South Carolina
171 Ashley Ave
Charleston, SC 29425
www.musc.edu
Phone: 843-792-2300
Fax: 843-792-0853

MUSC Medical Center of Medical University of South Carolina
171 Ashley Ave
Charleston, SC 29425
Phone: 843-792-2300
Fax: 843-792-8948

Ralph H Johnson Veterans Affairs Medical Center
109 Bee St
Charleston, SC 29401
Phone: 843-577-5011
Fax: 843-853-9167
TF: 888-878-6884

Roper Hospital
316 Calhoun St
Charleston, SC 29401
Phone: 843-724-2000
Fax: 843-724-2844

Roper Hospital North
2750 Speissegger Dr
North Charleston, SC 29405
Phone: 843-744-2110
Fax: 843-745-1797

Trident Medical Center
9330 Medical Plaza Dr
Charleston, SC 29406
Phone: 843-797-7000
Fax: 843-797-4958

Transportation

Airport(s)

Charleston International Airport (CHS)
13 miles NW of downtown (approx 20 minutes) . . .843-767-1100

Mass Transit

Downtown Area Shuttle
$.75 Base fare 843-724-7420
SCE&G City Bus
$.75 Base fare 843-747-0922

Rail/Bus

Amtrak Station
4565 Gaynor Ave
Charleston, SC 29405
Phone: 843-744-8264
TF: 800-872-7245

Utilities

Electricity
South Carolina Electric & Gas Co. 843-554-7234
www.goscana.com

Gas
South Carolina Electric & Gas Co. 843-554-7234
www.goscana.com

Water
Charleston Public Service Dept 843-724-3754
www.charleston.net/charlestoncity/pubservice.html

Garbage Collection/Recycling
Charleston County Recycling Center 843-720-7111
Charleston Sanitation Div 843-724-7364

Telecommunications

Telephone
BellSouth 800-336-0014
www.bellsouth.com

Cable Television
Berkeley Cable TV 843-761-8188
Comcast Cable 843-554-4100
Time Warner Cable 843-871-7000
www.timewarner.com
US Cable 843-559-2424

Internet Service Providers (ISPs)
World of Difference Inc 843-769-4488
www.awod.com

Banks

Bank of America
200 Meeting St
Charleston, SC 29401
Phone: 843-723-6819
Fax: 843-723-6850
TF: 800-333-6262

Bank of South Carolina
256 Meeting St
Charleston, SC 29402
Phone: 843-724-1500
Fax: 843-723-1473

Carolina First
276 E Bay St
Charleston, SC 29401
Phone: 843-577-4600
Fax: 843-723-7296

First Citizens Bank & Trust
182 Meeting St
Charleston, SC 29401
Phone: 843-577-4560
Fax: 843-722-5823

Shopping

Citadel Mall
2070 Sam Rittenberg Blvd
Charleston, SC 29407
E-mail: citadelmall@rejacobsgroup.com
www.shopyourmall.com/mall_welcome.asp?map=yes&mall_select=695
Phone: 843-766-8511

Northwoods Mall
2150 Northwoods Blvd Unit 60
North Charleston, SC 29406
E-mail: northwoodsmall@rejacobsgroup.com
www.shopyourmall.com/mall_welcome.asp?map=yes&mall_select=613
Phone: 843-797-3060
Fax: 843-797-8363

Shops at Charleston Place
130 Market St Charleston Place Hotel
Charleston, SC 29401
Phone: 843-722-4900

Media

Newspapers and Magazines

Moultrie News
PO Box 2014
Mount Pleasant, SC 29465
E-mail: eastcopper@aol.com
Phone: 843-849-1778
Fax: 843-849-0214

Post & Courier*
134 Columbus St
Charleston, SC 29403
E-mail: seima@postandcourier.com
www.charleston.net
Phone: 843-577-7111
Fax: 843-937-5579

**Indicates major daily newspapers*

Television

WCBD-TV Ch 2 (NBC)
210 W Coleman Blvd
Mount Pleasant, SC 29464
Phone: 843-884-2222
Fax: 843-881-3410

WCIV-TV Ch 4 (ABC)
PO Box 22165
Charleston, SC 29413
E-mail: newsroom@wciv.com
www.wciv.com
Phone: 843-881-4444
Fax: 843-849-2519

WCSC-TV Ch 5 (CBS)
2126 Charlie Hull Blvd
Charleston, SC 29414
www.wcsc5.com
Phone: 843-577-6397
Fax: 843-402-5744

WITV-TV Ch 7 (PBS)
PO Box 11000
Columbia, SC 29201
Phone: 803-737-3200
Fax: 803-737-3476

WTAT-TV Ch 24 (Fox)
4301 Arco Ln
Charleston, SC 29418
Phone: 843-744-2424
Fax: 843-554-9649

Radio

WAVF-FM 96.1 MHz (Rock)
1964 Ashley River Rd
Charleston, SC 29407
E-mail: comments@96wave.net
www.96wave.net
Phone: 843-852-9003
Fax: 843-852-9041

WMGL-FM 101.7 MHz (Urban)
2045 Spaulding Dr
Charleston, SC 29418
www.charlestonradio.com/magic
Phone: 843-308-9300
Fax: 843-308-9590

WPAL-FM 100.9 mHz (Urban)
1717 Wappoo Rd
Charleston, SC 29407
Phone: 843-763-6330
Fax: 843-769-4857

WQSC-AM 1340 kHz (Sports)
4995 LaCross Rd Suite 2200
North Charleston, SC 29418
Phone: 843-566-0074
Fax: 843-566-0806

WSSX-FM 95.1 MHz (AC)
1 Orange Grove Rd
Charleston, SC 29407
Phone: 843-556-5660
Fax: 843-763-0304

WSUY-FM 96.9 MHz (NAC)
1 Orange Grove Rd
Charleston, SC 29407
Phone: 843-556-5660
Fax: 843-763-0304

WTMA-AM 1250 kHz (N/T)
1 Orange Grove Rd
Charleston, SC 29407
Phone: 843-556-5660
Fax: 843-763-0304

WYBB-FM 98.1 MHz (CR)
59 Windermere Blvd
Charleston, SC 29407
E-mail: 98rock@awod.com
www.98rock.net
Phone: 843-769-4799
Fax: 843-769-4797

Attractions

The historic area in Charleston features beautiful original structures built at the turn of the 18th Century that serve as museums, shops, offices, and homes for Charleston's current residents. Among these is the Charleston Museum, which is America's oldest museum. Charleston's many historic churches reflect the diversity of spiritual beliefs and worship styles of the city's early residents. The historic area also includes the Market area and Waterfront Park, with a view of Charleston Harbor. Water tours of the harbor include stops at Fort Sumter and the U.S. Naval Base. Popular resorts in the Charleston area include Kiawah Island, noted for its award-winning golf courses, and Isle of Palms.

Aiken-Rhett House
48 Elizabeth St
Charleston, SC 29423
Phone: 843-723-1159

Audubon Swamp Garden
3550 Ashley River Rd Magnolia Plantation & Gardens
Charleston, SC 29414
E-mail: magnolia@internetx.net
www.magnoliaplantation.com
Phone: 843-571-1266
Fax: 843-571-5346
TF: 800-367-3517

Avery Research Center for African-American History & Culture
125 Bull St
Charleston, SC 29424
E-mail: netmgr@coax.net
www.coax.net/people/lwf/avery.htm
Phone: 843-953-7609
Fax: 843-953-7607

Best Friend Museum
31 Ann St
Charleston, SC 29403
Phone: 843-973-7269
Fax: 843-720-3999

Boone Hall Plantation
1235 Longpoint Rd
Charleston, SC 29464
Phone: 843-884-4371
Fax: 843-881-3642

Calhoun Mansion
16 Meeting St
Charleston, SC 29401
Phone: 843-722-8205

Cape Romain National Wildlife Refuge
5801 Hwy 17 N
Awendaw, SC 29429
southeast.fws.gov/caperomain
Phone: 843-928-3264
Fax: 843-928-3803

Charles Pinckney National Historic Site
1254 Long Point Rd
Mount Pleasant, SC 29464
www.nps.gov/chpi/
Phone: 843-881-5516
Fax: 843-881-7070

Charles Towne Landing
1500 Old Towne Rd
Charleston, SC 29407
Phone: 843-852-4200
Fax: 843-852-4205

Charleston Ballet Theatre
477 King St
Charleston, SC 29403
E-mail: tdominey@charlestonballet.com
www.charlestonballet.com
Phone: 843-723-7334
Fax: 843-723-9099

Charleston Ghost Walk
170 Church St Market Sq
Charleston, SC 29401
Phone: 843-577-5931

Charleston Museum
360 Meeting St
Charleston, SC 29403
www.charlestonmuseum.com
Phone: 843-722-2996
Fax: 843-722-1784

Charleston Stage Co
133 Church St Suite 7
Charleston, SC 29401
Phone: 843-577-5967
Fax: 843-577-5422

Charleston Symphony Orchestra
14 George St
Charleston, SC 29401
E-mail: info@charlestonsymphony.com
www.charlestonsymphony.com
Phone: 843-723-7528
Fax: 843-722-3463

Charleston Visitor Center
375 Meeting St
Charleston, SC 29402
Phone: 843-853-8000

Circular Congregation Church
150 Meeting St
Charleston, SC 29401
Phone: 843-577-6400

Citadel Archives & Museum
171 Moultrie St The Citadel
Charleston, SC 29409
Phone: 843-953-6846
Fax: 843-953-6956

City Marina
17 Lockwood Blvd
Charleston, SC 29401
Phone: 843-723-5098
Fax: 843-853-1840

College of Charleston
Saint Philip & George Sts
Charleston, SC 29401
Phone: 843-953-5507

Confederate Museum
34 Pitt St
Charleston, SC 29401
Phone: 800-774-0006

Congregation Beth Elohim
90 Hasell St
Charleston, SC 29401
Phone: 843-723-1090
Fax: 843-723-0537

Cypress Gardens
3030 Cypress Gardens Rd
Moncks Corner, SC 29461
Phone: 843-553-0515
Fax: 843-569-0644

Dock Street Theatre
135 Church St
Charleston, SC 29401
www.charlestonstage.com
Phone: 843-577-5967
Fax: 843-577-5422
TF: 800-454-7093

Drayton Hall
3380 Ashley River Rd
Charleston, SC 29414
www.draytonhall.org
Phone: 843-766-0188
Fax: 843-766-0878

Edmondston-Alston House
21 E Battery
Charleston, SC 29401
Phone: 843-722-7171

Emanuel African Methodist Episcopal Church
110 Calhoun St
Charleston, SC 29401
Phone: 843-722-2561

First (Scots) Presbyterian Church
53 Meeting St
Charleston, SC 29401
Phone: 843-722-8882
Fax: 843-722-8538

First Baptist Church
48 Meeting St
Charleston, SC 29401
Phone: 843-722-3896
Fax: 843-720-2175

Footlight Players
20 Queen St
Charleston, SC 29401
Phone: 843-722-7521

Fort Sumter National Monument
1214 Middle St
Sullivans Island, SC 29482
www.nps.gov/fosu/
Phone: 843-883-3123
Fax: 843-883-3910

French Protestant (Huguenot) Church
136 Church St
Charleston, SC 29401
Phone: 843-722-4385

Gibbes Museum of Art
135 Meeting St
Charleston, SC 29401
www.gibbes.com
Phone: 843-722-2706
Fax: 843-720-1682

Hall Gallery at City Hall
80 Broad St
Charleston, SC 29402
Phone: 843-724-3799

Heyward-Washington House
87 Church St
Charleston, SC 29401
Phone: 843-722-0354

Karpeles Manuscript Library Museum
68 Spring St
Charleston, SC 29403
www.rain.org/~karpeles/chr.html
Phone: 843-853-4651
Fax: 843-853-4651

Magnolia Plantation & Gardens
3550 Ashley River Rd
Charleston, SC 29414
E-mail: magnolia@internetx.net
www.magnoliaplantation.net
Phone: 843-571-1266
Fax: 843-571-5346
TF: 800-367-3517

Middleton Place
4300 Ashley River Rd
Charleston, SC 29414
www2.middletonplace.org
Phone: 843-556-6020
Fax: 843-766-4460

Nathaniel Russell House
51 Meeting St
Charleston, SC 29401
Phone: 843-724-8481

Old Bethel Methodist Church
222 Calhoun St
Charleston, SC 29401
Phone: 843-722-3470

Old Exchange & Provost Dungeon
122 E Bay St
Charleston, SC 29401
www.ccpl.org/ccl/exchange.html
Phone: 843-727-2165
Fax: 843-727-2163

Old Powder Magazine
79 Cumberland St
Charleston, SC 29401
Phone: 843-805-6730

Palmetto Islands County Park
444 Needlerush Pkwy
Mount Pleasant, SC 29464
Phone: 843-884-0832
Fax: 843-884-0254

Patriots Point Naval & Maritime Museum
Charleston Harbor 40 Patriots Point Rd
Mount Pleasant, SC 29464
www.state.sc.us/patpt/
Phone: 843-884-2727
Fax: 843-881-4232
TF: 800-248-3508

Postal Museum
Meeting & Broad Sts
Charleston, SC 29401
Phone: 843-853-8000

Rainbow Row
99-101 E Bay St
Charleston, SC 29401

Saint Andrews Parish Church
2604 Ashley River Rd
Charleston, SC 29401
Phone: 843-766-1541

Saint John's Lutheran Church
Clifford & Archdale Sts
Charleston, SC 29401
Phone: 843-723-2426
Fax: 843-577-2543

Saint Mary's Roman Catholic Church
89 Hasell St
Charleston, SC 29401
Phone: 843-722-7696
Fax: 843-577-5036

Saint Michael's Episcopal Church
Meeting & Broad Sts
Charleston, SC 29401
Phone: 843-723-0603
Fax: 843-724-7578

Shem Creek Maritime Museum
510 Mill St
Mount Pleasant, SC 29464
Phone: 843-849-9000
Fax: 843-884-5020

South Carolina Aquarium
57 Hasell St
Charleston, SC 29401
E-mail: seaquarium@awod.com
www.scaquarium.org
Phone: 843-720-1990
Fax: 843-720-3861

Washington Square
Meeting & Broad Sts
Charleston, SC 29401
Phone: 843-853-8000

White Point Gardens
2 Murray Blvd
Charleston, SC 29401
Phone: 843-724-7321

Sports Teams & Facilities

Charleston Battery (soccer)
1990 Daniel Island Rd Blackbaud Stadium
Daniel Island, SC 29492
www.charlestonbattery.com
Phone: 843-971-4625
Fax: 843-856-6958

Charleston Riverdogs (baseball)
360 Fishburne St
Charleston, SC 29403
E-mail: dogrus@riverdogs.com
www.awod.com/riverdogs
Phone: 843-577-3647
Fax: 843-723-2641

North Charleston Coliseum & Convention Center
5001 Coliseum Dr
North Charleston, SC 29418
Phone: 843-529-5050
Fax: 843-529-5010

South Carolina Stingrays (hockey)
3107 Firestone Rd
North Charleston, SC 29418
www.stingrayshockey.com
Phone: 843-744-2248
Fax: 843-744-2898

Annual Events

Battle of Secessionville (early November) 843-795-3049
Big Kahuna Tournament (early September) 843-588-3474
Blues Festival (early-mid-February)................ 843-762-9125
Carolina Day (late June).......................... 843-883-3123
Charleston Antiques Show (late October) 843-849-1949
Charleston Cup (early November) 843-766-6208
Charleston Maritime Harborfest (mid-April) 843-577-8878
Christmas in Charleston (December) 843-853-8000
Fall Candlelight Tours of Homes & Gardens (mid-September-late October).................. 843-722-4630
Festival of Houses & Gardens (mid-March-mid-April) 843-723-1623
Festival on the Fourth (July 4).................... 843-556-5660
Flowertown Festival (early April).................. 843-871-9622
Folly River Float Frenzy & Fish Fry (mid-August) 843-588-6663
Holiday Festival of Lights (early-November-early January) 843-853-8000
Low Country Cajun Festival (early-mid-April)....... 843-762-2172
LowCountry Blues Bash (early-mid-February) 800-868-8118
Moja Arts Festival (late September-early October).................. 843-724-7305
Plantation Christmas at Middleton Place (December).................................. 843-556-6020
Plantation Days (November)...................... 843-556-6020
Scottish Games & Highland Gathering (September) 843-884-4371
Southeastern Wildlife Exposition (February)........ 800-221-5273
Spoleto Festival USA (late May-early June)......... 843-722-2764
Summer Classic Horse Show (July) 843-768-2500
Taste of Charleston (October)..................... 843-577-4030
This Magic Moment (late June) 843-853-8000
World Grits Festival (late April).................. 843-563-2150

Charlotte, North Carolina

***County:* Mecklenburg**

CHARLOTTE is located in southern North Carolina's Piedmont region. Major cities within 100 miles include Winston-Salem, Greensboro, and Raleigh, North Carolina; and Greenville and Spartanburg, South Carolina.

Area (Land) .... 174.3 sq mi
Area (Water)................................ 0.3 sq mi
Elevation...................................... 700 ft
Latitude ....35-23-55 N
Longitude................................ 80-84-29 W
Time Zone ....EST
Area Code.. 704

Climate

Charlotte has a moderate climate with four distinct seasons. Winters are fairly mild, as the mountains shelter the area from extreme cold. Winter high temperatures average near 50 degrees, with lows in the low 30s. Snowfall is infrequent in Charlotte, averaging only six inches annually. Summers are long and warm, with average daytime high temperatures in the mid- to upper 80s; evenings cool down into the upper 60s. Precipitation is evenly distributed throughout the year in Charlotte, although March tends to be the wettest month and April the driest.

Average Temperatures & Precipitation

Temperatures

	Jan	Feb	Mar	Apr	May	Jun	Jul	Aug	Sep	Oct	Nov	Dec
High	49	53	62	71	78	86	89	88	82	72	63	52
Low	30	32	39	48	56	66	70	69	63	51	42	33

Precipitation

	Jan	Feb	Mar	Apr	May	Jun	Jul	Aug	Sep	Oct	Nov	Dec
Inches	3.7	3.8	4.4	2.7	3.8	3.4	3.9	3.7	3.5	3.4	3.2	3.5

History

The first European settlers in the Charlotte area, which was previously inhabited by the Catawba Indians, were hard-working people of Scotch-Irish decent who developed a small farming community that they named Charlotte in honor of Queen Charlotte, the wife of King George III of England. (Mecklenburg County was also named in her honor, after her German home town.) Charlotte was incorporated as a city in 1768 with a population of 276. During the Revolutionary War, Charlotte was referred to as a "veritable nest of hornets" by General Cornwallis, whose British troops chose to abandon the city after occupying it for less than three weeks due to constant attacks by Charlotte residents. This historical reference eventually led to the name of the city's professional basketball team, the Charlotte Hornets.

The discovery of gold in nearby Cabarrus County at the turn of the 19th Century aided the development of the region. In 1837 a branch of the U.S. Mint was established in Charlotte (the Mint ceased operation in 1913 and was reopened 23 years later as North Carolina's first art museum), and today the city is the nation's second largest financial center and the corporate home of First Union and BankAmerica. The textile industry, for which Charlotte is also well-known began there in the 19th Century with the invention of the cotton gin. The arrival of the railroad further enhanced Charlotte's potential to become a major transportation and distribution center. By the early 1900s, half of the nation's cotton mills were located within 100 miles of Charlotte and today the city remains an international leader in cotton yarn and textile production.

Charlotte has enjoyed continuous growth and prosperity throughout the 20th Century, especially during the 1970s and 80s when the city's population grew by more than 110,000. With a population exceeding a half million, Charlotte is the largest city in the Carolinas and one of the leading financial, transportation, and business centers in the United States.

Population

1990 Census 395,934
1998 Estimate.............................504,637
% Change 20.3
2005 Projection 748,688*

Racial/Ethnic Breakdown
White.................................... 65.6%
Black 31.8%
Other.................................... 2.6%
Hispanic Origin (may be of any race) 1.4%

Age Breakdown
Under 5 years............................. 7.5%
5 to 17.................................. 16.6%
18 to 20.................................. 4.3%
21 to 24.................................. 6.6%
25 to 34................................. 20.9%
35 to 44................................. 16.4%
45 to 54................................. 10.1%
55 to 64.................................. 7.8%
65 to 74.................................. 5.9%
75+ years 3.9%
Median Age................................32.1

Gender Breakdown
Male..................................... 47.5%
Female................................... 52.5%

** Information given is for Mecklenburg County.*

Government

Type of Government: Council-Manager

Charlotte City Clerk
600 E 4th St
Charlotte, NC 28202
Phone: 704-336-2247
Fax: 704-336-7588

Charlotte City Council
600 E 4th St
Charlotte, NC 28202
Phone: 704-336-3184
Fax: 704-336-6644

Charlotte City Hall
Charlotte-Mecklenburg Government Ctr
600 E 4th St
Charlotte, NC 28202
Phone: 704-336-2241
Fax: 704-336-6644

Charlotte City Manager
600 E 4th St
Charlotte, NC 28202
Phone: 704-336-2241
Fax: 704-336-6644

Charlotte Finance Dept
600 E 4th St
Charlotte, NC 28202
Phone: 704-336-2201
Fax: 704-336-6102

Charlotte Fire Dept
600 E 4th St 9th Fl
Charlotte, NC 28202
Phone: 704-336-2051
Fax: 704-336-4204

Charlotte Human Resources Dept
600 E 4th St 5th Fl
Charlotte, NC 28202
Phone: 704-336-2285
Fax: 704-336-6588

Charlotte Mayor
600 E 4th St
Charlotte, NC 28202
Phone: 704-336-2241
Fax: 704-336-3097

Charlotte Planning Dept
600 E 4th St
Charlotte, NC 28202
Phone: 704-336-2205
Fax: 704-336-5123

Charlotte Police Dept
601 E Trade St
Charlotte, NC 28202
Phone: 704-336-2337
Fax: 704-336-5714

Charlotte Solid Waste Services Dept
600 E 4th St 7th Fl
Charlotte, NC 28202
Phone: 704-336-2673
Fax: 704-353-0330

Charlotte Transportation Dept
600 E 4th St
Charlotte, NC 28202
Phone: 704-336-2261
Fax: 704-336-4400

Charlotte Utilities Dept
5100 Brookshire Blvd
Charlotte, NC 28216
Phone: 704-391-5070
Fax: 704-393-2219

Public Library of Charlotte & Mecklenburg County
310 N Tryon St
Charlotte, NC 28202
Phone: 704-336-2725
Fax: 704-336-2002

Important Phone Numbers

AAA....704-569-3600
American Express Travel....704-364-3373
Charlotte Regional Realtors Assn....704-372-0911
Dental Referral....704-376-0847
Driver's License Information....704-547-5787
Emergency....911
HotelDocs....800-468-3537
Info Net....704-845-4636
Mecklenburg Tax Collection....704-336-4600
Medical Referral....704-376-0847
North Carolina Revenue Dept....704-342-6124
Poison Control Center....704-379-5827
Time/Temp....704-375-6711
Travelers Aid....704-334-7288
Vehicle Registration Information....704-399-8306
Voter Registration Information....704-336-2133
Weather....704-570-9288

Information Sources

Better Business Bureau Serving Southern Piedmont Carolinas
5200 Park Rd Suite 202
Charlotte, NC 28209
www.charlotte.bbb.org
Phone: 704-527-0012
Fax: 704-525-7624

Carolinas Partnership
112 S Tryon St Suite 900
Charlotte, NC 28284
www.charlotteregion.com
Phone: 704-347-8942
Fax: 704-347-8981
TF: 800-554-4373

Charlotte Chamber of Commerce
PO Box 32785
Charlotte, NC 28232
www.charlottechamber.org
Phone: 704-378-1300
Fax: 704-374-1903

Charlotte Convention & Visitors Bureau
122 E Stonewall St
Charlotte, NC 28202
charlottecvb.org
Phone: 704-334-2282
Fax: 704-342-3972
TF: 800-722-1994

Charlotte Convention Center
501 S College St
Charlotte, NC 28202
www.charlotteconventionctr.com
Phone: 704-339-6000
Fax: 704-339-6111
TF: 800-432-7488

Charlotte Economic Development
Charlotte-Mecklenburg Government Ctr
600 E 4th St 8th Fl
Charlotte, NC 28202
www.ci.charlotte.nc.us/ciplanning
Phone: 704-336-3399
Fax: 704-336-5123

Mecklenburg County
600 E 4th St Charlotte-Mecklenburg Govt Ctr
Charlotte, NC 28202
www.charmeck.nc.us
Phone: 704-336-2472
Fax: 704-336-5887

Online Resources

4Charlotte.com
www.4charlotte.com

Anthill City Guide Charlotte
www.anthill.com/city.asp?city=charlotte

Area Guide Charlotte
charlotte.areaguides.net

Charlotte CityLink
www.usacitylink.com/citylink/charlotte

Charlotte Just Go
www.justgo.com/charlotte/

Charlotte Traveler's Friend
www.travelersfriend.com

Charlotte's Web
www.charweb.org/

CharlotteNet
www.charlottenet.com/

City Knowledge Charlotte
www.cityknowledge.com/nc_charlotte.htm

CitySearch Charlotte
charlotte.citysearch.com

CityTravelers.com Guide to Charlotte
www.citytravelers.com/charlotte.htm

Creative Loafing Charlotte
www.creativeloafing.com/charlotte/newsstand/current/index.html

DigitalCity Charlotte
home.digitalcity.com/charlotte

Excite.com Charlotte City Guide
www.excite.com/travel/countries/united_states/north_carolina/charlotte

Guest Guide Online
www.guestguideonline.com

Savvy Diner Guide to Charlotte Restaurants
www.savvydiner.com/charlotte/

Area Communities

Communities in the 13-county Charlotte region (Mecklenburg, Catawba, Cleveland, Iredell, Gaston, Cabarrus, Union, Stanly, Lincoln, Anson, and Rowan counties in North Carolina; and Lancaster and York counties in South Carolina) with populations greater than 20,000 include:

Concord
26 Union St S
Concord, NC 28026
Phone: 704-786-6161
Fax: 704-782-1331

Gastonia
PO Box 1748
Gastonia, NC 28053
Phone: 704-866-6719
Fax: 704-864-6607

Hickory
PO Box 398
Hickory, NC 28603
Phone: 828-323-7412
Fax: 828-323-7550

Kannapolis
PO Box 1199
Kannapolis, NC 28082
Phone: 704-938-5133
Fax: 704-938-5919

Monroe
PO Box 69
Monroe, NC 28111
Phone: 704-282-4501
Fax: 704-283-9098

Rock Hill
PO Box 11706
Rock Hill, SC 29731
Phone: 803-329-7012
Fax: 803-329-7038

Salisbury
217 S Main St
Salisbury, NC 28144
Phone: 704-638-5270
Fax: 704-638-5232

Statesville
301 S Center St
Statesville, NC 28677
Phone: 704-878-3585
Fax: 704-873-4167

Economy

A leading financial and industrial center for over a century, Charlotte has a strong and diverse economic base that ranges from agriculture to high finance. Fortune magazine recently named Charlotte as the city that has the #1 pro-business attitude in the nation. In addition to the financial institutions that call Charlotte their corporate home, other major U.S. companies have a presence in the Charlotte area include IBM, Philip Morris, Hoechst Celanese, and AT & T. A majority of Mecklenburg County residents are employed in service positions. Government also plays a role in Charlotte's economy—more than one-third of the area's 15 largest employers are government-related, among them North Carolina State Government and the U.S. Government.

Unemployment Rate	2.0%*
Per Capita Income	$20,997*
Median Family Income	$40,904*

** Information given is for Mecklenburg County.*

Principal Industries & Number of Wage Earners

Charlotte-Gastonia-Rock Hill MSA* - 1999

Construction & Mining	51,700
Finance, Insurance, & Real Estate	65,100
Government	94,700
Manufacturing	138,100
Retail Trade	135,400
Services	215,100
Transportation & Public Utilities	54,400
Wholesale Trade	58,300

** Information given is for the Charlotte-Gastonia-Rock Hill Metropolitan Statistical Area (MSA), which includes Cabarrus, Gaston, Lincoln, Mecklenburg, Rowan, and Union counties in North Carolina, and York County in South Carolina.*

Major Employers

Bank of America NA
101 S Tryon St
Charlotte, NC 28255
Phone: 888-279-3457
Fax: 704-386-9928

BellSouth Telecommunications Inc
4100 S Stream Blvd Suite 200
Charlotte, NC 28230
www.bellsouth.com
Phone: 800-767-2355

Carolinas Healthcare System
PO Box 32861
Charlotte, NC 28232
www.carolinas.org
Phone: 704-355-2000
Fax: 704-355-5073

Charlotte City Hall
Charlotte-Mecklenburg Government Ctr
600 E 4th St
Charlotte, NC 28202
www.ci.charlotte.nc.us
Phone: 704-336-2241
Fax: 704-336-6644

Charlotte Mecklenburg Schools
701 E 2nd St
Charlotte, NC 28202
www.cms.k12.nc.us
Phone: 704-343-6220
Fax: 704-343-7135

Duke Energy Corp
526 S Church St
Charlotte, NC 28202
www.duke-energy.com
Phone: 704-594-6200
Fax: 704-382-3781

First Union Corp
301 S Tryon St
Charlotte, NC 28288
E-mail: comments@firstunion.com
www.firstunion.com
Phone: 704-374-6161
Fax: 704-374-7934

Mecklenburg County
600 E 4th St Charlotte-Mecklenburg Govt Ctr
Charlotte, NC 28202
www.charmeck.nc.us
Phone: 704-336-2472
Fax: 704-336-5887

Novant Health
200 Hawthorne Ln
Charlotte, NC 28204
www.novanthealth.org
Phone: 704-384-4000
Fax: 704-384-5652

Ruddick Corp
1800 Two First Union Ctr
Charlotte, NC 28282
www.ruddickcorp.com
Phone: 704-372-5404
Fax: 704-372-6409

Solectron Technology Inc
PO Box 562148
Charlotte, NC 28256
www.solectron.com
Phone: 704-598-3300
Fax: 704-598-3333

US Airways Inc
PO Box 19004
Charlotte, NC 28219
www.usairways.com
Phone: 704-359-3000
Fax: 704-359-3203

US Postal Service
2901 S I-85 Service Rd
Charlotte, NC 28228
new.usps.com
Phone: 704-393-4444
Fax: 704-393-4405

Quality of Living Indicators

Total Crime Index....................53,417
(rates per 100,000 inhabitants)

Violent Crime
Murder/manslaughter.......... 84
Forcible rape.......... 263
Robbery..........2,517
Aggravated assault..........5,275

Property Crime
Burglary..........10,314
Larceny theft..........30,116
Motor vehicle theft..........4,848

Cost of Living Index..........100.6
(national average = 100)

Median Home Price..........$138,200

Education

Public Schools

Charlotte Mecklenburg Schools
701 E 2nd St
Charlotte, NC 28202
www.cms.k12.nc.us
Phone: 704-343-6220
Fax: 704-343-7135

Number of Schools
Elementary.......... 85
Middle.......... 28
High.......... 14

Student/Teacher Ratio
All Grades.......... 15.4:1

Private Schools

Number of Schools (all grades).......... 40+

Colleges & Universities

Barber-Scotia College
145 Cabarrus Ave W
Concord, NC 28025
www.barber-scotia.edu
Phone: 704-789-2900
Fax: 704-789-2911
TF: 800-610-0778

Belmont Abbey College
100 Belmont-Mt Holly Rd
Belmont, NC 28012
www.bac.edu/
Phone: 704-825-6700
Fax: 704-825-6670
TF: 888-222-0110

Central Piedmont Community College
PO Box 35009
Charlotte, NC 28235
www.cpcc.cc.nc.us
Phone: 704-330-2722
Fax: 704-330-5053

Davidson College
PO Box 1719
Davidson, NC 28036
E-mail: admission@davidson.edu
www.davidson.edu
Phone: 704-892-2000
Fax: 704-892-2016
TF: 800-768-0380

Johnson C Smith University
100 Beatties Ford Rd
Charlotte, NC 28216
www.jcsu.edu
Phone: 704-378-1000
Fax: 704-378-1242
TF: 800-782-7303

Lee University
1209 Little Rock Rd
Charlotte, NC 28214
E-mail: ecbc@msn.com
Phone: 704-394-2307
Fax: 704-393-3689

Queens College
1900 Selwyn Ave
Charlotte, NC 28274
www.queens.edu
Phone: 704-337-2200
Fax: 704-337-2503
TF: 800-849-0202

University of North Carolina Charlotte
9201 University City Blvd
Charlotte, NC 28223
www.uncc.edu
Phone: 704-547-2000
Fax: 704-510-6483

Wingate University
PO Box 159
Wingate, NC 28174
E-mail: admit@wingate.edu
www.wingate.edu
Phone: 704-233-8000
Fax: 704-233-8110
TF: 800-755-5550

Hospitals

Anson County Hospital
500 Morven Rd
Wadesboro, NC 28170
Phone: 704-694-5131
Fax: 704-694-3900

Carolinas Medical Center
PO Box 32861
Charlotte, NC 28232
www.carolinas.org/locations/hospitals/cmc.cfm
Phone: 704-355-2000
Fax: 704-355-5073

Catawba Memorial Hospital
810 Fairgrove Church Rd SE
Hickory, NC 28602
www.catawbamemorial.org
Phone: 828-326-3000
Fax: 828-326-3371

Cleveland Regional Medical Center
201 Grover St
Shelby, NC 28150
www.carolinas.org/locations/hospitals/cleveland
Phone: 704-487-3000
Fax: 704-487-3158

Davis Medical Center
PO Box 1823
Statesville, NC 28687
Phone: 704-873-0281
Fax: 704-838-7287

Frye Regional Medical Center
420 N Center St
Hickory, NC 28601
www.tenethealth.com/Frye
Phone: 828-322-6070
Fax: 828-324-0193

Gaston Memorial Hospital
2525 Court Dr
Gastonia, NC 28054
www.gastonhealthcare.org
Phone: 704-834-2000
Fax: 704-834-2500

Iredell Memorial Hospital
PO Box 1828
Statesville, NC 28687
Phone: 704-873-5661
Fax: 704-872-7924

Kings Mountain Hospital
706 W Kings St
Kings Mountain, NC 28086
www.carolinas.org/locations/hospitals/kings_mountain.cfm
Phone: 704-739-3601
Fax: 704-739-0800

Lake Norman Regional Medical Center
PO Box 3250
Mooresville, NC 28117
Phone: 704-663-1113
Fax: 704-660-4049

Lincoln Medical Center
PO Box 677
Lincolnton, NC 28093
www.lincolnmedical.org
Phone: 704-735-3071
Fax: 704-735-0584

Mercy Hospital
2001 Vail Ave
Charlotte, NC 28207
www.carolinas.org/locations/hospitals/mercy.cfm
Phone: 704-379-5000
Fax: 704-379-6056

Mercy Hospital South
10628 Park Rd
Charlotte, NC 28210
www.carolinas.org/locations/hospitals/mercy_south.cfm
Phone: 704-543-2000
Fax: 704-543-2010

NorthEast Medical Center
920 Church St N
Concord, NC 28025
www.northeastmedical.org
Phone: 704-783-3000
Fax: 704-783-1527
TF: 800-842-6868

Presbyterian Hospital in Charlotte
200 Hawthorne Ln
Charlotte, NC 28204
Phone: 704-384-4000
Fax: 704-384-4296

Presbyterian Hospital Matthews
1500 Matthews Township Pkwy
Matthews, NC 28105
Phone: 704-384-6570
Fax: 704-384-6515

Rowan Regional Medical Center
612 Mocksville Ave
Salisbury, NC 28144
Phone: 704-638-1000
Fax: 704-638-1288

Stanly Memorial Hospital
301 Yadkin St
Albemarle, NC 28001
Phone: 704-983-5111
Fax: 704-983-3414

Union Regional Medical Center
600 Hospital Dr
Monroe, NC 28111
www.carolinas.org/locations/hospitals/union.cfm
Phone: 704-283-3100
Fax: 704-296-4175

University Hospital
PO Box 560727
Charlotte, NC 28256
www.carolinas.org/locations/hospitals/university.cfm
Phone: 704-548-6000
Fax: 704-548-6236

Transportation

Airport(s)

Charlotte/Douglas International Airport (CLT)
7 miles W of downtown (approx 15 minutes) 704-359-4000

Mass Transit

Charlotte Transit System
$.80 Base fare 704-336-3366

Rail/Bus

Amtrak Station
1914 N Tryon St
Charlotte, NC 28206
Phone: 704-376-4416
TF: 800-872-7245

Greyhound/Trailways Bus Station
601 W Trade St
Charlotte, NC 28202
Phone: 704-372-0456

Utilities

Electricity
Duke Power 704-594-9400
www.dukepower.com

Gas
Piedmont Natural Gas Co 704-525-3882
www.piedmontng.com

Water
Charlotte/Mecklenburg Utilities Dept 704-336-2211

Garbage Collection/Recycling
Charlotte Solid Waste Services Dept............704-336-2673
www.ci.charlotte.nc.us/ciswaste

Telecommunications

Telephone
BellSouth 800-767-2355
www.bellsouth.com

Cable Television
Time Warner Cable 704-377-9600
www.twcarolina.com

Internet Service Providers (ISPs)
Carolina Internet 704-643-8330
www.caro.net
CetLink.Net 803-327-2754
www.cetlink.net
CT Communications Inc 704-782-7000
www.ctc.net
Internet of Western Carolina 704-861-1251
www.shelby.net
Vnet Internet Access Inc 704-334-3282
www.vnet.net
Wave Communications 828-326-0625
www.twave.net
WebServe Inc 704-556-7482
www.webserve.net

Banks

Bank of America NA
101 S Tryon St
Charlotte, NC 28255
Phone: 888-279-3457
Fax: 704-386-9928

Bank of Mecklenburg
2000 Randolph Rd
Charlotte, NC 28207
Phone: 704-375-2265
Fax: 704-347-5597

BB & T Bank
200 S College St
Charlotte, NC 28202
Phone: 704-954-1000
Fax: 704-954-1206
TF: 800-226-5228

Central Carolina Bank & Trust Co
101 S Kings Dr
Charlotte, NC 28204
Phone: 704-347-6092
Fax: 704-347-6179
TF: 800-422-2226

Centura Bank
2000 Randolph Rd
Charlotte, NC 28207
Phone: 704-331-1740
Fax: 704-343-9351

First Charter National Bank
5917 Cora St
Charlotte, NC 28216
Phone: 704-393-0126
Fax: 704-393-0213

First Citizens Bank & Trust Co
128 S Tryon St
Charlotte, NC 28202
Phone: 704-338-4000
Fax: 704-338-4037

First Union National Bank
301 S Charlotte St 2 First Union Plaza
Charlotte, NC 28288
Phone: 704-374-6161

Lincoln Bank of North Carolina
4500 Cameron Valley Pkwy
Charlotte, NC 28211
Phone: 704-365-2880
Fax: 704-362-0711

Mechanics & Farmers Bank
101 Beatties Ford Rd
Charlotte, NC 28216
Phone: 704-332-2121
Fax: 704-343-9003

Park Meridian Bank
6826 Morrison Blvd
Charlotte, NC 28211
Phone: 704-366-7275
Fax: 704-366-8165

SouthTrust Bank NA
112 S Tryon St Suite 100
Charlotte, NC 28284
Phone: 704-347-6777
Fax: 704-339-5143

Wachovia Bank NA
4525 Sharon Rd
Charlotte, NC 28211
Phone: 704-442-6400
Fax: 704-442-6415

Shopping

Cannon Village
200 West Ave
Kannapolis, NC 28081
www.cannonvillage.com
Phone: 704-938-3200
Fax: 704-932-4188
TF: 800-938-3200

Carolina Place Mall
11025 Carolina Place Pkwy
Pineville, NC 28134
www.shopcarolinaplace.com
Phone: 704-543-9300
Fax: 704-543-6355

Concord Mills
8111 Concord Mills Blvd
Concord, NC 28027
www.millscorp.com/concord/
Phone: 704-782-6700
TF: 877-626-4557

Eastland Mall
5471 Central Ave
Charlotte, NC 28212
Phone: 704-537-2626
Fax: 704-568-0291

Founder's Hall
100 N Tryon St Bank of America
Corporate Ctr
Charlotte, NC 28255
Phone: 704-386-0120
Fax: 704-386-1021

Market Place at Mint Hill
11237 Lawyers Rd
Charlotte, NC 28227
Phone: 704-545-3117
Fax: 704-545-3117

Midtown Square
401 S Independence Blvd Suite 800
Charlotte, NC 28204
Phone: 704-377-3467
Fax: 704-343-2541

SouthPark Mall
4400 Sharon Rd
Charlotte, NC 28211
E-mail: concierge@trammellcrow.com
www.southpark.com
Phone: 704-364-4411
Fax: 704-364-4913
TF: 888-364-4411

Specialty Shops on the Park
6401 Morrison Blvd
Charlotte, NC 28211
Phone: 704-366-9841

Media

Newspapers and Magazines

Business North Carolina Magazine
5435 77 Center Dr Suite 50
Charlotte, NC 28217
www.gocarolinas.com/partners/businessnc
Phone: 704-523-6987
Fax: 704-523-4211
TF: 800-604-6987

Charlotte Business Journal
120 W Morehead St Suite 2250
Charlotte, NC 28202
www.amcity.com/charlotte
Phone: 704-347-2340
Fax: 704-937-1102
TF: 800-948-5323

Charlotte Magazine
127 W Worthington Ave Suite 208
Charlotte, NC 28203
www.charlottemag.com
Phone: 704-335-7181
Fax: 704-335-3739

Charlotte Observer*
600 S Tryon St
Charlotte, NC 28202
www.charlotte.com
Phone: 704-358-5000
Fax: 704-358-5036
TF: 800-332-0686

Creative Loafing Charlotte
6112 Old Pineville Rd
Charlotte, NC 28217
E-mail: charlotte@creativeloafing.com
www.creativeloafing.com/charlotte/newsstand/current/index.html
Phone: 704-522-8334
Fax: 704-522-8088

Leader The
PO Box 30486
Charlotte, NC 28230
E-mail: editor@leadernews.com
www.leadernews.com
Phone: 704-331-4842
Fax: 704-347-0358

**Indicates major daily newspapers*

Television

WAXN-TV Ch 64 (Ind)
910 Fairview St
Kannapolis, NC 28083
www.gocarolinas.com/partners/action64
Phone: 704-933-9529
Fax: 704-932-3880

WBTV-TV Ch 3 (CBS)
1 Julian Price Pl
Charlotte, NC 28208
www.wbtv.com
Phone: 704-374-3500
Fax: 704-374-3889

WCCB-TV Ch 18 (Fox)
1 Television Pl
Charlotte, NC 28205
E-mail: stationinfo@fox18wccb.com
www.fox18wccb.com
Phone: 704-372-1800
Fax: 704-376-3415

WCNC-TV Ch 6 (NBC)
1001 Wood Ridge Ctr Dr
Charlotte, NC 28217
E-mail: wcnctv36@aol.com
www.wcnc.com
Phone: 704-329-3636
Fax: 704-357-4975

WFVT-TV Ch 55 (WB)
PO Box 668400
Charlotte, NC 28266
Phone: 704-398-0046
Fax: 704-393-8407

WHKY-TV Ch 14 (Ind)
PO Box 1059
Hickory, NC 28603
E-mail: whky@whky.com
www.whky.com
Phone: 828-322-5115
Fax: 828-322-8256

WJZY-TV Ch 46 (UPN)
3501 Performance Rd
Charlotte, NC 28214
www.upn46.com
Phone: 704-398-0046
Fax: 704-393-8407

WSOC-TV Ch 9 (ABC)
1901 N Tryon St
Charlotte, NC 28206
www.gocarolinas.com/partners/wsoctv
Phone: 704-338-9999
Fax: 704-335-4736

WTVI-TV Ch 42 (PBS)
3242 Commonwealth Ave
Charlotte, NC 28205
www.wtvi.org
Phone: 704-372-2442
Fax: 704-335-1358

Radio

WBAV-FM 101.9 MHz (Urban)
601 S Kings Dr Suite EE
Charlotte, NC 28204
www.v1019.com
Phone: 704-786-9111
Fax: 704-792-2334

WBT-AM 1110 kHz (N/T)
1 Julian Price Pl
Charlotte, NC 28208
www.wbt.com
Phone: 704-374-3500
Fax: 704-374-3889

WBT-FM 99.3 MHz (N/T)
1 Julian Price Pl
Charlotte, NC 28208
Phone: 704-374-3500
Fax: 704-374-3889

WCCJ-FM 92.7 MHz (NAC)
2303 W Moorehead St
Charlotte, NC 28208
www.wccj.com
Phone: 704-358-0211
Fax: 704-358-3752

WEND-FM 106.5 MHz (Alt)
801 E Morehead St Suite 200
Charlotte, NC 28202
www.1065.com
Phone: 704-376-1065
Fax: 704-334-9525

WFAE-FM 90.7 MHz (NPR)
8801 JM Keynes Dr Suite 91
Charlotte, NC 28262
www.wfae.org
Phone: 704-549-9323
Fax: 704-547-8851
TF: 800-876-9323

WFMX-FM 105.7 MHz (Ctry)
1117 Radio Rd
Statesville, NC 28677
E-mail: bbuck@vnet.net
www.wfmx.com
Phone: 704-872-6345
Fax: 704-873-6921

WFNZ-AM 610 kHz (Sports)
915 E 4th St
Charlotte, NC 28204
www.wfnz.com
Phone: 704-319-9369
Fax: 704-319-3934

WGFY-AM 1480 kHz (Misc)
4180 Pompano Rd
Charlotte, NC 28216
Phone: 704-393-1480
Fax: 704-393-5983

WGIV-AM 1600 kHz (Rel)
601 S Kings Dr
Charlotte, NC 28204
Phone: 704-333-0131
Fax: 704-792-2334

WGSP-AM 1310 kHz (Rel)
3719 Latrobe Dr Suite 860
Charlotte, NC 28211
Phone: 704-442-7277
Fax: 704-442-9518

WHVN-AM 1240 kHz (Rel)
5732 N Tryon St
Charlotte, NC 28213
Phone: 704-596-1240
Fax: 704-596-6939

WKKT-FM 96.9 MHz (Ctry)
801 Wood Ridge Center Dr
Charlotte, NC 28217
www.wkktfm.com
Phone: 704-714-9444
Fax: 704-332-8805
TF: 800-332-1029

WLNK-FM 107.9 MHz (AC)
1 Julian Price Pl
Charlotte, NC 28208
E-mail: sales@1079thelink.com
www.1079thelink.com
Phone: 704-374-3500
Fax: 704-374-3889

WLYT-FM 102.9 MHz (AC)
801 Wood Ridge Center Dr
Charlotte, NC 27217
Phone: 704-570-1029
Fax: 704-332-8805
TF: 800-332-1029

WMIT-FM 106.9 MHz (Rel)
PO Box 159
Black Mountain, NC 28711
www.brb.org/wmit.htm
Phone: 828-669-8477
Fax: 828-669-6983
TF: 800-293-1069

WNKS-FM 95.1 MHz (CHR)
137 S Kings Dr
Charlotte, NC 28204
E-mail: kiss951@mindspring.com
www.kiss951.com
Phone: 704-331-9510
Fax: 704-331-9140

WNMX-FM 106.1 MHz (Nost)
5732 N Tryon St
Charlotte, NC 28213
www.wmix106.com
Phone: 704-598-1480
Fax: 704-599-1061

WNOW-AM 1030 kHz (Span)
712 Rock Hill Church Rd
Matthews, NC 28104
E-mail: wnow@wnow.com
www.wnow.com
Phone: 704-332-8764
Fax: 704-882-1330

WOGR-AM 1540 kHz (Rel)
1501 N I-85 Service Rd
Charlotte, NC 28216
Phone: 704-393-1540
Fax: 704-393-1527

WPEG-FM 97.9 MHz (Urban)
601 S Kings Dr Suite EE
Charlotte, NC 28204
www.power98fm.com
Phone: 704-333-0131
Fax: 704-792-2334

WRCM-FM 91.9 MHz (Rel)
PO Box 17069
Charlotte, NC 28227
E-mail: newlife91.9@wrcm.org
www.wrcm.org
Phone: 704-821-9293

WRFX-FM 99.7 MHz (CR)
801 Wood Ridge Ctr Dr
Charlotte, NC 28217
wrfx.com
Phone: 704-714-9444
Fax: 704-332-8805
TF: 800-332-1029

WSOC-FM 103.7 MHz (Ctry)
4015 Stuart Andrew Blvd
Charlotte, NC 28217
www.wsocfm.com
Phone: 704-522-1103
Fax: 704-523-4800

WSSS-FM 104.7 MHz (CR)
4015 Stuart Andrew Blvd
Charlotte, NC 28217
www.star1047.com
Phone: 704-372-1104
Fax: 704-523-2444

WWMG-FM 96.1 MHz (Oldies)
801 E Morehead St Suite 200
Charlotte, NC 28202
www.magic961.com
Phone: 704-338-9600
Fax: 704-334-9525

WXRC-FM 95.7 MHz (Rock)
1515 Mockingbird Ln
Charlotte, NC 28209
www.957xrc.com
Phone: 704-527-0957
Fax: 704-527-2720

WYFQ-AM 930 kHz (Rel)
8030 Arrow Ridge Blvd
Charlotte, NC 28273
Phone: 704-291-7807
Fax: 704-291-7807

Attractions

Charlotte's Discovery Place is among the nation's top science museums. The museum features a wide variety of hands-on exhibits, The Charlotte Observer OMNIMAX Theatre, and the Kelly Space Voyager Planetarium—the largest planetarium in the world. Paramount's Carowinds amusement park is located just south of Charlotte on the state line between North and South Carolina. Southwest of the city is Kings Mountain National Military Park, site of a major battle of the American Revolution. In Charlotte, numerous city parks and nearby lakes offer recreational activities, and the Charlotte Motor Speedway hosts top racing events. Located between the Carolina beaches and the Great Smoky Mountains, with the spectacular Blue Ridge Mountains several hours to the west, an endless variety of recreational opportunities are available within a few hours of Charlotte.

Actor's Theatre of Charlotte
7th & College Sts Spirit Sq
Charlotte, NC 28202
www.actorstheatrecharlotte.org
Phone: 704-342-2251
Fax: 704-342-1229

Afro-American Cultural Center
401 N Meyers St
Charlotte, NC 28202
E-mail: afroamerican@mindspring.com
www.mindspring.com/~superboy/afroamerican
Phone: 704-374-1565
Fax: 704-374-9273

Backing Up Classics Motor Car Museum
4545 Concord Pkwy S
Harrisburg, NC 28075
Phone: 704-788-9494
Fax: 704-788-9495
TF: 888-736-2519

Charlotte Botanical Gardens & Sculpture Garden
Hwy 49 N University of North Carolina
Charlotte, NC 28223
Phone: 704-547-2555
Fax: 704-547-3128

Charlotte Choral Society
1900 Queens Rd
Charlotte, NC 28207
Phone: 704-374-1564
Fax: 704-372-8733

Charlotte City Ballet
9517 Monroe Rd Suite B
Charlotte, NC 28270
E-mail: charballet@aol.com
Phone: 704-708-4474

Charlotte Historic Trolley Museum
2104 South Blvd
Charlotte, NC 28203
Phone: 704-375-0850

Charlotte Metro Zoo
4400 Cook Rd
Rockwell, NC 28138
www.charlottemetrozoo.com
Phone: 704-279-6363
Fax: 704-279-7072

Charlotte Museum of History & Hezekiah Alexander Homesite
3500 Shamrock Dr
Charlotte, NC 28215
Phone: 704-568-1774
Fax: 704-566-1817

Charlotte Nature Museum
1658 Sterling Rd
Charlotte, NC 28209
www.gocarolinas.com/community/groups/nature
Phone: 704-372-6261
Fax: 704-337-2670
TF: 800-935-0553

Charlotte Philharmonic Orchestra
130 N Tryon St Blumenthal Performing Arts Ctr
Charlotte, NC 28202
E-mail: CharPhilOr@aol.com
www.charlottephilharmonic.org
Phone: 704-846-2788
Fax: 704-847-6043

Charlotte Regional Farmers Market
1801 Yorkmont Rd
Charlotte, NC 28217
Phone: 704-357-1269
Fax: 704-357-0708

Charlotte Repertory Theatre
129 W Trade St Suite 401
Charlotte, NC 28202
www.charlotterep.org
Phone: 704-333-8587
Fax: 704-333-0224

Charlotte Symphony Orchestra
201 S College St Suite 110
Charlotte, NC 28244
E-mail: charsym1@aol.com
www.charlottesymphony.org
Phone: 704-332-0468
Fax: 704-332-1963

Charlotte's Historic Walking Tour
128 S Tryon St
Charlotte, NC 28202
Phone: 704-376-1164

Children's Theatre of Charlotte
1017 E Morehead St
Charlotte, NC 28204
E-mail: info@ctcharlotte.org
www.ctcharlotte.org
Phone: 704-333-8983

Crowders Mountain State Park
522 Park Office Ln
Kings Mountain, NC 28086
Phone: 704-853-5375
Fax: 704-853-5391

Daniel Stowe Botanical Garden
6400 S New Hope Rd
Belmont, NC 28012
www.stowegarden.org
Phone: 704-825-4490
Fax: 704-825-4492

Discovery Place
301 N Tryon St
Charlotte, NC 28202
www.discoveryplace.org
Phone: 704-372-6261
Fax: 704-337-2670
TF: 800-935-0553

Energy Explorium
13339 Hagers Ferry Rd MG03E
Huntersville, NC 28078
Phone: 704-875-5600
Fax: 704-875-5602

Fieldcrest Cannon Textile Museum
200 West Ave
Kannapolis, NC 28081
Phone: 704-938-3200
Fax: 704-932-4188

Freedom Park
2435 Cumberland Ave
Charlotte, NC 28203
Phone: 704-336-2663

Hendrick Motorsports Museum
4400 Papa Joe Hendrick Blvd
Harrisburg, NC 28075
Phone: 704-455-0342

Historic Latta Plantation
5225 Sample Rd
Huntersville, NC 28078
www.lattaplantation.org
Phone: 704-875-2312

Historic Rosedale
3427 N Tryon St
Charlotte, NC 28206
Phone: 704-335-0325
Fax: 704-335-0384

James K Polk Memorial State Historic Site
308 S Polk St
Pineville, NC 28134
E-mail: polk1795@aol.com
www.ah.dcr.state.nc.us/sections/hs/polk/polk.htm
Phone: 704-889-7145

Kings Mountain National Military Park
2625 Park Rd
Blacksburg, SC 29702
www.nps.gov/kimo/
Phone: 864-936-7921
Fax: 864-936-9897

McAlpine Creek Greenway & Park
8711 Monroe Rd
Charlotte, NC 28212
Phone: 704-568-4044
Fax: 704-535-5454

McDowell Nature Preserve
15222 York Rd
Charlotte, NC 28278
Phone: 704-588-5224
Fax: 704-588-5226

Mint Museum of Art
2730 Randolph Rd
Charlotte, NC 28207
E-mail: comments@mintmuseum.org
www.mintmuseum.org
Phone: 704-337-2000
Fax: 704-337-2101

Mint Museum of Craft & Design
220 N Tryon St
Charlotte, NC 28202
www.mintmuseum.org/mmcd/index.htm
Phone: 704-337-2000
Fax: 704-337-2101

Monument of Valor
McDowell & 2nd Sts Marshall Pk
Charlotte, NC 28204

Museum of the New South
324 N College St
Charlotte, NC 28202
Phone: 704-333-1887
Fax: 704-333-1896

Neighborhood Theatre
511 E 36th St
Charlotte, NC 28205
E-mail: tickets@neighborhoodtheatre.com
www.neighborhoodtheatre.com
Phone: 704-358-9298
Fax: 704-373-0170

North Carolina Blumenthal Performing Arts Center
130 N Tryon St Suite 300
Charlotte, NC 28202
www.performingartsctr.org
Phone: 704-333-4686
Fax: 704-376-2289

North Carolina Dance Theatre
800 N College St
Charlotte, NC 28206
www.ncdance.org/index.html
Phone: 704-372-0101
Fax: 704-375-0260

Observer OMNIMAX Theatre
301 N Tryon St Discovery Pl
Charlotte, NC 28202
24.93.68.194/omniframe.htm
Phone: 704-372-6261
Fax: 704-337-2670
TF: 800-935-0553

Opera Carolina
345 N College St Suite 409
Charlotte, NC 28202
E-mail: operacar@charlotte.infi.net
www.operacarolina.com
Phone: 704-332-7177
Fax: 704-332-6448

Paramount's Carowinds
14523 Carowinds Blvd
Charlotte, NC 28241
www.carowinds.com
Phone: 704-588-2606
Fax: 704-588-5153
TF: 800-888-4386

Philip Morris USA
2321 Concord Pkwy S
Concord, NC 28027
Phone: 704-788-5000
Fax: 704-788-5099

Reed Gold Mine State Historic Site
9621 Reed Mine Rd
Stanfield, NC 28163
E-mail: reedmine@aol.com
Phone: 704-721-4653
Fax: 704-721-4657

Reedy Creek Park & Nature Preserve
2900 Rocky River Rd
Charlotte, NC 28215
Phone: 704-598-8857
Fax: 704-599-1770

Ribbon Walk Botanical Forest
4700 Hoyt Hinson Rd
Charlotte, NC 28269
Phone: 704-599-2600

Schiele Museum of Natural History & Planetarium
1500 E Garrison Blvd
Gastonia, NC 28054
www.schielemuseum.org
Phone: 704-866-6908
Fax: 704-866-6041

Spirit Square Center for the Arts
345 N College St
Charlotte, NC 28202
Phone: 704-348-5750
Fax: 704-348-5828
TF: 800-922-6431

Theatre Charlotte
501 Queens Rd
Charlotte, NC 28207
theatrecharlotte.org
Phone: 704-334-9128
Fax: 704-347-5216

Vietnam War Memorial Wall
1129 E 3rd St Thompson Pk
Charlotte, NC 28202
Phone: 704-336-4200

Wing Haven Garden & Bird Sanctuary
248 Ridgewood Ave
Charlotte, NC 28209
Phone: 704-331-0664
Fax: 704-331-9368

Sports Teams & Facilities

Carolina Panthers
800 S Mint St Ericsson Stadium
Charlotte, NC 28202
www.cpanthers.com
Phone: 704-358-7000
Fax: 704-358-7618

Charlotte Checkers (hockey)
2700 E Independence Blvd Independence Arena
Charlotte, NC 28205
www.gocheckers.com/
Phone: 704-342-4423
Fax: 704-377-4595

Charlotte Coliseum
100 Paul Buck Blvd
Charlotte, NC 28217
www.charlottecoliseum.com
Phone: 704-357-4700
Fax: 704-357-4757

Charlotte Eagles (soccer)
310 N Kings Dr Memorial Stadium
Charlotte, NC 28204
E-mail: charlotteeagles@compuserve.com
www.charlotteeagles.com
Phone: 704-841-8644
Fax: 704-841-8652

Charlotte Hornets
100 Paul Buck Blvd Charlotte Coliseum
Charlotte, NC 28217
www.nba.com/hornets
Phone: 704-357-0252
Fax: 704-357-0289

Charlotte Knights (baseball)
2280 Deerfield Dr
Fort Mill, SC 29715
www.aaaknights.com
Phone: 803-548-8050
Fax: 803-548-8055

Charlotte Motor Speedway
Hwy 29 N
Concord, NC 28026
www.charlottemotorspeedway.com
Phone: 704-455-3200
Fax: 704-455-3237

Charlotte Speed (soccer)
7310 N Kings Dr Charlotte Memorial Stadium
Charlotte, NC 28262
Phone: 704-721-6415
Fax: 704-721-6400

Charlotte Sting (basketball)
100 Paul Buck Blvd Charlotte Coliseum
Charlotte, NC 28217
www.wnba.com/sting
Phone: 704-357-0252
Fax: 704-329-4970

Ericsson Stadium
800 S Mint St
Charlotte, NC 28202
www.cpanthers.com/stadium/index.html
Phone: 704-358-7000
Fax: 704-358-7615

Grady Cole Center
310 N Kings Dr
Charlotte, NC 28204
Phone: 704-353-0200

Independence Arena
2700 E Independence Blvd
Charlotte, NC 28205
Phone: 704-335-3100

Memorial Stadium
310 N Kings Dr
Charlotte, NC 28204
Phone: 704-336-8979

North Carolina Auto Racing Hall of Fame
119 Knob Hill Rd Lakeside Pk
Mooresville, NC 28117
www.ncarhof.com
Phone: 704-663-5331
Fax: 704-663-6949

Annual Events

4th Ward Christmas Tour (early December) 704-372-0282
600 Festival The (early-late May)..................704-455-8888
African-American Heritage Celebration
(early May) 704-875-2312
Antiques Spectacular
(early April & early June & early November)......704-596-4643
AutoFair 1 (early April) 704-455-3200
Blooming Arts Festival (early May)................704-283-2784
Carolina Renaissance Festival
(early October-mid-November) 704-896-5555
Carolina's Carrousel Parade (late November) 800-231-4636

Center CityFest Outdoor Festival (late April) 704-483-6266
Charlotte Festival-New Plays in America Series (early March) 704-372-1000
Charlotte Film & Video Festival (early-mid-May) 704-337-2000
Charlotte International Auto Show (late September-early October)..................704-364-1078
Charlotte Observer Race Festival (early April) 704-358-5425
Charlotte Steeplechase Races (late April)...........704-423-3400
Christian Music Festival (late September)..........704-588-2600
Coca-Cola 600 (late May).........................704-455-3200
Country Christmas Classic Craft and Gift Show (late November)...............................704-596-4643
Festival in the Park (mid-September).............704-331-2700
Festival of Lights (late November-early January) 704-331-2701
Good Guys Southeastern Rod & Custom Car Show (late October)................................704-455-3200
Grandfather Mountain Highland Games (mid-July)...................................828-733-1333
Great American Antique & Collectible Spectacular (early April & early November)..................704-596-4643
Holiday Skylights Tree Lighting Ceremony (early December).............................704-378-1335
Home Depot Invitational (late April)...............704-846-4699
International Festival (late September)............704-547-2407
July 4th Fireworks (July 4).......................704-334-2282
Lake Norman Festival (mid-May).................704-664-3898
LakeFest (mid-September)........................704-892-1922
Latta Plantation Folklife Festival (mid-October).....704-875-2312
Latta Plantation Holiday Festival (late November)...704-875-2312
Latta Plantation Quilt & Needlework Show (mid-February)...............................704-875-2312
Legends Summer Shootout Auto Racing Series (June-August)................................704-455-3200
Loch Norman Highland Games (mid-April).........704-875-3113
Mid-Atlantic Boat Show (early February)...........704-339-6000
Mint Museum Home & Garden Tour (mid-April)....704-337-2095
Nascar Parade & Speed Street Festival (late May)...704-455-6814
National Balloon Rally & Hot Air Balloon Festival (mid-September) 704-873-2893
North American Karting Championships (early October)...............................704-455-3200
Qualifying Races for Winston No Bull Twin 25s (late May) 704-455-3200
Saint Patrick's Day Parade & Festival (mid-March) 704-542-6846
Shrine Bowl of the Carolinas (mid-December)......704-547-1414
Southeastern Origami Festival (late September) 704-375-3692
Southern Christmas Show (mid-late November) 704-376-6594
Southern Farm Show (early February).............704-376-6594
Southern Ideal Home Show (early April)...........704-376-6594
Southern Spring Show (late February-early March)....................704-376-6594
Taste of Charlotte (early May) 704-921-3337
WBT Skyshow (July 4)...........................704-374-3500
Winston Select (late May) 704-455-3200

Chattanooga, Tennessee

***County:* Hamilton**

CHATTANOOGA is located in the Tennessee River Valley in southeastern Tennessee just north of the Georgia border. Major cities within 100 miles include Knoxville, Tennessee; Atlanta, Georgia; and Huntsville, Alabama.

Area (Land) .... 118.4 sq mi
Area (Water)................................ 7.9 sq mi
Elevation....................................... 685 ft
Latitude ....34-99-72 N
Longitude................................ 85-23-86 W
Time Zone ....EST
Area Code....................................... 423

Climate

Chattanooga has a moderate climate with cool winters and hot summers. Winter high temperatures average around 50 degrees and lows average around 30. Snowfall is minimal, averaging less than five inches annually. Summer daytime high temperatures average in the upper 80s, but evenings cool down into the upper 60s. Afternoon thunderstorms help to moderate the summer heat. March is the wettest month in Chattanooga; October is the driest.

Average Temperatures & Precipitation

Temperatures

	Jan	Feb	Mar	Apr	May	Jun	Jul	Aug	Sep	Oct	Nov	Dec
High	47	52	62	71	79	86	89	88	82	72	61	51
Low	28	31	39	47	55	64	68	68	63	49	40	31

Precipitation

	Jan	Feb	Mar	Apr	May	Jun	Jul	Aug	Sep	Oct	Nov	Dec
Inches	4.9	4.8	6.0	4.3	4.4	3.5	4.9	3.5	4.2	3.2	4.6	5.2

History

The area surrounding Chattanooga was originally occupied by the Cherokee Indians from the early 1700s. It is believed that the city's name was derived from a Native American phrase meaning "pointed rock." During the early 19th Century, the establishment of a trading post called Ross's Landing by the leader of the Cherokee nation, Chief John Ross, and the creation of the Brainerd Mission helped the Chattanooga area become an educational and cultural center for the Cherokee Indians. In 1838, white settlers drove the Cherokees out of Ross's Landing, sending them to Oklahoma along the infamous "Trail of Tears," upon which 25 percent of the tribe perished. The new settlement, named Chattanooga, grew quickly as a port city on the Tennessee River. During the 1850's rail transportation began in Chattanooga, and the city became one of the most important railroad centers in the South. Many Civil War battles were fought in Chattanooga in 1863, including the Battle of Chickamauga, the Battle of Lookout Mountain ("Battle Above the Clouds"), and the Battle of Missionary Ridge. The city is filled with sites that commemorate Chattanooga's Civil War history, including Chickamauga and Chattanooga National Military Park, Chattanooga National Cemetery, and Lookout Mountain.

During the early part of the 20th Century, Chattanooga became famous as a railroad hub with the opening of Chattanooga's Terminal Station, sometimes referred to as the Chattanooga Choo-Choo, in 1909. In 1941, the same year that the song, "Chattanooga Choo-Choo" became a hit, the city became the geographic center of the seven-state region served by the Tennessee Valley Authority's power operations. TVA remains Chattanooga's largest employer, providing jobs for approximately 5,000 area residents.

The 1960s were difficult years for Chattanooga, filled with racial conflicts, high unemployment, and general urban decline. In 1990, 21 years after being dubbed the "worst polluted city in America," Chattanooga was recognized by the Environmental Protection Agency at the nation's best environmental turn-around story. More recently, Chattanooga has been undergoing a major revitalization that has resulted in improvements in every facet of life in the city. The "new" Chattanooga features better schools, safer neighborhoods, environment-friendly manufacturing and industrial development, and a renewed riverfront, complete with public parks, walking trails, and the $54 million Tennessee Aquarium that has generated hundreds of millions of dollars for the city's economy.

Population

1990 Census 152,393
1998 Estimate..............................147,790
% Change ....-3.0
2003 Projection 148,629

Racial/Ethnic Breakdown

White.................................... 65.0%
Black 33.7%
Other...................................... 1.3%
Hispanic Origin (may be of any race) 0.6%

Age Breakdown

Under 5 years............................. 6.8%
5 to 17.................................... 16.5%
18 to 20.................................... 4.7%
21 to 24.................................... 6.2%
25 to 34.................................. 16.3%
35 to 44.................................. 14.2%
45 to 54.................................. 10.0%
55 to 64.................................. 10.0%
65 to 74.................................... 8.4%
75+ years 6.8%
Median Age..................................34.7

Gender Breakdown
Male 46.2%
Female 53.8%

Government

Type of Government: Mayor-Council

Chattanooga City Attorney
801 Broad St 400 Pioneer Bank Bldg
Chattanooga, TN 37402
Phone: 423-757-5342
Fax: 423-756-0737

Chattanooga City Council
1000 Linsay St
Chattanooga, TN 37402
Phone: 423-757-5196
Fax: 423-757-4857

Chattanooga City Hall
100 E 11th St Suite 100
Chattanooga, TN 37402
Phone: 423-757-5152
Fax: 423-757-0005

Chattanooga Finance Dept
101 E 11th St Suite 102
Chattanooga, TN 37402
Phone: 423-757-5191
Fax: 423-757-5567

Chattanooga Fire Dept
910 Wisdom St
Chattanooga, TN 37406
Phone: 423-697-1455
Fax: 423-697-1441

Chattanooga Hamilton County Regional Planning Agency
100 City Hall Annex Suite 200
Chattanooga, TN 37402
Phone: 423-757-5216
Fax: 423-757-5532

Chattanooga Mayor
100 E 11th St
Chattanooga, TN 37402
Phone: 423-757-5152
Fax: 423-757-0005

Chattanooga Neighborhood Services Dept
1110 Market St Suite 333
Chattanooga, TN 37402
Phone: 423-757-5277
Fax: 423-757-0085

Chattanooga Parks & Recreation Dept
101 E 11th St Suite 216
Chattanooga, TN 37402
Phone: 423-757-5167
Fax: 423-757-5586

Chattanooga Personnel Dept
100 E 11th St Suite 302
Chattanooga, TN 37402
Phone: 423-757-5200
Fax: 423-757-5456

Chattanooga Police Dept
3300 Amnicola Hwy
Chattanooga, TN 37406
Phone: 423-698-9744
Fax: 423-493-2806

Chattanooga Public Works Dept
101 E 11th St
Chattanooga, TN 37402
Phone: 423-757-5110
Fax: 423-757-0586

Chattanooga Treasurer
101 E 11th St Rm 102
Chattanooga, TN 37402
Phone: 423-757-5191
Fax: 423-757-5567

Chattanooga-Hamilton County Bicentennial Library
1001 Broad St
Chattanooga, TN 37402
Phone: 423-757-5310

Important Phone Numbers

AAA 423-490-2000
American Express Travel 423-266-1893
ARTSline 423-756-2787
Chattanooga Assn of Realtors 423-698-8001
Chattanooga Property Tax Assessor 423-209-7300
Driver's License Information 423-634-6218
Emergency 911
Hamilton County Property Tax Assessor 423-209-7300
HotelDocs 800-468-3537
Poison Control Center 803-777-1117
Tennessee Dept of Revenue 423-634-6288
Time/Temp 423-265-1411
Vehicle Registration Information 423-209-6525
Voter Registration Information 423-209-7720

Information Sources

Better Business Bureau Serving Southeast Tennessee & Northwest Georgia
1010 Market St Suite 200
Chattanooga, TN 37402
www.chattanooga.bbb.org
Phone: 423-266-6144
Fax: 423-267-1924

Chattanooga Area Chamber of Commerce
1001 Market St
Chattanooga, TN 37402
www.chattanooga-chamber.com
Phone: 423-756-2121
Fax: 423-267-7242

Chattanooga Area Convention & Visitors Bureau
2 Broad St
Chattanooga, TN 37402
www.chattanooga.net/cvb
Phone: 423-756-8687
Fax: 423-265-1630
TF: 800-322-3344

Chattanooga Downtown Partnership
850 Market St Miller Plaza 2nd Fl
Chattanooga, TN 37402
www.downtownchattanooga.org
Phone: 423-265-0771
Fax: 423-265-6952

Chattanooga Hamilton County Regional Planning Agency
100 City Hall Annex Suite 200
Chattanooga, TN 37402
www.chcrpa.org
Phone: 423-757-5216
Fax: 423-757-5532

East Ridge Convention Center
1417 N Mack Smith Rd
Chattanooga, TN 37412
Phone: 423-899-6370
Fax: 423-899-5849

Hamilton County
County Courthouse Rm 201
Chattanooga, TN 37402
www.hamiltontn.gov
Phone: 423-209-6500
Fax: 423-209-6501

Online Resources

About.com Guide to Chattanooga
chattanooga.about.com/citiestowns/southeastus/chattanooga/mbody.htm

Anthill City Guide Chattanooga
www.anthill.com/city.asp?city=chattanooga

Area Guide Chattanooga
chattanooga.areaguides.net

Chattanooga CityLink
www.usacitylink.com/citylink/chatt/

Chattanooga Directory
www.vic.com/~smokyweb/chatt/

Chattanooga.TheLinks.com
chattanooga.thelinks.com

City Knowledge Chattanooga
www.cityknowledge.com/tn_chattanooga.htm

Excite.com Chattanooga City Guide
www.excite.com/travel/countries/united_states/tennessee/chattanooga

Guest Guide Online
www.guestguideonline.com

SurfNChattanooga
www.surfnchattanooga.com

Virtual Chattanooga
www.chattanooga.net/

Area Communities

Communities in the Chattanooga area with populations greater than 5,000 include:

Collegedale
4910 Swinyar Dr
Collegedale, TN 37315
Phone: 423-396-3135
Fax: 423-396-3138

East Ridge
1517 Tombras Ave
Chattanooga, TN 37412
Phone: 423-867-7711
Fax: 423-867-7340

Red Bank
3117 Dayton Blvd
Chattanooga, TN 37415
Phone: 423-877-1103
Fax: 423-877-1102

Signal Mountain
1111 Ridgeway Ave
Signal Mountain, TN 37377
Phone: 423-886-2177
Fax: 423-886-2939

Soddy-Daisy
9835 Dayton Pike
Soddy-Daisy, TN 37379
Phone: 423-332-5323
Fax: 423-332-5048

Economy

Services is the leading employment sector in the Chattanooga metropolitan area, and health care is among Chattanooga's largest service industries. The city's central location and access to several major highways also make it a major center for manufacturing and distribution. Major U.S. companies headquartered in the Chattanooga metro area include the Dixie Group Inc., Shaw Industries, and McKee Foods Corp. The area is also home to more than 30 environmental companies, and Chattanooga has become a major center for the research and development of electric transit vehicles.

Unemployment Rate 3.3%*
Per Capita Income $26,105*
Median Family Income $27,487

** Information given is for Hamilton County.*

Principal Industries & Number of Wage Earners

Chattanooga MSA* - February 2000

Industry	Wage Earners
Construction & Mining	9,100
Finance, Insurance, & Real Estate	16,600
Government	33,300
Manufacturing	53,700
Retail Trade	38,600
Services	57,800
Transportation, Communications, & Public Utilities	19,100
Wholesale Trade	10,100

** Information given is for the Chattanooga Metropolitan Statistical Area (MSA), which includes Hamilton and Marion counties in Tennessee; and Catoosa, Dade and Walker counties in Georgia.*

Major Employers

Blue Cross Blue Shield of Tennessee
801 Pine St
Chattanooga, TN 37402
E-mail: individual_sales@bcbst.com
www.bcbst.com
Phone: 423-755-5600
Fax: 423-755-2178
TF: 800-705-0391

Chattanooga City Hall
100 E 11th St Suite 100
Chattanooga, TN 37402
www.chattanooga.gov
Phone: 423-757-5152
Fax: 423-757-0005

CIGNA
1111 Market St MS BR6A
Chattanooga, TN 37402
www.cigna.com
Phone: 423-321-4400
Fax: 423-321-4861

Covenant Transport Inc
400 Birmingham Hwy
Chattanooga, TN 37419
www.covenanttransport.com
Phone: 423-821-1212
Fax: 423-821-5442
TF: 800-334-9686

DuPont EI de Nemours & Co Inc
4501 N Access Rd
Chattanooga, TN 37415
www.dupont.com/construction/
Phone: 423-875-7011
Fax: 423-875-7999

Erlanger Medical Center
975 E 3rd St
Chattanooga, TN 37403
www.erlanger.org
Phone: 423-778-7000
Fax: 423-778-7615

Hamilton County Dept of Education
6703 Bonny Oaks Dr
Chattanooga, TN 37421
Phone: 423-209-8400
Fax: 423-209-8539

McKee Foods Corp
PO Box 750
Collegedale, TN 37315
E-mail: comment@ccmail.mckee.com
www.mckeefoods.com
Phone: 423-238-7111
Fax: 423-238-7170
TF: 800-522-4499

Memorial Hospital
2525 Desales Ave
Chattanooga, TN 37404
www.memorial.org
Phone: 423-495-2525
Fax: 423-495-7726

North American Royalties Inc
200 E 8th St
Chattanooga, TN 37402
Phone: 423-265-3181
Fax: 423-756-3179

Olan Mills Inc
4325 Amnicola Hwy Box 23456
Chattanooga, TN 37422
www.olanmills.com
Phone: 423-622-5141
Fax: 423-622-8228
TF: 800-251-6323

Roper Corp
100 Manufacturers Rd
Chattanooga, TN 37405
Phone: 423-752-1234
Fax: 423-877-1102

Synthetic Industries Inc
PO Box 22788
Chattanooga, TN 37422
E-mail: fibermesh@sind.com
www.fibermesh.com
Phone: 423-892-8080
Fax: 423-499-0753

Tennessee Valley Authority
1101 Market St
Chattanooga, TN 37402
www.tva.gov
Phone: 423-751-2133
Fax: 423-751-8525

University of Tennessee Chattanooga
615 McCallie Ave
Chattanooga, TN 37403
www.utc.edu
Phone: 423-755-4662
Fax: 423-755-4157
TF: 800-882-6627

Quality of Living Indicators

Total Crime Index....................................16,099
(rates per 100,000 inhabitants)

Violent Crime
Murder/manslaughter........................... 22
Forcible rape 106
Robbery....................................... 593
Aggravated assault...........................1,979

Property Crime
Burglary 2,672
Larceny theft 9,244
Motor vehicle theft..........................1,483

Cost of Living Index....................................98.4
(national average = 100)

Median Home Price..................................$99,100

Education

Public Schools

Hamilton County Dept of Education
6703 Bonny Oaks Dr
Chattanooga, TN 37421
Phone: 423-209-8400
Fax: 423-209-8539

Number of Schools
Elementary.................................. 48
Middle 19
High... 14

Student/Teacher Ratio
All Grades 16.0:1

Private Schools

Number of Schools (all grades).................... 28+

Colleges & Universities

Chattanooga State Technical Community College
4501 Amnicola Hwy
Chattanooga, TN 37406
E-mail: joe@cstcc.chattanooga.net
Phone: 423-697-4400
Fax: 423-697-4709

Covenant College
14049 Scenic Hwy
Lookout Mountain, GA 30750
E-mail: conference@covenant.edu
www.covenant.edu
Phone: 706-820-1560
Fax: 706-820-0893

Lee University
PO Box 3450
Cleveland, TN 37320
www.leeuniversity.edu
Phone: 423-614-8000
Fax: 423-614-8016
TF: 800-533-9930

Southern Adventist University
4881 Taylor Cir
Collegedale, TN 37315
E-mail: pr@southern.edu
www.southern.edu
Phone: 423-238-2111
Fax: 423-238-3001
TF: 800-768-8437

Tennessee Temple University
1815 Union Ave
Chattanooga, TN 37404
www.tntemple.edu
Phone: 423-493-4100
Fax: 423-493-4497
TF: 800-553-4050

University of Tennessee Chattanooga
615 McCallie Ave
Chattanooga, TN 37403
www.utc.edu
Phone: 423-755-4662
Fax: 423-755-4157
TF: 800-882-6627

Hospitals

East Ridge Hospital
941 Spring Creek Rd
East Ridge, TN 37412
www.columbiachat.com/east/default.html
Phone: 423-894-7870
Fax: 423-855-3648

Erlanger Medical Center
975 E 3rd St
Chattanooga, TN 37403
www.erlanger.org
Phone: 423-778-7000
Fax: 423-778-7615

Memorial Hospital
2525 Desales Ave
Chattanooga, TN 37404
www.memorial.org
Phone: 423-495-2525
Fax: 423-495-7726

Parkridge Medical Center
2333 McCallie Ave
Chattanooga, TN 37404
www.parkridgemedicalcenter.com
Phone: 423-698-6061
Fax: 423-493-1558

Transportation

Airport(s)

Chattanooga Metropolitan Airport (CHA)
8 miles E of downtown (approx 20 minutes)......423-855-2200

Mass Transit

CARTA
$1.00 Base fare..............................423-629-1473

Downtown Electric Shuttle
Free 423-629-1411

Rail/Bus

Greyhound Bus Station
960 Airport Rd
Chattanooga, TN 37402
Phone: 423-892-1277
TF: 800-231-2222

Utilities

Electricity
Electric Power Board 423-756-2706
www.epb.net

Gas
Chattanooga Gas 423-490-4300
www.aglr.com

Water
Tennessee-American Water Co 423-755-7600

Garbage Collection/Recycling
Chattanooga Garbage & Trash Collection 423-757-5092
Chattanooga Recycle Center 423-697-1408

Telecommunications

Telephone
BellSouth 800-753-0223
www.bellsouth.com

Cable Television
Comcast Cablevision 423-855-4300

Internet Service Providers (ISPs)
Chattanooga Data Connection Inc 423-266-3369
www.cdc.net
Higher Service Technologies Inc 423-267-8867
www.highertech.net
Voyager Online LLC 423-209-2929
www.vol.com

Banks

AmSouth Bank
801 Broad St
Chattanooga, TN 37401
Phone: 423-755-6000
Fax: 423-755-6051

First Tennessee Bank NA
701 Market St
Chattanooga, TN 37402
Phone: 423-757-4034
Fax: 423-757-4021

First Volunteer Bank
728 Broad St
Chattanooga, TN 37402
Phone: 423-265-5001
Fax: 423-265-0609

Shopping

Eastgate Town Center
5600 Brainerd Rd
Chattanooga, TN 37411
Phone: 423-894-9199

Hamilton Place
2100 Hamilton Place Blvd
Chattanooga, TN 37421
Phone: 423-894-7177
Fax: 423-892-0765

Northgate Mall
5000 Hixson Pike
Chattanooga, TN 37415
Phone: 423-870-9521

Warehouse Row Factory Shops
1110 Market St
Chattanooga, TN 37402
Phone: 423-267-1111
Fax: 423-267-1129

Media

Newspapers and Magazines

Chattanooga Times*
PO Box 1447
Chattanooga, TN 37402
www.timesfreepress.com
Phone: 423-757-6497
Fax: 423-757-6383

**Indicates major daily newspapers*

Television

WDEF-TV Ch 12 (CBS)
3300 Broad St
Chattanooga, TN 37408
E-mail: news@wdef.com
www.wdef.com
Phone: 423-785-1200
Fax: 423-785-1273

WDSI-TV Ch 61 (Fox)
1101 E Main St
Chattanooga, TN 37408
E-mail: wdsi@fox61tv.com
www.fox61tv.com
Phone: 423-265-0061
Fax: 423-265-3636

WFLI-TV Ch 53 (UPN)
6024 Shallowford Rd Suite 100
Chattanooga, TN 37421
Phone: 423-893-9553
Fax: 423-893-9853

WRCB-TV Ch 3 (NBC)
900 Whitehall Rd
Chattanooga, TN 37405
E-mail: news@wrcbtv.com
Phone: 423-267-5412
Fax: 423-756-3148

WTCI-TV Ch 45 (PBS)
4411 Amnicola Hwy
Chattanooga, TN 37406
www.wtci-tv45.com
Phone: 423-629-0045
Fax: 423-698-8557

WTVC-TV Ch 9 (ABC)
PO Box 60028
Chattanooga, TN 37406
www.newschannel9.com
Phone: 423-757-7320
Fax: 423-757-7401

Radio

WDEF-AM 1370 kHz (N/T)
2615 S Broad St
Chattanooga, TN 37408
Phone: 423-321-6200
Fax: 423-321-6220

WDEF-FM 92.3 MHz (AC)
2615 S Broad St
Chattanooga, TN 37408
Phone: 423-321-6200
Fax: 423-321-6220

WDOD-FM 96.5 MHz (Rock)
2615 Broad St
Chattanooga, TN 37408
Phone: 423-321-6200
Fax: 423-321-6270

WGOW-AM 1150 kHz (N/T)
821 Pineville Rd
Chattanooga, TN 37405
E-mail: wgow@chattanooga.net
www.wgow.com
Phone: 423-756-6141
Fax: 423-266-3629

WGOW-FM 102.3 MHz (N/T)
821 Pineville Rd
Chattanooga, TN 37405
E-mail: wgow@chattanooga.net
www.wgow.com
Phone: 423-756-6141
Fax: 423-266-3629

WJTT-FM 94.3 MHz (Urban)
409 Chestnut St Suite A154
Chattanooga, TN 37402
power94.com
Phone: 423-265-9494
Fax: 423-266-2335

WMBW-FM 88.9 MHz (Rel)
PO Box 73026
Chattanooga, TN 37407
E-mail: wmbw@moody.edu
wmbw.mbn.org
Phone: 423-629-8900
Fax: 423-629-0021

WNOO-AM 1260 kHz (Rel)
1108 Hendricks St
Chattanooga, TN 37404
Phone: 423-698-8617
Fax: 423-629-0244

WSKZ-FM 106.5 MHz (Rock)
821 Pineville Rd
Chattanooga, TN 37405
E-mail: kz106@chattanooga.net
www.wskz.com
Phone: 423-756-6141
Fax: 423-266-3629

WUTC-FM 88.1 MHz (NPR)
615 McCallie Ave Dept 1151
Chattanooga, TN 37403
Phone: 423-755-4790
Fax: 423-785-2379

Attractions

Seven states can be seen from Rock City Gardens (named for its unusual rock formations), which is just one of several attractions on Lookout Mountain. Others include Ruby Falls, a 145-foot underground waterfall in a cavern in the heart of the mountain; the Incline Railway, which offers rides up and down the mountain and has a 72.7 percent grade near the top; and Point Park, located on the mountain's crest overlooking Chattanooga. In the city itself, in the center of Ross's Landing Park and Plaza, is the Tennessee Aquarium, the world's first freshwater aquarium. The railroad terminal-turned-vacation complex, the Chattanooga Choo Choo/Holiday Inn Complex, which includes restaurants, shops, sleeping rooms in railroad cars, a convention center, a trolley, gardens, and a largest-of-its-kind model railroad exhibit, stands as a reminder of Chattanooga's history as a railroad hub.

Backstage Playhouse Dinner Theater
3264 Brainerd Rd
Chattanooga, TN 37411
Phone: 423-629-1565
Fax: 423-629-7543

Ballet Tennessee
3202 Kelly's Ferry Rd
Chattanooga, TN 37419
Phone: 423-821-2055
Fax: 423-821-2156

Battles for Chattanooga Museum
1110 E Brow Rd
Chattanooga, TN 37350
Phone: 423-821-2812

Bessie Smith Performance Hall
200 ML King Blvd
Chattanooga, TN 37403
Phone: 423-757-0020
Fax: 423-267-1076

Chattanooga African-American Museum
200 E ML King Blvd
Chattanooga, TN 37401
Phone: 423-266-8658
Fax: 423-267-1076

Chattanooga National Cemetery
1200 Bailey Ave
Chattanooga, TN 37404
Phone: 423-855-6590
Fax: 423-855-6597

Chattanooga Nature Center
400 Garden Rd
Chattanooga, TN 37419
www.cdc.net/~nature
Phone: 423-821-1160
Fax: 423-821-1702

Chattanooga Regional History Museum
400 Chestnut St
Chattanooga, TN 37402
Phone: 423-265-3247
Fax: 423-266-9280

Chattanooga Symphony & Opera
630 Chestnut St
Chattanooga, TN 37402
E-mail: csoa@chattanooga.net
www.chattanoogasymphony.org
Phone: 423-267-8583
Fax: 423-265-6520

Chattanooga Theatre Centre
400 River St
Chattanooga, TN 37405
www.theatrecentre.com
Phone: 423-267-8534
Fax: 423-267-8617

Chickamauga & Chattanooga National Military Park
PO Box 2128
Fort Oglethorpe, GA 30742
www.nps.gov/chch/
Phone: 706-866-9241
Fax: 423-752-5215

Chickamauga & Chattanooga National Military Park
110 Point Park Rd
Lookout Mountain, TN 37350
Phone: 423-821-7786
Fax: 423-821-7788

Creative Discovery Museum
321 Chestnut St
Chattanooga, TN 37402
www.cdmfun.org
Phone: 423-756-2738
Fax: 423-267-9344

Flea Market-East Ridge
6725 Ringgold Rd
Chattanooga, TN 37412
Phone: 423-894-3960

Georgia Winery
447 High Point Dr
Chickamauga, GA 30707
Phone: 706-937-2177
Fax: 706-931-2851

Houston Museum of Decorative Arts
201 High St
Chattanooga, TN 37403
E-mail: houston@chattanooga.net
www.chattanooga.net/houston
Phone: 423-267-7176
Fax: 423-756-2156

Hunter Museum of American Art
10 Bluff View St
Chattanooga, TN 37403
E-mail: info@huntermuseum.org
www.huntermuseum.org/
Phone: 423-267-0968
Fax: 423-267-9844

IMAX 3D Theater
201 Chestnut St
Chattanooga, TN 37401
www.tennis.org/IMAX/imax.html
Phone: 423-266-4629
Fax: 423-756-1849
TF: 800-262-0695

International Towing & Recovery Hall of Fame & Museum
401 Broad St
Chattanooga, TN 37402
internationaltowingmuseum.org
Phone: 423-267-3132
Fax: 423-267-3132
TF: 800-231-6543

Lake Winnepesaukah Amusement Park
1730 Lakeview Dr
Rossville, GA 30741
E-mail: lakewinnie@worldnet.att.net
www.lakewinnie.com
Phone: 706-866-5681
Fax: 706-858-0497
TF: 877-525-3946

Lookout Mountain Incline Railway
827 E Brow Rd
Lookout Mountain, TN 37350
Phone: 423-821-4224
Fax: 423-821-9444

Lost Sea
140 Lost Sea Rd
Sweetwater, TN 37874
Phone: 423-337-6616
Fax: 423-337-0803

Messianic Museum
1928 Hamill Rd
Hixson, TN 37343
Phone: 423-876-8150
Fax: 423-876-8156
TF: 888-876-8150

National Knife Museum
7201 Shallowford Rd
Chattanooga, TN 37421
Phone: 423-892-5007
Fax: 423-899-9456

National Medal of Honor Museum of Military History
PO Box 11467
Chattanooga, TN 37401
www.smoky.com/medalofhonor
Phone: 423-267-1737
Fax: 423-266-7771

Raccoon Mountain Caverns
319 W Hills Dr
Chattanooga, TN 37419
E-mail: raccoon1@cdc.net
Phone: 423-821-9403
TF: 800-823-2267

River Gallery Sculpture Garden
400 E 2nd St
Chattanooga, TN 37403
Phone: 423-267-7353
Fax: 423-265-5944
TF: 800-374-2923

Rock City Gardens
1400 Patten Rd
Lookout Mountain, GA 30750
www.rockcitygardens.com
Phone: 706-820-2531
Fax: 706-820-2533

Ruby Falls-Lookout Mountain Caverns
1720 S Scenic Hwy
Chattanooga, TN 37409
E-mail: spunky@rubyfalls.com
www.rubyfalls.com
Phone: 423-821-2544
Fax: 423-821-6705

Southern Belle
201 Riverfront Pkwy Pier 2
Chattanooga, TN 37402
Phone: 423-266-4488
Fax: 423-265-9447
TF: 800-766-2784

Tennessee Aquarium
201 Chestnut St
Chattanooga, TN 37402
www.tennis.org
Phone: 423-265-0695
Fax: 423-267-3561
TF: 800-262-0695

Tennessee Valley Railroad
4119 Cromwell Rd
Chattanooga, TN 37421
www.tvrail.com
Phone: 423-894-8028
Fax: 423-894-8029

Tivoli Theatre
709 Broad St
Chattanooga, TN 37402
Phone: 423-757-5050
Fax: 423-757-5326

Warner Park Zoo
1254 E 3rd St
Chattanooga, TN 37404
zoo.chattanooga.org
Phone: 423-697-9722
Fax: 423-697-1331

Sports Teams & Facilities

Chattanooga Lookouts (baseball)
201 Power Alley BellSouth Park
Chattanooga, TN 37403
E-mail: lookouts@cyfx.com
www.lookouts.com
Phone: 423-267-2208
Fax: 423-267-4258

Annual Events

Chattanooga Traditional Jazz Festival (early May) . . .423-266-0944
Dixieland Excursions (April-November) 423-894-8028
Downtown Partnership Nightfall Concerts
(late May-late September) 423-265-0771
Enchanted Garden of Lights
(mid-November-early January) 423-756-8687
Fall Color Cruise & Folk Festival (late October) 423-892-0223
Hamilton County Fair (late September) 423-756-8687
Houston Museum's Antiques Show & Sale
(late February) 423-267-7176
Longhorn World Championship Rodeo
(early March) 423-266-6627
Pat Boone Celebrity Spectacular (mid-May). 423-842-5757
Praters Mill Country Fair (May & October) 423-756-8687
River Roast (mid-May) 423-266-7070
Riverbend Festival (mid-June) .423-265-4112
Taste of Chattanooga (early February) 423-265-4397
Wildflower Festival (early April). 423-821-1160

Chicago, Illinois

County: Cook

CHICAGO is located in northeastern Illinois along the shores of Lake Michigan. Major cities within 100 miles include Milwaukee, Wisconsin and South Bend, Indiana.

Area (Land) .... 224.9 sq mi
Area (Water)................................ 6.8 sq mi
Elevation...................................... 596 ft
Latitude ....41-88-50 N
Longitude................................ 87-65-00 W
Time Zone ....CST
Area Code.......................312, 630, 708, 773, 847

Climate

Chicago has a continental climate that is moderated by Lake Michigan. Winters are cold, with average temperatures in the 20s and an annual snowfall average of more than 40 inches. The cold winds off Lake Michigan have earned Chicago its famous nickname as "The Windy City." Summers are warm, with daytime highs averaging in the low 80s and nighttime low temperatures averaging around 60 degrees. Thunderstorms occur frequently in the summer. Skies are typically cloudy or partly cloudy year-round due to the "lake effect" caused by Lake Michigan. Areas lying close to Lake Michigan tend to be cooler in the summer and warmer in the winter than inland areas.

Average Temperatures & Precipitation

Temperatures

	Jan	Feb	Mar	Apr	May	Jun	Jul	Aug	Sep	Oct	Nov	Dec
High	29	34	46	59	70	80	84	82	75	63	48	34
Low	13	17	29	39	48	58	63	62	54	42	32	19

Precipitation

	Jan	Feb	Mar	Apr	May	Jun	Jul	Aug	Sep	Oct	Nov	Dec
Inches	1.5	1.4	2.7	3.6	3.3	3.8	3.7	4.2	3.8	2.4	2.9	2.5

History

Originally inhabited by the Sauk, Mesquakie, and Potawatomi tribes, the Chicago area was first explored by Jacques Marquette and Louis Joliet in 1673. At the time, the area was called "Checagou," a Native American phrase meaning wild onion, because of the abundance of wild onions that grew in the area. The first permanent settlement was established more than a century later, in 1779, by a Haitian fur trader named Jean Baptiste Point du Sable. Fort Dearborn was built by the U.S. Army in 1804 to protect the waterways in the area. The fort was destroyed Native Americans during the War of 1812, but was rebuilt in 1816.

The Chicago area began to grow rapidly after the opening of the Erie Canal in 1825. In 1837, Chicago was incorporated as a city with a population of 4,000. Chicago grew as an important trade center in the mid-19th Century, due in large part to the completion of the Illinois-Michigan Canal, which linked Lake Michigan, the Great Lakes, and the Mississippi River system in 1848; and the Transcontinental Railroad in 1869, which linked Chicago with San Francisco. The opening of the Union Stockyard in 1865 also helped to fuel the city's economy.

Immigrants from many different cultures, including Germans, Irish, Scandinavians, Italians, Poles, Czechs, Serbs, Russians, and Lithuanians, moved to Chicago seeking economic opportunities, and Chicago's diverse heritage is evident today in its many ethnic neighborhoods and cultural attractions. The Great Fire of 1871 that devastated nearly one-third of the city temporarily hampered the city's growth. The area damaged by fire was quickly rebuilt, and by the turn of the 20th Century, Chicago's population exceeded one million.

Over the course of the last century, Chicago has continued to grow as a financial, industrial, educational and cultural center, boasting three of the four largest futures exchanges in the U.S., the largest number of chemists and the second largest number of engineers in the country, several of the nation's top universities and business schools, and a number of world-renowned performing arts companies and museums. Chicago today, with a population of more than 2.8 million, is the third largest city in the United States.

Population

1990 Census 2,783,726
1998 Estimate............................2,802,079
% Change 0.7
2003 Projection 2,609,287

Racial/Ethnic Breakdown

White...................................43.4%
Black 39.1%
Other...................................15.5%
Hispanic Origin (may be of any race) 19.6%

Age Breakdown

Under 19 years............................27.5%
19 to 34.................................29.3%
35 to 49.................................18.8%
50 to 64.................................12.5%
65+ years 11.9%
Median Age.................................31.3

Gender Breakdown

Male....................................47.9%
Female..................................52.1%

Government

Type of Government: Mayor-Council

Chicago Buildings Dept
121 N La Salle St Rm 900
Chicago, IL 60602
Phone: 312-744-3400
Fax: 312-744-0682

Chicago City Clerk
121 N La Salle St Rm 107
Chicago, IL 60602
Phone: 312-744-6861
Fax: 312-744-1711

Chicago City Council
121 N La Salle St Rm 209
Chicago, IL 60602
Phone: 312-744-3081
Fax: 312-744-6824

Chicago City Hall
121 N La Salle St
Chicago, IL 60602
Phone: 312-744-4000
Fax: 312-744-4149

Chicago Finance Dept
121 N La Salle St Rm 501
Chicago, IL 60602
Phone: 312-744-7100
Fax: 312-744-0014

Chicago Fire Dept
121 N La Salle St Rm 105
Chicago, IL 60602
Phone: 312-744-6666
Fax: 312-744-2744

Chicago Human Services Dept
1615 W Chicago Ave
Chicago, IL 60622
Phone: 312-746-8545
Fax: 312-746-8973

Chicago Law Dept
121 N LaSalle St Rm 600
Chicago, IL 60602
Phone: 312-744-0200
Fax: 312-744-8538

Chicago Mayor
121 N La Salle St Rm 507
Chicago, IL 60602
Phone: 312-744-3300
Fax: 312-744-2324

Chicago Park District
425 E McFetridge Dr
Chicago, IL 60605
Phone: 312-742-7529
Fax: 312-747-6178

Chicago Personnel Dept
121 N LaSalle St Rm 1100
Chicago, IL 60602
Phone: 312-744-5394
Fax: 312-744-1521

Chicago Planning & Development Dept
121 N La Salle St Rm 1000
Chicago, IL 60602
Phone: 312-744-4471
Fax: 312-744-2271

Chicago Police Dept
1121 S State St Rm 400
Chicago, IL 60605
Phone: 312-747-5501
Fax: 312-747-2430

Chicago Public Library
400 S State St
Chicago, IL 60605
Phone: 312-747-4999
Fax: 312-747-4962

Chicago Streets & Sanitation Dept
121 N LaSalle St Rm 700
Chicago, IL 60602
Phone: 312-744-5000
Fax: 312-744-5317

Chicago Transit Authority
PO Box 3555
Chicago, IL 60654
Phone: 312-664-7200

Chicago Transportation Dept
30 N La Salle St Rm 1100
Chicago, IL 60602
Phone: 312-744-3674
Fax: 312-744-1200

Chicago Treasurer
121 N La Salle St Rm 206
Chicago, IL 60602
Phone: 312-744-3356
Fax: 312-744-3220

Chicago Water Dept
1000 E Ohio St
Chicago, IL 60611
Phone: 312-744-7001
Fax: 312-744-7119

Chicago Zoning Dept
121 N LaSalle St Rm 800
Chicago, IL 60602
Phone: 312-744-3508
Fax: 312-744-6552

Important Phone Numbers

AAA .312-372-1818
American Express Travel .312-435-2595
Chicago Assn of Realtors .312-222-2540
Chicago Fine Arts Hotline .312-346-3278
Chicago Music Alliance Hotline .312-987-1123
Cook County Treasurer's Office .312-443-6200
Dental Referral .312-836-7300
Driver's License/Vehicle Registration Information .312-793-1010
Emergency . 911
HotelDocs .800-468-3537
Illinois Dept of Revenue .800-732-8866
Jazz Hotline .312-427-3300
Medical Referral .312-670-2550
Music Alliance & Dance Coalition Hotline .312-987-9296
Poison Control Center .800-942-5969
Special Events Hotline .312-744-3370
Sportsbook Line .630-231-4600
Travelers Aid .312-629-4500
Voter Registration Information .312-269-7960
Weather .815-834-0675

Information Sources

Accenting Chicago Events & Tours Inc
225 N Michigan Ave 11th Fl
Chicago, IL 60601
Phone: 312-819-5363
Fax: 312-819-5366

Better Business Bureau Serving Chicago & Northern Illinois
330 N Wabash Ave Suite 2006
Chicago, IL 60611
www.chicago.bbb.org
Phone: 312-832-0500
Fax: 312-832-9985

Chicago Area Gay & Lesbian Chamber of Commerce
3713 N Halsted St
Chicago, IL 60613
www.glchamber.org
Phone: 773-871-4190
Fax: 773-871-1021
TF: 877-452-4262

Chicago Convention & Tourism Bureau
2301 S Lake Shore Dr McCormick Complex Lakeside Ctr
Chicago, IL 60616
www.chicago.il.org
Phone: 312-567-8500
Fax: 312-567-8533

Chicago International Visitors Center
820 N Michigan Ave Suite 515
Chicago, IL 60611
www.ivcc.org
Phone: 312-915-6380
Fax: 312-915-6381

Chicago Office of Tourism
78 E Washington St
Chicago, IL 60602
www.ci.chi.il.us/Tourism
Phone: 312-744-2400
Fax: 312-744-2947

Chicagoland Chamber of Commerce
330 N Wabash Ave 1 IBM Plaza Suite 2800
Chicago, IL 60611
www.chicagolandchamber.org
Phone: 312-494-6700
Fax: 312-494-0196

Cook County
118 N Clark St Rm 537
Chicago, IL 60602
www.co.cook.il.us
Phone: 312-443-6400
Fax: 312-443-4397

McCormick Place
2301 S Lake Shore Dr
Chicago, IL 60616
www.mccormickplace.com
Phone: 312-791-7000
Fax: 312-791-6227

Online Resources

4Chicago.com
www.4chicago.com

About.com Guide to Chicago North & Suburbs
chicagonorth.about.com/local/midwestus/chicagonorth

About.com Guide to Chicago West & Suburbs
chicagowest.about.com/local/midwestus/chicagowest

Anthill City Guide Chicago
www.anthill.com/city.asp?city=chicago

Area Guide Chicago
chicago.areaguides.net

Boulevards Chicago
www.boulevards.com/chicago/

Bradmans.com Chicago
www.bradmans.com/scripts/display_city.cgi?city=233

Chicago City Page
chicago.thelinks.com

Chicago CityLink
www.usacitylink.com/citylink/chicago

Chicago CityWomen
www.citywomen.com/chiwomen.htm

Chicago Footlights Performing Arts Guide
www.footlights.com

Chicago Graphic City Guide
www.futurecast.com/gcg/chicago.htm

Chicago Guide
www.chicago-guide.com/

Chicago Home Page
www.city-life.com/chicago

Chicago Metromix Arts & Entertainment Guide
www.metromix.com

Chicago NewCityNet
www.newcitynet.com

Chicago Reader
www.chireader.com

Chicago Web
www.chiweb.com/

City Insights Chicago
www.cityinsights.com/chicago.htm

City Knowledge Chicago
www.cityknowledge.com/il_chicago.htm

Cityhits Chicago
www.cityhits.com/chicago/

CitySearch Chicago
chicago.citysearch.com

CityTravelGuide.com Chicago
www.citytravelguide.com/chicago.htm

CuisineNet Chicago
www.cuisinenet.com/restaurant/chicago/index.shtml

DigitalCity Chicago
home.digitalcity.com/chicago

Excite.com Chicago City Guide
www.excite.com/travel/countries/united_states/illinois/chicago

Gayot's Guide Restaurant Search Chicago
www.perrier.com/restaurants/gayot.asp?area=CHI

HotelGuide Chicago
chicago.hotelguide.net

Lodging.com Chicago Illinois
www.lodging.com/auto/guides/chicago-area-il.html

Open World City Guides Chicago
www.worldexecutive.com/cityguides/chicago/

OutChicago Resource Guide
www.outchicago.org

Rough Guide Travel Chicago
travel.roughguides.com/content/511/

Savvy Diner Guide to Chicago Restaurants
www.savvydiner.com/chicago/

Time Out Chicago
www.timeout.com/chicago/

Virtual Voyages Chicago
www.virtualvoyages.com/usa/il/chicago/chicago.sht

WeekendEvents.com Chicago
www.weekendevents.com/CHICAGO/CHICAGO.HTM

Windy City Electronic Village
www.thewindycity.com/

Windy-City.com
www.windy-city.com/

Yahoo! Chicago
chi.yahoo.com

Area Communities

Communities with populations greater than 20,000 in the Greater Chicago area (Cook, DuPage, and Lake counties) include:

Addison
1 Friendship Plaza
Addison, IL 60101
Phone: 630-543-4100
Fax: 630-543-5593

Arlington Heights
33 S Arlington Heights Rd
Arlington Heights, IL 60005
Phone: 847-368-5000
Fax: 847-253-2524

Carol Stream
500 N Gary Ave
Carol Stream, IL 60188
Phone: 630-665-7050
Fax: 630-665-1064

Darien
1702 Plainfield Rd
Darien, IL 60561
Phone: 630-852-5000
Fax: 630-852-4709

Des Plaines
1420 Miner St
Des Plaines, IL 60016
Phone: 847-391-5300
Fax: 847-391-5378

Downers Grove
801 Burlington Civic Center
Downers Grove, IL 60515
Phone: 630-434-5500
Fax: 630-434-5571

Elk Grove Village
901 Wellington Ave
Elk Grove Village, IL 60007
Phone: 847-439-3900
Fax: 847-357-4044

Elmhurst
209 N York St
Elmhurst, IL 60126
Phone: 630-530-3000
Fax: 630-530-3014

Evanston
2100 Ridge Ave
Evanston, IL 60201
Phone: 847-866-2936
Fax: 847-448-0803

Glen Ellyn
535 Duane St
Glen Ellyn, IL 60137
Phone: 630-469-5000
Fax: 630-469-8849

Glendale Heights
300 E Fullerton Ave
Glendale Heights, IL 60139
Phone: 630-260-6000
Fax: 630-260-9728

Glenview
1225 Waukegan Rd
Glenview, IL 60025
Phone: 847-724-1700
Fax: 847-724-0916

Hanover Park
2121 W Lake St
Hanover Park, IL 60103
Phone: 630-372-4210
Fax: 630-372-4215

Highland Park
1707 St Johns Ave
Highland Park, IL 60035
Phone: 847-432-0800
Fax: 847-432-7625

Hoffman Estates
1900 Hassell Rd
Hoffman Estates, IL 60195
Phone: 847-882-9100
Fax: 847-882-2621

Lombard
255 E Wilson St
Lombard, IL 60148
Phone: 630-620-5700
Fax: 630-620-8222

Morton Grove
6101 Capulana St
Morton Grove, IL 60053
Phone: 847-965-4100
Fax: 847-965-4162

Mount Prospect
100 S Emerson St
Mount Prospect, IL 60056
Phone: 847-392-6000
Fax: 847-818-6954

Naperville
PO Box 3020
Naperville, IL 60566
Phone: 630-420-6018
Fax: 630-420-6083

Niles
1000 Civic Center Dr
Niles, IL 60714
Phone: 847-967-6100
Fax: 847-588-8050

Park Ridge
505 Butler Pl
Park Ridge, IL 60068
Phone: 847-318-5200
Fax: 847-318-5300

Rolling Meadows
3600 Kirchoff Rd
Rolling Meadows, IL 60008
Phone: 847-394-8500
Fax: 847-394-8710

Roselle
31 S Prospect St
Roselle, IL 60172
Phone: 630-980-2000
Fax: 630-980-8558

Schaumburg
101 Schaumburg Ct
Schaumburg, IL 60193
Phone: 847-895-4500
Fax: 847-895-7806

Skokie
5127 Oakton St
Skokie, IL 60077
Phone: 847-673-0500
Fax: 847-673-0525

Streamwood
301 E Irving Park Rd
Streamwood, IL 60107
Phone: 630-837-0200
Fax: 630-837-0242

Villa Park
20 S Ardmore Ave
Villa Park, IL 60181
Phone: 630-834-8500
Fax: 630-834-8967

Westmont
31 W Quincy St
Westmont, IL 60559
Phone: 630-968-0560
Fax: 630-829-4441

Wilmette
1200 Wilmette Ave
Wilmette, IL 60091
Phone: 847-251-2700
Fax: 847-853-7700

Woodridge
5 Plaza Dr
Woodridge, IL 60517
Phone: 630-852-7000
Fax: 630-719-0021

Economy

Chicago is the nation's leading center for confectionery and specialty food production and the second largest financial center. The area also ranks second in the country in publishing, and health services account for the largest number of people employed in the Chicago area. Services is Cook County's largest employment sector, followed by retail trade, and manufacturing. More than 40 Fortune 500 companies are headquartered in the Greater Chicago area, including Motorola, Amoco, and Kraft Foods.

In addition to the major employers listed below, the U.S. Government is the area's top employer, providing more than 67,000 jobs in various agencies; and the State of Illinois is among the top 15, employing more than 20,000 people.

Unemployment Rate 4.5%*
Per Capita Income.......................... $29,343*
Median Family Income...................... $30,707

** Information given is for Cook County.*

Principal Industries & Number of Wage Earners

Cook County - 1998

Agriculture/Other......................................14,600
Construction..115,300
Finance, Insurance, & Real Estate......................340,600
Government 371,900
Manufacturing 427,500
Mining 3,500
Retail Trade..462,200
Services 1,085,400
Transportation, Communications, & Public Utilities 197,900
Wholesale Trade.......................................174,200

Major Employers

Abbott Laboratories
100 Abbott Pk Rd
Abbott Park, IL 60064
www.abbott.com
Phone: 847-937-6100
Fax: 847-937-1511
TF: 800-323-9100

Advocate Health Care
2025 Windsor Dr
Oak Brook, IL 60523
www.advocatehealth.com
Phone: 630-572-9393
Fax: 630-572-9139

Ameritech Corp
30 S Wacker Dr
Chicago, IL 60606
E-mail: share.owners@ameritech.com
www.ameritech.com
Phone: 312-750-5000
Fax: 312-609-6307
TF: 800-257-0902

AT & T Corp
227 W Monroe St
Chicago, IL 60606
Phone: 312-441-2020

Bank One Corp
1 Bank One Plaza
Chicago, IL 60670
www.bankone.com
Phone: 312-732-4000
Fax: 847-488-4256

Chicago Board of Education
125 S Clark St
Chicago, IL 60603
www.cps.k12.il.us
Phone: 773-535-8000
Fax: 773-533-2690

Chicago City Hall
121 N La Salle St
Chicago, IL 60602
www.cityofchicago.org
Phone: 312-744-4000
Fax: 312-744-4149

Cook County
118 N Clark St Rm 537
Chicago, IL 60602
www.co.cook.il.us
Phone: 312-443-6400
Fax: 312-443-4397

Dominick's Finer Foods Inc
505 Railroad Ave
Northlake, IL 60164
www.dominicks.com
Phone: 708-562-1000

Jewel Food Stores Inc
1955 W North Ave
Melrose Park, IL 60160
www.jewelosco.com
Phone: 708-531-6000
Fax: 708-531-6390

Marshall Field & Co
111 N State St
Chicago, IL 60602
www.marshallfields.com
Phone: 312-781-1000
Fax: 312-781-4594

Motorola Inc
1301 E Algonquin Rd
Schaumburg, IL 60196
www.motorola.com
Phone: 847-576-5000
Fax: 847-538-3617
TF: 800-331-6456

Sears Roebuck & Co
3333 Beverly Rd
Hoffman Estates, IL 60179
www.sears.com
Phone: 847-286-2500

United Airlines Inc
PO Box 66100
Chicago, IL 60666
www.ual.com
Phone: 847-700-4000
Fax: 847-700-2214
TF: 800-241-6522

University of Chicago
5801 S Ellis Ave
Chicago, IL 60637
www.uchicago.edu
Phone: 773-702-1234
Fax: 773-702-0353

US Postal Service
433 W Harrison St
Chicago, IL 60607
new.usps.com
Phone: 312-983-8500
Fax: 312-983-6318

Quality of Living Indicators

Total Crime Index..................................252,399
(rates per 100,000 inhabitants)

Violent Crime
Murder/manslaughter.......................... 703
Forcible rape 2,387
Robbery.....................................23,117
Aggravated assault...........................36,740

Property Crime
Burglary 36,089
Larceny theft 121,537
Motor vehicle theft 31,826

Cost of Living Index..................................123.0
(national average = 100)

Median Home Price.................................$171,200

Education

Public Schools

Chicago Board of Education
125 S Clark St
Chicago, IL 60603
www.cps.k12.il.us
Phone: 773-535-8000
Fax: 773-533-2690

Number of Schools
Elementary/Middle 488
High....................................... 87

Student/Teacher Ratio
All Grades 20.4:1

Private Schools

Number of Schools (all grades) .... 200+

Colleges & Universities

American Academy of Art
332 S Michigan Ave Suite 300
Chicago, IL 60604
Phone: 312-461-0600
Fax: 312-294-9570

American Conservatory of Music
36 S Wabash Ave Suite 800
Chicago, IL 60603
E-mail: otto@shell.portal.com
Phone: 312-263-4161
Fax: 312-263-5832

American Islamic College
640 W Irving Park Rd
Chicago, IL 60613
Phone: 773-281-4700
Fax: 773-281-8552

Career Colleges of Chicago
11 E Adams St
Chicago, IL 60603
www.careerchi.com
Phone: 312-895-6300
Fax: 312-895-6301

Chicago State University
9501 S King Dr
Chicago, IL 60628
www.csu.edu
Phone: 773-995-2000
Fax: 773-995-3820

College of DuPage
425 22nd St
Glen Ellyn, IL 60137
www.cod.edu
Phone: 630-858-2800
Fax: 630-790-2686

College of Lake County
19351 W Washington St
Grayslake, IL 60030
www.clc.cc.il.us
Phone: 847-223-6601
Fax: 847-543-3061

Columbia College
600 S Michigan Ave
Chicago, IL 60605
www.colum.edu
Phone: 312-663-1600
Fax: 312-344-8024

Concordia University
7400 Augusta St
River Forest, IL 60305
E-mail: crfadmis@crf.cuis.edu
www.curf.edu
Phone: 708-771-8300
Fax: 708-209-3176
TF: 800-285-2668

DePaul University
1 E Jackson Blvd 9th Fl
Chicago, IL 60604
www.depaul.edu
Phone: 312-362-8000
Fax: 312-362-5749
TF: 800-433-7285

DeVRY Institute of Technology
3300 N Campbell Ave
Chicago, IL 60618
www.chi.devry.edu
Phone: 773-929-8500
Fax: 773-348-1780
TF: 800-659-4588

Dominican University
7900 W Division St
River Forest, IL 60305
www.dom.edu
Phone: 708-366-2490
Fax: 708-524-5990

East-West University
816 S Michigan Ave
Chicago, IL 60605
E-mail: seeyou@eastwest.edu
www.eastwest.edu
Phone: 312-939-0111
Fax: 312-939-0083

Elgin Community College
1700 Spartan Dr
Elgin, IL 60123
www.elgin.cc.il.us
Phone: 847-697-1000
Fax: 847-608-5458

Elmhurst College
190 S Prospect Ave
Elmhurst, IL 60126
E-mail: info@elmhurst.edu
www.elmhurst.edu
Phone: 630-617-3500
Fax: 630-617-5501
TF: 800-697-1871

Harold Washington College
30 E Lake St
Chicago, IL 60601
www.ccc.edu/hwashington
Phone: 312-553-6000
Fax: 312-553-6084

Harrington Institute of Interior Design
410 S Michigan Ave
Chicago, IL 60605
www.interiordesign.edu
Phone: 312-939-4975
Fax: 312-939-8005
TF: 877-939-4975

Harry S Truman College
1145 W Wilson Ave
Chicago, IL 60640
www.ccc.edu/truman/home.htm
Phone: 773-878-1700
Fax: 773-907-4464

Illinois Institute of Art
350 N Orleans St Suite 136-L
Chicago, IL 60654
www.ilia.aii.edu
Phone: 312-280-3500
Fax: 312-280-3528

Illinois Institute of Technology
3300 S Federal St
Chicago, IL 60616
www.iit.edu
Phone: 312-567-3000
Fax: 312-567-6939
TF: 800-448-2329

Industrial Engineering College
18 S Michigan Ave Suite 1006
Chicago, IL 60603
Phone: 312-372-1360
Fax: 312-236-2221

International Academy of Merchandising & Design
1 N State St
Chicago, IL 60602
www.iamd.edu
Phone: 312-980-9200
Fax: 312-541-3929
TF: 800-222-3369

ITT Technical Institute
375 W Higgins Rd
Hoffman Estates, IL 60195
www.itt-tech.edu
Phone: 847-519-9300
Fax: 847-519-0153

Joliet Junior College
1215 Houbolt Rd
Joliet, IL 60431
www.jjc.cc.il.us
Phone: 815-729-9020
Fax: 815-280-6740

Kendall College
2408 Orrington Ave
Evanston, IL 60201
www.kendall.edu
Phone: 847-866-1300
Fax: 847-733-7450

Kennedy-King College
6800 S Wentworth Ave
Chicago, IL 60621
www.ccc.edu/kennedyking/
Phone: 773-602-5000
Fax: 773-602-5247

Lewis University
Rt 53
Romeoville, IL 60446
www.lewisu.edu
Phone: 815-838-0500
Fax: 815-838-9456
TF: 800-897-9000

Lexington College
10840 S Western Ave
Chicago, IL 60643
E-mail: lexcollege@ameritech.net
Phone: 773-779-3800
Fax: 773-779-7450

Loyola University Chicago
820 N Michigan Ave
Chicago, IL 60611
E-mail: admissions@luc.edu
www.luc.edu
Phone: 312-915-6000
Fax: 312-915-6449
TF: 800-262-2373

Loyola University Chicago Mallinckrodt Campus
1041 Ridge Rd
Wilmette, IL 60091
Phone: 847-853-3000
Fax: 847-853-3375

Loyola University Chicago Mundelein College
6525 N Sheridan Rd
Chicago, IL 60626
www.luc.edu/schools/mundelein
Phone: 773-262-8100
Fax: 773-508-8008
TF: 800-756-9652

MacCormac College
506 S Wabash Ave
Chicago, IL 60605
Phone: 312-922-1884
Fax: 312-922-3196

Malcolm X College
1900 W Van Buren St
Chicago, IL 60612
cccweb1.ccc.edu/malcolmx/home.htm
Phone: 312-942-3000
Fax: 312-850-7092

Moody Bible Institute
820 N La Salle St
Chicago, IL 60610
www.moody.edu
Phone: 312-329-4000
Fax: 312-329-2099
TF: 800-356-6639

Moraine Valley Community College
10900 S 88th Ave
Palos Hills, IL 60465
www.moraine.cc.il.us
Phone: 708-974-4300
Fax: 708-974-0974

Morton College
3801 S Central Ave
Cicero, IL 60804
www.morton.cc.il.us
Phone: 708-656-8000
Fax: 708-656-9592

NAES College
2838 W Peterson Ave
Chicago, IL 60659
naes.indian.com
Phone: 773-761-5000
Fax: 773-761-3808

National College of Chiropractic
200 E Roosevelt Rd
Lombard, IL 60148
E-mail: HomePage@national.chiropractic.edu
www.national.chiropractic.edu
Phone: 630-629-2000
Fax: 630-889-6554
TF: 800-826-6285

National-Louis University
2840 Sheridan Rd
Evanston, IL 60201
www.nl.edu
Phone: 847-475-1100
Fax: 847-256-1057
TF: 800-443-5522

National-Louis University Chicago Campus
122 S Michigan Ave
Chicago, IL 60603
www.nl.edu/nlu_campuses/chicago.html#Chicago Campus
Phone: 312-621-9650
Fax: 312-621-1205
TF: 800-443-5522

North Central College
30 N Brainard St
Naperville, IL 60566
E-mail: ncadm@noctrl.edu
www.noctrl.edu
Phone: 630-637-5100
Fax: 630-637-5819
TF: 800-411-1861

North Park University
3225 W Foster Ave
Chicago, IL 60625
www.npcts.edu
Phone: 773-244-6200
Fax: 773-244-4953
TF: 800-888-6728

Northeastern Illinois University
5500 N St Louis Ave
Chicago, IL 60625
www.neiu.edu
Phone: 773-583-4050
Fax: 773-794-6243

Northwestern Business College
4829 N Lipps Ave
Chicago, IL 60630
Phone: 773-777-4220
Fax: 773-777-2861
TF: 800-396-5613

Northwestern University
1801 Hinman Ave
Evanston, IL 60208
E-mail: nuinfo@nwu.edu
www.nwu.edu
Phone: 847-491-3741
Fax: 847-491-5136

Oakton Community College
1600 E Golf Rd
Des Plaines, IL 60016
www.oakton.edu
Phone: 847-635-1600
Fax: 847-635-1706

Olive-Harvey College
10001 S Woodlawn Ave
Chicago, IL 60628
cccweb1.ccc.edu/oliveharvey
Phone: 773-568-3700
Fax: 773-291-6185

Prairie State College
202 S Halsted St
Chicago Heights, IL 60411
www.prairie.cc.il.us
Phone: 708-709-3500
Fax: 708-709-3951

Richard J Daley College
7500 S Pulaski Rd
Chicago, IL 60652
www.ccc.edu/daley
Phone: 773-838-7500
Fax: 773-838-7605

Robert Morris College Chicago Campus
401 S State St
Chicago, IL 60605
E-mail: enroll@rmcil.edu
www.rmcil.edu
Phone: 312-935-6800
Fax: 312-935-4440
TF: 800-225-1520

Roosevelt University
430 S Michigan Ave
Chicago, IL 60605
www.roosevelt.edu
Phone: 312-341-3500
Fax: 312-341-3523

Rush University
600 S Paulina St Rm 440
Chicago, IL 60612
E-mail: rushu@rush.edu
www.rushu.rush.edu
Phone: 312-942-7100
Fax: 312-942-2219

Saint Augustine College
1333-1345 W Argyle
Chicago, IL 60640
E-mail: info@staugustinecollege.edu
www.staugustinecollege.edu
Phone: 773-878-8756
Fax: 773-878-0932

Saint Xavier University
3700 W 103rd St
Chicago, IL 60655
www.sxu.edu
Phone: 773-298-3000
Fax: 773-779-9061

School of the Art Institute of Chicago
37 S Wabash Ave
Chicago, IL 60603
www.artic.edu/saic
Phone: 312-899-5100
Fax: 312-899-1840
TF: 800-232-7242

South Suburban College
15800 State St
South Holland, IL 60473
www.ssc.cc.il.us/
Phone: 708-596-2000
Fax: 708-210-5758
TF: 800-248-4772

Triton College
2000 N 5th Ave
River Grove, IL 60171
E-mail: triton@triton.cc.il.us
www.triton.cc.il.us
Phone: 708-456-0300
Fax: 708-583-3108

University of Chicago
5801 S Ellis Ave
Chicago, IL 60637
www.uchicago.edu
Phone: 773-702-1234
Fax: 773-702-0353

University of Illinois Chicago
1200 W Harrison St
Chicago, IL 60607
www.uic.edu
Phone: 312-996-3000
Fax: 312-413-7628

VanderCook College of Music
3140 S Federal St
Chicago, IL 60616
www.vandercook.edu
Phone: 312-225-6288
Fax: 312-225-5211
TF: 800-448-2655

West Suburban College of Nursing
Erie St & Austin Blvd
Oak Park, IL 60302
E-mail: wsadmis@crf.cuis.edu
www.curf.edu/~wscasseyp/wscn.htm
Phone: 708-763-6530
Fax: 708-763-1531

Wilbur Wright College
4300 N Narragansett Ave
Chicago, IL 60634
www.ccc.edu/wright/
Phone: 773-777-7900
Fax: 773-481-8185

William Rainey Harper College
1200 W Algonquin Rd
Palatine, IL 60067
www.harper.cc.il.us
Phone: 847-925-6000
Fax: 847-925-6044

Hospitals

Bethany Hospital
3435 W Van Buren St
Chicago, IL 60624
www.advocatehealth.com/sites/hospitals/beth/index.html
Phone: 773-265-7700
Fax: 773-265-3558

Children's Memorial Hospital
707 W Fullerton Ave
Chicago, IL 60614
www.childmmc.edu
Phone: 773-880-4000
Fax: 773-880-6954

Christ Hospital & Medical Center
4440 W 95th St
Oak Lawn, IL 60453
www.advocatehealth.com/sites/hospitals/chmc/index.html
Phone: 708-425-8000
Fax: 708-346-5012

Columbus Hospital
2520 N Lakeview Ave
Chicago, IL 60614
www.cath-health.org/columbushospita3618.cfm
Phone: 773-883-7300
Fax: 773-665-3861

Cook County Hospital
1835 W Harrison St
Chicago, IL 60612
Phone: 312-633-6000
Fax: 312-633-3070

Edgewater Medical Center
5700 N Ashland Ave
Chicago, IL 60660
Phone: 773-878-6000
Fax: 773-878-4431

Grant Hospital
550 W Webster Ave
Chicago, IL 60614
Phone: 773-883-3800
Fax: 773-883-5168

Holy Cross Hospital
2701 W 68th St
Chicago, IL 60629
Phone: 773-471-8000
Fax: 773-471-7460

Illinois Masonic Medical Center
836 W Wellington Ave
Chicago, IL 60657
www.immc.org
Phone: 773-975-1600
Fax: 773-296-5101

Loretto Hospital
645 S Central Ave
Chicago, IL 60644
Phone: 773-626-4300
Fax: 773-626-2613

Louis A Weiss Memorial Hospital
4646 N Marine Dr
Chicago, IL 60640
Phone: 773-878-8700
Fax: 773-564-5788

Loyola University Medical Center
2160 S 1st Ave
Maywood, IL 60153
www.lumc.edu
Phone: 708-216-9000
Fax: 708-216-6791

Lutheran General Hospital
1775 W Dempster St
Park Ridge, IL 60068
www.advocatehealth.com/sites/hospitals/luth/index.html
Phone: 847-696-2210
Fax: 847-723-5588

Mercy Hospital & Medical Center
2525 S Michigan Ave
Chicago, IL 60616
Phone: 312-567-2000
Fax: 312-328-7745

Methodist Hospital of Chicago
5025 N Paulina St
Chicago, IL 60640
Phone: 773-271-9040
Fax: 773-989-1537

Michael Reese Hospital
2929 S Ellis Ave
Chicago, IL 60616
www.michaelreese.com
Phone: 312-791-2000
Fax: 312-791-2299

Mount Sinai Hospital Medical Center of Chicago
California Ave & 15th St
Chicago, IL 60608
Phone: 773-542-2000
Fax: 773-257-6842

Naval Hospital
3001-A 6th St
Great Lakes, IL 60088
Phone: 847-688-4560
Fax: 847-688-5752

Northwestern Memorial Hospital
251 E Huron St
Chicago, IL 60611
www.nmh.org
Phone: 312-908-2000
Fax: 312-926-6199

Our Lady of Resurrection Medical Center
5645 W Addison St
Chicago, IL 60634
www.reshealth.org
Phone: 773-282-7000
Fax: 773-794-7651

Ravenswood Hospital Medical Center
4550 N Winchester Ave
Chicago, IL 60640
www.advocatehealth.com/sites/hospitals/ravn/index.html
Phone: 773-878-4300
Fax: 773-279-4181

Resurrection Medical Center
7435 W Talcott Ave
Chicago, IL 60631
Phone: 773-774-8000
Fax: 773-594-7987

Roseland Community Hospital
45 W 111th St
Chicago, IL 60628
Phone: 773-995-3000
Fax: 773-995-3151

Rush-Presbyterian-Saint Luke's Medical Center
1653 W Congress Pkwy
Chicago, IL 60612
www.rpslmc.edu
Phone: 312-942-5000
Fax: 312-942-3212

Saint Bernard Hospital & Health Care Center
326 W 64th St
Chicago, IL 60621
Phone: 773-962-3900
Fax: 773-602-3849

Saint Elizabeth's Hospital
1431 N Claremont Ave
Chicago, IL 60622
Phone: 773-278-2000
Fax: 312-850-5970

Saint Joseph Hospital & Health Care Center
2900 N Lake Shore Dr
Chicago, IL 60657
www.cath-health.org/saintjosephhosp3617.cfm
Phone: 773-665-3000
Fax: 773-665-3255

Saint Mary of Nazareth Hospital Center
2233 W Division St
Chicago, IL 60622
www.stmaryofnazareth.org
Phone: 312-770-2000
Fax: 312-770-3389

Shriners Hospitals for Children Chicago Unit
2211 N Oak Pk Ave
Chicago, IL 60707
www.shrinershq.org/Hospitals/Directry/chicago.html
Phone: 773-622-5400
Fax: 773-385-5453
TF: 800-237-5055

South Shore Hospital
8012 S Crandon Ave
Chicago, IL 60617
Phone: 773-768-0810
Fax: 773-768-8154

Trinity Hospital
2320 E 93rd St
Chicago, IL 60617
www.advocatehealth.com/sites/hospitals/trin/index.html
Phone: 773-978-2000
Fax: 773-933-6435

University of Chicago Hospitals
5841 S Maryland Ave
Chicago, IL 60637
www.uchospitals.edu
Phone: 773-702-1000
Fax: 773-702-9005

University of Illinois Hospital & Clinics
1740 W Taylor St Suite 1400
Chicago, IL 60612
www.uic.edu/hsc
Phone: 312-996-7000
Fax: 312-996-7049

Veterans Affairs Edward Hines Jr Hospital
PO Box 5000
Hines, IL 60141
Phone: 708-202-8387
Fax: 708-202-7998

Veterans Affairs Westside Medical Center
PO Box 8195
Chicago, IL 60680
Phone: 312-666-6500
Fax: 312-633-2195

Transportation

Airport(s)

Chicago Midway Airport (MDW)
9 miles SW of downtown (approx 45 minutes) 773-838-0600
Chicago O'Hare International Airport (ORD)
25 miles NW of downtown
(approx 30-45 minutes) 773-686-2200

Mass Transit

Chicago Transit Authority
$1.50 Base fare. 312-836-7000
L-Train
$1.50 Base fare. 312-836-7000

Rail/Bus

Amtrak Station
225 S Canal St Union Stn
Chicago, IL 60606
Phone: 800-872-7245

Greyhound Bus Station
630 W Harrison St
Chicago, IL 60607
Phone: 312-408-5971
TF: 800-231-2222

Utilities

Electricity
ComEd. 800-334-7661

Gas
Peoples Gas Light & Coke Co 312-240-7000

Water
Chicago Bureau of Water. 312-747-7956

Garbage Collection/Recycling
Chicago Streets & Sanitation Dept. 312-744-5000
www.cityofchicago.org/StreetsAndSan

Telecommunications

Telephone
Ameritech. 800-244-4444
www.ameritech.com

Cable Television

AT & T Cable Services 773-434-8710
www.cable.att.com

Prime Cable of Chicago 773-736-1800
www.primecablechi.com

Internet Service Providers (ISPs)

Ameritech Corp 312-750-5000
www.ameritech.com

Ameritech.net 800-638-8775
www.ameritech.net

Infinite Data Source Inc 312-255-5440
www.idsonline.com

InfoRamp Inc 312-577-6666
theramp.net

InterAccess Co 312-496-4400
www.interaccess.com

InterGlobal Communications 847-470-4920
www.igcom.net

Planet Group Inc 312-360-9588
www.pg.net

Ripco Communications Inc 773-477-6210
www.ripco.com

Verio Chicago 312-621-7400
home.verio.net/local/frontpage.cfm?AirportCode=ORD

Banks

Advance Bank
9200 S Commercial Ave
Chicago, IL 60617
Phone: 773-768-1400
Fax: 773-734-1534

Albany Bank & Trust Co NA
3400 W Lawrence Ave
Chicago, IL 60625
www.albanybank.com
Phone: 773-267-7300
Fax: 773-267-7337

Amalgamated Bank of Chicago
1 W Monroe St
Chicago, IL 60603
Phone: 312-822-3000
Fax: 312-822-3258
TF: 800-991-4254

American Metro Bank
4878 N Broadway
Chicago, IL 60640
Phone: 773-769-6868
Fax: 773-769-6288

American National Bank & Trust Co of Chicago
120 S La Salle St
Chicago, IL 60603
Phone: 312-661-5000
Fax: 312-661-6417

Argo FSB
2154 W Madison St
Chicago, IL 60612
Phone: 312-563-5500
Fax: 312-563-9396

Banco Popular North America
4000 W North Ave
Chicago, IL 60639
Phone: 773-772-8600
Fax: 773-292-4609

Bank of America NT & SA
231 S La Salle St
Chicago, IL 60697
Phone: 312-828-2345
Fax: 312-828-1974

Bank of Tokyo-Mitsubishi Ltd
227 W Monroe St Suite 2300
Chicago, IL 60606
Phone: 312-696-4500
Fax: 312-696-4530

Bank One NA
1 Bank One Plaza
Chicago, IL 60670
www.bankone.com
Phone: 312-732-4000
Fax: 847-488-4256

Broadway Bank
5960 N Broadway
Chicago, IL 60660
Phone: 773-989-2100
Fax: 773-989-4896

Citibank FSB
1 S Dearborn St
Chicago, IL 60603
Phone: 312-977-5000
Fax: 312-977-5000

Cole Taylor Bank
1965 N Milwaukee Ave
Chicago, IL 60647
E-mail: ctbnk@coletaylor.com
www.ctbnk.com
Phone: 773-927-7000
Fax: 773-278-2183

Corus Bank NA
4800 N Western Ave
Chicago, IL 60625
Phone: 773-388-5100
Fax: 773-388-5158

Firstar Bank Illinois
30 N Michigan Ave
Chicago, IL 60602
Phone: 312-641-1000
Fax: 312-641-2103

Harris Trust & Savings Bank
111 W Monroe St
Chicago, IL 60603
E-mail: newaccounts@harrisbank.com
www.harrisbank.com
Phone: 312-461-2121
Fax: 312-461-6640

LaSalle Bank NA
135 S LaSalle St
Chicago, IL 60603
E-mail: lsnb@ivi.net
www.lsnb.com
Phone: 312-443-2000
Fax: 312-904-6521

Manufacturers Bank
1200 N Ashland Ave
Chicago, IL 60622
www.manbk.com
Phone: 773-278-4040
Fax: 773-278-4066

Mid-City National Bank of Chicago
801 W Madison St
Chicago, IL 60607
Phone: 312-421-7600
Fax: 312-421-7612

Mid-Town Bank & Trust Co of Chicago
2021 N Clark St
Chicago, IL 60614
www.mtbchicago.com
Phone: 773-665-5000
Fax: 773-871-0879
TF: 877-665-5300

North Federal Savings Bank
100 W North Ave
Chicago, IL 60610
E-mail: northfedl@aol.com
www.northfederal.com
Phone: 312-664-4320
Fax: 312-664-4289

Northern Trust Co
50 S LaSalle St
Chicago, IL 60675
www.ntrs.com
Phone: 312-630-6000
Fax: 312-630-1779
TF: 888-289-6542

Old Kent Bank
233 S Wacker Dr
Chicago, IL 60606
Phone: 312-876-4200
Fax: 312-876-4184
TF: 800-653-5368

Pullman Bank & Trust Co
1000 E 111th St
Chicago, IL 60628
E-mail: marketing@pullmanbank.com
pullmanbank.com
Phone: 773-602-8200
Fax: 773-785-9755
TF: 800-785-5626

Saint Paul Federal Bank
6700 W North Ave
Chicago, IL 60707
www.stpaulbank.com
Phone: 773-622-5000
Fax: 773-804-2110
TF: 800-321-2265

South Shore Bank of Chicago
7054 S Jeffrey Blvd
Chicago, IL 60649
E-mail: accounts@sbk.com
www.sbk.com
Phone: 773-288-1000
Fax: 773-753-5699
TF: 800-669-7725

TCF National Bank of Illinois
4192 S Archer Ave
Chicago, IL 60632
Phone: 773-847-1140
Fax: 773-847-7791

University National Bank
1354 E 55th St
Chicago, IL 60615
E-mail: bank@uninatbk.com
www.uninatbk.com
Phone: 773-684-1200
Fax: 773-684-4560

Shopping

900 North Michigan Shops
900 N Michigan Ave
Chicago, IL 60611
Phone: 312-915-3916

Atrium Mall
100 W Randolph St
Chicago, IL 60601
Phone: 312-346-0777

Bloomingdale's
900 N Michigan Ave
Chicago, IL 60611
Phone: 312-440-4460
Fax: 312-440-4394

Carson Pirie Scott
1 S State St
Chicago, IL 60603
Phone: 312-641-7000
Fax: 312-641-7088

Century Shopping Centre
2828 N Clark St
Chicago, IL 60657
Phone: 773-929-8100

Charlestowne Mall
3800 E Main St
Saint Charles, IL 60174
Phone: 630-513-1120
Fax: 630-513-1459

Chicago Place
700 N Michigan Ave
Chicago, IL 60611
Phone: 312-266-7710
Fax: 312-266-8940

Chicago Ridge Mall
444 Chicago Ridge Mall Dr
Chicago Ridge, IL 60415
Phone: 708-422-0897
Fax: 708-499-6174

Chinatown
2169B S China Pl
Chicago, IL 60616
Phone: 312-326-5320
Fax: 312-326-5668

Evergreen Plaza
9730 S Western Ave
Evergreen Park, IL 60805
Phone: 708-422-5454
Fax: 708-422-9780

Fox Valley Center
195 Fox Valley Ctr
Aurora, IL 60504
Phone: 630-851-3000
Fax: 630-851-3683

Golf Mill Center
239 Golf Mill Ctr
Niles, IL 60714
Phone: 847-699-1070
Fax: 847-699-1593

Gurnee Mills Mall
6170 W Grand Ave
Gurnee, IL 60031
www.gurneemillsmall.com
Phone: 847-263-7500
Fax: 847-263-2423
TF: 800-937-7467

Hawthorn Center
122 Hawthorn Ctr
Vernon Hills, IL 60061
Phone: 847-362-2600
Fax: 847-362-2689

Lakehurst Mall
199 Lakehurst Rd
Waukegan, IL 60085
Phone: 847-473-0234

Lincoln Mall
208 Lincoln Mall Dr
Matteson, IL 60443
Phone: 708-747-5600
Fax: 708-747-5629

Lord & Taylor
835 N Michigan Ave
Chicago, IL 60611
Phone: 312-787-7400

Marshall Field & Co
111 N State St
Chicago, IL 60602
www.marshallfields.com
Phone: 312-781-1000
Fax: 312-781-4594

Navy Pier
600 E Grand Ave
Chicago, IL 60611
E-mail: npgeninfo@mpea.com
www.navypier.com
Phone: 312-595-7437
TF: 800-595-7437

Neiman Marcus
737 N Michigan Ave
Chicago, IL 60611
www.neimanmarcus.com
Phone: 312-642-5900
Fax: 312-642-9622

North Pier
401 E Illinois St
Chicago, IL 60611
Phone: 312-836-4300
Fax: 312-836-4329

Northbrook Court
2171 Northbrook Cr
Northbrook, IL 60062
Phone: 847-498-1770
Fax: 847-498-5194

Oakbrook Shopping Center
100 Oakbrook Ctr
Oak Brook, IL 60523
Phone: 630-573-0250
Fax: 630-573-0710

Old Orchard Center
34 Old Orchard Ctr Suite E34
Skokie, IL 60077
E-mail: info@oldorchard.com
www.oldorchard.com
Phone: 847-674-7070
Fax: 847-674-7083

Orland Square
288 Orland Sq
Orland Park, IL 60462
Phone: 708-349-6936
Fax: 708-349-8419

Randhurst Shopping Center
999 N Elmhurst Rd
Mount Prospect, IL 60056
www.randhurstmall.com
Phone: 847-259-0500
Fax: 847-259-0228

River Oaks Center Phone: 708-868-0600
96 River Oaks Dr Fax: 708-868-1402
Calumet City, IL 60409
www.shopsimon.com/smt/servlet/SMTMall?mid=190&pn=ENTRY&rs=0

Saks Fifth Avenue Phone: 312-944-6500
700 N Michigan Ave Fax: 312-944-3138
Chicago, IL 60611

Shops at the Mart Phone: 312-527-7990
222 Merchandise Mart Plaza Fax: 312-527-7058
Chicago, IL 60654

Spring Hill Mall Phone: 847-428-2200
1072 Spring Hill Mall Fax: 847-428-2219
West Dundee, IL 60118

Stratford Square Mall Phone: 630-351-9400
152 Stratford Sq Fax: 630-351-9769
Bloomingdale, IL 60108

Water Tower Place Phone: 312-440-3165
835-845 N Michigan Ave
Chicago, IL 60611

Woodfield Mall Phone: 847-330-1537
5 Woodfield Mall Fax: 847-330-0251
Schaumburg, IL 60173 TF: 800-847-9590
www.taubman.com/shopcen/htmfil/woodf/woodf.htm

Yorktown Shopping Center Phone: 630-629-7330
203 Yorktown Ctr Fax: 630-629-7334
Lombard, IL 60148
www.yorktowncenter.com

Media

Newspapers and Magazines

Bridgeport News Phone: 312-842-5883
3252 S Halstead St Fax: 312-842-5097
Chicago, IL 60608

Chicago Life Magazine Phone: 773-528-2737
PO Box 11311
Chicago, IL 60611
E-mail: chgolife@mcs.com

Chicago Magazine Phone: 312-222-8999
500 N Dearborn Ave Suite 1200 Fax: 312-222-0699
Chicago, IL 60610
www.chicagomag.com

Chicago NewCityNet Phone: 312-243-8786
770 N Halsted St Suite 208 Fax: 312-243-8802
Chicago, IL 60611
E-mail: info@newcitynet.com
www.newcitynet.com

Chicago Reader Phone: 312-828-0350
11 E Illinois St Fax: 312-828-0305
Chicago, IL 60611
E-mail: mail@chicagoreader.com
www.chicagoreader.com

Chicago Sun-Times* Phone: 312-321-3000
401 N Wabash Ave Fax: 312-321-3084
Chicago, IL 60611
E-mail: letters@suntimes.com
www.suntimes.com

Chicago Tribune* Phone: 312-222-3232
435 N Michigan Ave Fax: 312-222-2550
Chicago, IL 60611
www.chicago.tribune.com

Chicago's Northwest Side Press Phone: 773-286-6100
4937 N Milwaukee Ave Fax: 773-286-8151
Chicago, IL 60630

Crain's Chicago Business Phone: 312-649-5200
740 N Rush St Fax: 312-649-5415
Chicago, IL 60611 TF: 800-678-2724
www.crainschicagobusiness.com

Des Plaines Journal Phone: 847-299-5511
622 Graceland Ave Fax: 847-298-8549
Des Plaines, IL 60016
www.northstarnet.org/dpkhome/jtopics

Inside Lake View Phone: 773-878-7333
4710 N Lincoln Ave Fax: 773-878-0959
Chicago, IL 60625

Inside Lincoln Park Phone: 773-878-7333
4710 N Lincoln Ave Fax: 773-878-0959
Chicago, IL 60625

Inside Publications Phone: 773-878-7333
4710 N Lincoln Ave Fax: 773-878-0959
Chicago, IL 60625
E-mail: inside@suba.com
www.insideonline.com

Inside Ravenswood Phone: 773-878-7333
4710 N Lincoln Ave Fax: 773-878-0959
Chicago, IL 60625

Key: This Week in Chicago Phone: 312-943-0838
226 E Ontario St Suite 300 Fax: 312-664-6113
Chicago, IL 60611
www.keymag.com

Lombardian Phone: 630-627-7010
613 S Main St Fax: 630-627-7027
Lombard, IL 60148
E-mail: lombardian@aol.com
members.aol.com/lombardian/homepage.html

Morningstar Inc Phone: 312-696-6000
225 W Wacker Dr Fax: 312-696-6001
Chicago, IL 60606 TF: 800-735-0700
E-mail: joe@morningstar.net
www.morningstar.net

Naperville Sun Phone: 630-355-0063
1500 W Ogden Ave Fax: 630-416-5163
Naperville, IL 60540
www.copleynewspapers.com/sunpub/naper

North Loop News Phone: 773-283-7900
6008 W Belmont Ave Fax: 773-283-7761
Chicago, IL 60634

Where Chicago
1165 N Clark St Suite 302
Chicago, IL 60610
E-mail: wherechicago@insnet.com
www.wheremags.com/chicago.html
Phone: 312-642-1896
Fax: 312-642-5467

**Indicates major daily newspapers*

Television

WBBM-TV Ch 2 (CBS)
630 N McClurg Ct
Chicago, IL 60611
E-mail: wbbmch2@aol.com
Phone: 312-944-6000
Fax: 312-951-3878

WCIU-TV Ch 26 (Ind)
26 N Halsted St
Chicago, IL 60661
Phone: 312-705-2600
Fax: 312-705-2656

WCPX-TV Ch 38 (PAX)
541 N Fairbanks Ct Suite 800
Chicago, IL 60611
www.pax.net/WCPX
Phone: 312-410-9038
Fax: 312-467-9318

WFLD-TV Ch 32 (Fox)
205 N Michigan Ave
Chicago, IL 60601
www.foxchicago.com
Phone: 312-565-5532
Fax: 312-819-1332

WGBO-TV Ch 66 (Uni)
541 N Fairbanks Ct 11th Fl
Chicago, IL 60611
www.univision.net/stations/wgbo.htm
Phone: 312-670-1000
Fax: 312-494-6492

WGN-TV Ch 9 (WB)
2501 W Bradley Pl
Chicago, IL 60618
E-mail: wgn-tv@tribune.com
www.wgntv.com
Phone: 773-528-2311
Fax: 773-528-6050

WJYS-TV Ch 62 (Ind)
18600 S Oak Park Ave
Tinley Park, IL 60477
Phone: 708-633-0001
Fax: 708-633-0040

WLS-TV Ch 7 (ABC)
190 N State St
Chicago, IL 60601
Phone: 312-750-7777
Fax: 312-899-8019

WMAQ-TV Ch 5 (NBC)
454 N Columbus Dr NBC Tower
Chicago, IL 60611
www.nbc5.com
Phone: 312-836-5555
Fax: 312-527-5925

WPWR-TV Ch 50 (UPN)
2151 N Elston Ave
Chicago, IL 60614
Phone: 773-276-5050
Fax: 773-276-6477

WSNS-TV Ch 44 (Tele)
430 W Grant Pl
Chicago, IL 60614
Phone: 773-929-1200
Fax: 773-929-7269

WTTW-TV Ch 11 (PBS)
5400 N St Louis Ave
Chicago, IL 60625
E-mail: viewermail@wttw.com
www.wttw.com
Phone: 773-583-5000
Fax: 773-583-3046

WYCC-TV Ch 20 (Ind)
7500 S Pulaski Rd
Chicago, IL 60652
Phone: 773-838-7878
Fax: 773-581-2071

Radio

WAIT-AM 850 kHz (Nost)
8800 Rt 14
Crystal Lake, IL 60012
Phone: 815-459-7000
Fax: 312-755-1059

WBBM-AM 780 kHz (N/T)
630 N McClurg Ct
Chicago, IL 60611
E-mail: sales@wbbm.com
www.wbbm780.com
Phone: 312-944-6000
Fax: 312-951-3674

WBBM-FM 96.3 MHz (CHR)
630 N McClurg Ct
Chicago, IL 60611
E-mail: info@b96.com
www.b96.com
Phone: 312-944-6000
Fax: 312-951-1773

WBEZ-FM 91.5 MHz (NPR)
848 E Grand Ave
Chicago, IL 60611
www.a2z.com/wbez
Phone: 312-832-9150
Fax: 312-832-3100

WCKG-FM 105.9 MHz (N/T)
2 Prudential Plaza Suite 1059
Chicago, IL 60601
E-mail: wckg@aol.com
www.1059wckg.com
Phone: 312-240-7900
Fax: 312-565-3181

WDEK-FM 92.5 MHz (CHR)
737 N Michigan Ave Suite 1600
Chicago, IL 60611
Phone: 312-573-9400
Fax: 312-573-8058

WFMT-FM 98.7 MHz (Clas)
5400 N St Louis Ave
Chicago, IL 60625
E-mail: fine.arts@wfmt.com
www.wfmt.com
Phone: 773-279-2000
Fax: 773-279-2199

WGCI-AM 1390 kHz (Urban)
332 S Michigan Ave Suite 600
Chicago, IL 60604
Phone: 312-427-4800
Fax: 312-427-7410

WGCI-FM 107.5 MHz (Urban)
332 S Michigan Ave Suite 600
Chicago, IL 60604
Phone: 312-427-4800
Fax: 312-427-7410

WGN-AM 720 kHz (N/T)
435 N Michigan Ave
Chicago, IL 60611
E-mail: WGNfanAMU@aol.com
www.wgnradio.com
Phone: 312-222-4700
Fax: 312-222-5165

WIND-AM 560 kHz (Span)
625 N Michigan Ave Suite 300
Chicago, IL 60611
www.wind560.com
Phone: 312-751-5560
Fax: 312-654-0092

WJMK-FM 104.3 MHz (Oldies)
180 N Michigan Ave Suite 1200
Chicago, IL 60601
E-mail: wjmk@aol.com
www.wjmk.com
Phone: 312-977-1800
Fax: 312-977-1859

WKIE-FM 92.7 MHz (CHR)
737 N Michigan Ave Suite 1600
Chicago, IL 60611
Phone: 312-573-9400
Fax: 312-573-8058

WKQX-FM 101.1 MHz (Alt) Phone: 312-527-8348
Merchandise Mart Suite 1700 Fax: 312-245-0073
Chicago, IL 60654
E-mail: promotions@q101.com
stage.q101.com/new

WLEY-FM 107.9 MHz (Span) Phone: 312-920-9500
150 N Michigan Ave Suite 1040 Fax: 312-920-9515
Chicago, IL 60601
www.laley1079.com

WLIT-FM 93.9 MHz (AC) Phone: 312-329-9002
150 N Michigan Ave Suite 1135 Fax: 312-329-0267
Chicago, IL 60601
E-mail: administrator@wlit.com
www.wlit.com

WLS-AM 890 kHz (N/T) Phone: 312-984-0890
190 N State St Fax: 312-984-5305
Chicago, IL 60601
E-mail: wlslam@wlsam.com
www.wlsam.com

WLUP-FM 97.9 MHz (Rock) Phone: 312-440-5270
875 N Michigan Ave Suite 3750 Fax: 312-440-9377
Chicago, IL 60611
E-mail: wlup@aol.com
www.979theloop.com

WLXX-AM 1200 kHz (Span) Phone: 312-738-1200
625 N Michigan Ave 3rd Fl Fax: 312-654-0092
Chicago, IL 60611
www.wlxx.com

WMAQ-AM 670 kHz (Sports) Phone: 312-670-6767
455 N Cityfront Plaza NBC Tower 6th Fl Fax: 312-245-6098
Chicago, IL 60611
www.wmaqradio.com

WMVP-AM 1000 kHz (Sports) Phone: 312-980-1000
875 N Michigan Ave Suite 1510 Fax: 312-440-1993
Chicago, IL 60611
www.am1000.com

WNIB-FM 97.1 MHz (Clas) Phone: 312-633-9700
1140 W Erie St Fax: 312-633-9710
Chicago, IL 60622

WNND-FM 100.3 MHz (AC) Phone: 312-297-5100
1 Prudential Plaza Suite 2780 Fax: 312-297-5155
Chicago, IL 60601
www.windy100.com

WNUA-FM 95.5 MHz (NAC) Phone: 312-645-9550
444 N Michigan Ave Suite 300 Fax: 312-645-9645
Chicago, IL 60611
www.wnua.com

WOJO-FM 105.1 MHz (Span) Phone: 312-751-5560
625 N Michigan Ave Suite 300 Fax: 312-664-2472
Chicago, IL 60611
www.wojofm.com

WSCR-AM 1160 kHz (Sports) Phone: 773-777-1700
4949 W Belmont Ave Fax: 773-777-5031
Chicago, IL 60641

WTMX-FM 101.9 MHz (AC) Phone: 312-946-1019
1 Prudential Plaza Suite 2700 Fax: 312-946-4747
Chicago, IL 60601
www.wtmx.com

WUBT-FM 103.5 MHz (Oldies) Phone: 312-255-5100
875 N Michigan Ave Suite 4000 Fax: 312-440-9143
Chicago, IL 60611
www.1035thebeat.com

WUSN-FM 99.5 MHz (Ctry) Phone: 312-649-0099
875 N Michigan Ave Suite 1310 Fax: 312-664-3999
Chicago, IL 60611
E-mail: genmgr@us99mail.com
www.us99country.com

WVAZ-FM 102.7 MHz (Urban) Phone: 312-360-9000
800 S Wells St Suite 250 Fax: 312-360-9070
Chicago, IL 60607
www.v103.com

WVON-AM 1450 kHz (N/T) Phone: 773-247-6200
3350 S Kedzie Ave Fax: 773-247-5366
Chicago, IL 60623
www.wvon1450am.com

WXCD-FM 94.7 MHz (CR) Phone: 312-984-0890
190 N State St 8th Fl Fax: 312-984-5357
Chicago, IL 60601
E-mail: CD94.7@abc.com
www.cd947.com

WXRT-FM 93.1 MHz (Alt) Phone: 773-777-1700
4949 W Belmont Ave Fax: 773-777-5031
Chicago, IL 60641
E-mail: comments@wxrt.com
www.wxrt.com

WYPA-AM 820 kHz (Rel) Phone: 312-255-9972
401 N Wabash Ave Suite 608 Fax: 312-922-6120
Chicago, IL 60611

Attractions

Chicago is composed of many diverse neighborhoods, each offering different types of attractions. Its excellence in the arts is reflected in The Loop/Downtown area, which is home to the Chicago Architectural Foundation, Art Institute, Chicago Symphony, and many theaters. Along Lake Shore Drive one can visit the Museum of Science and Industry's thousands of exhibits demonstrating scientific principles and technical advances. The Chicago Cubs' Wrigley Field and the Lincoln Park Zoo are located in the Lincoln Park area. The Second City comedy group is located in the Old Town area, and one of the oldest art fairs in America is held here each summer. The world's largest marketplace, the Chicago Mercantile Exchange, and the world's largest oceanarium/aquarium, the Shedd Aquarium, and Navy Pier are also popular sites to visit. Just twenty minutes from Chicago is the Village of Oak Brook, which features the renowned architectural style of Frank Lloyd Wright.

ABA Museum of Law Phone: 312-988-6222
750 N Lake Shore Dr
Chicago, IL 60611

Adler Planetarium & Astronomy Museum
1300 S Lake Shore Dr
Chicago, IL 60605
E-mail: pr@adlernet.org
www.adlerplanetarium.org
Phone: 312-922-7827
Fax: 312-322-2257

Apollo Theater
2540 N Lincoln Ave
Chicago, IL 60614
Phone: 773-935-6100
Fax: 773-935-6214

Aragon Entertainment Center
1106 W Lawrence Ave
Chicago, IL 60640
Phone: 773-561-9500

Art Institute of Chicago Museum
111 S Michigan Ave
Chicago, IL 60603
www.artic.edu/aic/
Phone: 312-443-3600
Fax: 312-443-0849

Auditorium Theatre
50 E Congress Pkwy
Chicago, IL 60605
E-mail: information@auditoriumtheatre.org
www.auditoriumtheatre.org
Phone: 312-922-4046
Fax: 312-431-2360

Bailiwick Repertory Theater
1229 W Belmont Ave Bailiwick Arts Ctr
Chicago, IL 60657
E-mail: bailiwickr@aol.com
www.bailiwick.org
Phone: 773-883-1090
Fax: 773-525-3245

Ballet Chicago
185 N Wabash Ave Suite 2300
Chicago, IL 60601
Phone: 312-251-8838
Fax: 312-251-8840

Balzekas Museum of Lithuanian Culture
6500 S Pulaski Rd
Chicago, IL 60629
Phone: 773-582-6500
Fax: 773-582-5133

Brookfield Zoo
1st Ave & 31st St
Brookfield, IL 60513
www.brookfield-zoo.mus.il.us
Phone: 708-485-2200
Fax: 708-485-3532

Buckingham Fountain
Columbus Dr & Congress Pkwy Grant Pk
Chicago, IL 60605
Phone: 312-747-2200

Burnham Park
Lakefront at 18th Dr
Chicago, IL 60605
www.chicagoparkdistrict.com
Phone: 312-747-7009

Chicago Athenaeum Museum of Art Architecture & Design
190 S Roselle Rd
Schaumburg, IL 60193
www.chi-athenaeum.org
Phone: 847-895-3950
Fax: 847-895-3951

Chicago Board of Trade
141 W Jackson Blvd
Chicago, IL 60604
www.cbot.com
Phone: 312-435-3500
Fax: 312-341-3392
TF: 800-572-3276

Chicago Botanic Garden
1000 Lake Cook Rd
Glencoe, IL 60022
E-mail: cbglib@nslsilus.org
www.chicago-botanic.org
Phone: 847-835-5440
Fax: 847-835-4484

Chicago Chamber Orchestra
332 S Michigan Ave Suite 1143
Chicago, IL 60604
Phone: 312-922-5570

Chicago Children's Museum
700 E Grand Ave Suite 127
Chicago, IL 60611
www.chichildrensmuseum.org
Phone: 312-527-1000
Fax: 312-527-9082

Chicago Cultural Center
78 E Washington St
Chicago, IL 60602
www.ci.chi.il.us/Tourism/CultureCenterTour/
Phone: 312-346-3278
Fax: 312-744-2089

Chicago Historical Society
1601 N Clark St
Chicago, IL 60614
www.chicagohs.org
Phone: 312-642-4600
Fax: 312-266-2077

Chicago Mercantile Exchange
30 S Wacker Dr
Chicago, IL 60606
E-mail: info@cme.com
www.cme.com
Phone: 312-930-1000
Fax: 312-930-3016

Chicago Music Mart at De Paul Center
333 S State St
Chicago, IL 60604
www.chicagomusicmart.com
Phone: 312-362-6700
Fax: 312-362-5838

Chicago Opera Theater
70 E Lake St
Chicago, IL 60601
www.chicagooperatheater.org
Phone: 312-704-8420
Fax: 312-704-8421

Chicago Shakespeare Theater
800 E Grand Ave Navy Pier
Chicago, IL 60611
www.chicagoshakes.com
Phone: 312-595-5600
Fax: 312-595-5644

Chicago Sinfonietta
105 W Adams St Suite 3330
Chicago, IL 60603
Phone: 312-857-1062
Fax: 312-857-1007

Chicago Sports Hall of Fame
1150 N River Rd
Des Plaines, IL 60016
Phone: 847-294-1700
Fax: 847-635-1571

Chicago Stock Exchange
440 S LaSalle St
Chicago, IL 60605
www.chicagostockex.com
Phone: 312-663-2222
Fax: 312-663-2232

Chicago Symphony Orchestra
220 S Michigan Ave
Chicago, IL 60604
E-mail: info@chicagosymphony.org
www.chicagosymphony.org
Phone: 312-294-3000
Fax: 312-294-3035
TF: 800-223-7114

Chicago Theatre
175 N State St
Chicago, IL 60601
Phone: 312-443-1130
Fax: 312-263-9505

Chicago Zoological Park
3300 S Golf Rd
Brookfield, IL 60513
www.brookfield-zoo.mus.il.us
Phone: 708-485-0263
Fax: 708-485-3532

Chinatown Phone: 312-326-5320
2169B S China Pl Fax: 312-326-5668
Chicago, IL 60616

Civic Opera House Phone: 312-332-2244
20 N Wacker Dr Fax: 312-332-8120
Chicago, IL 60606
www.lyricopera.org

Clarke House Museum Phone: 312-745-0040
1827 S Indiana Ave Fax: 312-745-0077
Chicago, IL 60616

DisneyQuest Phone: 312-222-1300
10 W Ohio
Chicago, IL 60610
disney.go.com/DisneyQuest/Chicago/home.html

Downtown Thursday Nights Phone: 312-742-1171
20 N Michigan Ave
Chicago, IL 60602
www.dtnchicago.com

DuSable Museum of African American History Phone: 773-947-0600
740 E 56th Pl Fax: 773-947-0677
Chicago, IL 60637
www.dusablemuseum.org

Ernest Hemingway Museum Phone: 708-848-2222
200 N Oak Park Ave
Oak Park, IL 60303
hemingway.org

ESPN Zone Phone: 312-644-3776
43 E Ohio St
Chicago, IL 60611
espn.go.com/espninc/zone/chicago.html

Field Museum of Natural History Phone: 312-922-9410
1400 S Lake Shore Dr Fax: 312-427-7269
Chicago, IL 60605
www.fmnh.org

Ford Center for the Performing Arts/ Oriental Theatre Phone: 312-782-2004
24 W Randolph St Fax: 312-372-5427
Chicago, IL 60601

Frank Lloyd Wright Home & Studio Phone: 708-848-1976
931 Chicago Ave Fax: 708-848-1248
Oak Park, IL 60302
www.wrightplus.org

Garfield Park Conservatory Phone: 312-746-5100
300 N Central Park Ave
Chicago, IL 60624

Glessner House Museum Phone: 312-326-1480
1800 S Prairie Ave Fax: 312-326-1397
Chicago, IL 60616

Goodman Theatre Phone: 312-443-3800
200 S Columbus Dr Fax: 312-443-9201
Chicago, IL 60603

Grant Park Symphony Orchestra Phone: 312-742-7638
425 E McFetridge Dr Fax: 312-742-7662
Chicago, IL 60605
www.grantparkmusicfestival.com

Hancock Observatory Phone: 888-875-8439
875 N Michigan Ave
Chicago, IL 60611

Hellenic Museum & Cultural Center Phone: 312-726-1234
168 N Michigan Ave 4th Fl Fax: 312-726-8539
Chicago, IL 60601

Henry Crown Space Center OMNIMAX Theater Phone: 773-684-1414
5700 S Lake Shore Dr Fax: 773-684-7141
Chicago, IL 60637
E-mail: omnimax@msichicago.org
www.msichicago.org

Historic Pullman District Phone: 773-785-8181
11111 S Forrestville Ave Fax: 773-785-8182
Chicago, IL 60628

House of Blues Hotel Phone: 312-923-2000
330 N State St Fax: 312-527-3072
Chicago, IL 60610

Hubbard Street Dance Co Phone: 312-850-9744
1147 W Jackson Blvd Fax: 312-455-8240
Chicago, IL 60607

International Museum of Surgical Science Phone: 312-642-6502
1524 N Lake Shore Dr Fax: 312-642-9516
Chicago, IL 60610
E-mail: info@imss.org
www.imss.org

Irish American Heritage Center Phone: 773-282-7035
4626 N Knox Ave Fax: 773-282-0380
Chicago, IL 60630

Jackson Park Phone: 312-747-6187
6401 S Stony Island Ave
Chicago, IL 60637

Jane Adams Hull House Phone: 312-413-5353
800 S Halsted St Fax: 312-413-2092
Chicago, IL 60607

Joffrey Ballet of Chicago Phone: 312-739-0120
70 E Lake St Suite 1300 Fax: 312-739-0119
Chicago, IL 60601
E-mail: information@joffrey.com
www.joffrey.com

John G Shedd Aquarium Phone: 312-939-2426
1200 S Lake Shore Dr Fax: 312-939-8069
Chicago, IL 60605
www.sheddnet.org

John Hancock Center Phone: 312-751-3681
875 N Michigan Ave
Chicago, IL 60611
www.hancock-observatory.com

Lifeline Theatre Phone: 773-761-1772
6912 N Glenwood Ave Fax: 773-761-4582
Chicago, IL 60626
www.theatrechicago.com/lifeline

Lincoln Park Conservatory Phone: 312-742-7736
2400 N Stockton Dr Fax: 312-742-5619
Chicago, IL 60614

Lincoln Park Zoo
2001 N Clark St
Chicago, IL 60614
www.lpzoo.com
Phone: 312-742-2000
Fax: 312-742-2137

Lizzadro Museum of Lapidary Art
220 Cottage Hill Ave Wilder Pk
Elmhurst, IL 60126
Phone: 630-833-1616
Fax: 630-833-1225

Loews Cineplex IMAX Theatre
600 E Grand Ave Navy Pier
Chicago, IL 60611
www.cineplexodeon.com
Phone: 312-595-0090
Fax: 312-595-9212

Loop The Downtown District
State St
Chicago, IL 60602

Lyric Opera of Chicago
20 N Wacker Dr Civic Opera House
Suite 860
Chicago, IL 60606
Phone: 312-332-2244
Fax: 312-419-1459

Marriott's Lincolnshire Theatre
10 Marriott Dr
Lincolnshire, IL 60069
marriotthotels.com/CHILN
Phone: 847-634-0200
Fax: 847-634-7022

Mexican Fine Arts Center Museum
1852 W 19th St
Chicago, IL 60608
E-mail: coronel@mfacmchicago.org
www.mfacmchicago.org
Phone: 312-738-1503
Fax: 312-738-9740

Mordine & Co Dance Theatre
4730 N Sheridan Rd
Chicago, IL 60640
Phone: 773-989-3310
Fax: 312-344-8036

Morton Arboretum
4100 Illinois Rt 53
Lisle, IL 60532
E-mail: trees@mortonarb.org
www.mortonarb.org
Phone: 630-968-0074
Fax: 630-719-2463

Museum of Broadcast Communications
78 E Washington Ave St Chicago
Cultural Ctr
Chicago, IL 60602
www.mbcnet.org
Phone: 312-629-6000
Fax: 312-629-6009

Museum of Contemporary Art
220 E Chicago Ave
Chicago, IL 60611
www.mcachicago.org
Phone: 312-280-2660
Fax: 312-397-4095

Museum of Contemporary Photography
600 S Michigan Ave Columbia College
Chicago, IL 60605
Phone: 312-663-5554
Fax: 312-360-1656

Museum of Holography
1134 W Washington Blvd
Chicago, IL 60607
Phone: 312-226-1007

Museum of Science & Industry
5700 S Lake Shore Dr
Chicago, IL 60637
E-mail: msi@msichicago.org
www.msichicago.org
Phone: 773-684-1414
Fax: 773-684-7141
TF: 800-468-6674

Museum of the Chicago Academy of Sciences
2430 N Cannon Dr
Chicago, IL 60614
E-mail: cas@chias.org
www.chias.org
Phone: 773-549-0606
Fax: 773-755-5199

Music of the Baroque Chorus & Orchestra
100 N LaSalle St Suite 1610
Chicago, IL 60602
E-mail: baroque@baroque.org
www.baroque.org
Phone: 312-551-1415
Fax: 312-551-1444

National Vietnam Veterans Art Museum
1801 S Indiana Ave
Chicago, IL 60616
Phone: 312-326-0270

Navy Pier
600 E Grand Ave
Chicago, IL 60611
E-mail: npgeninfo@mpea.com
www.navypier.com
Phone: 312-595-7437
TF: 800-595-7437

New Maxwell Street Sunday Market
Canal St & Roosevelt Rd
Chicago, IL 60605
Phone: 312-922-3100

North Lakeside Cultural Center
6219 N Sheridan Rd
Chicago, IL 60660
Phone: 773-743-4477
Fax: 773-743-1484

North Pier
401 E Illinois St
Chicago, IL 60611
Phone: 312-836-4300
Fax: 312-836-4329

North Shore Center for the Performing Arts
9501 Skokie Blvd
Skokie, IL 60076
www.northshorecenter.org
Phone: 847-673-6300
Fax: 847-679-1879

Old Saint Patrick's Church
700 W Adams St
Chicago, IL 60661
Phone: 312-648-1021
Fax: 312-648-9025

Old Town
Wells St
Chicago, IL 60614

Old Town School of Folk Music
4544 N Lincoln Ave
Chicago, IL 60625
www.oldtownschool.org
Phone: 773-728-6000
Fax: 773-728-6999

Orchestra Hall
220 S Michigan Ave
Chicago, IL 60604
Phone: 312-294-3333
Fax: 312-294-3329
TF: 800-223-7114

Oriental Institute Museum
1155 E 58th St University of Chicago
Chicago, IL 60637
www-oi.uchicago.edu
Phone: 773-702-9514
Fax: 773-702-9853

Osaka Garden
5900 S Lake Shore Dr
Chicago, IL 60637
Phone: 312-747-2474

Paramount Arts Centre
23 E Galena Blvd
Aurora, IL 60506
www.paramountarts.com
Phone: 630-896-7676
Fax: 630-892-1084

Peace Museum
314 W Institute Pl
Chicago, IL 60610
www.peacemuseum.org
Phone: 312-440-1860
Fax: 312-440-1267

Peggy Notebaert Nature Museum
2430 Cannon Dr
Chicago, IL 60614
E-mail: cas@chias.org
www.chias.org
Phone: 773-549-0606
Fax: 773-755-5188

Performing Arts Chicago
410 S Michigan Ave Suite 911
Chicago, IL 60605
www.pachicago.org
Phone: 312-663-1628
Fax: 312-663-1043

Polish Museum of America
984 N Milwaukee Ave
Chicago, IL 60622
Phone: 773-384-3352
Fax: 773-384-3799
TF: 800-772-8632

Pullman Historic District/Hotel Florence Museum
11111 S Forrestville Ave
Chicago, IL 60628
www.pullmanil.org
Phone: 773-785-8181
Fax: 773-785-8182

Randolph A Phillip Pullman Porter Museum Gallery
10406 S Maryland Ave
Chicago, IL 60628
Phone: 773-928-3935

Rosehill Cemetery
5800 N Ravenswood Ave
Chicago, IL 60660
Phone: 773-561-5940

Rosemont Theatre
5400 N River Rd
Rosemont, IL 60018
Phone: 847-671-5100
Fax: 847-671-6405

Royal George Theatre Center
1641 N Halsted St
Chicago, IL 60614
Phone: 312-944-5626
Fax: 312-944-5627

Sears Tower
233 S Wacker Dr
Chicago, IL 60684
www.sears-tower.com
Phone: 312-875-9696

Second City Chicago
1608 N Wells St
Chicago, IL 60614
E-mail: bmk1616@aol.com
www.secondcity.com
Phone: 312-337-3992
Fax: 312-664-9837

Shattered Globe Theatre
2856 N Halsted St
Chicago, IL 60657
Phone: 773-404-1237
Fax: 773-404-8417

Six Flags Great America
542 N Rt 21
Gurnee, IL 60031
www.sixflags.com/greatamerica
Phone: 847-249-2133
Fax: 847-249-2390

South Shore Cultural Center
7059 S Shore Dr
Chicago, IL 60649
E-mail: cpdsite@enteract.com
www.chicagoparkdistrict.com
Phone: 312-747-2536
Fax: 312-747-6666

Spertus Museum
618 S Michigan Ave
Chicago, IL 60605
www.spertus.edu/Museum.html
Phone: 312-922-9012
Fax: 312-922-6406

Steppenwolf Theatre
1650 N Halsted St
Chicago, IL 60614
www.steppenwolf.org
Phone: 312-335-1650
Fax: 312-335-0440

Swedish American Museum
5211 N Clark St
Chicago, IL 60640
www.samac.org
Phone: 773-728-8111
Fax: 773-728-8870

Terra Museum of American Art
664 N Michigan Ave
Chicago, IL 60611
Phone: 312-664-3939
Fax: 312-664-2052

Ukranian National Museum
721 N Oakley St
Chicago, IL 60612
Phone: 312-421-8020

Water Tower Place
835-845 N Michigan Ave
Chicago, IL 60611
Phone: 312-440-3165

Sports Teams & Facilities

Arlington International Racecourse
2200 W Euclid Ave
Arlington Heights, IL 60006
www.arlingtonpark.com
Phone: 847-255-4300
Fax: 847-255-4331

Chicago Bears
Soldier Field
Chicago, IL 60616
www.chicagobears.com
Phone: 847-615-2327

Chicago Blackhawks
1901 W Madison St United Ctr
Chicago, IL 60612
www.chicagoblackhawks.com
Phone: 312-455-7000
Fax: 312-455-7041

Chicago Bluesmen (roller hockey)
33 E Palatine Rd
Prospect Heights, IL 60070
E-mail: chicagobluesmen@earthlink.net
www.chicagobluesmen.com
Phone: 847-419-1700
Fax: 847-419-1717

Chicago Bulls
1901 W Madison St United Ctr
Chicago, IL 60612
www.nba.com/bulls
Phone: 312-455-4000
Fax: 312-455-4198

Chicago Cobras (soccer)
35 W 945 Fieldcrest Dr
Saint Charles, IL 60175
www.chicagocobras.com
Phone: 630-377-3545
Fax: 630-377-0933

Chicago Cubs
1060 W Addison St Wrigley Field
Chicago, IL 60613
E-mail: comments@mail.cubs.com
www.cubs.com
Phone: 773-404-2827

Chicago Fire (soccer)
311 W Superior St Suite 444
Chicago, IL 60610
www.chicago-fire.com
Phone: 312-705-7200
Fax: 312-705-7393
TF: 888-657-3473

Chicago Freeze (hockey)
PO Box 1000
Batavia, IL 60510
E-mail: chgofreeze@aol.com
www.chicagofreeze.com
Phone: 630-262-0010
Fax: 630-262-9025

Chicago Motor Speedway
3301 S Laramie Ave
Cicero, IL 60804
www.chicagomotorspeedway.com
Phone: 773-242-2277
Fax: 773-242-2278

Chicago Sockers (soccer)
2121 S Goebbert Chicago Stingers Stadium
Arlington Heights, IL 60005
Phone: 847-670-5425
Fax: 847-670-5427

Chicago Stingers (soccer)
545 Consumers Ave
Palatine, IL 60067
E-mail: stingers@chicagosoccer.com
www.chicagosoccer.com
Phone: 847-394-9860
Fax: 847-394-9942

Chicago White Sox
333 W 35th St Comiskey Park
Chicago, IL 60616
www.chisox.com
Phone: 312-674-1000
Fax: 312-674-5140

Chicago Wolves (hockey)
6920 N Manheim Rd Rosemont Horizon
Rosemont, IL 60018
www.chicagowolves.com
Phone: 847-390-0404
Fax: 847-724-1652
TF: 800-843-9658

Comiskey Park
333 W 35th St
Chicago, IL 60616
www.chisox.com/comiskey/comiskey-main.asp
Phone: 312-674-1000
Fax: 312-674-5103

Hawthorne Race Course
3501 S Laramie Ave
Cicero, IL 60804
www.hawthorneracecourse.com
Phone: 708-780-3700
Fax: 708-780-3677
TF: 800-780-0701

Soldier Field
425 E McFetridge Dr
Chicago, IL 60605
www.soldierfield.net
Phone: 312-747-1285
Fax: 312-747-6694

Sportsman's Park Racetrack
3301 S Laramie Ave
Cicero, IL 60804
Phone: 773-242-1121
Fax: 773-652-0015

United Center
1901 W Madison St
Chicago, IL 60612
www.unitedcenter.com
Phone: 312-455-4500
Fax: 312-455-4511

Wrigley Field
1060 W Addison St
Chicago, IL 60613
Phone: 773-404-2827
Fax: 773-404-4129

Annual Events

Belmont Street Fair (early June) 773-868-3010
Berghoff Oktoberfest (mid-September) 312-427-3170
Celebrate on State Street (mid-June) 312-782-9160
Celtic Fest Chicago (mid-September) 312-744-3315
Chicago Air & Water Show (mid-August) 312-744-3370
Chicago Auto Show (mid-February) 312-744-3315
Chicago Blues Festival (early June) 312-744-3370
Chicago Country Music Festival (early July) 312-744-3315
Chicago Earth Day (April 22) 773-549-0606
Chicago Flower & Garden Show (mid-March) 312-321-0077
Chicago Gospel Music Festival (early June) 312-744-3315
Chicago International Film Festival (early-mid-October) 312-425-9400
Chicago Jazz Festival (early September) 312-744-3370
Chicago Park District Spring Flower Show (early April-early May) 312-742-7737
Chicago Underground Film Festival (early-mid-August) 773-327-3456
Chicago WinterBreak (early January-late March) 312-744-3315
Chinese New Year Parade (early February) 312-744-3315
Gay & Lesbian Pride Parade (late June) 773-348-8243
Gold Coast Art Fair (early August) 312-744-3315
Grant Park Music Festival (mid-June-mid-August) 312-742-7638
Halloween Happening (late October) 312-744-0566
LaSalle Banks Chicago Marathon (mid-October) 312-904-9800
Magnificent Mile Lights Festival (mid-November) .. 312-642-3570
Maple Syrup Festival (late March) 847-824-8360
Mayor's Cup Youth Soccer Fest (late July) 312-744-3315
Medinah Shrine Circus (mid-March) 312-266-5050
Old Town Art Fair (mid-June) 312-337-1938
Oz Festival (early August) 773-880-5200
Printers Row Book Fair (early June) 312-987-1980
Race to the Taste (early July) 312-744-3315
Saint Patrick's Day Celebration & Fireworks (mid-March) 312-942-9188
SOFA-Sculpture Objects & Functional Art (early November) 312-654-0870
South Side Irish Saint Patrick's Day Parade (mid-March) 773-239-7755
Taste of Chicago (late June-early July) 312-744-3370
Taste of Lincoln Avenue (late July) 312-744-3315
Taste of Polonia Festival (early September) 773-777-8898
Venetian Night (late July) 312-744-3315
Viva! Chicago Latin Music Festival (late August) 312-744-3370
Wells Street Art Festival (mid-June) 312-951-6106
World Music Fest Chicago (late September-early October) 312-744-3315

Cincinnati, Ohio

***County:* Hamilton**

CINCINNATI is located along the Ohio River in southwestern Ohio. Major cities within 100 miles include Columbus and Dayton, Ohio; Indianapolis, Indiana; and Lexington, Kentucky.

Area (Land)	77.2 sq mi
Area (Water)	1.6 sq mi
Elevation	683 ft
Latitude	39-16-19 N
Longitude	84-45-69 W
Time Zone	EST
Area Code	513

Climate

Cincinnati has a continental climate with cold winters and warm summers. Winter high temperatures average around 40 degrees and lows average in the mid-20s. Average annual sleet/snowfall is 24 inches. Summer daytime temperatures average in the mid-80s, while evenings cool down into the 60s. Most precipitation falls during the spring and summer months; summer thunderstorms are common.

Average Temperatures & Precipitation

Temperatures

	Jan	Feb	Mar	Apr	May	Jun	Jul	Aug	Sep	Oct	Nov	Dec
High	37	42	54	65	75	83	86	85	79	67	54	42
Low	22	25	34	44	54	62	66	64	58	46	37	27

Precipitation

	Jan	Feb	Mar	Apr	May	Jun	Jul	Aug	Sep	Oct	Nov	Dec
Inches	2.6	2.6	4.2	3.8	4.6	3.5	4.0	3.5	3.0	2.9	3.5	3.1

History

Originally part of the Miami Purchase, Cincinnati was founded in 1788 as a community called Losantiville, a name derived from Delaware Indian, French, Greek, and Latin phrases meaning "town opposite the mouth of the Licking River." In 1789, the U.S. Army built Fort Washington in the area. The city's name was changed to Cincinnati in 1790 in honor of the Revolutionary War organization founded by George Washington, the Society of Cincinnati. In 1819, Cincinnati was incorporated as a city and became the seat of Hamilton County.

With the introduction of steam navigation on the Ohio River in the early 1800s and the opening of the Miami Canal in 1827, the shipping industry prospered in Cincinnati. Railroads were introduced to the area in 1843, further increasing the city's accessibility, Cincinnati grew quickly as a manufacturing and distribution center. Many Germans were drawn to the area's beauty, which was reminiscent of the Rhine Valley. The city's German heritage is evident in Cincinnati today, with more than one-third of Greater Cincinnati's current population of German origin.

By the late 1800s, Cincinnati was the nation's eighth largest city. The city continued to grow rapidly during much of the 20th Century—in the years between 1910 and 1960, the city's population jumped from 363,591 to more than 500,000. Although the population has declined in recent years, Cincinnati remains an important center for manufacturing and trade.

Population

1990 Census	364,114
1998 Estimate	336,400
% Change	7.6
2005 Projection	2,048,000*

Racial/Ethnic Breakdown

White	60.5%
Black	37.9%
Other	1.6%
Hispanic Origin (may be of any race)	0.7%

Age Breakdown

Under 5 years	8.4%
5 to 17	16.7%
18 to 20	5.4%
21 to 24	7.6%
25 to 34	19.4%
35 to 44	13.0%
45 to 54	7.8%
55 to 64	7.8%
65 to 74	7.2%
75+ years	6.7%
Median Age	30.9

Gender Breakdown

Male	46.5%
Female	53.5%

** Information given is for the Greater Cincinnati Consolidated Metropolitan Statistical Area (CMSA), which includes the City of Cincinnati, the City of Hamilton, and the City of Middletown, as well as Butler, Brown, Clermont, Hamilton, and Warren counties in Ohio; Boone, Campbell, Kenton, Gallatin, Grant, and Pendleton counties in Kentucky; and Dearborn and Ohio counties in Indiana.*

Government

Type of Government: Council-Manager

Cincinnati City Council
801 Plum St Rm 308
Cincinnati, OH 45202

Phone: 513-352-3247
Fax: 513-352-2578

Cincinnati City Hall
801 Plum St
Cincinnati, OH 45202
Phone: 513-352-3000
Fax: 513-352-5201

Cincinnati City Manager
801 Plum St Rm 152
Cincinnati, OH 45202
Phone: 513-352-5200
Fax: 513-352-6284

Cincinnati City Planning Dept
805 Central Ave 2 Centennial Plaza Suite 720
Cincinnati, OH 45202
Phone: 513-352-4886
Fax: 513-352-4853

Cincinnati Economic Development Dept
805 Central Ave 2 Centennial Plaza Suite 710
Cincinnati, OH 45202
Phone: 513-352-3485
Fax: 513-352-6257

Cincinnati Finance Dept
801 Plum St Rm 250
Cincinnati, OH 45202
Phone: 513-352-3731
Fax: 513-352-1520

Cincinnati Fire Dept
430 Central Ave
Cincinnati, OH 45202
Phone: 513-352-6220
Fax: 513-352-1548

Cincinnati Law Dept
801 Plum St Rm 214
Cincinnati, OH 45202
Phone: 513-352-3334
Fax: 513-352-1515

Cincinnati Mayor
801 Plum St Rm 150
Cincinnati, OH 45202
Phone: 513-352-3250
Fax: 513-352-5201

Cincinnati Personnel Dept
805 Central Ave 2 Centennial Plaza Rm 200
Cincinnati, OH 45202
Phone: 513-352-2400
Fax: 513-352-5223

Cincinnati Police Dept
310 Ezzard Charles Dr
Cincinnati, OH 45214
Phone: 513-352-3536
Fax: 513-352-2949

Cincinnati Public Services Dept
805 Central Ave Suite 215
Cincinnati, OH 45202
Phone: 513-548-0321
Fax: 513-352-5497

Cincinnati Recreation Commission
805 Central Ave 2 Centennial Plaza Suite 800
Cincinnati, OH 45202
Phone: 513-352-4000
Fax: 513-352-1634

Cincinnati Water Works Dept
4747 Spring Grove Ave
Cincinnati, OH 45232
Phone: 513-591-7970
Fax: 513-591-6519

Public Library of Cincinnati & Hamilton County
800 Vine St
Cincinnati, OH 45202
Phone: 513-369-6900
Fax: 513-369-3123

Important Phone Numbers

AAA....513-762-3111
American Express Travel....513-241-1300
Cincinnati Board of Realtors....513-761-8800
Dial-the-Arts....513-684-4636
Driver's License Information....513-721-3271
Emergency....911
Hamilton County Auditor....513-946-4000
HotelDocs....800-468-3537
Medical Referral....888-749-3737
Ohio Dept of Taxation....513-852-3300
Poison Control Center....513-558-5111
Time/Temp....513-721-1700
Travelers Aid....513-762-5660
Vehicle Registration Information....614-752-7600
Visitor Information Line....800-246-2987
Voter Registration Information....513-632-7000
Weather....513-241-1010

Information Sources

Better Business Bureau Serving Southern Ohio Northern Kentucky & Southeastern Indiana
898 Walnut St 4th Fl
Cincinnati, OH 45202
www.cincinnati.bbb.org
Phone: 513-421-3015
Fax: 513-621-0907

Greater Cincinnati Chamber of Commerce
441 Vine St Carew Tower Suite 300
Cincinnati, OH 45202
www.gccc.com
Phone: 513-579-3100
Fax: 513-579-3102

Greater Cincinnati Convention & Visitors Bureau
300 W 6th St
Cincinnati, OH 45202
www.cincyusa.com
Phone: 513-621-2142
Fax: 513-621-5020
TF: 800-246-2987

Hamilton County
138 E Court St
Cincinnati, OH 45202
www.hamilton-co.org
Phone: 513-946-4400
Fax: 513-946-4444

Sabin Albert B Cincinnati Convention Center
525 Elm St
Cincinnati, OH 45202
www.cincycenter.com
Phone: 513-352-3750
Fax: 513-352-6226

Online Resources

4Cincinnati.com
www.4cincinnati.com

About.com Guide to Cincinnati
cincinnati.about.com/local/midwestus/cincinnati

Anthill City Guide Cincinnati
www.anthill.com/city.asp?city=cincinnati

Area Guide Cincinnati
cincinnati.areaguides.net

Best of Cincinnati
www.cinci.com/

Boulevards Cincinnati
www.boulevards.com/cities/cincinnati.html

CinciNet
www.cincinet.com

Cincinnati Atlas Online Guide
www.cincinnatlas.com/

Cincinnati CityBeat
www.citybeat.com

Cincinnati CityLink
www.usacitylink.com/citylink/cincinnati

Cincinnati Home Page
www.cincy.com

Cincinnati.com
www.cincinnati.com

City Knowledge Cincinnati
www.cityknowledge.com/oh_cincinnati.htm

CitySearch Cincinnati
cincinnati.citysearch.com

DigitalCity Cincinnati
home.digitalcity.com/cincinnati

Excite.com Cincinnati City Guide
www.excite.com/travel/countries/united_states/ohio/cincinnati

Insiders' Guide to Greater Cincinnati
www.insiders.com/cincinnati/

KEY Cincinnati City Guide
www.keycincinnati.com

Lodging.com Cincinnati Ohio
www.lodging.com/auto/guides/cincinnati-area-oh.html

Rough Guide Travel Cincinnati
travel.roughguides.com/content/476/

Area Communities

The Greater Cincinnati metropolitan area includes more than 100 communities in three states and 13 counties. Communities with populations greater than 10,000 include:

Anderson Township
7954 Beechmont Ave
Anderson Township, OH 45255
Phone: 513-474-5560
Fax: 513-474-5289

Blue Ash
4343 Cooper Rd
Blue Ash, OH 45242
Phone: 513-745-8500
Fax: 513-745-8594

Colerain Township
4300 Springdale Rd
Colerain Township, OH 45251
Phone: 513-741-8802
Fax: 513-741-9048

Covington
638 Madison Ave
Covington, KY 41011
Phone: 859-292-2160
Fax: 859-292-2137

Delhi Township
934 Neeb Rd
Delhi Township, OH 45233
Phone: 513-922-3111

Erlanger
505 Commonwealth Ave
Erlanger, KY 41018
Phone: 859-727-2525
Fax: 859-727-7944

Fairfield
5350 Pleasant Ave
Fairfield, OH 45014
Phone: 513-867-5374
Fax: 513-867-5329

Florence
8100 Ewing Blvd
Florence, KY 41042
Phone: 859-371-5491
Fax: 859-647-5436

Forest Park
1201 W Kemper Rd
Forest Park, OH 45240
Phone: 513-595-5200
Fax: 513-595-5285

Fort Thomas
130 N Fort Thomas Ave
Fort Thomas, KY 41075
Phone: 859-441-1055
Fax: 859-441-5104

Green Township
6303 Harrison Ave
Green Township, OH 45247
Phone: 513-574-4848
Fax: 513-574-6260

Hamilton
20 High St
Hamilton, OH 45011
Phone: 513-868-5834
Fax: 513-867-7335

Harrison Township
300 George St
Harrison, OH 45030
Phone: 513-367-2243
Fax: 513-367-3592

Independence
5247 Madison Pike
Independence, KY 41051
Phone: 859-356-5302
Fax: 859-356-6843

Lebanon
50 S Broadway St
Lebanon, OH 45036
Phone: 513-932-3060
Fax: 513-932-2493

Liberty Township
6400 Princeton Rd
Liberty Township, OH 45011
Phone: 513-777-4761
Fax: 513-777-4726

Mason
202 W Main St
Mason, OH 45040
Phone: 513-398-8010
Fax: 513-459-8784

Miami Township
112 S Miami Ave
Miami Township, OH 45002
Phone: 513-941-2466
Fax: 513-941-9307

Middletown
Donham Plaza
Middletown, OH 45042
Phone: 513-425-7836
Fax: 513-425-7792

Newport
998 Monmouth St
Newport, KY 41071
Phone: 859-292-3666
Fax: 859-292-3669

Norwood
4645 Montgomery Rd
Norwood, OH 45212
Phone: 513-458-4594
Fax: 513-458-4534

Reading
1000 Market St
Reading, OH 45215
Phone: 513-733-3725
Fax: 513-733-2077

Sharonville
10900 Reading Rd
Sharonville, OH 45241
Phone: 513-563-1144
Fax: 513-563-0617

Springdale
11700 Springfield Pike
Springdale, OH 45246
Phone: 513-346-5700
Fax: 513-346-5745

Springfield Township
9150 Winton Rd
Cincinnati, OH 45231
Phone: 513-522-1410
Fax: 513-729-0818

Sycamore Township
8540 Kenwood Rd
Sycamore Township, OH 45236
Phone: 513-791-8447
Fax: 513-792-8564

Symmes Township
9323 Union Cemetery Rd
Symmes Township, OH 45140
Phone: 513-683-6644
Fax: 513-683-6626

Union Township
4312 Glen Este-Wilhamsville Rd
Union Township, OH 45245
Phone: 513-752-1741
Fax: 513-752-5732

Economy

Greater Cincinnati is home to seven Fortune 500 companies, including Federated Department Stores, Inc., the Kroger Company, and Procter & Gamble, which is the world's largest manufacturer of soap and also the area's largest employer. Although Cincinnati has a diverse economy that includes finance and insurance companies, health services, and other types of business, manufacturing as well as wholesale and retail trade remain the city's most important industries. In addition to the major employers listed below, the U.S. Government and Ohio State Government are among the top 15, employing more than 13,500 and 3,600 area residents, respectively.

Unemployment Rate 3.2%*
Per Capita Income $25,855*
Median Family Income $54,800*

** Information given is for the Greater Cincinnati Consolidated Metropolitan Statistical Area (CMSA), which includes the City of Cincinnati, the City of Hamilton, and the City of Middletown, as well as Butler, Brown, Clermont, Hamilton, and Warren counties in Ohio; Boone, Campbell, Kenton, Gallatin, Grant, and Pendleton counties in Kentucky; and Dearborn and Ohio counties in Indiana.*

Principal Industries & Number of Wage Earners

Greater Cincinnati CMSA* - 2000

Construction 46,600
Finance, Insurance, & Real Estate 63,900
Government 123,900
Manufacturing 165,000
Retail Trade 186,300
Services 296,000
Transportation & Public Utilities 54,500
Wholesale Trade 68,500

** Information given is for the Greater Cincinnati Consolidated Metropolitan Statistical Area (CMSA), which includes the City of Cincinnati, the City of Hamilton, and the City of Middletown, as well as Butler, Brown, Clermont, Hamilton, and Warren counties in Ohio; Boone, Campbell, Kenton, Gallatin, Grant, and Pendleton counties in Kentucky; and Dearborn and Ohio counties in Indiana.*

Major Employers

AK Steel Corp
703 Curtis St
Middletown, OH 45043
www.aksteel.com
Phone: 513-425-6541
Fax: 513-425-2168

American Financial Group
1 E 4th St
Cincinnati, OH 45202
www.amfnl.com
Phone: 513-579-2121
Fax: 513-579-2580

CBS Personnel Services
www.cbs-companies.com
Phone: 513-651-3600

Children's Hospital Medical Center
3333 Burnet Ave
Cincinnati, OH 45229
www.cincinnatichildrens.org
Phone: 513-636-4200
Fax: 513-636-3733

Cincinnati Board of Education
PO Box 5381
Cincinnati, OH 45201
www.cpsboe.k12.oh.us
Phone: 513-475-7000
Fax: 513-475-4873

Cincinnati City Hall
801 Plum St
Cincinnati, OH 45202
www.ci.cincinnati.oh.us
Phone: 513-352-3000
Fax: 513-352-5201

Cinergy Corp
139 E 4th St
Cincinnati, OH 45202
www.cinergy.com
Phone: 513-421-9500
Fax: 513-287-4212

Delta Air Lines
201 E 4th St
Cincinnati, OH 45202
www.delta-air.com
Phone: 513-721-7000

Federated Department Stores Inc
7 W 7th St
Cincinnati, OH 45202
E-mail: info@federated-fds.com
www.federated-fds.com
Phone: 513-579-7000
Fax: 513-579-7555

Fifth Third Bank
38 Fountain Sq Plaza
Cincinnati, OH 45263
www.53.com
Phone: 513-579-5300
Fax: 513-762-7577

Frisch's Restaurants Inc
2800 Gilbert Ave
Cincinnati, OH 45206
www.frischs.com
Phone: 513-961-2660
Fax: 513-559-5160

GE Aircraft Engines
1 Neumann Way
Cincinnati, OH 45215
www.ge.com/aircraftengines
Phone: 513-243-2000
Fax: 513-552-2177

Hamilton County
138 E Court St
Cincinnati, OH 45202
www.hamilton-co.org
Phone: 513-946-4400
Fax: 513-946-4444

Kroger Co
1014 Vine St
Cincinnati, OH 45202
E-mail: investors@kroger.com
www.kroger.com
Phone: 513-762-4000
Fax: 513-762-1160

Procter & Gamble Co
1 Procter & Gamble Plaza
Cincinnati, OH 45202
www.pg.com
Phone: 513-983-1100
Fax: 513-983-4381

University of Cincinnati
2426 Clifton Ave
Cincinnati, OH 45221
E-mail: uc.web.general@uc.edu
www.uc.edu
Phone: 513-556-6000
Fax: 513-556-9684

Quality of Living Indicators

Total Crime Index....................................21,469
(rates per 100,000 inhabitants)

Violent Crime
Murder/manslaughter........................... 29
Forcible rape 236
Robbery....................................1,207
Aggravated assault...........................1,003

Property Crime
Burglary 4,332
Larceny theft 13,004
Motor vehicle theft 1,658

Cost of Living Index....................................98.3
(national average = 100)

Median Home Price.................................$119,900

Education

Public Schools

Cincinnati Board of Education
PO Box 5381
Cincinnati, OH 45201
www.cpsboe.k12.oh.us
Phone: 513-475-7000
Fax: 513-475-4873

Number of Schools
Elementary................................ 62
Middle 8
High....................................... 9

Student/Teacher Ratio
All Grades 15.8:1

Private Schools

Number of Schools (all grades).................. 100+

Colleges & Universities

Antonelli College
124 E 7th St
Cincinnati, OH 45202
Phone: 513-241-4338
Fax: 513-241-9396

Art Academy of Cincinnati
1125 Saint Gregory St
Cincinnati, OH 45202
www.artacademy.edu
Phone: 513-721-5205
Fax: 513-562-8778
TF: 800-323-5692

Athenaeum of Ohio
6616 Beechmont Ave
Cincinnati, OH 45230
E-mail: ath@mtsm.org
www.mtsm.org
Phone: 513-231-2223
Fax: 513-231-3254

Cincinnati Bible College & Seminary
2700 Glenway Ave
Cincinnati, OH 45204
www.cincybible.edu
Phone: 513-244-8100
Fax: 513-244-8140
TF: 800-949-4222

Cincinnati State Technical & Community College
3520 Central Pkwy
Cincinnati, OH 45223
www.cinstate.cc.oh.us/
Phone: 513-569-1500
Fax: 513-569-1562

Clermont College
4200 Clermont College Dr
Batavia, OH 45103
www.clc.uc.edu/
Phone: 513-732-5200
Fax: 513-732-5303

College of Mount Saint Joseph
5701 Delhi Rd
Cincinnati, OH 45233
E-mail: mountweb@mail.msj.edu
www.msj.edu
Phone: 513-244-4200
Fax: 513-244-4629

Miami University
500 E High St
Oxford, OH 45056
E-mail: admission@muohio.edu
www.muohio.edu
Phone: 513-529-1809
Fax: 513-529-1550

Miami University Hamilton Campus
1601 Peck Blvd
Hamilton, OH 45011
E-mail: helpdesk@ham.muohio.edu
www.ham.muohio.edu
Phone: 513-785-3000
Fax: 513-785-3145

Northern Kentucky University
Nunn Dr
Highland Heights, KY 41099
E-mail: admitnku@nku.edu
www.nku.edu
Phone: 859-572-5100
Fax: 859-572-5566
TF: 800-637-9948

Raymond Walters College
9555 Plainfield Rd
Cincinnati, OH 45236
www.rwc.uc.edu
Phone: 513-745-5600
Fax: 513-745-5768

Southern Ohio College
1011 Glendale Milford Rd
Cincinnati, OH 45215
www.socaec.com
Phone: 513-771-2424
Fax: 513-771-3413
TF: 800-888-1445

Southwestern College of Business Cincinnati
9910 Princeton-Glendale Rd
Cincinnati, OH 45246
Phone: 513-874-0432
Fax: 513-874-0123

The Union Institute
440 E McMillan St
Cincinnati, OH 45206
www.tui.edu
Phone: 513-861-6400
Fax: 513-861-0779
TF: 800-486-3116

Thomas More College
333 Thomas More Pkwy
Crestview Hills, KY 41017
www.thomasmore.edu
Phone: 859-341-5800
Fax: 859-344-3345
TF: 800-825-4557

University of Cincinnati
2426 Clifton Ave
Cincinnati, OH 45221
E-mail: uc.web.general@uc.edu
www.uc.edu
Phone: 513-556-6000
Fax: 513-556-9684

Xavier University
3800 Victory Pkwy
Cincinnati, OH 45207
www.xu.edu
Phone: 513-745-3000
Fax: 513-745-4319
TF: 800-344-4698

Hospitals

Bethesda North Hospital
10500 Montgomery Rd
Cincinnati, OH 45242
Phone: 513-745-1111
Fax: 513-745-1441

Bethesda Oak Hospital
619 Oak St
Cincinnati, OH 45206
Phone: 513-569-6111
Fax: 513-569-4065

Children's Hospital Medical Center
3333 Burnet Ave
Cincinnati, OH 45229
www.cincinnatichildrens.org
Phone: 513-636-4200
Fax: 513-636-3733

Christ Hospital
2139 Auburn Ave
Cincinnati, OH 45219
www.health-alliance.com/christ_control.html
Phone: 513-585-2000
Fax: 513-585-3200
TF: 800-527-8919

Clermont Mercy Hospital
3000 Hospital Dr
Batavia, OH 45103
Phone: 513-732-8200
Fax: 513-732-8550

Deaconess Hospital
311 Straight St
Cincinnati, OH 45219
www.deaconess-healthcare.com
Phone: 513-559-2100
Fax: 513-475-5251

Fort Hamilton Hospital
630 Eaton Ave
Hamilton, OH 45013
www.health-alliance.com/fort_control.html
Phone: 513-867-2000
Fax: 513-867-2620

Franciscan Hospital Mount Airy Campus
2446 Kipling Ave
Cincinnati, OH 45239
Phone: 513-853-5000
Fax: 513-541-4326

Franciscan Hospital Western Hills Campus
3131 Queen City Ave
Cincinnati, OH 45238
Phone: 513-389-5000
Fax: 513-389-5201

Good Samaritan Hospital
375 Dixmyth Ave
Cincinnati, OH 45220
Phone: 513-872-1400
Fax: 513-872-3435

Jewish Hospital
4777 E Galbraith Rd
Cincinnati, OH 45236
Phone: 513-686-3000
Fax: 513-686-3222

Mercy Hospital Anderson
7500 State Rd
Cincinnati, OH 45255
Phone: 513-624-4500
Fax: 513-624-4015

Mercy Hospital Hamilton
PO Box 418
Hamilton, OH 45012
Phone: 513-867-6400
Fax: 513-867-6521

Middletown Regional Hospital
105 McKnight Dr
Middletown, OH 45044
www.middletownhospital.org
Phone: 513-424-2111
Fax: 513-420-5688
TF: 800-338-4057

University of Cincinnati Hospital
234 Goodman St
Cincinnati, OH 45219
Phone: 513-584-1000
Fax: 513-584-3755

Veterans Affairs Medical Center
3200 Vine St
Cincinnati, OH 45220
Phone: 513-861-3100
Fax: 513-475-6500
TF: 888-267-7873

Transportation

Airport(s)

Cincinnati-Northern Kentucky International Airport (CVG)
13 miles SW of downtown (approx 15 minutes) . . .859-767-3151

Mass Transit

SORTA Bus
$.80 Base fare 513-621-4455
TANK Bus
$.75 Base fare 859-331-8265

Rail/Bus

Cincinnati Amtrak Station
1301 Western Ave
Cincinnati, OH 45203
Phone: 513-651-3337
TF: 800-872-7245

Greyhound/Trailways Bus Station
1005 Gilbert Ave
Cincinnati, OH 45202
Phone: 513-352-6012
TF: 800-231-2222

Utilities

Electricity
Cinergy Gas & Electric Co 513-421-9500
www.cinergy.com

Gas
Cinergy Gas & Electric Co 513-421-9500
www.cinergy.com

Water
Cincinnati Water Works 513-591-7700

Garbage Collection/Recycling
Cincinnati Dept of Public Works Sanitation Div . . .513-352-3691

Telecommunications

Telephone
Cincinnati Bell Telephone Co 513-565-2210

Cable Television
Adelphia Communications 513-941-7000
TCI Cablevision of Ohio 513-896-5455
Time Warner Cable 513-469-1112
www.twcincy.com
Warner Communications 513-489-5000

Internet Service Providers (ISPs)
Exodus Online Services 513-522-0011
www.eos.net
OneNet Communications 513-618-1000
www.one.net
Premier Internet 513-561-6245
www.cinti.net

Banks

Bank One NA
8044 Montgomery Rd Bank One Towers
Cincinnati, OH 45236
Phone: 513-985-5566
Fax: 513-985-5703
TF: 800-310-1111

Fifth Third Bank
38 Fountain Sq Plaza
Cincinnati, OH 45263
www.53.com
Phone: 513-579-5300
Fax: 513-762-7577

Firstar Bank NA
425 Walnut St
Cincinnati, OH 45202
Phone: 513-632-4234
Fax: 513-762-8847

Franklin Savings & Loan Co
4750 Ashwood Dr
Cincinnati, OH 45241
franklinsavings.com
Phone: 513-469-8000
Fax: 513-469-5360

PNC Bank NA
201 E 5th St
Cincinnati, OH 45202
Phone: 513-651-8032
Fax: 513-651-8050

Provident Bank
1 E 4th St
Cincinnati, OH 45202
Phone: 513-579-2036
Fax: 513-345-7216

Star Bank NA
425 Walnut St
Cincinnati, OH 45202
Phone: 513-632-4000
Fax: 513-632-5512

Sycamore National Bank
3209 W Galbraith Rd
Cincinnati, OH 45239
www.sycamorenationalbank.com
Phone: 513-741-7930
Fax: 513-741-0019

Winton Savings & Loan
5511 Cheviot Rd
Cincinnati, OH 45247
Phone: 513-385-3880
Fax: 513-741-5773

Shopping

Convention Place Mall
435 Elm St
Cincinnati, OH 45202
Phone: 513-421-2089

Eastgate Mall
4601 Eastgate Blvd
Cincinnati, OH 45245
E-mail: eastgatemall@rejacobsgroup.com
www.shopyourmall.com/mall_welcome.asp?map=yes&mall_select=655
Phone: 513-752-2290
Fax: 513-752-2499

Forest Fair Mall
1047 Forest Fair Dr
Cincinnati, OH 45240
Phone: 513-671-2929

Kenwood Towne Center
7875 Montgomery Rd
Cincinnati, OH 45236
E-mail: info@kenwoodcentre.com
www.kenwoodcentre.com
Phone: 513-745-9100
Fax: 513-745-9974

Merchants on Main Street
Over-the-Rhine Main betw Central Pkwy & Liberty St
Cincinnati, OH 45210
Phone: 513-241-2690

Northgate Mall
9501 Colerain Ave
Cincinnati, OH 45251
Phone: 513-385-5600
Fax: 513-385-5603

Saks Fifth Avenue
101 W 5th St
Cincinnati, OH 45202
Phone: 513-421-6800
Fax: 513-421-6416

Tower Place Mall
28 W 4th St
Cincinnati, OH 45202
Phone: 513-241-7700
Fax: 513-241-7770

Tri-County Mall
11700 Princeton Pike
Cincinnati, OH 45246
Phone: 513-671-0120
Fax: 513-671-2931

Media

Newspapers and Magazines

Cincinnati Business Courier
35 E 7th St Suite 700
Cincinnati, OH 45202
www.amcity.com/cincinnati
Phone: 513-621-6665
Fax: 513-621-2462

Cincinnati CityBeat
23 E 7th St Suite 617
Cincinnati, OH 45202
E-mail: letters@citybeat.com
www.citybeat.com
Phone: 513-665-4700
Fax: 513-665-4369

Cincinnati Downtowner
128 E 6th St
Cincinnati, OH 45202
Phone: 513-241-9906
Fax: 513-241-7235

Cincinnati Enquirer*
312 Elm St
Cincinnati, OH 45202
enquirer.com
Phone: 513-721-2700
Fax: 513-768-8340

Cincinnati Magazine
705 Central Ave 1 Centennial Plaza Suite 370
Cincinnati, OH 45202
Phone: 513-421-4300
Fax: 513-562-2746
TF: 800-837-4800

Cincinnati Post*
125 E Court St
Cincinnati, OH 45202
www.cincypost.com
Phone: 513-352-2000
Fax: 513-621-3962

Everybody's News
2530 Spring Grove Ave
Cincinnati, OH 45214
E-mail: enews@everybodys-news.com
www.everybodys-news.com
Phone: 513-361-0404
Fax: 513-287-8643

Fairfield Echo
5120 Dixie Hwy
Fairfield, OH 45014
www.fairfield-echo.com
Phone: 513-829-7900
Fax: 513-829-7950

Hilltop News-Press
5556 Cheviot Rd
Cincinnati, OH 45247
www.communitypress.com/papers/hilltop/paper.ssi
Phone: 513-923-3111
Fax: 513-923-1806

Northwest Press
5556 Cheviot Rd
Cincinnati, OH 45247
Phone: 513-923-3111
Fax: 513-923-1806

Ohio Magazine
62 E Broad St 2nd Fl
Columbus, OH 43215
www.ohiomagazine.com/
Phone: 614-461-5083
Fax: 614-461-5506
TF: 800-426-4624

Pulse-Journal
1066 Reading Rd
Mason, OH 45040
www.pulsejournal.com
Phone: 513-398-8856
Fax: 513-459-7965

Sunday Western Star
PO Box 29
Lebanon, OH 45036
E-mail: swtips@your.net.com
Phone: 513-932-3010
Fax: 513-932-6056

Western Hills Press
5556 Cheviot Rd
Cincinnati, OH 45247
Phone: 513-923-3111
Fax: 513-923-1806

**Indicates major daily newspapers*

Television

WCET-TV Ch 48 (PBS)
1223 Central Pkwy
Cincinnati, OH 45214
E-mail: comments_wcet@wcet.pbs.org
www.wcet.org
Phone: 513-381-4033
Fax: 513-381-7520

WCPO-TV Ch 9 (ABC)
500 Central Ave
Cincinnati, OH 45202
www.wcpo.com
Phone: 513-721-9900
Fax: 513-721-7717

WKRC-TV Ch 12 (CBS)
1906 Highland Ave
Cincinnati, OH 45219
www.wkrc.com
Phone: 513-763-5500
Fax: 513-421-3820

WLWT-TV Ch 5 (NBC)
1700 Young St
Cincinnati, OH 45210
E-mail: mail@wlwt.com
www.wlwt.com
Phone: 513-412-5000
Fax: 513-412-6121

WSTR-TV Ch 64 (WB)
5177 Fishwick Dr
Cincinnati, OH 45216
Phone: 513-641-4400
Fax: 513-242-2633

WXIX-TV Ch 19 (Fox)
635 W 7th St 19 Broadcast Plaza
Cincinnati, OH 45203
www.fox19.com
Phone: 513-421-1919
Fax: 513-421-3022

Radio

WAKW-FM 93.3 MHz (Rel)
6275 Collegevue Dr
Cincinnati, OH 45224
E-mail: wakw@eos.net
www.wakw.com
Phone: 513-542-3442
Fax: 513-542-9333

WBOB-AM 1160 kHz (Sports)
625 Eden Park Dr Suite 1050
Cincinnati, OH 45202
www.1160bob.com
Phone: 513-721-1050
Fax: 513-562-3060
TF: 800-561-1160

WCIN-AM 1480 kHz (Oldies)
3540 Reading Rd
Cincinnati, OH 45229
www.1480wcin.com
Phone: 513-281-7180
Fax: 513-281-6125

WCKY-AM 1360 kHz (Sports)
111 Saint Gregory St
Cincinnati, OH 45202
www.wcky.com
Phone: 513-421-9724
Fax: 513-241-0358

WEBN-FM 102.7 MHz (Rock)
1111 Saint Gregory St
Cincinnati, OH 45202
E-mail: webn@one.net
www.webn.com
Phone: 513-621-9326
Fax: 513-749-3299
TF: 800-616-9236

WGRR-FM 103.5 MHz (Oldies)
2060 Reading Rd
Cincinnati, OH 45202
www.wgrr1035.com
Phone: 513-699-5103
Fax: 513-699-5000

WGUC-FM 90.9 MHz (Clas)
1223 Central Pkwy
Cincinnati, OH 45214
www.wguc.org
Phone: 513-241-8282

WIZF-FM 100.9 MHz (Urban)
1821 Summit Rd Suite 400
Cincinnati, OH 45237
Phone: 513-679-6000
Fax: 513-679-6011

WKFS-FM 107.1 MHz (Alt)
1906 Highland Ave
Cincinnati, OH 45219
www.kiss107fm.com
Phone: 513-763-6499
Fax: 513-421-3299

WKRC-AM 550 kHz (N/T)
1111 Saint Gregory St
Cincinnati, OH 45202
www.55krc.com
Phone: 513-241-1550
Fax: 513-651-2555
TF: 800-852-7007

WKRQ-FM 101.9 MHz (CHR)
2060 Reading Rd
Cincinnati, OH 45202
Phone: 513-699-5102
Fax: 513-699-5000

WLW-AM 700 kHz (N/T)
1111 Saint Gregory St
Cincinnati, OH 45202
www.700wlw.com
Phone: 513-241-9597
Fax: 513-665-9700

WMOJ-FM 94.9 MHz (Oldies)
895 Central Ave Suite 900
Cincinnati, OH 45202
www.mojo949.com
Phone: 513-241-9500
Fax: 513-241-6689

WOFX-FM 92.5 MHz (CR)
1111 Saint Gregory St
Cincinnati, OH 45202
www.wofx.com
Phone: 513-621-9326
Fax: 513-784-1249

WRRM-FM 98.5 MHz (AC)
895 Central Ave Suite 900
Cincinnati, OH 45202
www.warm98.com
Phone: 513-241-9898
Fax: 513-241-6689

WSAI-AM 1530 kHz (Nost)
1111 Saint Gregory St
Cincinnati, OH 45202
www.wsai.com
Phone: 513-421-9724
Fax: 513-241-0358

WTSJ-AM 1050 kHz (Rel)
635 W 7th St Suite 400
Cincinnati, OH 45203
E-mail: wtsj@goodnews.net
www.wtsj.com
Phone: 513-579-1050
Fax: 513-421-0821

WUBE-AM 1230 kHz (Sports)
625 Eden Park Dr Suite 1050
Cincinnati, OH 45202
Phone: 513-721-1050
Fax: 513-621-2105
TF: 800-561-1160

WUBE-FM 105.1 MHz (Ctry)
625 Eden Park Dr Suite 1050
Cincinnati, OH 45202
Phone: 513-721-1050
Fax: 513-621-2105

WVMX-FM 94.1 MHz (AC)
1906 Highland Ave
Cincinnati, OH 45219
www.wvmx.com
Phone: 513-763-6499
Fax: 513-749-6499

WVXU-FM 91.7 MHz (NPR)
3800 Victory Pkwy
Cincinnati, OH 45207
E-mail: wvxu@xstarnet.com
www.xstarnet.com
Phone: 513-731-9898
Fax: 513-745-3483

WYGY-FM 96.5 MHz (Ctry)
625 Eden Park Dr Suite 1050
Cincinnati, OH 45202
Phone: 513-721-1050
Fax: 513-721-9949

Attractions

The riverfront city of Cincinnati serves as the home port of some of the only remaining overnight paddlewheel boats, and its "Majestic" is one of the last floating theaters in existence today. Cincinnati's Coliseum and Stadium also occupy the riverfront area. A popular outdoor attraction in Cincinnati, Mount Airy Forest's Garden of the States contains plant life from each of the 50 states. The Roebling Suspension Bridge on the Ohio river (built by John A. Roebling, who later built the Brooklyn Bridge) connects Cincinnati with Kentucky. Just east of the bridge is Covington, Kentucky, which features antebellum homes. The floating entertainment complex, Covington Landing, is located west of the bridge.

American Classical Music Hall of Fame & Museum
4 W 4th St Herschede Bldg
Cincinnati, OH 45202
E-mail: info@classicalhall.org
www.classicalhall.org
Phone: 513-621-3263
Fax: 513-381-4130
TF: 800-499-3263

Aronoff Center for the Arts
650 Walnut St
Cincinnati, OH 45202
www.cincinnatiarts.org
Phone: 513-721-3344
Fax: 513-977-4150

Arts Consortium
1515 Linn St
Cincinnati, OH 45214
Phone: 513-381-0645
Fax: 513-345-3743

Ault Park
3540 Principio at Observatory Ave
Cincinnati, OH 45208
Phone: 513-321-8439

Beach Waterpark
2590 Waterpark Dr
Mason, OH 45040
E-mail: thebeach@thebeachwaterpark.com
www.thebeachwaterpark.com
Phone: 513-398-2040
Fax: 513-398-6598

Children's Museum of Cincinnati
1301 Western Ave
Cincinnati, OH 45203
www.cincymuseum.org/cm.htm
Phone: 513-287-7000
Fax: 513-287-7079
TF: 800-733-2077

Cincinnati Art Museum
953 Eden Park Dr
Cincinnati, OH 45202
E-mail: cincyart@fuse.net
www.cincinnatiartmuseum.com
Phone: 513-721-5204
Fax: 513-721-0129

Cincinnati Ballet
1555 Central Pkwy
Cincinnati, OH 45214
www.cincinnatiballet.com
Phone: 513-621-5219
Fax: 513-621-4844

Cincinnati Chamber Orchestra
1406 Elm St
Cincinnati, OH 45210
www.cincinnati.com/cco/Welcome.html
Phone: 513-723-1182
Fax: 513-723-1057

Cincinnati Fire Museum
315 W Court St
Cincinnati, OH 45202
www.cincinet.com/firemuseum/
Phone: 513-621-5571

Cincinnati History Museum
1301 Western Ave Museum Ctr
Cincinnati, OH 45203
www.cincymuseum.org/chm.htm
Phone: 513-287-7000
Fax: 513-287-7029
TF: 800-733-2077

Cincinnati Museum Center
1301 Western Ave
Cincinnati, OH 45203
www.cincymuseum.org
Phone: 513-287-7000
Fax: 513-287-7029
TF: 800-733-2077

Cincinnati Museum of Natural History & Science
1301 Western Ave Museum Ctr
Cincinnati, OH 45203
E-mail: mnhs@fuse.net
www.cincymuseum.org/mnhs.htm
Phone: 513-287-7000
Fax: 513-287-7029
TF: 800-733-2077

Cincinnati Music Hall
1243 Elm St
Cincinnati, OH 45210
www.cincinnatiarts.org
Phone: 513-621-1919
Fax: 513-744-3345

Cincinnati Opera
1241 Elm St Music Hall
Cincinnati, OH 45210
E-mail: info@cincinnatiopera.com
www.cincyopera.com
Phone: 513-241-2742
Fax: 513-744-3520

Cincinnati Playhouse in the Park
962 Mt Adams Cir
Cincinnati, OH 45202
E-mail: playhous@one.net
www.cincyplay.com
Phone: 513-421-3888
Fax: 513-345-2254

Cincinnati Pops Orchestra
1241 Elm St Music Hall
Cincinnati, OH 45210
www.cincinnatipops.org
Phone: 513-381-3300
Fax: 513-744-3535

Cincinnati Shakespeare Festival
719 Race St
Cincinnati, OH 45202
E-mail: boxoffice@cincyshakes.com
www.cincyshakes.com
Phone: 513-381-2273
Fax: 513-381-2298

Cincinnati Symphony Orchestra
1241 Elm St Music Hall
Cincinnati, OH 45210
www.cincinnatisymphony.org
Phone: 513-621-1919
Fax: 513-744-3535

Cincinnati Zoo & Botanical Garden
3400 Vine St
Cincinnati, OH 45220
E-mail: feedback@cincyzoo.org
www.cincyzoo.org
Phone: 513-281-4701
Fax: 513-559-7790
TF: 800-944-4776

Civic Garden Center of Greater Cincinnati
2715 Reading Rd
Cincinnati, OH 45206
Phone: 513-221-0981
Fax: 513-221-0961

Coney Island
6201 Kellogg Ave
Cincinnati, OH 45228
www.coneyislandpark.com
Phone: 513-232-8230
Fax: 513-231-1352

Contemporary Arts Center
115 E 5th St
Cincinnati, OH 45202
Phone: 513-721-0390
Fax: 513-721-7418

Contemporary Dance Theatre
1805 Larch Ave
Cincinnati, OH 45224
Phone: 513-591-1222
Fax: 513-591-1222

Downtown Theatre Classics
9910 Humphrey Rd
Cincinnati, OH 45202
Phone: 513-745-9363
Fax: 513-745-9430

Eden Park
950 Eden Pk Dr
Cincinnati, OH 45202
www.cinci-parks.org/parks/text/eden.html
Phone: 513-352-4080
Fax: 513-352-4096

Ensemble Theatre of Cincinnati
1127 Vine St
Cincinnati, OH 45210
Phone: 513-421-3555
Fax: 513-562-4104

Fifth Third Bank Broadway Series
650 Walnut St Arnoff Ctr
Cincinnati, OH 45202
Phone: 513-241-2345
TF: 800-294-1816

Findlay Market
Elm & W Elder Sts
Cincinnati, OH 45202
www.findlaymarket.org
Phone: 513-352-6364
Fax: 513-352-4839

Fountain Square
5th & Walnut Sts
Cincinnati, OH 45216

Harriet Beecher Stowe House
2950 Gilbert Ave
Cincinnati, OH 45206
www.ohiohistory.org/places/stowe
Phone: 513-632-5120
Fax: 513-632-5114

Heritage Village
11450 Lebanon Pike
Cincinnati, OH 45241
Phone: 513-563-9484
Fax: 513-563-0914

Hudepohl-Schoenling Brewing Co
1599 Central Pkwy
Cincinnati, OH 45214
www.cincys-brewery.com
Phone: 513-241-4344
Fax: 513-357-5217

Krohn Conservatory
1501 Eden Park Dr
Cincinnati, OH 45202
Phone: 513-421-5707
Fax: 513-421-6007

Lindner Robert D Family Omnimax Theater
1301 Western Ave Museum Ctr
Cincinnati, OH 45203
www.cincymuseum.org/omni.htm
Phone: 513-287-7081
Fax: 513-287-7002
TF: 800-733-2077

Linton Music Series
1223 Central Pkwy
Cincinnati, OH 45214
Phone: 513-381-6868
Fax: 513-241-8456

Meier's Wine Cellars Inc
6955 Plainfield Rd
Silverton, OH 45236
E-mail: info@meierswinecellars.com
www.meierswinecellars.com
Phone: 513-891-2900
Fax: 513-891-6370
TF: 800-346-2941

Mount Airy Forest & Arboretum
5083 Colerain Ave
Cincinnati, OH 45202
Phone: 513-541-8176

National Underground Railroad Freedom Center
312 Elm St 20th Fl
Cincinnati, OH 45202
www.undergroundrailroad.com
Phone: 877-648-4838

Old Saint Mary's National Historic Site
123 E 13th St
Cincinnati, OH 45210
Phone: 513-721-2988

Paramount's Kings Island
PO Box 901
Kings Island, OH 45034
www.pki.com
Phone: 513-754-5700
Fax: 513-754-5725
TF: 800-288-0808

Riverbend Music Center
6295 Kellogg Ave
Cincinnati, OH 45230
Phone: 513-232-5882
Fax: 513-232-7577

Taft Museum of Art
316 Pike St
Cincinnati, OH 45202
www.taftmuseum.org
Phone: 513-241-0343
Fax: 513-241-7762

Taft Theatre
5th & Sycamore Sts
Cincinnati, OH 45202
www.taftevents.com
Phone: 513-721-8883
Fax: 513-721-2864

William Howard Taft National Historic Site
2038 Auburn Ave
Cincinnati, OH 45219
www.nps.gov/wiho/
Phone: 513-684-3262
Fax: 513-684-3627

Sports Teams & Facilities

Cincinnati Bengals
1 Paul Brown Stadium
Cincinnati, OH 45202
www.bengals.com
Phone: 513-621-3550
Fax: 513-621-3570

Cincinnati Cyclones (hockey)
100 Broadway
Cincinnati, OH 45202
www.cycloneshockey.com
Phone: 513-421-7825
Fax: 513-421-1210

Cincinnati Gardens
2250 Seymour Ave
Cincinnati, OH 45212
Phone: 513-631-7793
Fax: 513-631-2666

Cincinnati Mighty Ducks (hockey)
2250 Seymour Ave Cincinnati Gardens
Cincinnati, OH 45212
E-mail: duckinfo@cincinnatimightyducks.com
www.cincinnatimightyducks.com
Phone: 513-351-3999
Fax: 513-351-5898

Cincinnati Reds
Pete Rose Way Cinergy Field
Cincinnati, OH 45202
www.cincinnatireds.com
Phone: 513-421-4510
Fax: 513-421-7342
TF: 800-829-5353

Cincinnati Riverhawks (soccer)
5450 Kings Island Dr Galbreath Field
Mason, OH 45034
E-mail: hawks@riverhawks.com
www.riverhawks.com
Phone: 513-853-7070
Fax: 513-853-7079

Cinergy Field
100 Cinergy Field
Cincinnati, OH 45202
Phone: 513-421-4510
Fax: 513-421-7342

River Downs Race Track
6301 Kellogg Ave
Cincinnati, OH 45230
www.riverdowns.com
Phone: 513-232-8000
Fax: 513-232-1412

Turfway Park Racecourse
7500 Turfway Rd
Florence, KY 41042
E-mail: turfway@turfway.com
www.turfway.com
Phone: 859-371-0200
Fax: 859-647-4730
TF: 800-733-0200

Annual Events

All About Kids (mid-August) .513-621-2142
All-American Birthday Party (early July) .513-621-2142
Appalachian Festival (mid-May) .513-232-8230
Boofest (October) .513-287-7000
Celtic Music & Cultural Festival
(late September-early October) .513-533-4822
Cincinnati Auto Expo (mid-February) .513-281-0022
Cincinnati Flower Show (early May) .513-872-5194
Cincinnati Heart Mini-Marathon (late March) .513-281-4048
Cincinnati International Wine Festival
(mid-March) .513-723-9463
Cincinnati May Festival (late May) .513-381-3300
Cincinnati Saint Patrick Parade (mid-March) .513-251-2222
Coors Light Festival (late July) .800-452-3132
Enchanted Forest (mid-late October) .513-721-2905
Festival of Lights (late November-early January) .513-281-4700
Flying Pig Marathon (mid-May) .513-721-7447
Ford Dealer's Holiday Traditions Parade
(early December) .513-421-4440
Gold Star Chili Fest (mid-July) .513-579-3191
Hamilton County Fair (early August) .513-761-4224
Harvest Festival (late September) .513-281-4700
Holiday in Lights
(late November-late December) .513-287-7103
Jammin' on Main (mid-May) .513-621-6994
Ohio Renaissance Festival
(late August-mid-October) .513-897-7000
Oktoberfest Zinzinnati (mid-September) .513-579-3199
Oldiesfest (mid-late June) .513-321-8900
Riverfest (early September) .513-621-6994
Riverfront Stadium Festival (late July) .513-871-3900
Spiral Stakes Horseracing (March) .800-733-0200
Spring Floral Show (late February-mid-March) .513-352-4080
Summerfair (early June) .513-531-0050
Tall Stacks (mid-October) .513-744-8820
Taste of Cincinnati (late May) .513-579-3199
Taste of Findlay Market (late October) .513-241-0464

Cleveland, Ohio

***County:* Cuyahoga**

CLEVELAND is located in northeastern Ohio on the southern shore of Lake Erie. Major cities within 100 miles include Akron, Canton, and Toledo, Ohio.

Area (Land) .... 77.0 sq mi
Area (Water)............................... 5.1 sq mi
Elevation...................................... 680 ft
Latitude ....41-49-94 N
Longitude............................... 81-69-56 W
Time Zone ....EST
Area Code....................................... 216

Climate

Cleveland's climate is moderated by its location on Lake Erie. Winters are cold and overcast with average high temperatures in the mid-30s and lows in the high teens to mid-20s. The average annual snowfall in Cleveland is 54.6 inches. Summer days are warm, with average high temperatures in the high 70s to low 80s, while evening low temperatures cool down to around 60 degrees. June is the wettest month in Cleveland, while January is the driest.

Average Temperatures & Precipitation

Temperatures

	Jan	Feb	Mar	Apr	May	Jun	Jul	Aug	Sep	Oct	Nov	Dec
High	32	35	46	58	69	78	82	81	74	62	50	37
Low	18	19	28	37	47	57	61	60	54	44	35	25

Precipitation

	Jan	Feb	Mar	Apr	May	Jun	Jul	Aug	Sep	Oct	Nov	Dec
Inches	2.0	2.2	2.9	3.1	3.5	3.7	3.5	3.4	3.4	2.5	3.2	3.1

History

Originally part of the Connecticut Western Reserve, the Cleveland area was the site of a number of French and Native American trading posts during the 18th Century. The city itself was founded in 1796 by General Moses Cleaveland (after whom the city was named—the "a" was later dropped from the name), who was sent to survey the area for the Connecticut Land Company. Early growth in Cleveland was slow, but the opening of the Ohio Canal in 1832 stimulated commercial development in the area, and the city was incorporated four years later.

By the mid-19th Century, Cleveland had become an important commercial center, and the city's easy access to iron ore from the Lake Superior region and coal from Kentucky and West Virginia led to the development of numerous industries, including oil refining and steel production. During the Civil War, Cleveland served as an important manufacturing center for machinery, ships, and other war-related items. New industry in Cleveland created economic opportunities that drew large numbers of new settlers to the area—by 1910, Cleveland's population had grown from around 17,000 in 1850 to more than 500,000.

Racial tension, fires caused by industrial dumping, and economic decline plagued Cleveland during the mid-20th Century, resulting in a dramatic decline in the city's population. In recent years, however, Cleveland has taken steps to rebuild the city itself and its economy. Recent projects and improvements include a renovation of the city's lakefront area and the opening of two major attractions, the Rock and Roll Hall of Fame and Museum and the Great Lakes Science Center. With a population of more than 495,000, Cleveland today is Ohio's second largest city.

Population

1990 Census 505,616
1998 Estimate.............................495,817
% Change .... -1.9
2005 Projection 1,399,200*

Racial/Ethnic Breakdown

White.................................. 49.5%
Black 46.6%
Other.................................... 3.9%
Hispanic Origin (may be of any race) 4.6%

Age Breakdown

Under 5 years............................. 8.7%
5 to 17................................ 18.2%
18 to 20................................. 4.5%
21 to 24................................. 6.1%
25 to 34................................ 18.0%
35 to 44................................ 12.7%
45 to 54................................. 8.7%
55 to 64................................. 9.0%
65 to 74................................. 8.2%
75+ years 5.8%
Median Age................................31.9

Gender Breakdown

Male..................................... 46.9%
Female.................................. 53.1%

** Information given is for Cuyahoga County.*

Government

Type of Government: Mayor-Council

Cleveland City Council
601 Lakeside Ave Rm 216
Cleveland, OH 44114
Phone: 216-664-2848
Fax: 216-664-3837

Cleveland City Hall
601 Lakeside Ave
Cleveland, OH 44114
Phone: 216-664-2000
Fax: 216-664-3837

Cleveland City Planning Dept
601 Lakeside Ave Rm 501
Cleveland, OH 44114
Phone: 216-664-2210
Fax: 216-664-3281

Cleveland Community Development Dept
601 Lakeside Ave Rm 310
Cleveland, OH 44114
Phone: 216-664-4000
Fax: 216-664-4006

Cleveland Economic Development Dept
601 Lakeside Ave Rm 210
Cleveland, OH 44114
Phone: 216-664-2406
Fax: 216-664-3681

Cleveland Finance Dept
601 Lakeside Ave Rm 104
Cleveland, OH 44114
Phone: 216-664-2536
Fax: 216-664-2535

Cleveland Fire Div
1645 Superior Ave
Cleveland, OH 44114
Phone: 216-664-6397
Fax: 216-664-6816

Cleveland Law Dept
601 Lakeside Ave Rm 106
Cleveland, OH 44114
Phone: 216-664-2800
Fax: 216-420-8560

Cleveland Mayor
601 Lakeside Ave
Cleveland, OH 44114
Phone: 216-664-2220
Fax: 216-664-2815

Cleveland Parks Recreation & Properties Dept
500 Lakeside Ave
Cleveland, OH 44114
Phone: 216-664-2485
Fax: 216-664-4086

Cleveland Personnel & Human Resources Dept
601 Lakeside Ave Rm 121
Cleveland, OH 44114
Phone: 216-664-2493
Fax: 216-664-3489

Cleveland Police Div
1300 Ontario St
Cleveland, OH 44113
Phone: 216-623-5005
Fax: 216-623-5584

Cleveland Public Library
325 Superior Ave
Cleveland, OH 44114
Phone: 216-623-2800
Fax: 216-623-7050

Cleveland Public Utilities Dept
1201 Lakeside Ave
Cleveland, OH 44114
Phone: 216-664-2440
Fax: 216-664-3454

Important Phone Numbers

AAA 216-416-1912
American Express Travel 216-241-4575
Cleveland Area Board of Realtors 216-901-0130
Cleveland Treasurer 216-664-2240
Cuyahoga County Central Collection Agency 216-664-2070
Cuyahoga County Real Property Tax Dept 216-443-7420
Dental Referral 216-573-1181
Driver's License Information 216-941-8008
Emergency 911
HotelDocs 800-468-3537
Medical Referral 216-520-0110
Ohio State Taxation Dept 800-282-1780
Poison Control Center 216-231-4455
Road Conditions 800-394-7623
Time 216-931-1212
Vehicle Registration Information 216-431-1445
Voter Registration Information 216-443-3200
Weather 216-931-1212

Information Sources

Better Business Bureau Serving Northeast Ohio
2217 E 9th St Suite 200
Cleveland, OH 44115
www.cleveland.bbb.org
Phone: 216-241-7678
Fax: 216-861-6365

Cleveland Convention Center
500 Lakeside Ave
Cleveland, OH 44114
Phone: 216-348-2200
Fax: 216-348-2262
TF: 800-543-2489

Convention & Visitors Bureau of Greater Cleveland
50 Public Sq Terminal Tower Suite 3100
Cleveland, OH 44113
www.travelcleveland.com/
Phone: 216-621-4110
Fax: 216-621-5967
TF: 800-321-1001

Cuyahoga County
1219 Ontario St
Cleveland, OH 44114
www.cuyahoga.oh.us
Phone: 216-443-7000

Greater Cleveland Growth Assn
200 Tower City Ctr
Cleveland, OH 44113
www.clevelandgrowth.com
Phone: 216-621-3300
Fax: 216-621-6013
TF: 800-562-7121

International Exposition Center
6200 Riverside Dr
Cleveland, OH 44135
Phone: 216-265-7000
Fax: 216-267-7876

Online Resources

4Cleveland.com
www.4cleveland.com

About.com Guide to Cleveland
cleveland.about.com/local/midwestus/cleveland

Anthill City Guide Cleveland
www.anthill.com/city.asp?city=cleveland

Area Guide Cleveland
cleveland.areaguides.net

City Knowledge Cleveland
www.cityknowledge.com/oh_cleveland.htm

CitySearch Cleveland
cleveland.citysearch.com

Cleveland
www.clevelandohio.com

Cleveland Central
www.glwc.com/cleveland

Cleveland City Page
cleveland.thelinks.com

Cleveland Community Information
www.cwru.edu/cleveland.html

Cleveland Home Page
www.cleveland.oh.us

Cleveland Live
www.cleveland.com/

Cleveland Sites Online
cleveland.sitesonline.com

Cleveland's Neighborhood Link
little.nhlink.net/nhlink

DigitalCity Cleveland
home.digitalcity.com/cleveland

Excite.com Cleveland City Guide
www.excite.com/travel/countries/united_states/ohio/cleveland

Flats Net
www.flats.net/

Greater Cleveland Visitors Guide
www.cleve-visitors-guide.com/

Lodging.com Cleveland Ohio
www.lodging.com/auto/guides/cleveland-area-oh.html

Rough Guide Travel Cleveland
travel.roughguides.com/content/468/

Savvy Diner Guide to Cleveland Restaurants
www.savvydiner.com/cleveland/

Sun Newspapers
www.sunnews.com

Area Communities

Communities with populations greater than 20,000 in the six-county Cleveland Primary Metropolitan Statistical Area (Ashtabula, Cuyahoga, Geauga, Lake, Lorain, and Medina counties) include:

Ashtabula
4400 Main Ave
Ashtabula, OH 44004
Phone: 440-992-7103
Fax: 440-992-4515

Brook Park
6161 Engle Rd
Brook Park, OH 44142
Phone: 216-433-1300
Fax: 216-433-1511

Brunswick
4095 Center Rd
Brunswick, OH 44212
Phone: 330-225-9144
Fax: 330-273-8023

Cleveland Heights
40 Severance Cir
Cleveland, OH 44118
Phone: 216-291-4444
Fax: 216-291-5803

East Cleveland
14340 Euclid Ave
Cleveland, OH 44112
Phone: 216-681-5020
Fax: 216-681-2650

Eastlake
35150 Lake Shore Blvd
Eastlake, OH 44095
Phone: 440-951-1416
Fax: 440-951-9361

Elyria
328 Broad St
Elyria, OH 44035
Phone: 440-322-1829
Fax: 440-322-5956

Euclid
585 E 222nd St
Euclid, OH 44123
Phone: 216-289-2700
Fax: 216-289-2766

Garfield Heights
5407 Turney Rd
Garfield Heights, OH 44125
Phone: 216-475-1100
Fax: 216-475-1124

Lakewood
12650 Detroit Ave
Cleveland, OH 44107
Phone: 216-521-7580
Fax: 216-521-1379

Lorain
200 W Erie Ave
Lorain, OH 44052
Phone: 440-244-2286
Fax: 440-244-3927

Maple Heights
5353 Lee Rd
Maple Heights, OH 44137
Phone: 216-662-6000
Fax: 216-662-2880

Medina
132 N Elmwood Ave
Medina, OH 44256
Phone: 330-725-8861
Fax: 330-722-9045

Mentor
8500 Civic Center Blvd
Mentor, OH 44060
Phone: 440-255-1100
Fax: 440-974-5711

North Olmsted
5200 Dover Center Rd
North Olmsted, OH 44070
Phone: 440-777-8000
Fax: 440-777-5889

North Ridgeville
7307 Avon Belden Rd
North Ridgeville, OH 44039
Phone: 440-353-0819
Fax: 440-353-0052

North Royalton
13834 Ridge Rd
North Royalton, OH 44133
Phone: 440-237-5686
Fax: 440-237-5024

Parma
6611 Ridge Rd
Parma, OH 44129
Phone: 440-885-8000
Fax: 440-885-8192

Parma Heights
6281 Pearl Rd
Cleveland, OH 44130
Phone: 440-884-9600
Fax: 440-884-1802

Shaker Heights
3400 Lee Rd
Shaker Heights, OH 44120
Phone: 216-491-1400
Fax: 216-491-1465

Solon
34200 Bainbridge Rd
Solon, OH 44139
Phone: 440-248-1155
Fax: 440-349-6322

South Euclid
1349 S Green Rd
South Euclid, OH 44121
Phone: 216-381-0400
Fax: 216-291-4959

Strongsville
18688 Royalton Rd
Strongsville, OH 44136
Phone: 440-238-5720
Fax: 440-238-3001

Westlake
27216 Hilliard Blvd
Westlake, OH 44145
Phone: 440-871-3300
Fax: 440-835-6443

Willoughby
1 Public Sq
Willoughby, OH 44094
Phone: 440-951-2800
Fax: 440-953-4167

Economy

Although manufacturing and trade still play a vital role in Greater Cleveland's economy, in recent years the area's economic base has become more service-oriented. Approximately one-third of the Cleveland metro area's workforce is employed in service-related positions. Home of the world-renowned Cleveland Clinic, Cleveland is a leading center for medicine—health care is the leading industry in the services sector, employing more than 100,000 area residents. Government is also an important part of Cleveland's economic base—approximately 149,000 people are employed in government-related positions at the federal, state, and local levels in the Cleveland metro area.

Unemployment Rate 8.8%
Per Capita Income..........................$29,008*
Median Family Income......................$22,448

** Information given is for Cuyahoga County.*

Principal Industries & Number of Wage Earners

Cuyahoga County - 1998

Industry	Wage Earners
Agriculture	3,537
Construction	27,137
Finance, Insurance, & Real Estate	63,832
Government	82,721
Manufacturing	135,548
Mining	408
Services	252,360
Trade	194,400
Transportation & Public Utilities	34,887

Major Employers

American Greetings Corp
1 American Rd
Cleveland, OH 44144
E-mail: information@americangreetings.com
corporate.americangreetings.com
Phone: 216-252-7300
Fax: 216-252-6778
TF: 800-321-3040

Cleveland Clinic Foundation
9500 Euclid Ave
Cleveland, OH 44195
www.ccf.org
Phone: 216-444-2200
Fax: 216-444-0271
TF: 800-223-2273

Eaton Corp
1111 Superior Ave E Eaton Ctr
Cleveland, OH 44114
E-mail: corpcomm@eaton.com
www.eaton.com
Phone: 216-523-5000
Fax: 216-523-4787

Ferro Corp
1000 Lakeside Ave
Cleveland, OH 44114
www.ferro.com
Phone: 216-641-8580
Fax: 216-696-5784

Ford Motor Co
PO Box 9900
Brook Park, OH 44142
www.ford.com
Phone: 216-676-7000
Fax: 216-676-3064

General Motors Corp
5400 Chevrolet Blvd
Cleveland, OH 44102
www.gm.com/careers
Phone: 216-265-5000
Fax: 216-265-5915

KeyCorp
127 Public Sq
Cleveland, OH 44114
E-mail: boc_in1@keybank.com
www.keybank.com
Phone: 216-689-3000
Fax: 216-689-0991
TF: 888-539-2562

LTV Steel Co Inc
200 Public Sq
Cleveland, OH 44114
www.ltvsteel.com
Phone: 216-622-5000
Fax: 216-622-1013
TF: 888-937-3588

National City Corp
1900 E 9th St National City Ctr
Cleveland, OH 44114
www.national-city.com
Phone: 216-575-2000
Fax: 216-575-2353
TF: 800-622-6736

Parker Hannifin Corp
6035 Parkland Blvd
Cleveland, OH 44124
www.parker.com
Phone: 216-896-3000
Fax: 216-896-4000
TF: 800-272-7537

Progressive Corp
6300 Wilson Mills Rd
Mayfield Village, OH 44143
www1.progressive.com
Phone: 440-461-5000
Fax: 440-446-7436

Sherwin-Williams Co
101 Prospect Ave NW
Cleveland, OH 44115
www.sherwin.com
Phone: 216-566-2000
Fax: 216-566-3670

TRW Inc
1900 Richmond Rd
Cleveland, OH 44124
www.trw.com
Phone: 216-291-7000
Fax: 216-291-7629

University Hospitals of Cleveland
11100 Euclid Ave
Cleveland, OH 44106
www.uhhs.com
Phone: 216-844-1000
Fax: 216-844-8118

Quality of Living Indicators

Total Crime Index....................................33,573
(rates per 100,000 inhabitants)

Violent Crime

Murder/manslaughter........................... 76
Forcible rape 506
Robbery....................................3,038
Aggravated assault...........................2,429

Property Crime

Burglary 7,246
Larceny theft 12,868
Motor vehicle theft 7,410

Cost of Living Index 110.3
(national average = 100)

Median Home Price $125,100

Education

Public Schools

Cleveland Board of Education
1380 E 6th St
Cleveland, OH 44114
www.clevelandschools.org
Phone: 216-574-8500
Fax: 216-574-8193

Number of Schools
Elementary 82
Middle 25
High 17

Student/Teacher Ratio
All Grades 17.0:1

Private Schools

Number of Schools (all grades) .... 23+

Colleges & Universities

Baldwin-Wallace College
275 Eastland Rd
Berea, OH 44017
www.bw.edu
Phone: 440-826-2900
Fax: 440-826-3640

Bryant & Stratton Business Institute Parma
12955 Snow Rd
Parma, OH 44130
Phone: 216-265-3151
Fax: 216-265-0325
TF: 800-327-3151

Bryant & Stratton Career College Willoughby Hills
27557 Chardon Rd
Willoughby Hills, OH 44092
www.bryantstratton.edu/main/campusdesc/whills.htm
Phone: 440-944-6800
Fax: 440-944-9260

Bryant & Stratton College
1700 E 13th St
Cleveland, OH 44114
www.bryantstratton.edu
Phone: 216-771-1700
Fax: 216-771-7787

Case Western Reserve University
10900 Euclid Ave
Cleveland, OH 44106
E-mail: aurora@po.cwru.edu
www.cwru.edu
Phone: 216-368-2000
Fax: 216-368-5111
TF: 800-967-8898

Cleveland Institute of Art
11141 East Blvd
Cleveland, OH 44106
E-mail: info@cia.edu
www.cia.edu
Phone: 216-421-7400
Fax: 216-421-7438
TF: 800-223-4700

Cleveland Institute of Electronics
1776 E 17th St
Cleveland, OH 44114
E-mail: instruct@cie-uc.edu
Phone: 216-781-9400
Fax: 216-781-0331
TF: 800-243-6446

Cleveland Institute of Music
11021 East Blvd
Cleveland, OH 44106
www.cwru.edu/CIM/cimhome.html
Phone: 216-791-5000
Fax: 216-791-1530

Cleveland State University
1983 E 24th St
Cleveland, OH 44115
www.csuohio.edu
Phone: 216-687-2000
Fax: 216-687-9210
TF: 888-278-0440

Cuyahoga Community College Eastern Campus
4250 Richmond Rd
Cleveland, OH 44122
www.tri-c.cc.oh.us/EAST/Default.htm
Phone: 216-987-2024
Fax: 216-987-2214
TF: 800-954-8742

Cuyahoga Community College Metropolitan Campus
2900 Community College Ave
Cleveland, OH 44115
www.tri-c.cc.oh.us/Metro/Default.htm
Phone: 216-987-4000
Fax: 216-696-2567
TF: 800-954-8742

Cuyahoga Community College Western Campus
11000 Pleasant Valley Rd
Parma, OH 44130
www.tri-c.cc.oh.us/west/default.htm
Phone: 216-987-5154
Fax: 216-987-5071
TF: 800-954-8742

David N Myers College
112 Prospect Ave E
Cleveland, OH 44115
www.dnmyers.edu
Phone: 216-696-9000
Fax: 216-696-6430

John Carroll University
20700 N Park Blvd
University Heights, OH 44118
www.jcu.edu
Phone: 216-397-1886
Fax: 216-397-3098

Lake Erie College
391 W Washington St
Painesville, OH 44077
www.lakeerie.edu
Phone: 440-352-3361
Fax: 440-352-3533
TF: 800-533-4996

Lakeland Community College
7700 Clocktower Dr
Kirtland, OH 44094
www.lakeland.cc.oh.us
Phone: 440-953-7000
Fax: 440-953-9710
TF: 800-589-8520

Notre Dame College of Ohio
4545 College Rd
South Euclid, OH 44121
www.ndc.edu
Phone: 216-381-1680
Fax: 216-381-3802
TF: 877-632-6446

Sawyer College of Business Cleveland
13027 Lorain Ave
Cleveland, OH 44111
Phone: 216-941-7666
Fax: 216-941-1162

Ursuline College
2550 Lander Rd
Pepper Pike, OH 44124
E-mail: dgiaco@en.com
www.ursuline.edu/
Phone: 440-449-4200
Fax: 440-684-6138

Virginia Marti College of Fashion & Art
11724 Detroit Ave
Lakewood, OH 44107
Phone: 216-221-8584
Fax: 216-221-2311
TF: 800-473-4350

West Side Institute of Technology
9801 Walford Ave
Cleveland, OH 44102
Phone: 216-651-1656
Fax: 216-651-4077

Hospitals

Bedford Medical Center
44 Blaine Ave
Bedford, OH 44146
Phone: 440-439-2000
Fax: 440-232-0776

Cleveland Clinic Foundation
9500 Euclid Ave
Cleveland, OH 44195
www.ccf.org
Phone: 216-444-2200
Fax: 216-444-0271
TF: 800-223-2273

Deaconess Hospital of Cleveland
4229 Pearl Rd
Cleveland, OH 44109
Phone: 216-459-6300
Fax: 216-459-6746

Fairview General Hospital
18101 Lorain Ave
Cleveland, OH 44111
Phone: 216-476-7000
Fax: 216-476-4064
TF: 800-323-8434

Lake Hospital System
10 E Washington
Painesville, OH 44077
Phone: 440-354-2400
Fax: 440-354-4398

Lakewood Hospital
14519 Detroit Ave
Lakewood, OH 44107
Phone: 216-521-4200
Fax: 216-529-7161
TF: 800-521-3955

Lutheran Hospital
1730 W 25th St
Cleveland, OH 44113
Phone: 216-696-4300
Fax: 216-363-2012

Marymount Hospital
12300 McCracken Rd
Garfield Heights, OH 44125
Phone: 216-581-0500
Fax: 216-587-8212

Meridia Euclid Hospital
18901 Lake Shore Blvd
Euclid, OH 44119
www.meridia.com/advant.htm
Phone: 216-531-9000
Fax: 216-692-7488

Meridia Hillcrest Hospital
6780 Mayfield Rd
Mayfield Heights, OH 44124
www.meridia.com/advant.htm
Phone: 440-449-4500
Fax: 440-473-6405

Meridia Huron Hospital
13951 Terrace Rd
East Cleveland, OH 44112
www.meridia.com/advant.htm
Phone: 216-761-3300
Fax: 216-761-3529

Meridia South Pointe Hospital
4110 Warrensville Ctr Rd
Warrensville Heights, OH 44122
Phone: 216-491-6000
Fax: 216-491-7193

MetroHealth Medical Center
2500 MetroHealth Dr
Cleveland, OH 44109
www.metrohealth.org
Phone: 216-398-6000
Fax: 216-778-5226
TF: 800-554-5251

Saint John West Shore Hospital
29000 Center Ridge Rd
Westlake, OH 44145
www.sjws.net
Phone: 440-835-8000
Fax: 440-414-6401

Saint Vincent Charity Hospital
2351 E 22nd St
Cleveland, OH 44115
Phone: 216-861-6200
Fax: 216-363-3333

Southwest General Health Center
18697 Bagley Rd
Middleburg Heights, OH 44130
Phone: 440-816-8000
Fax: 440-816-8062

University Hospitals of Cleveland
11100 Euclid Ave
Cleveland, OH 44106
www.uhhs.com
Phone: 216-844-1000
Fax: 216-844-8118

Veterans Affairs Medical Center
10701 East Blvd
Cleveland, OH 44106
Phone: 216-791-3800
Fax: 216-421-3008

Transportation

Airport(s)

Cleveland Hopkins International Airport (CLE)
12 miles SW of downtown (approx 20 minutes) . . .216-265-6000

Mass Transit

Regional Transit Authority (RTA)
$1.25 Base fare 216-621-9500

Rail/Bus

Amtrak Station
200 Cleveland Memorial Shoreway NE
Cleveland, OH 44114
Phone: 216-696-5115
TF: 800-872-7245

Greyhound Bus Station
1465 Chester Ave
Cleveland, OH 44114
Phone: 216-781-0520
TF: 800-231-2222

Utilities

Electricity
Cleveland Public Power 216-664-4600
community.cleveland.com/cc/cpp

Gas
East Ohio Gas Co 216-432-3232
www.cng.com/eog/

Water
Cleveland Water Dept 216-664-3130

Garbage Collection/Recycling
Cleveland Waste Dept 216-664-3711

Telecommunications

Telephone
Ameritech 800-660-1000
www.ameritech.com

Cable Television
Cablevision Systems Corp 216-575-8000

Internet Service Providers (ISPs)
APK Net Ltd 216-241-7166
www.apk.net
Exchange Network Services Inc 216-615-9400
www.en.com
Internet Ohio 800-829-0024
www.ohio.net
Multiverse Inc 216-344-3080
www.multiverse.com
RMRC Ltd 440-269-3839
www.rmrc.net

Banks

Bank One NA
600 Superior Ave
Cleveland, OH 44114
Phone: 216-781-4437
Fax: 216-781-2238
TF: 800-310-1111

Charter One Bank FSB
1215 Superior Ave
Cleveland, OH 44114
www.charterone.com
Phone: 216-566-5300
Fax: 216-566-1465
TF: 800-553-8981

Dollar Bank FSB
614 Euclid Ave
Cleveland, OH 44114
Phone: 216-736-8990
Fax: 216-736-3954

Fifth Third Bank of Northwestern Ohio
200 Euclid Ave
Cleveland, OH 44114
Phone: 216-623-2700
Fax: 216-241-0262
TF: 800-972-3030

Firstar Bank NA
200 Public Sq
Cleveland, OH 44114
Phone: 216-623-4000

Firstmerit Bank NA
25 W Prospect Ave
Cleveland, OH 44115
Phone: 216-781-8100

Huntington National Bank
917 Euclid Ave
Cleveland, OH 44115
Phone: 216-515-6402

KeyBank NA
127 Public Sq
Cleveland, OH 44114
E-mail: boc_in1@keybank.com
www.keybank.com
Phone: 216-689-3000
Fax: 216-689-4037

National City Bank Cleveland
1900 E 9th St
Cleveland, OH 44114
Phone: 216-575-2000
Fax: 216-420-9512
TF: 888-622-4932

Ohio Savings Bank FSB
1801 E 9th St
Cleveland, OH 44114
www.ohiosavings.com
Phone: 216-622-4100
Fax: 216-622-4417
TF: 800-860-2025

Third Federal Savings & Loan Assn
7007 Broadway Ave
Cleveland, OH 44105
www.thirdfederal.com
Phone: 216-441-6000
Fax: 216-441-6034
TF: 800-944-7828

Shopping

Avenue The at Tower City Center
230 Huron Rd NW
Cleveland, OH 44113
www.towercitycenter.com/frame_shop.html
Phone: 216-771-0033

Beachcliff Market Square
19300 Detroit Rd
Rocky River, OH 44116
Phone: 440-333-5074
Fax: 440-331-2176

Beachwood Place
26300 Cedar Rd
Beachwood, OH 44122
www.beachwoodplace.com
Phone: 216-464-9460
Fax: 216-464-7939

Euclid Square Mall
100 Euclid Square Mall
Euclid, OH 44132
Phone: 216-731-8970

Flats The
1283 Riverbed St
Cleveland, OH 44113
www.voiceoftheflats.org
Phone: 216-566-1046
Fax: 216-566-0222

Galleria at Erieview
1301 E 9th St Suite 3333
Cleveland, OH 44114
E-mail: galleriaerieview@shopyourmall.com
www.shopyourmall.com/mall_welcome.asp?map=yes&mall_select=601
Phone: 216-861-4343
Fax: 216-861-0209

Great Lakes Mall
7850 Mentor Ave
Mentor, OH 44060
Phone: 440-255-6900
Fax: 440-255-0509

Great Northern Mall
4954 Great Northern Mall
North Olmsted, OH 44070
Phone: 440-734-6300
Fax: 440-734-8929

Midway Mall
3343 Midway Mall
Elyria, OH 44035
E-mail: midwaymall@rejacobsgroup.com
www.shopyourmall.com/mall_welcome.asp?map=yes&mall_select=612
Phone: 440-324-6610

Parmatown Mall
7899 W Ridgewood Dr
Parma, OH 44129
Phone: 440-885-5506
Fax: 440-884-9330

Randall Park Mall
20801 Miles Rd
Cleveland, OH 44128
Phone: 216-663-1250
Fax: 216-663-8750

Saks Fifth Avenue
26100 Cedar Rd
Beachwood, OH 44122
Phone: 216-292-5500
Fax: 216-292-4791

Severance Town Center
3640 Mayfield Rd
Cleveland, OH 44118
Phone: 216-381-7323
Fax: 216-381-4305

Shaker Square
13221 Shaker Sq
Cleveland, OH 44120
Phone: 216-991-8700
Fax: 216-991-8700

Southpark Center
500 Southpark Ctr
Strongsville, OH 44136
www.southparkcenter.com
Phone: 440-238-9000
Fax: 440-846-8323

Westgate Mall
3211 Westgate Mall
Cleveland, OH 44126
E-mail: westgatemall@rejacobsgroup.com
www.shopyourmall.com/mall_welcome.asp?map=yes&mall_select=605
Phone: 440-333-8336

Media

Newspapers and Magazines

Cleveland Free Times
1846 Coventry Rd Suite 100
Cleveland, OH 44118
E-mail: freetimes@freetimes.com
www.freetimes.com
Phone: 216-321-2300
Fax: 216-321-4456

Cleveland Magazine
1422 Euclid Ave Hanna Bldg Suite 730
Cleveland, OH 44115
www.clevelandmagazine.com
Phone: 216-771-2833
Fax: 216-781-6318

Clevescene
1 Playhouse Sq 1375 Euclid Ave #312
Cleveland, OH 44115
E-mail: scene@clevescene.com
www.clevescene.com
Phone: 216-241-7550
Fax: 216-241-6275

Crain's Cleveland Business
700 W St Clair Suite 310
Cleveland, OH 44113
E-mail: cle.crains@mail.multiverse.com
www.crainscleveland.com
Phone: 216-522-1383
Fax: 216-694-4264
TF: 888-909-9111

News Sun
5510 Cloverleaf Pkwy
Cleveland, OH 44125
www.sunnews.com
Phone: 216-524-0830
Fax: 216-986-2380

Parma Sun Post
32 Park St
Berea, OH 44017
www.sunnews.com
Phone: 440-243-3725
Fax: 440-243-4905

Plain Dealer*
1801 Superior Ave NE
Cleveland, OH 44114
www.cleveland.com
Phone: 216-999-4800
Fax: 216-999-6354
TF: 800-688-4802

Sun Herald
5510 Cloverleaf Pkwy
Valley View, OH 44125
www.sunnews.com
Phone: 216-524-0830
Fax: 216-524-7792

Sun Messenger
5510 Cloverleaf Pkwy
Valley View, OH 44125
Phone: 216-524-0830
Fax: 216-524-7792

Sun Scoop Journal
5510 Cloverleaf Pkwy
Valley View, OH 44125
www.sunnews.com
Phone: 216-524-0830
Fax: 216-524-7792

West Life
PO Box 45014
Westlake, OH 44145
E-mail: westlife@dceye.com
Phone: 440-871-5797
Fax: 440-871-3824

West Side Sun News
5510 Cloverleaf Pkwy
Cleveland, OH 44125
www.sunnews.com
Phone: 216-524-0830
Fax: 216-986-2380

**Indicates major daily newspapers*

Television

WBNX-TV Ch 55 (WB)
2690 State Rd
Cuyahoga Falls, OH 44223
www.wbnx.com
Phone: 330-922-5500
Fax: 330-929-2410

WEWS-TV Ch 5 (ABC)
3001 Euclid Ave
Cleveland, OH 44115
E-mail: news@newsnet5.com
www.newsnet5.com
Phone: 216-431-5555
Fax: 216-431-3666

WGGN-TV Ch 52 (Ind)
3809 Maple Ave
Castalia, OH 44824
Phone: 419-684-5311
Fax: 419-684-5378

WJW-TV Ch 8 (Fox)
5800 S Marginal Rd
Cleveland, OH 44103
E-mail: wjwfox8@en.com
Phone: 216-431-8888
Fax: 216-432-4239

WKYC-TV Ch 3 (NBC)
1403 E 6th St
Cleveland, OH 44114
E-mail: wkyc@aol.com
Phone: 216-344-3333
Fax: 216-344-3326

WMFD-TV Ch 68 (Ind)
2900 Park Ave W
Mansfield, OH 44906
E-mail: comments@wmfd.com
www.wmfd.com
Phone: 419-529-5900
Fax: 419-529-2319

WOIO-TV Ch 19 (CBS)
1717 E 12th St
Cleveland, OH 44114
www.woio.com
Phone: 216-771-1943
Fax: 216-436-5460

WUAB-TV Ch 43 (UPN)
1717 E 12th St
Cleveland, OH 44114
Phone: 216-771-1943
Fax: 216-515-7152
TF: 800-929-0132

WVIZ-TV Ch 25 (PBS)
4300 Brookpark Rd
Cleveland, OH 44134
www.wviz.org
Phone: 216-398-2800
Fax: 216-749-2560

Radio

WABQ-AM 1540 kHz (Rel)
8000 Euclid Ave
Cleveland, OH 44103
Phone: 216-231-8005
Fax: 216-421-0738

WCCD-AM 1000 kHz (Rel)
4 Summit Park Dr Suite 150
Independence, OH 44131
E-mail: office@wccdradio.com
www.wccdradio.com
Phone: 216-901-0921
Fax: 216-901-1104

WCLV-FM 95.5 MHz (Clas)
26501 Renaissance Pkwy
Cleveland, OH 44128
E-mail: wclv@wclv.com
www.wclv.com
Phone: 216-464-0900
Fax: 216-464-2206

WCPN-FM 90.3 MHz (NPR)
Cleveland Public Radio 3100 Chester Ave Suite 300
Cleveland, OH 44114
www.wcpn.org
Phone: 216-432-3700
Fax: 216-432-3681

WCRF-FM 103.3 MHz (Rel)
9756 Barr Rd
Cleveland, OH 44141
Phone: 440-526-1111
Fax: 440-526-1319

WDOK-FM 102.1 MHz (AC)
1 Radio Ln
Cleveland, OH 44114
www.wdok.com
Phone: 216-696-0123
Fax: 216-566-0764

WENZ-FM 107.9 MHz (Alt)
1041 Huron Rd
Cleveland, OH 44115
Phone: 216-861-0100
Fax: 216-696-0385

WERE-AM 1300 kHz (N/T)
820 W Superior
Cleveland, OH 44113
Phone: 216-579-1111
Fax: 216-575-9141

WGAR-FM 99.5 MHz (Ctry)
5005 Rockside Rd Suite 530
Cleveland, OH 44131
E-mail: wgarrequest@wgar.com
www.wgar.com
Phone: 216-328-9950
Fax: 216-328-9951

WHK-AM 1420 kHz (Rel)
4 Summit Park Dr Suite 150
Independence, OH 44131
E-mail: office@whkradio.com
www.whkradio.com
Phone: 216-901-0921

WJMO-AM 1490 kHz (Rel)
2510 Saint Clair Ave
Cleveland, OH 44114
Phone: 216-621-9566
Fax: 216-771-4164

WKNR-AM 1220 kHz (Sports)
9446 Broadview Rd
Cleveland, OH 44147
Phone: 440-838-1220
Fax: 440-838-1546

WMJI-FM 105.7 MHz (Oldies)
310 Lakeside Ave 6th Fl
Cleveland, OH 44113
www.wmji.com
Phone: 216-623-1105
Fax: 216-696-3299

WMMS-FM 100.7 MHz (Rock)
1660 W 2nd St 200 Skylight Office Tower
Cleveland, OH 44113
www.wmms.com
Phone: 216-781-9667
Fax: 216-771-1007

WMVX-FM 106.5 MHz (AC)
1660 W 2nd St Suite 200
Cleveland, OH 44113
www.wmvx.com
Phone: 216-781-9667
Fax: 216-771-1007

WNCX-FM 98.5 MHz (CR)
1041 Huron Rd
Cleveland, OH 44115
E-mail: wncx@wncx.com
www.wncx.com
Phone: 216-861-0100
Fax: 216-696-0385

WNWV-FM 107.3 MHz (NAC)
538 Broad St 4th Fl
Elyria, OH 44036
E-mail: thewave@wnwv.com
www.wnwv.com
Phone: 440-322-3761
Fax: 440-322-1536

WQAL-FM 104.1 MHz (AC)
1621 Euclid Ave Suite 1800
Cleveland, OH 44115
E-mail: qsales@wqal.com
www.wqal.com
Phone: 216-696-6666
Fax: 216-348-0104

WRMR-AM 850 kHz (Nost)
1 Radio Ln
Cleveland, OH 44114
Phone: 216-696-0123
Fax: 216-566-0764

WTAM-AM 1100 kHz (N/T)
1468 W 9th St Suite 805
Cleveland, OH 44113
www.wtam.com
Phone: 216-696-4444
Fax: 216-781-5143

WWMK-AM 1260 kHz (Misc)
1422 Euclid Ave Suite 604
Cleveland, OH 44115
Phone: 216-623-3500
Fax: 216-623-3501

WZAK-FM 93.1 MHz (Urban)
2510 St Clair Ave
Cleveland, OH 44114
www.wzak.com
Phone: 216-621-9300
Fax: 216-566-8238

WZJM-FM 92.3 MHz (Oldies)
2510 St Clair Ave
Cleveland, OH 44114
www.923thebeat.com
Phone: 216-621-9566
Fax: 216-771-4164

Attractions

Cleveland's Inner Harbor area is home to the Rock and Roll Hall of Fame and Museum, which features interactive displays, memorabilia, and live performances. Opened in 1995, the Rock and Roll Hall of Fame is the only Rock history museum in the entire world. New to Cleveland also is the Great Lakes Science Center, which features more than 350 interactive exhibits and an OMNIMAX theater. The Flats, an area along the Cuyahoga River, is known for its restaurants and nightclubs. Overlooking The Flats, in Town City Center, is The Avenue, which, along with The Galleria, are the premier shopping venues in the Cleveland. Other attractions include the Cleveland Museum of Art, Cleveland Museum of Natural History, and Cleveland Metroparks Zoo. A new baseball park, Jacobs Field, and basketball arena, Gund Arena, were also recently completed. Family amusements not far from Cleveland include Cedar Point amusement park in Sandusky and Sea World in Aurora.

African American Museum
1765 Crawford Rd
Cleveland, OH 44106
Phone: 216-791-1700
Fax: 216-791-1774

Brecksville Reservation
4101 Fulton Pkwy Cleveland Metroparks
Cleveland, OH 44144
Phone: 216-351-6300
Fax: 216-635-3286

Cain Park Theatre
Superior & Lee Rds Cain Pk
Cleveland Heights, OH 44118
Phone: 216-371-3000

Cedar Point Amusement Park
1 Cedar Point Dr
Sandusky, OH 44870
www.cedarpoint.com
Phone: 419-626-0830
Fax: 419-627-2200

Century Village
14653 E Park St
Burton, OH 44021
Phone: 440-834-1492
Fax: 440-834-4012

Cleveland Botanical Garden
11030 East Blvd
Cleveland, OH 44106
E-mail: info@cbgarden.org
www.cbgarden.org
Phone: 216-721-1600
Fax: 216-721-2056

Cleveland Center for Contemporary Art
8501 Carnegie Ave
Cleveland, OH 44106
www.contemporaryart.org
Phone: 216-421-8671
Fax: 216-421-0737

Cleveland Chamber Symphony
2001 Euclid Ave Cleveland State University
Cleveland, OH 44115
E-mail: xxrich@grail.csuohio.edu
www.csuohio.edu/ccs/
Phone: 216-687-9243
Fax: 216-687-9279

Cleveland Metroparks Zoo
3900 Wildlife Way
Cleveland, OH 44109
E-mail: cmzoomkt@interramp.com
www.clemetzoo.com
Phone: 216-661-6500
Fax: 216-661-3312

Cleveland Museum of Art
11150 East Blvd
Cleveland, OH 44106
E-mail: sas6@pocwru.edu
www.clemusart.com
Phone: 216-421-7340
Fax: 216-229-5095
TF: 888-262-7175

Cleveland Museum of Natural History
1 Wade Oval Dr University Cir
Cleveland, OH 44106
E-mail: wwwadmin@cmnh.org
www.cmnh.org/
Phone: 216-231-4600
Fax: 216-231-5919

Cleveland Opera
1422 Euclid Ave Suite 1052
Cleveland, OH 44115
E-mail: mail@clevelandopera.org
www.clevelandopera.org
Phone: 216-575-0903
Fax: 216-575-1918

Cleveland Orchestra
11001 Euclid Ave Severance Hall
Cleveland, OH 44106
www.clevelandorch.com
Phone: 216-231-7300
Fax: 216-231-0202
TF: 800-686-1141

Cleveland Play House
8500 Euclid Ave
Cleveland, OH 44106
E-mail: cphbox@en.com
www.cleveplayhouse.org
Phone: 216-795-7000
Fax: 216-795-7005

Cleveland Public Theatre
6415 Detroit Ave
Cleveland, OH 44102
www.en.com/cpt/
Phone: 216-631-2727
Fax: 216-631-2575

Cleveland San Jose Ballet
3615 Euclid Ave Suite 1A
Cleveland, OH 44115
www.csjballet.org
Phone: 216-426-2500
Fax: 216-426-2524

Cleveland Shakespeare Festival
1731 Coventry Rd Suite 2
Cleveland Heights, OH 44118
E-mail: info@cleveshakes.org
www.cleveshakes.org
Phone: 216-732-3311

Crawford Auto-Aviation Museum
10825 East Blvd
Cleveland, OH 44106
www.wrhs.org/sites/auto.htm
Phone: 216-721-5722
Fax: 216-721-0645

Cuyahoga Valley Scenic Railroad
1630 W Mill St
Peninsula, OH 44624
www.cvsr.com
Phone: 330-657-2000
Fax: 330-657-2080
TF: 800-468-4070

DanceCleveland
1501 Euclid Ave Playhouse Sqare Ctr
Cleveland, OH 44115
www.dancecleveland.org
Phone: 216-861-2213
Fax: 216-687-0022

Dittrick Museum of Medical History
11000 Euclid Ave
Cleveland, OH 44106
www.cwru.edu/chsl/hist_div.htm
Phone: 216-368-3648
Fax: 216-368-0165

Dobama Theater
1846 Coventry Rd
Cleveland, OH 44118
E-mail: dobama@multiverse.com
www.dobama.org
Phone: 216-932-6838
Fax: 216-932-3259

Dunham Tavern Museum
6709 Euclid Ave
Cleveland, OH 44103
Phone: 216-431-1060

Fairport Harbor Lakefront Park
2 Huntington Beach
Fairport Harbor, OH 44077
Phone: 440-639-7275

Flats The
1283 Riverbed St
Cleveland, OH 44113
www.voiceoftheflats.org
Phone: 216-566-1046
Fax: 216-566-0222

Great Lakes Brewing Co
2516 Market St
Cleveland, OH 44113
www.greatlakesbrewing.com
Phone: 216-771-4404
Fax: 216-771-4466

Great Lakes Science Center
601 Erieside Ave
Cleveland, OH 44114
www.greatscience.com
Phone: 216-694-2000
Fax: 216-696-2140

Great Lakes Theater Festival
1501 Euclid Ave
Cleveland, OH 44115
E-mail: mail@greatlakestheater.org
www.greatlakestheater.org
Phone: 216-241-5490
Fax: 216-241-6315

Hale Farm & Village
PO Box 296
Bath, OH 44210
www.wrhs.org/sites/hale.htm
Phone: 330-666-3711
Fax: 330-666-9497

Health Museum
8911 Euclid Ave
Cleveland, OH 44106
www.healthmuseum.org/
Phone: 216-231-5010
Fax: 216-231-5129

Hinckley Reservation
2191 Parker Rd
Cleveland, OH 44233
Phone: 216-351-6300

Holden Arboretum
9500 Sperry Rd
Kirtland, OH 44094
Phone: 440-256-1110
Fax: 440-256-1655

International Women's Air & Space Museum
1501 N Marginal Rd Burke Lakefront Airport Rm 165
Cleveland, OH 44114
E-mail: iwasm@ecr.net
www.iwasm.org
Phone: 216-623-1111
Fax: 216-623-1113

James A Garfield National Historic Site
8095 Mentor Ave Lawnfield
Mentor, OH 44060
www.nps.gov/jaga/
Phone: 440-255-8722
Fax: 440-255-8545

Lake Farmpark
8800 Chardon Rd
Kirtland, OH 44094
www.lakemetroparks.com/
Phone: 440-256-2112
Fax: 440-256-2147
TF: 800-366-3276

Lake View Cemetery
12316 Euclid Ave
Cleveland, OH 44106
Phone: 216-421-2665
Fax: 216-421-2415

Lyric Opera Cleveland
11021 East Blvd Cleveland Institute of Music
Cleveland, OH 44106
www.lyricoperacleveland.org
Phone: 216-231-2910
Fax: 216-231-5502

Mill Stream Run Reservation
9485 Eastland Rd
Strongsville, OH 44136
Phone: 440-234-6800

NASA Glenn Research Center
21000 Brookpark Rd MS 8-1
Cleveland, OH 44135
www.grc.nasa.gov
Phone: 216-433-4000
Fax: 216-433-8000

OMNIMAX Theater
601 Erieside Ave Great Lakes Science Ctr
Cleveland, OH 44114
www.glsc.org/geninfo.php3?class1=OmniMax&class2=All&class3=Intro
Phone: 216-694-2000
Fax: 216-696-2140

Playhouse Square Center
1501 Euclid Ave Suite 200
Cleveland, OH 44115
www.playhousesquare.com
Phone: 216-771-4444
Fax: 216-771-0217
TF: 800-888-9941

Polka Hall of Fame
291 E 22nd St Shore Cultural Ctr
Euclid, OH 44123
Phone: 216-261-3263

Rainbow Children's Museum
10730 Euclid Ave
Cleveland, OH 44106
www.museum4kids.com
Phone: 216-791-7114
Fax: 216-791-8838

Rock & Roll Hall of Fame & Museum
1 Key Plaza
Cleveland, OH 44114
E-mail: visit@rockhall.com
www.rockhall.com
Phone: 216-781-7625
Fax: 216-515-1283
TF: 800-349-7625

Rockefeller Park
E 88th St & ML King Jr Dr
Cleveland, OH 44108
Phone: 216-664-3103

Rocky River Reservation
Berea area betw Detroit Ave & Bagley Rd Cleveland Metroparks
Cleveland, OH 44144
Phone: 216-351-6300

Sea World of Ohio
1100 Sea World Dr
Aurora, OH 44202
www.seaworld.com/seaworld/sw_ohio/swoframe.html
Phone: 330-995-2121
Fax: 330-995-2115

Severance Hall
11001 Euclid Ave
Cleveland, OH 44106
www.clevelandorchestra.com/c-scripts/serve.pl?d=severance.html&c=tTqQ-sPqPpLG
Phone: 216-231-7300
Fax: 216-231-0202

Shaker Lakes Regional Nature Center
2600 S Park Blvd
Cleveland, OH 44120
Phone: 216-321-5935
Fax: 216-321-1869

Six Flags Ohio
1060 N Aurora Rd
Aurora, OH 44202
www.sixflags.com/ohio
Phone: 330-562-7131
Fax: 330-562-7020

Steamship William G Mather Museum
1001 E 9th St Pier
Cleveland, OH 44114
little.nhlink.net/wgm/wgmhome.html
Phone: 216-574-9053
Fax: 216-574-2536

Trinity Cathedral
2021 E 22nd St
Cleveland, OH 44115
community.cleveland.com/cc/trinity
Phone: 216-771-3630
Fax: 216-771-3657

Trolley Tours of Cleveland
Elm St & Winslow Ave Powerhouse
Cleveland, OH 44113
www.lollytrolley.com
Phone: 216-771-4484
TF: 800-848-0173

West Side Market
1979 W 25th St
Cleveland, OH 44113
Phone: 216-664-3368
Fax: 216-664-3390

Western Reserve Historical Society
10825 East Blvd
Cleveland, OH 44106
www.wrhs.org/
Phone: 216-721-5722
Fax: 216-721-9309

Sports Teams & Facilities

Cleveland Barons (hockey)
5310 Hauserman
Parma, OH 44130
Phone: 440-886-0512
Fax: 440-886-0512

Cleveland Browns
76 Lou Groza Blvd Cleveland Browns Stadium
Berea, OH 44017
www.clevelandbrowns.com
Phone: 440-891-5000
Fax: 440-891-5009
TF: 888-891-1999

Cleveland Browns Stadium
1085 West 3rd St
Cleveland, OH 44114
Phone: 440-891-5000
Fax: 440-824-3645
TF: 888-891-1999

Cleveland Caps (soccer)
7876 Broadview Rd
Parma, OH 44134
Phone: 216-901-1277
Fax: 216-901-9100

Cleveland Cavaliers
Gund Arena 1 Center Ct
Cleveland, OH 44115
www.nba.com/cavs
Phone: 216-420-2000
Fax: 216-420-2298
TF: 800-332-2287

Cleveland Crunch (soccer)
34200 Solon Rd 1 Crunch Pl
Solon, OH 44139
Phone: 440-349-2090
Fax: 440-349-0653

Cleveland Eclipse (soccer)
Foltz Industrial Pkwy Ehrnfelt Championship Field
Cleveland, OH 44136
Phone: 440-333-0981
Fax: 440-835-5405

Cleveland Indians
2401 Ontario St Jacobs Field
Cleveland, OH 44115
www.indians.com
Phone: 216-420-4200
Fax: 216-420-4624

Cleveland Junior Americans (hockey)
1616 9th Blvd
Lorain, OH 44052
E-mail: jrufo@centuryinter.net
Phone: 440-246-1075
Fax: 440-246-3113

Cleveland Lions (football)
3290 W 125th St
Cleveland, OH 44111
Phone: 216-741-2483
Fax: 216-661-8953

Cleveland Lumberjacks (hockey)
200 Huron Rd 1 Center Ice
Cleveland, OH 44115
www.jackshockey.com
Phone: 216-420-0000
Fax: 216-420-2520

Cleveland Rockers (basketball)
1 Center Ct Gund Arena
Cleveland, OH 44115
www.wnba.com/rockers
Phone: 216-420-2370
Fax: 216-420-2101

Gund Arena
1 Center Ct
Cleveland, OH 44115
www.gundarena.com
Phone: 216-420-2000
Fax: 216-420-2280
TF: 800-332-2287

Jacobs Field
2401 Ontario St
Cleveland, OH 44115
www.indians.com/jacobs/index.html
Phone: 216-420-4200
Fax: 216-420-4396

Northfield Park
10705 Northfield Rd
Northfield, OH 44067
www.northfieldpark.com
Phone: 330-467-4101
Fax: 330-468-2628

Thistledown Racing Club Inc
21501 Emery Rd
Cleveland, OH 44128
Phone: 216-662-8600
Fax: 216-662-5339

Annual Events

500,000 Country Lights (December) 800-366-3276
American & Canadian Sport Travel & Outdoor Show
(mid-March) 216-529-1300
American Indian Pow Wow (mid-June) 216-281-8480
American Legion Holiday Parade
(late November) 216-432-4046
Auto Rama (late January) 216-348-2200
Boo at the Zoo (late October) 216-661-6500
Cain Park Arts Festival (mid-July) 216-371-3000
Cleveland Christmas Connection
(late November-early December) 440-835-9627
Cleveland Grand Prix (late June-early July) 216-781-3500
Cleveland Home & Garden Show
(early-mid-February) 800-600-0307
Cleveland International Film Festival
(late March) 216-621-1374
Cleveland National Air Show (early September) 216-781-0747
Cleveland's Irish Cultural Festival (late July) 216-251-1711
Cuyahoga County Fair (mid-August) 800-321-1001
CVS-Cleveland Marathon (late April) 800-467-3826
Downtown Cleveland WinterFest
(early January-late February) 216-736-7799
EarthFest (April 22) 216-281-6468
Greater Cleveland Auto Show
(late February-early March) 216-676-6000
Greater Cleveland Golf Show
(mid-late February) 330-963-6963
Hale Farm Harvest Festival (mid-October) 800-589-9703
Haunted Hayrides (mid-October) 800-366-3276
Holiday Lights Festival (early-mid-December) 216-661-6500
Johnny Appleseed Festival (mid-September) 330-225-5577
Mid America Sail & Power Boat Show
(mid-late January) 216-676-6000
National Home & Garden Show
(early-mid-February) 216-676-6000
Ohio Arts & Crafts Christmas Festival
(late October) 440-243-0090
Ohio Irish Festival (late June) 440-779-6065
Oktoberfest (early September) 216-881-7773
Saint Patrick's Day Parade (mid-March) 216-621-4110
Shaker Apple Festival Weekend (early October) 216-921-1201
Shaker Square Holiday Lighting Ceremony
(late November) 216-991-8700
Ski Skate & Snowboard Show (early November) 216-676-6000
Taste of Cleveland (early September) 440-247-2722
Tri-C JazzFest (mid-April) 216-987-4400

Colorado Springs, Colorado

***County:* El Paso**

COLORADO SPRINGS is located in central Colorado at the base of Pike's Peak. Major cities within 100 miles include Pueblo, Denver, Golden, and Boulder, Colorado.

Area (Land) .... 183.2 sq mi
Area (Water)............................... 0.4 sq mi
Elevation...................................6,008 ft
Latitude ....38-83-39 N
Longitude.............................. 104-82-08 W
Time Zone .... MST
Area Code...................................... 719

Climate

Colorado Springs has a temperate dry climate. Winters are cold, with average high temperatures in the low to mid-40s and average lows in the mid- to high teens. The mountains to the west of the city protect the area from major heavy snowfalls—the average annual snowfall total is 40 inches. Summer days are warm, with average high temperatures in the low 80s, while evenings cool down dramatically into the low to mid-50s. July is the wettest month in Colorado Springs and January is the driest.

Average Temperatures & Precipitation

Temperatures

	Jan	Feb	Mar	Apr	May	Jun	Jul	Aug	Sep	Oct	Nov	Dec
High	41	45	50	60	69	79	84	81	74	64	51	42
Low	16	19	25	33	42	51	57	55	47	36	25	17

Precipitation

	Jan	Feb	Mar	Apr	May	Jun	Jul	Aug	Sep	Oct	Nov	Dec
Inches	0.3	0.4	0.9	1.2	2.2	2.3	2.9	3.0	1.3	0.8	0.5	0.5

History

The city known today as Colorado Springs was founded in 1870 by retired Civil War general and railroad developer William Jackson Palmer. Palmer's dream was to establish a city of temperance, unlike those typical of the Old West, that would be the most attractive place in the West with its spectacular scenery and mild climate. The following year, Palmer laid out his new community at the base of majestic Pike's Peak, fashioned after his native Tudor England (the new town was often referred to as "Little London," due to its resemblance to General Palmer's home town). Originally called Fountain Colony, the community's name was eventually changed to Colorado Springs.

The discovery of gold in nearby Cripple Creek in 1891 led to nearly two decades of financial prosperity and growth in the area. Colorado Springs became known as the "City of Millionaires" when prospectors who had made their fortunes in the gold mines built extravagant homes in the city. When the demand for gold declined in the early 1900s, the city focused on tourism to help revive the economy. In 1915, local businessman Spencer Penrose decided to capitalize on the rise of the automobile era by building a road to the top of Pike's Peak. The following year, he built the famous Broadmoor Hotel in Colorado Springs, which remains one of the leading hotels in the United States today.

In addition to its popularity as a leading tourist destination, Colorado Springs is also known for its military presence. In 1942, Camp Carson (now Fort Carson) was the first military base established in the area. (Fort Carson today is Colorado Springs' largest employer, providing jobs for more than 18,500 area residents.) In 1954, Colorado Springs was chosen as the site for the United States Air Force Academy, which began offering classes four years later. Other military operations in the Colorado Springs area include the North American Air Defense Command (NORAD), Peterson Air Force Base, and Falcon Air Force Base.

Over the second half of the 20th Century, Colorado Springs has experienced phenomenal growth, increasing in size from around 70,000 residents in 1950 to more than 344,000 today. Now Colorado's second largest city, Colorado Springs remains a popular tourist destination as well as an important center for national defense operations.

Population

1990 Census 280,430
1998 Estimate..............................344,987
% Change 23.0
2005 Projection 557,941*

Racial/Ethnic Breakdown

White.................................. 86.1%
Black 7.0%
Other................................... 6.9%
Hispanic Origin (may be of any race) 9.1%

Age Breakdown

Under 5 years............................ 8.4%
5 to 17................................ 18.4%
18 to 20................................ 4.4%
21 to 24................................ 6.6%
25 to 34............................... 20.1%
35 to 44............................... 16.3%
45 to 54................................ 9.6%
55 to 64................................ 7.1%
65 to 74................................ 5.6%
75+ years 3.6%
Median Age...............................31.1

Gender Breakdown
Male 49.1%
Female 50.9%

* *Information given is for El Paso County.*

Government

Type of Government: Council-Manager

Colorado Springs City Attorney
30 S Nevada Ave Suite 501
Colorado Springs, CO 80903
Phone: 719-385-5909
Fax: 719-578-6209

Colorado Springs City Clerk
PO Box 1575
Colorado Springs, CO 80901
Phone: 719-385-5901
Fax: 719-578-6431

Colorado Springs City Council
PO Box 1575
Colorado Springs, CO 80901
Phone: 719-385-5900
Fax: 719-578-6601

Colorado Springs City Hall
PO Box 1575
Colorado Springs, CO 80901
Phone: 719-385-5900
Fax: 719-578-6601

Colorado Springs City Planning Office
30 S Nevada Ave Suite 301
Colorado Springs, CO 80903
Phone: 719-385-5905
Fax: 719-578-6303

Colorado Springs Finance Dept
30 S Nevada Ave Suite 401
Colorado Springs, CO 80903
Phone: 719-385-5900
Fax: 719-578-6432

Colorado Springs Fire Dept
31 S Weber St
Colorado Springs, CO 80903
Phone: 719-385-5950
Fax: 719-578-6027

Colorado Springs Human Resources Dept
30 S Nevada Ave Suite 105
Colorado Springs, CO 80903
Phone: 719-385-5904
Fax: 719-578-6715

Colorado Springs Mayor
PO Box 1575
Colorado Springs, CO 80901
Phone: 719-385-5900
Fax: 719-578-6601

Colorado Springs Neighborhood Services Dept
30 S Nevada Ave Suite 302
Colorado Springs, CO 80903
Phone: 719-385-5911
Fax: 719-578-6543

Colorado Springs Parks & Recreation Dept
1401 Recreation Way
Colorado Springs, CO 80905
Phone: 719-385-5940
Fax: 719-578-6934

Colorado Springs Police Dept
705 S Nevada Ave
Colorado Springs, CO 80903
Phone: 719-444-7401
Fax: 719-578-6169

Colorado Springs Public Works Dept
30 S Nevada Ave Suite 405
Colorado Springs, CO 80903
Phone: 719-385-5907
Fax: 719-578-6255

Colorado Springs Utilities Dept
PO Box 1103
Colorado Springs, CO 80947
Phone: 719-448-8000
Fax: 719-448-8020

Important Phone Numbers

AAA 719-591-2222
Colorado Springs Sales Tax Div 719-385-5903
Colorado State Revenue Dept 303-232-2416
Driver's License Information 719-594-8701
El Paso County Treasurer 719-520-6666
Emergency 911
Events Line 719-635-1723
Medical Referral 719-444-2273
Non-emergency Police 719-444-7000
Pikes Peak Assn of Realtors 719-633-7718
Poison Control Center 719-776-5333
Time/Temp 719-630-1111
Vehicle Registration Information 719-520-6240
Voter Registration Information 719-520-6225
Weather 719-573-6846

Information Sources

Better Business Bureau Serving the Pike's Peak Region
25 N Wahsatch Ave
Colorado Springs, CO 80903
www.coloradosprings.bbb.org
Phone: 719-636-1155
Fax: 719-636-5078

Colorado Springs Chamber of Commerce
PO Box B
Colorado Springs, CO 80901
www.cscc.org
Phone: 719-635-1551
Fax: 719-635-1571

Colorado Springs City Auditorium
221 E Kiowa St
Colorado Springs, CO 80903
Phone: 719-578-6652
Fax: 719-635-7806

Colorado Springs City Planning Office
30 S Nevada Ave Suite 301
Colorado Springs, CO 80903
www.colorado-springs.com/PublicPlan/indexDHTML.htm
Phone: 719-385-5905
Fax: 719-578-6303

Colorado Springs Convention & Visitors Bureau
104 S Cascade Ave Suite 104
Colorado Springs, CO 80903
www.coloradosprings-travel.com
Phone: 719-635-7506
Fax: 719-635-4968
TF: 800-368-4748

El Paso County
200 S Cascade Ave
Colorado Springs, CO 80903
www.co.el-paso.co.us
Phone: 719-520-6200

Greater Colorado Springs Economic Development Corp
90 S Cascade Ave Suite 1050
Colorado Springs, CO 80903
www.coloradosprings.org
Phone: 719-471-8183
Fax: 719-471-9733

Online Resources

4ColoradoSprings.com
www.4coloradosprings.com

About.com Guide to Colorado Springs/Pueblo
coloradospring.about.com/local/mountainus/coloradosprings

Anthill City Guide Colorado Springs
www.anthill.com/city.asp?city=coloradosprings

Area Guide Colorado Springs
coloradosprings.areaguides.net

City Knowledge Colorado Springs
www.cityknowledge.com/co_colorado_springs.htm

Colorado Springs Page
www.cospgs.com/

Excite.com Colorado Springs City Guide
www.excite.com/travel/countries/united_states/colorado/colorado_springs

Lodging.com Colorado Springs Colorado
www.lodging.com/auto/guides/colorado_springs-co.html

Pikes Peak Country Attractions
www.pikes-peak.com/

Surf the Springs
www.csurf.com/

Virtual Voyages Colorado Springs
www.virtualvoyages.com/usa/co/co_spgs/co_spgs.sht

Welcome to Colorado Springs
www.coloradosprings.com/

Area Communities

Communities in the Colorado Springs area with populations greater than 5,000 include:

Fountain
116 S Main St
Fountain, CO 80817
Phone: 719-382-8521
Fax: 719-382-5194

Woodland Park
PO Box 9007
Woodland Park, CO 80863
Phone: 719-687-9246
Fax: 719-687-5232

Economy

The economy of the Colorado Springs area relies heavily on its strong military presence—four of El Paso County's top 10 employers are defense-related. Roughly half of the county's 15 largest employers are government-related, at the federal, state, and local levels. High-technology manufacturing has played an important role in Colorado Springs' economy since the late 1970s and early 80s. Major U.S. companies that have a presence in the Colorado Springs area include Hewlett-Packard, SCI Systems, and Compaq Computer Corporation. Telecommunications is also a growing industry in the area. A majority of El Paso County's workforce is employed in service-related positions. The tourism industry continues to thrive in the Pikes Peak region, generating more than 740 million dollars annually and providing jobs for 13,000 area residents. Non-profit organizations such as Focus On The Family, the National Olympic Committee, and Junior Achievement (all of which have their national headquarters in Colorado Springs) also contribute significantly to the local economy, employing more than 12,000 people in the region.

Unemployment Rate 3.8%*
Per Capita Income $26,269**
Median Family Income $48,000**

* *Information given is for El Paso County.*
** *Information given is for the Colorado Springs Metropolitan Statistical Area (MSA), which includes the City of Colorado Springs and El Paso County.*

Principal Industries & Number of Wage Earners

El Paso County - 1997

Industry	Wage Earners
Agricultural Services, Forestry, & Fishing	1,291
Construction	12,220
Finance, Insurance, & Real Estate	10,768
Manufacturing	24,049
Mining	233
Retail Trade	41,972
Services	74,819
Transportation & Public Utilities	11,106
Wholesale Trade	8,423

Major Employers

Academy School District #20
7610 N Union Blvd
Colorado Springs, CO 80920
Phone: 719-598-2566
Fax: 719-598-9534

Atmel Corp
1150 E Cheyenne Mountain Blvd
Colorado Springs, CO 80906
Phone: 719-576-3300
Fax: 719-540-1074

Broadmoor Resort & County Club
1 Lake Ave
Colorado Springs, CO 80906
E-mail: info@broadmoor.com
www.broadmoor.com
Phone: 719-634-7711
Fax: 719-577-5700
TF: 800-634-7711

Colorado Springs City Hall
PO Box 1575
Colorado Springs, CO 80901
E-mail: credlightning@ci.colospgs.co.us
www.colorado-springs.com
Phone: 719-385-5900
Fax: 719-578-6601

Colorado Springs School District #11
1115 N El Paso St
Colorado Springs, CO 80903
www.cssd11.k12.co.us
Phone: 719-520-2000
Fax: 719-577-4546

Compaq Computer Corp
305 Rockrimmon Blvd S
Colorado Springs, CO 80919
Phone: 719-548-2000
Fax: 719-592-5255

Current Inc
1025 E Woodmen Rd
Colorado Springs, CO 80920
E-mail: currentcustomerservice@current.com
www.currentinc.com
Phone: 719-594-4100
Fax: 719-531-6510
TF: 800-525-7170

Deluxe Business Forms
8245 N Union Blvd
Colorado Springs, CO 80920
www.deluxe.com
Phone: 719-528-5010
Fax: 800-858-2204
TF: 800-328-7205

El Paso County
200 S Cascade Ave
Colorado Springs, CO 80903
www.co.el-paso.co.us
Phone: 719-520-6200

Fort Carson
Fort Carson, CO 80913
www.carson.army.mil
Phone: 719-526-5811
Fax: 719-526-1021

FutureCall Telemarketing West One
2550 Tenderfoot Hill St
Colorado Springs, CO 80906
www.futurecallinc.com
Phone: 719-867-7100
Fax: 719-576-2521
TF: 888-388-8731

Hewlett-Packard Co
4920 Centennial Blvd
Colorado Springs, CO 80919
www.hp.com
Phone: 719-272-4200
Fax: 719-272-4350

Memorial Hospital
1400 E Boulder St
Colorado Springs, CO 80909
Phone: 719-365-5000
Fax: 719-365-6884

Penrose-Saint Francis Healthcare
2215 N Cascade Ave
Colorado Springs, CO 80907
Phone: 719-776-5000
Fax: 719-776-2770

Peterson Air Force Base
Peterson AFB, CO 80914
www.spacecom.af.mil
Phone: 719-556-2107
Fax: 719-556-2109

Quantum Corp
10125 Federal Dr
Colorado Springs, CO 80908
Phone: 719-536-5000
Fax: 719-536-5564

SCI Systems Inc
5525 Astrozon Blvd
Colorado Springs, CO 80916
Phone: 719-380-5800
Fax: 719-380-5888

Shriever Air Force Base
Falcon AFB, CO 80912
www.schriever.af.mil/
Phone: 719-567-1110
Fax: 719-567-6459

US Air Force Academy
2304 Cadet Dr Suite 200
USAF Academy, CO 80840
www.usafa.af.mil
Phone: 719-333-1110
Fax: 719-333-3012
TF: 800-443-9266

WorldCom Inc
2424 Garden of the Gods Rd
Colorado Springs, CO 80919
www.wcom.com
Phone: 719-592-1300
Fax: 719-535-5660

Quality of Living Indicators

Total Crime Index....................................20,922
(rates per 100,000 inhabitants)

Violent Crime
Murder/manslaughter............................ 8
Forcible rape 267
Robbery...................................... 511
Aggravated assault...........................1,145

Property Crime
Burglary 3,483
Larceny theft 14,211
Motor vehicle theft 1,297

Cost of Living Index....................................100.4
(national average = 100)

Median Home Price.................................$144,900

Education

Public Schools

Colorado Springs School District #11
1115 N El Paso St
Colorado Springs, CO 80903
www.cssd11.k12.co.us
Phone: 719-520-2000
Fax: 719-577-4546

Number of Schools
Elementary.................................. 39
Middle 9
High.. 5

Student/Teacher Ratio
All Grades 19.0:1

Private Schools

Number of Schools (all grades).................... 66+

Colleges & Universities

Beth-El College of Nursing
1420 Austin Bluffs Pkwy
Colorado Springs, CO 80933
E-mail: admrec@mail.uccs.edu
www.uccs.edu/~bethel
Phone: 719-262-4422
Fax: 719-262-4416

Blair College
828 Wooten Rd
Colorado Springs, CO 80915
blair-college.com
Phone: 719-574-1082
Fax: 719-574-4493

Colorado Baptist College
3615 Vickers Dr
Colorado Springs, CO 80918
Phone: 719-593-7887
Fax: 719-593-1798

Colorado College
14 E Cache La Poudre St
Colorado Springs, CO 80903
www.cc.colorado.edu/External.asp
Phone: 719-389-6000
Fax: 719-389-6816
TF: 800-542-7214

Colorado Technical College
4435 N Chestnut St
Colorado Springs, CO 80907
E-mail: admissions@cos.colotechu.edu
www.colotechu.edu
Phone: 719-598-0200
Fax: 719-598-3740

National American University Colorado Springs Campus
2577 N Chelton Rd
Colorado Springs, CO 80909
www.nationalcollege.edu/campussprings.html
Phone: 719-471-4205
Fax: 719-471-4751
TF: 888-471-4781

Pikes Peak Community College
5675 S Academy Blvd
Colorado Springs, CO 80906
E-mail: cover@ppcc.colorado.edu
www.ppcc.cccoes.edu
Phone: 719-576-7711
Fax: 719-540-7092
TF: 800-456-6847

University of Colorado Colorado Springs
PO Box 7150
Colorado Springs, CO 80933
E-mail: goldmine@uccs.edu
www.uccs.edu
Phone: 719-262-3000
Fax: 719-262-3116
TF: 800-990-8227

US Air Force Academy
2304 Cadet Dr Suite 200
USAF Academy, CO 80840
www.usafa.af.mil
Phone: 719-333-1110
Fax: 719-333-3012
TF: 800-443-9266

Hospitals

Memorial Hospital
1400 E Boulder St
Colorado Springs, CO 80909
Phone: 719-365-5000
Fax: 719-365-6884

Penrose-Saint Francis Healthcare
2215 N Cascade Ave
Colorado Springs, CO 80907
Phone: 719-776-5000
Fax: 719-776-2770

Transportation

Airport(s)

Colorado Springs Municipal Airport (COS)
14 miles E of downtown (approx 20 minutes).....719-550-1900

Mass Transit

Colorado Springs Transit
$1.25 Base fare................................719-385-7433

Rail/Bus

TNM & O/Greyhound Bus Station
120 S Weber St
Colorado Springs, CO 80903
Phone: 719-635-1505
TF: 800-231-2222

Utilities

Electricity
Colorado Springs Utility Dept 719-448-8000

Gas
Colorado Springs Utility Dept 719-448-8000

Water
Colorado Springs Utility Dept 719-448-8000

Garbage Collection/Recycling
BFI Waste Systems 719-591-5000
Recycle America-Colorado Springs 719-633-0426
Waste Management Inc 719-632-8877

Telecommunications

Telephone
Qwest.......................................800-244-1111
www.qwest.com

Cable Television
Adelphia Cable...............................719-633-6616

Internet Service Providers (ISPs)
Globalynk Internet Solutions Inc 800-369-6677
www.globalynk.com

Banks

Bank of the Rockies NA
4328 Edison Ave
Colorado Springs, CO 80915
Phone: 719-574-8060
Fax: 719-574-8075

Bank One Colorado NA
30 E Pikes Peak Ave
Colorado Springs, CO 80903
Phone: 719-227-6405
Fax: 719-227-6420

Cheyenne Mountain Bank
1580 E Cheyenne Mountain Blvd
Colorado Springs, CO 80906
Phone: 719-579-9150
Fax: 719-576-4534

Colorado Springs National Bank
3100 N Nevada Ave
Colorado Springs, CO 80907
Phone: 719-473-2000
Fax: 719-473-2025

KeyBank NA
1521 S 8th St
Colorado Springs, CO 80906
Phone: 719-471-1300
Fax: 719-471-1307

Norwest Bank Colorado NA
PO Box 400
Colorado Springs, CO 80901
Phone: 719-590-7740
Fax: 719-577-5376

Peoples National Bank
5175 N Academy Blvd
Colorado Springs, CO 80918
E-mail: bank@epeoples.com
www.epeoples.com
Phone: 719-488-8900
Fax: 719-488-0754

UMB Bank Colorado NA
150 E Pikes Peak Ave
Colorado Springs, CO 80903
Phone: 719-634-6000
Fax: 719-634-7932

US Bank NA
6 S Tejon St
Colorado Springs, CO 80903
Phone: 719-473-1333
Fax: 719-577-9741

Shopping

Castle Rock Factory Shops
5050 Factory Shop Blvd
Castle Rock, CO 80104
Phone: 303-688-4494
Fax: 303-688-2344

Chapel Hills Mall
1710 Briargate Blvd
Colorado Springs, CO 80920
www.mallibu.com
Phone: 719-594-0111
Fax: 719-594-6439

Citadel Mall
750 Citadel Dr E
Colorado Springs, CO 80909
Phone: 719-591-2900
Fax: 719-597-4839

Downtown Colorado Springs Shops
Colorado Springs, CO 80901
Phone: 719-632-0553

Historical Old Colorado City
W Colorado Ave betw 24th & 28th Sts
Colorado Springs, CO 80934
Phone: 719-577-4112

Nevada Avenue Antiques
405 S Nevada Ave
Colorado Springs, CO 80903
Phone: 719-473-3351

Media

Newspapers and Magazines

Colorado Springs Independent
121 E Pikes Peak #455
Colorado Springs, CO 80903
www.csindy.com
Phone: 719-577-4545
Fax: 719-577-4107

Gazette The*
PO Box 1779
Colorado Springs, CO 80903
E-mail: gtnews@usa.net
www.gazette.com
Phone: 719-632-5511
Fax: 719-636-0202

**Indicates major daily newspapers*

Television

KKTV-TV Ch 11 (CBS)
3100 N Nevada Ave
Colorado Springs, CO 80907
kktv.cbsnow.com
Phone: 719-634-2844
Fax: 719-634-3741

KOAA-TV Ch 5 & 30 (NBC)
2200 7th Ave
Pueblo, CO 81003
E-mail: news@koaa.com
www.koaa.com
Phone: 719-544-5781
Fax: 719-543-5052

KRDO-TV Ch 13 (ABC)
399 S 8th St
Colorado Springs, CO 80905
Phone: 719-632-1515
Fax: 719-475-0815

KTSC-TV Ch 8 (PBS)
2200 Bonforte Blvd
Pueblo, CO 81001
Phone: 719-543-8800
Fax: 719-549-2208
TF: 800-388-6183

KXRM-TV Ch 21 (Fox)
560 Wooten Rd
Colorado Springs, CO 80915
www.kxrm.com
Phone: 719-596-2100
Fax: 719-591-4180

Radio

KCCY-FM 96.9 MHz (Ctry)
3185 Janitell Rd Suite 100
Colorado Springs, CO 80906
E-mail: kccy@codenet.net
www.kccyfm.com
Phone: 719-538-9690
Fax: 719-538-4456

KCMN-AM 1530 kHz (Nost)
5050 Edison Ave Suite 218
Colorado Springs, CO 80915
Phone: 719-570-1530
Fax: 719-570-1007

KEPC-FM 89.7 MHz (AAA)
5675 S Academy Blvd Box C49
Colorado Springs, CO 80906
Phone: 719-540-7489
Fax: 719-540-7453

KILO-FM 94.3 MHz (Rock)
1805 E Cheyenne Rd
Colorado Springs, CO 80906
www.kilo943.com
Phone: 719-634-4896
Fax: 719-634-5837
TF: 800-727-5456

KKCS-AM 1460 kHz (N/T)
5145 Centennial Blvd Suite 200
Colorado Springs, CO 80919
www.hottalk1460.com
Phone: 719-594-9000
Fax: 719-594-9006

KKCS-FM 101.9 MHz (Ctry)
5145 Centennial Blvd Suite 200
Colorado Springs, CO 80919
E-mail: requestline@cs102fm.com
www.cs102fm.com
Phone: 719-594-9000
Fax: 719-594-9006

KKFM-FM 98.1 MHz (CR)
6805 Corporate Dr Suite 130
Colorado Springs, CO 80919
E-mail: info@kkfm.com
www.kkfm.com
Phone: 719-593-2700
Fax: 719-593-2727

KKLI-FM 106.3 MHz (AC)
2864 S Circle Dr Suite 150
Colorado Springs, CO 80906
E-mail: comments@kkli.com
kkli.com
Phone: 719-540-9200
Fax: 719-579-0882

KRCC-FM 91.5 MHz (NPR)
912 N Weber St
Colorado Springs, CO 80903
E-mail: krcc@cc.colorado.edu
www.krcc.org
Phone: 719-473-4801
Fax: 719-473-7863

KRDO-AM 1240 kHz (Sports)
3 S 7th St
Colorado Springs, CO 80905
Phone: 719-632-1515
Fax: 719-635-8455

KRDO-FM 95.1 MHz (AC)
3 S 7th St
Colorado Springs, CO 80905
Phone: 719-632-1515
Fax: 719-635-8455

KSKX-FM 105.5 MHz (NAC)
3 S 7th St
Colorado Springs, CO 80905
Phone: 719-632-1515
Fax: 719-635-8455

KTLF-FM 90.5 MHz (Rel)
1665 Briargate Blvd Suite 100
Colorado Springs, CO 80920
E-mail: lightpraise@ktlf.org
www.ktlf.org
Phone: 719-593-0600
Fax: 719-593-2399

KTWK-AM 740 kHz (Nost)
2864 S Circle Dr Suite 150
Colorado Springs, CO 80906
www.memory740.com
Phone: 719-540-9200
Fax: 719-527-9253

KVOR-AM 1300 kHz (N/T)
6805 Corporate Dr Suite 130
Colorado Springs, CO 80919
www.kvor.com
Phone: 719-593-2700
Fax: 719-593-2727

KVUU-FM 99.9 MHz (AC)
2864 S Circle Dr Suite 150
Colorado Springs, CO 80906
www.kvuu.com
Phone: 719-540-9200
Fax: 719-579-0882

KWYD-AM 1580 kHz (Rel)
PO Box 5668
Colorado Springs, CO 80931
www.kwyd.com
Phone: 719-392-4219
Fax: 719-392-3307

KYZX-FM 103.9 MHz (CR)
1805 E Cheyenne Rd
Colorado Springs, CO 80906
www.1039theeagle.com
Phone: 719-634-4896
Fax: 719-634-4837

Attractions

In 1893, a trip to the summit of Pike's Peak inspired Katharine Lee Bates to write the words to "America the Beautiful." The 14,110-foot peak, located just outside Colorado Springs, is accessible today by car, cog railway, or hiking path. The region's natural beauty is evident also in the Cave of the Winds, the Garden of the Gods, and the Royal Gorge Bridge area. Buckskin Joe Park, an Old West theme park, has often been used as a movie set, and the Pro Rodeo Hall of Fame chronicles the history of America's original sport. Other historic attractions in the area include the 46-room Miramont Castle and the Manitou Cliff Dwellers Museum, a prehistoric Indian preserve located in nearby Manitou Springs.

American Numismatic Assn Money Museum
818 N Cascade Ave
Colorado Springs, CO 80903
E-mail: anamus@money.org
www.money.org/moneymus.html
Phone: 719-632-2646
Fax: 719-634-4085
TF: 800-367-9723

Bear Creek Nature Center
245 Bear Creek Rd
Colorado Springs, CO 80906
Phone: 719-520-6387
Fax: 719-520-6388

Bent's Old Fort National Historic Site
35110 Hwy 194 E
La Junta, CO 81050
www.nps.gov/beol/
Phone: 719-383-5010
Fax: 719-383-5031

Carriage House Museum
16 Lake Cir
Colorado Springs, CO 80906
Phone: 719-634-7711

Cave of the Winds
Hwy 24 W
Manitou Springs, CO 80829
E-mail: info@caveofthewinds.com
www.caveofthewinds.com
Phone: 719-685-5444
Fax: 719-685-1712

Cheyenne Mountain Zoological Park
4250 Cheyenne Mountain Zoo Rd
Colorado Springs, CO 80906
www.cmzoo.org
Phone: 719-633-9925
Fax: 719-633-2254

Children's Museum of Colorado Springs
750 Citadel Dr E Suite 3116
Colorado Springs, CO 80909
E-mail: museum@usa.net
www.iex.net/cm
Phone: 719-574-0077
Fax: 719-574-0077

Colorado Music Hall
2475 E Pikes Peak Ave
Colorado Springs, CO 80909
Phone: 719-447-9797
Fax: 719-447-1893

Colorado Springs Choral Society
PO Box 2304
Colorado Springs, CO 80901
www.cschorale.org
Phone: 719-634-3737
Fax: 719-473-0077

Colorado Springs Dance Theatre
7 E Bijou St Suite 209
Colorado Springs, CO 80903
www.csdance.org
Phone: 719-630-7434
Fax: 719-442-2095

Colorado Springs Fine Arts Center
30 W Dale St
Colorado Springs, CO 80903
www.rmi.net/home/tour/colorado/cities/cosprgs/csfac.shtml
Phone: 719-634-5581
Fax: 719-634-0570

Colorado Springs Pioneers Museum
215 S Tejon St
Colorado Springs, CO 80903
Phone: 719-385-5990
Fax: 719-634-0570

Colorado Springs Symphony Orchestra
619 N Cascade Ave
Colorado Springs, CO 80903
E-mail: csso@access.usa.net
www.cssymphony.org
Phone: 719-633-4611
Fax: 719-633-6699

Curecanti National Recreation Area
102 Elk Creek
Gunnison, CO 81230
www.nps.gov/cure/
Phone: 970-641-2337
Fax: 970-641-3127

Florissant Fossil Beds National Monument
PO Box 185
Florissant, CO 80816
www.nps.gov/flfo/
Phone: 719-748-3253
Fax: 719-748-3164

Garden of the Gods Park
3130 N 30th St
Colorado Springs, CO 80904
www.pikes-peak.com/Garden/
Phone: 719-385-5940
Fax: 719-578-6934

Ghost Town Museum
400 S 21st St
Colorado Springs, CO 80904
Phone: 719-634-0696
Fax: 719-634-2435

Historical Old Colorado City
W Colorado Ave betw 24th & 28th Sts
Colorado Springs, CO 80934
Phone: 719-577-4112

Joe Buckskin Park & Railway
1193 County Rd 3A
Canon City, CO 81212
Phone: 719-275-5485
Fax: 719-275-6270

Magic Town
2418 W Colorado Ave
Colorado Springs, CO 80904
Phone: 719-471-9391

Manitou Cliff Dwellings Museum
Hwy 24 W
Manitou Springs, CO 80829
E-mail: cd@manitousprings.zzn.com
www.cliffdwellingsmuseum.com
Phone: 719-685-5242
Fax: 719-685-1562

May Natural History Museum & Museum of Space Exploration
710 Rock Creek Canyon Rd
Colorado Springs, CO 80926
E-mail: maymuseum@yahoo.com
www.maymuseum-camp-rvpark.com
Phone: 719-576-0450
Fax: 719-576-3644
TF: 800-666-3841

McAllister House Museum
423 N Cascade Ave
Colorado Springs, CO 80903
Phone: 719-635-7925

Miramont Castle Museum
9 Capitol Hill Ave
Manitou Springs, CO 80829
Phone: 719-685-1011
Fax: 719-685-1985
TF: 888-685-1011

Pike National Forest
601 S Weber St
Colorado Springs, CO 80903
www.fs.fed.us/r2/psicc
Phone: 719-636-1602
Fax: 719-477-4233

Pikes Peak Auto Hill Climb Museum
135 Manitou Ave
Manitou Springs, CO 80829
www.ppihc.com
Phone: 719-685-4400
Fax: 719-685-5885

Pikes Peak Center
190 S Cascade Ave
Colorado Springs, CO 80903
www.pikespeakcenter.org
Phone: 719-520-7453
Fax: 719-520-7462

Pikes Peak Cog Railway
515 Ruxton Ave
Manitou Springs, CO 80829
E-mail: cogtrain@mail.usa.net
www.cograilway.com/
Phone: 719-685-5401
Fax: 719-685-9033

Pikes Peak Highway Phone: 719-684-9383
Cascade, CO 80809

Pro Rodeo Hall of Fame & Museum of the American Cowboy Phone: 719-528-4764
101 Pro Rodeo Dr Fax: 719-548-4874
Colorado Springs, CO 80919
electricstores.com/Rodeo

Rock Ledge Ranch Phone: 719-578-6777
N 30th St & Gateway Rd
Colorado Springs, CO 80904

Rocky Mountain Motorcycle Museum & Hall of Fame Phone: 719-633-6329
302 E Arvada St Fax: 719-633-6329
Colorado Springs, CO 80906

Seven Falls Phone: 719-632-0765
2850 S Cheyenne Canyon Rd Fax: 719-632-0781
Colorado Springs, CO 80906

Smokebrush Center for Arts & Theater Phone: 719-444-0884
235 S Nevada Ave Fax: 719-471-7351
Colorado Springs, CO 80903
E-mail: info@smokebrush.org
www.smokebrush.org

Starsmore Discovery Center Phone: 719-578-6147
2120 S Cheyenne Canyon Rd Fax: 719-578-6149
Colorado Springs, CO 80906

University of Colorado Gallery of Contemporary Art Phone: 719-262-3567
1420 Austin Bluffs Pkwy Fax: 719-262-3183
Colorado Springs, CO 80918

US Olympic Center Complex Phone: 719-578-4500
1 Olympic Plaza Fax: 719-578-4677
Colorado Springs, CO 80909
www.usoc.org

US Olympic Hall of Fame Phone: 719-578-4618
1750 E Boulder St Fax: 719-578-4728
Colorado Springs, CO 80909
www.usoc.org

Western Museum of Mining & Industry Phone: 719-488-0880
1025 N Gate Rd Fax: 719-488-9261
Colorado Springs, CO 80921
E-mail: admin@wmmi.org
www.wmmi.org

World Figure Skating Museum & Hall of Fame Phone: 719-635-5200
20 1st St Fax: 719-635-9548
Colorado Springs, CO 80906
www.usfsa.org

Sports Teams & Facilities

Colorado Gold Kings (hockey) Phone: 719-579-9000
3185 Venetucci Blvd Fax: 719-579-7609
Colorado Springs, CO 80906
www.coloradogoldkings.com

Colorado Springs Sky Sox (baseball) Phone: 719-597-3000
4385 Tutt Blvd Sky Sox Stadium Fax: 719-597-2491
Colorado Springs, CO 80922
www.skysox.com/

Colorado Springs Stampede (soccer) Phone: 719-282-9452
8158 Lockport Dr Fax: 719-593-0900
Colorado Springs, CO 80920

Pikes Peak International Raceway Phone: 719-382-7223
16650 Midway Ranch Fax: 719-382-9180
Fountain, CO 80817 TF: 888-306-7223
www.ppir.com/

Rocky Mountain Greyhound Park Phone: 719-632-1391
3701 N Nevada Ave Fax: 719-632-1792
Colorado Springs, CO 80907
www.rmgp.com

Sky Sox Stadium Phone: 719-597-3000
4385 Tutt Blvd Fax: 719-597-2491
Colorado Springs, CO 80922
www.skysox.com/boxoffice/index.shtml

Annual Events

Balloon Classic (early September) 719-471-4833
Carnivale & Gumbo Cook-off (early February) 719-685-5089
Cavalcade of Music (early May).....................719-520-7469
Cinco de Mayo Celebration (early May).............719-262-3447
Clayfest & Mud Ball (mid-June)...................719-685-5089
Colorado Championship Chili Cook-off (early July) 719-593-2700
Colorado Springs Opera Festival (late July-early August).........................719-473-0073
Donkey Derby Days (late June) 719-689-3315
El Paso County Fair (late July) 719-575-8690
Fabulous Fourth (July 4).........................719-633-4611
Family Day & Antique Car Show (mid-September) 719-488-0880
Farmers' Market (July-September).................719-574-1283
First Night Pikes Peak (December 31) 719-471-9790
Food-A-Rama (early February) 719-576-4228
Gallery of Trees & Lights (December) 719-634-5581
Great Fruitcake Toss (early January) 719-685-5089
In Their Honor Parade & Air Show (early November).............................719-635-8803
July 4th on the 3rd (July 3) 719-635-8803
Kwanzaa Cultural Celebration (late December-early January)...................719-473-6566
Labor Day Arts & Crafts Festival (early September)...719-685-1008
Lone Feather Indian Council Pow Wow (mid-July) ...719-495-0798
Madrigal Christmas Celebration (late November-mid-December) 719-594-2237
Mountain Arts Festival (early August).............719-687-8298
National Little Britches Finals Rodeo (late July) 719-520-6711
Oktoberfest (early October).......................719-635-7506
Pikes Peak Auto Hill Climb (July 4) 719-685-4400
Pikes Peak Highland Games & Celtic Festival (mid-July) 719-481-4597
Pikes Peak Invitational Soccer Tournament (late June-early July)..........................719-590-9977
Pikes Peak or Bust Rodeo (early-mid-August) 719-520-7462
Pikes Peak or Bust Rodeo Parade (early August)....719-635-8803
Race to the Clouds (July 4)......................719-685-4400
Saint Patrick's Day Parade (mid-March) 719-635-8803
Taste of the Nation (early May) 719-528-6148
Territory Days Celebration (late May).............719-475-0955
Zebulon! A Festival of Arts (late June-late July) 719-475-2465

Columbia, South Carolina

***County:* Richland**

COLUMBIA is located in the Central Midlands of South Carolina at the confluence of the Broad, Saluda, and Congaree Rivers. Major cities within 100 miles include Spartanburg, South Carolina; Charlotte, North Carolina; and Augusta, Georgia.

Area (Land) .... 117.1 sq mi
Area (Water)................................ 1.9 sq mi
Elevation...................................... 213 ft
Latitude ....33-99-89 N
Longitude................................ 81-03-53 W
Time Zone ....EST
Area Code.. 803

Climate

Columbia has a temperate inland climate with four distinct seasons. Winters are generally mild with average high temperatures in the mid- to upper 50s, average lows around 30, and minimal snowfall. Summers are hot and humid with daytime high temperatures around 90 degrees and lows around 70. Thunderstorms are common during the summer months—July and August are the wettest months of the year; October and November are the driest.

Average Temperatures & Precipitation

Temperatures

	Jan	Feb	Mar	Apr	May	Jun	Jul	Aug	Sep	Oct	Nov	Dec
High	55	59	68	77	84	89	92	90	85	76	68	59
Low	22	34	42	49	58	66	70	69	69	50	42	35

Precipitation

	Jan	Feb	Mar	Apr	May	Jun	Jul	Aug	Sep	Oct	Nov	Dec
Inches	4.4	4.1	4.8	3.3	3.7	4.8	5.5	6.1	3.7	3.0	2.9	3.6

History

Originally inhabited by the Congaree Indians, the present-day city of Columbia was laid out in a two-square-mile grid in 1786 as South Carolina's new, centrally-located state capital. (Charleston, located along the South Carolina coast, had been the state's original capital city, but tensions between coastal settlers and inland settlers led the state to move the capital to the geographic center of the state.) Columbia's first state house, designed by John Hoban, bore a striking resemblance to the White House in Washington, DC, also designed by Hoban. Columbia thrived as a major center for cotton production during the 1800s, and was home to 8,000 people by the start of the Civil War. Much of the city of Columbia, including the original State Capitol Building was destroyed in February 1865 when the city was set afire by Union soldiers. The present State Capitol Building was under construction when the city was burned, and bronze stars have been placed on the building to indicate the marks left by General Sherman's cannons.

Columbia's residents worked diligently to rebuild the city following the Civil War, and by the early 1900s the new Columbia included a public school system, an African-American college (Allen University), nine railroad lines, and new industry spawned by fertilizer factories and textile mills that drew people to the area. World War I brought the creation of Camp Jackson (named for Andrew Jackson) to the area in 1917, and within a year, 70,000 U.S. troops were training at the base. Renamed Fort Jackson during World War II, the military installation remains the U.S. Army's largest initial entry training center and is one of the area's top five employers.

Columbia has been South Carolina's largest city since 1950, and the city has continued to grow as an industrial, financial, and transportation center. Columbia today is home to more than 110,000 people, and it is estimated that by the year 2010 the population of the Columbia metropolitan area will exceed 587,000.

Population

1990 Census 103,477
1998 Estimate.............................110,840
% Change 0.1
2010 Projection 331,880*

Racial/Ethnic Breakdown
White...................................50.9%
Black 46.6%
Other....................................7.7%
Hispanic Origin (may be of any race) 2.0%

Age Breakdown
Under 5 years.............................. 6.2%
5 to 17...................................13.5%
18 to 20..................................12.2%
21 to 24..................................10.8%
25 to 34..................................19.9%
35 to 44..................................13.0%
45 to 54................................... 6.7%
55 to 64................................... 6.0%
65 to 74................................... 6.6%
75+ years 5.3%
Median Age.................................28.4

Gender Breakdown
Male....................................46.6%
Female..................................53.4%

* *Information given is for Richland County.*

Government

Type of Government: Council-Manager

Columbia City Attorney
PO Box 667
Columbia, SC 29202
Phone: 803-733-8247
Fax: 803-733-8464

Columbia City Clerk
PO Box 147
Columbia, SC 29217
Phone: 803-733-8225
Fax: 803-733-8317

Columbia City Hall
PO Box 147
Columbia, SC 29217
Phone: 803-733-8200
Fax: 803-343-8719

Columbia City Manager
PO Box 147
Columbia, SC 29217
Phone: 803-733-8223
Fax: 803-733-8317

Columbia Community Development Dept
1225 Laurel St
Columbia, SC 29201
Phone: 803-733-8315
Fax: 803-988-8014

Columbia Economic Development Office
PO Box 147
Columbia, SC 29217
Phone: 803-733-8278
Fax: 803-988-8035

Columbia Finance Dept
PO Box 147
Columbia, SC 29217
Phone: 803-733-8256
Fax: 803-733-8237

Columbia Fire Dept
1800 Laurel St
Columbia, SC 29201
Phone: 803-733-8351
Fax: 803-733-8311

Columbia Mayor
PO Box 147
Columbia, SC 29217
Phone: 803-733-8221
Fax: 803-733-8633

Columbia Parks & Recreation Dept
1932 Calhoun St
Columbia, SC 29201
Phone: 803-733-8331
Fax: 803-343-8744

Columbia Personnel Dept
1737 Main St
Columbia, SC 29217
Phone: 803-733-8264
Fax: 803-343-8752

Columbia Planning Dept
1225 Laurel St
Columbia, SC 29217
Phone: 803-733-8343
Fax: 803-733-8312

Columbia Police Dept
1409 Lincoln St
Columbia, SC 29201
Phone: 803-733-8415
Fax: 803-733-8326

Columbia Public Works Dept
2910 Colonial Dr
Columbia, SC 29203
Phone: 803-733-8458
Fax: 803-733-8648

Columbia Water Dept
1225 Laurel St
Columbia, SC 29202
Phone: 803-733-8285
Fax: 803-733-8219

Important Phone Numbers

AAA 803-798-9205
Driver's License Information 803-737-4000
Emergency 911
Greater Columbia Assn of Realtors 803-771-8852
HotelDocs 800-468-3537
Medical Referral 803-765-1498
Poison Control Center 803-777-1117
Richland County Auditor 803-748-4955
South Carolina Taxpayer Service Center 803-898-5000
Time/Temp 803-714-9900
Travelers Aid Society 803-343-7071
Vehicle Registration Information 803-737-4000
Voter Registration Information 803-748-4944
Weather 803-822-8135

Information Sources

Better Business Bureau Serving Central South Carolina & the Charleston Area
PO Box 8326
Columbia, SC 29202
www.columbia.bbb.org
Phone: 803-254-2525
Fax: 803-779-3117

Central Carolina Economic Development Alliance
930 Richland St
Columbia, SC 29201
www.cceda.org
Phone: 803-733-1131
Fax: 803-733-1125

Columbia Community Development Dept
1225 Laurel St
Columbia, SC 29201
Phone: 803-733-8315
Fax: 803-988-8014

Columbia Economic Development Office
PO Box 147
Columbia, SC 29217
www.columbiasc.net/city/city1b.htm
Phone: 803-733-8278
Fax: 803-988-8035

Columbia Metropolitan Convention & Visitors Bureau
PO Box 15
Columbia, SC 29202
www.columbiasc.net
Phone: 803-254-0479
Fax: 803-799-6529
TF: 800-264-4884

Greater Columbia Chamber of Commerce
930 Richland St
Columbia, SC 29201
www.gcbn.com
Phone: 803-733-1110
Fax: 803-733-1149

Richland County
2020 Hampton St
Columbia, SC 29204
www.richlanddata.com
Phone: 803-748-4600
Fax: 803-748-4644

Online Resources

About.com Guide to Columbia
columbiasc.about.com/citiestowns/southeastus/columbiasc

Anthill City Guide Columbia
www.anthill.com/city.asp?city=columbia

Area Guide Columbia
columbiasc.areaguides.net

City Knowledge Columbia
www.cityknowledge.com/sc_columbia.htm

CityTravelers.com Guide to Columbia
www.citytravelers.com/columbia.htm

Columbia A to Z
www.columbiasouthcarolina.com/

Columbia Directory
www.scad.com/columbia/

Columbia Free Times
www.free-times.com/

Columbia Home Page
www.columbiasc.net/

Columbia Metropolitan Magazine
www.columbiametro.com/

Excite.com Columbia City Guide
www.excite.com/travel/countries/united_states/south_carolina/columbia

Area Communities

Communities in Greater Columbia with populations greater than 5,000 include:

Cayce
1800 12h St
Cayce, SC 29033
Phone: 803-796-9020
Fax: 803-796-9072

Forest Acres
PO Box 6587
Forest Acres, SC 29260
Phone: 803-782-9475
Fax: 803-782-3183

Irmo
PO Box 406
Irmo, SC 29063
Phone: 803-781-7050
Fax: 803-749-2743

Lexington
PO Box 397
Lexington, SC 29071
Phone: 803-359-4164
Fax: 803-359-4460

Newberry
PO Box 538
Newberry, SC 29108
Phone: 803-321-1000
Fax: 803-321-1003

West Columbia
1053 Center St
West Columbia, SC 29169
Phone: 803-791-1880
Fax: 803-739-6231

Economy

Columbia has a diverse economic base that ranges from high finance to food products manufacturing. Services, with health care accounting for one-fifth of service employment, and government are the largest employment sectors in the metro area. Government plays a primary role in Greater Columbia's economy. In addition to the major employers listed below, South Carolina State Government is the single largest employer in the area, providing jobs for more than 39,000 area residents. Federal government also ranks among the top five, employing more than 8,000 area residents in various offices.

Unemployment Rate 2.8%*
Per Capita Income $23,874*
Median Family Income $49,400*

** Information given is for Richland County.*

Principal Industries & Number of Wage Earners

Columbia Metropolitan Area* - 1999

Industry	Wage Earners
Construction & Mining	17,200
Finance, Insurance, & Real Estate	22,900
Government	75,700
Manufacturing	27,100
Retail Trade	51,000
Services	75,700
Transportation & Public Utilities	13,500
Wholesale Trade	17,500

** Information given is for the Columbia Metropolitan Area, which includes Lexington and Richland counties.*

Major Employers

Bank of America
1901 Main St
Columbia, SC 29201
Phone: 803-255-7555
Fax: 803-255-7550

Baptist Medical Center
1330 Taylor St
Columbia, SC 29220
Phone: 803-771-5010
Fax: 803-771-5462

BellSouth
250 Berryhill Rd Suite 300
Columbia, SC 29210
www.bellsouth.com
Phone: 803-750-2500
Fax: 803-750-2580

Blue Cross & Blue Shield of South Carolina
I-20 E & Alpine Rd
Columbia, SC 29219
E-mail: webinfo@bcbssc.com
www.bcbssc.com
Phone: 803-788-0222
Fax: 803-699-3792
TF: 800-845-3492

Columbia City Hall
PO Box 147
Columbia, SC 29217
www.columbiasc.net
Phone: 803-733-8200
Fax: 803-343-8719

Fort Jackson
Fort Jackson, SC 29207
jackson-www.army.mil
Phone: 803-751-7511
Fax: 803-751-3533

Mynd Corp
PO Box 10
Columbia, SC 29202
www.mynd.com
Phone: 803-333-4000
Fax: 803-333-5544

Palmetto Richland Memorial Hospital
5 Richland Medical Pk
Columbia, SC 29203
E-mail: info@rmh.edu
www.rmh.edu
Phone: 803-434-7000
Fax: 803-434-6982

Richland County
2020 Hampton St
Columbia, SC 29204
www.richlanddata.com
Phone: 803-748-4600
Fax: 803-748-4644

Richland County School District One
1616 Richland St
Columbia, SC 29201
www.richlandone.org
Phone: 803-733-6000
Fax: 803-253-5725

South Carolina Electric & Gas Co
Columbia, SC 29218
www.scana.com/sce&g
Phone: 803-748-3000
Fax: 803-217-8119

University of South Carolina
Columbia, SC 29208
E-mail: admissions-ugrad@sc.edu
www.sc.edu
Phone: 803-777-7000
Fax: 803-777-0302
TF: 800-922-9755

Wachovia Bank NA
1426 Main St
Columbia, SC 29226
www.wachovia.com
Phone: 803-765-3945
Fax: 803-988-4545
TF: 800-922-7750

Quality of Living Indicators

Total Crime Index .... na
(rates per 100,000 inhabitants)

Violent Crime
Murder/manslaughter 17
Forcible rape 72
Robbery 490
Aggravated assault 846

Property Crime
Burglary 1,281
Larceny theft .... na
Motor vehicle theft 740

Cost of Living Index 97.1
(national average = 100)

Median Home Price $109,500

Education

Public Schools

Richland County School District One
1616 Richland St
Columbia, SC 29201
www.richlandone.org
Phone: 803-733-6000
Fax: 803-253-5725

Number of Schools
Elementary 30
Middle 8
High 7
Other 6

Student/Teacher Ratio
All Grades 13.9:1

Private Schools

Number of Schools (all grades) .... 45+

Colleges & Universities

Allen University
1530 Harden St
Columbia, SC 29204
Phone: 803-254-4165
Fax: 803-376-5709

Benedict College
1600 Harden St
Columbia, SC 29204
Phone: 803-256-4220
Fax: 803-253-5167
TF: 800-868-6598

Columbia College
1301 Columbia College Dr
Columbia, SC 29203
Phone: 803-786-3012
Fax: 803-786-3674

Columbia International University
7435 Monticello Rd
Columbia, SC 29230
E-mail: publicrelations@ciu.edu
www.gospelcom.net/ciu/
Phone: 803-754-4100
Fax: 803-786-4209
TF: 800-777-2227

Columbia Junior College of Business
3810 Main St
Columbia, SC 29203
Phone: 803-799-9082
Fax: 803-799-9038

Midlands Technical College
PO Box 2408
Columbia, SC 29202
www.mid.tec.sc.us
Phone: 803-738-1400
Fax: 803-738-7784

Morris College
100 W College St
Sumter, SC 29150
www.morris.edu
Phone: 803-775-9371
Fax: 803-773-3687
TF: 800-778-1345

University of South Carolina
Columbia, SC 29208
E-mail: admissions-ugrad@sc.edu
www.sc.edu
Phone: 803-777-7000
Fax: 803-777-0302
TF: 800-922-9755

Hospitals

Baptist Medical Center
1330 Taylor St
Columbia, SC 29220
Phone: 803-771-5010
Fax: 803-771-5462

Lexington Medical Center
2720 Sunset Blvd
West Columbia, SC 29169
www.lexmed.com
Phone: 803-791-2000
Fax: 803-791-2483

Palmetto Richland Memorial Hospital
5 Richland Medical Pk
Columbia, SC 29203
www.rmh.edu
Phone: 803-434-7000
Fax: 803-434-6982

Providence Hospital
2435 Forest Dr
Columbia, SC 29204
www.provhosp.com
Phone: 803-256-5300
Fax: 803-256-5358

William Jennings Bryan Dorn Veterans Hospital
6439 Garners Ferry Rd
Columbia, SC 29209
Phone: 803-776-4000
Fax: 803-695-6799

Transportation

Airport(s)

Columbia Metropolitan Airport (CAE)
7-10 miles SW of downtown (approx 20 minutes) ... 803-822-5010

Mass Transit

SCE & G City Bus
$.75 Base fare 803-748-3019

Rail/Bus

Amtrak Station
850 Pulaski St
Columbia, SC 29201
Phone: 803-252-8246
TF: 800-872-7245

Greyhound Bus Station
2015 Gervais St
Columbia, SC 29204
Phone: 803-256-6465
TF: 800-231-2222

Utilities

Electricity
South Carolina Electric & Gas Co. 803-799-9000
www.goscana.com

Gas
South Carolina Electric & Gas Co. 803-799-9000
www.goscana.com

Water
Columbia Water Dept 803-733-8285

Garbage Collection/Recycling
Columbia Sanitation Dept 803-733-8456

Telecommunications

Telephone
BellSouth 800-336-0014
www.bellsouth.com

Cable Television
Benchmark Communications 803-736-9666
Time Warner Cable 803-252-2253
www.timewarner.com

Internet Service Providers (ISPs)
Conterra Communications Inc 803-733-2993
www.conterra.com
LogicSouth Inc 803-732-7757
www.logicsouth.com
Renaissance Interactive Inc 803-748-0506
www.ricommunity.com

Banks

Bank of America
1901 Main St
Columbia, SC 29201
Phone: 803-255-7555
Fax: 803-255-7550

Branch Banking & Trust Co of South Carolina
1901 Assembly St
Columbia, SC 29202
Phone: 803-251-1300
Fax: 803-251-1777
TF: 800-421-9899

Carolina First Bank
1501 Main St
Columbia, SC 29211
Phone: 803-540-2700
Fax: 803-540-2705

First Citizens Bank & Trust Co
1230 Main St
Columbia, SC 29201
Phone: 803-771-8700
Fax: 803-733-3480

Wachovia Bank NA
1426 Main St
Columbia, SC 29226
www.wachovia.com
Phone: 803-765-3945
Fax: 803-988-4545
TF: 800-922-7750

Shopping

Columbia Mall
7201 Two Notch Rd
Columbia, SC 29223
E-mail: columbiamall@rejacobsgroup.com
www.shopyourmall.com/mall_welcome.asp?map=yes&mall_select=611
Phone: 803-788-4676

Columbiana Centre Mall
100 Columbiana Cir
Columbia, SC 29212
Phone: 803-732-6255

Dutch Square Center
Broad River at Bush River Rd
Columbia, SC 29210
Phone: 803-772-3864

Market Pointe Mall
300-13 Outlet Pointe Blvd
Columbia, SC 29210
Phone: 803-798-8520
Fax: 803-798-8520

Old Mill Antique Mall
310 State St
West Columbia, SC 29169
Phone: 803-796-4229

Old Towne Antique Mall
2956 Broad River Rd
Columbia, SC 29210
Phone: 803-772-9335

Richland Fashion Mall
3400 Forest Dr
Columbia, SC 29204
Phone: 803-738-2995

Media

Newspapers and Magazines

State The*
PO Box 1333
Columbia, SC 29202
E-mail: cyberst@cyberstate.infi.net
www.thestate.com
Phone: 803-771-6161
Fax: 803-771-8430

**Indicates major daily newspapers*

Television

WACH-TV Ch 57 (Fox)
1400 Pickens St
Columbia, SC 29201
www.wach.com
Phone: 803-252-5757
Fax: 803-212-7270

WIS-TV Ch 10 (NBC)
1111 Bull St
Columbia, SC 29201
E-mail: wis-tv10@aol.com
www.wistv.com
Phone: 803-758-1218
Fax: 803-758-1278

WLTX-TV Ch 19 (CBS)
6027 Garner's Ferry Rd
Columbia, SC 29209
Phone: 803-776-3600
Fax: 803-776-1791

WOLO-TV Ch 25 (ABC)
5807 Shakespeare Rd
Columbia, SC 29223
E-mail: info@wolo.com
www.wolo.com
Phone: 803-754-7525
Fax: 803-754-6147

WQHB-TV Ch 63 (PAX)
PO Box 160
Sumter, SC 29151
www.pax.net/WQHB
Phone: 803-775-2817
Fax: 803-775-4486

Radio

WARQ-FM 93.5 MHz (Rock)
1900 Pineview Rd
Columbia, SC 29209
E-mail: rock935@aol.com
www.warq.com
Phone: 803-695-8680
Fax: 803-695-8605

WCOS-AM 1400 kHz (Sports)
56 Radio Ln
Columbia, SC 29210
www.allsportstalk.com
Phone: 803-772-5600
Fax: 803-798-5255

WLTR-FM 91.3 MHz (NPR)
1101 George Rogers Blvd
Columbia, SC 29201
Phone: 803-737-3420
Fax: 803-737-3552

WLTY-FM 96.7 MHz (AC)
PO Box 748
Columbia, SC 29202
Phone: 803-254-0967
Fax: 803-779-7572

WMFX-FM 102.3 MHz (Ctry)
1900 Pineview Rd
Columbia, SC 29209
Phone: 803-742-9639
Fax: 803-695-8605

WNOK-FM 104.7 MHz (CHR)
1300 Pickens St
Columbia, SC 29201
www.wnok.com
Phone: 803-771-0105
Fax: 803-779-7874

WOIC-AM 1230 kHz (Rel)
1900 Pineview Rd
Columbia, SC 29209
E-mail: sales@woic.com
www.woic.com
Phone: 803-776-1013
Fax: 803-695-8605

WQXL-AM 1470 kHz (Rel)
1303 Sunset Dr
Columbia, SC 29203
E-mail: wqxl@aol.com
Phone: 803-779-7911
Fax: 803-252-2158

WTCB-FM 106.7 MHz (AC)
PO Box 5106
Columbia, SC 29250
Phone: 803-796-7600
Fax: 803-796-9291

WVOC-AM 560 kHz (N/T)
PO Box 21567
Columbia, SC 29221
E-mail: mail@wvoc.com
www.wvoc.com
Phone: 803-772-5600
Fax: 803-798-5255

WWDM-FM 101.3 MHz (Urban)
PO Box 9127
Columbia, SC 29290
www.thebigdm.com
Phone: 803-776-1013
Fax: 803-695-8605

Attractions

Columbia has one of the top zoological parks in the U.S., Riverbanks Zoo, with more than 2,000 animals. Lake Murray is a popular outdoor recreation area for residents and visitors alike, with more than 540 miles of shoreline. Among the many antebellum historic homes and churches in Columbia is the First Baptist Church where the first secession convention opened in 1860. Another historic site in Columbia is the cottage built by Cecilia Mann, a black slave born in Charleston who bought her freedom and walked to Columbia.

Ashland Park
St Andrews Rd & I-26
Columbia, SC 29210
Phone: 803-256-9000

Carolina Ballet
914 Pulaski St
Columbia, SC 29201
Phone: 803-771-6303
Fax: 803-771-2625

Carolina Coliseum
701 Assembly St
Columbia, SC 29201
Phone: 803-777-5113
Fax: 803-777-5114

Cayce Historical Museum
1800 12th St
Cayce, SC 29033
Phone: 803-796-9020
Fax: 803-796-9072

Columbia City Ballet
1128 Taylor St
Columbia, SC 29201
E-mail: email@columbiacityballet.com
www.columbiacityballet.com
Phone: 803-799-7605
Fax: 803-799-7928
TF: 800-899-7408

Columbia Fire Department Museum
1800 Laurel St
Columbia, SC 29201
Phone: 803-733-8350
Fax: 803-733-8311

Columbia Marionette Theatre
401 Laurel St
Columbia, SC 29201
www.scescape.com/marionette
Phone: 803-252-7366
Fax: 803-252-7669

Columbia Museum of Art
PO Box 2068
Columbia, SC 29202
E-mail: ktucker@colmusart.org
www.colmusart.org
Phone: 803-799-2810
Fax: 803-343-2150

Columbia Riverfront Park & Historic Canal
312 Laurel St
Columbia, SC 29201
Phone: 803-733-8331

Confederate Relic Room & Museum
920 Sumter St
Columbia, SC 29201
www.state.sc.us/crr
Phone: 803-898-8095
Fax: 803-898-8099

Congaree Swamp National Monument
200 Caroline Sims Rd
Hopkins, SC 29061
www.nps.gov/cosw
Phone: 803-776-4396
Fax: 803-783-4241

Dreher Island State Park
3677 State Park Rd
Prosperity, SC 29127
Phone: 803-364-3530
Fax: 803-364-0756

Finlay Park
930 Laurel St
Columbia, SC 29201
Phone: 803-733-8331

First Baptist Church
1306 Hampton St
Columbia, SC 29201
Phone: 803-256-4251
Fax: 803-343-8584

Fort Jackson Museum
2179 Sumter St
Fort Jackson, SC 29207
Phone: 803-751-7419
Fax: 803-751-4434

Francis Marion-Sumter National Forest
4931 Broad River Rd
Columbia, SC 29212
www.fs.fed.us/r8/fms
Phone: 803-561-4000
Fax: 803-561-4004

Governor's Mansion & Green
800 Richland St
Columbia, SC 29201
Phone: 803-737-1710
Fax: 803-737-3860

Hampton-Preston Mansion & Garden
1615 Blanding St
Columbia, SC 29201
Phone: 803-252-1770

Keenan Ensor House
801 Wildwood Ave
Columbia, SC 29203
Phone: 803-733-8510

Koger Center for the Arts
1051 Greene St
Columbia, SC 29201
Phone: 803-777-7500
Fax: 803-777-9774

Lake Murray Tourism & Recreation Association
2184 N Lake Dr
Columbia, SC 29212
www.lakemurraycountry.com/
Phone: 803-781-5940
Fax: 803-781-6197

Longstreet Theatre
Greene & Sumter Sts
Columbia, SC 29201
Phone: 803-777-2551
Fax: 803-777-6669

Mann-Simons Cottage
1403 Richland St
Columbia, SC 29201
Phone: 803-252-7742

Memorial Park
Washington St
Columbia, SC 29201
Phone: 803-733-8331

Nickelodeon Theatre of the Columbia Film Society
937 Main St
Columbia, SC 29201
www.nickelodeon.org
Phone: 803-254-8234
Fax: 803-254-0299

Riverbanks Zoo & Botanical Garden
500 Wildlife Pkwy
Columbia, SC 29210
www.riverbanks.org
Phone: 803-779-8717
Fax: 803-253-6381

Robert Mills House
1618 Blanding St
Columbia, SC 29201
Phone: 803-252-7742
Fax: 803-929-7695

Seibels House
1601 Richland St
Columbia, SC 29201
Phone: 803-252-7742
Fax: 803-929-7695

Sesquicentennial State Park
9564 Two Notch Rd
Columbia, SC 29223
Phone: 803-788-2706
Fax: 803-788-2706

South Carolina Philharmonic Orchestra
1237 Gadsden St Suite 102
Columbia, SC 29201
E-mail: music@scphilharmonic.com
www.scphilharmonic.com
Phone: 803-771-7937
Fax: 803-771-0268

South Carolina State Capitol
Sumter St
Columbia, SC 29201
Phone: 803-734-2430

South Carolina State Museum
301 Gervais St
Columbia, SC 29202
www.museum.state.sc.us
Phone: 803-898-4978
Fax: 803-898-4917

Southeastern Regional Opera
914 Pulaski St
Columbia, SC 29201
Phone: 803-771-6303
Fax: 803-771-2625

State Farmers Market
1001 Bluff Rd
Columbia, SC 29201
Phone: 803-737-4664
Fax: 803-737-4667

Town Theatre
10125 Sumter St
Columbia, SC 29201
www.scescape.com/towntheatre/
Phone: 803-799-2510

Trustus Theatre
520 Lady St
Columbia, SC 29201
www.scescape.com/trustus/
Phone: 803-254-9732
Fax: 803-771-9153

University of South Carolina McKissick Museum
Pendleton & Bull Sts
Columbia, SC 29208
Phone: 803-777-7251
Fax: 803-777-2829

Woodrow Wilson's Boyhood Home
1705 Hampton St
Columbia, SC 29201
Phone: 803-252-7742
Fax: 803-929-7695

Workshop Theatre
1136 Bull St
Columbia, SC 29201
www.scescape.com/workshop/
Phone: 803-799-4876
Fax: 803-799-4876

Sports Teams & Facilities

Capital City Bombers (baseball)
301 S Assembly St Capital City Stadium
Columbia, SC 29201
www.bomberball.com
Phone: 803-254-4487
Fax: 803-256-4338

Annual Events

Carolina Classic Home & Garden Show (mid-March) 803-256-6238
Carolina Craftman Art Show (mid-March) 803-799-3387
Carolina Marathon (early February) 803-929-1996
Christmas Candlelight Tours (early December) 803-252-7742
Christmas Traditions (late November-late December) 803-779-8717
Columbia International Festival (late March-early April) 803-799-3452
Congaree Western Weekend Festival & Rodeo (early September) 803-755-2512
Greek Bake Sale (mid-April) 803-252-6758
Greek Festival (late September) 803-252-6758
Jubilee Festival of Heritage (mid-August) 803-252-7742
Labor Day Festival (early September) 803-345-1100
Lexington County Peach Festival (early July) 803-254-0479
Lights Before Christmas at the Zoo (December) 803-779-8717
Main Street Jazz (late May) 803-254-0479
Mayfest (early May) 803-254-0479
NatureFest (late April) 803-776-4396
Riverfest Celebration (mid-April) 803-254-0479

Saint Patrick's Day Festival (mid-March) 803-738-1499
South Carolina Oyster Festival (mid-March). 803-252-2128
South Carolina State Fair (early October) 803-254-0479
Vista After Five Spring Concerts
(early April-late May) 803-256-7501
Vista Lights (mid-November) 803-254-0479

Columbus, Ohio

***County:* Franklin**

COLUMBUS is located in central Ohio. Major cities within 100 miles include Akron, Cincinnati, and Dayton, Ohio.

Area (Land) .... 189.3 sq mi
Area (Water)................................ 2.1 sq mi
Elevation...................................... 780 ft
Latitude ....39-96-11 N
Longitude............................... 82-99-89 W
Time Zone ....EST
Area Code.. 614

Climate

Columbus has a changeable climate that is influenced by cold air masses coming down from Canada and warm air masses coming up from the Gulf of Mexico. Winters are typically cold, with temperatures averaging in the 20s and 30s and an average annual snowfall of 28 inches. Summers days are warm with high temperatures generally in the low 80s, but evenings cool down to around 60 degrees. Summer is the rainy season, with July being the wettest month—winter is the driest season.

Average Temperatures & Precipitation

Temperatures

	Jan	Feb	Mar	Apr	May	Jun	Jul	Aug	Sep	Oct	Nov	Dec
High	34	38	51	62	73	80	84	82	76	65	51	39
Low	19	21	31	40	50	58	63	61	55	43	34	25

Precipitation

	Jan	Feb	Mar	Apr	May	Jun	Jul	Aug	Sep	Oct	Nov	Dec
Inches	2.2	2.2	3.3	3.2	3.9	4.0	4.3	3.7	3.0	2.2	3.2	2.9

History

Originally settled by various Indian tribes known as Mound Builders for the earthen mounds they built along the banks of the Scioto River and Alum Creek, the area surrounding present-day Columbus was first developed in 1787 when Lucas Sullivant established the town of Franklinton on the west bank of the Scioto. In 1812, the newly formed state of Ohio decided to move the state capitol from Chillicothe, in southern Ohio, to a more central location. Columbus was established on the east bank of the Scioto, across from Franklinton (which was eventually absorbed by the new city), to serve as the state capital. By 1816, when the original state capitol building was completed, Columbus was home to 700 residents.

During the 1800s, new developments in transportation routes in Columbus, including the completion of a canal that linked the city to the Erie Canal, the National Road (U.S. Route 40) passing through the area, and the introduction of railroads, opened the door to the rest of the country, helping the area to grow as a major transportation, manufacturing, and distribution center. Columbus was incorporated as a city in 1834 with 5,000 residents. The city's population more than tripled in the following two decades. During the Civil War, Columbus served as a stop along the infamous Underground Railroad, and the city was also home to Camp Chase, a major Union Army induction/training center and prison. In the late 1800s, Columbus became known as the "Buggy Capital of the World," as more than 20,000 horse-drawn vehicles were produced by Columbus' nearly two dozen local manufacturers.

The city's population surged between 1880 and 1900, and by the year 1910 Columbus was home to nearly 200,000 people. The city has continued to grow throughout the 20th Century, due in large part to its diverse economic base, which relies on a combination of trade, manufacturing, government, and white collar jobs that has helped the city to thrive during even the most difficult economic times. Columbus today, with a population of more than 670,000, is the nation's 15th largest city.

Population

1990 Census 632,945
1998 Estimate.............................670,234
% Change 5.9
2003 Projection 685,319

Racial/Ethnic Breakdown

White...................................74.5%
Black 22.6%
Other 2.9%
Hispanic Origin (may be of any race) 0.9%

Age Breakdown

Under 18 years...........................23.4%*
18 to 44.................................48.8%*
45 to 64.................................17.8%*
65+ years 10.0%*
Median Age................................32.6

Gender Breakdown

Male.....................................48.7%*
Female..................................51.2%*

** Information given is for the Columbus Metropolitan Statistical Area (MSA), which includes the City of Columbus as well as Delaware, Fairfield, Franklin, Licking, Madison, Pickaway, and Union counties in Central Ohio.*

Government

Type of Government: Mayor-Council

Columbus City Attorney
90 W Broad St Rm 200
Columbus, OH 43215
Phone: 614-645-7385
Fax: 614-645-6949

Columbus City Clerk
90 W Broad St
Columbus, OH 43215
Phone: 614-645-7380
Fax: 614-645-6164

Columbus City Council
90 W Broad St
Columbus, OH 43215
Phone: 614-645-7380
Fax: 614-645-6164

Columbus City Hall
90 W Broad St
Columbus, OH 43215
Phone: 614-645-8100
Fax: 614-645-5880

Columbus Civil Service Commission
50 W Gay St
Columbus, OH 43215
Phone: 614-645-8300
Fax: 614-645-8334

Columbus Economic Development & Planning Services
109 N Front St
Columbus, OH 43215
Phone: 614-645-7574
Fax: 614-645-7855

Columbus Finance Dept
90 W Broad St 4th Fl
Columbus, OH 43215
Phone: 614-645-8200
Fax: 614-645-7139

Columbus Fire Div
3675 Parsons Ave
Columbus, OH 43207
Phone: 614-645-7533
Fax: 614-645-3040

Columbus Mayor
90 W Broad St Rm 247
Columbus, OH 43215
Phone: 614-645-7671
Fax: 614-645-8955

Columbus Metropolitan Library
96 S Grant Ave
Columbus, OH 43215
Phone: 614-645-2800
Fax: 614-645-2870

Columbus Planning Office
109 N Front St
Columbus, OH 43215
Phone: 614-645-8202
Fax: 614-645-1483

Columbus Police Div
120 Marconi Blvd
Columbus, OH 43215
Phone: 614-645-4600
Fax: 614-645-4551

Columbus Public Service Dept
90 W Broad St City Hall Rm 301
Columbus, OH 43215
Phone: 614-645-8290
Fax: 614-645-7805

Columbus Public Utilties Dept
910 Dublin Rd
Columbus, OH 43215
Phone: 614-645-6141
Fax: 614-645-8177

Columbus Recreation & Parks Dept
90 W Broad St 1st Fl
Columbus, OH 43215
Phone: 614-645-3300
Fax: 614-645-5801

Important Phone Numbers

AAA 614-431-7800
American Express Travel 614-228-6666
Columbus Board of Realtors 614-475-4000
Columbus Tax Information 614-645-7370
Driver's License Information 614-752-7600
Emergency 911
Franklin County Auditor 614-462-4663
HotelDocs 800-468-3537
Ohio State Dept of Taxation 614-466-3960
Poison Control Center 614-228-1323
Time/Temp 614-281-1111
Vehicle Registration Information 614-752-7500
Voter Registration Information 614-466-2585
Weather 614-469-1010

Information Sources

Better Business Bureau Serving Central Ohio
1335 Dublin Rd Suite 30-A
Columbus, OH 43215
www.columbus-oh.bbb.org
Phone: 614-486-6336
Fax: 614-486-6631
TF: 800-759-2400

Franklin County
369 S High St 3rd Fl
Columbus, OH 43215
www.co.franklin.oh.us
Phone: 614-462-3621
Fax: 614-462-4325

Greater Columbus Chamber of Commerce
37 N High St
Columbus, OH 43215
www.columbus-chamber.org
Phone: 614-221-1321
Fax: 614-221-9360
TF: 800-950-1321

Greater Columbus Convention & Visitors Bureau
90 N High St
Columbus, OH 43215
www.columbuscvb.org
Phone: 614-221-6623
Fax: 614-221-5618
TF: 800-354-2657

Greater Columbus Convention Center
400 N High St
Columbus, OH 43215
www.columbusconventions.com
Phone: 614-645-5000
Fax: 614-221-7239
TF: 800-626-0241

Greater Columbus Free-Net
1224 Kinnear Rd
Columbus, OH 43212
www.freenet.columbus.oh.us
Phone: 614-292-3200
Fax: 614-292-7168

Online Resources

4Columbus.com
www.4columbus.com

About.com Guide to Columbus
columbusoh.about.com/local/midwestus/columbusoh

Anthill City Guide Columbus
www.anthill.com/city.asp?city=columbus

Area Guide Columbus
columbusoh.areaguides.net

Central Ohio Source
www.sddt.com/~columbus

City Knowledge Columbus
www.cityknowledge.com/oh_columbus.htm

CitySearch Columbus
columbus.citysearch.com

Columbus Alive
www.alivewired.com

Columbus Home Page
www.columbus.net

Columbus Internet Directory
users1.ee.net/coldir/

Columbus Pages
www.columbuspages.com/

Columbus Super Site
www.columbus.org/

Columbus Webring
onart.digitalchainsaw.com/ccw1.htm

ColumbusTour
www.columbustour.com/

DigitalCity Columbus
home.digitalcity.com/columbus

Excite.com Columbus City Guide
www.excite.com/travel/countries/united_states/ohio/columbus

Out In Columbus
www.outincolumbus.com

Savvy Diner Guide to Columbus Restaurants
www.savvydiner.com/columbus/

Area Communities

Communities in the Columbus metro area with populations greater than 10,000 include:

Bexley
2242 E Main St
Columbus, OH 43209
Phone: 614-235-8694
Fax: 614-235-3420

Circleville
127 S Court St
Circleville, OH 43113
Phone: 740-477-2551
Fax: 740-477-8247

Delaware
1 S Sandusky St
Delaware, OH 43015
Phone: 740-368-1640
Fax: 740-368-1525

Dublin
5200 Emerald Pkwy
Dublin, OH 43017
Phone: 614-761-6500
Fax: 614-889-0740

Gahanna
200 S Hamilton Rd
Gahanna, OH 43230
Phone: 614-471-2563
Fax: 614-337-4381

Grove City
PO Box 427
Grove City, OH 43123
Phone: 614-871-6331
Fax: 614-871-6306

Hilliard
3800 Municipal Way
Hilliard, OH 43026
Phone: 614-876-7361
Fax: 614-876-0381

Lancaster
104 E Main St
Lancaster, OH 43130
Phone: 740-687-6600
Fax: 740-687-6698

Marysville
125 E 6th St
Marysville, OH 43040
Phone: 937-642-6015
Fax: 937-642-6045

Newark
40 W Main St
Newark, OH 43055
Phone: 740-349-6600
Fax: 740-349-6814

Pickerington
100 Lockville Rd
Pickerington, OH 43147
Phone: 614-837-3974
Fax: 614-833-2201

Reynoldsburg
7232 E Main St
Reynoldsburg, OH 43068
Phone: 614-866-6391
Fax: 614-866-8995

Upper Arlington
3600 Tremont Rd
Upper Arlington, OH 43221
Phone: 614-583-5030
Fax: 614-457-6620

Westerville
21 S State St
Westerville, OH 43081
Phone: 614-901-6400
Fax: 614-901-6401

Whitehall
360 S Yearling Rd
Whitehall, OH 43213
Phone: 614-338-3106
Fax: 614-237-0663

Worthington
6550 N High St
Worthington, OH 43085
Phone: 614-436-3100
Fax: 614-436-5966

Economy

Columbus is considered a world center for international trade, telecommunications, data processing, and material handling and shipping. Major corporations headquartered in the the area include CompuServe, Worthington Industries, and The Limited. In addition to the major employers listed below, Ohio State Government and the U.S. Government are ranked number one and two of the top 15, respectively, providing jobs for more than 44,000 residents in Central Ohio. The U.S. Postal Service also ranks among the top 15, providing employment for more than 6,000 Columbus metro area residents.

Unemployment Rate 2.5%*
Per Capita Income $41,357
Median Family Income $32,898

** Information given is for Franklin County.*

Principal Industries & Number of Wage Earners

Franklin County - 1998

Industry	Wage Earners
Agriculture	4,391
Construction	27,991
Finance, Insurance, & Real Estate	65,370
Government	88,862
Manufacturing	64,333
Mining	400
Services	194,582
Trade	180,141
Transportation & Public Utilities	33,334

Major Employers

Banc One Corp
800 E Broad St
Columbus, OH 43215
Phone: 614-248-5800
Fax: 614-248-1421

Columbus Public Schools
270 E State St
Columbus, OH 43215
www.columbus.k12.oh.us
Phone: 614-221-3228
Fax: 614-365-5814

Columumbus City Hall
90 W Broad St
Columbus, OH 43215
ci.columbus.oh.us
Phone: 614-645-8100
Fax: 614-645-5880

Defense Supply Center
3990 E Broad St
Columbus, OH 43213
www.dscc.dla.mil/
Phone: 614-692-3131
Fax: 614-692-1906

Franklin County
369 S High St 3rd Fl
Columbus, OH 43215
www.co.franklin.oh.us
Phone: 614-462-3621
Fax: 614-462-4325

Grant Riverside Methodist Hospitals
Grant Campus
111 S Grant Ave
Columbus, OH 43215
www.grmh.org
Phone: 614-566-9000
Fax: 614-566-8043

Honda of America Mfg Inc
24000 Honda Pkwy
Marysville, OH 43040
ohio.honda.com
Phone: 937-642-5000
Fax: 937-644-6543

Kroger Co
4111 Executive Pkwy
Westerville, OH 43081
www.kroger.com
Phone: 614-898-3200
Fax: 614-898-3520

Limited Inc
3 Limited Pkwy
Columbus, OH 43230
www.limited.com
Phone: 614-415-7000
Fax: 614-415-2491

Lucent Technologies Inc
6200 E Broad St
Columbus, OH 43213
www.lucent.com
Phone: 614-860-2000
Fax: 614-868-5483

Mount Carmel Health System
793 W State St
Columbus, OH 43222
Phone: 614-234-5000
Fax: 614-234-1281

National City Bank
155 E Broad St
Columbus, OH 43251
Phone: 614-463-7100
Fax: 614-463-7123
TF: 800-738-3888

Nationwide Insurance Enterprise
1 Nationwide Plaza
Columbus, OH 43215
www.nationwide.com
Phone: 614-249-7111
Fax: 614-249-7705
TF: 800-882-2822

Ohio State University
1800 Cannon Dr
Columbus, OH 43210
www.osu.edu
Phone: 614-292-6446
Fax: 614-292-4818

Riverside Hospital
3535 Olentangy River Rd
Columbus, OH 43214
Phone: 614-566-5000
Fax: 614-566-6760

Quality of Living Indicators

Total Crime Index....................61,292
(rates per 100,000 inhabitants)

Violent Crime
Murder/manslaughter.................. 71
Forcible rape 638
Robbery..................3,026
Aggravated assault..................2,020

Property Crime
Burglary 14,090
Larceny theft 34,625
Motor vehicle theft..................6,822

Cost of Living Index..................98.0
(national average = 100)

Median Home Price..................$125,000

Education

Public Schools

Columbus Public Schools
270 E State St
Columbus, OH 43215
www.columbus.k12.oh.us
Phone: 614-221-3228
Fax: 614-365-5814

Number of Schools
Elementary.................. 97
Middle 26
High.................. 22

Student/Teacher Ratio
All Grades 15.0:1

Private Schools

Number of Schools (all grades).................. 40+

Colleges & Universities

Bradford School
6170 Busch Blvd
Columbus, OH 43229
E-mail: bradford@bradfordschools.com
Phone: 614-846-9410
Fax: 614-846-9656
TF: 800-678-7981

Capital University
2199 E Main St
Columbus, OH 43209
www.capital.edu
Phone: 614-236-6011
Fax: 614-236-6926
TF: 800-289-6289

Columbus College of Art & Design
107 N 9th St
Columbus, OH 43215
E-mail: admissions@ccad.edu
www.ccad.edu
Phone: 614-224-9101
Fax: 614-222-4040

Columbus State Community College
550 E Spring St
Columbus, OH 43215
www.cscc.edu
Phone: 614-287-2400
Fax: 614-287-5117
TF: 800-621-6407

Denison University
100 S Bridge Rd
Granville, OH 43023
E-mail: admissions@denison.edu
www.denison.edu
Phone: 740-587-0810
Fax: 740-587-6306
TF: 800-336-4766

DeVRY Institute of Technology
1350 Alum Creek Dr
Columbus, OH 43209
www.devrycols.edu
Phone: 614-253-7291
Fax: 614-253-0843
TF: 800-426-2206

Franklin University
201 S Grant Ave
Columbus, OH 43215
www.franklin.edu
Phone: 614-341-6237
Fax: 614-224-8027
TF: 877-341-6300

Ohio Dominican College
1216 Sunbury Rd
Columbus, OH 43219
www.odc.edu
Phone: 614-253-2741
Fax: 614-252-0776
TF: 800-955-6446

Ohio State University
1800 Cannon Dr
Columbus, OH 43210
www.osu.edu
Phone: 614-292-6446
Fax: 614-292-4818

Otterbein College
1 Otterbein College
Westerville, OH 43081
www.otterbein.edu
Phone: 614-890-3000
Fax: 614-823-1200
TF: 800-488-8144

Hospitals

Children's Hospital
700 Children's Dr
Columbus, OH 43205
www.childrenshospital.columbus.oh.us
Phone: 614-722-2000
Fax: 614-722-5995

Doctors Hospital
1087 Dennison Ave
Columbus, OH 43201
www.doctors-10tv.com
Phone: 614-297-4000
Fax: 614-297-4116

Grant Riverside Methodist Hospitals
Grant Campus
111 S Grant Ave
Columbus, OH 43215
www.grmh.org
Phone: 614-566-9000
Fax: 614-566-8043

Mount Carmel East Hospital
6001 E Broad St
Columbus, OH 43213
Phone: 614-234-6000
Fax: 614-234-6408

Mount Carmel West Hospital
793 W State St
Columbus, OH 43222
www.mountcarmelhealth.com/pati/west.shtml
Phone: 614-234-5000
Fax: 614-234-5756

Ohio State University Medical Center
410 W 10th Ave
Columbus, OH 43210
www.acs.ohio-state.edu/osu/med-cent.html
Phone: 614-293-8000
Fax: 614-293-3535

Riverside Hospital
3535 Olentangy River Rd
Columbus, OH 43214
Phone: 614-566-5000
Fax: 614-566-6760

Saint Ann's Hospital
500 S Cleveland Ave
Westerville, OH 43081
www.mountcarmelhealth.com/pati/stan.shtml
Phone: 614-898-4000
Fax: 614-898-8668

University Hospital East
1492 E Broad St
Columbus, OH 43205
Phone: 614-257-3000
Fax: 614-257-3325

Transportation

Airport(s)

Port Columbus International Airport (CMH)
8 miles NE of downtown (approx 15 minutes) 614-239-4000

Mass Transit

COTA
$1.10 Base fare................................614-228-1776

Rail/Bus

Greyhound Bus Station
111 E Town St
Columbus, OH 43215
Phone: 614-221-2389
TF: 800-231-2222

Utilities

Electricity
American Electric Power Co Inc 614-223-1000
www.aep.com

Gas
Columbia Gas of Ohio Inc......................614-460-2222
www.columbiagasohio.com

Water
Columbus Water Dept 614-645-6186

Garbage Collection/Recycling
Columbus Refuse Collection Div................614-645-8774

Telecommunications

Telephone
Ameritech...................................800-660-1000
www.ameritech.com

Cable Television
Insight Communications.......................614-236-1200
Time Warner Cable...........................614-481-5050
www.twcol.com

Internet Service Providers (ISPs)
eNET 614-794-5971
www.ee.net
Greater Columbus Free-Net 614-292-3200
www.freenet.columbus.oh.us
NetSet Internet Services 614-527-9111
www.netset.com
NetWalk....................................614-621-9255
www.netwalk.com
NexTek Designs..............................740-349-0201
www.nextek.com
OARnet 614-728-8100
www.oar.net

Banks

Bank One NA
100 E Broad St
Columbus, OH 43215
Phone: 614-248-5601
Fax: 614-248-6463

Fifth Third Bank Central Ohio
21 E State St
Columbus, OH 43215
Phone: 614-341-2595
Fax: 614-341-2516

First City Bank
1885 Northwest Blvd
Columbus, OH 43212
Phone: 614-487-1010
Fax: 614-481-7294

Firstar Bank NA
62 E Broad St
Columbus, OH 43215
Phone: 614-221-2941
Fax: 614-222-8775
TF: 800-627-7827

Huntington National Bank
41 S High St
Columbus, OH 43215
www.huntington.com
Phone: 614-480-8300
Fax: 614-480-5746
TF: 800-480-2265

KeyBank NA Columbus District
88 E Broad St
Columbus, OH 43215
Phone: 614-460-3400
Fax: 614-365-3313
TF: 800-539-2968

National City Bank
155 E Broad St
Columbus, OH 43251
Phone: 614-463-7100
Fax: 614-463-7123
TF: 800-738-3888

Wheeling National Bank
6121 E Livingston Ave
Columbus, OH 43232
Phone: 614-759-0400
Fax: 614-759-0403

Shopping

Brice Outlet Mall
5891 Scarborough Blvd
Columbus, OH 43232
Phone: 614-847-1492
Fax: 614-847-1327

Columbus City Center
111 S 3rd St
Columbus, OH 43215
Phone: 614-221-4900
Fax: 614-469-5093
TF: 800-882-4900

Continent The
6076 Busch Blvd Suite 2
Columbus, OH 43229
Phone: 614-846-0418
Fax: 614-846-5599

Eastland Mall
2740B Eastland Mall
Columbus, OH 43232
E-mail: eastlandmall@rejacobsgroup.com
www.shopyourmall.com/mall_welcome.asp?map=yes&mall_select=616
Phone: 614-861-3232
Fax: 614-861-6279

Easton Town Center
4016 Townfair Way Suite 201
Columbus, OH 43219
Phone: 614-414-7300
Fax: 614-414-7311

Greater Columbus Antique Mall
1045 S High St
Columbus, OH 43206
Phone: 614-443-7858

Lazarus
141 S High St
Columbus, OH 43215
Phone: 614-463-2121
Fax: 614-463-3217

Marshall Field's
225 S 3rd St
Columbus, OH 43215
www.marshallfields.com
Phone: 614-227-6222
Fax: 614-227-6573

North Market
59 Spruce St
Columbus, OH 43215
www.northmarket.com/
Phone: 614-463-9664
Fax: 614-469-9323

Northland Mall
1711 Northland Way
Columbus, OH 43229
E-mail: northlandmall@rejacobsgroup.com
www.shopyourmall.com/mall_welcome.asp?map=yes&mall_select=604
Phone: 614-267-9258
Fax: 614-267-3449

Schottenstein
3251 Westerville Rd
Columbus, OH 43224
Phone: 614-471-4711
Fax: 614-471-5031

Westland Mall
4273 Broad St
Columbus, OH 43228
E-mail: westlandmall@rejacobsgroup.com
www.shopyourmall.com/mall_welcome.asp?map=yes&mall_select=617
Phone: 614-272-0012
Fax: 614-272-2688

Media

Newspapers and Magazines

Business First
471 E Broad St Suite 1500
Columbus, OH 43215
www.amcity.com/columbus
Phone: 614-461-4040
Fax: 614-365-2980

Columbus Alive
17 Brickel St
Columbus, OH 43215
E-mail: alive@alivewired.com
www.alivewired.com
Phone: 614-221-2449
Fax: 614-221-2456
TF: 888-254-8330

Columbus Dispatch*
34 S 3rd St
Columbus, OH 43215
E-mail: crow@cd.columbus.oh.us
www.dispatch.com
Phone: 614-461-5000
Fax: 614-461-7580

Columbus Monthly
5255 Sinclair Rd
Columbus, OH 43229
Phone: 614-888-4567
Fax: 614-848-3838

Delaware This Week
670 Lakeview Plaza Dr Suite 100
Delaware, OH 43815
E-mail: thisweek@infinet.com
www.thisweeknews.com
Phone: 740-548-4557
Fax: 740-548-4813

Dublin News
PO Box 29912
Columbus, OH 43229
Phone: 614-785-1212
Fax: 614-842-4760

Dublin Villager
PO Box 341890
Columbus, OH 43234
E-mail: thisweek@infinet.com
www.thisweeknews.com
Phone: 614-841-1781
Fax: 614-841-0436

Eastside Messenger
3378 Sullivant Ave
Columbus, OH 43204
Phone: 614-272-5422
Fax: 614-272-0684

Grove City Southwest Messenger
3378 Sullivant Ave
Columbus, OH 43204
Phone: 614-272-5422
Fax: 614-272-0684

Hilliard This Week
PO Box 341890
Columbus, OH 43234
www.thisweeknews.com
Phone: 614-841-1781
Fax: 614-841-0436

In the East Side This Week
PO Box 341890
Columbus, OH 43234
www.thisweeknews.com
Phone: 614-841-1781
Fax: 614-841-0436

Northland News
PO Box 29912
Columbus, OH 43229
Phone: 614-785-1212
Fax: 614-842-4760

Ohio Magazine
62 E Broad St 2nd Fl
Columbus, OH 43215
www.ohiomagazine.com/
Phone: 614-461-5083
Fax: 614-461-5506
TF: 800-426-4624

Reynoldsburg This Week
670 Lakeview Plaza Blvd Suite F
Columbus, OH 43085
www.thisweeknews.com
Phone: 614-841-1781
Fax: 614-841-0436

Southeast Messenger
3378 Sullivant Ave
Columbus, OH 43204
Phone: 614-272-5422
Fax: 614-272-0684

Southside This Week
PO Box 341890
Columbus, OH 43234
www.thisweeknews.com
Phone: 614-841-1781
Fax: 614-841-0436

This Week in Upper Arlington
PO Box 341890
Columbus, OH 43234
www.thisweeknews.com
Phone: 614-841-1781
Fax: 614-841-0436

Upper Arlington News
5257 Sinclair Rd
Columbus, OH 43229
Phone: 614-785-1212
Fax: 614-842-4760

Westerville News
PO Box 29912
Columbus, OH 43229
Phone: 614-785-1212
Fax: 614-842-4760

Westerville This Week
PO Box 341890
Columbus, OH 43234
E-mail: thisweek@infinet.com
www.thisweeknews.com
Phone: 614-841-1781
Fax: 614-841-0436

Westland News
PO Box 29912
Columbus, OH 43229
Phone: 614-785-1212
Fax: 614-842-4760

Westside Messenger
3378 Sullivant Ave
Columbus, OH 43204
Phone: 614-272-5422
Fax: 614-272-0684

Worthington This Week
PO Box 341890
Columbus, OH 43234
E-mail: thisweek@infinet.com
www.thisweeknews.com
Phone: 614-841-1781
Fax: 614-841-0436

**Indicates major daily newspapers*

Television

WBNS-TV Ch 10 (CBS)
770 Twin Rivers Dr
Columbus, OH 43215
www.wbns10tv.com
Phone: 614-460-3700
Fax: 614-460-2891

WCMH-TV Ch 4 (NBC)
3165 Olentangy River Rd
Columbus, OH 43202
E-mail: wcmh4@erinet.com
www.wcmh4.com
Phone: 614-263-4444
Fax: 614-263-0166

WOSU-TV Ch 34 (PBS)
2400 Olentangy River Rd
Columbus, OH 43210
www.wosu.org
Phone: 614-292-9678
Fax: 614-292-7625

WSFJ-TV Ch 51 (Ind)
10077 Jacksontown Rd SE
Thornville, OH 43076
www.wsfj.com
Phone: 740-323-0771
Fax: 740-323-3242

WSYX-TV Ch 6 (ABC)
1261 Dublin Rd
Columbus, OH 43215
Phone: 614-481-6666
Fax: 614-481-6624

WTTE-TV Ch 28 (Fox)
1261 Dubun Rd
Columbus, OH 43215
E-mail: viewer@wtte.com
www.wtte.com
Phone: 614-481-6666
Fax: 614-481-6624

WWHO-TV Ch 53 (UPN)
1160 Dublin Rd Suite 500
Columbus, OH 43215
www.paramountstations.com/WWHO
Phone: 614-485-5300
Fax: 614-485-5339

Radio

WAZU-FM 107.1 MHz (Rock)
2 Nationwide Plaza 10th Fl
Columbus, OH 43215
Phone: 614-227-9696
Fax: 614-461-1059

WBNS-AM 1460 kHz (Sports)
175 S 3rd St
Columbus, OH 43215
www.1460thefan.com
Phone: 614-460-3850
Fax: 614-460-2822

WBNS-FM 97.1 MHz (Oldies)
175 S 3rd St
Columbus, OH 43215
Phone: 614-460-3850
Fax: 614-460-3757

WBZX-FM 99.7 MHz (Rock)
1458 Dublin Rd
Columbus, OH 43215
E-mail: theblitz@wbzx.com
www.wbzx.com
Phone: 614-481-7800
Fax: 614-481-8070

WCBE-FM 90.5 MHz (NPR)
540 Jack Gibbs Blvd
Columbus, OH 43215
wcbe.org
Phone: 614-365-5555
Fax: 614-365-5060

WCKX-FM 107.5 MHz (Urban) Phone: 614-487-1444
1500 W 3rd Ave Suite 300 Fax: 614-487-5862
Columbus, OH 43212
www.wckx-fm.com

WCOL-FM 92.3 MHz (Ctry) Phone: 614-821-9265
2 Nationwide Plaza 10th Fl Fax: 614-221-9292
Columbus, OH 43215
E-mail: wcol@wcol.com
wcol.com

WEGE-FM 103.9 MHz (CR) Phone: 614-481-7800
1458 Dublin Rd Fax: 614-481-8070
Columbus, OH 43215

WFYI-AM 1230 kHz (N/T) Phone: 614-273-9344
1301 Dublin Rd Fax: 614-487-2559
Columbus, OH 43215
www.wfii.com

WHOK-FM 95.5 MHz (Ctry) Phone: 614-225-9465
2 Nationwide Plaza 10th Fl Fax: 614-677-0083
Columbus, OH 43215
E-mail: whok@whok.com
www.whok.com

WJZA-FM 103.5 MHz (NAC) Phone: 614-889-1043
655 Metro Pl S Suite 100 Fax: 614-717-9200
Dublin, OH 43017
www.columbusjazz.com

WJZK-FM 104.3 MHz (NAC) Phone: 614-889-1043
655 Metro Pl S Suite 100 Fax: 614-717-9200
Dublin, OH 43017
www.columbusjazz.com

WLVQ-FM 96.3 MHz (Rock) Phone: 614-227-9696
2 Nationwide Plaza 10th Fl Fax: 614-461-1059
Columbus, OH 43215
E-mail: qfm96@hotmail.com
www.qfm96.com

WMNI-AM 920 kHz (B/EZ) Phone: 614-481-7800
1458 Dublin Rd Fax: 614-481-8070
Columbus, OH 43215

WNCI-FM 97.9 MHz (CHR) Phone: 614-430-9624
6172 Busch Blvd Suite 2000 Fax: 614-847-0076
Columbus, OH 43229
www.wnci.com

WOSU-AM 820 kHz (NPR) Phone: 614-292-9678
2400 Olentangy River Rd Fax: 614-292-0513
Columbus, OH 43210
E-mail: wosu@osu.edu
www.wosu.org/main/am/news820.htm

WSNY-FM 94.7 MHz (AC) Phone: 614-451-2191
4401 Carriage Hill Ln Fax: 614-821-9595
Columbus, OH 43220
www.wsny.net

WTVN-AM 610 kHz (N/T) Phone: 614-486-6101
1301 Dublin Rd Fax: 614-487-2559
Columbus, OH 43215
www.wtvn.com

WVKO-AM 1580 kHz (Rel) Phone: 614-451-2191
4401 Carriage Hill Ln Fax: 614-451-1831
Columbus, OH 43220

WWCD-FM 101.1 MHz (Alt) Phone: 614-221-9923
503 S Front St Suite 101 Fax: 614-227-0021
Columbus, OH 43215
www.cd101.com

WXMG-FM 98.9 MHz (Oldies) Phone: 614-487-1444
1500 W 3rd Ave Suite 300 Fax: 614-487-5862
Columbus, OH 43212

WXST-FM 107.9 MHz (AC) Phone: 614-848-3108
1 Campus View Blvd Suite 335 Fax: 614-433-7108
Columbus, OH 43235
E-mail: comments@star1079.com
www.star1079.com

WZAZ-FM 105.7 MHz (Alt) Phone: 614-848-7625
6172 Busch Blvd Suite 2000 Fax: 614-847-9593
Columbus, OH 43229
www.1057channelz.com

Attractions

Ohio's history is preserved at the Ohio Historical Center and adjacent German Village, a restored district known for its beautifully renovated homes and live music. Columbus' commitment to historic preservation is also evident at Ohio Village, a recreation of a small 19th century town; and at the Santa Maria, a replica of Christopher Columbus's ship. Columbus is also home to the third-largest municipally owned zoo in the United States, the Columbus Zoo, which features a 100,000-gallon coral reef tank.

Anheuser-Busch Brewery Phone: 614-888-6644
700 Schrock Rd Fax: 614-847-6497
Columbus, OH 43229
www.anheuser-busch.com

BalletMet Columbus Phone: 614-229-4860
322 Mt Vernon Ave Fax: 614-224-3697
Columbus, OH 43215
www.balletmet.org

Center of Science & Industry (COSI) Phone: 614-228-2674
333 W Broad St Fax: 614-228-6363
Columbus, OH 43215 TF: 877-257-2674
www.cosi.org

Cloak & Dagger Dinner Theatre Phone: 614-523-9347
1048 Morse Rd Fax: 614-224-2326
Columbus, OH 43229 TF: 800-935-4548

Columbus Children's Theatre Phone: 614-224-6672
512 N Park St Fax: 614-224-8844
Columbus, OH 43215
E-mail: cctcolsoh@aol.com
www.colschildrenstheatre.org

Columbus Light Opera Phone: 614-461-8101
177 Naghten St Fax: 614-461-0806
Columbus, OH 43215
E-mail: lightopera@aol.com

Columbus Museum of Art
480 E Broad St
Columbus, OH 43215
E-mail: info@columbusart.mus.oh.us
www.columbusart.mus.oh.us
Phone: 614-221-6801
Fax: 614-221-0226

Columbus Symphony Orchestra
55 E State St
Columbus, OH 43215
www.csobravo.org
Phone: 614-228-9600
Fax: 614-224-7273

Columbus Zoo
9990 Riverside Dr
Powell, OH 43065
www.colszoo.org
Phone: 614-645-3400
Fax: 614-645-3465
TF: 800-666-5397

Contemporary American Theatre Co
77 S High St 2nd Fl
Columbus, OH 43215
www.catco.org
Phone: 614-461-0010
Fax: 614-461-4917

Franklin Park Conservatory & Botanical Garden
1777 E Broad St
Columbus, OH 43203
www.fpconservatory.org
Phone: 614-645-8733
Fax: 614-645-5921
TF: 800-241-7275

German Village
588 S 3rd St
Columbus, OH 43215
www.germanvillage.org
Phone: 614-221-8888
Fax: 614-222-4747

Griggs Park & Reservoir
2933 Riverside Dr
Columbus, OH 43221
Phone: 614-645-3300
Fax: 614-645-8839

Heritage Museum
530 E Town St
Columbus, OH 43215
Phone: 614-228-6515
Fax: 614-228-7809

Hoover Park & Reservoir
7001 Sunbury Rd
Columbus, OH 43081
Phone: 614-645-3300

Hopewell Culture National Historical Park
16062 SR-104
Chillicothe, OH 45601
www.nps.gov/hocu/
Phone: 740-774-1125
Fax: 740-774-1140

Inniswood Metro Gardens
940 S Hempstead Rd
Westerville, OH 43081
Phone: 614-895-6216
Fax: 614-895-6352

Jack Nicklaus Museum
5750 Memorial Dr
Dublin, OH 43017
Phone: 614-792-2353
Fax: 614-889-6026

Kelton House Museum
586 E Town St
Columbus, OH 43215
Phone: 614-464-2022
Fax: 614-464-3346

King Arts Complex
867 Mt Vernon Ave
Columbus, OH 43203
Phone: 614-645-5464
Fax: 614-645-3807

Motorcycle Hall of Fame Museum
13515 Yarmouth Dr
Pickerington, OH 43147
E-mail: melissak@ama-cycle.org
www.ama-cycle.org/museum/index.html
Phone: 614-856-1900
Fax: 614-856-2221
TF: 800-262-5646

Ohio Craft Museum
1665 W 5th Ave
Columbus, OH 43212
saso-oh.org/odc
Phone: 614-486-4402
Fax: 614-486-7110

Ohio Historical Center
1982 Velma Ave
Columbus, OH 43211
www.ohiohistory.org
Phone: 614-297-2300
Fax: 614-297-2411
TF: 800-686-6124

Ohio Statehouse
Broad & High Sts
Columbus, OH 43215
Phone: 614-466-2125

Ohio Theatre
55 E State St
Columbus, OH 43215
www.capa.com
Phone: 614-469-1045
Fax: 614-461-0429

Ohio Village
1982 Velma Ave
Columbus, OH 43211
Phone: 614-297-2300
Fax: 614-297-2358

Ohio Women's Hall of Fame
145 S Front St
Columbus, OH 43215
Phone: 614-466-4496
Fax: 614-466-7912

Olentangy Indian Caverns
1779 Home Rd
Delaware, OH 43015
E-mail: oic@olentangyindiancaverns.com
www.olentangyindiancaverns.com
Phone: 740-548-7917
Fax: 740-369-6466

Opera/Columbus
177 Naghten St
Columbus, OH 43215
www.operacols.org
Phone: 614-461-8101
Fax: 614-461-0806

Palace Theatre
34 W Broad St
Columbus, OH 43215
E-mail: info@capa.com
www.capa.com/Palace_Theatre.html
Phone: 614-469-1332
Fax: 614-460-2272

ProMusica Chamber Orchestra
243 N 5th St Suite 202
Columbus, OH 43215
Phone: 614-464-0066
Fax: 614-464-4141

Roscoe Village
381 Hill St
Coshocton, OH 43812
www.roscoevillage.com
Phone: 740-622-9310
Fax: 740-623-6555
TF: 800-877-1830

Saint Joseph Cathedral
212 E Broad St
Columbus, OH 43215
Phone: 614-224-1295

Santa Maria Replica
Marconi Blvd & W Broad St Battelle Riverfront Pk
Columbus, OH 43215
E-mail: info@santamaria.org
www.santamaria.org
Phone: 614-645-8760
Fax: 614-645-8748

Shadowbox Cabaret
232 E Spring St
Columbus, OH 43215
E-mail: genshad@netset.com
www.shadowboxcabaret.com
Phone: 614-265-7625
Fax: 614-224-9262
TF: 888-887-4236

Singing Buckeyes
400 Dublin Ave Suite 160
Columbus, OH 43215
www.harmonize.com/singingbuckeyes/
Phone: 614-221-4480
Fax: 877-219-5772

Slate Run Living Historical Farm
9130 Marcy Rd
Canal Winchester, OH 43110
Phone: 614-833-1880

Stuart Pimsler Dance & Theater
3000 E Main St
Columbus, OH 43209
E-mail: spdanth@aol.com
innerart.com/SPDT/dance.html
Phone: 614-461-0132
Fax: 614-461-0132

Thurber House
77 Jefferson Ave
Columbus, OH 43215
www.thurberhouse.org
Phone: 614-464-1032
Fax: 614-228-7445

Wexner Center for the Arts
1871 N High St Ohio State University
Columbus, OH 43210
E-mail: wexner@cgrg.ohio-state.edu
www.cgrg.ohio-state.edu/Wexner
Phone: 614-292-0330
Fax: 614-292-3369

Whetstone Park
3923 N High St
Columbus, OH 43214
Phone: 614-645-3217

Wyandot Lake Adventure Park
10101 Riverside Dr
Powell, OH 43065
www.sixflags.com/wyandotlake
Phone: 614-889-9283
Fax: 614-766-4753
TF: 800-328-9283

Sports Teams & Facilities

Beulah Park Race Track
3664 Grant Ave
Grove City, OH 43123
E-mail: hjcl@iwaynet.net
www.beulahpark.com
Phone: 614-871-9600
Fax: 614-871-0433
TF: 800-433-6905

Central Ohio Cows (baseball)
41 S Grant Ave
Columbus, OH 43215
E-mail: central.ohio.cows@mailexcite.com
Phone: 614-224-4534
Fax: 614-464-4730

Columbus All-Americans (baseball)
Lane Ave & Fred Taylor Dr Ohio State University Baseball Field
Columbus, OH 43201
Phone: 614-221-3151
Fax: 614-221-8196

Columbus Blue Jackets
150 E Wilson Bridge Rd
Worthington, OH 43085
www.bluejackets.com
Phone: 614-540-4625
Fax: 614-540-1189

Columbus Clippers (baseball)
1155 W Mound St
Columbus, OH 43223
E-mail: colsclippers@earthlink.net
www.clippersbaseball.com/
Phone: 614-462-5250
Fax: 614-462-3271

Columbus Crew (soccer)
1 Black & Gold Blvd
Columbus, OH 43211
E-mail: crew2739@aol.com
www.thecrew.com
Phone: 614-447-2739
Fax: 614-447-4109

Columbus Motor Speedway Inc
1845 Williams Rd
Columbus, OH 43207
E-mail: nascar@netwalk.com
www.columbusspeedway.com
Phone: 614-491-1047
Fax: 614-491-6010

National Trail Raceway
2650 National Rd SW
Hebron, OH 43025
E-mail: inquiry@nationaltrailraceway.com
www.nationaltrailraceway.com
Phone: 740-928-5706
Fax: 740-928-2922

Ohio Stadium
411 Woody Hayes Dr
Columbus, OH 43210
www.ohiostatebuckeyes.com
Phone: 614-292-7572
Fax: 614-292-0506

Scioto Downs
6000 S High St
Columbus, OH 43207
www.sciotodowns.com
Phone: 614-491-2515
Fax: 614-491-4626

Annual Events

All American Quarter Horse Congress
(early-mid-October) 740-943-2346
Asian Festival (late May) 614-292-0613
Capital Holiday Lights (December) 800-345-4386
Central Ohio Daffodil Society Show (mid-April) 614-645-8733
Central Ohio Rose Society Fall Show
(early September) 614-645-8733
Civil War Encampment (early-mid-September) 614-728-2698
Columbus Arts Festival (early June) 614-224-2606
Columbus International Festival
(early November) 614-228-4010
Columbus International Film & Video Festival
(late October) 614-841-1666
Columbus Marathon (late October) 614-794-1566
Comfest (late June-early July) 614-294-9511
Cruisin' on the Riverfront (late July) 614-258-1983
Equine Affaire-The Great American Horse Exposition
(early April) 740-845-0085
Festival Latino (mid-June) 614-645-7995
First Night Columbus (December 31) 614-481-0020
Jazz & Rib Fest (late July) 614-225-6922
Juneteenth Festival (mid-June) 614-299-4488
KidSpeak KidsFest (mid-September) 614-645-3314
Ohio State Fair (early-mid-August) 614-644-3247
Ohio State Fair Horse Show
(late July-late August) 614-644-4035
Oktoberfest (early September) 614-224-4300
PGA Memorial Tournament at Muirfield
(late May) 614-889-6700
Red White & Boom! (early July) 614-891-2666
Rhythm & Food: A Taste of Columbus
(late May) 614-221-6623
Rose Festival (early-mid-June) 614-645-3379
Saint Patrick's Day Parade (mid-March) 614-645-4375
Vintage Columbus (early-mid-June) 800-227-6972
Wildlight Wonderland
(late November-early January) 614-645-3550
Winterfair (early December) 614-486-7119

Corpus Christi, Texas

***County:* Nueces**

CORPUS CHRISTI is located in southeastern Texas, separated by the Gulf of Mexico by a series of barrier islands and Corpus Christi Bay. Major cities within 150 miles include San Antonio, Laredo, and Brownsville, Texas (Laredo and Brownsville lie on the U.S.-Mexican border).

Area (Land)	134.4 sq mi
Area (Water)	274.9 sq mi
Elevation	35 ft
Latitude	27-22-64 N
Longitude	97-96-15 W
Time Zone	CST
Area Code	361

Climate

Corpus Christi has a semitropical climate. Winters are mild, with average high temperatures in the mid- to upper 60s and lows in the mid- to upper 40s—snowfall is rare. Summers are hot and humid, with daytime high temperatures averaging in the low 90s, while Gulf breezes cool evening temperatures only into the mid-70s. September is the wettest month in Corpus Christi, while March is the driest.

Average Temperatures & Precipitation

Temperatures

	Jan	Feb	Mar	Apr	May	Jun	Jul	Aug	Sep	Oct	Nov	Dec
High	65	69	76	82	86	90	93	93	90	84	76	68
Low	45	48	55	63	70	73	75	75	72	64	56	48

Precipitation

	Jan	Feb	Mar	Apr	May	Jun	Jul	Aug	Sep	Oct	Nov	Dec
Inches	1.7	2.0	0.9	1.7	3.3	3.4	2.4	3.3	5.5	3.0	1.6	1.3

History

Although the town of Corpus Christi was not founded until 1839, the Bay area had been explored by the Spanish, Portuguese, English, and French and inhabited by Native Americans, buccaneers and pirates for centuries. The city began as a small trading post called Kinney's Trading Post or Kinney's Ranch (named after its founder Colonel Henry Lawrence Kinney), but was later renamed Corpus Christi after the adjoining bay. (The bay had been named more than 300 years earlier, in 1519, by Spanish conquistador Alonso Alvarez de Pineda on the Feast Day of Corpus Christi, a Latin phrase meaning "body of Christ".) During its early years, Corpus Christi grew primarily as an agricultural center. General Zachary Taylor and his troops spent the eight months from July of 1845 to March of 1846 at an encampment they had established on Corpus Christi Beach before heading south to fight in the Mexican War. During the war, the city became a transportation center.

Several years before Corpus Christi was incorporated as a city in 1852, the first port was established there, offering regular steamship service to New Orleans. The ship channel was quite shallow, and in 1860 the Corpus Christi Ship Channel Company was formed to dredge it, making Corpus Christi accessible to larger vessels and thereby paving the way for the city to become a major distribution center. In 1883, after the ship channel had been dredged to eight feet, the first cotton was shipped from Corpus Christi's port. Over the course of the next century, the ship channel was gradually dredged to its present depth of 45 feet. In the meantime, natural gas (in 1913) and oil (in 1930) were discovered in the Corpus Christi area. The petrochemical industry that developed from these discoveries shaped Corpus Christi's future, utilizing the city's access to the world via the Port of Corpus Christi (established in 1922), its ever-deepening ship channel, and the Gulf of Mexico.

Corpus Christi today is one of the leading petrochemical industrial centers in the United States. Major companies that have a presence in the area include CITGO, Celanese, Coastal, and Occidental Chemical Corporation. The Port of Corpus Christi is the nation's seventh largest port. Home to more than 281,000 people, the city's population is expected to exceed 320,000 by the year 2010.

Population

1990 Census	257,453
1998 Estimate	281,453
% Change	9.3
2010 Projection	327,786

Racial/Ethnic Breakdown

White	76.1%
Black	4.8%
Other	19.1%
Hispanic Origin (may be of any race)	50.4%

Age Breakdown

Under 5 years	8.3%
5 to 17	21.9%
18 to 20	4.5%
21 to 24	5.5%
25 to 34	17.7%
35 to 44	15.0%
45 to 54	9.2%
55 to 64	7.9%
65 to 74	6.1%
75+ years	4.0%
Median Age	30.6

Gender Breakdown

Male	48.8%
Female	51.2%

Government

Type of Government: Council-Manager

Corpus Christi City Attorney
1201 Leopard St
Corpus Christi, TX 78401
Phone: 361-880-3360
Fax: 361-880-3239

Corpus Christi City Council
1201 Leopard St
Corpus Christi, TX 78401
Phone: 361-880-3105
Fax: 361-880-3113

Corpus Christi City Hall
1201 Leopard St
Corpus Christi, TX 78401
Phone: 361-880-3000

Corpus Christi City Manager
1201 Leopard St
Corpus Christi, TX 78401
Phone: 361-880-3220
Fax: 361-880-3839

Corpus Christi City Secretary
1201 Leopard St
Corpus Christi, TX 78401
Phone: 361-880-3105
Fax: 361-880-3113

Corpus Christi Engineering Dept
1201 Leopard St
Corpus Christi, TX 78401
Phone: 361-880-3500
Fax: 361-880-3501

Corpus Christi Finance Dept
1201 Leopard St
Corpus Christi, TX 78401
Phone: 361-880-3600
Fax: 361-880-3601

Corpus Christi Fire Dept
201 N Chaparral Suite 300
Corpus Christi, TX 78401
Phone: 361-880-3900
Fax: 361-880-3954

Corpus Christi Human Resources Dept
1201 Loepard St 2nd Fl
Corpus Christi, TX 78401
Phone: 361-880-3315
Fax: 361-880-3322

Corpus Christi Mayor
1201 Leopard St
Corpus Christi, TX 78401
Phone: 361-880-3100
Fax: 361-880-3103

Corpus Christi Parks & Recreation Dept
1201 Leopard St
Corpus Christi, TX 78401
Phone: 361-880-3460
Fax: 361-880-3806

Corpus Christi Planning Dept
1201 Leopard St
Corpus Christi, TX 78401
Phone: 361-880-3560
Fax: 361-880-3590

Corpus Christi Police Dept
321 John Sartain St
Corpus Christi, TX 78401
Phone: 361-886-2604
Fax: 361-886-2607

Corpus Christi Public Libraries
805 Comanche St
Corpus Christi, TX 78401
Phone: 361-880-7000
Fax: 361-880-7005

Corpus Christi Water Dept
5352 Ayers St Bldg 8-A
Corpus Christi, TX 78415
Phone: 361-857-1881
Fax: 361-857-1889

Important Phone Numbers

AAA 800-222-4357
Corpus Christi Board of Realtors 361-991-8221
Driver's License Information 361-852-4669
Emergency 911
Highway Conditions 800-452-9292
HotelDocs 800-468-3537
Nueces County Tax Office 361-888-0230
Poison Control Center 800-764-7661
Texas Comptroller of Public Accounts 512-463-4000
Vehicle Registration Information 361-888-0459
Voter Registration Information 361-888-0404
Weather 361-289-1861

Information Sources

Better Business Bureau Serving the Coastal Bend of Texas
4301 Ocean Dr
Corpus Christi, TX 78412
www.caller.com/bbb
Phone: 361-852-4949
Fax: 361-852-4990

Corpus Christi Chamber of Commerce
1201 N Shoreline Blvd
Corpus Christi, TX 78401
www.corpuschristichamber.org
Phone: 361-881-1800
Fax: 361-888-5627
TF: 877-385-3437

Corpus Christi Convention & Visitors Bureau
1201 N Shoreline Blvd
Corpus Christi, TX 78401
www.corpuschristi-tx-cvb.org
Phone: 361-881-1888
Fax: 361-887-9023
TF: 800-766-2322

Corpus Christi Public Libraries
805 Comanche St
Corpus Christi, TX 78401
www.library.ci.corpus-christi.tx.us
Phone: 361-880-7000
Fax: 361-880-7005

Corpus Christi Tourist Information Center
PO Box 260185
Corpus Christi, TX 78426
Phone: 361-241-1464
Fax: 361-241-6312
TF: 800-766-2323

Greater Corpus Christi Business Alliance
1201 N Shoreline Blvd
Corpus Christi, TX 78401
Phone: 361-881-1888
Fax: 361-883-5027
TF: 800-678-6232

Memorial Coliseum
PO Box 9277 402 S Shoreline Dr
Corpus Christi, TX 78469
Phone: 361-884-8227
Fax: 361-884-1440

Nueces County
PO Box 2627
Corpus Christi, TX 78403
Phone: 361-888-0580
Fax: 361-888-0329

Online Resources

About.com Guide to Corpus Christi
corpuschristi.about.com/citiestowns/southwestus/corpuschristi/

Area Guide Corpus Christi
corpuschristi.areaguides.net

City Knowledge Corpus Christi
www.cityknowledge.com/tx_corpuschristi.htm

Corpus Christi.com
www.corpuschristi.com

Corpus Quest
www.corpusquest.com

Excite.com Corpus Christi City Guide
www.excite.com/travel/countries/united_states/texas/corpus_christi/

Lodging.com Corpus Christi Texas
www.lodging.com/auto/guides/corpus_christi-area-tx.html

Area Communities

Communities in the Corpus Christi Bay Area with populations greater than 5,000 include:

Alice
500 E Main St
Alice, TX 78332
Phone: 361-668-7210
Fax: 361-668-7292

Aransas Pass
PO Box 2000
Aransas Pass, TX 78335
Phone: 361-758-5301
Fax: 361-758-8188

Beeville
400 N Washington St
Beeville, TX 78102
Phone: 361-358-4641
Fax: 361-358-7355

Falfurrias
PO Box E
Falfurrias, TX 78355
Phone: 361-325-2420
Fax: 361-325-9784

Ingleside
PO Box 400
Ingleside, TX 78362
Phone: 361-776-2517

Kingsville
200 E Kleberg Ave
Kingsville, TX 78363
Phone: 361-595-8002
Fax: 361-595-8035

Mathis
411 E San Patricio Ave
Mathis, TX 78368
Phone: 361-547-3343
Fax: 361-547-3838

Portland
900 Moore Ave
Portland, TX 78374
Phone: 361-643-6501
Fax: 361-643-3747

Robstown
101 E Main Ave
Robstown, TX 78380
Phone: 361-387-4589
Fax: 361-387-9353

Rockport
PO Box 1059
Rockport, TX 78381
Phone: 361-729-2213
Fax: 361-729-6476

Sinton
PO Box 1395
Sinton, TX 78387
Phone: 361-364-2381
Fax: 361-364-3781

Economy

Although the petrochemical industry that dominated Corpus Christi's economy for more than a half century still plays a major role, the city's economic base has diversified significantly in recent years, and a majority of the area's workforce is employed in service-related positions. Tourism and health care have become leading industries in Corpus Christi (the Corpus Christi area hosts more than 4 million visitors a year who contribute a half billion dollars to the local economy). Government is also a leading employment sector in the area—six of Corpus Christi's ten largest employers are government-related, half of which are military establishments.

Unemployment Rate	6.1%*
Per Capita Income	$27,275**
Median Family Income	$29,855

** Information given is for the Corpus Christi Metropolitan Statistical Area (MSA), which includes Nueces and San Patricio counties.*
*** Information given is for Nueces County.*

Principal Industries & Number of Wage Earners

Corpus Christi MSA* - April 2000

Construction	12,800
Finance, Insurance, & Real Estate	6,300
Government	31,400
Manufacturing	13,200
Mining	1,900
Retail Trade	30,900
Services	49,500
Transportation & Public Utilities	6,900
Wholesale Trade	6,000

** Information given is for the Corpus Christi Metropolitan Statistical Area (MSA), which includes Nueces and San Patricio counties.*

Major Employers

APAC Customer Services
4525 Ayers Rd
Corpus Christi, TX 78415
www.apaccustomerservices.com
Phone: 361-696-8100
Fax: 361-696-8180

Bay Inc
1414 Corn Products Rd
Corpus Christi, TX 78469
Phone: 361-289-6600
Fax: 361-289-5005

Christus Spohn Hospital-Shoreline
600 Elizabeth St
Corpus Christi, TX 78404
www.christusspohn.com
Phone: 361-881-3000
Fax: 361-881-3738

Christus Spohn Memorial Hospital
2606 Hospital Blvd
Corpus Christi, TX 78405
www.spohnhealth.org
Phone: 361-902-4000
Fax: 361-902-4968

Columbia Healthcare Corp
6629 Woodridge Rd
Corpus Christi, TX 78414
Phone: 361-980-5200
Fax: 361-857-1407

Corpus Christi Army Depot
308 Crecy St
Corpus Christi, TX 78419
www.ccad.army.mil
Phone: 361-961-3626

Corpus Christi City Hall
1201 Leopard St
Corpus Christi, TX 78401
www.ci.corpus-christi.tx.us
Phone: 361-880-3000

Corpus Christi Independent School District
801 Leopard St
Corpus Christi, TX 78401
E-mail: feedback@familyeducation.com
www.familyeducation.com/home
Phone: 361-886-9001
Fax: 361-886-9209

First Data Corp
330 Opportunity Dr
Corpus Christi, TX 78405
www.firstdatacorp.com
Phone: 361-299-8115
Fax: 361-299-8101

HEB Grocery Co
4326 Kostoryz Rd
Corpus Christi, TX 78415
Phone: 361-857-1711

Koch Refining Co LP
PO Box 2608
Corpus Christi, TX 78403
Phone: 361-241-4811
Fax: 361-242-8676

Naval Air Station Corpus Christi
11101 D St
Corpus Christi, TX 78419
navaltx.navy.mil/nascc
Phone: 361-961-2811

Naval Air Station Kingsville
Kingsville, TX 79363
www.nask.navy.mil
Phone: 361-516-6136
Fax: 361-516-6875

Texas A & M University Kingsville
Campus Box 105
Kingsville, TX 78363
www.tamuk.edu
Phone: 361-593-2111
Fax: 361-593-3604

Wal-Mart Inc
1821 South Padre Island Dr
Corpus Christi, TX 78416
Phone: 361-854-0943
Fax: 361-814-2756

Quality of Living Indicators

Total Crime Index 20,375
(rates per 100,000 inhabitants)

Violent Crime
Murder/manslaughter 15
Forcible rape 194
Robbery 388
Aggravated assault 1,888

Property Crime
Burglary 3,521
Larceny theft 12,859
Motor vehicle theft 1,510

Cost of Living Index 94.6
(national average = 100)

Median Home Price $85,000

Education

Public Schools

Corpus Christi Independent School District
801 Leopard St
Corpus Christi, TX 78401
E-mail: feedback@familyeducation.com
www.familyeducation.com/home
Phone: 361-886-9001
Fax: 361-886-9209

Number of Schools
Elementary 40
Middle 12
High 5
Special 7

Student/Teacher Ratio
All Grades 16.3:1

Private Schools

Number of Schools (all grades) .... 20+

Colleges & Universities

Del Mar College East Campus
101 Baldwin Blvd
Corpus Christi, TX 78404
www.delmar.edu
Phone: 361-698-1200
Fax: 361-698-1182
TF: 800-652-3357

Texas A & M University Corpus Christi
6300 Ocean Dr
Corpus Christi, TX 78412
www.tamucc.edu
Phone: 361-825-6810
Fax: 361-825-5887
TF: 800-482-6822

Hospitals

Alice Regional Hospital
2500 E Main St
Alice, TX 78332
Phone: 361-664-4376
Fax: 361-660-5321

Christus Spohn Hospital Kleberg
1300 General Cabasos Blvd
Kingsville, TX 78363
www.spohnhealth.org
Phone: 361-595-1661
Fax: 361-595-9688

Christus Spohn Hospital-Shoreline
600 Elizabeth St
Corpus Christi, TX 78404
www.christusspohn.com
Phone: 361-881-3000
Fax: 361-881-3738

Christus Spohn Memorial Hospital
2606 Hospital Blvd
Corpus Christi, TX 78405
www.spohnhealth.org
Phone: 361-902-4000
Fax: 361-902-4968

Bay Area-Corpus Christi Medical Center
7101 S Padre Island Dr
Corpus Christi, TX 78412
Phone: 361-985-1200
Fax: 361-985-3670

Corpus Christi Medical Center
3315 S Alameda St
Corpus Christi, TX 78411
Phone: 361-857-1501
Fax: 361-857-5960

Driscoll Children's Hospital
3533 S Alameda St
Corpus Christi, TX 78411
www.driscollchildrens.org
Phone: 361-694-5000
Fax: 361-694-5317

Transportation

Airport(s)

Corpus Christi International Airport (CRP)
15 miles SW of downtown (approx 15 minutes) ... 361-289-0171

Mass Transit

B Ride Bus
$.50 Base fare 361-289-2600
RTA Trolley
$.50 base fare 361-289-2600
RTA Water Taxi
$1 Base fare 361-289-2600

Rail/Bus

Greyhound/Valley Transit Bus Station Phone: 361-882-2516
702 N Chaparral St
Corpus Christi, TX 78401

Utilities

Electricity
AEP/Central Power & Light Co 800-274-2611
www.aep.com

Gas
Corpus Christi Public Utilities 361-880-3400

Water
Corpus Christi Public Utilities 361-880-3400

Garbage Collection/Recycling
Corpus Christi Public Utilities 361-880-3400

Telecommunications

Telephone
Southwestern Bell Telephone Co. 361-967-6500
www.swbell.com

Cable Television
AT & T Cable Services 361-857-5000
www.cable.att.com

Internet Service Providers (ISPs)
CompuBasix 361-906-0111
www.davlin.net
Interconnect Services Inc 361-884-3447
www.interconnect.net

Banks

American National Bank Phone: 361-992-9900
5120 S Padre Island Dr Fax: 361-991-0084
Corpus Christi, TX 78411

Frost Bank Phone: 361-844-1128
2402 Leopard St Fax: 361-844-1134
Corpus Christi, TX 78403 TF: 800-562-6732

International Bank of Commerce Phone: 361-888-4000
221 S Shoreline Blvd Fax: 361-888-5243
Corpus Christi, TX 78401

Pacific Southwest Bank FSB Phone: 361-889-7700
606 N Carancahua St Suite 620 Fax: 361-889-7816
Corpus Christi, TX 78476 TF: 800-933-7224

Wells Fargo Bank Phone: 361-886-6550
615 Upper N Broadway Fax: 361-886-6562
Corpus Christi, TX 78477 TF: 800-224-7334

Shopping

Crossroads Shopping Village Phone: 361-991-4950
5830 McArdle St Fax: 361-991-9453
Corpus Christi, TX 78412

Lamar Park Shopping Center Phone: 361-854-8885
3817 S Alameda St Fax: 361-854-5889
Corpus Christi, TX 78411

Padre Island Park Co Phone: 361-949-9368
20420 Park Rd 22 Malaquite Beach Fax: 361-949-9368
Corpus Christi, TX 78418

Padre-Staples Mall Phone: 361-991-3755
5488 S Padre Island Dr Fax: 361-993-5631
Corpus Christi, TX 78411

Sunrise Mall Phone: 361-993-2900
5858 S Padre Island Dr
Corpus Christi, TX 78412

Water Street Market Phone: 361-881-9322
309 N Water St Fax: 361-881-9208
Corpus Christi, TX 78401

Media

Newspapers and Magazines

Caller-Times* Phone: 361-884-2011
PO Box 9136 Fax: 361-886-3732
Corpus Christi, TX 78469 TF: 800-827-2011
www.caller.com

South Texas Informer & Business Journal Phone: 361-857-6332
4455 S Padre Island Dr Suite 101 Fax: 361-857-6337
Corpus Christi, TX 78411

**Indicates major daily newspapers*

Television

KAJA-TV Ch 68 (Tele) Phone: 361-886-6101
409 S Staples Fax: 361-886-6116
Corpus Christi, TX 78401

KDF-TV Ch 47 (Fox) Phone: 361-886-6100
409 S Staples St Fax: 361-886-6116
Corpus Christi, TX 78401

KEDT-TV Ch 16 (PBS) Phone: 361-855-2213
4455 S Padre Island Dr Suite 38 Fax: 361-855-3877
Corpus Christi, TX 78411 TF: 800-307-5338
E-mail: mail@kedt.pbs.org
www.esc2.net/kedt/KEDT.htm

KIII-TV Ch 3 (ABC) Phone: 361-986-8300
5002 S Padre Island Dr Fax: 361-986-8440
Corpus Christi, TX 78411

KORO-TV Ch 28 (Uni) Phone: 361-883-2823
102 N Mesquite Fax: 361-883-2931
Corpus Christi, TX 78401

KRIS-TV Ch 6 (NBC) Phone: 361-886-6100
409 S Staples St Fax: 361-887-6666
Corpus Christi, TX 78401
E-mail: kris@trip.net
www.kristv.com/

KZTV-TV Ch 10 (CBS) Phone: 361-883-7070
301 Artesian St Fax: 361-884-8111
Corpus Christi, TX 78401

Radio

KEDT-FM 90.3 MHz (NPR) Phone: 361-855-2213
4455 S Padre Island Dr Suite 38 Fax: 361-855-3877
Corpus Christi, TX 78411 TF: 800-850-5717
www.kedt.org

KEYS-AM 1440 kHz (N/T)
2117 Leopard St
Corpus Christi, TX 78408
Phone: 361-882-7411
Fax: 361-882-9767

KFTX-FM 97.5 MHz (Ctry)
1520 S Port Ave
Corpus Christi, TX 78405
www.kftx.com
Phone: 361-883-5987
Fax: 361-883-3648
TF: 888-883-5389

KLTG-FM 96.5 MHz (CHR)
PO Box 898
Corpus Christi, TX 78403
Phone: 361-883-1600
Fax: 361-888-5685

KLUX-FM 89.5 MHz (B/EZ)
1200 Lantana St
Corpus Christi, TX 78407
Phone: 361-289-2487
Fax: 361-289-1420

KOUL-FM 103.7 MHz (Ctry)
1300 Antelope St
Corpus Christi, TX 78401
Phone: 361-883-1600
Fax: 361-888-5685

KZFM-FM 95.5 MHz (CHR)
PO Box 9757
Corpus Christi, TX 78469
E-mail: kzfm@aol.com
www.hotz95.com
Phone: 361-882-7411
Fax: 361-882-9767

Attractions

Located on the Texas coast, halfway between Houston and the U.S.-Mexican border, Corpus Christi sits on a bay surrounded by tropical islands, combining Texas traditions with the beaches and fishing of a Gulf resort. Port Aransas, a village on the tip of Mustang Island, is known for its great deep-sea fishing, and Conn Brown Harbor in Aransas Pass has the largest shrimping fleet on the Texas Coast. One can also go horseback riding on the beach at Mustang Island, or relax on the beaches at Padre Island National Seashore. (Similar activities are available in the Rockport-Fulton area, which is also an artist community.) In the city itself, popular sites include the Texas State Aquarium, which focuses exclusively on marine life of the Gulf of Mexico and Caribbean; the USS Lexington Museum-On-The Bay; and the life-size replicas of the Pinta, Nina, and Santa Maria docked in the Port of Corpus Christi.

Aransas National Wildlife Refuge
PO Box 100
Austwell, TX 77950
Phone: 361-286-3559
Fax: 361-286-3722

Art Center of Corpus Christi
100 Shoreline Dr
Corpus Christi, TX 78401
Phone: 361-884-6406
Fax: 361-884-8836

Asian Cultures Museum
1809 N Chaparral St
Corpus Christi, TX 78401
Phone: 361-882-2641
Fax: 361-882-5718

Bayfront Plaza Convention Center
1901 N Shoreline Blvd
Corpus Christi, TX 78401
Phone: 361-883-8543
Fax: 361-883-0788

Captain Clark's Flagship
People's Street T-Head Corpus Christi Marina
Corpus Christi, TX 78401
Phone: 361-884-8306

Conner John E Museum
905 W Santa Gertrudis St
Kingsville, TX 78363
Phone: 361-593-2810
Fax: 361-593-2112

Corpus Christi Ballet
1621 N Mesquite St
Corpus Christi, TX 78401
www.tamu.edu/ccballet/
Phone: 361-882-4588
Fax: 361-881-9291

Corpus Christi Botanical Gardens
8545 S Staples St
Corpus Christi, TX 78413
Phone: 361-852-2100
Fax: 361-852-7875

Corpus Christi Museum of Science & History
1900 N Chaparral St
Corpus Christi, TX 78401
www.ci.corpus-christi.tx.us/services/museum
Phone: 361-883-2862
Fax: 361-884-7392

Corpus Christi Symphony
1901 N Shoreline Blvd Selena Auditorium
Corpus Christi, TX 78401
Phone: 361-882-4091
Fax: 361-882-4132
TF: 877-286-6683

Corpus Christi Zoo
County Rd 33
Corpus Christi, TX 78403
Phone: 361-814-8000

French-Galvan House
1581 N Chaparral St
Corpus Christi, TX 78401
Phone: 361-883-0639
Fax: 361-883-0676

Fulton Mansion
317 Fulton Beach Rd
Rockport, TX 78382
Phone: 361-729-0386
Fax: 361-729-6581

Grande-Grossman House
1517 N Chaparral St
Corpus Christi, TX 78401
Phone: 361-887-0868
Fax: 361-887-9773

Gugenheim House
1601 N Chaparral St
Corpus Christi, TX 78401
Phone: 361-887-1601
Fax: 361-887-1602

Harbor Playhouse
1 Bayfront Pk
Corpus Christi, TX 78401
E-mail: boxoffic@harborplayhouse.com
www.harborplayhouse.com/
Phone: 361-888-7469
Fax: 361-888-4779

Henrietta Memorial Center
405 N 6th St
Kingsville, TX 78363
Phone: 361-595-1881
Fax: 361-592-3247

Heritage Park
1581 N Chaparral St
Corpus Christi, TX 78401
Phone: 361-883-0639
Fax: 361-883-0676

Jalufka-Govatos House
1513 N Chaparral St
Corpus Christi, TX 78401
Phone: 361-882-9226

King Ranch Inc
Hwy 141 W
Kingsville, TX 78363
www.king-ranch.com
Phone: 361-592-8055
Fax: 361-595-1344

Littles-Martin House
1519 N Chaparral St
Corpus Christi, TX 78401
Phone: 361-883-0639
Fax: 361-883-0676

McCampbell House
1501 N Chaparral St
Corpus Christi, TX 78401
Phone: 361-883-0639

Mustang Island State Park
Hwy 361
Port Aransas, TX 78373
Phone: 361-749-5246
Fax: 361-749-6455

Padre Island National Seashore
PO Box 181300
Corpus Christi, TX 78480
www.nps.gov/pais/
Phone: 361-949-8173
Fax: 361-949-8023

Palo Alto Battlefield National Historic Site
1623 Central Blvd
Brownsville, TX 78520
www.nps.gov/paal/
Phone: 956-541-2785
Fax: 956-541-6356

Port Aransas Park
321 Beach Rd Mustang Island
Port Aransas, TX 78412
Phone: 361-749-6117

Port of Corpus Christi
222 Power St
Corpus Christi, TX 78401
www.portofcorpuschristi.com
Phone: 361-882-5633
Fax: 361-882-7110
TF: 800-580-7110

Rockport Center for the Arts
902 Navigation Cir
Rockport, TX 78382
Phone: 361-729-5519
Fax: 361-729-3551

Ships of Christopher Columbus
1900 N Chaparral St
Corpus Christi, TX 78401
Phone: 361-883-2862
Fax: 361-884-7392

Sidbury House
1609 N Chaparral St
Corpus Christi, TX 78401
Phone: 361-883-0639
Fax: 361-883-0676

South Texas Institute for the Arts
1902 N Shoreline Blvd
Corpus Christi, TX 78401
E-mail: stiaweb@falcon.tamucc.edu
www.stia.org
Phone: 361-825-3500
Fax: 361-825-3520

Texas Maritime Museum
1202 Navigation Cir
Rockport, TX 78382
E-mail: tmm@2fords.net
Phone: 361-729-1271
Fax: 361-729-9938

Texas State Aquarium
2710 N Shoreline Blvd
Corpus Christi, TX 78402
E-mail: mermaid@txstateaq.org
www.txstateaq.org
Phone: 361-881-1200
Fax: 361-881-1257

USS Lexington Museum on the Bay
2914 N Shoreline Blvd
Corpus Christi, TX 78402
Phone: 361-888-4873
Fax: 361-883-8361

Xeriscape Learning Center & Design Garden
1900 N Chaparral St
Corpus Christi, TX 78401
Phone: 361-883-2862
Fax: 361-884-7392

Sports Teams & Facilities

Corpus Christi Greyhound Race Track
5302 Leopard St
Corpus Christi, TX 78408
www.corpuschristidogs.com
Phone: 361-289-9333
Fax: 361-289-4307

Corpus Christi IceRays (hockey)
402 S Shoreline Dr Memorial Coliseum
Corpus Christi, TX 78469
www.icerayshockey.com
Phone: 361-814-7825

Corpus Christi Speedway
SR-358 & SR-44
Corpus Christi, TX 78405
Phone: 361-289-8847

Memorial Coliseum
PO Box 9277 402 S Shoreline Dr
Corpus Christi, TX 78469
Phone: 361-884-8227
Fax: 361-884-1440

Annual Events

Annual Christmas Tree Forest (December) 361-980-3500
Artfest (mid-April) 361-884-6406
Bayfest (late September-early October) 361-887-0868
Beach to Bay Marathon (mid-May) 361-225-3338
Buccaneer Days & Rodeo (mid-April-early May).....361-882-3242
Corpus Christi Maritime Festival (May) 361-883-5011
Deep Sea Roundup (early July) 361-749-5919
Harbor Lights (December) 361-985-1555
La Feria De Las Flores (early August) 361-883-8543
Oysterfest (early March) 361-729-2388
Rockport Art Festival (early July) 361-729-6445
Rockport Seafair (early October) 800-242-3502
Shrimporee (September) 361-758-2750
South Texas Ranching Heritage Festival (February) 361-595-3712
Texas Jazz Festival (mid-October) 361-883-4500
US Open Windsurfing Regatta (late May) 361-985-1555

Dallas, Texas

***County:* Dallas**

DALLAS is located in the north central part of eastern Texas along the Trinity River. Major cities within 100 miles include Fort Worth, Garland, Irving, Arlington, Waco, and Wichita Falls, Texas.

Area (Land) .... 327 sq mi
Area (Water) .... 19.7 sq mi
Elevation .... 463 ft
Latitude .... 32-78-00 N
Longitude .... 96-81-00 W
Time Zone .... CST
Area Code 214, 972

Climate

Dallas has a continental climate. Winters are generally mild, with average high temperatures in the mid- to upper 50s and average lows in the mid- to upper 30s. Brief cold spells caused by polar air masses that move in from the Great Plains occur occasionally, but snowfall is minimal, averaging less than three inches annually. Summers are hot and humid, with average high temperatures in the mid-90s and average lows in the low to mid-70s. Thunderstorms are common during the spring months—May is the wettest month in Dallas, while January is the driest.

Average Temperatures & Precipitation

Temperatures

	Jan	Feb	Mar	Apr	May	Jun	Jul	Aug	Sep	Oct	Nov	Dec
High	55	60	69	77	84	91	96	96	88	78	67	58
Low	35	39	47	56	64	72	76	76	68	57	47	38

Precipitation

	Jan	Feb	Mar	Apr	May	Jun	Jul	Aug	Sep	Oct	Nov	Dec
Inches	1.8	2.3	3.2	3.9	5.0	3.5	2.4	2.3	3.6	3.9	2.4	1.9

History

The Dallas area was inhabited by various Native American tribes until 1841 when Tennessee lawyer John Neely Bryan established the first white settlement in the area. In 1846, the town was laid out and was named Dallas in honor of Vice President George Dallas. Dallas County was formed the same year, and in 1850, with a population of 430, the town became the county seat. Dallas was incorporated as a city in 1856. Early growth was slow, but the arrival of the railroad in 1872 linked Dallas with the rest of the United States, creating economic opportunities that drew settlers to the area. By 1900, the city's population had soared to more than 42,000.

The 20th Century was a time of phenomenal growth in Dallas—each decade saw the development of new industries that stimulated economic and population growth. Initially, agricultural trade dominated the economy. Finance became a major player in the city's economy in 1914 when Dallas was chosen as the site for one of the 12 regional U.S. Federal Reserve Banks. In 1910, urban planner George Kessler proposed a plan to create a levee system on the flood-prone Trinity River, which flowed through the city. A decade later, the Trinity River Reclamation Project began, resulting in a new business district for the city. During the 1920s, the commercial aviation industry developed when the city purchased World War I training field, Love Field. (Dallas would eventually become a leader in air transport—Dallas-Fort Worth International Airport was opened in 1973, became the headquarters of American Airlines six years later, and today ranks as the second busiest airport in the entire world.)

In 1930, the East Texas Oil Field—the world's largest deposit of oil at that time—was discovered east of Dallas. The city rapidly became a major center for the petroleum industry, as more than 500 new oil-related companies were established there within a year's time. Also during the 1930s, the high-technology industry took off in Dallas with the establishment of Geophysical Services Inc., a company that would later become industry giant Texas Instruments. The advent of World War II brought the defense and aviation manufacturing industry to the Dallas area, which has also continued to thrive.

In November 1963, Dallas became the site of one of the greatest tragedies in American history as shots were fired on the Presidential motorcade, killing President John F. Kennedy and injuring Texas Governor John Connally. President Kennedy's assassination sent shock waves throughout the world and, for a time, cast a shadow over Dallas' image.

The Dallas area is among the fastest growing metropolitan areas in the United States, increasing more than 40 percent from 1980 to 1995. One of the nation's leading commercial, financial, and distribution centers, the city of Dallas today is home to more than one million residents, making it the third largest city in Texas and the ninth largest city in the United States.

Population

1990 Census 1,007,618
1998 Estimate 1,075,894
% Change 6.8
2005 Projection 2,143,962*

Racial/Ethnic Breakdown

White 55.3%
Black 29.5%
Other 15.2%
Hispanic Origin (may be of any race) 20.9%

Age Breakdown

Under 5 years 8.1%
5 to 17 .... 16.9%
18 to 20 .... 4.3%

21 to 24.................................7.5%
25 to 34.................................22.4%
35 to 44.................................14.9%
45 to 54.................................9.1%
55 to 64.................................7.1%
65 to 74.................................5.6%
75+ years.................................4.1%
Median Age.................................30.6

Gender Breakdown

Male.................................49.1%
Female.................................50.9%

* *Information given is for Dallas County.*

Government

Type of Government: Council-Manager

Dallas City Council
1500 Marilla St Rm 5F-N
Dallas, TX 75201
Phone: 214-670-4050
Fax: 214-670-5117

Dallas City Hall
1500 Marilla St
Dallas, TX 75201
Phone: 214-670-3011

Dallas City Manager
1500 Marilla St Rm 4E-N
Dallas, TX 75201
Phone: 214-670-3296
Fax: 214-670-3946

Dallas City Secretary
1500 Marilla St Rm 5D-S
Dallas, TX 75201
Phone: 214-670-3738
Fax: 214-670-5029

Dallas Economic Development Dept
1500 Marilla St Rm 5C-S
Dallas, TX 75201
Phone: 214-670-1686
Fax: 214-670-0158

Dallas Fire Dept
1500 Marilla St Rm 7A-S
Dallas, TX 75201
Phone: 214-670-5466
Fax: 214-670-4564

Dallas Human Resources Dept
1500 Marilla St Rm 6A-N
Dallas, TX 75201
Phone: 214-670-3550
Fax: 214-670-3764

Dallas Mayor
1500 Marilla St Rm 5E-N
Dallas, TX 75201
Phone: 214-670-0773
Fax: 214-670-0646

Dallas Park & Recreation Dept
1500 Marilla St Rm 6F-N
Dallas, TX 75201
Phone: 214-670-4100
Fax: 214-670-4084

Dallas Planning & Development Dept
1500 Marilla St Rm 5D-N
Dallas, TX 75201
Phone: 214-670-4127
Fax: 214-670-5755

Dallas Police Dept
2014 Main St Rm 506
Dallas, TX 75201
Phone: 214-670-3698
Fax: 214-670-5507

Dallas Public Works Dept
320 E Jefferson Blvd
Dallas, TX 75203
Phone: 214-948-4200
Fax: 214-948-4239

Dallas Revenue & Taxation Div
1500 Marilla St Rm 2B-S
Dallas, TX 75201
Phone: 214-670-3442
Fax: 214-670-3360

Dallas Transportation Dept
320 E Jefferson Blvd
Dallas, TX 75203
Phone: 214-948-4650
Fax: 214-948-4239

Dallas Water Utilities Dept
1500 Marilla St Rm 4A N
Dallas, TX 75201
Phone: 214-670-3144
Fax: 214-670-3154

Jonsson J Eric Central Library
1515 Young St
Dallas, TX 75201
Phone: 214-670-1400
Fax: 214-670-7839

Important Phone Numbers

AAA.................................214-526-7911
American Express Travel.................................214-363-0214
Dallas Revenue & Taxation Div.................................214-670-3442
Dallas Central Appraisal District.................................214-631-0520
Dallas County Tax Office.................................214-653-7811
Dental Referral.................................214-526-3435
Driver's License Information.................................214-861-2125
Emergency.................................911
Greater Dallas Assn of Realtors.................................214-637-6660
Highway Conditions.................................800-452-9292
HotelDocs.................................800-468-3537
Medical Referral.................................214-320-7750
Poison Control Center.................................800-764-7661
Special Events Hotline.................................214-746-6679
Texas Comptroller of Public Accounts.................................800-252-5555
Travelers Aid.................................972-574-4420
Vehicle Registration Information.................................214-653-7621
Voter Registration Information.................................214-637-7937
Weather.................................214-787-1111

Information Sources

Better Business Bureau Serving Metropolitan Dallas & Northeast Texas
2001 Bryan St Suite 850
Dallas, TX 75201
www.dallas.bbb.org
Phone: 214-220-2000
Fax: 214-740-0321

Dallas Convention & Visitors Bureau
1201 Elm St Suite 2000
Dallas, TX 75270
www.dallascvb.com
Phone: 214-571-1000
Fax: 214-571-1008
TF: 800-232-5527

Dallas Convention Center
650 S Griffin St
Dallas, TX 75202
www.dallascc.com
Phone: 214-939-2700
Fax: 214-939-2795
TF: 877-850-2100

Dallas County
411 Elm St
Dallas, TX 75202
www.dallascounty.org
Phone: 214-653-7361
Fax: 214-653-7057

Dallas Market Center
2100 Stemmons Fwy Suite MS150
Dallas, TX 75207
www.dallasmarketcenter.com
Phone: 800-325-6587
Fax: 214-749-5464

Garland Chamber of Commerce
914 S Garland Ave
Garland, TX 75040
www.garlandchamber.org
Phone: 972-272-7551
Fax: 972-276-9261

Garland City Hall
200 N 5th St
Garland, TX 75040
www.ci.garland.tx.us
Phone: 972-205-2000
Fax: 972-205-2504

Garland Convention & Visitors Bureau
200 N 5th St
Garland, TX 75006
Phone: 972-205-2749
Fax: 972-205-2504

Garland Mayor
200 N 5th St 4th Fl
Garland, TX 75040
Phone: 972-205-2400
Fax: 972-205-2504

Garland Planning Dept
PO Box 469002
Garland, TX 75046
www.ci.garland.tx.us/cogplan.htm
Phone: 972-205-2445
Fax: 972-205-2474

Greater Dallas Chamber of Commerce
1201 Elm St Suite 2000
Dallas, TX 75270
www.gdc.org
Phone: 214-746-6600
Fax: 214-746-6799

Greater Irving Chamber of Commerce
3333 N MacArthur Blvd Suite 100
Irving, TX 75062
www.irving.net/chamber
Phone: 972-252-8484
Fax: 972-252-6710

Irving City Hall
825 W Irving Blvd
Irving, TX 75060
www.ci.irving.tx.us
Phone: 972-721-2600
Fax: 972-721-2384

Irving Community Development Dept
825 W Irving Blvd 2nd Fl
Irving, TX 75060
www.ci.irving.tx.us/CommDev/index.htm
Phone: 972-721-2424
Fax: 972-721-2422

Irving Convention & Visitors Bureau
3333 N MacArthur Blvd Suite 200
Irving, TX 75062
www.irvingtexas.com
Phone: 972-252-7476
Fax: 972-257-3153
TF: 800-247-8464

Irving Mayor
PO Box 152288
Irving, TX 75015
Phone: 972-721-2410
Fax: 972-721-2384

Irving Public Library System
801 W Irving Blvd
Irving, TX 75060
www.irving.lib.tx.us
Phone: 972-721-2606
Fax: 972-721-2463

Nicholson Memorial Library System
625 Austin St
Garland, TX 75040
www.ci.garland.tx.us/coglib1.htm
Phone: 972-205-2543
Fax: 972-205-2523

Online Resources

4Dallas.com
www.4dallas.com

About.com Guide to Dallas
dallas.about.com/local/southwestus/dallas

About.com Guide to Irving
irving.about.com/local/southwestus/irving

Access America Dallas
www.accessamer.com/dallas/

Anthill City Guide Dallas/Fort Worth
www.anthill.com/city.asp?city=dallas

Area Guide Dallas
dallas.areaguides.net

Area Guide Garland
garland.areaguides.net

Area Guide Irving
irving.areaguides.net

Boulevards Dallas
www.dallas.com

Bradmans.com Dallas
www.bradmans.com/scripts/display_city.cgi?city=234

City Knowledge Dallas
www.cityknowledge.com/tx_dallas.htm

City Knowledge Garland
www.cityknowledge.com/tx_garland.htm

Cityhits Dallas
www.cityhits.com/dallas/

CuisineNet Dallas
www.menusonline.com/cities/dallas/locmain.shtml

Dallas CityWomen
www.citywomen.com/dalwomen.htm

Dallas Entertainment Guide
www.wn.com/dallas

Dallas Fort Worth City Pages
dallas.thelinks.com

Dallas Fort Worth Metroplex Directory
www.flash.net/~dfwmet/

Dallas Gay/Lesbian Guide
www.cyberramp.net/~woofbyte/dfw_home.htm

Dallas Information
www.dallas.org

Dallas Observer
www.dallasobserver.com

Dallas Virtual Jewish Community
www.dvjc.org

Dallas-Fort Worth Texas
www.dallas-fort-worth.com

Dallas/Fort Worth Area Web
www.dfwareaweb.com/

DigitalCity Dallas-Fort Worth
home.digitalcity.com/dallas

Excite.com Dallas City Guide
www.excite.com/travel/countries/united_states/texas/dallas

Excite.com Garland City Guide
www.excite.com/travel/countries/united_states/texas/garland

Excite.com Irving City Guide
www.excite.com/travel/countries/united_states/texas/irving

GuideLive: Arts & Entertainment in Dallas & Fort Worth
www.guidelive.com

Hometown Dallas
www.hometowndallas.com

HotelGuide Dallas/Fort Worth
hotelguide.net/dfw

Irving.Net
www.irving.net/

Lodging.com Dallas-Fort Worth Texas
www.lodging.com/auto/guides/dallas_ft_worth-area-tx.html

MetroGuide Dallas/Fort Worth
metroguide.net/dfw

Open World City Guides Dallas
www.worldexecutive.com/cityguides/dallas/

Preservation Dallas
www.preservationdallas.org/

Rough Guide Travel Dallas
travel.roughguides.com/content/938/

Savvy Diner Guide to Dallas Restaurants
www.savvydiner.com/dallas/

Virtual Voyages Dallas-Fort Worth
www.virtualvoyages.com/usa/tx/dfw/dfw.sht

Yahoo! Dallas/Fort Worth
dfw.yahoo.com

YourDallas.com
www.yourdallas.com/

Area Communities

Communities in the Greater Dallas area (Collin, Dallas, Denton, Ellis, Kaufman, and Rockwall counties—Tarrant County communities are listed in the profile on Fort Worth) with populations greater than 10,000 include:

Addison
PO Box 9010
Addison, TX 75001
Phone: 972-450-7027
Fax: 972-450-7043

Allen
1 Allen Civic Plaza
Allen, TX 75013
Phone: 972-727-0100
Fax: 972-727-0165

Balch Springs
3117 Hickory Tree Rd
Balch Springs, TX 75180
Phone: 972-557-6070
Fax: 972-286-3683

Carrollton
PO Box 110535
Carrollton, TX 75011
Phone: 972-466-3000
Fax: 972-466-3252

Cedar Hill
PO Box 96
Cedar Hill, TX 75106
Phone: 972-291-5103
Fax: 972-291-5107

Coppell
255 Parkway Blvd
Coppell, TX 75019
Phone: 972-462-0022
Fax: 972-304-3673

Denton
215 E McKinney St
Denton, TX 76201
Phone: 940-349-8307
Fax: 940-349-8236

DeSoto
211 E Pleasant Run Rd
DeSoto, TX 75115
Phone: 972-230-9640
Fax: 972-230-5793

Duncanville
203 E Wheatland Rd
Duncanville, TX 75116
Phone: 972-780-5000
Fax: 972-780-5077

Ennis
115 W Brown St
Ennis, TX 75119
Phone: 972-875-1234
Fax: 972-875-9086

Farmers Branch
PO Box 819010
Farmers Branch, TX 75381
Phone: 972-247-3131
Fax: 972-341-6305

Flower Mound
2121 Cross Timbers Rd
Flower Mound, TX 75028
Phone: 972-724-0754
Fax: 972-539-3392

Frisco
6891 Main St
Frisco, TX 75034
Phone: 972-335-5555
Fax: 972-335-1959

Garland
200 N 5th St
Garland, TX 75040
Phone: 972-205-2000
Fax: 972-205-2504

Grand Prairie
317 College St
Grand Prairie, TX 75050
Phone: 972-237-8000
Fax: 972-237-8317

Highland Village
1000 Highland Village Rd
Highland Village, TX 75077
Phone: 972-317-2558
Fax: 972-317-0237

Irving
825 W Irving Blvd
Irving, TX 75060
Phone: 972-721-2600
Fax: 972-721-2384

Lancaster
211 N Henry St
Lancaster, TX 75146
Phone: 972-227-2111
Fax: 972-227-4032

Lewisville
PO Box 299002
Lewisville, TX 75029
Phone: 972-219-3400
Fax: 972-219-3412

McKinney
PO Box 517
McKinney, TX 75070
Phone: 972-542-2675
Fax: 972-542-0436

Mesquite
1515 N Galloway Ave
Mesquite, TX 75149
Phone: 972-216-6293
Fax: 972-216-6431

Plano
1520 Ave K
Plano, TX 75074
Phone: 972-941-7000
Fax: 972-423-9587

Richardson
PO Box 830309
Richardson, TX 75083
Phone: 972-744-4100
Fax: 972-744-5803

Rockwall
205 W Rusk St
Rockwall, TX 75087
Phone: 972-771-7700
Fax: 972-771-7727

Rowlett
PO Box 99
Rowlett, TX 75030
Phone: 972-412-6110
Fax: 972-412-6279

Terrell
201 E Nash St
Terrell, TX 75160
Phone: 972-551-6600
Fax: 972-551-6682

The Colony
6800 Main St
The Colony, TX 75056
Phone: 972-625-1756
Fax: 972-624-2298

University Park
3800 University Blvd
University Park, TX 75205
Phone: 214-363-1644
Fax: 214-987-5399

Waxahachie
PO Box 757
Waxahachie, TX 75168
Phone: 972-937-7330
Fax: 972-937-5518

Wylie
2000 N Hwy 78
Wylie, TX 75098
Phone: 972-442-8100
Fax: 972-442-8106

Economy

Approximately 6,000 companies, including 19 Fortune 500 and 16 Forbes 500 companies, have their corporate headquarters in Greater Dallas, making the area a leading center for business. Major U.S. corporations that have relocated to or expanded their operations in the Dallas area since 1980 include AT & T, Exxon, GTE, and JC Penney. The city and surrounding area has a healthy and diverse economic base that ranges from agriculture to finance, commercial aviation to international trade. The services sector accounts for the greatest number of jobs in the Dallas area, with healthcare, telecommunications, and tourism being major industries. Approximately one-quarter of the Dallas area's total workforce is employed in trade—Dallas is not only a leading domestic trade center, but as home to the North American Commission for Labor Cooperation (the only tri-national NAFTA office in the U.S.), the city is also a leader in the international marketplace.

Unemployment Rate	4.1%
Per Capita Income	$23,900*
Median Family Income	$31,925

** Information given is for the Dallas Primary Metropolitan Statistical Area (PMSA), which includes Collin, Dallas, Denton, Ellis, Henderson, Hunt, Kaufman, and Rockwall counties.*

Principal Industries & Number of Wage Earners

Dallas PMSA* - 1999

Construction	97,200
Finance, Insurance, & Real Estate	157,300
Government	208,100
Manufacturing	254,000
Mining	11,300
Services & Miscellaneous	584,600
Transportation, Communications, & Utilities	130,000
Wholesale & Retail Trade	457,200

** Information given is for the Dallas Primary Metropolitan Statistical Area (PMSA), which includes Collin, Dallas, Denton, Ellis, Henderson, Hunt, Kaufman, and Rockwall counties.*

Major Employers

AMR Corp
4333 Amon Carter Blvd
Fort Worth, TX 76155
www.amrcorp.com
Phone: 817-963-1234
Fax: 817-967-4162

AT & T
5501 LBJ Fwy
Dallas, TX 75240
www.att.com
Phone: 972-778-2000

Bank of America
1401 Elm St
Dallas, TX 75202
Phone: 888-279-3247
Fax: 214-508-8179

Baylor University Medical Center
3500 Gaston Ave
Dallas, TX 75246
www.baylorhealth.com
Phone: 214-820-0111
TF: 800-422-9567

Chase Bank of Texas NA
2200 Ross Ave
Dallas, TX 75201
Phone: 214-922-2300
Fax: 214-965-3767
TF: 800-882-7230

Children's Medical Center of Dallas
1935 Motor St
Dallas, TX 75235
www.childrens.com
Phone: 214-456-7000
Fax: 214-456-2197

Dallas City Hall
1500 Marilla St
Dallas, TX 75201
www.ci.dallas.tx.us
Phone: 214-670-3011

Dallas County
411 Elm St
Dallas, TX 75202
www.dallascounty.org
Phone: 214-653-7361
Fax: 214-653-7057

Dallas Independent School District
3700 Ross Ave
Dallas, TX 75204
www.dallasisd.org
Phone: 972-925-3700

Dallas Morning News
PO Box 655237
Dallas, TX 75265
E-mail: tdmned@cityview.com
www.dallasnews.com
Phone: 214-977-8222
Fax: 214-977-8319

Medical City Dallas
7777 Forest Ln
Dallas, TX 75230
Phone: 972-661-7000
Fax: 972-566-6248

Methodist Medical Center
PO Box 655999
Dallas, TX 75265
Phone: 214-947-8181
Fax: 214-947-3403

Northrop Grumman Corp Integrated Systems Sector
PO Box 655907
Dallas, TX 75265
www.northgrum.com/isa_www
Phone: 972-946-2011
Fax: 972-946-5761

Parkland Health & Hospital System
5201 Harry Hines Blvd
Dallas, TX 75235
www.swmed.edu/home_pages/parkland/
Phone: 214-590-8000
Fax: 214-590-8096

Presbyterian Healthcare System Div Texas Health Resources
8220 Walnut Hill Ln Suite 700
Dallas, TX 75231
Phone: 214-345-8500
Fax: 214-345-4999

Richland College
12800 Abrams Rd
Dallas, TX 75243
www.rlc.dcccd.edu
Phone: 972-238-6100
Fax: 972-238-6346

Southwest Airlines Co
2702 Love Field Dr
Dallas, TX 75235
www.southwest.com
Phone: 214-792-4000
Fax: 214-792-5015
TF: 800-435-9792

Southwestern Bell Telephone Co
208 S Akard Suite 3653
Dallas, TX 75202
www.swbell.com
Phone: 214-464-4949
Fax: 214-745-4146

Texas Instruments Inc
12500 TI Blvd
Dallas, TX 75243
E-mail: infomaster@ti.com
www.ti.com
Phone: 972-995-2011
TF: 800-336-5236

TXU Electric & Gas
1601 Bryan St
Dallas, TX 75201
E-mail: custinfo@txu.com
www.txu.com/residential
Phone: 214-812-4600
Fax: 214-812-5453
TF: 800-242-9113

United Parcel Service
10155 Monroe Dr
Dallas, TX 75229
www.upsjobs.com
Phone: 214-353-1084
Fax: 214-353-6565

University of Texas Southwestern Medical Center Dallas
5323 Harry Hines Blvd
Dallas, TX 75390
www.swmed.edu
Phone: 214-648-3404
Fax: 214-648-9809

US Postal Service Dallas District
951 W Bethel Rd
Coppell, TX 75099
new.usps.com
Phone: 972-393-6787
Fax: 972-393-6198

Veterans Affairs Medical Center
4500 S Lancaster Rd
Dallas, TX 75216
Phone: 214-857-1141
Fax: 214-857-1446

Quality of Living Indicators

Total Crime Index 104,944
(rates per 100,000 inhabitants)

Violent Crime
Murder/manslaughter 191
Forcible rape 663
Robbery 6,357
Aggravated assault 8,224

Property Crime
Burglary 19,629
Larceny theft 52,026
Motor vehicle theft 17,854

Cost of Living Index 100.3
(national average = 100)

Median Home Price $121,500

Education

Public Schools

Dallas Independent School District
3700 Ross Ave
Dallas, TX 75204
www.dallasisd.org
Phone: 972-925-3700

Number of Schools
Elementary 152
Middle 27
High 31
Other 9

Student/Teacher Ratio
All Grades 18.2:1

Private Schools

Number of Schools (all grades) .... 130+

Colleges & Universities

Amber University
1700 Eastgate Dr
Garland, TX 75041
www.amberu.edu
Phone: 972-279-6511
Fax: 972-279-9773

Arlington Baptist College
3001 W Division St
Arlington, TX 76012
www.abconline.edu
Phone: 817-461-8741
Fax: 817-274-1138

Art Institute of Dallas
8080 Park Ln
Dallas, TX 75231
www.aid.aii.edu
Phone: 214-692-8080
Fax: 214-692-6541
TF: 800-275-4243

Brookhaven College
3939 Valley View Ln
Farmers Branch, TX 75244
www.dcccd.edu/bhc/bhc-home.htm
Phone: 972-860-4700
Fax: 972-860-4886

Cedar Valley College
3030 N Dallas Ave
Lancaster, TX 75134
www.dcccd.edu/cvc/cvc.htm
Phone: 972-860-8200
Fax: 972-372-8207

Collin County Community College Central Park Campus
PO Box 8001
McKinney, TX 75070
www.ccccd.edu
Phone: 972-548-6790
Fax: 972-548-6702

Dallas Baptist University
3000 Mountain Creek Pkwy
Dallas, TX 75211
E-mail: info@dbu.edu
www.dbu.edu
Phone: 214-331-8311
Fax: 214-333-5447
TF: 800-460-1328

Dallas Christian College
2700 Christian Pkwy
Dallas, TX 75234
www.dallas.edu
Phone: 972-241-3371
Fax: 972-241-8021
TF: 800-688-1029

Dallas County Community College District System
701 Elm St
Dallas, TX 75202
www.dcccd.edu
Phone: 214-860-2125
Fax: 214-860-2009

DeVRY Institute of Technology
4800 Regent Blvd
Irving, TX 75063
E-mail: admissions@dal.devry.edu
www.dal.devry.edu
Phone: 972-929-6777
Fax: 972-929-6778
TF: 800-633-3879

Eastfield College
3737 Motley Dr
Mesquite, TX 75150
www.efc.dcccd.edu
Phone: 972-860-7002
Fax: 972-860-8306

El Centro College
Main & Lamar
Dallas, TX 75202
www.ecc.dcccd.edu/
Phone: 214-860-2037
Fax: 214-860-2233

Independent Baptist College
5101 Western Center Blvd
Fort Worth, TX 76137
Phone: 817-514-6364
Fax: 817-281-8257

ITT Technical Institute
2101 Water View Pkwy
Richardson, TX 75080
www.itt-tech.edu
Phone: 972-690-9100
Fax: 972-690-0853
TF: 888-488-5761

Mountain View College
4849 W Illinois Ave
Dallas, TX 75211
www.mvc.dcccd.edu
Phone: 214-860-8600
Fax: 214-860-8570

North Lake College
5001 N MacArthur Blvd
Irving, TX 75038
www.dcccd.edu/nlc/nlchp.htm
Phone: 972-273-3000
Fax: 972-273-3112

Northwood University Texas Campus
1114 W FM 1382
Cedar Hill, TX 75106
E-mail: info@northwood.edu
www.northwood.edu
Phone: 972-291-1541
Fax: 972-291-3824
TF: 800-927-9663

Paul Quinn College
3837 Simpson Stuart Rd
Dallas, TX 75241
Phone: 214-376-1000
Fax: 214-302-3613

Richland College
12800 Abrams Rd
Dallas, TX 75243
www.rlc.dcccd.edu
Phone: 972-238-6100
Fax: 972-238-6346

Southern Methodist University
6425 Boaz Ln
Dallas, TX 75275
www.smu.edu
Phone: 214-768-2000
Fax: 214-768-2507
TF: 800-323-0672

Southwestern Adventist University
100 W Hillcrest Dr
Keene, TX 76059
E-mail: illingworth@swac.edu
www.swac.edu
Phone: 817-645-3921
Fax: 817-556-4744
TF: 800-433-2240

Southwestern Assemblies of God University
1200 Sycamore St
Waxahachie, TX 75165
E-mail: info@sagu.edu
www.sagu.edu
Phone: 972-937-4010
Fax: 972-923-0006
TF: 888-937-7248

Southwestern Christian College
PO Box 10
Terrell, TX 75160
Phone: 972-524-3341
Fax: 972-563-7133
TF: 800-925-9357

Texas Woman's University
PO Box 425589
Denton, TX 76204
www.twu.edu
Phone: 940-898-2000
Fax: 940-898-2767

University of Dallas
1845 E Northgate Dr
Irving, TX 75062
acad.udallas.edu
Phone: 972-721-5000
Fax: 972-721-5017
TF: 800-628-6999

University of North Texas
PO Box 311277
Denton, TX 76203
E-mail: undergrad@abn.unt.edu
www.unt.edu
Phone: 940-565-2000
Fax: 940-565-2408

University of Texas Arlington
701 S Nedderman Dr
Arlington, TX 76019
www.uta.edu
Phone: 817-272-2011
Fax: 817-272-3435
TF: 800-687-2882

University of Texas Dallas
PO Box 830688
Richardson, TX 75083
www.utdallas.edu
Phone: 972-883-2111
Fax: 972-883-6803

Wade College
2300 Stemmons Fwy
Dallas, TX 75258
Phone: 214-637-3530
Fax: 214-637-0827
TF: 800-624-4850

Hospitals

Baylor Medical Center at Ellis
1405 W Jefferson St
Waxahachie, TX 75165
Phone: 972-923-7000

Baylor Medical Center at Garland
2300 Marie Curie Blvd
Garland, TX 75042
www.baylorhealth.com/garland/index.htm
Phone: 972-487-5000
Fax: 972-487-5005

Baylor Medical Center at Irving
1901 N MacArthur Blvd
Irving, TX 75061
www.bhcs.com/irving
Phone: 972-579-8100
Fax: 972-579-5290

Baylor Richardson Medical Center
401 W Campbell Rd
Richardson, TX 75080
www.bhcs.com/Richardson
Phone: 972-231-1441
Fax: 972-498-4883

Baylor University Medical Center
3500 Gaston Ave
Dallas, TX 75246
www.baylorhealth.com
Phone: 214-820-0111
TF: 800-422-9567

Charlton Methodist Hospital
3500 W Wheatland Rd
Dallas, TX 75237
www.mhd.com/cmh.html
Phone: 214-947-7777
Fax: 214-947-7525

Children's Medical Center of Dallas
1935 Motor St
Dallas, TX 75235
www.childrens.com
Phone: 214-456-7000
Fax: 214-456-2197

Dallas Southwest Medical Center
2929 S Hampton Rd
Dallas, TX 75224
Phone: 214-330-4611
Fax: 214-330-0199

Dallas-Fort Worth Medical Center
2709 Hospital Blvd
Grand Prairie, TX 75051
www.dfwmedicalcenter.com
Phone: 972-641-5000
Fax: 972-660-9589

Denton Community Hospital
207 N Bonnie Brae
Denton, TX 76201
www.dentonhospital.com
Phone: 940-898-7000
Fax: 940-898-7071

Denton Regional Medical Center
3535 S I-35 E
Denton, TX 76210
Phone: 940-384-3535
Fax: 940-384-4700

Doctors Hospital of Dallas
9440 Poppy Dr
Dallas, TX 75218
www.tenethealth.com/DoctorsDallas
Phone: 214-324-6100
Fax: 214-324-0612

Garland Community Hospital
2696 W Walnut St
Garland, TX 75042
Phone: 972-276-7116
Fax: 972-494-6913

Lake Pointe Medical Center
PO Box 1550
Rowlett, TX 75030
Phone: 972-412-2273
Fax: 972-475-8345

Medical Center of Lancaster
2600 W Pleasant Run Rd
Lancaster, TX 75146
Phone: 972-223-9600
Fax: 972-230-2966

Medical Center of Lewisville
500 W Main
Lewisville, TX 75057
Phone: 972-420-1000
Fax: 972-420-1073

Medical Center of Mesquite
1011 N Galloway Ave
Mesquite, TX 75149
Phone: 214-320-7000
Fax: 972-289-9468

Medical Center of Plano
3901 W 15th St
Plano, TX 75075
Phone: 972-596-6800
Fax: 972-519-1295

Medical City Dallas
7777 Forest Ln
Dallas, TX 75230
Phone: 972-661-7000
Fax: 972-566-6248

Mesquite Community Hospital
3500 Interstate 30
Mesquite, TX 75150
Phone: 972-698-3300
Fax: 972-698-2580

Methodist Medical Center
PO Box 655999
Dallas, TX 75265
Phone: 214-947-8181
Fax: 214-947-3403

North Central Medical Center
4500 Medical Ctr Dr
McKinney, TX 75069
Phone: 972-547-8000
Fax: 972-547-8008

Parkland Health & Hospital System
5201 Harry Hines Blvd
Dallas, TX 75235
www.swmed.edu/home_pages/parkland/
Phone: 214-590-8000
Fax: 214-590-8096

Presbyterian Hospital of Dallas
8200 Walnut Hill Ln
Dallas, TX 75231
Phone: 214-345-6789
Fax: 214-345-2350

Presbyterian Hospital of Kaufman
PO Box 310
Kaufman, TX 75142
Phone: 214-345-8463
Fax: 972-932-5425

Presbyterian Hospital of Plano
6200 W Parker Rd
Plano, TX 75093
Phone: 972-608-8000
Fax: 972-608-8111

RHD Memorial Medical Center
7 Medical Pkwy
Farmers Branch, TX 75234
www.tenethealth.com/RHDMemorial
Phone: 972-247-1000
Fax: 972-888-7090

Saint Paul Medical Center
5909 Harry Hines Blvd
Dallas, TX 75235
Phone: 214-879-1000
Fax: 214-879-6694

Texas Scottish Rite Hospital for Children
2222 Wellborn St
Dallas, TX 75219
Phone: 214-521-3168
Fax: 214-559-7612

Trinity Medical Center
4343 N Josey Ln
Carrollton, TX 75010
www.tenethealth.com/Trinity
Phone: 972-492-1010
Fax: 972-394-4783

Veterans Affairs Medical Center
4500 S Lancaster Rd
Dallas, TX 75216
Phone: 214-857-1141
Fax: 214-857-1446

Zale Lipshy University Hospital
5151 Harry Hines Blvd
Dallas, TX 75235
Phone: 214-590-3000
Fax: 214-590-3465

Transportation

Airport(s)

Dallas Love Field (DAL)
6 miles NW of downtown (approx 15 minutes) 214-670-6080
Dallas-Fort Worth International Airport (DFW)
16 miles NW of downtown Dallas
(approx 30 minutes) 972-574-8888

Mass Transit

DART Bus
$1 Base fare 214-979-1111
McKinney Avenue Trolley
$.75 Base fare 214-855-0006

Rail/Bus

Dallas Union Amtrak Station Phone: 214-653-1101
400 S Houston St
Dallas, TX 75202

Greyhound Bus Station Phone: 214-655-7082
205 S Lamar St TF: 800-231-2222
Dallas, TX 75202

Utilities

Electricity
TXU Electric & Gas 972-791-2888
www.txu.com/residential

Gas
TXU Electric & Gas 214-741-3750
www.txu.com/residential

Water
Dallas Water Dept 214-651-1441

Garbage Collection/Recycling
Dallas Sanitation Customer Service Dept 214-670-8613

Telecommunications

Telephone
Southwestern Bell 817-376-4200
www.swbell.com

Cable Television
AT & T Cable Services 214-328-5000
www.cable.att.com
Classic Cable 800-426-0528

Internet Service Providers (ISPs)
Allegiance Internet 972-490-7100
www.connect.net
AltiNet Inc 214-754-7177
www.altinet.net
Beam The 972-730-2326
www.thebeam.com
CapRock Internet Services 800-687-1600
www.caprock.com/internet
Cyberspace.com 888-285-5196
www.cyberspace.com
Excel Online 800-875-9235
www.excelonline.com
Internet America Inc 214-861-2950
www.airmail.net
Inturnet Inc 972-783-0066
www.intur.net
Masterlink Internet Business Systems 214-349-7873
www.masterlink.com
Nucentrix Broadband Networks 972-423-9494
www.nucentrix.com
Southwestern Bell Internet Services 888-792-4638
www.swbell.net
Texas Metronet Inc 972-705-2900
web.metronet.com
TopherNet Inc 972-733-0704
www.topher.net
Verio Texas 214-672-7267
home.verio.net/local/frontpage.cfm?AirportCode=DFW

Banks

Abrams Centre National Bank Phone: 972-238-9292
9330 LBJ Fwy Fax: 972-644-3812
Dallas, TX 75243
E-mail: yourbank@abramsbank.com
www.abramsbank.com

Bank of America Phone: 888-279-3247
1401 Elm St Fax: 214-508-8179
Dallas, TX 75202

Bank One Texas NA Phone: 214-290-2000
1717 Main St Fax: 214-290-3696
Dallas, TX 75201 TF: 800-695-1111

Bank United Phone: 214-348-9550
8541 Ferndale Rd Fax: 214-348-7421
Dallas, TX 75238

Chase Bank of Texas NA Phone: 214-922-2300
2200 Ross Ave Fax: 214-965-3767
Dallas, TX 75201 TF: 800-882-7230

Comerica Bank-Texas Phone: 214-953-1268
1919 Woodall Rogers Frwy Fax: 214-871-0313
Dallas, TX 75201

Compass Bank Phone: 214-706-8000
8080 N Central Expy
Dallas, TX 75206

Guaranty Federal Bank FSB Phone: 214-360-3360
8333 Douglas Ave Fax: 214-369-1004
Dallas, TX 75225 TF: 800-999-1726
www.gfbank.com

Provident Bank Phone: 972-458-0500
13760 Noel St Suite 100 Fax: 972-448-8480
Dallas, TX 75240

Texas Capital Bank NA Phone: 214-932-6700
2100 McKinney Ave Fax: 214-932-6701
Dallas, TX 75201 TF: 877-839-2265
E-mail: customerservice@texascapitalbank.com
www.texascapitalbank.com

Washington Mutual Bank Phone: 214-904-1760
5220 W Lovers Ln Fax: 214-358-2518
Dallas, TX 75209

Wells Fargo Bank NA Phone: 214-740-0099
1445 Ross Ave Fax: 214-953-0238
Dallas, TX 75202 TF: 800-869-3557

Shopping

Big Town Mall Phone: 214-327-4541
800 Big Town Shopping Center Fax: 214-320-2713
Mesquite, TX 75149

Collin Creek Mall
811 N Central Expy
Plano, TX 75075
www.collincreekmall.com
Phone: 972-422-1070
Fax: 972-881-1642

Coomers Mall
900 W Airport Fwy
Irving, TX 75062
Phone: 972-554-1882
Fax: 972-554-1782

Deep Ellum
2932 Main St Suite 101
Dallas, TX 75226
www.deepellumtx.com/
Phone: 214-748-4332
Fax: 214-741-4567

Galleria The
13350 Dallas Pkwy
Dallas, TX 75240
Phone: 972-702-7100
Fax: 972-702-7172

Grapevine Mills
3000 Grapevine Mills Pkwy
Grapevine, TX 76051
www.grapevinemills.com
Phone: 972-724-4904
Fax: 972-724-4920

Highland Park Village
Preston Rd & Mockingbird Ln
Dallas, TX 75205
www.hpvillage.com
Phone: 214-559-2740
Fax: 214-521-4326

Inwood Trade Center
1300 Inwood Rd
Dallas, TX 75247
Phone: 214-521-4777
Fax: 214-559-9795

Irving Mall
3880 Irving Mall
Irving, TX 75062
Phone: 972-255-0571
Fax: 972-570-7310

Love Field Antique Mall
6500 Cedar Springs
Dallas, TX 75235
Phone: 214-357-6500
Fax: 214-358-2188

McKinney Avenue Antique Market
2710 McKinney Ave
Dallas, TX 75204
Phone: 214-871-9803
Fax: 214-871-2463

Neiman Marcus
1618 Main St
Dallas, TX 75201
www.neimanmarcus.com
Phone: 214-741-6911
Fax: 214-573-6136
TF: 800-825-8000

Northpark Center
8687 N Central Expy
Dallas, TX 75231
Phone: 214-363-7441

Plaza of the Americas
700 N Pearl
Dallas, TX 75201
Phone: 214-720-8000
Fax: 214-571-6277

Plymouth Park Shopping Center
Irving Blvd at Story Rd
Irving, TX 75061
Phone: 972-790-3996
Fax: 972-790-8285

Quadrangle The
2828 Routh St
Dallas, TX 75201
Phone: 214-871-0878
Fax: 214-871-1136

Richardson Square Mall
501 S Plano Rd
Richardson, TX 75081
Phone: 972-783-0117

Saks Fifth Avenue
13550 Dallas Pkwy
Dallas, TX 75240
Phone: 972-458-7000

Southwest Center Mall
3662 W Camp Wisdom Rd
Dallas, TX 75237
Phone: 972-296-1491
Fax: 972-296-4220

Town East Mall
2063 Town East Mall
Mesquite, TX 75150
Phone: 972-270-4431
Fax: 972-686-8974

Valley View Center Mall
Preston Rd & LBJ Fwy
Dallas, TX 75240
Phone: 972-661-2425
Fax: 972-239-1344

Vista Ridge Mall
2401 S Stemmons Fwy
Lewisville, TX 75067
Phone: 972-315-0015
Fax: 972-315-3725

West End MarketPlace
603 Munger Ave
Dallas, TX 75202
Phone: 214-748-4801
Fax: 214-748-4803

Media

Newspapers and Magazines

D Magazine
1700 Commerce 18th Fl
Dallas, TX 75201
E-mail: feedback@dmagazine.com
www.dmagazine.com
Phone: 214-939-3636
Fax: 214-748-4153

Dallas Business Journal
10670 N Central Expy Suite 710
Dallas, TX 75231
www.amcity.com/dallas
Phone: 214-696-5959
Fax: 214-361-4045

Dallas Morning News*
PO Box 655237
Dallas, TX 75265
E-mail: tdmned@cityview.com
www.dallasnews.com
Phone: 214-977-8222
Fax: 214-977-8319

Dallas Observer
2130 Commerce
Dallas, TX 75201
www.dallasobserver.com
Phone: 214-757-9000
Fax: 214-757-8593

Fort Worth Star-Telegram*
PO Box 1870
Fort Worth, TX 76101
www.star-telegram.com
Phone: 817-390-7400
Fax: 817-390-7789

Irving News
1000 Ave 'H' E
Arlington, TX 76011
Phone: 817-695-0500
Fax: 817-695-0555

Metrocrest News
1720 Josey Ln Suite 100
Carrollton, TX 75006
Phone: 972-418-9999
Fax: 972-418-1620

Northside People
6116 N Central Expy Suite 230
Dallas, TX 75206
E-mail: people@peoplenewspapers.com
www.peoplenewspapers.com
Phone: 214-739-2244
Fax: 214-363-6948

**Indicates major daily newspapers*

Television

KDAF-TV Ch 33 (WB)
8001 John Carpenter Fwy
Dallas, TX 75247
www.wb33.com
Phone: 214-640-3300
Fax: 214-252-3379

KDFI-TV Ch 27 (Ind)
400 N Griffin St
Dallas, TX 75202
Phone: 214-637-2727
Fax: 214-720-3355

KDFW-TV Ch 4 (Fox)
400 N Griffin St
Dallas, TX 75202
Phone: 214-720-4444
Fax: 214-720-3263

KERA-TV Ch 13 (PBS)
3000 Harry Hines Blvd
Dallas, TX 75201
www.kera.org
Phone: 214-871-1390
Fax: 214-740-9369

KFWD-TV Ch 52 (Tele)
3000 W Story Rd
Irving, TX 75038
Phone: 972-255-5200
Fax: 972-258-1770

KLDT-TV Ch 55 (Ind)
2450 Rockbrook Dr
Lewisville, TX 75067
Phone: 972-316-2115
Fax: 972-316-1112

KMPX-TV Ch 29 (Ind)
PO Box 612066
Dallas, TX 75261
Phone: 817-571-1229
Fax: 817-571-7458

KPXD-TV Ch 68 (PAX)
800 W Airport Fwy Suite 750
Irving, TX 75062
www.pax.net/KPXD
Phone: 972-438-6868
Fax: 972-579-3045

KTVT-TV Ch 11 (CBS)
5233 Bridge St
Fort Worth, TX 76103
www.ktvt.com
Phone: 817-451-1111
Fax: 817-496-7739

KTXA-TV Ch 21 (UPN)
301 N Market St Suite 700
Dallas, TX 75202
www.paramountstations.com/KTXA
Phone: 214-743-2100
Fax: 214-743-2121

KUVN-TV Ch 23 (Uni)
2323 Bryan St Suite 1900
Dallas, TX 75201
www.univision.net/stations/kuvn.htm
Phone: 214-758-2300
Fax: 214-758-2324
TF: 800-494-5886

KXAS-TV Ch 5 (NBC)
3900 Barnett St
Fort Worth, TX 76103
www.kxas.com
Phone: 817-429-5555
Fax: 817-654-6325
TF: 800-232-5927

KXTX-TV Ch 39 (Ind)
3900 Harry Hines Blvd
Dallas, TX 75219
www.kxtx.com
Phone: 214-521-3900
Fax: 214-523-5946
TF: 800-465-5989

WFAA-TV Ch 8 (ABC)
606 Young St Communications Ctr
Dallas, TX 75202
www.wfaa.com
Phone: 214-748-9631
Fax: 214-977-6585

Radio

KBFB-FM 97.9 MHz (AC)
8235 Douglas Ave Suite 300
Dallas, TX 75225
E-mail: kbfb@kbfb.com
www.kbfb.com
Phone: 972-891-3400
Fax: 972-988-3292

KCBI-FM 90.9 MHz (Rel)
PO Box 619000
Dallas, TX 75261
E-mail: kcbi@kcbi.org
www.kcbi.org
Phone: 817-792-3800
Fax: 817-277-9929

KDGE-FM 94.5 MHz (Alt)
15851 N Dallas Pkwy Suite 1200
Addison, TX 75001
www.kdge.com
Phone: 972-770-7777
Fax: 972-770-7747

KDMM-AM 1150 (Rel)
7700 Carpenter Fwy 1st Fl
Dallas, TX 75247
Phone: 214-630-9400
Fax: 214-630-0060

KDMX-FM 102.9 MHz (AC)
14001 N Dallas Pkwy Suite 1210
Dallas, TX 75240
www.mix1029.com
Phone: 972-991-1029
Fax: 972-448-1029

KDXX-AM 1480 kHz (Span)
7700 Carpenter Fwy
Dallas, TX 75427
Phone: 214-630-8531
Fax: 214-920-2507

KEGG-AM 1560 KHz (N/T)
PO Box 497931
Garland, TX 75049
Phone: 903-645-4238
Fax: 903-645-3898

KEGL-FM 97.1 MHz (CR)
14001 N Dallas Pkwy Suite 1210
Dallas, TX 75240
www.kegl.com
Phone: 972-869-9700
Fax: 972-263-9710

KERA-FM 90.1 MHz (NPR)
3000 Harry Hines Blvd
Dallas, TX 75201
E-mail: kerafm@metronet.com
www.kera.org/
Phone: 214-871-1390
Fax: 214-740-9369

KESS-AM 1270 kHz (Span)
7700 Carpenter Fwy
Dallas, TX 75247
www.kess1270.com
Phone: 214-630-8531
Fax: 214-920-2507

KHKS-FM 106.1 MHz (CHR)
8235 Douglas Ave Suite 300
Dallas, TX 75225
www.1061kissfm.com
Phone: 214-891-3400
Fax: 214-692-9844

KHVN-AM 970 kHz (Rel)
7901 John Carpenter Fwy
Dallas, TX 75247
Phone: 214-630-3011
Fax: 214-905-5052

KKDA-AM 730 kHz (Oldies)
PO Box 530860
Grand Prairie, TX 75053
Phone: 972-263-9911
Fax: 972-558-0010

KKDA-FM 104.5 MHz (Urban)
PO Box 860
Grand Prairie, TX 75053
www.k104fm.com
Phone: 972-263-9911
Fax: 972-558-0010

KKZN-FM 93.3 MHz (AAA)
3500 Maple Ave Suite 1310
Dallas, TX 75219
www.933thezone.com
Phone: 214-526-7400
Fax: 214-787-1946

KLIF-AM 570 kHz (N/T)
3500 Maple Ave Suite 1600
Dallas, TX 75219
www.klif.com
Phone: 214-526-2400
Fax: 214-520-4343

KLTY-FM 100.7 MHz (Rel)
12900 Preston Rd Suite 100
Dallas, TX 75230
E-mail: klty@onramp.net
www.klty.com
Phone: 972-726-9941
Fax: 972-404-1451

KLUV-AM 1190 kHz (Oldies)
4131 N Central Expy Suite 700
Dallas, TX 75204
E-mail: promotions@kluv.com
www.kluv.com/kluv1190am.asp
Phone: 214-526-9870
Fax: 214-443-1570

KLUV-FM 98.7 MHz (Oldies)
4131 N Central Expy Suite 700
Dallas, TX 75204
E-mail: kluv@ix.netcom.com
www.kluv.com
Phone: 214-526-9870
Fax: 214-443-1570

KMEO-FM 96.7 MHz (AC)
2221 E Lamar Blvd Suite 400
Arlington, TX 76006
Phone: 817-695-3500
Fax: 817-695-3505

KNON-FM 89.3 MHz (Misc)
4415 Jacinto
Dallas, TX 75204
www.knon.org
Phone: 214-828-9500
Fax: 214-823-3051

KOAI-FM 107.5 MHz (NAC)
7901 Carpenter Fwy
Dallas, TX 75247
Phone: 214-630-3011
Fax: 214-688-7760

KPLX-FM 99.5 MHz (Ctry)
3500 Maple Ave Suite 1600
Dallas, TX 75219
E-mail: thewolf@flash.net
www.995thewolf.com
Phone: 214-526-2400
Fax: 214-520-4343

KRBV-FM 100.3 MHz (Urban)
7901 John Carpenter Fwy
Dallas, TX 75247
Phone: 214-630-3011
Fax: 214-688-7760

KRLD-AM 1080 kHz (N/T)
1080 Ballpark Way
Arlington, TX 76011
www.krld.com
Phone: 817-543-5400
Fax: 817-543-5572

KRNB-FM 105.7 MHz (AC)
621 NW 6th St
Grand Prairie, TX 75050
Phone: 972-263-9911
Fax: 972-558-0010

KRVA-AM 1600 kHz (Span)
5307 E Mockingbird Ln Suite 500
Dallas, TX 75206
Phone: 214-887-9107
Fax: 214-841-4215

KRVA-FM 106.9 MHz (Span)
5307 E Mockingbird Ln Suite 500
Dallas, TX 75206
Phone: 214-887-9107
Fax: 214-841-4215

KSCS-FM 96.3 MHz (Ctry)
2221 E Lamar Blvd Suite 400
Arlington, TX 76006
www.kscs.com
Phone: 817-640-1963
Fax: 817-654-9227

KSKY-AM 660 kHz (Rel)
4144 N Central Expy Suite 266
Dallas, TX 75204
E-mail: kskyradio@ksky.com
www.ksky.com
Phone: 214-827-5759
Fax: 214-827-7983

KTCK-AM 1310 kHz (N/T)
3500 Maple Ave Suite 1310
Dallas, TX 75219
www.theticket.com
Phone: 214-526-7400
Fax: 214-525-2525

KTCY-FM 104.9 MHz (Span)
7700 John Carpenter Fwy
Dallas, TX 75247
Phone: 214-630-9400
Fax: 214-630-0060

KTXQ-FM 102.1 MHz (Oldies)
4131 N Central Expy Suite 1200
Dallas, TX 75204
www.ktxq.com
Phone: 214-528-5500
Fax: 214-528-0747

KVIL-FM 103.7 MHz (AC)
9400 N Central Expy Suite 1600
Dallas, TX 75231
www.kvil.com
Phone: 214-691-1037
Fax: 214-891-7975

KVTT-FM 91.7 MHz (Rel)
11061 Shady Tr
Dallas, TX 75229
E-mail: kvtt@kvtt.org
www.kvtt.org
Phone: 214-351-6655
Fax: 214-351-6809

KWRD-FM 94.9 MHz (Rel)
545 E John Carpenter Fwy Suite 450
Irving, TX 75062
www.thewordfm.com
Phone: 972-402-9673
Fax: 972-869-4975

KYNG-FM 105.3 MHz (Ctry)
12201 Merit Dr Suite 930
Dallas, TX 75251
www.young-country.com
Phone: 972-716-7800
Fax: 972-716-7835

KZMP-AM 1540 kHz (Span)
5307 E Mockingbird Ln Suite 500
Dallas, TX 75206
Phone: 214-887-9107
Fax: 214-841-4215

KZMP-FM 101.7 MHz (Span)
5307 E Mockingbird Ln Suite 500
Dallas, TX 75206
Phone: 214-887-9107
Fax: 214-841-4215

KZPS-FM 92.5 MHz (CR)
15851 Dallas Pkwy Suite 1200
Addison, TX 75001
E-mail: balberts@iadfw.net
www.kzps.com
Phone: 972-770-7777
Fax: 972-770-7747

WBAP-AM 820 kHz (N/T)
2221 E Lamar Blvd Suite 400
Arlington, TX 76006
www.wbap.com
Phone: 817-640-1963
Fax: 817-654-9227

WRR-FM 101.1 MHz (Clas)
PO Box 159001
Dallas, TX 75315
www.wrr101.com
Phone: 214-670-8888
Fax: 214-670-8394

Attractions

Home to the largest urban arts district in America as well as hundreds of tourist attractions in the city and surrounding area, Dallas is a major center for culture and entertainment. The downtown area of Dallas includes Dealey Plaza and the former Texas School Book Depository from which Lee Harvey Oswald fired the shots that took the life of President John F. Kennedy in 1963. The sixth floor of the Depository now includes an exhibit that chronicles JFK's life. Located in the downtown area also is the West End Historic District, a popular restaurant and entertainment center; and just east of there is Deep Ellum, an area of trendy art galleries, restaurants, and clubs. The upscale area of North Dallas is known for its shopping. The Dallas area is also popular among sports enthusiasts, boasting four professional sports teams—the Dallas Cowboys football team, the Texas Rangers baseball team, the Dallas Mavericks basketball team, and the Dallas Stars hockey team.

In nearby Irving, Las Colinas, a European-style business-residential-entertainment area, contains the world's largest equestrian sculpture, Mustangs of Las Colinas, as well as a movie studio that offers tours, a world-class equestrian center, and many shops and restaurants. The Mandalay Canal Walk at Las Colinas allows visitors to stroll down cobblestone walkways beside the canal or explore the area in mahogany water taxis. Dallas Stadium, home of the World Champion Dallas Cowboys, and StarCenter Ice Arena, home of the Dallas Stars, are both located in Irving. In nearby Garland, Garland Center for the Performing Arts features a symphony orchestra, a civic theater, and summer musicals. The city's Winters Park hosts the annual U.S. National Softball Championships.

African American Museum
3536 Grand Ave Fair Pk
Dallas, TX 75210
Phone: 214-565-9026
Fax: 214-421-8204

Age of Steam Railroad Museum
1105 Washington St Fair Pk
Dallas, TX 75315
www.startext.net/homes/railroad/musmain.htm
Phone: 214-428-0101
Fax: 214-426-1937

American Museum of the Miniature Arts
2001 N Lamar St Suite 100
Dallas, TX 75202
E-mail: minimuseum@aol.com
www.minimuseum.org
Phone: 214-969-5502
Fax: 214-969-5997

Anita N Martinez Ballet Folklorico
4422 Live Oak
Dallas, TX 75204
www.anmbf.org
Phone: 214-828-0181
Fax: 214-828-0101

Bachman Lake Park
2750 Bachman Dr
Dallas, TX 75220
Phone: 214-670-6266
Fax: 214-670-6271

Bath House Cultural Center
521 E Lawther Dr
Dallas, TX 75218
E-mail: mail@bathhousecultural.com
www.bathhousecultural.com
Phone: 214-670-8749
Fax: 214-670-8751

Biblical Arts Center
7500 Park Ln
Dallas, TX 75225
www.biblicalarts.org
Phone: 214-691-4661
Fax: 214-691-4752

Carpenter Performance Hall
3333 N MacArthur Blvd
Irving, TX 75062
www.irving.net/iac/
Phone: 972-252-2787
Fax: 972-570-4962

Cavanaugh Flight Museum
4572 Claire Chennault Addison Airport
Addison, TX 75001
www.cavanaughflightmuseum.com
Phone: 972-380-8800
Fax: 972-248-0907

Cinemark IMAX Theater
11819 Webb Chapel Rd
Dallas, TX 75234
Phone: 972-888-2629
Fax: 972-241-5477

Conspiracy Museum
110 S Market St
Dallas, TX 75202
www.conspiracymuseum.com
Phone: 214-741-3040
Fax: 214-741-9339

Conte de Loyo Flamenco Theatre
3630 Harry Hines Blvd
Dallas, TX 75219
E-mail: flamenco@flash.net
www.flash.net/~flamenco
Phone: 214-521-0222
Fax: 214-559-4643

Dallas Aquarium
1st Ave & ML King Blvd Fair Pk
Dallas, TX 75226
E-mail: dallasaq@airmail.net
Phone: 214-670-8443
Fax: 214-670-8452

Dallas Arboretum & Botanical Garden
8617 Garland Rd
Dallas, TX 75218
Phone: 214-327-8263
Fax: 214-324-9801

Dallas Black Dance Theatre
2627 Flora St
Dallas, TX 75201
E-mail: dbdt@gte.net
www.dbdt.com
Phone: 214-871-2376
Fax: 214-871-2842
TF: 888-222-3238

Dallas Children's Theater
2215 Cedar Springs
Dallas, TX 75201
Phone: 214-978-0110

Dallas Communications Complex
6311 N O'Connor Rd
Irving, TX 75039
Phone: 972-869-7600
Fax: 972-869-7657

Dallas Farmers Market
1010 S Pearl
Dallas, TX 75201
Phone: 214-939-2808

Dallas Firefighters Museum
3801 Parry Ave
Dallas, TX 75226
Phone: 214-821-1500

Dallas Horticulture Center
3601 ML King Blvd Fair Pk
Dallas, TX 75210
E-mail: dhort@hotmail.com
www.startext.net/homes/dhc
Phone: 214-428-7476
Fax: 214-428-5338

Dallas Memorial Center for Holocaust Studies
7900 Northaven Rd
Dallas, TX 75230
Phone: 214-750-4654
Fax: 214-750-4672

Dallas Museum of Art
1717 N Harwood St
Dallas, TX 75201
www.dm-art.org
Phone: 214-922-1200
Fax: 214-954-0174

Dallas Museum of Natural History
3535 Grand Ave
Dallas, TX 75210
www.dallasdino.org
Phone: 214-421-3466
Fax: 214-428-4356

Dallas Nature Center
7171 Mountain Creek Pkwy
Dallas, TX 75249
E-mail: info@dallasnaturecenter.org
www.dallasnaturecenter.org
Phone: 972-296-1955
Fax: 972-296-0072

Dallas Opera
3102 Oak Lawn Ave Suite 450
Dallas, TX 75219
www.dallasopera.org
Phone: 214-443-1043
Fax: 214-443-1060

Dallas Science Place
1318 2nd Ave
Dallas, TX 75210
www.scienceplace.org
Phone: 214-428-5555
Fax: 214-428-2033

Dallas Symphony Orchestra
2301 Flora St Suite 300
Dallas, TX 75201
www.dalsym.com
Phone: 214-692-0203

Dallas Visual Art Center
2801 Swiss Ave Suite 100
Dallas, TX 75204
E-mail: dallasvisualart@startext.net
Phone: 214-821-2522
Fax: 214-821-9103

Dallas World Aquarium
1801 N Griffin St
Dallas, TX 75202
www.dwazoo.com
Phone: 214-655-1444
Fax: 214-720-2242

Dallas Zoo
650 S RL Thornton Fwy
Dallas, TX 75203
www.dallas-zoo.org
Phone: 214-670-6826
Fax: 214-670-7450

Deep Ellum
2932 Main St Suite 101
Dallas, TX 75226
www.deepellumtx.com/
Phone: 214-748-4332
Fax: 214-741-4567

Dr Pepper Bottling Co of Texas
2304 Century Ctr Blvd
Irving, TX 75062
www.drpep.com
Phone: 972-579-1024
Fax: 972-721-8147

Dupree Theater
3333 N MacArthur Blvd
Irving, TX 75062
www.irving.net/iac
Phone: 972-252-2787
Fax: 972-570-4962

Fair Park Dallas
1300 Robert B Cullum Blvd
Dallas, TX 75210
Phone: 214-670-8400
Fax: 214-670-8907

Freedman's Memorial Cemetery
Lemmon Ave & Central Expy
Dallas, TX 75201
Phone: 214-670-3284

Frontiers of Flight Museum
Mockingbird Ln & Cedar Springs Rd Love Field
Dallas, TX 75235
E-mail: fofm@iglobal.net
www.flightmuseum.com
Phone: 214-350-1651
Fax: 214-351-0101

Garland Civic Theatre
108 N 6th Stt
Garland, TX 75040
Phone: 972-485-8884
Fax: 972-487-2159

Garland Landmark Museum
200 Museum Plaza Dr
Garland, TX 75040
Phone: 972-205-2749

Garland Performing Arts Center
PO Box 469002
Garland, TX 75046
Phone: 972-205-2780
Fax: 972-205-2775

Garland Symphony Orchestra
1919 S Shiloh St Suite 101
Garland, TX 75042
E-mail: garlandsymphony@juno.com
Phone: 972-926-0611
Fax: 972-926-0811

Hall of State
3939 Grand Ave Fair Pk
Dallas, TX 75226
www.dallashistory.org/
Phone: 214-421-4500
Fax: 214-421-7500

Heritage House
303 S O'Connor Rd
Irving, TX 75060
Phone: 972-438-5775

International Museum of Cultures
7500 W Camp Wisdom Rd
Dallas, TX 75236
E-mail: imc_museum@sil.org
www.sil.org/imc/
Phone: 972-708-7406
Fax: 972-708-7341

Irving Arts Center
3333 N MacArthur Blvd
Irving, TX 75062
www.irving.net/iac
Phone: 972-252-7558
Fax: 972-570-4962

Irving Symphony Orchestra
3333 N MacArthur Blvd Carpenter Performance Hall
Irving, TX 75062
Phone: 972-831-8818
Fax: 972-831-8817

Kiest Park
3080 S Hampton Rd
Dallas, TX 75224
Phone: 214-670-1918

Lake Ray Hubbard
9501 Lakeview Pkwy
Rockwall, TX 75088
Phone: 972-475-2552

Las Colinas Equestrian Center
600 Royal Ln
Irving, TX 75039
Phone: 972-869-0600

Las Colinas Symphony Orchestra
1300 Walnut Hill Irving Art Center
Irving, TX 75038
Phone: 972-580-1566
Fax: 972-550-7954

Majestic Theatre
1925 Elm St
Dallas, TX 75201
Phone: 214-880-0137
Fax: 214-880-0097

Malibu SpeedZone
11130 Malibu Dr
Dallas, TX 75229
www.speedzone.com/dallas/dallas.html
Phone: 972-247-7223
Fax: 972-243-3170

Meadows Museum
6101 Bishop Blvd Southern Methodist University
Dallas, TX 75205
www.smu.edu/meadows/museum
Phone: 214-768-2516
Fax: 214-768-1688

Medieval Times Dinner & Tournament
2021 N Stemmons Fwy
Dallas, TX 75207
E-mail: dallas@medievaltimes.com
www.medievaltimes.com/TX_realm.htm
Phone: 214-761-1800
Fax: 214-761-1805
TF: 800-229-9900

Meyerson Morton H Symphony Center
2301 Flora St Suite 100
Dallas, TX 75201
Phone: 214-670-3600
Fax: 214-670-4334

Movie Studio at Las Colinas
6301 N O'Connor Blvd
Irving, TX 75039
Phone: 972-869-3456
Fax: 972-869-7728

Museum of the Americas
1717 N Harwood St
Dallas, TX 75201
Phone: 214-922-1200
Fax: 214-954-0174

Music Hall at Fair Park
909 1st Ave
Dallas, TX 75210
Phone: 214-565-1116
Fax: 214-565-0071

NASCAR Silicon Motor Speedway
13350 Dallas Pkwy Suite 3800
Dallas, TX 75240
Phone: 972-490-7223
Fax: 972-490-4240

Old City Park
1717 Gano St
Dallas, TX 75215
www.oldcitypark.org
Phone: 214-421-5141
Fax: 214-428-6351

Pace House
234 Museum Plaza Dr
Garland, TX 75040
Phone: 972-205-2780

Sammons Center for the Arts
3630 Harry Hines Blvd
Dallas, TX 75219
www.sammonsartcenter.org
Phone: 214-520-7789
Fax: 214-522-9174

Six Flags Over Texas
2201 Road to Six Flags
Arlington, TX 76011
www.sixflags.com/texas
Phone: 817-640-8900
Fax: 817-530-6040

Sixth Floor Museum
411 Elm St Dealey Plaza
Dallas, TX 75202
E-mail: jfk@jfk.org
www.jfk.org
Phone: 214-747-6660
Fax: 214-747-6662
TF: 888-485-4854

Skyline Ranch
1801 E Wheatland Rd
Dallas, TX 75241
E-mail: pitrehorse@aol.com
www.skylineranch.com
Phone: 972-224-8055
Fax: 972-224-7004

Southfork Ranch
3700 Hogge Rd
Parker, TX 75002
www.southforkranch.com
Phone: 972-442-7800
Fax: 972-442-5259
TF: 800-989-7800

Theatre Three
2800 Routh St
Dallas, TX 75201
E-mail: theatre3@airmail.net
www.vline.net/theatre3
Phone: 214-871-3300
Fax: 214-871-3139

TI Founders IMAX Theater
1318 2nd Ave Fair Pk
Dallas, TX 75210
www.scienceplace.org/imaxhome.htm
Phone: 214-428-5555
Fax: 214-428-4310

TILT Adventure Motion Theater
603 Munger Ave West End Marketplace
Dallas, TX 75202
Phone: 214-720-7276

West End MarketPlace
603 Munger Ave
Dallas, TX 75202
Phone: 214-748-4801
Fax: 214-748-4803

White Rock Lake Park
8300 Garland Rd
Dallas, TX 75238
Phone: 214-670-8895

Wilson Block Historic District
2922 Block of Swiss Ave
Dallas, TX 75204
www.preservationdallas.org/wilson.html
Phone: 214-821-3290
Fax: 214-821-3573

Sports Teams & Facilities

Ballpark in Arlington
1000 Ballpark Way Suite 400
Arlington, TX 76011
Phone: 817-273-5222
Fax: 817-273-5264
TF: 888-968-3927

Cotton Bowl
3750 Midway Dr
Dallas, TX 75215
Phone: 214-939-2222
Fax: 214-939-2224

Dallas Burn (soccer)
2602 McKinney Suite 200
Dallas, TX 75204
E-mail: theburnone@aol.com
www.burnsoccer.com
Phone: 214-979-0303
Fax: 214-979-1118

Dallas Convention Center
650 S Griffin St
Dallas, TX 75202
www.dallascc.com
Phone: 214-939-2750
Fax: 214-939-2795

Dallas Cowboys
2401 E Airport Fwy Texas Stadium
Irving, TX 75062
www.dallascowboys.com
Phone: 972-785-5000
Fax: 972-556-9304

Dallas Mavericks
777 Sports St Reunion Arena
Dallas, TX 75207
mavericks.nba.com
Phone: 214-748-1810
Fax: 214-741-6731
TF: 800-634-6287

Dallas Sidekicks (soccer)
777 Sports St Reunion Arena
Dallas, TX 75207
Phone: 214-653-0200
Fax: 214-741-6731

Dallas Stars
777 Sports St Reunion Arena
Dallas, TX 75207
www.dallasstarshockey.com
Phone: 214-939-2770
Fax: 214-939-2872

Lone Star Park at Grand Prairie
1000 Lone Star Pkwy
Grand Prairie, TX 75050
www.lonestarpark.com
Phone: 972-263-7223
Fax: 972-237-5109

North Texas Heat (soccer)
2001 Kelley Blvd Polk Football Stadium
Carrollton, TX 75006
E-mail: cdemarco@ntxsoccer.org
Phone: 972-492-7863
Fax: 972-242-3600

Reunion Arena
777 Sports St
Dallas, TX 75207
Phone: 214-939-2770
Fax: 214-939-2872

Texas Motor Speedway
3601 Hwy 114
Justin, TX 76247
E-mail: TMS_Guest_Feedback@texasmotorspeedway.com
www.texasmotorspeedway.com
Phone: 817-215-8500
Fax: 817-491-3749

Texas Motorplex
7500 W Hwy 287
Ennis, TX 75119
www.texasmotorplex.com
Phone: 972-878-2641
Fax: 972-878-1848

Texas Rangers
1000 Ballpark Way Ballpark at Arlington
Arlington, TX 76011
www.texasrangers.com
Phone: 817-273-5100
Fax: 817-273-5174
TF: 888-968-3927

Texas Rattlers (soccer)
12345 Inwood Rd Jesuit College
Dallas, TX 75244
www.texassoccer.net
Phone: 214-720-0285
Fax: 214-720-0595

Texas Stadium
2401 E Airport Fwy
Irving, TX 75062
www.dallascowboys.com/stadium/facts
Phone: 972-785-4000
Fax: 972-785-4709

Annual Events

A Ghostly Affair (late October) 972-790-8505
Annual Main Event (late October) 972-259-1249
Autumn Fest (late October) 972-205-2749
Barbecue Cook-Off (mid-October) 972-647-2331
Bedford Blues Festival & Arts Fair (early September) 214-855-1881
Christmas on the Square (December) 972-205-2749
Christmas Parade & Santa in the Park (late December) 972-259-7881
Cinco de Mayo Festival (early May) 972-721-2501
Cotton Bowl (January 1) 214-634-7525
Dallas Air Show (mid-September) 214-350-1651
Dallas Artfest (late May) 214-361-2011
Dallas Blooms (March-early April) 214-327-8263
Dallas Boat Show (early-mid-February) 972-714-0177
Dallas Home & Garden Show (early March) 800-654-1480
Dallas Morning News Dance Festival (late August-early September) 214-953-1977
Dallas Morning News Wine & Food Festival (mid-March) 214-887-9915
Dallas Summer Musicals (May-October) 214-421-0662
Dallas Video Festival (late March) 214-999-8999
Dallas' Taste the Nation (mid-April) 800-955-8278
Fourth of July Pops Concert & Fireworks (July 4) 972-831-8818
Garland Summer Musicals (June-July) 972-205-2790
Golden Gloves Tournament (mid-February) 214-670-8400
Greek Food Festival (late September) 972-991-1166
Independence Day Parade (July 4) 972-721-2501
Irving Heritage Festival (mid-June) 972-721-2424
It's a Gas Vintage Car Show (mid-October) 972-205-2749
Kidfilm Festival (mid-January) 214-821-6300
Labor Day Jubilee (late August-early September) 972-371-3789
Las Colinas Fall Horse Show (late September-early October) 972-869-0600
Las Colinas Horse Trials (late September-early October) 972-869-0600
Mesquite Rodeo (April-September) 972-285-8777
Montage (early September) 214-361-2011
Motocross (mid-April) 972-438-7676
National Championship Indian Pow Wow (early September) 214-571-1000
North Texas Hunter/Jumper Show (mid-October) ... 972-869-0600
North Texas Irish Festival (early March) 214-821-4174
Oasis Fireworks to Music (early July) 214-855-1881
Plano Balloon Festival (mid-September) 972-867-7566
Safari Days (late May) 214-670-5656
Saint Patrick's Day Parade (mid-March) 972-991-6677
Shakespeare Festival of Dallas (mid-June-late July) 214-559-2778
Southwestern Bell Cotton Bowl New Year's Eve Parade (December 31) 214-741-7185
Spring AutoFest (late April) 817-215-8500
Star Spangled 4th (July 4) 972-205-2749
State Fair of Texas (late September-mid-October) ... 214-565-9931
Taste of Dallas (early July) 214-741-7180
Taste of Irving (mid-August) 972-255-0572
Trick or Treat Trot (late October) 972-205-2749
USA Film Festival (late April) 214-821-6300
Waxahachie Scarborough Renaissance Fair (mid-April-early June) 972-938-1888
White Rock Marathon (early December) 214-528-2962

Dayton, Ohio

County: Montgomery

DAYTON is located in the Miami Valley in southwestern Ohio. Major cities within 100 miles include Springfield, Cincinnati, and Columbus, Ohio; and Muncie, Indiana.

Area (Land) .... 55.0 sq mi
Area (Water)............................... 0.9 sq mi
Elevation.................................... 757 ft
Latitude ....40-19-45 N
Longitude................................ 84-73-17 W
Time Zone ....EST
Area Code..................................... 937

Climate

Dayton has a continental climate that is influenced by the area's lack of natural barriers to shelter the city from extremes of hot and cold weather. Winters are cold, with average high temperatures in the mid- to upper 30s and average lows in the high teens to low 20s. The average annual snowfall in Dayton is 28.6 inches. Summer days are generally very warm, with average high temperatures in the mid-80s, while evenings cool down to around 60 degrees. May is the wettest month in Dayton; January is the driest.

Average Temperatures & Precipitation

Temperatures

	Jan	Feb	Mar	Apr	May	Jun	Jul	Aug	Sep	Oct	Nov	Dec
High	34	38	50	62	73	82	85	83	77	65	51	39
Low	18	21	31	41	51	59	63	61	55	44	34	24

Precipitation

	Jan	Feb	Mar	Apr	May	Jun	Jul	Aug	Sep	Oct	Nov	Dec
Inches	2.1	2.2	3.4	3.5	3.9	3.8	3.5	3.2	2.5	2.5	3.1	2.9

History

The site of numerous battles between the French and the Indians during much of the 18th Century, the Dayton area was eventually secured by American forces under the command of General "Mad Anthony" Wayne in 1790. The town of Dayton was founded in 1796 and named after one of its founding fathers, Revolutionary War hero General Jonathan Dayton. In 1805, Dayton was incorporated as a city. After the opening of the Miami Canal in 1829, which provided access to Cincinnati (and later Lake Erie), Dayton prospered as an industrial center, producing a wide variety of products that included iron casting, hats, flour, candles, soap, and furniture. In the three decades between 1910 and 1940, Dayton's population grew from 383 residents to 6,000. The arrival of railroad lines later in the century further stimulated industrial growth.

Dayton is also a city of inventions. The "Birthplace of Aviation," Dayton residents Wilbur and Orville Wright invented the world's first airplane there at the turn of the 20th Century, and the city was also the site of the first parachute jump, first solo instrument landing, and several other aviation-related events. In nearby Fairborn, Wright-Patterson Air Force Base (the U.S. Air Force's largest and oldest military installation) today is home to a $1 billion research facility that continues to pioneer innovations in the aerospace industry. Other technological innovations that came out of Dayton include the cash register, the ATM machine, and the liquid crystal display. Dayton was also the site of numerous advances in the automotive industry, including the automobile self-starter, anti-lock brakes, and road-sensing suspension systems that were first developed at General Motors plants in the area.

Dayton today remains an important center for manufacturing as well as invention. The Dayton area has one of the highest concentrations of technical experts in the entire world and ranks among the top 25 cities in the nation for number of patents awarded by the United States Patent and Trademark Office.

Population

1990 Census 182,005
1998 Estimate..............................167,475
% Change .... -8.0
2005 Projection 1,011,000*

Racial/Ethnic Breakdown
White....................................58.4%
Black 40.4%
Other 1.2%
Hispanic Origin (may be of any race) 0.7%

Age Breakdown
Under 5 years............................... 8.5%
5 to 17....................................17.4%
18 to 20..................................... 6.0%
21 to 24..................................... 7.3%
25 to 34....................................18.0%
35 to 44....................................13.0%
45 to 54..................................... 8.3%
55 to 64..................................... 8.5%
65 to 74..................................... 7.8%
75+ years 5.3%
Median Age..................................31.0

Gender Breakdown
Male.......................................47.6%
Female.....................................52.4%

** Information given is for the Dayton-Springfield Metropolitan Statistical Area (MSA), which includes the City of Dayton, the City of Springfield, as well as Clark, Greene, Miami, and Montgomery counties.*

Government

Type of Government: Commission-Manager

Dayton & Montgomery County Public Library
215 E 3rd St
Dayton, OH 45402
Phone: 937-227-9500
Fax: 937-227-9524

Dayton City Commission
101 W 3rd St
Dayton, OH 45402
Phone: 937-333-3636
Fax: 937-333-4297

Dayton City Hall
101 W 3rd St
Dayton, OH 45402
Phone: 937-333-3333
Fax: 937-333-4297

Dayton City Manager
101 W 3rd St
Dayton, OH 45402
Phone: 937-333-3600
Fax: 937-333-4298

Dayton Civil Service Board
130 W 2nd St Suite 710
Dayton, OH 45402
Phone: 937-333-2300
Fax: 937-333-2125

Dayton Economic Development Dept
101 W 3rd St Rm 430
Dayton, OH 45402
Phone: 937-333-3634
Fax: 937-333-4274

Dayton Finance Dept
101 W 3rd St 1st Fl
Dayton, OH 45402
Phone: 937-333-3578
Fax: 937-333-3557

Dayton Fire Dept
300 N Main St
Dayton, OH 45402
Phone: 937-333-4501
Fax: 937-333-4561

Dayton Mayor
101 W 3rd St
Dayton, OH 45402
Phone: 937-333-3636
Fax: 937-333-4299

Dayton Parks Recreation & Culture Dept
2013 W 3rd St
Dayton, OH 45417
Phone: 937-333-8400
Fax: 937-333-6019

Dayton Planning & Community Development Dept
101 W 3rd St 6th Fl
Dayton, OH 45402
Phone: 937-333-3670
Fax: 937-333-4281

Dayton Police Dept
335 W 3rd St
Dayton, OH 45402
Phone: 937-333-1082
Fax: 937-333-1321

Dayton Public Works Dept
101 W 3rd St
Dayton, OH 45402
Phone: 937-333-4070

Dayton Water Dept
320 W Monument Ave
Dayton, OH 45402
Phone: 937-333-3734
Fax: 937-228-2833

Important Phone Numbers

AAA.......................................937-224-2888
Dayton Area Board of Realtors 937-223-0900
Driver's License Information......................937-236-1763
Emergency 911
Montgomery County Auditor's Office Real Estate Dept.................................937-225-4326
Ohio Dept of Taxation...........................937-285-6220
Ohio Dept of Taxation Income Tax Div............937-285-6210
Poison Control Center 937-222-2227
Time..937-499-1212
Vehicle Registration Information 937-866-9511
Voter Registration Information....................937-225-5656
Weather.....................................937-258-2000

Information Sources

Better Business Bureau Serving Dayton/ Miami Valley
40 W 4th St Suite 1250
Dayton, OH 45402
www.dayton.bbb.org
Phone: 937-222-5825
Fax: 937-222-3338
TF: 800-776-5301

Dayton Area Chamber of Commerce
1 Chamber Plaza Suite 200
Dayton, OH 45402
www.daytonchamber.org
Phone: 937-226-1444
Fax: 937-226-8254

Dayton Convention Center
22 E 5th St
Dayton, OH 45402
www.daytoncenter.com
Phone: 937-333-4700
Fax: 937-333-4711
TF: 800-822-3498

Dayton/Montgomery County Convention & Visitors Bureau
1 Chamber Plaza Suite A
Dayton, OH 45402
www.daytoncvb.com
Phone: 937-226-8248
Fax: 937-226-8294
TF: 800-221-8235

Montgomery County
41 N Perry St
Dayton, OH 45422
www.co.montgomery.oh.us
Phone: 937-225-4000
Fax: 937-496-7220

Online Resources

4Dayton.com
www.4dayton.com

Anthill City Guide Dayton
www.anthill.com/city.asp?city=dayton

Area Guide Dayton
dayton.areaguides.net

City Knowledge Dayton
www.cityknowledge.com/oh_dayton.htm

Dayton Golf Online
www.daytongolf.com/

Dayton Home Page
www.dayton.net/dayton

Excite.com Dayton City Guide
www.excite.com/travel/countries/united_states/ohio/dayton

Area Communities

Dayton area communities with populations greater than 10,000 include:

Beavercreek
1368 Research Park Dr
Beavercreek, OH 45432
Phone: 937-426-5100
Fax: 937-427-5540

Centerville
100 W Spring Valley Rd
Centerville, OH 45458
Phone: 937-433-7151
Fax: 937-433-8221

Englewood
333 W National Rd
Englewood, OH 45322
Phone: 937-836-5106
Fax: 937-836-7426

Fairborn
44 W Hebble Ave
Fairborn, OH 45324
Phone: 937-754-3030
Fax: 937-879-7395

Franklin
35 E 4th St
Franklin, OH 45005
Phone: 513-746-9921
Fax: 513-746-1136

Huber Heights
6131 Taylorsville Rd
Huber Heights, OH 45424
Phone: 937-233-1423
Fax: 937-266-1272

Kettering
3600 Shroyer Rd
Kettering, OH 45429
Phone: 937-296-2550
Fax: 937-296-3242

Miamisburg
PO Box 0570
Miamisburg, OH 45343
Phone: 937-866-3303
Fax: 937-866-0891

Piqua
219 W Water St
Piqua, OH 45356
Phone: 937-778-2051
Fax: 937-778-0050

Springfield
76 E High St
Springfield, OH 45502
Phone: 937-324-7700
Fax: 937-328-3478

Troy
100 S Market St
Troy, OH 45373
Phone: 937-339-9601
Fax: 937-339-8601

Vandalia
333 James E Bohanan Memorial Dr
Vandalia, OH 45377
Phone: 937-898-5891
Fax: 937-898-6117

West Carrollton
300 E Central Ave
West Carrollton, OH 45449
Phone: 937-859-5783
Fax: 937-859-3366

Xenia
101 N Detroit St
Xenia, OH 45385
Phone: 937-376-7230
Fax: 937-374-1818

Economy

For more than a century, Dayton has been a center for industry and invention. Two companies responsible for making Dayton a city of innovation—General Motors and NCR Corp.—remain the area's two largest employers. Although manufacturing remains a vital part of Dayton's economy, the area's economic base has diversified significantly in recent years. Services is currently the largest employment sector, with health care being the leading service-related industry, employing some 33,000 Montgomery County residents. Government also plays an important role in Dayton's economy—one-third of Montgomery County's 15 largest employers are government-related.

Unemployment Rate 3.6%*
Per Capita Income.......................... $26,422*
Median Family Income...................... $52,400*

** Information given is for the Dayton-Springfield Metropolitan Statistical Area (MSA), which includes the City of Dayton, the City of Springfield, as well as Clark, Greene, Miami, and Montgomery counties.*

Principal Industries & Number of Wage Earners

Dayton-Springfield MSA* - 1999

Industry	Wage Earners
Communication & Utilities	5,800
Construction	17,900
Finance, Insurance, & Real Estate	18,800
Government	71,300
Manufacturing	95,800
Retail Trade	89,000
Services	142,500
Transportation	15,600
Wholesale Trade	21,400

** Information given is for the Dayton-Springfield Metropolitan Statistical Area (MSA), which includes the City of Dayton, the City of Springfield, as well as Clark, Greene, Miami, and Montgomery counties.*

Major Employers

Copeland Corp
1675 W Campbell Rd Box 669
Sidney, OH 45365
E-mail: info@copeland-corp.com
www.copeland-corp.com
Phone: 937-498-3011
Fax: 937-498-3887

Dayton City Hall
101 W 3rd St
Dayton, OH 45402
E-mail: cityinfo@ci.dayton.oh.us
www.ci.dayton.oh.us
Phone: 937-333-3333
Fax: 937-333-4297

Dayton City Schools
348 W 1st St
Dayton, OH 45402
www.dps.k12.oh.us
Phone: 937-461-3002
Fax: 937-542-3188

Dayton Power & Light Co
PO Box 1247
Dayton, OH 45401
E-mail: dplweb@waytogo.com
www.waytogo.com
Phone: 937-224-6000
Fax: 937-259-7385
TF: 800-929-8646

Elder-Beerman Stores Corp
PO Box 1448
Dayton, OH 45401
www.elder-beerman.com
Phone: 937-296-2700
Fax: 937-296-2948

Emery Worldwide
1 Emery Plaza Dr
Vandalia, OH 45377
www.emeryworld.com/eww/emeryweb/
Phone: 937-264-6500
Fax: 937-264-6069

Franciscan Medical Center
1 Franciscan Way
Dayton, OH 45408
Phone: 937-229-6000
Fax: 937-229-7093

General Motors Corp
3800 Springboro Pike
Dayton, OH 45439
www.gm.com/careers
Phone: 937-455-2471
Fax: 937-455-2919

Good Samaritan Hospital & Health Center
2222 Philadelphia Dr
Dayton, OH 45406
Phone: 937-278-2612
Fax: 937-276-7617

Grandview Hospital & Medical Center
405 W Grand Ave
Dayton, OH 45405
Phone: 937-226-3200
Fax: 937-461-0020

Miami Valley Hospital
1 Wyoming St
Dayton, OH 45409
Phone: 937-223-6192
Fax: 937-208-2225
TF: 800-544-0630

Montgomery County
41 N Perry St
Dayton, OH 45422
www.co.montgomery.oh.us
Phone: 937-225-4000
Fax: 937-496-7220

NCR Corp
1700 S Patterson Blvd
Dayton, OH 45479
www.ncr.com
Phone: 937-445-5000
Fax: 937-445-5617
TF: 800-531-2222

Reynolds & Reynolds Co
PO Box 2608
Dayton, OH 45401
E-mail: info@reyrey.com
www.reyrey.com
Phone: 937-485-2000
Fax: 937-485-4230
TF: 800-344-0996

University of Dayton
300 College Pk
Dayton, OH 45469
E-mail: admission@udayton.edu
www.udayton.edu
Phone: 937-229-1000
Fax: 937-229-4729
TF: 800-837-7433

US Postal Service
1111 E 5th St
Dayton, OH 45401
new.usps.com
Phone: 937-227-1105

Veterans Administration Medical Center
4100 W 3rd St
Dayton, OH 45417
Phone: 937-268-6511
Fax: 937-267-5374

Wright State University
3640 Colonel Glenn Hwy
Dayton, OH 45435
E-mail: cmdavis@desire.wright.edu
www.wright.edu
Phone: 937-775-3333
Fax: 937-775-5795
TF: 800-247-1770

Wright-Patterson Air Force Base
Wright-Patterson AFB, OH 45433
www.wpafb.af.mil
Phone: 937-257-1110

Quality of Living Indicators

Total Crime Index 15,997
(rates per 100,000 inhabitants)

Violent Crime
Murder/manslaughter 27
Forcible rape 181
Robbery 971
Aggravated assault 610

Property Crime
Burglary 3,653
Larceny theft 7,629
Motor vehicle theft 2,926

Cost of Living Index 101.4
(national average = 100)

Median Home Price $104,100

Education

Public Schools

Dayton City Schools
348 W 1st St
Dayton, OH 45402
www.dps.k12.oh.us
Phone: 937-461-3002
Fax: 937-542-3188

Number of Schools
Elementary 34
Middle 6
High 6

Student/Teacher Ratio
All Grades 15.1:1

Private Schools

Number of Schools (all grades) 68

Colleges & Universities

Antioch College
795 Livermore St
Yellow Springs, OH 45387
www.antioch-college.edu
Phone: 937-767-7331
Fax: 937-767-6473
TF: 800-543-9436

Cedarville College
PO Box 601
Cedarville, OH 45314
www.cedarville.edu
Phone: 937-766-2211
Fax: 937-766-7575
TF: 800-233-2784

Central State University
1400 Brush Row Rd
Wilberforce, OH 45384
E-mail: info@centralstate.edu
www.centralstate.edu
Phone: 937-376-6011
Fax: 937-376-6648
TF: 800-388-2781

Clark State Community College
570 E Leffel Ln
Springfield, OH 45505
www.clark.cc.oh.us
Phone: 937-325-0691
Fax: 937-328-6133

ITT Technical Institute
3325 Stop Eight Rd
Dayton, OH 45414
www.itt-tech.edu
Phone: 937-454-2267
Fax: 937-454-2278
TF: 800-568-3241

Kettering College of Medical Arts
3737 Southern Blvd
Kettering, OH 45429
www.kcma.edu
Phone: 937-296-7201
Fax: 937-296-4238
TF: 800-433-5262

Miami-Jacobs College
400 E 2nd St
Dayton, OH 45402
E-mail: miamijacob@miamijacobs.edu
www.miamijacobs.edu
Phone: 937-449-8277
Fax: 937-461-3384

Ohio Institute of Photography & Technology
2029 Edgefield Rd
Dayton, OH 45439
www.oipt.com
Phone: 937-294-6155
Fax: 937-294-2259
TF: 800-932-9698

RETS Tech Center
555 E Alex Bell Rd
Centerville, OH 45459
Phone: 937-433-3410
Fax: 937-435-6516
TF: 800-837-7387

Sinclair Community College
444 W 3rd St
Dayton, OH 45402
www.sinclair.edu
Phone: 937-512-2500
Fax: 937-512-2393

Southwestern College of Business Dayton
225 W First St
Dayton, OH 45402
Phone: 937-224-0061
Fax: 937-224-0065

University of Dayton
300 College Pk
Dayton, OH 45469
E-mail: admission@udayton.edu
www.udayton.edu
Phone: 937-229-1000
Fax: 937-229-4729
TF: 800-837-7433

Urbana University Dayton Campus
101 W Schantz Ave
Dayton, OH 45479
Phone: 937-298-3973

Wilberforce University
1055 N Bickett Rd
Wilberforce, OH 45384
www.wilberforce.edu
Phone: 937-376-2911
Fax: 937-376-4751
TF: 800-367-8568

Wright State University
3640 Colonel Glenn Hwy
Dayton, OH 45435
E-mail: cmdavis@desire.wright.edu
www.wright.edu
Phone: 937-775-3333
Fax: 937-775-5795
TF: 800-247-1770

Hospitals

Children's Medical Center
1 Children's Plaza
Dayton, OH 45404
www.cmc-dayton.org
Phone: 937-226-8300
Fax: 937-226-8326

Clinton Memorial Hospital
610 W Main St
Wilmington, OH 45177
Phone: 937-382-6611
Fax: 937-382-9408

Community Hospital
2615 E High St
Springfield, OH 45501
www.communityhospital.com
Phone: 937-325-0531
Fax: 937-328-9600

Franciscan Medical Center
1 Franciscan Way
Dayton, OH 45408
Phone: 937-229-6000
Fax: 937-229-7093

Good Samaritan Hospital & Health Center
2222 Philadelphia Dr
Dayton, OH 45406
Phone: 937-278-2612
Fax: 937-276-7617

Grandview Hospital & Medical Center
405 W Grand Ave
Dayton, OH 45405
Phone: 937-226-3200
Fax: 937-461-0020

Greene Memorial Hospital
1141 N Monroe Dr
Xenia, OH 45385
Phone: 937-372-8011
Fax: 937-376-6983

Kettering Medical Center
3535 Southern Blvd
Kettering, OH 45429
www.kmcnetwork.org
Phone: 937-298-4331
Fax: 937-296-4246

Mercy Medical Center
1343 N Fountain Blvd
Springfield, OH 45501
www.mercy-allyourcare.org
Phone: 937-390-5000
Fax: 937-390-5527

Miami Valley Hospital
1 Wyoming St
Dayton, OH 45409
Phone: 937-223-6192
Fax: 937-208-2225
TF: 800-544-0630

Middletown Regional Hospital
105 McKnight Dr
Middletown, OH 45044
www.middletownhospital.org
Phone: 513-424-2111
Fax: 513-420-5688
TF: 800-338-4057

Veterans Affairs Medical Center
4100 W 3rd St
Dayton, OH 45428
www.daytonvamc.com
Phone: 937-268-6511
Fax: 937-267-5331

Transportation

Airport(s)

Dayton International Airport (DAY)
5 miles N of downtown Dayton
(approx 5 minutes) 937-454-8200

Mass Transit

Miami Valley Regional Transit Authority
$1 Base fare 937-226-1144

Rail/Bus

Greyhound/Trailways Bus Station
111 E 5th St
Dayton, OH 45402
Phone: 937-224-1608
TF: 800-231-2222

Utilities

Electricity
Dayton Power & Light Co......................937-224-6000
www.waytogo.com

Gas
Dayton Power & Light Co......................937-224-6000
www.waytogo.com

Water
Dayton Div of Water Revenue 937-333-3550

Garbage Collection/Recycling
Dayton Waste Collection 937-333-4833

Telecommunications

Telephone
Ameritech 800-660-1000
www.ameritech.com

Cable Television
Time Warner Cable 937-294-6800
www.forerunner.net

Internet Service Providers (ISPs)
Crossroads of America X-press NETwork (COAX-NET) 937-890-8053
www.coax.net
Dayton Internet Services 937-586-2020
www.dayton.net
Dayton Network Access Co 937-463-5555
www.dnaco.net
Dayton Ohio Network (DONet) 937-256-7288
www.donet.com

Banks

Bank One NA
40 N Main St Kettering Tower
Dayton, OH 45401
Phone: 937-449-8803
Fax: 937-449-2060
TF: 800-333-1049

Fifth Third Bank
110 N Main St
Dayton, OH 45402
www.53.com
Phone: 937-227-6500
Fax: 937-449-2678
TF: 800-972-3030

Huntington National Bank
Courthouse Plaza SW Suite 200
Dayton, OH 45402
Phone: 937-443-5900
Fax: 937-443-5914

National City Bank of Dayton
6 N Main St
Dayton, OH 45412
Phone: 937-226-2175
Fax: 937-226-2023

Shopping

Dayton Mall
2700 Miamisburg Centerville Rd
Dayton, OH 45459
Phone: 937-433-9833
Fax: 937-433-5289

Elder-Beerman Courthouse Plaza
40 N Ludlow St
Dayton, OH 45401
Phone: 937-224-8000

Mall at Fairfield Commons
2727 Fairfield Commons
Beavercreek, OH 45431
Phone: 937-427-4300
Fax: 937-427-3668

Oregon Historic District
Dayton, OH 45402
Phone: 937-223-0538

Salem Mall
5200 Salem Ave
Dayton, OH 45426
Phone: 937-854-5000
Fax: 937-854-3463

Town & Country Shopping Center
Far Hills & Stroop Rd
Dayton, OH 45429
Phone: 937-293-7516
Fax: 937-293-5575

Media

Newspapers and Magazines

Centerville-Bellbrook Times
3085 Woodman Dr Suite 170
Kettering, OH 45420
Phone: 937-294-7000
Fax: 937-294-2981

Dayton Daily News*
45 S Ludlow St
Dayton, OH 45402
www.activedayton.com
Phone: 937-225-2000
Fax: 937-225-2489

Enon Messenger
1 Herald Sq
Fairborn, OH 45324
Phone: 937-878-3993
Fax: 937-878-8314

**Indicates major daily newspapers*

Television

WBDT-TV Ch 26 (Ind)
2675 Dayton Rd
Springfield, OH 45506
Phone: 937-323-0026
Fax: 937-323-1912

WDTN-TV Ch 2 (ABC)
4595 S Dixie Ave
Dayton, OH 45439
E-mail: wdtn@erinet.com
wdtn.com
Phone: 937-293-2101
Fax: 937-296-7147

WHIO-TV Ch 7 (CBS)
1414 Wilmington Ave
Dayton, OH 45420
www.activedayton.com/whiotv
Phone: 937-259-2111
Fax: 937-259-2024

WKEF-TV Ch 22 (NBC)
1731 Soldiers Home Rd
Dayton, OH 45418
E-mail: nbc22@erinet.com
www.nbc22.com
Phone: 937-263-2662
Fax: 937-268-2332

WPTD-TV Ch 16 (PBS)
110 S Jefferson St
Dayton, OH 45402
Phone: 937-220-1600
Fax: 937-220-1642

WRGT-TV Ch 45 (Fox)
45 Broadcast Plaza
Dayton, OH 45408
www.wrgt.com
Phone: 937-263-4500
Fax: 937-268-5265

Radio

WCTM-AM 1130 kHz (B/EZ)
320 Woodside Dr
West Alexandria, OH 45381
Phone: 937-456-3200

WDAO-AM 1210 kHz (Urban)
33 E 2nd St
Dayton, OH 45402
Phone: 937-222-9326
Fax: 937-461-6100

WFCJ-FM 93.7 MHz (Rel)
7331 Manning Rd
Miamisburg, OH 45342
www.wfcj.com
Phone: 937-866-2471
Fax: 937-866-2062

WGTZ-FM 92.9 MHz (CHR)
717 E David Rd
Dayton, OH 45429
www.erinet.com/wgtz
Phone: 937-294-5858
Fax: 937-297-5233

WHIO-AM 1290 kHz (N/T)
1414 Wilmington Ave
Dayton, OH 45420
E-mail: coxradio@erinet.com
www.activedayton.com/partners/whioam
Phone: 937-259-2111
Fax: 937-259-2144

WHKO-FM 99.1 MHz (Ctry)
1414 Wilmington Ave
Dayton, OH 45420
www.activedayton.com/partners/whkofm/
Phone: 937-259-2111
Fax: 937-259-2168

WING-AM 1410 kHz (N/T)
717 E David Rd
Dayton, OH 45429
www.wingam.com
Phone: 937-294-5858
Fax: 937-297-5233

WING-FM 102.9 MHz (CR)
717 E David Rd
Dayton, OH 45429
www.wingfm.com
Phone: 937-294-5858
Fax: 937-297-5233

WLQT-FM 99.9 MHz (AC)
101 Pine St
Dayton, OH 45402
E-mail: lite99@erinet.com
www.wlqt.com
Phone: 937-224-1137
Fax: 937-224-3667

WMMX-FM 107.7 MHz (AC)
101 Pine St
Dayton, OH 45402
E-mail: wmmx@erinet.com
www.wmmx.com
Phone: 937-224-1137
Fax: 937-224-3667

WONE-AM 980 kHz (Nost)
101 Pine St
Dayton, OH 45402
E-mail: wone@erinet.com
www.wone.com
Phone: 937-224-1137
Fax: 937-224-3667

WPFB-FM 105.9 MHz (Ctry)
4505 Central Ave
Middletown, OH 45044
www.amorefm.com
Phone: 513-422-3625
Fax: 513-424-9732

WROU-FM 92.1 MHz (Urban)
211 S Main St Fidelity Plaza Suite 1200
Dayton, OH 45402
E-mail: jams@wrou.com
www.wrou.com
Phone: 937-222-9768
Fax: 937-223-5687

WXEG-FM 103.9 MHz (Alt)
101 Pine St
Dayton, OH 45402
E-mail: thex1039@erinet.com
www.wxeg.com
Phone: 937-224-1137
Fax: 937-224-3667

Attractions

Beginning with Wilbur and Orville Wright, Dayton's history has centered on aviation. The Dayton Aviation National Historical Park, authorized in 1992, preserves the area's aviation heritage associated with the Wright Brothers, their inventions and developments in aviation, and the life and works of their friend and classmate, the poet Paul Laurence Dunbar. Each July, the world-famous U.S. Air and Trade Show, featuring more than 100 outdoor exhibits, is held in Dayton at Wright-Patterson Air Force Base. At the base also is the United States Air Force Museum, the world's largest military aviation museum, which has more than 200 historic aircraft and missiles.

Aullwood Audubon Center & Farm
1000 Aullwood Rd
Dayton, OH 45414
E-mail: aullwood@erinet.com
www.audubon.org/local/sanctuary/aullwood/
Phone: 937-890-7360
Fax: 937-890-2382

Aviation Trail Inc
22 S Williams St
Dayton, OH 45407
Phone: 937-443-0793

Carillon Historical Park
100 Carillon Blvd
Dayton, OH 45409
www.classicar.com/MUSEUMS/CARILLON/CARILLON.HTM
Phone: 937-293-2841
Fax: 937-293-5798

Carriage Hill MetroPark
7800 E Shull Rd Huber Heights
Dayton, OH 45424
Phone: 937-879-0461
Fax: 937-879-8904

Carriage Hills Farm Museum
7800 E Shull Rd
Dayton, OH 45424
Phone: 937-879-0461
Fax: 937-878-4243

Citizens Motorcar Co America's Packard Museum
420 S Ludlow St
Dayton, OH 45402
Phone: 937-226-1917
Fax: 937-224-1918

Cox Arboretum
6733 Springboro Pike
Dayton, OH 45449
Phone: 937-434-9005
Fax: 937-434-4361

Dayton Art Institute
456 Belmonte Pk N
Dayton, OH 45405
E-mail: info@daytonartinstitute.org
www.daytonartinstitute.org
Phone: 937-223-5277
Fax: 937-223-3140

Dayton Aviation National Historical Park
22 S Williams St
Dayton, OH 45409
www.nps.gov/daav/
Phone: 937-225-7705
Fax: 937-225-7706

Dayton Bach Society
300 College Pk
Dayton, OH 45469
E-mail: bach-soc@udayton.edu
www.udayton.edu/~bach-soc
Phone: 937-256-2224
Fax: 937-229-3916

Dayton Ballet
140 N Main St
Dayton, OH 45402
Phone: 937-449-5060
Fax: 937-461-8353

Dayton Contemporary Dance Co
126 N Main St Suite 240
Dayton, OH 45402
Phone: 937-228-3232
Fax: 937-223-6156

Dayton Cultural Center
216 N Main St
Dayton, OH 45402
Phone: 937-223-2489
Fax: 937-223-0795

Dayton Museum of Discovery
2600 DeWeese Pkwy
Dayton, OH 45414
E-mail: damuseum@gte.net
Phone: 937-275-7431
Fax: 937-275-5811

Dayton Opera
125 E 1st St Memorial Hall
Dayton, OH 45402
Phone: 937-228-0662
Fax: 937-228-9612

Dayton Philharmonic Orchestra
125 E 1st St Memorial Hall
Dayton, OH 45402
Phone: 937-224-3521
Fax: 937-223-9189

Dayton Visual Arts Center
40 W 4th St
Dayton, OH 45402
www.sinclair.edu/community/dvac/
Phone: 937-224-3822
Fax: 937-224-4356

Dunbar Paul Laurence House
219 Paul Laurence Dunbar St
Dayton, OH 45407
Phone: 937-224-7061
Fax: 937-224-7061

Eastwood MetroPark
Harshman Rd
Dayton, OH 45431
Phone: 937-426-8521

Five Rivers MetroParks
1375 E Siebenthaler Ave
Dayton, OH 45414
E-mail: metroparks@dayton.net
www.dayton.net/MetroParks/
Phone: 937-275-7275
Fax: 937-278-8849

Fraze Pavilion for the Performing Arts
695 Lincoln Pk Blvd Lincoln Park Ctr
Kettering, OH 45429
E-mail: fraze@dayton.net
Phone: 937-296-3300
Fax: 937-296-3302

Germantown MetroPark
6910 Boomershine Rd
Dayton, OH 45327
Phone: 937-855-7717

Human Race Theatre Co
126 N Main St
Dayton, OH 45419
E-mail: hrtheatre@aol.com
Phone: 937-461-3823
Fax: 937-461-7223

IMAX Theater
Springfield Pike US Air Force Museum
Wright-Patterson AFB, OH 45433
E-mail: afmfimax@donet.com
www.intecon.com/museum/imax/imax.html
Phone: 937-253-4629
Fax: 937-258-3816

Kettering-Moraine Museum & Historical Society
35 Moraine Cir S
Dayton, OH 45439
Phone: 937-299-2722

Miamisburg Mound State Memorial
Mound Ave
Miamisburg, OH 45342
Phone: 937-866-4532

National Afro-American Museum & Cultural Center
1350 Brush Row Rd
Wilberforce, OH 45384
www.ohiohistory.org/places/afroam/
Phone: 937-376-4944
Fax: 937-376-2007

Old Courthouse Museum & Montgomery County Historical Society
224 N Saint Claire St
Dayton, OH 45402
Phone: 937-228-6271
Fax: 937-331-7160

Paramount's Kings Island
PO Box 901
Kings Island, OH 45034
www.pki.com
Phone: 513-754-5700
Fax: 513-754-5725
TF: 800-288-0808

Patterson Homestead Museum & Rental Facility
1815 Brown St
Dayton, OH 45409
Phone: 937-222-9724
Fax: 937-222-0345

Possum Creek MetroPark
4901 Shank Rd
Dayton, OH 45418
Phone: 937-268-1312

Riverbend Arts Center
1301 E Siebenthaler Ave
Dayton, OH 45414
E-mail: artistvls@hotmail.com
www.riverbend-arts.org
Phone: 937-333-7000
Fax: 937-333-3158

Santa Clara Arts District
N Main St & Santa Clara Ave
Dayton, OH 45405
Phone: 937-278-4900

Sugarcreek MetroPark Preserve
7636 Wilmington-Dayton Pike
Dayton, OH 45459
Phone: 937-433-0004

SunWatch Indian Village Archaeological Park
2301 W River Rd
Dayton, OH 45418
Phone: 937-268-8199
Fax: 937-268-1760

Trapshooting Hall of Fame & Museum
601 W National Rd
Vandalia, OH 45377
Phone: 937-898-1945
Fax: 937-898-5472

US Air Force Museum
1100 Spaatz St Wright-Patterson Air Force Base
Dayton, OH 45433
www.wpafb.af.mil/museum
Phone: 937-255-3284
Fax: 937-255-3910

Victoria Theatre
138 N Main St
Dayton, OH 45402
www.victoriatheatre.com
Phone: 937-228-3630
Fax: 937-449-5068

Wegerzyn Horticultural Center & Stillwater Gardens
1301 E Siebenthaler Ave
Dayton, OH 45414
Phone: 937-277-6545
Fax: 937-277-6546

Wright Brothers Cycle Co
22 S Williams St
Dayton, OH 45407
Phone: 937-225-7705
Fax: 937-225-7706

Sports Teams & Facilities

Dayton Bombers (hockey)
3640 Colonel Glen Hwy Nutter Ctr Suite 417
Dayton, OH 45435
www.bombershockey.com
Phone: 937-775-4747
Fax: 937-775-4749
TF: 877-523-6684

Annual Events

A World A'Fair (mid-May) 937-233-0050
Art in the Park (late May) 937-278-0655
City Folk Festival (mid-June) 937-223-3655
Country Peddler Shows (late February & early June) 937-278-4776
Dayton Art Institute Oktoberfest (early October) 937-223-5277
Dayton Auto Show (mid-March) 937-333-4700
Dayton Black Cultural Festival (early July) 937-224-7100
Dayton Home & Garden Show (late March) 937-333-4700
Dayton Horse Show (late July-early August) 937-461-4740

Dayton Industrial Expo (late October) 937-333-4700
Dayton Sports Fishing Travel & Outdoor Show (mid-January).................................937-333-4700
Easter Eggstravaganza (early April)................937-226-8248
Family Fourth of July (July 4)....................937-224-1518
Fiesta Latino Americano (mid-June)...............937-296-3300
Fly City Music Festival (late August) 937-222-9768
Go 4th Celebration (July 4).......................937-296-3281
Grand American World Trapshooting Tournament (mid-August) 937-898-1945
Greek Festival (early September)..................937-224-0601
International Festival (late May-early June).........937-333-4700
Jazz at the Bend Jazz Festival (early September)....937-223-2489
MetroParks RiverFest (mid-October)...............937-278-8231
Miami Valley Boat Show (mid-January) 937-278-4776
Montgomery County Fair (early September) 937-224-1619
Oktoberfest (late September) 937-223-5277
SummerFest (late June)..........................937-268-8199
US Air & Trade Show (late July)..................937-898-5901
US Air Force Marathon (mid-September)...........937-255-3334
Women in Jazz Festival (late June)................937-461-5300
World Reggae Festival (early September)..........937-225-2333

Denver, Colorado

***County:* Denver**

DENVER is located in the High Plains of north central Colorado at the edge of the Rocky Mountains. Major cities within 100 miles include Aurora, Boulder, Colorado Springs, and Greeley, Colorado; and Cheyenne, Wyoming.

Area (Land) .... 153.3 sq mi
Area (Water)................................ 1.6 sq mi
Elevation....................................5,280 ft
Latitude ....39-66-77 N
Longitude............................... 104-83-54 W
Time Zone .... MST
Area Code....................................... 303

Climate

Denver's clear, dry climate is tempered by its location east of the Rocky Mountains, which protect it from extremes of hot and cold. Winters are cold but sunny, with average high temperatures in the mid-40s and lows in the mid- to high teens. The average annual snowfall in Denver is 60 inches. Summer days are warm, with average high temperatures in the mid-80s, while evenings cool down dramatically into the mid-50s. Precipitation is low throughout the year—May is the wettest month in Denver, while January is the driest.

Average Temperatures & Precipitation

Temperatures

	Jan	Feb	Mar	Apr	May	Jun	Jul	Aug	Sep	Oct	Nov	Dec
High	43	47	52	62	71	81	88	86	77	66	53	45
Low	16	20	26	35	44	52	59	57	48	36	25	17

Precipitation

	Jan	Feb	Mar	Apr	May	Jun	Jul	Aug	Sep	Oct	Nov	Dec
Inches	0.5	0.6	1.3	1.7	2.4	1.8	1.9	1.5	1.2	1.0	0.9	0.6

History

The town of Denver was founded in 1860 at the site of a trading post established two years earlier to supply prospectors of the Gold Rush that began at the confluence of the South Platte River and Cherry Creek. Prior to white settlement, the Denver area had been inhabited for thousands of years by the Arapahoe, Comanche, and Kiowa tribes and explored by Spaniards as early as the mid-1500s. During its early years, the city endured several disasters, including a fire, a flood, and a rash of Indian attacks.

Denver was chosen as the state capital of Colorado in 1867. With the arrival of the railroad three years later, the city became a regional transportation hub. By this time, many of the Native American tribes had been defeated, and white settlement flourished. Within two decades, Denver's population grew from fewer than 5,000 residents to more than 100,000. Successful gold and silver mining and processing fueled Denver's early economy, and in 1906 a U.S. Mint was established in the city.

The energy boom during the 1970s and 80s led to phenomenal growth in Denver—the city's population nearly doubled as more than 1,300 energy-related companies relocated to the area, bringing new economic opportunities. Now home to nearly 500,000 people, the "Mile High City" today is Colorado's largest city as well as the industrial, commercial, and financial center of the Rocky Mountain region.

Population

1990 Census 467,610
1998 Estimate.............................499,055
% Change 6.7

Racial/Ethnic Breakdown
White...................................72.1%
Black 12.8%
Other...................................15.1%
Hispanic Origin (may be of any race) 23.0%

Age Breakdown
Under 5 years..............................7.4%
5 to 17..................................14.6%
18 to 20..................................3.9%
21 to 24..................................5.9%
25 to 34.................................20.5%
35 to 44.................................16.5%
45 to 54..................................9.1%
55 to 64..................................8.2%
65 to 74..................................7.6%
75+ years 6.2%
Median Age.................................33.9

Gender Breakdown
Male....................................48.7%
Female..................................51.3%

Government

Type of Government: Strong Mayor-City Council

Denver Career Service Authority
110 16th St
Denver, CO 80202
Phone: 720-913-5612
Fax: 720-913-5720

Denver City Council
1437 Bannock St Rm 451
Denver, CO 80202
Phone: 303-640-3012
Fax: 303-640-2636

Denver City Hall
1437 Bannock St
Denver, CO 80202
Phone: 303-640-5555

Denver Clerk & Recorder
1437 Bannock St Rm 281
Denver, CO 80202
Phone: 303-640-7290
Fax: 303-640-3628

Denver Community Planning & Development Agency
200 W 14th Ave Suite 203
Denver, CO 80204
Phone: 303-640-2736
Fax: 303-572-4636

Denver Economic Development & International Trade Office
216 16th St Suite 1000
Denver, CO 80202
Phone: 303-640-7100
Fax: 303-640-7059

Denver Fire Dept
745 W Colfax Ave
Denver, CO 80204
Phone: 720-913-3414
Fax: 720-913-3583

Denver Mayor
1437 Bannock St Rm 350
Denver, CO 80202
Phone: 303-640-2721
Fax: 303-640-2329

Denver Medical Examiner
660 Bannock St
Denver, CO 80204
Phone: 303-436-7711
Fax: 303-436-7709

Denver Parks & Recreation Dept
2300 15th St Suite 150
Denver, CO 80202
Phone: 303-964-2500
Fax: 303-964-2559

Denver Police Dept
1331 Cherokee St
Denver, CO 80204
Phone: 720-913-6527
Fax: 720-913-7029

Denver Public Library
10 W 14th Ave Pkwy
Denver, CO 80204
Phone: 303-640-6200
Fax: 303-640-6143

Denver Public Works Dept
1437 Bannock St Rm 379
Denver, CO 80202
Phone: 303-640-2561
Fax: 303-640-2424

Denver Revenue Dept
144 W Colfax Annex III
Denver, CO 80202
Phone: 303-640-2262
Fax: 303-640-3218

Denver Water Board
1600 W 12th Ave
Denver, CO 80254
Phone: 303-628-6000
Fax: 303-628-6199

Important Phone Numbers

AAA 303-753-8800
American Express Travel 303-383-5050
Colorado State Revenue Dept 303-232-2416
Dental Referral 800-917-6453
Denver Assessment Div 303-640-3021
Denver Board of Realtors 303-756-0553
Denver Treasury Div 303-640-3792
Driver's License Information 303-937-9507
Emergency 911
HotelDocs 800-468-3537
Medical Referral 303-866-8000
Poison Control Center 303-739-1123
Road Conditions 303-639-1111
Time/Temp 303-443-1910
Travelers Aid 303-342-0400
Vehicle Registration Information 303-576-2882
Voter Registration Information 303-987-7080
Weather 303-871-1492

Information Sources

Arapahoe County
5334 S Prince St
Littleton, CO 80166
www.co.arapahoe.co.us
Phone: 303-795-4200
Fax: 303-794-4625

Aurora Chamber of Commerce
562 Sable Blvd Suite 200
Aurora, CO 80011
www.aurorachamber.org
Phone: 303-344-1500
Fax: 303-344-1564

Aurora City Hall
1470 S Havana St
Aurora, CO 80012
www.ci.aurora.co.us
Phone: 303-739-7000
Fax: 303-739-7520

Aurora Economic Development Council
562 Sable Blvd Suite 240
Aurora, CO 80011
www.auroraedc.com
Phone: 303-340-2101
Fax: 303-340-2111

Aurora Mayor
1470 S Havana St 8th Fl
Aurora, CO 80012
Phone: 303-739-7015
Fax: 303-739-7594

Aurora Public Library
14949 E Alameda Dr
Aurora, CO 80012
odyssey.aurora.lib.co.us
Phone: 303-739-6600
Fax: 303-739-6579

Better Business Bureau Serving the Denver-Boulder Metro Area
1780 S Bellaire St Suite 700
Denver, CO 80222
www.denver.bbb.org
Phone: 303-758-2100
Fax: 303-758-8321

Boulder Chamber of Commerce
2440 Pearl St
Boulder, CO 80302
chamber.boulder.net
Phone: 303-442-1044
Fax: 303-938-8837

Boulder City Hall
1777 Broadway
Boulder, CO 80302
www.ci.boulder.co.us
Phone: 303-441-3388
Fax: 303-441-4478

Boulder Convention & Visitors Bureau
2440 Pearl St
Boulder, CO 80302
visitor.boulder.net/
Phone: 303-442-2911
Fax: 303-938-8837
TF: 800-444-0447

Boulder County
2020 13th St West Wing 2nd Fl
Boulder, CO 80302
www.co.boulder.co.us
Phone: 303-441-3515
Fax: 303-441-4863

Boulder Mayor
1777 Broadway
Boulder, CO 80302
www.ci.boulder.co.us/council.html
Phone: 303-441-3002
Fax: 303-441-4478

Boulder Planning Dept
PO Box 791
Boulder, CO 80306
www.ci.boulder.co.us/planning
Phone: 303-441-3270
Fax: 303-441-3241

Boulder Public Library
1000 Canyon Blvd
Boulder, CO 80302
www.boulder.lib.co.us
Phone: 303-441-3100
Fax: 303-442-1808

Colorado Convention Center
700 14th St
Denver, CO 80202
denverconvention.com
Phone: 303-228-8000
Fax: 303-228-8104

Denver County
1437 Bannock St Suite 200
Denver, CO 80202
Phone: 303-640-2628
Fax: 303-640-3628

Denver Metro Convention & Visitors Bureau
1555 California St Suite 300
Denver, CO 80202
www.denver.org
Phone: 303-892-1112
Fax: 303-892-1636
TF: 800-645-3446

Greater Denver Chamber of Commerce
1445 Market St
Denver, CO 80202
www.den-chamber.org
Phone: 303-534-8500
Fax: 303-534-3200

Online Resources

4Denver.com
www.4denver.com

About.com Guide to Denver
denver.about.com/local/mountainus/denver

All of Boulder
www.allofboulder.com

Anthill City Guide Boulder
www.anthill.com/city.asp?city=boulder

Anthill City Guide Denver
www.anthill.com/city.asp?city=denver

Area Guide Boulder
boulder.areaguides.net

Area Guide Denver
denver.areaguides.net

Boulder Community Network
bcn.boulder.co.us

Boulder County Guide
www.boulderguide.com/

Boulder Info
www.boulderinfo.com/beta.html

Boulder Weekly
www.boulderweekly.com

Boulevards Denver
www.denver.com

Bradmans.com Denver
www.bradmans.com/scripts/display_city.cgi?city=235

City Knowledge Aurora
www.cityknowledge.com/co_aurora.htm

City Knowledge Boulder
www.cityknowledge.com/co_boulder.htm

City Knowledge Denver
www.cityknowledge.com/co_denver.htm

CitySearch Denver
denver.citysearch.com

Denver City Pages
denver.thelinks.com

Denver CityLink
www.usacitylink.com/citylink/denver

Denver Graphic City Guide
www.futurecast.com/gcg/denver.htm

Denver Online
www.denveronline.com/

Denver.sidewalk
denver.sidewalk.citysearch.com

DigitalCity Denver
home.digitalcity.com/denver

Do Denver
www.dodenver.com

Downtown Denver Guide
www.downtown-denver.com/

E.Central Big City Small Planet Denver Guide
www.ecentral.com/

Excite.com Aurora City Guide
www.excite.com/travel/countries/united_states/colorado/aurora

Excite.com Boulder City Guide
www.excite.com/travel/countries/united_states/colorado/boulder

Excite.com Denver City Guide
www.excite.com/travel/countries/united_states/colorado/denver

HotelGuide Denver
hotelguide.net/denver

Info Denver
infodenver.denver.co.us

Insiders' Guide to Boulder
www.insiders.com/boulder/index.htm

Insiders' Guide to Greater Denver
www.insiders.com/denver/

Lodging.com Aurora Colorado
www.lodging.com/auto/guides/aurora-co.html

Lodging.com Boulder Colorado
www.lodging.com/auto/guides/boulder-co.html

Lodging.com Denver Colorado
www.lodging.com/auto/guides/denver-area-co.html

MetroVille Denver
denver.metroville.com

Mile High City
milehighcity.com

Open World City Guides Denver
www.worldexecutive.com/cityguides/denver/

Rough Guide Travel Denver
travel.roughguides.com/content/1046/

Virtual Voyages Denver
www.virtualvoyages.com/usa/co/denver/denver.sht

Westword
www.westword.com

Area Communities

Communities in the Denver metropolitan area (Adams, Arapahoe, Boulder, Denver, Douglas, & Jefferson counties) with populations greater than 10,000 include:

Arvada
8101 Ralston Rd
Arvada, CO 80002
Phone: 303-421-2550
Fax: 303-431-3085

Aurora
1470 S Havana St
Aurora, CO 80012
Phone: 303-739-7000
Fax: 303-739-7520

Boulder
1777 Broadway
Boulder, CO 80302
Phone: 303-441-3388
Fax: 303-441-4478

Brighton
22 S 4th Ave
Brighton, CO 80601
Phone: 303-659-4050
Fax: 303-655-2047

Broomfield
1 Descombes Dr
Broomfield, CO 80020
Phone: 303-469-3301
Fax: 303-469-8554

Castle Rock
680 Wilcox St
Castle Rock, CO 80104
Phone: 303-660-1015
Fax: 303-660-1028

Commerce City
5291 E 60th Ave
Commerce City, CO 80022
Phone: 303-289-3611
Fax: 303-289-3688

Englewood
1000 Englewood Pkwy
Englewood, CO 80110
Phone: 303-762-2300
Fax: 303-789-1125

Golden
911 10th St
Golden, CO 80401
Phone: 303-384-8000
Fax: 303-384-8001

Lafayette
1290 S Public Rd
Lafayette, CO 80026
Phone: 303-665-5588
Fax: 303-665-2153

Lakewood
480 S Allison Pkwy
Lakewood, CO 80226
Phone: 303-987-7080
Fax: 303-987-7088

Littleton
2255 W Berry Ave
Littleton, CO 80165
Phone: 303-795-3780
Fax: 303-795-3819

Longmont
350 Kimbark St
Longmont, CO 80501
Phone: 303-651-8649
Fax: 303-651-8590

Louisville
749 Main St
Louisville, CO 80027
Phone: 303-666-6565
Fax: 303-666-4699

Northglenn
11701 Community Center Dr
Denver, CO 80233
Phone: 303-451-8326
Fax: 303-450-8708

Thornton
9500 Civic Center Dr
Thornton, CO 80229
Phone: 303-538-7200
Fax: 303-538-7562

Westminster
4800 W 92nd Ave
Westminster, CO 80031
Phone: 303-430-2400
Fax: 303-430-1809

Wheat Ridge
7500 W 29th Ave
Wheat Ridge, CO 80215
Phone: 303-234-5900
Fax: 303-234-5924

Economy

Denver is the industrial and commercial hub of the Rocky Mountain region. The metro area has a diverse economic base that ranges from livestock to aerospace. Services is the largest and fastest-growing employment sector in the metro area, accounting for nearly 30 percent of non-farm employment. Tourism is one of the area's leading service-related industries, generating roughly $2 billion of revenue in Denver each year. Government (federal, state, and local) is a vital part of the capital city's economic base as well, providing about 14 percent of total jobs in the metro area. In addition to being the governmental capital of Colorado, Denver is also the finance, insurance, and real estate capital of the state—approximately 70 percent of Colorado residents employed in this sector work in Denver metro area companies.

Unemployment Rate 3.2%**
Per Capita Income.......................... $33,727*
Median Family Income...................... $58,600**

** Information given is for Denver County.*
*** Information given in for the Denver Metropolitan Statistical Area (MSA) which includes Adams, Arapahoe, Boulder, Denver, Douglas, and Jefferson counties.*

Principal Industries & Number of Wage Earners

Denver County - 1997

Industry	Wage Earners
Agricultural Services, Forestry, & Fishing	1,235
Construction	14,251
Finance, Insurance, & Real Estate	36,112
Manufacturing	30,493
Mining	6,902
Retail Trade	55,867

Services 154,082
Wholesale Trade 31,312

Major Employers

Columbia/HealthONE · Phone: 303-788-2500
4643 S Ulster St Suite 1200
Denver, CO 80237

Coors Brewing Co · Phone: 303-279-6565 · Fax: 303-277-2611
PO Box 4030
Golden, CO 80401
www.coors.com

Denver Career Service Authority · Phone: 720-913-5612 · Fax: 720-913-5720
110 16th St
Denver, CO 80202
www.denvergov.org/dephome.asp?depid=30

Denver Public Schools · Phone: 303-764-3414 · Fax: 303-764-3201
900 Grant St
Denver, CO 80203
www.denver.k12.co.us

Kaiser-Hill Co/Rocky Flats Environmental Technology Site · Phone: 303-966-7000
10808 Hwy 93 Unit B
Golden, CO 80403
www.rfets.gov

King Soopers Inc · Phone: 303-778-3100 · Fax: 303-871-9274
PO Box 5567
Denver, CO 80217

Lockheed Martin Space Systems Co Astronautics Operations · Phone: 303-977-3000
PO Box 179 MS DC1020
Denver, CO 80201
www.ast.lmco.com

Lucent Technologies · Phone: 303-793-8200 · Fax: 303-793-8239
7979 E Tufts Avenue Pkwy
Denver, CO 80237
www.lucent.com

Public Service Co of Colorado · Phone: 303-571-7511 · Fax: 303-294-8533 · TF: 800-772-7858
PO Box 840
Denver, CO 80201
www.psco.com

Qwest · Phone: 303-391-8300 · Fax: 303-706-9905
1801 California St Suite 1700
Denver, CO 80202
www.qwest.com

Safeway Inc · Phone: 303-843-7600 · Fax: 303-843-7784
6900 S Yosemite St
Englewood, CO 80112
www.safeway.com

Quality of Living Indicators

Total Crime Index 27,027
(rates per 100,000 inhabitants)

Violent Crime
Murder/manslaughter 51
Forcible rape 320
Robbery 1,064
Aggravated assault 1,481

Property Crime
Burglary 5,900
Larceny theft 12,889
Motor vehicle theft 5,322

Cost of Living Index 102.1
(national average = 100)

Median Home Price $171,300

Education

Public Schools

Denver Public Schools · Phone: 303-764-3414 · Fax: 303-764-3201
900 Grant St
Denver, CO 80203
www.denver.k12.co.us

Number of Schools
Elementary 86
Middle 20
High 12

Student/Teacher Ratio
All Grades 23.2:1

Private Schools

Number of Schools (all grades) . . . . . . 27+

Colleges & Universities

Arapahoe Community College · Phone: 303-794-1550 · Fax: 303-797-5935
5900 S Santa Fe Dr
Littleton, CO 80160

Bel-Rea Institute of Animal Technology · Phone: 303-751-8700 · Fax: 303-751-9969 · TF: 800-950-8001
1681 S Dayton St
Denver, CO 80231
E-mail: admissions@bel-rea.com
www.bel-rea.com

Colorado Christian University · Phone: 303-963-3103 · Fax: 303-963-3201 · TF: 800-443-2484
180 S Garrison St
Lakewood, CO 80226
www.ccu.edu

Colorado Institute of Art · Phone: 303-837-0825 · Fax: 303-860-8520 · TF: 800-275-2420
1200 Lincoln St
Denver, CO 80203
www.aic.aii.edu

Colorado School of Mines · Phone: 303-273-3000 · Fax: 303-273-3278 · TF: 800-446-9488
1500 Illinois St
Golden, CO 80401
www.mines.colorado.edu

Community College of Aurora · Phone: 303-360-4700 · Fax: 303-360-4761
16000 E Centretech Pkwy
Aurora, CO 80011
www.ccac.edu

Community College of Denver · Phone: 303-556-2600 · Fax: 303-556-2431
PO Box 173363
Denver, CO 80217
www.ccd.cccoes.edu

Denver Automotive & Diesel College
460 S Lipan St
Denver, CO 80223
www.denverautodiesel.com
Phone: 303-722-5724
Fax: 303-778-8264
TF: 800-347-3232

Denver Technical College
925 S Niagara St
Denver, CO 80224
www.dtc.edu
Phone: 303-329-3000
Fax: 303-329-0955

Front Range Community College
3645 W 112th Ave
Westminster, CO 80030
frcc.cc.co.us
Phone: 303-466-8811
Fax: 303-466-1623

Metropolitan State College of Denver
1006 11th St
Denver, CO 80204
www.mscd.edu
Phone: 303-556-3058
Fax: 303-556-6345

Naropa University
2130 Arapahoe Ave
Boulder, CO 80302
E-mail: info@naropa.edu
www.naropa.edu
Phone: 303-444-0202
Fax: 303-444-0410

National American University Denver Campus
1325 S Colorado Blvd Suite 100
Denver, CO 80222
www.nationalcollege.edu/campusdenver.html
Phone: 303-758-6700
Fax: 303-758-6810

Parks College
9065 Grant St
Denver, CO 80229
Phone: 303-457-2757
Fax: 303-457-4030

Red Rocks Community College
13300 W 6th Ave
Lakewood, CO 80228
www.rrcc.cccoes.edu
Phone: 303-988-6160
Fax: 303-914-6666

Regis University
3333 Regis Blvd
Denver, CO 80221
www.regis.edu
Phone: 303-458-4100
Fax: 303-964-5534
TF: 800-388-2366

University of Colorado Boulder
Campus Box 30
Boulder, CO 80309
E-mail: homepage@colorado.edu
www.colorado.edu
Phone: 303-492-1411
Fax: 303-492-7115

University of Colorado Denver
Campus Box 167
Denver, CO 80217
www.cudenver.edu
Phone: 303-556-3287
Fax: 303-556-4838

University of Denver
2199 S University Blvd
Denver, CO 80208
www.du.edu
Phone: 303-871-2000
Fax: 303-871-4000
TF: 800-525-9495

Westwood College of Technology
7350 N Broadway
Denver, CO 80221
www.westwood.edu
Phone: 303-650-5050
Fax: 303-426-4647
TF: 800-875-6050

Yeshiva Toras Chaim Talmudical Seminary
1555 Stuart St
Denver, CO 80204
Phone: 303-629-8200
Fax: 303-623-5949

Hospitals

Boulder Community Hospital
1100 Balsam Ave
Boulder, CO 80301
www.bch.org
Phone: 303-440-2273
Fax: 303-440-2278

Centura Saint Anthony Hospital Central
4231 W 16th Ave
Denver, CO 80204
www.centura.org/facilities/denver/sac/sac.html
Phone: 303-629-3511
Fax: 303-629-2189

Children's Hospital
1056 E 19th Ave
Denver, CO 80218
www.tchden.org
Phone: 303-861-8888
Fax: 303-861-3992
TF: 800-624-6553

Children's Hospital
14406 E Evans Ave Suite 100
Aurora, CO 80014
Phone: 303-861-3916
Fax: 303-751-3195

Denver Health Medical Center
777 Bannock St
Denver, CO 80204
www.denverhealth.org
Phone: 303-436-6000
Fax: 303-436-5131

Exempla Healthcare/Lutheran Medical Center
8300 W 38th Ave
Wheat Ridge, CO 80033
Phone: 303-425-4500
Fax: 303-425-2595

Healthone Presbyterian-Saint Luke's Medical Center
1719 E 19th Ave
Denver, CO 80218
Phone: 303-839-6000
Fax: 303-839-7779

HealthOne Rose Medical Center
4567 E 9th Ave
Denver, CO 80220
www.rosemed.com
Phone: 303-320-2121
Fax: 303-320-2354

Medical Center of Aurora
700 Potomac St
Aurora, CO 80011
Phone: 303-363-7200
Fax: 303-337-9773

Medical Center of Aurora South Campus
1501 S Potomac St
Aurora, CO 80012
Phone: 303-695-2600
Fax: 303-695-2913

North Suburban Medical Center
9191 Grant St
Thornton, CO 80229
www.northsuburban.com
Phone: 303-451-7800
Fax: 303-457-6701

Porter Memorial Hospital
2525 S Downing St
Denver, CO 80210
Phone: 303-778-1955
Fax: 303-778-2424

Portercare Hospital Littleton
7700 S Broadway
Littleton, CO 80122
Phone: 303-730-8900
Fax: 303-798-9824

Provenant Saint Anthony Hospital North
2551 W 84th Ave
Westminster, CO 80030
Phone: 303-426-2151
Fax: 303-426-2155

Saint Joseph Hospital
1835 Franklin St
Denver, CO 80218
Phone: 303-837-7111
Fax: 303-837-7017

Swedish Medical Center
501 E Hampden Ave
Englewood, CO 80110
www.swedishhospital.com
Phone: 303-788-5000
Fax: 303-788-6313

University Hospital
4200 E 9th Ave
Denver, CO 80262
www.uchsc.edu/uh
Phone: 303-399-1211
Fax: 303-372-5857

Veterans Affairs Medical Center
1055 Clermont St
Denver, CO 80220
Phone: 303-399-8020
Fax: 303-393-4656
TF: 888-336-8262

Transportation

Airport(s)

Denver International Airport (DEN)
25 miles NE of downtown (approx 45 minutes) . . .303-342-2000

Mass Transit

RTD Bus
$1.25 Base fare. 303-299-6000

Rail/Bus

Amtrak Station
1701 Wynkoop St
Denver, CO 80202
Phone: 800-872-7245

Greyhound/Trailways Bus Station
1055 19th St
Denver, CO 80202
Phone: 303-293-6546
TF: 800-231-2222

Utilities

Electricity
Public Service Co of Colorado 303-623-1234
www.psco.com

Gas
Public Service Co of Colorado 303-623-1234
www.psco.com

Water
Denver Water. 303-628-6000
www.water.denver.co.gov

Garbage Collection/Recycling
Denver Recycles 303-640-1675
Denver Solid Waste Div. 303-640-2136

Telecommunications

Telephone
Qwest. 800-244-1111
www.qwest.com

Cable Television
AT & T Cable Services. 303-930-2000
www.cable.att.com

Internet Service Providers (ISPs)
Boulder Community Network. 303-492-8176
bcn.boulder.co.us
Colorado Internet Cooperative Assn 303-443-3786
www.coop.net
Expert Internet Service 303-326-0234
www.xpert.net
High Speed Access Corp 303-256-2000
www.hsacorp.net
Littleton Community Network 303-795-3727
www.littleton.org/LCN/
RMI.Net. 800-864-4344
www.rmi.net
SuperNet Inc 303-296-8202
www.sni.net
Verio Colorado 303-708-2239
home.verio.net/local/frontpage.cfm?AirportCode=DEN

Banks

Bank of Cherry Creek NA
3033 E 1st Ave
Denver, CO 80206
www.bankofcherrycreek.com
Phone: 303-394-5100
Fax: 303-394-5120

Bank of Denver
1534 California St
Denver, CO 80202
Phone: 303-572-3600
Fax: 303-623-0624

Bank One Colorado NA
1125 17th St
Denver, CO 80202
Phone: 303-244-3283
Fax: 303-244-5901
TF: 800-372-2651

Citywide Bank of Denver
12075 E 45th Ave
Denver, CO 80239
Phone: 303-365-8000
Fax: 303-365-8001

Commercial Federal Bank FSB
2720 S Colorado Blvd
Denver, CO 80222
Phone: 303-757-3367
Fax: 303-331-3756

KeyBank NA
3300 E 1st Ave
Denver, CO 80206
Phone: 303-321-1234
Fax: 303-331-0824

Liberty Savings Bank FSB
475 17th St
Denver, CO 80202
Phone: 303-295-7200
Fax: 303-295-7295

Mountain States Bank
1635 E Colfax Ave
Denver, CO 80218
Phone: 303-388-3641
Fax: 303-329-9415

Norwest Bank Colorado NA
1740 Broadway
Denver, CO 80274
Phone: 303-861-8811
Fax: 303-863-4605

UMB Bank Colorado NA
6900 E Hampden Ave
Denver, CO 80224
Phone: 303-758-2501
Fax: 303-758-6628

US Bank NA
PO Box 5168
Denver, CO 80217
Phone: 303-585-5000
Fax: 303-585-4721
TF: 800-872-2657

Wells Fargo Bank NA
633 17th St
Denver, CO 80270
Phone: 303-293-5963
Fax: 303-293-5163

Shopping

16th Street Mall
16th St betw Broadway & Market St
Denver, CO 80202
Phone: 303-534-6161
Fax: 303-534-2803

Aurora Mall
14200 E Alameda Ave
Aurora, CO 80012
Phone: 303-344-4120
Fax: 303-364-0308

Boulder Arts & Crafts Cooperative
1421 Pearl St
Boulder, CO 80302
Phone: 303-443-3683
Fax: 303-443-7998

Buckingham Square Shopping Center
1306 S Havana St
Aurora, CO 80012
Phone: 303-755-3232
Fax: 303-755-3234

Cherry Creek Shopping Center
3000 E 1st Ave
Denver, CO 80206
Phone: 303-388-3900
Fax: 303-377-7359

Colfax on the Hill District
Colfax Ave
Denver, CO 80218
Phone: 303-832-2086
Fax: 303-832-6761

Crossroads Mall
1600 28th St
Boulder, CO 80301
Phone: 303-444-0265
Fax: 303-449-5079

Denver Pavilions
500 16th St Suite 10
Denver, CO 80202
www.denverpavilions.com
Phone: 303-260-6000
Fax: 303-260-6080

Downtown Boulder Mall
Pearl St between 10th & 15th Sts
Boulder, CO 80302
Phone: 303-449-3774
Fax: 303-441-4130

Joslin's
7200 W Almeda Ave
Lakewood, CO 80226
Phone: 303-922-7575

Larimer Square
1400 Larimer Sq Suite 300
Denver, CO 80202
Phone: 303-534-2367
Fax: 303-623-1041

LoDo District
Lower Downtown
Denver, CO 80206
Phone: 303-295-1195

Shops at Tabor Center
1201 16th St Suite 120
Denver, CO 80202
Phone: 303-572-6868

Westminster Mall
5433 W 88th Ave
Westminster, CO 80031
Phone: 303-428-5634

Writer Square
1512 Larimer St Suite R-36
Denver, CO 80202
E-mail: info@writer-square.com
www.writer-square.com
Phone: 303-628-9056
Fax: 303-534-4559

Media

Newspapers and Magazines

Aurora Sentinel
10730 E Bethany Dr Suite 304
Aurora, CO 80014
E-mail: editor@aurorasentinel.com
www.aurorasentinel.com
Phone: 303-750-7555
Fax: 303-750-7699

Boulder County Business Report
3180 Sterling Cir Suite 201
Boulder, CO 80301
www.bcbr.com/
Phone: 303-440-4950
Fax: 303-440-8954

Boulder Daily Camera*
PO Box 591
Boulder, CO 80306
www.bouldernews.com/
Phone: 303-442-1202
Fax: 303-473-1175
TF: 800-783-1202

Boulder Weekly
690 S Lashley Ln
Boulder, CO 80303
E-mail: bweditor@tesser.com
www.boulderweekly.com
Phone: 303-494-5511
Fax: 303-494-2585

Colorado Daily*
5505 Central Ave
Boulder, CO 80301
www.codaily.com
Phone: 303-443-6272
Fax: 303-443-9357

Columbine Community Courier
PO Box 621093
Littleton, CO 80162
Phone: 303-933-2233
Fax: 303-933-4449

Denver Business Journal
1700 Broadway Suite 515
Denver, CO 80290
E-mail: denver@amcity.com
www.amcity.com/denver
Phone: 303-837-3500
Fax: 303-837-3535

Denver Post*
1560 Broadway
Denver, CO 80202
E-mail: letters@denverpost.com
www.denverpost.com
Phone: 303-820-1010
Fax: 303-820-1369
TF: 800-336-7678

Rocky Mountain News*
400 W Colfax Ave
Denver, CO 80204
E-mail: letters@denver-rmn.com
www.rockymountainnews.com
Phone: 303-892-5000
Fax: 303-892-2568

Westword
969 Broadway
Denver, CO 80203
www.westword.com
Phone: 303-296-7744
Fax: 303-296-5416

**Indicates major daily newspapers*

Television

KBDI-TV Ch 12 (PBS)
2900 Welton St 1st Fl
Denver, CO 80205
www.kbdi.org
Phone: 303-296-1212
Fax: 303-296-6650

KCEC-TV Ch 50 (Uni)
777 Grant St Suite 110
Denver, CO 80203
E-mail: kcecnews@aol.com
Phone: 303-832-0050
Fax: 303-832-3410

KCNC-TV Ch 4 (CBS)
1044 Lincoln St
Denver, CO 80203
E-mail: mailroom@kcncnews4.com
www.kcncnews4.com
Phone: 303-861-4444
Fax: 303-830-6380

KDVR-TV Ch 31 (Fox)
501 Wazee St
Denver, CO 80204
E-mail: feedback@fox31.com
www.fox31.com
Phone: 303-595-3131
Fax: 303-595-8312

KMGH-TV Ch 7 (ABC)
123 E Speer Blvd
Denver, CO 80203
E-mail: kmgh7@csn.net
www.kmgh.com
Phone: 303-832-7777
Fax: 303-832-0119

KPXC-TV Ch 59 (PAX)
3001 S Jamaica Ct
Aurora, CO 80014
www.pax.net/kpxc
Phone: 303-751-5959
Fax: 303-751-5993

KRMA-TV Ch 6 (PBS)
1089 Bannock St
Denver, CO 80204
E-mail: info@krma.org
www.krma.org
Phone: 303-892-6666
Fax: 303-620-5600

KSBS-TV Ch 63 (Tele)
2727 Bryant St Suite 430
Denver, CO 80211
Phone: 303-477-3031
Fax: 303-477-8287

KTVD-TV Ch 20 (UPN)
11203 E Peakview Ave
Englewood, CO 80111
Phone: 303-792-2020
Fax: 303-790-4633

KUSA-TV Ch 9 (NBC)
500 Speer Blvd
Denver, CO 80203
E-mail: kusa@9news.com
www.9news.com
Phone: 303-871-9999
Fax: 303-698-4700
TF: 800-338-5872

KWGN-TV Ch 2 (WB)
6160 S Wabash Way
Englewood, CO 80111
www.wb2.com
Phone: 303-740-2222
Fax: 303-740-2847

KWHD-TV Ch 53 (Ind)
12999 E Jamison Cir
Englewood, CO 80112
www.kwhd.com
Phone: 303-799-8853
Fax: 303-792-5303

Radio

KALC-FM 105.9 MHz (AC)
1200 17th St Suite 2300
Denver, CO 80202
alice106.com
Phone: 303-572-7000
Fax: 303-615-5393

KBCO-FM 97.3 MHz (AAA)
2500 Pearl St Suite 315
Boulder, CO 80302
www.kbco.com
Phone: 303-444-5600
Fax: 303-449-3057

KBPI-FM 106.7 MHz (Rock)
4695 S Monaco St
Denver, CO 80237
www.kbpi.com
Phone: 303-713-8000
Fax: 303-713-8743

KCFR-FM 90.1 MHz (NPR)
2249 S Josephine St
Denver, CO 80210
Phone: 303-871-9191
Fax: 303-733-3319

KCKK-FM 104.3 MHz (Ctry)
1095 S Monaco Pkwy
Denver, CO 80224
www.k1043.com
Phone: 303-321-0950
Fax: 303-320-0708

KEZW-AM 1430 kHz (Nost)
10200 E Girard Ave Suite B130
Denver, CO 80231
Phone: 303-696-1714
Fax: 303-696-0522

KGNU-FM 88.5 MHz (NPR)
PO Box 885
Boulder, CO 80306
www.kgnu.org
Phone: 303-449-4885

KHIH-FM 95.7 MHz (NAC)
4695 S Monaco St
Denver, CO 80237
www.khih.com
Phone: 303-713-8000
Fax: 303-713-8095

KHOW-AM 630 kHz (N/T)
4695 S Monaco St
Denver, CO 80237
www.khow.com
Phone: 303-713-8000
Fax: 303-713-8509

KIMN-FM 100.3 MHz (AC)
1560 Broadway Suite 1100
Denver, CO 80202
kimn100.com
Phone: 303-832-5665
Fax: 303-832-7000

KJMN-FM 92.1 MHz (Span)
5660 Greenwood Plaza Blvd Suite 400
Englewood, CO 80111
Phone: 303-721-9210
Fax: 303-721-1435

KKFN-AM 950 kHz (Sports)
1095 S Monaco Pkwy
Denver, CO 80224
Phone: 303-321-0950
Fax: 303-321-3383

KKHK-FM 99.5 MHz (CR)
10200 E Girard Ave Bldg B-130
Denver, CO 80231
www.thehawk.com
Phone: 303-696-1714
Fax: 303-696-0522

KLZ-AM 560 kHz (Rel)
2150 W 29th Ave Suite 300
Denver, CO 80211
Phone: 303-477-4636
Fax: 303-433-1555

KMXA-AM 1090 kHz (Span)
5660 Greenwood Plaza Blvd Suite 400
Englewood, CO 80111
Phone: 303-721-9210
Fax: 303-721-1435

KNUS-AM 710 kHz (N/T)
3131 S Vaughn Way Suite 601
Aurora, CO 80014
Phone: 303-750-5687
Fax: 303-696-8063

KOA-AM 850 kHz (N/T)
4695 S Monaco Ave
Denver, CO 80237
www.850koa.com
Phone: 303-713-8000
Fax: 303-892-4700

KOSI-FM 101.1 MHz (AC)
10200 E Girard Ave Suite B131
Denver, CO 80231
www.kosi101.com
Phone: 303-696-1714
Fax: 303-696-0522

KPOF-AM 910 kHz (Rel)
3455 W 83rd Ave
Westminster, CO 80031
E-mail: kpof@polnow.net
www.kpof.org
Phone: 303-428-0910
Fax: 303-429-0910

KQKS-FM 107.5 MHz (Urban)
1095 S Monaco Pkwy
Denver, CO 80224
Phone: 303-321-0950
Fax: 303-989-9081

KRFX-FM 103.5 MHz (CR)
1380 Lawrence St Suite 1300
Denver, CO 80204
E-mail: feedback@thefox.com
www.thefox.com
Phone: 303-893-3699
Fax: 303-534-7625

KTCL-FM 93.3 MHz (Alt)
1380 Lawrence St Suite 1300
Denver, CO 80204
www.ktcl.com
Phone: 303-623-9330
Fax: 303-534-7625

KTLK-AM 760 kHz (N/T)
1380 Lawrence St Suite 1300
Denver, CO 80204
Phone: 303-893-8500
Fax: 303-892-4700

KUVO-FM 89.3 MHz (NPR)
2900 Welton St Suite 200
Denver, CO 80205
E-mail: info@kuvo.org
www.kuvo.org
Phone: 303-480-9272
Fax: 303-291-0757

KVOD-AM 1280 kHz (Clas)
1560 Broadway Suite 1100
Denver, CO 80202
E-mail: info@kvod.com
www.kvod.com
Phone: 303-832-5665
Fax: 303-832-7000

KVOD-FM 92.5 MHz (Clas)
1560 Broadway Suite 1100
Denver, CO 80202
www.jammin925.com
Phone: 303-832-5665
Fax: 303-832-7000

KWAB-AM 1490 kHz (N/T)
3085 Bluff St
Boulder, CO 80301
Phone: 303-444-1490
Fax: 303-442-6544

KWBI-FM 91.1 MHz (Rel)
16075 W Belleview Ave
Morrison, CO 80465
E-mail: staff@kwbi.org
www.kwbi.org
Phone: 303-697-5924
Fax: 303-697-5944

KXKL-FM 105.1 MHz (Oldies)
1560 Broadway Suite 1100
Denver, CO 80202
www.kool105.net
Phone: 303-832-5665
Fax: 303-832-7000

KXPK-FM 96.5 MHz (Alt)
1200 17th St Suite 2300
Denver, CO 80202
E-mail: radio@thepeak.com
www.thepeak.com
Phone: 303-572-7000
Fax: 303-615-5393

KYGO-FM 98.5 MHz (Ctry)
1095 S Monaco Pkwy
Denver, CO 80224
www.kygo.com
Phone: 303-321-0950
Fax: 303-320-0708

Attractions

At the heart of Denver is the 16th Street Mall, a tree-lined pedestrian promenade that runs through the center of downtown. The Lower Downtown District (LoDo) features turn-of-the-century streetscaping, with art galleries, antique shops, unique restaurants, and jazz and dance clubs. Denver's City Park is home to the Denver Zoo, which has thousands of exotic animals in a natural setting, and the Denver Museum of Natural History. The Denver Art Museum covers seven floors and has some 40,000 works, including an extensive American Indian collection. Free tours are available of the U.S. Mint in Denver and of the Colorado State Capitol Building, which is modeled after the United States Capitol in Washington, DC, and features a panoramic view of the Rocky Mountains. (The Rockies are located just 12 miles west of the city.) Two other area attractions that feature spectacular views are Buffalo Bill's Grave at the top of Lookout Mountain and Red Rocks Amphitheatre, which is flanked by rugged sandstone rock formations that provide excellent acoustics. In nearby Boulder, Pearl Street Mall, the downtown historic preservation district which serves as that city's center, has restaurants, shops, park areas, and a range of activities and entertainment for both adults and children. Other historic sites in Boulder include the Chautauqua and Maple Hill districts, Whittier Neighborhood, and University Hill Neighborhood.

Arabian Horse Trust Museum
12000 Zuni St
Westminster, CO 80234
E-mail: information@arabianhorsetrust.com
www.arabianhorsetrust.com
Phone: 303-450-4710
Fax: 303-450-4707

Arapaho National Forest
2140 Yarmouth Ave
Boulder, CO 80301
www.fs.fed.us/arnf
Phone: 303-444-6600

Arvada Center for the Arts & Humanities
6901 Wadsworth Blvd
Arvada, CO 80003
Phone: 303-431-3939
Fax: 303-431-3083

Aurora Fox Arts Center
9900 E Colfax Ave
Aurora, CO 80010
Phone: 303-361-2910
Fax: 303-361-2909

Aurora History Museum
15001 E Alameda Dr
Aurora, CO 80012
www.ci.aurora.co.us/library/history.htm
Phone: 303-739-6660
Fax: 303-739-6657

Aurora Reservoir
5800 S Powhaton Rd
Aurora, CO 80016
Phone: 303-690-1286
Fax: 303-690-1654

Ballet Denver
3955 Tennyson St
Denver, CO 80212
Phone: 303-455-4974

Belleview Children's Farm
5001 S Inca Ave
Englewood, CO 80110
Phone: 303-798-6927

Black American West Museum & Heritage Center Phone: 303-292-2566
3091 California St Fax: 303-382-1981
Denver, CO 80205
E-mail: bawmhc@aol.com
www.coax.net/people/lwf/bawcal.htm

Boulder Ballet Phone: 303-442-6944
2590 Walnut St
Boulder, CO 80302
www.artstozoo.org/bb/

Boulder Museum of Contemporary Art Phone: 303-443-2122
1750 13th St Fax: 303-447-1633
Boulder, CO 80302
www.bmoca.org

Boulder Museum of History Phone: 303-449-3464
1206 Euclid Ave Fax: 303-938-8322
Boulder, CO 80302
bcn.boulder.co.us/arts/bmh

Boulder Philharmonic Orchestra Phone: 303-449-1343
17th St & University Ave Macky Auditorium Fax: 303-443-9203
Boulder, CO 80309
www.peakarts.org/main_bpo.htm

Boulder Reservoir Phone: 303-441-3461
5100 N 51st St Fax: 303-441-1807
Boulder, CO 80301

Boulder's Dinner Theater Phone: 303-449-6000
5501 Arapahoe Ave Fax: 303-442-5671
Boulder, CO 80303

Breckinridge Brewery Denver Phone: 303-297-3644
2220 Blake St Fax: 303-297-2341
Denver, CO 80205 TF: 800-910-2739

Broadway Brewing LLC Phone: 303-292-5027
2441 Broadway Fax: 303-296-0164
Denver, CO 80205

Buffalo Bill Memorial Museum Phone: 303-526-0744
987 1/2 Lookout Mountain Rd
Golden, CO 80401
www.buffalobill.org

Butterfly Pavilion & Insect Center Phone: 303-469-5441
6252 W 104th Ave Fax: 303-469-5442
Westminster, CO 80020
www.butterflies.org

Byers-Evans House & Denver History Museum Phone: 303-620-4933
1310 Bannock St
Denver, CO 80204
www.coloradohistory.org/byers-evans/default.asp

Celestial Seasonings Tea Phone: 303-581-1202
4600 Sleepytime Dr Fax: 303-581-1332
Boulder, CO 80301
www.celestialseasonings.com/whoweare/tourinfo/

Centennial House Phone: 303-739-6600
1671 Galena St
Aurora, CO 80010

Central City Opera House Assn Phone: 303-292-6500
621 17th St Suite 1601 Fax: 303-292-4958
Denver, CO 80293 TF: 800-851-8175
E-mail: boxoffice@centralcityopera.org
www.centralcityopera.org

Charles C Gates Planetarium Phone: 303-370-6351
2001 Colorado Blvd
Denver, CO 80205

Chautauqua Park Phone: 303-442-3282
900 Baseline Rd Fax: 303-449-0790
Boulder, CO 80302
www.chautauqua.com

Cherry Creek State Park Phone: 303-690-1166
4201 S Parker Rd Fax: 303-699-3864
Aurora, CO 80014
E-mail: chycrk@csn.net
parks.state.co.us/cherry_creek

Children's Museum of Denver Phone: 303-433-7444
2121 Children's Museum Dr Fax: 303-433-9520
Denver, CO 80211
www.artstozoo.org/cmd/

Collage Children's Museum Phone: 303-440-9894
2065 30th St Fax: 303-443-8040
Boulder, CO 80302
bcn.boulder.co.us/arts/collage

Colorado Ballet Phone: 303-837-8888
1278 Lincoln St Fax: 303-861-7174
Denver, CO 80203

Colorado Governor's Mansion Phone: 303-866-3682
8th & Logan Sts Fax: 303-866-5739
Denver, CO 80203

Colorado History Museum Phone: 303-866-3682
1300 Broadway Fax: 303-866-5739
Denver, CO 80203
E-mail: chssysop@usa.net
www.coloradohistory.org/colorado_history_museum/default.asp

Colorado Music Festival Orchestra Phone: 303-449-1397
1525 Spruce St Suite 101 Fax: 303-449-0071
Boulder, CO 80302
www.coloradomusicfest.com

Colorado Railroad Museum Phone: 303-279-4591
17155 W 44th Ave Fax: 303-279-4229
Golden, CO 80402 TF: 800-365-6263
E-mail: corrmus@aol.com
crrm.org

Colorado Sports Hall of Fame Phone: 303-620-8083
1445 Market St
Denver, CO 80202

Colorado State Capitol Phone: 303-866-2604
200 E Colfax Ave Rm 029 Fax: 303-866-2167
Denver, CO 80203

Colorado Symphony Orchestra Phone: 303-292-5566
821 17th St Suite 700 Fax: 303-293-2649
Denver, CO 80202
E-mail: info@coloradosymphony.com
www.indra.com/cso

Comanche Crossing Museum
56060 Colfax Ave Suite E
Strasburg, CO 80136
Phone: 303-622-4690

Coors Brewery
12th & Ford Sts
Golden, CO 80401
www.coors.com
Phone: 303-279-6565
Fax: 303-277-5723
TF: 800-642-6116

Dairy Center for the Arts
2590 Walnut St
Boulder, CO 80302
www.thedairy.org
Phone: 303-440-7826
Fax: 303-440-7104

Denver Art Museum
100 W 14th Avenue Pkwy
Denver, CO 80204
www.denverartmuseum.org
Phone: 303-640-2295
Fax: 303-640-5928

Denver Botanic Gardens
1005 York St
Denver, CO 80206
www.botanicgardens.org
Phone: 303-331-4000
Fax: 303-331-4013

Denver Center for the Performing Arts
14th & Curtis Sts
Denver, CO 80204
www.denvercenter.org
Phone: 303-893-4100
Fax: 303-893-3206

Denver Center Theatre Co
14th & Curtis Sts
Denver, CO 80204
Phone: 303-893-4100
Fax: 303-595-9634

Denver Firefighters Museum
1326 Tremont Pl
Denver, CO 80204
www.colorado2.com/museum
Phone: 303-892-1436
Fax: 303-892-1436

Denver Museum of Miniatures Dolls & Toys
1880 Gaylord St
Denver, CO 80206
Phone: 303-322-1053
Fax: 303-322-3704

Denver Museum of Natural History
2001 Colorado Blvd
Denver, CO 80205
www.dmnh.org
Phone: 303-370-6357
Fax: 303-331-6492
TF: 800-925-2250

Denver Performing Arts Complex
950 13th St
Denver, CO 80204
Phone: 303-640-2637
Fax: 303-572-4792

Denver Zoological Gardens
2300 Steele St
Denver, CO 80205
www.denverzoo.org
Phone: 303-376-4800
Fax: 303-376-4801

Eldorado Canyon State Park
PO Box B
Eldorado Springs, CO 80025
Phone: 303-494-3943
Fax: 303-499-2729

Fiske Planetarium & Science Center
Regent Dr University of Colorado Campus
Boulder, CO 80309
E-mail: planet@stripe.colorado.edu
www.colorado.edu/fiske
Phone: 303-492-5002
Fax: 303-492-1725

Four Mile Historic Park
715 S Forest St
Denver, CO 80246
Phone: 303-399-1859
Fax: 303-393-0788

Gateway Park Fun Center
4800 N 28th St
Boulder, CO 80301
E-mail: info@gatewayfunpark.com
www.gatewayfunpark.com
Phone: 303-442-4386
Fax: 303-448-0051

Golden Gate Canyon State Park
3873 Hwy 46
Golden, CO 80403
Phone: 303-582-3707
Fax: 303-582-3712

Golden Pioneer Museum
923 10th St
Golden, CO 80401
Phone: 303-278-7151
Fax: 303-278-2755

Heritage Square Music Hall
18301 W Colfax Ave Bldg D103
Golden, CO 80401
Phone: 303-279-7800

Historic Boulder
646 Pearl St
Boulder, CO 80302
Phone: 303-444-5192
Fax: 303-444-5309

Historic Boulder Walking Tours
646 Pearl St
Boulder, CO 80302
Phone: 303-449-5192

Historic Paramount Theatre
1621 Glenarm St
Denver, CO 80202
Phone: 303-825-4904
Fax: 303-741-1831

IMAX Theater
2001 Colorado Blvd Denver Museum of Natural History
Denver, CO 80205
www.dmnh.org/imax.htm
Phone: 303-370-6322
Fax: 303-331-6492

Interweave Dance Theatre
Broadway & University Blvd Charlotte York Irey Studio Theatre
Boulder, CO 80309
E-mail: montage@juno.com
bcn.boulder.co.us/arts/idt/idt.html
Phone: 303-449-0399

Lakeside Amusement Park
4601 Sheridan Blvd
Denver, CO 80212
E-mail: information@lakesideamusementpark.com
www.lakesideamusementpark.com
Phone: 303-477-1621
Fax: 303-455-1934

Larimer Square
1400 Larimer Sq Suite 300
Denver, CO 80202
Phone: 303-534-2367
Fax: 303-623-1041

Leanin' Tree Museum of Western Art
6055 Longbow Dr
Boulder, CO 80301
E-mail: jobs@leanintree.com
www.leanintree.com
Phone: 303-530-1442
Fax: 303-530-7283

LoDo District
Lower Downtown
Denver, CO 80206
Phone: 303-295-1195

Macky Auditorium
17th St & University Ave
Boulder, CO 80309
E-mail: macky@stripe.colorado.edu
www.colorado.edu/Macky
Phone: 303-492-8423
Fax: 303-492-1651

Mizel Museum of Judaica
560 S Monaco Pkwy
Denver, CO 80224
E-mail: museum@mizelmuseum.org
www.mizelmuseum.org
Phone: 303-333-4156
Fax: 303-331-8477

Molly Brown House
1340 Pennsylvania St
Denver, CO 80203
www.mollybrown.org
Phone: 303-832-4092
Fax: 303-832-2340

Museo de las Americas
861 Santa Fe Dr
Denver, CO 80204
www.museo.org
Phone: 303-571-4401
Fax: 303-607-9761

Museum of Contemporary Art Denver
1275 19th St
Denver, CO 80202
www.mocadenver.com
Phone: 303-298-7554
Fax: 303-298-7553

Museum of Outdoor Arts
7600 E Orchard Rd Suite 160-N
Englewood, CO 80111
www.fine-art.com/museum/moa.html
Phone: 303-806-0444
Fax: 303-741-1029

National Center for Atmospheric Research
PO Box 3000
Boulder, CO 80307
www.ncar.ucar.edu
Phone: 303-497-1000
Fax: 303-497-8610

Ocean Journey Aquarium
700 Water St US West Pk
Denver, CO 80211
www.oceanjourney.org
Phone: 303-561-4450
Fax: 303-561-4665

Opera Colorado
695 S Colorado Blvd Suite 20
Denver, CO 80246
E-mail: opera@ossinc.net
www.operacolo.org
Phone: 303-778-1500
Fax: 303-778-6533

Pearce-McAllister Cottage
1880 Gaylord St
Denver, CO 80201
Phone: 303-322-1053
Fax: 303-322-3704

Plains Conservation Center
21901 E Hampden Ave
Aurora, CO 80013
Phone: 303-693-3621

Red Rocks Amphitheater
12700 W Alameda Pkwy
Morrison, CO 80465
Phone: 303-640-2637
Fax: 303-295-4437

Robinson Parker Cleo Dance Theater
119 Park Ave W
Denver, CO 80205
E-mail: cleodance@aol.com
Phone: 303-295-1759
Fax: 303-295-1328

Rockies Brewing Co
2880 Wilderness Pl
Boulder, CO 80301
Phone: 303-444-8448
Fax: 303-444-4796

Rocky Mountain Arsenal National Wildlife Refuge
72nd & Quebec Sts
Commerce City, CO 80022
Phone: 303-289-0232
Fax: 303-289-0579

Rocky Mountain National Park
Estes Park, CO 80517
www.nps.gov/romo/
Phone: 970-586-1206
Fax: 970-586-1310

Rocky Mountain Quilt Museum
1111 Washington Ave
Golden, CO 80401
Phone: 303-277-0377
Fax: 303-215-1636

Sakura Square
1255 19th St
Denver, CO 80202
Phone: 303-295-0305
Fax: 303-295-0304

Six Flags Elitch Gardens
299 Walnut St
Denver, CO 80204
www.sixflags.com/elitchgardens
Phone: 303-595-4386
Fax: 303-534-2221

Swallow Hill Music Assn
71 E Yale Ave
Denver, CO 80210
Phone: 303-777-1003
Fax: 303-871-0527

Theatre on Broadway
13 S Broadway
Denver, CO 80209
Phone: 303-777-3292

Trianon Museum & Art Gallery
335 14th St
Denver, CO 80202
Phone: 303-623-0739

University of Colorado Art Galleries
University of Colorado Campus
Boulder, CO 80309
stripe.colorado.edu/~gallery/
Phone: 303-492-8300
Fax: 303-492-4886

University of Colorado Heritage Center
Old Main 3rd Fl
Boulder, CO 80309
Phone: 303-492-6329
Fax: 303-492-6799

University of Colorado Museum
Campus Box 218
Boulder, CO 80309
www.colorado.edu/CUMUSEUM/
Phone: 303-492-6892
Fax: 303-492-4195

Upstart Crow Theatre Co
2131 Arapahoe Ave
Boulder, CO 80302
www.serve.com/upstart/
Phone: 303-442-1415
Fax: 303-938-0376

US Mint
320 W Colfax Ave
Denver, CO 80204
www.usmint.gov
Phone: 303-405-4761
Fax: 303-405-4604

Water World
1800 W 89th Ave
Denver, CO 80221
www.hylandhills.org/waterworld.html
Phone: 303-427-7873
Fax: 303-650-7594

Wings Over the Rockies Air & Space Museum
7711 E Academy Blvd
Denver, CO 80230
E-mail: worm@dimensional.com
www.dimensional.com/~worm/
Phone: 303-360-5360
Fax: 303-360-5328

Writer Square
1512 Larimer St Suite R-36
Denver, CO 80202
E-mail: info@writer-square.com
www.writer-square.com
Phone: 303-628-9056
Fax: 303-534-4559

Youth Ballet Colorado Phone: 303-466-5685
555 Burbank St Suite J
Broomfield, CO 80020
E-mail: ybc@ibm.net
www.artstozoo.org/ybc

Sports Teams & Facilities

Arapahoe Park Race Track Phone: 303-690-2400
26000 E Quincy Ave Fax: 303-690-6730
Aurora, CO 80046
E-mail: arapahoe@wembleyusa.com
www.wembleyusa.com/arapahoe

Colorado Avalanche Phone: 303-405-1100
1000 Chopper Cir Pepsi Ctr Fax: 303-405-1315
Denver, CO 80204
www.coloradoavalanche.com

Colorado Comets (soccer) Phone: 303-288-1591
6200 Dahlia St Wembley Pk Stadium Fax: 303-289-1640
Commerce City, CO 80022
www.intermark.com/comets

Colorado National Speedway Phone: 303-665-4173
4281 Weld County Rd 10 Fax: 303-282-0729
Erie, CO 80516
E-mail: cns98@earthlink.net
www.coloradospeedway.com

Colorado Rapids (soccer) Phone: 303-299-1570
555 17th St Suite 3350 Fax: 303-299-1580
Denver, CO 80202 TF: 800-844-7777
E-mail: 103506.1147@compuserve.com
www.intermark.com/Rapids

Colorado Rockies Phone: 303-762-5437
2001 Blake St Coors Field Fax: 303-312-2219
Denver, CO 80205 TF: 800-388-7625
www.coloradorockies.com

Coors Field Phone: 303-312-2100
2001 Blake St Fax: 303-312-2219
Denver, CO 80205 TF: 800-388-7625
www.coloradorockies.com/coorsfield/default.asp

Denver Broncos Phone: 303-433-7466
1900 Eliot St Mile High Stadium Fax: 303-433-3414
Denver, CO 80204
www.denverbroncos.com

Denver Coliseum Phone: 303-295-4444
4600 Humboldt St Fax: 303-295-4467
Denver, CO 80216

Denver Diamonds (soccer) Phone: 303-986-5200
7112 W Jefferson Ave Suite 100 Fax: 303-986-5222
Lakewood, CO 80235

Denver Nuggets Phone: 303-893-3865
1000 Chopper Cir Pepsi Ctr Fax: 303-405-1315
Denver, CO 80204
www.nba.com/nuggets

Mile High Greyhound Park Phone: 303-288-1591
6200 Dahlia St Fax: 303-289-1640
Commerce City, CO 80022
E-mail: milehigh@wembleyusa.com
www.wembleyusa.com/milehigh

Mile High Stadium Phone: 303-458-4850
2755 W 175h Ave Fax: 303-458-4861
Denver, CO 80204
www.denverbroncos.com/offthefield/stadium/milehigh/index.html

Pepsi Center Phone: 303-893-3865
1000 Chopper Cir Fax: 303-575-1920
Denver, CO 80204 TF: 800-678-5440
www.pepsicenter.com

Annual Events

Blossoms of Lights
(early December-early January)..................303-331-4000
Bolder Boulder 10K (late May)....................303-444-7223
Boo at the Zoo (late October).....................303-376-4846
Boulder Art Fair (mid-July)........................303-449-3774
Boulder Artwalk (early December).................303-444-9106
Boulder Bach Festival (late January)...............303-494-3159
Boulder Creek Festival (late May) 303-449-3825
Boulder Fall Festival (early October) 303-449-3774
Buffalo Bill's Birthday Celebration
(late February)................................303-526-0744
Capitol Hill People's Fair (early June) 303-830-1651
Cherry Blossom Festival (late June)...............303-295-1844
Cherry Creek Arts Festival (July 4)................303-355-2787
Christmas in July (mid-July)......................303-770-0057
Cinco de Mayo Celebration (early May)............303-534-8342
Colorado Dance Festival
(early July-early August)........................303-442-7666
Colorado Indian Market & Western Art Roundup
(mid-January)................................806-355-1610
Colorado Irish Festival (late August)...............303-629-8777
Colorado Mahler Festival (mid-January)............303-447-0513
Colorado Music Festival (late June-early August)....303-449-1397
Colorado Performing Arts Festival
(early October)...............................720-913-8200
Colorado Scottish Festival (mid-August) 303-238-6524
Colorado Shakespeare Festival
(late June-late August) 303-492-0554
Colorado State Fair
(late August-early September)...................800-876-4567
Denver Auto Show (early March)...................303-831-1691
Denver Boat Show (early January).................303-228-8000
Denver International Film Festival
(mid-October)................................303-595-3456
Denver March Pow Wow (mid-late March)..........303-295-4444
Denver Pow Wow (mid-March)....................303-934-8045
Festival of Mountain & Plain: A Taste of Colorado
(early September) 303-534-6161
Gateway to the Rockies Festival
(mid-September) 303-361-6169
Great American Beer Festival (early October).......303-447-0816
Greek Festival (mid-June) 303-388-9314
Independence Day Celebration (July 4).............303-399-1859
International Buskerfest (late June) 303-534-6161
Juneteenth Festival (mid-June) 303-399-7138
Kids Spree (late July) 303-739-7181
Kinetic Conveyance Sculpture Challenge
(early May) 303-444-5600

Lights of December Parade (early December) 303-449-3774
Lyric Theatre Festival (July) 303-492-8008
Men's B Fast Pitch-ASA National Championship Tournament (late August) 303-695-7201
National Western Stock Show & Rodeo (early-mid-January) 303-297-1166
Oktoberfest (mid-September) 303-534-2367
Parade of Lights (early December). 303-534-6161
Pumpkin Fest (late October). 303-361-2936
Renaissance Festival (early June-early August) 303-688-6010
Riverfest (late August) 303-637-2645
Rocky Mountain Book Festival (mid-November). 303-839-8320
Rocky Mountain Children's Book Festival (mid-November). 303-839-8320
Saint Patrick's Day Parade (mid-March) 303-399-9226
Spirits of the Past (late October). 303-399-1859
Summer Nights (late June-late August) 303-534-2367
Taste of LoDo (mid-May). 303-458-6685
Theater in the Park (late July-early August) 303-770-2106
Wild Lights (December) 303-376-4800
Winter Park Jazz Festival (mid-July). 970-726-4118
Winterfest Weekends (late November-early January) 303-534-2367
World's Largest Christmas Lighting Display (early-late December) 303-640-2721

Des Moines, Iowa

County: **Polk**

DES MOINES is located at the confluence of the Des Moines River and the Raccoon River in central Iowa. Major cities within 150 miles include Ames, Cedar Rapids, and Iowa City, Iowa; and Omaha, Nebraska.

Area (Land)	75.3 sq mi
Area (Water)	1.5 sq mi
Elevation	803 ft
Latitude	41-60-06 N
Longitude	93-60-89 W
Time Zone	CST
Area Code	641

Climate

Des Moines has a continental climate with four distinct seasons. Winters are long and cold, with average high temperatures in the mid-30s and lows in the low to mid-teens. The average annual snowfall in Des Moines is 31.6 inches. Summer days are hot, with average high temperatures in the low to mid-80s, while evenings cool down into the low to mid-60s. Spring and summer are the rainy seasons in Des Moines, with June being the wettest month. January is the driest.

Average Temperatures & Precipitation

Temperatures

	Jan	Feb	Mar	Apr	May	Jun	Jul	Aug	Sep	Oct	Nov	Dec
High	28	34	47	62	73	82	87	84	76	64	48	33
Low	11	16	28	40	52	61	67	64	55	43	30	16

Precipitation

	Jan	Feb	Mar	Apr	May	Jun	Jul	Aug	Sep	Oct	Nov	Dec
Inches	1.0	1.1	2.3	3.4	3.7	4.5	3.8	4.2	3.5	2.6	1.8	1.3

History

Originally a military post established at the confluence of the Des Moines and Raccoon Rivers in 1843, Fort Des Moines was opened to white settlement in 1845. The community became the seat of Polk County in 1846 and was incorporated as a city in 1851. Six years later, in 1857, Fort Des Moines and neighboring East Des Moines were consolidated and renamed Des Moines, and the city was chosen as the new capital of Iowa (originally Iowa City). There are several conflicting stories as to where the name Des Moines originated. Some believe that the name was derived from the French words "de moyen," meaning "in the middle," referring to the river's location midway between the Mississippi and Missouri Rivers. Others believe that the river (and subsequently, the town) was named for the Moingounena Indians that inhabited the area, while yet another explanation attributes the name to the literal translation from the French "des moines," meaning "the monks," for the French missionaries that traversed the area.

Nicknamed the "Farm Capital of America," Des Moines grew primarily as a major U.S. agricultural center. Agriculture still plays a vital role in the area's economy, but Des Moines has also become known as a center for finance and insurance. Although the city suffered severe damage during the Midwest floods of 1993, Des Moines continues to grow and prosper. The city today is home to more than 191,000 people, making it Iowa's largest city .

Population

1990 Census	193,189
1998 Estimate	191,293
% Change	-1.0

Racial/Ethnic Breakdown

White	90.0%*
Black	4.9%*
Other	5.1%*
Hispanic Origin (may be of any race)	2.5%*

Age Breakdown

Under 5 years	7.8%
5 to 17	16.3%
18 to 20	5.1%
21 to 24	6.8%
25 to 34	19.0%
35 to 44	14.4%
45 to 54	9.0%
55 to 64	8.2%
65 to 74	7.3%
75+ years	6.1%
Median Age	32.3

Gender Breakdown

Male	47.8%*
Female	52.2%*

* *Information given is for Polk County.*

Government

Type of Government: Mayor-Council

Des Moines City Clerk
400 E 1st St 2nd Fl
Des Moines, IA 50309
Phone: 515-283-4209
Fax: 515-237-1645

Des Moines City Council
400 E 1st St 2nd Fl
Des Moines, IA 50309
Phone: 515-283-4944
Fax: 515-237-1645

Des Moines City Hall
400 E 1st St
Des Moines, IA 50309
Phone: 515-283-4500
Fax: 515-237-1300

Des Moines City Manager
400 E 1st St
Des Moines, IA 50309
Phone: 515-283-4141
Fax: 515-237-1300

Des Moines Community Development Dept
602 E 1st St
Des Moines, IA 50309
Phone: 515-283-4182
Fax: 515-237-1694

Des Moines Economic Development Office
400 E 1st St
Des Moines, IA 50309
Phone: 515-283-4004
Fax: 515-237-1667

Des Moines Finance Dept
400 E 1st St
Des Moines, IA 50309
Phone: 515-283-4921
Fax: 515-237-1670

Des Moines Fire Dept
900 Mulberry St
Des Moines, IA 50309
Phone: 515-283-4237
Fax: 515-283-4907

Des Moines Human Resources Dept
400 E 1st St Rm 103
Des Moines, IA 50309
Phone: 515-283-4213
Fax: 515-237-1680

Des Moines Mayor
400 E 1st St 2nd Fl
Des Moines, IA 50309
Phone: 515-283-4944
Fax: 515-237-1645

Des Moines Park & Recreation Dept
3226 University Ave
Des Moines, IA 50311
Phone: 515-237-1386
Fax: 515-237-1407

Des Moines Police Dept
25 E 1st St
Des Moines, IA 50309
Phone: 515-283-4800
Fax: 515-237-1665

Des Moines Public Works Dept
216 SE 5th St
Des Moines, IA 50307
Phone: 515-283-4950
Fax: 515-237-1655

Des Moines Traffic & Transportation Div
602 E 1st St Armory Bldg
Des Moines, IA 50309
Phone: 515-283-4973
Fax: 515-237-1640

Public Library of Des Moines
100 Locust St
Des Moines, IA 50309
Phone: 515-283-4152
Fax: 515-237-1654

Important Phone Numbers

AAA..........515-223-4104
American Express Travel..........515-247-7131
Dental Referral..........800-243-4444
Des Moines/Polk County Treasurer..........515-286-3060
Driver's License Information..........515-244-1052
Emergency..........911
Greater Des Moines Board of Realtors..........515-453-1064
HotelDocs..........800-468-3537
Iowa Dept of Revenue & Finance..........515-281-3114
Iowa Guest Hotline..........515-225-3655
Poison Control Center..........712-277-2222
Road Conditions..........515-288-1047
Time/Temp..........515-244-5611
Travelers Aid..........515-286-2088
Vehicle Registration Information..........515-286-3030
Voter Registration Information..........515-286-3247
Weather..........515-270-2614

Information Sources

Better Business Bureau Serving Central & Eastern Iowa
505 5th Ave Suite 950
Des Moines, IA 50309
www.desmoines.bbb.org
Phone: 515-243-8137
Fax: 515-243-2227
TF: 800-222-1600

Civic Center of Greater Des Moines
221 Walnut St
Des Moines, IA 50309
www.civiccenter.org
Phone: 515-243-0766
Fax: 515-243-1179

Greater Des Moines Convention & Visitors Bureau
601 Locust St Suite 222
Des Moines, IA 50309
www.desmoinesia.com
Phone: 515-286-4960
Fax: 515-244-9757
TF: 800-451-2625

Greater Des Moines Partnership
700 Locust St Suite 100
Des Moines, IA 50309
www.dmchamber.com
Phone: 515-286-4950
Fax: 515-286-4974
TF: 800-376-9059

Iowa Tourism Div
200 E Grand Ave
Des Moines, IA 50309
www.traveliowa.com
Phone: 515-242-4705
Fax: 515-242-4749
TF: 800-345-4692

Polk County
111 Court Ave
Des Moines, IA 50309
www.co.polk.ia.us
Phone: 515-286-3000
Fax: 515-286-3082

Polk County Convention Complex
501 Grand Ave
Des Moines, IA 50309
Phone: 515-242-2500
Fax: 515-242-2530

Online Resources

4DesMoines.com
www.4desmoines.com

About.com Guide to Des Moines
desmoines.about.com/local/midwestus/desmoines/index.htm

Anthill City Guide Des Moines
www.anthill.com/city.asp?city=desmoines

Area Guide Des Moines
desmoines.areaguides.net

City Knowledge Des Moines
www.cityknowledge.com/ia_desmoines.htm

Des Moines Site
www.desmoines-site.com

Excite.com Des Moines City Guide
www.excite.com/travel/countries/united_states/iowa/des_moines

Metro Arts Alliance
www.metroarts.org/

Area Communities

Greater Des Moines communities with populations greater than 5,000 include:

Altoona
407 8th St SE
Altoona, IA 50009
Phone: 515-967-5136
Fax: 515-967-0842

Ankeny
1605 N Ankeny Blvd
Ankeny, IA 50021
Phone: 515-965-6400
Fax: 515-965-6416

Clive
1900 NW 114th St
Clive, IA 50325
Phone: 515-223-6220
Fax: 515-278-0394

Indianola
110 N 1st St
Indianola, IA 50125
Phone: 515-961-9410
Fax: 515-961-9402

Johnston
6221 Merle Hay Rd
Johnston, IA 50131
Phone: 515-278-2344
Fax: 515-278-2033

Norwalk
705 North Ave
Norwalk, IA 50211
Phone: 515-981-0228
Fax: 515-981-0933

Perry
908 Willis Ave
Perry, IA 50220
Phone: 515-465-2481
Fax: 515-465-4862

Urbandale
3315 70th St
Urbandale, IA 50322
Phone: 515-278-3900
Fax: 515-278-3905

West Des Moines
4000 George M Mills Civic Pkwy
West Des Moines, IA 50265
Phone: 515-222-3600
Fax: 515-222-3640

Windsor Heights
1133 66th St
Windsor Heights, IA 50311
Phone: 515-279-3662
Fax: 515-279-3664

Economy

Agriculture has long been the primary industry in Des Moines, but as the headquarters of more than 60 insurance companies, it is also the third largest insurance center in the world. The Principal Financial Group, the holding company for Principal Life Insurance Company and Principal Mutual Life, is the area's largest employer, providing jobs for more than 8,000 area residents. Services is the leading employment sector in Des Moines, with health care and business services such as data processing being leading industries. Government also plays a vital role in the capital city's economy—more than 7,500 people in the Des Moines area are employed by Iowa State Government and another 26,000+ are employed in federal and local government positions.

Unemployment Rate 2.7%
Per Capita Income.........................$28,271*
Median Family Income.....................$32,772

** Information given is for Polk County.*

Principal Industries & Number of Wage Earners

Des Moines MSA* - 1998

Construction & Mining..................................12,400
Finance, Insurance, & Real Estate........................39,500
Government 34,300
Manufacturing 25,000
Retail Trade..50,800
Services 81,300
Transportation, Communication, & Public Utilities 14,500
Wholesale Trade.......................................21,600

** Information given is for the Des Moines Metropolitan Statistical Area (MSA), which includes Dallas, Polk, and Warren counties.*

Major Employers

Allied Insurance
701 5th Ave
Des Moines, IA 50391
www.alliedgroup.com
Phone: 515-280-4211
Fax: 515-280-4953
TF: 800-532-1436

Bridgestone/Firestone Inc
2nd Ave & Hoffman Ln
Des Moines, IA 50313
www.bridgestone-firestone.com
Phone: 515-243-1211
Fax: 515-235-4060

Central Iowa Health System
1200 Pleasant St
Des Moines, IA 50310
Phone: 515-241-5009
Fax: 515-241-8515

Communication Data Services
1901 Bell Ave
Des Moines, IA 50315
www.cdsfulfillment.com
Phone: 515-247-7500
Fax: 515-246-6687

Des Moines City Hall
400 E 1st St
Des Moines, IA 50309
www.ci.des-moines.ia.us
Phone: 515-283-4500
Fax: 515-237-1300

Des Moines Independent School District
1801 16th St
Des Moines, IA 50314
www.des-moines.k12.ia.us
Phone: 515-242-7911
Fax: 515-242-7891

EDS Inc
111 10th St
Des Moines, IA 50309
Phone: 515-237-4680
Fax: 515-237-4752

Foods Inc
4343 Merle Hay Rd
Des Moines, IA 50310
Phone: 515-278-1657
Fax: 515-278-0012
TF: 800-421-4355

Hy-Vee Inc
5820 Westown Pkwy
West Des Moines, IA 50266
www.hy-vee.com
Phone: 515-267-2800
Fax: 515-267-2817
TF: 800-289-8343

Mercy Hospital Medical Center
1111 6th Ave
Des Moines, IA 50314
www.mercydesmoines.org
Phone: 515-247-3121
Fax: 515-247-4259
TF: 800-637-2993

MidAmerican Energy Co
PO Box 657
Des Moines, IA 50303
www.midamericanenergy.com
Phone: 515-242-4300
Fax: 515-281-2981
TF: 800-338-8007

Pioneer Hi-Bred International Inc
400 Locust St Capital Sq Suite 800
Des Moines, IA 50309
www.pioneer.com
Phone: 515-248-4800
Fax: 515-248-4999
TF: 800-247-6803

Principal Financial Group
711 High St
Des Moines, IA 50392
www.principal.com
Phone: 515-247-5111
Fax: 515-283-5432
TF: 800-986-3343

Wellmark Blue Cross & Blue Shield of Iowa
636 Grand Ave
Des Moines, IA 50309
E-mail: customer_service@wellmark.com
www.wellmarkbcbs.com/about_us/companies/aboutbcbsi.htm
Phone: 515-245-4500
Fax: 515-245-4698
TF: 800-526-8995

Quality of Living Indicators

Total Crime Index 11,679
(rates per 100,000 inhabitants)

Violent Crime
- Murder/manslaughter 13
- Forcible rape 92
- Robbery 266
- Aggravated assault 374

Property Crime
- Burglary 1,609
- Larceny theft 8,492
- Motor vehicle theft 833

Cost of Living Index 92.0
(national average = 100)

Median Home Price $110,500

Education

Public Schools

Des Moines Independent School District
1801 16th St
Des Moines, IA 50314
www.des-moines.k12.ia.us
Phone: 515-242-7911
Fax: 515-242-7891

Number of Schools
- Elementary 42
- Middle 10
- High 5

Student/Teacher Ratio
- All Grades 13.5:1

Private Schools

Number of Schools (all grades) .... 10+

Colleges & Universities

American Institute of Business
2500 Fleur Dr
Des Moines, IA 50321
www.aib.edu
Phone: 515-244-4221
Fax: 515-244-6773
TF: 800-444-1921

Des Moines Area Community College
2006 S Ankeny Blvd
Ankeny, IA 50021
E-mail: marketing@dmacc.cc.ia.us
www.dmacc.cc.ia.us
Phone: 515-964-6200
Fax: 515-965-7054

Drake University
2507 University Ave
Des Moines, IA 50311
www.drake.edu
Phone: 515-271-2011
Fax: 515-271-2831
TF: 800-443-7253

Grand View College
1200 Grandview Ave
Des Moines, IA 50316
www.gvc.edu
Phone: 515-263-2800
Fax: 515-263-2974
TF: 800-444-6083

Simpson College
701 N 'C' St
Indianola, IA 50125
www.simpson.edu
Phone: 515-961-6251
Fax: 515-961-1870
TF: 800-362-2454

Hospitals

Broadlawns Medical Center
1801 Hickman Rd
Des Moines, IA 50314
www.broadlawns.org
Phone: 515-282-2200
Fax: 515-282-5785

Dallas County Hospital
610 10th St
Perry, IA 50220
Phone: 515-465-3547
Fax: 515-465-2922

Des Moines General Hospital
603 E 12th St
Des Moines, IA 50309
www.dmgeneral.com
Phone: 515-263-4200
Fax: 515-263-4699

Iowa Lutheran Hospital
700 E University Ave
Des Moines, IA 50316
Phone: 515-263-5612
Fax: 515-263-5295

Iowa Methodist Medical Center
1200 Pleasant St
Des Moines, IA 50309
Phone: 515-241-6212
Fax: 515-241-5994

Madison County Memorial Hospital
300 W Hutchings St
Winterset, IA 50273
Phone: 515-462-2373
Fax: 515-462-5008

Mary Greeley Medical Center
1111 Duff Ave
Ames, IA 50010
Phone: 515-239-2011
Fax: 515-239-2007

Mercy Hospital Medical Center
1111 6th Ave
Des Moines, IA 50314
www.mercydesmoines.org
Phone: 515-247-3121
Fax: 515-247-4259
TF: 800-637-2993

Veterans Affairs Medical Center Phone: 515-699-5999
3600 30th St Fax: 515-699-5862
Des Moines, IA 50310

Transportation

Airport(s)

Des Moines International Airport (DSM)
5 miles SE of downtown
(approx 10-15 minutes) 515-256-5050

Mass Transit

Des Moines Metropolitan Transit Authority
$1 Base fare 515-283-8100

Rail/Bus

Greyhound/Trailways Bus Station Phone: 800-231-2222
1107 Keosauqua Way
Des Moines, IA 50309

Utilities

Electricity
MidAmerican Energy Co 888-427-5632
www.midamericanenergy.com

Gas
MidAmerican Energy Co 888-427-5632
www.midamericanenergy.com

Water
Des Moines Water Works 515-283-8700

Garbage Collection/Recycling
Des Moines Garbage Collection 515-283-4595

Telecommunications

Telephone
Qwest.......................................800-244-1111
www.qwest.com

Cable Television
AT & T Cable Services.........................515-246-1890
www.cable.att.com

Internet Service Providers (ISPs)
Iowa Network Services Inc 515-830-0110
www.netins.net

Banks

Brenton Bank Phone: 800-820-0088
400 Locust St Suite 200 Fax: 515-237-5221
Des Moines, IA 50309

Commercial Federal Bank Phone: 515-246-0141
801 Grand Ave Suite 300 Fax: 515-246-0280
Des Moines, IA 50309

Firstar Bank Iowa NA Phone: 515-245-6100
503 Walnut St Fax: 515-245-6351
Des Moines, IA 50309 TF: 800-236-4462

West Des Moines State Bank Phone: 515-222-2300
1601 22nd St Fax: 515-222-2346
West Des Moines, IA 50266

Shopping

Historic Valley Junction Phone: 515-222-3642
217 5th St Fax: 515-274-8407
West Des Moines, IA 50265

Kaleidoscope at the Hub Phone: 515-243-3228
555-655 Walnut St
Des Moines, IA 50309

Locust Mall Phone: 515-282-1675
700 Locust St
Des Moines, IA 50309

Merle Hay Mall Phone: 515-276-8551
3800 Merle Hay Rd Fax: 515-276-9309
Des Moines, IA 50310

Southridge Mall Phone: 515-287-3880
1111 E Army Post Rd Fax: 515-287-0983
Des Moines, IA 50315

Valley West Mall Phone: 515-225-3631
1551 Valley West Dr Fax: 515-224-9935
West Des Moines, IA 50266

Media

Newspapers and Magazines

Des Moines Business Record Phone: 515-288-3336
100 4th St Fax: 515-288-0309
Des Moines, IA 50309
E-mail: pbc@mail.commonlink.com

Des Moines Register* Phone: 515-284-8000
PO Box 957 Fax: 515-286-2504
Des Moines, IA 50304
www.dmregister.com

Midwest Living Phone: 515-284-2662
1912 Grand Ave Fax: 515-284-3836
Des Moines, IA 50309 TF: 800-678-8093
E-mail: mwl@mdp.com
www.midwestliving.com

**Indicates major daily newspapers*

Television

KCCI-TV Ch 8 (CBS) Phone: 515-247-8888
888 9th St Fax: 515-244-0202
Des Moines, IA 50309
E-mail: kcci@kcci.com
www.kcci.com

KDIN-TV Ch 11 (PBS) Phone: 515-242-3100
6450 Corporate Dr Fax: 515-242-5830
Johnston, IA 50131
E-mail: webcomm2@iptv.org
www.iptv.org

KDSM-TV Ch 17 (Fox/UPN) Phone: 515-287-1717
4023 Fleur Dr Fax: 515-287-0064
Des Moines, IA 50321
E-mail: kdsm@commonlink.com
www.kdsmtv.com

WHO-TV Ch 13 (NBC)
1801 Grand Ave
Des Moines, IA 50309
E-mail: newscenter13@netins.net
www.whotv.com
Phone: 515-242-3500
Fax: 515-242-3796

WOI-TV Ch 5 (ABC)
3903 Westown Pkwy
West Des Moines, IA 50266
E-mail: woitv@ecity.net
www.woi-tv.com/
Phone: 515-457-9645
Fax: 515-457-1034

Radio

KBGG-AM 1700 kHz (N/T)
5161 Maple Dr
Des Moines, IA 50317
Phone: 515-262-9200
Fax: 515-261-6192

KDFR-FM 91.3 MHz (Rel)
PO Box 57023
Des Moines, IA 50317
Phone: 515-262-0449

KGGO-FM 94.9 MHz (CR)
3900 NE Broadway
Des Moines, IA 50317
E-mail: kggo@kggo.com
www.kggo.com
Phone: 515-265-6181
Fax: 515-265-8931

KIOA-FM 93.3 MHz (Oldies)
1416 Locust St
Des Moines, IA 50309
Phone: 515-280-1350
Fax: 515-280-3011

KLYF-FM 100.3 MHz (AC)
1801 Grand Ave
Des Moines, IA 50309
Phone: 515-242-3500
Fax: 515-242-3711

KSTZ-FM 102.5 MHz (AC)
1416 Locust St
Des Moines, IA 50309
Phone: 515-280-1350
Fax: 515-280-3011

KWKY-AM 1150 kHz (Rel)
PO Box 662
Des Moines, IA 50303
Phone: 515-981-0981
Fax: 515-981-0840

Attractions

Iowa's capital and largest city is also the birthplace of John Wayne and Mamie Doud Eisenhower. The city's skywalks, three miles of enclosed glass and concrete bridges connected at the second story level, make getting around downtown easy in any kind of weather. The Civic Center is home to the Des Moines Symphony, and the Des Moines Art Center is noted for its collection of 20th century art. Living History Farms in nearby Urbandale recreates Iowa's past in a 600-acre open-air museum. In Pella, the shops, homes, festivals, and events give visitors a taste of life in an Old World Dutch village. The state fairgrounds in Des Moines is the site of the annual Iowa State Fair, which has been held in Des Moines for more than a century, as well as the World Pork Expo, which is among the largest barbecue contests in the United States.

Adventureland Park
5091 NE 56th St
Altoona, IA 50009
www.adventureland-usa.com
Phone: 515-266-2121
Fax: 515-266-9831
TF: 800-532-1286

Blank Park Zoo
7401 SW 9th St
Des Moines, IA 50315
www.des-moines.ia.us/zoo
Phone: 515-285-4722
Fax: 515-285-1487

Boone & Scenic Valley Railroad
225 10th St
Boone, IA 50036
www.scenic-valleyrr.com
Phone: 515-432-4249
Fax: 515-432-4253
TF: 800-626-0319

Civic Music Assn
221 Walnut St
Des Moines, IA 50309
www.civicmusic.org
Phone: 515-288-8919
Fax: 515-243-1588

Court Avenue District
310 Court Ave
Des Moines, IA 50309
Phone: 515-243-2195
Fax: 515-243-2204

Des Moines Art Center
4700 Grand Ave
Des Moines, IA 50312
www.desmoinesartcenter.org
Phone: 515-277-4405
Fax: 515-271-0357

Des Moines Botanical Center
909 E River Dr
Des Moines, IA 50316
Phone: 515-242-2934
Fax: 515-242-2797

Des Moines Metro Opera
106 W Boston Ave
Indianola, IA 50125
E-mail: dmmopera@aol.com
Phone: 515-961-6221
Fax: 515-961-2994

Des Moines Symphony
221 Walnut St
Des Moines, IA 50309
www.dmsymphony.org
Phone: 515-243-1140
Fax: 515-243-1588

Eisenhower Mamie Doud Birthplace
709 Carroll St
Boone, IA 50036
Phone: 515-432-1896

Iowa Gold Star Museum
7700 NW Beaver Dr Camp Dodge
Johnston, IA 50131
www.guard.state.ia.us/pages/history/museum/iowa_gold_star_museumestablished.html
Phone: 515-252-4531
Fax: 515-252-4139

Iowa Historical Building
600 E Locust St
Des Moines, IA 50319
www.culturalaffairs.org
Phone: 515-281-5111
Fax: 515-282-0502

Iowa State Capitol
E 9th St & Grand Ave
Des Moines, IA 50319
Phone: 515-281-5591

John Wayne Birthplace
216 S 2nd St
Winterset, IA 50273
www.johnwaynebirthplace.org
Phone: 515-462-1044

Jordan House
2001 Fuller Rd
West Des Moines, IA 50265
Phone: 515-225-1286

Lake Red Rock
1105 Hwy T-15
Knoxville, IA 50138
www.lakeredrock.org
Phone: 641-828-7522
Fax: 641-828-7952

Living History Farms
2600 NW 111th St
Urbandale, IA 50322
www.ioweb.com/lhf/index.html
Phone: 515-278-5286
Fax: 515-278-9808

National Balloon Museum Phone: 515-961-3714
1601 N Jefferson St
Indianola, IA 50125

National Sprint Car Hall of Fame & Museum Phone: 641-842-6176
1 Sprint Capital Pl Fax: 641-842-6177
Knoxville, IA 50138
www.classicar.com/museums/sprint/sprint.htm

Pella Historical Village Phone: 641-628-4311
507 Franklin St Fax: 641-628-9192
Pella, IA 50219
E-mail: pellatt@kdsi.net
www.kdsi.net/~pellatt/

Polk County Heritage Gallery Phone: 515-286-3215
111 Court Ave Polk County Office Bldg
Des Moines, IA 50309

Salisbury House Foundation Phone: 515-274-1777
4025 Tonawanda Dr Fax: 515-274-0184
Des Moines, IA 50312
www.salisburyhouse.org

Saylorville Lake Phone: 515-964-0672
5600 NW 78th Ave
Johnston, IA 50131

Science Center of Iowa Phone: 515-274-6868
4500 Grand Ave Greenwood Pk Fax: 515-274-3404
Des Moines, IA 50312
www.sciowa.org

Sherman Hill National Historic District Phone: 515-284-5717
756 16th St
Des Moines, IA 50314

Sherman Hoyt Place Phone: 515-243-0913
1501 Woodland Ave Fax: 515-237-3582
Des Moines, IA 50309

Sleepy Hollow Sports Park Phone: 515-262-4100
4051 Dean Ave Fax: 515-262-6457
Des Moines, IA 50317

Smith Neal National Wildlife Refuge Phone: 515-994-3400
9981 Pacific St Fax: 515-994-3459
Prairie City, IA 50228

Terrace Hill-Governor's Mansion Phone: 515-281-3604
2300 Grand Ave
Des Moines, IA 50312
www.terracehill.org

Wallace House Foundation Phone: 515-243-7063
756 16th St Fax: 515-243-8927
Des Moines, IA 50314

Women's Army Corps Museum at Fort Des Moines Phone: 515-284-6005
225 E Army Post Rd Fax: 515-284-6125
Des Moines, IA 50315

Sports Teams & Facilities

Des Moines Buccaneers (hockey) Phone: 515-278-9757
7201 Hickman Rd Metro Arena Fax: 515-278-5401
Urbandale, IA 50322
www.bucshockey.org/

Des Moines Menace (soccer) Phone: 515-226-9890
50th St & Aurora Ave Cara McGrane Memorial Stadium Fax: 515-226-1595
Des Moines, IA 50325
E-mail: soccer@dmmenace.com
www.dmmenace.com

Iowa Barnstormers (football) Phone: 515-282-3596
833 5th Ave Veterans Memorial Auditorium Fax: 515-282-6449
TF: 888-786-7637
Des Moines, IA 50309
www.iowabarnstormers.com/

Iowa Cubs (baseball) Phone: 515-243-6111
350 SW 1st St Sec Taylor Stadium Fax: 515-243-5152
Des Moines, IA 50309
www.iowacubs.com/

Knoxville Raceway Phone: 641-842-5431
1000 N Lincoln St
Knoxville, IA 50138

Prairie Meadows Racetrack Phone: 515-967-1000
1 Prairie Meadows Dr Fax: 515-967-1253
Altoona, IA 50009 TF: 800-325-9015
www.prairiemeadows.com

Annual Events

Antique Jamboree
(mid-June & mid-August & mid-September)) 515-222-3642
Appaloosa Horse Show (mid-September) 515-262-3111
Autumn Festival & Craft Show (late October) 515-323-5444
Bass Masters Fishermen's Swap Meet & Boat Show
(late February) 515-262-3111
Block & Bridle Horse Show (late April) 515-262-3111
Christmas Walk (mid-November-late December) 641-628-2409
Covered Bridge Festival (mid-October) 515-462-1185
Craft Festival (late February) 515-276-8551
Des Moines Boat Tackle & Sports Show
(mid-January) 515-262-3111
Des Moines Home & Garden Show
(late February) 515-323-5444
Drake Relays Week (late April) 515-271-3711
Fall Classic Horse Show (early September) 515-262-3111
Fall Festival (mid-September) 641-628-2409
Festival of Lanterns
(mid-January-early February) 515-323-8900
Festival of Trees & Lights (late November) 515-241-6494
Firstar Eve (December 31) 515-245-6100
Fox Family Fair (early February) 515-323-5444
Happily Haunted Halloween Treasure Trail
(mid-late October) 515-323-8900
Holiday Lights & Holiday Wonderland
(December) 515-323-8900
Iowa Horse Fair (early April) 515-262-3111
Iowa Pork Congress (late January) 515-323-5444
Iowa Renaissance Festival (mid-September) 515-262-3111
Iowa Sports & Vacation Show
(late February-early March) 515-323-5444
Iowa State Fair (early-mid-August) 515-262-3111
Iowa Winter Beef Expo (mid-February) 515-262-3111
Kids Fest (early March) 515-288-1981
Mayor's Annual Ride for Trails (mid-April) 515-283-4500

Monster Jam (mid-January) 515-323-5444
National Balloon Classic (late July-early August) 515-961-8415
Potpourri Painters Craft Show (mid-March) 515-262-3111
Pufferbilly Days (early September) 800-266-6312
Skywalk Open Golf Tournament
(early February) 515-243-6625
Spring into the Past (late March) 515-281-6412
Two Rivers Art Expo (mid-November) 515-277-1511
Valley Arts Festival (mid-September) 515-225-6009
Wings Wheels & Water Festival
(late September) 515-964-0685
World of Wheels (early April) 515-323-5444
World Pork Expo (mid-June) 515-286-4960
World's Toughest Rodeo (late March) 515-323-5444

Detroit, Michigan

County: **Wayne**

DETROIT is located in southeastern Michigan across the Detroit River from Windsor, Ontario, Canada. Cities within 100 miles of Detroit include Flint and Lansing, Michigan; and London, Ontario, Canada.

Area (Land) .... 138.7 sq mi
Area (Water)................................ 4.2 sq mi
Elevation...................................... 600 ft
Latitude ....42-34-01 N
Longitude................................ 83-04-39 W
Time Zone ....EST
Area Code....................................... 313

Climate

Detroit is located in the North Temperate Zone. Winters are cold, with temperatures occasionally dipping below zero but averaging 23 degrees in January. The average snowfall amount for Detroit is 39 inches. Summers are warm, with July temperatures averaging 72 degrees, while temperatures in the 80s and 90s are common. Summer is also the rainy season in Detroit, with June being the wettest month.

Average Temperatures & Precipitation

Temperatures

	Jan	Feb	Mar	Apr	May	Jun	Jul	Aug	Sep	Oct	Nov	Dec
High	30	33	44	58	70	79	83	81	74	62	48	35
Low	16	18	27	37	47	56	61	60	53	41	32	21

Precipitation

	Jan	Feb	Mar	Apr	May	Jun	Jul	Aug	Sep	Oct	Nov	Dec
Inches	1.8	1.7	2.6	3.0	2.9	3.6	3.2	3.4	2.9	2.1	2.7	2.8

History

Originally a French village, the city of Detroit was founded by Antoine Lournet de La Mothe Cadillac under the orders of Louis XIV in 1701. The city's name was derived from the French phrase "Ville d'Etroit," meaning "city of the strait," as the village was established along the banks of the Detroit River. In its early years, Detroit was a Canadian city under French and British rule. General Anthony Wayne and his American troops occupied the Detroit area in 1796. General Wayne's victories against the Indians helped the United States of America gain sovereignty of the area at the turn of the 18th century. Wayne County was established in his honor, and many Americans settled there.

Three years after Detroit became a town in 1802, it was destroyed by fire. Over the course of the next decade, Judge Augustus Woodward and Governor William Hull worked to establish the territory of Michigan, rebuilding the city to act as the capital of the new territory. Detroit was incorporated as a city in 1815, and remained the capital until 1837 when Michigan gained its statehood.

Throughout the 1800s, Detroit was a major manufacturing center for transportation equipment such as railroad cars, engines, locomotives, and carriages. In 1896, the first car was built in Detroit by Henry Ford—the year 1900 marked the beginning of the automobile era, and Detroit earned its nickname "The Motor City." The three major American automobile manufacturers, Ford, General Motors Corp., and Chrysler Corp., all got their start in the Detroit area. The automobile industry drew large numbers of people to Detroit in the early 20th Century, and transportation equipment manufacturing remains one of the city's largest industries today.

Population

1990 Census 1,027,974
1998 Estimate..............................970,196
% Change .... -5.6

Racial/Ethnic Breakdown
White....................................21.6%
Black 75.7%
Other.....................................2.7%
Hispanic Origin (may be of any race) 2.8%

Age Breakdown
Under 5 years.............................. 9.1%
5 to 17...................................20.4%
18 to 20................................... 5.1%
21 to 24................................... 6.2%
25 to 34..................................16.5%
35 to 44..................................14.2%
45 to 54................................... 8.6%
55 to 64................................... 7.9%
65 to 74................................... 7.2%
75+ years 5.0%
Median Age.................................30.8

Gender Breakdown
Male.....................................46.4%
Female...................................53.6%

Government

Type of Government: Mayor-Council

Detroit Buildings & Safety Engineering Dept
2 Woodward Ave Rm 401
Detroit, MI 48226
Phone: 313-224-3251
Fax: 313-224-1467

Detroit City Clerk
2 Woodward Ave Rm 200
Detroit, MI 48226
Phone: 313-224-3260
Fax: 313-224-1466

Detroit City Council
2 Woodward Ave Rm 1340
Detroit, MI 48226
Phone: 313-224-3443
Fax: 313-224-4095

Detroit City Hall
2 Woodward Ave
Detroit, MI 48226
Phone: 313-224-3270

Detroit Finance Dept
2 Woodward Ave Rm 1200
Detroit, MI 48226
Phone: 313-224-2937
Fax: 313-224-4466

Detroit Fire Dept
250 W Larned St
Detroit, MI 48226
Phone: 313-596-2900
Fax: 313-596-1808

Detroit Human Resources Dept
2 Woodward Ave Rm 316
Detroit, MI 48226
Phone: 313-224-3700
Fax: 313-224-5609

Detroit Law Dept
660 Woodward Ave Suite 1650
Detroit, MI 48226
Phone: 313-224-4550
Fax: 313-224-5505

Detroit Mayor
2 Woodward Ave Rm 1126
Detroit, MI 48226
Phone: 313-224-3400
Fax: 313-224-4433

Detroit Planning & Development Dept
65 Cadillac Sq Suite 2300
Detroit, MI 48226
Phone: 313-224-2560
Fax: 313-224-1629

Detroit Police Dept
1300 Beaubien St
Detroit, MI 48226
Phone: 313-596-2200
Fax: 313-596-1450

Detroit Public Library
5201 Woodward Ave
Detroit, MI 48202
Phone: 313-833-1000
Fax: 313-832-0877

Detroit Public Works Dept
2 Woodward St Rm 513
Detroit, MI 48226
Phone: 313-224-3900

Detroit Recreation Dept
65 Cadillac Sq Suite 3900
Detroit, MI 48226
Phone: 313-224-1100
Fax: 313-224-1732

Detroit Transportation Dept
1301 E Warren Ave
Detroit, MI 48207
Phone: 313-933-1300
Fax: 313-833-5523

Detroit Water & Sewerage Dept
735 Randolph St
Detroit, MI 48226
Phone: 313-224-4800
Fax: 313-964-9580

Important Phone Numbers

AAA....313-336-1234
American Express Travel....248-642-3350
Dental Referral....313-871-3500
Detroit Board of Realtors....313-962-1313
Detroit Finance/Property Tax Div....313-224-3560
Driver's License/Vehicle Registration Information....313-869-1455
Emergency....911
HotelDocs....800-468-3537
Medical Referral....313-567-1640
Michigan Dept of Treasury....800-367-6263
Poison Control Center....313-745-5711
Time....248-472-1212
Travelers Aid....313-962-6740
Visitor Information Line....800-338-7648
Voter Registration Information....313-876-0190
Wayne County Taxpayer Information Line....313-224-5990

Information Sources

Ann Arbor Area Chamber of Commerce
425 S Main St Suite 103
Ann Arbor, MI 48104
www.annarborchamber.org/
Phone: 734-665-4433
Fax: 734-665-4191

Ann Arbor Area Convention & Visitors Bureau
120 W Huron St
Ann Arbor, MI 48104
www.annarbor.org
Phone: 734-995-7281
Fax: 734-995-7283
TF: 800-888-9487

Ann Arbor City Hall
100 N 5th Ave
Ann Arbor, MI 48107
www.ci.ann-arbor.mi.us
Phone: 734-994-2700
Fax: 734-994-8297

Ann Arbor Community Development Dept
PO Box 8647
Ann Arbor, MI 48107
www.ci.ann-arbor.mi.us/framed/commdev
Phone: 734-994-2912
Fax: 734-994-2915

Ann Arbor District Library
343 S 5th Ave
Ann Arbor, MI 48104
www.annarbor.lib.mi.us
Phone: 734-994-2333
Fax: 734-994-4762

Ann Arbor Mayor
PO Box 8647
Ann Arbor, MI 48107
Phone: 734-994-2766
Fax: 734-994-8297

Better Business Bureau Serving Detroit & Eastern Michigan
30555 Southfield Rd Suite 200
Southfield, MI 48076
www.detroit.bbb.org
Phone: 248-644-9100
Fax: 248-644-5026

Cobo Conference & Exhibition Center
1 Washington Blvd
Detroit, MI 48226
www.cobocenter.com
Phone: 313-877-8777
Fax: 313-877-8577

Greater Detroit Chamber of Commerce
1 Woodward Ave
Detroit, MI 48232
www.detroitchamber.com
Phone: 313-964-4000
Fax: 313-964-0531

Metropolitan Detroit Convention & Visitors Bureau
211 W Fort St Suite 1000
Detroit, MI 48226
www.visitdetroit.com
Phone: 313-202-1800
Fax: 313-202-1808
TF: 800-225-5389

Washtenaw County
PO Box 8645
Ann Arbor, MI 48107
www.co.washtenaw.mi.us
Phone: 734-996-3055
Fax: 734-994-2952

Wayne County
211 City-County Bldg
Detroit, MI 48226
www.waynecounty.com
Phone: 313-224-6262
Fax: 313-224-5364

Online Resources

4AnnArbor.com
www.4annarbor.com

4Detroit.com
www.4detroit.com

About.com Guide to Detroit
detroit.about.com/local/midwestus/detroit

Anthill City Guide Ann Arbor
www.anthill.com/city.asp?city=annarbor

Anthill City Guide Detroit
www.anthill.com/city.asp?city=detroit

Arborweb
www.arborweb.com

Area Guide Ann Arbor
annarbor.areaguides.net

Area Guide Detroit
detroit.areaguides.net

Boulevards Detroit
www.detroit.com

City Knowledge Ann Arbor
www.cityknowledge.com/mi_annarbor.htm

City Knowledge Detroit
www.cityknowledge.com/mi_detroit.htm

CitySearch Detroit
detroit.citysearch.com

Detroit City Pages
detroit.thelinks.com

Detroit CityLink
www.usacitylink.com/citylink/detroit

Detroit On-line Metro Directory
detroit.net

Detroit's Internet Metro Guide
www.metroguide.com/

DigitalCity Detroit
home.digitalcity.com/detroit

Electric Current Entertainment Magazine
www.ecurrent.com

Excite.com Ann Arbor City Guide
www.excite.com/travel/countries/united_states/michigan/ann_arbor

Excite.com Detroit City Guide
www.excite.com/travel/countries/united_states/michigan/detroit

Fabulous Ruins of Detroit
bhere.com/ruins/home.htm

InDetroit.com
www.indetroit.com

iNetDetroit
www.inetdetroit.com

Metro Detroit Area Guide
www.citysidewalks.com/detroitnew/frames17.htm

Metro On-Line Magazine
www.ddsi.com/metro/

MetroDine Detroit
www.metrodine.com/MetroDetroit/

Rough Guide Travel Detroit
travel.roughguides.com/content/483/

Area Communities

The Greater Detroit area encompasses eight counties and more than 250 municipalities. The city of Detroit alone has more than 200 neighborhoods. Select communities in the Greater Detroit area with populations exceeding 10,000 are listed below. Other communities in the area include Clinton Township, Westland, Taylor, Waterford, Canton Township, West Bloomfield, and Roseville.

Ann Arbor
100 N 5th Ave
Ann Arbor, MI 48107
Phone: 734-994-2700
Fax: 734-994-8297

Auburn Hills
1827 N Squirrel Rd
Auburn Hills, MI 48326
Phone: 248-370-9400
Fax: 248-370-9348

Berkley
3338 Coolidge Hwy
Berkley, MI 48072
Phone: 248-546-2470
Fax: 248-546-2428

Birmingham
PO Box 3001
Birmingham, MI 48012
Phone: 248-644-1800
Fax: 248-644-5614

Dearborn
13615 Michigan Ave
Dearborn, MI 48126
Phone: 313-943-2285
Fax: 313-943-2665

Farmington Hills
31555 11-Mile Rd
Farmington Hills, MI 48336
Phone: 248-474-6115
Fax: 248-474-5925

Grosse Pointe Farms
90 Kerby Rd
Grosse Pointe Farms, MI 48236
Phone: 313-885-6600
Fax: 313-885-0917

Livonia
33000 Civic Center Dr
Livonia, MI 48154
Phone: 734-466-2500
Fax: 734-421-1147

Madison Heights
300 W 13-Mile Rd
Madison Heights, MI 48071
Phone: 248-588-1200
Fax: 248-588-8442

Rochester Hills
1000 Rochester Hills Dr
Rochester Hills, MI 48309
Phone: 248-656-4600
Fax: 248-656-4744

Royal Oak
211 Williams St
Royal Oak, MI 48067
Phone: 248-544-6650
Fax: 248-546-1546

Saint Clair Shores
27600 Jefferson Circle Dr
Saint Clair Shores, MI 48081
Phone: 810-445-5240
Fax: 810-445-0469

Southfield
26000 Evergreen Rd
Southfield, MI 48076
Phone: 248-354-9380
Fax: 248-354-7937

Southgate
14400 Dix Toledo Hwy
Southgate, MI 48195
Phone: 734-246-1305
Fax: 734-246-1406

Sterling Heights
PO Box 8009
Sterling Heights, MI 48311
Phone: 810-446-2489
Fax: 810-276-4077

Troy
500 W Big Beaver Rd
Troy, MI 48084
Phone: 248-524-3300
Fax: 248-524-1770

Warren
29500 Van Dyke Ave
Warren, MI 48093
Phone: 810-574-4557
Fax: 810-574-4556

Wyandotte
3131 Biddle Ave
Wyandotte, MI 48192
Phone: 734-324-4500
Fax: 734-324-4568

Ypsilanti
1 S Huron St
Ypsilanti, MI 48197
Phone: 734-483-1100
Fax: 734-487-8742

Economy

The Greater Detroit workforce exceeds two million, with the majority of jobs in transportation equipment manufacturing and health services. Corporations headquartered in Detroit include Kmart, Stroh Brewery Co, American National Resources, and Federal Mogul. Fortune 500 companies in the Greater Detroit area include General Motors, Ford Motor, and DaimlerChrysler (Ford and General Motors are ranked number one and two on the list respectively).

Unemployment Rate 3.1%*
Per Capita Income $30,118*
Median Family Income $60,500*

** Information given is for the Detroit Metropolitan Statistical Area (MSA), which includes Lapeer, Macomb, Monroe, Oakland, Saint Clair, and Wayne counties.*

Principal Industries & Number of Wage Earners

Detroit MSA* - 1999

Construction & Mining 83,000
Finance, Insurance, & Real Estate 113,000
Government 231,000
Manufacturing 447,000
Private Services 667,000
Retail Trade 364,000
Transportation, Communications, & Utilities 95,000
Wholesale Trade 128,000

** Information given is for the Detroit Metropolitan Statistical Area (MSA), which includes Lapeer, Macomb, Monroe, Oakland, Saint Clair, and Wayne counties.*

Major Employers

Ameritech Michigan
444 Michigan Ave
Detroit, MI 48226
www.ameritech.com
Phone: 313-223-9900

CMS Energy Corp
330 Town Ctr Dr Suite 1100
Dearborn, MI 48126
E-mail: info@cmsenergy.com
www.cmsenergy.com
Phone: 313-436-9200
Fax: 313-982-9359

Comerica Inc
500 Woodward Ave
Detroit, MI 48226
www.comerica.com
Phone: 800-521-1190
Fax: 313-964-3752

DaimlerChrysler Corp
1000 Chrysler Dr
Auburn Hills, MI 48326
www.daimlerchrysler.com
Phone: 248-576-5741
Fax: 248-512-5143
TF: 800-992-1997

Detroit City Hall
2 Woodward Ave
Detroit, MI 48226
www.ci.detroit.mi.us
Phone: 313-224-3270

Detroit Edison Co
2000 2nd Ave
Detroit, MI 48226
www.detroitedison.com
Phone: 313-235-8000
Fax: 313-235-8828
TF: 800-477-4747

Detroit Medical Center
4201 St Antoine Blvd
Detroit, MI 48201
www.dmc.org
Phone: 313-745-8040
Fax: 313-745-8255

Detroit Public Schools
5057 Woodward Ave
Detroit, MI 48202
www.detroit.k12.mi.us
Phone: 313-494-1000
Fax: 313-494-1378

Ford Motor Co
PO Box 1899
Dearborn, MI 48121
www.ford.com
Phone: 313-322-3000

General Motors Corp
100 Renaissance Ctr
Detroit, MI 48265
www.gm.com
Phone: 313-556-5000
Fax: 313-556-5108
TF: 800-457-4522

Henry Ford Health System
1 Ford Pl
Detroit, MI 48202
www.henryfordhealth.org
Phone: 313-874-6000
Fax: 313-876-6099
TF: 800-492-9909

Kmart Corp
3100 W Big Beaver Rd
Troy, MI 48084
www.kmart.com
Phone: 248-643-1000
Fax: 248-643-5566
TF: 800-635-6278

Lear Seating Corp
4600 Nancy St
Detroit, MI 48212
Phone: 313-852-7800
Fax: 313-852-7852

Saint John Health System
22101 Moross Rd
Detroit, MI 48236
Phone: 313-343-4000
Fax: 313-343-7495

Quality of Living Indicators

Total Crime Index 117,911
(rates per 100,000 inhabitants)

Violent Crime
Murder/manslaughter 430
Forcible rape 858
Robbery 8,558
Aggravated assault 14,581

Property Crime
Burglary 21,516
Larceny theft 43,317
Motor vehicle theft 28,651

Cost of Living Index 114.0
(national average = 100)

Median Home Price $140,000

Education

Public Schools

Detroit Public Schools
5057 Woodward Ave
Detroit, MI 48202
www.detroit.k12.mi.us
Phone: 313-494-1000
Fax: 313-494-1378

Number of Schools
Elementary 174
Middle 49
High 37

Student/Teacher Ratio
All Grades 20.2:1

Private Schools

Number of Schools (all grades) .... 200+

Colleges & Universities

Baker College Auburn Hills Campus
1500 University Dr
Auburn Hills, MI 48326
E-mail: adm-ah@baker.edu
www.baker.edu/visit/auburn.html
Phone: 248-340-0600
Fax: 248-340-0608
TF: 888-429-0410

Center for Creative Studies College of Art & Design
201 E Kirby St
Detroit, MI 48202
www.ccscad.edu
Phone: 313-872-3118
Fax: 313-872-2739
TF: 800-952-2787

Cleary College
3601 Plymouth Rd
Ann Arbor, MI 48105
www.cleary.edu
Phone: 734-332-4477
Fax: 734-332-4646
TF: 800-589-1979

Concordia College
4090 Geddes Rd
Ann Arbor, MI 48105
E-mail: admissions@ccaa.edu
www.ccaa.edu
Phone: 734-995-7300
Fax: 734-995-4610
TF: 800-253-0680

Detroit College of Business
4801 Oakman Blvd
Dearborn, MI 48126
www.dcb.edu
Phone: 313-581-4400
Fax: 313-581-6822

Detroit College of Business Warren Campus
27500 Dequindre Rd
Warren, MI 48092
www.dcb.edu
Phone: 810-558-8700
Fax: 810-558-7868

Eastern Michigan University
Ypsilanti, MI 48197
www.emich.edu
Phone: 734-487-1849
Fax: 734-487-1484

Lawrence Technological University
21000 W 10-Mile Rd
Southfield, MI 48075
www.ltu.edu
Phone: 248-204-4000
Fax: 248-204-3188
TF: 800-225-5588

Lewis College of Business
17370 Meyers Rd
Detroit, MI 48235
www.lewiscollege.edu/index.html
Phone: 313-862-6300
Fax: 313-862-1027

Macomb Community College South Campus
14500 E 12-Mile Rd
Warren, MI 48093
E-mail: answer@macomb.cc.mi.us
www.macomb.cc.mi.us
Phone: 810-445-7000
Fax: 810-445-7140

Madonna University
36600 Schoolcraft Rd
Livonia, MI 48150
www.munet.edu
Phone: 734-432-5300
Fax: 734-432-5393
TF: 800-852-4951

Marygrove College
8425 W McNichols Rd
Detroit, MI 48221
www.marygrove.edu
Phone: 313-927-1200
Fax: 313-927-1345

Monroe County Community College
1555 S Raisinville Rd
Monroe, MI 48161
www.monroe.cc.mi.us
Phone: 734-242-7300
Fax: 734-242-9711

Oakland Community College
2480 Opdyke Rd
Bloomfield Hills, MI 48304
www.occ.cc.mi.us
Phone: 248-540-1500
Fax: 248-540-1841

Oakland Community College Auburn Hills Campus
2900 Featherstone Rd
Auburn Hills, MI 48326
www.occ.cc.mi.us/occ/ah.htm
Phone: 248-340-6500
Fax: 248-340-6507

Oakland Community College Royal Oak Campus
739 S Washington Ave
Royal Oak, MI 48067
www.occ.cc.mi.us/occ/ro.htm
Phone: 248-544-4900
Fax: 248-544-5517

Oakland Community College Southfield Campus
22322 Rutland Ave
Southfield, MI 48075
www.occ.cc.mi.us/occ/sf.htm
Phone: 248-552-2600
Fax: 248-552-2661

Oakland University
Walton Blvd & Squirrel Rd
Rochester, MI 48309
www.acs.oakland.edu
Phone: 248-370-2100
Fax: 248-370-4462

Rochester College
800 W Avon Rd
Rochester Hills, MI 48307
www.rc.edu
Phone: 248-651-5800
Fax: 248-218-2035
TF: 800-521-6010

Saint Mary's College
3535 Indian Trail
Orchard Lake, MI 48324
Phone: 248-682-1885
Fax: 248-683-0402

Schoolcraft College
18600 Haggerty Rd
Livonia, MI 48152
www.schoolcraft.cc.mi.us
Phone: 734-462-4400
Fax: 734-462-4553

University of Detroit Mercy
PO Box 19900
Detroit, MI 48219
www.udmercy.edu
Phone: 313-993-1000
Fax: 313-993-3326
TF: 800-635-5020

University of Michigan
503 Thompson St
Ann Arbor, MI 48109
www.umich.edu
Phone: 734-764-1817
Fax: 734-936-0740

University of Michigan Dearborn
4901 Evergreen Rd
Dearborn, MI 48128
www.umd.umich.edu
Phone: 313-593-5100
Fax: 313-436-9167

Washtenaw Community College
4800 E Huron River Dr
Ann Arbor, MI 48106
www.washtenaw.cc.mi.us
Phone: 734-973-3300
Fax: 734-677-5414

Wayne County Community College
801 W Fort St
Detroit, MI 48226
www.wccc.edu
Phone: 313-496-2500
Fax: 313-961-7842

Wayne State University
6050 Cass Ave
Detroit, MI 48202
E-mail: dsynder@cms.cc.wayne.edu
www.wayne.edu
Phone: 313-577-2424
Fax: 313-577-7536

William Tyndale College
35700 W 12-Mile Rd
Farmington Hills, MI 48331
Phone: 248-553-7200
Fax: 248-553-5963
TF: 800-483-0707

Hospitals

Bon Secours Hospital
468 Cadieux Rd
Grosse Pointe, MI 48230
Phone: 313-343-1000
Fax: 313-343-1297

Chelsea Community Hospital
775 S Main St
Chelsea, MI 48118
www.cch.org
Phone: 734-475-1311
Fax: 734-475-4066

Children's Hospital of Michigan
3901 Beaubien Blvd
Detroit, MI 48201
www.dmc.org/chm
Phone: 313-745-5437
Fax: 313-993-0389

Detroit Receiving Hospital & University Health Center
4201 Saint Antoine St
Detroit, MI 48201
Phone: 313-745-3100
Fax: 313-966-7206

Garden City Osteopathic Hospital
6245 N Inkster Rd
Garden City, MI 48135
www.gchosp.org
Phone: 734-421-3300
Fax: 734-421-3530

Harper Hospital
3990 John R St
Detroit, MI 48201
www.harperhospital.org/harper
Phone: 313-745-8040
Fax: 313-993-0635

Henry Ford Hospital
2799 W Grand Blvd
Detroit, MI 48202
Phone: 313-876-2600
Fax: 313-916-1410

Huron Valley Sinai Hospital
1 William Carls Dr
Commerce Township, MI 48382
Phone: 248-360-3300
Fax: 248-360-5022

Hutzel Hospital
4707 Saint Antoine St
Detroit, MI 48201
Phone: 313-745-7552
Fax: 313-993-0154

Providence Hospital
16001 W Nine-Mile Rd
Southfield, MI 48075
www.providence-hospital.org
Phone: 248-424-3000
Fax: 248-424-3035

Saint John Detroit Riverview Hospital
7733 E Jefferson Ave
Detroit, MI 48214
Phone: 313-499-3000
Fax: 313-499-4908

Saint John Health System Oakland Hospital
27351 Dequindre
Madison Heights, MI 48071
Phone: 248-967-7000
Fax: 248-967-7619

Saint John Hospital & Medical Center
22101 Moross Rd
Detroit, MI 48236
stjohn.org/StJohn/stjohnhospitalandmedicalcenter.cfm
Phone: 313-343-4000
Fax: 313-343-7532

Saint John Northeast Community Hospital
4777 E Outer Dr
Detroit, MI 48234
Phone: 313-369-9100
Fax: 313-369-5650

Saint Joseph Mercy-Oakland
900 Woodward Ave
Pontiac, MI 48341
www.mercyhealth.com/oakland
Phone: 248-858-3000
Fax: 248-858-3155

Sinai Grace Hospital
6071 W Outer Dr
Detroit, MI 48235
Phone: 313-966-3300
Fax: 313-966-3351

University of Michigan Health System
1500 E Medical Center Dr
Ann Arbor, MI 48109
www.med.umich.edu
Phone: 734-936-4000
Fax: 734-647-3273

Vencor Hospital Phone: 313-361-8000
2700 ML King Jr Blvd Fax: 313-361-8001
Detroit, MI 48208

Veterans Affairs Medical Center Phone: 734-769-7100
2215 Fuller Rd Fax: 734-761-7870
Ann Arbor, MI 48105

William Beaumont Hospital Phone: 248-551-5000
3601 W 13-Mile Rd Fax: 248-551-8446
Royal Oak, MI 48073
www.beaumont.edu

Transportation

Airport(s)

Detroit City Airport (DET)
6 miles E of downtown (approx 20 minutes) 313-852-6400
Detroit Metropolitan Airport (DTW)
20 miles SW of downtown (approx 30 minutes) . . .734-942-3685

Mass Transit

Detroit Dept of Transportation Bus
$1.25 Base fare 313-933-1300
Detroit Trolley
$.50 Base Fare 313-224-6449
People Mover
$.50 Base fare 313-962-7245
SMART Bus
$1.50 Base fare 313-962-5515

Rail/Bus

Amtrak Station Phone: 800-872-7245
11 W Baltimore Ave
Detroit, MI 48202

Greyhound/Trailways Bus Station Phone: 800-231-2222
1001 Howard St
Detroit, MI 48226

Utilities

Electricity
Detroit Edison 800-477-4747
www.detroitedison.com

Gas
Michigan Consolidated Gas Co 313-965-8000

Water
Detroit Water & Sewerage Dept 313-224-4800
www.ci.detroit.mi.us/dwsd

Garbage Collection/Recycling
Detroit Refuse & Bulk Collection 313-935-4700

Telecommunications

Telephone
Ameritech 800-345-6254
www.ameritech.com

Cable Television
Comcast 313-934-2600

Internet Service Providers (ISPs)
Computer Networking Services Inc 810-739-4800
www.compnetserv.com
ICNet 734-998-0090
www.ic.net
Izzy Dot Net Inc 734-973-2100
www.izzy.net
Merit Network Inc 734-764-9430
nic.merit.edu
Msen Inc 248-740-3400
www.msen.com
On Line Exchange 313-961-7100
www.ole.net
Verio Michigan 734-762-6000
home.verio.net/local/frontpage.cfm?AirportCode=DET

Banks

Bank One Michigan Phone: 313-225-1000
611 Woodward Ave Fax: 313-225-2371
Detroit, MI 48226

Comerica Bank Phone: 800-643-4418
500 Woodward Ave Fax: 313-222-4667
Detroit, MI 48226
www.comerica.com

First Federal of Michigan Phone: 313-965-1400
1001 Woodward Ave Fax: 313-965-5936
Detroit, MI 48226

First Independence National Bank of Detroit Phone: 313-256-8200
44 Michigan Ave Fax: 313-256-8456
Detroit, MI 48226
www.finb.com

First State Bank of East Detroit Phone: 810-775-5000
16100 E Nine-Mile Rd Fax: 810-773-7233
Eastpointe, MI 48021

Michigan National Bank Phone: 800-225-5662
25001 Michigan Ave Fax: 313-274-5460
Dearborn, MI 48124

National City Bank of Michigan/Illinois Phone: 800-925-9259
PO Box 2659 Fax: 313-596-8239
Detroit, MI 48231

NBD Bank Phone: 313-225-3774
611 Woodward Ave Fax: 313-225-3334
Detroit, MI 48226 TF: 800-225-5623

Shopping

Antiques Mall of Ann Arbor Phone: 734-663-8200
2739 Plymouth Rd
Ann Arbor, MI 48105

Briarwood Mall Phone: 734-769-9610
100 Briarwood Cir Fax: 734-769-2521
Ann Arbor, MI 48108

Depot Town Phone: 734-483-4444
E Cross & River Sts
Ypsilanti, MI 48198

Eastland Center
18000 Vernier Rd
Harper Woods, MI 48225
Phone: 313-371-1501
Fax: 313-371-3511

Fairlane Town Center
18900 Michigan Ave
Dearborn, MI 48126
Phone: 313-593-3330
Fax: 313-593-0572

Kerrytown Shops
407 N 5th Ave
Ann Arbor, MI 48104
Phone: 734-662-5008

Lakeside Mall
14000 Lakeside Cir
Sterling Heights, MI 48312
Phone: 800-334-5573

Laurel Park Place
37700 6 Mile Rd
Livonia, MI 48152
Phone: 734-462-1100
Fax: 734-462-6210

Macomb Mall
32100 Beaconsfield St
Roseville, MI 48066
Phone: 810-294-2816

Main Street Area
Main St betw William & Huron
Ann Arbor, MI 48104

New Center Place
3031 W Grand Blvd
Detroit, MI 48202
Phone: 313-874-4444
Fax: 313-874-5046

Northland Shopping Center
21500 Northwestern Hwy
Southfield, MI 48075
Phone: 248-569-6272
Fax: 248-569-0861

Oakland Mall
412 W 14 Mile Rd
Troy, MI 48083
Phone: 248-585-6000
Fax: 248-585-2440

Renaissance Center
200 Renaissance Ctr Suite 1200
Detroit, MI 48243
Phone: 313-568-5600
Fax: 313-568-5794

Somerset Collection
2800 W Big Beaver Rd
Troy, MI 48084
Phone: 248-643-6360
Fax: 248-643-4633

Summitt Place
315 N Telegraph Rd
Waterford, MI 48328
Phone: 248-682-0123
Fax: 248-682-1188

Tel Twelve Mall
28690 Telegraph Rd
Southfield, MI 48034
Phone: 248-354-0002
Fax: 248-353-1857

Twelve Oaks Mall
27500 Novi Rd
Novi, MI 48377
Phone: 248-348-9400
Fax: 248-348-9411

Media

Newspapers and Magazines

Ann Arbor News*
PO Box 1147
Ann Arbor, MI 48106
aa.mlive.com
Phone: 734-994-6989
Fax: 734-994-6879
TF: 800-466-6989

Birmingham Bloomfield Eccentric
805 E Maple
Birmingham, MI 48009
observer-eccentric.com/local/Birmingham/index.html
Phone: 248-644-1100
Fax: 248-644-1314

Connection The
96 Kercheval Ave
Grosse Pointe, MI 48236
Phone: 313-882-0294
Fax: 313-882-1585

Crain's Detroit Business
1400 Woodbridge St
Detroit, MI 48207
www.crainsdetroit.com
Phone: 313-446-6000
Fax: 313-446-1687

Dearborn Times-Herald
13730 Michigan Ave
Dearborn, MI 48126
Phone: 313-584-4000
Fax: 313-584-1357

Detroit Free Press*
600 W Fort St
Detroit, MI 48226
E-mail: city@freepr.com
www.freep.com
Phone: 313-222-6400
Fax: 313-222-5981
TF: 800-678-6400

Detroit News*
615 W Lafayette Blvd
Detroit, MI 48226
www.detnews.com
Phone: 313-222-6400
Fax: 313-222-2335
TF: 800-678-6400

Grosse Pointe News
96 Kercheval Ave
Grosse Pointe Farms, MI 48236
www.grossepointenews.com
Phone: 313-882-6900
Fax: 313-882-1585

Metro Times
733 Saint Antoine
Detroit, MI 48226
E-mail: metrotimes@metrotimes.com
www.metrotimes.com
Phone: 313-961-4060
Fax: 313-964-4849

Michigan Living
1 Auto Club Dr
Dearborn, MI 48126
E-mail: info@aaamich.com
www.leelanau.com/nmj/living
Phone: 313-336-1506
Fax: 313-336-0986

Taylor/Romulus News-Herald
1 Heritage Pl Suite 100
Southgate, MI 48195
E-mail: feedback@heritage.com
www.thenewsherald.com
Phone: 734-246-0800
Fax: 734-246-2727

Wyandotte/Trenton News-Herald
1 Heritage Pl Suite 100
Southgate, MI 48195
www.thenewsherald.com
Phone: 734-246-0800
Fax: 734-246-2727

**Indicates major daily newspapers*

Television

WADL-TV Ch 38 (Fox)
22590 15-Mile Rd
Clinton Township, MI 48035
Phone: 810-790-3838
Fax: 810-790-3841

WDIV-TV Ch 4 (NBC)
550 W Lafayette Blvd
Detroit, MI 48231
www.wdiv.com
Phone: 313-222-0444
Fax: 313-222-0592

WDWB-TV Ch 20 (WB)
27777 Franklin Rd Suite 1220
Southfield, MI 48034
www.wb20detroit.com
Phone: 248-355-2020
Fax: 248-355-0368

WJBK-TV Ch 2 (Fox)
PO Box 2000
Southfield, MI 48037
E-mail: contact@fox2detroit.com
www.wjbk.com
Phone: 248-557-2000
Fax: 248-552-0280

WKAR-TV Ch 23 (PBS)
MSU 212 Communications Arts Bldg
East Lansing, MI 48824
E-mail: mail@wkar.msu.edu
www.wkar.msu.edu/tv/index.htm
Phone: 517-432-9527
Fax: 517-353-7124

WKBD-TV Ch 50 (UPN)
26905 W 11-Mile Rd
Southfield, MI 48034
www.paramountstations.com/WKBD
Phone: 248-350-5050
Fax: 248-358-0977

WPXD-TV Ch 31 (PAX)
3975 Varsity Dr
Ann Arbor, MI 48108
www.pax.net/WPXD
Phone: 734-973-7900
Fax: 734-973-7906

WTVS-TV Ch 56 (PBS)
7441 2nd Ave
Detroit, MI 48202
E-mail: viewer_services@wtvs.pbs.org
www.wtvs.org
Phone: 313-873-7200
Fax: 313-876-8118

WWJ-TV Ch 62 (CBS)
300 River Pl Suite 6200
Detroit, MI 48207
Phone: 313-259-6288
Fax: 313-259-4585

WXYZ-TV Ch 7 (ABC)
20777 W 10-Mile Rd
Southfield, MI 48037
E-mail: talkback@wxyztv.com
www.detnow.com
Phone: 248-827-7777
Fax: 248-827-4454

Radio

CIDR-FM 93.9 MHz (AAA)
1640 Ouellette Ave
Windsor, ON N8X1L1
E-mail: sales@theriver939.com
www.smoothrock939.com
Phone: 313-961-9811
Fax: 313-961-1603

CIMX-FM 88.7 MHz (Alt)
1640 Ouellette Ave
Windsor, ON N8X1L1
Phone: 313-961-9811
Fax: 313-961-1603

CKLW-AM 800 kHz (N/T)
1640 Ouellette Ave
Windsor, ON N8X1L1
Phone: 313-961-9811
Fax: 313-961-1603

CKWW-AM 580 kHz (Nost)
1640 Ouellette Ave
Windsor, ON N8X1L1
Phone: 313-961-9811
Fax: 313-961-1603

WAAM-AM 1600 kHz (N/T)
4230 Packard Rd
Ann Arbor, MI 48108
E-mail: waam@aol.com
Phone: 734-971-1600
Fax: 734-973-2916

WCAR-AM 1090 kHz (Rel)
32500 Park Ln
Garden City, MI 48135
Phone: 734-525-1111
Fax: 734-525-3608

WCBN-FM 88.3 MHz (Misc)
530 Student Activities Bldg
Ann Arbor, MI 48109
wcbn.org
Phone: 734-763-3500
Fax: 734-647-3885

WCHB-FM 105.9 MHz (Urban)
2994 E Grand Blvd
Detroit, MI 48202
Phone: 313-871-0590
Fax: 313-871-8770

WCSX-FM 94.7 MHz (CR)
28588 Northwestern Hwy Suite 200
Southfield, MI 48034
www.wcsx.com
Phone: 248-945-9470
Fax: 248-355-3485

WDEO-AM 1290 kHz (Rel)
24 Frank Lloyd Wright Dr
Ann Arbor, MI 48106
Phone: 734-930-3177
Fax: 734-930-3101

WDET-FM 101.9 MHz (NPR)
4600 Cass Ave
Detroit, MI 48201
www.wdetfm.org
Phone: 313-577-4146
Fax: 313-577-1300

WDFN-AM 1130 kHz (Sports)
2930 E Jefferson Ave
Detroit, MI 48207
www.wdfn.com
Phone: 313-259-5440
Fax: 313-259-0560

WDRQ-FM 93.1 MHz (AC)
28411 Northwestern Hwy Suite 1000
Southfield, MI 48034
www.931wdrq.com
Phone: 248-354-9300
Fax: 248-354-1474

WDTJ-FM 105.9 MHz (Urban)
3250 Franklin St
Detroit, MI 48207
www.1059jamzdetroit.com
Phone: 313-259-2000
Fax: 313-259-7011

WEMU-FM 89.1 MHz (NPR)
PO Box 980350
Ypsilanti, MI 48198
www.wemu.org
Phone: 734-487-2229
Fax: 734-487-1015
TF: 888-299-8910

WGPR-FM 107.5 MHz (Urban)
3146 E Jefferson Ave
Detroit, MI 48207
E-mail: wgprsales@wgprdetroit.com
www.wgprdetroit.com
Phone: 313-259-8862
Fax: 313-259-6662

WGRV-FM 105.1 MHz (Urban)
1 Radio Plaza
Detroit, MI 48220
Phone: 248-414-5600
Fax: 248-399-5633

WIQB-FM 102.9 MHz (Alt)
24 Frank Lloyd Wright Dr Lobby D
Ann Arbor, MI 48106
www.rock103wiqb.com
Phone: 734-930-0103
Fax: 734-741-1071

WJLB-FM 97.9 MHz (Urban)
645 Griswold St Suite 633
Detroit, MI 48226
Phone: 313-965-2000
Fax: 313-965-3965

WJR-AM 760 kHz (N/T)
2100 Fisher Bldg
Detroit, MI 48202
www.760wjr.com
Phone: 313-875-4440
Fax: 313-875-9022

WKQI-FM 95.5 MHz (AC)
15401 W 10-Mile Rd
Detroit, MI 48237
www.q955.com
Phone: 248-967-3750
Fax: 248-967-0840

WKRK-FM 97.1 MHz (N/T)
15600 W 12-Mile Rd
Southfield, MI 48076
E-mail: wkrk@wkrk.com
www.wkrk.com
Phone: 248-395-9797
Fax: 248-423-7725

WMUZ-FM 103.5 MHz (Rel)
12300 Radio Pl
Detroit, MI 48228
E-mail: station@wmuz.com
www.wmuz.com
Phone: 313-272-3434
Fax: 313-272-5045

WMXD-FM 92.3 MHz (AC)
645 Griswold St Suite 633
Detroit, MI 48226
Phone: 313-965-2000
Fax: 313-965-3965

WNIC-FM 100.3 MHz (AC)
15001 Michigan Ave
Dearborn, MI 48126
www.wnic.com
Phone: 313-846-8500
Fax: 313-846-1068

WOMC-FM 104.3 MHz (Oldies)
2201 Woodward Heights
Detroit, MI 48220
E-mail: promo@womc.com
www.womc.com
Phone: 248-546-9600
Fax: 248-546-5446

WPLT-FM 96.3 MHz (Alt)
2100 Fisher Bldg
Detroit, MI 48202
E-mail: theplanet@planet963.com
www.planet963.com
Phone: 313-871-3030
Fax: 313-875-9636

WQBH-AM 1400 kHz (Urban)
645 Griswold Ave Suite 2050
Detroit, MI 48226
Phone: 313-965-4500
Fax: 313-965-4608

WQKL-FM 107.1 MHz (AC)
24 Frank Lloyd Wright Dr Lobby D
Ann Arbor, MI 48106
www.kool107.com
Phone: 734-930-0107
Fax: 734-741-1071

WRIF-FM 101.1 MHz (Rock)
1 Radio Plaza
Ferndale, MI 48220
www.wrif.com
Phone: 248-547-0101
Fax: 248-542-8800

WTKA-AM 1050 kHz (N/T)
24 Frank Lloyd Wright Dr Lobby D
Ann Arbor, MI 48106
www.wtka.com
Phone: 734-930-0107
Fax: 734-741-1071

WUOM-FM 91.7 MHz (NPR)
500 S State St 5000 LSA Bldg
Ann Arbor, MI 48109
E-mail: annat@umich.edu
www.umich.edu/~wuom/
Phone: 734-764-9210
Fax: 734-647-3488

WVMV-FM 98.7 MHz (NAC)
31555 W 14-Mile Rd Suite 102
Farmington Hills, MI 48334
Phone: 248-855-5100
Fax: 248-855-1302

WWBR-FM 102.7 MHz (AC)
850 Stephenson Hwy Suite 405
Troy, MI 48083
Phone: 248-589-7900
Fax: 248-589-8295

WWJ-AM 950 kHz (N/T)
26495 American Dr
Southfield, MI 48034
wwj.com
Phone: 248-455-7200
Fax: 248-304-4970

WWWW-FM 106.7 MHz (Ctry)
2930 E Jefferson Ave
Detroit, MI 48207
E-mail: alice1067email@yahoo.com
www.w4country.com
Phone: 313-259-4323
Fax: 313-259-9817

WXYT-AM 1270 kHz (N/T)
26495 American Dr
Southfield, MI 48034
www.wxyt.com
Phone: 248-455-7350
Fax: 248-455-7362

WYCD-FM 99.5 MHz (Ctry)
26555 Evergreen Rd Suite 675
Southfield, MI 48076
www.wycd.com
Phone: 248-799-0600
Fax: 248-358-9216

WYUR-AM 1310 kHz (Misc)
860 W Long Lake Rd
Bloomfield Hills, MI 48302
E-mail: wyursales@1310.com
www.1310.com
Phone: 248-433-9987
Fax: 248-258-5572

Attractions

Detroit's history as the "Automotive Capital of the World" can be seen in the area's many historical attractions, including the Henry Ford Museum and Greenfield Village, located in Dearborn. The Village is an indoor-outdoor museum that preserves 80 famous historic structures, among them Thomas Edison's laboratory, the bikeshop where the Wright Brothers' first airplane was built, and the farm where Henry Ford was born. Belle Isle Park, located in the Detroit River three miles southeast of the city center, is the nation's oldest and largest city island park. The park features an outdoor zoo that is open during the spring and summer months, as well as Whitcomb Conservatory, known for its orchid collections, and an aquarium that are open year-round. Greektown, located in southeast downtown Detroit, is one of the city's most popular entertainment districts. At the center of Greektown lies Trapper's Alley, the former fur center of the Midwest that has been transformed into a shopping center comprising numerous 500 year-old buildings enclosed under one roof.

ACT
35 E Grand River Ave
Detroit, MI 48226
Phone: 313-961-4336

Ann Arbor Art Center
117 W Liberty St
Ann Arbor, MI 48104
Phone: 734-994-8004
Fax: 734-994-3610

Ann Arbor Artisans & Farmers' Market
Catherine & 4th Ave 315D
Ann Arbor, MI 48104
www.arborlink.com/artisanmarket
Phone: 734-994-3276

Ann Arbor Civic Ballet
525 E Liberty St
Ann Arbor, MI 48104
Phone: 734-668-8066
Fax: 734-668-8066

Ann Arbor Civic Theatre
2275 Platt Rd
Ann Arbor, MI 48104
www.a2ct.org
Phone: 734-971-2228
Fax: 734-971-2769

Ann Arbor Hands-On Museum
220 E Ann St
Ann Arbor, MI 48104
www.aahom.org
Phone: 734-995-5439
Fax: 734-995-1188

Ann Arbor Ice Cube
2121 Oak Valley Dr
Ann Arbor, MI 48103
www.emich.edu/public/hockey/icecube.html
Phone: 734-213-1600
Fax: 734-213-7614

Ann Arbor Symphony Orchestra
603 E Liberty St Michigan Theater
Ann Arbor, MI 48104
www.wwnet.net/~a2so
Phone: 734-994-4801
Fax: 734-994-3949

Argus Planetarium
601 W Stadium Blvd
Ann Arbor, MI 48103
Phone: 734-994-1771
Fax: 734-994-2198

ArtVentures Art Center
117 W Liberty
Ann Arbor, MI 48104
Phone: 734-994-8004
Fax: 734-994-3610

Automotive Hall of Fame
21400 Oakwood Blvd
Dearborn, MI 48124
www.automotivehalloffame.org
Phone: 313-240-4000
Fax: 313-240-8641
TF: 888-298-4748

Belle Isle Park
E Grand Blvd & Jefferson Ave
Detroit, MI 48207
Phone: 313-852-4083

Belle Isle Zoo & Aquarium
Belle Isle Pk
Detroit, MI 48204
www.ring.com/zoo/belle.htm
Phone: 313-852-4083

Bentley Historical Library
1150 Beal Ave
Ann Arbor, MI 48109
E-mail: bentley.ref@umich.edu
www.umich.edu/~bhl
Phone: 734-764-3482
Fax: 734-936-1333

Bonstelle Theatre
3424 Woodward Ave
Detroit, MI 48202
Phone: 313-577-2960

Charles H Wright Museum of African American History
315 E Warren St
Detroit, MI 48201
www.maah-detroit.org
Phone: 313-494-5800
Fax: 313-494-5855

Chelsea Milling Co
PO Box 460
Chelsea, MI 48118
www.jiffymix.com
Phone: 734-475-1361
Fax: 734-475-4630

Chene Park
2600 E Atwater St
Detroit, MI 48207
Phone: 313-393-0292

Children's Museum
67 E Kirby St
Detroit, MI 48202
Phone: 313-873-8100
Fax: 313-873-3384

Cobblestone Farm Museum
2781 Packard Rd
Ann Arbor, MI 48108
Phone: 734-994-2928
Fax: 734-971-9415

Comic Opera Guild
3211 Packard Rd
Ann Arbor, MI 48108
Phone: 734-973-3264
Fax: 734-973-6281

Cranbrook House & Gardens
380 Lone Pine Rd
Bloomfield Hills, MI 48303
www.cranbrook.edu/museum/house.html
Phone: 248-645-3149
Fax: 248-645-3085

Cranbrook Institute of Science
1221 N Woodward Ave
Bloomfield Hills, MI 48304
Phone: 248-645-3260
Fax: 248-645-3050

Detroit Artists Market
300 River Pl Suite 1650
Detroit, MI 48207
E-mail: detroitartists@juno.com
Phone: 313-393-1770
Fax: 313-393-1772

Detroit Chamber Winds & Strings
755 W Big Beaver Rd Suite 214
Troy, MI 48084
E-mail: chambermusic@juno.com
www.chamberarts.org
Phone: 248-362-9329
Fax: 248-362-2628

Detroit Film Theatre
5200 Woodward Ave Detroit Institute of Arts
Detroit, MI 48202
www.dia.org
Phone: 313-833-2323
Fax: 313-833-9169

Detroit Gallery of Contemporary Crafts
Fisher Bldg Suite 104
Detroit, MI 48202
Phone: 313-873-7888

Detroit Historical Museum
5401 Woodward Ave
Detroit, MI 48202
www.detroithistorical.org
Phone: 313-833-1805
Fax: 313-833-5342

Detroit Institute of Arts
5200 Woodward Ave
Detroit, MI 48202
www.dia.org
Phone: 313-833-7900
Fax: 313-833-2357

Detroit Opera House
1526 Broadway
Detroit, MI 48226
www.motopera.org/doh
Phone: 313-961-3500
Fax: 313-237-3412

Detroit Repertory Theatre
13103 Woodrow Wilson St
Detroit, MI 48238
E-mail: DetRepTh@aol.com
Phone: 313-868-1347
Fax: 313-868-1705

Detroit Science Center
5020 John R St
Detroit, MI 48202
www.sciencedetroit.org
Phone: 313-577-8400
Fax: 313-832-1623

Detroit Symphony Orchestra
3711 Woodward Ave Orchestra Hall
Detroit, MI 48201
www.detnews.com/DSO
Phone: 313-576-5111
Fax: 313-576-5109

Detroit Symphony Orchestra Hall
3711 Woodward Ave
Detroit, MI 48201
E-mail: info@detroitsymphonyorchestra.com
Phone: 313-576-5100
Fax: 313-576-5101

Detroit Zoo
8450 W Ten-Mile Rd
Royal Oak, MI 48067
www.detroitzoo.org
Phone: 248-398-0903
Fax: 248-398-0504

Domino's Farm Petting Zoo
24 Frank Lloyd Wright Dr
Ann Arbor, MI 48106
Phone: 734-930-5032
Fax: 734-930-3012

Dossin Great Lakes Museum
100 Strand Dr Belle Isle
Detroit, MI 48207
www.detroithistorical.org/
Phone: 313-852-4051
Fax: 313-822-4610

Eastern Market
2934 Russell St
Detroit, MI 48207
Phone: 313-833-1560
Fax: 313-833-4831

Eddy Geology Center
16345 McClure Rd
Chelsea, MI 48118
Phone: 734-475-3170
Fax: 734-475-1830

Exhibit Museum of Natural History
1109 Geddes Ave University of Michigan
Ann Arbor, MI 48109
www.exhibits.lsa.umich.edu
Phone: 734-764-0478
Fax: 734-647-2767

Fisher Mansion
383 Lenox Ave
Detroit, MI 48215
Phone: 313-331-6740
Fax: 313-822-3748

Fisher Theatre
3011 W Grand Blvd
Detroit, MI 48202
www.fisherdetroit.com/frame1.html
Phone: 313-872-1000
Fax: 313-872-0632

Ford Edsel & Eleanor House
1100 Lake Shore Rd
Grosse Pointe Shores, MI 48236
E-mail: info@fordhouse.org
www.fordhouse.org
Phone: 313-884-4222
Fax: 313-884-5977

Ford Henry Estate-University of Michigan
4901 Evergreen Rd
Dearborn, MI 48128
www.umd.umich.edu/fairlane
Phone: 313-593-5590
Fax: 313-593-5243

Fox Theatre
2211 Woodward Ave
Detroit, MI 48201
Phone: 313-983-6611
Fax: 313-965-3599

Gallerie 454
15105 Kercheval Ave
Grosse Pointe Park, MI 48230
Phone: 313-822-4454
Fax: 313-822-3768

Gallup Park
3000 Fuller Rd
Ann Arbor, MI 48105
Phone: 734-994-2778

Gem Theater
333 Madison Ave
Detroit, MI 48226
Phone: 313-963-9800
Fax: 313-963-0889

Gerald R Ford Library
1000 Beal Ave
Ann Arbor, MI 48109
E-mail: library@fordlib.nara.gov
www.ford.utexas.edu
Phone: 734-741-2218
Fax: 734-741-2341

Gospel Music Hall of Fame & Museum
18301 W McNichols Rd
Detroit, MI 48219
www.gmhf.org
Phone: 313-592-0017
Fax: 313-592-8762

Graystone International Jazz Museum
1249 Washington Blvd Suite 201
Detroit, MI 48226
Phone: 313-963-3813

Greektown
400 Monroe St
Detroit, MI 48226
Phone: 313-963-3357
Fax: 313-963-2333

Greenfield Village
20900 Oakwood Blvd
Dearborn, MI 48124
www.hfmgv.org
Phone: 313-271-1620
Fax: 313-982-6230

Heidelberg Project
3658 Heidelberg St
Detroit, MI 48202
www.heidelberg.org
Phone: 313-537-8037

Henry Ford Museum
20900 Oakwood Blvd
Dearborn, MI 48124
www.hfmgv.org
Phone: 313-271-1620
Fax: 313-982-6244
TF: 800-835-5238

Herbarium of the University of Michigan
North University Bldg Rm 2001
Ann Arbor, MI 48109
Phone: 734-764-2407

Historic Hack House Museum
775 County St
Milan, MI 48160
Phone: 734-439-7522
Fax: 734-439-7522

Holocaust Memorial Center
6602 W Maple Rd
West Bloomfield, MI 48322
E-mail: info@holocaustcenter.org
holocaustcenter.org
Phone: 248-661-0840
Fax: 248-661-4204

IMAX Dome Theater
5020 John R St
Detroit, MI 48202
www.sciencedetroit.org/imax.html
Phone: 313-577-8400
Fax: 313-832-1623

Institute of African-American Arts
6559 W Grand River Ave
Detroit, MI 48208
Phone: 313-872-0332
Fax: 313-899-1662

International Institute of Metropolitan Detroit
111 E Kirby St
Detroit, MI 48202
Phone: 313-871-8600
Fax: 313-871-1651

Isle Royale National Park
800 East Lakeshore Dr
Houghton, MI 49931
www.nps.gov/isro/
Phone: 906-482-0986
Fax: 906-487-7170

Kelsey Museum of Archaeology
434 S State St University of Michigan
Ann Arbor, MI 48109
www.umich.edu/~kelseydb
Phone: 734-763-3559
Fax: 734-763-8976

Kempf House
312 S Division St
Ann Arbor, MI 48104
Phone: 734-994-4898

Kerrytown Concert House
415 N 4th Ave
Ann Arbor, MI 48104
Phone: 734-769-2999
Fax: 734-769-7791

Leslie Science Center
1831 Traver Rd
Ann Arbor, MI 48105
Phone: 734-662-7802
Fax: 734-997-1072

Lillie Park
Platt Rd
Ann Arbor, MI 48108
Phone: 734-996-3056

Majestic Theatre
4120 Woodward Ave
Detroit, MI 48201
Phone: 313-833-9700
Fax: 313-833-0314

Masonic Temple
500 Temple Ave
Detroit, MI 48201
Phone: 313-832-7100
Fax: 313-832-2922

Masonic Temple Theatre
500 Temple St
Detroit, MI 48201
www.fisherdetroit.com/frame3.html
Phone: 313-832-5900
Fax: 313-832-1047

Matthaei Botanical Gardens
1800 N Dixboro Rd
Ann Arbor, MI 48105
www.lsa.umich.edu/mbg/index.html
Phone: 734-998-7061
Fax: 734-998-6205

Meadow Brook Art Gallery
Oakland University Wilson Hall Rm 208
Rochester, MI 48309
Phone: 248-370-3005
Fax: 248-370-3108

Meadow Brook Hall
Oakland University
Rochester, MI 48309
Phone: 248-370-3140
Fax: 248-370-4260

MGM Grand Detroit Casino
1300 John C Lodge
Detroit, MI 48226
www.mgmgrand.com/detroit
Phone: 313-393-7777
Fax: 313-394-4210
TF: 877-888-2121

Michigan Opera Theatre
1526 Broadway
Detroit, MI 48226
detnews.com/mot
Phone: 313-961-3500
Fax: 313-237-3412

Michigan Sports Hall of Fame
1 Washington Blvd Cobo Conference Ctr
Detroit, MI 48226
Phone: 248-848-0252

Michigan Theater
603 E Liberty
Ann Arbor, MI 48104
www.michtheater.com/mt/
Phone: 734-668-8397
Fax: 734-668-7136

Moross House/Detroit Garden Center
1460 E Jefferson Ave
Detroit, MI 48207
Phone: 313-259-6363
Fax: 313-259-0107

MotorCity Casino
2901 Grand River Ave
Detroit, MI 48201
www.detroitentertainment.com
Phone: 313-237-7711
TF: 877-777-0711

Motown Museum
2648 W Grand Blvd
Detroit, MI 48208
E-mail: motownmus@aol.com
Phone: 313-875-2264
Fax: 313-875-2267

Music Hall Center for the Performing Arts
350 Madison St
Detroit, MI 48226
Phone: 313-963-7622
Fax: 313-963-2462

Nichols Aboretum
1610 Washington Heights University of Michigan
Ann Arbor, MI 48104
www.umich.edu/~snrewww/arb/
Phone: 734-998-9540
Fax: 734-998-9536

Old Mariners' Church
170 E Jefferson Ave
Detroit, MI 48226
Phone: 313-259-2206

Palmer Park
900 Merrill Plaisance
Detroit, MI 48203
Phone: 313-578-7600

Parker Mill County Park
4650 Geddes Rd
Ann Arbor, MI 48105
Phone: 734-971-6337
Fax: 734-971-6386

Pewabic Pottery
10125 E Jefferson Ave
Detroit, MI 48214
www.pewabic.com
Phone: 313-822-0954

Plowshares Theatre Co
2780 E Grand Blvd
Detroit, MI 48201
www.plowshares.org
Phone: 313-872-0279
Fax: 313-872-0067

Power Center for the Performing Arts
Huron & Fletcher
Ann Arbor, MI 48109
Phone: 734-763-3333

Renaissance Center
200 Renaissance Ctr Suite 1200
Detroit, MI 48243
Phone: 313-568-5600
Fax: 313-568-5794

River Rouge Park
22000 Joy Rd
Detroit, MI 48239
Phone: 313-852-4520

Riverside Arts Center
76 N Huron St
Ypsilanti, MI 48197
Phone: 734-480-2787

Saint Aubin Park & Marina
1900 E Atwater St
Detroit, MI 48207
Phone: 313-259-4677

Second City Detroit
2301 Woodward Ave
Detroit, MI 48201
E-mail: SCDet@aol.com
www.secondcity.com
Phone: 313-965-2222
Fax: 313-964-5833

Sharon Mills Winery
5701 Sharon Hollow Rd
Manchester, MI 48158
Phone: 734-428-9160

Spring Valley Trout Farm
12190 Island Lake Rd
Dexter, MI 48130
Phone: 734-426-4772
Fax: 734-426-2238

State Theatre
2115 Woodward Ave
Detroit, MI 48201
Phone: 313-961-5450
Fax: 313-965-6457

Stearn's Collection of Musical Instruments
1100 Baits Dr University of Michigan School of Music
Ann Arbor, MI 48109
Phone: 734-763-4389
Fax: 734-763-5097

Summit Observation Deck
Renaissance Ctr
Detroit, MI 48243
Phone: 313-568-8600

Towsley Margaret Dow Sports Museum
1200 S State St Schembechler Hall
Ann Arbor, MI 48109
Phone: 734-647-2583

University of Michigan Museum of Art
525 S State St
Ann Arbor, MI 48109
www.umich.edu/~umma/
Phone: 734-764-0395
Fax: 734-764-3731

Veterans Memorial Park
2150 Jackson Rd
Ann Arbor, MI 48103
Phone: 734-761-7240
Fax: 734-994-8988

Washtenaw County Park
2230 Platt Rd
Ann Arbor, MI 48107
Phone: 734-971-6337
Fax: 734-971-6386

Waterloo Recreation Area
16345 McClure Rd
Chelsea, MI 48118
Phone: 734-475-8307
Fax: 734-475-1830

Whitcomb Anna Scripps Conservatory
Belle Isle Pk
Detroit, MI 48207
Phone: 313-852-4065
Fax: 313-852-4074

Wild Swan Theater
416 W Huron St
Ann Arbor, MI 48103
E-mail: WildSwanTh@aol.com
comnet.org/wildswan
Phone: 734-995-0530
Fax: 734-668-7292

Yankee Air Museum
Willow Run Airport
Ypsilanti, MI 48197
www.yankeeairmuseum.org
Phone: 734-483-4030

Youtheatre
15600 JL Hudson Dr Suite B
Southfield, MI 48075
Phone: 248-557-4338
Fax: 248-557-4415

Ypsilanti Automotive Heritage Collection
100-112 E Cross St
Ypsilanti, MI 48198
Phone: 734-482-5200
Fax: 734-482-5200

Ypsilanti Historical Museum
220 N Huron St
Ypsilanti, MI 48197
www.hvcn.org/info/libyhma.html
Phone: 734-482-4990
Fax: 734-483-7481

Sports Teams & Facilities

Cobo Arena
301 Civic Center Dr
Detroit, MI 48226
Phone: 313-983-6616
Fax: 313-396-7994

Detroit Compuware Ambassadors (hockey)
14900 Beck Rd Compuware Sports Arena
Plymouth, MI 48170
www.compuwareambassadors.com
Phone: 734-453-6400
Fax: 734-453-3427

Detroit Lions
1200 Featherstone Rd Pontiac Silverdome
Pontiac, MI 48342
www.detroitlions.com
Phone: 248-335-4151
Fax: 248-322-2283

Detroit Pistons
The Palace at Auburn Hills 2 Championship Dr
Auburn Hills, MI 48326
www.nba.com/pistons
Phone: 248-377-0100
Fax: 248-377-4262

Detroit Red Wings
600 Civic Ctr Dr Joe Louis Arena
Detroit, MI 48226
www.detroitredwings.com
Phone: 313-396-7544
Fax: 313-567-0296

Detroit Rockers (soccer)
2 Championship Dr Palace of Auburn Hills
Auburn Hills, MI 48326
E-mail: rockersoc@aol.com
www.detroitrockers.com
Phone: 248-366-6254
Fax: 248-366-5317
TF: 877-519-5425

Detroit Shock (basketball)
2 Championship Dr Palace at Auburn Hills
Auburn Hills, MI 48326
www.wnba.com/shock
Phone: 248-377-0100
Fax: 248-377-3260

Detroit Tigers
2121 Trumbull Ave Tiger Stadium
Detroit, MI 48216
E-mail: tigers@detroittigers.com
www.detroittigers.com
Phone: 313-962-4000
TF: 800-221-2324

Detroit Vipers (hockey)
2 Championship Dr Palace at Auburn Hills
Auburn Hills, MI 48326
E-mail: info@detroitvipers.com
www.detroitvipers.com/
Phone: 248-377-0100
Fax: 248-377-2695

Joe Louis Arena
600 Civic Ctr Dr
Detroit, MI 48226
Phone: 313-396-7444
Fax: 313-396-7994

Michigan International Speedway
US-12
Brooklyn, MI 49230
www.mispeedway.com
Phone: 517-592-6672
Fax: 517-592-3848
TF: 800-354-1010

Michigan Stadium
Main & Stadium University of Michigan
Ann Arbor, MI 48109
Phone: 734-647-2583

Milan International Dragway
10860 Plank Rd
Milan, MI 48160
www.milandragway.com
Phone: 734-439-7368
Fax: 810-939-3366

Palace at Auburn Hills
2 Championship Dr
Auburn Hills, MI 48326
www.palacenet.com
Phone: 248-377-8222
Fax: 248-377-3260

Plymouth Whalers (hockey) Phone: 734-453-8400
14900 Beck Rd Compuware Sports Arena Fax: 734-453-4201
Plymouth, MI 48170
E-mail: hockey@compuworld.com
www.canoe.com/OHLStatsSeason/detroithome.html

Annual Events

African World Festival (mid-August)...............313-494-5800
America's Thanksgiving Day Parade
(late November)...............................313-923-7400
Ann Arbor Antiques Market (April-November) 734-995-7281
Ann Arbor Art Fair Extravaganza (mid-late July)....734-995-7281
Ann Arbor Blues & Jazz Festival
(early September) 734-995-7281
Ann Arbor Film Festival (early March).............734-668-8397
Ann Arbor Folk Music Festival (late January).......734-763-5750
Ann Arbor Spring Art Fair (mid-May)..............734-995-7281
Ann Arbor Summer Festival (late June-mid-July) ...734-647-2278
Ann Arbor Winter Art Fair (late October) 734-995-7281
APBA Gold Cup Thunderfest Races (early July).....313-331-7770
Art & Apples Craft Show (mid-September) 248-651-4110
Art on the Pointe (mid-June) 313-884-4222
Big Ten Run (late September) 734-994-0155
Builders Home & Detroit Flower Show
(late March) 248-737-4477
Christmas Flower Show & Open House
(December-mid-January) 313-852-4064
Detroit Aglow (mid-November)....................313-961-1403
Detroit Autorama (mid-February) 248-650-5560
Detroit Boat Show (early February)................734-261-0123
Detroit Festival of the Arts (mid-September) 313-577-5088
Detroit Riverfront Festivals (May-September).......313-202-1800
Eastern Market Flower Day (mid-May)............313-833-1560
Fall Chrysanthemum Show
(mid-October-late November) 313-852-4064
Fall Harvest Days
(late September-early October)..................313-271-1620
Festival of Trees (mid-late November) 313-745-0178
Ford Fleet Festival (late December) 313-852-4051
Ford House Holiday Tours (November-December)...313-884-4222
Frog Island Festival (late June) 734-761-1800
Greektown Art Fair (mid-May) 734-662-3382
Heritage Festival (mid-August)....................734-327-2051
International Freedom Festival
(late June-early July)..........................313-923-7400
Meadow Brook Music Festival (June-August) 248-377-0100
Mexicantown Mercado
(mid-June-early September) 313-967-9898
Michigan All-Morgan Horse Show (early July) 810-793-4583
Michigan State Fair
(late August-early September)...................313-369-8250
Michigan Tastefest (late June-early July) 313-872-0188
Montreux Detroit Jazz Festival (early September) ...313-963-7622
New Year Jubilee (December 31) 734-483-4444
North American International Auto Show
(mid-January)................................248-643-0250
Old Car Festival (mid-September) 313-271-1620
Original Old World Market (mid-October) 313-871-8600
Plymouth International Ice Sculpture Spectacular
(mid-January)................................734-459-6969
Pow Wow (early-mid-March).....................734-764-9044
Saint Patrick's Day Parade (mid-March) 313-963-5745
Summer Symphony (June-August) 734-677-4831
Tenneco Automotive Grand Prix of Detroit
(early June)..................................313-393-7749
Traditions of the Season
(late November-early January) 313-271-1620
Winter Carnival (mid-February) 734-994-2780
Zoo Boo-The Nighttime Zoo (late October).........248-541-5835

El Paso, Texas

***County:* El Paso**

EL PASO is located along the Rio Grande River in western Texas at the border of Mexico and New Mexico. Major cities within 100 miles include Las Cruces, New Mexico, and Ciudad Juarez, Chihuahua, Mexico.

Area (Land)	254.4 sq mi
Area (Water)	1.5 sq mi
Elevation	3,700 ft
Latitude	31-97-54 N
Longitude	106-60-50 W
Time Zone	MST
Area Code	915

Climate

El Paso has a dry desert climate. Winters are mild, with average high temperatures near 60, although lows can dip below freezing. Snowfall is rare, averaging less than five inches annually. Summer days are hot with high temperatures in the upper 90s, while evening temperatures drop dramatically into the mid- to upper 60s. El Paso has approximately 300 sunny days annually and relatively low humidity. September is the wettest month of the year in El Paso; April is the driest.

Average Temperatures & Precipitation

Temperatures

	Jan	Feb	Mar	Apr	May	Jun	Jul	Aug	Sep	Oct	Nov	Dec
High	56	62	70	79	87	97	96	94	87	78	66	58
Low	29	34	40	48	57	64	68	67	62	50	38	31

Precipitation

	Jan	Feb	Mar	Apr	May	Jun	Jul	Aug	Sep	Oct	Nov	Dec
Inches	0.4	0.4	0.3	0.2	0.3	0.7	1.5	1.6	1.7	0.8	0.4	0.6

History

The El Paso area was originally inhabited by various Native American tribes, including Tigua Indians. In 1598, Spanish conquistador Juan de Onate founded "El Paso del Rio del Norte" ("the pass through the river of the north") along the banks of the Rio Grande as a stopping point for travelers on El Camino Real (the Royal Highway), which ran from Mexico City to Santa Fe. The name of the city was later shortened to "El Paso." The city remained primarily under Spanish rule for the next 252 years, although Mexico, Texas, New Mexico, and the United States fought over control of El Paso throughout those years. In 1848, the city was divided between present-day Ciudad Juarez (El Paso's sister city across the Rio Grande in Mexico) and what was to become El Paso proper. The Chamizal Treaty of 1963 shifted this border, returning 700 acres to Mexico, and the Chamizal National Memorial in El Paso commemorates the settlement of this land dispute between the U.S. and Mexico. In 1850, El Paso officially became part of the state of Texas.

During the latter part of the 1800s, El Paso was a typical "Old West" town—several notorious gunfighters, including John Wesley Hardin, John Selman, and Marshall Dallas Stoudenmire were laid to rest at the city's Concordia Cemetery. El Paso grew quickly during the late 19th Century, due in large part to the opening of Fort Bliss in 1860. Originally established as a U.S. military outpost in 1848, Fort Bliss later became the largest cavalry post in the United States. The military presence of Fort Bliss ensured the nation that El Paso was safe for rail travel, and the Southern Pacific Railroad opened in the city in 1881. The railroad provided a gateway to the United States and to Mexico, thereby enabling El Paso to develop as a major center for international trade.

El Paso today, with more than 615,000 residents, is the fourth largest city in Texas and, with Ciudad Juarez, Mexico, forms the largest international metroplex in the world. Fort Bliss, which was instrumental in the development of the area, is presently the largest air defense center in the western world and one of El Paso's largest employers. One of the nation's fastest growing cities, the population of El Paso is expected to reach three-quarters of a million by the year 2010.

Population

1990 Census	515,342
1998 Estimate	615,032
% Change	19.3
2010 Projection	750,000

Racial/Ethnic Breakdown

White	76.9%
Black	3.4%
Other	19.7%
Hispanic Origin (may be of any race)	69.0%

Age Breakdown

Under 12 years	22.0%
12 to 19	15.0%
20 to 39	33.0%
40 to 59	19.0%
60+ years	11.0%
Median Age	28.7

Gender Breakdown

Male	48.0%
Female	52.0%

Government

Type of Government: Mayor-Council & County Commissioners Court

El Paso City Clerk
2 Civic Center Plaza
El Paso, TX 79901
Phone: 915-541-4127
Fax: 915-541-4306

El Paso City Council
2 Civic Ctr Plaza
El Paso, TX 79901
Phone: 915-541-4145
Fax: 915-541-4501

El Paso City Hall
2 Civic Center Plaza
El Paso, TX 79901
Phone: 915-541-4000
Fax: 915-541-4501

El Paso Community & Human Development Dept
2 Civic Center Plaza 9th Fl
El Paso, TX 79901
Phone: 915-541-4643
Fax: 915-541-4370

El Paso Economic Development Dept
2 Civic Center Plaza
El Paso, TX 79901
Phone: 915-533-4284
Fax: 915-541-1316

El Paso Fire Dept
8600 Montana Ave
El Paso, TX 79925
Phone: 915-771-1000
Fax: 915-771-1023

El Paso Mayor
2 Civic Center Plaza
El Paso, TX 79901
Phone: 915-541-4015
Fax: 915-541-4501

El Paso Parks & Recreation Dept
2 Civic Center Plaza 6th Fl
El Paso, TX 79901
Phone: 915-541-4331
Fax: 915-541-4355

El Paso Personnel Office
2 Civic Center Plaza 3rd Fl
El Paso, TX 79901
Phone: 915-541-4504
Fax: 915-541-4220

El Paso Planning Research & Development Office
2 Civic Center Plaza 8th Fl
El Paso, TX 79901
Phone: 915-541-4024
Fax: 915-541-4028

El Paso Police Dept
911 N Raynor St
El Paso, TX 79903
Phone: 915-564-7332
Fax: 915-564-7320

El Paso Public Library
501 N Oregon St
El Paso, TX 79901
Phone: 915-543-5401
Fax: 915-543-5410

El Paso Public Works Dept
2 Civic Center Plaza 6th Fl
El Paso, TX 79901
Phone: 915-541-4202
Fax: 915-541-4405

El Paso Water Utilities Public Service Board
1154 Hawkins Blvd
El Paso, TX 79925
Phone: 915-594-5500
Fax: 915-594-5699

Important Phone Numbers

AAA.........915-778-9521
American Express Travel.........915-532-8900
Driver's License Information.........915-855-2132
El Paso Tax Office.........915-546-2040
Emergency.........911
Greater El Paso Realtors Assn.........915-779-3521
Highway Conditions.........800-452-9292
Medical Referral.........800-327-9107
Poison Control Center.........800-764-7661
Texas Comptroller of Public Accounts.........512-463-4600
Time/Temp.........915-532-9911
Vehicle Registration Information.........915-546-2140
Voter Registration Information.........915-546-2154
Weather.........915-533-7744

Information Sources

Better Business Bureau Serving the El Paso Area
221 N Kansas St Suite 1101
El Paso, TX 79901
www.elpaso.bbb.org
Phone: 915-577-0191
Fax: 915-577-0209

El Paso Convention & Performing Arts Center
1 Civic Center Plaza
El Paso, TX 79901
Phone: 915-534-0600
Fax: 915-534-0686
TF: 800-351-6024

El Paso Convention & Visitors Bureau
1 Civic Center Plaza
El Paso, TX 79901
www.elpasocvb.com
Phone: 915-534-0696
Fax: 915-534-0687
TF: 800-351-6024

El Paso County
500 E San Antonio Ave
El Paso, TX 79901
www.co.el-paso.tx.us
Phone: 915-546-2000

Greater El Paso Chamber of Commerce
10 Civic Ctr Plaza
El Paso, TX 79901
www.elpaso.org
Phone: 915-534-0500
Fax: 915-534-0513

Online Resources

4ElPaso.com
www.4elpaso.com

Anthill City Guide El Paso
www.anthill.com/city.asp?city=elpaso

Area Guide El Paso
elpaso.areaguides.net

City Knowledge El Paso
www.cityknowledge.com/tx_elpaso.htm

Ciudad Juarez-El Paso
www.mexguide.net/juarez/

DesertUSA Guide to El Paso
www.desertusa.com/Cities/tx/tx_elpaso.html

El Paso Citi-Guide
www.citi-guide.com

El Paso Home Page
www.elpasotx.com/

El Paso Info Page
www.elpasoinfo.com

El Paso Restaurant Guide
www.elpaso-restaurants.com

El Paso Scene Online
www.epscene.com/

El Paso Texas.com
www.elpasotexas.com/

El Paso Webtree
www.webtree.com

Excite.com El Paso City Guide
www.excite.com/travel/countries/united_states/texas/el_paso

GuestLife El Paso
www.guestlife.com/elpaso/

Pass The
www.thepass.net

Road Runner El Paso
www.elp.rr.com/around_town/

Virtual El Paso
www.virtualelpaso.com/

Area Communities

Communities in the El Paso area with populations greater than 3,000 include:

Anthony Phone: 915-886-3944
PO Box 1269 Fax: 915-886-3115
Anthony, TX 79821

Horizon City Phone: 915-852-1046
14999 Darrington Rd Fax: 915-852-1005
Horizon City, TX 79927

Socorro Phone: 915-858-2915
124 S Horizon Blvd Fax: 915-858-9288
Socorro, TX 79927

Economy

El Paso's location on the U.S.-Mexican border has long made the city a major center for international trade, and trade remains the area's largest source of employment. Five of El Paso's top 15 employers represent the government sector—Fort Bliss, the City of El Paso, and the El Paso and Ysleta Independent School Districts each employ more than 5,000 area residents. Manufacturing also plays a major role in El Paso's economy—the city is the largest producer of apparel and sewn products (primarily denim jeans and boots) in the United States. Other products manufactured in El Paso include electrical components, medical equipment, and plastic injection molding. More than 70 Fortune 500 companies have divisions in the El Paso area. North American Philips Corp., located in Ciudad Juarez, Mexico, is also among El Paso's largest employers.

Unemployment Rate 8.3%
Per Capita Income.......................... $16,359*
Median Family Income...................... $34,100*

** Information given is for the El Paso Metropolitan Statistical Area (MSA), which includes the City of El Paso and El Paso County.*

Principal Industries & Number of Wage Earners

El Paso MSA* - June 2000

Construction & Mining................................13,600
Finance, Insurance, & Real Estate........................9,900
Government..55,100
Manufacturing..37,800
Retail Trade...47,400
Services...62,300
Transportation & Public Utilities.......................16,000
Wholesale Trade......................................12,900

** Information given is for the El Paso Metropolitan Statistical Area (MSA), which includes the City of El Paso and El Paso County.*

Major Employers

American Yazaki Corp Phone: 915-778-5373
12 Leigh Fisher Blvd Fax: 915-772-0532
El Paso, TX 79906

El Paso City Hall Phone: 915-541-4000
2 Civic Center Plaza Fax: 915-541-4501
El Paso, TX 79901
www.ci.el-paso.tx.us

El Paso County Phone: 915-546-2000
500 E San Antonio Ave
El Paso, TX 79901
www.co.el-paso.tx.us

El Paso Electric Co Phone: 915-543-5711
PO Box 982 Fax: 915-543-2299
El Paso, TX 79960 TF: 800-351-1621
www.epelectric.com

El Paso Independent School District Phone: 915-779-3781
6531 Boeing Dr Fax: 915-779-4280
El Paso, TX 79925
www.elpaso.k12.tx.us

Fort Bliss Phone: 915-568-2121
Fort Bliss, TX 79916 Fax: 915-568-1777
www.bliss.army.mil

Las Palmas Del Sol Regional Healthcare System Phone: 915-521-1200
1801 N Oregon St Fax: 915-521-1111
El Paso, TX 79902
www.laspalmashealth.com

Levi Strauss & Co Phone: 915-592-3999
11460 Pellicano Dr Fax: 915-593-8738
El Paso, TX 79936
www.levistrauss.com

Savane International Phone: 915-496-7000
PO Box 13800 Fax: 915-496-7338
El Paso, TX 79913
www.savane.com

Sierra Medical Center Phone: 915-747-4000
1625 Medical Center Dr Fax: 915-747-2550
El Paso, TX 79902

University of Texas El Paso Phone: 915-747-5000
500 W University Ave Fax: 915-747-5848
El Paso, TX 79968
www.utep.edu

Ysleta Independent School District
9600 Sims Dr
El Paso, TX 79925
Phone: 915-434-0251
Fax: 915-595-6827

Quality of Living Indicators

Total Crime Index 36,135
(rates per 100,000 inhabitants)

Violent Crime
Murder/manslaughter 14
Forcible rape 185
Robbery 715
Aggravated assault 3,366

Property Crime
Burglary 2,496
Larceny theft 27,052
Motor vehicle theft 2,307

Cost of Living Index 96.2
(national average = 100)

Median Home Price $78,100

Education

Public Schools

El Paso Independent School District
6531 Boeing Dr
El Paso, TX 79925
www.elpaso.k12.tx.us
Phone: 915-779-3781
Fax: 915-779-4280

Number of Schools
Elementary 53
Middle 13
High 12

Student/Teacher Ratio
All Grades 15.7:1

Private Schools

Number of Schools (all grades) .... 26+

Colleges & Universities

El Paso Community College Valle Verde Campus
PO Box 20500
El Paso, TX 79998
E-mail: postmaster@laguna.epcc.edu
www.epcc.edu
Phone: 915-831-2000
Fax: 915-831-2161

New Mexico State University
PO Box 30001 MSC-3A
Las Cruces, NM 88003
E-mail: admissions@nmsu.edu
www.nmsu.edu
Phone: 505-646-3121
Fax: 505-646-6330
TF: 800-662-6678

University of Texas El Paso
500 W University Ave
El Paso, TX 79968
www.utep.edu
Phone: 915-747-5000
Fax: 915-747-5848

Hospitals

Del Sol Medical Center
10301 Gateway W
El Paso, TX 79925
www.delsolmedicalcenter.com
Phone: 915-595-9000
Fax: 915-595-7224

Las Palmas Medical Center
1801 N Oregon St
El Paso, TX 79902
Phone: 915-521-1200
Fax: 915-544-5203

Providence Memorial Hospital
2001 N Oregon St
El Paso, TX 79902
Phone: 915-577-6011
Fax: 915-577-6109

RE Thomason General Hospital
4815 Alameda Ave
El Paso, TX 79905
Phone: 915-544-1200
Fax: 915-521-7612

Sierra Medical Center
1625 Medical Center Dr
El Paso, TX 79902
Phone: 915-747-4000
Fax: 915-747-2550

Transportation

Airport(s)

El Paso International Airport (ELP)
8 miles NE of downtown (approx 15 minutes) 915-772-4271

Mass Transit

Sun Metro
$1 Base fare 915-533-3333

Rail/Bus

El Paso Amtrak Station/Union Depot
700 San Francisco Ave
El Paso, TX 79901
Phone: 915-545-2247

Greyhound/Trailways Bus Station
200 W San Antonio St
El Paso, TX 79901
Phone: 915-532-2365
TF: 800-231-2222

Utilities

Electricity
El Paso Electric Co. 915-543-5970
www.epelectric.com

Gas
Southern Union Gas Co. 915-544-6300
www.southernunionco.com

Water
El Paso Water Utilities Public Service Board 915-594-5500
www.epwu.org

Garbage Collection/Recycling
El Paso Sanitation Dept 915-852-1005

Telecommunications

Telephone
Southwestern Bell 800-231-1997
www.swbell.com

Cable Television
Paragon Cable 915-772-4422

Internet Service Providers (ISPs)
Digital Zone The 915-751-0131
www.dzn.com

Banks

Bank of America Phone: 915-577-2415
416 N Stanton St Fax: 915-577-2020
El Paso, TX 79901

Bank of the West Phone: 915-532-1000
500 N Mesa St Fax: 915-747-1025
El Paso, TX 79901

Chase Bank of Texas NA Phone: 915-546-6500
201 E Main Dr
El Paso, TX 79901

Norwest Bank El Paso NA Phone: 915-532-9922
221 N Kansas St Fax: 915-546-4806
El Paso, TX 79901

State National Bank Phone: 915-485-9200
601 N Mesa Fax: 915-532-6735
El Paso, TX 79901
www.statenationalbank.com

Shopping

Bassett Center Phone: 915-772-7479
6101 Gateway Blvd W Suite M36 Fax: 915-778-9603
El Paso, TX 79925

Cielo Vista Mall Phone: 915-779-7070
8401 Gateway Blvd W Fax: 915-772-4926
El Paso, TX 79925

Sunland Park Mall Phone: 915-833-5595
750 Sunland Park Dr Fax: 915-584-0040
El Paso, TX 79912

Trevino Mall Phone: 915-591-0333
1323 Lee Trevino Dr
El Paso, TX 79936

Media

Newspapers and Magazines

El Paso Times* Phone: 915-546-6100
300 N Campbell St Times Plaza Fax: 915-546-6415
El Paso, TX 79901 TF: 800-351-6007
E-mail: elpasonews@elpasotimes.com
www.elpasotimes.com

**Indicates major daily newspapers*

Television

KCOS-TV Ch 13 (PBS) Phone: 915-747-6500
Education Bldg Rm 105 Fax: 915-747-6605
El Paso, TX 79902
www.kcostv.org

KDBC-TV Ch 4 (CBS) Phone: 915-532-6551
2201 Wyoming Ave Fax: 915-544-2591
El Paso, TX 79903
www.kdbc.com

KFOX-TV Ch 14 (Fox) Phone: 915-833-8585
6004 N Mesa Fax: 915-833-8717
El Paso, TX 79912
E-mail: fox14@whc.net

KINT-TV Ch 26 (Uni) Phone: 915-581-1126
5426 N Mesa Fax: 915-581-1393
El Paso, TX 79912
E-mail: feedback@kint.com
www.kint.com

KKWB-TV Ch 65 (WB) Phone: 915-532-6565
801 N Oregon St Fax: 915-532-6841
El Paso, TX 79902
www.kkwb.com

KMAZ-TV Ch 48 (Tele) Phone: 915-591-9595
10033 Carnegie Fax: 915-591-9896
El Paso, TX 79925

KTSM-TV Ch 9 (NBC) Phone: 915-532-5421
801 N Oregon St Fax: 915-544-0536
El Paso, TX 79902
E-mail: ktsmtv@whc.net
www.ktsm.com

KVIA-TV Ch 7 (ABC) Phone: 915-496-7777
4140 Rio Bravo St Fax: 915-532-0505
El Paso, TX 79902
E-mail: feedback@kvia.com
www.kvia.com

Radio

KAMA-AM 750 kHz (Span) Phone: 915-544-9797
2211 E Missouri Ave Suite S-300 Fax: 915-544-1247
El Paso, TX 79903

KAMZ-FM 93.1 MHz (AC) Phone: 915-544-7600
4150 Pinnacle St Suite 120 Fax: 915-532-0947
El Paso, TX 79902

KATH-FM 94.7 MHz (Ctry) Phone: 915-533-2400
5426 N Mesa Fax: 915-532-4970
El Paso, TX 79912
E-mail: cats@whc.net
www.catcountry947.com

KELP-AM 1590 kHz (Rel) Phone: 915-779-0016
6900 Commerce St Fax: 915-779-6641
El Paso, TX 79915
E-mail: info@kelpradio.com
www.kelpradio.com

KHEY-AM 690 kHz (Ctry) Phone: 915-566-9301
2419 N Piedras St Fax: 915-566-0928
El Paso, TX 79930
www.khey.com/khey_am/sportstic.html

KHEY-FM 96.3 MHz (Ctry) Phone: 915-566-9301
2419 N Piedras St Fax: 915-566-0928
El Paso, TX 79930
E-mail: y96@khey.com
www.khey.com/fm.html

KLAQ-FM 95.5 MHz (Rock) Phone: 915-544-8864
4150 Pinnacle St Suite 120 Fax: 915-544-9536
El Paso, TX 79902
E-mail: magic@klaq.com
www.klaq.com

KOFX-FM 92.3 MHz (Oldies)
5426 N Mesa
El Paso, TX 79912
Phone: 915-533-2400
Fax: 915-532-4970

KPRR-FM 102.1 MHz (CHR)
2419 N Piedras St
El Paso, TX 79930
www.kprr.com
Phone: 915-566-9301
Fax: 915-566-0928

KROD-AM 600 kHz (N/T)
4150 Pinnacle St Suite 120
El Paso, TX 79902
E-mail: infokrod@krod.com
www.krod.com
Phone: 915-544-8864
Fax: 915-544-9536

KTEP-FM 88.5 MHz (NPR)
500 W University Ave Cotton Memorial Bldg Rm 203
El Paso, TX 79968
E-mail: ktep@utep.edu
www.ktep.org
Phone: 915-747-5152
Fax: 915-747-5641

KTSM-AM 1380 kHz (N/T)
801 N Oregon St
El Paso, TX 79902
Phone: 915-532-5421
Fax: 915-544-5658

KTSM-FM 99.9 MHz (AC)
801 N Oregon St
El Paso, TX 79902
www.ktsmradio.com
Phone: 915-880-9909
Fax: 915-544-5658

Attractions

Several historic El Paso landmarks lie along El Camino Real, the oldest road in the United States, including the San Elizario Presidio, the Socorro Mission, and the Ysleta Mission, which is the oldest mission in Texas. El Paso also features the only Indian Reservation located in an urban area in the United States, the Tigua Indian Reservation. El Paso's Border Jumper Trolley makes hourly daytime trips into Ciudad Juarez, where visitors can enjoy bullfights, bargain shopping at enormous mercados, dining at fine restaurants, and sightseeing.

Americana Museum
5 Civic Center Plaza
El Paso, TX 79901
Phone: 915-542-0394

Amistad National Recreation Area
HCR 3 Box 5J
Del Rio, TX 78840
www.nps.gov/amis/
Phone: 830-775-7491
Fax: 830-775-7299

Ascarate Park
6900 Delta Dr
El Paso, TX 79905
Phone: 915-772-5605

Big Bend National Park
PO Box 129
Big Bend National Park, TX 79834
www.nps.gov/bibe/
Phone: 915-477-2251
Fax: 915-477-2357

Border Jumper Trolley
1 Civic Center Plaza
El Paso, TX 79901
www.borderjumper.com
Phone: 915-544-0062
Fax: 915-544-0002
TF: 800-259-6284

Chamizal National Memorial
800 S San Marcial St
El Paso, TX 79905
www.nps.gov/cham
Phone: 915-534-6668
Fax: 915-532-7240

El Paso Centennial Museum
University & Wiggins University of Texas
El Paso, TX 79968
E-mail: museum@mail.utep.edu
www.utep.edu/museum
Phone: 915-747-5565
Fax: 915-747-5411

El Paso Holocaust Museum & Study Center
401 Wallenberg Dr
El Paso, TX 79912
www.huntel.com/~ht2/holocst.html
Phone: 915-833-5656
Fax: 915-833-9523

El Paso Museum of Art
1 Art Festival Plaza
El Paso, TX 79901
Phone: 915-532-1707
Fax: 915-532-1010

El Paso Museum of History
12901 Gateway Blvd W
El Paso, TX 79927
Phone: 915-858-1928
Fax: 915-858-4591

El Paso Pro-Musica
6557 N Mesa St
El Paso, TX 79913
cs.utep.edu/elpaso/promusica.html
Phone: 915-833-9400
Fax: 915-833-9425

El Paso Symphony Orchestra
PO Box 180
El Paso, TX 79942
www.epso.org
Phone: 915-532-3776
Fax: 915-533-8162

El Paso Zoo
4001 E Paisano St
El Paso, TX 79905
www.elpasozoo.org
Phone: 915-544-1928

Fort Bliss Air Defense/Artillery Museum
Pleasanton Rd Fort Bliss Bldg 5000
El Paso, TX 79916
Phone: 915-568-5412
Fax: 915-568-6941

Fort Davis National Historic Site
PO Box 1456
Fort Davis, TX 79734
www.nps.gov/foda/
Phone: 915-426-3224
Fax: 915-426-3122

Franklin Mountain State Park
Transmountain Rd
El Paso, TX
Phone: 915-566-6441
Fax: 915-566-1849

Guadalupe Mountains National Park
HC 60 Box 400
Salt Flat, TX 79847
www.nps.gov/gumo/
Phone: 915-828-3251
Fax: 915-828-3269

Historic Mission Trail
Socorro Rd
El Paso, TX 79907
www.missiontrail.com
Phone: 915-534-0677

Hueco Tanks State Historical Park
6900 Hueco Tanks Rd #1
El Paso, TX 79936
www.tpwd.state.tx.us/park/hueco/hueco.htm
Phone: 915-857-1135
Fax: 915-857-3628

Indian Cliffs Ranch
I-10 & Fabens Exit
Fabens, TX 79838
Phone: 915-544-3200

Insights Science Museum
505 N Santa Fe St
El Paso, TX 79901
E-mail: insights@dzn.com
nasa.utep.edu/insights
Phone: 915-542-2990
Fax: 915-532-7416

Magoffin Homestead
1120 Magoffin Ave
El Paso, TX 79901
Phone: 915-533-5147
Fax: 915-544-4398

McKelligon Canyon
3 McKelligon Rd
El Paso, TX 79930
Phone: 915-565-6900
Fax: 915-565-6999

Rio Grande Wild & Scenic River
PO Box 129
Big Bend National Park, TX 79834
www.nps.gov/rigr
Phone: 915-477-2251
Fax: 915-477-1175

San Elizario Presidio of El Paso
1556 San Elizario Rd
El Paso, TX 79849
Phone: 915-851-2333

Skyline Park
5050 Yvette Ave
El Paso, TX 79924
Phone: 915-541-4331

Socorro Mission
328 S Nevarez St
El Paso, TX 79927
Phone: 915-859-7718

Speaking Rock Casino & Entertainment Center
122 S Old Pueblo Rd
El Paso, TX 79907
Phone: 915-860-7777
Fax: 915-860-7745

Tigua Indian Reservation
119 S Old Pueblo Rd
El Paso, TX 79907
Phone: 915-859-7913
Fax: 915-859-2988

US Border Patrol National Museum
4315 Transmountain Rd
El Paso, TX 79924
www.borderpatrolmuseum.org
Phone: 915-759-6060
Fax: 915-759-0992

Western Playland Amusement Park
6900 Delta St
El Paso, TX 79905
www.westernplayland.com
Phone: 915-772-3953
Fax: 915-778-9821

Wet 'N' Wild Waterworld
8804 S Desert Blvd
Anthony, TX 79821
E-mail: wetwild@wetwild.com
www.wetwild.com
Phone: 915-886-2222
Fax: 915-886-2341

Wilderness Park Museum
4301 Trans Mountain Rd
El Paso, TX 79924
Phone: 915-755-4332
Fax: 915-759-6824

Ysleta Mission
131 S Zaragosa Rd
El Paso, TX 79907
Phone: 915-859-9848
Fax: 915-860-9340

Sports Teams & Facilities

El Paso Buzzards (hockey)
4100 E Paisano Dr El Paso County Coliseum
El Paso, TX 79905
www.buzzards.com
Phone: 915-581-6666
Fax: 915-581-6650

El Paso Diablos (baseball)
9700 Gateway Blvd N Cohen Stadium
El Paso, TX 79924
www.diablos.com
Phone: 915-755-2000
Fax: 915-757-0671

El Paso Patriots (soccer)
6941 Industrial Ave
El Paso, TX 79915
E-mail: Info@patriout.usisl.com
www.elpaso-patriots.com
Phone: 915-771-6620
Fax: 915-778-8802

El Paso Speedway Park
14900 Montana Ave
El Paso, TX 79938
www.elpasospeedwaypark.com
Phone: 915-591-0966
Fax: 915-594-8687

Juarez Mexico Race Track
240 Thundergbird Dr Suite C
El Paso, TX 79912
Phone: 915-775-0555

Sun Bowl Stadium
2800 Sun Bowl Dr
El Paso, TX 79902
Phone: 915-747-5000
Fax: 915-747-5162

Sunland Park Race Track
1200 Futurity Dr
Sunland Park, NM 88063
E-mail: lucky@nmracing.com
www.nmracing.com/sunland.htm
Phone: 505-589-1131
Fax: 505-589-1518

Annual Events

A Christmas Fair (early November) 915-584-3511
Amigo Airsho (mid-October) 915-545-2865
Border Folk Festival (mid-October) 915-532-7273
El Paso Chamber Music Festival (mid-late January) 915-833-9400
Fiesta de las Flores (early September) 915-542-3464
First Thanksgiving Festival (late April) 915-534-0677
International Balloon Festival (late May) 915-886-2222
International Mariachi Festival (mid-September) 915-566-4066
Kermezaar Arts & Crafts Show (mid-October) 915-596-8337
Shakespeare on the Rocks Festival (early September-early October) 915-565-6900
Siglo de Oro Drama Festival (early-mid-March) 915-532-7273
Southwestern International Livestock Show & Rodeo (early-mid-February) 915-534-4229
Spring Square Dancing Festival (mid-March) 915-857-0232
Sun Carnival Football Classic (late December) 915-533-4416
Tour of Lights (mid-late December) 915-544-0062
Viva El Paso! (early June-late August) 915-565-6900

Eugene, Oregon

***County:* Lane**

EUGENE is located in the Willamette River Valley in western Oregon. Major cities within 100 miles include Salem and Portland, Oregon.

Area (Land) .... 38.0 sq mi
Area (Water).......... 0.0 sq mi
Elevation.......... 419 ft
Latitude .... 44-06-53 N
Longitude.......... 123-15-97 W
Time Zone .... PST
Area Code.......... 541

Climate

Eugene has a moderate climate featuring cool winters and warm summers. Winter daytime high temperatures average in the upper 40s to low 50s, with evening lows in the mid-30s. The average annual snowfall in the Eugene area is just over 47 inches. Summer days are warm, with average highs near 80 degrees, while evenings cool down into the low 50s. Summer is also the driest time of year in Eugene.

Average Temperatures & Precipitation

Temperatures

	Jan	Feb	Mar	Apr	May	Jun	Jul	Aug	Sep	Oct	Nov	Dec
High	46	51	56	61	57	74	82	82	76	65	52	46
Low	35	37	39	44	45	50	53	53	49	44	40	36

Precipitation

	Jan	Feb	Mar	Apr	May	Jun	Jul	Aug	Sep	Oct	Nov	Dec
Inches	7.9	5.6	5.5	3.1	2.2	1.4	0.5	1.1	1.7	3.4	8.3	8.6

History

Originally inhabited by the Kalapuya Indians, the first settlement in the area known today as Eugene was established in the late 1840s by Eugene Franklin Skinner. His cabin served initially as a trading post and in 1850 was authorized as a U.S. post office. With the help of Judge David Risdon, Skinner platted a new community called "Eugene City" in 1852. Later that year a flood devastated the area and a new site for Eugene City was chosen on higher ground, where early settlers harnessed the power of the nearby Willamette River and established a flour mill, a woolen mill, and sawmills.

Eugene City was incorporated in 1862, and in 1864, the same year the first telegraph lines reached the city, its name was changed to Eugene. The arrival of the Oregon-California Railway (now known as Southern Pacific) in 1871 helped to further fuel the city's growth and development. Because of its location in the fertile Willamette River Valley, Eugene prospered as a lumbering and agricultural center. To this day, Eugene is often referred to as the "lumber and wood products capital of the world." The University of Oregon was founded in Eugene in 1872, and more than a century later the university remains vital to the city's livelihood as one of the area's top employers.

The seat of Lane County, Eugene is now Oregon's second largest city, with a population of more than 128,000.

Population

1990 Census 112,733
1998 Estimate.......... 128,240
% Change 13.8
2005 Projection 352,000*

Racial/Ethnic Breakdown

White.......... 93.4%
Black 1.3%
Other.......... 5.3%
Hispanic Origin (may be of any race) 2.7%

Age Breakdown

Under 5 years.......... 6.0%
5 to 17.......... 15.3%
18 to 20.......... 7.8%
21 to 24.......... 9.1%
25 to 34.......... 16.4%
35 to 44.......... 17.3%
45 to 54.......... 9.0%
55 to 64.......... 6.5%
65 to 74.......... 6.9%
75+ years 5.8%
Median Age.......... 32.2

Gender Breakdown

Male.......... 48.1%
Female.......... 51.9%

** Information given is for Lane County*

Government

Type of Government: Council-Manager

Eugene City Attorney
101 E Broadway Suite 400
Eugene, OR 97401
Phone: 541-682-5080
Fax: 541-686-6564

Eugene City Council
777 Pearl St Suite 105
Eugene, OR 97401
Phone: 541-682-5010
Fax: 541-682-5414

Eugene City Hall
777 Pearl St
Eugene, OR 97401
Phone: 541-682-5010
Fax: 541-682-5414

Eugene City Manager
777 Pearl St Rm 105
Eugene, OR 97401
Phone: 541-682-5010
Fax: 541-682-5414

Eugene Financial Management Div
860 W Park St Suite 300
Eugene, OR 97401
Phone: 541-682-5022
Fax: 541-682-5802

Eugene Fire & EMS Dept
1705 W 2nd Ave
Eugene, OR 97402
Phone: 541-682-7100
Fax: 541-682-7116

Eugene Human Resource & Risk Services Dept
777 Pearl St Rm 101
Eugene, OR 97401
Phone: 541-682-5061
Fax: 541-682-6831

Eugene Mayor
777 Pearl St Rm 105
Eugene, OR 97401
Phone: 541-682-5010
Fax: 541-682-5414

Eugene Planning & Development Dept
99 W 10th Ave Rm 240
Eugene, OR 97401
Phone: 541-682-5443
Fax: 541-682-5593

Eugene Police Dept
777 Pearl St Rm 107
Eugene, OR 97401
Phone: 541-682-5111
Fax: 541-683-6804

Eugene Public Library
100 W 13th Ave
Eugene, OR 97401
Phone: 541-682-5450
Fax: 541-682-5898

Eugene Public Works Dept
858 Pearl St
Eugene, OR 97401
Phone: 541-682-5262
Fax: 541-682-6826

Eugene Recreation Services Div
99 W 10th St Suite 340
Eugene, OR 97401
Phone: 541-682-5333
Fax: 541-682-6834

Important Phone Numbers

AAA 541-484-0661
American Express Travel 503-484-1325
Dental Referral 541-686-1175
Driver's License/Vehicle Registration Information 541-686-7855
Emergency 911
Eugene Assn of Realtors 541-484-3043
Lane County Dept of Assessment & Taxation 541-682-4314
Medical Referral 541-868-1356
Oregon Dept of Revenue 503-378-4988
Poison Control Center 503-494-8968
Voter Registration Information 541-682-4234
Weather 541-484-1200

Information Sources

Better Business Bureau Serving Oregon & Western Washington
333 SW 5th Ave Suite 300
Portland, OR 97204
www.portland.bbb.org
Phone: 503-226-3981
Fax: 503-226-8200

Convention & Visitors Assn of Lane County Oregon
PO Box 10286
Eugene, OR 97440
www.cvalco.org
Phone: 541-484-5307
Fax: 541-343-6335
TF: 800-547-5445

Eugene Chamber of Commerce
PO Box 1107
Eugene, OR 97440
www.eugene-commerce.com
Phone: 541-484-1314
Fax: 541-484-4942

Eugene Planning & Development Dept
99 W 10th Ave Rm 240
Eugene, OR 97401
www.ci.eugene.or.us/PDD/PDDhome.htm
Phone: 541-682-5443
Fax: 541-682-5593

Eugene/Springfield Metropolitan Partnership Inc
1401 Willamette St 2nd Fl
Eugene, OR 97401
www.esmp.com
Phone: 541-686-2741
Fax: 541-686-2325

Lane County
125 E 8th Ave
Eugene, OR 97401
www.co.lane.or.us/
Phone: 541-682-4203
Fax: 541-682-3803

Lane County Fair & Convention Center
796 W 13th Ave
Eugene, OR 97402
www.atthefair.com
Phone: 541-682-4292
Fax: 541-682-3614

Online Resources

About.com Guide to Eugene
eugene.about.com/citiestowns/pacnwus/eugene

Anthill City Guide Eugene
www.anthill.com/city.asp?city=eugene

Area Guide Eugene
eugene.areaguides.net

City Knowledge Eugene
www.cityknowledge.com/or_eugene.htm

Eugene Free Community Network
www.efn.org/

Eugene Oregon Pages
www.efn.org/~sgazette/eugenehome.html

Eugene Weekly
www.eugeneweekly.com

Eugene.com
www.eugene.com

Excite.com Eugene City Guide
www.excite.com/travel/countries/united_states/oregon/eugene

Lodging.com Eugene Oregon
www.lodging.com/auto/guides/eugene-area-or.html

Planet Eugene Web Guide
www.planeteugene.com

WWWelcome to Eugene Oregon
www.el.com/To/Eugene

Area Communities

Communities in Lane County with populations greater than 5,000 include:

Cottage Grove
400 Main St
Cottage Grove, OR 97424
Phone: 541-942-3346
Fax: 541-942-1267

Creswell
PO Box 276
Creswell, OR 97426
Phone: 541-895-2531
Fax: 541-895-3647

Florence
PO Box 340
Florence, OR 97439
Phone: 541-997-3436
Fax: 541-997-6814

Junction City
PO Box 250
Junction City, OR 97448
Phone: 541-998-2153
Fax: 541-998-3140

Springfield
225 5th St
Springfield, OR 97477
Phone: 541-726-3700
Fax: 541-726-2363

Economy

Long regarded as a major lumbering center, Lane County's economic base has diversified significantly in recent years. Although the timber and wood products industry continues to play an important role in Eugene's economy, high-tech industries are currently experiencing the area's fastest job growth. Services is currently the largest employment sector in the Eugene/Springfield area, followed by retail trade and government. The U.S. Government is Lane County's largest employer, providing jobs for more than 3,600 residents in various agencies. The State of Oregon also ranks among the county's top ten employers, employing more than 1,300 people in Lane County.

Unemployment Rate 5.0%*
Per Capita Income $24,151*
Median Family Income $34,153

** Information given is for Lane County.*

Principal Industries & Number of Wage Earners

Eugene-Springfield MSA (Lane County) - May 2000

Industry	Wage Earners
Construction	7,000
Finance, Insurance, & Real Estate	7,300
Government	27,700
Manufacturing	23,300
Mining	200
Retail Trade	28,800
Services	38,900
Transportation, Communications, & Utilities	4,200
Wholesale Trade	6,800

Major Employers

Country Coach Inc
135 E 1st St
Junction City, OR 97448
www.countrycoach.com
Phone: 541-998-3720
Fax: 541-998-6291

Eugene City Hall
777 Pearl St
Eugene, OR 97401
E-mail: webweaver@ci.eugene.or.us
www.ci.eugene.or.us
Phone: 541-682-5010
Fax: 541-682-5414

Eugene School District #4J
200 N Monroe St
Eugene, OR 97402
schools.4j.lane.edu
Phone: 541-687-3123
Fax: 541-687-3692

HMT Technology Corp
3490 W 3rd Ave
Eugene, OR 97402
www.hmtt.com
Phone: 541-683-2355
Fax: 541-342-1757

Hyundai Semiconductor America
1830 Willow Creek Cir
Eugene, OR 97402
www.hsaeugene.com
Phone: 541-338-5000
Fax: 541-338-5200

Lane Community College
4000 E 30th Ave
Eugene, OR 97405
E-mail: lccpurch@class.org
lanecc.edu
Phone: 541-747-4501
Fax: 541-744-3995

Lane County
125 E 8th Ave
Eugene, OR 97401
www.co.lane.or.us/
Phone: 541-682-4203
Fax: 541-682-3803

McKenzie-Willamette Hospital
1460 G St
Springfield, OR 97477
www.mckweb.com
Phone: 541-726-4400
Fax: 541-726-4540

Peace Health Medical Group
1162 Willamette St
Eugene, OR 97401
Phone: 541-687-6000
Fax: 541-687-6050

Sacred Heart Medical Center
1255 Hilyard St
Eugene, OR 97401
www.peacehealth.org/Community/owv/WhoWeAreSHMC.htm
Phone: 541-686-7300
Fax: 541-686-3697
TF: 800-288-7444

Springfield School District #19
525 Mill St
Springfield, OR 97477
www.sps.lane.edu
Phone: 541-747-3331
Fax: 541-726-3315

University of Oregon
1585 E 13th Ave
Eugene, OR 97403
E-mail: uoadmit@oregon.uoregon.edu
www.uoregon.edu
Phone: 541-346-1000
Fax: 541-346-2548

Weyerhaeuser Co
PO Box 275
Springfield, OR 97477
www.weyerhaeuser.com
Phone: 541-746-2511
Fax: 541-741-5302

Quality of Living Indicators

Total Crime Index 10,222
(rates per 100,000 inhabitants)

Violent Crime

Murder/manslaughter	2
Forcible rape	48
Robbery	189
Aggravated assault	411

Property Crime
Burglary 1,775
Larceny theft 7,145
Motor vehicle theft 652

Cost of Living Index 97.0
(national average = 100)

Median Home Price $129,500

Education

Public Schools

Eugene School District #4J
200 N Monroe St
Eugene, OR 97402
schools.4j.lane.edu
Phone: 541-687-3123
Fax: 541-687-3692

Number of Schools
Elementary 32
Middle 8
High 5

Student/Teacher Ratio
All Grades 19.0:1

Private Schools

Number of Schools (all grades) 20

Colleges & Universities

Eugene Bible College
2155 Bailey Hill Rd
Eugene, OR 97405
www.ebc.edu
Phone: 541-485-1780
Fax: 541-343-5801

Gutenberg College
1883 University St
Eugene, OR 97403
E-mail: gutenberg@mckenziestudycenter.org
www.mckenziestudycenter.org/guten
Phone: 541-683-5141
Fax: 541-683-6997

Lane Community College
4000 E 30th Ave
Eugene, OR 97405
E-mail: lccpurch@class.org
lanecc.edu
Phone: 541-747-4501
Fax: 541-744-3995

Northwest Christian College
828 E 11th Ave
Eugene, OR 97401
Phone: 541-343-1641
Fax: 541-684-7323

University of Oregon
1585 E 13th Ave
Eugene, OR 97403
E-mail: uoadmit@oregon.uoregon.edu
www.uoregon.edu
Phone: 541-346-1000
Fax: 541-346-2548

Hospitals

McKenzie-Willamette Hospital
1460 G St
Springfield, OR 97477
www.mckweb.com
Phone: 541-726-4400
Fax: 541-726-4540

Peace Health Medical Group
1162 Willamette St
Eugene, OR 97401
Phone: 541-687-6000
Fax: 541-687-6050

Sacred Heart Medical Center
1255 Hilyard St
Eugene, OR 97401
www.peacehealth.org/Community/owv/WhoWeAreSHMC.htm
Phone: 541-686-7300
Fax: 541-686-3697
TF: 800-288-7444

Transportation

Airport(s)

Eugene Airport (EUG)
8 miles NW of downtown
(approx 15-20 minutes) 541-682-5430

Mass Transit

Lane Transit District
$1 Base fare 541-687-5555

Rail/Bus

Eugene Amtrak Station
433 Willamette St
Eugene, OR 97401
Phone: 541-687-0972
TF: 800-872-7245

Greyhound Bus Station
987 Pearl St
Eugene, OR 97401
Phone: 541-344-6265
TF: 800-231-2222

Utilities

Electricity
Eugene Water & Electric Board 541-484-6016
www.eweb.org

Gas
Northwest Natural Gas Co. 541-342-3661
www.nwnatural.com

Water
Eugene Water & Electric Board 541-484-6016
www.eweb.org

Garbage Collection/Recycling
ASW Disposal 541-485-4474
Countryside Disposal 541-687-1259
Lane Garbage Service 541-998-8072
Royal Refuse Service 541-688-5622
Sanipac 541-747-2121

Telecommunications

Telephone
Qwest 800-244-1111
www.qwest.com

Cable Television
AT & T Cable Services 541-484-3000
www.cable.att.com

Internet Service Providers (ISPs)
Bauer Communications 541-689-0893
www.bauercom.net
ClipperNet Corp 541-265-2051
www.clipper.net
Eugene Free-Net 541-484-9637
www.efn.org

Pond The 541-302-1295
www.pond.net
Willamette.Net LLC 541-465-3282
www.willamette.net

Banks

Centennial Bank Phone: 541-342-3969
675 Oak St Fax: 541-342-8126
Eugene, OR 97401

LibertyBank Phone: 541-681-4800
355 Goodpasture Island Rd Suite 200 Fax: 541-683-4261
Eugene, OR 97401

Pacific Continental Bank Phone: 541-686-8685
111 W 7th Ave Fax: 541-344-2843
Eugene, OR 97401

Wells Fargo Bank Phone: 541-465-5623
99 E Broadway Fax: 541-484-1755
Eugene, OR 97401 TF: 800-869-3557
www.wellsfargo.com

Shopping

Downtown Eugene Phone: 541-343-1117
betw 6th & 11th Sts & Charlton & High Sts
Eugene, OR 97401

Fifth Street Public Market Phone: 541-484-0383
296 E 5th St Fax: 541-686-1220
Eugene, OR 97401

Gateway Mall Phone: 541-747-6294
3000 Gateway St Fax: 541-747-5897
Springfield, OR 97477

Old Town Florence Phone: 541-997-3128
Bay St
Florence, OR 97439

Round Tu-it Gift Shop Phone: 541-942-9023
945 Gateway Blvd
Cottage Grove, OR 97424

Valley River Center Phone: 541-683-5513
Valley River Dr & Valley River Way Fax: 541-343-2478
Eugene, OR 97401

Media

Newspapers and Magazines

Register-Guard* Phone: 541-485-1234
3500 Chad Dr Fax: 541-683-7631
Eugene, OR 97408
www.registerguard.com

**Indicates major daily newspapers*

Television

KEVU-TV Ch 25 (UPN) Phone: 541-683-2525
2940 Chad Dr Fax: 541-683-8016
Eugene, OR 97408

KEZI-TV Ch 9 (ABC) Phone: 541-485-5611
PO Box 7009 Fax: 541-342-1568
Eugene, OR 97401
E-mail: kezi@efn.org
www.kezi.com

KLSR-TV Ch 34 (Fox) Phone: 541-683-2525
2940 Chad Dr Fax: 541-683-8016
Eugene, OR 97408

KMTR-TV Ch 16 (NBC) Phone: 541-746-1600
3825 International Ct Fax: 541-747-3429
Springfield, OR 97477
E-mail: info@nbc16.com
www.nbc16.com

KOPB-TV Ch 10 (PBS) Phone: 503-244-9900
7140 SW Macadam Ave Fax: 503-293-1919
Portland, OR 97219
E-mail: kopb@opb.org
www.opb.org/

KTVC-TV Ch 36 (PAX) Phone: 541-345-2119
4570 W 11th Ave Fax: 541-345-9376
Eugene, OR 97402
www.pax.net/KTVC

KVAL-TV Ch 13 (CBS) Phone: 541-342-4961
PO Box 1313 Fax: 541-342-2635
Eugene, OR 97440
E-mail: kval@rio.com
www.kval.com

Radio

KDUK-FM 104.7 MHz (CHR) Phone: 541-485-1120
1345 Olive St Fax: 541-484-5769
Eugene, OR 97401
www.kduk.com

KKNU-FM 93.1 MHz (Ctry) Phone: 541-686-9123
925 Country Club Rd Suite 200 Fax: 541-344-9424
Eugene, OR 97401
E-mail: salesmrb@kknu.com
www.kknu.com

KKXO-AM 1450 kHz (Nost) Phone: 541-484-9400
925 Country Club Rd Suite 200 Fax: 541-344-9424
Eugene, OR 97401

KMGE-FM 94.5 MHz (AC) Phone: 541-484-9400
925 Country Club Rd Suite 200 Fax: 541-344-9424
Eugene, OR 97401
www.kmge.com

KODZ-FM 99.1 MHz (Oldies) Phone: 541-485-1120
1345 Olive St Fax: 541-484-5769
Eugene, OR 97401

KPNW-AM 1120 kHz (N/T) Phone: 541-485-1120
1345 Olive St Fax: 541-484-5769
Eugene, OR 97401

KZEL-FM 96.1 MHz (CR) Phone: 541-342-7096
2100 W 11th Ave Suite 200 Fax: 541-484-6397
Eugene, OR 97402
www.96kzel.com

Attractions

Situated at the confluence of the Willamette and McKenzie Rivers, Eugene is surrounded by farmland, forests, and mountains. Three of the city's numerous parks are located along a river bank, and the city's extensive and innovative bike and jogging trails are ranked among the best in the U.S. The many recreational opportunities in the area range from golf to whitewater rafting. Cultural activities include performances by the Eugene Opera, Eugene Symphony, and Eugene Ballet Company, as well as musical and theatrical productions at the Community Center for the Performing Arts. Eugene is also home to the University of Oregon.

Actors Cabaret of Eugene
996 Willamette St
Eugene, OR 97401
Phone: 541-683-4368
TF: 800-310-4368

Camp Putt Adventure Golf Park
4006 Franklin Blvd
Eugene, OR 97403
Phone: 541-741-9828
Fax: 541-726-6038

Community Center for the Performing Arts
8th Ave & Lincoln St
Eugene, OR 97401
E-mail: wowhall@efn.org
www.efn.org/~wowhall
Phone: 541-687-2746

Dorris Ranch
S 2nd & Doris Sts
Springfield, OR 97477
Phone: 541-736-4544

Eugene Ballet Co
Hult Ctr for the Performing Arts One Eugene Ctr
Eugene, OR 97401
E-mail: eballet@pond.net
www.pond.net/~eballet/
Phone: 541-682-5000
Fax: 541-687-5745

Eugene Concert Choir
30 E Broadway Suite 122
Eugene, OR 97401
www.efn.org/~ecc/
Phone: 541-687-6865
Fax: 541-687-5745

Eugene Opera
PO Box 11200
Eugene, OR 97440
E-mail: eugeneop@aol.com
www.eugeneopera.com
Phone: 541-485-3985
Fax: 541-683-3783

Eugene Symphony
1 Eugene Centre
Eugene, OR 97401
Phone: 541-687-9487
Fax: 541-687-0527

Fifth Street Public Market
296 E 5th St
Eugene, OR 97401
Phone: 541-484-0383
Fax: 541-686-1220

Hinman Vineyards
27012 Briggs Hill Rd
Eugene, OR 97405
www.silvanridge.com
Phone: 541-345-1945
Fax: 541-345-6174

Hult Center for the Performing Arts
1 Eugene Ctr
Eugene, OR 97401
www.hultcenter.org
Phone: 541-682-5087
Fax: 541-682-5426

Kerns Maude Art Center
1910 E 15th Ave
Eugene, OR 97403
E-mail: mkac@efn.org
www.mkartcenter.org
Phone: 541-345-1571
Fax: 541-345-6248

Lane Arts Council
44 W Broadway Suite 304
Eugene, OR 97401
E-mail: lanearts.efn.org
www.efn.org/~laneartc
Phone: 541-485-2278
Fax: 541-485-2478

Lane County Historical Museum
740 W 13 Ave
Eugene, OR 97402
www.hometownonline.com/Historical_Museum/
Phone: 541-682-4242
Fax: 541-682-7361

Lane ESD Planetarium
2300 Leo Harris Pkwy
Eugene, OR 97401
E-mail: planetarium@lane.K12.or.us
www.efn.org/~esd_plt/
Phone: 541-687-7827

LaVelle Vineyards
89697 Sheffler Rd
Elmira, OR 97437
Phone: 541-935-9406
Fax: 541-935-7202

Orchard Point Park
27060 Clear Lake Rd
Eugene, OR 97402
Phone: 541-689-4926
Fax: 541-461-5865

Oregon Aviation & Space Museum
90377 Boeing Dr
Eugene, OR 97402
Phone: 541-461-1101
Fax: 541-461-1101

Oregon Coast Aquarium
2820 SE Ferry Slip Rd
Newport, OR 97365
E-mail: akh@aquarium.org
www.aquarium.org
Phone: 541-867-3474
Fax: 541-867-6846

Oregon Mozart Players
1 Eugene Centre Soreng Theatre - Hult Center for the Performing Arts
Eugene, OR 97401
Phone: 541-345-6648
Fax: 541-345-7849

Sea Lion Caves
91560 Hwy 101
Florence, OR 97439
E-mail: info@sealioncaves.com
www.sealioncaves.com
Phone: 541-547-3111
Fax: 541-547-3545

Springfield Museum
590 Main St
Springfield, OR 97477
Phone: 541-726-2300
Fax: 541-726-3689

University of Oregon Museum of Art
1430 Johnson Ln
Eugene, OR 97403
E-mail: info@uoma.uoregon.edu
uoma.uoregon.edu/
Phone: 541-346-3027
Fax: 541-346-0976

University of Oregon Museum of Natural History
1680 E 15th Ave
Eugene, OR 97403
oregon.uoregon.edu/~mnh
Phone: 541-346-3024
Fax: 541-346-5334

Willamette Science & Technology Center
2300 Leo Harris Pkwy
Eugene, OR 97401
E-mail: wistec@efn.org
www.efn.org/~wistec/
Phone: 541-682-7888
Fax: 541-484-9027

Sports Teams & Facilities

Eugene Emeralds (baseball)
2077 Willamette St Civic Stadium
Eugene, OR 97405
www.go-ems.com
Phone: 541-342-5367
Fax: 541-342-6089

Eugene Ice Hawks (hockey)
796 W 13th Ave Lane County Ice Arena
Eugene, OR 97402
www.proaxis.com/~oconnort/icehawks.html
Phone: 541-682-3615
Fax: 541-682-7368

Annual Events

Asian Kite Festival (mid-September) 541-687-9600
Bohemia Mining Days (late July) 541-942-6125
Centennial Bank Eugene Celebration (mid-September) 541-681-4108
Christmas Light Parade & Yule Fest (mid-December) 541-998-6154
Christmas Light Up the Valley (December) 541-896-3330
Coburg Antique Fair (early September) 541-688-1181
Coburg Classic Car Show (early August) 541-344-8081
Coburg Golden Years (mid-July) 541-484-5307
Cottage Grove Amateur Rodeo (early July) 541-942-2411
Creswell's Old Fashioned July 4th (July 4) 541-895-5161
Daffodil Drive Day (mid-March) 541-998-6154
Festival of Trees (December) 800-547-5445
Lane County Fair (mid-August) 541-682-4292
Mid-Winter Square Dance Festival (late January) 541-942-7539
Oregon Asian Celebration (mid-February) 541-687-9600
Oregon Bach Festival (late June-early July) 800-457-1486
Oregon Country Fair (mid-July) 541-343-4298
Oregon Dunes Mushers Mail Run (early March) 541-269-1269
Oregon Festival of American Music (early-mid-August) 800-248-1615
Rhododendron Festival & Parade (mid-May) 541-997-3128
Saturday Market (April-November) 541-686-8885
Scandinavian Festival (August) .541-998-6154
Spring Garden Tours (May) 800-726-3657
Ukrainian Celebration (early August) 541-726-7309
Whale Watching (November-March) 800-547-5445
Wildflower Festival (mid-May) .541-747-1504

Flint, Michigan

***County:* Genesee**

FLINT is located in southeastern Michigan. Major cities within 100 miles include Ann Arbor, Detroit, and Lansing, Michigan; and Toledo, Ohio.

Area (Land) .... 33.8 sq mi
Area (Water)............................... 0.4 sq mi
Elevation.................................... 750 ft
Latitude ....43-01-22 N
Longitude............................... 83-41-34 W
Time Zone ....EST
Area Code....................................... 810

Climate

Flint has a continental climate with four distinct seasons. Summers are warm, with average high temperatures around 80 degrees and lows near 60. Winters are cold with average temperatures in the 20s. An average of 40 inches of snow falls each year in Flint. August and September are the city's wettest months, while January and February are the driest.

Average Temperatures & Precipitation

Temperatures

	Jan	Feb	Mar	Apr	May	Jun	Jul	Aug	Sep	Oct	Nov	Dec
High	29	31	42	56	68	77	82	79	72	60	47	34
Low	14	16	26	36	46	55	60	58	51	41	32	21

Precipitation

	Jan	Feb	Mar	Apr	May	Jun	Jul	Aug	Sep	Oct	Nov	Dec
Inches	1.4	1.3	2.2	2.9	2.7	3.2	2.7	3.5	3.6	2.2	2.6	2.1

History

Flint was founded by European settlers in 1819 as a fur trading post, and by the mid-1800s Flint had grown as a lumbering center and was incorporated as a city. The lumber mills provided the materials necessary for carriage and wagon manufacturing, and by the turn of the 20th Century Flint's factories were producing more than 10,000 carriages annually.

Flint's reputation as the "Vehicle City" began in the early 1900s, with several auto makers making their debut in the city, including General Motors in 1908. GM's Buick, Chevrolet, and Fisher Body plants were all located in Flint, and the city became the nation's second largest producer of automobiles. Flint's population continued to grow during much of the 20th Century as many new residents, including European immigrants and African-Americans from the South, were drawn by the city's economic opportunities.

The late 1970s and the 1980s were difficult times for Flint. A decline in domestic automobile manufacturing led to the closure and relocation of many Flint plants, and this had a major impact on the city's economy. In recent years, Flint has diversified its economic base, with the health care industry rapidly gaining importance. Despite the plant closures of the past two decades, General Motors remains the city's largest employer and an integral part of Flint's economy.

Population

1990 Census 140,925
1998 Estimate..............................131,668
% Change .... -6.6

Racial/Ethnic Breakdown

White.................................... 49.5%
Black 47.9%
Other..................................... 2.6%
Hispanic Origin (may be of any race) 2.9%

Age Breakdown

Under 5 years.............................. 9.5%
5 to 17.................................. 20.9%
18 to 20.................................. 5.1%
21 to 24.................................. 6.3%
25 to 34................................. 17.6%
35 to 44................................. 13.5%
45 to 54.................................. 8.6%
55 to 64.................................. 7.8%
65 to 74.................................. 6.2%
75+ years 4.5%
Median Age.................................29.7

Gender Breakdown

Male..................................... 46.7%
Female.................................. 53.3%

Government

Type of Government: Mayor-Council

Flint City Clerk
1101 S Saginaw St
Flint, MI 48502
Phone: 810-766-7413
Fax: 810-766-7032

Flint City Council
1101 S Saginaw St
Flint, MI 48502
Phone: 810-766-7418
Fax: 810-766-7032

Flint City Hall
1101 S Saginaw St
Flint, MI 48502
Phone: 810-766-7015
Fax: 810-766-7218

Flint Community & Economic Development Dept
1101 S Saginaw St
Flint, MI 48502
Phone: 810-766-7436
Fax: 810-766-7351

Flint Finance Dept
1101 S Saganaw St
Flint, MI 48502
Phone: 810-766-7268
Fax: 810-766-7172

Flint Fire Dept
310 E 5th St
Flint, MI 48502
Phone: 810-762-7336
Fax: 810-762-7340

Flint Housing Commission
3820 Richfield Rd
Flint, MI 48506
Phone: 810-736-3050
Fax: 810-736-0158

Flint Legal Dept
1101 S Saginaw St Rm 307
Flint, MI 48502
Phone: 810-766-7146
Fax: 810-232-2114

Flint Mass Transportation Authority
1401 S Dort Hwy
Flint, MI 48503
Phone: 810-767-0100
Fax: 810-767-6580

Flint Mayor
1101 S Saginaw St
Flint, MI 48502
Phone: 810-766-7346
Fax: 810-766-7218

Flint Parks & Recreation Dept
120 E 5th St 2nd Fl
Flint, MI 48502
Phone: 810-766-7463
Fax: 810-766-7468

Flint Personnel Dept
1101 S Saginaw St
Flint, MI 48502
Phone: 810-766-7280
Fax: 810-766-7100

Flint Planning & Zoning Div
1101 S Saginaw St
Flint, MI 48502
Phone: 810-766-7355
Fax: 810-766-7351

Flint Police Dept
210 E 5th St
Flint, MI 48502
Phone: 810-237-6866
Fax: 810-237-6960

Flint Public Library
1026 E Kearsley St
Flint, MI 48502
Phone: 810-232-7111
Fax: 810-767-6740

Flint Public Works & Utilities Dept
1101 S Saginaw St
Flint, MI 48502
Phone: 810-766-7135
Fax: 810-766-7249

Flint Treasurer
1101 S Saginaw St
Flint, MI 48502
Phone: 810-766-7015
Fax: 810-238-8481

Important Phone Numbers

AAA .810-230-8890
American Express Travel .248-642-3350
Dental Referral .810-230-3790
Driver's License/Vehicle Registration Information .810-767-1993
Emergency 911
Entertainment Hot Line .810-232-2211
Flint Board of Realtors .810-767-6330
Flint Income Tax Div .810-766-7015
Genesee County Treasurer's Office .810-257-3054
Medical Referral .810-733-6260
Michigan Dept of Treasury .800-367-6263
Poison Control Center .313-745-5711
Time/Temp .810-743-4200
Voter Registration Information .810-766-7413
Weather .810-232-3333

Information Sources

Better Business Bureau Serving Detroit & Eastern Michigan
30555 Southfield Rd Suite 200
Southfield, MI 48076
www.detroit.bbb.org
Phone: 248-644-9100
Fax: 248-644-5026

Flint Area Chamber of Commerce
519 S Saginaw St Suite 200
Flint, MI 48502
www.flintchamber.org
Phone: 810-232-7101
Fax: 810-233-7437

Flint Area Convention & Visitors Bureau
519 S Saginaw St
Flint, MI 48502
flintcommercecenter.com
Phone: 810-232-8900
Fax: 810-232-1515
TF: 800-253-5468

Genesee County
900 S Saginaw St Rm 202
Flint, MI 48502
Phone: 810-257-3282
Fax: 810-257-3464

Online Resources

Anthill City Guide Flint
www.anthill.com/city.asp?city=flint

Area Guide Flint
flint.areaguides.net

Excite.com Flint City Guide
www.excite.com/travel/countries/united_states/michigan/flint

Area Communities

Communities in the Flint area with populations greater than 5,000 include:

Burton
4303 S Center Rd
Burton, MI 48519
Phone: 810-743-1500
Fax: 810-743-5060

Davison
PO Box 130
Davison, MI 48423
Phone: 810-653-2191
Fax: 810-653-9621

Fenton
301 S Leroy St
Fenton, MI 48430
Phone: 810-629-2261
Fax: 810-629-2004

Flushing
309 E Main St
Flushing, MI 48433
Phone: 810-659-5665
Fax: 810-659-0569

Grand Blanc
203 E Grand Blanc Rd
Grand Blanc, MI 48439
Phone: 810-694-1118

Economy

Flint is one of the nation's top centers for automobile and automotive parts manufacturing. General Motors employs more than 30,000 area residents at various divisions. Although manufacturing is vital to Genesee County's economy, services has recently become the area's largest employment sector. Health care is quickly becoming an important industry in Flint, with three of the city's top 15 employers in this field.

Unemployment Rate 4.9%*
Per Capita Income $23,947*
Median Family Income $50,900*

** Information given is for Genesee County.*

Principal Industries & Number of Wage Earners

Flint MSA (Genesee County) - 1999

Construction & Mining 7,400
Finance, Insurance, & Real Estate 6,600
Government 24,800
Manufacturing 35,100
Private Services 49,100
Retail Trade 35,800
Transportation, Communications, & Utilities 5,700
Wholesale Trade 8,500

Major Employers

Citizens Bank
328 S Saginaw St 1 Citizens Banking Ctr
Flint, MI 48502
www.cbclientsfirst.com
Phone: 810-766-7500
Fax: 810-766-7634
TF: 800-999-6949

General Motors Corp Delphi Automotive Systems Div
4800 S Saginaw St
Flint, MI 48501
Phone: 810-257-7775

General Motors Corp Metal Fab Div
G2238 W Bristol Rd
Flint, MI 48553
Phone: 810-236-3072
Fax: 810-236-5673

General Motors Corp Powertrain/ Components Div
902 E Hamilton Ave
Flint, MI 48550
www.gm.com/careers
Phone: 810-236-5143
Fax: 810-342-0741

General Motors Corp Powertrain/Flint V-6 Div
902 E Hamilton Ave
Flint, MI 48550
www.gm.com/careers
Phone: 810-236-0460
Fax: 810-236-4103

General Motors Corp Powertrain/V-8 Div
3248 Van Slyke Rd
Flint, MI 48552
www.gm.com/careers
Phone: 810-236-0460
Fax: 810-236-6197

General Motors Truck Group
G3100 Van Slyke Rd
Flint, MI 48551
Phone: 810-236-1393

Genesys Regional Medical Center Saint Joseph Campus
1 Genesys Pkwy
Grand Blanc, MI 48439
www.genesys.org/homegen.htm
Phone: 810-762-8000
Fax: 810-606-6915
TF: 888-606-6556

Hurley Medical Center
1 Hurley Plaza
Flint, MI 48503
www.hurleymc.com
Phone: 810-257-9000
Fax: 810-762-6585

McLaren Health Care Corp
G3235 Beecher Rd
Flint, MI 48532
www.mclaren.org
Phone: 810-342-1100
Fax: 810-342-1123

Quality of Living Indicators

Total Crime Index 14,576
(rates per 100,000 inhabitants)

Violent Crime
Murder/manslaughter 39
Forcible rape 137
Robbery 740
Aggravated assault 2,180

Property Crime
Burglary 3,718
Larceny theft 5,966
Motor vehicle theft 1,796

Cost of Living Index 107.2
(national average = 100)

Median Home Price $95,400

Education

Public Schools

Flint City School District
923 E Kearsley St
Flint, MI 48502
www.flintschools.com
Phone: 810-760-1000
Fax: 810-760-6790

Number of Schools
Elementary 26
Middle 15
High 5

Student/Teacher Ratio
All Grades 15.0:1

Private Schools

Number of Schools (all grades) .... 27+

Colleges & Universities

Baker College Flint Campus
1050 W Bristol Rd
Flint, MI 48507
E-mail: adm-fl@baker.edu
www.baker.edu/visit/flint.html
Phone: 810-767-7600
Fax: 810-766-4049

Charles Stewart Mott Community College
1401 E Court St
Flint, MI 48503
www.mcc.edu
Phone: 810-762-0200
Fax: 810-232-9442

University of Michigan Flint
303 E Kearsley St
Flint, MI 48502
www.flint.umich.edu
Phone: 810-762-3000
Fax: 810-762-3272
TF: 800-942-5636

Hospitals

Genesys Regional Medical Center Flint Osteopathic Campus
3921 Beecher Rd
Flint, MI 48532
Phone: 810-762-4000
Fax: 810-606-6605

Genesys Regional Medical Center Saint Joseph Campus
1 Genesys Pkwy
Grand Blanc, MI 48439
www.genesys.org/homegen.htm
Phone: 810-762-8000
Fax: 810-606-6915
TF: 888-606-6556

Hurley Medical Center
1 Hurley Plaza
Flint, MI 48503
www.hurleymc.com
Phone: 810-257-9000
Fax: 810-762-6585

McLaren Regional Medical Center
401 S Ballenger Hwy
Flint, MI 48532
Phone: 810-762-2000
Fax: 810-342-4912
TF: 800-821-6517

Transportation

Airport(s)

Bishop International Airport (FNT)
5 miles SW of downtown (approx 10 minutes) 810-235-6560

Mass Transit

Mass Transportation Authority
$1 Base fare 810-767-0100

Rail/Bus

Amtrak Station
1407 S Dort Hwy
Flint, MI 48503
Phone: 810-234-2659
TF: 800-872-7245

Greyhound Bus Station
615 N Harrison St
Flint, MI 48502
Phone: 810-232-1114
TF: 800-231-2222

Utilities

Electricity
Consumers Energy 810-235-1511
www.consumersenergy.com

Gas
Michgan Consolidated Gas Co 800-395-4005

Water
Flint Dept of Public Works & Utilities 810-766-7225

Garbage Collection/Recycling
Flint Dept of Public Works & Utilities Sanitation Div 810-766-7076
Flint Recycling Drop-Off Center 810-766-7076

Telecommunications

Telephone
Ameritech 800-445-9494
www.ameritech.com

Cable Television
Comcast Cablevision 810-235-9200

Internet Service Providers (ISPs)
Genesee Free-Net 810-230-9141
www.gfn.org
Internet Ramp The 810-720-7200
www.tir.com
Kodenet Inc 810-341-1474
www.kode.net

Banks

Chemical Bank Key State
3501 S Linden Rd
Flint, MI 48507
Phone: 810-733-6330
Fax: 810-733-7254

Citizens Bank
328 S Saginaw St 1 Citizens Banking Ctr
Flint, MI 48502
www.cbclientsfirst.com
Phone: 810-766-7500
Fax: 810-766-7634
TF: 800-999-6949

D & N Bank
G-6120 Fenton Rd
Flint, MI 48507
Phone: 810-232-3810
Fax: 810-232-2622
TF: 800-950-5540

Michigan National Bank
503 S Saginaw St
Flint, MI 48502
Phone: 800-225-5662
Fax: 810-762-5543

NBD Bank
111 E Court St
Flint, MI 48502
Phone: 800-225-5623
Fax: 810-237-3739

Old Kent Bank
G-5080 Corunna Rd
Flint, MI 48532
Phone: 810-762-4844
Fax: 810-235-8689

Republic Bank
G-3200 Beecher Rd
Flint, MI 48532
Phone: 810-732-3300
Fax: 810-732-3202

State Bank
1 Fenton Sq
Fenton, MI 48430
Phone: 800-729-6283
Fax: 810-629-3892

Shopping

Courtland Center
4190 E Court St
Burton, MI 48509
Phone: 810-744-0742
Fax: 810-742-6866

Genesee Valley Center
3341 Linden Rd S
Flint, MI 48507
Phone: 810-732-4000
Fax: 810-732-5437

Media

Newspapers and Magazines

Flint Journal*
200 E 1st St
Flint, MI 48502
E-mail: fj@flintj.com
fl.mlive.com
Phone: 810-766-6100
Fax: 810-767-7518
TF: 800-875-6300

**Indicates major daily newspapers*

Television

WEYI-TV Ch 25 (NBC)
2225 W Willard Rd
Clio, MI 48420
E-mail: weyi@aol.com
Phone: 810-687-1000
Fax: 810-687-4925

WFUM-TV Ch 28 (PBS)
University of Michigan
Flint, MI 48502
E-mail: wfum@list.flint.umich.edu
www.flint.umich.edu/wfum
Phone: 810-762-3028
Fax: 810-233-6017

WJRT-TV Ch 12 (ABC)
2302 Lapeer Rd
Flint, MI 48503
E-mail: wjrt@crif.com
Phone: 810-233-3130
Fax: 810-257-2812

WNEM-TV Ch 5 (CBS)
107 N Franklin
Saginaw, MI 48607
E-mail: wnem@concentric.net
www.wnem.com
Phone: 517-755-8191
Fax: 517-758-2110

WSMH-TV Ch 66 (Fox)
3463 W Pierson Rd
Flint, MI 48504
Phone: 810-785-8866
Fax: 810-785-8963

Radio

WCRZ-FM 107.9 MHz (AC)
3338 Bristol Rd
Burton, MI 48529
E-mail: wcrz@aol.com
Phone: 810-743-1080
Fax: 810-742-5170

WDZZ-FM 92.7 MHz (Urban)
6317 Taylor Dr
Flint, MI 48507
Phone: 810-238-7300
Fax: 810-238-7310

WFDF-AM 910 kHz (N/T)
6317 Taylor Dr
Flint, MI 48507
Phone: 810-238-7300
Fax: 810-238-7310

WFLT-AM 1420 kHz (Rel)
317 S Averill Ave
Flint, MI 48506
Phone: 810-239-5733
Fax: 810-239-7134

WFNT-AM 1470 kHz (N/T)
3338 Bristol Rd
Burton, MI 48529
Phone: 810-743-1080
Fax: 810-742-5170

WKCQ-FM 98.1 MHz (Ctry)
2000 Whittier St
Saginaw, MI 48601
Phone: 517-752-8161
Fax: 517-752-8102
TF: 800-262-0098

WWBN-FM 101.7 MHz (Rock)
3338 Bristol Rd
Burton, MI 48529
Phone: 810-743-1080
Fax: 810-742-5170

WWCK-AM 1570 kHz (CHR)
6317 Taylor Dr
Flint, MI 48507
Phone: 810-744-1570
Fax: 810-238-7310

WWCK-FM 105.5 MHz (CHR)
6317 Taylor Dr
Flint, MI 48507
Phone: 810-744-1570
Fax: 810-238-7310

Attractions

The seat of Genesee County, Flint was the original home of General Motors and is currently home to GM's Buick and Cadillac/Luxury Car divisions. The Alfred P. Sloan Museum presents Flint's history as an automotive center in a variety of exhibitions and special events, including the annual Summer Antique Auto Fair. Flint's Crossroads Village features 30 historic structures dating back to the mid-late 1800s where costumed performers demonstrate various facets of life in the 19th century. Visitors can tour the area by steam train or a paddlewheel river boat. Flint is also home to Michigan's largest planetarium, the Longway Planetarium, which features star shows and laser shows for visitors.

Buckham Alley Theater
512 Buckham Alley
Flint, MI 48502
Phone: 810-239-4477

Children's Museum
1602 W 3rd Ave
Flint, MI 48503
Phone: 810-767-5437
Fax: 810-767-4936

Crossroads Village & Huckleberry Railroad
6140 Bray Rd
Flint, MI 48506
www.geneseecountyparks.org/crossroadsvillage.htm
Phone: 810-736-7100
TF: 800-648-7275

Flint City Market
420 East Blvd
Flint, MI 48502
Phone: 810-766-7449

Flint Community Players
1220 E Kearsley St Bower Theater
Flint, MI 48503
Phone: 810-235-6963

Flint Cultural Center
1241 E Kearsley St Whiting Auditorium
Flint, MI 48503
E-mail: tickets@tir.com
www.flintculturalcenter.com
Phone: 810-237-7333
Fax: 810-237-7335
TF: 888-823-6837

Flint Institute of Arts
1120 E Kearsley St
Flint, MI 48503
www.flintarts.org
Phone: 810-234-1695
Fax: 810-234-1692

Flint Symphony Orchestra
1241 E Kearsley St Whiting Auditorium
Flint, MI 48503
Phone: 810-238-1350
Fax: 810-238-6385
TF: 800-395-4849

Flint Youth Theater
1220 E Kearsley St
Flint, MI 48503
Phone: 810-760-1018
Fax: 810-760-7420

For-Mar Nature Preserve & Arboretum
2142 N Genesee Rd
Burton, MI 48509
Phone: 810-789-8567

Genesee Belle
6140 Bray Rd
Flint, MI 48506
Phone: 810-736-7100
Fax: 810-736-7220
TF: 800-648-7275

Longway Robert T Planetarium
1310 E Kearsley St
Flint, MI 48503
flintcommercecenter.comlongway
Phone: 810-760-1181
Fax: 810-760-6774

Montrose Historical & Telephone Pioneer Museum
144 E Hickory St
Montrose, MI 48457
Phone: 810-639-6644

Sloan Alfred P Museum
1221 E Kearsley St
Flint, MI 48503
www.classicar.com/museums/sloan/sloan.htm
Phone: 810-760-1169
Fax: 810-760-5339

Stepping Stone Falls
5161 Branch Rd
Flint, MI 48506
Phone: 810-736-7100

University of Michigan-Flint Theater
303 E Kearsley St
Flint, MI 48502
Phone: 810-762-3230
Fax: 810-762-3687

Whaley Historical House
624 E Kearsley St
Flint, MI 48503
Phone: 810-235-6841
Fax: 810-235-4626

Sports Teams & Facilities

Flint Generals (hockey)
3501 Lapeer Rd IMA Sports Arena
Flint, MI 48503
www.flintgenerals.com
Phone: 810-742-9422
Fax: 810-742-5892

Mid-Michigan Bucks (soccer)
505 N Center Dr White Pines Stadium
Saginaw Township, MI 48706
E-mail: mmbucks@worldnet.att.net
home.att.net/~mmbucks
Phone: 517-781-6888

Sports Creek Raceway
4290 Morrish Rd
Swartz Creek, MI 48473
Phone: 810-635-3333
Fax: 810-635-9711

Annual Events

Antique Machine Show (early August) 800-648-7275
Civil War Weekend (late June) 800-648-7275
Country Music Fest (mid-June) 810-732-2040
Crim Festival of Races (late August)...............810-235-3396
Flint Art Fair (early-June).........................810-234-1695
Flint's Juneteenth Festival (mid-June).............810-766-7144
Fourth of July Festival (early July)................810-766-7463
Genesee County Fair (mid-late August) 810-687-0953
Honoring the Eagle Pow Wow (mid-July) 810-736-7100
Huckleberry Ghost Train (October)................810-736-7100
Michigan Renaissance Festival
(mid-August-late September)....................800-601-4848
Mott Community College Student Art Show
(May) 810-762-0474
Railfans Weekend (mid-August) 800-648-7275
Saint John Festival of Flags (late June)............810-653-2377
Septemberfest (early September) 810-686-9861
Summer Antique Auto Fair (late June) 810-760-1169

Fort Collins, Colorado

County: **Larimer**

FORT COLLINS is located along the Cache la Poudre River in the foothills of the Rocky Mountains of north central Colorado. Major cities within 100 miles include Denver and Boulder, Colorado and Cheyenne, Wyoming.

Area (Land) .... 41.2 sq mi
Area (Water).............................. 0.5 sq mi
Elevation.................................. 5,003 ft
Latitude .... 40-33-19 N
Longitude.............................. 105-04-06 W
Time Zone .... MST
Area Code....................................... 970

Climate

Fort Collins has a moderate climate with an annual average of approximately 300 days of sunshine. Winter days are cool, with average high temperatures in the low to mid-40s, while overnight lows dip into the teens. Fort Collins receives an average of around 50 inches of snow annually, with January being the snowiest month. Summer days are warm in Fort Collins, with average highs in the low to mid-80s, while evenings cool down into the 50s. April through July is the wettest time of the year in Fort Collins.

Average Temperatures & Precipitation

Temperatures

	Jan	Feb	Mar	Apr	May	Jun	Jul	Aug	Sep	Oct	Nov	Dec
High	41	46	52	61	70	80	86	83	75	64	51	42
Low	14	19	25	34	43	52	57	55	46	35	24	16

Precipitation

	Jan	Feb	Mar	Apr	May	Jun	Jul	Aug	Sep	Oct	Nov	Dec
Inches	0.4	0.4	1.4	1.8	2.7	1.9	1.8	1.3	1.3	1.0	0.7	0.5

History

The Fort Collins area was first settled in 1864 as Camp Collins, a military outpost of Fort Laramie that was built to guard the Overland Stage Route at the site of the present-day city of LaPorte. The outpost was named for U.S. Lt. Colonel William Collins, who commissioned the fort. Later that year, a flood destroyed the original location, and a new outpost was established a few miles southeast and renamed Fort Collins. By 1867 the fort had been abandoned, but the community that had formed around it remained. Five years later, with the establishment of the Larimer County Land improvement Company and the promise of irrigation systems, an agricultural colony was formed and the new town of Fort Collins was platted. Fort Collins was incorporated as a city in 1873.

Although Fort Collins' early progress was hampered by financial problems and insect plagues that destroyed local crops, the arrival of the Colorado Central Railroad opened the city up to new markets and subsequently helped fuel economic growth. The opening of the Agricultural College of Colorado (which would later become Colorado State University) in 1879 helped to spark Fort Collins' growth as an agricultural community. The creation of the college's Colorado Agricultural Experiment Station in 1888 eventually led to the development of Fort Collins' prosperous sugar beet industry during the 1890s. The sugar beet industry would fuel the city's economy for decades to come, attracting many new residents to the area, who came seeking jobs as field workers.

During the early 20th Century, Fort Collins continued to grow primarily as an agricultural community. In addition to the sugar industry, livestock feeding became a vital part of the city's economy. Although the Great Depression brought hard times to Fort Collins, the city experienced a post-World War II building boom. As a result, Fort Collins' population doubled in size between 1944 and 1955. In the decades that followed, the city's economy began to diversify as new industries developed in the area and the population continued to grow steadily.

Today, with a population exceeding 108,000, Fort Collins is Colorado's fifth largest and fastest-growing city. The seat of Larimer County, Fort Collins has also consistently ranked among the fastest-growing metropolitan areas in the U.S. for the past fifteen years.

Population

1990 Census 87,491
1998 Estimate.............................. 108,905
% Change 24.5
2010 Projection 137,600

Racial/Ethnic Breakdown

White...................................... 93.9%
Black 1.0%
Other....................................... 5.7%
Hispanic Origin (may be of any race) 7.1%

Age Breakdown

Under 5 years............................... 7.0%
5 to 17.................................... 15.4%
18 to 20................................... 10.6%
21 to 24................................... 11.6%
25 to 34................................... 19.5%
35 to 44................................... 15.8%
45 to 54.................................... 7.4%
55 to 64.................................... 5.0%
65 to 74.................................... 4.2%
75+ years 3.5%
Median Age................................... 27.8

Gender Breakdown

Male....................................... 49.6%
Female..................................... 50.4%

Government

Type of Government: Mayor-Council

Fort Collins Building & Zoning Div
281 N College Ave
Fort Collins, CO 80524
Phone: 970-221-6760
Fax: 970-224-6134

Fort Collins City Clerk
300 LaPorte Ave
Fort Collins, CO 80521
Phone: 970-221-6515
Fax: 970-221-6295

Fort Collins City Council
300 LaPorte Ave
Fort Collins, CO 80521
Phone: 970-221-6878
Fax: 970-224-6107

Fort Collins City Hall
300 LaPorte Ave
Fort Collins, CO 80521
Phone: 970-221-6500
Fax: 970-221-6329

Fort Collins City Manager
300 LaPorte Ave
Fort Collins, CO 80521
Phone: 970-221-6505
Fax: 970-224-6107

Fort Collins Human Resources Dept
200 W Mountain Ave Suite A
Fort Collins, CO 80522
Phone: 970-221-6535
Fax: 970-221-6238

Fort Collins Natural Resources Dept
281 N College Ave
Fort Collins, CO 80521
Phone: 970-221-6600
Fax: 970-224-6177

Fort Collins Parks & Recreation Dept
214 N Howes St
Fort Collins, CO 80521
Phone: 970-221-6640
Fax: 970-416-2100

Fort Collins Police Dept
300 W LaPorte Ave
Fort Collins, CO 80521
Phone: 970-221-6540
Fax: 970-224-6088

Fort Collins Poudre Fire Authority
102 Remington St
Fort Collins, CO 80524
Phone: 970-221-6570
Fax: 970-221-6635

Fort Collins Public Library
201 Peterson St
Fort Collins, CO 80524
Phone: 970-221-6742
Fax: 970-221-6398

Fort Collins Transportation Services
210 E Olive St
Fort Collins, CO 80524
Phone: 970-221-6608
Fax: 970-221-6239

Fort Collins Utility Services
PO Box 580
Fort Collins, CO 80522
Phone: 970-221-6700
Fax: 970-221-6619

Important Phone Numbers

AAA....970-223-1111
American Express Travel....970-484-5566
Colorado State Dept of Revenue Taxpayer Services Office....970-223-1097
Dental Referral....800-577-7317
Driver's License Information....970-223-3648
Emergency....911
Fort Collins Board of Realtors....970-223-2900
Larimer County Assessor....970-498-7050
Medical Referral....970-669-4640
Time/Temp....970-226-6060
Vehicle Registration Information....970-498-7878
Voter Registration Information....970-498-7820
Weather....970-484-8920

Information Sources

Better Business Bureau Serving the Mountain States
1730 S College Ave Suite 303
Fort Collins, CO 80525
www.rockymtn.bbb.org
Phone: 970-484-1348
Fax: 970-221-1239

Downtown Business Assn
19 Old Town Sq Suite 230
Fort Collins, CO 80524
www.downtownfortcollins.com
Phone: 970-484-6500
Fax: 970-484-2069

Fort Collins Area Chamber of Commerce
225 S Meldrum St
Fort Collins, CO 80521
www.fcchamber.org
Phone: 970-482-3746
Fax: 970-482-3774

Fort Collins Convention & Visitors Bureau
429 S Howes St Suite 101
Fort Collins, CO 80521
www.ftcollins.com
Phone: 970-482-5821
Fax: 970-493-8061
TF: 800-274-3678

Fort Collins Economic Developmment Corp
PO Box 1849
Fort Collins, CO 80522
www.fcedc.org
Phone: 970-221-0861
Fax: 970-221-5219

Larimer County
PO Box 1280
Fort Collins, CO 80522
www.co.larimer.co.us
Phone: 970-498-7000
Fax: 970-498-7830

Online Resources

Anthill City Guide Fort Collins
www.anthill.com/city.asp?city=fortcollins

Area Guide Fort Collins
fortcollins.areaguides.net

City Knowledge Fort Collins
www.cityknowledge.com/co_fort_collins.htm

Fort Collins Colorado Relocation Directory
www.frii.com/~lynne/colorado.html

Fort Collins Community Online
www.fortcollins.com

FortNet
www.fortnet.org

Area Communities

Communities in Larimer County with populations greater than 5,000 include:

Berthoud Phone: 970-532-3754
PO Box 1229 Fax: 970-532-0640
Berthoud, CO 80513

Estes Park Phone: 970-586-5331
PO Box 1200 Fax: 970-586-2816
Estes Park, CO 80517

Loveland Phone: 970-962-2000
500 E 3rd St Fax: 970-962-2901
Loveland, CO 80537

Economy

Despite Fort Collins' inception as an agricultural community, the city today has a diverse economic base and one of the strongest economies in the United States. The services, retail trade, manufacturing, and government sectors account for more than 80 percent of employment in Larimer County today. Playing a vital role in Fort Collins' development for more than a century, Colorado State University is Fort Collins' single largest employer, providing full-time jobs for more than 6,500 area residents.

Unemployment Rate 3.4%
Per Capita Income $19,089
Median Family Income $51,889

Principal Industries & Number of Wage Earners

Larimer County - 1998

Industry	Wage Earners
Agricultural Services, Forestry, & Fishing	1,842
Construction	8,159
Finance, Insurance, & Real Estate	3,991
Government	19,214
Manufacturing	19,747
Mining	252
Retail Trade	25,138
Services	26,772
Transportation, Communications, & Utilities	2,597
Wholesale Trade	2,733

Major Employers

Advanced Energy Industries Inc Phone: 970-221-4670
1625 Sharp Pt Dr Fax: 970-221-5583
Fort Collins, CO 80525
E-mail: support@ftc1.aei.com
www.advanced-energy.com

Anheuser-Busch Inc Phone: 970-490-4500
PO Box 20000 Fax: 970-490-4556
Fort Collins, CO 80524
www.anheuser-busch.com

Colorado State University Phone: 970-491-1101
Fort Collins, CO 80523 Fax: 970-491-7799
www.colostate.edu

Eastman Kodak Co Phone: 970-686-7611
9952 Eastman Park Dr Fax: 970-686-4236
Windsor, CO 80551
www.kodak.com

Fort Collins City Hall Phone: 970-221-6500
300 LaPorte Ave Fax: 970-221-6329
Fort Collins, CO 80521
www.ci.fort-collins.co.us

Hewlett-Packard Co Phone: 970-898-3754
3404 E Harmony Rd MS 81 Fax: 888-567-8329
Fort Collins, CO 80525
www.hp.com

Larimer County Phone: 970-498-7000
PO Box 1280 Fax: 970-498-7830
Fort Collins, CO 80522
www.co.larimer.co.us

LSI Logic Corp Phone: 970-223-5100
2001 Danfield Ct
Fort Collins, CO 80525
www.lsilogic.com

Poudre School District Phone: 970-482-7420
2407 LaPorte Ave Fax: 970-490-3514
Fort Collins, CO 80521
E-mail: info@psd.k12.co.us
www.psd.k12.co.us

Poudre Valley Hospital Phone: 970-495-7000
1024 S Lemay Ave Fax: 970-495-7603
Fort Collins, CO 80524 TF: 800-252-5784
www.pvhs.org

Waterpik Technologies Inc Phone: 970-484-1352
1730 E Prospect Rd Fax: 970-221-8715
Fort Collins, CO 80553
www.waterpik.com

Woodward Governor Co Phone: 970-482-5811
1000 E Drake Rd Fax: 970-498-3058
Fort Collins, CO 80525
www.woodward.com

Quality of Living Indicators

Total Crime Index 4,849
(rates per 100,000 inhabitants)

Violent Crime
Murder/manslaughter 3
Forcible rape 72
Robbery 35
Aggravated assault 279

Property Crime
Burglary 734
Larceny theft 3,504
Motor vehicle theft 222

Cost of Living Index 103.7
(national average = 100)

Median Home Price $85,400

Education

Public Schools

Poudre School District Phone: 970-482-7420
2407 LaPorte Ave Fax: 970-490-3514
Fort Collins, CO 80521
E-mail: info@psd.k12.co.us
www.psd.k12.co.us

Number of Schools
Elementary 29

Middle 8
High... 4

Student/Teacher Ratio
All Grades 23.0:1

Private Schools

Number of Schools (all grades) .... 8+

Colleges & Universities

Colorado Christian University Phone: 970-223-8505
3800 Automation Way Fax: 970-223-8964
Fort Collins, CO 80525 TF: 800-443-2484
www.ccu.edu

Colorado State University Phone: 970-491-1101
Fort Collins, CO 80523 Fax: 970-491-7799
www.colostate.edu

Front Range Community College
Larimer Campus Phone: 970-226-2500
4616 S Shields St Fax: 303-204-8365
Fort Collins, CO 80526
frcc.cc.co.us/la/index.html

National Technological University Phone: 970-495-6400
700 Centre Ave Fax: 970-498-0601
Fort Collins, CO 80526 TF: 800-582-9976
www.ntu.edu

Regis University Phone: 970-472-2200
1501 Academy Ct Fax: 970-472-2201
Fort Collins, CO 80524 TF: 800-390-0891
www.regis.edu

Hospitals

McKee Medical Center Phone: 970-669-4640
2000 Boise Ave Fax: 970-635-4066
Loveland, CO 80538
www.wphn.com/mckee.htm

Poudre Valley Hospital Phone: 970-495-7000
1024 S Lemay Ave Fax: 970-495-7603
Fort Collins, CO 80524 TF: 800-252-5784
www.pvhs.org

Transportation

Airport(s)

Denver International Airport (DEN)
65 miles SE of downtown Fort Collins
(approximately 75 minutes)..................... 303-342-2000
Fort Collins/Loveland Municipal Airport (FNL)
9 miles SE of downtown (approx 15 minutes)..... 970-962-2850

Mass Transit

Transfort
$.90 Base fare................................ 970-221-6620

Rail/Bus

Greyhound Bus Station Phone: 970-221-1327
501 Riverside Ave TF: 800-231-2222
Fort Collins, CO 80524

Utilities

Electricity
Fort Collins Utilities........................... 970-221-6785
www.ci.fort-collins.co.us/utilities

Gas
Public Service Co 800-772-7858

Water
Fort Collins Utilities........................... 970-221-6785
www.ci.fort-collins.co.us/utilities

Garbage Collection/Recycling
BFI of Northern Colorado...................... 970-223-0154
Waste Management of Northern Colorado........ 970-482-6319

Telecommunications

Telephone
Qwest.. 970-679-7000
www.qwest.com

Cable Television
AT & T Cable Services.......................... 970-493-7400
www.cable.att.com

Internet Service Providers (ISPs)
FortNet 970-224-5991
www.fortnet.org
Front Range Internet Inc 970-224-3668
www.frii.com

Banks

Bank One Colorado NA Phone: 970-662-7603
2000 S College Ave Fax: 970-484-7063
Fort Collins, CO 80525

First Community Industrial Bank Phone: 970-226-1080
2721 S College Ave Fax: 970-226-1096
Fort Collins, CO 80525

First National Bank Phone: 970-482-4861
205 W Oak St Fax: 970-495-9531
Fort Collins, CO 80521
www.1stnationalbank.com

First State Bank of Fort Collins Phone: 970-223-3535
2900 S College Ave Fax: 970-223-1557
Fort Collins, CO 80525
E-mail: talkback@firststatebankftc.com
www.firststatebankftc.com

Firstate Bank of Colorado Phone: 970-266-9090
3131 S College Ave Fax: 970-266-1022
Fort Collins, CO 80525

FirstBank of Northern Colorado Phone: 970-223-4000
1013 E Harmony Rd Fax: 970-282-3925
Fort Collins, CO 80525

KeyBank NA Phone: 970-482-3216
300 W Oak St Fax: 970-495-3310
Fort Collins, CO 80521

Norwest Bank Fort Collins Phone: 970-482-1100
401 S College Ave Fax: 970-482-1523
Fort Collins, CO 80524

Shopping

Foothills Fashion Mall
215 E Foothills Pkwy
Fort Collins, CO 80525
www.foothillsfashionmall.com
Phone: 970-226-5555
Fax: 970-226-5558

The Garment District
633 S College Ave
Fort Collins, CO 80524
Phone: 970-484-9212

Town Square Shopping Center
1228 W Elizabeth St
Fort Collins, CO 80521
Phone: 970-221-1805

Media

Newspapers and Magazines

Coloradoan The*
1212 Riverside Ave
Fort Collins, CO 80524
E-mail: news@coloradoan.com
www.coloradoan.com
Phone: 970-493-6397
Fax: 970-224-7899

Loveland Daily Reporter-Herald*
PO Box 59
Loveland, CO 80539
www.lovelandfyi.com
Phone: 970-669-5050
Fax: 970-667-1111
TF: 800-216-0680

Northern Colorado Business Report
201 S College Ave
Fort Collins, CO 80524
E-mail: ncbr@aol.com
www.ncbr.com
Phone: 970-221-5400
Fax: 970-221-5432

**Indicates major daily newspapers*

Television

KBDI-TV Ch 12 (PBS)
2900 Welton St 1st Fl
Denver, CO 80205
www.kbdi.org
Phone: 303-296-1212
Fax: 303-296-6650

KCEC-TV Ch 50 (Uni)
777 Grant St Suite 110
Denver, CO 80203
E-mail: kcecnews@aol.com
Phone: 303-832-0050
Fax: 303-832-3410

KCNC-TV Ch 4 (CBS)
1044 Lincoln St
Denver, CO 80203
E-mail: mailroom@kcncnews4.com
www.kcncnews4.com
Phone: 303-861-4444
Fax: 303-830-6380

KDVR-TV Ch 31 (Fox)
501 Wazee St
Denver, CO 80204
E-mail: feedback@fox31.com
www.fox31.com
Phone: 303-595-3131
Fax: 303-595-8312

KMGH-TV Ch 7 (ABC)
123 E Speer Blvd
Denver, CO 80203
E-mail: kmgh7@csn.net
www.kmgh.com
Phone: 303-832-7777
Fax: 303-832-0119

KRMA-TV Ch 6 (PBS)
1089 Bannock St
Denver, CO 80204
E-mail: info@krma.org
www.krma.org
Phone: 303-892-6666
Fax: 303-620-5600

KUSA-TV Ch 9 (NBC)
500 Speer Blvd
Denver, CO 80203
E-mail: kusa@9news.com
www.9news.com
Phone: 303-871-9999
Fax: 303-698-4700
TF: 800-338-5872

Radio

KCOL-AM 600 kHz (N/T)
1612 La Porte Ave
Fort Collins, CO 80521
E-mail: info@kcol.com
www.kcol.com
Phone: 970-482-5991
Fax: 970-482-5994

KGLL-FM 96.1 MHz (Ctry)
1612 La Porte Ave
Fort Collins, CO 80521
E-mail: info@kgll.com
www.kgll.com
Phone: 970-482-5991
Fax: 970-482-5994

KIIX-AM 1410 kHz (Sports)
1612 La Porte Ave
Fort Collins, CO 80521
Phone: 970-482-5991
Fax: 970-482-5994

KPAW-FM 107.9 MHz (AC)
1612 La Porte Ave
Fort Collins, CO 80521
E-mail: info@kpaw.com
www.kpaw.com
Phone: 970-482-5991
Fax: 970-482-5994

Attractions

The 70-mile-long Cache La Poudre is Colorado's only nationally designated "wild and scenic" river on which adventurers can enjoy rafting, fishing, and kayaking. Rocky Mountain National Park, with 266,906 acres of trails and mountain peaks, is just 35 miles from Fort Collins. For those who prefer indoor activities, the Anheuser-Busch Tour Center offers complimentary brewery tours highlighting the brewing process as well as the chance to see the world-famous Budweiser Clydesdales. Other activities available in Fort Collins include theatrical performances at the Bas Bleu Theatre Company, dance performances by the Canyon Concert Ballet, and classical music productions by the Fort Collins Symphony.

Alpine Family Fun Club
7824 S College Ave
Fort Collins, CO 80525
Phone: 970-669-4100

Anheuser-Busch Tour Center
2351 Busch Dr
Fort Collins, CO 80524
www.budweisertours.com
Phone: 970-490-4691

Arapaho & Roosevelt National Forests Visitor Center
1311 S College Ave
Fort Collins, CO 80524
www.fs.fed.us//arnf/
Phone: 970-498-2770

Avery House
328 W Mountain Ave
Fort Collins, CO 80521
www.fortnet.org/plf/
Phone: 970-221-0533

Bas Bleu Theatre Co Phone: 970-498-8949
216 Pine St
Fort Collins, CO 80524
E-mail: basbleu@csn.net

Big Horn Brewery Phone: 970-221-5954
1427 W Elizabeth St
Fort Collins, CO 80521

Buckhorn Llama Co Phone: 970-667-7411
7220 N County Rd 27
Loveland, CO 80538
E-mail: buckhorn@llamapack.com
www.llamapack.com

Budweiser Clydesdale Camera Saturdays Phone: 970-490-4691
2351 Busch Dr Anheuser-Busch Tour Ctr
Fort Collins, CO 80524

Canyon Concert Ballet Phone: 970-472-4156
1031 Conifer St Fax: 970-472-4158
Fort Collins, CO 80524
E-mail: info@ccballet.org
www.ccballet.org

Carousel Dinner Theatre Phone: 970-225-2555
3509 S Mason St Fax: 970-225-2389
Fort Collins, CO 80525 TF: 877-700-2555
E-mail: carousel@carouseltheatre.com
www.carouseltheatre.com

City Park Phone: 970-221-6660
1500 W Mulberry St Fax: 970-221-6849
Fort Collins, CO 80521

Colorado State University Environmental Learning Center Phone: 970-491-1661
2400 County Rd 9
Fort Collins, CO 80524

Colorado State University Hatton Gallery Phone: 970-491-7634
Colorado State University Visual Arts Bldg
Fort Collins, CO 80523

Contra Dances Phone: 970-493-8277
City Park Ctr NW Corner of Sheldon Lake
Fort Collins, CO 80524
E-mail: fotd@fortnet.org
www.fortnet.org/FoTD/Contras.html

Crystal Rapids Waterpark Phone: 970-663-1492
3601 E Eisenhower
Loveland, CO 80537

Discovery Center Science Museum Phone: 970-472-3990
703 E Prospect Rd Fax: 970-472-3997
Fort Collins, CO 80525
www.dcsm.org

Edora Park Phone: 970-221-6660
1420 E Stuart St Fax: 970-221-6849
Fort Collins, CO 80525

First Friday Old Town Gallery Walk Phone: 970-221-2383
Linden St
Fort Collins, CO 80524

Fort Collins Municipal Railway Phone: 970-482-8246
PO Box 635
Fort Collins, CO 80522

Fort Collins Museum Phone: 970-221-6738
200 Matthews St Fax: 970-416-2236
Fort Collins, CO 80524
www.ci.fort-collins.co.us/arts_culture/museum

Fort Collins Museum of Contemporary Art Phone: 970-482-2787
201 S College Ave Fax: 970-482-0804
Fort Collins, CO 80524
E-mail: fcmoca@frii.com
www.fcmoca.org

Fort Collins Symphony Phone: 970-482-4823
417 W Magnolia Lincoln Ctr Fax: 970-482-4858
Fort Collins, CO 80521
www.fcsymphony.org

Front Range Chamber Players Phone: 970-221-6730
417 W Magnolia St Lincoln Ctr Fax: 970-484-0424
Fort Collins, CO 80521

Grandview Cemetery Phone: 970-221-6810
1900 W Mountain Ave
Fort Collins, CO 80524

HC Berger Brewing Co Phone: 970-493-9044
1900 E Lincoln Ave Fax: 970-493-4508
Fort Collins, CO 80524
E-mail: info@hcberger.com
www.hcberger.com

Lincoln Center Phone: 970-221-6730
417 W Magnolia St Fax: 970-484-0424
Fort Collins, CO 80521

New Belgium Brewing Co Phone: 970-221-0524
500 Linden St Fax: 970-221-0535
Fort Collins, CO 80524
E-mail: nbb@newbelgium.com
www.newbelgium.com

Odell Brewing Co Phone: 970-498-9070
800 E Lincoln Ave Fax: 970-498-0706
Fort Collins, CO 80524
E-mail: odells@odells.com
www.odells.com

Open Stage Theatre & Co Phone: 970-484-5237
417 W Magnolia St Fax: 970-484-0424
Fort Collins, CO 80521

Rocky Mountain National Park Phone: 970-586-1206
Estes Park, CO 80517 Fax: 970-586-1310
www.nps.gov/romo

Strauss Cabin Phone: 970-679-4570
Horsetooth Rd & Country Rd 7
Fort Collins, CO 80524

The Farm at Lee Martinez Park Phone: 970-221-6665
600 S Sherwood St
Fort Collins, CO 80521

Walnut Street Gallery Phone: 970-221-2383
217 Linden St TF: 800-562-3387
Fort Collins, CO 80524
E-mail: rockout@walnutst.com
www.walnutst.com

Windswept Farm Phone: 970-484-1124
5537 N Country Rd 9
Fort Collins, CO 80524

Annual Events

1882 Fort Collins Waterworks Open House (mid-June) 970-221-0533
Anheuser-Busch Pumpkin Carving Contest (late October) 970-490-4691
Annual Garden Tour (late June) 970-224-0430
Boat Show (mid-March) 970-407-1866
Cinco de Mayo Celebration (early May) 970-484-6500
Colorado Brewers' Festival (late June) 970-484-6500
Colorado International Invitational Poster Exhibition (mid-September-late October) 970-491-7634
Concert Under the Stars (June-August) 970-484-6500
First Night Fort Collins (December 31) 970-484-6500
Fourth of July Celebration (July 4) 970-221-6790
Gem & Mineral Show (late March) 970-484-6752
Grateful Disc Spring Frisbee Festival (late April) 970-484-6932
Great Christmas Hall Artisans Fair (mid-November) 970-221-6735
Great Christmas Hall of Trees (mid-November) 970-221-6735
Historic Homes Tour (mid-September) 970-221-0533
Home & Garden Show (early March) 970-407-1866
Magic in the Rockies International Magic Show (early September) 970-484-7014
NewWestFest (late August) 970-484-6500
Northern Colorado Artists Association Annual Juried Art Show (mid-April-late May) 970-223-6450
Rendezvous & Skookum Day (mid-July) 970-221-6738
Saint Patrick's Day Parade (mid-March) 970-484-6500
Taste of Fort Collins (mid-June) 303-777-6887
Thanksgiving Day Run (late November) 970-224-2582
Victorian Christmas Open House (early December) 970-221-0533
WineFest (late May) 970-482-2700

Fort Lauderdale, Florida

***County:* Broward**

FORT LAUDERDALE is located on the southern Atlantic Coast, also known as the Gold Coast, of Florida. Major cities within 100 miles include West Palm Beach, Miami, and Fort Pierce, Florida.

Area (Land) .... 31.4 sq mi
Area (Water)................................ 4.3 sq mi
Elevation.. 8 ft
Latitude ....26-12-19 N
Longitude............................... 80-14-36 W
Time Zone ....EST
Area Code....................................... 954

Climate

Fort Lauderdale has a subtropical climate, with approximately 3,000 hours of sunshine each year and an average annual temperature of 76 degrees. Seasonal changes are mild due to ocean breezes influenced by the Gulf Stream and the prevailing southeasterly tradewinds that help to keep the temperature mild year-round. Summer is considered the "rainy season" in Fort Lauderdale, with June and September being the wettest months.

Average Temperatures & Precipitation

Temperatures

	Jan	Feb	Mar	Apr	May	Jun	Jul	Aug	Sep	Oct	Nov	Dec
High	77	78	80	83	86	88	90	90	89	86	81	78
Low	58	59	63	66	70	74	75	75	75	71	65	60

Precipitation

	Jan	Feb	Mar	Apr	May	Jun	Jul	Aug	Sep	Oct	Nov	Dec
Inches	2.2	2.8	2.7	3.3	6.6	9.6	6.6	6.8	7.6	6.3	3.9	2.1

History

Fort Lauderdale, Florida was named for Major William Lauderdale, who was dispatched to the area by the U.S. Army in 1838 to lead his Tennessee Volunteers in a war against the Seminole Indians. During the war, Lauderdale and his troops built three forts in the area, all of which were named Fort Lauderdale. Although the area is known to have been inhabited by the Tequesta Indians before 1450 B.C. and by the Seminole Indians for years before the Seminole Wars, the settlement boom that eventually led to Fort Lauderdale's ranking as one of the nation's most populous cities began in 1893 with the establishment of the area's first trading post, built by Frank Stranahan, who is sometimes referred to as the "father of modern Fort Lauderdale."

Fort Lauderdale was incorporated as a city in 1911. The population grew quickly during the real estate boom of the 1920's, during which numerous canals were dredged to create additional waterfront property in the area. Nicknamed the "Venice of America," Fort Lauderdale today has more than 300 miles of navigable waterways, rivers, and inlets.

The years following World War II marked another era of growth for the city, as many soldiers who had been stationed in the area fell in love with the city and returned to settle there after the war had ended. Today, the Greater Fort Lauderdale area is home to more than 1.5 million people, more than 153,000 of whom live in the City of Fort Lauderdale.

Population

1990 Census 149,238
1998 Estimate..............................153,728
% Change 3.0

Racial/Ethnic Breakdown

White.................................... 67.8%
Black 29.5%
Other..................................... 2.6%
Hispanic Origin (may be of any race) 8.6%

Age Breakdown

Under 5 years.............................. 6.1%
5 to 17.................................... 12.7%
18 to 24.................................... 8.6%
25 to 44................................... 34.8%
45 to 64................................... 20.1%
65+ years 17.7%
Median Age.................................39.0

Gender Breakdown

Male...................................... 50.1%
Female.................................... 49.9%

Government

Type of Government: City Manager-Commission

Broward County Library
100 S Andrews Ave
Fort Lauderdale, FL 33301
Phone: 954-357-7444

Fort Lauderdale City Attorney
100 N Andrews Ave
Fort Lauderdale, FL 33301
Phone: 954-761-5037
Fax: 954-761-5915

Fort Lauderdale City Clerk
100 N Andrews Ave 7th Fl
Fort Lauderdale, FL 33301
Phone: 954-761-5010
Fax: 954-761-5021

Fort Lauderdale City Commission
100 N Andrews Ave 8th Fl
Fort Lauderdale, FL 33301
Phone: 954-761-5003
Fax: 954-761-5667

Fort Lauderdale City Hall
100 N Andrews Ave
Fort Lauderdale, FL 33301
Phone: 954-761-5000
Fax: 954-761-5122

Fort Lauderdale City Manager
100 N Andrews Ave
Fort Lauderdale, FL 33301
Phone: 954-761-5013
Fax: 954-761-5021

Fort Lauderdale Community & Economic Development Dept
101 NE 3rd Ave 3rd Fl
Fort Lauderdale, FL 33301
Phone: 954-468-1515
Fax: 954-468-1500

Fort Lauderdale Finance Dept
100 N Andrews Ave 6th Fl
Fort Lauderdale, FL 33301
Phone: 954-761-5165
Fax: 954-761-5168

Fort Lauderdale Fire Rescue Dept
101 NE 3rd Ave Suite 500
Fort Lauderdale, FL 33301
Phone: 954-759-6800
Fax: 954-759-6843

Fort Lauderdale Mayor
100 N Andrews Ave 8th Fl
Fort Lauderdale, FL 33301
Phone: 954-761-5003
Fax: 954-761-5667

Fort Lauderdale Parks & Recreation Dept
1350 W Broward Blvd
Fort Lauderdale, FL 33312
Phone: 954-761-5346
Fax: 954-761-5650

Fort Lauderdale Personnel Div
100 N Andews Ave
Fort Lauderdale, FL 33301
Phone: 954-761-5300
Fax: 954-761-5315

Fort Lauderdale Police Dept
1300 W Broward Blvd
Fort Lauderdale, FL 33312
Phone: 954-761-5590
Fax: 954-759-6001

Fort Lauderdale Public Services Dept
949 NW 38th St
Fort Lauderdale, FL 33309
Phone: 954-492-7801
Fax: 954-492-7881

Important Phone Numbers

AAA 954-748-2700
Activity Line 954-527-5600
Broward Arts Line 954-357-5700
Broward County Revenue Collection Div 954-765-4600
Driver's License Information 954-327-6333
Emergency 911
Florida Dept of Revenue 954-967-1000
HotelDocs 800-468-3537
Poison Control Center 800-282-3171
Realtor Assn of Greater Fort Lauderdale 954-563-7261
Time/Temp 954-748-4444
Vehicle Registration Information 954-765-5050
Voter Registration Information 954-357-7050
Weather 954-748-4444

Information Sources

Broward County
115 S Andrews Ave Rm 421
Fort Lauderdale, FL 33301
www.co.broward.fl.us
Phone: 954-357-7000
Fax: 954-357-7295

Greater Fort Lauderdale Chamber of Commerce
512 NE 3rd Ave
Fort Lauderdale, FL 33301
www.ftlchamber.com
Phone: 954-462-6000
Fax: 954-527-8766

Greater Fort Lauderdale Convention & Visitors Bureau
1850 Eller Dr Suite 303
Fort Lauderdale, FL 33316
www.co.broward.fl.us/sunny.htm
Phone: 954-765-4466
Fax: 954-765-4467
TF: 800-356-1662

Greater Fort Lauderdale/Broward County Convention Center
1950 Eisenhower Blvd
Fort Lauderdale, FL 33316
www.co.broward.fl.us/convention-center.htm
Phone: 954-765-5900
Fax: 954-763-9551

Seflin Free-Net
100 S Andrews Ave
Fort Lauderdale, FL 33301
www.seflin.org
Phone: 954-357-7318
Fax: 954-357-6998

Online Resources

About.com Guide to Fort Lauderdale
fortlauderdale.about.com/local/southeastus/fortlauderdale

Anthill City Guide Fort Lauderdale
www.anthill.com/city.asp?city=ftlauderdale

Area Guide Fort Lauderdale
ftlauderdale.areaguides.net

Broward.com
www.broward.com

City Knowledge Fort Lauderdale
www.cityknowledge.com/fl_fortlauderdale.htm

City Link
www.clinkonline.com

CitySearch Miami/Fort Lauderdale
miami.citysearch.com

Come to the Sun Guide to South Florida
www.cometothesun.com

DigitalCity South Florida
home.digitalcity.com/southflorida

Essential Guide to Fort Lauderdale
www.ego.net/us/fl/fll/

Excite.com Fort Lauderdale City Guide
www.excite.com/travel/countries/united_states/florida/fort_lauderdale

Fort Lauderdale Connections
www.aesir.com/FtLauderdale/

Fort Lauderdale Florida
fortlauderdale-florida.com

Fort Lauderdale Florida Area Guide
beachbucks.com/ftl

Fort Lauderdale Gay & Lesbian Guide
www.southfloridafun.com/fortlauderdale/index.shtml

Fort Lauderdale Home Page
info.ci.ftlaud.fl.us

Fort Lauderdale Hotels & Discount Guide
www.flhotels.com/ftlauderdale/index.html

Fort Lauderdale Information Access
ft-lauderdale.info-access.com

Fort Lauderdale Information Network
www.gfl.com

Fort Lauderdale Night Guide
ft.lauderdale.nightguide.com

Fort Lauderdale Restaurant Guide
ft.lauderdale.diningguide.net

Fort Lauderdale Visitors Guide
www.introweb.com/fortlauderdale/mainmenu.htm

HotelGuide Fort Lauderdale
fort.lauderdale.hotelguide.net

InSouthFlorida.com
www.insouthflorida.com

Lodging.com Fort Lauderdale Florida
www.lodging.com/auto/guides/ft_lauderdale-area-fl.html

MetroGuide Fort Lauderdale
metroguide.net/fll

SoFla.com
www.sofla.com

Surf & Sun Beach Vacation Guide to Fort Lauderdale
www.surf-sun.com/fl-ft-lauderdale-main.htm

Area Communities

Communities in Greater Fort Lauderdale with populations greater than 10,000 include:

Coconut Creek
4800 W Copans Rd
Coconut Creek, FL 33063
Phone: 954-973-6770
Fax: 954-973-6794

Cooper City
PO Box 290910
Cooper City, FL 33329
Phone: 954-434-4300
Fax: 954-434-5099

Coral Springs
9551 W Sample Rd
Coral Springs, FL 33065
Phone: 954-344-1001
Fax: 954-344-1016

Dania Beach
100 W Dania Beach Blvd
Dania Beach, FL 33004
Phone: 954-921-8700
Fax: 954-921-2604

Davie
6591 Orange Dr
Davie, FL 33314
Phone: 954-797-1000
Fax: 954-797-2061

Deerfield Beach
150 NE 2nd Ave
Deerfield Beach, FL 33441
Phone: 954-480-4200
Fax: 954-480-4268

Hallandale
400 S Federal Hwy
Hallandale, FL 33009
Phone: 954-458-3251
Fax: 954-457-1342

Hollywood
2600 Hollywood Blvd
Hollywood, FL 33022
Phone: 954-921-3473
Fax: 954-921-3268

Lauderdale Lakes
4300 NW 36th St
Lauderdale Lakes, FL 33319
Phone: 954-731-1212
Fax: 954-733-5126

Lauderhill
2200 NW 55th Ave
Lauderhill, FL 33313
Phone: 954-739-0100
Fax: 954-730-3062

Lighthouse Point
PO Box 5100
Lighthouse Point, FL 33074
Phone: 954-943-6500
Fax: 954-784-3446

Margate
5790 Margate Blvd
Margate, FL 33063
Phone: 954-972-6454
Fax: 954-974-3191

Miramar
6700 Miramar Pkwy
Miramar, FL 33023
Phone: 954-967-1500
Fax: 954-967-1512

North Lauderdale
701 SW 71st Ave
North Lauderdale, FL 33068
Phone: 954-722-0900
Fax: 954-720-2064

Oakland Park
3650 NE 12th Ave
Oakland Park, FL 33334
Phone: 954-561-6250
Fax: 954-561-6299

Parkland
6600 University Dr
Parkland, FL 33067
Phone: 954-753-5040
Fax: 954-341-5161

Pembroke Pines
10100 Pines Blvd
Pembroke Pines, FL 33025
Phone: 954-431-4500
Fax: 954-437-1149

Plantation
400 NW 73rd Ave
Plantation, FL 33317
Phone: 954-797-2200
Fax: 954-797-2756

Pompano Beach
100 W Atlantic Blvd
Pompano Beach, FL 33060
Phone: 954-786-4600
Fax: 954-786-4504

Sunrise
10770 W Oakland Park Blvd
Sunrise, FL 33351
Phone: 954-741-2580
Fax: 954-746-3439

Tamarac
7525 NW 88th Ave
Tamarac, FL 33321
Phone: 954-724-1200
Fax: 954-724-2454

Wilton Manors
524 NE 21st Ct
Wilton Manors, FL 33305
Phone: 954-390-2100
Fax: 954-390-2199

Economy

Fort Lauderdale has a diverse economic base and is home to many leading U.S. companies. Major corporations headquartered in Fort Lauderdale include Alliance Entertainment, Alamo Rent A Car, and Microsoft's Latin Operations, and more than 80 Fortune 500 companies have divisions in the area. Services and trade are Greater Fort Lauderdale's leading employment sectors. With annual sales figures exceeding $14 million, Greater Fort Lauderdale is one of the top retail markets in the entire world. Tourism is also among the area's biggest industries. A large number of Greater Fort Lauderdale residents are also employed in various government positions. The Broward County School Board and county government are the area's largest and third largest employers, respectively.

Unemployment Rate 4.1%*
Per Capita Income $27,661*
Median Family Income $53,200*

** Information given is for the Fort Lauderdale Metropolitan Statistical Area (MSA), which includes the City of Fort Lauderdale and the remainder of Broward County.*

Principal Industries & Number of Wage Earners

Broward County - 1998

Agricultural Services, Forestry, & Fishing 6,081
Construction 34,697
Finance, Insurance, & Real Estate 46,313
Government 79,737
Manufacturing 39,737
Mining 138
Retail Trade 138,298
Services 197,964
Transportation, Communications, & Public Utilities 29,984
Wholesale Trade 38,594

Major Employers

Alamo Rent A Car Inc
PO Box 22776
Fort Lauderdale, FL 33335
www.goalamo.com
Phone: 954-320-4400
TF: 800-327-9633

American Express
777 American Expy
Fort Lauderdale, FL 33337
www.americanexpress.com
Phone: 954-503-3000
Fax: 954-503-3822

Broward County
115 S Andrews Ave Rm 421
Fort Lauderdale, FL 33301
www.co.broward.fl.us
Phone: 954-357-7000
Fax: 954-357-7295

Citrix Systems Inc
6400 NW 6th Way
Fort Lauderdale, FL 33309
www.citrix.com
Phone: 954-267-3000
Fax: 954-267-9319
TF: 800-393-1888

Florida Medical Center Hospital
5000 W Oakland Park Blvd
Fort Lauderdale, FL 33313
www.tenethealth.com/FloridaMedical
Phone: 954-735-6000
Fax: 954-735-0532
TF: 800-222-9355

Fort Lauderdale City Hall
100 N Andrews Ave
Fort Lauderdale, FL 33301
ci.ftlaud.fl.us
Phone: 954-761-5000
Fax: 954-761-5122

Memorial Regional Hospital
3501 Johnson St
Hollywood, FL 33021
www.memorialregional.com
Phone: 954-987-2000
Fax: 954-985-3412

North Broward Hospital District
303 SE 17th St
Fort Lauderdale, FL 33316
E-mail: clar80@nbhd.org
www.nbhd.org
Phone: 954-355-5100
Fax: 954-355-4966

Nova Southeastern University
3301 College Ave
Fort Lauderdale, FL 33314
E-mail: benny@nsu.acast.nova.edu
www.nova.edu
Phone: 954-262-7300
Fax: 954-262-3811
TF: 800-541-6682

Paychex Business Solutions
4000 Hollywood Blvd Suite 285
Hollywood, FL 33021
www.paychex.com
Phone: 954-986-2669
Fax: 954-986-2247

Publix Super Markets Inc
PO Box 407
Lakeland, FL 33802
www.publix.com
Phone: 863-688-1188
Fax: 863-284-5571

School Board of Broward County
600 SE 3rd Ave
Fort Lauderdale, FL 33301
www.browardschools.com
Phone: 954-765-6000

Spherion Corp
2050 Spectrum Blvd
Fort Lauderdale, FL 33309
www.spherion.com
Phone: 954-938-7600
Fax: 954-938-7666

Sun-Sentinel
200 E Las Olas Blvd
Fort Lauderdale, FL 33301
www.sun-sentinel.com
Phone: 954-356-4000
Fax: 954-356-4559
TF: 800-548-6397

Templeton Worldwide Inc
500 E Broward Blvd Suite 2100
Fort Lauderdale, FL 33394
Phone: 954-764-7390
Fax: 954-527-7329

Vacation Break USA
6400 N Andrews Ave Suite 200
Fort Lauderdale, FL 33309
Phone: 954-351-8500
Fax: 954-351-8510
TF: 800-633-2336

Winn-Dixie Stores Inc
1141 SW 12th Ave
Pompano Beach, FL 33069
E-mail: comments@winn-dixie.com
www.winn-dixie.com
Phone: 954-783-2700
Fax: 954-783-2896

Quality of Living Indicators

Total Crime Index 18,260
(rates per 100,000 inhabitants)

Violent Crime
Murder/manslaughter 16
Forcible rape 72
Robbery 935
Aggravated assault 751

Property Crime
Burglary 3,714
Larceny theft 10,418
Motor vehicle theft 2,354

Cost of Living Index..................................103.3
(national average = 100)

Median Home Price.................................$136,100

Education

Public Schools

School Board of Broward County
600 SE 3rd Ave
Fort Lauderdale, FL 33301
www.browardschools.com
Phone: 954-765-6000

Number of Schools
Elementary 127
Middle 33
High....................................... 22

Student/Teacher Ratio
All Grades 18.6:1

Private Schools

Number of Schools (all grades) .... 12+

Colleges & Universities

Art Institute of Fort Lauderdale
1799 SE 17th St
Fort Lauderdale, FL 33316
www.aifl.edu
Phone: 954-463-3000
Fax: 954-523-7676
TF: 800-275-7603

Broward Community College Downtown Center
225 E Las Olas Blvd
Fort Lauderdale, FL 33301
www.broward.cc.fl.us
Phone: 954-475-6500
Fax: 954-761-7466

Broward Community College North Campus
1000 Coconut Creek Pkwy
Coconut Creek, FL 33066
www.broward.cc.fl.us
Phone: 954-973-2240
Fax: 954-973-2247

Florida Atlantic University
777 Glades Rd
Boca Raton, FL 33431
E-mail: barton@fau.edu
www.fau.edu
Phone: 561-297-3000
Fax: 561-297-2758
TF: 800-299-4328

Florida Metropolitan University Fort Lauderdale College
1040 Bayview Dr
Fort Lauderdale, FL 33304
fmu.edu/784/f-784.htm
Phone: 954-568-1600
Fax: 954-568-2008
TF: 800-468-0168

ITT Technical Institute
3401 S University Dr
Fort Lauderdale, FL 33328
www.itt-tech.edu
Phone: 954-476-9300
Fax: 954-476-6889
TF: 800-488-7797

Lynn University
3601 N Military Trail
Boca Raton, FL 33431
E-mail: admission@lynn.edu
www.lynn.edu
Phone: 561-994-0770
Fax: 561-241-3552
TF: 800-544-8035

Nova Southeastern University
3301 College Ave
Fort Lauderdale, FL 33314
E-mail: benny@nsu.acast.nova.edu
www.nova.edu
Phone: 954-262-7300
Fax: 954-262-3811
TF: 800-541-6682

Prospect Hall School of Business
2620 Hollywood Blvd
Hollywood, FL 33020
E-mail: prospect@shadow.net
www.prospect.edu
Phone: 954-923-8100
Fax: 954-923-4297

Hospitals

Broward General Medical Center
1600 S Andrews Ave
Fort Lauderdale, FL 33316
www.nbhd.org/facility/bgmc.htm
Phone: 954-355-4400
Fax: 954-355-4410

Cleveland Clinic Hospital
2835 N Ocean Blvd
Fort Lauderdale, FL 33308
www4.clevelandclinic.org/florida/info/hospital.htm
Phone: 954-568-1000
Fax: 954-565-9928

Coral Springs Medical Center
3000 Coral Hills Dr
Coral Springs, FL 33065
www.nbhd.org/facility/csmc.htm
Phone: 954-344-3000
Fax: 954-344-3121

Florida Medical Center Hospital
5000 W Oakland Park Blvd
Fort Lauderdale, FL 33313
www.tenethealth.com/FloridaMedical
Phone: 954-735-6000
Fax: 954-735-0532
TF: 800-222-9355

Hollywood Medical Center
3600 Washington St
Hollywood, FL 33021
www.tenethealth.com/Hollywood
Phone: 954-966-4500
Fax: 954-985-6322

Holy Cross Hospital
4725 N Federal Hwy
Fort Lauderdale, FL 33308
www.holy-cross.com
Phone: 954-771-8000
Fax: 954-492-5777

Imperial Point Medical Center
6401 N Federal Hwy
Fort Lauderdale, FL 33308
Phone: 954-776-8500
Fax: 954-776-8609

Memorial Hospital Pembroke
2301 N University Dr
Pembroke Pines, FL 33024
www.memorialpembroke.com
Phone: 954-962-9650
Fax: 954-963-8036

Memorial Hospital West
703 N Flamingo Rd
Pembroke Pines, FL 33028
www.memorialwest.com
Phone: 954-436-5000
Fax: 954-433-7168

Memorial Regional Hospital
3501 Johnson St
Hollywood, FL 33021
www.memorialregional.com
Phone: 954-987-2000
Fax: 954-985-3412

North Ridge Medical Center
5757 N Dixie Hwy
Fort Lauderdale, FL 33334
www.tenethealth.com/NorthRidge
Phone: 954-776-6000
Fax: 954-938-3230

Northwest Medical Center
2801 N SR 7
Margate, FL 33063
Phone: 954-978-4008
Fax: 954-978-4019

Plantation General Hospital
401 NW 42nd Ave
Plantation, FL 33317
Phone: 954-587-5010
Fax: 954-587-3220

University Hospital
7201 N University Dr
Tamarac, FL 33321
Phone: 954-721-2200
Fax: 954-724-6567

Westside Regional Medical Center
8201 W Broward Blvd
Plantation, FL 33324
www.westsideregional.com
Phone: 954-473-6600
Fax: 954-452-2133

Transportation

Airport(s)

Fort Lauderdale/Hollywood International Airport (FLL)
5 miles S of downtown (approx 15 minutes) 954-359-6100
Palm Beach International Airport (PBI)
43 miles N of downtown Fort Lauderdale
(approx 60 minutes) 561-471-7412

Mass Transit

Broward County Transportation Authority
$1 Base fare 954-357-8400
Tri-Rail
fare varies with destination 800-874-7245
WaterBus
$1.75 Base fare 954-467-6677

Rail/Bus

Amtrak Station
200 SW 21st Terr
Fort Lauderdale, FL 33312
Phone: 954-587-6692

Greyhound Bus Station
515 NE 3rd St
Fort Lauderdale, FL 33301
Phone: 954-764-6551
TF: 800-231-2222

Utilities

Electricity
Florida Power & Light 954-797-5000
www.fpl.com

Gas
Teco Peoples Gas 954-763-8900
www.peoplesgas.com

Water
Fort Lauderdale Water Dept 954-761-5150

Garbage Collection/Recycling
Fort Lauderdale Garbage Collection/Recycling 954-771-0880

Telecommunications

Telephone
BellSouth Telecommunications Inc 954-780-2355
www.bellsouth.com

Cable Television
Advanced Cable Communications 954-753-0100
www.advancedcable.net
AT & T Cable Services 954-532-6000
Comcast Cable 954-527-6600

Internet Service Providers (ISPs)
Acquired Knowledge Systems Inc 954-525-2574
www.aksi.net
Advanced Cable Communications ISP Channel ... 888-326-9809
www.advancedcable.net/int_srv_0.html
Cybergate Inc 954-334-8000
www.gate.net
Seflin Free-Net 954-357-7318
www.seflin.org
Zimmerman Communications 954-584-0199
zim.net

Banks

American National Bank
4301 N Federal Hwy
Oakland Park, FL 33308
www.americannationalbank.com
Phone: 954-491-7788
Fax: 954-491-2833

BankAtlantic
1750 E Sunrise Blvd
Fort Lauderdale, FL 33304
E-mail: relocat@icanect.net
www.bankatlantic.com
Phone: 954-760-5000
Fax: 954-760-5595
TF: 800-741-1700

Citibank
500 E Broward Blvd
Fort Lauderdale, FL 33394
Phone: 800-374-9800

City National Bank of Florida
450 E Las Olas Blvd
Fort Lauderdale, FL 33301
Phone: 954-467-6667
Fax: 954-524-8247

Colonial Bank
600 S Andrews Ave
Fort Lauderdale, FL 33301
Phone: 954-462-6093
Fax: 954-764-6782

Comerica Bank
100 NE 3rd Ave Suite 100
Fort Lauderdale, FL 33301
Phone: 954-468-0600
Fax: 954-468-0615
TF: 800-225-6077

First Union National Bank
200 E Broward Blvd
Fort Lauderdale, FL 33301
Phone: 954-467-5111
Fax: 954-467-5240
TF: 800-275-3862

Gateway American Bank of Florida
1451 NW 62nd St Suite 212
Fort Lauderdale, FL 33309
Phone: 954-772-0005
Fax: 954-772-0254

NationsBank of Florida NA
100 SE 3rd Ave
Fort Lauderdale, FL 33394
Phone: 954-765-2000
Fax: 954-765-2820
TF: 800-299-2265

Northern Trust Bank of Florida NA
1100 E Las Olas Blvd
Fort Lauderdale, FL 33301
Phone: 954-527-0200

Regent Bank
1100 SE 3rd Ave
Fort Lauderdale, FL 33316
Phone: 954-474-5000
Fax: 954-765-5560

Republic Security Bank
110 E Broward Blvd
Fort Lauderdale, FL 33301
Phone: 954-522-1610
Fax: 954-262-8919

Southtrust Bank
225 N Federal Hwy
Pompano Beach, FL 33062
Phone: 954-786-9400
Fax: 954-782-9285

Sunniland Bank
424 W Sunrise Blvd
Fort Lauderdale, FL 33311
Phone: 954-764-8300
Fax: 954-462-7168

SunTrust Bank South Florida NA
501 E Las Olas Blvd
Fort Lauderdale, FL 33301
Phone: 954-766-2050
Fax: 954-765-7601
TF: 800-786-2265

Washington Mutual Bank
200 S Pine Island Rd
Plantation, FL 33324
Phone: 800-782-8875
Fax: 954-473-0266

Shopping

Beach Place Mall
17 S Fort Lauderdale Beach Blvd
Fort Lauderdale, FL 33316
Phone: 954-764-3460
Fax: 954-763-2527

Broward Mall
8000 W Broward Blvd
Plantation, FL 33388
Phone: 954-473-8100
Fax: 954-472-1389

Coral Square Mall
9469 W Atlantic Blvd
Coral Springs, FL 33071
Phone: 954-755-5550

Dania Beach Historic Antique Shopping District
Federal Hwy
Dania Beach, FL 33004
Phone: 954-927-1040

Fashion Mall
321 N University Dr
Plantation, FL 33324
Phone: 954-370-1884
Fax: 954-370-0571

Festival Flea Market Mall
2900 W Sample Rd
Pompano Beach, FL 33073
Phone: 954-979-4555
Fax: 954-968-3980

Galleria at Fort Lauderdale
2414 E Sunrise Blvd
Fort Lauderdale, FL 33304
Phone: 954-564-1015

Pembroke Lakes Mall
11401 Pines Blvd Suite 546
Pembroke Pines, FL 33026
Phone: 954-436-3520
Fax: 954-436-7992

Pompano Square Mall
2001 N Federal Hwy
Pompano Beach, FL 33062
Phone: 954-943-4683
Fax: 954-943-5469

Sawgrass Mills
12801 W Sunrise Blvd
Sunrise, FL 33323
www.sawgrassmillsmall.com
Phone: 954-846-2300
Fax: 954-846-2312
TF: 800-356-4557

Town Center at Boca Raton
6000 Glades Rd
Boca Raton, FL 33431
Phone: 561-368-6000
Fax: 561-338-0891

Media

Newspapers and Magazines

Broward News
767 S State Rd 7 Suite 1
Margate, FL 33068
Phone: 954-977-7770
Fax: 954-977-7779

City Link
200 E Las Olas Blvd Suite 1250
Fort Lauderdale, FL 33301
E-mail: citylink@clinkonline.com
www.clinkonline.com
Phone: 954-356-4943
Fax: 954-356-4949

Community News
5400 S University Dr Suite 605
Fort Lauderdale, FL 33328
Phone: 954-680-4460
Fax: 954-680-9965

Coral Springs/Parkland Forum
9660 W Sample Rd Suite 203
Coral Springs, FL 33065
Phone: 954-752-7474
Fax: 954-752-7855

Deerfield Beach-Lighthouse Point Observer
43 NE 2nd St
Deerfield Beach, FL 33441
Phone: 954-428-9045
Fax: 954-428-9096

Deerfield Times
601 Fairway Dr
Deerfield Beach, FL 33441
Phone: 954-698-6397
Fax: 954-429-1207
TF: 800-275-8820

Digest The
224 S Dixie Hwy
Hallandale, FL 33009
Phone: 954-457-8029
Fax: 954-457-1284
TF: 800-344-3780

Eastsider
PO Box 1189
Deerfield Beach, FL 33441
Phone: 954-698-6397
Fax: 954-429-1207
TF: 800-275-8820

Gold Coast
800 E Broward Blvd Cumberland Bldg Suite 506
Fort Lauderdale, FL 33301
Phone: 954-462-4488
Fax: 954-462-5588

Margate/Coconut Creek Forum
9660 W Sample Rd Suite 203
Coral Springs, FL 33065
Phone: 954-752-7474
Fax: 954-752-7855

Miami Herald Broward Edition*
1520 E Sunrise Blvd
Fort Lauderdale, FL 33304
Phone: 954-527-8940
Fax: 954-527-8955

Miami Metro Magazine
2800 Biscayne Blvd 11th Fl
Miami, FL 33137
E-mail: miametro@bellsouth.net
miamimetro.com
Phone: 305-755-9920
Fax: 305-755-9921
TF: 800-288-8388

New Times Broward Palm Beach
16 NE 4th St
Fort Lauderdale, FL 33301
E-mail: feedback@newtimesbpb.com
www.newtimesbpb.com
Phone: 954-233-1600
Fax: 954-233-1551

Pompano Ledger
2500 SE 5th Ct
Pompano Beach, FL 33062
E-mail: editor@pompanoledger.com
www.pompanoledger.com
Phone: 954-532-2000

South Florida Business Journal
4000 Hollywood Blvd Suite 695 South
Hollywood, FL 33021
www.amcity.com/southflorida
Phone: 954-359-2100
Fax: 954-359-2135

Sun-Sentinel*
200 E Las Olas Blvd
Fort Lauderdale, FL 33301
www.sun-sentinel.com
Phone: 954-356-4000
Fax: 954-356-4559
TF: 800-548-6397

Sunrise Times
601 Fairway Dr
Deerfield Beach, FL 33441
Phone: 954-698-6501
Fax: 954-429-1207

Tamarac/North Lauderdale Forum
PO Box 1189
Deerfield Beach, FL 33441
Phone: 954-698-6501
Fax: 954-698-6719

**Indicates major daily newspapers*

Television

WBZL-TV Ch 39 (WB)
2055 Lee St
Hollywood, FL 33020
E-mail: wb39@expressweb.com
www.wb39.com
Phone: 954-925-3939
Fax: 954-922-3965

WFOR-TV Ch 4 (CBS)
8900 NW 18th Terr
Miami, FL 33172
E-mail: news4@wfor.groupw.wec.com
wfor.cbsnow.com
Phone: 305-591-4444
Fax: 305-477-3040

WPBF-TV Ch 25 (ABC)
3970 RCA Blvd Suite 7007
Palm Beach Gardens, FL 33410
Phone: 561-694-2525
Fax: 561-624-1089

WPBT-TV Ch 2 (PBS)
14901 NE 20th Ave
Miami, FL 33181
www.channel2.org
Phone: 305-949-8321
Fax: 305-949-9772

WPEC-TV Ch 12 (CBS)
1100 Fairfield Dr
West Palm Beach, FL 33407
www.gopbi.com/partners/news12
Phone: 561-844-1212
Fax: 561-881-0731
TF: 800-930-9732

WPLG-TV Ch 10 (ABC)
3900 Biscayne Blvd
Miami, FL 33137
www.wplg.com/
Phone: 305-576-1010
Fax: 305-325-2480

WPTV-TV Ch 5 (NBC)
622 N Flagler Dr
West Palm Beach, FL 33401
E-mail: wptv@magg.net
www.wptv.com
Phone: 561-655-5455
Fax: 561-653-5719

WSVN-TV Ch 7 (Fox)
1401 79th St Cswy
Miami, FL 33141
E-mail: 7news@wsvn.com
www.wsvn.com
Phone: 305-751-6692
Fax: 305-757-2266

WTVJ-TV Ch 6 (NBC)
15000 SW 27 St
Miramar, FL 33027
www.nbc6.nbc.com
Phone: 954-622-6000
Fax: 954-622-6107

Radio

WAMR-FM 107.5 MHz (Span)
2828 Coral Way Suite 102
Miami, FL 33145
E-mail: comentarios@wamr.com
www.wamr.com
Phone: 305-447-1140
Fax: 305-643-1075

WAVS-AM 1170 kHz (Span)
6360 SW 41st Pl
Davie, FL 33314
Phone: 954-584-1170
TF: 888-854-9660

WBGG-FM 105.9 MHz (CR)
194 NW 187th St
Miami, FL 33169
E-mail: big106@big106fm.com
www.big106fm.com
Phone: 305-654-9494
Fax: 305-654-9090

WFLC-FM 97.3 MHz (AC)
2741 N 29th Ave
Hollywood, FL 33020
www.coastfm.com
Phone: 954-584-7117
Fax: 954-847-3223

WFTL-AM 1400 kHz (N/T)
1000 Corporate Dr Suite 330
Fort Lauderdale, FL 33334
Phone: 954-776-5300
Fax: 954-771-8176

WHQT-FM 105.1 MHz (Urban)
2741 N 29th Ave
Hollywood, FL 33020
www.hot105fm.com
Phone: 954-584-7117
Fax: 954-847-3223

WHYI-FM 100.7 MHz (CHR)
1975 E Sunrise Blvd Suite 400
Fort Lauderdale, FL 33304
www.y-100.com
Phone: 954-463-9299
Fax: 954-522-7002

WKIS-FM 99.9 MHz (Ctry)
9881 Sheridan St
Hollywood, FL 33024
E-mail: wkis@sefl.satelnet.org
www.wkis.com
Phone: 954-431-6200
Fax: 954-437-2466

WKPX-FM 88.5 MHz (Alt)
8000 NW 44th St
Sunrise, FL 33351
Phone: 954-572-1321
Fax: 954-572-1344

WLRN-FM 91.3 MHz (NPR)
172 NE 15th St
Miami, FL 33132
E-mail: radio@wlrn.org
www.wlrn.org/radio-fm
Phone: 305-995-1717
Fax: 305-995-2299

WLVE-FM 93.9 MHz (NAC)
194 NW 187th St
Miami, FL 33169
www.love94.com
Phone: 305-654-9494
Fax: 305-654-9090
TF: 800-603-9494

WMGE-FM 103.5 MHz (AC)
1975 E Sunrise Blvd Suite 400
Fort Lauderdale, FL 33304
www.megamiami.com
Phone: 954-463-9299
Fax: 954-462-5839

WPOW-FM 96.5 MHz (CHR)
20295 NW 2nd Ave
Miami, FL 33169
www.power96.com
Phone: 305-653-6796
Fax: 305-770-1456

WQAM-AM 560 kHz (Sports)
20295 NW 2nd Ave
Miami, FL 33169
wqam.com
Phone: 305-653-6796
Fax: 305-770-1456

WRMF-FM 97.9 MHz (AC)
2406 S Congress Ave
West Palm Beach, FL 33406
www.gopbi.com/partners/wrmf
Phone: 561-432-5100
Fax: 561-432-5111

WRTO-FM 98.3 MHz (Span)
2828 Coral Way Suite 102
Miami, FL 33145
E-mail: info@wrto.com
www.wrto.com
Phone: 305-447-1140
Fax: 305-445-8908

WSUA-AM 1260 kHz (Span)
2100 Coral Way
Miami, FL 33145
Phone: 305-285-1260
Fax: 305-858-5907

WTMI-FM 93.1 MHz (Clas)
3225 Aviation Ave
Miami, FL 33133
E-mail: wtmi@safari.net
www.wtmi.com
Phone: 305-856-9393
Fax: 305-854-0783

WXDJ-FM 95.7 MHz (Span)
1001 Ponce de Leon Blvd
Coral Gables, FL 33134
www.elzol95fm.com
Phone: 305-447-9595
Fax: 305-461-4466

WZTA-FM 94.9 MHz (Rock)
194 NW 187th St
Miami, FL 33169
www.949zeta.com
Phone: 305-654-9494
Fax: 305-654-9090

Attractions

Tourism is one of Fort Lauderdale's biggest industries—the city welcomes more than five million visitors each year. Fort Lauderdale is not only a top vacation destination itself, but it is also a gateway to the Bahamas and the Caribbean via Port Everglades, the world's second largest passenger cruise port. The city's world-famous beaches have recently been revitalized with a palm-lined oceanfront walk, the new Beach Place shopping complex, and a host of cafes and restaurants. The Downtown Fort Lauderdale area includes Riverwalk, a brick-lined promenade park along the banks of the New River; the Museum of Discovery and Science/Blockbuster IMAX Theater, which features hands-on exhibits, educational play areas for children, and a five-story high IMAX movie screen; the recently-built $55 million Broward Center for the Performing Arts; and the quaint shops of Las Olas Boulevard.

Anne Kolb Nature Center
751 Sheridan St
Hollywood, FL 33019
www.co.broward.fl.us/pri02300.htm
Phone: 954-926-2410
Fax: 954-926-2491

Art & Culture Center of Hollywood
1650 Harrison St
Hollywood, FL 33020
Phone: 954-921-3275
Fax: 954-921-3273

Bailey Hall
3501 SW Davie Rd
Fort Lauderdale, FL 33314
Phone: 954-475-6884

Beach Place Mall
17 S Fort Lauderdale Beach Blvd
Fort Lauderdale, FL 33316
Phone: 954-764-3460
Fax: 954-763-2527

Blockbuster 3D IMAX Theater
401 SW 2nd St
Fort Lauderdale, FL 33312
www.mods.org/imaxpage1.htm
Phone: 954-463-4629
Fax: 954-467-0046

Bonnet House
900 N Birch Rd
Fort Lauderdale, FL 33304
www.bonnethouse.com
Phone: 954-563-5393
Fax: 954-561-4174

Broward Center for the Performing Arts
201 SW 5th Ave
Fort Lauderdale, FL 33312
www.curtainup.org
Phone: 954-522-5334
Fax: 954-462-3541
TF: 800-564-9539

Broward County Historical Commission
151 SW 2nd St
Fort Lauderdale, FL 33301
www.co.broward.fl.us/history.htm
Phone: 954-765-4670
Fax: 954-765-4437

Buehler Planetarium
3501 SW Davie Rd
Davie, FL 33314
terra.broward.cc.fl.us/central/buehler
Phone: 954-475-6681
Fax: 954-475-2858

Butterfly World
3600 W Sample Rd Tradewinds Pk S
Coconut Creek, FL 33073
E-mail: gardens@butterflyworld.com
www.butterflyworld.com
Phone: 954-977-4400
Fax: 954-977-4501

Coral Ridge Concert Series
5555 N Federal Hwy
Fort Lauderdale, FL 33308
Phone: 954-491-1103
Fax: 954-491-7374

Coral Springs City Centre
2855 Coral Springs Dr
Coral Springs, FL 33065
E-mail: info@coralspringscitycentre.com
www.coralspringscitycentre.com
Phone: 954-344-5990
Fax: 954-344-5980

Everglades Holiday Park
2194 Griffin Rd
Fort Lauderdale, FL 33332
www.introweb.com/everglades
Phone: 954-434-8111
Fax: 954-434-4252

Fern Forest Nature Center
201 Lyons Rd S
Coconut Creek, FL 33063
www.co.broward.fl.us/pri01400.htm
Phone: 954-970-0150
Fax: 954-970-0111

Flamingo Gardens
3750 Flamingo Rd
Davie, FL 33330
www.flamingogardens.org
Phone: 954-473-2955
Fax: 954-473-1738

Florida Grand Opera
221 SW 3rd Ave
Fort Lauderdale, FL 33312
Phone: 954-728-9700
Fax: 954-728-9702

Florida Philharmonic
3401 NW 9th Ave
Fort Lauderdale, FL 33309
E-mail: admin@flaphil.com
www.flaphil.com
Phone: 954-561-2997
Fax: 954-561-1390
TF: 800-226-1812

Fort Lauderdale Beach
A1A betw 17th St & Sunrise Blvd
Fort Lauderdale, FL 33316
www.fortlauderdalebeach.com
Phone: 954-468-1595

Fort Lauderdale Children's Theater
640 N Andrews Ave
Fort Lauderdale, FL 33311
E-mail: flct@shadow.net
www.flct.org
Phone: 954-763-6901
Fax: 954-523-0507

Fort Lauderdale Historical Museum
231 SW 2nd Ave
Fort Lauderdale, FL 33301
Phone: 954-463-4433
Fax: 954-463-4434

Fort Lauderdale Historical Society
219 SW 2nd Ave
Fort Lauderdale, FL 33301
Phone: 954-463-4431
Fax: 954-463-4434

Fort Lauderdale Museum of Art
1 E Las Olas Blvd
Fort Lauderdale, FL 33301
www.museumofart.org
Phone: 954-525-5500
Fax: 954-524-6011

Fort Lauderdale Players
104 SE 1st St
Fort Lauderdale, FL 33301
E-mail: flplayers@aol.com
Phone: 954-760-7171
Fax: 954-761-5376

Fort Lauderdale Swap Shop
3291 W Sunrise Blvd
Fort Lauderdale, FL 33311
www.floridaswapshop.com
Phone: 954-791-7927
Fax: 954-583-8920

Fox Observatory
16001 W SR 84 Markham Pk
Sunrise, FL 33326
Phone: 954-384-0442
Fax: 954-389-2019

Gold Coast Jazz Society
901 E Las Olas Blvd Suite 201
Fort Lauderdale, FL 33301
E-mail: jmackle@omnigraphics.com
www.goldcoastjazz.org
Phone: 954-524-0805
Fax: 954-524-7041

Gold Coast Opera
2855 Coral Springs Dr Coral Springs City Centre
Coral Springs, FL 33065
Phone: 954-344-5990
Fax: 954-344-5980

Grand Prix Race-O-Rama
1801 NW 1st St
Dania Beach, FL 33004
E-mail: sales@grandprixflorida.com
Phone: 954-921-1411
Fax: 954-923-2604

Graves Museum of Archaeology & Natural History
481 S Federal Hwy
Dania Beach, FL 33044
Phone: 954-925-7770
Fax: 954-925-7064

Holiday Park
Federal Hwy & NE 8th St
Fort Lauderdale, FL 33304
Phone: 954-761-5385
Fax: 954-761-5650

Hugh Taylor Birch State Park
3109 E Sunrise Blvd
Fort Lauderdale, FL 33304
Phone: 954-564-4521
Fax: 954-762-3737

IGFA Fishing Hall of Fame & Museum
300 Gulf Stream Way
Dania Beach, FL 33004
Phone: 954-927-2628
Fax: 954-924-4299

International Swimming Hall of Fame
1 Hall of Fame Dr
Fort Lauderdale, FL 33316
E-mail: museum@ishof.org
www.ishof.org
Phone: 954-462-6536
Fax: 954-522-4521

Jungle Queen
801 Seabreeze Blvd Bahia Mar Yacht Basin
Fort Lauderdale, FL 33316
www.junglequeen.com
Phone: 954-462-5596
Fax: 954-832-9923

King-Cromartie House
229 SW 2nd Ave
Fort Lauderdale, FL 33301
Phone: 954-463-4431

Las Olas Boulevard
downtown Fort Lauderdale
Fort Lauderdale, FL 33301
E-mail: lasolas@lasolasonline.com
www.lasolasonline.com

Lloyd John U Beach State Recreation Area
6503 N Ocean Dr
Dania Beach, FL 33004
Phone: 954-924-3859
Fax: 954-923-2904

Lumonics Light/Sound Theater
3017 NW 60th St
Fort Lauderdale, FL 33309
www.lumonicslightandsound.com
Phone: 954-979-3161
Fax: 954-972-5802

Markham Park & Range
16001 W SR 84
Sunrise, FL 33326
www.co.broward.fl.us/pri01600.htm
Phone: 954-389-2000
Fax: 954-389-2019

Museum of Discovery & Science
401 SW 2nd St
Fort Lauderdale, FL 33312
www.mods.org
Phone: 954-467-6637
Fax: 954-467-0046

Native Indian Village
3551 N SR 7
Hollywood, FL 33021
Phone: 954-961-4519
Fax: 954-961-7221

Okalee Museum
5845 S SR-7
Fort Lauderdale, FL 33314
E-mail: museum@semtribe.com
www.seminoletribe.com/museum
Phone: 954-792-0745
Fax: 954-583-9893

Old Dillard Museum
1009 NW 4th St
Fort Lauderdale, FL 33311
Phone: 954-765-6952
Fax: 954-765-8899

Old Fort Lauderdale Museum of History
231 SW 2nd Ave
Fort Lauderdale, FL 33301
Phone: 954-463-4431
Fax: 954-463-4434

Parker Playhouse
707 NE 8th St
Fort Lauderdale, FL 33304
Phone: 954-763-2444
Fax: 954-461-3180

Pompano Beach Amphitheater
NE 6th St & 18th Ave
Pompano Beach, FL 33060
Phone: 954-946-2402

Port Everglades
1850 Eller Dr
Fort Lauderdale, FL 33316
www.co.broward.fl.us/port.htm
Phone: 954-523-3404
Fax: 954-525-1910

Quiet Waters Park
401 S Powerline Rd
Deerfield Beach, FL 33442
www.co.broward.fl.us/pri01800.htm
Phone: 954-360-1315
Fax: 954-360-1349

Riverwalk
Fort Lauderdale, FL 33301
Phone: 954-765-4466

Sawgrass Recreation Park
US 27 2 miles N of I-75
Fort Lauderdale, FL 33329
Phone: 954-389-0202

Sea Screamer Boat Rides
125 N Riverside Dr Sands Harbor Hotel
Pompano Beach, FL 33062
Phone: 954-566-9697

Secret Woods Nature Center
2701 W SR-84
Fort Lauderdale, FL 33312
www.co.broward.fl.us/pri01900.htm
Phone: 954-791-1030
Fax: 954-791-1092

Seminole Indian Bingo & Poker Casino
4150 N SR 7
Hollywood, FL 33021
Phone: 954-961-3220
Fax: 954-961-3401

Stranahan House
335 SE 6th Ave
Fort Lauderdale, FL 33301
Phone: 954-524-4736
Fax: 954-525-2838

Sunrise Musical Theater
Nob Hill Rd & Commercial Blvd
Sunrise, FL 33351
Phone: 954-741-7300
Fax: 954-749-4032

Topeekeegnee Yugnee Park
3300 N Park Rd
Hollywood, FL 33021
www.co.broward.fl.us/pri02200.htm
Phone: 954-985-1980
Fax: 954-961-5950

Tradewinds Park
3600 W Sample Rd
Coconut Creek, FL 33073
www.co.broward.fl.us/pri02000.htm
Phone: 954-968-3880
Fax: 954-968-3896

Tree Tops Park
3900 SW 100th Ave
Davie, FL 33328
www.co.broward.fl.us/pri02100.htm
Phone: 954-370-3750
Fax: 954-370-3770

War Memorial Auditorium
800 NE 8th St
Fort Lauderdale, FL 33304
Phone: 954-761-5380
Fax: 954-761-5361

Young at Art Children's Museum
11584 SR-84
Davie, FL 33325
Phone: 954-424-0085
Fax: 954-370-5057

Sports Teams & Facilities

Baltimore Orioles Spring Training (baseball)
5301 NW 12th Ave
Fort Lauderdale, FL 33309
www.theorioles.com
Phone: 954-776-1921
Fax: 954-776-9116

Dania Jai-Alai
301 E Dania Beach Blvd
Dania Beach, FL 33004
www.dania-jai-alai.com
Phone: 954-927-2841
Fax: 954-920-9095

Florida Bobcats (football)
1 Panther Pkwy National Car Rental Ctr
Sunrise, FL 33323
www.floridabobcats.com
Phone: 954-577-9009
Fax: 954-577-9008

Florida Marlins
2267 NW 199th St Pro Player Stadium
Miami, FL 33056
www.flamarlins.com
Phone: 305-626-7400
Fax: 305-626-7428

Florida Panthers
2555 Panther Pkwy National Car Rental Center
Sunrise, FL 33323
E-mail: flpanthers@flpanthers.com
www.flpanthers.com
Phone: 954-835-7000
Fax: 954-835-8012

Gulfstream Park
901 S Federal Hwy
Hallandale, FL 33009
www.gulfstreampark.com
Phone: 954-454-7000
Fax: 954-454-7827

Hollywood Greyhound Track
831 N Federal Hwy
Hallandale, FL 33009
www.hollywoodgreyhound.com
Phone: 954-454-9400
Fax: 954-457-4229

Miami Dolphins
2269 NW 199th St Pro Player Stadium
Miami, FL 33056
www.miamidolphins.com
Phone: 305-620-2578

Miami Heat
1 SE 3rd Ave American Airlines Arena Suite 2300
Miami, FL 33131
www.nba.com/heat
Phone: 305-577-4328
Fax: 305-789-5933

National Car Rental Center
2555 Panther Pkwy
Sunrise, FL 33323
www.national-ctr.com
Phone: 954-835-8000
Fax: 954-835-8012

Pompano Park Racing
1800 SW 3rd St
Pompano Beach, FL 33069
www.pompanopark.com
Phone: 954-972-2000
Fax: 954-970-3098

Pro Player Stadium
2269 NW 199th St
Miami, FL 33056
www.proplayer.com
Phone: 305-623-6100
Fax: 305-624-6403

Annual Events

Air & Sea Show (early May) 954-765-4466
Art a la Carte (October) 954-525-5500
Beethoven by the Beach (early July) 800-226-1812
Broward County Fair (late November) 954-963-3247
Cajun Zydeco Crawfish Festival (early May) 954-489-3255
Canadafest (early February). 954-921-3404
Chris Evert Pro-Celebrity Tennis Classic
(early December) 561-394-2400
Christmas on Las Olas (early December). 954-765-4466
Fiesta Tropical Mardi Gras Carnival
(late February) 954-922-9959
Florida Renaissance Festival
(late January-early March) 954-776-1642
Fort Lauderdale Billfish Tournament (late April). . . .954-563-0385
Fort Lauderdale International Auto Show
(March) 954-765-5933
Fort Lauderdale International Boat Show
(late October-early November) 954-764-7642
Fort Lauderdale International Film Festival
(late October-mid-November) 954-760-9898
Fort Lauderdale Seafood Festival (early April) 954-463-4431
Fort Lauderdale Spring Boat Show
(mid-late April). 954-764-7642
Greek Festival (February) 954-467-1515
Hollywood Beach Latinfest (mid-August) 954-921-3460
Hollywood Jazz Festival (mid-March) 954-921-3404
Irish Fest (mid-March). 954-946-1093
Las Olas Art Fair (early September) 954-472-3755
Las Olas Art Festival (early March). 954-525-5500
Light Up Fort Lauderdale (December 31). 954-765-4466
Micron PC Bowl (early January). 954-564-5000
NationsBank Starlight Musicals
(mid-June-late August). 954-627-6500
New River Boat Parade (mid-late December). 954-791-0202
New Riverfest (April) 954-765-4466
Pompano Beach Rainbow Festival (late July) 954-786-4111
Pompano Beach Seafood Festival (late April) 954-941-2940
Promenade in the Park (October) 954-525-5500
Riverwalk Blues Festival (early November) 954-761-5934
Riverwalk Winter Arts & Crafts Show
(mid-January). 954-761-5363
Saint Patrick's Day Parade & Festival
(mid-March) 954-921-3404
Seminole Tribal Festival (mid-February) 954-967-3706
Sistrunk Historical Festival (early February). 954-357-7514
Taste of Fort Lauderdale (late February) 954-485-3481
Viva Broward (mid-October) 954-527-0627
Winterfest Boat Parade (mid-December) 954-767-0686

Fort Wayne, Indiana

***County:* Allen**

FORT WAYNE is located in northeastern Indiana. Major cities within 100 miles include South Bend, Indiana and Kalamazoo, Michigan..

Area (Land) .... 62.7 sq mi
Area (Water).......... 0.2 sq mi
Elevation.......... 781 ft
Latitude .... 41-13-06 N
Longitude.......... 85-12-89 W
Time Zone .... EST
Area Code.......... 219

Climate

Fort Wayne's climate features four distinct seasons. Winters are cold and cloudy with average high temperatures in the low to mid-30s and average lows ranging from the mid-teens to low 20s. The average annual snowfall in Fort Wayne is 31 inches. Summer days are warm with high temperatures averaging in the low to mid-80s, while evenings cool down to near 60 degrees. June and July are the wettest months in Fort Wayne; January and February are the driest.

Average Temperatures & Precipitation

Temperatures

	Jan	Feb	Mar	Apr	May	Jun	Jul	Aug	Sep	Oct	Nov	Dec
High	30	34	46	60	71	81	85	82	76	63	49	36
Low	15	18	29	39	49	59	63	61	54	43	34	22

Precipitation

	Jan	Feb	Mar	Apr	May	Jun	Jul	Aug	Sep	Oct	Nov	Dec
Inches	1.9	1.9	2.9	3.4	3.4	3.6	3.5	3.4	2.7	2.5	2.8	2.9

History

Originally inhabited by Native Americans of the Miami tribe, the Fort Wayne area was first explored by European settlers as early as 1690. The town of Fort Wayne was founded in 1894 when General "Mad" Anthony Wayne built a fort at the confluence of the Maumee, Saint Joseph, and Saint Marys rivers. It was incorporated as a city 46 years later in 1840. The construction of the Wabash-Erie Canal in 1840 and the arrival of the railroad in 1852, linking the city with Pittsburgh and Chicago, stimulated growth in Fort Wayne.

In 1998 the city received an "All American City" award and has been designated as one of America's most livable cities. Fort Wayne today, with a population of more than 185,000, is Indiana's second largest city.

Population

1990 Census 195,680
1998 Estimate.......... 185,716
% Change .... -9.9

Racial/Ethnic Breakdown
White.......... 75.6%
Black 15.7%
Other.......... 8.7%
Hispanic Origin (may be of any race) 2.7%

Age Breakdown
Under 5 years.......... 8.1%
5 to 17.......... 18.3%
18 to 20.......... 4.6%
21 to 24.......... 6.5%
25 to 34.......... 18.7%
35 to 44.......... 14.0%
45 to 54.......... 8.6%
55 to 64.......... 7.9%
65 to 74.......... 7.3%
75+ years 6.1%
Median Age.......... 31.6

Gender Breakdown
Male.......... 44.7%
Female.......... 55.3%

Government

Type of Government: Mayor-City Council

Fort Wayne City Clerk
1 Main St Rm 122
Fort Wayne, IN 46802
Phone: 219-427-1208
Fax: 219-427-1371

Fort Wayne City Council
1 Main St Rm 122
Fort Wayne, IN 46802
Phone: 219-427-1221
Fax: 219-427-1371

Fort Wayne City Hall
1 Main St
Fort Wayne, IN 46802
Phone: 219-427-1111
Fax: 219-427-1115

Fort Wayne City Utilities Div
1 Main St Rm 280
Fort Wayne, IN 46802
Phone: 219-427-1381
Fax: 219-427-2540

Fort Wayne Community & Economic Development Div
1 Main St Rm 910
Fort Wayne, IN 46802
Phone: 219-427-1131
Fax: 219-427-1115

Fort Wayne Finance & Administration Div
1 Main St Rm 930
Fort Wayne, IN 46802
Phone: 219-427-1106
Fax: 219-427-1404

Fort Wayne Fire Dept
307 E Murray St
Fort Wayne, IN 46803
Phone: 219-427-1170
Fax: 219-427-1277

Fort Wayne Human Resources Office
1 Main St Rm 320
Fort Wayne, IN 46802
Phone: 219-427-1180
Fax: 219-427-1177

Fort Wayne Mayor
1 Main St
Fort Wayne, IN 46802
Phone: 219-427-1111
Fax: 219-427-1115

Fort Wayne Parks & Recreation Dept
705 E State Blvd
Fort Wayne, IN 46805
Phone: 219-427-6000
Fax: 219-427-6020

Fort Wayne Planning Dept
1 Main St Rm 800
Fort Wayne, IN 46802
Phone: 219-427-1140
Fax: 219-427-1132

Fort Wayne Police Dept
1320 E Creighton Ave
Fort Wayne, IN 46803
Phone: 219-427-1230
Fax: 219-427-1374

Fort Wayne Public Works Board
1 Main St Rm 920
Fort Wayne, IN 46802
Phone: 219-427-1109
Fax: 219-427-5553

Important Phone Numbers

AAA 219-484-1541
Allen County Treasurer 219-449-7693
Driver's License/Vehicle Registration Information ... 219-489-0690
Emergency 911
Fort Wayne Assn of Realtors 219-426-4700
Indiana State Revenue Dept 219-456-3476
Poison Control Center 800-382-9097
Time/Temp 219-422-0123
Voter Registration Information 219-449-7154
Weather 219-424-5050

Information Sources

Allen County
715 S Calhoun St County Courthouse Rm 201
Fort Wayne, IN 46802
www.co.allen.in.us
Phone: 219-449-7245
Fax: 219-449-7929

Allen County War Memorial Coliseum
4000 Parnell Ave
Fort Wayne, IN 46805
www.memorialcoliseum.com
Phone: 219-482-9502
Fax: 219-484-1637

Better Business Bureau Serving Northeastern Indiana
1203 Webster St
Fort Wayne, IN 46802
www.neindiana.bbb.org
Phone: 219-423-4433
Fax: 219-423-3301

Grand Wayne Center
120 W Jefferson Blvd
Fort Wayne, IN 46802
www.grandwayne.com
Phone: 219-426-4100
Fax: 219-420-9080

Greater Fort Wayne Chamber of Commerce
826 Ewing St
Fort Wayne, IN 46802
www.fwchamber.org
Phone: 219-424-1435
Fax: 219-426-7232

Online Resources

4FortWayne.com
www.4fortwayne.com

Anthill City Guide Fort Wayne
www.anthill.com/city.asp?city=fortwayne

Area Guide Fort Wayne
fortwayne.areaguides.net

City Knowledge Fort Wayne
www.cityknowledge.com/in_fortwayne.htm

Excite.com Fort Wayne City Guide
www.excite.com/travel/countries/united_states/indiana/fort_wayne

Ft-Wayne.Com
www.ft-wayne.com

InFortWayne.com
www.inftwayne.com/

Area Communities

Communities in the Fort Wayne metropolitan area (which encompasses Adams, Allen, DeKalb, Huntington, Wells, and Whitley counties) with populations greater than 5,000 include:

Auburn
210 E 9th St
Auburn, IN 46706
Phone: 219-925-5430
Fax: 219-925-8228

Bluffton
128 E Market St
Bluffton, IN 46714
Phone: 219-824-0612
Fax: 219-824-6041

Columbia City
112 S Chauncey St
Columbia City, IN 46725
Phone: 219-248-5112
Fax: 219-248-5105

Decatur
225 W Monroe St
Decatur, IN 46733
Phone: 219-724-4307
Fax: 219-724-7213

Garrett
130 S Randolph St
Garrett, IN 46738
Phone: 219-357-3836
Fax: 219-357-3146

Huntington
300 Cherry St
Huntington, IN 46750
Phone: 219-356-1400
Fax: 219-356-0344

New Haven
815 Lincoln Hwy E
New Haven, IN 46774
Phone: 219-749-5720
Fax: 219-493-6467

Economy

Manufacturing is the leading employment sector in the Fort Wayne metropolitan area. Goods produced in Fort Wayne include truck bodies, electrical equipment, and ice cream. The services sector is a close second based upon number of employees, and health service positions account for nearly one-third of all service-related jobs. Government is also an important component of Fort Wayne's economy—more than 27,000 area residents are employed in various agencies at the federal, state, and local levels.

Unemployment Rate 2.8%*
Per Capita Income..........................$24,890*
Median Family Income......................$51,900*

** Information given is for the Fort Wayne Metropolitan Statistical Area (MSA), which includes the City of Fort Wayne and Allen County.*

Principal Industries & Number of Wage Earners

Fort Wayne MSA* - 1999

Construction & Mining................................13,500
Finance, Insurance, & Real Estate.......................14,500
Government 26,300
Manufacturing 75,100
Retail Trade..48,400
Services 66,400
Transportation & Public Utilities 13,900
Wholesale Trade......................................16,800

** Information given is for the Fort Wayne Metropolitan Statistical Area (MSA), which includes Adams, Allen, Dekalb, Huntington, Wells, and Whitley counties.*

Major Employers

Allen County
715 S Calhoun St County Courthouse
Rm 201
Fort Wayne, IN 46802
www.co.allen.in.us
Phone: 219-449-7245
Fax: 219-449-7929

Dana Corp Spicer Axle Div
2100 W State St
Fort Wayne, IN 46808
www.dana.com/lightaxle
Phone: 219-483-7174
Fax: 219-481-3427

Fort Wayne City Hall
1 Main St
Fort Wayne, IN 46802
www.ci.ft-wayne.in.us
Phone: 219-427-1111
Fax: 219-427-1115

Fort Wayne Community Schools
1200 S Clinton St
Fort Wayne, IN 46802
www.fwcs.k12.in.us
Phone: 219-425-7200
Fax: 219-425-7757

GE Motors & Industrial Systems
1635 Broadway
Fort Wayne, IN 46802
www.ge.com/gemis
Phone: 219-439-2000
Fax: 219-439-2740
TF: 800-626-2004

General Motors Truck & Bus Group
12200 Lafayette Center Rd
Roanoke, IN 46783
Phone: 219-673-2000
Fax: 219-673-2698

Indiana University-Purdue University Fort Wayne
2101 E Coliseum Blvd
Fort Wayne, IN 46805
E-mail: violette@ipfw.indiana.edu
www.ipfw.indiana.edu
Phone: 219-481-6100
Fax: 219-481-6880

ITT Industries Aerospace/ Communications Div
PO Box 3700
Fort Wayne, IN 46801
Phone: 219-487-6000
Fax: 219-451-6033

Lincoln National Corp
200 E Berry St
Fort Wayne, IN 46802
E-mail: wcustomerservice@lnc.com
www.lfg.com
Phone: 219-455-2000
Fax: 219-455-4268
TF: 800-454-6265

Lutheran Hospital of Indiana
7950 W Jefferson Blvd
Fort Wayne, IN 46804
www.lutheran-hosp.com
Phone: 219-435-7001
Fax: 219-435-7632

North American Van Lines Inc
PO Box 988
Fort Wayne, IN 46801
www.northamerican-vanlines.com
Phone: 219-429-2511
Fax: 219-429-2374

Parkview Hospital
2200 Randallia Dr
Fort Wayne, IN 46805
www.parkview.com
Phone: 219-484-6636
Fax: 219-470-8218
TF: 888-856-2522

Scott's Food Stores Inc
4118 N Clinton St
Fort Wayne, IN 46805
www.scotts.com
Phone: 219-483-9537
Fax: 219-484-5034
TF: 800-428-7268

Shambaugh & Son Inc
7614 Opportunity Dr
Fort Wayne, IN 46825
www.shambaugh.com
Phone: 219-487-7777
Fax: 219-487-7701
TF: 800-234-9988

US Postal Service
1501 S Clinton St
Fort Wayne, IN 46802
new.usps.com
Phone: 219-427-7304

Quality of Living Indicators

Total Crime Index....................................12,388
(rates per 100,000 inhabitants)

Violent Crime
Murder/manslaughter........................... 20
Forcible rape 99
Robbery..................................... 538
Aggravated assault............................ 266

Property Crime
Burglary 1,665
Larceny theft 8,476
Motor vehicle theft 1,324

Cost of Living Index....................................95.5
(national average = 100)

Median Home Price..................................$92,200

Education

Public Schools

Fort Wayne Community Schools
1200 S Clinton St
Fort Wayne, IN 46802
www.fwcs.k12.in.us
Phone: 219-425-7200
Fax: 219-425-7757

Number of Schools
Elementary 53
Middle 16
High 11

Student/Teacher Ratio
Elementary 19.0:1
Middle 17.0:1
High 21.0:1

Private Schools

Number of Schools (all grades) .... 32+

Colleges & Universities

Indiana Institute of Technology
1600 E Washington Blvd
Fort Wayne, IN 46803
www.indtech.edu
Phone: 219-422-5561
Fax: 219-422-7696
TF: 888-666-8324

Indiana University-Purdue University Fort Wayne
2101 E Coliseum Blvd
Fort Wayne, IN 46805
E-mail: violette@ipfw.indiana.edu
www.ipfw.indiana.edu
Phone: 219-481-6100
Fax: 219-481-6880

International Business College
3811 Illinois Rd
Fort Wayne, IN 46804
Phone: 219-432-8702
Fax: 219-436-1896

ITT Technical Institute
4919 Coldwater Rd
Fort Wayne, IN 46825
www.itt-tech.edu
Phone: 219-484-4107
Fax: 219-484-0860
TF: 800-866-4488

Ivy Tech State College Fort Wayne
3800 N Anthony Blvd
Fort Wayne, IN 46805
www.ivy.tec.in.us/FortWayne
Phone: 219-482-9171
Fax: 219-480-2053
TF: 888-489-5463

Taylor University Fort Wayne Campus
1025 W Rudisill Blvd
Fort Wayne, IN 46807
www.tayloru.edu/fw/
Phone: 219-456-2111
Fax: 219-456-2119
TF: 800-233-3922

University of Saint Francis
2701 Spring St
Fort Wayne, IN 46808
E-mail: admiss@sf.edu
www.sfc.edu
Phone: 219-434-3100
Fax: 219-434-3183
TF: 800-729-4732

Hospitals

Lutheran Hospital of Indiana
7950 W Jefferson Blvd
Fort Wayne, IN 46804
www.lutheran-hosp.com
Phone: 219-435-7001
Fax: 219-435-7632

Parkview Hospital
2200 Randallia Dr
Fort Wayne, IN 46805
www.parkview.com
Phone: 219-484-6636
Fax: 219-470-8218
TF: 888-856-2522

Saint Joseph Medical Center
700 Broadway
Fort Wayne, IN 46802
Phone: 219-425-3000
Fax: 219-425-3222

Veterans Affairs Medical Center
2121 Lake Ave
Fort Wayne, IN 46805
Phone: 219-426-5431
Fax: 219-460-1336

Transportation

Airport(s)

Fort Wayne International Airport (FWA)
7 miles SW of downtown (approx 20-25 minutes) . . .219-747-4146

Mass Transit

PTC Bus
$1 Base fare 219-432-4546

Rail/Bus

Greyhound/Trailways Bus Station
929 Lafayette St
Fort Wayne, IN 46802
Phone: 219-423-9525
TF: 800-231-2222

Utilities

Electricity
American Electric Power 219-423-2331
www.aep.com

Gas
Northern Indiana Public Service Co 800-422-6199
www.nipsco.nisource.com

Water
Fort Wayne City Utilities 219-427-1234
www.ci.ft-wayne.in.us/city_utilities/index.htm

Garbage Collection/Recycling
Waste Management of Fort Wayne 219-749-9689

Telecommunications

Telephone
Verizon Communications 800-483-4000
www.verizon.com

Cable Television
Comcast Cablevision Inc 219-456-9000

Internet Service Providers (ISPs)
Corpis.com Inc 219-637-8910
www.corpis.com
CTLnet Internet Services 219-496-4300
www.ctlnet.com
SkyeNet 219-426-7701
skyenet.fwi.com
TEK Interactive Group Inc 219-459-2521
www.tekinteractive.com

Banks

Bank One
101 E Washington Blvd
Fort Wayne, IN 46802
Phone: 219-427-8333
Fax: 219-427-8667

Home Loan Bank SB
132 E Berry St
Fort Wayne, IN 46802
Phone: 219-422-3502
Fax: 219-426-7027

National City Bank
110 W Berry St
Fort Wayne, IN 46802
Phone: 219-426-0555
Fax: 219-461-6209

Norwest Bank Indiana NA
PO Box 960
Fort Wayne, IN 46801
Phone: 219-461-6000
Fax: 219-461-6392

Star Financial Bank
5854 N Clinton St
Fort Wayne, IN 46825
Phone: 219-467-5534
Fax: 219-467-5537

Shopping

Georgetown Mall
6426 Georgetown Ln
Fort Wayne, IN 46815
Phone: 219-749-0461

Glenbrook Square
4201 Coldwater Rd
Fort Wayne, IN 46805
Phone: 219-483-2119

Southtown Mall
7800 S Anthony Blvd
Fort Wayne, IN 46816
Phone: 219-447-4594

Media

Newspapers and Magazines

Journal Gazette*
600 W Main St
Fort Wayne, IN 46802
www.jg.net/jg/
Phone: 219-461-8222
Fax: 219-461-8648
TF: 800-444-3303

News-Sentinel*
600 W Main St
Fort Wayne, IN 46802
www.news-sentinel.com/ns
Phone: 219-461-8222
Fax: 219-461-8817

**Indicates major daily newspapers*

Television

WANE-TV Ch 15 (CBS)
2915 W State Blvd
Fort Wayne, IN 46808
E-mail: wane-tv@cris.com
www.wane.com
Phone: 219-424-1515
Fax: 219-424-6054

WFFT-TV Ch 55 (Fox)
3707 Hillegas Rd
Fort Wayne, IN 46808
E-mail: wfft@mail.fwi.com
www.wfft.com
Phone: 219-471-5555
Fax: 219-484-4331

WFWA-TV Ch 39 (PBS)
3632 Butler Rd
Fort Wayne, IN 46808
E-mail: tv39@wfwa.pbs.org
Phone: 219-484-8839
Fax: 219-482-3632

WKJG-TV Ch 33 (NBC)
2633 W State Blvd
Fort Wayne, IN 46808
www.nbc33.com
Phone: 219-422-7474
Fax: 219-422-7702

WPTA-TV Ch 21 (ABC)
3401 Butler Rd
Fort Wayne, IN 46808
E-mail: wpta@wpta.com
www.wpta.com
Phone: 219-483-0584
Fax: 219-484-8240

Radio

WAJI-FM 95.1 MHz (AC)
347 W Berry St Suite 600
Fort Wayne, IN 46802
www.waji.com
Phone: 219-423-3676
Fax: 219-422-5266

WBCL-FM 90.3 MHz (Rel)
1025 W Rudisill Blvd
Fort Wayne, IN 46807
E-mail: mail@wbcl.org
www.wbcl.org
Phone: 219-745-0576
Fax: 219-745-2001

WBNI-FM 89.1 MHz (NPR)
3204 Clairmont Ct
Fort Wayne, IN 46808
www.wbni.org
Phone: 219-452-1189
Fax: 219-452-1188

WBTU-FM 93.3 MHz (Ctry)
2100 Goshen Rd Suite 232
Fort Wayne, IN 46808
E-mail: info@b93hottestcountry.com
www.b93hottestcountry.com
Phone: 219-482-9288
Fax: 219-482-8655

WBYR-FM 98.9 MHz (Rock)
1005 Production Rd
Fort Wayne, IN 46808
www.wbyr.com
Phone: 219-471-5100
Fax: 219-471-5224

WMEE-FM 97.3 MHz (AC)
2915 Maples Rd
Fort Wayne, IN 46816
www.wmee.com
Phone: 219-447-5511
Fax: 219-447-7546

WXKE-FM 103.9 MHz (Rock)
2541 Goshen Rd
Fort Wayne, IN 46808
Phone: 219-484-0580
Fax: 219-482-5151

Attractions

One of Fort Wayne's newest attractions, Science Central, features a variety of fun and educational interactive exhibits, including a simulated space walk and a giant piano keyboard. The Foellinger-Freimann Botanical Conservatory (the largest passive solar conservatory in the midwestern United States) features educational programs as well as exhibits that simulate tropical, arid, and seasonal environments in which various types of flora and foliage can be observed and studied. The Lincoln Museum, located at the corporate headquarters of the Lincoln National Corporation in Fort Wayne, is home of the world's largest private collection of President Lincoln memorabilia. Fort Wayne also has an award-winning park system with more than 80 parks, playgrounds, and historical sites.

Allen County Courthouse
715 S Calhoun St
Fort Wayne, IN 46802
Phone: 219-449-7211
Fax: 219-449-7929

Arena Dinner Theater
719 Rockhill St
Fort Wayne, IN 46802
Phone: 219-493-1384

Artlink Visual Arts Gallery
437 E Berry St
Fort Wayne, IN 46802
Phone: 219-424-7195

Arts United of Greater Fort Wayne
114 E Superior St
Fort Wayne, IN 46802
Phone: 219-424-0646
Fax: 219-424-2783

Auburn Cord-Duesenberg Museum
1600 S Wayne St
Auburn, IN 46706
www.clearlake.com/auburn/
Phone: 219-925-1444
Fax: 219-925-6266

Cathedral of the Immaculate Conception Museum
1122 S Clinton St
Fort Wayne, IN 46802
Phone: 219-424-1485

Concordia Theological Seminary
6600 N Clinton St
Fort Wayne, IN 46825
www.ctsfw.edu
Phone: 219-452-2100
Fax: 219-452-2121

Embassy Theatre
125 W Jefferson Blvd
Fort Wayne, IN 46802
ft-wayne.com/theatres.html#embassy
Phone: 219-424-6287
Fax: 219-424-4806

Firefighters' Museum
226 W Washington Blvd
Fort Wayne, IN 46802
www.fwcvb.org/fire.html
Phone: 219-426-0051

First Presbyterian Theater
300 W Wayne St
Fort Wayne, IN 46802
Phone: 219-426-7421
Fax: 219-422-6329

Foellinger-Freimann Botanical Conservatory
1100 S Calhoun St
Fort Wayne, IN 46802
Phone: 219-427-6440
Fax: 219-427-6450

Fort Wayne Ballet
303 E Main St Performing Arts Center
Fort Wayne, IN 46802
Phone: 219-484-9646
Fax: 219-484-9647

Fort Wayne Children's Zoo
3411 Sherman Blvd
Fort Wayne, IN 46808
www.kidszoo.com
Phone: 219-427-6800
Fax: 219-427-6820

Fort Wayne Civic Theater
303 E Main St Performing Arts Ctr
Fort Wayne, IN 46802
E-mail: civic@fwa.cioe.com
www.fwcivic.org
Phone: 219-422-8641
Fax: 219-422-6699

Fort Wayne Dance Collective
437 E Berry St
Fort Wayne, IN 46802
Phone: 219-424-6574
Fax: 219-422-8712

Fort Wayne Historical Museum
302 E Berry St
Fort Wayne, IN 46802
E-mail: fwcvb@fwcvb.org
www.fwcvb.org/history.html
Phone: 219-426-2882
Fax: 219-424-4419

Fort Wayne Museum of Art
311 E Main St
Fort Wayne, IN 46802
www.art-museum-ftwayne.org
Phone: 219-422-6467
Fax: 219-422-1374

Fort Wayne Philharmonic Orchestra
303 E Main St Performing Arts Ctr
Fort Wayne, IN 46802
Phone: 219-744-1700
Fax: 219-456-8555

Fort Wayne Youtheatre
303 E Main St
Fort Wayne, IN 46802
Phone: 219-422-6900
Fax: 219-422-6900

Fox Island
7324 Yohne Rd
Fort Wayne, IN 46809
Phone: 219-449-3180
Fax: 219-449-3181

Headwaters Park
Superior & Clinton Sts
Fort Wayne, IN 46802
Phone: 219-425-5745
Fax: 219-425-5158

Heritage Trail Walking Tour
Downtown Ft Wayne
Fort Wayne, IN 46802
Phone: 219-426-5117
Fax: 219-426-5117

Jack D Diehm Museum of Natural History
600 Franke Park Dr
Fort Wayne, IN 46808
Phone: 219-427-6708

Lakeside Rose Garden
1400 Lake Ave
Fort Wayne, IN 46805
Phone: 219-427-6000
Fax: 219-427-6020

Lincoln Museum
200 E Berry St
Fort Wayne, IN 46802
www.thelincolnmuseum.org
Phone: 219-455-3864
Fax: 219-455-6922

Macedonian Tribune Museum
124 W Wayne St Suite 204
Fort Wayne, IN 46802
E-mail: mtfw@macedonian.org
www.macedonian.org
Phone: 219-422-5900
Fax: 219-422-1348

Science Central
1950 N Clinton St
Fort Wayne, IN 46805
Phone: 219-424-2413
Fax: 219-422-2899
TF: 800-442-6376

Swinney Homestead
1424 W Jefferson Blvd
Fort Wayne, IN 46802
Phone: 219-424-7212

Sports Teams & Facilities

Fort Wayne Fury (basketball)
4000 Parnell Ave Allen County War Memorial Coliseum
Fort Wayne, IN 46805
www.furyhoops.com
Phone: 219-471-3879
Fax: 219-471-9716

Fort Wayne Komets (hockey)
4000 Parnell Ave Allen County War Memorial Coliseum
Fort Wayne, IN 46805
www.komets.com/
Phone: 219-483-0011
Fax: 219-483-3899

Fort Wayne Wizards (baseball)
1616 E Coliseum Blvd Memorial Stadium
Fort Wayne, IN 46805
E-mail: info@wizzardsbaseball.com
www.fwi.com/wizards/
Phone: 219-482-6400

Annual Events

Allen County Fair (late July) 219-637-5818
Auburn Cord-Duesenberg Festival
(early September) 219-925-1444
Festival of Gingerbread
(late November-mid-December) 219-426-2882
Festival of Trees (late November-early December) 219-424-6287
Fort Wayne Hoosier Marathon (early-June) 219-749-7288
Gathering of the People (late July) 219-244-7702
Germanfest (mid-June). 219-436-4064
Greek Fest (late June) 219-489-0774
Hispanic American Festival (early September) 219-744-5129
Indiana Black Expo (early June) 219-422-6486
Indiana Highland Games (late July). 219-486-9543
Johnny Appleseed Festival (mid-September) 219-424-3700
National Print Exhibition (late May-early July). 219-424-7195
New Haven Canal Days (early June) 219-749-2972
Three Rivers Festival (mid-July) 219-745-5556

Fort Worth, Texas

***County:* Tarrant**

FORT WORTH is located in the north central part of eastern Texas. Major cities within 100 miles include Dallas, Arlington, Irving, Garland, Waco, and Wichita Falls, Texas.

Area (Land) .... 277.3 sq mi
Area (Water)............................... 6.4 sq mi
Elevation....................................... 670 ft
Latitude ....32-72-53 N
Longitude................................ 97-32-06 W
Time Zone ....CST
Area Code....................................... 817

Climate

Winters in Fort Worth are generally mild, with average high temperatures in the mid- to upper 50s and lows in the mid-30s. Occasionally, polar air masses make their way through the Great Plains, causing brief periods of cold weather, but snowfall is minimal in Fort Worth, averaging only 3.5 inches annually. Summers are hot and humid, with average high temperatures in the mid-90s and lows in the low 70s. Spring is the rainy season in Fort Worth—May is the wettest month of the year; December and January are the driest months.

Average Temperatures & Precipitation

Temperatures

	Jan	Feb	Mar	Apr	May	Jun	Jul	Aug	Sep	Oct	Nov	Dec
High	54	59	68	76	83	92	97	96	88	79	67	58
Low	33	37	46	55	63	70	74	74	67	56	45	36

Precipitation

	Jan	Feb	Mar	Apr	May	Jun	Jul	Aug	Sep	Oct	Nov	Dec
Inches	1.8	2.2	2.8	3.5	4.9	3.0	2.3	2.2	3.4	3.5	2.3	1.8

History

Fort Worth was founded in 1849 as an Army outpost established to protect settlers from Indian attacks. The town grew quickly as the last major stop along the Chisholm Trail, the main cattle drive that ran from the ranches in Texas to the slaughterhouses in Kansas. The arrival of the railroad in 1876, which may be credited in large part to Fort Worth residents who made contributions when the railroad company went bankrupt during the nation's economic depression, stimulated further growth and development as the town became a major meat processing and distribution center. In 1896, Fort Worth's first stock show was held in the city. A century later, the annual Southwestern Exposition and Livestock Show is among the country's largest livestock shows and rodeos.

Agriculture, primarily beef cattle and grain, played a large role in Fort Worth's economy through the first two decades of the 20th Century. The discovery of oil nearby in 1920 added a new dimension to Fort Worth's economic base, as the city was the last major commercial center before the oil fields of the western part of the state. Aviation-related industries have had a major impact on Fort Worth since World War II, when wartime industries including aircraft manufacturing brought economic opportunities to the city. The opening of Dallas/Fort Worth International Airport in 1973 also sparked economic and population growth in Fort Worth. The airport today is the second busiest in the world and American Airlines, whose corporate headquarters is located there, is Tarrant County's largest employer, providing jobs for more than 30,000 area residents.

With more than 490,000 residents, Fort Worth is the sixth largest city in Texas. Nearby Arlington, with a population of more than 306,000, is Texas' seventh largest city in terms of population, as well as the leading tourist destination in the state.

Population

1990 Census 447,619
1998 Estimate..............................491,801
% Change 9.9
2005 Projection 1,454,383*

Racial/Ethnic Breakdown

White.................................... 63.8%
Black 22.0%
Other.................................... 14.2%
Hispanic Origin (may be of any race) 19.5%

Age Breakdown

Under 5 years.............................. 8.7%
5 to 17.................................. 18.0%
18 to 20.................................. 4.7%
21 to 24.................................. 7.2%
25 to 34................................. 20.4%
35 to 44................................. 13.8%
45 to 54.................................. 8.5%
55 to 64.................................. 7.4%
65 to 74.................................. 6.4%
75+ years 4.8%
Median Age.................................30.3

Gender Breakdown

Male.................................... 49.2%
Female.................................. 50.8%

* *Information given is for Tarrant County.*

Government

Type of Government: Council-City Manager

Fort Worth City Council
1000 Throckmorton St 3rd Fl
Fort Worth, TX 76102

Phone: 817-871-6193
Fax: 817-871-6187

Fort Worth City Hall Phone: 817-871-8900
1000 Throckmorton St
Fort Worth, TX 76102

Fort Worth City Manager Phone: 817-871-6111
1000 Throckmorton St 3rd Fl Fax: 817-871-6134
Fort Worth, TX 76102

Fort Worth City Secretary Phone: 817-871-6150
1000 Throckmorton St 3rd Fl Fax: 817-871-6196
Fort Worth, TX 76102

Fort Worth Development Dept Phone: 817-871-7820
100 Throckmorton St Lower Level Fax: 817-871-8116
Fort Worth, TX 76102

Fort Worth Economic Development Office Phone: 817-871-6192
1000 Throckmorton St 3rd Fl Fax: 817-871-6134
Fort Worth, TX 76102

Fort Worth Finance Dept Phone: 817-871-8185
1000 Throckmorton St 3rd Fl Fax: 817-871-8966
Fort Worth, TX 76102

Fort Worth Fire Dept Phone: 817-871-6800
1000 Throckmorton St Fax: 817-871-6859
Fort Worth, TX 76102

Fort Worth Human Resources Dept Phone: 817-871-7772
1000 Throckmorton St Fax: 817-871-8869
Fort Worth, TX 76102

Fort Worth Mayor Phone: 817-871-6110
1000 Throckmorton St 3rd Fl Fax: 817-871-6187
Fort Worth, TX 76102

Fort Worth Parks & Community Services Dept Phone: 817-871-5700
2200 South Fwy Suite 2200 Fax: 817-871-5724
Fort Worth, TX 76115

Fort Worth Planning Dept Phone: 817-871-8000
1000 Throckmorton St Fax: 817-871-8016
Fort Worth, TX 76102

Fort Worth Police Dept Phone: 817-877-8385
350 W Belknap St Fax: 817-877-8270
Fort Worth, TX 76102

Fort Worth Public Library Phone: 817-871-7701
500 W 3rd St Fax: 817-871-7734
Fort Worth, TX 76102

Fort Worth Transportation & Public Works Dept Phone: 817-871-7800
1000 Throckmorton St Fax: 817-871-8092
Fort Worth, TX 76102

Fort Worth Water Dept Phone: 817-871-8220
PO Box 870 Fax: 817-871-8195
Fort Worth, TX 76101

Important Phone Numbers

AAA....................817-370-2503
American Express Travel....................817-738-5441
Driver's License Information....................817-238-9197
Emergency....................911
Events Hotline....................817-332-2000
Fort Worth Board of Realtors....................817-336-5165
Highway Conditions....................800-452-9292
Medical Referral....................817-732-2825
Poison Control Center....................800-764-7661
Tarrant County Tax Assessor/Collector....................817-884-1100
Texas Comptroller of Public Accounts....................800-252-5555
Travelers Aid....................972-574-4420
Vehicle Registration Information....................817-884-1100
Voter Registration Information....................817-884-1115
Weather....................214-787-1111

Information Sources

Arlington Chamber of Commerce Phone: 817-275-2613
316 W Main St Fax: 817-261-7535
Arlington, TX 76010 TF: 800-834-3928
www.chamber.arlingtontx.com

Arlington City Hall Phone: 817-275-3271
101 W Abram St Fax: 817-459-6199
Arlington, TX 76010
www.ci.arlington.tx.us

Arlington Community Center Phone: 817-465-6661
2800 S Center St Fax: 817-465-6663
Arlington, TX 76014

Arlington Convention & Visitors Bureau Phone: 817-265-7721
1905 E Randol Mill Rd Suite 650 Fax: 817-265-5640
Arlington, TX 76011 TF: 800-433-5374
www.acvb.org

Arlington Convention Center Phone: 817-459-5000
1200 Ballpark Way Fax: 817-459-5091
Arlington, TX 76011
www.ci.arlington.tx.us/aconvctr/

Arlington Mayor Phone: 817-459-6122
101 W Abram St Fax: 817-459-6120
Arlington, TX 76010
www.ci.arlington.tx.us/odom.html

Arlington Planning & Development Dept Phone: 817-459-6650
101 W Abram St Fax: 817-459-6671
Arlington, TX 76010
www.ci.arlington.tx.us/planning

Arlington Public Library Phone: 817-459-6900
101 E Abram St Fax: 817-459-6902
Arlington, TX 76010
www.pub-lib.ci.arlington.tx.us

Better Business Bureau Serving the Fort Worth Area Phone: 817-332-7585
1612 Summit Ave Suite 260 Fax: 817-882-0566
Fort Worth, TX 76102
www.fortworth.bbb.org

Fort Worth Chamber of Commerce Phone: 817-336-2491
777 Taylor St Suite 900 Fax: 817-877-4034
Fort Worth, TX 76102
www.fortworthcoc.org

Fort Worth Convention & Visitors Bureau
415 Throckmorton St
Fort Worth, TX 76102
www.fortworth.com
Phone: 817-336-8791
Fax: 817-336-3282
TF: 800-433-5747

Fort Worth/Tarrant County Convention Center
1111 Houston St
Fort Worth, TX 76102
www.fortworth.com/fwtccc.htm
Phone: 817-884-2222
Fax: 817-212-2756

Tarrant County
100 W Weatherford St
Fort Worth, TX 76196
www.tarrantcounty.com
Phone: 817-884-1195

Visitor Information Center
1905 E Randol Mill Rd
Arlington, TX 76011
Phone: 817-461-3888
Fax: 817-461-6689
TF: 800-342-4305

Online Resources

4FortWorth.com
www.4fortworth.com

Anthill City Guide Dallas/Fort Worth
www.anthill.com/city.asp?city=dallas

Area Guide Arlington
arlingtontx.areaguides.net

Arlington City Net
www.excite.com/travel/countries/united_states/texas/arlington

City Knowledge Arlington
www.cityknowledge.com/tx_arlington.htm

City Knowledge Fort Worth
www.cityknowledge.com/tx_fortworth.htm

Dallas Fort Worth City Pages
dallas.thelinks.com

Dallas Fort Worth Metroplex Directory
www.flash.net/~dfwmet/

Dallas-Fort Worth Texas
www.dallas-fort-worth.com

Dallas/Fort Worth Area Web
www.dfwareaweb.com/

DigitalCity Dallas-Fort Worth
home.digitalcity.com/dallas

Excite.com Fort Worth City Guide
www.excite.com/travel/countries/united_states/texas/fort_worth

Fort Worth CyberRodeo
www.cyberrodeo.com/fortworth

GuideLive: Arts & Entertainment in Dallas & Fort Worth
www.guidelive.com

HotelGuide Dallas/Fort Worth
hotelguide.net/dfw

Intro Fort Worth
www.introfortworth.com

Lodging.com Dallas-Fort Worth Texas
www.lodging.com/auto/guides/dallas_ft_worth-area-tx.html

MetroGuide Dallas/Fort Worth
metroguide.net/dfw

Virtual Voyages Dallas-Fort Worth
www.virtualvoyages.com/usa/tx/dfw/dfw.sht

Yahoo! Dallas/Fort Worth
dfw.yahoo.com

Area Communities

Communities in Tarrant County with populations greater than 10,000 include:

Arlington
101 W Abram St
Arlington, TX 76010
Phone: 817-275-3271
Fax: 817-459-6199

Bedford
2000 Forest Ridge Rd
Bedford, TX 76021
Phone: 817-952-2100
Fax: 817-952-2103

Benbrook
911 Winscott Rd
Benbrook, TX 76126
Phone: 817-249-3000
Fax: 817-249-0884

Euless
201 N Ector Dr
Euless, TX 76039
Phone: 817-685-1400
Fax: 817-685-1416

Grapevine
200 S Main St
Grapevine, TX 76051
Phone: 817-410-3000
Fax: 817-410-3002

Haltom City
5024 Broadway Ave
Haltom City, TX 76117
Phone: 817-222-7700
Fax: 817-834-7237

Hurst
1505 Precinct Line Rd
Hurst, TX 76054
Phone: 817-788-7000
Fax: 817-788-7009

Keller
158 S Main St
Keller, TX 76248
Phone: 817-431-1517
Fax: 817-431-5867

Mansfield
1305 E Broad St
Mansfield, TX 76063
Phone: 817-473-9371
Fax: 817-477-1416

North Richland Hills
PO Box 820609
North Richland Hills, TX 76182
Phone: 817-581-5500
Fax: 817-427-6016

Southlake
1725 E Southlake Blvd
Southlake, TX 76092
Phone: 817-481-5581
Fax: 817-488-6796

Watauga
7101 Whitley Rd
Watauga, TX 76148
Phone: 817-281-8047
Fax: 817-281-1991

White Settlement
214 Meadow Park Dr
White Settlement, TX 76108
Phone: 817-246-4971
Fax: 817-367-0885

Economy

Major U.S. corporations that call Fort Worth home include Burlington Northern-Santa Fe Corporation, Radio Shack, and Union Pacific Resource Company. Fort Worth has a diverse economy in which the aviation industry—both commercial aviation and aircraft manufacturing—plays a major role. One-third of Tarrant County's 15 largest employers, including the top three—American Airlines, Lockheed Martin, and Bell Helicopter Textron—are aviation-related. High-technology manufacturing and health care are also leading industries in the Fort Worth area.

Unemployment Rate 3.4%*
Per Capita Income.......................... $26,790*
Median Family Income...................... $55,300*

** Information given is for the Fort Worth-Arlington Metropolitan Statistica Area (MSA), which includes the City of Arlington, the City of Fort Worth, and Tarrant County.*

Principal Industries & Number of Wage Earners

Fort Worth-Arlington MSA* - June 2000

Industry	Wage Earners
Construction	45,100
Finance, Insurance, & Real Estate	37,700
Government	99,700
Manufacturing	112,500
Mining	4,000
Retail Trade	154,300
Services	220,200
Transportation & Public Utilities	77,500
Wholesale Trade	44,100

** Information given is for the Fort Worth-Arlington Metropolitan Statistica Area (MSA), which includes the City of Arlington, the City of Fort Worth, and Tarrant County.*

Major Employers

Alcon Laboratories Inc
6201 South Fwy
Fort Worth, TX 76134
www.alconlabs.com
Phone: 817-293-0450
Fax: 817-551-4030
TF: 800-757-9195

All Saints Health Systems
PO Box 31
Fort Worth, TX 76101
www.allsaints.com
Phone: 817-926-2544
Fax: 817-927-6226

American Airlines Inc
PO Box 619616
DFW Airport, TX 75261
www.aa.com
Phone: 817-963-1234
Fax: 817-967-4162
TF: 800-433-7300

Bell Helicopter Textron Inc
PO Box 482
Fort Worth, TX 76101
www.bellhelicopter.textron.com
Phone: 817-280-2011
Fax: 817-280-2321

Burlington Northern Santa Fe Corp
2650 Lou Menk Dr
Fort Worth, TX 76131
www.bnsf.com
Phone: 817-333-2000
Fax: 817-352-7924

Fort Worth City Hall
1000 Throckmorton St
Fort Worth, TX 76102
ci.fort-worth.tx.us
Phone: 817-871-8900

Fort Worth Independent School District
100 N University Dr
Fort Worth, TX 76107
www.fortworthisd.org
Phone: 817-871-2389
Fax: 817-871-2385

Fort Worth Star-Telegram
PO Box 1870
Fort Worth, TX 76101
www.star-telegram.com
Phone: 817-390-7400
Fax: 817-390-7789

Harris Methodist Fort Worth
1301 Pennsylvania Ave
Fort Worth, TX 76104
Phone: 817-882-2000
Fax: 817-882-3169

Lockheed Martin Aeronautics Co
PO Box 748
Fort Worth, TX 76101
www.lmtas.com
Phone: 817-777-2000
Fax: 817-777-2115

OnPoint
4201 Cambridge Rd
Fort Worth, TX 76155
E-mail: info@onpointcrm.com
www.onpointcrm.com
Phone: 817-355-8200
Fax: 817-354-8144
TF: 800-325-2580

RadioShack
100 Throckmorton St Suite 1800
Fort Worth, TX 76102
E-mail: rs.customer.relations@tandy.com
www.radioshack.com
Phone: 817-415-3011
Fax: 817-415-2774
TF: 800-843-7422

Sabre Inc
4255 Amon Carter Blvd
Fort Worth, TX 76155
www.sabre.com
Phone: 817-963-6400

Tarrant County
100 W Weatherford St
Fort Worth, TX 76196
www.tarrantcounty.com
Phone: 817-884-1195

Quality of Living Indicators

Total Crime Index.................................... 37,354
(rates per 100,000 inhabitants)

Violent Crime

Murder/manslaughter	67
Forcible rape	286
Robbery	1,447
Aggravated assault	2,446

Property Crime

Burglary	7,506
Larceny theft	21,703
Motor vehicle theft	3,899

Cost of Living Index....................................91.4
(national average = 100)

Median Home Price.................................$102,300

Education

Public Schools

Fort Worth Independent School District
100 N University Dr
Fort Worth, TX 76107
www.fortworthisd.org
Phone: 817-871-2389
Fax: 817-871-2385

Number of Schools
Elementary.................................. 70
Middle...................................... 22
High.. 13

Student/Teacher Ratio
All Grades................................ 17.8:1

Private Schools

Number of Schools (all grades)..................... 92

Colleges & Universities

Arlington Baptist College
3001 W Division St
Arlington, TX 76012
www.abconline.edu
Phone: 817-461-8741
Fax: 817-274-1138

ITT Technical Institute
551 Ryan Plaza Dr
Arlington, TX 76011
www.itttech.edu
Phone: 817-794-5100
Fax: 817-275-8446

Tarrant County Junior College
1500 Houston St
Fort Worth, TX 76102
www.tcjc.cc.tx.us
Phone: 817-515-5293
Fax: 817-515-5278

Tarrant County Junior College Southeast Campus
2100 TCJC Pkwy
Arlington, TX 76018
www.tcjc.cc.tx.us/se_campusindx.html
Phone: 817-515-3100
Fax: 817-515-3182

Texas Christian University
TCU Box 297013
Fort Worth, TX 76129
E-mail: admwww@tcuavm.is.tcu.edu
www.tcu.edu
Phone: 817-921-7000
Fax: 817-257-7268
TF: 800-828-3764

Texas Wesleyan University
1201 Wesleyan St
Fort Worth, TX 76105
E-mail: info@txwesleyan.edu
www.txwesleyan.edu
Phone: 817-531-4444
Fax: 817-531-4231
TF: 800-580-8980

University of Texas Arlington
701 S Nedderman Dr
Arlington, TX 76019
www.uta.edu
Phone: 817-272-2011
Fax: 817-272-3435
TF: 800-687-2882

Hospitals

All Saints Health Systems
PO Box 31
Fort Worth, TX 76101
www.allsaints.com
Phone: 817-926-2544
Fax: 817-927-6226

Arlington Memorial Hospital
800 W Randol Mill Rd
Arlington, TX 76012
www.phscare.org/hospitals/amh.htm
Phone: 817-548-6100
Fax: 817-548-6357

Baylor Medical Center at Grapevine
1650 W College St
Grapevine, TX 76051
Phone: 817-488-7546
Fax: 817-481-2962

Cook Children's Medical Center
801 7th Ave
Fort Worth, TX 76104
www.cookchildrens.org
Phone: 817-885-4000
Fax: 817-885-4229

Harris Methodist Fort Worth
1301 Pennsylvania Ave
Fort Worth, TX 76104
Phone: 817-882-2000
Fax: 817-882-3169

Harris Methodist Southwest
6100 Harris Pkwy
Fort Worth, TX 76132
Phone: 817-346-5050
Fax: 817-346-5117

Harris Methodist-HEB
1600 Hospital Pkwy
Bedford, TX 76022
Phone: 817-685-4000
Fax: 817-685-4890

Huguley Memorial Medical Center
11801 S Fwy
Fort Worth, TX 76134
Phone: 817-293-9110
Fax: 817-568-3269

Medical Center Arlington
3301 Matlock Rd
Arlington, TX 76015
Phone: 817-465-3241
Fax: 817-472-4878

North Hills Hospital
4401 Booth Calloway Rd
North richland Hills, TX 76180
Phone: 817-255-1000
Fax: 817-255-1998

Osteopathic Medical Center of Texas
1000 Montgomery St
Fort Worth, TX 76107
www.ohst.com
Phone: 817-731-4311
Fax: 817-735-6442

Plaza Medical Center
900 8th Ave
Fort Worth, TX 76104
Phone: 817-336-2100
Fax: 817-347-5796

Transportation

Airport(s)

Dallas-Fort Worth International Airport (DFW)
20 miles NE of downtown Forth Worth
(approx 35 minutes)...........................972-574-8888

Mass Transit

The 'T'-Fort Worth
$1 Base fare.................................817-215-8600

Rail/Bus

Amtrak Station
1501 Jones St
Fort Worth, TX 76102
Phone: 817-332-2931

Greyhound/Trailways Bus Station Phone: 817-429-3089
901 Commerce St TF: 800-231-2222
Fort Worth, TX 76102

Utilities

Electricity
TXU Electric & Gas 800-242-9113
www.txu.com/residential

Gas
TXU Electric & Gas 800-817-8877
www.txu.com/residential

Water
Fort Worth Water Dept 817-871-8200

Garbage Collection/Recycling
Fort Worth Waste Management Services 817-332-2251

Telecommunications

Telephone
Southwestern Bell.............................817-376-4200
www.swbell.com

Cable Television
Charter Communications.......................817-509-2225

Internet Service Providers (ISPs)
Access Zone 817-332-6448
web1.azone.net
AppLink Corp.................................817-481-5507
www.applink.net
DFW Internet Services Inc.....................817-332-5116
www.dfw.net
FastLane Communications 817-429-5263
www.fastlane.net
FlashNet Communications Inc..................817-332-8883
www.flash.net
ImagiNet Communications Ltd 817-516-0040
www.imagin.net
Spindlemedia Inc..............................817-332-5661
www.spindle.net
StarText (Fort Worth Star-Telegram) 817-390-7905
startext.net

Banks

Bank of America NA Phone: 800-247-6262
811 Lamar St
Fort Worth, TX 76102

Bank One Texas NA Phone: 817-884-4000
500 Throckmorton St Fax: 817-884-4907
Fort Worth, TX 76102 TF: 800-695-1111

Bank United Phone: 817-336-1666
343 Throckmorton St Fax: 817-336-1340
Fort Worth, TX 76102 TF: 800-366-7378

Chase Bank of Texas NA Phone: 817-878-7537
201 Main St
Fort Worth, TX 76102

First National Bank of Texas Phone: 817-294-9848
7300 S Hulen St Fax: 817-346-9762
Fort Worth, TX 76133

Frost National Bank Phone: 817-420-5200
777 Main St Fax: 817-420-5200
Fort Worth, TX 76102 TF: 800-513-7678

Guaranty Federal Bank FSB Phone: 817-731-7201
5701 Camp Bowie Blvd Fax: 817-731-6904
Fort Worth, TX 76107

Norwest Bank Texas NA Phone: 817-870-8200
100 Main St Fax: 817-870-8282
Fort Worth, TX 76102

Wells Fargo Bank NA Phone: 817-877-5588
315 W 7th St Fax: 817-877-0167
Fort Worth, TX 76102

Shopping

Antique Marketplace of Arlington Phone: 817-467-7030
3500 S Cooper St Fax: 817-468-7719
Arlington, TX 76015

Coomers Craft Mall Phone: 817-795-4433
2805 W Park Row Dr Fax: 817-795-4435
Arlington, TX 76013
www.coomers.com

Cooper Street Craft Mall Phone: 817-261-3184
1701 S Cooper St Fax: 817-861-4470
Arlington, TX 76010

Festival Marketplace Mall Phone: 817-213-1000
2900 Pioneer Pkwy Fax: 817-213-1010
Arlington, TX 76010

Fort Worth Outlet Square Phone: 817-390-3720
150 Throckmorton St Fax: 817-415-0284
Fort Worth, TX 76102
www.fwoutletsquare.com

Fort Worth Town Center Phone: 817-927-8459
4200 South Fwy Suite 100 Fax: 817-927-1833
Fort Worth, TX 76115

Hulen Mall Phone: 817-294-1200
4800 S Hulen St Fax: 817-370-0932
Fort Worth, TX 76132

Lincoln Square Phone: 214-750-1517
Hwy 157 & I-30 Fax: 214-373-7535
Arlington, TX 76011

Montgomery Street Antique Mall Phone: 817-735-9685
2601 Montgomery St Fax: 817-735-9379
Fort Worth, TX 76107

Neiman Marcus Phone: 817-738-3581
2100 Green Oaks Rd Fax: 817-732-0920
Fort Worth, TX 76116
www.neimanmarcus.com

North East Mall Phone: 817-284-3427
1101 Melbourne Rd Suite 1000 Fax: 817-595-4471
Hurst, TX 76053

North Hills Mall Phone: 817-589-2236
7624 Grapevine Hwy Fax: 817-284-9730
North Richland Hills, TX 76180

Parks at Arlington
3811 S Cooper St Suite 2206
Arlington, TX 76015
www.mallibu.com
Phone: 817-467-0200
Fax: 817-468-5356

Ridgmar Mall
2060 Green Oaks Rd
Fort Worth, TX 76116
Phone: 817-731-0856
Fax: 817-763-5146

Six Flags Mall
2911 E Division St
Arlington, TX 76011
Phone: 817-640-1641
Fax: 817-649-1825

Stripling & Cox
6370 Camp Bowie Blvd
Fort Worth, TX 76116
Phone: 817-738-7361
Fax: 817-377-5305

Sundance Square
512 Main St
Fort Worth, TX 76102
www.sundancesquare.com
Phone: 817-339-7777
Fax: 817-339-7216

Media

Newspapers and Magazines

Arlington Morning News*
1112 Copeland Rd Suite 400
Arlington, TX 76011
Phone: 817-461-6397
Fax: 817-436-4140

Business Press
314 Main St Suite 300
Fort Worth, TX 76102
www.dfwbusinesspress.com
Phone: 817-336-8300
Fax: 817-332-3038

Fort Worth Star-Telegram*
PO Box 1870
Fort Worth, TX 76101
www.star-telegram.com
Phone: 817-390-7400
Fax: 817-390-7789

FW Weekly
1204-B W 7th St
Fort Worth, TX 76102
E-mail: pub@fwweekly.com
www.fwweekly.com
Phone: 817-335-9559
Fax: 817-335-9575

Grapevine Sun
PO Box 400
Grapevine, TX 76099
E-mail: gvsun@gte.net
Phone: 817-488-8561
Fax: 817-488-5339

**Indicates major daily newspapers*

Television

KDAF-TV Ch 33 (WB)
8001 John Carpenter Fwy
Dallas, TX 75247
www.wb33.com
Phone: 214-640-3300
Fax: 214-252-3379

KDFI-TV Ch 27 (Ind)
400 N Griffin St
Dallas, TX 75202
Phone: 214-637-2727
Fax: 214-720-3355

KDFW-TV Ch 4 (Fox)
400 N Griffin St
Dallas, TX 75202
Phone: 214-720-4444
Fax: 214-720-3263

KDTN-TV Ch 2 (PBS)
3000 Harry Hines Blvd
Dallas, TX 75201
Phone: 214-871-1390
Fax: 214-754-0635

KERA-TV Ch 13 (PBS)
3000 Harry Hines Blvd
Dallas, TX 75201
www.kera.org
Phone: 214-871-1390
Fax: 214-740-9369

KFWD-TV Ch 52 (Tele)
3000 W Story Rd
Irving, TX 75038
Phone: 972-255-5200
Fax: 972-258-1770

KLDT-TV Ch 55 (Ind)
2450 Rockbrook Dr
Lewisville, TX 75067
Phone: 972-316-2115
Fax: 972-316-1112

KMPX-TV Ch 29 (Ind)
PO Box 612066
Dallas, TX 75261
Phone: 817-571-1229
Fax: 817-571-7458

KPXD-TV Ch 68 (PAX)
800 W Airport Fwy Suite 750
Irving, TX 75062
www.pax.net/KPXD
Phone: 972-438-6868
Fax: 972-579-3045

KTVT-TV Ch 11 (CBS)
5233 Bridge St
Fort Worth, TX 76103
www.ktvt.com
Phone: 817-451-1111
Fax: 817-496-7739

KTXA-TV Ch 21 (UPN)
301 N Market St Suite 700
Dallas, TX 75202
www.paramountstations.com/KTXA
Phone: 214-743-2100
Fax: 214-743-2121

KUVN-TV Ch 23 (Uni)
2323 Bryan St Suite 1900
Dallas, TX 75201
www.univision.net/stations/kuvn.htm
Phone: 214-758-2300
Fax: 214-758-2324
TF: 800-494-5886

KXAS-TV Ch 5 (NBC)
3900 Barnett St
Fort Worth, TX 76103
www.kxas.com
Phone: 817-429-5555
Fax: 817-654-6325
TF: 800-232-5927

KXTX-TV Ch 39 (Ind)
3900 Harry Hines Blvd
Dallas, TX 75219
www.kxtx.com
Phone: 214-521-3900
Fax: 214-523-5946
TF: 800-465-5989

WFAA-TV Ch 8 (ABC)
606 Young St Communications Ctr
Dallas, TX 75202
www.wfaa.com
Phone: 214-748-9631
Fax: 214-977-6585

Radio

KBFB-FM 97.9 MHz (AC)
8235 Douglas Ave Suite 300
Dallas, TX 75225
E-mail: kbfb@kbfb.com
www.kbfb.com
Phone: 972-891-3400
Fax: 972-988-3292

KCBI-FM 90.9 MHz (Rel)
PO Box 619000
Dallas, TX 75261
E-mail: kcbi@kcbi.org
www.kcbi.org
Phone: 817-792-3800
Fax: 817-277-9929

KDMX-FM 102.9 MHz (AC)
14001 N Dallas Pkwy Suite 1210
Dallas, TX 75240
www.mix1029.com
Phone: 972-991-1029
Fax: 972-448-1029

KEGL-FM 97.1 MHz (CR)
14001 N Dallas Pkwy Suite 1210
Dallas, TX 75240
www.kegl.com
Phone: 972-869-9700
Fax: 972-263-9710

KERA-FM 90.1 MHz (NPR)
3000 Harry Hines Blvd
Dallas, TX 75201
E-mail: kerafm@metronet.com
www.kera.org/
Phone: 214-871-1390
Fax: 214-740-9369

KESS-AM 1270 kHz (Span)
7700 Carpenter Fwy
Dallas, TX 75247
www.kess1270.com
Phone: 214-630-8531
Fax: 214-920-2507

KFJZ-AM 870 kHz (Span)
2214 E 4th St
Fort Worth, TX 76102
Phone: 817-336-7175
Fax: 817-338-1205

KKDA-AM 730 kHz (Oldies)
PO Box 530860
Grand Prairie, TX 75053
Phone: 972-263-9911
Fax: 972-558-0010

KKDA-FM 104.5 MHz (Urban)
PO Box 860
Grand Prairie, TX 75053
www.k104fm.com
Phone: 972-263-9911
Fax: 972-558-0010

KKZN-FM 93.3 MHz (AAA)
3500 Maple Ave Suite 1310
Dallas, TX 75219
www.933thezone.com
Phone: 214-526-7400
Fax: 214-787-1946

KLTY-FM 100.7 MHz (Rel)
12900 Preston Rd Suite 100
Dallas, TX 75230
E-mail: klty@onramp.net
www.klty.com
Phone: 972-726-9941
Fax: 972-404-1451

KLUV-FM 98.7 MHz (Oldies)
4131 N Central Expy Suite 700
Dallas, TX 75204
E-mail: kluv@ix.netcom.com
www.kluv.com
Phone: 214-526-9870
Fax: 214-443-1570

KPLX-FM 99.5 MHz (Ctry)
3500 Maple Ave Suite 1600
Dallas, TX 75219
E-mail: thewolf@flash.net
www.995thewolf.com
Phone: 214-526-2400
Fax: 214-520-4343

KRBV-FM 100.3 MHz (Urban)
7901 John Carpenter Fwy
Dallas, TX 75247
Phone: 214-630-3011
Fax: 214-688-7760

KRLD-AM 1080 kHz (N/T)
1080 Ballpark Way
Arlington, TX 76011
www.krld.com
Phone: 817-543-5400
Fax: 817-543-5572

KRNB-FM 105.7 MHz (AC)
621 NW 6th St
Grand Prairie, TX 75050
Phone: 972-263-9911
Fax: 972-558-0010

KSCS-FM 96.3 MHz (Ctry)
2221 E Lamar Blvd Suite 400
Arlington, TX 76006
www.kscs.com
Phone: 817-640-1963
Fax: 817-654-9227

KTNO-AM 1440 kHz (Rel)
3105 Arkansas Ln
Arlington, TX 76016
Phone: 817-469-1540
Fax: 817-261-2137

KTXQ-FM 102.1 MHz (Oldies)
4131 N Central Expy Suite 1200
Dallas, TX 75204
www.ktxq.com
Phone: 214-528-5500
Fax: 214-528-0747

KVIL-FM 103.7 MHz (AC)
9400 N Central Expy Suite 1600
Dallas, TX 75231
www.kvil.com
Phone: 214-691-1037
Fax: 214-891-7975

KYNG-FM 105.3 MHz (Ctry)
12201 Merit Dr Suite 930
Dallas, TX 75251
www.young-country.com
Phone: 972-716-7800
Fax: 972-716-7835

WBAP-AM 820 kHz (N/T)
2221 E Lamar Blvd Suite 400
Arlington, TX 76006
www.wbap.com
Phone: 817-640-1963
Fax: 817-654-9227

Attractions

Fort Worth is located just 34 miles from its sister city, Dallas. The area's cattle and cowboy history can be seen in the Stockyards Historic District of Fort Worth, which is also the home of Billy Bob's Texas, "the world's largest honky-tonk"—so large, in fact, that live bullriding is a featured event. The city is also home to the Cattleman's Museum, which features multimedia shows and life-size dioramas. Each winter the city hosts the Southwestern Exposition & Livestock Show and Rodeo, which draws nearly one million visitors annually. Other attractions in Fort Worth include the Fort Worth Botanic Garden, the Fort Worth Zoo, and the Amon Carter Museum, which features works by American artists, including the famous Southwestern artist, Georgia O'Keefe.

Fort Worth's neighbor, Arlington, is currently the number one tourist destination in Texas, due mainly to Six Flags Over Texas, a major theme park that features special events throughout the year. The Ballpark at Arlington is the home field of the Texas Rangers, drawing large numbers of sports fans to the city each season. The city's Air Combat School allows visitors to experience piloting a jet fighter using flight simulators.

Air Combat School
921 Six Flags Dr Suite 117
Arlington, TX 76011
www.aircombatschool.com
Phone: 817-640-1886

American Airlines CR Smith Museum
4601 Hwy 360 at FAA Rd
Fort Worth, TX 76155
Phone: 817-967-1560
Fax: 817-967-5737

Amon Carter Museum
500 Commerce St
Fort Worth, TX 76102
www.cartermuseum.org/
Phone: 817-738-1933
Fax: 817-332-7775

Antique Sewing Machine Museum
804 W Abram St
Arlington, TX 76013
Phone: 817-275-0971

Arlington Museum of Art
201 W Main St
Arlington, TX 76010
Phone: 817-275-4600
Fax: 817-860-4800

Arlington Skatium
5515 S Cooper St
Arlington, TX 76017
Phone: 817-784-6222
Fax: 817-784-6481

Ballpark in Arlington
1000 Ballpark Way
Arlington, TX 76011
Phone: 817-273-5222
Fax: 817-273-5174

Bass Performance Hall
4th & Calhoun Sts
Fort Worth, TX 76102
www.basshall.com
Phone: 817-212-4200
Fax: 817-810-9294

Billy Bob's Texas
2520 Rodeo Plaza
Fort Worth, TX 76106
Phone: 817-624-7117
Fax: 817-626-2340

Casa Mañana Theatre
3101 W Lancaster Ave
Fort Worth, TX 76107
Phone: 817-332-2272
Fax: 817-332-5711

Cattleman's Museum
1301 W 7th St
Fort Worth, TX 76102
Phone: 817-332-8551
Fax: 817-332-8749

Charles D Tandy Archaeological Museum
2001 W Seminary Dr
Fort Worth, TX 76115
Phone: 817-923-1921
Fax: 817-921-8765

Circle Theatre
230 W 4th St
Fort Worth, TX 76102
home.swbell.net/circleth
Phone: 817-877-3040
Fax: 817-877-3536

Cowtown Coliseum
121 E Exchange Ave
Fort Worth, TX 76106
www.cowtowncoliseum.com
Phone: 817-625-1025
Fax: 817-625-1148
TF: 888-269-8696

Creative Arts Theatre
1100 W Randol Mill Rd
Arlington, TX 76012
E-mail: cats@azone.net
www.creativearts.org
Phone: 817-861-2287
Fax: 817-274-0793

Eddleman-McFarland House Museum
1110 Penn St
Fort Worth, TX 76102
Phone: 817-332-5875
Fax: 817-332-5877

Fielder House Museum
1616 W Abram St
Arlington, TX 76013
www.fielderhouse.org
Phone: 817-460-4001
Fax: 817-460-1315

Fort Worth Ballet
6845 Green Oaks Rd
Fort Worth, TX 76116
Phone: 817-763-0207
Fax: 817-763-0624

Fort Worth Botanic Garden
3220 Botanic Garden Blvd
Fort Worth, TX 76107
Phone: 817-871-7686
Fax: 817-871-7638

Fort Worth Museum of Science & History
1501 Montgomery St
Fort Worth, TX 76107
E-mail: fwmsh1@metronet.com
www.fwmuseum.org
Phone: 817-732-1631
Fax: 817-732-7635
TF: 888-255-9300

Fort Worth Nature Center & Refuge
9601 Fossil Ridge Rd
Fort Worth, TX 76135
Phone: 817-237-1111
Fax: 817-237-1168

Fort Worth Opera
3505 W Lancaster
Fort Worth, TX 76107
E-mail: fwopera@startext.net
www.startext.net/interact/fwopera.htm
Phone: 817-731-0833
Fax: 817-731-0835

Fort Worth Symphony Orchestra
4th & Calhoun Sts Bass Performance Hall
Fort Worth, TX 76102
E-mail: ticks@fwsymphony.org
www.fwsymphony.org/
Phone: 817-665-6000
Fax: 817-665-6100

Fort Worth Theatre Inc
4401 Trail Lake Dr
Fort Worth, TX 76109
www.star-telegram.com/homes/fwt
Phone: 817-921-5300

Fort Worth Water Gardens
1502 Commerce St
Fort Worth, TX 76102
Phone: 817-871-7698
Fax: 817-871-5724

Fort Worth Zoological Park
1989 Colonial Pkwy
Fort Worth, TX 76110
www.fortworthzoo.com
Phone: 817-871-7000
Fax: 817-871-7012

Gateway Park
4501 E 1st St
Fort Worth, TX 76137
Phone: 817-871-7690
Fax: 817-335-1103

Hurricane Harbor
1800 E Lamar Blvd
Arlington, TX 76006
www.sixflags.com/hurricaneharbordallas
Phone: 817-265-3356
Fax: 817-265-9892

Imagisphere Children's Museum
7624 Grapevine Hwy Suite 716
North Richland Hills, TX 76180
E-mail: imaginc@imagisphere.com
www.imagisphere.org/
Phone: 817-589-9000
Fax: 817-589-1400

Johnnie High's Country Music Revue
224 N Center St
Arlington, TX 76011
Phone: 800-540-5127
Fax: 817-460-3913

Johnson Plantation Cemetery & Log Cabins
512 W Arkansas Ln
Arlington, TX 76014
Phone: 817-460-4001
Fax: 817-460-1315
TF: 800-433-5374

Jubilee Theatre
506 Main St
Fort Worth, TX 76102
www.jubileetheatre.org
Phone: 817-338-4411
Fax: 817-338-4206

Kimbell Art Museum
3333 Camp Bowie Blvd
Fort Worth, TX 76107
www.kimbellart.org
Phone: 817-332-8451
Fax: 817-877-1264

Lake Arlington
6300 W Arkansas La
Arlington, TX 76016
Phone: 817-451-6860
Fax: 817-451-4688

Legends of the Game Baseball Museum
1000 Ballpark Way
Arlington, TX 76011
Phone: 817-273-5023
Fax: 817-273-5093

Log Cabin Village
2100 Log Cabin Village Ln
Fort Worth, TX 76109
Phone: 817-926-5881
Fax: 817-922-0246

Mill Randol Park
1901 W Randol Mill Rd
Arlington, TX 76012
Phone: 817-459-5473

Modern Art Museum of Fort Worth
1309 Montgomery St
Fort Worth, TX 76107
www.mamfw.org
Phone: 817-738-9215
Fax: 817-735-1161

National Cowgirl Museum & Hall of Fame
111 W 4th St Suite 300
Fort Worth, TX 76102
www.cowgirl.net/
Phone: 817-336-4475
Fax: 817-336-2470
TF: 800-476-3263

Noble Planetarium
1501 Montgomery St Museum of Science & History
Fort Worth, TX 76107
www.fwmuseum.org/tnoble.html
Phone: 817-732-1631
Fax: 817-732-7635
TF: 888-255-9300

Omni Theater
1501 Montgomery St Museum of Science & History
Fort Worth, TX 76107
www.fwmuseum.org/tomni.html
Phone: 817-732-1631
Fax: 817-732-7635
TF: 888-255-9300

Palace of Wax & Ripley's Believe It or Not!
601 E Safari Pkwy
Grand Prairie, TX 75050
E-mail: lowcpm@onramp.net
www.ripleys.com/grandprairie.htm
Phone: 972-263-2391
Fax: 972-263-5954

Pate Museum of Transportation
Hwy 377 S of Fort Worth
Cresson, TX 76035
www.classicar.com/MUSEUMS/PATE/PATE.HTM
Phone: 817-396-4305
Fax: 800-827-0711

River Legacy Living Science Center
703 NW Green Oaks Blvd
Arlington, TX 76006
E-mail: rlegacy@arlington.net
www.riverlegacy.com
Phone: 817-860-6752
Fax: 817-860-1595

Sid Richarson Collection of Western Art
309 Main St
Fort Worth, TX 76102
E-mail: sidrmus@txcc.net
www.sidrmuseum.org
Phone: 817-332-6554
Fax: 817-332-8671

Six Flags Over Texas
2201 Road to Six Flags
Arlington, TX 76011
www.sixflags.com/texas
Phone: 817-640-8900
Fax: 817-530-6040

Sports Legacy Art Gallery
1000 Ballpark Way Suite 122
Arlington, TX 76011
Phone: 817-461-1994
Fax: 817-460-6068
TF: 800-659-9631

Stockyards Museum
131 E Exchange Ave
Fort Worth, TX 76106
Phone: 817-625-5087
Fax: 817-625-5083

Stockyards National Historic District
130 E Exchange St
Fort Worth, TX 76106
Phone: 817-624-4741
Fax: 817-625-9744

Stovall Park
2800 W Sublett Rd
Arlington, TX 76017
Phone: 817-459-5473

Sundance Square
512 Main St
Fort Worth, TX 76102
www.sundancesquare.com
Phone: 817-339-7777
Fax: 817-339-7216

Tarrant County Courthouse
100 W Weatherford St
Fort Worth, TX 76196
Phone: 817-884-1111
Fax: 817-884-1702

Theatre Arlington
305 W Main St
Arlington, TX 76010
E-mail: theatrearlington@theatrearlington.org
www.theatrearlington.org
Phone: 817-275-7661
Fax: 817-275-3370

Thistle Hill
1509 Pennsylvania Ave
Fort Worth, TX 76104
Phone: 817-336-1212
Fax: 817-335-5338

Traders Village
2602 Mayfield Rd
Grand Prairie, TX 75052
www.tradersvillage.com/gp1.html
Phone: 972-647-2331
Fax: 972-647-8585

Trinity Park
2401 N University Dr
Fort Worth, TX 76107
Phone: 817-871-7275

Vandergriff Park
2801 Matlock Rd
Arlington, TX 76015
Phone: 817-459-5473

Veterans Park
3600 W Arkansas Ln
Arlington, TX 76016
Phone: 817-459-5473

Vintage Flying Museum
505 NW 38th St Hanger 33 S Meacham Field
Fort Worth, TX 76106
E-mail: vfm@startext.net
www.startext.net/homes/vfm/
Phone: 817-624-1935
Fax: 817-485-4454

Will Rogers Memorial Center
3401 W Lancaster Ave
Fort Worth, TX 76107
Phone: 817-871-8150
Fax: 817-871-8170

Sports Teams & Facilities

Ballpark in Arlington
1000 Ballpark Way Suite 400
Arlington, TX 76011
Phone: 817-273-5222
Fax: 817-273-5264
TF: 888-968-3927

Fort Worth Brahmas (hockey)
1314 Lake St Suite 200
Fort Worth, TX 76102
E-mail: info@brahmas.com
www.brahmas.com
Phone: 817-336-4423
Fax: 817-336-3334

Lone Star Park at Grand Prairie
1000 Lone Star Pkwy
Grand Prairie, TX 75050
www.lonestarpark.com
Phone: 972-263-7223
Fax: 972-237-5109

Texas Motor Speedway
3601 Hwy 114
Justin, TX 76247
E-mail: TMS_Guest_Feedback@texasmotorspeedway.com
www.texasmotorspeedway.com
Phone: 817-215-8500
Fax: 817-491-3749

Texas Rangers
1000 Ballpark Way Ballpark at Arlington
Arlington, TX 76011
www.texasrangers.com
Phone: 817-273-5100
Fax: 817-273-5174
TF: 888-968-3927

Texas Rattlers (soccer)
12345 Inwood Rd Jesuit College
Dallas, TX 75244
www.texassoccer.net
Phone: 214-720-0285
Fax: 214-720-0595

Annual Events

Auto Swap Meet (early June)......................972-647-2331
Boar's Head & Yule Log Festival (January).........817-926-6631
Cardboard Boat Regatta (mid-April)................817-860-6752
Celebration of Lights (early-December) 817-459-6122
Christmas Fireworks to Music (late November).....214-855-1881
Country at Heart Art & Craft Show (mid-July)......817-459-5000
Cowtown Goes Green (March 17).................800-433-5747
Fort Worth Chisholm Trail Round-Up (mid-June) 817-625-7005
Fort Worth Cowtown Marathon & 10K Run (late February)................................817-735-2033
Fort Worth Fourth (July 4).......................800-433-5747
Fort Worth International Air Show (early October)...............................817-551-1967
Fort Worth RetroFest (mid-September-mid-November) 817-924-0492
Fourth of July Celebration (July 4) 817-459-6100
International Week (late March-early April).........817-272-2355
Juneteenth Celebration (mid-June) 800-433-5747
Last Great Gunfight (early February) 800-433-5747
Main Street Fort Worth Arts Festival (mid-late April)...............................817-336-2787
Mayfest (late April-early May).....................800-433-5747
National Championship Indian Pow Wow (early September) 972-647-2331
Neil Sperry's All Garden Show (late February-early March).....................817-459-5000
Oasis Fireworks to Music (early July)..............214-855-1881
Oktoberfest (early October).......................800-433-5747
Parade of Lights (late November-late December) 800-433-5747
Pioneer Days (mid-September)....................800-433-5747
Red Steagall Cowboy Gathering (late October) 800-433-5747
Shakespeare In the Park (June-July)...............800-433-5747
Southwestern Exposition & Livestock Show (mid-January-early February) 817-877-2400
Stockyards Championship Rodeo (early August-late November) 800-433-5747
Taste of Arlington (mid-September) 817-459-5000
Texas Brewers Festival (mid-October) 800-433-5747
Texas Indian Market (late March) 817-459-5000
Texas Scottish Festival & Games (early June) 817-654-2293
Yacht Club Regatta (early May)...................817-275-8074

Fresno, California

***County:* Fresno**

FRESNO is located in the San Joaquin Valley of central California. Major cities within 100 miles include Bakersfield and Modesto, California.

Area (Land) .... 99.1 sq mi
Area (Water)............................... 0.3 sq mi
Elevation.................................... 296 ft
Latitude ....36-84-09 N
Longitude.............................. 119-79-86 W
Time Zone .... PST
Area Code...................................... 559

Climate

The Fresno area has a moderate climate that varies by elevation, which ranges from 100 feet above sea level to 14,000 feet. The elevation of the city of Fresno is 296 feet. Winters there are generally mild, with average high temperatures ranging from the mid-50s to low 60s and lows ranging from the high 20s to the low 40s. Summer days are hot and dry, with average high temperatures reaching into the high 90s, while evenings cool down into the low to mid-60s. January is the wettest month in Fresno; July and August are the driest.

Average Temperatures & Precipitation

Temperatures

	Jan	Feb	Mar	Apr	May	Jun	Jul	Aug	Sep	Oct	Nov	Dec
High	54	62	67	75	84	93	99	97	90	80	65	54
Low	27	41	43	47	54	60	65	64	59	51	43	37

Precipitation

	Jan	Feb	Mar	Apr	May	Jun	Jul	Aug	Sep	Oct	Nov	Dec
Inches	2.0	1.8	1.9	1.0	0.3	0.1	0.0	0.0	0.2	0.5	1.4	1.4

History

The Fresno area was owned by Mexico until 1846, when the United States gained control of the land as a result of the Mexican-American War. Gold was discovered shortly thereafter, drawing many settlers to the region. Fresno County was established in 1856, and the town of Millerton was chosen as the county seat. Set in the central San Joaquin Valley, Fresno takes its name from the ash trees native to the area (Fresno is the Spanish word for "ash tree"). The town of Fresno was founded in 1872 when the Central Pacific Railroad chose the land as a site for a railroad telegraph office. The arrival of the railroad brought economic opportunities that led a number of Millerton residents to relocate to the new town. In 1885, Fresno was incorporated as a city and became the new centralized county seat.

Originally a dry, desert area, Fresno County was transformed into a fertile farming area through the development of irrigation canals called "church ditches" for Morris Church, who dug the first of these canals. Primary crops included grapes, grain, cotton, oranges, figs, and apples; and livestock, primarily cattle, was also an important part of Fresno's agricultural base. The lumber and mining industries also helped fuel Fresno's economy. Agriculture remains vital to the region's economic development—Fresno County today is one of the nation's leading agricultural regions, generating $3.5 billion in more than 250 commercial crops annually. In addition to its successful farming and agricultural processing industries, Fresno has also become a regional center for government and industry in central California. The City of Fresno today has more than 398,000 residents, a number that continues to grow steadily each year.

Population

1990 Census 354,091
1998 Estimate..............................398,133
% Change 12.4
2010 Projection 831,849*

Racial/Ethnic Breakdown

White....................................59.2%
Black 8.3%
Other....................................32.5%
Hispanic Origin (may be of any race) 29.9%

Age Breakdown

Under 5 years............................10.0%
5 to 17..................................21.7%
18 to 20..................................4.9%
21 to 24..................................7.1%
25 to 34.................................17.9%
35 to 44.................................13.9%
45 to 54..................................8.0%
55 to 64..................................6.4%
65 to 74..................................5.7%
75+ years 4.4%
Median Age...............................28.4

Gender Breakdown

Male.....................................48.6%
Female...................................51.4%

** Information given is for the Fresno Metropolitan Statistical Area (MSA), which includes the city of Fresno and the remainder of Fresno County.*

Government

Type of Government: Strong Mayor

Fresno City Clerk
2600 Fresno St
Fresno, CA 93721
Phone: 559-498-1321
Fax: 559-488-1005

Fresno City Council
2600 Fresno St
Fresno, CA 93721
Phone: 559-498-1560
Fax: 559-237-4010

Fresno City Hall
2600 Fresno St
Fresno, CA 93721
Phone: 559-498-4591
Fax: 559-488-1015

Fresno City Manager
2600 Fresno St 2nd Fl
Fresno, CA 93721
Phone: 559-489-2799
Fax: 559-488-1015

Fresno Development Dept
2600 Fresno St
Fresno, CA 93721
Phone: 559-498-1591
Fax: 559-498-1012

Fresno Finance Div
2600 Fresno St
Fresno, CA 93721
Phone: 559-498-1342
Fax: 559-488-4636

Fresno Fire Dept
450 M St
Fresno, CA 93721
Phone: 559-498-1542
Fax: 559-498-4261

Fresno Human Resources Div
2600 Fresno St 1st Fl
Fresno, CA 93721
Phone: 559-498-1575
Fax: 559-498-4775

Fresno Mayor
2600 Fresno St
Fresno, CA 93721
Phone: 559-498-1560
Fax: 559-488-1015

Fresno Parks Recreation & Community Services Dept
2326 Fresno St Rm 101
Fresno, CA 93721
Phone: 559-498-1145
Fax: 559-498-1588

Fresno Police Dept
2326 Mariposa St
Fresno, CA 93721
Phone: 559-498-1201

Fresno Public Utilities Dept
2600 Fresno St 1st Fl
Fresno, CA 93721
Phone: 559-498-4891
Fax: 559-498-1304

Fresno Public Works Dept
2600 Fresno St 4th Fl
Fresno, CA 93721
Phone: 559-498-1461
Fax: 559-488-1045

Fresno Transportation Dept
2401 N Ashley Way
Fresno, CA 93727
Phone: 559-498-4700
Fax: 559-251-4825

Fresno Water Management Div
1910 E University Ave
Fresno, CA 93703
Phone: 559-498-1458
Fax: 559-488-1024

Important Phone Numbers

AAA....800-222-4357
California State Franchise Tax Board....916-845-4300
Dental Referral....800-336-8478
Driver's License/Vehicle Registration Information...559-445-5469
Emergency....911
Fresno Assn of Realtors....559-226-4550
Fresno County Tax Collection Div....559-488-3482
FUN2DAY....559-222-8222
Medical Referral....559-449-2000
Poison Control Center....800-876-4766
Road Conditions....800-427-7623
Ski Report....559-233-3330
Time/Temp....559-592-8181
Voter Registration Information....559-488-3246
Weather....559-442-1212

Information Sources

Better Business Bureau Serving Central California
2519 W Shaw Ave Suite 106
Fresno, CA 93711
www.cencal.bbb.org
Phone: 559-222-8111
Fax: 559-228-6518

Fresno Chamber of Commerce
1649 Van Ness Ave Suite 103
Fresno, CA 93721
www.fresnochamber.com
Phone: 559-495-4800
Fax: 559-495-4811

Fresno Convention & Visitors Bureau
848 M St 3rd Fl
Fresno, CA 93721
www.fresnocvb.org
Phone: 559-233-0836
Fax: 559-445-0122
TF: 800-788-0836

Fresno Convention Center
848 M St
Fresno, CA 93721
www.ci.fresno.ca.us/convention
Phone: 559-498-1511
Fax: 559-488-4634

Fresno County
2281 Tulare St Rm 304 Hall of Records
Fresno, CA 93721
www.fresno.ca.gov
Phone: 559-488-1710
Fax: 559-488-1830

Fresno County Economic Development Corp
2344 Tulare St Suite 100
Fresno, CA 93721
Phone: 559-233-2564
Fax: 559-233-2156

Online Resources

4Fresno.com
www.4fresno.com

Anthill City Guide Fresno
www.anthill.com/city.asp?city=fresno

Area Guide Fresno
fresno.areaguides.net

Central Valley Internet Project
www.fresno.com/

Central Valley Online
www.fresno.com/cvonline/index.html

City Knowledge Fresno
www.cityknowledge.com/ca_fresno.htm

Excite.com Fresno City Guide
www.excite.com/travel/countries/united_states/california/fresno

Fresno Online
www.fresno-online.com

Hello Fresno
www.psnw.com/~deb/index.html

HomeFresno.com
www.homefresno.com

Tower 2000
www.tower2000.com/

Area Communities

Communities in Fresno County with populations greater than 5,000 include:

Clovis
1033 5th St
Clovis, CA 93612
Phone: 559-297-2300
Fax: 559-297-2552

Coalinga
155 W Durian St
Coalinga, CA 93210
Phone: 559-935-1533
Fax: 559-935-5912

Firebaugh
1575 11th St
Firebaugh, CA 93622
Phone: 559-659-2043
Fax: 559-659-3412

Huron
PO Box 339
Huron, CA 93234
Phone: 559-945-2241
Fax: 559-945-2609

Kerman
850 S Madera Ave
Kerman, CA 93630
Phone: 559-846-9384
Fax: 559-846-6199

Kingsburg
1401 Draper St
Kingsburg, CA 93631
Phone: 559-897-5821
Fax: 559-897-5568

Mendota
643 Quince St
Mendota, CA 93640
Phone: 559-655-4298
Fax: 559-655-4064

Orange Cove
633 6th St
Orange Cove, CA 93646
Phone: 559-626-5100
Fax: 559-626-4653

Parlier
1100 E Parlier Ave
Parlier, CA 93648
Phone: 559-646-3545
Fax: 559-646-0416

Reedley
1717 9th St
Reedley, CA 93654
Phone: 559-637-4200
Fax: 559-638-1093

Sanger
1700 7th St
Sanger, CA 93657
Phone: 559-875-2587
Fax: 559-875-8956

Selma
1710 Tucker St
Selma, CA 93662
Phone: 559-896-1064
Fax: 559-896-1068

Economy

Farming, as well as agriculture-related industries such as food processing, remains a vital part of Fresno County's economy, as it has for more than a century. Healthcare also has become a leading industry in Fresno. The city is the leading regional center for the industry between Los Angeles and San Francisco. Approximately half of the jobs in Fresno County's leading employment sector, services, are health care-related. Government is also a leading employer at the local, state, and federal levels in Fresno, which serves as the seat of Fresno County and is also home to the Internal Revenue Service's Western Processing Center.

Unemployment Rate 13.7%
Per Capita Income.......................... $19,946*
Median Family Income...................... $37,200*

** Information given is for the Fresno Metropolitan Statistical Area (MSA), which includes Fresno and Madera counties.*

Principal Industries & Number of Wage Earners

Fresno MSA* - 1999

Industry	Wage Earners
Construction	14,500
Farm Production	25,600
Finance, Insurance, & Real Estate	13,900
Government	67,000
Manufacturing	29,200
Mining	300
Retail Trade	51,500
Services	70,300
Transportation & Public Utilities	13,300
Wholesale Trade	14,900

** Information given is for the Fresno Metropolitan Statistical Area (MSA), which includes Fresno and Madera counties.*

Major Employers

Community Hospitals of Central California
PO Box 1232
Fresno, CA 93715
www.chsnet.com
Phone: 559-442-6000
Fax: 559-442-2450

Fresno Unified School District
2309 Tulare St
Fresno, CA 93721
fresno.k12.ca.us
Phone: 559-457-3000
Fax: 559-457-3528

Gottschalks Inc
7 River Park Pl E
Fresno, CA 93720
E-mail: gottschalks@gottschalks.com
www.gottschalks.com
Phone: 559-434-8000
Fax: 559-434-4806

Saint Agnes Medical Center
1303 E Herndon Ave
Fresno, CA 93720
Phone: 559-449-3000
Fax: 559-449-3990

State Center Community College District
1525 E Weldon Ave
Fresno, CA 93704
www.scccd.cc.ca.us
Phone: 559-226-0720
Fax: 559-229-7039

Sun-Maid Growers of California
13525 S Bethel Ave
Kingsburg, CA 93631
www.sun-maid.com
Phone: 559-896-8000
Fax: 559-897-6385
TF: 800-272-4746

University Medical Center
445 S Cedar Ave
Fresno, CA 93702
www.communitymedical.org/PatientServices/Facilities/umc.asp
Phone: 559-459-4000
Fax: 559-459-4787

Valley Children's Hospital Phone: 559-225-3000
9300 Valley Children's Pl Fax: 559-353-5161
Madera, CA 93638
www.valleychildrens.org

Valley Demonstration Service Phone: 559-225-6907
PO Box 13026 Fax: 559-225-6907
Fresno, CA 93650

Zacky Farms Phone: 559-486-2310
PO Box 122556 Fax: 559-443-2777
Fresno, CA 93778 TF: 800-999-8202
www.zacky.com

Quality of Living Indicators

Total Crime Index....................................32,075
(rates per 100,000 inhabitants)

Violent Crime
Murder/manslaughter........................... 32
Forcible rape 175
Robbery....................................1,394
Aggravated assault..........................2,649

Property Crime
Burglary 5,202
Larceny theft 16,948
Motor vehicle theft.........................5,671

Cost of Living Index..................................107.1
(national average = 100)

Median Home Price................................$135,000

Education

Public Schools

Fresno Unified School District Phone: 559-457-3000
2309 Tulare St Fax: 559-457-3528
Fresno, CA 93721
fresno.k12.ca.us

Number of Schools
Elementary................................ 61
Middle 14
High.. 12

Student/Teacher Ratio
All Grades 25.1:1

Private Schools

Number of Schools (all grades).................... 38+

Colleges & Universities

California Christian College Phone: 559-251-4215
4881 E University Ave Fax: 559-251-4231
Fresno, CA 93703
E-mail: cccfresno@aol.com
www.calchristiancollege.org

California State University Fresno Phone: 559-278-4240
5241 N Maple Ave Fax: 559-278-4812
Fresno, CA 93740
www.csufresno.edu

Fresno City College Phone: 559-442-4600
1101 E University Ave Fax: 559-237-4232
Fresno, CA 93741
www.fcc.cc.ca.us

Fresno Pacific University Phone: 559-453-2000
1717 S Chestnut Ave Fax: 559-453-5502
Fresno, CA 93702 TF: 800-660-6089
www.fresno.edu

Heald Business College Fresno Phone: 559-438-4222
255 W Bullard Ave Fax: 559-438-6368
Fresno, CA 93704 TF: 800-284-0844
www.heald.edu/CampusInfo/CampusInfo.asp?campus=FNB

State Center Community College District Phone: 559-226-0720
1525 E Weldon Ave Fax: 559-229-7039
Fresno, CA 93704
www.scccd.cc.ca.us

Hospitals

Clovis Community Medical Center Phone: 559-323-4000
2755 E Herndon Ave Fax: 559-324-3717
Clovis, CA 93611

Fresno Community Hospital & Medical Center Phone: 559-459-6000
2823 Fresno St Fax: 559-459-2450
Fresno, CA 93715

Saint Agnes Medical Center Phone: 559-449-3000
1303 E Herndon Ave Fax: 559-449-3990
Fresno, CA 93720

University Medical Center Phone: 559-459-4000
445 S Cedar Ave Fax: 559-459-4787
Fresno, CA 93702
www.communitymedical.org/PatientServices/Facilities/umc.asp

Valley Children's Hospital Phone: 559-225-3000
9300 Valley Children's Pl Fax: 559-353-5161
Madera, CA 93638
www.valleychildrens.org

Veterans Affairs Medical Center Phone: 559-225-6100
2615 E Clinton Ave Fax: 559-228-6911
Fresno, CA 93703

Transportation

Airport(s)

Fresno Air Terminal (FAT)
5 miles NE of downtown (approx 10 minutes) 559-498-4095

Mass Transit

Fresno Area Express
$1 Base fare 559-488-1122

Rail/Bus

Amtrak Station Phone: 559-486-7651
2650 Tulare St Bldg B TF: 800-872-7245
Fresno, CA 93721

Greyhound/Trailways Bus Station
1033 Broadway St
Fresno, CA 93721
Phone: 559-268-1829
TF: 800-231-2222

Utilities

Electricity
Pacific Gas & Electric Co 800-743-5000
www.pge.com

Gas
Pacific Gas & Electric Co 800-743-5000
www.pge.com

Water
Fresno Water Dept 559-498-1421

Garbage Collection/Recycling
Fresno Recycling Program 559-498-4678
Fresno Solid Waste Management Div...........559-498-1452

Telecommunications

Telephone
Pacific Bell..................................800-310-2355
www.pacbell.com

Cable Television
AT & T Cable Services.........................888-255-5789

Internet Service Providers (ISPs)
The Socket Internet Service....................559-437-1483
www.thesocket.com

Banks

Bank of America National Trust & Savings Assn
2611 S Cedar Ave
Fresno, CA 93725
Phone: 559-445-7321
Fax: 559-445-7395

Bank of the West
515 E Shaw Ave
Fresno, CA 93710
Phone: 559-221-4300
Fax: 559-221-6060

California Bank & Trust
7060 N Fresno St
Fresno, CA 93720
Phone: 559-438-2600
Fax: 559-438-2699

California Federal Bank
3141 N Cedar Ave
Fresno, CA 93703
Phone: 800-843-2265
Fax: 559-228-0934

Sanwa Bank California
2035 Fresno St
Fresno, CA 93721
Phone: 559-487-2101
Fax: 559-487-2118
TF: 888-467-2692

United Bank of California NA
7108 N Fresno St Suite 100
Fresno, CA 93720
Phone: 559-436-2700
Fax: 559-436-2720

United Security Bank
2151 W Shaw Ave
Fresno, CA 93711
Phone: 559-225-0101
Fax: 559-248-4929

Washington Mutual Bank
7160 N 1st St
Fresno, CA 93720
Phone: 559-437-1601
Fax: 559-437-1605

Wells Fargo Bank NA
1206 Van Ness Ave
Fresno, CA 93721
Phone: 559-442-6222
Fax: 559-233-3790

Westamerica Bank
1172 E Shaw Ave
Fresno, CA 93710
Phone: 559-221-2300
Fax: 559-221-2232
TF: 800-848-1088

Shopping

Fashion Fair Shopping Mall
645 E Shaw Ave
Fresno, CA 93726
Phone: 559-224-1591
Fax: 559-224-1040

Fig Garden Village
5082 N Palm Ave Suite A
Fresno, CA 93704
Phone: 559-226-4084
Fax: 559-226-7960

Fulton's Folly Antique Mall
920 E Olive Ave
Fresno, CA 93728
Phone: 559-268-3856

Macy's
4888 N Fresno St Fashion Fair Mall
Fresno, CA 93726
Phone: 559-228-3333

Manchester Center
1901 E Shields Ave Suite 243
Fresno, CA 93726
Phone: 559-227-1901
Fax: 559-227-1602

Sierra Vista Mall
Clovis & Shaw Aves
Clovis, CA 93612
Phone: 559-299-0660

Media

Newspapers and Magazines

Fresno Bee*
1626 'E' St
Fresno, CA 93786
E-mail: letters@fresnobee.com
www.fresnobee.com
Phone: 559-441-6111
Fax: 559-441-6436
TF: 800-877-7300

Kingsburg Recorder
1467 Marion St
Kingsburg, CA 93631
Phone: 559-897-2993
Fax: 559-897-4868

**Indicates major daily newspapers*

Television

KFSN-TV Ch 30 (ABC)
1777 G St
Fresno, CA 93706
Phone: 559-442-1170
Fax: 559-266-5024

KFTV-TV Ch 21 (Uni)
3239 W Ashlan Ave
Fresno, CA 93722
www.univision.net/stations/kftv.htm
Phone: 559-222-2121
Fax: 559-222-2890

KGMC-TV Ch 43 (Ind)
706 W Herndon Ave
Fresno, CA 93650
E-mail: cocolatv@psnw.com
www.cocolatv.com
Phone: 559-435-7000
Fax: 559-435-3201

KJEO-TV Ch 47 (CBS)
4880 N 1st St
Fresno, CA 93726
www.kjeo.com
Phone: 559-222-2411
Fax: 559-225-5305

KMPH-TV Ch 26 (Fox)
5111 E McKinley Ave
Fresno, CA 93727
Phone: 559-453-8850
Fax: 559-255-9626

KMSG-TV Ch 59 (Tele)
706 W Herndon Ave
Fresno, CA 93650
E-mail: corporate@kmsg59.com
www.kmsg59.com
Phone: 559-435-5900
Fax: 559-435-1448

KNXT-TV Ch 49 (Ind)
1550 N Fresno St
Fresno, CA 93703
Phone: 559-488-7440
Fax: 559-488-7444

KPXF-TV Ch 61 (PAX)
4910 E Clinton Ave Suite 107
Fresno, CA 93727
www.pax.net/KPXF
Phone: 559-255-1161
Fax: 559-255-1061

KSEE-TV Ch 24 (NBC)
5035 E McKinley Ave
Fresno, CA 93727
www.ksee24.com
Phone: 559-454-2424
Fax: 559-454-2485

KVPT-TV Ch 18 (PBS)
1544 Van Ness Ave
Fresno, CA 93721
www.kvpt.org
Phone: 559-266-1800
Fax: 559-650-1880
TF: 800-801-6500

Radio

KALZ-FM 102.7 MHz (AC)
4991 E McKinley Ave Suite 124
Fresno, CA 93727
Phone: 559-251-8614
Fax: 559-251-3347

KBOS-FM 94.9 MHz (CHR)
1066 E Shaw Ave
Fresno, CA 93710
www.kbos.com
Phone: 559-243-4300
Fax: 559-243-4301

KCBL-AM 1340 kHz (Sports)
1066 E Shaw Ave
Fresno, CA 93710
www.kcbl.com
Phone: 559-243-4300
Fax: 559-243-4301

KEZL-FM 96.7 MHz (Nost)
4991 E McKinley Ave Suite 124
Fresno, CA 93727
www.kezl.com
Phone: 559-251-8614
Fax: 559-251-3347

KFRR-FM 104.1 MHz (Alt)
1981 N Gateway Blvd Suite 101
Fresno, CA 93727
E-mail: newrock@lightspeed.net
www.newrock104.com
Phone: 559-255-1041
Fax: 559-456-8077

KFSO-FM 92.9 MHz (Oldies)
4991 E McKinley Ave Suite 124
Fresno, CA 93727
Phone: 559-251-8614
Fax: 559-251-3347

KGST-AM 1600 kHz (Span)
1110 E Olive Ave
Fresno, CA 93728
Phone: 559-497-1100
Fax: 559-497-1125

KJFX-FM 95.7 MHz (CR)
1981 N Gateway Blvd Suite 101
Fresno, CA 93727
www.957thefox.com
Phone: 559-255-1041
Fax: 559-456-8077

KJWL-FM 99.3 MHz (Nost)
675 Santa Fe
Fresno, CA 93727
www.kjwl.com
Phone: 559-497-5118
Fax: 559-595-9760

KKPW-FM 94.3 MHz (CHR)
2775 E Shaw Ave
Fresno, CA 93710
Phone: 559-292-9494
Fax: 559-294-0741

KLBN-FM 105.1 MHz (Span)
1110 E Olive Ave
Fresno, CA 93728
Phone: 559-497-1100
Fax: 559-497-1125

KMEG-FM 97.9 MHz (Oldies)
1071 W Shaw Ave
Fresno, CA 93711
Phone: 559-490-9800
Fax: 559-490-4199

KMGV-FM 97.9 MHz (Oldies)
1071 W Shaw Ave
Fresno, CA 93711
Phone: 559-490-5800
Fax: 559-490-4199

KMJ-AM 580 kHz (N/T)
1071 W Shaw Ave
Fresno, CA 93711
www.kmj58.com
Phone: 559-266-5800
Fax: 559-266-3714

KMPH-FM 107.5 MHz (N/T)
5087 E McKinley Ave
Fresno, CA 93727
www.kmphfm.com
Phone: 559-255-5600
Fax: 559-252-4522

KRNC-FM 105.9 MHz (Span)
1071 W Shaw Ave
Fresno, CA 93711
Phone: 559-490-0106
Fax: 559-490-5888

KRZR-FM 103.7 MHz (Rock)
1066 E Shaw Ave
Fresno, CA 93710
www.krzr.com
Phone: 559-243-4300
Fax: 559-243-4301

KSEQ-FM 97.1 MHz (CHR)
617 W Tulare Ave
Visalia, CA 93277
www.q97.com
Phone: 559-627-9710
Fax: 559-627-1590

KSKS-FM 93.7 MHz (Ctry)
1071 W Shaw Ave
Fresno, CA 93711
www.ksks.com
Phone: 559-490-5800
Fax: 559-490-5944

KSOF-FM 98.9 MHz (AC)
83 E Shaw Ave Suite 150
Fresno, CA 93727
www.ksof.com
Phone: 559-251-8614

KVPR-FM 89.3 MHz (NPR)
3437 W Shaw Ave
Fresno, CA 93711
Phone: 559-275-0764
Fax: 559-275-2202

KVSR-FM 101.1 MHz (AC)
1071 W Shaw Ave
Fresno, CA 93711
www.star101.com
Phone: 559-490-1011
Fax: 559-490-5990

KYNO-AM 1300 kHz (Sports)
1981 N Gateway Blvd Suite 101
Fresno, CA 93727
Phone: 559-255-1041
Fax: 559-456-8077

Attractions

Fresno's Blossom Trail includes more than 65 miles of orchards, vineyards, and citrus groves, as well as historical points of interest. Fresno is located near three national parks: Yosemite National Park, which includes the highest falls in North America; Sequoia National Park, home of the Giant Sequoia trees; and Kings Canyon, which features giant canyons, lakes, falls, and mountain meadows. Kings River, which flows through Kings Canyon, offers opportunities for whitewater rafting.

African American Historical & Cultural Museum
1857 Fulton St
Fresno, CA 93721
Phone: 559-268-7102
Fax: 559-268-7135

American Historical Society of Germans from Russia
3233 N West Ave
Fresno, CA 93705
E-mail: ahsgr@aol.com
www.ahsgr.org
Phone: 559-229-8287
Fax: 559-229-6078

Arte Americas
1630 Van Ness Ave
Fresno, CA 93721
Phone: 559-266-2623
Fax: 559-266-6904

Boyden Caverns
Hwy 180 Kings Canyon National Pk
Sequoia National Forest, CA 93633
E-mail: caverns@caverntours.com
www.caverntours.com/PAGES/Boyden.html
Phone: 209-736-2708

Chaffee Zoological Gardens of Fresno
894 W Belmont Ave
Fresno, CA 93728
E-mail: toucan@chaffeezoo.org
www.chaffeezoo.org
Phone: 559-498-4692
Fax: 559-264-9226

Club One Casino
1033 Van Ness Ave
Fresno, CA 93721
Phone: 559-497-3000
Fax: 559-237-2582

Discovery Center
1944 N Winery Ave
Fresno, CA 93703
E-mail: discoverycenter2@juno.com
Phone: 559-251-5533
Fax: 559-251-5531

Duncan Water Gardens
6901 E McKenzie Ave
Fresno, CA 93727
Phone: 559-252-1657

Forestiere Underground Gardens
5021 W Shaw Ave
Fresno, CA 93722
Phone: 559-271-0734

Fresno Art Museum
2233 N 1st St
Fresno, CA 93703
Phone: 559-441-4220
Fax: 559-441-4227

Fresno Ballet
1432 Fulton St
Fresno, CA 93721
Phone: 559-233-2623
Fax: 559-233-2670

Fresno Betsuin Buddhist Temple
1340 Kern St
Fresno, CA 93706
Phone: 559-442-4054
Fax: 559-442-1978

Fresno Metropolitan Museum of Art History & Science
1515 Van Ness Ave
Fresno, CA 93721
www.fresnomet.org
Phone: 559-441-1444
Fax: 559-441-8607

Fresno Philharmonic Orchestra
2610 W Shaw Ave Suite 103
Fresno, CA 93711
www.fresnophil.org/
Phone: 559-261-0600
Fax: 559-261-0700

Good Co Players Second Space Theater
928 E Olive Ave
Fresno, CA 93728
E-mail: gcplayers@lightspeed.net
www.tower2000.com/rockas-gcp/index2.html
Phone: 559-266-0211
Fax: 559-266-1342

Kearney Mansion Museum
7160 W Kearney Blvd
Fresno, CA 93706
www.valleyhistory.org
Phone: 559-441-0862
Fax: 559-441-1372

Kearney Park
Kearney Blvd
Fresno, CA 93706
Phone: 559-488-3004

Kings Canyon National Park
Three Rivers, CA 93271
www.nps.gov/seki
Phone: 559-565-3341
Fax: 559-565-3730

Legion of Valor Museum
2425 Fresno St Veterans Memorial Auditorium
Fresno, CA 93721
Phone: 559-498-0510
Fax: 559-498-3773

Meux Home Museum
1007 R St
Fresno, CA 93721
www.meux.mus.ca.us
Phone: 559-233-8007

Mexican Cultural Institute of Central California
2409 Merced St
Fresno, CA 93721
Phone: 559-445-2615
Fax: 559-495-0535

Nonini Winery
2640 N Dickenson
Fresno, CA 93722
Phone: 559-275-1936

Roeding Park
890 W Belmont Ave
Fresno, CA 93728
Phone: 559-498-1551
Fax: 559-498-1588

Roger Rocka's Dinner Theater
1226 N Wishon Ave
Fresno, CA 93728
www.tower2000.com/rockas-gcp/
Phone: 559-266-9494
TF: 800-808-7344

Rotary Storyland & Playland
890 W Belmont Ave Roeding Pk
Fresno, CA 93728
www.storyland.org
Phone: 559-264-2235
Fax: 559-495-1594

San Joaquin Gardens
5555 N Fresno St
Fresno, CA 93710
E-mail: sanjoaquin@abhow.com
Phone: 559-439-4770
Fax: 559-439-2457

Sanger Depot Museum
1770 7th St
Sanger, CA 93657
Phone: 559-875-5505
Fax: 559-875-9892

Sequoia National Park
47050 Generals Hwy
Three Rivers, CA 93271
www.nps.gov/seki/
Phone: 559-565-3341
Fax: 559-565-3730

Shin-Zen Japanese Friendship Gardens
7775 N Friant Rd
Fresno, CA 93710
Phone: 559-498-1551
Fax: 559-498 1588

Sierra National Forest
1600 Tollhouse Rd
Clovis, CA 93611
www.yosemite.com/forest/sierra/sierra.htm
Phone: 559-297-0706
Fax: 559-294-4809

Simonian Farms
2629 S Clovis Ave
Fresno, CA 93725
E-mail: simonian@fresno-online.com
www.fresno-online.com/simonian
Phone: 559-237-2294
Fax: 559-441-1198

Table Mountain Casino & Bingo
8184 Table Mountain Rd
Friant, CA 93626
Phone: 559-822-2485
Fax: 559-822-2084

Theatre Three
1544 Fulton St
Fresno, CA 93721
www.theatre3.com
Phone: 559-486-3333

Tower Theatre for the Performing Arts
815 E Olive Ave
Fresno, CA 93728
Phone: 559-485-9050
Fax: 559-485-3941

Warnors Theatre
1400 Fulton St
Fresno, CA 93721
Phone: 559-264-6863
Fax: 559-264-5643

Wild Water Adventures
11413 E Shaw Ave
Clovis, CA 93611
E-mail: wildwater@mail.com
www.wildwater1.com
Phone: 559-297-6540
Fax: 559-297-6549

Woodward Park
7775 Friant Rd
Fresno, CA 93710
Phone: 559-498-1551
Fax: 559-498-1588

Yosemite Mountain Sugar Pine Railroad
56001 Hwy 41
Fish Camp, CA 93623
www.ymsprr.com
Phone: 559-683-7273
Fax: 559-683-8307

Yosemite National Park
PO Box 577
Yosemite National Park, CA 95389
www.yosemitepark.com
Phone: 209-372-0200

Sports Teams & Facilities

Fresno Bandits (football)
PO Box 72
Fresno, CA 93707
Phone: 559-264-9249
Fax: 559-264-9246

Fresno Falcons (hockey)
700 M St Fresno Selland Arena
Fresno, CA 93701
www.fresnofalcons.com
Phone: 559-264-7644
Fax: 559-497-6077

Selland Arena
700 M St Fresno Convention Ctr
Fresno, CA 93721
www.ci.fresno.ca.us/convention/selland.html
Phone: 559-498-1511
Fax: 559-488-4634

Annual Events

Carnival (early March) .559-441-4220
Civil War Revisited (early October) .559-441-0862
Clovis Rodeo (late April) .559-299-8838
Easton May Day Celebration (early May) .559-233-0836
Fresno County Blossom Trail
(md-February-mid-March) .559-233-0836
Fresno Fair (early-mid-October). .559-453-3247
Hmong National New Year
(late December-early January). .559-252-8782
Kingsburg Gun Shoot (late June) .559-897-1111
Kingsburg Summer Band Concerts Under the Stars
(late June-early August) .559-897-1111
Kwanzaa Festival (late December-early January). .559-268-7102
Mariachi Festival (late March) .559-455-5761
Miss California Pageant (late June-early July). .559-233-0836
Obon Odori Festival (early July) .559-442-4054
Raisin Bowl Regatta (early May) .559-822-2332
Renaissance Festival (late October). .559-436-3434
Sanger Blossom Days Festival (early March) .559-875-4575
Sanger Grape Bowl Festival
(late September-early October). .559-875-4575
Shaver Lake Fishing Derby (mid-June) .559-841-3350
Sudz in the City (mid-late May). .559-266-9982
Tower Arts Festival (mid-May). .559-498-8560
William Saroyan Festival (late April). .559-221-1441

Grand Rapids, Michigan

***County:* Kent**

GRAND RAPIDS is located in southwestern central Michigan along the Grand River. Major cities within 100 miles include Lansing and Flint, Michigan; Milwaukee, Wisconsin; and South Bend, Indiana.

Area (Land)	44.3 sq mi
Area (Water)	0.7 sq mi
Elevation	657 ft
Latitude	42-95-80 N
Longitude	85-68-44 W
Time Zone	EST
Area Code	616

Climate

Grand Rapids' climate is greatly influenced by nearby Lake Michigan. Winters are cold, with average high temperatures around 30 degrees and average lows in the mid- to upper teens, but the lake prevents prolonged periods of extreme cold. Heavy snowfall is common, with annual averages over 60 inches. Summer days are warm, with highs in the lower 80s, but evenings cool down into the mid-to-upper 50s. September is Grand Rapid's wettest month.

Average Temperatures & Precipitation

Temperatures

	Jan	Feb	Mar	Apr	May	Jun	Jul	Aug	Sep	Oct	Nov	Dec
High	29	32	43	57	69	79	83	81	72	60	46	34
Low	15	16	25	35	46	55	60	58	50	39	30	21

Precipitation

	Jan	Feb	Mar	Apr	May	Jun	Jul	Aug	Sep	Oct	Nov	Dec
Inches	1.8	1.4	2.6	3.4	3.1	3.7	3.2	3.6	4.2	2.8	3.3	2.9

History

Named for the rapids in the Grand River, which flows through the heart of the city, Grand Rapids was originally inhabited by various Native American tribes, including the Ottawa. During the early 1800's French and British settlers came to the Grand Rapids area and traded metal and textile goods with the Ottawa in exchange for fur pelts. The first permanent white settlement was established in 1825 by Baptist Minister Isaac McCoy. The following year Frenchman Louis Campau established a trading post in the area. Settlers were drawn to Grand Rapids because of the area's rich farmland and successful trade, and because of the Grand River's potential to provide power for water wheels and turbines for factories. The area's first furniture factory was established in 1836, and Grand Rapids later gained recognition as the "Furniture Capital of America."

Grand Rapids was incorporated as a city in 1850, with a population of nearly 3,000, and it continued to grow as a major furniture manufacturing and distribution center. During the mid-1940s, Grand Rapids became the campaign headquarters for Gerald R. Ford, a resident of the city who ran for Congress, eventually becoming the House minority leader. Ford became the President of the United States in 1974, after the resignations of President Richard Nixon and Vice President Spiro Agnew. He also ran in the 1976 presidential election, but was defeated.

Today, Grand Rapids is recognized as the world's largest manufacturer of office furniture. Top office furniture manufacturers headquartered in the Grand Rapids area include Steelcase, which is one of Kent County's largest employers. With a population of more than 185,000, Grand Rapids is Michigan's second largest city.

Population

1990 Census	189,126
1998 Estimate	185,437
% Change	-2.0

Racial/Ethnic Breakdown

White	76.7%
Black	18.6%
Other	4.7%
Hispanic Origin (may be of any race)	4.5%

Age Breakdown

Under 5 years	9.4%
5 to 17	18.1%
18 to 20	5.6%
21 to 24	7.2%
25 to 34	19.5%
35 to 44	13.1%
45 to 54	7.2%
55 to 64	6.9%
65 to 74	6.7%
75+ years	6.4%
Median Age	29.8

Gender Breakdown

Male	47.5%
Female	52.5%

Government

Type of Government: Commission-Manager

Grand Rapids City Attorney
300 Monroe Ave NW Rm 620
Grand Rapids, MI 49503
Phone: 616-456-3181
Fax: 616-456-4569

Grand Rapids City Clerk
300 Monroe Ave NW
Grand Rapids, MI 49503
Phone: 616-456-3014
Fax: 616-456-4607

Grand Rapids City Commission
300 Monroe Ave NW
Grand Rapids, MI 49503
Phone: 616-456-3035
Fax: 616-456-3111

Grand Rapids City Hall
300 Monroe Ave NW
Grand Rapids, MI 49503
Phone: 616-456-3000
Fax: 616-456-3111

Grand Rapids City Income Tax Dept
300 Monroe Ave NW
Grand Rapids, MI 49503
Phone: 616-456-3415
Fax: 616-456-4540

Grand Rapids City Manager
300 Monroe Ave NW
Grand Rapids, MI 49503
Phone: 616-456-3166
Fax: 616-456-3111

Grand Rapids Fire Dept
38 LaGrave Ave SE
Grand Rapids, MI 49503
Phone: 616-456-3900
Fax: 616-456-3898

Grand Rapids Human Resources Dept
300 Monroe Ave NW Rm 880
Grand Rapids, MI 49503
Phone: 616-456-3176
Fax: 616-456-3728

Grand Rapids Mayor
300 Monroe Ave NW
Grand Rapids, MI 49503
Phone: 616-456-3168
Fax: 616-456-3111

Grand Rapids Parks & Recreation Dept
201 Market Ave SW
Grand Rapids, MI 49503
Phone: 616-456-3696
Fax: 616-456-4567

Grand Rapids Planning Dept
300 Monroe Ave NW
Grand Rapids, MI 49503
Phone: 616-456-3031
Fax: 616-456-4568

Grand Rapids Police Dept
333 Monroe Ave NW
Grand Rapids, MI 49503
Phone: 616-456-3403
Fax: 616-456-3406

Grand Rapids Public Library
60 Library Plaza NE
Grand Rapids, MI 49503
Phone: 616-456-3600
Fax: 616-456-3619

Grand Rapids Streets & Sanitation Dept
201 Market Ave SW
Grand Rapids, MI 49503
Phone: 616-456-3232
Fax: 616-456-4561

Grand Rapids Treasurer
300 Monroe Ave NW Rm 220
Grand Rapids, MI 49503
Phone: 616-456-3020
Fax: 616-456-3413

Grand Rapids Water Dept
1101 Monroe Ave NW
Grand Rapids, MI 49503
Phone: 616-456-3200
Fax: 616-456-4466

Important Phone Numbers

AAA....................616-364-6111
Driver's License/Vehicle Registration Information ...616-363-8778
Emergency.................... 911
Grand Rapids Treasurer....................616-456-3020
Grand Rapids City Income Tax Dept....................616-456-3415
Grand Rapids Assn of Realtors....................616-940-8200
Grand Rapids Events Line....................616-451-3866
HotelDocs....................800-468-3537
Kent County Treasurer....................616-336-3641
Michigan Dept of Treasury & Tax Help Service......800-487-7000
Poison Control Center....................800-764-7661
Time....................616-459-1212
Voter Registration Information....................616-456-3010
Weather....................616-776-1234

Information Sources

Better Business Bureau Serving Western Michigan
40 Pearl St NW Suite 354
Grand Rapids, MI 49503
www.grandrapids.bbb.org
Phone: 616-774-8236
Fax: 616-774-2014

Grand Center
245 Monroe Ave NW
Grand Rapids, MI 49503
www.grandcenter.com/grand.htm
Phone: 616-742-6600
Fax: 616-742-6590

Grand Rapids Area Chamber of Commerce
111 Pearl St NW
Grand Rapids, MI 49503
www.grandrapids.org
Phone: 616-771-0300
Fax: 616-771-0318
TF: 800-376-6437

Grand Rapids/Kent County Convention & Visitors Bureau
140 Monroe Ctr Suite 300
Grand Rapids, MI 49503
www.grcvb.org
Phone: 616-459-8287
Fax: 616-459-7291
TF: 800-678-9859

Kent County
300 Monroe Ave NW
Grand Rapids, MI 49503
www.co.kent.mi.us/
Phone: 616-336-3550
Fax: 616-336-2885

Online Resources

4GrandRapids.com
www.4grandrapids.com

Anthill City Guide Grand Rapids
www.anthill.com/city.asp?city=grandrapids

Area Guide Grand Rapids
grandrapids.areaguides.net

City Knowledge Grand Rapids
www.cityknowledge.com/mi_grandrapids.htm

DigitalCity Grand Rapids
www.digitalcity.com/grandrapids

Excite.com Grand Rapids City Guide
www.excite.com/travel/countries/united_states/michigan/grand_rapids

Grand Happenings Community Calendar
www.grand-rapids.mi.us/calendar/

Area Communities

Communities with populations greater than 15,000 in the Grand Rapids area (Kent and Ottawa counties) include:

Byron Township
8085 Byron Center Ave SW
Byron, MI 49315
Phone: 616-878-9104
Fax: 616-878-3980

Cascade Township
2865 Thornhills Ave SE
Grand Rapids, MI 49546
Phone: 616-949-1500
Fax: 616-949-3918

Gaines Township
1685 68th St SE
Caledonia, MI 49316
Phone: 616-698-7980
Fax: 616-698-2490

Georgetown Township
1515 Baldwin St
Jenison, MI 49428
Phone: 616-457-2340
Fax: 616-457-3670

Grandville
3195 Wilson Ave SW
Grandville, MI 49418
Phone: 616-530-4977
Fax: 616-530-4984

Holland
270 River Ave
Holland, MI 49423
Phone: 616-355-1300
Fax: 616-355-1490

Holland Township
353 120th Ave
Holland, MI 49424
Phone: 616-396-2345
Fax: 616-396-2537

Kentwood
4900 Breton Ave SE
Kentwood, MI 49508
Phone: 616-698-9610
Fax: 616-554-0796

Park Township
52 152nd Ave
Holland, MI 49424
Phone: 616-399-4520
Fax: 616-399-8540

Plainfield Township
PO Box 365
Belmont, MI 49306
Phone: 616-364-8466
Fax: 616-364-6537

Walker
4243 Remembrance Rd NW
Grand Rapids, MI 49544
Phone: 616-791-6865
Fax: 616-793-6881

Wyoming
1155 28th St SW
Wyoming, MI 49509
Phone: 616-530-7296
Fax: 616-530-7200

Economy

Greater Grand Rapids has a diverse economic base that includes agriculture (Kent County has nearly 1,200 farms), health care, and manufacturing. Manufacturing is the largest employment sector in the Grand Rapids metro area, followed by wholesale trade and private services. Furniture is one of the area's leading products, and Steelcase is one of Kent County's largest employers, providing jobs for more than 9,500 area residents. Fabricated metal and industrial equipment are also among the area's primary products.

Unemployment Rate 3.1%*
Per Capita Income.......................... $28,820*
Median Family Income..................... $32,049

** Information given is for Kent County.*

Principal Industries & Number of Wage Earners

Grand Rapids-Muskegon-Holland MSA* - 1999

Construction 26,700
Finance, Insurance, & Real Estate 22,400
Government 56,000
Manufacturing 160,300
Mining 400
Private Services 143,800
Retail Trade.. 106,400
Transportation, Communications & Utilities 20,600
Wholesale Trade.. 145,700

** Information given is for the Grand Rapids-Muskegon-Holland Metropolitan Statistical Area (MSA), which includes Allegan, Kent, Muskegon, and Ottawa counties.*

Major Employers

Amway Corp
7575 Fulton St E
Ada, MI 49355
www.amway.com
Phone: 616-787-6000
Fax: 616-787-5675
TF: 800-544-7167

Benteler Automotive
3721 Hagen Dr SE
Grand Rapids, MI 49548
www.benteler.de/engl/At/AtIx.htm
Phone: 616-245-4607
Fax: 616-247-5910

D & W Food Centers Inc
PO Box 878
Grand Rapids, MI 49588
www.dwfoodcenters.com
Phone: 616-940-3580
Fax: 616-940-3159

General Motors Corp
300 36th St SW
Grand Rapids, MI 49548
www.gm.com/careers
Phone: 616-246-2750
Fax: 616-246-3150

Grand Rapids City Hall
300 Monroe Ave NW
Grand Rapids, MI 49503
www.grand-rapids.mi.us
Phone: 616-456-3000
Fax: 616-456-3111

Grand Rapids Community College
143 Bostwick Ave NE
Grand Rapids, MI 49503
www.grcc.cc.mi.us
Phone: 616-234-4000
Fax: 616-234-3907

Grand Rapids Public Schools
1331 Franklin St SE
Grand Rapids, MI 49506
grps.k12.mi.us
Phone: 616-771-2000
Fax: 616-771-2104

Herman Miller Inc
PO Box 302
Zeeland, MI 49464
www.hmiller.com
Phone: 616-654-3000
Fax: 616-654-5385

Kent County
300 Monroe Ave NW
Grand Rapids, MI 49503
www.co.kent.mi.us/
Phone: 616-336-3550
Fax: 616-336-2885

Meijer Inc
2929 Walker Ave NW
Grand Rapids, MI 49544
www.meijer.com
Phone: 616-453-6711
Fax: 616-791-2572

Old Kent Financial Corp
1 Vandenberg Ctr
Grand Rapids, MI 49503
E-mail: okfc.hr@oldkent.com
www.oldkent.com
Phone: 616-771-5000
Fax: 616-771-0015

Saint Mary's Health Services
200 Jefferson St SE
Grand Rapids, MI 49503
www.mercyhealth.com/smhs
Phone: 616-752-6090
Fax: 616-732-3004

Spectrum Health DeVos Children's Hospital
100 Michigan St NE
Grand Rapids, MI 49503
www.spectrum-health.org/devos/dvchindex2.htm
Phone: 616-391-1774
Fax: 616-391-2780

Spectrum Health East Campus
1840 Wealthy St SE
Grand Rapids, MI 49506
www.spectrum-health.org
Phone: 616-774-7444
Fax: 616-391-2780

Steelcase Inc
PO Box 1967
Grand Rapids, MI 49501
www.steelcase.com
Phone: 616-247-2710
Fax: 616-247-2256
TF: 888-783-3522

Quality of Living Indicators

Total Crime Index 14,502
(rates per 100,000 inhabitants)

Violent Crime
Murder/manslaughter 23
Forcible rape 71
Robbery 624
Aggravated assault 1,611

Property Crime
Burglary 3,151
Larceny theft 7,799
Motor vehicle theft 1,223

Cost of Living Index 107.6
(national average = 100)

Median Home Price $106,700

Education

Public Schools

Grand Rapids Public Schools
1331 Franklin St SE
Grand Rapids, MI 49506
grps.k12.mi.us
Phone: 616-771-2000
Fax: 616-771-2104

Number of Schools
Elementary 53
Middle 6
High 4

Student/Teacher Ratio
All Grades 20.5:1

Private Schools

Number of Schools (all grades) .... 30+

Colleges & Universities

Aquinas College
1607 Robinson Rd SE
Grand Rapids, MI 49506
www.aquinas.edu
Phone: 616-459-8281
Fax: 616-732-4487
TF: 800-678-9593

Calvin College
3201 Burton St SE
Grand Rapids, MI 49546
E-mail: admissions@calvin.edu
www.calvin.edu
Phone: 616-957-6000
Fax: 616-957-8551
TF: 800-688-0122

Cornerstone College
1001 E Beltline Ave NE
Grand Rapids, MI 49525
www.cornerstone.edu
Phone: 616-949-5300
Fax: 616-222-1400
TF: 800-787-9778

Davenport College
415 E Fulton St
Grand Rapids, MI 49503
www.davenport.edu/grandrapids
Phone: 616-451-3511
Fax: 616-732-1167
TF: 800-632-9569

Grace Bible College
1011 Aldon SW
Wyoming, MI 49509
E-mail: info@gbcol.edu
www.gbcol.edu
Phone: 616-538-2330
Fax: 616-538-0599
TF: 800-968-1887

Grand Rapids Community College
143 Bostwick Ave NE
Grand Rapids, MI 49503
www.grcc.cc.mi.us
Phone: 616-234-4000
Fax: 616-234-3907

Kendall College of Art & Design
111 Division Ave N
Grand Rapids, MI 49503
www.kcad.edu
Phone: 616-451-2787
Fax: 616-451-9867
TF: 800-676-2787

Reformed Bible College
3333 East Beltline Ave NE
Grand Rapids, MI 49525
E-mail: admissions@reformed.edu
www.reformed.edu
Phone: 616-222-3000
Fax: 616-222-3045
TF: 800-511-3749

Hospitals

Holland Community Hospital
602 Michigan Ave
Holland, MI 49423
www.hoho.org
Phone: 616-392-5141
Fax: 616-394-3528

Metropolitan Hospital
1919 Boston St SE
Grand Rapids, MI 49506
Phone: 616-252-7200
Fax: 616-252-7365

Saint Mary's Health Services
200 Jefferson St SE
Grand Rapids, MI 49503
www.mercyhealth.com/smhs
Phone: 616-752-6090
Fax: 616-732-3004

Spectrum Health DeVos Children's Hospital
100 Michigan St NE
Grand Rapids, MI 49503
www.spectrum-health.org/devos/dvchindex2.htm
Phone: 616-391-1774
Fax: 616-391-2780

Spectrum Health East Campus
1840 Wealthy St SE
Grand Rapids, MI 49506
www.spectrum-health.org
Phone: 616-774-7444
Fax: 616-391-2780

Transportation

Airport(s)

Kent County International Airport (GRR)
6 miles SE of downtown (approx 20 minutes).....616-336-4500

Mass Transit

Grand Rapids Area Transit Authority (GRATA)
$1.25 Base fare.................................616-776-1100

Rail/Bus

Amtrak Station
Market & Wealthy Sts
Grand Rapids, MI 49503
Phone: 800-872-7245

Greyhound Bus Station
190 Wealthy St SW
Grand Rapids, MI 49503
Phone: 616-456-1709
TF: 800-231-2222

Utilities

Electricity
Consumers Energy.............................800-477-5050
www.consumersenergy.com

Gas
Michgan Consolidated Gas Co..................800-395-4005

Water
Grand Rapids Water Dept.......................616-771-1200

Garbage Collection/Recycling
Grand Rapids Refuse Collection.................616-456-3232

Telecommunications

Telephone
Ameritech....................................800-468-3949
www.ameritech.com

Cable Television
AT & T Cable Services..........................616-977-2200
www.cable.att.com
Cable Michigan................................800-545-0994
Lowell Cable System...........................616-897-8405

Internet Service Providers (ISPs)
Internet 2000 Inc.............................616-532-8425
www.i2k.com
Iserv Corp....................................616-493-3720
www.iserv.net
Macatawa Area Community Network.............616-394-4689
freenet.macatawa.org

Banks

Bank West
2185 Three-Mile Rd NW
Grand Rapids, MI 49544
Phone: 616-785-3400
Fax: 616-785-3590

Comerica Bank
99 Monroe Ave Suite 100
Grand Rapids, MI 49503
Phone: 800-654-4456
Fax: 616-451-9298

Grand Bank
126 Ottawa Ave NW Suite 100
Grand Rapids, MI 49503
www.grandbank.com
Phone: 616-235-7000
Fax: 616-235-2160

Huntington Bank
173 Ottawa Ave NW
Grand Rapids, MI 49503
Phone: 616-771-6256
Fax: 616-235-5904
TF: 800-480-2265

National City Corp
171 Monroe Ave
Grand Rapids, MI 49503
Phone: 616-771-8701
Fax: 616-454-2979

Old Kent Bank
111 Lyon St
Grand Rapids, MI 49503
Phone: 616-771-5000
Fax: 616-771-4672
TF: 800-652-2657

Shopping

Breton Village Shopping Center
1830 Breton Rd SE
Grand Rapids, MI 49506
Phone: 616-949-4141
Fax: 616-949-0414

Gaslight Village
Wealthy St-betw Bretton Rd & Lovett Ave
East Grand Rapids, MI 49506
Phone: 616-459-8287

Holland Outlet Center
12330 James St
Holland, MI 49424
Phone: 616-396-1808
Fax: 616-396-5993

Monroe Mall
Monroe Ave btwn Pearl & Lewis Sts
Grand Rapids, MI 49503
Phone: 616-459-8287

Woodland Shopping Center
3195 28th St SE
Grand Rapids, MI 49512
Phone: 616-949-0010
Fax: 616-949-7348

Media

Newspapers and Magazines

Ada/Cascade/Forest Hills Advance
PO Box 9
Jenison, MI 49429
Phone: 616-669-2700
Fax: 616-669-4848

Grand Rapids Business Journal
549 Ottawa Ave NW
Grand Rapids, MI 49503
www.grbj.com
Phone: 616-459-0555
Fax: 616-459-4800

Grand Rapids Press*
155 Michigan St NW
Grand Rapids, MI 49503
gr.mlive.com
Phone: 616-459-1400
Fax: 616-222-5409

Grand Valley Advance
PO Box 9
Jenison, MI 49429
E-mail: advancenews@juno.com
Phone: 616-669-2700
Fax: 616-669-1162

Kentwood Advance
PO Box 9
Jenison, MI 49429
Phone: 616-669-2700
Fax: 616-669-4848

Northfield Advance
PO Box 9
Jenison, MI 49429
Phone: 616-669-2700
Fax: 616-669-4848

Walker/Westside Advance
PO Box 9
Jenison, MI 49429
Phone: 616-669-2700
Fax: 616-669-4848

Wyoming Advance
PO Box 9
Jenison, MI 49429
Phone: 616-669-2700
Fax: 616-669-4848

**Indicates major daily newspapers*

Television

WGVU-TV Ch 35 (PBS)
301 W Fulton St
Grand Rapids, MI 49504
www.wgvu.org/tv.html
Phone: 616-771-6666
Fax: 616-771-6625

WLLA-TV Ch 64 (Ind)
PO Box 3157
Kalamazoo, MI 49003
Phone: 616-345-6421
Fax: 616-345-5665

WOOD-TV Ch 8 (NBC)
PO Box B
Grand Rapids, MI 49501
E-mail: woodtv8@aol.com
www.woodtv.com
Phone: 616-456-8888
Fax: 616-456-5755

WOTV-TV Ch 41 (ABC)
5200 W Dickman Rd
Battle Creek, MI 49015
E-mail: wotv@wotv.com
www.wotv.com
Phone: 616-968-9341
Fax: 616-966-6837

WTLJ-TV Ch 54 (Ind)
10290 48th Ave
Allendale, MI 49401
Phone: 616-895-4154
Fax: 616-892-4401

WWMT-TV Ch 3 (CBS)
590 W Maple St
Kalamazoo, MI 49008
www.wwmt.com
Phone: 616-388-3333
Fax: 616-388-8322

WXMI-TV Ch 17 (Fox)
3117 Plaza Dr NE
Grand Rapids, MI 49525
www.wxmi.com
Phone: 616-364-8722
Fax: 616-364-8506

WZPX-TV Ch 43 (Ind)
2610 Horizon Dr Suite E
Grand Rapids, MI 49546
www.wzpxtv.com
Phone: 616-222-4343
Fax: 616-493-2677

WZZM-TV Ch 13 (ABC)
645 Three-Mile Rd NW
Grand Rapids, MI 49544
E-mail: wzzmtv@aol.com
Phone: 616-785-1313
Fax: 616-785-1301

Radio

WBBL-AM 1340 kHz (Sports)
60 Monroe Ctr 10th Fl
Grand Rapids, MI 49503
www.wbbl.com
Phone: 616-456-5461
Fax: 616-451-3299

WBCT-FM 93.7 MHz (Ctry)
77 Monroe Ctr Suite 1000
Grand Rapids, MI 49503
www.b93.com
Phone: 616-459-1919
Fax: 616-732-3330

WCSG-FM 91.3 MHz (Rel)
1159 E Beltline Ave NE
Grand Rapids, MI 49525
E-mail: wcsgfm@aol.com
www.wcsg.org
Phone: 616-942-1500
Fax: 616-942-7078
TF: 800-968-4543

WCUZ-FM 101.3 kHz (Ctry)
77 Monroe Ctr NW Suite 1000
Grand Rapids, MI 49503
www.wcuz.com
Phone: 616-459-1919
Fax: 616-242-9373

WGRD-FM 97.9 MHz (Rock)
38 W Fulton St
Grand Rapids, MI 49503
www.wgrd.com
Phone: 616-459-4111
Fax: 616-454-5530

WGVU-AM 1480 kHz (NPR)
Grand Valley State University 301 W Fulton St
Grand Rapids, MI 49504
E-mail: wgvu@gvsu.edu
www.wgvu.org/radio.html
Phone: 616-771-6666
Fax: 616-336-7204
TF: 800-442-2771

WGVU-FM 88.5 MHz (NPR)
301 W Fulton St
Grand Rapids, MI 49504
E-mail: wgvu@gvsu.edu
www.wgvu.org/radio.html
Phone: 616-771-6666
Fax: 616-336-7204

WKLQ-FM 94.5 MHz (Rock)
60 Monroe Ctr
Grand Rapids, MI 49503
www.wklq.com
Phone: 616-774-8461
Fax: 616-774-0351
TF: 800-968-9450

WMFN-AM 640 kHz (Sports)
2422 Burton SE
Grand Rapids, MI 49546
Phone: 616-949-8585
Fax: 616-949-9262
TF: 800-380-0064

WMJH-AM 810 kHz (Nost)
2422 Burton St
Grand Rapids, MI 49546
Phone: 616-949-8585
Fax: 616-949-9262
TF: 800-380-0064

WOOD-FM 105.7 MHz (AC)
77 Monroe Ctr Suite 1000
Grand Rapids, MI 49503
www.woodradio.com
Phone: 616-459-1919
Fax: 616-732-3330

Attractions

Grand Rapids is home to Michigan's largest general museum, the Public Museum of Grand Rapids/Van Andel Museum Center, which features a restored 1928 carousel as well as numerous examples of Grand Rapids craftsmanship in furniture making. Among the various exhibits there is a large collection of furniture that includes designs by Frank Lloyd Wright. In addition, a completely restored Wright home can be seen at the Meyer May House in Grand Rapids. Originally built in 1908, this prairie style house has been reproduced in exact detail by its present owner, Steelcase, Inc. The Gerald R. Ford Museum in Grand Rapids honors the nation's 38th president, who was one of the city's most famous residents. New renovations opened in April 1997 include a holographic tour of the White House.

Amway Corp Tours
7575 Fulton St E
Ada, MI 49355
Phone: 616-787-6701
Fax: 616-787-7102

Ball John Zoological Garden
1300 W Fulton
Grand Rapids, MI 49504
www.ring.com/zoo/ballzoo5.htm
Phone: 616-336-4300
Fax: 616-336-3907

Blandford Nature Center
1715 Hillburn Ave NW
Grand Rapids, MI 49504
E-mail: staff@grmuseum.org
www.grmuseum.org/blnfrd.htm
Phone: 616-453-6192
Fax: 616-456-2204

BOB The (Big Old Building)
20 Monroe Ave
Grand Rapids, MI 49503
E-mail: thebob@thebob.com
www.thebob.com
Phone: 616-356-2000
Fax: 616-493-2011

Broadway Theatre Guild
161 Ottawa Ave NW Suite 603
Grand Rapids, MI 49503
E-mail: live@iserv.net
www.bwaygr.org
Phone: 616-235-6285
Fax: 616-235-6282

Calvin College Center Art Gallery
Calvin College
Grand Rapids, MI 49546
Phone: 616-957-6271
Fax: 616-957-8551

Chaffee Roger B Planetarium
272 Pearl Ave NW
Grand Rapids, MI 49504
Phone: 616-456-3977
Fax: 616-456-3873

Community Circle Theatre
1300 W Fulton St
Grand Rapids, MI 49504
Phone: 616-456-5929
Fax: 616-456-8540

DeGraaf Nature Center
600 Graafschap Rd
Holland, MI 49423
Phone: 616-355-1057
Fax: 616-355-1069

Fish Ladder Sculpture
Scribner Ave
Grand Rapids, MI 49503
Phone: 616-459-8287

Gaslight Village
Wealthy St-betw Bretton Rd & Lovett Ave
East Grand Rapids, MI 49506
Phone: 616-459-8287

Gerald R Ford Museum
303 Pearl St NW Suite 126
Grand Rapids, MI 49504
E-mail: information.museum@fordmus.nara.gov
www.ford.utexas.edu
Phone: 616-451-9263
Fax: 616-451-9570

Grand Lady Riverboat
4243 Indian Mounds Dr
Grandville, MI 49418
www.river-boat.com
Phone: 616-457-4837
Fax: 616-457-2231

Grand Rapids Art Museum
155 Division Ave N
Grand Rapids, MI 49503
E-mail: gram@iserv.net
www.gram.mus.mi.us
Phone: 616-459-4677
Fax: 616-459-8491

Grand Rapids Ballet Co
233 E Fulton St Suite 126
Grand Rapids, MI 49503
E-mail: grballet@grballet.org
www.grballet.org
Phone: 616-454-4771
Fax: 616-454-0672

Grand Rapids Children's Museum
22 Sheldon Ave NE
Grand Rapids, MI 49503
E-mail: grcm@hotmail.com
www.grcm.org
Phone: 616-235-4726
Fax: 616-235-4728

Grand Rapids Civic Theatre
30 N Division Ave
Grand Rapids, MI 49503
www.grct.org
Phone: 616-222-6650
Fax: 616-222-6660

Grand Rapids Symphony Orchestra
169 Louis Campau Promenade Suite 1
Grand Rapids, MI 49503
www.grsymphony.org/
Phone: 616-454-9451
Fax: 616-454-7477

Heritage Hill Historic District
126 College Ave SE
Grand Rapids, MI 49503
E-mail: heritage@iserv.net
www.heritagehill.gen.mi.us/
Phone: 616-459-8950
Fax: 616-459-2409

LeMontueux Vineyard & Winery
2365 8 Mile Road NW
Grand Rapids, MI 49544
Phone: 616-784-4554
Fax: 616-784-4554

Meijer Frederik Gardens
1000 E Beltline Rd
Grand Rapids, MI 49525
www.meijergardens.org/home.html
Phone: 616-957-1580
Fax: 616-957-5792

Meyer May House
450 Madison Ave SE
Grand Rapids, MI 49503
Phone: 616-246-4821

Monroe Mall
Monroe Ave btwn Pearl & Lewis Sts
Grand Rapids, MI 49503
Phone: 616-459-8287

Opera Grand Rapids
161 Ottawa Ave NW Suite 207
Grand Rapids, MI 49503
Phone: 616-451-2741
Fax: 616-451-4587

Public Museum of Grand Rapids
272 Pearl St NW Van Andel Museum Ctr
Grand Rapids, MI 49504
E-mail: staff@grmuseum.org
www.grmuseum.org
Phone: 616-456-3977
Fax: 616-456-3873

Saugatuck Dune Rides
6495 Washington Rd
Saugutuck, MI 49453
Phone: 616-857-2253

Urban Institute for Contemporary Arts
41 Sheldon Blvd SE
Grand Rapids, MI 49503
www.uica.org/
Phone: 616-454-7000
Fax: 616-454-7013

Voigt House Victorian Museum
115 College Ave SE
Grand Rapids, MI 49503
E-mail: staff@grmuseum.org
www.grmuseum.org/voigt.htm
Phone: 616-456-4600
Fax: 616-456-4603

Windmill Island
7th & Lincoln Aves
Holland, MI 49423
Phone: 616-355-1030
Fax: 616-355-1035

Sports Teams & Facilities

Grand Rapids Griffins (hockey)
130 W Fulton St Van Andel Arena
Grand Rapids, MI 49503
E-mail: info@grgriffins.com
www.grgriffins.com/
Phone: 616-774-4585
Fax: 616-336-5464
TF: 800-246-2539

Grand Rapids Hoops (basketball)
130 W Fulton St Van Andel Arena
Grand Rapids, MI 49503
E-mail: admin@grhoops.com
www.grhoops.com
Phone: 616-458-7788
Fax: 616-458-2123

Grand Rapids Rampage (soccer)
25 Ionia Ave SW Suite 300
Grand Rapids, MI 49503
www.grrampage.com
Phone: 616-559-1871
Fax: 616-774-2337

Grattan Raceway Park
7201 Lessiter
Belding, MI 48809
Phone: 616-691-7221
Fax: 616-691-7449

Van Andel Arena
130 W Fulton St
Grand Rapids, MI 49503
www.vanandelarena.com
Phone: 616-742-6600
Fax: 616-742-6197

West Michigan Explosion (soccer)
1001 E Beltline SE Cornerstone College Soccer Field
Grand Rapids, MI 49505
Phone: 616-957-2500
Fax: 616-957-0369

West Michigan Whitecaps (baseball)
4500 W River Dr Old Kent Pk
Comstock Park, MI 49321
E-mail: whitecaps@gr.cns.net
www.whitecaps-baseball.com/
Phone: 616-784-4131
Fax: 616-784-4911

Annual Events

African American Festival (mid-June) 616-245-5756
Buffalo Days (mid-June) 616-784-4853
Celebration on the Grand (early September) 616-456-3696
Christmas Around the World (late November-late December)..................616-957-1580
Downtown Discovery Days (mid-October) 616-774-7124
East Rotary Antique Fair & Sale (mid-April) 616-243-5333
Festa Italiana (early August).......................616-456-3178
Festival of the Arts (June)........................616-459-2787
Foremost Insurance Championship (late August-early September)..................616-235-0943
Germanfest (late August)..........................616-364-0456
Grand Center Boat Show (mid-February)..........616-530-1919
Grand Rapids Jazz & Blues Festival (late July) 616-774-7124
Grand Regatta (mid-July)..........................616-364-5150
Grand Valley Artist Reeds Lake Art Festival (late June)...................................616-458-0315
Grand Valley Indian Pow Wow (early September)....616-364-4697
Hispanic Festival (mid-September) 616-742-0200
Kent Harvest Trails (late September-mid-October)..................616-452-4647
Klein Rodeo (early September)....................616-887-9945
Labor Day Parade and Rally (early September)......616-241-6555
Parade of Homes (late May-early June & late September-early October)................................616-281-2021
Polish Harvest Festival (mid-August) 616-452-3363
Pulaski Days Celebration (early October)...........616-459-8287
Riverside Arts & Craft Fair (mid-August) 616-454-7900
Saint Patrick's Day Parade (mid-March) 616-247-5127
Saladin Shrine Circus (mid-late March)............616-957-4100
Summer in the City (mid-June-late August) 616-774-7124
Three Fires Indian Pow Wow (mid-June)...........616-458-8759
Tulip Time (early-mid-May).......................800-822-2770
Victorian Christmas at Voigt House (mid-November-early January) 616-456-4600
West Michigan Home & Garden Show (early March) 616-530-1919
Zoo Goes Boo (late October)......................616-336-4300

Greensboro, North Carolina

***County:* Guilford**

GREENSBORO is located in the Piedmont Triad region of central North Carolina. Major cities within 100 miles include Winston-Salem, Chapel Hill, Raleigh/Durham, and Charlotte, North Carolina.

Area (Land) .... 79.8 sq mi
Area (Water)............................... 1.6 sq mi
Elevation.................................... 939 ft
Latitude ....36-07-25 N
Longitude............................... 79-79-22 W
Time Zone ....EST
Area Code...................................... 336

Climate

Greensboro's climate is moderated by the Brushy and Blue Ridge Mountains to the west of the area. Winters are cool, with average high temperatures in the upper 40s to low 50s and average lows near 30 degrees. The average annual snowfall in Greensboro is just over nine inches. Summers are warm and humid, with average high temperatures in the mid-80s and lows in the mid-60s. Precipitation is fairly evenly distributed throughout the year in Greensboro—July tends to be the wettest month, while April is the driest.

Average Temperatures & Precipitation

Temperatures

	Jan	Feb	Mar	Apr	May	Jun	Jul	Aug	Sep	Oct	Nov	Dec
High	47	51	60	70	77	84	87	86	80	70	61	51
Low	27	29	37	46	55	63	67	66	60	47	39	31

Precipitation

	Jan	Feb	Mar	Apr	May	Jun	Jul	Aug	Sep	Oct	Nov	Dec
Inches	3.2	3.3	3.7	2.8	4.0	3.8	4.5	3.9	3.5	3.5	3.0	3.4

History

The Greensboro area was first settled in the mid-18th Century by Quakers, Scotch-Irish, and Germans who migrated to the region from the northern colonies. In 1767, the area was the site of an important Revolutionary War battle led by General Nathanael Greene, the Battle of Guilford Courthouse, which significantly weakened the British forces. The town of Greensborough (named after the Revolutionary War general—the name was later shortened to Greensboro) was founded in 1808 as the new, centralized county seat of Guilford County.

The new town grew quickly as a commercial center for the surrounding agricultural region. The textile industry for which Greensboro has become famous began in 1828 when Henry Humphries established North Carolina's first steampowered cotton mill. The arrival of the North Carolina Railroad lines in 1856 further developed Greensboro's potential to become a leading commercial, industrial, and distribution center.

During the Civil War, Greensboro served the Confederacy as a transportation center and repository. At the same time, Greensboro also served as a major stop along the Underground Railroad (from the 1830s until after the War), due in large part to the efforts of resident anti-slavery advocate Vestal Coffin and his cousin Levi. A century later, in 1960, the city became the focus of a major Civil Rights movement when four African-American students from North Carolina Agricultural and Technical State University sat down at a "whites only" lunch counter in downtown Greensboro and demanded service—an event that prompted a nationwide non-violent "sit-in."

With a population that exceeds 197,000, Greensboro today is North Carolina's third largest city and an important regional center for commerce and industry in the state's Piedmont Triad. Home to Burlington Industries and several other U.S. textile giants, the Greensboro area remains a national leader in textile production, continuing a tradition that began more than 150 years ago.

Population

1990 Census 183,894
1998 Estimate.............................197,910
% Change 6.9
2005 Projection 415,525*

Racial/Ethnic Breakdown

White...................................63.8%
Black 33.9%
Other....................................2.3%
Hispanic Origin (may be of any race) 1.0%

Age Breakdown

Under 5 years.............................. 6.5%
5 to 17.................................. 14.9%
18 to 20.................................. 7.1%
21 to 24.................................. 8.2%
25 to 34.................................. 18.3%
35 to 44.................................. 15.3%
45 to 54.................................. 9.6%
55 to 64.................................. 8.3%
65 to 74.................................. 6.9%
75+ years 4.9%
Median Age.................................32.2

Gender Breakdown

Male................................... 46.4%
Female.................................. 53.6%

** Information given is for Guilford County.*

Government

Type of Government: Council-Manager

Greensboro Business Assistance & Development Office
PO Box 3136
Greensboro, NC 27402
Phone: 336-373-2668
Fax: 336-373-2117

Greensboro City Clerk
PO Box 3136
Greensboro, NC 27402
Phone: 336-373-2397
Fax: 336-373-2117

Greensboro City Council
PO Box 3136
Greensboro, NC 27402
Phone: 336-373-2396
Fax: 336-373-2117

Greensboro City Hall
300 W Washington St
Greensboro, NC 27402
Phone: 336-373-2000

Greensboro Finance Dept
PO Box 3136
Greensboro, NC 27402
Phone: 336-373-2077
Fax: 336-373-2138

Greensboro Fire Dept
1514 N Church St
Greensboro, NC 27405
Phone: 336-373-2356
Fax: 336-373-2936

Greensboro Housing & Community Development Dept
PO Box 3136
Greensboro, NC 27402
Phone: 336-373-2349
Fax: 336-412-6315

Greensboro Mayor
PO Box 3136
Greensboro, NC 27402
Phone: 336-373-2396
Fax: 336-373-2117

Greensboro Parks & Recreation Dept
1001 4th St
Greensboro, NC 27405
Phone: 336-373-2574
Fax: 336-373-2060

Greensboro Personnel Dept
PO Box 3136
Greensboro, NC 27402
Phone: 336-373-2065
Fax: 336-373-2511

Greensboro Planning Dept
PO Box 3136
Greensboro, NC 27402
Phone: 336-373-2144
Fax: 336-412-6315

Greensboro Police Dept
PO Box 3136
Greensboro, NC 27402
Phone: 336-373-2450
Fax: 336-333-6060

Greensboro Public Library
219 N Church St
Greensboro, NC 27402
Phone: 336-373-2474
Fax: 336-333-6781

Greensboro Transportation Dept
PO Box 3136
Greensboro, NC 27402
Phone: 336-373-2332
Fax: 336-412-6171

Greensboro Water Resources Dept
PO Box 3136
Greensboro, NC 27402
Phone: 336-373-2055
Fax: 336-412-6305

Important Phone Numbers

AAA 336-852-0506
American Express Travel Services 336-668-5000
Driver's License Information 336-334-5745
Emergency 911
Greensboro Regional Realtors Assn 336-854-5868
Guilford County Tax Collector 336-373-3362
Medical Referral 336-832-8000
North Carolina Dept of Revenue 919-733-7211
North Carolina Dept of Revenue Individual Income Div 919-733-4684
Poison Control Center 800-848-6946
Vehicle Registration Information 336-379-7980
Voter Registration Information 336-373-3836
Weather 919-515-8209

Information Sources

Better Business Bureau Serving Central North Carolina
3608 W Friendly Ave
Greensboro, NC 27410
www.greensboro.bbb.org
Phone: 336-852-4240
Fax: 336-852-7540

Greater Greensboro Merchants Assn
225 Commerce Pl
Greensboro, NC 27401
www.greensboro.com/gma/
Phone: 336-378-6350
Fax: 336-378-6272
TF: 800-288-7408

Greensboro Area Chamber of Commerce
342 N Elm St Suite 100
Greensboro, NC 27401
www.greensboro.org
Phone: 336-275-8675
Fax: 336-230-1867

Greensboro Area Convention & Visitors Bureau
317 S Greene St
Greensboro, NC 27401
www.greensboronc.org
Phone: 336-274-2282
Fax: 336-230-1183
TF: 800-344-2282

Greensboro Cultural Center at Festival Park
200 N Davie St
Greensboro, NC 27401
Phone: 336-373-2712
Fax: 336-373-2659

Guilford County
PO Box 3427
Greensboro, NC 27402
www.co.guilford.nc.us/
Phone: 336-373-3383
Fax: 336-333-6833

Online Resources

Anthill City Guide Greensboro
www.anthill.com/city.asp?city=greensboro

Area Guide Greensboro
greensboro.areaguides.net

City Knowledge Greensboro
www.cityknowledge.com/nc_greensboro.htm

CityTravelers.com Guide to Greensboro
www.citytravelers.com/greensboro.htm

Depot The
www.thedepot.com

DigitalCity Greensboro
home.digitalcity.com/greensboro

ESP Magazine
www.espmagazine.com

Excite.com Greensboro City Guide
www.excite.com/travel/countries/united_states/north_carolina/greensboro

Welcome to Greensboro
www.hickory.nc.us/ncnetworks/grb-intr.html

Wire The
www.thewire.org

Area Communities

Incorporated communities in the Greensboro area (Guilford and Alamance counties) with populations greater than 10,000 include:

Burlington
PO Box 1358
Burlington, NC 27216
Phone: 336-222-5000
Fax: 336-229-3120

Graham
PO Box 357
Graham, NC 27253
Phone: 336-570-6700
Fax: 336-570-6703

High Point
PO Box 230
High Point, NC 27261
Phone: 336-883-3298
Fax: 336-883-3052

Economy

Greensboro's economy is fueled by the textile industry, and the city is the corporate home of three of the nation's leading textile producers, Burlington Industries, Cone Mills, and Guilford Mills. Although education, health care, government, and communications contribute to Greensboro's economy, textile manufacturing dominates the area's economic base, accounting for more than 20 percent of total manufacturing employment. Other important industries in the surrounding Piedmont Triad region include furniture manufacturing, for which nearby High Point is world-renowned, and tobacco processing.

Unemployment Rate	2.4%*
Per Capita Income	$27,560*
Median Family Income	$49,300*

* *Information given is for Guilford County.*

Principal Industries & Number of Wage Earners

Greensboro/Winston-Salem/High Point MSA* - 1999

Construction & Mining	34,800
Finance, Insurance, & Real Estate	35,300
Government	71,800
Manufacturing	158,600
Retail Trade	113,000
Services	180,100
Transportation & Public Utilities	35,000
Wholesale Trade	35,400

* *Information given is for the Greensboro/Winston-Salem/High Point Metropolitan Statistical Area (MSA), which includes Alamance, Davidson, Davie, Forsyth, Guilford, Randolph, Stokes, and Yadkin counties.*

Major Employers

American Express
7701 Airport Center Dr
Greensboro, NC 27409
www.americanexpress.com
Phone: 336-668-5000
Fax: 336-668-5832

AMP Inc
3700 Reidsville Rd
Winston-Salem, NC 27052
www.amp.com
Phone: 336-720-9222
Fax: 336-727-5621

Bank of America
101 W Friendly Ave
Greensboro, NC 27401
Phone: 336-805-3669
Fax: 336-805-3250

Cone Mills Corp
3101 N Elm St
Greensboro, NC 27408
www.cone.com
Phone: 336-379-6220
Fax: 336-379-6287
TF: 800-763-0123

Greensboro City Hall
300 W Washington St
Greensboro, NC 27402
www.ci.greensboro.nc.us
Phone: 336-373-2000

Guilford County
PO Box 3427
Greensboro, NC 27402
www.co.guilford.nc.us/
Phone: 336-373-3383
Fax: 336-333-6833

Guilford County Schools
712 N Eugene St
Greensboro, NC 27401
E-mail: www@guilford.k12.nc.us
www.guilford.k12.nc.us
Phone: 336-370-8100
Fax: 336-370-8398

Guilford Mills Inc
4925 W Market St
Greensboro, NC 27407
www.guilfordmills.com
Phone: 336-316-4000
Fax: 336-316-4059
TF: 800-277-0987

High Point Regional Hospital
601 N Elm St
High Point, NC 27262
Phone: 336-878-6000
Fax: 336-878-6130

Lorillard
2525 E Market St
Greensboro, NC 27401
www.lorillard.net
Phone: 336-335-6600
Fax: 336-335-6917
TF: 800-282-7084

Moses Cone Health System
1200 N Elm St
Greensboro, NC 27401
www.mosescone.com
Phone: 336-832-7400
Fax: 336-574-7591

Sears Roebuck & Co
3200 W Friendly Ave
Greensboro, NC 27408
Phone: 336-632-3300
Fax: 336-632-3290

United Parcel Service
3009 Executive Dr
Greensboro, NC 27406
www.upsjobs.com
Phone: 336-271-0456
Fax: 336-271-0455

University of North Carolina Greensboro
1000 Spring Garden St
Greensboro, NC 27402
E-mail: undergrad_admissions@uncg.edu
www.uncg.edu
Phone: 336-334-5000
Fax: 336-334-4180

US Postal Service
201 N Murrow Blvd
Greensboro, NC 27420
new.usps.com
Phone: 336-370-1184
Fax: 336-370-9614

Quality of Living Indicators

Total Crime Index....................15,531
(rates per 100,000 inhabitants)

Violent Crime
Murder/manslaughter.......... 19
Forcible rape 105
Robbery.......... 758
Aggravated assault.......... 938

Property Crime
Burglary 3,198
Larceny theft 9,174
Motor vehicle theft..........1,339

Cost of Living Index..........97.9
(national average = 100)

Median Home Price..........$124,800

Education

Public Schools

Guilford County Schools
712 N Eugene St
Greensboro, NC 27401
E-mail: www@guilford.k12.nc.us
www.guilford.k12.nc.us
Phone: 336-370-8100
Fax: 336-370-8398

Number of Schools
Elementary.......... 61
Middle 17
High.......... 14

Student/Teacher Ratio
All Grades 15.4:1

Private Schools

Number of Schools (all grades).......... 33

Colleges & Universities

Bennett College
900 E Washington St
Greensboro, NC 27401
E-mail: bcinfo@bennett1.bennett.edu
www.bennett.edu
Phone: 336-273-4431
Fax: 336-378-0511
TF: 800-413-5323

Elon College
PO Box 398
Elon College, NC 27244
www.elon.edu
Phone: 336-584-9711
Fax: 336-538-3986

Greensboro College
815 W Market St
Greensboro, NC 27401
E-mail: admissions@gborocollege.edu
www.gborocollege.edu
Phone: 336-272-7102
Fax: 336-378-0154
TF: 800-346-8226

Guilford College
5800 W Friendly Ave
Greensboro, NC 27410
www.guilford.edu
Phone: 336-316-2100
Fax: 336-316-2954
TF: 800-992-7759

Guilford Technical Community College
PO Box 309
Jamestown, NC 27282
E-mail: kirklands@gtcc.cc.nc.us
technet.gtcc.cc.nc.us/
Phone: 336-334-4822
Fax: 336-819-2022

High Point University
833 Montlieu Ave
High Point, NC 27262
acme.highpoint.edu
Phone: 336-841-9000
Fax: 336-841-4599

North Carolina A & T State University
1601 E Market St
Greensboro, NC 27411
www.ncat.edu
Phone: 336-334-7500
Fax: 336-334-7478

University of North Carolina Greensboro
1000 Spring Garden St
Greensboro, NC 27402
E-mail: undergrad_admissions@uncg.edu
www.uncg.edu
Phone: 336-334-5000
Fax: 336-334-4180

Hospitals

High Point Regional Hospital
601 N Elm St
High Point, NC 27262
Phone: 336-878-6000
Fax: 336-878-6130

Moses H Cone Memorial Hospital
1200 N Elm St
Greensboro, NC 27401
www.mosescone.com
Phone: 336-832-7000
Fax: 336-832-8236

Wesley Long Community Hospital
501 N Elam Ave
Greensboro, NC 27402
Phone: 336-832-1000
Fax: 336-832-0529

Women's Hospital of Greensboro
801 Green Valley Rd
Greensboro, NC 27408
Phone: 336-832-6500
Fax: 336-274-9408

Transportation

Airport(s)

Piedmont Triad International Airport (GSO)
10 miles W of downtown (approx 20 minutes) 336-665-5600

Mass Transit

Greensboro Transit Authority
$1 Base fare 336-332-6440

Rail/Bus

Amtrak Station
2603 Oakland Ave
Greensboro, NC 27403
Phone: 336-855-3382
TF: 800-872-7245

Greyhound Bus Station
501 W Lee St
Greensboro, NC 27406
Phone: 336-272-8950
TF: 800-231-2222

Utilities

Electricity
Duke Power Co .336-378-9451
www.dukepower.com

Gas
Piedmont Natural Gas Co .336-378-1845
www.piedmontng.com

Water
Greensboro Water Dept .336-375-2227

Garbage Collection/Recycling
Greensboro Solid Waste Management Div .336-373-2035

Telecommunications

Telephone
BellSouth .800-767-2355
www.bellsouth.com

Cable Television
Time-Warner Cable .336-379-0200

Internet Service Providers (ISPs)
Internet/MCR Corp .336-544-4500
www.netmcr.com
Netpath/Stratonet Inc .336-226-0425
www.netpath.net

Banks

Bank of America
1616 E Bessemer Ave
Greensboro, NC 27405
Phone: 336-805-3050
Fax: 336-274-8613
TF: 800-333-6262

BB & T Bank
201 W Market St
Greensboro, NC 27401
Phone: 336-433-4000
Fax: 336-433-4009

Central Carolina Bank & Trust Co
3227 Battleground Ave
Greensboro, NC 27408
Phone: 336-373-5018
Fax: 336-282-1705
TF: 800-422-2226

Centura Bank
2301 Battleground Ave
Greensboro, NC 27408
Phone: 336-271-5840
Fax: 336-271-5850

First Union National Bank
3305 Battleground Ave
Greensboro, NC 27410
Phone: 336-574-5880
Fax: 336-574-5883
TF: 800-733-3862

Mutual Community Savings Bank
100 S Murrow Blvd
Greensboro, NC 27401
Phone: 336-373-8500
Fax: 336-373-1204
TF: 888-366-6272

Wachovia Bank NA
1204 Bradford Pkwy
Greensboro, NC 27407
Phone: 336-856-5200
Fax: 336-856-5240
TF: 800-922-4684

Shopping

Four Seasons Town Centre
400 Four Seasons Town Centre
Greensboro, NC 27407
E-mail: fourseas@nr.infi.net
www.shopfourseasons.com
Phone: 336-299-9200
Fax: 336-299-9969

Friendly Center
3110 Kathleen Ave
Greensboro, NC 27408
www.friendlycenter.com/
Phone: 336-292-2789
Fax: 336-292-4297

Oak Hollow Mall
921 Eastchester Dr
High Point, NC 27262
Phone: 336-886-6255
Fax: 336-886-6257

Old Downtown Greensborough
Elm St
Greensboro, NC 27406
Phone: 336-274-2282

State Street Station
408 1/2 State St
Greensboro, NC 27405
www.statestreetstation.com
Phone: 336-275-8586

Media

Newspapers and Magazines

News & Record*
200 E Market St
Greensboro, NC 27420
www.thedepot.com
Phone: 336-373-7000
Fax: 336-373-7382
TF: 800-553-6880

Triad Style
106 S Church St
Greensboro, NC 27401
E-mail: tstyle@nr.insi.net
Phone: 336-373-7083
Fax: 336-373-7323
TF: 800-553-6880

**Indicates major daily newspapers*

Television

WBFX-TV Ch 20 (WB)
622G Guilford College Rd
Greensboro, NC 27409
Phone: 336-547-0020
Fax: 336-547-8144

WFMY-TV Ch 2 (CBS)
1615 Phillips Ave
Greensboro, NC 27405
E-mail: fmy2@aol.com
www.wfmy.com
Phone: 336-379-9369
Fax: 336-273-9433

WGHP-TV Ch 8 (Fox)
PO Box HP-8
High Point, NC 27261
www.fox8wghp.com
Phone: 336-841-8888
Fax: 336-841-5169

WUNC-TV Ch 4 (PBS)
PO Box 14900
Research Triangle Park, NC 27709
E-mail: viewer@unctv.org
www.unctv.org
Phone: 919-549-7000
Fax: 919-549-7043
TF: 800-906-5050

WUNL-TV Ch 26 (PBS)
PO Box 14900
Research Triangle Park, NC 27709
Phone: 919-549-7000
Fax: 919-549-7201

WUPN-TV Ch 48 (UPN)
3500 Myer Lee Dr
Winston-Salem, NC 27101
www.wxlv.com/WUPN-48
Phone: 336-274-4848
Fax: 336-722-6289

WXII-TV Ch 12 (NBC)
700 Coliseum Dr
Winston-Salem, NC 27116
E-mail: newschannel12@wxii.com
www.wxii.com
Phone: 336-721-9944
Fax: 336-721-0856

Radio

WJMH-FM 102.1 MHz (Urban) Phone: 336-605-5200
7819 National Service Rd Suite 401 Fax: 336-605-5219
Greensboro, NC 27409

WKRR-FM 92.3 MHz (Rock) Phone: 336-274-8042
192 E Lewis St Fax: 336-274-1629
Greensboro, NC 27406
www.rock92.com

WKSI-FM 98.7 MHz (AC) Phone: 336-275-9895
221 W Meadowview Rd Fax: 336-275-6236
Greensboro, NC 27406
www.987thepoint.com

WKZL-FM 107.5 MHz (CHR) Phone: 336-274-8042
192 E Lewis St Fax: 336-274-1629
Greensboro, NC 27406
www.1075kzl.com

WMQX-FM 93.1 MHz (Oldies) Phone: 336-605-5200
7819 National Service Rd Suite 401 Fax: 336-605-5221
Greensboro, NC 27409

WNAA-FM 90.1 MHz (Urban) Phone: 336-334-7936
North Carolina A & T State University Fax: 336-334-7960
Price Hall Suite 200
Greensboro, NC 27411
E-mail: whaafm@aurora.ncat.edu
wnaalive.ncat.edu

WPET-AM 950 kHz (Rel) Phone: 336-275-9738
221 W Meadowview Rd Fax: 336-275-2090
Greensboro, NC 27406
E-mail: wpet@netmcr.com

WQFS-FM 90.9 MHz (Alt) Phone: 336-316-2352
17714 Founders Hall
Greensboro, NC 27410

WQMG-AM 1510 kHz (Rel) Phone: 336-605-5200
7819 National Service Rd Fax: 336-605-0138
Greensboro, NC 27409

WQMG-FM 97.1 MHz (CR) Phone: 336-605-5200
7819 National Service Rd Fax: 336-605-0138
Greensboro, NC 27409

WUAG-FM 103.1 MHz (Misc) Phone: 336-334-5450
University of North Carolina Taylor Bldg Fax: 336-334-5168
Greensboro, NC 27402

Attractions

Guilford Courthouse National Military Park, located on Guilford Battleground, is a popular tourist attraction in Greensboro, and the Greensboro Historical Museum includes displays on Greensboro natives William Sydney Porter (O. Henry) and Dolly Madison. Other local attractions include the Blandwood Mansion, home of former North Carolina governor John Motley Morehead; the Colonial Heritage Center at Tannenbaum Park; five art galleries at the Greensboro Cultural Center; the Charlotte Hawkins Brown Memorial, which honors her efforts in African-American education; and the Mattye Reed African Heritage Museum, which houses 3,500 art and craft items from more than 30 African nations, New Guinea, and Haiti. In nearby Jamestown are Castle McCulloch, a restored 19th Century gold refinery; and Mendenhall Plantation, a Quaker plantation that has a false-bottomed wagon which was used to transport slaves on the Underground Railroad.

Barn Dinner Theatre Phone: 336-292-2211
120 Stage Coach Trail Fax: 336-294-8663
Greensboro, NC 27409 TF: 800-668-1764
www.barndinner.com

Bicentennial Gardens Phone: 336-373-2199
1105 Hobbs Rd Fax: 336-299-7940
Greensboro, NC 27408

Blandwood Mansion Phone: 336-272-5003
447 W Washington St
Greensboro, NC 27401
www.blandwood.org

Broach Theatre Phone: 336-378-9300
520-C S Elm St Fax: 336-378-9301
Greensboro, NC 27406

Carolina Model Railroaders Phone: 336-656-7968
300 E Washington St The Depot
Greensboro, NC 27401

Carolina Theatre Phone: 336-333-2600
310 S Greene St Fax: 336-333-2604
Greensboro, NC 27401
E-mail: cartheatre@aol.com
www.carolinatheatre.com

Castle McCulloch Phone: 336-887-5413
6000 Kersey Valley Rd Fax: 336-887-5429
Jamestown, NC 27282
E-mail: castlemcc@juno.com
www.castlemcculloch.com

Charlotte Hawkins Brown Memorial State Historic Site Phone: 336-449-4846
6136 Burlington Rd Fax: 336-449-0176
Sedalia, NC 27342
www.netpath.net/~chb/

Chinqua-Penn Plantation Phone: 336-349-7069
2138 Wentworth St Fax: 336-342-4863
Reidsville, NC 27320 TF: 800-948-0847
www.chinquapenn.com/

Community Theatre of Greensboro Phone: 336-333-7470
200 N Davie St Fax: 336-333-2607
Greensboro, NC 27401
www.wirecom.com/ctg/

Country Park Phone: 336-373-2574
3902 Nathanael Greene Dr Fax: 336-545-5342
Greensboro, NC 27455

Green Hill Center for North Carolina Art Phone: 336-333-7460
200 N Davie St Fax: 336-333-2612
Greensboro, NC 27401
E-mail: info@greenhillcenter.org
greenhillcenter.org

Greensboro Arboretum Phone: 336-373-2199
W Wendover Ave & Market St Fax: 336-299-7940
Greensboro, NC 27403

Greensboro Ballet
200 Davie St Greensboro Cultural Ctr
Greensboro, NC 27401
Phone: 336-333-7480
Fax: 336-333-7482

Greensboro Children's Museum
220 N Church St
Greensboro, NC 27401
www.gcmuseum.com
Phone: 336-574-2898
Fax: 336-574-3810

Greensboro Cultural Center at Festival Park
200 N Davie St
Greensboro, NC 27401
Phone: 336-373-2712
Fax: 336-373-2659

Greensboro Historical Museum
130 Summit Ave
Greensboro, NC 27401
Phone: 336-373-2043
Fax: 336-373-2204

Greensboro Opera Co
1834 Pembroke Rd Suite 7
Greensboro, NC 27408
www.greensboro.com/goc
Phone: 336-273-9472
Fax: 336-273-9481

Greensboro Symphony Orchestra
200 N Davie St Suite 328
Greensboro, NC 27401
www.greensborosymphony.org
Phone: 336-335-5456
Fax: 336-335-5580

Greensboro War Memorial Auditorium
1921 W Lee St
Greensboro, NC 27403
Phone: 336-373-7400
Fax: 336-373-2170

Guilford College Art Gallery
5800 W Friendly Ave Hege Library
Greensboro, NC 27410
Phone: 336-316-2438

Guilford Courthouse National Military Park
2332 New Garden Rd
Greensboro, NC 27410
www.nps.gov/guco/
Phone: 336-288-1776
Fax: 336-282-2296

Hagan Stone Park
5920 Hagan Stone Park Rd
Greensboro, NC 27313
Phone: 336-373-2574
Fax: 336-674-7410

Hester Park
3615 Deutzia St
Greensboro, NC 27407
Phone: 336-373-2937
Fax: 336-299-2195

International Civil Rights Center & Museum
134 S Elm St
Greensboro, NC 27401
www.sitinmovement.org
Phone: 336-274-9199
Fax: 336-274-6244

Livestock Players Musical Theatre
310 S Greene St Carolina Theatre
Greensboro, NC 27401
Phone: 336-373-2728
Fax: 336-373-2659

Mattye Reed African Heritage Museum
Dudley Bldg A&T State University
Greensboro, NC 27411
Phone: 336-334-3209
Fax: 336-334-4378

Mendenhall Plantation
603 W Main St
Jamestown, NC 27282
Phone: 336-454-3819

Natural Science Center
4301 Lawndale Dr
Greensboro, NC 27455
E-mail: nscg@greensboro.com
www.greensboro.com/sciencecenter
Phone: 336-288-3769
Fax: 336-288-2531

North Carolina Tennis Hall of Fame
3802 Jaycee Park Dr
Greensboro, NC 27455
www.nctennis.com
Phone: 336-852-8577
Fax: 336-852-7334

North Carolina Zoological Park
4401 Zoo Pkwy
Asheboro, NC 27203
www.nczoo.org
Phone: 336-879-7000
Fax: 336-879-2891

Old Downtown Greensborough
Elm St
Greensboro, NC 27406
Phone: 336-274-2282

Old Mill of Guilford
1340 NC 68 N
Oak Ridge, NC 27310
Phone: 336-643-4783

Piedmont Triad Farmers Market
2914 Sandy Ridge Rd
Colfax, NC 27235
www.agr.state.nc.us/markets/facilit/farmark/triad/index.htm
Phone: 336-605-9157
Fax: 336-605-9401

Richard Petty Museum
311 Branson Mill Rd
Randleman, NC 27317
Phone: 336-495-1143
Fax: 336-498-4334

Tannenbaum Park & Colonial Heritage Center
2200 New Garden Rd
Greensboro, NC 27410
www.ci.greensboro.nc.us/leisure/tannenbaum
Phone: 336-545-5315
Fax: 336-545-5314

Weatherspoon Art Gallery
Spring Garden & Tate Sts
Greensboro, NC 27402
www.uncg.edu/wag
Phone: 336-334-5770
Fax: 336-334-5907

Wet 'n Wild Emerald Pointe Water Park
3910 S Holden Rd
Greensboro, NC 27406
E-mail: sales@emeraldpointe.com
www.emeraldpointe.com
Phone: 336-852-9721
Fax: 336-852-2391

Sports Teams & Facilities

Carolina Dynamo (soccer)
2920 School Pk Rd High Point Athletic Complex
High Point, NC 27265
E-mail: colleenk@northstate.net
www.carolinadynamo.com
Phone: 336-869-1022
Fax: 336-869-1190

Carolina Hurricanes (hockey)
1400 Edwards Mill Rd Entertainment Sports Arena
Greensboro, NC 27607
www.caneshockey.com
Phone: 919-467-7825
Fax: 919-861-2310

Greensboro Bats (baseball)
510 Yanceyville St War Memorial Stadium
Greensboro, NC 27405
www.greensborobats.com
Phone: 336-333-2287
Fax: 336-273-7350

Greensboro Coliseum
1921 W Lee St
Greensboro, NC 27403
E-mail: gsoarena@interpath.com
www.greensborocoliseum.com
Phone: 336-373-7400
Fax: 336-373-2170

Greensboro Generals (hockey)
1921 W Lee St Greensboro Coliseum
Greensboro, NC 27403
Phone: 336-218-5428
Fax: 336-373-2170

Piedmont Spark (soccer)
2920 School Park Rd High Point Athletic Complex
High Point, NC 27265
Phone: 336-869-1022
Fax: 336-869-1190

Annual Events

African American Heritage Festival (early June).....336-449-4846
African-American Arts Festival (mid-January) 336-373-7523
Artists Hang-Up & Put-Down (mid-late March).....336-333-7460
Boo at the Zoo (late October).....................800-488-0444
Carolina Blues Festival (mid-May)................336-274-2282
Charlotte Hawkins Brown Gravesite Ceremonies (early June)..................................336-449-4846
Chili Championship & Rubber Duck Regatta (mid-September) 800-443-4093
City Stage Street Festival (early October) 336-274-2282
Eastern Music Festival (late June-early August).....336-333-7450
Eastern Music Festival Wine Tasting (late March) 336-333-7450
Fun Fourth Festival (early July) 336-274-2282
Greater Greensboro Chrysler Classic (late April) 800-999-5446
Greensboro Agricultural Fair (mid-late September) 336-373-7400
Greensboro Gun Show (late August)...............336-674-9287
GYC Carnival (early May).........................336-373-2173
Holiday of Lights (early January).................919-839-2443
Ice Cream Festival (mid-July)....................336-379-8748
Native American Pow Wow (mid-September)........336-273-8686
Oak Ridge Easter Horse Show (mid-April) 336-643-4151
Re-Enactment of the Battle of Guilford Courthouse (mid-March) 336-545-5315
Rock Festival (late August) 336-288-3769
Seafest (mid-February)...........................336-288-3769
Serendipity Weekend (mid-April) 336-316-2301
State Games of North Carolina (late June) 800-277-8763
Street Rod Safari (mid-April) 800-488-0444
Tacky Country Frolic (early September)............336-349-4576
Tannenbaum Park Colonial Fair (mid-November).............................336-545-5315
Tulip Days at Chinqua-Penn Plantation (April) 336-349-4576
US Hot Rod Monster Jam (late January) 336-373-7400

Greenville, South Carolina

County: **Greenville**

GREENVILLE is located in the foothills of the Blue Ridge Mountains in northwestern South Carolina. Major cities within 100 miles include Asheville and Charlotte, North Carolina, and Columbia, South Carolina.

Area (Land) .... 25.1 sq mi
Area (Water)............................... 0.1 sq mi
Elevation.................................... 966 ft
Latitude ....34-84-81 N
Longitude............................... 82-40-64 W
Time Zone ....EST
Area Code..................................... 864

Climate

Greenville's climate is moderated by its proximity to the Blue Ridge Mountains and features four distinct seasons. Summer days are hot, with average high temperatures in the upper 80s, while evenings cool down into the mid- to upper 60s. Winters are generally mild, with high temperatures in the lower 50s and lows in the low 30s. Snowfall is rare. March is the wettest month in Greenville.

Average Temperatures & Precipitation

Temperatures

	Jan	Feb	Mar	Apr	May	Jun	Jul	Aug	Sep	Oct	Nov	Dec
High	50	54	64	72	79	86	88	87	81	72	63	53
Low	30	32	40	48	56	64	68	67	61	49	41	33

Precipitation

	Jan	Feb	Mar	Apr	May	Jun	Jul	Aug	Sep	Oct	Nov	Dec
Inches	4.1	4.4	5.4	3.9	4.4	4.8	4.6	4.0	4.0	4.0	3.7	4.1

History

Originally inhabited by Cherokee Indians, the area known today as Greenville was founded as a trading post by Captain Richard Pearis in the mid-1700s. Greenville County was established in 1786, and the village chosen as the county seat in 1797 was called Pleasantburg. In 1831, the name of the county seat was changed to Greenville and the village was chartered by state law.

During the 1820s, three mills opened in the Greenville area, and the city grew quickly as a major center for textile manufacturing. By 1869, 2,000 people inhabited the Greenville area, and Greenville was incorporated as a city in 1907. Like most southern cities, Greenville struggled through difficult economic times during the Civil War; however, the city's textile industry began to flourish once again after Reconstruction. In 1915, the city hosted the first Southern Textile Exposition and shortly thereafter proclaimed itself the "Textile Center of the South." Greenville remains one of the country's leading textile manufacturing centers today, although other industries have gained importance in recent years. Greenville County, with a population greater than 358,000, is South Carolina's most populous county, and it is also part of one of the fastest-growing metropolitan areas in the United States.

Population

1990 Census 58,256
1998 Estimate...............................56,436
% Change .... -3.1
2015 Projection 375,500*

Racial/Ethnic Breakdown

White.................................... 63.6%
Black 35.2%
Other 1.2%
Hispanic Origin (may be of any race) 1.0%

Age Breakdown

Under 5 years.............................. 6.9%
5 to 17.................................. 15.0%
18 to 20.................................. 6.7%
21 to 24.................................. 7.4%
25 to 34................................. 18.0%
35 to 44................................. 13.7%
45 to 54.................................. 8.5%
55 to 64.................................. 7.8%
65 to 74.................................. 8.8%
75+ years 7.0%
Median Age.................................32.6

Gender Breakdown

Male..................................... 45.5%
Female................................... 54.5%

** Information given is for Greenville County.*

Government

Type of Government: Council-Manager

Greenville City Attorney
PO Box 2207
Greenville, SC 29602
Phone: 864-467-4420
Fax: 864-467-4424

Greenville City Clerk
PO Box 2207
Greenville, SC 29602
Phone: 864-467-4431
Fax: 864-467-5725

Greenville City Council
PO Box 2207
Greenville, SC 29602
Phone: 864-467-4431
Fax: 864-467-5725

Greenville City Hall
206 S Main St
Greenville, SC 29601
Phone: 864-467-4500
Fax: 864-467-5725

Greenville City Manager
PO Box 2207
Greenville, SC 29602
Phone: 864-467-5700
Fax: 864-467-5725

Greenville Community Services Dept
22 W Broad St
Greenville, SC 29602
Phone: 864-467-4449
Fax: 864-467-4466

Greenville Economic Development Dept
PO Box 2207
Greenville, SC 29602
Phone: 864-467-4401
Fax: 864-467-5744

Greenville Finance Dept
PO Box 2207
Greenville, SC 29602
Phone: 864-467-4536
Fax: 864-467-4597

Greenville Fire Dept
22 W Broad St
Greenville, SC 29601
Phone: 864-467-4447
Fax: 864-467-5790

Greenville Human Resources Dept
PO Box 2207
Greenville, SC 29602
Phone: 864-467-4530
Fax: 864-467-5722

Greenville Mayor
PO Box 2207
Greenville, SC 29602
Phone: 864-467-4590
Fax: 864-467-5725

Greenville Police Dept
4 McGee St
Greenville, SC 29601
Phone: 864-467-5310
Fax: 864-467-4317

Greenville Public Works Dept
360 S Hudson St
Greenville, SC 29601
Phone: 864-467-4335
Fax: 864-467-4303

Important Phone Numbers

AAA....864-240-3010
American Express Travel....864-292-9970
Driver's License Information....864-260-2205
Emergency....911
Greenville Board of Realtors....864-672-4427
Greenville County Auditor....864-467-7040
HotelDocs....800-468-3537
Poison Control Center....803-777-1117
South Carolina Taxpayer Service Center....803-898-5000
Time/Temp....864-233-3000
Vehicle Registration Information....800-442-1368
Voter Registration Information....864-467-7250
Weather....864-233-3000

Information Sources

Better Business Bureau Serving Central South Carolina & the Charleston Area
PO Box 8326
Columbia, SC 29202
www.columbia.bbb.org
Phone: 803-254-2525
Fax: 803-779-3117

Greater Greenville Chamber of Commerce
24 Cleveland St
Greenville, SC 29601
Phone: 864-242-1050
Fax: 864-282-8509

Greater Greenville Convention & Visitors Bureau
206 S Main St
Greenville, SC 29601
www.greatergreenville.com
Phone: 864-421-0000
Fax: 864-421-0005
TF: 800-351-7180

Greenville County
305 E North St Courthouse Suite 224
Greenville, SC 29601
www.co.greenville.sc.us
Phone: 864-467-8551
Fax: 864-467-8540

Palmetto Exposition Center
PO Box 5823
Greenville, SC 29606
www.palmettoexpo.com
Phone: 864-233-2562
Fax: 864-233-0619

Online Resources

4Greenville.com
www.4greenville.com

About.com Guide to Greenville
greenville.about.com/citiestowns/southeastus/greenville

Anthill City Guide Greenville
www.anthill.com/city.asp?city=greenville

Area Guide Greenville
greenvillesc.areaguides.net

City Knowledge Greenville
www.cityknowledge.com/sc_greenville.htm

CityTravelers.com Guide to Greenville
www.citytravelers.com/gsp.htm

Creative Loafing Online Greenville/Spartanburg
www.creativeloafing.com/greenville/newsstand/current/

Excite.com Greenville City Guide
www.excite.com/travel/countries/united_states/south_carolina/greenville

Greenville Directory
www.scad.com/greenvil

Greenville North Carolina Information Directory
www.greenvillenc.net

Area Communities

Communities in the Greater Greenville area with populations greater than 10,000 include:

Easley
PO Box 466
Easley, SC 29641
Phone: 864-855-7900
Fax: 864-855-7905

Greer
106 S Main St
Greer, SC 29650
Phone: 864-848-2150
Fax: 864-848-2157

Mauldin
5 E Butler Rd
Mauldin, SC 29662
Phone: 864-288-4910
Fax: 864-297-3411

Simpsonville
118 NE Main St
Simpsonville, SC 29681
Phone: 864-967-9526
Fax: 864-967-9530

Economy

Greenville is one of the nation's top centers for textile manufacturing—manufacturing is the largest employment sector in the metropolitan area, with textiles as the primary product. Greenville County is also a major engineering center, with more engineers per capita than any other U.S. county. A number of Fortune 500 companies, including Lockheed Martin, General Electric, and Fluor Daniel, are headquartered or have divisions in the Greenville area.

Unemployment Rate 3.1%
Per Capita Income $27,131*
Median Family Income $33,997

** Information given is for Greenville County.*

Principal Industries & Number of Wage Earners

Greenville-Spartanburg-Anderson Metropolitan Area* - 1999

Construction & Mining................................32,100
Finance, Insurance, & Real Estate 16,300
Government 59,900
Manufacturing 118,700
Retail Trade...94,400
Services 107,600
Transportation & Public Utilities 20,200
Wholesale Trade......................................28,500

** Information given is for the Greenville-Spartanburg-Anderson Metropolitan Area, which includes Anderson, Cherokee, Greenville, Pickens, and Spartanburg counties.*

Major Employers

Bi-Lo Inc Phone: 864-234-1600
PO Box 99 Fax: 864-987-8472
Mauldin, SC 29662
E-mail: bilo_feedback@aholdusa.com
www.bi-lo.com

Bob Jones University Phone: 864-242-5100
1700 Wade Hampton Blvd Fax: 864-242-2543
Greenville, SC 29614
www.bju.edu

Cryovac Div Sealed Air Corp Phone: 864-433-2000
100 Rogers Bridge Rd Bldg A Fax: 864-433-2689
Duncan, SC 29334 TF: 800-845-7551

Fluor Daniel Phone: 864-281-4400
100 Fluor Daniel Dr Fax: 864-281-4938
Greenville, SC 29607
www.fluordanielconsulting.com

GE Gas Turbine Phone: 864-254-2282
PO Box 648 Fax: 864-254-2228
Greenville, SC 29602
www.gepower.com

Greenville County Phone: 864-467-8551
305 E North St Courthouse Suite 224 Fax: 864-467-8540
Greenville, SC 29601
www.co.greenville.sc.us

Greenville County School District Phone: 864-241-3100
301 E Camperdown Way Fax: 864-241-3109
Greenville, SC 29601
E-mail: infoline@greenville.k12.sc.us
www.greenville.k12.sc.us

Greenville Hospital System Phone: 864-455-7000
701 Grove Rd Fax: 864-455-8434
Greenville, SC 29605
www.ghs.org

Greenville Technical College Phone: 864-250-8000
PO Box 5616 Fax: 864-250-8534
Greenville, SC 29606 TF: 800-723-0673
www.greenvilletech.com

JPS Industries Inc Phone: 864-239-3900
555 N Pleasantburg Dr Suite 202 Fax: 864-271-9939
Greenville, SC 29607

KEMET Electronics Corp Phone: 864-963-6300
PO Box 5928 Fax: 864-963-6322
Greenville, SC 29606
E-mail: capmaster@kemet.com
www.kemet.com

Lockheed Martin Aircraft & Logistics Centers Phone: 864-422-6395
107 Frederick St Fax: 864-422-6398
Greenville, SC 29607
lmalc.external.lmco.com

Michelin North America Phone: 864-458-5000
PO Box 19001 Fax: 800-423-2987
Greenville, SC 29602 TF: 800-847-3435
E-mail: webtire@us.michelin.com
www.michelin.com

Saint Francis Hospital Phone: 864-255-1000
1 St Francis Dr Fax: 864-255-1013
Greenville, SC 29601

WorldCom Inc Phone: 864-676-1000
50 International Dr Fax: 864-676-3434
Greenville, SC 29615
www.wcom.com

Quality of Living Indicators

Total Crime Index......................................5,871
(rates per 100,000 inhabitants)

Violent Crime
Murder/manslaughter............................ 10
Forcible rape 47
Robbery....................................... 219
Aggravated assault............................. 581

Property Crime
Burglary 857
Larceny theft 3,810
Motor vehicle theft 347

Cost of Living Index....................................99.8
(national average = 100)

Median Home Price..................................$113,800

Education

Public Schools

Greenville County School District Phone: 864-241-3100
301 E Camperdown Way Fax: 864-241-3109
Greenville, SC 29601
E-mail: infoline@greenville.k12.sc.us
www.greenville.k12.sc.us

Number of Schools
Elementary 54
Middle 16
High 14

Student/Teacher Ratio
All Grades 15.9:1

Private Schools

Number of Schools (all grades) .... 65+

Colleges & Universities

Bob Jones University
1700 Wade Hampton Blvd
Greenville, SC 29614
www.bju.edu
Phone: 864-242-5100
Fax: 864-242-2543

Clemson University
102 Sikes Hall
Clemson, SC 29634
E-mail: mikeh@clemson.edu
www.clemson.edu
Phone: 864-656-3311
Fax: 864-656-2464

Furman University
3300 Poinsett Hwy
Greenville, SC 29613
www.furman.edu
Phone: 864-294-2000
Fax: 864-294-3127

Greenville Technical College
PO Box 5616
Greenville, SC 29606
www.greenvilletech.com
Phone: 864-250-8000
Fax: 864-250-8534
TF: 800-723-0673

North Greenville College
7801 N Tigerville Rd
Tigerville, SC 29688
E-mail: admissions@ngc.edu
www.ngc.edu
Phone: 864-977-7000
Fax: 864-977-7021
TF: 800-468-6642

Southern Wesleyan College
907 Wesleyan Dr
Central, SC 29630
E-mail: admissions@swu.edu
www.swu.edu
Phone: 864-644-5000
Fax: 864-644-5900
TF: 800-282-8798

Hospitals

Baptist Medical Center Easley
200 Fleetwood Dr
Easley, SC 29640
Phone: 864-855-7200
Fax: 864-855-7521

Greenville Memorial Hospital
701 Grove Rd
Greenville, SC 29605
Phone: 864-455-7000
Fax: 864-455-8434

Saint Francis Hospital
1 St Francis Dr
Greenville, SC 29601
Phone: 864-255-1000
Fax: 864-255-1013

Shriners Hospitals for Children Greenville Unit
950 W Faris Rd
Greenville, SC 29605
www.shrinershq.org/Hospitals/Directry/greenville.html
Phone: 864-271-3444
Fax: 864-271-4471
TF: 800-591-7564

Transportation

Airport(s)

Greenville-Spartanburg Airport (GSP)
12 miles NE of downtown Greenville
(approx 25 minutes) 864-877-7426

Mass Transit

Greenville Transit Authority
$1 Base fare 864-467-5000

Rail/Bus

Amtrak Station
1120 W Washington St
Greenville, SC 29601
Phone: 864-255-4221
TF: 800-872-7245

Greyhound Bus Station
100 W McBee Ave
Greenville, SC 29601
Phone: 864-235-3513
TF: 800-231-2222

Utilities

Electricity
Duke Power 864-242-3261
www.dukepower.com

Gas
Piedmont Natural Gas Co 864-232-5141
www.piedmontng.com

Water
Greenville Water System 864-241-6000

Garbage Collection/Recycling
Greenville Recycling 864-467-8300
Greenville Sanitation Dept 864-467-4345

Telecommunications

Telephone
BellSouth 800-336-0014
www.bellsouth.com

Cable Television
Charter Communications 864-271-8526

Internet Service Providers (ISPs)
Global Vision Inc 864-241-0901
www.globalvision.net

Banks

American Federal Bank FSB
300 E McBee Ave
Greenville, SC 29601
Phone: 864-255-7000
Fax: 864-255-7504
TF: 888-232-9980

Bank of America
7 N Laurens St
Greenville, SC 29601
Phone: 864-271-5600

Carolina First Bank
102 S Main St
Greenville, SC 29601
Phone: 864-255-7900
Fax: 864-239-6401

First Citizens Bank & Trust
75 Beattie Pl 2 Liberty Sq
Greenville, SC 29601
Phone: 864-255-3700
Fax: 864-255-3737

First Union National Bank
PO Box 1329
Greenville, SC 29602
Phone: 864-255-8000
Fax: 864-255-8068
TF: 800-473-3862

Regions Bank
PO Box 17308
Greenville, SC 29606
Phone: 864-233-7989
Fax: 864-235-6636
TF: 800-734-4667

Shopping

Augusta Commons
2222 Augusta St
Greenville, SC 29605
Phone: 864-232-5669

Foothills Factory Stores
I-26 & New Cut Rd
Spartanburg, SC 29301
Phone: 864-574-8587

Greenville Mall
1025 Woodruff Rd
Greenville, SC 29607
Phone: 864-297-8800
Fax: 864-281-0359

Haywood Mall
700 Haywood Rd
Greenville, SC 29607
Phone: 864-288-0511
Fax: 864-297-6018

Little Stores of West End
315 Augusta St
Greenville, SC 29601
Phone: 864-467-1770

McAlister Square
225 S Pleasantburg Dr
Greenville, SC 29607
Phone: 864-232-6204

Media

Newspapers and Magazines

Greenville Magazine
225 S Pleasantburg Dr Suite D-2
Greenville, SC 29607
E-mail: gmag@greenvillemagazine.com
www.greenvillemagazine.com
Phone: 864-271-1105
Fax: 864-271-1165

Greenville News*
PO Box 1688
Greenville, SC 29602
E-mail: newsletters@greenville.infi.net
greenvilleonline.com
Phone: 864-298-4100
Fax: 864-298-4395
TF: 800-274-7879

**Indicates major daily newspapers*

Television

WASV-TV Ch 62 (UPN)
1293 Hendersonville Rd Suite 12
Asheville, NC 28803
Phone: 828-277-0902
Fax: 828-277-5060

WFBC-TV Ch 40 (Ind)
288 Macon Ave
Asheville, NC 28804
E-mail: contact@wfbc.com
www.wfbc.com
Phone: 828-255-0013
Fax: 828-255-4612
TF: 800-288-8813

WGGS-TV Ch 16 (Ind)
3409 Rutherford Rd
Taylors, SC 29687
Phone: 864-244-1616
Fax: 864-292-8481
TF: 800-849-3683

WHNS-TV Ch 21 (Fox)
21 Interstate Ct
Greenville, SC 29615
E-mail: fox21@whns.com
www.whns.com
Phone: 864-288-2100
Fax: 864-297-0728

WNEG-TV Ch 32 (CBS)
100 Boulevard
Toccoa, GA 30577
E-mail: wnegtv@bellsouth.net
www.toccoa.net/hosted/ch32/ch32.htm
Phone: 706-886-0032
Fax: 706-886-7033

WRET-TV Ch 49 (PBS)
PO Box 4069
Spartanburg, SC 29305
www.wret.org
Phone: 864-503-9371
Fax: 864-503-3615

WRLK-TV Ch 35 (PBS)
1101 George Rogers Blvd
Columbia, SC 29201
Phone: 803-737-3200
Fax: 803-737-3526

WSPA-TV Ch 7 (CBS)
PO Box 1717
Spartanburg, SC 29304
E-mail: newschannel7@wspa.com
www.wspa.com
Phone: 864-576-7777
Fax: 864-587-5430
TF: 800-207-6397

WYFF-TV Ch 4 (NBC)
505 Rutherford St
Greenville, SC 29609
E-mail: wyff@aol.com
www.wyff.com/
Phone: 864-242-4404
Fax: 864-240-5305

Radio

WESC-FM 92.5 MHz (Ctry)
223 W Stone Ave
Greenville, SC 29609
www.wescfm.com
Phone: 864-242-4660
Fax: 864-271-5029

WFBC-FM 93.7 MHz (CHR)
501 Rutherford St
Greenville, SC 29609
Phone: 864-271-9200
Fax: 864-241-4387

WGVL-AM 1440 kHz (Ctry)
7 N Laurens St Suite 700
Greenville, SC 29601
Phone: 864-242-1005
Fax: 864-271-3830

WJMZ-FM 107.3 MHz (Urban)
220 N Main St Suite 402
Greenville, SC 29602
www.wjmz.com
Phone: 864-235-1073
Fax: 864-370-3403

WMUU-AM 1260 kHz (Rel)
920 Wade Hampton Blvd
Greenville, SC 29609
E-mail: wmuu@bju.edu
www.bju.edu/wmuu
Phone: 864-242-6240
Fax: 864-370-3829

WMUU-FM 94.5 MHz (B/EZ)
920 Wade Hampton Blvd
Greenville, SC 29609
E-mail: wmuu@bju.edu
www.bju.edu/wmuu
Phone: 864-242-6240
Fax: 864-370-3829

WMYI-FM 102.5 MHz (AC)
7 N Laurens St Suite 700
Greenville, SC 29601
www.wmyi.com
Phone: 864-235-1025
Fax: 864-242-1025

WROQ-FM 101.1 MHz (CR)
7 N Laurens St Suite 700
Greenville, SC 29601
www.wroq.com
Phone: 864-242-0101
Fax: 864-298-0067

WTPT-FM 93.3 MHz (Rock)
223 W Stone Ave
Greenville, SC 29609
www.93planet.com
Phone: 864-242-4660
Fax: 864-271-5029

Attractions

Upstate South Carolina is home to many scenic points of interest, including the foothills of the Blue Ridge Mountains, Chattooga National Wild and Scenic River, as well as numerous other rivers, lakes, and waterfalls. Located approximately 30 miles southwest of Greenville, the 250 acres of the Clemson University Botanical Gardens include wildflower, fern, and bog gardens containing hundreds of species native to South Carolina. The Sacred Art Museum at Bob Jones University in Greenville features religious art dating from the 13th century, including works by Rembrandt, Reubens, Titian, and Van Dyck; and the area of the city known as Little Stores of West-End is a unique shopping village of specialty stores. Greenville's 126-acre Cleveland Park includes the Fernwood Nature Trail, the Greenville Zoo, the Major Rudolf Anderson Memmoria, and the Vietnam War Memorial.

16th South Carolina Volunteers Museum of the Confederate History
15 Boyce Ave
Greenville, SC 29601
www.scaevola.com/16thregiment
Phone: 864-421-9039

Bob Jones University Artist Series & University Classic Players
1700 Wade Hampton Blvd
Greenville, SC 29614
Phone: 864-242-5100
Fax: 864-242-3923

Bob Jones University Collection of Sacred Art
Bob Jones University 1700 Wade Hampton Blvd
Greenville, SC 29614
Phone: 864-242-5100
Fax: 864-233-9829

Center Stage-South Carolina!
501 River St
Greenville, SC 29601
Phone: 864-233-6733
Fax: 864-233-3901

Christ Episcopal Church
10 N Church St
Greenville, SC 29601
Phone: 864-271-8773
Fax: 864-242-0879

Cleveland Park
Downtown Greenville-E Washington St
Greenville, SC 29601
Phone: 864-467-4355
Fax: 864-467-5735
TF: 800-849-4339

Cowpens National Battlefield
4001 Chesnee Hwy
Gaffney, SC 29341
www.nps.gov/cowp/
Phone: 864-461-2828
Fax: 864-461-7795

Downtown Baptist Church
101 W McBee Ave
Greenville, SC 29601
Phone: 864-235-5746
Fax: 864-370-3827

First Presbyterian Church
200 W Washington St
Greenville, SC 29601
Phone: 864-235-0496

Fort Hill-The John C Calhoun House
Fort Hill St
Clemson, SC 29634
Phone: 864-656-2475

Furman University Theatre
3300 Poinsett Hwy
Greenville, SC 29613
Phone: 864-294-2125

Gassaway Mansion
106 Dupont Dr
Greenville, SC 29607
Phone: 864-271-0188

Greenville Ballet
100 S Main St Peace Center for the Performing Arts
Greenville, SC 29601
Phone: 864-235-6456

Greenville County Historical Society
211 E Washington St
Greenville, SC 29601
Phone: 864-233-4103

Greenville County Museum of Art
420 College St
Greenville, SC 29601
www.greenvillemuseum.org
Phone: 864-271-7570
Fax: 864-271-7579

Greenville Little Theatre
444 College St
Greenville, SC 29601
www.greenvillelittletheatre.com
Phone: 864-233-6238
Fax: 864-233-6237

Greenville Symphony Orchestra
PO Box 10002
Greenville, SC 29603
Phone: 864-232-0344
Fax: 864-467-3113

Greenville Zoo
150 Cleveland Pk Dr
Greenville, SC 29601
www.greenvillezoo.org
Phone: 864-467-4300
Fax: 864-467-4314

Historic Greenville Foundation
123 W Broad St
Greenville, SC 29601
Phone: 864-467-3100
Fax: 864-467-3133

Historic Reedy River Falls Park
Corner of S Main St & Camperdown Way
Greenville, SC 29601
Phone: 864-467-4355
Fax: 864-467-6662

Kilgore-Lewis House
560 N Academy St
Greenville, SC 29601
Phone: 864-232-3020

Little Stores of West End
315 Augusta St
Greenville, SC 29601
Phone: 864-467-1770

Ninety Six National Historic Site
1103 Hwy 248 S
Ninety Six, SC 29666
www.nps.gov/nisi/
Phone: 864-543-4068
Fax: 864-543-2058

Nippon Cultural Center
500 Congaree Rd
Greenville, SC 29607
Phone: 864-288-8471
Fax: 864-288-8018

Paris Mountain State Park
2401 State Park Rd
Greenville, SC 29609
Phone: 864-244-5565
Fax: 864-244-5565

Peace Center for the Performing Arts
101 W Broad St
Greenville, SC 29601
www.peacecenter.org
Phone: 864-467-3030
Fax: 864-467-3040

Reedy River Falls Historic Park
123 W Broad St
Greenville, SC 29601
Phone: 864-467-4350

Roper Mountain Science Center
402 Roper Mountain Rd
Greenville, SC 29615
www.ropermountain.org
Phone: 864-281-1188
Fax: 864-458-7034

Scuffletown USA
603 Scuffletown Rd
Simpsonville, SC 29681
Phone: 864-967-2276
Fax: 864-967-4499

Shoeless Joe Jackson Memorial Park
406 West Ave
Greenville, SC 29611
Phone: 864-288-6470

South Carolina Botanical Garden
102 Garden Trail Clemson University
Clemson, SC 29634
E-mail: scbg@clemson.edu
virtual.clemson.edu/groups/scbg
Phone: 864-656-3405
Fax: 864-656-6230

South Carolina Children's Theatre
106 Augusta St
Greenville, SC 29601
Phone: 864-235-2885
Fax: 864-235-0208

Thompson Gallery
3300 Poinsett Hwy Furman University
Greenville, SC 29613
Phone: 864-294-2074

Warehouse Theatre
37 Augusta St
Greenville, SC 29601
www.warehousetheatre.com
Phone: 864-235-6948

Wesley John United Methodist Church
101 E Court St
Greenville, SC 29601
Phone: 864-232-6903

Wild Water Ltd Rafting Trips
1251 Academy Rd
Long Creek, SC 29658
Phone: 864-647-9587
Fax: 864-647-5361
TF: 800-451-9972

Sports Teams & Facilities

Bi-Lo Center
650 N Academy St
Greenville, SC 29601
www.bilocenter.com
Phone: 864-241-3800
Fax: 864-241-3872

Greenville Braves (baseball)
1 Braves Ave Greenville Municipal Stadium
Greenville, SC 29607
www.gbraves.com
Phone: 864-299-3456
Fax: 864-277-7369

Greenville Grrrowl (hockey)
650 N Academy St Bi-Lo Ctr Arena
Greenville, SC 29601
www.grrrowl.com
Phone: 864-467-4777
Fax: 864-241-3872

Annual Events

Antiques Extravaganza (mid-August) 864-233-2562
Art in the Park (mid-September) 864-467-6627
Aunt Het Festival (early October) 864-862-2586
Back to Nature Festival (mid-October) 864-288-6470
Boat RV & Sport Show (early February) 864-233-2562
Boo in the Zoo Festival (late October) 864-467-4300
Christmas Light Show
(late November-late December) 800-717-0023
Country Corn Festival (mid-July) 864-322-8565
Fall for Greenville-A Taste of Our Town
(mid-October) 864-467-5781
First Night Greenville (December 31) 864-467-5780
Freedom Weekend Aloft Balloon Race
(Memorial Day weekend) 864-232-3700
Halloween Spooktacular (late October) 864-288-6470
Holiday Fair (early December) 864-233-2562
Main Street Jazz (early April-early October) 864-467-5780
Michelin Cycling Classic (mid-October) 864-467-6627
Music on the Mountain (June-August) 864-288-6470
River Place Arts Festival (early May) 864-467-5780
Thursday Night Downtown Alive
(April-October) 864-467-8089

Hartford, Connecticut

***County:* Hartford**

HARTFORD is located in central Connecticut in the Connecticut River Valley. Major cities within 100 miles include New Haven, Stamford, and Bridgeport, Connecticut; New York, New York; Boston and Springfield, Massachusetts; and Providence, Rhode Island.

Area (Land) .... 17.3 sq mi
Area (Water)............................... 0.7 sq mi
Elevation....................................... 50 ft
Latitude ....41-76-36 N
Longitude............................... 72-68-56 W
Time Zone ....EST
Area Code....................................... 860

Climate

Hartford's moderate climate features frequently changing weather patterns. Winters are cold, with average high temperatures in the mid-30s and lows in the high teens to near 20 degrees. The average annual snowfall in Hartford is 42 inches. Summer days are warm and humid, with average high temperatures in the low to mid-80s, while evenings cool down into the upper 50s and low 60s. May tends to be wettest month in Hartford, while February is the driest.

Average Temperatures & Precipitation

Temperatures

	Jan	Feb	Mar	Apr	May	Jun	Jul	Aug	Sep	Oct	Nov	Dec
High	33	36	47	60	72	80	85	83	75	64	51	38
Low	16	19	28	38	48	57	62	60	52	41	33	21

Precipitation

	Jan	Feb	Mar	Apr	May	Jun	Jul	Aug	Sep	Oct	Nov	Dec
Inches	3.4	3.2	3.6	3.9	4.1	3.8	3.2	3.7	3.8	3.6	4.0	3.9

History

Originally inhabited by the Saukiog tribe, the area known today as Hartford was first settled by Europeans in 1633 as a Dutch fur trading post called "The House of Hope." Three years later, a group of Puritans led by Reverend Thomas Hooker arrived in the area and transformed "The House of Hope" into a permanent English settlement, which Hooker renamed Hartford after of the English birthplace (Hertford) of his assistant, Reverend Samuel Stone. In 1662, Hartford was chosen as the capital of the Connecticut Colony, a duty it shared with New Haven between the years of 1701 and 1873. One of the most notable events in Hartford history occurred in 1687 when local colonists hid Connecticut's charter inside a tree (which came to be known as the Charter Oak) to prevent the colony from falling under the authority of New England's governor, Sir Edmond Andros. Today a plaque marks the place where the Charter Oak once stood (the actual tree was blown down in the mid-1800s). Hartford was incorporated as a city in 1784.

During its earliest years, Hartford's economy centered around agriculture, but the village soon became an important manufacturing and trade center along the Connecticut River. The insurance industry that Hartford has become famous for began as a response to the needs of the many factories in the area. From the founding of the Hartford Fire Insurance Company in 1810, Hartford has become known as the "Insurance Capital of the World" and is home to six of the nation's largest insurance companies. Hartford is also known as the birthplace of the nation's oldest continuously-published newspaper, the Hartford Courant, which was established in 1764; and for the revolver, which was invented in Hartford in 1836 by Samuel Colt, whose company, the Colt Firearms Factory, pioneered the concepts of mass production and interchangeable parts. Among Hartford's noted one-time residents are authors Mark Twain and Harriet Beecher Stowe, whose homes have become historical attractions in the city, as well as Hartford native, Noah Webster, compiler of the nation's first dictionary.

With a population of more than 131,000, Hartford today is Connecticut's second largest city, and, aided by an ongoing downtown revitalization project that began more than two decades ago, is a major financial and commercial center in the U.S.

Population

1990 Census 139,739
1998 Estimate.............................131,523
% Change .... -5.9
2005 Projection 133,570

Racial/Ethnic Breakdown

White.................................... 40.0%
Black 38.9%
Other.................................... 21.1%
Hispanic Origin (may be of any race) 31.6%

Age Breakdown

Under 5 years.............................. 8.5%
5 to 17.................................. 18.9%
18 to 20.................................. 6.6%
21 to 24.................................. 8.7%
25 to 34................................. 19.7%
35 to 44................................. 13.0%
45 to 54.................................. 8.1%
55 to 64.................................. 6.6%
65 to 74.................................. 5.4%
75+ years 4.5%
Median Age................................28.4

Gender Breakdown

Male.................................... 47.7%
Female................................... 52.3%

Government

Type of Government: Council-Manager

Hartford City Council
550 Main St
Hartford, CT 06103
Phone: 860-543-8510
Fax: 860-722-6591

Hartford City Hall
550 Main St
Hartford, CT 06103
Phone: 860-522-4888
Fax: 860-722-6591

Hartford City Manager
550 Main St
Hartford, CT 06103
Phone: 860-543-8520
Fax: 860-722-6619

Hartford City Treasurer
10 Prospect St Suite 208
Hartford, CT 06103
Phone: 860-543-8530
Fax: 860-722-6127

Hartford Finance Dept
550 Main St Rm 303
Hartford, CT 06103
Phone: 860-543-8550
Fax: 860-722-6024

Hartford Fire Dept
275 Pearl St
Hartford, CT 06103
Phone: 860-722-8200
Fax: 860-722-8205

Hartford Health Dept
131 Coventry St
Hartford, CT 06112
Phone: 860-543-8800
Fax: 860-722-6719

Hartford Housing & Community Development Dept
10 Prospect St 4th Fl
Hartford, CT 06103
Phone: 860-543-8640
Fax: 860-722-6630

Hartford Mayor
550 Main St 2nd Fl
Hartford, CT 06103
Phone: 860-543-8500
Fax: 860-722-6606

Hartford Personnel Dept
550 Main St
Hartford, CT 06103
Phone: 860-543-8590
Fax: 860-722-8042

Hartford Police Dept
50 Jennings Rd
Hartford, CT 06120
Phone: 860-527-6300
Fax: 860-722-8270

Hartford Public Library
500 Main St
Hartford, CT 06103
Phone: 860-543-8628
Fax: 860-722-6900

Hartford Public Works Dept
525 Main St
Hartford, CT 06103
Phone: 860-543-8625
Fax: 860-722-6164

Hartford Town & City Clerk
550 Main St
Hartford, CT 06103
Phone: 860-543-8581
Fax: 860-722-8041

Important Phone Numbers

AAA 860-236-5864
Connecticut Dept of Revenue Services 860-297-5962
Dental Referral 860-523-8657
Driver's License/Vehicle Registration Information 860-263-5700
Emergency 911
Events Line 860-522-6400
Greater Hartford Assn of Realtors 860-561-1800
Hartford Tax Dept 860-543-8565
HotelDocs 800-468-3537
Poison Control Center 800-343-2722
Time/Temp 203-366-4242
Voter Registration Information 860-543-8585
Weather 203-366-4242

Information Sources

Better Business Bureau Serving Connecticut
821 N Main St Ext
Wallingford, CT 06492
www.connecticut.bbb.org
Phone: 203-269-2700
Fax: 203-269-3124

Greater Hartford Convention & Visitors Bureau
1 Civic Center Plaza
Hartford, CT 06103
www.grhartfordcvb.com
Phone: 860-728-6789
Fax: 860-293-2365
TF: 800-446-7811

Hartford Civic Center
1 Civic Center Plaza
Hartford, CT 06103
www.hartfordciviccenter.com
Phone: 860-249-6333
Fax: 860-241-4226

Metro Hartford Chamber of Commerce
250 Constitution Plaza
Hartford, CT 06103
www.metrohartford.com
Phone: 860-525-4451
Fax: 860-293-2592

Online Resources

4Hartford.com
www.4hartford.com

About.com Guide to Hartford
hartford.about.com/local/newenglandus/hartford

Area Guide Hartford
hartford.areaguides.net

City Knowledge Hartford
www.cityknowledge.com/ct_hartford.htm

DigitalCity Hartford
home.digitalcity.com/hartford

Downtown Hartford Page
hartforddowntown.com

Excite.com Hartford City Guide
www.excite.com/travel/countries/united_states/connecticut/hartford

Hartford Events Calendar
www.eventscalendar.com

Hartford Home Page
www.state.ct.us/MUNIC/HARTFORD/hartford.htm

XenonArts
www.xenonarts.com/

Area Communities

Communities in Greater Hartford with populations greater than 20,000 include:

East Hartford
740 Main St
East Hartford, CT 06108
Phone: 860-291-7100
Fax: 860-289-0831

Enfield
820 Enfield St
Enfield, CT 06082
Phone: 860-253-6440
Fax: 860-253-6331

Farmington
1 Monteith Dr
Farmington, CT 06032
Phone: 860-673-8200
Fax: 860-675-7140

Glastonbury
2155 Main St
Glastonbury, CT 06033
Phone: 860-652-7710
Fax: 860-652-7505

Manchester
41 Center St
Manchester, CT 06040
Phone: 860-647-3037
Fax: 860-647-3029

New Britain
27 W Main St
New Britain, CT 06051
Phone: 860-826-3344
Fax: 860-826-3348

Newington
131 Cedar St
Newington, CT 06111
Phone: 860-665-8510
Fax: 860-665-8507

Simsbury
PO Box 495
Simsbury, CT 06070
Phone: 860-658-3200
Fax: 860-658-3206

South Windsor
1540 Sullivan Ave
South Windsor, CT 06074
Phone: 860-644-2511
Fax: 860-644-3781

Vernon
14 Park Pl
Vernon, CT 06066
Phone: 860-872-8591

West Hartford
50 S Main St
West Hartford, CT 06107
Phone: 860-523-3100
Fax: 860-523-3200

Wethersfield
505 Silas Deane Hwy
Wethersfield, CT 06109
Phone: 860-721-2801
Fax: 860-721-2994

Windsor
275 Broad St
Windsor, CT 06095
Phone: 860-688-3675
Fax: 860-285-1909

Economy

Known as the "Insurance Capital of the World," Hartford's economy has been fueled by the insurance industry for nearly two hundred years. Major U.S. insurance companies that have their corporate headquarters in Greater Hartford include the Travelers Insurance Companies, Aetna Life & Casualty, and CIGNA Corporation. Although the insurance industry has played a vital role in Hartford's economy for centuries, it is only one component of the region's diverse economic base. Services, manufacturing, and retail trade are, in fact, Hartford County's largest employment sectors, and Greater Hartford is rapidly becoming an important center for high-technology manufacturing and health care, which are currently the region's fastest-growing industries.

Unemployment Rate	2.2%
Per Capita Income	$32,035
Median Family Income	$59,600

Principal Industries & Number of Wage Earners

Hartford County - 1997

Agricultural Services, Forestry, & Fishing	2,160
Construction	23,061
Finance, Insurance, & Real Estate	70,023
Manufacturing	75,181
Mining	399
Retail Trade	77,523
Services	150,086
Transportation & Public Utilities	24,507
Wholesale Trade	30,722

Major Employers

ABB C-E Services
2000 Day Hill Rd
Windsor, CT 06095
Phone: 860-688-1911
Fax: 860-285-5606

ADVO Inc
1 Univac Ln
Windsor, CT 06095
www.advo.com
Phone: 860-285-6100
Fax: 860-285-6412

Aetna Inc
151 Farmington Ave
Hartford, CT 06156
E-mail: aetna.general@aetna1.sprint.com
www.aetna.com
Phone: 860-273-0123
Fax: 860-273-8909
TF: 800-872-3862

CIGNA Healthcare
900 Cottage Grove Rd
Hartford, CT 06002
www.cigna.com/health.html
Phone: 860-726-6000

Dexter Corp
1 Elm St
Windsor Locks, CT 06096
www.dexter.com
Phone: 860-654-8300
Fax: 860-292-7673
TF: 800-733-9833

Fleet National Bank
777 Main St
Hartford, CT 06115
Phone: 860-986-4336
Fax: 860-986-4350

Hartford City Hall
550 Main St
Hartford, CT 06103
ci.hartford.ct.us
Phone: 860-522-4888
Fax: 860-722-6591

Hartford Hospital
80 Seymour St
Hartford, CT 06102
www.harthosp.org
Phone: 860-545-5000
Fax: 860-545-4335

Northeast Utilities
107 Selden St
Berlin, CT 06037
E-mail: nucommunications@nu.com
www.nu.com
Phone: 860-665-5000
Fax: 860-444-4241

Phoenix Mutual Life Insurance Co
1 American Row
Hartford, CT 06115
www.phl.com
Phone: 860-403-1000
Fax: 860-403-5855

Saint Francis Hospital & Medical Center
114 Woodland St
Hartford, CT 06105
www.stfranciscare.org/index.htm
Phone: 860-714-4000
Fax: 860-714-8062
TF: 800-993-4312

Stanley Works
1000 Stanley Dr
New Britain, CT 06053
E-mail: corporate@mail.stanleyworks.com
www.stanleyworks.com
Phone: 860-225-5111
Fax: 860-827-3895
TF: 800-262-2161

Travelers Property Casualty Corp
1 Tower Sq
Hartford, CT 06183
www.travelerspc.com
Phone: 860-277-0111
Fax: 860-277-1970

United Technologies Corp Hamilton Standard Div
1 Hamilton Rd
Windsor Locks, CT 06096
E-mail: generalinterest@hamilton-standard.com
www.hamilton-standard.com
Phone: 860-654-6000
Fax: 860-654-5060

University of Connecticut
2131 Hillside Rd
Storrs, CT 06269
www.uconn.edu
Phone: 860-486-2000
Fax: 860-486-1476

University of Connecticut Health Center
263 Farmington Ave
Farmington, CT 06030
www.uchc.edu
Phone: 860-679-1000
Fax: 860-679-2267

University of Hartford
200 Bloomfield Ave
West Hartford, CT 06117
www.hartford.edu
Phone: 860-768-4100
Fax: 860-768-4961
TF: 800-947-4303

US Airways Inc
2345 Crystal Dr Crystal Pk 4
Arlington, VA 22227
www.usairways.com
Phone: 703-872-7000
Fax: 703-294-5097
TF: 800-428-4322

Quality of Living Indicators

Total Crime Index....................11,955
(rates per 100,000 inhabitants)

Violent Crime
Murder/manslaughter.......... 25
Forcible rape.......... 62
Robbery.......... 846
Aggravated assault.......... 718

Property Crime
Burglary..........1,762
Larceny theft..........6,932
Motor vehicle theft..........1,610

Cost of Living Index..........123.0
(national average = 100)

Median Home Price..........$150,700

Education

Public Schools

Hartford Public Schools
153 Market St
Hartford, CT 06103
www.hartfordschools.org
Phone: 860-722-8500
Fax: 860-722-8502

Number of Schools
Elementary.......... 28
Middle.......... 3
High.......... 3

Student/Teacher Ratio
All Grades.......... 14.0:1

Private Schools

Number of Schools (all grades).......... 19+

Colleges & Universities

Asnuntuck Community-Technical College
170 Elm St
Enfield, CT 06082
www.asctc.commnet.edu
Phone: 860-253-3000
Fax: 860-253-3016

Capital Community-Technical College
61 Woodland St
Hartford, CT 06105
webster.commnet.edu
Phone: 860-520-7800
Fax: 860-520-7906

Central Connecticut State University
1615 Stanley St
New Britain, CT 06050
Phone: 860-832-3200
Fax: 860-832-2295

Hartford College for Women
1265 Asylum Ave
Hartford, CT 06105
www.hartford.edu/uofh/hcw_s.html
Phone: 860-236-1215
Fax: 860-768-5693

Hartford Seminary
77 Sherman St
Hartford, CT 06105
E-mail: drollins@ursa.hartnet.org
www.hartsem.edu
Phone: 860-509-9500
Fax: 860-509-9509

Manchester Community-Technical College
PO Box 1046
Manchester, CT 06045
www.mcc.commnet.edu
Phone: 860-646-4900
Fax: 860-647-6328

Saint Joseph College
1678 Asylum Ave
West Hartford, CT 06117
www.sjc.edu
Phone: 860-232-4571
Fax: 860-233-5695
TF: 800-285-6565

Trinity College
300 Summit St
Hartford, CT 06106
E-mail: publicrelations@trincoll.edu
www.trincoll.edu
Phone: 860-297-2000
Fax: 860-297-2275

Tunxis Community College
271 Scott Swamp Rd
Farmington, CT 06032
www.tunxis.commnet.edu
Phone: 860-677-7701
Fax: 860-676-8906

University of Hartford
200 Bloomfield Ave
West Hartford, CT 06117
www.hartford.edu
Phone: 860-768-4100
Fax: 860-768-4961
TF: 800-947-4303

Hospitals

Bristol Hospital
Brewster Rd
Bristol, CT 06010
www.bristolhospital.org
Phone: 860-585-3000
Fax: 860-585-3058

Connecticut Children's Medical Center
282 Washington St
Hartford, CT 06106
www.ccmckids.org
Phone: 860-545-9000
Fax: 860-545-8560

Hartford Hospital
80 Seymour St
Hartford, CT 06102
www.harthosp.org
Phone: 860-545-5000
Fax: 860-545-4335

Manchester Memorial Hospital
71 Haynes St
Manchester, CT 06040
www.echn.org/mmh.htm
Phone: 860-646-1222
Fax: 860-647-4797

Mount Sinai Campus
500 Blue Hills Ave
Hartford, CT 06112
www.stfranciscare.org/about/sinai.htm
Phone: 860-714-2611
Fax: 860-714-8544

New Britain General Hospital
100 Grand St
New Britain, CT 06050
www.nbgh.org
Phone: 860-224-5011
Fax: 860-224-5740

Rockville General Hospital
31 Union St
Vernon, CT 06066
Phone: 860-872-0501
Fax: 860-872-6056

Saint Francis Hospital & Medical Center
114 Woodland St
Hartford, CT 06105
www.stfranciscare.org/index.htm
Phone: 860-714-4000
Fax: 860-714-8062
TF: 800-993-4312

University of Connecticut Health Center
John Dempsey Hospital
263 Farmington Ave
Farmington, CT 06030
www.uchc.edu
Phone: 860-679-2000
Fax: 860-679-4515

Veterans Administration Medical Center
555 Willard Ave
Newington, CT 06111
Phone: 860-666-6951
Fax: 860-667-6764

Transportation

Airport(s)

Bradley International Airport (BDL)
12 miles N of downtown Hartford
(approx 15 minutes) 860-292-2000

Mass Transit

CT Transit
$1 Base fare 860-525-9181

Rail/Bus

Amtrak Station
1 Union Pl Union Stn
Hartford, CT 06103
Phone: 860-727-1776
TF: 800-872-7245

Greyhound Bus Station
1 Union Pl Union Stn
Hartford, CT 06103
Phone: 860-522-9267
TF: 800-231-2222

Utilities

Electricity
Northeast Utilities 800-286-2000
www.nu.com

Gas
Connecticut Natural Gas Corp 860-727-3000
www.ctgcorp.com

Water
Metropolitan District Commission 860-278-0127

Garbage Collection/Recycling
McCauley Enterprises 860-724-4575

Telecommunications

Telephone
Southern New England Telephone Co 800-453-7638
www.snet.com

Cable Television
AT & T Cable Services 860-505-6248
www.cable.att.com
Cox Communications 860-432-6000

Internet Service Providers (ISPs)
NETPLEX 860-233-1111
www.ntplx.net

Banks

Advest Bank & Trust
90 State House Sq
Hartford, CT 06103
www.advest.com/bank/index.htm
Phone: 860-509-3000
Fax: 860-509-3571
TF: 800-541-3566

First International Bank
280 Trumbull St
Hartford, CT 06103
Phone: 860-727-0700
Fax: 860-525-2083

Fleet Bank
777 Main St
Hartford, CT 06115
Phone: 860-986-2000
Fax: 860-986-4350
TF: 800-841-4000

Mechanics Savings Bank
100 Pearl St
Hartford, CT 06103
Phone: 860-293-4000
Fax: 860-692-4148

Sovereign Bank
100 Pearl St
Hartford, CT 06103
Phone: 860-757-3405
Fax: 860-757-3910
TF: 877-768-2265

Shopping

Civic Center Mall & Pratt Street Shops
1 Civic Center Plaza
Hartford, CT 06103
Phone: 860-275-6100
Fax: 860-275-6110

Enfield Square Mall
90 Elm St
Enfield, CT 06082
E-mail: Email:info@enfieldsquaremall.com
www.enfieldsquaremall.com/
Phone: 860-745-7000
Fax: 860-745-3007

Richardson Building
942 Main St
Hartford, CT 06103
Phone: 860-525-9711

State House Square
10 State House Sq
Hartford, CT 06103
Phone: 860-241-0100
Fax: 860-549-5301

Westfarms Mall
500 Westfarms Mall
Farmington, CT 06032
Phone: 860-561-3420
Fax: 860-521-8682

Media

Newspapers and Magazines

East Hartford Gazette
1171 Main St
East Hartford, CT 06108
Phone: 860-289-6468
Fax: 860-289-6469

Hartford Advocate
100 Constitution Plaza
Hartford, CT 06103
www.hartfordadvocate.com
Phone: 860-548-9300
Fax: 860-548-9335

Hartford Courant*
285 Broad St
Hartford, CT 06115
E-mail: readerep@courant.com
www.hartfordcourant.com
Phone: 860-241-6200
Fax: 860-241-3865
TF: 800-472-7377

Hartford News
191 Franklin Ave
Hartford, CT 06114
E-mail: ssmedia@townusa.com
www.hartfordnews.com
Phone: 860-296-6128
Fax: 860-296-8769

Reminder The
PO Box 210
Vernon, CT 06066
www.remindernet.com
Phone: 860-875-3366
Fax: 860-872-4614

River East News Bulletin
PO Box 373
Glastonbury, CT 06033
Phone: 860-633-4691
Fax: 860-657-3258

**Indicates major daily newspapers*

Television

WBNE-TV Ch 59 (WB)
8 Elm St
New Haven, CT 06510
E-mail: feedback@wb59.com
www.wb59.com
Phone: 203-782-5900
Fax: 203-782-5995

WEDH-TV Ch 24 (PBS)
240 New Britain Ave
Hartford, CT 06106
Phone: 860-278-5310
Fax: 860-278-2157

WFSB-TV Ch 3 (CBS)
3 Constitution Plaza
Hartford, CT 06103
www.wfsb.com
Phone: 860-728-3333
Fax: 860-728-0263

WHPX-TV Ch 26 (PAX)
Shaws Cove 3 Suite 226
New London, CT 06320
www.pax.net/whpx
Phone: 860-444-2626
Fax: 860-440-2601

WTIC-TV Ch 61 (Fox)
1 Corporate Ctr
Hartford, CT 06103
www.fox61.com
Phone: 860-527-6161
Fax: 860-293-0178

WTNH-TV Ch 8 (ABC)
8 Elm St
New Haven, CT 06510
E-mail: wtnh@aol.com
www.wtnh.com
Phone: 203-784-8888
Fax: 203-789-2010

WTXX-TV Ch 20 (UPN)
1 Corporate Ctr
Hartford, CT 06103
Phone: 860-527-6161
Fax: 860-520-6578

WVIT-TV Ch 30 (NBC)
1422 New Britain Ave
West Hartford, CT 06110
www.wvit.com
Phone: 860-521-3030
Fax: 860-521-4860

Radio

WCCC-AM 1290 kHz (Rock)
1039 Asylum Ave
Hartford, CT 06105
Phone: 860-525-1069
Fax: 860-246-9084

WCCC-FM 106.9 MHz (Rock)
1039 Asylum Ave
Hartford, CT 06105
Phone: 860-525-1069
Fax: 860-246-9084

WDRC-AM 1360 kHz (Nost)
869 BlueHills Ave
Bloomfield, CT 06002
www.wdrc.com
Phone: 860-243-1115
Fax: 860-286-8257

WDRC-FM 102.9 MHz (Oldies)
869 BlueHills Ave
Bloomfield, CT 06002
www.wdrc.com
Phone: 860-243-1115
Fax: 860-286-8257

WFAN-AM 660 kHz (Sports)
34-12 36th St
Astoria, NY 11106
Phone: 718-706-7690
Fax: 718-706-6481

WHCN-FM 105.9 MHz (CR)
10 Columbus Blvd
Hartford, CT 06106
Phone: 860-723-6080
Fax: 860-723-6106

WKSS-FM 95.7 MHz (CHR)
10 Columbus Blvd
Hartford, CT 06106
www.kiss957.com
Phone: 860-723-6160
Fax: 860-723-6195

WLAT-AM 1230 kHz (Span)
86 Cedar St
Hartford, CT 06106
Phone: 860-524-0001
Fax: 860-548-1922

WMRQ-FM 104.1 MHz (Alt)
10 Columbus Blvd
Hartford, CT 06106
E-mail: feedback@radio104.com
www.radio104.com
Phone: 860-723-6040
Fax: 860-723-6078

WNEZ-AM 910 kHz (Urban)
86 Cedar St
Hartford, CT 06106
Phone: 860-524-0001
Fax: 860-548-1922

WPKT-FM 90.5 MHz (NPR)
240 New Britain Ave
Hartford, CT 06106
Phone: 860-278-5310
Fax: 860-278-2157

WPOP-AM 1410 kHz (Sports)
10 Columbus Blvd
Hartford, CT 06106
Phone: 860-723-6160
Fax: 860-723-6195

WRCH-FM 100.5 MHz (AC)
10 Executive Dr
Farmington, CT 06032
www.wrch.com
Phone: 860-677-6700
Fax: 860-678-7053

WTIC-AM 1080 kHz (N/T)
10 Executive Dr
Farmington, CT 06032
www.wtic.com
Phone: 860-677-6700
Fax: 860-284-9842

WTIC-FM 96.5 MHz (AC)
10 Executive Dr
Farmington, CT 06032
E-mail: wticamfm@tiac.net
www.ticfm.com/
Phone: 860-677-6700
Fax: 860-284-9650

WWYZ-FM 92.5 MHz (Ctry)
10 Columbus Blvd
Hartford, CT 06106
www.wwyz.com
Phone: 860-723-6120
Fax: 860-723-6159

WZMX-FM 93.7 MHz (CR)
10 Executive Dr
Farmington, CT 06032
www.wzmx.com
Phone: 860-677-6700
Fax: 860-677-6799

Attractions

Historical attractions in Hartford include the Raymond E. Baldwin Museum of Connecticut History, which features Connecticut's original charter dating back to 1662; the nation's oldest State House; and the former homes of notable Hartford residents Mark Twain and Harriet Beecher Stowe. Hartford's Wadsworth Atheneum, established during the 1840s as America's first public art museum, has become known as one of the top museums in the country, featuring nearly 50,000 objects spanning five centuries of art from around the globe. Professionally trained guides in downtown Hartford assist visitors who lose their way.

Artists Collective
1200 Albany Ave
Hartford, CT 06112
Phone: 860-527-3205
Fax: 860-527-2979

Austin Arts Center
300 Summit St
Hartford, CT 06106
www.trincoll.edu/~aac
Phone: 860-297-2199
Fax: 860-297-5380

Bushnell Park Carousel
Elm & Jewell Sts Bushnell Pk
Hartford, CT 06106
Phone: 860-246-7739

Bushnell Performing Arts Center
166 Capitol Ave
Hartford, CT 06106
E-mail: info@bushnell.org
www.bushnell.org
Phone: 860-987-5900
Fax: 860-987-6080
TF: 888-824-2874

Center Church & Ancient Burying Ground
60 Gold St
Hartford, CT 06103
Phone: 860-249-5631
Fax: 860-246-3915

Charter Oak Landing Cruises
Charter Oak Landing
Hartford, CT
www.deeprivernavigation.com
Phone: 860-526-4954
Fax: 860-526-2322

Christ Church Cathedral
45 Church St
Hartford, CT 06103
E-mail: ccc@tiac.net
www.cccathedral.org
Phone: 860-527-7231
Fax: 860-527-5313

Connecticut Historical Society
1 Elizabeth St
Hartford, CT 06105
E-mail: cthist@ix.netcom.com
www.hartnet.org/~chs/
Phone: 860-236-5621
Fax: 860-236-2664

Connecticut Opera Assn
226 Farmington Ave
Hartford, CT 06105
E-mail: connopera@aol.com
www.connecticutopera.org
Phone: 860-527-0713
Fax: 860-293-1715

Connecticut State Capitol
210 Capitol Ave
Hartford, CT 06106
www.cga.state.ct.us
Phone: 860-240-0222

Constitution Plaza
State & Market Sts
Hartford, CT 06103
Phone: 860-527-7011
Fax: 860-527-6577

Dance Connecticut
224 Farmington Ave
Hartford, CT 06105
Phone: 860-525-9396
Fax: 860-249-8116

Edward E King Museum
840 Main St
East Hartford, CT 06108
Phone: 860-289-6429
Fax: 860-291-9166

Elizabeth Park Rose Gardens
Prospect & Asylum Aves
Hartford, CT 06102
Phone: 860-242-0017
Fax: 860-242-0017

Goodwin Park
Maple Ave & South St
Hartford, CT 06106
Phone: 860-547-1426
Fax: 860-722-6497

Governor's Residence
990 Prospect Ave
Hartford, CT 06105
Phone: 860-566-4840

Harriett Beecher Stowe House
77 Forest St
Hartford, CT 06105
E-mail: stowelib@hartnet.org
www.hartnet.org/~stowe/stowe_house.html
Phone: 860-525-9317
Fax: 860-522-9259

Hartford Children's Theater
PO Box 2547
Hartford, CT 06146
Phone: 860-249-7970
Fax: 860-548-0783

Hartford Chorale
200 Bloomfield Ave Hartt School
West Hartford, CT 06117
E-mail: nhinchee@hickoryhill.com
www.hartfordchorale.org
Phone: 860-547-1982
Fax: 860-768-4441

Hartford Police Museum
101 Pearl St
Hartford, CT 06103
Phone: 860-722-6152

Hartford Stage Co
50 Church St
Hartford, CT 06103
E-mail: stagehartford@worldnet.att.net
www.hartfordstage.org
Phone: 860-527-5151
Fax: 860-247-8243

Hartford Symphony Orchestra
166 Capitol Ave Bushnell Memorial Hall
Hartford, CT 06106
Phone: 860-244-2999
Fax: 860-249-5430

Isham-Terry House
211 High St
Hartford, CT 06112
Phone: 860-247-8996
Fax: 860-249-4907

Lincoln Theater
200 Bloomfield Ave University of Hartford Campus
West Hartford, CT 06117
Phone: 860-768-4228
Fax: 860-768-4229
TF: 800-274-8587

Mark Twain House
351 Farmington Ave
Hartford, CT 06105
www.hartnet.org/~twain
Phone: 860-247-0998
Fax: 860-278-8148

Meadows Music Theatre
61 Savitt Way
Hartford, CT 06120
E-mail: info@meadowsmusic.com
www.meadowsmusic.com
Phone: 860-548-7370
Fax: 860-548-7386

Menczer Museum of Medicine & Dentistry
230 Scarborough St
Hartford, CT 06105
Phone: 860-236-5613
Fax: 860-236-8401

Museum of American Political Life
200 Bloomfield Ave University of Hartford
West Hartford, CT 06117
www.hartford.edu/polmus/polmus1.html
Phone: 860-768-4090
Fax: 860-768-5159

New Britain Museum of American Art
56 Lexington St
New Britain, CT 06052
www.nbmaa.org
Phone: 860-229-0257
Fax: 860-229-3445

Old State House
800 Main St
Hartford, CT 06103
Phone: 860-522-6766
Fax: 860-522-2812

Pump House Gallery
Bushnell Pk
Hartford, CT 06106
Phone: 860-722-6536

Raymond E Baldwin Museum of Connecticut History
231 Capitol Ave
Hartford, CT 06106
www.cslib.org/museum.htm
Phone: 860-566-3056
Fax: 860-566-2133

Soldiers & Sailors Memorial Arch
Trinity St Bushnell Pk
Hartford, CT 06106
www.bushnellpark.org/poi/smarch.html
Phone: 860-728-6789
Fax: 860-722-6514

TheaterWorks
233 Pearl St
Hartford, CT 06103
Phone: 860-527-7838
Fax: 860-525-0758

Wadsworth Atheneum
600 Main St
Hartford, CT 06103
www.hartnet.org/~wadsworth
Phone: 860-278-2670
Fax: 860-527-0803

Sports Teams & Facilities

Connecticut Pride (basketball)
21 Waterville Rd
Avon, CT 06001
E-mail: ctpride@ctpride.com
www.ctpride.com/
Phone: 860-678-8156
Fax: 860-674-2639
TF: 888-887-7433

Connecticut Wolves (soccer)
635 S Main St Veterans Memorial Stadium
New Britain, CT 06050
E-mail: connecticutwolves@yahoo.com
www.ct-wolves.com
Phone: 860-223-0710
Fax: 860-223-2759

Hartford Coliseum
1 Civic Center Plaza Hartford Civic Ctr
Hartford, CT 06103
Phone: 860-249-6333
Fax: 860-241-4226

New Britain Rock Cats (baseball)
S Main St New Britain Stadium
New Britain, CT 06051
www.minorleaguebaseball.com/teams/east-nbr.php3
Phone: 860-224-8383
Fax: 860-225-6267

New England Sea Wolves (football)
1 Civic Center Plaza Hartford Civic Ctr
Hartford, CT 06103
www.neseawolves.com
Phone: 860-246-7825
Fax: 860-240-7618

Norwich Navigators (baseball)
14 Stott Ave Dodd Stadium
Norwich, CT 06360
www.gators.com
Phone: 860-887-7962
Fax: 860-886-5996
TF: 800-644-2867

Annual Events

Big Bass Tournaments
(late May-early September) 860-713-3131
Family Day Festival (mid-August) 860-722-6567
Farmington Antique Weekend
(early September & early June) 800-793-4480
Festival of Jazz (late July).........................800-332-7829
Festival of Light (late November-late December) 860-728-6789
First Night Hartford (December 31) 860-728-3089
Greater Hartford Marathon (early October) 860-525-3435
Greater Hartford Open (late June-early July)........860-246-4446
Hartford Flower Show (mid-February) 860-529-2123
Head to the New Riverfront Regatta
(mid-October).................................860-713-3131
Hebron Maple Festival (early March)...............860-244-8181
Music Under the Stars Concert Series
(early June-late September).....................860-713-3131
Nutmeg State Games (late July-early August).......860-528-4588
Podunk Blue Grass Music Festival (late July).......860-282-8241
Riverfest (early July).............................860-713-3131
Taste of Hartford (mid-June) 860-728-3089

Honolulu, Hawaii

***County:* Honolulu**

HONOLULU is located on the southern coast of the Hawaiian island of Oahu. Major cities within 100 miles include Kahalui, Maui, Hawaii.

Area (Land) . . . . 82.8 sq mi
Area (Water). . . . . 19.4 sq mi
Elevation. . . . . 18 ft
Latitude . . . . .20-73-46 N
Longitude. . . . . 156-44-75 W
Time Zone . . . . .Hawaii
Area Code. 808

Climate

Honolulu has a tropical climate that features warm temperatures throughout the year. Summer daytime temperatures average in the upper 80s, with evening temperatures cooling down into the low to mid-70s. Winters are very mild, with average highs near 80 degrees and lows dipping only into the mid- to upper 60s. Late autumn through winter is the wettest time of the year in Hawaii, while summer is the driest. Despite it's location in the middle of the Pacific Ocean, Hawaii is rarely affected by tropical storms.

Average Temperatures & Precipitation

Temperatures

	Jan	Feb	Mar	Apr	May	Jun	Jul	Aug	Sep	Oct	Nov	Dec
High	80	81	82	83	85	87	88	89	89	87	84	81
Low	66	65	67	69	70	72	74	74	74	72	70	67

Precipitation

	Jan	Feb	Mar	Apr	May	Jun	Jul	Aug	Sep	Oct	Nov	Dec
Inches	3.6	2.2	2.2	1.5	1.1	0.5	0.6	0.4	0.8	2.3	3.0	3.8

History

The Hawaiian Islands were originally inhabited by Polynesians, possibly as early as the first century A.D. Although it is the subject of some debate, it is believed that the area known today as Honolulu was first settled in 1100 A.D. In 1778, Captain James Cook became the first European to arrive in the Hawaiian Islands, but Honolulu Harbor was not discovered by western explorers until Captain William Brown arrived in 1794. Around the turn of the 19th Century, the islands were united into a kingdom and ruled by King Kamehameha I. In 1804, King Kamehameha moved his court from the island of Hawaii to Waikiki, and in 1809, relocated once again to present-day downtown Honolulu. Early explorers referred to the harbor as Brown's Harbor, but the name "Honolulu," which means "sheltered harbor," soon came into common use.

An influx of Europeans and Americans during the 1800s westernized the Hawaiian Islands. The newcomers introduced the Hawaiians to Christianity, education, economics and politics. Unfortunately, the immigrants also introduced new diseases to the native population, and many Hawaiians perished as a result. Honolulu flourished as the islands' major port and the center for the Pacific whaling industry. The islands were temporarily ruled by the British, but became a sovereign kingdom again in 1843. Seven years later, Honolulu was proclaimed the capital of the kingdom by King Kamehameha III. In 1893, the monarchy, then ruled by Queen Liliuokalani, was overthrown, and the following year the Republic of Hawaii was established. Honolulu and other areas of the islands were annexed by the United States in 1898, and Hawaii became a territory of the U.S in 1900. The County of Oahu was incorporated in 1905, and was renamed the City and County of Honolulu two years later.

During the early 20th Century, Honolulu grew as a center for pineapple and sugar production, cattle ranching and tourism. Defense also became important to the area economy when the U.S. Navy established their Pacific headquarters at Pearl Harbor. Honolulu was thrust into the spotlight when the Japanese attacked Pearl Harbor on December 7, 1941, signaling the beginning of the United States' involvement in World War II. Pearl Harbor served as an important Pacific military base throughout the war. In 1959, Hawaii became the nation's 50th state, and Honolulu was chosen as it's capital.

Today, the City and County of Honolulu, which encompasses the island of Oahu and some surrounding islets, is home to more than 860,000 people. More than 395,000 of Honolulu's population live in the city itself, which is technically a "Census Designated Place," rather than an incorporated community, as are the remaining cities on the island. Honolulu remains the governmental and economic center of the State of Hawaii, and is also one of the world's most popular tourist destinations.

Population

1990 Census 377,059
1998 Estimate. 395,789
% Change 5.0

Racial/Ethnic Breakdown

White. 26.7%
Black 1.3%
Other. 72.0%
Hispanic Origin (may be of any race) 4.6%

Age Breakdown

Under 5 years. 5.5%
5 to 17. . . . . 13.6%
18 to 20. . . . . 4.0%
21 to 24. . . . . 6.1%
25 to 34. . . . . 17.6%
35 to 44. . . . . 16.2%
45 to 54. . . . . 10.8%
55 to 64. . . . . 10.3%

65 to 74 .... 9.8%
75+ years 6.2%
Median Age 36.9

Gender Breakdown
Male 49.4%
Female 50.6%

Government

Type of Government: Mayor-Council

Honolulu Budget & Fiscal Services Dept
530 S King St Rm 208
Honolulu, HI 96813
Phone: 808-523-4616
Fax: 808-523-4771

Honolulu City Clerk
530 S King St Rm 100
Honolulu, HI 96813
Phone: 808-523-4291
Fax: 808-527-6888

Honolulu City Council
530 S King St Rm 202
Honolulu, HI 96813
Phone: 808-527-5654
Fax: 808-523-4220

Honolulu City Hall
530 S King St
Honolulu, HI 96813
Phone: 808-523-4385

Honolulu Community Services Dept
715 S King St Rm 111
Honolulu, HI 96813
Phone: 808-527-6269
Fax: 808-527-5498

Honolulu Environmental Services Dept
650 S King St 3rd Fl
Honolulu, HI 96813
Phone: 808-527-6663
Fax: 808-527-6675

Honolulu Fire Dept
3375 Koapaka St Suite H425
Honolulu, HI 96819
Phone: 808-831-7771
Fax: 808-831-7777

Honolulu Human Resources Dept
550 S King St
Honolulu, HI 96813
Phone: 808-523-4809
Fax: 808-527-5563

Honolulu Mayor
530 S King St
Honolulu, HI 96813
Phone: 808-523-4141
Fax: 808-527-5552

Honolulu Medical Examiner Dept
835 Iwilei Rd
Honolulu, HI 96817
Phone: 808-527-6777
Fax: 808-524-8797

Honolulu Parks & Recreation Dept
650 S King St
Honolulu, HI 96813
Phone: 808-527-6343
Fax: 808-523-4054

Honolulu Planning & Permitting Dept
650 S King St 8th Fl
Honolulu, HI 96813
Phone: 808-523-4432
Fax: 808-523-4950

Honolulu Police Dept
801 S Beretania St
Honolulu, HI 96813
Phone: 808-529-3111
Fax: 808-529-3030

Honolulu Transportation Services Dept
711 Kapiolani Blvd Suite 1200
Honolulu, HI 96813
Phone: 808-523-4125
Fax: 808-523-4730

Honolulu Water Supply Board
630 S Beretania St
Honolulu, HI 96843
Phone: 808-527-6180
Fax: 808-533-2714

Important Phone Numbers

AAA 808-593-2221
American Express Travel 808-946-7741
Dental Referral 808-593-7956
Driver's License/Vehicle Registration Information ... 808-532-7700
Emergency 911
Hawaii State Tax Office Taxpayer Service Branch 800-222-3229
Honolulu Board of Realtors 808-732-3000
Honolulu Real Property Tax Office 808-523-4856
HotelDocs 800-468-3537
Medical Referral 808-536-7702
Poison Control Center 808-941-4411
Travelers Aid 808-926-8274
Voter Registration Information 808-523-4293
Weather 808-973-5286

Information Sources

Better Business Bureau Serving Hawaii
1132 Bishop St Suite 1507
Honolulu, HI 96813
www.hawaii.bbb.org
Phone: 808-536-6956
Fax: 808-523-2335

Hawaii Chamber of Commerce
1132 Bishop St Suite 402
Honolulu, HI 96813
www.cochawaii.com
Phone: 808-545-4300
Fax: 808-545-4369

Hawaii Visitors & Convention Bureau
2270 Kalakaua Ave Suite 801
Honolulu, HI 96815
www.gohawaii.com
Phone: 808-923-1811
Fax: 808-924-0290
TF: 800-464-2924

Honolulu County
530 S King St
Honolulu, HI 96813
www.co.honolulu.hi.us
Phone: 808-523-4352
Fax: 808-527-6888

Neal S Blaisdel Center
777 Ward Ave
Honolulu, HI 96814
Phone: 808-527-5400
Fax: 808-527-5499

Online Resources

4Honolulu.com
www.4honolulu.com

About.com Guide to Honolulu/Oahu
honolulu.about.com/local/alaskahawaii/honolulu

Access America Honolulu
www.accessamer.com/honolulu_oahu/

Area Guide Honolulu
honolulu.areaguides.net

Boulevards Honolulu
www.honolulu.com

City Knowledge Honolulu
www.cityknowledge.com/hi_honolulu.htm

Excite.com Honolulu City Guide
www.excite.com/travel/countries/united_states/hawaii/honolulu

Gayot's Guide Restaurant Search Hawaii
www.perrier.com/restaurants/gayot.asp?area=HAW

HotelGuide Honolulu
hotelguide.net/honolulu

Rough Guide Travel Honolulu
travel.roughguides.com/content/1623/

Area Communities

Communities (Census Designated Places) in Honolulu County with populations greater than 10,000 include Eva Beach, Halawa, Kailua, Kaneohe, Mililani Town, Mokapu, Pearl City, Schofield Barracks, Wahiawa, Waimalu, Waipahu, and Waipio.

Economy

Honolulu is the economic center for the State of Hawaii. Government plays a dominant role in the area's economy - not only is Honolulu the state capital and the county seat, the city and surrounding area are also home to three military installations - Pearl Harbor Naval Base, Hickam Air Force Base, and Tripler Army Medical Center. A world-renowned vacation destination, tourism continues to have a major impact on Honolulu's economy-nearly 17,000 people in the City and County of Honolulu are employed in the hotel industry alone. Retail trade is the area's third largest employment sector, providing jobs for more than 79,000 on Oahu.

Unemployment Rate	5.4%*
Per Capita Income	$27,259*
Median Family Income	$45,227*

** Information given is for the City & County of Honolulu.*

Principal Industries & Number of Wage Earners

Honolulu MSA* - 1999

Construction & Mining	15,900
Finance, Insurance & Real Estate	27,950
Government	90,500
Manufacturing	12,750
Retail Trade	79,650
Services & Miscellaneous	124,000
Transportation, Communications, & Utilities	31,850
Wholesale Trade	16,900

** Information given is for the Honolulu Metropolitan Statistical Area (MSA), which includes the City and County of Honolulu.*

Major Employers

Alexander & Baldwin Inc
822 Bishop St
Honolulu, HI 96813
E-mail: invrel@alexanderbaldwin.com
www.alexanderbaldwin.com
Phone: 808-525-6611
Fax: 808-525-6652

BancWest Corp
PO Box 3200
Honolulu, HI 96847
www.bancwestcorp.com
Phone: 808-525-7000
Fax: 808-525-8753
TF: 800-488-2265

City & County of Honolulu
530 S King St
Honolulu, HI 96813
www.co.honolulu.hi.us
Phone: 808-523-4352
Fax: 808-527-6888

Cutter Automotive Team
1311 Kapiolani Blvd Suite 200
Honolulu, HI 96814
Phone: 808-592-5401
Fax: 808-592-5460

Duty Free Shoppers Hawaii
3375 Koapaka St Suite 200
Honolulu, HI 96819
Phone: 808-837-3000
Fax: 808-837-3490

Hawaii Medical Service Assn
818 Keeaumoku St
Honolulu, HI 96814
www.hmsa.com
Phone: 808-948-6111
Fax: 808-948-5567

Hawaiian Airlines Inc
3375 Koapaka St Suite G350
Honolulu, HI 96819
www.hawaiianair.com
Phone: 808-835-3700
Fax: 808-835-3690
TF: 800-367-5320

Hawaiian Electric Industries Inc
900 Richards St
Honolulu, HI 96813
www.hei.com
Phone: 808-543-5662
Fax: 808-543-7966

JTB Hawaii
2155 Kalakaua Ave 9th Fl
Honolulu, HI 96815
Phone: 808-922-0200
Fax: 808-922-3473

Kapiolani Health
55 Merchant St 23rd Fl
Honolulu, HI 96813
www.kapiolani.org
Phone: 808-535-7401
Fax: 808-535-7550

Kyo-Ya Co Ltd
2255 Kalakaua Ave 2nd Fl
Honolulu, HI 96815
Phone: 808-931-8600
Fax: 808-923-0892

Liberty House of Hawaii
1450 Ala Moana Blvd
Honolulu, HI 96814
E-mail: customer.service@libertyhouse.com
www.libertyhouse.com
Phone: 808-941-2345
Fax: 808-945-8700
TF: 800-654-9970

Outrigger Hotels & Resorts
2375 Kuhio Ave
Honolulu, HI 96815
www.outrigger.com
Phone: 808-921-6600
Fax: 808-921-6655
TF: 800-688-7444

Pacific Century Financial Corp
130 Merchant St
Honolulu, HI 96813
Phone: 808-537-8272
Fax: 808-538-8131

Queen's Health Systems
1099 Alakea St Suite 1100
Honolulu, HI 96813
www.queens.org
Phone: 808-532-6100
Fax: 808-532-6118

Servco Pacific Inc
PO Box 2788
Honolulu, HI 96803
www.servco.com
Phone: 808-521-6511
Fax: 808-523-3937

Straub Clinic & Hospital
888 S King St
Honolulu, HI 96813
www.straubhealth.com
Phone: 808-522-4000
Fax: 808-522-4111

Tesoro Hawaii Corp
PO Box 3379
Honolulu, HI 96842
www.energypeople.com
Phone: 808-547-3111
Fax: 808-547-3145

Verizon Communications
PO Box 2200
Honolulu, HI 96841
www.verizon.com
Phone: 808-643-3343
Fax: 808-546-6194

Quality of Living Indicators

Total Crime Index....47,453*
(rates per 100,000 inhabitants)

Violent Crime
Murder/manslaughter.... 17*
Forcible rape 242*
Robbery....1,052*
Aggravated assault....1,031*

Property Crime
Burglary 7,692*
Larceny theft 32,669*
Motor vehicle theft....4,750*

** Information given is for the City & County of Honolulu.*

Cost of Living Index....184.0
(national average = 100)

Median Home Price....$290,000

Education

Public Schools

Hawaii Dept of Education
PO Box 2360
Honolulu, HI 96804
www.k12.hi.us
Phone: 808-586-3230
Fax: 808-586-3234

Number of Schools
Elementary.... 174
Middle 30
High.... 35

Student/Teacher Ratio
All Grades 18.1:1

Private Schools

Number of Schools (all grades).... 90+

Colleges & Universities

Chaminade University
3140 Waialae Ave
Honolulu, HI 96816
E-mail: cuhadm@lava.net
www.chaminade.edu
Phone: 808-735-4711
Fax: 808-739-4647
TF: 800-735-3733

Hawaii Pacific University
1164 Bishop St Suite 200
Honolulu, HI 96813
E-mail: admissions@hpu.edu
www.hpu.edu
Phone: 808-544-0237
Fax: 808-544-1136
TF: 800-669-4724

Heald Business College Honolulu
1500 Kapiolani Blvd
Honolulu, HI 96814
Phone: 808-955-1500
Fax: 808-955-6964

Kapiolani Community College
4303 Diamond Head Rd
Honolulu, HI 96816
www.kcc.hawaii.edu
Phone: 808-734-9559
Fax: 808-734-9545

University of Hawaii Honolulu Community College
874 Dillingham Blvd
Honolulu, HI 96817
www.hcc.hawaii.edu
Phone: 808-845-9129
Fax: 808-845-9173

University of Hawaii Manoa
2444 Dole St
Honolulu, HI 96822
www.uhm.hawaii.edu
Phone: 808-956-8111
Fax: 808-956-4148
TF: 800-823-9771

Hospitals

Kaiser Permanente Medical Center
3288 Moanalua Rd
Honolulu, HI 96819
Phone: 808-834-5333
Fax: 808-834-3990

Kuakini Medical Center
347 N Kuakini St
Honolulu, HI 96817
Phone: 808-536-2236
Fax: 808-547-9547

Queen's Medical Center
1301 Punchbowl St
Honolulu, HI 96813
www.queens.org
Phone: 808-538-9011
Fax: 808-537-7851

Saint Francis Medical Center
2230 Liliha St
Honolulu, HI 96817
www.sfhs-hi.org
Phone: 808-547-6011
Fax: 808-547-6296

Straub Clinic & Hospital
888 S King St
Honolulu, HI 96813
www.straubhealth.com
Phone: 808-522-4000
Fax: 808-522-4111

Transportation

Airport(s)

Honolulu International Airport (HNL)
5 miles NW of downtown (approx 15 minutes)....808-836-6413

Mass Transit

Bus The
$1 Base fare 808-848-4500

Utilities

Electricity
Hawaiian Electric Co Inc....808-543-7311
www.heco.com

Gas
The Gas Co....808-526-0066

Water
Honolulu Board of Water Supply....808-532-6510

Garbage Collection/Recycling
Honolulu Refuse Div 808-523-4424

Telecommunications

Telephone
Verizon Communications 808-643-3343
www.verizon.com

Cable Television
Oceanic Cablevision 808-625-8100

Internet Service Providers (ISPs)
FlexNet Inc. 808-539-3790
www.flex.com
GST Hawaii OnLine 808-791-1000
www.gst.net
Hula Net Inc. 808-522-9393
www.hula.net
internet@dvantage Inc 808-522-0615
www.iav.com
LavaNet Inc 808-545-5282
www.lava.net
Oahu Internet 808-527-2000
www.oahu.net
Pacific Global Communications Inc 808-521-1455
www.pacificglobal.net
PixiNet 808-522-9396
www.pixi.com
SliderNET 808-539-3792
www.slider.net
ViAlta.com Inc 808-523-7988
www.vizip.com

Banks

American Savings Bank FSB
915 Fort St
Honolulu, HI 96813
Phone: 808-531-6262
Fax: 808-846-4655
TF: 800-272-2566

Bank of Hawaii
111 S King St
Honolulu, HI 96813
www.boh.com
Phone: 808-538-4171
Fax: 808-693-1285
TF: 888-643-3888

Bank of Honolulu
841 Bishop St
Honolulu, HI 96813
Phone: 808-543-3700
Fax: 808-543-3747

Central Pacific Bank
220 S King St
Honolulu, HI 96813
www.cpbi.com
Phone: 808-544-0500
Fax: 808-531-2982

City Bank
201 Merchant St
Honolulu, HI 96813
Phone: 808-535-2500
Fax: 808-546-2435

First Hawaiian Bank
999 Bishop St
Honolulu, HI 96813
www.fhb.com
Phone: 808-525-7153
Fax: 808-525-8708
TF: 800-843-8411

Hawaii National Bank
45 N King St
Honolulu, HI 96817
Phone: 808-528-7711
Fax: 808-528-7773

Shopping

Ala Moana Shopping Center
1450 Ala Moana Blvd
Honolulu, HI 96814
www.alamoana.com
Phone: 808-955-9517
Fax: 808-946-2216

Aloha Tower Marketplace
1 Aloha Tower Dr
Honolulu, HI 96813
E-mail: olc@olaha.net
www.alohatower.com/
Phone: 808-528-5700
Fax: 808-524-8334

Hilo Hattie Store of Hawaii
700 N Nimitz Hwy
Honolulu, HI 96817
Phone: 808-537-2926

International Marketplace
2330 Kalakaua Ave Suite 200
Honolulu, HI 96815
Phone: 808-971-2080
Fax: 808-971-2090

Koko Marina Shopping Center
7192 Kalanianaole Hwy Suite G205
Honolulu, HI 96825
Phone: 808-395-4737
Fax: 808-396-8656

Liberty House of Hawaii
1450 Ala Moana Blvd
Honolulu, HI 96814
E-mail: customer.service@libertyhouse.com
www.libertyhouse.com
Phone: 808-941-2345
Fax: 808-945-8700
TF: 800-654-9970

Pearlridge Center
231 Pearlridge Ctr
Aiea, HI 96701
Phone: 808-488-0981
Fax: 808-488-9456

Royal Hawaiian Heritage Jewelry
1525 Kalakaua Ave
Honolulu, HI 96826
www.rhhj.com
Phone: 808-942-7474
Fax: 808-942-5454

Royal Hawaiian Shopping Center
2201 Kalakaua Ave
Honolulu, HI 96815
Phone: 808-922-0588
Fax: 808-922-0961

Waikele Premium Outlet
94790 Lumiaina St
Waipahu, HI 96797
Phone: 808-676-5656
Fax: 808-676-9700

Waikiki Town Center
2301 Kuhio Ave Suite 304
Honolulu, HI 96815
Phone: 808-922-2724
Fax: 808-924-7168

Ward Centre
1200 Ala Moana Blvd
Honolulu, HI 96814
www.victoriaward.com
Phone: 808-591-8411
Fax: 808-596-4919

Media

Newspapers and Magazines

Hawaii Art News & Directory
PO Box 586
Kahuku, HI 96731
E-mail: artnews@lava.net
www.hawaiiartnews.com
Phone: 808-293-5683
Fax: 808-293-5314

Honolulu Advertiser* Phone: 808-525-8000
PO Box 3110 Fax: 808-525-8037
Honolulu, HI 96802
www.thehonoluluadvertiser.com

Honolulu Magazine Phone: 808-524-7400
36 Merchant St Fax: 808-531-2306
Honolulu, HI 96813 TF: 800-272-5245
E-mail: honmag@pixi.com
honpub.com/hnl/hnlintro.htm

Honolulu Star-Bulletin* Phone: 808-525-8000
PO Box 3080 Fax: 808-523-8509
Honolulu, HI 96802
E-mail: editor@starbulletin.com
www.starbulletin.com

Island Business Phone: 808-524-7400
36 Merchant St Fax: 808-531-2306
Honolulu, HI 96813 TF: 800-788-4230
www.honpub.com

**Indicates major daily newspapers*

Television

KBFD-TV Ch 32 (Ind) Phone: 808-521-8066
1188 Bishop St PH 1 Fax: 808-521-5233
Honolulu, HI 96813
www.kbfd.com

KGMB-TV Ch 9 (CBS) Phone: 808-973-5462
1534 Kapiolani Blvd Fax: 808-941-8153
Honolulu, HI 96814
www.kgmb.com

KHET-TV Ch 10 (PBS) Phone: 808-973-1000
2350 Dole St Fax: 808-973-1090
Honolulu, HI 96822
E-mail: e_mail@khet.pbs.org
www.khet.org

KHNL-TV Ch 13 (NBC) Phone: 808-847-3246
150-B Puuhale Rd Fax: 808-845-3616
Honolulu, HI 96819
www.khnl.com

KHON-TV Ch 2 (Fox) Phone: 808-591-4278
1170 Auahi St Fax: 808-593-2418
Honolulu, HI 96814
E-mail: khon@pixi.com
www.khon.com

KIKU-TV Ch 20 (Ind) Phone: 808-847-2021
197 Sand Island Access Rd Suite 2021 Fax: 808-841-3326
Honolulu, HI 96819
E-mail: kikutv@lava.net
www.kikutv.com

KITV-TV Ch 4 (ABC) Phone: 808-593-4444
1290 Ala Moana Blvd Fax: 808-593-9446
Honolulu, HI 96814
E-mail: news4@kitv.com
www.kitv.com

KPXO-TV Ch 66 (PAX) Phone: 808-591-1275
875 Waimanu St Suite 601 Fax: 808-591-1409
Honolulu, HI 96813
www.pax.net/KPXO

Radio

KAIM-FM 95.5 MHz (Rel) Phone: 808-735-2424
3555 Harding Ave Fax: 808-735-2428
Honolulu, HI 96816
E-mail: kaim@kaimradio.org
www.kaimradio.org

KCCN-AM 1420 kHz (Misc) Phone: 808-536-2728
900 Fort St Mall Suite 400 Fax: 808-536-2528
Honolulu, HI 96813

KCCN-FM 100.3 MHz (CHR) Phone: 808-536-2728
900 Fort St Suite 700 Fax: 808-536-2528
Honolulu, HI 96813
E-mail: info@kccnfm100.com
www.kccnfm100.com

KGMZ-AM 1460 kHz (Oldies) Phone: 808-254-3596
970 N Kalaheo Ave Suite C-107 Fax: 808-254-3299
Kailua, HI 96734
www.oldiesradio.net

KGMZ-FM 107.9 MHz (Oldies) Phone: 808-254-3596
970 N Kalaheo Ave Suite C-107 Fax: 808-254-3299
Kailua, HI 96734
www.oldiesradio.net

KHNR-AM 650 kHz (NPR) Phone: 808-533-0065
560 N Nimitz Hwy Suite 114-B Fax: 808-528-5467
Honolulu, HI 96817
E-mail: khnr@gte.net
home1.gte.net/khnr

KHPR-FM 88.1 MHz (NPR) Phone: 808-955-8821
738 Kaheka St Fax: 808-942-5477
Honolulu, HI 96814
E-mail: hpr@lava.net
www.hawaiipublicradio.org

KHVH-AM 830 kHz (N/T) Phone: 808-521-8383
345 Queen St Suite 601 Fax: 808-531-0083
Honolulu, HI 96813

KIKI-AM 990 kHz (CHR) Phone: 808-841-8300
650 Iwilei Rd Suite 400 Fax: 808-550-9510
Honolulu, HI 96817

KIKI-FM 93.9 MHz (CHR) Phone: 808-531-4602
345 Queen St Suite 601 Fax: 808-531-4606
Honolulu, HI 96813

KKHN-FM 102.7 MHz (Ctry) Phone: 808-591-9369
1833 Kalakaua Ave Suite 500 Fax: 808-591-9349
Honolulu, HI 96815
E-mail: kkhn@hawaiiradio.com
www.kkhn.net

KLHT-AM 1040 kHz (Rel) Phone: 808-524-1040
1190 Nuuanu Ave Fax: 808-524-0998
Honolulu, HI 96817

KNDI-AM 1270 kHz (Rel) Phone: 808-946-2844
1734 S King St Fax: 808-947-3531
Honolulu, HI 96826

KORL-FM 99.5 MHz (AC) Phone: 808-591-9369
1833 Kalakaua Ave Suite 500 Fax: 808-593-8946
Honolulu, HI 96815
www.korl.net

KPOI-FM 97.5 MHz (Alt) Phone: 808-591-9369
711 Kapiolani Blvd Suite 1193 Fax: 808-591-9349
Honolulu, HI 96813

KQMQ-AM 690 kHz (CHR) Phone: 808-591-9369
1833 Kalakaua Ave Suite 500 Fax: 808-591-9349
Honolulu, HI 96815
www.hawaiiradio.com

KQMQ-FM 93.1 MHz (CHR) Phone: 808-591-9369
1833 Kalakaua Ave Suite 500 Fax: 808-591-9349
Honolulu, HI 96815
www.hawaiiradio.com

KRTR-FM 96.3 MHz (AC) Phone: 808-254-3596
970 N Kalaheo Ave Suite C-107 Fax: 808-254-3299
Kailua, HI 96734
www.krater96.com

KSSK-AM 590 kHz (AC) Phone: 808-550-9200
650 Iwilei Rd Suite 400 Fax: 808-550-9288
Honolulu, HI 96817
E-mail: kssk@pixi.com
www.ksskradio.com

KSSK-FM 92.3 MHz (AC) Phone: 808-550-9200
650 Iwilei Rd Suite 400 Fax: 808-550-9288
Honolulu, HI 96817
www.ksskradio.com

KUCD-FM 101.9 MHz (Jazz) Phone: 808-841-8300
1505 Dillingham Blvd Suite 208 Fax: 808-842-1019
Honolulu, HI 96817

KUMU-AM 1500 kHz (AC) Phone: 808-947-1500
765 Amana St Suite 206 Fax: 808-947-1506
Honolulu, HI 96814
www.kumu.com

KUMU-FM 94.7 MHz (B/EZ) Phone: 808-947-1500
765 Amana St Suite 206 Fax: 808-947-1506
Honolulu, HI 96814
www.kumu.com

KXME-FM 104.3 MHz (CHR) Phone: 808-254-3596
970 N Kalaheo Ave Suite C-107 Fax: 808-254-3299
Kailua, HI 96734
E-mail: programdirector@xtremehawaii.com
www.xtremeradiohawaii.com

Attractions

Located on the island of Oahu, Honolulu attracts close to five million visitors a year. The city and surrounding areas offer a variety of attractions, including world-famous Waikiki Beach, Diamond Head State Park, and Waimea Falls Park, with archaeological sites and several varieties of exotic tropical flora. Outdoor recreational activities such as rainforest hikes, outrigger canoe rides, and volcano climbs are all available within an hour's drive from Honolulu. At Pearl Harbor, one can see the USS Arizona Memorial as well as the USS Bowfin, an actual WWII submarine. The National Memorial Cemetery of the Pacific, the resting place for more than 25,000 servicemen and women, provides a panoramic view of the Harbor, Waikiki, and Honolulu.

Ala Moana Regional Park Phone: 808-523-4182
1201 Ala Moana Blvd Fax: 808-523-4054
Honolulu, HI 96814

Aloha Tower Marketplace Phone: 808-528-5700
1 Aloha Tower Dr Fax: 808-524-8334
Honolulu, HI 96813
E-mail: olc@olaha.net
www.alohatower.com/

Arizona Memorial Museum Assn Phone: 808-422-5664
1 Arizona Memorial Pl
Honolulu, HI 96818
E-mail: azmemph@aol.com
members.aol.com/azmemph

Bishop Museum Phone: 808-847-3511
1525 Bernice St Fax: 808-841-8968
Honolulu, HI 96817
www.bishop.hawaii.org

Blaisdell Neal S Center Concert Hall Phone: 808-527-5400
777 Ward Ave Fax: 808-527-5499
Honolulu, HI 96814
www.co.honolulu.hi.us/Depts/aud/blaisd/concert

Children's Discovery Center Phone: 808-524-5437
111 Ohe St Fax: 808-524-5433
Honolulu, HI 96813

Diamond Head State Park Phone: 808-587-0300
Diamond Head Rd & 18th Ave Fax: 808-587-0311
Honolulu, HI 96809

Dole Cannery Square Phone: 808-528-2236
650 Iwilei Rd Fax: 808-531-3159
Honolulu, HI 96817

Dole Plantation Phone: 808-621-8408
64-1550 Kamehameha Hwy Fax: 808-621-1926
Wahiawa, HI 96786

Foster Botanical Garden Phone: 808-522-7066
50 N Vineyard Blvd Fax: 808-522-7050
Honolulu, HI 96817

Hawaii Army Museum Society Phone: 808-955-9552
Fort Derussy Fax: 808-941-3617
Honolulu, HI 96815
www.aloha-lestweforget.com

Hawaii Contemporary Museum Phone: 808-526-0232
2411 Makiki Heights Dr Fax: 808-536-5973
Honolulu, HI 96822
www.tcmhi.org

Hawaii IMAX Theatre Phone: 808-923-4629
325 Seaside Ave Fax: 808-923-2707
Honolulu, HI 96815

Hawaii Okinawa Center Phone: 808-676-5400
94-587 Ukee St
Waipahu, HI 96797

Hawaii Opera Theatre Phone: 808-596-7372
987 Waimanu St Fax: 808-596-0379
Honolulu, HI 96814

Hawaii State Ballet Phone: 808-947-2755
1418 Kaplolani Blvd
Honolulu, HI 96814

Hawaii's Plantation Village
94-695 Waipahu St
Waipahu, HI 96797
Phone: 808-677-0110
Fax: 808-676-6727

Hawaiian Waters Adventure Park
400 Farrington Hwy
Kapolei, HI 96707
E-mail: reservations@hawaiianwaters.com
www.hawaiianwaters.com
Phone: 808-674-9283

Honolulu Academy of Arts
900 S Beretania St
Honolulu, HI 96814
www.honoluluacademy.org/
Phone: 808-532-8700
Fax: 808-532-8787

Honolulu Botanical Gardens
50 N Vineyard Blvd
Honolulu, HI 96817
Phone: 808-522-7060
Fax: 808-522-7050

Honolulu Dance Theatre
3041 Manoa Rd
Honolulu, HI 96822
E-mail: hdt@pixi.com
www.pixi.com/~hdt
Phone: 808-988-3202
Fax: 808-988-5199

Honolulu Symphony Orchestra
650 Iwilei Rd Suite 202
Honolulu, HI 96817
Phone: 808-524-0815
Fax: 808-524-1507

Honolulu Zoo
151 Kapahulu Ave
Honolulu, HI 96815
www.honoluluzoo.org/
Phone: 808-971-7175
Fax: 808-971-7173

Iolani Palace
PO Box 2259
Honolulu, HI 96804
alaike.lcc.hawaii.edu/openstudio/iolani
Phone: 808-538-1471
Fax: 808-532-1051

Japanese Cultural Center of Hawaii
2454 S Beretania St
Honolulu, HI 96826
www.jcch.com
Phone: 808-945-7633
Fax: 808-944-1123

Judiciary History Center
417 S King St
Honolulu, HI 96813
www.jhchawaii.org
Phone: 808-539-4999
Fax: 808-539-4996

Kapiolani Regional Park
2805 Monsarrat Ave
Honolulu, HI 96815
Phone: 808-523-4182

Mission Houses Museum
553 S King St
Honolulu, HI 96813
E-mail: mlm@lava.net
www.lava.net/~mhm/main.htm
Phone: 808-531-0481
Fax: 808-545-2280

National Memorial Cemetery of the Pacific
2177 Puowaina Dr
Honolulu, HI 96813
Phone: 808-532-3720
Fax: 808-532-3756

Pacific Aerospace Museum
Honolulu International Airport
Honolulu, HI 96819
Phone: 808-839-0777
Fax: 808-836-3267

Paradise Cove Luau
92-1089 Aliinui Dr
Kapolei, HI 96707
www.paradisecovehawaii.com
Phone: 808-973-5828
Fax: 808-679-0007
TF: 800-775-2683

Polynesian Cultural Center
55-370 Kamehameha Hwy
Laie, HI 96762
www.polynesia.com
Phone: 808-293-3000
Fax: 808-293-3027

Pu'uhonua O Honaunau National Historical Park
PO Box 129
Honaunau, HI 96726
www.nps.gov/puho/
Phone: 808-328-2326
Fax: 808-328-9485

Queen Emma Summer Palace
2913 Pali Hwy
Honolulu, HI 96817
Phone: 808-595-3167
Fax: 808-595-4395

Royal Hawaiian Hotel Luau
2259 Kalakaua Ave
Honolulu, HI 96815
Phone: 808-931-7194
Fax: 808-931-7188
TF: 800-325-3535

Sea Life Park
41-202 Kalanianaole Hwy
Waimanalo, HI 96795
E-mail: slp@atlantisadventures.com
www.atlantisadventures.com/slp
Phone: 808-259-7933
Fax: 808-259-7373

Sheraton's Spectacular Polynesian Revue
120 Kaiulani Ave 2nd Fl
Honolulu, HI 96815
Phone: 808-931-4660
Fax: 808-931-4653

Tropic Lightning Museum
Schofield Barracks Carter Hall Waianae Ave
Honolulu, HI 96857
Phone: 808-655-0438
Fax: 808-655-8301

US Army Museum of Hawaii
Fort DeRussy
Waikiki, HI 96815
Phone: 808-438-2821
Fax: 808-438-2819

USS Arizona Memorial
1 Arizona Memorial Pl
Honolulu, HI 96818
www.nps.gov/usar/
Phone: 808-422-2772
Fax: 808-541-3168

USS Bowfin Submarine Museum & Park
11 Arizona Memorial Dr
Honolulu, HI 96818
E-mail: bowfin@aloha.net
www.aloha.net/~bowfin/
Phone: 808-423-1341
Fax: 808-422-5201

USS Missouri Memorial
1 Arizona Memorial Pl USS Bowfin Submarine Museum
Honolulu, HI 96818
www.ussmissouri.com
Phone: 808-423-2263
Fax: 808-423-0700
TF: 888-877-6477

Waikiki Aquarium
2777 Kalakaua Ave
Honolulu, HI 96815
waquarium.mic.hawaii.edu
Phone: 808-923-9741
Fax: 808-923-1771

Waikiki Beach
Honolulu, HI 96815
Phone: 808-923-1811
Fax: 808-924-0290

Waimea Valley Park
59-864 Kamehameha Hwy
Haleiwa, HI 96712
www.atlantisadventures.com/wv
Phone: 808-638-8511
Fax: 808-638-7900

Wyland Galleries Hawaii
66-150 Kamehameha Hwy
Haleiwa, HI 96712
Phone: 808-637-7498
Fax: 808-637-3700

Sports Teams & Facilities

Blaisdell Center Arena
777 Ward Ave
Honolulu, HI 96814
www.co.honolulu.hi.us/Depts/aud/blaisd/arena/index.htm
Phone: 808-527-5400
Fax: 808-527-5499

Hawaii Island Movers (baseball)
Rainbow Stadium University of Hawaii
Honolulu, HI 96817
Phone: 808-832-4805
Fax: 808-841-2321

Annual Events

Ala Wai Challenge (late January) .808-923-1800
Aloha Bowl (December 25) .808-947-4141
Aloha Festivals O'ahu (mid-late September) .808-589-1771
Bank of Hawaii Ki Ho Alu Festival (mid-August) .808-537-8615
Bankoh Nawahineokekai Championship Long Distance Canoe Races (September-October) .808-537-8658
Bud Light Tin Man Triathalon (mid-July) .808-923-1811
Cherry Blossom Festival Culture & Craft Fair (early March) .808-949-2255
Cinco de Mayo Fun Run & Festival (early May) .808-854-5434
Downtown Faire (early May) .808-521-8941
Fancy Fair (mid-June) .808-531-0481
Festival of Trees (late November-early December) .808-547-4397
Great Hawaiian Rubber Duckie Race (late March) .808-532-6744
Hawaii International Film Festival (November) .808-528-3456
Hawaii International Jazz Festival (mid-July) .808-941-9974
Hawaii Mardi Gras Celebration (late February) .808-923-1811
Hawaii Public Radio Wine Classic Tasting & Auction (early March) .808-955-8821
Hawaii World Music Fest (late November) .808-550-2000
Hawaiian Scottish Festival & Games (early April) .808-235-7605
Honolulu Downtown Jazz Festival (mid-February) .808-923-1811
Honolulu Festival & Parade (mid-March) .808-922-0254
Honolulu International Bed Race Festival (late April) .808-923-1811
Honolulu Marathon (mid-December) .808-734-7200
Hula Bowl (late January) .808-947-4141
Ironman Triathlon (October) .808-329-0063
King Kamehameha Celebration Floral Parade (mid-June) .808-586-0333
King Kamehameha Day Celebration (mid-June) .808-935-9338
Lei Day Celebration (early May) .808-266-7654
Made in Hawaii Festival (mid-August) .808-533-1292
Matsuri in Hawaii Festival (mid-June) .808-926-0647
Merrie Monarch Festival (early April) .808-935-9168
Narcissus Festival (January-February) .808-923-1811
Narcissus Festival/Night in Chinatown (late January) .808-533-3181
NFL Pro Bowl (early February) .808-486-9500
Outrigger Hotels Hawaiian Oceanfest (late May-early June) .808-521-4322
Pacific Handcrafters Guild Christmas Festival of Art & Fine Crafts (early December) .808-637-1248
Pan-Pacific Festival Matsuri in Hawaii Celebration (mid-June) .808-923-0492
Rainbow Classic (late December) .808-956-6501
Saint Patrick's Day Parade (March 17) .808-923-1811
Taste of Honolulu (late June) .808-536-1015
Triple Crown of Surfing (mid-November-mid-December) .808-637-4558
Warrior Society Pow Wow (early May) .808-947-3206
World Invitational Hula Festival (early-mid-November) .808-486-3185

Houston, Texas

County: **Harris**

HOUSTON is located in southeastern Texas, 50 miles from the Gulf of Mexico. Major cities within 100 miles include Beaumont and Galveston, Texas.

Area (Land) .... 527.1 sq mi
Area (Water)............................... 21.8 sq mi
Elevation.. 55 ft
Latitude ....29-76-31 N
Longitude................................ 95-36-31 W
Time Zone ....CST
Area Code...................................713, 281

Climate

Houston has a marine climate that is greatly influenced by its proximity to the Gulf of Mexico. Gulf breezes moderate the temperature throughout the year. Humidity is high during the summer months, when high temperatures average in the low 90s. Summer evening temperatures cool down to around 70 degrees. Winters are generally mild, with average high temperatures ranging from the low 60s to the low 70s. Winter low temperatures generally average in the 40s. May and June are the wettest months in Houston; February and March are the driest.

Average Temperatures & Precipitation

Temperatures

	Jan	Feb	Mar	Apr	May	Jun	Jul	Aug	Sep	Oct	Nov	Dec
High	61	65	71	78	85	90	90	93	93	88	81	72
Low	40	43	50	58	64	64	71	72	72	68	58	50

Precipitation

	Jan	Feb	Mar	Apr	May	Jun	Jul	Aug	Sep	Oct	Nov	Dec
Inches	3.3	3.0	2.9	3.2	5.2	5.0	3.6	3.5	4.9	4.3	3.8	3.5

History

Named in honor of Texas Revolutionary hero General Sam Houston, the city of Houston was founded in 1836 by brothers Augustus and John Allen. Their intent was to create a city and make it the capital of the Republic of Texas. Houston indeed served as the state's capital from its incorporation in 1837 until 1840, when Austin was chosen as the new capital city due to its more centralized location. After losing its position as the state capital, Houston was left to find an alternate source of economic growth. Over the course of the next 74 years, the city (located 50 miles inland from the Gulf of Mexico) developed its potential to become a major distribution center. The Buffalo Bayou was transformed into the Houston Ship Channel, which linked Houston with the Gulf of Mexico via the Port of Houston, thus opening the door for international trade. A system of railroads linked Houston with other major cities in the United States, and the city became a major center for distribution.

In the early 1900s, oil was discovered in East Texas, and Houston became a major world center for the energy industry. Oil refineries sprang up along the Houston Ship Channel during the 1920s and '30s, and Houston's economy flourished and its population soared. In 1930, Houston was home to 292,352 residents, and by 1955 the population had reached one million. During the oil boom of the 1970s, Houston led the nation in housing starts, as the oil industry began to spill over into other sectors of the economy, including real estate, banking, and services.

Nicknamed "Space City," Houston is also well-known as an aerospace center. During the early 1960's the city became a leader in aerospace research with the opening of NASA's Johnson Space Center, located just outside the city, which is the nucleus of the United States' manned space flight program. It was from that facility that the first words spoken from the surface of the moon on July 29, 1969 were broadcast throughout the world.

Houston's population continues to grow steadily. Now home to more than 1.7 million people, Houston is the largest city in the state of Texas and the fourth largest city in the United States.

Population

1990 Census 1,630,864
1998 Estimate............................ 1,786,691
% Change 8.0
2005 Projection 4,433,600*

Racial/Ethnic Breakdown

White.................................. 52.6%
Black 28.1%
Other.................................. 19.3%
Hispanic Origin (may be of any race) 27.6%

Age Breakdown

Under 5 years............................ 8.3%
5 to 17................................. 18.4%
18 to 20................................. 4.8%
21 to 24................................. 7.2%
25 to 34................................ 20.8%
35 to 44................................ 15.4%
45 to 54................................. 9.5%
55 to 64................................. 7.3%
65 to 74................................. 5.0%
75+ years 3.2%
Median Age...............................30.4

Gender Breakdown

Male.................................. 49.6%
Female................................. 50.4%

** Information given is for the Houston Primary Metropolitan Statistical Area (PMSA), which includes Chambers, Fort Bend, Harris, Liberty, Montgomery, and Waller counties.*

Government

Type of Government: Mayor-Council

Houston City Council
PO Box 1562
Houston, TX 77251
Phone: 713-247-2099
Fax: 713-247-2676

Houston City Hall
901 Bagby St
Houston, TX 77002
Phone: 713-247-1000
Fax: 713-247-3439

Houston City Secretary
PO Box 1562
Houston, TX 77251
Phone: 713-247-1840
Fax: 713-247-1907

Houston Finance & Administration Dept
611 Walker St Suite 2532
Houston, TX 77002
Phone: 713-837-9888
Fax: 713-837-9879

Houston Fire Dept
1205 Dart St
Houston, TX 77007
Phone: 713-247-5000
Fax: 713-247-5081

Houston Housing & Community Development Dept
601 Sawyer 4th Fl
Houston, TX 77007
Phone: 713-868-8300
Fax: 713-868-8306

Houston Human Resources Dept
611 Walker St
Houston, TX 77002
Phone: 713-837-9300
Fax: 713-837-9486

Houston Legal Dept
PO Box 1562
Houston, TX 77251
Phone: 713-247-2745
Fax: 713-247-1195

Houston Mayor
901 Bagby St 3rd Fl
Houston, TX 77002
Phone: 713-247-2200
Fax: 713-247-2355

Houston Parks & Recreation Dept
2999 S Wayside Dr
Houston, TX 77023
Phone: 713-845-1000
Fax: 713-845-1262

Houston Planning & Development Dept
PO Box 1562
Houston, TX 77251
Phone: 713-837-7701
Fax: 713-837-7921

Houston Police Dept
1200 Travis St
Houston, TX 77002
Phone: 713-247-5420
Fax: 713-247-5543

Houston Public Library
500 McKinney St
Houston, TX 77002
Phone: 713-236-1313

Houston Public Utilities Div
PO Box 1560
Houston, TX 77097
Phone: 713-371-1400
Fax: 713-371-1130

Houston Public Works & Engineering Dept
611 Walker St
Houston, TX 77002
Phone: 713-837-0050

Important Phone Numbers

AAA.....713-524-1851
American Express Travel.....713-658-1114
Dental Referral.....713-961-4337
Driver's License Information.....713-681-6187
Emergency.....911
Harris County Tax Assessor & Collector.....713-224-1919
Highway Conditions.....800-452-9292
HISD Property Tax Information.....713-892-7700
HotelDocs.....800-468-3537
Houston Board of Realtors.....713-629-1900
Medical Referral.....713-794-6000
Poison Control Center.....800-764-7661
Texas State Property Tax Board.....800-252-9121
Texas State Sales Tax Information.....713-868-9112
Time/Temp.....713-529-4444
Travelers Aid.....713-526-8300
Vehicle Registration Information.....713-224-1919
Voter Registration Information.....713-224-1919
Weather.....713-529-4444

Information Sources

Better Business Bureau Serving Houston
5225 Katy Fwy Suite 500
Houston, TX 77007
www.bbbhou.org
Phone: 713-868-9500
Fax: 713-867-4947

Brown George R Convention Center
1001 Avenida de Las Americas
Houston, TX 77010
Phone: 713-853-8001
Fax: 713-853-8090
TF: 800-427-4697

Greater Houston Convention & Visitors Bureau
901 Bagby St
Houston, TX 77002
www.houston-guide.com/
Phone: 713-437-5200
Fax: 713-227-6336
TF: 800-446-8786

Greater Houston Partnership
1200 Smith St Suite 700
Houston, TX 77002
www.houston.org
Phone: 713-844-3600
Fax: 713-844-0200

Harris County
1001 Preston St
Houston, TX 77002
www.co.harris.tx.us
Phone: 713-755-5000
Fax: 713-755-4977

Online Resources

4Houston.com
www.2houston.com

About.com Guide to Houston: Downtown
houston.about.com/local/southwestus/houston

About.com Guide to Houston: Northwest
houstonnw.about.com/citiestowns/southwestus/houstonnw

Annual Guide for the Arts
www.guide4arts.com/tx/

Anthill City Guide Houston
www.anthill.com/city.asp?city=houston

Area Guide Houston
houston.areaguides.net

Around Houston Index & Directory
aroundhouston.com

Bradmans.com Houston
www.bradmans.com/scripts/display_city.cgi?city=236

City Knowledge Houston
www.cityknowledge.com/tx_houston.htm

CitySearch Houston
houston.citysearch.com

CuisineNet Houston
www.menusonline.com/cities/houston/locmain.shtml

DigitalCity Houston
home.digitalcity.com/houston

Excite.com Houston City Guide
www.excite.com/travel/countries/united_states/texas/houston

Gay Web Resource Guide to Houston
www.houstongayweb.com/

HotelGuide Houston
hotelguide.net/houston

Houston City Pages
houston.thelinks.com

Houston Eats
www.webside.com/eats

Houston Interactive Map & Guide
www.houstonet.com/

Houston Relocation Council
pmadt.com/houreloc

HoustonSites
www.houstonsites.com

Lodging.com Houston Texas
www.lodging.com/auto/guides/houston-area-tx.html

Official Guide to Houston
houston-guide.com

Rough Guide Travel Houston
travel.roughguides.com/content/909/

Texas On-Line
www.texas-on-line.com/graphic/houston.htm

Virtual Voyages Houston
www.virtualvoyages.com/usa/tx/houston/houston.sht

Area Communities

Communities in the the Houston Primary Metropolitan Statistical Area (PMSA), which includes Chambers, Fort Bend, Harris, Liberty, Montgomery, and Waller counties, with populations greater than 10,000 include:

Baytown
PO Box 424
Baytown, TX 77522
Phone: 281-422-8281
Fax: 281-420-6586

Bellaire
7008 S Rice Ave
Bellaire, TX 77401
Phone: 713-662-8222
Fax: 713-662-8212

Conroe
PO Box 3066
Conroe, TX 77305
Phone: 936-539-4431
Fax: 936-525-4777

Deer Park
PO Box 700
Deer Park, TX 77536
Phone: 281-479-2394
Fax: 281-478-7217

Friendswood
910 S Friendswood Dr
Friendswood, TX 77546
Phone: 281-996-3200
Fax: 281-482-6491

Galena Park
2000 Clinton Dr
Galena Park, TX 77547
Phone: 713-672-2556
Fax: 713-672-1840

Humble
114 W Higgins St
Humble, TX 77338
Phone: 281-446-3061
Fax: 281-446-3912

La Porte
PO Box 1115
La Porte, TX 77572
Phone: 281-471-5020
Fax: 281-471-7168

Missouri City
1522 Texas Pkwy
Missouri City, TX 77459
Phone: 281-261-4260
Fax: 281-261-4233

Pasadena
1211 Southmore Ave
Pasadena, TX 77502
Phone: 713-477-1511
Fax: 713-472-0144

Pearland
3519 Liberty Dr
Pearland, TX 77581
Phone: 281-485-2411
Fax: 281-652-1706

Richmond
402 Morton St
Richmond, TX 77469
Phone: 281-342-5456
Fax: 281-232-8626

Rosenberg
PO Box 32
Rosenberg, TX 77471
Phone: 281-344-3318
Fax: 281-344-3333

South Houston
1018 Dallas St
South Houston, TX 77587
Phone: 713-947-7700
Fax: 713-947-2213

Stafford
2610 S Main St
Stafford, TX 77477
Phone: 281-261-3900
Fax: 281-261-3994

Sugar Land
PO Box 110
Sugar Land, TX 77487
Phone: 281-275-2700
Fax: 281-275-2712

West University Place
3800 University Blvd
West University Place, TX 77005
Phone: 713-668-4441
Fax: 713-349-2705

Economy

Houston has a diverse economic base, and 13 Fortune 500 as well as 25 Forbes 500 companies have their corporate headquarters there. The city is a world center for the energy industry, and many of the nation's top companies, including Shell Oil and Conoco, are headquartered there. Houston is also a major engineering center—many of the nation's top firms have their corporate headquarters or divisions in the area, including Halliburton Brown & Root, which is Houston's largest private employer. Health care and research are also important industries in Houston. Texas Medical Center, the largest medical center in the world, is located in the city. The complex covers 675 acres and comprises nearly 40 non-profit institutions and more than 100 permanent buildings. The Center's Texas Heart Institute is known for its excellence in research and medical training.

Unemployment Rate 4.1%
Per Capita Income..........................$19,235
Median Family Income......................$36,094

Principal Industries & Number of Wage Earners

Houston PMSA* - 1998

Construction..137,300
Finance, Insurance, & Real Estate......................106,100
Government 256,200
Manufacturing 219,500
Mining..69,200
Retail Trade...320,500
Services 608,200
Transportation, Communications, & Public Utilities 140,800
Wholesale Trade....................................130,300

** Information given is for the Houston Primary Metropolitan Statistical Area (PMSA), which includes Chambers, Fort Bend, Harris, Liberty, Montgomery, and Waller counties.*

Major Employers

Compaq Computer Corp
PO Box 692000
Houston, TX 77269
www.compaq.com
Phone: 281-370-0670
Fax: 281-514-1740
TF: 800-652-6672

Continental Airlines Inc
1600 Smith St
Houston, TX 77002
www.continental.com
Phone: 713-324-5000
Fax: 713-324-5940
TF: 800-525-0280

Exxon Mobil Corp
5959 Las Colinas Blvd
Irving, TX 75039
www.exxon.mobil.com
Phone: 972-444-1000
Fax: 972-444-1348

Foley's
1110 Main St
Houston, TX 77002
www.mayco.com/fo/index.jsp
Phone: 713-405-7035
Fax: 713-651-6698
TF: 800-527-7147

Halliburton Brown & Root Inc
4100 Clinton Dr
Houston, TX 77020
www.halliburton.com
Phone: 713-676-3011
Fax: 713-676-4109

HCA Healthcare Co
7400 Fannin Suite 650
Houston, TX 77054
Phone: 713-852-1500
Fax: 713-852-1599

Houston Independent School District
3830 Richmond Ave
Houston, TX 77027
www.houstonisd.org
Phone: 713-892-6000
Fax: 713-892-6061

Kroger Co
16770 Imperial Valley Dr
Houston, TX 77060
www.kroger.com
Phone: 713-507-4800
Fax: 713-422-8044

Memorial Hermann Healthcare System
7600 Beechnut St
Houston, TX 77074
www.mhhs.org
Phone: 713-776-5500
Fax: 713-776-5665

Randall's Food Markets Inc
PO Box 4506
Houston, TX 77210
www.randalls.com
Phone: 713-268-3500
Fax: 713-268-3684
TF: 800-420-5385

Reliant Energy Inc
PO Box 1700
Houston, TX 77251
www.reliantenergy.com
Phone: 713-207-3000
Fax: 713-207-0050

Shell Oil Co
PO Box 2463
Houston, TX 77252
www.shellus.com
Phone: 713-241-6161
Fax: 713-241-4044
TF: 800-248-4257

Southwestern Bell Telephone Co
9051 Park W Suite 1165
Houston, TX 77063
www.swbell.com
Phone: 713-638-7200
Fax: 713-972-7387
TF: 800-613-5627

University of Texas Houston MD Anderson Cancer Center
1515 Holcombe Blvd
Houston, TX 77030
utmdacc.mda.uth.tmc.edu
Phone: 713-792-2121
Fax: 713-792-7573

University of Texas Medical Branch Hospitals
301 University Blvd
Galveston, TX 77555
www.utmb.edu
Phone: 409-772-1011
Fax: 409-772-5119

Quality of Living Indicators

Total Crime Index....................................131,776
(rates per 100,000 inhabitants)

Violent Crime
Murder/manslaughter.......................... 241
Forcible rape 748
Robbery.....................................8,350
Aggravated assault..........................12,180

Property Crime
Burglary 24,744
Larceny theft 66,068
Motor vehicle theft..........................19,445

Cost of Living Index 95.1
(national average = 100)

Median Home Price $105,300

Education

Public Schools

Houston Independent School District
3830 Richmond Ave
Houston, TX 77027
www.houstonisd.org
Phone: 713-892-6000
Fax: 713-892-6061

Number of Schools
Elementary 174
Middle 35
High 29
Other 51

Student/Teacher Ratio
All Grades 18.2:1

Private Schools

Number of Schools (all grades) . . . . . 200+

Colleges & Universities

Alvin Community College
3110 Mustang Rd
Alvin, TX 77511
E-mail: admiss@flipper.alvin.cc.tx.us
www.alvin.cc.tx.us
Phone: 281-331-6111
Fax: 281-388-4929

Art Institute of Houston
1900 Yorktown
Houston, TX 77056
www.aih.aii.edu
Phone: 713-623-2040
Fax: 713-966-2700
TF: 800-275-4244

College of the Mainland
1200 Amburn Rd
Texas City, TX 77591
www.mainland.cc.tx.us
Phone: 409-938-1211
Fax: 409-938-3126

Galveston College
4015 Ave Q
Galveston, TX 77550
E-mail: psanger@tusk.gc.edu
www.gc.edu
Phone: 409-763-6551
Fax: 409-762-0667

Houston Baptist University
7502 Fondren Rd
Houston, TX 77074
www.hbu.edu
Phone: 281-649-3000
Fax: 281-649-3217

Houston Community College (System)
PO Box 7849
Houston, TX 77270
E-mail: postmaster@hccs.cc.tx.us
www.hccs.cc.tx.us
Phone: 713-869-5021
Fax: 713-863-0529

ITT Technical Institute
15621 Blue Ash Dr Suite 160
Houston, TX 77090
www.itt-tech.edu
Phone: 281-873-0512
Fax: 281-873-0518
TF: 800-879-6486

Kingwood College
20000 Kingwood Dr
Kingwood, TX 77339
kcweb.nhmccd.edu
Phone: 281-312-1600
Fax: 281-312-1477
TF: 800-883-7939

Lee College
200 Lee Dr
Baytown, TX 77522
E-mail: clightfo@lee.edu
www.lee.edu
Phone: 281-427-5611
Fax: 281-425-6831

North Harris Montgomery Community College District
250 North Sam Houston Pkwy E
Houston, TX 77060
www.nhmccd.cc.tx.us
Phone: 281-260-3500
Fax: 281-260-3513

Rice University
PO Box 1892
Houston, TX 77251
E-mail: admi@rice.edu
www.rice.edu
Phone: 713-527-8101
Fax: 713-737-5646

San Jacinto College North
5800 Uvalde Rd
Houston, TX 77049
www.sjcd.cc.tx.us/overview/north.htm
Phone: 281-458-4050
Fax: 281-459-7125

San Jacinto College South
13735 Beamer Rd
Houston, TX 77089
www.sjcd.cc.tx.us/overview/south.htm
Phone: 281-922-3431
Fax: 281-922-3485

Texas Southern University
3100 Cleburne St
Houston, TX 77004
www.tsu.edu
Phone: 713-313-7011
Fax: 713-527-7318

Tomball College
30555 Tomball Pkwy
Tomball, TX 77375
wwwtc.nhmccd.edu
Phone: 281-351-3300
Fax: 281-351-3384

University of Houston
4800 Calhoun Rd
Houston, TX 77004
E-mail: admissions@uh.edu
www.uh.edu
Phone: 713-743-1000
Fax: 713-743-9633

University of Houston Clear Lake
2700 Bay Area Blvd
Houston, TX 77058
www.cl.uh.edu
Phone: 281-283-7600
Fax: 281-283-2530

University of Saint Thomas
3800 Montrose Blvd
Houston, TX 77006
E-mail: postmaster@basil.stthom.edu
basil.stthom.edu
Phone: 713-522-7911
Fax: 713-525-3558
TF: 800-856-8565

University of Texas Health Science Center at Houston
7000 Fannin St
Houston, TX 77225
E-mail: cwis@oac.hsc.uth.tmc.edu
www.uth.tmc.edu
Phone: 713-500-4472
Fax: 713-500-3805

Hospitals

Bayou City Medical Center
6700 Belaire Blvd
Houston, TX 77004
www.tenethealth.com/Sharpstown
Phone: 713-623-2500
Fax: 713-522-6723

Bellaire Medical Center
5314 Dashwood St
Houston, TX 77081
Phone: 713-512-1200
Fax: 713-512-1412

Cypress Fairbanks Medical Center
10655 Steepletop Dr
Houston, TX 77065
www.tenethealth.com/CypressFairbanks
Phone: 281-890-4285
Fax: 281-890-5341

Doctors Hospital Parkway
233 W Parker Rd
Houston, TX 77076
Phone: 281-765-2600
Fax: 281-765-7512

East Houston Medical Center
13111 East Fwy
Houston, TX 77015
Phone: 713-393-2000
Fax: 713-393-2714

Hermann Hospital
6411 Fannin St
Houston, TX 77030
www.mhhs.org/locations/mher/mher.html
Phone: 713-704-4000
Fax: 713-704-4498

Houston Northwest Medical Center
710 FM 1960 W
Houston, TX 77090
www.reddingmedicalcenter.com/HoustonNorthwest/yh
Phone: 281-440-1000
Fax: 281-440-2666

Kingwood Medical Center
22999 US Hwy 59
Kingwood, TX 77339
Phone: 281-359-7500
Fax: 281-348-1310

Memorial City Medical Center
920 Frostwood Dr
Houston, TX 77024
www.mhcs.org/locations/mhmc/mhmc.html
Phone: 713-932-3000
Fax: 713-827-4096

Memorial Hospital Southwest
7600 Beechnut St
Houston, TX 77074
www.mhcs.org/locations/mhsw/mhsw.html
Phone: 713-776-5000
Fax: 713-776-5766

Methodist Diagnostic Center Hospital
6447 Main St
Houston, TX 77030
www.methodisthealth.com/Diagnostic
Phone: 713-790-0790
Fax: 713-796-6587

North Houston Medical Center
7333 North Fwy
Houston, TX 77076
Phone: 713-692-3014

Saint Joseph Hospital
1919 La Branch St
Houston, TX 77002
Phone: 713-757-1000
Fax: 713-657-7173

Saint Luke's Episcopal Hospital
6720 Bertner
Houston, TX 77032
www.sleh.com
Phone: 713-791-2011
Fax: 713-794-6182

Spring Branch Medical Center
8850 Long Pt St
Houston, TX 77055
Phone: 713-467-6555
Fax: 713-722-3771

Texas Children's Hospital
6621 Fannin
Houston, TX 77030
www.texaschildrenshospital.org
Phone: 713-770-1000
Fax: 713-770-1005
TF: 800-364-5437

Veterans Affairs Medical Center
2002 Holcombe Blvd
Houston, TX 77030
Phone: 713-791-1414
Fax: 713-794-7182

West Houston Medical Center
12141 Richmond Ave
Houston, TX 77082
Phone: 281-558-3444
Fax: 281-558-7169
TF: 800-265-8624

Transportation

Airport(s)

Bush Intercontinental Airport (IAH)
22 miles N of downtown (approx 30 minutes).....281-233-3000
William P Hobby Airport (HOU)
8 miles SE of downtown (approx 25 minutes).....713-640-3000

Mass Transit

Metropolitan Transit
$1 Base fare 713-635-4000
Metropolitan Transit Downtown Trolleys
Free 713-635-4000

Rail/Bus

Greyhound/Trailways Bus Station
2121 Main St
Houston, TX 77002
Phone: 713-759-6565
TF: 800-231-2222

Houston Amtrak Station
902 Washington Ave
Houston, TX 77002
Phone: 713-224-1577

Utilities

Electricity
Reliant Energy HL & P.........................713-207-7777
www.hlp.com

Gas
Entex Inc...................................713-659-2111
entex.reliantenergy.com

Water
Houston Public Utilities Div....................713-371-1400
www.ci.houston.tx.us/departme/works/utilities

Garbage Collection/Recycling
Garbage Collection - Northeast..................713-699-1113
Garbage Collection - Northwest..................713-956-6589
Garbage Collection - Southeast..................713-928-6258
Garbage Collection - Southwest..................713-551-7300
Recycling Hotline...........................713-837-9130

Telecommunications

Telephone
Southwestern Bell.............................713-638-7200
www.swbell.com

Cable Television
Time Warner Cable............................713-462-9000
www.twchouston.com/index3.html

Internet Service Providers (ISPs)
Black Box...................................281-480-2685
www.blkbox.com
Compass Net Inc.............................713-776-0022
www.compassnet.com

DomiNet 713-613-4800
www.domi.net
Electrotex 713-526-3456
www.electrotex.com
First Internet 713-963-0712
www.firstnethou.com
Houston Internet Connect Inc 713-780-4070
www.hic.net
InfoHighway International Inc 281-447-7025
www.infohwy.com
Insync Internet Services Inc 713-407-7000
www.insync.net
Mediawest Online 713-223-9378
www.mediawest.com
NeoSoft Inc 713-830-3300
www.neosoft.com
Net One 713-688-9111
www.net1.net
Netropolis Communications Corp 713-977-9779
www.netropolis.net
Networks On-Line Inc 713-554-7100
www.nol.net
OrbitWorld Network 281-286-5625
www.orbitworld.net
PDQ.net 713-830-3100
www.pdq.net
WT.net 713-965-0485
www.wt.net

Banks

American Bank
1600 Smith St Suite 300
Houston, TX 77002
E-mail: info@americanbk.com
www.americanbk.com
Phone: 713-951-7100
Fax: 713-951-7172

Bank of America NA
700 Louisiana St
Houston, TX 77002
Phone: 888-279-3247
Fax: 713-247-6161

Bank of Houston
5115 S Main St
Houston, TX 77002
Phone: 713-529-4881
Fax: 713-529-9131

Bank One Texas NA
910 Travis
Houston, TX 77002
Phone: 713-751-6132
Fax: 713-751-6420
TF: 800-695-1111

Bank United
3200 Southwest Fwy Suite 1600
Houston, TX 77027
E-mail: stockvm@bankunited.com
www.bankunited.com
Phone: 713-543-6500
Fax: 713-543-6883
TF: 800-366-7378

Central Bank
55 Waugh Dr
Houston, TX 77007
Phone: 713-868-5577
Fax: 713-868-3317

Chase Bank of Texas NA
712 Main St
Houston, TX 77002
Phone: 713-216-4865
Fax: 713-216-2269
TF: 800-235-8522

Compass Bank
24 Greenway Plaza
Houston, TX 77046
Phone: 713-621-3336

Frost National Bank
601 Jefferson St
Houston, TX 77002
Phone: 713-652-7600
Fax: 713-652-7641

Guaranty Federal Bank FSB
1201 Louisiana St Suite 118
Houston, TX 77002
Phone: 713-658-0885
Fax: 713-659-4166

MetroBank NA
9600 Bellaire Blvd
Houston, TX 77036
E-mail: metrobank@metrobank-na.com
www.metrobank-na.com
Phone: 713-776-3876
Fax: 713-776-8068

Prime Bank
1220 Northwest Fwy
Houston, TX 77092
Phone: 713-209-6600
Fax: 713-209-6699
TF: 800-942-2265

SouthTrust Bank NA
9601 Katy Fwy Suite 100
Houston, TX 77024
Phone: 713-932-4150

Southwest Bank of Texas NA
4400 Post Oak Pkwy
Houston, TX 77027
www.swbanktx.com
Phone: 713-235-8800
Fax: 713-235-8816
TF: 800-287-0301

Union Planters Bank NA
999 N Shepherd Dr
Houston, TX 77008
Phone: 713-867-7400

Washington Mutual Bank NA
10850 Bellaire Blvd
Houston, TX 77072
Phone: 281-498-2233
Fax: 281-879-8286

Wells Fargo Bank
1000 Louisiana St
Houston, TX 77002
Phone: 800-411-4932
Fax: 713-739-1035

Shopping

Almeda Mall
12200 Gulf Fwy
Houston, TX 77075
Phone: 713-944-1010
Fax: 713-944-5948

Centre at Post Oak
5000 Westheimer Rd
Houston, TX 77056
Phone: 713-866-6923

Conroe Outlet Center
1111 League Line Rd
Conroe, TX 77303
www.primeoutlets.com/Conroe/index.html
Phone: 936-756-0999

Deerbrook Mall
20131 Hwy 59 N
Humble, TX 77338
Phone: 281-446-5300
Fax: 281-446-1921

First Colony Mall
16535 Southwest Fwy Suite 1
Sugar Land, TX 77479
Phone: 281-265-6123
Fax: 281-265-6124

Foley's
1110 Main St
Houston, TX 77002
www.mayco.com/fo/index.jsp
Phone: 713-405-7035
Fax: 713-651-6698
TF: 800-527-7147

Galleria The
5075 Westheimer Rd
Houston, TX 77056
Phone: 713-621-1907

Greenspoint Mall
208 Greenspoint Mall
Houston, TX 77060
Phone: 281-875-4201
Fax: 281-873-7144

Gulfgate Mall
7100 Gulf Fwy
Houston, TX 77087
Phone: 713-643-5777

Highland Village Shopping Center
3900 & 4000 block of Westheimer
Houston, TX 77027
Phone: 713-850-3100
Fax: 713-850-3190

Memorial City Mall
900 S Gessner Rd Suite 303
Houston, TX 77024
Phone: 713-464-8640
Fax: 713-464-7845

Meyerland Plaza Shopping Center
4700 Beechnut St
Houston, TX 77096
Phone: 713-664-1166

Northline Shopping Center
4400 North Fwy
Houston, TX 77022
Phone: 713-692-6131
Fax: 713-692-7543

Northwest Mall
9800 Hempstead Rd
Houston, TX 77092
Phone: 713-681-1303
Fax: 713-681-4362

Old Town Spring
Spring Cypress Rd
Spring, TX 77373
E-mail: otspl@oldtownspringtx.com
www.oldtownspringtx.com
Phone: 281-353-9310
Fax: 281-288-6674
TF: 800-653-8696

Park Shops
1200 McKinney Houston Ctr
Houston, TX 77010
www.houstoncenter.com
Phone: 713-759-1442

Pavilion The on Post Oak
1800 Post Oak Blvd Suite 240
Houston, TX 77056
Phone: 713-622-7979
Fax: 713-622-6843

River Oaks Antiques Center
2030 Westheimer Rd
Houston, TX 77098
E-mail: roac1@riveroaksantiques.com
www.riveroaksantiques.com
Phone: 713-520-8238
TF: 800-520-7622

River Oaks Shopping Center
1964 W Gray St
Houston, TX 77019
Phone: 713-866-6936

Sharpstown Center
7500 Bellaire Blvd
Houston, TX 77036
Phone: 713-777-1111
Fax: 713-777-7924

Town & Country Center
800 W Sam Houston Pkwy N
Houston, TX 77024
Phone: 713-468-1565
Fax: 713-468-0328

Traders Village Flea Market
7979 N Eldridge Rd
Houston, TX 77041
E-mail: tvh@flash.net
www.tradersvillage.com/hn1.html
Phone: 281-890-5500

Upper Kirby District
3015 Richmond Ave Suite 200
Houston, TX 77098
www.upperkirby.com
Phone: 713-524-8000
Fax: 713-524-2786

Uptown Park
1000 Uptown Park Blvd
Houston, TX 77056
Phone: 713-840-8474

West Oaks Mall
1000 West Oaks Mall
Houston, TX 77082
E-mail: info@shopwestoaksmall.com
www.shopwestoaksmall.com
Phone: 281-531-1332
Fax: 281-531-1579

Willowbrook Mall
2000 Willowbrook Mall
Houston, TX 77070
Phone: 281-890-8000
Fax: 281-890-3109

Media

Newspapers and Magazines

Houston Business Journal
1001 West Loop S Suite 650
Houston, TX 77027
E-mail: houston@amcity.com
www.amcity.com/houston
Phone: 713-688-8811
Fax: 713-968-8025

Houston Chronicle*
801 Texas Ave
Houston, TX 77002
E-mail: hci@chron.com
www.chron.com
Phone: 713-220-7171
Fax: 713-220-6806
TF: 800-735-3800

Houston Forward Times
PO Box 2962
Houston, TX 77001
E-mail: forwardt@flash.net
www.forwardtimes.com
Phone: 713-526-4727
Fax: 713-526-3170

Houston LifeStyle Magazine
10707 Corporate Dr Suite 170
Stafford, TX 77477
www.fortbendpublishing.com
Phone: 281-240-2445
Fax: 281-240-5079

Houston Press
1621 Milam Suite 100
Houston, TX 77002
E-mail: letters@houstonpress.com
www.houstonpress.com
Phone: 713-280-2400
Fax: 713-280-2444

Humble Sun
PO Box 1389
Humble, TX 77347
Phone: 281-446-1071
Fax: 281-446-6901

Leader The
PO Box 924487
Houston, TX 77292
Phone: 713-686-8494
Fax: 713-686-0970

Pearland Journal
PO Box 1830
Pearland, TX 77588
www.westwardcommllc.com/pearlandj
Phone: 281-485-2785
Fax: 281-485-4464

**Indicates major daily newspapers*

Television

KHOU-TV Ch 11 (CBS)
1945 Allen Pkwy
Houston, TX 77019
E-mail: 11listens@khou.com
www.khou.com
Phone: 713-526-1111
Fax: 713-520-7763

KHTV-TV Ch 39 (WB) Phone: 713-781-3939
7700 Westpark Dr Fax: 713-781-3441
Houston, TX 77063
www.khtv.com

KNWS-TV Ch 51 (Ind) Phone: 713-974-5151
8440 Westpark Dr Fax: 713-974-5188
Houston, TX 77063

KPRC-TV Ch 2 (NBC) Phone: 713-222-2222
PO Box 2222 Fax: 713-771-4930
Houston, TX 77252
E-mail: news2@kprc.com
www.kprc.com

KPXB-TV Ch 49 (PAX) Phone: 281-820-4900
256 N Sam Houston Pkwy E Suite 49 Fax: 281-820-4840
Houston, TX 77060

KRIV-TV Ch 26 (Fox) Phone: 713-479-2600
4261 Southwest Fwy Fax: 713-479-2859
Houston, TX 77027

KTBU-TV Ch 55 (Ind) Phone: 713-864-0455
7026 Old Katy Rd Suite 201 Fax: 713-864-1993
Houston, TX 77024

KTMD-TV Ch 48 (Tele) Phone: 713-974-4848
3903 Stoney Brook St Fax: 713-974-5875
Houston, TX 77063
E-mail: t48gm@ktmd.com
www.ktmd.com

KTRK-TV Ch 13 (ABC) Phone: 713-666-0713
3310 Bissonnet St Fax: 713-664-0013
Houston, TX 77005
E-mail: ktrktv@aol.com
www.ktrk.com

KTXH-TV Ch 20 (UPN) Phone: 713-661-2020
8950 Kirby Dr Fax: 713-665-3909
Houston, TX 77054
www.paramountstations.com/KTXH

KUHT-TV Ch 8 (PBS) Phone: 713-748-8888
4513 Cullen Blvd Fax: 713-749-8216
Houston, TX 77004
E-mail: postmaster@kuht.uh.edu
www.kuht.uh.edu

KXLN-TV Ch 45 (Uni) Phone: 713-662-4545
9440 Kirby Dr Fax: 713-668-9057
Houston, TX 77054
www.univision.net/stations/kxln.htm

Radio

KBME-AM 790 kHz (Nost) Phone: 713-526-5874
510 Lovett Blvd Fax: 713-630-3666
Houston, TX 77006

KBXX-FM 97.9 MHz (CHR) Phone: 713-623-2108
24 Greenway Plaza Suite 1508 Fax: 713-623-0344
Houston, TX 77046
www.kbxx.com

KENR-AM 1070 kHz (Rel) Phone: 713-260-3600
6161 Savoy St Suite 1200 Fax: 713-260-3628
Houston, TX 77036

KEYH-AM 850 kHz (Span) Phone: 713-993-8000
1980 Post Oak Blvd Suite 1500 Fax: 713-933-8050
Houston, TX 77056

KHMX-FM 96.5 MHz (AC) Phone: 713-790-0965
1990 Post Oak Blvd Suite 2300 Fax: 713-586-8080
Houston, TX 77056 TF: 800-683-0965
E-mail: mix965@khmx.com
www.khmx.com

KIKK-AM 650 kHz (Ctry) Phone: 713-881-5957
24 E Greenway Plaza Suite 1900 Fax: 713-881-5997
Houston, TX 77046

KIKK-FM 95.7 MHz (Ctry) Phone: 713-881-5100
24 Greenway Plaza Suite 1900 Fax: 713-881-5999
Houston, TX 77046
www.youngcountry957.com

KILT-AM 610 kHz (Sports) Phone: 713-881-5100
24 Greenway Plaza Suite 1900 Fax: 713-881-5199
Houston, TX 77046
www.star610kilt.com

KILT-FM 100.3 MHz (Ctry) Phone: 713-881-5100
24 Greenway Plaza Suite 1900 Fax: 713-881-5199
Houston, TX 77046
E-mail: kilt@kilt.com
www.kilt.com

KJOJ-FM 103.3 MHz (Rel) Phone: 281-588-4800
11767 Katy Fwy Suite 1170 Fax: 281-884-4820
Houston, TX 77079

KKBQ-FM 92.9 MHz (Ctry) Phone: 713-961-0093
3050 Post Oak Blvd Suite 1250 Fax: 713-963-1293
Houston, TX 77056
www.kkbq.com

KKHT-FM 106.9 MHz (Rel) Phone: 713-260-3600
6161 Savoy St Suite 1200 Fax: 713-260-3628
Houston, TX 77036
E-mail: kkht@kkht.com
www.kkht.com/

KKRW-FM 93.7 MHz (CR) Phone: 713-830-8000
350 Post Oak Blvd 12th Fl Fax: 713-830-8099
Houston, TX 77056
www.kkrw.com

KKTL-FM 97.1 MHz (Alt) Phone: 713-968-1000
1990 Post Oak Blvd Suite 2300 Fax: 713-968-1070
Houston, TX 77056

KLAT-AM 1010 kHz (N/T) Phone: 713-868-4344
1415 North Loop W Suite 400 Fax: 713-407-1400
Houston, TX 77008

KLDE-FM 94.5 MHz (Oldies) Phone: 713-622-5533
5353 W Alabama St Suite 410 Fax: 713-963-0590
Houston, TX 77056
www.klde.com

KLOL-FM 101.1 MHz (Rock) Phone: 713-526-6855
510 Lovett Blvd Fax: 713-630-3555
Houston, TX 77006
E-mail: klol@klol.com
www.klol.com

KLTN-FM 102.9 MHz (Span)
1415 North Loop W Suite 1400
Houston, TX 77008
Phone: 713-407-1415
Fax: 713-407-1400

KLTN-FM 93.3 MHz (Span)
1415 North Loop W Suite 400
Houston, TX 77008
Phone: 713-868-4344
Fax: 713-407-1400

KLTO-FM 104.9 MHz (Span)
1415 North Loop W Suite 400
Houston, TX 77008
Phone: 713-868-4344
Fax: 713-407-1400

KMJQ-FM 102.1 MHz (Urban)
24 Greenway Plaza Suite 1508
Houston, TX 77046
www.kmjq.com
Phone: 713-623-2108
Fax: 713-623-0106

KODA-FM 99.1 MHz (AC)
3050 Post Oak Blvd 12th Fl
Houston, TX 77056
www.sunny99.com
Phone: 713-830-8000
Fax: 713-830-8099

KOVA-FM 104.9 MHz (Span)
1415 N Loop W Suite 400
Houston, TX 77008
Phone: 713-407-1415
Fax: 713-407-1400

KOVE-FM 100.7 MHz (Span)
1415 North Loop West Suite 400
Houston, TX 77008
Phone: 713-407-1415
Fax: 713-407-1400

KPRC-AM 950 kHz (N/T)
11767 Katy Fwy Suite 1170
Houston, TX 77079
Phone: 281-588-4800
Fax: 281-588-4820

KQQK-FM 106.5 MHz (Span)
1980 Post Oak Blvd Suite 1500
Houston, TX 77056
Phone: 713-993-8000
Fax: 713-993-8003

KRBE-FM 104.1 MHz (CHR)
9801 Westheimer Rd Suite 700
Houston, TX 77042
E-mail: mailbox@krbe.com
www.krbe.com
Phone: 713-266-1000
Fax: 713-954-2344

KRTS-FM 92.1 MHz (Clas)
1600 Smith St Suite 5100
Houston, TX 77002
E-mail: krts@krts.com
www.krts.com
Phone: 713-921-5787
Fax: 713-651-0267

KRTX-AM 980 kHz (Span)
1415 N Loop W Suite 400
Houston, TX 77008
Phone: 713-407-1415
Fax: 713-407-1400

KRTX-FM 100.7 MHz (Span)
1415 N Loop W Suite 400
Houston, TX 77008
Phone: 713-407-1415
Fax: 713-407-1400

KSEV-AM 700 kHz (N/T)
11767 Katy Fwy Suite 1170
Houston, TX 77079
Phone: 281-588-4800
Fax: 281-588-4820

KTBZ-FM 107.5 MHz (Rock)
1990 Post Oak Blvd Suite 2300
Houston, TX 77056
E-mail: thebuzz@thebuzz.com
www.thebuzz.com
Phone: 713-968-1000
Fax: 713-968-1070

KTJM-FM 98.5 MHz (Oldies)
24 Greenway Plaza Suite 1508
Houston, TX 77046
ktjm.com
Phone: 713-623-2108
Fax: 713-623-8173

KTRH-AM 740 kHz (N/T)
PO Box 1520
Houston, TX 77251
www.ktrh.com
Phone: 713-526-5874
Fax: 713-630-3666

KUHF-FM 88.7 MHz (NPR)
3801 Cullen Blvd Communications Bldg Suite 101
Houston, TX 77004
E-mail: gsmith@uh.edu
www.uh.edu/campus/kuhf
Phone: 713-743-0887
Fax: 713-743-0868

KVPU-FM 91.3 MHz (NPR)
PO Box 156
Prairie View, TX 77446
Phone: 936-857-4511

KXTJ-FM 107.9 MHz (Span)
1980 Post Oak Blvd Suite 1500
Houston, TX 77056
Phone: 713-993-8000
Fax: 713-965-0108

Attractions

Near downtown Houston is 401-acre Hermann Park, which includes the Houston Zoological Park and Japanese Friendship Gardens, riding trails, the Museum of Natural Science, and the Mecom Rockwell Fountain, one of the city's most beautiful structures. Houston's Western heritage is celebrated every February at the Houston Livestock Show and Rodeo. The event is held at the Astrodome and lasts 17 days. Approximately 25 miles southeast of Houston is Space Center Houston, which includes NASA's Johnson Space Center.

AD Players
2710 W Alabama St
Houston, TX 77098
Phone: 713-526-2721
Fax: 713-439-0905

Aerial Theater at Bayou Place
520 Texas Ave
Houston, TX 77002
webadv.chron.com/display/a/aerialtheater/index.html
Phone: 713-230-1666
Fax: 713-230-1669

Alley Theatre
615 Texas Ave
Houston, TX 77002
www.alleytheatre.com
Phone: 713-228-9341
Fax: 713-222-6542
TF: 800-259-2553

American Cowboy Museum
11822 Almeda St
Houston, TX 77045
Phone: 713-433-4441
Fax: 713-433-4441

Armand Bayou Nature Center
8500 Bay Area Blvd
Houston, TX 77258
Phone: 281-474-2551
Fax: 281-474-2552

Astrodome
8400 Kirby Dr
Houston, TX 77054
www.astros.com/dome.htm
Phone: 713-799-9555
Fax: 713-799-9840

Baker Burke Planetarium
1 Hermann Circle Dr
Houston, TX 77030
www.hmns.org/hmns/planetarium.html
Phone: 713-639-4600
Fax: 713-523-4125

Battleship Texas SHS
3527 Battleground Rd
La Porte, TX 77571
Phone: 281-479-2411
Fax: 281-479-4197

Bayou Bend Museum
1 Westcott St
Houston, TX 77007
Phone: 713-639-7750
Fax: 713-639-7770

Big Thicket National Preserve
3785 Milam St
Beaumont, TX 77701
www.nps.gov/bith/
Phone: 409-839-2689
Fax: 409-839-2599

CG Jung Educational Center of Houston
5200 Montrose Blvd
Houston, TX 77006
www.cgjunghouston.org
Phone: 713-524-8253
Fax: 713-524-8096

Children's Museum of Houston
1500 Binz St
Houston, TX 77004
E-mail: childrensmuseum@cmhouston.org
www.cmhouston.org
Phone: 713-522-1138
Fax: 713-522-5747

Contemporary Arts Museum
5216 Montrose Blvd
Houston, TX 77006
www.camh.org/
Phone: 713-284-8250
Fax: 713-284-8275

Cullen Park
19008 Saums Rd
Houston, TX 77023
Phone: 713-845-1111

Da Camera of Houston
1427 Branard
Houston, TX 77006
www.dacamera.com
Phone: 713-524-7601
Fax: 713-524-4148

Ensemble Theatre
3535 Main St
Houston, TX 77002
Phone: 713-520-0055
Fax: 713-520-1269

Forbidden Gardens
23500 Franz Rd
Katy, TX 77493
Phone: 281-347-8000
Fax: 281-347-8080

Fort Bend Museum
500 Houston St
Richmond, TX 77469
www.fortbendmuseum.org
Phone: 281-342-6478
Fax: 281-342-2439

George Ranch Historical Park
10215 FM 762
Richmond, TX 77469
www.georgeranch.org/
Phone: 281-545-9212
Fax: 281-343-9316

Hermann Park
6001 Fannin St
Houston, TX 77004
Phone: 713-845-1000
Fax: 713-845-1201

Holocaust Museum Houston
5401 Caroline St
Houston, TX 77004
www.hmh.org
Phone: 713-942-8000
Fax: 713-942-7953

Houston Arboretum & Nature Center
4501 Woodway
Houston, TX 77024
www.neosoft.com/~arbor
Phone: 713-681-8433
Fax: 713-681-1191

Houston Ballet
1921 W Bell St
Houston, TX 77019
www.neosoft.com/~ballet
Phone: 713-523-6300
Fax: 713-523-4038

Houston Fire Museum
2403 Milam St
Houston, TX 77006
www.houstonfiremuseum.org
Phone: 713-524-2526
Fax: 713-520-7566

Houston Grand Opera Assn
510 Preston Suite 500
Houston, TX 77002
www.hgo.com
Phone: 713-546-0200
Fax: 713-247-0906
TF: 800-626-7372

Houston Museum of Natural Science
1 Hermann Circle Dr Hermann Pk
Houston, TX 77030
www.hmns.org
Phone: 713-639-4600
Fax: 713-639-4761

Houston Symphony Orchestra
615 Louisiana St Suite 102
Houston, TX 77002
E-mail: hso@iwi.net
www.housym.org
Phone: 713-224-4240
Fax: 713-222-7024

Houston Zoological Gardens
1513 N MacGregor St
Houston, TX 77030
www.houstonzoo.org
Phone: 713-284-1300
Fax: 713-284-1329

IMAX 3D Theater
1 Hope Blvd Moody Gardens
Galveston, TX 77554
Phone: 409-744-4673
Fax: 409-744-1631
TF: 800-582-4673

Jesse H Jones Hall for the Performing Arts
615 Louisiana St
Houston, TX 77002
Phone: 713-227-3974
Fax: 713-228-9629

Lawndale Art & Performance Center
4912 Main St
Houston, TX 77002
E-mail: lawndale@neosoft.com
www.neosoft.com/~lawndale/
Phone: 713-528-5858
Fax: 713-528-4140

Lone Star Flight Museum
2002 Terminal Dr
Galveston, TX 77554
www.lsfm.org
Phone: 409-740-7722
Fax: 409-740-7612

Malibu Grand Prix
1105 W Loop North
Houston, TX 77055
Phone: 713-688-5273
Fax: 713-680-0603

Memorial Park
Loop 610 at Memorial Dr
Houston, TX 77024
Phone: 713-845-1111

Menil The Collection Museum
1515 Sul Ross St
Houston, TX 77006
www.menil.org/
Phone: 713-525-9400
Fax: 713-525-9444

Miller Outdoor Theatre
PO Box 1562
Houston, TX 77251
www.ci.houston.tx.us/departme/parks/millerschedule.htm
Phone: 713-284-8351

Moody Gardens
1 Hope Blvd
Galveston, TX 77554
www.moodygardens.com/
Phone: 409-744-4673
Fax: 409-744-1631
TF: 800-582-4673

Museum of Fine Arts
1001 Bissonnet St
Houston, TX 77005
www.mfah.org
Phone: 713-639-7300
Fax: 713-639-7784
TF: 888-733-6324

Museum of Health & Medical Science
1515 Hermann Dr
Houston, TX 77004
E-mail: lblanch@mhms.org
www.mhms.org
Phone: 713-521-1515
Fax: 713-526-1434

National Museum of Funeral History
415 Barren Springs Dr
Houston, TX 77090
www.nmfh.org
Phone: 281-876-3063
Fax: 281-876-4403

Old Town Spring
Spring Cypress Rd
Spring, TX 77373
E-mail: otspl@oldtownspringtx.com
www.oldtownspringtx.com
Phone: 281-353-9310
Fax: 281-288-6674
TF: 800-653-8696

Port of Houston
PO Box 2562
Houston, TX 77252
www.portofhouston.com
Phone: 713-670-2400
Fax: 713-670-2429
TF: 800-688-3625

Rice University Art Gallery
6100 S Main Rice University
Houston, TX 77005
www.ruf.rice.edu/~ruag/
Phone: 713-348-6069
Fax: 713-348-5980

Richmond Avenue Entertainment District
5600-6500 Block of Richmond Ave
Houston, TX 77257
Phone: 713-974-4686
Fax: 713-975-0565

Sam Houston Park
1100 Bagby St
Houston, TX 77002
Phone: 713-655-1912
Fax: 713-655-7527

San Jacinto Battleground
3523 Hwy 134
La Porte, TX 77571
www.tpwd.state.tx.us/park/battlesh/battlesh.htm
Phone: 281-479-2431
Fax: 281-479-5618

Space Center Houston
1601 Nasa Rd 1
Houston, TX 77058
www.spacecenter.org
Phone: 281-244-2100
Fax: 281-283-7724
TF: 800-972-0369

Spring Historical Museum
403 Main St Old Town Spring
Spring, TX 77373
Phone: 281-651-0055

Stages Repertory Theatre
3201 Allen Pkwy Suite 101
Houston, TX 77019
Phone: 713-527-8243
Fax: 713-527-8669

Theatre Under the Stars
2600 Southwest Fwy Suite 600
Houston, TX 77098
www.tuts.com/
Phone: 713-558-2600
Fax: 713-558-2650
TF: 800-678-5440

Traders Village Flea Market
7979 N Eldridge Rd
Houston, TX 77041
E-mail: tvh@flash.net
www.tradersvillage.com/hn1.html
Phone: 281-890-5500

Upper Kirby District
3015 Richmond Ave Suite 200
Houston, TX 77098
www.upperkirby.com
Phone: 713-524-8000
Fax: 713-524-2786

Uptown Park
1000 Uptown Park Blvd
Houston, TX 77056
Phone: 713-840-8474

WaterWorld USA
9001 Kirby Dr
Houston, TX 77054
www.sixflags.com/houston
Phone: 713-799-8404
Fax: 713-799-1491

Wortham IMAX Theatre
1 Hermann Cir Dr Houston Museum of Natural Science
Houston, TX 77030
www.hmns.org
Phone: 713-639-4629
Fax: 713-523-4125

Wortham Theater Center
510 Preston St
Houston, TX 77002
Phone: 713-237-1439
Fax: 713-237-9313

Sports Teams & Facilities

Battleground Speedway
I-10 & Exit 787
Highlands, TX 77562
Phone: 713-946-7223
TF: 800-722-3464

Compaq Center
10 E Greenway Plaza
Houston, TX 77046
Phone: 713-843-3900
Fax: 713-843-3986

Gulf Greyhound Park
1000 FM 2004
La Marque, TX 77568
www.gulfgreyhound.com
Phone: 800-275-2946

Houston Aeros (hockey)
3100 Wilcrest Suite 260
Houston, TX 77042
E-mail: wwwaeros@aeros.com
www.aeros.com
Phone: 713-974-7825
Fax: 713-361-7900

Houston Astros
501 Crawford Enron Field
Houston, TX 77002
E-mail: twinspin@astros.com
www.astros.com
Phone: 713-259-8000
Fax: 713-259-8456

Houston Comets (basketball)
10 Greenway Plaza Compaq Ctr
Houston, TX 77046
www.wnba.com/comets
Phone: 713-627-9622
Fax: 713-963-7315

Houston Hotshots (soccer)
8400 Kirby Dr The Astrodome
Houston, TX 77054
E-mail: hotshots@neosoft.com
www.houstonhotshots.com
Phone: 713-468-5100
Fax: 713-799-9743

Houston Hurricanes (soccer)
13755 Main St Butler Stadium
Houston, TX 77035
E-mail: info@hurricanesprosoccer.com
www.hurricanesprosoccer.com
Phone: 281-647-6285
Fax: 281-859-8839

Houston Raceway Park
2525 FM 565
Baytown, TX 77522
E-mail: feedback@houstonraceway.com
www.houstonraceway.com
Phone: 281-383-2666
Fax: 281-383-3777

Houston Rockets
2 Greenway Plaza Suite 400
Houston, TX 77046
www.nba.com/rockets
Phone: 713-627-3865
Fax: 713-963-7315

Houston Speedway
Mt Houston Rd & SR-8
The Woodlands, TX 77387
Phone: 281-458-1972
Fax: 281-458-2052

Houston Thunderbears (football)
10 Greenway Plaza Compaq Ctr
Houston, TX 77046
www.thunderbears.com
Phone: 713-627-9622
Fax: 713-963-7315

Houston Tornado's
13755 S Main St Butler Stadium
Houston, TX 77035
www.houstontornados.com
Phone: 281-456-8732
Fax: 281-456-0289

Sam Houston Race Park
7575 North Sam Houston Pkwy W
Houston, TX 77064
www.shrp.com/
Phone: 281-807-8700
Fax: 281-807-8777

Annual Events

Asian-American Festival
(mid-October & mid-May) 713-339-3688
Bayou City Art Festival
(late March & mid-October) 713-521-0133
Christmas Candlelight Tours (early December) 713-655-1912
Cinco de Mayo Festival (May 5) 713-437-5200
Fall Motor Fest (early November) 281-890-5500
Festa Italiana (mid-October).......................713-524-4222
Fotofest (early March-early April) 713-223-5522
Freedom Festival (July 4) 713-621-8600
Greek Festival (early October) 713-526-5377
Hot Air Balloon Festival (late August) 281-488-7676
Houston International Boat Sport & Travel Show
(mid-January).................................713-526-6361
Houston International Festival (early-mid-April) 713-654-8808
Houston International Jazz Festival
(early August).................................713-839-7000
Houston Livestock Show & Rodeo
(mid-February-early March).....................713-791-9000
Houston Methodist Hospital Marathon
(mid-January).................................713-957-3453
Houston Shakespeare Festival (early-mid-August)...713-284-8350
International Quilt Festival
(late October-early November) 713-781-6864
Japan Festival (April) 713-963-0121
Juneteenth Celebration (mid-June) 713-437-5200
Mayor's Official Downtown Houston Holiday Celebration
(early December)..............................713-845-1267
Oktoberfest (early October).......................281-890-5500
Texas Crawfish Festival (mid-late May) 281-353-9310
Texas Renaissance Festival
(early October-mid-November) 800-458-3435
Texian Market Days (late October) 281-343-0218
Thanksgiving Day Parade (late November)..........713-654-8808
Uptown Tree Lighting Ceremony
(late November)...............................713-621-2011
Wings Over Houston Airshow (mid-October) 713-644-1018
World Championship Bar-B-Que Contest
(mid-February)................................713-791-9000
Worldfest Houston International Film Festival
(early-mid-April) 713-965-9955

Huntsville, Alabama

***County:* Madison**

HUNTSVILLE is located in northeastern Alabama between the Tennessee River and the Appalachian Mountains. Major cities within 100 miles include Birmingham, Alabama and Chattanooga and Nashville, Tennessee.

Area (Land)	145.4 sq mi
Area (Water)	0.3 sq mi
Elevation	641 ft
Latitude	34-71-88 N
Longitude	86-56-82 W
Time Zone	CST
Area Code	256

Climate

Huntsville's climate features four distinct seasons. Winter days are generally mild, with average high temperatures near 50 degrees, while evening lows average around 30. Snowfall is minimal in Huntsville, averaging four inches annually. Summer days are very warm, with average highs in the upper 80s, while evenings cool down into the mid- to upper 60s. March is the wettest month of the year in Huntsville; October is the driest.

Average Temperatures & Precipitation

Temperatures

	Jan	Feb	Mar	Apr	May	Jun	Jul	Aug	Sep	Oct	Nov	Dec
High	48	54	63	73	79	87	89	89	83	73	62	53
Low	29	33	41	49	57	65	69	68	62	49	41	33

Precipitation

	Jan	Feb	Mar	Apr	May	Jun	Jul	Aug	Sep	Oct	Nov	Dec
Inches	5.2	4.9	6.6	4.9	5.1	4.1	4.9	3.5	4.1	3.3	4.9	5.9

History

The Huntsville area was originally a Cherokee hunting ground until the United States Government acquired the land by treaty in 1805. At that time, John Hunt, after whom the town was named founded Huntsville. Within three years, more than 300 people had moved to the area and Madison County was formed. In 1810, Huntsville was chosen as the seat of Madison County, and the town was called Twickenham. The following year, the city was incorporated and renamed Huntsville after its founding father. Huntsville served as the temporary state capital of Alabama for a few months in 1819. Union troops occupied Huntsville during the Civil War, however the city was spared the mass destruction that many southern towns were forced to endure. Throughout the 1800s and well into the 20th Century, the city grew as an agricultural trade and distribution center, with cotton being its primary product.

At the beginning of World War II, the Huntsville area became the site of Redstone Arsenal, an Army chemical plant that produced chemical weapon and other ammunition. The event that propelled Huntsville to become the high technology center that it is today occurred in 1950. That year, the Army consolidated its missiles and rocket research and chose Redstone as the prime facility. By the end of the decade, Dr. Wernher Von Braun and his team of more than 100 German rocket scientists that had come to call the arsenal home had developed the nation's first rocket, the Redstone. During the 1960s, the newly formed National Aeronautics and Space Administration (NASA) established the Marshall Space Flight Center in the Huntsville area. In less than 20 years, Huntsville's population had grown from just over 16,400 in 1950 to 50,000. Von Braun's team of scientists went on to develop numerous rockets for NASA, including the Saturn V, the powerful rocket that transported 3 astronauts into space and resulted in Neil Armstrong's famous walk on the Moon on July 15, 1969. Huntsville today is home to more than 175,000 people. This aerospace center has become known as "America's Space Capital" and "Rocket City, USA." Both the U.S. Army Missile Command, located at Redstone Arsenal and NASA's Marshall Space Flight Center remain among the city's largest employers. Huntsville has also become a center for other types of high technology research and development, including electronics and telecommunications.

Population

1990 Census	159,880
1998 Estimate	175,979
% Change	10.1
2004 Projection	291,479*

Racial/Ethnic Breakdown

White	72.6%
Black	24.4%
Other	3.0%
Hispanic Origin (may be of any race)	1.2%

Age Breakdown

Under 5 years	6.6%
5 to 17	16.6%
18 to 20	5.5%
21 to 24	6.9%
25 to 34	18.7%
35 to 44	14.5%
45 to 54	11.7%
55 to 64	9.6%
65 to 74	6.3%
75+ years	3.7%
Median Age	32.6

Gender Breakdown

Male	48.6%
Female	51.4%

** Information given is for Madison County.*

Government

Type of Government: Mayor-City Council

Huntsville City Clerk/Treasurer
PO Box 308
Huntsville, AL 35804
Phone: 256-427-5090
Fax: 256-427-5095

Huntsville City Council
PO Box 308
Huntsville, AL 35804
Phone: 256-427-5011
Fax: 256-427-5020

Huntsville City Hall
308 Fountain Cir
Huntsville, AL 35801
Phone: 256-427-5000
Fax: 256-427-5257

Huntsville Community Development Div
120 E Holmes Ave
Huntsville, AL 35801
Phone: 256-427-5400
Fax: 256-427-5431

Huntsville Finance Dept
308 Fountain Cir
Huntsville, AL 35801
Phone: 256-427-5080
Fax: 256-427-5064

Huntsville Fire Dept
PO Box 308
Huntsville, AL 35804
Phone: 256-427-7401
Fax: 256-427-7437

Huntsville Human Resources Dept
PO Box 308
Huntsville, AL 35804
Phone: 256-427-5248
Fax: 256-427-5245

Huntsville Mayor
PO Box 308
Huntsville, AL 35804
Phone: 256-427-5000
Fax: 256-427-5257

Huntsville Police Dept
PO Box 2085
Huntsville, AL 35804
Phone: 256-427-7001
Fax: 256-427-7141

Huntsville Public Transportation Div
100 Church St
Huntsville, AL 35801
Phone: 256-427-6811
Fax: 256-427-6869

Huntsville Public Works Dept
PO Box 308
Huntsville, AL 35804
Phone: 256-883-3944
Fax: 256-883-3961

Huntsville Recreation Services Div
308 Fountain Cir
Huntsville, AL 35801
Phone: 256-427-5230
Fax: 256-427-5223

Huntsville Urban Development Dept
PO Box 308
Huntsville, AL 35804
Phone: 256-427-5100
Fax: 256-535-4236

Huntsville-Madison County Public Library
915 Monroe St
Huntsville, AL 35801
Phone: 256-532-5940
Fax: 256-532-5997

Important Phone Numbers

AAA....................256-539-7493
Alabama Dept of Revenue....................256-922-1082
American Express Travel....................256-539-0671
Driver's License Information....................256-539-0681
Emergency....................911
Huntsville Board of Realtors....................256-536-3334
Madison County Sales Tax Office....................256-532-3498
Madison County Tax Assessor's Office....................256-532-3350
Poison Control Center....................800-462-0800
Time/Temp....................256-721-0034
Vehicle Registration Information....................256-532-3310
Voter Registration Information....................256-532-3510
Weather....................256-533-1990

Information Sources

Better Business Bureau Serving Northern Alabama
PO Box 383
Huntsville, AL 35804
www.northalabama.bbb.org
Phone: 256-533-1640
Fax: 256-533-1177

Chamber of Commerce of Huntsville/ Madison County
PO Box 408
Huntsville, AL 35804
www.hsvchamber.org
Phone: 256-535-2000
Fax: 256-535-2015

Huntsville/Madison County Convention & Visitor's Bureau
700 Monroe St
Huntsville, AL 35801
www.huntsville.org
Phone: 256-551-2230
Fax: 256-551-2324
TF: 800-772-2348

Madison County
100 Northside Sq
Huntsville, AL 35801
www.co.madison.al.us
Phone: 256-532-3327
Fax: 256-532-6977

Von Braun Civic Center
700 Monroe St
Huntsville, AL 35801
www.vbcc.com
Phone: 256-533-1953
Fax: 256-551-2203

Online Resources

About.com Guide to Huntsville
huntsville.about.com/citiestowns/southeastus/huntsville

Area Guide Huntsville
huntsville.areaguides.net

City Knowledge Huntsville
www.cityknowledge.com/al_huntsville.htm

Excite.com Huntsville City Guide
www.excite.com/travel/countries/united_states/alabama/huntsville

Huntsville Virtual Times
hsv.com

Lodging.com Huntsville Alabama
www.lodging.com/auto/guides/huntsville-al.html

RocketCity.com
www.rocketcity.com/

Area Communities

Communities in the Huntsville metropolitan area with populations greater than 10,000 include:

Athens
PO Box 1089
Athens, AL 35612
Phone: 256-233-8720
Fax: 256-233-8721

Decatur
402 Lee St NE
Decatur, AL 35601
Phone: 256-355-7410
Fax: 256-351-2362

Madison
100 Hughes Rd
Madison, AL 35758
Phone: 256-772-5600
Fax: 256-772-5668

New Hope
PO Box 419
New Hope, AL 35760
Phone: 256-723-2616
Fax: 256-723-5845

Economy

The Huntsville area has a continually diversifying economic base. The three leading employment sectors in the metro area are services, government, and manufacturing. A major U.S. center for high-technology research and development and manufacturing, Huntsville's economy continues to rely heavily on aerospace and other high tech industries. In addition to the U.S. Army and NASA, many leading high-tech manufacturers have a presence in the Huntsville area, including SCI Systems and Motorola.

Unemployment Rate 2.9%*
Per Capita Income.......................... $25,304*
Median Family Income...................... $39,708

** Information given is for Madison County.*

Principal Industries & Number of Wage Earners

Huntsville MSA* - 1999

Finance, Insurance, & Real Estate 5,000
Government 40,200
Manufacturing 35,300
Mining & Construction..................................6,600
Retail Trade...30,500
Services 52,200
Transportation & Public Utilities 4,500
Wholesale Trade...6,200

** Information given is for the Huntsville Metropolitan Statistical Area (MSA), which includes Limestone and Madison counties.*

Major Employers

Alabama A & M University
4900 Meridian St
Huntsville, AL 35811
www.aamu.edu
Phone: 256-851-5000
Fax: 256-851-5034

AVEX Electronics Inc
4807 Bradford Dr NW
Huntsville, AL 35805
E-mail: info@avex.com
www.avex.com
Phone: 256-722-6000
Fax: 256-722-7428

BAMSI Inc
PO Box 8395
Redstone Arsenal, AL 35808
Phone: 256-544-7979
Fax: 256-544-1801

Boeing Co
PO Box 240002
Huntsville, AL 35824
www.boeing.com
Phone: 256-461-2121

DaimlerChrysler Corp
PO Box 240001
Huntsville, AL 35824
www.daimlerchrysler.com
Phone: 256-464-1200
Fax: 256-464-2279

Dunlop Tire Corp
PO Box 1141
Huntsville, AL 35824
www.dunloptire.com
Phone: 256-772-9631
Fax: 256-772-1299

Huntsville Board of Education
200 White St NE
Huntsville, AL 35801
www.hsv.k12.al.us/dept/merts/admin/board/
Phone: 256-532-4600
Fax: 256-532-4853

Huntsville City Hall
308 Fountain Cir
Huntsville, AL 35801
www.ci.huntsville.al.us
Phone: 256-427-5000
Fax: 256-427-5257

Huntsville Hospital System
101 Sivley Rd SW
Huntsville, AL 35801
E-mail: burri@mktg-pr.hhsys.org
www.hhsys.org
Phone: 256-533-8020
Fax: 256-517-8416

Intergraph Corp
1 Madison Industrial Pk
Huntsville, AL 35894
E-mail: info@intergraph.com
www.intergraph.com
Phone: 256-730-2000
Fax: 256-730-7898
TF: 800-345-4856

Marshall George C Space Flight Center
NASA
MSFC, AL 35812
www.msfc.nasa.gov
Phone: 256-544-2121
Fax: 256-544-5852

SCI Systems Inc
2101 W Clinton Ave
Huntsville, AL 35805
www.sci.com
Phone: 256-882-4800
Fax: 256-882-4804

Teledyne Brown Engineering
PO Box 070007
Huntsville, AL 35807
www.tbe.com
Phone: 256-726-1000
Fax: 256-726-3570
TF: 800-933-2091

University of Alabama Huntsville
301 Sparkman Dr
Huntsville, AL 35899
www.uah.edu
Phone: 256-890-6120
Fax: 256-890-6073
TF: 800-824-2255

US Army Aviation & Missile Command
AMSAM-RD
Redstone Arsenal, AL 35898
ard.huji.ac.il/1025.htm
Phone: 256-876-3322
Fax: 256-876-9142

Quality of Living Indicators

Total Crime Index....................................11,716
(rates per 100,000 inhabitants)

Violent Crime
Murder/manslaughter............................ 11
Forcible rape 92
Robbery.. 301
Aggravated assault............................. 841

Property Crime
Burglary 1,848
Larceny theft 7,521
Motor vehicle theft 1,102

Cost of Living Index 90.9
(national average = 100)

Median Home Price $115,100

Education

Public Schools

Huntsville Board of Education
200 White St NE
Huntsville, AL 35801
www.hsv.k12.al.us/dept/merts/admin/board/
Phone: 256-532-4600
Fax: 256-532-4853

Number of Schools
Elementary 28
Middle 11
High 5

Student/Teacher Ratio
Grades K-5 .... 22.0:1
Grades 6-8 .... 15.0:1
Grades 9-12 .... 15.0:1

Private Schools

Number of Schools (all grades) 26

Colleges & Universities

Alabama A & M University
4900 Meridian St
Huntsville, AL 35811
www.aamu.edu
Phone: 256-851-5000
Fax: 256-851-5034

Calhoun Community College
6250 Hwy 31 N
Tanner, AL 35671
www.calhoun.cc.al.us
Phone: 256-306-2500
Fax: 256-306-2885
TF: 800-626-3628

JF Drake State Technical College
3421 Meridian St N
Huntsville, AL 35811
E-mail: dstc28@hotmail.com
www.dstc.cc.al.us
Phone: 256-539-8161
Fax: 256-539-6439

Oakwood College
7000 Adventist Blvd
Huntsville, AL 35896
www.oakwood.edu
Phone: 256-726-7000
Fax: 256-726-7154
TF: 800-824-5312

Southeastern Institute of Technology
200 Sparkman Dr
Huntsville, AL 35807
Phone: 256-837-9726

University of Alabama Huntsville
301 Sparkman Dr
Huntsville, AL 35899
www.uah.edu
Phone: 256-890-6120
Fax: 256-890-6073
TF: 800-824-2255

Hospitals

Athens-Limestone Hospital
700 W Market St
Athens, AL 35611
www.alhosp.com
Phone: 256-233-9292
Fax: 256-233-9277

Crestwood Medical Center
1 Hospital Dr
Huntsville, AL 35801
crestwoodmedcenter.com
Phone: 256-882-3100
Fax: 256-880-4246

Decatur General Hospital
1201 7th St SE
Decatur, AL 35601
www.decaturgeneral.org
Phone: 256-341-2000
Fax: 256-341-2648

Huntsville Hospital System
101 Sivley Rd SW
Huntsville, AL 35801
www.hhsys.org
Phone: 256-533-8020
Fax: 256-517-8416

Parkway Medical Center Hospital
1874 Beltline Rd SW
Decatur, AL 35601
www.parkway-pavilion.com
Phone: 256-350-2211
Fax: 256-350-8415

Transportation

Airport(s)

Huntsville International Airport (HSV)
12 miles W of downtown (approx 20 minutes) 256-772-9395

Mass Transit

Huntsville Public Transit
$1 Base fare 256-532-7433

Rail/Bus

Greyhound Bus Station
601 Monroe St NW
Huntsville, AL 35801
Phone: 256-534-1681
TF: 800-231-2222

Utilities

Electricity
Huntsville Utilities 256-535-1200
www.hsvutil.org

Gas
North Alabama Gas 256-772-0227
www.nagd.com

Water
Madison County Water Dept 256-532-1659

Garbage Collection/Recycling
Huntsville Recycling Hotline 256-830-2467
Madison County Waste Control 256-532-3718

Telecommunications

Telephone
BellSouth 800-753-3320
www.bellsouth.com

Cable Television
Comcast Cablevision 256-859-7800
Knology 256-533-5353
www.knology.com

Internet Service Providers (ISPs)
HiWAAY Information Services 256-533-4296
www.hiwaay.net

Banks

Colonial Bank
101 Governors Dr
Huntsville, AL 35801
Phone: 256-551-4700
Fax: 256-551-4800
TF: 800-533-0655

Compass Bank
114 Governors Dr
Huntsville, AL 35801
Phone: 256-532-6273
Fax: 256-532-6277
TF: 800-239-1166

Regions Bank
216 West Side Sq
Huntsville, AL 35801
Phone: 256-535-0100
Fax: 256-535-0338
TF: 800-734-4667

SouthTrust Bank of Huntsville NA
409 Madison St SE
Huntsville, AL 35801
Phone: 256-533-3600
Fax: 256-551-4009

Shopping

Madison Square Mall
5901 University Dr
Huntsville, AL 35806
Phone: 256-830-5407

Market Square Mall
721 Clinton Ave W
Huntsville, AL 35804
Phone: 256-533-3414
Fax: 256-533-3454

Parkway City Mall
2801 Memorial Pkwy S
Huntsville, AL 35801
Phone: 256-533-0700
Fax: 256-533-9349

Media

Newspapers and Magazines

Huntsville Times*
2317 S Memorial Pkwy
Huntsville, AL 35801
www.al.com/hsvtimes/hsv.html
Phone: 256-532-4000
Fax: 256-532-4420
TF: 800-239-5271

**Indicates major daily newspapers*

Television

WAAY-TV Ch 31 (ABC)
1000 Monte Sano Blvd SE
Huntsville, AL 35801
www.waaytv.com
Phone: 256-533-3131
Fax: 256-533-5191

WAFF-TV Ch 48 (NBC)
1414 Memorial Pkwy N
Huntsville, AL 35801
www.waff.com
Phone: 256-533-4848
Fax: 256-534-4101

WHIQ-TV Ch 25 (PBS)
2112 11th Ave S Suite 400
Birmingham, AL 35205
www.aptv.org/InsideAPT/WHIQ25.html
Phone: 205-328-8756
Fax: 205-251-2192

WHNT-TV Ch 19 (CBS)
PO Box 19
Huntsville, AL 35804
www.whnt19.com
Phone: 256-533-1919
Fax: 256-536-9468

WZDX-TV CH 54 (Fox)
1309 N Memorial Pkwy
Huntsville, AL 35801
www.fox54.com
Phone: 256-533-5454
Fax: 256-533-5315

Radio

WAHR-FM 99.1 MHz (AC)
2714 Lawrence Ave SW
Huntsville, AL 35805
E-mail: wahr@hiwaay.net
www.star99.fm
Phone: 256-536-1568
Fax: 256-536-4416

WDJL-AM 1000 kHz (Oldies)
6420 Stringfield Rd
Huntsville, AL 35806
Phone: 256-852-1223
Fax: 256-852-1900

WEUP-AM 1600 kHz (Urban)
2609 Jordan Ln NW
Huntsville, AL 35806
Phone: 256-837-9387
Fax: 256-837-9404

WEUP-FM 92.1 MHz (Urban)
2609 Jordan Ln NW
Huntsville, AL 35806
Phone: 256-837-9387
Fax: 256-837-9404

WJAB-FM 90.9 MHz (NPR)
PO Box 1687
Normal, AL 35762
E-mail: mburns@asnaam.aamu.edu
Phone: 256-851-5795
Fax: 256-851-5907

WLOR-AM 1550 kHz (Urban)
2523 Bronco Cir NW
Huntsville, AL 35816
Phone: 256-721-0035
Fax: 256-722-0318

WLRH-FM 89.3 MHz (NPR)
John Wright Dr University of Alabama-Huntsville
Huntsville, AL 35899
www.wlrh.org
Phone: 256-895-9574
Fax: 256-830-4577

WNDA-FM 95.1 MHz (Rel)
2407 9th Ave SW
Huntsville, AL 35805
E-mail: wnda@juno.com
www.wnda.com
Phone: 256-534-2433

WOCG-FM 90.1 MHz (Rel)
7000 Adventist Blvd
Huntsville, AL 35896
E-mail: wocg@oakwood.edu
www.oakwood.edu/wocg
Phone: 256-726-7418
Fax: 256-726-7417

WTAK-FM 106.1 MHz (CR)
401 14th St SE
Decatur, AL 35601
www.wtak.com
Phone: 256-353-1811
Fax: 256-353-2470

WTKI-AM 1450 kHz (N/T)
2305 Holmes Ave
Huntsville, AL 35816
www.wtki1450.com
Phone: 256-533-1450
Fax: 256-536-4349

Attractions

Huntsville's past as a cotton processing center and seat of government is preserved in the Twickenham Historic District, Huntsville Depot Museum, and Alabama's Constitution Village, a living history museum. Since 1950, however, the city has been known as a center for space technology. The U.S. Space and Rocket Center, the world's largest space attraction, offers hands-on astronaut training exhibits, as well as displays of many NASA spacecraft. The Center includes the Space Museum, Rocket and Shuttle parks, the Spacedome Theater, the U.S. Space Camp and Academy, and a bus tour of NASA's George C. Marshall Space Flight Center.

Alabama's Constitution Village Phone: 256-564-8100
109 Gates Ave Fax: 256-564-8151
Huntsville, AL 35801 TF: 800-678-1819

Burritt Museum & Park Phone: 256-536-2882
3101 Burritt Dr Fax: 256-532-1784
Huntsville, AL 35801
E-mail: bm-recep@ci.huntsville.al.us
ci.huntsville.al.us/Burritt

Harrison Brothers Hardware Store Phone: 256-536-3631
124 Southside Sq
Huntsville, AL 35801

Historic Huntsville Depot Phone: 256-564-8100
320 Church St Fax: 256-564-8151
Huntsville, AL 35801 TF: 800-678-1819
www.earlyworks.com

Huntsville Art League Phone: 256-534-3860
2801 S Memorial Pkwy Gallery
Huntsville, AL 35801

Huntsville Museum of Art Phone: 256-535-4350
300 Church St S Fax: 256-532-1743
Huntsville, AL 35801
www.hsv.tis.net/hma

Huntsville Opera Theater Phone: 256-881-4796
700 Monroe St Von Braun Center Playhouse
Huntsville, AL 35802
fly.hiwaay.net/~mbeutjer/hot.html

Huntsville Symphony Orchestra Phone: 256-539-4818
PO Box 2400 Fax: 256-539-4819
Huntsville, AL 35804
E-mail: hso@ro.com
www.hso.org

Huntsville/Madison County Botanical Garden Phone: 256-830-4447
4747 Bob Wallace Ave Fax: 256-830-5314
Huntsville, AL 35805
E-mail: vmhurst@traveller.com
www.hsvbg.org/

Limestone Zoological Park & Exotic Wildlife Refuge Phone: 256-230-0330
30193 Nick Davis Rd Fax: 256-230-0990
Harvest, AL 35749
E-mail: wildside@garply.com
www.garply.com/~wildside/

Little River Canyon National Preserve Phone: 256-997-9239
PO Box 45 Fax: 256-997-9153
Fort Payne, AL 35967
www.nps.gov/liri

Madison County Nature Trail Phone: 256-883-9501
5000 Nature Trail Rd
Huntsville, AL 35803

Maple Hill Cemetery Phone: 256-427-5730
203 Maple Hill Dr Fax: 256-427-5733
Huntsville, AL 35801

Monte Sano State Park Phone: 256-534-3757
5105 Nolen Ave Fax: 256-539-7069
Huntsville, AL 35801

Russell Cave National Monument Phone: 256-495-2672
3729 County Rd 98 Fax: 256-495-9220
Bridgeport, AL 35740
www.nps.gov/ruca/

Twickenham Historic District Phone: 256-551-2230
Downtown Huntsville
Huntsville, AL 35801

US Space & Rocket Center Phone: 256-837-3400
1 Tranquility Base Fax: 256-837-6137
Huntsville, AL 35805 TF: 800-637-7223
E-mail: joeb@spacecamp.com
www.ussrc.com/

Weeden House Museum Phone: 256-536-7718
300 Gates Ave SE
Huntsville, AL 35801

Sports Teams & Facilities

Huntsville Channel Cats (hockey) Phone: 256-551-2383
700 Monroe St Fax: 256-551-2382
Huntsville, AL 35801
www.channelcats.net

Huntsville Speedway Phone: 256-882-9191
357 Hegia Burrow Rd Fax: 256-882-9131
Huntsville, AL 35803
E-mail: dstewart@traveller.com
www.huntsvillespeedway.com

Huntsville Stars (baseball) Phone: 256-882-2562
3125 Leeman Ferry Rd Joe Davis Stadium Fax: 256-880-0801
Huntsville, AL 35801
www.huntsvillestars.com

Annual Events

Big Spring Jam (late September) 256-533-5723
Black Arts Festival (late June) 256-837-9387
Civil War Living History Weekend (early November & early May) 256-536-2882
Cotton Row Run (late May) 256-533-4757
Down Home Blues Festival (late May) 256-536-4312
Galaxy of Lights (late November-early January) 256-830-4447
Huntsville Pilgrimage (early May) 256-533-5723
Indian Heritage Festival (mid-October) 256-536-2882
Living History Weekends (June-August) 256-536-2882
Northeast Alabama State Fair (early-mid-September) 256-533-5723
Old Fashioned Trade Day (early September) 256-536-0097
Panoply-Huntsville's Festival of the Arts (late April) 256-519-2787
Rocket City Marathon (early December) 256-828-6207
Sorghum & Harvest Festival (early November) 256-536-2882
State Fiddling Bluegrass Convention (mid-September) 256-859-4470
Under the Christmas Tree (mid-November) 256-533-1953

Indianapolis, Indiana

County: **Marion**

INDIANAPOLIS is located in central Indiana along the banks of the White River. Major cities within 100 miles include Terre Haute, Indiana; Louisville, Kentucky; and Dayton, Ohio.

Area (Land) .... 361.7 sq mi
Area (Water)................................ 6.6 sq mi
Elevation...................................... 717 ft
Latitude .... 39-71-43 N
Longitude................................ 86-09-35 W
Time Zone .... EST
Area Code.. 317

Climate

Indianapolis has a temperate climate with four distinct seasons. Winters are cold, with average high temperatures in the mid- to upper 30s and lows in the high teens to low 20s. The average annual snowfall in Indianapolis is 23 inches. Summer days are warm, with average high temperatures in the mid-80s, while evenings cool down into the low to mid-60s. Precipitation is fairly evenly distributed throughout the year—July tends to be the wettest month and January is the driest.

Average Temperatures & Precipitation

Temperatures

	Jan	Feb	Mar	Apr	May	Jun	Jul	Aug	Sep	Oct	Nov	Dec
High	34	38	51	63	74	83	86	84	78	66	52	39
Low	17	21	32	42	52	61	65	63	56	44	34	23

Precipitation

	Jan	Feb	Mar	Apr	May	Jun	Jul	Aug	Sep	Oct	Nov	Dec
Inches	2.3	2.5	3.8	3.7	4.0	3.5	4.5	3.6	2.9	2.6	3.2	3.3

History

Indianapolis was founded in 1821 after being chosen as the new, centralized location for Indiana State Government (which had originally been located in Corydon). The city was platted by engineer Alexander Ralston, who had assisted noted architect Pierre l'Enfant in planning the nation's capital, Washington DC. Indianapolis officially became the capital of Indiana in 1825.

Early development in Indianapolis was fairly slow until 1830, when the National Road reached the city. The railroad soon followed, and with the city's accessibility and central location in the midst of a rich agricultural region, Indianapolis soon became an agricultural processing, manufacturing, and transportation hub. By the mid-1800s, immigrants of various ethnic groups, including Irish, Germans, Italians, and Eastern Europeans as well as African-Americans from the southern United States, were drawn in large numbers to the city, seeking the economic opportunities created by industry. Indianapolis was incorporated as a city in 1847, and during the 1850s the city's population more than doubled.

Government has played a critical role in Indianapolis' economy throughout the city's history. In 1970, the city implemented legislation called Unigov, by which the City of Indianapolis and Marion County were consolidated to form one government body. This event greatly increased Indianapolis' boundaries, population, and tax base, and ultimately improved the city's economy.

Throughout the years, Indianapolis has remained a major commercial, manufacturing, and transportation center. Home to one of the country's top universities—Indiana University-Purdue University at Indianapolis—as well as numerous cultural organizations, sports teams, and the world-famous Indianapolis 500, the city has also emerged as a leading center for education, entertainment, and culture. With a population exceeding 740,000, Indianapolis is presently the 13th largest city in the United States.

Population

1990 Census 731,311
1998 Estimate............................. 741,304
% Change 1.4

Racial/Ethnic Breakdown
White.. 75.8%
Black 22.6%
Other.. 1.6%
Hispanic Origin (may be of any race) 1.1%

Age Breakdown
Under 5 years................................ 8.0%
5 to 17... 17.7%
18 to 20.. 4.2%
21 to 24.. 6.4%
25 to 34....................................... 20.1%
35 to 44....................................... 14.6%
45 to 54.. 9.3%
55 to 64.. 8.3%
65 to 74.. 6.7%
75+ years 4.8%
Median Age.................................... 31.7

Gender Breakdown
Male.. 47.5%
Female... 52.5%

Government

Type of Government: Mayor-Council (consolidated)

Indianapolis Capital Asset Management Dept
200 E Washington St Suite 2360
Indianapolis, IN 46204
Phone: 317-327-4700
Fax: 317-327-4577

Indianapolis City Hall
200 E Washington St
Indianapolis, IN 46204
Phone: 317-327-4348
Fax: 317-327-3980

Indianapolis City-County Council
200 E Washington St Suite 241
Indianapolis, IN 46204
Phone: 317-327-4242
Fax: 317-327-4230

Indianapolis Clerk of Council
200 E Washington St Rm W122
Indianapolis, IN 46204
Phone: 317-327-4740
Fax: 317-327-3893

Indianapolis Economic Development Div
200 E Washington St Rm 2001
Indianapolis, IN 46204
Phone: 317-327-5402
Fax: 317-327-5858

Indianapolis Fire Dept
555 N New Jersey St
Indianapolis, IN 46204
Phone: 317-327-6041
Fax: 317-327-6043

Indianapolis Human Resources Div
200 E Washington St Rm 1541
Indianapolis, IN 46204
Phone: 317-327-5200

Indianapolis Mayor
200 E Washington St Suite 2501
Indianapolis, IN 46204
Phone: 317-327-3601
Fax: 317-327-3980

Indianapolis Metropolitan Development Dept
200 E Washington St Rm 2042
Indianapolis, IN 46204
Phone: 317-327-3698
Fax: 317-327-5858

Indianapolis Parks & Recreation Dept
200 E Washington St Suite 2301
Indianapolis, IN 46204
Phone: 317-327-7275
Fax: 317-327-7033

Indianapolis Planning Div
200 E Washington St Suite 1841
Indianapolis, IN 46204
Phone: 317-327-5151
Fax: 317-327-5103

Indianapolis Police Dept
50 N Alabama St
Indianapolis, IN 46204
Phone: 317-327-3282
Fax: 317-327-3289

Indianapolis Public Works Dept
200 E Washington St Rm 2460
Indianapolis, IN 46204
Phone: 317-327-4000
Fax: 317-327-4954

Indianapolis Solid Waste Div
2700 S Belmont Ave
Indianapolis, IN 46221
Phone: 317-327-5684

Indianapolis-Marion County Public Library
40 E Saint Clair St
Indianapolis, IN 46204
Phone: 317-269-1700
Fax: 317-269-1768

Important Phone Numbers

AAA 317-923-1500
American Express Travel 317-237-2230
Dental Referral 317-471-8131
Driver's License/Vehicle Registration Information 317-923-3867
Emergency 911
HotelDocs 800-468-3537
Indiana Revenue Dept 317-233-4015
Marion County Tax Information Line 317-327-4444
Metropolitan Indianapolis Board of Realtors 317-956-5000
Poison Control Center 317-929-2323
Time/Temp 317-635-5959
Voter Registration Information 317-232-3939
Weather 317-635-5959

Information Sources

Better Business Bureau Serving Central Indiana
22 E Washington St Suite 200
Indianapolis, IN 46204
www.indianapolis.bbb.org
Phone: 317-488-2222
Fax: 317-488-2224

Indiana Convention Center & RCA Dome
100 S Capitol Ave
Indianapolis, IN 46225
www.iccrd.com
Phone: 317-262-3410
Fax: 317-262-3685

Indianapolis Chamber of Commerce
320 N Meridian St Suite 200
Indianapolis, IN 46204
www.indychamber.com
Phone: 317-464-2200
Fax: 317-464-2217
TF: 800-333-4492

Indianapolis City Center
201 S Capitol Ave Pan Am Plaza Suite 200
Indianapolis, IN 46225
www.indy.org
Phone: 317-237-5200
Fax: 317-237-5211
TF: 800-323-4639

Indianapolis Convention & Visitors Assn
200 S Capitol Ave 1 RCA Dome Suite 100
Indianapolis, IN 46225
www.indy.org
Phone: 317-639-4282
Fax: 317-639-5273
TF: 800-323-4639

Indianapolis Economic Development Corp
41 E Washington St Suite 310
Indianapolis, IN 46204
www.iedc.com
Phone: 317-236-6262
Fax: 317-236-6275
TF: 877-236-4332

Marion County
200 E Washington St W-122 City County Bldg
Indianapolis, IN 46204
www.indygov.org/county
Phone: 317-327-3200
Fax: 317-327-4757

Online Resources

4Indianapolis.com
www.4indianapolis.com

About.com Guide to Indianapolis
indianapolis.about.com/local/midwestus/indianapolis

Anthill City Guide Indianapolis
www.anthill.com/city.asp?city=indianapolis

Area Guide Indianapolis
indianapolis.areaguides.net

Boulevards Indianapolis
www.indianapolis.com

City Knowledge Indianapolis
www.cityknowledge.com/in_indianapolis.htm

DigitalCity Indianapolis
home.digitalcity.com/indianapolis

Excite.com Indianapolis City Guide
www.excite.com/travel/countries/united_states/indiana/indianapolis

Front Page
www.indianapolis.org/menu1.htm

Gateway to Greater Indianapolis
www.bit-wise.com/magic

Gay & Lesbian Indianapolis
www.gayindy.org

Go Indy
www.goindy.com

Greater Indianapolis
www.greaterindy.com

Indianapolis Connect
www.indplsconnect.com/

Indianapolis Online
www.indianapolis.in.us

Indy Links
www.indylinks.com

Indy.com
www.indy.com

IndyMall
www.indymall.com/

IndySearch
www.indysearch.com/

InIndianapolis.com
www.inindy.com/

Lodging.com Indianapolis Indiana
www.lodging.com/auto/guides/indianapolis-area-in.html

Area Communities

Communities in the Indianapolis metropolitan area (including Boone, Hamilton, Hancock, Hendricks, Johnson, Madison, Marion, Morgan, and Shelby counties) with populations greater than 10,000 include:

Anderson
120 E 8th St
Anderson, IN 46016
Phone: 765-648-6075
Fax: 765-648-5910

Beech Grove
806 Main St
Beech Grove, IN 46107
Phone: 317-784-3003
Fax: 317-788-4976

Brownsburg
80 E Vermont St
Brownsburg, IN 46112
Phone: 317-852-1120
Fax: 317-852-1135

Carmel
1 Civic Sq
Carmel, IN 46032
Phone: 317-571-2400
Fax: 317-571-2410

Fishers
1 Municipal Dr
Fishers, IN 46038
Phone: 317-595-3140
Fax: 317-595-3115

Franklin
55 W Madison St
Franklin, IN 46131
Phone: 317-736-3609
Fax: 317-736-7244

Greenfield
110 S State St
Greenfield, IN 46140
Phone: 317-462-8515
Fax: 317-462-8614

Lawrence
9001 E 59th St Suite 301
Lawrence, IN 46226
Phone: 317-545-6191
Fax: 317-549-4830

Lebanon
201 E Main St
Lebanon, IN 46052
Phone: 765-482-1201
Fax: 765-482-8883

Martinsville
59 S Jefferson St
Martinsville, IN 46151
Phone: 765-342-6012
Fax: 765-342-6725

Noblesville
16 S 10th St
Noblesville, IN 46060
Phone: 317-773-4614
Fax: 317-776-6363

Plainfield
PO Box 65
Plainfield, IN 46168
Phone: 317-839-2561
Fax: 317-838-5236

Shelbyville
44 W Washington St
Shelbyville, IN 46176
Phone: 317-392-5103
Fax: 317-392-5158

Speedway
1450 N Lynhurst Dr
Speedway, IN 46224
Phone: 317-241-2566
Fax: 317-240-1322

Economy

Indianapolis has a diverse economic base that ranges from automotive parts manufacturing to education to professional and amateur sports. Government has long been a vital component of Indianapolis' economic base. Local, state, and federal government are the top three employers in the nine-county Indianapolis Metropolitan Statistical Area, providing jobs for more than 102,000 area residents in various agencies. Services is the area's largest employment sector, with healthcare being the largest service industry. Retail trade and manufacturing also play important roles in Indianapolis' economy. The city is the corporate home of pharmaceutical manufacturing giant Eli Lilly and Company, which is the area's fifth largest employer.

Unemployment Rate 2.7%*
Per Capita Income.......................... $18,151*
Median Family Income...................... $35,054*

** Information given is for Marion County.*

Principal Industries & Number of Wage Earners

Marion County - 1998

Agriculture & Services 174,149
Construction 27,653
Finance 45,463
Manufacturing 82,118
Mining 212
Retail Trade 104,886
Transportation, Communications, & Public Utilities 41,711
Wholesale Trade 41,088

Major Employers

Clarian Health Partners Inc Phone: 317-929-2000
PO Box 1367 Fax: 317-929-1867
Indianapolis, IN 46206
www.clarian.com/

Community Hospital North Phone: 317-849-6262
7150 Clearvista Dr Fax: 317-588-7957
Indianapolis, IN 46256

Community Hospitals East Phone: 317-355-1411
1500 N Ritter Ave Fax: 317-351-7723
Indianapolis, IN 46219
www.commhospindy.org

Delphi Energy & Chaise Phone: 765-646-2000
2900 S Scatterfield Rd Fax: 765-646-3989
Anderson, IN 46013
www.delphiauto.com

General Motors Corp Allison Transmission Div Phone: 317-242-5000
4700 W 10th St Fax: 317-242-3123
Indianapolis, IN 46222

Guide Corp Phone: 765-644-5511
2915 Pendleton Ave Fax: 765-641-5345
Anderson, IN 46016

Indiana University-Purdue University Indianapolis Phone: 317-274-5555
425 University Blvd Fax: 317-278-1862
Indianapolis, IN 46202
www.iupui.edu

Indianapolis City Hall Phone: 317-327-4348
200 E Washington St Fax: 317-327-3980
Indianapolis, IN 46204
www.indygov.org

Indianapolis Public Schools Phone: 317-226-4411
120 E Walnut St Fax: 317-226-4936
Indianapolis, IN 46204
www.ips.k12.in.us

Kroger Co Central Marketing Area Phone: 317-579-8100
5960 Castleway West Dr Fax: 317-579-8080
Indianapolis, IN 46250

Lilly Eli & Co Phone: 317-276-2000
Lilly Corporate Ctr Fax: 317-276-9117
Indianapolis, IN 46285 TF: 800-545-5979
www.lilly.com

Marsh Supermarkets Inc Phone: 317-594-2100
9800 Crosspoint Blvd Fax: 317-594-2704
Indianapolis, IN 46256
www.marsh.net

Rolls-Royce Corp Phone: 317-230-2000
2001 S Tibbs Ave Fax: 317-230-5100
Indianapolis, IN 46241

Saint Vincent Hospital & Health Systems Phone: 317-338-2345
2001 W 86th St Fax: 317-338-7005
Indianapolis, IN 46260
www.stvincent.org

Quality of Living Indicators

Total Crime Index 40,397*
(rates per 100,000 inhabitants)

Violent Crime
Murder/manslaughter 112*
Forcible rape 424*
Robbery 2,598*
Aggravated assault 4,579*

Property Crime
Burglary 9,971*
Larceny theft 17,279*
Motor vehicle theft 5,434*

** Information given is for Indianapolis/Marion County.*

Cost of Living Index 96.2
(national average = 100)

Median Home Price $110,900

Education

Public Schools

Indianapolis Public Schools Phone: 317-226-4411
120 E Walnut St Fax: 317-226-4936
Indianapolis, IN 46204
www.ips.k12.in.us

Number of Schools
Elementary 52
Middle 16
High 5
Alternative 4

Student/Teacher Ratio
All Grades 16.7:1

Private Schools

Number of Schools (all grades) .... 70+

Colleges & Universities

Butler University Phone: 317-940-8000
4600 Sunset Ave Fax: 317-940-8150
Indianapolis, IN 46208 TF: 800-368-6852
E-mail: Admission@Butler.edu
www.butler.edu

Franklin College
501 E Monroe St
Franklin, IN 46131
E-mail: broshears@delta.franklincoll.edu
www.franklincoll.edu
Phone: 317-738-8000
Fax: 317-736-6030
TF: 800-852-0232

Indiana Business College
802 N Meridian St
Indianapolis, IN 46204
www.indianabusinesscollege.com
Phone: 317-264-5656
Fax: 317-634-0471
TF: 800-999-9229

Indiana University-Purdue University Indianapolis
425 University Blvd
Indianapolis, IN 46202
www.iupui.edu
Phone: 317-274-5555
Fax: 317-278-1862

ITT Technical Institute
9511 Angola Ct
Indianapolis, IN 46268
Phone: 317-875-8640
Fax: 317-875-8641
TF: 800-937-4488

Ivy Tech State College Central Indiana
1 W 26th St
Indianapolis, IN 46208
www.ivy.tec.in.us/Indianapolis
Phone: 317-921-4882
Fax: 317-921-4753

Lincoln Technical Institute
1201 Stadium Dr
Indianapolis, IN 46202
www.lincolntech.com
Phone: 317-632-5553
Fax: 317-687-0475
TF: 800-554-4465

Marian College
3200 Cold Spring Rd
Indianapolis, IN 46222
www.marian.edu
Phone: 317-955-6000
Fax: 317-955-6401

Martin University
2171 Avondale Pl
Indianapolis, IN 46218
www.martin.edu
Phone: 317-543-3235
Fax: 317-543-4790

University of Indianapolis
1400 E Hanna Ave
Indianapolis, IN 46227
www.uindy.edu
Phone: 317-788-3368
Fax: 317-788-3300
TF: 800-232-8634

Hospitals

Community Hospital South
1402 E County Line Rd S
Indianapolis, IN 46227
Phone: 317-887-7000
Fax: 317-877-4670

Community Hospitals East
1500 N Ritter Ave
Indianapolis, IN 46219
www.commhospindy.org
Phone: 317-355-1411
Fax: 317-351-7723

Indiana University Medical Center
550 N University Blvd
Indianapolis, IN 46202
www.iupui.edu/home/medcentr.html
Phone: 317-274-5000
Fax: 317-274-6777

Methodist Hospital of Indiana
1701 N Senate Blvd
Indianapolis, IN 46202
Phone: 317-929-2000
Fax: 317-929-6188
TF: 800-248-1199

Richard L Roudebush Veterans Affairs Medical Center
1481 W 10th St
Indianapolis, IN 46202
Phone: 317-554-0000
Fax: 317-554-0028

Saint Francis Hospital & Health Centers
1600 Albany St
Beech Grove, IN 46107
www.stfrancis-indy.org
Phone: 317-787-3311
Fax: 317-782-6731

Saint Vincent Carmel Hospital
13500 N Meridian St
Carmel, IN 46032
Phone: 317-573-7000

Saint Vincent Hospital & Health Systems
2001 W 86th St
Indianapolis, IN 46260
www.stvincent.org
Phone: 317-338-2345
Fax: 317-338-7005

Westview Hospital
3630 Guion Rd
Indianapolis, IN 46222
Phone: 317-924-6661
Fax: 317-920-7551

Winona Memorial Hospital
3232 N Meridian St
Indianapolis, IN 46208
Phone: 317-924-3392
Fax: 317-927-2875

Wishard Health Services
1001 W 10th St
Indianapolis, IN 46202
Phone: 317-639-6671
Fax: 317-630-6947

Women's Hospital
8111 Township Line Rd
Indianapolis, IN 46260
Phone: 317-875-5994
Fax: 317-554-6807

Transportation

Airport(s)

Indianapolis International Airport (IND)
10 miles SW of downtown (approx 10 minutes) . . .317-487-9594

Mass Transit

Metro
$1 Base fare 317-635-3344

Rail/Bus

Greyhound/Trailways Bus Station
350 S Illinois St
Indianapolis, IN 46204
Phone: 317-267-3076
TF: 800-231-2222

Indianapolis Amtrak Station
350 S Illinois St
Indianapolis, IN 46225
Phone: 317-263-0550
TF: 800-872-7245

Utilities

Electricity
Indianapolis Power & Light Co 317-261-8261
www.ipalco.com

Gas
Citizens Gas & Coke Utility .317-924-3311
www.citizensgas.com

Water
Indianapolis Water Co 317-639-1501
www.iwcr.com/IWC.html

Garbage Collection/Recycling
Indianapolis Solid Waste Div 317-327-5684
www.indygov.org/dpw/solid_waste.htm

Telecommunications

Telephone

Ameritech....................................800-223-9960
www.ameritech.com

Cable Television

Comcast Cablevision...........................317-872-2225
Time Warner Cable............................317-632-2288
www.timewarner.com

Internet Service Providers (ISPs)

IndyNet.......................................317-251-5208
www.indy.net
Internet Indiana..............................317-876-5638
www.in.net
IQuest Internet Inc...........................317-259-5050
www.iquest.net
Net Direct Inc................................317-251-5252
www.netdirect.net
SCICAN.......................................765-349-4458
www.scican.net

Banks

Fifth Third Bank Indiana
130 E Market St
Indianapolis, IN 46204
Phone: 317-237-8000
Fax: 317-237-8150
TF: 800-972-3030

First Chicago NBD Bank
1 Indiana Sq
Indianapolis, IN 46266
Phone: 317-266-6000
Fax: 317-266-5626
TF: 800-548-3600

First Indiana Bank
135 N Pennsylvania St First Indiana Plaza
Indianapolis, IN 46204
www.firstindiana.com
Phone: 317-269-1200
Fax: 317-269-1341
TF: 800-888-8586

Harrington Bank FSB
9775 Fall Creek Rd
Indianapolis, IN 46256
Phone: 317-845-9619

Huntington National Bank
8520 N Center Run Dr
Indianapolis, IN 46250
Phone: 317-849-8909
Fax: 317-849-8915

KeyBank NA
10 W Market St
Indianapolis, IN 46204
Phone: 317-464-8008
Fax: 317-464-8038

National City Bank Indiana
101 W Washington St
Indianapolis, IN 46255
Phone: 317-267-7000
Fax: 317-267-6156

Union Federal Bank
45 N Pennsylvania St
Indianapolis, IN 46204
www.unionfedbank.com
Phone: 317-269-4700
Fax: 317-269-4857
TF: 800-284-8585

Union Planters Bank NA
1 Indiana Sq
Indianapolis, IN 46204
Phone: 317-221-6040
Fax: 317-221-6043

Shopping

Castleton Square Mall
6020 E 82nd St
Indianapolis, IN 46250
Phone: 317-849-9993
Fax: 317-849-4689

Circle Centre Mall
49 W Maryland St
Indianapolis, IN 46204
Phone: 317-681-8000
Fax: 317-681-5697

Fountain Square
1105 E Prospect St
Indianapolis, IN 46203
E-mail: info@fountainsquareindy.com
www.fountainsquareindy.com
Phone: 317-686-6010
Fax: 317-686-6002

Glendale Center
6101 N Keystone Ave
Indianapolis, IN 46220
Phone: 317-251-9281
Fax: 317-255-5107

Greenwood Park Mall
1251 US Hwy 31
Greenwood, IN 46142
Phone: 317-881-6758
Fax: 317-887-8606

Indianapolis City Market
222 E Market St
Indianapolis, IN 46204
E-mail: citymarket@iquest.net
www.indianapoliscitymarket.com
Phone: 317-634-9266
Fax: 317-637-6814

Indianapolis Downtown Antique Mall
1044 Virginia Ave
Indianapolis, IN 46203
Phone: 317-635-5336
Fax: 317-635-5336

Keystone at the Crossing
8701 Keystone Crossing Blvd
Indianapolis, IN 46240
Phone: 317-574-4000

Lafayette Square Mall
3919 Lafayette Rd
Indianapolis, IN 46254
Phone: 317-291-6390

LS Ayres & Co
6020 E 82nd St
Indianapolis, IN 46250
Phone: 317-579-2900
Fax: 317-579-2932

Shops at 52nd Street
652 E 52nd St
Indianapolis, IN 46205
Phone: 317-283-3753
Fax: 317-283-0053

Southport Antique Mall
2028 E Southport Rd
Indianapolis, IN 46227
E-mail: antique@iquest.net
Phone: 317-786-8246
Fax: 317-786-9926

Washington Square Mall
10202 E Washington St
Indianapolis, IN 46229
Phone: 317-899-4567
Fax: 317-897-9428

Media

Newspapers and Magazines

Carmel News Tribune
PO Box 1478
Noblesville, IN 46060
Phone: 317-773-1210
Fax: 317-598-6360

Hendricks County Flyer
PO Box 6
Plainfield, IN 46168
www.flyergroup.com
Phone: 317-839-5129
Fax: 317-839-6546

Indiana Business Magazine
1000 Waterway Blvd
Indianapolis, IN 46202
E-mail: info@indianabusiness.com
www.indianabusiness.com
Phone: 317-692-1200
Fax: 317-692-4250

Indianapolis Business Journal
41 E Washington St Suite 200
Indianapolis, IN 46204
www.ibj.com
Phone: 317-634-6200
Fax: 317-263-5406

Indianapolis Monthly
40 Monument Cir Suite 100
Indianapolis, IN 46204
Phone: 317-237-9288
Fax: 317-684-2080
TF: 888-403-9005

Indianapolis Star*
307 N Pennsylvania St
Indianapolis, IN 46204
E-mail: stareditor@starnews.com
www.starnews.com
Phone: 317-633-1240
Fax: 317-633-1038
TF: 800-669-7827

Lebanon Reporter The
117 E Washington St
Lebanon, IN 46052
Phone: 765-482-4650
Fax: 765-482-4652

NUVO Newsweekly
811 E Westfield Blvd
Indianapolis, IN 46220
E-mail: nuvo@nuvo.net
www.nuvo-online.com
Phone: 317-254-2400
Fax: 317-254-2405

Westside Community News
551 S Fleming
Indianapolis, IN 46241
Phone: 317-241-7363
Fax: 317-240-6397

**Indicates major daily newspapers*

Television

WAV-TV Ch 53 (Ind)
6264 La Pas Trail
Indianapolis, IN 46268
Phone: 317-293-9600
Fax: 317-328-3870

WFYI-TV Ch 20 (PBS)
1401 N Meridian St
Indianapolis, IN 46202
www.wfyi.org
Phone: 317-636-2020
Fax: 317-633-7418

WHMB-TV Ch 40 (Ind)
10511 Greenfield Ave
Noblesville, IN 46060
www.lesea.com/whmb.htm
Phone: 317-773-5050
Fax: 317-776-4051

WISH-TV Ch 8 (CBS)
1950 N Meridian St
Indianapolis, IN 46202
E-mail: wishmail@wish-tv.com
www.wish-tv.com
Phone: 317-923-8888
Fax: 317-931-2242

WNDY-TV Ch 23 (UPN)
4551 W 16th St
Indianapolis, IN 46222
www.upn23.com
Phone: 317-241-2388
Fax: 317-381-6975

WRTV-TV Ch 6 (ABC)
1330 N Meridian St
Indianapolis, IN 46202
www.6news.com
Phone: 317-635-9788
Fax: 317-269-1445

WTBU-TV Ch 69 (Ind)
2835 N Illinois St
Indianapolis, IN 46208
www.wtbu.butler.edu
Phone: 317-940-9828
Fax: 317-940-5971

WTHR-TV Ch 13 (NBC)
1000 N Meridian St
Indianapolis, IN 46204
E-mail: 13news@wthr.com
www.wthr.com
Phone: 317-636-1313
Fax: 317-636-3717

WTTV-TV Ch 4 (WB)
3490 Bluff Rd
Indianapolis, IN 46217
E-mail: wb4@wb4.com
www.ttv.com
Phone: 317-782-4444
Fax: 317-780-5464

WXIN-TV Ch 59 (Fox)
1440 N Meridian St
Indianapolis, IN 46202
www.wxin.com
Phone: 317-632-5900
Fax: 317-687-6534

Radio

WBKS-FM 106.7 MHz (Urban)
6264 La Pas Trail
Indianapolis, IN 46268
www.wbksradio.com
Phone: 317-293-9600
Fax: 317-328-3870

WENS-FM 97.1 MHz (AC)
40 Monument Cir Suite 600
Indianapolis, IN 46204
www.wens.com
Phone: 317-266-9700
Fax: 317-684-2021

WFBQ-FM 94.7 MHz (CR)
6161 Fall Creek Rd
Indianapolis, IN 46220
www.wfbq.com
Phone: 317-257-7565
Fax: 317-253-6501

WFMS-FM 95.5 MHz (Ctry)
6810 N Shadeland Ave
Indianapolis, IN 46220
E-mail: info@wfms.com
www.wfms.com
Phone: 317-842-9550
Fax: 317-577-3361

WFYI-FM 90.1 MHz (NPR)
1401 N Meridian St
Indianapolis, IN 46202
www.wfyi.org
Phone: 317-636-2020
Fax: 317-633-7433

WGLD-FM 104.5 MHz (Oldies)
6810 N Shadeland Ave
Indianapolis, IN 46220
www.gold1045.com
Phone: 317-842-9550
Fax: 317-921-1996

WGRL-FM 93.9 MHz (Ctry)
6810 N Shadeland Ave
Indianapolis, IN 46220
www.939thebear.com
Phone: 317-842-9550
Fax: 317-577-3361

WHHH-FM 96.3 MHz (CHR)
6264 La Pas Trail
Indianapolis, IN 46268
www.whhh.com
Phone: 317-293-9600
Fax: 317-328-3870

WIBC-AM 1070 kHz (N/T)
40 Monument Cir Suite 400
Indianapolis, IN 46204
www.wibc.com
Phone: 317-266-9422
Fax: 317-684-2022

WKKG-FM 101.5 MHz (Ctry)
3212 Washington St
Columbus, IN 47203
www.wkkg.com
Phone: 812-372-4448
Fax: 812-372-1061
TF: 877-269-1015

WKLU-FM 101.9 MHz (CR)
733 N Green St
Brownsburg, IN 46112
www.oldies102wqfe.com
Phone: 317-852-9119
Fax: 317-852-8018

WMYS-AM 1430 kHz (Nost)
9245 N Meridian St Suite 300
Indianapolis, IN 46260
www.wmys.com
Phone: 317-816-4000
Fax: 317-816-4030

WNAP-FM 93.1 MHz (CR)
40 Monument Cir Suite 600
Indianapolis, IN 46204
E-mail: buzzard@wnap.com
www.wnap.com
Phone: 317-236-9300
Fax: 317-684-2024

WNDE-AM 1260 kHz (Sports)
6161 Fall Creek Rd
Indianapolis, IN 46220
www.wnde.com
Phone: 317-257-7565
Fax: 317-253-6501

WRZX-FM 103.3 MHz (Alt)
6161 Fall Creek Rd
Indianapolis, IN 46220
www.wrzx.com
Phone: 317-257-7565
Fax: 317-253-6501

WTLC-AM 1310 kHz (Rel)
40 Monument Cir 1 Emmis Plaza Suite 500
Indianapolis, IN 46204
www.wtlc.com
Phone: 317-955-9852
Fax: 317-684-2010

WTLC-FM 105.7 MHz (Urban)
40 Monument Cir 1 Emmis Plaza Suite 500
Indianapolis, IN 46204
www.wtlc.com
Phone: 317-955-9852
Fax: 317-684-2010

WTPI-FM 107.9 MHz (AC)
9245 N Meridian St Suite 300
Indianapolis, IN 46260
www.wtpi.com
Phone: 317-816-4000
Fax: 317-816-4060

WTTS-FM 92.3 MHz (AAA)
400 One City Centre
Bloomington, IN 47404
www.wttsfm.com
Phone: 812-332-3366
Fax: 812-331-4570

WXIR-FM 98.3 MHz (Rel)
4802 E 62nd St
Indianapolis, IN 46220
www.love98radio.com
Phone: 317-255-5484
Fax: 317-255-4452

WXLW-AM 950 kHz (Rel)
54 Monument Cir Suite 250
Indianapolis, IN 46204
www.wxlw.com
Phone: 317-655-9999
Fax: 317-655-9995

WYJZ-FM 100.9 MHz (Jazz)
6264 La Pas Trail
Indianapolis, IN 46268
www.wyjzradio.com
Phone: 317-293-9600
Fax: 317-328-3870

WZPL-FM 99.5 MHz (CHR)
9245 N Meridian St Suite 300
Indianapolis, IN 46260
www.wzpl.com
Phone: 317-816-4000
Fax: 317-816-4060

Attractions

The world-renowned Indy 500 automobile race attracts more than 350,000 spectators to Indianapolis every May, and the Brickyard 400 is held there each August. Indianapolis is also home to the world's largest Children's Museum; and the Eiteljorg Museum of American Indians and Western Art, the President Benjamin Harrison Home, Murat Temple, and Connor Prairie (a living history museum set in a restored 1836 village) are also a part of the Indianapolis cultural scene. The 60,500 seat RCA Dome (formerly called the Hoosier Dome) is home to the Indianapolis Colts football team and the National Track and Field Hall of Fame, and the new Indiana Basketball Hall of Fame is just 48 miles from Indianapolis, in the city of New Castle.

American Cabaret Theatre
401 E Michigan St
Indianapolis, IN 46204
E-mail: cabaret@indy.net
www.americancabarettheatre.com
Phone: 317-631-0334
Fax: 317-686-5443
TF: 800-375-8887

Anthenaeum The
401 E Michigan St
Indianapolis, IN 46204
Phone: 317-630-4569

Ballet International
502 N Capitol Ave Suite B
Indianapolis, IN 46204
Phone: 317-637-8979
Fax: 317-637-1637

Billie Creek Village & Inn
RR 2 Box 27
Rockville, IN 47872
www.billiecreek.org
Phone: 765-569-3430
Fax: 765-569-3582

Children's Museum of Indianapolis
3000 N Meridian St
Indianapolis, IN 46208
E-mail: tcmi@childrensmuseum.org
www.childrensmuseum.org
Phone: 317-924-5431
Fax: 317-920-2001
TF: 800-826-5431

Christ Church Cathedral
125 Monument Cir
Indianapolis, IN 46204
www.christcathedralindy.com
Phone: 317-636-4577
Fax: 317-635-1040

Christel DeHaan Fine Arts Center
1400 E Hanna Ave University of Indianapolis
Indianapolis, IN 46227
Phone: 317-788-3211
Fax: 317-788-3300
TF: 800-232-8634

Clowes Memorial Hall at Butler University
4600 Sunset Ave
Indianapolis, IN 46208
Phone: 317-940-9696
Fax: 317-940-8456

Conner Prairie Pioneer Settlement
13400 Allisonville Rd
Fishers, IN 46038
www.connerprairie.org
Phone: 317-776-6000
Fax: 317-776-6014
TF: 800-966-1836

Crispus Attucks Museum
1140 ML King Jr St
Indianapolis, IN 46202
Phone: 317-226-4611

Deer Creek Music Center
12880 E 146th St
Noblesville, IN 46060
www.deercreekconcerts.com
Phone: 317-776-3337
Fax: 317-773-5996

Eagle Creek Park
7840 W 56th St
Indianapolis, IN 46254
Phone: 317-327-7110
Fax: 317-327-7122

Easley Winery
205 N College Ave
Indianapolis, IN 46202
Phone: 317-636-4516

Edyvean Repertory Theatre
1400 E Hanna Ave Ransburg Auditorium
Indianapolis, IN 46227
E-mail: ert@indy.net
www.edyvean.org
Phone: 317-788-2072
Fax: 317-788-2079
TF: 800-807-7732

Eiteljorg Museum of American Indian & Western Art
500 W Washington St
Indianapolis, IN 46204
Phone: 317-636-9378
Fax: 317-264-1724

Fountain Square
1105 E Prospect St
Indianapolis, IN 46203
E-mail: info@fountainsquareindy.com
www.fountainsquareindy.com
Phone: 317-686-6010
Fax: 317-686-6002

Freetown Village
Indianapolis State Museum 202 N Alabama St
Indianapolis, IN 46204
E-mail: freetown@ameritech.net
Phone: 317-631-1870
Fax: 317-631-0224

Gaia Wines Contemporary Winery
608 Massachusetts Ave
Indianapolis, IN 46204
E-mail: gaiawines@aol.com
www.gaiawines.com
Phone: 317-634-9463
Fax: 317-634-0269

Garfield Park
2345 Pagoda Dr
Indianapolis, IN 46203
Phone: 317-327-7220
Fax: 317-327-7235

Garfield Park Conservatory & Sunken Gardens
2450 Shelby St
Indianapolis, IN 46203
Phone: 317-327-7184
Fax: 317-327-7268

Hilbert Circle Theatre
45 Monument Cir
Indianapolis, IN 46204
Phone: 317-262-1110
Fax: 317-262-1159
TF: 800-366-8457

Historic Ransom Place Museum & Heritage Learning Center
830 Dr ML King Jr St
Indianapolis, IN 46202
Phone: 317-632-2340
Fax: 317-685-2760

Hook's Historical Drug Store & Pharmacy Museum
1180 E 38th St Indiana State Fairgrounds
Indianapolis, IN 46205
E-mail: hookamerx@aol.com
Phone: 317-924-1503
Fax: 317-951-2224
TF: 877-924-5886

IMAX 3D Theater
650 W Washington St White River State Pk
Indianapolis, IN 46204
Phone: 317-233-4629
Fax: 317-232-0749

Indiana Basketball Hall of Fame
1 Hall of Fame Ct
New Castle, IN 47362
E-mail: inbkbhof@ecic.cioe.com
www.hoopshall.com
Phone: 765-529-1891
Fax: 765-529-0273

Indiana Historical Society
450 W Ohio St
Indianapolis, IN 46202
www.indianahistory.org
Phone: 317-232-1882
Fax: 317-233-3109

Indiana Medical History Museum
3045 W Vermont St
Indianapolis, IN 46222
www.imhm.org
Phone: 317-635-7329
Fax: 317-635-7349

Indiana Repertory Theatre
140 W Washington St
Indianapolis, IN 46204
E-mail: indianarep@indianarep.com
www.indianarep.com
Phone: 317-635-5277
Fax: 317-236-0767

Indiana State Capitol
200 W Washington St
Indianapolis, IN 46204
Phone: 317-233-5293

Indiana State House
200 W Washington St Rm 206
Indianapolis, IN 46204
Phone: 317-232-4567
Fax: 317-232-3443

Indiana State Museum
202 N Alabama St
Indianapolis, IN 46204
www.ai.org/ism/
Phone: 317-232-1637
Fax: 317-232-7090

Indianapolis Art Center
820 E 67th St
Indianapolis, IN 46220
www.indplsartcenter.org
Phone: 317-255-2464
Fax: 317-254-0486

Indianapolis Artsgarden
110 W Washington St
Indianapolis, IN 46204
www.indyarts.org
Phone: 317-631-3301
Fax: 317-624-2559
TF: 800-965-2787

Indianapolis Civic Theatre
1200 W 38th St
Indianapolis, IN 46208
www.civictheatre.org
Phone: 317-923-4597
Fax: 317-923-3548

Indianapolis Motor Speedway & Hall of Fame Museum
4790 W 16th St
Indianapolis, IN 46222
www.indyracingleague.com
Phone: 317-484-6747
Fax: 317-484-6449

Indianapolis Museum of Art
1200 W 38th St
Indianapolis, IN 46208
E-mail: ima@starnews.com
www.ima-art.org
Phone: 317-923-1331
Fax: 317-926-8931

Indianapolis Opera
250 E 38 St
Indianapolis, IN 46205
www.indyopera.org
Phone: 317-283-3531
Fax: 317-923-5611

Indianapolis Symphony Orchestra
45 Monument Cir
Indianapolis, IN 46204
E-mail: cello@in.net
www.indyorch.org
Phone: 317-262-1100
Fax: 317-262-1159
TF: 800-366-8457

Indianapolis Zoo
1200 W Washington St
Indianapolis, IN 46222
www.indyzoo.com
Phone: 317-630-2001
Fax: 317-630-5153

James Whitcomb Riley Museum Home
528 Lockerbie St
Indianapolis, IN 46202
Phone: 317-631-5885
Fax: 317-955-0619

JI Holcomb Observatory & Planetarium
4600 Sunset Ave Butler University
Indianapolis, IN 46208
Phone: 317-940-9333
Fax: 317-940-9951

Madame Walker Theatre Center
617 Indiana Ave
Indianapolis, IN 46202
www.mmewalkertheatre.org
Phone: 317-236-2099
Fax: 317-236-2097

Morris-Butler House
1204 N Park Ave
Indianapolis, IN 46202
E-mail: info@historiclandmarks.org
www.historiclandmarks.org/M-B%20House.htm
Phone: 317-636-5409
Fax: 317-636-2630

Murat Temple
510 N New Jersey St
Indianapolis, IN 46204
Phone: 317-635-2433
Fax: 317-686-4199

National Art Museum of Sport
850 W Michigan St University Pl at IUPUI
Indianapolis, IN 46202
namos.iupui.edu
Phone: 317-274-3627
Fax: 317-274-3878

NCAA Hall of Champions Visitors Center
1802 Alonzo Watford Sr Dr
Indianapolis, IN 46202
Phone: 317-917-6222
Fax: 317-917-6888
TF: 800-735-6222

Philharmonic Orchestra of Indianapolis
17 W Market St Suite 910
Indianapolis, IN 46204
www.iupui.edu/it/dentlib/concerts.html
Phone: 317-916-0178

President Benjamin Harrison Memorial Home
1230 N Delaware St
Indianapolis, IN 46202
E-mail: harrison@surf-ici.com
www.surf-ici.com/harrison
Phone: 317-631-1898
Fax: 317-632-5488

Scottish Rite Cathedral
650 N Meridian St
Indianapolis, IN 46204
Phone: 317-262-3100
Fax: 317-262-3124
TF: 800-489-3579

USS Indianapolis Memorial
Walnut St Footbridge
Indianapolis, IN 46204
Phone: 317-232-7615
Fax: 317-233-4285

War Memorials Plaza
431 N Meridian St
Indianapolis, IN 46204
Phone: 317-232-7615
Fax: 317-233-4285

Warren Performing Arts Center
9301 E 18th St
Indianapolis, IN 46229
Phone: 317-898-9722
Fax: 317-532-6440

White River State Park
801 W Washington St
Indianapolis, IN 46204
E-mail: wrsp@inwhiteriver.com
www.inwhiteriver.com
Phone: 317-233-2434
Fax: 317-634-4508
TF: 800-665-9056

Sports Teams & Facilities

Churchill Downs Sports Spectrum
110 W Washington St
Indianapolis, IN 46204
Phone: 317-656-7223
Fax: 317-656-7250

Conseco Fieldhouse
125 S Pennsylvania St
Indianapolis, IN 46204
www.consecofieldhouse.com
Phone: 317-917-2500
Fax: 317-917-2599

Hoosier Park
4500 Dan Patch Cir
Anderson, IN 46013
www.hoosierpark.com
Phone: 765-642-7223
Fax: 765-644-0467
TF: 800-526-7223

Indiana Blast (soccer)
1502 W 16th St Kuntz Memorial Stadium
Indianapolis, IN 46250
E-mail: blastblaze@aol.com
indianablast.com/blast
Phone: 317-585-9203
Fax: 317-585-9205

Indiana Blaze
1502 W 16th St Kuntz Memorial Stadium
Indianapolis, IN 46250
E-mail: blastblaze@aol.com
www.indianablast.com
Phone: 317-585-9203
Fax: 317-585-9205

Indiana Pacers
300 E Market St Market Square Arena
Indianapolis, IN 46204
www.nba.com/pacers
Phone: 317-917-2500

Indianapolis Colts
100 S Capitol Ave RCA Dome
Indianapolis, IN 46225
www.colts.com
Phone: 317-297-7000
Fax: 317-297-7010

Indianapolis Ice (hockey)
1202 E 38th St Pepsi Coliseum
Indianapolis, IN 46205
www.indyice.org
Phone: 317-925-4423
Fax: 317-931-4511

Indianapolis Indians (baseball)
501 W Maryland St
Indianapolis, IN 46225
E-mail: indians@indyindians.com
www.indyindians.com
Phone: 317-269-3545
Fax: 317-269-3541

Indianapolis Motor Speedway
4790 W 16th St
Indianapolis, IN 46222
www.indyracingleague.com
Phone: 317-484-6747
Fax: 317-484-6759

Indianapolis Raceway Park
10267 Hwy 136
Indianapolis, IN 46234
www.goracing.com/indy
Phone: 317-293-7223
Fax: 317-291-4220

Pepsi Coliseum
1202 E 38th St Indiana State Fairgrounds
Indianapolis, IN 46205
Phone: 317-927-7500
Fax: 317-927-7695

RCA Dome
100 S Capitol Ave
Indianapolis, IN 46225
www.iccrd.com
Phone: 317-262-3410
Fax: 317-262-3685

Annual Events

4th Fest (July 4) 317-633-6363
500 Festival (May) 800-638-4296
Africafest (mid-August) 317-923-1331
Animals & All that Jazz (August)..................317-630-2001
Brickyard 400 (early August) 317-481-8500
Broad Ripple Art Fair (early May) 317-255-2464
Carquest World of Wheels (early February).........317-236-6515
Celebration of Lights (late November) 317-237-2222
Children's Folk Dance Festival (early May).........317-327-7066
Circle City Classic (early October).................317-237-5222
Circle City Grand National Rodeo (early January)....317-917-2500
Circlefest (late July) 317-237-2222
Earth Day Indiana Festival (April 22)..............317-767-3672
Fall Home Show (late October) 317-927-7500
Freedom Fest (July 4) 317-633-6363
Greek Festival (mid-September)...................317-283-3816
Halloween ZooBoo (late October)..................317-630-2001
Harrison Victorian Christmas (December)..........317-631-1898
Heartland Film Festival (late October).............317-464-9405
Hoosier Classic (late December)...................317-917-2727
Hoosier Horse Fair & Expo (mid-April)............317-927-7500
Hoosier Storytelling Festival (late September) 317-255-7628
Indian Market (late June).........................317-636-9378
Indiana Avenue Jazz Festival (mid-August).........317-236-2099
Indiana Black Expo (mid-July)....................317-925-2702
Indiana Flower & Patio Show (mid-March).........317-576-9933
Indiana Motorcycle & Watercraft Expo
(late January) 317-546-4344
Indiana State Fair (mid-August)...................317-927-7500
Indianapolis 500 (late May).......................317-481-8500
Indianapolis Boat Sport & Travel Show
(late February)................................317-546-4344
Indianapolis Home Show
(late January-early February)....................317-927-7500
Indy Festival (May) 317-237-3400
Italian Festival (mid-June)........................317-636-4478
IU Basketball Classic (early December) 317-262-3410
Juneteenth Celebration (mid-June) 317-334-3322
Maple Fair (late February-early March).............765-569-3430
Merry Prairie Days (December) 317-773-0666
Middle Eastern Festival (mid-June)................317-547-9356
Oktoberfest (early-mid-September) 317-888-6940
Penrod Arts Fair (mid-September) 317-252-9895
RCA Championships (mid-August) 317-632-4100
Saint Patrick's Day Parade (mid-March) 317-236-6515
Some Like it Hot Chili Cookoff (mid-September)....317-636-9378
Strawberry Festival (mid-June)....................317-636-4577
Talbott Street Art Fair (mid-June).................800-323-4639
Winterland Holiday Light Display
(late November-early January) 765-664-3918

Jackson, Mississippi

County: **Hinds**

JACKSON is located in central Mississippi, approximately 45 miles east of the Mississippi River and 145 miles north of the Gulf of Mexico. Major cities within 100 miles include Vicksburg and Meridian, Mississippi.

Area (Land) .... 100.6 sq mi
Area (Water)................................ 1.9 sq mi
Elevation...................................... 294 ft
Latitude ....32-29-32 N
Longitude................................ 90-18-96 W
Time Zone ....CST
Area Code....................................... 601

Climate

Jackson's climate is strongly influenced by air masses from the Gulf of Mexico, which result in warm, humid weather much of the year. Summers are hot, with high temperatures averaging in the low 90s. Winters are generally mild, with highs near 60 degrees and low temperatures in the 30s. Snowfall is rare. Although winter and spring are typically Jackson's wettest seasons, the hurricane season (June-November) can bring tropical storms that produce large amounts of rain during the summer and fall.

Average Temperatures & Precipitation

Temperatures

	Jan	Feb	Mar	Apr	May	Jun	Jul	Aug	Sep	Oct	Nov	Dec
High	56	60	69	77	84	91	92	92	88	79	69	60
Low	33	36	44	52	60	67	71	70	64	50	42	36

Precipitation

	Jan	Feb	Mar	Apr	May	Jun	Jul	Aug	Sep	Oct	Nov	Dec
Inches	5.2	4.7	5.8	5.6	5.1	3.2	4.5	3.8	3.6	3.3	4.8	5.9

History

In 1821 a trading post called LeFleur's Bluff, located along the west bank of the Pearl River, was chosen as the new, centrally-located capital of Mississippi (Natchez was the former state capital). The city was renamed Jackson in honor of Major General Andrew Jackson, and the first of Mississippi's three capitol buildings was completed in 1822. The second "Old Capitol" building, completed in 1840, remained in use until 1903 when the New Capitol building was erected. Today, both the Old Capitol (which houses Mississippi's Historical Museum) and the New Capitol are major tourist attractions in Jackson. The Governor's Mansion in Jackson, completed in 1842, is the second oldest building of its kind in the United States and is listed on the National Register of Historic Places. Jackson's City Hall, completed in 1846, still houses the city's municipal government offices, more than 150 years later.

During the Civil War, Jackson was burned three times by Union Troops—so many buildings were destroyed that at one point only brick chimneys were left standing (hence Jackson's nickname, "Chimneyville"). However, the city was rebuilt and by the turn of the 20th Century was home to approximately 7,000 people.

Jackson's location, midway between Memphis and New Orleans to the north and south and Atlanta and Dallas to the east and west, has helped it grow as a distribution center. Jackson today, with a population exceeding 188,000, is Mississippi's largest city.

Population

1990 Census 196,637
1998 Estimate..............................188,419
% Change .... -6.8
2010 Projection 251,456*

Racial/Ethnic Breakdown
White.................................... 43.4%
Black 55.6%
Other..................................... 1.0%
Hispanic Origin (may be of any race) 4.0%

Age Breakdown
Under 5 years.............................. 7.8%
5 to 17.................................. 19.8%
18 to 20.................................. 5.7%
21 to 24.................................. 6.5%
25 to 34................................. 17.7%
35 to 44................................. 14.3%
45 to 54.................................. 8.8%
55 to 64.................................. 7.8%
65 to 74.................................. 6.6%
75+ years 4.0%
Median Age.................................30.8

Gender Breakdown
Male..................................... 46.3%
Female................................... 43.7%

** Information given is for Hinds County.*

Government

Type of Government: Mayor-Council

Jackson City Attorney
455 E Capitol St
Jackson, MS 39205
Phone: 601-960-1799
Fax: 601-960-1756

Jackson City Clerk
219 S President St
Jackson, MS 39201
Phone: 601-960-1035
Fax: 601-960-1032

Jackson City Council
PO Box 17
Jackson, MS 39205
Phone: 601-960-1033
Fax: 601-960-1032

Jackson City Hall
219 S President St
Jackson, MS 39201
Phone: 601-960-1084
Fax: 601-960-2193

Jackson Finance Div
200 S President St 6th Fl
Jackson, MS 39205
Phone: 601-960-1019
Fax: 601-960-1600

Jackson Fire Dept
555 S West St
Jackson, MS 39201
Phone: 601-960-1392
Fax: 601-960-2198

Jackson Human & Cultural Services Dept
350 Woodrow Wilson Blvd Suite 311
Jackson, MS 39213
Phone: 601-368-7409
Fax: 601-960-1572

Jackson Mayor
219 S President St
Jackson, MS 39201
Phone: 601-960-1084
Fax: 601-960-2193

Jackson Parks & Recreation Dept
350 W Woodrow Wilson Dr Suite 311
Jackson, MS 39213
Phone: 601-368-7053
Fax: 601-960-1576

Jackson Personnel Management Dept
218 S President St
Jackson, MS 39201
Phone: 601-960-1053
Fax: 601-960-1043

Jackson Planning & Development Dept
200 S President St 2nd Fl
Jackson, MS 39201
Phone: 601-960-1993
Fax: 601-960-2208

Jackson Police Dept
327 E Pascagoula St
Jackson, MS 39205
Phone: 601-960-1234
Fax: 601-960-1247

Jackson Public Works Dept
200 S President St
Jackson, MS 39201
Phone: 601-960-1175
Fax: 601-960-1174

Jackson Water/Sewer Utilities Div
PO Box 23092
Jackson, MS 39225
Phone: 601-368-7002
Fax: 601-960-1130

Jackson/Hinds Library System
300 N State St
Jackson, MS 39201
Phone: 601-968-5811
Fax: 601-968-5806

Important Phone Numbers

AAA....601-957-8484
Driver's License Information....601-987-1287
Emergency....911
Hinds County Tax Assessor....601-968-6616
Hinds County Tax Collector....601-968-6599
HotelDocs....800-468-3537
Jackson Realtors Assn....601-948-1332
Mississippi State Tax Commission....601-923-7000
Poison Control Center....601-354-7660
Time/Temp....601-355-9311
Vehicle Registration Information....601-968-6587
Voter Registration Information....601-968-6640
Weather....601-936-2189

Information Sources

Better Business Bureau Serving Mississippi
PO Box 12745
Jackson, MS 39236
www.bbbmississippi.org
Phone: 601-987-8282
Fax: 601-987-8285

Hinds County
PO Box 686
Jackson, MS 39205
www.co.hinds.ms.us
Phone: 601-968-6501
Fax: 601-968-6794

Metro Economic Development Alliance
PO Box 3318
Jackson, MS 39207
www.metroeda.com
Phone: 601-948-3111
Fax: 601-352-5539
TF: 800-566-5267

Metro Jackson Convention & Visitors Bureau
921 N President St
Jackson, MS 39202
www.visitjackson.com
Phone: 601-960-1891
Fax: 601-960-1827
TF: 800-354-7695

MetroJackson Chamber of Commerce
PO Box 22548
Jackson, MS 39225
www.metrochamber.com
Phone: 601-948-7575
Fax: 601-352-5539

Mississippi Trade Mart
1200 E Mississippi St
Jackson, MS 39205
Phone: 601-354-7051

Online Resources

About.com Guide to Jackson
jackson.about.com/citiestowns/southeastus/jackson

Area Guide Jackson
jacksonms.areaguides.net

City Knowledge Jackson
www.cityknowledge.com/ms_jackson.htm

Excite.com Jackson City Guide
www.excite.com/travel/countries/united_states/mississippi/jackson

Area Communities

Communities in the Jackson metropolitan area (which includes Hinds, Madison, and Rankin counties) with populations greater than 10,000 include:

Brandon
201 N College St
Brandon, MS 39042
Phone: 601-825-5021
Fax: 601-825-1015

Canton
226 E Peace St
Canton, MS 39046
Phone: 601-859-4331
Fax: 601-859-4379

Clinton
PO Box 156
Clinton, MS 39060
Phone: 601-924-5462
Fax: 601-925-4605

Madison
PO Box 40
Madison, MS 39130
Phone: 601-856-7116
Fax: 601-856-8786

Pearl
2420 Old Brandon Rd
Pearl, MS 39208
Phone: 601-932-2262
Fax: 601-932-3568

Ridgeland
PO Box 217
Ridgeland, MS 39158
Phone: 601-856-7113
Fax: 601-856-7819

Economy

Government plays a dominant role in Jackson's economy, with more than 35,000 area residents employed by federal, state, and local agencies. Hinds County's largest employment sector is services, followed by wholesale and retail trade. Telecommunications is also important to the local economy - the Jackson metropolitan area is home to two major U.S. telecommunications companies, MCI WorldCom and SkyTel Communications. The area is also one of the top distribution centers in the southern United States.

Unemployment Rate 4.5%
Per Capita Income.......................... $22,186*
Median Family Income...................... $28,401

** Information given is for Hinds County.*

Principal Industries & Number of Wage Earners

Hinds County - 1999

Construction.. 6,150
Finance, Insurance, & Real Estate....................... 11,660
Government 35,290
Manufacturing 10,270
Mining 280
Services 45,750
Transportation & Public Utilities 10,390
Wholesale & Retail Trade............................... 36,420

Major Employers

Belhaven College
1500 Peachtree St
Jackson, MS 39202
www.belhaven.edu
Phone: 601-968-5928
Fax: 601-968-9998
TF: 800-960-5940

Delphi Automotive Systems Corp
Packard Electric Systems Div
PO Box 260
Clinton, MS 39060
Phone: 601-924-7411
Fax: 601-925-2390

Hinds County
PO Box 686
Jackson, MS 39205
www.co.hinds.ms.us
Phone: 601-968-6501
Fax: 601-968-6794

Jackson City Hall
219 S President St
Jackson, MS 39201
www.city.jackson.ms.us/CityHall/default.htm
Phone: 601-960-1084
Fax: 601-960-2193

Jackson Public School District
622 S President St
Jackson, MS 39201
www.jackson.k12.ms.us
Phone: 601-960-8852
Fax: 601-960-8895

Mindbender New Media
517 Keywood Cir Suite 2A
Jackson, MS 39208
www.mindbender.net
Phone: 601-853-0211
Fax: 601-853-1088

Mississippi College
200 College St
Clinton, MS 39058
E-mail: admissions@mc.edu
www.mc.edu
Phone: 601-925-3000
Fax: 601-925-3950
TF: 800-738-1236

Parkway Properties Inc
PO Box 24647
Jackson, MS 39225
E-mail: mail@parkwayco.com
www.parkwayco.com
Phone: 601-948-4091
Fax: 601-949-4077
TF: 800-748-1667

RealityChek
4735 Old Canton Rd 1 LeFleur's Sq
Jackson, MS 39211
www.acc-software.com
Phone: 601-932-5227
Fax: 601-939-0501

SkyTel Communications Inc
200 S Lamar St
Jackson, MS 39201
E-mail: skyuser@skyten.com
www.skytel.com
Phone: 601-944-1300
Fax: 601-944-7094
TF: 800-801-2480

Tyson Foods
238 Wilmington St
Jackson, MS 39207
www.tyson.com
Phone: 601-372-7441
Fax: 601-371-4909

University of Mississippi Medical Center
2500 N State St
Jackson, MS 39216
umcnews.com
Phone: 601-984-1000
Fax: 601-984-4125

WorldCom Inc
500 Clinton Ctr Dr
Clinton, MS 39056
E-mail: investor@wcom.com
www.wcom.com
Phone: 601-460-5600
Fax: 601-460-8269
TF: 800-844-1009

Quality of Living Indicators

Total Crime Index.................................... 20,072
(rates per 100,000 inhabitants)

Violent Crime
Murder/manslaughter............................ 45
Forcible rape 248
Robbery.. 1,096
Aggravated assault.............................. 691

Property Crime
Burglary 4,814
Larceny theft 9,703
Motor vehicle theft 3,475

Cost of Living Index.................................... 89.3
(national average = 100)

Median Home Price.................................. $95,100

Education

Public Schools

Jackson Public School District
622 S President St
Jackson, MS 39201
www.jackson.k12.ms.us
Phone: 601-960-8852
Fax: 601-960-8895

Number of Schools
Elementary 38
Middle 10
High 8

Student/Teacher Ratio
All Grades 15.9:1

Private Schools

Number of Schools (all grades) .... 12+

Colleges & Universities

Belhaven College
1500 Peachtree St
Jackson, MS 39202
www.belhaven.edu
Phone: 601-968-5928
Fax: 601-968-9998
TF: 800-960-5940

Jackson College of Ministries
1555 Beasley Rd
Jackson, MS 39206
E-mail: jcm@jcm.edu
www.jcm.edu
Phone: 601-981-1611
Fax: 601-982-5121

Jackson State University
1400 John R Lynch St
Jackson, MS 39217
E-mail: gblakley@ccaix.jsums.edu
ccaix.jsums.edu
Phone: 601-979-2121
Fax: 601-979-2948
TF: 800-682-5390

Millsaps College
1701 N State St
Jackson, MS 39210
E-mail: hinesfw@okra.millsaps.edu
www.millsaps.edu
Phone: 601-974-1000
Fax: 601-974-1059
TF: 800-352-1050

Mississippi College
200 College St
Clinton, MS 39058
E-mail: admissions@mc.edu
www.mc.edu
Phone: 601-925-3000
Fax: 601-925-3950
TF: 800-738-1236

Tougaloo College
500 W County Line Rd
Tougaloo, MS 39174
E-mail: information@mail.tougaloo.edu
www.tougaloo.edu
Phone: 601-977-7700
Fax: 601-977-6185
TF: 888-424-2566

Hospitals

Baptist Health Systems Inc
1225 N State St
Jackson, MS 39202
www.mbhs.org
Phone: 601-968-1000
Fax: 601-968-1149
TF: 800-948-6262

Central Mississippi Medical Center
1850 Chadwick Dr
Jackson, MS 39204
www.hma-corp.com/ms7.html
Phone: 601-376-1000
Fax: 601-376-2821
TF: 800-844-0919

River Oaks Hospital
PO Box 5100
Jackson, MS 39296
Phone: 601-932-1030
Fax: 601-936-2275

Saint Dominic-Jackson Memorial Hospital
969 Lakeland Dr
Jackson, MS 39216
www.health-futures.org/stdom.html
Phone: 601-982-0121
Fax: 601-364-6800

University of Mississippi Medical Center
2500 N State St
Jackson, MS 39216
umcnews.com
Phone: 601-984-1000
Fax: 601-984-4125

Veterans Affairs Medical Center
1500 E Woodrow Wilson Dr
Jackson, MS 39216
www.health-futures.org/va.html
Phone: 601-362-4471
Fax: 601-364-1286

Transportation

Airport(s)

Jackson International Airport (JAN)
10 miles E of downtown (approx 10 minutes) 601-939-5631

Mass Transit

JATRAN
$1 Base fare 601-948-3840

Rail/Bus

Amtrak Station
300 W Capitol St
Jackson, MS 39201
Phone: 601-355-6350
TF: 800-872-7245

Greyhound Bus Station
201 S Jefferson St
Jackson, MS 39201
Phone: 601-353-6342

Utilities

Electricity
Entergy Mississippi 601-368-5000
www.entergy.com

Gas
Mississippi Valley Gas Co 601-961-6600
www.mvgas.com

Water
Jackson Water/Sewer Utilities Div 601-368-7002
www.city.jackson.ms.us/CityHall/water.htm

Garbage Collection/Recycling
Jackson Solid Waste Div 601-960-1193

Telecommunications

Telephone
BellSouth 800-622-6146
www.bellsouth.com

Cable Television
Time Warner Cablevision 601-982-0922
www.timewarner.com

Internet Service Providers (ISPs)
Ayrix Technologies Inc 601-718-1000
www.ayrix.net
Internet Doorway Inc 601-969-1434
www.netdoor.com

Banks

BancorpSouth Bank
525 E Capitol St
Jackson, MS 39201
Phone: 601-354-4500
Fax: 601-944-3621
TF: 888-797-7711

Deposit Guaranty National Bank
210 E Capitol St 1 Deposit Guaranty Plaza
Jackson, MS 39201
www.dgb.com
Phone: 601-354-8211
Fax: 601-354-8369
TF: 800-748-8500

Trustmark National Bank
248 E Capitol St
Jackson, MS 39201
www.trustmark.com
Phone: 601-354-5111
Fax: 601-354-5030
TF: 800-844-2000

Union Planters Bank of Central Mississippi
329 E Capital St
Jackson, MS 39201
Phone: 601-969-6100
Fax: 601-969-6173

Shopping

Fairground Antique Flea Market
900 High St
Jackson, MS 39225
Phone: 601-353-5327

Highland Village Shopping Center
4500 I-55 N
Jackson, MS 39211
Phone: 601-982-5861
Fax: 601-362-6922

Metrocenter Mall
3645 Hwy 80 W
Jackson, MS 39209
Phone: 601-969-7633

Northpark Mall
1200 E County Line Rd
Ridgeland, MS 39157
Phone: 601-957-3744

Westland Plaza Shopping Center
Ellis & Robinson Rds
Jackson, MS 39204
Phone: 601-948-7786

Media

Newspapers and Magazines

Clarion-Ledger*
201 S Congress St
Jackson, MS 39201
www.clarionledger.com
Phone: 601-961-7000
Fax: 601-961-7211
TF: 800-367-3384

Mississippi
5 Lakeland Cir
Jackson, MS 39216
Phone: 601-982-8418
Fax: 601-982-8447

Mississippi Business Journal
5120 Galaxie Dr
Jackson, MS 39206
E-mail: mbj@msbusiness.com
www.msbusiness.com
Phone: 601-364-1000
Fax: 601-364-1007

Northside Sun
PO Box 16709
Jackson, MS 39236
Phone: 601-957-1122
Fax: 601-957-1533

**Indicates major daily newspapers*

Television

WAPT-TV Ch 16 (ABC)
7616 Channel 16 Way
Jackson, MS 39209
E-mail: wapt@misnet.com
www.wapt.com
Phone: 601-922-1607
Fax: 601-922-1663

WDBD-TV Ch 40 (Fox)
7440 Channel 16 Way
Jackson, MS 39209
www.fox40wdbd.com
Phone: 601-922-1234
Fax: 601-922-0268

WJTV-TV Ch 12 (CBS)
1820 TV Rd
Jackson, MS 39204
www.wjtv.com
Phone: 601-372-6311
Fax: 601-373-8401

WLBT-TV Ch 3 (NBC)
715 S Jefferson St
Jackson, MS 39201
E-mail: news@wlbt.com
www.wlbt.com
Phone: 601-948-3333
Fax: 601-355-7830

WMPN-TV Ch 29 (PBS)
3825 Ridgewood Rd
Jackson, MS 39211
www.etv.state.ms.us
Phone: 601-432-6565
Fax: 601-432-6746

Radio

WIIN-AM 780 kHz (Oldies)
265 High Point Dr
Ridgeland, MS 39157
Phone: 601-956-0102
Fax: 601-978-3980

WJDX-AM 620 kHz (Sports)
PO Box 31999
Jackson, MS 39286
E-mail: thescore@netdoor.com
www.wjdx.com
Phone: 601-982-1062
Fax: 601-362-1905

WJKK-FM 98.7 MHz (AC)
269 High Point Dr
Ridgeland, MS 39157
www.98mix.com
Phone: 601-956-0102
Fax: 601-978-3980

WJNT-AM 1180 kHz (N/T)
PO Box 1248
Jackson, MS 39215
www.wjnt.com
Phone: 601-366-1150
Fax: 601-366-1627

WJSU-FM 88.5 MHz (NPR)
1400 Lynch St
Jackson, MS 39217
ccaix.jsums.edu/~wjsufm
Phone: 601-968-2140
Fax: 601-968-2878

WJXN-FM 92.1 kHz (Rel)
PO Box 24387
Jackson, MS 39205
Phone: 601-944-1450
Fax: 601-944-1450

WMPN-FM 91.3 MHz (NPR)
3825 Ridgewood Rd
Jackson, MS 39211
Phone: 601-432-6565
Fax: 601-432-6746

WMPR-FM 90.1 MHz (Urban)
1018 Pecan Park Cir
Jackson, MS 39209
Phone: 601-948-5835
Fax: 601-948-6162

WMSI-FM 102.9 MHz (Ctry)
PO Box 31999
Jackson, MS 39286
E-mail: sales@miss103.com
www.miss103.com
Phone: 601-982-1062
Fax: 601-362-8270

WSTZ-FM 106.7 MHz (CR)
1375 Beasley Rd
Jackson, MS 39206
www.z106.com
Phone: 601-982-1062
Fax: 601-362-1905

WTYX-FM 94.7 MHz (CR) Phone: 601-957-3000
222 Beasley Rd Fax: 601-956-0370
Jackson, MS 39206
E-mail: mail94@arrow94.com
www.arrow94.com

WYOY-FM 101.7 MHz (CHR) Phone: 601-956-0102
265 High Point Dr Fax: 601-978-3980
Ridgeland, MS 39157

Attractions

Many of Jackson's museums, including the Mississippi Museum of Art and the Jim Buck Ross Mississippi Agriculture and Forestry Museum, are located in the downtown area of the city. The Ross Museum has ten old Mississippi farm buildings, a working farm, and a 1920s crossroads town on the premises. The Governor's Mansion in Jackson has served as the official home of the Mississippi first family since its completion in 1842 and is open for public tours. The Natchez Trace Parkway runs through Jackson, and the Ross R. Barnett Reservoir is located on this portion of the 400-mile parkway. The Reservoir has a wide range of picnic and water sports areas.

Alamo Theater Phone: 601-352-3365
333 N Farish St
Jackson, MS 39202

Armed Forces Museum Phone: 601-558-2757
Hwy 49
Camp Shelby, MS 39407

Ballet Magnificat Phone: 601-977-1001
5406 I-55 N Fax: 601-977-8948
Jackson, MS 39211
E-mail: bmag@teclink.net
www.balletmagnificat.com

Ballet Mississippi Phone: 601-960-1560
201 E Pascagoula St Suite 106 Fax: 601-960-2135
Jackson, MS 39205

City of Jackson Fire Museum Phone: 601-960-2433
355 Woodrow Wilson Blvd Fax: 601-960-2432
Jackson, MS 39213
www.city.jackson.ms.us/Fire/pfsed_museum.html

Davis Planetarium Phone: 601-960-1550
201 E Pascagoula St Fax: 601-960-1555
Jackson, MS 39201

Farish Street Historical District Phone: 601-949-4000
300 N Farish St Fax: 601-949-9919
Jackson, MS 39202
E-mail: farish1@bellsouth.net

Governor's Mansion Phone: 601-359-3175
300 E Capitol St Fax: 601-359-6473
Jackson, MS 39201

Jackson Municipal Art Gallery Phone: 601-960-1582
839 N State St
Jackson, MS 39202

Jackson Zoological Park Phone: 601-352-2580
2918 W Capitol St Fax: 601-352-2594
Jackson, MS 39209
www.ayrix.net/jacksonzoo

Jim Buck Ross Mississippi Agriculture & Forestry Museum/National Agricultural Aviation Museum Phone: 601-354-6113
1150 Lakeland Dr Fax: 601-982-4292
Jackson, MS 39216 TF: 800-844-8687
www.lnstar.com/agmuseum/

LeFleur's Bluff State Park Phone: 601-987-3923
2140 Riverside Dr Fax: 601-354-6930
Jackson, MS 39202

Manship House Phone: 601-961-4724
420 E Fortification St Fax: 601-354-6043
Jackson, MS 39202

Mississippi Archives & History Library Phone: 601-359-6876
100 S State St Fax: 601-359-6964
Jackson, MS 39201
E-mail: refdesk@mdah.state.ms.us
mdah.state.ms.us

Mississippi Museum of Art Phone: 601-960-1515
201 E Pascagoula St Fax: 601-960-1505
Jackson, MS 39201
www.msmuseumart.org

Mississippi Museum of Natural Science Phone: 601-354-7303
2148 Riverside Dr Fax: 601-354-7227
Jackson, MS 39202
www.mdwfp.state.ms.us/museum

Mississippi Opera Phone: 601-960-2300
201 E Pascagoula St Thalia Mara Hall Fax: 601-960-1526
Jackson, MS 39201

Mississippi Petrified Forest Phone: 601-879-8189
124 Forest Park Rd
Jackson, MS 39209

Mississippi Sports Hall of Fame Phone: 601-982-8264
1152 Lakeland Dr Fax: 601-982-4702
Jackson, MS 39216 TF: 800-280-3263
E-mail: info@msfame.com
www.msfame.com

Mississippi State Capitol Phone: 601-359-3114
400 High St
Jackson, MS 39205

Mississippi State Historical Museum Phone: 601-359-6920
100 S State St Fax: 601-359-6981
Jackson, MS 39201
www.mdah.state.ms.us/musetxt.html#capitol

Mississippi Symphony Orchestra Phone: 601-960-1565
PO Box 2052 Fax: 601-960-1564
Jackson, MS 39225
www.msorchestra.com

Municipal Art Gallery Phone: 601-960-1582
839 N State St
Jackson, MS 39202

Museum of the Southern Jewish Experience Phone: 601-362-6357
PO Box 16528 Fax: 601-366-6293
Jackson, MS 39236
E-mail: information@msje.org
www.msje.org

Mynelle Gardens
4736 Clinton Blvd
Jackson, MS 39209
www.lnstar.com/mynelle/
Phone: 601-960-1894
Fax: 601-922-5759

New Stage Theatre
1100 Carlisle St
Jackson, MS 39202
www.newstagetheatre.com
Phone: 601-948-3531
Fax: 601-948-3538

Oaks House Museum
823 N Jefferson St
Jackson, MS 39202
Phone: 601-353-9339

Rapids on the Reservoir
PO Box 6020
Brandon, MS 39047
E-mail: rapids@rapidswaterpark.net
www.rapidswaterpark.net
Phone: 601-992-0500
Fax: 601-992-0531

Smith Robertson Museum & Cultural Center
528 Bloom St
Jackson, MS 39202
Phone: 601-960-1457
Fax: 601-960-2070

Thalia Mara Hall
255 E Pascagoula St
Jackson, MS 39205
Phone: 601-960-1537
Fax: 601-960-1583

Vicksburg National Military Park
3201 Clay St
Vicksburg, MS 39180
www.nps.gov/vick/
Phone: 601-636-0583
Fax: 601-636-9497

War Memorial Building
100 State St
Jackson, MS 39201
Phone: 601-354-7207

Sports Teams & Facilities

Coliseum The
Mississippi State Fairgrounds 1207 Mississippi St
Jackson, MS 39202
www.mdac.state.ms.us/coliseum.htm
Phone: 601-961-4000
Fax: 601-354-6545

Jackson Chargers (soccer)
2240 E Westbrook Dr Sports Club Stadium
Jackson, MS 39211
E-mail: ajd-ins@teclink.net
members.aol.com/JxnCharger/index.html
Phone: 601-991-0047
Fax: 601-956-7529

Veterans Memorial Stadium
2531 N State St
Jackson, MS 39296
www.ms-veteransstadium.com
Phone: 601-354-6021
Fax: 601-354-6019

Annual Events

Capital City Football Classic (mid-November) 601-960-1891
Celtic Fest (early September) 601-960-1891
Chimneyville Crafts Festival (early December) 601-981-0019
Dixie National Livestock Show & Rodeo (late January-mid-February) 601-961-4000
Farish Street Festival (late September) 601-960-2384
Festival of Christmas Trees (December) 601-960-1457
Gem & Mineral Show (late February).............601-961-4000
Harvest Festival (early November)................601-354-6113
Hog Wild In June (late June) 601-354-6113
Holiday Jubilee (early December)..................601-960-1891
Hot Air Balloon Race (early July)..................601-859-1307
International Crawfish Festival (early May).........601-354-6113
Jackson County Fair (mid-October)................228-762-6043
Jubilee Jam (mid-May)...........................601-960-2008
Mal's Saint Paddy's Day Parade (mid-March) 601-984-1109
Mississippi State Fair (early-mid-October)..........601-961-4000
Mistletoe Marketplace (early November)...........601-960-1891
Old Fashioned Independence Day (July 4)..........601-354-6113
Pioneer Indian Festival (late October) 601-856-7546
Scottish Highland Games (late August) 601-960-1891
Sky Parade (late August-early September) 601-982-8088
Spring Festival at Mynelle Garden (late March) 601-960-1894
WellsFest (late September) 601-353-0658
Zoo Blues (early May)............................601-960-1891

Jacksonville, Florida

County: **Duval**

JACKSONVILLE is located along the Saint Johns River in northeastern Florida's First Coast region. Major cities within 100 miles include Saint Augustine, Gainesville, and Daytona Beach, Florida.

Area (Land) .... 773.8 sq mi
Area (Water).............................. 144.4 sq mi
Elevation....................................... 19 ft
Latitude .... 30-33-09 N
Longitude................................ 81-65-62 W
Time Zone .... EST
Area Code....................................... 904

Climate

Jacksonville has a subtropical climate, and breezes off the Atlantic Ocean moderate its temperature throughout the year. Winters are mild, with high temperatures in the mid-60s and lows in the mid-40s. Summer days are hot, with high temperatures averaging around 90 degrees, while evenings cool down to around 70. Summer is the rainy season in Jacksonville, with August being the wettest month; November is the driest.

Average Temperatures & Precipitation

Temperatures

	Jan	Feb	Mar	Apr	May	Jun	Jul	Aug	Sep	Oct	Nov	Dec
High	64	67	73	79	85	89	91	91	87	80	74	67
Low	41	43	49	55	62	69	72	72	69	59	50	43

Precipitation

	Jan	Feb	Mar	Apr	May	Jun	Jul	Aug	Sep	Oct	Nov	Dec
Inches	3.3	3.9	3.7	2.8	3.6	5.7	5.6	7.9	7.1	2.9	2.2	2.7

History

The Jacksonville area was first settled by French Huguenots in 1562, but the settlers abandoned the region shortly thereafter as Spain, Great Britain, France, and the Timucua Indians fought for control of the area. In the early 1800s, the site of present-day downtown Jacksonville was a grazing land for cattle called "Cowford." In 1822, Isaiah D. Hart founded a town in Cowford and renamed the area Jacksonville in honor of Andrew Jackson, who was the territorial governor of Florida at that time. After he became President of the United States, Jackson made the town a port of entry in 1831, and Jacksonville was incorporated the following year.

In 1864, Jacksonville was the site of Florida's only major Civil War battle, the Battle of Olustee. Jacksonville survived the war, but the decades that followed brought difficult times to the city. In 1888, a yellow fever epidemic struck the area, killing hundreds of people and driving thousands more out of the city. Thirteen years later, in 1901, the Great Jacksonville Fire destroyed much of the downtown area. The city was rebuilt and Jacksonville became a major shipbuilding center during the early 1900s.

Jacksonville has grown steadily during the 20th Century. By the end of World War II, the area was home to three military bases, Mayport Naval Station, Naval Air Station Jacksonville, and Naval Air Station Cecil Field, all of which remain important to the city's economy today. In 1968, Jacksonville and Duval County formed a consolidated government, making the city the nation's largest in square mileage. Today, Jacksonville is an important center for finance, insurance, and health care. With a population of more than 693,000 people, Jacksonville is Florida's largest city and the 14th largest city in the United States.

Population

1990 Census 635,230
1998 Estimate.............................. 693,630
% Change 9.2
2005 Projection 787,000

Racial/Ethnic Breakdown

White.................................... 72.3%*
Black 25.0%*
Other...................................... 2.7%*
Hispanic Origin (may be of any race) 3.0%*

Age Breakdown

Under 6 years............................ 10.0%*
6 to 11.................................... 8.7%*
12 to 17................................... 7.9%*
18 to 24................................... 9.5%*
25 to 34.................................. 17.3%*
35 to 44.................................. 16.4%*
45 to 54.................................. 11.7%*
55 to 64................................... 7.6%*
65+ years 10.9%*
Median Age.................................. 33*

Gender Breakdown

Male...................................... 48.5%*
Female.................................... 51.5%*

** Information given is for Duval County.*

Government

Type of Government: Mayor-Council

Jacksonville Administration & Finance Dept
117 W Duval St Suite 300
Jacksonville, FL 32202
Phone: 904-630-1298
Fax: 904-630-3615

Jacksonville City Council
117 W Duval St
Jacksonville, FL 32202
Phone: 904-630-1377
Fax: 904-630-2906

Jacksonville City Hall
117 W Duval St
Jacksonville, FL 32202
Phone: 904-630-1178

Jacksonville Community Services Dept
117 W Duval St Suite 210
Jacksonville, FL 32202
Phone: 904-630-3632
Fax: 904-630-3639

Jacksonville Economic Development Commission
220 E Bay St 14th Fl
Jacksonville, FL 32202
Phone: 904-630-1858
Fax: 904-630-2919

Jacksonville Electric Authority
21 W Church St 16th Fl
Jacksonville, FL 32202
Phone: 904-632-5200
Fax: 904-665-7366

Jacksonville Fire & Rescue Dept
515 N Julia St
Jacksonville, FL 32202
Phone: 904-798-1140
Fax: 904-798-0010

Jacksonville Human Resources Div
117 W Duval St Suite 100
Jacksonville, FL 32206
Phone: 904-630-1111
Fax: 904-630-1108

Jacksonville Mayor
117 W Duval St
Jacksonville, FL 32202
Phone: 904-630-1776
Fax: 904-630-2391

Jacksonville Medical Examiner
2100 Jefferson St
Jacksonville, FL 32206
Phone: 904-630-0977
Fax: 904-630-0964

Jacksonville Parks Recreation & Entertainment Dept
851 N Market St
Jacksonville, FL 32202
Phone: 904-630-3500
Fax: 904-630-3567

Jacksonville Planning & Development Dept
128 E Forsyth St Suite 700
Jacksonville, FL 32202
Phone: 904-630-1900
Fax: 904-630-2912

Jacksonville Public Library
122 N Ocean St
Jacksonville, FL 32202
Phone: 904-630-1994
Fax: 904-630-2431

Jacksonville Public Works Dept
220 E Bay St Rm 1207
Jacksonville, FL 32202
Phone: 904-630-1665
Fax: 904-630-2909

Jacksonville Sheriff's Office
501 E Bay St
Jacksonville, FL 32202
Phone: 904-630-2120
Fax: 904-630-2107

Important Phone Numbers

AAA.......904-398-0564
American Express Travel.......904-642-1701
Driver's License Information.......904-777-2120
Duval County Tax Collector.......904-630-1916
Emergency.......911
Florida Dept of Revenue.......904-359-6070
HotelDocs.......800-468-3537
Jacksonville Ad Valorem (Property) Tax Information.......904-630-2020
Jacksonville Assn of Realtors.......904-396-1323
Poison Control Center.......800-282-3171
Time/Temp.......904-387-4545
Vehicle Registration Information.......904-630-1916
Voter Registration Information.......904-630-1410
Weather.......904-741-4311

Information Sources

Better Business Bureau Serving Northeast Florida
7820 Arlington Expy Suite 147
Jacksonville, FL 32211
www.jacksonville.bbb.org
Phone: 904-721-2288
Fax: 904-721-7373

Duval County
117 W Duval St
Jacksonville, FL 32202
Phone: 904-630-1178

Jacksonville Chamber of Commerce
3 Independent Dr
Jacksonville, FL 32202
www.jacksonvillechamber.org
Phone: 904-366-6600
Fax: 904-632-0617

Jacksonville Convention & Visitors Bureau
201 E Adams St
Jacksonville, FL 32202
www.jaxcvb.com
Phone: 904-798-9111
Fax: 904-798-9103
TF: 800-733-2668

Osborn Prime F Convention Center
1000 Water St
Jacksonville, FL 32204
www.jaxevents.com/osborn.html
Phone: 904-630-4000
Fax: 904-630-4029

Saint Augustine & Saint Johns County Chamber of Commerce
1 Riberia St
Saint Augustine, FL 32084
www.staugustinechamber.com
Phone: 904-829-5681
Fax: 904-829-6477

Saint Augustine City Hall
75 King St
Saint Augustine, FL 32084
www.ci.st-augustine.fl.us
Phone: 904-825-1010
Fax: 904-825-1051

Saint Augustine Mayor
75 King St City Hall
Saint Augustine, FL 32084
www.ci.st-augustine.fl.us/Departments/Mayors_Office/mayors_office.html
Phone: 904-825-2941
Fax: 904-825-1096

Saint Augustine Visitor Information Center
10 S Castillo Dr
Saint Augustine, FL 32084
Phone: 904-825-1000
Fax: 904-825-1096

Saint Johns County
PO Box 300
Saint Augustine, FL 32085
www.co.st-johns.fl.us
Phone: 904-823-2500
Fax: 904-823-2294

Saint Johns County Convention & Visitors Bureau
88 Riberia St Suite 400
Saint Augustine, FL 32084
www.oldcity.com/vcb
Phone: 904-829-1711
Fax: 904-829-6149
TF: 800-653-2489

Saint Johns County Public Library
1960 N Ponce de Leon Blvd
Saint Augustine, FL 32084
Phone: 904-823-2650
Fax: 904-823-2656

Tourist & Development Council
88 Riberia St Suite 400
Saint Augustine, FL 32084
Phone: 904-823-2680
Fax: 904-829-6149
TF: 800-653-2489

Online Resources

About.com Guide to Jacksonville
jacksonville.about.com/local/southeastus/jacksonville

Access America Saint Augustine
www.accessamer.com/staugustine/

All-Florida Visitors Guide to Saint Augustine
www.florida-accommodations.com/StAugustine

Anthill City Guide Jacksonville
www.anthill.com/city.asp?city=jacksonvillefl

Area Guide Jacksonville
jacksonville.areaguides.net

Best Read Guide Jacksonville
bestreadguide.com/jacksonville

Best Read Guide Saint Augustine
www.bestreadguide.com/staugustine

City Knowledge Jacksonville
www.cityknowledge.com/fl_jacksonville.htm

DigitalCity Jacksonville
home.digitalcity.com/jacksonville

Excite.com Jacksonville City Guide
www.excite.com/travel/countries/united_states/florida/jacksonville

Excite.com Saint Augustine City Guide
www.excite.com/travel/countries/united_states/florida/st_augustine

History of Saint Augustine
macserver.stjohns.k12.fl.us/history/history.html

HotelGuide Jacksonville
hotelguide.net/jacksonville

Info Person Guide to Saint Augustine
www.infoperson.com

Jacksonville City Info
www.scalise.com/jax/cityinfo.htm

Jacksonville CityLink
www.usacitylink.com/citylink/jackvill

Jacksonville.TheLinks.com
jacksonville.thelinks.com

Lodging.com Jacksonville Florida
www.lodging.com/auto/guides/jacksonville-area-fl.html

Lodging.com Saint Augustine Florida
www.lodging.com/auto/guides/st_augustine-area-fl.html

Online City Guide to Saint Augustine
www.onlinecityguide.com/fl/staugustine/

Planet Jax
www.planetjax.com/

Saint Augustine Travel Guide
www.2000floridatravel.com/staugustine

Surf & Sun Beach Vacation Guide to Jacksonville
www.surf-sun.com/fl-jacksonville-main.htm

Surf & Sun Beach Vacation Guide to Saint Augustine
www.surf-sun.com/fl-st-augustine-main.htm

Virtual Saint Augustine
www.aug.com/virtual/virtual.html

Welcome to the First Coast
www.welcometo.com

Area Communities

Communities in the Jacksonville metropolitan area (Duval, Clay, Nassau, and Saint Johns counties) with populations greater than 5,000 include:

Atlantic Beach
800 Seminole Rd
Atlantic Beach, FL 32233
Phone: 904-247-5800
Fax: 904-247-5805

Fernandina Beach
204 Ash St
Fernandina Beach, FL 32034
Phone: 904-277-7305
Fax: 904-277-7308

Jacksonville Beach
11 N 3rd St
Jacksonville Beach, FL 32250
Phone: 904-247-6268
Fax: 904-247-6276

Neptune Beach
116 1st St
Neptune Beach, FL 32266
Phone: 904-270-2400
Fax: 904-270-2417

Orange Park
2042 Park Ave
Orange Park, FL 32073
Phone: 904-264-9565
Fax: 904-278-3025

Saint Augustine
75 King St
Saint Augustine, FL 32084
Phone: 904-825-1010
Fax: 904-825-1051

Economy

Jacksonville is a major financial and insurance center in the southeastern United States, with several major U.S. companies headquartered in the city. Government, including the U.S. Military, plays an important role in Jacksonville's economy, employing more than 50,000 civilians and military personnel. Health care is also a growing industry in Jacksonville, which is home to more than 25 general and specialty hospitals.

Unemployment Rate 3.5%
Per Capita Income..........................$24,751*
Median Family Income......................$48,800*

** Information given is for the Jacksonville Metropolitan Statistical Area (MSA), which includes the city of Jacksonville, Clay, Duval, Nassau and Saint Johns counties.*

Principal Industries & Number of Wage Earners

Duval County - 1998

Agriculture, Forestry, & Fishing....3,157
Construction....23,182
Finance, Insurance, & Real Estate....50,736
Government....50,430
Manufacturing....31,063
Mining....218
Retail Trade....72,998
Services....122,540
Transportation, Communications, & Public Utilities....30,359
Wholesale Trade....25,788

Major Employers

AT & T Universal Card Services
8787 Baypine Rd
Jacksonville, FL 32256
www.att.com/ucs
Phone: 904-954-7500
Fax: 904-954-7816

Bank of America NA
50 N Laura St
Jacksonville, FL 32202
Phone: 904-791-5808
Fax: 904-791-7433
TF: 800-299-2265

Baptist/Saint Vincent Health System
800 Prudential Dr
Jacksonville, FL 32207
Phone: 904-202-4000
Fax: 904-202-1789

BellSouth
8171 Baymeadows Way W
Jacksonville, FL 32256
www.bellsouth.com
Phone: 904-443-6800

Blue Cross & Blue Shield of Florida
PO Box 1798
Jacksonville, FL 32231
www.bcbsfl.com
Phone: 904-791-6111
Fax: 904-905-8126
TF: 800-876-2227

CSX Transportation
500 Water St
Jacksonville, FL 32202
www.csxt.com
Phone: 904-359-3100
Fax: 904-359-1832

First Union-Florida
225 Water St 11th Fl
Jacksonville, FL 32202
www.firstunion.com
Phone: 904-361-3020
Fax: 904-361-5888

Naval Air Station Jacksonville
Jacksonville, FL 32212
www.nasjax.navy.mil/
Phone: 904-542-2345

Naval Aviation Depot
US Hwy 17 Naval Air Station
Jacksonville, FL 32212
Phone: 904-542-2805

Publix Super Markets Inc
9786 W Beaver St
Jacksonville, FL 32220
Phone: 904-781-8600
Fax: 904-693-6111

University Medical Center
655 W 8th St
Jacksonville, FL 32209
Phone: 904-549-5000
Fax: 904-549-4821

Vistakon Johnson & Johnson Vision Products Inc
4500 Salisbury Rd
Jacksonville, FL 32216
www.jnjvision.com
Phone: 904-443-1000
Fax: 904-443-1083
TF: 800-874-5278

Winn-Dixie Stores Inc
5050 Edgewood Ct
Jacksonville, FL 32254
E-mail: comments@winn-dixie.com
www.winn-dixie.com
Phone: 904-783-5000
Fax: 904-783-5294

Quality of Living Indicators

Total Crime Index....54,725
(rates per 100,000 inhabitants)

Violent Crime
Murder/manslaughter....74
Forcible rape....521
Robbery....2,051
Aggravated assault....5,467

Property Crime
Burglary....10,849
Larceny theft....30,472
Motor vehicle theft....5,291

Cost of Living Index....95.8
(national average = 100)

Median Home Price....$95,200

Education

Public Schools

Duval County School System
1701 Prudential Dr
Jacksonville, FL 32207
www.educationcentral.org
Phone: 904-390-2000
Fax: 904-390-2395

Number of Schools
Elementary....100
Middle....22
High....18

Student/Teacher Ratio
All Grades....18.0:1

Private Schools

Number of Schools (all grades)....90+

Colleges & Universities

Edward Waters College
1658 Kings Rd
Jacksonville, FL 32209
www.ewc.edu
Phone: 904-366-6576
Fax: 904-366-2760

First Coast Technical Institute
2980 Collins Ave
Saint Augustine, FL 32095
www.fcti.org
Phone: 904-824-4401
Fax: 904-824-6750

Flagler College
74 King St
Saint Augustine, FL 32084
E-mail: info@flagler.com
www.flagler.edu
Phone: 904-829-6481
Fax: 904-826-0094

Florida Community College at Jacksonville Downtown Campus
101 W State St
Jacksonville, FL 32202
www.fccj.cc.fl.us
Phone: 904-633-8100
Fax: 904-633-8105

ITT Technical Institute
6600 Youngerman Cir Suite 10
Jacksonville, FL 32244
www.itt-tech.edu
Phone: 904-573-9100
Fax: 904-573-0512
TF: 800-318-1264

Jacksonville University
2800 University Blvd N
Jacksonville, FL 32211
E-mail: admissions@junix.ju.edu
junix.ju.edu
Phone: 904-744-3950
Fax: 904-745-7012
TF: 800-225-2027

Jones College
5353 Arlington Expy
Jacksonville, FL 32211
www.jones.edu
Phone: 904-743-1122
Fax: 904-743-4446
TF: 800-331-0176

Saint Johns River Community College Saint Augustine Campus
2990 College Dr
Saint Augustine, FL 32095
Phone: 904-808-7400
Fax: 904-808-7420

Saint Leo College
2990 College Dr
Saint Augustine, FL 32095
Phone: 904-824-7030

University of North Florida
4567 St Johns Bluff Rd S
Jacksonville, FL 32224
E-mail: osprey@unf.edu
www.unf.edu
Phone: 904-620-1000
Fax: 904-620-2414

University of Saint Augustine
1 University Blvd
Saint Augustine, FL 32086
E-mail: info@usa.edu
www.usa.edu
Phone: 904-826-0084
Fax: 904-826-0085
TF: 800-241-1027

Hospitals

Baptist Medical Center
800 Prudential Dr
Jacksonville, FL 32207
www.baptist-stvincents.com/Hospitals/bmc.htm
Phone: 904-393-2000
Fax: 904-202-1216

Flagler Hospital
400 Health Park Blvd
Saint Augustine, FL 32086
www.flaglerhospital.org
Phone: 904-829-5155
Fax: 904-819-4904

Memorial Hospital ofJacksonville
3625 University Blvd S
Jacksonville, FL 32216
Phone: 904-399-6111
Fax: 904-399-6382

Orange Park Medical Center
2001 Kingsley Ave
Orange Park, FL 32073
www.opmedical.com
Phone: 904-276-8500
Fax: 904-276-8710

Saint Luke's Hospital
4201 Belfort Rd
Jacksonville, FL 32216
Phone: 904-296-3700
Fax: 904-296-4615

Saint Vincent's Medical Center
1800 Barrs St
Jacksonville, FL 32204
www.baptist-stvincents.com/Hospitals/stvin.htm
Phone: 904-308-7300
Fax: 904-308-7326

Shands Jacksonville
580 W 8th St
Jacksonville, FL 32209
Phone: 904-798-8000
Fax: 904-366-7044

University Medical Center
655 W 8th St
Jacksonville, FL 32209
Phone: 904-549-5000
Fax: 904-549-4821

Transportation

Airport(s)

Jacksonville International Airport (JAX)
15 miles N of downtown (approx 20 minutes).....904-741-4902

Mass Transit

Jacksonville Transit Authority Bus
$.75 Base fare.................................904-630-3100
Skyway Express
$.35 Base fare.................................904-630-3110

Rail/Bus

Amtrak Station
3570 Clifford Ln
Jacksonville, FL 32209
Phone: 904-766-5110
TF: 800-872-7245

Greyhound/Trailways Bus Station
10 N Pearl St
Jacksonville, FL 32202
Phone: 904-356-9976
TF: 800-231-2222

Utilities

Electricity
Jacksonville Electric Authority..................904-632-5200
www.jea.com

Gas
Peoples Gas 904-739-1211
www.peoplesgas.com

Water
Jacksonville Electric Authority..................904-632-5200
www.jea.com

Garbage Collection/Recycling
Waste Management............................904-260-0605

Telecommunications

Telephone
BellSouth 904-443-6800
www.bellsouth.com

Cable Television
AT & T Cable Services.........................904-680-8000

Internet Service Providers (ISPs)
AugLink Communications Inc 904-824-1660
www.aug.com

FDN.com....904-425-6100
www.fdn.com
First Coast On-Line Inc....904-633-9888
www.fcol.com
MediaOne Internet Road Runner....888-339-3160
www.mediaonerr.com

Banks

AmSouth Bank
51 W Bay St
Jacksonville, FL 32202
Phone: 904-281-2640
Fax: 904-281-2649

Bank of America NA
50 N Laura St
Jacksonville, FL 32202
Phone: 904-791-5808
Fax: 904-791-7433
TF: 800-299-2265

Compass Bank
3740 Beach Blvd
Jacksonville, FL 32207
Phone: 904-564-8000
Fax: 904-564-8050

First Guaranty Bank & Trust Co of Jacksonville
1234 King St
Jacksonville, FL 32204
www.firstguarantybank.com
Phone: 904-384-7541
Fax: 904-381-7040

First Union-Florida
225 Water St 11th Fl
Jacksonville, FL 32202
www.firstunion.com
Phone: 904-361-3020
Fax: 904-361-5888

Marine National Bank of Jacksonville
300 W Adams St
Jacksonville, FL 32202
Phone: 904-350-7500
Fax: 904-350-7540

SouthTrust Bank of Northeast Florida NA
1301 Riverplace Blvd
Jacksonville, FL 32207
Phone: 904-798-6300
Fax: 904-798-6306

SunTrust Bank North Florida NA
200 W Forsyth St
Jacksonville, FL 32202
Phone: 904-632-2900
Fax: 904-632-2897

Shopping

Avenues The
10300 Southside Blvd
Jacksonville, FL 32256
Phone: 904-363-3054
Fax: 904-363-3058

Jacksonville Landing
2 Independent Dr
Jacksonville, FL 32202
E-mail: info@jacksonvillelanding.com
www.jacksonvillelanding.com
Phone: 904-353-1188
Fax: 904-353-1558

Jacobson's
9911 Old Baymeadows Rd
Jacksonville, FL 32256
Phone: 904-642-5000
Fax: 904-642-7640

Lightner Antique Mall
75 King St
Saint Augustine, FL 32085
Phone: 904-824-2874
Fax: 904-824-2712

One King Street
1 King St
Saint Augustine, FL 32084
Phone: 904-829-6939

Orange Park Mall
1910 Wells Rd
Orange Park, FL 32073
Phone: 904-269-2422
Fax: 904-269-9440

Ponce de Leon Mall
2121 US Hwy 1 S
Saint Augustine, FL 32086
www.poncemall.com
Phone: 904-797-5324
Fax: 904-797-5324

Regency Square Mall
9501 Arlington Expy Suite 100
Jacksonville, FL 32225
Phone: 904-725-1220
Fax: 904-724-7109

Saint Augustine Outlet Center
2700 SR-16 Suite 200
Saint Augustine, FL 32092
Phone: 904-825-1555
Fax: 904-825-0474

Worth Antiques Gallery
1316 Beach Blvd
Jacksonville, FL 32250
Phone: 904-249-6000
Fax: 904-241-3547

Media

Newspapers and Magazines

Clay Today
1564 Kingsley Ave
Orange Park, FL 32073
Phone: 904-264-3200
Fax: 904-269-6958

Florida Times-Union*
PO Box 1949
Jacksonville, FL 32231
www.times-union.com
Phone: 904-359-4111
Fax: 904-359-4478
TF: 800-472-6397

Folio Weekly
9456 Philips Hwy Suite 11
Jacksonville, FL 32256
E-mail: themail@folioweekly.com
www.folioweekly.com
Phone: 904-260-9770
Fax: 904-260-9773

Jacksonville Business Journal
1200 River Pl Blvd Suite 201
Jacksonville, FL 32207
E-mail: jacksonville@amcity.com
www.amcity.com/jacksonville
Phone: 904-396-3502
Fax: 904-396-5706

Jacksonville Daily Record
10 N Newnan St
Jacksonville, FL 32202
E-mail: sales@jaxdailyrecord.com
www.jaxdailyrecord.com
Phone: 904-356-2466
Fax: 904-353-2628

Jacksonville Magazine
1032 Hendricks Ave
Jacksonville, FL 32207
Phone: 904-396-8666
Fax: 904-396-0926
TF: 800-962-0214

Northeast Florida Advocate
8905 Castle Blvd
Jacksonville, FL 32208
Phone: 904-766-5298
Fax: 904-766-5542

Saint Augustine Record*
158 Cordova St
Saint Augustine, FL 32084
www.staugustine.com
Phone: 904-824-6105
Fax: 904-829-6664

**Indicates major daily newspapers*

Television

WAWS-TV Ch 30 (Fox)
11700 Central Pkwy
Jacksonville, FL 32224
Phone: 904-642-3030
Fax: 904-646-0115

WJCT-TV Ch 7 (PBS)
100 Festival Park Ave
Jacksonville, FL 32202
Phone: 904-353-7770
Fax: 904-354-6846

WJWB-TV Ch 17 (WB)
9117 Hogan Rd
Jacksonville, FL 32216
Phone: 904-641-1700
Fax: 904-641-0306

WJXT-TV Ch 4 (CBS)
4 Broadcast Pl
Jacksonville, FL 32247
E-mail: news@wjxt.com
www.wjxt.com
Phone: 904-399-4000
Fax: 904-393-9822

WJXX-TV Ch 25 (ABC)
PO Box 551000
Jacksonville, FL 32255
E-mail: info@wjxx.com
www.wjxx.com/new
Phone: 904-332-2525
Fax: 904-332-2418

WTEV-TV Ch 47 (UPN)
11700 Central Pkwy
Jacksonville, FL 32224
Phone: 904-646-4747
Fax: 904-646-0115

WTLV-TV Ch 12 (NBC)
1070 E Adams St
Jacksonville, FL 32202
Phone: 904-354-1212
Fax: 904-633-8899

Radio

WAOC-AM 1420 kHz (N/T)
567 Lewis Point Rd Ext
Saint Augustine, FL 32086
Phone: 904-797-4444
Fax: 904-797-3446

WAPE-FM 95.1 MHz (CHR)
9090 Hogan Rd
Jacksonville, FL 32216
E-mail: thebigape@wape951.com
www.wape951.com
Phone: 904-725-9273
Fax: 904-641-3297

WAYL-FM 91.9 MHz (CHR)
1485 US 1 S
Saint Augustine, FL 32086
E-mail: waylfm@aug.com
www.wayl.com
Phone: 904-829-9200
Fax: 904-829-9202

WBGB-FM 106.5 MHz (Rel)
8386 Baymeadows Rd Suite 107
Jacksonville, FL 32256
E-mail: sales@1065thepromise.com
www.1065thepromise.com
Phone: 904-636-0507
Fax: 904-730-5040

WBWL-AM 600 kHz (Sports)
6869 Lenox Ave
Jacksonville, FL 32205
www.wbwl.com
Phone: 904-783-3711
Fax: 904-786-1529

WCGL-AM 1360 kHz (Rel)
6050-6 Moncries Rd
Jacksonville, FL 32209
www.wcgl1360.com
Phone: 904-766-9955
Fax: 904-765-9214

WEJZ-FM 96.1 MHz (AC)
1896 Corporate Square Blvd
Jacksonville, FL 32216
Phone: 904-727-9696
Fax: 904-721-9322

WFCF-FM 88.5 MHz (Misc)
PO Box 1027 Flagler College
Saint Augustine, FL 32085
Phone: 904-829-6481
Fax: 904-829-3471

WFKS-FM 99.9 MHz (AC)
801 W Granada Blvd Suite 201
Ormond Beach, FL 32174
www.radiokiss.com
Phone: 904-672-9210
Fax: 904-677-2252

WFOY-AM 1240 kHz (N/T)
1 Radio Rd
Saint Augustine, FL 32084
www.oldcity.com/wfoy
Phone: 904-829-3416
Fax: 904-829-8051

WFSJ-FM 97.9 MHz (NAC)
8386 Baymeadows Rd Suite 107
Jacksonville, FL 32256
E-mail: sales@wfsj.com
www.wfsj.com
Phone: 904-636-0507
Fax: 904-730-5040

WFYV-FM 104.5 MHz (Rock)
9090 Hogan Rd
Jacksonville, FL 32216
E-mail: wfyv105@cybermax.net
www.wfyv105.com
Phone: 904-642-1055
Fax: 904-641-3297

WIYD-AM 1260 kHz (Ctry)
900 River St
Palatka, FL 32177
Phone: 904-325-4556
Fax: 904-328-5161

WJAX-AM 1220 kHz (Nost)
5353 Arlington Expy
Jacksonville, FL 32211
Phone: 904-743-2400

WJBT-FM 92.7 MHz (Urban)
10592 E Balmoral Cir Suite 1
Jacksonville, FL 32218
www.wjbt.com
Phone: 904-696-1015
Fax: 904-714-4487

WJCT-FM 89.9 MHz (NPR)
100 Festival Pk Ave
Jacksonville, FL 32202
E-mail: wjct@wjct.org
www.wjct.org/Stereo90
Phone: 904-353-7770
Fax: 904-358-6352

WJGR-AM 1320 kHz (N/T)
5555 Radio Ln
Jacksonville, FL 32205
www.wjgr.com
Phone: 904-388-7711
Fax: 904-384-0859

WKLN-AM 1170 kHz (N/T)
2820 Lewis Speedway
Saint Augustine, FL 32084
E-mail: wkln@aug.com
www.wkln.com
Phone: 904-825-0009
Fax: 904-825-4371

WKQL-FM 96.9 MHz (Oldies)
6869 Lenox Ave
Jacksonville, FL 32205
E-mail: coolfm@wkql969.com
www.wkql969.com
Phone: 904-783-3711
Fax: 904-786-1529

WKTZ-FM 90.9 MHz (B/EZ)
5353 Arlington Expy
Jacksonville, FL 32211
Phone: 904-743-2400

WMXQ-FM 102.9 MHz (AC)
6869 Lenox Ave
Jacksonville, FL 32205
E-mail: info@wmxq103.com
www.wmxq103.com
Phone: 904-783-3711
Fax: 904-786-1529

WNCM-FM 88.1 MHz (Rel)
2361 Cortez Rd
Jacksonville, FL 32246
E-mail: contact@fm88.org
www.fm88.org
Phone: 904-641-9626
Fax: 904-645-9626

WNZS-AM 930 kHz (Sports)
8386 Baymeadows Rd Suite 107
Jacksonville, FL 32256
www.wnzs.com
Phone: 904-636-0507
Fax: 904-636-7971

WOKV-AM 690 kHz (N/T)
6869 Lenox Ave
Jacksonville, FL 32205
www.wokv.com
Phone: 904-783-3711
Fax: 904-786-1529

WPLA-FM 93.3 MHz (Alt)
8386 Baymeadows Rd Suite 107
Jacksonville, FL 32256
E-mail: planet@planet93.com
www.planet93.com
Phone: 904-636-0507
Fax: 904-730-5040

WPLK-AM 800 kHz (Nost)
1501 Reid St
Palatka, FL 32177
Phone: 904-325-5800
Fax: 904-328-8725

WQIK-FM 99.1 MHz (Ctry)
5555 Radio Ln
Jacksonville, FL 32205
www.wqik.com
Phone: 904-388-7711
Fax: 904-384-0859

WROO-FM 107.3 MHz (Ctry)
8386 Baymeadows Rd Suite 107
Jacksonville, FL 32256
www.roostercountry107.com
Phone: 904-636-0507
Fax: 904-636-0522

WSOL-FM 101.5 MHz (AC)
10592 Balmoral Cir E Suite 1
Jacksonville, FL 32218
www.v1015.com
Phone: 904-696-1015
Fax: 904-696-1011

WSOS-FM 94.1 MHz (Nost)
2715 Stratton Blvd
Saint Augustine, FL 32084
www.wsosfm.com
Phone: 904-824-0833
Fax: 904-825-0105

WSVE-AM 1280 kHz (Rel)
4343 Spring Grove
Jacksonville, FL 32209
Phone: 904-768-1211
Fax: 904-768-5115

WVOJ-AM 970 kHz (N/T)
2427 University Blvd N
Jacksonville, FL 32211
Phone: 904-743-6234
Fax: 904-745-0331

WYGV-FM 105.5 MHz (Oldies)
567 Lewis Point Rd Ext
Saint Augustine, FL 32086
Phone: 904-797-4444
Fax: 904-797-3446

WZAZ-AM 1400 kHz (Rel)
10592 Balmoral Cir E Suite 1
Jacksonville, FL 32218
Phone: 904-696-1015
Fax: 904-696-1011

WZNZ-AM 1460 kHz (N/T)
8386 Baymeadows Rd Suite 107
Jacksonville, FL 32256
E-mail: programming@wznz.com
www.wznz.com
Phone: 904-636-0507
Fax: 904-636-0533

Attractions

Jacksonville's Atlantic beaches, Saint Johns River, and numerous lakes provide a variety of recreational opportunities, including boating, fishing, swimming, surfing, and sunbathing. Jacksonville Landing and the Riverwalk near the Saint John's River are popular sites for festivals and cultural events. North of the city is historic Fernandina Beach, featuring 19th Century mansions; and on Fort George Island, Kingsley Plantation provides a glimpse of life on a 19th century sea island cotton plantation.

3D World
28 San Marco Ave
Saint Augustine, FL 32084
Phone: 904-824-1220
Fax: 904-824-1226

Adventure Landing
1944 Beach Blvd
Jacksonville, FL 32250
www.adventurelanding.com
Phone: 904-246-4386
Fax: 904-249-1018

Alexander Brest Museum
2800 University Blvd N Jacksonville University
Jacksonville, FL 32211
Phone: 904-744-3950
Fax: 904-745-7375

Alhambra Dinner Theatre
12000 Beach Blvd
Jacksonville, FL 32246
Phone: 904-641-1212

Amelia Island Museum of History
233 S 3rd St
Fernandina Beach, FL 32034
E-mail: aimh@net-magic.net
Phone: 904-261-7378
Fax: 904-261-9701

Anastasia State Park
1340 A1A S
Saint Augustine, FL 32084
Phone: 904-461-2033
Fax: 904-461-2006

Anheuser-Busch Brewery
111 Busch Dr
Jacksonville, FL 32218
www.anheuser-busch.com
Phone: 904-751-8118
Fax: 904-751-8095

Castillo De San Marcos National Monument
1 S Castillo Dr
Saint Augustine, FL 32084
www.nps.gov/casa
Phone: 904-829-6506
Fax: 904-823-9388

Cumberland Island National Seashore
PO Box 806
Saint Marys, GA 31558
www.nps.gov/cuis/
Phone: 912-882-4336
Fax: 912-882-6284

Cummer Museum of Art & Gardens
829 Riverside Ave
Jacksonville, FL 32204
www.cummer.org
Phone: 904-356-6857
Fax: 904-353-4101

Favor-Dykes State Park
US 1 S & I-95
Saint Augustine, FL 32086
Phone: 904-794-0997
Fax: 904-794-1378

Florida Ballet
123 E Forsyth St Florida Theatre of Performing Arts
Jacksonville, FL 32202
Phone: 904-353-7518

Florida National Pavilion & Metropolitan Park
1410 Gator Bowl Blvd
Jacksonville, FL 32202
Phone: 904-630-0837
Fax: 904-630-0538

Florida Theatre of Performing Arts
128 E Forsyth St Suite 300
Jacksonville, FL 32202
E-mail: StillCool@70.fl-theatre-jax.com
Phone: 904-355-5661
Fax: 904-358-1874

Fort Caroline National Memorial
12713 Fort Caroline Rd
Jacksonville, FL 32225
www.nps.gov/foca
Phone: 904-641-7155
Fax: 904-641-3798

Fort Clinch State Park
2601 Atlantic Ave
Fernandina Beach, FL 32034
Phone: 904-277-7274
Fax: 904-277-7225

Fort Matanzas National Monument
8635 A1A S
Saint Augustine, FL 32080
www.nps.gov/foma
Phone: 904-471-0116
Fax: 904-471-7605

Government House Museum
48 King St
Saint Augustine, FL 32084
Phone: 904-825-5033
Fax: 904-825-5096

Guana River State Park
2690 S Ponte Vedra Blvd
Ponte Vedra Beach, FL 32082
Phone: 904-825-5071
Fax: 904-825-6829

Hanna Kathryn Abbey Park
500 Wonderwood Dr
Jacksonville, FL 32233
www.coj.net/fun/parks.htm#kathr
Phone: 904-249-4700
Fax: 904-247-8688

Historic Villages of St Augustine
254-A San Marco Ave
Saint Augustine, FL 32084
E-mail: toursaug@aug.com
Phone: 904-824-8874
Fax: 904-824-6848

Huguenot Memorial Park
10980 Heckscher Dr
Jacksonville, FL 32226
Phone: 904-251-3335
Fax: 904-251-3019

Jacksonville Landing
2 Independent Dr
Jacksonville, FL 32202
E-mail: info@jacksonvillelanding.com
www.jacksonvillelanding.com
Phone: 904-353-1188
Fax: 904-353-1558

Jacksonville Maritime Museum
1015 Museum Cir Unit 2
Jacksonville, FL 32207
www.jaxmarmus.com
Phone: 904-398-9011
Fax: 904-398-7248

Jacksonville Museum of Modern Art
PO Box 40248
Jacksonville, FL 32203
Phone: 904-366-6911
Fax: 904-366-6901

Jacksonville Symphony Orchestra
300 W Water St Suite 200
Jacksonville, FL 32202
www.jaxsymphony.org
Phone: 904-354-5479
Fax: 904-354-9238

Jacksonville Zoo
8605 Zoo Pkwy
Jacksonville, FL 32218
www.jaxzoo.org
Phone: 904-757-4463
Fax: 904-757-4315

Karpeles Manuscript Library Museum
101 W 1st St
Jacksonville, FL 32206
www.rain.org/~karpeles/jax.html
Phone: 904-356-2992
Fax: 904-356-4338

Kingsley Plantation
11676 Palmetto Ave
Jacksonville, FL 32226
Phone: 904-251-3537
Fax: 904-251-3577

Lightner Museum
75 King St
Saint Augustine, FL 32084
Phone: 904-824-2874
Fax: 904-824-2712

Limelight Theatre
1681 US 1 S
Saint Augustine, FL 32086
Phone: 904-825-1164
Fax: 904-825-4662

Little Talbot Island State Park
12157 Heckscher Dr
Jacksonville, FL 32226
Phone: 904-251-2320
Fax: 904-251-2325

Museum of Science & History of Jacksonville
1025 Museum Cir
Jacksonville, FL 32207
Phone: 904-396-7062
Fax: 904-396-5799

Museum of Southern History
4304 Herschel St
Jacksonville, FL 32210
Phone: 904-388-3574

Museum of Weapons & History
81-C King St Suite C
Saint Augustine, FL 32084
Phone: 904-829-3727

Okefenokee National Wildlife Refuge
Rt 2 Box 3330
Folkston, GA 31537
Phone: 912-496-3331
Fax: 912-496-3332

Old Jail Museum
167 San Marco Ave
Saint Augustine, FL 32084
Phone: 904-829-3800
Fax: 904-829-6678
TF: 800-397-4071

Oldest House The Gonzales-Alvarez House
14 Saint Francis St
Saint Augustine, FL 32084
E-mail: oldhouse@aug.com
Phone: 904-824-2872
Fax: 904-824-2569

Oldest Wooden School House
14 Saint George St
Saint Augustine, FL 32084
Phone: 904-824-0192
Fax: 904-826-1913
TF: 888-653-7245

Olustee Battlefield State Historic Site
Hwy 90
Olustee, FL 32072
Phone: 904-397-4331

Pablo Historical Park
425 Beach Blvd
Jacksonville Beach, FL 32250
Phone: 904-246-0093
Fax: 904-246-8641

Peña-Peck House Museum
143 Saint George St
Saint Augustine, FL 32084
Phone: 904-829-5064

Ponce de Leon's Fountain of Youth
11 Magnolia Ave
Saint Augustine, FL 32084
Phone: 904-829-3168
Fax: 904-826-1913
TF: 800-356-8222

Pope Duval Park Phone: 904-630-3500
17575 W Beaver St
Jacksonville, FL 32209

Potter's Wax Museum Phone: 904-829-9056
17 King St Fax: 904-824-3434
Saint Augustine, FL 32084

Ripley's Believe It or Not! Museum Phone: 904-824-1606
19 San Marco Ave Fax: 904-829-1790
Saint Augustine, FL 32084
www.staugustine-ripleys.com

River City Opry Phone: 904-448-8120
300 W Water St Times Union Ctr for the Performing Arts Fax: 904-448-2672
Jacksonville, FL 32202

Riverwalk Phone: 904-630-0837
1000 Museum Dr Fax: 904-630-0538
Jacksonville, FL 32202

Saint Augustine Alligator Farm Phone: 904-824-3337
999 Anastasia Blvd Fax: 904-829-6677
Saint Augustine, FL 32084
E-mail: alligator@aug.com
www.alligatorfarm.com

Saint Augustine Ampitheater Phone: 904-829-1711
1340 A1A S
Saint Augustine, FL 32084

Saint Augustine Historical Society Phone: 904-824-2872
271 Charlotte St Fax: 904-824-2569
Saint Augustine, FL 32084

Saint Augustine Historical Trolley Tours Phone: 904-829-3800
167 San Marco Ave Fax: 904-829-6678
Saint Augustine, FL 32084 TF: 800-397-4071

Saint Augustine Lighthouse & Museum Phone: 904-829-0745
81 Lighthouse Ave Fax: 904-829-0745
Saint Augustine, FL 32084
E-mail: stauglh@aug.com
www.stauglight.com/

Saint Augustine National Cemetery Phone: 352-793-7740
104 Marine St
Saint Augustine, FL 32084

Saint Augustine Sightseeing Trains Phone: 904-829-6545
170 San Marco Ave Fax: 904-829-6548
Saint Augustine, FL 32084 TF: 800-226-6545
E-mail: trains@aug.com
www.redtrains.com/

Saint Johns Audubon Society Phone: 904-797-5997
PO Box 965
Saint Augustine, FL 32094

San Sebastian Winery Phone: 904-826-1594
157 King St Fax: 904-826-1595
Saint Augustine, FL 32084 TF: 888-352-9463

Spanish Quarter Museum Phone: 904-825-6830
29 Saint George St Fax: 904-825-6874
Saint Augustine, FL 32084

Talbot Islands Geopark Phone: 904-251-2320
12157 Heckscher Dr Fax: 904-251-2325
Jacksonville, FL 32226
www.dep.state.fl.us/parks/BigTalbot

Theodore Roosevelt Area Phone: 904-641-7155
13165 Mount Pleasant Rd Fax: 904-221-5248
Jacksonville, FL 32225

Timucuan Ecological & Historic Preserve Phone: 904-641-7155
12713 Fort Caroline Rd Fort Caroline National Memorial Fax: 904-641-3798
Jacksonville, FL 32225
www.nps.gov/timu/

Tree Hill-Jacksonville's Nature Center Phone: 904-724-4646
7152 Lone Star Rd Fax: 904-724-9132
Jacksonville, FL 32211
E-mail: thnc@mediaone.net
www.treehill.org

Washington Oaks State Gardens Phone: 904-446-6780
6400 N Oceanshore Blvd Fax: 904-446-6781
Palm Coast, FL 32137

World Golf Hall of Fame Phone: 904-940-4000
21 World Golf Pl Fax: 904-940-4393
Saint Augustine, FL 32092 TF: 800-948-4746
www.wgv.com

World Golf Village IMAX Theater Phone: 904-940-4123
21 World Golf Pl World Golf Village Fax: 904-940-4374
Saint Augustine, FL 32084
www.wgv.com/wgv/main.nsf/allframesets/wgv200f.html

Sports Teams & Facilities

Alltel Stadium Phone: 904-633-6000
1 Alltel Stadium Pl Fax: 904-633-6050
Jacksonville, FL 32202 TF: 800-618-8005
E-mail: tcharde@ccse.net
www.jaxevents.com/alltel.html

Jacksonville Cyclones (soccer) Phone: 904-278-9232
1201 E Duval St Samuel Wolfson Pk Fax: 904-278-9556
Jacksonville, FL 32202
E-mail: cyclones@cyclonesoccer.com
www.cyclonesoccer.com

Jacksonville Jade (soccer) Phone: 904-262-1722
4831 Greenland Rd Mandarin High School Stadium Fax: 904-262-3223
Jacksonville, FL 32256
E-mail: jacksonvillejade@socceramerica.net
www.jaxjade.com

Jacksonville Jaguars Phone: 904-633-2000
1 Alltel Stadium Pl Alltel Stadium Fax: 904-633-6338
Jacksonville, FL 32202
www.jaguarsnfl.com

Jacksonville Kennel Club Phone: 904-646-0001
1440 N McDuff Ave Fax: 904-646-0420
Jacksonville, FL 32254
www.jaxkennel.com

Jacksonville Lizard Kings (hockey)
1145 E Adams St Veterans Memorial Coliseum
Jacksonville, FL 32201
Phone: 904-358-7825
Fax: 904-630-3913
E-mail: lizard@lizardkings.com
www.lizardkings.com

Jacksonville Veterans Memorial Coliseum
1145 E Adams St
Jacksonville, FL 32202
Phone: 904-630-3905
Fax: 904-630-3913

Saint Augustine Speedway
900 Big Oak Rd
Saint Augustine, FL 32095
Phone: 904-825-2886
Fax: 904-824-2889
E-mail: info@staugustinespeedway.com
www.staugustinespeedway.com

Annual Events

18th Century Christmas Caroling (mid-December) . . .904-829-1711
A Taste of Jacksonville/Blessing of the Fleet (late March) 904-798-9111
American Music Festival (September-June) 904-354-5547
Ancient City King Fish Tournament (mid-July) 904-471-2730
Antique Car Show (late May) 904-471-0341
Atlantic Shakespeare Festival (mid-August) 904-471-1965
Beach Bash (early June) 904-461-2000
Blessing of the Fleet (late March) 904-825-1010
Blue Water Tournament (late May) 904-829-5676
British Night Watch (early December) 904-829-1711
Cabbage & Potato Festival (late April) 904-692-1420
Cannon Firing Season (late May-early September) 904-829-6506
Caribbean Carnival (early November) 904-798-9111
Carols by Candlelight (early December) 904-461-2000
Celebrate Ponte Vedra (May) 904-280-0614
Celebration of Centuries (mid-May-mid-June) 800-653-2489
Christmas Tour of Homes (early December) 904-829-1711
Conch House Challenge (late August) 904-824-4347
Confederate Encampment (late January) 904-829-6506
Days In Spain (early September) 904-825-1010
Drake's Raid (early June) 904-829-1711
Earth Day Celebration (late April) 904-808-7009
Easter Parade (early April) 904-829-2992
Easter Sunday Promenade (early April) 904-829-2992
EPIC Celebration of Spring (mid-April) 904-829-3295
Fall Arts & Crafts Festival (late November) 904-829-1711
Fine Art & Jazz Show (early May) 888-352-9463
Flight to Freedom (late February) 904-461-2000
Founder's Day (early September) 904-825-1010
Fourth of July Celebration (July 4) 800-653-2489
Gamble Rogers Folk Festival (late April-early May) . . .904-794-0222
Gate River Run (early March) 904-739-1917
Gator Bowl (early January) 904-798-9111
Grand Illumination (early December) 904-460-9368
Great Chowder Debate (early November) 904-829-8646
Greater Jacksonville Agricultural Fair (mid-late October) 904-353-0535
Greater Jacksonville Kingfish Tournament (mid-July) 904-798-9111
Greek Landing Day Festival (late June) 904-829-8205
Halloween Nights (late October) 904-471-9010
Hispanic Heritage Folk Festival (mid-October) 904-751-0533
Historic Homes & Gardens Tour (late April) 904-389-2449
Historic Inns & Garden Tour (mid-April) 904-829-3295
Holiday by the Sea Festival (early December) 904-751-0533
Hot Times in the Old Town (early May) 904-829-1711
Jacksonville Boat-A-Rama (early February) 904-724-3003
Jacksonville Downtown Countdown (December 31) 904-630-3520
Jacksonville Jazz Festival (early-mid-November) 904-353-7770
Jacksonville Light Parade (late November) 904-798-9111
Jacksonville Pro Rodeo (July) 904-630-3900
Jacksonville Scottish Highland Games (late February) 904-641-1119
Jacksonville Spring Fair (late March) 904-358-6336
Jacksonville Wine Experience (early April) 904-358-6336
July Fourth Celebration (July 4) 904-630-3520
King Neptune Seafood Festival (early April) 904-249-3972
Kingbuster Fishing Tournament (mid-June) 904-992-9600
Kuumba Festival (late May) 904-353-2270
La Fiesta de Navidad (mid-December) 904-829-1711
Las Posadas Celebration (mid-December) 904-826-0209
Legends of Golf Tournament (mid-March) 904-940-0321
Light Up Jacksonville Tree Lighting (late November) 904-353-1188
Lighthouse Festival & 5K Run (mid-March) 904-829-0745
Lincolnville Festival (early November) 904-829-8379
Luminaries in the Plaza (early-mid-December) 800-653-2489
Matanzas 5K & Fun Run (late January) 904-739-1917
Mayport/Fort George Seafood Festival (mid-March) 904-249-9336
Memorial Weekend Cathedral Festival (late May) 904-797-1563
Menendez Day & Festival (mid-February) 904-825-1010
Mother's Day Arts & Crafts Show (early May) 904-471-7731
Mug Race (early May) 904-264-4094
Native American Pow Wow (late February) 904-829-2201
Nature Photo Contest (early May-mid-July) 904-824-3337
New Year's Eve Rockin' the River Festival (December 31) 904-798-1700
Nights of Lights Festival (late November-late January) 904-829-5681
Passion Play (mid-late March-early April) 904-794-1544
Players Championship The (late March) 904-285-7888
Regatta of Lights (mid-December) 800-653-2489
Riverside Arts & Music Festival (early September) . . .904-389-2449
Saint Augustine Beach Run (mid-April) 904-829-1711
Saint Augustine Christmas Parade (early December) 904-829-5681
Saint Augustine Flower, Garden & Art Show (mid-April) 904-829-3295
Saint Johns County Fair (mid-March) 904-829-5681
Seafood Festival (early April) 904-824-1978
Spanish Night Watch (mid-June) 904-797-7217
Spring Arts & Crafts Festival (late March) 904-829-1711
Springing the Blues Festival (early April) 904-249-3972
Tale Tellers of Saint Augustine (mid-January) 904-471-0179
Taste of Saint Augustine (mid-April) 904-829-3295
Torch Light Tour (early Feb-early April) 904-829-6506
Union Encampment (mid-March) 904-829-6506
Victorian Spring (late April) 904-825-5033
Vilano Bridge Run (early May) 904-824-1761
Winter Dance Festival (mid-January) 904-829-1617
World of Nations (early May) 904-630-0837

Kansas City, Missouri

County: **Jackson**

KANSAS CITY, Missouri is located at the confluence of the Missouri and Kansas Rivers in the northwestern part of the state. Major cities within 100 miles include Columbia and Jefferson City, Missouri; and Kansas City, Topeka, and Manhattan, Kansas.

Area (Land) .... 154.7 sq mi
Area (Water)................................ 2.4 sq mi
Elevation...................................... 800 ft
Latitude ....39-09-00 N
Longitude................................ 94-57-00 W
Time Zone ....CST
Area Code....................................... 816

Climate

Kansas City's climate has four distinct seasons and an average of 223 days of sunshine per year. Winters are cold, with average high temperatures ranging from the mid-30s to low 40s and average low temperatures near 20 degrees. Kansas City receives an average of 20 inches of snow annually. Summer days are very warm, with average highs in the mid- to upper 80s, while evenings cool down into the mid-60s. May is the wettest month in Kansas City; January and February are the driest.

Average Temperatures & Precipitation

Temperatures

	Jan	Feb	Mar	Apr	May	Jun	Jul	Aug	Sep	Oct	Nov	Dec
High	35	41	53	65	74	83	89	86	78	68	53	39
Low	17	22	33	44	54	63	68	66	57	46	34	22

Precipitation

	Jan	Feb	Mar	Apr	May	Jun	Jul	Aug	Sep	Oct	Nov	Dec
Inches	1.1	1.1	2.5	3.1	5.0	4.7	4.4	4.0	4.9	3.3	1.9	1.6

History

The area known today as Kansas City was founded by French fur traders in 1821 as a settlement called "Westport Landing," which served as the terminus of both the Santa Fe and the Oregon Trails. Westport Landing's location along the Missouri River also facilitated the area's development as an important trade center. The settlement was incorporated as a town in 1850 and incorporated as the City of Kansas three years later (the current name, "Kansas City," was adopted in 1889).

The city continued to grow as a commercial and transportation hub, especially after the arrival of the railroad linking it to Saint Louis in 1865 and the construction of the Hannibal Bridge across the Missouri River four years later. Agriculture and livestock production, an industry that Kansas City has become famous for, were important mainstays of the city's early economy.

The automotive industry gained importance in Kansas City after the turn of the century, and today the city is one of largest producers of automobiles in the U.S. Kansas City also became the national center for the greeting card industry when Hallmark was established there in 1910. Economic opportunities created by new industry drew large numbers of new residents to Kansas City. In the years between 1910 and 1960, the population nearly doubled, rising from just under 250,000 to more than 475,000.

Located in the heart of the nation, Kansas City remains one of the nation's top commercial and transportation centers. Although the city's population has declined in recent decades, it is once again on the rise. Kansas City today, with a population of more than 441,000, is Missouri's largest city.

Population

1990 Census 434,829
1998 Estimate..............................441,574
% Change 1.6

Racial/Ethnic Breakdown
White....................................72.4%*
Black 22.4%*
Other 5.2%*
Hispanic Origin (may be of any race) 3.4%*

Age Breakdown
Under 18 years............................25.8%
18 to 24...................................8.7%
25 to 34.................................16.4%
35 to 49.................................22.4%
50+ years 26.7%
Median Age..................................33.5

Gender Breakdown
Male.....................................47.6%
Female...................................52.4%

* *Information given is for Jackson County.*

Government

Type of Government: Council-Manager

Kansas City City Clerk
414 E 12th St 25th Fl
Kansas City, MO 64106
Phone: 816-513-3360
Fax: 816-513-3353

Kansas City City Council
414 E 12th St 24th Fl
Kansas City, MO 64106
Phone: 816-513-1368
Fax: 816-513-1612

Kansas City City Hall Phone: 816-513-3600
414 E 12th St
Kansas City, MO 64106

Kansas City City Manager Phone: 816-513-1408
414 E 12th St 29th Fl Fax: 816-513-1363
Kansas City, MO 64106

Kansas City City Planning & Development Dept Phone: 816-513-1407
414 E 12th St 15th Fl Fax: 816-513-2838
Kansas City, MO 64106

Kansas City Finance Dept Phone: 816-513-1173
414 E 12th St 3rd Fl Fax: 816-513-1174
Kansas City, MO 64106

Kansas City Fire Dept Phone: 816-513-1724
414 E 12th St 22nd Fl Fax: 816-513-1734
Kansas City, MO 64106

Kansas City Human Resources Dept Phone: 816-513-1914
414 E 12th St 12th Fl Fax: 816-513-2639
Kansas City, MO 64106

Kansas City Law Dept Phone: 816-513-1342
414 E 12th St 28th Fl Fax: 816-513-3133
Kansas City, MO 64106

Kansas City Mayor Phone: 816-513-3500
414 E 12th St 29th Fl Fax: 816-513-3518
Kansas City, MO 64106

Kansas City Parks & Recreation Dept Phone: 816-513-7500
4600 E 63rd St Fax: 816-513-7719
Kansas City, MO 64130

Kansas City Police Dept Phone: 816-234-5000
1125 Locust St Fax: 816-234-5013
Kansas City, MO 64106

Kansas City Public Library Phone: 816-701-3400
311 E 12th St Fax: 816-701-3401
Kansas City, MO 64106

Kansas City Public Works Dept Phone: 816-513-2627
414 E 12th St 20th Fl Fax: 816-513-2615
Kansas City, MO 64106

Kansas City Water Services Dept Phone: 816-513-2171
414 E 12th St 5th Fl Fax: 816-513-2085
Kansas City, MO 64106

Important Phone Numbers

AAA....816-931-5252
American Express Travel....816-531-9114
Dental Referral....816-737-5353
Driver's License Information....816-889-2461
Emergency....911
Events Bureau Fun Phone....816-691-3800
HotelDocs....800-468-3537
Jazz Hotline....816-753-5277
Kansas City Finance Dept Revenue Div....816-513-1120
Kansas City Finance Dept Tax Information....816-513-1173
Medical Referral....816-531-8432
Metropolitan Kansas City Board of Realtors....816-242-4200
Missouri Dept of Revenue Taxpayer Services & Collections....816-889-2944
Poison Control Center....816-234-3434
Time/Temp....816-844-4444
Vehicle Registration Information....816-889-2461
Voter Registration Information....816-842-4820
Weather....913-384-5555

Information Sources

Better Business Bureau Serving Greater Kansas City Phone: 816-421-7800
306 E 12th St Suite 1024 Fax: 816-472-5442
Kansas City, MO 64106
www.kansascity.bbb.org

Convention & Visitors Bureau of Greater Kansas City Phone: 816-221-5242
1100 Main St Suite 2550 Fax: 816-691-3805
Kansas City, MO 64105 TF: 800-767-7700
www.visitkc.com

Greater Kansas City Chamber of Commerce Phone: 816-221-2424
911 Main St Suite 2600 Fax: 816-221-7440
Kansas City, MO 64105
www.kcity.com

Independence Chamber of Commerce Phone: 816-252-4745
PO Box 1077 Fax: 816-252-4917
Independence, MO 64051
www.independencechamber.com

Independence City Hall Phone: 816-325-7000
111 E Maple Ave Fax: 816-325-7012
Independence, MO 64050
www.ci.independence.mo.us

Independence Community Development Dept Phone: 816-325-7425
111 E Maple Ave Fax: 816-325-7400
Independence, MO 64050
www.ci.independence.mo.us/comdev.htm

Independence Mayor Phone: 816-325-7027
111 E Maple Ave City Hall Fax: 816-325-7012
Independence, MO 64050
www.ci.independence.mo.us/officials.htm

Independence Tourism Dept Phone: 816-325-7111
111 E Maple Ave Fax: 816-325-7400
Independence, MO 64050 TF: 800-810-4700
www.ci.independence.mo.us/tourism

Jackson County Phone: 816-881-1626
200 S Main St 2nd Fl Fax: 816-881-4473
Independence, MO 64050

Kansas City (KS) City Hall Phone: 913-573-5000
701 N 7th St Municipal Office Bldg Fax: 913-573-5005
Kansas City, KS 66101
www.wycokck.org

Kansas City (KS) Economic Development Phone: 913-573-5730
701 N 7th St Rm 421 Fax: 913-573-5745
Kansas City, KS 66101

Kansas City (KS) Mayor
701 N 7th St Municipal Office Bldg
Suite 926
Kansas City, KS 66101
www.wycokck.org/html/officials.htm
Phone: 913-573-5010
Fax: 913-573-5020

Kansas City Convention Center
301 W 13th St
Kansas City, MO 64105
www.kcconvention.com
Phone: 816-513-5000
Fax: 816-513-5001
TF: 800-821-7060

Kansas City Kansas Area Chamber of Commerce
PO Box 171337
Kansas City, KS 66117
www.kckacc.com
Phone: 913-371-3070
Fax: 913-371-3732

Kansas City Kansas Public Library
625 Minnesota Ave
Kansas City, KS 66101
www.kckpl.lib.ks.us
Phone: 913-551-3280
Fax: 913-551-3216

Kansas City Kansas/Wyandotte County Convention & Visitors Bureau
727 Minnesota Ave
Kansas City, KS 66117
www.kckcvb.org
Phone: 913-321-5800
Fax: 913-371-3732
TF: 800-264-1563

Mid-Continent Public Library
15616 E 24 Hwy
Independence, MO 64050
www.mcpl.lib.mo.us
Phone: 816-836-5200
Fax: 816-521-7253

Reardon Jack Civic Center
500 Minnesota Ave
Kansas City, KS 66101
Phone: 913-371-1610
Fax: 913-342-6160

Wyandotte County
710 N 7th St
Kansas City, KS 66101
www.wyandottecountyks.com
Phone: 913-573-2800
Fax: 913-321-0237

Online Resources

4Independence.com
www.4independence.com

4KansasCity.com
www.4kansascity.com

About.com Guide to Kansas City
kansascity.about.com/citiestowns/midwestus/kansascity

Access America Kansas City
www.accessamer.com/kansascity/

Anthill City Guide Independence
www.anthill.com/city.asp?city=independence

Anthill City Guide Kansas City
www.anthill.com/city.asp?city=kansascity

Area Guide Independence
independence.areaguides.net

Area Guide Kansas City
kansascity.areaguides.net

City Knowledge Independence
www.cityknowledge.com/mo_independence.htm

City Knowledge Kansas City
www.cityknowledge.com/mo_kansascity.htm

CuisineNet Kansas City
www.menusonline.com/cities/kansas_city/locmain.shtml

DigitalCity Kansas City
www.digitalcity.com/kansascity

Excite.com Independence City Guide
www.excite.com/travel/countries/united_states/missouri/independence

Excite.com Kansas City City Guide
www.excite.com/travel/countries/united_states/missouri/kansas_city

Gazette Weekly Newspaper Online
www.gazetteweekly.com

Greater Kansas City Civic Center
worldmall.com/wmcc/wmcc.htm

Independence Bed & Breakfast Directory
bbchannel.previewtravel.com/USA/Missouri/Independence.asp

Independence-Missouri.com
www.independence-missouri.com

Kansas City Jazz Ambassador Magazine
www.jazzkc.org

KansasCity.Com
www.kansascity.com/

KansasCity.TheLinks.com
kansascity.thelinks.com

Lodging.com Independence Missouri
www.lodging.com/auto/guides/independence-mo.html

Virtual Kansas City
www.virtualkansascity.com/

Webcrafter's KC Metro
webcrafters.com/kcmetro

Area Communities

Communities in the Kansas City metropolitan area (including Cass, Clay, Clinton, Jackson, Lafayette, Platte, and Ray counties in Missouri; and Johnson, Leavenworth, Miami, and Wyandotte counties in Kansas) with populations greater than 10,000 include:

Belton
506 Main St
Belton, MO 64012
Phone: 816-331-4331
Fax: 816-322-4620

Blue Springs
903 W Main St
Blue Springs, MO 64015
Phone: 816-228-0110
Fax: 816-228-7592

Excelsior Springs
201 E Broadway St
Excelsior Springs, MO 64024
Phone: 816-630-0752
Fax: 816-630-4424

Gladstone
7010 N Holmes St
Gladstone, MO 64118
Phone: 816-436-2200
Fax: 816-436-2228

Grandview
1200 Main St
Grandview, MO 64030
Phone: 816-763-3900
Fax: 816-763-3902

Independence
111 E Maple Ave
Independence, MO 64050
Phone: 816-325-7000
Fax: 816-325-7012

Kansas City (KS)
701 N 7th St Municipal Office Bldg
Kansas City, KS 66101
Phone: 913-573-5000
Fax: 913-573-5005

Leavenworth
100 N 5th St
Leavenworth, KS 66048
Phone: 913-682-9201
Fax: 913-758-0180

Leawood
4800 Town Center Dr
Leawood, KS 66211
Phone: 913-339-6700
Fax: 913-339-6781

Lee's Summit
10 NE Tudor Rd
Lees Summit, MO 64086
Phone: 816-969-7392
Fax: 816-969-7521

Lenexa
PO Box 14888
Lenexa, KS 66285
Phone: 913-492-8800
Fax: 913-477-7504

Liberty
101 E Kansas Ave
Liberty, MO 64068
Phone: 816-781-7100
Fax: 816-792-6091

Merriam
9000 W 62nd Terr
Merriam, KS 66202
Phone: 913-722-3330
Fax: 913-722-0238

Olathe
126 S Cherry St
Olathe, KS 66061
Phone: 913-782-2600
Fax: 913-393-6203

Overland Park
8500 Santa Fe Dr
Shawnee Mission, KS 66212
Phone: 913-895-6000
Fax: 913-895-5009

Prairie Village
7700 Mission Rd
Prairie Village, KS 66208
Phone: 913-381-6464
Fax: 913-381-7755

Raytown
10000 E 59th St
Raytown, MO 64133
Phone: 816-737-6000
Fax: 816-737-6050

Shawnee
11110 Johnson Dr
Shawnee Mission, KS 66203
Phone: 913-631-2500
Fax: 913-631-7351

Economy

Kansas City's diverse economic base ranges from the automotive assembly and livestock industries that have sustained the city for centuries to telecommunications. Major U.S. corporations headquartered in Greater Kansas City include Sprint, Farmland Industries, and Hallmark Cards. Two of Kansas City's largest employers, AT & T and Ford Motor Company (both of which provide jobs for more than 5,000 area residents at various offices throughout Greater Kansas City), are among dozens of other corporate giants that have a presence in the area. Services is currently Greater Kansas City's largest employment sector, representing more than 30 percent of the metropolitan area's total labor market. Government also plays a vital role in the region's economy—the federal government and state governments of both Missouri and Kansas are among the Greater Kansas City's largest employers.

Unemployment Rate	3.5%*
Per Capita Income	$24,807*
Median Family Income	$32,969

** Information given is for Jackson County.*

Principal Industries & Number of Wage Earners

Kansas City MSA* - 1999

Construction & Mining	51,600
Finance, Insurance, & Real Estate	70,500
Government	133,800
Manufacturing	107,100
Retail Trade	168,100
Services	286,800
Transportation, Communication, & Utilities	80,600
Wholesale Trade	65,500

** Information given is for the Kansas City Metropolitan Statistical Area (MSA), which includes Cass, Clay, Clinton, Jackson, Lafayette, Platte, and Ray counties.*

Major Employers

AT & T
1100 Walnut Town Pavillion 3rd Fl
Kansas City, MO 64106
www.att.com
Phone: 816-654-5627

Ford Motor Co
Hwy 69
Kansas City, MO 64119
www.ford.com
Phone: 816-459-1249

Fort Leavenworth
Fort Leavenworth, KS 66027
leav-www.army.mil
Phone: 913-684-4021
Fax: 913-684-3624

Hallmark Cards Inc
2501 McGee St
Kansas City, MO 64108
www.hallmark.com
Phone: 816-274-5111
Fax: 816-274-5061
TF: 800-425-5627

Health Midwest
2304 E Meyer Blvd Suite A21
Kansas City, MO 64132
www.healthmidwest.org
Phone: 816-276-9297
Fax: 816-276-9222

Kansas City City Hall
414 E 12th St
Kansas City, MO 64106
www.kcmo.org
Phone: 816-513-3600

Kansas City Missouri School District
2000 NE 46th St
Kansas City, MO 64116
www.kcmsd.k12.mo.us
Phone: 816-413-5000
Fax: 816-418-7712

Saint Luke's Hospital
4401 Wornall Rd
Kansas City, MO 64111
www.saint-lukes.org/about/stlukes.html
Phone: 816-932-2000
Fax: 816-932-5971

Shawnee Mission Medical Center
9100 W 74th St
Shawnee Mission, KS 66204
www.saintlukes.org
Phone: 913-676-2000
Fax: 913-789-3178

Southwestern Bell
500 E 8th St Rm 1232
Kansas City, MO 64106
www.swbell.com
Phone: 816-275-2497

Sprint Corp
2330 Shawnee Mission Pkwy
Westwood, KS 66205
www.sprint.com
Phone: 913-624-3000
Fax: 913-624-2455
TF: 800-877-4020

University of Kansas Medical Center
3901 Rainbow Blvd
Kansas City, KS 66160
www.kumc.edu/Pulse
Phone: 913-588-1270
Fax: 913-588-1280

Quality of Living Indicators

Total Crime Index 51,634
(rates per 100,000 inhabitants)

Violent Crime
Murder/manslaughter 111
Forcible rape 330
Robbery 2,479
Aggravated assault 4,840

Property Crime
Burglary 8,611
Larceny theft 28,513
Motor vehicle theft 6,750

Cost of Living Index 98.2
(national average = 100)

Median Home Price $120,700

Education

Public Schools

Kansas City Missouri School District
2000 NE 46th St
Kansas City, MO 64116
www.kcmsd.k12.mo.us
Phone: 816-413-5000
Fax: 816-418-7712

Number of Schools
Elementary 55
Middle 12
High 11

Student/Teacher Ratio
All Grades 18.0:1

Private Schools

Number of Schools (all grades) .... 60+

Colleges & Universities

Avila College
11901 Wornall Rd
Kansas City, MO 64145
E-mail: admissions@mail.avila.edu
www.avila.edu
Phone: 816-942-8400
Fax: 816-942-3362
TF: 800-462-8452

Brown Mackie College
100 E Santa Fe St Suite 300
Olathe, KS 66061
www.bmcaec.com
Phone: 913-768-1900
Fax: 913-768-0555
TF: 800-635-9101

Calvary Bible College & Seminary
15800 Calvary Rd
Kansas City, MO 64147
www.calvary.edu
Phone: 816-322-0110
Fax: 816-331-4474
TF: 800-326-3960

Concorde Career Colleges Inc
5800 Foxridge Dr Mission Corporate Ctr
Suite 500
Mission, KS 66202
www.concordecareercolleges.com
Phone: 913-831-9977
Fax: 913-831-6556
TF: 800-515-1007

DeVRY Institute of Technology
11224 Holmes Rd
Kansas City, MO 64131
www.kc.devry.edu
Phone: 816-941-0430
Fax: 816-941-0896
TF: 800-821-3766

Donnelly College
608 N 18th St
Kansas City, KS 66102
www.donnelly.cc.ks.us
Phone: 913-621-6070
Fax: 913-621-0354

Finlay Engineering College
7 E 79th Terr
Kansas City, MO 64114
Phone: 816-523-6030

Graceland College
1401 W Truman Rd
Independence, MO 64050
Phone: 816-833-0524
Fax: 816-833-2990
TF: 800-833-0524

Kansas City Art Institute
4415 Warwick Blvd
Kansas City, MO 64111
Phone: 816-472-4852
Fax: 816-802-3309
TF: 800-522-5224

Kansas City Kansas Community College
7250 State Ave
Kansas City, KS 66112
www.kckcc.cc.ks.us
Phone: 913-334-1100
Fax: 913-596-9648

Longview Community College
500 SW Longview Rd
Lee's Summit, MO 64081
www.longview.cc.mo.us
Phone: 816-672-2000
Fax: 816-672-2040

Maple Woods Community College
2601 NE Barry Rd
Kansas City, MO 64156
www.kcmetro.cc.mo.us/maplewoods/mwhome.html
Phone: 816-437-3000
Fax: 816-437-3049

MidAmerica Nazarene University
2030 E College Way
Olathe, KS 66062
www.mnu.edu
Phone: 913-782-3750
Fax: 913-791-3481
TF: 800-800-8887

National American University Kansas City Campus
4200 Blue Ridge Blvd
Kansas City, MO 64133
www.nationalcollege.edu/campuskansas.html
Phone: 816-353-4554
Fax: 816-353-1176

Park College Independence Campus
2200 Hwy 291 S
Independence, MO 64057
www.park.edu
Phone: 816-252-9065
Fax: 816-252-4161

Penn Valley Community College
3201 SW Trafficway
Kansas City, MO 64111
www.kcmetro.cc.mo.us/pennvalley
Phone: 816-759-4000
Fax: 816-759-4161

Rockhurst College
1100 Rockhurst Rd
Kansas City, MO 64110
E-mail: wadsworth@vax2.rockhurst.edu
www.rockhurst.edu
Phone: 816-501-4000
Fax: 816-501-4588
TF: 800-842-6776

University of Missouri Kansas City
5100 Rockhill Rd
Kansas City, MO 64110
E-mail: catalog-admin@smtpgate.umkc.edu
www.umkc.edu
Phone: 816-235-1000
Fax: 816-235-5544

Vatterott College
8955 E 38th Terr
Kansas City, MO 64129
www.vatterott-college.com
Phone: 816-252-3997
Fax: 816-252-0645
TF: 800-466-3997

Hospitals

Baptist Medical Center
6601 Rockhill Rd
Kansas City, MO 64131
www.healthmidwest.org/Hospitals_and_Services/Baptist_Medical_Center/
Phone: 816-276-7000
Fax: 816-926-2266

Bethany Medical Center
51 N 12th St
Kansas City, KS 66102
Phone: 913-281-8400
Fax: 913-281-8494

Children's Mercy Hospital
2401 Gillham Rd
Kansas City, MO 64108
www.cmh.edu
Phone: 816-234-3000
Fax: 816-842-6107

Independence Regional Health Center
1509 W Truman Rd
Independence, MO 64050
Phone: 816-836-8100
Fax: 816-836-6003

Liberty Hospital
2525 Glenn Hendren Dr
Liberty, MO 64069
Phone: 816-781-7200
Fax: 816-792-7117

Medical Center of Independence
17203 E 23rd St
Independence, MO 64057
www.healthmidwest.org/Hospitals_and_Services/Medical_Center_of_Independence
Phone: 816-478-5000
Fax: 816-478-5383

Menorah Medical Center
5721 W 119th St
Overland Park, KS 66209
www.healthmidwest.org/Hospitals_and_Services/Menorah_Medical_Center/
Phone: 913-498-6000
Fax: 913-345-3716

North Kansas City Hospital
2800 Clay Edwards Dr
North Kansas City, MO 64116
Phone: 816-691-2000
Fax: 816-346-7192

Olathe Medical Center
20333 W 151st St
Olathe, KS 66061
www.omci.com
Phone: 913-791-4200
Fax: 913-791-4454

Overland Park Regional Medical Center
10500 Quivira Rd
Overland Park, KS 66215
www.overlandparkregional.com
Phone: 913-541-5000
Fax: 913-541-5484

Providence Medical Center
8929 Parallel Pkwy
Kansas City, KS 66112
Phone: 913-596-4000
Fax: 913-596-4098

Research Medical Center
2316 E Meyer Blvd
Kansas City, MO 64132
Phone: 816-276-4000
Fax: 816-276-4387

Saint Joseph Health Center
1000 Carondelet Dr
Kansas City, MO 64114
Phone: 816-942-4400
Fax: 816-943-4560

Saint Luke's Hospital
4401 Wornall Rd
Kansas City, MO 64111
www.saint-lukes.org/about/stlukes.html
Phone: 816-932-2000
Fax: 816-932-5971

Saint Mary's Hospital of Blue Springs
201 W RD Mize Rd
Blue Springs, MO 64014
Phone: 816-228-5900
Fax: 816-655-5395

Shawnee Mission Medical Center
9100 W 74th St
Shawnee Mission, KS 66204
www.saintlukes.org
Phone: 913-676-2000
Fax: 913-789-3178

Trinity Lutheran Hospital
3030 Baltimore Ave
Kansas City, MO 64108
www.healthmidwest.org/Hospitals_and_Services/Trinity_Lutheran_Hospital
Phone: 816-751-4600
Fax: 816-751-4692

Truman Medical Center East
7900 Lee's Summit Rd
Kansas City, MO 64139
www.trumed.org/departments/east/East.html
Phone: 816-373-4415
Fax: 816-478-7500

Truman Medical Center West
2301 Holmes St
Kansas City, MO 64108
Phone: 816-556-3000
Fax: 816-556-3882

University of Kansas Medical Center
3901 Rainbow Blvd
Kansas City, KS 66160
www.kumc.edu/Pulse
Phone: 913-588-1270
Fax: 913-588-1280

Veterans Affairs Medical Center
4801 E Linwood Blvd
Kansas City, MO 64128
Phone: 816-861-4700
Fax: 816-922-3331
TF: 800-525-1483

Transportation

Airport(s)

Kansas City International Airport (MCI)
25 miles NW of downtown (approx 30 minutes) . . .816-243-5237

Mass Transit

Gray Line
$6 Base fare 816-221-3399
KCATA Metro Bus
$.90 Base fare 816-221-0660

Rail/Bus

Amtrak Station
2200 Main St
Kansas City, MO 64108
Phone: 816-421-3622
TF: 800-872-7245

Greyhound Bus Station
1101 Troost St
Kansas City, MO 64106
Phone: 816-221-2885
TF: 800-231-2222

Utilities

Electricity
Kansas City Power & Light 816-471-5275
www.kcpl.com

Gas
Missouri Gas Energy 816-756-5252
www.southernunionco.com/mge/

Water
Kansas City Missouri Water & Pollution Control Dept 816-513-2182

Garbage Collection/Recycling
Kansas City Solid Waste Div .816-513-3490

Telecommunications

Telephone
Southwestern Bell Telephone Co 800-246-4999
www.swbell.com

Cable Television
Time Warner Cable 816-358-8833
www.twckc.com

Internet Service Providers (ISPs)
SkyNET Corp 816-421-2626
www.sky.net
Sound Advice Ltd 816-436-5206
www.sound.net

Banks

Bank Midwest NA
1100 Main St Suite 350
Kansas City, MO 64105
www.bankmw.com
Phone: 816-471-9800
Fax: 816-472-5668

Bank of America NA
1200 Main St
Kansas City, MO 64105
Phone: 888-279-3121
Fax: 816-979-7424

Blue Ridge Bank & Trust Co
4240 Blue Ridge Blvd Suite 100
Kansas City, MO 64133
E-mail: marketing@blueridgebank.net
www.blueridgebank.net
Phone: 816-358-5000
Fax: 816-356-7530

Central Bank of Kansas City
2301 Independence Ave
Kansas City, MO 64124
Phone: 816-483-1210
Fax: 816-483-2586

Commerce Bank NA
1000 Walnut St
Kansas City, MO 64106
E-mail: mymoney@commercebank.com
www.commercebank.com
Phone: 816-234-2000
Fax: 816-234-2799
TF: 800-453-2265

First Federal Bank FSB
6900 N Executive Dr
Kansas City, MO 64120
E-mail: questions@firstfedbankkc.com
www.firstfedbankkc.com
Phone: 816-241-7800
Fax: 816-245-4187

Mercantile Bank of Kansas City
1101 Walnut Tower
Kansas City, MO 64106
www.mercantile.com/kansas
Phone: 816-472-6372
Fax: 816-871-2326
TF: 800-963-6372

Missouri Bank & Trust Co
1044 Main St
Kansas City, MO 64105
Phone: 816-881-8200
Fax: 816-881-8236

UMB Bank NA
1010 Grand Blvd
Kansas City, MO 64106
www.umb.com
Phone: 816-860-7000
Fax: 816-421-5411
TF: 800-821-2171

Shopping

39th Street Corridor
39th & Bell Sts
Kansas City, MO 64111
Phone: 816-561-5411

Antioch Shopping Center
5307 Center Mall Antioch & Vivion Rds
Kansas City, MO 64119
Phone: 816-454-1200

Bannister Mall
5600 E Bannister Rd
Kansas City, MO 64137
E-mail: info@shopbannister.com
www.shopbannister.com
Phone: 816-763-6900
Fax: 816-763-3920

City Market/River Market
20 E 5th St Suite 201
Kansas City, MO 64106
E-mail: mktg@kc-citymarket.com
www.kc-citymarket.com
Phone: 816-842-1271

Country Club Plaza
450 Ward Pkwy
Kansas City, MO 64112
E-mail: plaza@unicom.net
www.countryclubplaza.com
Phone: 816-753-0100
Fax: 816-753-4625

Crown Center
2450 Grand Ave
Kansas City, MO 64108
www.crowncenter.com
Phone: 816-274-8444
Fax: 816-545-6595

Dillard's
8800 Ward Pkwy
Kansas City, MO 64114
Phone: 816-363-8800

Great Mall of the Great Plains
20700 W 151st St
Olathe, KS 66061
Phone: 888-386-6255

Hall's
200 E 25th St
Kansas City, MO 64108
Phone: 816-274-8111
Fax: 816-274-4471

Independence Center
2035 Independence Center Dr
Independence, MO 64057
Phone: 816-795-8600
Fax: 816-795-7836

Independence Square
Main St betw Walnut St & Truman Rd
Independence, MO 64050

Indian Springs Marketplace
4601 State Ave
Kansas City, KS 66102
Phone: 913-287-9393
Fax: 913-287-4367

Jones Store
9757 Metcalf
Overland Park, KS 66212
www.mayco.com/js/index.jsp
Phone: 913-652-8651
Fax: 913-652-7438
TF: 800-821-2146

Metcalf South Shopping Center
9635 Metcalf Ave
Overland Park, KS 66212
Phone: 913-649-2277
Fax: 913-649-2295

Metro North Mall
400 NW Barry Rd
Kansas City, MO 64155
Phone: 816-436-7800
Fax: 816-436-9952

Mission Center Mall
4801 Johnson Dr
Shawnee Mission, KS 66205
Phone: 913-262-3000
Fax: 913-262-3622

Oak Park Mall
11461 W 95th St
Overland Park, KS 66214
www.thenewoakparkmall.com
Phone: 913-888-4400
Fax: 913-888-0843

River Market Antique Mall
115 W 5th St
Kansas City, MO 64105
Phone: 816-221-0220

Saks Fifth Avenue
444 Nichols Rd
Kansas City, MO 64112
Phone: 816-931-6000
Fax: 816-753-4564

Town Pavilion
1111 Main St Suite 218
Kansas City, MO 64105
Phone: 816-472-9600
Fax: 816-474-0693

Ward Parkway Shopping Center
8600 Ward Pkwy
Kansas City, MO 64114
Phone: 816-363-3545

Westport Historic District
Broadway & Westport Rd
Kansas City, MO 64111
Phone: 816-756-2789
Fax: 816-756-2919

Westport Square
435 Westport Rd
Kansas City, MO 64111
www.westporttoday.com
Phone: 816-756-2789

Media

Newspapers and Magazines

Examiner The*
410 S Liberty St
Independence, MO 64050
examiner.net
Phone: 816-254-8600
Fax: 816-836-3805

Kansas City Business Journal
1101 Walnut St Suite 800
Kansas City, MO 64106
E-mail: kansascity@amcity.com
www.amcity.com/kansascity
Phone: 816-421-5900
Fax: 816-472-4010

Kansas City Star*
1729 Grand Blvd
Kansas City, MO 64108
E-mail: starstaff@kcstar.com
www.kcstar.com
Phone: 816-234-4141
Fax: 816-234-4926
TF: 800-726-2340

Liberty Sun News
12 N Main St
Liberty, MO 64068
Phone: 816-781-1044
Fax: 816-781-1755

Northland News
12 N Main St
Liberty, MO 64068
Phone: 816-781-1044
Fax: 816-792-5979

PitchWeekly
3535 Broadway Suite 400
Kansas City, MO 64111
E-mail: pitch@pitch.com
www.pitch.com
Phone: 816-561-6061
Fax: 816-756-0502

Raytown Dispatch-Tribune
7007 NE Parvin Rd
Kansas City, MO 64117
Phone: 816-454-9660
Fax: 816-452-5889

Raytown Post
PO Box 9338
Raytown, MO 64133
Phone: 816-353-5545

Wednesday Magazine
20 E Gregory St
Kansas City, MO 64114
Phone: 816-454-9660
Fax: 816-822-1856

**Indicates major daily newspapers*

Television

KCPT-TV Ch 19 (PBS)
125 E 31st St
Kansas City, MO 64108
E-mail: kcpt@tv19.kcpt.org
www.kcpt.org
Phone: 816-756-3580
Fax: 816-931-2500

KCTV-TV Ch 5 (CBS)
PO Box 5555
Kansas City, MO 64109
E-mail: kctv@kctv.com
www.kctv.com
Phone: 913-677-5555
Fax: 913-677-7243

KCWE-TV Ch 29 (UPN)
1049 Central
Kansas City, MO 64105
Phone: 816-221-2900
Fax: 816-760-9149

KMBC-TV Ch 9 (ABC)
1049 Central St
Kansas City, MO 64105
www.kmbc.com
Phone: 816-221-9999
Fax: 816-421-4163

KMCI-TV Ch 38 (Ind)
2951 Four Wheel Dr
Lawrence, KS 66047
www.kmci.com
Phone: 785-749-3388
Fax: 785-749-3377

KPXE-TV Ch 50 (PAX)
3101 Broadway Suite 570
Kansas City, MO 64111
www.pax.net/kpxe
Phone: 816-924-5050
Fax: 816-931-1818

KSHB-TV Ch 41 (NBC)
4720 Oak St
Kansas City, MO 64112
E-mail: news@kshb.com
www.kshb.com
Phone: 816-753-4141
Fax: 816-932-4145

KSMO-TV Ch 62 (WB)
10 E Cambridge Dr Suite 300
Kansas City, KS 66103
Phone: 913-621-6262
Fax: 913-621-4703

WDAF-TV Ch 4 (Fox)
3030 Summit St
Kansas City, MO 64108
www.wdaftv4.com
Phone: 816-753-4567
Fax: 816-561-4181

Radio

KBEQ-FM 104.3 MHz (Ctry)
4717 Grand Ave Suite 600
Kansas City, MO 64112
www.youngcountryq104.com
Phone: 816-531-2535
Fax: 816-531-7327

KCCV-AM 760 kHz (Rel)
10550 Barkley St Suite 112
Overland Park, KS 66212
Phone: 913-642-7600
Fax: 913-642-2424

KCFX-FM 101.1 MHz (Rock)
5800 Foxridge Dr
Mission, KS 66202
www.kcfx.com
Phone: 913-514-3000
Fax: 913-514-3003

KCHZ-FM 95.7 MHz (CHR)
4240 Blue Ridge Blvd Suite 820
Kansas City, MO 64133
Phone: 816-356-2400
Fax: 816-356-2479

KCIY-FM 106.5 MHz (Nost)
5800 Foxridge Dr Suite 600
Mission, KS 66202
www.kciy1065.com
Phone: 913-514-3000
Fax: 913-514-3003

KCMO-AM 710 kHz (N/T)
4935 Belinder Rd
Westwood, KS 66205
www.kcmoam.com
Phone: 913-677-8998
Fax: 913-677-8901

KCMO-FM 94.9 MHz (Oldies)
4935 Belinder Rd
Westwood, KS 66205
www.oldies95.com
Phone: 913-677-8998
Fax: 913-677-8901

KCUR-FM 89.3 MHz (NPR)
4825 Troost Ave Suite 202
Kansas City, MO 64110
E-mail: kcur@smtpgate.umkc.edu
www.umkc.edu/kcur
Phone: 816-235-1551
Fax: 816-235-2864

KCWJ-AM 1030 kHz (Rel)
544 E 99th St
Kansas City, MO 64131
www.kcwj.com
Phone: 816-942-7772
Fax: 816-942-7774

KCXL-AM 1140 kHz (N/T)
310 S La Frenz Rd
Liberty, MO 64068
E-mail: kcxl@kcxl.com
www.kcxl.com
Phone: 816-792-1140
Fax: 816-792-8258

KEXS-AM 1090 kHz (Rel)
201 Industrial Park Rd
Excelsior Springs, MO 64024
Phone: 816-630-1090
Fax: 816-630-6063

KFEZ-AM 1340 kHz (Nost)
1212 Baltimore St
Kansas City, KS 64105
Phone: 816-421-1900
Fax: 816-471-1320
TF: 800-266-1190

KFKF-FM 94.1 MHz (Ctry)
4717 Grand Ave Suite 600
Kansas City, MO 64112
E-mail: kfkf@kansascity.com
sites.kansascity.com/kfkf
Phone: 816-753-4000
Fax: 816-753-4045

KGGN-AM 890 kHz (Rel)
1734 E 63rd St Suite 600
Kansas City, MO 64110
Phone: 816-333-0092
Fax: 816-363-8120

KKFI-FM 90.1 MHz (Misc)
900 1/2 Westport Rd 2nd Fl
Kansas City, MO 64111
Phone: 816-931-3122
Fax: 816-931-7078

KKLO-AM 1410 kHz (Rel)
481 Muncie Rd
Leavenworth, KS 66048
E-mail: kklo@tfs.net
www.kklo.com
Phone: 913-351-1410

KLJC-FM 88.5 MHz (Rel)
15800 Calvary Rd
Kansas City, MO 64147
E-mail: kljc@kljc.org
www.kljc.org
Phone: 816-331-8700
Fax: 816-303-1553

KMBZ-AM 980 kHz (N/T)
4935 Belinder Rd
Westwood, KS 66205
www.kmbz.com
Phone: 913-236-9800
Fax: 913-677-8901

KMXV-FM 93.3 MHz (CHR)
508 Westport Rd
Kansas City, MO 64111
www.mix93.com
Phone: 816-756-5698
Fax: 816-531-2550

KNRX-FM 107.3 MHz (Urban)
4240 Blue Ridge Blvd Suite 820
Kansas City, MO 64133
E-mail: comments@1073thex.com
www.1073thex.com
Phone: 816-353-7600
Fax: 816-353-2300

KPHN-AM 1190 kHz (N/T)
1212 Baltimore St
Kansas City, KS 64105
E-mail: mail@kphn1190.com
www.kphn1190.com
Phone: 816-421-1900
Fax: 816-471-1320

KPRS-FM 103.3 MHz (Urban) Phone: 816-763-2040
11131 Colorado Ave Fax: 816-966-1055
Kansas City, MO 64137
E-mail: 103@kprs.com
www.kprs.com

KPRT-AM 1590 kHz (Rel) Phone: 816-763-2040
11131 Colorado Ave Fax: 816-966-1055
Kansas City, MO 64137
E-mail: 1590@kprt.com
www.kprt.com

KQRC-FM 98.9 MHz (Rock) Phone: 913-514-3000
5800 Foxridge Rd Fax: 913-514-3303
Mission, KS 66205
www.989therock.com

KSRC-FM 102.1 MHz (AC) Phone: 816-561-9102
508 Westport Rd Suite 202 Fax: 816-531-2550
Kansas City, MO 64111
E-mail: request@star102.net
www.star102.net

KUDL-FM 98.1 MHz (AC) Phone: 913-236-9800
4935 Belinder Rd Fax: 913-677-8981
Westwood, KS 66205
www.kudl.com

KXTR-FM 96.5 MHz (Clas) Phone: 913-514-3000
5800 Foxridge Dr Fax: 913-514-3003
Mission, KS 66202

KYYS-FM 99.7 MHz (Rock) Phone: 913-677-8998
4935 Belinder Rd Fax: 913-677-8901
Westwood, KS 66205
www.kyys.com

WDAF-AM 610 kHz (Ctry) Phone: 913-677-8998
4935 Belinder Rd Fax: 913-677-8901
Westwood, KS 66205
www.wdaf.com

WHB-AM 810 kHz (Sports) Phone: 816-836-8326
10841 E 28th St Fax: 816-836-2111
Independence, MO 64052
www.810whb.com

Attractions

Some of the oldest buildings in Kansas City are located in the unique historic district of Westport. A center for outfitting and Indian trade in the 1850s, Westport is now home to shopping areas built from preserved old building facades. Its Pioneer Park traces the district's role in the founding of Kansas City. In contrast, Kansas City's ultra-modern Crown Center complex is a "city within a city," with live theater, 80 shops and restaurants, ice-skating facilities, and the Hallmark Visitors Center. An event which brings thousands of visitors to Kansas City each autumn is the American Royal Livestock, Horse Show and Rodeo, the largest combined show of its kind in the country. The home of President Harry S Truman and his Library and Museum are located in the nearby town of Independence. Across the Missouri River, visitors can learn about Kansas City, Kansas' Eastern European heritage at the Strawberry Hill Museum and Cultural Center, and families with children can enjoy hands-on learning at the Children's Museum of Kansas City.

1827 Log Courthouse Phone: 816-325-7111
107 W Kansas Ave
Independence, MO 64050

1859 Jail Marshal's Home & Museum Phone: 816-252-1892
217 N Main St Fax: 816-252-7792
Independence, MO 64050

39th Street Corridor Phone: 816-561-5411
39th & Bell Sts
Kansas City, MO 64111

Airline History Museum Phone: 816-421-3401
480 NW Richards Rd Fax: 816-421-3421
Kansas City, MO 64116 TF: 800-513-9484
www.saveaconnie.org

Alexander Majors Historic House & Museum Phone: 816-333-5556
8201 State Line Rd
Kansas City, MO 64114

American Heartland Theatre Phone: 816-842-0202
2450 Grand Blvd Suite 314 Fax: 816-842-1881
Kansas City, MO 64108

American Jazz Museum Phone: 816-474-8463
1616 E 18th St Fax: 816-474-0074
Kansas City, MO 64108
E-mail: scheduling@americanjazzmuseum.com
www.americanjazzmuseum.com

American Royal Museum & Visitors Center Phone: 816-221-9800
1701 American Royal Ct Fax: 816-221-8189
Kansas City, MO 64102
E-mail: mericanroyal@americanroyal.com
www.americanroyal.com

Arabia Steamboat Museum Phone: 816-471-1856
400 Grand Blvd Fax: 816-471-1616
Kansas City, MO 64106 TF: 800-471-1856
E-mail: info@1856.com
www.1856.com

Benjamin Ranch on the Santa Fe Trail Phone: 816-761-5055
6401 E 87th St Fax: 816-761-7400
Kansas City, MO 64138 TF: 800-437-2624

Bingham-Waggoner Estate Phone: 816-461-3491
313 W Pacific Ave Fax: 816-461-1540
Independence, MO 64050

Bingham-Waggoner Historical Society Phone: 816-461-3491
313 W Pacific Ave Fax: 816-461-1540
Independence, MO 64050

Black Archives of Mid-America Phone: 816-483-1300
2033 Vine St Fax: 816-483-1341
Kansas City, MO 64108
www.blackarchives.org

Boulevard Brewing Co Phone: 816-474-7095
2501 Southwest Blvd Fax: 816-474-1722
Kansas City, MO 64108

Brown John Statue Phone: 913-371-7489
27th St & Sewell Ave
Kansas City, KS 66104

Bruce R Watkins Cultural Heritage Center
3700 Blue Pkwy
Kansas City, MO 64130
Phone: 816-784-4444
Fax: 816-784-4448

Cave Spring Interpretive Center
8701 E Gregory Blvd
Kansas City, MO 64133
Phone: 816-358-2283

Children's Museum of Kansas City
4601 State Ave
Kansas City, KS 66102
www.geocities.com/~kidmuzm
Phone: 913-287-8888
Fax: 913-287-8888

Cool Crest Family Fun Center
10735 Hwy 40 E
Independence, MO 64050
E-mail: info@coolcrest.com
www.coolcrest.com
Phone: 816-358-0088
Fax: 816-358-7980

Coterie Theatre
2450 Grand Blvd
Kansas City, MO 64108
www.crowncenter.com/coterie.html
Phone: 816-474-6552
Fax: 816-474-7112

Country Club Plaza
450 Ward Pkwy
Kansas City, MO 64112
E-mail: plaza@unicom.net
www.countryclubplaza.com
Phone: 816-753-0100
Fax: 816-753-4625

Crown Center
2450 Grand Ave
Kansas City, MO 64108
www.crowncenter.com
Phone: 816-274-8444
Fax: 816-545-6595

Excelsior Springs Historical Museum
101 E Broadway
Excelsior Springs, MO 64024
Phone: 816-630-3712
Fax: 816-630-3712

Federal Reserve Bank Visitors Center
925 Grand Ave
Kansas City, MO 64198
Phone: 816-881-2200
Fax: 816-881-2568

Flamingo Hilton Casino
1800 E Front St
Kansas City, MO 64120
Phone: 816-855-7777
Fax: 816-855-4188
TF: 800-946-8711

Fleming Park/Lake Jacomo
22807 Woods Chapel Rd Jackson County Parks & Recreation
Blue Springs, MO 64015
Phone: 816-795-8200
Fax: 816-795-1234

Folly Theater
300 W 12th St
Kansas City, MO 64105
Phone: 816-474-4444
Fax: 816-842-8709

Fort Osage National Historic Landmark
105 Osage St
Sibley, MO 64088
Phone: 816-795-8200
Fax: 816-795-7938

Gem Theater Cultural & Performing Arts Center
1615 E 18th St
Kansas City, MO 64108
Phone: 816-842-4538
Fax: 816-842-8379

Grinter Place Museum
1420 S 78th St
Kansas City, KS 66111
Phone: 913-299-0373

Hallmark Visitors Center
2501 McGee
Kansas City, MO 64108
Phone: 816-274-3613
Fax: 816-274-3148

Harrah's Casino Hotel North Kansas City
1 Riverboat Dr
North Kansas City, MO 64116
www.harrahs.com/tour/tour_northkc.html
Phone: 816-472-7777
Fax: 816-472-7778
TF: 800-427-7247

Harris-Kearney House
4000 Baltimore St
Kansas City, MO 64111
Phone: 816-561-1821

Harry S Truman Home
219 N Delaware St
Independence, MO 64050
Phone: 816-254-9929

Harry S Truman Presidential Library & Museum
500 W Hwy 24
Independence, MO 64050
E-mail: library@truman.nara.gov
www.trumanlibrary.org
Phone: 816-833-1400
Fax: 816-833-4368

Hodge Park
7000 NE Barry Rd
Kansas City, MO 64156
Phone: 816-792-2655

Huron Indian Cemetery
7th & Minnesota Sts
Kansas City, KS 66101
Phone: 913-321-5800

Independence Square
Main St betw Walnut St & Truman Rd
Independence, MO 64050

Jackson County Historical Society Archives
112 W Lexington Ave Rm 103
Independence, MO 64050
E-mail: info@jchs.org
www.jchs.org
Phone: 816-252-7454
Fax: 816-252-8146

James Country Mercantile
111 N Main St
Liberty, MO 64068
Phone: 816-781-9473
Fax: 816-781-1470

John Wornall House Museum
146 W 61st Terr
Kansas City, MO 64113
E-mail: jwornall@crn.org
Phone: 816-444-1858
Fax: 816-361-8165

Kaleidoscope
PO Box 419580
Kansas City, MO 64141
Phone: 816-274-8301
Fax: 816-274-3148

Kansas City Ballet
1601 Broadway
Kansas City, MO 64108
www.kcballet.org
Phone: 816-931-2232
Fax: 816-931-1172

Kansas City Board of Trade
4800 Main St Suite 303
Kansas City, MO 64112
E-mail: kcbt@kcbt.com
www.kcbt.com
Phone: 816-753-7500
Fax: 816-753-3944
TF: 800-821-5228

Kansas City Museum
3218 Gladstone Blvd
Kansas City, MO 64123
www.kcmuseum.com
Phone: 816-483-8300
Fax: 816-483-9912
TF: 800-556-9372

Kansas City Music Hall
301 W 13th St
Kansas City, MO 64105
Phone: 816-513-5000
Fax: 816-513-5002
TF: 800-821-7060

Kansas City Symphony
1020 Central St Suite 300
Kansas City, MO 64105
E-mail: symphony-info@kcsymphony.org
www.kcsymphony.org
Phone: 816-471-1100
Fax: 816-471-0976

Kansas City Zoological Gardens
6700 Zoo Dr
Kansas City, MO 64132
www.kansascityzoo.org
Phone: 816-513-5700
Fax: 816-784-3909

Kemper Museum of Contemporary Art
4420 Warwick Blvd
Kansas City, MO 64111
www.kemperart.org
Phone: 816-753-5784
Fax: 816-753-5806

Korean-Vietnam War Memorial
91st & Leavenworth Rd
Kansas City, KS 66109
Phone: 913-299-0550

Lakeside Nature Center
4701 E Gregory Blvd
Kansas City, MO 64132
Phone: 816-516-8960

Leila's Hair Museum
815 W 23rd St
Independence, MO 64050
Phone: 816-252-4247

Liberty Memorial Museum & Archives
100 W 26th St
Kansas City, MO 64108
www.libertymemorialmuseum.org
Phone: 816-931-0749
Fax: 816-221-8981

Longview Lake Park
11100 View High Dr
Kansas City, MO 64134
Phone: 816-795-8200
Fax: 816-795-1234

Lyric Opera of Kansas City
1029 Central St
Kansas City, MO 64105
E-mail: mail@kc-opera.org
kc-opera.org
Phone: 816-471-4933
Fax: 816-471-0602

Martin City Melodrama
13440 Holmes Rd
Kansas City, MO 64145
Phone: 816-942-7576

Midland Theatre
1228 Main St
Kansas City, MO 64105
www.amctheatres.com/theatres/kc_midland/index.html
Phone: 816-471-8600
Fax: 816-221-1127

Missouri Repertory Theatre
4949 Cherry St
Kansas City, MO 64110
cctr.umkc.edu/user/gkeathley/missouri.htm
Phone: 816-235-2700
Fax: 816-235-5367
TF: 888-502-2700

Missouri Town 1855
8010 E Park Rd Fleming Pk
Blue Springs, MO 64015
Phone: 816-795-8200

Mormon Visitors Center
937 W Walnut St
Independence, MO 64050
Phone: 816-836-3466
Fax: 816-252-6256

Museums at 18th & Vine
1616 E 18th St
Kansas City, MO 64108
Phone: 816-474-8463
Fax: 816-474-0074

National Agricultural Center & Hall of Fame
630 Hall of Fame Dr
Bonner Springs, KS 66012
Phone: 913-721-1075
Fax: 913-721-1202

National Frontier Trails Center
318 W Pacific Ave
Independence, MO 64050
E-mail: fdesk@indepmo.org
www.frontiertrailscenter.com
Phone: 816-325-7575
Fax: 816-325-7479

Negro Leagues Baseball Museum
1616 E 18th St
Kansas City, MO 64108
E-mail: nlmuseum@hotmail.com
www.nlbm.com
Phone: 816-221-1920
Fax: 816-221-8424

Nelson-Atkins Museum of Art
4525 Oak St
Kansas City, MO 64111
www.nelson-atkins.org
Phone: 816-561-4000
Fax: 816-561-7154

Oceans of Fun
8200 NE Parvin Rd
Kansas City, MO 64161
E-mail: info@worldsoffun.com
www.worldsoffun.com/_oof/index.htm
Phone: 816-454-4545
Fax: 816-454-4655

Osage Honey Farms Inc
222 Santa Fe St
Sibley, MO 64088
Phone: 816-650-5637

Owens George Nature Park
1601 S Speck Rd
Independence, MO 64057
Phone: 816-257-1760

Pioneer Spring Cabin
Truman & Noland Rds
Independence, MO 64050
Phone: 816-325-7111

Plaza Riverwalk Boat Cruise
Wyandotte St & Ward Pkwy
Kansas City, MO 64112
Phone: 816-741-3410

Powell Gardens
1609 US Hwy 50 NW
Kingsville, MO 64061
www.powellgardens.org
Phone: 816-697-2600
Fax: 816-697-3576

Quality Hill Playhouse
303 W 10th St
Kansas City, MO 64141
www.qhpkc.org
Phone: 816-421-1700
Fax: 816-221-6556

Quindaro Ruins & Underground Railroad
27th St & Sewell Ave
Kansas City, KS 66104
Phone: 913-321-5800

Rosedale Memorial Arch
35th St & Booth
Kansas City, KS 66103
Phone: 913-677-5097

Saint Mary's Episcopal Church
1307 Holmes St
Kansas City, MO 64106
Phone: 816-842-0975
Fax: 816-221-2371

Science City at Union Station
30 W Pershing Rd
Kansas City, MO 64108
www.sciencecity.com
Phone: 816-460-2222
TF: 877-724-2489

Shoal Creek Living History Museum
7000 NE Barry Rd Hodge Pk
Kansas City, MO 64156
Phone: 816-792-2655
Fax: 816-792-3469

Soldiers & Sailors Memorial Hall
600 N 7th St
Kansas City, KS 66101
Phone: 913-371-7555
Fax: 913-371-2025

Spencer Museum of Art
1301 Mississippi St University of Kansas
Lawrence, KS 66045
www.ukans.edu/~sma
Phone: 785-864-4710
Fax: 785-864-3112

Sprint IMAX Theater
6800 Zoo Dr Deramus Education Pavilion
Kansas City, MO 64132
Phone: 816-513-4629
Fax: 816-513-5850

Starlight Theatre
4600 Starlight Rd Swope Pk
Kansas City, MO 64132
E-mail: starlight@kcstarlight.com
www.kcstarlight.com
Phone: 816-363-7827
Fax: 816-361-6398

Station Casino Kansas City
3200 N Station Dr
Kansas City, MO 64161
www.kansascitystation.com
Phone: 816-414-7000
Fax: 816-414-7221
TF: 800-499-4961

Strawberry Hill Museum & Cultural Center
720 N 4th St
Kansas City, KS 66101
Phone: 913-371-3264

Swope Park
Swope Pkwy & Meyer Blvd
Kansas City, MO 64132
Phone: 816-221-5242

Thomas Hart Benton Home & Studio Historic Site
3616 Belleview St
Kansas City, MO 64111
Phone: 816-931-5722

Toy & Miniature Museum
5235 Oak St
Kansas City, MO 64112
Phone: 816-333-2055
Fax: 816-333-2055

Truman Harry S National Historic Site
223 N Main St
Independence, MO 64050
www.nps.gov/hstr
Phone: 816-254-2720
Fax: 816-254-4491

Unicorn Theatre
3828 Main St
Kansas City, MO 64111
Phone: 816-531-7529
Fax: 816-531-0421

Union Cemetery
227 E 28th St
Kansas City, MO 64108
Phone: 816-472-4990

University of Missouri-Kansas City Gallery of Art
5100 Rockhill Rd
Kansas City, MO 64110
www.umkc.edu/gallery
Phone: 816-235-1502
Fax: 816-235-6528

Vaile Mansion
1500 N Liberty Ave
Independence, MO 64050
Phone: 816-325-7430

Vietnam Veterans Memorial
43rd St & Broadway
Kansas City, MO 64111
Phone: 816-561-8387

Westport Historic District
Broadway & Westport Rd
Kansas City, MO 64111
Phone: 816-756-2789
Fax: 816-756-2919

Westport Square
435 Westport Rd
Kansas City, MO 64111
www.westporttoday.com
Phone: 816-756-2789

Worlds of Fun
4545 Worlds of Fun Ave
Kansas City, MO 64161
E-mail: info@worldsoffun.com
www.worldsoffun.com
Phone: 816-454-4545
Fax: 816-454-4655

Wyandotte County Historical Society & Museum
631 N 126th St
Bonner Springs, KS 66012
E-mail: wycomus@toto.net
Phone: 913-721-1078
Fax: 913-721-1394

Wyandotte County Lake & Park
91st & Leavenworth Rd
Kansas City, KS 66109
Phone: 913-299-0550
Fax: 913-299-9051

Wyandotte Players
7250 State Ave
Kansas City, KS 66112
Phone: 913-596-9690

Sports Teams & Facilities

Arrowhead Stadium
1 Arrowhead Dr
Kansas City, MO 64129
www.kcchiefs.com/fanfair/arrowhead.asp
Phone: 816-920-9300
Fax: 816-923-4719

Kansas City Attack (soccer)
1800 Genessee St Kemper Arena
Kansas City, MO 64102
E-mail: info@kcattack.com
www.kcattack.com
Phone: 816-474-2255
Fax: 816-474-2255

Kansas City Blades (hockey)
1800 Genessee St Kemper Arena
Kansas City, MO 64102
www.kcblades.com
Phone: 816-842-1063
Fax: 816-842-5610

Kansas City Brass (soccer)
135th & Switzer Sts Blue Valley District Activites Ctr
Overland Park, KS 66225
Phone: 913-262-2227
Fax: 913-451-9607

Kansas City Chiefs
1 Arrowhead Dr Arrowhead Stadium
Kansas City, MO 64129
www.kcchiefs.com
Phone: 816-920-9300
Fax: 816-920-4315
TF: 800-676-5488

Kansas City Royals Phone: 816-921-8000
1 Royal Way Kauffman Stadium Fax: 816-921-5775
Kansas City, MO 64129
www.kcroyals.com

Kansas City Wizards (soccer) Phone: 816-472-4625
1 Arrowhead Dr Arrowhead Stadium Fax: 816-472-0299
Kansas City, MO 64105
www.kcwizards.com

Kauffman Ewing M Stadium Phone: 816-921-8000
1 Royal Way Fax: 816-924-0347
Kansas City, MO 64129
www.kcroyals.com/kauffmanstadium/kauffman_stadium.html

Kemper Arena Phone: 816-274-6222
1800 Genessee St Fax: 816-472-0306
Kansas City, MO 64102 TF: 800-634-3942

Lakeside Speedway Phone: 913-299-2040
5615 Wolcott Dr Fax: 913-299-1105
Kansas City, KS 66109
E-mail: I70Lake@discoverynet.com
www.lakesidespeedway.com

Municipal Auditorium Arena Phone: 816-513-5000
301 W 13th St Suite 100 Fax: 816-513-5001
Kansas City, MO 64105 TF: 800-821-7060

Woodlands Race Track Phone: 913-299-9797
9700 Leavenworth Rd Fax: 913-299-9804
Kansas City, KS 66109

Annual Events

Abdallah Shrine Rodeo (mid-August) 913-362-5300
American Royal Barbecue Contest (early October)...............................816-221-9800
American Royal Livestock Horse Show & Rodeo (late October-early November) 800-821-5857
Avenue Area Christmas Lighting Ceremony (mid-November)..............................913-371-0065
Best Little Arts & Crafts Show in Independence (mid-late November)...........................816-325-7370
Bingham-Waggoner Antique & Craft Fair (early July) 816-461-3491
Bingham-Waggoner Fashion Show (mid-March) 816-461-3491
Bingham-Waggoner Quilt Show (September) 816-461-3491
Blue Devil Barbecue Cookoff (mid-May)............913-321-5800
Brookside Art Annual (early March) 816-523-0091
Brookside Saint Patrick's Day Warm-Up Parade (mid-March) 816-523-5553
Central Avenue Parade (late September)...........913-371-4511
Children's Day at Fort Osage National Historic Landmark (early August) 816-795-8200
Children's Day at Missouri Town 1855 (early June)...................................816-795-8200
Cinco de Mayo Celebration (early May)............816-221-4747
Dawg Days Animal Fair Craft Show & Flea Market (early August)...............................816-252-0608
Enchanted Forest (late October) 816-257-1760
Ethnic Enrichment Festival (late August) 816-842-7530
Excelsior Springs Waterfest (October) 816-792-7691
Farm & Flower Festival (late April) 816-252-0608
Farm Heritage Days (mid-July) 913-721-1075
Farmer's Market Saturdays (early May-late October)........................816-252-0608
Fiesta Hispana (mid-September) 816-765-1992
Flint Knap-In (mid-May & mid-September).........816-795-8200
Fort Osage Militia Muster (mid-October)...........816-795-8200
Frontier Christmas (early December) 816-795-8200
Frontier Fright Night (late October)...............816-795-8200
Greater Kansas City Auto Show (early March) 816-871-3700
Greek Festival (September).......................816-942-9100
Grinter Applefest (late September) 913-321-5800
Harry S Truman Appreciation Ceremony (early August)................................816-833-1400
Heartland of America Shakespeare Festival (late June-mid-July) 816-531-7728
Highland Games & Scottish Festival (early June).................................913-432-6823
Historic Site Trolley Tours (early May) 816-325-7111
Holiday Open House (early November).............816-252-0608
Independence Day at Fort Osage National Historic Landmark (July 4).........................816-795-8200
Independence Day at Missouri Town 1855 (July 4) 816-795-8200
Juneteenth Celebrations (mid-June) 816-483-1300
Kansas City Blues & Jazz Festival (late July).......800-530-5266
Kansas City Home Show (late March).............816-942-8800
Kansas City Jaycees Rodeo (early July).............816-761-5055
Kansas City Parade of Homes (late April-mid-May) 816-942-8800
Kansas City Saint Patrick's Day Parade (March 17) 816-931-7373
Kansas Day at the American Royal (early November).............................816-221-9800
Kiki's Crawfish Fiesta (early June) 816-842-1271
Lighting of Jackson County Courthouse & Queen City Christmas Tree (early November) 816-252-0608
Missouri Town Christmas Celebration (mid-December).............................816-795-8200
Missouri Town Fall Festival (early October) 816-795-8200
National Wildlife Art Show (late March-early April) 913-451-7691
North Kansas City Barbecue & Funfest (early June).................................816-274-6000
Plaza Fine Arts Fair (late September)..............816-753-0100
Plaza Lighting Ceremony (late November)..........816-753-0100
Polski Day (early May) 913-321-5800
Presidential Wreath Laying (May 8)................816-833-1400
Renaissance Festival (early September-mid-October).................800-373-0357
Santa's Express (early-mid-December).............913-721-1075
Santa-Cali-Gon Days Festival (early September).....816-252-4745
Santa-Cali-Gon Quilt Show (early September) 816-325-7370
Settlers' Day (early June) 816-792-2655
Silver City Celebration (early October) 913-321-5800
Snake Saturday Parade & Festival (mid-March).....816-274-6000
Spirit Festival (Labor Day weekend) 816-221-4444
Spirit of Christmas Past Homes Tour (late November-late December)..................816-461-3491
Spirits of the Past (late October)..................816-795-8200
Strawberry Festival (early June)...................816-252-9098

Tiblow Days (late August) 913-321-5800
Trick 'n Treat & Halloween Parade
(late October)..................................816-252-4745
Truman Birthday Celebration (May 8)..............816-252-0608
Truman Health Walk (early May)..................816-833-2088
Turner Days (mid-October)........................913-287-7500
Vaile Tea Party (late March) 816-461-5135
Windows on the Past (early December) 816-795-8200
Wyandotte County Fair (late July-early August) 913-788-7898
Wyandotte Days (mid-October)....................913-321-5800

Knoxville, Tennessee

County: **Knox**

KNOXVILLE is located in eastern Tennessee. Major cities within 100 miles include Chattanooga and Johnson City, Tennessee.

Area (Land) .... 77.2 sq mi
Area (Water)............................... 1.7 sq mi
Elevation.................................... 889 ft
Latitude ....35-96-06 N
Longitude................................ 83-92-08 W
Time Zone ....EST
Area Code...................................... 865

Climate

Knoxville's climate features four distinct seasons. The mountains surrounding Knoxville moderate temperatures, keeping periods of extreme heat or cold brief. Winter high temperatures average near 50 degrees, with lows in the upper 20s. Annual snowfall averages 13 inches. Summer days are warm, featuring daytime high temperatures in the mid- to upper 80s and cool evenings in the mid-60s. March is the wettest month in Knoxville; October is the driest.

Average Temperatures & Precipitation

Temperatures

	Jan	Feb	Mar	Apr	May	Jun	Jul	Aug	Sep	Oct	Nov	Dec
High	46	51	61	70	78	85	87	87	81	71	60	50
Low	26	29	37	45	53	62	66	65	59	46	38	30

Precipitation

	Jan	Feb	Mar	Apr	May	Jun	Jul	Aug	Sep	Oct	Nov	Dec
Inches	4.2	4.1	5.1	3.7	4.1	4.0	4.7	3.1	3.1	2.8	3.8	4.5

History

The city known today as Knoxville began as a settlement called "White's Fort," founded by General James White in the late 1700s. The area was originally part of the Cherokee territory, but the tribe ceded the rights to the land in a 1791 treaty. The following year, the town of White's Fort was platted and renamed Knoxville in honor of Henry Knox, George Washington's Secretary of War. Knoxville served as the first capital of the newly established state of Tennessee from 1796 until 1812. The city was incorporated in 1815 and grew quickly as a supply point for travelers en route to the West. By the year 1850, Knoxville was home to more than 2,000 people.

During the Civil War, Knoxville residents' sympathies were divided between the North and the South. Initially, the Confederacy dominated the area; but after winning a battle fought at Fort Sanders in November 1863, Union forces took control of Knoxville. The city continued to grow and prosper in the years following the Civil War. During the latter part of the 19th Century, Knoxville's population tripled over a 20-year period.

Power generation has played a major role in Knoxville's development during the 20th Century. The city is surrounded by seven of the "Great Lakes of the South" created by the hydroelectric dams of the Tennessee Valley Authority. The formation of the Tennessee Valley Authority's electric power operations during the 1930s led to a population explosion in Knoxville, as new economic opportunities drew thousands of newcomers to the area. During World War II, the Knoxville metropolitan area became a center for nuclear power research, with the establishment of the top secret "Manhatten Project" in nearby Oak Ridge.

Knoxville gained worldwide attention when it hosted the 1982 World's Fair, which featured exhibits from more than 90 corporations from 22 countries around the globe and attracted more than 11 million visitors to the city. Knoxville today is home to more than 165,000 people.

Population

1990 Census 165,039
1998 Estimate..............................165,540
% Change .... -2.5
2005 Projection 389,865*

Racial/Ethnic Breakdown

White.................................... 82.7%
Black 15.8%
Other 1.5%
Hispanic Origin (may be of any race) 0.7

Age Breakdown

Under 5 years.............................. 6.0%
5 to 17.................................. 13.8%
18 to 21.................................. 7.6%
21 to 24.................................. 9.0%
25 to 34................................. 17.9%
35 to 44................................. 13.1%
45 to 44.................................. 8.5%
55 to 64.................................. 8.6%
65 to 74.................................. 8.5%
75+ years 6.9%
Median Age.................................32.4

Gender Breakdown

Male.................................... 46.7%
Female.................................. 53.3%

** Information given is for Knox County.*

Government

Type of Government: Mayor-Council

Knoxville City Council
PO Box 1631
Knoxville, TN 37901
Phone: 865-215-2075
Fax: 865-215-4269

Knoxville City Hall
400 Main St
Knoxville, TN 37902
Phone: 865-215-2000

Knoxville City Recorder
PO Box 1631
Knoxville, TN 37901
Phone: 865-215-2075
Fax: 865-215-4269

Knoxville Civil Service Dept
400 Main St Rm 569
Knoxville, TN 37902
Phone: 865-215-2106
Fax: 865-215-4270

Knoxville Development Dept
400 Main St Rm 505
Knoxville, TN 37902
Phone: 865-215-4545
Fax: 865-215-4547

Knoxville Finance Dept
PO Box 1631
Knoxville, TN 37901
Phone: 865-215-2086
Fax: 865-215-2277

Knoxville Fire Dept
900 Hill Ave Suite 430
Knoxville, TN 37915
Phone: 865-595-4480
Fax: 865-595-4482

Knoxville Law Dept
400 Main St Rm 699
Knoxville, TN 37902
Phone: 865-215-2050
Fax: 865-215-2643

Knoxville Mayor
PO Box 1631
Knoxville, TN 37901
Phone: 865-215-2040
Fax: 865-215-2978

Knoxville Metropolitan Planning Commission
400 Main St Suite 403 City-County Bldg
Knoxville, TN 37902
Phone: 865-215-2500
Fax: 865-215-2068

Knoxville Parks & Recreation Dept
400 Main St Rm 303
Knoxville, TN 37902
Phone: 865-215-2090
Fax: 865-215-2408

Knoxville Police Dept
800 E Church Ave
Knoxville, TN 37927
Phone: 865-215-7000
Fax: 865-215-7412

Knoxville Public Service Dept
PO Box 1631
Knoxville, TN 37901
Phone: 865-215-2060
Fax: 865-215-4688

Knoxville Utilities Board
626 S Gay St
Knoxville, TN 37902
Phone: 865-524-2911

Important Phone Numbers

AAA 865-637-1910
Driver's License Information 865-966-4350
Emergency 911
Knox County Tax Office 865-215-2305
Knoxville Board of Realtors 865-584-8647
Knoxville City Tax Office 865-215-2084
Knoxvoice Events Line 865-525-9900
Medical Referral 865-673-3678
Poison Control Center 865-544-9400
Tennessee Revenue Dept 615-253-0600
Time/Temp 865-521-6300
Vehicle Registration Information 865-215-2385
Visitors Information 865-523-7263
Voter Registration Information 865-215-2480
Weather 865-521-6300

Information Sources

Better Business Bureau Serving Greater East Tennessee
PO Box 10327
Knoxville, TN 37939
www.knoxville.bbb.org
Phone: 865-522-2552
Fax: 865-637-8042

Knox County
PO Box 1566
Knoxville, TN 37901
Phone: 865-215-2000
Fax: 865-215-3655

Knoxville Area Chamber Partnership
601 W Summit Hill Suite 300
Knoxville, TN 37902
www.knoxville.org
Phone: 865-637-4550
Fax: 865-523-2071

Knoxville Convention & Visitors Bureau
601 W Summit Hill Dr Suite 200B
Knoxville, TN 37902
www.knoxville.org
Phone: 865-523-7263
Fax: 865-673-4400
TF: 800-727-8045

Knoxville Convention Exhibition Center
PO Box 2603
Knoxville, TN 37901
Phone: 865-544-5371
Fax: 865-544-5376

Online Resources

4Knoxville.com
www.4knoxville.com

About Knoxville
www.knoxvilletennessee.com

About.com Guide to Knoxville
knoxville.about.com/local/southeastus/knoxville

Anthill City Guide Knoxville
www.anthill.com/city.asp?city=knoxville

Area Guide Knoxville
knoxville.areaguides.net

DiningGuide Fort Lauderdale
fort.lauderdale.diningguide.net

Excite.com Knoxville City Guide
www.excite.com/travel/countries/united_states/tennessee/knoxville

KnoxFirst
www.knoxfirst.com/

Knoxville Directory
www.vic.com/~smokyweb/knox/

Knoxville Tourist Bureau
www.goknox.com

Knoxville-Oak Ridge Regional Network
www.korrnet.org/

Knoxville-TN.com
www.knoxville-tn.com/

Kvine Online Knoxville
www.kvine.com/

Metro Pulse
www.metropulse.com

Area Communities

Communities in the Knoxville metropolitan area with populations greater than 5,000 include:

Alcoa
441 N Hall Rd
Alcoa, TN 37701
Phone: 865-981-4135
Fax: 865-981-4103

Clinton
100 Bowling St
Clinton, TN 37716
Phone: 865-457-0424
Fax: 865-457-4651

Farragut
11408 Municipal Center Dr
Farragut, TN 37922
Phone: 865-966-7057
Fax: 865-675-2096

Jefferson City
112 W Broadway Blvd
Jefferson City, TN 37760
Phone: 865-475-4363
Fax: 865-475-8224

Lenoir City
600 E Broadway St
Lenoir City, TN 37771
Phone: 865-986-2715
Fax: 865-988-5143

Maryville
400 W Broadway Ave
Maryville, TN 37801
Phone: 865-981-1300
Fax: 865-981-1301

Oak Ridge
PO Box 1
Oak Ridge, TN 37831
Phone: 865-425-3432
Fax: 865-425-3409

Sevierville
120 Church St
Sevierville, TN 37864
Phone: 865-453-5504
Fax: 865-453-5518

Economy

Services is the largest employment sector in the Knoxville metropolitan area and health care is one of Knoxville's leading industries—four of the area's top employers are health-related. Government is also a major employment sector in the Knoxville area -state and local agencies provide residents with more than 19,000 jobs, more than 12,000 of which are in public education. The Tennessee Valley Authority remains one of Knoxville's largest employers, employing some 1,900 area residents.

Unemployment Rate	2.6%*
Per Capita Income	$24,688*
Median Family Income	$26,131

** Information given is for Knox County.*

Principal Industries & Number of Wage Earners

Knoxville MSA* - 1998

Construction	16,200
Finance, Insurance, & Real Estate	14,600
Government	54,700
Manufacturing	48,200
Services	88,200
Trade	87,300
Transporation, Communications, & Public Utilities	14,200

** Information given is for the Knoxville Metropolitan Statistical Area (MSA), which includes Anderson, Blount, Knox, Louden, Sevier, and Union counties.*

Major Employers

Aluminum Co of America
900 S Gay St
Knoxville, TN 37902
Phone: 865-594-4700
Fax: 865-594-4615

Baptist Health System of East Tennessee
137 Blount Ave
Knoxville, TN 37920
Phone: 865-632-5099
Fax: 865-632-5086

Brunswick Corp Sea Ray Group
2600 Sea Ray Blvd
Knoxville, TN 37914
www.searay.com
Phone: 865-522-4181
Fax: 865-971-6434
TF: 800-772-6287

Clayton Homes Inc
5000 Clayton Rd
Maryville, TN 37804
E-mail: recruiting@clayton.net
www.clayton.net
Phone: 865-380-3000
Fax: 865-380-3788

Covenant Health Alliance
100 Fort Sanders Blvd W
Knoxville, TN 37922
Phone: 865-531-5555
Fax: 865-531-5272

Denso Mfg Tennessee
1720 Robert C Jackson Dr
Maryville, TN 37801
www.denso-int.com/c01.asp
Phone: 865-982-7000
Fax: 865-981-5262

Dollywood Inc
1020 Dollywood Ln
Pigeon Forge, TN 37863
www.dollywood.com
Phone: 865-428-9400
Fax: 865-428-9494

Knox County
PO Box 1566
Knoxville, TN 37901
Phone: 865-215-2000
Fax: 865-215-3655

Knox County Public Schools
PO Box 2188
Knoxville, TN 37901
www.korrnet.org/kcschool/
Phone: 865-594-1801
Fax: 865-594-1909

Knoxville City Hall
400 Main St
Knoxville, TN 37902
www.ci.knoxville.tn.us
Phone: 865-215-2000

Lockheed Martin Energy Systems
PO Box 2009 MS 8019
Oak Ridge, TN 37831
E-mail: w5u@y12.doe.gov
www.y12.doe.gov/lmes
Phone: 865-576-5454
Fax: 865-576-9444

Saint Mary's Medical Center
900 E Oak Hill Ave
Knoxville, TN 37917
www.mercy.com/stmarys/index.htm
Phone: 865-545-8000
Fax: 865-545-3037

Tennessee Valley Authority
400 W Summit Hill Dr
Knoxville, TN 37902
www.tva.gov
Phone: 865-632-2101
Fax: 865-632-6609

University of Tennessee
Knoxville, TN 37996
www.utk.edu
Phone: 865-974-1000
Fax: 865-974-6435
TF: 800-221-8657

University of Tennessee Medical Center
1924 Alcoa Hwy
Knoxville, TN 37920
www.utmck.edu/library
Phone: 865-544-9000
Fax: 865-544-9429

Quality of Living Indicators

Total Crime Index....................................9,469
(rates per 100,000 inhabitants)

Violent Crime
Murder/manslaughter.......................... 20
Forcible rape 66
Robbery..................................... 567
Aggravated assault........................... 739

Property Crime
Burglary 1,381
Larceny theft 5,336
Motor vehicle theft..........................1,360

Cost of Living Index....................................96.9
(national average = 100)

Median Home Price................................$108,300

Education

Public Schools

Knox County Public Schools
PO Box 2188
Knoxville, TN 37901
www.korrnet.org/kcschool/
Phone: 865-594-1801
Fax: 865-594-1909

Number of Schools
Elementary 50
Middle 14
High....................................... 12
Other 8

Student/Teacher Ratio
All Grades 20.0:1

Private Schools

Number of Schools (all grades)..................... 28

Colleges & Universities

Carson-Newman College
1646 S Russell Ave
Jefferson City, TN 37760
www.cn.edu
Phone: 865-475-9061
Fax: 865-471-3502
TF: 800-678-9061

ITT Technical Institute
10208 Technology Dr
Knoxville, TN 37932
www.itt-tech.edu
Phone: 865-671-2800
Fax: 865-671-2811
TF: 800-671-2801

Johnson Bible College
7900 Johnson Dr
Knoxville, TN 37998
E-mail: jbc@jbc.edu
www.jbc.edu
Phone: 865-573-4517
Fax: 865-579-2337
TF: 800-827-2122

Knoxville College
901 College St
Knoxville, TN 37921
falcon.nest.kxcol.edu
Phone: 865-524-6500
Fax: 865-524-6686
TF: 800-743-5669

Maryville College
502 E Lamar Alexander Pkwy
Maryville, TN 37804
www.maryvillecollege.edu
Phone: 865-981-8000
Fax: 865-981-8005
TF: 800-597-2687

Pellissippi State Technical Community College
10915 Hardin Valley Rd
Knoxville, TN 37933
www.pstcc.cc.tn.us
Phone: 865-694-6400
Fax: 865-539-7217
TF: 800-548-6925

Tennessee Institute of Electronics
3203 Tazewell Pike
Knoxville, TN 37918
Phone: 865-688-9422
Fax: 865-688-2419

University of Tennessee
Knoxville, TN 37996
www.utk.edu
Phone: 865-974-1000
Fax: 865-974-6435
TF: 800-221-8657

Walters State Community College
500 S Davy Crockett Pkwy
Morristown, TN 37813
www.wscc.cc.tn.us
Phone: 423-585-2600
Fax: 423-585-2631
TF: 800-225-4770

Hospitals

Baptist Hospital of East Tennessee
137 Blount Ave
Knoxville, TN 37920
Phone: 865-632-5011
Fax: 865-632-5086

East Tennessee Children's Hospital
2018 Clinch Ave
Knoxville, TN 37916
www.etch.com
Phone: 865-546-7711
Fax: 865-541-8343

Fort Sanders Regional Medical Center
1901 Clinch Ave SW
Knoxville, TN 37916
www.covenanthealth.com/aboutus/fsrmc.html
Phone: 865-541-1111
Fax: 865-541-2851

Fort Sanders-Parkwest Medical Center
9352 Park West Blvd
Knoxville, TN 37923
www.covenanthealth.com/aboutus/fspw.html
Phone: 865-693-5151
Fax: 865-531-4420

Saint Mary's Medical Center
900 E Oak Hill Ave
Knoxville, TN 37917
www.mercy.com/stmarys/index.htm
Phone: 865-545-8000
Fax: 865-545-3037

University of Tennessee Medical Center Phone: 865-544-9000
1924 Alcoa Hwy Fax: 865-544-9429
Knoxville, TN 37920
www.utmck.edu/library

Transportation

Airport(s)

McGhee Tyson Airport (TYS)
13 miles S of downtown (approx 35 minutes) 865-970-2773

Mass Transit

KAT
$1 Base fare 865-546-3752

Rail/Bus

Greyhound Bus Station Phone: 865-522-5144
100 Magnolia Ave NE TF: 800-231-2222
Knoxville, TN 37917

Utilities

Electricity
Knoxville Utilities Board 865-524-2911
www.ci.knoxville.tn.us/departments/kub.htm

Gas
Knoxville Utilities Board 865-524-2911
www.ci.knoxville.tn.us/departments/kub.htm

Water
Knoxville Utilities Board 865-524-2911
www.ci.knoxville.tn.us/departments/kub.htm

Garbage Collection/Recycling
BFI Waste Systems 865-522-0078

Telecommunications

Telephone
BellSouth 800-753-0223
www.bellsouth.com

Cable Television
Charter Communications.......................865-544-0099
Comcast Cable 865-637-5411

Internet Service Providers (ISPs)
Esper Systems...............................865-633-9650
www.esper.com
Virtual Interactive Ctr 865-470-7851
www.vic.com

Banks

Bank of America Phone: 865-541-6130
9375 Kingston Pike Fax: 865-694-5009
Knoxville, TN 37922

First Tennessee Bank Phone: 865-971-2114
800 S Gay St Fax: 865-971-2025
Knoxville, TN 37929

Home Federal Bank of Tennessee FSB Phone: 865-546-0330
515 Market St Fax: 865-541-6962
Knoxville, TN 37902
www.homefedtn.com

SunTrust Bank East Tennessee NA Phone: 865-544-2250
700 E Hill Ave Fax: 865-524-5956
Knoxville, TN 37915

Shopping

Bearden Antique Mall Phone: 865-584-1521
310 Mohican St
Knoxville, TN 37919

Homespun Craft & Antique Mall Phone: 865-671-3444
11523 Kingston Pike Fax: 865-671-0301
Knoxville, TN 37922

Knoxville Center Phone: 865-544-1500
3000-A Mall Rd N
Knoxville, TN 37924

Pigeon Forge Factory Mall Phone: 865-428-2828
2850 Parkway
Pigeon Forge, TN 37864

West Town Mall Phone: 865-693-0292
7600 Kingston Pike Fax: 865-531-0503
Knoxville, TN 37919

Media

Newspapers and Magazines

Knoxville News-Sentinel* Phone: 865-523-3131
208 W Church Ave Fax: 865-342-6400
Knoxville, TN 37902 TF: 800-237-5821
www.knoxnews.com

Metro Pulse Phone: 865-522-5399
505 Market St Fax: 865-522-2955
Knoxville, TN 37902
E-mail: info@metropulse.com
www.metropulse.com

Press Enterprise Phone: 865-675-6397
11863 Kingston Pike Fax: 865-675-1675
Knoxville, TN 37922
E-mail: pressent@aol.com

**Indicates major daily newspapers*

Television

WATE-TV Ch 6 (ABC) Phone: 865-637-6666
1306 Broadway NE Fax: 865-525-4091
Knoxville, TN 37917
E-mail: coverage@wate.com
www.wate.com

WBIR-TV Ch 10 (NBC) Phone: 865-637-1010
1513 Hutchinson Ave Fax: 865-637-6380
Knoxville, TN 37917

WSJK-TV Ch 2 (PBS) Phone: 865-595-0220
1611 E Magnolia Fax: 865-595-0300
Knoxville, TN 37917

WTNZ-TV Ch 43 (Fox) Phone: 865-693-4343
9000 Executive Pk Dr Bldg D Suite 300 Fax: 865-691-6904
Knoxville, TN 37923
E-mail: programming@wtnzfox43.com
www.wtnzfox43.com

WVLT-TV Ch 8 (CBS) Phone: 865-450-8888
6516 Papermill Dr Fax: 865-450-8869
Knoxville, TN 37919
www.volunteertv.com

Radio

WHJM-AM 1180 kHz (N/T) Phone: 865-546-4653
802 S Central Ave Fax: 865-637-7133
Knoxville, TN 37902

WIMZ-FM 103.5 MHz (CR) Phone: 865-525-6000
1100 Sharps Ridge Rd Fax: 865-525-2000
Knoxville, TN 37917

WITA-AM 1490 kHz (Rel) Phone: 865-588-2974
7212 Kingston Pike
Knoxville, TN 37919

WIVK-FM 107.7 MHz (Ctry) Phone: 865-588-6511
4711 Old Kingston Pike Fax: 865-588-3725
Knoxville, TN 37919
www.wivk.com

WJXB-FM 97.5 MHz (AC) Phone: 865-525-6000
1100 Sharps Ridge Rd Fax: 865-525-2000
Knoxville, TN 37917
www.b975.com/

WMYU-FM 102.1 MHz (Oldies) Phone: 865-693-1020
8419 Kingston Pike Fax: 865-693-8493
Knoxville, TN 37919

WNFZ-FM 94.3 MHz (Alt) Phone: 865-525-6000
1100 Sharps Ridge Rd Fax: 865-525-2000
Knoxville, TN 37919

WNOX-FM 99.1 MHz (N/T) Phone: 865-558-9900
4711 Old Kingston Pike Fax: 865-558-4218
Knoxville, TN 37919

WOKI-FM 100.3 MHz (CR) Phone: 865-588-6511
4711 Old Kingston Pike Fax: 865-558-4218
Knoxville, TN 37919

WUOT-FM 91.9 MHz (NPR) Phone: 865-974-5375
209 Communications Bldg Fax: 865-974-3941
Knoxville, TN 37996
sunsite.utk.edu/wuot

Attractions

The Knoxville area is home to the nation's most visited national park, Great Smoky Mountains National Park. Located 45 minutes from Knoxville, the park features more than 510,000 acres of natural splendor and provides a variety of recreational opportunities, including hiking, camping, and wildlife viewing. Also located within the park's boundaries is Cades Cove, which features original log cabins, churches, and cemeteries dating back to the 1800s. In addition to numerous historic homes and sites in Knoxville that chronicle the city's Revolutionary and Civil War history, the East Tennessee Discovery Center and the Knoxville Zoo are popular attractions. Other attractions in the area include Dolly Parton's Dollywood in Pigeon Forge and the mountain resort town of Gatlinburg, located at the north entrance to Great Smoky Mountains National Park.

American Museum of Science & Energy Phone: 865-576-3200
300 S Tulane Ave Fax: 865-576-6024
Oak Ridge, TN 37830
E-mail: info@amse.org
www.kornet.org/amse/

Andrew Johnson National Historic Site Phone: 423-638-3551
PO Box 1088 Fax: 423-638-9194
Greeneville, TN 37744
www.nps.gov/anjo/

Armstrong-Lockett House Phone: 865-637-3163
2728 Kingston Pike
Knoxville, TN 37919

Beck Cultural Exchange Center Inc Phone: 865-524-8461
1927 Dandridge Ave Fax: 865-524-8462
Knoxville, TN 37915
E-mail: beckcec@korrnet.org
www.korrnet.org/beckcec

Big South Fork National River & Recreation Area Phone: 423-569-9778
4564 Leatherwood Rd Fax: 423-569-5505
Oneida, TN 37841
www.nps.gov/biso/

Bijou Theatre Phone: 865-522-0832
803 S Gay St Fax: 865-522-0238
Knoxville, TN 37902
www.bijoutheatre.com

Blount Mansion Phone: 865-525-2375
200 W Hill Ave Fax: 865-546-5315
Knoxville, TN 37901
E-mail: blount96@korrnet.org
www.korrnet.org/blount96/

Brown Clarence Theatre Phone: 865-974-5161
1714 Andy Holt Blvd
Knoxville, TN 37996

Carousel Theatre Phone: 865-974-5161
1714 Andy Holt Ave
Knoxville, TN 37996

Children's Museum of Oak Ridge Phone: 865-482-1074
461 W Outer Dr Fax: 865-481-4889
Oak Ridge, TN 37830
newsite.com/cmor

Chilhowee Park Phone: 865-215-1450
3301 E Magnolia Ave Fax: 865-215-1455
Knoxville, TN 37914

Confederate Memorial Hall Phone: 865-522-2371
3148 Kingston Pike
Knoxville, TN 37919

Cumberland Gap National Historical Park Phone: 606-248-2817
PO Box 1848 Fax: 606-248-7276
Middlesboro, KY 40965
www.nps.gov/cuga/

Dollywood Inc Phone: 865-428-9400
1020 Dollywood Ln Fax: 865-428-9494
Pigeon Forge, TN 37863
www.dollywood.com

East Tennessee Discovery Center Phone: 865-594-1494
516 N Beaman St Chilhowee Pk Fax: 865-594-1469
Knoxville, TN 37914
web.utk.edu/~loganj/etdc

East Tennessee Historical Society Museum Phone: 865-215-8828
600 Market St Fax: 865-215-8819
Knoxville, TN 37902
www.east-tennessee-history.org/museum/mushome.htm

Ewing Gallery of Art & Architecture Phone: 865-974-3200
1715 Volunteer Blvd
Knoxville, TN 37996
E-mail: spangler@utk.edu

Farragut Folklife Museum Phone: 865-966-7057
11408 Municipal Center Dr Fax: 865-675-2096
Farragut, TN 37922
www.farragut.tn.us/arts.html

Frank H McClung Museum Phone: 865-974-2144
1327 Circle Park Dr University of Tennessee Fax: 865-974-3827
Knoxville, TN 37996
E-mail: museum@utkux.utcc.utk.edu
mcclungmuseum.utk.edu

Great Smoky Mountains National Park Phone: 865-436-1200
107 Park Headquarters Rd Fax: 865-436-1220
Gatlinburg, TN 37738
www.nps.gov/grsm/

Ijams Nature Center Phone: 865-577-4717
2915 Island Home Ave Fax: 865-577-1683
Knoxville, TN 37917
E-mail: ijams@nxs.net
www.ijams.org

Knox County Old Gray Cemetery Phone: 865-522-1424
543 N Broadway
Knoxville, TN 37901

Knox County Regional Farmers' Market Phone: 865-524-3276
4700 New Harvest Ln Fax: 865-522-4833
Knoxville, TN 37918

Knoxville Ballet Phone: 865-544-0495
500 E Church Ave Civic Auditorium
Knoxville, TN 37902
E-mail: cityballet@nxs.net
www.knoxballet.org

Knoxville Museum of Art Phone: 865-525-6101
1050 World Fair Park Dr Fax: 865-546-3635
Knoxville, TN 37916
E-mail: kma@esper.com
www.knoxart.org

Knoxville Opera Co Phone: 865-523-8712
612 E Depot Ave Fax: 865-524-7384
Knoxville, TN 37917
www.knoxvilleopera.com

Knoxville Symphony Orchestra Phone: 865-523-1178
PO Box 360 Fax: 865-546-3766
Knoxville, TN 37901

Knoxville Zoo Phone: 865-637-5331
3333 Woodbine Ave Fax: 865-637-1943
Knoxville, TN 37914
www.knoxville-zoo.org

Laurel Theatre & Jubilee Center Phone: 865-522-5851
1538 Laurel Ave
Knoxville, TN 37916
E-mail: jubilee@korrnet.org
www.korrnet.org/jca

Lost Sea Phone: 423-337-6616
140 Lost Sea Rd Fax: 423-337-0803
Sweetwater, TN 37874

Mabry-Hazen House Phone: 865-522-8661
1711 Dandridge Ave Fax: 865-522-8471
Knoxville, TN 37915
www.korrnet.org/mabry

Marble Springs Phone: 865-573-5508
1220 W Governor John Sevier Hwy
Knoxville, TN 37920

Museum of Appalachia Phone: 865-494-7680
2877 Andersonville Hwy Fax: 865-494-8957
Clinton, TN 37716

Obed Wild & Scenic River Phone: 423-346-6294
208 N Maiden St Fax: 423-346-3362
Wartburg, TN 37887
www.nps.gov/obed/

Old City District
Jackson Ave E & Central St S
Knoxville, TN 37915

Ramsey House Phone: 865-546-0745
2614 Thorngrove Pike
Knoxville, TN 37914

South's Finest Chocolate Factory Phone: 865-522-2049
1060 World's Fair Park Dr World's Fair Pk Fax: 865-522-0874
Knoxville, TN 37916 TF: 800-682-4449
E-mail: choc@chocolatelovers.com
www.chocolatelovers.com

Star of Knoxville Riverboat Phone: 865-522-4630
300 Neyland Dr Fax: 865-522-5941
Knoxville, TN 37902 TF: 800-509-2628

Sunsphere Phone: 865-523-4228
810 W Clinch Ave
Knoxville, TN 37902

Tennessee Children's Dance Ensemble Phone: 865-588-8842
4216 Sutherland Ave
Knoxville, TN 37919
www.korrnet.org/tcde

Tennessee Riverboat Co Phone: 865-525-7827
300 Neyland Dr Volunteer Landing Fax: 865-522-5941
Knoxville, TN 37902 TF: 800-509-2628
E-mail: capt@tnriverboat.com
www.tnriverboat.com

Tennessee Stage Co Phone: 865-546-4280
1060 World's Fair Park Dr
Knoxville, TN 37916

Tennessee Theater
604 S Gay St
Knoxville, TN 37902
Phone: 865-522-1174
Fax: 865-637-2141

University of Tennessee Music Hall
1741 Volunteer Blvd
Knoxville, TN 37996
Phone: 865-974-3241
Fax: 865-974-1941

Victorian Houses
11th St & Laurel Ave
Knoxville, TN 37916
Phone: 865-525-7619

White James Fort
205 E Hill Ave
Knoxville, TN 37915
Phone: 865-525-6514
Fax: 865-525-6514

Sports Teams & Facilities

Knoxville Smokies (baseball)
633 Jesamine St Bill Meyer Stadium
Knoxville, TN 37917
E-mail: info@smokiesbaseball.com
www.smokiesbaseball.com
Phone: 865-637-9494
Fax: 865-523-9913

Annual Events

Artfest (early September-late October) 865-523-7543
Boomsday (early September). 865-693-1020
Christmas in the City
(late November-late December). 865-215-4248
Dogwood Arts Festival (early-late April). 865-637-4561
Fantasy of Trees (late November) 865-541-8385
Foothills Craft Guild Fall Show & Sale
(mid-November). 865-544-5371
Fourth of July Celebration & Anvil Shoot
(early July) 865-494-7680
International Jubilee Festival (early June). 865-522-5851
Knoxville Boat Show (early March). 865-588-1233
Knoxville Western Film Festival (late April) 865-522-2600
Kuumba Festival (early June). .865-525-0961
Ragin' Cajun Cookout (mid-May). 865-558-9040
Smoky Mountain Marathon (late February). 865-588-7465
Statehood Day Celebration (early June) 865-525-2375
Tennessee Fall Homecoming (early October) 865-494-7680
Tennessee Valley Fair (mid-September) 865-637-5840

Lafayette, Louisiana

County: **Lafayette Parish**

LAFAYETTE is located in the Acadiana region of south central Louisiana along the Vermilion River. Major cities within 100 miles include Baton Rouge and Lake Charles, Louisiana.

Area (Land)	40.9 sq mi
Area (Water)	0.1 sq mi
Elevation	42 ft
Latitude	30-12-19 N
Longitude	91-59-15 W
Time Zone	CST
Area Code	337

Climate

Lafayette has a moderated subtropical climate that features hot, humid summers and cool winters. Winter high temperatures average in the low 60s, with lows in the low to mid-40s. With temperatures dropping below freezing only a few days each year, snowfall is rare in Lafayette. Summer high temperatures average near 90 degrees, with average lows in the low to mid-70s. Summer is the rainiest time of year in Lafayette, with afternoon thunderstorms an almost daily occurrence from June through August. The city's proximity to the Gulf of Mexico also makes it susceptible to hurricanes. Hurricane season runs from June through November.

Average Temperatures & Precipitation

Temperatures

	Jan	Feb	Mar	Apr	May	Jun	Jul	Aug	Sep	Oct	Nov	Dec
High	60	63	71	79	85	90	91	90	87	80	71	64
Low	41	44	51	59	65	71	74	73	69	58	50	44

Precipitation

	Jan	Feb	Mar	Apr	May	Jun	Jul	Aug	Sep	Oct	Nov	Dec
Inches	5.0	4.3	4.1	4.1	5.2	5.1	7.0	5.4	5.4	3.8	3.8	5.4

History

The area of southern Louisiana known today as Lafayette was originally inhabited by the cannibalistic Attakapas Indians. The first white settlers, the Acadians, arrived in the area in 1763. (At that time the region was under Spanish rule.) The Acadians were French-speaking people from Nova Scotia who had been exiled from their Canadian homeland by the British for failing to pledge their allegiance to Great Britain. In 1821, land was donated to the Catholic congregation by Jean Moulton, a successful cotton planter and Acadian immigrant, and Saint John's Church was established there. A new town, Vermilionville (named for its location along the Vermilion River), was designed around the church. In 1823 Lafayette Parish, named for the Marquis de Lafayette, a French general who fought in the American Revolution, was established. Mouton donated more land to Vermilionville to build a courthouse, and the town became the parish seat. Vermilionville was incorporated in 1836 and began to grow as an agricultural community and religious center. The city was reincorporated 33 years later, in 1869. During the Civil War the area was devastated by yellow fever, but the population and the local economy recovered during the 1880s with the arrival of the railroad, which had been extended from New Orleans to Houston. In 1884 Vermilionville's name was officially changed to Lafayette.

Due to the city's proximity to the oil reserves in the Gulf of Mexico, the oil and gas industry became a major player in Lafayette's economy during the 1940s, and the petroleum industry remains important to the area's economy today. With a population of more than 113,000, Lafayette is currently Louisiana's fourth largest city.

Population

1990 Census	101,865
1998 Estimate	113,615
% Change	11.5
2004 Projection	196,588*

Racial/Ethnic Breakdown

White	70.8%
Black	27.2%
Other	2.0%
Hispanic Origin (may be of any race)	1.7%

Age Breakdown

Under 5 years	7.5%
5 to 17	18.9%
18 to 20	6.4%
21 to 24	7.7%
25 to 34	17.8%
35 to 44	14.9%
45 to 54	9.1%
55 to 64	8.2%
65 to 74	5.7%
75+ years	3.8%
Median Age	30.4

Gender Breakdown

Male	48.1%
Female	51.9%

** Information given is for Lafayette Parish.*

Government

Type of Government: President-Council (consolidated)

Lafayette Administrative Services Dept
705 W University Ave
Lafayette, LA 70506

Phone: 337-291-8354
Fax: 337-291-8437

Lafayette City Hall Phone: 337-291-8200
705 W University Ave
Lafayette, LA 70502

Lafayette City-Parish Council Phone: 337-291-8800
1010 Lafayette St Fax: 337-291-8822
Lafayette, LA 70501

Lafayette City-Parish President Phone: 337-291-8300
705 W University Ave City Hall Fax: 337-291-8399
Lafayette, LA 70502

Lafayette Clerk of the Council Phone: 337-291-8810
1010 Lafayette St Fax: 337-291-8399
Lafayette, LA 70501

Lafayette Community Development Dept Phone: 337-291-8402
705 W University Ave Fax: 337-291-8415
Lafayette, LA 70501

Lafayette Fire Dept Phone: 337-291-8703
300 E Vermilion St Fax: 337-291-8787
Lafayette, LA 70501

Lafayette Lafayette Utilities System Phone: 337-291-8348
1314 Walker Rd Fax: 337-291-5995
Lafayette, LA 70506

Lafayette Legal Dept Phone: 337-291-8015
PO Box 2907 Fax: 337-237-9638
Lafayette, LA 70502

Lafayette Parks & Recreation Dept Phone: 337-291-8361
500 Girard Park Dr Fax: 337-291-8389
Lafayette, LA 70506

Lafayette Planning Zoning & Codes Dept Phone: 337-291-8013
101 E Cypress St Fax: 337-291-8492
Lafayette, LA 70501

Lafayette Police Dept Phone: 337-291-8654
900 E University Ave Fax: 337-291-5665
Lafayette, LA 70503

Lafayette Public Works Dept Phone: 337-291-8500
1515 E University Ave Fax: 337-291-5696
Lafayette, LA 70501

Lafayette Traffic Engineering & Transportation Dept Phone: 337-291-8545
1515 E University Ave Fax: 337-291-5693
Lafayette, LA 70501

Important Phone Numbers

AAA..........504-838-7500
American Express Travel..........337-233-6990
Driver's License Information..........225-922-1175
Emergency..........911
Lafayette Board of Realtors..........337-233-0086
Lafayette Parish Tax Assessor..........337-291-7080
Louisiana Dept of Revenue & Taxation..........337-262-5455
Poison Control Center..........504-345-5554
Time/Temp..........337-394-9744
Vehicle Registration Information..........337-262-1807
Voter Registration Information..........337-291-7140

Information Sources

Better Business Bureau Serving Acadiana Phone: 337-981-3497
100 Huggins Rd Fax: 337-981-7559
Lafayette, LA 70506
www.lafayette.bbb.org

Greater Lafayette Chamber of Commerce Phone: 337-233-2705
804 E St Mary Blvd Fax: 337-234-8671
Lafayette, LA 70503
www.lafchamber.org

Lafayette City-Parish President Phone: 337-291-8300
705 W University Ave City Hall Fax: 337-291-8399
Lafayette, LA 70502

Lafayette Convention & Visitors Commission Phone: 337-232-3737
PO Box 52066 Fax: 337-232-0161
Lafayette, LA 70505 TF: 800-346-1958
www.lafayettetravel.com

Lafayette Parish Phone: 337-233-0150
PO Box 2009 Fax: 337-269-6392
Lafayette, LA 70502

Online Resources

4Lafayette.com
www.4lafayette.com

Area Guide Lafayette
lafayettela.areaguides.net

CajunFun.com
www.cajunfun.com

Excite.com Lafayette City Guide
www.excite.com/travel/countries/united_states/louisiana/lafayette

Guide to Acadiana
www.webcom.com/~gumbo/cajun-home.html

Lodging.com Lafayette Louisiana
www.lodging.com/auto/guides/lafayette-la.html

Online City Guide to Lafayette
www.olcg.com/la/lafayette/index.html

USA Hotel Guide Lafayette
www.usahotelguide.com/states/louisiana/lafayette

Area Communities

Communities in Lafayette Parish with populations greater than 1,000 include:

Broussard Phone: 337-837-6681
416 E Main St Fax: 337-837-8121
Broussard, LA 70518

Carencro Phone: 337-896-8481
210 E Saint Peter St Fax: 337-896-0890
Carencro, LA 70520

Scott Phone: 337-233-1130
420 Lions Club Rd Fax: 337-233-0240
Scott, LA 70583

Youngsville
305 Iberia St
Youngsville, LA 70592
Phone: 337-856-4181
Fax: 337-856-8863

Economy

Located in the eight-parish metro area known as Acadiana, Lafayette has a diverse economic base. Acadiana's top 10 private companies include a jewelry manufacturer, a food distributor, a food manufacturer, two automobile dealerships, a medical transportation company, and several petroleum-related companies. The oil and gas industry continues to play an important role in the local economy, with 10% of the area's workforce employed in the mining sector. However, services is currently the area's largest employment sector, followed by retail trade and government.

Unemployment Rate 3.6%*
Per Capita Income.......................... $19,142*
Median Family Income...................... $32,991

** Information given is for Lafayette Parish.*

Principal Industries & Number of Wage Earners

Lafayette MSA* - May 2000

Construction... 9,400
Finance, Insurance, & Real Estate 6,400
Government 25,300
Manufacturing 15,000
Mining 12,400
Retail Trade.. 33,600
Services 44,300
Transportation 9,200
Wholesale Trade.. 9,700

** Information given is for the Lafayette Metropolitan Statistical Area (MSA), which includes Lafayette, Acadia, Saint Landry, and Saint Martin parishes.*

Major Employers

Acadian Ambulance & Air Med Services Inc
PO Box 98000
Lafayette, LA 70509
www.acadian.com
Phone: 337-267-3333
Fax: 337-291-3326
TF: 800-259-3333

Ace Transportation Inc
PO Box 91714
Lafayette, LA 70509
Phone: 337-837-4567
Fax: 337-837-1423
TF: 800-451-9844

Frank's Casing Crew & Rental Tools Inc
PO Box 51729
Lafayette, LA 70505
www.frankscasing.com
Phone: 337-233-0303
Fax: 337-572-2462

Kergan Brothers Inc
PO Box 80154
Lafayette, LA 70598
Phone: 337-988-5301
Fax: 337-988-5305

Lafayette City Hall
705 W University Ave
Lafayette, LA 70502
www.lafayettegov.org
Phone: 337-291-8200

Lafayette General Medical Center
1214 Coolidge Blvd
Lafayette, LA 70503
www.lafayettegeneral.org
Phone: 337-289-7991
Fax: 337-289-7911

Lafayette Parish School System
PO Drawer 2158
Lafayette, LA 70502
www.lft.k12.la.us
Phone: 337-236-6800
Fax: 337-236-6963

Offshore Logistics Inc
224 Rue De Jean
Lafayette, LA 70508
E-mail: marketing@olog.com
www.olog.com
Phone: 337-233-1221
Fax: 337-235-6678

Our Lady of Lourdes Regional Medical Center
611 Saint Landry St
Lafayette, LA 70506
E-mail: info@lourdes.net
www.lourdes.net
Phone: 337-289-2000
Fax: 337-289-2681

Petroleum Helicopters Inc
PO Box 90808
Lafayette, LA 70509
www.phihelico.com
Phone: 337-235-2452
Fax: 337-235-3424
TF: 800-235-2452

Stuller Settings Inc
PO Box 87777
Lafayette, LA 70598
E-mail: info@stuller.com
www.stuller.com
Phone: 337-837-4100
Fax: 337-981-1655
TF: 800-877-7777

Super K Mart
3300 Ambassador Caffery Pkwy
Lafayette, LA 70506
Phone: 337-988-6900
Fax: 337-988-3484

University Medical Center
2390 W Congress St
Lafayette, LA 70506
Phone: 337-261-6000
Fax: 337-261-6660

University of Southwestern Louisiana
104 University Cir
Lafayette, LA 70504
www.usl.edu
Phone: 337-482-1000
Fax: 337-482-6195
TF: 800-752-6553

Quality of Living Indicators

Total Crime Index.. 8,617
(rates per 100,000 inhabitants)

Violent Crime
Murder/manslaughter.............................. 7
Forcible rape 51
Robbery.. 206
Aggravated assault............................... 552

Property Crime
Burglary 1,524
Larceny theft 5,648
Motor vehicle theft 629

Cost of Living Index 96.3
(national average = 100)

Median Home Price $65,000

Education

Public Schools

Lafayette Parish School System
PO Drawer 2158
Lafayette, LA 70502
www.lft.k12.la.us
Phone: 337-236-6800
Fax: 337-236-6963

Number of Schools
Elementary 23
Middle 11
High 5

Student/Teacher Ratio
All Grades 17.8:1

Private Schools

Number of Schools (all grades) 24

Colleges & Universities

University of Southwestern Louisiana
104 University Cir
Lafayette, LA 70504
www.usl.edu
Phone: 337-482-1000
Fax: 337-482-6195
TF: 800-752-6553

Hospitals

Lafayette General Medical Center
1214 Coolidge Blvd
Lafayette, LA 70503
www.lafayettegeneral.org
Phone: 337-289-7991
Fax: 337-289-7911

Our Lady of Lourdes Regional Medical Center
611 Saint Landry St
Lafayette, LA 70506
www.lourdes.net
Phone: 337-289-2000
Fax: 337-289-2681

Transportation

Airport(s)

Lafayette Regional Airport (LFT)
1 mile SE of downtown (approx 20 minutes) 337-266-4400

Mass Transit

Lafayette Transit System
$.45 Base fare 337-291-8570

Rail/Bus

Greyhound Bus Station
315 Lee Ave
Lafayette, LA 70501
Phone: 337-233-6750
TF: 800-231-2222

Utilities

Electricity
Lafayette Utilities System 337-291-8280
www.lafayettegov.org/index.cfm

Gas
Reliant Energy ENTEX 337-232-4194
entex.reliantenergy.com
Trans-Louisiana Gas Co. 888-852-2424
www.transla.com

Water
Lafayette Utilities System 337-291-8280
www.lafayettegov.org/index.cfm

Garbage Collection/Recycling
Waste Management of Acadiana 337-261-0430

Telecommunications

Telephone
BellSouth 800-832-0679
www.bellsouth.com

Cable Television
Cox Communications 337-232-6323
www.cox.com

Internet Service Providers (ISPs)
Net-Connect Ltd 337-234-4396
www.net-connect.net

Banks

Bank One
800 W Pinhook Rd
Lafayette, LA 70503
Phone: 337-236-7118
Fax: 337-236-7280
TF: 800-777-8837

First Louisiana National Bank
2701 Moss St
Lafayette, LA 70501
Phone: 337-268-9600
Fax: 337-268-5112

Gulf Coast Bank
4310 Johnston St
Lafayette, LA 70503
Phone: 337-989-1133
Fax: 337-989-2172
TF: 800-722-5363

Hibernia National Bank
213 W Vermilion St
Lafayette, LA 70501
Phone: 337-268-4521
Fax: 337-268-4564
TF: 800-562-9007

Iberia Bank
2130 Kaliste Saloom Rd
Lafayette, LA 70508
Phone: 337-988-4438
Fax: 337-981-5987

Mid South National Bank
102 Versailles Blvd
Lafayette, LA 70501
www.midsouthbank.com
Phone: 337-237-8343
Fax: 337-267-4316
TF: 800-213-2265

Regions Bank
5711 S Johnston St
Lafayette, LA 70503
Phone: 337-988-0703
Fax: 337-988-2358
TF: 800-734-4667

Shopping

Acadiana Mall
5725 Johnston St
Lafayette, LA 70503
Phone: 337-984-8240
Fax: 337-981-4896

Acadiana Market
1693 Creswell Ln
Lafayette, LA 70570
Phone: 337-942-6111

Jefferson Street Market Phone: 337-233-2589
538 Jefferson St Fax: 337-237-8882
Lafayette, LA 70501

Lafayette Antique Market Phone: 337-981-9884
3108 Johnston St
Lafayette, LA 70503

Media

Newspapers and Magazines

Daily Advertiser The* Phone: 337-289-6300
PO Box 3268 Fax: 337-289-6443
Lafayette, LA 70502
E-mail: acasmg@aol.com
www.acadiananow.com/advrtsr2.html

Lifestyle Lafayette Phone: 337-988-4607
1720 Kaliste Saloom Rd Suite B-1 Fax: 337-983-0150
Lafayette, LA 70508
E-mail: lifestyle@1stnet.com

Times of Acadiana Phone: 337-237-3560
201 Jefferson St Fax: 337-233-7484
Lafayette, LA 70501

**Indicates major daily newspapers*

Television

KADN-TV Ch 15 (Fox) Phone: 337-237-1500
1500 Eraste Landry Rd Fax: 337-237-2237
Lafayette, LA 70506
www.kadn.com

KATC-TV Ch 3 (ABC) Phone: 337-235-3333
1103 Eraste Landry Rd Fax: 337-234-3580
Lafayette, LA 70506
www.katc.com

KLFY-TV Ch 10 (CBS) Phone: 337-981-4823
1808 Eraste Landry Rd Fax: 337-984-8323
Lafayette, LA 70506
www.klfy.com

KLPB-TV Ch 24 (PBS) Phone: 225-767-5660
7733 Parkins Rd Fax: 225-767-4277
Baton Rouge, LA 70810
E-mail: comments@lpb.org
www.lpb.org

KPLC-TV Ch 7 (NBC) Phone: 337-439-9071
PO Box 1490 Fax: 337-437-7600
Lake Charles, LA 70602
E-mail: kplc@aol.com

Radio

KAJN-FM 102.9 MHz (Rel) Phone: 337-783-1560
110 W 3rd St Fax: 337-783-1674
Crowley, LA 70526

KANE-AM 1240 kHz (Oldies) Phone: 337-365-3434
2316 E Main St Fax: 337-367-5385
New Iberia, LA 70560

KEUN-AM 1490 kHz (Ctry) Phone: 337-457-3041
330 W Laurel Ave Fax: 337-457-3081
Eunice, LA 70535

KFMV-FM 105.5 MHz (Urban) Phone: 337-233-4262
413 Jefferson St Fax: 337-235-9681
Lafayette, LA 70501

KFRA-AM 1390 kHz (Rel) Phone: 337-233-4262
413 Jefferson St Fax: 337-235-9681
Lafyaette, LA 70501

KFTE-FM 96.5 MHz (Rock) Phone: 337-232-2242
1749 Bertrand Dr Fax: 337-235-4181
Lafayette, LA 70506

KFXZ-FM 106.3 MHz (Rel) Phone: 337-981-0106
3225 Ambassador Caffrey Pkwy Fax: 337-988-0443
Lafayette, LA 70506

KJCB-AM 770 kHz (Urban) Phone: 337-233-4262
413 Jefferson St Fax: 337-235-9681
Lafayette, LA 70501

KMDL-FM 97.3 MHz (Ctry) Phone: 337-232-2242
1749 Bertrand Dr Fax: 337-235-4181
Lafayette, LA 70506

KNEK-FM 104.7 MHz (Urban) Phone: 337-981-0106
3225 Ambassador Caffery Pkwy Fax: 337-988-0443
Lafayette, LA 70506

KNIR-AM 1360 kHz (Nost) Phone: 337-365-6651
145 W Main St Fax: 337-365-6314
New Iberia, LA 70560

KPEL-AM 1420 kHz (N/T) Phone: 337-233-7003
1749 Bertrand Dr Fax: 337-234-7360
Lafayette, LA 70506

KROF-AM 960 kHz (B/EZ) Phone: 337-893-2531
9525 US Hwy 167 Fax: 337-893-2569
Abbeville, LA 70510

KROF-FM 105.1 MHz (Oldies) Phone: 337-893-2531
9525 US Hwy 167 Fax: 337-893-2569
Abbeville, LA 70510

KRRQ-FM 95.5 MHz (Urban) Phone: 337-981-0106
3225 Ambassador Caffrey Pkwy Fax: 337-988-0443
Lafayette, LA 70506

KRVS-FM 88.7 MHz (NPR) Phone: 337-482-5668
104 E University Martin Bldg Rm 319 Fax: 337-482-5908
Lafayette, LA 70503
E-mail: krvs@usl.edu
krvs.usl.edu

KRXZ-FM 107.9 MHz (CR) Phone: 337-233-7003
1749 Bertrand Dr Fax: 337-234-7360
Lafayette, LA 70506

KSIG-AM 1450 kHz (B/EZ) Phone: 337-783-2520
320 N Parkerson Ave Fax: 337-783-5744
Crowley, LA 70526

KSJY-FM 90.9 MHz (Rel) Phone: 337-572-9909
614 Acadian Hills Ln Fax: 337-572-9920
Lafayette, LA 70507

KSLO-AM 1230 kHz (Ctry) Phone: 337-942-2633
PO Box 1150 Fax: 337-942-2635
Opelousas, LA 70571

KSMB-FM 94.5 MHz (CHR) Phone: 337-232-2632
202 Galbert Rd Fax: 337-233-3779
Lafayette, LA 70506
www.ksmb.com

KTDY-FM 99.9 MHz (AC) Phone: 337-233-6000
1749 Bertrand Dr Fax: 337-234-7360
Lafayette, LA 70506
E-mail: ktdy@aol.com

KVOL-AM 1330 kHz (Sports) Phone: 337-233-1330
202 Galbert Rd Fax: 337-233-3779
Lafayette, LA 70506

KVOL-FM 105.9 MHz (Sports) Phone: 337-233-1330
202 Galbert Rd Fax: 337-233-3779
Lafayette, LA 70506

KXKC-FM 99.1 MHz (Ctry) Phone: 337-365-6651
145 W Main St Fax: 337-365-6314
New Iberia, LA 70560
E-mail: kxkc@kxkc.com
www.kxkc.com

Attractions

Louisiana is the only state in the U.S. with a dominant French culture, dating back to the 1700s. Acadian immigrants from Canada, now known as Cajuns, and migrants direct from French countries have kept their French heritage alive, preserving their culture in language, music, and food. This heritage is celebrated each April at the Festival International de Louisiane in Lafayette, Louisiana. One of Louisiana's biggest festivals, it features international musicians, artists, storytellers, theater performers, and crafters, each celebrating the French heritage and influence in Louisiana. The Cajun and Creole culture is also showcased at Vermilionville, a 23-acre attraction in Lafayette that features a living history exhibit, Cajun music, a gift shop, and an art gallery.

Acadian Village Phone: 337-981-2489
200 Greenleaf St Fax: 337-988-4554
Lafayette, LA 70506 TF: 800-962-9133

Alexandre Mouton House/Lafayette Museum Phone: 337-234-2208
1122 Lafayette St
Lafayette, LA 70501

Artists Alliance Gallery Phone: 337-233-7518
551 Jefferson St
Lafayette, LA 70501
www.metacadiana.com/alliance

Artists of Acadiana Gallery Phone: 337-233-4077
1600 Surrey St Vermilionville
Lafayette, LA 70508

Children's Museum of Acadiana Phone: 337-232-8500
201 E Congress St Fax: 337-232-8167
Lafayette, LA 70501

Chretien Point Plantation Phone: 337-662-5876
665 Chretien Point Rd Fax: 337-662-5876
Sunset, LA 70584 TF: 800-880-7050

Girard Park Phone: 337-291-8379
500 Girard Park Cir Fax: 337-291-8389
Lafayette, LA 70503

Heymann Performing Arts Center Phone: 337-291-5540
1373 S College Rd Fax: 337-291-5580
Lafayette, LA 70503

Jean Lafitte National Historical Park/ Acadian Cultural Center Phone: 337-232-0789
501 Fisher Rd Fax: 337-232-5740
Lafayette, LA 70508
www.nps.gov/jela

Kart Ranch Family Fun Center Phone: 337-837-5278
508 Youngsville Hwy 89 Fax: 337-837-4078
Lafayette, LA 70592
www.kartranch.com

Lafayette Art Gallery Phone: 337-269-0363
412 Travis St Acadiana Symphony Cultural Ctr
Lafayette, LA 70503

Lafayette Museum Phone: 337-234-2208
1122 Lafayette St Fax: 337-234-2208
Lafayette, LA 70501

Lafayette Natural History Museum & Planetarium Phone: 337-291-5544
637 Girard Park Dr Fax: 337-291-5464
Lafayette, LA 70503
E-mail: magasin@1stnet.com
www.lnhm.org

Rodrigue Gallery Phone: 337-232-6398
1206 Jefferson St
Lafayette, LA 70501

Saint John The Evangelist Museum Phone: 337-232-1322
914 Saint John St Fax: 337-232-1379
Lafayette, LA 70502

University Art Museum Phone: 337-231-5326
E Lewis St USL Campus Fletcher Hall Fax: 337-482-5907
Lafayette, LA 70504

Vermilionville Phone: 337-233-4077
1600 Surrey St Fax: 337-233-1694
Lafayette, LA 70508 TF: 800-992-2968

Zoo of Arcadiana Phone: 337-837-4325
116 Lakeview Dr Fax: 337-837-4253
Broussard, LA 70518

Sports Teams & Facilities

Bayou Bullfrogs (baseball) Phone: 337-233-0998
201 Reinhardt Dr ML Tigue Moore Field Fax: 337-237-3539
Lafayette, LA 70506
E-mail: frogs@txproball.com
www.txproball.com/frogs

Cajundome Phone: 337-265-2100
444 Cajundome Blvd Fax: 337-265-2311
Lafayette, LA 70506

Louisiana Hockeyplex Phone: 337-896-2042
3067 NW Evangeline Thwy Fax: 337-896-2047
Carencro, LA 70520
E-mail: administrator@lahockeyplex.com
www.lahockeyplex.com

Louisiana IceGators (hockey)
444 Cajundome Blvd Cajundome
Lafayette, LA 70506
www.icegators.com
Phone: 337-234-4423
Fax: 337-232-1254

Rapides Rangers (football)
600 Lorie Ave
Lafayette, LA 70507
www.rapidesrangers.com
Phone: 318-442-1272
Fax: 337-896-7652
TF: 888-422-9682

Annual Events

Acadiana Culinary Classic (early November) 337-265-2100
Cajun & Creole Christmas (December)............337-232-3808
Cajun Fun Fest (early May).......................337-365-1540
Cajun Heartland State Fair (late May-early June)....337-265-2100
Catfish Festival (mid-late March).................337-826-3627
Children's Carnival (late February) 337-845-4217
Children's Mardi Gras Parade (late February)......337-232-3808
Christmas at Vermilionville (December)...........337-233-4077
Christmas Renaissance "Festival of Light"
(early December) 337-232-1267
Christmas Under the Lamppost
(early December) 337-828-3817
Downtown Alive!
(April-June & September-November).............337-291-5566
Festival International de Louisiane (late April)......337-232-8086
Festivals Acadiens (mid-late September) 337-232-3808
Fourth Futurity Festival (early July)...............337-896-7223
Herb Fest (mid-April).............................337-232-3737
King's Court (late February)......................337-291-5566
King's Parade (mid-February)....................337-232-3808
Kwanzaa Celebration
(late December-early January)..................337-233-4758
La Fete de Vermilionville (mid-April) 337-233-4077
Lafayette Christmas Parade (early December).......337-232-3808
Le Cajun Music Awards Festival
(early-mid-August).............................337-232-3808
Le Festival de Mardi Gras à Lafayette
(mid-February)...............................337-265-3904
Mardi Gras Association Parade (late February)......337-232-3808
Saint Ignatius Rainbeau Festival
(mid-late March) 337-662-3325
Zydeco Extravaganza (late May) 337-234-9695

Lansing, Michigan

***County:* Ingham**

LANSING is located in south central Michigan. Major cities within 100 miles include Detroit, Flint, Kalamazoo, and Muskegon, Michigan.

Area (Land) .... 32.8 sq mi
Area (Water) .... 0.2 sq mi
Elevation .... 860 ft
Latitude .... 42-72-43 N
Longitude .... 84-56-13 W
Time Zone .... EST
Area Code 517

Climate

Lansing's climate ranges from continental (due to its central location in the state) to semi-marine (due to its proximity to the Great Lakes), depending on prevailing weather conditions. Winters tend to be cold and cloudy, with average high temperatures near 30 degrees and lows in the teens. The average annual snowfall in Lansing is 52 inches. Summer days are warm, with average high temperatures in the high 70s to low 80s, while evenings cool down into the mid- to high 50s. Precipitation is distributed fairly evenly throughout the year—June tends to be the wettest month in Lansing, while February is the driest.

Average Temperatures & Precipitation

Temperatures

	Jan	Feb	Mar	Apr	May	Jun	Jul	Aug	Sep	Oct	Nov	Dec
High	29	32	43	57	69	78	83	80	72	59	46	34
Low	13	14	25	35	45	55	59	57	50	39	31	19

Precipitation

	Jan	Feb	Mar	Apr	May	Jun	Jul	Aug	Sep	Oct	Nov	Dec
Inches	1.5	1.4	2.3	2.8	2.6	3.7	2.5	3.2	3.6	2.1	2.6	2.3

History

Lansing was founded in the 1840s by a group of settlers from Lansing, New York who came to the area with the belief that they had purchased land there. Although the pioneers discovered that the transaction existed only on paper, they decided to start a settlement there, naming it after their home town. In 1847, Lansing was chosen as the new state capital (formerly located in Detroit). At that time, the town consisted of little more than a log cabin and a sawmill, and Lansing became known as the "Capital in the Wilderness." The town was incorporated in 1859.

Industrial development in Lansing began during the 1860s with the arrival of the railroad. During the 1880s, Ransom E. Olds and Frank G. Clark produced the first automobile in the Lansing area, and by the turn of the century automobile production had become a vital part of the city's economy. The automobile industry remains important to Lansing today. General Motors, the area's largest private employer, has several plants in the area, and Lansing is home to the company's Oldsmobile Division. The city currently has a population of more than 127,000, making Lansing Michigan's fifth largest city.

Population

1990 Census 127,321
1998 Estimate 127,825
% Change 0.4
2010 Projection 123,223

Racial/Ethnic Breakdown
White 73.9%
Black 18.6%
Other 7.5%
Hispanic Origin (may be of any race) 7.9%

Age Breakdown
Under 5 years 9.2%
5 to 17 .... 18.2%
18 to 20 .... 4.5%
21 to 24 .... 7.8%
25 to 34 .... 20.9%
35 to 44 .... 14.8%
45 to 54 .... 8.2%
55 to 64 .... 6.8%
65 to 74 .... 5.6%
75+ years 4.0%
Median Age 29.7

Gender Breakdown
Male 47.4%
Female 52.6%

Government

Type of Government: Mayor-Council

Lansing City Attorney
124 W Michigan Ave 5th Fl
Lansing, MI 48933
Phone: 517-483-4320
Fax: 517-483-4081

Lansing City Clerk
124 W Michigan Ave
Lansing, MI 48933
Phone: 517-483-4133
Fax: 517-377-0068

Lansing City Council
124 W Michigan Ave 10th Fl
Lansing, MI 48933
Phone: 517-483-4177
Fax: 517-483-7630

Lansing City Hall
124 W Michigan Ave
Lansing, MI 48933
Phone: 517-483-4000

Lansing City Treasurer
124 W Michigan Ave 1st Fl
Lansing, MI 48933
Phone: 517-483-4112
Fax: 517-483-6084

Lansing Finance Dept
124 W Michigan Ave 8th Fl
Lansing, MI 48933
Phone: 517-483-4500
Fax: 517-483-4524

Lansing Fire Dept
120 E Shiawassee St
Lansing, MI 48933
Phone: 517-483-4200
Fax: 517-483-4488

Lansing Mayor
124 W Michigan Ave 9th Fl
Lansing, MI 48933
Phone: 517-483-4141
Fax: 517-483-6066

Lansing Parks & Recreation Dept
318 N Capitol Ave
Lansing, MI 48933
Phone: 517-483-4277
Fax: 517-483-6062

Lansing Personnel Services Dept
124 W Michigan Ave 4th Fl
Lansing, MI 48933
Phone: 517-483-4004
Fax: 517-483-6064

Lansing Planning & Neighborhood Development Dept
316 N Capitol Ave Suite D-1
Lansing, MI 48933
Phone: 517-483-4066
Fax: 517-483-6036

Lansing Police Dept
120 W Michigan Ave
Lansing, MI 48933
Phone: 517-483-4600
Fax: 517-377-0035

Lansing Public Library
401 S Capitol Ave
Lansing, MI 48933
Phone: 517-325-6400
Fax: 517-367-6333

Lansing Public Services Dept
124 W Michigan Ave Rm 732
Lansing, MI 48933
Phone: 517-483-4455
Fax: 517-483-6082

Important Phone Numbers

AAA .517-699-3515
American Express Travel .517-787-5200
Artsline .517-372-4636
Driver's License/Vehicle Registration Information .517-322-1460
Emergency 911
Greater Lansing Assn of Realtors .517-323-4090
Lansing City Income Tax Administrator .517-483-4121
Lansing Property Assessment Div .517-483-4020
Michigan Revenue Bureau .517-373-3196
Michigan State Tax Tribunal .517-334-6521
Poison Control Center .800-764-7661
Time .517-487-1212
Voter Registration Information .517-483-4133
Weather .517-321-7576

Information Sources

Better Business Bureau Serving Western Michigan
40 Pearl St NW Suite 354
Grand Rapids, MI 49503
www.grandrapids.bbb.org
Phone: 616-774-8236
Fax: 616-774-2014

Greater Lansing Convention & Visitors Bureau
1223 Turner St
Lansing, MI 48906
www.lansing.org
Phone: 517-487-6800
Fax: 517-487-5151
TF: 800-648-6630

Ingham County
PO Box 179
Mason, MI 48854
www.ingham.org
Phone: 517-676-7204
Fax: 517-676-7254

Lansing Center
333 E Michigan Ave
Lansing, MI 48933
www.lansingcenter.com
Phone: 517-483-7400
Fax: 517-483-7439

Lansing Regional Chamber of Commerce
300 E Michigan Ave Suite 300
Lansing, MI 48933
www.lansingchamber.org/
Phone: 517-487-6340
Fax: 517-484-6910

Online Resources

4Lansing.com
www.4lansing.com

Anthill City Guide Lansing
www.anthill.com/city.asp?city=lansing

Area Guide Lansing
lansing.areaguides.net

City Knowledge Lansing
www.cityknowledge.com/mi_lansing.htm

Excite.com Lansing City Guide
www.excite.com/travel/countries/united_states/michigan/lansing

Lansing.com
lansing.com

Lansing.TheLinks.com
lansing.thelinks.com

Area Communities

Communities in the Greater Lansing region with populations greater than 10,000 include:

Delhi Township
2074 Aurelius Rd
Holt, MI 48842
Phone: 517-694-2136
Fax: 517-694-1289

Delta Township
7710 W Saginaw
Lansing, MI 48917
Phone: 517-323-8500
Fax: 517-323-8599

DeWitt Township
1401 W Hervison Rd
DeWitt, MI 48820
Phone: 517-668-0270
Fax: 517-668-0277

East Lansing
410 Abbott Rd
East Lansing, MI 48823
Phone: 517-337-1731
Fax: 517-337-1607

Meridian Township
5151 Marsh Rd
Okemos, MI 48864
Phone: 517-349-1200
Fax: 517-349-0506

Mount Pleasant
401 N Main St
Mount Pleasant, MI 48858
Phone: 517-773-7971
Fax: 517-773-4691

Owosso
301 W Main St
Owosso, MI 48867
Phone: 517-725-0500
Fax: 517-723-8854

Economy

For more than a century, the automobile industry has played a dominant role in Lansing's economy. General Motors is Lansing's largest private employer, providing jobs for 16,000 area residents at area manufacturing plants, including the company's Oldsmobile Division, which is based in Lansing. As the capital of Michigan, Lansing's economy is also fueled by government—nearly half of Greater Lansing's top 15 employers are government-related. Employing 20,000 people, the State of Michigan is the region's single-largest employer. Other important industries in the Lansing region include retail trade and health care.

Unemployment Rate 3.1%*
Per Capita Income.......................... $24,296**
Median Family Income..................... $31,576

** Information given is for the Lansing Metropolitan Area, which includes Eaton, Clinton, and Ingham counties.*
*** Information given is for Ingham County.*

Principal Industries & Number of Wage Earners

Lansing Metropolitan Area* - 1998

Industry	Wage Earners
Construction & Mining	9,400
Finance, Insurance, & Real Estate	14,100
Government	30,400
Manufacturing	28,500
Retail Trade	44,100
Services	58,200
Transportation, Communications, & Utilities	6,100
Wholesale Trade	9,500

** Information given is for the Lansing Metropolitan Area, which includes Eaton, Clinton, and Ingham counties.*

Major Employers

EDS Corp
905 Southland St
Lansing, MI 48910
www.eds.com/careers/
Phone: 517-885-3800
Fax: 517-885-3411

General Motors Corp Oldsmobile Div
200 Renaissance Ctr
Detroit, MI 48265
E-mail: oldsheidi@aol.com
www.oldsmobile.com
Phone: 313-556-5000
TF: 800-442-6537

Ingham County
PO Box 179
Mason, MI 48854
www.ingham.org
Phone: 517-676-7204
Fax: 517-676-7254

Ingham Regional Medical Center
401 W Greenlawn Ave
Lansing, MI 48910
www.irmc.org
Phone: 517-334-2121
Fax: 517-334-2047

Jackson National Life Insurance Co
5901 Executive Dr
Lansing, MI 48911
www.jacksonnational.com
Phone: 517-394-3400
Fax: 517-394-5908
TF: 800-644-4565

Lansing City Hall
124 W Michigan Ave
Lansing, MI 48933
ci.lansing.mi.us
Phone: 517-483-4000

Lansing Community College
521 N Washington Sq
Lansing, MI 48901
www.lansing.cc.mi.us
Phone: 517-483-1957
Fax: 517-483-9668
TF: 800-644-4522

Lansing School District
519 W Kalamazoo St
Lansing, MI 48933
scnc.lsd.k12.mi.us
Phone: 517-325-6000
Fax: 517-325-7345

Meijer Inc
2929 Walker Ave NW
Grand Rapids, MI 49544
www.meijer.com
Phone: 616-453-6711
Fax: 616-791-2572

Michigan National Bank
124 W Allegan St
Lansing, MI 48933
Phone: 800-225-5662
Fax: 517-377-3037

Michigan State University
250 Administration Bldg
East Lansing, MI 48824
E-mail: admis@pilot.msu.edu
wxweb.msu.edu
Phone: 517-355-1855
Fax: 517-353-1647

Peckham Vocational Industries
2822 N MLK Jr Blvd
Lansing, MI 48906
www.peckham.org
Phone: 517-323-2400
Fax: 517-319-8490

Sparrow Health System
1215 E Michigan Ave
Lansing, MI 48912
E-mail: sparrow@www.sparrow.com
www.sparrow.com
Phone: 517-483-2700
Fax: 517-483-3747

US Postal Service
4800 Collins Rd
Lansing, MI 48924
new.usps.com
Phone: 517-337-8711
Fax: 517-337-8734

Quality of Living Indicators

Total Crime Index.................................... 7,606
(rates per 100,000 inhabitants)

Violent Crime
Murder/manslaughter............................ 5
Forcible rape 112
Robbery.................................... 253
Aggravated assault............................ 802

Property Crime
Burglary 1,269
Larceny theft 4,728
Motor vehicle theft 437

Cost of Living Index 85.0
(national average = 100)

Median Home Price $105,200

Education

Public Schools

Lansing School District
519 W Kalamazoo St
Lansing, MI 48933
scnc.lsd.k12.mi.us
Phone: 517-325-6000
Fax: 517-325-7345

Number of Schools
Elementary 33
Middle 4
High 3
Specialty 4

Student/Teacher Ratio
All Grades 19.7:1

Private Schools

Number of Schools (all grades) . . . . 25+

Colleges & Universities

Davenport College
220 E Kalamazoo St
Lansing, MI 48933
E-mail: laadmissions@davenport.edu
www.davenport.edu/lansing
Phone: 517-484-2600
Fax: 517-484-9719
TF: 800-686-1600

Great Lakes Christian College
6211 W Willow Hwy
Lansing, MI 48917
E-mail: glcc@glcc.edu
www.glcc.edu
Phone: 517-321-0242
Fax: 517-321-5902
TF: 800-937-4522

Lansing Community College
521 N Washington Sq
Lansing, MI 48901
www.lansing.cc.mi.us
Phone: 517-483-1957
Fax: 517-483-9668
TF: 800-644-4522

Michigan State University
250 Administration Bldg
East Lansing, MI 48824
E-mail: admis@pilot.msu.edu
wxweb.msu.edu
Phone: 517-355-1855
Fax: 517-353-1647

Hospitals

Ingham Regional Medical Center
401 W Greenlawn Ave
Lansing, MI 48910
www.irmc.org
Phone: 517-334-2121
Fax: 517-334-2047

Ingham Regional Medical Center Pennsylvania Campus
2727 S Pennsylvania St
Lansing, MI 48910
Phone: 517-372-8220
Fax: 517-372-0098

Saint Lawrence Hospital & Healthcare Services
1210 W Saginaw St
Lansing, MI 48915
Phone: 517-372-3610
Fax: 517-377-0467

Sparrow Health System
1215 E Michigan Ave
Lansing, MI 48912
www.sparrow.com
Phone: 517-483-2700
Fax: 517-483-3747

Transportation

Airport(s)

Capital City Airport (LAN)
5 miles NW of downtown (approx 10 minutes) 517-321-6121

Mass Transit

Capital Area Transportation Authority
$1 Base fare 517-394-1000

Rail/Bus

Amtrak Station
1240 S Harrison Rd
East Lansing, MI 48823
Phone: 517-332-5051
TF: 800-872-7245

Greyhound Bus Station
420 S Grand Ave
Lansing, MI 48933
Phone: 517-482-0673
TF: 800-231-2222

Utilities

Electricity
Consumers Energy 800-477-5050
www.consumersenergy.com
Lansing Board of Water & Light 517-371-6006
www.lbwl.com

Gas
Consumers Energy 800-477-5050
www.consumersenergy.com

Water
Lansing Board of Water & Light 517-371-6006
www.lbwl.com

Garbage Collection/Recycling
Lansing Garbage Collection & Disposal 517-483-4400

Telecommunications

Telephone
Ameritech 800-345-6254
www.ameritech.com

Cable Television
AT & T Cable Services 517-394-0001
www.cable.att.com

Internet Service Providers (ISPs)
ACD.net Internet Services 517-333-0900
www.acd.net

Banks

Bank One
201 Washington Sq S
Lansing, MI 48933
Phone: 517-487-1037
Fax: 517-487-5472

Capitol National Bank
200 Washington Sq N
Lansing, MI 48933
Phone: 517-484-5080
Fax: 517-374-2559

Citizens Bank
2201 E Grand River
Lansing, MI 48912
Phone: 800-825-7200
Fax: 517-371-8869

Michigan National Bank
124 W Allegan St
Lansing, MI 48933
Phone: 800-225-5662
Fax: 517-377-3037

National City Bank
120 N Washington Sq
Lansing, MI 48933
Phone: 517-334-1600
Fax: 517-334-5370

Old Kent Bank
112 E Allegan St
Lansing, MI 48933
Phone: 517-371-2911
Fax: 517-371-1491
TF: 800-304-0434

Shopping

Central Park Place
5100 Marsh Rd
Okemos, MI 48864
Phone: 517-349-5450
Fax: 517-349-7192

Lansing Factory Outlet Stores
1161 E Clark Rd
DeWitt, MI 48820
Phone: 517-669-2624

Lansing Mall
5330 W Saginaw Hwy
Lansing, MI 48917
www.lansingmall.com
Phone: 517-321-3534

Meridian Mall
1982 W Grand River Ave
Okemos, MI 48864
www.meridianmall.com
Phone: 517-349-2030
Fax: 517-349-7737

Washington Square Mall
Washington Sq & Michigan Ave
Lansing, MI 48933
Phone: 517-487-3322
Fax: 517-487-5889

Williamston Area Antique District
E & W Grand River Ave & N & S Putnam St
Williamston, MI 48895
Phone: 517-655-2622

Media

Newspapers and Magazines

Greater Lansing Business Monthly
614 Seymour Ave
Lansing, MI 48933
E-mail: glbm@lansing.net
www.businessmonthly.com/
Phone: 517-487-1714
Fax: 517-487-9597

Independent Advisor
1907 W M-21
Owosso, MI 48867
Phone: 517-723-1118
Fax: 517-725-1834

Lansing State Journal*
120 E Lenawee St
Lansing, MI 48919
www.lansingstatejournal.com
Phone: 517-377-1000
Fax: 517-377-1298
TF: 800-433-6946

Michigan Out-of-Doors
PO Box 30235
Lansing, MI 48909
www.mucc.org/michigan_out_of_doors/mood.html
Phone: 517-371-1041
Fax: 517-371-1505
TF: 800-777-6720

**Indicates major daily newspapers*

Television

WILX-TV Ch 10 (NBC)
500 American Rd
Lansing, MI 48911
www.wilxnbc10.com
Phone: 517-393-0110
Fax: 517-393-9180

WKAR-TV Ch 23 (PBS)
MSU 212 Communications Arts Bldg
East Lansing, MI 48824
E-mail: mail@wkar.msu.edu
www.wkar.msu.edu/tv/index.htm
Phone: 517-432-9527
Fax: 517-353-7124

WLAJ-TV Ch 53 (ABC)
5815 S Pennsylvania Ave
Lansing, MI 48911
www.wlaj.com/
Phone: 517-394-5300
Fax: 517-887-0077

WLNS-TV Ch 6 (CBS)
2820 E Saginaw St
Lansing, MI 48912
www.wlns.com
Phone: 517-372-8282
Fax: 517-374-7610

WSYM-TV Ch 47 (Fox)
600 W Saint Joseph St Suite 47
Lansing, MI 48933
Phone: 517-484-7747
Fax: 517-484-3144

WZPX-TV Ch 43 (Ind)
2610 Horizon Dr Suite E
Grand Rapids, MI 49546
www.wzpxtv.com
Phone: 616-222-4343
Fax: 616-493-2677

Radio

WILS-AM 1320 kHz (Nost)
PO Box 25008
Lansing, MI 48909
Phone: 517-393-1320
Fax: 517-393-0882

WJIM-AM 1240 kHz (N/T)
3420 Pine Tree Rd
Lansing, MI 48911
Phone: 517-394-7272
Fax: 517-393-9757
TF: 800-286-9546

WKAR-AM 870 kHz (NPR)
Michigan State University 283 Communication Arts Bldg
East Lansing, MI 48824
wkar.msu.edu/
Phone: 517-355-6540
Fax: 517-353-7124

WKAR-FM 90.5 MHz (NPR)
283 Communications Arts & Sciences Michigan State University
East Lansing, MI 48824
E-mail: mail@wkar.msu.edu
wkar.msu.edu/radio/index.htm
Phone: 517-355-6540
Fax: 517-353-7124

WMMQ-FM 94.9 MHz (CR)
3200 Pine Tree Rd
Lansing, MI 48911
www.wmmq.com
Phone: 517-393-1010
Fax: 517-393-4041

WVFN-AM 730 kHz (Sports)
3420 Pine Tree Rd
Lansing, MI 48911
Phone: 517-394-7272
Fax: 517-393-9757

WXIK-FM 94.1 MHz (Ctry)
2495 N Cedar St
Holt, MI 48842
Phone: 517-699-0994
Fax: 517-699-1880
TF: 800-786-7106

WXLA-AM 1180 kHz (AC)
1011 Northcrest Rd Suite 4
Lansing, MI 48906
Phone: 517-484-9600
Fax: 517-484-9699

Attractions

One of the top science museums in the United States, Impression 5 Science Center, is situated along Museum Drive in downtown Lansing. This is also the starting point for Planet Walk, a model of the solar system that stretches across 8,000 feet of the River Trail along the Grand River in Lansing. Other attractions in this area include the Riverwalk Theatre, Michigan Museum of Surveying, and R.E. Olds Transportation Museum. The State Capitol Building, originally designed by architect Elijah E. Meyers, has recently undergone extensive renovation in order to restore its original Victorian design, thereby earning its new designation as a National Historic Landmark.

Abrams Planetarium
Shaw Ln & Science Rd Michigan State University
East Lansing, MI 48824
www.pa.msu.edu/abrams
Phone: 517-355-4676
Fax: 517-432-3838

Adado Louis F Riverfront Park & Trail System
201 E Shiawasee St
Lansing, MI 48933
Phone: 517-483-4277
Fax: 517-483-6062

Arts Council of Greater Lansing
425 S Grand Ave Center for the Arts
Lansing, MI 48933
E-mail: artscouncil@lansing.com
www.lansing.com/artscouncil
Phone: 517-372-4636
Fax: 517-484-2564

Beal WJ Botanical Garden
Michigan State University
East Lansing, MI 48824
www.cpp.msu.edu/beal
Phone: 517-355-9582
Fax: 517-432-1090

BoarsHead Michigan Public Theater
425 S Grand Ave Center for the Arts
Lansing, MI 48933
E-mail: boarshead@voyager.net
www.boarshead.org
Phone: 517-484-7805
Fax: 517-484-2564

Burchfield Park
881 Grovenburg Rd
Holt, MI 48842
Phone: 517-676-2233
Fax: 517-694-2958

Butterfly House
Bogue St Plant & Soil Science Bldg
East Lansing, MI 48824
Phone: 517-355-0348
Fax: 517-353-0890

Cooley Gardens
225 W Main St
Lansing, MI 48933
Phone: 517-483-4277

Country Mill
4648 Otto Rd
Charlotte, MI 48813
E-mail: sales@thecountrymill.com
www.countrymill.com/
Phone: 517-543-1019

Fenner Carl G Nature Center
2020 E Mt Hope Rd
Lansing, MI 48910
Phone: 517-483-4224
Fax: 517-377-0012

Frances Park
2600 Moores River Dr
Lansing, MI 48911
Phone: 517-483-4277
Fax: 517-483-6062

Greater Lansing Symphony Orchestra
230 N Washington Sq Suite 100
Lansing, MI 48933
www.lansingsymphony.org
Phone: 517-487-5001
Fax: 517-487-0210

Impression 5 Science Center
200 Museum Dr
Lansing, MI 48933
www.impression5.org
Phone: 517-485-8116
Fax: 517-485-8125

Ingham County Courthouse
PO Box 319
Mason, MI 48854
Phone: 517-676-7213
Fax: 517-676-7230

Kresge Art Museum
Michigan State University
East Lansing, MI 48824
www.msu.edu/unit/kamuseum/
Phone: 517-355-7631
Fax: 517-355-6577

Lansing Art Gallery
425 S Grand Ave Center for the Arts
Lansing, MI 48933
Phone: 517-374-6400
Fax: 517-484-2564

Lansing Civic Players
2300 E Michigan Ave
Lansing, MI 48912
Phone: 517-484-9115
Fax: 517-484-7440

Ledges The
133 Fitzgerald Park Dr
Grand Ledge, MI 48837
Phone: 517-627-7351

Malcolm X Homesite
ML King Jr Blvd
Lansing, MI 48911

Meridian Historical Village
5151 Marsh Rd Meridian Township Central Park
Okemos, MI 48864
Phone: 517-347-7300

Michigan Library & Historical Center
717 W Allegan St
Lansing, MI 48918
www.sos.state.mi.us/history/history.html
Phone: 517-373-3559
Fax: 517-373-0851

Michigan State Capitol
Capitol & Michigan Aves
Lansing, MI 48913
Phone: 517-373-2348

Michigan State University Museum
W Circle Dr
East Lansing, MI 48824
museum.cl.msu.edu
Phone: 517-355-2370
Fax: 517-432-2846

Michigan Women's Historical Center & Hall of Fame
213 W Main St
Lansing, MI 48933
E-mail: mwhfame@leslie.k12.mi.us
scnc.leslie.k12.mi.us/~mwhfame
Phone: 517-484-1880
Fax: 517-372-0170

Museum of Surveying
220 S Museum Dr
Lansing, MI 48933
www.surveyhistory.org
Phone: 517-484-6605
Fax: 517-484-3711

Nokomis Learning Center
5153 Marsh Rd
Okemos, MI 48864
E-mail: cameron@nokomis.org
www.nokomis.org
Phone: 517-349-5777
Fax: 517-349-8560

Opera Co of Mid-Michigan
215 S Washington Sq
Lansing, MI 48933
Phone: 517-482-1431

Planet Walk
Lansing, MI 48933
Phone: 517-487-6800

Potter Park Zoo
1301 S Pennsylvania Ave
Lansing, MI 48912
E-mail: potterpark@ci.lansing.mi.us
www.ci.lansing.mi.us/depts/zoo/zoo.html
Phone: 517-483-4221
Fax: 517-483-6065

RE Olds Transportation Museum
240 Museum Dr
Lansing, MI 48933
Phone: 517-372-0422
Fax: 517-372-2901

Riverwalk Theatre
228 Museum Dr
Lansing, MI 48933
www.comnet.org/riverwalktheatre
Phone: 517-482-5700
Fax: 517-482-9812

Snow's Sugar Bush
3188 Plains Rd
Mason, MI 48854
Phone: 517-676-2442

Spotlight Theatre
3804 E Grand Ledge Hwy Fitzgerald Pk
Grand Ledge, MI 48837
Phone: 517-627-5444
Fax: 517-627-2977

Telephone Pioneer Museum
221 N Washington Sq
Lansing, MI 48933
Phone: 517-487-6800

Turner-Dodge House & Park
100 E North St
Lansing, MI 48906
Phone: 517-483-4220
Fax: 517-483-6081

Wharton Center for the Performing Arts
Michigan State University
East Lansing, MI 48824
E-mail: wharton@pilot.msu.edu
web.msu.edu/wharton/
Phone: 517-432-2000
Fax: 517-353-5329
TF: 800-942-7866

Woldumar Nature Center
5739 Old Lansing Rd
Lansing, MI 48917
www.woldumar.org
Phone: 517-322-0030
Fax: 517-322-9394

Sports Teams & Facilities

Lansing Lugnuts (baseball)
505 E Michigan Ave Oldsmobile Pk
Lansing, MI 48912
E-mail: lugnuts@tcimet.net
www.lansinglugnuts.com
Phone: 517-485-4500
Fax: 517-485-4518
TF: 800-945-6887

Annual Events

Bluegrass Music Festival (mid-August) 517-589-8097
Car/Capital Celebration (late August)...............517-372-0529
Central Michigan Boat Show (late January).........517-485-2309
East Lansing Art Festival (late May)...............517-337-1731
Festeve (December 31)...........................517-483-4499
Festival of Trees (late November) 517-483-7400
Home & Garden Show (mid-March) 517-686-0660
Ingham County Fair (late July-early August)........517-676-2428
Island Art Fair (early August).....................517-627-9843
Lansing Jazzfest (early August) 517-371-4600
LPGA Tournament (late August) 517-336-2220
Mexican Fiesta (Memorial Day Weekend)...........517-394-4639
Michigan Parades Into the 21st Century (mid-May) 517-323-2000
National Folk Festival (mid-August) 517-355-2370
Old Town Lansing Art & Octoberfest (mid-October).................................517-487-3322
Wonderland of Lights (late November-late December)..................517-363-4730

Las Cruces, New Mexico

County: **Doña Ana**

LAS CRUCES is located east of the Rio Grande in the Mesilla Valley of south central New Mexico. Major cities within 100 miles include El Paso, Texas and Juarez, Mexico.

Area (Land) .... 37.5 sq mi
Area (Water).............................. 0.1 sq mi
Elevation.................................. 3,896 ft
Latitude .... 32-17-22 N
Longitude.............................. 106-55-19 W
Time Zone .... MST
Area Code.................................. 505

Climate

Las Cruces has a moderate climate with abundant sunshine and low humidity. Summer days are hot, with average high temperatures in the 90s, while evenings cool down into the 60s. Winter high temperatures average in the upper 50s to low 60s, with lows in the upper 20s. Snowfall is minimal, averaging three inches annually. Las Cruces is fairly dry, with less than 10 inches of rain each year.

Average Temperatures & Precipitation

Temperatures

	Jan	Feb	Mar	Apr	May	Jun	Jul	Aug	Sep	Oct	Nov	Dec
High	57	62	69	77	85	94	94	91	86	78	66	58
Low	26	30	36	43	51	60	67	64	58	45	34	27

Precipitation

	Jan	Feb	Mar	Apr	May	Jun	Jul	Aug	Sep	Oct	Nov	Dec
Inches	0.5	0.4	0.2	0.2	0.3	0.7	1.4	2.3	1.4	0.9	0.5	0.7

History

Centuries before the city known today as Las Cruces was settled, it was inhabited by various Indian tribes, including the Mogollons as early as 1450 and, later, the Apaches. In 1598, Don Juan Onate and his soldiers passed through the Mesilla Valley on the Camino Real en route from Mexico to Santa Fe. The group introduced the valley's early inhabitants to Christianity and the written word, and they also brought the first horses and cattle to the area. European colonization soon followed, and the Spanish established the area's first settlement, Doña Ana.

The Mesilla Valley area was originally part of Mexico until the Treaty of Guadeloupe Hidalgo granted the land to the United States in 1848 at the end of the Mexican-American War. Once the area became part of the U.S., Lt. Delos Bennett Sackett was sent by the Army to protect the area from Apaches and desperados, and new settlers began to arrive. At the request of Doña Ana's leader, Don Pablo Melendres, Sackett laid out a new community, Las Cruces, to accommodate the influx of new residents. The origin of the name "Las Cruces" (meaning "the crosses" in Spanish) is the subject of much debate. Some believe that the community was named for the crosses that marked the graves of travelers killed during Apache attacks, while others believe that the name was chosen because of the community's location at the crossroads of the U.S. and Mexico.

The 1880s also saw the arrival of the Santa Fe Railroad, which helped to fuel Las Cruces' growth, and the establishment of Las Cruces College, an agricultural college that later became New Mexico State University. Established as a pueblo in 1907, Las Cruces was not incorporated as a city until 1946. The 1940s proved to be a pivotal decade in Las Cruces history. Government replaced agriculture as the driving force behind Las Cruces' economy. In 1945, White Sands Missile Range, the largest overland test range in the United States, was established in Doña Ana County. Today, White Sands remains an important research and testing facility for the U.S. Military, NASA, and for civilian contractors and is one of the area's largest employers.

The seat of Doña Ana County, Las Cruces today is home to more than 76,000 residents. Las Cruces is also among the nation's fastest growing metropolitan areas.

Population

1990 Census 62,360
1998 Estimate.............................. 76,102
% Change 22.0
2020 Projection 120,000

Racial/Ethnic Breakdown

White.................................. 88.2%
Black 1.9%
Other.................................. 9.9%
Hispanic Origin (may be of any race) 46.9%

Age Breakdown

Under 5 years.............................. 7.8%
5 to 17.................................. 19.0%
18 to 20.................................. 5.6%
21 to 24.................................. 8.7%
25 to 34.................................. 17.3%
35 to 44.................................. 13.3%
45 to 54.................................. 8.9%
55 to 64.................................. 8.1%
65 to 74.................................. 6.7%
75+ years 4.6%
Median Age.................................. 30.0

Gender Breakdown

Male.................................. 49.0%
Female.................................. 51.0%

Government

Type of Government: City Manager-Council

Las Cruces City Attorney
PO Box 20000
Las Cruces, NM 88004
Phone: 505-541-2128
Fax: 505-541-2017

Las Cruces City Council
200 N Church St
Las Cruces, NM 88001
Phone: 505-541-2066
Fax: 505-541-2183

Las Cruces City Hall
200 N Church St
Las Cruces, NM 88001
Phone: 505-541-2000

Las Cruces Finance Dept
200 N Church St
Las Cruces, NM 88001
Phone: 505-541-2050
Fax: 505-541-2039

Las Cruces Fire Dept
201 E Picacho Ave
Las Cruces, NM 88001
Phone: 505-528-3473
Fax: 505-528-4082

Las Cruces Human Resources Dept
575 S Alameda Blvd
Las Cruces, NM 88001
Phone: 505-528-3100
Fax: 505-528-3020

Las Cruces Mayor
200 N Church St
Las Cruces, NM 88001
Phone: 505-541-2067
Fax: 505-541-2077

Las Cruces Parks & Recreation Dept
1600 E Hadley Ave
Las Cruces, NM 88001
Phone: 505-541-2553
Fax: 505-541-2636

Las Cruces Planning Dept
575 S Alameda Blvd
Las Cruces, NM 88004
Phone: 505-528-3222

Las Cruces Police Dept
217 E Picacho Ave
Las Cruces, NM 88001
Phone: 505-528-4089
Fax: 505-528-4136

Las Cruces Transit Div
1501-A E Hadley Ave
Las Cruces, NM 88001
Phone: 505-541-2500
Fax: 505-541-2545

Las Cruces Utilities Dept
PO Box 20000
Las Cruces, NM 88004
Phone: 505-528-3500
Fax: 505-528-3513

Important Phone Numbers

AAA....505-523-5681
American Express Travel....505-521-1400
Doña Ana County Tax Assessor....505-647-7400
Doña Ana County Treasurer....505-647-7433
Driver's License/Vehicle Registration Information....505-524-6215
Emergency....911
Las Cruces Assn of Realtors....505-524-0658
Medical Referral....505-841-1777
New Mexico Taxation & Revenue Dept....505-524-6225
Poison Control Center....800-432-6866
Voter Registration Information....505-647-7429

Information Sources

Better Business Bureau Serving New Mexico
2625 Pennsylvania NE Suite 2050
Albuquerque, NM 87110
www.bbbnm.com
Phone: 505-346-0110
Fax: 505-346-0696
TF: 800-873-2224

Doña Ana County
180 W Amador Ave
Las Cruces, NM 88001
chilepepper.co.dona-ana.nm.us
Phone: 505-525-6600
Fax: 505-647-7224

Las Cruces Chamber of Commerce
760 W Picacho Ave
Las Cruces, NM 88005
lascruces.org/chamber
Phone: 505-524-1968
Fax: 505-527-5546

Las Cruces Convention & Visitors Bureau
211 N Water St
Las Cruces, NM 88001
www.lascrucescvb.org
Phone: 505-541-2444
Fax: 505-541-2164
TF: 800-343-7827

Mesilla Valley Economic Development Alliance
2345 E Nevada St
Las Cruces, NM 88001
www.mveda.com
Phone: 505-525-2852
Fax: 505-523-5707

Online Resources

4LasCruces.com
www.4lascruces.com

City Knowledge Las Cruces
www.cityknowledge.com/nm_lascruces.htm

Excite.com Las Cruces City Guide
www.excite.com/travel/countries/united_states/new_mexico/las_cruces

Las Cruces Citi-Guide
www.citi-guide.com/lascruces/index.htm

Las Cruces CityGuide
cityguide.lycos.com/southwest/LasCrucesNM.html

Las Cruces Information Center
www.zianet.com/snm/ricruces.htm

Lodging.com Las Cruces New Mexico
www.lodging.com/auto/guides/las_cruces-nm.html

Mesilla-Valley.Net
arteffects.com/mesilla

Online City Guide to Las Cruces
www.olcg.com/nm/lascruces/index.html

Area Communities

Incorporated communities in Doña Ana County with populations greater than 1,000 include:

Hatch
PO Box 220
Hatch, NM 87937
Phone: 505-267-5216
Fax: 505-267-1135

Mesilla
PO Box 10
Mesilla, NM 88046
Phone: 505-524-3262
Fax: 505-541-6327

Sunland Park
3800 McNutt Rd
Sunland Park, NM 88063
Phone: 505-589-7565
Fax: 505-589-1222

Economy

Government, at the federal, state, and local levels, is the dominant player in Las Cruces' economy. White Sands Missile Range (www.wsmr.army.mil) is the area's largest Federal Government employer, providing jobs for approximately 6,000 people, most of whom live in the Las Cruces area. The facility is also Doña Ana County's most lucrative employer, bringing more than $200 million into the community. Area educational institutions, including New Mexico State University and the local school districts, employ a large percentage of the county's government workers. Services and retail trade are the area's second and third largest employment sectors.

Unemployment Rate 9.1%
Per Capita Income.......................... $14,923*
Median Family Income...................... $28,011

* *Information given is for Doña Ana County.*

Principal Industries & Number of Wage Earners

Doña Ana County - 1998

Contract Construction 3,150
Finance, Insurance, & Real Estate 1,993
Government 18,757
Manufacturing 2,906
Retail Trade.. 9,772
Services & Miscellaneous 12,739
Transportation & Public Utilities 1,973
Wholesale Trade.. 1,214

Major Employers

Doña Ana County Phone: 505-525-6600
180 W Amador Ave Fax: 505-647-7224
Las Cruces, NM 88001
chilepepper.co.dona-ana.nm.us

Gadsden Independent School District Phone: 505-882-6200
PO Drawer 70 Fax: 505-882-6250
Anthony, NM 88021

Las Cruces City Hall Phone: 505-541-2000
200 N Church St
Las Cruces, NM 88001
www.las-cruces.org

Las Cruces Public Schools Phone: 505-527-5800
505 S Main St Fax: 505-527-6658
Las Cruces, NM 88001
lcps.k12.nm.us

McDonald's Phone: 505-524-2912
PO Box 2797 Fax: 505-524-8375
Las Cruces, NM 88004
www.mcdonalds.com/corporate/careers

Memorial Medical Center Phone: 505-522-8641
2450 S Telshor Blvd Fax: 505-521-5050
Las Cruces, NM 88011
www.mmclc.org

NASA JSC White Sands Test Facility Phone: 505-524-5773
PO Box 20 Fax: 505-524-5798
Las Cruces, NM 88004
www.wstf.nasa.gov

New Mexico State University Phone: 505-646-3121
PO Box 30001 MSC-3A Fax: 505-646-6330
Las Cruces, NM 88003 TF: 800-662-6678
E-mail: admissions@nmsu.edu
www.nmsu.edu

Verizon Communications Phone: 505-523-6186
1673 E Lohman Ave Fax: 505-524-0559
Las Cruces, NM 88001
www.verizon.com

Wal-Mart Phone: 505-523-2204
571 Walton Blvd Fax: 505-523-6650
Las Cruces, NM 88001
www.walmartstores.com

Quality of Living Indicators

Total Crime Index..................................... 6,472
(rates per 100,000 inhabitants)

Violent Crime
Murder/manslaughter............................ 8
Forcible rape 60
Robbery.. 102
Aggravated assault.............................. 371

Property Crime
Burglary 1,185
Larceny theft 4,547
Motor vehicle theft 185

Cost of Living Index.................................. 100.1
(national average = 100)

Median Home Price.................................. $67,800

Education

Public Schools

Las Cruces Public Schools Phone: 505-527-5800
505 S Main St Fax: 505-527-6658
Las Cruces, NM 88001
lcps.k12.nm.us

Number of Schools
Elementary................................. 21
Middle 7
High.. 4

Student/Teacher Ratio
All Grades 18.1:1

Private Schools

Number of Schools (all grades)..................... 3+

Colleges & Universities

Doña Ana Branch Community College Phone: 505-527-7500
Box 30001 Dept 3DA Fax: 505-527-7515
Las Cruces, NM 88003 TF: 800-903-7503
dabcc-www.nmsu.edu

New Mexico State University Phone: 505-646-3121
PO Box 30001 MSC-3A Fax: 505-646-6330
Las Cruces, NM 88003 TF: 800-662-6678
E-mail: admissions@nmsu.edu
www.nmsu.edu

Hospitals

Memorial Medical Center Phone: 505-522-8641
2450 S Telshor Blvd Fax: 505-521-5050
Las Cruces, NM 88011
www.mmclc.org

Mesilla Valley Hospital Phone: 505-382-3500
3751 Del Rey Blvd Fax: 505-382-3071
Las Cruces, NM 88012

Transportation

Airport(s)

El Paso International Airport (ELP)
44 miles SE of downtown Las Cruces
(approx 50 minutes) 915-772-4271
Las Cruces International Airport (LRU)
7 miles W of downtown (approx 15 minutes) 505-524-2762

Mass Transit

Las Cruces Transit Dept
$.50 Base fare....505-541-2500

Rail/Bus

Greyhound Bus Station Phone: 505-524-8518
490 N Valley Dr TF: 800-231-2222
Las Cruces, NM 88005

Utilities

Electricity
El Paso Electric Co.....505-526-5555
www.epelectric.com

Gas
City of Las Cruces Utilities....505-541-2111

Water
City of Las Cruces Utilities....505-541-2111

Garbage Collection/Recycling
City of Las Cruces Utilities....505-541-2111

Telecommunications

Telephone
Qwest....800-244-1111
www.qwest.com

Cable Television
TCI of Las Cruces....505-523-2531

Internet Service Providers (ISPs)
ZiaNet Inc....505-522-1234
www.zianet.com

Banks

Bank of the Rio Grande NA Phone: 505-525-8960
2535 S Telshor Blvd Fax: 505-522-5075
Las Cruces, NM 88011
www.bank-riogrande.com

Citizens Bank Phone: 505-522-1000
2200 Missouri Ave Fax: 505-522-1000
Las Cruces, NM 88001
www.citizenslc.com

Community First Phone: 505-527-6200
201 N Church St Fax: 505-527-6250
Las Cruces, NM 88001 TF: 800-218-4954

First Federal Savings Bank Phone: 505-522-2664
1800 S Telshor Blvd Fax: 505-522-5416
Las Cruces, NM 88011 TF: 800-432-4412

First Savings Bank Phone: 505-521-7931
2804 N Telshor Blvd Fax: 505-521-7906
Las Cruces, NM 88011 TF: 800-555-6895

First Security Bank Phone: 505-526-7350
1375 E Boutz Rd Fax: 505-526-7349
Las Cruces, NM 88001 TF: 800-683-5670

Matrix Capital Bank Phone: 505-524-7748
277 E Amador Ave Fax: 505-523-2542
Las Cruces, NM 88011
www.matrix-capital.com

State National Bank Phone: 505-523-5920
225 E Idaho Ave Fax: 505-523-5922
Las Cruces, NM 88004

Wells Fargo Bank Phone: 505-527-0551
700 N Main St Fax: 505-527-0557
Las Cruces, NM 88001 TF: 800-396-2265

White Sands Federal Credit Union Phone: 505-647-4500
2190 E Lohman Ave Fax: 505-647-4540
Las Cruces, NM 88001
www.wsfcu.org

Shopping

Mesilla Valley Mall Phone: 505-522-1001
700 Telshor Blvd
Las Cruces, NM 88011

Monte Vista Shopping Center Phone: 505-526-2281
2205 S Main St Fax: 505-526-4249
Las Cruces, NM 88001

Media

Newspapers and Magazines

Las Cruces Bulletin Phone: 505-524-8061
PO Box 637 Fax: 505-526-4621
Las Cruces, NM 88004
E-mail: bulletin@zianet.com
www.zianet.com/Bulletin

Las Cruces Sun-News* Phone: 505-541-5400
256 W Las Cruces Ave Fax: 505-541-5499
Las Cruces, NM 88005 TF: 800-745-5851
www.newschoice.com/Newspapers/MidStates/LasCruces

Southern New Mexico Magazine Phone: 505-382-0408
7440 Arroyo Seco Fax: 505-382-0428
Las Cruces, NM 88011
www.zianet.com/redsky

**Indicates major daily newspapers*

Television

KDBC-TV Ch 4 (CBS) Phone: 915-532-6551
2201 Wyoming Ave Fax: 915-544-2591
El Paso, TX 79903
www.kdbc.com

KFOX-TV Ch 14 (Fox) Phone: 915-833-8585
6004 N Mesa Fax: 915-833-8717
El Paso, TX 79912
E-mail: fox14@whc.net

KKWB-TV Ch 65 (WB) Phone: 915-532-6565
801 N Oregon St Fax: 915-532-6841
El Paso, TX 79902
www.kkwb.com

KRWG-TV Ch 22 (PBS) Phone: 505-646-2222
Jordan St Milton Hall Rm 100 Fax: 505-646-1924
Las Cruces, NM 88003
E-mail: viewer@krwg.pbs.org
www.nmsu.edu/~krwgtv

KTSM-TV Ch 9 (NBC) Phone: 915-532-5421
801 N Oregon St Fax: 915-544-0536
El Paso, TX 79902
E-mail: ktsmtv@whc.net
www.ktsm.com

KVIA-TV Ch 7 (ABC) Phone: 915-496-7777
4140 Rio Bravo St Fax: 915-532-0505
El Paso, TX 79902
E-mail: feedback@kvia.com
www.kvia.com

Radio

KFNA-AM 1060 kHz (Span) Phone: 915-542-2969
2211 Missouri St Suite 237 Fax: 915-542-2958
El Paso, TX 79903

KGRT-AM 570 kHz (Ctry) Phone: 505-524-8588
3401 W Picacho St Fax: 505-524-8580
Las Cruces, NM 88005

KGRT-FM 103.9 MHz (Ctry) Phone: 505-524-8588
3401 W Picacho St Fax: 505-524-8580
Las Cruces, NM 88005
E-mail: kgrt@zianet.com

KHEY-AM 690 kHz (Ctry) Phone: 915-566-9301
2419 N Piedras St Fax: 915-566-0928
El Paso, TX 79930
www.khey.com/khey_am/sportstic.html

KMVR-FM 104.9 MHz (AC) Phone: 505-526-2496
1832 W Amador Fax: 505-523-3918
Las Cruces, NM 88005

KOBE-AM 1450 kHz (N/T) Phone: 505-526-2496
1832 W Amador Fax: 505-523-3918
Las Cruces, NM 88005

KROD-AM 600 kHz (N/T) Phone: 915-544-8864
4150 Pinnacle St Suite 120 Fax: 915-544-9536
El Paso, TX 79902
E-mail: infokrod@krod.com
www.krod.com

KROL-FM 99.5 MHz (Rel) Phone: 915-779-0016
6900 Commerce St Fax: 505-523-2212
El Paso, TX 79915

KRWG-FM 90.7 MHz (NPR) Phone: 505-646-4525
PO Box 3000 Fax: 505-646-1974
Las Cruces, NM 88003
E-mail: krwgfm@nmsu.edu
www.krwgfm.org/index.htm

KSNM-FM 98.7 MHz (B/EZ) Phone: 505-525-9298
1355 E California St Fax: 505-525-9419
Las Cruces, NM 88001

KVLC-FM 101.1 MHz (Oldies) Phone: 505-527-1111
105 E Idaho Ave Suite B Fax: 505-527-1100
Las Cruces, NM 88002
E-mail: kvlc@zianet.com
www.zianet.com/kvlc

KXDA-FM 103.1 MHz (CR) Phone: 505-525-9298
1355 E California St Fax: 505-525-9419
Las Cruces, NM 88001

Attractions

The Old Mesilla area of Las Cruces was the site of Billy the Kid's trial, sentencing, and escape, and is now a popular attraction featuring shops, restaurants, and cultural events. Part of Las Cruces' original town site can still be found at the Mesquite Street-Original Townsite Historic District. La Cueva, a natural cave located about 11 miles east of Las Cruces, was first home to ancient Mogollon Indians, then later inhabited by an eccentric Italian nobleman known as the Hermit at La Cueva. Another nearby attraction is Fort Selden State Monument. The fort is the former home of the Buffalo Soldiers, the famous Black Calvary who protected the Mesilla Valley from Indian attacks New Mexico State University houses the largest contemporary art gallery in south central New Mexico and contains over 1,800 19th Century Mexican retablos.

Branigan Cultural Center Phone: 505-541-2155
500 N Water St Fax: 505-525-3645
Las Cruces, NM 88001
www.lascruces-culture.org/html/branigan_cultural_center.html

Dripping Springs Recreation Area Phone: 505-525-4300
University Ave
Las Cruces, NM 88005

Fort Selden State Monument Phone: 505-526-8911
1280 Ft Selden Rd
Radium Springs, NM 88054

Historical Lawmen Museum Phone: 505-525-1911
1725 Marquess St Fax: 505-647-7800
Las Cruces, NM 88005

Hubbard Museum of the American West Phone: 505-378-4142
841 Hwy 70 W Fax: 505-378-4166
Ruidoso Downs, NM 88346

La Cueva Phone: 505-522-1219
Drippings Springs Rd
Las Cruces, NM 88001

La Viña Winery Phone: 505-882-7632
4201 Hwy 28
La Union, NM 88021

Las Cruces Chamber Ballet Phone: 505-523-7325
224 N Campo St
Las Cruces, NM 88001

Las Cruces Community Theater Phone: 505-523-1200
313 N Downtown Mall Fax: 505-525-0015
Las Cruces, NM 88001
www.zianet.com/lcct

Las Cruces Museum of Fine Art & Culture Phone: 505-541-2155
490 N Water St
Las Cruces, NM 88001
www.lascruces-culture.org/fine-art-museum/

Las Cruces Museum of Natural History Phone: 505-541-2155
700 Telshor Blvd
Las Cruces, NM 88001
E-mail: mnh@zianet.com
www.nmsu.edu/Museum

Las Cruces Symphony Phone: 505-646-3709
New Mexico State University MSC-3F Fax: 505-646-1086
Horshoe Espina
Las Cruces, NM 88004
www.nmsu.edu/LCSO

Leasburg Dam State Park Phone: 505-524-4068
Leasburg State Park Rd
Radium Springs, NM 88054

Log Cabin Museum Phone: 505-541-2155
Lucero & Main Sts
Las Cruces, NM 88001
www.lascruces-culture.org/html/log_cabin_museum.html

Mesilla Valley Fine Arts Gallery Phone: 505-522-2933
1322 Mesilla Valley Mall 700 Telshor Blvd
Las Cruces, NM 88011

New Mexico Farm & Ranch Heritage Museum Phone: 505-522-4100
4100 Dripping Springs Rd Fax: 505-522-3085
Las Cruces, NM 88011

New Mexico State University Art Gallery Phone: 505-646-2545
MSC 3572 NMSU PO Box 30001
Las Cruces, NM 88003

New Mexico State University Museum Phone: 505-646-3739
University Ave & Solano St Kent Hall
Las Cruces, NM 88003

Our Lady at the Foot of the Cross Shrine Phone: 505-541-2444
Lohman Ave & Water St
Las Cruces, NM 88001

San Augustin Pass & Aguirre Spring Recreational Area Phone: 505-525-4300
Hwy 70
Las Cruces, NM 88012

Space Murals Museum Phone: 505-382-0977
12450 Hwy 70 E
Las Cruces, NM 88012

Volunteer Memorial Sculpture Garden Phone: 505-541-2155
500 N Water St
Las Cruces, NM 88001
www.lascruces-culture.org/html/sculpture_garden.html

Zohn Hershel Theatre Phone: 505-646-4515
New Mexico State University Campus
Las Cruces, NM 88003

Sports Teams & Facilities

Ruidoso Downs Racing Inc Phone: 505-378-4431
1461 Hwy 70 W Fax: 505-378-4631
Ruidoso Downs, NM 88346

Southern New Mexico Speedway Phone: 505-524-7913
3530 W Picacho Ave Fax: 505-541-6398
Las Cruces, NM 88005
www.snmspeedway.com

Annual Events

Arts Hop (mid-September)........................505-523-6403
Baylor Pass Mountain Trail Run (mid-November)..............................505-524-7824
Burn Lake Triathalon (mid-July) 505-541-2554
Christmas Carols & Luminaries on the Plaza (December 24) 505-524-3262
Christmas in July (mid-July).....................505-528-3276
Christmas Lights Guided Night Walk (mid-December)..............................505-524-8032
Cinco de Mayo Fiesta (early May)..................505-524-3262
Dearholt Desert Trail Run (mid-January) 505-524-7824
Diez y Sies de Septembre Fiesta (mid-September) 505-524-3262
Fort Selden Frontier Days (mid-April) 505-526-8911
Fourth of July Celebration (July 4) 505-528-3149
Frontier Days (mid-late April) 505-526-8911
Gus Macker 3-on-3 Basketball Tournament (April) 505-523-2681
Harvest of Fun (mid-September) 505-528-3276
Independence Day Run (July 4) 505-541-2554
Juneteenth Celebration (mid-late June) 505-522-5152
La Viña Wine Festival (early October)..............505-882-7632
Las Cruces International Mariachi Conference (mid-November)..............................505-523-2681
MVTC Triathalon (mid-April) 505-524-7824
New Mexico Wine & Chile War Festival (late May) 505-646-4543
Nostalgia Club Antique & Collectible Show (mid-September & mid-March)..................505-526-8624
Nutcracker Suite (mid-November).................505-523-7325
Oktoberfest Volksmarch (late September) 505-523-7325
Old Fashion Christmas (mid-December) 505-528-3276
Picacho Street Antique & Collectible Flea Market (late May) 505-526-8624
Renaissance Craftfaire (early November) 505-523-6403
Run Old Mesilla (late March) 505-524-7824
Saint Genevieve's Antique & Craft Show (late November)..............................505-526-8624
San Juan Fiesta (late June).......................505-526-8171
Serra Club Antique & Collectible Show (early June)..................................505-526-8624
Southern New Mexico State Fair (late September) 505-524-8612
Turkey Trot (late November)......................505-524-7824
Whole Enchilada Fiesta (early October) 505-524-6832

Las Vegas, Nevada

***County:* Clark**

LAS VEGAS is located in the southern tip of Nevada. Major cities within 100 miles include Boulder City, Nevada and Kingman, Arizona.

Area (Land) .... 83.3 sq mi
Area (Water)............................... 0.1 sq mi
Elevation.................................2,020 ft
Latitude ....36-17-50 N
Longitude.............................. 115-13-64 W
Time Zone ....PST
Area Code...................................... 702

Climate

Las Vegas has a typical desert climate characterized by low humidity, high daytime temperatures and cool evening temperatures. Average summer high temperatures exceed 100 degrees, while evening temperatures drop sharply into the low to mid-70s. Winters are mild, with highs near 60 degrees and lows in the mid-30s. Monthly precipitation totals average a half-inch or less.

Average Temperatures & Precipitation

Temperatures

	Jan	Feb	Mar	Apr	May	Jun	Jul	Aug	Sep	Oct	Nov	Dec
High	57	63	69	78	88	100	106	103	95	82	67	58
Low	34	39	44	51	60	69	76	74	66	54	43	34

Precipitation

	Jan	Feb	Mar	Apr	May	Jun	Jul	Aug	Sep	Oct	Nov	Dec
Inches	0.5	0.5	0.4	0.2	0.3	0.1	0.4	0.5	0.3	0.2	0.3	0.4

History

Originally settled by Native Americans of the Paiute tribe, Las Vegas (Spanish for "the meadows") was named by Spanish explorers who visited the area in the 1840s. The first white settlement in Las Vegas was established during the 1850s by Mormon missionaries. In 1864, the U.S. Army built Fort Baker in the Las Vegas area to protect the westward route to California. During its early years, Las Vegas was developed primarily as an agricultural center for raising livestock.

The railroad, introduced to Las Vegas in 1905, helped to further develop the area, and the city was incorporated in 1911. The early 1900s brought some hardships to Las Vegas, including two devastating floods and a financial crisis that destroyed the area's mining industry. However, two key events in 1931 led to the development of modern-day Las Vegas—the Hoover Dam was constructed along the Colorado River; and gambling was legalized in the state of Nevada. Las Vegas' first casino opened in 1946, and within 30 years, the city's daily gambling revenues exceeded one million dollars.

Sometimes referred to as the "Monte Carlo of the West," present-day Las Vegas is world-renowned as a major gaming and resort center, hosting more than 33 million visitors annually. Boasting more than 120,000 hotel rooms, the city is home to hundreds of hotels, motels, resorts, and casinos, including the world's largest, the $1.85 billion MGM Grand. More than 404,000 people live in Las Vegas, and nearly half of that number are employed in tourism-related industries. One of the nation's fastest growing metropolitan areas, Las Vegas' plentiful job opportunities and favorable tax climate (no state, local, or corporate income taxes) continue to attract thousands of new residents to the area each year.

Population

1990 Census 258,204
1998 Estimate..............................404,288
% Change 56.2
2010 Projection 1,874,431*

Racial/Ethnic Breakdown
White......................................78.4%
Black......................................11.4%
Other......................................10.2%
Hispanic Origin (may be of any race)........12.5%

Age Breakdown
Under 5 years...............................8.3%
5 to 17....................................16.7%
18 to 20....................................3.9%
21 to 24....................................6.2%
25 to 34...................................19.6%
35 to 44...................................15.4%
45 to 54...................................10.7%
55 to 64....................................8.9%
65 to 74....................................6.9%
75+ years...................................3.4%
Median Age..................................32.6

Gender Breakdown
Male.......................................48.4%
Female.....................................51.6%

* *Information given is for Clark County.*

Government

Type of Government: Council-Manager

Las Vegas Business Development Office
400 Las Vegas Blvd S
Las Vegas, NV 89101
Phone: 702-229-6551
Fax: 702-385-3128

Las Vegas City Attorney
400 E Stewart Ave 9th Fl
Las Vegas, NV 89101
Phone: 702-229-6590
Fax: 702-386-1749

Las Vegas City Clerk
400 Stewart Ave
Las Vegas, NV 89101
Phone: 702-229-6311
Fax: 702-382-4803

Las Vegas City Council
400 Stewart Ave 10th Fl
Las Vegas, NV 89101
Phone: 702-229-6405
Fax: 702-382-8558

Las Vegas City Hall
400 Stewart Ave
Las Vegas, NV 89101
Phone: 702-229-6011

Las Vegas Finance & Business Services Dept
400 Stewart Ave 6th Fl
Las Vegas, NV 89101
Phone: 702-229-6321
Fax: 702-383-0769

Las Vegas Fire Dept
500 N Casino Ctr Blvd
Las Vegas, NV 89101
Phone: 702-383-2888
Fax: 702-384-1667

Las Vegas Human Resources Dept
416 N 7th St
Las Vegas, NV 89101
Phone: 702-229-6315
Fax: 702-385-1259

Las Vegas Leisure Services Dept
749 Veterans Memorial Dr
Las Vegas, NV 89101
Phone: 702-229-6297
Fax: 702-383-6306

Las Vegas Mayor
400 Stewart Ave
Las Vegas, NV 89101
Phone: 702-229-6241
Fax: 702-385-7960

Las Vegas Metropolitan Police Dept
3141 E Sunrise Ave
Las Vegas, NV 89101
Phone: 702-229-3111
Fax: 702-229-2729

Las Vegas Planning & Development Dept
731 S 4th St
Las Vegas, NV 89101
Phone: 702-229-6301
Fax: 702-385-7268

Las Vegas Public Works Dept
400 Stewart Ave
Las Vegas, NV 89101
Phone: 702-229-6276
Fax: 702-382-0848

Las Vegas-Clark County Library District
833 Las Vegas Blvd N
Las Vegas, NV 89101
Phone: 702-382-3493
Fax: 702-382-1280

Important Phone Numbers

AAA....702-870-9171
American Express Travel....702-876-1410
Clark County Assessor's Office....702-455-3882
Driver's License/Vehicle Registration Information...702-486-4368
Emergency....911
Entertainment Line....702-225-5554
Events Line....702-892-7576
Greater Las Vegas Assn of Realtors....702-732-8177
Highway Conditions....775-793-1313
HotelDocs....800-468-3537
Medical Referral....702-739-9989
Nevada State Dept of Taxation....702-486-2300
Poison Control Center....702-732-4989
Time/Temp....702-248-4800
Travelers Aid....702-369-4357
Voter Registration Information....702-455-8683
Weather....702-248-4800

Information Sources

Better Business Bureau Serving Southern Nevada
5595 W Spring Mountain Rd
Las Vegas, NV 89146
www.lasvegas.bbb.org
Phone: 702-440-3003
Fax: 702-320-4560

Clark County
200 S 3rd St
Las Vegas, NV 89101
www.co.clark.nv.us
Phone: 702-455-3156
Fax: 702-455-4929

Las Vegas Chamber of Commerce
3720 Howard Hughes Pkwy
Las Vegas, NV 89109
www.lvchamber.com
Phone: 702-735-1616
Fax: 702-735-2011

Las Vegas Convention & Visitors Authority
3150 Paradise Rd
Las Vegas, NV 89109
www.lasvegas24hours.com
Phone: 702-892-0711
Fax: 702-892-2824
TF: 800-332-5333

Las Vegas Convention Center
3150 Paradise Rd
Las Vegas, NV 89109
Phone: 702-892-0711
Fax: 702-892-2824
TF: 800-332-5333

Nevada Development Authority
3773 Howard Hughes Pkwy Suite 140 S
Las Vegas, NV 89109
www.nevadadevelopment.org
Phone: 702-791-0000
Fax: 702-796-6483
TF: 888-668-2937

Online Resources

4LasVegas.com
www.4lasvegas.com

About.com Guide to Las Vegas
lasvegas.about.com/local/southwestus/lasvegas

Access America Las Vegas
lasvegas.accessamer.com

Anthill City Guide Las Vegas
www.anthill.com/city.asp?city=lasvegas

Area Guide Las Vegas
lasvegas.areaguides.net

Best Read Guide Las Vegas
bestreadguide.com/lasvegas

Casino City Casino Directory
www.casinocity.com/

City Knowledge Las Vegas
www.cityknowledge.com/nv_lasvegas.htm

CitySearch Las Vegas
lasvegas.citysearch.com

CityTravelGuide.com Las Vegas
www.citytravelguide.com/las-vegas.htm

DesertUSA Guide to Las Vegas
www.desertusa.com/Cities/nv/lasvegas.html

DigitalCity Las Vegas
home.digitalcity.com/lasvegas

Excite.com Las Vegas City Guide
www.excite.com/travel/countries/united_states/nevada/las_vegas

Fabulous Las Vegas
www.intermind.net/im/lasvegas.html

Gay Las Vegas
www.gayvegas.com/

Gayot's Guide Restaurant Search Las Vegas
www.perrier.com/restaurants/gayot.asp?area=LSV

HotelGuide Las Vegas
lasvegas.hotelguide.net

In-Vegas.com
www.in-vegas.com/

Info Las Vegas
www.ilv.com

InfoVegas
www.infovegas.com/

Insider Viewpoint of Las Vegas
www.insidervlv.com/

Insiders' Guide to Las Vegas
www.insiders.com/lasvegas/

Las Vegas Entertainment Guide
www.lvindex.com

Las Vegas Golf Guide
las-vegas-golf.com

Las Vegas Leisure Guide
www.pcap.com/lasvegas.html

Las Vegas Life
www.lasvegaslife.com/

Las Vegas Online Entertainment Guide
www.lvol.com

Lasvegas.com
www.lasvegas.com/

Locals Love Las Vegas
www.localslovelasvegas.com

Lodging.com Las Vegas Nevada
www.lodging.com/auto/guides/las_vegas-area-nv.html

MetroGuide Las Vegas
lasvegas.metroguide.net

MetroVille Las Vegas
lasvegas.metroville.com

Move to Las Vegas Relocation Directory
www.movetolasvegas.com

Night on the Town
www.nightonthetown.com/

Online City Guide to Las Vegas
www.olcg.com/nv/lasvegas/index.html

Rough Guide Travel Las Vegas
travel.roughguides.com/content/1280/

Savvy Diner Guide to Las Vegas Restaurants
www.savvydiner.com/lasvegas/

Time Out Las Vegas
www.timeout.com/lasvegas/

Vegas Deluxe
www.vegasdeluxe.com

Vegas Pages
vegaspages.com/

Vegas.com
www.vegas.com/

VegasGuide.com
www.vegasguide.com

Virtual Vegas
www.virtualvegas.com

Virtual Voyages Las Vegas
www.virtualvoyages.com/usa/nv/vegas/vegas.sht

What's On in Las Vegas Magazine
www.whats-on.com/

Area Communities

Communities in the Las Vegas area with populations greater than 10,000 include:

Boulder City
PO Box 61350
Boulder City, NV 89006
Phone: 702-293-9208
Fax: 702-293-9245

Henderson
240 S Water St
Henderson, NV 89015
Phone: 702-565-2323
Fax: 702-565-3273

Mesquite
10 E Mesquite Blvd
Mesquite, NV 89027
Phone: 702-346-5295
Fax: 702-346-2908

North Las Vegas
2200 Civic Center Dr
North Las Vegas, NV 89030
Phone: 702-633-1000
Fax: 702-649-3846

Economy

Tourism and conventions dominate Las Vegas' economy—the city hosts more than 33 million tourists and more than 3 million convention delegates annually. Eleven of Clark County's top 15 employers are hotels and/or casinos, and more than 164,000 area residents are employed in tourism-related industries. Government also plays an important role in the Las Vegas economy. In addition to the major employers listed below, Nevada State Government is among the area's largest.

Unemployment Rate 4.4%*
Per Capita Income $26,212*
Median Family Income $35,300

** Information given is for Clark County.*

Principal Industries & Number of Wage Earners

Clark County - 1998

Construction 65,202
Finance, Insurance, & Real Estate 31,033
Government 62,859
Manufacturing 19,380
Mining 695
Retail Trade 105,764
Services 271,716
Transportation, Communications, & Public Utilities 32,331
Wholesale Trade 20,306

Major Employers

Bally's Las Vegas Casino & Resort Phone: 702-739-4111
PO Box 93898 Fax: 702-739-4405
Las Vegas, NV 89193 TF: 800-634-3434
www.ballyslv.com

Bellagio Hotel & Casino Phone: 702-693-7111
3600 Las Vegas Blvd S Fax: 702-693-8546
Las Vegas, NV 89109 TF: 888-987-6667
www.bellagiolasvegas.com

Caesars Palace Phone: 702-731-7110
3570 Las Vegas Blvd S Fax: 702-731-6636
Las Vegas, NV 89109 TF: 800-634-6661
www.caesars.com/palace/default.html

Clark County Phone: 702-455-3156
200 S 3rd St Fax: 702-455-4929
Las Vegas, NV 89101
www.co.clark.nv.us

Clark County School District Phone: 702-799-5311
2832 E Flamingo Rd Fax: 702-799-5505
Las Vegas, NV 89121
www.ccsd.net

Excalibur Hotel & Casino Phone: 702-597-7777
3850 Las Vegas Blvd S Fax: 702-597-7009
Las Vegas, NV 89109 TF: 800-937-7777
www.excalibur-casino.com

Luxor Hotel & Casino Phone: 702-262-4000
3900 Las Vegas Blvd S Fax: 702-262-4404
Las Vegas, NV 89119 TF: 800-288-1000
www.luxor.com

Mandalay Resort Group Phone: 702-632-7777
3950 Las Vegas Blvd Fax: 702-632-8805
Las Vegas, NV 89119 TF: 877-632-7700
www.mandalayresortgroup.com

MGM Grand Hotel & Casino Phone: 702-891-1111
3799 Las Vegas Blvd S Fax: 702-891-3036
Las Vegas, NV 89109 TF: 800-929-1111
www.mgmgrand.com

Mirage The Phone: 702-791-7111
3400 Las Vegas Blvd S Fax: 702-791-7414
Las Vegas, NV 89109 TF: 800-627-6667
www.themirage.com

Rio Suite Hotel & Casino Phone: 702-252-7777
3700 W Flamingo Rd Fax: 702-579-6565
Las Vegas, NV 89103 TF: 888-746-7482
E-mail: riorita@playrio.com
www.playrio.com

Treasure Island Phone: 702-894-7111
3300 Las Vegas Blvd S Fax: 702-894-7414
Las Vegas, NV 89109
www.treasureislandlasvegas.com

University of Nevada Las Vegas Phone: 702-895-3011
4505 S Maryland Pkwy Fax: 702-895-1118
Las Vegas, NV 89154 TF: 800-334-8658
E-mail: witter@ccmail.nevada.edu
www.unlv.edu

Venetian Casino Resorts LLC Phone: 702-733-5000
3355 Las Vegas Blvd S Fax: 702-733-5190
Las Vegas, NV 89109 TF: 888-283-6423
www.venetian.com

Quality of Living Indicators

Total Crime Index 47,828
(rates per 100,000 inhabitants)

Violent Crime
Murder/manslaughter 109
Forcible rape 532
Robbery 3,121
Aggravated assault 2,371

Property Crime
Burglary 10,130
Larceny theft 21,793
Motor vehicle theft 9,772

Cost of Living Index 104.6
(national average = 100)

Median Home Price $130,800

Education

Public Schools

Clark County School District Phone: 702-799-5311
2832 E Flamingo Rd Fax: 702-799-5505
Las Vegas, NV 89121
www.ccsd.net

Number of Schools
Elementary 151
Middle 35
High 31

Student/Teacher Ratio
All Grades 19.3:1

Private Schools

Number of Schools (all grades) .... 25+

Colleges & Universities

Community College of Southern Nevada
Cheyenne Campus Phone: 702-651-4000
3200 E Cheyenne Ave Fax: 702-643-1474
North Las Vegas, NV 89030
www.ccsn.nevada.edu/general/campuses/Cheyenne

University of Nevada Las Vegas Phone: 702-895-3011
4505 S Maryland Pkwy Fax: 702-895-1118
Las Vegas, NV 89154 TF: 800-334-8658
E-mail: witter@ccmail.nevada.edu
www.unlv.edu

Hospitals

Desert Springs Hospital Phone: 702-733-8800
2075 E Flamingo Rd Fax: 702-369-7836
Las Vegas, NV 89119
www.valleyhealthsystem.org/facilities/desert

Saint Rose Dominican Hospital Phone: 702-564-2622
102 E Lake Mead Dr Fax: 702-564-4699
Henderson, NV 89015

Sunrise Hospital & Medical Center Phone: 702-731-8000
3186 S Maryland Pkwy Fax: 702-731-8668
Las Vegas, NV 89109
www.sunrisehospital.com

University Medical Center Phone: 702-383-2000
1800 W Charleston Blvd Fax: 702-383-2067
Las Vegas, NV 89102
www.umc-cares.org

Valley Hospital Medical Center Phone: 702-388-4000
620 Shadow Ln Fax: 702-388-4636
Las Vegas, NV 89106

Transportation

Airport(s)

McCarran International Airport (LAS)
7 miles S of downtown (approx 20 minutes) 702-261-5743

Mass Transit

Citizens Area Transit
$1.50 Base fare................................702-228-7433
Freemont Street Downtown Neighborhood Trolley
$.50 Base fare.................................702-229-6025
Strip The Trolley
$1.30 Base fare................................702-382-1404

Rail/Bus

Greyhound Bus Station Phone: 702-384-8009
200 S Main St TF: 800-231-2222
Las Vegas, NV 89101

Utilities

Electricity
Nevada Power Co...............................702-367-5555
www.nevadapower.com

Gas
Southwest Gas Corp...........................702-365-1555
www.swgas.com

Water
Las Vegas Valley Water District.................702-870-4194

Garbage Collection/Recycling
Republic Services 702-735-5151

Telecommunications

Telephone
Sprint 702-244-7400
www.sprint.com

Cable Television
Cox Communications...........................702-383-4000
www.cox.com

Internet Service Providers (ISPs)
@wizard.com 702-317-2001
www.wizard.com
Access Nevada Inc.............................702-294-0480
www.accessnv.com
Skylink Networks Inc..........................702-260-0900
www.skylink.net

Banks

American Bankcorp Phone: 702-891-8700
4335 Industrial Rd Fax: 702-891-8787
Las Vegas, NV 89103

Bank of America NA Phone: 702-386-1000
300 S 4th St Fax: 702-654-7820
Las Vegas, NV 89101 TF: 800-388-2265

Bank of Commerce Phone: 702-876-7429
5811 W Sahara Ave Fax: 702-889-8212
Las Vegas, NV 89146
E-mail: info@bankofcommerce-nevada.com
www.bankofcommerce-nevada.com

Bank of the West Phone: 702-733-2199
1771 E Flamingo Rd Suite 213-A Fax: 702-733-4967
Las Vegas, NV 89119

BankWest of Nevada Phone: 702-248-4200
2700 W Sahara Ave Fax: 702-362-2026
Las Vegas, NV 89102

Business Bank of Nevada Phone: 702-220-3302
6085 W Twain Ave Fax: 702-220-3807
Las Vegas, NV 89103

California Federal Bank FSB Phone: 800-843-2265
103 S Rainbow Blvd
Las Vegas, NV 89128

Citibank Nevada NA Phone: 702-796-7379
3900 Paradise Rd Suite M Fax: 702-796-8239
Las Vegas, NV 89109

Colonial Bank Phone: 702-258-9990
2820 W Charleston Blvd Suite 5 Fax: 702-870-6313
Las Vegas, NV 89102

Community Bank of Nevada
1400 S Rainbow Blvd
Las Vegas, NV 89146
Phone: 702-878-0700
Fax: 702-878-1060

First Republic Bank
6700 W Charleston Blvd
Las Vegas, NV 89146
Phone: 702-880-3700
Fax: 702-880-3600

First Security Bank of Nevada
530 Las Vegas Blvd S
Las Vegas, NV 89101
Phone: 702-952-7681
Fax: 702-952-7685

Nevada First Bank
2800 W Sahara Ave Suite 1-A
Las Vegas, NV 89102
Phone: 702-310-4000
Fax: 702-310-4040

Nevada State Bank
201 S 4th St
Las Vegas, NV 89101
Phone: 702-383-4111
Fax: 702-383-4307
TF: 800-727-4743

Pioneer Citizens Bank of Nevada
8400 W Lake Mead Blvd
Las Vegas, NV 89128
Phone: 702-242-1279
Fax: 702-242-5573

Silver State Bank
170 S Rainbow Blvd
Las Vegas, NV 89128
Phone: 702-968-8400
Fax: 702-968-8415

Sun West Bank
5830 W Flamingo Rd
Las Vegas, NV 89103
Phone: 702-949-2265
Fax: 702-949-2299

US Bank NA
801 E Charleston Blvd
Las Vegas, NV 89104
Phone: 702-387-1919
Fax: 702-382-9062
TF: 800-872-2657

Wells Fargo Bank NA
3300 W Sahara Ave
Las Vegas, NV 89102
Phone: 702-765-3009
Fax: 702-765-3035

Shopping

Bally's Shopping Arcade
3645 Las Vegas Blvd S
Las Vegas, NV 89109
Phone: 702-739-4111

Belz Factory Outlet World
7400 Las Vegas Blvd S
Las Vegas, NV 89123
Phone: 702-896-5599
Fax: 702-896-4626

Boulevard Mall
3528 S Maryland Pkwy
Las Vegas, NV 89109
E-mail: blvdmall@vegas.infi.net
www.blvdmall.com
Phone: 702-735-8268
Fax: 702-732-9197

Fantastic Indoor Swap Meet
1717 S Decatur Blvd
Las Vegas, NV 89102
Phone: 702-877-0087
Fax: 702-877-3102

Fashion Show Mall
3200 Las Vegas Blvd S
Las Vegas, NV 89109
www.thefashionshow.com/
Phone: 702-369-8382
Fax: 702-369-1613

Forum Shops at Caesars Palace
3500 Las Vegas Blvd S
Las Vegas, NV 89109
Phone: 702-893-4800
Fax: 702-893-3009

Galleria at Sunset
1300 W Sunset Rd
Henderson, NV 89014
Phone: 702-434-0202
Fax: 702-434-0259

Las Vegas Factory Stores
9155 Las Vegas Blvd S Suite 200
Las Vegas, NV 89123
Phone: 702-897-9090
Fax: 702-897-9094

Masquerade Village
3700 W Flamingo Rd Rio Suite Hotel
Las Vegas, NV 89103
Phone: 702-252-7777

Meadows Mall
4300 Meadows Ln
Las Vegas, NV 89107
Phone: 702-878-4849
Fax: 702-878-3138

Media

Newspapers and Magazines

Las Vegas Business Press
3335 Wynn Rd
Las Vegas, NV 89102
Phone: 702-871-6780
Fax: 702-871-3740

Las Vegas Review-Journal*
PO Box 70
Las Vegas, NV 89125
www.lvrj.com
Phone: 702-383-0211
Fax: 702-383-4676

Las Vegas Sun*
800 S Valley View Blvd
Las Vegas, NV 89107
www.lasvegassun.com
Phone: 702-385-3111
Fax: 702-383-7264

Las Vegas Weekly
2290 Corporate Circle Dr Suite 250
Henderson, NV 89014
E-mail: lasvegas@lasvegasweekly.com
www.lasvegasweekly.com
Phone: 702-990-2400
Fax: 702-990-2424

**Indicates major daily newspapers*

Television

KBLR-TV Ch 39 (Tele)
5000 W Oakey Suite B-2
Las Vegas, NV 89146
Phone: 702-258-0039
Fax: 702-258-0556

KFBT-TV Ch 33 (Ind)
3830 S Jones Blvd
Las Vegas, NV 89103
E-mail: ch33inc@aol.com
pax.net/KFBT
Phone: 702-873-0033
Fax: 702-382-1351

KINC-TV Ch 15 (Uni)
500 Pilot Rd Suite D
Las Vegas, NV 89119
Phone: 702-434-0015
Fax: 702-434-0527

KLAS-TV Ch 8 (CBS)
3228 Channel 8 Dr
Las Vegas, NV 89109
E-mail: klas@infi.net
www.klas-tv.com
Phone: 702-792-8888
Fax: 702-734-7437

KLVX-TV Ch 10 (PBS)
4210 Channel 10 Dr
Las Vegas, NV 89119
www.klvx.org
Phone: 702-799-1010
Fax: 702-799-5586

KTNV-TV Ch 13 (ABC) Phone: 702-876-1313
3355 S Valley View Blvd Fax: 702-876-2237
Las Vegas, NV 89102
E-mail: ktnv13@ktnv.com
www.ktnv.com

KVBC-TV Ch 3 (NBC) Phone: 702-642-3333
PO Box 44169 Fax: 702-657-3152
Las Vegas, NV 89116
E-mail: ch3@kvbc.com
www.wherenewscomesfirst.com

KVVU-TV Ch 5 (Fox) Phone: 702-435-5555
25 TV 5 Dr Fax: 702-451-4220
Henderson, NV 89014
www.kvvutv.com

KVWB-TV Ch 21 (WB) Phone: 702-382-2121
3830 S Jones Blvd Fax: 702-382-1351
Las Vegas, NV 89103
E-mail: info@wb21.com
www.wb21.com

Radio

KBAD-AM 920 kHz (Sports) Phone: 702-876-1460
4660 S Decatur Blvd Fax: 702-876-6685
Las Vegas, NV 89103

KBOX-AM 1280 (Span) Phone: 702-732-1664
953 E Sahara Ave Suite 255 Fax: 702-732-1937
Las Vegas, NV 89104

KCEP-FM 88.1 MHz (NPR) Phone: 702-648-4218
330 W Washington Ave Fax: 702-647-0803
Las Vegas, NV 89106
www.kcepfm88.com

KDWN-AM 720 kHz (N/T) Phone: 702-385-7212
1 Main St Fax: 702-385-7990
Las Vegas, NV 89101
E-mail: kdwn@kdwn.com
www.kdwn.com

KENO-AM 1460 kHz (Sports) Phone: 702-876-1460
4660 S Decatur Blvd Fax: 702-876-6685
Las Vegas, NV 89103

KFMS-AM 1410 kHz (Ctry) Phone: 702-732-7753
1130 Desert Inn Rd Fax: 702-732-4890
Las Vegas, NV 89109

KFMS-FM 101.9 MHz (Ctry) Phone: 702-732-7753
1130 E Desert Inn Rd Fax: 702-792-9018
Las Vegas, NV 89109
www.kfms.com

KISF-FM 103.5 (Span) Phone: 702-795-1035
6767 W Tropicana Ave Suite 102 Fax: 702-284-6403
Las Vegas, NV 89103
www.lanueva1035.com

KJUL-FM 104.3 MHz (Nost) Phone: 702-730-0300
1455 E Tropicana Ave Suite 800 Fax: 702-736-8447
Las Vegas, NV 89119
E-mail: kjul@kjul.com
www.kjul.com

KKLZ-FM 96.3 MHz (CR) Phone: 702-739-9600
1455 E Tropicana Ave Suite 800 Fax: 702-736-8447
Las Vegas, NV 89119
www.kklz.net

KKVV-AM 1060 kHz (Rel) Phone: 702-731-5588
3185 S Highland Dr Suite 13 Fax: 702-731-5851
Las Vegas, NV 89109
E-mail: kkvvradio@aol.com
www.kkvv.com

KLAV-AM 1230 kHz (N/T) Phone: 702-796-1230
1810 Weldon Pl Fax: 702-796-7433
Las Vegas, NV 89104
E-mail: klavradio@aol.com
www.klav1230am.com

KLSQ-AM 870 kHz (Span) Phone: 702-367-3322
6767 W Tropicana Ave Suite 102 Fax: 702-284-6475
Las Vegas, NV 89103

KLUC-FM 98.5 MHz (Rock) Phone: 702-253-9800
6655 Sahara Ave Suite D208 Fax: 702-889-7398
Las Vegas, NV 89146
E-mail: music@kluc.com
www.kluc.com

KMXB-FM 94.1 MHz (AC) Phone: 702-889-5100
6655 W Sahara Ave Suite C-216 Fax: 702-257-2936
Las Vegas, NV 89102
www.mix941.fm

KMZQ-FM 100.5 MHz (AC) Phone: 702-889-5100
6655 W Sahara Ave Suite C-216 Fax: 702-257-2936
Las Vegas, NV 89102

KNPR-FM 89.5 MHz (NPR) Phone: 702-258-9895
1289 S Torrey Pines Dr Fax: 702-258-5646
Las Vegas, NV 89146
E-mail: info@knpr.org
www.knpr.org

KNUU-AM 970 kHz (N/T) Phone: 702-735-8644
1455 E Tropicana Ave Suite 101 Fax: 702-735-8184
Las Vegas, NV 89119

KOMP-FM 92.3 MHz (Rock) Phone: 702-876-1460
4660 S Decatur Blvd Fax: 702-876-6685
Las Vegas, NV 89103
E-mail: komp@infi.net
www.komp.com/komp/

KQOL-FM 93.1 MHz (Oldies) Phone: 702-732-7753
1130 E Desert Inn Rd Fax: 702-792-0573
Las Vegas, NV 89109
www.kqol.com

KSFN-AM 1140 kHz (Oldies) Phone: 702-253-9800
6655 W Sahara Ave Suite D-208 Fax: 702-889-7384
Las Vegas, NV 89146

KSNE-FM 106.5 MHz (AC) Phone: 702-732-7753
1130 E Desert Inn Rd Fax: 702-734-1065
Las Vegas, NV 89109
www.ksne.com

KSTJ-FM 105.5 MHz (AC) Phone: 702-730-0300
1455 E Tropicana Ave Suite 800 Fax: 702-736-8447
Las Vegas, NV 89119
www.star1055.net

KVBC-FM 105.1 MHz (N/T) Phone: 702-657-3105
1500 Foremaster Ln Fax: 702-657-3442
Las Vegas, NV 89101

KWNR-FM 95.5 MHz (Ctry) Phone: 702-732-7753
1130 E Desert Inn Rd Fax: 702-733-0433
Las Vegas, NV 89109
www.kwnr.com

KXNT-AM 840 kHz (N/T) Phone: 702-364-8400
6655 W Sahara Ave Suite D-208 Fax: 702-889-7384
Las Vegas, NV 89146
www.kxnt.com

KXPT-FM 97.1 MHz (CR) Phone: 702-876-1460
4660 S Decatur Blvd Fax: 702-876-1886
Las Vegas, NV 89103
www.point97.com

KXTE-FM 107.5 MHz (Alt) Phone: 702-257-1075
6655 W Sahara Ave Suite C202 Fax: 702-889-7575
Las Vegas, NV 89146
www.xtremeradio.com

Attractions

The Strip in Las Vegas features many of the casinos, luxury hotels, nightclubs, and big name entertainers' shows that have made the city famous. While names like Bally's and Caesars Palace are widely recognized, newer and larger hotels have recently gained public attention. The Luxor is a 30-story pyramid hotel and casino with three levels of entertainment; and at Treasure Island visitors are greeted with an authentic pirate battle. Now the world's largest hotel, Las Vegas' MGM Grand has more than 5,000 rooms and a 33-acre theme park. Other attractions in the Las Vegas area include Hoover Dam and the Lake Mead National Recreation Area.

Adventuredome Phone: 702-734-0410
2880 Las Vegas Blvd S Fax: 702-792-2846
Las Vegas, NV 89109
E-mail: info@adventuredome.com
www.adventuredome.com

Bonnie Springs Ranch Phone: 702-875-4191
1 Gunfighter Ln Fax: 702-875-4424
Las Vegas, NV 89004
E-mail: springs@vegas.net
www.bonniesprings.com

Boulder City/Hoover Dam Museum Phone: 702-294-1988
1305 Arizona St Fax: 702-294-4380
Boulder City, NV 89005

Caesars Palace Omnimax Theater Phone: 702-731-7900
3570 Las Vegas Blvd S
Las Vegas, NV 89109

Cirque du Soleil 'O' Phone: 702-693-7790
c/o Bellagio Hotel 3600 Las Vegas Blvd S Fax: 702-693-7768
Las Vegas, NV 89109
www.cirquedusoleil.com/en/piste/o/index.html

Cirque du Soleil Mystère Phone: 702-894-7790
c/o Treasure Island at the Mirage 3300 Las Vegas Blvd S Fax: 702-894-7789
Las Vegas, NV 89109
www.cirquedusoleil.com/en/piste/mystere/index.html

Clark County Museum Phone: 702-455-7955
1830 S Boulder Hwy Fax: 702-455-7948
Henderson, NV 89015

Ethel M Chocolate Factory Phone: 702-458-8864
2 Cactus Garden Dr Fax: 800-392-2587
Henderson, NV 89014 TF: 800-438-4356
www.ethelm.com

Floyd Lamb State Park Phone: 702-486-5413
9200 Tule Springs Rd Fax: 702-486-5423
Las Vegas, NV 89131

Freemont Street Experience Phone: 702-678-5777
Fremont St-betw Main St & Las Vegas Blvd Fax: 702-678-5611
Las Vegas, NV 89101 TF: 800-249-3559
www.pcap.com/frmntexp.htm

Guinness World of Records Museum Phone: 702-792-3766
2780 Las Vegas Blvd S Fax: 702-792-0530
Las Vegas, NV 89109

Ham Artemus W Concert Hall Phone: 702-895-3535
4505 Maryland Pkwy PO Box 455005 Fax: 702-895-4714
Las Vegas, NV 89154
E-mail: romito@nevada.edu
pac.nevada.edu

Hoover Dam Phone: 702-293-8367
Rt 93
Boulder City, NV 89006
www.hooverdam.com

Imperial Palace Auto Collection Phone: 702-731-3311
3535 Las Vegas Blvd S Fax: 702-369-7430
Las Vegas, NV 89109

Lake Mead National Recreation Area Phone: 702-293-8920
601 Nevada Hwy Fax: 702-293-8936
Boulder City, NV 89005
www.nps.gov/lame/

Las Vegas Art Museum Phone: 702-360-8000
9600 W Sahara Ave Fax: 702-360-8080
Las Vegas, NV 89117
www.lastplace.com/EXHIBITS/LVAM/index.htm

Las Vegas Natural History Museum Phone: 702-384-3466
900 Las Vegas Blvd N Fax: 702-384-5343
Las Vegas, NV 89101
vegaswebworld.com/lvnathistory

Lee's Ron World of Clowns Phone: 702-434-1700
330 Carousel Pkwy Fax: 702-434-4310
Henderson, NV 89014

Liberace Museum Phone: 702-798-5595
1775 E Tropicana Ave Fax: 702-798-7386
Las Vegas, NV 89119
www.liberace.org/museum.html

Lied Discovery Children's Museum Phone: 702-382-3445
833 Las Vegas Blvd N Fax: 702-382-0592
Las Vegas, NV 89101

Lost City Museum of Archeology Phone: 702-397-2193
721 S Moapa Valley Blvd Fax: 702-397-8987
Overton, NV 89040
enos.comnett.net/~kolson

Luxor IMAX Theatre Phone: 702-262-4555
3900 Las Vegas Blvd S
Las Vegas, NV 89119
www.luxor.com/imax.html#imax

Madame Tussaud's Wax Museum Phone: 702-733-5000
3355 Las Vegas Blvd S Venetian Hotel & Casino
Las Vegas, NV 89109

Magic & Movie Hall of Fame Phone: 702-737-1343
3555 S Las Vegas Blvd Fax: 702-737-3846
Las Vegas, NV 89109

MGM Grand Adventures Theme Park Phone: 702-891-7979
3799 Las Vegas Blvd S Fax: 702-891-7831
Las Vegas, NV 89109

Nevada Ballet Theatre Phone: 702-898-6306
1651 Inner Cir Fax: 702-804-0364
Las Vegas, NV 89134

Nevada Dance Theater Phone: 702-895-2787
4505 S Maryland Pkwy Performing Arts Center
Las Vegas, NV 89154

Nevada Opera Theatre Phone: 702-699-9775
4080 Paradise Rd Suite 15 Fax: 702-699-9831
Las Vegas, NV 89109

Nevada State Museum & Historical Society Phone: 702-486-5205
700 Twin Lakes Dr Fax: 702-486-5172
Las Vegas, NV 89107
dmla.clan.lib.nv.us/docs/museums/lv/vegas.htm

Old Las Vegas Mormon Fort State Historic Park Phone: 702-486-3511
500 E Washington Blvd
Las Vegas, NV 89158

Red Rock Canyon National Conservation Area Phone: 702-363-1921
HCR 33 Box 5500 Fax: 702-363-6779
Las Vegas, NV 89124

Shark Reef at Mandalay Bay Phone: 702-632-7777
3950 Las Vegas Blvd S Fax: 702-632-7234
Las Vegas, NV 89119 TF: 877-632-7000
www.mandalaybay.com

Southern Nevada Zoological Society Phone: 702-648-5955
1775 N Rancho Dr Fax: 702-648-5955
Las Vegas, NV 89106

Treasure Island Phone: 702-894-7111
3300 Las Vegas Blvd S Fax: 702-894-7414
Las Vegas, NV 89109
www.treasureislandlasvegas.com

University of Nevada Las Vegas Barrick Museum of Natural History Phone: 702-895-3381
4505 S Maryland Pkwy Fax: 702-895-3094
Las Vegas, NV 89154
hrcweb.lv-hrc.nevada.edu

University of Nevada Las Vegas Performing Arts Center Phone: 702-895-2787
4505 Maryland Pkwy Fax: 702-895-1940
Las Vegas, NV 89154
pac.nevada.edu

Valley of Fire State Park Phone: 702-397-2088
I-15 N to exit 75
Overton, NV 89040

Wet 'n Wild Phone: 702-734-0088
2601 NW Las Vegas Blvd Fax: 702-765-9777
Las Vegas, NV 89109
www.wetnwild.com/las-vegas

Whipple Reed Cultural Arts Center Phone: 702-229-6211
821 Las Vegas Blvd N Fax: 702-382-5199
Las Vegas, NV 89101

World of Coca-Cola Las Vegas Phone: 702-270-5975
3785 Las Vegas Blvd S Fax: 702-740-5439
Las Vegas, NV 89109 TF: 800-720-2653

Sports Teams & Facilities

Las Vegas Motor Speedway Phone: 702-644-4444
7000 N Las Vegas Blvd Fax: 702-632-8015
Las Vegas, NV 89115 TF: 800-644-4444
E-mail: media@lvms.com
www.lvms.com

Las Vegas Stars (baseball) Phone: 702-386-7200
850 Las Vegas Blvd N Cashman Field Fax: 702-386-7214
Las Vegas, NV 89101
E-mail: jsacc@lasvegasstars.com
www.lasvegasstars.com

Las Vegas Thunder (hockey) Phone: 702-798-7825
4505 S Maryland Pkwy Thomas & Mack Ctr Fax: 702-798-9464
Las Vegas, NV 89154

MGM Grand Garden Arena Phone: 702-891-7800
3799 Las Vegas Blvd S Fax: 702-891-7831
Las Vegas, NV 89109 TF: 800-929-1111

Thomas & Mack Center/Sam Boyd Stadium Phone: 702-895-3761
4505 S Maryland Pkwy Box 45000 Fax: 702-895-1099
Las Vegas, NV 89154 TF: 800-406-2566
www.thomasandmack.com

Annual Events

Big League Weekends (early April) 702-386-7200
Columbus Day Parade (mid-October) 702-892-0711
Comdex Computer Show (mid-November)..........781-449-6600
Fremont Street Holiday Festival (late November)..............................800-249-3559
International Food Festival (May) 702-258-8961
International Mariachi Festival (mid-September) 800-637-1006
Las Vegas Bowl (late December) 702-895-3900
Las Vegas International Bike Festival & Expo (mid-October)................................702-792-9430
Las Vegas International Marathon & Half-Marathon (February)..................................702-876-3870
Las Vegas Invitational PGA Golf Tournament (mid-May) 702-242-3000

Las Vegas Jaycees State Fair (early October)........702-457-8832
Las Vegas Mardi Gras (mid-February)..............702-678-5777
Las Vegas Senior Classic (late April)...............702-242-3000
National Finals Rodeo (early-mid-December) 702-895-3900
Native American Arts Festival (early April) 702-455-7955
Parade of Lights (early December).................702-293-2034
Winston Cup Race (early March) 702-644-4444
World Series of Poker (late April-mid-May).........702-366-7397

Lexington, Kentucky

***County:* Fayette**

LEXINGTON is located in the Bluegrass region of north central Kentucky. Major cities within 100 miles include Frankfort and Louisville, Kentucky and Cincinnati, Ohio.

Area (Land) .... 284.5 sq mi
Area (Water)................................ 1.0 sq mi
Elevation...................................... 983 ft
Latitude ....38-04-92 N
Longitude................................ 84-50-03 W
Time Zone ....EST
Area Code.. 859

Climate

Lexington's climate features four distinct seasons. Winters are cold, with average daytime temperatures in the upper 30s to low 40s, and average nighttime lows in the mid-20s. On average, Lexington receives just over 16 inches of snow annually. Summer days are warm, with average highs in the mid-80s, while evenings cool down comfortably into the mid-60s. Precipitation is distributed fairly evenly throughout the year.

Average Temperatures & Precipitation

Temperatures

	Jan	Feb	Mar	Apr	May	Jun	Jul	Aug	Sep	Oct	Nov	Dec
High	39	44	55	66	74	83	86	85	78	67	55	44
Low	22	25	35	44	54	62	66	64	58	46	37	28

Precipitation

	Jan	Feb	Mar	Apr	May	Jun	Jul	Aug	Sep	Oct	Nov	Dec
Inches	2.9	3.2	4.4	3.9	4.5	3.7	5.0	3.9	3.2	2.6	3.4	4.0

History

The area known today as Lexington was founded in 1775 as a campsite at McConnell Springs by a group of frontiersman led by Colonel Robert Patterson. The settlement was named for the first battle of the American Revolution, the Battle of Lexington (Massachusetts), which had occurred only a few months earlier. At the time of Lexington's founding, the region was known as the Kentucky District of Virginia. In 1780, the Virginia Legislature divided the district into three counties, one of which was named Fayette County in honor of French war hero and supporter of the American Revolution, Marquis de Lafayette, and Lexington was chosen as its county seat. Virginia released the district in 1792, and Kentucky was granted statehood. The first Kentucky State Legislature met in Lexington later that year.

Lexington was incorporated as a city in 1832. Often referred to as the "Athens of the West," the city grew as a cultural, industrial, and trade center. Although hemp was Lexington's primary crop during its early years, tobacco gained dominance after the 1870s and Lexington soon became the largest burley tobacco market in the world.

Lexington continued to grow throughout the 20th Century, and in 1974 the City of Lexington and Fayette County governments merged to form Kentucky's first and only consolidated urban county government. With a population exceeding 241,000 today, Lexington-Fayette County is Kentucky's second largest city. Lexington stands today as the educational, health care, retail, industrial, and cultural center of Kentucky's Bluegrass region.

Population

1990 Census 225,366*
1998 Estimate..............................241,749*
% Change 7.3*
2010 Projection 257,621

Racial/Ethnic Breakdown
White....................................83.8%
Black 13.8%
Other 2.4%
Hispanic Origin (may be of any race) 1.3%

Age Breakdown
Under 17 years............................21.4%
18 to 24.................................14.0%
25 to 44.................................35.1%
45 to 64.................................19.6%
65+......................................9.8%
Median Age................................32.0

Gender Breakdown
Male.....................................48.0%
Female...................................52.0%

** Information given is for Lexington-Fayette County.*

Government

Type of Government: Mayor-County Council (consolidated)

Lexington Chief Administrative Officer
200 E Main St 12th Fl
Lexington, KY 40507
Phone: 859-258-3155
Fax: 859-258-3894

Lexington City Hall
200 E Main St Fayette Government Ctr
Lexington, KY 40507
Phone: 859-258-3000
Fax: 859-258-3250

Lexington Coroner
247 E 2nd St
Lexington, KY 40507
Phone: 859-252-5691
Fax: 859-259-1858

Lexington Council Clerk
200 E Main St 1st Fl
Lexington, KY 40507
Phone: 859-258-3393
Fax: 859-258-3393

Lexington Finance Dept
200 E Main St
Lexington, KY 40507
Phone: 859-258-3300
Fax: 859-258-3385

Lexington Fire & Emergency Services Div
219 E 3rd St
Lexington, KY 40508
Phone: 859-231-5649
Fax: 859-281-6136

Lexington Human Resources Div
200 E Main St 2nd Fl
Lexington, KY 40507
Phone: 859-258-3051
Fax: 859-258-3059

Lexington Law Dept
200 E Main St 11th Fl
Lexington, KY 40507
Phone: 859-258-3500
Fax: 859-258-3538

Lexington Mayor
200 E Main St Fayette Government Ctr
Lexington, KY 40507
Phone: 859-258-3100
Fax: 859-258-3194

Lexington Parks & Recreation Div
545 N Upper St
Lexington, KY 40508
Phone: 859-288-2900
Fax: 859-254-0142

Lexington Planning Div
200 E Main St Fayette Government Ctr
Lexington, KY 40507
Phone: 859-258-3160
Fax: 859-258-3163

Lexington Police Div
150 E Main St
Lexington, KY 40507
Phone: 859-258-3600
Fax: 859-258-3574

Lexington Public Library
140 E Main St
Lexington, KY 40507
Phone: 859-231-5500
Fax: 859-231-5598

Lexington Public Works Dept
200 E Main St 9th Fl
Lexington, KY 40507
Phone: 859-258-3400
Fax: 859-258-3403

Lexington Urban County Council
200 E Main St
Lexington, KY 40507
Phone: 859-258-3200
Fax: 859-258-3838

Important Phone Numbers

AAA.......859-233-1111
Driver's License Information.......859-246-2151
Emergency.......911
Kentucky Revenue Cabinet.......502-564-4581
Lexington-Bluegrass Assn of Realtors.......859-276-3503
Lexington-Fayette Div of Revenue.......859-258-3340
Medical Referral.......859-272-6099
Poison Control Center.......800-722-5725
Time/Temp.......859-259-2333
Vehicle Registration Information.......859-253-3344
Voter Registration Information.......859-255-7563
Weather.......859-253-4444

Information Sources

Better Business Bureau Serving Central & Eastern Kentucky
1460 Newton Pike
Lexington, KY 40511
www.lexington.bbb.org
Phone: 859-259-1008
Fax: 859-259-1639

Fayette County
162 E Main St
Lexington, KY 40507
Phone: 859-253-3344
Fax: 859-231-9619

Greater Lexington Chamber of Commerce
330 E Main St Suite 100
Lexington, KY 40507
www.lexchamber.com
Phone: 859-254-4447
Fax: 859-233-3304

Lexington Convention & Visitors Bureau
301 E Vine St
Lexington, KY 40507
www.visitlex.com/
Phone: 859-233-7299
Fax: 859-254-4555
TF: 800-845-3959

Lexington Convention Center
430 W Vine St
Lexington, KY 40507
www.lexingtoncenter.com/lexpo/lexpo.htm
Phone: 859-233-4567
Fax: 859-253-2718

Online Resources

4Lexington.com
www.4lexington.com

About.com Guide to Lexington
lexington.about.com/local/southeastus/lexington

Anthill City Guide Lexington
www.anthill.com/city.asp?city=lexington

Area Guide Lexington
lexington.areaguides.net

City Knowledge Lexington
www.cityknowledge.com/ky_lexington.htm

DigitalCity Lexington
home.digitalcity.com/lexington

Excite.com Lexington City Guide
www.excite.com/travel/countries/united_states/kentucky/lexington

Insiders' Guide to Greater Lexington & the Kentucky Bluegrass
www.insiders.com/lexington-ky

Lex Info
www.lexinfo.com/

Lexington CityLink
www.usacitylink.com/citylink/lexing

Lexington Kentucky
lexington-kentucky.com

Lexington Online
www.lexington-on-line.com/

METROSPIN
www.metrospin.com

Area Communities

Communities in the seven-county Lexington Metropolitan Statistical Area (Fayette, Bourbon, Clark, Jessamine, Madison, Scott and Woodford counties) with populations greater than 10,000 include:

Berea
212 Chestnut St
Berea, KY 40403
Phone: 859-986-8528
Fax: 859-986-7657

Georgetown
100 Court St
Georgetown, KY 40324
Phone: 502-863-9800
Fax: 502-863-9810

Nicholasville
500 N Main St
Nicholasville, KY 40356
Phone: 859-885-4334
Fax: 859-885-9476

Richmond
239 Main St
Richmond, KY 404475
Phone: 859-623-1000
Fax: 859-623-7816

Winchester
32 N Wall St
Winchester, KY 40391
Phone: 859-744-6292
Fax: 859-744-7450

Economy

The Lexington area has a sound economy and a diverse economic base. Major corporations with a presence in the Lexington area include Toyota, Lexmark, General Electric, and Raytheon. Services is the area's largest employment sector, with healthcare one of the leading industries - four of the area's top 15 employers are healthcare-related. Wholesale and retail trade combined represent Lexington's second largest employment sector, followed by government. The University of Kentucky is the area's single largest employer, providing jobs for more than 10,500 area residents.

Unemployment Rate 1.8%*
Per Capita Income.........................$29,933**
Median Family Income.....................$42,500*

** Information given is for the Lexington Metropolitan Statistical Area (MSA), which includes Fayette, Bourbon, Clark, Jessamine, Madison, Scott and Woodford counties.*
*** Information given is for Fayette County.*

Principal Industries & Number of Wage Earners

Fayette County - 1998

Industry	Wage Earners
Contract Construction	8,907
Finance, Insurance, & Real Estate	7,797
Manufacturing	18,891
Mining & Quarrying	181
Other	3,092
Services	47,885
State & Local Government	24,122
Transportation, Communications, & Utilities	8,364
Wholesale/Retail Trade	41,591

Major Employers

Central Baptist Hospital
1740 Nicholasville Rd
Lexington, KY 40503
www.centralbap.com
Phone: 859-275-6100
Fax: 859-260-6935

Chandler Medical Center
800 Rose St University of Kentucky
Lexington, KY 40536
www.mc.uky.edu
Phone: 859-323-5000
Fax: 859-257-2184

Dillard's
2349 Richmond Rd
Lexington, KY 40502
Phone: 859-269-3611
Fax: 859-269-3611

Eastern Kentucky University
521 Lancaster Ave
Richmond, KY 40475
www.eku.edu
Phone: 859-622-1000
Fax: 859-622-1020
TF: 800-465-9191

Fayette County Public Schools
701 E Main St
Lexington, KY 40502
www.fayette.k12.ky.us
Phone: 859-281-0100
Fax: 859-281-0271

Johnson Controls Inc
1 Quality Dr
Georgetown, KY 40324
www.careermosaic.com/cm/jc/
Phone: 502-863-3910
Fax: 502-863-0701

Kentucky Utilities Co
1 Quality St
Lexington, KY 40507
www.kuenergy.com
Phone: 859-255-2100
Fax: 859-367-1190
TF: 800-981-0600

Lexington-Fayette Urban County Government
200 E Main St Fayette Government Ctr
Lexington, KY 40507
www.lfucg.com
Phone: 859-258-3000
Fax: 859-258-3250

Lexmark International Inc
740 W New Circle Rd
Lexington, KY 40550
www.lexmark.com
Phone: 859-232-2000
Fax: 859-232-1886
TF: 800-539-6275

Osram Sylvania Inc
1000 Tyrone Pike
Versailles, KY 40383
www.sylvania.com/aboutus/humres/
Phone: 859-873-7351
Fax: 859-873-4803

Saint Joseph Hospital
1 St Joseph Dr
Lexington, KY 40504
www.sjhlex.org/sjh
Phone: 859-313-1000
Fax: 859-313-3001

Toyota Motor Mfg Kentucky Inc
1001 Cherry Blossom Way
Georgetown, KY 40324
Phone: 502-868-2000
Fax: 502-868-2007

Trane Co
1515 Mercer Rd
Lexington, KY 40511
www.trane.com/corporate/
Phone: 859-259-2500
Fax: 859-259-2595

University of Kentucky
100 Funkhouser Bldg
Lexington, KY 40506
E-mail: rmills@pop.uky.edu
www.uky.edu
Phone: 859-257-9000
Fax: 859-257-3823

Veterans Affairs Medical Center Lexington
2250 Leestown Rd
Lexington, KY 40511
Phone: 859-233-4511
Fax: 859-281-4970

Quality of Living Indicators

Total Crime Index....................................14,842
(rates per 100,000 inhabitants)

Violent Crime
Murder/manslaughter.......................... 24
Forcible rape 143
Robbery...................................... 530
Aggravated assault...........................1,216

Property Crime
Burglary 2,483
Larceny theft 9,522
Motor vehicle theft 924

Cost of Living Index....................................97.4
(national average = 100)

Median Home Price................................$111,900

Education

Public Schools

Fayette County Public Schools
701 E Main St
Lexington, KY 40502
www.fayette.k12.ky.us
Phone: 859-281-0100
Fax: 859-281-0271

Number of Schools
Elementary 35
Middle 11
High.. 5
Technology Schools 2

Student/Teacher Ratio
All Grades 16.9:1

Private Schools

Number of Schools (all grades).................... 20+

Colleges & Universities

Asbury College
1 Macklem Dr
Wilmore, KY 40390
E-mail: admissions@asbury.edu
www.asbury.edu
Phone: 859-858-3511
Fax: 859-858-3921
TF: 800-888-1818

Berea College
101 Chestnut St
Berea, KY 40404
E-mail: Claude_Hammond@berea.edu
www.berea.edu
Phone: 859-985-3000
Fax: 859-985-3512
TF: 800-326-5948

Centre College of Kentucky
600 W Walnut St
Danville, KY 40422
E-mail: admission@centre.edu
www.centre.edu
Phone: 859-238-5200
Fax: 859-238-5373
TF: 800-423-6236

Eastern Kentucky University
521 Lancaster Ave
Richmond, KY 40475
www.eku.edu
Phone: 859-622-1000
Fax: 859-622-1020
TF: 800-465-9191

Fugazzi College
407 Marquis Ave
Lexington, KY 40502
Phone: 859-266-0401
Fax: 859-268-2118

Georgetown College
400 E College St
Georgetown, KY 40324
E-mail: admissions@gtc.georgetown.ky.us
www.georgetowncollege.edu
Phone: 502-863-8000
Fax: 502-868-8891
TF: 800-788-9985

Lexington Community College
Cooper Dr 203 Oswald Bldg
Lexington, KY 40506
E-mail: lccweb@pop.uky.edu
www.uky.edu/LCC
Phone: 859-257-4872
Fax: 859-257-2634

National Business College
628 E Main St
Lexington, KY 40508
www.nationalbusiness.edu
Phone: 859-253-0621
Fax: 859-233-3054

Transylvania University
300 N Broadway
Lexington, KY 40508
E-mail: admsapp@music.transy.edu
www.transy.edu
Phone: 859-233-8300
Fax: 859-233-8797
TF: 800-872-6798

University of Kentucky
100 Funkhouser Bldg
Lexington, KY 40506
E-mail: rmills@pop.uky.edu
www.uky.edu
Phone: 859-257-9000
Fax: 859-257-3823

Hospitals

Central Baptist Hospital
1740 Nicholasville Rd
Lexington, KY 40503
www.centralbap.com
Phone: 859-275-6100
Fax: 859-260-6935

Chandler Medical Center
800 Rose St University of Kentucky
Lexington, KY 40536
www.mc.uky.edu
Phone: 859-323-5000
Fax: 859-257-2184

Saint Joseph Hospital
1 St Joseph Dr
Lexington, KY 40504
www.sjhlex.org/sjh
Phone: 859-313-1000
Fax: 859-313-3001

Saint Joseph Hospital East
150 N Eagle Creek Dr
Lexington, KY 40509
Phone: 859-268-4800
Fax: 859-268-3766

Samaritan Hospital
310 S Limestone St
Lexington, KY 40508
Phone: 859-252-6612
Fax: 859-226-7101

Shriners Hospitals for Children Lexington Unit
1900 Richmond Rd
Lexington, KY 40502
www.shrinershq.org/Hospitals/Directry/lexington.html
Phone: 859-266-2101
Fax: 859-268-5636
TF: 800-668-4634

Veterans Affairs Medical Center Lexington
2250 Leestown Rd
Lexington, KY 40511
Phone: 859-233-4511
Fax: 859-281-4970

Transportation

Airport(s)

Blue Grass Airport (LEX)
5 miles W of downtown (approx 15 minutes) 859-425-3114

Mass Transit

LexTran
$.80 Base fare.................................859-252-4936

Rail/Bus

Greyhound Bus Station
477 New Circle Rd
Lexington, KY 40511
Phone: 859-299-8804
TF: 800-231-2222

Utilities

Electricity
Kentucky Utilities Co 859-255-2100
www.kuenergy.com

Gas
Columbia Gas of Kentucky 859-288-0200
www.columbiagasky.com

Water
Kentucky-American Water Co...................859-268-6300

Garbage Collection/Recycling
Lexington-Fayette Solid Waste Div 859-425-2255

Telecommunications

Telephone
Verizon Communications.......................859-253-4000
www.verizon.com

Cable Television
Insight.......................................859-268-1134

Internet Service Providers (ISPs)
Mikrotec Internet Services 859-266-5925
www.mis.net

Banks

Bank One Lexington NA
201 E Main St
Lexington, KY 40507
Phone: 859-231-2696
Fax: 859-231-2175

Central Bank & Trust Co
300 W Vine St
Lexington, KY 40507
Phone: 859-253-6222
Fax: 859-253-6100
TF: 800-637-6884

Community Trust Bank
100 E Vine St
Lexington, KY 40507
Phone: 859-389-5350
Fax: 859-233-1320

Firstar Bank
2020 Nicholasville Rd
Lexington, KY 40503
Phone: 859-232-8199
Fax: 859-232-8164

National City Bank Kentucky
301 E Main St
Lexington, KY 40507
Phone: 859-281-5100
Fax: 859-281-5238

PNC Bank
200 W Vine St
Lexington, KY 40507
Phone: 859-281-0400
Fax: 859-281-0459

Shopping

Bluegrass Bazaar
246 Walton Ave
Lexington, KY 40502
Phone: 859-259-0303

Civic Center Shops
410 West Vine St
Lexington, KY 40507
www.lexingtoncenter.com/shops.htm
Phone: 859-233-4567

Dudley Square
380 S Mill & Maxwell St
Lexington, KY 40508

Factory Stores of America
401 Outlet Center Dr
Georgetown, KY 40324
www.factorystores.com/
Phone: 502-868-0682
Fax: 502-868-0686

Fayette Mall
3401 Nicholasville Rd
Lexington, KY 40503
E-mail: fayettemall@rejacobsgroup.com
www.shopyourmall.com/mall_welcome.asp?map=yes&mall_select=665
Phone: 859-272-3493
Fax: 859-273-6376

Lexington Mall
2349 Richmond Rd
Lexington, KY 40502
Phone: 859-269-5393

Mall at Lexington Green
161 Lexington Green Cir
Lexington, KY 40503
Phone: 859-245-1513

Patchen Village
153-154 Patchen Dr
Lexington, KY 40517
Phone: 859-266-6664

Triangle Center
325 W Main St
Lexington, KY 40507
Phone: 859-231-1085

Turfland Mall
2033 Turfland Mall
Lexington, KY 40504
Phone: 859-276-4411
Fax: 859-277-2892

Victorian Square
401 W Main St
Lexington, KY 40507
Phone: 859-252-7575
Fax: 859-254-4496

Media

Newspapers and Magazines

Lexington Herald-Leader*
100 Midland Ave
Lexington, KY 40508
E-mail: hledit@lex.infi.net
www.kentuckyconnect.com/heraldleader
Phone: 859-231-3100
Fax: 859-254-9738
TF: 800-274-7355

**Indicates major daily newspapers*

Television

WDKY-TV Ch 56 (Fox)
836 Euclid Ave
Lexington, KY 40502
Phone: 859-269-5656
Fax: 859-269-3774

WKLE-TV Ch 46 (PBS)
600 Cooper Dr
Lexington, KY 40502
Phone: 859-258-7000
Fax: 859-258-7399

WKYT-TV Ch 27 (CBS)
2851 Winchester Rd
Lexington, KY 40509
E-mail: fbme52a@prodigy.com
www.wkyt.com
Phone: 859-299-0411
Fax: 859-293-1578

WLEX-TV Ch 18 (NBC)
1065 Russell Cave Rd
Lexington, KY 40505
E-mail: wlex@mis.net
www.wlextv.com
Phone: 859-259-1818
Fax: 859-255-2418

WTVQ-TV Ch 36 (ABC)
6940 Man O War Blvd
Lexington, KY 40509
www.wtvq.com
Phone: 859-233-3600
Fax: 859-293-5002

Radio

WBUL-FM 98.1 MHz (Ctry)
2601 Nicholasville Rd
Lexington, KY 40503
Phone: 859-422-1000
Fax: 859-422-1038

WEKU-FM 88.9 MHz (NPR)
521 Lancaster Ave 102 Perkins Bldg-EKU
Richmond, KY 40475
E-mail: weku@acs.eku.edu
www.weku.org
Phone: 859-622-1660
Fax: 859-622-6276
TF: 800-621-8890

WGKS-FM 96.9 MHz (AC)
PO Box 11788
Lexington, KY 40578
Phone: 859-233-1515
Fax: 859-233-1517

WKQQ-FM 100.1 MHz (CR)
2601 Nicholasville Rd
Lexington, KY 40503
E-mail: catduvh@aol.com
www.wkqq.com
Phone: 859-422-1000
Fax: 859-422-1038

WLAP-AM 630 kHz (Sports)
2601 Nicholasville Rd
Lexington, KY 40503
Phone: 859-422-1000
Fax: 859-422-1038

WLRO-FM 101.5 MHz (CR)
300 W Vine St
Lexington, KY 40507
Phone: 859-253-5900
Fax: 859-253-5903

WMXL-FM 94.5 MHz (AC)
2601 Nicholasville Rd
Lexington, KY 40503
Phone: 859-422-1000
Fax: 859-422-1038

WUKY-FM 91.3 MHz (NPR)
340 McVey Hall University of Kentucky
Lexington, KY 40506
E-mail: wuky913@ukcc.uky.edu
wuky.uky.edu
Phone: 859-257-3221
Fax: 859-257-6291

WVLK-FM 92.9 MHz (Ctry)
300 W Vine St
Lexington, KY 40507
E-mail: k93@mis.net
www.k93.com
Phone: 859-253-5900
Fax: 859-253-5903

Attractions

The Kentucky Horse Park at Lexington is a 1,032-acre working farm and park devoted to the horse. Features there include two museums, films, a stable of equine champions, walking and horse-drawn tours, and year-round shows and events. One such event is the Southern Lights Holiday Festival, which begins the day after Thanksgiving and runs through January 1 each year, featuring some 750,000 lights with animated holiday and horse scenes along a two-and-a-half-mile drive. Thoroughbred racing is available at Keeneland Race Course in Lexington, with harness racing at the Red Mile Harness Track. A number of historic sites in Lexington offer guided tours to visitors, including: Ashland, the Henry Clay Estate; Hopemont, the Hunt-Morgan House; the Mary Todd Lincoln house, where President Lincoln's wife spent her girlhood; and Waveland, an antebellum plantation house built in the 1840s. Lexington also has several shopping areas, including Victorian Square in the downtown area and Dudley Square, a restored 1881 school building with shops featuring antiques, prints, quilts, collectibles, and other unique items.

American Saddle Horse Museum
4093 Iron Works Pkwy
Lexington, KY 40511
E-mail: asbfan@aol.com
www.lexinfo.com/museum/saddle.html
Phone: 859-259-2746
Fax: 859-255-4909
TF: 800-829-4438

ArtsPlace
161 N Mill St
Lexington, KY 40507
www.lexarts.org
Phone: 859-255-2951
Fax: 859-255-2787

Ashland-The Henry Clay Estate
120 Sycamore Rd
Lexington, KY 40502
www.henryclay.org
Phone: 859-266-8581

Aviation Museum of Kentucky
Hangar Dr Blue Grass Airport
Lexington, KY 40544
www.aviationky.org
Phone: 859-231-1219
Fax: 859-381-8739

Bluegrass Scenic Railroad & Museum
Beasley Rd Woodford County Pk
Versailles, KY 40383
Phone: 859-873-2476
Fax: 859-223-2363

Cathedral of Christ the King
299 Colony Blvd
Lexington, KY 40502
Phone: 859-268-2861

Flag Fork Herb Farms
900 N Broadway
Lexington, KY 40505
Phone: 859-233-7381

Headley-Whitney Museum
4435 Old Frankfort Pike
Lexington, KY 40510
www.headley-whitney.org
Phone: 859-255-6653
Fax: 859-255-8375

Hopemont-The Hunt-Morgan House
201 N Mill St
Lexington, KY 40508
Phone: 859-233-3290

Hummel Arnim D Planetarium
Eastern Kentucky University
Richmond, KY 40475
Phone: 859-622-1547
Fax: 859-622-6205

Jacobson Park
4051 Athens-Boonesboro Rd
Lexington, KY 40515
Phone: 859-288-2900

Kentucky Horse Center
3380 Paris Pike
Lexington, KY 40511
E-mail: info@khc.org
www.khc.org
Phone: 859-293-1853
Fax: 859-299-1284

Kentucky Horse Park
4089 Iron Works Pike
Lexington, KY 40511
www.imh.org/khp/hp1.html
Phone: 859-233-4303
Fax: 859-254-0253

Kentucky Theater
214 E Main St
Lexington, KY 40507
E-mail: kytheatr@mis.net
Phone: 859-231-6997
Fax: 859-231-7924

Labrot & Graham Distillery
7855 McCracken Pike
Versailles, KY 40383
Phone: 859-879-1812
Fax: 859-879-1946
TF: 800-542-1812

Lexington Ballet
161 N Mill St
Lexington, KY 40507
Phone: 859-233-3925

Lexington Cemetery
833 W Main St
Lexington, KY 40508
Phone: 859-255-5522

Lexington Children's Museum
401 W Main St Suite 309
Lexington, KY 40507
Phone: 859-258-3253
Fax: 859-258-3255

Lexington Opera House
401 W Short St
Lexington, KY 40508
www.lfucg.com/opera.htm
Phone: 859-233-4567
Fax: 859-253-2718

Lexington Philharmonic
161 N Mill St
Lexington, KY 40507
Phone: 859-233-4226
Fax: 859-233-7896

Loudoun House
209 Castlewood Dr
Lexington, KY 40505
www.lexingtonartleague.org
Phone: 859-254-7024
Fax: 859-254-7214

Mary Todd Lincoln House
578 W Main St
Lexington, KY 40507
Phone: 859-233-9999

Masterson Station Park
3051 Leestown Rd
Lexington, KY 40511
Phone: 859-288-2900

McConnell Springs
416 Quarry Dr
Lexington, KY 40504
Phone: 859-225-4073

Raven Run Nature Sanctuary
5888 Jacks Creek Rd
Lexington, KY 40515
Phone: 859-272-6105

Senator John Pope House
326 Grosvenor Ave
Lexington, KY 40508
Phone: 859-254-7673

Shaker Village of Pleasant Hill
3501 Lexington Rd
Harrodsburg, KY 40330
www.shakervillageky.org
Phone: 859-734-5411
Fax: 859-734-5411
TF: 800-734-5611

Shillito Park
3399 Brunswick Dr
Lexington, KY 40503
Phone: 859-288-2900

University of Kentucky Art Museum
Rose & Euclid Sts
Lexington, KY 40506
www.uky.edu/artmuseum
Phone: 859-257-5716
Fax: 859-323-1994

University of Kentucky Museum of Anthropology
211 Lafferty Hall
Lexington, KY 40506
Phone: 859-257-1944
Fax: 859-323-3686

Waveland Historical Site
225 Waveland Museum Ln
Lexington, KY 40514
Phone: 859-272-3611
Fax: 859-245-4269

Woodland Park
601 E High St
Lexington, KY 40508
Phone: 859-288-2900

Sports Teams & Facilities

Keeneland Race Course
4201 Versailles Rd
Lexington, KY 40510
E-mail: keeneland@keeneland.com
www.keeneland.com
Phone: 859-254-3412
Fax: 859-288-4348
TF: 800-456-3412

Kentucky Thoroughblades (hockey)
430 W Vine St Rupp Arena
Lexington, KY 40507
E-mail: hockey@thoroughblades.com
www.thoroughblades.com/
Phone: 859-259-1996
Fax: 859-252-3684
TF: 888-259-1996

Red Mile Harness Track
1200 Red Mile Rd
Lexington, KY 40504
www.tattersallsredmile.com
Phone: 859-255-0752
Fax: 859-231-0217

Rupp Arena
430 W Vine St
Lexington, KY 40507
E-mail: comments@rupparena.com
www.lexingtoncenter.com/rupp/rupp_arena.htm
Phone: 859-233-4567
Fax: 859-253-2718

Annual Events

All-Arabian Combined Classic I & II (early September) 859-233-4303
Bluegrass Classic Dog Show (early September) 859-527-3865
Bluegrass Festival Hunter/Jumper Show (mid-late August) 859-266-6937
Bluegrass State Games (mid-March & mid-late July) 859-255-0336
Boy's Sweet Sixteen Tournament (mid-March) 859-233-3535
Breyerfest (late July) 859-233-4303
Champagne Run Hunter/Jumper Show (mid-March) 859-263-4638

Festival of the Bluegrass (mid-June) 859-846-4995
Festival of the Horse
(late September-early October).................502-863-2547
Great American Brass Band Festival (early June) ...800-755-0076
Harvest Festival (late September) 859-257-3221
High Hope Steeplechase (mid-May)................859-255-5727
July 4th Festival (early July).....................859-258-3123
Kentucky Arabian Horse Assn Annual Show
(early April).................................502-241-5244
Kentucky Guild of Artists & Craftsmen Spring Fair
(mid-May & mid-October) 859-986-3192
Kentucky High School Rodeo Assn Annual Rodeo
(late May) 270-395-4889
Kentucky Hunter/Jumper Assn Show
(late August)................................859-266-6937
Kentucky National Hunter/Jumper Show
(late September) 859-233-4303
Lexington Christmas Parade (early December)......859-231-7335
Lexington Egyptian Event (early June)............859-231-0771
Lexington Lions Club Bluegrass Fair
(early March) 859-233-1465
Lexington Shakespeare Festival (July) 859-266-4423
Mayfest (early May)...............................859-231-7335
Memorial Stakes Day Chili Cook-off (late May) 859-255-0752
Mid-America Miniature Horse Assn Julep Cup
(mid-July) 800-848-1224
Mid-South Regional Pony Club Rally (late June) 502-244-1797
Paso Fino Festival of the Bluegrass (mid-June).....270-345-2501
Polo at the Park (June-October)...................859-233-4303
Red Mile Harness Racing Grand Circuit Meet
(late September-early October).................859-255-0752
Rolex Kentucky Three Day Event (late April) 859-254-8123
Roots & Heritage Festival (early September) 859-231-2611
Saint Patrick's Day Parade (mid-March) 859-278-7349
Sheiks & Shreiks Arabian Fun Show
(early November).............................859-987-3190
Southern Lights Holiday Festival
(late November-late December).................859-255-5727
Woodland Art Fair (mid-August) 859-254-7024

Lincoln, Nebraska

County: **Lancaster**

LINCOLN is located in southeastern Nebraska. Major cities within 100 miles include Omaha, Nebraska and Council Bluffs, Iowa.

Area (Land) .... 63.3 sq mi
Area (Water).... 0.8 sq mi
Elevation.... 1,176 ft
Latitude .... 40-80-00 N
Longitude.... 96-66-67 W
Time Zone .... CST
Area Code.... 402

Climate

Lincoln's climate features four distinct seasons. Winters are cold, with average high temperatures in the 30s and lows dipping into the teens. An average of 26 inches of snow falls each year in Lincoln. Summers are warm, with average daytime highs in the upper 80s to near 90 degrees and lows in the low to mid-60s. May and June are the wettest months in Lincoln; January is the driest.

Average Temperatures & Precipitation

Temperatures

	Jan	Feb	Mar	Apr	May	Jun	Jul	Aug	Sep	Oct	Nov	Dec
High	32	38	50	64	74	85	90	87	77	67	50	36
Low	10	15	27	39	50	60	66	63	53	41	27	15

Precipitation

	Jan	Feb	Mar	Apr	May	Jun	Jul	Aug	Sep	Oct	Nov	Dec
Inches	0.5	0.7	2.1	2.8	3.9	3.9	3.2	3.4	3.5	2.1	1.3	0.9

History

The area known today as Lincoln began as a salt basin that drew Native Americans of various tribes to the area. Before refrigeration, salt was important for preserving food, and by the 1850s salt companies began sending representatives to the area to investigate the possibility of harvesting salt. One of these representatives was Captain W.T. Donovan of Lancaster, Pennsylvania. He became one of the area's first white settlers and also helped the territorial legislature choose a site and a name for a new county. In 1859 the community of Lancaster, named for Captain Donovan's hometown, was established as the seat of Lancaster County.

Although Omaha was the original seat of Nebraska's territorial government, it was practically inaccessible to people living south of the Platte River. The "South Platters" proposed moving the capital farther west, and Lancaster was chosen as the new site. The new capital was originally going to be renamed "Capital City," but an Omaha Democratic Senator proposed naming the new capital Lincoln, after President Abraham Lincoln. His suggestion was an attempt to sway South Platte Democrats to oppose relocating the capital to their area, as the president was not highly regarded during the post-Civil War years. Despite the name change, South Platters voted unanimously for the capital's relocation, and in 1867 Lincoln became the capital of the newly admitted State of Nebraska. Lincoln was incorporated as a village in 1869.

Lincoln was home to U.S. Representative William Jennings Bryan, who vied unsuccessfully for the U.S. presidency three times (in 1896, 1900, and 1908), and the city grew as a political center in Nebraska. By the turn of the century Lincoln had also become a major railroad hub and meat packing center. Today, with a population of more than 213,000, Lincoln is Nebraska's second largest city.

Population

1990 Census 191,972
1998 Estimate.... 213,088
% Change 11.0
2005 Projection 248,175*

Racial/Ethnic Breakdown
White.... 94.5%
Black 2.4%
Other.... 3.1%
Hispanic Origin (may be of any race) 2.0%

Age Breakdown
Under 5 years.... 7.2%
5 to 17.... 16.2%
18 to 20.... 7.5%
21 to 24.... 9.0%
25 to 34.... 18.8%
35 to 44.... 15.0%
45 to 54.... 8.4%
55 to 64.... 7.0%
65 to 74.... 5.9%
75+ years 5.1%
Median Age.... 30.3

Gender Breakdown
Male.... 48.6%
Female.... 51.4%

* *Information given is for Lancaster County.*

Government

Type of Government: Mayor-Council

Lincoln City Attorney
575 S 10th St
Lincoln, NE 68508
Phone: 402-441-7286
Fax: 402-441-8812

Lincoln City Clerk Phone: 402-441-7438
555 S 10th St Fax: 402-441-8325
Lincoln, NE 68508

Lincoln City Council Phone: 402-441-7515
555 S 10th St Fax: 402-441-6533
Lincoln, NE 68508

Lincoln City Hall Phone: 402-441-7171
555 S 10th St Fax: 402-441-8325
Lincoln, NE 68508

Lincoln City Libraries Phone: 402-441-8500
136 S 14th St Fax: 402-441-8586
Lincoln, NE 68508

Lincoln City Treasurer Phone: 402-441-7458
555 S 10th St Fax: 402-441-8325
Lincoln, NE 68508

Lincoln Finance Dept Phone: 402-441-7411
555 S 10th St Fax: 402-441-8325
Lincoln, NE 68508

Lincoln Fire Dept Phone: 402-441-8350
1801 Q St Fax: 402-441-7098
Lincoln, NE 68508

Lincoln Mayor Phone: 402-441-7511
555 S 10th St Suite 208 Fax: 402-441-7120
Lincoln, NE 68508

Lincoln Parks & Recreation Dept Phone: 402-441-7847
2740 A St Fax: 402-441-8706
Lincoln, NE 68502

Lincoln Personnel Dept Phone: 402-441-7517
555 S 10th St Rm 107 Fax: 402-441-8748
Lincoln, NE 68508

Lincoln Planning Dept Phone: 402-441-7491
555 S 10th St Rm 213 Fax: 402-441-6377
Lincoln, NE 68508

Lincoln Police Dept Phone: 402-441-7204
575 S 10th St Fax: 402-441-8492
Lincoln, NE 68508

Lincoln Public Works/Utilities Dept Phone: 402-441-7566
555 S 10th St Fax: 402-441-8609
Lincoln, NE 68508

Lincoln Urban Development Dept Phone: 402-441-7864
129 N 10th St Rm 110 Fax: 402-441-8711
Lincoln, NE 68508

Important Phone Numbers

AAA....402-474-2229
American Express Travel....402-291-4131
Driver's License Information....402-471-2823
Emergency....911
HotelDocs....800-468-3537
Lancaster County Assessor....402-441-7463
Lancaster County Treasurer....402-441-7425
Lincoln Board of Realtors....402-441-3620
Medical Referral....402-441-8000
Nebraska Taxpayer Assistance....800-742-7474
Poison Control Center....803-777-1117
Time/Temp....402-476-9211
Vehicle Registration Information....402-441-7497
Voter Registration Information....402-441-7311
Weather....402-475-6100

Information Sources

Better Business Bureau Serving Southern Nebraska Phone: 402-476-8855
3633 'O' St Suite 1 Fax: 402-476-8221
Lincoln, NE 68510
www.lincoln.bbb.org

Lancaster County Phone: 402-441-7481
555 S 10th St Fax: 402-441-8728
Lincoln, NE 68508
interlinc.ci.lincoln.ne.us

Lincoln Chamber of Commerce Phone: 402-436-2350
PO Box 83006 Fax: 402-436-2360
Lincoln, NE 68501
www.lcoc.com

Lincoln Convention & Visitors Bureau Phone: 402-434-5335
1135 M St Suite 200 Fax: 402-436-2360
Lincoln, NE 68508 TF: 800-423-8212
www.lincoln.org/cvb/

Nebraska Travel & Tourism Div Phone: 402-471-3791
PO Box 98907 Fax: 402-471-3026
Lincoln, NE 68509 TF: 800-228-4307
www.visitnebraska.org

Pershing Auditorium Phone: 402-441-8744
226 Centennial Mall South Fax: 402-441-7913
Lincoln, NE 68508

Online Resources

Anthill City Guide Lincoln
www.anthill.com/city.asp?city=lincoln

Area Guide Lincoln
lincoln.areaguides.net

City Knowledge Lincoln
www.cityknowledge.com/ne_lincoln.htm

Discover Lincoln
yp.lincoln.alltel.com/lincoln

Downtown Lincoln Assn
www.downtownlincoln.org

Excite.com Lincoln City Guide
www.excite.com/travel/countries/united_states/nebraska/lincoln

LincNet
www.lincnet.com

Lincoln Guide
www.lincolnguide.com

Lincoln Online
lincoln.inetnebr.com

Lincoln Picture Tour
db.4w.com/lincolntour

Lincoln Yellow Pages
yp.aliant.com

Strictly Business Online
www.zaa.com/online/

Surf Lincoln!
www2.lincolnonline.com/lol/IntroLincolnOnline.html

Area Communities

Communities in Lancaster County with populations greater than 1,000 include:

Hickman Phone: 402-792-2212
PO Box 27 Fax: 402-792-2210
Hickman, NE 68372

Waverly Phone: 402-786-2312
14130 Lancashire Fax: 402-786-2490
Waverly, NE 68462

Economy

Serving as Nebraska's political center for more than a century, government (at the federal, state, and local levels), remains Lincoln's single largest employer. Lincoln is also an important center for the insurance industry - several of the city's top employers are insurance companies. Services is the city's second largest employment sector, followed by retail trade and manufacturing. Major manufacturers with a presence in Lincoln include Goodyear, Kawasaki, and Novartis.

Unemployment Rate	2.3%*
Per Capita Income	$24,602*
Median Family Income	$53,000*

** Information given is for Lancaster County.*

Principal Industries & Number of Wage Earners

Lincoln MSA (Lancaster County) - 1999

Construction & Mining	7,318
Finance, Insurance, & Real Estate	10,778
Government	33,645
Manufacturing	18,155
Retail Trade	26,253
Services (Except Domestic)	41,135
Transportation & Public Utilities	9,293
Wholesale Trade	5,674

Major Employers

Ameritas Life Insurance Corp Phone: 402-467-1122
5900 'O' St Fax: 402-467-7935
Lincoln, NE 68510 TF: 800-283-9588
www.ameritas.com

Blue Cross & Blue Shield of Nebraska Phone: 402-458-4800
1233 Lincoln Mall Fax: 402-477-2952
Lincoln, NE 68508

Bryan LGH Medical Center Phone: 402-475-1011
2300 S 16th St Fax: 402-481-5273
Lincoln, NE 68502
www.bryan.org

Bryan LGH Medical Center East Phone: 402-489-0200
1600 S 48th St Fax: 402-483-8306
Lincoln, NE 68506
www.bryan.org

Burlington Northern & Santa Fe Railway Phone: 402-458-7700
201 N 7th St Fax: 402-458-7660
Lincoln, NE 68508
www.bnsf.com/about_bnsf/html/employment.html

Cornhusker Bank Phone: 402-434-2265
1101 Cornhusker Hwy Fax: 402-434-2262
Lincoln, NE 68521

Gallup Organization Inc Phone: 402-489-9000
300 S 68th Street Pl Fax: 402-486-6243
Lincoln, NE 68510 TF: 800-288-8592

Goodyear Tire & Rubber Co Phone: 402-466-8311
4021 N 56th St Fax: 402-467-8191
Lincoln, NE 68504
www.goodyear.com/about/employ/

Kawasaki Motors Mfg Corp Phone: 402-476-6600
6600 NW 27th St Fax: 402-476-6672
Lincoln, NE 68524
www.kawasaki.com

Lancaster County Phone: 402-441-7481
555 S 10th St Fax: 402-441-8728
Lincoln, NE 68508
interlinc.ci.lincoln.ne.us

Lincoln Benefit Life/Surety Life Insurance Co Phone: 402-475-4061
2940 S 84th St Fax: 402-328-6112
Lincoln, NE 68506

Lincoln City Hall Phone: 402-441-7171
555 S 10th St Fax: 402-441-8325
Lincoln, NE 68508
www.ci.lincoln.ne.us

Lincoln Electric System Phone: 402-475-4211
PO Box 80869 Fax: 402-475-3152
Lincoln, NE 68501
E-mail: info@les.com
www.les.lincoln.ne.us

Lincoln Public Schools Phone: 402-436-1000
5901 O St Fax: 402-436-1620
Lincoln, NE 68510
www.lps.org

Novartis Consumer Health Phone: 402-464-6311
PO Box 83288 Fax: 402-467-8833
Lincoln, NE 68501
www.info.novartis.com/ch

University of Nebraska Lincoln Phone: 402-472-7211
501 N 14th St Fax: 402-472-9040
Lincoln, NE 68588 TF: 800-742-8800
E-mail: nuhusker@unl.edu
www.unl.edu

Quality of Living Indicators

Total Crime Index....................................13,399
(rates per 100,000 inhabitants)

Violent Crime
Murder/manslaughter............................ 9
Forcible rape 82
Robbery...................................... 162
Aggravated assault............................ 965

Property Crime
Burglary 1,886
Larceny theft 9,782
Motor vehicle theft............................ 513

Cost of Living Index...................................103.1
(national average = 100)

Median Home Price.................................$101,100

Education

Public Schools

Lincoln Public Schools
5901 O St
Lincoln, NE 68510
www.lps.org
Phone: 402-436-1000
Fax: 402-436-1620

Number of Schools
Elementary................................. 36
Middle 10
High.. 4

Student/Teacher Ratio
All Grades 15.3:1

Private Schools

Number of Schools (all grades).................... 25+

Colleges & Universities

Concordia University
800 N Columbia Ave
Seward, NE 68434
E-mail: admiss@seward.cune.edu
www.cune.edu
Phone: 402-643-3651
Fax: 402-643-4073
TF: 800-535-5494

Doane College
1014 Boswell Ave
Crete, NE 68333
www.doane.edu
Phone: 402-826-2161
Fax: 402-826-8600
TF: 800-333-6263

Lincoln School of Commerce
1821 K St
Lincoln, NE 68508
www.lscadvantage.com
Phone: 402-474-5315
Fax: 402-474-5302
TF: 800-742-7738

Nebraska Wesleyan University
5000 St Paul Ave
Lincoln, NE 68504
www.nebrwesleyan.edu
Phone: 402-466-2371
Fax: 402-465-2179
TF: 800-541-3818

Southeast Community College-Lincoln
8800 'O' St
Lincoln, NE 68520
Phone: 402-437-2500
Fax: 402-437-2404
TF: 800-642-4075

Union College
3800 S 48th St
Lincoln, NE 68506
www.ucollege.edu
Phone: 402-488-2331
Fax: 402-486-2566
TF: 800-228-4600

University of Nebraska Lincoln
501 N 14th St
Lincoln, NE 68588
E-mail: nuhusker@unl.edu
www.unl.edu
Phone: 402-472-7211
Fax: 402-472-9040
TF: 800-742-8800

Hospitals

Bryan LGH Medical Center
2300 S 16th St
Lincoln, NE 68502
www.bryan.org
Phone: 402-475-1011
Fax: 402-481-5273

Bryan LGH Medical Center East
1600 S 48th St
Lincoln, NE 68506
www.bryan.org
Phone: 402-489-0200
Fax: 402-483-8306

Saint Elizabeth Regional Medical Center
555 S 70th St
Lincoln, NE 68510
www.stez.org/sermc
Phone: 402-489-7181
Fax: 402-486-8973

Veterans Affairs Medical Center
600 S 70th St
Lincoln, NE 68510
Phone: 402-489-3802
Fax: 402-486-7840

Transportation

Airport(s)

Lincoln Municipal Airport (LNK)
5 miles NW of downtown (approx 15 minutes) 402-474-2770

Mass Transit

STARTRAN
$.85 Base fare.................................402-476-1234

Rail/Bus

Amtrak Station
201 N 7th St
Lincoln, NE 68508
Phone: 402-476-1295
TF: 800-872-7245

Greyhound Bus Station
940 'P' St
Lincoln, NE 68508
Phone: 402-474-1071
TF: 800-231-2222

Utilities

Electricity
Lincoln Electric System........................402-475-4211
www.les.lincoln.ne.us

Gas
Peoples Natural Gas 800-303-0752

Water
Lincoln Water System 402-441-7551

Garbage Collection/Recycling
Lincoln Solid Waste Management 402-474-6814

Telecommunications

Telephone
ALLTEL.....................................402-436-4321
www.alltel.com

Cable Television
Time Warner Cable............................402-421-0300
www.cablelinc.com

Internet Service Providers (ISPs)
Internet Nebraska.............................402-434-8680
www.inetnebr.com

Banks

Cornhusker Bank
1101 Cornhusker Hwy
Lincoln, NE 68521
Phone: 402-434-2265
Fax: 402-434-2262

First Federal Lincoln Bank
1235 'N' St
Lincoln, NE 68508
E-mail: info@fflb.com
www.fflb.com
Phone: 402-475-0521
Fax: 402-473-6242

Union Bank & Trust Co
3643 S 48th St
Lincoln, NE 68506
www.ubt.com
Phone: 402-488-0941
Fax: 402-483-8156
TF: 800-828-2441

US Bank NA
233 S 13th St
Lincoln, NE 68508
Phone: 402-434-1690
Fax: 402-434-1108
TF: 800-872-2657

Shopping

East Park Plaza Shopping Center
220 N 66th St
Lincoln, NE 68510
Phone: 402-467-3703
Fax: 402-467-4859

Gateway Mall
6100 'O' St
Lincoln, NE 68505
E-mail: gatewaymall@rejacobsgroup.com
www.shopyourmall.com/mall_welcome.asp?map=yes&mall_select=633
Phone: 402-464-3196

Historic Haymarket District
downtown-betw 9th & 'P' Sts
Lincoln, NE 68508
Phone: 402-435-7496

Meridian Park
6900 'O' St
Lincoln, NE 68510
Phone: 402-467-6996
Fax: 402-441-5805

Media

Newspapers and Magazines

Lincoln Journal-Star*
PO Box 81609
Lincoln, NE 68501
E-mail: feedback@nebweb.com
www.nebweb.com/ljs
Phone: 402-475-4200
Fax: 402-473-7291
TF: 800-742-7315

**Indicates major daily newspapers*

Television

KETV-TV Ch 7 (ABC)
2665 Douglas St
Omaha, NE 68131
Phone: 402-345-7777
Fax: 402-978-8922

KLKN-TV Ch 8 (ABC)
3240 S 10th St
Lincoln, NE 68502
Phone: 402-434-8000
Fax: 402-436-2236

KOLN-TV Ch 10 (CBS)
PO Box 30350
Lincoln, NE 68503
Phone: 402-467-4321
Fax: 402-467-9210

KPTM-TV Ch 42 (Fox)
4625 Farnam St
Omaha, NE 68132
Phone: 402-558-4200
Fax: 402-554-4279

KUON-TV Ch 12 (PBS)
1800 N 33rd St
Lincoln, NE 68583
Phone: 402-472-3611
Fax: 402-472-1785

WOWT-TV Ch 6 (NBC)
3501 Farnam St
Omaha, NE 68131
www.wowt.com
Phone: 402-346-6666
Fax: 402-233-7880

Radio

KFOR-AM 1240 kHz (AC)
6900 Van Dorn St Suite 11
Lincoln, NE 68506
www.kfor1240.com
Phone: 402-483-5100
Fax: 402-483-4095

KFRX-FM 102.7 MHz (CHR)
6900 Van Dorn St Suite 11
Lincoln, NE 68506
www.kfrxfm.com
Phone: 402-483-5100
Fax: 402-483-4095

KKNB-FM 104.1 MHz (AC)
4630 Antelope Creek Rd
Lincoln, NE 68506
www.kknb.com
Phone: 402-483-1517
Fax: 402-489-9989

KRKR-FM 95.1 MHz (CR)
6900 Van Dorn St Suite 11
Lincoln, NE 68506
www.krkrfm.com
Phone: 402-483-5100
Fax: 402-483-4095

KUCV-FM 90.9 MHz (NPR)
1800 N 33rd St
Lincoln, NE 68583
Phone: 402-472-2200
Fax: 402-472-2403

KZKX-FM 96.9 MHz (Ctry)
4630 Antelope Creek Rd Suite 200
Lincoln, NE 68506
www.kzkx.com
Phone: 402-488-9601
Fax: 402-489-9989

Attractions

The University of Nebraska is located in the capital city of Lincoln. On its grounds is the University of Nebraska State Museum, also known as "Elephant Hall" due to its large collection of extinct animals that once roamed the Great Plains. The University's Cornhusker football team is consistently ranked as one of the top teams in the country. The city's Pioneers Park and Nature Center has a toboggan run and cross-country ski area, as well as live outdoor animal exhibits of bison, white-tailed deer, and red foxes. Twenty minutes from Lincoln, visitors can hike the natural prairies at Nine-Mile Prairie.

American Historical Society of Germans from Russia
631 D St
Lincoln, NE 68502
E-mail: ahsgr@aol.com
www.ahsgr.org
Phone: 402-474-3363
Fax: 402-474-7229

Elder Art Gallery
N 50th St & Huntington Ave Wesleyan University Rogers Center for Fine Art
Lincoln, NE 68504
Phone: 402-465-2230

Folsom Children's Zoo & Botanical Gardens
1222 S 27th St
Lincoln, NE 68502
www.aza.org/folsom/
Phone: 402-475-6741
Fax: 402-475-6572

Governor's Mansion
1425 'H' St
Lincoln, NE 68508
Phone: 402-471-3466
Fax: 402-471-2329

Great Plains Art Collection
215 Love Library
Lincoln, NE 68588
www.unl.edu/plains/artcol.html
Phone: 402-472-6220
Fax: 402-472-2960

Historic Haymarket District
downtown-betw 9th & 'P' Sts
Lincoln, NE 68508
Phone: 402-435-7496

Homestead National Monument of America
Rt 3 Box 47
Beatrice, NE 68310
www.nps.gov/home/
Phone: 402-223-3514
Fax: 402-228-4231

Hyde Memorial Observatory
2740 A St
Lincoln, NE 68502
www.blackstarpress.com/arin/hyde/
Phone: 402-441-7895
Fax: 402-441-8706

Kennard Thomas P House
1627 H St
Lincoln, NE 68508
Phone: 402-471-4764

Lentz Center for Asian Cultures
14th & U Sts 329 Merrill Hall University of Nebraska
Lincoln, NE 68588
www.unl.edu/finearts/lentz.html
Phone: 402-472-5841
Fax: 402-472-8899

Lied Center for Performing Arts
301 N 12th St
Lincoln, NE 68588
www.unl.edu/lied/
Phone: 402-472-4700
Fax: 402-472-4730

Lincoln Botanical Garden & Arboretum
University of Nebraska 1340 N 17th St
Lincoln, NE 68588
E-mail: unlbga@cwis.unl.edu
www.unl.edu/unlbga/
Phone: 402-472-2679
Fax: 402-472-9615

Lincoln Children's Museum
13th & 'O' Sts
Lincoln, NE 68508
Phone: 402-477-4000
Fax: 402-477-2004

Lincoln Community Playhouse
2500 S 56th St
Lincoln, NE 68506
Phone: 402-489-7529
Fax: 402-489-1035

Lincoln Symphony Orchestra
5225 S 16th St
Lincoln, NE 68542
Phone: 402-423-2211
Fax: 402-423-5220

Mueller Planetarium
University of Nebraska Morrill Hall Rm 213
Lincoln, NE 68588
www.spacelaser.com/
Phone: 402-472-2641
Fax: 402-472-8899

Museum of Nebraska History
131 Centennial Mall N
Lincoln, NE 68508
www.nebraskahistory.org/sites/mnh/index.htm
Phone: 402-471-4754
Fax: 402-471-3314
TF: 800-833-6747

National Museum of Roller Skating
4730 South St
Lincoln, NE 68506
www.rollerskatingmuseum.com
Phone: 402-483-7551
Fax: 402-483-1465

Nebraska Historical Society
1500 R St
Lincoln, NE 68501
E-mail: nshs@inetnebr.com
www.nebraskahistory.org
Phone: 402-471-3270
Fax: 402-471-3100

Nebraska Repertory Theatre
12th & R Sts Howell Theatre
Lincoln, NE 68588
Phone: 402-472-2073

Nebraska State Capitol
1445 K St
Lincoln, NE 68509
Phone: 402-471-0448

Pioneers Park & Nature Center
Van Dorn St & Coddington Ave
Lincoln, NE 68522
Phone: 402-441-7895
Fax: 402-441-6468

Sheldon Memorial Art Gallery
12th & R Sts
Lincoln, NE 68588
E-mail: feedback@sheldon.unl.edu
sheldon.unl.edu/
Phone: 402-472-2461
Fax: 402-472-4258

University of Nebraska State Museum
14th & U Sts
Lincoln, NE 68588
www-museum.unl.edu/
Phone: 402-472-2642
Fax: 402-472-8899

University Place Art Center
2601 N 48th St
Lincoln, NE 68504
Phone: 402-466-8692
Fax: 402-466-3786

Sports Teams & Facilities

Eagle Raceway
238th & 'O' Sts
Eagle, NE 68347
www.eagleraceway.com
Phone: 402-420-7223
Fax: 402-488-2766

Lincoln Stars (hockey)
1800 State Fair Park Dr
Lincoln, NE 68508
www.lincolnstars.com
Phone: 402-474-7827
Fax: 402-474-7831

Annual Events

Annual Square & Round Dance Festival (early May) 402-434-5335
Arts in General (mid-November) 402-481-5117
Boat Sport & Travel Show (early February) 402-466-8102

Boo at the Zoo (late October) 402-475-6741
Downtown Performance Series (May-September) 402-434-6900
Gem & Mineral Show (late March) 402-472-7564
Haymarket Farmers Market (May-October) 402-434-6906
Haymarket Heydays (mid-June) 402-434-6906
Holidays in the Haymarket
(mid-November-mid-December) 402-434-6900
Home Garden & Leisure Show (mid-March) 402-474-5371
Jazz in June (June) 402-472-2540
July Jamm (late July) 402-434-6900
Lancaster County Fair & Rodeo
(late July-early August) 402-441-6545
Lincoln Marathon & Half Marathon (early May) 402-434-5335
Midwest Invitational Tournament (mid-March) 402-434-9217
Nebraska Builders Home & Garden Show
(mid-February) 402-423-4225
Nebraska State Fair
(late August-early September) 402-474-5371
Shrine Circus (mid-late March) 402-474-6890
Spring Affair (late April) 402-472-2679
Star City Holiday Parade Weekend Festival
(early December) 402-441-7391
Taste of Nebraska (mid-April) 402-483-2630
Victorian Holidays Past (December) 402-471-4764
Winter Lights (late November) 402-475-6741

Little Rock, Arkansas

County: Pulaski

LITTLE ROCK is located in central Arkansas along the Arkansas River. The only major city within 100 miles is Pine Bluff, Arkansas.

Area (Land) .... 102.9 sq mi
Area (Water)................................ 0.3 sq mi
Elevation...................................... 291 ft
Latitude ....34-74-64 N
Longitude................................ 92-28-94 W
Time Zone ....CST
Area Code....................................... 501

Climate

Little Rock's continental climate has four distinct seasons. Winters are fairly cool, with average high temperatures near 50 degrees and lows near 30; however arctic air masses from the north can bring periods of very cold weather. Snowfall is infrequent, averaging only 5.2 inches a year. Summer days are hot and humid, with average high temperatures near 90 degrees, while evenings cool down to about 70. Precipitation is distributed fairly evenly throughout the year in Little Rock—April is the wettest month and August is the driest.

Average Temperatures & Precipitation

Temperatures

	Jan	Feb	Mar	Apr	May	Jun	Jul	Aug	Sep	Oct	Nov	Dec
High	49	54	64	73	81	89	92	91	85	75	63	53
Low	29	33	42	51	59	67	72	70	64	51	42	33

Precipitation

	Jan	Feb	Mar	Apr	May	Jun	Jul	Aug	Sep	Oct	Nov	Dec
Inches	3.4	3.6	4.9	5.5	5.2	3.6	3.6	3.3	4.1	3.8	5.2	4.8

History

Originally inhabited by the Quapaw people, the area known today as Little Rock was first explored by the French in 1721. Explorer Bernard de la Harpe established a trading post along the Arkansas River, and settlement in the area began in the early 1800s. Little Rock was given its name by French settlers who called the city "La Petite Roche" in order to distinguish it from larger rock outcroppings along the Arkansas River. In 1821, the community became the capital of Arkansas Territory, and 15 years later Little Rock was incorporated as a city, retaining its status as the capital of the newly admitted state of Arkansas.

After the Civil War, the arrival of the railroad helped Little Rock grow as an agricultural center, with cotton and grain being the primary crops, and as an important regional transportation center. In 1956, Little Rock was the site of civil unrest as Arkansas' governor attempted to prevent the integration (which had been ordered by the Supreme Court two years earlier) of the city's all-white high school. The turmoil final came to an end when the federal government intervened, and the school was desegregated. In the decades that followed, the federal government once again helped shape Little Rock's future by implementing a federal navigation project on the Arkansas River. The project was completed in 1969, and this helped the city to develop as an important inland port, which in turn stimulated further growth and development. From the 1980s until 1993, Little Rock was the home of U.S. President (then Arkansas Governor) Bill Clinton.

Little Rock today remains an important center for commerce, manufacturing, and distribution. With a population of more than 175,000, Little Rock is Arkansas' largest city.

Population

1990 Census 175,727
1998 Estimate..............................175,303
% Change .... -0.2

Racial/Ethnic Breakdown

White.................................... 64.7%
Black 34.0%
Other.....................................2.3%
Hispanic Origin (may be of any race) 0.8%

Age Breakdown

Under 5 years.............................. 7.2%
5 to 17.................................. 17.6%
18 to 20.................................. 4.2%
21 to 24.................................. 6.3%
25 to 34.................................. 18.7%
35 to 44.................................. 16.0%
45 to 54.................................. 9.6%
55 to 64.................................. 7.8%
65 to 74.................................. 6.9%
75+ years 5.6%
Median Age................................32.8

Gender Breakdown

Male..................................... 46.4%
Female................................... 53.6%

Government

Type of Government: Council-City Manager

Central Arkansas Library System
100 Rock St
Little Rock, AR 72201

Phone: 501-918-3000
Fax: 501-375-7451

Little Rock Board of Directors
500 W Markham St Rm 203
Little Rock, AR 72201
Phone: 501-371-4516
Fax: 501-371-4498

Little Rock Central Arkansas Transit Authority
901 Maple St
North Little Rock, AR 72114
Phone: 501-375-6717
Fax: 501-375-6812

Little Rock City Clerk
500 W Markham St Rm 200
Little Rock, AR 72201
Phone: 501-371-4765
Fax: 501-371-4498

Little Rock City Hall
500 W Markham St
Little Rock, AR 72201
Phone: 501-371-4500

Little Rock City Manager
500 W Markham St Rm 203
Little Rock, AR 72201
Phone: 501-371-4510
Fax: 501-371-4498

Little Rock Finance Dept
500 W Markham St Rm 208
Little Rock, AR 72201
Phone: 501-371-4806
Fax: 501-244-5446

Little Rock Fire Dept
624 S Chester St
Little Rock, AR 72201
Phone: 501-918-3700
Fax: 501-371-4485

Little Rock Human Resources Dept
500 W Markham St Suite 130W
Little Rock, AR 72201
Phone: 501-371-4590
Fax: 501-371-4496

Little Rock Mayor
500 W Markham St Rm 203
Little Rock, AR 72201
Phone: 501-371-4791
Fax: 501-371-4498

Little Rock Parks & Recreation Dept
500 W Markham St Rm 108
Little Rock, AR 72201
Phone: 501-371-4770
Fax: 501-371-6832

Little Rock Planning & Development Dept
723 W Markham St
Little Rock, AR 72201
Phone: 501-371-4790
Fax: 501-371-6863

Little Rock Police Dept
700 W Markham St
Little Rock, AR 72201
Phone: 501-371-4621
Fax: 501-371-4892

Little Rock Public Works Dept
701 W Markham St
Little Rock, AR 72201
Phone: 501-371-4475
Fax: 501-371-4843

Little Rock Water Commission
PO Box 1789
Little Rock, AR 72203
Phone: 501-377-1255
Fax: 501-377-1244

Important Phone Numbers

AAA..........501-223-9222
Arkansas Dept of Finance & Administration..........501-682-7104
Arkansas Dept of Finance & Administration Income Tax Div..........501-682-7250
Dental Referral..........501-771-7650
Driver's License Information..........501-682-7058
Emergency..........911
HotelDocs..........800-468-3537
Little Rock Realtors Assn..........501-225-1987
Medical Referral..........501-227-8478
Pulaski County Assessor..........501-340-6170
Pulaski County Collector..........501-340-6040
State Highway Road Conditions..........501-569-2374
Telefun Events..........501-372-3399
Time/Temp..........501-376-8111
Vehicle Registration Information..........501-682-4692
Voter Registration Information..........501-340-8683
Weather..........501-371-7777

Information Sources

Better Business Bureau Serving Arkansas
1415 S University Ave
Little Rock, AR 72204
www.arkansas.bbb.org
Phone: 501-664-7274
Fax: 501-664-0024

Greater Little Rock Chamber of Commerce
101 S Spring St Suite 200
Little Rock, AR 72201
www.littlerockchamber.com
Phone: 501-374-4871
Fax: 501-374-6018

Little Rock Convention & Visitors Bureau
PO Box 3232
Little Rock, AR 72203
www.littlerock.com/lrcvb/
Phone: 501-376-4781
Fax: 501-374-2255
TF: 800-844-4781

Pulaski County
401 W Markham St Suite 102
Little Rock, AR 72201
www.co.pulaski.ar.us
Phone: 501-340-8431
Fax: 501-340-8420

Statehouse Convention Center
Markham & Main Sts 1 Statehouse Plaza
Little Rock, AR 72201
www.littlerock.com/facilities/statehouse_convention.html
Phone: 501-376-4781
Fax: 501-376-7833
TF: 800-844-4781

Online Resources

4LittleRock.com
www.4littlerock.com

About.com Guide to Little Rock
littlerock.about.com/citiestowns/southeastus/littlerock

Anthill City Guide Little Rock
www.anthill.com/city.asp?city=littlerock

Area Guide Little Rock
littlerock.areaguides.net

Arkansas Times
www.arktimes.com

City Knowledge Little Rock
www.cityknowledge.com/ar_littlerock.htm

Excite.com Little Rock City Guide
www.excite.com/travel/countries/united_states/arkansas/little_rock

Little Rock CityLink
www.usacitylink.com/citylink/lit-rock

Little Rock Free Press
www.aristotle.net/FREEP

Little Rock Info
www.littlerockinfo.com

Lodging.com Little Rock Arkansas
www.lodging.com/auto/guides/little_rock-area-ar.html

Area Communities

Communities in the Greater Little Rock Metropolitan Statistical Area (Pulaski, Faulkner, Lonoke, and Saline counties) with populations greater than 10,000 include:

Benton
114 S East St
Benton, AR 72015
Phone: 501-776-5900
Fax: 501-776-5910

Cabot
101 N 2nd St
Cabot, AR 72023
Phone: 501-843-3566
Fax: 501-941-3127

Conway
1201 Oak St
Conway, AR 72032
Phone: 501-450-6100
Fax: 501-450-6109

Jacksonville
PO Box 126
Jacksonville, AR 72078
Phone: 501-982-3181
Fax: 501-985-0168

North Little Rock
PO Box 5757
North Little Rock, AR 72119
Phone: 501-340-5318
Fax: 501-340-5469

Sherwood
2199 E Kiehl Ave
Sherwood, AR 72120
Phone: 501-835-5319
Fax: 501-835-1274

Economy

Little Rock's diverse economic base ranges from food and cosmetics manufacturing to telecommunications. Major U.S. corporations that call Little Rock home include Dillard Department Stores, TCBY, and ALLTEL. Many of Little Rock's top employers are government-related, including the metropolitan area's two largest employers, the State of Arkansas and the U.S. Government, which provide jobs for nearly 35,000 area residents. Services is currently Little Rock's largest employment sector, with health care being the primary industry.

Unemployment Rate 3.4%*
Per Capita Income $26,104*
Median Family Income $45,900*

** Information given is for the Little Rock-North Little Rock Metropolitan Statistical Area (MSA), which includes Faulkner, Lonoke, Pulaski, and Saline counties.*

Principal Industries & Number of Wage Earners

Little Rock-North Little Rock MSA* - 1999

Construction & Mining 15,600
Finance, Insurance, & Real Estate 18,200
Government 60,200
Manufacturing 32,800
Services 92,800
Trade 72,400
Transportation & Public Utilities 21,400

** Information given is for the Little Rock-North Little Rock Metropolitan Statistical Area (MSA), which includes Faulkner, Lonoke, Pulaski, and Saline counties.*

Major Employers

ALLTEL Corp
1 Allied Dr
Little Rock, AR 72202
www.alltel.com
Phone: 501-905-8000
Fax: 501-905-8487
TF: 800-255-8351

Arkansas Blue Cross Blue Shield
PO Box 2181
Little Rock, AR 72203
www.arkbluecross.com
Phone: 501-378-2000
Fax: 501-378-3796
TF: 800-238-8379

Arkansas Children's Hospital
800 Marshall St
Little Rock, AR 72202
www.ach.uams.edu
Phone: 501-320-1100
Fax: 501-320-4777

Baptist Medical Center
9601 I-630 Exit 7
Little Rock, AR 72205
Phone: 501-202-2000
Fax: 501-202-1159

Dillard's Inc
PO Box 486
Little Rock, AR 72203
www.dillards.com
Phone: 501-376-5200
Fax: 501-399-7271

Little Rock Air Force Base
Little Rock AFB, AR 72099
Phone: 501-987-3131
Fax: 501-987-6978

Pulaski County Special School District
925 E Dixon Rd
Little Rock, AR 72206
Phone: 501-490-2000
Fax: 501-490-0483

Saint Vincent Health Systems
2 St Vincent Cir
Little Rock, AR 72205
Phone: 501-660-3000
Fax: 501-660-2329

Southwestern Bell Telephone Co
700 W 29th St
North Little Rock, AR 72114
www.swbell.com
Phone: 501-371-9700
Fax: 501-373-1432

Union Pacific Railroad Co
800 Pike Ave
North Little Rock, AR 72114
www.uprr.com/uprr/business/hr/
Phone: 501-373-2288
Fax: 501-373-2449

University of Arkansas for Medical Sciences
4301 W Markham St
Little Rock, AR 72205
www.uams.edu
Phone: 501-686-7000
Fax: 501-686-8365

University of Arkansas Little Rock
2801 S University Ave
Little Rock, AR 72204
www.ualr.edu
Phone: 501-569-3000
Fax: 501-569-8956

Veterans Affairs Medical Center
4300 W 7th St
Little Rock, AR 72205
Phone: 501-257-1000
Fax: 501-257-5404

Quality of Living Indicators

Total Crime Index 18,515
(rates per 100,000 inhabitants)

Violent Crime
Murder/manslaughter 25
Forcible rape 144
Robbery 763
Aggravated assault 1,145

Property Crime
Burglary 3,675
Larceny theft 11,456
Motor vehicle theft 1,307

Cost of Living Index 94.7
(national average = 100)

Median Home Price $91,200

Education

Public Schools

Little Rock School District
810 W Markham
Little Rock, AR 72201
www.lrsd.k12.ar.us
Phone: 501-324-2000
Fax: 501-327-2032

Number of Schools
Elementary 35
Middle 8
High 5

Student/Teacher Ratio
All Grades 15.9:1

Private Schools

Number of Schools (all grades) .... 68+

Colleges & Universities

Arkansas Baptist College
1600 Bishop St
Little Rock, AR 72202
Phone: 501-374-7856
Fax: 501-372-0321

Philander Smith College
812 W 13th St
Little Rock, AR 72202
Phone: 501-375-9845
Fax: 501-370-5225
TF: 800-446-6772

Shorter College
604 N Locust St
North Little Rock, AR 72114
Phone: 501-374-6305
Fax: 501-374-9333

University of Arkansas Little Rock
2801 S University Ave
Little Rock, AR 72204
www.ualr.edu
Phone: 501-569-3000
Fax: 501-569-8956

University of Central Arkansas
201 Donaghey Ave
Conway, AR 72035
E-mail: admission@ecom.uca.edu
www.uca.edu
Phone: 501-450-5000
Fax: 501-450-5228
TF: 800-243-8245

Hospitals

Arkansas Children's Hospital
800 Marshall St
Little Rock, AR 72202
www.ach.uams.edu
Phone: 501-320-1100
Fax: 501-320-4777

Baptist Medical Center
9601 I-630 Exit 7
Little Rock, AR 72205
Phone: 501-202-2000
Fax: 501-202-1159

Baptist Memorial Medical Center
1 Pershing Cir
North Little Rock, AR 72114
Phone: 501-202-3000
Fax: 501-202-3489

Saint Vincent Doctors Hospital
6101 St Vincent Cir
Little Rock, AR 72205
Phone: 501-661-4000
Fax: 501-661-3959
TF: 800-265-8624

Saint Vincent Health Systems
2 St Vincent Cir
Little Rock, AR 72205
Phone: 501-660-3000
Fax: 501-660-2329

Southwest Hospital
11401 I-30
Little Rock, AR 72209
Phone: 501-455-7100
Fax: 501-455-7399

University of Arkansas for Medical Sciences
4301 W Markham St
Little Rock, AR 72205
www.uams.edu
Phone: 501-686-7000
Fax: 501-686-8365

Veterans Affairs Medical Center
4300 W 7th St
Little Rock, AR 72205
Phone: 501-257-1000
Fax: 501-257-5404

Transportation

Airport(s)

Little Rock National Airport/Adams Field (LIT)
3 miles E of downtown (approx 12-15 minutes) 501-372-3439

Mass Transit

Central Arkansas Transit
$1 Base fare 501-375-1163
River Cities Trolley Shuttle
$.25 Base fare 501-375-1163

Rail/Bus

Amtrak Station
1400 Markham St
Little Rock, AR 72201
Phone: 501-372-6841
TF: 800-872-7245

Greyhound Bus Station
118 E Washington St
North Little Rock, AR 72114
Phone: 501-372-3007
TF: 800-231-2222

Utilities

Electricity
Entergy 800-368-3749
www.entergy.com

Gas
Arkansas Louisiana Gas Co 501-372-7552

Water
Little Rock Municipal Water Works.............501-372-5161

Garbage Collection/Recycling
Little Rock Solid Waste Collection Dept.........501-888-2208

Telecommunications

Telephone
Southwestern Bell.............................800-324-7699
www.swbell.com

Cable Television
Comcast Cablevision...........................501-376-5700

Internet Service Providers (ISPs)
ALLTEL Internet Services......................501-661-8000
www.alltel.net
Aristotle Internet Access.......................501-374-4638
www.aristotle.net
Con.neCt Internet.............................501-450-6006
www.conwaycorp.net
World Lynx...................................501-954-9090
www.cei.net

Banks

Metropolitan National Bank Phone: 501-377-7600
111 Center St Fax: 501-377-7640
Little Rock, AR 72201
www.metbank.com

NationsBank Phone: 501-378-1000
200 W Capitol Ave Fax: 501-378-1204
Little Rock, AR 72201

One National Bank Phone: 501-370-4400
300 W Capitol Ave Fax: 501-370-4505
Little Rock, AR 72201

Pulaski Bank & Trust Co Phone: 501-661-7700
5800 R St Fax: 501-661-7867
Little Rock, AR 72207

Regions Bank Phone: 501-371-7000
400 W Capitol Ave Fax: 501-371-7413
Little Rock, AR 72201 TF: 800-482-8430

Shopping

Dillard's Phone: 501-376-5200
1600 Cantrella Rd
Little Rock, AR 72201

McCain Mall Phone: 501-758-6340
3929 McCain Blvd Fax: 501-758-0131
Little Rock, AR 72116

Park Plaza Mall Phone: 501-664-4956
6000 W Markham St Fax: 501-666-2115
Little Rock, AR 72205
www.parkplazamall.com

River Market Phone: 501-375-2552
400 E Markham St Fax: 501-375-5559
Little Rock, AR 72201

University Mall Phone: 501-664-3724
300 S University Ave
Little Rock, AR 72205

Media

Newspapers and Magazines

Arkansas Business Journal Phone: 501-372-1443
PO Box 3686 Fax: 501-375-0933
Little Rock, AR 72203 TF: 888-322-6397
www.abnews.com/

Arkansas Democrat-Gazette* Phone: 501-378-3400
PO Box 2221 Fax: 501-372-3908
Little Rock, AR 72203 TF: 800-482-1121
E-mail: news@arkdg.com
www.ardemgaz.com

Arkansas Times Phone: 501-375-2985
201 E Markham Suite 200 Fax: 501-375-3623
Little Rock, AR 72201
E-mail: arktimes@arktimes.com
www.arktimes.com

**Indicates major daily newspapers*

Television

KARK-TV Ch 4 (NBC) Phone: 501-340-4444
201 W 3rd St Fax: 501-375-1961
Little Rock, AR 72201
E-mail: news4@kark.com
www.kark.com

KATV-TV Ch 7 (ABC) Phone: 501-372-7777
401 S Main St Fax: 501-324-7852
Little Rock, AR 72201
E-mail: tv7@katv.com
www.katv.com

KETS-TV Ch 2 (PBS) Phone: 501-682-2386
350 S Donaghey St
Conway, AR 72032

KLRT-TV Ch 16 (Fox) Phone: 501-225-0016
11711 W Markham St Fax: 501-225-0428
Little Rock, AR 72211
www.klrt.com

KTHV-TV Ch 11 (CBS) Phone: 501-376-1111
PO Box 269 Fax: 501-376-1645
Little Rock, AR 72203

Radio

KABF-FM 88.3 MHz (Misc) Phone: 501-372-6119
2101 S Main St Fax: 501-376-3952
Little Rock, AR 72206

KARN-AM 920 kHz (N/T) Phone: 501-661-7500
4021 W 8th St Fax: 501-661-7519
Little Rock, AR 72204
E-mail: newsradio@karn.com

KDDK-FM 106.7 MHz (Ctry) Phone: 501-227-9696
8114 Cantrell Rd 3rd Fl Fax: 501-228-9547
Little Rock, AR 72227

KDRE-FM 101.1 MHz (B/EZ)
1 Shackleford Dr Suite 400
Little Rock, AR 72211
Phone: 501-219-2400
Fax: 501-221-3955

KHTE-FM 106.3 MHz (CHR)
1 Shackleford Dr Suite 400
Little Rock, AR 72211
Phone: 501-219-2400
Fax: 501-221-3955

KIPR-FM 92.3 MHz (Urban)
415 N McKinley Suite 920
Little Rock, AR 72205
Phone: 501-663-0092
Fax: 501-664-9201

KITA-AM 1440 kHz (Rel)
723 W 14th St
Little Rock, AR 72202
Phone: 501-375-1440
Fax: 501-375-0947

KKPT-FM 94.1 MHz (CR)
2400 Cottondale Ln
Little Rock, AR 72202
www.kkpt.com
Phone: 501-664-9410
Fax: 501-664-5871

KLAL-FM 107.7 MHz (Alt)
415 N McKinley Suite 920
Little Rock, AR 72202
Phone: 501-663-0092
Fax: 501-664-6524

KLEC-FM 96.5 MHz (AC)
1 Shackleford Dr Suite 400
Little Rock, AR 72211
Phone: 501-219-2400
Fax: 501-221-3955

KLIH-AM 1250 kHz (Rel)
1429 Merrill Dr
Little Rock, AR 72211
Phone: 501-221-0100
Fax: 501-221-1293

KOKY-FM 94.9 MHz (Urban)
415 N McKinley Suite 920
Little Rock, AR 72205
Phone: 501-663-0092
Fax: 501-664-9201

KOLL-FM 94.9 MHz (Oldies)
8114 Cantrell Rd 3rd Fl
Little Rock, AR 72227
Phone: 501-227-9696
Fax: 501-228-9547

KSSN-FM 95.7 MHz (Ctry)
8114 Cantrell Rd
Little Rock, AR 72227
www.kssn.com/
Phone: 501-227-9696
Fax: 501-228-9547

KSYG-FM 103.7 MHz (N/T)
2400 Cottondale Ln
Little Rock, AR 72202
www.ksyg.com
Phone: 501-661-1037
Fax: 501-664-5871

KUAR-FM 89.1 MHz (NPR)
2801 S University Ave
Little Rock, AR 72204
E-mail: kuar@ualr.edu
www.ualr.edu/~kuar/
Phone: 501-569-8485
Fax: 501-569-8488

KURB-FM 98.5 MHz (AC)
1429 Merrill Dr
Little Rock, AR 72211
www.b98.com
Phone: 501-221-0100
Fax: 501-221-1293

KVLO-FM 102.9 MHz (AC)
1429 Merrill Dr
Little Rock, AR 72211
www.k-love.com
Phone: 501-221-0100
Fax: 501-221-1293

KYFX-FM 99.5 MHz (Urban)
415 N McKinley St Suite 610
Little Rock, AR 72205
Phone: 501-666-9499
Fax: 501-666-9699

Attractions

The Quapaw Quarter in Little Rock, named for the Arkansas native Quapaw Indians, contains some of the city's oldest structures, including some that date from before the Civil War. In Quapaw Quarter's MacArthur Park, the Arkansas Art Center features a 389-seat theater, a library, and an extensive collection of drawings and traveling exhibits in its five galleries (including one children's gallery). The Art Center also offers classes in the visual and performing arts. Across the Arkansas River in North Little Rock is the Old Mill that was used in the opening scene of "Gone With the Wind."

Arkansas Arts Center
501 E 9th St
Little Rock, AR 72202
Phone: 501-372-4000
Fax: 501-375-8053

Arkansas Museum of Discovery
500 E Markham St Suite 150
Little Rock, AR 72201
E-mail: mod@aristotle.net
www.amod.org
Phone: 501-396-7050
Fax: 501-396-7054

Arkansas Repertory Theater
601 Main St
Little Rock, AR 72203
E-mail: tickets@therep.org
www.therep.org
Phone: 501-378-0405
Fax: 501-378-0012

Arkansas State Capitol
Capitol Ave & Woodlane Dr
Little Rock, AR 72201
Phone: 501-682-5080

Arkansas Symphony Orchestra
PO Box 7328
Little Rock, AR 72217
Phone: 501-666-1761
Fax: 501-666-3193

Arkansas Territorial Restoration
200 E 3rd St
Little Rock, AR 72201
E-mail: info@dah.state.ar.us
www.heritage.state.ar.us/atr/her_atr.html
Phone: 501-324-9351
Fax: 501-324-9345

Ballet Arkansas
7509 Cantrell Rd
Little Rock, AR 72207
Phone: 501-664-9509
Fax: 501-664-0833

Breckling Julius Riverfront Park
Cumberland & LaHarpe Sts
Little Rock, AR 72201
Phone: 501-371-4770

Central High Museum Visitor Center
2125 W 14th St
Little Rock, AR 72202
E-mail: chmuseum@swbell.net
home.swbell.net/chmuseum
Phone: 501-374-1957
Fax: 501-376-4728

Children's Museum of Arkansas
1400 W Markham St Suite 200
Little Rock, AR 72201
www.aristotle.net/kidsonline/
Phone: 501-374-6655
Fax: 501-374-4746

Community Theater of Little Rock
13401 Chenal Pkwy Capital Keyboard Theatre
Little Rock, AR 72211
Phone: 501-663-9494

Decorative Arts Museum
411 E 7th St
Little Rock, AR 72202
Phone: 501-396-0357

Hillcrest Historic District
Kavanaugh & Beechwood Sts
Little Rock, AR 72201
www.hillcrest-lr.org/
Phone: 501-376-4781

IMAX Theater
3301 E Roosevelt Rd
Little Rock, AR 72206
www.aerospaced.org
Phone: 501-376-4629
Fax: 501-244-4906

Julius Breckling Park
Laharpe/Cantrell & Markham St
Little Rock, AR 72201
Phone: 501-375-2552

Little Rock Zoo
1 Jonesboro Dr
Little Rock, AR 72205
www.littlerockzoo.com
Phone: 501-666-2406
Fax: 501-666-7040

MacArthur Park
9th St & Commerce
Little Rock, AR 72202
Phone: 501-371-4770

North Shore Riverwalk
Riverfront Dr
North Little Rock, AR 72114
Phone: 501-758-1424

Old Mill
Lakeshore Dr & Fairway Ave
North Little Rock, AR 72216
Phone: 501-791-8537

Old State House
300 W Markham St
Little Rock, AR 72201
E-mail: info@oldstatehouse.org
www.oldstatehouse.org
Phone: 501-324-9685
Fax: 501-324-9688

Opera Theatre at Wildwood
20919 Denny Rd
Little Rock, AR 72223
E-mail: parkinfo@wildwoodpark.org
www.wildwoodpark.org
Phone: 501-821-7275
Fax: 501-821-7280
TF: 888-278-7727

Pinnacle Mountain State Park
11901 Pinnacle Valley Rd
Roland, AR 72135
Phone: 501-868-5806
Fax: 501-868-5018

Quapaw Quarter
1315 S Scott St
Little Rock, AR 72202
Phone: 501-371-0075
Fax: 501-374-8142

Robinson Center
400 W Markham St
Little Rock, AR 72201
www.littlerock.com/facilities/robinson.html
Phone: 501-376-4781
Fax: 501-374-2255
TF: 800-844-4781

Spirit Riverboat Excursions
PO Box 579
North Little Rock, AR 72114
Phone: 501-376-4150

Toltec Mounds State Park
490 Toltec Mounds Rd
Scott, AR 72142
Phone: 501-961-9442
Fax: 501-961-9221

University of Arkansas at Little Rock Planetarium
2801 S University Ave
Little Rock, AR 72204
Phone: 501-569-3259
Fax: 501-569-3314

University of Arkansas Little Rock Gallery
2801 S University Ave
Little Rock, AR 72204
Phone: 501-569-3183
Fax: 501-569-8775

Villa Marre
1320 S Scott St
Little Rock, AR 72202
E-mail: qqa@quapaw.com
www.quapaw.com/villa_marre.html
Phone: 501-371-0075
Fax: 501-374-8142

War Memorial Park
Markham Rd & Fair Pk
Little Rock, AR 72201
Phone: 501-371-4770

Wild River Country Water Park
6820 Crystal Hill Rd
North Little Rock, AR 72118
Phone: 501-753-8600
Fax: 501-753-0277

Wildwood Park for the Performing Arts
20919 Denny Rd
Little Rock, AR 72223
E-mail: parkinfo@wildwoodpark.org
www.wildwoodpark.org
Phone: 501-821-7275
Fax: 501-821-7280
TF: 888-278-7727

Sports Teams & Facilities

ALLTEL Arena
1 ALLTEL Arena Way
North Little Rock, AR 72114
www.alltelarena.com
Phone: 501-340-5660
Fax: 501-340-5668

Arkansas Glacier Cats
2600 Howard St Barton Coliseum
Little Rock, AR 72216
www.glaciercats.com
Phone: 501-374-7825
Fax: 501-374-1225

Arkansas Riverblades (hockey)
1 ALLTEL Arena Way
North Little Rock, AR 72114
www.riverblades.com
Phone: 501-975-2327

Arkansas Travelers (baseball)
War Memorial Pk Ray Winder Field
Little Rock, AR 72205
E-mail: travs@travs.com
www.travs.com
Phone: 501-664-1555
Fax: 501-664-1834

Barton Coliseum
2600 Howard St
Little Rock, AR 72216
E-mail: arkfair@alltell.net
www.arkfairgrounds.com
Phone: 501-372-8341
Fax: 501-372-4197

War Memorial Stadium
Markham & Fair Park
Little Rock, AR 72205
Phone: 501-663-6385
Fax: 501-663-6387

Annual Events

Arkansas Flower & Garden Show
(late February) 501-821-4000
Arkansas Holiday Light Up & Laser Show
(late November-late December) 800-844-4781
Arkansas Marine Expo (mid-January) 501-455-1001
Arkansas River Blues Festival (mid-September) 501-376-4781
Arkansas State Fair (early October) 501-372-8341

Arkansas Territorial Restoration Arts & Crafts Festival (early May) .501-376-4781
Burns Park Arts & Crafts Fair (late September) .800-643-4000
Children's Festival of the Arts (late September) .501-758-1424
Christmas Showcase Arkansas (late November-early December) .501-376-4781
Decorative Arts Forum (mid-March) .501-372-4000
Depression Glass Show & Sale (late February) .501-375-0435
Eagle Awareness Days (mid-January) .501-727-5441
Eagle Watch Barge Tours (January-February) .501-868-5806
Festival of Trees (late November) .501-664-8573
Great Southern Gun & Knife Show (late October) .888-325-4482
Holiday House (mid-November) .501-666-0658
Juneteenth Celebration (mid-June) .501-376-4781
Martin Luther King Jr Holiday Celebration (mid-January) .501-324-9333
Pops On The River (July 4) .501-376-4781
Quapaw Quarter Spring Tour of Homes (early May) .501-376-4781
Riverfest (late May) .501-255-3378
Summer Shakespeare Festival (mid-late August) .501-376-4781
Summerset (early September) .501-758-1424
Timberfest (early October) .870-942-3021
Toadsuck Daze (early May) .501-376-4781
Toughman Contest (late March) .501-376-4781
Wildwood Festival of Music & the Arts (June) .501-821-7275
Wildwood Jazz Festival (early June) .501-821-7275
Zoo Days (mid-late August) .501-666-2406

Los Angeles, California

***County:* Los Angeles**

LOS ANGELES is located in southern California, and the five-county (Los Angeles, Orange, Riverside, San Bernardino, and Ventura) Los Angeles metropolitan area extends from the Pacific Coast to the mountains of south central California, covering more than 34,000 square miles. Major cities within 100 miles of Los Angeles include Santa Barbara, Palm Springs, and San Diego, California; and Tijuana, Mexico.

Area (Land)	469.3 sq mi
Area (Water)	29.1 sq mi
Elevation	330 ft
Latitude	34-05-22 N
Longitude	118-24-28 W
Time Zone	PST
Area Code	213, 310, 818

Climate

Los Angeles has a Mediterranean/semi-tropical climate, with pleasant weather much of the year. Winters are mild, with high temperatures averaging 66 degrees and lows in the upper 40s, and snowfall is rare. Summer days are warm, with average high temperatures in the mid-70s, while evenings cool down into the low 60s. Summer is also the dry season in Los Angeles, with no significant rainfall on record for the months of June and July. February is the wettest month of the year in Los Angeles, with an average precipitation total of only 2.5 inches.

Average Temperatures & Precipitation

Temperatures

	Jan	Feb	Mar	Apr	May	Jun	Jul	Aug	Sep	Oct	Nov	Dec
High	66	66	66	67	69	72	75	77	77	74	70	66
Low	48	49	51	53	56	60	63	64	63	59	53	48

Precipitation

	Jan	Feb	Mar	Apr	May	Jun	Jul	Aug	Sep	Oct	Nov	Dec
Inches	2.4	2.5	2.0	0.7	0.1	0.0	0.0	0.2	0.3	0.3	1.8	1.7

History

Originally inhabited by Native Americans representing some 30 tribes, the region known today as the Los Angeles metropolitan area was first explored by Europeans in 1769. Early Spanish explorers, led by Gaspar de Portola, recognized the potential of the area, with its fertile soil and water resources, to become the site of a settlement. The Spaniards named the river that flowed through the area El Rio de Nuestra Señora la Reina de Los Angeles de Porciuncula (The River of Our Lady the Queen of Angels of Porciuncula). On September 4, 1781, the city founded there was initially given the same name as the river. The city was founded by a group of Mexican settlers known as "Los Pobladores," who had been sent to the area under the direction of the Spanish governor of California, Felipe de Neve. The city later became known as Ciudad de Los Angeles ("City of Angels"), and eventually Los Angeles.

Los Angeles remained under Spanish rule from the time of its founding until Mexico took control of the area in 1822. Twenty-five years later, in 1847, the United States took possession of Los Angeles, and the following year California became a U.S. territory as a result of the Treaty of Guadelupe. In 1850, Los Angeles was incorporated as a city.

Development was slow in Los Angeles until the arrival of the Southern Pacific and Santa Fe Railroads (in 1876 and 1885, respectively), which linked the area with other populated areas of the country. During the late 19th and early 20th century, Los Angeles became a major citrus growing region, and with its ideal location and pleasant climate, the area also developed as a resort area. By 1900 Los Angeles had a population of slightly more than 100,000 residents.

The city of Los Angeles began to grow in population as well as area during the early 1900s. As construction projects were completed in outlying areas, many towns were annexed into Los Angeles. One such project was the completion of a harbor in San Pedro on the Pacific coast that was to be used as L.A.'s port. The growth of the oil industry and the birth of the entertainment industry in Hollywood during the 1920s caused Los Angeles' population to double during that decade. In the 1940s, economic opportunities brought about by wartime industries, such as aircraft manufacturing, led to further population growth in Los Angeles during and immediately after World War II. The mid-1980s also brought a surge in population to the Los Angeles area in the form of immigrants from Asia and Central America (primarily Mexico). Today, nearly 40 percent of Los Angeles' 3.5 million residents are of Hispanic Origin.

Los Angeles is the nation's second most populous city as well as one of the leading commercial, financial, international trade, manufacturing, and transportation centers in the United States. The five-county Los Angeles metropolitan area, which includes Los Angeles (the nation's most populous county), Orange, Riverside, San Bernardino, and Ventura counties, is currently home to more than 15 million people.

Population

1990 Census	3,485,557
1998 Estimate	3,597,556
% Change	3.2
2010 Projection	11,274,600*

Racial/Ethnic Breakdown

White	52.8%
Black	14.0%
Other	33.2%
Hispanic Origin (may be of any race)	39.9%

Age Breakdown

Under 5 years 8.1%
5 to 17 .... 16.7%
18 to 20 .... 5.2%
21 to 24 .... 7.9%
25 to 34 .... 20.7%
35 to 44 .... 15.0%
45 to 54 .... 9.2%
55 to 64 .... 7.2%
65 to 74 .... 5.8%
75+ years 4.2%
Median Age 30.7

Gender Breakdown

Male 50.2%
Female 49.8%

** Information given is for Los Angeles County.*

Government

Type of Government: Mayor-Council

Los Angeles Building & Safety Dept
201 N Figueroa St
Los Angeles, CA 90012
Phone: 213-977-6941
Fax: 213-977-5950

Los Angeles City Attorney
200 N Main St Rm 1800
Los Angeles, CA 90012
Phone: 213-485-5408
Fax: 213-680-3634

Los Angeles City Clerk
200 N Main St Rm 607
Los Angeles, CA 90012
Phone: 213-485-5708
Fax: 213-473-5212

Los Angeles City Council
200 N Main St Rm 615
Los Angeles, CA 90012
Phone: 213-485-5708
Fax: 213-237-0636

Los Angeles City Hall
200 N Main St
Los Angeles, CA 90012
Phone: 213-485-2121

Los Angeles Community Development Dept
215 W 6th St
Los Angeles, CA 90014
Phone: 213-485-1617
Fax: 213-485-2291

Los Angeles Controller
215 W 6th St 8th Fl
Los Angeles, CA 90014
Phone: 213-485-2496
Fax: 213-628-6467

Los Angeles Cultural Affairs Dept
433 S Spring St 10th Fl
Los Angeles, CA 90013
Phone: 213-485-2433
Fax: 213-847-2601

Los Angeles Fire Dept
200 N Main St Rm 1020
Los Angeles, CA 90012
Phone: 213-485-6003
Fax: 213-485-8247

Los Angeles Harbor Dept
425 S Palos Verdes St
San Pedro, CA 90731
Phone: 310-732-7678
Fax: 310-547-4611

Los Angeles Mayor
200 N Main St City Hall Rm 800
Los Angeles, CA 90012
Phone: 213-847-2489
Fax: 213-485-1286

Los Angeles Personnel Dept
700 E Temple St
Los Angeles, CA 90012
Phone: 213-847-9240
Fax: 213-847-9377

Los Angeles Planning Dept
221 N Figueroa St Rm 1640
Los Angeles, CA 90012
Phone: 213-580-1168
Fax: 213-580-1176

Los Angeles Police Dept
150 N Los Angeles St
Los Angeles, CA 90012
Phone: 213-485-3202
Fax: 213-847-0676

Los Angeles Public Library
630 W 5th St
Los Angeles, CA 90071
Phone: 213-228-7000
Fax: 213-228-7429

Los Angeles Public Works Dept
433 S Spring St Suite 600
Los Angeles, CA 90013
Phone: 213-485-3376
Fax: 213-847-3163

Los Angeles Recreation & Parks Dept
200 N Main St Rm 1330
Los Angeles, CA 90012
Phone: 213-473-6833
Fax: 213-978-0014

Los Angeles Transportation Dept
221 N Figueroa St Suite 500
Los Angeles, CA 90012
Phone: 213-580-1177
Fax: 213-580-1188

Los Angeles Water & Power Dept
111 N Hope St Rm 1550
Los Angeles, CA 90012
Phone: 213-367-4211
Fax: 213-367-1438

Important Phone Numbers

AAA 213-741-3686
American Express Travel 310-542-8631
California State Franchise Tax Board 916-845-4300
Dental Referral 213-380-7669
Driver's License/Vehicle Registration Information 213-744-2000
Emergency 911
HotelDocs 800-468-3537
Info Line 323-686-0950
Los Angeles Assn of Realtors 310-967-8800
Los Angeles County Assessor 213-974-3211
Los Angeles County Property Tax Information System (PROPTAX) 213-974-2111
Poison Control Center 800-876-4766
Time 323-853-1212
Travelers Aid 310-646-2270
Voter Registration 562-462-2748
Weather 213-554-1212

Information Sources

Anaheim Chamber of Commerce
100 S Anaheim Blvd Suite 300
Anaheim, CA 92805
anaheimchamber.org
Phone: 714-758-0222
Fax: 714-758-0468

Anaheim City Hall
200 S Anaheim Blvd
Anaheim, CA 92805
www.anaheim.net
Phone: 714-765-5247
Fax: 714-765-5164

Anaheim Convention Center
800 W Katella Ave
Anaheim, CA 92802
www.anaheimresort.com
Phone: 714-765-8900
Fax: 714-765-8965

Anaheim Mayor
200 S Anaheim Blvd 7th Fl
Anaheim, CA 92805
Phone: 714-765-5247
Fax: 714-765-5164

Anaheim Planning Dept
200 S Anaheim Blvd Suite 162
Anaheim, CA 92805
www.anaheim.net/depts_servc/planning
Phone: 714-765-5139
Fax: 714-765-5280

Anaheim Public Library
500 W Broadway
Anaheim, CA 92805
www.anaheim.net/comm_svc/apl
Phone: 714-765-1880
Fax: 714-765-1730

Anaheim/Orange County Visitor & Convention Bureau
800 W Katella Ave
Anaheim, CA 92802
www.anaheimoc.org
Phone: 714-765-8888
Fax: 714-991-8963

Better Business Bureau Serving Los Angeles
3727 W 6th St Suite 607
Los Angeles, CA 90020
www.la.bbb.org
Phone: 213-251-9984
Fax: 213-251-9986

Better Business Bureau Serving Los Angeles Orange Riverside & San Bernardino Counties
PO Box 970
Colton, CA 92324
www.la.bbb.org
Phone: 909-825-7280
Fax: 909-825-6246

Better Business Bureau Serving Placentia
550 W Orangethorpe Ave
Placentia, CA 92870
www.la.bbb.org
Phone: 714-985-8900
Fax: 714-985-8920

Better Business Bureau Serving Southern California
17609 Ventura Blvd Suite LL03
Encino, CA 91316
www.la.bbb.org
Phone: 818-386-5514
Fax: 818-386-5513

Catalina Island Information
PO Box 217
Avalon, CA 90704
www.catalina.com
Phone: 310-510-1520
Fax: 310-510-7606

Downtown Long Beach Associates
1 World Trade Ctr Suite 300
Long Beach, CA 90831
Phone: 562-436-4259
Fax: 562-435-5653

Garden Grove Chamber of Commerce
12866 Main St Suite 102
Garden Grove, CA 92840
www.gardengrovechamber.org
Phone: 714-638-7950
Fax: 714-636-6672

Garden Grove City Hall
11222 Acacia Pkwy
Garden Grove, CA 92842
www.ci.garden-grove.ca.us
Phone: 714-741-5000
Fax: 714-741-5205

Garden Grove Community Development Dept
11222 Acacia Pkwy
Garden Grove, CA 92840
www.ci.garden-grove.ca.us/internet/commdev.html
Phone: 714-741-5120
Fax: 714-741-5136

Garden Grove Mayor
11222 Acacia Pkwy
Garden Grove, CA 92840
Phone: 714-741-5100
Fax: 714-741-5044

Garden Grove Regional Library
11200 Stanford Ave
Garden Grove, CA 92840
www.ocpl.org/ggregnal/ggreg.htm
Phone: 714-530-0711
Fax: 714-530-0961

Garden Grove Visitors Bureau
12866 Main St Suite 102
Garden Grove, CA 92840
Phone: 714-638-7950
Fax: 714-636-6672

Glendale Chamber of Commerce
200 S Louise St
Glendale, CA 91205
www.glendalechamber.com
Phone: 818-240-7870
Fax: 818-240-2872

Glendale City Hall
613 E Broadway
Glendale, CA 91206
www.ci.glendale.ca.us
Phone: 818-548-2090
Fax: 818-241-5386

Glendale Civic Auditorium
1401 N Verdugo Rd
Glendale, CA 91208
www.ci.glendale.ca.us/civicaud
Phone: 818-548-2147
Fax: 818-543-0793

Glendale Community Development & Housing Dept
141 N Glendale Ave Rm 202
Glendale, CA 91206
www.ci.glendale.ca.us/nhood-services/commdev.html
Phone: 818-548-2060
Fax: 818-548-3724

Glendale Mayor
613 E Broadway Suite 200
Glendale, CA 91206
Phone: 818-548-4844
Fax: 818-547-6740

Glendale Public Library
222 E Harvard St
Glendale, CA 91205
library.ci.glendale.ca.us
Phone: 818-548-2021
Fax: 818-548-7225

Greater Oxnard & Harbors Tourism Bureau
200 W 7th St
Oxnard, CA 93030
www.oxnardtourism.com
Phone: 805-385-7545
Fax: 805-385-7571
TF: 800-269-6273

Greater Riverside Chamber of Commerce
3685 Main St Suite 350
Riverside, CA 92501
www.riverside-chamber.com
Phone: 909-683-7100
Fax: 909-683-2670

Huntington Beach Chamber of Commerce
2100 Main St Suite 200
Huntington Beach, CA 92648
www.hbchamber.org
Phone: 714-536-8888
Fax: 714-960-7654

Huntington Beach City Hall
2000 Main St
Huntington Beach, CA 92648
www.ci.huntington-beach.ca.us
Phone: 714-536-5511
Fax: 714-374-1557

Huntington Beach Conference & Visitors Bureau
101 Main St Suite 2A
Huntington Beach, CA 92648
www.hbvisit.com/
Phone: 714-969-3492
Fax: 714-969-5592

Huntington Beach Economic Development Dept
PO Box 190
Huntington Beach, CA 92648
www.hbbiz.com
Phone: 714-536-5582
Fax: 714-375-5087

Huntington Beach Mayor
2000 Main St
Huntington Beach, CA 92648
Phone: 714-536-5553
Fax: 714-536-5233

Huntington Beach Public Library
7111 Talbert Ave
Huntington Beach, CA 92648
www.hbpl.org
Phone: 714-842-4481
Fax: 714-375-5180

Long Beach Business Development Center
200 Pine Ave 4th Fl
Long Beach, CA 90802
www.ci.long-beach.ca.us/bdc/bdc
Phone: 562-570-3800
Fax: 562-570-3897

Long Beach City Hall
333 W Ocean Blvd
Long Beach, CA 90802
www.ci.long-beach.ca.us
Phone: 562-570-6555

Long Beach Convention & Entertainment Center
300 E Ocean Blvd
Long Beach, CA 90802
www.longbeachcc.com
Phone: 562-436-3636
Fax: 562-436-9491

Long Beach Convention & Visitors Bureau
1 World Trade Ctr Suite 300
Long Beach, CA 90831
www.golongbeach.org
Phone: 562-436-3645
Fax: 562-435-5653
TF: 800-452-7829

Long Beach Mayor
333 W Ocean Blvd
Long Beach, CA 90802
www.ci.long-beach.ca.us/mayor-council/mayor.htm
Phone: 562-570-6309
Fax: 562-570-6538

Long Beach Public Library
101 Pacific Ave
Long Beach, CA 90822
www.lbpl.org
Phone: 562-570-7500
Fax: 562-570-7408

Los Angeles Area Chamber of Commerce
350 S Bixel St
Los Angeles, CA 90017
www.lachamber.org
Phone: 213-580-7500
Fax: 213-580-7511

Los Angeles Convention & Exhibition Center
1201 S Figueroa St
Los Angeles, CA 90015
www.lacclink.com
Phone: 213-741-1151
Fax: 213-765-4266
TF: 800-448-7775

Los Angeles Convention & Visitors Bureau
633 W 5th St Suite 6000
Los Angeles, CA 90071
www.lacvb.com
Phone: 213-624-7300
Fax: 213-624-9746
TF: 800-228-2452

Los Angeles County
500 W Temple St
Los Angeles, CA 90012
www.co.la.ca.us
Phone: 213-974-1311

Orange County
12 Civic Center Plaza
Santa Ana, CA 92702
www.oc.ca.gov
Phone: 714-834-2500
Fax: 714-834-2675

Oxnard
721 S 'A' St
Oxnard, CA 93030
www.oxnardedc.com
Phone: 805-385-7444
Fax: 805-385-7452
TF: 800-422-6332

Oxnard Chamber of Commerce
400 S 'A' St
Oxnard, CA 93030
www.oxnardchamber.org
Phone: 805-385-8860
Fax: 805-487-1763

Oxnard City Hall
305 W 3rd St
Oxnard, CA 93030
www.ci.oxnard.ca.us/cityhall.html
Phone: 805-385-7803
Fax: 805-385-7806

Oxnard Community Development Dept
305 W 3rd St
Oxnard, CA 93030
www.ci.oxnard.ca.us/econdev.html
Phone: 805-385-7857
Fax: 805-385-7408

Oxnard Mayor
300 W 3rd St
Oxnard, CA 93030
Phone: 805-385-7430
Fax: 805-385-7595

Oxnard Public Library
251 S 'A' St
Oxnard, CA 93030
www.oxnard.org
Phone: 805-385-7500
Fax: 805-385-7526

Riverside City & County Public Library
3581 Mission Inn Ave
Riverside, CA 92501
www.ci.riverside.ca.us/library
Phone: 909-862-5201
Fax: 909-826-5407

Riverside City Hall
3900 Main St
Riverside, CA 92522
www.ci.riverside.ca.us
Phone: 909-826-5312
Fax: 909-826-5470

Riverside Convention & Visitors Bureau
3737 6th St
Riverside, CA 92501
www.riversidecb.com
Phone: 909-222-4700
Fax: 909-222-4712

Riverside Convention Center
3443 Orange St
Riverside, CA 92501
Phone: 909-787-7950
Fax: 909-222-4706

Riverside County
4080 Lemon St 12th Fl
Riverside, CA 92501
www.co.riverside.ca.us
Phone: 909-955-1100
Fax: 909-955-1105

Riverside Development Dept
3900 Main St 5th Fl
Riverside, CA 92522
www.ci.riverside.ca.us/devdept
Phone: 909-826-5649
Fax: 909-826-5744

Riverside Mayor
3900 Main St
Riverside, CA 92522
www.ci.riverside.ca.us/mayor/Default.htm
Phone: 909-826-5551
Fax: 909-826-2543

San Bernardino Area Chamber of Commerce
PO Box 658
San Bernardino, CA 92402
www.sbachamber.org
Phone: 909-885-7515
Fax: 909-384-9979

San Bernardino City Hall
300 N 'D' St
San Bernardino, CA 92418
www.ci.san-bernardino.ca.us
Phone: 909-384-5133
Fax: 909-384-5067

San Bernardino Convention & Visitors Bureau
201 N 'E' St Suite 103
San Bernardino, CA 92401
san-bernardino.org
Phone: 909-889-3980
Fax: 909-888-5998
TF: 800-867-8366

San Bernardino County
222 W Hospitality Ln
San Bernardino, CA 92415
www.co.san-bernardino.ca.us
Phone: 909-387-8306
Fax: 909-376-8940

San Bernardino Economic Development Agency
201 N 'E' St Suite 301
San Bernardino, CA 92401
www.sanbernardino-eda.org
Phone: 909-663-1044
Fax: 909-888-9413

San Bernardino Mayor
300 N 'D' St
San Bernardino, CA 92418
Phone: 909-384-5051
Fax: 909-384-5067

San Bernardino Public Library
555 W 6th St
San Bernardino, CA 92410
e2.empirenet.com/~sbpl
Phone: 909-381-8201
Fax: 909-381-8229

Santa Ana Chamber of Commerce
PO Box 205
Santa Ana, CA 92702
www.santaanacc.com
Phone: 714-541-5353
Fax: 714-541-2238

Santa Ana City Hall
20 Civic Center Plaza
Santa Ana, CA 92701
www.ci.santa-ana.ca.us
Phone: 714-647-6900
Fax: 714-649-6954

Santa Ana Community Development Agency
PO Box 1988
Santa Ana, CA 92702
www.ci.santa-ana.ca.us/departments/cda/default.htm
Phone: 714-647-5360
Fax: 714-647-6549

Santa Ana Mayor
20 Civic Center Plaza
Santa Ana, CA 92701
www.ci.santa-ana.ca.us/mayor/default.htm
Phone: 714-647-6900
Fax: 714-647-6954

Santa Ana Public Library
26 Civic Center Plaza
Santa Ana, CA 92701
www.ci.santa-ana.ca.us/departments/library/default.htm
Phone: 714-647-5250
Fax: 714-647-5356

Ventura County
800 S Victoria Ave
Ventura, CA 93009
www.ventura.org/vencnty.htm
Phone: 805-654-2267
Fax: 805-662-6343

Online Resources

4LA.com
www.4la.com

4LongBeach.com
www.4longbeach.com

4OrangeCounty.com
www.4orangecounty.com

4Riverside.com
www.4riverside.com

4SantaAna.com
www.4santaana.com

@LA
www.at-la.com

About Los Angeles
www.thewebstation.com/OgardTravel/losangeles/

About.com Guide to Hollywood
hollywood.about.com/citiestowns/caus/hollywood/mbody.htm

About.com Guide to San Gabriel Valley
sangabriel.about.com/citiestowns/caus/sangabriel/mbody.htm

About.com Guide to Santa Monica
santamonica.about.com/citiestowns/caus/santamonica/mbody.htm

Anaheim CityLink
www.usacitylink.com/citylink/anaheim

Annual Guide for the Arts
www.guide4arts.com/la/

Anthill City Guide Anaheim
www.anthill.com/city.asp?city=anaheim

Anthill City Guide Glendale
www.anthill.com/city.asp?city=glendale

Anthill City Guide Long Beach
www.anthill.com/city.asp?city=longbeach

Anthill City Guide Los Angeles
www.anthill.com/city.asp?city=losangeles

Anthill City Guide Oxnard
www.anthill.com/city.asp?city=oxnard

Anthill City Guide Riverside
www.anthill.com/city.asp?city=riverside

Anthill City Guide San Bernardino
www.anthill.com/city.asp?city=sanbernardino

Area Guide Anaheim
anaheim.areaguides.net

Area Guide Long Beach
longbeach.areaguides.net

Area Guide Los Angeles
losangeles.areaguides.net

Area Guide Riverside
riverside.areaguides.net

ArtScene
artscenecal.com/index.html

Boulevards Los Angeles
www.losangeles.com

Bradmans.com Los Angeles
www.bradmans.com/scripts/display_city.cgi?city=237

Calendar Live
calendarlive.com

City Knowledge Anaheim
www.cityknowledge.com/ca_anaheim.htm

City Knowledge Garden Grove
www.cityknowledge.com/ca_garden_grove.htm

City Knowledge Glendale
www.cityknowledge.com/ca_glendale.htm

City Knowledge Huntington Beach
www.cityknowledge.com/ca_huntington_beach.htm

City Knowledge Long Beach
www.cityknowledge.com/ca_longbeach.htm

City Knowledge Los Angeles
www.cityknowledge.com/ca_losangeles.htm

City Knowledge Oxnard
www.cityknowledge.com/ca_oxnard.htm

CityTravelGuide.com Los Angeles
www.citytravelguide.com/los-angeles.htm

CuisineNet Los Angeles
www.cuisinenet.com/restaurant/los_angeles/index.shtml

DigitalCity Los Angeles
home.digitalcity.com/losangeles

Excite.com Anaheim City Guide
www.excite.com/travel/countries/united_states/california/anaheim

Excite.com Garden Grove City Guide
www.excite.com/travel/countries/united_states/california/garden_grove/

Excite.com Huntington Beach City Guide
www.excite.com/travel/countries/united_states/california/huntington_beach

Excite.com Long Beach City Guide
www.excite.com/travel/countries/united_states/california/long_beach

Excite.com Los Angeles City Guide
www.excite.com/travel/countries/united_states/california/los_angeles

Excite.com Oxnard City Guide
www.excite.com/travel/countries/united_states/california/oxnard

Excite.com Riverside City Guide
www.excite.com/travel/countries/united_states/california/riverside

Excite.com San Bernardino City Guide
www.excite.com/travel/countries/united_states/california/san_bernardino

Excite.com Santa Ana City Guide
www.excite.com/travel/countries/united_states/california/santa_ana

Garden Grove On Line
www.gardengrove.com/

Gayot's Guide Restaurant Search Los Angeles
www.perrier.com/restaurants/gayot.asp?area=LSA

Glendale City Net
www.excite.com/travel/countries/united_states/california/glendale

Glendale Community Wire Service
www.cwire.com/glendale/

Glendale On-Line
glendale-online.com

GlendaleAccess.com
www.glendaleaccess.com

HotelGuide Anaheim
hotelguide.net/anaheim

HotelGuide Los Angeles
losangeles.hotelguide.net

Huntington Beach News
hb.quik.com/jperson

Huntington Beach Online
www.hbonline.com/

InOrangeCounty.com
www.inorangecounty.com

LA Dining
ladining.com

LA Directory
www.ladir.com/

LA Loop
www.smart1.net/laloop/

LA Weekly
www.laweekly.com

La.com
www.la.com

LA2nite.com
www.la2nite.com

LAHarbor.com
laharbor.com

Lodging.com Los Angeles California
www.lodging.com/auto/guides/los_angeles-area-ca.html

Long Beach Jewish Community Web Site
jcclb.org

Long Beach Virtual Village
www.lngbch.com

Los Angeles California
www.los-angeles-california.com

Los Angeles CityWomen
www.citywomen.com/lawomen.htm

Los Angeles Culture Net
home.lacn.org/LACN

Los Angeles Downtown News
losangelesdowntown.com

Los Angeles Graphic City Guide
www.futurecast.com/gcg/la.htm

LosAngeles.TheLinks.com
losangeles.thelinks.com

Open World City Guides Los Angeles
www.worldexecutive.com/cityguides/los_angeles/

Orange County's Premier Website
www.ocpremier.com

Rough Guide Travel Los Angeles
travel.roughguides.com/content/1300/

San Bernardino.com
www.sanbernardino.com

Savvy Diner Guide to Los Angeles Restaurants
www.savvydiner.com/losangeles/

Search Los Angeles
www.searchlosangeles.com

Surf & Sun Beach Vacation Guide to Huntington Beach
www.surf-sun.com/ca-huntington-main.htm

Surf & Sun Beach Vacation Guide to Long Beach
www.surf-sun.com/ca-long-beach-main.htm

Surf & Sun Beach Vacation Guide to Los Angeles
www.surf-sun.com/ca-los-angeles-main.htm

Surf City
surfcity.huntington-beach.ca.us/

Surf City Web
www.surfcityweb.com

Time Out Los Angeles
www.timeout.com/losangeles/

Virtual Voyages Los Angeles
www.virtualvoyages.com/usa/ca/l_a/l_a.sht

WeekendEvents.com Los Angeles
www.weekendevents.com/LOSANGEL/la.html

Westside Story Newspaper
www.westsidestory.com

Yahoo! Los Angeles
www.la.yahoo.com

Area Communities

Incorporated communities with populations greater than 100,000 in the five-county Los Angeles metropolitan area include:

Anaheim
200 S Anaheim Blvd
Anaheim, CA 92805
Phone: 714-765-5247
Fax: 714-765-5164

Corona
815 W 6th St
Corona, CA 92882
Phone: 909-736-2201
Fax: 909-736-2399

Costa Mesa
77 Fair Dr
Costa Mesa, CA 92626
Phone: 714-754-5223

El Monte
11333 Valley Blvd
El Monte, CA 91731
Phone: 626-580-2016
Fax: 626-580-2274

Fontana
8353 Sierra Ave
Fontana, CA 92335
Phone: 909-350-7605
Fax: 909-350-6613

Fullerton
303 W Commonwealth Ave
Fullerton, CA 92832
Phone: 714-738-6300
Fax: 714-525-8071

Garden Grove
11222 Acacia Pkwy
Garden Grove, CA 92842
Phone: 714-741-5000
Fax: 714-741-5205

Glendale
613 E Broadway
Glendale, CA 91206
Phone: 818-548-2090
Fax: 818-241-5386

Huntington Beach
2000 Main St
Huntington Beach, CA 92648
Phone: 714-536-5511
Fax: 714-374-1557

Inglewood
1 W Manchester Blvd
Inglewood, CA 90301
Phone: 310-412-5111
Fax: 310-412-8788

Irvine
1 Civic Center Plaza
Irvine, CA 92606
Phone: 949-724-6000
Fax: 949-724-6045

Lancaster
44933 N Fern Ave
Lancaster, CA 93534
Phone: 661-723-6000
Fax: 661-723-6141

Long Beach
333 W Ocean Blvd
Long Beach, CA 90802
Phone: 562-570-6555

Moreno Valley
14177 Frederick St
Moreno Valley, CA 92553
Phone: 909-413-3001
Fax: 909-413-3009

Ontario
303 E 'B' St
Ontario, CA 91764
Phone: 909-986-1151
Fax: 909-395-2070

Orange
300 E Chapman Ave
Orange, CA 92866
Phone: 714-744-5500
Fax: 714-744-5515

Oxnard
305 W 3rd St
Oxnard, CA 93030
Phone: 805-385-7803
Fax: 805-385-7806

Palmdale
38300 Sierra Hwy
Palmdale, CA 93550
Phone: 661-267-5100
Fax: 661-267-5122

Pasadena
100 N Garfield Ave
Pasadena, CA 91109
Phone: 626-744-4124
Fax: 626-744-3921

Pomona
505 S Garey Ave
Pomona, CA 91766
Phone: 909-620-2311
Fax: 909-620-3710

Rancho Cucamonga
10500 Civic Center Dr
Rancho Cucamonga, CA 91730
Phone: 909-477-2700
Fax: 909-477-2849

Riverside
3900 Main St
Riverside, CA 92522
Phone: 909-826-5312
Fax: 909-826-5470

San Bernardino
300 N 'D' St
San Bernardino, CA 92418
Phone: 909-384-5133
Fax: 909-384-5067

Santa Ana
20 Civic Center Plaza
Santa Ana, CA 92701
Phone: 714-647-6900
Fax: 714-649-6954

Santa Clarita
23920 Valencia Blvd Suite 300
Santa Clarita, CA 91355
Phone: 661-259-2489

Simi Valley
2929 TAPO Canyon Rd
Simi Valley, CA 93063
Phone: 805-583-6700
Fax: 805-583-6300

Thousand Oaks
2100 E Thousand Oaks Blvd
Thousand Oaks, CA 91362
Phone: 805-449-2100
Fax: 805-449-2150

Torrance
3031 Torrance Blvd
Torrance, CA 90503
Phone: 310-328-5310
Fax: 310-618-2931

Economy

Although Los Angeles has long been associated with the entertainment industry, the metropolitan area has a diverse economic base that ranges from agriculture to the aerospace industry. The area is, in fact, one of California's leading agricultural and commercial fishing regions—primary products include fruits, nuts, fresh-cut flowers, tuna, anchovy, and mackerel. Other major industries in the Los Angeles metropolitan area include business and financial services, aerospace, tourism, health services, wholesale trade, and international trade. Services is, by far, Los Angeles County's largest employment sector—service-related positions account for more than twice as many jobs as retail positions, and retail trade is the county's second largest employment sector.

Unemployment Rate 6.2%
Per Capita Income $26,773*
Median Family Income $51,300*

** Information given is for the Los Angeles-Long Beach Metropolitan Statistical Area (MSA), which includes the City of Los Angeles, the City of Long Beach, the City of Burbank, the City of Pasadena, the City of Pomona, and Los Angeles County.*

Principal Industries & Number of Wage Earners

Los Angeles County - 1999

Industry	Wage Earners
Construction	121,900
Finance, Insurance, & Real Estate	230,100
Government	549,500
Manufacturing	663,800
Mining	4,500
Retail Trade	605,800
Services	1,323,700
Transportation & Public Utilities	229,300
Wholesale Trade	276,800

Major Employers

California Federal Bank
5660 Wilshire Blvd
Los Angeles, CA 90036
www.calfed.com
Phone: 800-843-2265

California Hospital Medical Center
1401 S Grand Ave
Los Angeles, CA 90015
www.chmcla.com
Phone: 213-748-2411
Fax: 213-742-5725

Capitol Records
1750 N Vine St
Hollywood, CA 90028
hollywoodandvine.com
Phone: 323-462-6252
Fax: 323-469-0384

Cedars-Sinai Medical Center
8700 Beverly Blvd
Los Angeles, CA 90048
www.csmc.edu
Phone: 310-855-5000
Fax: 310-967-0105
TF: 800-233-2771

Children's Hospital of Los Angeles
4650 Sunset Blvd
Los Angeles, CA 90027
www.childrenshospitalla.org
Phone: 323-660-2450
Fax: 323-666-3809
TF: 800-877-2452

Chuck Fries Productions
1880 Century Pk E Suite 315
Los Angeles, CA 90067
Phone: 310-203-9520
Fax: 310-203-9520

Dames & Moore Inc
911 Wilshire Blvd Suite 700
Los Angeles, CA 90017
www.dames.com
Phone: 213-683-1560
Fax: 213-996-2290

Gleason Corp/Ace Products Inc
10474 Santa Monica Blvd Suite 400
Los Angeles, CA 90025
Phone: 310-470-6001
Fax: 310-470-4121

Hanna-Barbera Productions Inc
3400 Cahuenga Blvd
Hollywood, CA 90068
Phone: 323-851-5000
Fax: 323-969-1201

Hughes Electronics Corp Phone: 310-364-6000
2000 E El Segundo Blvd
El Segundo, CA 90245
E-mail: corpcomm@hughes.com
www.hughes.com

Los Angeles City Hall Phone: 213-485-2121
200 N Main St
Los Angeles, CA 90012
www.ci.la.ca.us

Los Angeles Community College District Phone: 213-891-2000
770 Wilshire Blvd Fax: 213-891-2035
Los Angeles, CA 90017
www.laccd.edu

Los Angeles County Phone: 213-974-1311
500 W Temple St
Los Angeles, CA 90012
www.co.la.ca.us

Los Angeles Unified School District Phone: 213-625-6000
450 N Grand Ave Fax: 213-628-9701
Los Angeles, CA 90012
www.lausd.k12.ca.us

Northrop Grumman Corp Phone: 310-553-6262
1840 Century Pk E Fax: 310-553-2076
Los Angeles, CA 90067
www.northrop-grumman.com

Paramount Pictures Phone: 323-956-5000
5555 Melrose Ave Fax: 323-862-8528
Los Angeles, CA 90038
www.paramount.com

Pardee Construction Co Phone: 310-475-3525
10880 Wilshire Blvd Suite 1900 Fax: 310-446-1291
Los Angeles, CA 90024

Queen of Angels Hollywood Presbyterian Medical Center Phone: 323-913-4800
1300 N Vermont Ave Fax: 323-644-4411
Los Angeles, CA 90027
bloodlessdoctors.com

University of California Los Angeles Phone: 310-825-4321
405 Hilgard Ave Fax: 310-206-1206
Los Angeles, CA 90095
www.ucla.edu

University of Southern California Phone: 213-740-2311
University Pk Fax: 213-740-6364
Los Angeles, CA 90089
www.usc.edu

Unocal Corp Phone: 310-726-7600
2141 Rosecrans Ave Fax: 310-726-7872
El Segundo, CA 90245
E-mail: askus@www.unocal.com
www.unocal.com

Young's Market Co LLC Phone: 714-283-4933
2164 N Batavia St Fax: 714-283-6175
Orange, CA 92865
www.youngsmarket.com

Quality of Living Indicators

Total Crime Index....................................183,706
(rates per 100,000 inhabitants)

Violent Crime
Murder/manslaughter.......................... 426
Forcible rape 1,395
Robbery...................................15,835
Aggravated assault..........................31,545

Property Crime
Burglary 26,067
Larceny theft 79,997
Motor vehicle theft.........................28,441

Cost of Living Index....................................123.1
(national average = 100)

Median Home Price................................$205,300

Education

Public Schools

Los Angeles Unified School District Phone: 213-625-6000
450 N Grand Ave Fax: 213-628-9701
Los Angeles, CA 90012
www.lausd.k12.ca.us

Number of Schools
Elementary................................ 420
Middle 72
High....................................... 49

Student/Teacher Ratio
All Grades 23.0:1

Private Schools

Number of Schools (all grades).................. 100+

Colleges & Universities

American Academy of Dramatic Arts Phone: 626-229-9777
600 Playhouse Alley Fax: 626-229-9977
Pasadena, CA 91101 TF: 800-222-2867
www.aada.org

American Film Institute Phone: 323-856-7600
2021 N Western Ave Fax: 323-467-4578
Los Angeles, CA 90027 TF: 800-999-4234
www.afionline.org

American InterContinental University Los Angeles Phone: 310-302-2000
12655 W Jefferson Blvd Fax: 310-302-2002
Los Angeles, CA 90066 TF: 800-333-2652
E-mail: info@aiuniv.edu
www.aiuniv.edu

Art Center College of Design Phone: 626-396-2200
1700 Lida St Fax: 626-405-9104
Pasadena, CA 91103
www.artcenter.edu

Azusa Pacific University
1915 W Orangewood Ave
Orange, CA 92868
E-mail: uc@apu.edu
www.apu.edu
Phone: 714-935-9697
Fax: 714-935-0356
TF: 800-825-5278

Azusa Pacific University
901 E Alosta Ave
Azusa, CA 91702
www.apu.edu
Phone: 626-969-3434
Fax: 626-969-7180

Brooks College
4825 E Pacific Coast Hwy
Long Beach, CA 90804
E-mail: admin@brookscollege.edu
www.brookscollege.edu
Phone: 562-498-2441
Fax: 562-597-7412
TF: 800-421-3775

California Baptist College
8432 Magnolia Ave
Riverside, CA 92504
www.calbaptist.edu
Phone: 909-689-5771
Fax: 909-343-4525
TF: 877-228-8866

California Institute of Technology
1200 E California Blvd
Pasadena, CA 91125
E-mail: ugadmissions@caltech.edu
www.caltech.edu
Phone: 626-395-6811
Fax: 626-683-3026
TF: 800-568-8324

California Institute of the Arts
24700 McBean Pkwy
Valencia, CA 91355
www.calarts.edu
Phone: 661-255-1050
Fax: 661-254-8352
TF: 800-545-2787

California International University
3130 Wilshire Blvd
Los Angeles, CA 90010
E-mail: dean@ciula.edu
www.ciula.edu
Phone: 213-381-3719
Fax: 213-381-6990

California State University Fullerton
800 N State College Blvd
Fullerton, CA 92831
www.fullerton.edu
Phone: 714-278-2011
Fax: 714-278-2300

California State University Long Beach
1250 Bellflower Blvd
Long Beach, CA 90840
www.csulb.edu
Phone: 562-985-4111
Fax: 562-985-4973

California State University Los Angeles
5151 State University Dr
Los Angeles, CA 90032
www.calstatela.edu
Phone: 323-343-3000
Fax: 323-343-3888

California State University San Bernardino
5500 University Pkwy
San Bernardino, CA 92407
www.csusb.edu
Phone: 909-880-5000
Fax: 909-880-7021

Cerritos College
11110 Alondra Blvd
Norwalk, CA 90650
E-mail: info@cerritos.edu
www.cerritos.edu
Phone: 562-860-2451
Fax: 562-467-5068

Chaffey College
5885 Haven Ave
Rancho Cucamonga, CA 91737
www.chaffey.cc.ca.us
Phone: 909-987-1737
Fax: 909-941-2783

Chapman University
1 University Dr
Orange, CA 92866
E-mail: low@chapman.edu
www.chapman.edu
Phone: 714-997-6815
Fax: 714-997-6713
TF: 800-282-7759

Citrus College
1000 W Foothill Blvd
Glendora, CA 91741
www.citrus.cc.ca.us
Phone: 626-963-0323
Fax: 626-914-8618

City University of Los Angeles
PO Box 4277
Inglewood, CA 90309
E-mail: info@cula.com
www.cula.edu
Phone: 310-671-0783
Fax: 310-671-0572
TF: 800-262-8388

Coastline Community College
11460 Warner Ave
Fountain Valley, CA 92708
coastline.cccd.edu
Phone: 714-546-7600
Fax: 714-241-6288

College of Oceaneering
272 S Fries Ave
Wilmington, CA 90744
E-mail: admissions@diveco.com
diveco.com
Phone: 310-834-2501
Fax: 310-834-7132
TF: 800-432-3483

College of the Canyons
26455 N Rockwell Canyon Rd
Santa Clarita, CA 91355
E-mail: pio660@coc.cc.ca.us
www.coc.cc.ca.us
Phone: 661-259-7800
Fax: 661-254-7996

Columbia College Hollywood
18618 Oxnard St
Tarzana, CA 91356
www.columbiacollege.edu
Phone: 818-345-8414
Fax: 818-345-9053

Compton Community College
1111 E Artesia Blvd
Compton, CA 90221
www.compton.cc.ca.us
Phone: 310-637-2660
Fax: 310-900-1695

Cypress College
9200 Valley View St
Cypress, CA 90630
www.cypress.cc.ca.us
Phone: 714-484-7000
Fax: 714-484-7446

DeVRY Institute of Technology
3880 Kilroy Airport Way
Long Beach, CA 90806
www.lb.devry.edu
Phone: 562-427-4162
Fax: 562-427-3512
TF: 800-597-1333

Don Bosco Technical Institute
1151 San Gabriel Blvd
Rosemead, CA 91770
Phone: 626-307-6500
Fax: 626-940-2000

East Los Angeles College
1301 Cesar Chavez Ave
Monterey Park, CA 91754
E-mail: east@laccd.cc.ca.us
www.laccd.edu/college.htm#EAST
Phone: 323-265-8650
Fax: 323-265-8688

El Camino College
16007 Crenshaw Blvd
Torrance, CA 90506
www.elcamino.cc.ca.us
Phone: 310-532-3670
Fax: 310-660-3818

Eubanks Conservatory of Music & Arts Phone: 323-291-7821
4928 S Crenshaw Blvd
Los Angeles, CA 90043

Fashion Institute of Design & Merchandising Phone: 213-624-1200
919 S Grand Ave Fax: 213-624-4777
Los Angeles, CA 90015 TF: 800-421-0127
E-mail: fidm@fidm.com
www.fidm.com

Glendale Community College Phone: 818-240-1000
1500 N Verdugo Rd Fax: 818-551-5255
Glendale, CA 91208
E-mail: gparker@glendale.cc.ca.us
www.glendale.cc.ca.us

Golden West College Phone: 714-892-7711
15744 Golden West St Fax: 714-895-8960
Huntington Beach, CA 92647
E-mail: mposner@mail.gwc.cccd.edu
www.gwc.cccd.edu

Hebrew Union College Los Angeles Phone: 213-749-3424
3077 University Ave Fax: 213-747-6128
Los Angeles, CA 90007
cwis.usc.edu/dept/huc-la

International Christian University & Seminary Phone: 213-381-0081
2853 W 7th St Fax: 213-381-0010
Los Angeles, CA 90005

ITT Technical Institute Phone: 310-380-1555
20050 S Vermont Ave Fax: 310-380-1557
Torrance, CA 90502 TF: 800-388-3368
www.itt-tech.edu

ITT Technical Institute Phone: 818-364-5151
12669 Encinitas Ave Fax: 818-364-5150
Sylmar, CA 91342 TF: 800-363-2086
www.itt-tech.edu

ITT Technical Institute Phone: 714-535-3700
525 N Muller Ave Fax: 714-535-1802
Anaheim, CA 92801
www.itt-tech.edu

ITT Technical Institute Phone: 909-889-3800
630 E Brier Dr Suite 150 Fax: 909-888-6970
San Bernardino, CA 92408 TF: 800-888-3801
www.itt-tech.edu

La Sierra University Phone: 909-785-2000
4700 Pierce St Fax: 909-785-2447
Riverside, CA 92515
E-mail: dulerodr@lasierra.edu
www.lasierra.edu

Loma Linda University Phone: 909-824-4300
11234 Anderson St Fax: 909-824-4577
Loma Linda, CA 92354
www.llu.edu

Long Beach City College Phone: 562-938-4111
4901 E Carson St Fax: 562-420-4118
Long Beach, CA 90808
E-mail: rschultz@lbcc.cc.ca.us
www.lbcc.cc.ca.us

Los Angeles City College Phone: 323-953-4000
855 N Vermont Ave Fax: 323-953-4294
Los Angeles, CA 90029
citywww.lacc.cc.ca.us

Los Angeles Community College District Phone: 213-891-2000
770 Wilshire Blvd Fax: 213-891-2035
Los Angeles, CA 90017
www.laccd.edu

Los Angeles Harbor College Phone: 310-522-8200
1111 Figueroa Pl Fax: 310-834-1882
Wilmington, CA 90744
E-mail: woodg@laccd.cc.ca.us
www.lahc.cc.ca.us

Los Angeles Mission College Phone: 818-364-7600
13356 Eldridge Ave Fax: 818-364-7755
Sylmar, CA 91342
www.lamission.cc.ca.us

Los Angeles Pierce College Phone: 818-347-0551
6201 Winnetka Ave Fax: 818-710-9844
Woodland Hills, CA 91371
www.piercecollege.com

Los Angeles Trade-Technical College Phone: 213-744-9500
400 W Washington Blvd Fax: 213-748-7334
Los Angeles, CA 90015
E-mail: tradetech@laccd.cc.ca.us
www.lattc.cc.ca.us

Los Angeles Valley College Phone: 818-947-2600
5800 Fulton Ave Fax: 818-947-2610
Valley Glen, CA 91401
E-mail: jakme@bigfoot.com
www.lavc.cc.ca.us

Loyola Marymount University Phone: 310-338-2700
7900 Loyola Blvd Fax: 310-338-2797
Los Angeles, CA 90045
E-mail: bweinste@lmumail.lmu.edu
www.lmu.edu

Marymount College Palos Verdes Phone: 310-377-5501
30800 Palos Verdes Dr E Fax: 310-377-6223
Rancho Palos Verdes, CA 90275
E-mail: admissions@marymountpv.edu
www.marymountpv.edu

Mount Saint Mary's College Phone: 310-476-2237
12001 Chalon Rd Fax: 310-954-4259
Los Angeles, CA 90049 TF: 800-999-9893
www.msmc.la.edu

Mount Saint Mary's College Doheny Campus Phone: 213-746-0450
10 Chester Pl Fax: 213-477-2569
Los Angeles, CA 90007
www.msmc.la.edu

Mount San Antonio College Phone: 909-594-5611
1100 N Grand Ave Fax: 909-468-4068
Walnut, CA 91789
www.mtsac.edu

National University Phone: 714-429-5300
765 The City Dr Fax: 714-429-5307
Orange, CA 92868 TF: 800-628-8648
www.nu.edu

Occidental College
1600 Campus Rd
Los Angeles, CA 90041
www.oxy.edu
Phone: 323-259-2500
Fax: 323-259-2958
TF: 800-825-5262

Otis College of Art & Design
9045 Lincoln Blvd
Los Angeles, CA 90045
www.otisart.edu
Phone: 310-665-6820
Fax: 310-665-6821
TF: 800-527-6847

Oxnard College
4000 S Rose Ave
Oxnard, CA 93033
www.oxnard.cc.ca.us
Phone: 805-488-0911
Fax: 805-986-5806

Pacific Southern University
9581 W Pico Blvd
Los Angeles, CA 90035
Phone: 310-551-0304
Fax: 310-277-5280
TF: 888-477-8872

Pacific Western University
600 N Sepulveda Blvd
Los Angeles, CA 90049
www.pwu.com
Phone: 310-471-0306
Fax: 310-471-6456
TF: 800-423-3244

Pasadena City College
1570 E Colorado Blvd
Pasadena, CA 91106
www.paccd.cc.ca.us
Phone: 626-585-7123
Fax: 626-585-7915

Pepperdine University
24255 Pacific Coast Hwy
Malibu, CA 90263
www.pepperdine.edu
Phone: 310-456-4000
Fax: 310-456-4758

Rancho Santiago Community College District Office
2323 N Broadway
Santa Ana, CA 92706
www.rancho.cc.ca.us
Phone: 714-480-7484
Fax: 714-796-3939

Rio Hondo College
3600 Workman Mill Rd
Whittier, CA 90601
www.rh.cc.ca.us/
Phone: 562-692-0921
Fax: 562-692-8318

Riverside Community College Riverside City Campus
4800 Magnolia Ave
Riverside, CA 92506
E-mail: webmstr@rccd.cc.ca.us
www.rccd.cc.ca.us
Phone: 909-222-8000
Fax: 909-222-8036

Ryokan College
11965 Venice Blvd Suite 304
Los Angeles, CA 90066
www.ryokan.edu
Phone: 310-390-7560
Fax: 310-391-9756

San Bernardino Valley College
701 S Mt Vernon Ave
San Bernardino, CA 92410
sbvc.sbccd.cc.ca.us
Phone: 909-888-6511
Fax: 909-889-4988

Santa Ana College Garden Grove Center
11277 Garden Grove Blvd
Garden Grove, CA 92843
Phone: 714-564-5570

Santa Monica College
1900 Pico Blvd
Santa Monica, CA 90405
www.smc.edu
Phone: 310-450-5150
Fax: 310-434-3645

South Baylo University
1126 Norris Brookhurst St
Anaheim, CA 92801
E-mail: admin@southbaylo.edu
southbaylo.edu
Phone: 714-533-1495
Fax: 714-533-6040

Southern California Institute of Architecture
5454 Beethoven St
Los Angeles, CA 90066
Phone: 310-574-1123
Fax: 310-574-3801

Taft William Howard University
201 E Sandpointe Ave
Santa Ana, CA 92707
E-mail: admissions@taftu.edu
www.taftu.edu
Phone: 714-850-4800
Fax: 714-708-2082
TF: 800-882-4555

University of California Los Angeles
405 Hilgard Ave
Los Angeles, CA 90095
www.ucla.edu
Phone: 310-825-4321
Fax: 310-206-1206

University of California Riverside
900 University Ave
Riverside, CA 92521
www.ucr.edu
Phone: 909-787-1012
Fax: 909-787-5836

University of Judaism
15600 Mulholland Dr
Los Angeles, CA 90077
E-mail: admissions@uj.edu
www.uj.edu
Phone: 310-476-9777
Fax: 310-471-3657
TF: 888-853-6763

University of Southern California
University Pk
Los Angeles, CA 90089
www.usc.edu
Phone: 213-740-2311
Fax: 213-740-6364

University of West Los Angeles
1155 W Arbor Vitae St
Inglewood, CA 90301
Phone: 310-215-3339
Fax: 310-342-5296

West Los Angeles College
4800 Freshman Dr
Culver City, CA 90230
www.wlac.cc.ca.us
Phone: 310-287-4200
Fax: 310-841-0396

West Orange College
12865 Main St Suite 105
Garden Grove, CA 92840
Phone: 714-530-5000
Fax: 714-530-5003

Whittier College
13406 E Philadelphia St
Whittier, CA 90601
www.whittier.edu
Phone: 562-907-4200
Fax: 562-907-4870

William Carey International University
1539 E Howard St
Pasadena, CA 91104
E-mail: admissions@wciu.edu
www.wciu.edu
Phone: 626-797-1200
Fax: 626-398-2111

Woodbury University
7500 Glenoaks Blvd
Burbank, CA 91510
E-mail: admissions@vaxb.woodbury.edu
www.woodburyu.edu
Phone: 818-767-0888
Fax: 818-767-7520
TF: 800-784-9663

Hospitals

Alhambra Hospital
100 S Raymond Ave
Alhambra, CA 91801
Phone: 626-570-1606
Fax: 626-570-8825

Anaheim Memorial Hospital
1111 W La Palma Ave
Anaheim, CA 92801
Phone: 714-774-1450
Fax: 714-999-6122

Anaheim Memorial Outpatient Tower
1830 W Romneya Dr
Anaheim, CA 92801
Phone: 714-491-5200
Fax: 714-491-5310

Antelope Valley Hospital
1600 W Ave J
Lancaster, CA 93534
Phone: 661-949-5000
Fax: 661-949-5510

Arrowhead Regional Medical Center
400 N Pepper Ave
Colton, CA 92324
Phone: 909-580-1000
Fax: 909-580-6196

Bay Harbor Hospital
1437 W Lomita Blvd
Harbor City, CA 90710
Phone: 310-325-1221
Fax: 310-534-3286

Bellflower Doctors Medical Center
9542 E Artesia Blvd
Bellflower, CA 90706
Phone: 562-925-8355
Fax: 562-925-4413

Beverly Hospital
309 W Beverly Blvd
Montebello, CA 90640
www.beverly.org
Phone: 323-726-1222
Fax: 323-725-4353

Brotman Medical Center
3828 Delmas Terr
Culver City, CA 90231
www.tenethealth.com/Brotman
Phone: 310-836-7000
Fax: 310-202-4141

California Hospital Medical Center
1401 S Grand Ave
Los Angeles, CA 90015
www.chmcla.com
Phone: 213-748-2411
Fax: 213-742-5725

Cedars-Sinai Medical Center
8700 Beverly Blvd
Los Angeles, CA 90048
www.csmc.edu
Phone: 310-855-5000
Fax: 310-967-0105
TF: 800-233-2771

Centinela Hospital Medical Center
555 E Hardy St
Inglewood, CA 90301
www.tenethealth.com/Centinela
Phone: 310-673-4660
Fax: 310-673-0400

Century City Hospital
2070 Century Park E
Los Angeles, CA 90067
www.tenethealth.com/CenturyCity
Phone: 310-553-6211
Fax: 310-201-6723

Chapman Medical Center
2601 E Chapman Ave
Orange, CA 92869
Phone: 714-633-0011
Fax: 714-633-1014

Children's Hospital of Los Angeles
4650 Sunset Blvd
Los Angeles, CA 90027
www.childrenshospitalla.org
Phone: 323-660-2450
Fax: 323-666-3809
TF: 800-877-2452

Children's Hospital of Orange County
455 S Main St
Orange, CA 92868
www.choc.com
Phone: 714-997-3000
Fax: 714-289-4559

Chino Valley Medical Center
5451 Walnut Ave
Chino, CA 91710
www.cvmc.com
Phone: 909-464-8600
Fax: 909-464-8882

Coastal Communities Hospital
2701 S Bristol St
Santa Ana, CA 92704
www.tenethealth.com/CoastalCommunities
Phone: 714-754-5454
Fax: 714-754-5538

Columbia West Hills Medical Center
7300 Medical Center Dr
West Hills, CA 91307
Phone: 818-676-4000
Fax: 818-712-4173

Community Hospital of San Bernardino
1805 Medical Center Dr
San Bernardino, CA 92411
www.communityhospitalsb.org/community_sanbern/default.asp
Phone: 909-887-6333
Fax: 909-887-6468

Community Memorial Hospital
147 N Brent St
Ventura, CA 93003
www.cmhhospital.com
Phone: 805-652-5011
Fax: 805-652-5031

Daniel Freeman Marina Hospital
4650 Lincoln Blvd
Marina del Rey, CA 90292
www.danielfreeman.org
Phone: 310-823-8911
Fax: 310-574-7854

Daniel Freeman Memorial Hospital
333 N Prairie Ave
Inglewood, CA 90301
Phone: 310-674-7050
Fax: 310-419-8273

Desert Hospital
1150 N Indian Canyon Dr
Palm Springs, CA 92262
Phone: 760-323-6511
Fax: 760-323-6859

Downey Regional Medical Center
11500 Brookshire Ave
Downey, CA 90241
www.drmc-inc.org
Phone: 562-904-5000
Fax: 562-904-5309

East Los Angeles Doctors Hospital
4060 Whittier Blvd
Los Angeles, CA 90023
Phone: 323-268-5514
Fax: 323-266-1256

Eisenhower Medical Center
39000 Bob Hope Dr
Rancho Mirage, CA 92270
Phone: 760-340-3911
Fax: 760-773-4396

Encino Tarzana Regional Medical Center Encino Campus
16237 Ventura Blvd
Encino, CA 91436
Phone: 818-995-5000
Fax: 818-907-8630

Encino Tarzana Regional Medical Center Tarzana Campus
18321 Clark St
Tarzana, CA 91356
Phone: 818-881-0800
Fax: 818-708-5382

Foothill Presbyterian Hospital Morris L Johnston Memorial
250 S Grand Ave
Glendora, CA 91741
Phone: 626-963-8411
Fax: 626-857-3290

Fountain Valley Regional Hospital & Medical Center
17100 Euclid St
Fountain Valley, CA 92708
www.fountainvalleyhospital.com
Phone: 714-966-7200
Fax: 714-966-8039

Garden Grove Hospital & Medical Center
12601 Garden Grove Blvd
Garden Grove, CA 92843
www.tenethealth.com/GardenGrove
Phone: 714-537-5160
Fax: 714-741-3322

Garfield Medical Center
525 N Garfield Ave
Monterey Park, CA 91754
www.tenethealth.com/Garfield
Phone: 626-573-2222
Fax: 626-571-8972

Glendale Adventist Medical Center
1509 Wilson Terr
Glendale, CA 91206
www.serve.com/easy/db/gamc/WelcometoGlenda.html
Phone: 818-409-8000
Fax: 818-546-5650

Glendale Memorial Hospital & Health Center
1420 S Central Ave
Glendale, CA 91204
www.glendalememorial.com
Phone: 818-502-1900
Fax: 818-246-4104

Good Samaritan Hospital
1225 Wilshire Blvd
Los Angeles, CA 90017
www.goodsam.org
Phone: 213-977-2121
Fax: 213-482-2770

Granada Hills Community Hospital
10445 Balboa Blvd
Granada Hills, CA 91344
Phone: 818-360-1021
Fax: 818-360-6451

Greater El Monte Community Hospital
1701 Santa Anita Ave
South El Monte, CA 91733
Phone: 626-579-7777
Fax: 626-350-0368

Hemet Valley Medical Center
1117 E Devonshire Ave
Hemet, CA 92543
www.valleyhealthsystem.com/hemmain.htm
Phone: 909-652-2811
Fax: 909-765-4988

Henry Mayo Newhall Memorial Hospital
23845 W McBean Pkwy
Valencia, CA 91351
www.henrymayo.com
Phone: 661-253-8000
Fax: 661-253-8897

Hoag Memorial Hospital Presbyterian
1 Hoag Dr
Newport Beach, CA 92663
www.hoag.org
Phone: 949-645-8600
Fax: 949-760-5593

Huntington Beach Hospital
17772 Beach Blvd
Huntington Beach, CA 92647
Phone: 714-842-1473
Fax: 714-843-5038

Huntington East Valley Hospital
150 W Alosta Ave
Glendora, CA 91740
Phone: 626-335-0231
Fax: 626-335-5082

Huntington Memorial Hospital
100 W California Blvd
Pasadena, CA 91109
www.huntingtonhospital.com
Phone: 626-397-5000
Fax: 626-397-2980

Inland Valley Regional Medical Center
36485 Inland Valley Dr
Wildomar, CA 92595
www.ivrmc.com
Phone: 909-677-1111
Fax: 909-677-9754

Irvine Regional Hospital
16200 Sand Canyon Ave
Irvine, CA 92618
www.tenethealth.com/Irvine
Phone: 949-753-2000
Fax: 949-753-2131

Jerry L Pettis Memorial Veterans Affairs Medical Center
11201 Benton St
Loma Linda, CA 92357
Phone: 909-825-7084
Fax: 909-422-3106
TF: 800-741-8387

John F Kennedy Memorial Hospital
47-111 Monroe St
Indio, CA 92201
www.tenethealth.com/JFKMemorial
Phone: 760-347-6191
Fax: 760-775-8014

Kaiser Foundation Hospital
9400 E Rosecrans Ave
Bellflower, CA 90706
Phone: 562-461-3000
Fax: 562-461-6108

Kaiser Foundation Hospital
5601 De Soto Ave
Woodland Hills, CA 91365
Phone: 818-719-2000
Fax: 818-719-2363

Kaiser Permanente Hospital
441 N Lakeview Ave
Anaheim, CA 92807
Phone: 714-279-4000
Fax: 714-279-4647
TF: 800-464-4000

Kaiser Permanente Los Angeles Medical Center
4867 Sunset Blvd
Los Angeles, CA 90027
Phone: 323-783-4011
Fax: 323-783-7227

Kaiser Permanente Medical Center
9961 Sierra Ave
Fontana, CA 92335
Phone: 909-427-5000
Fax: 909-427-4256

Kaiser Permanente Medical Center
13652 Cantara St
Panorama City, CA 91402
Phone: 818-375-2000
Fax: 818-375-3480

Kaiser Permanente Medical Center
25825 S Vermont Ave
Harbor City, CA 90710
Phone: 310-325-5111
Fax: 310-517-2234
TF: 800-464-4000

Kaiser Permanente Medical Center-West Los Angeles
6041 Cadillac Ave
Los Angeles, CA 90034
Phone: 323-857-2000
Fax: 323-857-4501
TF: 800-954-8000

Kaiser Permanente Riverside Medical Center
10800 Magnolia Ave
Riverside, CA 92505
Phone: 909-353-2000
Fax: 909-353-4611
TF: 800-464-4000

La Palma Intercommunity Hospital
7901 Walker St
La Palma, CA 90623
Phone: 714-670-7400
Fax: 714-670-6004

LAC-Harbor-UCLA Medical Center
1000 W Carson St
Torrance, CA 90509
Phone: 310-222-2345
Fax: 310-328-9624

LAC-King-Drew Medical Center
12021 S Wilmington Ave
Los Angeles, CA 90059
Phone: 310-668-5011
Fax: 310-631-2717

LAC-University of Southern California Medical Center
1200 N State St
Los Angeles, CA 90033
Phone: 323-226-2622
Fax: 323-226-6518

Lakewood Regional Medical Center
PO Box 6070
Lakewood, CA 90714
www.tenethealth.com/Lakewood
Phone: 562-531-2550
Fax: 562-602-0083

Lancaster Community Hospital
43830 N 10th St West
Lancaster, CA 93534
Phone: 661-948-4781
Fax: 661-949-9783

Little Company of Mary Hospital
4101 Torrance Blvd
Torrance, CA 90503
Phone: 310-540-7676
Fax: 310-540-8408

Loma Linda University Community Medical Center
25333 Barton Rd
Loma Linda, CA 92354
Phone: 909-796-0167
Fax: 909-796-6628

Loma Linda University Medical Center
11234 Anderson St
Loma Linda, CA 92354
www.llu.edu
Phone: 909-558-4000
Fax: 909-558-0149

Long Beach Community Medical Center
1720 Termino Ave
Long Beach, CA 90804
www.lbcommunity.com
Phone: 562-498-1000
Fax: 562-498-4630

Long Beach Memorial Medical Center
2801 Atlantic Ave
Long Beach, CA 90806
Phone: 562-933-2000
Fax: 562-933-1336

Los Alamitos Medical Center
3751 Katella Ave
Los Alamitos, CA 90720
www.tenethealth.com/LosAlamitos
Phone: 562-598-1311
Fax: 562-596-0254

Los Angeles Community Hospital
4081 E Olympic Blvd
Los Angeles, CA 90023
Phone: 323-267-0477
Fax: 323-264-3703

Los Angeles Metropolitan Medical Center
2231 S Western Ave
Los Angeles, CA 90018
Phone: 323-737-7372
Fax: 323-734-0963

Los Robles Regional Medical Center
215 W Janss Rd
Thousand Oaks, CA 91360
Phone: 805-497-2727
Fax: 805-370-4498

Memorial Hospital of Gardena
1145 W Redondo Beach Blvd
Gardena, CA 90247
Phone: 310-532-4200
Fax: 310-538-6680

Methodist Hospital of Southern California
300 W Huntington Dr
Arcadia, CA 91007
www.methodisthospital.com
Phone: 626-445-4441
Fax: 626-821-6968

Midway Hospital Medical Center
5925 San Vincente Blvd
Los Angeles, CA 90019
www.midwayhospital.com/home/home.cfm
Phone: 323-938-3161
Fax: 323-932-5061
TF: 800-827-8599

Northridge Hospital Medical Center-Roscoe Blvd Campus
18300 Roscoe Blvd
Northridge, CA 91328
www.nhmc-roscoe.org
Phone: 818-885-8500
Fax: 818-885-5365

Northridge Hospital Medical Center-Sherman Way Campus
14500 Sherman Cir
Van Nuys, CA 91405
www.nhmc-shermanway.org
Phone: 818-997-0101
Fax: 818-908-8607

Olive View Medical Center
14445 Olive View Dr
Sylmar, CA 91342
Phone: 818-364-1555
Fax: 818-364-4206

Orange Coast Memorial Medical Center
9920 Talbert Ave
Fountain Valley, CA 92708
www.memorialcare.com
Phone: 714-962-4677
Fax: 714-378-7079

Orange County Community Hospital of Buena Park
6850 Lincoln Ave
Buena Park, CA 90620
Phone: 714-827-1161
Fax: 714-826-5158

Pacific Hospital of Long Beach
2776 Pacific Ave
Long Beach, CA 90806
Phone: 562-595-1911
Fax: 562-427-8072

Parkview Community Hospital Medical Center
3865 Jackson St
Riverside, CA 92503
Phone: 909-688-2211
Fax: 909-352-5471

Placentia-Linda Community Hospital
1301 Rose Dr
Placentia, CA 92670
Phone: 714-993-2000
Fax: 714-961-8427

Pomona Valley Hospital Medical Center
1798 N Garey Ave
Pomona, CA 91767
www.pvhmc.org
Phone: 909-865-9500
Fax: 909-865-9796

Presbyterian Intercommunity Hospital
12401 E Washington Blvd
Whittier, CA 90602
Phone: 562-698-0811
Fax: 562-698-1728

Providence Holy Cross Medical Center
15031 Rinaldi St
Mission Hills, CA 91345
Phone: 818-365-8051
Fax: 818-898-4569

Providence Saint Joseph Medical Center
501 S Buena Vista St
Burbank, CA 91505
Phone: 818-843-5111
Fax: 818-843-0641

Queen of Angels Hollywood Presbyterian Medical Center
1300 N Vermont Ave
Los Angeles, CA 90027
bloodlessdoctors.com
Phone: 323-913-4800
Fax: 323-644-4411

Queen of the Valley Hospital
1115 S Sunset Ave
West Covina, CA 91790
Phone: 626-962-4011
Fax: 626-814-2524

Riverside Community Hospital
4445 Magnolia Ave
Riverside, CA 92501
Phone: 909-788-3000
Fax: 909-788-3174

Riverside County Regional Medical Center
26520 Cactus Ave
Moreno Valley, CA 92555
Phone: 909-486-4000
Fax: 909-486-4475

Robert F Kennedy Medical Center
4500 W 116th St
Hawthorne, CA 90250
Phone: 310-973-1711
Fax: 310-219-3715

Saddleback Memorial Medical Center
24451 Health Center Dr
Laguna Hills, CA 92653
Phone: 949-837-4500
Fax: 949-452-3467

Saint Bernardine Medical Center
2101 N Waterman Ave
San Bernardino, CA 92404
Phone: 909-883-8711
Fax: 909-881-7600

Saint Francis Medical Center
3630 E Imperial Hwy
Lynwood, CA 90262
Phone: 310-603-6000
Fax: 310-604-0864

Saint John's Hospital & Health Center
1328 22nd St
Santa Monica, CA 90404
Phone: 310-829-5511
Fax: 310-449-5230

Saint John's Regional Medical Center
1600 N Rose Ave
Oxnard, CA 93030
Phone: 805-988-2500
Fax: 805-981-4495

Saint Joseph Hospital
1100 W Stewart Dr
Orange, CA 92868
Phone: 714-633-9111
Fax: 714-744-8668

Saint Jude Medical Center
101 E Valencia Mesa Dr
Fullerton, CA 92835
Phone: 714-992-3000
Fax: 714-992-3029

Saint Luke Medical Center
2632 E Washington Blvd
Pasadena, CA 91107
Phone: 626-797-1141
Fax: 626-797-0948

Saint Mary Medical Center
1050 Linden Ave
Long Beach, CA 90813
Phone: 562-491-9000
Fax: 562-491-7962

Saint Vincent Medical Center
2131 W 3rd St
Los Angeles, CA 90057
www.stvincentmedicalcenter.com
Phone: 213-484-7111
Fax: 213-484-9304

San Antonio Community Hospital
999 San Bernardino Rd
Upland, CA 91786
www.sach.org
Phone: 909-985-2811
Fax: 909-920-4730

San Dimas Community Hospital
1350 West Covina Blvd
San Dimas, CA 91773
Phone: 909-599-6811
Fax: 909-599-0629

San Gabriel Valley Medical Center
438 W Las Tunas Dr
San Gabriel, CA 91776
www.sgvmc.org
Phone: 626-289-5454
Fax: 626-299-3190

San Pedro Peninsula Hospital
1300 W 7th St
San Pedro, CA 90732
Phone: 310-832-3311
Fax: 310-514-5403

Santa Ana Hospital Medical Center
1901 N Fairview St
Santa Ana, CA 92706
Phone: 714-554-1653
Fax: 714-265-3450

Santa Martha Hospital
319 N Humphreys Ave
Los Angeles, CA 90022
Phone: 323-266-6500
Fax: 323-260-8518
TF: 800-477-7889

Santa Monica UCLA Medical Center
1250 16th St
Santa Monica, CA 90404
Phone: 310-319-4000
Fax: 310-319-4534

Santa Teresita Hospital
819 Buena Vista St
Duarte, CA 91010
www.santa-teresita.org
Phone: 626-359-3243
Fax: 626-932-3443

Sepulveda Veterans Affairs Medical Center
16111 Plummer St
North Hills, CA 91343
Phone: 818-891-7711
Fax: 818-895-5884
TF: 800-516-4567

Sherman Oaks Hospital & Health Center
4929 Van Nuys Blvd
Sherman Oaks, CA 91403
Phone: 818-981-7111
Fax: 818-907-4557

Shriners Hospitals for Children Los Angeles Unit
3160 Geneva St
Los Angeles, CA 90020
www.shrinershq.org/Hospitals/Directry/losangeles.html
Phone: 213-388-3151
Fax: 213-387-7528
TF: 800-237-5055

Simi Valley Hospital & Health Care Services
2975 N Sycamore Dr
Simi Valley, CA 93065
Phone: 805-527-2462
Fax: 805-526-9655

South Coast Medical Center
31872 Coast Hwy
South Laguna, CA 92651
Phone: 949-499-1311
Fax: 949-499-7529

Suburban Medical Center
16453 S Colorado Ave
Paramount, CA 90723
Phone: 562-531-3110
Fax: 562-531-4671

Temple Community Hospital
235 N Hoover St
Los Angeles, CA 90004
Phone: 213-382-7252
Fax: 213-389-4559

Torrance Memorial Medical Center
3330 Lomita Blvd
Torrance, CA 90505
torrancememorial.org
Phone: 310-325-9110
Fax: 310-784-4801

UCLA Medical Center
10833 Le Conte Ave
Los Angeles, CA 90095
www.medctr.ucla.edu
Phone: 310-825-9111
Fax: 310-825-9179

University of California Irvine Medical Center
101 City Dr S
Orange, CA 92868
Phone: 714-456-6011
Fax: 714-456-7927

Valley Presbyterian Hospital
15107 Vanowen St
Van Nuys, CA 91405
Phone: 818-782-6600
Fax: 818-902-5701

Vencor Hospital
200 Hospital Cir
Westminster, CA 92683
www.vencor.com
Phone: 714-893-4541
Fax: 714-894-3407

Ventura County Medical Center
3291 Loma Vista Rd
Ventura, CA 93003
Phone: 805-652-6058
Fax: 805-652-6188

Verdugo Hills Hospital
1812 Verdugo Blvd
Glendale, CA 91208
www.verdugohillshospital.org
Phone: 818-790-7100
Fax: 818-952-4616

Veterans Affairs Medical Center
5901 E 7th St
Long Beach, CA 90822
Phone: 562-494-2611
Fax: 562-494-5972
TF: 888-769-8387

Veterans Affairs Medical Center
11301 Wilshire Blvd
Los Angeles, CA 90073
Phone: 310-478-3711
Fax: 310-268-3494

Victor Valley Hospital
15248 11th St
Victorville, CA 92392
Phone: 760-245-8691
Fax: 760-245-8824

West Anaheim Medical Center
3033 W Orange Ave
Anaheim, CA 92804
Phone: 714-827-3000
Fax: 714-229-6813

Western Medical Center
1001 N Tustin Ave
Santa Ana, CA 92705
Phone: 714-835-3555
Fax: 714-953-3613
TF: 800-777-7464

Western Medical Center Anaheim
1025 S Anaheim Blvd
Anaheim, CA 92805
Phone: 714-533-6220
Fax: 714-563-2839

White Memorial Medical Center
1720 Cesar E Chavez Ave
Los Angeles, CA 90033
Phone: 323-268-5000
Fax: 323-265-5065

Whittier Hospital Medical Center
9080 Colima Rd
Whittier, CA 90605
Phone: 562-945-3561
Fax: 562-464-2930

Transportation

Airport(s)

Burbank-Glendale-Pasadena Airport (BUR)
15 miles NW of downtown Los Angeles
(approx 45 minutes) 818-840-8840
Los Angeles International Airport (LAX)
17 miles SW of downtown (approx 45 minutes) 310-646-5252

Mass Transit

DASH Shuttle Bus
$.25 Base fare 818-808-2273
MTA Bus
$1.35 Base fare 213-626-4455

Rail/Bus

Amtrak Station
800 N Alameda St
Los Angeles, CA 90012
Phone: 213-683-6729
TF: 800-872-7245

Greyhound/Trailways Bus Station
1716 E 7th St
Los Angeles, CA 90021
Phone: 213-629-8536
TF: 800-231-2222

Utilities

Electricity
Los Angeles Water & Power Dept 213-367-4211
www.ladwp.com
Southern California Edison Co 626-302-1212
www.sce.com

Gas
Gas Co The 800-427-2200

Water
Los Angeles Water & Power Dept 213-367-4211
www.ladwp.com
Metropolitan Water District of Southern California 213-217-6000

Garbage Collection/Recycling
Public Works Trash Collection Div 213-473-7999

Telecommunications

Telephone
Pacific Bell 800-310-2355
www.pacbell.com
Verizon Communications 800-483-4000
www.verizon.com

Cable Television
Adelphia Cable 626-333-4265
AT & T Cable Services 888-255-5789
Comcast Cablevision 714-680-4070
Cox Communications 949-720-2020
www.cox.com

Internet Service Providers (ISPs)
aNet Communications Inc 310-360-7620
www.artnet.net
Cogent Software Inc 626-585-2788
www.cogent.net
CruzNet 714-680-6600
www.cruznet.net
DeltaNet 714-490-2000
www.deltanet.com
ExoCom Internet 714-991-1919
www.exo.com
Infospec.net 805-446-2219
www.ispec.net
InteleNet Communications Inc 949-851-8250
www.intelenet.net
Keyway Internet Access (Keyway Network Systems) 909-933-3650
www.keyway.net
KTB Internet Online 818-240-6600
www.ktb.net
LA Internet 310-231-3595
www.lainet.com
Liberty Information Network 714-996-7777
www.liberty.com
Loop Internet Switch Co 323-465-1311
www.loop.com
Neptune.Net 949-864-0017
www.neptune.net
NetworkOne Internet Inc 661-723-2700
www.networkone.net

PE.net 909-320-7800
www.pe.net
Quantum Networking Solutions Inc.............661-538-2028
www.qnet.com
TST On Ramp 909-620-7724
www.tstonramp.com
Verio Los Angeles 213-624-9346
home.verio.net/local/frontpage.cfm?AirportCode=LAX
Verio Southern California 949-450-8400
home.verio.net/local/frontpage.cfm?AirportCode=IRV
WareNet.....................................949-367-9862
www.ware.net

Banks

Bank of America NA Phone: 213-228-2805
555 S Flower St
Los Angeles, CA 90071

California Bank & Trust Phone: 213-229-4000
101 S San Pedro St
Los Angeles, CA 90012

California Commerce Bank Phone: 800-222-1234
2029 Century Pk E 42nd Fl Fax: 310-203-3594
Los Angeles, CA 90067
www.ccbusa.com

California Federal Bank FSB Phone: 800-843-2265
624 S Grand Ave Fax: 213-622-4017
Los Angeles, CA 90017

City National Bank Phone: 310-282-7820
2029 Century Pk E B-Level Fax: 310-282-7815
Los Angeles, CA 90067 TF: 800-773-7100

First Federal Bank of California FSB Phone: 323-655-4450
464 N Fairfax Ave Fax: 323-655-5698
Los Angeles, CA 90036

Mercantile National Bank Phone: 310-277-2265
1840 Century Pk E Fax: 310-201-0869
Los Angeles, CA 90067

Union Bank of California NA Phone: 213-236-5000
445 S Figueroa St
Los Angeles, CA 90071

Washington Mutual Bank FA Phone: 213-624-1403
888 W 7th St Fax: 213-624-5741
Los Angeles, CA 90017

Wells Fargo Bank NA Phone: 213-614-2707
707 Wilshire Blvd Fax: 213-614-2718
Los Angeles, CA 90017 TF: 800-869-3557

Shopping

Anaheim Festival Phone: 714-283-3535
8020 E Santa Ana Canyon Rd Fax: 714-283-0525
Anaheim, CA 92808

Anaheim Indoor Marketplace Phone: 714-999-0888
1440 S Anaheim Blvd Fax: 714-999-0885
Anaheim, CA 92805

Anaheim Plaza Phone: 714-635-3431
530 N Euclid St Fax: 714-758-1374
Anaheim, CA 92801

Arco Plaza Phone: 213-485-9595
505 S Flower St Fax: 213-622-5059
Los Angeles, CA 90071

Belmont Shore Phone: 562-436-3645
2nd St-betw Livingston & Bayshore Drs
Long Beach, CA 90803

Beverly Center Phone: 310-854-0070
8500 Beverly Blvd
West Hollywood, CA 90048

Block at Orange Phone: 714-769-4000
20 City Blvd W Fax: 714-769-4011
Orange, CA 92868
www.theblockatorange.com

Brea Mall Phone: 714-990-2732
1065 Brea Mall Fax: 714-990-5048
Brea, CA 92821

Broadway Plaza Phone: 213-624-2891
7th & Flower Sts Fax: 213-688-0176
Los Angeles, CA 90017

Buena Park Mall Phone: 714-828-7722
8308 On The Mall Fax: 714-761-0748
Buena Park, CA 90620

Canyon Crest Towne Centre Phone: 909-686-8000
5225 Canyon Crest Dr
Riverside, CA 92507

Carousel Mall Phone: 909-884-0106
295 Carousel Mall Fax: 909-885-6893
San Bernardino, CA 92401

Centerpoint Mall Phone: 805-487-1142
2655 Saviers Rd
Oxnard, CA 93033

Century City Shopping Center & Marketplace Phone: 310-553-5300
10250 Santa Monica Blvd Fax: 310-553-3812
West Los Angeles, CA 90067

Citadel Outlet Collection Phone: 323-888-1220
5675 E Telegraph Rd Fax: 323-888-0311
City of Commerce, CA 90040
www.citadelfactorystores.com

Cooper Building Phone: 213-622-1139
860 S Los Angeles St Fax: 213-629-5484
Los Angeles, CA 90014

Del Amo Fashion Center Phone: 310-542-8525
3525 Carson St Fax: 310-793-9235
Torrance, CA 90503
torranceweb.com/dafc

Fashion Island Shopping Center Phone: 949-721-2000
401 Newport Ctr Dr Fax: 949-720-3350
Newport Beach, CA 92660
www.fashionisland-nb.com

Fox Hills Mall Phone: 310-390-7833
6000 Sepulveda Blvd Fax: 310-391-9576
Culver City, CA 90230

Fullerton Metro Center
1301-1577 S Harbor Blvd & 104-250 W Orangethorpe Blvd
Fullerton, CA 92632
Phone: 714-427-5977
Fax: 714-427-5922

Galleria at South Bay
1815 Hawthorne Blvd Suite 201
Redondo Beach, CA 90278
www.sobaygalleria.com
Phone: 310-371-7546
Fax: 310-371-0103

Galleria at Tyler
1299 Galleria at Tyler St
Riverside, CA 92503
Phone: 909-351-3112
Fax: 909-351-3139

Garden Grove Shopping Center
Garden Grove & Harbor Blvds
Garden Grove, CA 92840
Phone: 949-650-9737

Garden Promenade
Chapman Ave & Brookhurst St
Garden Grove, CA 92845

Giorgio Beverly Hills
327 N Rodeo Dr
Beverly Hills, CA 90210
Phone: 310-274-0200
Fax: 310-315-3182

Glendale Galleria
2148 Glendale Galleria
Glendale, CA 91210
E-mail: mallinfo@glendalegalleria.com
www.glendalegalleria.com
Phone: 818-240-9481
Fax: 818-547-9398

Golden West Swap Meet
15744 Golden West St
Huntington Beach, CA 92647
Phone: 714-898-7927
Fax: 714-895-8944

Harbor Town & Country Center
12913 Harbor Blvd
Garden Grove, CA 92840
Phone: 949-650-9737

Harris & Frank Inc
17629 Ventura Blvd
Encino, CA 91316
Phone: 818-783-3125
Fax: 818-783-2693

Historic Main Street
Main St & Garden Grove Blvd
Garden Grove, CA 92840

Huntington Beach Mall
7777 Edinger Ave
Huntington Beach, CA 92647
Phone: 714-897-2533
Fax: 714-894-7686

Huntington Harbour Mall
Warner Ave & Algonquin St
Huntington Beach, CA 92649

Inland Center Mall
500 Inland Center Dr
San Bernardino, CA 92408
Phone: 909-884-7268
Fax: 909-381-5380

Japanese Village Plaza
335 E 2nd St Suite 220
Los Angeles, CA 90012
Phone: 213-622-2033
Fax: 213-627-9095

JC Penney
333 W Colorado St
Glendale, CA 91210
Phone: 818-240-8700

Loehmann's Five Points Plaza
18593 Main St
Huntington Beach, CA 92648
Phone: 714-841-0036
Fax: 714-843-5776

Long Beach Plaza
451 Long Beach Blvd
Long Beach, CA 90802
Phone: 562-435-8686

Los Angeles City Mall
201 N Los Angeles St
Los Angeles, CA 90012
Phone: 213-847-5927
Fax: 213-847-5891

Los Cerritos Center
239 Los Cerritos Ctr
Cerritos, CA 90703
Phone: 562-860-0341
Fax: 562-860-5289

Main Street Downtown
201 N 'E' St
San Bernardino, CA 92401
Phone: 909-381-5037
Fax: 909-888-2576

Main Street Mall
5th St & University Ave
Riverside, CA 92501
Phone: 909-781-7335

Main Street Shopping
Pacific Coast Hwy & Main St
Huntington Beach, CA 92648
Phone: 714-969-3492

MainPlace Santa Ana
2800 N Main St
Santa Ana, CA 92705
Phone: 714-547-7000
Fax: 714-547-2643

Mall of Orange
2298 N Orange Mall
Orange, CA 92865
Phone: 714-998-0440
Fax: 714-998-6378

Marina Pacifica
6272 E Pacific Coast Hwy Suite D
Long Beach, CA 90803
Phone: 562-598-2728
Fax: 562-431-8413

Marketplace The
6400 Pacific Coast Hwy
Long Beach, CA 90803
Phone: 562-431-6282

Media City Center
201 E Magnolia Blvd
Burbank, CA 91501
Phone: 818-566-8556
Fax: 818-566-7936

Montebello Town Center
2134 Montebello Town Ctr
Montebello, CA 90640
Phone: 323-722-1776
Fax: 323-722-1268

Nordstrom
200 W Broadway
Glendale, CA 91210
Phone: 818-502-9922
Fax: 818-502-0109

Oaks The
222 W Hillcrest Dr
Thousand Oaks, CA 91360
Phone: 805-495-4628
Fax: 805-495-9656

Old World Village
7561 Center Ave
Huntington Beach, CA 92647
Phone: 714-898-3033

Ontario Mills
1 Mills Cir Suite 1
Ontario, CA 91764
ontariomills.com
Phone: 909-484-8300
Fax: 909-484-8306

Oxnard Factory Outlet Phone: 805-485-2244
2000 Outlet Center Dr Suite 222 Fax: 805-485-3303
Oxnard, CA 93030

Pacific View Mall Phone: 805-642-5530
3301 E Main St Fax: 805-654-1521
Ventura, CA 93003
www.shoppacificview.com

Peters Landing Phone: 562-592-2126
16400 Pacific Coast Hwy Fax: 562-592-5382
Huntington Beach, CA 92649

Picadilly Circus Phone: 562-435-3511
1126 Queens Hwy
Long Beach, CA 90802

Plaza at West Covina Phone: 626-960-1881
112 Plaza Dr Fax: 626-337-3337
West Covina, CA 91790
www.westcovina.shoppingtown.com

Ports O'Call Village Phone: 310-732-7696
Berth 77 P7A Fax: 310-547-5389
San Pedro, CA 90731

Queen Mary Seaport Phone: 562-435-3511
1126 Queens Hwy Fax: 562-437-4531
Long Beach, CA 90802 TF: 800-437-2934
E-mail: queenmary@qte.net
www.queenmary.com/

Riverside Marketplace Phone: 909-715-3400
Main St Fax: 909-715-3404
Riverside, CA 92501

Riverside Plaza Phone: 909-683-1030
3690 Central Ave
Riverside, CA 92506

Robinsons-May Phone: 213-683-1144
920 W 7th St Fax: 213-683-2764
Los Angeles, CA 90017

Santa Anita Fashion Park Phone: 626-445-3116
400 S Baldwin Ave Fax: 626-446-9320
Arcadia, CA 91007

Sears Roebuck & Co Phone: 818-507-7200
236 N Central Ave
Glendale, CA 91203

Seventh Marketplace Phone: 213-955-7150
735 S Figueroa St Citicorp Plaza
Los Angeles, CA 90017

Shoreline Village Phone: 562-435-2668
419-R Shoreline Village Dr Fax: 562-435-6445
Long Beach, CA 90802
E-mail: management@shorelinevillage.com
www.shorelinevillage.com

South Coast Plaza Phone: 714-435-2000
3333 Bristol St Fax: 714-540-7334
Costa Mesa, CA 92626
E-mail: info@southcoastplaza.com
www.southcoastplaza.com

Talbot's Phone: 213-624-2377
848 W 7th St
Los Angeles, CA 90017

Ventura Harbor Village Phone: 805-644-0169
1583 Spinnaker Dr Suite 215 Fax: 805-644-1684
Ventura, CA 93001

Westminster Mall Phone: 714-898-2558
1025 Westminster Mall Fax: 714-892-8824
Westminster, CA 92683

Media

Newspapers and Magazines

Anaheim Bulletin Phone: 714-634-1567
1771 S Lewis St Fax: 714-704-3714
Anaheim, CA 92805

Beverly Hills 213 Phone: 310-275-8850
9777 Wilshire Blvd Suite 707 Fax: 310-275-1341
Beverly Hills, CA 90212

Covina Highlander Press Courier Phone: 626-962-8811
1210 N Azusa Canyon Rd Fax: 626-854-8719
West Covina, CA 91790

East Los Angeles/Brooklyn Belvedere Comet Phone: 323-263-5743
2500 S Atlantic Blvd Bldg A Fax: 323-263-9169
Los Angeles, CA 90040

Foothill Leader Phone: 818-249-8090
3527-A N Verdugo Rd Fax: 818-249-6563
Glendale, CA 91208

Fullerton News-Tribune Phone: 714-634-1567
1771 S Lewis St Fax: 714-704-3714
Anaheim, CA 92805

Garden Grove Journal Phone: 714-539-6018
12866 Main St Suite 203 Fax: 714-892-7052
Garden Grove, CA 92840
www.ggjournal.com

Glendora Press Phone: 626-854-8700
1210 N Azusa Canyon Rd Fax: 626-854-8719
West Covina, CA 91790

Hollywood Independent Phone: 323-932-6397
4201 Wilshire Blvd Suite 600 Fax: 323-932-8285
Los Angeles, CA 90010
E-mail: laingroup@aol.com

Huntington Beach Independent Phone: 714-965-3030
18682 Beach Blvd Suite 160 Fax: 714-965-7174
Huntington Beach, CA 92648
www.latimes.com/tcn/indynews

Independent The Phone: 714-965-3030
18682 Beach Blvd Suite 160 Fax: 714-965-7174
Huntington Beach, CA 92648

Inland Empire Magazine Phone: 909-682-3026
3769 Tibbetts St Suite A Fax: 909-682-0246
Riverside, CA 92506

La Opinion*
PO Box 15268
Los Angeles, CA 90015
www.laopinion.com
Phone: 213-622-8332
Fax: 213-896-2171

LA Weekly
6715 Sunset Blvd
Los Angeles, CA 90028
E-mail: laweekly@aol.com
www.laweekly.com
Phone: 323-465-4414
Fax: 323-465-0444

Los Angeles Business Journal
5700 Wilshire Blvd Suite 170
Los Angeles, CA 90036
www.labusinessjournal.com
Phone: 323-549-5225
Fax: 323-549-5255

Los Angeles Downtown News
1264 W 1st St
Los Angeles, CA 90026
E-mail: realpeople@downtownnews.com
www.ladowntownnews.com
Phone: 213-481-1448
Fax: 213-250-4617

Los Angeles Magazine
11100 Santa Monica Blvd 7th Fl
Los Angeles, CA 90025
www.lamag.com
Phone: 310-312-2270
Fax: 310-312-2285

Los Angeles Times*
Times Mirror Sq
Los Angeles, CA 90053
www.latimes.com
Phone: 213-237-5000
Fax: 213-237-4712
TF: 800-528-4637

Los Angeles Times Orange County*
1375 Sunflower Ave
Costa Mesa, CA 92626
www.latimes.com/editions/orange
Phone: 714-966-5600
Fax: 714-966-5600

New Times Los Angeles
1950 Sawtelle Blvd Suite 200
Los Angeles, CA 90025
E-mail: letters@newtimesla.com
www.newtimesla.com
Phone: 310-477-0403
Fax: 310-477-8428

Orange City News
1771 S Lewis St
Anaheim, CA 92805
Phone: 714-634-1567
Fax: 714-704-3714

Orange County Business Journal
2600 Michelson Dr Suite 170
Irvine, CA 92612
Phone: 949-833-8373
Fax: 949-833-8751

Orange County Register*
625 N Grand Ave
Santa Ana, CA 92701
www.ocregister.com
Phone: 714-835-1234
Fax: 714-565-3681

Orange County Reporter
600 W Santa Ana Blvd Suite 205
Santa Ana, CA 92701
Phone: 714-543-2027
Fax: 714-542-6841

Pasadena Weekly
50 S Delacey Ave Suite 200
Pasadena, CA 91105
E-mail: editorial@pasadenaweekly.com
www.pasadenaweekly.com
Phone: 626-584-1500
Fax: 626-795-0149

Press-Enterprise*
PO Box 792
Riverside, CA 92502
E-mail: comments@pe.net
www.pe.net
Phone: 909-684-1200
Fax: 909-782-7572

Press-Telegram*
604 Pine Ave
Long Beach, CA 90844
www.ptconnect.com
Phone: 562-435-1161
Fax: 562-437-7892

Rialto Record
PO Box 6247
San Bernardino, CA 92412
Phone: 909-381-9898
Fax: 909-384-0406

Riverside County Record
PO Box 3187
Riverside, CA 92519
Phone: 909-685-6191
Fax: 909-685-2961

San Dimas/La Verne Highlander
1210 N Azusa Canyon Rd
West Covina, CA 91790
Phone: 626-854-8700
Fax: 626-854-8719

Southern California
3769 Tibbetts Ave Suite A
Riverside, CA 92506
Phone: 909-682-3026
Fax: 909-682-0246

Sun The*
399 N 'D' St
San Bernardino, CA 92401
E-mail: mail@sbcsun.com
www.sbcsun.com
Phone: 909-889-9666
Fax: 909-885-8741

Tustin News
615 N Grand Ave
Santa Ana, CA 92701
Phone: 714-796-7072
Fax: 714-796-6098

Tustin Weekly
PO Box C-19512
Irvine, CA 92623
E-mail: iwneditor@aol.com
Phone: 949-261-2435
Fax: 949-833-3281

Ventura County Reporter
1567 Spinnaker Dr Suite 202
Ventura, CA 93001
E-mail: vcreporter@aol.com
Phone: 805-658-2244
Fax: 805-658-7803

Ventura County Star*
5250 Ralston St
Ventura, CA 93003
www.staronline.com
Phone: 805-650-2900
Fax: 805-650-2950

West Covina Highlander
1210 N Azusa Canyon Rd
West Covina, CA 91790
Phone: 626-962-8811
Fax: 626-338-9157

Where Los Angeles Magazine
3679 Motor Ave Suite 300
Los Angeles, CA 90034
E-mail: wherela@aol.com
www.wherela.com
Phone: 310-280-2880
Fax: 310-280-2890

Yorba Linda Star
1771 S Lewis St
Anaheim, CA 92805
Phone: 714-634-1567
Fax: 714-704-3714

**Indicates major daily newspapers*

Television

KABC-TV Ch 7 (ABC)
4151 Prospect Ave
Los Angeles, CA 90027
E-mail: abc7@abc.com
abcnews.go.com/local/kabc
Phone: 310-557-3200
Fax: 310-557-3360

KADY-TV Ch 63 (UPN)
950 Flynn Rd
Camarillo, CA 93012
Phone: 805-388-0081
Fax: 805-388-9693

KCAL-TV Ch 9 (Ind)
5515 Melrose Ave
Hollywood, CA 90038
E-mail: news@kcal.com
www.kcal.com
Phone: 323-467-5459
Fax: 323-464-2526

KCBS-TV Ch 2 (CBS)
6121 Sunset Blvd
Los Angeles, CA 90028
www.kcbs2.com
Phone: 323-460-3000
Fax: 323-460-3733

KCET-TV Ch 28 (PBS)
4401 Sunset Blvd
Los Angeles, CA 90027
www.kcet.org
Phone: 323-666-6500
Fax: 323-953-5523

KCOP-TV Ch 13 (UPN)
915 N La Brea Ave
Los Angeles, CA 90038
www.upn13.com
Phone: 323-851-1000
Fax: 323-850-1265

KDOC-TV Ch 56 (Ind)
18021 Cowan
Irvine, CA 92614
Phone: 949-442-9800
Fax: 949-261-5956

KHIZ-TV Ch 64 (Ind)
15605 Village Dr
Victorville, CA 92394
Phone: 760-241-5888
Fax: 760-241-0056

KJLA-TV Ch 57 (Ind)
18344 Oxnard St Suite 210
Tarzana, CA 91356
Phone: 818-757-7583
Fax: 818-757-7533

KLCS-TV Ch 58 (Ind)
1061 W Temple St
Los Angeles, CA 90012
E-mail: info@klcs.org
www.klcs.org
Phone: 213-625-6958
Fax: 213-481-1019

KMEX-TV Ch 34 (Uni)
6701 Center Dr W 15th Fl
Los Angeles, CA 90045
www.kmex.com
Phone: 310-216-3434
Fax: 310-348-3493

KNBC-TV Ch 4 (NBC)
3000 W Alameda Ave
Burbank, CA 91523
www.knbc4la.com
Phone: 818-840-4444
Fax: 818-840-3535

KPXN-TV Ch 30 (PAX)
10880 Wilshire Blvd Suite 1200
Los Angeles, CA 90024
Phone: 310-234-2230
Fax: 310-234-4035

KRCA-TV Ch 62 (Ind)
1813 Victory Pl
Burbank, CA 91504
Phone: 818-563-5722
Fax: 818-972-2694

KSCI-TV Ch 18 (Ind)
1990 S Bundy Dr Suite 850
Los Angeles, CA 90025
Phone: 310-478-1818
Fax: 310-207-1508
TF: 800-841-1818

KTLA-TV Ch 5 (WB)
5800 W Sunset Blvd
Los Angeles, CA 90028
www.ktla.com
Phone: 323-460-5500
Fax: 323-460-5333

KTTV-TV Ch 11 (Fox)
1999 S Bundy Dr
West Los Angeles, CA 90025
E-mail: talkback@fox11la.com
www.fox11la.com
Phone: 310-584-2000
Fax: 310-584-2023

KVEA-TV Ch 52 (Tele)
1139 Grand Central Ave
Glendale, CA 91201
E-mail: airway@kvea.com
www.kvea.com
Phone: 818-502-5700
Fax: 818-247-2561

KWHY-TV Ch 22 (Ind)
5545 Sunset Blvd
Los Angeles, CA 90028
Phone: 323-466-5441
Fax: 323-603-4226

Radio

KABC-AM 790 kHz (N/T)
3321 S La Cienega Blvd
Los Angeles, CA 90016
www.kabc.com
Phone: 310-840-4900
Fax: 310-838-5222

KACD-FM 103.1 MHz (AAA)
1425 5th St
Santa Monica, CA 90401
E-mail: channel1031@yahoo.com
www.channel1031.com
Phone: 310-451-1031
Fax: 310-395-8736

KACE-FM 103.9 MHz (Oldies)
610 S Ardmore Ave
Los Angeles, CA 90005
Phone: 213-427-1039
Fax: 213-380-4214

KBIG-FM 104.3 MHz (AC)
330 N Brand Blvd Suite 800
Glendale, CA 91203
www.kbig104.com
Phone: 818-546-1043
Fax: 818-637-2267

KBUA-FM 94.3 MHz (Span)
5724 Hollywood Blvd
Hollywood, CA 90028
Phone: 323-461-9300
Fax: 323-461-9946

KBUE-FM 105.5 MHz (Span)
5724 Hollywood Blvd
Hollywood, CA 90028
Phone: 323-461-9300
Fax: 323-461-9946

KCAL-AM 1410 kHz (Span)
1950 S Sunwest Ln Suite 302
San Bernardino, CA 92408
Phone: 909-825-5020
Fax: 909-884-5844

KCAL-FM 96.7 MHz (Rock)
1940 Orange Tree Ln Suite 200
Redlands, CA 92374
www.kcalfm.com
Phone: 909-793-3554
Fax: 909-793-3094

KCAQ-FM 104.7 MHz (CHR)
2284 S Victoria Ave Suite 2M
Oxnard, CA 93003
Phone: 805-289-1400
Fax: 805-644-4257

KCBS-FM 93.1 MHz (CR)
6121 Sunset Blvd
Los Angeles, CA 90028
www.arrowfm.com
Phone: 323-460-3000
Fax: 323-463-9270

KCLU-FM 88.3 MHz (NPR)
60 W Olsen Rd
Thousand Oaks, CA 91360
www.kclu.org
Phone: 805-493-3900
Fax: 805-493-3982

KCMG-FM 100.3 MHz (Oldies)
6500 Wilshire Blvd Suite 650
Los Angeles, CA 90048
www.mega100fm.com
Phone: 323-852-1003
Fax: 323-866-1260

KCRW-FM 89.9 MHz (NPR)
1900 Pico Blvd
Santa Monica, CA 90405
E-mail: info@kcrw.org
kcrw.org
Phone: 310-450-5183
Fax: 310-450-7172

KCXX-FM 103.9 MHz (Alt)
740 W 4th St
San Bernardino, CA 92410
www.x1039.com/
Phone: 909-384-1039
Fax: 909-888-7302

KDAR-FM 98.3 MHz (N/T)
500 Esplanade Dr Suite 1500
Oxnard, CA 93030
E-mail: info@kdar.com
www.kdar.com
Phone: 805-485-8881
Fax: 805-656-5330

KDB-FM 93.7 MHz (Clas)
23 W Micheltorena St
Santa Barbara, CA 93101
E-mail: info@kdb.com
www.kdb.com
Phone: 805-966-4131
Fax: 805-966-4788

KDIF-AM 1440 kHz (Span)
1465 Spruce St Suite A
Riverside, CA 92507
Phone: 909-784-4210
Fax: 909-784-4213

KEZY-AM 1190 kHz (N/T)
1190 E Ball Rd
Anaheim, CA 92805
Phone: 714-776-1190
Fax: 714-774-1631

KFI-AM 640 kHz (N/T)
610 S Ardmore Ave
Los Angeles, CA 90005
www.kfi640.com
Phone: 213-385-0101
Fax: 213-389-7640

KFRG-FM 95.1 MHz (Ctry)
900 E Washington St Suite 315
Colton, CA 92324
E-mail: thefrog@kfrog.com
www.kfrog.com
Phone: 909-825-9525
Fax: 909-825-0441
TF: 888-560-3764

KFSG-FM 96.3 MHz (Rel)
1910 W Sunset Blvd Suite 480
Los Angeles, CA 90026
E-mail: comments@kfsg.com
www.kfsg.com
Phone: 213-483-5374
Fax: 213-484-8304

KFWB-AM 980 kHz (N/T)
6230 Yucca St
Hollywood, CA 90028
E-mail: quake@kfwb.groupw.wec.com
www.kfwb.com
Phone: 323-462-5392
Fax: 323-871-4670

KGGI-FM 99.1 MHz (CHR)
2001 Iowa Ave Suite 200
Riverside, CA 92507
Phone: 909-684-1991
Fax: 909-274-4949

KHAY-FM 100.7 (Ctry)
1376 Walter St
Ventura, CA 93003
www.khay.com
Phone: 805-642-8595
Fax: 805-656-5838

KHWY-FM 98.9 MHz (AC)
1611 E Main St
Barstow, CA 92311
Phone: 760-256-0326
Fax: 760-256-9507

KIEV-AM 870 kHz (N/T)
701 N Brand Blvd Suite 550
Glendale, CA 91203
www.kiev870.com
Phone: 818-244-8483
Fax: 818-551-1110

KIIS-FM 102.7 MHz (CHR)
3400 Riverside Dr Suite 800
Burbank, CA 91505
www.kiisfm.com
Phone: 818-845-1027
Fax: 818-295-6466
TF: 800-520-1027

KJLH-FM 102.3 MHz (Urban)
161 N La Brea Ave
Inglewood, CA 90301
E-mail: 1023kjlh@earthlink.net
www.kjlhradio.com
Phone: 310-330-5550
Fax: 310-330-5555

KKBT-FM 92.3 MHz (Urban)
5900 Wilshire Blvd Suite 1900
Los Angeles, CA 90036
www.thebeatla.com
Phone: 323-634-1800
Fax: 323-634-1888
TF: 888-520-9292

KKDD-AM 1290 kHz (Misc)
2001 Iowa Ave Suite 200
Riverside, CA 92507
www.radiodisney.com
Phone: 909-684-1991
Fax: 909-274-4949

KKGO-FM 105.1 MHz (Clas)
1500 Cotner Ave
Los Angeles, CA 90025
www.kkgofm.com
Phone: 310-478-5540
Fax: 310-478-4189

KKLA-FM 99.5 MHz (N/T/Rel)
701 N Brand Blvd Suite 550
Glendale, CA 91203
E-mail: info@kkla.com
www.kkla.com
Phone: 818-956-5552
Fax: 818-551-1110

KLAC-AM 570 kHz (Nost)
330 N Brand Blvd Suite 800
Glendale, CA 91203
www.570klac.com
Phone: 818-546-1043
Fax: 818-637-2267

KLAX-FM 97.9 MHz (Span)
10281 W Pico Blvd
Los Angeles, CA 90064
Phone: 310-203-0900
Fax: 310-203-8989

KLON-FM 88.1 MHz (NPR)
1288 N Bellflower Blvd
Long Beach, CA 90815
E-mail: jazzave@klon.org
klon.org
Phone: 562-985-5566
Fax: 562-597-8453

KLOS-FM 95.5 MHz (Rock)
3321 S La Cienega Blvd
Los Angeles, CA 90016
www.955klos.com
Phone: 310-840-4900
Fax: 310-558-7685

KLSX-FM 97.1 MHz (N/T)
3580 Wilshire Blvd
Los Angeles, CA 90010
www.realradio.com
Phone: 213-383-4222
Fax: 213-386-3649

KLVE-FM 107.5 MHz (Span)
1645 N Vine St Suite 200
Hollywood, CA 90028
www.klve.com
Phone: 323-465-3171
Fax: 323-461-9973

KLYY-FM 107.1 MHz (Alt)
1888 Century Pk E Suite 200
Los Angeles, CA 90067
Phone: 626-351-9107
Fax: 626-351-6218

KMLT-FM 92.7 MHz (AC)
99 Long Ct Suite 200
Thousand Oaks, CA 91360
E-mail: info@92.7fm.com
www.lite92.7fm.com
Phone: 805-497-8511
Fax: 805-497-8514

KMZT-FM 105.1 MHz (Clas)
1500 Cotner Ave
Los Angeles, CA 90025
Phone: 310-478-5540
Fax: 310-479-2183

KNX-AM 1070 kHz (N/T)
6121 Sunset Blvd
Los Angeles, CA 90028
www.knx1070.com
Phone: 323-460-3000
Fax: 323-460-3767

KOLA-FM 99.9 MHz (Oldies)
1940 Orange Tree Ln Suite 200
Redlands, CA 92374
www.kola-fm.com
Phone: 909-793-3554
Fax: 909-798-6627

KORG-AM 1190 kHz (N/T)
1190 E Ball Rd
Anaheim, CA 92805
Phone: 714-776-1190
Fax: 714-774-1631

KOST-FM 103.5 MHz (AC)
610 S Ardmore Ave
Los Angeles, CA 90005
Phone: 213-427-1035
Fax: 213-385-0281
TF: 800-929-5678

KOXR-AM 910 kHz (Span)
418 W 3rd St
Oxnard, CA 93030
Phone: 805-487-0444
Fax: 805-487-2117

KPCC-FM 89.3 MHz (NPR)
1570 E Colorado Blvd
Pasadena, CA 91106
www.kpcc.org
Phone: 626-585-7000
Fax: 626-585-7916

KPRO-AM 1570 kHz (Rel)
7351 Lincoln Ave
Riverside, CA 92504
Phone: 909-688-1570
Fax: 909-688-7009

KPWR-FM 105.9 MHz (CHR)
2600 W Olive Ave Suite 850
Burbank, CA 91505
Phone: 818-953-4200
Fax: 818-848-0961

KROQ-FM 106.7 MHz (Alt)
3500 W Olive Ave
Burbank, CA 91505
E-mail: likewecare@kroq.com
www.kroq.com
Phone: 818-567-1067
Fax: 818-841-5903

KRTH-FM 101.1 MHz (Oldies)
5901 Venice Blvd
Los Angeles, CA 90034
www.k-earth101.com
Phone: 323-937-5230
Fax: 323-936-3427

KSCA-FM 101.9 MHz (Span)
1645 N Vine St
Hollywood, CA 90028
www.lanueva1019.com
Phone: 323-465-3171
Fax: 323-461-9973

KSGN-FM 89.7 MHz (Rel)
11498 Pierce St
Riverside, CA 92505
www.goodnewsradio.com
Phone: 909-687-5746
Fax: 909-785-2288

KSSE-FM 97.5 MHz (Span)
3450 Wilshire Blvd Suite 820
Los Angeles, CA 90010
Phone: 213-251-1011
Fax: 213-251-1033

KSZZ-AM 590 kHz (Span)
1950 S Sunwest Ln Suite 302
San Bernardino, CA 92408
Phone: 909-825-5020
Fax: 909-884-5844

KTNQ-AM 1020 kHz (Span)
1645 N Vine St Suite 200
Hollywood, CA 90028
Phone: 323-465-3171
Fax: 323-461-9973

KTWV-FM 94.7 MHz (NAC)
8944 Lindblade St
Culver City, CA 90232
E-mail: wave@ktwv.cbs.com
www.947wave.com
Phone: 310-840-7100
Fax: 310-815-1129

KUCR-FM 88.3 MHz (Misc)
University of California
Riverside, CA 92521
www.kucr.org
Phone: 909-787-3737
Fax: 909-787-3240

KUSC-FM 91.5 MHz (NPR)
3716 S Hope St Suite 262
Los Angeles, CA 90007
E-mail: kusc@kusc.org
www.kusc.org
Phone: 213-514-1400
Fax: 213-747-9400

KVCR-FM 91.9 MHz (NPR)
701 Mt Vernon Ave
San Bernardino, CA 92410
E-mail: hometeam@kvcr.pbs.org
Phone: 909-888-6511
Fax: 909-885-2116

KVEN-AM 1450 kHz (N/T)
1376 Walter St
Ventura, CA 93003
E-mail: info@kven.com
www.kven.com
Phone: 805-642-8595
Fax: 805-656-5838

KVTA-AM 1520 kHz (N/T)
2284 S Victoria Ave Suite 2-G
Oxnard, CA 93003
E-mail: am1520kvta@hotmail.com
Phone: 805-289-1400
Fax: 805-644-7906

KWIZ-FM 96.7 MHz (Span)
3101 W 5th St
Santa Ana, CA 92703
Phone: 714-554-5000
Fax: 714-554-9362

KWRP-FM 96.1 MHz (Nost)
475 W Stetson Ave Suite U
Hemet, CA 92543
www.kwrp-fm.com
Phone: 909-929-5088
Fax: 909-658-8822

KXFG-FM 92.9 MHz (Ctry) Phone: 909-825-9525
900 E Washington St Suite 315 Fax: 909-825-0441
Colton, CA 92324

KXRS-FM 105.7 MHz (Span) Phone: 909-925-9000
2615 W Devonshire Ave Fax: 909-658-4843
Hemet, CA 92545

KXSB-FM 101.7 MHz (Span) Phone: 909-925-9000
2615 W Devonshire Ave Fax: 909-658-4843
Hemet, CA 92545

KYSR-FM 98.7 MHz (AC) Phone: 818-955-7000
3500 W Olive Ave Suite 250 Fax: 818-955-6436
Burbank, CA 91505
www.star987.com

KZLA-FM 93.9 MHz (Ctry) Phone: 323-882-8000
7755 Sunset Blvd Fax: 323-874-9494
Los Angeles, CA 90046 TF: 800-977-1939
E-mail: kzla@kzla.net
www.kzla.net

XTRA-AM 1150 kHz (Sports) Phone: 818-845-1027
3400 Riverside Dr Suite 800 Fax: 818-295-6466
Burbank, CA 91505
www.xtrasports1150.com

Attractions

El Pueblo de Los Angeles Historic Park, the site of the original pueblo from which the "City of Angels" evolved, is located in the downtown area of Los Angeles and contains the restored plaza, the original church (still in use today) from which the city takes its name, and Olvera Street, an authentic Mexican marketplace. Los Angeles is perhaps best known as the movie and television capital of the world, and visitors can tour both movie and TV studios or take a stroll down the Walk of Fame on Hollywood Boulevard, where the hand- and footprints of famous stars are impressed in the sidewalk outside Mann's Chinese Theatre. Other popular area attractions include miles of beaches; the Santa Monica Pier, with its vintage 1910 carousel; Chinatown; the Rancho La Brea Tar Pits; and Rodeo Drive in Beverly Hills, known for its exclusive shops and boutiques.

The world-famous Disneyland theme park is located in nearby Anaheim, and the Queen Mary ocean liner (now a hotel and tourist site) is in Long Beach. Near Los Angeles also is Huntington Beach, considered a surfer's paradise, while the San Gabriel Mountains in the San Bernardino area offer a number of ski resorts. Some of the other attractions located among the many communities that surround Los Angeles include Historic Downtown Santa Ana; the museums and restaurants at Channel Islands Harbor in Oxnard; and the Galleria Mall in Glendale, which is Southern California's largest (and highest sales tax-generating) mall.

ABC Inc Phone: 310-557-7777
2040 Ave of the Stars
Century City, CA 90067

Adventure City Phone: 714-236-9300
10200 Beach Blvd Fax: 714-827-2992
Stanton, CA 90680
E-mail: adventurecity@prodigy.net
www.adventurecity.com

Agua Mansa Cemetery Museum Phone: 909-370-2091
2001 Agua Mansa Rd W
Colton, CA 92324

Ahmanson Theatre Phone: 213-628-2772
135 N Grand Ave Music Center of Los Angeles County Fax: 213-972-7224
Los Angeles, CA 90012
E-mail: ahmanson_manager@ctgla.com
www.taperahmanson.com/1999-2000/index-ahmanson.html

Air Combat USA Phone: 714-522-7590
230 N Dale Pl Fax: 714-522-7592
Fullerton, CA 92833 TF: 800-522-7590
www.aircombatusa.com

Albinger Archaeological Museum Phone: 805-648-5823
113 E Main St
Ventura, CA 93001

Alex Theatre Phone: 818-243-2809
216 N Brand Blvd Fax: 818-243-3622
Glendale, CA 91203
theatre.glendale.ca.us/alex/

Alternative Repertory Theatre Phone: 714-836-7929
125 N Broadway Suite B
Santa Ana, CA 92701
E-mail: glcplt@concentric.net
www.concentric.net/~glcplt/

American Jazz Philharmonic Phone: 310-845-1900
PO Box 34575 Fax: 310-845-1909
Los Angeles, CA 90034
www.amjazzphil.org

American Wilderness Zoo & Aquarium Phone: 909-481-6604
4557 Mills Cir Fax: 909-987-9584
Ontario, CA 91764
www.wildernesszoo.com

Anaheim Museum Phone: 714-778-3301
241 S Anaheim Blvd Fax: 714-778-6740
Anaheim, CA 92805

Angeles National Forest Phone: 626-574-1613
701 N Santa Anita Ave Fax: 626-574-5233
Arcadia, CA 91006
www.r5.fs.fed.us/angeles

Aquarium of the Pacific Phone: 562-590-3100
100 Aquarium Way Fax: 562-951-1629
Long Beach, CA 90802
www.aquariumofpacific.org/

Armand Hammer Museum of Art & Cultural Center Phone: 310-443-7000
10899 Wilshire Blvd Fax: 310-443-7099
Los Angeles, CA 90024
artscenecal.com/UCLAHammerMsm.html

Art Association Gallery Phone: 805-648-1235
700 E Santa Clara St
Ventura, CA 93001

Asistencia Mission Phone: 909-793-5402
26930 Barton Rd Fax: 909-798-8585
Redlands, CA 92373

Atlantis Play Center Phone: 714-892-6015
9301 Westminster Ave
Garden Grove, CA 92844

Ballet Folklorico de Mexico
10801 National Blvd Suite 220
Los Angeles, CA 90064
www.balletfolkloricotours.com
Phone: 310-474-4443
Fax: 310-446-9531

Ballet Folklorico de Riverside
8859 Philbin Ave
Riverside, CA 92503
Phone: 909-354-8872

Bear Mountain Ski & Golf Resort
43101 Gold Mine Dr
Big Bear Lake, CA 92315
www.bearmtn.com
Phone: 909-585-2519
Fax: 909-585-6805

Beattle George F Planetarium
701 S Mt Vernon Ave
San Bernardino, CA 92410
Phone: 909-888-6511
Fax: 909-889-4988

Benedict Castle
5445 Chicago Ave
Riverside, CA 92507
Phone: 909-683-4241
Fax: 909-682-3754

Block at Orange
20 City Blvd W
Orange, CA 92868
www.theblockatorange.com
Phone: 714-769-4000
Fax: 714-769-4011

Bolsa Chica Ecological Reserve
3842 Warner Ave
Huntington Beach, CA 92649
Phone: 714-846-1114

Bowers Kidseum
1802 N Main St
Santa Ana, CA 92706
www.nativecreative.com/kidseum/
Phone: 714-480-1520
Fax: 714-480-0053

Bowers Museum of Cultural Art
2002 N Main St
Santa Ana, CA 92706
www.bowers.org/
Phone: 714-567-3600
Fax: 714-567-3603

Box Springs Mountain Park
9699 Box Springs Mountain Rd
Moreno Valley, CA 92557
Phone: 909-955-4310

Brand Library & Art Center
1601 W Mountain St
Glendale, CA 91201
library.ci.glendale.ca.us/brand
Phone: 818-548-2051

Brand Park
1601 W Mountain St
Glendale, CA 91201
Phone: 818-548-2147

Buena Park Civic Theater
8150 Knott Ave
Buena Park, CA 90620
Phone: 714-562-3888
Fax: 714-827-9782

California African Museum
600 State Dr Exposition Pk
Los Angeles, CA 90037
www.caam.ca.gov
Phone: 213-744-7432
Fax: 213-744-2050

California Botanic Gardens
University of California Riverside
Riverside, CA 92521
Phone: 909-787-4650
Fax: 909-787-4437

California Citrus State Historic Park
9400 Dufferin Ave
Riverside, CA 92503
Phone: 909-780-6222
Fax: 909-780-6073

California Museum of Photography
3824 Main St
Riverside, CA 92501
www.cmp.ucr.edu
Phone: 909-784-3686

California Plaza
350 S Grand Ave Suite A4
Los Angeles, CA 90071
E-mail: events@grandperformances.org
www.grandperformances.org
Phone: 213-687-2190
Fax: 213-687-2191

California Science Center
700 State Dr
Los Angeles, CA 90037
www.casciencectr.org
Phone: 213-744-7400
Fax: 213-744-2650

California Theatre of Performing Arts
562 W 4th St
San Bernardino, CA 92401
www.theatricalarts.com
Phone: 909-386-7361
Fax: 909-885-8672

Carnegie Art Museum
424 S C St
Oxnard, CA 93030
www.vcnet.com/carnart
Phone: 805-385-8157
Fax: 805-483-3654

Casa Adobe De San Rafael
1330 Dorothy Dr
Glendale, CA 91202
Phone: 818-548-2147
Fax: 818-543-0793

Castle Amusement Park
3500 Polk St
Riverside, CA 92505
E-mail: info@castlepark.com
www.castlepark.com
Phone: 909-785-3000
Fax: 909-785-4177

CBS Studio
7800 Beverly Blvd
Los Angeles, CA 90036
www.cbs.com
Phone: 323-575-2345
Fax: 323-651-5900

Channel Islands Ballet
800 Hobson Way
Oxnard, CA 93030
Phone: 805-486-2424
Fax: 805-483-7303

Channel Islands Harbor
2731 S Victoria Ave Visitor Information
Oxnard, CA 93035
Phone: 805-985-4852
Fax: 805-985-7952

Channel Islands National Park
1901 Spinnaker Dr
Ventura, CA 93001
E-mail: chis_interpretation@nps.gov
www.nps.gov/chis/
Phone: 805-658-5700
Fax: 805-658-5799

Crest Kimberly House & Gardens
1325 Prospect Dr
Redlands, CA 92373
www.kimberlycrest.com
Phone: 909-792-2111

Crystal Cathedral
12141 Lewis St
Garden Grove, CA 92840
www.crystalcathedral.org
Phone: 714-971-4000
Fax: 714-750-3836

Descanso Gardens
1418 Descanso Dr
La Canada, CA 91011
www.descanso.com/
Phone: 818-952-4401
Fax: 818-790-3291

Discovery Museum
3101 W Harvard St
Santa Ana, CA 92704
Phone: 714-540-0404
Fax: 714-540-1932

Discovery Science Center
2500 N Main St
Santa Ana, CA 92705
www.go2dsc.org
Phone: 714-542-2823
Fax: 714-542-2828

Disneyland
PO Box 3232
Anaheim, CA 92803
disney.go.com/Disneyland
Phone: 714-781-4565

El Dorado East Regional Park & Nature Center
7550 E Spring St
Long Beach, CA 90815
Phone: 562-570-1745
Fax: 562-570-8530

El Dorado Park West
2800 Studebaker Rd
Long Beach, CA 90815
Phone: 562-570-1765

Elysian Park
929 Academy Rd
Los Angeles, CA 90012
Phone: 323-226-1402
Fax: 323-226-1400

Ennis-Brown House
2655 Glendower Ave
Los Angeles, CA 90027
E-mail: ennisbrn@primenet.com
www.ennisbrownhouse.org
Phone: 323-660-0607
Fax: 323-660-3646

Fairmount Park
2601 Fairmount Blvd
Riverside, CA 92501
Phone: 909-715-3440

Fiesta Village
1405 E Washington Rd
Colton, CA 92324
Phone: 909-824-1111
Fax: 909-423-0192

First Congregational Church
3504 Mission Inn Ave
Riverside, CA 92501
Phone: 909-684-2494
Fax: 909-778-0309

Forest Lawn Museum
1712 S Glendale Ave
Glendale, CA 91205
Phone: 323-240-3131
Fax: 323-551-5329
TF: 800-204-3131

Found Theatre
251 E 7th St
Long Beach, CA 90813
Phone: 562-433-3363
Fax: 562-433-3363

Galaxy Concert Theatre
3503 Harbor Blvd
Santa Ana, CA 92704
www.galaxytheatre.com/
Phone: 714-957-0600
Fax: 714-957-6605

Garden Grove Playhouse
12001 Saint Mark St
Garden Grove, CA 92845
Phone: 714-897-5122

Gene Autry Western Heritage Museum
4700 Western Heritage Way
Los Angeles, CA 90027
E-mail: autry@autry-museum.org
Phone: 323-667-2000
Fax: 323-660-5721

General Phineas Banning Residence Museum
401 E M St
Wilmington, CA 90744
banning.org
Phone: 310-548-7777
Fax: 310-548-2644

Gibbs Norma Brandel Park
Graham Pl-betw Warner & Heil Sts
Huntington Beach, CA 92649
Phone: 714-536-5486

Glen Helen Regional Park
2555 Glen Helen Pkwy
San Bernardino, CA 92407
Phone: 909-880-2522
Fax: 909-880-2659

Glendale Centre Theater
324 N Orange St
Glendale, CA 91203
Phone: 818-244-8481
Fax: 818-244-5042

Glendale Symphony Orchestra
401 N Brand Blvd Suite 520
Glendale, CA 91203
glendale-online.com/entertainment/gso
Phone: 818-500-8720
Fax: 818-500-8014

Grier-Musser Museum
403 S Bonnie Brae Ave
Los Angeles, CA 90057
www.isi.edu/sims/sheila/gm.html
Phone: 213-413-1814

Griffith Observatory
2800 E Observatory Rd Griffith Pk
Los Angeles, CA 90027
www.griffithobs.org
Phone: 323-664-1181
Fax: 323-663-4323

Griffith Park
Los Feliz Blvd & Riverside Dr
Los Angeles, CA 90027
Phone: 213-485-8775
Fax: 213-485-8775

Grove Theater Center
12852 Main St
Garden Grove, CA 92840
E-mail: gtc@gtc.org
www.gtc.org
Phone: 714-741-9554
Fax: 714-741-9560

Gull Wings Children's Museum
418 W 4th St
Oxnard, CA 93030
Phone: 805-483-3005

Heritage House (Riverside)
8193 Magnolia Ave
Riverside, CA 92504
Phone: 909-689-1333

Heritage House (San Bernardino)
796 'D' St
San Bernardino, CA 92401
Phone: 909-883-0750

Heritage Square
715 S 'A' St
Oxnard, CA 93030
Phone: 805-483-7960
Fax: 805-486-4299

Heritage Square Museum
3800 Homer St
Los Angeles, CA 90031
Phone: 626-449-0193
Fax: 626-304-9652

Historic Downtown Santa Ana
downtown
Santa Ana, CA 92701
Phone: 714-558-2791

Historic French Park
901 N French St
Santa Ana, CA 92702
Phone: 714-571-4200

Historic Main Street
Main St & Garden Grove Blvd
Garden Grove, CA 92840

Historical Glass Museum Phone: 909-798-0868
1157 N Orange St
Redlands, CA 92373

Hobby City Doll & Toy Museum Phone: 714-527-2323
1238 S Beach Blvd Fax: 714-236-9762
Anaheim, CA 92804

Hollywood Bowl Phone: 323-850-2000
2301 N Highland Ave Fax: 323-850-2155
Los Angeles, CA 90068
www.hollywoodbowl.org/

Huntington Beach Arts Center Phone: 714-374-1650
538 Main St Fax: 714-374-1654
Huntington Beach, CA 92648

Huntington Beach Central Park Phone: 714-536-5486
Golden West St
Huntington Beach, CA 92648

Huntington Beach Pier Phone: 714-536-5281
Pacific Coast Hwy & Main St
Huntington Beach, CA 92648

Huntington Beach Playhouse Phone: 714-375-0696
7111 Talbert Ave Fax: 714-847-0457
Huntington Beach, CA 92648
www.user-friendly.com/playhouse/hb.html

Hurricane Harbor Phone: 661-255-4100
26101 Magic Mountain Pkwy
Valencia, CA 91355
www.sixflags.com/hurricaneharborla

IMAX Theater Phone: 213-744-2014
700 State Dr Exposition Pk
Los Angeles, CA 90037

Inland Empire Symphony Assn Phone: 909-381-5388
362 W Court St Fax: 909-381-5380
San Bernardino, CA 92401

International City Theatre Phone: 562-495-4595
1 World Trade Ctr PO Box 32069 Fax: 714-969-9639
Long Beach, CA 90832

International Surfing Museum Phone: 714-960-3483
411 Olive Ave Fax: 714-960-1434
Huntington Beach, CA 92648
www.surfingmuseum.org

J Paul Getty Museum Phone: 310-440-7300
1200 Getty Center Dr Fax: 310-440-6949
Los Angeles, CA 90049
www.getty.edu

Japanese American National Museum Phone: 213-625-0414
369 E 1st St Fax: 213-625-1770
Los Angeles, CA 90012 TF: 800-461-5266
www.lausd.k12.ca.us/janm/

Jensen-Alvarado Historic Ranch & Museum Phone: 909-369-6055
4307 Briggs St
Riverside, CA 92509

Joshua Tree National Park Phone: 760-367-5500
74485 National Park Dr Fax: 760-367-6392
Twentynine Palms, CA 92277
www.nps.gov/jotr/

Jurupa Mountains Cultural Center Phone: 909-685-5818
7621 Granite Hill Dr Fax: 909-685-1240
Riverside, CA 92509
E-mail: jmcc@dreamsoft.com
www.the-jmcc.org

Just Plain Dancin' & Company Phone: 909-681-6930
6515 Clay
Riverside, CA 92509

Kaye Museum of Miniatures Phone: 323-937-6464
5900 Wilshire Blvd East Wing Fax: 323-937-2126
Los Angeles, CA 90036
www.museumofminiatures.com

Kidspace A Participatory Museum Phone: 626-449-9144
390 S El Molino Ave Fax: 626-449-9985
Pasadena, CA 91101

Knott's Berry Farm Phone: 714-827-1776
8039 Beach Blvd Fax: 714-220-5200
Buena Park, CA 90620
E-mail: info@knotts.com
www.knotts.com

Life Arts Center Phone: 909-784-5849
3485 University Ave
Riverside, CA 92501

Lincoln Memorial Shrine Phone: 909-798-7636
125 W Vine St Fax: 909-798-7566
Redlands, CA 92373

Long Beach Arts Phone: 562-435-5995
447 Long Beach Blvd
Long Beach, CA 90802

Long Beach Museum of Art Phone: 562-439-2119
2300 E Ocean Blvd Fax: 562-439-3587
Long Beach, CA 90803
www.lbma.org

Long Beach Opera Phone: 562-439-2580
PO Box 14895
Long Beach, CA 90853

Long Beach Playhouse Phone: 562-494-1616
5021 E Anaheim St Fax: 562-494-1014
Long Beach, CA 90804
www.longbeachplayhouse.com

Long Beach Symphony Orchestra Phone: 562-436-3203
555 E Ocean Blvd Suite 106 Fax: 562-491-3599
Long Beach, CA 90802
E-mail: lbso@lbso.org
www.lbso.org

Los Angeles Ballet Phone: 213-833-3610
PO Box 712462 Fax: 714-991-8050
Los Angeles, CA 90071

Los Angeles Chamber Orchestra Phone: 213-622-7001
611 W 6th St Suite 2710 Fax: 213-955-2071
Los Angeles, CA 90017
E-mail: lachamber@aol.com
www.laco.org

Los Angeles Children's Museum
310 N Main St
Los Angeles, CA 90012
Phone: 213-687-8801
Fax: 213-687-0319

Los Angeles County Museum of Art
5905 Wilshire Blvd
Los Angeles, CA 90036
www.lacma.org
Phone: 323-857-6111
Fax: 323-857-4702

Los Angeles Farmers Market
6333 W 3rd St
Los Angeles, CA 90036
E-mail: info@farmersmarketla.com
www.farmersmarketla.com/
Phone: 323-933-9211

Los Angeles Master Chorale
135 N Grand Ave Music Center of Los Angeles County
Los Angeles, CA 90012
E-mail: lamc@lamc.org
www.lamc.org
Phone: 213-626-0624
Fax: 213-626-0196

Los Angeles Opera
135 N Grand Ave
Los Angeles, CA 90012
E-mail: contact@laopera.org
www.laopera.org
Phone: 213-972-7219
Fax: 213-687-3490

Los Angeles Philharmonic Assn
135 N Grand Ave
Los Angeles, CA 90012
www.laphil.org
Phone: 213-972-7300
Fax: 213-617-3065

Los Angeles Zoo
5333 Zoo Dr
Los Angeles, CA 90027
E-mail: lazooed@ix.netcom.com
www.lazoo.org
Phone: 323-666-4650
Fax: 323-662-9786

Main Street Downtown
201 N 'E' St
San Bernardino, CA 92401
Phone: 909-381-5037
Fax: 909-888-2576

Main Street Mall
5th St & University Ave
Riverside, CA 92501
Phone: 909-781-7335

Mann's Chinese Theatre
6925 Hollywood Blvd
Hollywood, CA 90028
Phone: 323-461-3331
Fax: 323-463-0879

Manzanar National Historic Site
PO Box 579
Death Valley, CA 92328
www.nps.gov/manz
Phone: 760-786-2331
Fax: 760-786-3283

March Field Air Museum
22550 Van Buren Blvd March Air Reserve Base
Riverside, CA 92518
E-mail: info@marchfield.org
www.marchfield.org
Phone: 909-697-6600
Fax: 909-697-6605

Medieval Times Dinner & Tournament
7662 Beach Blvd
Buena Park, CA 90620
E-mail: buenapark@medievaltimes.com
www.medievaltimes.com/CA_realm.htm
Phone: 714-521-4740
Fax: 714-670-2721
TF: 800-899-6600

Miller Earl Burns Japanese Garden
1250 Bellflower Blvd
Long Beach, CA 90840
Phone: 562-985-8885
Fax: 562-985-8884

Mission Inn Museum
3649 Mission Inn Ave
Riverside, CA 92501
Phone: 909-788-9556
Fax: 909-341-6574

Mojave National Preserve
222 E Main St Suite 202
Barstow, CA 92311
www.nps.gov/moja
Phone: 760-255-8800
Fax: 760-255-8809

Movieland Wax Museum
7711 Beach Blvd
Buena Park, CA 90620
E-mail: sales@waxmuseum.com
www.movielandwaxmuseum.com
Phone: 714-522-1155
Fax: 714-739-9668

Museum of Contemporary Art
250 S Grand Ave California Plaza
Los Angeles, CA 90012
www.moca.org
Phone: 213-621-2766
Fax: 213-620-8674

Museum of Latin American Art
628 Alamitos Ave
Long Beach, CA 90802
www.molaa.com
Phone: 562-437-1689
Fax: 562-437-7043

Museum of Neon Art
501 W Olympic Blvd
Los Angeles, CA 90015
E-mail: info@neonmona.org
neonmona.org
Phone: 213-489-9918
Fax: 213-489-9932

Museum of Tolerance
9760 W Pico Blvd Wiesenthal Ctr
Los Angeles, CA 90035
www.wiesenthal.com
Phone: 310-553-8403
Fax: 310-772-7655

Music Center of Los Angeles
135 N Grand Ave
Los Angeles, CA 90012
www.performingartscenterla.org
Phone: 213-972-7200
Fax: 213-972-7474

Natural History Museum of Los Angeles County
900 Exposition Blvd
Los Angeles, CA 90007
E-mail: info@nhm.org
www.nhm.org
Phone: 213-763-3466
Fax: 213-746-2999

NBC Studio
3000 W Alameda Ave
Burbank, CA 91523
Phone: 818-840-4444
Fax: 818-840-3535

NBC Studios
3000 W Alameda Ave
Burbank, CA 91523
Phone: 818-840-3537

New West Symphony
800 Hobson Way
Oxnard, CA 93030
Phone: 805-486-2424
Fax: 805-483-7303

Newland House Museum
19820 Beach Blvd
Huntington Beach, CA 92648
Phone: 714-962-5777

Old Courthouse Museum
211 W Santa Ana Blvd
Santa Ana, CA 92701
Phone: 714-834-3703
Fax: 714-834-2280

Olivas Adobe Historical Park
4200 Olivas Park Dr
Ventura, CA 93001
Phone: 805-644-4346

Opera Pacific
18025 Sky Pk E Suite H
Irvine, CA 92614
Phone: 949-474-4488
Fax: 949-474-4442

Orange County Crazies
Santa Ana Blvd & Bush St
Santa Ana, CA 92701
Phone: 714-550-9890
Fax: 714-550-0825

Orange County Museum of Art (Newport Beach)
850 San Clemente Dr
Newport Beach, CA 92660
ocartsnet.org/ocma
Phone: 949-759-1122
Fax: 949-759-5623

Orange County Museum of Art (Costa Mesa)
3333 Bristol St South Coast Plaza
Costa Mesa, CA 92626
Phone: 714-662-3366
Fax: 714-662-3818

Orange County Performing Arts Center
600 Town Ctr Dr
Costa Mesa, CA 92626
www.ocpac.org
Phone: 714-556-2121
Fax: 714-556-0156

Oxnard Performing Arts Center
800 Hobson Way
Oxnard, CA 93030
Phone: 805-486-2424
Fax: 805-483-7303

Pacific Chorale
1221 E Dyer Rd Suite 230
Santa Ana, CA 92705
E-mail: sing@pacific-chorale.org
www.pacific-chorale.org
Phone: 714-662-2345
Fax: 714-662-2395

Pacific Symphony Orchestra
1231 E Dyer Rd Suite 200
Santa Ana, CA 92705
E-mail: pso@pso.org
www.pso.org
Phone: 714-755-5788
Fax: 714-755-5789

Page George C Museum at La Brea Tar Pits
5801 Wilshire Blvd
Los Angeles, CA 90036
www.tarpits.org
Phone: 323-857-6311
Fax: 323-933-3974

Paramount Film & TV Studios
5555 Melrose Ave
Los Angeles, CA 90038
www.paramount.com
Phone: 323-956-1777
Fax: 323-862-8534

Pasadena Center
300 E Green St
Pasadena, CA 91101
www.pasadenacenter.org
Phone: 626-793-2122
Fax: 626-793-8014

Pasadena Symphony
300 Green St Civic Auditorium Suite 260
Pasadena, CA 91101
www.pasadenasymphony.org
Phone: 626-793-7172
Fax: 626-793-7180

Performing Arts Center of Los Angeles County
135 N Grand Ave
Los Angeles, CA 90012
www.performingartscenterla.org
Phone: 213-972-7211
Fax: 213-481-1176

Petersen Automotive Museum
6060 Wilshire Blvd
Los Angeles, CA 90036
www.petersen.org
Phone: 323-930-2277
Fax: 323-930-6642

Pharaoh's Lost Kingdom Theme Park
1101 N California St
Redlands, CA 92374
E-mail: pharaoh@pharaohslostkingdom.com
www.pharaohslostkingdom.com
Phone: 909-335-7275
Fax: 909-307-2622

Plaza Garibaldi Dinner Theater
1490 S Anaheim Blvd
Anaheim, CA 92805
Phone: 714-758-9014
Fax: 714-758-9110

Port Hueneme Museum
220 N Market St
Port Hueneme, CA 93041
Phone: 805-488-2023
Fax: 805-488-6993

Ports O'Call Village
Berth 77 P7A
San Pedro, CA 90731
Phone: 310-732-7696
Fax: 310-547-5389

Queen Mary Seaport
1126 Queens Hwy
Long Beach, CA 90802
E-mail: queenmary@qte.net
www.queenmary.com/
Phone: 562-435-3511
Fax: 562-437-4531
TF: 800-437-2934

Rancho Jurupa Regional Park
4800 Crestmore Rd
Riverside, CA 92519
Phone: 909-684-7032

Rancho Los Alamitos
6400 E Bixby Hill Rd
Long Beach, CA 90815
www.ci.long-beach.ca.us/park/rancho.htm
Phone: 562-431-3541
Fax: 562-430-9694

Rancho Los Cerritos
4600 Virginia Rd
Long Beach, CA 90807
www.ci.long-beach.ca.us/park/ranchlc.htm
Phone: 562-570-1755
Fax: 562-570-1893

Recreation Park
4900 E 7th St
Long Beach, CA 90804
Phone: 562-570-3100

Redlands Bowl
PO Box 466
Redlands, CA 92373
Phone: 909-793-7316
Fax: 909-793-5086

Ripley's Believe It or Not! Museum (Hollywood)
6780 Hollywood Blvd
Hollywood, CA 90028
E-mail: hollywood@ripleys.com
www.ripleys.com/hollywood.htm
Phone: 323-466-6335
Fax: 323-466-6512

Ripley's Believe It or Not! Museum (Buena Park)
7850 Beach Blvd
Buena Park, CA 90620
E-mail: sales@waxmuseum.com
www.movielandwaxmuseum.com/rip.html
Phone: 714-522-1152
Fax: 714-739-9668

Riverside Art Museum
3425 Mission Inn Ave
Riverside, CA 92501
Phone: 909-684-7111
Fax: 909-684-7332

Riverside Arts Foundation
3485 Mission Inn Ave Municipal Auditorium
Riverside, CA 92501
www.ci.riverside.ca.us/arts_foundation/
Phone: 909-680-1345
Fax: 909-680-1348

Riverside Ballet Theater
3840 Lemon St Aurea Vista Hotel
Riverside, CA 92501
Phone: 909-787-7850
Fax: 909-686-1240

Riverside Community Players
4026 14th St
Riverside, CA 92501
Phone: 909-369-1200
Fax: 909-369-1261

Riverside County Philharmonic
3485 Mission Inn Ave Municipal Auditorium
Riverside, CA 92501
Phone: 909-787-0251
Fax: 909-787-8933

Riverside Marketplace
Main St
Riverside, CA 92501
Phone: 909-715-3400
Fax: 909-715-3404

Riverside Municipal Museum
3580 Mission Inn Ave
Riverside, CA 92501
www.ci.riverside.ca.us/museum
Phone: 909-826-5273
Fax: 909-369-4970

Saint Joseph Ballet
1810 N Main St
Santa Ana, CA 92706
Phone: 714-541-8314
Fax: 714-541-2150

Saint Luke's Episcopal Church
Atlantic Ave & 7th St
Long Beach, CA 90813
Phone: 562-436-4047

San Bernardino County Museum
2024 Orange Tree Ln
Redlands, CA 92374
www.co.san-bernardino.ca.us/museum
Phone: 909-307-2669
Fax: 909-307-0539
TF: 888-247-3344

San Bernardino National Forest
1824 S Commercenter Cir
San Bernardino, CA 92408
Phone: 909-383-5588
Fax: 909-383-5770

San Bernardino Symphony
562 W 4th St California Theatre
San Bernardino, CA 92401
Phone: 909-381-5388
Fax: 909-381-5380

San Manuel Indian Bingo & Casino
5797 N Victoria Ave
Highland, CA 92346
E-mail: slengel@sanmanuel.com
www.sanmanuel.com
Phone: 909-864-5050
Fax: 909-862-0682
TF: 800-359-2464

Santa Ana Historic Preservation Society
500 N Sycamore St
Santa Ana, CA 92706
Phone: 714-547-9645

Santa Ana Zoo
1801 E Chestnut Ave
Santa Ana, CA 92701
www.santaanazoo.org
Phone: 714-835-7484

Santa Barbara Museum of Art
1130 State St
Santa Barbara, CA 93101
www.sbmuseart.org
Phone: 805-963-4364
Fax: 805-966-6840

Santa Barbara Museum of Natural History
2559 Puesta Del Sol Rd
Santa Barbara, CA 93105
www.sbnature.org
Phone: 805-682-4711
Fax: 805-569-3170

Santa Monica Mountains National Recreation Area
401 W Hillcrest Dr
Thousand Oaks, CA 91360
www.nps.gov/samo/
Phone: 805-370-2301
Fax: 805-370-1850

Seabee Museum
1000 23rd Ave Bldg 99
Port Hueneme, CA 93043
Phone: 805-982-5163
Fax: 805-982-5595

Sherman Indian High School Indian Museum
9010 Magnolia Ave
Riverside, CA 92503
www.shermanindianmuseum.org
Phone: 909-276-6719
Fax: 909-276-6336

Shoreline Village
419-R Shoreline Village Dr
Long Beach, CA 90802
E-mail: management@shorelinevillage.com
www.shorelinevillage.com
Phone: 562-435-2668
Fax: 562-435-6445

Six Flags Magic Mountain
26101 Magic Mountain Pkwy
Valencia, CA 91355
www.sixflags.com/magicmountain
Phone: 661-255-4100
Fax: 661-255-4815

South Coast Botanic Garden
26300 Crenshaw Blvd
Palos Verdes, CA 90274
Phone: 310-544-6815
Fax: 310-544-6820

South Coast Chorale
PO Box 92524
Long Beach, CA 90809
Phone: 562-439-6919

Southwest Museum
234 Museum Dr
Los Angeles, CA 90065
E-mail: swmuseum@annex.com
www.southwestmuseum.org
Phone: 323-221-2164
Fax: 323-224-8223

Special Place A
1003 E Highland Ave
San Bernardino, CA 92404
Phone: 909-881-1201

Stanley Ranch Museum
12174 Euclid St PO Box 4297
Garden Grove, CA 92842
Phone: 714-530-8871

Sturges Center for the Fine Arts
780 N 'E' St
San Bernardino, CA 92410
Phone: 909-384-5415
Fax: 909-384-5449

Theatre LA
644 S Figueroa St
Los Angeles, CA 90017
www.theatrela.org
Phone: 213-614-0556
Fax: 213-614-0561

Theatre-by-the-Sea Phone: 805-985-4852
3890 Channel Islands Blvd
Oxnard, CA 93035

Tustin Area Historical Society Museum Phone: 714-731-5701
395 El Camino Real
Tustin, CA 92780

Universal Studios Hollywood Phone: 818-622-3801
100 Universal City Plaza Fax: 818-866-1516
Universal City, CA 91608
E-mail: execdesk@mca.com
www.universalstudios.com/unicity/thehill.html

University Art Museum Phone: 562-985-5761
1250 Bellflower Blvd CSULB Fax: 562-985-7602
Long Beach, CA 90840

Ventura County Maritime Museum Phone: 805-984-6260
2731 S Victoria Ave Fax: 805-984-5970
Oxnard, CA 93035

Ventura County Museum of History & Art Phone: 805-653-0323
100 E Main St Fax: 805-653-5267
Ventura, CA 93001

Warner Bros Studios Phone: 818-954-1744
4000 Warner Blvd Fax: 818-954-2089
Burbank, CA 91522

Watts Towers Phone: 213-847-4646
1727 E 107th St Fax: 323-564-7030
Los Angeles, CA 90002

Wells Fargo History Museum Phone: 213-253-7166
333 S Grand Ave Fax: 213-680-2269
Los Angeles, CA 90071
www.wellsfargohistory.com

Westminster Museum Phone: 714-891-2597
8612 Westminster Blvd
Westminster, CA 92683

Wild Bill's Wild West Phone: 714-522-6414
7600 Beach Blvd Fax: 714-521-1176
Buena Park, CA 90620 TF: 800-883-1546

Wiltern Theatre Phone: 213-388-1400
3790 Wilshire Blvd Fax: 213-388-0242
Los Angeles, CA 90010

World Museum of Natural History Phone: 909-785-2209
4700 Pierce St La Sierra University Fax: 909-785-2091
Riverside, CA 92515

World Trade Center Phone: 213-489-3337
350 S Figueroa St Suite 233 Fax: 213-680-1878
Los Angeles, CA 90071

Yorba Regional Park Phone: 714-970-1460
7600 E La Palma Ave Fax: 714-970-7892
Anaheim, CA 92807

Zimmer Discovery Children's Museum Phone: 323-857-0072
5870 W Olympic Blvd Fax: 323-965-1758
Los Angeles, CA 90036

Sports Teams & Facilities

Anaheim Angels Phone: 714-940-2000
2000 Gene Autry Way Edison International Field Fax: 714-940-2001
Anaheim, CA 92806
www.angelsbaseball.com

Arrowhead Pond of Anaheim Phone: 714-704-2400
2695 E Katella Ave Fax: 714-704-2443
Anaheim, CA 92806
www.arrowheadpond.com

California Speedway Phone: 909-429-5000
9300 Cherry Ave Fax: 909-429-5500
Fontana, CA 91719 TF: 800-944-7223
www.californiaspeedway.com

Dodger Stadium Phone: 323-224-1351
1000 Elysian Park Ave Fax: 323-224-1399
Los Angeles, CA 90012

Edison International Field Phone: 714-940-2000
2000 Gene Autry Way Fax: 714-940-2001
Anaheim, CA 92806
www.angelsbaseball.com/edisonfield

Long Beach Arena Phone: 562-436-3636
300 E Ocean Blvd Fax: 562-436-9491
Long Beach, CA 90802

Long Beach Ice Dogs (hockey) Phone: 562-423-3647
300 E Ocean Blvd Long Beach Arena Fax: 562-437-5116
Long Beach, CA 90802
www.icedogshockey.com

Los Alamitos Race Course Phone: 714-236-4400
4961 Katella Ave
Los Alamitos, CA 90720
www.webworldinc.com/larace/laqhr

Los Angeles Avengers (football) Phone: 310-473-7999
865 S Figueroa St STAPLES Ctr Fax: 310-473-7790
Los Angeles, CA 90017
E-mail: info@laavengers.com
www.laavengers.com

Los Angeles Clippers Phone: 213-748-8000
1111 S Figueroa St Staples Ctr Fax: 213-745-0494
Los Angeles, CA 90015
www.nba.com/clippers

Los Angeles Dodgers Phone: 323-224-1400
1000 Elysian Park Ave Dodger Stadium Fax: 323-224-1269
Los Angeles, CA 90012
www.dodgers.com

Los Angeles Galaxy (soccer) Phone: 310-445-1260
1640 S Sepulveda Blvd Suite 114 Fax: 310-445-1270
Los Angeles, CA 90025
E-mail: falozano@aol.com

Los Angeles Kings Phone: 310-419-3160
865 S Figueroa St Staples Ctr Fax: 310-673-8927
Los Angeles, CA 90017
E-mail: tickets@lakings.com
www.lakings.com

Los Angeles Lakers
865 S Figueroa St Staples Ctr
Los Angeles, CA 90017
www.nba.com/lakers
Phone: 310-426-6000
Fax: 310-742-7782

Los Angeles Sparks (basketball)
3900 W Manchester Blvd Great Western Forum
Inglewood, CA 90306
www.wnba.com/sparks
Phone: 310-419-3131

Los Angeles Sports Arena
3939 S Figueroa St
Los Angeles, CA 90037
Phone: 213-748-6136
Fax: 213-746-9636

Mighty Ducks of Anaheim
2695 E Katella Ave Arrowhead Pond of Anaheim
Anaheim, CA 92806
www.mightyducks.com
Phone: 714-704-2700
Fax: 714-704-2913

Orange County Waves (soccer)
602 N Flower St Eddie West Field
Santa Ana, CA 92702
www.ocwavesoccer.com
Phone: 949-250-9283
Fax: 949-348-4601

Playa Grande Polo Club
18381 Goldenwest St
Huntington Beach, CA 92648
Phone: 714-842-7656

San Bernardino Stampede (baseball)
280 'E' St
San Bernardino, CA 92401
E-mail: lerxst@stampedebaseball.com
www.stampedebaseball.com/
Phone: 909-888-9922
Fax: 909-888-5251

San Fernando Valley Heroes (soccer)
7955 San Fernando Rd
Sun Valley, CA 91352
Phone: 818-768-0965
Fax: 818-768-5213

San Gabriel Valley Highlanders (soccer)
536 N Glen Oaks Blvd
Burbank, CA 91501
Phone: 818-242-9110
Fax: 818-556-6427

Santa Anita Park
285 W Huntington Dr
Arcadia, CA 91007
E-mail: sainfo@santaanita.com
www.santaanita.com
Phone: 626-574-7223
Fax: 626-446-9565

Staples Center
865 S Figueroa St
Los Angeles, CA 90017
www.staplescenterla.com
Phone: 213-742-7340
Fax: 213-742-7282

Annual Events

Academy Awards (late March).....310-247-3000
AFI International Film Festival (late October).....323-856-7707
African Marketplace & Cultural Faire (late August-early September).....323-734-1164
Aloha Concert Jam (late June).....562-436-3645
Alpine Village Oktoberfest (early September-late October).....310-327-4384
Anaheim Harvest Festivals (late October).....707-778-6300
Anaheim Street International Festival (early October).....562-436-3645
Antique Car Parade (August).....714-571-4200
Apple Blossom Festival Weekend (April).....909-797-6833
Beach Charities BeachFest (early May).....949-376-6942
Belmont Shore Car Show (mid-September).....562-434-3066
Belmont Shore Christmas Parade (early December).....562-434-3066
Bob Marley Reggae Festival (mid-February).....562-436-3661
Cajun & Zydeco Festival (late July).....562-427-3713
California 500 (late October).....909-429-5000
California Plaza's Moonlight Concerts (June-October).....213-687-2159
California Strawberry Festival (mid-May).....805-385-7545
Celebration of the Whales (mid-February-mid-March).....805-985-4852
Celtic Lands Faire (early October).....805-486-2424
Channel Islands Harbor Boat Show (late July-early August).....805-985-4852
Cherry Festival (early June).....909-845-9541
Cherry Valley Cherry Festival (early June).....909-845-8466
Chinese New Year's Parade in Chinatown (mid-February).....213-617-0396
Christmas Fantasy Parade (late November-early January).....714-781-4560
Christmas on Main Street (mid-November).....909-781-7335
Christmas Parade (early December).....909-885-3268
Christmas Tree Lighting & Holiday Kick-off (early December).....909-381-5037
Cinco de Mayo (Oxnard) (early May).....805-486-0266
Cinco de Mayo (Riverside) (early May).....909-340-5906
Cinco de Mayo Celebration (Anaheim) (early May).....714-765-5274
Cinco de Mayo Celebrations (Los Angeles) (early May).....213-628-1274
Cinco de Mayo Celebration (Santa Ana) (early May).....714-571-4200
Civil War Reenactment (Labor Day weekend).....714-962-5777
Concerts in the Park (July-August).....909-780-6222
Concours d'Elegance (early June).....714-842-4481
Concours on Rodeo (late June).....310-858-6100
Crystal Cathedral Glory of Christmas (late November-December).....714-544-5679
Crystal Cathedral Glory of Easter (early-late April).....714-544-5679
Days of Verdugo Festival (mid-October).....818-240-2464
Distance Derby (mid-August).....714-536-5486
Duck-A-Thon (mid-May).....714-374-1951
Earth Day Heal the Bay (mid-April).....310-581-4188
Family Village Festival (late October).....909-787-7678
Fantasy in the Sky (June-September).....714-781-4560
Festival of Lights (November).....909-781-7335
Festival of Philippine Arts & Culture (early September).....213-389-3050
Festival of Trees (late November).....909-875-8756
Fiesta Broadway Cinco de Mayo Celebration (late April).....310-914-0015
Fiesta de las Artes (late May).....310-376-0951
Floral Park Home & Garden Tour (late April).....714-543-3218
Flying U Rodeo (early February).....714-704-2400
Four Moons Pow Wow (early June).....909-823-6150
Fourth of July Celebration (July 4).....909-384-5031
Galaxy of Gems Show (late November).....805-525-5415
Garden Grove Strawberry Festival (late May).....714-638-0981

Golden Dragon Parade (mid-February) 213-617-0396
Grammy Awards (late February) 310-392-3777
Grand Prix of Long Beach (early April) 562-436-9953
Grapes & Gourmet Wine & Food Festival (early July) 909-384-5426
Great American Irish Fair & Music Festival (mid-June) 818-503-2511
Grecian Festival (early September) 562-494-8929
Grey Whale Migration (September-December) 805-985-4852
Griffith Park Light Festival (late November-late December) 323-913-4688
Harvest Fair (early-mid-November) 909-384-5426
Harvest Festival (Anaheim) (mid-August) 714-940-2074
Harvest Festival (Long Beach) (early September) 562-436-3661
Harvest Festival (Riverside) (mid-September) 707-778-6300
Heritage Square Summer Concert Series (late June-late August) 805-483-7960
Hollywood Christmas Parade (late November) 323-469-8311
Huntington Beach Summer Surf Contest (late September) 714-536-5486
Huntington Harbour Cruise of Lights (mid-late December) 714-840-7542
Independence Day Celebration (July 4) 909-683-7100
Independence Day Parade (July 4) 714-536-5486
International Sea Festival (August) 562-570-3100
Intertribal Marketplace at Southwest Museum (early November) 323-221-2164
Israeli Festival (mid-May) 818-757-0123
Kaleidoscope Festival (late April) 562-985-2288
KLON Blues Festival (Labor Day weekend) 562-985-1686
Korean Festival (early-October) 714-741-3310
LA Fiesta Broadway (late April) 310-914-8308
Las Posadas Candlelight Procession (mid-December) 213-628-1274
Long Beach Blues Festival (early September) 562-985-5566
Long Beach Jazz Festival (early August) 562-436-7794
Long Beach Lesbian & Gay Pride Festival (mid-May) 800-354-7743
Long Beach Renaissance Arts Festival (late August) 562-570-5333
Long Beach Sea Festival (August) 562-570-3100
Los Angeles Bach Festival (mid-March) 213-385-1345
Los Angeles City's Birthday Celebration (early September) 213-485-9777
Los Angeles County Fair (mid-September-early October) 909-623-3111
Los Angeles Gay & Lesbian Pride Celebration (late June) 323-686-0950
Los Angeles Gospel Festival (late May) 626-793-8983
Los Angeles Marathon (early March) 310-444-5544
Los Angeles Music Week (early December) 310-670-6898
Los Angeles Shakespeare Festival (late June-early July) 213-489-4127
Lotus Festival (early July) 213-624-7300
Main Street International Music Festival (early June) 909-381-5037
Malibu Art Festival (late July) 310-456-9025
Mariachi Festival (early May) 800-269-6273
Mariachi USA Festival (mid-June) 323-848-7717
Martin Luther King Celebration & Parade (mid-January) 562-570-6816
Mexican Independence Festival (mid-September) 714-571-4200
Miss San Bernardino Pageant (mid-March) 909-889-3980
Mission Inn 5K/10K Run (mid-November) 909-781-8241
Multi-Cultural Festival (late October) 805-385-7434
National Orange Show (late May) 909-888-6788
New Year's Eve Blues & Reggae Cruise & Fireworks (December 31) 562-799-7000
New Year's Eve Gala on Queen Mary (December 31) 562-435-3511
New Year's Eve on Pine Square (December 31) 562-436-4259
Nisei Week Japanese Festival (late July-early August) 213-687-7193
NoHo Theater & Arts Festival (late June) 818-508-5155
Oasis del Espiritu Santo Convention (late February-early March) 805-486-2424
Obon Festival (mid-July) 805-483-5948
Oktoberfest (mid-September-early November) 714-563-4166
Old Pasadena Jazz Fest (early July) 213-624-7300
Old Pasadena Summer Fest (late May) 626-797-6803
Old World Village Oktoberfest (mid-September-late October) 714-895-8020
Orange County Fair (mid-July) 714-708-3247
Orange County Wine Festival (early October) 714-530-0430
Outfest-Los Angeles Gay & Lesbian Film Festival (mid-July) 323-960-9200
Oxnard's HomeTown Christmas Parade (early December) 805-385-7545
Pacific Shoreline Marathon (late January) 949-766-1428
Page Museum's Fossil Excavation at La Brea Tar Pits (mid-July-mid-September) 323-934-7243
Pageant of the Masters/Festival of the Arts (early July-late August) 949-494-1145
Pan African Film Festival (mid-late February) 213-896-8221
Pan African Fine Art Festival (mid-late February) 213-896-8221
Parade of a Thousand Lights (late December) 562-435-4093
Parade of Lights (early December) 800-269-6273
Parks & Recreation Holiday Craft Fair (early December) 909-381-5037
Playboy Jazz Festival (mid-June) 310-449-4070
Point Mugu Air Show (late April) 805-989-8548
Port Hueneme Harbor Days (early October) 800-269-6273
Queen Mary Scottish Festival (mid-February) 562-435-3511
Red Ribbon Week & Downtown Parade (late October) 909-885-0509
Renaissance Pleasure Faire (early May-late June) 800-523-2473
Riverside County Fair & National Date Festival (mid-late February) 760-863-8247
Riverside Dickens Festival (early February) 909-781-3168
Riverside Orange Blossom Festival (late April) 909-715-3400
Rose Bowl Game (early January) 626-449-4100
Rose Show & Sale (late October) 714-998-1521
Route 66 Rendezvous (mid-September) 909-889-3980
San Bernardino County Fair (mid-May) 760-951-2200
Sawdust Festival (late June-late August) 949-494-3030
Scandinavian Festival (early October) 323-661-4273
Seabee Days Celebration (late June) 805-982-4493
Shakespeare on the Square (August) 909-381-5037
Ship Model Expo & Sale (December) 805-984-6260
Soap Box Derby (mid-May) 909-888-6788
South Bay Greek Festival (early October) 310-540-2434

Southern California Home & Garden Show (mid-late August)..............................714-978-8888
Spring Fest (mid-May)...........................626-282-5767
Spring Festival of Flowers (late March-mid-April) 818-952-4400
Star of Bethlehem (December)....................714-547-7000
Strawberry Classic Golf Tournament (late April) 805-983-4653
Summer Horse Classic (early-mid-August) 714-536-5258
Summer Nights at the Ford (mid-June-early September) 213-974-1396
Surf City Festival (late July)......................949-215-8008
Taste of Ventura County Food & Wine Festival (October)....................................805-985-4852
Tet Festival (late January)........................714-775-6820
Thai Cultural Day (mid-late September)............310-827-2910
Tournament of Roses Parade (January 1) 626-795-9311
Tournament of Roses Parade & Rose Bowl (January 1) 626-449-4100
UCLA Jazz & Reggae Festival (late May)...........310-825-9912
UCLA Pow Wow (early May) 310-206-7513
Valley Fair (mid-June) 818-557-1600
Venice Art Walk (mid-late May) 310-392-9255
Ventura County Boat Show (late July) 805-985-4852
Ventura County Fair (early-mid-August)............805-648-3376
Village Classic & Vintage Car Show (late May)......909-337-2533
Western Art Show & Sale (late March) 909-270-5632
Western Little League Tournament (mid-August) 909-887-6444
Whale Watching (January-March)..................562-436-3645

Louisville, Kentucky

***County:* Jefferson**

LOUISVILLE is located in western Kentucky along the Ohio River. Major cities within 100 miles include Lexington, Kentucky and Cincinnati, Ohio.

Area (Land) .... 62.1 sq mi
Area (Water)............................... 4.5 sq mi
Elevation..................................... 462 ft
Latitude ....38-25-42 N
Longitude................................ 85-75-94 W
Time Zone ....EST
Area Code.. 502

Climate

Louisville's continental climate features cold winters and warm, humid summers. Average winter high temperatures range from the low to mid-40s and lows average in the mid-20s. Snowfall is infrequent in Louisville, averaging only 17 inches annually. Summer days are warm, with average high temperatures in the mid-80s, while evenings cool down into the mid-60s. March is the wettest month in Louisville; October is the driest.

Average Temperatures & Precipitation

Temperatures

	Jan	Feb	Mar	Apr	May	Jun	Jul	Aug	Sep	Oct	Nov	Dec
High	40	45	56	67	76	84	87	86	80	69	57	45
Low	23	27	36	45	55	63	67	66	59	46	37	29

Precipitation

	Jan	Feb	Mar	Apr	May	Jun	Jul	Aug	Sep	Oct	Nov	Dec
Inches	2.9	3.3	4.7	4.2	4.6	3.5	4.5	3.5	3.2	2.7	3.7	3.6

History

The city known today as Louisville was founded by George Rogers Clark in 1778 as a settlement on Corn Island in the Ohio River. The community was moved the following year to its present location at the Falls of the Ohio River (which are now covered by a man-made lake), and in 1780 was named Louisville in honor of Louis XVI of France.

Early development in Louisville was slow, but by 1820 the city had become an important inland port on the Ohio River. The completion of a canal around the Falls in 1830 further stimulated development in the newly chartered city, and industry and commerce thrived following the arrival of the railroad in 1850. The city became an important transportation center and served as a Union stronghold during the Civil War. The first Kentucky Derby, an event for which Louisville has become famous, was held in the city in 1875.

Although Louisville has endured numerous hardships since the late 19th Century (including two devastating tornadoes, a flood, and a general decline in population as a result of the suburbanization of industry and the economic recession of the 1970s and '80s), the city has managed to rebuild. Louisville is presently Kentucky's largest city with a population of more than 255,000.

Population

1990 Census 269,555
1998 Estimate.............................255,045
% Change ....-5.4
2010 Projection 707,981*

Racial/Ethnic Breakdown

White....................................69.1%
Black 29.6%
Other 1.3%
Hispanic Origin (may be of any race) 0.7%

Age Breakdown

Under 5 years.............................. 6.8%
5 to 17...................................16.6%
18 to 20.................................. 4.4%
21 to 24.................................. 5.8%
25 to 34.................................17.6%
35 to 44.................................14.0%
45 to 54.................................. 8.8%
55 to 64.................................. 9.5%
65 to 74.................................. 9.1%
75+ years 7.5%
Median Age.................................34.3

Gender Breakdown

Male....................................46.2%
Female..................................53.8%

* *Information given is for Jefferson County.*

Government

Type of Government: Mayor-Board of Aldermen

Louisville Board of Aldermen
601 W Jefferson St 3rd Fl
Louisville, KY 40202
Phone: 502-574-3521
Fax: 502-574-4420

Louisville Business Services Office
600 W Main St 4th Fl
Louisville, KY 40202
Phone: 502-574-3051
Fax: 502-574-3026

Louisville City Hall
601 W Jefferson St
Louisville, KY 40202
Phone: 502-574-3333

Louisville Clerk of the Board
601 W Jefferson St
Louisville, KY 40202
Phone: 502-574-3902
Fax: 502-574-4420

Louisville Employee Relations Dept
609 W Jefferson St
Louisville, KY 40202
Phone: 502-574-3601
Fax: 502-574-4413

Louisville Finance & Budget Dept
611 W Jefferson St
Louisville, KY 40202
Phone: 502-574-3211
Fax: 502-574-4384

Louisville Fire Div
1135 W Jefferson St
Louisville, KY 40203
Phone: 502-574-3701
Fax: 502-574-2929

Louisville Free Public Library
301 York St
Louisville, KY 40203
Phone: 502-574-1600
Fax: 502-574-1657

Louisville Law Dept
601 W Jefferson St
Louisville, KY 40202
Phone: 502-574-3511
Fax: 502-574-4215

Louisville Mayor
601 W Jefferson St 1st Fl
Louisville, KY 40202
Phone: 502-574-3061
Fax: 502-574-4201

Louisville Neighborhoods Dept
200 S 7th St Suite 200
Louisville, KY 40202
Phone: 502-574-3380
Fax: 502-574-4227

Louisville Parks Dept
1297 Trevilan Way
Louisville, KY 40213
Phone: 502-456-8100
Fax: 502-456-8111

Louisville Police Div
633 W Jefferson St
Louisville, KY 40202
Phone: 502-574-7660
Fax: 502-574-2450

Louisville Public Works Dept
601 W Jefferson St Rm 216
Louisville, KY 40202
Phone: 502-574-3111
Fax: 502-574-3849

Important Phone Numbers

AAA 502-582-2222
American Express Travel 502-585-2368
Dental Referral 502-459-7971
Driver's License Information 502-595-4405
Emergency 911
HotelDocs 800-468-3537
Kentucky Revenue Cabinet 502-595-4512
Louisville Board of Realtors 502-894-9860
Louisville Property Evaluation Administration 502-574-6860
Medical Referral 502-587-4912
Poison Control Center 502-589-8222
Time/Temp 502-585-5961
Travelers Aid 502-584-8186
Vehicle Registration Information 502-574-5700
Voter Registration Information 502-574-6100
Weather 502-585-1212

Information Sources

Better Business Bureau Serving Louisville Southern Indiana & Western Kentucky
844 S 4th St
Louisville, KY 40203
www.ky-in.bbb.org
Phone: 502-583-6546
Fax: 502-589-9940

Greater Louisville Inc
600 W Main St
Louisville, KY 40202
www.greaterlouisville.com
Phone: 502-625-0000
Fax: 502-625-0211

Jefferson County
527 W Jefferson St
Louisville, KY 40202
www.co.jefferson.ky.us
Phone: 502-574-5700
Fax: 502-574-5566

Kentucky International Convention Center
221 4th St
Louisville, KY 40202
Phone: 502-595-3141
Fax: 502-584-9711
TF: 800-701-5831

Louisville & Jefferson County Convention & Visitors Bureau
400 S 1st St
Louisville, KY 40202
www.louisville-visitors.com
Phone: 502-584-2121
Fax: 502-584-6697
TF: 800-792-5595

Online Resources

4Louisville.com
www.2louisville.com

About.com Guide to Louisville
louisville.about.com/local/southeastus/louisville

Anthill City Guide Louisville
www.anthill.com/city.asp?city=louisville

Area Guide Louisville
louisville.areaguides.net

City Knowledge Louisville
www.cityknowledge.com/ky_louisville.htm

Excite.com Louisville City Guide
www.excite.com/travel/countries/united_states/kentucky/louisville

Insiders' Guide to Greater Louisville
www.insiders.com/louisville/index.htm

introLouisville
www.introlouisville.com

Links @ Louisville
www.johnpaul.com/links/

Louisville Kentucky
louisville-kentucky.com

Louisville Scene
www.louisvillescene.com

Louisville.com
www.louisville.com

Louisville.net
www.louisville.net

Area Communities

Incorporated communities with populations greater than 10,000 in the seven-county (Bullitt, Jefferson, and Oldham counties in Kentucky and Clark, Floyd, Harrison, and Scott counties in Indiana) Louisville metropolitan area include:

Clarksville Phone: 812-288-7155
2000 Broadway St Fax: 812-283-1536
Clarksville, IN 47129

Jeffersontown Phone: 502-267-8333
10416 Watterson Trail Fax: 502-267-0547
Jeffersontown, KY 40299

Jeffersonville Phone: 812-285-6200
501 E Court Ave Fax: 812-285-6426
Jeffersonville, IN 47131

New Albany Phone: 812-948-5336
City/County Bldg Fax: 812-948-1596
New Albany, IN 47150

Saint Matthews Phone: 502-895-9444
3940 Grandview Ave Fax: 502-895-0510
Saint Matthews, KY 40207

Shively Phone: 502-449-5000
3920 Dixie Hwy Fax: 502-449-5004
Shively, KY 40216

Economy

For more than 175 years Louisville has served as an important regional transportation center. Package delivery/air cargo giant United Parcel Service is the Louisville area's largest employer, providing jobs for more than 16,000 area residents. Services is currently the largest employment sector in the area—one-third of the region's top 15 private employers are health-care related, and the city is also home to one of the nation's largest HMOs, Humana. In addition, Louisville's diverse manufacturing base includes appliances, trucks, Braille books, cigarettes, and pork products. The city is also the largest producer of bourbon whiskey and in the world.

Unemployment Rate 3.7%*
Per Capita Income.......................... $29,473*
Median Family Income...................... $25,805

** Information given is for Jefferson County.*

Principal Industries & Number of Wage Earners

Jefferson County - 1998

Agricultural Services, Forestry, & Fishing 1,881
Construction 20,917
Finance, Insurance, & Real Estate 33,265
Manufacturing 63,144
Mining 312
Retail Trade 80,663
Services 136,792
Transportation & Public Utilities 31,152
Wholesale Trade 28,329

Major Employers

Bank One Kentucky NA Phone: 502-566-2002
416 W Jefferson St Fax: 502-566-3614
Louisville, KY 40202

Baptist Hospital East Phone: 502-897-8100
4000 Kresge Way Fax: 502-897-8500
Louisville, KY 40207
www.baptisteast.com

Caritas Health Services Phone: 502-361-6000
1850 Bluegrass Ave Fax: 502-361-6799
Louisville, KY 40215
www.caritas.com/body.cfm?id=36865

Catholic Archdiocese of Louisville Phone: 502-585-3291
212 E College St Fax: 502-585-2466
Louisville, KY 40203
www.archlou.org

Ford Motor Co Kentucky Truck Plant Phone: 502-429-2000
3001 Chamberlain Ln Fax: 502-429-2960
Louisville, KY 40241

Ford Motor Co Louisville Assembly Plant Phone: 502-364-3673
Fern Valley Rd & Grade Ln Fax: 502-364-3641
Louisville, KY 40213

GE Appliances Phone: 502-452-4311
Appliance Pk Fax: 502-452-0739
Louisville, KY 40225 TF: 800-626-2000
www.ge.com/appliances

Humana Inc Phone: 502-580-1000
500 W Main St Fax: 502-580-3690
Louisville, KY 40202 TF: 800-486-2620
www.humana.com

Jewish Hospital Phone: 502-587-4011
217 E Chestnut St Fax: 502-587-4598
Louisville, KY 40202
E-mail: info@jhhs.org
www.jhhs.org

Kroger Co Phone: 502-423-4800
10168 Linn Station Rd Fax: 502-423-4162
Louisville, KY 40232
www.kroger.com

LG & E Energy Corp Phone: 502-627-2000
220 W Main St Fax: 502-627-2549
Louisville, KY 40202 TF: 800-331-7370
E-mail: lgeenergy@lgeenergy.com
www.lgeenergy.com

Norton Healthcare Phone: 502-629-8400
200 E Chestnut St Fax: 502-629-8417
Louisville, KY 40232
E-mail: info@nortonhealthcare.com
www.nortonhealthcare.com

Publishers Printing Co Phone: 502-543-2251
PO Box 37500 Fax: 502-955-5586
Louisville, KY 40233 TF: 800-627-5801
www.pubpress.com

Sears Roebuck & Co
4807 Outer Loop
Louisville, KY 40219
Phone: 502-966-1198
Fax: 502-966-1169

United Parcel Service
1400 N Hurstbourne Pkwy
Louisville, KY 40223
www.upsjobs.com
Phone: 502-329-3000
Fax: 502-329-3046

Quality of Living Indicators

Total Crime Index....................................15,317
(rates per 100,000 inhabitants)

Violent Crime
Murder/manslaughter............................ 37
Forcible rape 62
Robbery....................................1,158
Aggravated assault............................. 959

Property Crime
Burglary 3,418
Larceny theft 7,683
Motor vehicle theft 2,000

Cost of Living Index....................................96.5
(national average = 100)

Median Home Price.................................$109,700

Education

Public Schools

Jefferson County Public Schools
PO Box 34020
Louisville, KY 40232
www.jefferson.k12.ky.us
Phone: 502-485-3228
Fax: 502-485-3991

Number of Schools
Elementary 87
Middle 23
High.. 20

Student/Teacher Ratio
All Grades 17.0:1

Private Schools

Number of Schools (all grades).................. 100+

Colleges & Universities

Bellarmine College
2001 Newburg Rd
Louisville, KY 40205
www.bellarmine.edu
Phone: 502-452-8000
Fax: 502-452-8002
TF: 800-274-4723

Indiana University Southeast Campus
4201 Grant Line Rd
New Albany, IN 47150
E-mail: dcampbel@ius.indiana.edu
www.ius.indiana.edu
Phone: 812-941-2000
Fax: 812-941-2595

Jefferson Community College
109 E Broadway
Louisville, KY 40202
www.jcc.uky.edu
Phone: 502-584-0181
Fax: 502-585-4425

Louisville Bible College
PO Box 91046
Louisville, KY 40291
E-mail: loubibcol@juno.com
Phone: 502-231-5221
Fax: 502-231-5222

Louisville Technical Institute
3901 Atkinson Square Dr
Louisville, KY 40218
www.louisvilletech.com
Phone: 502-456-6509
Fax: 502-456-2341
TF: 800-844-6528

RETS Electronic Institute
300 Highrise Dr
Louisville, KY 40213
www.retsaec.com
Phone: 502-968-7191
Fax: 502-968-1727
TF: 800-999-7387

Simmons Bible College
1811 Dumesnil St
Louisville, KY 40210
Phone: 502-776-1443
Fax: 502-776-2227

Spalding University
851 S 4th St
Louisville, KY 40203
www.spalding.edu
Phone: 502-585-9911
Fax: 502-585-7128
TF: 800-896-8941

Sullivan College
3101 Bardstown Rd
Louisville, KY 40205
E-mail: admissions@sullivan.edu
www.sullivan.edu
Phone: 502-456-6504
Fax: 502-456-0040
TF: 800-844-1354

University of Louisville
2301 S 3rd St
Louisville, KY 40292
E-mail: admitme@ulkyvm.louisville.edu
www.louisville.edu
Phone: 502-852-5555
Fax: 502-852-6526
TF: 800-334-8635

Hospitals

Audubon Hospital
1 Audobon Plaza Dr
Louisville, KY 40217
Phone: 502-636-7111
Fax: 502-636-7399

Baptist Hospital East
4000 Kresge Way
Louisville, KY 40207
www.baptisteast.com
Phone: 502-897-8100
Fax: 502-897-8500

Caritas Medical Center
1850 Bluegrass Ave
Louisville, KY 40215
www.caritas.com/body.cfm?id=36865
Phone: 502-361-6000
Fax: 502-361-6799

Jewish Hospital
217 E Chestnut St
Louisville, KY 40202
www.jhhs.org
Phone: 502-587-4011
Fax: 502-587-4598

Norton Hospital
200 E Chestnut St
Louisville, KY 40202
Phone: 502-629-8000
Fax: 502-629-7591

Norton Southwest Hospital
9820 3rd Street Rd
Louisville, KY 40272
Phone: 502-933-8100
Fax: 502-933-8278

Norton Suburban Hospital
4001 Dutchmans Ln
Louisville, KY 40207
Phone: 502-893-1000
Fax: 502-893-1289

Tri-County Baptist Hospital
1025 New Moody Ln
LaGrange, KY 40031
www.tri-countybaptist.com
Phone: 502-222-5388
Fax: 502-222-3411
TF: 888-222-8071

University of Louisville Hospital
545 S Jackson St
Louisville, KY 40202
Phone: 502-562-3000
Fax: 502-562-3831

Vencor Hospital Louisville
1313 St Anthony Pl
Louisville, KY 40204
Phone: 502-587-7001
Fax: 502-425-4448

Veterans Affairs Medical Center
800 Zorn Ave
Louisville, KY 40206
Phone: 502-895-3401
Fax: 502-894-6155

Transportation

Airport(s)

Louisville International Airport (SDF)
5 miles S of downtown (approx 5 minutes) 502-368-6524

Mass Transit

TARC
$1 Base fare 502-585-1234

Rail/Bus

Greyhound Bus Station
720 W Muhammad Ali Blvd
Louisville, KY 40203
Phone: 502-561-2801
TF: 800-231-2222

Utilities

Electricity
Louisville Gas & Electric Co (LG & E) 502-589-1444
www.lgeenergy.com

Gas
Louisville Gas & Electric Co (LG & E) 502-589-1444
www.lgeenergy.com

Water
Louisville Water Co............................502-583-6610

Garbage Collection/Recycling
Louisville Garbage Collection/Recycling Information 502-574-3333

Telecommunications

Telephone
BellSouth 800-477-4459
www.bellsouth.com

Cable Television
Insight Communications.......................502-448-7750

Internet Service Providers (ISPs)
BluegrassNet 502-589-4638
www.bluegrass.net
CAS-Com Internet Services 502-635-7979
www.cas-com.net
IgLou Internet Services........................502-966-3848
www.iglou.com
KA.NET Internet Services......................502-992-0324
www.ka.net
WinNet Communications Inc 502-815-7000
www.win.net

Banks

Bank One Kentucky NA
416 W Jefferson St
Louisville, KY 40202
Phone: 502-566-2002
Fax: 502-566-3614

Firstar Bank
1 Financial Sq
Louisville, KY 40202
Phone: 502-562-6000
Fax: 502-562-6659

Mid-America Bank of Louisville & Trust Co
500 W Broadway
Louisville, KY 40202
Phone: 502-589-3351
Fax: 502-562-5403
TF: 800-925-0810

National City Bank
PO Box 36000
Louisville, KY 40233
Phone: 502-581-4200
Fax: 814-437-4106
TF: 800-727-8686

PNC Bank Kentucky
500 W Jefferson St
Louisville, KY 40202
Phone: 502-581-2100
Fax: 502-581-2792

Stock Yards Bank & Trust Co
1040 E Main St
Louisville, KY 40206
www.syb.com
Phone: 502-582-2571
Fax: 502-589-2855
TF: 800-625-9066

Shopping

Bashford Manor Mall
3600 Bardstown Rd & Hikes Ln
Louisville, KY 40218
Phone: 502-459-9600

Galleria The
4th Ave & Liberty St
Louisville, KY 40202
Phone: 502-584-7170
Fax: 502-584-7185

Jefferson Mall
4801 Outerloop Rd
Louisville, KY 40219
E-mail: jeffersonmall@rejacobsgroup.com
www.shopyourmall.com/mall_welcome.asp?map=yes&mall_select=690
Phone: 502-968-4101

Kentucky Art & Craft Gallery
609 W Main St
Louisville, KY 40202
Phone: 502-589-0102
Fax: 502-589-0154

Lazarus
7900 Shelbyville Rd
Louisville, KY 40222
Phone: 502-423-3212
Fax: 502-423-3317

Louisville Antique Mall
900 Goss Ave
Louisville, KY 40217
Phone: 502-635-2852

Mall Saint Matthews
5000 Shelbyville Rd
Louisville, KY 40207
Phone: 502-893-0311
Fax: 502-897-5849

Oxmoor Center
7900 Shelbyville Rd
Louisville, KY 40222
www.oxmoorcenter.com
Phone: 502-426-3000
Fax: 502-425-3417

Media

Newspapers and Magazines

Business First
501 S 4th St Suite 130
Louisville, KY 40202
www.amcity.com/louisville
Phone: 502-583-1731
Fax: 502-587-1703

Courier-Journal*
PO Box 740031
Louisville, KY 40201
www.courier-journal.com
Phone: 502-582-4011
Fax: 502-582-4200
TF: 800-765-4011

Louisville Eccentric Observer
600 E Main St Suite 102
Louisville, KY 40202
www.louisville.com/leo
Phone: 502-895-9770
Fax: 502-895-9779

Louisville Magazine
137 W Muhammad Ali Blvd Suite 101
Louisville, KY 40202
E-mail: loumag@louisville.com
www.louisville.com/loumag
Phone: 502-625-0100
Fax: 502-625-0109

**Indicates major daily newspapers*

Television

WAVE-TV Ch 3 (NBC)
725 S Floyd St
Louisville, KY 40203
E-mail: wave3mail@msn.com
www.wave3.com
Phone: 502-585-2201
Fax: 502-561-4105

WBNA-TV Ch 21 (PAX)
3701 Fern Valley Rd
Louisville, KY 40219
E-mail: info@wbna.com
www.wbna.com
Phone: 502-964-2121
Fax: 502-966-9692

WDRB-TV Ch 41 (Fox)
1 Independence Sq
Louisville, KY 40203
E-mail: administration@fox41.com
www.fox41.com
Phone: 502-584-6441
Fax: 502-589-5559

WFTE-TV Ch 58 (UPN)
5257 S Skyline Dr
Floyds Knobs, IN 47119
Phone: 812-948-5800
Fax: 812-949-9365

WHAS-TV Ch 11 (ABC)
PO Box 1100
Louisville, KY 40201
E-mail: info@whas11.com
www.whas11.com
Phone: 502-582-7840
Fax: 502-582-7279

WKMJ-TV Ch 68 (PBS)
600 Cooper Dr
Lexington, KY 40502
Phone: 859-258-7000
Fax: 859-258-7390
TF: 800-432-0951

WKPC-TV Ch 15 (PBS)
600 Cooper Dr
Lexington, KY 40502
Phone: 859-258-7000
Fax: 859-258-7390

WLKY-TV Ch 32 (CBS)
PO Box 6205
Louisville, KY 40206
E-mail: wlky@iglou.com
www.wlky.com/
Phone: 502-893-3671
Fax: 502-896-0725

Radio

WAMZ-FM 97.5 MHz (Ctry)
4000 One Radio Dr
Louisville, KY 40218
www.wamz.com
Phone: 502-479-2222
Fax: 502-479-2227

WAVG-AM 1450 kHz (Ctry)
PO Box 726
Jeffersonville, IN 47130
www.wavg.com
Phone: 812-285-5055
Fax: 812-285-5060

WBLO-FM 104.3 MHz (Urban)
520 S 4th St Suite 300
Louisville, KY 40202
Phone: 502-625-1220
Fax: 502-625-1255

WDJX-FM 99.7 MHz (AC)
612 S 4th Ave Suite 100
Louisville, KY 40202
Phone: 502-589-4800
Fax: 502-587-0212

WFIA-AM 900 kHz (N/T)
520 S 4th St 2nd Fl
Louisville, KY 40202
Phone: 502-625-1220
Fax: 502-625-1255

WFPK-FM 91.9 MHz (NPR)
619 S 4th St
Louisville, KY 40202
E-mail: wfpk@iglou.com
Phone: 502-814-6500
Fax: 502-814-6599

WFPL-FM 89.3 MHz (NPR)
619 S 4th St
Louisville, KY 40202
E-mail: wfpl@iglou.com
Phone: 502-814-6500
Fax: 502-814-6599

WGZB-FM 96.5 MHz (Urban)
520 S 4th Ave 2nd Fl
Louisville, KY 40202
Phone: 502-625-1220
Fax: 502-625-1255

WHAS-AM 840 kHz (N/T)
4000 One Radio Dr
Louisville, KY 40218
E-mail: info@whas.com
www.whas.com
Phone: 502-479-2222
Fax: 502-479-2224

WKJK-AM 1080 kHz (Nost)
4000 One Radio Dr
Louisville, KY 40218
www.wkjk.com
Phone: 502-479-2222
Fax: 502-479-2225

WLKY-AM 970 kHz (N/T)
1918 Mellwood Ave
Louisville, KY 40206
Phone: 502-893-3671
Fax: 502-893-7725

WLLV-AM 1240 kHz (Rel)
2001 W Broadway Suite 13
Louisville, KY 40203
Phone: 502-776-1240
Fax: 502-776-1250

WLOU-AM 1350 kHz (Rel)
2001 W Broadway Dale Plaza
Louisville, KY 40203
Phone: 502-776-1350
Fax: 502-776-1250

WLRS-FM 102.3 MHz (Alt)
520 S 4th Ave 2nd Fl
Louisville, KY 40202
Phone: 502-625-1220
Fax: 502-625-1255

WMHX-FM 103.9 (NAC)
612 S 4th Ave Suite 100
Louisville, KY 40202
Phone: 502-589-4800
Fax: 502-587-0212

WMJM-FM 101.3 MHz (Oldies)
520 S 4th Ave 2nd Fl
Louisville, KY 40203
Phone: 502-625-1220
Fax: 502-625-1255

WMPI-FM 105.3 MHz (Ctry)
22 E McClain Ave
Scottsburg, IN 47170
E-mail: wmpi@seidata.com
www.wmpi.com
Phone: 812-752-3688
Fax: 812-752-2345

WQMF-FM 95.7 MHz (CR)
4000 One Radio Dr
Louisville, KY 40218
www.wqmf.com
Phone: 502-479-2222
Fax: 502-479-2227

WRKA-FM 103.1 MHz (Oldies)
612 4th Ave
Louisville, KY 40202
www.wrka.com
Phone: 502-589-4800
Fax: 502-587-0212

WRVI-FM 105.9 MHz (Rel)
10001 Linn Station Rd Suite 416
Louisville, KY 40223
Phone: 502-339-9470
Fax: 502-423-3161

WSFR-FM 107.7 MHz (CR)
612 S 4th Ave Suite 100
Louisville, KY 40202
Phone: 502-589-4800
Fax: 502-587-0212

WTFX-FM 100.5 MHz (Rock)
4000 One Radio Dr
Louisville, KY 40218
Phone: 502-479-2222
Fax: 502-479-2227

WTMT-AM 620 kHz (Sports)
162 W Broadway
Louisville, KY 40202
Phone: 502-583-6200
Fax: 502-589-2979

WULV-FM 102.3 MHz (AC)
520 S 4th St Suite 300
Louisville, KY 40202
Phone: 502-625-1220
Fax: 502-625-1255

WVEZ-FM 106.9 MHz (AC)
612 S 4th Ave Suite 100
Louisville, KY 40202
www.wvez.com
Phone: 502-589-4800
Fax: 502-587-0212

WWKY-AM 790 kHz (N/T)
4000 One Radio Dr
Louisville, KY 40218
www.wwky.com
Phone: 502-479-2222
Fax: 502-479-2227

WYBL-FM 93.1 MHz (Ctry)
4000 One Radio Dr
Louisville, KY 40218
www.931thebull.com
Phone: 502-479-2222
Fax: 502-479-2227

Attractions

Nicknamed the "Run for the Roses" and often referred to as "the greatest two minutes in sports," the Kentucky Derby is held at Louisville's Churchill Downs each year on the first Saturday in May. Long known as the city's main social event, the oldest race in continuous existence in the U.S. is preceded by the two-week-long Kentucky Derby Festival, which includes parades, concerts, sports tournaments, and the Great Steamboat Race. The Kentucky Derby Museum is located next to Churchill Downs and has an outdoor paddock for the thoroughbreds on its grounds. Interesting sites at the University of Louisville include the Photo Archives, one of the largest collections of photographs in the country; and the original town charter signed by Thomas Jefferson. Slugger Park, manufacturer of Louisville Slugger baseball bats, and the Belle of Louisville, the oldest Mississippi sternwheeler in the country, are also located in Louisville.

Actors Theatre of Louisville
316 W Main St
Louisville, KY 40202
E-mail: actors@aye.net
www.actorstheatre.org
Phone: 502-584-1265
Fax: 502-561-3300

American Printing House for the Blind
1839 Frankfort Ave
Louisville, KY 40206
E-mail: info@aph.org
www.aph.org
Phone: 502-895-2405
Fax: 502-899-2274
TF: 800-223-1839

Belle of Louisville
401 W River Rd
Louisville, KY 40214
www.co.jefferson.ky.us/AttractionsBelle.html
Phone: 502-574-2355
Fax: 502-574-3030

Brennan House Historic Home
631 S 5th St
Louisville, KY 40202
Phone: 502-540-5145
Fax: 502-587-6481

Broadway Series
611 W Main St
Louisville, KY 40202
www.broadwayseries.com
Phone: 502-584-7469
Fax: 502-584-2703
TF: 800-294-1849

Brown Theater
315 W Broadway
Louisville, KY 40202
Phone: 502-562-0188

Bunbury Theatre
112 S 7th St
Louisville, KY 40202
Phone: 502-585-5306

Cathedral Heritage Foundation
429 W Muhammad Ali Blvd Suite 100
Louisville, KY 40202
www.cathedral-heritage.org
Phone: 502-583-3100
Fax: 502-583-8524

Cave Hill Cemetery & Arboretum
701 Baxter Ave
Louisville, KY 40204
Phone: 502-451-5630
Fax: 502-451-5655

Cherokee Park
Eastern Pkwy & Cherokee Rd
Louisville, KY 40204
Phone: 502-456-8100

Colonel Harland Sanders Museum
1441 Gardiner Ln
Louisville, KY 40213
Phone: 502-874-8353
Fax: 502-874-8792

Conrad-Caldwell House
1402 St James Ct
Louisville, KY 40208
Phone: 502-636-5023

Farmington Historic Home
3033 Bardstown Rd
Louisville, KY 40205
Phone: 502-452-9920
Fax: 502-456-1976

Filson Club Historical Society
1310 S 3rd St
Louisville, KY 40208
www.filsonclub.org
Phone: 502-635-5083
Fax: 502-635-5086

IMAX Theater
727 W Main St
Louisville, KY 40202
www.lsclouienet.org/imax.htm
Phone: 502-561-6100
Fax: 502-561-6145

Iroquois Park
Taylor Blvd & South Pkwy
Louisville, KY 40214
Phone: 502-456-8100

Kentucky Art & Craft Gallery
609 W Main St
Louisville, KY 40202
Phone: 502-589-0102
Fax: 502-589-0154

Kentucky Center for the Arts
501 W Main St
Louisville, KY 40202
E-mail: kca@sitesonthe.net
www.kca.org
Phone: 502-562-0100
Fax: 502-562-0150
TF: 800-775-7777

Kentucky Derby Museum
704 Central Ave
Louisville, KY 40208
E-mail: info@derbymuseum.org
www.derbymuseum.org
Phone: 502-634-0676
Fax: 502-636-5855
TF: 800-273-3729

Kentucky Opera Assn
101 S 8th St
Louisville, KY 40202
Phone: 502-584-4500
Fax: 502-584-7484

Locust Grove Historic Home
561 Blankenbaker Ln
Louisville, KY 40207
E-mail: lghh@locustgrove.org
www.locustgrove.org
Phone: 502-897-9845
Fax: 502-897-0103

Louisville Ballet
315 E Main St
Louisville, KY 40202
E-mail: louballet1@ka.net
www.louisvilleballet.org
Phone: 502-583-3150
Fax: 502-583-0006

Louisville Chorus
6303 Fern Valley Pass
Louisville, KY 40228
www.fastzone.com/chorus
Phone: 502-968-6300
Fax: 502-962-1094

Louisville Fire History & Learning Center
3228 River Park Dr
Louisville, KY 40211
Phone: 502-574-3731

Louisville Nature Center
3745 Illinois Ave
Louisville, KY 40213
Phone: 502-458-1328
Fax: 502-458-0232

Louisville Orchestra
300 W Main St Suite 100
Louisville, KY 40202
www.louisvilleorchestra.org
Phone: 502-587-8681
Fax: 502-589-7870

Louisville Science Center
727 W Main St
Louisville, KY 40202
www.lsclouienet.org
Phone: 502-561-6100
Fax: 502-561-6145

Louisville Slugger Museum
800 W Main St
Louisville, KY 40202
www.slugger.com/museum
Phone: 502-588-7228
Fax: 502-585-1179

Louisville Zoological Garden
1100 Trevilian Way
Louisville, KY 40213
www.iglou.com/louzoo
Phone: 502-459-2181
Fax: 502-459-2196

Music Theatre Louisville
624 W Main St
Louisville, KY 40202
Phone: 502-589-4060
Fax: 502-589-0741

Old Louisville Historic District
1340 S 4th St
Louisville, KY 40208
Phone: 502-635-5244

Palace Theatre
625 4th Ave
Louisville, KY 40202
www.louisvillepalace.com
Phone: 502-583-4555
Fax: 502-583-9955

Riverside Farnsley-Moremen House
7410 Moorman Rd
Louisville, KY 40272
www.co.jefferson.ky.us/AttractionsRiverside.html
Phone: 502-935-6809

Shawnee Park
Broadway & SW Pkwy
Louisville, KY 40233
Phone: 502-456-8100

Six Flags Kentucky Kingdom
937 Phillips Ln
Louisville, KY 40209
www.sixflags.com/kentuckykingdom
Phone: 502-366-2231
Fax: 502-366-8746
TF: 800-727-3267

Speed JB Art Museum
2035 S 3rd St
Louisville, KY 40208
www.speedmuseum.org
Phone: 502-634-2700
Fax: 502-636-2899

Thomas Edison House
729-31 E Washington St
Louisville, KY 40202
Phone: 502-585-5247
Fax: 502-585-5247

University of Louisville Photo Archives
Ekstrom Library University of Louisville
Louisville, KY 40292
Phone: 502-852-6752
Fax: 502-852-8734

Whitehall
3110 Lexington Rd
Louisville, KY 40206
Phone: 502-897-2944
Fax: 502-897-7737

Sports Teams & Facilities

Cardinal Stadium/Freedom Hall
937 Phillips Ln Kentucky Fair & Exposition Ctr
Louisville, KY 40209
Phone: 502-367-5000
Fax: 502-367-5139

Churchill Downs Inc
700 Central Ave
Louisville, KY 40208
www.churchilldowns.com
Phone: 502-636-4400
Fax: 502-636-4430

Kentucky Fair & Expo Center
937 Phillips Ln
Louisville, KY 40209
www.kyfairexpo.org
Phone: 502-367-5000
Fax: 502-367-5139

Louisville Motor Speedway Phone: 502-966-2277
1900 Outer Loop Fax: 502-969-8582
Louisville, KY 40219
E-mail: info@louisvillespeedway.com
www.louisvillespeedway.com

Louisville RiverBats (baseball) Phone: 502-212-2287
401 E Main St Louisville Slugger Field
Louisville, KY 40202
E-mail: info@batsbaseball.com
www.batsbaseball.com

Annual Events

Autumn Fest (early October) 502-583-3577
Cherokee Triangle Art Fair (late April).............502-451-3534
Corn Island Storytelling Festival
(mid-September) 502-582-3732
Derby City Square Dance Festival (mid-May) 502-367-5000
Derby Festival Great Balloon Glow (late April)......502-584-6383
Derby Festival Great Balloon Race (late April) 502-584-6383
Derby Festival Great Steamboat Race (May 3) 502-584-6383
Derby Festival KyDzFest (late April)...............502-584-6383
Derby Festival Pegasus Parade (May 4) 502-584-6383
Derby Festival Planes of Thunder (mid-April) 502-584-6383
Dickens on Main Street (late November) 502-574-3333
DinnerWorks (mid-January-mid-February).........502-896-2146
Humana Festival of New American Plays
(late February-late March)......................502-584-1265
Kentucky Derby (early May) 502-582-3732
Kentucky Derby Festival (late March-early May).....800-928-3378
Kentucky Golf Show (mid-January)................502-367-5000
Kentucky Oaks (early May) 502-636-4400
Kentucky Reggae Festival (late May)...............502-583-0333
Kentucky Shakespeare Festival
(mid-June-mid-July) 502-583-8738
Kentucky State Fair (late August) 502-582-3732
Light Up Louisville International Festival
(late February & early June)....................502-584-2121
Louisville Art & Blues Festival (early July).........502-896-2146
Mid-America Trucking Show (late March) 502-367-5000
National City Music Weekend (late July)............502-348-5237
National Farm Machinery Show & Tractor Pull
(mid-February)...............................502-367-5000
National Gun Days
(early February & early June)...................502-367-5000
Revolutionary War Encampment (early April).......502-896-2433
Saint James Court Art Show (early October) 502-635-1842
Sport Boat & Vacation Show
(late January-early February)....................502-367-5000
Strassenfest (early July)..........................502-561-3440
Strictly Bluegrass Festival (mid-September)........502-582-3732
Thunder over Louisville (mid-April) 502-584-6383

Madison, Wisconsin

***County:* Dane**

MADISON is located in south central Wisconsin along the banks of Lake Mendota and Lake Monona. Major cities within 100 miles include Milwaukee and Janesville, Wisconsin and Dubuque, Iowa.

Area (Land)	57.8 sq mi
Area (Water)	16.0 sq mi
Elevation	863 ft
Latitude	43-04-23 N
Longitude	89-22-55 W
Time Zone	CST
Area Code	608

Climate

Madison's climate is characterized by long, cold winters and pleasant summers. Winter high temperatures average below freezing, in the mid- to upper 20s, and lows average around 10 degrees. Snowfall is plentiful, with more than an inch on the ground approximately 60 percent of the time from mid-December through March. Summer high temperatures average around 80 degrees, while evening lows dip into the upper 50s. Summer is the rainy season in Madison, with August being the wettest month.

Average Temperatures & Precipitation

Temperatures

	Jan	Feb	Mar	Apr	May	Jun	Jul	Aug	Sep	Oct	Nov	Dec
High	25	30	42	57	69	78	82	79	72	60	44	30
Low	7	11	23	34	44	54	60	57	48	38	27	14

Precipitation

	Jan	Feb	Mar	Apr	May	Jun	Jul	Aug	Sep	Oct	Nov	Dec
Inches	1.1	1.1	2.2	2.9	3.1	3.7	3.4	4.0	3.4	2.2	2.1	1.8

History

Originally inhabited by Native Americans of the Winnebago tribe, Madison was founded in 1836 by territorial Judge James Doty, who had purchased and platted the land seven years earlier. Doty persuaded the territorial legislature to designate his city as the site for the new capital of the Wisconsin Territory (Belmont was the original location), and he named the city in honor of U.S. President James Madison. The Village of Madison was incorporated in 1846 with a population of around 600 people. Wisconsin became a state in 1848 with Madison as its capital. By the time Madison was incorporated as a city in 1856, the capital's population had grown to more than 6,800 people, due in large part to the new railroad linking the city with Milwaukee. Early settlers included Yankees from the East, as well as German, Irish, and Norwegian immigrants.

The 1900s brought new economic opportunities to Madison, drawing more ethnic groups to the area from other parts of the United States and Europe. State and county government expanded and new industries were established in the area. During the 1920s, Oscar Mayer, which remains one of the area's largest employers, began operations in Madison, and the city grew as a center for meat processing. The expansion of the University of Wisconsin also contributed greatly to Madison's growth during the 20th Century. Today, the university is Madison's largest employer, providing jobs for more than 26,000 area residents.

In 1996, Money Magazine named Madison the "Best Place to Live in America." The city consistently has one of the lowest crime rates in the nation among cities of similar size. Madison is currently home to more than 209,000 people, and the city continues to grow at a steady pace. By the year 2010, Madison's population is expected to exceed 219,000.

Population

1990 Census	190,766
1998 Estimate	209,306
% Change	9.7
2010 Projection	219,909

Racial/Ethnic Breakdown

White	89.5%
Black	4.2%
Other	6.3%
Hispanic Origin (may be of any race)	2.0%

Age Breakdown

Under 5 years	6.2%
5 to 17	12.4%
18 to 20	10.0%
21 to 24	12.0%
25 to 34	20.4%
35 to 44	15.4%
45 to 54	8.1%
55 to 64	6.2%
65 to 74	5.1%
75+ years	4.2%
Median Age	29.3

Gender Breakdown

Male	48.8%
Female	51.2%

Government

Type of Government: Mayor-Aldermanic

Madison City Attorney
210 ML King Jr Blvd Rm 401
Madison, WI 53709

Phone: 608-266-4511
Fax: 608-267-8715

Madison City Clerk
210 ML King Jr Blvd Rm 103
Madison, WI 53709
Phone: 608-266-4601
Fax: 608-266-4666

Madison City Hall
210 ML King Jr Blvd
Madison, WI 53709
Phone: 608-266-4611

Madison Common Council
210 ML King Jr Blvd Rm 417
Madison, WI 53709
Phone: 608-266-4071
Fax: 608-267-8669

Madison Community & Economic Development Unit
PO Box 2983
Madison, WI 53701
Phone: 608-266-4222
Fax: 608-267-8739

Madison Fire Dept
325 W Johnson St
Madison, WI 53703
Phone: 608-266-4420
Fax: 608-267-1100

Madison Human Resources Dept
210 ML King Jr Blvd Rm 501
Madison, WI 53709
Phone: 608-266-4615
Fax: 608-267-1115

Madison Mayor
210 ML King Jr Blvd Rm 403
Madison, WI 53709
Phone: 608-266-4611
Fax: 608-267-8671

Madison Parks Div
215 ML King Jr Blvd Rm 120
Madison, WI 53713
Phone: 608-266-4711
Fax: 608-266-1162

Madison Planning & Development Dept
PO Box 2985
Madison, WI 53701
Phone: 608-266-4635
Fax: 608-267-8739

Madison Police Dept
211 S Carroll St
Madison, WI 53703
Phone: 608-266-4022
Fax: 608-266-4855

Madison Public Library
201 W Mifflin St
Madison, WI 53703
Phone: 608-266-6300
Fax: 608-266-4338

Madison Transportation Div
PO Box 2986
Madison, WI 53701
Phone: 608-266-4761
Fax: 608-267-1158

Madison Treasurer
210 ML King Jr Blvd Rm 107
Madison, WI 53709
Phone: 608-266-4771
Fax: 608-266-4666

Madison Water Utility Office
523 E Main St
Madison, WI 53703
Phone: 608-266-4652
Fax: 608-266-4426

Important Phone Numbers

AAA 800-236-1300
Dane County Treasurer 608-266-4151
Driver's License/Vehicle Registration Information 608-266-1466
Emergency 911
HotelDocs 800-468-3537
Madison Assessor's Office 608-266-4545
Poison Control Center 608-262-3702
Realtors Assn of South Central Wisconsin 608-240-2800
Time/Temp 608-255-1234
Voter Registration Information 608-266-4601
Weather 608-936-1212
Wisconsin Dept of Revenue Div of Income Sales & Excise Tax 608-266-1911

Information Sources

Better Business Bureau Serving Wisconsin
PO Box 2190
Milwaukee, WI 53201
www.wisconsin.bbb.org
Phone: 414-273-1600
Fax: 414-224-0881

Dane County
210 ML King Jr Blvd Rm 112
Madison, WI 53709
www.co.dane.wi.us
Phone: 608-266-4121

Dane County Exposition Center
1919 Expo Way
Madison, WI 53713
www.co.dane.wi.us/expo/expo.html
Phone: 608-267-3976
Fax: 608-267-0146

Greater Madison Chamber of Commerce
615 E Washington Ave
Madison, WI 53703
www.greatermadisonchamber.com
Phone: 608-256-8348
Fax: 608-256-0333

Greater Madison Convention & Visitors Bureau
615 E Washington Ave
Madison, WI 53703
www.visitmadison.com
Phone: 608-255-2537
Fax: 608-258-4950
TF: 800-373-6376

Madison Civic Center
211 State St
Madison, WI 53703
www.madcivic.org
Phone: 608-266-6550
Fax: 608-266-4864

Monona Terrace Community & Convention Center
1 John Nolan Dr
Madison, WI 53703
www.mononaterrace.com
Phone: 608-261-4000
Fax: 608-261-4049

Online Resources

4Madison.com
www.4madison.com

About.com Guide to Madison
madison.about.com/local/midwestus/madison

All-Info Madison
www.all-info.com/

Anthill City Guide Madison
www.anthill.com/city.asp?city=madison

Area Guide Madison
madison.areaguides.net

At Home in Madison
www.athomein.com

Boulevards Madison
www.boulevards.com/cities/madison.html

City Knowledge Madison
www.cityknowledge.com/wi_madison.htm

Excite.com Madison City Guide
www.excite.com/travel/countries/united_states/wisconsin/madison

Insiders' Guide to Madison
www.insiders.com/madison/index.htm

Mad About Madison
www.ci.madison.wi.us/madabout.html

Madison Area Guide
www.wistrails.com/guide/

Madison Business Internet Guide
www.abcon.com/ablinks.html

Madison Online
www.netphoria.com/mol/

Madison's Online Magazine
www.link-here.com

Madison.com
www.madison.com

Surf Madison
www.mabb.com

Area Communities

Communities in the Madison area with populations greater than 10,000 include:

Fitchburg — Phone: 608-270-4200; Fax: 608-270-4212
5520 Lacy Rd
Fitchburg, WI 53711

Middleton — Phone: 608-827-1050; Fax: 608-827-1057
7426 Hubbard Ave
Middleton, WI 53562

Stoughton — Phone: 608-873-6677; Fax: 608-873-5519
381 E Main St
Stoughton, WI 53589

Sun Prairie — Phone: 608-837-2511; Fax: 608-825-6879
300 E Main St
Sun Prairie, WI 53590

Economy

Madison has a diverse economic base that ranges from agriculture (nearly one-sixth of all Wisconsin farms are in Greater Madison) to insurance to research and development. Government is the largest employment sector in Dane County, with more than 73,000 area residents employed at the federal, state, and local levels—more than 30,000 jobs are provided by the University of Wisconsin Madison, making the institution Madison's largest employer. Major U.S. companies headquartered in Madison include Rayovac Corporation and American Mutual Insurance.

Unemployment Rate 1.5%*
Per Capita Income $30,214*
Median Family Income $61,400*

** Information given is for the Madison Metropolitan Statistical Area (MSA), which includes the City of Madison and Dane County.*

Principal Industries & Number of Wage Earners

Madison MSA (Dane County) - 1999

Industry	Wage Earners
Construction & Mining	14,000
Finance, Insurance, & Real Estate	23,000
Government	73,100
Manufacturing	30,400
Retail Trade	48,500
Services	72,000
Transportation & Public Utilities	9,500
Wholesale Trade	12,700

Major Employers

American Family Mutual Insurance Co — Phone: 608-249-2111; Fax: 608-243-4921; TF: 800-374-0008
6000 American Pkwy
Madison, WI 53783
www.amfam.com

CUNA Mutual Group — Phone: 608-238-5851; Fax: 608-238-0830; TF: 800-937-2644
5910 Mineral Point Rd
Madison, WI 53705
E-mail: custhelp@cunamutual.com
www.cunamutual.com

Dane County — Phone: 608-266-4121
210 ML King Jr Blvd Rm 112
Madison, WI 53709
www.co.dane.wi.us

Madison Area Technical College — Phone: 608-246-6100; Fax: 608-246-6880
3550 Anderson St
Madison, WI 53704
www.madison.tec.wi.us

Madison City Hall — Phone: 608-266-4611
210 ML King Jr Blvd
Madison, WI 53709
www.ci.madison.wi.us

Madison Gas & Electric Co — Phone: 608-252-7000; Fax: 608-252-7098; TF: 800-245-1125
133 S Blair St
Madison, WI 53703
www.mge.com

Madison Metropolitan School District — Phone: 608-266-6270; Fax: 608-267-1626
545 W Dayton St
Madison, WI 53703
E-mail: cburch@madison.k12.wi.us
www.madison.k12.wi.us

Meriter Health Services Inc — Phone: 608-284-6836; Fax: 608-267-6568
202 S Park St
Madison, WI 53715
www.pplusmeriter.com/mhs/index.htm

Nicolet Instrument Corp — Phone: 608-276-6100; Fax: 608-273-6880
5225 Verona Rd
Madison, WI 53711
E-mail: nicinfo@nicolet.com
www.nicolet.com

Oscar Mayer Foods Corp
PO Box 7188
Madison, WI 53707
www.oscar-mayer.com
Phone: 608-241-3311
Fax: 608-242-6102

Rayovac Corp
601 Rayovac Dr
Madison, WI 53711
E-mail: consumers@rayovac.com
www.rayovac.com
Phone: 608-275-3340
Fax: 608-275-4577
TF: 800-237-7000

Saint Mary's Hospital Medical Center
707 S Mills St
Madison, WI 53715
www.stmarysmadison.com
Phone: 608-251-6100
Fax: 608-258-6327

Stoughton Trailers Inc
416 S Academy St
Stoughton, WI 53589
E-mail: sales@stoughton-trailers.com
www.stoughton-trailers.com
Phone: 608-873-2500
Fax: 608-873-2575

University of Wisconsin Hospital & Clinics
600 Highland Ave
Madison, WI 53792
www.medicine.wisc.edu
Phone: 608-263-6400
Fax: 608-263-9830

University of Wisconsin Madison
716 Langdon St
Madison, WI 53706
E-mail: on.wisconsin@mail.admin.wisc.edu
www.wisc.edu
Phone: 608-262-1234
Fax: 608-262-1429

Wisconsin Physician Service Insurance Co
PO Box 8190
Madison, WI 53708
www.wpsic.com
Phone: 608-221-4711
Fax: 608-223-3609

Quality of Living Indicators

Total Crime Index 7,891
(rates per 100,000 inhabitants)

Violent Crime
Murder/manslaughter 4
Forcible rape 85
Robbery 264
Aggravated assault 362

Property Crime
Burglary 1,355
Larceny theft 5,219
Motor vehicle theft 602

Cost of Living Index 104.7
(national average = 100)

Median Home Price $136,500

Education

Public Schools

Madison Metropolitan School District
545 W Dayton St
Madison, WI 53703
E-mail: cburch@madison.k12.wi.us
www.madison.k12.wi.us
Phone: 608-266-6270
Fax: 608-267-1626

Number of Schools
Elementary 29
Middle 11
High 4

Student/Teacher Ratio
All Grades 13.2:1

Private Schools

Number of Schools (all grades) 32

Colleges & Universities

Edgewood College
855 Woodrow St
Madison, WI 53711
www.edgewood.edu
Phone: 608-257-4861
Fax: 608-663-3291
TF: 800-444-4861

Herzing College of Technology
1227 N Sherman Ave
Madison, WI 53704
E-mail: mailbag@msn.herzing.edu
www.herzing.edu/madison/home.htm
Phone: 608-249-6611
Fax: 608-249-8593
TF: 800-582-1227

Madison Area Technical College
3550 Anderson St
Madison, WI 53704
www.madison.tec.wi.us
Phone: 608-246-6100
Fax: 608-246-6880

University of Wisconsin Colleges
780 Regent St
Madison, WI 53708
www.uwc.edu
Phone: 608-262-1783
Fax: 608-262-7872

University of Wisconsin Madison
716 Langdon St
Madison, WI 53706
E-mail: on.wisconsin@mail.admin.wisc.edu
www.wisc.edu
Phone: 608-262-1234
Fax: 608-262-1429

Hospitals

Meriter Hospital
202 S Park St
Madison, WI 53715
www.meriter.com/meriter/mhs/index.htm
Phone: 608-267-6000
Fax: 608-267-6419

Saint Mary's Hospital Medical Center
707 S Mills St
Madison, WI 53715
www.stmarysmadison.com
Phone: 608-251-6100
Fax: 608-258-6327

University of Wisconsin Hospital & Clinics
600 Highland Ave
Madison, WI 53792
www.medicine.wisc.edu
Phone: 608-263-6400
Fax: 608-263-9830

William S Middleton Memorial Veterans Hospital
2500 Overlook Terr
Madison, WI 53705
Phone: 608-256-1901
Fax: 608-262-7095

Transportation

Airport(s)

Dane County Regional Airport (MSN)
5 miles NE of downtown (approx 15 minutes) 608-246-3380

Mass Transit

Madison Metro Transit
$1.25 Base fare. 608-266-4466

Rail/Bus

Greyhound Bus Station
2 S Bedford St
Madison, WI 53703
Phone: 608-257-3050
TF: 800-231-2222

Utilities

Electricity
Madison Gas & Electric Co. .608-252-7000
www.mge.com

Gas
Madison Gas & Electric Co. .608-252-7000
www.mge.com

Water
Madison Water Utility. 608-266-4641

Garbage Collection/Recycling
Madison Dept of Sanitation .608-246-4532

Telecommunications

Telephone
Ameritech 800-924-1000
www.ameritech.com

Cable Television
Charter Communications. 608-274-3511
Sky Cable 608-271-6999

Internet Service Providers (ISPs)
Chorus Communications Group LLC 608-231-9098
www.chorus.net
DANEnet. 608-274-3107
danenet.wicip.org
FullFeed Communications 608-246-4239
www.fullfeed.com
SupraNet Communications Inc 608-836-0282
www.supranet.com
TDSNET 800-358-3648
www.tds.net/tdsnet
WiscNet. 608-265-6761
www.wiscnet.net

Banks

Bank One Madison
1965 Atwood Ave
Madison, WI 53704
Phone: 608-246-2333
Fax: 608-246-2326
TF: 800-947-1111

Bankers' Bank
7700 Mineral Point Rd
Madison, WI 53717
www.bankersbankusa.com
Phone: 608-833-5550
Fax: 608-829-5590

Firstar Bank Wisconsin
1 S Pinckney St on the Square
Madison, WI 53703
Phone: 608-252-4000
Fax: 608-252-7621
TF: 800-347-7827

M & I Bank of Southern Wisconsin
1 W Main St
Madison, WI 53703
www.mibank.com
Phone: 608-252-5800
Fax: 608-252-5880
TF: 888-464-5463

Shopping

Antiques Mall of Madison
4748 Cottage Grove Rd
Madison, WI 53716
Phone: 608-222-2049
Fax: 608-222-2261

East Towne Mall
151 E Washington Ave
Madison, WI 53704
E-mail: easttownmall@rejacobsgroup.com
www.shopyourmall.com/mall_welcome.asp?map=yes&mall_select=610
Phone: 608-244-1501
Fax: 608-244-8306

Hilldale Mall
702 N Midvale Mall
Madison, WI 53705
Phone: 608-238-6640
Fax: 608-238-7338

Lands' End Outlet
209 Junction Rd
Madison, WI 53717
Phone: 608-833-3343
Fax: 608-833-3491

State Street District
State & Gorham Sts
Madison, WI 53703
www.state-st.com/
Phone: 608-255-2537

West Towne Mall
66 West Towne Way
Madison, WI 53719
E-mail: westtownemall@rejacobsgroup.com
www.shopyourmall.com/mall_welcome.asp?map=yes&mall_select=606
Phone: 608-833-6330
Fax: 608-833-5878

Media

Newspapers and Magazines

Capital Times*
1901 Fish Hatchery Rd
Madison, WI 53713
E-mail: tctvoice@captimes.madison.com
www.thecapitaltimes.com
Phone: 608-252-6400
Fax: 608-252-6445

In Business Magazine
2718 Dryden Dr
Madison, WI 53704
Phone: 608-246-3599
Fax: 608-246-3597

Isthmus
101 King St
Madison, WI 53703
E-mail: edit@isthmus.com
www.thedailypage.com
Phone: 608-251-5627
Fax: 608-251-2165

Wisconsin State Journal*
1901 Fish Hatchery Rd
Madison, WI 53713
www.madison.com/wsj
Phone: 608-252-6100
Fax: 608-252-6119

Wisconsin Trails
1131 Mills St
Black Earth, WI 53515
E-mail: info@wistrails.com
www.wistrails.com/magazine.html
Phone: 608-767-8000
Fax: 608-767-5444
TF: 800-236-8088

**Indicates major daily newspapers*

Television

WHA-TV Ch 21 (PBS)
821 University Ave
Madison, WI 53706
www.wpt.org
Phone: 608-263-2121
Fax: 608-263-9763

WISC-TV Ch 3 (CBS)
PO Box 44965
Madison, WI 53744
E-mail: talkback@wisctv.com
www.wisctv.com
Phone: 608-271-4321
Fax: 608-271-0800

WKOW-TV Ch 27 (ABC)
5727 Tokay Blvd
Madison, WI 53719
E-mail: 27listens@wkowtv.com
www.wkowtv.com
Phone: 608-274-1234
Fax: 608-274-9514

WMSN-TV Ch 47 (Fox)
7847 Big Sky Dr
Madison, WI 53719
www.fox47.com
Phone: 608-833-0047
Fax: 608-833-5055

WMTV-Ch 15 (NBC)
615 Forward Dr
Madison, WI 53711
www.nbc15.com
Phone: 608-274-1515
Fax: 608-271-5194

Radio

WERN-FM 88.7 MHz (NPR)
821 University Ave
Madison, WI 53706
www.wpr.org
Phone: 608-264-9600
Fax: 608-264-9622

WHA-AM 970 kHz (NPR)
821 University Ave
Madison, WI 53706
www.wpr.org
Phone: 608-263-3970
Fax: 608-263-9763

WHLA-FM 90.3 MHz (N/T)
821 University Ave
Madison, WI 53706
Phone: 608-263-3970
Fax: 608-263-9763

WIBA-FM 101.5 MHz (CR)
PO Box 99
Madison, WI 53701
www.wiba.com
Phone: 608-274-5450
Fax: 608-274-5521

WJJO-FM 94.1 MHz (Rock)
2740 Ski Ln
Madison, WI 53713
www.wjjo.com/
Phone: 608-273-1000
Fax: 608-271-8182

WMGN-FM 98.1 MHz (AC)
2740 Ski Ln
Madison, WI 53713
www.magic98.com
Phone: 608-273-1000
Fax: 608-271-8182
TF: 800-708-0098

WMLI-FM 96.3 MHz (AC)
2651 Fish Hatchery Rd
Madison, WI 53711
E-mail: lite@madcity.com
www.softrock963.com
Phone: 608-274-1070
Fax: 608-274-5521

WTSO-AM 1070 kHz (N/T)
2651 S Fish Hatchery Rd
Madison, WI 53711
Phone: 608-274-1070
Fax: 608-274-5521

WWQM-FM 106.3 MHz (Ctry)
2740 Ski Ln
Madison, WI 53713
www.q106.com
Phone: 608-271-6611
Fax: 608-271-0400

Attractions

The center of the city of Madison lies on an eight-block-wide isthmus between Lakes Mendota and Monona. Much of the city's activity is focused around the lakes, where one can rent canoes, fish year round, and hike, roller skate, or bike on numerous paths. State Street, with its array of boutiques, galleries, coffee houses, and ethnic restaurants, links the State Capitol to the University of Wisconsin campus. This prominent Big Ten University has the acclaimed Elvehjem Museum of Art and the University Arboretum, with more than 1,200 acres of natural plant and animal communities. Just west of Madison is Blue Mound State Park. The Park's lookout tower, located along the nearly 40-mile Military Ridge Trail, affords a perfect view of the area's rolling hills. Little Norway, a restored 1856 Norwegian homestead, is also west of the city.

American Players Theater
5950 Golf Course Rd
Spring Green, WI 53588
www.americanplayers.org
Phone: 608-588-7401
Fax: 608-588-7085

Barrymore Theatre
2090 Atwood Ave
Madison, WI 53704
Phone: 608-241-8633
Fax: 608-241-8861

Blue Mound State Park
4350 Mounds Park Rd
Blue Mounds, WI 53517
www.dnr.state.wi.us
Phone: 608-437-5711

Broom Street Theatre
1119 Williamson St
Madison, WI 53703
www.geocities.com/~broomstreet
Phone: 608-244-8338

Cave of the Mounds
2975 Cave of the Mounds Rd
Blue Mounds, WI 53517
Phone: 608-437-3038
Fax: 608-437-4181

CTM Madison Family Theatre Co
228 State St
Madison, WI 53703
E-mail: marketing@theatreforall.com
www.theatreforall.com
Phone: 608-255-2080
Fax: 608-255-6760

Dance Wisconsin
6332 Monona Dr
Madison, WI 53716
www.dancewisconsin.com
Phone: 608-221-4535
Fax: 608-221-4535

Elvehjem Museum of Art
800 University Ave University of Wisconsin
Madison, WI 53706
www.uwpd.wisc.edu/elvehjem.htm
Phone: 608-263-2246
Fax: 608-263-8188

Governor Nelson State Park
5140 County Hwy M
Waunakee, WI 53597
Phone: 608-831-3005

House on the Rock
5754 Hwy 23
Spring Green, WI 53588
www.thehouseontherock.com
Phone: 608-935-3639
Fax: 608-935-9472

Lake Kegonsa State Park
2405 Door Creek Rd
Stoughton, WI 53589
Phone: 608-873-9695
Fax: 608-873-0674
TF: 888-947-2757

Little Norway
3576 Hwy JG N
Blue Mounds, WI 53517
www.littlenorway.com
Phone: 608-437-8211
Fax: 608-437-7827

Luma Theatre of Light
4535 Helgesen Dr
Madison, WI 53718
E-mail: firstlight@globaldialog.com
www.lumatheatre.com
Phone: 608-222-0077
Fax: 608-226-0028

Madison Art Center
211 State St
Madison, WI 53703
E-mail: mac@itis.com
www.madisonartcenter.org
Phone: 608-257-0158
Fax: 608-257-5722

Madison Children's Museum
100 State St
Madison, WI 53703
E-mail: mcm@terracom.net
www.kidskiosk.org
Phone: 608-256-6445
Fax: 608-256-3226

Madison Geology Museum
1215 W Dayton St University of Wisconsin Weeks Hall
Madison, WI 53706
E-mail: kwwestph@facstaff.wisc.edu
Phone: 608-262-2399
Fax: 608-262-0693

Madison Opera
211 State St Oscar Mayer Theatre
Madison, WI 53703
E-mail: stanke@madisonopera.org
www.madisonopera.org
Phone: 608-238-8085
Fax: 608-233-3431

Madison Repertory Theater
122 State St Suite 201
Madison, WI 53703
E-mail: madisonrep@aol.com
www.madstage.com
Phone: 608-256-0029
Fax: 608-256-7433

Madison Symphony Orchestra
211 N Carroll St
Madison, WI 53703
www.madisonsymphony.org
Phone: 608-257-3734
Fax: 608-258-2315

Mitby Theatre
3550 Anderson St
Madison, WI 53704
mitbytheater.madison.tec.wi.us
Phone: 608-243-4000
Fax: 608-243-4011

Olbrich Botanical Gardens
3330 Atwood Ave
Madison, WI 53704
www.olbrich.org/
Phone: 608-246-4551
Fax: 608-246-4719

Oscar Mayer Theater
211 State St Madison Civic Ctr
Madison, WI 53703
Phone: 608-266-9055
Fax: 608-261-9975

State Historical Museum of Wisconsin
30 N Carroll St
Madison, WI 53703
E-mail: shsmuseum@mail.shsw.wisc.edu
www.shsw.wisc.edu/museum
Phone: 608-264-6555
Fax: 608-264-6575

State Street District
State & Gorham Sts
Madison, WI 53703
www.state-st.com/
Phone: 608-255-2537

Swiss Historical Village
612 7th Ave
New Glarus, WI 53574
Phone: 608-527-2317

Taliesin
Hwy 23 & Hwy C
Spring Green, WI 53588
www.taliesinpreservation.org
Phone: 608-588-7900
Fax: 608-588-7514

University of Wisconsin Arboretum
1207 Seminole Hwy
Madison, WI 53711
Phone: 608-263-7888
Fax: 608-262-5209

Vilas Henry Park Zoo
702 S Randall Ave
Madison, WI 53715
E-mail: zoo@abcon.com
www.vilaszoo.com
Phone: 608-266-4732
Fax: 608-266-5923

Wisconsin Chamber Orchestra
22 N Carroll St Suite 104
Madison, WI 53703
E-mail: wco@midplains.net
www.jupitercc.com/wco/
Phone: 608-257-0638
Fax: 608-257-0611

Wisconsin Dance Ensemble
6320 Monona Dr Suite 319
Madison, WI 53716
Phone: 608-222-5552
Fax: 608-222-5662

Wisconsin Dells
701 Superior St
Wisconsin Dells, WI 53965
www.dells.com/index-a.html
Phone: 608-254-8088
Fax: 608-254-4293
TF: 800-223-3557

Wisconsin State Capitol
Capitol Sq
Madison, WI 53702
Phone: 608-266-0382

Wisconsin Union Art Collection & Theater Galleries
800 Langdon St Room 507
Madison, WI 53706
E-mail: union@macc.wisc.edu
www.wisc.edu/union
Phone: 608-262-5969
Fax: 608-262-8862

Wisconsin Union Theater
800 Langdon St
Madison, WI 53706
www.wisc.edu/union/mu/muarts/wut/wut.html
Phone: 608-262-2201

Wisconsin Veterans Museum Phone: 608-264-6086
30 W Mifflin St Fax: 608-264-7615
Madison, WI 53703
badger.state.wi.us/agencies/dva/museum/wvmmain.html

Sports Teams & Facilities

Madison Black Wolf (baseball) Phone: 608-244-5666
2920 N Sherman Ave Warner Pk Fax: 608-244-6996
Madison, WI 53704
E-mail: madwolf@madwall.com
www.madwolf.com

Madison Kodiaks (hockey) Phone: 608-250-2611
1881 Expo Mall E Dane County Coliseum Fax: 608-250-2614
Madison, WI 53713
www.co.dane.wi.us/expo/newhockey.html

Madison Mad Dogs (football) Phone: 608-294-1460
1881 Expo Mall E Dane County Coliseum Fax: 608-294-1464
Madison, WI 53713 TF: 888-316-3647
E-mail: bganther@ganther.com
www.indoorfootballleague.com/madison.html

Annual Events

Art Fair off the Square (mid-July)................608-798-4811
Audubon Art Fair (early May)....................608-255-2473
Badger State Summer Games (mid-late June) 608-226-4780
Capital City Jazz Festival (late April)..............608-877-4171
Capitol Christmas Pageant (early December)........608-849-9529
Concerts in the Gardens (June-August) 608-246-4551
Concerts on the Square (late June-late July).......608-257-0638
Cows on the Concourse (early June)..............608-221-8698
Crazy Legs Run (late April).......................608-263-7894
Dane County Fair (mid-July).....................608-224-6455
Dane County Farmers' Market
(late April-early November) 920-563-5037
Executive Residence Christmas Tours
(December)..................................608-266-3554
Executive Residence Public Tours
(April-August)................................608-266-3554
Fall Festival (mid-October) 608-437-5914
Firstar Eve (December 31) 608-255-2537
Garden Expo (mid-February).....................608-262-5255
Halloween at the Zoo (late October) 608-266-4732
Heroes Madison Marathon (late May) 608-256-9922
Holiday Art Fair (late November).................608-257-0158
Holiday Fantasy of Lights
(late November-early January) 608-222-7630
Holiday Flower & Train Show (December) 608-246-4718
Hometown USA Festival (mid-June)...............608-831-5696
International Children's Film Festival (March)......608-266-9055
International Holiday Festival (mid-November) 608-266-6550
Isthmus Jazz Festival (early October).............608-266-6550
Jingle Bell Run (mid-December) 608-221-9800
June Jam (early June)............................608-276-6606
Kites on Ice (early February) 608-831-1725
Kwanzaa Holiday Marketplace (late November)......608-255-9600
Madison Folk Music Festival (early May)...........608-836-8422
Madison Holiday Parade (late November)...........608-831-1725
Maxwell Street Days (mid-July) 608-266-6033
Midwest Horse Fair (mid-April) 608-267-3976
Mount Horeb Art Fair (mid-July)..................608-437-5914
National Mustard Day (early August)...............608-437-3986
Paddle & Portage (late July)......................608-255-1008
Rhapsody in Bloom (mid-June) 608-246-4550
Rhythm & Booms (early July) 800-951-2264
Spring Flower Show (mid-March) 608-246-4550
Summer Concerts in the Gardens
(early June-mid-August)........................608-246-4551
Taste of Madison (early September) 800-373-6376
Triangle Ethnic Fest (mid-August) 800-373-6376
Tuesday Noon Concerts (June-September)..........608-266-0382
Umbrella Daze (mid-July) 608-423-3780
Wednesday Farmers' Market (May-late October).....920-563-5037
Willy Street Fair (mid-September)................608-256-3527
Winter Art Festival (mid-November)...............608-798-4811
Winter Concerts in the Gardens (January-March)....608-246-4551
Wisconsin Quarter Horse Show
(mid-late August).............................608-267-3976
World Dairy Expo
(late September-early October)..................608-224-6455
Zor Shrine Circus (mid-February)................608-274-2260

Memphis, Tennessee

***County:* Shelby**

MEMPHIS is located on the Chickasaw Bluffs in southwestern Tennessee along the banks of the Mississippi River. Major cities within 100 miles include Little Rock, Arkansas and Clarksdale and Oxford, Mississippi.

Area (Land)	256.0 sq mi
Area (Water)	15.1 sq mi
Elevation	254 ft
Latitude	35-08-46 N
Longitude	90-03-13 W
Time Zone	CST
Area Code	901

Climate

Memphis has a moderate climate that changes frequently due to the influence of weather patterns moving north from the Gulf of Mexico and south from Canada. Winters are fairly cold, with average high temperatures around 50 degrees and average lows in the low 30s. Snowfall is rare in Memphis, averaging only 5.3 inches annually. Summer days are hot, with average high temperatures near 90 degrees, while evening temperatures drop into the high 60s to low 70s. April is the wettest month in Memphis; October is the driest.

Average Temperatures & Precipitation

Temperatures

	Jan	Feb	Mar	Apr	May	Jun	Jul	Aug	Sep	Oct	Nov	Dec
High	49	54	63	73	81	89	92	91	84	74	62	53
Low	31	35	43	52	61	69	73	71	65	52	43	35

Precipitation

	Jan	Feb	Mar	Apr	May	Jun	Jul	Aug	Sep	Oct	Nov	Dec
Inches	3.7	4.4	5.4	5.5	5.0	3.6	3.8	3.4	3.5	3.0	5.1	5.7

History

Originally inhabited by the Chickasaw people, the area known today as Memphis was first explored by Europeans as early as the mid-1500s. The French built a fort at the site of present-day Memphis in 1739, and over the course of the 18th Century control of the land shifted from the French to the British to the Americans. In 1818 the U.S. gained control of the territory when the Chickasaw ceded the land to the U.S. Government. The city of Memphis was founded the following year by Andrew Jackson, John Overton, and James Winchester, who named the new city on the Mississippi Memphis after the Egyptian city on the Nile.

Incorporated as a town in 1826, Memphis grew quickly as an important trade center on the Mississippi, and by the time it was incorporated as a city in 1849, Memphis had become one of the nation's busiest ports. Cotton was (and continues to be) an important commodity in Memphis. During the American Civil War, the city served as a Confederate military center until it was captured by Union troops in 1862. Memphis also served as the temporary state capital for a short time during the war and was one of the few Southern cities that had not been destroyed by war's end.

Devastation came to the city in another form—yellow fever—during the 1870s. Numerous epidemics resulted in the death of more than 5,000 Memphis residents and forced hundreds of others to flee. By 1879, only one-third of the people who called Memphis home at the beginning of the decade remained in the city, and Memphis was forced to surrender its city charter and declare bankruptcy. During the late 19th Century, the remaining residents of Memphis worked to revive the city—bonds were sold to finance sanitation, drainage, and transportation projects, and a merchants exchange was formed to help diversify the economy. The city regained its charter in 1893. E.H. "Boss" Crump (who served as mayor from 1910-1915, but continued to work toward improving the city through the 1950s) is credited with boosting the quality and number of city services, improving industry (and thereby employment) in the city, and helping Memphis achieve financial security.

During the 20th Century, Memphis gained recognition as a music capital. The Blues were born in Memphis in 1909 when African-American musician W.C. Handy wrote the very first Blues song, "Memphis Blues." Four decades later, a young musician named Elvis Presley was discovered in Memphis, and the city became known as the birthplace of yet another new genre of music, Rock 'n' Roll. Presley's former estate, Graceland, remains one of Memphis' biggest tourist attractions.

Memphis continues to thrive as one of the nation's leading distribution centers and remains an important regional commercial center for the vast farmland surrounding the Mississippi Delta. With a population of more than 603,000, Memphis is Tennessee's largest city.

Population

1990 Census	618,652
1998 Estimate	603,507
% Change	-2.4
2003 Projection	897,343*

Racial/Ethnic Breakdown

White	43.4%
Black	54.1%
Other	2.5%
Hispanic Origin (may be of any race)	0.7%

Age Breakdown

Under 5 years	8.1%
5 to 17	18.7%
18 to 20	4.9%
21 to 24	6.5%

25 to 34 .... 17.9%
35 to 44 .... 14.2%
45 to 54 .... 9.0%
55 to 64 .... 8.4%
65 to 74 .... 7.1%
75+ years 5.1%
Median Age 31.5

Gender Breakdown
Male 46.1%
Female 53.9%

** Information given is for Shelby County.*

Government

Type of Government: Mayor-Council

Memphis Center City Commission
114 N Main St Crump Bldg
Memphis, TN 38103
Phone: 901-575-0540
Fax: 901-575-0541

Memphis Chief Administrative Officer
125 N Main St Rm 308
Memphis, TN 38103
Phone: 901-576-6586
Fax: 901-576-6555

Memphis City Attorney
125 N Main St Rm 314
Memphis, TN 38103
Phone: 901-576-6614
Fax: 901-576-6524

Memphis City Council
125 N Main St Rm 514
Memphis, TN 38103
Phone: 901-576-6786
Fax: 901-576-6796

Memphis City Hall
125 N Main St
Memphis, TN 38103
Phone: 901-576-6500

Memphis Finance Div
125 N Main St Rm 368
Memphis, TN 38103
Phone: 901-576-6657
Fax: 901-576-6193

Memphis Fire Services Div
65 S Front St
Memphis, TN 38103
Phone: 901-527-1400
Fax: 901-527-9516

Memphis Housing & Community Development Div
701 N Main St
Memphis, TN 38107
Phone: 901-576-7300
Fax: 901-576-7318

Memphis Human Resources Div
125 N Main St Suite 406
Memphis, TN 38103
Phone: 901-576-6571
Fax: 901-576-6482

Memphis Mayor
125 N Main St Suite 700
Memphis, TN 38103
Phone: 901-576-6000
Fax: 901-576-6012

Memphis Park Commission
2599 Avery Ave
Memphis, TN 38112
Phone: 901-454-5600
Fax: 901-454-5275

Memphis Planning & Development Div
125 N Main St
Memphis, TN 38103
Phone: 901-576-7197
Fax: 901-576-7188

Memphis Police Dept
201 Poplar Ave
Memphis, TN 38103
Phone: 901-545-5700
Fax: 901-545-3877

Memphis Public Services Div
125N Main St Suite 200
Memphis, TN 39103
Phone: 901-576-6564
Fax: 901-576-6259

Memphis Public Works Div
125 N Main St Rm 608
Memphis, TN 38103
Phone: 901-576-6742
Fax: 901-576-7116

Memphis/Shelby County Public Library
1850 Peabody Ave
Memphis, TN 38104
Phone: 901-725-8855
Fax: 901-725-8883

Important Phone Numbers

AAA 901-761-5371
American Express Travel 901-291-1400
Driver's License Information 901-543-7920
Emergency 911
Events Line 901-753-5847
HotelDocs 800-468-3537
Medical Referral 901-362-8677
Memphis Area Assn of Realtors 901-685-2100
Memphis Treasury Dept 901-576-6306
Poison Control Center 901-528-6048
Tennessee Taxpayer Services Dept Corporate Franchise Tax Information 901-537-2902
Tennessee Taxpayer Services Dept State Income/Sales Tax Information 901-537-2904
Time/Temp 901-526-5261
Travelers Aid 901-525-5466
Vehicle Registration Information 901-545-4244
Voter Registration Information 901-545-4121
Weather 901-544-0399

Information Sources

Better Business Bureau Serving West Tennessee North Mississippi & Eastern Arkansas
PO Box 17036
Memphis, TN 38187
www.memphis.bbb.org
Phone: 901-759-1300
Fax: 901-757-2997

Memphis Area Chamber of Commerce
PO Box 224
Memphis, TN 38101
www.memphischamber.com
Phone: 901-543-3500
Fax: 901-543-3510

Memphis Center City Commission
114 N Main St Crump Bldg
Memphis, TN 38103
www.downtownmemphis.com
Phone: 901-575-0540
Fax: 901-575-0541

Memphis Convention & Visitors Bureau
47 Union Ave
Memphis, TN 38103
www.memphistravel.com
Phone: 901-543-5300
Fax: 901-543-5350
TF: 800-873-6282

Memphis Cook Convention Center
255 N Main St
Memphis, TN 38103
www.memphisconvention.com
Phone: 901-576-1200
Fax: 901-576-1212
TF: 800-726-0915

Memphis Visitors Information Center
119 N Riverside Dr
Memphis, TN 38103
Phone: 901-543-5333
Fax: 901-543-5335

Shelby County
160 N Main St Suite 619
Memphis, TN 38103
www.co.shelby.tn.us
Phone: 901-545-4301
Fax: 901-545-4283

Online Resources

4Memphis.com
www.4memphis.com

About.com Guide to Memphis
memphis.about.com/citiestowns/southeastus/memphis

Area Guide Memphis
memphis.areaguides.net

Boulevards Memphis
www.memphis.com

City Knowledge Memphis
www.cityknowledge.com/tn_memphis.htm

DigitalCity Memphis
home.digitalcity.com/memphis

Downtown Memphis
www.downtownmemphis.com/

Excite.com Memphis City Guide
www.excite.com/travel/countries/united_states/tennessee/memphis

IntroMemphis
www.intromemphis.com

LocalPaper@Memphis
www.localpaper.com

Memphis Community Network
www.memphis.acn.net/

Memphis Connection
www.memphisconnection.com/

Memphis Flyer
www.memphisflyer.com

Memphis Guide
www.memphisguide.com/

MemphisNet
www.memphisnet.com/

Mid-South Citizen Site
www.lunaweb.com/index.htm

Rough Guide Travel Memphis
travel.roughguides.com/content/747/

Search Memphis
www.searchmemphis.com/

Area Communities

Communities in the Memphis area with populations greater than 10,000 include:

Bartlett
6400 Stage Rd
Bartlett, TN 38134
Phone: 901-385-6400
Fax: 901-385-5514

Collierville
101 Walnut St
Collierville, TN 38017
Phone: 901-853-3200
Fax: 901-853-3230

Germantown
1930 S Germantown Rd
Germantown, TN 38138
Phone: 901-757-7261

Millington
7930 Nelson Rd
Millington, TN 38053
Phone: 901-872-2211
Fax: 901-872-4113

Economy

Memphis is one of the nation's leading distribution centers. It is the corporate home of Federal Express, which is the city's largest employer, providing jobs for some 29,500 area residents. Services and trade are currently the Memphis metropolitan area's largest employment sectors. Health care is the leading service industry in Memphis. Baptist Memorial Health Care System, the world's largest not-for-profit hospital, is based in Memphis and is currently the area's sixth largest employer. Agribusiness is also a vital industry in the city, which remains an important trade center for the fertile Mississippi Delta region.

Unemployment Rate 3.7%*
Per Capita Income.......................... $27,300
Median Family Income...................... $48,600*

* *Information given is the Memphis, Tennessee/Arkansas/Mississippi Metropolitan Statistical Area (MSA), which includes the City of Memphis, Shelby County, and Tipton County in Tennessee; and the City of West Memphis, Crittenden County, and DeSoto County in Arkansas.*

Principal Industries & Number of Wage Earners

Shelby County - 1998

Agricultural Services, Forestry, & Fishing 3,018
Construction... 21,796
Finance, Insurance, & Real Estate 25,155
Government 50,016
Manufacturing 47,804
Services 138,394
Trade 121,063
Transportation, Communications, & Public Utilities 63,734

Major Employers

Baptist Memorial Health Care System
899 Madison Ave
Memphis, TN 38103
Phone: 901-227-2727
Fax: 901-226-3731

Cleo Inc
4025 Viscount Ave
Memphis, TN 38118
www.cleowrap.com
Phone: 901-369-6300
Fax: 901-362-1099
TF: 800-289-2536

Federal Express Corp
2005 Corporate Plaza
Memphis, TN 38132
www.fedex.com
Phone: 901-369-3600
Fax: 901-224-8700
TF: 800-463-3339

First Tennessee Bank NA
165 Madison Ave
Memphis, TN 38103
Phone: 901-523-4444
Fax: 901-523-4145
TF: 800-999-0110

Kroger Co
800 Ridge Lake Blvd
Memphis, TN 38101
www.kroger.com
Phone: 901-765-4100
Fax: 901-765-4228

Memphis City Board of Education
2597 Avery Ave
Memphis, TN 38112
E-mail: comm@memphis-schools.k12.tn.us
www.memphis-schools.k12.tn.us
Phone: 901-325-5300
Fax: 901-325-5322

Memphis City Hall
125 N Main St
Memphis, TN 38103
www.ci.memphis.tn.us
Phone: 901-576-6500

Methodist Hospitals of Memphis
1265 Union Ave
Memphis, TN 38104
Phone: 901-726-7000
Fax: 901-726-7927

Northwest Airlines
2491 Winchester Rd
Memphis, TN 38116
Phone: 901-922-8568
Fax: 901-922-8507

Regional Medical Center at Memphis
877 Jefferson Ave
Memphis, TN 38103
www.the-med.com
Phone: 901-545-7100
Fax: 901-545-8315

Shelby County
160 N Main St Suite 619
Memphis, TN 38103
www.co.shelby.tn.us
Phone: 901-545-4301
Fax: 901-545-4283

Shelby County School System
160 S Hollywood
Memphis, TN 38112
Phone: 901-325-7900
Fax: 901-325-7920

University of Memphis
Memphis, TN 38152
www.memphis.edu
Phone: 901-678-2040
Fax: 901-678-3053
TF: 800-669-2678

University of Tennessee Memphis
800 Madison Ave
Memphis, TN 38163
www.utmem.edu
Phone: 901-448-5000
Fax: 901-448-7772

Veterans Affairs Medical Center
1030 Jefferson Ave
Memphis, TN 38104
Phone: 901-523-8990
Fax: 901-577-7286

Wal-Mart Stores Inc
1280 S Germantown Pkwy
Germantown, TN 38138
Phone: 901-758-1591
Fax: 901-758-8759

Quality of Living Indicators

Total Crime Index....................................51,034
(rates per 100,000 inhabitants)

Violent Crime
Murder/manslaughter.......................... 119
Forcible rape 688
Robbery....................................3,715
Aggravated assault.............................4,081

Property Crime
Burglary 13,005
Larceny theft 21,756
Motor vehicle theft 7,670

Cost of Living Index....................................92.6
(national average = 100)

Median Home Price.................................$111,300

Education

Public Schools

Memphis City Board of Education
2597 Avery Ave
Memphis, TN 38112
E-mail: comm@memphis-schools.k12.tn.us
www.memphis-schools.k12.tn.us
Phone: 901-325-5300
Fax: 901-325-5322

Number of Schools
Elementary................................ 103
Middle 14
High....................................... 6

Student/Teacher Ratio
All Grades 17.9:1

Private Schools

Number of Schools (all grades).................... 86+

Colleges & Universities

Christian Brothers University
650 East Pkwy S
Memphis, TN 38104
E-mail: admissions@bucs.cbu.edu
www.cbu.edu
Phone: 901-321-3000
Fax: 901-321-3494
TF: 800-288-7576

Crichton College
PO Box 757830
Memphis, TN 38175
Phone: 901-367-9800
Fax: 901-367-3866
TF: 800-960-9777

LeMoyne-Owen College
807 Walker Ave
Memphis, TN 38126
www.mecca.org/LOC/page/LOC.html
Phone: 901-774-9090
Fax: 901-942-6272
TF: 800-737-7778

Memphis College of Art Overton Park
1930 Poplar Ave
Memphis, TN 38107
www.mca.edu
Phone: 901-726-4085
Fax: 901-272-6830
TF: 800-727-1088

Rhodes College
2000 North Pkwy
Memphis, TN 38112
E-mail: adminfo@rhodes.edu
www.rhodes.edu
Phone: 901-843-3000
Fax: 901-843-3719
TF: 800-844-5969

Rust College
150 E Rust Ave
Holly Springs, MS 38635
www.rustcollege.edu
Phone: 662-252-4661
Fax: 662-252-6107

Shelby State Community College
PO Box 40568
Memphis, TN 38174
Phone: 901-333-5000
Fax: 901-333-5920

State Technical Institute Memphis
5983 Macon Cove
Memphis, TN 38134
E-mail: postmaster@stim.tec.tn.us
www.stim.tec.tn.us
Phone: 901-383-4100
Fax: 901-383-4503
TF: 888-832-4937

Tri-State Baptist College
6001 Goodman Rd
Walls, MS 38680
Phone: 662-781-7777
Fax: 662-781-7777

University of Memphis
Memphis, TN 38152
www.memphis.edu
Phone: 901-678-2040
Fax: 901-678-3053
TF: 800-669-2678

University of Tennessee Memphis
800 Madison Ave
Memphis, TN 38163
www.utmem.edu
Phone: 901-448-5000
Fax: 901-448-7772

Hospitals

Baptist Memorial Hospital East Memphis
6019 Walnut Grove Rd
Memphis, TN 38120
Phone: 901-226-5000
Fax: 901-226-5618

Baptist Memorial Hospital Medical Center
899 Madison Ave
Memphis, TN 38146
Phone: 901-227-2727
Fax: 901-227-5650

Delta Medical Center
3000 Getwell Rd
Memphis, TN 38118
Phone: 901-369-8500
Fax: 901-369-8503

Le Bonheur Children's Medical Center
50 N Dunlap Ave
Memphis, TN 38103
Phone: 901-572-3000
Fax: 901-572-4586

Methodist Germantown Hospital
7691 Poplar Ave
Germantown, TN 38138
Phone: 901-754-6418
Fax: 901-757-6669

Methodist Hospital Central
1265 Union Ave
Memphis, TN 38104
www.methodisthealth.org/facilities/memphis.htm#Central
Phone: 901-726-7000
Fax: 901-726-7339

Methodist Hospital North
3960 New Covington Pike
Memphis, TN 38128
www.methodisthealth.org/facilities/memphis.htm#North
Phone: 901-384-5200
Fax: 901-384-5582

Methodist Hospital South
1300 Wesley Dr
Memphis, TN 38116
www.methodisthealth.org/facilities/memphis.htm#South
Phone: 901-346-3700
Fax: 901-346-3766

Regional Medical Center at Memphis
877 Jefferson Ave
Memphis, TN 38103
www.the-med.com
Phone: 901-545-7100
Fax: 901-545-8315

Saint Francis Hospital
5959 Park Ave
Memphis, TN 38119
www.tenethealth.com/SaintFrancis
Phone: 901-765-1000
Fax: 901-765-1799

Saint Jude Children's Research Hospital
332 N Lauderdale St
Memphis, TN 38105
www.stjude.org
Phone: 901-495-3300
Fax: 901-495-3123

University of Tennessee Bowld Hospital
951 Court Ave
Memphis, TN 38103
Phone: 901-448-4108
Fax: 901-448-4054

Veterans Affairs Medical Center
1030 Jefferson Ave
Memphis, TN 38104
Phone: 901-523-8990
Fax: 901-577-7286

Transportation

Airport(s)

Memphis International Airport (MEM)
10 miles SE of downtown (approx 20 minutes)....901-922-8000

Mass Transit

Main Street Trolley
$.50 Base fare.................................901-274-6282
MATA
$1.10 Base fare...............................901-274-6282

Rail/Bus

Greyhound Bus Station
203 Union Ave
Memphis, TN 38105
Phone: 901-523-9003
TF: 800-231-2222

Memphis Amtrak Station
545 S Main St
Memphis, TN 38103
Phone: 901-526-0052
TF: 800-872-7245

Utilities

Electricity
Memphis Light Gas & Water 901-528-4011
www.mlgw.com

Gas
Memphis Light Gas & Water 901-528-4011
www.mlgw.com

Water
Memphis Light Gas & Water 901-528-4011
www.mlgw.com

Garbage Collection/Recycling
City Beautiful Commission....................901-576-6900
Memphis Public Works Div Solid Waste Management...............................901-576-6730

Telecommunications

Telephone
BellSouth 800-766-9115
www.bellsouth.com

Cable Television
Time Warner Communications..................901-365-1770
www.timewarner.com

Internet Service Providers (ISPs)
WorldSpice Technologies Inc...................901-527-9300
www.wspice.com

Banks

Bank of America NA
200 Madison Ave
Memphis, TN 38103
Phone: 901-529-6005
Fax: 901-529-6057

First American National Bank
117 S Main St
Memphis, TN 38103
Phone: 901-684-3338

First Tennessee Bank NA
165 Madison Ave
Memphis, TN 38103
Phone: 901-523-4444
Fax: 901-523-4145
TF: 800-999-0110

National Bank of Commerce
1 Commerce Sq
Memphis, TN 38150
E-mail: nbc@wspice.com
www.nbcbank.com
Phone: 901-523-3434
Fax: 901-523-3310

Regions Bank
5384 Poplar Ave
Memphis, TN 38119
Phone: 901-766-2700
Fax: 901-766-2856
TF: 800-690-5857

SouthTrust Bank NA
6445 Poplar Ave
Memphis, TN 38119
Phone: 901-537-1320
Fax: 901-537-1334

Tri-State Bank of Memphis
180 S Main St
Memphis, TN 38103
Phone: 901-525-0384
Fax: 901-526-8608

Union Planters National Bank
6200 Poplar Ave
Memphis, TN 38122
www.unionplanters.com
Phone: 901-580-6000
Fax: 901-580-5491

Shopping

Chickasaw Oaks Plaza
3092 Poplar Ave
Memphis, TN 38111
Phone: 901-794-3022

Dillard's
4430 American Way
Memphis, TN 38118
Phone: 901-363-0063

Goldsmith's
4545 Poplar Ave
Memphis, TN 38117
Phone: 901-766-4199

Hickory Ridge Mall
6075 Winchester Rd
Memphis, TN 38115
E-mail: info@hickoryridge.com
www.hickoryridge.com
Phone: 901-795-8844
Fax: 901-363-8471

Laurelwood Shopping Center
Poplar Ave & Perkins Rd
Memphis, TN 38117
Phone: 901-794-6022

Mall of Memphis
Perkins Rd & American Way
Memphis, TN 38118
Phone: 901-362-9315

Oak Court Mall
Poplar Ave & Perkins Rd
Memphis, TN 38117
Phone: 901-682-8928
Fax: 901-763-4528

Raleigh Springs Mall
3384 Austin Peay Hwy
Memphis, TN 38128
Phone: 901-388-4300
Fax: 901-388-6970

Regalia The
Poplar Ave & Ridgeway
Memphis, TN 38119
Phone: 901-767-0100
Fax: 901-766-4299

Sanderlin Shopping Centre
5101 Sanderlin Ave
Memphis, TN 38117
Phone: 901-763-2288

Shops of Saddle Creek
Poplar Ave & Farmington/West St
Germantown, TN 38138
Phone: 901-761-7604
Fax: 901-761-5325

Southland Mall
1215 Southland Mall
Memphis, TN 38116
Phone: 901-346-1210
Fax: 901-398-3501

Whitehaven Plaza
Elvis Presley Blvd & Raines Rd
Memphis, TN 38116
Phone: 901-458-8922
Fax: 901-458-7668

Wolfchase Galleria
2760 N Germantown Pkwy
Memphis, TN 38133
E-mail: info@wolfchasegalleria.com
www.wolfchasegalleria.com
Phone: 901-381-2769
Fax: 901-388-5542

Media

Newspapers and Magazines

Commercial Appeal*
495 Union Ave
Memphis, TN 38103
www.gomemphis.com
Phone: 901-529-2345
Fax: 901-529-2522
TF: 800-444-6397

Dateline Memphis
3100 Walnut Grove Rd Suite 402
Memphis, TN 38111
www.memphisdateline.com
Phone: 901-327-8986
Fax: 901-327-6442

Memphis Business Journal
88 Union Ave Suite 102
Memphis, TN 38103
www.amcity.com/memphis
Phone: 901-523-1000
Fax: 901-526-5240

Memphis Flyer
460 Tennessee St
Memphis, TN 38103
E-mail: letters@memphisflyer.com
www.memphisflyer.com
Phone: 901-521-9000
Fax: 901-521-0129

Memphis Magazine
460 Tennessee St
Memphis, TN 38103
E-mail: memflyer@aol.com
www.memphismagazine.com
Phone: 901-521-9000
Fax: 901-521-0129

**Indicates major daily newspapers*

Television

WBUY-TV Ch 40 (TBN)
PO Box 38421
Memphis, TN 38183
Phone: 901-521-9289
Fax: 901-521-9989

WHBQ-TV Ch 13 (Fox)
485 S Highland St
Memphis, TN 38111
E-mail: news@fox13whbq.com
www.fox13whbq.com
Phone: 901-320-1313
Fax: 901-320-1366

WKNO-TV Ch 10 (PBS)
900 Getwell Rd
Memphis, TN 38111
E-mail: wknopi@wkno.org
www.wkno.org
Phone: 901-458-2521
Fax: 901-325-6505

WLMT-TV Ch 30 (UPN)
2701 Union Ave Ext
Memphis, TN 38112
www.upn30memphis.com
Phone: 901-323-2430
Fax: 901-452-1820

WMC-TV Ch 5 (NBC)
1960 Union Ave
Memphis, TN 38104
www.wmcstations.com/wmctv
Phone: 901-726-0555
Fax: 901-278-7633

WPTY-TV Ch 24 (ABC)
2701 Union Ave
Memphis, TN 38112
E-mail: newsdesk@abc24.com
www.abc24.com
Phone: 901-323-2430
Fax: 901-452-1820

WREG-TV Ch 3 (CBS)
803 Channel Three Dr
Memphis, TN 38103
E-mail: wreg@wreg.com
www.wreg.com
Phone: 901-543-2333
Fax: 901-543-2167

Radio

KJMS-FM 101.1 MHz (Urban)
112 Union Ave
Memphis, TN 38115
www.smooth101.com
Phone: 901-527-0101
Fax: 901-529-9557

KWAM-AM 990 kHz (Rel)
112 Union Ave
Memphis, TN 38103
www.am990.com
Phone: 901-527-5926
Fax: 901-527-1393

KXHT-FM 107.1 MHz (Urban)
6080 Mt Moriah Blvd
Memphis, TN 38115
www.hot107.com
Phone: 901-375-9324
Fax: 901-375-5889

WBBP-AM 1480 kHz (Rel)
250 E Raines Rd
Memphis, TN 38109
www.wbbp.org/wbbphome.htm
Phone: 901-278-7878
Fax: 901-344-0038

WCRV-AM 640 kHz (Rel)
555 Perkins Rd Ext Suite 201
Memphis, TN 38117
Phone: 901-763-4640
Fax: 901-763-4920

WDIA-AM 1070 kHz (AC)
112 Union Ave
Memphis, TN 38103
E-mail: promo@am1070wdia.com
www.am1070wdia.com
Phone: 901-529-4300
Fax: 901-529-9557

WEGR-FM 102.7 MHz (CR)
203 Beale St Suite 200
Memphis, TN 38103
www.rock103.com
Phone: 901-578-1103
Fax: 901-525-8054

WGKX-FM 105.9 MHz (Ctry)
965 Ridgelake Blvd Suite 102
Memphis, TN 38120
E-mail: news@wgkx.com
www.wgkx.com
Phone: 901-682-1106
Fax: 901-767-9531

WHBQ-AM 560 kHz (Sports)
6080 Mt Moriah Rd Ext
Memphis, TN 38115
www.sports56whbq.com
Phone: 901-375-9324
Fax: 901-795-4454

WHRK-FM 97.1 MHz (Urban)
112 Union Ave
Memphis, TN 38103
www.k97fm.com
Phone: 901-529-4397
Fax: 901-527-3455

WJCE-AM 680 kHz (Urban)
5904 Ridgeway Ctr Pkwy
Memphis, TN 38120
Phone: 901-767-0104
Fax: 901-767-0582

WKNO-FM 91.1 MHz (NPR)
900 Getwell Rd
Memphis, TN 38111
E-mail: wknofm@aol.com
www.wknofm.org
Phone: 901-325-6544
Fax: 901-325-6506

WLOK-AM 1340 kHz (Rel)
363 S 2nd St
Memphis, TN 38103
E-mail: staff@wlok.com
www.wlok.com
Phone: 901-527-9565
Fax: 901-528-0335

WMC-AM 790 kHz (N/T)
1960 Union Ave
Memphis, TN 38104
E-mail: talk@wmcstations.com
www.wmcstations.com/am790/
Phone: 901-726-0555
Fax: 901-722-5643

WMC-FM 99.7 MHz (AC)
1960 Union Ave
Memphis, TN 38104
E-mail: info@wmcstations.com
www.wmcstations.com/fm100/
Phone: 901-726-0555
Fax: 901-272-9618

WMFS-FM 92.9 MHz (Rock)
1632 Sycamore View
Memphis, TN 38134
www.wmfs.com
Phone: 901-383-9637
Fax: 901-373-1478
TF: 800-929-9637

WOGY-FM 94.1 MHz (Ctry)
5904 Ridgeway Center Pkwy
Memphis, TN 38120
E-mail: froggy94@accessus.net
www.froggy94.com
Phone: 901-683-9400
Fax: 901-682-2804

WOWW-AM 1430 kHz (Misc)
6080 Mt Moriah Rd Ext
Memphis, TN 38115
Phone: 901-375-9324
Fax: 901-375-5889

WPLX-AM 1170 kHz (B/EZ)
6655 Poplar Ave Suite 200
Germantown, TN 38138
Phone: 901-751-1513
Fax: 901-751-1501

WREC-AM 600 kHz (N/T)
203 Beale St Suite 200
Memphis, TN 38103
E-mail: comments@wrecradio.com
www.wrecradio.com
Phone: 901-578-1160
Fax: 901-525-8054

WRVR-FM 104.5 MHz (AC)
5904 Ridgeway Center Pkwy
Memphis, TN 38120
E-mail: river104@wrvr.com
www.wrvr.com
Phone: 901-767-0104
Fax: 901-767-0582

WRXQ-FM 95.7 MHz (Oldies)
203 Beale St Suite 200
Memphis, TN 38103
E-mail: wrxq96x@aol.com
www.96x.com
Phone: 901-578-1100
Fax: 901-578-1132

WSRR-FM 98.1 MHz (CR)
965 Ridgelake Blvd Suite 102
Memphis, TN 38120
www.star98memphis.com
Phone: 901-680-9898
Fax: 901-680-0482

Attractions

Memphis received its name from General James Winchester, who was inspired by the Nile-like Mississippi River to name the area for the Egyptian city of Memphis, and today the banks of the Mississippi are home to a 32-story sports/entertainment/music complex called The Pyramid. Between Riverside Drive and Danny Thomas Boulevard is Memphis' Beale Street, the "Birthplace of the Blues," where W.C. Handy first wrote Blues music of the Mississippi Delta. But Memphis is perhaps best known as the city where Elvis Presley began his musical career. Thousands of people visit his home, Graceland, each year, and the city remembers "The King" every August on the anniversary of his death with memorial celebrations.

Alex Haley House Museum
200 S Church St
Henning, TN 38041
Phone: 901-738-2240
Fax: 901-738-2585

Art Museum of the University of Memphis
3750 Norriswood Ave Communication & Fine Arts Bldg
Memphis, TN 38152
www.people.memphis.edu/~artmuseum/amhome.html
Phone: 901-678-2224
Fax: 901-678-5118

Ballet Memphis
7950 Trinity Rd
Memphis, TN 38018
www.balletmemphis.org
Phone: 901-737-7457
Fax: 901-737-7037

Beale Street Historic District
Downtown Memphis
Memphis, TN 38103
E-mail: bluesmaster@bealestreet.com
www.bealestreet.com
Phone: 901-543-5333
Fax: 901-543-5335

Burkle Estate Museum
826 N 2nd St
Memphis, TN 38107
Phone: 901-527-3427
Fax: 901-527-8784

Center for Southern Folklore
209 Beale St
Memphis, TN 38103
Phone: 901-525-3655
Fax: 901-525-3945

Children's Museum of Memphis
2525 Central Ave
Memphis, TN 38104
E-mail: children@cmom.com
www.cmom.com/
Phone: 901-458-2678
Fax: 901-458-4033

Chucalissa Indian Village
1987 Indian Village Dr
Memphis, TN 38109
www.people.memphis.edu/~chucalissa/
Phone: 901-785-3160
Fax: 901-785-0519

Circuit Playhouse
1705 Poplar Ave
Memphis, TN 38104
Phone: 901-726-4656
Fax: 901-272-7530

Clough-Hanson Gallery Rhodes College
2000 North Pkwy
Memphis, TN 38112
Phone: 901-843-3442

Cooper Young Entertainment District
892 S Cooper St
Memphis, TN 38104
E-mail: cydc@bellsouth.net
Phone: 901-272-1459
Fax: 901-272-1455

Crystal Shrine Grotto
5668 Poplar Ave Memorial Park Cemetery
Memphis, TN 38119
Phone: 901-767-8930
Fax: 901-763-2442

Davies Manor House
9336 Davies Plantation Rd
Memphis, TN 38133
Phone: 901-386-0715

Dixon Gallery & Gardens
4339 Park Ave
Memphis, TN 38117
E-mail: info@dixon.org
www.dixon.org/
Phone: 901-761-5250
Fax: 901-682-0943

Fire Museum of Memphis
118 Adams Ave
Memphis, TN 38103
E-mail: gwitt@memphisonline.com
www.firemuseum.com
Phone: 901-320-5650
Fax: 901-529-8422

Fuller State Recreation Park
1500 Mitchell Rd
Memphis, TN 38109
Phone: 901-543-7581
Fax: 901-785-8485

Germantown Performing Arts Centre
1801 Exeter Rd
Germantown, TN 38138
E-mail: info@gpacweb.com
Phone: 901-751-7500
Fax: 901-751-7514

Graceland (Elvis Presley Mansion)
3734 Elvis Presley Blvd
Memphis, TN 38116
E-mail: graceland@memphisonline.com
www.elvis-presley.com/
Phone: 901-332-3322
Fax: 901-344-3131
TF: 800-238-2000

Historic Elmwood Cemetery
824 S Dudley St
Memphis, TN 38104
Phone: 901-774-3212
Fax: 901-774-0085

Hunt-Phelan Home
533 Beale St
Memphis, TN 38103
www.hunt-phelan.com
Phone: 901-525-8225
Fax: 901-542-5042
TF: 800-350-9009

Libertyland
940 Early Maxwell Blvd
Memphis, TN 38104
E-mail: llweb@libertyland.com
www.libertyland.com
Phone: 901-274-1776
Fax: 901-274-8804

Lichterman Nature Center
1680 Lynfield Rd
Memphis, TN 38119
E-mail: more_info@memphismuseums.org
www.memphismuseums.org/nature.htm
Phone: 901-767-7322
Fax: 901-682-3050

Lindenwood Concerts
2400 Union Ave
Memphis, TN 38112
www.lroom.org
Phone: 901-458-1652
Fax: 901-458-0145

Magevney House
198 Adams Ave
Memphis, TN 38103
E-mail: more-info@memphismuseums.org
www.memphismuseums.org/magevney.htm
Phone: 901-526-4464

Main Street Trolley
547 N Main St
Memphis, TN 38105
Phone: 901-577-2640
Fax: 901-577-2660

Mallory Neely House
652 Adams Ave
Memphis, TN 38105
E-mail: more_info@memphismuseums.org
www.memphismuseums.org/mallory.htm
Phone: 901-523-1484
Fax: 901-526-8666

Martin Luther King Riverside Park
Riverside & Pkwy
Memphis, TN 38112
Phone: 901-454-5200

Mason Temple Church of God in Christ
930 Mason St
Memphis, TN 38126
Phone: 901-947-9330

Meeman Shelby State Park
910 Riddick Rd
Millington, TN 38053
Phone: 901-876-5215
Fax: 901-873-3217

Memphis Belle B-17 Bomber
125 N Front St Mud Island
Memphis, TN 38103
E-mail: belle@memphisbelle.com
www.memphisbelle.com/
Phone: 901-576-7241
TF: 800-507-6507

Memphis Botanic Garden
750 Cherry Rd
Memphis, TN 38117
Phone: 901-685-1566
Fax: 901-682-1561

Memphis Brooks Museum of Art
1934 Poplar Ave Overton Pk
Memphis, TN 38104
www.brooksmuseum.org
Phone: 901-544-6200
Fax: 901-725-4071

Memphis Music Hall of Fame
97 S 2nd St
Memphis, TN 38103
Phone: 901-525-4007
Fax: 901-525-6576

Memphis Pink Palace Museum & Planetarium
3050 Central Ave
Memphis, TN 38111
E-mail: more_info@memphismuseums.org
www.memphismuseums.org
Phone: 901-320-6320
Fax: 901-320-6391

Memphis Queen River Excursions
45 S Riverside Dr
Memphis, TN 38103
E-mail: mqueen@memphisqueen.com
www.memphisqueen.com/
Phone: 901-527-5694
Fax: 901-524-5757
TF: 800-221-6197

Memphis Symphony Orchestra
3100 Walnut Grove Rd Suite 501
Memphis, TN 38111
Phone: 901-324-3627
Fax: 901-324-3698

Memphis Transportation Museum
125 N Rowlett St
Collierville, TN 38017
Phone: 901-683-2266

Memphis Zoo & Aquarium
2000 Galloway St
Memphis, TN 38112
E-mail: jheizer@memphiszoo.org
www.memphiszoo.org
Phone: 901-726-4787
Fax: 901-725-9305

Mississippi River Museum
125 N Front St
Memphis, TN 38103
www.mudisland.com/museum.html
Phone: 901-576-7230
Fax: 901-576-6666
TF: 800-507-6507

Mud Island
125 N Front St
Memphis, TN 38103
www.mudisland.com
Phone: 901-576-7241
Fax: 901-576-6666
TF: 800-507-6507

National Civil Rights Museum
450 Mulberry St
Memphis, TN 38103
www.mecca.org/~crights
Phone: 901-521-9699
Fax: 901-521-9740

National Ornamental Metal Museum
374 Metal Museum Dr
Memphis, TN 38106
Phone: 901-774-6380
Fax: 901-774-6382

Opera Memphis
4097 S MSU B St Suite 1
Memphis, TN 38152
Phone: 901-678-2706
Fax: 901-678-3506

Orpheum Theatre
203 S Main St
Memphis, TN 38173
www.orpheum-memphis.com
Phone: 901-525-7800
Fax: 901-526-0829

Overton Park
2080 Poplar Ave
Memphis, TN 38104
Phone: 901-454-5200

Overton Square Entertainment District
Madison & Cooper Sts
Memphis, TN 38104
Phone: 901-278-6300
Fax: 901-278-0145

Playhouse on the Square
51 S Cooper St
Memphis, TN 38104
Phone: 901-726-4656
Fax: 901-272-7530

Pyramid Arena
1 Auction Ave
Memphis, TN 38105
www.pyramidarena.com
Phone: 901-521-9675
Fax: 901-528-0153

Rainbow Works
387 S Main St
Memphis, TN 38103
Phone: 901-521-0400
Fax: 901-521-8310

Saint Mary's Catholic Church & Grotto of Lourdes
155 Market St
Memphis, TN 38105
Phone: 901-522-9420

Shelby Farms
7171 Mullins Station Rd Shelby Park
Memphis, TN 38134
Phone: 901-382-4250

Sun Studio
706 Union Ave
Memphis, TN 38103
E-mail: sun@wspice.com
www.sunstudio.com/
Phone: 901-521-0664
Fax: 901-525-8055

Theatre Memphis
630 Perkins Ext
Memphis, TN 38117
www.theatrememphis.org
Phone: 901-682-8601
Fax: 901-763-4096

Union Planters IMAX Theater
3050 Central Ave Pink Palace Museum
Memphis, TN 38111
E-mail: more_info@memphismuseums.org
www.memphismuseums.org/imax.htm
Phone: 901-320-6320
Fax: 901-320-6391

WC Handy Museum
352 Beale St
Memphis, TN 38103
Phone: 901-522-1556
Fax: 901-527-8784

Wonders: The Memphis International Cultural Series
119 S Main St Suite C-180
Memphis, TN 38103
E-mail: peruinfo@wonders.org
www.wonders.org
Phone: 901-521-2644
Fax: 901-521-2647
TF: 800-263-6744

Woodruff Fontaine House
680 Adams Ave
Memphis, TN 38105
Phone: 901-526-1469
Fax: 901-526-4531

Sports Teams & Facilities

Adelphia Coliseum
1 Titans Way
Nashville, TN 37213
www.titansonline.com/adelphia
Phone: 615-565-4000

Liberty Bowl Memorial Stadium
335 S Hollywood St
Memphis, TN 38104
Phone: 901-729-4344
Fax: 901-276-2756

Memphis International Motorsports Park
5500 Taylor Forge Dr
Millington, TN 38053
Phone: 901-358-7223
Fax: 901-358-7274

Memphis Riverkings (hockey)
315 S Hollywood Bldg E
Memphis, TN 38104
www.riverkings.com
Phone: 901-278-9009
Fax: 901-274-3209
TF: 888-748-3754

Mid-South Coliseum
996 Early Maxwell Blvd
Memphis, TN 38104
www.midsouthcoliseum.com
Phone: 901-274-3982
Fax: 901-276-8653

Southland Greyhound Park
1550 Ingram Blvd
West Memphis, AR 72301
www.southlandgreyhound.com
Phone: 870-735-3670
Fax: 870-732-8335
TF: 800-467-6182

Tennessee Titans
1 Titans Way Adelphia Coliseum
Nashville, TN 37213
www.titansonline.com
Phone: 615-673-1500
Fax: 615-673-1524
TF: 888-313-8326

Annual Events

Africa in April Cultural Awareness Festival (mid-April) 901-947-2133
Arts in the Park (mid-October) 901-761-1278
Beale Street Music Festival (early May) 901-525-4611
Beale Street New Year's Eve Celebration (December 31) 901-526-0110
Carnival Memphis (early-mid-June) 901-278-0243
Choctaw Indian Cultural Festival (early August) 901-785-3160
Christmas at Graceland (late November-early January) 800-238-2000
Dr Martin Luther King Jr Celebration/Birthday (mid-late January) 901-525-2458
Ducks Unlimited Great Outdoors Festival (early June) 901-758-3711
Elvis Presley International Tribute Week (early-mid-August) 901-332-3322
First Tennessee Memphis Marathon (early December) 800-893-7223
Germantown Charity Horse Show (early June) 901-753-6441
Information Open House (early April) 901-333-4116
Irish International Street Party (March 17) 901-522-9596
Juneteenth Freedom Festival (mid-June) 901-385-4943
Kwanzaa Celebration (December) 901-521-9699
Liberty Bowl (late December) 901-795-7700
Memphis Boat Show (mid-January) 901-684-6211
Memphis Christmas Parade (early December) 901-575-0540
Memphis in May International Festival (May) 901-525-4611
Memphis Italian Festival (early June) 901-767-6949
Memphis Kemet Jubilee (early May) 901-774-1118
Memphis Music & Heritage Festival (early September) 901-525-3655
Mid-South Fair (late September-early October) 901-274-8800
Native American Days (late October) 901-785-3160
NeighborFest (late April-early May) 901-526-6627
New Year's Eve Festival (December 31) 901-526-0110
Pink Palace Crafts Fair (early October) 901-320-6320
Southern Heritage Classic (mid-September) 901-398-6655
Spring's Best Plant Sale (mid-April) 901-685-1566
Zydeco Festival (mid-February) 901-529-0999

Miami, Florida

County: Miami-Dade

MIAMI is located on the southeastern coast of Florida. Major cities within 100 miles include Key Largo, Fort Lauderdale, and West Palm Beach, Florida.

Area (Land) .... 35.6 sq mi
Area (Water).............................. 19.4 sq mi
Elevation.................................... 11 ft
Latitude ....25-83-11 N
Longitude.............................. 80-27-80 W
Time Zone ....EST
Area Code.................................... 305

Climate

Miami's subtropical climate provides mild temperatures year-round. Although cold fronts occasionally cause temperatures to dip into the 40s during the winter months, the average low temperature during the winter is around 60 degrees. Winter highs average in the mid-70s. Summers are hot and humid, with average high temperatures in the upper 80s and lows in the mid-70s. Summer is also considered the "rainy season" in Miami, with June being the wettest month.

Average Temperatures & Precipitation

Temperatures

	Jan	Feb	Mar	Apr	May	Jun	Jul	Aug	Sep	Oct	Nov	Dec
High	75	77	79	82	85	88	89	89	88	85	80	77
Low	59	60	64	68	72	75	76	76	76	72	67	62

Precipitation

	Jan	Feb	Mar	Apr	May	Jun	Jul	Aug	Sep	Oct	Nov	Dec
Inches	2.0	2.1	2.4	2.9	6.2	9.3	5.7	7.6	7.6	5.6	2.7	1.8

History

Inhabited by the Tequesta people more than 10,000 years ago, the area known today as Miami was first explored by Spaniards in the early 1500s, and South Florida remained under Spanish rule until 1821, when the United States gained control of the territory. Among the area's earliest inhabitants were Bahamians who came to South Florida in the early 1800s to reap the treasures of ships that had sunk along the Great Florida Reef. The Seminole tribe also inhabited the Miami area during the early part of the 19th Century, but they eventually retreated into the Everglades after many years of war with the non-Indian residents. The first European community was established in the Coconut Grove area of Miami in 1884 by Charles and Isabella Peacock, an English couple who opened a hotel there.

The City of Miami was established in 1896 after local resident and visionary Julia Tuttle persuaded Henry Flagler to extend his railroad south from West Palm Beach to Miami. At the time of its incorporation, Miami's population totaled 1,500. Flagler also built the Royal Palm Hotel in Miami and began running steamships between the city and Nassau, Bahamas, Key West, and Havana, Cuba. These events marked the beginning of Miami's growth as a resort area, as well as the city's reputation as the "Cruise Capital of the World."

The real estate boom of the 1920s led to a surge in the area's population as new neighborhoods were developed in the surrounding areas, Miami's population quadrupled during the early part of that decade. The latter part of the 1920s, however, brought devastation to the area in the form of a hurricane in 1926 as well as an economic depression. Even during the Depression, however, positive events were taking place in Miami—Pan American Airways began service between Miami and Latin America, and a new group of predominantly Jewish residents began building hotels along Miami Beach, which contributed to the area's economy. Those hotels have become known as the "Art Deco District" of Miami Beach, which is one of the area's leading tourist attractions. Other 20th Century events that contributed to the growth of Miami include the establishment of military training bases in the area during World War II, which brought thousands of soldiers to the area who remained in Miami after the war. In 1959, thousands of Cuban exiles fled to Miami when their homeland was taken over by dictator Fidel Castro.

Today Miami is a leading center for international business, trade, and finance. The city remains a leading tourist destination, and the Port of Miami is one of the top passenger ports in the world. In recent years, Miami's South Beach area has become a mecca for the fashion, film, and music industries and is considered one of the "trendiest" places in the nation. Rich in ethnic diversity, Miami is Florida's second largest city with a population exceeding 368,000 people, more than 65 percent of whom are Hispanic. The Greater Miami area is home to more than two million people.

Population

1990 Census 358,648
1998 Estimate.............................368,624
% Change 2.8

Racial/Ethnic Breakdown

White.................................... 65.6%
Black 27.4%
Other..................................... 7.0%
Hispanic Origin (may be of any race) 62.5%

Age Breakdown

Under 5 years.............................. 7.1%
5 to 17.................................. 15.9%
18 to 20.................................. 3.8%
21 to 24.................................. 5.5%
25 to 34................................. 16.2%
35 to 44................................. 13.2%
45 to 54................................. 10.8%

55 to 64 .... 10.8%
65 to 74 .... 9.1%
75+ years 7.5%
Median Age 36.0

Gender Breakdown
Male 48.3%
Female 51.7%

Government

Type of Government: Executive Mayor

Miami Building & Zoning Dept
Miami Riverside Ctr 444 SW 2nd Ave 4th Fl
Miami, FL 33130
Phone: 305-416-1100
Fax: 305-416-2168

Miami City Attorney
444 SW 2nd Ave 10th Fl
Miami, FL 33130
Phone: 305-416-1800
Fax: 305-416-1801

Miami City Clerk
3500 Pan American Dr
Miami, FL 33133
Phone: 305-250-5360
Fax: 305-858-1610

Miami City Hall
3500 Pan American Dr
Miami, FL 33133
Phone: 305-250-5300
Fax: 305-854-4001

Miami City Manager
444 SW 2nd Ave 10th Fl
Miami, FL 33130
Phone: 305-416-1025
Fax: 305-416-1191

Miami Community Development Dept
Miami Riverside Center 444 SW 2nd Ave 2nd Fl
Miami, FL 33130
Phone: 305-416-2080
Fax: 305-416-2090

Miami Finance Dept
444 SW 2nd Ave 6th Fl
Miami, FL 33130
Phone: 305-416-1330
Fax: 305-416-1987

Miami Fire-Rescue Dept
444 SW 2nd Ave 10th FL
Miami, FL 33130
Phone: 305-416-1600
Fax: 305-416-1680

Miami Human Resources Dept
444 SW 2nd Ave 7th Fl
Miami, FL 33130
Phone: 305-416-2100
Fax: 305-416-2115

Miami Management & Budget Dept
444 SW 2nd Ave 5th Fl
Miami, FL 33130
Phone: 305-416-1500
Fax: 305-416-2150

Miami Mayor
3500 Pan American Dr
Miami, FL 33133
Phone: 305-250-5300
Fax: 305-854-4001

Miami Parks & Recreation Dept
444 SW 2nd Ave 8th Fl
Miami, FL 33130
Phone: 305-416-1300
Fax: 305-416-2154

Miami Planning & Development Dept
444 SW 2nd Ave
Miami, FL 33130
Phone: 305-416-1400
Fax: 305-416-2156

Miami Police Dept
400 NW 2nd Ave
Miami, FL 33128
Phone: 305-579-6565
Fax: 305-372-4609

Miami Public Works Dept
444 SW 2nd Ave
Miami, FL 33130
Phone: 305-416-1200
Fax: 305-416-2153

Miami Solid Waste Dept
1290 SW 20th St
Miami, FL 33142
Phone: 305-575-5107
Fax: 305-575-5138

Important Phone Numbers

American Express Travel 305-865-5959
Driver's License Information 305-229-6333
Emergency 911
Florida Dept of Revenue 305-470-5001
HotelDocs 800-468-3537
Metro Dade Tax Collection Dept 305-270-4916
Miami-Dade Consumer Services 305-375-4222
Poison Control Center 800-282-3171
Realtor Assn of Miami 305-468-7000
Time/Temp 305-324-8811
Vehicle Registration Information 305-375-3591
Voter Registration Information 305-375-4600
Weather 305-229-4522

Information Sources

Beacon Council
80 SW 8th St Suite 2400
Miami, FL 33130
www.beaconcouncil.com
Phone: 305-579-1300
Fax: 305-375-0271

Greater Miami Chamber of Commerce
1601 Biscayne Blvd
Miami, FL 33132
www.greatermiami.com
Phone: 305-350-7700
Fax: 305-374-6902
TF: 888-660-5955

Greater Miami Convention & Visitors Bureau
701 Brickell Ave Suite 2700
Miami, FL 33131
www.miamiandbeaches.com
Phone: 305-539-3000
Fax: 305-539-3113
TF: 800-933-8448

Hialeah Chamber of Commerce & Industries
1840 W 49th St Suite 410
Hialeah, FL 33012
www.hialeahchamber.com
Phone: 305-828-9898
Fax: 305-828-9777

Hialeah City Council
501 Palm Ave 3rd Fl
Hialeah, FL 33010
www.ci.hialeah.fl.us/council
Phone: 305-883-5805
Fax: 305-883-5814

Hialeah City Hall
501 Palm Ave
Hialeah, FL 33010
www.ci.hialeah.fl.us
Phone: 305-883-5820
Fax: 305-883-5814

Hialeah Mayor
501 Palm Ave
Hialeah, FL 33010
www.ci.hialeah.fl.us/mayor
Phone: 305-883-5800
Fax: 305-883-5992

Hialeah-Dade Development Inc
501 Palm Ave
Hialeah, FL 33010
www.hddi.org
Phone: 305-884-1219
Fax: 305-884-1740

Hialeah-Miami Springs-Northwest Dade Area Chamber of Commerce
59 W 5th St
Hialeah, FL 33010
www.hialeahnwdade.com
Phone: 305-887-1515
Fax: 305-887-2453

Kennedy John F Library
190 W 49th St
Hialeah, FL 33012
www.ci.hialeah.fl.us/library
Phone: 305-821-2700
Fax: 305-818-9144

Miami Beach Chamber of Commerce
420 Lincoln Rd Ste 2D
Miami Beach, FL 33139
www.sobe.com/miamibeachchamber
Phone: 305-672-1270
Fax: 305-538-4336

Miami Beach Convention Center
1901 Convention Center Dr
Miami Beach, FL 33139
ci.miami-beach.fl.us
Phone: 305-673-7311
Fax: 305-673-7435

Miami Convention Center
400 SE 2nd Ave
Miami, FL 33131
Phone: 305-579-6341
Fax: 305-372-2919

Miami-Dade County
111 NW 1st St Suite 220
Miami, FL 33128
www.co.miami-dade.fl.us
Phone: 305-375-5124
Fax: 305-375-5569

Online Resources

4Miami.com
www.4miami.com

About.com Guide to Miami/Miami Beach
miami.about.com/citiestowns/southeastus/miami

Anthill City Guide Miami
www.anthill.com/city.asp?city=miami

Area Guide Miami
miami.areaguides.net

Bradmans.com Miami
www.bradmans.com/scripts/display_city.cgi?city=238

City Knowledge Miami
www.cityknowledge.com/fl_miami.htm

CitySearch Miami/Fort Lauderdale
miami.citysearch.com

CityTravelGuide.com Miami
www.citytravelguide.com/miami.htm

Come to the Sun Guide to South Florida
www.cometothesun.com

CuisineNet Miami
www.cuisinenet.com/restaurant/miami/index.shtml

DigitalCity South Florida
home.digitalcity.com/southflorida

Dining Guide Miami
miami.diningguide.net

Excite.com Miami City Guide
www.excite.com/travel/countries/united_states/florida/miami

Gayot's Guide Restaurant Search Miami
www.perrier.com/restaurants/gayot.asp?area=MIA

Go Miami
www.cnet1.com/gomiami/

Goodnight Miami
www.goodnight.net

HotelGuide Miami
miami.hotelguide.net

I-95 Exit Information Guide Miami
www.usastar.com/i95/cityguide/touristguide.htm

InSouthFlorida.com
www.insouthflorida.com

Lodging.com Hialeah Florida
www.lodging.com/auto/guides/hialeah-fl.html

Lodging.com Miami Florida
www.lodging.com/auto/guides/miami-area-fl.html

MetroGuide Miami
miami.metroguide.net

Miami Beach Florida
miami-beach-florida.com

Miami City Web Online
www.miamicity.com

Miami CityWomen
www.citywomen.com/miamwomen.htm

Miami Event Guide
miami.eventguide.com

Miami Gay & Lesbian Guide
www.southfloridafun.com/miami/index.shtml

Miami Metroparks
www.metro-dade.com/parks/

Miami Regional Guide
www.buybeach.com/access/miami.htm

Miami VR
www.miamivr.com/

Miami's Tiki
miamifl.metatiki.com

Miami.com
www.miami.com

Miami.TheLinks.com
miami.thelinks.com

Open World City Guides Miami
www.worldexecutive.com/cityguides/miami/

Rough Guide Travel Miami
travel.roughguides.com/content/819/

SoFla.com
www.sofla.com

Southbeach.com
www.southbeach.com/

SouthBeach.org
southbeach.org

Surf & Sun Beach Vacation Guide to Miami Beach
www.surf-sun.com/fl-miami-main.htm

Time Out Miami
www.timeout.com/miami/

Virtual Voyages Miami
www.virtualvoyages.com/usa/fl/miami/miami.sht

WeekendEvents.com Miami
www.weekendevents.com/misccity/miami/miami.html

Yahoo! Miami
miami.yahoo.com

Area Communities

Incorporated communities in the Greater Miami area with populations greater than 10,000 include:

Coral Gables Phone: 305-446-6800
405 Biltmore Way Fax: 305-460-5309
Miami, FL 33134

Hialeah Phone: 305-883-5820
501 Palm Ave Fax: 305-883-5814
Hialeah, FL 33010

Hialeah Gardens Phone: 305-558-4114
10001 NW 87th Ave Fax: 305-362-7155
Hialeah Gardens, FL 33016

Homestead Phone: 305-247-1801
790 N Homestead Blvd Fax: 305-246-2736
Homestead, FL 33030

Miami Beach Phone: 305-673-7411
1700 Convention Center Dr Fax: 305-673-7254
Miami Beach, FL 33139

Miami Shores Phone: 305-795-2207
10050 NE 2nd Ave Fax: 305-756-8972
Miami Shores, FL 33138

Miami Springs Phone: 305-885-4581
201 Westward Dr Fax: 305-885-0437
Miami Springs, FL 33166

North Miami Phone: 305-893-6511
776 NE 125th St Fax: 305-899-0497
North Miami, FL 33161

North Miami Beach Phone: 305-947-7581
17011 NE 19th Ave Fax: 305-787-6026
North Miami Beach, FL 33162

Opa-Locka Phone: 305-688-4611
777 Sharazad Blvd Fax: 305-953-2834
Opa Locka, FL 33054

South Miami Phone: 305-663-6340
6130 Sunset Dr Fax: 305-663-6348
South Miami, FL 33143

Sweetwater Phone: 305-221-0411
500 SW 109th Ave Fax: 305-221-2541
Sweetwater, FL 33174

Economy

For nearly a century, the tourism industry has helped to fuel the economy of Greater Miami, which today hosts more than eight million visitors annually. Service-related positions currently comprise approximately 30% of the total job market in Miami-Dade County. Alhough tourism remains a vital part the area's economic base, Greater Miami's economy has diversified significantly in recent decades. International finance and trade are important industries—Greater Miami is home to more than 300 multinational corporations. Government also plays an important role in Greater Miami's economy; federal and state government are Miami-Dade County's third and fourth largest employers respectively, employing more than 35,000 area residents. Local government accounts for more than 30,000 other jobs.

Unemployment Rate 5.6%*
Per Capita Income.......... $23,919*
Median Family Income.......... $42,400*

** Information given is for Miami Metropolitan Statistical Area (MSA), which includes the City of Miami and Miami-Dade County.*

Principal Industries & Number of Wage Earners

Miami-Dade County - 1998

Industry	Wage Earners
Agricultural Services, Forestry, & Fishing	11,485
Construction	33,102
Finance, Insurance, & Real Estate	65,702
Manufacturing	72,719
Mining	319
Retail Trade	170,023
Services	290,909
Transportation, Communications, & Public Utilities	84,452
Wholesale Trade	76,910

Major Employers

American Airlines Phone: 817-963-1234
PO Box 619616 Fax: 817-967-4380
DFW Airport, TX 75261
www.aacareers.com

Baptist Health Systems of South Florida Phone: 305-273-2555
6855 Red Rd Fax: 305-273-2452
Coral Gables, FL 33143
E-mail: corporatepr@baptisthealth.net
www.baptisthealth.net

BellSouth Telecommunications Inc-Florida Phone: 305-347-5300
150 W Flagler St Fax: 305-530-5324
Miami, FL 33130

Burdines
22 E Flagler St
Miami, FL 33131
www.burdinesflorida.com
Phone: 305-835-5151
Fax: 305-577-2234

Carnival Corp
3655 NW 87th Ave
Miami, FL 33178
Phone: 305-599-2600
Fax: 305-406-4700

Florida Power & Light Co
PO Box 029100
Miami, FL 33102
www.fpl.com
Phone: 305-552-3552
Fax: 800-888-1860

Jackson Memorial Hospital
1611 NW 12th Ave
Miami, FL 33136
www.um-jmh.org
Phone: 305-585-1111
Fax: 305-326-1974

K-Mart
14091 SW 88th St
Miami, FL 33186
Phone: 305-385-5970
Fax: 305-387-2499

Lennar Corp
700 NW 107th Ave Suite 400
Miami, FL 33172
www.lennar.com
Phone: 305-559-4000
Fax: 305-226-4158

MasTec Inc
3155 NW 77th Ave
Miami, FL 33122
www.mastec.com
Phone: 305-599-1800
Fax: 305-406-1960
TF: 800-444-7797

Miami City Hall
3500 Pan American Dr
Miami, FL 33133
ci.miami.fl.us
Phone: 305-250-5300
Fax: 305-854-4001

Miami-Dade County
111 NW 1st St Suite 220
Miami, FL 33128
www.co.miami-dade.fl.us
Phone: 305-375-5124
Fax: 305-375-5569

Miami-Dade County Public Schools
1450 NE 2nd Ave Rm 912
Miami, FL 33132
dcps.dade.k12.fl.us
Phone: 305-995-1430
Fax: 305-995-1488

Mount Sinai Medical Center
4300 Alton Rd
Miami Beach, FL 33140
www.mountsinaimiami.org
Phone: 305-674-2121
Fax: 305-674-2007

Publix Super Markets Inc
PO Box 407
Lakeland, FL 33802
www.publix.com
Phone: 863-688-1188
Fax: 863-284-5571

University of Miami
1252 Memorial Dr
Coral Gables, FL 33146
www.miami.edu
Phone: 305-284-4323
Fax: 305-284-2507

Winn-Dixie Stores Inc
1141 SW 12th Ave
Pompano Beach, FL 33069
E-mail: comments@winn-dixie.com
www.winn-dixie.com
Phone: 954-783-2700
Fax: 954-783-2896

Quality of Living Indicators

Total Crime Index....................44,922
(rates per 100,000 inhabitants)

Violent Crime
Murder/manslaughter.......... 86
Forcible rape 140
Robbery..........3,797
Aggravated assault..........5,482

Property Crime
Burglary 7,831
Larceny theft 20,905
Motor vehicle theft..........6,681

Cost of Living Index..........107.7
(national average = 100)

Median Home Price..........$134,600

Education

Public Schools

Miami-Dade County Public Schools
1450 NE 2nd Ave Rm 912
Miami, FL 33132
dcps.dade.k12.fl.us
Phone: 305-995-1430
Fax: 305-995-1488

Number of Schools
Elementary.......... 210
Middle 49
High.......... 47

Student/Teacher Ratio
All Grades 19.5:1

Private Schools

Number of Schools (all grades).......... 155+

Colleges & Universities

ATI Health Education Center
1395 NW 167 St Suite 200
Miami, FL 33169
E-mail: ati1@aticareertraining.com
www.aticareertraining.com
Phone: 305-628-1000
Fax: 305-628-1461
TF: 800-275-2725

Barry University
11300 NE 2nd Ave
Miami Shores, FL 33161
www.barry.edu
Phone: 305-899-3000
Fax: 305-899-2971
TF: 800-756-6000

Florida International University
11200 SW 8th St
Miami, FL 33199
www.fiu.edu
Phone: 305-348-2000
Fax: 305-348-3648

Florida Memorial College
15800 NW 42nd Ave
Miami, FL 33054
www.fmc.edu
Phone: 305-626-3600
Fax: 305-623-1462
TF: 800-822-1362

Florida National College
4162 W 12th Ave
Hialeah, FL 33012
www.florida-national.edu
Phone: 305-821-3333
Fax: 305-362-0595

International Fine Arts College
1737 N Bayshore Dr
Miami, FL 33132
www.ifac.edu
Phone: 305-373-4684
Fax: 305-374-7946
TF: 800-225-9023

Miami-Dade Community College Kendall Campus
11011 SW 104th St
Miami, FL 33176
www.kendall.mdcc.edu
Phone: 305-237-2000
Fax: 305-237-2964

Miami-Dade Community College North Campus
11380 NW 27th Ave
Miami, FL 33167
E-mail: info@mail.north.mdcc.edu
www.mdcc.edu
Phone: 305-237-1000
Fax: 305-237-8070

Miami-Dade Community College North Campus-Hialeah Branch
1776 W 49th St
Hialeah, FL 33012
Phone: 305-237-8700
Fax: 305-237-1812

National School of Technology Inc
12000 Biscayne Blvd Suite 302
North Miami, FL 33181
www.national-school-tech.edu
Phone: 305-893-0005
Fax: 305-893-9913

Saint Thomas University
16400 NW 32nd Ave
Miami, FL 33054
www.stu.edu
Phone: 305-625-6000
Fax: 305-628-6591
TF: 800-367-9010

Trinity International University South Florida Campus
500 NE 1st Ave
Miami, FL 33132
E-mail: tcmadm@tiu.edu
www.trin.edu/miami/index.html
Phone: 305-577-4600
Fax: 305-577-4612

University of Miami
1252 Memorial Dr
Coral Gables, FL 33146
www.miami.edu
Phone: 305-284-4323
Fax: 305-284-2507

Whitman Education Group Inc
4400 Biscayne Blvd
Miami, FL 33137
Phone: 305-575-6514
Fax: 305-575-6535
TF: 800-445-6108

Hospitals

Baptist Hospital of Miami
8900 N Kendall Dr
Miami, FL 33176
www.baptisthealth.net/Hospitals/HomePage/0,1024,1,00.html
Phone: 305-596-6503
Fax: 305-598-5960

Cedars Medical Center
1400 NW 12th Ave
Miami, FL 33136
www.cedarsmed.com
Phone: 305-325-5511
Fax: 305-325-5100

Coral Gables Hospital
3100 Douglas Rd
Coral Gables, FL 33134
www.tenethealth.com/CoralGables
Phone: 305-445-8461
Fax: 305-441-6879

HealthSouth Doctors' Hospital
5000 University Dr
Coral Gables, FL 33146
Phone: 305-666-2111
Fax: 305-669-2289

Hialeah Hospital
651 E 25th St
Hialeah, FL 33013
www.hialeahhosp.com
Phone: 305-693-6100
Fax: 305-835-4252

Jackson Memorial Hospital
1611 NW 12th Ave
Miami, FL 33136
www.um-jmh.org
Phone: 305-585-1111
Fax: 305-326-1974

Kendall Medical Center
11750 Bird Rd
Miami, FL 33175
Phone: 305-223-3000
Fax: 305-229-2481

Mercy Hospital
3663 S Miami Ave
Miami, FL 33133
www.mercymiami.com
Phone: 305-854-4400
Fax: 305-285-2967

Miami Children's Hospital
3100 SW 62nd Ave
Miami, FL 33155
www.mch.com
Phone: 305-666-6511
Fax: 305-665-1576

Mount Sinai Medical Center
4300 Alton Rd
Miami Beach, FL 33140
www.mountsinaimiami.org
Phone: 305-674-2121
Fax: 305-674-2007

North Shore Medical Center
1100 NW 95th St
Miami, FL 33150
www.tenethealth.com/NorthShoreMedical
Phone: 305-835-6000
Fax: 305-694-3693

Palm Springs General Hospital
1475 W 49th St
Hialeah, FL 33012
Phone: 305-558-2500
Fax: 305-558-8679

Palmetto General Hospital
2001 W 68th St
Hialeah, FL 33016
www.tenethealth.com/Palmetto
Phone: 305-823-5000
Fax: 305-364-2173

Pan American Hospital
5959 NW 7th St
Miami, FL 33126
www.pahnet.org/hospital.html
Phone: 305-264-1000
Fax: 305-265-6536

Parkway Regional Medical Center
160 NW 170th St
North Miami Beach, FL 33169
Phone: 305-654-5050
Fax: 305-654-5083

South Miami Hospital
6200 SW 73rd St
Miami, FL 33143
www.baptisthealth.net/Hospitals/HomePage/0,1024,2,00.html
Phone: 305-661-4611
Fax: 305-663-5025

South Shore Hospital & Medical Center
630 Alton Rd
Miami Beach, FL 33139
Phone: 305-672-2100
Fax: 305-534-2643

Veterans Affairs Medical Center Phone: 305-324-4455
1201 NW 16th St Fax: 305-324-3407
Miami, FL 33125

Transportation

Airport(s)

Miami International Airport (MIA)
7 miles NW of downtown (approx 20 minutes) 305-876-7515

Mass Transit

Electric Wave Shuttle
Free 305-535-9160
Metrobus
$1.25 Base fare 305-770-3131
Metromover
$.25 Base fare 305-770-3131
Metrorail
$1.25 Base fare 305-770-3131
Tri-Rail
fare varies with destination 800-874-7245

Rail/Bus

Amtrak Station Phone: 305-835-1222
8303 NW 37th Ave Miami Station TF: 800-872-7245
Miami, FL 33147

Greyhound Bus Station Phone: 305-379-7403
700 Biscayne Blvd TF: 800-231-2222
Miami, FL 33132

Utilities

Electricity
Florida Power & Light 305-442-8770
www.fpl.com

Gas
City Gas Co of Florida 305-691-8710
Peoples Gas 305-944-1933
www.peoplesgas.com

Water
Miami-Dade Water & Sewer 305-665-7471
www.co.miami-dade.fl.us/wasd

Garbage Collection/Recycling
Miami Recycling Program 305-365-0978
Miami Solid Waste Dept 305-575-5107

Telecommunications

Telephone
BellSouth Telecommunications Inc 800-753-0710
www.bellsouth.com

Cable Television
Miami-Dade County Cable Communications Licensing Div 305-375-3677

Internet Service Providers (ISPs)
Internet Providers of Florida 305-273-7978
www.fla.net
Netpoint Communications Inc 305-891-1955
www.netpoint.net
Netrox Inc 305-374-3031
www.netrox.net
Netrus 305-717-3221
www.netrus.net
Shadow Information Services 305-594-3450
www.shadow.net

Banks

Bank of America NA Phone: 305-350-6350
1 SE 3rd Ave TF: 800-299-2265
Miami, FL 33131

BankAtlantic FSB Phone: 305-374-1776
2 S Biscayne Blvd Fax: 305-381-9671
Miami, FL 33131

Citibank FSB Phone: 800-374-9800
120 S Biscayne Blvd Fax: 305-530-3250
Miami, FL 33131

Colonial Bank Phone: 305-669-7440
7545 N Kendall Dr Fax: 305-662-6634
Miami, FL 33156

First Union National Bank Phone: 305-789-4710
200 S Biscayne Blvd Fax: 305-789-4700
Miami, FL 33131 TF: 800-275-3862

Hamilton Bank NA Phone: 305-717-5500
3750 NW 87th Ave Fax: 305-717-5560
Miami, FL 33178

Mellon United National Bank Phone: 305-358-4334
1399 SW 1st Ave Fax: 305-381-6320
Miami, FL 33130

Ocean Bank Phone: 305-442-2660
780 NW 42nd Ave Fax: 305-444-8153
Miami, FL 33126
www.oceanbank.com

Peoples Bank of Commerce Phone: 305-696-0700
3275 NW 79th St Fax: 305-835-7345
Miami, FL 33147

SunTrust Bank Miami NA Phone: 305-591-6000
777 Brickell Ave Fax: 305-577-5028
Miami, FL 33131

Union Planters Bank NA Phone: 305-536-1550
1221 Brickell Ave Fax: 305-374-0409
Miami, FL 33131

Washington Mutual Bank FA Phone: 305-220-6876
8700 SW Coral Way Fax: 305-220-6886
Miami, FL 33165

Shopping

Aventura Mall Phone: 305-935-1110
19501 Biscayne Blvd Fax: 305-935-9360
Aventura, FL 33180
www.shopaventuramall.com

Bal Harbour Shops Phone: 305-866-0311
9700 Collins Ave Fax: 305-866-5235
Bal Harbour, FL 33154
www.balharbourshops.com

Bayside Marketplace
401 Biscayne Blvd
Miami, FL 33132
E-mail: info@baysidemarketplace.com
www.baysidemarketplace.com
Phone: 305-577-3344
Fax: 305-577-0306

CocoWalk
3015 Grand Ave Suite 118
Coconut Grove, FL 33133
E-mail: comments@cocowalk.com
www.cocowalk.com
Phone: 305-444-0777
Fax: 305-441-8936

Cutler Ridge Mall
20505 S Dixie Hwy
Miami, FL 33189
Phone: 305-235-8562
Fax: 305-235-7956

Dadeland Mall
7535 N Kendall Dr
Miami, FL 33156
Phone: 305-665-6226
Fax: 305-665-5012

Downtown Miami Shopping District
Biscayne Blvd to 3rd Ave & SE 1st to NE 3rd Sts
Miami, FL 33131
Phone: 305-379-7070
Fax: 305-379-7222

Falls The Shopping Center
US Hwy 1 & 136th St
Miami, FL 33176
www.thefallsshoppingcenter.com
Phone: 305-255-4570

Mall at 163rd Street
1421 NE 163rd St
Miami, FL 33162
Phone: 305-944-7132
Fax: 305-947-1429

Mall of the Americas
7795 W Flagler St
Miami, FL 33144
Phone: 305-261-8772
Fax: 305-262-4060

Miami International Mall
1455 NW 107th Ave
Miami, FL 33172
Phone: 305-593-1775
Fax: 305-591-4210

Omni International Mall
1601 Biscayne Blvd
Miami, FL 33132
Phone: 305-374-6664
Fax: 305-374-6118

Opa Locka Hialeah Flea Market
12705 NW 42nd Ave
Opa Locka, FL 33054
Phone: 305-688-0500
Fax: 305-687-8312

Palm Springs Mile
555 Palm Springs Mile
Hialeah, FL 33012
Phone: 305-821-7111

Streets of Mayfair
2911 Grand Ave Suite 2A
Coconut Grove, FL 33133
www.streetsofmayfair.com
Phone: 305-448-1700
Fax: 305-448-1641

Westland Mall
1675 W 49th St
Hialeah, FL 33012
Phone: 305-823-9310

Media

Newspapers and Magazines

Daily Business Review
1 SE 3rd Ave Suite 900
Miami, FL 33131
www.floridabiz.com
Phone: 305-347-6672
Fax: 305-347-6678
TF: 800-777-7300

Diario Las Americas*
2900 NW 39th St
Miami, FL 33142
www.diariolasamericas.com
Phone: 305-633-3341
Fax: 305-635-7668
TF: 800-327-4210

El Nuevo Herald*
1 Herald Plaza
Miami, FL 33132
E-mail: digit@elherald.com
www.elherald.com
Phone: 305-376-3535
Fax: 305-376-2378

El Sol de Hialeah
436 Palm Ave
Hialeah, FL 33010
www.elsoldehialeah.com
Phone: 305-885-5111
Fax: 305-887-8324

Kendall News Gazette
6796 SW 62nd Ave
South Miami, FL 33143
Phone: 305-669-7355
Fax: 305-661-0954

La Voz de La Calle
4696 E 10th Ct
Hialeah, FL 33013
Phone: 305-687-5555
Fax: 305-681-0500

Miami Herald*
1 Herald Plaza
Miami, FL 33132
E-mail: nationalnews@herald.com
www.herald.com
Phone: 305-350-2111
Fax: 305-376-5287

Miami Metro Magazine
2800 Biscayne Blvd 11th Fl
Miami, FL 33137
E-mail: miametro@bellsouth.net
miamimetro.com
Phone: 305-755-9920
Fax: 305-755-9921
TF: 800-288-8388

Miami New Times
2800 Biscayne Blvd Suite 100
Miami, FL 33137
E-mail: editorial@miami-newtimes.com
www.miaminewtimes.com
Phone: 305-576-8000
Fax: 305-571-7676

Miami Today
PO Box 1368
Miami, FL 33101
Phone: 305-358-2663
Fax: 305-358-4811

Ocean Drive Magazine
404 Washington Ave Suite 650
Miami Beach, FL 33139
www.oceandrive.com
Phone: 305-532-2544
Fax: 305-532-4366

South Florida Business Journal
4000 Hollywood Blvd Suite 695 South
Hollywood, FL 33021
www.amcity.com/southflorida
Phone: 954-359-2100
Fax: 954-359-2135

**Indicates major daily newspapers*

Television

WAMI-TV Ch 69 (USA)
605 Lincoln Rd 2nd Fl
Miami Beach, FL 33139
E-mail: wami@miamiusa.com
Phone: 305-373-6900
Fax: 305-604-0406

WBFS-TV Ch 33 (UPN)
16550 NW 52nd Ave
Miami, FL 33014
www.paramountstations.com/WBFS
Phone: 305-621-3333
Fax: 305-628-3448

WBZL-TV Ch 39 (WB)
2055 Lee St
Hollywood, FL 33020
E-mail: wb39@expressweb.com
www.wb39.com
Phone: 954-925-3939
Fax: 954-922-3965

WFOR-TV Ch 4 (CBS)
8900 NW 18th Terr
Miami, FL 33172
E-mail: news4@wfor.groupw.wec.com
wfor.cbsnow.com
Phone: 305-591-4444
Fax: 305-477-3040

WLRN-TV Ch 17 (PBS)
172 NE 15th St
Miami, FL 33132
E-mail: info@wlrn.org
wlrn.org/tv
Phone: 305-995-1717
Fax: 305-995-2299

WLTV-TV Ch 23 (Uni)
9405 NW 41st St
Miami, FL 33178
www.univision.net/stations/wltv.htm
Phone: 305-470-2323
Fax: 305-471-4236

WPBT-TV Ch 2 (PBS)
14901 NE 20th Ave
Miami, FL 33181
www.channel2.org
Phone: 305-949-8321
Fax: 305-949-9772

WPLG-TV Ch 10 (ABC)
3900 Biscayne Blvd
Miami, FL 33137
www.wplg.com/
Phone: 305-576-1010
Fax: 305-325-2480

WPXM-TV Ch 35 (PAX)
11900 Biscayne Blvd Suite 760
Miami, FL 33181
www.pax.net/wpxm
Phone: 305-895-1835
Fax: 305-895-7935

WSCV-TV Ch 51 (Tele)
2340 W 8th Ave
Hialeah, FL 33010
E-mail: info@wscv.com
www.wscv.com
Phone: 305-888-5151
Fax: 305-889-7651
TF: 800-688-8851

WSVN-TV Ch 7 (Fox)
1401 79th St Cswy
Miami, FL 33141
E-mail: 7news@wsvn.com
www.wsvn.com
Phone: 305-751-6692
Fax: 305-757-2266

WTVJ-TV Ch 6 (NBC)
15000 SW 27 St
Miramar, FL 33027
www.nbc6.nbc.com
Phone: 954-622-6000
Fax: 954-622-6107

WWFD-TV Ch 8 (Ind)
16502 NW 52nd Ave
Miami, FL 33014
Phone: 305-621-3688
Fax: 305-621-5181

Radio

WAMR-FM 107.5 MHz (Span)
2828 Coral Way Suite 102
Miami, FL 33145
E-mail: comentarios@wamr.com
www.wamr.com
Phone: 305-447-1140
Fax: 305-643-1075

WAQI-AM 710 kHz (N/T)
2828 Coral Way
Miami, FL 33145
E-mail: info@waqi.com
www.waqi.com/
Phone: 305-445-4020
Fax: 305-443-3601

WAVS-AM 1170 kHz (Span)
6360 SW 41st Pl
Davie, FL 33314
Phone: 954-584-1170
TF: 888-854-9660

WAXY-AM 790 kHz (N/T)
20450 NW 2nd Ave
Miami, FL 33169
www.waxy.com
Phone: 305-653-8811
Fax: 305-652-5385

WBGG-FM 105.9 MHz (CR)
194 NW 187th St
Miami, FL 33169
E-mail: big106@big106fm.com
www.big106fm.com
Phone: 305-654-9494
Fax: 305-654-9090

WCMQ-FM 92.3 MHz (Span)
1001 Ponce de Leon Blvd
Coral Gables, FL 33134
Phone: 305-444-9292
Fax: 305-461-4951

WDNA-FM 88.9 MHz (Nost)
4848 SW 74th Ct
Miami, FL 33155
www.wdna.org
Phone: 305-662-8889
Fax: 305-662-1975

WEDR-FM 99.1 MHz (Urban)
3790 NW 167th St
Miami, FL 33055
www.wedrfm.com
Phone: 305-623-7711
Fax: 305-624-2736

WFLC-FM 97.3 MHz (AC)
2741 N 29th Ave
Hollywood, FL 33020
www.coastfm.com
Phone: 954-584-7117
Fax: 954-847-3223

WHQT-FM 105.1 MHz (Urban)
2741 N 29th Ave
Hollywood, FL 33020
www.hot105fm.com
Phone: 954-584-7117
Fax: 954-847-3223

WHYI-FM 100.7 MHz (CHR)
1975 E Sunrise Blvd Suite 400
Fort Lauderdale, FL 33304
www.y-100.com
Phone: 954-463-9299
Fax: 954-522-7002

WINZ-AM 940 kHz (N/T)
194 NW 187th St
Miami, FL 33169
www.supertalk940.com
Phone: 305-654-9494
Fax: 305-654-9090

WIOD-AM 610 kHz (N/T)
194 NW 187th St
Miami, FL 33169
E-mail: wiod610@ix.netcom.com
www.wiod.com
Phone: 305-654-9494
Fax: 305-690-9090

WKIS-FM 99.9 MHz (Ctry)
9881 Sheridan St
Hollywood, FL 33024
E-mail: wkis@sefl.satelnet.org
www.wkis.com
Phone: 954-431-6200
Fax: 954-437-2466

WLQY-AM 1320 kHz (Misc)
11645 Biscayne Blvd Suite 102-B
North Miami, FL 33181
Phone: 305-891-1729
Fax: 305-891-1583

WLRN-FM 91.3 MHz (NPR)
172 NE 15th St
Miami, FL 33132
E-mail: radio@wlrn.org
www.wlrn.org/radio-fm
Phone: 305-995-1717
Fax: 305-995-2299

WLVE-FM 93.9 MHz (NAC)
194 NW 187th St
Miami, FL 33169
www.love94.com
Phone: 305-654-9494
Fax: 305-654-9090
TF: 800-603-9494

WLYF-FM 101.5 MHz (AC)
20450 NW 2nd Ave
Miami, FL 33169
www.wlyf.com
Phone: 305-653-8811
Fax: 305-652-5385
TF: 877-790-1015

WMBM-AM 1490 kHz (Rel)
814 1st St
Miami Beach, FL 33139
E-mail: wmbm@wmbm.com
www.wmbm.com
Phone: 305-672-1100
Fax: 305-673-1194

WMGE-FM 103.5 MHz (AC)
1975 E Sunrise Blvd Suite 400
Fort Lauderdale, FL 33304
www.megamiami.com
Phone: 954-463-9299
Fax: 954-462-5839

WMXJ-FM 102.7 MHz (Oldies)
20450 NW 2nd Ave
Miami, FL 33169
E-mail: majic@gate.net
www.wmxj.com
Phone: 305-651-1027
Fax: 305-652-1888

WPOW-FM 96.5 MHz (CHR)
20295 NW 2nd Ave
Miami, FL 33169
www.power96.com
Phone: 305-653-6796
Fax: 305-770-1456

WQAM-AM 560 kHz (Sports)
20295 NW 2nd Ave
Miami, FL 33169
wqam.com
Phone: 305-653-6796
Fax: 305-770-1456

WQBA-AM 1140 kHz (N/T)
2828 Coral Way Suite 102
Miami, FL 33145
E-mail: info@wqba.com
www.wqba.com
Phone: 305-447-1140
Fax: 305-441-2454

WRMA-FM 106.7 MHz (Span)
1001 Ponce de Leon Blvd
Coral Gables, FL 33134
Phone: 305-444-9292
Fax: 305-461-0987

WRTO-FM 98.3 MHz (Span)
2828 Coral Way Suite 102
Miami, FL 33145
E-mail: info@wrto.com
www.wrto.com
Phone: 305-447-1140
Fax: 305-445-8908

WSUA-AM 1260 kHz (Span)
2100 Coral Way
Miami, FL 33145
Phone: 305-285-1260
Fax: 305-858-5907

WTMI-FM 93.1 MHz (Clas)
3225 Aviation Ave
Miami, FL 33133
E-mail: wtmi@safari.net
www.wtmi.com
Phone: 305-856-9393
Fax: 305-854-0783

WWFE-AM 670 kHz (Span)
330 SW 27th Ave Suite 207
Miami, FL 33135
www.lapoderosa.com
Phone: 305-541-3300
Fax: 305-541-7470

WXDJ-FM 95.7 MHz (Span)
1001 Ponce de Leon Blvd
Coral Gables, FL 33134
www.elzol95fm.com
Phone: 305-447-9595
Fax: 305-461-4466

WZTA-FM 94.9 MHz (Rock)
194 NW 187th St
Miami, FL 33169
www.949zeta.com
Phone: 305-654-9494
Fax: 305-654-9090

Attractions

One of the unique city neighborhoods that make up Miami is Little Havana, with Cuban cuisine and coffees and Calle Ocho, one of the largest Hispanic festivals in the nation. The city's Little Haiti area offers authentic Creole food and a Caribbean Marketplace, while Coconut Grove is home to CocoWalk, a stretch of open air stores, cafes, and bars, and the Coconut Grove Arts Festival, one of the country's largest outdoor art shows. Across Biscayne Bay is Miami's sister city, Miami Beach, a resort area recognized for its Art Deco District. Designated as a National Historic District, the old art deco buildings have been restored to their neon and pastel colors. Overlooking the bay is Miami Beach's Bayside, a 16-acre complex with shops, entertainment, and restaurants. Hialeah, a suburb northwest of Miami, is home to the Hialeah Park race track, which is known as "one of the world's most beautiful race tracks" and is listed on the National Register of Historic Places. The racetrack has won a number of awards for its architecture, historical significance, and aesthetic appeal.

American Police Hall of Fame & Museum
3801 Biscayne Blvd
Miami, FL 33137
E-mail: policeinfo@aphf.org
www.aphf.org
Phone: 305-573-0070
Fax: 305-573-9819

Ancient Spanish Monastery
16711 W Dixie Hwy
North Miami Beach, FL 33160
Phone: 305-945-1462
Fax: 305-945-6986

Art Center South Florida
924 Lincoln Rd Suite 205
Miami Beach, FL 33139
Phone: 305-674-8278
Fax: 305-674-8772

Art Museum at Florida International University
SW 8th St & 107th Ave University Pk PC110
Miami, FL 33199
www.fiu.edu/museum.html
Phone: 305-348-2890
Fax: 305-348-2762

Atrium Gallery
16400 NW 32nd Ave Saint Thomas University
Miami, FL 33054
Phone: 305-628-6660
Fax: 305-628-6703

Barnacle State Historic Site
3485 Main Hwy
Coconut Grove, FL 33133
E-mail: barnacle@gate.net
www.gate.net/~barnacle
Phone: 305-448-9445
Fax: 305-448-7484

Bass Museum of Art
2121 Park Ave
Miami Beach, FL 33139
ci.miami-beach.fl.us/newcity/culture/bass.html
Phone: 305-673-7530
Fax: 305-673-7062

Bayside Marketplace
401 Biscayne Blvd
Miami, FL 33132
E-mail: info@baysidemarketplace.com
www.baysidemarketplace.com
Phone: 305-577-3344
Fax: 305-577-0306

Biscayne National Park
9700 SW 328th St
Homestead, FL 33033
www.nps.gov/bisc/
Phone: 305-230-1144
Fax: 305-230-1190

Biscayne Nature Center
4000 Crandon Blvd
Key Biscayne, FL 33149
Phone: 305-642-9600
Fax: 305-642-5050

Caleb Joseph Auditorium
5400 NW 22nd Ave
Miami, FL 33142
Phone: 305-636-2350
Fax: 305-638-5625

Cape Florida State Recreation Area
1200 S Crandon Blvd
Key Biscayne, FL 33149
Phone: 305-361-5811
Fax: 305-365-0003

Coconut Grove Playhouse
3500 Main Hwy
Coconut Grove, FL 33133
www.cgplayhouse.com/
Phone: 305-442-4000
Fax: 305-443-6369

CocoWalk
3015 Grand Ave Suite 118
Coconut Grove, FL 33133
E-mail: comments@cocowalk.com
www.cocowalk.com
Phone: 305-444-0777
Fax: 305-441-8936

Coral Castle
28655 S Dixie Hwy
Homestead, FL 33030
www.coralcastle.com
Phone: 305-248-6344
Fax: 305-248-6344

Crandon Park
4000 Crandon Blvd
Key Biscayne, FL 33149
Phone: 305-361-5421

Dry Tortugas National Park
40001 SR-9336 Everglades National Park
Homestead, FL 33034
www.nps.gov/drto/
Phone: 305-242-7700
Fax: 305-242-7728

Eden of the Everglades
903 Dupont Rd
Everglades City, FL 34139
Phone: 941-695-2800
Fax: 941-695-4506
TF: 800-543-3367

Everglades Alligator Farm
40351 SW 192nd Ave
Homestead, FL 33090
E-mail: gatorfarmr@aol.com
www.everglades.com
Phone: 305-247-2628
Fax: 305-248-9711

Everglades National Park
40001 SR-9336
Homestead, FL 33034
www.nps.gov/ever/home.htm
Phone: 305-242-7700
Fax: 305-242-7711

Everglades Safari Park
26700 Tamiami Trail
Miami, FL 33194
Phone: 305-226-6923
Fax: 305-554-5666

Fairchild Tropical Garden
10901 Old Cutler Rd
Miami, FL 33156
www.ftg.org
Phone: 305-667-1651
Fax: 305-661-8953

Florida Grand Opera
1200 Coral Way
Miami, FL 33145
www.fgo.org
Phone: 305-854-1643
Fax: 305-856-1042
TF: 800-741-1010

Florida Pioneer Museum
826 N Krome Ave
Florida City, FL 33034
Phone: 305-246-9531

Fruit & Spice Park
24801 SW 187th Ave
Homestead, FL 33031
E-mail: fsp@co.miami-dade.fl.us
Phone: 305-247-5727
Fax: 305-245-3369

GableStage
1200 Anastasia Ave Biltmore Hotel
Coral Gables, FL 33134
Phone: 305-445-1119
Fax: 305-445-8645

Gator Park
24050 SW 8th St
Miami, FL 33184
www.gatorpark.com
Phone: 305-559-2255
TF: 800-559-2205

Gold Coast Railroad Museum
12450 SW 152nd St
Miami, FL 33177
www.goldcoast-railroad.org
Phone: 305-253-0063
Fax: 305-233-4641

Greynolds Park
17530 W Dixie Hwy
North Miami Beach, FL 33160
Phone: 305-945-3425
Fax: 305-945-3428

Gusman Center for the Performing Arts
174 E Flagler St
Miami, FL 33131
Phone: 305-374-2444
Fax: 305-374-0303

Historical Museum of Southern Florida
101 W Flagler St
Miami, FL 33130
E-mail: hasf@ix.netcom.com
www.historical-museum.org/
Phone: 305-375-1492
Fax: 305-375-1609

Holocaust Memorial
1933-1945 Meridian Ave
Miami Beach, FL 33139
Phone: 305-538-1663
Fax: 305-538-2423

Ichimura Miami Japan Garden
Watson Island & MacArthur Cswy
Miami Beach, FL 33139
Phone: 305-858-5016
Fax: 305-860-3922

IGFA Fishing Hall of Fame & Museum
300 Gulf Stream Way
Dania Beach, FL 33004
Phone: 954-927-2628
Fax: 954-924-4299

IMAX Theatre at Sunset Place
5701 Sunset Dr Suite 134
South Miami, FL 33143
www.imax.com/miami
Phone: 305-663-4629
Fax: 305-740-0611

Jackie Gleason Theater of the Performing Arts
1700 Washington Ave
Miami Beach, FL 33139
www.gleasontheater.com
Phone: 305-673-7300
Fax: 305-538-6810

James L Knight International Center
400 SE Second Ave
Miami, FL 33131
Phone: 305-372-4634
Fax: 305-372-2919

John Pennekamp Coral Reef State Park
Mile Marker 102.5
Key Largo, FL 33037
www.dep.state.fl.us/parks/District_5/JohnPennekamp
Phone: 305-451-1202

Latin American Art Museum
4006 Aurora St
Coral Gables, FL 33146
E-mail: hispmuseum@aol.com
www.latinoweb.com/museo
Phone: 305-444-7060
Fax: 305-261-6996

Lincoln Theatre
541 Lincoln Rd
Miami Beach, FL 33139
Phone: 305-673-3330
Fax: 305-673-6749

Lowe Art Museum University of Miami
1301 Stanford Dr
Coral Gables, FL 33124
www.lowemuseum.org
Phone: 305-284-3535
Fax: 305-284-2024

Malibu Grand Prix
7775 NW 8th St
Miami, FL 33126
Phone: 305-266-2100
Fax: 305-262-2251

Merrick House
907 Coral Way
Coral Gables, FL 33134
Phone: 305-460-5361
Fax: 305-443-8820

Miami Art Museum
101 W Flagler St
Miami, FL 33130
www.miamiartmuseum.org
Phone: 305-375-3000
Fax: 305-375-1725

Miami Brewing Co
9292 NW 101st St
Miami, FL 33178
E-mail: reef@shadow.net
www.hurricanereef.com
Phone: 305-888-6505
Fax: 305-888-8868

Miami Chamber Symphony
1314 Miller Dr Gusman Concert Hall
Coral Gables, FL 33146
Phone: 305-858-3500
Fax: 305-857-5001

Miami Children's Museum
701 Arena Blvd
Miami, FL 33143
www.mcmuseum.org
Phone: 305-373-5439
Fax: 305-373-5431

Miami City Ballet
2200 Liberty Ave
Miami Beach, FL 33139
www.miamicityballet.org
Phone: 305-929-7000

Miami Metrozoo
12400 SW 152nd St
Miami, FL 33177
www.metro-dade.com/parks/metrozoo.htm
Phone: 305-251-0400
Fax: 305-378-6381

Miami Museum of Science
3280 S Miami Ave
Miami, FL 33129
www.miamisci.org
Phone: 305-646-4200
Fax: 305-646-4300

Miami Seaquarium
4400 Rickenbacker Cswy
Miami, FL 33149
www.miamiseaquarium.com
Phone: 305-361-5705
Fax: 305-361-6077

Miccosukee Indian Village & Airboat Tours
PO Box 440021
Miami, FL 33144
www.miccosukeetribe.com
Phone: 305-223-8380
Fax: 305-223-1011

Monkey Jungle
14805 SW 216th St
Miami, FL 33170
www.monkeyjungle.com
Phone: 305-235-1611

Museum of Contemporary Art
770 NE 125th St
North Miami, FL 33161
www.mocanomi.com
Phone: 305-893-6211
Fax: 305-891-1472

National Historic District
1001 Ocean Dr
Miami Beach, FL 33139
Phone: 305-672-2014
Fax: 305-672-4319

New World Symphony
541 Lincoln Rd
Miami Beach, FL 33139
E-mail: email@nws.org
www.nws.org
Phone: 305-673-3330
Fax: 305-673-6749
TF: 800-597-3331

North Miami Beach Performing Arts Theater
17011 NE 19th Ave
North Miami Beach, FL 33162
Phone: 305-948-2990
Fax: 305-787-6040

Oleta River State Recreation Area
3400 NE 163rd St
North Miami Beach, FL 33160
Phone: 305-919-1846
Fax: 305-919-1845

Parrot Jungle & Gardens
11000 SW 57th Ave
Miami, FL 33156
E-mail: parrots@parrotjungle.com
parrotjungle.com
Phone: 305-666-7834
Fax: 305-661-2230

Space Transit Planetarium
3280 S Miami Ave
Miami, FL 33129
E-mail: bdishong@miamisci.org
www.miamisci.org
Phone: 305-854-4242
Fax: 305-854-2239

Stardancer Casino
Pier B Miami Beach Marina
Miami Beach, FL 33139
Phone: 305-538-8300
Fax: 305-538-2909

Venetian Pool
2701 DeSoto Blvd
Coral Gables, FL 33134
www.venetianpool.com
Phone: 305-460-5356
Fax: 305-460-5357

Vizcaya Museum & Gardens
3251 S Miami Ave
Miami, FL 33129
Phone: 305-250-9133
Fax: 305-285-2004

Weeks Air Museum
14710 SW 128th St Tamiami Airport
Miami, FL 33196
www.weeksairmuseum.com
Phone: 305-233-5197
Fax: 305-232-4134

Wolfsonian Museum
1001 Washington Ave
Miami Beach, FL 33139
Phone: 305-531-1001
Fax: 305-531-2133

Ziff Jewish Museum of Florida
301 Washington Ave
Miami Beach, FL 33139
E-mail: jmofmosaic@aol.com
www.jewishmuseum.com
Phone: 305-672-5044
Fax: 305-672-5933

Sports Teams & Facilities

American Airlines Arena
1 SE 3rd Ave Suite 2300
Miami, FL 33131
www.aaarena.com
Phone: 786-577-4328
Fax: 786-777-1607

Calder Race Course Inc
21001 NW 27th Ave
Miami, FL 33056
E-mail: marketing@calderracecourse.com
www.calderracecourse.com
Phone: 305-625-1311
Fax: 305-620-2569
TF: 800-333-3227

Flagler Greyhound Track
401 NW 38th Ct
Miami, FL 33126
E-mail: generalinfo@flaglerdogs.com
www.flaglerdogs.com
Phone: 305-649-3000
Fax: 305-631-4525

Florida Panthers
2555 Panther Pkwy National Car Rental Center
Sunrise, FL 33323
E-mail: flpanthers@flpanthers.com
www.flpanthers.com
Phone: 954-835-7000
Fax: 954-835-8012

Gulfstream Park
901 S Federal Hwy
Hallandale, FL 33009
www.gulfstreampark.com
Phone: 954-454-7000
Fax: 954-454-7827

Hialeah Park Race Course
2200 E 4th Ave
Hialeah, FL 33011
www.hialeahpark.com
Phone: 305-885-8000
Fax: 305-887-8006

Hialeah Speedway
3300 W Okeechobee Rd
Hialeah, FL 33012
Phone: 305-821-6644
Fax: 305-556-9858

Miami Arena
721 NW 1st Ave
Miami, FL 33136
www.miamiarena.com
Phone: 305-530-4400
Fax: 305-530-4429

Miami Breakers (soccer)
Alton Rd & 12th Ave Flamingo Pk
Miami Beach, FL 33138
Phone: 305-532-5080
Fax: 305-532-0508

Miami Dolphins
2269 NW 199th St Pro Player Stadium
Miami, FL 33056
www.miamidolphins.com
Phone: 305-620-2578

Miami Fusion (soccer)
2200 Commercial Blvd Suite 104
Fort Lauderdale, FL 33309
www.miamifusion.com
Phone: 954-739-2501
Fax: 954-733-6105

Miami Heat
1 SE 3rd Ave American Airlines Arena Suite 2300
Miami, FL 33131
www.nba.com/heat
Phone: 305-577-4328
Fax: 305-789-5933

Miami Jai-Alai
3500 NW 37th Ave
Miami, FL 33142
E-mail: miajaili@netrunner.net
www.fla-gaming.com/miami
Phone: 305-633-6400
Fax: 305-633-4386

Miami Tango (soccer)
10651 NW 19th St
Miami, FL 33172
Phone: 305-593-6033
Fax: 305-594-3973

Orange Bowl Stadium
1501 NW 3rd St
Miami, FL 33125
Phone: 305-643-7100
Fax: 305-643-7115

Pro Player Stadium
2269 NW 199th St
Miami, FL 33056
www.proplayer.com
Phone: 305-623-6100
Fax: 305-624-6403

Annual Events

4th of July at Bayfront Park (July 4) 305-358-7550
Arabian Nights Festival (early May)................305-688-4611
Art Deco Weekend Festival (mid-January)..........305-672-2014
Art Expo (early January) 305-558-1758
Banyan Arts & Crafts Festival (mid-November).....305-444-7270
Beaux Arts Festival of the Arts (mid-January)......305-284-3535
Big Orange New Year's Eve Celebration (December 31)...............................305-358-7550
Bob Marley Festival (mid-February) 305-358-7550
Calle Ocho Festival (early March) 305-644-8888
Caribbean Festival (mid-October)..................305-653-1877
Carnaval Miami (early March).....................305-644-8888
Coconut Grove Arts Festival (mid-February)........305-447-0401
Colombian Festival (mid-July) 305-358-8858
Columbus Day Regatta (mid-October)..............305-858-3320
Dade Heritage Days (mid-March-mid-May) 305-358-9572
Dade Radio Tropical Hamboree Show (early February).............................305-642-4139
Doral-Ryder Open (late February-early March)......305-477-4653
Earth Day Festival (early May)....................305-372-6798
Ericsson Open (late March-early April).............305-442-3367
February Home Show (early February).............305-579-3311
Festival Miami (mid-September-late October).......305-284-4940
Flamingo Stakes (early April).....................305-885-8000
Florida Dance Festival (mid-late June).............800-252-0808
Florida Derby (mid-March) 305-931-7223
Grand Prix of Miami (late March) 305-230-7223
Great Sunrise Balloon Race & Festival (early May) 305-275-3317
Greater Miami Race for the Cure (mid-October).....305-666-7223
Hialeah Spring Festival (late February-early March).....................305-828-9898
Hispanic Heritage Festival (October)...............305-541-5023

Hispanic Heritage Month (October)................305-687-2671
Holiday Country Craft Show (late November).......305-821-1130
Homestead Championship Rodeo
(early February)..............................305-247-3515
International Hispanic Theatre Festival
(early-mid-June)..............................305-445-8877
International Mango Festival (mid-July)............305-667-1651
Italian Renaissance Festival (mid-March) 305-250-9133
Key Biscayne 4th of July Parade & Fireworks
(July 4) 305-365-8901
Key Biscayne Art Festival (late January) 305-365-0120
King Mango Strut (December 26) 305-445-1865
King Orange Jamboree Parade (December 31) 305-371-4600
Kwanzaa Celebration (December 8)................305-380-6233
La Settimana del Cinema Italiano (mid-January) 305-861-2000
Martin Luther King Jr Parade & Festival
(January).....................................305-835-2464
Metropolitan South Florida Fishing Tournament
(December-mid-May)...........................305-569-0066
Miami Beach Festival of the Arts
(early February)..............................305-672-1272
Miami Billfish Tournament (early April) 305-598-2525
Miami Book Fair International (mid-November).....305-237-3258
Miami Film Festival (late February) 305-377-3456
Miami International Boat Show (mid-February).....305-531-8410
Miami International Map Fair (early February)......305-375-1492
Miami International Orchid Show (early March) 305-444-8484
Miami Reggae Festival (mid-October).............305-891-2944
Miami-Dade County Fair & Exposition
(mid-March-early April) 305-223-7060
Miami/Bahamas Goombay Festival (early June) 305-372-9966
Miccosukee Tribe's Indian Arts Festival
(late December-early January)...................305-223-8380
National Children's Theatre Festival
(mid-January).................................305-444-9293
Ocean Drive Street Festival (mid-January) 305-672-2014
Orange Bowl (early January)......................305-371-4600
Original Miami Beach Antique Show
(late January-early February)...................305-754-4931
Outdoor Festival of the Arts (early February).......305-673-7577
Redlands Natural Arts Festival (mid-January).......305-247-5727
Roots & Culture Festival (late May) 305-756-5627
Saint Stephen's Arts & Crafts Show
(mid-February)...............................305-558-1758
Santa's Enchanted Forest
(late November-early January) 305-893-0090
South Beach Film Festival (late April)............305-532-1233
South Florida International Auto Show
(early-mid-November)..........................305-947-5950
South Miami Art Festival (early November) 305-661-1621
Spring Plant Sale (late April) 305-667-1651
Springtime Harvest Festival (late April)...........305-375-1492
Subtropics Music Festival (mid-March-mid-May)....305-867-3752
Taste of the Beach (late October) 305-672-1270
Taste of the Grove (late January)..................305-444-7270
Tropical Agricultural Fiesta (mid-July).............305-248-3311
West Indian Carnival Extravaganza
(mid-October).................................305-539-3034
Widener Handicap (late March)....................305-885-8000

Milwaukee, Wisconsin

***County:* Milwaukee**

MILWAUKEE is located at the confluence of the Kinnikinic, Menomonee, and Milwaukee Rivers in southeastern Wisconsin on the western shore of Lake Michigan. Major cities within 100 miles include Green Bay and Madison, Wisconsin; and Chicago, Illinois.

Area (Land) .... 96.0 sq mi
Area (Water)............................... 0.8 sq mi
Elevation.................................... 634 ft
Latitude ....43-03-89 N
Longitude.............................. 87-90-64 W
Time Zone ....CST
Area Code...................................... 414

Climate

Milwaukee's climate is influenced by its proximity to Lake Michigan, which helps moderate temperatures year-round. Winters are cold—daytime high temperatures average below freezing in the upper 20s and low 30s, with lows in the teens. The average annual snowfall in Milwaukee is 47 inches. Summer days are warm, with average highs in the low 80s, and evening temperatures cool down to around 60 degrees. April, July, and August are the wettest months in Milwaukee; February is the driest.

Average Temperatures & Precipitation

Temperatures

	Jan	Feb	Mar	Apr	May	Jun	Jul	Aug	Sep	Oct	Nov	Dec
High	27	32	43	57	70	80	84	82	74	61	47	33
Low	12	16	27	37	47	57	63	61	54	43	32	19

Precipitation

	Jan	Feb	Mar	Apr	May	Jun	Jul	Aug	Sep	Oct	Nov	Dec
Inches	1.6	1.5	2.7	3.5	2.8	3.2	3.5	3.5	3.4	2.4	2.5	2.3

History

The name "Milwaukee" is derived from the Native American phrase meaning "where the waters meet." This name was given to the present-day city of Milwaukee by Native Americans who originally inhabited the area because of its location at the confluence of the Kinnikinic, Menomonee, and Milwaukee Rivers. Jesuit missionary Father Jacques Marquette was among the first whites to explore the area in 1674, and in the years that followed, fur trappers arrived to utilize the area's natural resources. The first white settlement in the Milwaukee area was established in 1818 by Solomon Juneau. Although Native Americans remained in the region for several years, their disagreement with the European idea of land ownership eventually led to the Blackhawk War of 1832. The white settlers were victorious, and many of Milwaukee's Native American inhabitants were driven from the area.

In 1846, Juneau's community joined with two other neighboring communities to form the city of Milwaukee. Industry developed quickly in the city, facilitated by the arrival of the railroad in 1851. Economic opportunities drew large numbers of European immigrants, including Irish, Czechs, Dutch, Austrians, Norwegians, Britons, and later, Poles and Italians, to the city, but the largest number of immigrants, by far, came from Germany. By 1850, one-third of the city's population was German, and Milwaukee was often referred to as the "German Athens of America" and, by the end of the 19th Century, the "second Berlin." Although the city's first brewery was actually established by Welshmen, the German's were instrumental in developing the industry for which Milwaukee has become famous.

By the turn of the century, Milwaukee's population had skyrocketed from less than 20,000 in 1850 to more than 285,000. Industry flourished during the early 1900s, drawing African-Americans from the South and Hispanics from Mexico seeking economic opportunities in the city's factories. After a lag in growth and development during the Great Depression, new wartime industries that emerged in Milwaukee during World War II caused another surge in population during the 1940s and '50s. With the opening of the Saint Lawrence Seaway in 1959, the city became a major international seaport. The recession of the 1970s and early '80s led to a decline in Milwaukee's economy and, consequently, its population, but in recent years, Milwaukee has worked toward rebuilding its economy by diversifying its economic base. With a population of more than 578,000, Milwaukee is presently Wisconsin's largest city.

Population

1990 Census 628,088
1998 Estimate..............................578,364
% Change .... -7.9
2005 Projection 662,144

Racial/Ethnic Breakdown

White.................................... 63.4%
Black 30.5%
Other...................................... 6.1%
Hispanic Origin (may be of any race) 6.3%

Age Breakdown

Under 5 years............................. 8.6%
5 to 17.................................. 18.8%
18 to 20................................... 5.1%
21 to 24................................... 7.1%
25 to 34................................. 19.0%
35 to 44................................. 13.4%
45 to 54................................... 7.9%
55 to 64................................... 7.7%
65 to 74................................... 6.8%
75+ years 5.6%
Median Age.................................30.3

Gender Breakdown
Male....47.3%
Female....52.7%

Government

Type of Government: Mayor-Common Council

Milwaukee Administration Dept
200 E Wells St Rm 606
Milwaukee, WI 53202
Phone: 414-286-3508
Fax: 414-286-8547

Milwaukee City Attorney
200 E Wells St Rm 800
Milwaukee, WI 53202
Phone: 414-286-2601
Fax: 414-286-8550

Milwaukee City Clerk
200 E Wells St Rm 205
Milwaukee, WI 53202
Phone: 414-286-2221
Fax: 414-286-3456

Milwaukee City Development Dept
809 N Broadway
Milwaukee, WI 53202
Phone: 414-286-5900
Fax: 414-286-5507

Milwaukee City Hall
200 E Wells St
Milwaukee, WI 53202
Phone: 414-286-2150
Fax: 414-286-3245

Milwaukee City Treasurer
200 E Wells St Rm 103
Milwaukee, WI 53202
Phone: 414-286-2240
Fax: 414-286-3186

Milwaukee Common Council
200 E Wells St
Milwaukee, WI 53202
Phone: 414-286-2221
Fax: 414-286-3456

Milwaukee Economic Development Div
809 N Broadway
Milwaukee, WI 53202
Phone: 414-286-5840
Fax: 414-286-5778

Milwaukee Fire Dept
711 W Wells St
Milwaukee, WI 53233
Phone: 414-286-8948
Fax: 414-286-8996

Milwaukee Mayor
200 E Wells St City Hall Rm 201
Milwaukee, WI 53202
Phone: 414-286-2200
Fax: 414-286-3191

Milwaukee Neighborhood Services Dept
814 W Wisconsin Ave
Milwaukee, WI 53233
Phone: 414-286-3441
Fax: 414-286-8667

Milwaukee Police Dept
951 N James Lovel St
Milwaukee, WI 53233
Phone: 414-933-4444
Fax: 414-935-7120

Milwaukee Public Library
814 W Wisconsin Ave
Milwaukee, WI 53233
Phone: 414-286-3000
Fax: 414-286-2137

Milwaukee Public Works Dept
841 N Broadway Rm 516
Milwaukee, WI 53202
Phone: 414-286-3300
Fax: 414-286-8110

Milwaukee Water Works
841 N Broadway Rm 402
Milwaukee, WI 53202
Phone: 414-286-2870
Fax: 414-286-8723

Important Phone Numbers

AAA....262-796-8960
American Express Travel....414-332-3157
Dental Referral....800-503-3682
Driver's License Information....414-266-1000
Emergency....911
Greater Milwaukee Events....800-554-1448
HotelDocs....800-468-3537
Medical Referral....262-544-2745
Metropolitan Assn of Realtors....414-778-4929
Milwaukee Assessor....414-286-3651
Milwaukee County Treasurer....414-278-4045
Poison Control Center....414-266-2222
Time....414-844-1414
Travelers Aid....414-449-4777
Vehicle Registration Information....414-266-1000
Voter Registration Information....414-286-8683
Weather....414-936-1212
Wisconsin Dept of Revenue....414-227-4000

Information Sources

Better Business Bureau Serving Wisconsin
PO Box 2190
Milwaukee, WI 53201
www.wisconsin.bbb.org
Phone: 414-273-1600
Fax: 414-224-0881

Greater Milwaukee Convention & Visitors Bureau
510 W Kilbourn Ave
Milwaukee, WI 53203
www.milwaukee.org
Phone: 414-273-3950
Fax: 414-273-5596
TF: 800-231-0903

Metropolitan Milwaukee Assn of Commerce
756 N Milwaukee St
Milwaukee, WI 53202
www.mmac.org
Phone: 414-287-4100
Fax: 414-271-7753

Midwest Express Center
400 W Wisconsin Ave
Milwaukee, WI 53203
www.wcd.org/site/home/fac/mid_exp_cen/main.html
Phone: 414-908-6000
Fax: 414-908-6010

Milwaukee County
901 N 9th St
Milwaukee, WI 53233
www.co.milwaukee.wi.us
Phone: 414-278-4067

Online Resources

4Milwaukee.com
www.2milwaukee.com

About.com Guide to Milwaukee
milwaukee.about.com/local/midwestus/milwaukee

Boulevards Milwaukee
www.milwaukee.com

City Knowledge Milwaukee
www.cityknowledge.com/wi_milwaukee.htm

DigitalCity Milwaukee
home.digitalcity.com/milwaukee

Discover Milwaukee
www.discovermilwaukee.com

Excite.com Milwaukee City Guide
www.excite.com/travel/countries/united_states/wisconsin/milwaukee

Explore Milwaukee
www.exploremilwaukee.com

Lodging.com Milwaukee Wisconsin
www.lodging.com/auto/guides/milwaukee-area-wi.html

Milwaukee Footlights Performing Arts Guide
www.footlights.com

Milwaukee Home Page
www.execpc.com/~trilux

Milwaukee.TheLinks.com
milwaukee.thelinks.com

Rough Guide Travel Milwaukee
travel.roughguides.com/content/526/

Area Communities

Communities with populations greater than 10,000 in the Greater Milwaukee area (Kenosha, Milwaukee, Ozaukee, Racine, Walworth, Washington, and Waukesha counties) include:

Brookfield
645 N Janacek Rd
Brookfield, WI 53045
Phone: 262-796-3788
Fax: 262-796-0339

Brown Deer
4800 W Green Brook Dr
Brown Deer, WI 53223
Phone: 414-371-3000
Fax: 414-371-3045

Caledonia
6922 Nicholson Rd
Caledonia, WI 53108
Phone: 262-835-4451
Fax: 262-835-2388

Cedarburg
PO Box 49
Cedarburg, WI 53012
Phone: 262-375-7600
Fax: 262-375-7906

Cudahy
5050 S Lake Dr
Cudahy, WI 53110
Phone: 414-769-2204
Fax: 414-769-2257

Franklin
9229 W Loomis Rd
Franklin, WI 53132
Phone: 414-425-7500
Fax: 414-425-6428

Germantown
PO Box 337
Germantown, WI 53022
Phone: 262-250-4740
Fax: 262-253-8255

Glendale
5909 N Milwaukee River Pkwy
Glendale, WI 53209
Phone: 414-228-1718
Fax: 414-228-1724

Grafton
PO Box 125
Grafton, WI 53024
Phone: 262-375-5300
Fax: 262-375-5304

Greendale
6500 Northway
Greendale, WI 53129
Phone: 414-423-2100
Fax: 414-423-2107

Greenfield
7325 W Forest Home Ave
Greenfield, WI 53220
Phone: 414-543-5500
Fax: 414-543-0591

Kenosha
625 52nd St
Kenosha, WI 53140
Phone: 262-653-4000
Fax: 262-653-4010

Menomonee Falls
W156 N8480 Pilgrim Rd
Menomonee Falls, WI 53051
Phone: 262-255-8300
Fax: 262-532-4219

Mequon
11333 N Cedarburg Rd
Mequon, WI 53092
Phone: 262-242-3100
Fax: 262-242-9655

Mount Pleasant
6126 Durand Ave
Racine, WI 53406
Phone: 262-554-8750
Fax: 262-554-6785

Muskego
PO Box 749
Muskego, WI 53150
Phone: 262-679-4100
Fax: 262-679-4106

New Berlin
3805 S Casper Dr
New Berlin, WI 53151
Phone: 262-786-8610
Fax: 262-786-6121

Oak Creek
8640 S Howell Ave
Oak Creek, WI 53154
Phone: 414-768-6500
Fax: 414-768-9587

Oconomowoc
W359 N6812 Brown St
Oconomowoc, WI 53066
Phone: 262-567-0251
Fax: 262-567-0252

Pewaukee
W 240 N 3065 Pewaukee Rd
Pewaukee, WI 53072
Phone: 262-691-0770
Fax: 262-691-1798

Pleasant Prairie
9915 39th Ave
Pleasant Prairie, WI 53158
Phone: 262-694-1400
Fax: 262-694-4734

Port Washington
100 W Grand Ave
Port Washington, WI 53074
Phone: 262-284-5585
Fax: 262-284-7224

Racine
730 Washington Ave
Racine, WI 53403
Phone: 262-636-9101
Fax: 262-636-9570

Shorewood
3930 N Murray Ave
Shorewood, WI 53211
Phone: 414-963-6990
Fax: 414-963-6909

South Milwaukee
2424 15th Ave
South Milwaukee, WI 53172
Phone: 414-762-2222
Fax: 414-762-3272

Waukesha
201 Delafield St
Waukesha, WI 53188
Phone: 262-524-3500
Fax: 262-524-3888

Wauwatosa
7725 W North Ave
Wauwatosa, WI 53213
Phone: 414-471-8400
Fax: 414-479-8989

West Allis
7525 W Greenfield Ave
West Allis, WI 53214
Phone: 414-302-8200
Fax: 414-302-8321

West Bend
1115 S Main St
West Bend, WI 53095
Phone: 262-335-5100
Fax: 262-335-5164

Whitefish Bay
5300 N Marlborough Dr
Whitefish Bay, WI 53217
Phone: 414-962-6690
Fax: 414-962-5651

Whitewater
PO Box 178
Whitewater, WI 53190
Phone: 262-473-0500
Fax: 262-473-0509

Economy

With an increasingly diverse economic base that ranges from dairy products to high-tech electronic equipment, Milwaukee is a leading U.S. industrial, commercial, and transportation center. Major U.S. corporations that have their headquarters in Milwaukee include Northwestern Mutual Life Insurance Company, Manpower Temporary Services, Briggs & Stratton, Harley Davidson, Johnson Controls, Quad Graphics, and Miller Brewing Company. Long known as the "Beer Capital of the World," Milwaukee remains one of the world's leading producers of malt beverages; however, the city's economy is no longer dominated by the brewing industry, which today accounts for only one percent of the area's total workforce. Although manufacturing continues to play an important role in Milwaukee's economy, services has become the area's largest employment sector—accounting for more than 30 percent of Greater Milwaukee's total workforce, with many of these jobs in the health care field.

Unemployment Rate 2.9%*
Per Capita Income..........................$25,535*
Median Family Income......................$28,292

** Information given is for Milwaukee County.*

Principal Industries & Number of Wage Earners

Milwaukee-Waukesha MSA* - 1999

Industry	Wage Earners
Construction & Mining	33,700
Finance, Insurance, & Real Estate	58,800
Government	90,700
Manufacturing	174,400
Retail Trade	135,900
Services	279,900
Transportation & Public Utilities	40,400
Wholesale Trade	49,800

** Information given is for the Milwaukee-Waukesha Metropolitan Statistical Area (MSA), which includes Milwaukee, Ozaukee, Washington, and Waukesha counties.*

Major Employers

Ameritech Wisconsin
722 N Broadway
Milwaukee, WI 53202
Phone: 262-549-7102

Aurora Health Care Inc
3000 W Montana St
Milwaukee, WI 53234
www.aurorahealthcare.com
Phone: 414-647-3000
Fax: 414-647-3494

Briggs & Stratton Corp
PO Box 702
Milwaukee, WI 53201
www.briggsandstratton.com
Phone: 414-259-5333
Fax: 414-259-9594
TF: 800-444-7774

Covenant Health Care Systems
PO Box 14970 1126 S 70th St
Milwaukee, WI 53214
Phone: 414-456-2300
Fax: 414-456-2363

Firstar Corp
777 E Wisconsin Ave
Milwaukee, WI 53202
www.firstar.com
Phone: 414-765-4321
Fax: 414-765-5677
TF: 800-236-6777

Horizon Healthcare Corp
2300 N Mayfair Rd Suite 550
Milwaukee, WI 53226
www.horizonhealth.com
Phone: 414-257-3888
Fax: 414-257-3433

Journal Communications Inc
333 W State St
Milwaukee, WI 53203
www.jc.com
Phone: 414-224-2000
Fax: 414-224-2469
TF: 800-456-5943

Kohl's Corp
N 56 West 17000 Ridgewood Dr
Menomonee Falls, WI 53051
www.kohls.com
Phone: 262-703-7000
Fax: 262-703-6373
TF: 800-837-6644

Marshall & Ilsley Corp
770 N Water St
Milwaukee, WI 53202
www.micorp.com
Phone: 414-765-7801
Fax: 414-765-7899

Milwaukee City Hall
200 E Wells St
Milwaukee, WI 53202
www.ci.mil.wi.us
Phone: 414-286-2150
Fax: 414-286-3245

Milwaukee County
901 N 9th St
Milwaukee, WI 53233
www.co.milwaukee.wi.us
Phone: 414-278-4067

Milwaukee Public Schools
5225 W Vliet St
Milwaukee, WI 53208
E-mail: justta@mail.milwaukee.k12.wi.us
www.milwaukee.k12.wi.us
Phone: 414-475-8393
Fax: 414-475-8722

Quad/Graphics Inc
N63 W23075 Hwy 74
Sussex, WI 53089
E-mail: qgraphics@qgraph.com
www.quadgraphics.com
Phone: 414-566-6000
Fax: 414-246-5123

Rockwell Automation
PO Box 2086
Milwaukee, WI 53201
E-mail: rsprovan@abpost.remnet.ab.com
www.ab.com
Phone: 414-671-2000
Fax: 414-382-4444

Quality of Living Indicators

Total Crime Index....................................46,058
(rates per 100,000 inhabitants)

Violent Crime
Murder/manslaughter.......................... 124
Forcible rape 269
Robbery.....................................3,134
Aggravated assault...........................2,531

Property Crime
Burglary 6,462
Larceny theft 26,124
Motor vehicle theft..........................7,414

Cost of Living Index...................................105.4
(national average = 100)

Median Home Price................................$135,300

Education

Public Schools

Milwaukee Public Schools
5225 W Vliet St
Milwaukee, WI 53208
E-mail: justta@mail.milwaukee.k12.wi.us
www.milwaukee.k12.wi.us
Phone: 414-475-8393
Fax: 414-475-8722

Number of Schools
Elementary................................ 105
Middle 23
High.. 21
K-8... 11
K-12.. 1

Student/Teacher Ratio
All Grades 17.3:1

Private Schools

Number of Schools (all grades).................. 150+

Colleges & Universities

Alverno College
3400 S 43rd St
Milwaukee, WI 53234
E-mail: alvadmsh@execpc.com
www.alverno.edu
Phone: 414-382-6100
Fax: 414-382-6354
TF: 800-933-3401

Bryant & Stratton Career College
1300 N Jackson St
Milwaukee, WI 53202
www.bryantstratton.edu/main/campusdesc/mil.htm
Phone: 414-276-5200
Fax: 414-276-3930

Cardinal Stritch University
6801 N Yates Rd
Milwaukee, WI 53217
www.stritch.edu
Phone: 414-410-4000
Fax: 414-410-4239
TF: 800-347-8822

Carroll College
100 N East Ave
Waukesha, WI 53186
www.cc.edu
Phone: 262-547-1211
Fax: 262-524-7139
TF: 800-227-7655

Carthage College
2001 Alford Pk Dr
Kenosha, WI 53140
www.carthage.edu
Phone: 262-551-8500
Fax: 262-551-5762
TF: 800-351-4058

Columbia College of Nursing
2121 E Newport Ave
Milwaukee, WI 53211
www.ccon.edu
Phone: 414-961-3530
Fax: 414-961-4121

Concordia University Wisconsin
12800 N Lake Shore Dr
Mequon, WI 53097
www.cuw.edu
Phone: 262-243-5700
Fax: 262-243-4545

ITT Technical Institute
6300 W Layton Ave
Greenfield, WI 53220
www.itt-tech.edu
Phone: 414-282-9494
Fax: 414-282-9698

Marquette University
1442 W Wisconsin Ave
Milwaukee, WI 53233
www.mu.edu
Phone: 414-288-7700
Fax: 414-288-3764

Milwaukee Area Technical College
700 W State St
Milwaukee, WI 53233
www.milwaukee.tec.wi.us
Phone: 414-297-6600
Fax: 414-297-7990

Milwaukee Institute of Art & Design
273 E Erie St
Milwaukee, WI 53202
www.miad.edu
Phone: 414-276-7889
Fax: 414-291-8077
TF: 888-749-6423

Milwaukee School of Engineering
1025 N Broadway St
Milwaukee, WI 53202
E-mail: explore@msoe.edu
www.msoe.edu
Phone: 414-277-7300
Fax: 414-277-7475
TF: 800-332-6763

Mount Mary College
2900 N Menomonee River Pkwy
Milwaukee, WI 53222
E-mail: mktg@mtmary.edu
www.mtmary.edu
Phone: 414-258-4810
Fax: 414-256-0180
TF: 800-321-6265

University of Wisconsin Colleges Waukesha County
1500 University Dr
Waukesha, WI 53188
E-mail: uwwak@uwc.edu
www.uwc.edu/waukesha/
Phone: 262-521-5210
Fax: 262-521-5491

University of Wisconsin Milwaukee
PO Box 749
Milwaukee, WI 53201
E-mail: dgm@bfs.uwm.edu
www.uwm.edu
Phone: 414-229-1122
Fax: 414-229-6940

Wisconsin Lutheran College
8800 W Bluemound Rd
Milwaukee, WI 53226
E-mail: admissions@wlc.edu
www.wlc.edu
Phone: 414-443-8800
Fax: 414-443-8514
TF: 888-947-5884

Hospitals

All Saints Health Care Phone: 262-636-4011
3801 Spring St Fax: 262-631-8039
Racine, WI 53405
www.all-saints.com

Children's Hospital of Wisconsin Phone: 414-266-2000
PO Box 1997 Fax: 414-266-2179
Milwaukee, WI 53201
www.chw.org

Columbia Hospital Phone: 414-961-3300
2025 E Newport Ave Fax: 414-961-8712
Milwaukee, WI 53211
www.columbia-stmarys.com/html/columbia.shtml

Community Memorial Hospital Phone: 262-251-1000
PO Box 408 Fax: 262-253-7169
Menomonee Falls, WI 53052
www.communitymemorial.com

Elmbrook Memorial Hospital Phone: 262-785-2000
19333 W North Ave Fax: 262-785-2444
Brookfield, WI 53045
www.covhealth.org/affiliat/elmbr.html

Froedtert Memorial Lutheran Hospital Phone: 414-259-3000
9200 W Wisconsin Ave Fax: 414-259-8910
Milwaukee, WI 53226
www.froedtert.com

Kenosha Hospital & Medical Center Phone: 262-656-2011
6308 8th Ave Fax: 262-656-2124
Kenosha, WI 53143

Lakeland Medical Center Phone: 262-741-2000
W3985 County Rd NN Fax: 262-741-2759
Elkhorn, WI 53121
www.aurorahealthcare.org/facilities/sites/0008/0008.htm

Memorial Hospital Phone: 262-763-2411
252 McHenry St Fax: 262-763-0309
Burlington, WI 53105

Memorial Hospital of Oconomowoc Phone: 262-569-9400
791 Summit Ave Fax: 262-569-0545
Oconomowoc, WI 53066

Northwest General Hospital Phone: 414-447-8543
5310 W Capitol Dr Fax: 414-447-8589
Milwaukee, WI 53216

Saint Francis Hospital Phone: 414-647-5000
3237 S 16th St Fax: 414-647-5565
Milwaukee, WI 53215
www.covhealth.org/affiliat/sfh.html

Saint Joseph's Community Hospital Phone: 262-334-5533
551 S Silverbrook Dr Fax: 262-334-8575
West Bend, WI 53095

Saint Joseph's Hospital Phone: 414-447-2000
5000 W Chambers St Fax: 414-447-2768
Milwaukee, WI 53210
www.covhealth.org/affiliat/sjh.html

Saint Luke's Hospital Phone: 262-636-2011
1320 Wisconsin Ave Fax: 262-636-2494
Racine, WI 53403

Saint Luke's Medical Center Phone: 414-649-6000
2900 W Oklahoma Ave Fax: 414-649-5562
Milwaukee, WI 53215
www.aurorahealthcare.org/facilities/sites/0001/0001.htm

Saint Luke's South Hospital Phone: 414-769-9000
5900 S Lake Dr Fax: 414-489-4171
Cudahy, WI 53110

Saint Mary's Hospital Phone: 414-291-1000
2323 N Lake Dr Fax: 414-291-1208
Milwaukee, WI 53211
www.columbia-stmarys.com/html/stmarysmil.shtml

Saint Mary's Hospital Ozaukee Phone: 262-243-7300
1311 N Port Washington Rd Fax: 262-243-7331
Mequon, WI 53097
www.columbia-stmarys.com/html/stmarysoz.shtml

Saint Michael Hospital Phone: 414-527-8000
2400 W Villard Ave Fax: 414-527-8461
Milwaukee, WI 53209
www.covhealth.org/affiliat/smh.html

Sinai Samaritan Medical Center Phone: 414-219-2000
945 N 12th St Fax: 414-219-6735
Milwaukee, WI 53201 TF: 888-414-7762
www.aurorahealthcare.org/facilities/sites/0012/0012.htm

Veterans Affairs Medical Center Phone: 414-384-2000
5000 W National Ave Fax: 414-382-5319
Milwaukee, WI 53295 TF: 888-469-6614

Waukesha Memorial Hospital Phone: 262-928-1000
725 American Ave Fax: 262-928-4995
Waukesha, WI 53188 TF: 800-326-2011

West Allis Memorial Hospital Phone: 414-328-6000
8901 W Lincoln Ave Fax: 414-328-8515
West Allis, WI 53227
www.aurorahealthcare.org/facilities/sites/0006/0006.htm

Transportation

Airport(s)

General Mitchell International Airport (MKE)
11 miles S of downtown (approx 15 minutes) 414-747-5300

Mass Transit

Milwaukee County Transit System
$1.35 Base fare. 414-344-4550

Rail/Bus

Greyhound Bus Station Phone: 414-272-2259
606 N James Lovell St TF: 800-231-2222
Milwaukee, WI 53233

Milwaukee Amtrak Station Phone: 414-271-0840
433 W St Paul Ave TF: 800-872-7245
Milwaukee, WI 53203

Utilities

Electricity
Wisconsin Electric 414-221-2949
www.wisconsinelectric.com

Gas
Wisconsin Electric 414-221-2949
www.wisconsinelectric.com
Wisconsin Gas Co 414-385-7000
www.wisconsingas.co

Water
Milwaukee Water Works 414-286-2830

Garbage Collection/Recycling
Milwaukee Sanitation 414-286-3341

Telecommunications

Telephone
Ameritech 800-924-1000
www.ameritech.com

Cable Television
Time Warner Cable 414-771-8400
www.timewarnerwi.com

Internet Service Providers (ISPs)
AcroNet Professional Internet Services Inc 262-697-2220
www.acronet.net
ExecPC Internet 262-789-4200
home.execpc.com
Internet Dynamics Corp 262-473-7700
www.idcnet.net
Mix Communications 414-319-4200
www.mixcom.com

Banks

Bank One Wisconsin
111 E Wisconsin Ave
Milwaukee, WI 53202
Phone: 414-765-3000
Fax: 414-765-0553
TF: 800-947-1111

Firstar Bank Milwaukee NA
777 E Wisconsin Ave
Milwaukee, WI 53202
Phone: 414-765-4321
Fax: 414-287-3439

M & I Marshall & Ilsley Bank
770 N Water St
Milwaukee, WI 53202
E-mail: mibank@mibank.com
www.miweb.com
Phone: 414-765-7700
Fax: 414-765-7436

Mutual Savings Bank
4949 W Brown Deer Rd
Milwaukee, WI 53223
Phone: 414-354-1500
Fax: 414-362-6196
TF: 800-261-6888

North Shore Bank FSB
4414 N Oakland Ave
Milwaukee, WI 53211
Phone: 414-964-6710
Fax: 414-332-4295

Norwest Bank Wisconsin NA
100 E Wisconsin Ave
Milwaukee, WI 53202
Phone: 414-224-3775
Fax: 414-224-3790

Tri-City National Bank
7213 N Teutonia Ave
Milwaukee, WI 53209
Phone: 414-351-7280
Fax: 414-351-2859

US Bank NA
201 W Wisconsin Ave
Milwaukee, WI 53259
Phone: 414-227-6000
Fax: 414-227-5979

Shopping

Bayshore Mall
5900 N Port Washington Rd
Milwaukee, WI 53217
Phone: 414-332-8136

Boston Store
331 W Wisconsin Ave
Milwaukee, WI 53203
Phone: 414-347-4141
Fax: 414-347-5337

East Town
770 N Jefferson St
Milwaukee, WI 53202
www.easttown.com
Phone: 414-271-1416
Fax: 414-271-6401

Grand Avenue Mall
275 W Wisconsin Ave
Milwaukee, WI 53203
Phone: 414-224-0384
Fax: 414-224-0849

Historic Third Ward
219 N Milwaukee St 3rd Fl
Milwaukee, WI 53202
www.milwaukee-htw.org
Phone: 414-273-1173
Fax: 414-273-2205

Mayfair Mall
2500 N Mayfair Rd
Milwaukee, WI 53226
Phone: 414-771-1300

Northridge Mall
7700 W Brown Deer Rd
Milwaukee, WI 53223
Phone: 414-354-2900
Fax: 414-354-0951

Northridge Shopping Center
7700 W Brown Deer Rd
Milwaukee, WI 53223
Phone: 414-354-1804
Fax: 414-354-0951

Old World Third Street
Wisconsin Ave & 3rd St
Milwaukee, WI 53203
Phone: 414-273-3950

Regency Mall
5538 Durand Ave
Racine, WI 53406
E-mail: regencymall@rejacobsgroup.com
www.shopyourmall.com/mall_welcome.asp?map=yes&mall_select=625
Phone: 262-554-7979
Fax: 262-554-7477

Southridge Mall
5300 S 76th St
Greendale, WI 53129
Phone: 414-421-1102
Fax: 414-421-0492

Media

Newspapers and Magazines

Bulletin The
715-58th St Lower Level
Kenosha, WI 53140
Phone: 262-656-1101
Fax: 262-657-8455
TF: 800-846-1101

Business Journal of Milwaukee
600 W Virginia St Suite 500
Milwaukee, WI 53204
www.bizjournals.com/milwaukee
Phone: 414-278-7788
Fax: 414-278-7028

Exclusively Yours Magazine
740 N Plankinton Ave Suite 500
Milwaukee, WI 53203
Phone: 414-271-4270
Fax: 414-271-0383

Milwaukee Courier
PO Box 06279
Milwaukee, WI 53206
Phone: 414-449-4860
Fax: 414-449-4872

Milwaukee Journal Sentinel*
333 W State St
Milwaukee, WI 53203
www.jsonline.com
Phone: 414-224-2000
Fax: 414-224-2047

Milwaukee Magazine
417 E Chicago St
Milwaukee, WI 53202
E-mail: milmag@qgraph.com
www.milwaukeemagazine.com
Phone: 414-273-1101
Fax: 414-273-0016
TF: 800-662-4818

Shepherd Express
413 N 2nd St
Milwaukee, WI 53203
www.shepherd-express.com
Phone: 414-276-2222
Fax: 414-276-3312

Shepherd Express Metro
413 N 2nd St
Milwaukee, WI 53203
E-mail: ctyed@aol.com
shepherd-express.com
Phone: 414-276-2222
Fax: 414-276-3312

**Indicates major daily newspapers*

Television

WCGV-TV Ch 24 (UPN)
4041 N 35th St
Milwaukee, WI 53216
Phone: 414-874-1824
Fax: 414-874-1899

WDJT-TV Ch 58 (CBS)
809 S 60th St
Milwaukee, WI 53214
E-mail: news@cbs58.com
www.cbs58.com
Phone: 414-777-5800
Fax: 414-777-5802

WISN-TV Ch 12 (ABC)
759 N 19th St
Milwaukee, WI 53233
E-mail: news@wisn.com
www.wisn.com
Phone: 414-342-8812
Fax: 414-342-7505

WITI-TV Ch 6 (Fox)
9001 N Green Bay Rd
Milwaukee, WI 53217
Phone: 414-355-6666
Fax: 414-362-2141

WJJA-TV Ch 49 (Ind)
4311 E Oakwood Rd
Oak Creek, WI 53154
Phone: 414-764-4953
Fax: 414-764-5190

WMVS-TV Ch 10 (PBS)
1036 N 8th St
Milwaukee, WI 53233
www.mptv.org
Phone: 414-271-1036
Fax: 414-297-7536

WMVT-TV Ch 36 (PBS)
1036 N 8th St
Milwaukee, WI 53233
www.mptv.org
Phone: 414-271-1036
Fax: 414-297-7536

WPXE-TV Ch 55 (PAX)
700 W Virginia St Suite 605
Milwaukee, WI 53204
www.pax.net/wpxe
Phone: 414-278-5500
Fax: 414-278-5501

WTMJ-TV Ch 4 (NBC)
720 E Capitol Dr
Milwaukee, WI 53212
www.touchtmj4.com
Phone: 414-332-9611
Fax: 414-967-5378

WVCY-TV Ch 30 (Ind)
3434 W Kilbourn Ave
Milwaukee, WI 53208
E-mail: tv30@vcyamerica.org
www.vcyamerica.org/wvcytv30.html
Phone: 414-935-3000
Fax: 414-935-3015

WVTV-TV Ch 18 (WB)
4041 N 35th St
Milwaukee, WI 53216
Phone: 414-874-1824
Fax: 414-874-1899

Radio

WAUK-AM 1510 kHz (Sports)
1801 Coral Dr
Waukesha, WI 53186
www.doubleplay1510.com
Phone: 262-544-6800
Fax: 262-544-1705

WEZY-FM 92.1 MHz (B/EZ)
4201 Victory Ave
Racine, WI 53405
Phone: 262-634-3311
Fax: 262-634-6515

WFMR-FM 98.3 MHz (Clas)
5407 W McKinley Ave
Milwaukee, WI 53208
E-mail: feedback@wfmr.com
www.wfmr.com
Phone: 414-799-9830
Fax: 414-978-9008

WHAD-FM 90.7 MHz (NPR)
111 E Kilbourn Ave Suite 1650
Milwaukee, WI 53202
E-mail: whad@execpc.com
www.wpr.org
Phone: 414-227-2040
Fax: 414-227-2043

WISN-AM 1130 kHz (N/T)
759 N 19th St
Milwaukee, WI 53233
www.radio1130online.com
Phone: 414-342-1111
Fax: 414-342-4734

WJMR-FM 106.9 MHz (Oldies)
5407 W McKinley Ave
Milwaukee, WI 53208
E-mail: jamminstudio@jammin1069.com
www.jammin1069.com
Phone: 414-454-0800
Fax: 414-454-0877

WJYI-AM 1340 kHz (Rel)
5407 W McKinley Ave
Milwaukee, WI 53208
www.joy1340.com
Phone: 414-454-0900
Fax: 414-978-9001

WJZI-FM 93.3 MHz (NAC)
2979 N Mayfair Rd
Milwaukee, WI 53222
www.wjzi.com
Phone: 414-778-1933
Fax: 414-771-3036

WKKV-FM 100.7 MHz (Urban)
PO Box 20920
Milwaukee, WI 53220
E-mail: info@v100.com
www.v100.com
Phone: 414-321-1007
Fax: 414-546-9654

WKLH-FM 96.5 MHz (CR)
5407 W McKinley Ave
Milwaukee, WI 53208
www.wklh.com
Phone: 414-454-0900
Fax: 414-978-9001

WKTI-FM 94.5 MHz (AC)
720 E Capitol Dr
Milwaukee, WI 53212
E-mail: info@wkti.com
www.wkti.com
Phone: 414-332-9611
Fax: 414-967-5266

WLTQ-FM 97.3 MHz (AC)
759 N 19th St
Milwaukee, WI 53233
www.light97.net
Phone: 414-342-1111
Fax: 414-342-9730

WLUM-FM 102.1 MHz (Rock)
2979 N Mayfair Rd
Milwaukee, WI 53222
www.rock102one.com/2000
Phone: 414-771-1021
Fax: 414-771-3036
TF: 800-899-1021

WLZR-FM 102.9 MHz (Rock)
5407 W McKinley Ave
Milwaukee, WI 53208
www.lazer103.com
Phone: 414-454-0900
Fax: 414-978-9001

WMCS-AM 1290 kHz (Urban)
4222 W Capitol Dr
Milwaukee, WI 53216
www.1290wmcs.com
Phone: 414-444-1290
Fax: 414-444-1409

WMIL-FM 106.1 MHz (Ctry)
12100 W Howard Ave
Greenfield, WI 53228
E-mail: fm106@execpc.com
www.fm106.com
Phone: 414-545-8900
Fax: 414-546-9654
TF: 800-709-1061

WMYX-FM 99.1 MHz (AC)
11800 W Grange Ave
Hales Corners, WI 53130
Phone: 414-529-1250
Fax: 414-529-2122

WNOV-AM 860 kHz (Urban)
3815 N Teutonia Ave
Milwaukee, WI 53206
Phone: 414-449-9668
Fax: 414-449-9945

WOKY-AM 920 kHz (Nost)
12100 W Howard Ave
Greenfield, WI 53228
Phone: 414-545-5920
Fax: 414-546-9657

WRIT-FM 95.7 MHz (Oldies)
12100 W Howard Ave
Greenfield, WI 53228
Phone: 414-545-8900
Fax: 414-546-9654

WTMJ-AM 620 kHz (N/T)
720 E Capitol Dr
Milwaukee, WI 53212
www.620wtmj.com
Phone: 414-332-9611
Fax: 414-967-5298

WUWM-FM 89.7 MHz (NPR)
161 W Wisconsin Ave Suite 1000LL
Milwaukee, WI 53203
www.uwm.edu/WUWM
Phone: 414-229-4664
Fax: 414-270-1297

WXSS-FM 103.7 MHz (CHR)
11800 W Grange Ave
Hales Corners, WI 53130
Phone: 414-529-1250
Fax: 414-529-2122

Attractions

Milwaukee's many breweries have earned it a reputation as the "Beer Capital of the World," and visitors to the city can tour the facilities of Pabst, Miller, or Schlitz brewing companies. Milwaukee is notorious for its harsh winters, but the Mitchell Park Horticultural Conservatory is a haven from the cold. It houses three domes—tropical, arid, and show—which feature seasonal shows and year-round exhibits. Spring and summer are the best times of year for a visit to the Milwaukee County Zoo or a drive along Lake Michigan.

America's Black Holocaust Museum
2233 N 4th St
Milwaukee, WI 53212
Phone: 414-264-2500
Fax: 414-264-0112

Beer Museum The
PO Box 309
Milwaukee, WI 53201
Phone: 262-821-8004
Fax: 262-965-3281

Betty Brinn Children's Museum
929 E Wisconsin Ave
Milwaukee, WI 53202
E-mail: kiplade@execpc.com
www.bbcmkids.org
Phone: 414-291-0888
Fax: 414-291-0906

Boerner Botanical Gardens
5879 S 92nd St
Hales Corners, WI 53130
E-mail: schuck@csd.uwm.edu
www.uwm.edu/Dept/Biology/Boerner/
Phone: 414-425-1130
Fax: 414-425-8679

Brown Deer Park
7835 N Green Bay Rd
Milwaukee, WI 53209
Phone: 414-352-7502

Charles Allis Art Museum
1801 N Prospect Ave
Milwaukee, WI 53202
Phone: 414-278-8295
Fax: 414-278-0335

City Ballet Theatre Inc
3908 W Capitol Dr
Milwaukee, WI 53216
E-mail: cbt@pitnet.net
Phone: 414-445-3006
Fax: 414-578-1588

Discovery World Museum of Science Economics & Technology
815 N James Lovell St
Milwaukee, WI 53233
www.braintools.org
Phone: 414-765-9966
Fax: 414-765-0311

East Town
770 N Jefferson St
Milwaukee, WI 53202
www.easttown.com
Phone: 414-271-1416
Fax: 414-271-6401

First Stage Milwaukee
929 N Water St Marcus Ctr
Milwaukee, WI 53202
Phone: 414-273-2314
Fax: 414-273-5595

Florentine Opera of Milwaukee
735 N Water St Suite 1315
Milwaukee, WI 53202
E-mail: info@florentineopera.com
www.florentineopera.com
Phone: 414-291-5700
Fax: 414-291-5706

Greene Memorial Museum
3209 N Maryland Ave Lapham Hall UWM Campus
Milwaukee, WI 53211
Phone: 414-229-4561
Fax: 414-229-5452

Historic Third Ward
219 N Milwaukee St 3rd Fl
Milwaukee, WI 53202
www.milwaukee-htw.org
Phone: 414-273-1173
Fax: 414-273-2205

Humphrey IMAX Dome Theater
800 W Wells St
Milwaukee, WI 53201
E-mail: hamilton@humphreyimax.com
www.humphreyimax.com
Phone: 414-319-4629

International Clown Hall of Fame Inc
161 W Wisconsin Ave
Milwaukee, WI 53203
Phone: 414-319-0848
Fax: 414-319-1070

Kettle Moraine Scenic Steam Train
Hwy 83
North Lake, WI 53064
Phone: 262-782-8074

Kilbourntown House
4400 N Estabrook Dr Estabrook Pk
Milwaukee, WI 53211
www.milwaukeecountyhistsoc.org
Phone: 414-273-8288

Lakefront Brewery Inc
1872 N Commerce St
Milwaukee, WI 53212
www.lakefront-brewery.com
Phone: 414-372-8800
Fax: 414-372-4400

Lincoln Park
1301 W Hampton Ave
Milwaukee, WI 53209
Phone: 414-332-1350

Marcus Center for the Performing Arts
929 N Water St
Milwaukee, WI 53202
www.milwaukeearts.org
Phone: 414-273-7206
Fax: 414-273-0649

Miller Brewing Co
3939 W Highland Blvd
Milwaukee, WI 53208
www.millerbrewing.com
Phone: 414-931-2000
Fax: 414-931-3735

Milwaukee Art Museum
750 N Lincoln Memorial Dr
Milwaukee, WI 53202
E-mail: asktheartist@mam.org
www.mam.org
Phone: 414-224-3200
Fax: 414-271-7588

Milwaukee Ballet
929 N Waters St Marcus Ctr for the Performing Arts
Milwaukee, WI 53202
www.milwaukeeballet.org
Phone: 414-643-7677
Fax: 414-649-4066

Milwaukee Chamber Theatre
158 N Broadway Broadway Theatre Ctr
Milwaukee, WI 53202
www.chamber-theatre.com
Phone: 414-276-8842
Fax: 414-277-4477

Milwaukee County Historical Society
910 N Old World 3rd St
Milwaukee, WI 53203
Phone: 414-273-8288
Fax: 414-273-3268

Milwaukee County Sports Complex
6000 W Ryan Rd
Franklin, WI 53132
Phone: 414-421-9733
Fax: 414-421-6353

Milwaukee County War Memorial
750 N Lincoln Memorial Dr Rm 315
Milwaukee, WI 53202
Phone: 414-273-5533
Fax: 414-273-2455

Milwaukee County Zoo
10001 W Bluemound Rd
Milwaukee, WI 53226
www.execpc.com/~cwzoo
Phone: 414-771-3040
Fax: 414-256-5410

Milwaukee Public Museum
800 W Wells St
Milwaukee, WI 53233
www.mpm.edu
Phone: 414-278-2700
Fax: 414-278-6100

Milwaukee Repertory Theater
108 E Wells St
Milwaukee, WI 53202
www.milwaukeerep.com/mrt.htm
Phone: 414-224-9490
Fax: 414-224-9097

Milwaukee Symphony Orchestra
330 E Kilbourn Ave Suite 900
Milwaukee, WI 53202
www.milwaukeesymphony.org
Phone: 414-291-6010
Fax: 414-291-7610

Mitchell Gallery of Flight
5300 S Howell Ave Mitchell International Airport
Milwaukee, WI 53207
Phone: 414-747-5300
Fax: 414-747-4525

Mitchell Park Conservatory
524 S Layton Blvd
Milwaukee, WI 53215
E-mail: schuck@csd.uwm.edu
www.uwm.edu/Dept/Biology/domes
Phone: 414-649-9830
Fax: 414-649-8616

Old Mill District
210 S Water St
Watertown, WI 53094
Phone: 920-262-2348
Fax: 920-262-2382

Old World Third Street
Wisconsin Ave & 3rd St
Milwaukee, WI 53203
Phone: 414-273-3950

Old World Wisconsin
S 103 West 37890 Hwy 67
Eagle, WI 53119
E-mail: owwvisit@idcnet.com
Phone: 262-594-6300
Fax: 262-594-6342

Pabst Mansion
2000 W Wisconsin Ave
Milwaukee, WI 53233
E-mail: pabstman@execpc.com
www.pabstmansion.com
Phone: 414-931-0808
Fax: 414-931-1005

Pabst Theater
144 E Wells St
Milwaukee, WI 53202
Phone: 414-286-3665
Fax: 414-286-2154

Patrick & Beatrice Haggerty Museum of Art
13th & Clybourn Sts Marquette University
Milwaukee, WI 53223
E-mail: haggertym@vms.csd.mu.edu
www.marquette.edu/haggerty
Phone: 414-288-7290
Fax: 414-288-5415

Potawatomi Bingo Casino
1721 W Canal St
Milwaukee, WI 53233
www.paysbig.com
Phone: 414-645-6888
Fax: 414-645-6866

Present Music Phone: 414-271-0711
1840 N Farwell Ave Fax: 414-271-7998
Milwaukee, WI 53202

Riveredge Nature Center Phone: 262-375-2715
4458 W Hawthorne Dr Box 26 Fax: 262-375-2714
Newburg, WI 53060

Riverside Theatre Phone: 414-224-3000
116 W Wisconsin Ave Fax: 414-224-3019
Milwaukee, WI 53203
E-mail: theatrerob@aol.com

Saint Joan of Arc Chapel Phone: 414-288-6873
14th St & Wisconsin Ave Fax: 414-288-3696
Milwaukee, WI 53233
www.marquette.edu/campus/joanarc.html

Saint Josaphat Basilica Phone: 414-645-5623
6th St & Lincoln Ave Fax: 414-385-3270
Milwaukee, WI 53215

Schlitz Audubon Center Phone: 414-352-2880
1111 E Brown Deer Rd Fax: 414-352-6091
Milwaukee, WI 53217

Skylight Opera Theatre Phone: 414-291-7811
158 N Broadway Fax: 414-291-7815
Milwaukee, WI 53202
www.skylightopera.com

Sprecher Brewing Co Phone: 414-964-2739
701 W Glendale Ave Fax: 414-964-2462
Glendale, WI 53209
www.sprecherbrewery.com

Villa Terrace Decorative Arts Museum Phone: 414-271-3656
2220 N Terrace Ave Fax: 414-271-3986
Milwaukee, WI 53202

Wehr Nature Center Phone: 414-425-8550
9701 W College Ave Fax: 414-425-6992
Franklin, WI 53132

Whitnall Park Phone: 414-257-6100
5879 S 92nd St
Hales Corners, WI 53130

Wisconsin Black Historical Society Museum Phone: 414-372-7677
2620 W Center St Fax: 414-372-4888
Milwaukee, WI 53206
wbhsm.org

Wisconsin Conservatory of Music Phone: 414-276-5760
1845 N Fairwell Ave Suite 200 Fax: 414-276-6076
Milwaukee, WI 53202
www.wcmusic.org

Wisconsin Maritime Museum Phone: 920-684-0218
75 Maritime Dr Fax: 920-684-0219
Manitowoc, WI 54220

Wisconsin's Ethnic Settlement Trail Phone: 414-961-2110
5900 N Port Washington Rd Fax: 414-961-2110
Milwaukee, WI 53217

Sports Teams & Facilities

Bradley Center Phone: 414-227-0400
1001 N 4th St Fax: 414-227-0497
Milwaukee, WI 53203

Dairyland Greyhound Park Phone: 262-657-8200
5522 104th Ave Fax: 262-657-8231
Kenosha, WI 53144 TF: 800-233-3357
E-mail: dgpsimul@execpc.com
www.dairylandgreyhoundpark.com

Great Lakes Dragway Phone: 262-878-3783
18411 1st St Fax: 262-878-4462
Union Grove, WI 53182 TF: 888-324-7683

Green Bay Packers Phone: 920-496-5719
1265 Lombardi Ave Lambeau Field Fax: 920-496-5738
Green Bay, WI 54304
www.packers.com

Milwaukee Admirals (hockey) Phone: 414-227-0550
1001 N 4th St Bradley Ctr Fax: 414-227-0568
Milwaukee, WI 53203 TF: 800-927-6630
E-mail: comments@milwaukeeadmirals.com
www.milwaukeeadmirals.com

Milwaukee Auditorium Phone: 414-908-6000
500 W Kilbourne Ave Fax: 414-908-6010
Milwaukee, WI 53203
www.wcd.org/site/home/fac/are/main.html

Milwaukee Brewers Phone: 414-933-9000
201 S 46th St Milwaukee County Stadium
Milwaukee, WI 53201
www.milwaukeebrewers.com

Milwaukee Bucks Phone: 414-227-0500
1001 N 4th St Bradley Ctr Fax: 414-227-0543
Milwaukee, WI 53203
www.nba.com/bucks

Milwaukee County Stadium Phone: 414-933-4114
201 S 46th St Fax: 414-933-7111
Milwaukee, WI 53214 TF: 800-933-7890
www.milwaukeebrewers.com

Milwaukee Mile Phone: 414-453-8277
7722 W Greenfield Ave Fax: 414-453-9920
West Allis, WI 53214
E-mail: feedback@milmile.com
www.milmile.com

Milwaukee Mustangs (football) Phone: 414-272-1555
1001 N 4th St Bradley Ctr Fax: 414-272-3891
Milwaukee, WI 53203
E-mail: mustangsmail@milwaukeemustangs.com
www.milwaukeemustangs.com

Milwaukee Rampage (soccer) Phone: 414-358-2655
7101 W Good Hope Rd Uihlein Soccer Pk Fax: 414-358-2618
Milwaukee, WI 53223
E-mail: bear@milwaukeerampage.com
www.milwaukeerampage.com

Milwaukee Wave (soccer) Phone: 262-241-7500
10201 N Port Washington Rd Suite 200 Fax: 262-241-7506
Mequon, WI 53092
www.milwaukeewave.com

Uihlein Soccer Park
7101 W Good Hope Rd
Milwaukee, WI 53223
Phone: 414-358-2678
Fax: 414-358-2572

Wilmot Speedway
Kenosha County Fairgrounds
Wilmot, WI 53192
Phone: 847-395-0500
Fax: 847-395-0363

Annual Events

African World Festival (early August) 414-372-4567
Bastille Days (mid-July)..........................414-271-1416
Bavarian Volksfest (late June)....................414-462-9147
Boerner in Bloom (late June) 414-529-1870
CajunFest (early-mid-June) 414-476-7303
Christmas in the Country
(mid-November-early December) 262-377-9620
Christmas in the Ward (early December)..........414-273-1173
Cinco de Mayo Festival (mid-May)................414-671-5700
Downtown Saint Patrick's Day Parade
(March 17) 414-276-6696
Festa Italiana (mid-July) 920-232-2192
Firstar Eve Celebration (December 31)............414-765-6500
Gen Con Game Fair (early August) 800-529-3976
German Fest (late July) 414-464-9444
Grape Lakes Food & Wine Festival (mid-May) 414-224-3850
Great Circus Parade Week (mid-July) 608-355-9450
Greater Milwaukee Auto Show
(late February-early March)....................414-908-6000
Greater Milwaukee Open (early-mid-July)...........414-540-3800
Harvest Fair (late September)....................414-266-7000
Holiday Craft & Gift Show (late November) 414-321-2100
Holiday Folk Fair (mid-November) 414-225-6225
Indian Summer Festival (early September).........414-774-7119
International Arts Festival (February).............414-273-3950
Jazz in the Park (early June-mid-September) 414-271-1416
Juneteenth Day (mid-June).......................414-372-3770
Lakefront Festival of the Arts (mid-June) 414-224-3850
Mexican Fiesta (late August)......................414-383-7066
Milwaukee Boat Show (mid-February) 414-908-6000
Milwaukee Christmas Parade (mid-November) 414-273-3950
Milwaukee Highland Games (early June) 262-796-0807
Milwaukee Irish Fest (mid-August) 414-476-3378
Milwaukee à la Carte (mid-August) 414-771-3040
Oktoberfest (September) 414-964-4221
Polish Fest (late June)...........................414-529-2140
PrideFest (early-mid-June) 414-645-3378
Rainbow Summer (early June-late August) 414-273-7121
RiverSplash (early June) 414-297-9855
Senior Fest (early June)..........................414-647-6040
Shermanfest-Milwaukee's Premier Blues Festival
(late June)...................................414-444-9803
South Shore Water Frolics (mid-July) 414-224-2753
Spring Craft & Gift Show (mid-March) 414-321-2100
Strawberry Festival (late June)....................800-827-8020
Summerfest (late June-early July).................800-837-3378
TosaFest (mid-September)........................414-476-5300
US International Snow Sculpting Competition
(late January) 414-476-5573
Wisconsin State Fair (early August) 414-266-7000

Minneapolis, Minnesota

***County:* Hennepin**

MINNEAPOLIS-SAINT PAUL is located at the confluence of the Minnesota and Mississippi Rivers in southeastern Minnesota. Major cities within 100 miles include Mankato, Rochester, and Saint Cloud, Minnesota; and Eau Claire, Wisconsin.

Area (Land)	54.9 sq mi
Area (Water)	3.5 sq mi
Elevation	838 ft
Latitude	44-98-00 N
Longitude	93-26-36 W
Time Zone	CST
Area Code	612

Climate

Minneapolis has a continental climate that features four distinct seasons. Winters are long and cold, with average high temperatures in the mid-20s and lows in the single digits. The average annual snowfall in Minneapolis is just under 50 inches, which is not especially high for a northern city, but sustained periods of low temperatures cause the snow to remain on the ground for a longer period of time. Summers are pleasant, with average daytime high temperatures around 70 degrees and lows near 60. Summer is also considered the rainy season in Minneapolis—June is the wettest month of the year, while February is the driest.

Average Temperatures & Precipitation

Temperatures

	Jan	Feb	Mar	Apr	May	Jun	Jul	Aug	Sep	Oct	Nov	Dec
High	21	27	39	57	69	79	84	81	71	59	41	26
Low	3	9	23	36	48	58	63	60	50	39	25	10

Precipitation

	Jan	Feb	Mar	Apr	May	Jun	Jul	Aug	Sep	Oct	Nov	Dec
Inches	1.0	0.9	1.9	2.4	3.4	4.1	3.5	3.6	2.7	2.2	1.6	1.1

History

The "Twin Cities" of Minneapolis and Saint Paul, as they are known today, developed on land that was originally inhabited by the Dakota (Sioux) tribe. The area was first explored by Europeans in 1680, when Franciscan priest Father Louis Hennepin (after whom Hennepin County was later named) and two companions visited the area, discovering the falls that they would later name the Falls of Saint Anthony. The area east of the Mississippi River belonged to the French until 1803, when it became the property of the United States with the signing of the Louisiana Purchase. In the early 19th Century, President Thomas Jefferson ordered the construction of what would later become Fort Snelling at the confluence of the Mississippi and Minnesota Rivers. In 1837, the Native Americans ceded a portion of their land in the region to the United States, paving the way for white settlement.

The present-day city of Saint Paul was the first community to develop in the area. Originally a French village known as "Pig's Eye Landing," the city was renamed in 1841 at the request of Father Lucien Galtier, who built a chapel in the city dedicated to Saint Paul. Further cessions of Native American land during the 1850s included land to the west of the Mississippi River where the new community of Minneapolis (the Native American word for water "minne"—and the Greek word for city—"polis") developed. The economies of both cities relied heavily on the lumber and flour milling industries, but the area also served as an important port on the Mississippi River.

For much of the remainder of the 19th Century, Minneapolis and Saint Paul vied for dominance. Initially, Saint Paul had a greater population and it was chosen as the capital of the Minnesota Territory (and later the State of Minnesota). By 1880, however, Minneapolis' population had surpassed that of its twin city, due in large part to its highly successful flour milling industry, which included two of the nation's leading companies, Pillsbury and General Mills (originally known as Washburn-Crosby Milling). Many European immigrants, primarily Scandinavians, settled in the Twin Cities area during the late 1800s and early 1900s.

Around 1920, a decline in the lumber and flour milling industries that had sustained Minneapolis-Saint Paul's early economy led both cities to diversify their economic base. For much of the 20th Century, improvements in transportation—from a successful electric streetcar service at the turn of the century to the construction of an extensive freeway system during the 1960s—also stimulated growth in the Twin Cities area, allowing for the development of suburban communities. Today, more than half of Minnesota's entire 4.7 million population resides in the Twin Cities metropolitan area. Home to more than 351,000 people, Minneapolis today is Minnesota's largest city; Saint Paul, with a population of more than 257,000 is the second largest city in the state.

Population

1990 Census	368,383
1998 Estimate	351,731
% Change	-4.5

Racial/Ethnic Breakdown

White	78.4%
Black	13.0%
Other	8.6%
Hispanic Origin (may be of any race)	2.1%

Age Breakdown

Under 5 years	7.4%
5 to 17	13.3%
18 to 20	5.1%

21 to 24 .... 8.4%
25 to 34 .... 23.3%
35 to 44 .... 15.8%
45 to 54 .... 7.7%
55 to 64 .... 6.2%
65 to 74 .... 6.3%
75+ years 6.6%
Median Age 31.7

Gender Breakdown
Male 48.5%
Female 51.5%

Government

Type of Government: Mayor-Council

Minneapolis City Attorney
333 S 7th St Suite 300
Minneapolis, MN 55402
Phone: 612-673-2010
Fax: 612-673-3811

Minneapolis City Clerk
350 S 5th St Rm 304
Minneapolis, MN 55415
Phone: 612-673-2215
Fax: 612-673-3812

Minneapolis City Council
350 S 5th St Rm 307
Minneapolis, MN 55415
Phone: 612-673-2200
Fax: 612-673-3940

Minneapolis City Hall
350 S 5th St
Minneapolis, MN 55415
Phone: 612-673-2215
Fax: 612-673-2185

Minneapolis Finance Dept
350 S 5th St Rm 325M
Minneapolis, MN 55415
Phone: 612-673-2577
Fax: 612-673-2042

Minneapolis Fire Dept
350 S 5th St Rm 230
Minneapolis, MN 55415
Phone: 612-673-2890
Fax: 612-673-2828

Minneapolis Human Resources Dept
250 S 4th St Rm 100
Minneapolis, MN 55415
Phone: 612-673-2282

Minneapolis Mayor
350 S 5th St Rm 331
Minneapolis, MN 55415
Phone: 612-673-2100
Fax: 612-673-2305

Minneapolis Park & Recreation Board
400 S 4th St Suite 200
Minneapolis, MN 55415
Phone: 612-661-4800
Fax: 612-661-4777

Minneapolis Planning Dept
350 S 5th St Rm 210
Minneapolis, MN 55415
Phone: 612-673-2597
Fax: 612-673-2728

Minneapolis Police Dept
350 S 5th St Rm 130
Minneapolis, MN 55415
Phone: 612-673-2853
Fax: 612-673-2613

Minneapolis Public Library
300 Nicollet Mall
Minneapolis, MN 55401
Phone: 612-630-6000
Fax: 612-630-6210

Minneapolis Public Works Dept
350 S 5th St Rm 203
Minneapolis, MN 55415
Phone: 612-673-2443
Fax: 612-673-3565

Minneapolis Transportation Div
350 S 5th St Rm 233
Minneapolis, MN 55415
Phone: 612-673-2411
Fax: 612-673-2149

Minneapolis Water Works
250 S 4th St Public Health Bldg Rm 206
Minneapolis, MN 55415
Phone: 612-673-5600
Fax: 612-673-3723

Important Phone Numbers

AAA 952-927-2727
American Express Travel 612-343-5500
Connection The 952-922-9000
Dental Referral 952-892-5050
Driver's License/Vehicle Registration Information .. 612-348-8240
Emergency 911
Hennepin County Assessor 612-348-3011
HotelDocs 800-468-3537
Medical Referral 651-697-3333
Minneapolis Area Assn of Realtors 952-933-9020
Minnesota Revenue Dept 651-296-3781
Poison Control Center 612-347-3141
Road Conditions 651-405-6030
Saint Paul Area Assn of Realtors 651-774-5206
Time 763-512-1111
Voter Registration Information 612-673-2070
Weather 763-512-1111

Information Sources

Better Business Bureau Serving Minnesota & North Dakota
2706 Gannon Rd
Saint Paul, MN 55116
www.minnesota.bbb.org
Phone: 651-699-1111
Fax: 651-699-7665

Greater Minneapolis Chamber of Commerce
81 S 9th St Suite 200
Minneapolis, MN 55402
www.tc-chamber.org
Phone: 612-370-9132
Fax: 612-370-9195

Greater Minneapolis Convention & Visitors Assn
33 S 6th St Multifoods Tower Suite 4000
Minneapolis, MN 55402
www.minneapolis.org
Phone: 612-661-4700
Fax: 612-335-5839
TF: 800-445-7412

Hennepin County
300 S 6th St
Minneapolis, MN 55487
www.co.hennepin.mn.us
Phone: 612-348-3000

Minneapolis Convention Center
1301 2nd Ave S
Minneapolis, MN 55403
www.mplsconvctr.org
Phone: 612-335-6000
Fax: 612-335-6757

Ramsey County
15 W Kellogg Blvd Rm 250
Saint Paul, MN 55102
www.co.ramsey.mn.us
Phone: 651-266-8000
Fax: 651-266-8039

RiverCentre
175 W Kellogg Blvd
Saint Paul, MN 55102
www.rivercentre.org
Phone: 651-265-4800
Fax: 651-265-4899

Saint Paul Area Chamber of Commerce
332 Minnesota St Suite N-205
Saint Paul, MN 55101
www.saintpaulchamber.com
Phone: 651-223-5000
Fax: 651-223-5119

Saint Paul City Hall
15 W Kellogg Blvd
Saint Paul, MN 55102
www.stpaul.gov
Phone: 651-266-8500

Saint Paul Convention & Visitors Bureau
175 W Kellogg Blvd RiverCentre Suite 502
Saint Paul, MN 55102
www.stpaulcvb.org
Phone: 651-265-4900
Fax: 651-265-4999
TF: 800-627-6101

Saint Paul Mayor
15 W Kellogg Blvd Rm 390
Saint Paul, MN 55102
www.stpaul.gov/mayor
Phone: 651-266-8510
Fax: 651-266-8513

Saint Paul Planning & Economic Development Dept
25 W 4th St
Saint Paul, MN 55102
www.stpaul.gov/depts/ped
Phone: 651-266-6700
Fax: 651-228-3261

Saint Paul Public Library
90 W 4th St
Saint Paul, MN 55102
www.stpaul.lib.mn.us
Phone: 651-266-7000
Fax: 651-292-6141

Online Resources

4Minneapolis.com
www.4minneapolis.com

About.com Guide to Minneapolis/Saint Paul
minneapolis.about.com/local/midwestus/minneapolis

Area Guide Minneapolis
minneapolis.areaguides.net

Area Guide Saint Paul
stpaul.areaguides.net

Boulevards Minneapolis
www.boulevards.com/cities/minneapolis.html

City Knowledge Minneapolis
www.cityknowledge.com/mn_minneapolis.htm

City Knowledge Saint Paul
www.cityknowledge.com/mn_stpaul.htm

City Wide Guide
www.citywideguide.com

CitySearch Twin Cities
twincities.citysearch.com

DigitalCity Twin Cities
home.digitalcity.com/twincities

Excite.com Minneapolis City Guide
www.excite.com/travel/countries/united_states/minnesota/minneapolis

Excite.com Saint Paul City Guide
www.excite.com/travel/countries/united_states/minnesota/saint_paul

Insiders' Guide to the Twin Cities
www.insiders.com/twin-cities/

Lodging.com Twin Cities Minnesota
www.lodging.com/auto/guides/twin_cities-area-mn.html

Minneapolis City Pages
minneapolis.thelinks.com

Minneapolis FAQ
scc.net/~peter/MPLSFAQ.html

Minneapolis-Saint Paul City Guide
www.tgimaps.com/marketplace/cityguide/

Minneapolis-Saint Paul CityWomen
www.citywomen.com/minnwomen.htm

Mpls.com
www.mpls.com/

Rough Guide Travel Minneapolis
travel.roughguides.com/content/538/

Rough Guide Travel Saint Paul
travel.roughguides.com/content/11184/

Saint Paul City Guide
www.saint-paul.com

Saint Paul Neighborhood Network
www.spnn.org/

Savvy Diner Guide to Minneapolis-Saint Paul Restaurants
www.savvydiner.com/minneapolis/

Twin Cities Global Connection
www.tcglobal.com

Twin Cities Internet Guide & Directory
www.tcigd.com/

Twin Cities Just Go
www.justgo.com/twincities

Twin Cities Restaurant Guide
dine.com/twin

TwinCities.com
www.twincities.com

Yahoo! Twin Cities
minn.yahoo.com

Area Communities

Communities in the Twin Cities metropolitan area (including Hennepin, Ramsey, Carver, Dakota, Scott, Washington, and Anoka counties) with populations greater than 20,000 include:

Andover
1685 Crosstown Blvd NW
Andover, MN 55304
Phone: 763-755-5100
Fax: 763-755-8923

Apple Valley
14200 Cedar Ave
Apple Valley, MN 55124
Phone: 952-953-2500
Fax: 952-953-2515

Blaine
9150 Central Ave NE
Blaine, MN 55434
Phone: 612-784-6700
Fax: 612-785-6156

Bloomington
2215 W Old Shakopee Rd
Bloomington, MN 55431
Phone: 952-948-8782
Fax: 952-948-8789

Brooklyn Center
6301 Shingle Creek Pkwy
Brooklyn Center, MN 55430
Phone: 763-569-3300
Fax: 763-569-3494

Brooklyn Park
5200 85th Ave N
Brooklyn Park, MN 55443
Phone: 763-424-8000
Fax: 763-493-8391

Burnsville
100 Civic Center Pkwy
Burnsville, MN 55337
Phone: 952-895-4490
Fax: 952-895-4404

Champlin
11955 Champlin Dr
Champlin, MN 55316
Phone: 763-421-8100
Fax: 763-421-5256

Coon Rapids
11155 Robinson Dr
Coon Rapids, MN 55433
Phone: 763-755-2880

Crystal
4141 Douglas Dr N
Crystal, MN 55422
Phone: 763-531-1000
Fax: 763-531-1188

Eagan
3830 Pilot Knob Rd
Eagan, MN 55122
Phone: 651-681-4600
Fax: 651-681-4612

Eden Prairie
8080 Mitchell Rd
Eden Prairie, MN 55344
Phone: 952-949-8300
Fax: 952-949-8390

Edina
4801 W 50th St
Edina, MN 55424
Phone: 952-927-8861
Fax: 952-826-0390

Fridley
6431 University Ave NE
Fridley, MN 55432
Phone: 763-571-3450
Fax: 763-571-1287

Golden Valley
7800 Golden Valley Rd
Golden Valley, MN 55427
Phone: 763-593-8000
Fax: 763-593-8109

Inver Grove Heights
8150 Barbara Ave
Inver Grove Heights, MN 55077
Phone: 651-450-2500
Fax: 651-450-2502

Lakeville
20195 Holyoke Ave
Lakeville, MN 55044
Phone: 952-469-4431
Fax: 952-985-4499

Maple Grove
PO Box 1180
Maple Grove, MN 55311
Phone: 763-494-6000
Fax: 763-494-6420

Maplewood
1830 County Rd 'B' E
Maplewood, MN 55109
Phone: 651-770-4500
Fax: 651-770-4506

Minnetonka
14600 Minnetonka Blvd
Minnetonka, MN 55345
Phone: 952-939-8200
Fax: 952-939-8244

New Brighton
803 5th Ave NW
New Brighton, MN 55112
Phone: 651-638-2100
Fax: 651-638-2044

New Hope
4401 Xylon Ave N
New Hope, MN 55428
Phone: 763-531-5100
Fax: 763-531-5136

Oakdale
1584 Hadley Ave N
Oakdale, MN 55128
Phone: 651-739-5086
Fax: 651-730-2820

Plymouth
3400 Plymouth Blvd
Plymouth, MN 55447
Phone: 763-509-5050
Fax: 763-509-5060

Richfield
6700 Portland Ave
Richfield, MN 55423
Phone: 612-861-9700
Fax: 612-861-9749

Saint Louis Park
5005 Minnetonka Blvd
Saint Louis Park, MN 55416
Phone: 952-924-2525
Fax: 952-924-2175

Saint Paul
15 W Kellogg Blvd
Saint Paul, MN 55102
Phone: 651-266-8500

Shoreview
4600 Victoria St N
Saint Paul, MN 55126
Phone: 651-490-4600
Fax: 651-490-4699

White Bear Lake
4701 Hwy 61 N
White Bear Lake, MN 55110
Phone: 651-429-8526
Fax: 651-429-8500

Woodbury
8301 Valley Creek Rd
Woodbury, MN 55125
Phone: 651-739-5972
Fax: 651-731-5791

Economy

The Twin Cities metropolitan area has a diverse economic base that ranges from agriculture to high-technology, and with over 1,300 technology-intensive companies, the Minneapolis-Saint Paul metro area has one of the largest concentrations of high-technology businesses in the country. Twelve Minnesota-based Fortune 500 companies are headquartered in the Minneapolis-Saint Paul metro area and major U.S. companies also located in the Twin Cities include Dayton Hudson, Minnesota Mining & Manufacturing (3M), Supervalu, Northwest Airlines, General Mills, and Cargill. Services, retail trade, and manufacturing are the area's largest employment sectors. Government also plays a vital role in the Twin Cities' economy—the State of Minnesota and the U.S. government rank numbers 1 and 3 respectively on the area's largest employers list, providing jobs for nearly 80,000 area residents collectively. Hennepin County and the City of Minneapolis also rank among Minneapolis-Saint Paul's 15 largest employers.

Unemployment Rate 1.6%
Per Capita Income $33,561*
Median Family Income $63,600*

** Information given is for the Minneapolis/Saint Paul, Minnesota/Wisconsin Metropolitan Statistical Area (MSA), which includes the City of Bloomington, the City of Minneapolis, the City of Saint Paul, Anoka Conty, Carver County, Chisago County, Dakota County, Hennepin County, Isanti County, Ramsey County, Scott County, Washington County, and Wright County in Minnesota; and Saint Croix County in Wisconsin.*

Principal Industries & Number of Wage Earners

Hennepin County - 1998

Agricultural Services, Forestry, & Fishing 3,431
Construction 27,317
Finance, Insurance, & Real Estate 81,892
Government 82,624
Manufacturing 122,701
Mining 77
Retail Trade 140,242
Services 268,238
Transportation, Communications, & Public Utilities 55,076
Wholesale Trade 63,458

Major Employers

Allina Health System
PO Box 9310
Minneapolis, MN 55440
www.allina.com
Phone: 952-992-2000
Fax: 952-992-3998

American Express Financial Advisors Inc
IDS Tower 10
Minneapolis, MN 55440
www.americanexpress.com/advisors
Phone: 612-671-3131
Fax: 612-671-8880
TF: 800-328-8300

Carlson Cos Inc
PO Box 59159
Minneapolis, MN 55459
www.carlson.com
Phone: 763-212-1000
Fax: 763-212-5020

Fairview Hospital & Healthcare Services
2450 Riverside Ave S
Minneapolis, MN 55454
fairview.org
Phone: 612-672-6000
Fax: 612-672-4098
TF: 800-328-4661

Healtheast
559 Capitol Blvd Suite 6-South
Saint Paul, MN 55103
Phone: 651-232-2300
Fax: 651-232-2315

Hennepin County
300 S 6th St
Minneapolis, MN 55487
www.co.hennepin.mn.us
Phone: 612-348-3000

Minneapolis City Hall
350 S 5th St
Minneapolis, MN 55415
E-mail: opa@ci.minneapolis.mn.us
www.ci.mpls.mn.us
Phone: 612-673-2215
Fax: 612-673-2185

Northern States Power Co
414 Nicollet Mall
Minneapolis, MN 55401
E-mail: inquire@nspco.com
www.nspco.com
Phone: 612-330-5500
Fax: 612-330-2900
TF: 800-328-8226

Northwest Airlines Corp
5101 Northwest Dr
Saint Paul, MN 55111
www.nwa.com/corpinfo
Phone: 612-726-2111
Fax: 612-726-0776
TF: 800-225-2525

SUPERVALU Inc
11840 Valley View Rd
Minneapolis, MN 55344
www.supervalu.com
Phone: 952-828-4000
Fax: 952-828-8998
TF: 888-256-2800

Target Corp
777 Nicollet Mall
Minneapolis, MN 55402
www.targetcorp.com
Phone: 612-370-6948
Fax: 612-370-6675
TF: 800-440-0680

University of Minnesota Twin Cities
231 Pillsbury Dr SE
Minneapolis, MN 55455
E-mail: admissions@tc.umn.edu
www.umn.edu
Phone: 612-625-5000
Fax: 612-624-6037
TF: 800-752-1000

US Bancorp
601 2nd Ave S
Minneapolis, MN 55402
www.usbank.com
Phone: 612-973-1111
Fax: 651-244-7488

Quality of Living Indicators

Total Crime Index 30,737
(rates per 100,000 inhabitants)

Violent Crime
Murder/manslaughter 47
Forcible rape 451
Robbery 2,096
Aggravated assault 2,349

Property Crime
Burglary 5,562
Larceny theft 16,366
Motor vehicle theft 3,866

Cost of Living Index 101.7
(national average = 100)

Median Home Price $138,700

Education

Public Schools

Minneapolis Public Schools
807 NE Broadway
Minneapolis, MN 55413
E-mail: answers@mpls.k12.mn.us
www.mpls.k12.mn.us
Phone: 612-668-0000
Fax: 612-627-2182

Number of Schools
Elementary 65
Middle 8
High 7

Student/Teacher Ratio
All Grades 18.4:1

Private Schools

Number of Schools (all grades) .... 70+

Colleges & Universities

Anoka-Ramsey Community College Phone: 763-427-2600
11200 Mississippi Blvd NW Fax: 763-422-3341
Coon Rapids, MN 55433
E-mail: trallela@an.cc.mn.us
www.an.cc.mn.us

Apostolic Bible Institute Inc Phone: 651-739-7686
6944 Hudson Blvd N Fax: 651-730-8669
Saint Paul, MN 55128
E-mail: abi@mm.com
www.apostolic.org

Art Institute of Minnesota Phone: 612-332-3361
15 S 9th St Fax: 612-332-3934
Minneapolis, MN 55402 TF: 800-777-3643
www.aii.edu

Augsburg College Phone: 612-330-1000
2211 Riverside Ave Fax: 612-330-1649
Minneapolis, MN 55454 TF: 800-788-5678
E-mail: admissions@augsburg.edu
www.augsburg.edu

Bethel College & Seminary Phone: 651-638-6400
3900 Bethel Dr Fax: 651-638-6001
Saint Paul, MN 55112 TF: 800-255-8706
E-mail: mrussell@homer.bethel.edu
www.bethel.edu

Brown Institute Phone: 651-905-3400
1440 Northland Dr Fax: 651-905-3550
Mendota Heights, MN 55120 TF: 800-627-6966
www.brown-institute.com

Century College Phone: 651-779-3200
3300 Century Ave Fax: 651-773-1796
White Bear Lake, MN 55110 TF: 800-228-1978
www.century.cc.mn.us

College of Saint Catherine Phone: 651-690-6000
2004 Randolph Ave Fax: 651-690-6024
Saint Paul, MN 55105 TF: 800-945-4599
E-mail: admissions@stkate.edu
www.stkate.edu

College of Saint Catherine Minneapolis Phone: 651-690-7700
601 25th Ave S Fax: 651-690-7849
Minneapolis, MN 55454

Concordia University Phone: 651-641-8278
275 Syndicate St N Fax: 651-659-0207
Saint Paul, MN 55104 TF: 800-333-4705
E-mail: admiss@luther.csp.edu
www.csp.edu

Hamline University Phone: 651-523-2800
1536 Hewitt Ave Fax: 651-523-2458
Saint Paul, MN 55104 TF: 800-753-9753
E-mail: admis@seq.hamline.edu
www.hamline.edu

Inver Hills Community College Phone: 651-450-8501
2500 80th St E Fax: 651-450-8677
Inver Grove Heights, MN 55076
www.ih.cc.mn.us

Macalester College Phone: 651-696-6000
1600 Grand Ave Fax: 651-696-6724
Saint Paul, MN 55105 TF: 800-231-7974
E-mail: admissions@macalstr.edu
www.macalstr.edu

Medical Institute of Minnesota Phone: 952-844-0064
5503 Green Valley Dr Fax: 952-844-0472
Bloomington, MN 55437
E-mail: info@mim.tec.mn.us
www.mim.tec.mn.us

Metropolitan State University Phone: 651-772-7777
700 E 7th St Fax: 651-772-7738
Saint Paul, MN 55106
www.metrostate.edu

Minneapolis College of Art & Design Phone: 612-874-3760
2501 Stevens Ave S Fax: 612-874-3702
Minneapolis, MN 55404 TF: 800-874-6223
E-mail: admissions@mn.mcad.edu
www.mcad.edu

Minneapolis Community College Phone: 612-341-7000
1501 Hennepin Ave Fax: 612-341-7075
Minneapolis, MN 55403
E-mail: mctcinfo@mi.cc.mn.us

National American University Saint Paul Campus Phone: 651-644-1265
1380 Energy Ln Suite 13 Fax: 651-644-0690
Saint Paul, MN 55108
www.nationalcollege.edu/campuspaul.html

NEI College of Technology Phone: 763-781-4881
825-41st Ave NE Fax: 763-782-7329
Columbia Heights, MN 55421 TF: 800-777-7634
www.neicoltech.org

Normandale Community College Phone: 952-832-6000
9700 France Ave S Fax: 952-832-6571
Bloomington, MN 55431
www.nr.cc.mn.us

North Central University Phone: 612-332-3491
910 Elliot Ave S Fax: 612-343-4778
Minneapolis, MN 55404 TF: 800-289-6222
E-mail: postmaster@northcentral.edu
www.northcentral.edu

North Hennepin Community College Phone: 763-424-0702
7411 85th Ave N Fax: 763-424-0929
Brooklyn Park, MN 55445
www.nh.cc.mn.us

Northwest Technical Institute Phone: 952-944-0080
11995 Singletree Ln Fax: 952-944-9274
Eden Prairie, MN 55344 TF: 800-443-4223
www.nwtech.org

Northwestern College Phone: 651-631-5100
3003 Snelling Ave N Fax: 651-631-5680
Saint Paul, MN 55113 TF: 800-827-6827
www.nwc.edu

Saint Paul Technical College Phone: 651-221-1300
235 Marshall Ave Fax: 651-221-1416
Saint Paul, MN 55102 TF: 800-227-6029
www.sptc.tec.mn.us

University of Minnesota Twin Cities Phone: 612-625-5000
231 Pillsbury Dr SE Fax: 612-624-6037
Minneapolis, MN 55455 TF: 800-752-1000
E-mail: admissions@tc.umn.edu
www.umn.edu

University of Saint Thomas Phone: 651-962-5000
2115 Summit Ave Fax: 651-962-6160
Saint Paul, MN 55105 TF: 800-328-6819
www.stthomas.edu

Hospitals

Abbott Northwestern Hospital Phone: 612-863-4000
800 E 28th St Fax: 612-863-5667
Minneapolis, MN 55407
www.abbottnorthwestern.com

Children's Hospitals & Clinics Minneapolis Phone: 612-813-6100
2525 Chicago Ave Fax: 612-813-6531
Minneapolis, MN 55404
www.childrenshc.org

Children's Hospitals & Clinics Saint Paul Phone: 651-220-6000
345 N Smith Ave Fax: 651-220-7180
Saint Paul, MN 55102
www.childrenshc.org

Fairview-University Medical Center Riverside Campus Phone: 612-672-6000
2450 Riverside Ave Fax: 612-672-4582
Minneapolis, MN 55454

Fairview-University Medical Center University Campus Phone: 612-626-3000
420 SE Delaware St Fax: 612-273-6685
Minneapolis, MN 55455 TF: 800-688-5252
www.fairview.org/pps/fumc

Hennepin County Medical Center Phone: 612-347-2121
701 Park Ave Fax: 612-904-4216
Minneapolis, MN 55415
www.co.hennepin.mn.us/wmedctr.html

Methodist Hospital HealthSystem Minnesota Phone: 952-993-5000
6500 Excelsior Blvd Fax: 952-993-5273
Saint Louis Park, MN 55426
www.healthsystemminnesota.com/Methodist_Hospital/methodist_hospital.html

North Memorial Health Care Phone: 763-520-5200
3300 Oakdale Ave N Fax: 763-520-1454
Robbinsdale, MN 55422
www.nmmc.com

Regions Hospital Phone: 651-221-3456
640 Jackson St Fax: 651-221-3643
Saint Paul, MN 55101 TF: 800-332-5720
www.regionshospital.com

Ridgeview Medical Center Phone: 952-442-2191
500 S Maple St Fax: 952-442-6543
Waconia, MN 55387

Saint John's Hospital Phone: 651-232-7000
1575 Beam Ave Fax: 651-232-7697
Maplewood, MN 55109
www.healtheast.org

Saint Joseph's Hospital Phone: 651-232-3000
69 W Exchange St Fax: 651-232-4352
Saint Paul, MN 55102
www.healtheast.org

United Hospital Phone: 651-220-8000
333 N Smith Ave Fax: 651-220-5189
Saint Paul, MN 55102
www.unitedhospital.com

Unity Hospital Phone: 763-421-2222
550 Osborne Rd NE Fax: 763-780-6783
Fridley, MN 55432

Veterans Affairs Medical Center Phone: 612-725-2000
1 Veterans Dr Fax: 612-725-2270
Minneapolis, MN 55417
pet.med.va.gov:8080

Transportation

Airport(s)

Minneapolis-Saint Paul International Airport (MSP)
10 miles SE of downtown Minneapolis
(approx 20 minutes) 612-726-5500

Mass Transit

Como-Harriet Streetcar Line
$1.25 Base fare...............................651-228-0263
Metropolitan Transit
$1 Base fare 612-373-3333

Rail/Bus

Greyhound Bus Station Phone: 612-371-3334
1100 Hawthorne Ave TF: 800-231-2222
Minneapolis, MN 55403

Utilities

Electricity
North Saint Paul Electric 651-770-4450
Northern States Power Co.......................800-622-4677
www.nspco.com

Gas
Minnegasco Inc 612-372-4727
www.minnegasco.com
Northern States Power Co.......................800-622-4677
www.nspco.com

Water
Minneapolis Water Works 612-673-1114

Garbage Collection/Recycling
Minneapolis Solid Waste & Recycling Div........612-673-2917

Telecommunications

Telephone

Qwest....800-244-1111
www.qwest.com

Cable Television

AT & T Cable Services....651-222-3333
Time Warner Cable....763-522-2000
www.timewarner.com

Internet Service Providers (ISPs)

Backpack Software Inc (BPSI)....651-645-7550
www.bpsi.net
Bitstream Underground Inc....612-321-9290
www.bitstream.net
Enterprise Network Systems (ENS)....651-683-9141
www.ens.net
gofast.net....651-291-1890
gofast.net
GoldenGate Internet Services....763-574-2200
www.goldengate.net
InterNetwork Services Inc.....763-391-7300
www.inet-serv.com
Minnesota MicroNet....952-882-7711
www.mm.com
MinnNet Communications Inc....612-338-8863
www.minn.net
MN Inter.Net....952-882-2990
www.mninter.net
Onvoy....952-944-9885
www.onvoy.net
Orbis Internet Services Inc....651-603-9030
www.orbis.net
pcOnline Internet Services....651-647-6774
www.pconline.com
Protocol Communications Inc....612-623-9900
www.protocom.com
Real Time Enterprises Inc....952-943-8700
www.real-time.com
Sihope Communications....952-829-9667
www.sihope.com
SkyPoint Communications Inc.....763-417-0227
www.skypoint.com
StarNet Communications Inc....612-333-1505
www.winternet.com
Twin Cities Free-Net....651-256-2112
freenet.msp.mn.us
US Internet Corp.....651-222-4638
www.usinternet.com
Vector Internet Services Inc....612-288-0880
www.visi.com

Banks

Franklin National Bank of Minneapolis
2100 Blaisdell Ave
Minneapolis, MN 55404
Phone: 612-874-6000
Fax: 612-874-7978

National City Bank of Minneapolis
651 Nicollet Mall
Minneapolis, MN 55402
Phone: 612-904-8000
Fax: 612-904-8010

Northeast Bank
77 Broadway St NE
Minneapolis, MN 55413
Phone: 612-379-8811
Fax: 612-362-3262

Norwest Bank Minnesota NA
6th St & Marquette Ave
Minneapolis, MN 55479
Phone: 612-667-1234
Fax: 612-667-0288

Resource Trust Bank
730 2nd Ave S Suite 1400
Minneapolis, MN 55402
Phone: 612-371-9332
Fax: 612-336-1388

Ridgedale State Bank
1200 Nicollet Mall
Minneapolis, MN 55403
Phone: 612-332-8890
Fax: 612-333-8547

Riverside Bank
1801 Riverside Ave
Minneapolis, MN 55454
Phone: 612-341-3505
Fax: 612-341-3576

TCF National Bank Minnesota
801 Marquette Ave
Minneapolis, MN 55402
www.tcfbank.com
Phone: 612-661-6500
Fax: 612-661-8271
TF: 800-328-0728

US Bank NA
601 2nd Ave S
Minneapolis, MN 55402
www.usbank.com
Phone: 612-973-1111
Fax: 612-973-4645
TF: 800-872-2657

Shopping

Burnsville Center
1178 Burnsville Ctr
Burnsville, MN 55306
www.burnsvillecenter.com
Phone: 952-435-8182
Fax: 952-892-5073

Calhoun Square Shopping Center
3001 Hennepin Ave S
Minneapolis, MN 55408
www.calhounsquare.com/
Phone: 612-824-1240
Fax: 612-824-4930

Carriage Hill Plaza
350 Saint Peter St
Saint Paul, MN 55102
Phone: 651-848-0533

City Center
40 S 7th St
Minneapolis, MN 55402
Phone: 612-372-1234

Dayton's
700 Nicollet Mall
Minneapolis, MN 55402
Phone: 612-375-2200
Fax: 612-375-3878

Dayton's
411 Cedar St
Saint Paul, MN 55101
Phone: 651-292-5222

Galtier Plaza
175 5th St E Suite 315
Saint Paul, MN 55101
Phone: 651-297-6734
Fax: 651-297-6287

Gaviidae Common
651 Nicollet Mall
Minneapolis, MN 55402
Phone: 612-372-1222
Fax: 612-372-1239

Grand Avenue
1043 Grand Ave Box 315
Saint Paul, MN 55105
www.grandave.com/
Phone: 651-699-0029
Fax: 651-699-7775

Knollwood Mall
8332 Hwy 7
Saint Louis Park, MN 55426
Phone: 952-933-8041
Fax: 952-933-7660

Lafayette Square Shopping Center
1990 Christensen Ave
West Saint Paul, MN 55118
Phone: 651-455-7100

Mall of America
60 E Broadway
Bloomington, MN 55425
E-mail: info@mallofamerica.com
www.mallofamerica.com
Phone: 952-883-8810
Fax: 952-883-8886

Mall of Saint Paul
1817 Selby Ave
Saint Paul, MN 55104
Phone: 651-647-6163

Maplewood Mall
I-694 & White Bear Ave
Saint Paul, MN 55106
Phone: 651-770-5020

Minneapolis City Center
40 S 7th St
Minneapolis, MN 55402
Phone: 612-372-1200

Norwest Center
55 E 5th St
Saint Paul, MN 55101
Phone: 651-221-1949
Fax: 651-221-0540

Oakdale Mall
7166 10th St N
Saint Paul, MN 55128
Phone: 651-739-4893

Phalen New Market
1345 E Magnolia Ave
Saint Paul, MN 55106
Phone: 651-771-2504
Fax: 651-771-1063

Prime Outlet Center
Hwy I-94 & County Rd 19
Woodbury, MN 55129
Phone: 651-735-9060
Fax: 651-735-9235

Ridgedale Center
12401 Wayzata Blvd
Minnetonka, MN 55305
www.ridgedalecenter.com
Phone: 952-541-4864
Fax: 952-540-0154

Rosedale Center
Hwy 36 & Fairview Ave
Roseville, MN 55113
E-mail: shop@rosedalecenter.com
Phone: 651-638-3553
Fax: 651-638-3599

Saint Anthony Main Shopping & Entertainment Center
125 SE Main St
Minneapolis, MN 55414
Phone: 612-378-1226
Fax: 651-646-0230

Southdale Center
10 Southdale Ctr
Edina, MN 55435
E-mail: shopping@southdalecenter.com
www.southdalecenter.com
Phone: 952-925-7874
Fax: 952-925-7856

Town Square
445 Minnesota St
Saint Paul, MN 55101
Phone: 651-227-3307
Fax: 651-291-5922

World Trade Center
30 E 7th St Suite 2600
Saint Paul, MN 55101
Phone: 651-291-5900
Fax: 651-291-5922

Media

Newspapers and Magazines

City Pages
401 N 3rd St Suite 550
Minneapolis, MN 55401
E-mail: letters@citypages.com
www.citypages.com
Phone: 612-375-1015
Fax: 612-372-3737

Corporate Report Minnesota
527 Marquette Ave S Suite 300
Minneapolis, MN 55402
Phone: 612-338-4288
Fax: 612-573-6300

Finance & Commerce
730 2nd Ave S Peavey Bldg Suite 100
Minneapolis, MN 55402
www.finance-commerce.com
Phone: 612-333-4244
Fax: 612-333-3243

Lakeville Life & Times
PO Box 549
Lakeville, MN 55044
Phone: 952-469-2181
Fax: 952-469-2184

Minneapolis-Saint Paul
220 S 6th St Suite 500
Minneapolis, MN 55402
E-mail: edit@mspcommunications.com
www.mspmag.com
Phone: 612-339-7571
Fax: 612-339-5806

Minneapolis-Saint Paul CityBusiness
527 Marquette Ave Suite 400
Minneapolis, MN 55402
E-mail: twincities@amcity.com
www.amcity.com/twincities
Phone: 612-288-2141
Fax: 612-288-2121

Plymouth Sun Sailor
13911 Ridgedale Dr Suite 110
Minnetonka, MN 55305
www.mnsun.com
Phone: 763-546-7474
Fax: 763-546-7484

Saint Louis Park Sun Sailor
13911 Ridgedale Dr Suite 110
Minnetonka, MN 55305
www.wcco.com/community/sun/articles/sl/new
Phone: 763-546-7474
Fax: 763-546-7484

Saint Paul Pioneer Press*
345 Cedar St
Saint Paul, MN 55101
E-mail: feedback@pioneerplanet.infi.net
www.pioneerplanet.com
Phone: 651-222-5011
Fax: 651-228-5500

Shoreview/Arden Hills Bulletin
PO Box 120608
New Brighton, MN 55112
Phone: 651-633-2777
Fax: 651-633-3846

Skyway News
10001 Wayzata Blvd
Minnetonka, MN 55402
Phone: 612-375-9222
Fax: 612-375-9208

Star Tribune*
425 Portland Ave S
Minneapolis, MN 55488
E-mail: roberts@startribune.com
www.startribune.com
Phone: 612-673-4000
Fax: 612-673-4359
TF: 800-827-8742

**Indicates major daily newspapers*

Television

KARE-TV Ch 11 (NBC)
8811 Olson Memorial Hwy
Minneapolis, MN 55427
www.kare11.com
Phone: 763-546-1111
Fax: 763-546-8606

KMSP-TV Ch 9 (UPN)
11358 Viking Dr
Eden Prairie, MN 55344
E-mail: upn9@kmsp9.com
www.kmsp.com
Phone: 952-944-9999
Fax: 952-942-0286

KMWB-TV Ch 23 (WB)
1640 Como Ave
Saint Paul, MN 55108
Phone: 651-646-2300
Fax: 651-646-1220

KPXM-TV Ch 41 (PAX)
PO Box 407
Big Lake, MN 55309
www.pax.net/kpxm
Phone: 763-263-8666
Fax: 763-263-6600

KSTP-TV Ch 5 (ABC)
3415 University Ave SE
Saint Paul, MN 55114
www.kstp.com
Phone: 651-646-5555
Fax: 651-642-4409

KTCA-TV Ch 2 (PBS)
172 E 4th St
Saint Paul, MN 55101
www.ktca.org
Phone: 651-222-1717
Fax: 651-229-1282

KTCI-TV Ch 17 (PBS)
172 E 4th St
Saint Paul, MN 55101
Phone: 651-222-1717
Fax: 651-229-1282

WCCO-TV Ch 4 (CBS)
90 S 11th St
Minneapolis, MN 55403
E-mail: wccotv@wcco.com
www.wcco.com/partners/tv/index.html
Phone: 612-339-4444
Fax: 612-330-2767

WFTC-TV Ch 29 (Fox)
1701 Broadway St NE
Minneapolis, MN 55413
E-mail: feedback@fox29.com
www.fox29.com
Phone: 612-379-2929
Fax: 612-379-2900

Radio

KDWB-FM 101.3 MHz (CHR)
100 N 6th St Suite 306C
Minneapolis, MN 55403
www.kdwb.com
Phone: 612-340-9000
Fax: 612-340-9560

KEEY-FM 102.1 MHz (Ctry)
7900 Xerxes Ave S Suite 102
Minneapolis, MN 55431
E-mail: k102@pclink.com
www.k102.com
Phone: 952-820-4200
Fax: 952-820-4223

KFAN-AM 1130 kHz (Sports)
7900 Xerxes Ave S Suite 102
Minneapolis, MN 55431
E-mail: kfan@pclink.com
www.kfan.com
Phone: 952-820-4300
Fax: 952-820-4256

KLBB-AM 1400 kHz (Nost)
331 11th St S Suite 31
Minneapolis, MN 55404
E-mail: info@klbb.com
Phone: 612-321-7200
Fax: 612-321-7202

KMOJ-FM 89.9 MHz (Urban)
501 Bryant Ave N
Minneapolis, MN 55405
E-mail: live@kmoj.com
www.kmoj.com
Phone: 763-377-0594
Fax: 763-377-6919

KNOW-FM 91.1 MHz (NPR)
45 E 7th St
Saint Paul, MN 55101
access.mpr.org/stations/ksjnknow/index.html
Phone: 651-290-1500
Fax: 651-290-1295

KQQL-FM 107.9 MHz (Oldies)
60 S 6th St Suite 930
Minneapolis, MN 55402
www.kool108.com
Phone: 612-333-8118
Fax: 612-333-1616

KQRS-FM 92.5 MHz (CR)
917 N Lilac Dr
Golden Valley, MN 55422
E-mail: kqcrew@mnvirtmall.com
www.92kqrs.com
Phone: 763-545-5601
Fax: 763-595-4940

KSTP-AM 1500 kHz (N/T)
3415 University Ave
Saint Paul, MN 55114
www.am1500.com
Phone: 651-647-1500
Fax: 651-647-2904
TF: 877-615-1500

KSTP-FM 94.5 MHz (AC)
3415 University Ave
Saint Paul, MN 55114
Phone: 651-642-4141
Fax: 651-642-4148

KTCJ-AM 690 kHz (Ctry)
7900 Xerxes Ave S Suite 102
Minneapolis, MN 55431
Phone: 952-820-4200
Fax: 952-820-4223

KTCZ-FM 97.1 MHz (AAA)
100 N 6th St Suite 306-C
Minneapolis, MN 55403
www.cities97.com
Phone: 612-339-0000
Fax: 612-333-2997

KXXR-FM 93.7 MHz (Rock)
917 N Lilac Dr
Golden Valley, MN 55422
E-mail: 93x@sidewalk.com
www.93x.com
Phone: 763-545-5601
Fax: 763-595-4940

KZNR-FM 105.1 MHz (Alt)
917 N Lilac Dr
Golden Valley, MN 55422
Phone: 763-545-5601
Fax: 763-595-4940

KZNZ-FM 105.7 MHz (Alt)
917 N Lilac Dr
Golden Valley, MN 55422
E-mail: mail@zone105.com
www.zone105.com
Phone: 763-545-5601
Fax: 763-595-4940

WCAL-FM 89.3 MHz (NPR)
1520 St Olaf Ave
Northfield, MN 55057
E-mail: wcal@stolaf.edu
www.stolaf.edu/wcal/
Phone: 612-798-9225
Fax: 612-798-8614
TF: 888-798-9225

WCCO-AM 830 kHz (N/T)
625 2nd Ave S
Minneapolis, MN 55402
E-mail: wcco830@ibsys.com
www.wcco.com
Phone: 612-370-0611
Fax: 612-370-0159

WLOL-FM 100.3 MHz (CR)
16 S 6th St Suite 930
Minneapolis, MN 55402
Phone: 612-330-0100
Fax: 612-330-0897

WLTE-FM 102.9 MHz (AC)
625 2nd Ave S Suite 500
Minneapolis, MN 55402
www.wlte.com
Phone: 612-339-1029
Fax: 612-339-5653

WRQC-FM 100.3 MHz (Rock)
60 S 6th St Suite 930
Minneapolis, MN 55402
Phone: 612-330-0100
Fax: 612-330-0897

WWTC-AM 1280 kHz (N/T)
5501 Excelsior Blvd
Minneapolis, MN 55416
Phone: 952-926-1280
Fax: 952-926-8014

WXPT-FM 104.1 MHz (Alt)
7001 France Ave S Suite 200
Edina, MN 55435
www.1041thepoint.com
Phone: 952-836-1041
Fax: 952-915-6781

Attractions

The Mississippi Mile winds through downtown Minneapolis, with parkways, biking and walking paths, and picnic areas all along the banks of the River. From the James J. Hill Stone Bridge one can view the Mississippi, Saint Anthony Falls, and the surrounding historic district. Fort Snelling State Park, a stone fortress where guides recreate army life of the 1820s, also overlooks the River. In the nearby city of Bloomington is the Mall of America, the largest shopping complex in the U.S. A total of 32 Fortune 500 companies, including Honeywell and General Mills, have their corporate headquarters in Minneapolis and the surrounding Twin Cities area.

Saint Paul is the state capital of Minnesota and the "Twin City" of Minneapolis. The city is known for its magnificent architecture, and the State Capitol building boasts the largest unsupported marble dome in the world. Summit Avenue in Saint Paul is known for its beautiful Victorian mansions, and the architecture of the acclaimed Ordway Music Theatre has been compared to the great concert halls of Europe. Saint Paul is also home to the largest fairgrounds in the United States, the Minnesota State Fairgrounds, where the city hosts the annual Minnesota State Fair each August.

Alexander Ramsey House
265 S Exchange St
Saint Paul, MN 55102
www.mnhs.org/places/sites/arh/index.html
Phone: 651-296-0100
Fax: 651-296-0100

American Swedish Institute
2600 Park Ave
Minneapolis, MN 55407
E-mail: information@americanswedishinst.org
www.americanswedishinst.org/
Phone: 612-871-4907
Fax: 612-871-8682
TF: 800-579-3336

Ard Godfrey House
28 University Ave SE
Minneapolis, MN 55414
Phone: 612-870-8001
Fax: 612-813-5336

Bakken Library & Museum
3537 Zenith Ave S
Minneapolis, MN 55416
www.thebakken.org
Phone: 952-927-6508
Fax: 952-927-7265

Baseball Hall of Fame
910 3rd Ave S
Minneapolis, MN 55415
Phone: 612-375-9707
TF: 888-375-9707

Carriage Hill Plaza
350 Saint Peter St
Saint Paul, MN 55102
Phone: 651-848-0533

Children's Theatre Co
2400 3rd Ave S
Minneapolis, MN 55404
E-mail: info@childrenstheatre.org
www.childrenstheatre.org/
Phone: 612-874-0400
Fax: 612-874-8119

Como Ordway Memorial Japanese Garden
1325 Aida Pl
Saint Paul, MN 55103
Phone: 651-487-8240
Fax: 651-487-8255

Como Park
Lexington Pkwy & Como
Saint Paul, MN 55102
www.stpaul.gov/depts/parks/userguide/comopark.html
Phone: 651-266-6400

Como Park Zoo & Conservatory
Midway Pkwy & Kaufman Dr
Saint Paul, MN 55103
Phone: 651-487-8200
Fax: 651-487-8203

Crosby Park
Shepard Rd & Gannon
Saint Paul, MN 55104
Phone: 651-632-5111
Fax: 651-632-5115

Dakota County Historical Museum
130 3rd Ave N
South Saint Paul, MN 55075
Phone: 651-451-6260
Fax: 651-552-7265

Dodge Nature Center
365 W Marie Ave
West Saint Paul, MN 55118
Phone: 651-455-4531
Fax: 651-455-2575

Ethnic Dance Theatre
2337 Central Ave NE
Minneapolis, MN 55418
Phone: 763-782-3970
Fax: 763-782-3970

Farmers' Market
290 E 5th St
Saint Paul, MN 55101
E-mail: spmkweb@aol.com
www.stpaulfarmersmarket.com
Phone: 651-227-8101

Fitzgerald Theater
10 E Exchange St
Saint Paul, MN 55101
E-mail: fitzgerald@mpr.org
www.fitzgeraldtheater.com
Phone: 651-290-1200
Fax: 651-290-1195

Fort Snelling State Park
Hwys 5 & 55
Minneapolis, MN 55111
www.mnhs.org/places/sites/hfs/index.html
Phone: 612-725-2413

Foshay Tower Observation Deck & Museum
821 Marquette Ave
Minneapolis, MN 55402
Phone: 612-359-3030
Fax: 612-359-3034

Gibbs Farm Museum
2097 W Larpenteur Ave
Saint Paul, MN 55113
www.rchs.com/gbbsfm2.htm
Phone: 651-646-8629

Governor's Residence
1006 Summit Ave
Saint Paul, MN 55115
Phone: 651-297-8177

Great American History Theatre
30 10th St E
Saint Paul, MN 55101
E-mail: info@historytheatre.com
Phone: 651-292-4323
Fax: 651-292-4322

Guthrie Theater
725 Vineland Pl
Minneapolis, MN 55403
Phone: 763-377-2224
Fax: 612-375-8721
TF: 877-447-8243

Harriet Island
Plato Ave & Waubasha St
Saint Paul, MN 55102
Phone: 651-266-6400
Fax: 651-292-7405

Hennepin History Museum
2303 3rd Ave S
Minneapolis, MN 55404
Phone: 612-870-1329
Fax: 612-870-1320

Hey City Theater
824 Hennepin Ave
Minneapolis, MN 55403
E-mail: heycitythr@aol.com
Phone: 612-333-9202
Fax: 612-333-9195
TF: 800-476-2786

Hidden Falls Park
Magoffin Ave & Mississippi River Blvd
Saint Paul, MN 55104
Phone: 651-488-7291

Hidden Falls/Crosby Farm Park
1313 Hidden Falls Dr
Saint Paul, MN 55116
Phone: 651-266-6400
Fax: 651-292-7405

Historic Fort Snelling
Hwy 55 E of Airport
Saint Paul, MN 55111
www.mnhs.org/places/sites/hfs/index.html
Phone: 612-726-1171

Historic Orpheum Theatre
910 Hennepin Ave
Minneapolis, MN 55403
Phone: 612-339-0075
Fax: 612-339-3909

Historic State Theatre
805 Hennepin Ave
Minneapolis, MN 55403
Phone: 612-339-0075
Fax: 612-339-3909

Humphrey Forum
301 19th Ave S
Minneapolis, MN 55455
Phone: 612-624-5799
Fax: 612-625-3513

Imation IMAX Theatre
12000 Zoo Blvd
Apple Valley, MN 55124
www.imax3d.com
Phone: 952-431-4629
Fax: 952-997-9744

Indian Mounds Park
Mounds Blvd & Earl St
Saint Paul, MN 55106
Phone: 651-266-6400
Fax: 651-292-7405

James Ford Bell Museum of Natural History
10 Church St SE
Minneapolis, MN 55455
www.umn.edu/bellmuse/
Phone: 612-624-7083
Fax: 612-626-7704

James J Hill House
240 Summit Ave
Saint Paul, MN 55102
www.mnhs.org/places/sites/jjhh/index.html
Phone: 651-297-2555
Fax: 651-297-5655
TF: 888-727-8386

John H Stevens House
4901 Minnehaha Ave
Minneapolis, MN 55417
Phone: 612-722-2220

Jungle Theater
2951 Lindale Ave S
Minneapolis, MN 55408
Phone: 612-822-7063
Fax: 612-822-9408

Knott's Camp Snoopy
5000 Center Ct
Bloomington, MN 55425
www.campsnoopy.com
Phone: 952-883-8500
Fax: 952-883-8683

Lake Harriet
4135 W Lake Harriet Pkwy
Minneapolis, MN 55415
Phone: 612-661-4806
Fax: 612-661-4789

Landmark Center
75 W 5th St
Saint Paul, MN 55102
Phone: 651-292-3225
Fax: 651-292-3272

Lowertown District
Downtown Saint Paul-E of Jackson St
Saint Paul, MN 55101
www.lowertown.org
Phone: 651-227-9131

Macphail Center for the Arts
1128 LaSalle Ave
Minneapolis, MN 55403
Phone: 612-321-0100
Fax: 612-321-9740

Mall of America
60 E Broadway
Bloomington, MN 55425
E-mail: info@mallofamerica.com
www.mallofamerica.com
Phone: 952-883-8810
Fax: 952-883-8886

Mears Park
6th St & Sibley
Saint Paul, MN 55101
Phone: 651-266-6400

Minneapolis Grain Exchange
400 S 4th St Rm 130
Minneapolis, MN 55415
E-mail: mgex@ix.netcom.com
www.mgex.com
Phone: 612-338-6212
Fax: 612-339-1155
TF: 800-827-4746

Minneapolis Institute of Arts
2400 3rd Ave S
Minneapolis, MN 55404
E-mail: miagen@artsmia.org
www.artsmia.org
Phone: 612-870-3000
Fax: 612-870-3004
TF: 888-642-2787

Minneapolis Planetarium
300 Nicollet Mall
Minneapolis, MN 55401
ast1.spa.umn.edu/Outreach/planetarium.html
Phone: 612-630-6150
Fax: 612-630-6180

Minneapolis Sculpture Garden
726 Vineland Pl
Minneapolis, MN 55403
Phone: 612-370-3996
Fax: 612-370-4882

Minnehaha Falls
4825 Minnehaha Ave S
Minneapolis, MN 55417
Phone: 612-661-4800

Minnehaha Princess Depot
4926 Hiawatha Ave Minnehaha Falls
Minneapolis, MN 55417
E-mail: minnehahadepot@mnhs.org
www.mnhs.org/places/sites/md/index.html
Phone: 651-228-0263
Fax: 651-228-9412

Minnesota Air Guard Museum
670 General Miller Dr Minnesota Air Guard Base
Saint Paul, MN 55111
www.mnangmuseum.org
Phone: 612-713-2523
Fax: 612-713-2525

Minnesota Brewing Co
882 W 7th St
Saint Paul, MN 55102
E-mail: info@grainbelt.com
www.grainbelt.com
Phone: 651-228-9173
Fax: 651-290-8211

Minnesota Children's Museum
10 W 7th St
Saint Paul, MN 55102
E-mail: membership@mcm.org
www.mcm.org
Phone: 651-225-6001
Fax: 651-225-6006

Minnesota Historical Society
345 Kellogg Blvd W
Saint Paul, MN 55102
www.mnhs.org
Phone: 651-296-6126
Fax: 651-296-1004
TF: 800-657-3773

Minnesota Museum of American Art
75 W 5th St
Saint Paul, MN 55102
www.mtn.org/MMAA
Phone: 651-292-4355
Fax: 651-292-4340

Minnesota Opera
345 Washington St Ordway Music Theatre
Saint Paul, MN 55102
E-mail: mithu@mnopera.org
www.mnopera.org
Phone: 612-333-6669
Fax: 612-333-0869

Minnesota Opera Co
620 N 1st St
Minneapolis, MN 55401
www.bitstream.net/theatre/opera.htm
Phone: 612-333-2700
Fax: 612-333-0869

Minnesota Orchestra
1111 Nicollet Mall Orchestra Hall
Minneapolis, MN 55403
E-mail: info@mnorch.org
www.mnorch.org
Phone: 612-371-5600
Fax: 612-371-0838

Minnesota Sinfonia
1820 Stevens Ave S Suite E
Minneapolis, MN 55403
Phone: 612-871-1701
Fax: 612-871-1701

Minnesota State Capitol
75 Constitution Ave
Saint Paul, MN 55155
E-mail: statecapitol@mnhs.org
www.mnhs.org/places/sites/msc/index.html
Phone: 651-296-2739

Minnesota Transportation Museum
193 Pennsylvania Ave
Saint Paul, MN 55101
www.mtmuseum.org
Phone: 651-228-0263
Fax: 651-228-9412
TF: 800-711-2591

Minnesota Valley National Wildlife Refuge
3815 E 80th St
Bloomington, MN 55425
www.fws.gov/r3pao/mn_vall
Phone: 952-854-5900
Fax: 952-725-3279

Minnesota Vietnam Veterans' Memorial
State Capitol Grounds
Saint Paul, MN 55082
Phone: 651-777-0686

Minnesota Zoo
13000 Zoo Blvd
Apple Valley, MN 55124
www.mnzoo.com
Phone: 952-431-9200
Fax: 952-431-9300
TF: 800-366-7811

Mississippi Mile
125 SE Main St
Minneapolis, MN 55414
Phone: 612-673-5123

Museum of Questionable Medical Devices
201 SE Main St
Minneapolis, MN 55414
E-mail: quack@mtn.org
www.mtn.org/~quack
Phone: 612-379-4046
Fax: 763-540-9999

Music Box Theatre
1407 Nicollet Ave
Minneapolis, MN 55403
Phone: 612-871-1414

Music in the Park Series
2129 Commonwealth Ave St Anthony Pk
Saint Paul, MN 55108
E-mail: jahchamber@aol.com
www.musicintheparkseries.org
Phone: 651-644-4234
Fax: 651-644-8152

Mystic Lake Casino
2400 Mystic Lake Blvd
Prior Lake, MN 55372
www.mysticlake.com
Phone: 952-445-9000
Fax: 952-496-7280
TF: 800-262-7799

North Star Opera
312 N Hamline Ave EM Pearson Theatre
Saint Paul, MN 55104
Phone: 651-698-5386

Old Muskego Church
2481 Como Ave
Saint Paul, MN 55108
Phone: 651-641-3456

Ordway Music Theatre
345 Washington St
Saint Paul, MN 55102
www.ordway.org/
Phone: 651-224-4222
Fax: 651-282-3160

Orpheum Theatre
910 Hennepin Ave
Minneapolis, MN 55402
E-mail: groupsales@orpheum.com
www.state-orpheum.com
Phone: 612-373-5600
Fax: 612-339-3909

Our Lady of Lourdes Church
1 Lourdes Pl
Minneapolis, MN 55414
Phone: 612-379-2259

Park Square Theatre Co
20 W 7th Pl
Saint Paul, MN 55102
www.bitstream.net/theatre/psquare.htm
Phone: 651-291-7005
Fax: 651-291-9180

Pavek Museum of Broadcasting
3515 Raleigh Ave
Saint Louis Park, MN 55416
www.pavekmuseum.org
Phone: 952-926-8198
Fax: 952-926-9761

Penumbra Theatre
270 N Kent St
Saint Paul, MN 55102
Phone: 651-224-4601
Fax: 651-224-7074

Plymouth Music Series of Minnesota
1900 Nicollet Ave
Minneapolis, MN 55403
www.plymouthmusic.org
Phone: 763-547-1451
Fax: 763-547-1484

Purcell Cutts House
2328 Lake Pl
Minneapolis, MN 55405
Phone: 612-870-3131

Rice Park
5th & Market Sts
Saint Paul, MN 55102
Phone: 651-266-6400

Riverplace
1 Main St SE Suite 204
Minneapolis, MN 55414
Phone: 612-379-2438
Fax: 612-379-4120

Saint Anthony Main Shopping & Entertainment Center
125 SE Main St
Minneapolis, MN 55414
Phone: 612-378-1226
Fax: 651-646-0230

Saint Paul Chamber Orchestra
408 Saint Peter St Hamm Bldg Suite 500
Saint Paul, MN 55102
www.stpaulchamberorchestra.org
Phone: 651-292-3248
Fax: 651-292-3281

Saint Paul's Cathedral
239 Selby Ave
Saint Paul, MN 55102
Phone: 651-228-1766

Schubert Club Musical Instrument Museum
75 W 5th St
Saint Paul, MN 55102
www.schubert.org/museum.html
Phone: 651-292-3267
Fax: 651-292-4317

Science Museum of Minnesota
120 W Kellogg Blvd
Saint Paul, MN 55102
www.smm.org
Phone: 651-221-9444
Fax: 651-221-9448

Seventh Place Plaza
7th Pl-betw Wabasha & Saint Peter Sts
Saint Paul, MN 55102
Phone: 651-225-9002

Summit Brewing Co
910 Montreal Cir
Saint Paul, MN 55102
Phone: 651-265-7800
Fax: 651-265-7801

Theodore Wirth Park
Wirth Pkwy & Plymouth Ave N
Minneapolis, MN 55422
Phone: 612-661-4806
Fax: 612-661-4789

Town Square
445 Minnesota St
Saint Paul, MN 55101
Phone: 651-227-3307
Fax: 651-291-5922

Town Square Park
7th & Minnesota Sts
Saint Paul, MN 55101
Phone: 651-227-3307
Fax: 651-227-5908

Valleyfair
1 Valleyfair Dr
Shakopee, MN 55379
www.valleyfair.com
Phone: 952-445-7600
Fax: 952-445-1539
TF: 800-386-7433

Wabasha Street Caves
215 S Wabasha St
Saint Paul, MN 55107
Phone: 651-224-1191
Fax: 651-224-0059

Walker Art Center
725 Vineland Pl
Minneapolis, MN 55403
www.walkerart.org
Phone: 612-375-7600
Fax: 612-375-7618

Weisman Art Museum
333 E River Rd
Minneapolis, MN 55455
hudson.acad.umn.edu
Phone: 612-625-9494
Fax: 612-625-9630

Westwood Hills Nature Center
8300 W Franklin Ave
Saint Louis Park, MN 55426
Phone: 952-924-2544
Fax: 763-797-9691

William L McKnight 3M Omnitheater
120 W Kellogg Blvd
Saint Paul, MN 55102
www.smm.org/omni
Phone: 651-221-9444
Fax: 651-221-9433

World Trade Center
30 E 7th St Suite 2600
Saint Paul, MN 55101
Phone: 651-291-5900
Fax: 651-291-5922

Zenon Dance Co
528 Hennepin Ave Suite 400
Minneapolis, MN 55403
Phone: 612-338-1101
Fax: 612-338-2479

Sports Teams & Facilities

Hubert H Humphrey Metrodome
900 S 5th St
Minneapolis, MN 55415
E-mail: 105521.764@compuserve.com
Phone: 612-332-0386
Fax: 612-332-8334

Midway Stadium
1771 Energy Park Dr
Saint Paul, MN 55108
Phone: 651-644-6512
Fax: 651-644-1627

Minnesota Thunder (soccer)
1700 105th Ave NE National Sports Ctr
Blaine, MN 55449
E-mail: info@mnthunder.com
www.mnthunder.com
Phone: 763-785-3668
Fax: 763-785-5999

Minnesota Timberwolves
600 1st Ave N Target Ctr
Minneapolis, MN 55403
www.nba.com/timberwolves
Phone: 612-337-3865
Fax: 612-673-1699

Minnesota Twins
34 Kirby Puckett Pl
Minneapolis, MN 55415
E-mail: twins@mntwins.com
www.mntwins.com
Phone: 612-338-9467
Fax: 612-375-7473
TF: 800-338-9467

Minnesota Vikings
900 S 5th St Hubert H Humphrey Metrodome
Minneapolis, MN 55415
www.vikings.com
Phone: 612-333-8828
Fax: 612-333-0458

Raceway Park
1 Checkered Flag Blvd
Shakopee, MN 55379
www.goracewaypark.com
Phone: 952-445-2257
Fax: 952-445-5500

Saint Paul Saints (baseball)
1771 Energy Park Dr Midway Stadium
Saint Paul, MN 55108
E-mail: funsgood@spsaints.com
spsaints.com/
Phone: 651-644-6659
Fax: 651-644-1627

Target Center
600 1st Ave N
Minneapolis, MN 55403
E-mail: mail@targetcenter.com
www.targetcenter.com
Phone: 612-673-1300
Fax: 612-673-1370

Annual Events

Alive After Five Concerts (June) 612-338-3807
American Craft Council Craft Expo (mid-April) 651-224-7361
An Irish Celebration (mid-March) 651-292-3225
Bavarian Sommerfest (late June) 651-439-7128
Bloomington Jazz Festival (mid-August) 952-948-8877
Capital City Lights (November-February) 651-265-4900
Capital New Year (December 31) 952-920-9054
Cinco de Mayo Mexican Fiesta (early May) 651-222-6347
Civil War Weekend (mid-June) 612-726-1171
Classic Cars on Wabasha (June-mid-October) 651-266-8989
Country Folk Art Show (mid-September) 651-642-2200
Dayton's Bachman's Flower Show (mid-late March) 612-375-3018
Eagle Creek Rendezvous (late May) 952-445-6900
Easter Egg-Stravaganza (mid-April) 952-883-8600
Fall Colors Art Festival (early October) 651-439-4001
Fall Home & Garden Show (mid-October) 612-335-6000
Farmers Market on Nicollet Mall (May-October) 612-338-3807
Festival of Nations (early May) 651-647-0191
Fur Trade Weekend 1827 (mid-August) 612-725-2413
Gaslight Tours (late January-early February) 651-297-2555
Grand Meander (early December) 651-699-0029
Hill House Holidays (mid-late December) 651-297-2555
Holiday Bazaar (late November-early December) 651-292-3230
Holidays at the Zoo (December) 952-431-9298
Hollidazzle Parades (late November-December) 612-338-3807
International Film Fest (early April-mid-May) 202-724-5613
Juneteenth Festival (mid-June) 612-375-7622
Main Street Days (mid-May) 952-931-0132
Mayday Parade & Festival (early May) 612-721-2535
Midsommar Celebration & Scandinavian Art Fair (mid-June) 612-871-4907
Midwest Fall Antique Auto Show (early October) 651-642-2200
Minneapolis Aquatennial (mid-July) 612-661-4700
Minnesota 4-H Horse Show (late September) 651-642-2200
Minnesota Fringe Theater Festival (late July-early August) 612-823-6005
Minnesota Renaissance Festival (mid-August-late September) 952-445-7361
Minnesota State Fair (late August-early September) 651-642-2200
New Year's Eve Fireworks Celebration (December 31) 612-673-5123
Northwest Sports Show (early-mid-March) 612-827-5833
Oktoberfest (mid-late September) 651-439-7128
Oyster & Guinness Festival (late August) 612-904-1000
Rondo Days Festival (mid-July) 651-646-6597
Saint Paul Art Crawl (early October & late April) 651-292-4373
Saint Paul Ice Fishing & Winter Sports Show (early December) 651-265-4900
Saint Paul Winter Carnival (late January-early February) 651-223-4710
Scottish Ramble & Highland Dance Competition (mid-February) 651-292-3276
Semstone Truck Rodeo (mid-September) 651-642-2200
Ski Snowmobile & Winter Sports Show (mid-November) 612-335-6000
Sommerfest (July) 612-661-4700
Spring Babies (early-mid-April) 952-431-9213
Spring Festival Arts & Crafts Affair (early April) 952-445-7223
Stone Arch Festival of the Arts (mid-June) 612-378-1226
Summit Avenue Walking Tours (May-September) 651-297-2555
Taste of Minnesota (early July) 651-772-9980
Thursday Night Live Outdoor Concerts (July) 651-774-5422
Twin Cities Juneteenth Celebration (mid-June) 763-529-5553
Twin Cities Marathon (early October) 612-673-0778
Twin Cities Ribfest (late July) 612-673-1300
Uptown Art Fair (early August) 612-661-4700
Viennese Sommerfest (July) 612-371-5656
Warehouse District Group Show (early March) 612-344-1700
Western Saddle Club Horse Show (late September) 651-642-2200
Winter on the Hill (late January-early February) 651-297-2555

Mobile, Alabama

***County:* Mobile**

MOBILE is located in southwestern Alabama where the Mobile River flows into Mobile Bay, 30 miles north of the Gulf of Mexico. Major cities within 100 miles include Pensacola, Florida; and Biloxi and Pascagoula, Mississippi.

Area (Land)	118.0 sq mi
Area (Water)	38.6 sq mi
Elevation	16 ft
Latitude	30-69-42 N
Longitude	88-04-31 W
Time Zone	CST
Area Code	334

Climate

Mobile's climate is influenced by the city's proximity to the Gulf of Mexico. Winters are mild, with average high temperatures in the low 60s and lows in the low 40s. Summers are hot and humid, with average daytime high temperatures in the low 90s and evening lows in the low 70s. August is the wettest month of the year in Mobile; October is the driest.

Average Temperatures & Precipitation

Temperatures

	Jan	Feb	Mar	Apr	May	Jun	Jul	Aug	Sep	Oct	Nov	Dec
High	60	64	71	79	85	90	91	91	87	80	70	63
Low	40	43	50	57	64	71	73	73	69	57	49	43

Precipitation

	Jan	Feb	Mar	Apr	May	Jun	Jul	Aug	Sep	Oct	Nov	Dec
Inches	4.8	5.5	6.4	4.5	5.7	5.0	6.9	7.0	5.9	2.9	4.1	5.3

History

The city of Mobile was originally founded (in 1702) by Jean Baptiste LeMoyne, Sieur de Bienville several miles north of its present location as "Fort Louis de Mobile." The settlement was moved to the mouth of the Mobile River nine years later when high flood waters drove the early residents of Fort Louis de Mobile from their homes. The settlement also served as the capital of French Louisiana until 1718. Over the course of 50 years (1763-1813), control of Mobile shifted from France to Great Britain to Spain before the United States finally gained control of the region in 1813. The following year, in 1814, Mobile was incorporated as a city.

During the 19th century, Mobile grew quickly as port city, with cotton its leading commodity. The city continued to serve as a port for much of the Civil War, until the Battle of Mobile Bay in 1864. Mobile Bay was also the site where Confederate torpedoes sank the ironclad Tecumseh, on which Admiral David Farragut said, "Damn the torpedoes! Full speed ahead!" The city itself was not captured by Union troops until 1865. The city also served as an important military center during World Wars I and II, building and repairing battleships and shipping supplies to the U.S. troops overseas.

The Mobile metropolitan area today is an important commercial and industrial center, and the Port of Mobile is among the nation's busiest seaports. Home to more than 202,000 people, Mobile is Alabama's second largest city.

Population

1990 Census	196,263
1998 Estimate	202,181
% Change	1.1
2003 Projection	202,820

Racial/Ethnic Breakdown

White	59.6%
Black	38.9%
Other	1.5%
Hispanic Origin (may be of any race)	1.0%

Age Breakdown

Under 5 years	7.6%
5 to 19	22.1%
20 to 34	24.5%
35 to 54	23.5%
55 to 64	8.6%
65 to 74	7.9%
75+ years	5.8%
Median Age	32.5

Gender Breakdown

Male	46.4%
Female	55.6%

Government

Type of Government: Mayor-Council

Mobile Administrative Services Div
PO Box 1827
Mobile, AL 36633
Phone: 334-208-7806
Fax: 334-208-7548

Mobile City Clerk
PO Box 1827
Mobile, AL 36633
Phone: 334-208-7209
Fax: 334-208-7576

Mobile City Council
PO Box 1827
Mobile, AL 36633
Phone: 334-208-7411
Fax: 334-208-7482

Mobile City Hall
PO Box 1827
Mobile, AL 36633
Phone: 334-208-7411
Fax: 334-208-7482

Mobile Finance Div
PO Box 1827
Mobile, AL 36633
Phone: 334-208-7407
Fax: 334-208-7756

Mobile Fire-Rescue Dept
701 Saint Francis St
Mobile, AL 36602
Phone: 334-208-7351
Fax: 334-208-5813

Mobile Human Resources Dept
PO Box 1827
Mobile, AL 36633
Phone: 334-208-7832
Fax: 334-208-7153

Mobile Legal Dept
PO Box 1827
Mobile, AL 36633
Phone: 334-208-7416
Fax: 334-208-7322

Mobile Mayor
PO Box 1827
Mobile, AL 36633
Phone: 334-208-7395
Fax: 334-208-7548

Mobile Parks & Recreation Dept
2301 Airport Blvd
Mobile, AL 36606
Phone: 334-441-1600
Fax: 334-478-5072

Mobile Police Dept
2460 Government Blvd
Mobile, AL 36606
Phone: 334-208-1700
Fax: 334-298-1725

Mobile Public Library
700 Government St
Mobile, AL 36602
Phone: 334-208-7073
Fax: 334-208-5865

Mobile Public Works Dept
770 Gayle St
Mobile, AL 36604
Phone: 334-208-2900
Fax: 334-208-2926

Mobile Urban Development Dept
PO Box 1827
Mobile, AL 36633
Phone: 334-208-7198
Fax: 334-208-7896

Important Phone Numbers

AAA.....334-265-1237
Alabama Revenue Dept.....334-344-4737
American Express Travel.....334-476-5095
Driver's License Information.....334-242-4371
Emergency.....911
Mobile Area Assn of Realtors.....334-479-8654
Mobile County Revenue Commissioner.....334-690-8530
Poison Control Center.....800-462-0800
Time/Temp.....334-660-0044
Vehicle Registration Information.....334-242-9056
Voter Registration Information.....334-690-8586
Weather.....334-478-6666

Information Sources

Better Business Bureau Serving Southern Alabama
PO Box 2008
Mobile, AL 36652
www.mobile.bbb.org
Phone: 334-433-5494
Fax: 334-438-3191

Mobile Area Chamber of Commerce
451 Government St
Mobile, AL 36602
www.mobcham.org
Phone: 334-433-6951
Fax: 334-432-1143

Mobile Convention & Visitors Corp
1 S Water St
Mobile, AL 36602
www.mobile.org
Phone: 334-208-2000
Fax: 334-208-2060
TF: 800-566-2453

Mobile Convention Center
1 S Water St
Mobile, AL 36602
Phone: 334-208-2100
Fax: 334-208-2150
TF: 800-566-2453

Mobile County
205 Government St
Mobile, AL 36644
www.acan.net/government/local/county
Phone: 334-690-8700
Fax: 334-690-5079

Online Resources

About.com Guide to Mobile
mobile.about.com/citiestowns/southeastus/mobile

Alabama Community Access Network
www.maf.mobile.al.us

Area Guide Mobile
mobile.areaguides.net

Excite.com Mobile City Guide
www.excite.com/travel/countries/united_states/alabama/mobile

Harbinger The
entropy.me.usouthal.edu/harbinger

InMobile.com
www.inmobile.com

Lodging.com Mobile Alabama
www.lodging.com/auto/guides/mobile-area-al.html

Mobile Home Page
cityshowcase.com/mobile

Mobile Today
www.wimi.com/mobile

Mobile.TheLinks.com
mobile.thelinks.com

Area Communities

Communities in the Mobile metropolitan area (Mobile and Baldwin counties) with populations greater than 5,000 include:

Bay Minette
PO Box 1208
Bay Minette, AL 36507
Phone: 334-580-1619
Fax: 334-580-2573

Chickasaw
224 N Craft Hwy
Chickasaw, AL 36611
Phone: 334-452-6463
Fax: 334-452-6468

Daphne
PO Box 400
Daphne, AL 36526
Phone: 334-621-9000
Fax: 334-626-3008

Fairhope
161 N Section St
Fairhope, AL 36532
Phone: 334-928-2136
Fax: 334-928-6776

Foley
407 E Laurel Ave
Foley, AL 36535
Phone: 334-943-1545
Fax: 334-952-4014

Prichard
216 E Prichard Ave
Prichard, AL 36610
Phone: 334-452-7860
Fax: 334-452-7886

Saraland
716 Hwy 43 S
Saraland, AL 36571
Phone: 334-675-5103
Fax: 334-679-5560

Satsuma
5668 2nd St
Satsuma, AL 36572
Phone: 334-675-1440
Fax: 334-675-1442

Economy

The Mobile metropolitan area is a regional center for commerce and industry. Major U.S. corporations that have a presence in the Mobile area include Ciba Specialty Chemicals, International Paper Company, and Kimberly Clark. The city has served as an important seaport for more than a century, shipping a variety of goods, from minerals and agricultural products from the area's rich farmland to man-made chemicals and paper products. Services is the metropolitan area's leading employment sector, with the trade sector a close second. Healthcare is the leading service-related industry in Mobile, with four of the 10 largest employers representing that industry.

Unemployment Rate 3.8%
Per Capita Income..........................$18,516
Median Family Income......................$28,220

Principal Industries & Number of Wage Earners

Mobile Metropolitan Area* - 1998

Construction & Mining.................................18,300
Finance, Insurance, & Real Estate........................9,900
Government 32,900
Manufacturing 28,000
Services 62,900
Transportation & Public Utilities 12,800
Wholesale & Retail Trade..............................60,000

* *Information given is for the Mobile Metropolitan Area, which includes Mobile and Baldwin counties.*

Major Employers

Ciba Specialty Chemicals
PO Box 95307
McIntosh, AL 36553
www.cibasc.com/es/es_01.asp
Phone: 334-944-2202
Fax: 334-436-5032

Delchamps Inc
3226 B Dauphin St
Mobile, AL 36606
Phone: 334-478-2505
Fax: 334-478-7447

Kimberly-Clark Corp
200 Bay Bridge Rd
Mobile, AL 36652
www.kc-careers.com
Phone: 334-330-3000
Fax: 334-452-6318

Mobile City Hall
PO Box 1827
Mobile, AL 36633
www.ci.mobile.al.us
Phone: 334-208-7411
Fax: 334-208-7482

Mobile County
205 Government St
Mobile, AL 36644
www.acan.net/government/local/county
Phone: 334-690-8700
Fax: 334-690-5079

Mobile County School System
PO Box 1327
Mobile, AL 36633
www.mcpss.com
Phone: 334-690-8083
Fax: 334-690-8344

Mobile Infirmary Medical Center
PO Box 2144
Mobile, AL 36652
www.mimc.com
Phone: 334-431-2400
Fax: 334-435-2543

Providence Hospital
6801 Airport Blvd
Mobile, AL 36608
E-mail: info@providencehospital.org
www.providencehospital.org
Phone: 334-633-1000
Fax: 334-633-1529

Saad Enterprises
6207 Cottage Hill Rd Suite G
Mobile, AL 36609
Phone: 334-380-3800
Fax: 334-380-3807

Springhill Memorial Hospital
3719 Dauphin St
Mobile, AL 36608
www.springhillmemorial.com
Phone: 334-344-9630
Fax: 334-460-5298

University of South Alabama
307 University Blvd
Mobile, AL 36688
www.usouthal.edu
Phone: 334-460-6101
Fax: 334-460-7023
TF: 800-872-5247

University of South Alabama Doctors Hospital
1700 Center St
Mobile, AL 36604
www.southalabama.edu/usacwh
Phone: 334-415-1000
Fax: 334-415-1001

University of South Alabama Medical Center
2451 Fillingim St
Mobile, AL 36617
www.usahospitals.org
Phone: 334-471-7000
Fax: 334-470-1672

US Army Corps of Engineers
109 Saint Joseph St
Mobile, AL 36602
Phone: 334-471-5966
Fax: 334-690-2505

Quality of Living Indicators

Total Crime Index.....................................18,357
(rates per 100,000 inhabitants)

Violent Crime
Murder/manslaughter........................... 36
Forcible rape 71
Robbery....................................... 877
Aggravated assault............................ 524

Property Crime
Burglary 4,438
Larceny theft 10,510
Motor vehicle theft 1,901

Cost of Living Index 93.8
(national average = 100)

Median Home Price $93,300

Education

Public Schools

Mobile County School System
PO Box 1327
Mobile, AL 36633
www.mcpss.com
Phone: 334-690-8083
Fax: 334-690-8344

Number of Schools
Elementary 58
Middle 23
High 17

Student/Teacher Ratio
All Grades 19.4:1

Private Schools

Number of Schools (all grades) 42

Colleges & Universities

Bishop State Community College
351 N Broad St
Mobile, AL 36603
E-mail: info@bscc.cc.al.us
www.bscc.cc.al.us
Phone: 334-690-6412
Fax: 334-438-2463

Bishop State Community College Southwest Campus
925 Dauphin Island Pkwy
Mobile, AL 36605
E-mail: info@bscc.cc.al.us
www.bscc.cc.al.us/sw_camp.htm
Phone: 334-479-7476
Fax: 334-473-2049

Spring Hill College
4000 Dauphin St
Mobile, AL 36608
www.shc.edu
Phone: 334-380-4000
Fax: 334-460-2186
TF: 800-742-6704

University of Mobile
5735 College Pkwy
Mobile, AL 36613
E-mail: adminfo@maf.mobile.al.us
www.umobile.edu
Phone: 334-675-5990
Fax: 334-442-2498
TF: 800-946-7267

University of South Alabama
307 University Blvd
Mobile, AL 36688
www.usouthal.edu
Phone: 334-460-6101
Fax: 334-460-7023
TF: 800-872-5247

Hospitals

Mercy Medical
101 Villa Dr
Daphne, AL 36526
www.mercymedical.com
Phone: 334-626-2694
Fax: 334-621-4331

Mobile Infirmary Medical Center
PO Box 2144
Mobile, AL 36652
www.mimc.com
Phone: 334-431-2400
Fax: 334-435-2543

Providence Hospital
6801 Airport Blvd
Mobile, AL 36608
www.providencehospital.org
Phone: 334-633-1000
Fax: 334-633-1529

Springhill Memorial Hospital
3719 Dauphin St
Mobile, AL 36608
www.springhillmemorial.com
Phone: 334-344-9630
Fax: 334-460-5298

University of South Alabama Doctors Hospital
1700 Center St
Mobile, AL 36604
www.southalabama.edu/usacwh
Phone: 334-415-1000
Fax: 334-415-1001

University of South Alabama Medical Center
2451 Fillingim St
Mobile, AL 36617
www.usahospitals.org
Phone: 334-471-7000
Fax: 334-470-1672

Transportation

Airport(s)

Mobile Regional Airport (MOB)
14 miles W of downtown (approx 30 minutes) 334-633-0313

Mass Transit

Mobile Transit Authority
$1.25 Base fare 334-344-5656

Rail/Bus

Amtrak Station
11 Government St
Mobile, AL 36602
Phone: 334-432-4052
TF: 800-872-7245

Greyhound Bus Station
2545 Government Blvd
Mobile, AL 36602
Phone: 334-478-6089
TF: 800-231-2222

Utilities

Electricity
Alabama Power Co 800-245-2244
www.southernco.com/site/alapower

Gas
Mobile Gas Service Corp 334-476-8052
www.mobile-gas.com

Water
Mobile Water/Sewer System 334-694-3130

Garbage Collection/Recycling
Mobile Public Works Dept 334-208-2900

Telecommunications

Telephone
BellSouth 800-753-3320
www.bellsouth.com

Cable Television
Comcast Cablevision 334-476-7600

Internet Service Providers (ISPs)
Zebra.Net 334-634-1000
www.zebra.net

Banks

AmSouth Bank Phone: 334-434-3270
7860 Airport Blvd Fax: 334-434-3274
Mobile, AL 36608 TF: 800-267-6884

Regions Bank Phone: 334-690-1212
106 Saint Francis St Fax: 334-690-1030
Mobile, AL 36602

South Alabama Bank Phone: 334-431-7800
100 Saint Joseph St Fax: 334-431-7851
Mobile, AL 36602
E-mail: southalabama@southalabamabank.com
www.southalabamabank.com

SouthTrust Bank of Alabama NA Phone: 334-431-9200
61 Saint Joseph St Fax: 334-431-9256
Mobile, AL 36602

Shopping

Bel Air Mall Phone: 334-473-8623
3299 Bel Air Mall Fax: 334-476-5722
Mobile, AL 36606

Cotton City Antique Mall Phone: 334-479-9747
2012 Airport Blvd
Mobile, AL 36606

Mobile Festival Centre Phone: 334-341-0500
3725 Airport Blvd Fax: 334-343-0829
Mobile, AL 36608

Springdale Mall Phone: 334-471-1945
3250 Airport Blvd Fax: 334-479-1374
Mobile, AL 36606
www.springdalemall.com

Media

Newspapers and Magazines

Mobile Register* Phone: 334-433-1551
PO Box 2488 Fax: 334-434-8662
Mobile, AL 36652 TF: 800-239-1340
E-mail: register@dibbs.net
www.mobileregister.com/

**Indicates major daily newspapers*

Television

WALA-TV Ch 10 (Fox) Phone: 334-434-1010
210 Government St Fax: 334-434-1073
Mobile, AL 36602

WEAR-TV Ch 3 (ABC) Phone: 850-456-3333
4990 Mobile Hwy Fax: 850-455-0159
Pensacola, FL 32506
E-mail: news@weartv.com
www.wear.pensacola.com

WEIQ-TV Ch 42 (PBS) Phone: 205-328-8756
2112 11th Ave S
Birmingham, AL 35205
www.aptv.org/InsideAPT/WEIQ42.html

WJTC-TV Ch 44 (UPN) Phone: 334-602-1544
661 Azalea Rd Fax: 334-602-1547
Mobile, AL 36609
www.wjtc.com

WKRG-TV Ch 5 (CBS) Phone: 334-479-5555
555 Broadcast Dr Fax: 334-473-8130
Mobile, AL 36606 TF: 800-957-4885
E-mail: tv5@wkrg.com
www.wkrg.com

WPMI-TV Ch 15 (NBC) Phone: 334-602-1500
661 Azalea Rd Fax: 334-602-1550
Mobile, AL 36609
E-mail: nbc15@wpmi.com
www.wpmi.com

Radio

WABB-FM 97.5 MHz (CHR) Phone: 334-432-5572
1551 Springhill Ave Fax: 334-438-4044
Mobile, AL 36604
www.wabb.com

WBHY-FM 88.5 MHz (Rel) Phone: 334-473-8488
PO Box 1328 Fax: 334-473-8854
Mobile, AL 36633
www.goforth.org

WBLX-FM 92.9 MHz (Urban) Phone: 334-652-2000
1 Office Pk Suite 416 Fax: 334-652-2001
Mobile, AL 36609
www.93blx.com

WGOK-AM 900 kHz (Rel) Phone: 334-432-9900
1 Office Pk Suite 215 Fax: 334-434-6596
Mobile, AL 36609

WHIL-FM 91.3 MHz (NPR) Phone: 334-380-4685
PO Box 8509 Fax: 334-460-2189
Mobile, AL 36689
www.whil.org

WKSJ-FM 94.9 MHz (Ctry) Phone: 334-450-0100
555 Broadcast Dr 3rd Fl Fax: 334-473-6662
Mobile, AL 36606

WRKH-FM 96.1 MHz (CR) Phone: 334-450-0100
555 Broadcast Dr 3rd Fl Fax: 334-473-6662
Mobile, AL 36606
www.961therocket.com

Attractions

Mobile's beautiful azaleas are featured each year at the city's Azalea Trail Festival. Depending on when blooms peak, every March or April visitors can view a 27-mile long trail of the city's most colorful floral displays. Azaleas are also featured at the Bellingrath Gardens and Home, along with 65 acres of various other flowers that bloom during all four seasons. The estate is the former home of Coca-Cola bottling pioneer Walter D. Bellingrath and contains one of the finest antiques collections in the Southeast. Mobile Bay is the site of the USS Alabama Battleship Memorial Park, which includes the USS

Alabama (WWII battleship), USS Drum (WWII submarine), and the B-52 bomber "Calamity Jane." South of Mobile, across the bay, are the white sand beaches and resort hotels of Gulf Shores.

Bellingrath Gardens & Home Phone: 334-973-2217
12401 Bellingrath Garden Rd Fax: 334-973-0540
Theodore, AL 36582
E-mail: bellingrath@juno.com
www.zebra.net/~wlee/bellingrath.html

Big Zion African Methodist Episcopal Church Phone: 334-433-8431
112 S Bayou St
Mobile, AL 36602

Bragg-Mitchell Mansion Phone: 334-471-6364
1906 Springhill Ave Fax: 334-478-3800
Mobile, AL 36607
www.azaleacity.com/BraggMitchell

Carlen House Phone: 334-470-7768
54 S Carlen St Fax: 334-470-7768
Mobile, AL 36606

Cathedral of the Immaculate Conception Phone: 334-434-1565
2 S Claiborne St
Mobile, AL 36602

Chickasabogue Park Phone: 334-452-8496
760 Aldock Rd Fax: 334-457-0541
Mobile, AL 36613

Conde-Charlotte House Phone: 334-432-4722
104 Theatre St
Mobile, AL 36602

Dauphin Island Phone: 334-861-5524
S end of Hwy 193 Fax: 334-861-2154
Dauphin Island, AL 36528 TF: 877-532-8744
www.dauphinisland.cc

Dauphin Island Sea Lab Estuarium Phone: 334-861-2141
101 Bienville Blvd Fax: 334-861-4646
Dauphin Island, AL 36528
www.disl.org

Exploreum Imax Theater Phone: 334-208-6883
65 Government St Fax: 334-208-6889
Mobile, AL 36602
www.exploreum.net/imax.html

Exploreum Museum of Science Phone: 334-208-6883
65 Government St Fax: 334-208-6889
Mobile, AL 36602 TF: 877-625-4386
www.exploreum.net

Fleamarket Mobile Phone: 334-633-7533
401 Schillinger Rd N Fax: 334-639-0570
Mobile, AL 36608
www.fleamarketmobile.com

Fort Conde Phone: 334-434-7304
150 S Royal St Fax: 334-208-7659
Mobile, AL 36602

Fort Gaines Historic Site Phone: 334-861-6992
E end of Dauphin Island
Dauphin Island, AL 36528

Government Street Presbyterian Church Phone: 334-432-1749
300 Government St Fax: 334-434-9324
Mobile, AL 36602

Historic Blakeley Park Phone: 334-580-0005
33707 Hwy 225 Fax: 334-580-0005
Spanish Fort, AL 36527
E-mail: blakeley@siteone.com
www.siteone.com/tourist/blakeley/index.html

Mobile Ballet Phone: 334-342-2241
4351 Dowtowner Loop N Fax: 334-344-5421
Mobile, AL 36609
olympus.asms.net/ballet

Mobile Botanical Gardens Phone: 334-342-0555
5151 Museum Dr Langan Pk
Mobile, AL 36602

Mobile Medical Museum Phone: 334-434-5055
1504 Springhill Ave Fax: 334-434-3752
Mobile, AL 36604

Mobile Museum of Art Phone: 334-208-5200
PO Box 8426 Fax: 334-208-5201
Mobile, AL 36689

Mobile Museum of Art Downtown Gallery Phone: 334-694-0533
300 Dauphin St
Mobile, AL 36602
www.mobilemuseumofart.com

Mobile Opera Inc Phone: 334-476-7372
PO Box 66633 Fax: 334-476-7373
Mobile, AL 36660
www.mobileopera.org

Mobile Theatre Guild Phone: 334-433-7513
14 N Lafayette St
Mobile, AL 36604

Museum of the City of Mobile Phone: 334-434-7569
355 Government St Fax: 334-208-7686
Mobile, AL 36602

National African-American Archives & Museum Phone: 334-433-8511
564 ML King Ave Fax: 334-433-4265
Mobile, AL 36603

Oakleigh Period House Museum Phone: 334-432-1281
350 Oakleigh Pl Fax: 334-432-8843
Mobile, AL 36604
E-mail: info@historicmobile.org
www.historicmobile.org

Phoenix Fire Museum Phone: 334-434-7554
203 S Claiborne St Fax: 334-434-7686
Mobile, AL 36602

Playhouse in the Park Phone: 334-344-1537
Mobile Municipal Park
Mobile, AL 36608

Richards-DAR House Phone: 334-434-7320
256 N Joachim St Fax: 334-208-7321
Mobile, AL 36603

Saenger Theatre
6 S Joachim St
Mobile, AL 36602
Phone: 334-433-2787
Fax: 334-433-2087

Southern Belle/Alabama Cruises
12402 Bellingrath Gardens Rd
Theodore, AL 36582
Phone: 334-973-1244
Fax: 334-973-1255

USS Alabama Battleship Memorial Park
2703 Battleship Pkwy
Mobile, AL 36602
www.ussalabama.com
Phone: 334-432-5951

Waterville USA
906 Gulf Shores Pkwy
Gulf Shores, AL 36542
E-mail: wville@gulftel.com
www.watervilleusa.com
Phone: 334-948-2106
Fax: 334-948-7918

Sports Teams & Facilities

Ladd-Peebles Stadium
1621 Virginia St
Mobile, AL 36604
Phone: 334-208-2500
Fax: 334-208-2514

Mobile BayBears (baseball)
755 Bolling Brothers Blvd Hank Aaron Stadium
Mobile, AL 36606
E-mail: baybears@mobilebaybears.com
www.mobilebaybears.com
Phone: 334-479-2327
Fax: 334-476-1147

Mobile Greyhound Park
7101 Old Pascagoula Rd
Theodore, AL 36582
E-mail: mgp7101@bellsouth.net
www.mobilegreyhoundpark.com
Phone: 334-653-5000
Fax: 334-653-9185

Mobile International Speedway
7800 Park Blvd
Irvington, AL 36544
www.mobilespeedway.com/
Phone: 334-957-2026
Fax: 334-957-2063

Mobile Mysticks (hockey)
401 Civic Center Dr
Mobile, AL 36602
E-mail: mysticks@mysticks.com
www.mysticks.com
Phone: 334-208-7825
Fax: 334-208-7931

Annual Events

A Taste of the Colony (mid-March) 334-861-6992
Africatown Folk Festival (March) 334-470-7730
Alabama Deep Sea Fishing Rodeo (mid-July) 334-470-7730
Azalea Trail Run & Festival (late March) 334-473-7223
Bayfest Music Festival (early October) 334-470-7730
Blessing of the Fleet at Bayou la Batre (May) 334-824-2415
Candlelight Christmas at Oakleigh (early December) 334-415-2000
Christmas at Fort Gaines (early December) 334-861-6992
Christmas in Mobile Festival Arts & Crafts Show (late December) 334-415-2100
Christmas Jubilee (late November) 334-415-2000
Colonial Isle Dauphine (early October) 334-861-6992
Craft Bugs Holiday Fantasy (late November) 334-470-7730
Dauphin Island Regatta (late April) 334-470-7730
Dauphin Island Spring Festival (early May) 334-861-5525
Deep South Dulcimer Festival (early November) 334-452-8496
Delchamps Senior Bowl (mid-January) 334-438-2276
First Night Mobile (December 31) 334-470-7730
Greater Gulf State Fair (mid-late October) 334-470-7730
International Carnival (mid-November) 334-470-7730
Junior League Christmas Jubilee (mid-November) 334-471-3348
Labor Day Invitational Billfish Tournament (late August-early September) 334-343-1619
Mardi Gras (February-March) 334-470-7730
Mobile Fourth of July Celebration (July 4) 334-470-7730
Mobile Historic Homes Tours (mid-March) 334-470-7730
Mobile International Festival (mid-November) 334-470-7730
Mobile Jazz Festival (mid-April) 334-470-7730
National Shrimp Festival (October) 334-968-6904
Providence Festival of Flowers (mid-March) 334-639-2050
Renaissance Festival (mid-November) 334-861-6992
Senior Bowl (January) 334-470-7730
September Celebration (September) 334-470-7730
Taste of Mobile (April) 334-415-2000
Thunder on the Bay (mid-May) 334-861-6992
Women's Encampment (early November) 334-861-6992

Modesto, California

County: **Stanislaus**

MODESTO is located in the San Joaquin Valley of north central California. Major cities within 100 miles include Stockton, Sacramento, San Jose, and San Francisco, California.

Area (Land) .... 30.2 sq mi
Area (Water) .... 0.2 sq mi
Elevation .... 87 ft
Latitude .... 37-39-35 N
Longitude .... 120-59-38 W
Time Zone .... PST
Area Code 209

Climate

Modesto's temperate climate features four distinct seasons. Winters are cool, with average high temperatures ranging from the low 50s to the low 60s and lows averaging around 40 degrees. January is the wettest month of the year in Modesto. Summer days are hot, with highs reaching into the 90s, while evenings cool down to near 60 degrees. Summer is also the driest time of year in Modesto - the area typically receives less than an inch of rain from May to September.

Average Temperatures & Precipitation

Temperatures

	Jan	Feb	Mar	Apr	May	Jun	Jul	Aug	Sep	Oct	Nov	Dec
High	54	62	67	74	82	79	94	94	88	78	64	53
Low	37	41	43	47	51	57	60	59	56	50	43	37

Precipitation

	Jan	Feb	Mar	Apr	May	Jun	Jul	Aug	Sep	Oct	Nov	Dec
Inches	2.2	1.8	2.1	1.0	0.2	0.1	0.1	0.1	0.3	0.7	1.9	1.7

History

Originally inhabited by Native Americans who lived along the banks of the river that flowed through the San Joaquin Valley, the area known today as Modesto was first explored in 1806 by Spanish explorer Gabriel Moraga and his party. The arrival of the explorers triggered a clash between Mexican officials and the natives, led by Chief Estanislao, that lasted nearly 40 years. Once peace was made, white settlement began in the area and the river was named the Estanislao River in honor of the chief. This was eventually changed to Stanislaus after an early mapmaker accidentally misspelled the river's name on a map.

The Gold Rush of 1849 drew thousands of pioneers to north central California, and cities began to spring up all over the region. Stanislaus County was established in 1854, and 16 years later, in 1870, the Central Pacific Railroad established a new rail town named Ralston near the Stanislaus River. Ralston's name was soon changed to Modesto, the Spanish word for "modesty," and the new city became the seat of Stanislaus County the following year. Located in the fertile San Joaquin Valley, the city grew quickly as an agricultural center, and by 1872 Stanislaus County had become the top wheat production center in the United States. Modesto was incorporated in 1884 and had grown to a city of 2,000 by the early 20th Century.

Modesto's success as an agricultural hub was dependent on a steady supply of water, and unpredictable rainfall led to alternating periods of floods and droughts that threatened the area's economic livelihood. However, by 1903 a new system of canal irrigation had been completed in the city, and Modesto's agricultural base began to thrive once again. The availability of reliable irrigation led to diversification of the area's crops, and almonds, walnuts, grapes, peaches, and tomatoes have since become major crops. The importance of this development in Modesto's history is reflected in the city's motto, "Water, Wealth, Commitment, Health."

With a population that now exceeds 182,000, Modesto today is the largest city in Stanislaus County and continues to flourish as one of California's leading agricultural centers.

Population

1990 Census 164,746
1998 Estimate 182,016
% Change 10.5
2005 Projection 249,400

Racial/Ethnic Breakdown
White 80.6%
Black 2.7%
Other 16.7%
Hispanic Origin (may be of any race) 16.3%

Age Breakdown
Under 5 years 9.0%
5 to 17 .... 21.2%
18 to 20 .... 4.1%
21 to 24 .... 5.4%
25 to 34 .... 18.0%
35 to 44 .... 15.6%
45 to 54 .... 9.3%
55 to 64 .... 6.9%
65 to 74 .... 6.1%
75+ years 4.4%
Median Age 30.8

Gender Breakdown
Male 48.5%
Female 51.5%

Government

Type of Government: Council-Manager

Modesto Business Development Office
PO Box 642
Modesto, CA 95353
Phone: 209-571-5566
Fax: 209-491-5798

Modesto City Attorney
PO Box 642
Modesto, CA 95353
Phone: 209-577-5284
Fax: 209-544-8260

Modesto City Clerk
PO Box 642
Modesto, CA 95353
Phone: 209-577-5396
Fax: 209-571-5152

Modesto City Council
PO Box 642
Modesto, CA 95353
Phone: 209-571-5169
Fax: 209-571-5586

Modesto City Hall
1010 10th St
Modesto, CA 95354
Phone: 209-577-5200
Fax: 209-571-5152

Modesto City Manager
PO Box 642
Modesto, CA 95353
Phone: 209-577-5223
Fax: 209-571-5128

Modesto Community Development Dept
PO Box 642
Modesto, CA 95353
Phone: 209-571-5566
Fax: 209-491-5798

Modesto Disaster Preparedness Office
610 11th St
Modesto, CA 95354
Phone: 209-572-9596
Fax: 209-578-9591

Modesto Engineering & Transportation Dept
PO Box 642
Modesto, CA 95353
Phone: 209-577-5429
Fax: 209-571-5521

Modesto Finance Dept
PO Box 642
Modesto, CA 95353
Phone: 209-577-5369
Fax: 209-571-5880

Modesto Fire Dept
600 11th St
Modesto, CA 95354
Phone: 209-572-9590
Fax: 209-578-9591

Modesto Housing & Neighborhoods Div
PO Box 642
Modesto, CA 95353
Phone: 209-577-5245
Fax: 209-544-3982

Modesto Mayor
1010 10th St
Modesto, CA 95354
Phone: 209-577-5230
Fax: 209-571-5586

Modesto Personnel Dept
PO Box 642
Modesto, CA 95353
Phone: 209-577-5402
Fax: 209-571-5813

Modesto Police Dept
PO Box 1746
Modesto, CA 95353
Phone: 209-572-9501
Fax: 209-572-9669

Modesto Recreation & Neighborhoods Dept
PO Box 642
Modesto, CA 95353
Phone: 209-577-5344
Fax: 209-579-5077

Modesto Utilities Div
PO Box 642
Modesto, CA 95353
Phone: 209-577-5395
Fax: 209-491-5920

Important Phone Numbers

AAA.......209-523-9171
American Express Travel.......209-571-5606
California State Franchise Tax Board.......916-845-4300
Central Valley Assn of Realtors.......209-858-1700
Dental Referral.......209-522-1530
Driver's License/Vehicle Registration Information.......209-576-6305
Emergency.......911
Medical Referral.......209-523-9151
Poison Control Center.......800-876-4766
Stanislaus County Assessor.......209-525-6461
Stanislaus County Treasurer & Tax Collector.......209-525-6388
Voter Registration Information.......209-525-5200
Weather.......209-982-1793

Information Sources

Better Business Bureau Serving the Mid Counties
11 S San Joaquin St Suite 803
Stockton, CA 95202
www.stockton.bbb.org
Phone: 209-948-4880
Fax: 209-465-6302

Modesto Centre Plaza
10th & K St
Modesto, CA 95354
Phone: 209-577-6444
Fax: 209-544-6729

Modesto Chamber of Commerce
1114 J St
Modesto, CA 95353
www.modchamber.org
Phone: 209-577-5757
Fax: 209-577-2673

Modesto Convention & Visitors Bureau
1114 J St
Modesto, CA 95353
www.modestocvb.org/
Phone: 209-571-6480
Fax: 209-571-6486
TF: 800-266-4282

Stanislaus County
PO Box 1670
Modesto, CA 95353
www.co.stanislaus.ca.us
Phone: 209-525-5251
Fax: 209-525-5210

Online Resources

Anthill City Guide Modesto
www.anthill.com/city.asp?city=modesto

Excite.com Modesto City Guide
www.excite.com/travel/countries/united_states/california/modesto

Modesto Community
www.cityofturlock.com/modesto

Area Communities

Communities in Stanislaus County with populations greater than 10,000 include:

Ceres
2720 2nd St
Ceres, CA 95307
Phone: 209-538-5755
Fax: 209-538-5780

Oakdale
280 N 3rd Ave
Oakdale, CA 95361
Phone: 209-847-3031
Fax: 209-847-6834

Patterson
33 S Del Puerto Ave
Patterson, CA 95363
Phone: 209-892-2041
Fax: 209-892-6119

Riverbank
6707 3rd St
Riverbank, CA 95367
Phone: 209-869-7101
Fax: 209-869-7100

Turlock
156 S Broadway
Turlock, CA 95380
Phone: 209-668-5540
Fax: 209-668-5668

Economy

Agriculture remains a vital part of Modesto's economy, and Stanislaus County consistently ranks among the nation's largest centers for agricultural production, generating more than $1.3 million in gross annual income from agriculture. However, although it plays a major role, agricultural jobs account for only 10% of Stanislaus County's total workforce. Services is currently the area's largest employment sector, followed by retail trade and manufacturing.

Unemployment Rate 12.9%*
Per Capita Income $19,650*
Median Family Income $33,021*

** Information given is for Stanislaus County.*

Principal Industries & Number of Wage Earners

Modesto MSA (Stanislaus County) - 1999

Industry	Wage Earners
Construction	9,300
Farm (Production & Services)	16,200
Finance, Insurance, & Real Estate	4,500
Government	23,800
Manufacturing	25,800
Retail Trade	28,600
Services	36,600
Transportation & Public Utilities	5,600
Wholesale Trade	7,400

Major Employers

Basic Vegetable Products
705 E Whitmore Ave
Modesto, CA 95358
www.basicveg.com
Phone: 209-538-1071
Fax: 209-538-5423
TF: 800-358-9195

Doctors Medical Center
PO Box 4138
Modesto, CA 95352
www.tenethealth.com/DMCModesto
Phone: 209-578-1211
Fax: 209-576-3896

E & J Gallo Winery
PO Box 1130
Modesto, CA 95353
www.gallo.com/USA
Phone: 209-341-3111
Fax: 209-341-3307

Frito-Lay Co Inc
600 Garner Rd
Modesto, CA 95357
www.fritolay.com
Phone: 209-544-5400
Fax: 209-544-5576

Memorial Hospitals Assn
1700 Coffee Rd
Modesto, CA 95355
Phone: 209-526-4500
Fax: 209-576-7385

Modesto Bee
PO Box 5156
Modesto, CA 95352
www.modbee.com
Phone: 209-578-2000
Fax: 209-578-2207
TF: 800-776-4233

Modesto City Hall
1010 10th St
Modesto, CA 95354
www.ci.modesto.ca.us
Phone: 209-577-5200
Fax: 209-571-5152

Modesto City Schools
426 Locust St
Modesto, CA 95351
www.monet.k12.ca.us
Phone: 209-576-4011
Fax: 209-576-4846

Modesto Junior College
435 College Ave
Modesto, CA 95350
www.gomjc.org
Phone: 209-575-6498
Fax: 209-575-6666

Procter & Gamble Paper Products Co
PO Box 4368
Modesto, CA 95352
www.pg.com/careers/index.htm
Phone: 209-538-5000
Fax: 209-538-5135

Stanislaus County
PO Box 1670
Modesto, CA 95353
www.co.stanislaus.ca.us
Phone: 209-525-5251
Fax: 209-525-5210

Sutter-Gould Medical Foundation
600 Coffee Rd
Modesto, CA 95355
www.sutterhealth.org
Phone: 209-524-1211
Fax: 209-572-2618

Tri Valley Growers
2801 Finch Rd
Modesto, CA 95354
www.trivalleygrowers.com
Phone: 209-572-5200
Fax: 209-572-5641

Quality of Living Indicators

Total Crime Index 10,048
(rates per 100,000 inhabitants)

Violent Crime
Murder/manslaughter 5
Forcible rape 71
Robbery 290
Aggravated assault 626

Property Crime
Burglary 1,851
Larceny theft 5,936
Motor vehicle theft 1,269

Cost of Living Index 160.0
(national average = 100)

Median Home Price $129,100

Education

Public Schools

Modesto City Schools
426 Locust St
Modesto, CA 95351
www.monet.k12.ca.us
Phone: 209-576-4011
Fax: 209-576-4846

Number of Schools
Elementary 23
Junior High 3
Middle 1
High 5

Student/Teacher Ratio
Elementary/Middle 20.4:1
High 24.2:1

Private Schools

Number of Schools (all grades) .... 13+

Colleges & Universities

Chapman University Phone: 209-545-1234
3600 Sisk Rd Suite 5A Fax: 209-545-0596
Modesto, CA 95356

Modesto Junior College Phone: 209-575-6498
435 College Ave Fax: 209-575-6666
Modesto, CA 95350
www.gomjc.org

Yosemite Community College District Phone: 209-575-6498
435 College Ave Fax: 209-575-6666
Modesto, CA 95350
www.yosemite.cc.ca.us

Hospitals

Doctors Medical Center Phone: 209-578-1211
PO Box 4138 Fax: 209-576-3896
Modesto, CA 95352
www.tenethealth.com/DMCModesto

Memorial Hospitals Assn Phone: 209-526-4500
1700 Coffee Rd Fax: 209-576-7385
Modesto, CA 95355

Stanislaus Medical Center Phone: 209-558-7000
830 Scenic Dr Fax: 209-558-8320
Modesto, CA 95350

Transportation

Airport(s)

Modesto City Airport (MOD)
3 miles E of downtown (approx 10 minutes) 209-577-5318

Mass Transit

MAX Bus
$.80 Base fare 209-521-1274

Rail/Bus

Amtrak Station Phone: 800-872-7245
1700 Held Dr
Modesto, CA 95355

Greyhound Bus Station Phone: 209-526-4314
1001 9th St TF: 800-231-2222
Modesto, CA 95354

Utilities

Electricity
Modesto Irrigation District 209-526-7373
www.mid.org

Gas
Pacific Gas & Electric Co 800-743-5000
www.pge.com

Water
Modesto Utilities Div 209-577-5395

Garbage Collection/Recycling
Modesto Utilities Div 209-577-5395

Telecommunications

Telephone
Pacific Bell 800-310-2355
www.pacbell.com

Cable Television
Cable One 209-577-3500

Internet Service Providers (ISPs)
American InfoMetrics Inc 209-549-8333
www.ainet.com

Banks

Bank of America Phone: 209-578-6016
1601 'I' St Fax: 209-578-6060
Modesto, CA 95354

Bank of the West Phone: 209-529-4355
1335 Yosemite Blvd Fax: 209-529-4023
Modesto, CA 95354

California Federal Bank Phone: 209-526-9912
2929 McHenry Ave Fax: 209-522-8858
Modesto, CA 95354

Delta National Bank Phone: 209-527-3700
2711 McHenry Ave Fax: 209-527-0820
Modesto, CA 95350

Farmers & Merchants Bank of California Phone: 209-577-8311
3001 McHenry Ave Fax: 209-524-3935
Modesto, CA 95350

Guaranty Federal Bank Phone: 209-526-1811
1101 J St Fax: 209-526-8433
Modesto, CA 95358

Pacific State Bank Phone: 209-577-2265
2020 Standiford Ave Suite H Fax: 209-571-6095
Modesto, CA 95350

Sanwa Bank California Phone: 209-521-8060
3600 McHenry Ave Fax: 209-521-7458
Modesto, CA 95356

Union Bank of California NA Phone: 209-576-2000
1124 J St Fax: 209-576-2025
Modesto, CA 95354

Union Safe Deposit Bank
901 H St
Modesto, CA 95354
Phone: 209-529-9300
Fax: 209-521-7761

US Bank
2008 McHenry Ave
Modesto, CA 95350
Phone: 209-524-5454
Fax: 209-526-0262

Wells Fargo Bank
1120 K St
Modesto, CA 95354
Phone: 209-578-6805
Fax: 209-526-8163

Westamerica Bank
1524 McHenry Ave
Modesto, CA 95350
Phone: 209-572-8580
Fax: 209-572-8593

Shopping

Downtown Improvement District
PO Box 1428
Modesto, CA 95353
Phone: 209-529-9303
Fax: 209-529-2143

McHenry Village
1700 McHenry Ave Suite 25
Modesto, CA 95350
Phone: 209-523-6473
Fax: 209-523-1282

Vintage Faire Mall
3401 Dale Rd
Modesto, CA 95356
www.shopvintagefairemall.com
Phone: 209-527-3401
Fax: 209-525-8827

Media

Newspapers and Magazines

Modesto Bee*
PO Box 5156
Modesto, CA 95352
www.modbee.com
Phone: 209-578-2000
Fax: 209-578-2207
TF: 800-776-4233

**Indicates major daily newspapers*

Television

KCRA-TV Ch 3 (NBC)
3 Television Cir
Sacramento, CA 95814
www.kcra.com
Phone: 916-446-3333
Fax: 916-441-4050

KMAX-TV Ch 31 (UPN)
500 Media Pl
Sacramento, CA 95815
www.paramountstations.com/KMAX
Phone: 916-925-3100
Fax: 916-921-3050

KNSO-TV Ch 51 (WB)
142 N 9th St Suite 8
Modesto, CA 95350
Phone: 209-529-5100
Fax: 209-575-4547

KOVR-TV Ch 13 (CBS)
2713 KOVR Dr
West Sacramento, CA 95605
www.kovr.com
Phone: 916-374-1313
Fax: 916-374-1304

KTXL-TV Ch 40 (Fox)
4655 Fruitridge Rd
Sacramento, CA 95820
Phone: 916-454-4422
Fax: 916-739-0559

KVIE-TV Ch 6 (PBS)
2595 Capitol Oaks Dr
Sacramento, CA 95833
E-mail: member@kvie.org
www.kvie.org
Phone: 916-929-5843
Fax: 916-929-7367

KXTV-TV Ch 10 (ABC)
400 Broadway
Sacramento, CA 95818
E-mail: kxtv10@kxtv10.com
www.kxtv10.com
Phone: 916-441-2345
Fax: 916-447-6107

Radio

KATM-FM 103.3 MHz (Ctry)
1581 Cummins Dr Suite 135
Modesto, CA 95358
www.katm.com
Phone: 209-523-7756
Fax: 209-522-2061
TF: 800-262-1986

KCIV-FM 99.9 MHz (Rel)
1031 15th St Suite 1
Modesto, CA 95354
Phone: 209-524-8999
Fax: 209-524-9088
TF: 800-743-5248

KEST-AM 970 kHz (Sports)
1581 Cummins Dr Suite 135
Modesto, CA 95358
Phone: 209-523-7756
Fax: 209-522-2061

KFIV-AM 1360 kHz (N/T)
3600 Sisk Rd Suite 2B
Modesto, CA 95356
Phone: 209-545-5585
Fax: 209-545-5588

KHOP-FM 95.1 MHz (Rock)
1581 Cummins Dr Suite 135
Modesto, CA 95358
E-mail: feedback@khop.com
www.khop.com
Phone: 209-523-7756
Fax: 209-522-2061
TF: 800-262-1986

KJSN-FM 102.3 MHz (AC)
3600 Sisk Rd Suite 2B
Modesto, CA 95356
Phone: 209-545-5585
Fax: 209-545-5588

KLOC-AM 920 kHz (Span)
1620 N Carpenter Rd Suite D41
Modesto, CA 95351
Phone: 209-521-5562
Fax: 209-529-1528

KVFX-FM 96.7 MHz (Rock)
3600 Sisk Rd Suite 2B
Modesto, CA 95356
Phone: 209-521-9797
Fax: 209-521-9844

Attractions

Modesto's legacy as an agricultural center carries over into its attractions. Visitors and residents alike can take advantage of a number of "Taste 'n Sample" tours offered by local agricultural producers, including Blue Diamond Growers, Hillman Cheese Company, and Hershey's. Historical attractions in Modesto include Miller's California Ranch, which has rare farm equipment and vehicles dating back to the 1880s, as well as an old-fashioned general store. The ornamental Modesto arch, erected in 1912, still stands today across I street, displaying the city's motto in white lights which are illuminated every evening.

Big Bear Park
13400 Yosemite Blvd
Waterford, CA 95386
www.campgrounds.com/bigbear
Phone: 209-874-1984
Fax: 209-874-4544

Blue Diamond Growers Store Phone: 209-545-3222
4800 Sisk Rd Fax: 209-545-6215
Salida, CA 95356

Castle Air Museum Phone: 209-723-2178
5050 Santa Fe Dr Fax: 209-723-0323
Atwater, CA 95301
E-mail: cam@elite.net
www.elite.net/castle-air

Central California Art League Art Center Phone: 209-529-3369
1402 'I' St
Modesto, CA 95354
www.ainet.com/ccal/

Central West Ballet Co Phone: 209-576-8957
3125 McHenry Ave Suite D Fax: 209-576-1308
Modesto, CA 95350
www.centralwestballet.com

Delicato Vineyards Phone: 209-824-3600
12001 S Hwy 99 Fax: 209-824-3400
Manteca, CA 95336
E-mail: wine@delicato.com
www.delicato.com

Great Valley Museum of Natural History Phone: 209-575-6196
1100 Stoddard Ave Fax: 209-575-6410
Modesto, CA 95350

Hershey's Visitors Center Phone: 209-848-8126
120 S Sierra Ave Fax: 209-847-2622
Oakdale, CA 95361
www.hersheys.com/visit/oakdale

McHenry Mansion Phone: 209-577-5344
906 15th St Fax: 209-579-5077
Modesto, CA 95353

McHenry Museum Phone: 209-577-5366
1402 'I' St Fax: 209-491-4407
Modesto, CA 95354
www.invsn.com/mchenry/museum/introduction.html

Miller's California Ranch Phone: 209-522-1781
9425 Yosemite Blvd & Hwy 132
Modesto, CA 95357

Modesto Arch Phone: 209-577-5757
9th & 'I' Sts
Modesto, CA 95353

Modesto Civic Theatre Phone: 209-526-5505
1307 J St State Theatre
Modesto, CA 95353

Modesto Performing Arts Phone: 209-524-9777
2633 El Greco Dr Fax: 209-524-5654
Modesto, CA 95354

Modesto Symphony Orchestra Phone: 209-523-4156
3509 Coffee Rd Suite D-1 Fax: 209-523-0201
Modesto, CA 95355
www.modestosymphony.org

Pure Joy at the Bloomingcamp Ranch Phone: 209-847-1412
10528 Hwy 120 Fax: 209-845-8519
Oakdale, CA 95361

Saint Stan's Brewery Phone: 209-524-2337
821 L St Fax: 209-524-4827
Modesto, CA 95354

State Theatre Phone: 209-527-4697
1307 J St Fax: 209-575-0554
Modesto, CA 95354
www.thestate.ainet.com

Townsend Opera Players Phone: 209-572-2867
605 H St Fax: 209-579-0532
Modesto, CA 95354
E-mail: top@ainet.com
www.townsendoperaplayers.com

Yosemite National Park Phone: 209-372-0200
PO Box 577
Yosemite National Park, CA 95389
www.yosemitepark.com

Sports Teams & Facilities

Modesto A's (baseball) Phone: 209-572-4487
601 Neece Dr John Thurman Field Fax: 209-572-4490
Modesto, CA 95351
www.minorleaguebaseball.com/teams/cal-mod.php3

Stanislaus County Cruisers (soccer) Phone: 209-531-1403
1511 Crows Landing Rd Fax: 209-531-2358
Modesto, CA 95351
E-mail: modcruz@wac.com
www.wac.com/~modcruz

Annual Events

1st Annual American Graffiti Car Show
(mid-June) 888-746-9763
Antiques & Collectibles Show & Sale
(mid-February & late November) 209-571-6480
Central Valley Renaissance Festival (mid-May) 209-571-6480
Cinco de Mayo Celebration (early May) 209-571-6480
Delicato Vineyards Grape Stomp (late August) 209-239-1215
Greek Food Festival (mid-September) 209-522-7694
International Festival
(late September-early October) 209-521-3852
July 4th Parade & Festival (July 4) 209-571-6480
Knight's Ferry Peddler's Fair
(mid-April-mid May) 209-881-3217
Manteca Pumpkin Festival (early October) 209-823-6121
Modesto Christmas Parade (early December) 209-571-6480
Modesto Farmers Market
(late May-late November) 209-632-9322
Modesto Home Show (mid-September) 209-473-7733
Oakdale Chocolate Festival (mid-May) 209-847-2244
Oktoberfest (late September) 209-577-5757
Ripon Almond Blossom Festival (late February) 209-571-6480
Riverbank Cheese & Wine Exposition
(mid-October) 209-869-4541
Saint Patrick's Jazz Bash (mid-March) 209-869-3280
Scandi Fest (late September) 209-667-1452
Scottish Games & Gathering of the Clans
(early June) 209-538-0821
Spring Art Show (mid-May) 209-529-3369
Tracy Dry Bean Festival (early August) 209-835-2131

Montgomery, Alabama

***County:* Montgomery**

MONTGOMERY is located on the Alabama River in central Alabama. Major cities within 100 miles include Birmingham and Auburn, Alabama and Columbus, Georgia.

Area (Land) .... 135.0 sq mi
Area (Water)............................... 0.8 sq mi
Elevation.................................... 250 ft
Latitude ....32-36-67 N
Longitude............................... 86-30-00 W
Time Zone ....CST
Area Code...................................... 334

Climate

Montgomery has a mild, temperate climate. Summers are warm, with average daytime highs near 90 degrees and lows near 70. Winters are generally mild, with average high temperatures ranging from the mid-50s to low 60s, and average lows in the mid- to upper 30s. Snowfall is rare in Montgomery. Precipitation is distributed fairly evenly throughout the year - March tends to be the wettest month in Montgomery, while October is normally the driest.

Average Temperatures & Precipitation

Temperatures

	Jan	Feb	Mar	Apr	May	Jun	Jul	Aug	Sep	Oct	Nov	Dec
High	56	61	69	76	83	89	91	90	87	78	69	60
Low	36	39	46	53	61	68	72	71	66	53	45	39

Precipitation

	Jan	Feb	Mar	Apr	May	Jun	Jul	Aug	Sep	Oct	Nov	Dec
Inches	4.7	5.5	6.3	4.5	3.9	3.9	5.2	3.7	4.1	2.5	4.1	5.2

History

Originally inhabited by Alabamu Indians (early ancestors of the Creek tribe), the city of Montgomery was established in 1819 with the consolidation of two local settlements and was named for Revolutionary War General Richard Montgomery. Located along the banks of the Alabama River, which proved to be important for both transportation and trade, and also in the heart of Alabama's rich farming area known as the "black belt," Montgomery grew quickly as a center for commerce and agriculture, with cotton being the leading crop. In 1847 the state capital was relocated from Tuscaloosa to Montgomery.

During the 1860s Montgomery became known as the "Cradle of the Confederacy," serving as the capital for the Confederate States of America during the Civil War. In 1861 Jefferson Davis was sworn in as president of the Confederacy. Montgomery was captured by Union troops in April 1865.

Nearly a century later, Montgomery was thrust into the national spotlight once again—this time as the site of civil rights demonstrations. In December 1955 Rosa Parks refused to give up her seat on a city bus in Montgomery, sparking a year-long boycott, led by Martin Luther King Jr., of the city's segregated bus system. This event marked one of the first major victories for the civil rights movement. Four years later Dr. King ended the Civil Rights march from Selma on the steps of the capital in Montgomery.

Today, life is much more peaceful in Alabama's capital city. In 1998 Money Magazine named Montgomery one of the best medium-sized cities in U.S. in its annual ranking of the "Best Places to Live in America." Montgomery is currently home to more than 197,000 people, making it Alabama's third largest city and the second fastest-growing city in the state.

Population

1990 Census 190,350
1998 Estimate..............................197,014
% Change 3.5
2003 Projection 237,037*

Racial/Ethnic Breakdown
White.................................... 56.5%
Black 42.3%
Other..................................... 1.2%
Hispanic Origin (may be of any race) 0.8%

Age Breakdown
Under 5 years.............................. 7.9%
5 to 17................................... 19.8%
18 to 20................................... 5.3%
21 to 24................................... 6.0%
25 to 34.................................. 17.3%
35 to 44.................................. 14.9%
45 to 54................................... 9.3%
55 to 64................................... 7.9%
65 to 74................................... 6.7%
75+ years 5.0%
Median Age.................................31.5

Gender Breakdown
Male...................................... 46.5%
Female.................................... 53.5%

** Information given is for Montgomery County.*

Government

Type of Government: Mayor-Council

Montgomery City Attorney
PO Box 1111
Montgomery, AL 36101
Phone: 334-241-2050
Fax: 334-241-2600

Montgomery City Clerk
PO Box 1111
Montgomery, AL 36101
Phone: 334-241-2096
Fax: 334-241-2056

Montgomery City Council
PO Box 1111
Montgomery, AL 36101
Phone: 334-241-2096
Fax: 334-241-2056

Montgomery City Hall
103 N Perry St
Montgomery, AL 36104
Phone: 334-241-4400
Fax: 334-241-2266

Montgomery City-County Public Library
245 High St
Montgomery, AL 36104
Phone: 334-240-4999
Fax: 334-240-4980

Montgomery Community Development Dept
PO Box 1111
Montgomery, AL 36101
Phone: 334-241-2996
Fax: 334-241-4432

Montgomery Finance Dept
PO Box 1111
Montgomery, AL 36101
Phone: 334-241-2025
Fax: 334-241-2266

Montgomery Fire Dept
PO Box 1111
Montgomery, AL 36101
Phone: 334-241-2983
Fax: 334-241-2611

Montgomery Mayor
PO Box 1111
Montgomery, AL 36101
Phone: 334-241-2000
Fax: 334-241-2600

Montgomery Parks & Recreation Dept
1010 Forest Ave
Montgomery, AL 36106
Phone: 334-241-4731
Fax: 334-241-2301

Montgomery Personnel Dept
PO Box 1111
Montgomery, AL 36101
Phone: 334-241-2675
Fax: 334-241-2219

Montgomery Planning Controls Dept
103 N Perry St
Montgomery, AL 36104
Phone: 334-241-2722
Fax: 334-241-2017

Montgomery Police Dept
PO Box 159
Montgomery, AL 36101
Phone: 334-241-2810
Fax: 334-241-2333

Montgomery Sanitation Dept
934 N Ripley St
Montgomery, AL 36104
Phone: 334-241-2566
Fax: 334-241-2566

Important Phone Numbers

AAA....334-265-1237
Alabama Dept of Revenue....334-242-1000
Driver's License Information....334-272-8868
Emergency....911
HotelDocs....800-468-3537
Medical Referral....334-286-3463
Montgomery Area Assn of Realtors....334-396-0256
Montgomery County Revenue Commission....334-832-1220
Poison Control Center....800-462-0800
Time/Temp....334-262-8871
Travelers Aid....334-269-0488
Vehicle Registration Information....334-832-1233
Voter Registration Information....334-832-1215
Weather....205-945-7000

Information Sources

Better Business Bureau Serving Central Alabama & the Wiregrass Area
1210 20th St S
Birmingham, AL 35205
www.birmingham-al.bbb.org
Phone: 205-558-2238
Fax: 205-558-2239

Montgomery Area Chamber of Commerce
41 Commerce St
Montgomery, AL 36104
www.montgomerychamber.org
Phone: 334-834-5200
Fax: 334-265-4745

Montgomery Civic Center
300 Bibb St
Montgomery, AL 36104
www.civic-center.ci.montgomery.al.us
Phone: 334-241-2100
Fax: 334-241-2117

Montgomery County
PO Box 1667
Montgomery, AL 36102
Phone: 334-832-4950
Fax: 334-832-2533

Montgomery Visitors Center
300-A Water St Union Station
Montgomery, AL 36104
Phone: 334-262-0013
Fax: 334-261-1111

Online Resources

About.com Guide to Montgomery
montgomery.about.com/citiestowns/southeastus/montgomery

Area Guide Montgomery
montgomery.areaguides.net

City Knowledge Montgomery
www.cityknowledge.com/al_montgomery.htm

Excite.com Montgomery City Guide
www.excite.com/travel/countries/united_states/alabama/montgomery

Lodging.com Montgomery Alabama
www.lodging.com/auto/guides/montgomery-al.html

Mainstreet USA Montgomery
www.mainstreetusa.com/al/montgomery

Montgomery Area Information Site
www.bwsolutions.com/montgomery/

Online Montgomery
www.montgomery-al.com

Area Communities

Communities in the Montgomery Metropolitan Statistical Area (MSA), which includes Montgomery, Autauga, and Elmore counties, with populations greater than 10,000 include:

Millbrook
3821 Grandview Rd
Millbrook, AL 36054
Phone: 334-285-6428
Fax: 334-285-6460

Prattville
101 W Main St
Prattville, AL 36067
Phone: 334-365-9997
Fax: 334-361-3608

Tallassee
3 Freeman Ave
Tallassee, AL 36078
Phone: 334-283-6571
Fax: 334-283-3335

Wetumpka
212 S Main St
Wetumpka, AL 36092
Phone: 334-567-5147
Fax: 334-567-1307

Economy

Montgomery is not only the governmental center for the state of Alabama, it is also a major regional trade and transportation hub. Services is currently the area's largest employment sector, with healthcare being the leading industry, representing approximately one-third of all service-related jobs in Montgomery County. Home to Alabama's state government, a military base and two state university campuses, government remains important to the city's economy. The State of Alabama is Montgomery's single largest employer, providing jobs for 19,000 area residents.

Unemployment Rate 3.1%
Per Capita Income.......................... $24,103*
Median Family Income...................... $43,700**

** Information given is for Montgomery County.*
*** Information given is for the Montgomery Metropolitan Area, which includes Montgomery, Autauga, and Elmore counties.*

Principal Industries & Number of Wage Earners

Montgomery MSA* - 1999

Finance, Insurance, & Real Estate 10,700
Government 37,300
Manufacturing 18,600
Mining & Construction................................. 8,700
Services 45,000
Trade 38,500
Transportation & Public Utilities 7,300

** Information given is for the Montgomery Metropolitan Statistical Area (MSA), which includes Montgomery, Autauga, and Elmore counties.*

Major Employers

Alabama State University
915 S Jackson St
Montgomery, AL 36101
www.alasu.edu
Phone: 334-229-4100
Fax: 334-229-4984
TF: 800-253-5037

Alfa Insurance
PO Box 11000
Montgomery, AL 36191
E-mail: marketing@alfains.com
www.alfains.com
Phone: 334-288-3900
Fax: 334-288-0905

Auburn University Montgomery
7300 University Dr
Montgomery, AL 36117
www.aum.edu
Phone: 334-244-3000
Fax: 334-244-3721
TF: 800-227-2649

Baptist Health
2105 E South Blvd
Montgomery, AL 36116
Phone: 334-288-2100
Fax: 334-286-5602

Electronic Data Systems (EDS)
2743 Gunter Park Dr N Suites A & B
Montgomery, AL 36109
www.eds.com/careers/
Phone: 334-277-8445
Fax: 334-277-3622

Jackson Hospital & Clinic Inc
1725 Pine St
Montgomery, AL 36106
www.jackson.org
Phone: 334-293-8000
Fax: 334-293-8934

Maxwell Air Force Base
Maxwell AFB, AL 36112
E-mail: dpope@max1.au.af.mil
Phone: 334-953-3800
Fax: 334-953-3379

Montgomery City Hall
103 N Perry St
Montgomery, AL 36104
montgomery.al.us
Phone: 334-241-4400
Fax: 334-241-2266

Montgomery Public Schools
307 S Decatur St
Montgomery, AL 36104
www.mps.k12.al.us
Phone: 334-223-6700
Fax: 334-269-3076

Regions Bank
8 Commerce St
Montgomery, AL 36104
Phone: 334-832-8011
Fax: 334-832-8107

Regions Mortgage Inc
PO Box 669
Montgomery, AL 36101
Phone: 334-223-3701
Fax: 334-223-3453
TF: 800-392-5669

Rheem Mfg Co
PO Box 244020
Montgomery, AL 36124
rheem.com/index.html
Phone: 334-260-1500
Fax: 334-260-1420

US Postal Service
6701 Winton Blount Blvd
Montgomery, AL 36119
new.usps.com
Phone: 334-244-7553
Fax: 334-244-7573

Winn-Dixie Montgomery Inc
1550 Jackson Ferry Rd
Montgomery, AL 36104
Phone: 334-240-6200
Fax: 334-240-6221

Quality of Living Indicators

Total Crime Index.................................... 15,407
(rates per 100,000 inhabitants)

Violent Crime
Murder/manslaughter........................... 26
Forcible rape 120
Robbery...................................... 591
Aggravated assault............................ 846

Property Crime
Burglary 3,165
Larceny theft 9,259
Motor vehicle theft 1,400

Cost of Living Index....................................97.6
(national average = 100)

Median Home Price..................................$99,100

Education

Public Schools

Montgomery Public Schools Phone: 334-223-6700
307 S Decatur St Fax: 334-269-3076
Montgomery, AL 36104
www.mps.k12.al.us

Number of Schools
Elementary.................................. 33
Jr. High/Middle 11
High....................................... 7

Student/Teacher Ratio
All Grades 16.4:1

Private Schools

Number of Schools (all grades).................... 15+

Colleges & Universities

Alabama State University Phone: 334-229-4100
915 S Jackson St Fax: 334-229-4984
Montgomery, AL 36101 TF: 800-253-5037
www.alasu.edu

Auburn University Montgomery Phone: 334-244-3000
7300 University Dr Fax: 334-244-3721
Montgomery, AL 36117 TF: 800-227-2649
www.aum.edu

Faulkner University Phone: 334-272-5820
5345 Atlanta Hwy Fax: 334-260-6137
Montgomery, AL 36109 TF: 800-879-9816
www.faulkner.edu

Huntingdon College Phone: 334-833-4497
1500 E Fairview Ave Fax: 334-833-4347
Montgomery, AL 36106 TF: 800-763-0313
www.huntingdon.edu

John M Patterson State Technical College Phone: 334-288-1080
3920 Troy Hwy Fax: 334-284-9357
Montgomery, AL 36116
E-mail: jptech@montgomerymindstring.com
www.jptech.cc.al.us

South College Phone: 334-263-1013
122 Commerce St Fax: 334-262-7326
Montgomery, AL 36104
www.southcollege.edu/campus_mont.htm

Southern Christian University Phone: 334-277-2277
1200 Taylor Rd Fax: 334-387-3878
Montgomery, AL 36117
E-mail: scuniversity@mindspring.com
www.southernchristian.edu

Trenholm State Technical College Phone: 334-832-9000
1225 Air Base Blvd Fax: 334-832-9777
Montgomery, AL 36108
www.tstc.cc.al.us

Troy State University Phone: 334-670-3100
University Ave Fax: 334-670-3733
Troy, AL 36082
www.troyst.edu

Hospitals

Baptist Medical Center South Phone: 334-288-2100
2105 E South Blvd Fax: 334-286-5602
Montgomery, AL 36116

Jackson Hospital Phone: 334-293-8000
1725 Pine St Fax: 334-293-8934
Montgomery, AL 36106
www.jackson.org

Transportation

Airport(s)

Montgomery Regional Airport (MGM)
7 miles SW of downtown (approx 15 minutes) 334-281-5040

Mass Transit

Montgomery Area Transit System
$1.50 Base fare...............................334-262-7321

Rail/Bus

Greyhound Bus Station Phone: 334-286-0120
950 W South Blvd
Montgomery, AL 36105

Utilities

Electricity
Alabama Power Co 800-245-2244
www.southernco.com/site/alapower

Gas
Alagasco 334-263-2341
www.alagasco.com

Water
Montgomery Water & Sanitary Sewer Board......334-206-1600

Garbage Collection/Recycling
Montgomery Sanitation 334-241-2750

Telecommunications

Telephone
BellSouth 800-753-3320
www.bellsouth.com
Knology of Montgomery.......................334-356-1000
www.knology.com

Cable Television
AT & T Cable Services........................334-271-1414
www.cable.att.com
Knology of Montgomery.......................334-356-1000
www.knology.com

Internet Service Providers (ISPs)
Novazone Inc 334-263-0506
novazone.com
World Media Inc 334-832-4811
www.worlddomain.com

Banks

Aliant Bank
PO Box 135
Montgomery, AL 36101
Phone: 334-270-3000
Fax: 334-270-3013
TF: 800-949-5666

Amsouth Bank
201 Monroe St
Montgomery, AL 36104
Phone: 334-834-9500
Fax: 334-240-1397
TF: 800-333-7485

Colonial Bank
1 Commerce St
Montgomery, AL 36104
www.hsv.tis.net/colonial
Phone: 334-240-5000
Fax: 334-954-1131

Compass Bank
3480 Eastern Blvd
Montgomery, AL 36116
Phone: 334-409-7453
Fax: 334-409-7312

First Tuskegee Bank
100 Commerce St
Montgomery, AL 36104
Phone: 334-262-0800
Fax: 334-265-4333

Regions Bank
8 Commerce St
Montgomery, AL 36104
Phone: 800-734-4667
Fax: 334-832-8913

Southtrust Bank
210 Water St Union Station
Montgomery, AL 36104
Phone: 334-270-2340
Fax: 334-270-2345
TF: 800-239-2300

Sterling Bank
4121 Carmichael Rd Suite 100
Montgomery, AL 36106
E-mail: info@sterlingmontgomery.com
www.sterlingmontgomery.com
Phone: 334-279-7800
Fax: 334-244-4429

Shopping

Eastdale Mall
5501 Atlanta Hwy
Montgomery, AL 36117
Phone: 334-277-7359
Fax: 334-277-1386

Montgomery Mall
Southern Blvd & McGehee Rd
Montgomery, AL 36116
Phone: 334-284-1533
Fax: 334-281-4618

Media

Newspapers and Magazines

Montgomery Advertiser*
PO Box 1000
Montgomery, AL 36101
www.accessmontgomery.com
Phone: 334-262-1611
Fax: 334-261-1521

Montgomery Independent
1810 W 5th St
Montgomery, AL 36106
www.the-independent.com
Phone: 334-265-7323
Fax: 334-265-7320

**Indicates major daily newspapers*

Television

WAIQ-TV Ch 26 (PBS)
1255 Madison Ave
Montgomery, AL 36107
www.aptv.org/InsideAPT/WAIQ26.html
Phone: 334-264-9900
Fax: 334-264-7045

WAKA-TV Ch 8 (CBS)
3020 East Blvd
Montgomery, AL 36116
E-mail: waka@mindspring.com
www.waka.com
Phone: 334-279-8787
Fax: 334-272-6444

WCOV-TV Ch 20 (Fox)
PO Box 250045
Montgomery, AL 36125
E-mail: wcovtv20@mont.mindspring.com
www.wcov.com
Phone: 334-288-7020
Fax: 334-288-5414

WHOA-TV Ch 32 (ABC)
3251 Harrison Rd
Montgomery, AL 36109
www.whoa32.com
Phone: 334-270-3200
Fax: 334-271-6348

WSFA-TV Ch 12 (NBC)
PO Box 251200
Montgomery, AL 36125
E-mail: wsfanews12@aol.com
www.wsfa.com
Phone: 334-288-1212
Fax: 334-613-8303

Radio

WACV-AM 1170 kHz (N/T)
PO Box 210723
Montgomery, AL 36121
Phone: 334-244-1170
Fax: 334-244-1176

WBAM-FM 98.9 MHz (CHR)
PO Box 210519
Montgomery, AL 36121
www.star989.com
Phone: 334-213-0598
Fax: 334-279-9563

WHHY-FM 101.9 MHz (CHR)
1 Commerce St Suite 300
Montgomery, AL 36104
www.y102montgomery.com
Phone: 334-264-2288
Fax: 334-834-9102

WLBF-FM 89.1 MHz (Rel)
PO Box 210789
Montgomery, AL 36121
E-mail: spaceradio@mindsprung.com
Phone: 334-271-8900
Fax: 334-260-8962

WLWI-FM 92.3 MHz (Ctry)
1 Commerce St Suite 300
Montgomery, AL 36104
www.wlwi.com
Phone: 334-240-9274
Fax: 334-240-9219

WMSP-AM 740 kHz (Sports)
1 Commerce St Suite 300
Montgomery, AL 36104
www.sportsradio740.com
Phone: 334-240-9274
Fax: 334-240-9219

WNZZ-AM 950 kHz (B/EZ)
1 Commerce St Suite 300
Montgomery, AL 36104
Phone: 334-240-9274
Fax: 334-240-9219

WRWO-FM 96.1 MHz (AC)
PO Box 210723
Montgomery, AL 36121
Phone: 334-244-0961
Fax: 334-279-9563

WVAS-FM 90.7 MHz (NPR)
915 S Jackson St
Montgomery, AL 36101
Phone: 334-229-4287
Fax: 334-269-4995

WXFX-FM 95.1 MHz (Rock)
PO Box 250210
Montgomery, AL 36125
Phone: 334-264-2288
Fax: 334-834-9102

Attractions

Montgomery is the birthplace of the Civil War, and of the modern Civil Rights Movement. A Civil Rights Memorial at the Southern Poverty Law Center in Montgomery chronicles key events and lists the names of 40 people who died in the struggle for racial equality between 1955 and 1968. (The Memorial was designed by Maya Lin, the artist who designed the Vietnam Veterans Memorial in Washington, DC.) Another reminder of this era is the Dexter Avenue King Memorial Baptist Church, the first pulpit of Dr. King and the center of the Montgomery bus boycott. Other attractions in Montgomery include the final resting place, as well as a life-size statue, of country music singer Hank Williams; and the one-time home of F. Scott Fitzgerald and his wife Zelda, a Montgomery native. North of the city is the Jasmine Hill Gardens and Outdoor Museum, which features a 17-acre garden and an extensive collection of fountains, pools, and Greek statuary, as well as an 1830s cottage.

Alabama Artists Gallery Phone: 334-242-4076
201 Monroe St Suite 110 Fax: 334-240-3269
Montgomery, AL 36104

Alabama Dance Theatre Phone: 334-241-2590
1018 Madison Ave Fax: 334-241-2504
Montgomery, AL 36104
www.freenet.tlh.fl.us/ADT/

Alabama Dept of Archives & History Public Services Div Phone: 334-242-4363
624 Washington Ave Fax: 334-240-3433
Montgomery, AL 36130

Alabama Shakespeare Festival Phone: 334-271-5353
Wynton M Blount Cultural Pk Fax: 334-271-5348
Montgomery, AL 36117 TF: 800-841-4273
E-mail: pr4bard@wsnet.com
www.asf.net

Alabama State Capitol Phone: 334-242-3750
600 Dexter Ave Fax: 334-242-2788
Montgomery, AL 36130

Alabama War Memorial Phone: 334-262-6638
120 N Jackson St Fax: 334-262-9694
Montgomery, AL 36104 TF: 800-234-5544
E-mail: alabamaamericanlegion@att.net

Civil Rights Memorial Phone: 334-264-0286
400 Washington Ave
Montgomery, AL 36104

Davis Theatre for the Performing Arts Phone: 334-241-9567
251 Montgomery St Fax: 334-241-9756
Montgomery, AL 36104
www.tsum.edu/davis

Dexter Avenue King Memorial Baptist Church Phone: 334-263-3970
454 Dexter Ave Fax: 334-263-3970
Montgomery, AL 36104

Eufaula National Wildlife Refuge Phone: 334-687-4065
509 Old State Hwy 165 Fax: 334-687-5906
Eufaula, AL 36027

Executive Mansion Phone: 334-834-3022
1142 S Perry St Fax: 334-240-3466
Montgomery, AL 36104

Faulkner University Dinner Theatre Phone: 334-260-6190
5345 Atlanta Hwy
Montgomery, AL 36109

First White House of the Confederacy Phone: 334-242-1861
644 Washington Ave
Montgomery, AL 36104

Fitzgerald F Scott & Zelda Museum Phone: 334-264-4222
919 Felder Ave
Montgomery, AL 36106

Folmar Anita P Youth Art Gallery Phone: 334-241-2787
1018 Madison Ave Fax: 334-241-2504
Montgomery, AL 36104

Gayle WA Planetarium Phone: 334-241-4799
1010 Forest Ave Fax: 334-240-4309
Montgomery, AL 36106
www.tsum.edu/planet

Horseshoe Bend National Military Park Phone: 256-234-7111
11288 Horseshoe Bend Rd Fax: 256-329-9905
Daviston, AL 36256
www.nps.gov/hobe/

Jasmine Hill Gardens & Outdoor Museum Phone: 334-567-6463
3001 Jasmine Hill Rd Fax: 334-567-6466
Wetumpka, AL 36093
E-mail: jasminehill@jasminehill.com
www.jasminehill.org

Loard Leon Gallery of Fine Arts Phone: 334-270-9010
2781 Zelda Rd Fax: 334-270-0150
Montgomery, AL 36106

Maxwell Air Force Base Phone: 334-953-2014
Air Base Blvd & Day St Fax: 334-953-3379
Montgomery, AL 36112
www.maxwell.af.mil

Montgomery Ballet Phone: 334-409-0522
6009 E Shirley Ln Fax: 334-409-2311
Montgomery, AL 36117

Montgomery Museum of Fine Arts Phone: 334-244-5700
1 Museum Dr Fax: 334-244-5774
Montgomery, AL 36117
E-mail: mmfa@wsnet.com
www.fineartsmuseum.com

Montgomery State Farmers Market Phone: 334-242-5350
1655 Federal Dr Fax: 334-240-3275
Montgomery, AL 36107 TF: 800-243-4769

Montgomery Symphony Orchestra Phone: 334-240-4004
250 Montgomery St Davis Theatre Fax: 334-240-4034
Montgomery, AL 36104

Montgomery Zoo Phone: 334-240-4900
2301 Coliseum Pkwy Fax: 334-240-4916
Montgomery, AL 36110
www.mindspring.com/~zoonet/montgome/montgome.html

Old Alabama Town Phone: 334-240-4500
301 Columbus St Fax: 334-240-4519
Montgomery, AL 36104 TF: 888-240-1850
www.mindspring.com/~olaltown/

Tuskegee Institute National Historic Site
1212 Old Montgomery Rd
Tuskegee Institute, AL 36088
www.nps.gov/tuin/
Phone: 334-727-3200
Fax: 334-727-4597

Sports Teams & Facilities

Crampton Bowl Stadium
1022 Madison Ave
Montgomery, AL 36104
Phone: 334-240-4200
Fax: 334-241-2301

Garrett Coliseum
1555 Federal Dr
Montgomery, AL 36107
agencies.state.al.us/garrett
Phone: 334-242-5597
Fax: 334-240-3242

Montgomery Motorsports Park
2600 N Belt Dr
Montgomery, AL 36110
Phone: 334-260-9660
Fax: 334-260-9320

VictoryLand Greyhound Racing
Exit 22 off I-85
Shorter, AL 36075
E-mail: victoryland@worldaccess.com
www.victoryland.com
Phone: 334-269-6087
Fax: 334-727-0737

Annual Events

Alabama Highland Games (late September)........334-361-4571
Blue-Gray All Star Football Classic (December).....334-265-1266
Blue-Gray Intercollegiate Tennis Championship (mid-March)........334-271-7001
Broadway Under the Stars (late August)........334-240-4004
Calico Fort Arts & Crafts Fair (early April)........334-227-3250
Christmas on the River Parade (early December)........800-252-2262
Festival in the Park (early October)........334-241-2300
Flimp Festival (early May)........334-244-5700
Greek Festival (early May)........334-263-1366
Jubilee CityFest (late May)........334-834-7220
Montgomery State Farmers Market Day (mid-July)........334-242-5350
NCAA Division II National Baseball Championship (late May)........334-241-2300
Oktoberfest (early October)........334-272-6527
South Alabama State Fair (early October)........334-272-6831
Taste of Montgomery (November)........334-277-1840
Turkey Day Classic Parade (late November)........334-229-4100
World Championship Rodeo (mid-March)........334-265-1867

Naples, Florida

***County:* Collier**

NAPLES is located on the southwest coast of Florida. Major cities within 150 miles include Fort Myers, Fort Lauderdale, Sarasota, and Miami, Florida.

Area (Land) .... 13.5 sq mi
Area (Water)............................... 2.4 sq mi
Elevation.. 9 ft
Latitude ....26-08-41 N
Longitude.............................. 81-47-41 W
Time Zone ....EST
Area Code.. 941

Climate

Naples' climate features mild temperatures year-round. Summer days are very warm, with average high temperatures in the low-90s, while evenings cool down into the low 70s. Summer is also the rainy season in Naples - most of the annual precipitation falls between June and September. Winters are mild, with average high temperatures in the mid- to upper 70s and lows in the mid-50s. December is the driest month of the year in Naples.

Average Temperatures & Precipitation

Temperatures

	Jan	Feb	Mar	Apr	May	Jun	Jul	Aug	Sep	Oct	Nov	Dec
High	76	77	81	85	88	90	91	92	91	87	82	78
Low	53	54	58	61	66	71	72	73	72	67	61	55

Precipitation

	Jan	Feb	Mar	Apr	May	Jun	Jul	Aug	Sep	Oct	Nov	Dec
Inches	1.7	2.2	2.3	1.5	4.1	8.6	7.8	8.2	8.4	3.1	1.8	1.4

History

Originally inhabited by the Calusa Indians during the 1700s, the area known today as Naples was also first explored by Europeans during the 16th Century. Spaniard Ponce de Leon was the first European to visit Florida's southwest coast. The Seminole Indians arrived in the area during the mid-1800s, and many Seminoles still inhabit the interior sections of South Florida today. The city's first white settlers, Roger Gordon and Joe Wiggins, arrived during the 1860s. The area's mild climate and good fishing had often been compared to the Italian city of Naples, leading to the city's present name. In 1887, the city of Naples was founded by Walter N. Haldeman, owner of a Kentucky newspaper, the Louisville Courier Journal. Haldeman is also credited with building Naples' 600-foot T-shaped pier, as well as Palm Cottage, which served as a hotel for years before becoming the current headquarters of the Collier County Historical Society and one of the city's leading historical tourist attractions. During its early years, Naples was primarily a quiet fishing village, although it quickly gained a reputation as a popular winter resort.

In 1923 entrepreneur Barron Gift Collier founded Collier County, and Everglades City, which is located south of Naples, served as its first county seat. Collier was instrumental in the construction of the Tamiami Trail, a road running from Miami on the southeast coast of Florida, across the Everglades and up the west coast to Tampa. The completion of the Tamiami Trail in 1928 and the arrival of the railroad helped to spark the growth of Naples. In 1966, the county seat was relocated to Naples.

Although Naples remains a relatively small city, it is becoming more popular as a place for relocation. In 1996, Money Magazine named Naples one of the "Five Best Small Places to Live in America." Today, Naples is home to more than 19,000 people.

Population

1990 Census 19,505
1998 Estimate...............................19,404
% Change .... -0.5
2005 Projection 327,900*

Racial/Ethnic Breakdown

White.......................................93.9%
Black 5.6%
Other 0.5%
Hispanic Origin (may be of any race) 2.1%

Age Breakdown

Under 5 years...............................2.9%
5 to 17.......................................7.4%
18 to 20.....................................1.9%
21 to 24.....................................2.4%
25 to 34.....................................7.6%
35 to 44.....................................9.5%
45 to 54....................................10.9%
55 to 64....................................15.5%
65 to 74....................................23.2%
75+ years 18.7%
Median Age..................................41.0*

Gender Breakdown

Male..45.5%
Female......................................54.5%

** Information given is for Collier County.*

Government

Type of Government: Mayor-Council

Naples Building & Zoning Div
735 8th St S
Naples, FL 34102
Phone: 941-434-4640
Fax: 941-434-4652

Naples City Attorney
735 8th St S
Naples, FL 34102
Phone: 941-434-4606
Fax: 941-434-4748

Naples City Clerk
735 8th St S
Naples, FL 34102
Phone: 941-434-4701
Fax: 941-434-4704

Naples City Council
735 8th St S
Naples, FL 34102
Phone: 941-434-4601
Fax: 941-434-4855

Naples City Hall
735 8th St S
Naples, FL 34102
Phone: 941-434-4717
Fax: 941-434-4659

Naples City Manager
735 8th St S
Naples, FL 34102
Phone: 941-434-4610
Fax: 941-434-4620

Naples Community Services Dept
280 13th St N
Naples, FL 34102
Phone: 941-434-4680
Fax: 941-262-5640

Naples Engineering Dept
735 8th St S 2nd Fl
Naples, FL 34102
Phone: 941-434-4655
Fax: 941-434-5359

Naples Human Resources Dept
735 8th St S
Naples, FL 34102
Phone: 941-434-4670
Fax: 941-434-4864

Naples Mayor
735 8th St S
Naples, FL 34102
Phone: 941-434-4601
Fax: 941-434-4855

Naples Natural Resources Dept
735 8th St S
Naples, FL 34102
Phone: 941-434-4655
Fax: 941-434-4620

Naples Planning Dept
801 8th Ave S
Naples, FL 34102
Phone: 941-434-4626
Fax: 941-434-4627

Naples Police & Emergency Services Dept
355 13th St N
Naples, FL 34102
Phone: 941-434-4790
Fax: 941-262-5354

Naples Public Works Dept
380 13th St N
Naples, FL 34102
Phone: 941-434-4745
Fax: 941-430-7154

Important Phone Numbers

AAA.....941-594-5006
American Express Travel.....941-262-3300
Collier County Property Appraiser.....941-774-8141
Collier County Tax Collector.....941-774-8171
Dental Referral.....813-931-3018
Driver's License Information.....941-417-6358
Emergency.....911
Florida Dept of Revenue.....941-436-1050
Medical Referral.....941-436-5430
Naples Area Board of Realtors.....941-597-1666
Poison Control Center.....800-282-3171
Time/Temp.....941-594-1234
Vehicle Registration Information.....941-774-8177
Voter Registration Information.....941-774-8450
Weather.....941-594-1234

Information Sources

Collier County
3301 Tamiami Trail E
Naples, FL 34112
www.co.collier.fl.us
Phone: 941-774-8383
Fax: 941-774-4010

Consumer Protection Agency
407 S Calhoun St 2nd Fl Mayo Bldg
Tallahassee, FL 32399
www.800helpfla.com
Phone: 850-488-2221
Fax: 850-487-4177

Economic Development Council
3050 N Horseshoe Dr Suite 120
Naples, FL 34104
www.swfloridabusiness.com
Phone: 941-263-8989
Fax: 941-263-6021

Naples Area Chamber of Commerce
895 5th Ave S
Naples, FL 34102
www.naples-online.com
Phone: 941-263-1858
Fax: 941-435-9910

Online Resources

Area Guide Naples
naples.areaguides.net

Best of Naples
www.bestof.net/naples/

City Knowledge Naples
www.cityknowledge.com/fl_naples.htm

DiningGuide Naples
diningguide.net/naples

Excite.com Naples City Guide
www.excite.com/travel/countries/united_states/florida/naples

HotelGuide Naples
hotelguide.net/naples

Lodging.com Naples Florida
www.lodging.com/auto/guides/naples-area-fl.html

MetroGuide Naples
metroguide.net/naples

Naples & Southwest Florida Guide
www.naplesnet.com/naples2/index.html

Naples CityLink
usacitylink.com/citylink/fl/naples/default.html

Naples Florida
www.naples-florida.com

Naples Florida Visitor Information
www.azinet.com/Naples

Naples.com
www.naples.com

Online City Guide to Naples
www.olcg.com/fl/naples/index.html

Surf & Sun Beach Vacation Guide to Naples
www.surf-sun.com/fl-naples-main.htm

Welcome to Naples Florida
www.naplesnet.com/naples/naples.htm

Area Communities

Marco Island is the only other incorporated community in Collier County with a population exceeding 10,000. Unincorporated communities in Collier County with populations greater than 10,000 include Immokalee and Golden Gate.

Marco Island Phone: 941-389-5000
950 N Collier Blvd Suite 308 Fax: 941-389-4359
Marco Island, FL 34145

Economy

Naples' economic base ranges from agriculture to hospitality. Collier County's agriculture industry, which includes tomato, citrus, winter vegetable, and cattle farming, generates nearly $400 million in revenue annually. Naples also remains a popular winter resort destination, as it has for more than a century - the county population increases by more than 40 percent during the winter tourist season. Several of the area's top employers are hotels and resorts, but the Collier County School Board is the area's single largest employer, providing jobs for more than 3,300 area residents.

Unemployment Rate 4.1%
Per Capita Income.......................... $42,813*
Median Family Income...................... $48,800*

** Information given is for Collier County.*

Principal Industries & Number of Wage Earners

Collier County - 1998

Industry	Wage Earners
Agricultural Services, Forestry & Fishing	7,700
Construction	9,971
Finance, Insurance, & Real Estate	5,524
Manufacturing	2,661
Mining	36
Retail Trade	21,243
Services	30,785
Transportation, Communications, & Public Utilities	2,377
Wholesale Trade	2,755

Major Employers

Barron Collier Co Phone: 941-657-3602
1320 N 15th St Fax: 941-657-2337
Immokalee, FL 34142

Bentley Village Classic Residence by Hyatt Phone: 941-598-3153
561 Bentley Village Ct Fax: 941-598-3357
Naples, FL 34110
www.azstarnet.com/devel/hyatt/index.htm

Boran Craig Barber Construction Co Inc Phone: 941-643-3343
3606 Enterprise Ave Fax: 941-643-4548
Naples, FL 34104

Collier County Phone: 941-774-8383
3301 Tamiami Trail E Fax: 941-774-4010
Naples, FL 34112
www.co.collier.fl.us

Collier County School Board Phone: 941-643-2700
3710 Estey Ave Fax: 941-436-6500
Naples, FL 34104
www.collier.k12.fl.us

Collier County Sherriff's Office Phone: 941-774-4434
3301 Tamiami Trail E Bldg J Fax: 941-793-9181
Naples, FL 34112
E-mail: ccsofla@colliersheriff.org
www.colliersheriff.org

Collier Enterprises Phone: 941-261-4455
3003 Tamiami Trail N Suite 400 Fax: 941-263-4437
Naples, FL 34103
www.collierenterprises.com

First Union Bank Phone: 941-591-7848
5801 Pelican Bay Blvd Fax: 941-591-7917
Naples, FL 34108

Naples Daily News Phone: 941-262-3161
1075 Central Ave Fax: 941-263-4816
Naples, FL 34102
E-mail: info@naplesnews.com
www.naplesnews.com

NCH Healthcare System Phone: 941-436-5000
350 7th St N Fax: 941-436-5914
Naples, FL 34102
E-mail: info@nchhcs.org
www.nchhcs.org

Publix Super Markets Inc Phone: 863-688-1188
PO Box 407 Fax: 863-284-5571
Lakeland, FL 33802
www.publix.com

Registry Resort Phone: 941-597-3232
475 Seagate Dr Fax: 941-594-6310
Naples, FL 34103 TF: 800-247-9810
www.registryhotels.com

Ritz-Carlton Naples Phone: 941-598-3300
280 Vanderbilt Beach Rd Fax: 941-598-6690
Naples, FL 34108 TF: 800-241-3333
www.ritzcarlton.com/html_prop/resort.asp?Property_ID=12&PageNo=9

Wal-Mart Discount Cities Phone: 941-793-5517
3451 Tamiami Trail E Fax: 941-793-3022
Naples, FL 34112

Winn-Dixie Stores Inc Phone: 954-783-2700
1141 SW 12th Ave Fax: 954-783-2896
Pompano Beach, FL 33069
E-mail: comments@winn-dixie.com
www.winn-dixie.com

Quality of Living Indicators

Total Crime Index..................................... 1,247
(rates per 100,000 inhabitants)

Violent Crime
Murder/manslaughter............................ -

Forcible rape 1
Robbery...................................... 17
Aggravated assault.............................. 68

Property Crime
Burglary 200
Larceny theft 910
Motor vehicle theft............................. 51

Cost of Living Index....................................98.4
(national average = 100)

Median Home Price.................................$249,600

Education

Public Schools

Collier County School Board Phone: 941-643-2700
3710 Estey Ave Fax: 941-436-6500
Naples, FL 34104
www.collier.k12.fl.us

Number of Schools
Elementary................................. 20
Middle 7
High.. 4

Student/Teacher Ratio
All Grades 16.6:1

Private Schools

Number of Schools (all grades)..................... 8+

Colleges & Universities

International College Phone: 941-774-4700
2654 Tamiami Trail E Fax: 941-774-4593
Naples, FL 34112 TF: 800-466-8017
www.internationalcollege.edu

Hospitals

Naples Community Hospital Phone: 941-436-5000
350 7th St N Fax: 941-436-5914
Naples, FL 34102
www.nchhcs.org

North Collier Hospital Phone: 941-513-7000
11190 Health Park Blvd Fax: 941-513-7779
Naples, FL 34110

Transportation

Airport(s)

Naples Municipal Airport (APF)
5 miles SE of downtown (approx 15 minutes).....941-643-1415
Southwest Florida International Airport (RSW)
35 miles N of downtown Naples
(approx 45 minutes) 941-768-4321

Rail/Bus

Greyhound Bus Station Phone: 941-774-5660
2669 Davis Blvd TF: 800-231-2222
Naples, FL 34104

Utilities

Electricity
Florida Power & Light.........................941-262-1322
www.fpl.com

Water
Naples Water Dept 941-434-4717

Garbage Collection/Recycling
Naples Solid Waste Div 941-434-4747

Telecommunications

Telephone
Sprint 800-699-0728
www.sprint.com

Cable Television
AT & T Cable Services.........................941-793-9600

Internet Service Providers (ISPs)
CyberStreet Inc 941-334-4484
www.cyberstreet.com
Naples Free-Net...............................941-774-4007
www.naples.net
Venture Net 941-261-1768
www.intventure.net

Banks

AmSouth Bank Phone: 941-261-5522
4851 Tamiami Trail Fax: 941-261-2476
Naples, FL 34103

Atlantic States Bank Phone: 941-435-1333
5010 N Airport Pulling Rd Fax: 941-435-1277
Naples, FL 34105

Bank of America Phone: 941-436-1960
796 5th Ave S Fax: 941-643-4213
Naples, FL 34102

Citizens Community Bank of Florida Phone: 941-775-0074
5101 Tamiami Trail E Fax: 941-775-7854
Naples, FL 34113
www.ccbank.com

Community Bank of Naples NA Phone: 941-649-1500
5150 Tamiami Trail N Fax: 941-649-1411
Naples, FL 34103 TF: 888-649-1500
www.communitybankofnaples.com

Fifth Third Bank of Florida Phone: 941-430-5300
4099 Tamiami Trail N Fax: 941-430-5343
Naples, FL 34101 TF: 800-972-3030
www.53.com

First National Bank of Naples Phone: 941-262-7600
900 Goodlette Rd N Fax: 941-262-5294
Naples, FL 34101 TF: 800-262-7600

First Union National Bank Phone: 941-435-3120
900 5th Ave S Fax: 941-435-3127
Naples, FL 34102 TF: 800-275-3862

Gulf Coast National Bank Phone: 941-261-4262
3838 Tamiami Trail N Fax: 941-261-2990
Naples, FL 34103 TF: 800-648-4262

PNC Bank FSB
3003 Tamiami Trail N Suite 100
Naples, FL 34103
Phone: 941-643-7960
Fax: 941-643-7966

SouthTrust Bank NA
811 Vanderbilt Beach Rd
Naples, FL 34108
Phone: 941-598-1001
Fax: 941-598-3152
TF: 800-239-9987

World Savings Bank
8877 Tamiami Trail N
Naples, FL 34108
Phone: 941-514-1766

Shopping

5th Avenue South
5th Ave S betw 1st & 9th Sts
Naples, FL 34102
www.fifthavenuesouth.com
Phone: 941-435-3742
Fax: 941-435-0994

Coastland Center Mall
1900 9th St N
Naples, FL 34102
Phone: 941-262-2323
Fax: 941-262-5125

Greentree Center
2346 Immokalee Rd
Naples, FL 34110
Phone: 941-566-1100
Fax: 941-566-1764

Pavilion Shopping Center
823 Vanderbilt Beach Rd
Naples, FL 34108
Phone: 941-592-7720
Fax: 941-592-7822

Prime Outlets at Naples
7222 Isle of Capri Rd Suite 121
Naples, FL 34114
www.primeretail.com/naples
Phone: 941-775-8083
Fax: 941-775-8415
TF: 888-545-7196

Third Street South Shopping District
Third Street betw Broad & 14th Aves S
Naples, FL 34102

Tin City Waterfront Marketplace
1200 5th Ave S
Naples, FL 34102
E-mail: info@tin-city.com
www.tin-city.com
Phone: 941-262-4200
Fax: 941-262-5966

Village on Venetian Bay
4200 Gulf Shore Blvd
Naples, FL 34103
www.naples.com/village
Phone: 941-261-6100
Fax: 941-262-6315

Village Plaza Shopping Center
2377 Davis Blvd
Naples, FL 34104
Phone: 941-774-3338

Waterside Shops at Pelican Bay
5415 N Tamiami Tr Suite 320
Naples, FL 34108
www.watersideshops.net
Phone: 941-598-1605
Fax: 941-598-1773

Media

Newspapers and Magazines

Naples Daily News*
1075 Central Ave
Naples, FL 34102
E-mail: info@naplesnews.com
www.naplesnews.com
Phone: 941-262-3161
Fax: 941-263-4816

Naples Illustrated
1250 Tamiami Trail N Suite 304
Naples, FL 34102
Phone: 941-434-6966
Fax: 941-435-0409
TF: 800-308-7346

**Indicates major daily newspapers*

Television

WBBH-TV Ch 20 (NBC)
3719 Central Ave
Fort Myers, FL 33901
www.nbc-2.com
Phone: 941-939-2020
Fax: 941-936-7771

WEVU-TV Ch 7 (UPN)
301 Tower Rd
Naples, FL 34113
www.wevutv.com
Phone: 941-793-9603
Fax: 941-793-3957

WFTX-TV Ch 36 (Fox)
621 SW Pine Island Rd
Cape Coral, FL 33991
Phone: 941-574-3636
Fax: 941-574-2025

WGCU-TV Ch 30 (PBS)
10501 FGCU Blvd
Fort Myers, FL 33965
Phone: 941-590-2300
Fax: 941-590-2310

WINK-TV Ch 11 (CBS)
2824 Palm Beach Blvd
Fort Myers, FL 33916
Phone: 941-334-1111
Fax: 941-334-0744

WTVK-TV Ch 46 (WB)
3451 Bonita Bay Blvd Suite 101
Bonita Springs, FL 34134
Phone: 941-498-4600
Fax: 941-498-0146

WZVN-TV Ch 26 (ABC)
3719 Central Ave
Fort Myers, FL 33901
Phone: 941-939-2020
Fax: 941-936-7771

Radio

WARO-FM 94.5 MHz (CR)
2824 Palm Beach Blvd
Fort Myers, FL 33916
Phone: 941-479-5506
Fax: 941-332-0767

WAVV-FM 101.1 MHz (B/EZ)
11800 Tamiami Trail E
Naples, FL 34113
Phone: 941-775-9288
Fax: 941-793-7000

WAYJ-FM 88.7 MHz (Rel)
1860 Boyscout Dr Suite 202
Fort Myers, FL 33907
E-mail: wayj@wayfm.com
wayfm.com/wayj
Phone: 941-936-1929
Fax: 941-936-5433
TF: 888-936-1929

WCKT-FM 107.1 MHz (Ctry)
4110 Center Pointe Dr Suite 212
Fort Myers, FL 33916
www.wckt.com
Phone: 941-275-5107
Fax: 941-275-8684

WGCU-FM 90.1 MHz (NPR)
10501 FGCU Blvd
Fort Myers, FL 33965
wgcufm.fgcu.edu
Phone: 941-590-2500
Fax: 941-590-2511

WGUF-FM 98.9 MHz (N/T)
2640 Golden Gate Pkwy Suite 316
Naples, FL 34105
Phone: 941-435-9100
Fax: 941-435-9106

WINK-AM 1240 kHz (N/T)
2824 Palm Beach Blvd
Fort Myers, FL 33916
Phone: 941-334-1111
Fax: 941-332-0767

WJBX-FM 99.3 MHz (Alt)
12995 S Cleveland Ave Suite 258
Fort Myers, FL 33907
Phone: 941-275-9980
Fax: 941-275-5611

WJST-FM 106.3 MHz (Nost)
12995 S Cleveland Ave Suite 258
Fort Myers, FL 33907
Phone: 941-275-9980
Fax: 941-275-5611

WNOG-AM 1270 kHz (N/T)
333 8th St S
Naples, FL 34102
Phone: 941-263-4600
Fax: 941-263-6525

WODX-AM 1480 kHz (B/EZ)
1112 1/2 N Collier Blvd
Marco Island, FL 34145
E-mail: wodx@wodx.com
www.wodx.com
Phone: 941-394-5353
Fax: 941-642-6970

WOLZ-FM 95.3 MHz (Oldies)
7290 College Pkwy Suite 200
Fort Myers, FL 33907
Phone: 941-275-0095
Fax: 941-275-3299

WQNU-FM 105.5 MHz (Ctry)
4110 Center Pointe Dr Suite 212
Fort Myers, FL 33916
E-mail: mts1055@aol.com
www.wqnu.com
Phone: 941-275-5107
Fax: 941-275-8684

WSGL-FM 104.7z (AC)
2640 Golden Gate Pkwy Suite 316
Naples, FL 34105
Phone: 941-435-9100
Fax: 941-435-9106

WSOR-FM 90.9 MHz (Rel)
940 Tarpon St
Fort Myers, FL 33916
Phone: 941-334-1393
Fax: 941-334-0596

WSRX-FM 89.5 MHz (Rel)
2132 Shadowlawn Dr
Naples, FL 34112
www.praisefm.com
Phone: 941-775-8950
Fax: 941-774-5889

WWGR-FM 101.9 MHz (Ctry)
4210 Metro Pkwy Suite 210
Fort Myers, FL 33916
www.gatorcountry1019.com
Phone: 941-936-2599
Fax: 941-936-0977

Attractions

Naples is renowned for its pristine beaches along the Gulf, as well as its lakes, rivers, and bays, so it's not surprising that fishing is a popular sport there. Shelling is also a popular local activity, especially in the nearby resort areas of Sanibel and Marco Islands, which are noted for their white sand beaches and abundance of seashells. Though rare in the rest of the world, left-handed shells (snail shells with openings on the left) are common along beaches in the Naples area. Just east of Naples, in the interior section of Florida lies the Everglades, which is home to such species of wildlife as manatees, pelicans, Florida panthers, alligators, and sea turtles. These and other animals and birds can be viewed at a number of area attractions, including Big Cypress National Preserve, Corkscrew Swamp Sanctuary, and, of course, Everglades National Park. Airboat or swamp buggy rides offer visitors the opportunity for a close-up look at alligators and shore birds.

Barefoot Beach Preserve
Hickory Blvd & Bonita Beach Rd
Bonita Springs, FL 34134

Big Cypress Gallery
52388 Tamiami Trail
Ochopee, FL 34141
www.clydebutcher.com
Phone: 941-695-2428
Fax: 941-695-2670
TF: 888-999-9113

Big Cypress National Preserve
62105 E Tamiami Trail
Ochopee, FL 34141
www.nps.gov/bicy/
Phone: 941-695-4111
Fax: 941-695-3007

Briggs Nature Center
401 Shell Island Rd
Naples, FL 34113
www.conservancy.org
Phone: 941-775-8569
Fax: 941-775-5139

Cambier Park
755 Ace Ave S
Naples, FL 34102
Phone: 941-434-4690
Fax: 941-434-3049

Caribbean Gardens & Jungle Larry's Zoological Park
1590 Goodlette-Frank Rd
Naples, FL 34102
www.caribbeangardens.com/
Phone: 941-262-5409
Fax: 941-262-6866

Clam Pass County Park
Seagate Dr
Naples, FL 34103
Phone: 941-353-0404
Fax: 941-353-1002

Collier County Museum
3301 Tamiami Trail E
Naples, FL 34112
www.colliermuseum.com
Phone: 941-774-8476
Fax: 941-774-8580

Collier-Seminole State Park
20200 Tamiami Trail E
Naples, FL 34114
Phone: 941-394-3397
Fax: 941-394-5113

Conservancy Nature Center
1450 Merrihue Dr
Naples, FL 34102
www.conservancy.org
Phone: 941-262-0304
Fax: 941-262-0672

Corkscrew Swamp Sanctuary
375 Sanctuary Rd W
Naples, FL 34120
www.audubon.org/local/sanctuary/corkscrew/index.html
Phone: 941-348-9151
Fax: 941-348-9155

DeBruyne Fine Art
275 Broad Ave S
Naples, FL 34102
E-mail: sales@debruynefineart.com
www.debruynefineart.com
Phone: 941-262-4551
Fax: 941-262-4051

Delnor-Wiggins Pass State Recreation Area
11100 Gulfshore Dr
Naples, FL 34108
Phone: 941-597-6196
Fax: 941-597-8223

East Naples Community Park
3500 Thomasson Dr
Naples, FL 34112
Phone: 941-793-4414
Fax: 941-793-7358

Eden of the Everglades
903 Dupont Rd
Everglades City, FL 34139
Phone: 941-695-2800
Fax: 941-695-4506
TF: 800-543-3367

Fleischmann Park
1600 Fleischmann Blvd
Naples, FL 34102
Phone: 941-434-4692
Fax: 941-434-3044

Florida Sports Park
PO Box 990010
Naples, FL 34116
www.florida-sports-park.com
Phone: 941-774-2701
Fax: 941-774-4118
TF: 800-897-2701

King Richard's Family Fun Park
6780 N Airport-Pulling Rd
Naples, FL 34109
Phone: 941-598-1666
Fax: 941-514-7164

Lowdermilk Park
Banyan Blvd at Gulf Shore Blvd N
Naples, FL 34102
Phone: 941-434-4698

Naples Art Association-Von Leibig Art Center
585 Park St
Naples, FL 34102
www.naplesartcenter.org
Phone: 941-262-6517
Fax: 941-262-5404

Naples Depot
1051 5th Ave S
Naples, FL 34102
Phone: 941-262-1776
Fax: 941-262-5119

Naples Horse & Carriage
1450 Whippoorwill Ln
Naples, FL 34105
Phone: 941-649-1210

Naples Philharmonic Center for the Arts
5833 Pelican Bay Blvd
Naples, FL 34108
www.naplesphilcenter.org
Phone: 941-597-1900
Fax: 941-597-7856

Naples Players
701 5th Ave S Sugden Community Theatre
Naples, FL 34102
E-mail: theatre@naples.net
gator.naples.net/presents/theatre
Phone: 941-263-7990
Fax: 941-434-7772

Naples Princess Cruise Line
1001 10th Ave S
Naples, FL 34102
E-mail: naplesprin@aol.com
www.naplesprincesscruises.com
Phone: 941-649-2275
Fax: 941-649-7357

Naples Trolley Tours
1010 6th Ave S
Naples, FL 34102
www.naples-trolley.com
Phone: 941-262-7300
Fax: 941-262-6967

Palm Cottage
137 12th Ave S
Naples, FL 34102
Phone: 941-261-8164
Fax: 941-435-1438

Philharmonic Center for the Arts Galleries
5833 Pelican Bay Blvd
Naples, FL 34108
www.naplesphilcenter.org
Phone: 941-597-1111
Fax: 941-597-8163

Shaw Gallery of Naples
761 Fifth Ave S
Naples, FL 34102
E-mail: info@shawgallery.com
www.shawgallery.com
Phone: 941-261-7828
Fax: 941-261-6108
TF: 888-406-1369

Sugden Community Theatre
701 5th Ave S
Naples, FL 34102
E-mail: theatre@naples.net
gator.naples.net/presents/theatre/np_newth.htm
Phone: 941-263-7990
Fax: 941-434-7772

Teddy Bear Museum
2511 Pine Ridge Rd
Naples, FL 34109
www.teddymuseum.com
Phone: 941-598-2711
Fax: 941-598-9239

Tin City Waterfront Marketplace
1200 5th Ave S
Naples, FL 34102
E-mail: info@tin-city.com
www.tin-city.com
Phone: 941-262-4200
Fax: 941-262-5966

Veterans Community Park
1900 Immokalee Rd
Naples, FL 34110
Phone: 941-566-2367
Fax: 941-566-8128

Village on Venetian Bay
4200 Gulf Shore Blvd
Naples, FL 34103
www.naples.com/village
Phone: 941-261-6100
Fax: 941-262-6315

Sports Teams & Facilities

Naples/Fort Myers Greyhound Track
10601 Bonita Beach Rd
Bonita Springs, FL 34135
E-mail: nfmgreyhound@tntonline.com
www.nfmgreyhound.com
Phone: 941-992-2411
Fax: 941-947-9244

Annual Events

American Street Craft Show (early September) 941-435-3742
Art Encounter (February) 941-262-6517
Art in the Park (November-May) 941-262-6517
Christmas Walk & Festival of Lights (early December) 941-435-3742
Classic Swamp Buggy Races (early March & mid-late May & late October) 941-774-2701
Collier County Fair (mid-January) 941-455-1444
Fourth of July Festival (July 4) 941-434-4717
Grand Millenium Parade (early December) 941-435-3742
Lunar Festival (mid-April) 941-992-2184
Millennium Lifestyle & Business Expo (early-mid-May) 941-435-3742
Naples Invitational Art Fest (late January) 941-263-1667
Naples National Art Festival (late February) 941-262-6517
Naples Saint Patrick's Day Parade (mid-March) 941-774-6086
Naples/Fort Myers Bluegrass Jam (mid-March) 941-992-2184
National Art Association Founders Exhibit (March) 941-262-6517
Octoberfest & Sidewalk Sale (late October) 941-435-3742
Spring Plant & Garden Festival (mid-March) 941-643-7275
Summerjazz on the Gulf (May-September) 941-261-2222
Swamp Buggy Parade (mid-late October) 941-774-2701
Thanksgiving Weekend Festival (late November) 941-435-3742
World Orchid Symposium (late October) 941-261-2222

Nashville, Tennessee

***County:* Davidson**

NASHVILLE is located along the Cumberland River in central Tennessee. Major cities within 100 miles include Clarksville and Columbia, Tennessee; and Bowling Green, Kentucky.

Area (Land)	473.3 sq mi
Area (Water)	23.7 sq mi
Elevation	440 ft
Latitude	36-16-58 N
Longitude	86-78-44 W
Time Zone	CST
Area Code	615

Climate

Nashville's moderate climate features four distinct seasons. Winter days are cool, with average high temperatures near 50 degrees, while evening temperatures dip into the upper 20s or low 30s. Snowfall is minimal in Nashville, averaging little more than 9 inches annually. Summer days are very warm, with average highs in the upper 80s, while evenings cool down comfortably into the mid- to upper 60s. March and May are the wettest months in Nashville; October is the driest.

Average Temperatures & Precipitation

Temperatures

	Jan	Feb	Mar	Apr	May	Jun	Jul	Aug	Sep	Oct	Nov	Dec
High	46	51	61	71	79	87	90	88	83	73	60	50
Low	27	30	39	48	57	65	69	68	61	48	40	31

Precipitation

	Jan	Feb	Mar	Apr	May	Jun	Jul	Aug	Sep	Oct	Nov	Dec
Inches	3.6	3.8	4.9	4.4	4.9	3.6	4.0	3.5	3.5	2.6	4.1	4.6

History

Originally a hunting ground for the Cherokee, Chickasaw, Choctow, Creek, and Shawnee tribes, the region known today as Nashville was once the site of a trading post called French Lick established by French Canadian fur traders during the late 17th and early 18th centuries. The first permanent settlement in the region was established in 1779 by a group of pioneers (many of them North Carolinians) led by James Robertson. They named the settlement Fort Nashborough (a name that was changed five years later to Nashville) in honor of Revolutionary War General Francis Nash. The settlers drew up a document for self-government known as the Cumberland Compact, which was enacted the following year in 1780. Twenty-six years later Nashville was incorporated as a city.

Located on the Cumberland River and also serving as the northern terminus of the Natchez Trace, Nashville grew as a center for commerce, with cotton its primary export. Nashville's legacy as a publishing center began when the first book was published there in 1810; the first music—a book of hymns known as Western Harmony—was published there 14 years later. In 1843, Nashville was chosen as the permanent state capital of Tennessee. In 1862 the city became the first southern capital to be captured by Union troops during the Civil War.

In the 1920s, Nashville gained recognition as the "Country Music Capital of the World." The Grand Ole Opry began broadcasting country music radio programs in 1925 from the city, and today Nashville ranks among the top U.S. cities for the recording industry. The 1930s marked the beginning of a period of rapid industrial growth in Nashville, as inexpensive power became available from the Tennessee Valley Authority. In 1963, the governments of the City of Nashville and Davidson County were consolidated to form a metropolitan government. Now home to more than 510,000 people, Nashville is Tennessee's second largest city.

Population

1990 Census	488,366
1998 Estimate	510,274
% Change	4.5
2005 Projection	558,770*

Racial/Ethnic Breakdown

White	73.8%
Black	24.3%
Other	1.9%
Hispanic Origin (may be of any race)	0.9%

Age Breakdown

Under 5 years	7.1%
5 to 17	15.8%
18 to 20	5.0%
21 to 24	6.8%
25 to 34	20.7%
35 to 44	15.5%
45 to 54	9.7%
55 to 64	8.1%
65 to 74	6.5%
75+ years	4.9%
Median Age	32.3

Gender Breakdown

Male	47.4%
Female	52.6%

* *Information given is for Davidson County.*

Government

Type of Government: Mayor-Metropolitan Council (consolidated)

Nashville City Hall
102 Metro Courthouse
Nashville, TN 37201
Phone: 615-862-5000
Fax: 615-862-6784

Nashville Economic Development Office
117 Union St
Nashville, TN 37201
Phone: 615-862-6026
Fax: 615-862-6025

Nashville Electric Service
1214 Church St
Nashville, TN 37203
Phone: 615-747-3911
Fax: 615-747-3854

Nashville Finance Dept
222 3rd Ave N Suite 110
Nashville, TN 37201
Phone: 615-862-6210
Fax: 615-880-2810

Nashville Fire Dept
500 2nd Ave N
Nashville, TN 37201
Phone: 615-862-5421
Fax: 615-862-5419

Nashville Legal Dept
204 Metro Courthouse
Nashville, TN 37201
Phone: 615-862-6341
Fax: 615-862-6352

Nashville Mayor
107 Metro Courthouse
Nashville, TN 37201
Phone: 615-862-6000
Fax: 615-862-6040

Nashville Metro Transit Authority
130 Nestor St
Nashville, TN 37210
Phone: 615-862-5969
Fax: 615-862-6208

Nashville Metropolitan Clerk
205 Metro Courthouse
Nashville, TN 37201
Phone: 615-862-6770
Fax: 615-862-6774

Nashville Metropolitan Council
102 Metro Courthouse
Nashville, TN 37201
Phone: 615-862-6780
Fax: 615-862-6784

Nashville Parks & Recreation Dept
211 Union St Cnetennial Park
Nashville, TN 37201
Phone: 615-826-8400
Fax: 615-862-8414

Nashville Personnel Dept
222 3rd Ave N Suite 200
Nashville, TN 37201
Phone: 615-862-6640
Fax: 615-862-6654

Nashville Planning Commission
730 2nd Ave S
Nashville, TN 37201
Phone: 615-862-7150
Fax: 615-862-7209

Nashville Police Dept
200 James Robertson Pkwy
Nashville, TN 37201
Phone: 615-862-7301
Fax: 615-862-7787

Nashville Public Library
225 Polk Ave
Nashville, TN 37203
Phone: 615-862-5800
Fax: 615-880-2605

Nashville Public Works Dept
750 S 5th St
Nashville, TN 37206
Phone: 615-862-8700
Fax: 615-862-8799

Nashville Water & Sewerage Services Dept
1600 2nd Ave N
Nashville, TN 37208
Phone: 615-862-4505
Fax: 615-862-4929

Important Phone Numbers

AAA	615-333-4840
American Express Travel	615-385-3535
Driver's License Information	615-251-5303
Emergency	911
HotelDocs	800-468-3537
Information Line	615-244-9393
Metropolitan Nashville-Davidson County Trustee	615-862-6330
Nashville Board of Realtors	615-254-7516
Poison Control Center	615-936-2034
Tennessee Revenue Dept	615-253-0600
Time/Temp	615-259-2222
Travelers Aid	615-780-9472
Vehicle Registration Information	615-862-6050
Voter Registration Information	615-862-8800
Weather	615-244-9393

Information Sources

Better Business Bureau Serving Middle Tennessee
PO Box 198436
Nashville, TN 37219
www.middletennessee.bbb.org
Phone: 615-242-4222
Fax: 615-250-4245

Davidson County
205 Metro Courthouse
Nashville, TN 37201
www.nashville.org/index.html
Phone: 615-862-6770
Fax: 615-862-6774

Nashville Chamber of Commerce
161 4th Ave N
Nashville, TN 37219
www.nashvillechamber.com
Phone: 615-259-4755
Fax: 615-256-3074
TF: 800-657-6910

Nashville Convention & Visitors Bureau
161 4th Ave N
Nashville, TN 37219
www.nashvillecvb.com
Phone: 615-259-4730
Fax: 615-244-6278
TF: 800-657-6910

Nashville Convention Center
601 Commerce St
Nashville, TN 37203
www.nashvilleconventionctr.com
Phone: 615-742-2000
Fax: 615-742-2014

Nashville Tourist Information Center
Broadway St & 5th Ave
Nashville, TN 37203
Phone: 615-259-4747
Fax: 615-259-4747

Online Resources

4Nashville.com
www.4nashville.com

About.com Guide to Nashville
nashville.about.com/local/southeastus/nashville

Area Guide Nashville
nashville.areaguides.net

Best Read Guide Nashville
bestreadguide.com/nashville

Boulevards Nashville
www.boulevards.com/cities/nashville.html

City Knowledge Nashville
www.cityknowledge.com/tn_nashville.htm

CitySearch Nashville
nashville.citysearch.com

Country.Com
www.country.com

DigitalCity Nashville
home.digitalcity.com/nashville

Excite.com Nashville City Guide
www.excite.com/travel/countries/united_states/tennessee/nashville

Insiders' Guide to Nashville
www.insiders.com/nashville/

Jackson-Crockett's Nashville Guide
www.hermitage.com/nashville.html

Lodging.com Nashville Tennessee
www.lodging.com/auto/guides/nashville-area-tn.html

Nashville Best Read Guide
bestreadguide.com/nashville

Nashville City Pages
nashville.thelinks.com

Nashville Directory
www.nashvilledirectory.com/

Nashville Scene
www.nashscene.com

Nashville.Net
www.nashville.net

NashvilleLife.com
www.nashvillelife.com

Nashvillenet.com
www.nashvillenet.com/

Rough Guide Travel Nashville
travel.roughguides.com/content/758/

WeekendEvents.com Nashville
www.weekendevents.com/misccity/nashville/nashville.htm

Area Communities

Communities with populations greater than 10,000 in the eight-county (Cheatham, Davidson, Dickson, Robertson, Rutherford, Sumner, Williamson, and Wilson) Nashville metropolitan area include:

Brentwood
PO Box 788
Brentwood, TN 37024
Phone: 615-371-0060
Fax: 615-370-4767

Dickson
202 S Main St
Dickson, TN 37055
Phone: 615-441-9508
Fax: 615-446-4806

Franklin
109 3rd Ave S
Franklin, TN 37064
Phone: 615-791-3217
Fax: 615-790-0469

Gallatin
132 W Main St
Gallatin, TN 37066
Phone: 615-452-5400
Fax: 615-451-5916

Hendersonville
1 Executive Park Dr
Hendersonville, TN 37075
Phone: 615-822-1000
Fax: 615-264-5327

La Vergne
5093 Murfreesboro Rd
La Vergne, TN 37086
Phone: 615-793-6295
Fax: 615-793-6025

Lebanon
200 Castle Heights Ave N
Lebanon, TN 37087
Phone: 615-443-2839
Fax: 615-443-2851

Murfreesboro
111 W Vine St
Murfreesboro, TN 37130
Phone: 615-893-5210
Fax: 615-849-2679

Smyrna
315 S Lowry St
Smyrna, TN 37167
Phone: 615-459-2553
Fax: 615-355-5715

Springfield
405 N Main St
Springfield, TN 37172
Phone: 615-382-2200
Fax: 615-382-1612

Economy

The Nashville metropolitan area's diverse economic base ranges from automobile and appliance manufacturing to book publishing and higher education. With the largest concentration of health care management firms in the U.S., including the corporate headquarters for Columbia/HCA Health Care, Nashville is a major regional hub for the health care industry. Other major U.S. corporations that have a presence in the Nashville area include Saturn Corporation, Nissan Motor Manufacturing, Bridgestone/Firestone, Service Merchandise, and Ingram Industries. Nashville is also home to Gaylord Entertainment, which owns many of the music-related attractions in the city, including the Opryland USA theme park, the TNN and CMT cable television networks, and the Grand Ole Opry itself. The music industry plays both a direct role and an indirect role in the area's economy, providing jobs for more than 25,000 area residents at recording studios and other businesses, as well as drawing millions of visitors annually to "Music City USA." Government also plays an important role in the Nashville metropolitan area's economy—more than 83,000 area residents are employed in government-related positions. In addition to the major employers listed below, the U.S. Government is among Nashville's employers, providing jobs for more than 11,000 people in various offices throughout the metro area.

Unemployment Rate 2.8%*
Per Capita Income.......................... $30,723*
Median Family Income...................... $34,009

** Information given is for Davidson County.*

Principal Industries & Number of Wage Earners

Nashville MSA* - 1998

Construction & Mining................................33,700
Finance, Insurance, & Real Estate........................39,500
Government...83,200
Manufacturing.......................................96,000
Retail & Wholesale Trade............................155,700

Services 198,900
Transportation, Communications, & Public Utilities 31,600

** Information given is for the Nashville Metropolitan Statistical Area (MSA), which includes Chatham, Davidson, Dickson, Robertson, Rutherford, Sumner, Williamson, and Wilson counties.*

Major Employers

BBA Reemay Inc
70 Old Hickory Blvd
Old Hickory, TN 37138
www.reemay.com
Phone: 615-847-7000
Fax: 615-847-7068

BellSouth
333 Commerce St
Nashville, TN 37201
www.bellsouth.com/employment
Phone: 615-401-4000

Gaylord Entertainment Co
1 Gaylord Dr
Nashville, TN 37214
www.gaylordentertainment.com
Phone: 615-316-6000
Fax: 615-316-6060

General Motors Corp Saturn Corp Div
100 Saturn Pkwy
Spring Hill, TN 37174
www.saturncars.com
Phone: 931-486-5000
TF: 800-553-6000

HCA-The Healthcare Co
1 Park Plaza
Nashville, TN 37203
www.hcahealthcare.com
Phone: 615-344-9551
Fax: 615-344-5722

Kroger Co
2620 Elm Hill Pike
Nashville, TN 37214
www.kroger.com
Phone: 615-871-2400
Fax: 615-871-2799

Metropolitan Nashville & Davidson County Schools
2601 Bransford Ave
Nashville, TN 37204
www.nashville.k12.tn.us
Phone: 615-259-8400
Fax: 615-259-8576

Nissan Motor Manufacturing Corp USA
983 Nissan Dr
Smyrna, TN 37167
Phone: 615-459-1400
Fax: 615-459-1555

Saint Thomas Health Services
4220 Harding Rd
Nashville, TN 37205
www.saintthomas.org
Phone: 615-222-2111
Fax: 615-222-5970

Shoney's Inc
1727 Elm Hill Pike
Nashville, TN 37210
www.shoneys.com
Phone: 615-391-5201
Fax: 615-231-2498
TF: 877-377-2233

Tennessee State Department of Personnel
James K Polk Bldg 2nd Fl
Nashville, TN 37243
www.state.tn.us/personnel/
Phone: 615-741-2958
Fax: 615-532-0728

United Parcel Service
705 Massman Dr
Nashville, TN 37210
www.upsjobs.com
Phone: 615-885-8481
Fax: 615-885-8446

Vanderbilt University
2305 West End Ave
Nashville, TN 37203
E-mail: admissions@vanderbilt.edu
www.vanderbilt.edu
Phone: 615-322-7311
Fax: 615-343-7765
TF: 800-288-0432

Vanderbilt University Medical Center
1211 22nd Ave S
Nashville, TN 37232
www.mc.vanderbilt.edu
Phone: 615-322-5000
Fax: 615-343-5555
TF: 800-288-7777

Quality of Living Indicators

Total Crime Index 46,457
(rates per 100,000 inhabitants)

Violent Crime
Murder/manslaughter 68
Forcible rape 460
Robbery 1,960
Aggravated assault 5,918

Property Crime
Burglary 6,962
Larceny theft 26,100
Motor vehicle theft 4,989

Cost of Living Index 95.5
(national average = 100)

Median Home Price $116,400

Education

Public Schools

Metropolitan Nashville & Davidson County Schools
2601 Bransford Ave
Nashville, TN 37204
www.nashville.k12.tn.us
Phone: 615-259-8400
Fax: 615-259-8576

Number of Schools
Elementary 68
Middle 33
High 11

Student/Teacher Ratio
All Grades 15.3:1

Private Schools

Number of Schools (all grades) . . . . 55+

Colleges & Universities

Aquinas College
4210 Harding Rd
Nashville, TN 37205
www.aquinas-tn.edu
Phone: 615-297-7545
Fax: 615-297-7970

Belmont University
1900 Belmont Blvd
Nashville, TN 37212
E-mail: Warren@Belmont.Edu
www.belmont.edu
Phone: 615-460-6000
Fax: 615-460-5434
TF: 800-563-6765

Cumberland University
1 Cumberland Sq
Lebanon, TN 37087
www.cumberland.edu
Phone: 615-444-2562
Fax: 615-444-2569

David Lipscomb University
3901 Granny White Pike
Nashville, TN 37204
Phone: 615-269-1000
Fax: 615-269-1804
TF: 800-333-4358

Draughons Junior College
PO Box 17386
Nashville, TN 37217
Phone: 615-361-7555
Fax: 615-367-2736

Fisk University
1000 17th Ave N
Nashville, TN 37208
E-mail: gwash@dubois.fisk.edu
www.fisk.edu
Phone: 615-329-8500
Fax: 615-329-8715
TF: 800-443-3474

Free Will Baptist Bible College
3606 West End Ave
Nashville, TN 37205
www.fwbbc.edu
Phone: 615-383-1340
Fax: 615-269-6028
TF: 800-763-9222

ITT Technical Institute
441 Donelson Pike
Nashville, TN 37214
www.itt-tech.edu
Phone: 615-889-8700
Fax: 615-872-7209
TF: 800-331-8386

John A Gupton College
1616 Church St
Nashville, TN 37203
www.guptoncollege.com
Phone: 615-327-3927
Fax: 615-321-4518

Nashville State Technical Institute
120 White Bridge Rd
Nashville, TN 37209
www.nsti.tec.tn.us
Phone: 615-353-3333
Fax: 615-353-3243

O'More College of Design
423 S Margin St
Franklin, TN 37064
www.omorecollege.edu
Phone: 615-794-4254
Fax: 615-790-1662

Tennessee State University
3500 John A Merritt Blvd
Nashville, TN 37209
www.tnstate.edu
Phone: 615-963-5000
Fax: 615-963-2929

Trevecca Nazarene University
333 Murfreesboro Rd
Nashville, TN 37210
www.trevecca.edu
Phone: 615-248-1200
Fax: 615-248-7406
TF: 888-210-4868

Vanderbilt University
2305 West End Ave
Nashville, TN 37203
E-mail: admissions@vanderbilt.edu
www.vanderbilt.edu
Phone: 615-322-7311
Fax: 615-343-7765
TF: 800-288-0432

Hospitals

Baptist Hospital
2000 Church St
Nashville, TN 37236
www.baptist-hosp.org
Phone: 615-329-5555
Fax: 615-340-4606

Centennial Medical Center
2300 Patterson St
Nashville, TN 37203
www.centennialmedctr.com
Phone: 615-342-1000
Fax: 615-342-1045
TF: 800-251-8200

HCA Southern Hills Medical Center
391 Wallace Rd
Nashville, TN 37211
Phone: 615-781-4000
Fax: 615-781-4611

Metropolitan Nashville General Hospital
1818 Albion St
Nashville, TN 37208
Phone: 615-341-4000
Fax: 615-341-4617

Saint Thomas Health Services
4220 Harding Rd
Nashville, TN 37205
www.saintthomas.org
Phone: 615-222-2111
Fax: 615-222-5970

Skyline Medical Center
3441 Dickerson Pike
Nashville, TN 37207
Phone: 615-756-1000

Tennessee Christian Medical Center
500 Hospital Dr
Madison, TN 37115
www.tcmconline.com
Phone: 615-865-2373
Fax: 615-860-6311

Vanderbilt University Medical Center
1211 22nd Ave S
Nashville, TN 37232
www.mc.vanderbilt.edu
Phone: 615-322-5000
Fax: 615-343-5555
TF: 800-288-7777

Veterans Affairs Medical Center
1310 24th Ave S
Nashville, TN 37212
Phone: 615-327-4751
Fax: 615-340-2317

Transportation

Airport(s)

Nashville International Airport (BNA)
8 miles SE of downtown (approx 20 minutes).....615-275-1600

Mass Transit

Metropolitan Transit Authority
$1.45 Base fare................................615-862-5950
Nashville Trolley
$1 Base fare.................................615-862-5950

Rail/Bus

Greyhound Bus Station
200 8th Ave S
Nashville, TN 37203
Phone: 615-255-3556
TF: 800-231-2222

Utilities

Electricity
Nashville Electric Service......................615-747-3911
www.nespower.com

Gas
Nashville Gas Co.............................615-734-0665
www.nashvillegas.com

Water
Metro Dept of Water & Sewage Services.........615-862-4600

Garbage Collection/Recycling
Metropolitan Dept of Public Works.............615-862-8750

Telecommunications

Telephone
BellSouth 800-766-9115
www.bellsouth.com

Cable Television
InterMedia 615-244-5990
Tennessee Cable Telecommunications Assn 615-256-7037

Internet Service Providers (ISPs)
EdgeNet Media LLC 615-371-3848
www.edge.net
Heart of Tennessee Computer Communications 615-895-7737
www.hotcc.com
Telalink Corp 615-321-9100
www.telalink.net

Banks

AmSouth Bank Phone: 615-291-5285
333 Union St
Nashville, TN 37201

Bank of America NA Phone: 888-279-3121
1 Bank of America Plaza
Nashville, TN 37239

First Union National Bank Phone: 615-251-9200
150 4th Ave N Fax: 615-251-9323
Nashville, TN 37219

National Bank of Commerce Phone: 615-871-7000
221 4th Ave N Fax: 615-871-7011
Nashville, TN 37219

Regions Bank Phone: 615-242-2255
315 Union St Fax: 615-254-0616
Nashville, TN 37201

SouthTrust Bank NA Phone: 615-880-4000
230 4th Ave N Fax: 615-880-4004
Nashville, TN 37219

SunTrust Bank Nashville NA Phone: 615-748-4000
201 4th Ave N Fax: 615-748-5071
Nashville, TN 37219

Union Planters Bank NA Phone: 615-244-0571
401 Union St Fax: 615-726-4375
Nashville, TN 37219

Shopping

100 Oaks Mall Phone: 615-383-6002
719 Thompson Ln Fax: 615-383-1050
Nashville, TN 37204

Bellevue Center Phone: 615-646-8690
7620 Hwy 70 S
Nashville, TN 37221

CoolSprings Galleria Phone: 615-771-2128
1800 Galleria Blvd Fax: 615-771-2127
Brentwood, TN 37067
www.coolspringsgalleria.com

Dillard's Phone: 615-297-0971
2126 Abbott Martin Rd
Nashville, TN 37215

Factory Stores of America Phone: 615-885-5140
2434 Music Valley Dr
Nashville, TN 37214
www.factorystores.com/

Green Hills Antique Mall Phone: 615-383-3893
4108 Hillsboro Rd Fax: 615-383-4886
Nashville, TN 37215

Harding Mall Phone: 615-833-6327
4050 Nolensville Rd Fax: 615-833-0247
Nashville, TN 37211

Mall at Green Hills Phone: 615-298-5478
2126 Abbott Martin Rd
Nashville, TN 37215

Nashville Arcade Phone: 615-255-1034
4th Ave N & 5th Ave N
Nashville, TN 37219

Rivergate Mall Phone: 615-859-3456
1000 Two-Mile Pkwy Suite 1 Fax: 615-851-9656
Goodlettsville, TN 37072
www.rivergate-mall.com

Media

Newspapers and Magazines

Dickson Herald Phone: 615-446-2811
PO Box 587 Fax: 615-446-5560
Dickson, TN 37056

Nashville Business Journal Phone: 615-248-2222
222 2nd Ave N Suite 610 Fax: 615-248-6246
Nashville, TN 37202
www.nashbiz.com/

Nashville Scene Phone: 615-244-7989
2120 8th Ave S Fax: 615-244-8578
Nashville, TN 37204
E-mail: editor@nashvillescene.com
www.nashscene.com

Tennessean* Phone: 615-259-8800
1100 Broadway Fax: 615-259-8093
Nashville, TN 37203 TF: 800-342-8237
www.tennessean.com

**Indicates major daily newspapers*

Television

WDCN-TV Ch 8 (PBS) Phone: 615-259-9325
161 Rains Ave Fax: 615-248-6120
Nashville, TN 37203
www.wdcn.org

WKRN-TV Ch 2 (ABC) Phone: 615-259-2200
441 Murfreesboro Rd Fax: 615-248-7329
Nashville, TN 37210
E-mail: wkrntv@edge.ercnet.com
www.wkrn.com/

WNAB-TV Ch 58 (WB)
3201 Dickerson Pike
Nashville, TN 37207
Phone: 615-650-5858
Fax: 615-650-5859

WNPX-TV Ch 28 (PAX)
209 10th Ave S Suite 349
Nashville, TN 37203
www.pax.net/wnpx
Phone: 615-726-2828
Fax: 615-726-2854

WSMV-TV Ch 4 (NBC)
5700 Knob Rd
Nashville, TN 37209
www.wsmv.com
Phone: 615-353-4444
Fax: 615-353-2343

WTVF-TV Ch 5 (CBS)
474 James Robertson Pkwy
Nashville, TN 37219
www.newschannel5.com
Phone: 615-244-5000
Fax: 615-244-9883

WUXP-TV Ch 30 (UPN)
631 Mainstream Dr
Nashville, TN 37228
local.upn30.citysearch.com
Phone: 615-259-5630
Fax: 615-259-3962

WZTV-TV Ch 17 (Fox)
631 Mainstream Dr
Nashville, TN 37228
local.fox17.citysearch.com
Phone: 615-244-1717
Fax: 615-259-3962

Radio

WAMB-AM 1160 kHz (Nost)
1617 Lebanon Rd
Nashville, TN 37210
Phone: 615-889-1960

WGFX-FM 104.5 MHz (Oldies)
506 2nd Ave S
Nashville, TN 37210
www.arrow1045.com
Phone: 615-244-9533
Fax: 615-259-1271

WJXA-FM 92.9 MHz (AC)
504 Rosedale Ave
Nashville, TN 37211
Phone: 615-259-9696
Fax: 615-259-4594

WKDF-FM 103.3 MHz (Ctry)
PO Box 101604
Nashville, TN 37224
Phone: 615-244-9533
Fax: 615-259-1271

WLAC-AM 1510 kHz (N/T)
55 Music Sq W
Nashville, TN 37203
E-mail: 1510@wlac.com
www.wlac.com
Phone: 615-256-0555
Fax: 615-242-4826

WMDB-AM 880 kHz (Urban)
3051 Stokers Ln
Nashville, TN 37218
Phone: 615-255-2876

WNAH-AM 1360 kHz (Rel)
44 Music Sq E
Nashville, TN 37203
E-mail: wnah@wnah.com
www.wnah.com
Phone: 615-254-7611
Fax: 615-255-9624

WNRQ-FM 105.9 MHz (CR)
55 Music Sq W
Nashville, TN 39203
E-mail: therock@1059.com
www.1059.com
Phone: 615-256-0555
Fax: 615-242-4826

WNSR-AM 560 kHz (Sports)
435 37th Ave N
Nashville, TN 37209
E-mail: wnsr@aol.com
www.wnsr.com
Phone: 615-844-1039
Fax: 615-777-2284

WPLN-FM 90.3 MHz (NPR)
630 Mainstream Dr
Nashville, TN 37228
www.wpln.org
Phone: 615-760-2903
Fax: 615-760-2904

WQQK-FM 92.1 MHz (Urban)
50 Music Sq W Suite 901
Nashville, TN 37203
Phone: 615-321-1067
Fax: 615-321-5771

WQZQ-FM 102.5 MHz (CHR)
1824 Murfreesboro Rd
Nashville, TN 37217
www.1025theparty.com
Phone: 615-399-1029
Fax: 615-399-1023

WRLG-FM 94.1 MHz (AAA)
401 Church St 30th Fl
Nashville, TN 37219
wrlg.com
Phone: 615-242-5600
Fax: 615-242-9877

WRLT-FM 100.1 MHz (AAA)
401 Church St L & C Tower 30th Fl
Nashville, TN 37219
E-mail: comments@wrlt.com
www.wrlt.com
Phone: 615-242-5600
Fax: 615-242-9877

WRMX-FM 96.3 MHz (Oldies)
504 Rosedale Ave
Nashville, TN 37211
Phone: 615-259-9696
Fax: 615-259-4594

WRVW-FM 107.5 MHz (CHR)
55 Music Sq W
Nashville, TN 37203
www.1075theriver.com
Phone: 615-664-2400
Fax: 615-664-2457

WSIX-FM 97.9 MHz (Ctry)
55 Music Sq W
Nashville, TN 37203
www.wsix.com
Phone: 615-664-2400
Fax: 615-664-2457

WSM-AM 650 kHz (Ctry)
2644 McGavock Pike
Nashville, TN 37214
www.650wsm.com
Phone: 615-889-6595
Fax: 615-871-5982

WSM-FM 95.5 MHz (Ctry)
2644 McGavock Pike
Nashville, TN 37214
www.nashville95.com
Phone: 615-889-6595
Fax: 615-871-5982

WVOL-AM 1470 kHz (Urban)
50 Music Sq W Suite 901
Nashville, TN 37203
Phone: 615-321-1067
Fax: 615-321-5771

WWTN-FM 99.7 MHz (N/T)
107 Music City Cir Suite 203
Nashville, TN 37214
www.997wtn.com
Phone: 615-885-9986
Fax: 615-885-9900

WYYB-FM 93.7 MHz (Misc)
401 Church St 30th Fl
Nashville, TN 37219
Phone: 615-242-5600
Fax: 615-242-9877

WZPC-FM 102.9 MHz (Ctry)
1824 Murfreesboro Rd
Nashville, TN 37217
www.1029thebuzz.com
Phone: 615-399-1029
Fax: 615-399-1023

WZTO-FM 101.1 MHz (Rel)
10 Music Cir E
Nashville, TN 37203
E-mail: win@theoneonline.com
www.theoneonline.com
Phone: 615-256-0555
Fax: 615-242-4826

Attractions

The name Nashville is synonymous with country music—Opryland theme park's Grand Ole Opry House has launched some of the most famous names in the industry and is the broadcast site for the nation's oldest continuous radio show. Nashville is also the only city in the U.S. with a cable television network that uses the city's name, The Nashville Network. The city is also home to Andrew Jackson's estate, The Hermitage. Its 660 acres include a museum and formal gardens, as well as the burial place of Jackson and his wife, Rachel. The Parthenon in Nashville's Centennial Park is a reproduction of the original Greek structure and contains regional and national art collections, as well as a 42-foot statue of the goddess Athena.

328 Performance Hall
328 4th Ave S
Nashville, TN 37201
www.328performancehall.com
Phone: 615-259-3288
Fax: 615-244-6565

Belle Meade Plantation
5025 Harding Rd
Nashville, TN 37205
Phone: 615-356-0501
Fax: 615-356-2336
TF: 800-270-3991

Belmont Mansion
1900 Belmont Blvd
Nashville, TN 37212
Phone: 615-460-5459
Fax: 615-460-5688

Bicentennial Mall State Park
598 James Robertson Pkwy
Nashville, TN 37243
Phone: 615-741-5280
Fax: 615-532-2683

Carnton Plantation
1345 Carnton Ln
Franklin, TN 37064
Phone: 615-794-0903
Fax: 615-794-6563

Carter House
1140 Columbia Ave
Franklin, TN 37064
Phone: 615-791-1861
Fax: 615-794-1327

Centennial Park
West End Ave-betw 25th & 28th Aves
Nashville, TN 37201
Phone: 615-862-8431

Chaffin's Barn Dinner Theatre
8204 Hwy 100
Nashville, TN 37221
www.dinnertheatre.com
Phone: 615-646-9977
Fax: 615-662-5439

Cheekwood-Tennessee Botanical Gardens & Museum of Art
1200 Forrest Park Dr
Nashville, TN 37205
www.cheekwood.org
Phone: 615-356-8000
Fax: 615-353-2156

Country Music Hall of Fame & Museum
4 Music Sq E
Nashville, TN 37203
www.country.com/hof/hof-f.html
Phone: 615-416-2001
Fax: 615-255-2245

Cumberland Caverns
1437 Cumberland Caverns Rd
McMinnville, TN 37110
www.cumberlandcaverns.com
Phone: 931-668-4396
Fax: 931-668-5382

Cumberland Science Museum
800 Fort Negley Blvd
Nashville, TN 37203
www.csmisfun.com
Phone: 615-862-5160
Fax: 615-401-5086

Darkhorse Theater
4610 Charlotte Ave
Nashville, TN 37209
E-mail: info@darkhorsetheater.com
www.darkhorsetheater.com
Phone: 615-297-7113
Fax: 615-665-3336

Edwin Warner Park
50 Vaughn Rd
Nashville, TN 37201
Phone: 615-862-8400

Fort Donelson National Battlefield
PO Box 434
Dover, TN 37058
www.nps.gov/fodo/
Phone: 931-232-5706
Fax: 931-232-6331

General Jackson Showboat
2802 Opryland Dr
Nashville, TN 37214
Phone: 615-889-6611
Fax: 615-871-5772

Grand Ole Opry
2804 Opryland Dr
Nashville, TN 37214
www.grandoleopry.com
Phone: 615-889-3060
Fax: 615-871-5719

Grand Ole Opry Museum
2802 Opryland Dr
Nashville, TN 37214
Phone: 615-889-6611
Fax: 615-871-5772

Hartzler-Towner Multicultural Museum
1008 19th Ave S
Nashville, TN 37212
Phone: 615-340-7500
Fax: 615-340-7463

Hermitage The: Home of Andrew Jackson
4580 Rachel's Ln
Hermitage, TN 37076
E-mail: info@thehermitage.com
www.thehermitage.com
Phone: 615-889-2941
Fax: 615-889-9289

Historic Rock Castle
139 Rock Castle Ln
Hendersonville, TN 37075
Phone: 615-824-0502
Fax: 615-824-0502

Historic Travellers Rest
636 Farrell Pkwy
Nashville, TN 37220
Phone: 615-832-8197
Fax: 615-832-8169

Jim Reeves Museum
1023 Joyce Ln
Nashville, TN 37216
Phone: 615-776-5656
Fax: 615-776-5357

Museum of Beverage Containers & Advertising
1055 Ridgecrest Dr
Millersville, TN 37072
E-mail: info@nostalgiaville.com
www.gono.com/cc/museum.htm
Phone: 615-859-5236
Fax: 615-859-5238

Music City Queen Phone: 615-889-6611
Opryland USA Riverfront Pk
Nashville, TN 37203

Music Valley Car Museum Phone: 615-885-7400
2611 McGavock Pike
Nashville, TN 37214

Music Valley Wax Museum of the Stars Phone: 615-883-3612
2515 McGavock Pike
Nashville, TN 37214

Nashville Ballet Phone: 615-244-7233
2976 Sidco Dr Fax: 615-242-1741
Nashville, TN 37204

Nashville Children's Theatre Phone: 615-254-9103
724 2nd Ave S
Nashville, TN 37210
www.nct-dragonsite.org

Nashville Network The (TNN) Phone: 615-883-7000
2806 Opryland Dr Fax: 615-457-9660
Nashville, TN 37214

Nashville Opera Phone: 615-832-5242
3628 Trousdale Dr Suite D Fax: 615-832-5243
Nashville, TN 37204
E-mail: nashopera@nashvilleopera.org
www.nashvilleopera.org

Nashville Symphony Phone: 615-255-5600
209 10th Ave S Suite 448 Fax: 615-255-5656
Nashville, TN 37203
www.nashvillesymphony.com

Nashville Toy Museum Phone: 615-883-8870
2613-B McGavock Pike Fax: 615-391-0556
Nashville, TN 37214

Nashville Zoo Phone: 615-833-1534
3777 Nolensville Rd Fax: 615-333-0728
Nashville, TN 37211
www.nashvillezoo.org

Oscar Farris Agricultural Museum Phone: 615-837-5197
440 Hogan Rd Fax: 615-837-5194
South Nashville, TN 37204

Parthenon The Phone: 615-862-8431
West End & N 25th Aves Centennial Pk Fax: 615-880-2265
Nashville, TN 37201
E-mail: info@parthenon.org
www.parthenon.org

Percy Warner Park Phone: 615-862-8400
2500 Old Hickory Blvd
Nashville, TN 37201

Radnor Lake State Natural Area Phone: 615-373-3467
1160 Otter Creek Rd Fax: 615-373-7893
Nashville, TN 37220

Ryman Auditorium Phone: 615-254-1445
116 5th Ave N Fax: 615-251-1026
Nashville, TN 37219

Shiloh National Military Park Phone: 901-689-5275
1055 Pittsburg Landing Rd Fax: 901-689-5450
Shiloh, TN 38376
www.nps.gov/shil/

Stones River National Battlefield Phone: 615-893-9501
3501 Old Nashville Hwy Fax: 615-893-9508
Murfreesboro, TN 37129
www.nps.gov/stri/

Tennessee Dance Theatre Phone: 615-248-3262
615 5th Ave S Fax: 615-256-3576
Nashville, TN 37203

Tennessee Fox Trot Carousel Phone: 615-254-7020
1st & Broadway Sts Riverfront Pk
Nashville, TN 37203

Tennessee Performing Arts Center Phone: 615-782-4000
505 Deaderick St Fax: 615-782-4001
Nashville, TN 37219
www.tpac.org

Tennessee Repertory Theatre Phone: 615-244-4878
427 Chestnut St Fax: 615-244-1232
Nashville, TN 37203
E-mail: therep@hammock.com
therep.hammock.com/

Tennessee State Capitol Phone: 615-741-1621
Charlotte Ave Fax: 615-532-9711
Nashville, TN 37243

Tennessee State Museum Phone: 615-741-2692
505 Deaderick St Fax: 615-741-7231
Nashville, TN 37243 TF: 800-407-4324

Texas Troubadour Theatre Phone: 615-885-0028
2416 Music Valley Dr Suite 107 Fax: 615-316-9269
Nashville, TN 37214
www.etrs.net/theatre.htm

Travellers Rest Plantation House & Grounds Phone: 615-832-8197
636 Farrell Pkwy Fax: 615-832-8169
Nashville, TN 37220

Upper Room Chapel & Museum Phone: 615-340-7207
1908 Grand Ave Fax: 615-340-7293
Nashville, TN 37212

Van Vechten Gallery Phone: 615-329-8720
Jackson St & DB Todd Blvd Fisk University Fax: 615-329-8544
Nashville, TN 37208

Vanderbilt University Fine Arts Gallery Phone: 615-322-0605
23rd & West End Aves Fax: 615-343-1382
Nashville, TN 37203
www.vanderbilt.edu/ans/finearts/gallery.html

Willie Nelson & Friends Showcase Museum Phone: 615-885-1515
2613A McGavock Pike Fax: 615-885-0733
Nashville, TN 37214

Sports Teams & Facilities

Adelphia Coliseum
1 Titans Way
Nashville, TN 37213
www.titansonline.com/adelphia
Phone: 615-565-4000

Gaylord Entertainment Center
501 Broadway
Nashville, TN 37203
E-mail: info@nashvillearena.com
www.nashvillearena.com
Phone: 615-770-2000
Fax: 615-770-2010

Music City Raceway
3302 Ivy Point Rd
Goodlettsville, TN 37072
E-mail: racersrick@msn.com
www.musiccityraceway.com
Phone: 615-876-0981
Fax: 615-264-0362

Nashville Kats (football)
5th & Broadway Nashville Arena
Nashville, TN 37201
E-mail: editor@katsfan.com
www.katsfan.com
Phone: 615-254-5287
Fax: 615-843-5206

Nashville Municipal Auditorium
417 4th Ave N
Nashville, TN 37201
E-mail: munaud@nashville.org
www.nashville.org/ma
Phone: 615-862-6390
Fax: 615-862-6394

Nashville Predators
501 Broadway Nashville Arena
Nashville, TN 37203
E-mail: info@nashvillepredators.com
www.nashvillepredators.com
Phone: 615-770-7825

Nashville Sounds (baseball)
534 Chestnut St Herschel Greer Stadium
Nashville, TN 37203
www.nashsounds.com
Phone: 615-242-4371
Fax: 615-256-5684

Nashville Speedway USA
Wedgewood Ave & Nolensville Rd
Nashville, TN 37203
www.nashvillespeedway.com
Phone: 615-726-1818
Fax: 615-726-0691

Tennessee Rhythm (soccer)
1314 Columbia Ave Battle Ground Stadium
Franklin, TN 37064
E-mail: tennesseefc@aol.com
www.rhythmsoccer.com
Phone: 615-591-9545
Fax: 615-591-2130

Tennessee Titans
1 Titans Way Adelphia Coliseum
Nashville, TN 37213
www.titansonline.com
Phone: 615-673-1500
Fax: 615-673-1524
TF: 888-313-8326

Annual Events

A Country Christmas (early November-late December) 615-871-6169
African Street Festival (mid-September) 615-299-0412
American Artisan Festival (mid-June)..............615-298-4691
Americana Sampler Craft Folk Art & Antique Show (early August)................................615-227-2080
Antiques & Garden Show of Nashville (early-mid-February)...........................615-352-1282
Belle Meade Fall Fest (mid-September) 615-356-0501
Boo at the Zoo (mid-late October).................615-371-8462
Chet Atkins' Musician Days (early April) 615-256-9596
Colonial Fair Day (early May).....................615-859-7979
Dancin' in the District (mid-May-late August) 615-256-9596
Grand Ole Opry Birthday Celebration (mid-October)................................615-889-6611
Heart of Country Antiques Show (mid-February)....615-883-2211
Historic Edgefield Tour of Homes (late May) 615-226-3340
Independence Day Celebration (July 4).............615-862-8400
International Country Music Fan Fair (mid-June) 615-889-7503
Iroquois Steeplechase (mid-May)..................615-322-7450
Italian Street Fair (early September)...............615-255-5600
L'Été du Vin (late July) 615-341-7300
Longhorn World Championship Rodeo (mid-November)..............................800-357-6336
Main Street Festival (late April)...................615-791-9924
NAIA Powwow (late October) 615-726-0806
Nashville Boat & Sport Show (mid-January)........615-742-2000
Nashville Lawn & Garden Show (early March) 615-352-3863
Nashville's Country Holidays (mid-November-late December) 615-259-4700
Oktoberfest (mid-October)........................615-256-2729
TACA Fall Crafts Fair (late September) 615-665-0502
Tennessee Crafts Fair (early May).................615-665-0502
Tennessee Renaissance Festival (early-late May) 615-259-4747
Tennessee State Fair (early-mid-September)........615-862-8980
Tennessee Walking Horse National Celebration (late August-early September)...................931-684-5915
Tin Pan South (early April)......................615-251-3472
Wildflower Fair (late March-early April) 615-353-2148

New Haven, Connecticut

County: **New Haven**

NEW HAVEN is located in south central Connecticut on Long Island Sound at the mouth of the Quinnipiac River. Major cities within 100 miles include Hartford, Connecticut; Providence, Rhode Island; Springfield, Massachusetts; and New York, New York.

Area (Land) .... 18.9 sq mi
Area (Water)............................... 1.4 sq mi
Elevation...................................... 25 ft
Latitude ....41-30-81 N
Longitude............................... 72-92-86 W
Time Zone ....EST
Area Code...................................... 203

Climate

New Haven's climate features four distinct seasons. Winters are cold, with average high temperatures in the upper 30s and lows in the mid-20s. The average annual snowfall in New Haven is 26 inches. Summers are generally mild, with average daytime high temperatures in the upper 70s and low 80s and evening lows in the low to mid-60s. Precipitation is fairly evenly distributed throughout the year in New Haven. May is the wettest month, while February is the driest.

Average Temperatures & Precipitation

Temperatures

	Jan	Feb	Mar	Apr	May	Jun	Jul	Aug	Sep	Oct	Nov	Dec
High	36	38	46	57	67	76	82	81	74	64	53	41
Low	22	23	31	40	50	59	66	65	58	47	38	28

Precipitation

	Jan	Feb	Mar	Apr	May	Jun	Jul	Aug	Sep	Oct	Nov	Dec
Inches	3.2	3.0	3.8	3.8	3.9	3.5	3.8	3.3	3.1	3.1	3.8	3.5

History

One of the nation's first planned communities, New Haven was founded in 1638 by a group of Puritans led by John Davenport and Theophilus Eaton. Originally called Quinnipiac, the colony was renamed New Haven two years later. New Haven remained an independent colony until 1665 when it was absorbed by the Connecticut Colony. Together with Hartford, New Haven served as the joint capital of Connecticut from 1701 to 1875. In its early years, the colony was primarily a farming and seafaring community. New Haven became an important educational center in 1716 when Yale University was established there. The colony was raided and partially burned by the British during the American Revolution in 1779; five years later, in 1784, New Haven was incorporated as a city.

During the 19th century, New Haven became an important trade and industrial hub as immigrants from Europe began settling in the area. Inventors who called New Haven home during that era include Eli Whitney, Noah Webster, and Charles Goodyear. During the 20th Century, New Haven has gained recognition for its efforts towards urban renewal—the first antipoverty program in U.S. history was implemented in New Haven in 1962. Connecticut's third largest city, with a population of more than 123,000, New Haven today remains a leading U.S. center for transportation, education, manufacturing, and trade.

Population

1990 Census 130,474
1998 Estimate..............................123,189
% Change .... -5.6

Racial/Ethnic Breakdown

White.......................................53.9%
Black 36.1%
Other 10.0%
Hispanic Origin (may be of any race) 13.2%

Age Breakdown

Under 5 years.............................. 7.8%
5 to 17.....................................15.9%
18 to 20.................................... 7.7%
21 to 24.................................... 9.3%
25 to 34....................................20.2%
35 to 44....................................12.8%
45 to 54.................................... 7.7%
55 to 64.................................... 6.3%
65 to 74.................................... 6.4%
75+ years 5.9%
Median Age...................................29.2

Gender Breakdown

Male...47.0%
Female.......................................53.0%

Government

Type of Government: Mayor-Board of Aldermen

New Haven Board of Aldermen
165 Church St
New Haven, CT 06510
Phone: 203-946-8370
Fax: 203-946-7476

New Haven Business Development Office
165 Church St 6th Fl
New Haven, CT 06510
Phone: 203-946-7060
Fax: 203-946-4866

New Haven Children & Family Services Dept
165 Church St
New Haven, CT 06510
Phone: 203-946-6442
Fax: 203-946-8587

New Haven City Clerk
200 Orange St
New Haven, CT 06510
Phone: 203-946-8346
Fax: 203-946-6974

New Haven City Hall
165 Church St
New Haven, CT 06510
Phone: 203-946-8339
Fax: 203-946-6974

New Haven Finance Dept
200 Orange St
New Haven, CT 06502
Phone: 203-946-8300
Fax: 203-946-7244

New Haven Fire Dept
PO Box 374
New Haven, CT 06502
Phone: 203-946-6222
Fax: 203-946-6221

New Haven Free Public Library
133 Elm St
New Haven, CT 06510
Phone: 203-946-8130
Fax: 203-946-8699

New Haven Human Resources Dept
200 Orange St 4th Fl
New Haven, CT 06510
Phone: 203-946-8252
Fax: 203-946-7166

New Haven Mayor
165 Church St
New Haven, CT 06510
Phone: 203-946-8200
Fax: 203-946-7683

New Haven Parks Recreation & Trees Dept
720 Edgewood Ave
New Haven, CT 06515
Phone: 203-946-8025
Fax: 203-946-8024

New Haven Planning Dept
165 Church St
New Haven, CT 06510
Phone: 203-946-6353
Fax: 203-946-7815

New Haven Police Dept
1 Union Ave
New Haven, CT 06519
Phone: 203-946-6333
Fax: 203-946-7294

New Haven Public Works Dept
34 Middletown Ave
New Haven, CT 06513
Phone: 203-946-7700
Fax: 203-946-7357

Important Phone Numbers

AAA....203-281-1133
American Express Travel....203-772-0060
Connecticut Dept of Revenue Services....203-287-8243
Driver's License/Vehicle Registration Information....860-263-5700
Emergency....911
Greater New Haven Assn of Realtors....203-234-7700
HotelDocs....800-468-3537
New Haven Property Tax Information....203-946-7073
New Haven Tax Office....203-946-6428
Poison Control Center....800-343-2722
Time....203-777-4647
Travelers Aid....203-495-7437
Voter Registration Information....203-946-8034

Information Sources

Better Business Bureau Serving Connecticut
821 N Main St Ext
Wallingford, CT 06492
www.connecticut.bbb.org
Phone: 203-269-2700
Fax: 203-269-3124

Greater New Haven Chamber of Commerce
900 Chapel St 10th Fl
New Haven, CT 06510
www.newhavenchamber.com
Phone: 203-787-6735
Fax: 203-782-4329

Greater New Haven Convention & Visitors Bureau
59 Elm St
New Haven, CT 06510
www.newhavencvb.org/
Phone: 203-777-8550
Fax: 203-782-7755
TF: 800-332-7829

Online Resources

About.com Guide to New Haven
newhaven.about.com/citiestowns/newenglandus/newhaven/mbody.htm

Area Guide New Haven
newhaven.areaguides.net

DigitalCity Hartford
home.digitalcity.com/hartford

Excite.com New Haven City Guide
www.excite.com/travel/countries/united_states/connecticut/new_haven

New Haven Web
www.newhavenweb.com

Area Communities

Communities in Greater New Haven with populations greater than 10,000 include:

Branford
PO Box 150
Branford, CT 06405
Phone: 203-488-8394
Fax: 203-481-5561

Cheshire
84 S Main St
Cheshire, CT 06410
Phone: 203-271-6660
Fax: 203-271-6664

East Haven
250 Main St
East Haven, CT 06512
Phone: 203-468-3204
Fax: 203-468-3372

Guilford
31 Park St
Guilford, CT 06437
Phone: 203-453-8015
Fax: 203-453-8467

Hamden
2372 Whitney Ave
Hamden, CT 06518
Phone: 203-287-2500
Fax: 203-287-2501

Madison
8 Campus Dr
Madison, CT 06443
Phone: 203-245-5602
Fax: 203-245-5609

Milford
70 W River St
Milford, CT 06460
Phone: 203-783-3200

North Branford
PO Box 287
North Branford, CT 06471
Phone: 203-315-6000
Fax: 203-315-6025

North Haven
18 Church St
North Haven, CT 06473
Phone: 203-239-5321
Fax: 203-234-2130

Orange
617 Orange Center Rd
Orange, CT 06477
Phone: 203-891-2122
Fax: 203-891-2185

Wallingford
45 S Main St
Wallingford, CT 06492
Phone: 203-294-2070
Fax: 203-294-2073

West Haven
355 Main St
West Haven, CT 06516
Phone: 203-937-3500
Fax: 203-937-3705

Economy

Greater New Haven has a diverse economic base ranging from hardware manufacturing to finance. Services is the largest employment sector in New Haven, with health care and educational services being the leading industries. World-renowned Yale University and Yale-New Haven Hospital are New Haven's two largest employers, and the Hospital of Saint Raphael and Southern Connecticut State University also rank among the top 10. Trade and manufacturing—the industries that have fueled the area's economy for nearly two centuries—also remain leading employment sectors. Principal products include metal goods, chemicals, and printed materials.

Unemployment Rate 2.1%
Per Capita Income $40,928
Median Family Income $58,500*

** Information given is for New Haven County.*

Principal Industries & Number of Wage Earners

City of New Haven - June 1998

Construction 1,140
Finance, Insurance, & Real Estate 3,690
Government 10,150
Manufacturing 5,790
Retail Trade 6,700
Services 39,020
Wholesale Trade 1,430

Major Employers

Hospital of Saint Raphael
1450 Chapel St
New Haven, CT 06511
www.srhs.org
Phone: 203-789-3000
Fax: 203-789-3359
TF: 800-662-2366

Knights of Columbus
1 Columbus Plaza
New Haven, CT 06510
www.kofc.org
Phone: 203-772-2130
Fax: 203-773-3000

Metro North
347 Madison Ave
New York, NY 10017
Phone: 212-340-3000
Fax: 212-340-3499

Sargent Mfg Co
100 Sargent Dr
New Haven, CT 06511
Phone: 203-562-2151
Fax: 203-499-6840

SNET Corp
310 Orange St
New Haven, CT 06510
www.snet.com
Phone: 203-771-5200
Fax: 203-772-4855
TF: 800-453-7638

Southern Connecticut State University
501 Crescent St
New Haven, CT 06515
www.scsu.ctstateu.edu
Phone: 203-392-5200
Fax: 203-392-5727

United Illuminating Co
PO Box 1564
New Haven, CT 06506
www.uinet.com
Phone: 203-499-2000
Fax: 203-499-3664
TF: 800-722-5584

US Repeating Arms Co
344 Winchester Ave
New Haven, CT 06511
www.winchester-guns.com
Phone: 203-789-5000
Fax: 203-789-5552

Yale University
PO Box 208234 Yale Stn
New Haven, CT 06520
www.yale.edu
Phone: 203-432-4771
Fax: 203-432-7329

Yale-New Haven Hospital
20 York St
New Haven, CT 06504
info.med.yale.edu/ynhh
Phone: 203-688-4242
Fax: 203-688-4319

Quality of Living Indicators

Total Crime Index 13,255
(rates per 100,000 inhabitants)

Violent Crime
Murder/manslaughter 15
Forcible rape 66
Robbery 825
Aggravated assault 1,195

Property Crime
Burglary 2,147
Larceny theft 7,510
Motor vehicle theft 1,497

Cost of Living Index 123.0
(national average = 100)

Median Home Price $145,700

Education

Public Schools

New Haven Public Schools
54 Meadow St
New Haven, CT 06519
www.nhps.net
Phone: 203-946-8811
Fax: 203-946-8805

Number of Schools
Elementary 28
Middle 10
High 8

Student/Teacher Ratio
All Grades 15.4:1

Private Schools

Number of Schools (all grades) .... 18+

Colleges & Universities

Albertus Magnus College Phone: 203-773-8550
700 Prospect St Fax: 203-773-3117
New Haven, CT 06511
E-mail: admissions@albertus.edu
www.albertus.edu

Gateway Community-Technical College Phone: 203-789-7071
60 Sargent Dr Fax: 203-867-6057
New Haven, CT 06511
www.gwctc.commnet.edu

Naugatuck Valley Community-Technical College Phone: 203-575-8040
750 Chase Pkwy Fax: 203-575-8096
Waterbury, CT 06708
www.nvctc.commnet.edu

Paier College of Art Inc Phone: 203-287-3031
20 Gorham Ave Fax: 203-287-3021
Hamden, CT 06514
E-mail: info@paierart.com
www.paierart.com

Quinnipiac College Phone: 203-288-5251
275 Mt Carmel Ave Fax: 203-582-8906
Hamden, CT 06518 TF: 800-462-1944
www.quinnipiac.edu

Southern Connecticut State University Phone: 203-392-5200
501 Crescent St Fax: 203-392-5727
New Haven, CT 06515
www.scsu.ctstateu.edu

University of New Haven Phone: 203-932-7000
300 Orange Ave Fax: 203-931-6093
West Haven, CT 06516 TF: 800-342-5864
www.newhaven.edu

Yale University Phone: 203-432-4771
PO Box 208234 Yale Stn Fax: 203-432-7329
New Haven, CT 06520
www.yale.edu

Hospitals

Hospital of Saint Raphael Phone: 203-789-3000
1450 Chapel St Fax: 203-789-3359
New Haven, CT 06511 TF: 800-662-2366
www.srhs.org

Milford Hospital Phone: 203-876-4000
300 Seaside Ave Fax: 203-876-4198
Milford, CT 06460
www.milfordhospital.org

Veterans Affairs Connecticut Health Care System Phone: 203-932-5711
950 Campbell Ave Fax: 203-937-3868
West Haven, CT 06516

Yale-New Haven Hospital Phone: 203-688-4242
20 York St Fax: 203-688-4319
New Haven, CT 06504
info.med.yale.edu/ynhh

Transportation

Airport(s)

Tweed-New Haven Regional Airport (HVN)
3 1/2 miles SE of downtown
(approx 10 minutes) 203-466-8833

Mass Transit

CT Transit
$1 Base fare 203-624-0151

Rail/Bus

Greyhound Bus Station Phone: 203-772-2470
50 Union Ave TF: 800-231-2222
New Haven, CT 06519

Metro-North/Amtrak/Shore Line Railroad Phone: 203-773-6176
50 Union Ave New Haven Union Stn
New Haven, CT 06519

Utilities

Electricity
United Illuminating Co 203-499-2000
www.uinet.com

Gas
Southern Connecticut Gas Co 203-786-6111
www.naturalgas.com/scg/

Water
Regional Water Authority 203-624-6671
www.rwater.com

Garbage Collection/Recycling
New Haven Public Works Dept 203-946-8149
New Haven Recycling Office 203-946-8053

Telecommunications

Telephone
SNET Corp 203-771-5200
www.snet.com

Cable Television
AT & T Cable Services 888-824-2273
www.cable.att.com
Comcast Cable 203-865-0096

Internet Service Providers (ISPs)
i-conn 203-821-2575
www.iconn.net
PCNet 860-278-1188
www.pcnet.com

Banks

Bank of Boston NA
123 Church St
New Haven, CT 06510
Phone: 800-788-5000
Fax: 401-276-1443

Citizens Bank
209 Church St
New Haven, CT 06510
Phone: 203-498-3600
Fax: 203-624-0288

First Union National Bank
205 Church St
New Haven, CT 06510
Phone: 203-773-0500
Fax: 203-787-1501

Hudson United Bank
2 Whitney Ave
New Haven, CT 06510
Phone: 203-776-6033
Fax: 203-782-3603

New Haven Savings Bank
195 Church St
New Haven, CT 06510
www.nhsb.com
Phone: 203-787-1111
Fax: 203-784-5059

Webster Bank
80 Elm St
New Haven, CT 06510
Phone: 203-782-4588
Fax: 203-782-4536
TF: 800-325-2424

Shopping

Boulevard Flea Market
520 Ella T Grasso Blvd
New Haven, CT 06519
Phone: 203-772-1447

Chapel Square Mall
900 Chapel St
New Haven, CT 06510
Phone: 203-777-6661
Fax: 203-674-2976

Connecticut Post Mall
1201 Boston Post Rd
Milford, CT 06460
connecticutpost.shoppingtown.com
Phone: 203-878-6837
Fax: 203-874-5812

Media

Newspapers and Magazines

Milford Reporter
PO Box 5339
Milford, CT 06460
Phone: 203-876-6800
Fax: 203-877-4772

New Haven Advocate
1 Long Wharf Dr
New Haven, CT 06511
www.newhavenadvocate.com
Phone: 203-789-0010
Fax: 203-787-1418

New Haven Register*
40 Sargent Dr
New Haven, CT 06511
www.ctcentral.com
Phone: 203-789-5200
Fax: 203-865-7894

Stratford Bard
PO Box 5339
Milford, CT 06460
Phone: 203-876-6800
Fax: 203-877-4772

**Indicates major daily newspapers*

Television

WEDH-TV Ch 24 (PBS)
240 New Britain Ave
Hartford, CT 06106
Phone: 860-278-5310
Fax: 860-278-2157

WFSB-TV Ch 3 (CBS)
3 Constitution Plaza
Hartford, CT 06103
www.wfsb.com
Phone: 860-728-3333
Fax: 860-728-0263

WTIC-TV Ch 61 (Fox)
1 Corporate Ctr
Hartford, CT 06103
www.fox61.com
Phone: 860-527-6161
Fax: 860-293-0178

WTNH-TV Ch 8 (ABC)
8 Elm St
New Haven, CT 06510
E-mail: wtnh@aol.com
www.wtnh.com
Phone: 203-784-8888
Fax: 203-789-2010

WVIT-TV Ch 30 (NBC)
1422 New Britain Ave
West Hartford, CT 06110
www.wvit.com
Phone: 860-521-3030
Fax: 860-521-4860

Radio

WAVZ-AM 1300 kHz (Nost)
495 Benham St
Hamden, CT 06514
www.wavz.com
Phone: 203-248-8814
Fax: 203-281-2795

WELI-AM 960 kHz (N/T)
495 Benham St
Hamden, CT 06514
www.weli.com
Phone: 203-281-9600
Fax: 203-407-4652

WKCI-FM 101.3 MHz (CHR)
495 Benham St
Hamden, CT 06514
E-mail: comments@kc101.com
www.kc101.com
Phone: 203-248-8814
Fax: 203-281-2795

WPLR-FM 99.1 MHz (Rock)
1191 Dixwell Ave
Hamden, CT 06514
www.wplr.com
Phone: 203-287-9070
Fax: 203-287-8997

WYBC-FM 94.3 MHz (Urban)
165 Elm St
New Haven, CT 06520
www.wybc.com/fm/index.html
Phone: 203-432-4118
Fax: 203-432-4117

Attractions

The Yale University Art Gallery in New Haven is the nation's oldest college art museum, with 75,000 pieces from ancient Egypt to present day. Yale's Beinecke Rare Book and Manuscript Library features the Gutenberg Bible, a sunken sculpture garden, and translucent marble "windows." Also part of Yale University, the Peabody Museum of Natural History, one of the nation's oldest and largest natural history museums, features the Pulitzer Prize-winning mural The Age of Reptiles, as well as a variety of exhibits on subjects ranging from meteorites to Connecticut birds. The Shubert Performing Arts Center in New Haven has been called the "Birthplace of the Nation's Greatest Hits" (including My Fair Lady and A Streetcar Named Desire); and the New Haven Symphony Orchestra is the fourth-oldest symphony in the U.S.

Alliance Theatre at University of New Haven
300 Orange Ave Dodds Hall
West Haven, CT 06516
Phone: 203-932-7085

Ansonia Nature & Recreation Center
10 Deerfield Rd
Ansonia, CT 06401
E-mail: ansnaturecenter@snet.net
Phone: 203-736-9360
Fax: 203-734-1672

Beinecke Rare Book & Manuscript Library at Yale
121 Wall St Yale University
New Haven, CT 06511
Phone: 203-432-2977
Fax: 203-432-4047

Boulevard Flea Market
520 Ella T Grasso Blvd
New Haven, CT 06519
Phone: 203-772-1447

Chamber Music Society at Yale
435 College St School of Music
New Haven, CT 06520
Phone: 203-432-4158

Connecticut Children's Museum
22 Wall St
New Haven, CT 06511
Phone: 203-562-5437
Fax: 203-787-9414

Edgerton Park-Greenbrier Greenhouse & Crosby Conservatory
75 Cliff St
New Haven, CT 06511
Phone: 203-777-1886
Fax: 203-787-7804

Eli Whitney Museum
915 Whitney Ave
Hamden, CT 06517
www.eliwhitney.org/
Phone: 203-777-1833
Fax: 203-777-1229

Ethnic Historical Archives Center
501 Crescent St
New Haven, CT 06515
Phone: 203-392-6126

Fairmount Theatre
33 Main St
New Haven, CT 06512
Phone: 203-467-3832
Fax: 203-467-3832

Fort Nathan Hale & Black Rock Fort
36 Woodward Ave
New Haven, CT 06512
Phone: 203-946-8790

Knights of Columbus Museum
1 Columbus Plaza
New Haven, CT 06510
Phone: 203-772-2130

Lighthouse Point Park
2 Lighthouse Rd
New Haven, CT 06512
Phone: 203-946-8005

Long Wharf Theatre
222 Sargent Dr
New Haven, CT 06511
www.longwharf.org
Phone: 203-787-4282
Fax: 203-776-2287

Lyman John Performing Arts Center
501 Crescent St
New Haven, CT 06515
Phone: 203-392-6154
Fax: 203-392-6158

Milford's Wharf Lane Complex
34 High St
Milford, CT 06460
Phone: 203-874-2664

New England Academy of Theatre
3013 Dixwell Ave
Hamden, CT 06518
E-mail: neactors@aol.com
www.neatct.org
Phone: 203-458-7671

New Haven Colony Historical Society
114 Whitney Ave
New Haven, CT 06510
Phone: 203-562-4183
Fax: 203-562-2002

New Haven Crypt
250 Temple St
New Haven, CT 06511
Phone: 203-787-0121
Fax: 203-787-2187

New Haven Symphony Orchestra
Yale University Woolsey Hall
New Haven, CT 06510
Phone: 203-776-1444
Fax: 203-789-8907

Orchestra New England
College & Elm Sts Battell Chapel Yale University
New Haven, CT 06510
Phone: 203-932-7180
Fax: 203-934-8379

Palace Theatre
246 College St
New Haven, CT 06510
Phone: 203-789-2120
Fax: 203-789-0347

Pardee-Morris House
325 Lighthouse Rd
New Haven, CT 06512
Phone: 203-562-4183
Fax: 203-562-2002

Peabody Museum of Natural History
170 Whitney Ave Yale University
New Haven, CT 06520
www.peabody.yale.edu/
Phone: 203-432-3750
Fax: 203-432-9816

Shore Line Trolley Museum
17 River St
East Haven, CT 06512
E-mail: berasltm@aol.com
www.bera.org
Phone: 203-467-6927
Fax: 203-467-7635

Shubert Performing Arts Center
247 College St
New Haven, CT 06510
E-mail: shubert@shubert.com
www.shubert.com
Phone: 203-624-1825
Fax: 203-789-2286

West Rock Ridge State Park
Wintergreen Ave
New Haven, CT 06515
Phone: 203-789-7498
Fax: 203-789-7498

Yale Center for British Art
1080 Chapel St
New Haven, CT 06520
www.yale.edu/ycba
Phone: 203-432-2800
Fax: 203-432-9695

Yale University Art Gallery
1111 Chapel St
New Haven, CT 06520
www.yale.edu/artgallery
Phone: 203-432-0600
Fax: 203-432-7159

Yale University Collection of Musical Instruments
15 Hillhouse Ave
New Haven, CT 06520
Phone: 203-432-0822
Fax: 203-432-8342

Yale University Theatre
222 York St
New Haven, CT 06510
Phone: 203-432-1234
Fax: 203-432-8337

Sports Teams & Facilities

Milford Jai-Alai
311 Old Gate Ln
Milford, CT 06460
www.jaialai.com
Phone: 203-877-4211
Fax: 203-878-2317
TF: 800-243-9660

New Haven Coliseum
275 S Orange St
New Haven, CT 06510
Phone: 203-772-4200
Fax: 203-503-6015

New Haven Ravens (baseball)
252 Derby Ave Yale Field
West Haven, CT 06510
www.ravens.com
Phone: 203-782-1666
Fax: 203-782-3150

Annual Events

Blessing of the Fleet (early June) 203-777-8550
Celebrate New Haven Fourth (early July)...........203-946-7821
Celebration of American Crafts
(early November-late December) 203-562-4927
Cider and Donuts Festival (mid-September) 203-777-8550
Fair on the Green (early June)....................203-874-1982
Fall Festival & Chili Cookoff (mid-September)......203-387-7700
Film Fest New Haven (early April) 203-481-6789
Freddie Fixer Parade & Festival (early-mid-May)....203-389-1119
Gem & Mineral Show (mid-June) 203-929-3404
Goldenbells Festival (mid-late April)...............203-281-4768
International Festival of Arts & Ideas
(mid-June-early July) 203-498-1212
Kite Fly & Spring Festival (early May).............203-230-5226
May Fest: A Day of Arts, Crafts, & Entertainment
(early May) 203-287-2546
Meet the Artists & Artisans
(mid-May & early October) 203-874-5672
New England Arts and Crafts Festival (mid-July)....203-878-6647
North Haven Agricultural Fair
(early-mid-September) 203-239-3700
Pilot Pen International Tennis Tournament
(late August).................................203-776-7331
Rolling Thunder Monster Truck Tour
(early January)...............................203-772-4200
Saint Andrew's Italian Festival (late June) 203-865-9846
Saint Anthony's Feast (mid-June).................203-624-1418
Saint Barbara Greek Festival (early September).....203-795-1347
Saint Francis Strawberry Festival (mid-June).......203-294-1112
Savin Rock Festival (late July)....................203-937-3511
SNET Jazz Festival (August)......................203-946-7821
UI Fantasy of Lights
(mid-November-early January) 203-777-2000
Winterfest (early February).......................203-378-2700
Wooster Square Cherry Blossom Festival
(mid-April) 203-865-5842

New Orleans, Louisiana

County: Orleans Parish

NEW ORLEANS is located on Lake Ponchartrain near the mouth of the Mississippi River in southeastern Louisiana. Major cities within 100 miles include Baton Rouge, Louisiana; Gulfport, Biloxi, and Pascagoula, Mississippi; and Mobile, Alabama.

Area (Land)	180.6 sq mi
Area (Water)	169.6 sq mi
Elevation	5 ft
Latitude	29-95-44 N
Longitude	90-07-50 W
Time Zone	CST
Area Code	504

Climate

Surrounded by several bodies of water, New Orleans' location produces warm, humid weather. Winters are mild, with average high temperatures in the low to mid-60s and lows in the low to mid-40s. Snowfall is rare in New Orleans. Summers are hot and humid, with average high temperatures near 90 degrees and lows in the low 70s. Thunderstorms are common during the summer, which is the rainy season in New Orleans. August is the wettest month, while October is the driest.

Average Temperatures & Precipitation

Temperatures

	Jan	Feb	Mar	Apr	May	Jun	Jul	Aug	Sep	Oct	Nov	Dec
High	61	64	72	79	84	89	91	90	87	79	71	64
Low	42	44	52	58	65	71	73	73	70	59	51	45

Precipitation

	Jan	Feb	Mar	Apr	May	Jun	Jul	Aug	Sep	Oct	Nov	Dec
Inches	5.1	6.0	4.9	4.5	4.6	5.8	6.1	6.2	5.5	3.1	4.4	5.8

History

The area known today as New Orleans was first visited by Europeans in 1541, when a group of Spanish explorers led by Hernando de Soto discovered the Mississippi River. In 1682, French explorer Robert Cavalier de La Salle claimed the Mississippi River territory for France. At the turn of the 18th century, French brothers Pierre le Moyne d'Iberville and Jean Baptiste Le Moyne de Bienville arrived in southeastern "Louisiane" (as the territory was named) with some 200 settlers. They established a colony there, naming it Nouvelle Orleans in honor of the regent of France, duc d'Orleans. During the 18th Century, control of the Louisiana Territory shifted between France and Spain, but in 1803, shortly after France had regained control of the territory, Napoleon sold the land to the United States through the Louisiana Purchase.

New Orleans was incorporated as a city in 1805. The city had served as the capital of the Louisiana Territory and Spanish Louisiana, and it also served as the state capital of Louisiana from the time it was granted statehood in 1812 until 1849 (except for a brief period between 1830 and 1831). New Orleans' location near the mouth of the Mississippi River enabled the city to grow as an important center for trade, with cotton and sugarcane the area's primary commodities. Hundreds of thousands of people were drawn by the region's plentiful economic opportunities, and New Orleans' population skyrocketed from 75,000 in 1810 to 700,000 a half-century later. By the 1850s, New Orleans had become the third largest city in the U.S.

During the Civil War, the port city served as a vital military center. Originally part of the Confederacy, New Orleans was captured by Union troops early in the war. Although the Civil War led to a period of economic decline in the region, by the early 1900s New Orleans was once again a bustling commercial hub. The oil and gas industry has been a primary contributor to the region's economy for much of the 20th Century.

The New Orleans metro area remains an important commercial and industrial center, and the Port of New Orleans is among the busiest in the U.S. Rich in heritage and culture, as well as the site of the famous annual Mardi Gras celebration, New Orleans is also a major tourist destination. With a population of more than 465,000 people, New Orleans today is Louisiana's largest city.

Population

1990 Census	496,938
1998 Estimate	465,538
% Change	-6.3
2005 Projection	481,520*

Racial/Ethnic Breakdown

White	34.9%
Black	61.9%
Other	3.2%
Hispanic Origin (may be of any race)	3.5%

Age Breakdown

Under 5 years	7.8%
5 to 17	19.7%
18 to 20	5.1%
21 to 24	6.3%
25 to 34	16.9%
35 to 44	14.3%
45 to 54	8.9%
55 to 64	8.0%
65 to 74	7.4%
75+ years	5.6%
Median Age	31.6

Gender Breakdown
Male 46.5%
Female 53.5%

** Information given is for Orleans Parish.*

Government

Type of Government: Mayor-Council

New Orleans City Council
1300 Perdido St 2nd Fl W
New Orleans, LA 70112
Phone: 504-565-6300
Fax: 504-565-6332

New Orleans City Hall
1300 Perdido St
New Orleans, LA 70112
Phone: 504-565-6000

New Orleans City Planning Commission
1300 Perdido St Rm 9W03
New Orleans, LA 70112
Phone: 504-565-7000
Fax: 504-565-7915

New Orleans Civil Service Dept
1300 Perdido St Rm 7W03
New Orleans, LA 70112
Phone: 504-565-6800
Fax: 504-565-7678

New Orleans Clerk of Council
1300 Perdido St Rm 1E09
New Orleans, LA 70112
Phone: 504-565-6393
Fax: 504-565-6387

New Orleans Economic Development Div
1515 Poydras St Suite 1200
New Orleans, LA 70112
Phone: 504-565-8100
Fax: 504-565-8108

New Orleans Finance Dept
1300 Perdido St Rm 3E06
New Orleans, LA 70112
Phone: 504-565-6600
Fax: 504-565-6603

New Orleans Fire Dept
317 Decatur St
New Orleans, LA 70130
Phone: 504-565-7800
Fax: 504-565-7848

New Orleans Law Dept
1300 Perdido St Rm 5E03
New Orleans, LA 70112
Phone: 504-565-6200
Fax: 504-565-7691

New Orleans Mayor
1300 Perdido St
New Orleans, LA 70112
Phone: 504-565-6400
Fax: 504-565-8076

New Orleans Police Dept
715 S Broad St Suite 501
New Orleans, LA 70119
Phone: 504-826-2727
Fax: 504-827-3598

New Orleans Public Library
219 Loyola Ave
New Orleans, LA 70112
Phone: 504-596-2550
Fax: 504-596-2609

New Orleans Public Works Dept
1300 Perdido St Rm 6W03
New Orleans, LA 70112
Phone: 504-565-6844
Fax: 504-565-6848

New Orleans Recreation Dept
1344 Poydras St Suite 700
New Orleans, LA 70119
Phone: 504-299-4170
Fax: 504-299-4197

New Orleans Sewerage & Water Board
625 Saint Joseph St
New Orleans, LA 70165
Phone: 504-585-2000
Fax: 504-585-2455

New Orleans Utilities Dept
1300 Perdido Rm 2W89
New Orleans, LA 70112
Phone: 504-565-6260
Fax: 504-565-6449

Important Phone Numbers

AAA 800-926-4222
American Express Travel 504-586-8201
Dental Referral 504-834-6449
Driver's License Information 504-483-4610
Emergency 911
HotelDocs 800-468-3537
Louisiana Dept of Revenue & Taxation 504-568-5233
Medical Referral 504-456-5000
New Orleans Metro Assn of Realtors 504-885-3200
New Orleans Treasury Dept 504-565-6703
Poison Control Center 800-256-9822
Travelers Aid Society 504-525-8726
Vehicle Registration Information 225-925-6146
Voter Registration Information 504-565-7135
Weather 504-828-4000

Information Sources

Better Business Bureau Serving Greater New Orleans
1539 Jackson Ave Suite 400
New Orleans, LA 70130
www.neworleans.bbb.org
Phone: 504-581-6222
Fax: 504-524-9110

Ernest N Morial Convention Center
900 Convention Center Blvd
New Orleans, LA 70130
Phone: 504-582-3023
Fax: 504-582-3088

Jefferson Parish
PO Box 9
Gretna, LA 70054
www.jeffparish.net
Phone: 504-364-2600
Fax: 504-364-2633

Jefferson Parish Library
4747 W Napoleon Ave
Metairie, LA 70001
www.jefferson.lib.la.us
Phone: 504-838-1100
Fax: 504-838-1117

Jefferson Parish Tourist Information Center
2828 Loyola Dr
Kenner, LA 70062
Phone: 504-468-7527
Fax: 504-471-2155

Metairie Community Development Dept
1221 Elmwood Pk Blvd Suite 605
Jefferson, LA 70123
www.jeffparish.net/departments/d-cdev.html
Phone: 504-736-6262
Fax: 504-736-6425

Metairie Parish President
1221 Elmwood Pk Blvd Suite 1002
Jefferson, LA 70123
Phone: 504-736-6400
Fax: 504-736-6638

New Orleans & River Region Chamber of Commerce
601 Poydras St Suite 1700
New Orleans, LA 70130
chamber.gnofn.org
Phone: 504-527-6900
Fax: 504-527-6950

New Orleans Metropolitan Convention & Visitors Bureau
1520 Sugar Bowl Dr
New Orleans, LA 70112
www.neworleanscvb.com
Phone: 504-566-5011
Fax: 504-566-5046
TF: 800-672-6124

New Orleans Visitor Center
1520 Sugar Bowl Dr
New Orleans, LA 70112
www.neworleanscvb.com
Phone: 504-566-5011
Fax: 504-566-5046

Orleans Parish
1300 Perdido St Rm 9-E-06
New Orleans, LA 70112
Phone: 504-565-6570

Online Resources

4NewOrleans.com
www.4neworleans.com

About.com Guide to New Orleans
neworleans.about.com/local/southeastus/neworleans

Area Guide New Orleans
neworleans.areaguides.net

BigEasy.com Guide to New Orleans
www.bigeasy.com

City Knowledge New Orleans
www.cityknowledge.com/la_neworleans.htm

CitySearch New Orleans
neworleans.citysearch.com

CityTravelGuide.com New Orleans
www.citytravelguide.com/new-orleans.htm

CrescentCity.com
www.crescentcity.com/

CuisineNet New Orleans
www.menusonline.com/cities/new_orleans/locmain.shtml

DigitalCity New Orleans
home.digitalcity.com/neworleans

Discover New Orleans
www.discoverneworleans.com/

Excite.com New Orleans City Guide
www.excite.com/travel/countries/united_states/louisiana/new_orleans

Experience New Orleans
www.neworleansweb.org/

French Quarter
www.frenchquarter.com

Gambit Weekly
www.bestofneworleans.com

Gateway New Orleans
www.gatewayno.com/

Gay New Orleans
www.gayneworleans.com

Gayot's Guide Restaurant Search New Orleans
www.perrier.com/restaurants/gayot.asp?area=NOR

Gumbo Pages
www.gumbopages.com

HotelGuide New Orleans
new.orleans.hotelguide.net

Lodging.com Metairie Louisiana
www.lodging.com/auto/guides/metairie-la.html

Lodging.com New Orleans Louisiana
www.lodging.com/auto/guides/new_orleans-area-la.html

Metairie.com
www.metairie.com

New Orleans 2fun.com
www.2fun.com

New Orleans CityLink
www.usacitylink.com/citylink/new-orleans/

New Orleans Connection
www.neworleansla.com

New Orleans from A to Z
www.neworleansatoz.com/home.htm

New Orleans Guide
nola.accesscom.net

New Orleans Home Page
www.neworleans.com

New Orleans LA Live
www.nolalive.com

New Orleans Online
www.neworleansonline.com

New Orleans Times & Directory
www.gna.com

New Orleans Visitors Guide
www.compucast.com/acquaint.html

New Orleans à la Net
www.alanet.com

Nitebeat Guide to Nightlife
www.nitebeat.com/

OffBeat Magazine
www.offbeat.com

Open World City Guides New Orleans
www.worldexecutive.com/cityguides/new_orleans/

Rough Guide Travel New Orleans
travel.roughguides.com/content/883/

Time Out New Orleans
www.timeout.com/neworleans/

Virtual New Orleans
www.virtualneworleans.com/

Virtual Voyages New Orleans
www.virtualvoyages.com/usa/la/n_o/n_o.sht

WeekendEvents.com New Orleans
www.weekendevents.com/neworleans/norleans.html

Area Communities

Incorporated communities in the seven-parish New Orleans/River Region (Jefferson, Orleans, Plaquemines, Saint Bernard, Saint Charles, Saint James, and Saint John the Baptist parishes) with populations greater than 10,000 are listed below. Another prominent, yet unincorporated, community in the New Orleans area is Metairie, which is in fact the region's second-largest community (next to New Orleans) with a population of more than 150,000.

Grenta
PO Box 404
Grenta, LA 70054
Phone: 504-363-1500
Fax: 504-363-1509

Harahan
6437 Jefferson Hwy
New Orleans, LA 70123
Phone: 504-737-6383
Fax: 504-737-6384

Kenner
1801 Williams Blvd
Kenner, LA 70062
Phone: 504-468-7200
Fax: 504-468-6633

Westwego
419 Ave A
Westwego, LA 70094
Phone: 504-341-3424
Fax: 504-341-8941

Economy

New Orleans' economy ranges from finance to higher education to aerospace. One of the nation's busiest ports, the Port of New Orleans plays a vital role not only in the region's economy, but in Louisiana's economy as a whole—10% of the state's entire workforce is employed in port-related activities. Despite a decline during the 1980s, the oil and gas industry also remains an important part of New Orleans' economic base. Major U.S. petroleum companies that have a presence in New Orleans and the River Region include Shell, ExxonMobil, and BP. New Orleans' economy has diversified significantly since the oil boom of the 1980s, and services is currently the largest employment sector in the area. Tourism and health care are among the region's fastest-growing industries.

Unemployment Rate 5.1%*
Per Capita Income $23,553*
Median Family Income $22,182

** Information given is for Orleans Parish (which is coextensive with the City of New Orleans).*

Principal Industries & Number of Wage Earners

New Orleans MSA* - 1999

Industry	Wage Earners
Construction	32,600
Finance, Insurance, & Real Estate	30,800
Government	104,000
Manufacturing	49,800
Mining	13,300
Retail Trade	116,400
Services	196,200
Transportation, Communications, & Public Utilities	40,800
Wholesale Trade	36,400

** Information given is for the New Orleans Metropolitan Statistical Area (MSA), which includes Jefferson, Orleans, Plaquemines, Saint Bernard, Saint Charles, Saint James, Saint John the Baptist, and Saint Tammany parishes.*

Major Employers

Exxon Mobil Corp
PO Box 61707
New Orleans, LA 70161
www.exxon.mobil.com/working/index.html
Phone: 504-561-3636

Hibernia Corp
313 Carondelet St
New Orleans, LA 70130
E-mail: mailus@hiberniabank.com
www.hiberniabank.com
Phone: 504-533-2858
Fax: 504-533-2297

Lockheed Martin Space Systems Co Michoud Operations
13800 Old Gentilly Rd
New Orleans, LA 70129
www.lmco.com/michoud
Phone: 504-257-3311
Fax: 504-257-4431

Louisiana State University Medical Center
433 Bolivar St
New Orleans, LA 70112
Phone: 504-568-4808
Fax: 504-568-4704

Loyola University
6363 St Charles Ave
New Orleans, LA 70118
www.loyno.edu
Phone: 504-865-2011
Fax: 504-865-3383
TF: 800-456-9652

Naval Air Station New Orleans
400 Russell Ave
New Orleans, LA 70143
www.nasjrb.nola.navy.mil
Phone: 504-678-3264
Fax: 504-678-3244

Orleans Parish School Board
3510 General Degaulle Dr
New Orleans, LA 70114
Phone: 504-365-8800
Fax: 504-365-8733

Shell Offshore Inc
701 Poydras St
New Orleans, LA 70139
Phone: 504-588-6161
Fax: 504-588-0077

Touro Infirmary
1401 Foucher St
New Orleans, LA 70115
www.touro.com
Phone: 504-897-7011
Fax: 504-897-8446

Tulane University
6823 St Charles Ave
New Orleans, LA 70118
E-mail: Undergrad.Admission@tulane.edu
www.tulane.edu
Phone: 504-865-5000
Fax: 504-862-8715

Tulane University Medical Center
1415 Tulane Ave
New Orleans, LA 70112
www.mcl.tulane.edu
Phone: 504-588-5263
Fax: 504-582-7973
TF: 800-588-5800

University of New Orleans
2000 Lakeshore Dr
New Orleans, LA 70148
E-mail: help_desk@uno.edu
www.uno.edu
Phone: 504-280-6000
Fax: 504-280-5522
TF: 800-256-5866

Whitney National Bank
228 St Charles Ave
New Orleans, LA 70130
Phone: 504-586-7272
Fax: 504-586-7383
TF: 800-347-7272

Quality of Living Indicators

Total Crime Index.....35,762
(rates per 100,000 inhabitants)

Violent Crime
Murder/manslaughter..... 159
Forcible rape..... 280
Robbery.....2,733
Aggravated assault.....2,760

Property Crime
Burglary.....5,626
Larceny theft.....17,086
Motor vehicle theft.....7,118

Cost of Living Index.....96.8
(national average = 100)

Median Home Price.....$109,100

Education

Public Schools

Orleans Parish School Board
3510 General Degaulle Dr
New Orleans, LA 70114
Phone: 504-365-8800
Fax: 504-365-8733

Number of Schools
Elementary..... 81
Middle..... 17
High..... 20
Other..... 10

Student/Teacher Ratio
All Grades..... 18.5:1

Private Schools

Number of Schools (all grades)..... 75+

Colleges & Universities

Concordia University
3229 36th St
Metairie, LA 70001
Phone: 504-828-3802
Fax: 504-828-2008

Delgado Community College
615 City Park Ave
New Orleans, LA 70119
www.dcc.edu
Phone: 504-483-4216
Fax: 504-483-4386

Dillard University
2601 Gentilly Blvd
New Orleans, LA 70122
www.dillard.edu
Phone: 504-283-8822
Fax: 504-286-4895
TF: 877-240-3838

Elaine P Nunez Community College
3710 Paris Rd
Chalmette, LA 70043
Phone: 504-278-7350
Fax: 504-278-7353

Loyola University
6363 St Charles Ave
New Orleans, LA 70118
www.loyno.edu
Phone: 504-865-2011
Fax: 504-865-3383
TF: 800-456-9652

Nicholls State University
906 E 1st St
Thibodaux, LA 70301
E-mail: nichweb@mail.nich.edu
www.nich.edu
Phone: 504-446-8111
Fax: 504-448-4929
TF: 877-642-4655

Our Lady of Holy Cross College
4123 Woodland Dr
New Orleans, LA 70131
www.olhcc.edu
Phone: 504-394-7744
Fax: 504-391-2421
TF: 800-259-7744

Southeast College of Technology
321 Veterans Memorial Blvd
Metairie, LA 70005
www.sctno.com
Phone: 504-948-7246
Fax: 504-831-6803

Southern University New Orleans
6400 Press Dr
New Orleans, LA 70126
www.suno.edu
Phone: 504-286-5000
Fax: 504-286-5131

Tulane University
6823 St Charles Ave
New Orleans, LA 70118
E-mail: Undergrad.Admission@tulane.edu
www.tulane.edu
Phone: 504-865-5000
Fax: 504-862-8715

University of New Orleans
2000 Lakeshore Dr
New Orleans, LA 70148
E-mail: help_desk@uno.edu
www.uno.edu
Phone: 504-280-6000
Fax: 504-280-5522
TF: 800-256-5866

Xavier University of Louisiana
7325 Palmetto St
New Orleans, LA 70125
E-mail: apply@mail.xula.edu
www.xula.edu
Phone: 504-486-7411
Fax: 504-482-1508

Hospitals

Chalmette Medical Center
9001 Patricia St
Chalmette, LA 70043
www.cmcuhs.com
Phone: 504-620-6000
Fax: 504-620-6162

Children's Hospital
200 Henry Clay Ave
New Orleans, LA 70118
www.chnola.org
Phone: 504-899-9511
Fax: 504-896-9708

Doctors Hospital of Jefferson
4320 Houma Blvd
Metairie, LA 70006
www.tenethealth.com/DoctorsJefferson
Phone: 504-849-4000
Fax: 504-846-3004

East Jefferson General Hospital
4200 Houma Blvd
Metairie, LA 70006
www.eastjeffhospital.org
Phone: 504-454-4000
Fax: 504-456-8151

Kenner Regional Medical Center
180 W Esplanade Ave
Kenner, LA 70065
Phone: 504-468-8600
Fax: 504-464-8256

Lakeland Medical Center
6000 Bullard Ave
New Orleans, LA 70128
Phone: 504-241-6335
Fax: 504-243-3370

Lakeside Hospital
4700 I-10 Service Rd
Metairie, LA 70001
Phone: 504-885-3333
Fax: 504-780-4374

Meadowcrest Hospital
2500 Belle Chasse Hwy
Gretna, LA 70056
www.tenethealth.com/Meadowcrest
Phone: 504-392-3131
Fax: 504-391-5498

Medical Center of Louisiana at New Orleans
1532 Tulane Ave
New Orleans, LA 70112
Phone: 504-568-2311
Fax: 504-568-2028

Memorial Medical Center
2700 Napoleon Ave Baptist Campus
New Orleans, LA 70115
Phone: 504-899-9311
Fax: 504-897-4418

Ochsner Foundation Hospital
1516 Jefferson Hwy
New Orleans, LA 70121
www.ochsner.org
Phone: 504-842-3000
Fax: 504-842-3434
TF: 800-928-6247

Pendleton Memorial Methodist Hospital
5620 Read Blvd
New Orleans, LA 70127
Phone: 504-244-5100
Fax: 504-244-5841

River Parishes Hospital
500 Rue de Sante
LaPlace, LA 70068
Phone: 504-652-7000
Fax: 504-652-5161

Saint Charles General Hospital
3700 St Charles Ave
New Orleans, LA 70115
www.tenethealth.com/StCharles
Phone: 504-899-7441
Fax: 504-899-3174

Saint Cloud Medical Center
3419 St Claude Ave
New Orleans, LA 70117
Phone: 504-948-8200
Fax: 504-948-8208

Touro Infirmary
1401 Foucher St
New Orleans, LA 70115
www.touro.com
Phone: 504-897-7011
Fax: 504-897-8446

Tulane University Medical Center
1415 Tulane Ave
New Orleans, LA 70112
www.mcl.tulane.edu
Phone: 504-588-5263
Fax: 504-582-7973
TF: 800-588-5800

University Hospital of Medical Center of Louisiana
2021 Perdido St
New Orleans, LA 70112
Phone: 504-588-3000
Fax: 504-524-7584

Veterans Affairs Medical Center
1601 Perdido St
New Orleans, LA 70112
Phone: 504-568-0811
Fax: 504-619-4110
TF: 800-935-8387

West Jefferson Medical Center
1101 Medical Center Blvd
Marrero, LA 70072
Phone: 504-347-5511
Fax: 504-349-1319

Transportation

Airport(s)

New Orleans International Airport (MSY)
14 miles NW of downtown (approx 20 minutes) . . .504-464-0831

Mass Transit

Mass Transit RTA
$1.25 Base fare 504-248-3900

Rail/Bus

Amtrak Station
1001 Loyola Ave
New Orleans, LA 70113
Phone: 504-528-1610
TF: 800-872-7245

Greyhound/Trailways Bus Station
1001 Loyola Ave
New Orleans, LA 70113
Phone: 504-525-6075
TF: 800-231-2222

Utilities

Electricity
Entergy 800-368-3749
www.entergy.com

Gas
Entergy 800-368-3749
www.entergy.com

Water
New Orleans Sewerage & Water Board 504-529-2837

Garbage Collection/Recycling
Orleans Parish Sanitation Dept 504-299-3673

Telecommunications

Telephone
BellSouth 800-832-0679
www.bellsouth.com

Cable Television
Cox Communications 504-304-7345
www.cox.com

Internet Service Providers (ISPs)
Greater New Orleans Free-Net (GNOFN) 504-539-9242
www.gnofn.org
Verio New Orleans 504-636-3800
home.verio.net/local/frontpage.cfm?AirportCode=MSY

Banks

AmSouth Bank
321 St Charles Ave
New Orleans, LA 70130
Phone: 504-838-4533
Fax: 504-525-4072

Bank of Louisiana
300 St Charles Ave
New Orleans, LA 70130
Phone: 504-592-0600
Fax: 504-592-0606

Bank One Louisiana NA
201 St Charles Ave
New Orleans, LA 70170
Phone: 504-623-8413
Fax: 504-623-8416
TF: 800-777-8837

Crescent Bank & Trust
1100 Poydras St Suite 100
New Orleans, LA 70163
Phone: 504-556-5950
Fax: 504-552-4467

Dryades Savings Bank FSB
231 Carondelet St Suite 200
New Orleans, LA 70130
Phone: 504-581-5891
Fax: 504-598-7233

Federal Reserve Bank
525 St Charles Ave
New Orleans, LA 70130
Phone: 504-593-3200
Fax: 504-593-5831
TF: 800-562-9023

First Bank & Trust
909 Poydras St Suite 100
New Orleans, LA 70112
Phone: 504-584-5900
Fax: 504-584-5902

Greater New Orleans Homestead FSB
5435 Magazine St
New Orleans, LA 70115
Phone: 504-897-9751

Gulf Coast Bank & Trust Co
200 St Charles Ave
New Orleans, LA 70130
Phone: 504-581-4561
Fax: 504-392-3031

Hibernia National Bank
313 Carondelet St
New Orleans, LA 70112
E-mail: mailus@hiberniabank.com
www.hiberniabank.com
Phone: 504-533-3333
Fax: 504-533-2367
TF: 800-562-9007

Iberia Bank
9300 Jefferson Hwy
New Orleans, LA 70123
Phone: 504-363-7873
Fax: 504-363-7973

Liberty Bank & Trust Co
1950 St Bernard Ave
New Orleans, LA 70116
Phone: 504-941-6471
Fax: 504-483-6654

Omni Bank
330 Carondelet St
New Orleans, LA 70130
Phone: 504-833-2900
Fax: 504-841-2183

Regions Bank
301 St Charles Ave
New Orleans, LA 70130
Phone: 504-584-1382
Fax: 504-565-3109
TF: 800-888-1655

Schwegmann Bank & Trust Co
6600 Franklin Ave
New Orleans, LA 70122
Phone: 504-883-5132
Fax: 504-883-5135

United Bank & Trust Co
2714 Canal St Suite 100
New Orleans, LA 70119
Phone: 504-827-0060
Fax: 504-827-0059

Whitney National Bank
228 St Charles Ave
New Orleans, LA 70130
Phone: 504-586-7272
Fax: 504-586-7383
TF: 800-347-7272

Shopping

Canal Place
333 Canal St
New Orleans, LA 70130
Phone: 504-522-9200
Fax: 504-522-0866

Clearview Shopping Center
4436 Veterans Memorial Blvd
Metairie, LA 70006
Phone: 504-885-0202
Fax: 504-885-4100

Esplanade The
1401 W Esplanade Ave
Kenner, LA 70065
Phone: 504-468-6116
Fax: 504-466-9502

French Market Corp
1008 N Peters St
New Orleans, LA 70116
Phone: 504-522-2621
Fax: 504-596-3419

Jackson Brewery Mall
600 Decatur St
New Orleans, LA 70130
Phone: 504-566-7245

Lakeside Shopping Center
3301 Veterans Memorial Blvd
Metairie, LA 70002
Phone: 504-835-8000
Fax: 504-831-1170

Macy's
1400 Poydras St
New Orleans, LA 70112
Phone: 504-592-5985

New Orleans Centre
1400 Poydras St
New Orleans, LA 70112
Phone: 504-568-0000
Fax: 504-595-8870

Plaza Shopping Center
5700 Read Blvd
New Orleans, LA 70127
Phone: 504-246-1500
Fax: 504-246-9222

Riverwalk Marketplace
1 Poydras St Suite 101
New Orleans, LA 70130
www.riverwalkmarketplace.com
Phone: 504-522-1555
Fax: 504-586-8532

Rosedale Mall
3780 Veterans Memorial Blvd
Metairie, LA 70002
Phone: 504-455-3678
Fax: 504-455-3373

Royal Street District
828 Royal St
New Orleans, LA 70116
www.royalstreetguild.com
Phone: 504-524-1260
Fax: 504-393-9117

Saks Fifth Avenue
301 Canal St
New Orleans, LA 70130
Phone: 504-524-2200
Fax: 504-529-2323

Slidell Factory Stores
1000 Caruso Blvd
Slidell, LA 70461
Phone: 504-646-0756
Fax: 504-646-0758

Uptown Square
200 Broadway St
New Orleans, LA 70118
Phone: 504-866-4513

Westgate Shopping Center
4941 Yale St
Metairie, LA 70006
Phone: 504-455-1283

Media

Newspapers and Magazines

Gambit Weekly
3923 Bienville St
New Orleans, LA 70119
E-mail: response@gambitweekly.com
www.bestofneworleans.com
Phone: 504-486-5900
Fax: 504-483-3159

Louisiana Life
111 Veterans Memorial Blvd Suite 1810
Metairie, LA 70005
www.neworleans.com/lalife/
Phone: 504-834-9292
Fax: 504-838-7700
TF: 877-221-3512

New Orleans City Business
111 Veterans Memorial Blvd Suite 1810
Metairie, LA 70005
E-mail: citybiz@nopg.com
citybusiness.neworleans.com
Phone: 504-834-9292
Fax: 504-832-3550

New Orleans Magazine
111 Veterans Memorial Blvd Suite 1810
Metairie, LA 70005
www.neworleans.com/no_magazine/
Phone: 504-831-3731
Fax: 504-838-7700

Times-Picayune*
3800 Howard Ave
New Orleans, LA 70140
www.nola.com
Phone: 504-826-3279
Fax: 504-826-3007
TF: 800-925-0000

Where New Orleans Magazine
528 Wilkinson Row
New Orleans, LA 70130
E-mail: wneworlean@aol.com
www.whereneworleans.com
Phone: 504-522-6468
Fax: 504-522-0018

**Indicates major daily newspapers*

Television

WDSU-TV Ch 6 (NBC)
846 Howard Ave
New Orleans, LA 70113
E-mail: wdsu@comm.net
www.wdsu.com
Phone: 504-679-0600
Fax: 504-679-0733

WGNO-TV Ch 26 (ABC)
2 Canal St World Trade Ctr Suite 2800
New Orleans, LA 70130
E-mail: wgno-tv@tribune.com
www.abc26.com
Phone: 504-581-2600
Fax: 504-619-6332

WHNO-TV Ch 20 (Ind)
1100 S Jefferson Davis Pkwy
New Orleans, LA 70125
www.whno.com
Phone: 504-822-1920
Fax: 504-822-2060

WLAE-TV Ch 32 (PBS)
2929 S Carrollton Ave
New Orleans, LA 70118
E-mail: info@wlae.pbs.org
www.pbs.org/wlae/
Phone: 504-866-7411
Fax: 504-861-5186

WNOL-TV Ch 38 (WB)
1400 Poydras St Suite 745
New Orleans, LA 70112
E-mail: wnol@comm.net
www.wnol.com
Phone: 504-525-3838
Fax: 504-569-0908

WPXL-TV Ch 49 (PAX)
3900 Veterans Blvd Suite 202
Metairie, LA 70002
www.pax.net/WPXL
Phone: 504-887-9795
Fax: 504-887-1518

WUPL-TV Ch 54 (UPN)
3850 N Causeway Blvd Suite 454
Metairie, LA 70002
www.paramountstations.com/WUPL
Phone: 504-828-5454
Fax: 504-828-5455

WVUE-TV Ch 8 (Fox)
1025 S Jefferson Davis Pkwy
New Orleans, LA 70125
Phone: 504-486-6161
Fax: 504-483-1212

WWL-TV Ch 4 (CBS)
1024 N Rampart St
New Orleans, LA 70116
www.wwltv.com
Phone: 504-529-4444
Fax: 504-529-6472

WYES-TV Ch 12 (PBS)
916 Navarre Ave
New Orleans, LA 70124
E-mail: assist@wyes.pbs.org
www.pbs.org/wyes/
Phone: 504-486-5511
Fax: 504-483-8408

Radio

KKND-FM 106.7 MHz (Alt)
929 Howard Ave 2nd Fl
New Orleans, LA 70113
www.1067theend.com
Phone: 504-679-7300
Fax: 504-679-7345

KMEZ-FM 102.9 MHz (Urban)
201 Saint Charles Suite 201
New Orleans, LA 70170
Phone: 504-581-7002
Fax: 504-566-4857

KUMX-FM 104.1 MHz (CHR)
929 Howard Ave 2nd Fl
New Orleans, LA 70113
E-mail: request@themixmail.com
www.themix1041.com
Phone: 504-679-7300
Fax: 504-679-7358

WBOK-AM 1230 kHz (Rel)
1639 Gentilly Blvd
New Orleans, LA 70119
Phone: 504-943-4600
Fax: 504-944-4662

WBSN-FM 89.1 MHz (Rel)
3939 Gentilly Blvd
New Orleans, LA 70126
E-mail: info@lifesongs.com
www.wbsn.com
Phone: 504-286-3600
Fax: 504-286-3580

WBYU-AM 1450 kHz (B/EZ)
201 St Charles Ave
New Orleans, LA 70170
Phone: 504-581-7002
Fax: 504-566-4857

WCKW-FM 92.3 MHz (Rock)
3501 N Causeway Blvd Suite 700
Metairie, LA 70002
www.wckw.com
Phone: 504-831-8811
Fax: 504-831-8885

WEZB-FM 97.1 MHz (CHR)
3525 N Causeway Blvd Suite 1053
New Orleans, LA 70002
Phone: 504-834-9587
Fax: 504-834-9689

WGSO-AM 990 kHz (N/T)
111 Veterans Memorial Blvd Suite 1800
Metairie, LA 70005
www.wgsoradio.com
Phone: 504-834-9292
Fax: 504-838-7700

WLMG-FM 101.9 MHz (AC)
3525 N Causeway Blvd Suite 1053
Metairie, LA 70002
E-mail: info@magic1019.com
www.magic1019.com
Phone: 504-834-9587
Fax: 504-833-8560

WLNO-AM 1060 kHz (Rel)
401 Whitney Ave
Gretna, LA 70056
E-mail: wlno@communique.net
www.wlno.com
Phone: 504-362-9800
Fax: 504-362-5541

WLTS-FM 105.3 MHz (AC)
3525 N Causeway Blvd Suite 1053
Metairie, LA 70002
Phone: 504-834-9587
Fax: 504-833-8560

WNOE-FM 101.1 MHz (Ctry)
929 Howard Ave
New Orleans, LA 70113
www.wnoe.com
Phone: 504-679-7300
Fax: 504-679-7345

WODT-AM 1280 kHz (Urban)
2228 Gravier St
New Orleans, LA 70119
Phone: 504-827-6000
Fax: 504-827-6048

WQUE-FM 93.3 MHz (Urban)
2228 Gravier St
New Orleans, LA 70119
E-mail: email@q93mail.com
www.q93.com
Phone: 504-827-6000
Fax: 504-827-6045

WRNO-FM 99.5 MHz (CR)
201 St Charles Ave Suite 201
New Orleans, LA 70170
www.wrno.com
Phone: 504-581-7002
Fax: 504-566-4857

WSHO-AM 800 kHz (Rel)
1001 Howard Ave Suite 4304
New Orleans, LA 70113
E-mail: wsho@compuserve.com
www.wsho.com
Phone: 504-527-0800
Fax: 504-527-0881

WSMB-AM 1350 kHz (Sports)
1450 Poydras St Suite 440
New Orleans, LA 70112
Phone: 504-593-2100
Fax: 504-593-1850

WTIX-FM 94.3 MHz (Oldies)
4539 I-10 Service Rd 3rd Fl
Metairie, LA 70006
Phone: 504-454-9000
Fax: 504-454-9506

WTKL-FM 95.7 MHz (Oldies)
1450 Poydras Suite 440
New Orleans, LA 70112
www.kool957.com
Phone: 504-593-6376
Fax: 504-593-1865

WVOG-AM 600 kHz (Rel)
2730 Loumor Ave
Metairie, LA 70001
Phone: 504-831-6941

WWL-AM 870 kHz (N/T)
1450 Poydras St Suite 440
New Orleans, LA 70112
www.wwl870am.com
Phone: 504-593-6376
Fax: 504-593-1850

WWNO-FM 89.9 MHz (NPR)
University of New Orleans Lake Front Campus
New Orleans, LA 70148
E-mail: wwno@www.uno.edu
wwno.uno.edu
Phone: 504-280-7000
Fax: 504-280-6061

WWOZ-FM 90.7 MHz (Urban)
1201 Saint Philip St
New Orleans, LA 70116
E-mail: wwoz@gnofn.org
www.wwoz.org
Phone: 504-568-1239
Fax: 504-558-9332

WYLD-AM 940 kHz (Rel)
2228 Gravier St
New Orleans, LA 70119
Phone: 504-827-6000
Fax: 504-827-6048

WYLD-FM 98.5 MHz (Urban)
2228 Gravier St
New Orleans, LA 70119
www.wyldfm.com
Phone: 504-827-6000
Fax: 504-827-6045

Attractions

New Orleans is a unique blend of several distinct cultures, and the legacy of its Cajun, Creole, and Santo Domingan heritage is reflected in the city's music, food, architecture, and religion. The 100 square blocks of the Historic French Quarter, with its wrought iron balconies and secluded courtyards, offer exotic Creole cuisine and some of the area's finest jazz, especially along Bourbon Street. The Saint Charles Avenue streetcar travels to the more formal Uptown area, with its Garden District of pre-Civil War homes. Along River Avenue, as well as in outlying areas, are many restored plantations and "Louisiana cottages." Each year people come from all over the country to celebrate Mardi Gras in New Orleans, and the two weeks before Lent are filled with non-stop parties, parades, costume balls, and street festivals. In late April, the city hosts the annual Jazz and Heritage Festival.

American Italian Renaissance Foundation Museum
537 S Peters St
New Orleans, LA 70130
www.airf.com
Phone: 504-522-7294
Fax: 504-522-1657

Aquarium of the Americas
1 Canal St
New Orleans, LA 70130
Phone: 504-565-3033
Fax: 504-565-3010
TF: 800-774-7394

Audubon Institute
PO Box 4327
New Orleans, LA 70178
www.auduboninstitute.org
Phone: 504-861-2537
Fax: 504-866-0819

Audubon Park
6500 Magazine St
New Orleans, LA 70118
www.auduboninstitute.org/html/parks_audubon.html
Phone: 504-565-3020

Audubon Zoological Gardens
PO Box 5327
New Orleans, LA 70178
www.auduboninstitute.org/html/aa_zoomain.html
Phone: 504-581-5629
Fax: 504-565-3865

Bally's Casino
1 Stars & Stripes Blvd
New Orleans, LA 70126
www.ballysno.com
Phone: 504-248-3200
Fax: 504-248-3283
TF: 800-572-2559

BAND-Black Arts National Diaspora Inc
1530 N Claiborne Ave
New Orleans, LA 70116
E-mail: band@gnofn.org
www.gnofn.org/~band
Phone: 504-949-2263
Fax: 504-949-6052
TF: 888-535-2263

Bayou Segnette State Park
7777 Westbank Expy
Westwego, LA 70094
www.crt.state.la.us/crt/parks/bayouseg/byusegne.htm
Phone: 504-736-7140
Fax: 504-436-4788
TF: 888-677-2296

Cajun Queen Riverboat
Canal St Wharf
New Orleans, LA 70130
www.bigeasy.com/rivercruises/cajunqueenmad.htm
Phone: 504-529-4567
Fax: 504-524-6265
TF: 800-445-4109

Cane River Creole National Historical Park & Heritage Area
4386 Hwy 494
Natchez, LA 71456
www.nps.gov/cari/
Phone: 318-352-0383
Fax: 318-352-4549

Cannes Brulee Native American Center
303 Williams Blvd Rivertown
Kenner, LA 70062
Phone: 504-468-7231
Fax: 504-471-2159
TF: 800-473-6789

Carousel Gardens in City Park
Dreyfus Ave
New Orleans, LA 70124
Phone: 504-482-4888
Fax: 504-483-9412

Celebration Station Entertainment Complex
5959 Veterans Memorial Blvd
Metairie, LA 70003
www.celebrationstation.com
Phone: 504-887-7888
Fax: 504-888-8404

Children's Castle
503 Williams Blvd Rivertown
Kenner, LA 70062
Phone: 504-468-7231
Fax: 504-471-2159
TF: 800-473-6789

City Park
1 Palm Dr
New Orleans, LA 70124
Phone: 504-482-4888
Fax: 504-483-9412

Confederate Museum
929 Camp St
New Orleans, LA 70130
www.confederatemuseum.com
Phone: 504-523-4522

Contemporary Arts Center
900 Camp St
New Orleans, LA 70130
www.cacno.org
Phone: 504-523-1216
Fax: 504-528-3828

Cytec Louisiana Wildlife & Fisheries Museum
303 Williams Blvd Rivertown
Kenner, LA 70062
Phone: 504-468-7231
Fax: 504-471-2159

Daily Living Science Center
409 Williams Blvd
Kenner, LA 70062
Phone: 504-468-7231
Fax: 504-468-7599

Delta Festival Ballet
3850 N Causeway Blvd Suite 119
Metairie, LA 70002
Phone: 504-836-7166
Fax: 504-836-7167

Delta Queen Steamboat Co
1380 Port of New Orleans Pl Robin Street Wharf
New Orleans, LA 70130
www.deltaqueen.com
Phone: 504-586-0631
Fax: 504-585-0630
TF: 800-543-7637

Destrehan Plantation
13034 River Rd
Destrehan, LA 70047
E-mail: destplan@aol.com
www.destrehanplantation.org
Phone: 504-764-9315
Fax: 504-725-1929

Elms Mansion
3029 St Charles Ave
New Orleans, LA 70115
www.elmsmansion.com
Phone: 504-895-5493
Fax: 504-899-3231

Entergy IMAX Theater
1 Canal St Aquarium of the Americas
New Orleans, LA 70130
www.auduboninstitute.org/html/aa_imaxmain.html
Phone: 504-565-3033

Fine Arts Gallery of New Orleans
636 Burdette St
New Orleans, LA 70118
www.fineartsgallery.com
Phone: 504-866-4287
Fax: 504-866-4287

Freeport Memoran Daily Living Science Center
409 Williams Blvd Rivertown
Kenner, LA 70062
Phone: 504-468-7231
Fax: 504-471-2159
TF: 800-473-6789

Gallery for Fine Photography
322 Royal St
New Orleans, LA 70130
www.agallery.com
Phone: 504-568-1313
Fax: 504-568-1322

Gallier House Museum
1132 Royal St
New Orleans, LA 70116
E-mail: hggh@gnofn.org
www.gnofn.org/~hggh/
Phone: 504-525-5661
Fax: 504-568-9735

Harrah's Casino Hotel New Orleans
512 S Peter St
New Orleans, LA 70130
www.harrahsneworleans.com
Phone: 504-533-6000
TF: 800-427-7247

Hermann-Grima House
820 Saint Louis St
New Orleans, LA 70112
www.gnofn.org/~hggh
Phone: 504-525-5661
Fax: 504-568-9735

Historic New Orleans Collection
533 Royal St
New Orleans, LA 70130
E-mail: hnocinfo@hnoc.org
www.hnoc.org/
Phone: 504-523-4662
Fax: 504-598-7108

House of Broel's Historic Mansion & Dollhouse Museum
2220 St Charles Ave
New Orleans, LA 70130
www.houseofbroel.com
Phone: 504-525-1000
Fax: 504-524-6775

Jackson Barracks Military Museum
6400 St Claude Ave
New Orleans, LA 70146
E-mail: jbmuseum@cmq.com
www.la.ngb.army.mil/jbmm.htm
Phone: 504-278-8242
Fax: 504-278-8614

Jean Lafitte National Historical Park & Preserve
365 Canal St Suite 2400
New Orleans, LA 70130
www.nps.gov/jela/
Phone: 504-589-3882
Fax: 504-589-3851

Lil' Cajun Swamp Tours
Hwy 301
Crown Point, LA 70072
Phone: 504-689-3213
Fax: 504-689-3213
TF: 800-689-3213

Longue Vue House & Gardens
7 Bamboo Rd
New Orleans, LA 70124
www.longuevue.com
Phone: 504-488-5488
Fax: 504-486-7015

Louisiana Children's Museum
420 Julia St
New Orleans, LA 70130
www.lcm.org
Phone: 504-523-1357
Fax: 504-529-3666

Louisiana Nature Center
PO Box 870610
New Orleans, LA 70187
www.auduboninstitute.org/html/aa_lancmain.html
Phone: 504-246-5672
Fax: 504-242-1889

Louisiana Philharmonic Orchestra
305 Baronne St Suite 600
New Orleans, LA 70112
E-mail: lpo@gnofn.org
www.gnofn.org/~lpo/index.html
Phone: 504-523-6530
Fax: 504-595-8468

Louisiana State Museum
751 Chartres St
New Orleans, LA 70116
lsm.crt.state.la.us
Phone: 504-568-6968
Fax: 504-568-4995
TF: 800-568-6968

Louisiana Toy Train Museum
519 Williams Blvd Rivertown
Kenner, LA 70062
Phone: 504-468-7231
Fax: 504-471-2159

Louisiana Wildlife Museum
303 Williams Blvd Rivertown
Kenner, LA 70062
Phone: 504-468-7231
Fax: 504-471-2159

Mahalia Jackson Theatre of Performing Arts
801 N Rampart St
New Orleans, LA 70116
Phone: 504-565-7470
Fax: 504-565-7477

Mardi Gras World
233 Newton St Take free ferry from Canal St
New Orleans, LA 70114
www.mardigrasday.com/world.html
Phone: 504-361-7821
Fax: 504-361-3164
TF: 800-362-8213

Mississippi River Cruises
Toulouse St Wharf
New Orleans, LA 70130
Phone: 800-233-2628

Musée Conti-Wax Museum of Louisiana Legends
917 Rue Conti French Quarter
New Orleans, LA 70112
E-mail: sales@get-waxed.com
www.get-waxed.com
Phone: 504-525-2605
Fax: 504-566-7636

Natchez Steamboat
2 Canal St
New Orleans, LA 70130
E-mail: natchez@nosteamboat.com
www.nosteamboat.com
Phone: 504-586-8777
Fax: 504-587-0708
TF: 800-233-2628

National D-Day Museum
945 Magazine St
New Orleans, LA 70130
E-mail: info@ddaymuseum.org
www.ddaymuseum.org
Phone: 504-527-6012
Fax: 504-527-6088

New Orleans Historic Voodoo Museum
724 Dumaine St
New Orleans, LA 70116
E-mail: voodoo@voodoomuseum.com
www.voodoomuseum.com/
Phone: 504-522-5223
Fax: 504-523-8591

New Orleans Jazz National Historical Park
365 Canal St Suite 2400
New Orleans, LA 70130
www.nps.gov/neor/
Phone: 504-589-4806
Fax: 504-589-3865

New Orleans Museum of Art
1 Collins Diboll Cir
New Orleans, LA 70124
www.noma.org
Phone: 504-488-2631
Fax: 504-484-6662

New Orleans Opera Assn
305 Baronne St Suite 500
New Orleans, LA 70112
www.neworleansopera.org
Phone: 504-529-2278
Fax: 504-529-7668
TF: 800-881-4459

New Orleans Pharmacy Museum
514 Chartres St
New Orleans, LA 70130
E-mail: info@pharmacymuseum.org
www.pharmacymuseum.org
Phone: 504-565-8027
Fax: 504-565-8028

New Orleans School of Glass Works & Printmaking Studio
727 Magazine St
New Orleans, LA 70130
Phone: 504-529-7277
Fax: 504-539-5417

Old Absinthe House Bar
400 Bourbon St
New Orleans, LA 70130
Phone: 504-525-8108

Pitot House Museum
1440 Moss St
New Orleans, LA 70119
Phone: 504-482-0312
Fax: 504-482-0312

Pontchartrain Astronomy Society Observatory
409 Williams Blvd Rivertown
Kenner, LA 70062
Phone: 504-468-7231
Fax: 504-471-2159

Preservation Hall
726 Saint Peters St
New Orleans, LA 70116
www.preservationhall.com
Phone: 504-522-2841
Fax: 504-558-9192

Rivertown USA
405 Williams Blvd
Kenner, LA 70062
www.kenner.la.us
Phone: 504-468-7231

Riverwalk
1 Poydras St Suite 101
New Orleans, LA 70130
Phone: 504-522-1555
Fax: 504-586-8532

Saenger Theatre of the Creative & Performing Arts
143 N Rampart St
New Orleans, LA 70112
www.saengertheatre.com
Phone: 504-525-1052
Fax: 504-569-1533

Saint Louis Cathedral
615 Père Antoine Alley
New Orleans, LA 70116
Phone: 504-525-9585
Fax: 504-525-9583

Saints Hall of Fame Museum
409 Williams Blvd Rivertown
Kenner, LA 70062
www.kenner.la.us/saints.html
Phone: 504-468-7231
Fax: 504-471-2159

Southern Rep Theatre
333 Canal St
New Orleans, LA 70130
www.southernrep.com
Phone: 504-861-8163
Fax: 504-861-5875

Treasure Chest Casino
5050 Williams Blvd
Kenner, LA 70065
www.treasurechest.com
Phone: 504-443-8000
Fax: 504-443-8104
TF: 800-298-0711

Treasure Chest Casino Presents Mardi Gras Museum
421 Williams Blvd Rivertown
Kenner, LA 70062
Phone: 504-468-7231
Fax: 504-471-2159
TF: 800-473-6789

Sports Teams & Facilities

Fair Grounds Race Course
1751 Gentilly Blvd
New Orleans, LA 70119
www.fgno.com
Phone: 504-944-5515
Fax: 504-944-1211
TF: 800-786-0010

Kiefer Uno Lakefront Arena
6801 Franklin Ave
New Orleans, LA 70122
Phone: 504-280-7222
Fax: 504-280-7178

Louisiana Superdome
Sugar Bowl Dr
New Orleans, LA 70112
www.superdome.com
Phone: 504-587-3663
Fax: 504-587-3848
TF: 800-756-7074

New Orleans Arena
1501 Girod St
New Orleans, LA 70113
E-mail: arenaticketing@superdome.com
www.neworleansarena.com
Phone: 504-846-5959

New Orleans Brass (hockey)
1600 Girod St New Orleans Arena
New Orleans, LA 70113
www.brasshockey.com
Phone: 504-522-7825
Fax: 504-523-7295

New Orleans Saints
Sugar Bowl Dr Louisiana Superdome
New Orleans, LA 70112
www.neworleanssaints.com
Phone: 504-731-1700
Fax: 504-731-1888
TF: 800-241-3011

New Orleans Zephyrs (baseball)
6000 Airline Dr Zephyr Field
Metairie, LA 70003
www.insideneworleans.com/zephyrs
Phone: 504-734-5155
Fax: 504-734-5118

Annual Events

Bayou Classic Football Game (late November) 504-587-3663
Boo at the Zoo (late October) 504-861-2537
Celebration in the Oaks (late November-early January) 504-488-2896
Celtic Nations Heritage Festival of Louisiana (late October) 504-486-1113
Chinese New Year Festival (late January) 504-482-6682
Christmas in July (late July) 504-465-9985
Christmas Tree Lighting (early December) 504-363-1580
Christmas Village (late November-mid-December) 504-468-7293
Collector's Festival (late September) 504-363-1580
Compaq Classic of New Orleans (early May) 504-831-4653
Crescent City Classic (mid-April) 504-861-8686
Destrehan Plantation Fall Festival (mid-November) 504-764-9315
Earth Fest (late March) 504-861-2537
Essence Music Festival (early July) 504-523-5652
Family Day (early October) 504-468-7293
French Quarter Festival (mid-April) 504-522-5730
Fête d'Amérique (late May) 504-581-9569
Go Fourth on the River (July 4) 504-528-9994
Great French Market Tomato Festival (early June) 504-522-2621
Greek Festival (late May) 504-282-0259
Gretna Heritage Festival (early October) 504-363-1580
Gumbo Festival (mid-October) 504-436-4712
Halloween in New Orleans (late October) 800-672-6124
Holly Jolly Christmas Bonfires (mid-December) 504-468-7293
Jeff Fest (mid-October) 504-888-2900
Los Islenos Festival (late March) 504-682-0862
Louisiana Black Heritage Festival (mid-March) 504-827-0112
Louisiana Crawfish Festival (early May) 337-332-6655
Louisiana Railroad Festival (mid-November) 504-363-1580
Louisiana Shrimp & Petroleum Festival (late August-early September) 504-385-0703
Lundi Gras (mid-February) 504-566-5005
Mardi Gras (late February) 504-566-5011
Mensaje's Spanish Festival (mid-October-early November) 504-468-7527
New Orleans Boat Show (early February) 504-846-4446
New Orleans Christmas (December) 504-522-5730
New Orleans Film & Video Festival (early-mid-October) 504-523-3818
New Orleans Jazz & Heritage Festival (late April-early May) 504-522-4786
New Orleans Wine & Food Experience (mid-July) 504-529-9463
New Year's Eve Countdown (December 31) 504-566-5011
Nokia Sugar Bowl Mardi Gras Marathon (early February) 504-525-8573
Oktoberfest (late September-late October) 504-566-5011
Pet Fest (late September) 504-734-7590
Reggae Riddums International Arts Festival (mid-June) 504-367-1313
Saint Joseph's Day Festivities (mid-March) 504-522-7294
Saint Patrick's Day Parade (mid-March) 504-525-5169
Spring Fiesta (mid-March) 504-581-1367
Sugar Bowl (January) 504-525-8573
Swamp Festival (early-mid-October) 504-861-2537
Sweet Arts & Beaux Arts Ball (mid-February) 504-528-3805
Tennessee Wiliams/New Orleans Literary Festival (late March) 504-581-1144
Veteran's Day Program (November 11) 504-363-1580
Westwego Festival (mid-September) 504-436-0812
Winn-Dixie Showdown (late February) 504-587-3663

New York, New York

County: **New York**

NEW YORK CITY is located in southeastern New York State on the Hudson and East Rivers and New York Bay. New York City is composed of five boroughs, each of which is coextensive with a county in New York State. These include Brooklyn (Kings County), Bronx (Bronx County), Manhattan (New York County), Queens (Queens County), and Staten Island (Richmond County). Major cities within 100 miles include Newark, New Jersey; Philadelphia, Pennsylvania; and Bridgeport, Norwalk, and Hartford, Connecticut.

Area (Land)	308.9 sq mi
Area (Water)	159.0 sq mi
Elevation	87 ft
Latitude	40-45-06 N
Longitude	73-59-39 W
Time Zone	EST
Area Code	212, 718

Climate

New York City has a continental climate that is strongly influenced by its proximity to the Atlantic Ocean. Winters are cold, with average high temperatures in the upper 30s and low 40s, and average lows in the high 20s. The average annual snowfall in New York City is just under 30 inches. The ocean's influence, however, keeps periods of extreme cold relatively short. Summers are warm and very humid, with average highs in the low 80s and lows in the mid-60s, but the sea breezes help to bring relief from prolonged periods of extreme heat. July is the wettest month in New York City; February is the driest.

Average Temperatures & Precipitation

Temperatures

	Jan	Feb	Mar	Apr	May	Jun	Jul	Aug	Sep	Oct	Nov	Dec
High	37	39	48	59	70	79	84	82	75	64	53	42
Low	26	27	35	44	54	63	69	68	61	51	42	31

Precipitation

	Jan	Feb	Mar	Apr	May	Jun	Jul	Aug	Sep	Oct	Nov	Dec
Inches	3.0	2.9	3.6	3.8	3.8	3.6	4.1	3.8	3.4	3.0	3.8	3.4

History

Originally inhabited by the Algonquian and Iroquois tribes, the area known today as New York City was first explored by Europeans in the early 16th Century when Italian navigator Giovanni da Verrazano visited the area. In 1609, the Dutch sent Henry Hudson to explore the region via the river that now bears his name. Fifteen years later, the Dutch West India Company established a colony called New Netherlands in the area, and in 1625 a Dutch trading post named New Amsterdam was established at the tip of Manhattan Island. Permanent white settlement began in the area the following year. Further colonization took place during the mid-1600s in the surrounding region as four other settlements were established—Bronx (located north of Manhattan, attached to the mainland), Staten Island (located southwest of Manhattan across New York Bay), Brooklyn, and Queens (both of which are located southeast of Manhattan on the western portion of Long Island). Control of New Amsterdam shifted between the Dutch and the English during the mid-17th Century, until the signing of the Treaty of Westminster in 1674, at which time the English gained permanent control and renamed the settlement "New York."

With its sheltered harbor, New York gradually developed as a maritime trade center. In 1776, during the American Revolution, the settlement was occupied by British troops as a result of the Battle of Long Island and remained so until the end of the war. New York City served as the capital of the United States for a brief period, from 1789-1790, by which time it had already become the largest city in the country. It also served as the state capital of New York until 1797.

The 19th Century was a time of phenomenal growth in New York City. The opening of the Erie Canal in 1825, which linked the Hudson River to the Great Lakes region, stimulated the growth and development of the finance, insurance, and manufacturing industries in New York City. About that time, a massive influx of European immigrants began arriving in New York, primarily from Germany, Ireland, and Italy. Between 1820 and 1850, the city's population quadrupled in size. Immigration continued throughout the 19th Century, as hundreds of thousands of foreigners entered the country through New York City, many of them settling in the area. By the late 1800s, the origin of the dominant ethnic groups arriving in New York shifted from western Europe to eastern and southern Europe and China. The various ethnic groups tended to congregate in specific areas, and many neighborhoods in New York's boroughs still have a distinct ethnic flavor.

During the late 19th Century, Manhattan was linked with its neighboring islands by a number of suspension bridges, the first of which—the world-famous Brooklyn Bridge—was built in 1883 by noted engineers John and Washington Roebling. This new wave of bridge construction led to the consolidation in 1898 of the five boroughs—Manhattan, Brooklyn, Bronx, Queens, and Staten Island—that comprise present-day New York City. (Staten Island was accessible only by ferry until the Verrazano-Narrows Bridge was completed in 1964, linking the Island with Brooklyn). Growth continued into the 20th Century, and New York's population became increasingly diverse, as African-Americans from the southern United States as well as Puerto Ricans and other Latin American and Caribbean immigrants poured into the city. New York City is considered one of the most ethnically diverse cities in the entire world.

Today, the federally-defined New York Consolidated Metropolitan Statistical Area (CMSA), which includes a large portion of southeastern New York State, northern New Jersey, and southwestern Connecticut, is home to more than 20 million people. With a population of more than 7.4 million people, New York is the largest city in the United States and the fourth largest in the world. The city also stands as a major U.S. and international center for finance, industry, trade, communications, tourism, and transportation.

Population

1990 Census 7,322,564
1998 Estimate 7,420,166
% Change 1.3

Racial/Ethnic Breakdown
- White 52.3%
- Black 28.7%
- Other 19.0%
- Hispanic Origin (may be of any race) 24.4%

Age Breakdown
- Under 5 years 7.0%
- 5 to 17 .... 16.1%
- 18 to 20 .... 4.3%
- 21 to 24 .... 6.3%
- 25 to 34 .... 18.7%
- 35 to 44 .... 15.2%
- 45 to 54 .... 10.6%
- 55 to 64 .... 8.8%
- 65 to 74 .... 7.3%
- 75+ years 5.8%
- Median Age 33.7

Gender Breakdown
- Male 46.9%
- Female 53.1%

Government

Type of Government: Mayor-Council

New York Borough President - Bronx
851 Grand Concourse
Bronx, NY 10451
Phone: 718-590-3500
Fax: 718-590-3537

New York Borough President - Brooklyn
209 Joralemon St
Brooklyn, NY 11201
Phone: 718-802-3900
Fax: 718-802-3959

New York Borough President - Manhattan
1 Centre St 19th Fl
New York, NY 10007
Phone: 212-669-8300
Fax: 212-669-3380

New York Borough President - Queens
120-55 Queens Blvd
Kew Gardens, NY 11424
Phone: 718-286-3000
Fax: 718-286-2885

New York Borough President - Staten Island
120 Borough Hall
Staten Island, NY 10301
Phone: 718-816-2000
Fax: 718-816-2026

New York Buildings Dept
60 Hudson St 14th Fl
New York, NY 10013
Phone: 212-312-8100
Fax: 212-312-8065

New York Business Services Dept
110 William St
New York, NY 10038
Phone: 212-513-6300
Fax: 212-618-8991

New York Chief Medical Examiner
520 1st Ave
New York, NY 10016
Phone: 212-447-2030
Fax: 212-447-2716

New York City Clerk
1 Centre St Rm 265
New York, NY 10007
Phone: 212-669-8898
Fax: 212-669-3300

New York City Council
City Hall
New York, NY 10007
Phone: 212-788-7100
Fax: 212-788-7207

New York City Hall
Broadway & Murray Sts
New York, NY 10007
Phone: 212-788-3000
Fax: 212-788-7476

New York City Planning Dept
22 Reade St
New York, NY 10007
Phone: 212-720-3300
Fax: 212-720-3219

New York Citywide Personnel Services Div
1 Centre St 17th Fl
New York, NY 10007
Phone: 212-487-5627

New York Cultural Affairs Dept
330 W 42nd St 14th Fl
New York, NY 10036
Phone: 212-643-7770
Fax: 212-643-7780

New York Finance Dept
1 Centre St Rm 500
New York, NY 10007
Phone: 212-669-4855
Fax: 212-669-2275

New York Fire Dept
9 Metrotech
Brooklyn, NY 11201
Phone: 718-999-2000
Fax: 718-999-0103

New York Law Dept
100 Church St
New York, NY 10007
Phone: 212-788-0303
Fax: 212-788-0367

New York Mayor
Broadway & Murray Sts City Hall
New York, NY 10007
Phone: 212-788-3000
Fax: 212-788-7476

New York Parks & Recreation Dept
830 5th Ave 3rd Fl
New York, NY 10021
Phone: 212-360-8111
Fax: 212-360-1329

New York Police Dept
1 Police Plaza
New York, NY 10038
Phone: 212-374-6710
Fax: 212-374-0265

New York Public Library
476 5th Ave
New York, NY 10018
Phone: 212-930-0800
Fax: 212-930-0572

New York Transportation Dept
40 Worth St
New York, NY 10013
Phone: 212-442-7000
Fax: 212-442-7347

Important Phone Numbers

AAA 212-586-1166

American Express Travel 212-687-3700
Broadway Shows (Information) 212-563-2929
Driver's License/Vehicle Registration Information ... 518-473-5595
Emergency 911
HotelDocs 800-468-3537
Medical Referral 212-420-4000
New York City Dept of Finance 718-935-9500
New York State Dept of Taxation & Finance 800-225-5829
Poison Control Center 212-764-7667
Real Estate Board of New York 212-532-3100
Travelers Aid 718-656-4870
Voter Registration Information 212-868-3692
Weather 631-924-0517

Information Sources

Auditorium at Equitable Center Phone: 212-314-4004
787 7th Ave Fax: 212-314-4001
New York, NY 10019

Better Business Bureau Serving Metropolitan New York Phone: 212-533-6200
257 Park Ave S 4th Fl Fax: 212-477-4912
New York, NY 10010
www.newyork.bbb.org

Better Business Bureau Serving Metropolitan New York Mid-Hudson Region Phone: 914-428-1230
30 Glenn St Fax: 914-428-6030
White Plains, NY 10603
www.newyork.bbb.org

Better Business Bureau Serving Northern New Jersey Phone: 973-581-1313
400 Lanidex Plaza Fax: 973-581-7022
Parsippany, NJ 07054
www.parsippany.bbb.org

Grand Prospect Hall Phone: 718-788-0777
263 Prospect Ave Fax: 718-788-0404
Brooklyn, NY 11215
www.grandprospect.com

Hudson County Phone: 201-795-6112
583 Newark Ave Brennan Courthouse Fax: 201-795-2581
Jersey City, NJ 07306

Hudson County Chamber of Commerce Phone: 201-653-7400
574 Summit Ave Suite 404 Fax: 201-798-3886
Jersey City, NJ 07306

Hudson County Division of Cultural & Heritage Affairs Phone: 201-459-2070
583 Newark Ave William Brennan Courthouse Fax: 201-792-0729
Jersey City, NJ 07306

Javits Jacob K Convention Center Phone: 212-216-2000
655 W 34th St Fax: 212-216-2588
New York, NY 10001
www.javitscenter.com

Jersey City City Hall Phone: 201-547-5000
280 Grove St Fax: 201-547-5461
Jersey City, NJ 07302
www.cityofjerseycity.com

Jersey City Economic Development Div Phone: 201-547-5070
30 Montgomery St Fax: 201-547-6566
Jersey City, NJ 07302
www.cityofjerseycity.com/docs/hedc.html

Jersey City Mayor Phone: 201-547-5200
280 Grove St Fax: 201-547-4288
Jersey City, NJ 07302
www.cityofjerseycity.com/docs/mayor.htm

Jersey City Public Library Phone: 201-547-4500
472 Jersey Ave Fax: 201-547-4584
Jersey City, NJ 07302

Manhattan Center Studios Phone: 212-279-7740
311 W 34th St Fax: 212-465-2367
New York, NY 10001
www.mcstudios.com

New York City Partnership & Chamber of Commerce Phone: 212-493-7500
1 Battery Park Plaza Fax: 212-344-3344
New York, NY 10004
www.nycp.org

New York Convention & Visitors Bureau Phone: 212-484-1200
810 7th Ave 3rd Fl Fax: 212-484-1222
New York, NY 10019 TF: 800-692-8474
www.nycvisit.com

New York County Phone: 212-374-8359
60 Centre St
New York, NY 10007

Westchester County Phone: 914-285-3080
110 Dr ML King Jr Blvd Fax: 914-285-3172
White Plains, NY 10601
www.co.westchester.ny.us

Yonkers Chamber of Commerce Phone: 914-963-0332
20 S Broadway Suite 1207 Fax: 914-963-0455
Yonkers, NY 10701
www.yonkerschamber.com

Yonkers City Hall Phone: 914-377-6000
40 S Broadway City Hall Fax: 914-377-6029
Yonkers, NY 10701
www.cityofyonkers.com

Yonkers Economic Development Office Phone: 914-377-6797
40 S Broadway Rm 416 Fax: 914-377-6003
Yonkers, NY 10701

Yonkers Mayor Phone: 914-377-6300
40 S Broadway City Hall Fax: 914-377-6048
Yonkers, NY 10701
www.cityofyonkers.com/mayor.html

Yonkers Public Library Phone: 914-337-1500
7 Main St Fax: 914-963-0868
Yonkers, NY 10701
wlsmail.wls.lib.ny.us/libs/yonkers/ypl_home.htm

Online Resources

4NY.com
www.4ny.com

@New York Newsletter
www.news-ny.com

About.com Guide to Brooklyn
brooklyn.about.com/citiestowns/midlanticus/brooklyn/mbody.htm

About.com Guide to Downtown New York
nycdowntown.about.com/citiestowns/midlanticus/nycdowntown/mbody.htm

About.com Guide to Long Island
longisland.about.com/citiestowns/midlanticus/longisland/mbody.htm

About.com Guide to New York
nycdowntown.about.com/local/midlanticus/nycdowntown

About.com Guide to New York: East Village
eastvillage.about.com/citiestowns/midlanticus/eastvillage/mbody.htm

About.com Guide to New York: Harlem/Uptown
harlem.about.com/citiestowns/midlanticus/harlem/mbody.htm

About.com Guide to New York: Queens
queens.about.com/citiestowns/midlanticus/queens/mbody.htm

About.com Guide to New York: Upper East Side
uppereastside.about.com/citiestowns/midlanticus/uppereastside/mbody.htm

About.com Guide to New York: Upper West Side
upperwestside.about.com/citiestowns/midlanticus/upperwestside/mbody.htm

Access America New York City
www.accessamer.com/newyorkcity/

All New York City Super Resource Guide
www.allny.com/

Alliance for Downtown New York
www.downtownny.com

Anthill City Guide Jersey City
www.anthill.com/city.asp?city=jerseycity

Anthill City Guide Midtown Manhattan
www.anthill.com/city.asp?city=midtown

Area Guide Jersey City
jerseycity.areaguides.net

Area Guide New York
newyork.areaguides.net

Boulevards New York
www.boulevards.com/cities/newyork.html

Bradmans.com New York
www.bradmans.com/scripts/display_city.cgi?city=240

City Insights New York
www.cityinsights.com/newyork.htm

City Knowledge New York
www.cityknowledge.com/ny_newyork.htm

Cityguide NYC
www.cityguideny.com/

Cityhits New York
www.cityhits.com/newyork/

CitySearch NYC
newyork.citysearch.com

CityTravelGuide.com New York
www.citytravelguide.com/new-york.htm

CuisineNet New York
www.cuisinenet.com/restaurant/new_york/index.shtml

DigitalCity New York
home.digitalcity.com/newyork

Excite.com Jersey City City Guide
www.excite.com/travel/countries/united_states/new_jersey/jersey_city

Excite.com New York City Guide
www.excite.com/travel/countries/united_states/new_york/new_york

Gayot's Guide Restaurant Search New York
www.perrier.com/restaurants/gayot.asp?area=NYC

GoldenNYC.com
www.goldennyc.com/

Guide to New York's Nightlife
models.com/night

HotelGuide New York
newyork.hotelguide.net

Hotres.com NYC
hotres.com

Lodging.com Yonkers New York
www.lodging.com/auto/guides/yonkers-ny.html

Long Island Home Page
www.webscope.com/li/info.html

Most New York
www.mostnewyork.com

New York City CityWomen
www.citywomen.com/nycwomen.htm

New York City Guide
www.nycguide.net/

New York City Insider
www.theinsider.com/nyc

New York City Reference
www.panix.com/clay/nyc

New York Graphic City Guide
www.futurecast.com/gcg/newyork.htm

New York Now
nynow.com

New York Rock Magazine
www.nyrock.com/

New York Subway Finder
www.krusch.com/nysf.html

New York Today
www.nytoday.com

NewYork.TheLinks.com
newyork.thelinks.com

NYC Culture Guide & Calendar
www.allianceforarts.org

NYCTourist.com
www.nyctourist.com

Online City Guide to Yonkers
www.olcg.com/ny/yonkers/index.html

Open World City Guides New York City
www.worldexecutive.com/cityguides/new_york/

PaperMag
www.papermag.com/

Rough Guide Travel New York City
travel.roughguides.com/content/4/

Savvy Diner Guide to New York Restaurants
www.savvydiner.com/newyork/

Time Out New York
www.timeout.com/newyork/

Village Alliance
www.villagealliance.org/

Virtual Voyages New York City
www.virtualvoyages.com/usa/ny/nyc/nyc.sht

WeekendEvents.com New York
www.weekendevents.com/NEWYORK/newyork.html

Yahoo! New York
ny.yahoo.com

Area Communities

Communities in the New York City metropolitan area with populations greater than 20,000 (including Bronx, Kings, Nassau, New York, Queens, Richmond, Suffolk, and Westchester counties in New York; and Bergen and Hudson counties in New Jersey) include:

Bayonne
630 Ave C
Bayonne, NJ 07002
Phone: 201-858-6000
Fax: 201-858-6077

Bergenfield
198 N Washington Ave
Bergenfield, NJ 07621
Phone: 201-387-4055
Fax: 201-387-6737

Bronx
851 Grand Concourse Rm 118
Bronx, NY 10451
Phone: 718-590-3500
Fax: 718-590-8122

Brooklyn
209 Joralemon St
Brooklyn, NY 11201
Phone: 718-802-3700
Fax: 718-802-3959

Cliffside Park
525 Palisade Ave
Cliffside Park, NJ 07010
Phone: 201-945-3456
Fax: 201-945-9823

Englewood
210 N Van Brunt St
Englewood, NJ 07631
Phone: 201-871-6611
Fax: 201-567-4395

Fair Lawn
8-01 Fair Lawn Ave
Fair Lawn, NJ 07410
Phone: 201-796-1700
Fax: 201-475-1581

Fort Lee
309 Main St
Fort Lee, NJ 07024
Phone: 201-592-3546
Fax: 201-592-1657

Freeport
46 N Ocean Ave
Freeport, NY 11520
Phone: 516-377-2200
Fax: 516-771-4127

Garden City
351 Stewart Ave
Garden City, NY 11530
Phone: 516-742-5800
Fax: 516-742-5223

Garfield
111 Outwater Ln
Garfield, NJ 07026
Phone: 973-340-2001
Fax: 973-340-5183

Hackensack
65 Central Ave
Hackensack, NJ 07601
Phone: 201-646-3901
Fax: 201-646-8059

Harrison
1 Heineman Pl
Harrison, NY 10528
Phone: 914-835-2000
Fax: 914-835-3075

Hempstead
99 Nichols Ct
Hempstead, NY 11550
Phone: 516-489-3400
Fax: 516-483-4313

Hoboken
94 Washington St
Hoboken, NJ 07030
Phone: 201-420-2071
Fax: 201-420-2085

Jersey City
280 Grove St
Jersey City, NJ 07302
Phone: 201-547-5000
Fax: 201-547-5461

Kearny
402 Kearny Ave
Kearny, NJ 07032
Phone: 201-955-7979
Fax: 201-998-6069

Lindenhurst
430 S Wellwood Ave
Lindenhurst, NY 11757
Phone: 631-957-7500
Fax: 631-957-4605

Lodi
1 Memorial Dr
Lodi, NJ 07644
Phone: 973-365-4005
Fax: 973-365-1723

Manhattan
1 Centre St Suite 19S
New York, NY 10007
Phone: 212-669-8300
Fax: 212-669-4900

Mount Vernon
1 Roosevelt Sq
Mount Vernon, NY 10550
Phone: 914-665-2300
Fax: 914-665-2496

New Rochelle
515 North Ave
New Rochelle, NY 10801
Phone: 914-654-2150
Fax: 914-654-2357

Ossining
16 Croton Ave
Ossining, NY 10562
Phone: 914-762-8428
Fax: 914-762-7710

Paramus
Jockish Sq
Paramus, NJ 07652
Phone: 201-265-2100
Fax: 201-265-0086

Peekskill
840 Main St
Peekskill, NY 10566
Phone: 845-737-3400
Fax: 845-734-4233

Port Chester
10 Pearl St
Port Chester, NY 10573
Phone: 914-939-2200
Fax: 914-937-3169

Queens
120-55 Queens Blvd
Kew Gardens, NY 11424
Phone: 718-286-2870
Fax: 718-286-2885

Ridgewood
131 N Maple Ave
Ridgewood, NJ 07451
Phone: 201-670-5505
Fax: 201-652-7623

Rockville Centre
1 College Place
Rockville Centre, NY 11570
Phone: 516-678-9300
Fax: 516-678-9225

Staten Island
10 Richmond Terr
Staten Island, NY 10301
Phone: 718-816-2000
Fax: 718-816-2026

Union City
3715 Palisade Ave
Union City, NJ 07087
Phone: 201-348-5731
Fax: 201-348-5728

Valley Stream
123 S Central Ave
Valley Stream, NY 11582
Phone: 516-825-4205
Fax: 516-825-2879

West New York
428 60th St
West New York, NJ 07093
Phone: 201-295-5090
Fax: 201-861-2576

White Plains
255 Main St
White Plains, NY 10601
Phone: 914-422-1411
Fax: 914-422-1395

Yonkers
40 S Broadway City Hall
Yonkers, NY 10701
Phone: 914-377-6000
Fax: 914-377-6029

Economy

New York has long been one of the leading financial centers in the world—nearly half of New York City's 25 largest employers are financial companies. Corporate giants in the industry that have their headquarters in Manhattan include Chase Manhattan, Citicorp, Merrill Lynch, J.P. Morgan & Co., and Prudential Securities. Services is currently New York City's largest employment sector, providing jobs for more than 1.4 million people in the metro area. New York City is also a world leader in international trade, transportation, and tourism, all of which contribute significantly to the city's economy.

Unemployment Rate 6.7%
Per Capita Income $36,316*
Median Family Income $34,360

** Information given is for the New York City Primary Metropolitan Statistical Area (PMSA), which includes Bronx, Kings/Brooklyn, New York/Manhattan, Queens and Richmond/Staten Island counties.*

Principal Industries & Number of Wage Earners

New York City PMSA* - March 2000

Industry	Wage Earners
Construction	113,400
Finance, Insurance, & Real Estate	487,800
Government	567,000
Manufacturing	247,200
Mining	300
Retail Trade	417,900
Services	1,422,800
Transportation & Public Utilities	207,800
Wholesale Trade	190,900

** Information given is for the New York City Primary Metropolitan Statistical Area (PMSA), which includes Bronx, Kings/Brooklyn, New York/Manhattan, Queens and Richmond/Staten Island counties.*

Major Employers

AMR Corp
4333 Amon Carter Blvd
Fort Worth, TX 76155
www.amrcorp.com
Phone: 817-963-1234
Fax: 817-967-4162

AXA Financial Inc
1290 Ave of the Americas
New York, NY 10104
www.axa-financial.com
Phone: 212-554-1234

Bank of New York Co Inc
1 Wall St
New York, NY 10286
E-mail: comments@bankofny.com
www.bankofny.com
Phone: 212-495-1784
Fax: 212-635-1799

Beth Israel Medical Center
1st Ave & 16th St
New York, NY 10003
www.bethisraelny.org/
Phone: 212-420-2000
Fax: 212-420-2881

Chase Manhattan Corp
270 Park Ave
New York, NY 10017
www.chase.com
Phone: 212-552-2222
Fax: 212-638-7421

Citigroup Inc
153 E 53rd St
New York, NY 10043
www.citibank.com/citigroup
Phone: 212-559-1000
Fax: 212-559-5138

Columbia University
W 116th St & Broadway
New York, NY 10027
www.columbia.edu
Phone: 212-854-1754
Fax: 212-854-2000

Consolidated Edison Co of New York
4 Irving Pl
New York, NY 10003
E-mail: pa@coned.com
www.coned.com
Phone: 212-460-4600
Fax: 212-260-8647

Deutsche Bank AG
31 W 52nd St
New York, NY 10019
Phone: 212-250-2500
Fax: 212-469-3872

Federated Department Stores Inc
11 Penn Plaza
New York, NY 10001
www.federated-fds.com
Phone: 212-494-6000
Fax: 212-494-6825

Goldman Sachs & Co
85 Broad St
New York, NY 10004
www.gs.com
Phone: 212-902-1000
Fax: 212-902-1513
TF: 800-323-5678

Marsh & McLennan Cos Inc
1166 Ave of the Americas
New York, NY 10036
www.marshmac.com
Phone: 212-345-5000
Fax: 212-345-4808

Merrill Lynch & Co Inc
250 Vesey St World Financial Ctr North Tower
New York, NY 10281
www.merrilllynch.com
Phone: 212-449-1000
Fax: 212-449-8665
TF: 800-338-2814

Montefiore Medical Center
111 E 210th St
Bronx, NY 10467
www.montefiore.org
Phone: 718-920-4321
Fax: 718-920-6049

Morgan Stanley Dean Witter & Co
1585 Broadway
New York, NY 10036
E-mail: genlfeedback@msdw.com
www.msdw.com
Phone: 212-761-4000
Fax: 212-761-0086
TF: 800-223-2440

Mount Sinai Medical Center
100th St & 5th Ave
New York, NY 10029
www.mountsinai.org
Phone: 212-241-6500
Fax: 212-348-6583

New York City Board of Education
110 Livingston St
Brooklyn, NY 11201
www.nycenet.edu
Phone: 718-935-2000
Fax: 718-935-5368

New York City Hall
Broadway & Murray Sts
New York, NY 10007
www.ci.nyc.ny.us
Phone: 212-788-3000
Fax: 212-788-7476

New York Presbyterian Hospital
525 E 68th St
New York, NY 10021
E-mail: publicaffairs@mail.med.cornell.edu
www.nyp.org
Phone: 212-746-5454
Fax: 212-746-8565

New York University
22 Washington Sq N
New York, NY 10011
www.nyu.edu
Phone: 212-998-4500
Fax: 212-995-4902

PricewaterhouseCoopers LLP
1301 Ave of the Americas
New York, NY 10019
www.pwcglobal.com/us
Phone: 212-259-1000
Fax: 212-259-1301

Time Warner Inc
75 Rockefeller Plaza 4th Fl
New York, NY 10019
www.timewarner.com/corp
Phone: 212-484-8000
Fax: 212-275-3048

Verizon Communications
1095 Ave of the Americas
New York, NY 10036
www.verizon.com
Phone: 212-395-2121
Fax: 212-921-9233
TF: 800-621-9900

Quality of Living Indicators

Total Crime Index....................................299,523
(rates per 100,000 inhabitants)

Violent Crime
Murder/manslaughter.......................... 671
Forcible rape 1,702
Robbery....................................36,100
Aggravated assault..........................40,511

Property Crime
Burglary 40,469
Larceny theft 140,377
Motor vehicle theft..........................36,693

Cost of Living Index....................................231.8
(national average = 100)

Median Home Price..................................$203,200

Education

Public Schools

New York City Board of Education
110 Livingston St
Brooklyn, NY 11201
www.nycenet.edu
Phone: 718-935-2000
Fax: 718-935-5368

Number of Schools
Elementary................................. 675
Middle 197
High....................................... 213
Special Education 60

Student/Teacher Ratio
All Grades 17.7:1

Private Schools

Number of Schools (all grades).................... 900+

Colleges & Universities

Adelphi University
1 South Ave
Garden City, NY 11530
www.adelphi.edu
Phone: 516-877-3000
Fax: 516-877-3039
TF: 800-233-5744

Albert A List College of Jewish Studies
3080 Broadway
New York, NY 10027
www.jtsa.edu/academic/lc
Phone: 212-678-8832
Fax: 212-678-8947

American Academy McAllister Institute of Funeral Service
450 W 56th St
New York, NY 10019
Phone: 212-757-1190
Fax: 212-765-5923

American Academy of Dramatic Arts
120 Madison Ave
New York, NY 10016
E-mail: aada@va.pubnix.com
www.aada.org
Phone: 212-686-9244
Fax: 212-545-7934
TF: 800-463-8990

Audrey Cohen College
75 Varick St
New York, NY 10013
www.audrey-cohen.edu
Phone: 212-343-1234
Fax: 212-343-7399

Barnard College Columbia University
3009 Broadway
New York, NY 10027
www.barnard.columbia.edu/
Phone: 212-854-5262
Fax: 212-854-6220

Berkeley College New York
3 E 43rd St
New York, NY 10017
E-mail: nycampus@berkeley.org
www.berkeleycollege.edu
Phone: 212-986-4343
Fax: 212-697-3371
TF: 800-446-5400

Boricua College
3755 Broadway
New York, NY 10032
Phone: 212-694-1000
Fax: 212-694-1015

Bradford School
8 E 40th St
New York, NY 10016
Phone: 212-686-9040
Fax: 212-686-9171

Bramson ORT College
69-30 Austin St
Forest Hills, NY 11375
www.bramsonort.org
Phone: 718-261-5800
Fax: 718-459-6565

City University of New York Bernard M Baruch College
151 E 25th St
New York, NY 10010
E-mail: udgbb@cunyvm.cuny.edu
www.baruch.cuny.edu
Phone: 212-802-2222
Fax: 212-802-2190

City University of New York Borough of Manhattan Community College
199 Chambers St Rm S-300
New York, NY 10007
www.bmcc.cuny.edu
Phone: 212-346-8105
Fax: 212-346-8110

City University of New York City College
138th St & Convent Ave
New York, NY 10031
www.ccny.cuny.edu/
Phone: 212-650-7000
Fax: 212-650-6417

City University of New York College of Staten Island
2800 Victory Blvd
Staten Island, NY 10314
www.csi.cuny.edu
Phone: 718-982-2000
Fax: 718-982-2500

City University of New York Herbert H Lehman College
250 Bedford Park Blvd W
Bronx, NY 10468
www.lehman.cuny.edu
Phone: 718-960-8000
Fax: 718-960-8712

City University of New York Hostos Community College
500 Grand Concourse
Bronx, NY 10451
www.hostos.cuny.edu
Phone: 718-518-4444
Fax: 718-518-6643

City University of New York Hunter College
695 Park Ave
New York, NY 10021
www.hunter.cuny.edu/
Phone: 212-772-4000
Fax: 212-650-3336

City University of New York John Jay College of Criminal Justice
445 W 59th St
New York, NY 10019
www.jjay.cuny.edu/
Phone: 212-237-8000
Fax: 212-237-8742

City University of New York Kingsborough Community College
2001 Oriental Blvd
Brooklyn, NY 11235
www.kbcc.cuny.edu
Phone: 718-368-5000
Fax: 718-368-5024

City University of New York LaGuardia Community College
31-10 Thomson Ave
Long Island City, NY 11101
www.lagcc.cuny.edu
Phone: 718-482-5000
Fax: 718-482-5599

City University of New York Medgar Evers College
1650 Bedford Ave
Brooklyn, NY 11225
Phone: 718-270-4900
Fax: 718-270-6188

City University of New York Queens College
65-30 Kissena Blvd
Flushing, NY 11367
E-mail: admissions@qc.edu
www.qc.edu
Phone: 718-997-5000
Fax: 718-997-5617

City University of New York Queensborough Community College
222-05 56th Ave
Bayside, NY 11364
Phone: 718-631-6262
Fax: 718-281-5069

City University of New York York College
94-20 Guy R Brewer Blvd
Jamaica, NY 11451
E-mail: admissions@york.cuny.edu
www.york.cuny.edu
Phone: 718-262-2000
Fax: 718-262-2601

Cochran School of Nursing
967 N Broadway
Yonkers, NY 10701
www.riversidehealth.org/stjohns/html/nursing.html
Phone: 914-964-4283
Fax: 914-964-4971

College of Aeronautics
86-01 23rd Ave
East Elmhurst, NY 11369
www.aero.edu
Phone: 718-429-6600
Fax: 718-779-2231
TF: 800-776-2376

College of Insurance
101 Murray St
New York, NY 10007
www.tci.edu
Phone: 212-962-4111
Fax: 212-964-3381
TF: 800-356-5146

College of Mount Saint Vincent
6301 Riverdale Ave
Riverdale, NY 10471
www.cmsv.edu
Phone: 718-405-3200
Fax: 718-549-7945

College of New Rochelle
29 Castle Pl
New Rochelle, NY 10805
E-mail: cnr2@pppmail.nyser.net
www.cnr.edu
Phone: 914-632-5300
Fax: 914-654-5554
TF: 800-933-5923

Columbia University
W 116th St & Broadway
New York, NY 10027
www.columbia.edu
Phone: 212-854-1754
Fax: 212-854-2000

Concordia College
171 White Plains Rd
Bronxville, NY 10708
www.concordia-ny.edu
Phone: 914-337-9300
Fax: 914-395-4636
TF: 800-937-2655

Cooper Union College
30 Cooper Sq
New York, NY 10003
www.cooper.edu
Phone: 212-353-4100
Fax: 212-353-4343

Eugene Lang College
65 W 11th St
New York, NY 10011
E-mail: lang@newschool.edu
www.newschool.edu/academic/lang
Phone: 212-229-5799
Fax: 212-229-5625

Fashion Institute of Technology
227 W 27th St
New York, NY 10001
www.fitnyc.edu
Phone: 212-217-7675
Fax: 212-217-7481
TF: 800-468-6348

Fordham University
441 E Fordham Rd
Bronx, NY 10458
www.fordham.edu
Phone: 718-817-1000
Fax: 718-367-9404
TF: 800-367-3426

Hebrew Union College
1 W 4th St
New York, NY 10012
www.huc.edu
Phone: 212-674-5300
Fax: 212-388-1720

Helene Fuld School of Nursing
1879 Madison Ave
New York, NY 10035
Phone: 212-423-1000
Fax: 212-427-2453

Hofstra University
100 Hofstra University
Hempstead, NY 11549
E-mail: hofstra@hofstra.edu
www.hofstra.edu
Phone: 516-463-6700
Fax: 516-463-5100
TF: 800-463-7872

Hudson County Community College
162 Sip Ave
Jersey City, NJ 07306
www.hudson.cc.nj.us
Phone: 201-656-2020
Fax: 201-714-2136

Institute of Design & Construction
141 Willoughby St
Brooklyn, NY 11201
Phone: 718-855-3661
Fax: 718-852-5889

Interboro Institute
450 W 56th St
New York, NY 10019
www.interboro.com
Phone: 212-399-0091
Fax: 212-765-5772

Iona College
715 North Ave
New Rochelle, NY 10801
www.iona.edu
Phone: 914-633-2000
Fax: 914-633-2096

Juilliard School
60 Lincoln Ctr Plaza
New York, NY 10023
www.juilliard.edu
Phone: 212-799-5000
Fax: 212-769-6420

Katharine Gibbs School
200 Park Ave
New York, NY 10166
www.gibbs-ny.com
Phone: 212-867-9300
Fax: 212-338-9606
TF: 800-567-3877

Laboratory Institute of Merchandising
12 E 53rd St
New York, NY 10022
E-mail: limcollege@usa.pipeline.com
www.limcollege.edu
Phone: 212-752-1530
Fax: 212-832-6708
TF: 800-677-1323

Long Island University Brooklyn Campus
University Plaza
Brooklyn, NY 11201
www.brooklyn.liunet.edu/cwis/bklyn/bklyn.html
Phone: 718-488-1000
Fax: 718-780-4097

Manhattan College
4513 Manhattan College Pkwy
Bronx, NY 10471
www.mancol.edu
Phone: 718-862-8000
Fax: 718-862-8019

Manhattan School of Music
601 W 122nd St
New York, NY 10027
www.msmnyc.edu
Phone: 212-749-2802
Fax: 212-749-5471

Mannes College of Music
150 W 85th St
New York, NY 10024
www.newschool.edu/academic/mannes.htm
Phone: 212-580-0210
Fax: 212-580-1738
TF: 800-292-3040

Marymount Manhattan College
221 E 71st St
New York, NY 10021
marymount.mmm.edu
Phone: 212-517-0400
Fax: 212-517-0413
TF: 800-627-9668

Mercy College Bronx Campus
50 Antin Pl
Bronx, NY 10462
www.mercynet.edu
Phone: 718-518-7710
Fax: 718-518-7879

Molloy College
1000 Hempstead Ave
Rockville Centre, NY 11571
E-mail: tufan01@molloy.edu
www.molloy.edu
Phone: 516-678-5000
Fax: 516-256-2247
TF: 800-229-1020

Monroe College
2501 Jerome Ave
Bronx, NY 10468
www.monroecoll.edu
Phone: 718-933-6700
Fax: 718-364-3552
TF: 800-556-6676

New Jersey City University
2039 JFK Blvd
Jersey City, NJ 07305
www.njcu.edu
Phone: 201-200-2000
Fax: 201-200-2044
TF: 888-441-6528

New York Career Institute
15 Park Row
New York, NY 10038
E-mail: admissions@nyci.com
www.nyci.com
Phone: 212-962-0002
Fax: 212-608-8210

New York Institute of Technology New York City Campus
1855 Broadway
New York, NY 10023
Phone: 212-261-1500
Fax: 212-261-1704
TF: 800-345-6948

New York School of Interior Design
170 E 70th St
New York, NY 10021
E-mail: admissions@nysid.edu
www.nysid.edu
Phone: 212-472-1500
Fax: 212-472-1867
TF: 800-336-9743

New York University
22 Washington Sq N
New York, NY 10011
www.nyu.edu
Phone: 212-998-4500
Fax: 212-995-4902

Pace University
1 Pace Plaza
New York, NY 10038
www.pace.edu
Phone: 212-346-1200
Fax: 212-346-1040

Parsons School of Design
2 W 13th St
New York, NY 10011
E-mail: parsadm@newschool.edu
www.parsons.edu
Phone: 212-229-8900
Fax: 212-929-2456
TF: 800-252-0852

Phillips Beth Israel School of Nursing
310 E 22nd St 9th Floor
New York, NY 10010
Phone: 212-614-6108
Fax: 212-614-6109

Plaza Business Institute
74-09 37th Ave
Jackson Heights, NY 11372
E-mail: info@plazacollege.edu
www.plazacollege.edu
Phone: 718-779-1430
Fax: 718-779-7423

Polytechnic University
6 Metrotech Ctr
Brooklyn, NY 11201
E-mail: admub@duke.poly.edu
www.poly.edu
Phone: 718-260-3600
Fax: 718-260-3136

Pratt Institute
200 Willoughby Ave
Brooklyn, NY 11205
E-mail: info@pratt.edu
www.pratt.edu
Phone: 718-636-3600
Fax: 718-636-3670
TF: 800-331-0834

Saint Francis College
180 Remsen St
Brooklyn, NY 11201
www.stfranciscollege.edu
Phone: 718-522-2300
Fax: 718-522-1274

Saint John's University
8000 Utopia Pkwy
Jamaica, NY 11439
www.stjohns.edu
Phone: 718-969-8000
Fax: 718-990-1677

Saint John's University Staten Island Campus
300 Howard Ave
Staten Island, NY 10301
www.stjohns.edu
Phone: 718-447-4343
Fax: 718-390-4298

Saint Joseph's College
245 Clinton Ave
Brooklyn, NY 11205
Phone: 718-636-6800
Fax: 718-636-7245

Saint Peter's College
2641 JFK Blvd
Jersey City, NJ 07306
www.spc.edu
Phone: 201-915-9000
Fax: 201-451-0036
TF: 888-772-9933

Saint Thomas Aquinas College
125 Rt 340
Sparkill, NY 10976
www.stac.edu
Phone: 845-359-9500
Fax: 845-359-8136

School of Visual Arts
209 E 23rd St
New York, NY 10010
www.sva.edu
Phone: 212-592-2000
Fax: 212-592-2116
TF: 800-436-4204

State University of New York Maritime College
6 Pennyfield Ave Fort Schuyler
Bronx, NY 10465
E-mail: sunymarit@aol.com
www.sunymaritime.edu
Phone: 718-409-7200
Fax: 718-409-7465

State University of New York Nassau Community College
1 Education Dr
Garden City, NY 11530
E-mail: info@sunynassau.edu
www.sunynassau.edu
Phone: 516-572-7500
Fax: 516-572-9743

Taylor Business Institute
269 W 40th St
New York, NY 10018
Phone: 212-302-4000
Fax: 212-302-2624
TF: 800-959-9999

Technical Career Institutes
320 W 31st St
New York, NY 10001
E-mail: admissions@tciedu.com
www.tciedu.com
Phone: 212-594-4000
Fax: 212-629-3937
TF: 800-878-8246

Touro College
27-33 W 23rd St
New York, NY 10010
www.touro.edu
Phone: 212-463-0400
Fax: 212-627-9542

US Merchant Marine Academy
Steamboat Rd
Kings Point, NY 11024
www.usmma.edu
Phone: 516-773-5000
Fax: 516-773-5390
TF: 800-732-6267

Wagner College
1 Campus Rd
Staten Island, NY 10301
www.wagner.edu
Phone: 718-390-3411
Fax: 718-390-3105
TF: 800-221-1010

Webb Institute
Crescent Beach Rd
Glen Cove, NY 11542
E-mail: admissions@webb-institute.edu
www.webb-institute.edu
Phone: 516-671-2213
Fax: 516-674-9838

Westchester Business Institute
325 Central Ave
White Plains, NY 10606
www.wbi.org
Phone: 914-948-4442
Fax: 914-948-8216
TF: 800-333-4924

Yeshiva University
500 W 185th St
New York, NY 10033
www.yu.edu
Phone: 212-960-5400
Fax: 212-960-0055

Hospitals

Bayley Seton Hospital
75 Vanderbilt Ave
Staten Island, NY 10304
Phone: 718-354-6000
Fax: 718-354-6011

Bellevue Hospital Center
462 1st Ave
New York, NY 10016
Phone: 212-562-4141
Fax: 212-562-4036

Beth Israel Medical Center
1st Ave & 16th St
New York, NY 10003
www.bethisraelny.org/
Phone: 212-420-2000
Fax: 212-420-2881

Beth Israel Medical Center Kings Highway Div
3201 Kings Hwy
Brooklyn, NY 11234
Phone: 718-252-3000
Fax: 718-252-2233

Beth Israel Medical Center Singer Div
170 East End Ave
New York, NY 10128
Phone: 212-870-9000
Fax: 212-870-9404

Bronx-Lebanon Hospital Center
1276 Fulton Ave
Bronx, NY 10456
www.bronxcare.org
Phone: 718-590-1800
Fax: 718-901-6251

Brookdale Hospital Medical Center
1 Brookdale Plaza
Brooklyn, NY 11212
www.brookdalehospital.com
Phone: 718-240-5000
Fax: 718-240-5042

Brooklyn Hospital Center
121 DeKalb Ave
Brooklyn, NY 11201
www.tbh.org
Phone: 718-250-8000

Cabrini Medical Center
227 E 19th St
New York, NY 10003
www.cabrininy.org
Phone: 212-995-6000
Fax: 212-995-7444
TF: 800-222-7464

Catholic Medical Center Mary Immaculate Hospital
152-11 89th Ave
Queens, NY 11432
Phone: 718-558-2000
Fax: 718-558-2383

Catholic Medical Center of Brooklyn & Queens
88-25 153rd St
Jamaica, NY 11432
Phone: 718-558-6900
Fax: 718-558-7286

Catholic Medical Center Saint John's Queens Hospital
90-02 Queens Blvd
Elmhurst, NY 11373
Phone: 718-558-1000
Fax: 718-558-1945

Catholic Medical Center Saint Joseph's Hospital
158-40 79th Ave
Flushing, NY 11366
Phone: 718-558-6200
Fax: 718-558-5073

Catholic Medical Center Saint Mary's Hospital of Brooklyn
170 Buffalo Ave
Brooklyn, NY 11213
Phone: 718-221-3000
Fax: 718-221-3181

Christ Hospital
176 Palisade Ave
Jersey City, NJ 07306
www.christhospital.org
Phone: 201-795-8200
Fax: 201-795-8796

Coney Island Hospital
2601 Ocean Pkwy
Brooklyn, NY 11235
Phone: 718-616-3000
Fax: 718-616-4439

Flushing Hospital Medical Center
45th Ave at Parsons Blvd
Flushing, NY 11355
Phone: 718-670-5000
Fax: 718-670-4587

Harlem Hospital Center
506 Lenox Ave
New York, NY 10037
Phone: 212-939-1000
Fax: 212-939-1974

Interfaith Medical Center
555 Prospect Pl
Brooklyn, NY 11238
Phone: 718-935-7000
Fax: 718-935-7109

Jacobi Medical Center
1400 Pelham Pkwy S
Bronx, NY 10461
Phone: 718-918-8141
Fax: 718-918-4607

Jamaica Hospital Medical Center
8900 Van Wyck Expy
Jamaica, NY 11418
www.jamaicahospital.org
Phone: 718-206-6000
Fax: 718-657-0545

Jersey City Medical Center
50 Baldwin Ave
Jersey City, NJ 07304
Phone: 201-915-2000
Fax: 201-915-2002

Kings County Hospital Center
451 Clarkson Ave
Brooklyn, NY 11203
Phone: 718-245-3131
Fax: 718-245-4494

Kingsbrook Jewish Medical Center
585 Schenectady Ave
Brooklyn, NY 11203
Phone: 718-604-5000
Fax: 718-604-5595

Lenox Hill Hospital
100 E 77th St
New York, NY 10021
www.lenoxhillhospital.org
Phone: 212-434-2000
Fax: 212-434-3434

Lincoln Medical & Mental Health Center
234 E 149th St
Bronx, NY 10451
Phone: 718-579-5000
Fax: 718-579-5974

Long Island Jewish Medical Center
270-05 76th Ave
New Hyde Park, NY 11040
www.lij.edu
Phone: 718-470-7000
Fax: 718-470-6724

Lutheran Medical Center
150 55th St
Brooklyn, NY 11220
Phone: 718-630-7000
Fax: 718-630-8228

Maimonides Medical Center
4802 10th Ave
Brooklyn, NY 11219
www.maimonidesmed.org
Phone: 718-283-6000
Fax: 718-283-8553

Metropolitan Hospital Center
1901 1st Ave
New York, NY 10029
Phone: 212-423-6262
Fax: 212-423-7207

Montefiore Medical Center
111 E 210th St
Bronx, NY 10467
www.montefiore.org
Phone: 718-920-4321
Fax: 718-920-6049

Mount Sinai Medical Center
100th St & 5th Ave
New York, NY 10029
www.mountsinai.org
Phone: 212-241-6500
Fax: 212-348-6583

New York Downtown Hospital
170 William St
New York, NY 10038
Phone: 212-312-5000
Fax: 212-312-5977

New York Hospital Medical Center of Queens
56-45 Main St
Flushing, NY 11355
Phone: 718-670-1021
Fax: 718-358-1196

New York Methodist Hospital
506 6th St
Brooklyn, NY 11215
Phone: 718-780-3000
Fax: 718-780-3770

New York Presbyterian Hospital
525 E 68th St
New York, NY 10021
www.nyp.org
Phone: 212-746-5454
Fax: 212-746-8565

New York University Medical Center
550 1st Ave
New York, NY 10016
www.med.nyu.edu
Phone: 212-263-7300
Fax: 212-263-8960

North Central Bronx Hospital
7424 Kossuth Ave
Bronx, NY 10467
Phone: 718-519-5000
Fax: 718-519-4902

North General Hospital
1879 Madison Ave
New York, NY 10035
Phone: 212-423-4000
Fax: 212-423-4204

North Shore University Hospital at Forest Hills
102-01 66th Rd
Forest Hills, NY 11375
www.northshorelij.com/visit/foresthills.htm
Phone: 718-830-4000
Fax: 718-830-4168

Our Lady of Mercy Medical Center
600 E 233rd St
Bronx, NY 10466
www.ourladyofmercy.com
Phone: 718-920-9000
Fax: 718-920-9977

Our Lady of Mercy Medical Center Florence D'Urso Pavilion
1870 Pelham Park Way S
Bronx, NY 10461
Phone: 718-430-6000
Fax: 718-430-6011

Peninsula Hospital Center
51-15 Beach Channel Dr
Far Rockaway, NY 11691
Phone: 718-734-2000
Fax: 718-734-2699

Queens Hospital Center
82-68 164th St
Jamaica, NY 11432
Phone: 718-883-3000
Fax: 718-883-6156

Saint Barnabas Hospital
4422 3rd Ave
Bronx, NY 10457
Phone: 718-960-9000
Fax: 718-960-3132

Saint Clare's Hospital & Health Center
415 W 51st St
New York, NY 10019
Phone: 212-586-1500
Fax: 212-459-8316

Saint Francis Hospital
25 McWilliams Pl
Jersey City, NJ 07302
Phone: 201-418-1000
Fax: 201-418-2011

Saint Joseph's Medical Center
127 S Broadway
Yonkers, NY 10701
Phone: 914-378-7000
Fax: 914-965-4838

Saint Luke's-Roosevelt Hospital Center
1111 Amsterdam Ave
New York, NY 10025
www.slrhc.org
Phone: 212-523-4000
Fax: 212-523-1981

Saint Vincent's Hospital & Medical Center of New York
153 W 11th St
New York, NY 10011
Phone: 212-604-7000
Fax: 212-604-2100

Sisters of Charity Medical Center-Saint Vincent's Campus
355 Bard Ave
Staten Island, NY 10310
www.schsi.org
Phone: 718-876-1234
Fax: 718-876-1322

Staten Island University Hospital
475 Seaview Ave
Staten Island, NY 10305
www.siuh.edu
Phone: 718-226-9000
Fax: 718-226-8966

University Hospital of Brooklyn
450 Clarkson Ave
Brooklyn, NY 11203
Phone: 718-270-1000
Fax: 718-270-1941

Veterans Affairs Medical Center
423 E 23rd St
New York, NY 10010
Phone: 212-686-7500
Fax: 212-951-3375

Victory Memorial Hospital
699 92nd St
Brooklyn, NY 11228
Phone: 718-567-1234
Fax: 718-567-1002

Yonkers General Hospital
2 Park Ave
Yonkers, NY 10703
www.riversidehealth.org/yonkers/yonkers.html
Phone: 914-964-7300
Fax: 914-964-7311

Transportation

Airport(s)

John F Kennedy International Airport (JFK)
15 miles SE of downtown New York
(approx 30 minutes) 718-244-4444

LaGuardia Airport (LGA)
8 miles NE of downtown New York
(approx 45 minutes) 718-476-5000

Newark International Airport (EWR)
16 miles SW of downtown New York
(approx 45 minutes) 973-961-6000

Mass Transit

New York City Transit Authority Bus/Subway
$1.50 Base fare 718-330-1234

Rail/Bus

Amtrak Station
7th Ave & 31st St
New York, NY 10001
Phone: 800-872-7245

Grand Central Station Phone: 212-340-3000
89 E 42nd St
New York, NY 10017

Port Authority Bus Terminal Phone: 212-564-8484
625 8th Ave
New York, NY 10018

Utilities

Electricity
Con Edison....800-752-6633
www.conedison.com

Gas
Con Edison....800-752-6633
www.conedison.com

Water
New York Water Supply....212-442-1904

Garbage Collection/Recycling
New York City Dept of Sanitation....212-219-8090

Telecommunications

Telephone
Verizon Communications....212-890-2350
www.verizon.com

Cable Television
Cablevision....718-991-6000
Staten Island Cable....718-816-8686
Time Warner Cable of New York City....212-674-9100
www.twcnyc.com

Internet Service Providers (ISPs)
Cloud 9 Consulting Inc....914-696-4000
www.cloud9.net
Cybernex Inc....201-270-4196
www.cybernex.net
Cyburban Link....914-397-0500
www.cyburban.com
Digital Telemedia Inc....212-625-5300
www.dti.net
Echo Communications Group Inc....212-292-0900
www.echonyc.com
el Net....212-966-3141
www.el.net
ExecNet Information Systems....914-665-0600
www.execnet.com
Gillette Global Network Inc....212-906-0100
www.ggn.com
Hudsonet Internet Services....201-217-8284
www.hudsonet.com
I-2000 Inc....212-422-1951
www.i-2000.com
IDT Corp....201-928-1000
www.idt.net
Ingress Enterprises Inc....212-488-1088
www.ingress.com
Insight Communications Co Inc....212-371-2266
www.insight-com.com
Intercom Online Inc....212-378-2202
www.intercom.com
Internet Channel....212-243-5200
www.inch.com
Internet QuickLink Corp....212-475-0882
www.quicklink.com
Interport Communications Corp....646-414-6929
www.interport.com
Maestro Technologies Inc....212-293-1655
www.maestro.com
MetConnect.com....877-469-2477
www.metconnect.com
Network Data Link Inc....718-935-1337
www.ndl.net
New York Connect.Net Ltd....212-293-2620
www.nyct.net
NY WEBB Inc....212-242-4912
www.webb.com
Octet Media....212-475-6393
www.octet.com
Outernet Inc (bway.net)....212-982-9800
www.bway.net
Panix Public Access Unix....212-741-4400
www.panix.com
Peak Access....800-340-7325
www.peakaccess.net
Redgoose Inc....212-627-5400
www.redgoose.net
SPEEDUS.COM Inc....718-567-4300
www.speedus.com
Stealth Communications Inc....212-232-2020
www.stealth.net
Together Foundation....212-319-4043
www.together.org
TSI Broadband....212-730-2210
www.tsibroadband.net
TunaNet....212-220-4242
www.infohouse.com
Verio New York City....212-691-5767
home.verio.net/local/frontpage.cfm?AirportCode=LGA
Walrus Internet....212-406-5000
www.walrus.com
Way Communications....212-843-2400
www.way.com

Banks

Amalgamated Bank of New York Phone: 212-255-6200
11-15 Union Sq W Fax: 212-462-3705
New York, NY 10003

Atlantic Bank of New York Phone: 212-967-7425
960 Ave of the Americas Fax: 212-563-2729
New York, NY 10001

Bank Leumi USA Phone: 917-542-2343
579 5th Ave Fax: 212-599-7579
New York, NY 10017

Bank of America Phone: 212-390-2000
1 World Trade Ctr Fax: 212-390-2560
New York, NY 10048

Bank of New York Phone: 212-635-1005
1 Wall St Fax: 212-635-1200
New York, NY 10286

Chase Manhattan Bank NA Phone: 212-552-2222
1 Chase Manhattan Plaza Fax: 212-270-1043
New York, NY 10081

Chinese American Bank Phone: 212-966-3303
77 Bowery Fax: 212-966-3396
New York, NY 10002

Citibank NA
399 Park Ave
New York, NY 10043
www.citibank.com
Phone: 212-559-7299
Fax: 212-559-7373

Dime Savings Bank of New York FSB
589 5th Ave
New York, NY 10017
www.dime.com
Phone: 212-326-6170
Fax: 212-326-6194
TF: 800-843-3463

Excel Bank NA
400 Park Ave
New York, NY 10022
Phone: 212-605-6500
Fax: 212-605-6065

Fleet Bank NA
50 Bayard St
New York, NY 10013
Phone: 212-406-4711
Fax: 212-406-4728

Fuji Bank & Trust Co
2 World Trade Ctr 79th Fl
New York, NY 10048
www.fujibank.co.jp
Phone: 212-898-2400
Fax: 212-321-9408

HSBC Bank USA
140 Broadway
New York, NY 10005
Phone: 212-658-1647

Israel Discount Bank of New York
511 5th Ave
New York, NY 10017
Phone: 212-551-8500
Fax: 212-370-9623

Merchants Bank of New York
275 Madison Ave
New York, NY 10016
Phone: 212-973-6600
Fax: 212-973-6663

Morgan Guaranty Trust Co of New York
60 Wall St
New York, NY 10260
Phone: 212-483-2323
Fax: 212-648-5230

Royal Bank of Canada
1 Liberty Plaza
New York, NY 10006
E-mail: feedback@www.royalbank.com
www.royalbank.com
Phone: 212-428-6200
Fax: 212-428-2329

Safra National Bank of New York
546 5th Ave
New York, NY 10036
Phone: 212-704-5500
Fax: 212-704-5527
TF: 800-223-2311

Sterling National Bank
425 Park Ave
New York, NY 10022
Phone: 212-935-1440
Fax: 212-935-1646

Shopping

Annex Outdoor Antiques Fair & Flea Market
25th St & Avenue of the Americas
New York, NY 10010
Phone: 212-243-5343

Barney's
660 Madison Ave
New York, NY 10021
www.barneys.com
Phone: 212-826-8900
Fax: 212-833-2260

Bergdorf Goodman Inc
754 5th Ave
New York, NY 10019
Phone: 212-753-7300
Fax: 212-872-8616

Bloomingdale's
1000 3rd Ave
New York, NY 10022
E-mail: comments@bloomingdales.com
www.bloomingdales.com
Phone: 212-705-2000
Fax: 212-705-2502
TF: 800-950-0047

Bruckner Boulevard Antique District
Bruckner Blvd
Bronx, NY 10454
Phone: 718-292-3113
Fax: 718-292-3115

Citicorp Center
53rd St & Lexington Ave
New York, NY 10022
Phone: 212-559-6758
Fax: 212-486-1969

Cross Country Shopping Center
6K Mall Walk
Yonkers, NY 10704
Phone: 914-968-9570

Cross Country Square Shopping Center
750 Central Park
Yonkers, NY 10704
Phone: 914-968-5734

FAO Schwarz
767 5th Ave
New York, NY 10153
www.fao.com
Phone: 212-644-9400
Fax: 212-826-1826

Green Acres Mall
2034 Green Acres Mall
Valley Stream, NY 11581
Phone: 516-561-7360
Fax: 516-561-8370

Historic Orchard Street Shopping District
261 Broome St
New York, NY 10002
www.orchardstreet.org
Phone: 212-226-9010
Fax: 212-226-8161
TF: 800-825-8374

Hudson Mall
Rt 440
Jersey City, NJ 07304
Phone: 201-432-0119
Fax: 201-432-4731

Journal Square
Kennedy Blvd
Jersey City, NJ 07306

Kings Plaza Shopping Center
Flatbush & C Aves
Brooklyn, NY 11234
Phone: 718-253-6842
Fax: 718-951-8857

Loehmann's
5740 Broadway
Riverdale, NY 10463
Phone: 718-543-6420
Fax: 718-543-6449

Lord & Taylor
424 5th Ave
New York, NY 10018
www.mayco.com/lt/index.jsp
Phone: 212-391-3344
Fax: 212-391-3265

Manhattan Mall
33rd St & Avenue of the Americas
New York, NY 10001
Phone: 212-465-0500
Fax: 212-465-0603

Newport Center Mall
30 Mall Dr W
Jersey City, NJ 07310
Phone: 201-626-2025
Fax: 201-626-2033

Saks Fifth Avenue
611 5th Ave
New York, NY 10022
Phone: 212-753-4000
Fax: 212-940-4849

South Street Seaport Market Place
19 Fulton St
New York, NY 10038
www.southstseaport.org
Phone: 212-732-8257
Fax: 212-964-8056

Tiffany & Co
727 5th Ave
New York, NY 10022
www.tiffany.com
Phone: 212-755-8000
Fax: 212-605-4465
TF: 800-526-0649

Media

Newspapers and Magazines

Bay News
1733 Sheepshead Bay Rd
Brooklyn, NY 11235
Phone: 718-769-4400
Fax: 718-769-5048

Brooklyn Heights Press & Cobble Hill News
30 Henry St
Brooklyn, NY 11201
Phone: 718-858-2300
Fax: 718-858-4483

Crain's New York Business
711 3rd Ave
New York, NY 10017
www.crainsny.com
Phone: 212-210-0100
Fax: 212-210-0799
TF: 800-283-2724

Harbor Watch (Metro New York)
1733 Sheepshead Bay Rd
Brooklyn, NY 11235
Phone: 718-769-4400
Fax: 718-769-5048

Hoboken Reporter
1400 Washington St
Hoboken, NJ 07030
Phone: 201-798-7800
Fax: 201-798-0018

Hudson Reporter
PO Box 3069
Hoboken, NJ 07030
Phone: 201-798-7800
Fax: 201-798-0018

Jersey Journal*
30 Journal Sq
Jersey City, NJ 07306
www.nj.com
Phone: 201-653-1000
Fax: 201-653-1414

Journal News*
1 Gannett Dr
White Plains, NY 10604
www.nyjournalnews.com
Phone: 914-694-9300
Fax: 914-694-3535
TF: 800-942-1010

Journal of Commerce*
2 World Trade Ctr 27th Fl
New York, NY 10048
www.joc.com
Phone: 212-837-7000
Fax: 212-837-7035
TF: 800-223-0243

Kings Courier
1733 Sheepshead Bay Rd
Brooklyn, NY 11235
Phone: 718-769-4400
Fax: 718-769-5048

Manhattan
330 W 56th St Suite 3G
New York, NY 10019
Phone: 212-265-7970
Fax: 212-265-8052

New Jersey Business Magazine
310 Passaic Ave
Fairfield, NJ 07004
E-mail: njbmag@intac.com
www.njbmagazine.com/
Phone: 973-882-5004
Fax: 973-882-4648

New York
444 Madison Ave
New York, NY 10022
www.newyorkmag.com
Phone: 212-508-0700
TF: 800-678-0900

New York Harbor Watch
1733 Sheepshead Bay Rd
Brooklyn, NY 11235
Phone: 718-769-4400
Fax: 718-769-5048
TF: 800-564-5433

New York Observer
54 E 64th St
New York, NY 10021
E-mail: comments@observer.com
www.observer.com
Phone: 212-755-2400
Fax: 212-688-4889

New York Post*
1211 Ave of the Americas
New York, NY 10036
E-mail: nypost@aol.com
www.nypostonline.com
Phone: 212-930-8000
Fax: 212-930-8540

New York Press
333 7th Ave 14th Fl
New York, NY 10001
www.nypress.com
Phone: 212-244-2282
Fax: 212-244-9864

New York Times*
229 W 43rd St
New York, NY 10036
www.nytimes.com
Phone: 212-556-1234
Fax: 212-556-8828

Our Town Newspaper
242 W 30th St 5th Fl
New York, NY 10001
Phone: 212-268-8600
Fax: 212-268-2935

People's Weekly World
239 W 23rd St
New York, NY 10011
E-mail: pww@pww.org
www.hartford-hwp.com/cp-usa/pww.html
Phone: 212-924-2523
Fax: 212-645-5436

Ridgewood News
41 Oak St
Ridgewood, NJ 07450
Phone: 201-843-0500
Fax: 201-612-7992

Staten Island Register
2100 Clove Rd
Staten Island, NY 10305
Phone: 718-447-4700
Fax: 718-816-7719

Village Voice
36 Cooper Sq
New York, NY 10003
E-mail: ads@villagevoice.com
www.villagevoice.com
Phone: 212-475-3300
Fax: 212-475-8944
TF: 800-875-2997

Villager The
80 8th Ave Suite 200
New York, NY 10011
E-mail: vilpaper@aol.com
www.thevillager.com
Phone: 212-229-1890
Fax: 212-229-2790

Where New York
810 7th Ave 4th Fl
New York, NY 10019
E-mail: info@wheremags.com
www.wheremags.com/wheremag.nsf/Cities/NewYork
Phone: 212-636-2700
Fax: 212-636-2747

**Indicates major daily newspapers*

Television

WABC-TV Ch 7 (ABC)
7 Lincoln Sq
New York, NY 10023
abcnews.go.com/local/wabc
Phone: 212-456-7777
Fax: 212-456-2381

WCBS-TV Ch 2 (CBS)
524 W 57th St
New York, NY 10019
www.cbs2ny.com
Phone: 212-975-4321
Fax: 212-975-9387

WHSI-TV Ch 67 (Ind)
PO Box 609
Central Islip, NY 11722
Phone: 631-582-6700
Fax: 631-582-8337

WLNY-TV Ch 55 (Ind)
270 S Service Rd
Melville, NY 11747
Phone: 631-777-8855
Fax: 631-420-4822

WMBC-TV Ch 63 (Ind)
500 Weldon Rd
Lake Hopatcong, NJ 07849
Phone: 973-697-0063
Fax: 973-697-5515

WNBC-TV Ch 4 (NBC)
30 Rockefeller Plaza
New York, NY 10112
E-mail: nbc4ny@nbc.com
www.newschannel4.com
Phone: 212-664-4444
Fax: 212-664-2994

WNET-TV Ch 13 (PBS)
450 W 33rd St
New York, NY 10001
E-mail: webinfo@www.wnet.org
www.wnet.org
Phone: 212-560-1313
Fax: 212-560-1314

WNJU-TV Ch 47 (Tele)
47 Industrial Ave
Teterboro, NJ 07608
E-mail: redaccion@noticiero47.net
www.noticiero47.net
Phone: 201-288-5550
Fax: 201-288-0129

WNYE-TV Ch 25 (PBS)
112 Tillary St
Brooklyn, NY 11201
E-mail: wnyemail@wnye.pbs.org
www.wnye.nycenet.edu
Phone: 718-250-5800
Fax: 718-855-8863

WNYW-TV Ch 5 (Fox)
205 E 67th St
New York, NY 10021
Phone: 212-452-5555
Fax: 212-249-1182

WPIX-TV Ch 11 (WB)
220 E 42nd St
New York, NY 10017
E-mail: wpix11@aol.com
www.wpix.com
Phone: 212-949-1100
Fax: 212-210-2591

WPXN-TV Ch 31 (PAX)
1330 Ave of the Americas 35th Fl
New York, NY 10019
www.pax.net/WPXN
Phone: 212-757-3100
Fax: 212-956-0951

WRNN-TV Ch 62 (Ind)
721 Broadway
Kingston, NY 12401
www.rnntv.com
Phone: 845-339-6200
Fax: 845-339-6264

WWOR-TV Ch 9 (UPN)
9 Broadcast Plaza
Secaucus, NJ 07096
www.upn9.com
Phone: 201-348-0009
Fax: 201-330-3777

WXTV-TV Ch 41 (Uni)
500 Frank W Burr Blvd 6th Fl
Teaneck, NJ 07666
www.univision.net/stations/wxtv.htm
Phone: 201-287-4141
Fax: 201-287-9427

Radio

WABC-AM 770 kHz (N/T)
2 Penn Plaza 17th Fl
New York, NY 10121
E-mail: postmaster@wabcradio.com
www.wabcradio.com
Phone: 212-613-3800
Fax: 212-947-1340

WALK-FM 97.5 MHz (AC)
66 Colonial Dr
Patchogue, NY 11772
E-mail: walkie@walkradio.com
www.walkradio.com
Phone: 631-475-5200
Fax: 631-475-9016

WAXQ-FM 104.3 MHz (CR)
1180 6th Ave 5th Fl
New York, NY 10036
classicq104.amfmi.com
Phone: 212-575-1043
Fax: 212-302-7814

WBAB-FM 102.3 MHz (Rock)
555 Sunrise Hwy
West Babylon, NY 11704
E-mail: wbab@wbab.com
www.wbab.com
Phone: 631-587-1023
Fax: 631-587-1282

WBGO-FM 88.3 MHz (NPR)
54 Park Pl
Newark, NJ 07102
E-mail: jazz88@wbgo.org
www.wbgo.org
Phone: 973-624-8880
Fax: 973-824-8888

WBLI-FM 106.1 MHz (CHR)
555 Sunrise Hwy
West Babylon, NY 11704
www.wbli.com
Phone: 631-669-9254
Fax: 631-376-0812

WBLS-FM 107.5 MHz (Urban)
3 Park Ave
New York, NY 10016
www.wbls.com
Phone: 212-447-1000
Fax: 212-447-5197

WBZO-FM 103.1 MHz (Oldies)
900 Walt Whitman Rd
Melville, NY 11747
E-mail: b103@prodigy.com
www.b103.com
Phone: 631-423-6740
Fax: 631-423-6750

WCAA-FM 105.9 MHz (Span)
485 Madison Ave 3rd Fl
New York, NY 10022
Phone: 212-310-6000
Fax: 212-888-3694

WCBS-AM 880 kHz (N/T)
51 W 52nd St
New York, NY 10019
www.cbsnewyork.com/now/section/0,1636,10100-207,00.shtml
Phone: 212-975-4321
Fax: 212-975-1893

WCBS-FM 101.1 MHz (Oldies)
51 W 52nd St
New York, NY 10019
wcbsfm.com
Phone: 212-975-4321
Fax: 212-975-9123

WDRE-FM 98.5 MHz (Alt)
1103 Stewart Ave
Garden City, NY 11530
Phone: 516-222-1103
Fax: 516-222-1391

WFME-FM 94.7 MHz (Rel)
289 Mount Pleasant Ave
West Orange, NJ 07052
Phone: 973-736-3600
Fax: 973-736-4832
TF: 800-543-1495

WFUV-FM 90.7 MHz (NPR)
Fordham University
Bronx, NY 10458
E-mail: thefolks@wfuv.org
www.wfuv.org
Phone: 718-817-4550
Fax: 718-817-5595

WGSM-AM 740 kHz (Nost)
1055 Franklin Ave
Garden City, NY 11530
Phone: 516-294-8400
Fax: 516-746-0034

WHFM-FM 95.3 MHz (Rock)
430 Main St Suite 102
Center Moriches, NY 11934
Phone: 631-283-9500
Fax: 631-283-9506

WHLI-AM 1100 kHz (Nost)
1055 Franklin Ave
Garden City, NY 11530
www.whli.com
Phone: 516-294-8400
Fax: 516-746-0034

WHTZ-FM 100.3 MHz (CHR)
230 Park Ave Suite 605
New York, NY 10169
E-mail: z100radio@aol.com
www.z100.com
Phone: 212-239-2300
Fax: 212-239-2308
TF: 800-242-0100

WINS-AM 1010 kHz (N/T)
888 7th Ave 10th Fl
New York, NY 10106
www.1010wins.com
Phone: 212-397-1010
Fax: 212-247-7918

WKJY-FM 98.3 MHz (AC)
1055 Franklin Ave
Garden City, NY 11530
www.kjoy.com
Phone: 516-294-8400
Fax: 516-746-0025

WKTU-FM 103.5 MHz (CHR)
525 Washington Blvd 16th Fl
Jersey City, NJ 07310
E-mail: info@ktu.com
www.ktu.com
Phone: 201-420-3700
Fax: 201-420-3770

WLIB-AM 1190 kHz (N/T)
3 Park Ave
New York, NY 10016
E-mail: info@wlib.com
www.wlib.com
Phone: 212-447-1000
Fax: 212-447-5193

WLIR-FM 92.7 MHz (Alt)
1103 Stewart Ave
Garden City, NY 11530
www.wlir.com
Phone: 516-222-1104
Fax: 516-222-1391

WLTW-FM 106.7 MHz (AC)
1133 Ave of the Americas 34th Fl
New York, NY 10036
E-mail: contact@1067litefm.com
www.1067litefm.com
Phone: 212-603-4600
Fax: 212-603-4602

WMJC-FM 94.3 MHz (Ctry)
900 Walt Whitman Rd
Melville, NY 11747
www.wmjc.com
Phone: 631-423-6740
Fax: 631-423-6750

WNEW-FM 102.7 MHz (N/T)
888 7th Ave 9th Fl
New York, NY 10106
E-mail: feedback@wnew.com
www.wnew.com
Phone: 212-489-1027
Fax: 212-957-9639

WNJR-AM 1430 kHz (Misc)
1 Riverfront Plaza Suite 345
Newark, NJ 07102
Phone: 973-642-8000
Fax: 973-642-5208

WNYC-AM 820 kHz (NPR)
1 Centre St
New York, NY 10007
E-mail: emailus@wnyc.org
www.wnyc.org
Phone: 212-669-7800
Fax: 212-553-0626

WNYC-FM 93.9 kHz (NPR)
1 Centre St
New York, NY 10007
E-mail: news@wnyc.org
www.wnyc.org
Phone: 212-669-7800
Fax: 212-553-0626

WOR-AM 710 kHz (N/T)
1440 Broadway
New York, NY 10018
www.wor710.com
Phone: 212-642-4500
Fax: 212-921-4204

WPAT-AM 930 kHz (Misc)
449 Broadway 2nd Fl
New York, NY 10013
Phone: 212-966-1059
Fax: 212-966-9580

WPAT-FM 93.1 MHz (Span)
26 W 56th St
New York, NY 10019
Phone: 212-541-9200
Fax: 212-333-7642

WPLJ-FM 95.5 MHz (AC)
2 Penn Plaza 17th Fl
New York, NY 10121
www.plj.com
Phone: 212-613-8900
Fax: 212-613-8956

WQCD-FM 101.9 MHz (NAC)
395 Hudson St 7th Fl
New York, NY 10014
www.cd1019.com
Phone: 212-352-1019
Fax: 212-929-8559

WQHT-FM 97.1 MHz (Urban)
395 Hudson St 7th Fl
New York, NY 10014
www.hot97.com
Phone: 212-229-9797
Fax: 212-929-8559

WQXR-FM 96.3 MHz (Clas)
122 5th Ave
New York, NY 10011
E-mail: wqxr963fm@aol.com
www.wqxr.com
Phone: 212-633-7600
Fax: 212-633-7666

WRKS-FM 98.7 MHz (Urban)
395 Hudson St 7th Fl
New York, NY 10014
Phone: 212-242-9870
Fax: 212-242-0706

WSKQ-FM 97.9 MHz (Span)
26 W 56th St
New York, NY 10019
E-mail: info@lamega.com
www.lamega.com
Phone: 212-541-9200
Fax: 212-333-7642

WTJM-FM 105.1 MHz (Oldies)
1120 Ave of the Americas 18th Fl
New York, NY 10036
E-mail: mix105ny@aol.com
www.jammin105.com
Phone: 212-704-1051
Fax: 212-398-3299

WXRK-FM 92.3 MHz (Alt)
40 W 57th St 14th Fl
New York, NY 10019
E-mail: wxrk923@aol.com
www.krockradio.com
Phone: 212-314-9230
Fax: 212-314-9340

Attractions

From Wall Street to Coney Island, New York is considered one of the world's largest and most exciting cities. Manhattan Island is considered "downtown" and is the site of most of the city's attractions and events. New York's famous skyline includes the twin towers of the World Trade Center and the Empire State Building, which offers an impressive view of the city from its observation deck. Among the city's most popular attractions are the Statue of Liberty, Central Park, and Broadway shows. Other visitor favorites include the New York Public Library, Macy's and Tiffany's, trendy Greenwich Village, SoHo, and Times Square.

Abagail Adams Smith Museum & Gardens
421 E 61st St
New York, NY 10021
www.fieldtrip.com/ny/28386878.htm
Phone: 212-838-6878
Fax: 212-838-7390

Afro-American Historical Society Museum
1841 Kennedy Blvd
Jersey City, NJ 07305
Phone: 201-547-5262
Fax: 201-547-5392

Ailey Alvin American Dance Theater
211 W 61st St 3rd Fl
New York, NY 10023
www.alvinailey.org
Phone: 212-767-0590
Fax: 212-767-0625

Alice Austen House Museum & Garden
2 Hylan Blvd
Staten Island, NY 10305
Phone: 718-816-4506
Fax: 718-815-3959

Ambassador Theatre
215 W 49th St
New York, NY 10019
Phone: 212-239-6200
TF: 800-432-7250

American Ballet Theatre
890 Broadway 3rd Fl
New York, NY 10003
www.abt.org
Phone: 212-477-3030
Fax: 212-254-5938

American Bible Society
1865 Broadway
New York, NY 10023
www.americanbible.org
Phone: 212-408-1200
Fax: 212-408-1512
TF: 800-322-4253

American Composers Orchestra
1775 Broadway Suite 525
New York, NY 10019
E-mail: amcomporch@aol.com
www.americancomposers.org
Phone: 212-977-8495
Fax: 212-977-8995

American Craft Museum
40 W 53rd St
New York, NY 10019
www.fieldtrip.com/ny/29563535.htm
Phone: 212-956-3535
Fax: 212-459-0926

American Indian Dance Theatre
223 E 61st St
New York, NY 10021
Phone: 212-308-9555
Fax: 212-826-0724

American Museum of Natural History
175-208 Central Pk W
New York, NY 10024
www.amnh.org
Phone: 212-769-5000
Fax: 212-769-5199

American Museum of the Moving Image
3601 35th Ave
Astoria, NY 11106
www.ammi.org
Phone: 718-784-4520
Fax: 718-784-4681

American Museum-Hayden Planetarium
81st St & Central Pk W
New York, NY 10024
www.amnh.org/rose
Phone: 212-769-5900
Fax: 212-769-5007

American Numismatic Society
Broadway & 155th St
New York, NY 10032
E-mail: info@amnumsoc.org
www.amnumsoc.org
Phone: 212-234-3130
Fax: 212-234-3381

American Symphony Orchestra
850 7th Ave Suite 503
New York, NY 10019
E-mail: amsymphony@aol.com
www.americansymphony.org
Phone: 212-581-1365
Fax: 212-489-7188

Americas Society
680 Park Ave
New York, NY 10021
www.americas-society.org
Phone: 212-249-8950
Fax: 212-249-5868

Andreas Space Planetarium
511 Warburton Ave Hudson River Museum of Westchester
Yonkers, NY 10701
www.hrm.org/Planetarium/planetarium.html
Phone: 914-963-4550
Fax: 914-963-8558

Apollo Theatre
253 W 125th St
New York, NY 10027
Phone: 212-531-5300
Fax: 212-749-2743

Avery Fisher Hall
W 65th St & Broadway
New York, NY 10023
www.lincolncenter.org
Phone: 212-875-5030
Fax: 212-875-5027

Ballet Hispanico of New York
167 W 89th St
New York, NY 10024
Phone: 212-362-6710
Fax: 212-362-7809

Barrymore Theatre
243 W 47th St
New York, NY 10036
Phone: 212-239-6200
TF: 800-432-7250

Bartow-Pell Mansion Museum
895 Shore Rd Pelham Bay Pk
Bronx, NY 10464
www.fieldtrip.com/ny/88851461.htm
Phone: 718-885-1461
Fax: 718-885-9164

Belasco Theatre
111 W 44th St
New York, NY 10036
Phone: 212-239-6200
TF: 800-432-7250

Belvedere Castle
830 5th Ave Mid Park 79th St
New York, NY 10021
Phone: 212-772-0210

Booth Theatre
222 W 45th St
New York, NY 10036
Phone: 212-239-6200
TF: 800-432-7250

Broadhurst Theatre
235 W 44th St
New York, NY 10036
Phone: 212-239-6200
TF: 800-432-7250

Broadway Theatre
1681 Broadway
New York, NY 10019
www.broadwaytheater.com/
Phone: 212-239-6200
TF: 800-432-7250

Bronx County Historical Society
3309 Bainbridge Ave
Bronx, NY 10467
www.bronxhistoricalsociety.org
Phone: 718-881-8900
Fax: 718-881-4827

Bronx Museum of the Arts
1040 Grand Concourse
Bronx, NY 10456
www.fieldtrip.com/ny/86816000.htm
Phone: 718-681-6000
Fax: 718-681-6181

Bronx Zoo Wildlife Conservation Park
2300 Southern Blvd
Bronx, NY 10460
www.wcs.org/zoos/bronxzoo
Phone: 718-220-5100
Fax: 718-220-2685

Brooklyn Academy of Music
30 Lafayette Ave
Brooklyn, NY 11217
www.bam.org
Phone: 718-636-4111
Fax: 718-636-4179

Brooklyn Botanic Garden
1000 Washington Ave
Brooklyn, NY 11225
www.bbg.org
Phone: 718-623-7200
Fax: 718-857-2430

Brooklyn Children's Museum
145 Brooklyn Ave
Brooklyn, NY 11213
www.fieldtrip.com/ny/87354400.htm
Phone: 718-735-4400
Fax: 718-604-7442

Brooklyn Museum of Art
200 Eastern Pkwy
Brooklyn, NY 11238
www.brooklynart.org
Phone: 718-638-5000
Fax: 718-638-3731

Brooklyn Philharmonic Orchestra
1 Hanson Pl Suite 1806
Brooklyn, NY 11243
Phone: 718-622-5555
Fax: 718-622-3774

Brooks Atkinson Theatre
256 W 47th St
New York, NY 10036
Phone: 212-307-4100
TF: 800-755-4000

Bryant Park
betw 40th & 42nd Sts & betw 5th & 6th Aves
New York, NY 10018
E-mail: bprc@urbanmgt.com
www.bryantpark.org
Phone: 212-768-4242
Fax: 212-719-3499

Carnegie Hall
154 W 57th St
New York, NY 10019
www.carnegiehall.org
Phone: 212-247-7800
Fax: 212-581-6539

Castle Clinton National Monument
Battery Park
New York, NY 10004
www.nps.gov/cacl/
Phone: 212-344-7220

Cathedral Church of Saint John the Divine
1047 Amsterdam Ave
New York, NY 10025
E-mail: stjohn@interport.net
www.stjohndivine.org
Phone: 212-316-7540
Fax: 212-932-7348

Central Park
830 5th Ave
New York, NY 10021
www.centralpark.org
Phone: 212-360-8111
Fax: 212-360-1329

Central Park Wildlife Conservation Center
5th Ave & 64th St
New York, NY 10021
www.wcs.org/zoos/wildlifecenters/centralpark
Phone: 212-861-6030

Central Railroad Terminal
Audrey Zapp Dr Liberty State Park
Jersey City, NJ 07304
Phone: 201-915-3400
Fax: 201-915-3413

Chelsea Piers Sports & Entertainment Complex
W 23rd St & Hudson River
New York, NY 10011
www.chelseapiers.com
Phone: 212-336-6666
Fax: 212-336-6808

Children's Museum of Manhattan
212 W 83rd St
New York, NY 10024
E-mail: mail@cmom.org
www.cmom.org
Phone: 212-721-1223
Fax: 212-721-1127

Children's Museum of the Arts
182 Lafayette St
New York, NY 10013
Phone: 212-941-9198

Church of the Transfiguration
1 E 29th St
New York, NY 10016
E-mail: transfig@ix.netcom.com
www.littlechurch.org
Phone: 212-684-6770
Fax: 212-684-1662

Citicorp Center
53rd St & Lexington Ave
New York, NY 10022
Phone: 212-559-6758
Fax: 212-486-1969

City Center
130 W 56th St
New York, NY 10019
www.citycenter.org
Phone: 212-247-0430
Fax: 212-246-9778

Cloisters Museum
Fort Tryon Pk
New York, NY 10040
www.fieldtrip.com/ny/29233700.htm
Phone: 212-923-3700
Fax: 212-795-3640

Conservatory Garden
5th Ave & 105th St Central Pk
New York, NY 10029
www.centralpark.org
Phone: 212-860-1382

Cooper-Hewitt National Design Museum (Smithsonian Institution)
2 E 91st St
New York, NY 10128
www.si.edu/ndm
Phone: 212-849-8300
Fax: 212-849-8401

Cort Theatre
138 W 48th St
New York, NY 10036
Phone: 212-239-6200
TF: 800-432-7250

Cunningham Merce Dance Co
55 Bethune St
New York, NY 10014
E-mail: cdfmerce@delphi.com
www.merce.org
Phone: 212-255-8240
Fax: 212-633-2453

Dahesh Museum
601 5th Ave
New York, NY 10017
E-mail: education@daheshmuseum.org
www.daheshmuseum.org
Phone: 212-759-0606
Fax: 212-759-1235

Dance Theatre of Harlem Inc
466 W 152nd St
New York, NY 10031
E-mail: DnseHarlem@aol.com
www.dancetheatreofharlem.com
Phone: 212-690-2800
Fax: 212-690-8736

DIA Center for the Arts
548 W 22nd St
New York, NY 10011
www.diacenter.org
Phone: 212-989-5566
Fax: 212-989-4055

Duffy Theatre
1553 Broadway
New York, NY 10036
Phone: 212-695-3401

Dyckman House
215 Nagle Ave
New York, NY 10034
Phone: 212-569-7300
Fax: 212-304-1642

Empire State Building
350 5th Ave Suite 3210
New York, NY 10118
E-mail: info@esbnyc.com
www.esbnyc.com
Phone: 212-736-3100
Fax: 212-967-6167

ESPN Zone New York
1472 Broadway
New York, NY 10036
Phone: 212-921-3776

Eugene O'Neill Theatre
230 W 49th St
New York, NY 10036
Phone: 212-239-6200
TF: 800-432-7250

Federal Hall National Memorial
26 Wall St
New York, NY 10005
www.nps.gov/feha/
Phone: 212-825-6888
Fax: 212-825-6874

Forbes Magazine Galleries
62 5th Ave
New York, NY 10011
Phone: 212-206-5548

Ford Center for the Performing Arts
213 W 42nd St
New York, NY 10036
Phone: 212-307-4100
TF: 800-755-4000

Frick Collection
1 E 70th St
New York, NY 10021
www.frick.org
Phone: 212-288-0700
Fax: 212-628-4417

Gateway National Recreation Area
Headquarters Bldg 69 Floyd Bennett Field
Brooklyn, NY 11234
www.nps.gov/gate/
Phone: 718-338-3687
Fax: 718-338-3560

General Grant National Memorial
Riverside Dr & W 122nd St
New York, NY 10027
www.nps.gov/gegr
Phone: 212-666-1640
Fax: 212-932-9631

Gershwin Theatre
222 W 51st St
New York, NY 10019
Phone: 212-307-4100
TF: 800-755-4000

Golden Theatre
252 W 45th St
New York, NY 10036
Phone: 212-239-6200

Gracie Mansion
88th St & East End Ave
New York, NY 10128
Phone: 212-570-4751

Graham Martha Dance Center
440 Lafayette St
New York, NY 10003
Phone: 212-832-9166
Fax: 212-223-0351

Green Flea Market Saturdays
E 67th St-betw 1st Ave & York St
New York, NY 10024
Phone: 212-721-0900

Green Flea Market Sundays
Columbus Ave-betw 76th & 77th Sts
New York, NY 10024
Phone: 212-721-0900
Fax: 212-721-6934

Guggenheim Museum SoHo
575 Broadway
New York, NY 10012
www.guggenheim.org
Phone: 212-423-3500
Fax: 212-360-4340

Hamilton Grange National Memorial
287 Convent Ave
New York, NY 10031
www.nps.gov/hagr/
Phone: 212-283-5154

Harbor Defense Museum
Fort Hamilton
Brooklyn, NY 11252
Phone: 718-630-4349

Helen Hayes Theatre
240 W 44th St
New York, NY 10036
Phone: 212-239-6200
TF: 800-432-7250

Historic Richmond Town
441 Clarke Ave
Staten Island, NY 10306
Phone: 718-351-1611
Fax: 718-351-6057

Home of Franklin D Roosevelt National Historic Site
519 Albany Post Rd
Hyde Park, NY 12538
www.nps.gov/hofr/
Phone: 845-229-9115
Fax: 845-229-0739

Hudson River Museum of Westchester
511 Warburton Ave
Yonkers, NY 10701
www.hrm.org
Phone: 914-963-4550
Fax: 914-963-8558

Imperial Theatre
249 W 45th St
New York, NY 10036
Phone: 212-239-6200
TF: 800-432-7250

International Center of Photography
1130 5th Ave
New York, NY 10128
www.icp.org/
Phone: 212-860-1777
Fax: 212-360-6490

Intrepid Sea-Air-Space Museum
W 46th St & 12th Ave Pier 86
New York, NY 10036
E-mail: marketing@intrepid-museum.com
www.intrepid-museum.com
Phone: 212-245-0072
Fax: 212-245-7289

Jacques Marchais Museum of Tibetan Art
338 Lighthouse Ave
Staten Island, NY 10306
Phone: 718-987-3500
Fax: 718-351-0402

Jamaica Bay Wildlife Refuge
Gateway National Recreation Area Headquarters Bldg 69 Floyd Bennett Field
Brooklyn, NY 11234
Phone: 718-318-4340
Fax: 718-318-4338

Jersey City Museum
472 Jersey Ave
Jersey City, NJ 07302
Phone: 201-547-4514

Jewish Museum
1109 5th Ave
New York, NY 10128
www.thejewishmuseum.org
Phone: 212-423-3200
Fax: 212-423-3232

Kingsland Homestead
143-35 37th Ave
Flushing, NY 11354
www.preserve.org/queens/kingsland.htm
Phone: 718-939-0647
Fax: 718-539-9885

Kodak OMNI Theater
251 Phillip St
Jersey City, NJ 07305
Phone: 201-451-0006
Fax: 201-451-6383

Lehman Center for the Performing Arts
250 Bedford Park Blvd W
Bronx, NY 10468
Phone: 718-960-8232
Fax: 718-960-8233

Liberty Science Center
251 Phillip St
Jersey City, NJ 07305
www.lsc.org
Phone: 201-451-0006
Fax: 201-451-6383

Liberty State Park
Morris Pesin Dr
Jersey City, NJ 07305
Phone: 201-915-3400
Fax: 201-915-3408

Liberty Street Gallery
225 Liberty St World Financial Ctr
New York, NY 10281
Phone: 212-945-0505

Lincoln Center for the Performing Arts
70 Lincoln Ctr Plaza
New York, NY 10023
www.lincolncenter.org
Phone: 212-875-5223
Fax: 212-875-5242

Long Island Children's Museum
550 Stewart Ave
Garden City, NY 11530
www.516web.com/museum/licm.htm
Phone: 516-222-0217
Fax: 516-222-0225

Longacre Theatre
220 W 48th St
New York, NY 10036
Phone: 212-239-6200
TF: 800-432-7250

Lower East Side Tenement Museum
90 Orchard St
New York, NY 10002
www.wnet.org/archive/tenement/
Phone: 212-431-0233
Fax: 212-431-0402

Lunt-Fontanne Theatre
205 W 46th St
New York, NY 10036
Phone: 212-307-4100
TF: 800-755-4000

Lyceum Theatre
149 W 45th St
New York, NY 10036
Phone: 212-239-6200
TF: 800-432-7250

Majestic Theatre
245 W 44th St
New York, NY 10036
Phone: 212-239-6200
TF: 800-432-7250

Manhattan Lyric Opera
435 E 77th St
New York, NY 10021
E-mail: tmo68@musicentral.com
musicentral.com/manhattanlyric
Phone: 212-879-0144
Fax: 212-753-0757

Manhattan Philharmonic
70 W 36th St Suite 305
New York, NY 10018
www.midamerica-music.com/manhattan/home.html
Phone: 212-239-0205
Fax: 212-563-5587

Manhattan Theatre Club Inc
311 W 43rd St 8th Fl
New York, NY 10036
E-mail: questions@mtc-nyc.org
www.mtc-nyc.org
Phone: 212-399-3000
Fax: 212-399-4329

Marquis Theatre
211 W 45th St Marriott Marquis Hotel
New York, NY 10036
Phone: 212-307-4100
TF: 800-755-4000

Martin Beck Theatre
302 W 45th St
New York, NY 10036
Phone: 212-239-6200
TF: 800-432-7250

Medieval Times Dinner & Tournament
720 7th Ave
New York, NY 10036
www.medievaltimes.com/NY_realm.htm
Phone: 212-586-9096
Fax: 212-586-9251

Metropolitan Museum of Art
1000 5th Ave
New York, NY 10028
E-mail: visitorservices@metmuseum.org
www.metmuseum.org
Phone: 212-879-5500
Fax: 212-570-3879

Metropolitan Opera Assn Inc
64th St & Broadway Lincoln Ctr
New York, NY 10023
E-mail: metinfo@visionfoundry.com
www.metopera.org
Phone: 212-799-3100
Fax: 212-870-7416

Minskoff Theatre
200 W 45th St
New York, NY 10036
Phone: 212-307-4100
TF: 800-755-4000

Morris Mark Dance Group
225 Lafayette St Suite 504
New York, NY 10012
E-mail: info@mmdg.org
www.mmdg.org
Phone: 212-219-3660
Fax: 212-219-3960

Morris-Jumel Museum
65 Jumel Terr at 160th St
New York, NY 10032
Phone: 212-923-8008
Fax: 212-923-8947

Museo del Barrio
1230 5th Ave
New York, NY 10029
www.elmuseo.org
Phone: 212-831-7272
Fax: 212-831-7927

Museum for African Art
593 Broadway
New York, NY 10012
www.fieldtrip.com/ny/29661313.htm
Phone: 212-966-1313
Fax: 212-966-1432

Museum of American Financial History
28 Broadway
New York, NY 10004
www.mafh.org
Phone: 212-908-4110
Fax: 212-908-4601

Museum of American Folk Art
555 W 57th St 13th Fl
New York, NY 10019
www.folokartmuseum.org
Phone: 212-977-7170
Fax: 212-977-8134

Museum of American Illustration
128 E 63rd St
New York, NY 10021
www.fieldtrip.com/ny/28382560.htm
Phone: 212-838-2560
Fax: 212-838-2561
TF: 800-746-8738

Museum of Jewish Heritage
18 1st Pl Battery Park City
New York, NY 10004
www.mjhnyc.org
Phone: 212-968-1800
Fax: 212-968-1368

Museum of Modern Art
11 W 53rd St
New York, NY 10019
E-mail: comments@moma.org
www.moma.org
Phone: 212-708-9400
Fax: 212-333-1251

Museum of Television & Radio
25 W 52nd St
New York, NY 10019
www.mtr.org
Phone: 212-621-6600
Fax: 212-621-6700

Museum of the American Piano
211 W 58th St
New York, NY 10019
E-mail: pmuseum@pianomuseum.com
www.pianomuseum.com
Phone: 212-246-4646
Fax: 212-245-5432

Museum of the City of New York
1220 5th Ave
New York, NY 10029
E-mail: mcny@mcny.org
www.mcny.org
Phone: 212-534-1672
Fax: 212-534-5974

Music Box Theatre
239 W 45th St
New York, NY 10036
Phone: 212-239-6200
TF: 800-432-7250

Music Hall at Snug Harbor Cultural Center
1000 Richmond Terr
Staten Island, NY 10301
www.snug-harbor.org
Phone: 718-448-2500
Fax: 718-815-0198

National Academy of Design Museum
1083 5th Ave
New York, NY 10128
www.nationalacademy.org
Phone: 212-369-4880
Fax: 212-360-6795

National Museum of the American Indian (Smithsonian Institution)
1 Bowling Green
New York, NY 10004
www.si.edu/nmai
Phone: 212-514-3700
Fax: 212-514-3800
TF: 800-242-6624

Nederlander Theatre
208 W 41st St
New York, NY 10036
Phone: 212-307-4100
TF: 800-755-4000

Neil Simon Theatre
250 W 52nd St
New York, NY 10019
Phone: 212-307-4100
TF: 800-755-4000

New Amsterdam Theatre
214 W 42nd St
New York, NY 10036
Phone: 212-307-4100
TF: 800-755-4000

New Museum of Contemporary Art
583 Broadway
New York, NY 10012
E-mail: newmu@newmuseum.org
www.newmuseum.org
Phone: 212-219-1222
Fax: 212-431-5328

New York Aquarium
Boardwalk & W 8th St Coney Island
Brooklyn, NY 11224
www.wcs.org/zoos/aquarium
Phone: 718-265-3474
Fax: 718-265-2660

New York Botanical Garden
200th St & Kazimiroff Blvd
Bronx, NY 10458
www.nybg.org
Phone: 718-817-8700
Fax: 718-220-6504

New York Chamber Ensemble
475 Riverside Dr Rm 621
New York, NY 10115
Phone: 212-870-2439

New York Chamber Symphony
130 W 56th St Suite 70
New York, NY 10019
www.nycs.org
Phone: 212-262-6927
Fax: 212-246-3204

New York City Ballet
20 Lincoln Ctr Plaza New York State Theatre 4th Fl
New York, NY 10023
www.nycballet.com
Phone: 212-870-5656
Fax: 212-870-4244
TF: 800-580-8730

New York City Fire Museum
278 Spring St
New York, NY 10013
Phone: 212-691-1303
Fax: 212-924-0430

New York City Opera
20 Lincoln Ctr Plaza New York State Theater
New York, NY 10023
www.nycopera.com
Phone: 212-870-5600
Fax: 212-724-1120

New York Hall of Science
47-01 111th St Flushing Meadows
Corona Park, NY 11368
www.nyhallsci.org
Phone: 718-699-0005
Fax: 718-699-1341

New York Historical Society
2 W 77th St
New York, NY 10024
www.nyhistory.org
Phone: 212-873-3400
Fax: 212-874-8706

New York Philharmonic
10 Lincoln Ctr Plaza Avery Fisher Hall
New York, NY 10023
E-mail: nyphil@pegasusnet.com
www.nyphilharmon.org
Phone: 212-875-5000
Fax: 212-875-5717

New York Pops Orchestra
881 7th Ave Suite 903
New York, NY 10019
E-mail: nypops@aol.com
www.newyorkpops.org
Phone: 212-765-7677
Fax: 212-315-3199

New York Public Library for the Performing Arts
521 W 43rd St
New York, NY 10036
www.nypl.org/research/lpa/lpa.html
Phone: 212-870-1650
Fax: 212-870-1794

New York Skyride
350 5th Ave
New York, NY 10118
www.skyride.com
Phone: 212-564-2224
Fax: 212-564-0652

New York State Theater
63rd St & Columbus Ave
New York, NY 10023
Phone: 212-870-5570
Fax: 212-870-5693

New York Stock Exchange Visitors Center
20 Broad St 3rd Fl
New York, NY 10005
Phone: 212-656-5162
Fax: 212-656-2010

New York Transit Museum
Boerum Pl & Schermerhorn St Subway Stn
Brooklyn, NY 11201
www.fieldtrip.com/ny/83303060.htm
Phone: 718-243-8601
Fax: 718-522-2339

Opera Orchestra of New York
239 W 72nd St Suite 2R
New York, NY 10023
E-mail: oony@tiac.net
www.oony.org
Phone: 212-799-1982
Fax: 212-721-9170

Orchestra of Saint Luke's
330 W 42nd St 9th Fl
New York, NY 10036
www.stlukes.cc
Phone: 212-594-6100
Fax: 212-594-3291

Orpheus Chamber Orchestra
490 Riverside Dr
New York, NY 10027
www.orpheusnyc.com
Phone: 212-896-1700
Fax: 212-896-1717
TF: 800-677-4387

Palace Theatre
1564 Broadway
New York, NY 10036
Phone: 212-307-4100
TF: 800-755-4000

Papp Joseph Public Theater
425 Lafayette St
New York, NY 10003
www.publictheater.org
Phone: 212-539-8500
Fax: 212-539-8505

Pelham Bay Park
Bruckner Blvd & Middletown & Shore Rds
Bronx, NY 10464
Phone: 718-430-1890

Philipse Manor Hall
29 Warburton Ave
Yonkers, NY 10701
Phone: 914-965-4027
Fax: 914-965-6485

Plymouth Theatre
236 W 45th St
New York, NY 10036
Phone: 212-239-6200
TF: 800-432-7250

Poe Edgar Allan Cottage
E Kingsbridge Rd Grand Concourse
Bronx, NY 10467
Phone: 718-881-8900

Police Academy Museum
25 Broadway 2nd FL
New York, NY 10004
www.nycpolicemuseum.org
Phone: 212-301-4440

Prospect Park Wildlife Center
450 Flatbush Ave
Brooklyn, NY 11225
www.wcs.org/zoos/wildlifecenters/prospectpark
Phone: 718-399-7339
Fax: 718-399-7337

Queens Botanical Garden
43-50 Main St
Flushing, NY 11355
Phone: 718-886-3800
Fax: 718-463-0263

Queens County Farm Museum
7350 Little Neck Pkwy Floral Pk
Queens, NY 11004
E-mail: queensfarm@citysoftinc.com
www.queensfarm.org
Phone: 718-347-3276
Fax: 718-347-3243

Queens Museum of Art
Flushing Meadows Corona Pk
Flushing, NY 11368
www.queensmuse.org
Phone: 718-592-9700
Fax: 718-592-5778

Queens Wildlife Center
111th St & 53rd Ave
Flushing Meadows, NY 11368
www.wcs.org/zoos/wildlifecenters/queens
Phone: 718-271-7761

Radio City Music Hall
1260 Ave of the Americas
New York, NY 10020
www.radiocity.com
Phone: 212-632-4000

Richard Rodgers Theatre
226 W 46th St
New York, NY 10036
Phone: 212-307-4100
TF: 800-755-4000

Riverside Church
120th St & Riverside Dr
New York, NY 10027
www.theriversidechurchny.org
Phone: 212-870-6700
Fax: 212-870-6800

Riverside Park
Hudson River betw 72nd & 155th Sts
New York, NY 10023
Phone: 212-408-0264

Rockefeller Center
630 5th Ave
New York, NY 10111
Phone: 212-332-6500

Roundabout Theatre Co
231 W 39th St Suite 1200
New York, NY 10018
www.roundabouttheatre.org
Phone: 212-869-8400

Royale Theatre
242 W 45th St
New York, NY 10036
Phone: 212-239-6200
TF: 800-432-7250

Rye Playland Park
Playland Pkwy
Rye, NY 10580
Phone: 914-925-2701
Fax: 914-925-2757

Saint James Theatre
246 W 44th St
New York, NY 10036
Phone: 212-239-6200
TF: 800-432-7250

Saint Patrick's Cathedral
14 E 51st St
New York, NY 10022
Phone: 212-753-2261

Saint Paul's Church National Historic Site
897 S Columbus Ave
Mount Vernon, NY 10550
www.nps.gov/sapa/
Phone: 914-667-4116
Fax: 914-667-3024

Santana Carlota Spanish Dance Co
154 Christopher St Suite 3D
New York, NY 10014
flamenco-vivo.org
Phone: 212-229-9754
Fax: 212-229-1085

Sherwood House
340 Tuckahoe Rd
Yonkers, NY 10710
Phone: 914-965-0401
Fax: 914-965-0401

Shubert Theatre
225 W 44th St
New York, NY 10036
Phone: 212-239-6200
TF: 800-432-7250

Skyscraper Museum
16 Wall St
New York, NY 10005
Phone: 212-968-1961
Fax: 212-766-1324

Snug Harbor Cultural Center
1000 Richmond Terr
Staten Island, NY 10301
community.silive.com/cc/snugharbor
Phone: 718-448-2500
Fax: 718-442-8534

Solomon R Guggenheim Museum
1071 5th Ave
New York, NY 10128
www.guggenheim.org
Phone: 212-423-3500
Fax: 212-423-3640

Sony IMAX Theatre
1998 Broadway
New York, NY 10023
www.theatres.sre.sony.com/
Phone: 212-336-5020
Fax: 212-336-5055

Sony Wonder Technology Lab
550 Madison Ave Sony Plaza
New York, NY 10022
wondertechlab.sony.com
Phone: 212-833-8100
Fax: 212-833-4445

South Street Seaport Market Place
19 Fulton St
New York, NY 10038
www.southstseaport.org
Phone: 212-732-8257
Fax: 212-964-8056

Stardust Theatre
1650 Broadway
New York, NY 10019
Phone: 212-239-6200
TF: 800-432-7250

Staten Island Botanical Garden
1000 Richmond Terr
Staten Island, NY 10301
E-mail: sibg@erols.com
www.sibg.org
Phone: 718-273-8200
Fax: 718-442-3645

Staten Island Institute of Arts & Sciences
75 Stuyvesant Pl
Staten Island, NY 10301
Phone: 718-727-1135
Fax: 718-273-5683

Staten Island Zoo
614 Broadway Staten Island Zoo
Staten Island, NY 10310
Phone: 718-442-3101
Fax: 718-981-8711

Statue of Liberty National Monument & Ellis Island
Liberty Island
New York, NY 10004
www.nps.gov/stli
Phone: 212-363-3200
Fax: 212-363-6304

Studio Museum in Harlem
144 W 125th St
New York, NY 10027
www.studiomuseuminharlem.org
Phone: 212-864-4500
Fax: 212-864-4800

Symphony for United Nations
170 West End Ave Suite 27-L
New York, NY 10023
Phone: 631-723-2251

Theodore Roosevelt Birthplace National Historic Site
28 E 20th St
New York, NY 10003
www.nps.gov/thrb/
Phone: 212-260-1616
Fax: 212-677-3587

Top of the World Observation Deck
2 World Trade Ctr Suite 1520
New York, NY 10048
E-mail: info@wtc-top.com
www.wtc-top.com
Phone: 212-323-2340
Fax: 212-323-2352

Ukrainian Museum
203 2nd Ave
New York, NY 10003
E-mail: ukrmus@aol.com
brama.com/ukrainian_museum
Phone: 212-228-0110
Fax: 212-228-1947

United Nations
1st Ave & 42nd St
New York, NY 10017
E-mail: ecu@un.org
www.un.org
Phone: 212-963-1234
Fax: 212-371-4360

Untermyer Park
285 Nepperhan Ave
Yonkers, NY 10701
Phone: 914-377-6450
Fax: 914-377-6428

Van Cortlandt Park
Broadway & W 242nd St
Bronx, NY 10463
Phone: 718-430-1890

Vanderbilt Mansion National Historic Site
4097 Albany Post Rd
Hyde Park, NY 12538
www.nps.gov/vama
Phone: 845-229-9115
Fax: 845-229-0739

Via Max
37 W 65th St
New York, NY 10023
Phone: 212-874-6700
Fax: 212-877-1146
TF: 800-462-9278

Virginia Theatre
245 W 52nd St
New York, NY 10019
Phone: 212-239-6200
TF: 800-432-7250

Vivian Beaumont Theatre
150 W 65th St
New York, NY 10023
Phone: 212-239-6200
TF: 800-432-7250

Walter Kerr Theatre
219 W 48th St
New York, NY 10036
Phone: 212-239-6200
TF: 800-432-7250

Wave Hill Garden
W 249th St & Independence Ave
Bronx, NY 10471
Phone: 718-549-3200

Whitney Museum of American Art
945 Madison Ave
New York, NY 10021
www.echonyc.com/~whitney
Phone: 212-570-3600
Fax: 212-570-7729

Winter Garden Theatre
1634 Broadway
New York, NY 10019
Phone: 212-239-6200
TF: 800-432-7250

World Trade Center
2 World Trade Ctr
New York, NY 10048
Phone: 212-435-4170

Yeshiva University Museum
15 W 16th St
New York, NY 10011
www.yu.edu/museum
Phone: 212-294-8330
Fax: 212-294-8335

Yonkers Education & Cultural Arts Center
1109 N Broadway
Yonkers, NY 10701
Phone: 914-376-8286
Fax: 914-376-8288

Sports Teams & Facilities

Aqueduct Race Track
Rockaway Blvd & 108th St Ozone Pk
Ozone Park, NY 11417
www.nyracing.com/aqueduct
Phone: 718-641-4700
Fax: 718-835-5246
TF: 800-522-5554

Belmont Park Race Track
2150 Hempstead Tpke
Elmont, NY 11003
www.nyracing.com/belmont/
Phone: 516-488-6000
Fax: 516-488-6016

Brooklyn Knights (soccer)
125-08 Flatlands Ave Jefferson Field
Brooklyn, NY 11208
E-mail: knightsocr@aol.com
www.brooklynknights.com
Phone: 718-621-1900
Fax: 718-621-1332

Giants Stadium
50 State Hwy 120
East Rutherford, NJ 07073
Phone: 201-935-8500
Fax: 201-935-7121

Long Island Lady Riders (soccer)
Evergreen Ave Michael J Tully Jr Stadium
New Hyde Park, NY 11753
E-mail: ridersmail@aol.com
ladyriders.com
Phone: 516-735-2277
Fax: 516-735-2288

Long Island Rough Riders (soccer)
3 Court House Dr EAB Park
Central Islip, NY 11722
E-mail: info@rough-riders.com
www.rough-riders.com
Phone: 631-940-3825

Madison Square Garden
2 Pennsylvania Plaza
New York, NY 10121
www.thegarden.com
Phone: 212-465-6000
Fax: 212-465-6092

New Brunswick Brigade (soccer)
Joyce Kilmer Ave Memorial Stadium
New Brunswick, NJ 08901
Phone: 732-517-0278
Fax: 732-517-0278

New Brunswick Power (soccer)
Joyce Kilmer Ave Memorial Stadium
New Brunswick, NJ 08901
Phone: 732-517-0278
Fax: 732-517-0278

New Jersey Devils
50 Rt 120 N Continental Airlines Arena
East Rutherford, NJ 07073
www.newjerseydevils.com
Phone: 201-935-6050
Fax: 201-935-2127
TF: 800-653-3845

New Jersey Nets
50 Rt 120 N Continental Airlines Arena
East Rutherford, NJ 07073
www.nba.com/nets
Phone: 201-935-3900
Fax: 201-507-8128

New York Freedom (soccer)
Charles Lindbergh Blvd Mitchel Athletic Complex
Uniondale, NY 11553
Phone: 631-940-3825
Fax: 631-940-3800

New York Giants
50 State Hwy 120 Giants Stadium
East Rutherford, NJ 07073
www.giants.com
Phone: 201-935-8111
Fax: 201-939-4134

New York Islanders
1255 Hempstead Tpke Nassau Coliseum
Uniondale, NY 11553
Phone: 516-794-9300

New York Jets
50 State Hwy 120 Giants Stadium
East Rutherford, NJ 07073
www.newyorkjets.com
Phone: 201-935-8500

New York Knicks
2 Penn Plaza Madison Square Garden
New York, NY 10121
www.nba.com/knicks
Phone: 212-465-6000
Fax: 212-465-6062

New York Liberty (basketball)
2 Penn Plaza Madison Square Garden
New York, NY 10121
www.wnba.com/liberty
Phone: 212-465-6005
Fax: 212-465-6250

New York Magic (soccer)
218th St & Broadway Columbia University Stadium
New York, NY 10034
Phone: 212-447-0932
Fax: 212-447-0932

New York Mets
123-01 Roosevelt Ave Shea Stadium
Flushing, NY 11368
www.newyorkmets.com
Phone: 718-507-8499

New York Rangers
2 Penn Plaza Madison Square Garden
New York, NY 10121
www.newyorkrangers.com
Phone: 212-465-6741
Fax: 212-465-6494

New York Yankees
161st St & River Ave Yankee Stadium
Bronx, NY 10451
www.yankees.com
Phone: 718-293-6000
Fax: 718-293-4841

New York/New Jersey MetroStars (soccer)
1 Harmon Plaza 3rd Fl
Secaucus, NJ 07094
E-mail: kickstuff@aol.com
www.metrostars.com
Phone: 201-583-7000
Fax: 201-583-7055

North Jersey Imperials (soccer)
Sprague Field Montclair State University Campus
Montclair, NJ 07042
E-mail: info@njimperials.com
www.njimperials.com
Phone: 201-729-1500
Fax: 201-729-1511
TF: 888-542-5794

Westchester Flames (soccer)
112 W Boston Post Rd
Mamaroneck, NY 10543
Phone: 718-626-6767
Fax: 718-267-0282

Yankee Stadium
161st St & River Ave
Bronx, NY 10451
www.yankees.com
Phone: 718-293-4300
Fax: 718-293-8431

Yonkers Raceway
Yonkers & Central Park Aves
Yonkers, NY 10704
Phone: 914-968-4200
Fax: 914-968-4479

Annual Events

4th of July Concert in Battery Park (July 4)........212-835-2789
5th Avenue Art & Antiques Show (mid-October)....212-249-4865
9th Avenue International Food Festival (mid-May)..........212-581-7217
African Film Festival (mid-late April)..............718-638-5000
American Crafts Festival (mid-June)...............212-875-5000
Art Expo New York (early March) 212-216-2000
Artists' Studio Tour (late October) 201-547-6969
Bell Atlantic Jazz Festival (early-mid-June).........212-219-3006
Belmont Stakes (early June)......................718-641-4700
Big Apple Circus (late October-mid-January)........212-268-2500
Brooklyn Botanical Garden Center Flower Sale (early May) 718-623-7200
Bryant Park Summer Film Festival (mid-June-mid-August)..........212-512-5700
Cathedral Arts Festival (mid-March)...............201-659-2211
Celebrate Brooklyn Festival (July-late August) 718-855-7882
Chinese New Year Celebrations (early-mid-February)..........212-431-9740
Chrysanthemum & Bonsai Festival (mid-October)..........718-817-8700
Crafts on Columbus (late April-early May)..........212-866-2239
Cultural Arts Festival (mid-June)..................201-547-5522
Earth Day New York (April 22)....................212-922-0048
Egyptian Festival (early September) 201-547-5522
Empire State Building Holiday Lights (early December-early January)..........212-736-3100
First Night New York (December 31) 212-883-2420
Gen Art Film Festival (late April-early May) 212-290-0312
Great July 4th Festival (July 4) 212-809-4900
Greek Festival (early September) 201-547-5522
Greenwich Village Halloween Parade (late October)..........845-758-5519
Irish Festival (late September)....................201-547-5522
Italian Festival (early October)....................201-547-5522
JVC Jazz Festival (mid-late June)..................212-501-1390
Korean Festival (late September)..................201-547-5522
Lincoln Center Family Art Show (mid-December-early January)..........212-875-5151
Lincoln Center Festival (early-late July)............212-875-5000
Macy's Fireworks Celebration (July 4) 212-695-4400
Macy's Thanksgiving Day Parade (late November)..........212-494-5432
Mostly Mozart Festival (early-late August)..........212-875-5030
National Black Fine Art Show (late January)........212-777-5218
National Horse Show (early November) 516-484-1865
New Year's Eve Celebration & Ball Drop in Times Square (December 31)..........212-768-1560
New York Film Festival (late September-early October)..........212-875-5610
New York Lesbian & Gay Film Festival (early-mid-June)..........212-254-7228
New York Marathon (early November)..............212-860-4455
New York National Boat Show (early-mid-January)..........212-984-7070
New York Restaurant & Food Service Show (mid-March)..........212-216-2000
New York Underground Film Festival (mid-March)..........212-675-1137
Outsider Art Fair (late January)...................212-777-5218
Passports to Off Broadway Theatres (February-April)..........212-768-1818
Paul Winter's Winter Solstice Celebration (mid-December)..........212-662-2133
Radio City Christmas Spectacular (early November-early January)..........212-247-4777
Rockefeller Center Christmas Tree Lighting (late November)..........212-332-6500
Saint Patrick's Day Parade (mid-March) 212-484-1222
Seaworthy Saturdays (September-June) 212-245-0072
Shakespeare in the Park (late June-mid-July).......212-539-8500
SummerStage (mid-June-mid-August) 212-360-2777
Untermyer Performing Arts Festival (late July-late August)..........914-377-6442
US Open Tennis Championships (late August-mid-September)..........718-760-6200
Washington Square Music Festival (mid-late July)..........212-431-1088

Welcome Back to Brooklyn Festival (mid-June) 718-855-7882
Westchester County Fair (late May-early June)......914-968-4200
Wine Spectator Wine Experience (late October).....212-684-4224

Winter Wildlife Holiday Lights
(late November-early January) 718-367-1010
Yonkers Hudson Riverfest (late September) 914-377-3378

Norfolk, Virginia

***County:* Independent City**

NORFOLK is located on the Virginia Peninsula in the southeastern part of the state—the region is sometimes referred to as "Hampton Roads" or the "Tidewater." Major cities within 100 miles include Williamsburg and Richmond, Virginia.

Area (Land) .... 53.8 sq mi
Area (Water).............................. 42.5 sq mi
Elevation.. 12 ft
Latitude ....36-85-10 N
Longitude................................ 76-27-84 W
Time Zone ....EST
Area Code.. 757

Climate

Norfolk has a mild climate, and its central location on the Atlantic Coast is generally protected from major storms that affect the Northeast and hurricanes that affect the Southeast. Winter high temperatures average near 50 degrees, with low temperatures in the low 30s. Norfolk's annual snowfall totals average just over seven and a half inches. Summers are characterized by warm days, with highs in the mid-80s, and pleasant evenings, with lows averaging in the upper 60s. Summer is also the rainy season in Norfolk, with July being the wettest month.

Average Temperatures & Precipitation

Temperatures

	Jan	Feb	Mar	Apr	May	Jun	Jul	Aug	Sep	Oct	Nov	Dec
High	47	50	58	67	75	83	86	85	80	70	61	52
Low	31	32	39	47	57	65	70	69	64	53	44	35

Precipitation

	Jan	Feb	Mar	Apr	May	Jun	Jul	Aug	Sep	Oct	Nov	Dec
Inches	3.8	3.5	3.7	3.1	3.8	3.8	5.1	4.8	3.9	3.2	2.9	3.2

History

The oldest city in southeastern Virginia's Hampton Roads region, Norfolk was originally chartered in 1682 on a 50-acre parcel of land that had been purchased in exchange for 10,000 pounds of tobacco. In 1736, Norfolk's population had reached 1,000, making it Virginia's largest city to date. The area grew quickly due to its successful tobacco industry and foreign trade. By 1769, Norfolk was home to 6,000 people. Over the course of the next century, Norfolk experienced waves of both prosperity and misfortune.

The American Revolution brought difficult times to Hampton Roads. Norfolk was completely destroyed by fire during the early months of 1776—two-thirds of the city had been destroyed as a result of an 11-hour assault by British soldiers on New Year's Day, and the colonists themselves burned the remainder of the city to prevent the British from occupying the area. Norfolk was characterized as the most devastated community in the Colonies following the Revolutionary War. After the war had ended, Norfolk was rebuilt and regained its position as a major seaport until trade restrictions brought about by the War of 1812 halted growth in the area, but improved land transportation routes in the region in the early 1800s renewed development. Norfolk was incorporated in 1845, and the area prospered until the 1850s. Troubled times returned to Norfolk during the summer of 1855, when a yellow fever epidemic resulted in the death of 2,000 residents and the closure of many area businesses. In the decade that followed, the city had to contend with the occupation of Union troops during the Civil War. After Reconstruction, Norfolk resumed its successful foreign trade. Cotton had become an important commodity, but coal quickly surpassed cotton, and Hampton Roads soon became the world's largest coal port.

Norfolk has enjoyed steady growth during the 20th Century. The Jamestown Exhibition, a major national event commemorating the 300th anniversary of the founding of Jamestown, the country's first settlement, was held in 1907 at Sewell's Point, located 10 miles from downtown Norfolk. During World War I, the site of the Jamestown Exhibition was transformed into Norfolk Naval Base, which would become the largest naval base in the world. The economic opportunities created by the development of Norfolk Naval Base, other military installations, and various new manufacturing plants in the area caused a population explosion in Norfolk—the city's population jumped from 67,452 residents in 1910 to 115,777 in 1920. The presence of U.S. Navy in Norfolk helped the city to remain strong throughout the century—through the Great Depression and both World Wars—and the military remains an important part of the city's present economy. Norfolk today, with a population of more than 215,000, is Virginia's second largest city.

Population

1990 Census 261,250
1998 Estimate.............................215,215
% Change ....-17.6
2010 Projection 215,003

Racial/Ethnic Breakdown

White.................................... 56.7%
Black 39.0%
Other..................................... 4.3%
Hispanic Origin (may be of any race) 2.9%

Age Breakdown

Under 5 years.............................. 8.3%
5 to 17.................................. 14.7%
18 to 20................................... 9.1%
21 to 24................................. 12.7%
25 to 34................................. 19.9%
35 to 44................................. 11.8%

45 to 54 .... 6.6%
55 to 64 .... 6.5%
65 to 74 .... 6.4%
75+ years 4.1%
Median Age 27.4

Gender Breakdown
Male 53.3%
Female 46.7%

Government

Type of Government: Council-Manager

Norfolk City Attorney
810 Union St Rm 908
Norfolk, VA 23510
Phone: 757-664-4529
Fax: 757-664-4201

Norfolk City Clerk
810 Union St Rm 1006
Norfolk, VA 23510
Phone: 757-664-4268
Fax: 757-664-4290

Norfolk City Council
810 Union St Rm 1006
Norfolk, VA 23510
Phone: 757-664-4268
Fax: 757-664-4290

Norfolk City Hall
810 Union St
Norfolk, VA 23510
Phone: 757-664-4000
Fax: 757-664-4006

Norfolk City Manager
810 Union St Rm 1101
Norfolk, VA 23510
Phone: 757-664-4242
Fax: 757-664-4239

Norfolk Development Dept
500 E Main St Rm 1500
Norfolk, VA 23510
Phone: 757-664-4338
Fax: 757-664-4315

Norfolk Finance Dept
810 Union St Rm 1003
Norfolk, VA 23510
Phone: 757-664-4346
Fax: 757-664-4064

Norfolk Fire & Paramedical Services
100 Brooke Ave Suite 500
Norfolk, VA 23510
Phone: 757-664-6600
Fax: 757-624-6832

Norfolk Human Resources Dept
810 Union St Rm 100
Norfolk, VA 23510
Phone: 757-664-4486
Fax: 757-664-4492

Norfolk Mayor
810 Union St Rm 1109
Norfolk, VA 23510
Phone: 757-664-4679
Fax: 757-441-2909

Norfolk Neighborhood & Leisure Services Dept
501 Boush St
Norfolk, VA 23510
Phone: 757-441-2400
Fax: 757-441-5423

Norfolk Planning Dept
810 Union St Rm 508
Norfolk, VA 23510
Phone: 757-664-4747
Fax: 757-664-4748

Norfolk Police Dept
100 Brooke Ave
Norfolk, VA 23510
Phone: 757-664-3277
Fax: 757-664-3278

Norfolk Public Library
301 E City Hall Ave
Norfolk, VA 23510
Phone: 757-664-7323
Fax: 757-664-7320

Norfolk Public Works Dept
810 Union St 7th Fl
Norfolk, VA 23510
Phone: 757-664-4655
Fax: 757-664-4603

Norfolk Utilities Dept
400 Granby St
Norfolk, VA 23510
Phone: 757-664-6701
Fax: 757-664-6707

Important Phone Numbers

AAA 757-622-5634
American Express Travel 757-622-6692
Dental Referral 757-491-4626
Driver's License/Vehicle Registration Information ... 757-461-1919
Emergency 911
Medical Referral 800-736-8272
Norfolk Commissioner of Revenue 757-441-2277
Norfolk Real Estate Assessor 757-664-4732
Poison Control Center 800-552-6337
Time 757-622-9311
Travelers Aid 757-622-7017
Virginia Peninsula Assn of Realtors 757-599-5222
Virginia State Sales Tax Office 757-455-3810
Voter Registration Information 757-664-4353
Weather 757-666-1212

Information Sources

Better Business Bureau Serving Greater Hampton Roads
586 Virginian Dr
Norfolk, VA 23505
www.hamptonroadsbbb.org
Phone: 757-531-1300
Fax: 757-531-1388

Chesapeake (Independent City)
PO Box 15225
Chesapeake, VA 23328
www.chesapeake.va.us
Phone: 757-382-6151
Fax: 757-382-6678

Chesapeake City Hall
306 Cedar Rd
Chesapeake, VA 23322
www.chesapeake.va.us
Phone: 757-382-6241
Fax: 757-382-8749

Chesapeake Conference Center
900 Greenbrier Cir
Chesapeake, VA 23320
www.chesapeakeconference.com
Phone: 757-382-2500
Fax: 757-382-2525

Chesapeake Economic Development Dept
501 Independence Pkwy Suite 200
Chesapeake, VA 23320
www.chesapeake.va.us/economic/econindex.html
Phone: 757-382-8040
Fax: 757-382-8050
TF: 888-224-3782

Chesapeake Mayor
PO Box 15225
Chesapeake, VA 23328
www.chesapeake.va.us/communty/mayor/mayor.html
Phone: 757-382-6462
Fax: 757-382-6678

Chesapeake Public Communications Dept
306 Cedar Rd
Chesapeake, VA 23322
www.chesapeake.va.us
Phone: 757-382-6241
Fax: 757-382-8538

Chesapeake Public Library
298 Cedar Rd
Chesapeake, VA 23322
www.chesapeake.lib.va.us
Phone: 757-382-6576
Fax: 757-382-8567

Hampton Roads Chamber of Commerce
420 Bank St
Norfolk, VA 23501
www.hrccva.com
Phone: 757-622-2312
Fax: 757-622-5563

Newport News (Independent City)
2400 Washington Ave
Newport News, VA 23607
www.newport-news.va.us
Phone: 757-926-8411
Fax: 757-926-3503

Newport News Development Div
2400 Washington Ave
Newport News, VA 23607
Phone: 757-926-8428
Fax: 757-926-3504

Newport News Mayor
2400 Washington Ave
Newport News, VA 23607
www.newport-news.va.us
Phone: 757-926-8403
Fax: 757-926-3546

Newport News Public Library
110 Main St
Newport News, VA 23601
www.newport-news.va.us/library
Phone: 757-591-4858
Fax: 757-591-7425

Newport News Tourism Development Office
2400 Washington Ave 7th Fl
Newport News, VA 23607
www.newport-news.org
Phone: 757-926-3561
Fax: 757-926-6901
TF: 888-493-7386

Norfolk (Independent City)
1101 City Hall Bldg
Norfolk, VA 23510
www.city.norfolk.va.us
Phone: 757-664-4242
Fax: 757-664-4239

Norfolk Scope Cultural & Convention Center
201 E Brambleton Ave
Norfolk, VA 23501
www.norfolkscope.com
Phone: 757-664-6464
Fax: 757-664-6990

Virginia Beach (Independent City)
2401 Courthouse Dr Municipal Ctr Bldg 1
Virginia Beach, VA 23456
www.virginia-beach.va.us
Phone: 757-427-4242
Fax: 757-427-4135

Virginia Beach Central Library
4100 Virginia Beach Blvd
Virginia Beach, VA 23452
www.virginia-beach.va.us/services/library/system/central.htm
Phone: 757-431-3001
Fax: 757-431-3018

Virginia Beach City Hall
Municipal Ctr Bldg 22
Virginia Beach, VA 23456
www.virginia-beach.va.us
Phone: 757-427-4111

Virginia Beach Convention And Visitor Bureau
2101 Parks Ave Suite 500
Virginia Beach, VA 23451
www.vbfun.com
Phone: 757-437-4700
Fax: 757-437-4747
TF: 800-700-7702

Virginia Beach Economic Development Dept
1 Columbus Ctr Suite 300
Virginia Beach, VA 23462
www.virginia-beach.va.us/dept/econdev
Phone: 757-437-6464
Fax: 757-499-9894
TF: 800-989-4567

Virginia Beach Mayor
2401 Courthouse Dr Municipal Ctr Rm 234
Virginia Beach, VA 23456
Phone: 757-427-4581
Fax: 757-426-5699

Virginia Beach Pavilion Convention Center
1000 19th St
Virginia Beach, VA 23451
www.vabeach.com/pavilion/
Phone: 757-437-7600
Fax: 757-422-8860

Virginia Beach Visitors Information Center
2100 Parks Ave
Virginia Beach, VA 23451
www.city.virginia-beach.va.us
Phone: 757-437-4888
Fax: 757-437-4918
TF: 800-446-8038

Virginia Peninsula Chamber of Commerce
1919 Commerce Dr Suite 320
Hampton, VA 23666
www.vpcc.org
Phone: 757-262-2000
Fax: 757-262-2009
TF: 800-556-1822

Online Resources

4Norfolk.com
www.4norfolk.com

Anthill City Guide Norfolk
www.anthill.com/city.asp?city=norfolk

Area Guide Chesapeake
chesapeake.areaguides.net

Area Guide Norfolk
norfolk.areaguides.net

Area Guide Virginia Beach
virginiabeach.areaguides.net

City Knowledge Norfolk
www.cityknowledge.com/va_norfolk.htm

City Knowledge Virginia Beach
www.cityknowledge.com/va_virginia_beach.htm

DigitalCity Hampton Roads
hamptonroads.digitalcity.com

Essential Guide to Virginia Beach
www.ego.net/us/va/vb/index.htm

Excite.com Chesapeake City Guide
www.excite.com/travel/countries/united_states/virginia/chesapeake

Excite.com Newport News City Guide
www.excite.com/travel/countries/united_states/virginia/newport_news

Excite.com Norfolk City Guide
www.excite.com/travel/countries/united_states/virginia/norfolk

Excite.com Virginia Beach City Guide
www.excite.com/travel/countries/united_states/virginia/virginia_beach

Festevents
www.festeventsva.org

Insiders' Guide to Virginia's Chesapeake
www.insiders.com/chesapeake-va/

Lodging.com Virginia Beach Virginia
www.lodging.com/auto/guides/virginia_beach-area-va.html

Norfolk CityLink
www.usacitylink.com/citylink/norfolk

Norfolk Visitors' Guide
www.vgnet.com/norfolk/

Sunny Day Guide Virginia Beach
www.sunnydayguides.com/vb/

Surf & Sun Beach Vacation Guide to Norfolk
www.surf-sun.com/va-norfolk-main.htm

Surf & Sun Beach Vacation Guide to Virginia Beach
www.surf-sun.com/va-virginia-beach-main.htm

Virginia Beach
emporium.turnpike.net/~ntravel/vabeach/fun.htm

Virginia Beach Net
www.vabeach.com/

Virginia Beach Online
www.vabeachonline.com

Virginia Beach Visitor's Guide
www.vgnet.com/VirginiaBeach/index_r.html

Area Communities

Communities in the Hampton Roads region with populations greater than 50,000 include:

Chesapeake Phone: 757-382-6241
306 Cedar Rd Fax: 757-382-8749
Chesapeake, VA 23322

Hampton Phone: 757-727-6392
22 Lincoln St Fax: 757-728-3037
Hampton, VA 23669

Newport News Phone: 757-926-8411
2400 Washington Ave Fax: 757-926-3503
Newport News, VA 23607

Portsmouth Phone: 757-393-8641
801 Crawford St Fax: 757-393-5241
Portsmouth, VA 23704

Suffolk Phone: 757-925-6344
PO Box 1858 Fax: 757-925-6386
Suffolk, VA 23439

Virginia Beach Phone: 757-427-4111
Municipal Ctr Bldg 22
Virginia Beach, VA 23456

Economy

Nearly 30 percent of Norfolk's workforce is employed in service-related positions, including healthcare, which is rapidly becoming a leading industry in southeastern Virginia. (In fact, five of Norfolk's top 15 companies are healthcare-related.) The area's second largest employment sector is government—the U.S. Military provides jobs for more than 70,000 military personnel and civilians at various military installations in the area, including the Norfolk Naval Base. A related industry, shipbuilding, is also important to the Hampton Roads economy, with Newport News Shipbuilding among the area's largest employers. In addition, the Hampton Roads area hosts more than four million visitors annually, contributing some $2 billion to the local economy each year.

Unemployment Rate 4.9%
Per Capita Income.......................... $20,221
Median Family Income...................... $32,446

Principal Industries & Number of Wage Earners

City of Norfolk - 3rd Quarter 1998

Agriculture 577
Construction.. 5,965
Finance, Insurance, & Real Estate 9,506
Government 33,715
Manufacturing 13,771
Services 42,972
Trade 28,465
Transportation 11,330

Major Employers

Bank of America NA Phone: 757-441-4770
1 Commercial Pl Fax: 757-441-4579
Norfolk, VA 23510

Bernard C Harris Publishing Inc Phone: 757-455-3460
16 Center Dr Fax: 757-455-2947
Norfolk, VA 23502
www.bcharrispub.com/jobs

Bon Secours DePaul Medical Center Phone: 757-489-5000
150 Kingsley Ln Fax: 757-489-3509
Norfolk, VA 23505
www.bonsecours.org/hamptonroads/facilities/fac-depaul.htm

Children's Hospital of the King's Daughters Phone: 757-668-7000
601 Children's Ln Fax: 757-668-8050
Norfolk, VA 23507
www.chkd.org

FHC Health Systems Phone: 757-459-5100
240 Corporate Blvd Fax: 757-459-5219
Norfolk, VA 23502
www.fhchealthsystems.com

Ford Motor Co Inc Phone: 757-494-2000
2424 Ford Dr Fax: 757-494-5678
Norfolk, VA 23523
www.ford.com

Landmark Communications Inc
150 W Brambleton Ave
Norfolk, VA 23510
www.landmarkcom.com
Phone: 757-446-2010
Fax: 757-446-2489
TF: 800-446-2004

Medical College of Hampton Roads
358 Mowbray Arch Suite 101
Norfolk, VA 23507
Phone: 757-446-6043
Fax: 757-446-6158

Naval Station Norfolk
1530 Gilbert St
Norfolk, VA 23511
naval-station.norfolk.va.us
Phone: 757-444-0000
Fax: 757-445-1953

Newport News Shipbuilding Inc
4101 Washington Ave
Newport News, VA 23607
www.nns.com
Phone: 757-380-2000
Fax: 757-380-3114

Norfolk Southern Corp
3 Commercial Pl
Norfolk, VA 23510
www.nscorp.com
Phone: 757-629-2600
Fax: 757-664-5269
TF: 800-635-5768

Sentara Health System
6015 Poplar Hall Dr
Norfolk, VA 23502
www.sentara.com
Phone: 757-455-7000
Fax: 757-466-7083

USAA
5800 Northampton Blvd
Norfolk, VA 23502
/www.usaa.com
Phone: 757-461-5188

Virginia Natural Gas Inc
5100 E Virginia Beach Blvd
Norfolk, VA 23502
www.cng.com/vng/Welcome.html
Phone: 757-466-5400
Fax: 757-466-5437

Virginia Power
2700 Cromwell Dr
Norfolk, VA 23509
www.vapower.com
Phone: 800-730-7230

Quality of Living Indicators

Total Crime Index....................16,188
(rates per 100,000 inhabitants)

Violent Crime
Murder/manslaughter.......... 32
Forcible rape 158
Robbery.......... 732
Aggravated assault.......... 646

Property Crime
Burglary 2,214
Larceny theft 11,137
Motor vehicle theft..........1,269

Cost of Living Index..........99.2
(national average = 100)

Median Home Price..........$113,500

Education

Public Schools

Norfolk Public Schools
800 E City Hall Ave
Norfolk, VA 23510
www.norfolk.k12.ma.us
Phone: 757-441-2107
Fax: 757-441-2802

Number of Schools
Elementary.......... 36
Middle 8
High.......... 6
Alternative.......... 2

Student/Teacher Ratio
All Grades 13.0:1

Private Schools

Number of Schools (all grades).......... 25+

Colleges & Universities

Bryant & Stratton Career College Virginia Beach
301 Center Point Dr
Virginia Beach, VA 23462
www.bryantstratton.edu
Phone: 757-499-7900
Fax: 757-499-9977

Christopher Newport University
1 University Pl
Newport News, VA 23606
E-mail: admit@cnu.edu
www.cnu.edu
Phone: 757-594-7000
Fax: 757-594-7333
TF: 800-333-4268

College of William & Mary
PO Box 8795
Williamsburg, VA 23187
E-mail: ccharr@facstaff.wm.edu
www.wm.edu
Phone: 757-221-4000
Fax: 757-221-1242

Hampton University
Hampton, VA 23668
www.hamptonu.edu
Phone: 757-727-5000
Fax: 757-727-5998
TF: 800-624-3328

ITT Technical Institute
863 Glenrock Rd
Norfolk, VA 23502
www.itt-tech.edu
Phone: 757-466-1260
Fax: 757-466-7630
TF: 800-253-8324

Norfolk State University
700 Park Ave
Norfolk, VA 23504
www.nsu.edu
Phone: 757-683-8396
Fax: 757-823-2078

Old Dominion University
Hampton Blvd
Norfolk, VA 23529
E-mail: aos100s@shawnee.oa.odu.edu
web.odu.edu
Phone: 757-683-3000
Fax: 757-683-3255
TF: 800-348-7926

Tabernacle Baptist Bible College & Theological Seminary
717 N Whitehurst Landing Rd
Virginia Beach, VA 23464
Phone: 757-420-5476
Fax: 757-424-3014

Thomas Nelson Community College Phone: 757-825-2700
99 Thomas Nelson Dr Fax: 757-825-2763
Hampton, VA 23666
www.tncc.cc.va.us

Tidewater Community College Chesapeake Campus Phone: 757-822-5100
1428 Cedar Rd Fax: 757-822-5122
Chesapeake, VA 23322
www.tc.cc.va.us

Tidewater Community College Portsmouth Campus Phone: 757-822-2124
7000 College Dr Fax: 757-686-5173
Portsmouth, VA 23703
www.tc.cc.va.us

Tidewater Community College Virginia Beach Campus Phone: 757-822-7100
1700 College Crescent Fax: 757-427-7041
Virginia Beach, VA 23456
www.tc.cc.va.us/campuses/vabeach.htm

Virginia Wesleyan College Phone: 757-455-3200
1584 Wesleyan Dr Fax: 757-461-5238
Norfolk, VA 23502 TF: 800-737-8684
www.vwc.edu

Hospitals

Bon Secours DePaul Medical Center Phone: 757-489-5000
150 Kingsley Ln Fax: 757-489-3509
Norfolk, VA 23505
www.bonsecours.org/hamptonroads/facilities/fac-depaul.htm

Bon Secours Maryview Medical Center Phone: 757-398-2200
3636 High St Fax: 757-397-2446
Portsmouth, VA 23707

Chesapeake General Hospital Phone: 757-482-6100
736 Battlefield Blvd N Fax: 757-482-6184
Chesapeake, VA 23327
www.chesgh.org

Children's Hospital of the King's Daughters Phone: 757-668-7000
601 Children's Ln Fax: 757-668-8050
Norfolk, VA 23507
www.chkd.org

Mary Immaculate Hospital Phone: 757-886-6600
2 Bernardine Dr Fax: 757-886-6751
Newport News, VA 23602
www.mihospital.com

Riverside Regional Medical Center Phone: 757-594-2000
500 J Clyde Morris Blvd Fax: 757-594-4495
Newport News, VA 23601
www.riverside-online.com/rrmc.htm

Sentara Bayside Hospital Phone: 757-363-6100
800 Independence Blvd Fax: 757-363-6650
Virginia Beach, VA 23455
www.sentara.com/hospitals/sentara_bayside.html

Sentara Leigh Hospital Phone: 757-466-6000
830 Kempsville Rd Fax: 757-466-6765
Norfolk, VA 23502
www.sentara.com/hospitals/sentara_leigh.html

Sentara Norfolk General Hospital Phone: 757-668-3000
600 Gresham Dr Fax: 757-668-2256
Norfolk, VA 23507
www.sentara.com/hospitals/sentara_norfolk.html

Sentara Virginia Beach General Hospital Phone: 757-395-8000
1060 First Colonial Rd Fax: 757-395-6106
Virginia Beach, VA 23454 TF: 800-736-8272
www.sentara.com/hospitals/virginiabeach.html

Transportation

Airport(s)

Norfolk International Airport (ORF)
8 miles NE of downtown (approx 15 minutes) 757-857-3351

Mass Transit

Hampton Roads Regional Transit
$1.50 Base fare. 757-222-6100

Rail/Bus

Greyhound Bus Station Phone: 757-625-2608
701 Monticello Ave TF: 800-231-2222
Norfolk, VA 23510

Utilities

Electricity
Virginia Power 888-667-3000
www.vapower.com

Gas
Virginia Natural Gas 757-466-5550
www.cng.com/vng/Welcome.html

Water
Norfolk Utilities. 757-664-6701

Garbage Collection/Recycling
Hampton Roads Sanitation District 757-460-2261
Southeastern Public Service Authority (Recycling) 757-548-2256

Telecommunications

Telephone
Verizon Communications. 757-954-6222
www.verizon.com

Cable Television
Cox Communications 757-224-4269
www.cox.com
Falcon Cable TV 757-539-2312

Internet Service Providers (ISPs)
Eagles Nest Ltd 757-466-9200
www.eaglesnest.crosslink.net
Exis Net Inc. 757-552-1009
www.exis.net
Great Bridge Internet Inc 757-482-1383
www.gr8brdg.net

InfiNet....................................757-622-4289
www.infi.net
NetFX Inc...................................757-369-2600
www.nfx.net
PICUS LLC..................................888-852-1617
www.picusnet.com
Pinnacle Online..............................757-455-5959
www.pinn.net
Sevanet....................................757-594-7092
www.seva.net

Banks

Bank of America NA Phone: 757-441-4770
1 Commercial Pl Fax: 757-441-4579
Norfolk, VA 23510

Bank of the Commonwealth Phone: 757-446-6900
403 Boush St Fax: 757-446-6929
Norfolk, VA 23510

Branch Banking & Trust Co of Virginia Phone: 757-858-1223
109 Main St
Norfolk, VA 23510

CENIT Bank Phone: 757-446-6600
225 W Olney Rd Fax: 757-446-6643
Norfolk, VA 23510
www.cenit.com

Essex Savings Bank FSB Phone: 757-893-1300
Koger Ctr Bldg 9 Suite 200 Fax: 757-466-2827
Norfolk, VA 23502
www.essexbancorp.com

First Union National Bank Phone: 757-628-0458
999 Waterside Dr
Norfolk, VA 23510

First Virginia Bank-Hampton Roads Phone: 757-628-6600
PO Box 3097 Fax: 757-628-6619
Norfolk, VA 23514

Heritage Bank & Trust Phone: 757-523-2672
841 N Military Hwy Fax: 757-523-2677
Norfolk, VA 23502 TF: 800-790-6691

Wachovia Bank NA Phone: 757-640-5000
World Trade Ctr Suite 100
Norfolk, VA 23510

Shopping

Altschul's Phone: 757-622-2317
427 Granby St Fax: 757-622-5514
Norfolk, VA 23510

Chesapeake Square Mall Phone: 757-488-9636
4200 Portsmouth Blvd Fax: 757-465-5590
Chesapeake, VA 23321

Ghent Phone: 757-664-6620
Colley Ave & 21st St
Norfolk, VA 23517

Greenbrier Mall Phone: 757-424-7300
1401 Greenbrier Pkwy Fax: 757-420-8048
Chesapeake, VA 23320

Historic Hilton Village Phone: 757-596-5630
10000 Block of Warwick Blvd
Newport News, VA 23602

Janaf Shopping Center Phone: 757-461-4954
5900 E Virginia Beach Blvd Fax: 757-459-2229
Norfolk, VA 23502

La Promenade Phone: 757-422-8839
1860 Laskin Rd
Virginia Beach, VA 23454

Lynnhaven Mall Phone: 757-340-9340
701 S Lynnhaven Pkwy Fax: 757-463-8150
Virginia Beach, VA 23452

Military Circle Mall Phone: 757-461-1940
880 N Military Hwy
Norfolk, VA 23502

Newmarket Center Phone: 757-838-9500
110 Newmarket Fair Fax: 757-825-0243
Newport News, VA 23605

Ocean View Shopping Center Phone: 757-627-8611
179 W Ocean View Ave
Norfolk, VA 23503

Patrick Henry Mall Phone: 757-249-4305
12300 Jefferson Ave Fax: 757-249-2730
Newport News, VA 23602

Pembroke Mall Phone: 757-497-6255
4582 Pembroke Mall Fax: 757-671-8546
Virginia Beach, VA 23462
E-mail: pembmll@infi.net
www.pembrokemall.com

Tower Mall Phone: 757-488-4453
4040 Victory Blvd Fax: 757-465-5889
Portsmouth, VA 23701

Waterside The Phone: 757-627-3300
333 Waterside Dr Fax: 757-627-3981
Norfolk, VA 23510

Media

Newspapers and Magazines

Chesapeake Bay Magazine Phone: 410-263-2662
1819 Bay Ridge Ave Suite 158 Fax: 410-267-6924
Annapolis, MD 21403 TF: 800-584-5066

Daily Press* Phone: 757-247-4600
7505 Warwick Blvd Fax: 757-245-8618
Newport News, VA 23607
E-mail: letters@dailypress.com
www.dailypress.com

Port Folio Phone: 757-363-2400
5700 Thurston Ave Suite 133 Fax: 757-363-1767
Virginia Beach, VA 23455
www.portfolioweekly.com

Virginia Business Magazine Phone: 804-649-6999
411 E Franklin St Suite 105 Fax: 804-649-6311
Richmond, VA 23219
virginiabusiness.com

Virginian-Pilot*
PO Box 449
Norfolk, VA 23501
E-mail: pilot@infi.net
www.pilotonline.com
Phone: 757-446-2000
Fax: 757-446-2414
TF: 800-446-2004

**Indicates major daily newspapers*

Television

WAVY-TV Ch 10 (NBC)
300 Wavy St
Portsmouth, VA 23704
E-mail: wavy10p@infi.net
www.wavy.com
Phone: 757-393-1010
Fax: 757-397-8279

WGNT-TV Ch 27 (UPN)
1318 Spratley St
Portsmouth, VA 23704
E-mail: upn27@paramount.com
www.paramountstations.com/WGNT
Phone: 757-393-2501
Fax: 757-399-3303

WHRO-TV Ch 15 (PBS)
5200 Hampton Blvd
Norfolk, VA 23508
E-mail: info@whro.org
www.whro.org
Phone: 757-889-9400
Fax: 757-489-0007

WPXV-TV Ch 49 (PAX)
230 Clearfield Ave Suite 104
Virginia Beach, VA 23462
www.pax.net/WPXV
Phone: 757-490-1249
Fax: 757-499-1679

WTKR-TV Ch 3 (CBS)
PO Box 300
Norfolk, VA 23501
www.wtkr.com
Phone: 757-446-1000
Fax: 757-446-1376

WTVZ-TV Ch 33 (WB)
900 Granby St
Norfolk, VA 23510
Phone: 757-622-3333
Fax: 757-623-1541

WVBT-TV Ch 43 (Fox)
243 Wavy St
Portsmouth, VA 23704
www.wvbt.com
Phone: 757-393-4343
Fax: 757-393-7615

WVEC-TV Ch 13 (ABC)
613 Woodis Ave
Norfolk, VA 23510
wvec.com
Phone: 757-625-1313
Fax: 757-628-5855

Radio

WAFX-FM 106.9 MHz (CR)
870 Greenbrier Cir Suite 399
Chesapeake, VA 23320
E-mail: gm@1069thefox.com
www.wafx.com
Phone: 757-366-9900
Fax: 757-366-0022

WCMS-AM 1050 kHz (Ctry)
900 Commonwealth Pl
Virginia Beach, VA 23464
E-mail: wcms@wcms.com
Phone: 757-424-1050
Fax: 757-424-3479

WCMS-FM 100.5 MHz (Ctry)
900 Commonwealth Pl
Virginia Beach, VA 23464
E-mail: wcms@wcms.com
www.wcms.com
Phone: 757-424-1050
Fax: 757-424-3479

WFOG-FM 92.9 MHz (AC)
5589 Greenwich Rd Suite 200
Virginia Beach, VA 23462
Phone: 757-671-1000
Fax: 757-671-1010

WGH-AM 1310 kHz (Sports)
5589 Greenwich Rd Suite 200
Virginia Beach, VA 23462
Phone: 757-671-1000
Fax: 757-671-1010

WGH-FM 97.3 MHz (Ctry)
5589 Greenwich Rd Suite 200
Virginia Beach, VA 23462
www.eagle97.com
Phone: 757-671-1000
Fax: 757-671-1010

WGOI-AM 1230 kHz (B/EZ)
870 Greenbrier Cir Suite 399
Chesapeake, VA 23320
E-mail: wnor99a@aol.com
Phone: 757-366-9900
Fax: 757-366-0022

WGPL-AM 1350 kHz (Rel)
645 Church St Suite 400
Norfolk, VA 23510
Phone: 757-622-4600
Fax: 757-624-6515

WHRO-FM 90.3 MHz (Clas)
5200 Hampton Blvd
Norfolk, VA 23508
www.whro.org/903_WHRO_FM
Phone: 757-889-9400
Fax: 757-489-0007

WHRV-FM 89.5 MHz (NPR)
5200 Hampton Blvd
Norfolk, VA 23508
Phone: 757-889-9400
Fax: 757-489-0007

WJCD-FM 105.3 MHz (NAC)
1003 Norfolk Sq
Norfolk, VA 23502
E-mail: cd105.3@wjcd.com
wjcd.com
Phone: 757-466-0009
Fax: 757-466-9523

WKOC-FM 93.7 MHz (AAA)
999 Waterside Dr Dominion Tower
Suite 500
Norfolk, VA 23510
E-mail: thecoast@exis.net
thecoast.com
Phone: 757-640-8500
Fax: 757-622-6397

WNIS-AM 790 kHz (N/T)
999 Waterside Dr Dominion Tower
Suite 500
Norfolk, VA 23510
E-mail: wnis@exis.net
wnis.exis.net
Phone: 757-640-8500
Fax: 757-622-6397

WNOR-FM 98.7 MHz (Rock)
870 Greenbrier Cir Suite 399
Chesapeake, VA 23320
E-mail: gm@fm99.com
www.fm99.com
Phone: 757-366-9900
Fax: 757-366-0022

WNSB-FM 91.1 MHz (NPR)
700 Park Ave Suite 129
Norfolk, VA 23504
E-mail: wnsb@vger.nsu.edu
Phone: 757-823-9672
Fax: 757-823-2385

WNVZ-FM 104.5 MHz (CHR)
236 Clearfield Ave Suite 206
Virginia Beach, VA 23462
www.z104.com
Phone: 757-497-2000
Fax: 757-456-5458

WOWI-FM 102.9 MHz (Urban)
1003 Norfolk Sq
Norfolk, VA 23502
www.103jamz.com
Phone: 757-466-0009
Fax: 757-466-7043

WPCE-AM 1400 kHz (Rel)
645 Church St Suite 400
Norfolk, VA 23510
Phone: 757-622-4600
Fax: 757-624-6515

WPTE-FM 94.9 MHz (AC)
236 Clearfield Ave Suite 206
Virginia Beach, VA 23462
www.pointradio.com
Phone: 757-497-2000
Fax: 757-473-1100

WROX-FM 96.1 MHz (Alt)
999 Waterside Dr Dominion Tower
Suite 500
Norfolk, VA 23510
E-mail: 96X@exis.net
www.96x.exis.net
Phone: 757-640-8500
Fax: 757-640-8552

WSVV-FM 92.1 MHz (CHR)
1003 Norfolk Sq
Norfolk, VA 23502
Phone: 757-466-0009
Fax: 757-466-7043

WSVY-FM 107.7 MHz (Urban)
1003 Norfolk Sq
Norfolk, VA 23502
Phone: 757-466-0009
Fax: 757-466-0082

WTAR-AM 850 kHz (N/T)
999 Waterside Dr 500 Dominion Tower
Norfolk, VA 23510
wtar.exis.net
Phone: 757-640-8500
Fax: 757-640-8552

WVKL-FM 95.7 MHz (Oldies)
236 Clearfield Ave Suite 206
Virginia Beach, VA 23462
Phone: 757-497-2000
Fax: 757-456-5458

WWDE-FM 101.3 MHz (AC)
236 Clearfield Ave Suite 206
Virginia Beach, VA 23462
www.2wd.com
Phone: 757-497-2000
Fax: 757-456-5458

WXEZ-FM 94.1 MHz (AC)
4026 George Washington Hwy
Yorktown, VA 23692
www.ez94.com
Phone: 757-898-9494
Fax: 757-898-9401

Attractions

Norfolk's harbor, rivers, and the Chesapeake Bay make it the center of the Virginia Waterfront. These waters are the site of Norfolk Naval Base, the largest naval installation in the world and home port to more than 100 ships. The Waterside Marketplace overlooks the Elizabeth River, where one can see a daily parade of Navy vessels, sailboats, and tugboats. The downtown Norfolk waterfront is also home to NAUTICUS, the National Maritime Center, which features multimedia shows, virtual reality experiences, ship tours, laser shows, and other activities. Spanning 17.6 miles across the water is the Chesapeake Bay Bridge-Tunnel, touted as one of the "Seven Wonders of the Modern World."

Norfolk's neighboring Hampton Roads communities also offer a wide variety of attractions. The largest private shipyard in the world, Newport News Shipbuilding, is located in nearby Newport News, which has been a leader in the shipbuilding industry since the turn of the century. Historical sites in Newport News include a number of Civil War sites, the War Memorial Museum of Virginia, and the Victory Arch through which U.S. troops marched to celebrate the Allied victory following World War I. Located adjacent to Norfolk on the Atlantic Coast, Virginia Beach's 26 miles of beaches along the Atlantic Ocean and Chesapeake Bay make the city a popular resort area. In addition to the many beachfront hotels and attractions, Virginia Beach is also home to Virginia's most visited state park, Seashore State Park, which offers a variety of outdoor recreational opportunities. The Great Dismal Swamp Wildlife Refuge in nearby Suffolk is home to many species of birds, black bears, bobcats, foxes, and white-tailed deer.

Arts Center of the Portsmouth Museums
420 High St
Portsmouth, VA 23704
Phone: 757-393-8543
Fax: 757-393-5228

Atlantic Wildfowl Heritage Museum
1113 Atlantic Ave
Virginia Beach, VA 23451
E-mail: wmuseum@aol.com
www.pilot.infi.net/~raven/wildfowl.html
Phone: 757-437-8432
Fax: 757-437-9055

Back Bay National Wildlife Refuge
4005 Sandpiper Rd
Virginia Beach, VA 23456
Phone: 757-721-2412
Fax: 757-721-6141

Blue Moon Cruises
600 Laskin Rd
Virginia Beach, VA 23451
Phone: 757-422-2900
Fax: 757-491-9007

Chesapeake Bay Bridge-Tunnel
PO Box 111
Cape Charles, VA 23310
Phone: 757-331-2960

Chesapeake Fine Arts Commission
PO Box 15225
Chesapeake, VA 23328
Phone: 757-382-6411
Fax: 757-382-8418

Chesapeake Planetarium
Shea Dr
Chesapeake, VA 23320
Phone: 757-547-0153
Fax: 757-547-0279

Children's Museum of Virginia
221 High St
Portsmouth, VA 23704
Phone: 757-393-8393
Fax: 757-393-9276

Christian Broadcasting Network
977 Centerville Tpke
Virginia Beach, VA 23463
Phone: 757-579-7000

Chrysler Hall
215 St Pauls Blvd
Norfolk, VA 23510
Phone: 757-664-6464
Fax: 757-664-6690

Chrysler Museum of Art
245 W Olney Rd
Norfolk, VA 23510
www.chrysler.org
Phone: 757-664-6200
Fax: 757-664-6201

Colonial National Historical Park
Colonial Pkwy & Rt 238
Yorktown, VA 23690
www.nps.gov/colo/
Phone: 757-898-3400
Fax: 757-898-3400

Contemporary Art Center of Virginia
2200 Parks Ave
Virginia Beach, VA 23451
www.cacv.org
Phone: 757-425-0000
Fax: 757-425-8186

d'Art Center Phone: 757-625-4211
125 College Pl
Norfolk, VA 23510
sites.communitylink.org/dArt

False Cape State Park Phone: 757-426-7128 Fax: 757-426-0055
4001 Sandpiper Rd
Virginia Beach, VA 23456
www.state.va.us/~dcr/parks/falscape.htm

First Landing State Park Phone: 757-412-2300 Fax: 757-412-2315 TF: 800-933-7275
2500 Shore Dr
Virginia Beach, VA 23451
www.state.va.us/~dcr/parks/1stland.htm

Fort Norfolk Phone: 757-625-1720
810 Front St
Norfolk, VA 23508

Fort Story Phone: 757-422-7164 Fax: 757-422-7750
N Atlantic Ave
Virginia Beach, VA 23459

General Douglas MacArthur Memorial Phone: 757-441-2965 Fax: 757-441-5389
MacArthur Sq
Norfolk, VA 23510
E-mail: macmem@norfolk.infi.net
sites.communitylink.org/mac/

Generic Theater Phone: 757-441-2160 Fax: 757-441-2729
912 W 21st St
Norfolk, VA 23517
E-mail: generic@whro.net
www.generictheater.org

Great Dismal Swamp National Wildlife Refuge Phone: 757-986-3705
3100 Desert Rd
Suffolk, VA 23439
E-mail: R5RW_GDSNWR@mail.fws.gov

Hermitage Foundation Museum Phone: 757-423-2052 Fax: 757-423-1604
7637 N Shore Rd
Norfolk, VA 23505

Hill House Phone: 757-393-0241
221 North St
Portsmouth, VA 23704

Hunter House Victorian Museum Phone: 757-623-9814
240 W Freemason St
Norfolk, VA 23510

Huntington Tugboat Museum Phone: 757-627-4884
1 Waterside Dr National Maritime Ctr
Norfolk, VA 23510

Hurrah Players Phone: 757-627-5437 Fax: 757-623-7418
935 Woodrow Ave
Norfolk, VA 23517
E-mail: hurrah@pilot.infi.net
www.hurrahplayers.com

IMAX Theater (Hampton) Phone: 757-727-0800 Fax: 757-727-0898
600 Settlers Landing Rd
Hampton, VA 23669
www.vasc.org/imax.html

IMAX Theater (Virginia Beach) Phone: 757-437-4949 Fax: 757-437-4976
717 General Booth Blvd Virginia Marine Science Museum
Virginia Beach, VA 23451

Jones Matthew House Phone: 757-898-5090
Taylor & Harrison Rds Fort Eustis
Newport News, VA 23604

Land Francis House Phone: 757-431-4000 Fax: 757-431-3733
3131 Virginia Beach Blvd
Virginia Beach, VA 23452

Lee Hall Mansion Phone: 757-888-3371
163 Yorktown Rd
Newport News, VA 23603
www.leehall.org

Lightship Museum Phone: 757-393-8741
Water St & London Slip
Portsmouth, VA 23704

Little Theater of Virginia Beach Phone: 757-428-9233
24th St & Barberton Dr
Virginia Beach, VA 23451

Little Theatre of Norfolk Phone: 757-627-8551
801 Claremont Ave
Norfolk, VA 23507

Lynnhaven House Phone: 757-460-1688 Fax: 757-456-0351
4401 Wishart Rd
Virginia Beach, VA 23455

Lynnhaven Seafood Marina & Dockside Inn Restaurant Phone: 757-481-7211 Fax: 757-481-1533
3311 Shore Dr
Virginia Beach, VA 23451

Mariners' Museum Phone: 757-596-2222 Fax: 757-591-7310
100 Museum Dr
Newport News, VA 23606
E-mail: info@mariner.org
www.mariner.org

Moses Myers House Phone: 757-664-6200 Fax: 757-441-2329
331 Bank St
Norfolk, VA 23510

Mount Trashmore Park Phone: 757-490-8551 Fax: 757-473-5187
300 Edwin Dr
Virginia Beach, VA 23462

NAUTICUS The National Maritime Center Phone: 757-664-1000 Fax: 757-623-1287
1 Waterside Dr
Norfolk, VA 23510
www.nauticus.org

Naval Amphibious Base Little Creek Phone: 757-462-7923 Fax: 757-462-3144
2600 Tarawa Ctr Suite 112
Norfolk, VA 23512

Newport News Park Phone: 757-888-3333
13564 Jefferson Ave
Newport News, VA 23603

Newsome House Museum & Cultural Center
2803 Oak Ave
Newport News, VA 23607
Phone: 757-247-2380
Fax: 757-928-6754

Norfolk Botanical Gardens
6700 Azalea Garden Rd
Norfolk, VA 23518
Phone: 757-441-5830
Fax: 757-853-8294

Norfolk Chamber Consort
Hampton Blvd Chandler Recital Hall
Norfolk, VA 23529
Phone: 757-440-1803
Fax: 757-440-1964

Norfolk Naval Air Station
9079 Hampton Blvd
Norfolk, VA 23511
www.pinn.net/~navytour/
Phone: 757-444-7955

Northwest River Park
1733 Indian Creek Rd
Chesapeake, VA 23322
Phone: 757-421-7151
Fax: 757-421-0134

Old Cape Henry Lighthouse
N Atlantic Ave Fort Story
Virginia Beach, VA 23459
Phone: 757-422-9421

Old Coast Guard Station
24th St & Oceanfront
Virginia Beach, VA 23451
E-mail: old_coast@va-beach.com
www.vabeach.com/old_coast/index.html
Phone: 757-422-1587
Fax: 757-491-8609

Peninsula Community Theatre
11056 Warwick Blvd
Newport News, VA 23601
Phone: 757-595-5728

Peninsula Fine Arts Center
101 Museum Dr
Newport News, VA 23606
E-mail: pfac@whro.org
Phone: 757-596-8175
Fax: 757-596-0807

Portsmouth Naval Shipyard Museum
PO Box 248
Portsmouth, VA 23705
Phone: 757-393-8591
Fax: 757-393-5244

Princess Anne Park
3475 Princess Anne Rd
Virginia Beach, VA 23456
Phone: 757-563-1100

Riddick's Folly
510 N Main St
Suffolk, VA 23434
E-mail: riddicksfolly@prodigy.net
groups.hamptonroads.com/riddicksfolly
Phone: 757-934-1390

Saint Luke's Historic Church
14477 Benns Church Blvd
Smithfield, VA 23430
Phone: 757-357-3367

Saint Paul's Church
201 St Pauls Blvd
Norfolk, VA 23510
Phone: 757-627-4353

Spirit of Norfolk Cruises
100 W Plume St Suite 106
Norfolk, VA 23510
www.spiritcruises.com/norfolk/location.asp
Phone: 757-625-1463
Fax: 757-625-1321

Thoroughgood Adam House
1636 Parish Rd
Virginia Beach, VA 23455
Phone: 757-460-7588
Fax: 757-460-7644

Time Machine
1606 Atlantic Ave
Virginia Beach, VA 23451
Phone: 757-491-6876

US Army Transportation Museum
Bldg 300 Besson Hall
Fort Eustis, VA 23604
E-mail: atzfptm@eustis.army.mil
www.eustis.army.mil/dptmsec/museum.htm
Phone: 757-878-1182
Fax: 757-878-5656

Victory Arch
West Ave & 25th St
Newport News, VA 23607

Virginia Air & Space Center/Hampton Roads History Center
600 Settlers Landing Rd
Hampton, VA 23669
www.vasc.org
Phone: 757-727-0800
Fax: 757-727-0898
TF: 800-296-0800

Virginia Ballet Theater
134 W Olney Rd
Norfolk, VA 23510
Phone: 757-622-4822
Fax: 757-622-7904

Virginia Beach Farmer's Market
3640 Dam Neck Rd
Virginia Beach, VA 23456
Phone: 757-427-4395
Fax: 757-427-4364

Virginia Living Museum
524 J Clyde Morris Blvd
Newport News, VA 23601
www.valivingmuseum.org
Phone: 757-595-1900
Fax: 757-599-4897

Virginia Marine Science Museum
717 General Booth Blvd
Virginia Beach, VA 23451
E-mail: vmsm@infi.net
www.va-beach.com/va-marine-science-museum/
Phone: 757-425-3474
Fax: 757-437-4976

Virginia Opera
PO Box 2580
Norfolk, VA 23501
www.vaopera.org
Phone: 757-627-9545
Fax: 757-622-0058

Virginia Sports Hall of Fame
420 High St
Portsmouth, VA 23704
Phone: 757-393-8031
Fax: 757-393-5228

Virginia Stage Co
Monticello & Tazewell Sts
Norfolk, VA 23514
E-mail: boxoffice@vastage.com
www.vastage.com
Phone: 757-627-6988
Fax: 757-628-5958

Virginia Symphony
208 E Plume St
Norfolk, VA 23501
Phone: 757-623-2310
Fax: 757-627-6546

Virginia War Museum
9285 Warwick Blvd
Newport News, VA 23607
Phone: 757-247-8523
Fax: 757-247-8627

Virginia Zoological Park
3500 Granby St
Norfolk, VA 23504
E-mail: vazoo@whro.org
sites.communitylink.org/vazoo/
Phone: 757-441-2706
Fax: 757-624-1106

Waterside The
333 Waterside Dr
Norfolk, VA 23510
Phone: 757-627-3300
Fax: 757-627-3981

Wild Water Rapids
849 General Booth Blvd
Virginia Beach, VA 23451
Phone: 757-422-0718
Fax: 757-425-0970
TF: 800-678-9453

Willoughby-Baylor House
601 E Freemason St
Norfolk, VA 23510
Phone: 757-664-6296

Sports Teams & Facilities

Hampton Coliseum
1000 Coliseum Dr
Hampton, VA 23666
www.hampton.va.us/coliseum
Phone: 757-838-5650
Fax: 757-838-2595

Hampton Roads Admirals (hockey)
201 E Brambleton Ave Scope Arena
Norfolk, VA 23510
E-mail: hradmirals@erols.com
www.hradmirals.com
Phone: 757-640-1212

Hampton Roads Mariners (soccer)
2181 Landstown Rd Virginia Beach Sportsplex
Virginia Beach, VA 23456
Phone: 757-430-8873
Fax: 757-430-8803

Hampton Roads Piranhas (soccer)
2181 Landstown Rd Virginia Beach Sportsplex
Virginia Beach, VA 23456
Phone: 757-405-6022
Fax: 757-431-3259

Langley Speedway
3165 N Armstead Ave
Hampton, VA 23666
www.langleyspeedway.com
Phone: 757-865-1100
Fax: 757-865-1147

Norfolk Scope
201 E Brambleton Ave Scope Arena
Norfolk, VA 23510
www.norfolkscope.com
Phone: 757-664-6464
Fax: 757-664-6990

Norfolk Tides (baseball)
150 Park Ave Harbor Park Stadium
Norfolk, VA 23510
www.gohamptonroads.com/partners/tides
Phone: 757-622-2222
Fax: 757-624-9090

Annual Events

A Fare for the Arts (late August) .757-393-5327
A Newsome House Christmas (December) .757-247-2360
AFR'AM Fest (late May) .757-456-1743
American Music Festival (early September) .757-437-4800
Annual 4th In the Park (July) .757-543-5721
Annual Civil War Re-enactment (late April) .757-887-1862
Art Explosure (early May) .757-622-4262
Artful Giving & Home for the Holidays (mid-November-early January) .757-596-8175
Bark in the Park (early October) .757-382-6411
Battle of Great Bridge Reenactment (early December) .757-382-6411
Bayou Boogaloo & Cajun Food Festival (mid-August) .757-441-2345
Beach Music Weekend (mid-May) .757-491-7866
Beef Fest (mid-September) .757-487-6122
Big Band Weekend (late May) .757-491-7866
Blues & Brews Festival (late October) .757-463-1940
Boardwalk Art Show (mid-June) .757-425-0000
Celebration in Lights (late November-early January) .757-926-8451
Chesapeake Eggstravaganza (late March) .757-382-8466
Chesapeake Holiday Wonderland (late November-early December) .757-482-6241
Chesapeake Jubilee (mid-April) .757-482-4848
Christmas in the Field Civil War Re-enactment (mid-December) .757-887-1862
Cinco de Mayo Celebration (early May) .757-491-7866
Civil War Days (early September) .757-382-6591
Cock Island Race (early June) .757-393-9933
Concerts at the Point (May-June) .757-441-2345
Crawford Bay Crew Classic (late March) .757-393-9933
Elizabeth River Run (mid-May) .757-421-2602
Ella Fitzgerald Music Festival (late April) .757-594-8752
Elvis is Everywhere Festival (early June) .800-446-8038
Fall Festival (early October) .888-493-7386
First Night Norfolk (December 31) .757-441-2345
Garden of Lights Holiday Festival (late November-early January) .757-441-5830
Great American Food Fest (early October) .757-382-6159
Great American Picnic (July 4) .757-441-2345
Greek Festival (mid-May) .757-440-0500
Hampton Bay Days Festival (mid-September) .757-727-6122
Harborfest (mid-June) .757-441-2345
Holiday Lights at the Beach (mid-November-early January) .757-491-7866
Holiday Tree Lighting (late November) .757-382-6241
Holidays in the City (late November-early December) .757-441-2345
Holly Festival (mid-late November) .757-668-7098
Indian River Craft Show (mid-November) .757-382-8464
International Azalea Festival-Norfolk (mid-April) .757-664-2525
Jubilee on the James (mid-June) .757-926-8451
King-Lincoln Music Festival (late August) .757-926-8451
Kwanzaa Celebrations (late December) .757-382-6411
Labor Day Celebration (early September) .757-382-6411
Men's Pro-Am Volleyball Tournament (mid-August) .757-437-4882
Mid-Atlantic Sports & Boat Show (mid-February) .757-491-7866
Mid-Atlantic Wildfowl Festival (early March) .757-437-8432
Monsters on the Beach Truck Expo (mid-October) .757-491-7866
Neptune Festival & Air Show (late September) .757-498-0215
Ocean View Beach Festival (mid-May) .757-583-0000
October Oyster Roast (mid-October) .888-493-7386
Peanut Festival (mid-October) .757-539-6751
Peninsula Fine Arts Center Juried Exhibition (late August-early November) .757-596-8175
Pontiac American Musical Festival (early September) .757-491-7866
Pungo Strawberry Festival (late May) .757-721-6001
Reggae on the River (early September) .757-441-2345
Seawall Festival (mid-June) .757-393-5327

Shamrock Sportsfest Marathon (mid-March) 757-481-5090
Sheep to Shawl (mid-April).......................757-382-6591
ShowDeo (early September) 757-427-6020
Spring Carnival (late April).......................757-441-2118
Star of Wonder (late November-early January) 757-595-1900
Stardust Ball (late May)..........................757-382-2330
Stars in the Sky (July 4) 757-926-8451
Stockley Gardens Art Festival (mid-May)...........757-625-6161
Town Point Air Show & 4th of July Celebration
(early July) 757-441-2345
Town Point Jazz & Blues Festival (mid-May).......757-441-2345
Town Point Virginia Wine Festival
(mid-October)................................757-441-2345
Virginia Beach East Coast Surfing Championships
(late August).................................800-861-7873
Virginia Children's Festival (late October)..........757-441-2345
Virginia International Waterfront Arts Festival
(late April-late May)...........................757-664-6492
Whale Watching (late December-early March).......757-437-4949
Wildlife Arts Festival (late January)................757-595-1900
Yuletides at the Mariners Museum
(late December) 757-596-2222

Oklahoma City, Oklahoma

***County:* Oklahoma**

OKLAHOMA CITY is located in central Oklahoma along the banks of the North Canadian River. The only major city within 100 miles is Tulsa, Oklahoma.

Area (Land) .... 352.3 sq mi
Area (Water) .... 5.6 sq mi
Elevation .... 1,207 ft
Latitude .... 35-46-22 N
Longitude .... 97-52-04 W
Time Zone .... CST
Area Code 405

Climate

Oklahoma City has a continental climate that has some influence from the Gulf of Mexico. Winters are generally mild, with high temperatures averaging around 50 degrees and lows in the upper 20s. The average annual snowfall is nine inches. Summers are long, hot, and humid, with average high temperatures in the low 90s and lows in the 70s. Oklahoma City averages 3,000 hours of sunshine each year. May is the wettest month in the city, while January is the driest.

Average Temperatures & Precipitation

Temperatures

	Jan	Feb	Mar	Apr	May	Jun	Jul	Aug	Sep	Oct	Nov	Dec
High	47	52	62	72	79	87	93	93	84	74	60	50
Low	25	30	39	49	58	66	71	70	62	50	39	29

Precipitation

	Jan	Feb	Mar	Apr	May	Jun	Jul	Aug	Sep	Oct	Nov	Dec
Inches	1.1	1.6	2.7	2.8	5.2	4.3	2.6	2.6	3.8	3.2	2.0	1.4

History

The Oklahoma Territory was originally inhabited by various Native American tribes, many of whom had been relocated there from other parts of the country, but two million acres of land, commonly known as the "Unassigned Lands," had not been claimed by any tribe. President Rutherford B. Hayes scheduled for this parcel of land to be opened for settlement by whites at noon on April 22, 1889. Thousands of pioneers gathered at the boundaries of the "Unassigned Lands" the night before, and some sneaked past the army patrols to stake out prime land. These people were known as the "Sooners," hence Oklahoma's nickname the "Sooner State." At 12 o'clock sharp the following day a single cannon shot signaled the start of the Great Land Run, and nearly 10,000 settlers staked claimed to land on the site of the present Oklahoma City, which is sometimes referred to as the "city born in a day."

The city was incorporated in 1890 and developed primarily as an agricultural center. The arrival of the railroad in the late 1800s also spawned growth. Oklahoma became a state in 1907, and three years later local leaders petitioned for the state capital to be moved from Guthrie to Oklahoma City. In 1910, Oklahoma City, with a population of 64,000, became the capital of the state of Oklahoma by popular vote. The State Capitol building, dedicated in 1917, is one of the few in the nation that does not have a dome, as the state's war-time budget and shortage of materials did not allow for elaborate design.

The event that sparked great economic development in Oklahoma City occurred on December 4, 1928, when oil was discovered in the city. In the years that followed, oil wells sprang up at sites throughout the city, including the grounds of the State Capitol. Although the oil industry has lost its dominance in the area as Oklahoma City's economy diversified through the years, it still remains a significant part of the city's overall economy, employing more than 7,000 area residents.

In 1995, tragedy struck Oklahoma City when a truck carrying a bomb exploded outside the Alfred P. Murrah Federal Building, killing more than 168 men, women, and children. Deemed the most deadly terrorist bombing in United States history, the event devastated the community, both physically and emotionally. Today, a memorial stands at the site of the Alfred P. Murrah bombsite to honor those who lost their lives. The determination and strong community spirit of Oklahoma City's residents has helped the city to rebuild itself in the face of tragedy.

Population

1990 Census 444,724
1998 Estimate 472,221
% Change 6.2
2005 Projection 1,102,000*

Racial/Ethnic Breakdown

White 77.8%
Black 16.0%
Other 6.2%
Hispanic Origin (may be of any race) 5.0%

Age Breakdown

Under 5 years 7.8%
5 to 17 .... 18.2%
18 to 20 .... 4.2%
21 to 24 .... 6.0%
25 to 34 .... 18.7%
35 to 44 .... 15.0%
45 to 54 .... 10.0%
55 to 64 .... 8.4%
65 to 74 .... 6.8%
75+ years 5.1%
Median Age 32.4

Gender Breakdown
Male 48.2%
Female 51.8%

** Information given is for the Oklahoma City Metropolitan Statistical Area (MSA), which includes the City of Norman, the City of Oklahoma City, the City of Shawnee, as well as Canadian, Cleveland, Logan, McClain, Oklahoma, and Pottawatomie counties.*

Government

Type of Government: Council-Manager

Oklahoma City City Clerk
200 N Walker Ave
Oklahoma City, OK 73102
Phone: 405-297-2394
Fax: 405-297-3121

Oklahoma City City Council
200 N Walker Ave 3rd Fl
Oklahoma City, OK 73102
Phone: 405-297-3884
Fax: 405-297-3003

Oklahoma City City Hall
200 N Walker Ave
Oklahoma City, OK 73102
Phone: 405-297-2578
Fax: 405-297-2570

Oklahoma City City Manager
200 N Walker Ave 3rd Fl
Oklahoma City, OK 73102
Phone: 405-297-2345
Fax: 405-297-2570

Oklahoma City Finance Dept
100 N Walker Ave
Oklahoma City, OK 73102
Phone: 405-297-2506
Fax: 405-297-2332

Oklahoma City Fire Dept
820 NW 5th St
Oklahoma City, OK 73106
Phone: 405-297-3314
Fax: 405-297-3329

Oklahoma City Mayor
200 N Walker Ave
Oklahoma City, OK 73102
Phone: 405-297-2424
Fax: 405-297-2570

Oklahoma City Municipal Counselor
200 N Walker Ave 4th & 5th Fls
Oklahoma City, OK 73102
Phone: 405-297-2451
Fax: 405-297-2118

Oklahoma City Parks & Recreation Dept
420 W Main St Suite 210
Oklahoma City, OK 73102
Phone: 405-297-3882
Fax: 405-297-3175

Oklahoma City Personnel Dept
420 W Main St Suite 110
Oklahoma City, OK 73102
Phone: 405-297-2530
Fax: 405-297-2137

Oklahoma City Planning Dept
420 W Main St 9th Fl
Oklahoma City, OK 73102
Phone: 405-297-2623
Fax: 405-297-1631

Oklahoma City Police Dept
701 Colcord Dr
Oklahoma City, OK 73102
Phone: 405-297-1000
Fax: 405-297-1466

Oklahoma City Public Works Dept
420 W Main St Suite 700
Oklahoma City, OK 73102
Phone: 405-297-2508
Fax: 405-297-2117

Oklahoma City Transit Services Dept
300 SW 7th St
Oklahoma City, OK 73109
Phone: 405-297-2601
Fax: 405-297-2111

Oklahoma City Water & Wastewater Utilities Dept
420 W Main St Suite 500
Oklahoma City, OK 73102
Phone: 405-297-2422
Fax: 405-297-3813

Important Phone Numbers

AAA 405-943-9922
American Express Travel 800-528-4800
Driver's License Information 405-425-2026
Emergency 911
Medical Referral 405-843-5619
Oklahoma Assn of Realtors 405-848-9944
Oklahoma County Treasurer 405-278-1300
Oklahoma State Tax Commission 405-521-3125
Poison Control Center 405-271-5454
Time/Temp 405-599-1234
Travelers Aid 405-232-5507
Vehicle Registration Information 405-521-3221
Voter Registration Information 405-278-1515
Weather 405-478-3377

Information Sources

Better Business Bureau Serving Central Oklahoma
17 S Dewey Ave
Oklahoma City, OK 73102
www.oklahomacity.bbb.org
Phone: 405-239-6081
Fax: 405-235-5891

Greater Oklahoma City Chamber of Commerce
123 Park Ave
Oklahoma City, OK 73102
www.okcchamber.com
Phone: 405-297-8900
Fax: 405-297-8916
TF: 800-616-1114

Myriad Convention Center
1 Myriad Gardens
Oklahoma City, OK 73102
www.myriadevents.com
Phone: 405-297-3300
Fax: 405-297-1683
TF: 800-654-3676

Oklahoma City Convention & Visitors Bureau
189 W Sheridan St
Oklahoma City, OK 73102
www.okccvb.org
Phone: 405-297-8910
Fax: 405-297-8888
TF: 800-225-5652

Oklahoma County
320 Robert S Kerr Ave
Oklahoma City, OK 73102
www.oklahomacounty.org
Phone: 405-270-0082
Fax: 405-278-1852

Online Resources

About.com Guide to Oklahoma City
oklahomacity.about.com/local/southwestus/oklahomacity

Area Guide Oklahoma City
oklahomacity.areaguides.net

City Knowledge Oklahoma City
www.cityknowledge.com/ok_oklahomacity.htm

Connect Oklahoma
www.connectok.com

DigitalCity Oklahoma City
home.digitalcity.com/oklahomacity

Excite.com Oklahoma City City Guide
www.excite.com/travel/countries/united_states/oklahoma/oklahoma_city

Oklahoma City Community Web Site
www.oklahomacity.com

Oklahoma City Online
okconline.com

Area Communities

Communities in the Oklahoma City area with populations greater than 20,000 include:

Del City
4517 SE 29th St
Del City, OK 73115
Phone: 405-671-2800
Fax: 405-671-2897

Edmond
PO Box 2970
Edmond, OK 73083
Phone: 405-359-4500
Fax: 405-359-4512

Midwest City
PO Box 10570
Midwest City, OK 73140
Phone: 405-739-1201
Fax: 405-739-1208

Moore
301 N Broadway
Moore, OK 73160
Phone: 405-793-5200
Fax: 405-793-5107

Norman
201 W Gray St Suite A
Norman, OK 73069
Phone: 405-366-5402
Fax: 405-366-5389

Economy

Oklahoma City's diverse economic base features industries ranging from agriculture to aerospace technology. Government plays a major role in the capital city's economy, with Oklahoma State Government being the area's largest employer, providing more than 38,000 jobs. Local and federal government agencies, educational institutions, and the military are major employers as well. Health care is also an important industry, with more than 25,000 area residents employed in the field.

Unemployment Rate 3.8%
Per Capita Income.......................... $23,236*
Median Family Income...................... $43,300**

** Information given is for Oklahoma County.*
*** Information given is for the Oklahoma City Metropolitan Statistical Area (MSA), which includes the City of Norman, the City of Oklahoma City, the City of Shawnee, as well as Canadian, Cleveland, Logan, McClain, Oklahoma, and Pottawatomie counties.*

Principal Industries & Number of Wage Earners

Oklahoma County - 1997

Agriculture, Forestry, & Fishing.......................... 1,719
Construction.. 14,279
Finance, Insurance & Real Estate......................... 22,264
Manufacturing 42,425
Mining 8,992
Retail Trade.. 67,924
Services 126,454
Transporation & Public Utilities......................... 20,828
Wholesale Trade....................................... 24,155

Major Employers

Dayton Tire Co
PO Box 24011
Oklahoma City, OK 73124
Phone: 405-280-3000
Fax: 405-280-3309

FAA Mike Monroney Aeronautical Center
6500 S MacArthur Blvd
Oklahoma City, OK 73169
www.mmac.jccbi.gov/MMAC/
Phone: 405-954-3011
Fax: 405-954-3548

Fleming Cos Inc
PO Box 26647
Oklahoma City, OK 73126
E-mail: fleming@ionet.net
www.fleming.com
Phone: 405-840-7200
Fax: 405-840-7242

General Motors Corp
7447 SE 74th St
Oklahoma City, OK 73135
www.gm.com/careers
Phone: 405-733-6011
Fax: 405-733-6328

Hertz Corp
3817 NW Expressway St
Oklahoma City, OK 73112
Phone: 405-721-6440
Fax: 405-280-4839

Integris Baptist Medical Center
3300 Northwest Expy
Oklahoma City, OK 73112
Phone: 405-949-3011
Fax: 405-949-3573

OG & E Electric Services
PO Box 321
Oklahoma City, OK 73101
www.oge.com
Phone: 405-553-3000
Fax: 405-553-3165

Oklahoma City City Hall
200 N Walker Ave
Oklahoma City, OK 73102
www.okc-cityhall.org
Phone: 405-297-2578
Fax: 405-297-2570

Oklahoma City Public Schools
900 N Klein Ave
Oklahoma City, OK 73106
Phone: 405-297-6522
Fax: 405-297-6580

Oklahoma Health Center
PO Box 26901
Oklahoma City, OK 73104
Phone: 405-271-4000
Fax: 405-271-3925

Saint Anthony Hospital
1000 N Lee St
Oklahoma City, OK 73101
www.saintsok.com
Phone: 405-272-7000
Fax: 405-272-6781
TF: 800-227-6964

Seagate Technology Inc
PO Box 12313
Oklahoma City, OK 73157
Phone: 405-324-3000
Fax: 405-324-3234

Tinker Air Force Base
Tinker AFB, OK 73145
Phone: 405-739-2026
Fax: 405-739-2882

University of Oklahoma
1000 Asp Ave
Norman, OK 73019
www.ou.edu
Phone: 405-325-0311
Fax: 405-325-7124

US Postal Service
3030 NW Expressway St
Oklahoma City, OK 73198
new.usps.com
Phone: 405-553-6211
Fax: 405-553-6106

Quality of Living Indicators

Total Crime Index 44,153
(rates per 100,000 inhabitants)

Violent Crime
Murder/manslaughter 56
Forcible rape 398
Robbery 1,064
Aggravated assault 2,553

Property Crime
Burglary 8,038
Larceny theft 28,414
Motor vehicle theft 3,630

Cost of Living Index 91.5
(national average = 100)

Median Home Price $84,200

Education

Public Schools

Oklahoma City Public Schools
900 N Klein Ave
Oklahoma City, OK 73106
Phone: 405-297-6522
Fax: 405-297-6580

Number of Schools
Elementary 54
Middle 7
High 6

Student/Teacher Ratio
All Grades 15.9:1

Private Schools

Number of Schools (all grades) 73

Colleges & Universities

Hillsdale Free Will Baptist College
PO Box 7208
Moore, OK 73153
E-mail: go-saints@hillsdale.org
www.hc.edu
Phone: 405-912-9000
Fax: 405-912-9050

Mid-America Bible College
3500 SW 119th St
Oklahoma City, OK 73170
E-mail: mbcinfo@mabc.edu
www.mabc.edu
Phone: 405-691-3800
Fax: 405-692-3165

Oklahoma Christian University of Science & Arts
2501 E Memorial Blvd
Edmond, OK 73013
E-mail: info@oc.edu
www.oc.edu
Phone: 405-425-5000
Fax: 405-425-5208
TF: 800-877-5010

Oklahoma City Community College
7777 S May Ave
Oklahoma City, OK 73159
www.okc.cc.ok.us
Phone: 405-682-1611
Fax: 405-682-7521

Oklahoma City University
2501 N Blackwelder Ave
Oklahoma City, OK 73106
E-mail: uadmissions@frodo.okcu.edu
frodo.okcu.edu
Phone: 405-521-5000
Fax: 405-521-5916
TF: 800-633-7242

Oklahoma State University Oklahoma City
900 N Portland Ave
Oklahoma City, OK 73107
www.osuokc.edu
Phone: 405-947-4421
Fax: 405-945-3277

Rose State College
6420 SE 15th St
Midwest City, OK 73110
www.rose.cc.ok.us
Phone: 405-733-7311
Fax: 405-736-0309

Southern Nazarene University
6729 NW 39th Expy
Bethany, OK 73008
www.snu.edu
Phone: 405-789-6400
Fax: 405-491-6320
TF: 800-648-9899

Southwestern College of Christian Ministry
7210 NW 39th Expy
Bethany, OK 73008
Phone: 405-789-7661
Fax: 405-495-0078

University of Central Oklahoma
100 N University Dr
Edmond, OK 73034
E-mail: aix1@ucok.edu
www.ucok.edu
Phone: 405-341-2980
Fax: 405-341-4964

University of Oklahoma
1000 Asp Ave
Norman, OK 73019
www.ou.edu
Phone: 405-325-0311
Fax: 405-325-7124

University of Sciences & Arts of Oklahoma
PO Box 82345
Chickasha, OK 73018
www.usao.edu
Phone: 405-224-3140
Fax: 405-522-3176
TF: 800-933-8726

Hospitals

Deaconess Hospital
5501 N Portland Ave
Oklahoma City, OK 73112
Phone: 405-946-5581
Fax: 405-604-6153

Edmond Medical Center
1 S Bryant St
Edmond, OK 73034
Phone: 405-341-6100
Fax: 405-359-5500

Hillcrest Health Center
2129 SW 59th St
Oklahoma City, OK 73119
www.hillcrest.com
Phone: 405-685-6671
Fax: 405-680-2237

Integris Baptist Medical Center
3300 Northwest Expy
Oklahoma City, OK 73112
Phone: 405-949-3011
Fax: 405-949-3573

Integris Southwest Medical Center of Oklahoma
Phone: 405-636-7000
Fax: 405-636-7881
4401 S Western Ave
Oklahoma City, OK 73109

Mercy Health Center
Phone: 405-755-1515
Fax: 405-752-3750
4300 W Memorial Rd
Oklahoma City, OK 73120

Norman Regional Hospital
Phone: 405-307-1000
Fax: 405-307-1304
PO Box 1308
Norman, OK 73070

Presbyterian Medical Center
Phone: 405-271-5100
Fax: 405-271-5977
700 NE 13th St
Oklahoma City, OK 73104

Saint Anthony Hospital
Phone: 405-272-7000
Fax: 405-272-6781
TF: 800-227-6964
1000 N Lee St
Oklahoma City, OK 73101
www.saintsok.com

University Hospitals
Phone: 405-271-5656
Fax: 405-271-3888
PO Box 26307
Oklahoma City, OK 73126

Veterans Affairs Medical Center
Phone: 405-270-0501
Fax: 405-270-1586
921 NE 13th St
Oklahoma City, OK 73104

Transportation

Airport(s)

Will Rogers World Airport (OKC)
10 miles SW of downtown (approx 20 minutes) . . .405-680-3200

Mass Transit

Metro Transit
$1 Base fare 405-235-7433
Water Taxi of Oklahoma
$5 Base fare 405-234-8294

Rail/Bus

Union Bus Station
Phone: 405-235-6425
427 W Sheridan Ave
Oklahoma City, OK 73102

Utilities

Electricity
Oklahoma Gas & Electric Co 405-272-9741
www.oge.com

Gas
Oklahoma Natural Gas Co 405-551-6602
www.ong.com

Water
Oklahoma City Utility Customer Service 405-297-2833

Garbage Collection/Recycling
Oklahoma City Solid Waste Management 405-749-3092

Telecommunications

Telephone
Southwestern Bell Telephone 405-236-6611
www.swbell.com

Cable Television
Cox Communications 405-348-5750
www.cox.com

Internet Service Providers (ISPs)
InterCON Inc 405-302-5166
www.icon.net
Internet Access Plus Inc 405-848-4424
www.netplus.net
Internet Shop 405-848-7000
www.theshop.net
ioNet Inc 405-270-0999
www.ionet.net
Questar Information Systems Inc 405-848-3228
www.qns.com
Telepath Systems Inc 405-321-1900
www.telepath.com

Banks

BancFirst Corp
Phone: 405-270-1000
Fax: 405-270-1089
PO Box 26788
Oklahoma City, OK 73126
www.bancfirst.com

Bank of America NA
Phone: 888-279-3247
211 N Robinson Ave
Oklahoma City, OK 73102

Bank of Oklahoma NA
Phone: 405-272-2000
Fax: 405-272-2458
201 Robert S Kerr Ave
Oklahoma City, OK 73102
www.bankofoklahoma.com

Bank One Oklahoma NA
Phone: 405-231-6000
Fax: 405-231-6908
100 N Broadway Ave
Oklahoma City, OK 73102

Bankers Bank
Phone: 405-848-8877
Fax: 405-842-4524
TF: 800-522-9220
5801 N Broadway Parragon Bldg Suite 300
Oklahoma City, OK 73118

Commercial Federal Bank FSB
Phone: 405-722-0959
Fax: 405-722-0994
5757 Northwest Expy
Oklahoma City, OK 73132

Guaranty Bank & Trust Co
Phone: 405-945-8100
Fax: 405-858-8118
3333 Northwest Expy
Oklahoma City, OK 73112

National Bank of Commerce
Phone: 405-748-9100
Fax: 405-748-9191
13401 N Pennsylvania Ave
Oklahoma City, OK 73120
www.nbcok.com

UMB Oklahoma Bank
Phone: 405-239-5800
Fax: 405-239-5932
1217 S Agnew Ave
Oklahoma City, OK 73108

Shopping

50 Penn Place
Phone: 405-848-7940
Fax: 405-848-5921
1900 Northwest Expy
Oklahoma City, OK 73118

Bricktown
Phone: 405-236-8666
Fax: 405-236-8669
315 E Sheridan Ave
Oklahoma City, OK 73104
www.bricktown-ok.com/

Crossroads Mall
7000 Crossroads Blvd
Oklahoma City, OK 73149
Phone: 405-631-4421
Fax: 405-634-1503

Dillard's
7000 Crossroads Blvd
Oklahoma City, OK 73149
Phone: 405-634-6569
Fax: 405-634-6975

Heritage Park Mall
6801 E Reno Ave
Midwest City, OK 73110
Phone: 405-737-1472
Fax: 405-737-5546

Mayfair Village
NW 50th & May Ave
Oklahoma City, OK 73112
Phone: 405-721-2797
Fax: 405-721-5956

Penn Square Mall
1901 Northwest Expy
Oklahoma City, OK 73118
E-mail: info@shoppenn.com
www.shoppenn.com
Phone: 405-842-4424
Fax: 405-842-4676

Quail Springs Mall
2501 W Memorial Rd
Oklahoma City, OK 73134
www.quailspringsmall.com
Phone: 405-755-6530
Fax: 405-751-8344

Media

Newspapers and Magazines

Daily Oklahoman*
PO Box 25125
Oklahoma City, OK 73125
www.oklahoman.net
Phone: 405-475-3311
Fax: 405-475-3183
TF: 800-375-6397

Journal Record Oklahoma City*
222 N Robinson St
Oklahoma City, OK 73102
www.journalrecord.com
Phone: 405-235-3100
Fax: 405-278-6907

Oklahoma Gazette
3701 N Shartel Ave
Oklahoma City, OK 73154
E-mail: publisher@okgazette.com
www.okgazette.com
Phone: 405-528-6000
Fax: 405-528-4600

Oklahoma Today Magazine
15 N Robinson Ave Colcord Bldg Suite 100
Oklahoma City, OK 73102
E-mail: oktpublisher@otrd.state.ok.us
www.oklahomatoday.com
Phone: 405-521-2496
Fax: 405-522-4588
TF: 800-777-1793

**Indicates major daily newspapers*

Television

KAUT-TV Ch 43 (UPN)
11901 N Eastern Ave
Oklahoma City, OK 73131
Phone: 405-478-4300
Fax: 405-516-4343

KETA-TV Ch 13 (PBS)
7403 N Kelley St
Oklahoma City, OK 73111
www.oeta.onenet.net
Phone: 405-848-8501
Fax: 405-841-9216

KFOR-TV Ch 4 (NBC)
444 E Britton Rd
Oklahoma City, OK 73114
E-mail: news@kfor.com
www.kfor.com
Phone: 405-478-1212
Fax: 405-478-6337

KOCB-TV Ch 34 (WB)
1501 NE 85th St
Oklahoma City, OK 73131
E-mail: kocb@telepath.com
www.kocb.com
Phone: 405-478-3434
Fax: 405-478-1027

KOCO-TV Ch 5 (ABC)
1300 E Britton Rd
Oklahoma City, OK 73131
E-mail: koco@ionet.net
www.ionet.net/koco
Phone: 405-478-3000
Fax: 405-478-6675

KOKH-TV Ch 25 (Fox)
1228 E Wilshire Blvd
Oklahoma City, OK 73111
E-mail: prgramming@fox25.net
www.kokh.com
Phone: 405-843-2525
Fax: 405-478-4343

KOPX-TV Ch 62 (PAX)
13424 Railway Dr
Oklahoma City, OK 73114
www.pax.net/KOPX
Phone: 405-751-6800
Fax: 405-751-6867

KSBI-TV Ch 52 (Ind)
PO Box 26404
Oklahoma City, OK 73126
www.ksbitv.com
Phone: 405-631-7335
Fax: 405-631-7367

KWTV-TV Ch 9 (CBS)
7401 N Kelley Ave
Oklahoma City, OK 73111
E-mail: mailroom@kwtv.com
www.kwtv.com
Phone: 405-843-6641
Fax: 405-841-9989

Radio

KATT-FM 100.5 MHz (Rock)
4045 NW 64th St Suite 600
Oklahoma City, OK 73116
www.katt.com
Phone: 405-848-0100
Fax: 405-848-1915

KGOU-FM 106.3 MHz (NPR)
780 Van Vleet Oval
Norman, OK 73019
www.kgou.org/
Phone: 405-325-3388
Fax: 405-325-7129

KJYO-FM 102.7 MHz (CHR)
PO Box 1000
Oklahoma City, OK 73101
Phone: 405-840-5271
Fax: 405-858-1435

KKNG-FM 93.3 MHz (Ctry)
5105 W Shields Blvd
Oklahoma City, OK 73129
www.kkng.com
Phone: 405-616-5500
Fax: 405-616-5505

KMGL-FM 104.1 MHz (AC)
400 E Britton Rd
Oklahoma City, OK 73114
E-mail: info@magic104.com
www.magic104.com
Phone: 405-478-5104
Fax: 405-478-0448

KOMA-AM 1520 kHz (Oldies)
400 E Britton Rd
Oklahoma City, OK 73114
E-mail: thegoodguys@komaradio.com
www.komaradio.com
Phone: 405-794-4000
Fax: 405-793-0514

KOMA-FM 92.5 MHz (Oldies) Phone: 405-794-4000
820 SW 4th St Fax: 405-793-0514
Moore, OK 73160
E-mail: thegoodguys@komaradio.com
www.komaradio.com

KQCV-AM 800 kHz (Rel) Phone: 405-521-0800
1919 N Broadway Fax: 405-521-1391
Oklahoma City, OK 73103

KQSR-FM 94.7 MHz (AC) Phone: 405-840-5271
50 Penn Pl Suite 1000 Fax: 405-858-1435
Oklahoma City, OK 73118

KRXO-FM 107.7 MHz (CR) Phone: 405-794-4000
400 E Britton Rd Fax: 405-793-0514
Oklahoma City, OK 73114
www.krxo.com

KTNT-FM 97.9 MHz (NAC) Phone: 405-848-0100
4045 NW 64th St Suite 600 Fax: 405-843-5288
Oklahoma City, OK 73116
www.ktnt.com

KTOK-AM 1000 kHz (N/T) Phone: 405-840-5271
50 Penn Pl Fax: 405-858-1435
Oklahoma City, OK 73118

KTST-FM 101.9 MHz (Ctry) Phone: 405-528-5543
101 NE 28th St Fax: 405-525-3832
Oklahoma City, OK 73105
E-mail: twister@thetwister.com
www.thetwister.com

KVSP-AM 1140 kHz (Urban) Phone: 405-425-4100
1528 NE 23rd St Fax: 405-424-8811
Oklahoma City, OK 73111
www.kvsp.com/KVSP/kvsp.htm

KXXY-FM 96.1 MHz (Ctry) Phone: 405-528-5543
101 NE 28th St Fax: 405-525-3832
Oklahoma City, OK 73105
www.kxy.com

KYIS-FM 98.9 MHz (AC) Phone: 405-848-0100
4045 NW 64th St Suite 330 Fax: 405-843-5288
Oklahoma City, OK 73116
www.kyis.com

Attractions

Oklahoma City's Omniplex entertainment complex includes three museums—the Kirkpatrick Science and Air Space Museum, the International Photography Hall of Fame, and the Red Earth Indian Center—that feature more than 300 hands-on exhibits, as well as gardens, greenhouses, a planetarium, a museum shop, and a café. Bricktown, part of Oklahoma City's historic downtown area, has become one of the city's most popular entertainment districts, featuring a host of shops and restaurants in a turn-of-the-century setting. Authentic western boots and clothing are hand-made at Stockyards City, site of the Oklahoma National Stockyards, where more than one million head of cattle are auctioned off each year. Other Oklahoma City attractions include the National Cowboy Hall of Fame and Western Heritage Center, and Myriad Gardens/Crystal Bridge Tropical Conservatory, which features plant life from tropical locations around the globe and a 35-foot waterfall.

45th Infantry Division Museum Phone: 405-424-5313
2145 NE 36th St Fax: 405-424-3748
Oklahoma City, OK 73111
www.45thdivisionmuseum.com

Ballet Oklahoma Phone: 405-843-9898
7421 N Classen Blvd Fax: 405-843-9894
Oklahoma City, OK 73116
www.balletoklahoma.com

Black Liberated Arts Center Phone: 405-232-2522
201 Channing Sq Fax: 405-840-0061
Oklahoma City, OK 73102

Bricktown Phone: 405-236-8666
315 E Sheridan Ave Fax: 405-236-8669
Oklahoma City, OK 73104
www.bricktown-ok.com/

Canterbury Choral Society Phone: 405-232-7464
428 W California St Fax: 405-232-7465
Oklahoma City, OK 72102

Carpenter Square Theatre Phone: 405-232-6500
400 W Main St Fax: 405-232-6502
Oklahoma City, OK 73101
www.carpentersquare.com

Chickasaw National Recreation Area Phone: 580-622-3165
PO Box 201 Fax: 580-622-6931
Sulphur, OK 73086
www.nps.gov/chic/

City Arts Center Phone: 405-951-0000
3000 Pershing Blvd Fax: 405-951-0003
Oklahoma City, OK 73107
E-mail: cacoct@ix.netcom.com
www.cityartscenter.com

Civic Center Music Hall Phone: 405-297-2584
201 Channing Sq Suite 100 Fax: 405-297-3890
Oklahoma City, OK 73102
www.okc-cityhall.org/CivicCenter

Earlywine Park Phone: 405-297-2211
3101 SW 119th St & May Ave Fax: 405-297-3657
Oklahoma City, OK 73170

Enterprise Square USA Phone: 405-425-5030
2501 E Memorial Rd Fax: 405-425-5108
Oklahoma City, OK 73136
www.esusa.org

Frontier City Theme Park Phone: 405-478-2412
11501 Northeast Expy Fax: 405-478-3104
Oklahoma City, OK 73131
www.sixflags.com/frontiercity

Governor's Mansion Phone: 405-521-9211
820 NE 23rd St Fax: 405-521-1198
Oklahoma City, OK 73105

Harn Homestead & 1889er Museum Phone: 405-235-4058
313 NE 16th St Fax: 405-235-4041
Oklahoma City, OK 73104

Historic Paseo Artist District Phone: 405-525-2688
NW 30th & Dewey Ave Fax: 405-525-3133
Oklahoma City, OK 73103
www.okclive.com/paseo/

International Photography Hall of Fame & Museum
2100 NE 52nd St
Oklahoma City, OK 73111
E-mail: info@iphf.org
iphf.org
Phone: 405-424-4055
Fax: 405-424-4058

Jewel Box Theatre
3700 N Walker Ave
Oklahoma City, OK 73118
Phone: 405-521-1786
Fax: 405-525-6562

Kirkpatrick Science & Air Space Museum
2100 NE 52nd St
Oklahoma City, OK 73111
E-mail: omniplex@ionet.net
www.ionet.net/~omniplex/index.shtml
Phone: 405-602-6664
Fax: 405-602-3768
TF: 800-532-7652

Lake Overholser
10th St & Overholser Dr
Oklahoma City, OK 73102
Phone: 405-297-2211

Lyric Theatre of Oklahoma
4444 N Classen Blvd Suite 103
Oklahoma City, OK 73118
www.lyrictheatreokc.com
Phone: 405-524-9312
Fax: 405-524-9316

Martin Park Nature Center
5000 W Memorial Rd
Oklahoma City, OK 73142
Phone: 405-755-0676
Fax: 405-749-3072

Myriad Botanical Gardens/Crystal Bridge Tropical Conservatory
100 Myriad Gardens
Oklahoma City, OK 73102
www.okccvb.org/attractions/myrgard/myrgard.html
Phone: 405-297-3995
Fax: 405-297-3620

National Cowboy Hall of Fame & Western Heritage Center
1700 NE 63rd St
Oklahoma City, OK 73111
www.cowboyhalloffame.org
Phone: 405-478-2250
Fax: 405-478-2046

National Softball Hall of Fame & Museum
2801 NE 50th St
Oklahoma City, OK 73111
E-mail: info@softball.org
www.softball.org
Phone: 405-424-5266
Fax: 405-424-3855

Oklahoma City Art Museum at the Fairgrounds
3113 Pershing Blvd
Oklahoma City, OK 73107
E-mail: info@okcartmuseum.com
www.okcartmuseum.com
Phone: 405-946-4477
Fax: 405-946-7671
TF: 800-579-9278

Oklahoma City Philharmonic
428 W California Ave Suite 210
Oklahoma City, OK 73102
www.okcphilharmonic.org/
Phone: 405-232-7575
Fax: 405-232-4353

Oklahoma City Zoo
2101 NE 50th St
Oklahoma City, OK 73111
www.okczoo.com
Phone: 405-424-3344
Fax: 405-425-0207

Oklahoma Firefighters Museum
2716 NE 50th St
Oklahoma City, OK 73111
www.okccvb.org/attractions/firefighters/firemus.htm
Phone: 405-424-3440
Fax: 405-424-1032

Oklahoma Heritage Center
201 NW 14th St
Oklahoma City, OK 73103
E-mail: oha@telepath.com
www.telepath.com/oha/weddings.html
Phone: 405-235-4458
Fax: 405-235-2714

Oklahoma Opry
404 W Commerce St
Oklahoma City, OK 73109
E-mail: scarberry@thor.net
Phone: 405-632-8322

Oklahoma State Capitol
2300 N Lincoln Blvd
Oklahoma City, OK 73105
Phone: 405-521-3356

Omniplex
2100 NE 52nd St
Oklahoma City, OK 73111
E-mail: omniplex@ionet.net
www.ionet.net/~omniplex/index.shtml
Phone: 405-602-6664
Fax: 405-602-3768
TF: 800-532-7652

Overholser Mansion
405 NW 15th St
Oklahoma City, OK 73103
Phone: 405-528-8485

Prairie Dance Theatre
2100 NE 52nd St
Oklahoma City, OK 73111
Phone: 405-424-2249

Red Earth Indian Center
2100 NE 52nd St
Oklahoma City, OK 73111
Phone: 405-427-5228
Fax: 405-427-8079

Rogers Will Park
36th St & N Portland Ave
Oklahoma City, OK 73112
Phone: 405-943-0827

Stage Center
400 W Sheridan Ave
Oklahoma City, OK 73102
www.stagecenter.com
Phone: 405-270-4801
Fax: 405-270-4806

Stars & Stripes Park
3701 S Lake Hefner Pkwy
Oklahoma City, OK 73102
Phone: 405-297-2211

State Fair Park
500 Land Rush St
Oklahoma City, OK 73107
www.oklafair.org/
Phone: 405-948-6700
Fax: 405-948-6828

State Museum of History
2100 N Lincoln Blvd Wiley Post Historical Bldg
Oklahoma City, OK 73105
www.ok-history.mus.ok.us
Phone: 405-521-2491
Fax: 405-521-2492

Stockyards & Cowtown
2501 Exchange Ave
Oklahoma City, OK 73108
E-mail: cfreeze777@aol.com
www.onsy.com
Phone: 405-235-8675
Fax: 405-236-3277

Trosper Park Phone: 405-297-2211
SE 25th St & Eastern Ave
Oklahoma City, OK 73102

White Water Bay Phone: 405-943-9687
3908 W Reno Ave Fax: 405-947-3714
Oklahoma City, OK 73107
www.sixflags.com/whitewaterbay

World of Wings Pigeon Center Phone: 405-478-5155
2300 NE 63rd St TF: 800-882-1586
Oklahoma City, OK 73111

World Organization of China Painters Museum Phone: 405-521-1234
2641 NW 10th St Fax: 405-521-1265
Oklahoma City, OK 73107
E-mail: wocporg@theshop.net
www.theshop.net/wocporg/

Sports Teams & Facilities

Oklahoma City Blazers (hockey) Phone: 405-235-7825
119 N Robinson Ave Suite 230 Fax: 405-272-9875
Oklahoma City, OK 73102
E-mail: info@okcblazers.com
www.okcblazers.com

Oklahoma RedHawks (baseball) Phone: 405-218-1000
2 S Mickey Mantle Dr Fax: 405-218-1001
Oklahoma City, OK 73104
www.redhawksbaseball.com

Oklahoma Wranglers (football) Phone: 405-236-0131
1 Myriad Gardens Myriad Convention Ctr Fax: 405-236-0139
Oklahoma City, OK 73102
www.okwranglers.com

Remington Park Race Track Phone: 405-424-1000
1 Remington Pl Fax: 405-425-3297
Oklahoma City, OK 73111
E-mail: rp-mis@remingtonpark.com
www.remingtonpark.com

State Fair Arena Phone: 405-948-6700
333 Gorden Cooper Blvd Fax: 405-948-6821
Oklahoma City, OK 73107
www.oklafair.org

State Fair Speedway Phone: 405-948-6796
500 Land Rush St Fax: 405-948-6828
Oklahoma City, OK 73107
www.na-motorsports.com/Tracks/StateFair.html

Annual Events

89ers Days PRCA Rodeo (late April)..............800-595-7433
Aerospace America International Air Show (mid-June) 405-685-9546
All-College Basketball Tournament (late December)..............................800-225-5652
An Affair of the Heart Craft Show (early February & late October) 405-948-6704
Arts Festival Oklahoma (early September)..........405-682-7536
BalloonFest (mid-August) 405-794-4000
Big 12 Baseball Tournament (mid-May)............800-225-5652
Bullnanza (early February) 800-234-3393
Celebration of African-American Heritage (early February)..............................405-951-0000
Centennial Horse Show (mid-late April)...........405-557-9400
Cowboy Chuckwagon Gathering (late May) 405-478-2250
Crystal Lights Holiday Display (late November-late December).................405-297-3995
Deep Deuce Jazz Festival (early October) 405-524-3800
Festival of the Arts (late April)....................405-297-8910
Fourth of July Festival (July 4) 800-225-5652
Grand National Morgan Horse Show (early October)...............................800-225-5652
Heritage Hills Historic Homes Tour (mid-October)................................405-528-8485
Holiday Treefest (late November-early January) 405-602-6664
International Arabian Horse Show (late July).......405-948-6700
International Finals Rodeo (mid-January) 405-235-6540
Lazy E Spring Barrel Futurity (early April).........800-595-7433
National Appaloosa Horse Show (late June-mid-July) 405-297-8938
National Finals Steer Roping (late October) 800-595-7433
National Reining Horse Derby (mid-May) 405-297-8938
Oklahoma City Home & Garden Show (early April)...................................405-948-6704
Oklahoma Farm Show (mid-April).................405-948-6704
Oklahoma State Fair (mid-September-early October).................800-225-5652
Paseo Arts Festival (late May) 405-525-2688
Prairie Circuit Finals Rodeo (mid-November).......800-595-7433
Prix De West Invitational Exhibition & Sale (mid-June) 405-478-2250
Red Earth Native American Cultural Festival (mid-June) 405-427-5228
Sooner State Summer Games (June) 405-235-4222
Southwest Street Rod Nationals (mid-July).........405-948-6700
Sportsfest (early February) 405-235-4222
Spring Fair & Livestock Exposition (late March)....405-948-6704
Spring Festival of the Arts (late April).............405-270-4848
Sunday Twilight Concert Series (June-late August)............................405-270-4848
Timed Event Championship of the World (mid-March)................................405-282-7433
WinterTales Storytelling Festival (mid-February)....405-270-4848
World Championship Barrel Racing Futurity (early December).............................405-948-6704
World Championship Quarter Horse Show (mid-November).............................800-225-5652

Olympia, Washington

***County:* Thurston**

OLYMPIA is located at the southern tip of Puget Sound in western Washington State. Major cities within 100 miles include Seattle and Tacoma, Washington.

Area (Land)	16.1 sq mi
Area (Water)	1.8 sq mi
Elevation	100 ft
Latitude	47-02-70 N
Longitude	122-93-91 W
Time Zone	PST
Area Code	360

Climate

Olympia has a moderate climate. Winters are cool and wet, with average low temperatures in the mid-40s to near 50 degrees and lows in the low 30s. Approximately 18 inches of snow falls annually in Olympia, on average. November through March is the wettest time of the year. Summer days are warm and fairly dry, with average high temperatures in the mid-70s, while evenings cool down dramatically into the mid- to upper 40s. July is Olympia's driest month.

Average Temperatures & Precipitation

Temperatures

	Jan	Feb	Mar	Apr	May	Jun	Jul	Aug	Sep	Oct	Nov	Dec
High	44	50	54	59	65	71	77	77	71	61	50	44
Low	32	33	34	36	41	46	49	50	45	39	35	32

Precipitation

	Jan	Feb	Mar	Apr	May	Jun	Jul	Aug	Sep	Oct	Nov	Dec
Inches	8.0	5.8	5.0	3.3	2.1	1.6	0.8	1.3	2.3	4.3	8.1	8.1

History

Originally inhabited by Salish Indians of the Chehalis, Nisqually, and Squaxin tribes, the area at the southern tip of Puget Sound was first explored by Europeans in 1792. The area was not settled, however, until 1846, when Levi Lathrop Smith and Edmund Sylvester founded the town of Smithfield. Several years later, Sylvester platted the new town, and soon after its name was changed to Olympia for the city's spectacular view of the nearby Olympic Mountains.

In 1852 Olympia became the county seat of Thurston County. Olympia's location at the southernmost access to Puget Sound from the Columbia River soon made it an important center of maritime commerce. In 1853, with a population nearing 1,000, Olympia was chosen as the capital of the newly established Washington Territory. At that time, Thurston County was the most populous county in Washington and remained so until the 1870s when major railroad lines bypassed the city, selecting Tacoma as their western terminus. Olympia remained the capital city when Washington became a state in 1889, but in the decades that followed other cities vied for the seat of state government. Although Olympia had grown rapidly as a lumber processing center in the years following World War II, the expansion of state government brought new economic opportunities that drew new residents to the area.

Today the Olympia area continues to enjoy steady growth. The Thurston County communities of Lacey and Tumwater have grown by more than 50 percent in the past decade and, although it is no longer Washington's most populous county, it is among the fastest growing in the state. With a population exceeding 39,000, Olympia is currently Thurston County's largest city.

Population

1990 Census	33,729
1998 Estimate	39,188
% Change	16.2
2005 Projection	56,134

Racial/Ethnic Breakdown

White	92.0%
Black	1.2%
Other	6.8%
Hispanic Origin (may be of any race)	2.6%

Age Breakdown

Under 5 years	6.4%
5 to 17	16.2%
18 to 20	4.0%
21 to 24	6.4%
25 to 34	17.0%
35 to 44	17.5%
45 to 54	10.3%
55 to 64	7.6%
65 to 74	7.9%
75+ years	6.7%
Median Age	35.0

Gender Breakdown

Male	47.4%
Female	52.6%

Government

Type of Government: Council-Manager

Olympia Administrative Services Dept
PO Box 1967
Olympia, WA 98507
Phone: 360-753-8325
Fax: 360-753-8165

Olympia City Council
PO Box 1967
Olympia, WA 98507
Phone: 360-753-8450
Fax: 360-709-2791

Olympia City Hall Phone: 360-753-8447
900 Plum St SE Fax: 360-753-8165
Olympia, WA 98501

Olympia City Manager Phone: 360-753-8450
PO Box 1967 Fax: 360-709-2791
Olympia, WA 98507

Olympia Community Planning & Development Dept Phone: 360-753-8314
PO Box 1967 Fax: 360-753-8087
Olympia, WA 98507

Olympia Fire Dept Phone: 360-753-8458
100 Eastside St Fax: 360-753-8054
Olympia, WA 98501

Olympia Human Resources Dept Phone: 360-753-8442
900 Plum St SE Fax: 360-753-8165
Olympia, WA 98501

Olympia Legal Dept Phone: 360-753-8449
PO Box 1967 Fax: 360-709-2791
Olympia, WA 98507

Olympia Mayor Phone: 360-753-8450
PO Box 1967 Fax: 360-709-2791
Olympia, WA 98507

Olympia Parks & Recreation Dept Phone: 360-753-8380
PO Box 1967 Fax: 360-753-8334
Olympia, WA 98507

Olympia Police Dept Phone: 360-753-8300
PO Box 1967 Fax: 360-753-8143
Olympia, WA 98507

Olympia Public Works Dept Phone: 360-753-8426
PO Box 1967 Fax: 360-754-9268
Olympia, WA 98507

Olympia Treasurer Phone: 360-753-8325
PO Box 1967 Fax: 360-709-2791
Olympia, WA 98507

Important Phone Numbers

AAA 360-357-5561
Dental Referral 800-917-6453
Driver's License/Vehicle Registration Information 360-902-3770
Emergency 911
Medical Referral 360-352-1417
Olympia-Thurston County Assn of Realtors 360-491-3910
Poison Control Center 800-732-6985
Thurston County Assessor 360-786-5410
Thurston County Treasurer 360-786-5550
Voter Registration Information 360-786-5224
Washington State Dept of Revenue 800-647-7706
Weather 360-357-6453

Information Sources

Better Business Bureau Serving Oregon & Western Washington Phone: 206-431-2222
4800 S 188th St Suite 222 Fax: 206-431-2211
SeaTac, WA 98188
www.seatac.bbb.org

Economic Development Council of Thurston County Phone: 360-754-6320
721 Columbia SW Fax: 360-586-5493
Olympia, WA 98501
www.thurstonedc.com

Olympia/Thurston County Chamber of Commerce Phone: 360-357-3362
PO Box 1427 Fax: 360-357-3376
Olympia, WA 98507
www.olympiachamber.com

State Capitol Visitor Center Phone: 360-586-3460
14th & Capitol Way Fax: 360-586-4636
Olympia, WA 98504

Thurston County Phone: 360-786-5430
2000 Lakeridge Dr SW Bldg 2 Fax: 360-754-4060
Olympia, WA 98502
www.halcyon.com/thurston/

Online Resources

Anthill City Guide Olympia
www.anthill.com/city.asp?city=olympia

Area Guide Olympia
olympia.areaguides.net

City Knowledge Olympia
www.cityknowledge.com/wa_olympia.htm

Excite.com Olympia City Guide
www.excite.com/travel/countries/united_states/washington/olympia

Olympia Online
www.olympiaonline.com

Online Highways Travel Guide to Olympia
www.ohwy.com/wa/o/olympia.htm

Welcome to Olympia Washington
www.city-olympia.com/

Area Communities

Communities in Thurston County with populations greater than 10,000 include:

Lacey Phone: 360-491-3214
PO Box 3400 Fax: 360-438-2669
Lacey, WA 98509

Tumwater Phone: 360-754-5855
555 Israel Rd SW Fax: 360-754-4126
Tumwater, WA 98501

Economy

The Olympia area's economic base ranges from forestry to health care. Federal, state, and local government continues to play a vital role in the Capital Region's economy. Government is Thurston County's largest employment sector, accounting for more than 40 percent of the county's workforce. Washington State Government is the single largest employer in Thurston County, providing jobs for more than 21,600 residents. Federal Government also ranks among the top five, employing more than 900 people in various agencies. Services is the county's second largest employment sector, with health care being the leading industry - four of the area's top 15 employers are health care-related.

Unemployment Rate 4.9%*
Per Capita Income $26,607*
Median Family Income $37,441

** Information given is for Thurston County.*

Principal Industries & Number of Wage Earners

Thurston County - 1998

Agriculture, Forestry, & Fishing 1,975
Construction 3,449
Finance, Insurance, & Real Estate 2,981
Government 31,832
Manufacturing 2,077
Mining 68
Retail Trade 14,031
Services 18,310
Transportation & Public Utilities 2,077
Wholesale Trade 2,160

Major Employers

Capital Medical Center
3900 Capital Mall Dr SW
Olympia, WA 98502
Phone: 360-754-5858
Fax: 360-956-2574

Evergreen State College
2700 Evergreen Pkwy NW
Olympia, WA 98505
www.evergreen.edu
Phone: 360-866-6000
Fax: 360-866-6680

Group Health Cooperative
521 Wall St
Seattle, WA 98121
E-mail: info@ghc.org
www.ghc.org
Phone: 206-448-5643
Fax: 206-448-2361
TF: 888-901-4636

Home Depot
1325 Fones Rd SE
Olympia, WA 98501
www.homedepot.com
Phone: 360-412-1900
Fax: 360-412-8807

Intercity Transit
PO Box 659
Olympia, WA 98507
www.intercitytransit.com
Phone: 360-786-8585
Fax: 360-357-6184

Memorial Clinic
500 Lilly Rd NE
Olympia, WA 98506
Phone: 360-456-1122
Fax: 360-413-8898

Miller Brewing Co
PO Box 947
Olympia, WA 98507
Phone: 360-754-5000
Fax: 360-754-5166

Olympia City Hall
900 Plum St SE
Olympia, WA 98501
E-mail: cityhall@ci.olympia.wa.us
www.ci.olympia.wa.us
Phone: 360-753-8447
Fax: 360-753-8165

Olympia School District #111
1113 Legion Way SE
Olympia, WA 98501
kids.osd.wednet.edu
Phone: 360-753-8850
Fax: 360-753-8822

Panorama Corp
1751 Circle Ln SE
Lacey, WA 98503
www.panoramacity.org
Phone: 360-456-0111
Fax: 360-438-5901

Providence Saint Peter Hospital
413 NE Lilly Rd
Olympia, WA 98506
Phone: 360-491-9480
Fax: 360-493-7089
TF: 888-492-9480

Safeway Stores
3215 Harrison Ave NW
Olympia, WA 98502
Phone: 360-357-9377
Fax: 360-352-3504

South Puget Sound Community College
2011 Mottman Rd SW
Olympia, WA 98512
www.spscc.ctc.edu
Phone: 360-754-7711
Fax: 360-664-4336

The Olympian
PO Box 407
Olympia, WA 98507
www.theolympian.com
Phone: 360-754-5400
Fax: 360-357-0202

Thurston County
2000 Lakeridge Dr SW Bldg 2
Olympia, WA 98502
E-mail: comment@co.thurston.wa.us
www.halcyon.com/thurston/
Phone: 360-786-5430
Fax: 360-754-4060

Quality of Living Indicators

Total Crime Index 33,840
(rates per 100,000 inhabitants)

Violent Crime
Murder/manslaughter .... -
Forcible rape 30
Robbery 67
Aggravated assault 53

Property Crime
Burglary 437
Larceny theft 2,194
Motor vehicle theft 222

Cost of Living Index 107.2
(national average = 100)

Median Home Price $123,800

Education

Public Schools

Olympia School District #111
1113 Legion Way SE
Olympia, WA 98501
kids.osd.wednet.edu
Phone: 360-753-8850
Fax: 360-753-8822

Number of Schools
Elementary 12
Middle 4
High 2

Student/Teacher Ratio
All Grades 21.0:1

Private Schools

Number of Schools (all grades).................... 16

Colleges & Universities

Evergreen State College Phone: 360-866-6000
2700 Evergreen Pkwy NW Fax: 360-866-6680
Olympia, WA 98505
www.evergreen.edu

South Puget Sound Community College Phone: 360-754-7711
2011 Mottman Rd SW Fax: 360-664-4336
Olympia, WA 98512
www.spscc.ctc.edu

Hospitals

Capital Medical Center Phone: 360-754-5858
3900 Capital Mall Dr SW Fax: 360-956-2574
Olympia, WA 98502

Providence Saint Peter Hospital Phone: 360-491-9480
413 NE Lilly Rd Fax: 360-493-7089
Olympia, WA 98506 TF: 888-492-9480

Transportation

Airport(s)

Seattle-Tacoma International Airport (SEA)
45 miles NW of downtown Olympia
(approx 60 minutes) 206-431-4444

Mass Transit

Capitol Shuttle
free...360-786-1881
Intercity Transit
$.60 Base fare................................360-786-1881

Rail/Bus

Amtrak Station Phone: 360-923-4602
6600 Yelm Hwy SE TF: 800-872-7245
Lacey, WA 98513

Greyhound Bus Station Phone: 360-357-5541
107 E 7th St TF: 800-231-2222
Olympia, WA 98501

Utilities

Electricity
Puget Sound Energy 425-454-2000
www.psechoice.com

Gas
Puget Sound Energy 425-454-2000
www.psechoice.com

Water
Olympia Utilities.............................360-753-8340

Garbage Collection/Recycling
Olympia Utilities.............................360-753-8340

Telecommunications

Telephone
Qwest.......................................800-244-1111
www.qwest.com

Cable Television
AT & T Cable Services.........................360-357-3364
www.cable.att.com

Internet Service Providers (ISPs)
Connect Corp................................360-528-2020
www.connectcorp.net
WLN Internet Services.........................360-923-4000
www.wln.com

Banks

Continental Savings Bank Phone: 360-438-4200
720 Lilly Rd Fax: 360-438-1106
Olympia, WA 98501

Heritage Bank FSB Phone: 360-943-1500
201 W 5th Ave Fax: 360-943-8046
Olympia, WA 98501

KeyBank NA Phone: 360-753-8533
3611 Martin Way E Fax: 360-753-8536
Olympia, WA 98506

West Coast Bank Phone: 360-754-2400
2850 Harrison Ave NW Fax: 360-956-0866
Olympia, WA 98502 TF: 800-847-4983

Shopping

Capital Mall Phone: 360-754-8017
324 Capital Mall Dr
West Olympia, WA 98502

Centralia Square Phone: 360-736-6406
201 S Pearl St
Centralia, WA 98531

South Sound Center Mall Phone: 360-491-6850
691 Sleater Kinney Rd SE Suite 100
Lacey, WA 98503

Media

Newspapers and Magazines

Olympian The* Phone: 360-754-5400
PO Box 407 Fax: 360-357-0202
Olympia, WA 98507
www.theolympian.com

South Sound Business Examiner Phone: 360-956-3133
204 N Quince St Suite 200 Fax: 360-956-3135
Olympia, WA 98506

**Indicates major daily newspapers*

Television

KCPQ-TV Ch 13 (Fox) Phone: 206-674-1313
1813 Westlake Ave N Fax: 206-674-1777
Seattle, WA 98109
E-mail: reception@kcpq.com
www.kcpq.com

KCTS-TV Ch 9 (PBS) Phone: 206-728-6463
401 Mercer St Fax: 206-443-6691
Seattle, WA 98109
E-mail: viewer@kcts.org
www.kcts.org

KING-TV Ch 5 (NBC) Phone: 206-448-5555
333 Dexter Ave N Fax: 206-448-4525
Seattle, WA 98109
E-mail: kingtv@king5.com
www.king5.com

KIRO-TV Ch 7 (CBS) Phone: 206-728-7777
2807 3rd Ave Fax: 206-441-4840
Seattle, WA 98121
E-mail: kironews7@kiro-tv.com
www.kirotv.com

KOMO-TV Ch 4 (ABC) Phone: 206-443-4000
100 4th Ave N Fax: 206-443-3422
Seattle, WA 98109
www.komotv.com

KSTW-TV Ch 11 (UPN) Phone: 253-572-5789
PO Box 11411 Fax: 253-272-7581
Tacoma, WA 98411
E-mail: kstw98d@prodigy.com
www.paramountstations.com/KSTW

Radio

KGY-AM 1240 kHz (AC) Phone: 360-943-1240
1240 NE Washington St Fax: 360-352-1222
Olympia, WA 98501
E-mail: kgyeng@kgyradio.com
www.kgyradio.com

KGY-FM 96.9 kHz (Ctry) Phone: 360-943-1240
1240 NE Washington St Fax: 360-352-1222
Olympia, WA 98501
E-mail: kgyeng@kgyradio.com
www.kgyradio.com

KXXO-FM 96.1 MHz (AC) Phone: 360-943-9937
119 N Washington St Fax: 360-352-3643
Olympia, WA 98501
E-mail: admin@mixx96.com
www.mixx96.com

Attractions

Situated at the southern end of Puget Sound, with Seattle to the north and Mount Saint Helens to the south, Olympia serves as a gateway to the Olympic Peninsula and the beaches of the Pacific Ocean. The Olympic Mountains from which the city derives its name rise across the water west of the city, with Mount Rainier and the Cascades to the east. Nisqually National Wildlife Refuge and nearby Wolf Haven provide homes to a variety of wildlife. Wolf Haven is a sanctuary for abandoned or displaced captive-born wolves and currently houses 40 wolves. Nisqually residents include owls, ducks, salmon, and small mammals, and the Refuge's mixed conifer forests on bluffs above the delta serve as perches for bald eagle and osprey and as a nesting site for blue herons.

Bigelow House Phone: 360-753-1215
918 Glass Ave NE
Olympia, WA 98506

Executive Mansion Phone: 360-586-8687
14th Ave & Capitol Way Capitol Campus
Olympia, WA 98504

Hands On Children's Museum Phone: 360-956-0818
106 11th Ave SW Fax: 360-754-8626
Olympia, WA 98501
www.hocm.org

Japanese Garden Phone: 360-753-8380
1010 Plum St SE
Olympia, WA 98501

Little Creek Casino Phone: 360-427-7711
W 91 Hwy 108 Fax: 360-427-7868
Shelton, WA 98584 TF: 800-667-7711

Miller Brewing Co Phone: 360-754-5177
Custer Way & Schmidt Pl Fax: 360-754-5252
Tumwater, WA 98501

Millersylvania State Park Phone: 360-753-1519
12245 Tilley Rd S Fax: 360-664-2180
Olympia, WA 98512

Nisqually National Wildlife Refuge Phone: 360-753-9467
100 Brown Farm Rd Fax: 360-534-9302
Olympia, WA 98516

Nisqually Reach Nature Center Phone: 360-459-0387
4949 D'Milluhr Rd NE
Olympia, WA 98516

Olympia Farmers Market Phone: 360-352-9096
7010 N Capitol Way
Olympia, WA 98501
www.farmers-market.org/

Olympia Film Society Phone: 360-754-6670
416 Washington St SE Fax: 360-943-9100
Olympia, WA 98501
E-mail: ofs@olywa.net
www.olywa.net/ofs

Olympia Little Theatre Phone: 360-786-9484
1925 Miller Ave NE
Olympia, WA 98506
www.olympialittletheater.org

Olympia Symphony Orchestra Phone: 360-753-0074
512 Washington St SE Washington Ctr Fax: 360-753-4735
for the Performing Arts
Olympia, WA 98501

Rainbow Falls State Park Phone: 360-291-3767
4008 State Hwy 6 TF: 800-233-0321
Chehalis, WA 98532

Tenino Depot Museum Phone: 360-264-4321
339 West Park South Thurston County
Historical Society
Tenino, WA 98589

Tolmie State Park Phone: 360-456-6464
8 miles NE of Olympia Johnson Pt TF: 800-233-0321
Olympia, WA 98512

Tumwater Falls Park Phone: 360-943-2550
Deschutes St
Tumwater, WA 98502

Washington Center for the Performing Arts
512 Washington St SE
Olympia, WA 98501
E-mail: info@washingtoncenter.com
Phone: 360-753-8586
Fax: 360-754-1177

Washington State Capital Museum
211 W 21st Ave
Olympia, WA 98501
Phone: 360-753-2580
Fax: 360-586-8322

Washington State Capitol
PO Box 41034
Olympia, WA 98504
Phone: 360-586-8687
Fax: 360-664-9647

Wolf Haven International
3111 Offut Lake Rd
Tenino, WA 98589
E-mail: wolfhvn@aol.com
www.wolfhaven.org
Phone: 360-264-4695
Fax: 360-264-4639

Annual Events

Capital Food & Wine Festival (late March) 360-438-4366
Capital Lakefair (mid-July).........................360-586-3460
Greater Olympia Dixieland Jazz Festival (early July) 360-754-8129
Harbor Days (September) 360-352-4557
Music in the Park (July-August)...................360-357-8948
Olympia Film Festival (mid-late October) 360-754-6670
Oregon Trail Days (late July) 360-264-5075
Parade of Lighted Ships (early December)..........360-357-6767
Shakespeare Festival (late May-August) 360-943-9492
Super Saturday (June) 360-866-6000
Thurston County Fair (late July-early August) 360-786-5453
Winterfest in Historic Tenino (early December).....360-264-5855
Wooden Boat Festival (mid-May) 360-943-5404
Yelm Prairie Days (mid-July) 360-458-3492

Omaha, Nebraska

County: **Douglas**

OMAHA is located along the eastern Nebraska border. Major cities within 100 miles include Lincoln, Nebraska and Council Bluffs and Sioux City, Iowa.

Area (Land) .... 100.6 sq mi
Area (Water) .... 3.0 sq mi
Elevation .... 1,040 ft
Latitude .... 41-25-86 N
Longitude .... 95-93-75 W
Time Zone .... CST
Area Code 402

Climate

Omaha's climate features cold winters and warm summers. Winter high temperatures average in the low 30s, and lows average in the low to mid- teens. An average of 30 inches of snow falls each year in Omaha. Summer days are warm, with high temperatures in the low to mid 80s, while evening temperatures dip into the low to mid-60s. Spring and summer are the rainy seasons in Omaha, with May being the wettest month. Winter is the dry season.

Average Temperatures & Precipitation

Temperatures

	Jan	Feb	Mar	Apr	May	Jun	Jul	Aug	Sep	Oct	Nov	Dec
High	30	35	48	62	73	82	87	84	75	64	48	33
Low	11	17	28	40	52	61	67	64	55	43	30	16

Precipitation

	Jan	Feb	Mar	Apr	May	Jun	Jul	Aug	Sep	Oct	Nov	Dec
Inches	0.7	0.8	2.1	2.7	4.4	3.9	3.3	3.2	3.7	2.4	1.4	0.9

History

Nebraska's largest city, Omaha was founded in 1854 by the Council Bluffs and Nebraska Ferry Company in an effort to expand the Council Bluffs area (the city served as an outfitting post for pioneers heading west to California during the Gold Rush). The town was originally called "Omaha City" and was incorporated in 1857. The city's population jumped from around 300 in 1855 to nearly 5,000 in 1865. Nebraska became a state in 1870, and the following year the name of the city was changed to Omaha. Over the course of the next decade, Omaha continued to grow as the first rail lines to cross the Missouri River were laid in the area. The Union Pacific Railroad established its headquarters in Omaha in 1869, and the city remains one of the nation's top rail centers. By 1880, Omaha's population exceeded 30,000.

Omaha's reputation as an insurance center began in the 1880s. More than a century later, the present-day Omaha is home to more than 20 insurance companies, including Mutual of Omaha, the largest provider of individual and family health insurance in the United States. Farming was also important to Omaha's early economy, and in 1898 the city held the Trans-Mississippi Exhibition, marking the beginning of the "Golden Age" for Nebraska farmers. Agriculture remained important well into the 20th Century, as Omaha became the leading meat supplier in the United States. In 1917, Boys Town, a refuge for abused, abandoned, neglected, and handicapped children was founded in Omaha by Father Edward J. Flanagan. Today, Boys Town has satellite locations across the U.S. and helps more than 17,000 children each year.

Omaha currently has more than 371,000 residents. In recent years, the city has been named one of the safest cities in the United States among those of a similar size. With a low cost of living and plentiful job opportunities (the city is ranked among the top 15 metropolitan areas in the nation with the lowest employment rates), Omaha is quickly becoming a leading destination for relocation.

Population

1990 Census 335,719
1998 Estimate 371,291
% Change 7.8
2010 Projection 483,780*

Racial/Ethnic Breakdown

White 83.5%
Black 14.2%
Other 2.3%
Hispanic Origin (may be of any race) 6.1%

Age Breakdown

Under 5 years 7.2%
5 to 17 .... 18.5%
18 to 24 .... 10.9%
25 to 34 .... 15.4%
35 to 44 .... 15.5%
45 to 54 .... 12.4%
55 to 64 .... 8.3%
65 to 74 .... 6.7%
75+ years 5.1%
Median Age 33.6

Gender Breakdown

Male 47.9%
Female 52.1%

* *Information given is for Douglas County.*

Government

Type of Government: Mayor-Council

Omaha City Attorney
1819 Farman St Rm 804
Omaha, NE 68183
Phone: 402-444-5115
Fax: 402-444-5125

Omaha City Clerk Phone: 402-444-5552
1819 Farnam St Rm LC-1 Fax: 402-444-5263
Omaha, NE 68183

Omaha City Council Phone: 402-444-5520
1819 Farnham St Rm LC1 Fax: 402-444-5263
Omaha, NE 68183

Omaha City Hall Phone: 402-444-7000
1819 Farnam St
Omaha, NE 68183

Omaha Finance Dept Phone: 402-444-5478
1819 Farnam St 10th Fl Fax: 402-444-5423
Omaha, NE 68183

Omaha Fire Dept Phone: 402-444-5700
1516 Jackson St Fax: 402-444-6378
Omaha, NE 68102

Omaha Marketing & Business Development Office Phone: 402-444-5546
1819 Farnam St Rm 304 Fax: 402-444-7963
Omaha, NE 68183

Omaha Mayor Phone: 402-444-5000
1819 Farnam St Suite 300 Fax: 402-444-6059
Omaha, NE 68183

Omaha Parks Recreation & Public Property Dept Phone: 402-444-5900
1819 Farman St Rm 701 Fax: 402-444-4921
Omaha, NE 68183

Omaha Personnel Dept Phone: 402-444-5300
1819 Farnam St Suite 506 Fax: 402-444-5314
Omaha, NE 68183

Omaha Planning Dept Phone: 402-444-5150
1819 Farnam St 11th Fl Fax: 402-444-6140
Omaha, NE 68183

Omaha Police Dept Phone: 402-444-5600
505 S 15th St Fax: 402-444-4225
Omaha, NE 68102

Omaha Public Library Phone: 402-444-4800
215 S 15th St Fax: 402-444-4504
Omaha, NE 68102

Omaha Public Works Dept Phone: 402-444-5220
1819 Farnam St Rm 602 Fax: 402-444-5248
Omaha, NE 68183

Important Phone Numbers

AAA 402-390-1010
American Express Travel 402-697-5300
Dental Referral 800-336-8478
Douglas County Assessor 402-444-6713
Driver's License Information 402-595-2038
Emergency 911
Events Line 402-444-6800
HotelDocs 800-468-3537
Medical Referral 402-393-1415
Nebraska State Dept of Revenue 402-595-2065
Omaha Area Board of Realtors 402-493-2995
Poison Control Center 402-390-5555
Road Conditions 800-906-9069
Time/Temp 402-342-8463
Vehicle Registration Information 402-444-7103
Voter Registration Information 402-444-7200
Weather 402-392-1111

Information Sources

Better Business Bureau Serving Northern Nebraska & Southwest Iowa Phone: 402-391-7612
2237 N 91st Ct Fax: 402-391-7535
Omaha, NE 68134
www.omahabbb.org

Douglas County Phone: 402-444-7000
1819 Farnum St Fax: 402-444-5263
Omaha, NE 68183
www.co.douglas.ne.us

Greater Omaha Chamber of Commerce Phone: 402-346-5000
1301 Harney St Fax: 402-346-7050
Omaha, NE 68102
www.accessomaha.com

Greater Omaha Convention & Visitors Bureau Phone: 402-444-4660
6800 Mercy Rd Suite 202 Fax: 402-444-4511
Omaha, NE 68106 TF: 800-332-1819
www.visitomaha.com

Omaha Civic Auditorium Phone: 402-444-4750
PO Box 719 Fax: 402-444-4739
Omaha, NE 68101

Online Resources

4Omaha.com
www.4omaha.com

Anthill City Guide Omaha
www.anthill.com/city.asp?city=omaha

Area Guide Omaha
omaha.areaguides.net

City Atlas
www.cityatlas.com/

City Knowledge Omaha
www.cityknowledge.com/ne_omaha.htm

DiscoverOmaha.com
www.discoveromaha.com

Excite.com Omaha City Guide
www.excite.com/travel/countries/united_states/nebraska/omaha

Omaha Home Page
omahafreenet.org

Omaha Internet Site
www.radiks.net/omasite

Omaha Link
www.omaha.org

Omaha Page
www.novia.net/~cmeyers/omaha.html

Surf Omaha
www.surfomaha.com/

Area Communities

Communities within the Omaha metropolitan area (which includes Cass, Douglas, Washington, and Sarpy counties in Nebraska and Pottawattamie County in Iowa) with populations of 5,000 or more include:

Bellevue
210 W Mission Ave
Bellevue, NE 68005
Phone: 402-293-3023
Fax: 402-293-3058

Blair City
218 S 16th St
Blair, NE 68008
Phone: 402-426-4191
Fax: 402-426-4195

Council Bluffs
209 Pearl St
Council Bluffs, IA 51503
Phone: 712-328-4601
Fax: 712-328-2137

La Vista
8116 Park View Blvd
La Vista, NE 68128
Phone: 402-331-4343
Fax: 402-331-4375

Papillion
122 E 3rd St
Papillion, NE 68046
Phone: 402-597-2000
Fax: 402-339-0670

Ralston
5500 S 77th St
Ralston, NE 68127
Phone: 402-331-6677
Fax: 402-331-4553

Economy

Omaha has one of the lowest unemployment rates among U.S. metropolitan areas, averaging 2.6 percent in 1999. Services, primarily business services, is Omaha's leading employment sector. The city is home to First Data Corp., the one of the country's largest third-party providers of credit card processing services. Government is also a major employer, providing jobs for more than 35,000 area residents at various educational institutions, at Offutt Air Force Base, and at the local government level. Home to more than 20 insurance companies, including the corporate headquarters for Mutual of Omaha, the City of Omaha is one of the nation's top insurance centers. Other Fortune 500 companies that have their headquarters in Omaha include ConAgra, Berkshire Hathaway, and Peter Kiewit Sons'.

Unemployment Rate 2.8%*
Per Capita Income $18,784
Median Family Income $42,779

** Information given is for Douglas County.*

Principal Industries & Number of Wage Earners

Douglas County - 1999

Construction & Mining 17,062
Finance, Insurance, & Real Estate 32,903
Government 35,516
Manufacturing 32,515
Retail Trade 55,404
Services 115,205
Transportation, Communications, & Utilities 19,715
Wholesale Trade 24,315

Major Employers

Alegent Health
1010 N 96th St
Omaha, NE 68114
Phone: 402-343-4343
Fax: 402-343-4316

Alegent Health Bergen Medical Center
7500 Mercy Rd
Omaha, NE 68124
Phone: 402-398-6060
Fax: 402-398-6920

Baker's Supermarket Inc
8420 W Dodge Rd Suite 400
Omaha, NE 68114
Phone: 402-397-4321
Fax: 402-398-0390

First Data Corp
10825 Farnam Dr
Omaha, NE 63154
www.firstdatacorp.com
Phone: 402-777-2000
Fax: 402-222-7303

Lucent Technologies
120 & I Sts
Omaha, NE 68137
www.lucent.com
Phone: 402-691-3000
Fax: 402-691-4897

Methodist Health System
8511 W Dodge Rd
Omaha, NE 68114
www.bestcare.org
Phone: 402-354-4844
Fax: 402-354-4819

Mutual of Omaha Cos
Mutual of Omaha Plaza
Omaha, NE 68175
E-mail: newscenter@mutualofomaha.com
www.mutualofomaha.com
Phone: 402-342-7600
Fax: 402-351-2775
TF: 800-775-6000

Nebraska Health System
42nd & Dewey Ave
Omaha, NE 68105
www.nhsnet.org/home.html
Phone: 402-552-2000
Fax: 402-552-3063

Odyssey Staffing Inc
5012 L St
Omaha, NE 68117
Phone: 402-731-1466
Fax: 402-731-0954

Offutt Air Force Base
Offutt AFB, NE 68113
www.offutt.af.mil
Phone: 402-294-1110
Fax: 402-294-7172

Omaha City Hall
1819 Farnam St
Omaha, NE 68183
www.ci.omaha.ne.us
Phone: 402-444-7000

Omaha Public Schools
3215 Cuming St
Omaha, NE 68131
www.ops.org
Phone: 402-557-2222
Fax: 402-557-2319

Oriental Trading Co Inc
5455 S 90th St
Omaha, NE 68127
E-mail: staff@oriental.com
www.oriental.com
Phone: 402-596-1200
Fax: 402-331-3873
TF: 800-225-6440

Union Pacific Railroad Co
1416 Dodge St
Omaha, NE 68179
www.uprr.com
Phone: 402-271-5000
Fax: 402-271-2256
TF: 888-870-8777

University of Nebraska Medical Center
985230 Nebraska Medical Ctr
Omaha, NE 68198
www.unmc.edu
Phone: 402-559-4000
Fax: 402-559-5498
TF: 800-642-1095

Quality of Living Indicators

Total Crime Index....................................26,245
(rates per 100,000 inhabitants)

Violent Crime
Murder/manslaughter........................... 34
Forcible rape 174
Robbery...................................... 960
Aggravated assault...........................3,445

Property Crime
Burglary 3,516
Larceny theft 14,530
Motor vehicle theft..........................3,586

Cost of Living Index....................................94.7
(national average = 100)

Median Home Price.................................$109,400

Education

Public Schools

Omaha Public Schools
3215 Cuming St
Omaha, NE 68131
www.ops.org
Phone: 402-557-2222
Fax: 402-557-2319

Number of Schools
Elementary................................. 58
Middle 10
High.. 7

Student/Teacher Ratio
All Grades 16.0:1

Private Schools

Number of Schools (all grades).................... 60+

Colleges & Universities

Clarkson College
101 S 42nd St
Omaha, NE 68131
E-mail: admiss@clrkcol.crhsnet.edu
www.clarksoncollege.edu
Phone: 402-552-3100
Fax: 402-552-6057
TF: 800-647-5500

College of Saint Mary
1901 S 72nd St
Omaha, NE 68124
E-mail: enroll@csm.edu
www.csm.edu
Phone: 402-399-2400
Fax: 402-399-2412
TF: 800-926-5534

Creighton University
2500 California Plaza
Omaha, NE 68178
www.creighton.edu
Phone: 402-280-2700
Fax: 402-280-2685
TF: 800-282-5835

Dana College
2848 College Dr
Blair, NE 68008
www.dana.edu
Phone: 402-426-9000
Fax: 402-426-7386

Grace University
1311 S 9th St
Omaha, NE 68108
www.graceu.edu
Phone: 402-449-2800
Fax: 402-341-9587
TF: 800-383-1422

ITT Technical Institute
9814 M St
Omaha, NE 68127
www.itt-tech.edu
Phone: 402-331-2900
Fax: 402-331-9495
TF: 800-677-9260

Metropolitan Community College
PO Box 3777
Omaha, NE 68103
www.mccneb.edu
Phone: 402-457-2400
Fax: 402-457-2395
TF: 800-228-9553

Midland Lutheran College
900 N Clarkson St
Fremont, NE 68025
E-mail: kahnk@admin.mlc.edu
www.mlc.edu
Phone: 402-721-5480
Fax: 402-721-0250
TF: 800-642-8382

Nebraska College of Business
3350 N 90th St
Omaha, NE 68134
E-mail: admissions@ncbedu.com
www.ncbedu.com
Phone: 402-572-8500
Fax: 402-573-1341
TF: 800-642-1456

Omaha College of Health Careers
225 N 80th St
Omaha, NE 68114
Phone: 402-392-1300
Fax: 402-392-2828
TF: 800-865-8628

University of Nebraska Omaha
6001 Dodge St
Omaha, NE 68182
www.unomaha.edu
Phone: 402-554-2200
Fax: 402-554-3472
TF: 800-858-8648

Hospitals

Alegent Health Bergen Medical Center
7500 Mercy Rd
Omaha, NE 68124
Phone: 402-398-6060
Fax: 402-398-6920

Childrens Hospital
8301 Dodge St
Omaha, NE 68114
www.chsomaha.org
Phone: 402-354-5400
Fax: 402-354-5443

Immanuel Medical Center
6901 N 72nd St
Omaha, NE 68122
Phone: 402-572-2121
Fax: 402-572-3177

Jennie Edmundson Memorial Hospital
933 E Pierce St
Council Bluffs, IA 51503
Phone: 712-328-6000
Fax: 712-328-6288

Midlands Community Hospital
11111 S 84th St
Papillion, NE 68046
Phone: 402-593-3000
Fax: 402-593-3324

Nebraska Methodist Hospital
8303 Dodge St
Omaha, NE 68114
Phone: 402-390-4000
Fax: 402-354-8735

NHS Clarkson Hospital Phone: 402-552-2000
4350 Dewey Ave Fax: 402-552-2152
Omaha, NE 68106

Saint Joseph Hospital Phone: 402-449-4000
601 N 30th St Fax: 402-449-4337
Omaha, NE 68131
www.tenethealth.com/SaintJoseph

University of Nebraska Medical Center Phone: 402-559-4000
985230 Nebraska Medical Ctr Fax: 402-559-5498
Omaha, NE 68198 TF: 800-642-1095
www.unmc.edu

Veterans Affairs Medical Center Phone: 402-346-8800
4101 Woolworth Ave Fax: 402-977-5635
Omaha, NE 68105

Transportation

Airport(s)

Eppley Airfield (OMA)
5 miles NE of downtown (approx 10 minutes) 402-422-6800

Mass Transit

MAT
$.90 Base fare....402-341-0800

Rail/Bus

Amtrak Station Phone: 402-342-1501
1003 S 9th St TF: 800-872-7245
Omaha, NE 68108

Greyhound Bus Station Phone: 402-341-1906
1601 Jackson St TF: 800-231-2222
Omaha, NE 68102

Utilities

Electricity
Omaha Public Power District....402-552-5548
www.oppd.com

Gas
Metropolitan Utilities District....402-554-6666
www.mudomaha.com

Water
Metropolitan Utilities District....402-554-6666
www.mudomaha.com

Garbage Collection/Recycling
Deffenbaugh Disposal Service....402-731-3333

Telecommunications

Telephone
Qwest....800-244-1111
www.qwest.com

Cable Television
Cox Communications....402-330-6770
www.cox.com
Qwest Telechoice....402-691-1999

Internet Service Providers (ISPs)
Nebraska On-Ramp Inc....402-827-9090
www.neonramp.com
Novia Internetworking....402-895-2633
www.novia.net
Radiks Internet Access....402-346-4026
www.radiks.net
Synergy Communications Inc....402-346-4638
www.synergy.net

Banks

American National Bank Phone: 402-399-5000
8990 W Dodge Rd Fax: 402-399-5057
Omaha, NE 68114
E-mail: customerservice@anbank.com
www.anbank.com

Commercial Federal Bank FSB Phone: 402-554-9200
2120 S 72nd St Fax: 402-554-9330
Omaha, NE 68124 TF: 800-228-5023

First Federal Lincoln Bank Phone: 402-554-8108
9628 M St Fax: 402-554-8126
Omaha, NE 68127

First National Bank of Omaha Phone: 402-341-0500
1620 Dodge St Fax: 402-636-6033
Omaha, NE 68102

First Westroads Bank Inc Phone: 402-330-7200
10855 W Dodge Rd Fax: 402-330-8272
Omaha, NE 68154
E-mail: wpavl@fwrb.com
www.fwrb.com

Great Western Bank Phone: 402-551-4310
6015 NW Radial Hwy Fax: 402-391-1856
Omaha, NE 68104 TF: 800-952-2039
E-mail: info@greatwesternbank.com
www.greatwesternbank.com

Mid City Bank Inc Phone: 402-558-8000
304 S 42nd St Fax: 402-558-2996
Omaha, NE 68131

Norwest Bank Nebraska NA Phone: 402-536-2420
1919 Douglas St Fax: 402-536-2317
Omaha, NE 68103 TF: 800-440-7878
www.norwest.com

Omaha State Bank Phone: 402-333-9100
12100 W Center Rd Fax: 402-333-9787
Omaha, NE 68144 TF: 877-968-7672
E-mail: osbinfo@omahastate.com
www.omahastate.com

US Bank NA Phone: 402-348-6000
1700 Farnam St Fax: 402-348-6741
Omaha, NE 68102

Shopping

Countryside Village Shopping Center Phone: 402-391-2200
87th & Pacific Sts Fax: 402-391-3084
Omaha, NE 68114

Crossroads Mall Phone: 402-397-2343
7400 Dodge St Fax: 402-393-3765
Omaha, NE 68114

Dillard's Phone: 402-392-0333
7400 Dodge St Fax: 402-392-2410
Omaha, NE 68114

Market Place Mall Phone: 402-346-4930
12th & Jackson Sts
Omaha, NE 68102

Meadowlark Antique Mall Phone: 402-896-0800
10700 Sapp Bros Dr Fax: 402-894-9527
Omaha, NE 68138

Montclair Shopping Center Phone: 402-333-7373
132nd St & W Center Rd
Omaha, NE 68144

Nebraska Crossing Factory Stores Phone: 402-332-4940
14333 S Hwy 31 TF: 800-746-7632
Gretna, NE 68028

Oak View Mall Phone: 402-330-3332
144th St & W Center Rd Fax: 402-330-3255
Omaha, NE 68144

Old Market Phone: 402-346-4445
Harney & Jackson Sts & 10th & 13th Sts Fax: 402-346-4449
Omaha, NE 68102

One Pacific Place Phone: 402-399-8049
103rd & Pacific Sts
Omaha, NE 68114
www.onepacificplace.com

Regency Court Phone: 402-393-8474
120 Regency Pkwy
Omaha, NE 68114

Rockbrook Village Phone: 402-390-0890
108th & W Center Rd Fax: 402-393-7341
Omaha, NE 68144

Southroads Mall Phone: 402-733-7777
1001 Fort Crook Rd N Fax: 402-733-3796
Bellevue, NE 68005

Westroads Mall Phone: 402-397-2398
10000 California St Fax: 402-397-6701
Omaha, NE 68114

Westwood Plaza Phone: 402-333-7373
W Center Rd-betw 120th & 125th Sts
Omaha, NE 68144

Younkers Department Store Phone: 402-399-6638
7200 Dodge St Fax: 402-399-6671
Omaha, NE 68114

Media

Newspapers and Magazines

Bellevue Leader Phone: 402-733-7300
PO Box 1219 Fax: 402-733-9116
Bellevue, NE 68005

Midlands Business Journal Phone: 402-330-1760
PO Box 24245 Fax: 402-333-4659
Omaha, NE 68124
www.mbj.com

Omaha Magazine Phone: 402-596-1105
PO Box 461208 Fax: 402-592-2798
Omaha, NE 68046
www.omahamagazine.com

Omaha Reader Phone: 402-341-7323
4807 Dodge St Fax: 402-341-6967
Omaha, NE 68132
E-mail: reader@synergy.net
www.thereader.com

Omaha World-Herald* Phone: 402-444-1000
1334 Dodge St Fax: 402-345-0183
Omaha, NE 68102 TF: 800-284-6397
www.omaha.com

**Indicates major daily newspapers*

Television

KETV-TV Ch 7 (ABC) Phone: 402-345-7777
2665 Douglas St Fax: 402-978-8922
Omaha, NE 68131

KMTV-TV Ch 3 (CBS) Phone: 402-592-3333
10714 Mockingbird Dr Fax: 402-592-4714
Omaha, NE 68127

KPTM-TV Ch 42 (Fox) Phone: 402-558-4200
4625 Farnam St Fax: 402-554-4279
Omaha, NE 68132

KXVO-TV Ch 15 (WB) Phone: 402-554-1500
4625 Farnam St Fax: 402-554-4290
Omaha, NE 68132

KYNE-TV Ch 26 (PBS) Phone: 402-554-2516
6001 Dodge St Fax: 402-554-2440
Omaha, NE 68182

WOWT-TV Ch 6 (NBC) Phone: 402-346-6666
3501 Farnam St Fax: 402-233-7880
Omaha, NE 68131
www.wowt.com

Radio

KCTY-FM 106.9 MHz (AAA) Phone: 402-553-2489
5011 Capitol Ave Suite 300 Fax: 402-561-9467
Omaha, NE 68132
www.1069thecity.com

KEFM-FM 96.1 MHz (AC) Phone: 402-558-9696
105 S 70th St Fax: 402-558-3036
Omaha, NE 68132

KESY-AM 1420 kHz (AC) Phone: 402-556-6700
4807 Dodge St
Omaha, NE 68132

KEZO-FM 92.3 MHz (Rock) Phone: 402-592-5300
11128 John Galt Blvd Fax: 402-592-4538
Omaha, NE 68137
E-mail: the_rock_station@z92.com
www.z92.com

KFAB-AM 1110 kHz (N/T) Phone: 402-556-8000
5010 Underwood Ave Fax: 402-556-5791
Omaha, NE 68132
www.kfab.com

KGOR-FM 99.9 MHz (Oldies)
5010 Underwood Ave
Omaha, NE 68132
E-mail: kgor@kgor.com
www.kgor.com
Phone: 402-556-2323
Fax: 402-556-8937

KIOS-FM 91.5 MHz (NPR)
3230 Burt St
Omaha, NE 68131
E-mail: kiosinfo@kios.org
www.kios.org
Phone: 402-557-2777
Fax: 402-557-2559

KKCD-FM 105.9 MHz (CR)
11128 John Galt Blvd
Omaha, NE 68137
E-mail: cd105@cd105.com
www.cd105.com
Phone: 402-592-5300
Fax: 402-592-6605

KOIL-AM 1290 kHz (Nost)
1001 Farnam St
Omaha, NE 68102
Phone: 402-342-2000
Fax: 402-342-7041

KOSR-AM 1490 kHz (N/T)
11128 John Galt Blvd Suite 192
Omaha, NE 68137
E-mail: sports1490@sports1490.com
www.sports1490.com
Phone: 402-592-5300
Fax: 402-592-9434

KQCH-FM 97.7 MHz (Urban)
11128 John Galt Blvd Suite 192
Omaha, NE 68137
Phone: 402-592-5300
Fax: 402-592-9434

KQKQ-FM 98.5 MHz (CHR)
1001 Farnam-on-the-Mall
Omaha, NE 68102
www.sweet98.com
Phone: 402-342-2000
Fax: 402-342-9367

KSRZ-FM 104.5 MHz (AC)
11128 John Galt Blvd Suite 192
Omaha, NE 68137
E-mail: star@104star.com
www.104star.com
Phone: 402-592-5300
Fax: 402-592-6605

KXKT-FM 103.7 MHz (Ctry)
5010 Underwood Ave
Omaha, NE 68132
www.kxkt.com
Phone: 402-561-2000
Fax: 402-556-8937

WOW-FM 94.1 MHz (Ctry)
5030 N 72nd St
Omaha, NE 68134
wowradio.com
Phone: 402-573-5900
Fax: 402-573-0138

Attractions

Although perhaps best known as the home of Boys Town, Omaha is also site of the Strategic Air Command headquarters (SAC), which has a museum in nearby Bellevue, Nebraska; and is the birthplace of former president Gerald Ford. The Mormon Pioneer Monument in Omaha commemorates the final resting place of more than 600 Mormon emigrants who died during the winter of 1846-47 while camped in the area that is now part of metropolitan Omaha.

Aksarben Aquarium
21502 W Hwy 31
Gretna, NE 68028
Phone: 402-332-3901
Fax: 402-332-5853

Belle Riverboat
State Recreation Area
Brownville, NE 68321
Phone: 402-342-3553

Bemis Center for Contemporary Arts
724 S 12th St
Omaha, NE 68102
www.novia.net/bemis
Phone: 402-341-7130
Fax: 402-341-9791

Blue Barn Theatre
614 S 11th St
Omaha, NE 68102
Phone: 402-345-1576

Bluffs Run Casino
2701 23rd Ave
Council Bluffs, IA 51501
www.bluffsrun.com
Phone: 712-323-2500
Fax: 712-322-9354
TF: 800-238-2946

Boys Town
13628 Flanagan Blvd
Boys Town, NE 68010
www.ffbh.boystown.org/
Phone: 402-498-1140
Fax: 402-498-1194
TF: 800-448-3000

Carter Levi Park
809 Carter Lake Shore Dr
Omaha, NE 68183
Phone: 402-444-5900

Creighton University Mainstage & Studio Theatre
2500 California Plaza
Omaha, NE 68178
Phone: 402-280-2636
Fax: 402-280-2700

Cunningham Glenn Lake
8660 Lake Cunningham Rd
Omaha, NE 68183
Phone: 402-444-5900

Dodge NP Memorial Park
11001 John J Pershing Dr
Omaha, NE 68183
Phone: 402-444-5900

Doorly Henry Zoo & Aquarium
3701 S 10th St
Omaha, NE 68107
www.omaha.org/oma/zoo.htm
Phone: 402-733-8401
Fax: 402-733-4415

Durham Western Heritage Museum
801 S 10th St
Omaha, NE 68108
Phone: 402-444-5071
Fax: 402-444-5397

El Museo Latino
4701 S 25th St
Omaha, NE 68107
Phone: 402-731-1137
Fax: 402-733-7012

Florence Mill
9102 N 30th St
Omaha, NE 68112
Phone: 402-551-1233

Fontenelle Forest Nature Center
1111 Bellevue Blvd N
Bellevue, NE 68005
Phone: 402-731-3140
Fax: 402-731-2403

Fort Atkinson
Hwy 75
Fort Calhoun, NE 68023
Phone: 402-468-5611

Freedom Park US Naval Museum
2497 Freedom Park Rd
Omaha, NE 68110
Phone: 402-345-1959
Fax: 402-345-3418

Fremont/Elkhorn Valley Railroad
1835 N Somers Ave
Fremont, NE 68025
Phone: 402-727-0615
Fax: 402-727-0615

Fun Plex
7003 Q St
Omaha, NE 68117
Phone: 402-331-8436
TF: 800-353-4180

General Crook House
5730 N 30th St Bldg 11B
Omaha, NE 68111
Phone: 402-455-9990
Fax: 402-453-9448

Gerald R Ford Birth Site
3212 Woolworth Ave
Omaha, NE 68105
Phone: 402-444-5900

Gerald R Ford Conservation Center
1326 S 32nd St
Omaha, NE 68105
Phone: 402-595-1180
Fax: 402-595-1178

Grande Olde Players
2339 N 90th St
Omaha, NE 68114
Phone: 402-397-5262

Great Plains Black History Museum
2213 Lake St
Omaha, NE 68111
Phone: 402-345-2212
Fax: 402-345-2256

Heartland of America Park & Fountain
8th & Douglas Sts
Omaha, NE 68102
Phone: 402-444-7275

Historic Florence
8502 N 30th St
Omaha, NE 68112
Phone: 402-453-4462

Historic Florence Bank & Depot Museum
8502 N 30th St
Omaha, NE 68112
Phone: 402-453-4280

Joslyn Art Museum
2200 Dodge St
Omaha, NE 68102
E-mail: info@joslyn.org
www.joslyn.org
Phone: 402-342-3300
Fax: 402-342-2376

Kenefick Park
1212 Abbott Dr
Omaha, NE 68110
Phone: 402-444-5955

Kountze Mallory Planetarium
67th & Dodge Sts Durham Science Ctr
Omaha, NE 68182
Phone: 402-554-2219

Leahy Gene Mall Park
14th & Farnam Sts
Omaha, NE 68102
Phone: 402-444-5955
Fax: 402-444-6838

Lewis & Clark National Historic Trail
1709 Jackson St National Park Service
Omaha, NE 68102
Phone: 402-221-3471
Fax: 402-221-3461

Lozier IMAX Theatre
3704 S 10th St
Omaha, NE 68107
Phone: 402-733-8401
Fax: 402-733-7868

Memorial Park
60th & Underwood Sts
Omaha, NE 68132
Phone: 402-444-5955

Mormon Pioneer Monument at Winter Quarter
3215 State St
Omaha, NE 68112
E-mail: mormontrailcenter@juno.com
Phone: 402-453-9372
Fax: 402-453-1538

Mount Vernon Gardens
13th & Y Sts
Omaha, NE 68107
Phone: 402-444-5955
Fax: 402-444-6838

Neale Woods Nature Center
14323 Edith Marie Ave
Omaha, NE 68112
Phone: 402-453-5615
Fax: 402-453-0724

Nebraska Jewish Historical Museum
333 S 132nd St
Omaha, NE 68154
Phone: 402-334-6441
Fax: 402-334-1330

Old Market
Harney & Jackson Sts & 10th & 13th Sts
Omaha, NE 68102
Phone: 402-346-4445
Fax: 402-346-4449

Omaha Botanical Gardens
5th & Cedar Sts
Omaha, NE 68107
Phone: 402-333-2359

Omaha Children's Museum
500 S 20th St
Omaha, NE 68102
www.ocm.org
Phone: 402-342-6164
Fax: 402-342-6165

Omaha Community Playhouse
6915 Cass St
Omaha, NE 68132
www.omahaplayhouse.com
Phone: 402-553-0800
Fax: 402-553-6288
TF: 888-782-4338

Omaha Symphony Orchestra
1605 Howard St
Omaha, NE 68102
E-mail: bravo@omahasymphony.org
www.omahasymphony.org/
Phone: 402-342-3836
Fax: 402-342-3819

Omaha Theater Co for Young People
2001 Farnam St Rose Blumkin Performing Arts Ctr
Omaha, NE 68102
www.otcyp.org
Phone: 402-345-4849
Fax: 402-344-7255

Opera Omaha
1625 Farnam St Suite 100
Omaha, NE 68102
Phone: 402-346-0357
Fax: 402-346-7323
TF: 877-346-7372

Orpheum Theatre
409 S 16th St
Omaha, NE 68102
Phone: 402-444-4750
Fax: 402-444-6201

Prospect Hill Cemetery
3202 Parker St
Omaha, NE 68111
Phone: 402-556-6057

Red Barn Opry Showhouse
10318 Sapp Bros Dr
Omaha, NE 68138
Phone: 402-895-5939

Shelterbelt Theatre Phone: 402-293-7023
3225 1/2 California St
Omaha, NE 68131

Strategic Air Command (SAC) Museum Phone: 402-944-3100
28210 W Park Hwy Fax: 402-944-3160
Ashland, NE 68003 TF: 800-358-5029
www.sacmuseum.org

Sports Teams & Facilities

Aksarben Coliseum/Event Center Phone: 402-561-7000
6800 Mercy Rd Suite 100 Fax: 402-561-7012
Omaha, NE 68106 TF: 800-228-6001
E-mail: office@aksarbenomaha.com

Horsemen's Park Phone: 402-731-2900
6303 Q St
Omaha, NE 68117

Omaha Beef (football) Phone: 402-558-4849
1804 Capitol Ave Civic Auditorium Fax: 402-558-5996
Omaha, NE 68102
E-mail: omaha@beeffootball.com
www.beeffootball.com

Omaha Golden Spikes (baseball) Phone: 402-734-2550
1202 Bert Murphy Ave Rosenblatt Stadium Fax: 402-734-7166
Omaha, NE 68107
E-mail: omahabaseball@goldenspikes.com
www.goldenspikes.com

Omaha Lancers (hockey) Phone: 402-561-7001
6800 Mercy Rd Aksarben Coliseum Fax: 402-561-7019
Omaha, NE 68106

Sunset Speedway Phone: 402-493-5271
114th & State Sts Fax: 402-493-0181
Omaha, NE 68134
www.sunsetspeedway.com

Annual Events

Autumn Festival-An Arts & Crafts Affair
(early November) 402-331-2889
Cathedral Flower Festival (late January) 402-558-3100
Holiday Wildlights
(late November-late December) 402-733-8401
Jazz on the Green (early July-August) 402-342-3300
Midwest Boat Show (early-mid-January) 402-393-3339
NCAA World Series (mid-June) 402-422-1212
Nebraska Shakespeare Festival
(mid-June-early July) 402-280-2391
Old Fashioned Memorial Day Observance
(late May) 402-553-1770
Omaha Classic (early August) 402-399-1800
Omaha Sports Show (late February) 402-393-3339
Renaissance Faire of the Midlands
(early-mid-June) 402-345-5401
River City Roundup & Rodeo (late September) 402-554-9602
Rockbrook Village Art Fair (early-mid-September) . . . 402-390-0890
SeptemberFest (late August-early September) 402-346-4800
Shakespeare on the Green (late June-early July) 402-444-4660
Spring Festival-An Arts & Crafts Affair
(early April) 402-331-2889
Summer Arts Festival (late June) 402-896-5976
Taste of Omaha (early June) 402-346-8003
Westfair! (late July) 712-323-7722
Wings & Wetlands Festival (early May) 402-731-3140

Orlando, Florida

County: Orange

ORLANDO is located in central Florida. Major cities within 100 miles include Daytona Beach, Tampa, and Saint Petersburg, Florida.

Area (Land)	67.3 sq mi
Area (Water)	4.7 sq mi
Elevation	106 ft
Latitude	28-53-81 N
Longitude	81-37-94 W
Time Zone	EST
Area Code	407

Climate

Orlando has a mild climate with abundant sunshine. Although cold fronts occasionally bring brief periods of cold weather to the area, winters are generally mild, with average high temperatures in the low 70s and lows in the low 50s. Summers are hot and humid, with average highs in the low 90s and lows in the low 70s. Summer is also the rainy season in Orlando, and afternoon thunderstorms are common. June and July are the wettest months in Orlando, while April is the driest.

Average Temperatures & Precipitation

Temperatures

	Jan	Feb	Mar	Apr	May	Jun	Jul	Aug	Sep	Oct	Nov	Dec
High	71	73	78	83	88	91	92	92	90	85	79	73
Low	49	50	55	59	66	72	73	73	72	66	58	51

Precipitation

	Jan	Feb	Mar	Apr	May	Jun	Jul	Aug	Sep	Oct	Nov	Dec
Inches	2.3	3.0	3.2	1.8	3.6	7.3	7.3	6.8	6.0	2.4	2.3	2.2

History

Originally inhabited by Native Americans of the Timucuan Tribe, the land known today as Orlando was first settled by whites around 1843. In the years prior to white settlement, the area served as a military post during the Second Seminole War (1835-1842). Around 1850, one of the area's earliest settlers, Aaron Jernigan from Georgia, built a stockade on the western shore of Lake Holden. The community that grew up around the stockade was named Jernigan, and in 1856, Jernigan became the seat of Orange County. The following year, the town was renamed Orlando. Although there is some debate as to where the name Orlando originated, it is widely believed that the community was named in honor of Orlando Reeves, a soldier who had lost his life there during the Second Seminole War.

During its early years, Orlando grew as an agricultural community, with cattle and cotton being its primary products. In 1865, the citrus farming industry that the region has become famous for was established, as the first commercial groves were planted that year. In the early 1870s, the area's cotton crops were destroyed by heavy rains, and citrus took over as a primary crop. Orlando was incorporated as a city in 1875, with 85 residents.

In 1880, the South Florida Railroad reached Orlando, spurring industrial development and creating economic opportunities that drew more settlers to the area. In 1895 a freeze destroyed a majority of the area's citrus groves, and, unaware of the fact that such extreme dips in temperature were a rarity, many citrus farmers abandoned their land. However, by the early part of the 20th Century the citrus industry had bounced back, and the landowners who had chosen to remain in Central Florida benefited tremendously. Citrus groves eventually dominated Orlando's farmland, forcing the cattle industry to move further south.

During the 1950s, development in Orlando was stimulated by the growth of Cape Canaveral, located nearby on the east coast in Cocoa Beach. The Martin Company, a missile manufacturer, established a plant in Orlando in 1955, and Lockheed Martin (as the company is known today) remains one of the area's leading employers. But the event that really launched Orlando occurred in 1971, when Walt Disney's Magic Kingdom theme park opened there. In the years since Walt Disney World opened, growth in the area has been phenomenal. Now, one of the leading tourist destinations in the world, the Orlando metropolitan area has more than 1.5 million residents, more than 181,000 of whom live in the city of Orlando.

Population

1990 Census	164,674
1998 Estimate	181,175
% Change	10.0
2005 Projection	196,863

Racial/Ethnic Breakdown

White	68.8%
Black	26.9%
Other	4.3%
Hispanic Origin (may be of any race)	8.7%

Age Breakdown

Under 5 years	6.8%
5 to 17	14.1%
18 to 20	7.9%
21 to 24	8.4%
25 to 34	22.6%
35 to 44	13.8%
45 to 54	8.0%
55 to 64	7.0%
65 to 74	6.3%
75+ years	5.0%
Median Age	30.2

Gender Breakdown
Male 50.3%
Female 49.7%

Government

Type of Government: Mayor-Council

Orlando Chief Administrative Officer
400S Orange Ave 3rd Fl
Orlando, FL 32801
Phone: 407-246-2226
Fax: 407-246-3342

Orlando City Clerk
400 S Orange Ave
Orlando, FL 32801
Phone: 407-246-2251
Fax: 407-246-3010

Orlando City Commission
400 S Orange Ave
Orlando, FL 32801
Phone: 407-246-2382
Fax: 407-246-3010

Orlando City Hall
400 S Orange Ave
Orlando, FL 32801
Phone: 407-246-2221
Fax: 407-246-2842

Orlando Community & Youth Services Dept
649 W Livingston St
Orlando, FL 32801
Phone: 407-246-2288
Fax: 407-246-2875

Orlando Downtown Development Board
100 S Orange Ave 9th Fl
Orlando, FL 32801
Phone: 407-246-2555
Fax: 407-246-2848

Orlando Economic Development Office
300 S Orange Ave 3rd Fl
Orlando, FL 32801
Phone: 407-246-2821
Fax: 407-246-3342

Orlando Finance Dept
400 S Orange Ave 4th Fl
Orlando, FL 32801
Phone: 407-246-2341
Fax: 407-246-2707

Orlando Fire Dept
400 S Orange Ave 7th Fl
Orlando, FL 32801
Phone: 407-246-2390
Fax: 407-246-2512

Orlando Human Resources Dept
400 S Orange Ave 1st Fl
Orlando, FL 32801
Phone: 407-246-2235
Fax: 407-246-2019

Orlando Legal Affairs Office
400 S Orange Ave 3rd Fl
Orlando, FL 32801
Phone: 407-246-2295
Fax: 407-246-2854

Orlando Mayor
400 S Orange Ave
Orlando, FL 32801
Phone: 407-246-2221
Fax: 407-246-2842

Orlando Planning & Development Dept
400 S Orange Ave
Orlando, FL 32801
Phone: 407-246-2269
Fax: 407-246-2895

Orlando Police Dept
100 S Hughey Ave
Orlando, FL 32801
Phone: 407-246-2401
Fax: 407-246-2732

Orlando Public Works Dept
400 S Orange Ave
Orlando, FL 32801
Phone: 407-246-2266
Fax: 407-246-2892

Important Phone Numbers

AAA 407-894-3333
American Express Travel 407-843-0004
Dental Referral 407-894-9798
Driver's License Information 407-275-4059
Emergency 911
Florida Dept of Revenue 407-623-1141
Greater Orlando Assn of Realtors 407-422-5143
HotelDocs 800-468-3537
Medical Referral 407-897-1700
Orange County Tax Collector's Office 407-836-2700
Poison Control Center 800-282-3171
Time 407-646-3131
Vehicle Registration Information 407-836-4145
Voter Registration Information 407-836-2070
Weather 321-255-2900

Information Sources

Better Business Bureau Serving Central Florida
151 Wymore Rd Suite 100
Altamonte Springs, FL 32714
www.orlando.bbb.org
Phone: 407-621-3300
Fax: 407-786-2625

Official Visitor Center
8723 International Dr Suite 101
Orlando, FL 32819
Phone: 407-363-5871
Fax: 407-354-0874

Orange County
PO Box 1393
Orlando, FL 32802
www.citizens-first.co.orange.fl.us
Phone: 407-836-7350
Fax: 407-836-5879

Orange County Convention Center
9800 International Dr
Orlando, FL 32819
www.orlandoconvention.com
Phone: 407-345-9800
Fax: 407-345-9876

Orlando Centroplex & Expo Center
500 W Livingston St
Orlando, FL 32801
www.orlandocentroplex.com
Phone: 407-849-2000
Fax: 407-423-3482

Orlando Regional Chamber of Commerce
PO Box 1234
Orlando, FL 32802
www.orlando.org
Phone: 407-425-1234
Fax: 407-839-5020

Orlando/Orange County Convention & Visitors Bureau
6700 Forum Dr Suite 100
Orlando, FL 32821
www.go2orlando.com
Phone: 407-363-5871
Fax: 407-370-5022
TF: 800-643-9492

Online Resources

4Orlando.com
www.4orlando.com

About.com Guide to Orlando
orlando.about.com/citiestowns/southeastus/orlando

Access America Orlando
orlando.accessamer.com

Area Guide Orlando
orlando.areaguides.net

City Knowledge Orlando
www.cityknowledge.com/fl_orlando.htm

CitySearch Orlando
orlando.citysearch.com

CityTravelGuide.com Orlando
www.citytravelguide.com/orlando.htm

DigitalCity Orlando
home.digitalcity.com/orlando

DiningGuide Orlando
orlando.diningguide.net

Downtown Orlando
www.downtownorlando.com/

Essential Guide to Orlando
www.ego.net/us/fl/orlando/

EventGuide Orlando
orlando.eventguide.com

Events Guide Orlando
eventguide.com/mco

Excite.com Orlando City Guide
www.excite.com/travel/countries/united_states/florida/orlando

Florida Vacation Store
www.floridavacationstore.com

Go2Orlando
www.go2orlando.com

HotelGuide Orlando
orlando.hotelguide.net

Index 411 Orlando
www.index411.com/orlando/01003a.htm

Inside Central Florida
www.insidecentralflorida.com

Lodging.com Orlando Florida
www.lodging.com/auto/guides/orlando-area-fl.html

MetroGuide Orlando
metroguide.net/orlando

Open World City Guides Orlando
www.worldexecutive.com/cityguides/orlando/

Orl.com
www.orl.com/

Orlando
www.iu.net/orlando

Orlando Connections
www.aesir.com/Orlando/Welcome.html

Orlando Golf Guide
orlando-golf.com

Orlando Graphic City Guide
www.futurecast.com/gcg/orlando.htm

Orlando Holiday Choice
www.holiday-choice.com

Orlando Hotel Source
www.hotelorlando.com

Orlando Online
orlandoonline.com

Orlando Travel
www.orlandotravel.com/

Slant The
www.theslant.com/

Virtual Voyages Orlando
www.virtualvoyages.com/usa/fl/orlando/orlando.sht

Area Communities

Communities with populations greater than 10,000 in the four-county (Orange, Osceola, Seminole, and Lake) Orlando metropolitan area include:

Altamonte Springs
225 Newburyport Ave
Altamonte Springs, FL 32701
Phone: 407-830-3801
Fax: 407-830-4421

Apopka
PO Box 1229
Apopka, FL 32712
Phone: 407-703-1700
Fax: 407-703-1725

Casselberry
95 Triplet Lake Dr
Casselberry, FL 32707
Phone: 407-262-7700
Fax: 407-262-7745

Eustis
PO Drawer 68
Eustis, FL 32727
Phone: 352-483-5430
Fax: 352-357-2971

Kissimmee
101 N Church St
Kissimmee, FL 34741
Phone: 407-847-2821
Fax: 407-847-8369

Lady Lake
409 Fennell Blvd
Lady Lake, FL 32159
Phone: 352-751-1500
Fax: 352-751-1510

Leesburg
PO Box 490630
Leesburg, FL 34749
Phone: 352-728-9705
Fax: 352-728-9734

Longwood
175 W Warren Ave
Longwood, FL 32750
Phone: 407-260-3440
Fax: 407-260-3419

Ocoee
150 N Lakeshore Dr
Ocoee, FL 34761
Phone: 407-656-2322
Fax: 407-656-8504

Oviedo
400 Alexandria Blvd
Oviedo, FL 32765
Phone: 407-977-6000
Fax: 407-977-6009

Saint Cloud
1300 9th St
Saint Cloud, FL 34769
Phone: 407-957-7300
Fax: 407-892-5110

Sanford
PO Box 1788
Sanford, FL 32772
Phone: 407-330-5600
Fax: 407-330-5606

Winter Park
401 S Park Ave
Winter Park, FL 32789
Phone: 407-599-3292
Fax: 407-599-3436

Winter Springs
1126 E State Rd 434
Winter Springs, FL 32708
Phone: 407-327-1800
Fax: 407-327-6912

Economy

Hosting more than 24 million visitors annually, Orlando's economy is dominated by its booming tourism industry, which contributes more than $10 billion each year. Although tourism plays a primary role, the economic base in the Orlando metropolitan area ranges from citrus farming to construction, aerospace equipment manufacturing to finance. As it has for more than a century, agribusiness continues to play an important (albeit small) role in the area's economy—citrus fruit, cattle, and dairy products are the area's primary products. The Orlando metropolitan area has also become a leading center for high-technology, and nearly 80 percent of the total growth in the manufacturing sector since 1980 has been in the high-tech field. Services is the largest employment sector in the Orlando area, representing more than 40 percent of the total workforce. Major companies that have their corporate headquarters in and around Orlando include the American Automobile Association, Correct Craft, TG Lee, and Tupperware. Other U.S. corporate giants that have a presence in the Orlando area include AT & T, Lockheed Martin, and Westinghouse Electric Corporation.

Unemployment Rate 3.1%*
Per Capita Income..........................$23,373**
Median Family Income......................$48,100**

** Information given is for Orange County.*
*** Information given is for the Orlando Metropolitan Statistical Area (MSA), which includes the city of Orlando, Orange, Osceola, and Seminole counties.*

Principal Industries & Number of Wage Earners

Orange County - 1998

Agricultural Services, Forestry, & Fishing 8,662
Construction..26,797
Finance, Insurance, & Real Estate 32,852
Manufacturing 36,845
Mining 80
Retail Trade..96,290
Services 245,092
Transportation, Communications, & Public Utilities 32,922
Wholesale Trade.......................................31,723

Major Employers

AT & T
850 Trafalgar Ct
Maitland, FL 32751
www.att.com
Phone: 800-505-2162

Central Florida Investments Inc
5601 Windover Dr
Orlando, FL 32819
www.westgateresorts.com/aboutwr.html
Phone: 407-351-3383
Fax: 407-352-8935
TF: 800-925-9999

Florida Hospital Medical Center
601 E Rollins St
Orlando, FL 32803
www.flhosp.org/locations/FHsouth/index.htm
Phone: 407-896-6611
Fax: 407-897-1755

Lockheed Martin Information Systems
12506 Lake Underhill Rd
Orlando, FL 32825
www.lmco.com/lmis
Phone: 407-306-1000
Fax: 407-306-7225

Lockheed Martin Missiles & Fire Control Orlando
5600 Sand Lake Rd
Orlando, FL 32819
www.missilesandfirecontrol.com
Phone: 407-356-2000
Fax: 407-356-2010

Orange County
PO Box 1393
Orlando, FL 32802
www.citizens-first.co.orange.fl.us
Phone: 407-836-7350
Fax: 407-836-5879

Orange County Public Schools
445 W Amelia St
Orlando, FL 32801
www.ocps.k12.fl.us
Phone: 407-317-3200
Fax: 407-317-3392

Orlando Regional Healthcare System
1414 Kuhl Ave
Orlando, FL 32806
www.orhs.org
Phone: 407-841-5111
Fax: 407-649-6845

Publix Super Markets Inc
PO Box 407
Lakeland, FL 33802
www.publix.com
Phone: 863-688-1188
Fax: 863-284-5571

Seminole County Public Schools
400 E Lake Mary Blvd
Sanford, FL 32773
nt1.scps.k12.fl.us
Phone: 407-320-0000
Fax: 407-320-0284

SunTrust Bank Central Florida NA
200 S Orange Ave
Orlando, FL 32801
Phone: 407-237-4141
Fax: 407-237-6910
TF: 800-432-4760

Universal Studios Florida
1000 Universal Studios Plaza
Orlando, FL 32819
www.uescape.com/studios/attractions/
Phone: 407-363-8000
Fax: 407-363-8006

US Postal Service
10401 Post Office Blvd
Orlando, FL 32862
new.usps.com
Phone: 407-850-6203
Fax: 407-826-5642

Walt Disney World Co
PO Box 10000
Lake Buena Vista, FL 32830
www.disneyworld.com
Phone: 407-824-2222

Winn-Dixie Stores Inc
3015 Coastline Dr
Orlando, FL 32808
E-mail: comments@winn-dixie.com
www.winn-dixie.com
Phone: 407-578-4000
Fax: 407-578-4090

Quality of Living Indicators

Total Crime Index....................................25,421
(rates per 100,000 inhabitants)

Violent Crime
Murder/manslaughter........................... 25
Forcible rape 203
Robbery....................................1,123
Aggravated assault............................2,737

Property Crime
Burglary 3,995
Larceny theft 15,089
Motor vehicle theft...........................2,249

Cost of Living Index....................................97.7
(national average = 100)

Median Home Price.................................$105,300

Education

Public Schools

Orange County Public Schools Phone: 407-317-3200
445 W Amelia St Fax: 407-317-3392
Orlando, FL 32801
www.ocps.k12.fl.us

Number of Schools
Elementary................................. 98
Middle 27
High...................................... 13

Student/Teacher Ratio
All Grades 16.3:1

Private Schools

Number of Schools (all grades).................. 186+

Colleges & Universities

Crane Institute of America Inc Phone: 407-875-6969
1063 Maitland Ctr Commons Suite 100 Fax: 407-875-1126
Maitland, FL 32751 TF: 800-832-2726
E-mail: craneinstitute@msn.com

Florida Christian College Phone: 407-847-8966
1011 Bill Beck Blvd Fax: 407-847-3925
Kissimmee, FL 34744 TF: 888-468-6322
www.fcc.edu

Florida Metropolitan University Orlando College-North Phone: 407-628-5870
5421 Diplomat Cir Fax: 407-628-1344
Orlando, FL 32810 TF: 800-628-5870
fmu.edu/767/f-767.htm

Full Sail Center for the Recording Arts Phone: 407-679-6333
3300 University Blvd Suite 160 Fax: 407-678-0070
Winter Park, FL 32792 TF: 800-226-7625
E-mail: admissions@fullsail.com
www.fullsail.com

Rollins College Phone: 407-646-2000
1000 Holt Ave Fax: 407-646-1502
Winter Park, FL 32789
www.rollins.edu

Seminole Community College Phone: 407-328-4722
100 Weldon Blvd Fax: 407-328-2395
Sanford, FL 32773
www.seminole.cc.fl.us

Southern College Phone: 407-273-1000
5600 Lake Underhill Rd Fax: 407-273-0492
Orlando, FL 32807
E-mail: postmaster@southern.edu
southern.edu

University of Central Florida Phone: 407-823-2000
4000 Central Florida Blvd Fax: 407-823-5652
Orlando, FL 32816
www.ucf.edu

Valencia Community College Phone: 407-299-5000
PO Box 3028 Fax: 407-293-8839
Orlando, FL 32802
valencia.cc.fl.us/

Hospitals

Central Florida Regional Hospital Phone: 407-321-4500
1401 W Seminole Blvd Fax: 407-324-4790
Sanford, FL 32771

Florida Hospital Altamonte Phone: 407-830-4321
601 E Altamonte Dr Fax: 407-767-2399
Altamonte Springs, FL 32701

Florida Hospital East Orlando Phone: 407-277-8110
7727 Lake Underhill Rd Fax: 407-281-8697
Orlando, FL 32822

Florida Hospital Medical Center Phone: 407-896-6611
601 E Rollins St Fax: 407-897-1755
Orlando, FL 32803
www.flhosp.org/locations/FHsouth/index.htm

Florida Hospital Waterman Phone: 352-589-3333
201 N Eustis St Fax: 352-589-3481
Eustis, FL 32726

Health Central Phone: 407-296-1000
10000 W Colonial Dr Fax: 407-521-3406
Ocoee, FL 34761
www.health-central.org

Leesburg Regional Medical Center Phone: 352-365-4545
600 E Dixie Ave Fax: 352-323-5009
Leesburg, FL 34748 TF: 800-889-3755

Orlando Regional Lucerne Phone: 407-649-6111
818 Main Ln Fax: 407-649-6194
Orlando, FL 32801

Orlando Regional Medical Center Phone: 407-841-5111
1414 Kuhl Ave Fax: 407-425-5093
Orlando, FL 32806

Orlando Regional South Seminole Hospital Phone: 407-767-1200
555 W State Rd 434 Fax: 407-767-5913
Longwood, FL 32750

Osceola Regional Medical Center Phone: 407-846-2266
700 W Oak St Fax: 407-518-3684
Kissimmee, FL 34741

Sand Lake Hospital
9400 Turkey Lake Rd
Orlando, FL 32819
Phone: 407-351-8500
Fax: 407-351-8569

Transportation

Airport(s)

Orlando International Airport (MCO)
8 miles SE of downtown (approx 20 minutes).....407-825-2001

Mass Transit

Tri County Transit Authority
$1 Base fare 407-841-8240

Rail/Bus

Amtrak Auto Train
600 Persimmon Ave
Sanford, FL 32771
Phone: 407-330-6066
TF: 800-872-7245

Amtrak Station
1400 Sligh Blvd
Orlando, FL 32806
Phone: 407-425-9411
TF: 800-872-7245

Greyhound Bus Station
555 John Young Pkwy
Orlando, FL 32805
Phone: 407-292-3407
TF: 800-231-2222

Utilities

Electricity
Florida Power Corp............................407-629-1010

Gas
Peoples Gas System...........................407-425-4661

Water
Orlando Utilities Commission 407-423-9018

Garbage Collection/Recycling
Orlando Solid Waste Management Bureau........407-246-2314

Telecommunications

Telephone
BellSouth Telecommunications Inc 800-753-0710
www.bellsouth.com

Cable Television
Time Warner Communications..................407-291-2500
www.twcentralflorida.com

Internet Service Providers (ISPs)
Florida Digital Network Inc (FDN)..............407-835-0300
www.floridadigital.net
Internet Access Group.........................407-786-1145
www.iag.net
MPI Net.......................................407-660-7900
www.mpinet.net
Verio Central Florida 407-648-9060
home.verio.net/local/frontpage.cfm?AirportCode=MCO
World Ramp Inc 407-740-5987
zeus.worldramp.net

Banks

AmSouth Bank of Florida
111 N Orange Ave
Orlando, FL 32801
Phone: 407-246-8900
Fax: 407-849-0034

First Union National Bank
20 N Orange Ave
Orlando, FL 32802
Phone: 407-649-5079
Fax: 407-649-5513

NationsBank
390 N Orange Ave
Orlando, FL 32801
Phone: 407-420-2800
Fax: 407-236-5250

Republic Bank
255 S Orange Ave
Orlando, FL 32801
Phone: 407-841-3333
Fax: 407-649-1620
TF: 800-386-5454

SunTrust Bank Central Florida NA
200 S Orange Ave
Orlando, FL 32801
Phone: 407-237-4141
Fax: 407-237-6910
TF: 800-432-4760

Washington Mutual Bank
2700 S Orange Ave
Orlando, FL 32806
Phone: 407-423-0515
Fax: 407-352-5934
TF: 800-782-8875

Shopping

Altamonte Mall
451 Altamonte Ave
Altamonte Springs, FL 32701
www.altamontemall.com
Phone: 407-830-4422
Fax: 407-830-0872

Belz Factory Outlet World
5401 W Oakridge Rd
Orlando, FL 32819
Phone: 407-352-9611
Fax: 407-351-3873

Church Street Market
55 W Church St
Orlando, FL 32801
Phone: 407-872-3500

Colonial Plaza Mall
2560 E Colonial Dr
Orlando, FL 32803
Phone: 407-894-3601

Crossroads of Lake Buena Vista
SR 535 & I-4
Lake Buena Vista, FL 32830
Phone: 407-827-7300

Florida Mall
8001 S Orange Blossom Trail
Orlando, FL 32809
Phone: 407-851-6255

Goodings International Plaza
8255 International Dr
Orlando, FL 32819
Phone: 407-354-2200

Lake Buena Vista Factory Stores
15591 S Apopka Vineland Rd
Orlando, FL 32821
Phone: 407-238-9301

Market Street at Celebration
I-4 & US Hwy 192 E
Orlando, FL 32801
www.celebrationfl.com/market_street/home.html
Phone: 407-566-3448

Mercado The
8445 International Dr
Orlando, FL 32819
www.themercado.com
Phone: 407-345-9337
Fax: 407-345-1072

Old Town
5770 W Irlo Bronson Memorial Hwy
Kissimmee, FL 34746
Phone: 407-396-4888
Fax: 407-396-0348
TF: 800-843-4202

Orlando Fashion Square
3201 E Colonial Dr
Orlando, FL 32803
Phone: 407-896-1131
Fax: 407-894-8381

Park Avenue Shopping District
150 N New York Ave
Winter Park, FL 32789
Phone: 407-644-8281
Fax: 407-644-7826

Seminole Towne Center
200 Towne Ctr Cir
Sanford, FL 32771
www.shopsimon.com/smt/servlet/SMTMall?mid=122&pn=ENTRY&rs=0
Phone: 407-323-2262
Fax: 407-323-2464

West Oaks Mall
9401 W Colonial Dr
Ocoee, FL 34761
Phone: 407-294-2775
Fax: 407-294-0760

Media

Newspapers and Magazines

Orlando Business Journal
315 E Robinson St Suite 250
Orlando, FL 32801
www.amcity.com/orlando
Phone: 407-649-8470
Fax: 407-649-8469

Orlando Magazine
225 S Westmont Dr Suite 1100
Altamonte Springs, FL 32704
E-mail: orlandomag@aol.com
www.orlandomag.com
Phone: 407-767-8338
Fax: 407-767-8348
TF: 800-243-0609

Orlando Sentinel*
633 N Orange Ave
Orlando, FL 32801
www.orlandosentinel.com
Phone: 407-420-5000
Fax: 407-420-5350
TF: 800-669-5757

Orlando Weekly
807 S Orlando Ave Suite R
Winter Park, FL 32789
E-mail: orlandoweekly@aminc.com
www.orlandoweekly.com
Phone: 407-645-5888
Fax: 407-645-2547

Osceola News-Gazette
PO Box 422068
Kissimmee, FL 34742
E-mail: osceolang@aol.com
www.oscnewsgazette.com
Phone: 407-846-7600
Fax: 407-846-8516

**Indicates major daily newspapers*

Television

WBSF-TV Ch 43 (Ind)
4450-L Enterprise Ct
Melbourne, FL 32934
Phone: 321-254-4343
Fax: 321-242-0863

WESH-TV Ch 2 (NBC)
1021 N Wymore Rd
Winter Park, FL 32789
E-mail: wesh@intersrv.com
www.wesh.com
Phone: 407-645-2222
Fax: 407-539-7948

WFTV-TV Ch 9 (ABC)
490 E South St
Orlando, FL 32801
E-mail: news@wftv.com
www.insidecentralflorida.com/partners/wftv
Phone: 407-841-9000
Fax: 407-481-2891

WKCF-TV Ch 18 (WB)
31 Skyline Dr
Lake Mary, FL 32746
E-mail: wb18wkcf@wb18.com
www.wb18.com
Phone: 407-670-3018
Fax: 407-647-4163

WKMG-TV Ch 6 (CBS)
4466 N John Young Pkwy
Orlando, FL 32804
www.wkmg.com
Phone: 407-291-6000
Fax: 407-298-2122

WMFE-TV Ch 24 (PBS)
11510 E Colonial Dr
Orlando, FL 32817
www.pbs.org/wmfe/
Phone: 407-273-2300
Fax: 407-273-3613

WOFL-TV Ch 35 (Fox)
35 Skyline Dr
Lake Mary, FL 32746
E-mail: wofl@wofl.com
www.wofl.com
Phone: 407-644-3535
Fax: 407-333-0234

WOPX-TV Ch 56 (PAX)
7091 Grand National Dr Suite 100
Orlando, FL 32819
www.pax.net/WOPX
Phone: 407-370-5600
Fax: 407-370-5656

WRBW-TV Ch 65 (UPN)
2000 Universal Studios Plaza Suite 200
Orlando, FL 32819
E-mail: wrbw@wrbw.com
www.wrbw.com
Phone: 407-248-6500
Fax: 407-248-6520

WTGL-TV Ch 52 (Ind)
653 W Michigan St
Orlando, FL 32805
tv52.org
Phone: 407-423-5200
Fax: 407-422-0120

Radio

WCFB-FM 94.5 MHz (AC)
4192 N John Young Pkwy
Orlando, FL 32804
Phone: 407-294-2945
Fax: 407-297-7595

WDBO-AM 580 kHz (N/T)
4192 N John Young Pkwy
Orlando, FL 32804
www.insidecentralflorida.com/partners/580wdbo
Phone: 407-295-5858
Fax: 407-291-4879

WHOO-AM 990 kHz (Nost)
200 S Orange Ave Suite 2240
Orlando, FL 32801
Phone: 407-422-9696
Fax: 407-422-0917

WHTQ-FM 96.5 MHz (CR)
200 S Orange Ave Suite 2240
Orlando, FL 32801
www.whtq.com
Phone: 407-422-9890
Fax: 407-425-9696

WJHM-FM 101.9 MHz (Urban)
1800 Pembrook Dr Suite 400
Orlando, FL 32810
E-mail: fm102jamz@aol.com
www.wjhm.com
Phone: 407-919-1000
Fax: 407-919-1329

WJRR-FM 101.1 MHz (Rock)
2500 Maitland Ctr Pkwy Suite 401
Maitland, FL 32751
www.wjrr.com
Phone: 407-916-7800
Fax: 407-916-7406

WLOQ-FM 103.1 MHz (NAC)
170 W Fairbanks Ave Suite 200
Winter Park, FL 32789
E-mail: general@wloq.com
www.wloq.com
Phone: 407-647-5557
Fax: 407-647-4495

WMFE-FM 90.7 MHz (NPR)
11510 E Colonial Dr
Orlando, FL 32817
E-mail: wmfe@magicnet.net
www.pbs.org/wmfe
Phone: 407-273-2300
Fax: 407-273-8462

WMGF-FM 107.7 MHz (AC)
PO Box 107
Maitland, FL 32794
Phone: 407-916-7800
Fax: 407-916-7406

WMMO-FM 98.9 MHz (AC)
200 S Orange Ave Suite 2240
Orlando, FL 32801
www.wmmo.com
Phone: 407-422-9890
Fax: 407-423-9666

WOCL-FM 105.9 MHz (Oldies)
1800 Pembrook Dr Suite 400
Orlando, FL 32810
cool1059.com
Phone: 407-919-1000
Fax: 407-919-9329

WOMX-FM 105.1 MHz (AC)
1800 Pembrook Dr Suite 400
Orlando, FL 32810
www.mix1051.com
Phone: 407-919-1000
Fax: 407-919-1140

WPCV-FM 97.5 MHz (Ctry)
404 W Lime St
Lakeland, FL 33815
E-mail: wpcv@wpcv.com
www.wpcv.com
Phone: 863-682-8184
Fax: 863-683-2409

WPYO-FM 95.3 MHz (CHR)
3701 N John Young Pkwy Suite 102
Orlando, FL 32804
Phone: 407-299-9595
Fax: 407-290-1302

WQTM-AM 540 kHz (Sports)
2500 Maitland Ctr Pkwy Suite 401
Maitland, FL 32751
E-mail: programdirector@540theteam.com
www.540theteam.com
Phone: 407-916-7800
Fax: 407-916-7406

WSHE-FM 100.3 MHz (AC)
2500 Maitland Ctr Pkwy Suite 401
Maitland, FL 32751
E-mail: wshe@broadcast.com
Phone: 407-916-7800
Fax: 407-916-7406

WTKS-FM 104.1 MHz (N/T)
2500 Maitland Ctr Pkwy Suite 401
Maitland, FL 32751
E-mail: real104@magicnet.net
www.wtks.com
Phone: 407-916-7800
Fax: 407-916-7511

WTLN-AM 950 kHz (Rel)
400 W Lake Brantley Rd
Altamonte Springs, FL 32714
E-mail: am950wtln@aol.com
www.wtln.com
Phone: 407-682-9494
Fax: 407-682-7005

WUCF-FM 89.9 MHz (NPR)
4000 Central Florida Blvd Bldg 75 Rm 130
Orlando, FL 32816
E-mail: wucf@pegasus.cc.ucf.edu
wucf.ucf.edu
Phone: 407-823-0899
Fax: 407-823-6364

WWKA-FM 92.3 MHz (Ctry)
4192 N John Young Pkwy
Orlando, FL 32804
Phone: 407-298-9292
Fax: 407-291-4879

WWNZ-AM 740 kHz (N/T)
2500 Maitland Ctr Pkwy Suite 401
Maitland, FL 32751
Phone: 407-916-7800
Fax: 407-916-7402

WXXL-FM 106.7 MHz (CHR)
1800 Pembrook Dr Suite 400
Orlando, FL 32810
www.wxxl.com
Phone: 407-919-1000
Fax: 407-332-9613

Attractions

Since the opening of Walt Disney World in 1971, Orlando has been a top vacation spot for travelers from all over the world. In addition to the Magic Kingdom and EPCOT, the park area also encompasses Disney-MGM Studios, River Country, Disney's Typhoon Lagoon and Blizzard Beach aquatic parks, and Pleasure Island. Also in the surrounding Orlando area are Universal Studios Florida, the largest working film studio outside Hollywood; Sea World; Cypress Gardens; and Splendid China theme park, with more than 60 scaled-down models of the greatest landmarks in China. Besides its many theme parks, restaurants, and hotels, Orlando also has several fine museums, more than 100 golf courses, fishing, water skiing, horseback riding, and hot-air ballooning. The Kennedy Space Center is on the Atlantic coast in nearby Cocoa Beach.

Bok Tower Gardens
1151 Tower Blvd
Lake Wales, FL 33853
www.boktower.org
Phone: 863-676-1408
Fax: 863-676-6770

Canaveral National Seashore
308 Julia St
Titusville, FL 32796
www.nps.gov/cana
Phone: 321-267-1110
Fax: 321-264-2906

Carr Bob Performing Arts Centre
401 W Livingston St
Orlando, FL 32801
www.orlandocentroplex.com
Phone: 407-849-2000
Fax: 407-843-0758

Charles Hosmer Morse Museum of American Art
445 N Park Ave
Winter Park, FL 32789
www.morsemuseum.org
Phone: 407-645-5311
Fax: 407-647-1284

Church Street Station
129 W Church St
Orlando, FL 32801
churchstreetstation.com
Phone: 407-422-2434
Fax: 407-872-7960

Cirque du Soleil La Nouba
PO Box 22157
Lake Buena Vista, FL 32830
www.cirquedusoleil.com/en/piste/lanouba/index.html
Phone: 407-934-9200
Fax: 407-934-9148

Civic Theatre of Central Florida
1001 E Princeton St
Orlando, FL 32803
Phone: 407-896-7365
Fax: 407-897-3284

Cornell Fine Arts Museum
1000 Holt Ave
Winter Park, FL 32789
www.rollins.edu/cfam
Phone: 407-646-2526
Fax: 407-646-2524

Cypress Gardens Phone: 863-324-2111
2641 S Lake Summit Dr Fax: 863-324-7946
Winter Haven, FL 33884
www.cypressgardens.com/

Disney Institute Phone: 407-827-1100
1960 Magnolia Way Fax: 407-827-4100
Lake Buena Vista, FL 32830 TF: 800-282-9282
www.disneyinstitute.com

Disney's Wide World of Sports Phone: 407-939-1500
700 Victory Way Fax: 407-939-2070
Kissimmee, FL 34747
asp.disney.go.com/disneyworld/db/wideworldofsports/index.asp

Disney-MGM Studios Theme Park Phone: 407-824-4321
PO Box 10000
Lake Buena Vista, FL 32830
asp.disney.go.com/disneyworld/db/seetheworld/themeparks/facilities/index.asp?id=78

DisneyQuest Phone: 407-828-4600
PO Box 10000
Lake Buena Vista, FL 32830
disney.go.com/DisneyQuest/Orlando/home.html

Downtown Disney Phone: 407-939-7727
Hotel Plaza Blvd
Lake Buena Vista, FL 32830

Downtown Farmers' Market Phone: 407-246-2555
Church St
Orlando, FL 32801

Enzian Theater Phone: 407-629-1088
1300 S Orlando Ave Fax: 407-629-6870
Maitland, FL 32751
www.enzian.org

Florida Symphony Youth Orchestra Phone: 407-999-7800
1111 N Orange Ave Fax: 407-999-7849
Orlando, FL 32804
www.fsyo.org

Flying Tigers Warbird Air Museum Phone: 407-933-1942
231 N Hoagland Blvd Fax: 407-933-7843
Kissimmee, FL 34741
E-mail: kittyhwk@earthlink.net
www.warbirdmuseum.com

Fun at Flea World Phone: 407-330-1792
4311 Hwy 17-92
Sanford, FL 32773

Gatorland Phone: 407-855-5496
14501 S Orange Blossom Trail Fax: 407-240-9389
Orlando, FL 32837 TF: 800-393-5297
www.i3.net/1-800-FL-VILLA/gatorland

Green Meadows Petting Farm Phone: 407-846-0770
1365 S Poinciana Blvd Fax: 407-870-8644
Kissimmee, FL 34746

IMAX Theater Phone: 321-452-2121
Kennedy Space Center Visitor Ctr
Kennedy Space Center, FL 32899
www.kennedyspacecenter.com/html/imax.html

Jungle Adventures Phone: 407-568-1354
26205 E Hwy 50 Fax: 407-568-0038
Christmas, FL 32709
E-mail: jungleadventures@aol.com

Jungleland Phone: 407-396-1012
4580 W US Hwy 192 Fax: 407-396-1013
Kissimmee, FL 34746

Kennedy Space Center Spaceport USA Phone: 321-452-0300
Kennedy Space Center, FL 32899 Fax: 321-452-3043

King Henry's Feast Phone: 407-351-5151
8984 International Dr Fax: 407-351-3593
Orlando, FL 32819 TF: 800-883-8181

Leu Harry P Botanical Gardens Phone: 407-246-2620
1920 N Forest Ave Fax: 407-246-2849
Orlando, FL 32803
www.ci.orlando.fl.us/departments/leu_gardens/

Maitland Art Center Phone: 407-539-2181
231 W Packwood Ave Fax: 407-539-1198
Maitland, FL 32751

Malibu Grand Prix Phone: 407-351-7093
5863 American Way
Orlando, FL 32819

Mark Two Dinner Theater Phone: 407-843-6275
3376 Edgewater Dr Fax: 407-843-1510
Orlando, FL 32804 TF: 800-726-6275

Market Street at Celebration Phone: 407-566-3448
I-4 & US Hwy 192 E
Orlando, FL 32801
www.celebrationfl.com/market_street/home.html

Medieval Times Dinner & Tournament Phone: 407-396-1518
4510 E Hwy 192
Kissimmee, FL 34746
E-mail: kissimmee@medievaltimes.com
www.medievaltimes.com/FL_realm.htm

Mercado The Phone: 407-345-9337
8445 International Dr Fax: 407-345-1072
Orlando, FL 32819
www.themercado.com

Movie Rider Phone: 407-352-0050
8815 International Dr TF: 800-998-4418
Orlando, FL 32819

Mystery Fun House Phone: 407-351-3359
5767 Major Blvd Fax: 407-351-5657
Orlando, FL 32819

Nickelodeon Studios Phone: 407-363-8500
3000 Universal Studios Plaza Fax: 407-363-8590
Orlando, FL 32819
www.uescape.com/studios

Old Town Phone: 407-396-4888
5770 W Irlo Bronson Memorial Hwy Fax: 407-396-0348
Kissimmee, FL 34746 TF: 800-843-4202

Orange County Historical Museum Phone: 407-897-6350
812 E Rollins St Fax: 407-897-6409
Orlando, FL 32803

Orlando Broadway Series
201 S Orange Ave Suite 101
Orlando, FL 32801
Phone: 407-423-9999
Fax: 407-841-4738
TF: 800-950-4647

Orlando Museum of Art
2416 N Mills Ave
Orlando, FL 32803
www.omart.org
Phone: 407-896-4231
Fax: 407-894-4314

Orlando Opera
1111 N Orange Ave
Orlando, FL 32804
www.orlandoopera.org
Phone: 407-426-1717
Fax: 407-426-1705
TF: 800-336-7372

Orlando Philharmonic Orchestra
812 E Rollins St
Orlando, FL 32803
www.orlandophil.org
Phone: 407-896-6700

Orlando Science Center
777 E Princeton St
Orlando, FL 32803
E-mail: cosmicnews@aol.com
www.osc.org
Phone: 407-514-2000
Fax: 407-514-2277

Pleasure Island
PO Box 10000
Lake Buena Vista, FL 32830
Phone: 407-934-7781
Fax: 407-363-6017

Pointe Orlando
9101 International Dr Suite 1040
Orlando, FL 32819
www.pointeorlandofl.com
Phone: 407-248-2838
Fax: 407-248-0078

Richard Petty Driving Experience
3450 N World Dr
Lake Buena Vista, FL 32830
Phone: 407-939-0130
Fax: 407-939-0137
TF: 800-237-3889

Ripley's Believe It or Not! Museum
8201 International Dr
Orlando, FL 32819
www.ripleysorlando.com
Phone: 407-363-4418

Sea World of Florida
7007 Sea World Dr
Orlando, FL 32821
E-mail: sea.world@bev.net
www.seaworld.com/seaworld/sw_florida/swfframe.html
Phone: 407-351-3600
Fax: 407-363-2256
TF: 800-327-2424

Silver Springs
PO Box 370
Silver Springs, FL 34489
www.silversprings.com
Phone: 352-236-2121
Fax: 352-236-1732
TF: 800-234-7458

Skull Kingdom
5933 American Way
Orlando, FL 32819
E-mail: info@skullkingdom.com
www.skullkingdom.com
Phone: 407-354-1564
Fax: 407-354-1567

Southern Ballet Theatre
1111 N Orange Ave Suite 4
Orlando, FL 32804
www.southernballet.org
Phone: 407-426-1733
Fax: 407-426-1734

Splendid China
3000 Splendid China Blvd
Kissimmee, FL 34747
www.floridasplendidchina.com
Phone: 407-396-7111
Fax: 407-397-8845
TF: 800-244-6226

Terror on Church Street
135 S Orange Ave
Orlando, FL 32801
members.tripod.com/~tocs
Phone: 407-649-1912

Tom Reilly Vintage Aircraft
231 N Hoagland Blvd
Kissimmee, FL 34741
E-mail: warbirds@warbirdmuseum.com
www.warbirdmuseum.com
Phone: 407-847-7477
Fax: 407-933-7843

Tosohatchee State Reserve
3365 Taylor Creek Rd
Christmas, FL 32709
Phone: 407-568-5893

Universal Cineplex
Universal Studios CityWalk 1000
Universal Studios Plaza
Orlando, FL 32819
www.uescape.com/citywalk/cineplex/main.html
Phone: 407-354-5998

Universal Studios CityWalk
1000 Universal Studios Plaza
Orlando, FL 32819
E-mail: guestservices@universalstudios.com
www.uescape.com/citywalk
Phone: 407-363-8000
TF: 888-837-2273

Universal Studios Florida
1000 Universal Studios Plaza
Orlando, FL 32819
www.uescape.com/studios/attractions/
Phone: 407-363-8000
Fax: 407-363-8006

Universal Studios Islands of Adventure
1000 Universal Studios Plaza
Orlando, FL 32819
E-mail: guestservices@universalflorida.com
www.uescape.com/islands
Phone: 407-363-8000
TF: 888-837-2273

Walt Disney World Animal Kingdom
PO Box 10000
Lake Buena Vista, FL 32830
asp.disney.go.com/disneyworld/db/seetheworld/themeparks/facilities/index.asp?id=93
Phone: 407-824-4321

Walt Disney World Blizzard Beach
3250 Buena Vista Dr W
Lake Buena Vista, FL 32830
disney.go.com/DisneyWorld/Recreation/Rec51.html
Phone: 407-824-4321

Walt Disney World Boardwalk
2101 Epcot Resorts Blvd PO Box 10000
Lake Buena Vista, FL 32830
disney.go.com/DisneyWorld/Entertainment/Rec510.html
Phone: 407-939-5100
Fax: 407-939-5150

Walt Disney World Epcot Center
PO Box 10000
Lake Buena Vista, FL 32830
asp.disney.go.com/disneyworld/db/seetheworld/themeparks/facilities_epcot/index.asp?id=47
Phone: 407-824-4321
Fax: 407-828-5400

Walt Disney World Magic Kingdom
PO Box 10000
Lake Buena Vista, FL 32830
disney.go.com/disneyworld
Phone: 407-824-4321

Water Mania
6073 W Hwy 192
Kissimmee, FL 34747
www.watermania-florida.com
Phone: 407-396-2626
Fax: 407-396-8125
TF: 800-527-3092

Wekiwa Springs State Park
1800 Wekiwa Cir
Apopka, FL 32712
Phone: 407-884-2009
Fax: 407-884-2014

Wet 'n Wild Inc
6200 International Dr
Orlando, FL 32819
E-mail: getwet@wetnwild.com
www.wetnwild.com/orlando
Phone: 407-351-1800
Fax: 407-363-1147
TF: 800-992-9453

WonderWorks
9067 International Dr
Orlando, FL 32819
Phone: 407-351-8800
Fax: 407-352-6624

World of Orchids
2501 Old Lake Wilson Rd
Kissimmee, FL 34747
E-mail: info@a-world-of-orchids.com
www.a-world-of-orchids.com
Phone: 407-396-1887
Fax: 407-396-4177

Sports Teams & Facilities

Atlanta Braves Spring Training (baseball)
Disney's Wide World of Sports Stadium 700 S Victory Way
Kissimmee, FL 34747
Phone: 407-938-3500

Central Florida Kraze (soccer)
PO Box 621566
Oviedo, FL 32762
E-mail: weeksend@bellsouth.net
www.orlandosoccer.org
Phone: 407-365-2319
Fax: 407-366-9026

Cleveland Indians Spring Training (baseball)
Chain O'Lakes Park
Winter Haven, FL 33880
Phone: 863-291-5803
Fax: 863-299-4491

Cocoa Expos (soccer)
500 Friday Rd Cocoa Expo Sports Ctr
Cocoa, FL 32926
E-mail: xsoccer@palmnet.net
Phone: 321-639-3976
Fax: 321-504-3716

Houston Astros Spring Training (baseball)
Osceola County Stadium 1000 Bill Beck Blvd
Kissimmee, FL 34744
Phone: 407-933-6500
Fax: 407-847-6237

Kissimmee Cobras (baseball)
1000 Bill Beck Blvd
Kissimmee, FL 34744
Phone: 407-933-5500
Fax: 407-847-6237

Orlando Jackals (hockey)
600 W Amelia St Orlando Arena
Orlando, FL 32801
E-mail: pky@jackals.inspace.net
Phone: 561-241-9880

Orlando Magic
600 W Amelia St TD Waterhouse Centre
Orlando, FL 32801
www.nba.com/magic
Phone: 407-896-2442
Fax: 407-428-3201

Orlando Nighthawks (soccer)
803 Live Oak Dr N
Rockledge, FL 32955
Phone: 321-631-0691
Fax: 321-631-9656

Orlando Predators (football)
400 W Church St
Orlando, FL 32801
Phone: 407-648-4444
Fax: 407-648-8101

Orlando Rays (baseball)
287 S Tampa Ave Tinker Field
Orlando, FL 32805
E-mail: orays@aol.com
www.insidecentralflorida.com/sports/orlandorays/
Phone: 407-872-7593

Orlando Solar Bears (hockey)
600 W Amelia St Orlando Arena
Orlando, FL 32801
Phone: 407-872-7825

Orlando-Seminole Jai Alai
6405 S Hwy 17-92
Fern Park, FL 32730
E-mail: jannouncer@orlandojaialai.com
www.orlandojaialai.com
Phone: 407-339-6221

Sanford-Orlando Kennel Club
301 Dog Track Rd
Longwood, FL 32750
Phone: 407-831-1600
Fax: 407-831-3997

Seminole Greyhound Park
2000 Seminola Blvd
Casselberry, FL 32707
Phone: 407-699-4510
Fax: 407-695-9115

TD Waterhouse Centre
600 W Amelia St
Orlando, FL 32801
Phone: 407-849-2000
Fax: 407-849-2329

Annual Events

Bach Music Festival (late February) 407-646-2182
Central Florida Fair (late February-early March) 407-295-3247
Epcot International Flower & Garden Show (mid April-late May) 407-824-4321
Epcot International Food & Wine Festival (late October-late November) 407-824-4321
Festival of the Masters (mid-November)............407-824-4321
Fiesta in the Park (early November) 407-649-3152
Florida Citrus Bowl (January 1)...................407-423-2476
Florida Film Festival (mid-late June) 407-629-1088
Halloween Horror Nights (October)................800-447-0675
Maitland Arts & Fine Crafts Festival (mid-April) 407-644-0741
Orlando Craft Fair (early October).................407-860-0092
Orlando Scottish Highland Games (mid-January)...............................407-699-4510
Orlando's Singing Christmas Trees (mid-December).............................407-425-2555
Orlando-UCF Shakespeare Festival (October-May)...407-245-0985
Silver Spurs Rodeo (mid-February & early October).................800-847-4052
Summer Festival (late June).......................407-943-7992
Surf Expo (mid-January & mid-September) 407-345-9800
Walt Disney World Fourth of July Celebration (July 4) 407-824-2222
Walt Disney World Marathon (early January) 407-939-7810
Walt Disney World National Car Rental Golf Classic (late October)................................407-824-2250
Winter Park Sidewalk Arts Festival (mid-March) 407-644-8281

Philadelphia, Pennsylvania

County: **Philadelphia**

PHILADELPHIA is located in southeastern Pennsylvania at the confluence of the Delaware and Schuylkill Rivers. Cities within 100 miles include Allentown and Harrisburg, Pennsylvania; Trenton, New Jersey; New York, New York; and Baltimore, Maryland.

Area (Land) .... 135.1 sq mi
Area (Water)................................ 7.5 sq mi
Elevation....................................... 40 ft
Latitude ....39-95-22 N
Longitude................................ 75-16-42 W
Time Zone ....EST
Area Code.. 215

Climate

Philadelphia's winter high temperatures average around 40 degrees and lows average in the mid-20s. The average annual snowfall is over 20 inches. Summer daytime high temperatures average in the upper 80s, but evenings cool down into the low-to-mid 60s. The city's proximity to the Atlantic Ocean helps to moderate temperatures, keeping periods of extreme hot or cold weather brief. Precipitation is spread fairly evenly throughout the year.

Average Temperatures & Precipitation

Temperatures

	Jan	Feb	Mar	Apr	May	Jun	Jul	Aug	Sep	Oct	Nov	Dec
High	38	41	52	63	73	82	86	85	78	66	55	43
Low	23	24	33	42	53	62	67	66	59	46	38	28

Precipitation

	Jan	Feb	Mar	Apr	May	Jun	Jul	Aug	Sep	Oct	Nov	Dec
Inches	3.2	2.8	3.5	3.6	3.8	3.7	4.3	3.8	3.4	2.6	3.3	3.4

History

Philadelphia, the "City of Brotherly Love," was founded by Quaker William Penn in 1682 and was the first city in the world where religious freedom was guaranteed. The city became the capital of the newly formed colony of Pennsylvania the following year and remained the capital until 1799. Although Philadelphia's earliest residents were primarily Quakers, by the time the city was incorporated in 1701 settlers of various backgrounds, including Germans, Dutch, Scottish, and Irish inhabited the city.

Philadelphia was one of the most important cities in American history. The city became the site of the colonies' first free library, hospital, and learned society, all of which were founded by Benjamin Franklin, one of the city's most famous residents. Philadelphia was the site of several key events of the American Revolution, including the meeting of the First and Second Continental Congress in 1774 and 1775, and the signing of The Declaration of Independence on July 4, 1776. The U.S. Constitution was drafted in the city the following year. Philadelphia also acted as the seat of the national government for the majority of the period from 1776 to 1800.

Philadelphia thrived as a commercial and industrial center through the 1800s, and by the mid-19th Century Philadelphia was home to a half-million people. The city strongly supported the abolitionist movement and was a major industrial supplier for the Union during the Civil War. The first international fair, the Centennial Exhibition, was held in Philadelphia in 1876, commemorating the nation's 100th birthday. The city was also a center of attention on July 4, 1976, during the country's Bicentennial celebration.

Today, with more than 1.4 million residents, Philadelphia is Pennsylvania's largest city and the fifth largest city in the United States. Greater Philadelphia, which includes the City of Philadelphia and neighboring counties in Pennsylvania and New Jersey, is one of the top commercial, industrial, financial, and educational centers in the nation.

Population

1990 Census 1,585,577
1998 Estimate............................ 1,436,287
% Change .... -9.4
2005 Projection 1,491,116*

Racial/Ethnic Breakdown

White.................................... 53.5%
Black 39.8%
Other..................................... 6.7%
Hispanic Origin (may be of any race) 5.6%

Age Breakdown

Under 5 years.............................. 7.3%
5 to 17.................................. 16.6%
18 to 20................................... 4.8%
21 to 24................................... 6.8%
25 to 34.................................. 17.5%
35 to 44.................................. 13.5%
45 to 54................................... 9.3%
55 to 64................................... 9.0%
65 to 74................................... 8.7%
75+ years 6.5%
Median Age.................................33.2

Gender Breakdown

Male..................................... 46.5%
Female................................... 53.5%

** Information given is for Philadelphia County.*

Government

Type of Government: Mayor-Council

Free Library of Philadelphia
1901 Vine St
Philadelphia, PA 19103
Phone: 215-686-5322
Fax: 215-563-3628

Philadelphia City Council
494 City Hall
Philadelphia, PA 19107
Phone: 215-686-3412
Fax: 215-563-3162

Philadelphia City Hall
City Hall
Philadelphia, PA 19107
Phone: 215-686-1776

Philadelphia City Planning Commission
1515 Arch St 13th Fl
Philadelphia, PA 19102
Phone: 215-683-4615
Fax: 215-683-4630

Philadelphia Commerce Dept
1515 Arch St 12th Fl
Philadelphia, PA 19102
Phone: 215-683-2000
Fax: 215-683-2097

Philadelphia Finance Dept
1401 JFK Blvd Rm 1330
Philadelphia, PA 19102
Phone: 215-686-6140
Fax: 215-568-1947

Philadelphia Fire Dept
240 Spring Garden St
Philadelphia, PA 19123
Phone: 215-686-1300
Fax: 215-922-3952

Philadelphia Law Dept
1515 Arch St 15th Fl
Philadelphia, PA 19102
Phone: 215-683-5000
Fax: 215-683-5069

Philadelphia Licenses & Inspections Dept
1401 JFK Blvd 11th Fl
Philadelphia, PA 19102
Phone: 215-686-2400
Fax: 215-686-2500

Philadelphia Mayor
215 City Hall
Philadelphia, PA 19107
Phone: 215-686-2181
Fax: 215-686-2180

Philadelphia Personnel Dept
1401 JFK Blvd 15th Fl
Philadelphia, PA 19102
Phone: 215-686-0880
Fax: 215-686-2317

Philadelphia Police Dept
700 Race St Rm 311
Philadelphia, PA 19106
Phone: 215-686-3128

Philadelphia Public Health Dept
1101 Market St 8th Fl
Philadelphia, PA 19103
Phone: 215-686-5000
Fax: 215-685-5398

Philadelphia Recreation Dept
1515 Arch St 10th Fl
Philadelphia, PA 19102
Phone: 215-683-3600
Fax: 215-683-3599

Philadelphia Water Dept
1101 Market St 5th Fl
Philadelphia, PA 19107
Phone: 215-592-6103
Fax: 215-685-4915

Important Phone Numbers

AAA.......................................215-864-5000
Airport Medical Emergencies.....................215-937-3111
American Express Travel 215-592-9211
Dental Referral.................................800-917-6453
Driver's License Information.....................717-391-6190
Emergency 911
Greater Philadelphia Assn of Realtors 215-925-2607
HotelDocs 800-468-3537
Medical Referral................................215-563-5343
Pennsylvania Dept of Revenue....................215-560-2056
Philadelphia Revenue Dept........................215-686-6600
Poison Control Center 215-386-2100
Time...610-846-1212
Travelers Aid Society............................215-523-7580
Vehicle Registration Information 717-391-6190
Voter Registration Information....................215-686-1500
Weather 610-936-1212

Information Sources

Better Business Bureau Serving Eastern Pennsylvania
1608 Walnut St Suite 600
Philadelphia, PA 19103
www.easternpa.bbb.org
Phone: 215-985-9313
Fax: 215-893-9312

Greater Philadelphia Chamber of Commerce
200 S Broad St Suite 700
Philadelphia, PA 19102
www.gpcc.com
Phone: 215-545-1234
Fax: 215-790-3600

Pennsylvania Convention Center
1101 Arch St
Philadelphia, PA 19107
www.paconvention.com
Phone: 215-418-4700
Fax: 215-418-4747
TF: 800-428-9000

Philadelphia Convention & Visitors Bureau
1515 Market St Suite 2020
Philadelphia, PA 19102
www.libertynet.org/phila-visitor
Phone: 215-636-3300
Fax: 215-636-3327
TF: 800-537-7676

Philadelphia County
City Hall
Philadelphia, PA 19107
Phone: 215-686-1776

Online Resources

4Philadelphia.com
www.4philadelphia.com

About.com Guide to Philadelphia
philadelphia.about.com/local/midlanticus/philadelphia

Access America Philadelphia
www.accessamer.com/philadelphia/

Anthill City Guide Philadelphia
www.anthill.com/city.asp?city=philadelphia

Area Guide Philadelphia
philadelphia.areaguides.net

Boulevards Philadelphia
www.philadelphia.com

Bradmans.com Philadelphia
www.bradmans.com/scripts/display_city.cgi?city=241

City Knowledge Philadelphia
www.cityknowledge.com/pa_philadelphia.htm

CitySearch Philadelphia
philadelphia.citysearch.com

CityTravelGuide.com Philadelphia
www.citytravelguide.com/philadelphia.htm

CuisineNet Philadelphia
www.cuisinenet.com/restaurant/philadelphia/

DigitalCity Philadelphia
www.digitalcity.com/philadelphia/

Essential Guide to Philadelphia
www.ego.net/us/pa/phl/index.htm

Excite.com Philadelphia City Guide
www.excite.com/travel/countries/united_states/pennsylvania/philadelphia

InPhiladelphia.com
www.inphiladelphia.com

Philadelphia City Pages
philadelphia.thelinks.com

Philadelphia City Paper
www.citypaper.net

Philadelphia CityWomen
www.citywomen.com/philwomen.htm

Philadelphia Interactive
www.nealcomm.com/pi/index.htm

Philadelphia Liberty Net
www.libertynet.org

Philadelphia Night Life
www.phillynightlife.com

Philadelphia Online
www.philly.com

Philadelphia's Center City District
www.centercityphila.org/

Philanet.com
philanet.com

Philly Web
www.phillyweb.com/

Phillyfriend.com
www.phillyfriend.com

Rough Guide Travel Philadelphia
travel.roughguides.com/content/332/

Savvy Diner Guide to Philadelphia Restaurants
www.savvydiner.com/philadelphia/

Time Out Philadelphia
www.timeout.com/philadelphia/

Virtual Philly
www.virtualphilly.com/

Area Communities

Communities in the Greater Philadelphia region (which includes Bucks, Chester, Delaware, Montgomery, and Philadelphia counties in Pennsylvania; and Burlington, Camden, and Gloucester counties in New Jersey) with populations of 30,000 or more include:

Abington Township
1176 Old York Rd
Abington, PA 19001
Phone: 215-884-5000
Fax: 215-884-8271

Bensalem Township
2400 Byberry Rd
Bensalem, PA 19020
Phone: 215-633-3600
Fax: 215-633-3609

Camden
PO Box 95120
Camden, NJ 08101
Phone: 856-757-7000
Fax: 856-757-7220

Cheltenham Township
8230 Old York Rd
Elkins Park, PA 19027
Phone: 215-887-1000
Fax: 215-887-1561

Cherry Hill Township
820 Mercer St
Cherry Hill, NJ 08002
Phone: 856-665-6500
Fax: 856-488-7854

Chester
36 E 5th St
Chester, PA 19013
Phone: 610-447-7700
Fax: 610-447-7706

Evesham Township
984 Tuckerton Rd
Marlton, NJ 08053
Phone: 856-983-2900
Fax: 856-985-3695

Falls Township
188 Lincoln Hwy Suite 100
Fairless Hills, PA 19030
Phone: 215-949-9000
Fax: 215-949-9013

Gloucester Township
1261 Chews Landing-Clementon Rd
Laurel Springs, NJ 08021
Phone: 856-228-4000
Fax: 856-374-3527

Haverford Township
2325 Darby Rd
Havertown, PA 19083
Phone: 610-446-9403
Fax: 610-446-3930

Horsham Township
1025 Horsham Rd
Horsham, PA 19044
Phone: 215-643-3131
Fax: 215-643-0448

Lower Makefield Township
1100 Edgewood Rd
Yardley, PA 19067
Phone: 215-493-3646
Fax: 215-493-3053

Lower Merion Township
75 E Lancaster Ave
Ardmore, PA 19003
Phone: 610-649-4000
Fax: 610-645-6331

Middletown Township
2140 Trenton Rd
Levittown, PA 19056
Phone: 215-943-0300
Fax: 215-943-9937

Mount Laurel Township
100 Mount Laurel Rd
Mount Laurel, NJ 08054
Phone: 856-234-0001
Fax: 856-234-8621

Northampton Township
55 Township Rd
Richboro, PA 18954
Phone: 215-357-6800
Fax: 215-357-1251

Pemberton Township
500 Pemberton-Browns Mills Rd
Pemberton, NJ 08068
Phone: 609-894-8201
Fax: 609-894-2703

Pennsauken Township
5605 N Crescent Blvd
Pennsauken, NJ 08110
Phone: 856-665-1000
Fax: 856-665-7602

Ridley Township
100 E Macdade Blvd
Ridley, PA 19033
Phone: 610-534-4800
Fax: 610-534-2545

Upper Darby Township
100 Garrett Rd
Upper Darby, PA 19082
Phone: 610-352-4100
Fax: 610-734-7709

Warminster Township
401 Henry Ave
Warminster, PA 18976
Phone: 215-443-5414
Fax: 215-443-2761

Washington Township
PO Box 1106
Turnersville, NJ 08012
Phone: 856-589-0696
Fax: 856-589-9177

Willingboro Township
1 Salem Rd
Willingboro, NJ 08046
Phone: 609-877-2200
Fax: 609-835-0782

Winslow Township
125 S Rte 73
Braddock, NJ 08037
Phone: 609-567-0700
Fax: 609-567-0500

Economy

Greater Philadelphia's economic base ranges from higher education to high finance. Major U.S. corporations headquartered in Philadelphia include Cigna, Comcast, and ARAMARK. The Philadelphia region has the nation's second largest concentration of healthcare resources, including more than 120 hospitals and more than 125 pharmaceutical, biotechnology and medical technology companies. Home to more than 300 research and development establishments, Greater Philadelphia also has one of the largest concentrations of research institutions in the United States. Government also plays a primary role in Philadelphia's economy - the U.S. Government is the county's single largest employer and Pennsylvania State Government ranks number 10 on Philadelphia County's top employers list.

Unemployment Rate 5.7%*
Per Capita Income.......................... $24,769*
Median Family Income...................... $30,140

** Information given is for Philadelphia County.*

Principal Industries & Number of Wage Earners

Philadelphia County - 1998

Industry	Wage Earners
Agriculture	837
Construction	11,503
Finance, Insurance, & Real Estate	51,740
Manufacturing	56,868
Retail Trade	91,355
Services	275,661
Transportation & Utilities	46,378
Wholesale Trade	22,774

Major Employers

Acme Markets Inc
75 Valley Stream Pkwy
Malvern, PA 19355
www.acmemarkets.com
Phone: 610-889-4000
Fax: 610-889-3039
TF: 800-767-2312

Albert Einstein Healthcare Network
5501 Old York Rd
Philadelphia, PA 19141
www.einstein.edu
Phone: 215-456-7890
Fax: 215-456-6424

ARAMARK Corp
1101 Market St Aramark Tower
Philadelphia, PA 19107
www.aramark.com
Phone: 215-238-3000
Fax: 215-238-3333
TF: 800-999-8989

Cardone Industries Inc
5501 Whitaker Ave
Philadelphia, PA 19124
E-mail: cardone@cardoneonline.com
www.cardoneonline.com
Phone: 215-912-3000
Fax: 215-912-3700

Children's Hospital of Philadelphia
34th St & Civic Center Blvd
Philadelphia, PA 19104
www.chop.edu
Phone: 215-590-1000
Fax: 215-590-1413

First Union
123 S Broad St
Philadelphia, PA 19109
www.firstunion.com
Phone: 215-985-6000
Fax: 215-670-6719

Independence Blue Cross
1901 Market St
Philadelphia, PA 19103
www.ibx.com
Phone: 215-241-2400
Fax: 215-241-3237

Pennsylvania Hospital
800 Spruce St
Philadelphia, PA 19107
www.pahosp.com
Phone: 215-829-3000
Fax: 215-829-6363

Philadelphia City Hall
City Hall
Philadelphia, PA 19107
www.phila.gov
Phone: 215-686-1776

Philadelphia Newspapers Inc
400 N Broad St
Philadelphia, PA 19130
Phone: 215-854-2000
Fax: 215-854-2991

School District of Philadelphia
21st St & Benjamin Franklin Pkwy
Philadelphia, PA 19103
www.phila.k12.pa.us
Phone: 215-299-2940
Fax: 215-299-8831

Southeastern Pennsylvania Transportation Authority
1234 Market St
Philadelphia, PA 19107
www.septa.org
Phone: 215-580-4000
Fax: 215-580-3655

Temple University
1801 N Broad St
Philadelphia, PA 19122
www.temple.edu
Phone: 215-204-7000
Fax: 215-204-5694

Tenet Healthsystem Philadelphia Inc
1500 Market St Centre Sq W Tower Mail Rm 24th Fl
Philadelphia, PA 19102
Phone: 215-255-7401
Fax: 215-832-2092

Thomas Jefferson University
1025 Walnut St
Philadelphia, PA 19107
www.tju.edu
Phone: 215-955-6000
Fax: 215-503-7241
TF: 800-247-6933

University of Pennsylvania
3451 Walnut St
Philadelphia, PA 19104
E-mail: regist@pobox.upenn.edu
www.upenn.edu
Phone: 215-898-5000
Fax: 215-898-9670

US Airways Inc
2345 Crystal Dr Crystal Pk 4
Arlington, VA 22227
www.usairways.com
Phone: 703-872-7000
Fax: 703-294-5097
TF: 800-428-4322

Quality of Living Indicators

Total Crime Index 104,658
(rates per 100,000 inhabitants)

Violent Crime
Murder/manslaughter 292
Forcible rape 934
Robbery 11,104
Aggravated assault 10,701

Property Crime
Burglary 14,042
Larceny theft 49,874
Motor vehicle theft 17,711

Cost of Living Index 116.9
(national average = 100)

Median Home Price $124,800

Education

Public Schools

School District of Philadelphia
21st St & Benjamin Franklin Pkwy
Philadelphia, PA 19103
www.phila.k12.pa.us
Phone: 215-299-2940
Fax: 215-299-8831

Number of Schools
Elementary 176
Middle 42
High 39
Special 6

Student/Teacher Ratio
All Grades 19.4:1

Private Schools

Number of Schools (all grades) .... 45+

Colleges & Universities

American College
270 S Bryn Mawr Ave
Bryn Mawr, PA 19010
www.amercoll.edu
Phone: 610-526-1000
Fax: 610-526-1310

Antonelli Institute
300 Montgomery Ave
Erdenheim, PA 19038
E-mail: admissions@antonelli.org
www.antonelli.org
Phone: 215-836-2222
Fax: 215-836-2794
TF: 800-722-7871

Art Institute of Philadelphia
1622 Chestnut St
Philadelphia, PA 19103
www.aii.edu
Phone: 215-567-7080
Fax: 215-246-3339
TF: 800-275-2474

Beaver College
450 S Easton Rd
Glenside, PA 19038
www.beaver.edu
Phone: 215-572-2900
Fax: 215-572-4049
TF: 888-232-8373

Berean Institute
1901 W Girard Ave
Philadelphia, PA 19130
Phone: 215-763-4833
Fax: 215-236-6011

Bryn Athyn College of the New Church
PO Box 717
Bryn Athyn, PA 19009
www.newchurch.org
Phone: 215-938-2543
Fax: 215-938-2658

Bryn Mawr College
101 N Merion Ave
Bryn Mawr, PA 19010
E-mail: agiardin@brynmawr.edu
www.brynmawr.edu
Phone: 610-526-5000
Fax: 610-526-7471

Cabrini College
610 King of Prussia Rd
Radnor, PA 19087
E-mail: admit@cabrini.edu
www.cabrini.edu
Phone: 610-902-8100
Fax: 610-902-8508
TF: 800-848-1003

Chestnut Hill College
9601 Germantown Ave
Philadelphia, PA 19118
www.chc.edu
Phone: 215-248-7000
Fax: 215-248-7082
TF: 800-248-0052

Cheyney University of Pennsylvania
Cheyney, PA 19319
www.cheyney.edu
Phone: 610-399-2000
Fax: 610-399-2099
TF: 800-243-9639

CHI Institute
2641 Westchester Pike
Broomall, PA 19008
Phone: 610-353-7630
Fax: 610-359-1370

Community College of Philadelphia
1700 Spring Garden St
Philadelphia, PA 19130
www.ccp.cc.pa.us
Phone: 215-751-8000
Fax: 215-751-8001

Curtis Institute of Music
1726 Locust St
Philadelphia, PA 19103
www.curtis.edu
Phone: 215-893-5252
Fax: 215-893-9065

Delaware County Community College
901 S Media Line Rd
Media, PA 19063
www.dccc.edu
Phone: 610-359-5000
Fax: 610-359-5343

Drexel University
3141 Chestnut St
Philadelphia, PA 19104
E-mail: admissions@post.drexel.edu
www.drexel.edu
Phone: 215-895-2000
Fax: 215-895-5939
TF: 800-237-3935

Eastern College
1300 Eagle Rd
Saint Davids, PA 19087
E-mail: ugadm@eastern.edu
www.eastern.edu
Phone: 610-341-5800
Fax: 610-341-1723

Gwynedd-Mercy College
PO Box 901
Gwynedd Valley, PA 19437
www.gmc.edu
Phone: 215-646-7300
Fax: 215-641-5556
TF: 800-342-5462

Hahnemann University of the Health Sciences
245 N 15th St
Philadelphia, PA 19102
www.mcphu.edu
Phone: 215-762-8288
Fax: 215-762-6194

Harcum College
750 Montgomery Ave
Bryn Mawr, PA 19010
E-mail: enroll@harcum.edu
www.harcum.edu
Phone: 610-525-4100
Fax: 610-526-6147
TF: 800-345-2600

Haverford College
370 W Lancaster Ave
Haverford, PA 19041
www.haverford.edu
Phone: 610-896-1000
Fax: 610-896-1224

Holy Family College
Grant & Frankford Aves
Philadelphia, PA 19114
www.hfc.edu
Phone: 215-637-7700
Fax: 215-281-1022

Hussian School of Art
1118 Market St
Philadelphia, PA 19107
www.hussianart.edu
Phone: 215-981-0900
Fax: 215-864-9115

Immaculata College
1145 King Rd
Immaculata, PA 19345
www.immaculata.edu
Phone: 610-647-4400
Fax: 610-251-1668
TF: 888-777-2780

La Salle University
1900 W Olney Ave
Philadelphia, PA 19141
E-mail: webadmin@lasalle.edu
www.lasalle.edu
Phone: 215-951-1000
Fax: 215-951-1656

Lincoln Technical Institute
9191 Torresdale Ave
Philadelphia, PA 19136
Phone: 215-335-0800
Fax: 215-335-1443

Manor Junior College
700 Fox Chase Rd
Jenkintown, PA 19046
manor.edu
Phone: 215-885-2360
Fax: 215-576-6564

Montgomery County Community College Central Campus
340 DeKalb Pike
Blue Bell, PA 19422
www.mc3.edu
Phone: 215-641-6300
Fax: 215-641-6516

Moore College of Art & Design
20th & Race Sts
Philadelphia, PA 19103
www.moore.edu
Phone: 215-568-4515
Fax: 215-568-8017
TF: 800-523-2025

Peirce College
1420 Pine St
Philadelphia, PA 19102
E-mail: peirce@libertynet.org
www.peirce.edu/index.html
Phone: 215-545-6400
Fax: 215-546-5996
TF: 888-467-3472

Pennco Tech
3815 Otter St
Bristol, PA 19007
E-mail: admissions@penncotech.com
www.penncotech.com
Phone: 215-824-3200
Fax: 215-785-1945
TF: 800-579-9399

Pennsylvania Institute of Technology
800 Manchester Ave
Media, PA 19063
E-mail: info@pit.edu
www.pit.edu
Phone: 610-565-7900
Fax: 610-892-1510
TF: 800-422-0025

Pennsylvania State University Abington Campus
1600 Woodland Rd
Abington, PA 19001
www.abington.psu.edu
Phone: 215-881-7300
Fax: 215-881-7317

Philadelphia College of Bible
200 Manor Ave
Langhorne, PA 19047
www.pcb.edu
Phone: 215-752-5800
Fax: 215-702-4248
TF: 800-366-0049

Philadelphia College of Textiles & Science
4201 Henry Ave
Philadelphia, PA 19144
E-mail: admissions@philacol.edu
www.philacol.edu
Phone: 215-951-2700
Fax: 215-951-2907
TF: 800-951-7287

Rosemont College
1400 Montgomery Ave
Rosemont, PA 19010
www.rosemont.edu
Phone: 610-527-0200
Fax: 610-527-0341
TF: 800-331-0708

Rutgers The State University of New Jersey Camden Campus
311 N 5th St
Camden, NJ 08102
E-mail: camden@asb-ugadm.rutgers.edu
camden-www.rutgers.edu
Phone: 856-225-1766
Fax: 856-225-6495

Saint Joseph's University
5600 City Ave
Philadelphia, PA 19131
www.sju.edu
Phone: 610-660-1000
Fax: 610-660-1314

Swarthmore College
500 College Ave
Swarthmore, PA 19081
www.swarthmore.edu
Phone: 610-328-8000
Fax: 610-328-8673
TF: 800-667-3110

Temple University
1801 N Broad St
Philadelphia, PA 19122
www.temple.edu
Phone: 215-204-7000
Fax: 215-204-5694

Thomas Jefferson University
1025 Walnut St
Philadelphia, PA 19107
www.tju.edu
Phone: 215-955-6000
Fax: 215-503-7241
TF: 800-247-6933

University of Pennsylvania
3451 Walnut St
Philadelphia, PA 19104
E-mail: regist@pobox.upenn.edu
www.upenn.edu
Phone: 215-898-5000
Fax: 215-898-9670

University of the Arts
320 S Broad St
Philadelphia, PA 19102
E-mail: emuarts@netaxs.com
www.uarts.edu
Phone: 215-717-6000
Fax: 215-717-6045
TF: 800-616-2787

University of the Sciences
600 S 43rd St
Philadelphia, PA 19104
www.pcps.edu
Phone: 215-596-8800
Fax: 215-895-1100

Valley Forge Military Academy & College
1001 Eagle Rd
Wayne, PA 19087
www.vfmac.edu
Phone: 610-989-1200
Fax: 610-688-1545
TF: 800-234-8362

Villanova University
800 Lancaster Ave
Villanova, PA 19085
www.villanova.edu
Phone: 610-519-4500
Fax: 610-519-6450
TF: 800-338-7927

Widener University
1 University Pl
Chester, PA 19013
www.widener.edu
Phone: 610-499-4000
Fax: 610-499-4676

Williamson Free School of Mechanical Trades
106 S New Middletown Rd
Media, PA 19063
E-mail: wiltech@libertynet.org
www.libertynet.org/wiltech
Phone: 610-566-1776
Fax: 610-566-6502

Hospitals

Albert Einstein Medical Center
5501 Old York Rd
Philadelphia, PA 19141
www.einstein.edu/aehn/aemed_center.html
Phone: 215-456-7010
Fax: 215-456-6199

Chestnut Hill Hospital
8835 Germantown Ave
Philadelphia, PA 19118
www.chh.org/hospital.html
Phone: 215-248-8200
Fax: 215-248-8053

Children's Hospital of Philadelphia
34th St & Civic Center Blvd
Philadelphia, PA 19104
www.chop.edu
Phone: 215-590-1000
Fax: 215-590-1413

City Avenue Hospital
4150 City Avenue
Philadelphia, PA 19131
Phone: 215-871-1000
Fax: 215-871-1230

Episcopal Hospital
100 E Lehigh Ave
Philadelphia, PA 19125
Phone: 215-427-7000
Fax: 215-427-3191

Frankford Hospital of the City of Philadelphia
Knights & Red Lion Rds
Philadelphia, PA 19114
Phone: 215-612-4000
Fax: 215-612-4942

Graduate Hospital
1800 Lombard St
Philadelphia, PA 19146
Phone: 215-893-2000
Fax: 215-893-7205

Hahnemann University Hospital Center City
Broad & Vine Sts
Philadelphia, PA 19102
Phone: 215-762-7000
Fax: 215-762-3895

Hospital Health System University of Pennsylvania
3400 Spruce St
Philadelphia, PA 19104
www.med.upenn.edu
Phone: 215-662-4000
Fax: 215-662-2599

Jeanes Hospital
7600 Central Ave
Philadelphia, PA 19111
www.jeanes.com
Phone: 215-728-2000
Fax: 215-728-2118

Methodist Hospital
2301 S Broad St
Philadelphia, PA 19148
Phone: 215-952-9000
Fax: 215-952-9933

Nazareth Hospital
2601 Holme Ave
Philadelphia, PA 19152
Phone: 215-335-6000
Fax: 215-335-7620

Neumann Medical Center
1741 Frankford Ave
Philadelphia, PA 19125
Phone: 215-291-2000
Fax: 215-291-2028

North Philadelphia Health Systems Saint Joseph Hospital
16th St at Girard Ave
Philadelphia, PA 19130
Phone: 215-787-9000
Fax: 215-787-9558

Northeastern Hospital of Philadelphia
2301 E Allegheny Ave
Philadelphia, PA 19134
Phone: 215-291-3000
Fax: 215-291-3611

Parkview Hospital
1331 E Wyoming Ave
Philadelphia, PA 19124
Phone: 215-537-7400
Fax: 215-537-7680

Pennsylvania Hospital
800 Spruce St
Philadelphia, PA 19107
www.pahosp.com
Phone: 215-829-3000
Fax: 215-829-6363

Presbyterian Medical Center of Philadelphia
39th & Market Sts
Philadelphia, PA 19104
Phone: 215-662-8000
Fax: 215-662-9850

Roxborough Memorial Hospital
5800 Ridge Ave
Philadelphia, PA 19128
Phone: 215-483-9900
Fax: 215-487-4546

Saint Agnes Medical Center
1900 S Broad St
Philadelphia, PA 19145
Phone: 215-339-4100
Fax: 215-339-0482

Saint Christopher's Hospital for Children
Erie Ave & Front St
Philadelphia, PA 19134
Phone: 215-427-5000
Fax: 215-427-4444

Shriners Hospitals for Children Philadelphia Unit
3551 N Broad St
Philadelphia, PA 19140
Phone: 215-430-4000
Fax: 215-430-4079
TF: 800-281-4050
www.shrinershq.org/Hospitals/Directory/philadelphia.html

Temple University Hospital
3401 N Broad St
Philadelphia, PA 19140
Phone: 215-707-2000
Fax: 215-707-3261
www.health.temple.edu/tuh

Thomas Jefferson University Hospital
111 S 11th St
Philadelphia, PA 19107
Phone: 215-955-6000
Fax: 215-955-5207
www.jeffersonhealth.org/tjuh

Veterans Affairs Medical Center
University & Woodland Aves
Philadelphia, PA 19104
Phone: 215-823-5800
Fax: 215-823-5109
TF: 800-949-1001

Transportation

Airport(s)

Philadelphia International Airport (PHL)
7 miles SW of downtown (approx 30 minutes) 215-937-6937

Mass Transit

Philly Phlash
$1.50 Base fare 215-474-5274
Port Authority Transit
$.85 Base fare 215-922-4600
RiverLink Ferry Service
$5 Base fare 215-925-5465
SEPTA
$1.60 Base fare 215-580-7800

Rail/Bus

30th Street Amtrak Station
30th & Market Sts
Philadelphia, PA 19104
Phone: 215-349-2135
TF: 800-872-7245

Greyhound Bus Station
1001 Filbert St
Philadelphia, PA 19107
Phone: 215-931-4075
TF: 800-231-2222

Utilities

Electricity
PECO Energy Co. 215-841-4000
www.peco.com

Gas
PECO Energy Co. 215-841-4000
www.peco.com

Water
Philadelphia Water Dept 215-685-6121

Garbage Collection/Recycling
Philadelphia Sanitation Dept 215-686-5560

Telecommunications

Telephone
Verizon Communications 215-571-7050
www.verizon.com

Cable Television
Comcast Digital Cable 215-673-6600
Time Warner Cable 215-581-6100
www.timewarner.com

Internet Service Providers (ISPs)
Comcast Commercial Online 888-638-4338
www.comcastwork.com
Comcast Online Communications 215-981-8531
www.comcastonline.com
Coolnet Internet Services Inc. 215-330-3200
www.coolnet.net
DirectWeb Inc 856-787-4300
www.directweb.com
Health Sciences Libraries Consortium 215-222-1532
www.hslc.org
Internet-Gateway 856-983-0066
www.net-gate.com
InterStat Inc 856-234-2900
www.interstat.net
Southern New Jersey Internet Providers Inc 856-662-8640
www.snip.net
Verio Philadelphia 215-682-0100
home.verio.net/local/frontpage.cfm?AirportCode=PHL

Banks

Beneficial Mutual Savings Bank
1200 Chestnut St
Philadelphia, PA 19107
E-mail: bsb@libertynet.org
www.beneficialsavings.com
Phone: 215-864-6000
Fax: 215-864-6018
TF: 888-784-8490

Commonwealth Bank
6537 Castor Ave
Philadelphia, PA 19149
Phone: 215-289-9696
Fax: 215-289-0249

First Bank of Philadelphia
1632 Walnut St
Philadelphia, PA 19103
Phone: 215-790-9000
Fax: 215-790-5208

First Union Bank
123 S Broad St
Philadelphia, PA 19109
www.firstunion.com
Phone: 215-985-6000
Fax: 215-670-6719

Firstrust Savings Bank
1931 Cottman Ave
Philadelphia, PA 19111
Phone: 215-722-2000
Fax: 215-725-1614
TF: 800-220-2265

Jefferson Bank
31 S 18th St
Philadelphia, PA 19103
Phone: 215-564-5040

PNC Bank NA
4th & Market Sts
Philadelphia, PA 19106
Phone: 215-351-4324
Fax: 215-351-4328

Sovereign Bank
8623 Germantown Ave
Philadelphia, PA 19119
Phone: 215-247-7660
Fax: 215-247-3839

Summit Bank
9501 Bustleton Ave
Philadelphia, PA 19115
Phone: 215-464-6431
Fax: 215-464-6755

United Bank of Philadelphia
714 Market St
Philadelphia, PA 19106
Phone: 215-829-2265
Fax: 215-829-2269

Shopping

Chestnut Hill Shopping District
7900-8700 Germantown Ave
Philadelphia, PA 19118
Phone: 215-247-6696
Fax: 215-247-5680

Court & Plaza at King of Prussia
160 N Gulph Rd
King of Prussia, PA 19406
Phone: 610-265-5727

Franklin Mills
1455 Franklin Mills Cir
Philadelphia, PA 19114
www.franklin-mills-mall.com
Phone: 215-632-1500
Fax: 215-632-7888
TF: 800-336-6255

Gallery at Market East
9th & Market Sts
Philadelphia, PA 19107
Phone: 215-925-7162
Fax: 215-440-0116

Jewelers' Row
Sansom St-betw 9th & 7th Sts
Philadelphia, PA 19107
Phone: 215-636-1666

King of Prussia Plaza
1600 N Gulf Rd
King of Prussia, PA 19406
www.shopking.com
Phone: 610-768-6420
Fax: 610-265-1640

Market Place East
701 Market St
Philadelphia, PA 19106
Phone: 215-592-8905

Oxford Valley Mall
2300 E Lincoln Hwy
Langhorne, PA 19047
E-mail: info@oxfordvalleymall.com
www.oxfordvalleymall.com
Phone: 215-752-0222
Fax: 215-752-2869

Rittenhouse Row
1830 Rittenhouse Sq
Philadelphia, PA 19103
Phone: 215-735-4899

Roosevelt Mall
2329 Cottman Ave
Philadelphia, PA 19149
Phone: 215-331-2000
Fax: 215-331-5771

Shops at Liberty Place
1625 Chestnut St
Philadelphia, PA 19103
Phone: 215-851-9055
Fax: 215-851-9154

Shops at The Bellevue
Broad & Walnut Sts
Philadelphia, PA 19102
Phone: 215-875-8350

South Street Antiques Market
615 S 6th St
Philadelphia, PA 19147
Phone: 215-592-0256

South Street Shopping District
South St-betw Front & 8th Sts
Philadelphia, PA 19147
Phone: 215-636-1666

Media

Newspapers and Magazines

Bucks County Tribune
390 Easton Rd
Horsham, PA 19044
Phone: 215-675-6600

Central Record
PO Box 1027
Medford, NJ 08055
Phone: 609-654-5000
Fax: 609-654-8237

Courier Post/This Week
PO Box 5300
Cherry Hill, NJ 08034
Phone: 856-663-4200
Fax: 856-663-7664

Germantown Courier
7169 Germantown Ave
Philadelphia, PA 19119
Phone: 215-248-7580
Fax: 215-848-9160

Leader The
2385 W Cheltenham Ave Suite 182
Philadelphia, PA 19150
Phone: 215-885-4111
Fax: 215-885-0226

Main Line Life
110 Ardmore Ave
Ardmore, PA 19003
Phone: 610-896-9555
Fax: 610-896-9560

Mount Airy Times Express
7169 Germantown Ave
Philadelphia, PA 19119
Phone: 215-248-7580
Fax: 215-248-7585

News of Delaware County
Manoa Shopping Ctr
Havertown, PA 19083
Phone: 610-446-8700
Fax: 610-446-1883

Northeast Breeze
9999 Gantry Rd
Philadelphia, PA 19115
Phone: 215-969-5100
Fax: 215-969-7650

Philadelphia Business Journal
400 Market St Suite 300
Philadelphia, PA 19106
E-mail: philadelphia@amcity.com.
www.amcity.com/philadelphia/index.html
Phone: 215-238-1450
Fax: 215-238-1466

Philadelphia City Paper
123 Chestnut St 3rd Fl
Philadelphia, PA 19106
E-mail: adinfo@citypaper.net
www.citypaper.net
Phone: 215-735-8444
Fax: 215-599-0634

Philadelphia Daily News*
PO Box 7788
Philadelphia, PA 19101
E-mail: dailynews.opinion@phillynews.com
www.phillynews.com/pdn
Phone: 215-854-2000
Fax: 215-854-5910

Philadelphia Inquirer*
PO Box 8263
Philadelphia, PA 19101
E-mail: Inquirer.opinion@phillynews.com
www.phillynews.com/inq
Phone: 215-854-2000
Fax: 215-854-5099

Philadelphia Magazine
1818 Market St
Philadelphia, PA 19103
E-mail: mail@phillymag.com
www.phillymag.com
Phone: 215-564-7700
Fax: 215-656-3500
TF: 800-777-1003

Philadelphia Weekly
1701 Walnut St
Philadelphia, PA 19103
E-mail: mail@philadelphiaweekly.com
www.philadelphiaweekly.com
Phone: 215-563-7400
Fax: 215-563-6799

Progress of Montgomery County
390 Easton Rd
Horsham, PA 19044
Phone: 215-675-8250

Review The
6220 Ridge Ave
Philadelphia, PA 19128
www.ausinc.com/ing
Phone: 215-483-7300
Fax: 215-483-2073

Suburban Advertiser
PO Box 409
Wayne, PA 19087
www.waynesuburban.com/jrc-html/papers/localnews_p60.html
Phone: 610-688-3000
Fax: 610-964-1346

Where Philadelphia Magazine
301 S 19th St Suite 1-C
Philadelphia, PA 19103
Phone: 215-893-5100
Fax: 215-893-5105

**Indicates major daily newspapers*

Television

KYW-TV Ch 3 (CBS)
101 S Independence Mall E
Philadelphia, PA 19106
www.kyw.com
Phone: 215-238-4700
Fax: 215-238-4783
TF: 800-238-4700

WCAU-TV Ch 10 (NBC)
10 Monument Rd
Bala Cynwyd, PA 19004
www.nbc10.com
Phone: 610-668-5510
Fax: 610-668-3700

WGTW-TV Ch 48 (Ind)
3900 Main St
Philadelphia, PA 19127
Phone: 215-930-0482
Fax: 215-930-0496

WHYY-TV Ch 12 (PBS)
150 N 6th St
Philadelphia, PA 19106
E-mail: talkback@whyy.org
whyy.org
Phone: 215-351-1200
Fax: 215-351-0398

WMGM-TV Ch 40 (NBC)
1601 New Rd
Linwood, NJ 08221
E-mail: wmgmtv@acy.digex.net
www.wmgmtv.com
Phone: 609-927-4440
Fax: 609-927-7014

WPHL-TV Ch 17 (WB)
5001 Wynnefield Ave
Philadelphia, PA 19131
E-mail: wb17philly@aol.com
www.wb17.com
Phone: 215-878-1700
Fax: 215-879-7682

WPPX-TV Ch 61 (PAX)
520 N Columbus Blvd
Philadelphia, PA 19123
www.pax.net/wppx
Phone: 215-923-2661
Fax: 215-923-2677

WPSG-TV Ch 57 (UPN)
420 N 20th St
Philadelphia, PA 19130
E-mail: upn57@paramount.com
www.paramountstations.com/WPSG
Phone: 215-563-5757
Fax: 215-563-5786

WPVI-TV Ch 6 (ABC)
4100 City Line Ave
Philadelphia, PA 19131
abcnews.go.com/local/wpvi
Phone: 215-878-9700
Fax: 215-581-4530

WTVE-TV Ch 51 (Tele)
1729 N 11th St
Reading, PA 19604
Phone: 610-921-9181
Fax: 610-921-9139
TF: 800-458-7659

WTXF-TV Ch 29 (Fox)
330 Market St
Philadelphia, PA 19106
www.foxphiladelphia.com
Phone: 215-925-2929
Fax: 215-925-2420

WWAC-TV Ch 53 (Ind)
19 S New York Ave
Atlantic City, NJ 08401
Phone: 609-344-5030
Fax: 609-347-4758

Radio

KYW-AM 1060 kHz (N/T)
101 S Independence Mall E
Philadelphia, PA 19106
www.kyw1060.com
Phone: 215-238-4700
Fax: 215-238-4657

WBEB-FM 101.1 MHz (AC)
10 Presidential Blvd
Bala Cynwyd, PA 19004
www.b101radio.com
Phone: 610-667-8400
Fax: 610-667-6795

WDAS-AM 1480 kHz (Rel)
23 W City Line Ave
Bala Cynwyd, PA 19004
Phone: 610-617-8500
Fax: 610-617-2576

WDAS-FM 105.3 MHz (Urban)
23 W City Line Ave
Bala Cynwyd, PA 19004
Phone: 610-617-8500
Fax: 610-617-2576

WEJM-FM 95.7 MHz (AC)
1 Bala Plaza Suite 424
Bala Cynwyd, PA 19004
www.jammingold957.com
Phone: 610-667-8500
Fax: 610-771-9610

WHAT-AM 1340 kHz (N/T)
2471 N 54th St Suite 220
Philadelphia, PA 19131
www.what1340.com
Phone: 215-581-5161
Fax: 215-581-5185

WHYY-FM 90.9 MHz (NPR)
150 N 6th St
Philadelphia, PA 19106
www.whyy.org/91FM/index.html
Phone: 215-351-9200
Fax: 215-351-3352

WIOQ-FM 102.1 MHz (CHR)
1 Bala Plaza Suite 243
Bala Cynwyd, PA 19004
E-mail: wmq102@q102philly.com
q102philly.amfmi.com
Phone: 610-667-8100
Fax: 610-668-4657

WIP-AM 610 kHz (Sports)
441 N 5th St
Philadelphia, PA 19123
Phone: 215-922-5000
Fax: 215-922-2364

WJJZ-FM 106.1 MHz (NAC)
440 Domino Ln
Philadelphia, PA 19128
wjjz.amfmi.com
Phone: 215-508-1200
Fax: 215-508-4466

WMGK-FM 102.9 MHz (CR)
1 Bala Plaza Suite 339
Bala Cynwyd, PA 19004
E-mail: programdirector@wmgk.com
www.wmgk.com
Phone: 610-667-8500
Fax: 610-664-9610

WMMR-FM 93.3 MHz (Rock)
1 Bala Plaza Suite 424
Bala Cynwyd, PA 19004
www.wmmr.com
Phone: 610-771-0933
Fax: 610-771-9610

WOGL-FM 98.1 MHz (Oldies)
10 Monument Rd
Bala Cynwyd, PA 19004
www.wogl.com
Phone: 610-668-5900
Fax: 610-668-5977

WPEN-AM 950 kHz (Nost)
1 Bala Plaza Suite 339
Bala Cynwyd, PA 19004
www.wpen.com
Phone: 610-667-8500
Fax: 610-664-9610

WPHI-FM 103.9 MHz (Urban)
100 Old York Rd Suite 2260
Jenkintown, PA 19046
Phone: 215-884-9400
Fax: 215-884-2608

WPHT-AM 1210 kHz (N/T)
10 Monument Rd
Bala Cynwyd, PA 19004
Phone: 610-668-5800
Fax: 610-668-5888

WPLY-FM 100.3 MHz (Alt)
1003 Baltimore Pike
Media, PA 19063
www.y100.com
Phone: 610-565-8900
Fax: 610-565-6024

WPST-FM 97.5 MHz (CHR)
619 Alexander Rd 3rd Fl
Princeton, NJ 08540
www.wpst.com
Phone: 609-419-0300
Fax: 609-419-0143

WRTI-FM 90.1 MHz (NPR)
2020 N 13th St
Philadelphia, PA 19122
Phone: 215-204-8405
Fax: 215-204-4870

WUSL-FM 98.9 MHz (Urban)
440 Domino Ln
Philadelphia, PA 19128
www.power99.com
Phone: 215-483-8900
Fax: 215-483-5930

WWDB-FM 96.5 MHz (N/T)
166 E Levering Mill Rd
Bala Cynwyd, PA 19004
Phone: 610-668-4400
Fax: 610-668-4453

WXTU-FM 92.5 MHz (Ctry)
555 City Line Ave Suite 330
Bala Cynwyd, PA 19004
E-mail: comments@wxtu.com
www.wxtu.com
Phone: 610-667-9000
Fax: 610-667-5978

WYSP-FM 94.1 MHz (Rock)
101 S Independence Mall E
Philadelphia, PA 19106
E-mail: wysp94@aol.com
www.94wysp.com
Phone: 215-625-9460
Fax: 215-625-6555

WYXR-FM 104.5 MHz (AC)
1 Bala Plaza Suite 243 W
Bala Cynwyd, PA 19004
Phone: 610-668-0750
Fax: 610-668-8253

Attractions

Philadelphia is sometimes referred to as the "Cradle of the Nation." The city's Waterfront and Independence National Historic Park includes Independence Hall, where the Declaration of Independence and the Constitution were signed; Independence Square, where the Declaration of Independence was first read aloud; the Liberty Bell Pavilion, where the famous symbol of liberty is kept; and Congress Hall, where the U.S. Congress met when Philadelphia was the nation's capital. Located here also is Carpenter's Hall, where the First Continental Congress met in 1774, and Christ Church, where many of the founding fathers worshipped; many are buried in the Christ Church Burial Ground. Other area attractions include the houses where Thomas Jefferson drafted the Declaration of Independence and Betsy Ross sewed the first American flag; and the U.S. Mint. Less than an hour away is Valley Forge National Historical Park.

Academy of Natural Sciences Museum
1900 Benjamin Franklin Pkwy
Philadelphia, PA 19103
www.acnatsci.org/
Phone: 215-299-1000
Fax: 215-299-1028

African-American Museum in Philadelphia
701 Arch St
Philadelphia, PA 19106
www.aampmuseum.org
Phone: 215-574-0380
Fax: 215-574-3110

American Swedish Historical Museum
1900 Pattison Ave
Philadelphia, PA 19145
E-mail: ashm@libertynet.org
www.libertynet.org/~ashm/
Phone: 215-389-1776
Fax: 215-389-7701

Arch Street Meeting House
320 Arch St
Philadelphia, PA 19106
Phone: 215-627-2667

Arden Theatre Co
40 N 2nd St
Philadelphia, PA 19106
E-mail: ardenthco@aol.com
www.libertynet.org/arden
Phone: 215-922-8900
Fax: 215-922-7011

Athenaeum of Philadelphia
219 S 6th St
Philadelphia, PA 19106
E-mail: athena@libertynet.org
www.libertynet.org/athena/
Phone: 215-925-2688
Fax: 215-925-3755

AVA Opera Theatre
1920 Spruce St
Philadelphia, PA 19103
E-mail: info@avaopera.com
www.avaopera.com
Phone: 215-735-1685
Fax: 215-732-2189

Balch Institute for Ethnic Studies
18 S 7th St
Philadelphia, PA 19106
E-mail: balchlib@balchinstitute.org
www.libertynet.org/balch/
Phone: 215-925-8090
Fax: 215-925-8195

Barnes Foundation Museum & Arboretum
300 N Latch's Ln
Merion, PA 19066
Phone: 610-667-0290
Fax: 610-664-4026

Betsy Ross House
239 Arch St
Philadelphia, PA 19106
www.libertynet.org/iha/betsy
Phone: 215-627-5343
Fax: 215-686-1256

Blockbuster-Sony Waterfront Music Centre
1 Harbour Blvd
Camden, NJ 08103
www.ecentre.com
Phone: 856-365-1300
Fax: 856-365-1062

Blue Cross River Rink at Penn's Landing
121 N Columbus Blvd
Philadelphia, PA 19106
www.pennslandingcorp.com
Phone: 215-925-7465
Fax: 215-923-9202

Carpenter's Hall
320 Chestnut St
Philadelphia, PA 19106
Phone: 215-925-0167
Fax: 215-925-3880

Christ Church in Philadelphia
20 N American St
Philadelphia, PA 19106
Phone: 215-922-1695
Fax: 215-922-3578

Civil War Library & Museum
1805 Pine St
Philadelphia, PA 19103
www.libertynet.org/~cwlm/library.html
Phone: 215-735-8196
Fax: 215-735-3812

Congregation Mikveh Israel
44 N 4th St
Philadelphia, PA 19106
Phone: 215-922-5446
Fax: 215-922-1550

Dorney Park & Wildwater Kingdom
3830 Dorney Park Rd
Allentown, PA 18104
E-mail: info@dorneypark.com
www.dorneypark.com
Phone: 610-395-3724
Fax: 610-391-7685
TF: 800-551-5656

Eastern State Penitentiary Historic Site
22nd St & Fairmount Ave
Philadelphia, PA 19130
E-mail: e-state@libertynet.org
www.easternstate.com
Phone: 215-236-3300

Edgar Allan Poe National Historic Site
532 N 7th St
Philadelphia, PA 19123
www.nps.gov/edal/
Phone: 215-597-8780

Elfreth's Alley Museum
126 Elfreth's Alley
Philadelphia, PA 19106
Phone: 215-574-0560
Fax: 215-922-7869

Fairmount Park
Benjamin Franklin Pkwy
Philadelphia, PA 19131
Phone: 215-685-0000
Fax: 215-878-9859

Fireman's Hall
147 N 2nd St
Philadelphia, PA 19106
Phone: 215-923-1438

Fleisher Art Memorial
719 Catherine St
Philadelphia, PA 19147
www.fleisher.org
Phone: 215-922-3456

Franklin Court
313 Walnut St
Philadelphia, PA 19106
Phone: 215-597-2761

Franklin Institute Science Museum
222 N 20th St
Philadelphia, PA 19103
www.fi.edu
Phone: 215-448-1200
Fax: 215-448-1235

Germantown Historical Society
5501 Germantown Ave
Philadelphia, PA 19144
Phone: 215-844-0514
Fax: 215-844-2831

Historic Bartram's Garden
54th St & Lindbergh Blvd
Philadelphia, PA 19143
Phone: 215-729-5281
Fax: 215-729-1047

Historic New Hope
1 W Mechanic St
New Hope, PA 18938
www.newhopepa.com
Phone: 215-862-5030
Fax: 215-862-5245

Historic Olde Saint Augustine's Church
243 N Lawrence St
Philadelphia, PA 19106
Phone: 215-627-1838

Historic Saint George's United Methodist Church
235 N 4th St
Philadelphia, PA 19106
Phone: 215-925-7788

Historical Society of Pennsylvania
1300 Locust St
Philadelphia, PA 19107
E-mail: hsppr@aol.com
www.libertynet.org/~pahist/
Phone: 215-732-6201
Fax: 215-732-2680

Hopewell Furnace National Historic Site
2 Mark Bird Ln
Elverson, PA 19520
www.nps.gov/hofu/
Phone: 610-582-8773
Fax: 610-582-2768

Independence Brewing Co
1000 E Comly St
Philadelphia, PA 19149
Phone: 215-537-2337
Fax: 215-537-4677

Independence Hall & Congress Hall
Chestnut St-betw 5th & 6th Sts
Philadelphia, PA 19106
www.nps.gov/inde/
Phone: 215-597-8974

Independence National Historical Park
313 Walnut St
Philadelphia, PA 19106
www.nps.gov/inde/
Phone: 215-597-8787
Fax: 215-597-1548

Independence Seaport Museum
211 S Columbus Blvd
Philadelphia, PA 19106
E-mail: seaport@libertynet.org
www.libertynet.org/seaport/
Phone: 215-925-5439
Fax: 215-925-6713

Institute of Contemporary Art
118 S 36th St University of Pennsylvania
Philadelphia, PA 19104
E-mail: icaup@pobox.upenn.edu
www.upenn.edu/ica/
Phone: 215-898-7108
Fax: 215-898-5050

Italian Market
9th St-betw Christian & Washington Sts
Philadelphia, PA 19147
Phone: 215-922-5557
Fax: 215-922-5723

Japanese House & Garden
West Fairmount Pk
Philadelphia, PA 19103
E-mail: jhg@libertynet.org
www.libertynet.org/~jhg
Phone: 215-878-5097
Fax: 215-878-1276

Kent Atwater Museum-History Museum of Philadelphia
15 S 7th St
Philadelphia, PA 19106
www.philadelphiahistory.org
Phone: 215-922-3031
Fax: 215-922-0708

Liberty Bell Pavilion
Market & 5th Sts
Philadelphia, PA 19106
Phone: 215-597-8975
Fax: 215-597-0042

Longwood Gardens
1001 Longwood Rd
Kennett Square, PA 19348
www.longwoodgardens.com
Phone: 610-388-1000
Fax: 610-388-2183
TF: 800-737-5500

Mann Center for the Performing Arts
123 S Broad St Suite 1930
Philadelphia, PA 19109
www.manncenter.org
Phone: 215-546-7900
Fax: 215-546-9524

Mario Lanza Museum
416 Queen St Settlement Music School
Philadelphia, PA 19147
Phone: 215-468-3623
Fax: 215-468-1903

Merriam Theater
250 S Broad St
Philadelphia, PA 19102
Phone: 215-732-5997
Fax: 215-732-1396

Morris Arboretum of the University of Pennsylvania
100 Northwestern Ave
Philadelphia, PA 19118
Phone: 215-247-5882
Fax: 215-248-4439

Mummers Museum
1100 S 2nd St
Philadelphia, PA 19147
E-mail: mummersmus@aol.com
riverfrontmummers.com/mummersmuseum.html
Phone: 215-336-3050
Fax: 215-389-5630

National Museum of American Jewish History
55 N 5th St
Philadelphia, PA 19106
E-mail: nmajh@nmajh.org
www.nmajh.org
Phone: 215-923-3811
Fax: 215-923-0763

National Shrine of Saint John Neumann
1019 N 5th St
Philadelphia, PA 19123
Phone: 215-627-3080
Fax: 215-627-3296
TF: 888-315-1860

New Jersey State Aquarium
1 Riverside Dr
Camden, NJ 08103
www.njaquarium.org
Phone: 856-365-3300
Fax: 856-365-3311

Old City Gallery & Cultural District
303 Cherry St
Philadelphia, PA 19106
Phone: 215-238-9576

Opera Co of Philadelphia
Broad & Locust Sts Academy of Music
Philadelphia, PA 19102
E-mail: tix@operaphilly.com
www.operaphilly.com
Phone: 215-928-2110
Fax: 215-928-2112

Painted Bride Art Center
230 Vine St
Philadelphia, PA 19106
www.paintedbride.org
Phone: 215-925-9914
Fax: 215-925-7402

Penn's Landing
Columbus Blvd & Chestnut St Great Plaza
Philadelphia, PA 19106
www.pennslandingcorp.com/
Phone: 215-923-8181
Fax: 215-923-2801

Pennsylvania Academy of the Fine Arts Museum
118 N Broad St
Philadelphia, PA 19102
www.pafa.org/museum
Phone: 215-972-7600
Fax: 215-567-2429

Pennsylvania Ballet
1101 S Broad St
Philadelphia, PA 19147
E-mail: info@paballet.org
www.paballet.org
Phone: 215-551-7000
Fax: 215-551-7224

Philadelphia Academy of Music
Broad & Locust Sts
Philadelphia, PA 19102
www.philorch.org
Phone: 215-893-1935
Fax: 215-893-1933
TF: 800-457-8354

Philadelphia Chamber Music Society
135 S 18th St
Philadelphia, PA 19103
E-mail: mail@pcmsnet.org
www.pcmsnet.org
Phone: 215-569-8587
Fax: 215-569-9497

Philadelphia Dance Co
9 N Preston St
Philadelphia, PA 19104
Phone: 215-387-8200
Fax: 215-387-8203

Philadelphia Museum of Art
26th & Benjamin Franklin Pkwy
Philadelphia, PA 19130
www.philamuseum.org/
Phone: 215-763-8100
Fax: 215-236-4465

Philadelphia Orchestra
260 S Broad St 16th Fl
Philadelphia, PA 19102
www.philorch.org
Phone: 215-893-1900
Fax: 215-893-1948

Philadelphia Zoological Garden
3400 W Girard Ave
Philadelphia, PA 19104
www.phillyzoo.org
Phone: 215-243-1100
Fax: 215-243-5385

Philadelphia's Vietnam Veterans Memorial
Delaware & Spruce Sts
Philadelphia, PA 19104
razeinnovations.com/memorial1/
Phone: 215-535-0643

Physick House
321 S 4th St
Philadelphia, PA 19106
Phone: 215-925-7866
Fax: 215-925-9707

Please Touch Museum
210 N 21st St
Philadelphia, PA 19103
E-mail: mmarketing@pleasetouchmuseum.org
www.pleasetouchmuseum.org
Phone: 215-963-0666
Fax: 215-963-0424

Polish American Cultural Center Museum
308 Walnut St
Philadelphia, PA 19106
E-mail: mail@polishamericancenter.org
www.polishamericancenter.org
Phone: 215-922-1700
Fax: 215-922-1518

Powel House
244 S 3rd St
Philadelphia, PA 19106
Phone: 215-627-0364

Presbyterian Historical Society
425 Lombard St
Philadelphia, PA 19147
Phone: 215-627-1852
Fax: 215-627-0509

Quaker Information Center
1501 Cherry St
Philadelphia, PA 19102
E-mail: quakerinfo@afsc.org
www.afsc.org/qic.htm
Phone: 215-241-7024
Fax: 215-567-2096

Reading Terminal Market
12th & Arch Sts
Philadelphia, PA 19107
Phone: 215-922-2317
Fax: 215-922-2040

Rodin Museum
22nd & Benjamin Franklin Pkwy
Philadelphia, PA 19130
www.rodinmuseum.org/
Phone: 215-763-8100
Fax: 215-236-4465

Rosenbach Museum & Library
2010 DeLancey Pl
Philadelphia, PA 19103
www.rosenbach.org
Phone: 215-732-1600
Fax: 215-545-7529

Society Hill
Walnut, S 5th, Lombard & S 2nd Sts
Philadelphia, PA 19106

Society Hill Playhouse
507 S 8th St
Philadelphia, PA 19147
www.societyhillplayhouse.com
Phone: 215-923-0210
Fax: 215-923-1789

Stenton Museum
4601 N 18th St
Philadelphia, PA 19140
Phone: 215-329-7312
Fax: 215-329-7312

Stephen Girard Collection
2101 S College Ave Founder's Hall
Philadelphia, PA 19121
Phone: 215-787-2602
Fax: 215-787-2725

Thaddeus Kosciuszko National Memorial
313 Walnut St Independence National Historical Pk
Philadelphia, PA 19106
www.nps.gov/thko
Phone: 215-597-7120
Fax: 215-597-1416

Tuttleman Omniverse Theater
222 N 20th St
Philadelphia, PA 19103
E-mail: webteam@www.fi.edu
www.fi.edu/tfi/info/omnivers.html
Phone: 215-448-1200
Fax: 215-444-1235

University of Pennsylvania Museum of Archaeology & Anthropology
33rd & Spruce Sts
Philadelphia, PA 19104
www.upenn.edu/museum
Phone: 215-898-4000
Fax: 215-898-0657

US Mint
5th & Arch Sts
Philadelphia, PA 19106
www.usmint.gov/
Phone: 215-408-0114
Fax: 215-408-2700

Valley Forge National Historical Park
PO Box 953
Valley Forge, PA 19482
www.nps.gov/vafo/
Phone: 610-783-1011
Fax: 610-783-1088

Wagner Free Institute of Science
1700 W Montgomery Ave
Philadelphia, PA 19121
Phone: 215-763-6529
Fax: 215-763-1299

Walnut Street Theatre
825 Walnut St
Philadelphia, PA 19107
www.wstonline.org
Phone: 215-574-3550
Fax: 215-574-3598

Wilma Theater
Broad & Spruce Sts
Philadelphia, PA 19107
www.libertynet.org/wilma/
Phone: 215-546-7824
Fax: 215-893-0895

Woodlands The
4000 Woodland Ave
Philadelphia, PA 19104
Phone: 215-386-2181
Fax: 215-386-2431

Sports Teams & Facilities

First Union Center
Broad St & Pattison Ave
Philadelphia, PA 19148
Phone: 215-336-3600
Fax: 215-389-9579

Philadelphia 76ers
3601 S Broad St First Union Ctr
Philadelphia, PA 19148
www.nba.com/sixers/
Phone: 215-339-7676
Fax: 215-339-7680

Philadelphia Eagles
3501 S Broad St Veterans Stadium
Philadelphia, PA 19148
www.eaglesnet.com
Phone: 215-463-2500
Fax: 215-339-5464

Philadelphia Flyers
3601 S Broad St First Union Ctr
Philadelphia, PA 19148
www.philadelphiaflyers.com
Phone: 215-465-4500
Fax: 215-389-9403

Philadelphia Kixx (soccer)
3601 S Broad St The Spectrum
Philadelphia, PA 19148
E-mail: kixxsoccer@aol.com
kixxonline.com
Phone: 215-952-5499
Fax: 215-952-5488
TF: 888-888-5499

Philadelphia Phantoms (hockey)
3601 S Broad St The Spectrum
Philadelphia, PA 19148
www.phantomshockey.com
Phone: 215-465-4522
Fax: 215-952-5245

Philadelphia Phillies
3601 S Broad St Veterans Stadium
Philadelphia, PA 19148
E-mail: phans@phillies.com
www.phillies.com
Phone: 215-463-1000
Fax: 215-463-9434

Philadelphia Wings (lacrosse)
3601 S Broad St First Union Ctr
Philadelphia, PA 19148
Phone: 215-389-9464
Fax: 215-389-9506

Veterans Stadium
3501 S Broad St
Philadelphia, PA 19148
Phone: 215-685-1500
Fax: 215-463-9878

Annual Events

Advanta Tennis Championships for Women (mid-November) .610-828-5777
Bach Festival of Philadelphia (October-April) .215-247-2224
Book & Cook Fair (mid-March) .215-636-1666
Chestnut Hill Garden Festival Blooms (late April-early May) .215-247-6696
Chocolate Festival (mid-February) .215-925-7465
Devon Horse Show & Country Fair (late May-early June) .610-964-0550
Festival of Fountains (late May-early September) .610-388-1000
First Union Jam on the River (late May) .215-636-1666
First Union US Pro Championship The (mid-June) .215-973-3580
Flower & Garden Festival (early May) .215-794-4000
Historic Houses in Flower (late April) .215-763-8100
Jam Festival (late May) .215-629-3237
Junior Jazz Weekend (mid-February) .215-963-0667
Manayunk Arts Fest (late June) .215-482-9565
Maple Syrup Festival (late March) .215-922-2317
Market Street East Holiday Festival (late December) .215-636-1666
Midsommarfest (early June) .215-389-1776
Mummers Parade (January 1) .215-336-3050
Odunde African Street Festival & Marketplace (mid-June) .215-732-8508
PECO Energy Jazz Festival (October-November) .215-636-4433
Penn Relays (late April) .215-898-6128
Pennsylvania Fair (mid-May) .215-639-9000
Philadelphia Boat Show (mid-January) .610-449-9910
Philadelphia Festival of World Cinema (late April-early May) .215-895-6571
Philadelphia Flower Show (early March) .215-418-4700
Philadelphia Folk Festival (late August) .215-242-0150
Philadelphia International Film Festival (mid-late July) .215-879-8209
Philadelphia Museum of Art Craft Show (late October-early November) .215-684-7930
Philadelphia Open House Tours (late April-mid-May) .215-928-1188
Purim Festival (late March) .215-923-3811
Renninger Antique (late February) .610-337-4000
Rittenhouse Square Fine Arts Annual (early June) .877-689-4112
Springside School Antiques Show (mid-April) .215-247-7200
US Hot Rod Grand Slam Monster Jam (mid-February) .215-336-3600
Welcome America (late June-early July) .800-770-5883
Yo Philadelphia Festival (early September) .215-925-7465

Phoenix, Arizona

County: **Maricopa**

PHOENIX is located in the Salt River Valley in central Arizona, a region often referred to as the "Valley of the Sun." Major cities within 100 miles include Glendale, Mesa, Scottsdale, Tempe, and Tuscon, Arizona.

Area (Land)	419.9 sq mi
Area (Water)	0.2 sq mi
Elevation	1,090 ft
Latitude	33-44-83 N
Longitude	112-07-33 W
Time Zone	MST
Area Code	602

Climate

Phoenix has a dry desert climate that features more than 300 sunny days a year. Winter days are mild, with average high temperatures in the high 60s to low 70s, while evenings cool down into the low to mid-40s. Summer days are hot, with temperatures averaging just above 100 degrees, but very low humidity makes the high temperatures seem more bearable. Summer evening temperatures cool down into the 70s. August and December are the wettest months of the year in Phoenix, with only one inch of rain—May and June are the driest, with only .1 inch.

Average Temperatures & Precipitation

Temperatures

	Jan	Feb	Mar	Apr	May	Jun	Jul	Aug	Sep	Oct	Nov	Dec
High	66	71	76	85	94	104	106	104	98	88	75	66
Low	41	45	49	55	64	73	81	79	73	61	49	42

Precipitation

	Jan	Feb	Mar	Apr	May	Jun	Jul	Aug	Sep	Oct	Nov	Dec
Inches	0.7	0.7	0.9	0.2	0.1	0.1	0.8	1.0	0.9	0.7	0.7	1.0

History

As early as the first century A.D., the area known today as Phoenix was inhabited by Native Americans who built an extensive irrigation system that helped sustain their agricultural society for several hundred years before the tribe simply vanished. (Prolonged drought is suspected as the cause of the tribe's extinction.) Several centuries later, roving Native Americans who came across the ruins of the prehistoric civilization referred to the original settlers as "Hohokam" (a name meaning "the people who have gone").

White settlement began in the Valley of the Sun during the late 1860s on the banks of the Salt River, when pioneer Jack Swilling visited the fertile but arid area and established an irrigation system there. Phoenix was founded in 1870 and named by an early settler who predicted that, like the bird of legend, the city would rise from the ashes of ancient Hohokam Indian ruins. The City of Phoenix was incorporated in 1881, and eight years later, Phoenix became the capital of the Arizona Territory.

Early development in Phoenix can be attributed to farming, ranching, and mining. The construction of the Roosevelt Dam in 1911 sparked growth in the area, as water and electric power became more readily available. When Arizona was granted statehood in 1912, Phoenix remained the capital city. During the 20th Century, Phoenix, with its pleasant year-round climate, also gained popularity as a resort and vacation destination. The establishment of several air bases in the region during World War II also stimulated development in the Phoenix metropolitan area.

More than three million people now make their home in the Valley of the Sun, with more than 1.1 million residing in the city of Phoenix.

Population

1990 Census	984,309
1998 Estimate	1,198,064
% Change	21.3
2005 Projection	3,330,000*

Racial/Ethnic Breakdown

White	81.6%
Black	5.2%
Other	13.2%
Hispanic Origin (may be of any race)	20.0%

Age Breakdown

Under 5 years	8.5%
5 to 17	18.6%
18 to 20	4.5%
21 to 24	6.2%
25 to 34	19.5%
35 to 44	15.6%
45 to 54	9.9%
55 to 64	7.4%
65 to 74	5.9%
75+ years	3.8%
Median Age	31.1

Gender Breakdown

Male	49.5%
Female	50.5%

* *Information given is for Maricopa County.*

Government

Type of Government: Council-Manager

Phoenix City Clerk
200 W Washington St 15th Fl
Phoenix, AZ 85003
Phone: 602-262-6811
Fax: 602-495-5847

Phoenix City Council Phone: 602-262-4469
200 W Washington St 11th Fl Fax: 602-495-2036
Phoenix, AZ 85003

Phoenix City Hall Phone: 602-262-6659
200 W Washington St
Phoenix, AZ 85003

Phoenix Community & Economic Development Dept Phone: 602-262-5040
200 W Washington St 20th Fl Fax: 602-495-5097
Phoenix, AZ 85003

Phoenix Finance Dept Phone: 602-262-7166
251 W Washington St 9th Fl Fax: 602-495-5605
Phoenix, AZ 85003

Phoenix Fire Dept Phone: 602-262-6002
150 S 12th St Fax: 602-262-4429
Phoenix, AZ 85034

Phoenix Mayor Phone: 602-262-7111
200 W Washington St 11th Fl Fax: 602-495-5583
Phoenix, AZ 85003

Phoenix Parks Recreations & Library Dept Phone: 602-262-6862
200 W Washington St 16th Fl Fax: 602-534-3787
Phoenix, AZ 85003

Phoenix Personnel Dept Phone: 602-262-6609
135 N 2nd Ave Fax: 602-534-2602
Phoenix, AZ 85003

Phoenix Planning Dept Phone: 602-262-7131
200 W Washington St 2nd Fl Fax: 602-495-0563
Phoenix, AZ 85003

Phoenix Police Dept Phone: 602-262-6747
620 W Washington St Fax: 602-495-0356
Phoenix, AZ 85003

Phoenix Public Library Phone: 602-262-4636
1221 N Central Ave Fax: 602-261-8751
Phoenix, AZ 85004

Phoenix Public Transit Dept Phone: 602-262-7242
302 N 1st Ave Suite 700 Fax: 602-495-2002
Phoenix, AZ 85003

Phoenix Public Works Dept Phone: 602-262-7251
101 S Central Ave Suite 500 Fax: 602-534-9864
Phoenix, AZ 85004

Phoenix Water Services Dept Phone: 602-262-6627
200 W Washington St 9th Fl Fax: 602-495-5542
Phoenix, AZ 85003

Important Phone Numbers

AAA 602-274-1116
American Express Travel 480-949-7000
Arizona Revenue Dept 602-255-3381
Dental Referral 602-957-4864
Driver's License/Vehicle Registration Information 602-255-0072
Emergency 911
HotelDocs 800-468-3537
Maricopa County Assessor's Office 602-506-3406
Maricopa County Treasurer 602-506-8511
Medical Referral 602-252-2015
Phoenix Assn of Realtors 602-246-1012
Poison Control Center 602-253-3334
Time/Temp 602-265-5550
Visitor Hotline 602-252-5588
Voter Registration Information 602-506-1511
Weather 602-265-5550

Information Sources

Better Business Bureau Serving Central Northeast Northwest & Southwest Arizona Phone: 602-264-1721
4428 N 12th St Fax: 602-263-0997
Phoenix, AZ 85014
www.phoenix.bbb.org

Glendale Chamber of Commerce Phone: 623-937-4754
PO Box 249 Fax: 623-937-3333
Glendale, AZ 85311 TF: 800-437-8669
www.glendaleazchamber.org

Glendale City Hall Phone: 623-930-2000
5850 W Glendale Ave Fax: 623-915-2690
Glendale, AZ 85301
www.ci.glendale.az.us

Glendale Economic Development Dept Phone: 623-930-2988
5850 W Glendale Ave Fax: 623-931-5730
Glendale, AZ 85301
www.ci.glendale.az.us/localgov/economic_dev

Glendale Mayor Phone: 623-930-2260
5850 W Glendale Ave Fax: 623-937-2764
Glendale, AZ 85301

Glendale Public Library Phone: 623-930-3530
5959 W Brown St Fax: 623-842-4209
Glendale, AZ 85302
www.lib.ci.glendale.az.us

Greater Phoenix Chamber of Commerce Phone: 602-254-5521
201 N Central Ave Suite 2700 Fax: 602-495-8913
Phoenix, AZ 85073
www.phoenixchamber.com

Greater Phoenix Convention & Visitors Bureau Phone: 602-254-6500
400 E Van Buren St 1 Arizona Ctr Suite 600 Fax: 602-253-4415
Phoenix, AZ 85004 TF: 877-266-5749
www.arizonaguide.com/phxcvb

Maricopa County Phone: 602-506-3415
301 W Jefferson St 10th Fl Fax: 602-506-6402
Phoenix, AZ 85003
www.maricopa.gov

Mesa Chamber of Commerce Phone: 480-969-1307
120 N Center St Fax: 480-827-0727
Mesa, AZ 85201
www.arizonaguide.com/cities/mesa/index.html

Mesa City Hall Phone: 480-644-2011
55 N Center St Fax: 480-644-2418
Mesa, AZ 85201
www.ci.mesa.az.us

Mesa Community & Conference Center Phone: 480-644-2178
201 N Center Fax: 480-644-2617
Mesa, AZ 85201

Mesa Convention & Visitors Bureau Phone: 480-827-4700
120 N Center St Fax: 480-827-0727
Mesa, AZ 85201 TF: 800-283-6372
www.arizonaguide.com/mesa

Mesa Mayor Phone: 480-644-2388
PO Box 1466 Fax: 480-644-2175
Mesa, AZ 85211
www.ci.mesa.az.us/citymgt/mc_mayor.htm

Mesa Neighborhood Services Dept Phone: 480-644-2387
PO Box 1466 Fax: 480-644-4842
Mesa, AZ 85211

Mesa Public Library Phone: 480-644-2702
64 E 1st St Fax: 480-644-3490
Mesa, AZ 85201
www.ci.mesa.az.us/library

Phoenix Civic Plaza Convention Center Phone: 602-262-7272
225 E Adams St Fax: 602-495-3642
Phoenix, AZ 85004 TF: 800-282-4842
www.ci.phoenix.az.us/civplaza.html

Scottsdale Chamber of Commerce Phone: 480-945-8481
7343 Scottsdale Mall Fax: 480-947-4523
Scottsdale, AZ 85251 TF: 800-877-1117
www.scottsdalechamber.com

Scottsdale City Hall Phone: 480-312-2414
3939 N Drinkwater Blvd Fax: 480-312-2738
Scottsdale, AZ 85251
www.ci.scottsdale.az.us

Scottsdale Convention & Visitor's Bureau Phone: 480-945-8481
7343 Scottsdale Mall Fax: 480-947-4523
Scottsdale, AZ 85251 TF: 800-877-1117
www.arizonaguide.com/cities/scottsdale/index.html

Scottsdale Economic Development Dept Phone: 480-312-7601
7447 E Indian School Rd Fax: 480-312-2672
Scottsdale, AZ 85251
www.ci.scottsdale.az.us/economic

Scottsdale Mayor Phone: 480-312-2433
3939 N Drinkwater Blvd Fax: 480-312-2738
Scottsdale, AZ 85251
www.ci.scottsdale.az.us/welcome/mayor.asp

Scottsdale Public Library System Phone: 480-312-2474
3839 N Drinkwater Blvd Fax: 480-312-7993
Scottsdale, AZ 85251
library.ci.scottsdale.az.us

Tempe Chamber of Commerce Phone: 480-967-7891
PO Box 28500 Fax: 480-966-5365
Tempe, AZ 85285
www.tempechamber.org

Tempe City Hall Phone: 480-967-2001
PO Box 5002 Fax: 480-350-8996
Tempe, AZ 85280
www.tempe.gov

Tempe Convention & Visitors Bureau Phone: 480-894-8158
51 W 3rd St Suite 105 Fax: 480-968-8004
Tempe, AZ 85281 TF: 800-283-6734
www.arizonaguide.com/cities/tempe/index.html

Tempe Development Services Dept Phone: 480-350-8340
PO Box 5002
Tempe, AZ 85280
www.tempe.gov/tdsi

Tempe Mayor Phone: 480-350-8865
PO Box 5002 Fax: 480-350-8996
Tempe, AZ 85280
www.tempe.gov/manager/mayor.htm

Tempe Public Library Phone: 480-350-5500
3500 S Rural Rd Fax: 480-350-5544
Tempe, AZ 85282
www.tempe.gov/library

Online Resources

4Phoenix.com
www.4phoenix.com

About.com Guide to Phoenix
phoenix.about.com/local/southwestus/phoenix

Anthill City Guide Mesa
www.anthill.com/city.asp?city=mesa

Anthill City Guide Phoenix
www.anthill.com/city.asp?city=phoenix

Area Guide Phoenix
phoenix.areaguides.net

Arizona Guide to Glendale
www.arizonaguide.com/clients/glendale/

Boulevards Phoenix
www.boulevards.com/cities/phoenix.html

City Knowledge Mesa
www.cityknowledge.com/az_mesa.htm

City Knowledge Phoenix
www.cityknowledge.com/az_phoenix.htm

City Knowledge Scottsdale
www.cityknowledge.com/az_scottsdale.htm

City Knowledge Tempe
www.cityknowledge.com/az_tempe.htm

CitySearch Phoenix
phoenix.citysearch.com

DesertUSA Guide to Phoenix
www.desertusa.com/Cities/az/city_phoenixAZ.html

DesertUSA Guide to Scottsdale
www.desertusa.com/Cities/az/city_scottsdaleAZ.html

DigitalCity Phoenix
home.digitalcity.com/phoenix

Excite.com Mesa City Guide
www.excite.com/travel/countries/united_states/arizona/mesa

Excite.com Phoenix City Guide
www.excite.com/travel/countries/united_states/arizona/phoenix

Excite.com Tempe City Guide
www.excite.com/travel/countries/united_states/arizona/tempe

Glendale City Net
www.excite.com/travel/countries/united_states/arizona/glendale

HotelGuide Phoenix
hotelguide.net/phoenix

Insiders' Guide to Phoenix
www.insiders.com/phoenix/

Lodging.com Mesa Arizona
www.lodging.com/auto/guides/mesa-az.html

Lodging.com Tempe Arizona
www.lodging.com/auto/guides/tempe-az.html

Metrowise Phoenix
www.metrowise.com

Phoenix Guide
www.phoenixaz.com

Phoenix New Times
www.phoenixnewtimes.com

Phoenix Online
www.phoenixonline.com/

Phoenix Traveller
www.thetraveller.com

Phoenix-Best.com
www.phoenix-best.com

Phoenix.TheLinks.com
phoenix.thelinks.com

Rough Guide Travel Phoenix
travel.roughguides.com/content/1197/

Savvy Diner Guide to Phoenix-Scottsdale Restaurants
www.savvydiner.com/phoenix/

Scottsdale Arizona
scottsdale-arizona.com

Scottsdale Directory
www.scottsdaledirectory.com

Scottsdale Golf Guide
scottsdale-golf.com

Tempe City News
www.tempe.gov/events.htm

Tempe in Touch
www.tempe.gov

Tempe Net
www.tempe.net

Ultimate Arizona Vacation Guide
www.webcreationsetc.com/Azguide/Phoenix/

Virtual City Entertainment Magazine On-line
www.opus1.com/emol/phoenix/phoenix.html

Virtual Voyages Phoenix
www.virtualvoyages.com/usa/az/phoenix/phoenix.sht

WeekendEvents.com Phoenix
www.weekendevents.com/misccity/phoenix/phoenix.htm

Area Communities

Communities in the Phoenix metropolitan area with populations greater than 10,000 are listed below. Another prominent, yet unincorporated, community in the Valley of the Sun is Sun City/Sun City West, a retirement community of nearly 60,000 people that is located northwest of Phoenix.

Apache Junction
1001 N Idaho Rd
Apache Junction, AZ 85219
Phone: 480-982-8002
Fax: 480-982-7018

Avondale
525 N Central Ave
Avondale, AZ 85323
Phone: 623-932-2400
Fax: 623-932-2205

Buckeye
100 N Apache Rd Suite A
Buckeye, AZ 85326
Phone: 623-386-4691
Fax: 623-386-7832

Chandler
55 N Arizona Pl Suite 301
Chandler, AZ 85225
Phone: 480-782-2220
Fax: 480-782-2209

Fountain Hills
16836 E Palisades Blvd
Fountain Hills, AZ 85268
Phone: 480-837-2003
Fax: 480-837-3145

Gilbert
1025 S Gilbert Rd
Gilbert, AZ 85296
Phone: 480-503-6000
Fax: 480-497-4943

Glendale
5850 W Glendale Ave
Glendale, AZ 85301
Phone: 623-930-2000
Fax: 623-915-2690

Mesa
55 N Center St
Mesa, AZ 85201
Phone: 480-644-2011
Fax: 480-644-2418

Paradise Valley
6401 E Lincoln Dr
Paradise Valley, AZ 85253
Phone: 480-948-7411
Fax: 480-951-3715

Peoria
8401 W Monroe St
Peoria, AZ 85345
Phone: 623-773-7000
Fax: 623-773-7304

Scottsdale
3939 N Drinkwater Blvd
Scottsdale, AZ 85251
Phone: 480-312-2414
Fax: 480-312-2738

Tempe
PO Box 5002
Tempe, AZ 85280
Phone: 480-967-2001
Fax: 480-350-8996

Economy

The Phoenix metropolitan area's diverse economic base ranges from agriculture and mining to finance and high-technology manufacturing. Major U.S. corporations that have a presence in the area include Motorola, Bank One, America West Airlines, and Intel. As the state capital and the seat of Maricopa County, government plays an important role in Phoenix's economy—four of the area's top 10 employers are government-related. Services is currently Maricopa County's largest employment sector, followed by retail trade, government, and manufacturing. The construction industry is also thriving in the Valley of the Sun, as recent improvements in economic development have resulted in numerous business expansions and relocations in the Phoenix metropolitan area, creating the need for both business and residential construction. Tourism is a vital part of the economy as well, contributing approximately $3.8 billion dollars annually.

Unemployment Rate 2.8%
Per Capita Income.......................... $26,686*
Median Family Income...................... $50,200*

** Information given is for the Phoenix-Mesa Metropolitan Statistical Area (MSA), which includes Maricopa County and the cities of Mesa, Phoenix, Scottsdale, and Tempe.*

Principal Industries & Number of Wage Earners

Maricopa County - 1999

Construction 113,000
Finance, Insurance, & Real Estate 122,600
Government 172,600
Manufacturing 167,400
Mining 900
Services 457,000
Trade 359,200
Transportation & Public Utilities 78,800

Major Employers

America West Airlines Inc
4000 E Sky Harbor Blvd
Phoenix, AZ 85034
www.americawest.com
Phone: 480-693-0800
Fax: 480-693-5546
TF: 800-363-2542

American Express Travel Related Services
20022 N 31st Ave
Phoenix, AZ 85027
travel.americanexpress.com/travel
Phone: 623-492-8100
Fax: 623-492-3637
TF: 800-528-4800

Banc One Arizona Corp
241 N Central Ave
Phoenix, AZ 85004
Phone: 602-221-2900
Fax: 602-221-2095
TF: 800-877-0608

Honeywell Inc
402 S 36th St
Phoenix, AZ 85034
www.honeywell.com/careers
Phone: 602-231-1000
Fax: 602-231-3982

Honeywell Space & Aviation Control
PO Box 21111
Phoenix, AZ 85036
www.sac.honeywell.com
Phone: 602-436-2311
Fax: 602-436-2252

Intel Corp
5000 W Chandler Blvd
Chandler, AZ 85226
www.intel.com
Phone: 480-554-8080

Maricopa County
301 W Jefferson St 10th Fl
Phoenix, AZ 85003
www.maricopa.gov
Phone: 602-506-3415
Fax: 602-506-6402

Mesa Public Schools
549 N Stapley Dr
Mesa, AZ 85203
www.mpsaz.org
Phone: 480-472-0000
Fax: 480-472-0422

ON Semiconductor
5005 E McDowell Rd
Phoenix, AZ 85008
www.onsemiconductor.com
Phone: 602-244-6600

Phoenix City Hall
200 W Washington St
Phoenix, AZ 85003
www.ci.phoenix.az.us
Phone: 602-262-6659

Qwest
5090 N 40th St
Phoenix, AZ 85018
www.qwest.com
Phone: 602-351-6000

Safeway Inc Phoenix Div
2750 S Priest Dr
Tempe, AZ 85282
www.safeway.com
Phone: 480-894-4100

Samaritan Health Systems of Phoenix
1441 N 12th St
Phoenix, AZ 85006
www.samaritan.edu
Phone: 602-495-4000
Fax: 602-495-4559

US Postal Service
4949 E Van Buren St
Phoenix, AZ 85026
new.usps.com
Phone: 800-275-8777

Wells Fargo Bank Arizona NA
100 W Washington St
Phoenix, AZ 85003
Phone: 602-378-4690
Fax: 602-528-1088
TF: 800-869-3557

Quality of Living Indicators

Total Crime Index.................................... 104,734
(rates per 100,000 inhabitants)

Violent Crime
Murder/manslaughter.......................... 185
Forcible rape 346
Robbery....................................... 3,764
Aggravated assault............................ 5,906

Property Crime
Burglary 18,733
Larceny theft 57,957
Motor vehicle theft 17,843

Cost of Living Index 102.3
(national average = 100)

Median Home Price $126,400

Education

Public Schools

Phoenix Elementary District
1817 N 7th St
Phoenix, AZ 85006
www.phxelem.k12.az.us
Phone: 602-257-3755
Fax: 602-257-6077

Phoenix Union High School District
4502 N Central Ave
Phoenix, AZ 85012
www.phxhs.k12.az.us
Phone: 602-271-3100
Fax: 602-271-3510

Number of Schools
Elementary 18
Middle 2
High 6

Student/Teacher Ratio
Grades K-8 .... 18.0:1 (Phoenix Elementary District)
Grades 9-12 .. 17.8:1 (Phoenix Union High School District)

Private Schools

Number of Schools (all grades) .... 100+

Colleges & Universities

American Indian College of the Assemblies of God
10020 N 15th Ave
Phoenix, AZ 85021
Phone: 602-944-3335
Fax: 602-943-8299
TF: 800-933-3828

Arizona State University
Tempe, AZ 85287
E-mail: ugradadm@asuvm.inre.asu.edu
www.asu.edu
Phone: 480-965-9011
Fax: 480-965-3610

Arizona State University West Campus
PO Box 37100
Phoenix, AZ 85069
www.west.asu.edu
Phone: 602-543-5500
Fax: 602-543-8312

DeVRY Institute of Technology
2149 W Dunlap Ave
Phoenix, AZ 85021
www.devry-phx.edu
Phone: 602-870-9222
Fax: 602-331-1494
TF: 800-528-0250

GateWay Community College
108 N 40th St
Phoenix, AZ 85034
www.gwc.maricopa.edu
Phone: 602-392-5000
Fax: 602-392-5329

Glendale Community College
6000 W Olive Ave
Glendale, AZ 85302
E-mail: info@gc.maricopa.edu
www.gc.maricopa.edu
Phone: 623-845-3000
Fax: 623-845-3303

Grand Canyon University
3300 W Camelback Rd
Phoenix, AZ 85017
www.grand-canyon.edu
Phone: 602-249-3300
Fax: 602-589-2580
TF: 800-800-9776

International Baptist College
2150 E Southern Ave
Tempe, AZ 85282
Phone: 480-838-7070
Fax: 480-838-5432
TF: 800-422-4858

ITT Technical Institute
4837 E McDowell Rd
Phoenix, AZ 85008
www.itt-tech.edu
Phone: 602-231-0871
Fax: 602-267-8727
TF: 800-879-4881

Lamson Junior College
1126 N Scottsdale Rd
Tempe, AZ 85281
E-mail: admissions@lamsonjc.com
www.lamsonjc.com
Phone: 480-898-7000
Fax: 480-967-6645
TF: 800-898-7017

Mesa Community College
1833 W Southern Ave
Mesa, AZ 85202
www.mc.maricopa.edu
Phone: 480-461-7000
Fax: 480-461-7804

Ottawa University
2340 W Mission Ln
Phoenix, AZ 85021
www.ottawa.edu/phoenix/index.html
Phone: 602-371-1188
Fax: 602-371-0035
TF: 800-235-9586

Ottawa University
13402 N Scottsdale Rd Suite B170
Scottsdale, AZ 85254
www.ottawa.edu/phoenix
Phone: 480-998-2297
Fax: 602-371-0035

Ottawa University
4545 S Wendler Dr Suite 105
Tempe, AZ 85282
www.ottawa.edu
Phone: 602-438-4468
Fax: 602-438-4571
TF: 800-235-9586

Paradise Valley Community College
18401 N 32nd St
Phoenix, AZ 85032
www.pvc.maricopa.edu
Phone: 602-787-6500
Fax: 602-787-7025

Phoenix College
1202 W Thomas Rd
Phoenix, AZ 85013
www.pc.maricopa.edu
Phone: 602-264-2492
Fax: 602-285-7813

Rainstar College
4130 N Goldwater Blvd
Scottsdale, AZ 85251
www.rainstargroup.com
Phone: 480-423-0375
Fax: 480-945-9824

Rio Salado Community College
2323 W 14th St
Tempe, AZ 85281
www.rio.maricopa.edu
Phone: 480-517-8000
Fax: 480-517-8199

Scottsdale Community College
9000 E Chaparral Rd
Scottsdale, AZ 85256
www.sc.maricopa.edu
Phone: 480-423-6000
Fax: 480-423-6200

South Mountain Community College
7050 S 24th St
Phoenix, AZ 85040
E-mail: montano@smc.maricopa.edu
www.smc.maricopa.edu
Phone: 602-243-8000
Fax: 602-243-8199

Southwest Institute of Arts
1402 N Miller Rd
Scottsdale, AZ 85257
Phone: 480-994-9244
Fax: 480-994-3228

Southwestern College
2625 E Cactus Rd
Phoenix, AZ 85032
E-mail: swc@netwrx.net
Phone: 602-992-6101
Fax: 602-404-2159
TF: 800-247-2697

Sweetwater Bible College
PO Box 5640
Glendale, AZ 85312
Phone: 602-978-5511
Fax: 602-588-3586

University of Phoenix
4605 E Elwood St
Phoenix, AZ 85040
www.uophx.edu
Phone: 480-966-7400
Fax: 480-303-5874

Western International University
9215 N Black Canyon Hwy
Phoenix, AZ 85021
www.wintu.edu
Phone: 602-943-2311
Fax: 602-371-8637

Hospitals

Arrowhead Community Hospital
18701 N 67th Ave
Glendale, AZ 85308
www.baptisthealth.com/family/in_services/arrowhead.html
Phone: 623-561-1000
Fax: 623-561-7142

Carl T Hayden Veterans Affairs Medical Center
650 E Indian School Rd
Phoenix, AZ 85012
Phone: 602-277-5551
Fax: 602-222-6435

Chandler Regional Hospital
475 S Dobson Rd
Chandler, AZ 85224
elmo.netnation.com/~evrhs/crh/crhhome.htm
Phone: 480-963-4561
Fax: 480-899-5548

Charter Desert Vista Hospital
570 W Brown Rd
Mesa, AZ 85201
Phone: 480-962-3900
Fax: 480-827-0412

Del E Webb Memorial Hospital
14502 W Meeker Blvd
Sun City West, AZ 85375
www.sunhealth.org/webb
Phone: 623-214-4000
Fax: 623-214-4105

Desert Samaritan Medical Center
1400 S Dobson Rd
Mesa, AZ 85202
www.samaritanaz.com/centers/desert_sam.html
Phone: 480-835-3000
Fax: 480-835-8711

Glendale Family Health Center
5141 W Lamar Rd
Glendale, AZ 85301
Phone: 623-931-9361
Fax: 623-344-6701

Good Samaritan Regional Medical Center
1111 E McDowell Rd
Phoenix, AZ 85006
Phone: 602-239-2000
Fax: 602-239-3749

Lincoln John C Hospital North Mountain
250 E Dunlap Ave
Phoenix, AZ 85020
Phone: 602-943-2381
Fax: 602-997-8972

Maricopa Medical Center
2601 E Roosevelt St
Phoenix, AZ 85008
www.maricopa.gov/medcenter/mmc.html
Phone: 602-344-5011
Fax: 602-344-5190

Maryvale Hospital Medical Center
5102 W Campbell Ave
Phoenix, AZ 85031
Phone: 623-848-5000
Fax: 623-848-5337

Mesa General Hospital Medical Center
515 N Mesa Dr
Mesa, AZ 85201
Phone: 480-969-9111
Fax: 480-969-0095

Mesa Lutheran Hospital
525 W Brown Rd
Mesa, AZ 85201
Phone: 480-834-1211
Fax: 480-461-2915

Paradise Valley Hospital
3929 E Bell Rd
Phoenix, AZ 85032
Phone: 602-867-1881
Fax: 602-867-5657

Phoenix Baptist Hospital & Medical Center
2000 W Bethany Home Rd
Phoenix, AZ 85015
www.baptisthealth.com/family/in_services/pbh.html
Phone: 602-249-0212
Fax: 602-246-5979

Phoenix Children's Hospital
1111 E McDowell Rd
Phoenix, AZ 85006
www.phxchildrens.com
Phone: 602-239-5920
Fax: 602-239-3522

Phoenix Memorial Hospital
1201 S 7th Ave
Phoenix, AZ 85007
Phone: 602-258-5111
Fax: 602-824-3383

Piper Kenneth Health Center
9007 E Shea Blvd
Scottsdale, AZ 85260
Phone: 480-860-8140

Saint Joseph's Hospital & Medical Center
350 W Thomas Rd
Phoenix, AZ 85013
Phone: 602-406-3000
Fax: 602-406-6143

Saint Luke's Medical Center
1800 E Van Buren St
Phoenix, AZ 85006
Phone: 602-251-8100
Fax: 602-251-8487

Scottsdale Healthcare Osborn
7400 E Osborn Rd
Scottsdale, AZ 85251
Phone: 480-675-4000
Fax: 480-675-4072

Scottsdale Memorial Hospital-North
9003 E Shea Blvd
Scottsdale, AZ 85260
Phone: 480-860-3000
Fax: 480-860-3510

Tempe Saint Luke's Hospital
1500 S Mill Ave
Tempe, AZ 85281
Phone: 480-968-9411
Fax: 480-784-5630

Thunderbird Samaritan Medical Center
5555 W Thunderbird Rd
Glendale, AZ 85306
www.samaritanaz.com/centers/thunderbird_sam.html
Phone: 602-588-5555
Fax: 602-588-5498

US Public Health Service Phoenix Indian Medical Center
4212 N 16th St
Phoenix, AZ 85016
Phone: 602-263-1200
Fax: 602-263-1618
TF: 877-733-7462

Valley Lutheran Hospital
6644 Baywood Ave
Mesa, AZ 85206
Phone: 480-981-2000
Fax: 480-981-4198

Walter O Boswell Memorial Hospital Phone: 623-977-7211
10401 Thunderbird Blvd Fax: 623-876-5595
Sun City, AZ 85351

Transportation

Airport(s)

Phoenix Sky Harbor International Airport (PHX)
3 miles SE of downtown (approx 15 minutes).....602-273-3300

Mass Transit

DASH Shuttle
$.30 Base fare.................................602-253-5000
Valley Metro
$1.25 Base fare................................602-253-5000

Rail/Bus

Greyhound Bus Station Phone: 602-389-4200
2115 E Buckeye Rd TF: 800-231-2222
Phoenix, AZ 85034

Utilities

Electricity
Arizona Public Service Co......................602-371-7171
about.apsc.com
Salt River Project.............................602-236-8888
www.srpnet.com

Gas
Southwest Gas Corp...........................602-861-1999
www.swgas.com

Water
Phoenix Water Services Dept..................602-262-6251

Garbage Collection/Recycling
Phoenix Public Works Dept....................602-262-7251

Telecommunications

Telephone
Qwest..602-678-9800
www.qwest.com

Cable Television
Cable America...............................480-461-0715
Cable Communications........................623-582-6518
Sun Lakes Cable..............................480-895-8084

Internet Service Providers (ISPs)
AzTeC Computing.............................480-965-4156
aztec.asu.edu
Crossroads Communications...................480-831-2800
www.xroads.com
Evergreen Internet Inc.......................480-926-4500
www.evergreen.com
FASTQ Communications........................602-553-8966
www.amug.org
First Internet...............................480-839-1070
www.firstinter.net
GetNet.......................................602-651-7000
www.getnet.com
PCSLINK (Phoenix Computer Specialists).......602-265-9188
www.pcslink.com
Systems Solutions Inc.........................602-955-5566
www.syspac.com
Winstar GoodNet..............................480-648-1000
www.goodnet.com

Banks

Bank of America NT & SA Phone: 602-594-2371
101 N 1st Ave Fax: 602-594-4376
Phoenix, AZ 85003 TF: 800-284-8491
www.bofa.com

Bank One Arizona NA Phone: 602-221-4724
241 N Central Ave Fax: 602-221-2152
Phoenix, AZ 85004 TF: 800-877-0608

First Arizona Savings FSB Phone: 480-481-8500
3333 E Camelback Rd Suite 240 Fax: 480-481-8515
Phoenix, AZ 85018

Firstar Metropolitan Bank & Trust Phone: 602-230-1233
3800 N Central Ave Fax: 602-277-6806
Phoenix, AZ 85012

M & I Thunderbird Bank Phone: 602-241-6500
1 E Camelback Rd Fax: 602-241-6584
Phoenix, AZ 85012

Northern Trust Bank of Arizona NA Phone: 602-468-1650
2398 E Camelback Rd Suite 400 Fax: 602-912-8665
Phoenix, AZ 85016

Valley Commerce Bank Phone: 602-840-5550
5050 N 44th St Fax: 602-840-6022
Phoenix, AZ 85018

Wells Fargo Bank Arizona NA Phone: 602-378-4690
100 W Washington St Fax: 602-528-1088
Phoenix, AZ 85003 TF: 800-869-3557

Shopping

Arizona Mills Phone: 480-491-7300
5000 Arizona Mills Cir Fax: 480-491-7400
Tempe, AZ 85282
www.arizonamillsmall.com

Arrowhead Towne Center Phone: 623-979-7777
7700 W Arrowhead Towne Ctr Fax: 623-979-4447
Glendale, AZ 85308

Biltmore Fashion Park Phone: 602-955-8400
24th St & Camelback Rd
Phoenix, AZ 85016
www.shopbiltmore.com

Borgata of Scottsdale Phone: 480-998-1822
6166 N Scottsdale Rd
Scottsdale, AZ 85253

Dillard's Phone: 623-849-0100
7621 W Thomas Rd
Phoenix, AZ 85033

Dillard's Phone: 480-833-7777
1435 W Southern Ave Fax: 480-833-4311
Mesa, AZ 85202

DMB Centerpoint Phone: 480-829-7778
660 S Mill Ave Suite 160 Fax: 480-966-5096
Tempe, AZ 85281

Downtown Tempe
398 S Mill Ave Suite 210
Tempe, AZ 85281
Phone: 480-921-2300

el Pedregal
34505 N Scottsdale Rd
Scottsdale, AZ 85262
Phone: 480-488-1072
Fax: 480-488-5915

Factory Stores of America
2050 S Roslyn Pl
Mesa, AZ 85208
www.factorystores.com/
Phone: 480-984-0697
TF: 800-772-8336

Fiesta Mall
2104 Fiesta Mall
Mesa, AZ 85202
Phone: 480-833-4121
Fax: 480-834-8462

Fifth Avenue Area Shops
7087 E 5th Ave
Scottsdale, AZ 85251
Phone: 480-945-0962

Hilton Village
6166 N Scottsdale Rd
Scottsdale, AZ 85253
Phone: 480-998-1822
Fax: 480-998-7581

Indoor SwapMart
5115 N 27th Ave
Phoenix, AZ 85017
Phone: 602-246-9600

Macy's Fiesta Mall
4000 Fiesta Mall
Mesa, AZ 85202
Phone: 480-835-2100

Mervyn's
800 E Southern Rd
Tempe, AZ 85282
Phone: 480-894-9281
Fax: 480-894-9281

Metrocenter
9617 Metro Pkwy W Suite 1001
Phoenix, AZ 85051
E-mail: metro@westcor.com
www.westcor.com/met
Phone: 602-997-2641
Fax: 602-870-9983

Old Towne Shopping District
58th & Glendale Aves
Glendale, AZ 85301

Park Central Mall
3121 N 3rd Ave
Phoenix, AZ 85013
Phone: 602-264-5575

Pinnacle of Scottsdale
23733 N Scottsdale Rd
Scottsdale, AZ 85255
Phone: 480-585-8869
Fax: 480-502-6102

Prime Outlet at New River
4250 W Anthem Way
Phoenix, AZ 85086
Phone: 623-465-9500
Fax: 623-465-9516

Saks Fifth Avenue
2446 E Camelback Rd
Phoenix, AZ 85016
Phone: 602-955-8000
Fax: 602-468-0189

Scottsdale Fashion Square
7014 E Camelback Rd
Scottsdale, AZ 85251
Phone: 480-990-7800
Fax: 480-423-1455

Scottsdale Seville
NE Corner of Scottsdale Rd & Indian Bend
Scottsdale, AZ 85253
Phone: 480-905-8110
Fax: 480-905-8120

Shops at Arizona Center
400 E Van Buren St Suite 550
Phoenix, AZ 85004
Phone: 602-271-4000

Shops at Rawhide
23023 N Scottsdale Rd
Scottsdale, AZ 85255
www.rawhide.com/shopping.html
Phone: 480-502-1880
Fax: 480-502-1301
TF: 800-527-1880

Superstition Springs Center
6555 E Southern Ave
Mesa, AZ 85206
E-mail: ssc@westcor.com
www.westcor.com/ssc
Phone: 480-396-2570
Fax: 480-830-7693

Wigwam Outlet Stores
I-10 & Litchfield Rd
Phoenix, AZ 85338
Phone: 623-935-9733
Fax: 623-935-9588

Media

Newspapers and Magazines

Ahwatukee Foothills News
10631 S 51st St
Phoenix, AZ 85044
E-mail: afn@netzone.com
www.ahwatukee.com/afn
Phone: 480-496-0665
Fax: 480-893-1684

Apache Junction Independent
201 W Apache Trail Suite 708
Apache Junction, AZ 85220
Phone: 480-982-7799
Fax: 480-671-0016

Arizona Business Gazette
PO Box 194
Phoenix, AZ 85001
www.azcentral.com
Phone: 602-444-7300
Fax: 602-444-7363

Arizona Republic*
PO Box 1950
Phoenix, AZ 85001
www.azcentral.com
Phone: 602-444-8000
Fax: 602-444-8044
TF: 800-331-9303

Business Journal of Phoenix
3030 N Central Ave Suite 1500
Phoenix, AZ 85012
www.bizjournals.com/phoenix
Phone: 602-230-8400
Fax: 602-230-0955

Chandler Independent
325 E Elliott Rd Suite 21
Chandler, AZ 85225
Phone: 480-497-0048
Fax: 480-926-1019

East Mesa Independent
201 W Apache Trail Suite 708
Apache Junction, AZ 85220
Phone: 480-497-0048
Fax: 480-671-0016

Paradise Valley Independent
11000 N Scottsdale Rd Suite 210
Scottsdale, AZ 85254
Phone: 480-483-0977
Fax: 480-948-0496

Phoenix Magazine
4041 N Central Ave Suite 530
Phoenix, AZ 85012
Phone: 602-234-0840
Fax: 602-277-7857
TF: 800-888-5621

Phoenix New Times
1201 E Jefferson St
Phoenix, AZ 85034
E-mail: newtimes@newtimes.com
www.phoenixnewtimes.com
Phone: 602-271-0040
Fax: 602-495-9954

Scottsdale Progress Tribune*
7525 E Camelback Rd
Scottsdale, AZ 85252
www.aztrib.com
Phone: 480-941-2300
Fax: 480-970-2360

Tribune*
120 W 1st Ave
Mesa, AZ 85210
www.aztrib.com
Phone: 480-898-6500
Fax: 480-898-6463
TF: 800-272-2460

Where Scottsdale Magazine
4383 N 75th St Suite 103
Scottsdale, AZ 85251
Phone: 480-481-9981
Fax: 480-481-9979

**Indicates major daily newspapers*

Television

KAET-TV Ch 8 (PBS)
PO Box 871405
Tempe, AZ 85287
E-mail: kaet@asu.edu
www.kaet.asu.edu
Phone: 480-965-3506
Fax: 480-965-1000

KASW-TV Ch 61 (WB)
5555 N 7th Ave
Phoenix, AZ 85013
Phone: 480-661-6161
Fax: 480-207-3277

KDRX-TV Ch 64 (Tele)
4001 E Broadway Suite 11
Phoenix, AZ 85040
Phone: 602-470-0507
Fax: 602-470-0810

KNXV-TV Ch 15 (ABC)
515 N 44th St
Phoenix, AZ 85008
E-mail: news15@primenet.com
www.knxv.com
Phone: 602-273-1500
Fax: 602-685-3000

KPHO-TV Ch 5 (CBS)
4016 N Black Canyon Hwy
Phoenix, AZ 85017
www.kpho.com
Phone: 602-264-1000
Fax: 602-650-0761

KPNX-TV Ch 12 (NBC)
1101 N Central Ave
Phoenix, AZ 85004
Phone: 602-257-1212
Fax: 602-257-6619

KSAZ-TV Ch 10 (Fox)
511 W Adams St
Phoenix, AZ 85003
Phone: 602-257-1234
Fax: 602-262-0177

KTVK-TV Ch 3 (Ind)
5555 N 7th Ave
Phoenix, AZ 85013
E-mail: feedback@azfamily.com
Phone: 602-207-3333
Fax: 602-207-3477

KTVW-TV Ch 33 (Uni)
3019 E Southern Ave
Phoenix, AZ 85040
www.univision.net/stations/ktvw.htm
Phone: 602-243-3333
Fax: 602-276-8658

KUSK-TV Ch 7 (Ind)
3211 Tower Rd
Prescott, AZ 86305
E-mail: sauro@kusk.com
www.kusk.com
Phone: 520-778-6770
Fax: 520-445-5210

KUTP-TV Ch 45 (UPN)
4630 S 33rd St
Phoenix, AZ 85040
www.kutp.com
Phone: 602-268-4500
Fax: 602-276-4082

Radio

KBAQ-FM 89.5 MHz (NPR)
1435 S Dobson St
Mesa, AZ 85202
Phone: 480-834-5627
Fax: 480-835-5925

KDDJ-FM 100.3 MHz (Alt)
4745 N 7th St Suite 410
Phoenix, AZ 85014
Phone: 602-266-1360
Fax: 602-263-4844

KDKB-FM 93.3 MHz (Rock)
1167 W Javelina Ave
Mesa, AZ 85210
E-mail: rock@kdkb.com
www.kdkb.com
Phone: 480-897-9300
Fax: 480-897-1964

KEDJ-FM 106.3 MHz (Alt)
4745 N 7th St Suite 410
Phoenix, AZ 85014
www.accessarizona.com/partners/kedj/home.html
Phone: 602-266-1360
Fax: 602-263-4844

KESZ-FM 99.9 MHz (AC)
5555 N 7th Ave Suite B-300
Phoenix, AZ 85013
Phone: 602-207-9999
Fax: 602-207-3177

KFYI-AM 910 kHz (N/T)
631 N 1st Ave
Phoenix, AZ 85003
www.accessarizona.com/partners/kfyi/
Phone: 602-258-6161
Fax: 602-817-1199

KHEP-AM 1280 kHz (Rel)
100 W Clarendon Ave Suite 720
Phoenix, AZ 85013
Phone: 602-234-1280
Fax: 602-234-1586

KJZZ-FM 91.5 MHz (NPR)
1435 S Dobson Rd
Mesa, AZ 85202
www.kjzz.org
Phone: 480-834-5627
Fax: 480-835-5925

KKFR-FM 92.3 MHz (CHR)
631 N First Ave
Phoenix, AZ 85003
www.power92fm.com
Phone: 602-258-6161
Fax: 602-817-1199

KKLT-FM 98.7 MHz (AC)
5300 N Central Ave
Phoenix, AZ 85012
Phone: 602-274-6200
Fax: 602-266-3858

KLNZ-FM 103.5 MHz (Span)
1641 E Osborn Rd Suite 8
Phoenix, AZ 85016
Phone: 602-266-2005
Fax: 602-279-2921

KMLE-FM 107.9 MHz (Ctry)
645 E Missouri Ave Suite 244
Phoenix, AZ 85012
www.kmle108.com
Phone: 602-264-0108
Fax: 602-230-2116

KMVP-AM 860 kHz (Sports)
5300 N Central Ave
Phoenix, AZ 85012
Phone: 602-274-6200
Fax: 602-266-3858

KMXP-FM 96.9 MHz (AC)
645 E Missouri Ave Suite 360
Phoenix, AZ 85012
www.mix969.com
Phone: 602-279-5577
Fax: 602-230-2781

KNIX-FM 102.5 MHz (Ctry)
600 E Gilbert Dr
Tempe, AZ 85281
Phone: 480-966-6236
Fax: 480-921-6365

KOOL-FM 94.5 MHz (Oldies)
4745 N 7th St Suite 210
Phoenix, AZ 85014
www.koolradio.com
Phone: 602-956-9696
Fax: 602-285-1450

KOY-AM 1230 kHz (AC)
840 N Central Ave
Phoenix, AZ 85004
Phone: 602-258-8181
Fax: 602-420-9916

KPTY-FM 103.9 MHz (CHR)
7434 E Stetson Dr Suite 265
Scottsdale, AZ 85251
Phone: 480-423-9255
Fax: 480-423-9382

KSLX-AM 1440 kHz (CR)
4343 E Camelback Rd Suite 200
Phoenix, AZ 85018
www.kslx.com
Phone: 480-941-1007
Fax: 602-808-2288

KSLX-FM 100.7 MHz (CR)
4343 E Camelback Rd Suite 200
Phoenix, AZ 85018
www.kslx.com
Phone: 480-941-1007
Fax: 602-808-2288

KTAR-AM 620 kHz (N/T)
5300 N Central Ave
Phoenix, AZ 85012
E-mail: talk@ktarmail.com
www.ktar620.com
Phone: 602-274-6200
Fax: 602-266-3858

KUPD-FM 97.9 MHz (Rock)
1900 W Carmen St
Tempe, AZ 85283
E-mail: kupd@netzone.com
www.98kupd.com
Phone: 480-838-0400
Fax: 480-820-8469

KVVA-FM 107.1 MHz (Span)
1641 E Osborn Rd Suite 8
Phoenix, AZ 85016
Phone: 602-266-2005
Fax: 602-279-2921

KYOT-FM 95.5 MHz (Nost)
840 N Central Ave
Phoenix, AZ 85004
www.kyot.com
Phone: 602-258-8181
Fax: 602-440-6530

KZON-FM 101.5 MHz (CHR)
840 N Central Ave
Phoenix, AZ 85004
www.kzon.com
Phone: 602-258-8181
Fax: 602-440-6530

KZZP-FM 104.7 MHz (CHR)
645 E Missouri Ave Suite 360
Phoenix, AZ 85012
www.kzzp.com
Phone: 602-279-5577
Fax: 602-230-2781

Attractions

Camelback Mountain, the most prominent landmark in Phoenix, and the Echo Canyon Recreation Area feature sheer red cliffs, the Praying Monk rock formation, and the famous camel's silhouette. Pueblo Grande Museum and Cultural Park is the site of Hohokam ruins that were occupied A.D. 1 through A.D. 1450, with permanent exhibits that feature material excavated from the site. The Heard Museum has an extensive collection of both primitive and modern Native American art. The city's 16,500-acre South Mountain Park is the largest municipal park in the world, with more than 300 specimens of plant life; and the Desert Botanical Garden has an extensive collection of desert plants. Air tours of the scenic areas near the Valley of the Sun, including trips to the Grand Canyon, can be chartered from Phoenix.

Arizona Hall of Fame Museum
1101 W Washington St
Phoenix, AZ 85007
www.dlapr.lib.az.us/museum/hof.htm
Phone: 602-255-2110
Fax: 602-255-3314

Arizona Historical Society Museum
1300 N College Ave
Tempe, AZ 85281
E-mail: ahs@ahs.lib.az.us
www.tempe.gov/ahs
Phone: 480-929-0292
Fax: 480-967-5450

Arizona Mining & Mineral Museum
1502 W Washington St
Phoenix, AZ 85007
Phone: 602-255-3791
Fax: 602-255-3777

Arizona Museum for Youth
35 N Robson St
Mesa, AZ 85201
Phone: 480-644-2468
Fax: 480-644-2466

Arizona Opera Co
4600 N 12th St
Phoenix, AZ 85014
Phone: 602-266-7464

Arizona Performing Arts LLC
2101 E Broadway Suite 7
Tempe, AZ 85282
E-mail: info@murderinkproductions.com
www.murderinkproductions.com
Phone: 480-967-6800
Fax: 480-967-6888

Arizona Science Center
600 E Washington St
Phoenix, AZ 85004
www.azscience.org/
Phone: 602-716-2000
Fax: 602-716-2099

Arizona State Capitol Museum
1700 W Washington St
Phoenix, AZ 85007
E-mail: campus@dlapr.lib.az.us
www.dlapr.lib.az.us/museum/capitol.htm
Phone: 602-542-4675
Fax: 602-542-4690

Arizona State University Art Museum
10th St & Mill Ave Nelson Fine Arts Ctr
Arizona State University
Tempe, AZ 85287
asuam.fa.asu.edu
Phone: 480-965-2787
Fax: 480-965-5254

Arizona State University Gallery of Design
Architecture & Environmental Design
South Bldg PO Box 871905
Tempe, AZ 85287
Phone: 480-965-8169
Fax: 480-965-1594

Arizona State University Life Sciences Center
300 E University Dr Life Sciences Bldg C
Tempe, AZ 85287
Phone: 480-965-3571
Fax: 480-965-2519

Arizona State University Meteorite Collection
Center for Meteorite Studies Physical Science Bldg Suite C151 MS 872504
Tempe, AZ 85287
Phone: 480-965-3576

Arizona State University Museum of Anthropology
Anthropology Bldg
Tempe, AZ 85287
Phone: 480-965-6213
Fax: 480-965-7671

Arizona State University Museum of Geology
Dept of Geology Physical Sciences Bldg F 686
Tempe, AZ 85287
Phone: 480-965-5081
Fax: 480-965-8102

Arizona State University Planetarium
Tempe, AZ 85287
Phone: 480-965-6891
Fax: 480-965-7331

Arizona State University's Kerr Cultural Center
6110 N Scottsdale Rd
Scottsdale, AZ 85253
www.asukerr.com
Phone: 480-965-5377
Fax: 480-483-9646

Arizona Temple Visitors Center
525 E Main St
Mesa, AZ 85204
Phone: 480-964-7164
Fax: 480-964-7789

Arizona Theatre Co
502 W Roosevelt St
Phoenix, AZ 85003
www.aztheatreco.org
Phone: 602-256-6899
Fax: 602-256-7399

Ballet Arizona
3645 E Indian School Rd
Phoenix, AZ 85018
www.balletarizona.citysearch.com
Phone: 602-381-0184
Fax: 602-381-0189

Big Surf
1500 N McClintock Rd
Tempe, AZ 85281
Phone: 480-947-2477
Fax: 480-423-9737

Biosphere 2
32540 S Biosphere Rd
Oracle, AZ 85623
www.bio2.edu
Phone: 520-896-6200
Fax: 520-896-6471

Buffalo Museum of America
10261 N Scottsdale Rd
Scottsdale, AZ 85253
Phone: 480-951-1022
Fax: 480-991-6162

Camelback Mountain & Echo Canyon Recreation Area
5700 N Echo Canyon Pkwy
Phoenix, AZ 85018
Phone: 602-256-3220

Casa Grande Ruins National Monument
1100 Ruins Dr
Coolidge, AZ 85228
www.nps.gov/cagr/
Phone: 520-723-3172
Fax: 520-723-7209

Catlin Court Historic District
7141 N 58th Ave
Glendale, AZ 85301
Phone: 623-937-4754

Cerreta Candy Co
5345 W Glendale Ave
Glendale, AZ 85301
www.cerreta.com
Phone: 623-930-9000
Fax: 623-930-9085

Champlin Fighter Aircraft Museum
4636 E Fighter Aces Dr
Mesa, AZ 85215
www.ci.mesa.az.us/airport/museum.htm
Phone: 480-830-4540
Fax: 480-830-4543

Chandler Center for the Arts
250 N Arizona Ave
Chandler, AZ 85224
Phone: 480-782-2680
Fax: 480-782-2684

Childsplay
132 E 6th St Suite 106
Tempe, AZ 85281
E-mail: childsplayaz@juno.com
www.tempe.gov/childsplay
Phone: 480-350-8101
Fax: 480-350-8584

Computing Commons Gallery
Palm Walk & Orange Mall Computing Commons Rm 140
Tempe, AZ 85287
Phone: 480-965-3609
Fax: 480-965-8698

Confederate Air Force Museum
2017 N Greenfield Rd Falcon Field
Mesa, AZ 85215
www.arizonawingcaf.org
Phone: 480-924-1940
Fax: 480-981-1945

CrackerJax Family Fun & Sports Park
16001 N Scottsdale Rd
Scottsdale, AZ 85254
Phone: 480-998-2800
Fax: 480-998-8544

Deer Valley Rock Art Center
3711 W Deer Valley Rd
Phoenix, AZ 85308
E-mail: dvrac@asu.edu
www.asu.edu/clas/anthropology/dvrac
Phone: 623-582-8007
Fax: 623-582-8831

Desert Botanical Garden
1201 N Galvin Pkwy
Phoenix, AZ 85008
E-mail: dbgadmin@dbg.org
www.dbg.org
Phone: 480-941-1225
Fax: 480-481-8124

DMB Centerpoint
660 S Mill Ave Suite 160
Tempe, AZ 85281
Phone: 480-829-7778
Fax: 480-966-5096

Encanto Park
2605 N 15th Ave
Phoenix, AZ 85007
Phone: 602-262-6412

Enchanted Island Amusement Park
1202 W Encanto Blvd Encanto Pk
Phoenix, AZ 85007
E-mail: enchantedisland@uswest.net
www.enchantedisland.com
Phone: 602-254-2020
Fax: 602-254-1264

Fiddlesticks Family Fun Park & Atlantis Laser Odyssey
8800 E Indian Bend Rd
Scottsdale, AZ 85250
www.fiddlesticksaz.com
Phone: 480-951-6060
Fax: 480-951-4065

Fiddlesticks-Family Fun Park
1155 W Elliott Rd
Tempe, AZ 85284
Phone: 480-961-0800
Fax: 480-961-0427

Fleischer Museum
17207 N Perimeter Dr
Scottsdale, AZ 85255
www.fleischer.org
Phone: 480-585-3108
Fax: 480-585-2225
TF: 800-528-1179

Fort McDowell Casino
PO Box 18359
Fountain Hills, AZ 85269
www.fortmcdowellcasino.com
Phone: 480-837-1424
Fax: 480-837-4756
TF: 800-843-3678

Frank Lloyd Wright Home-Taliesin
12621 Frank Lloyd Wright Blvd
Scottsdale, AZ 85261
www.arizonaguide.com/taliesinwest
Phone: 480-860-2700
Fax: 480-860-8472

Gammage Auditorium
Mill Rd & Apache Blvd Arizona State University
Tempe, AZ 85287
Phone: 480-965-4050
Fax: 480-965-2243

Goldfield Ghost Town & Mine
Hwy 88
Apache Junction, AZ 85219
Phone: 480-983-0333

Golfland/SunSplash
155 W Hampton Ave
Mesa, AZ 85210
www.golfland-sunsplash.com
Phone: 480-834-8318

Grady Gammage Memorial Auditorium
Mill Ave & Apache Blvd
Tempe, AZ 85287
www.asugammage.com
Phone: 480-965-3434
Fax: 480-965-3583

Grand Canyon IMAX Theatre
Hwy 64 & US 180 S Entrance
Grand Canyon, AZ 86023
E-mail: imax@thecanyon.com
www.imaxtheatre.com/grandcanyon/
Phone: 520-638-2203
Fax: 520-638-2807

Grand Canyon National Park
PO Box 129
Grand Canyon, AZ 86023
E-mail: info@thecanyon.com
www.thecanyon.com/nps
Phone: 520-638-7888

Hackett House
95 W 4th St
Tempe, AZ 85281
Phone: 480-350-8181

Hall of Flame Museum of Firefighting
6101 E Van Buren St
Phoenix, AZ 85008
www.hallofflame.org
Phone: 602-275-3473
Fax: 602-275-0896

Heard Museum
2301 N Central Ave
Phoenix, AZ 85004
www.heard.org
Phone: 602-252-8840
Fax: 602-252-9757

Herberger Theater Center
222 E Monroe St
Phoenix, AZ 85004
E-mail: herberger@nonline.com
www.herbergertheater.org
Phone: 602-254-7399
Fax: 602-258-9521

Hohokam Pima National Monument
1100 Ruins Dr Casa Grande Ruins National Monument
Coolidge, AZ 85228
Phone: 520-723-3172
Fax: 520-723-7209

Hoo-hoogam Ki Museum
10005 E Osborn Rd Salt River Indian Reservation
Scottsdale, AZ 85256
Phone: 480-850-8190
Fax: 480-890-8961

MacDonald's Ranch
26540 N Scottsdale Rd
Scottsdale, AZ 85255
www.macdonaldsranch.com
Phone: 480-585-0239
Fax: 480-585-1519

Mat Corner The
1020 S Mill Ave
Tempe, AZ 85281
Phone: 480-966-2055

Max's Dinner Theater
6727 N 47th Ave
Glendale, AZ 85301
Phone: 623-937-1671
Fax: 623-931-4611

McCormick-Stillman Railroad Park
7301 E Indian Bend Rd
Scottsdale, AZ 85250
www.ci.scottsdale.az.us/mccormickpark/
Phone: 480-312-2312
Fax: 480-312-7001

Mesa Arts Center
155 N Center St
Mesa, AZ 85201
Phone: 480-644-2056
Fax: 480-644-2901

Mesa Historical Museum
2345 N Horne St
Mesa, AZ 85203
Phone: 480-835-7358
Fax: 480-835-1442

Mesa Southwest Museum
53 N MacDonald St
Mesa, AZ 85201
Phone: 480-644-2169
Fax: 480-644-3424

Mesa Symphony Orchestra
201 N Centre St Mesa Ampitheatre
Mesa, AZ 85201
Phone: 480-897-2121
Fax: 480-897-2121

Mesa Youtheatre
155 N Center Mesa Arts Center
Mesa, AZ 85211
Phone: 480-644-2681
Fax: 480-644-2901

Museo Chicano
147 E Adams St
Phoenix, AZ 85004
Phone: 602-257-5536

Mystery Castle
800 E Mineral Rd
Phoenix, AZ 85040
Phone: 602-268-1581

Northlight Gallery
Tyler & Forest Malls Arizona State University
Tempe, AZ 85287
Phone: 480-965-6517
Fax: 480-965-8338

Orpheum Theatre
203 W Adams St
Phoenix, AZ 85003
Phone: 602-252-9678
Fax: 602-252-1223

Out of Africa Wildlife Park
9736 N Fort McDowell Rd
Scottsdale, AZ 85264
www.outofafricapark.com
Phone: 480-837-7779
Fax: 480-837-7379

Paolo Soleri Windbells Historic Site
6433 Doubletree Ranch Rd
Scottsdale, AZ 85253
Phone: 480-948-6145
Fax: 480-998-4312
TF: 800-752-3187

Papago Park
625 N Galvin Pkwy
Phoenix, AZ 85032
Phone: 602-256-3220

Park of the Canals
1710 N Horne
Mesa, AZ 85201
Phone: 480-827-4700

Petersen House Museum
1414 W Southern Ave
Tempe, AZ 85282
Phone: 480-350-5100
Fax: 480-350-5150

Phoenix Art Museum
1625 N Central Ave
Phoenix, AZ 85004
E-mail: info@phxart.org
www.azcentral.com/community/phxart/home.html
Phone: 602-257-1880
Fax: 602-253-8662

Phoenix Civic Plaza
111 N 3rd St
Phoenix, AZ 85004
www.ci.phoenix.az.us/civplaza.html
Phone: 602-262-6225
Fax: 602-495-3642
TF: 800-282-4842

Phoenix Heritage Square
115 N 6th St
Phoenix, AZ 85004
www.accessarizona.com/community/groups/hhssquare
Phone: 602-262-5071
Fax: 602-534-1786

Phoenix Mountains Preserve
17642 N 40th St
Phoenix, AZ 85032
Phone: 602-262-6696

Phoenix Museum of History
105 N 5th St
Phoenix, AZ 85004
Phone: 602-253-2734
Fax: 602-253-2348

Phoenix Police Museum
101 S Central Ave Suite 100
Phoenix, AZ 85004
Phone: 602-534-7278

Phoenix Symphony Orchestra
455 N 3rd St Suite 390
Phoenix, AZ 85004
E-mail: info@phoenixsymphony.com
www.phoenixsymphony.com
Phone: 602-495-1117
Fax: 602-253-1772
TF: 800-776-9080

Phoenix Zoo
455 N Galvin Pkwy
Phoenix, AZ 85008
E-mail: zooqna@thephxzoo.com
www.phoenixzoo.org
Phone: 602-273-1341
Fax: 602-273-7078

Pioneer Arizona Living History Museum
3901 W Pioneer Rd
Phoenix, AZ 85086
www.pioneer-arizona.com
Phone: 623-465-1052
Fax: 623-465-1029

PlayHouse Theatre for Children
7402 W Alexandria Way
Peoria, AZ 85381
E-mail: ptcaz@aol.com
members.aol.com/ptcaz/Main.html
Phone: 623-487-9434
Fax: 623-487-9476

Pueblo Grande Museum & Cultural Park
4619 E Washington St
Phoenix, AZ 85034
www.arizonaguide.com/pueblogrande
Phone: 602-495-0901
Fax: 602-495-5645
TF: 877-706-4408

Rawhide 1880s Western Town
23023 N Scottsdale Rd
Scottsdale, AZ 85255
www.rawhide.com
Phone: 480-502-5600
Fax: 480-502-1301

Rawhide Saloon
23023 N Scottsdale Rd
Scottsdale, AZ 85255
www.rawhide.com
Phone: 480-502-5600
Fax: 480-502-1301

Red River Music Hall
730 N Mill Ave
Tempe, AZ 85281
E-mail: info@redrivermusichall.com
www.redrivermusichall.com
Phone: 480-829-0607
Fax: 480-829-1552
TF: 800-466-6779

Sahuaro Ranch Park
5850 W Glendale Ave
Glendale, AZ 85301
Phone: 623-930-2820
Fax: 623-931-9651

Scottsdale Center for the Arts
7380 E 2nd St
Scottsdale, AZ 85251
E-mail: info@sccarts.org
scottsdalearts.org/sca/
Phone: 480-994-2787
Fax: 480-874-4699

Scottsdale Historical Museum
7333 E Civic Center Mall
Scottsdale, AZ 85251
Phone: 480-945-4499
Fax: 480-970-3251

Scottsdale Museum of Contemporary Art
7380 E 2nd St
Scottsdale, AZ 85251
E-mail: info@sccarts.org
scottsdalearts.org/smoca/
Phone: 480-874-4644
Fax: 480-874-4699

Scottsdale Symphony Orchestra
3817 N Brown Ave
Scottsdale, AZ 85251
E-mail: sso@scotsymph.org
www.scotsymph.org
Phone: 480-945-8071
Fax: 480-946-8770

Scottsdale Thursday Night Art Walk
Main St
Scottsdale, AZ 85251
www.scottsdalegalleries.com
Phone: 480-990-3939

Shemer Arts Center & Museum
5005 E Camelback Rd
Phoenix, AZ 85018
Phone: 602-262-4727
Fax: 602-262-1605

Sirrine House
160 N Center St
Mesa, AZ 85201
Phone: 480-644-2760

South Mountain Park
10919 S Central Ave
Phoenix, AZ 85040
Phone: 602-495-0222
Fax: 602-495-0212

South Mountain Park/Preserve
10919 S Central Ave
Phoenix, AZ 85040
Phone: 602-261-8457
Fax: 602-495-0212

Squaw Peak Recreation Area Phone: 602-262-7901
2701 E Squaw Peak Dr Fax: 602-262-4763
Phoenix, AZ 85032

Stagebrush Theatre Phone: 480-990-7405
7020 E 2nd St Fax: 480-990-2182
Scottsdale, AZ 85251

Sundome Center for the Performing Arts Phone: 623-584-3118
19403 RH Johnson Blvd Fax: 623-584-7947
Sun City West, AZ 85375

Tempe Historical Museum Phone: 480-350-5100
809 E Southern Ave Fax: 480-350-5150
Tempe, AZ 85282
www.tempe.gov/museum/archives.htm

Tempe Little Theatre Phone: 480-350-8388
132 E 6th St Fax: 480-350-8584
Tempe, AZ 85281

Tempe Performing Arts Center Phone: 480-350-8101
132 E 6th St Fax: 480-350-8584
Tempe, AZ 85281

Thompson Boyce Southwestern Arboretum Phone: 520-689-2632
37615 Hwy 60 Fax: 520-689-5858
Superior, AZ 85273
ag.arizona.edu/BTA

Tonto National Monument Phone: 520-467-2241
Hwy 88 Fax: 520-467-2225
Roosevelt, AZ 85545
www.nps.gov/tont/

WestWorld Equestrian Center Phone: 480-312-6802
16601 N Pima Rd Fax: 480-312-6803
Scottsdale, AZ 85260

Wrigley Mansion Phone: 602-955-4079
2501 E Telawa Trail Fax: 602-956-8439
Phoenix, AZ 85016
www.wrigleymansionclub.com

Sports Teams & Facilities

America West Arena Phone: 602-379-2000
201 E Jefferson St Fax: 602-379-7857
Phoenix, AZ 85004
www.americawestarena.com

Anaheim Angels Spring Training (baseball) Phone: 480-350-5265
Alameda Dr & 48th St Fax: 480-350-5059
Tempe, AZ 85282

Apache Greyhound Park Phone: 480-982-2371
2551 W Apache Trail Fax: 480-983-0013
Apache Junction, AZ 85220

Arizona Cardinals Phone: 602-379-0101
8701 S Hardy Dr Fax: 602-379-1819
Tempe, AZ 85284
www.azcardinals.com

Arizona Diamondbacks Phone: 602-462-6500
401 E Jefferson St Bank One Ballpark Fax: 602-462-6600
Phoenix, AZ 85004
www.azdiamondbacks.com

Arizona Rattlers (football) Phone: 602-379-7878
201 E Jefferson St America West Arena Fax: 602-514-8303
Phoenix, AZ 85004
www.azrattlers.com

Arizona Sahuaros (soccer) Phone: 623-516-2133
1630 E Southern Ave MEsa Jack Rabbit Stadium Fax: 623-492-0602
Mesa, AZ 85204
E-mail: mark@sahuaros.com
www.azsahuaros.com

Arizona Thunder (soccer) Phone: 602-263-5425
1826 W McDowell Rd Arizona Veterans Memorial Coliseum Fax: 602-263-7730
Phoenix, AZ 85007
www.arizonathunder.com

Arizona Veterans Memorial Coliseum & Exposition Center Phone: 602-252-6771
1826 W McDowell Rd Suite 100 Fax: 602-251-0528
Phoenix, AZ 85007

Bank One Ballpark Phone: 602-462-6500
401 E Jefferson St Fax: 602-462-6600
Phoenix, AZ 85004
www.azdiamondbacks.com/bob/index.shtml?seating_chart2.shtml

Chicago Cubs Spring Training (baseball) Phone: 480-964-4467
1235 N Center St
Mesa, AZ 85201
www.cubspringtraining.com

Firebird International Raceway Park Phone: 602-268-0200
Maricopa Rd & I-10 Fax: 520-796-0531
Chandler, AZ 85226
E-mail: info@firebirdraceway.com
www.firebirdraceway.com

Harlem Globetrotters International Inc Phone: 602-258-0000
400 E Van Buren St Suite 300 Fax: 602-258-5925
Phoenix, AZ 85004 TF: 800-641-4667
www.harlemglobetrotters.com

Manzanita Speedway Phone: 602-276-9401
3417 W Broadway Rd Fax: 602-276-3174
Phoenix, AZ 85041
E-mail: manzyspeed@earthlink.net
www.manzanitaspeedway.com

Milwaukee Brewers Spring Training (baseball) Phone: 623-245-5555
3600 N 51st Ave Maryvale Baseball Pk
Phoenix, AZ 85031

Phoenix Coyotes Phone: 480-473-5600
9375 E Bell Rd Fax: 480-473-5699
Scottsdale, AZ 85260
www.nhlcoyotes.com/home.shtml

Phoenix Greyhound Park Phone: 602-273-7181
3801 E Washington St Fax: 602-273-6176
Phoenix, AZ 85034
www.phxgp.com

Phoenix International Raceway
455 N 3rd St Suite 340
Phoenix, AZ 85004
www.phoenixintlraceway.com
Phone: 602-252-3833
Fax: 602-254-4622

Phoenix Mercury (basketball)
201 E Jefferson St America West Arena
Phoenix, AZ 85004
www.wnba.com/mercury
Phone: 602-252-9622
Fax: 602-514-8303

Phoenix Suns
201 E Jefferson St America West Arena
Phoenix, AZ 85004
www.nba.com/suns
Phone: 602-379-7800
Fax: 602-379-7922

San Francisco Giants Spring Training (baseball)
Scottsdale Stadium 7408 E Osborn Rd
Scottsdale, AZ 85251
Phone: 480-990-7972

Scottsdale Scorpions (baseball)
7402 E Osborn Rd Scottsdale Stadium
Scottsdale, AZ 85251
Phone: 480-496-6700
Fax: 480-496-6384

Scottsdale Stadium
7408 East Osborn Rd
Scottsdale, AZ 85251
Phone: 480-312-2580

Sun Devil Stadium
Stadium Dr & 6th St Arizona State University
Tempe, AZ 85287
www.thesundevils.com
Phone: 480-965-5062
Fax: 480-965-7663

Turf Paradise Racetrack
1501 W Bell Rd
Phoenix, AZ 85023
www.turfparadise.com
Phone: 602-942-1101
Fax: 602-588-2002

Annual Events

A Family A Fair (early April) 623-930-2820
Acorn's Spring Antique Show & Sale (late March) 480-830-2660
Air Show Spectacular (mid-March) 480-988-1013
Annual Quilt Show (mid-January-mid-March) 623-939-5782
Arizona Quarter Horse Amateur Horse Show (mid-January) 480-312-6802
Arizona Renaissance Festival (early February-late March) 520-463-2700
Arizona Scottish Highland Games (late February) 602-431-0095
Arizona Special Olympics Summer Games (early May) 602-230-1200
Arizona Spring Super Classic Circuit (early April) 480-312-6802
Arizona State Fair (early-late October) 602-252-6771
Arizona Stock Show & Rodeo (late December-early January) 602-258-8568
Arizona Woodcarvers Show (late November) 480-895-7036
Arizona's Cactus League Spring Training (March) . . . 480-969-1307
ARR Desert Classic Marathon (mid-February) 623-933-2425
Blues Blast (late February) 480-644-2242
Borgata Farmers Market (October-April) 480-998-1822
Chandler Ostrich Festival (mid-March) 480-963-4571
Cinco de Mayo Celebrations (Mesa) (early May) 480-644-2230
Cinco de Mayo Festival (Phoenix) (early May) 602-279-4669
Community Bank Concerts (June-July) 623-930-2820
Coors Light World Finals Drag Boat Racing (late October) 602-268-0200
Copper World Classic Auto Racing (late January-early February) 602-252-3833
Country Thunder USA (late April) 480-966-9920
Cowboy Artists of America Exhibition (mid-October-mid-November) 602-257-1880
Dia de los Muertos Festival (early November) 480-833-5875
Easter Pageant (mid-late April) 480-964-7164
Equine Spectacular (early March) 480-502-5600
Fall Festival of the Arts (early December) 480-967-4877
Fiesta Bowl (early January) 480-350-0900
Fiesta Bowl Duck Race (early October) 480-350-0900
Fiesta Bowl Parade (late December) 480-350-0900
Fiesta of Lights (mid-December) 602-261-8604
Fountain Festival of the Arts & Crafts (early November) 480-837-1654
Fountain Hills Festival of Arts & Crafts (mid-November) 480-837-1654
Fountain Hills Great Fair (late February) 480-837-1654
Fourth of July Celebration (Glendale) (July 4) 623-937-4754
Fourth of July Celebration (Tempe) (July 4) 480-967-7891
French Week in Arizona (mid-November) 602-262-6169
Front Porch Festival (late-September) 623-435-0556
Gilbert Days (mid-late November) 480-380-8399
Glendale Jazz Festival (late-April) 623-930-2960
Grand Canyon State Games (mid-June) 480-517-9700
Holiday Out West Arts & Crafts Festival (late November) 480-488-2014
Hot Air Balloon Race & Thunderbird Balloon Classic (early November) 480-312-6802
Independence Day Celebrations (July 4) 480-644-2011
Indy Racing League Phoenix 200 (late March) 602-252-2227
Insight.com Bowl (late December) 480-350-0900
July 4th Festivities (July 4) 602-256-4125
Jump into Spring Hunter Jumper Horse Show (late March) 480-312-6802
Juried Fine Arts Competition (late March-late April) 623-939-5782
Knix Spring Rodeo Connection at Rawhide (early May-late June) 480-502-5600
Lost Dutchman Days (late February) 480-982-3141
Maricopa County Fair (mid-April) 602-252-0717
Merry-Go-Round Horse Show (mid-October) 480-312-6802
Mesa Day (early March) 480-644-2351
Mesa Southwest Antique Guild Show & Sale (mid-May) 602-943-1766
Mill Avenue Masquerade (October 31) 480-967-4877
Music by Moonlight Thursday Night Concert Series (mid-April-late June) 480-488-1072
Native American Pow Wow (mid-October) 480-644-2169
New Year's Eve Block Party (December 31) 480-894-8158
Parada Del Sol Parade (late January) 480-990-3179
Peach Festival (mid-May) 480-987-3333
Performances in the Park (late April) 623-937-4754
Phoenix Open Golf Tournament (late January) 602-870-0163
PRCA Pro Rodeo Series (mid-April) 480-502-5600
Pueblo Grande Indian Market (mid-December) 602-495-0901
Queen Creek Potato Festival (late May) 480-987-3333

Rawhide's Rollickin' New Year's Eve
(December 31) 480-502-5600
Region 7 All-Arabian Championship Horse Show
(late April-early May) 480-312-6802
Sahuaro Ranch Days (early November) 623-939-5782
Scottsdale Arabian Horse Show
(mid-late February) 480-312-6802
Scottsdale Arts Festival (mid-March) 480-994-2787
Scottsdale Celebration of Fine Art
(mid-January-late March) 480-443-7695
Scottsdale Culinary Festival (mid-April) 480-945-7193
Scottsdale Desert Festival of Fine Art
(early February) 480-837-5637
Southwest Salsa Challenge (late April) 602-955-3947
Spring Festival of the Arts
(late March-early April) 480-967-4877
Spring POW WOW Competition (mid-April) 480-965-5224
Tempe's Fantasy of Lights
(late November-early January) 480-894-8158
Tempe's Thanksgiving Soccer Tournament
(late November) 480-966-4053
Territorial Days (mid-February) 480-644-2351
Tumbleweed Christmas Tree Lighting Ceremony
(December) 480-782-2727
Valley of the Sun Polka Festival (mid-February) 602-237-4024
Victorian Holiday (mid-December) 602-262-5029

Pittsburgh, Pennsylvania

County: **Allegheny**

PITTSBURGH is located in southwestern Pennsylvania where the Allegheny and Monongahela Rivers join to form the Ohio River. Major cities within 100 miles include Akron, Cleveland, and Youngstown, Ohio; and Morgantown and Wheeling, West Virginia.

Area (Land) .... 55.6 sq mi
Area (Water)................................ 2.7 sq mi
Elevation...................................... 770 ft
Latitude .... 40-36-31 N
Longitude................................ 79-86-87 W
Time Zone .... EST
Area Code....................................... 412

Climate

Pittsburgh has a continental climate with four distinct seasons. Winters are cold, with average high temperatures in the mid- to upper 30s and lows near 20 degrees. The average annual snowfall in Pittsburgh is just over 40 inches. Summer days are warm, with average high temperatures near 80 degrees, while evenings cool down to around 60. July is the wettest month of the year in Pittsburgh, while February and October are the driest.

Average Temperatures & Precipitation

Temperatures

	Jan	Feb	Mar	Apr	May	Jun	Jul	Aug	Sep	Oct	Nov	Dec
High	34	37	49	60	71	79	83	81	74	63	50	39
Low	19	20	30	39	48	57	62	60	54	42	34	24

Precipitation

	Jan	Feb	Mar	Apr	May	Jun	Jul	Aug	Sep	Oct	Nov	Dec
Inches	2.5	2.4	3.4	3.2	3.6	3.7	3.8	3.2	3.0	2.4	2.9	2.9

History

Originally an Iroquois village, the area known today as Pittsburgh served as a fur trading post during the late 1600s. In the early 1750s, the French built Fort Duquesne in the area, which was destroyed by the British and rebuilt as Fort Pitt (the largest outpost in North America) later in the decade. The settlement that developed around Fort Pitt (named for then British Prime Minister William Pitt) eventually became known as the borough of Pittsburgh.

The area surrounding Pittsburgh was rich in mineral resources, and the community's location at the point where the Allegheny and Monongahela Rivers meet to form the Ohio River enabled the city to grow as an important industrial center. Incorporated as a city in 1816, Pittsburgh quickly became a leading supplier of iron, glass, and coke. Industrial growth was further stimulated by the completion of the Pennsylvania Canal and the arrival of the Portage Railroad, both of which linked Pittsburgh with Philadelphia. The steel industry that Pittsburgh has become famous for began in 1873 when Andrew Carnegie established his first steel mill in the city. By the early part of the 20th Century, the city produced three-quarters of the steel used in the United States.

By the mid-1900s, Pittsburgh was plagued by air pollution and frequent flooding, including a devastating flood in 1936. In the 1940s, the first of two major redevelopment projects was implemented (the second was implemented three decades later in the '70s) in an effort to remedy these problems. The 1980s brought massive economic decline to Pittsburgh, as the city's steel industry was adversely affected by the increase in foreign steel production. In the past decade, however, Pittsburgh has emerged as not only a center for industry, but also as a center for transportation, finance, medicine, education, and culture. Home to more than 340,000 people, Pittsburgh today is Pennsylvania's second largest city.

Population

1990 Census 369,879
1998 Estimate.............................. 340,520
% Change .... -7.9

Racial/Ethnic Breakdown

White.................................... 72.1%
Black 25.8%
Other 2.1%
Hispanic Origin (may be of any race) 0.9%

Age Breakdown

Under 5 years.............................. 6.2%
5 to 17.................................. 13.7%
18 to 20.................................. 6.5%
21 to 24.................................. 7.5%
25 to 34................................. 16.9%
35 to 44................................. 13.2%
45 to 54.................................. 8.5%
55 to 64.................................. 9.6%
65 to 74................................. 10.1%
75+ years 7.8%
Median Age................................. 34.6

Gender Breakdown

Male..................................... 46.4%
Female................................... 53.6%

Government

Type of Government: Mayor-Council

Carnegie Library of Pittsburgh
4400 Forbes Ave
Pittsburgh, PA 15213
Phone: 412-622-3116
Fax: 412-622-6278

Pittsburgh City Clerk
414 Grant St Rm 510
Pittsburgh, PA 15219
Phone: 412-255-2138
Fax: 412-255-2821

Pittsburgh City Council
414 Grant St Rm 510
Pittsburgh, PA 15219
Phone: 412-255-2142
Fax: 412-255-2821

Pittsburgh City Hall
414 Grant St
Pittsburgh, PA 15219
Phone: 412-255-2621
Fax: 412-255-2821

Pittsburgh City Planning Dept
200 Ross St Robin Civic Bldg 4th fl
Pittsburgh, PA 15219
Phone: 412-255-2201
Fax: 412-255-2838

Pittsburgh Finance Dept
414 Grant St Rm 200
Pittsburgh, PA 15219
Phone: 412-255-2576
Fax: 412-255-8649

Pittsburgh Fire Bureau
100 Grant St Public Safety Bldg 6th Fl
Pittsburgh, PA 15219
Phone: 412-255-2870
Fax: 412-255-8839

Pittsburgh Law Dept
414 Grant St Rm 313
Pittsburgh, PA 15219
Phone: 412-255-2015
Fax: 412-255-2285

Pittsburgh Mayor
414 Grant St Rm 512
Pittsburgh, PA 15219
Phone: 412-255-2626
Fax: 412-255-2687

Pittsburgh Parks & Recreation Dept
414 Grant St Rm 400
Pittsburgh, PA 15219
Phone: 412-255-2539
Fax: 412-255-2307

Pittsburgh Personnel Dept & Civil Service Commission
414 Grant St Rm 431
Pittsburgh, PA 15219
Phone: 412-255-2710
Fax: 412-255-4736

Pittsburgh Police Bureau
100 Grant St 7th Fl
Pittsburgh, PA 15219
Phone: 412-255-2814
Fax: 412-255-2909

Pittsburgh Public Works Dept
611 2nd Ave
Pittsburgh, PA 15219
Phone: 412-255-2790
Fax: 412-255-8981

Pittsburgh Water & Sewer Authority
441 Smithfield St
Pittsburgh, PA 15222
Phone: 412-255-8949
Fax: 412-255-2304

Important Phone Numbers

AAA....................412-363-5100
American Express Travel....................412-391-3202
Dental Referral....................800-917-6453
Driver's License Information....................724-832-3277
Emergency....................911
Events Line....................800-366-0093
HotelDocs....................800-468-3537
Medical Referral....................412-321-5030
Pennsylvania Revenue Dept....................412-565-7540
Pittsburgh Finance Dept....................412-255-2541
Pittsburgh Finance Dept Real Estate Div....................412-255-2567
Poison Control Center....................412-681-6669
Realtors Assn of Greater Pittsburgh....................412-261-5200
Time/Temp....................412-391-9500
Travelers Aid....................412-281-5474
Vehicle Registration Information....................717-787-3184
Voter Registration Information....................412-350-4500
Weather....................412-936-1212

Information Sources

Allegheny County
436 Grant St County Courthouse
Pittsburgh, PA 15219
info.co.allegheny.pa.us
Phone: 412-350-5300
Fax: 412-350-3581

Better Business Bureau Serving Western Pennsylvania
300 6th Ave Suite 100-UL
Pittsburgh, PA 15222
www.pittsburgh.bbb.org
Phone: 412-456-2700
Fax: 412-456-2739

David L Lawrence Convention Center
1001 Penn Ave
Pittsburgh, PA 15222
www.pgh-conventionctr.com
Phone: 412-565-6000
Fax: 412-565-6008
TF: 800-222-5200

Greater Pittsburgh Chamber of Commerce
425 6th Ave
Pittsburgh, PA 15219
www.pittsburghchamber.com
Phone: 412-392-4500
Fax: 412-392-4520
TF: 800-843-8772

Greater Pittsburgh Convention & Visitors Bureau
425 6th Ave 30th Fl
Pittsburgh, PA 15219
www.pittsburgh-cvb.org
Phone: 412-281-7711
Fax: 412-644-5512
TF: 800-359-0758

Online Resources

4Pittsburgh.com
www.4pittsburgh.com

About.com Guide to Pittsburgh
pittsburgh.about.com/local/midlanticus/pittsburgh

Access America Pittsburgh
www.accessamer.com/pittsburgh/

Anthill City Guide Pittsburgh
www.anthill.com/city.asp?city=pittsburgh

Area Guide Pittsburgh
pittsburgh.areaguides.net

Boulevards Pittsburgh
www.boulevards.com/cities/pittsburgh.html

City Knowledge Pittsburgh
www.cityknowledge.com/pa_pittsburgh.htm

CitySearch Pittsburgh
pittsburgh.citysearch.com

Cyburgh Pittsburgh
www.cyburgh.com/

DigitalCity Pittsburgh
home.digitalcity.com/pittsburgh

Discover Pittsburgh!
trfn.clpgh.org/Local

Excite.com Pittsburgh City Guide
www.excite.com/travel/countries/united_states/pennsylvania/pittsburgh

Greater Pittsburgh Museum Council
huntbot.andrew.cmu.edu/GPMC/GPghMusCouncil.html

In Pittsburgh Newsweekly
www.inpgh.com

Marbles E-Zine
www.sgi.net/marbles

OnTv: Pittsburgh's Community Webstation
www.ontv.com/

Pittsburgh City Pages
pittsburgh.thelinks.com

Pittsburgh City Paper
www.pghcitypaper.com

Pittsburgh Guide
www.pghguide.com/

Pittsburgh Travel Aid
www.nb.net/~tsalacri/pghtrav.html

Pittsburgh's South Side
betatesters.com/penn/sahside

Pittsburgh.Net
www.pittsburgh.net

Practical Pittsburgher
www.cs.cmu.edu/practical.html

Real Pittsburgh.com
www.realpittsburgh.com

ShopPittsburgh.net
www.shoppittsburgh.net

Telerama's Virtual Tour of Pittsburgh
web.lm.com/pittsburgh.html

Three Rivers Free-Net
trfn.pgh.pa.us/

Area Communities

Communities in the five-county (Allegheny, Beaver, Butler, Washington, and Westmoreland) Pittsburgh metropolitan area with populations greater than 10,000 include:

Aliquippa
581 Franklin Ave
Aliquippa, PA 15001
Phone: 724-375-5188
Fax: 724-375-4594

Beaver Falls
715 15th St
Beaver Falls, PA 15010
Phone: 724-847-2800
Fax: 724-847-4748

Bethel Park
5100 W Library Ave
Bethel Park, PA 15102
Phone: 412-831-6800
Fax: 412-831-8675

Butler
140 W North St
Butler, PA 16001
Phone: 724-285-4124
Fax: 724-285-6880

Butler Township
6 Chesapeake St
Lyndora, PA 16045
Phone: 724-283-3430
Fax: 724-282-2142

Center Township
224 Center Grange Rd
Aliquippa, PA 15001
Phone: 724-774-0271
Fax: 724-774-6055

Cranberry Township
2525 Rochester Rd
Cranberry Township, PA 16066
Phone: 724-776-4806
Fax: 724-776-5488

Derry Township
650 Derry Rd
Derry, PA 15627
Phone: 724-539-2961
Fax: 724-694-5860

Greensburg
416 S Main St
Greensburg, PA 15601
Phone: 724-838-4324
Fax: 724-838-4350

Hempfield Township
Woodward Dr RD 6 Bx 500
Greensburg, PA 15601
Phone: 724-834-7232
Fax: 724-834-5510

Hopewell Township
1700 Clark Blvd
Aliquippa, PA 15001
Phone: 724-378-1460
Fax: 724-378-3034

Lower Burrell
2800 Bethel St
Lower Burrell, PA 15068
Phone: 724-335-9875
Fax: 724-335-9881

McCandless
9955 Grubbs Rd
Wexford, PA 15090
Phone: 412-364-0616
Fax: 412-364-5066

McKeesport
201 Lysle Blvd
McKeesport, PA 15132
Phone: 412-675-5030
Fax: 412-675-5049

Monroeville
2700 Monroeville Blvd
Monroeville, PA 15146
Phone: 412-856-1000
Fax: 412-856-3366

Mount Lebanon
710 Washington Rd
Pittsburgh, PA 15228
Phone: 412-343-3400
Fax: 412-343-3753

Mount Pleasant Township
PO Box 158
Mammoth, PA 15664
Phone: 724-423-5653
Fax: 724-423-1122

Murrysville
4100 Sardis Rd
Murrysville, PA 15668
Phone: 724-327-2100
Fax: 724-327-2881

New Kensington
301 11th St
New Kensington, PA 15068
Phone: 724-337-4523
Fax: 724-337-6911

North Huntingdon
11279 Center Hwy
North Huntingdon, PA 15642
Phone: 724-863-3806
Fax: 724-863-9568

Penn Hills
12245 Frankstown Rd
Penn Hills, PA 15235
Phone: 412-795-3500
Fax: 412-798-2109

Penn Township
PO Box 452
Harrison City, PA 15636
Phone: 724-744-2171
Fax: 724-744-2172

Peters Township
610 E McMurray Rd
McMurray, PA 15317
Phone: 724-941-4180
Fax: 724-942-5022

Ross Township
5325 Perrysville Ave
Pittsburgh, PA 15229
Phone: 412-931-7055
Fax: 412-931-7062

Shaler Township
300 Whetzel Rd
Glenshaw, PA 15116
Phone: 412-486-9700
Fax: 412-487-4107

Unity Township
1104 Beatty County Rd
Latrobe, PA 15650
Phone: 724-539-2546
Fax: 724-539-7088

Washington
55 W Maiden St
Washington, PA 15301
Phone: 724-223-4209
Fax: 724-223-4229

Wilkinsburg
605 Ross Ave
Wilkensburg, PA 15221
Phone: 412-244-2900
Fax: 412-244-8642

Economy

Pittsburgh has a healthy, diverse economy that ranges from finance to food product manufacturing. Major U.S. corporations that are headquartered in the area include USX Corporation, Alcoa, Westinghouse Electric, H.J. Heinz, PPG Industries, and PNC Bank. The steel, iron, and glass industries that fueled Pittsburgh's economy for more than a century play a much smaller role in the area's present economy. Home to more than 2,500 high-tech firms, as well as several university-based research centers, Pittsburgh's fastest-growing industry today is high-technology. Services is currently the area's largest employment sector, with health care being a major industry—more than 56,000 area residents are employed in hospitals alone. Pittsburgh has become a major center for medical research and biotechnology and is among the nation's leaders in organ transplants. Government also plays an important role in southwestern Pennsylvania's economy, employing more than 124,000 people at the federal, state, and local levels—the U.S. Government is Allegheny County's largest employer, providing jobs for more than 14,000 area residents.

Unemployment Rate	3.7%**
Per Capita Income	$29,328*
Median Family Income	$42,700**

** Information given is for Allegheny County.*
*** Information given is for the Pittsburgh Metropolitan Statistical Area (MSA), which includes the City of Pittsburgh, Allegheny County, Beaver County, Butler County, Washington County, & Westmoreland County.*

Principal Industries & Number of Wage Earners

Pittsburgh MSA* - June 2000

Construction	61,800
Finance, Insurance, & Real Estate	68,200
Government	124,300
Manufacturing	139,400
Mining	4,500
Retail Trade	204,200
Services	391,800
Transportation & Public Utilities	68,700
Wholesale Trade	59,600

** Information given is for the Pittsburgh Metropolitan Statistical Area (MSA), which includes the City of Pittsburgh, Allegheny County, Beaver County, Butler County, Washington County, & Westmoreland County.*

Major Employers

Alcoa Inc
201 Isabella St
Pittsburgh, PA 15212
www.alcoa.com
Phone: 412-553-4545
Fax: 412-553-4498

Allegheny County
436 Grant St County Courthouse
Pittsburgh, PA 15219
info.co.allegheny.pa.us
Phone: 412-350-5300
Fax: 412-350-3581

Commonwealth of Pennsylvania State Civil Service
300 Liberty Ave State Office Bldg
Pittsburgh, PA 15222
www.scsc.state.pa.us
Phone: 412-565-7666

HJ Heinz Co
600 Grant St 60th Fl
Pittsburgh, PA 15219
www.heinz.com
Phone: 412-456-5700
Fax: 412-456-6128

Marconi Corp
1000 Fore Dr
Pittsburgh, PA 15086
www.marconi.com
Phone: 724-742-4444
Fax: 724-742-7777
TF: 888-404-0444

May Co Kaufmann's Div
400 5th Ave
Pittsburgh, PA 15219
Phone: 412-232-2212
Fax: 412-232-2936

Medrad Inc
1 Medrad Dr
Indianola, PA 15051
E-mail: info@medrad.com
www.medrad.com
Phone: 412-767-2400
Fax: 412-767-4295
TF: 800-633-7231

PNC Financial Services Group Inc
249 5th Ave 1 PNC Plaza
Pittsburgh, PA 15222
www.pnc.com
Phone: 412-762-2000
Fax: 412-762-2256
TF: 877-762-2000

PPG Industries Inc
1 PPG Pl
Pittsburgh, PA 15272
E-mail: corporate@ppg.com
www.ppg.com
Phone: 412-434-3131
Fax: 412-434-2011

University of Pittsburgh Phone: 412-624-4141
4200 5th Ave Fax: 412-648-8815
Pittsburgh, PA 15260
E-mail: hrpitt+@pitt.edu
www.pitt.edu

University of Pittsburgh Medical Center Phone: 412-648-6000
200 Lothrop St Fax: 412-647-5125
Pittsburgh, PA 15213
www.upmc.edu

US Airways Inc Phone: 412-472-7000
Pittsburgh International Airport
Pittsburgh, PA 15231
www.usair.com/corporate/jobs

USX Corp Phone: 412-433-1121
600 Grant St Fax: 412-433-5733
Pittsburgh, PA 15219
www.usx.com

Quality of Living Indicators

Total Crime Index 21,286
(rates per 100,000 inhabitants)

Violent Crime
Murder/manslaughter 48
Forcible rape 138
Robbery 1,581
Aggravated assault 1,312

Property Crime
Burglary 3,115
Larceny theft 11,895
Motor vehicle theft 3,197

Cost of Living Index 109.5
(national average = 100)

Median Home Price $89,900

Education

Public Schools

Pittsburgh Public Schools Phone: 412-622-3500
341 S Bellefield Ave Fax: 412-622-7973
Pittsburgh, PA 15213
E-mail: publicaf@pps.pgh.pa.us
www.pps.pgh.pa.us

Number of Schools
Elementary 57
Middle 19
High 10

Student/Teacher Ratio
All Grades 15.1:1

Private Schools

Number of Schools (all grades) .... 54+

Colleges & Universities

Art Institute of Pittsburgh Phone: 412-263-6600
526 Penn Ave Fax: 412-263-6667
Pittsburgh, PA 15222 TF: 800-275-2470
www.aii.edu

Carlow College Phone: 412-578-6000
3333 5th Ave Fax: 412-578-6668
Pittsburgh, PA 15213 TF: 800-333-2275
E-mail: ehof@carlow.edu
www.carlow.edu

Carnegie Mellon University Phone: 412-268-2000
5000 Forbes Ave Warner Hall Fax: 412-268-7838
Pittsburgh, PA 15213
E-mail: undergraduate-admissions+@CMU.edu
www.cmu.edu

Chatham College Phone: 412-365-1100
Woodland Rd Fax: 412-365-1609
Pittsburgh, PA 15232 TF: 800-837-1290
www.chatham.edu

Community College of Allegheny County Allegheny Campus Phone: 412-237-2525
808 Ridge Ave Fax: 412-237-4581
Pittsburgh, PA 15212
www.ccac.edu

Community College of Allegheny County Boyce Campus Phone: 724-327-1327
595 Beatty Rd Fax: 724-325-6859
Monroeville, PA 15146
www.ccac.edu

Community College of Allegheny County North Campus Phone: 412-366-7000
8701 Perry Hwy Fax: 412-369-3635
Pittsburgh, PA 15237

Dean Institute of Technology Phone: 412-531-4433
1501 W Liberty Ave Fax: 412-531-4435
Pittsburgh, PA 15226
E-mail: deantech@earthlink.net

Duff's Business Institute Phone: 412-261-4520
110 9th St Fax: 412-261-4546
Pittsburgh, PA 15222 TF: 888-279-3314
duffs-institute.com

Duquesne University Phone: 412-396-6000
600 Forbes Ave Fax: 412-396-5644
Pittsburgh, PA 15282 TF: 800-456-0590
E-mail: mclaughc@duq2.cc.duq.edu
www.duq.edu

Geneva College Phone: 724-846-5100
3200 College Ave Fax: 724-847-6776
Beaver Falls, PA 15010 TF: 800-847-8255
www.geneva.edu

ICM School of Business Phone: 412-261-2647
10 Wood St Fax: 412-261-0998
Pittsburgh, PA 15222 TF: 800-441-5222
www.icmschool.com

La Roche College Phone: 412-367-9300
9000 Babcock Blvd Fax: 412-536-1062
Pittsburgh, PA 15237
www.laroche.edu

Penn Technical Institute Phone: 412-232-3547
110 9th St Fax: 412-355-7904
Pittsburgh, PA 15222

Pennsylvania State University Beaver Campus
100 University Dr
Monaca, PA 15061
www.br.psu.edu
Phone: 724-773-3500
Fax: 724-773-3658

Pennsylvania State University Delaware County Campus
25 Yearsley Mill Rd
Media, PA 19063
www.de.psu.edu
Phone: 610-892-1350
Fax: 610-892-1357

Pennsylvania State University McKeesport Campus
4000 University Dr
McKeesport, PA 15132
www.mk.psu.edu
Phone: 412-675-9000
Fax: 412-675-9056

Pennsylvania State University New Kensington Campus
3550 7th Street Rd Rt 780
Upper Burrell, PA 15068
www.nk.psu.edu
Phone: 724-334-6000
Fax: 724-334-6111

Pittsburgh Institute of Aeronautics
PO Box 10897
Pittsburgh, PA 15236
E-mail: admissions@piainfo.org
www.piainfo.org
Phone: 412-462-9011
Fax: 412-466-0513
TF: 800-444-1440

Pittsburgh Institute of Mortuary Science Inc
5808 Baum Blvd
Pittsburgh, PA 15206
E-mail: pims5805@aol.com
www.p-i-m-s.com
Phone: 412-362-8500
Fax: 412-362-1684
TF: 800-933-5808

Pittsburgh Technical Institute
635 Smithfield St
Pittsburgh, PA 15222
E-mail: pti@fujinet
Phone: 412-471-1011
Fax: 412-232-3945

Point Park College
201 Wood St
Pittsburgh, PA 15222
www.ppc.edu
Phone: 412-391-4100
Fax: 412-391-1980

Robert Morris College
881 Narrows Run Rd
Moon Township, PA 15108
www.robert-morris.edu
Phone: 412-262-8200
Fax: 412-299-2425
TF: 800-762-0097

Slippery Rock University
Slippery Rock, PA 16057
E-mail: dms@sruvm.sru.edu
www.sru.edu
Phone: 724-738-9000
Fax: 724-738-2913
TF: 800-929-4778

Triangle Tech Inc
1940 Perrysville Ave
Pittsburgh, PA 15214
Phone: 412-359-1000
Fax: 412-359-1012
TF: 800-874-8324

University of Pittsburgh
4200 5th Ave
Pittsburgh, PA 15260
E-mail: hrpitt+@pitt.edu
www.pitt.edu
Phone: 412-624-4141
Fax: 412-648-8815

Hospitals

Allegheny General Hospital
320 E North Ave
Pittsburgh, PA 15212
www.allhealth.edu
Phone: 412-359-3131
Fax: 412-359-4108

Allegheny Valley Hospital
1301 Carlisle St
Natrona Heights, PA 15065
Phone: 724-224-5100
Fax: 724-226-7490

Braddock Medical Center
400 Holland Ave
Braddock, PA 15104
Phone: 412-636-5000
Fax: 412-636-5398

Butler Memorial Hospital
911 E Brady St
Butler, PA 16001
Phone: 724-283-6666
Fax: 724-284-4645

Canonsburg General Hospital
100 Medical Blvd
Canonsburg, PA 15317
Phone: 724-745-6100
Fax: 724-873-5876

Children's Hospital of Pittsburgh
3705 5th Ave
Pittsburgh, PA 15213
www.chp.edu
Phone: 412-692-5325
Fax: 412-692-8509

Citizens General Hospital
651 4th Ave
New Kensington, PA 15068
Phone: 724-337-3541
Fax: 724-334-2072

Forbes Regional Hospital
2570 Haymaker Rd
Monroeville, PA 15146
Phone: 412-858-2000
Fax: 412-858-2979

Jeannette District Memorial Hospital
600 Jefferson Ave
Jeannette, PA 15644
Phone: 724-527-3551
Fax: 724-527-9430

Jefferson Hospital
Coal Valley Rd
Pittsburgh, PA 15236
Phone: 412-469-5000
Fax: 412-469-7062

Latrobe Area Hospital
121 W 2nd Ave
Latrobe, PA 15650
www.lah.com
Phone: 724-537-1000
Fax: 724-532-6073

McKeesport Hospital
1500 5th Ave
McKeesport, PA 15132
Phone: 412-664-2000
Fax: 412-664-2309

Medical Center The
1000 Dutch Ridge Rd
Beaver, PA 15009
Phone: 724-728-7000
Fax: 724-728-5322

Mercy Hospital of Pittsburgh
1400 Locust St
Pittsburgh, PA 15219
www.mercylink.org
Phone: 412-232-8111
Fax: 412-232-7380

Mercy Providence Hospital
1004 Arch St
Pittsburgh, PA 15212
Phone: 412-323-5600
Fax: 412-323-5646

Monongahela Valley Hospital
1163 Country Club Rd
Monongahela, PA 15063
www.monvalleyhospital.com
Phone: 724-258-1000
Fax: 724-258-1421

Monsour Medical Center
70 Lincoln Way E
Jeannette, PA 15644
Phone: 724-527-1511
Fax: 724-527-0613

Ohio Valley General Hospital
25 Heckel Rd
McKees Rocks, PA 15136
Phone: 412-777-6161
Fax: 412-777-6806

Saint Clair Hospital
1000 Bower Hill Rd
Pittsburgh, PA 15243
www.stclair.org
Phone: 412-561-4900
Fax: 412-572-6580

Saint Francis Central Hospital
1200 Centre Ave
Pittsburgh, PA 15219
Phone: 412-562-3000
Fax: 412-261-5575

Saint Francis Medical Center
400 45th St
Pittsburgh, PA 15201
www.sfhs.edu/sfmc
Phone: 412-622-4343
Fax: 412-688-3447

University of Pittsburgh Medical Center
200 Lothrop St
Pittsburgh, PA 15213
www.upmc.edu
Phone: 412-648-6000
Fax: 412-647-5125

University of Pittsburgh Medical Center Beaver Valley
2500 Hospital Dr
Aliquippa, PA 15001
www.upmc.edu/BeaverValley/default.htm
Phone: 724-857-1212
Fax: 724-857-1298

University of Pittsburgh Medical Center Shadyside
5230 Centre Ave
Pittsburgh, PA 15232
www.upmc.edu/SHADYSIDE
Phone: 412-623-2121
Fax: 412-683-7539

University of Pittsburgh Medical Center South Side
2000 Mary St
Pittsburgh, PA 15203
Phone: 412-488-5550
Fax: 412-488-5748

UPMC Passavant Hospital
9100 Babcock Blvd
Pittsburgh, PA 15237
www.upmc.edu/Passavant/default.htm
Phone: 412-367-6700
Fax: 412-367-5498

UPMC Saint Margaret
815 Freeport Rd
Pittsburgh, PA 15215
www.upmc.edu/StMargaret
Phone: 412-784-4000
Fax: 412-784-4008

Veterans Affairs Medical Center
325 New Castle Rd
Butler, PA 16001
Phone: 724-287-4781
Fax: 724-477-5019

Veterans Affairs Medical Center
7180 Highland Dr
Pittsburgh, PA 15206
Phone: 412-365-4900
Fax: 412-365-5105

Washington Hospital
155 Wilson Ave
Washington, PA 15301
Phone: 724-225-7000
Fax: 724-229-2188

Western Pennsylvania Hospital
4800 Friendship Ave
Pittsburgh, PA 15224
www.westpennhospital.com
Phone: 412-578-5000
Fax: 412-578-4321

Westmoreland Regional Hospital
532 W Pittsburgh St
Greensburg, PA 15601
www.westmoreland.org
Phone: 724-832-4000
Fax: 724-832-5051

Transportation

Airport(s)

Greater Pittsburgh International Airport (PIT)
18 miles W of downtown (approx 25 minutes) 412-472-3525

Mass Transit

Port Authority Transit
$1.25 Base fare. 412-442-2000
T Light Rail Transit
$1.25 Base fare. 412-442-2000

Rail/Bus

Greyhound Bus Station
11th & Liberty Aves
Pittsburgh, PA 15222
Phone: 412-392-6513
TF: 800-231-2222

Pittsburgh Amtrak Station
1100 Liberty Ave
Pittsburgh, PA 15222
Phone: 412-471-6172
TF: 800-872-7245

Utilities

Electricity
Duquesne Light Co. 888-393-7100
www.duquesnelight.com

Gas
Columbia Gas of Pennsylvania 412-344-9800
www.columbiagaspamd.com
Equitable Gas Co. 412-395-3050
www.equitablegas.com
People's Natural Gas Co 412-244-2626

Water
Pittsburgh Water & Sewer Authority 412-255-2423

Garbage Collection/Recycling
Pittsburgh Bureau of Environmental Services 412-255-2780

Telecommunications

Telephone
Verizon Communications. 215-571-7050
www.verizon.com

Cable Television
AT & T Cable Services. 412-771-1300
www.cable.att.com

Internet Service Providers (ISPs)
CityNet Inc. 412-481-5406
www.city-net.com
Helicon On-Line 724-439-8805
www.hhs.net
Stargate Industries Inc 412-316-7827
www.stargate.net
Telerama Public Access Internet. 412-688-3200
www.telerama.com
Three Rivers Free-Net 412-622-8862
trfn.clpgh.org

Verio Pennsylvania 412-688-1750
home.verio.net/local/frontpage.cfm?AirportCode=PIT
Westmoreland Online Inc 724-830-4900
www.westol.com
Zoom Internet Service..........................724-482-4480
www.zbzoom.net

Banks

Allegheny Valley Bank of Pittsburgh Phone: 412-781-0318
5137 Butler St Fax: 412-781-6474
Pittsburgh, PA 15201
www.avbpgh.com

Dollar Bank FSB Phone: 412-261-4900
PO Box 765 Fax: 412-261-8535
Pittsburgh, PA 15230
E-mail: customerservice@dollarbank.com
www.dollarbank.com

Great American Federal Savings & Loan Assn Phone: 412-882-9800
4750 Clairton Blvd Fax: 412-882-5866
Pittsburgh, PA 15236 TF: 888-423-9400
www.greatamericanfederal.com

Mellon Bank NA Phone: 412-234-5000
500 Grant St 1 Mellon Bank Ctr Fax: 412-236-4491
Pittsburgh, PA 15258 TF: 800-635-5662
www.mellon.com

National City Bank of Pennsylvania Phone: 412-644-8111
300 4th Ave Fax: 412-644-8781
Pittsburgh, PA 15278

NorthSide Bank Phone: 412-231-6900
100 Federal St Fax: 412-231-3584
Pittsburgh, PA 15212

Parkvale Savings Bank Phone: 412-373-7200
4220 William Penn Hwy Fax: 412-373-1570
Monroeville, PA 15146
www.parkvale.com

PNC Bank NA Phone: 412-762-2000
249 5th Ave 1 PNC Plaza Fax: 412-762-5798
Pittsburgh, PA 15222 TF: 888-762-2265
www.pncbank.com

Spring Hill Savings Bank FSB Phone: 412-231-0809
1 North Shore Ctr Suite 120 Fax: 412-231-8203
Pittsburgh, PA 15212

Three Rivers Bank & Trust Co Phone: 412-382-1000
PO Box 10915 Fax: 412-664-8980
Pittsburgh, PA 15236

Shopping

Arcade Shops at Fifth Avenue Place Phone: 412-456-7800
120 5th Ave Fax: 412-456-7810
Pittsburgh, PA 15222

Century III Mall Phone: 412-653-1220
3075 Clairton Rd Fax: 412-655-0202
West Mifflin, PA 15123

East Carson Street Shopping District Phone: 412-481-0651
E Carson St-betw 8th & 25th Sts Fax: 412-481-2624
Pittsburgh, PA 15203

Kaufmann's Phone: 412-232-2000
400 5th Ave Fax: 412-232-2141
Pittsburgh, PA 15219
www.mayco.com/kf/index.jsp

Monroeville Mall Phone: 412-243-8511
200 Mall Blvd Fax: 412-372-0205
Monroeville, PA 15146

North Hills Village Phone: 412-366-2250
4801 McKnight Rd Fax: 412-366-5418
Pittsburgh, PA 15237

Ross Park Mall Phone: 412-369-4400
1000 Ross Park Mall Dr Fax: 412-369-4408
Pittsburgh, PA 15237
www.shopsimon.com/smt/servlet/SMTMall?mid=158&pn=ENTRY&rs=0

Saks Fifth Avenue Phone: 412-263-4800
513 Smithfield St Fax: 412-263-4880
Pittsburgh, PA 15222

Shops of One Oxford Centre Phone: 412-391-5300
301 Grant St Fax: 412-391-5309
Pittsburgh, PA 15219

South Hills Village Phone: 412-831-2900
301 South Hills Village
Pittsburgh, PA 15241

Station Square Phone: 412-261-2811
1 Station Square Dr Fax: 412-261-2825
Pittsburgh, PA 15219
www.stationsquare.com

Westmoreland Mall Phone: 724-836-5025
Rt 30 E Fax: 724-836-4825
Greensburg, PA 15601

Media

Newspapers and Magazines

Almanac The Phone: 724-941-7725
395 Valley Brook Rd Fax: 724-941-8685
McMurray, PA 15317
www.thealmanac.net

Cranberry Journal Phone: 724-776-4422
20232 Perry Hwy Fax: 724-776-4492
Cranberry Township, PA 16066
www.ghplus.com

Pittsburgh Business Times Phone: 412-481-6397
2313 E Carson St Suite 200 Fax: 412-481-9956
Pittsburgh, PA 15203
www.amcity.com/pittsburgh/

Pittsburgh City Paper Phone: 412-316-3342
650 Smithfield St Suite 2200 Fax: 412-316-3388
Pittsburgh, PA 15222
E-mail: info@pgcitypaper.com
www.pghcitypaper.com

Pittsburgh Magazine
4802 5th Ave
Pittsburgh, PA 15213
www.pittsburghmag.com/mag/index.html
Phone: 412-622-6440
Fax: 412-622-7066
TF: 800-495-7323

Pittsburgh Post-Gazette*
34 Blvd of the Allies
Pittsburgh, PA 15222
www.post-gazette.com
Phone: 412-263-1100
Fax: 412-391-8452

Pittsburgh Tribune-Review*
503 Martindale St 503 DL Clark Bldg
Pittsburgh, PA 15212
triblive.com
Phone: 412-321-6460
Fax: 412-320-7965
TF: 800-433-3045

**Indicates major daily newspapers*

Television

KDKA-TV Ch 2 (CBS)
1 Gateway Ctr
Pittsburgh, PA 15222
www.kdka.com
Phone: 412-575-2200
Fax: 412-575-2871

WCWB-TV Ch 22 (WB)
3474 William Penn Hwy
Pittsburgh, PA 15235
Phone: 412-829-9788
Fax: 412-829-0313

WPGH-TV Ch 53 (Fox)
750 Ivory Ave
Pittsburgh, PA 15214
Phone: 412-931-5300
Fax: 412-931-8029

WPXI-TV Ch 11 (NBC)
11 Television Hill
Pittsburgh, PA 15214
www.realpittsburgh.com/partners/wpxi
Phone: 412-237-1100
Fax: 412-327-4900

WQED-TV Ch 13 (PBS)
4802 5th Ave
Pittsburgh, PA 15213
www.wqed.org
Phone: 412-622-1300
Fax: 412-622-6413

WTAE-TV Ch 4 (ABC)
400 Ardmore Blvd
Pittsburgh, PA 15221
www.wtaetv.com
Phone: 412-242-4300
Fax: 412-244-4628

Radio

KDKA-AM 1020 kHz (N/T)
1 Gateway Ctr
Pittsburgh, PA 15222
www.kdkaradio.com
Phone: 412-575-2200
Fax: 412-575-2424

KQV-AM 1410 kHz (N/T)
650 Smithfield St Centre City Towers
Pittsburgh, PA 15222
E-mail: kqvradio@trib.infi.net
www.kqv.com
Phone: 412-562-5900
Fax: 412-562-5903

WAMO-AM 860 kHz (Urban)
960 Penn Ave Suite 200
Pittsburgh, PA 15222
www.wamo.com
Phone: 412-471-2181
Fax: 412-456-4066

WAMO-FM 106.7 MHz (Urban)
960 Penn Ave Suite 200
Pittsburgh, PA 15222
www.wamo.com
Phone: 412-471-2181
Fax: 412-391-3559

WASP-FM 94.9 MHz (Ctry)
National City Bank Bldg 7th Fl
Uniontown, PA 15401
Phone: 724-430-0949
Fax: 724-430-9265

WBZZ-FM 93.7 MHz (CHR)
651 Holiday Dr Foster Plaza 2nd Fl
Pittsburgh, PA 15220
www.b94fm.com
Phone: 412-920-9400
Fax: 412-920-9449

WDSY-FM 107.9 MHz (Ctry)
651 Holiday Dr Foster Plaza 2nd Fl
Pittsburgh, PA 15220
E-mail: promoy108@y108.com
www.y108.com
Phone: 412-920-9400
Fax: 412-920-9449

WDUQ-FM 90.5 MHz (NPR)
Duquesne University
Pittsburgh, PA 15282
E-mail: info@wduq.org
www.wduq.org
Phone: 412-396-6030
Fax: 412-396-5601

WDVE-FM 102.5 MHz (Rock)
200 Fleet St
Pittsburgh, PA 15220
www.dve.com
Phone: 412-937-1441
Fax: 412-937-0323

WJAS-AM 1320 kHz (Nost)
900 Parish St 3rd Fl
Pittsburgh, PA 15220
Phone: 412-875-4800
Fax: 412-875-9570

WJJJ-FM 104.7 MHz (Oldies)
200 Fleet St Suite 300
Pittsburgh, PA 15220
Phone: 412-937-1441
Fax: 412-937-9239

WLTJ-FM 92.9 MHz (AC)
650 Smithfield St Suite 2200
Pittsburgh, PA 15222
E-mail: info@wltj.net
www.wltj.com
Phone: 412-316-3342
Fax: 412-316-3388

WOGG-FM 103.5 MHz (Ctry)
123 Blaine Rd
Brownsville, PA 15417
Phone: 724-938-2000
Fax: 724-938-7824

WORD-FM 101.5 MHz (Rel)
7 Parkway Ctr Suite 625
Pittsburgh, PA 15220
www.wordwpit.com
Phone: 412-937-1500
Fax: 412-937-1576

WPHH-FM 96.1 MHz (AC)
200 Fleet St
Pittsburgh, PA 15220
Phone: 412-937-1441
Fax: 412-937-9239

WPTT-AM 1360 kHz (N/T)
900 Parish St 3rd Fl
Pittsburgh, PA 15220
Phone: 412-875-9500
Fax: 412-875-9474

WQED-FM 89.3 MHz (NPR)
4802 5th Ave
Pittsburgh, PA 15213
E-mail: radio@wqed.org
www.wqed.org/fm/index.html
Phone: 412-622-1436
Fax: 412-622-7073

WRRK-FM 96.9 MHz (CR)
650 Smithfield St Suite 2200
Pittsburgh, PA 15222
E-mail: quinn@sgi.net
www.rrk.com
Phone: 412-316-3342
Fax: 412-316-3388

WSHH-FM 99.7 MHz (AC)
900 Parish St 3rd Fl
Pittsburgh, PA 15220
www.wshh.com
Phone: 412-875-9500
Fax: 412-875-9474

WTAE-AM 1250 kHz (Sports)
400 Ardmore Blvd
Pittsburgh, PA 15221
www.wtaeradio.com
Phone: 412-731-0996
Fax: 412-244-4596

WWSW-AM 970 kHz (Oldies)
1 Allegheny Sq Suite 800
Pittsburgh, PA 15212
www.realpittsburgh.com/partners/3ws
Phone: 412-323-5300
Fax: 412-323-5313

WWSW-FM 94.5 MHz (Oldies)
1 Allegheny Sq Suite 800
Pittsburgh, PA 15212
E-mail: oldies@3wsradio.com
www.realpittsburgh.com/partners/3ws
Phone: 412-323-5300
Fax: 412-323-5313

WXDX-FM 105.9 MHz (Alt)
200 Fleet St
Pittsburgh, PA 15220
www.wxdx.com
Phone: 412-937-1441
Fax: 412-937-9239

WYEP-FM 91.3 MHz (NPR)
2313 E Carson St
Pittsburgh, PA 15203
E-mail: info@wyep.org
www.wyep.org
Phone: 412-381-9131
Fax: 412-381-9126

WZPT-FM 100.7 MHz (Oldies)
651 Holiday Dr Foster Plaza 2nd Fl
Pittsburgh, PA 15220
www.1007.com
Phone: 412-920-9400
Fax: 412-920-9449

Attractions

Pittsburgh is situated at the point where the Allegheny and Monongahela rivers meet to form the great Ohio River, and these waterways inspired the name for Three Rivers Stadium, home of the Pittsburgh Steelers and Pittsburgh Pirates, which is located across the Allegheny from downtown on the North Side. The Andy Warhol Museum and Carnegie Science Center are also located in this part of town. Across the Monongahela from downtown are the shops and restaurants of Station Square; further down the river is the South Side, which has coffee houses, jazz clubs, ethnic neighborhoods, and antique dealers. East of downtown Pittsburgh, in the neighborhood of Oakland, are the Carnegie Museums of Art and Natural History. A ride to the top of Mount Washington on either the Duquesne or the Monongahela Incline affords a spectacular view of the entire city.

Allegheny Portage Railroad National Historic Site
110 Federal Park Rd
Gallitzin, PA 16641
E-mail: alpo_visitor_center@nps.gov
www.nps.gov/alpo
Phone: 814-886-6150
Fax: 814-886-6117

American Wind Symphony Orchestra
550 Plains Church Rd
Mars, PA 16046
Phone: 724-934-8334
Fax: 724-742-2897

Andy Warhol Museum
117 Sandusky St
Pittsburgh, PA 15212
E-mail: warhol@alphaclp.clpgh.org
www.warhol.org
Phone: 412-237-8300
Fax: 412-237-8340

Benedum Center for the Performing Arts
719 Liberty Ave
Pittsburgh, PA 15222
Phone: 412-456-6666
Fax: 412-456-2694

Carnegie Library
4400 Forbes Ave
Pittsburgh, PA 15213
www.clpgh.org/clp
Phone: 412-622-3131
Fax: 412-622-6278

Carnegie Museum of Art
4400 Forbes Ave
Pittsburgh, PA 15213
www.cmoa.org
Phone: 412-622-3131
Fax: 412-622-6258

Carnegie Museum of Natural History
4400 Forbes Ave
Pittsburgh, PA 15213
www.clpgh.org/cmnh
Phone: 412-622-3131
Fax: 412-622-6258

Carnegie Music Hall
4400 Forbes Ave
Pittsburgh, PA 15213
Phone: 412-622-3360
Fax: 412-688-8664

Carnegie Science Center
1 Allegheny Ave
Pittsburgh, PA 15212
www.carnegiesciencecenter.org
Phone: 412-237-3400
Fax: 412-237-3375

Cathedral of Learning's Nationality Rooms
4200 5th Ave University of Pittsburgh
Pittsburgh, PA 15260
www.pitt.edu/~bdobler/rooms/countries/natrooms.html
Phone: 412-624-6000
Fax: 412-624-4214

City Theatre Co
13th & Bingham Sts
Pittsburgh, PA 15203
www.citytheatre-pgh.org
Phone: 412-431-2489

Dance Alloy
5530 Penn Ave
Pittsburgh, PA 15206
E-mail: alloy@telerama.im.com
Phone: 412-363-4321
Fax: 412-363-4320

Duquesne Incline
1220 Grandview Ave
Pittsburgh, PA 15211
E-mail: cablecar@incline.cc
www.incline.cc
Phone: 412-381-1665

Fallingwater
Rt 381
Mill Run, PA 15464
Phone: 724-329-8501
Fax: 724-329-0553

Fort Necessity National Battlefield
1 Washington Pkwy
Farmington, PA 15437
www.nps.gov/fone
Phone: 724-329-5512
Fax: 724-329-8682

Fort Pitt Museum
101 Commonwealth Pl
Pittsburgh, PA 15222
Phone: 412-281-9284
Fax: 412-281-1417

Frick Art & Historical Center
7227 Reynolds St
Pittsburgh, PA 15208
E-mail: info@frickart.org
www.frickart.org
Phone: 412-371-0600
Fax: 412-371-6140

Frick Park
S Braddock & Forbes Aves
Pittsburgh, PA 15221
Phone: 412-241-7190
Fax: 412-371-7141

Friendship Hill National Historic Site
Rd 1 Box 149-A
Point Marion, PA 15474
www.nps.gov/frhi
Phone: 724-725-9190
Fax: 724-725-1999

Hartwood Mansion
215 Saxonburg Blvd
Pittsburgh, PA 15238
Phone: 412-767-9200

Heinz Hall for the Performing Arts
600 Penn Ave
Pittsburgh, PA 15222
www.pittsburghsymphony.org/pghsymph.nsf/web/heinz.html
Phone: 412-392-4800
Fax: 412-392-4910

Heinz Memorial Chapel
5th & Bellefield Aves University of Pittsburgh
Pittsburgh, PA 15260
Phone: 412-624-4157
Fax: 412-624-4155

Highland Park
Highland Ave & Stanton St
Pittsburgh, PA 15206
Phone: 412-255-2365
Fax: 412-255-8981

Johnstown Flood National Memorial
733 Lake Rd
Saint Michael, PA 15951
www.nps.gov/jofl/
Phone: 814-495-4643
Fax: 814-495-7181

Kennywood Park
4800 Kennywood Blvd
West Mifflin, PA 15122
www.kennywood.com
Phone: 412-461-0500
Fax: 412-464-0719

Mattress Factory
500 Sampsonia Way
Pittsburgh, PA 15212
E-mail: info@mattress.org
www.mattress.org
Phone: 412-231-3169
Fax: 412-322-2231

Monongahela Incline
W Carson & Smithfield Sts
Pittsburgh, PA 15233
Phone: 412-442-2000

National Aviary in Pittsburgh
Allegheny Commons West
Pittsburgh, PA 15212
E-mail: ntlaviary@aol.com
www.aviary.org
Phone: 412-323-7234
Fax: 412-321-4364
TF: 800-972-2473

Old Economy Village
14th & Church Sts
Ambridge, PA 15003
www.beavercounty.net/oldeconomy
Phone: 724-266-4500
Fax: 724-266-7506

Phipps Conservatory & Botanical Gardens
1 Schenley Pk
Pittsburgh, PA 15213
E-mail: phipps@phipps.pgh.pa.us
www.phipps.conservatory.org
Phone: 412-622-6915
Fax: 412-622-7363

Pittsburgh Ballet Theatre
2900 Liberty Ave
Pittsburgh, PA 15201
artsnet.heinz.cmu.edu/pbt
Phone: 412-281-0360
Fax: 412-281-9901

Pittsburgh Brewing Co
3340 Liberty Ave
Pittsburgh, PA 15201
E-mail: info@pittsburghbrewingco.com
www.pittsburghbrewingco.com
Phone: 412-682-7400
Fax: 412-692-1189

Pittsburgh Center for the Arts
6300 5th Ave
Pittsburgh, PA 15232
www.pghcenarts.net
Phone: 412-361-0873
Fax: 412-361-8338

Pittsburgh Chamber Music Society
4400 Forbes Ave Carnegie Music Hall
Pittsburgh, PA 15213
E-mail: pcms@trfn.clpgh.org
trfn.clpgh.org/pcms/
Phone: 412-624-4129

Pittsburgh Children's Museum
10 Childrens Way
Pittsburgh, PA 15212
E-mail: info@pittsburghkids.org
www.pittsburghkids.org
Phone: 412-322-5059
Fax: 412-322-4932

Pittsburgh Civic Light Opera
719 Liberty Ave
Pittsburgh, PA 15222
E-mail: mail@pittsburghclo.org
www.pittsburghclo.org
Phone: 412-281-3973
Fax: 412-281-5339

Pittsburgh Opera
801 Penn Ave
Pittsburgh, PA 15222
E-mail: pghopera@pghopera.org
www.pghopera.org
Phone: 412-281-0912
Fax: 412-281-4324

Pittsburgh Public Theater
621 Penn Ave
Pittsburgh, PA 15222
E-mail: pittpublic@aol.com
www.ppt.org
Phone: 412-316-1600
Fax: 412-316-8219

Pittsburgh Symphony Orchestra
600 Penn Ave Heinz Hall for the Performing Arts
Pittsburgh, PA 15222
www.pittsburghsymphony.org
Phone: 412-392-4800
Fax: 412-392-3311

Pittsburgh Zoo & Aquarium
1 Wild Pl
Pittsburgh, PA 15206
zoo.pgh.pa.us
Phone: 412-665-3639
Fax: 412-665-3661
TF: 800-474-4966

PPG Wintergarden
Stanwix St & 4th Ave
Pittsburgh, PA 15222
Phone: 412-434-1900
Fax: 412-434-1901

Rangos Omnimax Theater
1 Allegheny Ave Carnegie Science Ctr
Pittsburgh, PA 15212
carnegiesciencecenter.org/family_omnimax.asp
Phone: 412-237-3400
Fax: 412-237-3375

River City Brass Band
PO Box 6436
Pittsburgh, PA 15212
E-mail: moreinfo@rcbb.com
www.rcbb.com
Phone: 412-322-7222
Fax: 412-322-6821

Riverview Park
Riverview Ave
Pittsburgh, PA 15214
Phone: 412-255-2539

Sandcastle Water Park Phone: 412-462-6666
1000 Sandcastle Dr Fax: 412-464-0719
West Homestead, PA 15120
www.sandcastlewaterpark.com

Schenley Park Phone: 412-255-2539
Schenley & Overlook Drs
Pittsburgh, PA 15213

Senator John Heinz Pittsburgh Regional History Center Phone: 412-454-6000
1212 Smallman St Fax: 412-454-6028
Pittsburgh, PA 15222
E-mail: hswp@hswp.org
www.pghhistory.org

Silver Eye Center for Photography Phone: 412-431-1810
1015 E Carson St Fax: 412-431-5777
Pittsburgh, PA 15203

Soldiers & Sailors Memorial Hall Phone: 412-621-4253
4141 5th Ave Fax: 412-683-9339
Pittsburgh, PA 15213
E-mail: ssmh@clpgh.org

Station Square Phone: 412-261-2811
1 Station Square Dr Fax: 412-261-2825
Pittsburgh, PA 15219
www.stationsquare.com

Stephen C Foster Memorial Phone: 412-624-4100
Forbes Ave University of Pittsburgh Fax: 412-624-7447
Pittsburgh, PA 15260
E-mail: dlr@pitt.edu
www.library.pitt.edu/libraries/cam/cam.html

Trinity Cathedral Phone: 412-232-6404
328 6th Ave Fax: 412-232-6408
Pittsburgh, PA 15222

Sports Teams & Facilities

Ladbroke at The Meadows Phone: 724-225-9300
Race Track Rd Fax: 724-225-9556
Meadow Lands, PA 15347
www.latm.com

Mellon Arena Phone: 412-642-1800
66 Mario Lemieux Pl Fax: 412-642-1925
Pittsburgh, PA 15219
www.civicarena.com

Pittsburgh CrosseFire (lacrosse) Phone: 412-642-1935
66 Mario Lemieux Pl Mellon Arena Fax: 412-201-9121
Pittsburgh, PA 15219
www.pittsburghcrossefire.com

Pittsburgh Penguins Phone: 412-642-1300
66 Mario Lemieux Pl Mellon Arena Fax: 412-642-1316
Pittsburgh, PA 15219
www.pittsburghpenguins.com

Pittsburgh Pirates Phone: 412-321-2827
600 Stadium Cir Three Rivers Stadium Fax: 412-323-1724
Pittsburgh, PA 15212
E-mail: talkback@pirates.usa.com
www.pirateball.com

Pittsburgh Riverhounds (soccer) Phone: 412-381-4625
Church Rd Bethel Pk Stadium Fax: 412-481-2529
Bethel Park, PA 15102
E-mail: cheasley@riverhounds.com
riverhounds.com

Pittsburgh Steelers Phone: 412-323-1200
300 Stadium Cir Three Rivers Stadium Fax: 412-323-1393
Pittsburgh, PA 15212 TF: 800-832-6883
steelershome.com

Three Rivers Stadium Phone: 412-321-0650
400 Stadium Cir Fax: 412-321-1436
Pittsburgh, PA 15212
www.3riversstadium.com

Annual Events

Celebration of Lights-Hartwood
(November-January) 800-366-0093
Christmas Arts & Crafts Show (late November). 412-856-8100
City of Pittsburgh Marathon (early May) 412-647-7866
Downtown Pittsburgh Sparkles
(early December-early January). 888-744-3378
First Night Pittsburgh (December 31) 888-744-3378
Greater Pittsburgh Renaissance Festival
(late June). 412-281-7711
Halloween Happenings (late October) 412-622-6914
Head of the Ohio Regatta (early October) 412-232-7506
Juneteenth Celebration (mid-June) 412-281-7711
Light-Up Weekend (mid-November). 888-744-3378
Maple Sugar Fest (late March) .412-422-6558
Mellon Jazz Festival (mid-late June) 800-366-0093
Penn's Colony Festival & Marketplace
(mid-late September) 412-487-6922
Pittsburgh Children's Festival (mid-May) 412-321-5520
Pittsburgh Folk Festival (late May). 800-366-0093
Pittsburgh International Lesbian & Gay Film Festival
(mid-October). 412-232-3277
Pittsburgh Irish Festival (mid-September) 412-661-1221
Pittsburgh Three Rivers Regatta (early August) 412-875-4841
Pittsburgh Vintage Grand Prix (mid-July) 800-366-0093
Pittsburgh Zoo Holiday Lights Festival
(December-early January) 412-665-3639
Saint Patrick's Day Parade (mid-March) 412-621-0600
Science & Engineering Fair (mid-March) 412-237-1821
Shadyside Summer Arts & Jazz Festival
(early August). 412-681-2809
Snowbird Festival (early-mid-December) 412-323-7235
Southside Summer Street Spectacular
(mid-July) 412-481-0651
Sparkle Season (late November-early January) 412-566-4190
Spring Flower Show (late March-mid-April) 412-622-6915
Station Square Festival (early June) 412-621-7223
Summerfest (mid-August). 412-562-9900
Three Rivers Arts Festival (early-mid-June) 412-281-8723
Three Rivers Film Festival
(early-mid-November). 412-681-5449
US Beer & Music Festival (late June). 412-562-9900
Westmoreland Arts & Heritage Festival
(early July) 724-834-7474
Winter Flower Show
(late November-early January) 412-622-6915

Winterfest (early February) 814-352-7777
WTAE-TV4 Summerfest (late June) 412-462-6666
Zoo Lights (early December-early January) 412-665-3640
ZooBoo for Kid's Sake (late October) 412-665-3640

Portland, Oregon

County: **Multnomah**

PORTLAND is located in northwestern Oregon along the Columbia and Willamette Rivers. Major cities within 100 miles include Salem and Eugene, Oregon; and Vancouver and Olympia, Washington.

Area (Land) .... 124.0 sq mi
Area (Water)................................ 9.7 sq mi
Elevation....................................... 77 ft
Latitude ....45-52-36 N
Longitude............................... 122-67-50 W
Time Zone ....PST
Area Code....................................... 503

Climate

Portland has a mild climate due to the sheltering effect of the Coast Range to the west of the city and the Cascades to the east. Winters are cloudy and wet, but temperatures remain fairly mild, with average highs in the upper 40s and lows in the mid-30s. Snowfall is minimal in Portland, averaging only 6.6 inches annually. Summer days are warm, with average high temperatures in the upper 70s, while evenings cool down into the mid-50s. December is the wettest month in Portland, while July is the driest.

Average Temperatures & Precipitation

Temperatures

	Jan	Feb	Mar	Apr	May	Jun	Jul	Aug	Sep	Oct	Nov	Dec
High	45	51	56	61	67	74	80	80	75	64	53	46
Low	34	36	39	41	47	53	57	57	52	45	40	35

Precipitation

	Jan	Feb	Mar	Apr	May	Jun	Jul	Aug	Sep	Oct	Nov	Dec
Inches	5.4	3.9	3.6	2.4	2.1	1.5	0.6	1.1	1.8	2.7	5.3	6.1

History

When members of the Lewis and Clark expedition first visited the area now known as Portland in 1806, the land was inhabited by Native Americans of the Chinook tribe. However, much of the area's native population was destroyed during an outbreak of malaria some thirty years later. White settlement began in the area during the 1840s when a tract of land was purchased by New Englanders Asa Lovejoy of Boston, Massachusetts and Francis W. Pettygrove of Portland, Maine. The landowners flipped a coin to determine whose hometown would be honored when naming the new town, and Pettygrove won the coin toss. Portland was incorporated as a city in 1851.

In its early years, Portland served as an outfitting post for miners during the California, Alaska, and Klondike gold rushes. Located on the Columbia and Willamette Rivers, Portland developed quickly as a center for commerce, with lumber and grain from the surrounding rich agricultural region as its major exports. The arrival of the first transcontinental railroad during the 1880s stimulated growth and development in the area, as did the establishment of facilities built in the 1930s to utilize the hydroelectric power generated by the area's two rivers. In the past two decades, several redevelopment projects and environmental programs have been implemented, modernizing the city and improving the overall quality of life in the Portland area.

Portland is still one of the nation's leading trade centers, as well as an important manufacturing and distribution hub. Known for its abundant natural resources, as well as its natural beauty, the Portland metropolitan area continues to grow and prosper, with a population of more than 1.8 million. Now home to more than 503,000 people, the city of Portland is Oregon's largest.

Population

1990 Census 438,882
1998 Estimate..............................503,891
% Change 3.7
2010 Projection 2,201,228*

Racial/Ethnic Breakdown

White...................................84.3%
Black 7.6%
Other 8.1%
Hispanic Origin (may be of any race) 3.2%

Age Breakdown

Under 5 years.............................6.9%
5 to 17.................................15.0%
18 to 20..................................4.1%
21 to 24..................................6.1%
25 to 34.................................18.8%
35 to 44.................................17.7%
45 to 54..................................9.3%
55 to 64..................................7.5%
65 to 74..................................7.8%
75+ years 6.8%
Median Age................................34.5

Gender Breakdown

Male....................................48.3%
Female..................................51.7%

** Information given is for the Portland/Vancouver Primary Metropolitan Statistical Area (PMSA), which includes Clackamas, Columbia, Multnomah, Washington, and Yamhill counties in Oregon; and Clark County in Washington.*

Government

Type of Government: Mayor-Commission

Portland City Attorney
1221 SW Fourth Ave Suite 430
Portland, OR 97204
Phone: 503-823-4047
Fax: 503-823-3089

Portland City Council
1221 SW 4th Ave Suite 210
Portland, OR 97204
Phone: 503-823-4682
Fax: 503-823-4040

Portland City Hall
1221 SW 4th Ave
Portland, OR 97204
Phone: 503-823-4000

Portland Development Commission
1900 SW 4th Ave Suite 7000
Portland, OR 97201
Phone: 503-823-3200
Fax: 503-823-3368

Portland Environmental Services Bureau
1120 SW 5th Ave Rm 100
Portland, OR 97204
Phone: 503-823-7769
Fax: 503-823-6995

Portland Finance & Administration Office
1120 SW 5th Ave Rm 1250
Portland, OR 97204
Phone: 503-823-5288
Fax: 503-823-5384

Portland Fire Bureau
55 SW Ash St
Portland, OR 97204
Phone: 503-823-3700
Fax: 503-823-3710

Portland Housing & Community Development Bureau
421 SW 6th Ave Suite 1100A
Portland, OR 97204
Phone: 503-823-2375
Fax: 503-823-2387

Portland Human Resources Bureau
1120 SW 5th Ave Suite 404
Portland, OR 97204
Phone: 503-823-3572
Fax: 503-823-4156

Portland Mayor
1221 SW 4th Ave Rm 340
Portland, OR 97204
Phone: 503-823-4120
Fax: 503-823-3588

Portland Parks & Recreation Dept
1120 SW 5th Ave Suite 1302
Portland, OR 97204
Phone: 503-823-7529
Fax: 503-823-5297

Portland Planning Bureau
1900 SW 4th Ave Rm 4100
Portland, OR 97201
Phone: 503-823-7700
Fax: 503-823-7800

Portland Police Bureau
1111 SW 2nd Ave
Portland, OR 97204
Phone: 503-823-4636
Fax: 503-823-0342

Portland Transportation Office
1120 SW 5th Ave Rm 800
Portland, OR 97204
Phone: 503-823-5185
Fax: 503-823-7576

Portland Water Bureau
1120 SW 5th Ave Suite 600
Portland, OR 97204
Phone: 503-823-7555
Fax: 503-823-6133

Important Phone Numbers

AAA....503-222-6734
American Express Travel....503-226-2961
Driver's License/Vehicle Registration Information...503-299-9999
Emergency....911
HotelDocs....800-468-3537
Medical Referral....503-335-3500
Multnomah County Assessment & Taxation....503-248-3326
Oregon Dept of Revenue....503-378-4988
Poison Control Center....503-494-8968
Portland Metropolitan Assn of Realtors....503-228-6595
Rose Quarter Event Hotline....503-321-3211
Voter Registration Information....503-248-3720
Weather....503-243-7575

Information Sources

Better Business Bureau Serving Oregon & Western Washington
333 SW 5th Ave Suite 300
Portland, OR 97204
www.portland.bbb.org
Phone: 503-226-3981
Fax: 503-226-8200

Clark County
PO Box 5000
Vancouver, WA 98666
www.co.clark.wa.us
Phone: 360-699-2292
Fax: 360-397-6099

Columbia River Economic Development Council
100 E Columbia Way
Vancouver, WA 98661
www.credc.org
Phone: 360-694-5006
Fax: 360-694-9927

Fort Vancouver Regional Library
1007 E Mill Plain Blvd
Vancouver, WA 98663
www.fvrl.org
Phone: 360-695-1561
Fax: 360-693-2681
TF: 800-750-9876

Greater Vancouver Chamber of Commerce
404 E 15th St Suite 11
Vancouver, WA 98663
www.vancouverusa.com
Phone: 360-694-2588
Fax: 360-693-8279

Multnomah County
1021 SW 4th Ave
Portland, OR 97204
www.multnomah.lib.or.us
Phone: 503-248-3511
Fax: 503-306-5773

Oregon Convention Center
777 NE ML King Jr Blvd
Portland, OR 97232
www.oregoncc.org
Phone: 503-235-7575
Fax: 503-235-7417
TF: 800-791-2250

Portland Metropolitan Chamber of Commerce
221 NW 2nd Ave
Portland, OR 97209
pdxchamber.org
Phone: 503-228-9411
Fax: 503-228-5126

Portland Oregon Visitors Assn
26 SW Salmon St 3 World Trade Ctr
Portland, OR 97204
www.pova.com
Phone: 503-275-9750
Fax: 503-275-9774
TF: 800-962-3700

Vancouver City Hall
210 E 13th St
Vancouver, WA 98660
www.ci.vancouver.wa.us
Phone: 360-696-8121
Fax: 360-696-8049

Vancouver Mayor
210 E 13th St
Vancouver, WA 98668
www.ci.vancouver.wa.us/govern.htm
Phone: 360-696-8211
Fax: 360-696-8049

Online Resources

4Portland.com
www.4portland.com

About.com Guide to Portland
portlandor.about.com/local/pacnwus/portlandor

Anthill City Guide Portland
www.anthill.com/city.asp?city=portland

Area Guide Portland
portlandor.areaguides.net

Boulevards Portland
www.boulevards.com/portland-or/

Cascade Link
www.cascadelink.org

City Knowledge Portland
www.cityknowledge.com/or_portland.htm

City Knowledge Vancouver
www.cityknowledge.com/wa_vancouver.htm

CitySearch Portland
katu.citysearch.com

CuisineNet Portland
www.cuisinenet.com/restaurant/portland/index.shtml

DigitalCity Portland
home.digitalcity.com/portland

Excite.com Vancouver City Guide
www.excite.com/travel/countries/united_states/washington/vancouver

Insiders' Guide to Portland
www.insiders.com/portland/

Lodging.com Vancouver Washington
www.lodging.com/auto/guides/vancouver-wa.html

Online City Guide to Vancouver
www.onlinecityguide.com/wa/vancouver

Portland City Net
www.excite.com/travel/countries/united_states/oregon/portland

Portland Essential Links
www.el.com/To/Portland/Links/

Portland Low-Budget Guide
www.hevanet.com/chezxx/low-rent/

Portland Oregon
www.ohwy.com/or/p/portland.htm

Portland Practical Guide
www.teleport.com/~repmail/pdxprat.html

Portland.TheLinks.com
portland.thelinks.com

Rough Guide Travel Portland
travel.roughguides.com/content/1553/

Savvy Diner Guide to Portland Restaurants
www.savvydiner.com/portland/

Southwest Washington Community Network
www.swwcn.org

Vancouver Network
www.vanusa.net

Vancouver USA Metro Area
www.mkt-place.com/market/vanusa/vanintro.html

Welcome to Portland
www.el.com/To/Portland

Willamette Week
www.wweek.com

Area Communities

Communities in the six-county (Multnomah, Washington, Clackamas, Columbia, and Yamhill counties in Oregon; and Clark county in Washington) Portland metropolitan area with populations greater than 10,000 include:

Beaverton
4755 SW Griffith Dr
Beaverton, OR 97005
Phone: 503-526-2497
Fax: 503-526-2479

Camas
PO Box 1055
Camas, WA 98607
Phone: 360-834-6864
Fax: 360-834-1535

Canby
PO BOx 930
Canby, OR 97013
Phone: 503-266-4021
Fax: 503-266-7961

Forest Grove
PO Box 326
Forest Grove, OR 97116
Phone: 503-992-3200
Fax: 503-992-3207

Gladstone
525 Portland Ave
Gladstone, OR 97027
Phone: 503-656-5225
Fax: 503-650-8938

Gresham
1333 NW Eastman Pkwy
Gresham, OR 97030
Phone: 503-661-3000
Fax: 503-665-7692

Hillsboro
123 W Main St
Hillsboro, OR 97123
Phone: 503-681-6113
Fax: 503-681-6232

Lake Oswego
PO Box 369
Lake Oswego, OR 97034
Phone: 503-635-0270
Fax: 503-635-0269

McMinnville
230 NE 2nd St
McMinnville, OR 97128
Phone: 503-434-7302
Fax: 503-472-4104

Milwaukie
10722 SE Main St
Milwaukie, OR 97222
Phone: 503-659-5171
Fax: 503-652-4433

Newberg
PO Box 970
Newberg, OR 97132
Phone: 503-538-9421
Fax: 503-537-5013

Oregon City
PO Box 3040
Oregon City, OR 97045
Phone: 503-657-0891
Fax: 503-657-3339

Tigard
13125 SW Hall Blvd
Tigard, OR 97223
Phone: 503-639-4171
Fax: 503-684-7297

Troutdale
104 SE Kibling Ave
Troutdale, OR 97060
Phone: 503-665-5175
Fax: 503-667-6403

Tualatin
PO Box 369
Tualatin, OR 97062
Phone: 503-692-2000
Fax: 503-692-5421

Vancouver
210 E 13th St
Vancouver, WA 98660
Phone: 360-696-8121
Fax: 360-696-8049

West Linn
22500 Salamo Rd
West Linn, OR 97068
Phone: 503-657-0331
Fax: 503-650-9041

Wilsonville
30000 SW Town Center Loop E
Wilsonville, OR 97070
Phone: 503-682-1011
Fax: 503-682-1012

Economy

Portland's economic base ranges from lumber processing to finance. A major U.S. gateway to the Pacific Rim, Portland is a thriving center for trade—the Port of Portland is one of the leading ports on the west coast both in exports and overall volume. Excellent rail and highway connections further enhance the area's distribution capabilities. Services is currently Portland's largest employment sector, with health care being a leading industry—three of the metropolitan area's 10 largest private-sector employers are healthcare organizations. High technology is another rapidly-growing industry in the Portland area, with employment growing by 65 percent in the field between 1990 and 1998.

Unemployment Rate 5.2%*
Per Capita Income $28,466*
Median Family Income $32,424

** Information given is for Multnomah County.*

Principal Industries & Number of Wage Earners

Portland/Vancouver PMSA* - 1999

Construction 52,200
Finance, Insurance, & Real Estate 66,600
Government 122,700
Manufacturing 145,100
Mining & Quarrying 1,200
Retail Trade 167,000
Services 268,200
Transportation & Public Utilities 55,100
Wholesale Trade 67,700

** Information given is for the Portland/Vancouver Primary Metropolitan Statistical Area (PMSA), which includes Clackamas, Columbia, Multnomah, Washington, and Yamhill counties in Oregon; and Clark County in Washington.*

Major Employers

Albertsons Inc
17001 NE San Rafael
Portland, OR 97230
www1.albertsons.com/corporate
Phone: 503-251-9500
Fax: 503-251-9541

Fort James Corp
401 NE Adams St
Camas, WA 98607
www.fortjames.com
Phone: 360-817-4500

Fred Meyer Inc
3800 SE 22nd Ave
Portland, OR 97202
www.fredmeyer.com
Phone: 503-232-8844
TF: 800-858-9202

Freightliner Corp
4747 N Channel Ave
Portland, OR 97217
E-mail: customerhelp@freightliner.com
www.freightliner.com
Phone: 503-735-8000
Fax: 503-735-8921
TF: 800-385-4357

Hewlett-Packard Co
PO Box 8906
Vancouver, WA 98668
www.hp.com
Phone: 360-212-8110
Fax: 360-212-3035
TF: 800-447-0200

Intel Corp Communications Products Group
5200 NE Elam Young Pkwy
Hillsboro, OR 97124
www.intel.com
Phone: 503-696-8080

Kaiser Permanente
500 NE Multnomah St Suite 100
Portland, OR 97232
Phone: 503-813-2800
Fax: 503-813-4733

Legacy Health System
1919 NW Lovejoy St
Portland, OR 97209
E-mail: contact@lhs.org
www.legacyhealth.org
Phone: 503-225-8600
Fax: 503-225-8777

Nike Inc
1 Bowerman Dr
Beaverton, OR 97005
www.nikebiz.com
Phone: 503-671-6453
Fax: 503-671-6300
TF: 800-344-6453

Precision Castparts Corp
4650 SW Macadam Ave Suite 300
Portland, OR 97201
www.precast.com
Phone: 503-417-4800
Fax: 503-417-4817

Providence Health System
1235 NE 47th St Suite 299
Portland, OR 97213
www.providence.org
Phone: 503-215-4700
Fax: 503-215-4703

Qwest
421 SW Oak
Portland, OR 97204
www.qwest.com
Phone: 503-242-6365

Safeway Inc Portland Div
PO Box 523
Clackamas, OR 97015
www.safeway.com
Phone: 503-656-1461
Fax: 503-657-6341

Tektronix Inc
14200 SW Karl Brawn Dr PO Box 500
Beaverton, OR 97077
www.tektronix.com.
Phone: 503-627-7111
Fax: 503-627-5227
TF: 800-835-6100

US Bancorp Piper Jaffray Inc
101 SW Main Suite 1040
Portland, OR 97204
Phone: 503-248-1345
Fax: 503-224-1802

Wells Fargo Bank
1300 SW 5th Ave
Portland, OR 97201
www.wellsfargo.com
Phone: 503-886-3340
Fax: 503-886-3480

Quality of Living Indicators

Total Crime Index....................................41,399
(rates per 100,000 inhabitants)

Violent Crime
Murder/manslaughter........................... 35
Forcible rape 340
Robbery....................................1,418
Aggravated assault...........................4,501

Property Crime
Burglary 6,107
Larceny theft 24,308
Motor vehicle theft 4,690

Cost of Living Index....................................111.7
(national average = 100)

Median Home Price.................................$165,100

Education

Public Schools

Portland Public Schools
PO Box 3107
Portland, OR 97208
www.pps.k12.or.us
Phone: 503-916-2000
Fax: 503-916-3107

Number of Schools
Elementary................................. 62
Middle 17
High....................................... 10

Student/Teacher Ratio
All Grades 19.3:1

Private Schools

Number of Schools (all grades) 37

Colleges & Universities

Art Institute of Portland
2000 SW 5th Ave
Portland, OR 97201
Phone: 503-228-6528
Fax: 503-525-8331
TF: 888-228-6528

Cascade College
9101 E Burnside St
Portland, OR 97216
www.cascade.edu
Phone: 503-255-7060
Fax: 503-257-1222
TF: 800-550-7678

Clackamas Community College
19600 S Molalla Ave
Oregon City, OR 97045
www.clackamas.cc.or.us
Phone: 503-657-8400
Fax: 503-650-6654

Clark College
1800 E McLoughlin Blvd
Vancouver, WA 98663
E-mail: grotsd@ooi.clark.edu
www.clark.edu
Phone: 360-694-6521
Fax: 360-992-2876

Concordia University
2811 NE Holman St
Portland, OR 97211
E-mail: cu-admissions@cu-portland.edu
www.cu-portland.edu
Phone: 503-288-9371
Fax: 503-280-8531
TF: 800-321-9371

George Fox University
414 N Meridian St
Newberg, OR 97132
www.georgefox.edu
Phone: 503-538-8383
Fax: 503-538-7234
TF: 800-765-4369

ITT Technical Institute
6035 NE 78th Ct
Portland, OR 97218
www.itt-tech.edu
Phone: 503-255-6500
Fax: 503-255-6135
TF: 800-234-5488

Lewis & Clark College
0615 SW Palatine Hill Rd
Portland, OR 97219
www.lclark.edu
Phone: 503-244-6161
Fax: 503-768-7055

Mount Hood Community College
26000 SE Stark St
Gresham, OR 97030
www.mhcc.cc.or.us
Phone: 503-667-6422
Fax: 503-491-7388

Oregon Health Sciences University
3181 SW Sam Jackson Park Rd
Portland, OR 97201
www.ohsu.edu
Phone: 503-494-8311
Fax: 503-494-4812

Pacific Northwest College of Art
1241 NW Johnson St
Portland, OR 97209
www.pnca.edu
Phone: 503-226-4391
Fax: 503-226-3587

Pacific University
2043 College Way
Forest Grove, OR 97116
www.pacificu.edu
Phone: 503-357-6151
Fax: 503-359-2975
TF: 800-635-0561

Portland Community College Sylvania
12000 SW 49th Ave
Portland, OR 97219
www.pcc.edu
Phone: 503-244-6111
Fax: 503-977-4740

Portland State University
PO Box 751
Portland, OR 97207
E-mail: askadm@osa.pdx.edu
www.pdx.edu
Phone: 503-725-3000
Fax: 503-725-5525
TF: 800-547-8887

Reed College
3203 SE Woodstock Blvd
Portland, OR 97202
E-mail: admission@reed.edu
www.reed.edu
Phone: 503-771-1112
Fax: 503-777-7553
TF: 800-547-4750

University of Portland
5000 N Willamette Blvd
Portland, OR 97203
E-mail: info@uofport.edu
www.uofport.edu
Phone: 503-943-7911
Fax: 503-943-7315
TF: 800-227-4568

Warner Pacific College
2219 SE 68th Ave
Portland, OR 97215
E-mail: admiss@warnerpacific.edu
www.warnerpacific.edu
Phone: 503-775-4366
Fax: 503-517-1352
TF: 800-582-7885

Washington State University Vancouver
14204 NE Salmon Creek Ave
Vancouver, WA 98686
E-mail: admissions@vancouver.wsu.edu
www.vancouver.wsu.edu
Phone: 360-546-9779
Fax: 360-546-9030

Hospitals

Adventist Medical Center
10123 SE Market St
Portland, OR 97216
www.adventisthealthnw.com/portland
Phone: 503-257-2500
Fax: 503-261-6638

Kaiser Permanente Medical Center
10180 SE Sunnyside Rd
Clackamas, OR 97015
Phone: 503-652-2880
Fax: 800-813-2000

Legacy Emanuel Hospital & Health Center
2801 N Gantenbein Ave
Portland, OR 97227
Phone: 503-413-2200
Fax: 503-413-2756

Legacy Good Samaritan Hospital
1015 NW 22nd Ave
Portland, OR 97210
Phone: 503-229-7711
Fax: 503-413-8016

Legacy Meridian Park Hospital
19300 SW 65th Ave
Tualatin, OR 97062
Phone: 503-692-1212
Fax: 503-692-2478

Legacy Mount Hood Medical Center
24800 SE Stark St
Gresham, OR 97030
Phone: 503-667-1122
Fax: 503-674-1608

Oregon Health Sciences University
3181 SW Sam Jackson Park Rd
Portland, OR 97201
www.ohsu.edu
Phone: 503-494-8311
Fax: 503-494-4812

Providence Medical Center
4805 NE Glisan St
Portland, OR 97213
Phone: 503-215-1111
Fax: 503-215-6349

Providence Saint Vincent Medical Center
9205 SW Barnes Rd
Portland, OR 97225
Phone: 503-216-1234
Fax: 503-216-4141

Southwest Washington Medical Center
PO Box 1600
Vancouver, WA 98668
www.swmedctr.com
Phone: 360-514-2000
Fax: 360-514-3035

Tuality Community Hospital
335 SE 8th Ave
Hillsboro, OR 97123
Phone: 503-681-1111
Fax: 503-681-1608

Veterans Affairs Medical Center
3710 US Veterans Hospital Rd
Portland, OR 97201
Phone: 503-220-8262
Fax: 503-402-2909

Willamette Falls Hospital
1500 Division St
Oregon City, OR 97045
Phone: 503-656-1631
Fax: 503-650-6807

Woodland Park Hospital
10300 NE Hancock St
Portland, OR 97220
Phone: 503-257-5500
Fax: 503-257-5672

Transportation

Airport(s)

Portland International Airport (PDX)
9 miles NE of downtown (approx 20 minutes) 503-460-4040

Mass Transit

MAX Light Rail Line
$1.10 Base fare................................503-238-7433
Tri-Met
$1.10 Base fare................................503-238-7433

Rail/Bus

Greyhound Bus Station
550 NW 6th Ave
Portland, OR 97209
Phone: 503-243-2357
TF: 800-231-2222

Portland Amtrak Station
800 NW 6th Ave
Portland, OR 97209
Phone: 503-273-4871
TF: 800-872-7245

Utilities

Electricity
PacifiCorp..................................888-221-7070
www.pacificorp.com
Portland General Electric......................503-228-6322
www.portlandgeneral.com

Gas
Northwest Natural Gas Co......................503-226-4212
www.nwnatural.com

Water
Portland Water & Sewer.......................503-823-7770

Garbage Collection/Recycling
Metro Recycling Information Center............503-234-3000
Portland Curbside Hotline & Referral..........503-823-7202

Telecommunications

Telephone
Qwest.......................................800-244-1111
www.qwest.com

Cable Television
AT & T Cable Services........................503-230-2000
www.cable.att.com

Internet Service Providers (ISPs)

aracnet.com 503-626-7696
www.aracnet.com
CyberNet Northwest Inc........................503-205-4767
www.cnnw.net
EasyStreet Online Services.....................503-646-8400
www.easystreet.com
Europa Communications Inc 503-222-9508
www.europa.com
Hevanet Communications 503-228-3520
www.hevanet.com
Internet Partners Inc..........................503-690-2700
www.ipinc.net
Involved Inc 503-226-4006
www.involved.com
Northwest.com................................503-639-2727
www.northwest.com
One World Internetworking Inc.................541-758-1112
www.oneworld.com
Pacifier Computers............................360-693-2116
www.pacifier.com
PCs Made Easy LLC 503-639-0828
www.pcez.com
PlaNet Access Inc.............................503-537-9976
www.planacc.com
Teleport Internet Services......................503-223-0076
www.teleport.com
THIS Computer Solution 360-696-9453
www.this.com
Transport Logic...............................503-243-1940
www.transport.com
Verio Portland 503-227-5665
home.verio.net/local/frontpage.cfm?AirportCode=PDX

Banks

American State Bank
2737 NE ML King Jr Blvd
Portland, OR 97212
Phone: 503-282-2216
Fax: 503-282-5751

Bank of America Oregon
121 SW Morrison St Suite 170
Portland, OR 97204
Phone: 503-275-2222
Fax: 503-275-0903

Bank of the Northwest
888 SW 5th Ave Suite 600
Portland, OR 97204
Phone: 503-417-8800
Fax: 503-417-8888

Bank of the West
401 SW 5th Ave
Portland, OR 97204
Phone: 503-221-2122

KeyBank NA Oregon District
1222 SW 6th Ave Suite 200
Portland, OR 97204
Phone: 503-790-7690
Fax: 503-790-7693
TF: 800-539-2968

Northern Bank of Commerce
1001 SW 5th Ave Suite 250
Portland, OR 97204
Phone: 503-222-9164
Fax: 503-222-0501

Sterling Savings Bank
4728 NE Sandy Blvd
Portland, OR 97213
Phone: 503-287-2076
Fax: 503-287-1409

US Bank NA
321 SW 6th Ave
Portland, OR 97204
Phone: 503-275-5122
Fax: 503-275-4193

Washington Mutual Bank
2364 W Burnside St Suite E-1
Portland, OR 97210
Phone: 503-238-3366
Fax: 503-238-3538

Shopping

Clackamas Town Center
12000 SE 82nd Ave
Portland, OR 97266
www.clackamastowncenter.com
Phone: 503-653-6913
Fax: 503-653-7357

Galleria
921 SW Morrison St
Portland, OR 97205
Phone: 503-228-2748

Hawthorne Boulevard
Hawthorne Blvd-betw 12th & 55th Aves
Portland, OR 97293
Phone: 503-774-2832
Fax: 503-788-0412

Jantzen Beach SuperCenter
1405 Jantzen Beach Ctr
Portland, OR 97217
Phone: 503-289-5555
Fax: 503-289-2642

Lloyd Center
2201 Lloyd Ctr
Portland, OR 97232
Phone: 503-282-2511
Fax: 503-280-9407

Meier & Frank Department Stores
621 SW 5th Ave
Portland, OR 97204
www.mayco.com/mf/index.jsp
Phone: 503-223-0512
Fax: 503-241-5783
TF: 800-452-6323

Multnomah Village
SW 35th Ave & Capitol Hwy
Portland, OR 97219
Phone: 503-245-4014

Nordstrom
701 SW Broadway
Portland, OR 97205
Phone: 503-224-6666
Fax: 503-299-2822

Pendleton Woolen Mill & Outlet Store
2 17th St
Washougal, WA 98671
Phone: 360-835-1118
TF: 800-568-2480

Pendleton Woolen Mills Inc
PO Box 3030
Portland, OR 97208
E-mail: wool@pendleton-usa.com
www.pendleton-usa.com
Phone: 503-226-4801
Fax: 503-535-5599
TF: 800-760-4844

Pioneer Place
888 SW 5th Ave Suite 410
Portland, OR 97204
Phone: 503-228-5800
Fax: 503-228-5864

Portland Saturday Market
1st & Front Sts under Burnside Bridge
Portland, OR 97209
Phone: 503-222-6072
Fax: 503-222-0254

Portland Skidmore Fountain Market
120 SW Ankeny St Suite 200
Portland, OR 97204
Phone: 503-228-2392
Fax: 503-228-0576

Powell's City of Books
1005 W Burnside St
Portland, OR 97209
E-mail: help@powells.com
www.powells.com
Phone: 800-878-7323
Fax: 503-227-4631

Stars Antique Mall
7027 SE Milwaukee Ave
Portland, OR 97202
Phone: 503-239-0346
Fax: 503-872-9724

Vancouver Mall
8700 NE Vancouver Mall Dr
Vancouver, WA 98662
Phone: 360-892-6255
Fax: 360-892-0124

Washington Square Shopping Center
9585 SW Washington Square Rd
Tigard, OR 97223
www.shopwashingtonsquare.com
Phone: 503-639-8860
Fax: 503-620-5612

Water Tower at Johns Landing
5331 SW Macadam Ave
Portland, OR 97201
Phone: 503-228-9431
Fax: 503-228-9473

Media

Newspapers and Magazines

Business Journal of Portland
PO Box 14490
Portland, OR 97293
www.bizjournals.com/portland
Phone: 503-274-8733
Fax: 503-227-2650

Columbian*
PO Box 180
Vancouver, WA 98666
www.columbian.com
Phone: 360-694-3391
Fax: 360-699-6033
TF: 800-743-3391

Daily Journal of Commerce*
PO Box 10127
Portland, OR 97296
E-mail: subscriptions@djc-or.com
www.djc-or.com
Phone: 503-226-1311
Fax: 503-224-7140

Hillsboro Argus
PO Box 588
Hillsboro, OR 97123
E-mail: argus@imagine.com
Phone: 503-648-1131
Fax: 503-648-9191

Oregonian*
1320 SW Broadway
Portland, OR 97201
www.oregonlive.com
Phone: 503-221-8100
Fax: 503-227-5306
TF: 800-826-0376

Vancouver Business Journal
2525 E Fourth Plain Blvd
Vancouver, WA 98661
E-mail: editorial@vbjusa.com
www.vbjusa.com
Phone: 360-695-2442
Fax: 360-695-3056

Willamette Week
822 SW 10th Ave
Portland, OR 97225
www.wweek.com
Phone: 503-243-2122
Fax: 503-243-1115

**Indicates major daily newspapers*

Television

KATU-TV Ch 2 (ABC)
2153 NE Sandy Blvd
Portland, OR 97232
local.katu.citysearch.com
Phone: 503-231-4222
Fax: 503-231-4263

KGW-TV Ch 8 (NBC)
1501 SW Jefferson St
Portland, OR 97201
www.kgw.com
Phone: 503-226-5000
Fax: 503-226-4448

KOIN-TV Ch 6 (CBS)
222 SW Columbia St
Portland, OR 97201
E-mail: koin06a@prodigy.com
www.koin.com
Phone: 503-464-0600
Fax: 503-464-0717

KOPB-TV Ch 10 (PBS)
7140 SW Macadam Ave
Portland, OR 97219
E-mail: kopb@opb.org
www.opb.org/
Phone: 503-244-9900
Fax: 503-293-1919

KPDX-TV Ch 49 (Fox)
910 NE ML King Jr Blvd
Portland, OR 97232
www.kpdx.com
Phone: 503-239-4949
Fax: 503-239-6184

KPTV-TV Ch 12 (UPN)
211 SE Caruthers St
Portland, OR 97214
www.kptv.com
Phone: 503-230-1200
Fax: 503-230-1065

KPXG-TV Ch 22 (PAX)
54 SW Yamhill St
Portland, OR 97204
www.pax.net/KPXG
Phone: 503-222-2221
Fax: 503-222-3732

KWBP-TV Ch 32 (WB)
10255 SW Arctic Dr
Beaverton, OR 97005
Phone: 503-644-3232
Fax: 503-626-3576
TF: 800-347-4947

Radio

KBBT-FM 107.5 kHz (AC)
2040 SW 1st Ave
Portland, OR 97201
www.thebeat.com
Phone: 503-222-1011
Fax: 503-222-2047
TF: 800-567-1075

KBMS-AM 1480 kHz (Urban)
601 Main St Suite 600
Vancouver, WA 98660
Phone: 360-699-1881

KBNP-AM 1410 kHz (Misc)
278 SW Arthur St
Portland, OR 97201
E-mail: kbnp@kbnp.com
www.kbnp.com
Phone: 503-223-6769

KBOO-FM 90.7 MHz (Misc)
20 SE 8th Ave
Portland, OR 97214
E-mail: general@kboo.org
www.kboo.org
Phone: 503-231-8032
Fax: 503-231-7145

KBPS-FM 89.9 MHz (Clas)
515 NE 15th Ave
Portland, OR 97232
www.kbps.org
Phone: 503-916-5828
Fax: 503-916-2642

KBVM-FM 88.3 MHz (Rel)
5000 N Willamette Blvd Suite 44
Portland, OR 97203
E-mail: info@kbvm.com
www.kbvm.com
Phone: 503-285-5200

KEWS-AM 620 kHz (N/T)
4949 SW Macadam Ave
Portland, OR 97201
www.620knews.com
Phone: 503-225-1190
Fax: 503-227-5873

KEX-AM 1190 kHz (N/T)
4949 SW Macadam Ave
Portland, OR 97201
www.1190kex.com
Phone: 503-225-1190
Fax: 503-224-3216

KFXX-AM 910 kHz (Sports)
0700 SW Bancroft St
Portland, OR 97201
E-mail: kfxx@kfxx.com
www.kfxx.com
Phone: 503-223-1441
Fax: 503-223-6909

KGON-FM 92.3 MHz (CR)
0700 SW Bancroft St
Portland, OR 97201
www.kgon.com
Phone: 503-223-1441
Fax: 503-223-6909

KINK-FM 101.9 MHz (AAA)
1501 SW Jefferson St
Portland, OR 97201
E-mail: kinkfm102@kinkfm102.com
www.kinkfm102.com
Phone: 503-226-5080
Fax: 503-226-4578

KKCW-FM 103.3 MHz (AC)
5005 SW Macadam Ave
Portland, OR 97201
www.k103.com
Phone: 503-222-5103
Fax: 503-222-0030

KKGT-AM 1150 kHz (N/T)
15240 SE 82nd Dr
Clackamas, OR 97015
www.greattalk1150am.com
Phone: 503-222-1150
Fax: 503-722-9111

KKJZ-FM 106.7 MHz (NAC)
222 SW Columbia Ave Suite 350
Portland, OR 97201
www.kkjz.com
Phone: 503-223-0300
Fax: 503-497-2333

KKRZ-FM 100.3 MHz (CHR)
4949 SW Macadam Ave
Portland, OR 97201
E-mail: hlg@z100portland.com
www.z100portland.com
Phone: 503-226-0100
Fax: 503-295-9281

KKSN-AM 1520 kHz (Nost)
0700 SW Bancroft St
Portland, OR 97201
www.sunny1520.com
Phone: 503-226-9791
Fax: 503-243-3299

KKSN-FM 97.1 MHz (Oldies)
888 SW 5th Ave Suite 790
Portland, OR 97204
www.kisnfm.com
Phone: 503-226-9791
Fax: 503-243-3299

KNRK-FM 94.7 MHz (Alt)
0700 SW Bancroft St
Portland, OR 97201
www.knrk.com
Phone: 503-223-1441
Fax: 503-223-6909

KOPB-FM 91.5 MHz (NPR)
7140 SW Macadam Ave
Portland, OR 97219
E-mail: audience_services@opb.org
www.opb.org
Phone: 503-293-1905
Fax: 503-293-1919

KPDQ-FM 93.7 MHz (Rel)
5110 SE Stark St
Portland, OR 97215
www.kpdq.com
Phone: 503-231-7800
Fax: 503-238-7202

KRSK-FM 105.1 MHz (AC)
0700 SW Bancroft St
Portland, OR 97201
www.rosie105.com
Phone: 503-223-1441
Fax: 503-223-6909
TF: 888-733-5105

KUFO-FM 101.1 MHz (Rock)
2040 SW 1st Ave
Portland, OR 97201
www.kufo.com
Phone: 503-222-1011
Fax: 503-222-2047

KUPL-FM 98.7 MHz (Ctry)
222 SW Columbia Ave Suite 350
Portland, OR 97221
www.kupl.com
Phone: 503-223-0300
Fax: 503-497-2336

KVAN-AM 1550 kHz (N/T)
7710 NE Vancouver Mall Dr
Vancouver, WA 98662
E-mail: feedback@kvan.com
www.kvan.com
Phone: 360-944-1550
Fax: 360-944-6679

KWJJ-FM 99.5 MHz (Ctry)
2000 SW 1st Ave Suite 300
Portland, OR 97201
www.kwjj.com
Phone: 503-228-4393
Fax: 503-227-3938

KXJM-FM 95.5 MHz (Urban)
0234 SW Bancroft St
Portland, OR 97201
www.jamminfm.com
Phone: 503-243-7595
Fax: 503-417-7661

KXL-AM 750 kHz (N/T)
0234 SW Bancroft St
Portland, OR 97201
www.kxl.com
Phone: 503-243-7595
Fax: 503-417-7661

Attractions

Portland's location and climate are ideal for roses and have earned Portland it's nickname, the "City of Roses." The International Rose Test Garden in Portland has more than 10,000 rose bushes with some 400 varieties of roses, and a 24-day Festival of Roses is held in Portland every year. Just 50 miles east of the city is Mount Hood National Forest, with facilities for skiing, camping, hiking, fishing, and horseback riding. Along the coast, during the winter and spring, whale watching is a popular pastime. Other points of interest in the Portland area include the Pendleton Woolen Mills, Multnomah Falls, and Crown Point State Park.

Altman Gallery
210 W Evergreen Blvd
Vancouver, WA 98660
Phone: 360-695-9298

American Advertising Museum
5035 SE 24th Ave
Portland, OR 97202
www.admuseum.org/
Phone: 503-226-0000
Fax: 503-238-6674

Artists Repertory Theatre
1516 SW Alder St
Portland, OR 97205
www.artistsrep.org
Phone: 503-241-9807
Fax: 503-241-8268

Battle Ground Lake State Park
18002 NE 249th St
Battle Ground, WA 98604
Phone: 360-687-4621
Fax: 360-666-8158
TF: 800-233-0321

Berry Botanic Garden
1505 SW Summerville Ave
Portland, OR 97219
E-mail: bbg@agora.rdrop.com
www.berrybot.org
Phone: 503-636-4112
Fax: 503-636-7496

Blitz-Weinhard Brewing Co
1133 W Burnside St
Portland, OR 97209
Phone: 503-222-4351
Fax: 503-229-4689

BridgePort Brewing Co
1318 NW Northrup St
Portland, OR 97209
E-mail: brewmaster@firkin.com
www.firkin.com
Phone: 503-241-7179
Fax: 503-241-0625

Cedar Creek Grist Mill & Covered Bridge
Grist Mill Rd
Woodland, WA 98674
Phone: 360-225-8532

Chamber Music Northwest
522 SW 5th Ave Suite 725
Portland, OR 97204
E-mail: info@cmnw.org
www.teleport.com/~cmnw/
Phone: 503-223-3202
Fax: 503-294-1690

Clark County Historical Museum
1511 Main St
Vancouver, WA 98660
Phone: 360-695-4681

Columbia River Gorge Information
405 Port Way Ave
Hood River, OR 97031
Phone: 541-386-2000
Fax: 541-386-2057

Covington House
4201 Main St
Vancouver, WA 98663
Phone: 360-695-6750

Crown Point State Park's Vista House
40700 E Historic Columbia River Hwy
Corbett, OR 97019
E-mail: friends@vistahouse.com
www.vistahouse.com
Phone: 503-695-2230
Fax: 503-695-2250

Downtown Vancouver Assn
609 Main St
Vancouver, WA 98660
Phone: 360-693-2978

First Avenue Gallery
205 SW 1st
Portland, OR 97204
Phone: 503-222-3850
Fax: 503-222-1475

Forest Park
Newberry Rd-betw NW Skyline & St Helens Rd
Portland, OR 97210
Phone: 503-823-2223
Fax: 503-823-5297

Fort Vancouver National Historic Site
612 E Reserve St
Vancouver, WA 98661
www.nps.gov/fova/
Phone: 360-696-7655
Fax: 360-696-7657
TF: 800-832-3599

Frenchman's Bar Regional Park
9612 NW Lower River Rd
Vancouver, WA 98660
Phone: 360-735-8839

General Howard House
750 Andresen St
Vancouver, WA 98661
Phone: 360-992-1820

Gifford Pinchot National Forest
10600 NE 51st St
Vancouver, WA 98682
www.fs.fed.us/gpnf/
Phone: 360-891-5001
Fax: 360-891-5045

Grant House Folk Art Center
1101 Officers Row
Vancouver, WA 98661
Phone: 360-694-5252

Great Western Malting Co
PO Box 1529
Vancouver, WA 98668
Phone: 360-693-3661
Fax: 360-696-8354

Grotto The
Sandy Blvd & NE 85th Ave
Portland, OR 97220
E-mail: grottog1@tdeport.com
www.thegrotto.org
Phone: 503-254-7371
Fax: 503-254-7948

Imago Theatre
17 SE 8th Ave
Portland, OR 97214
www.imagotheatre.com
Phone: 503-231-3959
Fax: 503-239-5248

International Rose Test Garden
4000 SW Kingston Dr
Portland, OR 97201
Phone: 503-823-3636

Japanese Garden
PO Box 3847
Portland, OR 97208
Phone: 503-223-4070
Fax: 503-223-8303

Kaiser Henry J Shipyard Memorial & Interpretive Center
Columbia Way Marine Pk
Vancouver, WA 98661
Phone: 360-696-8173
Fax: 360-696-8009

Leverich Park
E 39th & M Sts
Vancouver, WA 98660
Phone: 360-696-8171

Lewisville County Park
26411 NE Lewisville Hwy
Vancouver, WA
Phone: 360-696-8171

Lloyd Center
2201 Lloyd Ctr
Portland, OR 97232
Phone: 503-282-2511
Fax: 503-280-9407

Marshall House & Gift Shop
1301 Officers Row
Vancouver, WA 98661
Phone: 360-693-3103

McMenamins Breweries Inc
1624 NW Glisan St
Portland, OR 97209
www.mcmenamins.com/Brewing
Phone: 503-223-0109
Fax: 503-294-0837

Mount Hood National Forest
16400 Champion Way
Sandy, OR 97055
Phone: 503-668-1700
Fax: 503-668-1641

Mount Saint Helens National Volcanic Monument Headquarters
42218 NE Yale Bridge Rd
Amboy, WA 98601
www.fs.fed.us/gpnf/mshnvm
Phone: 360-247-3900
Fax: 360-247-3901

Multnomah Village
SW 35th Ave & Capitol Hwy
Portland, OR 97219
Phone: 503-245-4014

Musical Theatre Co
531 SE 14th Ave
Portland, OR 97214
www.rdrop.com/~mluce/tmc.html
Phone: 503-224-8730
Fax: 503-224-5123

Northwest Afrikan American Ballet
PO Box 11143
Portland, OR 97211
Phone: 503-287-8852
Fax: 503-287-8852

Oaks Amusement Park
SE Spokane St
Portland, OR 97202
www.oakspark.com
Phone: 503-233-5777
Fax: 503-236-9143

OMNIMAX Theater
1945 SE Water Ave
Portland, OR 97214
www.omsi.edu/explore/omnimax/
Phone: 503-797-4640
Fax: 503-797-4500

Oregon Ballet Theater
1120 SW 10th Ave
Portland, OR 97205
www.obt.org
Phone: 503-227-0977
Fax: 503-227-4186
TF: 888-922-5538

Oregon Children's Theatre
SW 3rd & Clay Sts Civic Auditorium
Portland, OR 97205
www.octc.org
Phone: 503-228-9571
Fax: 503-228-3545

Oregon City Trolley
1726 Washington St
Oregon City, OR 97045
Phone: 503-657-0891
Fax: 503-657-7892
TF: 800-424-3002

Oregon Historical Society
1200 SW Park Ave
Portland, OR 97205
E-mail: orhist@ohs.org
www.ohs.org
Phone: 503-222-1741
Fax: 503-221-2035

Oregon Maritime Center & Museum
113 SW Naito Pkwy
Portland, OR 97204
E-mail: omcm@teleport.com
www.teleport.com/~omcm/index.shtml
Phone: 503-224-7724
Fax: 503-224-7767

Oregon Military Museum
10101 SE Clackamas Rd Bldg 6101
Clackamas, OR 97015
Phone: 503-557-5336
Fax: 503-557-5202

Oregon Museum of Science & Industry
1945 SE Water Ave
Portland, OR 97214
www.omsi.edu
Phone: 503-797-4000
Fax: 503-797-4500

Oregon Sports Hall of Fame & Museum
321 SW Salmon St
Portland, OR 97204
Phone: 503-227-7466
Fax: 503-227-6925

Oregon Symphony Orchestra
921 SW Washington St Suite 200
Portland, OR 97205
www.orsymphony.org
Phone: 503-228-4294
Fax: 503-228-4150
TF: 800-228-7343

Oregon Zoo
4001 SW Canyon Rd
Portland, OR 97221
E-mail: hartlinej@metro.dst.or.us
www.zooregon.org
Phone: 503-226-1561
Fax: 503-226-6836

Parkersville National Historic Site
24 S 'A' St
Washougal, WA 98671
Phone: 360-834-4792
Fax: 360-835-2197

Pearson Air Museum
1115 E 5th St
Vancouver, WA 98661
E-mail: pearson@pacifier.com
www.pearsonairmuseum.org
Phone: 360-694-7026
Fax: 360-694-0824

Pendleton Woolen Mill & Outlet Store
2 17th St
Washougal, WA 98671
Phone: 360-835-1118
TF: 800-568-2480

Photographic Image Gallery
240 SW 1st Ave
Portland, OR 97204
www.photographicimage.com
Phone: 503-224-3543
Fax: 503-224-3607

Pioneer Courthouse Square
715 SW Morrison Suite 702
Portland, OR 97205
www.pioneersquare.citysearch.com
Phone: 503-223-1613
Fax: 503-222-7425

Pittock Mansion
3229 NW Pittock Dr
Portland, OR 97210
Phone: 503-823-3624
Fax: 503-823-3619

Pomeroy Living History Farm
20902 NE Lucia Falls Rd
Yacolt, WA 98675
Phone: 360-686-3537

Port of Vancouver
3103 Lower River Rd
Vancouver, WA 98660
E-mail: povinfo@portvanusa.com
www.portvanusa.com
Phone: 360-693-3611
Fax: 360-735-1565

Portland Art Museum
1219 SW Park Ave
Portland, OR 97205
E-mail: paminfo@pam.org
www.pam.org
Phone: 503-226-2811
Fax: 503-226-4842

Portland Audubon Society
5151 NW Cornell Rd
Portland, OR 97210
Phone: 503-292-6855
Fax: 503-292-1021

Portland Brewers Guild
510 NW 3rd Ave
Portland, OR 97209
Phone: 503-295-1862
Fax: 503-226-4895
TF: 800-440-2537

Portland Brewing Co
2730 NW 31st Ave
Portland, OR 97210
portlandbrew.com
Phone: 503-226-7623
Fax: 503-226-2702
TF: 800-356-2017

Portland Center for the Performing Arts
1111 SW Broadway
Portland, OR 97205
www.pcpa.com
Phone: 503-248-4335
Fax: 503-274-7490

Portland Center Stage
1111 SW Broadway
Portland, OR 97205
E-mail: prmanager@pcs.org
www.pcs.org
Phone: 503-274-6588
Fax: 503-228-7058

Portland Childen's Museum
3037 SW 2nd Ave
Portland, OR 97201
www.parks.ci.portland.or.us/parks
Phone: 503-823-2227
Fax: 503-823-3667

Portland Institute for Contemporary Art
219 NW 12th Ave Suite 100
Portland, OR 97209
www.pica.org/
Phone: 503-242-1419
Fax: 503-243-1167

Portland Opera Assn
1515 SW Morrison St
Portland, OR 97205
www.portlandopera.org
Phone: 503-241-1401
Fax: 503-241-4212

Portland Saturday Market
1st & Front Sts under Burnside Bridge
Portland, OR 97209
Phone: 503-222-6072
Fax: 503-222-0254

Portland Skidmore Fountain Market
120 SW Ankeny St Suite 200
Portland, OR 97204
Phone: 503-228-2392
Fax: 503-228-0576

Powell Butte Nature Park
SE 162nd & Powell Blvd
Portland, OR 97204
Phone: 503-823-2223

Powell's City of Books
1005 W Burnside St
Portland, OR 97209
E-mail: help@powells.com
www.powells.com
Phone: 800-878-7323
Fax: 503-227-4631

Ridgefield National Wildlife Refuge
301 N 3rd Ave
Ridgefield, WA 98642
Phone: 360-887-4106
Fax: 360-887-4109

Rocket City Neon Advertising Museum
1554 NE 3rd Ave
Camas, WA 98607
E-mail: david@rocketcityneon.com
www.rocketcityneon.com
Phone: 360-834-6366
Fax: 360-834-6366

Rogue Ales Co
2320 OSU Dr
Newport, OR 97365
E-mail: roguedawg@rogueales.com
www.rogueales.com
Phone: 541-867-3660
Fax: 541-867-3260
TF: 800-489-5482

Royal Durst Theater
3101 Main St
Vancouver, WA 98663
Phone: 360-737-4284
Fax: 360-696-5227

Salishan Vineyards
35011 N Fork Ave
LaCenter, WA 98629
Phone: 360-263-2713

Salmon Creek Regional Park
1112 NE 117th St
Vancouver, WA 98685
Phone: 360-735-8839

Steigerwald Lake National Wildlife Refuge
36062 SR-14
Stevenson, WA 98648
Phone: 509-427-5208
Fax: 509-427-4707

Tears of Joy Puppet Theatre
601 Main St Suite 403
Vancouver, WA 98660
Phone: 360-695-0477
Fax: 360-695-0438

Two Rivers Heritage Museum
001 16th St
Washougal, WA 98671
Phone: 360-835-8742

Vancouver Lake Park
6801 NW Lower River Rd
Vancouver, WA 98660
Phone: 360-696-8171

Vancouver Symphony Orchestra
3101 Main St Vancouver School of the Arts
Vancouver, WA 98660
Phone: 360-735-7278

Washington Park
SW Park Pl-Hwy 26
Portland, OR 97204
Phone: 503-823-2223

Water Resources Education Center
4600 SE Columbia Way
Vancouver, WA 98668
www.ci.vancouver.wa.us/watercenter
Phone: 360-696-8478

Water Tower at Johns Landing
5331 SW Macadam Ave
Portland, OR 97201
Phone: 503-228-9431
Fax: 503-228-9473

Wendel Museum of Animal Conservation
8303 SE Evergreen Hwy
Vancouver, WA 98664
Phone: 360-694-8651
Fax: 360-254-3698

Widmer Brothers Brewing Co
929 N Russell St
Portland, OR 97227
www.widmer.com
Phone: 503-281-2437
Fax: 503-281-1496

Willamette Shore Trolley
311 N State St
Lake Oswego, OR 97034
Phone: 503-222-2226

World Forestry Center
4033 SW Canyon Rd
Portland, OR 97221
www.teleport.com/~wfc/
Phone: 503-228-1367
Fax: 503-228-4608

Sports Teams & Facilities

Multnomah Greyhound Park
PO Box 9
Fairview, OR 97024
E-mail: mgp@ez2winmgp.com
www.ez2winmgp.com/
Phone: 503-667-7700
Fax: 503-667-4852
TF: 800-888-7576

Portland Civic Stadium
1844 SW Morrison St
Portland, OR 97205
Phone: 503-248-4345
Fax: 503-221-3983

Portland Fire
1 Center Ct Suite 150 Rose Garden
Portland, OR 97227
www.wnba.com/Fire
Phone: 503-234-9291
Fax: 503-736-2138

Portland International Raceway
1940 N Victory Blvd
Portland, OR 97217
E-mail: indytrax@teleport.com
www.teleport.com/~pir
Phone: 503-823-7223
Fax: 503-823-5896

Portland Meadows Horse Track
1001 N Schmeer Rd
Portland, OR 97217
E-mail: tnpm@portlandmeadows.com
www.portlandmeadows.com
Phone: 503-285-9144
Fax: 503-286-9763
TF: 800-944-3127

Portland Pythons (soccer)
1 Center Ct Rose Garden
Portland, OR 97227
www.portlandpythons.com
Phone: 503-684-5425
Fax: 503-639-8084

Portland Rockies (baseball)
1844 SW Morrison St Civic Stadium
Portland, OR 97205
www.portlandrockies.com
Phone: 503-223-2837
Fax: 503-223-2948

Portland Trail Blazers
1 Center Ct Memorial Coliseum
Portland, OR 97227
www.nba.com/blazers
Phone: 503-234-9291
Fax: 503-736-2187

Portland Winter Hawks (hockey)
1 Center Ct Memorial Coliseum
Portland, OR 97208
E-mail: hawks@teleport.com
www.winterhawks.com
Phone: 503-238-6366
Fax: 503-238-7629

Rose Garden
1 Center Ct
Portland, OR 97227
www.rosequarter.com
Phone: 503-797-9617
Fax: 503-736-2191

Vancouver Indoor Sports Arena
3315 NE 112th Ave
Vancouver, WA 98682
Phone: 360-254-8453

Annual Events

Amboy Territorial Days Celebration (early-mid-July) 360-686-3383
America's Largest Christmas Bazaar (late November-early December) 503-736-5200
An Olde-Fashioned Fourth (early July) 360-686-3537
Antique Aircraft Fly-In (early July) 360-694-7026
Bite-A Taste of Portland (mid-August) 503-248-0600
Camas Days (late July) 360-834-2472
Candlelight Tour (mid-September) 360-696-7655
Christmas at Fort Vancouver (mid-December) 360-696-7655
Christmas at the Pittock Mansion (late November-late December) 503-823-3624
Christmas Ships Parade (December) 503-275-9750
Cinco de Mayo Celebration (early May) 503-222-9807
Clark County Fair (early-mid-August) 360-737-6180
Clark County Rural Heritage Fair (mid-July) 360-687-4554
Earth Action Day (mid-April) 360-696-8478
Evening Concerts at the Zoo (mid-June-mid-August) 503-226-1561
Festa Italiana (late August) 503-771-0310
Festival of Lights at the Grotto (late November-late December) 503-254-7371
Fort James Health & Safety Fair (early May) 360-834-3021
Fort Vancouver Brigade Encampment (mid-July) 360-696-7655
Fort Vancouver Days Celebration (early-mid-July) 360-696-8171
Fort Vancouver Fourth of July Celebration (July 4) 360-693-5481
Founders Day (late August) 360-696-7655
Greek Festival (early October) 503-234-0468
Harvest Days Celebration (mid-July) 360-687-1510
Hazel Dell Parade of Bands (mid-May) 360-576-1195
Herb Festival (mid-May) 360-686-3537
Heritage Weekend (early May) 360-699-5288
Hollywood Video Winter Wonderland Celebration of Lights (late November-early January) 503-232-3000
Home & Garden Idea Fair (late April) 360-992-3231
Homowo Festival of African Arts (mid-August) 503-288-3025
Indian Art Northwest (late May) 503-224-8650
International Discovery Walk Festival (late April) 360-892-6758
International Film Festival (mid-February-early March) 503-221-1156
LaCenter Summer Our Days Festival (late July) 360-263-7168
Mount Hood Jazz Festival (early August) 503-232-3000
Mount Tum Tum Native American Indian Encampment (early July) 360-247-5235
North by Northwest Music Festival (early-mid-September) 512-467-7979
Oregon Brewers Festival (late July) 503-778-5917
Oregon Shakespeare Festival (February-October) 541-482-2111
Oregon State Fair (late August-early September) 503-378-3247
Our Days Festival (late July) 360-263-8850
Portland Arts Festival (June) 503-227-2681
Portland Creative Conference (mid-September) 503-234-1641
Portland Marathon (late September) 503-226-1111
Portland Rose Festival & Grand Floral Parade (early June) 503-227-2681
Portland Scottish Highland Games (mid-July) 503-293-8501
Queen Victoria's Birthday (late May) 360-696-7655
River Rhythms & Chili Cook-Off (early-mid-July) 360-696-8171
Rose Festival Airshow (late June) 503-227-2681
Rose Show (late June) 360-693-6822
Seafarer's International Festival (late July) 360-694-9300
Seafood & Wine Festival (late February) 800-262-7844
Spring Beer Fest (late April) 503-246-4503
Spring Castles Programs (early March-early June) 360-992-1821
Spring Dance (late May) 360-694-7026
Starlight Parade (early June) 503-227-2681
Sturgeon Festival (late May) 360-696-8478
Tulip Festival (late April) 503-228-5108
Vancouver Farmers Market Saturdays (April-October) 360-737-8298
Washington County Fair & Rodeo (early August) 503-648-1416
Waterfront Blues Festival (early July) 503-973-3378
Zoolights (December) 503-226-1561

Providence, Rhode Island

***County:* Providence**

PROVIDENCE is located at the head of the Narragansett Bay along the Providence River in northeastern Rhode Island. Major cities within 100 miles include Newport and Pawtucket, Rhode Island; Boston, Worcester, and Fall River, Massachusetts; and Hartford and New Haven, Connecticut.

Area (Land) .... 18.5 sq mi
Area (Water)............................... 2.1 sq mi
Elevation....................................... 24 ft
Latitude ....41-82-39 N
Longitude............................... 71-41-33 W
Time Zone ....EST
Area Code....................................... 401

Climate

Providence's climate features four distinct seasons and is strongly influenced by the city's proximity to Narragansett Bay and the Atlantic Ocean. Winters are generally cold, but temperatures are moderated by the marine influence. Winter high temperatures average in the upper 30s, and low temperatures average in the low 20s. The average annual snowfall in Providence is 35 inches. Summer days are warm yet pleasant due to the seabreeze, with average high temperatures near 80 degrees and evening low temperatures near 60. Precipitation is fairly evenly distributed throughout the year in Providence—November and December tend to be the wettest months in the city, while July is the driest.

Average Temperatures & Precipitation

Temperatures

	Jan	Feb	Mar	Apr	May	Jun	Jul	Aug	Sep	Oct	Nov	Dec
High	37	38	46	57	67	77	82	81	74	64	53	41
Low	19	21	29	38	47	57	63	62	54	43	35	24

Precipitation

	Jan	Feb	Mar	Apr	May	Jun	Jul	Aug	Sep	Oct	Nov	Dec
Inches	3.9	3.6	4.1	4.1	3.8	3.3	3.2	3.6	3.5	3.7	4.4	4.4

History

Providence was founded in 1635 by Roger Williams, a Puritan leader from Boston who had been banished from Massachusetts for his religious beliefs. He and a group of his fellow believers established the settlement, which they named in honor of God's providence, as a haven from religious and political persecution. In 1644, Providence gained its charter and became a part of the Colony of Providence Plantations (Rhode Island's official title). The land on which Providence was established was originally inhabited by the Narragansett tribe. Hostilities between the Native Americans and the white settlers mounted throughout the mid-17th Century, culminating in King Philip's War (King Philip was a Native American chief) in 1675, during which much of Providence was destroyed.

By the early 1700s, Providence had been rebuilt and transformed into a thriving port city, with rum and molasses from the West Indies and Africa being the primary imports. The city was also involved in the slave trade. In 1764, Brown University, one of the nation's oldest institutions of higher education, was established in Providence. During the American Revolution, Brown University's University Hall served as quarters for American and French troops. In May of 1776, the Rhode Island Independence Act was signed in Providence two months before the signing of the Declaration of Independence. Incorporated as a city in 1831, Providence grew quickly as a manufacturing hub noted for its production of silverware, jewelry, and textiles. In 1854, Providence was chosen, along with Newport, to serve as the joint state capital of Rhode Island, an honor the two cities shared until 1900, when Providence became the sole capital city.

Nearly a century later, Providence is both the seat of state government and of Providence County. The city also remains one of New England's leading industrial centers, and with a population of more than 150,000, is Rhode Island's largest city.

Population

1990 Census 160,728
1998 Estimate.............................150,890
% Change .... -6.1

Racial/Ethnic Breakdown

White.................................... 70.0%
Black 15.0%
Other.................................... 15.0%
Hispanic Origin (may be of any race) 16.0%

Age Breakdown

Under 5 years.............................. 8.0%
5 to 17.................................. 16.0%
18 to 24................................. 18.0%
25 to 44................................. 30.0%
45 to 54.................................. 7.0%
55 to 64.................................. 7.0%
65+ years 14.0%
Median Age................................29.3

Gender Breakdown

Male..................................... 48.0%
Female................................... 52.0%

Government

Type of Government: Mayor-Council

Providence City Clerk
25 Dorrance St
Providence, RI 02903

Phone: 401-421-7740
Fax: 401-421-6492

Providence City Council
25 Dorrance St
Providence, RI 02903
Phone: 401-521-7477
Fax: 401-521-3920

Providence City Hall
25 Dorrance St
Providence, RI 02903
Phone: 401-421-7740

Providence Finance Dept
25 Dorrance St
Providence, RI 02903
Phone: 401-421-7740
Fax: 401-621-8102

Providence Fire Dept
209 Fountain St
Providence, RI 02903
Phone: 401-421-1293
Fax: 401-274-8508

Providence Mayor
25 Dorrance St
Providence, RI 02903
Phone: 401-421-7740
Fax: 401-274-8240

Providence Personnel Office
25 Dorrance St 4th Fl
Providence, RI 02903
Phone: 401-421-7740

Providence Planning & Development Dept
400 Westminster St
Providence, RI 02903
Phone: 401-351-4300
Fax: 401-351-9533

Providence Police Dept
209 Fountain St
Providence, RI 02903
Phone: 401-272-3121
Fax: 401-453-3766

Providence Public Library
225 Washington St
Providence, RI 02903
Phone: 401-455-8000
Fax: 401-455-8080

Providence Public Works Dept
700 Allens Ave
Providence, RI 02905
Phone: 401-467-7950
Fax: 401-941-2567

Providence Recreation Dept
1 Recreation Way
Providence, RI 02904
Phone: 401-421-7740
Fax: 401-455-8860

Providence School Dept
797 Westminster St
Providence, RI 02903
Phone: 401-456-9100
Fax: 401-456-9292

Providence Treasurer's Dept
25 Dorrance St
Providence, RI 02903
Phone: 401-421-7740

Providence Water Supply Board
552 Academy Ave
Providence, RI 02908
Phone: 401-521-6300
Fax: 401-331-5081

Important Phone Numbers

AAA....401-272-7100
American Express Travel....401-274-2900
Driver's License/Vehicle Registration Information....401-222-2970
Emergency....911
Medical Referral....401-456-4636
Poison Control Center....401-444-5727
Providence Tax Assessor....401-421-5900
Providence Tax Collection....401-331-5252
Rhode Island Assn of Realtors....401-785-3650
Rhode Island Taxation Div....401-222-1040
Travelers Aid of Rhode Island....401-521-2255
Voter Registration Information....401-421-0495
Weather....401-277-7777

Information Sources

Better Business Bureau Serving Rhode Island
120 Lavan St
Warwick, RI 02888
www.rhodeisland.bbb.org
Phone: 401-785-1212
Fax: 401-785-3061

Greater Providence Chamber of Commerce
30 Exchange Terr
Providence, RI 02903
www.provchamber.com
Phone: 401-521-5000
Fax: 401-751-2434

Newport City Hall
43 Broadway
Newport, RI 02840
www.cityofnewport.com
Phone: 401-846-9600
Fax: 401-848-5750

Newport County
45 Washington Sq
Newport, RI 02840
Phone: 401-841-8330

Newport County Chamber of Commerce
45 Valley Rd
Middletown, RI 02842
www.newportchamber.com
Phone: 401-847-1600
Fax: 401-849-5848

Newport County Convention & Visitors Bureau
23 America's Cup Ave
Newport, RI 02840
www.gonewport.com
Phone: 401-849-8048
Fax: 401-849-0291
TF: 800-326-6030

Newport Marina & Event Center
4 Commercial Wharf
Newport, RI 02840
Phone: 401-846-1600
Fax: 401-847-9262

Newport Mayor
43 Broadway
Newport, RI 02840
Phone: 401-846-9600
Fax: 401-848-5750

Newport Planning Zoning & Development Dept
43 Broadway
Newport, RI 02840
www.cityofnewport.com/nwplan.html
Phone: 401-846-9600
Fax: 401-848-5750

Newport Public Library
300 Spring St
Newport, RI 02840
www.wsii.com/rhodeisl/users/newp_lib/Index.htm
Phone: 401-847-8720
Fax: 401-842-0841

Providence Civic Center
1 LaSalle Sq
Providence, RI 02903
www.provcc.com
Phone: 401-331-0700
Fax: 401-751-6792

Providence County
1 Dorrance Plaza
Providence, RI 02903
Phone: 401-458-5200
Fax: 401-222-3462

Providence Warwick Convention & Visitors Bureau
1 W Exchange St
Providence, RI 02903
www.providencecvb.com/
Phone: 401-274-1636
Fax: 401-351-2090
TF: 800-233-1636

Rhode Island Convention Center
1 Sabin St
Providence, RI 02903
www.guidetori.com
Phone: 401-458-6000
Fax: 401-458-6500

Rhode Island Economic Development Corp
1 W Exchange St
Providence, RI 02903
www.riedc.com
Phone: 401-222-2601
Fax: 401-222-2102

Rhode Island Tourism Div
1 West Exchange St
Providence, RI 02903
visitrhodeisland.com
Phone: 401-222-2601
Fax: 401-222-2102
TF: 800-556-2484

Online Resources

4Providence.com
www.4providence.com

About.com Guide to Providence
providence.about.com/citiestowns/newenglandus/providence/mbody.htm

Area Guide Newport
newportri.areaguides.net

Area Guide Providence
providence.areaguides.net

Best Read Guide Newport
www.newportri.com/

City Knowledge Providence
www.cityknowledge.com/ri_providence.htm

DigitalCity Providence
home.digitalcity.com/providence

Excite.com Newport City Guide
www.excite.com/travel/countries/united_states/rhode_island/newport

Excite.com Providence City Guide
www.excite.com/travel/countries/united_states/rhode_island/providence

Federal Hill Gazette
www.fedhillgazette.com/

Guide to Antique Shops in Newport
www.drawrm.com/dealers.htm

Guide to Newport
www.mswebpros.com

I-95 Exit Information Guide Providence
www.usastar.com/i95/cityguide/providence.htm

Lodging.com Newport Rhode Island
www.lodging.com/auto/guides/newport-area-ri.html

Newport Online
www.newportonline.com

Newport Rhode Island
www.bbsnet.com/Newport/newport.html

Newport RI On-line Guide
members.aol.com/newporters

Providence CityLink
usacitylink.com/providen/

Rough Guide Travel Newport
travel.roughguides.com/content/392/

Rough Guide Travel Providence
travel.roughguides.com/content/391/

Surf & Sun Beach Vacation Guide to Newport
www.surf-sun.com/ri-newport-main.htm

Visit Newport
www.visitnewport.com

Area Communities

Communities in Rhode Island with populations greater than 20,000 include:

Bristol
10 Court St
Bristol, RI 02809
Phone: 401-253-7000
Fax: 401-253-1570

Coventry
1670 Flat River Rd
Coventry, RI 02816
Phone: 401-821-6400
Fax: 401-822-9132

Cranston
869 Park Ave
Cranston, RI 02910
Phone: 401-461-1000
Fax: 401-461-9650

Cumberland
PO Box 7
Cumberland, RI 02864
Phone: 401-728-2400
Fax: 401-724-3311

East Providence
145 Taunton Ave
East Providence, RI 02914
Phone: 401-435-7500
Fax: 401-435-7501

Johnston
1385 Hartford Ave
Johnston, RI 02919
Phone: 401-351-6618
Fax: 401-331-4271

Newport
43 Broadway
Newport, RI 02840
Phone: 401-846-9600
Fax: 401-848-5750

North Kingstown
80 Boston Neck Rd
North Kingstown, RI 02852
Phone: 401-294-3331
Fax: 401-885-7373

North Providence
2000 Smith St
North Providence, RI 02911
Phone: 401-232-0900
Fax: 401-233-1409

Pawtucket
137 Roosevelt Ave
Pawtucket, RI 02860
Phone: 401-728-0500
Fax: 401-728-8932

South Kingstown
PO Box 31
Wakefield, RI 02880
Phone: 401-789-9331
Fax: 401-789-5280

Warwick
3275 Post Rd
Warwick, RI 02886
Phone: 401-738-2000
Fax: 401-738-6639

West Warwick
1170 Main St
West Warwick, RI 02893
Phone: 401-822-9200
Fax: 401-822-9252

Westerly
45 Broad St
Westerly, RI 02891
Phone: 401-348-2500
Fax: 401-348-2571

Woonsocket
169 Main St
Woonsocket, RI 02895
Phone: 401-762-6400
Fax: 401-765-0022

Economy

Providence is Rhode Island's primary industrial center. Nicknamed the "Jewelry Capital of the World," Rhode Island has long been recognized for its jewelry and silverware production, and manufacturing of these and other products continues to play an important role in Providence's economy. Major U.S. manufacturers that have their corporate headquarters in the Providence area include A.T. Cross, Hasbro, and Textron. Services is the largest employment sector in Providence County. With six major hospitals in the city and surrounding area, health care is the leading service industry in Providence. Higher education, retail trade, finance, and the insurance industry are also important contributors to the area's economy. In addition to the major employers listed below, Rhode Island State Government and the U.S. Government are among the top 15.

Unemployment Rate 6.1%
Per Capita Income $26,953*
Median Family Income $39,490

** Information given is for Providence County.*

Principal Industries & Number of Wage Earners

City of Providence - 1998

Industry	Wage Earners
Agriculture, Forestry, & Fisheries	98
Construction	2,415
Finance, Insurance, & Real Estate	9,904
Manufacturing	14,229
Retail Trade	10,681
Services	53,728
Transportation, Communications, & Utilities	4,014
Wholesale Trade	4,381

Major Employers

Amica Mutual Insurance Co
PO Box 6008
Providence, RI 02940
www.amica.com
Phone: 401-334-6000
Fax: 401-334-1491
TF: 800-622-6422

Brown University
Providence, RI 02912
E-mail: Admission_Undergraduate@Brown.Edu
www.brown.edu
Phone: 401-863-1000
Fax: 401-863-9300

Care New England
45 Willard Ave
Providence, RI 02905
Phone: 401-453-7900
Fax: 401-453-7686

CVS Corp
1 CVS Dr
Woonsocket, RI 02895
www.cvs.com
Phone: 401-765-1500
Fax: 401-770-6949
TF: 800-666-0500

Diocese of Providence
1 Cathedral Sq
Providence, RI 02903
Phone: 401-278-4500
Fax: 401-831-1947

Memorial Hospital of Rhode Island
111 Brewster St
Pawtucket, RI 02860
www.mhri.org
Phone: 401-729-2000
Fax: 401-722-0198

Our Lady of Fatima Hospital
200 High Service Ave
North Providence, RI 02904
www.saintjosephri.com
Phone: 401-456-3000
Fax: 401-456-3824

Providence City Hall
25 Dorrance St
Providence, RI 02903
www.providenceri.com
Phone: 401-421-7740

Providence School District
797 Westminster St
Providence, RI 02903
www.providenceri.com/education/education.html
Phone: 401-456-9100
Fax: 401-456-9292

Rhode Island Hospital
593 Eddy St
Providence, RI 02903
www.lifespan.org/partners/rih
Phone: 401-444-4000
Fax: 401-444-8161

Roger Williams Medical Center
825 Chalkstone Ave
Providence, RI 02908
E-mail: rwmc@aol.com
www.rwmc.com
Phone: 401-456-2000
Fax: 401-456-6988

Stop & Shop Cos Inc
1385 Hancock St
Quincy, MA 02169
www.stopandshop.com
Phone: 781-380-8000
Fax: 617-770-8190

Verizon Communications
234 Washington St
Providence, RI 02903
www.verizon.com
Phone: 401-455-4500
Fax: 401-455-4548

Quality of Living Indicators

Total Crime Index 12,156
(rates per 100,000 inhabitants)

Violent Crime

Murder/manslaughter	26
Forcible rape	80
Robbery	463
Aggravated assault	572

Property Crime
Burglary....2,101
Larceny theft....6,637
Motor vehicle theft....2,277

Cost of Living Index....116.0
(national average = 100)

Median Home Price....$128,800

Education

Public Schools

Providence School District
797 Westminster St
Providence, RI 02903
www.providenceri.com/education/education.html
Phone: 401-456-9100
Fax: 401-456-9292

Number of Schools
Elementary....22
Middle....6
High....6
Alternative High....1
Vocational....1
Special Education....1

Student/Teacher Ratio
All Grades....16.5:1

Private Schools

Number of Schools (all grades)....30+

Colleges & Universities

Brown University
Providence, RI 02912
E-mail: Admission_Undergraduate@Brown.Edu
www.brown.edu
Phone: 401-863-1000
Fax: 401-863-9300

Bryant College
1150 Douglas Pike
Smithfield, RI 02917
E-mail: postmaster@research1.bryant.edu
www.bryant.edu
Phone: 401-232-6000
Fax: 401-232-6741
TF: 800-622-7001

Community College of Rhode Island Flanagan Campus
1762 Louisquissett Pike
Lincoln, RI 02865
www.ccri.cc.ri.us
Phone: 401-333-7000
Fax: 401-333-7111

Community College of Rhode Island Knight Campus
400 East Ave
Warwick, RI 02886
Phone: 401-825-1000
Fax: 401-825-2394

Johnson & Wales University
8 Abbott Park Pl
Providence, RI 02903
www.jwu.edu
Phone: 401-598-1000
Fax: 401-598-2948
TF: 800-342-5598

New England Institute of Technology
2500 Post Rd
Warwick, RI 02886
www.neit.edu
Phone: 401-467-7744
Fax: 401-738-5122
TF: 800-736-7744

Providence College
River Ave
Providence, RI 02918
www.providence.edu
Phone: 401-865-1000
Fax: 401-865-2826
TF: 800-721-6444

Rhode Island College
600 Mt Pleasant Ave
Providence, RI 02908
E-mail: admissions@grog.ric.edu
www.ric.edu
Phone: 401-456-8000
Fax: 401-456-8817

Rhode Island School of Design
2 College St
Providence, RI 02903
E-mail: admissions@risd.edu
www.risd.edu
Phone: 401-454-6100
Fax: 401-454-6309

Roger Williams University
1 Old Ferry Rd
Bristol, RI 02809
www.rwu.edu
Phone: 401-253-1040
Fax: 401-254-3557

Salve Regina University
100 Ochre Point Ave
Newport, RI 02840
www.salve.edu
Phone: 401-847-6650
Fax: 401-848-2823
TF: 800-467-2583

University of Rhode Island
Kingston, RI 02881
www.uri.edu
Phone: 401-874-1000
Fax: 401-874-5523

Hospitals

Emma Pendleton Bradley Hospital
1011 Veterans Memorial Pkwy
East Providence, RI 02915
Phone: 401-432-1000
Fax: 401-432-1500

Miriam Hospital
164 Summit Ave
Providence, RI 02906
www.lifespan.org/partners/tmh
Phone: 401-793-2500
Fax: 401-331-6496

Newport Hospital
11 Friendship St
Newport, RI 02840
www.lifespan.org/partners/nh
Phone: 401-846-6400
Fax: 401-845-1088

Our Lady of Fatima Hospital
200 High Service Ave
North Providence, RI 02904
www.saintjosephri.com
Phone: 401-456-3000
Fax: 401-456-3824

Rhode Island Hospital
593 Eddy St
Providence, RI 02903
www.lifespan.org/partners/rih
Phone: 401-444-4000
Fax: 401-444-8161

Roger Williams Medical Center
825 Chalkstone Ave
Providence, RI 02908
www.rwmc.com
Phone: 401-456-2000
Fax: 401-456-6988

South County Hospital
100 Kenyon Ave
Wakefield, RI 02879
www.schospital.com
Phone: 401-782-8000
Fax: 401-783-6330

Veterans Affairs Medical Center
830 Chalkstone Ave
Providence, RI 02908
Phone: 401-273-7100
Fax: 401-457-3370

Transportation

Airport(s)

Theodore Francis Green State Airport (PVD)
7 miles S of downtown Providence
(approx 15 minutes) 401-737-4000

Mass Transit

Rhode Island Public Transit
$1.25 Base fare 401-781-9400

Rail/Bus

Amtrak Station
100 Gaspee St
Providence, RI 02903
Phone: 401-727-7379
TF: 800-872-7245

Bonanza Bus Station
1 Bonanza Way
Providence, RI 02904
Phone: 401-751-8800
TF: 888-751-8800

Utilities

Electricity
Narragansett Electric Co 401-784-4000
www.narragansett.com

Gas
Providence Gas Co 401-831-8800

Water
Providence Water Supply Board 401-521-6300
www.provwater.com

Garbage Collection/Recycling
Providence Public Works Dept 401-467-7950

Telecommunications

Telephone
Verizon Communications 401-525-3830
www.verizon.com

Cable Television
Cox Cable 401-828-2288

Internet Service Providers (ISPs)
IDS World Network 401-384-6000
www.ids.net
Log On America Inc 401-453-6100
www.loa.com
Ocean State Free-Net 401-272-5388
osfn.rhilinet.gov
RIconneCT Internet Services 401-596-7341
www.riconnect.com

Banks

Bank Rhode Island
195 Taunton Ave
East Providence, RI 02914
Phone: 401-435-8700
Fax: 401-435-8710

Citizens Bank
870 Westminster St
Providence, RI 02903
Phone: 401-456-7000
Fax: 401-456-7278
TF: 800-922-9999

Citizens Bank of Rhode Island
1 Citizens Plaza
Providence, RI 02903
Phone: 401-456-7000
Fax: 401-455-5715
TF: 800-922-9999

First Bank & Trust Co
180 Washington St
Providence, RI 02903
Phone: 401-421-3600
Fax: 401-861-6221

Fleet National Bank
111 Westminster St
Providence, RI 02903
www.fleet.com
Phone: 401-278-6000
Fax: 401-278-6523
TF: 800-445-4542

Union Bank
1565 Mineral Spring Ave
North Providence, RI 02904
Phone: 401-353-8910
Fax: 401-353-8938

Shopping

Ann & Hope Inc
1 Ann & Hope Way
Cumberland, RI 02864
Phone: 401-722-1000
Fax: 401-725-7190

Aquidneck Centre
99 E Main Rd
Middletown, RI 02842
Phone: 401-849-6800
Fax: 401-849-7863

Arcade The
65 Weybosset St
Providence, RI 02903
Phone: 401-598-1199

Bannister's Wharf
1 Bannister's Wharf
Newport, RI 02840
www.bannisterswharf.com
Phone: 401-846-4500
Fax: 401-849-8750

Bellevue Gardens Shopping Center
Bellevue Ave
Newport, RI 02840

Catalog Fashion Outlet
1689 Post Rd
Warwick, RI 02888
Phone: 401-738-5145

Fall River Factory Outlet District
Rt 24 N & 195
Fall River, RI 02721
Phone: 800-424-5519
Fax: 508-677-4956

Garden City Center
Sockanosset Rd & Reservoir Ave
Cranston, RI 02920
Phone: 401-942-2800

Newport Mall
199 Connell Hwy
Newport, RI 02840

Providence Place Mall
1 Providence Pl
Providence, RI 02903
www.oso.com/partners/ppm
Phone: 401-270-1000
Fax: 401-270-1001

Rhode Island Mall
650 Bald Hill Rd
Warwick, RI 02886
Phone: 401-828-7651

Shops at Brick Marketplace
Thames St & America's Cup Ave
Newport, RI 02840
Phone: 401-849-8048

Warwick Mall
400 Baldhill Rd Suite 100
Warwick, RI 02886
Phone: 401-739-7500
Fax: 401-732-6052

Wayland Square
Medway & Waterman St
Providence, RI 02903
Phone: 401-751-1177

Media

Newspapers and Magazines

Newport Daily News*
101 Malbone Rd
Newport, RI 02840
Phone: 401-849-3300
Fax: 401-849-3306

Newport Mercury
101 Malbone Rd
Newport, RI 02840
Phone: 401-849-3300
Fax: 401-849-3306

Newport This Week
38 Bellevue Ave
Newport, RI 02840
www.newportthisweek.com/
Phone: 401-847-7766
Fax: 401-846-4974

Providence Business News
300 Richmond St Suite 202
Providence, RI 02903
E-mail: editor@pbn.com
www.pbn.com
Phone: 401-273-2201
Fax: 401-274-0270

Providence Journal-Bulletin*
75 Fountain St
Providence, RI 02902
www.projo.com
Phone: 401-277-7000
Fax: 401-277-7346

Providence Phoenix
150 Chestnut St
Providence, RI 02903
E-mail: providence-feedback@phx.com
www.providencephoenix.com
Phone: 401-273-6397
Fax: 401-273-0920

Rhode Island Monthly
280 Kinsley Ave
Providence, RI 02903
www.rimonthly.com/
Phone: 401-421-2552
Fax: 401-831-5624

**Indicates major daily newspapers*

Television

WJAR-TV Ch 10 (NBC)
23 Kenney Dr
Cranston, RI 02920
E-mail: mail.box10@nbc.com
www.nbc10wjar.com
Phone: 401-455-9100
Fax: 401-455-9140

WLNE-TV Ch 6 (ABC)
10 Orms St
Providence, RI 02904
www.abc6.com
Phone: 401-453-8000
Fax: 401-453-8092

WLWC-TV Ch 28 (WB)
10 Dorrance St Suite 805
Providence, RI 02903
Phone: 401-351-8828
Fax: 401-351-0222

WNAC-TV Ch 64 (Fox)
25 Catamore Blvd
East Providence, RI 02914
E-mail: fox64@fox64.com
www.fox64.com
Phone: 401-438-7200
Fax: 401-431-1012

WPRI-TV Ch 12 (CBS)
25 Catamore Blvd
East Providence, RI 02914
E-mail: wpri@wpri.com
www.wpri.com
Phone: 401-438-7200
Fax: 401-431-1012

WPXQ-TV Ch 69 (PAX)
1 Richmond Sq
Providence, RI 02906
www.pax.net/WPXQ
Phone: 401-453-6969
Fax: 401-453-6901

WSBE-TV Ch 36 (PBS)
50 Park Ln
Providence, RI 02907
www.wsbe.org
Phone: 401-222-3636
Fax: 401-222-3407

Radio

WADK-AM 1540 kHz (N/T)
15 Dr Marcus Wheatland Blvd
Newport, RI 02840
www.wadk.com
Phone: 401-846-1540
Fax: 401-846-1598

WAKX-FM 102.7 MHz (CHR)
1110 Central Ave
Pawtucket, RI 02861
Phone: 401-723-1063
Fax: 401-725-8609

WALE-AM 990 kHz (N/T)
1185 N Main St
Providence, RI 02904
Phone: 401-521-0990
Fax: 401-521-5077

WBRU-FM 95.5 MHz (Alt)
88 Benevolent St
Providence, RI 02906
www.wbru.com
Phone: 401-272-9550
Fax: 401-272-9278

WBSM-AM 1420 kHz (N/T)
22 Sconticut Neck Rd
Fairhaven, MA 02719
Phone: 508-993-1767
Fax: 508-999-1420

WCTK-FM 98.1 MHz (Ctry)
75 Oxford St
Providence, RI 02905
Phone: 401-467-4366
Fax: 401-941-2983

WDOM-FM 91.3 MHz (Urban)
Providence College River Ave
Providence, RI 02918
Phone: 401-865-2460

WFHN-FM 107.1 MHz (CHR)
22 Sconticut Neck Rd
Fairhaven, MA 02719
Phone: 508-993-1767
Fax: 508-999-1420

WHCK-FM 99.7 MHz (CR)
1502 Wampanoag Trail
East Providence, RI 02915
E-mail: lzevon@amaltd.com
Phone: 401-433-4200
Fax: 401-433-1183

WHJJ-AM 920 kHz (N/T)
115 Eastern Ave
East Providence, RI 02914
Phone: 401-438-6110
Fax: 401-438-3520

WHJY-FM 94.1 MHz (Rock)
115 Eastern Ave
East Providence, RI 02914
www.whjy.com
Phone: 401-438-6110
Fax: 401-438-3520

WHKK-FM 100.3 MHz (CR)
1502 Wampanoag Trail
East Providence, RI 02915
E-mail: bgwotb1003@aol.com
Phone: 401-433-4200
Fax: 317-433-1183

WKSO-AM 790 kHz (Sports)
1502 Wampanoag Trail
East Providence, RI 02915
Phone: 401-433-4200
Fax: 401-224-4295

WLKW-AM 550 kHz (Nost)
1110 Central Ave
Pawtucket, RI 02861
Phone: 401-723-1063
Fax: 401-725-8609
TF: 877-728-0550

WPMZ-AM 1110 kHz (Span)
1270 Mineral Springs Ave
North Providence, RI 02904
Phone: 401-726-8413
Fax: 401-726-8649

WPRO-AM 630 kHz (N/T)
1502 Wampanoag Trail
East Providence, RI 02915
Phone: 401-433-4200
Fax: 401-433-5967

WPRO-FM 92.3 MHz (CHR)
1502 Wampanoag Trail
East Providence, RI 02915
Phone: 401-433-4200
Fax: 401-433-5967

WRKO-AM 680 kHz (N/T)
116 Huntington Ave
Boston, MA 02116
www.wrko.com
Phone: 617-236-6800
Fax: 617-236-6890

WSNE-FM 93.3 MHz (AC)
100 Boyd Ave
East Providence, RI 02914
www.wsne.com/
Phone: 401-438-9300
Fax: 401-434-4243

WWBB-FM 101.5 MHz (Oldies)
75 Oxford St 3rd Fl
Providence, RI 02905
E-mail: oldiesb101@aol.com
www.b101.com
Phone: 401-781-9979
Fax: 401-781-9329

WWKX-FM 106.3 MHz (CHR)
1110 Central Ave
Pawtucket, RI 02861
Phone: 401-723-1063
Fax: 401-725-8609

WWLI-FM 105.1 MHz (AC)
1502 Wampanoag Trail
East Providence, RI 02915
www.lite105.com
Phone: 401-433-4200
Fax: 401-433-1183

WWRX-FM 103.7 MHz (CR)
75 Oxford St
Providence, RI 02905
www.wrx.com
Phone: 401-781-9979
Fax: 401-781-9329

WZRA-FM 99.7 MHz (CR)
1502 Wampanoag Trail
East Providence, RI 02915
Phone: 401-433-4200
Fax: 401-224-4295

WZRI-FM 100.3 MHz (CR)
1502 Wampanoag Trail
East Providence, RI 02915
www.z100providence.com
Phone: 401-433-4200
Fax: 401-224-4295

Attractions

Rhode Island's capital was founded by Roger Williams in 1635 as a haven for religious dissenters and free thinkers. Today, several attractions in Providence are situated along the Roger Williams Heritage Trail, including Colonial homes along Benefit Street (also called the "Mile of History"), prestigious Brown University, Rhode Island School of Design Museum of Art, the State Capitol (an important architectural landmark), and Roger Williams Park, which has its own planetarium, zoo, and natural history museum. Outdoor concerts are held at the Park's Benedict Temple to Music. Shopping along the Trail is available at The Arcade, the country's oldest indoor shopping center.

Aldrich House-Museum of Rhode Island History
110 Benevolent St
Providence, RI 02906
www.rihs.org
Phone: 401-331-8575
Fax: 401-351-0127

Arcade The
65 Weybosset St
Providence, RI 02903
Phone: 401-598-1199

Artillery Co of Newport Military Museum
23 Clarke St
Newport, RI 02840
www.newportartillery.org/museum.html
Phone: 401-846-8488
Fax: 401-846-3311

AS220 Center for Arts
115 Empire St
Providence, RI 02903
www.as220.org
Phone: 401-831-9327
Fax: 401-454-7445

Astors' Beechwood Mansion
580 Bellevue Ave
Newport, RI 02840
www.astors-beechwood.com
Phone: 401-846-3772
Fax: 401-849-6998

Banner Trail Trolley Tour
10 Nate Whipple Hwy
Cumberland, RI 02864
Phone: 401-658-3400
Fax: 401-658-3411
TF: 800-888-4661

Bannister's Wharf
1 Bannister's Wharf
Newport, RI 02840
www.bannisterswharf.com
Phone: 401-846-4500
Fax: 401-849-8750

Bayard Ewing Building
231 S Main St
Providence, RI 02903
Phone: 401-454-6280
Fax: 401-454-6299

Belcourt Castle
657 Bellevue Ave
Newport, RI 02840
Phone: 401-846-0669
Fax: 401-846-5345

Bell David Winton Gallery
64 College St
Providence, RI 02912
Phone: 401-863-2932
Fax: 401-863-9323

Breakers Stable & Carriage House
Bateman & Coggeshall Ave
Newport, RI 02840
www.newportmansions.org/html/bsch.html
Phone: 401-847-1000
Fax: 401-847-1361

Breakers The
Ochre Point Ave
Newport, RI 02840
www.newportmansions.org/html/breakers.html
Phone: 401-847-1000
Fax: 401-847-1361

Brenton Point State Park
Ocean Dr
Newport, RI 02840
Phone: 401-847-2400
Fax: 401-841-9821

Brown AnnMary Memorial
21 Brown St
Providence, RI 02912
Phone: 401-863-1994

Brown John House
52 Power St
Providence, RI 02906
www.rihs.org
Phone: 401-331-8575
Fax: 401-751-2307

Cathedral of Saint John
271 N Main St
Providence, RI 02903
Phone: 401-331-4622
Fax: 401-831-8425

Cathedral of Saints Peter & Paul
30 Fenner St Cathedral Sq
Providence, RI 02903
Phone: 401-331-2434
Fax: 401-331-2435

Chateau-Sur-Mer
Bellevue Ave
Newport, RI 02840
www.newportmansions.org/html/csm.html
Phone: 401-847-1000
Fax: 401-847-1361

Continental Sloop Providence War Ship
India Point Pk
Providence, RI 02903
E-mail: info@sloopprovidence.org
www.sloopprovidence.org
Phone: 401-274-7447
Fax: 401-751-0121

Culinary Archives & Museum at Johnson & Wales University
315 Harborside Blvd
Providence, RI 02905
Phone: 401-598-2805
Fax: 401-598-2807

Edward King House
35 King St
Newport, RI 02840
Phone: 401-846-7426
Fax: 401-846-5308

Elms The
Bellevue Ave
Newport, RI 02840
www.newportmansions.org/html/elms.html
Phone: 401-847-1000
Fax: 401-847-1361

Festival Ballet
5 Hennessey Ave
North Providence, RI 02911
Phone: 401-353-1129
Fax: 401-353-8853

First Baptist Church in America
75 N Main St
Providence, RI 02903
Phone: 401-454-3418
Fax: 401-421-4095

Fort Adams State Park
Harrison Ave
Newport, RI 02840
www.moonbase.com/davemann/ftadams
Phone: 401-847-2400
Fax: 401-841-9821

Governor Henry Lippitt House Museum
199 Hope St
Providence, RI 02906
Phone: 401-453-0688
Fax: 401-453-8221

Governor Stephen Hopkins House
15 Hopkins St
Providence, RI 02903
Phone: 401-421-0694

Green Animals
Cory's Ln
Portsmouth, RI 02871
www.newportmansions.org/html/animals.html
Phone: 401-847-1000
Fax: 401-847-1361

Groundwerx Dance Theater
95 Empire St
Providence, RI 02903
E-mail: groundwerx@as220.org
www.as220.org/groundwerx
Phone: 401-454-4564
Fax: 401-454-4564

Haffenreffer Museum of Anthropology
300 Tower St
Bristol, RI 02809
www.brown.edu/Facilities/Haffenreffer
Phone: 401-253-8388
Fax: 401-253-1198

Hay John Library
20 Prospect St Brown University
Providence, RI 02912
Phone: 401-863-2146

Hunter House
54 Washington St
Newport, RI 02840
www.newportmansions.org/html/hunter.html
Phone: 401-847-1000
Fax: 401-847-1361

International Tennis Hall of Fame & Museum
194 Bellevue Ave
Newport, RI 02840
E-mail: ithf@aol.com
www.tennisfame.org
Phone: 401-849-3990
Fax: 401-849-8780
TF: 800-457-1144

King Roger Gallery of Fine Art
21 Bowen's Wharf
Newport, RI 02840
E-mail: rking@rkingfinearts.com
www.rkingfinearts.com
Phone: 401-847-4359
Fax: 401-846-4096

Kingscote
424 Bellevue Ave
Newport, RI 02840
www.newportmansions.org/html/kingscote.html
Phone: 401-847-1000
Fax: 401-847-1361

La Gondola River Tours
1 Citizens Plaza
Providence, RI 02903
Phone: 401-421-8877

Marble House
Bellevue Ave
Newport, RI 02840
www.newportmansions.org/html/marble.html
Phone: 401-847-1000
Fax: 401-847-1361

Museum of Newport History at the Brick Market
127 Thames St
Newport, RI 02840
www.newporthistorical.com
Phone: 401-841-8770
Fax: 401-846-1853

Museum of Yachting
Fort Adams State Pk
Newport, RI 02840
www.moy.org
Phone: 401-847-1018
Fax: 401-847-8320

Nature's Best Dairy
2032 Plainfield Pike
Cranston, RI 02921
Phone: 401-946-1122
Fax: 401-946-9960

Naval War College Museum
Coasters Harbor Island
Newport, RI 02841
www.visitnewport.com/buspages/navy
Phone: 401-841-4052
Fax: 401-841-7689

Newport Art Museum
76 Bellevue Ave
Newport, RI 02840
Phone: 401-848-8200
Fax: 401-848-8205

Newport Casino
194 Bellevue Ave
Newport, RI 02840
Phone: 401-849-3990
Fax: 401-849-8780

Newport Historical Society
575 Thames St
Newport, RI 02840
Phone: 401-846-0813
Fax: 401-846-1853

Norman Bird Sanctuary
583 Third Beach Rd
Middletown, RI 02842
E-mail: info@normanbirdsanctuary.org
www.normanbirdsanctuary.org
Phone: 401-846-2577
Fax: 401-846-2772

Old State House
150 Benefit St
Providence, RI 02903
Phone: 401-222-2678

Pendleton House
224 Benefit St
Providence, RI 02903
Phone: 401-454-6500
Fax: 401-454-6556

Perishable Theatre
95 Empire St
Providence, RI 02903
www.as220.org/perishable/
Phone: 401-331-2695
Fax: 401-331-7811

Prescott Farm
2009 W Main Rd
Middletown, RI 02842
Phone: 401-847-6230

Providence Athenaeum
251 Benefit St
Providence, RI 02903
www.providenceathenaeum.org/
Phone: 401-421-6970
Fax: 401-421-2860

Providence Children's Museum
100 South St
Providence, RI 02903
E-mail: provcm@childrenmuseum.org
www.childrenmuseum.org
Phone: 401-273-5437
Fax: 401-273-1004

Providence Jewelry Museum
1 Spectacle St
Providence, RI 02910
Phone: 401-781-3100
Fax: 401-781-2890

Providence Performing Arts Center
220 Weybosset St
Providence, RI 02903
www.ppacri.org/
Phone: 401-421-2787
Fax: 401-421-5767

Providence Preservation Society
21 Meeting St Shakespeare's Head
Providence, RI 02903
Phone: 401-831-7440
Fax: 401-831-8583

Redwood Library & Athenaeum
50 Bellevue Ave
Newport, RI 02840
www.redwood1747.org
Phone: 401-847-0292
Fax: 401-841-5680

Rhode Island Black Heritage Society
229 Westminster St
Providence, RI 02903
Phone: 401-751-3490
Fax: 401-751-0040

Rhode Island Historical Society
110 Benevolent St
Providence, RI 02906
www.rihs.org
Phone: 401-331-8575
Fax: 401-751-7930

Rhode Island Philharmonic Orchestra
222 Richmond St Suite 112
Providence, RI 02903
www.ri-philharmonic.org
Phone: 401-831-3123
Fax: 401-831-4577

Rhode Island School of Design Museum of Art
224 Benefit St
Providence, RI 02903
Phone: 401-454-6501
Fax: 401-454-6556

Rhode Island School of Design Woods-Gerry Gallery
62 Prospect St
Providence, RI 02903
Phone: 401-454-6141
Fax: 401-454-6608

Rhode Island State Archives
337 Westminster St
Providence, RI 02903
Phone: 401-222-2353
Fax: 401-222-3199

Rhode Island State Capitol
82 Smith St
Providence, RI 02903
E-mail: comments@sec.state.ri.us
www.state.ri.us
Phone: 401-222-2357
Fax: 401-222-1356

Roger Williams National Memorial
282 N Main St
Providence, RI 02903
www.nps.gov/rowi/
Phone: 401-521-7266
Fax: 401-521-7239

Roger Williams Park Museum of Natural History
Roger Williams Pk
Providence, RI 02905
www.osfn.org/museum
Phone: 401-785-9450
Fax: 401-461-5146

Roger Williams Park Zoo
1000 Elmwood Ave
Providence, RI 02907
users.ids.net/~rwpz
Phone: 401-785-3510
Fax: 401-941-3988

Rose Island Lighthouse
365 Thames St
Newport, RI 02840
www.roseislandlighthouse.org
Phone: 401-847-4242
Fax: 401-847-7262

Rosecliff
Bellevue Ave
Newport, RI 02840
www.newportmansions.org/html/rosecliff.html
Phone: 401-847-1000
Fax: 401-847-1361

Saint Mary's Church
12 William St
Newport, RI 02840
Phone: 401-847-0475

Sakonnet Vineyards
162 W Main Rd
Little Compton, RI 02837
E-mail: sakonnetri@aol.com
www.sakonnetwine.com
Phone: 401-635-8486
Fax: 401-635-2101
TF: 800-919-4637

Sandra Feinstein-Gamm Theatre
31 Elbow St
Providence, RI 02903
www.sfgt.org
Phone: 401-831-2919
Fax: 401-831-8635

Thames Science Center
77 Long Wharf
Newport, RI 02840
www.thamesscience.org
Phone: 401-849-6966
Fax: 401-849-7144
TF: 800-587-2872

Touro Synagogue National Historic Site
85 Touro St
Newport, RI 02840
www.tourosynagogue.org
Phone: 401-847-4794
Fax: 401-847-8121

Trinity Repertory Co
201 Washington St
Providence, RI 02903
www.trinityrep.com/
Phone: 401-351-4242
Fax: 401-751-5577

Wanton-Lyman-Hazard House
17 Broadway
Newport, RI 02840
www.newporthistorical.org/the1.htm
Phone: 401-846-0813
Fax: 401-846-1853

Warwick Museum of Art
3259 Post Rd
Warwick, RI 02886
Phone: 401-737-0010

Waterplace Park
American Express Way & Memorial Blvd
Providence, RI 02903
Phone: 401-274-1636

Wayland Square
Medway & Waterman St
Providence, RI 02903
Phone: 401-751-1177

White Horse Tavern
26 Marlborough St
Newport, RI 02840
Phone: 401-849-3600
Fax: 401-849-7317

Whitehorne Samuel House
416 Thames St
Newport, RI 02840
Phone: 401-849-7300
Fax: 401-849-0125

Williams Betsey Cottage
Roger Williams Pk
Providence, RI 02905
Phone: 401-785-9451
Fax: 401-461-5146

Sports Teams & Facilities

Newport Grand Jai Alai
150 Admiral Kalbfus Rd
Newport, RI 02840
newportgrand.com
Phone: 401-849-5000
Fax: 401-846-0290

Pawtucket Red Sox (baseball)
1 Columbus Ave McCoy Stadium
Pawtucket, RI 02860
E-mail: pawsox@worldnet.att.net
www.pawsox.com
Phone: 401-724-7300
Fax: 401-723-7620

Providence Bruins (hockey)
1 LaSalle Sq Providence Civic Ctr
Providence, RI 02903
www.canoe.ca/AHLProvidence/
Phone: 401-273-5000
Fax: 401-273-5004

Rhode Island Rays
44 Border Dr
Wakefield, RI 02879
Phone: 401-789-7477
Fax: 401-782-1652

Rhode Island Stingrays (soccer)
201 Mercer St Pierce Memorial Stadium
East Providence, RI 02914
E-mail: info@stingraysoccer.com
www.stingraysoccer.com
Phone: 401-351-8455
Fax: 401-438-9702

Annual Events

Ben & Jerry's Newport Folk Festival (early August) ... 401-847-3700
Black Ships Festival (mid-July) ... 401-846-2720
Bowen's Wharf Waterfront Seafood Festival (mid-October) ... 401-849-2243
Christmas in Newport (December) ... 401-849-6454
Christmas Tree Lighting (early December) ... 401-849-2243
Classic Yacht Regatta (early September) ... 401-847-1018
Craft Fair (late November) ... 401-847-3213
Festival of Historic Houses (mid-June) ... 401-831-7440
Fiesta Italiana (early October) ... 401-849-8048
First Night Providence (December 31) ... 401-521-1166
Great Chowder Cook-off (early-mid-June) ... 401-846-1600
Harvest Fair (early October) ... 401-846-2577
Heritage Day Festival (mid-September) ... 401-222-2669
Holiday Tours in Historic Providence (mid-December) ... 401-831-8587
July 3rd Clambake (July 3) ... 401-847-1441
Latin Christmas Carol Celebration (early December) ... 401-863-2123
Newport Flower Show (mid-July) ... 401-847-1000
Newport International Boat Show (mid-September) ... 401-846-1115
Newport International Polo Series (early June-mid-September) ... 401-847-7090
Newport Irish Heritage Month (March) ... 401-845-9123
Newport Jazz Festival (early August) ... 401-847-3700
Newport Music Festival (early July) ... 401-846-1133
Newport Winter Festival (mid-late February) ... 401-847-7666
Octoberfest (early October) ... 401-846-1600
Providence Auto Show (mid-January) ... 401-274-1636
Providence Boat Show (late January) ... 401-458-6000
Providence Walking Tours (early July-late September) ... 401-831-7440
Rhode Island Spring Flower & Garden Show (mid-February) ... 401-458-6000
Secret Garden Tour (mid-June) ... 401-847-0514
Small Boat Regatta (mid-July) ... 401-847-1018
Taste of Newport (early November) ... 401-849-2300
Taste of Rhode Island (late September) ... 401-846-1600
Victorian Christmas Feast (mid-December) ... 401-846-3772
Water Fire Providence (mid-May-late December) ... 401-331-3624
We Rose for Rose Regatta (mid-September) ... 401-847-4242

Provo, Utah

***County:* Utah**

PROVO is located in the Utah Valley at the foot of the Wasatch Mountains in north central Utah. Major cities within 100 miles include Salt Lake City and Ogden, Utah.

Area (Land) .... 38.6 sq mi
Area (Water)................................. 2.1 sq mi
Elevation.....................................4,549 ft
Latitude ....40-24-88 N
Longitude............................... 111-64-79 W
Time Zone .... MST
Area Code... 801

Climate

Provo has a moderate climate, with hot summers and cold winters. Summer daytime highs can reach into the 90s, while lows cool down into the 50s and 60s. Winter high temperatures average near 40 degrees, with lows often dipping into the low 20s. Although more than five feet of snow falls in the neighboring Wasatch Mountains, the Utah Valley averages less than two feet of snow annually. Precipitation is distributed fairly evenly throughout the year.

Average Temperatures & Precipitation

Temperatures

	Jan	Feb	Mar	Apr	May	Jun	Jul	Aug	Sep	Oct	Nov	Dec
High	36	44	52	61	72	83	92	89	79	66	51	38
Low	19	25	31	38	46	55	64	62	51	40	31	22

Precipitation

	Jan	Feb	Mar	Apr	May	Jun	Jul	Aug	Sep	Oct	Nov	Dec
Inches	1.1	1.2	1.9	2.1	1.8	0.9	0.8	0.9	1.3	1.4	1.3	1.4

History

Originally inhabited by the Timpanogos Utes (Ute Indians), the Utah Valley was first explored in 1776 by Spanish missionaries. In the years that followed, others traveled through the area, including French-Canadian fur trapper Etienne Proveau, after whom the city of Provo was named. The Utah Valley was not settled until March of 1849, when members of the Church of Jesus Christ of Latter Day Saints (also known as the Mormons) arrived in the area. Fort Utah was the first settlement established along the Provo River. A few miles away, Provo was established by church president Brigham Young and incorporated as a city later that year.

In 1875, the Mormon leader established Brigham Young Academy in Provo as an educational institution where religion was intermingled with secular education. Today, Brigham Young University (renamed in 1903) is one of the most highly regarded universities in the country. It is also the Utah Valley's single largest employer, providing jobs for more than 16,000 area residents.

Although Provo was originally established as an agricultural community, the city and surrounding area today is among the nation's leading high-technology centers. Provo's excellent quality of life, including low employment rates, a business-friendly economic climate, and well-regarded educational system, has helped the city to become Utah's fastest growing city, as well as the 15th fastest-growing city in the United States.

With a population exceeding 110,000, Provo is currently Utah's second largest city. In recent years, Provo has consistently been named as one of the country's most livable places, ranking in the top twenty of Money Magazine's "Best Places to Live in America" for the past five years.

Population

1990 Census 86,835
1998 Estimate...............................110,419
% Change 27.2
2005 Projection 392,725*

Racial/Ethnic Breakdown
White......................................94.1%
Black.......................................0.2%
Other.......................................5.7%
Hispanic Origin (may be of any race).........4.2%

Age Breakdown
Under 5 years...............................9.3%
5 to 17....................................16.3%
18 to 20...................................15.8%
21 to 24...................................20.8%
25 to 34...................................17.1%
35 to 44....................................6.2%
45 to 54....................................4.3%
55 to 64....................................3.8%
65 to 74....................................3.6%
75+ years 2.9%
Median Age.................................22.7

Gender Breakdown
Male.......................................48.5%
Female.....................................51.5%

** Information given is for Utah County.*

Government

Type of Government: Mayor-Council

Provo City Attorney
PO Box 1849
Provo, UT 84603
Phone: 801-852-6140
Fax: 801-852-6150

Provo City Council
PO Box 1849
Provo, UT 84603
Phone: 801-852-6120
Fax: 801-852-6121

Provo City Hall
351 W Center St
Provo, UT 84601
Phone: 801-852-6000

Provo City Library
425 W Center St
Provo, UT 84601
Phone: 801-852-6650
Fax: 801-852-6670

Provo City Recorder
PO Box 1849
Provo, UT 84603
Phone: 801-852-6524
Fax: 801-852-6530

Provo City Treasurer
PO Box 1849
Provo, UT 84603
Phone: 801-852-6521
Fax: 801-852-6530

Provo Community Development Dept
351 W Center St
Provo, UT 84603
Phone: 801-852-6400
Fax: 801-852-6417

Provo Economic Development Dept
PO Box 1849
Provo, UT 84603
Phone: 801-852-6161
Fax: 801-375-1469

Provo Finance Dept
PO Box 1849
Provo, UT 84603
Phone: 801-852-6506
Fax: 801-852-6513

Provo Fire Dept
PO Box 1849
Provo, UT 84603
Phone: 801-852-6300
Fax: 801-852-6309

Provo Human Resources Dept
351 W Center St
Provo, UT 84601
Phone: 801-852-6180
Fax: 801-852-6190

Provo Mayor
351 W Center St
Provo, UT 84601
Phone: 801-852-6100
Fax: 801-852-6107

Provo Parks & Recreation Dept
PO Box 1849
Provo, UT 84603
Phone: 801-852-6601
Fax: 801-852-6648

Provo Police Dept
PO Box 1849
Provo, UT 84603
Phone: 801-852-6200
Fax: 801-377-7315

Provo Public Works Dept
PO Box 1849
Provo, UT 84603
Phone: 801-852-6770
Fax: 801-852-6778

Important Phone Numbers

AAA.......801-225-4801
Driver's License Information.......801-227-8090
Emergency.......911
Medical Referral.......800-515-2220
Poison Control Center.......800-456-7707
Road Conditions.......801-964-6000
Time/Temp.......801-373-9120
Utah County Assessor.......801-370-8286
Utah County Board of Realtors.......801-226-3777
Utah State Tax Commission.......800-662-4335
Vehicle Registration Information.......800-368-8824
Voter Registration Information.......801-370-8128
Weather.......801-975-4499

Information Sources

Better Business Bureau Serving Utah
5673 S Redwood Rd
Salt Lake City, UT 84123
www.saltlakecity.bbb.org
Phone: 801-892-6009
Fax: 801-892-6002

Mountainland Travel Region Office
586 E 800 North
Orem, UT 84097
www.mountainland.org
Phone: 801-229-3800
Fax: 801-229-3801

Provo/Orem Chamber of Commerce
51 S University Ave Suite 215
Provo, UT 84601
www.thechamber.org
Phone: 801-379-2555
Fax: 801-379-2557

Utah County
125 N 100 West
Provo, UT 84601
www.co.utah.ut.us
Phone: 801-429-1000
Fax: 801-429-1033

Utah County Convention & Visitors Bureau
51 S University Ave Suite 111
Provo, UT 84601
www.utahvalley.org/cvb
Phone: 801-370-8393
Fax: 801-370-8050
TF: 800-222-8824

Utah Valley Economic Development Assn
100 E Center St Suite 3200
Provo, UT 84606
www.utahvalley.org/uveda
Phone: 801-370-8100
Fax: 801-370-8105

Online Resources

Anthill City Guide Provo/Orem
www.anthill.com/city.asp?city=provoorem

City Knowledge Provo
www.cityknowledge.com/ut_provo.htm

Excite.com Provo City Guide
www.excite.com/travel/countries/united_states/utah/provo

Area Communities

Communities in the Utah Valley with populations greater than 10,000 include:

American Fork
31 N Church St
American Fork, UT 84003
Phone: 801-763-3004
Fax: 801-763-3004

Lehi
153 N 100 East
Lehi, UT 84043
Phone: 801-768-7100
Fax: 801-768-7101

Orem
56 N State St
Orem, UT 84057
Phone: 801-229-7000
Fax: 801-229-7031

Payson
439 W Utah Ave
Payson, UT 84651
Phone: 801-465-5200
Fax: 801-465-5208

Pleasant Grove
70 S 100 East
Pleasant Grove, UT 84062
Phone: 801-785-5045
Fax: 801-785-8925

Spanish Fork
30 S 100 West
Spanish Fork, UT 84660
Phone: 801-798-5000
Fax: 801-798-5005

Springville
50 S Main St
Springville, UT 84663
Phone: 801-489-2700
Fax: 801-489-2709

Economy

The Utah Valley currently has one of the fastest-growing economies in the United States. Provo was ranked 4th in the U.S. for forecasted job growth in Money Magazine's 2000 "Best Places to Live" list. The area has become one of the country's top high-technology centers, with the nation's third-largest concentration of software firms. More than 400 high-tech companies, which employ over 10% of the area's total workforce, have a presence in the Provo area. Although high-technology plays a major role in Provo's economic growth, services and trade are currently the two leading employment sectors in Utah County. Education is a vital part of the Utah Valley economy-five of the top fifteen employers are education-related, including the area's largest employer, Brigham Young University.

Unemployment Rate 3.1%*
Per Capita Income.......................... $17,500*
Median Family Income...................... $15,465

** Information given is for Utah County.*

Principal Industries & Number of Wage Earners

Utah County - 1999

Construction..10,748
Finance, Insurance, & Real Estate........................4,481
Government..19,491
Manufacturing..19,453
Mining.. 38
Services...56,074
Trade..32,985
Transportation, Communications, & Utilities...............2,335

Major Employers

Alpine School District
575 N 100 East
American Fork, UT 84003
www.alpine.k12.ut.us
Phone: 801-756-8400
Fax: 801-756-8490

Convergys Corp
1409 N Research Way Bldg J
Orem, UT 84097
www.convergys.com
Phone: 801-765-7171
Fax: 801-765-7059

Geneva Steel
PO Box 2500
Provo, UT 84603
E-mail: comments@geneva.com
www.geneva.com
Phone: 801-227-9000
Fax: 801-227-9454
TF: 800-877-9990

IHC Health Care Services
1034 N 500 West
Provo, UT 84605
www.ihc.com
Phone: 801-373-7850
Fax: 801-357-7146

Marketing Ally Teleservices
501 N 900 E
Provo, UT 84606
E-mail: sales@marketingally.com
www.marketingally.com
Phone: 801-374-8709
Fax: 801-374-0779
TF: 800-400-4042

Modus Media International Holdings Inc
690 Canton St
Westwood, MA 02090
E-mail: marketing_mmi@modusmedia.com
www.modusmedia.com
Phone: 781-407-2000
Fax: 781-407-3836
TF: 888-996-6387

Nebo School District
350 S Main St
Spanish Fork, UT 84660
www.nebo.edu
Phone: 801-798-4000
Fax: 801-798-4010

Nestlé USA Food Group Inc
815 W Raymond Klauck Way
Springville, UT 84663
www.nestleusa.com
Phone: 801-489-8621
Fax: 801-489-1820

Novell Inc
1800 S Novell Pl
Provo, UT 84606
www.novell.com
Phone: 801-861-7000
Fax: 801-373-6798
TF: 800-453-1267

Nu Skin Enterprises Inc
75 W Center St
Provo, UT 84601
www.nuskin.com
Phone: 801-345-6100
Fax: 801-345-5999

Provo School District
280 W 940 N
Provo, UT 84604
www.provo.k12.ut.us
Phone: 801-374-4800
Fax: 801-374-4808

US Postal Service
95 W 100 South
Provo, UT 84601
new.usps.com
Phone: 800-275-8777
Fax: 801-375-6944

Utah County
125 N 100 West
Provo, UT 84601
www.co.utah.ut.us
Phone: 801-429-1000
Fax: 801-429-1033

Utah Valley State College
800 W University Pkwy
Orem, UT 84058
E-mail: info@www.uvsc.edu
www.uvsc.edu
Phone: 801-222-8000
Fax: 801-225-4677

Quality of Living Indicators

Total Crime Index....................................3,602
(rates per 100,000 inhabitants)

Violent Crime
Murder/manslaughter................................-
Forcible rape.................................... 45
Robbery.. 20
Aggravated assault............................... 75

Property Crime
Burglary 595
Larceny theft 2,666
Motor vehicle theft 201

Cost of Living Index 96.0
(national average = 100)

Median Home Price $98,300

Education

Public Schools

Provo School District
280 W 940 N
Provo, UT 84604
www.provo.k12.ut.us
Phone: 801-374-4800
Fax: 801-374-4808

Number of Schools
Elementary 13
Middle 3
High 4

Student/Teacher Ratio
All Grades 22.7:1

Private Schools

Number of Schools (all grades) .... 7+

Colleges & Universities

Brigham Young University
D-238 ASB
Provo, UT 84602
E-mail: admissions@byu.edu
www.byu.edu
Phone: 801-378-1211
Fax: 801-378-2320

Utah Valley State College
800 W University Pkwy
Orem, UT 84058
E-mail: info@www.uvsc.edu
www.uvsc.edu
Phone: 801-222-8000
Fax: 801-225-4677

Hospitals

Utah Valley Regional Medical Center
1034 N 500 West
Provo, UT 84604
Phone: 801-373-7850
Fax: 801-374-8220

Transportation

Airport(s)

Salt Lake City International Airport (SLC)
50 miles N of downtown Provo
(approx 80 minutes) 801-575-2400

Mass Transit

Utah Transit Authority
$1 Base fare 801-375-4636

Utilities

Electricity
Provo City Utilities 801-379-6820
www.provo.org/util/

Gas
Questar Gas Co 800-323-5517
www.questarcorp.com

Water
Provo City Utilities 801-379-6820
www.provo.org/util/

Garbage Collection/Recycling
Provo City Utilities 801-379-6820
www.provo.org/util/

Telecommunications

Telephone
Qwest 801-237-5511
www.qwest.com

Cable Television
AT & T Cable Services 801-377-8600
www.cable.att.com
Provo Cable 801-377-1360

Internet Service Providers (ISPs)
Fibernet Corp 801-223-9939
www.fiber.net
Internet Servers Inc 801-224-9346
www.iserver.com

Banks

Bonneville Bank
1675 N 200 West
Provo, UT 84604
Phone: 801-374-9500
Fax: 801-377-1036

Central Bank
75 N University Ave
Provo, UT 84603
Phone: 801-375-1000
Fax: 801-377-7637

Far West Bank
201 E Center St
Provo, UT 84606
Phone: 801-342-6000
Fax: 801-377-3351

Wells Fargo Bank
66 E 1650 North
Provo, UT 84604
Phone: 801-375-1929
Fax: 801-377-6578

Zions First National Bank
1060 N University Ave
Provo, UT 84604
Phone: 801-375-9995
Fax: 801-370-4124

Shopping

Provo Town Square
51 S University Ave
Provo, UT 84601
Phone: 801-379-2555

University Mall
1229 S State St
Orem, UT 84058
Phone: 801-224-0694

Media

Newspapers and Magazines

Daily Herald*
PO Box 717
Provo, UT 84603
www.daily-herald.com
Phone: 801-373-5050
Fax: 801-373-5489
TF: 800-880-8075

**Indicates major daily newspapers*

Television

KBYU-TV Ch 11 (PBS)
2000 Ironton Blvd Brigham Young University
Provo, UT 84606
E-mail: kbyu@byu.edu
www.kbyu.org/tv
Phone: 801-378-8450
Fax: 801-378-8478

KSL-TV Ch 5 (NBC)
PO Box 1160
Salt Lake City, UT 84110
E-mail: eyewitness@ksl.com
www.ksl.com/TV/
Phone: 801-575-5555
Fax: 801-575-5560

KSTU-TV Ch 13 (Fox)
5020 W Amelia Earhart Dr
Salt Lake City, UT 84116
www.fox13.com
Phone: 801-532-1300
Fax: 801-537-5335

KTVX-TV Ch 4 (ABC)
1760 Fremont Dr
Salt Lake City, UT 84104
E-mail: news@4utah.com
www.4utah.com
Phone: 801-975-4444
Fax: 801-975-4442

KUTV-TV Ch 2 (CBS)
2185 S 3600 West
West Valley City, UT 84119
www.kutv.com
Phone: 801-973-3000
Fax: 801-973-3349

Radio

KALL-AM 910 kHz (N/T)
2801 S Decker Lake Dr
West Valley City, UT 84119
www.kall910.com
Phone: 801-575-5255
Fax: 801-908-1499

KBEE-FM 98.7 MHz (AC)
434 Bearcat Dr
Salt Lake City, UT 84115
E-mail: pdirector@b987.com
www.b987.com
Phone: 801-485-6700
Fax: 801-487-5369

KBER-FM 101.1 MHz (Rock)
434 Bearcat Dr
Salt Lake City, UT 84115
www.kber.com
Phone: 801-485-6700
Fax: 801-487-5369

KEYY-AM 1450 kHz (Rel)
307 S 1600 West
Provo, UT 84601
E-mail: mail@keyy.com
www.keyy.com
Phone: 801-374-5210
Fax: 801-374-2910

KISN-FM 97.1 MHz (AC)
4001 S 700 East Suite 800
Salt Lake City, UT 84101
Phone: 801-303-4100
Fax: 801-303-4112

KNRS-AM 570 kHz (Nost)
2801 S Decker Lake Dr
Salt Lake City, UT 84119
Phone: 801-908-1300
Fax: 801-908-1459

KOSY-FM 106.5 (Nost)
280 S 400 West Suite 200
Salt Lake City, UT 84101
Phone: 801-303-4100
Fax: 801-303-4112

KRAR-FM 106.9 MHz (Rock)
4455 S 5500 West
Hooper, UT 84315
Phone: 801-731-9000
Fax: 801-731-9666

KUBL-FM 93.3 MHz (Ctry)
434 Bearcat Dr
Salt Lake City, UT 84115
E-mail: bull@xmission.com
Phone: 801-485-6700
Fax: 801-487-5369

KZHT-FM 94.9 MHz (CHR)
2801 S Decker Lake Dr
Salt Lake City, UT 84119
www.949zht.com
Phone: 801-908-1300
Fax: 801-908-1449

Attractions

Scenic drives provide the best opportunity to view the attractions of Provo and the Utah County area. The Provo Canyon Byway winds through Provo Canyon all the way to Heber Valley. At the west end of Provo Canyon, Squaw Peak Trail offers views of the Utah Valley and a high-altitude mountain bike trek across the front of the Wasatch Mountains. Accessible also from the Byway are the Bridal Veil Falls and Skytram. The steepest passenger tram in the world, the Skytram provides aerial views of the double cataract falls, which drop 607 feet. At the top of Provo Canyon is Deer Creek Reservoir, a popular site for fishing, boating, and waterskiing. The Provo Canyon Byway continues past another scenic drive known as the Alpine Look Scenic Backway. The Backway is 24 miles long and accesses Timpanogos Cave National Monument, Mount Timpanogos hiking trails, and Robert Redford's Sundance Resort.

Brigham Young University Earth Science Museum
1683 N Canyon Rd
Provo, UT 84602
cpms.byu.edu/ESM
Phone: 801-378-3680
Fax: 801-378-7911

Brigham Young University Museum of Arts
North Campus Dr
Provo, UT 84602
www.byu.edu/moa
Phone: 801-378-8200
Fax: 801-378-8222

Brigham Young University Museum of Peoples & Cultures
700 N 100 East
Provo, UT 84602
Phone: 801-378-6112
Fax: 801-378-7123

Crandall Historical Printing Museum
275 E Center St
Provo, UT 84606
Phone: 801-377-7777
Fax: 801-374-3333

Fort Utah
200 N Geneva Rd
Provo, UT 84601
Phone: 801-379-6600

Hale Family Theater
225 W 400 North
Orem, UT 84057
E-mail: hcto@inet-1.com
www.haletheater.com
Phone: 801-226-8600
Fax: 801-852-3189

Heber Valley Historic Railroad
450 S 600 West
Heber City, UT 84032
E-mail: hebervalleyrr@shadowlink.net
www.hebervalleyrr.org
Phone: 435-654-5601
Fax: 435-654-3709

Historic County Court House
51 S University Ave
Provo, UT 84606
Phone: 801-370-8393

McCurdy Historical Doll Museum
246 N 100 East
Provo, UT 84606
Phone: 801-377-9935

Monte L Bean Life Science Museum
290 Monte L Bean Museum Bldg
Provo, UT 84602
Phone: 801-378-5051
Fax: 801-378-3733

Northpark Museum
500 W 600 North
Provo, UT 84601
Phone: 801-377-7078

Provo Canyon
N Hwy 189
Provo, UT 84606
Phone: 801-370-8393

Provo Historic Buildings (Tour)
Provo, UT 84606
Phone: 801-370-8393

Provo Theatre Co
105 E 100 North
Provo, UT 84606
Phone: 801-379-0600

Seven Peaks Water Park
1330 E 300 North
Provo, UT 84606
www.sevenpeaks.com
Phone: 801-373-8777
Fax: 801-373-8791

Springville Museum of Art
126 E 400 South
Springville, UT 84663
E-mail: sma@nebo.edu
www.shs.nebo.edu/museum/museum.html
Phone: 801-489-2727
Fax: 801-489-2739

Sundance Ski Resort
North Fork Provo Canyon
Provo, UT 84604
www.sundance.net
Phone: 801-225-4107
TF: 800-892-1600

Timpanogos Cave National Monument
RR 3 Box 200
American Fork, UT 84003
www.nps.gov/tica/
Phone: 801-756-5239
Fax: 801-756-5661

Trafalga Family Fun Center
168 S 1200 West
Orem, UT 84058
Phone: 801-224-6000

Uinta National Forest
88 W 100 North
Provo, UT 84601
Phone: 801-342-5200
Fax: 801-342-5144

Utah Lake State Park
4400 W Center
Provo, UT 84601
Phone: 801-375-0731
Fax: 801-373-4215

Utah Valley Symphony
50 S University Ave Provo LDS Tabernacle
Provo, UT 84601
Phone: 801-377-6995

Valley Center Playhouse
780 N 200 East
Lindon, UT 84042
Phone: 801-785-1186

Annual Events

Alpine Days (mid-August) 801-756-6347
America's Freedom Festival
(mid-June-early July) 801-370-8019
Highland Fling (early August). .801-370-8393
Lehi Roundup (late June) 801-370-8393
Park City Art Festival (early August). 435-649-8882
Pioneer Day Celebrations (mid-July). 800-541-4955
Santaquin Cherry Days (late July-early August) 801-370-8393
Spanish Fork Fiesta Days (late July) 801-370-8393
Springville Art City Days (mid-June) 801-370-8393
Sundance Institute Film Festival (late January). 801-328-3456
Swiss Days (late August). 435-654-3666
Torchlight Parade (late December) 435-649-8111
World Dance & Music Folkfest (early July). 801-489-2726

Raleigh, North Carolina

***County:* Wake**

RALEIGH is located in central North Carolina, 150 miles west of the Atlantic Ocean and 190 miles east of the Great Smoky Mountains. Major cities within 100 miles include Durham, Chapel Hill, Greensboro, and Winston-Salem, North Carolina.

Area (Land) .... 88.1 sq mi
Area (Water)............................... 0.7 sq mi
Elevation.................................... 363 ft
Latitude ....35-77-38 N
Longitude............................... 78-63-31 W
Time Zone ....EST
Area Code...................................... 919

Climate

Raleigh's climate has four distinct seasons. Winters are generally mild, as the mountains to the west of the city help to block much of the cold air brought in by fronts. Winter high temperatures average around 50 degrees, with lows near 30. Annual snowfall totals average just over seven inches. Summer days are warm and humid with high temperatures in the mid- to upper 80s, while evenings cool down into the upper 60s. July and August are the wettest months in Raleigh; April is the driest.

Average Temperatures & Precipitation

Temperatures

	Jan	Feb	Mar	Apr	May	Jun	Jul	Aug	Sep	Oct	Nov	Dec
High	49	53	62	72	79	85	88	87	81	72	63	53
Low	29	31	39	46	55	64	68	68	61	48	40	32

Precipitation

	Jan	Feb	Mar	Apr	May	Jun	Jul	Aug	Sep	Oct	Nov	Dec
Inches	3.5	3.7	3.8	2.6	3.9	3.7	4.0	4.0	3.2	2.9	3.0	3.2

History

Originally inhabited by the Tuscarora people, the site of present-day Raleigh was chosen in 1788 as the site for the new capital on a whim of the North Carolina General Assembly that the seat of government should be located within ten miles of Isaac Hunter's tavern. The city was established in 1792 and named for explorer Sir Walter Raleigh. The original State Capitol was completed in 1794, but was destroyed by fire in 1831. A new State Capitol was completed in 1840, and the building is one of Raleigh's most popular historical attractions today. During the Civil War, in April 1865, Raleigh was captured by General Sherman and occupied by Union troops.

During Raleigh's early years, the city grew as a center for government, and the area's thriving tobacco industry also helped to fuel the economy. Research Triangle Park, the nation's largest planned research park (6,000+-acres) and one of the nation's leading centers for scientific research and development, has had a major impact on the area's economy since its formation in 1961. The Park consolidates the scientific resources of the University of North Carolina in Chapel Hill, Duke University in Durham, and North Carolina State University in Raleigh. It is also home to the U.S. Environmental Protection Agency, and more than 50 high technology companies and R & D firms, including IBM, Glaxo-Wellcome, and Northern Telecom, have their corporate headquarters or divisions in the Triangle. The economic opportunities created by the development of Research Triangle Park led to a population explosion in the area, and the Greater Raleigh area today is home to more than three-quarters of a million people, 259,000 of whom live in the city of Raleigh.

Population

1990 Census 212,092
1998 Estimate.............................259,423
% Change 18.5
2005 Projection 1,181,000*

Racial/Ethnic Breakdown

White....................................67.8%
Black 27.0%
Other.....................................5.2%
Hispanic Origin (may be of any race) 1.4%

Age Breakdown

Under 5 years.............................6.2%
5 to 17..................................13.4%
18 to 20..................................7.3%
21 to 24.................................10.3%
25 to 34.................................22.5%
35 to 44.................................15.8%
45 to 54..................................9.0%
55 to 64..................................6.6%
65 to 74..................................5.2%
75+ years 3.6%
Median Age...............................30.3

Gender Breakdown

Male.....................................47.5%
Female...................................52.5%

* *Information given is for the Raleigh-Durham-Chapel Hill Metropolitan Statistical Area (MSA), which includes the City of Chapel Hill, the City of Durham, the City of Raleigh, as well as Durham, Franklin, Ornage, and Wake counties.*

Government

Type of Government: Council-Manager

Raleigh City Clerk
PO Box 590
Raleigh, NC 27602
Phone: 919-890-3040
Fax: 919-890-3164

Raleigh City Council
PO Box 590
Raleigh, NC 27602
Phone: 919-890-3050
Fax: 919-890-3058

Raleigh City Hall
222 W Hargett St
Raleigh, NC 27601
Phone: 919-890-3000
Fax: 919-890-3180

Raleigh City Manager
222 W Hargett St
Raleigh, NC 27601
Phone: 919-890-3070
Fax: 919-890-3080

Raleigh Community Development Dept
310 W Martin St
Raleigh, NC 27602
Phone: 919-857-4330
Fax: 919-857-4359

Raleigh Community Services Dept
310 W Martin St Suite 201
Raleigh, NC 27602
Phone: 919-831-6100
Fax: 919-831-6123

Raleigh Finance Dept
PO Box 590
Raleigh, NC 27602
Phone: 919-890-3215
Fax: 919-890-3052

Raleigh Fire Dept
PO Box 590
Raleigh, NC 27602
Phone: 919-831-6115
Fax: 919-831-6180

Raleigh Mayor
PO Box 590
Raleigh, NC 27602
Phone: 919-890-3050
Fax: 919-890-3058

Raleigh Parks & Recreation Dept
222 W Hargett St Rm 608
Raleigh, NC 27602
Phone: 919-890-3285
Fax: 919-890-3299

Raleigh Personnel Dept
222 W Hargett St Rm 101
Raleigh, NC 27601
Phone: 919-890-3315
Fax: 919-890-3845

Raleigh Planning Dept
222 W Hargett St 4th Fl
Raleigh, NC 27601
Phone: 919-890-3125
Fax: 919-890-3690

Raleigh Police Dept
PO Box 590
Raleigh, NC 27602
Phone: 919-890-3385
Fax: 919-890-3525

Raleigh Public Utilities Operations
3304 Lake Woodard Dr
Raleigh, NC 27604
Phone: 919-890-3400
Fax: 919-890-3600

Raleigh Transportation Dept
PO Box 590
Raleigh, NC 27602
Phone: 919-890-3430
Fax: 919-890-3451

Important Phone Numbers

AAA.........919-832-0543
Dental Referral.........800-917-6453
Driver's License Information.........919-733-4540
Emergency......... 911
HotelDocs.........800-468-3537
Medical Referral.........800-362-8677
North Carolina Dept of Revenue.........919-733-3991
Raleigh Board of Realtors.........919-654-5400
Travelers Aid Society.........919-821-1348
Vehicle Registration Information.........919-715-7000
Voter Registration Information.........919-856-6240
Wake County Revenue Collector.........919-856-5400
Weather.........919-515-8225

Information Sources

Better Business Bureau Serving Eastern North Carolina
3125 Poplarwood Ct Suite 308
Raleigh, NC 27604
www.raleigh-durham.bbb.org
Phone: 919-688-6143
Fax: 919-954-0622

Capital Area Visitor Center
301 N Blount St
Raleigh, NC 27601
Phone: 919-733-3456
Fax: 919 733-1991

Durham City Hall
101 City Hall Plaza
Durham, NC 27701
www.ci.durham.nc.us
Phone: 919-560-4100

Durham City/County Planning Dept
101 City Hall Plaza
Durham, NC 27701
www.ci.durham.nc.us/planning
Phone: 919-560-4137
Fax: 919-560-4641

Durham Convention & Visitors Bureau
101 E Morgan St
Durham, NC 27701
dcvb.durham.nc.us
Phone: 919-687-0288
Fax: 919-683-9555
TF: 800-446-8604

Durham County
200 E Main St
Durham, NC 27701
www.co.durham.nc.us
Phone: 919-560-0000
Fax: 919-560-0020

Durham County Library
PO Box 3809
Durham, NC 27702
ils.unc.edu/nclibs/durham/dclhome.htm
Phone: 919-560-0220
Fax: 919-560-0106

Durham Mayor
101 City Hall Plaza
Durham, NC 27701
Phone: 919-560-4333
Fax: 919-560-4801

Greater Durham Chamber of Commerce
300 W Morgan St Suite 1400
Durham, NC 27701
www.herald-sun.com/dcc/
Phone: 919-682-2133
Fax: 919-688-8351

Greater Raleigh Chamber of Commerce
800 S Salisbury St
Raleigh, NC 27601
www.raleighchamber.org
Phone: 919-664-7000
Fax: 919-664-7099

Greater Raleigh Convention & Visitors Bureau
421 Fayetteville St Mall Suite 1505
Raleigh, NC 27601
www.raleighcvb.org
Phone: 919-834-5900
Fax: 919-831-2887
TF: 800-849-8499

Raleigh Convention & Conference Center
500 Fayetteville Street Mall
Raleigh, NC 27601
www.raleighconvention.com
Phone: 919-831-6011
Fax: 919-831-6013

Wake County
PO Box 550 Suite 1100
Raleigh, NC 27602
www.co.wake.nc.us
Phone: 919-856-6160
Fax: 919-856-6168

Online Resources

4RaleighDurham.com
www.4raleighdurham.com

About.com Guide to Raleigh/Durham
raleighdurham.about.com/citiestowns/southeastus/raleighdurham

Anthill City Guide Durham
www.anthill.com/city.asp?city=durham

Anthill City Guide Raleigh
www.anthill.com/city.asp?city=raleigh

Area Guide Durham
durham.areaguides.net

City Knowledge Durham
www.cityknowledge.com/nc_durham.htm

City Knowledge Raleigh
www.cityknowledge.com/nc_raleigh.htm

CitySearch the Triangle
triangle.citysearch.com

DigitalCity Raleigh/Durham
home.digitalcity.com/raleigh

Excite.com Durham City Guide
www.excite.com/travel/countries/united_states/north_carolina/durham

Excite.com Raleigh City Guide
www.excite.com/travel/countries/united_states/north_carolina/raleigh

Guest Guide Online
www.guestguideonline.com

introRaleigh
www.raleigh.acn.net/

Lodging.com Raleigh-Durham North Carolina
www.lodging.com/auto/guides/raleigh-durham-area-nc.html

Raleigh CityLink
www.usacitylink.com/citylink/raleigh

Raleigh North Carolina
raleigh-north-carolina.com

Raleigh Online
www.webs4you.com/raleigh

Virtual Raleigh
www.virtualraleigh.com/

Welcome to Durham
ncnet.com/ncnw/dur-intr.html

Welcome to Raleigh
www.hickory.nc.us/ncnetworks/ral-intr.html

Area Communities

Communities in the Greater Raleigh area (including Wake, Durham, and Orange counties) with populations greater than 5,000 include:

Apex
PO Box 250
Apex, NC 27502
Phone: 919-362-7300
Fax: 919-362-0954

Carrboro
301 W Main St
Carrboro, NC 27510
Phone: 919-942-8541
Fax: 919-968-7737

Cary
PO Box 8005
Cary, NC 27512
Phone: 919-469-4006
Fax: 919-460-4929

Chapel Hill
306 N Columbia St
Chapel Hill, NC 27516
Phone: 919-968-2743
Fax: 919-969-2063

Durham
101 City Hall Plaza
Durham, NC 27701
Phone: 919-560-4100

Fuquay-Varina
401 Old Honeycutt Rd
Fuquay-Varina, NC 27526
Phone: 919-552-3178
Fax: 919-552-7481

Garner
PO Box 446
Garner, NC 27529
Phone: 919-772-4688
Fax: 919-662-8874

Wake Forest
401 Elm Ave
Wake Forest, NC 27587
Phone: 919-554-6190
Fax: 919-554-6195

Economy

Raleigh's diverse economic base ranges from agriculture to high technology. Greater Raleigh has been a hub for scientific research and development since the establishment of Research Triangle Park (located 20 minutes from downtown Raleigh) during the 1960s—today, the Triangle's many high-tech companies employ thousands of area residents. Healthcare is an important industry in the Triangle. Nearby Durham has been dubbed the "City of Medicine," and the Raleigh/Durham metropolitan area ranks sixth in the nation for number of physicians per capita. Government is also among the area's top employment sectors, providing jobs for more than 62,000 people at the state and local levels. North Carolina State Government is the area's largest employer, providing more than 23,000 jobs in the Greater Raleigh area.

Unemployment Rate 1.6%**
Per Capita Income $30,394**
Median Family Income $54,700*

** Information given is for Wake County.*
*** Information given is for the Raleigh-Durham-Chapel Hill Metropolitan Statistical Area (MSA), which includes the City of Chapel Hill, the City of Durham, the City of Raleigh, Durham County, Franklin County, Ornage County, and Wake County.*

Principal Industries & Number of Wage Earners

Wake County - 1998

Industry	Wage Earners
Agricultural Services, Forestry, & Fishing	3,935
Construction	24,883
Finance, Insurance, & Real Estate	19,027
Government	62,584
Manufacturing	27,383
Mining	445
Retail Trade	64,273
Services	113,537
Transportation, Communications, & Public Utilities	21,481
Wholesale Trade	22,398

Major Employers

American Airlines Southeastern Reservation Center
500 Gregson Dr
Cary, NC 27511
Phone: 919-460-4000
Fax: 919-460-4160

CP & L Energy Inc
411 Fayetteville St
Raleigh, NC 27602
www.cplc.com
Phone: 919-546-6111
Fax: 919-546-7784

International Business Machines Corp
3039 Cornwallis Rd
Research Triangle Park, NC 27709
Phone: 919-543-5221
Fax: 800-262-2494

Nortel Networks Corp
4001 E Chapel Hill-Nelson Hwy
Research Triangle Park, NC 27709
Phone: 919-992-5000
Fax: 800-546-8092

North Carolina State Government
1331 Mail Service Ctr
Raleigh, NC 27699
Phone: 919-733-7934
Fax: 919-733-0653

North Carolina State University
4700 Hillsborough St
Raleigh, NC 27695
E-mail: undergrad_admissions@ncsu.edu
www.ncsu.edu
Phone: 919-515-2011
Fax: 919-515-5039

Raleigh City Hall
222 W Hargett St
Raleigh, NC 27601
www.raleigh-nc.org
Phone: 919-890-3000
Fax: 919-890-3180

Research Triangle Institute
PO Box 12194
Research Triangle Park, NC 27709
E-mail: listen@rti.org
www.rti.org
Phone: 919-541-6000
Fax: 919-541-6506

Rex Healthcare
4420 Lake Boone Trail
Raleigh, NC 27607
www.rexhealth.com
Phone: 919-783-3100
Fax: 919-784-3387

SAS Institute Inc
SAS Campus Dr
Cary, NC 27513
www.sas.com
Phone: 919-677-8000
Fax: 919-677-4444

Wake County
PO Box 550 Suite 1100
Raleigh, NC 27602
www.co.wake.nc.us
Phone: 919-856-6160
Fax: 919-856-6168

Wake County Public School System
3600 Wake Forest Rd
Raleigh, NC 27609
www.wcpss.net
Phone: 919-850-1600
Fax: 919-850-1963

Wake Medical Center
3000 New Bern Ave
Raleigh, NC 27610
Phone: 919-350-8000
Fax: 919-350-2847

Winn-Dixie Stores Raleigh Inc
PO Box 8000
Clayton, NC 27520
E-mail: comments@winn-dixie.com
www.winn-dixie.com
Phone: 919-550-7100
Fax: 919-550-7169

Quality of Living Indicators

Total Crime Index 18,671
(rates per 100,000 inhabitants)

Violent Crime
- Murder/manslaughter 16
- Forcible rape 92
- Robbery 738
- Aggravated assault 1,184

Property Crime
- Burglary 3,459
- Larceny theft 11,847
- Motor vehicle theft 1,135

Cost of Living Index 100.8
(national average = 100)

Median Home Price $165,000

Education

Public Schools

Wake County Public School System
3600 Wake Forest Rd
Raleigh, NC 27609
www.wcpss.net
Phone: 919-850-1600
Fax: 919-850-1963

Number of Schools
- Elementary 69
- Middle 21
- High 15

Student/Teacher Ratio
- All Grades 16.5:1

Private Schools

Number of Schools (all grades) .... 51+

Colleges & Universities

Duke University
2138 Campus Dr Box 90586
Durham, NC 27708
E-mail: askduke@admissions.duke.edu
www.duke.edu
Phone: 919-684-3214
Fax: 919-681-8941

Durham Technical Community College
1637 E Lawson St
Durham, NC 27703
www.dtcc.cc.nc.us
Phone: 919-686-3300
Fax: 919-686-3396

Meredith College
3800 Hillsborough St
Raleigh, NC 27607
E-mail: admission@meredith.edu
www.meredith.edu
Phone: 919-760-8600
Fax: 919-760-2348
TF: 800-637-3348

North Carolina Central University
1801 Fayetteville St
Durham, NC 27707
www.nccu.edu
Phone: 919-560-6298
Fax: 919-530-7625
TF: 877-667-7533

North Carolina State University
4700 Hillsborough St
Raleigh, NC 27695
E-mail: undergrad_admissions@ncsu.edu
www.ncsu.edu
Phone: 919-515-2011
Fax: 919-515-5039

Peace College
15 E Peace St
Raleigh, NC 27604
www.peace.edu
Phone: 919-508-2000
Fax: 919-508-2326
TF: 800-732-2347

Saint Augustine's College
1315 Oakwood Ave
Raleigh, NC 27610
www.st-aug.edu
Phone: 919-516-4000
Fax: 919-516-5805
TF: 800-948-1126

Shaw University
118 E South St
Raleigh, NC 27601
www.shawuniversity.edu
Phone: 919-546-8200
Fax: 919-546-8271
TF: 800-214-6683

University of North Carolina Chapel Hill
2200 Jackson Hall
Chapel Hill, NC 27599
E-mail: uadm@email.unc.edu
www.unc.edu
Phone: 919-962-2211
Fax: 919-962-9149

Wake Technical Community College
9101 Fayetteville Rd
Raleigh, NC 27603
wtcc-gw.wake.tec.nc.us
Phone: 919-662-3500
Fax: 919-779-3360

Hospitals

Duke University Medical Center
PO Box 3708
Durham, NC 27710
www.mc.duke.edu
Phone: 919-684-5414
Fax: 919-681-8921

Durham Regional Hospital
3643 N Roxboro Rd
Durham, NC 27704
www.drh.duhs.duke.edu
Phone: 919-470-4000
Fax: 919-470-7394

Raleigh Community Hospital
3400 Wake Forest Rd
Raleigh, NC 27609
Phone: 919-954-3000
Fax: 919-954-3900

Rex Healthcare
4420 Lake Boone Trail
Raleigh, NC 27607
www.rexhealth.com
Phone: 919-783-3100
Fax: 919-784-3387

Veterans Affairs Medical Center
508 Fulton St
Durham, NC 27705
Phone: 919-286-0411
Fax: 919-286-6855

Wake Medical Center
3000 New Bern Ave
Raleigh, NC 27610
Phone: 919-350-8000
Fax: 919-350-2847

Transportation

Airport(s)

Raleigh-Durham International Airport (RDU)
12 miles NW of downtown Raleigh
(approx 15 minutes) 919-840-2100

Mass Transit

Capital Area Transit
$.75 Base fare 919-828-7228

Rail/Bus

Amtrak Station
320 W Cabarrus St
Raleigh, NC 27601
Phone: 919-833-7594
TF: 800-872-7245

Greyhound Bus Station
314 W Jones St
Raleigh, NC 27603
Phone: 919-834-8275
TF: 800-231-2222

Utilities

Electricity
Carolina Power & Light 800-452-2777
www.cplc.com

Gas
Public Service Co of North Carolina Inc 877-776-2427

Water
Raleigh Water Dept 919-890-3245

Garbage Collection/Recycling
Raleigh Recycling 919-831-6194
Raleigh Trash Pickup 919-831-6890

Telecommunications

Telephone
BellSouth 800-767-2355
www.bellsouth.com

Cable Television
Time Warner Cable 919-832-2225
www.twc-nc.com

Internet Service Providers (ISPs)
Business Telecommunications Inc (BTI) 919-510-7000
www.btitele.com
NTRnet Systems Inc 919-484-0504
www.ntrnet.net
Triangle Internet Co 919-872-8435
www.tico.com

Banks

First Citizens Bank & Trust Co
239 Fayetteville Street Mall
Raleigh, NC 27602
Phone: 919-755-7000
Fax: 919-716-7379

First Union Bank
601 Oberlin Rd
Raleigh, NC 27605
Phone: 919-881-6324
Fax: 919-571-3843

NationsBank
6300 Falls of Neuse Rd
Raleigh, NC 27615
Phone: 919-829-6690
Fax: 919-876-1377

Wachovia Bank NA
227 Fayetteville St
Raleigh, NC 27601
Phone: 919-755-7872
Fax: 919-755-7924

Shopping

Cameron Village
1900 Cameron St
Raleigh, NC 27605
Phone: 919-821-1350

Carolina Antique Mall
2050 Clark Ave
Raleigh, NC 27605
Phone: 919-833-8227

Cary Town Center
1105 Walnut St
Cary, NC 27511
Phone: 919-460-1053

City Market
300/200 Parham St
Raleigh, NC 27601
Phone: 919-828-4555

Crabtree Valley Mall
4325 Glenwood Ave
Raleigh, NC 27612
www.crabtree-valley-mall.com
Phone: 919-787-2506
Fax: 919-787-7108

Crossroads Plaza
US 1 & Hwy 64
Cary, NC 27511
Phone: 919-233-8087
Fax: 919-233-6931

Fairgrounds Flea Market
1025 Blue Ridge Rd
Raleigh, NC 27607
Phone: 919-829-3533

Magnolia Marketplace
651 Cary Towne Blvd
Cary, NC 27511
Phone: 919-319-0505
Fax: 919-319-1619

North Hills Mall & Plaza
4217 Six Forks Rd
Raleigh, NC 27609
www.shopnorthhillsmall.com
Phone: 919-787-9042
Fax: 919-881-0530

Northgate Mall
1058 W Club Blvd
Durham, NC 27701
www.ngatemall.com
Phone: 919-286-4400
Fax: 919-286-3948

Prime Outlets at Morrisville
1001 Airport Blvd
Morrisville, NC 27560
Phone: 919-380-8700
Fax: 919-380-8661

South Square Mall
4001 Chapel Hill Blvd
Durham, NC 27707
Phone: 919-493-2451

State Farmers Market
1201 Agriculture St
Raleigh, NC 27603
Phone: 919-733-7417

Willow Park Antique Mall & Galleries
4422 Durham-Chapel Hill Blvd
Durham, NC 27707
Phone: 919-493-3923

Media

Newspapers and Magazines

Business Leader
3801 Wake Forest Rd Suite 102
Raleigh, NC 27609
E-mail: editor@businessleader.com
www.businessleader.com
Phone: 919-872-7077
Fax: 919-872-1590

Chapel Hill News
PO Box 870
Chapel Hill, NC 27514
www.chapelhillnews.com
Phone: 919-932-2000
Fax: 919-968-4953
TF: 800-365-6115

Herald-Sun*
PO Box 2092
Durham, NC 27702
E-mail: www@herald-sun.com
www.herald-sun.com
Phone: 919-419-6500
Fax: 919-419-6889
TF: 800-672-0061

Independent Weekly
PO Box 2690
Durham, NC 27715
E-mail: sioux@indyweek.com
Phone: 919-286-1972
Fax: 919-286-4274

News & Observer*
215 S McDowell St
Raleigh, NC 27601
E-mail: naostaff@nando.com
www.news-observer.com
Phone: 919-829-4500
Fax: 919-829-4529

Triangle Business Journal
1305 Navaho Dr Suite 401
Raleigh, NC 27609
www.amcity.com/triangle
Phone: 919-878-0010
Fax: 919-790-6885

**Indicates major daily newspapers*

Television

WFPX-TV Ch 62 (PAX)
PO Box 62
Lumber Bridge, NC 28357
Phone: 910-843-3884
Fax: 910-843-2873

WKFT-TV Ch 40 (Ind)
230 Donaldson St
Fayetteville, NC 28301
Phone: 910-323-4040
Fax: 910-323-3924

WLFL-TV Ch 22 (WB)
3012 Highwoods Blvd Suite 101
Raleigh, NC 27604
E-mail: wlfl22@nando.net
Phone: 919-872-9535
Fax: 919-878-3877

WNCN-TV Ch 17 (NBC)
1205 Front St
Raleigh, NC 27609
www.nbc17.com
Phone: 919-836-1717
Fax: 919-836-1747

WRAL-TV Ch 5 (CBS)
2619 Western Blvd
Raleigh, NC 27606
www.wral-tv.com
Phone: 919-821-8555
Fax: 919-821-8541

WRAZ-TV Ch 50 (Fox)
512 S Mangum St
Durham, NC 27701
www.fox50.com
Phone: 919-595-5050
Fax: 919-595-5028
TF: 877-369-5050

WRDC-TV Ch 28 (UPN)
3012 Highwoods Blvd Suite 101
Raleigh, NC 27604
Phone: 919-872-2854
Fax: 919-790-6991

WRPX-TV Ch 47 (PAX)
3209 Gresham Lake Rd Suite 160
Raleigh, NC 27615
Phone: 919-872-4748
Fax: 919-872-4766

WTVD-TV Ch 11 (ABC)
PO Box 2009
Durham, NC 27702
www.newschannel11abc.com
Phone: 919-683-1111
Fax: 919-687-4373
TF: 800-467-4440

WUNC-TV Ch 4 (PBS)
PO Box 14900
Research Triangle Park, NC 27709
E-mail: viewer@unctv.org
www.unctv.org
Phone: 919-549-7000
Fax: 919-549-7043
TF: 800-906-5050

Radio

WDCG-FM 105.1 MHz (CHR)
3100 Smoketree Ct Suite 700
Raleigh, NC 27604
E-mail: prism@interpath.com
Phone: 919-871-1051
Fax: 919-954-8561

WDNC-AM 620 kHz (N/T)
407 Blackwell St
Durham, NC 27701
www.wdnc.com
Phone: 919-687-6580
Fax: 919-688-0180

WDTF-AM 570 kHz (Rel)
3012 Highwoods Blvd Suite 201
Raleigh, NC 27604
www.570wdtf.com
Phone: 919-954-1550
Fax: 919-875-1126

WFTK-AM 1030 kHz (Rel)
707 Leon St
Durham, NC 27704
Phone: 919-781-1030
Fax: 919-220-0006

WFXC-FM 107.1 MHz (AC)
8001-101 Creedmoor Rd
Raleigh, NC 27613
E-mail: info@foxy107-104.com
www.foxy107-104.com
Phone: 919-848-9736
Fax: 919-863-4857

WFXK-FM 104.3 MHz (Urban)
8001-101 Creedmoor Rd
Raleigh, NC 27613
E-mail: info@foxy107-104.com
www.foxy107-104.com
Phone: 919-848-9736
Fax: 919-844-3947

WKIX-FM 96.9 MHz (Ctry)
5706 New Chapel Hill Rd
Raleigh, NC 27607
Phone: 919-851-2711
Fax: 919-859-1482

WKNC-FM 88.1 MHz (Rock)
Box 8607
Raleigh, NC 27607
E-mail: sales@wknc.org
wknc.org
Phone: 919-515-2401
Fax: 919-513-2693

WKXU-FM 101.1 MHz (Ctry)
PO Box 1119
Burlington, NC 27216
Phone: 336-584-0126
Fax: 336-584-0739
TF: 800-272-6404

WNCU-FM 90.7 MHz (NPR)
PO Box 19875
Durham, NC 27707
www.wncu.com
Phone: 919-560-9628
Fax: 919-530-7975

WNNL-FM 103.9 MHz (Rel)
8001-101 Creedmoor Rd
Raleigh, NC 27613
Phone: 919-790-1035
Fax: 919-863-4856

WPTF-AM 680 kHz (N/T)
3012 Highwoods Blvd Suite 200
Raleigh, NC 27604
www.wptf.com
Phone: 919-876-0674
Fax: 919-790-8369

WQDR-FM 94.7 MHz (Ctry)
3012 Highwoods Blvd Suite 200
Raleigh, NC 27604
Phone: 919-876-0674
Fax: 919-790-8893

WQOK-FM 97.5 MHz (Urban)
8001-101 Creedmoor Rd
Raleigh, NC 27613
Phone: 919-790-1035
Fax: 919-863-4862

WRAL-FM 101.5 MHz (AC)
PO Box 10100
Raleigh, NC 27605
E-mail: wralfm@interpath.com
www.wralfm.com
Phone: 919-890-6101
Fax: 919-890-6146

WRBZ-AM 850 kHz (N/T)
5000 Falls of Neuse Rd Suite 308
Raleigh, NC 27609
E-mail: manager@850thebuzz.com
www.wrbz.com/
Phone: 919-875-9100
Fax: 919-875-9080

WRCQ-FM 103.5 MHz (Rock)
1009 Drayton Rd
Fayetteville, NC 28303
Phone: 910-860-1401
Fax: 910-860-4360

WRDU-FM 106.1 MHz (CR)
3100 Smoketree Ct Suite 700
Raleigh, NC 27604
E-mail: wrdu@capstar-raleigh.com
www.rdu.citysearch.com
Phone: 919-876-1061
Fax: 919-876-2929

WRSN-FM 93.9 MHz (AC)
3100 Smoketree Ct Suite 700
Raleigh, NC 27604
Phone: 919-871-1051
Fax: 919-954-8561

WSHA-FM 88.9 MHz (Jazz)
118 E South St
Raleigh, NC 27601
www.wshafm.org
Phone: 919-546-8430
Fax: 919-546-8315

WSRC-AM 1410 kHz (Rel)
3202 Guess Rd
Durham, NC 27705
Phone: 919-477-7999
Fax: 919-477-9811

WTRG-FM 100.7 MHz (Oldies)
3100 Smoketree Ct Suite 700
Raleigh, NC 27604
www.oldies.citysearch.com
Phone: 919-876-1007
Fax: 919-876-2929

WUNC-FM 91.5 MHz (NPR)
University of North Carolina Swain Hall
Box 0915
Chapel Hill, NC 27599
E-mail: wunc@unc.edu
wunc.citysearch.com
Phone: 919-966-5454
Fax: 919-966-5955

WXDU-FM 88.7 MHz (Alt)
PO Box 90689
Durham, NC 27708
E-mail: wxdu@duke.edu
www.wxdu.duke.edu
Phone: 919-684-2957
Fax: 919-684-3260

Attractions

The North Carolina State Capitol, built more than 150 years ago in the Greek Revival style, is a National Historic Landmark and one of Raleigh's most popular historical attractions. Other areas of historic interest in the city include Historic Oakwood, a preserved Victorian neighborhood established in the 1870s that is listed on the National Register of Historic Places; and the Governor's (Executive) Mansion, another example of Victorian architecture from the late 19th Century. The State Museum of Natural Sciences, as well as the North Carolina Symphony Orchestra, are based in Raleigh. Each October, Raleigh hosts the North Carolina State Fair, featuring livestock competitions, handmade crafts, and amusement rides.

African American Cultural Complex
119 Sunnybrook Rd
Raleigh, NC 27610
www.aaccmuseum.org
Phone: 919-231-0625
Fax: 919-212-3598

Artspace
201 E Davie St
Raleigh, NC 27601
triangle.citysearch.com/E/V/RDUNC/1000/00/59
Phone: 919-821-2787
Fax: 919-821-0383

Bennett Place State Historic Site
4409 Bennett Memorial Rd
Durham, NC 27705
E-mail: bennettplace@mindspring.com
Phone: 919-383-4345
Fax: 919-383-4349

Bond Metro Park
801 High House Rd
Cary, NC 27513
Phone: 919-469-4100

Borden Building
820 Clay St
Raleigh, NC 27605
Phone: 919-831-6430

Capital City Bicycle Motocross Race Track
516 Dennis Ave Lions Pk
Raleigh, NC 27604
Phone: 919-831-6995

Carolina Ballet
2914 Kildaire Farm Rd
Cary, NC 27511
www.carolinaballet.com
Phone: 919-510-8945
Fax: 919-363-7728

Center Stage
Cates Ave Talley Student Ctr
Raleigh, NC 27695
E-mail: centerstage@ncsu.edu
www.fis.ncsu.edu/Center_Stage
Phone: 919-513-3030
Fax: 919-515-1406

Contemporary Art Museum
336 Fayetteville St Mall 4th Fl
Raleigh, NC 27602
www.camnc.org
Phone: 919-836-0088
Fax: 919-836-2239

Downtown Durham Historic District & Brightleaf Square
Market St
Durham, NC 27701
Phone: 919-682-9229

Duke Homestead State Historic Site & Tobacco Museum
2828 Duke Homestead Rd
Durham, NC 27705
metalab.unc.edu/maggot/dukehome/index.html
Phone: 919-477-5498
Fax: 919-479-7092

Duke Memorial United Methodist Church
504 W Chapel Hill St
Durham, NC 27701
Phone: 919-683-3467
Fax: 919-682-3349

Duke Sarah P Gardens
Anderson St betw Erwin Rd & Campus Dr
Durham, NC 27708
Phone: 919-684-3698
Fax: 919-684-8861

Duke University Chapel
Chapel Dr Duke University West Campus
Durham, NC 27706
www.chapel.duke.edu/
Phone: 919-681-1704

Duke University Institute of the Arts Gallery
109 Bivins Bldg
Durham, NC 27708
www.duke.edu/web/dia/
Phone: 919-660-3356
Fax: 919-684-8906

Duke University Museum of Art
N Buchanan Blvd & Trinity Ave
Durham, NC 27701
www.duke.edu/duma
Phone: 919-684-5135
Fax: 919-681-8624

Duke University Primate Center
3705 Erwin Rd
Durham, NC 27705
E-mail: primate@acpub.duke.edu
www.duke.edu/web/primate
Phone: 919-489-3364
Fax: 919-490-5394

Durant Nature Park
8305 Camp Durant Rd
Raleigh, NC 27614
Phone: 919-870-2871

Durham Symphony
120 Morris St
Durham, NC 27701
Phone: 919-560-2736

Eno River State Park
6101 Cole Mill Rd
Durham, NC 27705
Phone: 919-383-1686
Fax: 919-382-7378

Executive Mansion
200 N Blount St
Raleigh, NC 27601
Phone: 919-733-3456

Falls Lake State Recreation Area
13304 Creedmoor Rd
Wake Forest, NC 27587
Phone: 919-676-1027
Fax: 919-773-3499

Funtasia Family Fun Park
4350 Garrett Rd
Durham, NC 27707
Phone: 919-493-8973
Fax: 919-489-5772

Hayti Heritage Center
804 Old Fayetteville St
Durham, NC 27702
Phone: 919-683-1709
Fax: 919-682-5869

Haywood Hall House & Gardens
211 New Bern Pl
Raleigh, NC 27601
Phone: 919-832-8357

Hemlock Bluffs Nature Preserve
2616 Kildaire Farm Rd
Cary, NC 27511
Phone: 919-387-5980

Historic Oak View County Park
4028 Carya Dr
Raleigh, NC 27610
Phone: 919-250-1013
Fax: 919-250-1262

Historic Oakwood
519 Oakwood Ave
Raleigh, NC 27601
Phone: 919-834-0887

Historic Stagville
PO Box 71217
Durham, NC 27722
Phone: 919-620-0120
Fax: 919-620-0422

Historic Trolley Tours
1 Mimosa St Mordecai Historic Pk
Raleigh, NC 27604
Phone: 919-834-4844
Fax: 919-834-7314

Hugh Mangum Museum of Photography
5101 N Roxboro Rd
Durham, NC 27704
Phone: 919-471-1623
Fax: 919-560-4021

JC Raulston Arboretum
4301 Beryl Rd
Raleigh, NC 27606
arb.ncsu.edu
Phone: 919-515-3132
Fax: 919-515-7747

Joel Lane House Museum & Gardens
Saint Mary's & W Hargett Sts
Raleigh, NC 27603
Phone: 919-833-3431

Lake Crabtree County Park
1400 Aviation Pkwy
Morrisville, NC 27560
Phone: 919-460-3390

Lake Johnson Park
5600 Avent Ferry Rd
Raleigh, NC 27606
Phone: 919-233-2121

Lake Wheeler
6404 Lake Wheeler Rd
Raleigh, NC 27603
Phone: 919-662-5704

Laurel Hills Park
3808 Edwards Mill Rd
Raleigh, NC 27612
Phone: 919-420-2383

Moores Creek National Battlefield
40 Patriots Hall Dr
Currie, NC 28435
www.nps.gov/mocr/
Phone: 910-283-5591
Fax: 910-283-5351

Mordecai Ellen Gardens
Mimosa St & Wake Forest Rd
Raleigh, NC 27604
E-mail: cappresinc@aol.com
Phone: 919-834-4844
Fax: 919-834-7314

Mordecai Historic Park
1 Mimosa St
Raleigh, NC 27604
Phone: 919-834-4844
Fax: 919-834-7314

Morehead Planetarium
E Franklin St UNC Chapel Hill Campus Box 3480
Chapel Hill, NC 27599
E-mail: mhplanet@unc.edu
www.unc.edu/depts/mhplanet/
Phone: 919-962-1236
Fax: 919-962-1238

National Opera Co
PO Box 12800
Raleigh, NC 27605
www.operabase.com/level1/nara.html
Phone: 919-890-6083
Fax: 919-890-6279

North Carolina Central University Art Museum
1801 Fayetteville St
Durham, NC 27705
Phone: 919-560-6211

North Carolina Museum of Art
2110 Blue Ridge Rd
Raleigh, NC 27607
ncartmuseum.org
Phone: 919-839-6262
Fax: 919-733-8034

North Carolina Museum of History
5 E Edenton St
Raleigh, NC 27601
nchistory.dcr.state.nc.us/museums
Phone: 919-715-0200
Fax: 919-733-8655

North Carolina Museum of Life & Science
433 Murray Ave
Durham, NC 27704
www.ncmls.org
Phone: 919-220-5429
Fax: 919-220-5575

North Carolina Railroad Museum
SR 1011
New Hill, NC 27562
Phone: 919-362-5416

North Carolina State Archives
109 E Jones St
Raleigh, NC 27601
www.ah.dcr.state.nc.us
Phone: 919-733-3952
Fax: 919-733-1354

North Carolina State Capitol
1 E Edenton St
Raleigh, NC 27601
www.ah.dcr.state.nc.us/sections/capitol/default.htm
Phone: 919-733-4993
Fax: 919-715-4030

North Carolina State Museum of Natural Sciences
11 W Jones St
Raleigh, NC 27603
www.naturalsciences.org
Phone: 919-733-7450
Fax: 919-733-1573

North Carolina Symphony Orchestra
2 E South St Memorial Auditorium
Raleigh, NC 27601
www.ncsymphony.org
Phone: 919-733-2750
Fax: 919-733-9920

North Carolina Theatre
1 E South St Memorial Auditorium
Raleigh, NC 27601
www.nctheatre.com
Phone: 919-831-6941
Fax: 919-831-6951

North Carolina Theatre
309 W Morgan St Royall Ctr for the Arts
Durham, NC 27701
www.nctheatre.com
Phone: 919-560-3040
Fax: 919-560-3065

Oakwood Cemetery
701 Oakwood Ave
Raleigh, NC 27601
Phone: 919-832-6077
Fax: 919-832-2982

Page-Walker Arts & History Center
119 Ambassador Loop
Cary, NC 27513
Phone: 919-460-4963
Fax: 919-469-4344

Patterson's Mill Country Store
5109 Farrington Rd
Chapel Hill, NC 27514
Phone: 919-493-8149

Pullen Park
520 Ashe Ave
Raleigh, NC 27606
Phone: 919-831-6468

Raleigh City Museum
220 Fayetteville St Mall Suite 100
Raleigh, NC 27601
www.raleighcitymuseum.org
Phone: 919-832-3775
Fax: 919-832-3085

Raleigh Contemporary Gallery
323 Blake St
Raleigh, NC 27601
Phone: 919-828-6500
Fax: 919-828-6500

Raleigh Ensemble Players Theatre Co
201 E Davie St
Raleigh, NC 27601
www.realtheatre.org
Phone: 919-832-9607
Fax: 919-821-0383

Raleigh Little Theatre
301 Pogue St
Raleigh, NC 27607
www.mindspring.com/~rallittletheatre/
Phone: 919-821-4579
Fax: 919-821-7961

Raleigh Municipal Rose Garden
301 Pogue St
Raleigh, NC 27607
Phone: 919-821-4579

Research Triangle Park
2 Hanes Dr
Research Triangle Park, NC 27709
E-mail: parkinfo@rtp.org
www.rtp.org
Phone: 919-549-8181
Fax: 919-549-8246

Saint Augustine's College Chapel
1315 Oakwood Ave
Raleigh, NC 27610
Phone: 919-516-4189

Sertoma Arts Center
1400 W Millbrook Rd
Raleigh, NC 27612
Phone: 919-420-2329

Shelley Lake
1400 W Millbrook Rd Sertoma Park
Raleigh, NC 27612
Phone: 919-420-2331

Silver Lake Waterpark
5300 Tyron Rd
Raleigh, NC 27606
Phone: 919-851-1683

Spring Hill House
705 Barbours Dr
Raleigh, NC 27603
Phone: 919-733-5454
Fax: 919-733-1029

State Farmers Market
1201 Agriculture St
Raleigh, NC 27603
Phone: 919-733-7417

State Legislative Building
16 W Jones St
Raleigh, NC 27601
Phone: 919-733-7928
Fax: 919-733-2599

Theatre in the Park
107 Pullen Rd
Raleigh, NC 27607
www.tip.dreamhost.com
Phone: 919-831-6058
Fax: 919-831-9475

Triangle Opera
309 Morgan St Carolina Theatre
Durham, NC 27701
www.triangleopera.org
Phone: 919-956-7744
Fax: 919-956-7788

Tucker House
418 N Person St
Raleigh, NC 27601
Phone: 919-831-6009

Umstead William B State Park
8801 Glenwood Ave
Raleigh, NC 27612
Phone: 919-571-4170

Walnut Creek Amphitheatre
3801 Rock Quarry Rd
Raleigh, NC 27610
E-mail: info@alltelpavilion.com
www.alltelpavilion.com
Phone: 919-831-6400
Fax: 919-831-6415

West Point on the Eno City Park
5101 N Roxboro Rd
Durham, NC 27704
Phone: 919-471-1623

Wheels Recreation Park
715 N Hoover Rd
Durham, NC 27703
Phone: 919-598-1944

Sports Teams & Facilities

Carolina Cobras (football)
1400 Edwards Mill Rd Raleigh
Entertainment & Sports Arena
Raleigh, NC 27607
www.cobrasfootball.com
Phone: 919-281-0400
Fax: 919-281-0410
TF: 877-426-2727

Carolina Mudcats (baseball)
1501 North Carolina Hwy Five County
Stadium
Zebulon, NC 27597
www.gomudcats.com
Phone: 919-269-2287
Fax: 919-269-4940

Raleigh Capital Express (soccer)
7700 Perry Creek Rd Wral Field
Raleigh, NC 27616
www.raleighexpress.com
Phone: 919-781-7259
Fax: 919-786-1778

Raleigh Wings (soccer)
7700 Perry Creek Rd Championship Field
Raleigh, NC 27603
E-mail: info@raleighwings.com
www.raleighwings.com
Phone: 919-848-8412
Fax: 919-848-4657

Annual Events

Air Expo (early May) 919-840-2100
American Dance Festival (mid-June-late July) 919-684-6402
Artsplosure Jazz & Arts Festival (mid-May) 919-832-8699
Bass & Saltwater Fishing Expo (early January) 336-855-0208
Bimbe Festival (late May) 919-560-4355
Brightleaf Festival (early October) 919-365-6318
Brightleaf Music Workshop & Finale
(late June-early August) 919-493-0385
Bull Durham Blues Festival (mid-September) 919-683-1709
Buy.com Carolina Classic (early May) 919-380-0011
Capitol's July 4th Celebration (early July) 919-733-4994
Carolian Power & Sailboat Show (mid-February) 336-855-0208

Carolina Christmas Show (mid-late November) 919-831-6011
Carolina Fall Boat Show (early September).........336-855-0208
Celebration of the Outdoors (early May)............919-552-1410
Centerfest (mid-September) 919-560-2722
Christmas Celebration on the Mall
(early December)..............................919-733-4994
Civil War Living History (mid-April)...............919-733-4994
CROP Walk (late March).........................919-688-3843
Double Take Film Festival (early April)...........919-660-3699
Edible Arts Festival of Food & Art (early June).....919-560-2787
Farmers Market Festival (early July)...............919-733-7417
Festival for the Eno (early July)...................919-477-4549
First Night Raleigh (December 31)................919-832-8699
Great Raleigh Road Race (early May) 919-831-6061
Greater Raleigh Antique Show
(early March & mid-November)................919-782-5782
Grecian Festival (mid-September).................919-781-4548
Home & Garden Show (mid-February).............919-831-6061
International Auto Show (late February)...........919-831-6061
International Festival (early October).............919-834-5900
KwanzaaFest (early January)......................919-560-2729
Lazy Daze Festival (late August) 919-469-4061
Living Christmas Tree (mid-December)............919-832-2257
Native American Celebration (early November)......919-733-7450
Native American Pow Wow (mid-February).........919-286-3366
Natural History Halloween (late October)...........919-733-7450
North Carolina International Jazz Festival
(late January-late April)........................919-660-3300
North Carolina State Fair (mid-October)...........919-733-2145
North Carolina State Farmers Market Festival
(early July)...................................919-733-7417
Oktoberfest (late September)......................919-834-5900
Old Reliable Run (mid-November).................919-829-4843
Pine Cone's Old Time Bluegrass Music Festival
(early May)...................................919-990-1900
Raleigh Antiques Extravaganza (mid-January)......336-924-8337
Raleigh Christmas Parade (late November).........919-420-0120
Run for the Roses (mid-February).................919-231-0714
Saint Patrick's Day Parade (mid-March)...........919-846-9739
Southern Ideal Home Show
(mid-April & late September)...................919-851-2911
Summer Festival of Creative Arts
(late May-mid-August).........................919-684-4741
Tarheel Regatta (early June)......................919-662-5704
Triangle Triumph Road Race (late September)......919-990-7938

Reno, Nevada

***County:* Washoe**

RENO is located in western Nevada along the banks of the Truckee River. Major cities within 100 miles include Sparks and Carson City, Nevada.

Area (Land) .... 57.5 sq mi
Area (Water).............................. 0.2 sq mi
Elevation.................................. 4,498 ft
Latitude .... 39-52-97 N
Longitude.............................. 119-81-28 W
Time Zone .... PST
Area Code..................................... 775

Climate

Reno's climate offers four distinct seasons, with significant variation in high and low temperatures. While summer daytime high temperatures can reach the low 90s, nighttime lows generally drop to near 50 degrees. Winter high temperatures average in the mid- 40s to near 50, with lows in the low 20s. Reno receives an average of just over 26 inches of snow annually, however the neighboring areas in the Sierra Nevada's can receive as much as 250 inches annually. The average annual rainfall in Reno is less than eight inches.

Average Temperatures & Precipitation

Temperatures

	Jan	Feb	Mar	Apr	May	Jun	Jul	Aug	Sep	Oct	Nov	Dec
High	45	52	56	64	73	83	92	90	80	69	54	46
Low	21	24	29	33	40	47	51	50	41	33	27	20

Precipitation

	Jan	Feb	Mar	Apr	May	Jun	Jul	Aug	Sep	Oct	Nov	Dec
Inches	1.1	1.0	0.7	0.4	0.7	0.5	0.3	0.3	0.4	0.4	0.9	1.0

History

Originally inhabited by the Washoe and Paiute Indians, settlement did not begin in the area known today as Reno until the 1850s, when gold was discovered in California. The first settlement, called Lake's Crossing, was established in 1859 when a toll bridge was built across the Truckee River, drawing pioneers from the east in search of fortune. The greatest silver strike in U.S. history, the Comstock Lode, took place in nearby Virginia City later that year. This discovery prompted pioneers headed west to stop and settle in the area, and it drew new prospectors by the thousands.

During the Civil War, silver from the Comstock Lode provided financial support for the Union. In 1868, Lakes Crossing was renamed Reno in honor of General Jesse Reno. In addition to silver, the arrival of the railroad during the 1860s also helped to fuel the area's growth. The legalization of gambling in Nevada in 1869 (although it was banned for several years during the early 1900s) would prove to be a significant event in the future growth and development of the area.

In 1903, Reno was incorporated as a city. During the late 1920s, a transcontinental highway was built through Reno, and the Reno Arch was erected across Virginia Street to welcome visitors to the city. Today "the Biggest Little City in the World," a slogan created by a local contest winner in 1929, with its myriad hotels and casinos and its proximity to Lake Tahoe, has become one of the leading tourist destinations in the United States, hosting more than five million visitors annually.

The seat of Washoe County, Reno today is Nevada's second largest city, with a population exceeding 163,000. The Reno-Sparks metropolitan area, which includes the two cities plus the unincorporated areas of Washoe County, is currently home to more than 300,000 people and ranks among the fastest-growing metropolitan areas in the nation.

Population

1990 Census 134,230
1998 Estimate............................. 163,334
% Change 21.7
2002 Projection 179,386

Racial/Ethnic Breakdown

White.................................... 86.1%
Black 2.9%
Other.................................... 11.0%
Hispanic Origin (may be of any race) 11.1%

Age Breakdown

Under 5 years.............................. 7.2%
5 to 17.................................. 13.6%
18 to 20................................... 4.9%
21 to 24................................... 7.4%
25 to 34.................................. 20.2%
35 to 44.................................. 16.1%
45 to 54.................................. 10.4%
55 to 64................................... 8.4%
65 to 74................................... 7.4%
75+ years 4.4%
Median Age................................. 33.3

Gender Breakdown

Male..................................... 50.8%
Female................................... 49.2%

Government

Type of Government: Council-Manager

Reno City Attorney
PO Box 1900
Reno, NV 89505
Phone: 775-334-2050
Fax: 775-334-2420

Reno City Clerk
PO Box 7
Reno, NV 89504
Phone: 775-334-2030
Fax: 775-334-2432

Reno City Council
PO Box 1900
Reno, NV 89505
Phone: 775-334-2020
Fax: 775-334-2097

Reno City Hall
490 S Center St
Reno, NV 89501
Phone: 775-334-2020
Fax: 775-334-2097

Reno City Manager
PO Box 1900
Reno, NV 89505
Phone: 775-334-2020
Fax: 775-334-2097

Reno Community Development Dept
PO Box 1900
Reno, NV 89505
Phone: 775-334-2060
Fax: 775-334-2043

Reno Finance Dept
PO Box 1900
Reno, NV 89505
Phone: 775-334-2080
Fax: 775-334-2409

Reno Fire Dept
PO Box 1900
Reno, NV 89505
Phone: 775-334-2300
Fax: 775-334-3826

Reno Human Resources Dept
490 S Center St
Reno, NV 89501
Phone: 775-334-2285
Fax: 775-334-2045

Reno Mayor
PO Box 1900
Reno, NV 89505
Phone: 775-334-2001
Fax: 775-334-2097

Reno Parks Recreation & Community Services Dept
100 Washington St Suite 200
Reno, NV 89503
Phone: 775-334-2262
Fax: 775-334-2449

Reno Police Dept
PO Box 1900
Reno, NV 89505
Phone: 775-334-2100
Fax: 775-334-3890

Reno Public Works Dept
350 S Center St Suite 400
Reno, NV 89501
Phone: 775-334-2350
Fax: 775-334-2490

Important Phone Numbers

AAA 775-826-8800
American Express Travel 775-689-7700
Driver's License/Vehicle Registration Information 775-688-2368
Emergency 911
HotelDocs 800-468-3537
Nevada Dept of Taxation 775-687-4820
Poison Control Center 775-982-4129
Reno-Sparks Assn of Realtors 775-823-8800
Road Conditions 775-688-2500
Time 775-844-1212
Voter Registration Information 775-328-3670
Washoe County Treasurer 775-328-2550
Weather 775-793-1300

Information Sources

Better Business Bureau Serving Northern Nevada
991 Bible Way
Reno, NV 89502
www.reno.bbb.org
Phone: 775-322-0657
Fax: 775-322-8163

Carson City (Independent City)
201 N Carson St
Carson City, NV 89701
www.carson-city.nv.us
Phone: 775-887-2100
Fax: 775-887-2286

Carson City Area Chamber of Commerce
1900 S Carson St Suite 100
Carson City, NV 89701
www.carsoncitychamber.com
Phone: 775-882-1565
Fax: 775-882-4179

Carson City City Hall
201 N Carson St
Carson City, NV 89701
www.carson-city.nv.us
Phone: 775-887-2100
Fax: 775-887-2286

Carson City Community Development Dept
2621 Northgate Ln Suite 62
Carson City, NV 89706
Phone: 775-887-2180
Fax: 775-887-2278

Carson City Convention & Visitors Bureau
1900 S Carson St Suite 200
Carson City, NV 89701
www.carson-city.org
Phone: 775-687-7410
Fax: 775-687-7416
TF: 800-638-2321

Carson City Library
900 N Roop St
Carson City, NV 89701
Phone: 775-887-2247
Fax: 775-887-2273

Carson City Mayor
201 N Carson St Suite 2
Carson City, NV 89701
Phone: 775-887-2100
Fax: 775-887-2286

Nevada State Chamber of Commerce
1 E 1st St 16th Fl
Reno, NV 89501
www.reno-sparkschamber.org
Phone: 775-686-3030
Fax: 775-686-3038

Reno-Sparks Convention & Visitors Authority
4590 S Virginia St
Reno, NV 89502
www.playreno.com
Phone: 775-827-7600
Fax: 775-827-7686
TF: 800-443-1482

Reno-Sparks Convention Center
4590 S Virginia St
Reno, NV 89502
Phone: 775-827-7600
Fax: 775-827-7713

Washoe County
PO Box 11130
Reno, NV 89520
www.co.washoe.nv.us
Phone: 775-328-3260
Fax: 775-328-3582

Online Resources

About.com Guide to Reno/Tahoe
renotahoe.about.com/citiestowns/southwestus/renotahoe

Anthill City Guide Carson City
www.anthill.com/city.asp?city=carsoncity

Anthill City Guide Reno
www.anthill.com/city.asp?city=reno

Area Guide Carson City
carsoncity.areaguides.net

Area Guide Reno
reno.areaguides.net

City Knowledge Reno
www.cityknowledge.com/nv_reno.htm

Excite.com Carson City City Guide
www.excite.com/travel/countries/united_states/nevada/carson_city/

Excite.com Reno City Guide
www.excite.com/travel/countries/united_states/nevada/reno

HotelGuide Reno/Sparks
hotelguide.net/reno

Insiders' Guide to Reno & Lake Tahoe
www.insiders.com/reno-tahoe/index.htm

Lodging.com Carson City Nevada
www.lodging.com/auto/guides/carson_city-nv.html

Lodging.com Reno Nevada
www.lodging.com/auto/guides/reno-area-nv.html

NevadaNet.com
www.nevadanet.com

Reno Nevada
reno-nevada.com

Reno Nevada Guide
www.renonv.com

Reno Pages
www.renopages.com/

Reno-Tahoe Territory
www.renotahoe.com

Reno.Net
www.reno.net/

Virtual Voyages Reno
www.virtualvoyages.com/usa/nv/reno/reno.sht

Area Communities

Most of the communities surrounding Reno are unincorporated. Incorporated cities in the Reno area include:

Carson City
201 N Carson St
Carson City, NV 89701
Phone: 775-887-2100
Fax: 775-887-2286

South Lake Tahoe
1052 Tata Ln
South Lake Tahoe, CA 96150
Phone: 530-542-6000
Fax: 530-544-8657

Sparks
431 Prater Way
Sparks, NV 89431
Phone: 775-353-2350
Fax: 775-353-2489

Economy

Greater Reno/Sparks has a diverse economic base that ranges from high-technology to tourism to mining. Major corporations that have a presence in the Reno area include Amazon.com, International Game Technology, General Motors, and Ralston Foods Inc. Services is the area's largest employment sector, with nearly half of all service jobs in the hotels/gaming/recreation industry. Trade and government are the area's second and third largest employment sectors. The State of Nevada is among Reno/Sparks' 15 largest employers, providing jobs for more than 1,800 area residents in various agencies.

Unemployment Rate	3.7%*
Per Capita Income	$33,040*
Median Family Income	$36,200

** Information given is for Washoe County.*

Principal Industries & Number of Wage Earners

Reno MSA (Washoe County) - 1998

Construction	12,969
Finance, Insurance & Real Estate	8,354
Government	21,645
Manufacturing	13,642
Mining	513
Retail Trade	29,113
Services	68,491
Transportation, Communications, & Utilities	11,665
Wholesale Trade	12,023

Major Employers

Atlantis Casino Resort
3800 S Virginia St
Reno, NV 89502
E-mail: mkt@atlantis.reno.nv.us
atlantiscasino.com
Phone: 775-825-4700
Fax: 775-826-7860
TF: 800-723-6500

Circus Circus Hotel & Casino Reno
500 N Sierra St
Reno, NV 89503
www.circusreno.com
Phone: 775-329-0711
Fax: 775-328-9652
TF: 800-648-5010

Eldorado Hotel Casino
345 N Virginia St
Reno, NV 89501
www.eldoradoreno.com
Phone: 775-786-5700
Fax: 775-322-7124
TF: 800-648-5966

Harrah's Casino Hotel Reno
219 N Center St
Reno, NV 89501
Phone: 775-786-3232
Fax: 775-788-2815
TF: 800-427-7247

International Game Technology
9295 Prototype Dr
Reno, NV 89511
www.igtonline.com
Phone: 775-448-7777
Fax: 775-448-1600

John Ascuaga's Nugget Hotel Casino
1100 Nugget Ave
Sparks, NV 89431
janugget.com
Phone: 775-356-3300
Fax: 775-356-4198
TF: 800-648-1177

Peppermill Hotel & Casino
2707 S Virginia St
Reno, NV 89502
E-mail: hotel@sierra.net
www.peppermillcasinos.com
Phone: 775-826-2121
Fax: 775-826-5205
TF: 800-282-2444

Reno City Hall
490 S Center St
Reno, NV 89501
www.cityofreno.com
Phone: 775-334-2020
Fax: 775-334-2097

Reno Hilton by Marriott
2500 E 2nd St
Reno, NV 89595
www.renohilton.net
Phone: 775-789-2000
Fax: 775-789-1677
TF: 800-736-6386

Saint Mary's Regional Medical Center
235 W 6th St
Reno, NV 89503
www.saintmarysreno.com
Phone: 775-323-2041
Fax: 775-770-3260

Silver Legacy Resort & Casino
407 N Virginia St
Reno, NV 89501
www.silverlegacy.com
Phone: 775-329-4777
Fax: 775-325-7474
TF: 800-687-8733

University of Nevada Reno
1664 N Virginia St
Reno, NV 89557
www.unr.edu
Phone: 775-784-1110
Fax: 775-784-1146

Washoe County
PO Box 11130
Reno, NV 89520
www.co.washoe.nv.us
Phone: 775-328-3260
Fax: 775-328-3582

Washoe County School District
425 E 9th St
Reno, NV 89520
www.washoe.k12.nv.us
Phone: 775-348-0200
Fax: 775-348-0397

Washoe Medical Center
77 Pringle Way
Reno, NV 89520
www.washoehealth.com/careers
Phone: 775-982-4100
Fax: 775-982-4111

Quality of Living Indicators

Total Crime Index 9,416
(rates per 100,000 inhabitants)

Violent Crime
Murder/manslaughter 14
Forcible rape 88
Robbery 358
Aggravated assault 397

Property Crime
Burglary 1,557
Larceny theft 6,266
Motor vehicle theft 736

Cost of Living Index 110.5
(national average = 100)

Median Home Price $150,600

Education

Public Schools

Washoe County School District
425 E 9th St
Reno, NV 89520
www.washoe.k12.nv.us
Phone: 775-348-0200
Fax: 775-348-0397

Number of Schools
Elementary 58
Middle 11
High 11

Student/Teacher Ratio
Elementary 22.5:1
Secondary 25.5:1

Private Schools

Number of Schools (all grades) .... 24+

Colleges & Universities

Morrison College
140 Washington St
Reno, NV 89503
www.morrison.edu
Phone: 775-323-4145
Fax: 775-323-8495

Truckee Meadows Community College
7000 Dandini Blvd
Reno, NV 89512
E-mail: costa_lisa@tmcc.edu
www.tmcc.edu
Phone: 775-673-7042
Fax: 775-673-7028

University of Nevada Reno
1664 N Virginia St
Reno, NV 89557
www.unr.edu
Phone: 775-784-1110
Fax: 775-784-1146

Western Nevada Community College
2201 W College Pkwy
Carson City, NV 89703
www.wncc.nevada.edu
Phone: 775-445-3277
Fax: 775-887-3141
TF: 800-748-5690

Hospitals

Carson Tahoe Hospital
775 Fleischmann Way
Carson City, NV 89703
www.carson-tahoehospital.com
Phone: 775-882-1361
Fax: 775-885-4523

Ioannis A Lougaris Veterans Affairs Medical Center
1000 Locust St
Reno, NV 89502
Phone: 775-786-7200
Fax: 775-328-1464
TF: 888-838-6256

Northern Nevada Medical Center
2375 E Prater Way
Sparks, NV 89434
www.nnmc.com
Phone: 775-331-7000
Fax: 775-331-3399

Saint Mary's Regional Medical Center
235 W 6th St
Reno, NV 89503
www.saintmarysreno.com
Phone: 775-323-2041
Fax: 775-770-3260

Washoe Medical Center
77 Pringle Way
Reno, NV 89520
www.washoehealth.com/careers
Phone: 775-982-4100
Fax: 775-982-4111

Transportation

Airport(s)

Reno-Tahoe International Airport (RNO)
5 miles SE of downtown (approx 15 minutes).....775-328-6400

Mass Transit

Citifare
$1.25 Base fare.....775-348-7433

Rail/Bus

Amtrak Station
135 E Commercial Row
Reno, NV 89501
Phone: 800-872-7245

Greyhound Bus Station
155 Stevenson St
Reno, NV 89503
Phone: 775-322-2970
TF: 800-231-2222

Utilities

Electricity
Sierra Pacific Power Co.....775-834-4444
www.sierrapacific.com

Gas
Sierra Pacific Power Co.....775-834-4444
www.sierrapacific.com

Water
Sierra Pacific Power Co.....775-834-4444
www.sierrapacific.com

Garbage Collection/Recycling
Reno Disposal Services/Sparks Sanitation Co.....775-329-8822

Telecommunications

Telephone
Nevada Bell.....877-469-2355
www.nevadabell.com

Cable Television
AT & T Cable Services.....775-850-8555
www.cable.att.com

Internet Service Providers (ISPs)
Great Basin Internet Services.....775-348-7299
www.greatbasin.net
SourceNet Corp.....775-332-3200
www.source.net

Banks

Bank of America
5905 S Virginia St
Reno, NV 89502
Phone: 775-688-8900
Fax: 775-688-8908

Bank of the West
4950 Kietzke Ln
Reno, NV 89509
Phone: 775-689-2300
Fax: 775-689-2333
TF: 800-488-2265

Heritage Bank of Nevada
1401 S Virginia St
Reno, NV 89502
Phone: 775-348-1000
Fax: 775-348-1022

Pioneer Citizens Bank of Nevada
1 W Liberty
Reno, NV 89505
Phone: 775-688-7950
Fax: 775-688-7963

US Bank
300 S Virginia St
Reno, NV 89501
Phone: 775-688-6620
Fax: 775-348-2730
TF: 800-872-2657

Shopping

Carson Mall
1313 S Carson St
Carson City, NV 89701
Phone: 775-882-3395

Frontier Antique Mall
3rd & Currey Sts
Carson City, NV 89703
Phone: 775-887-1466

Meadowood Mall
Virginia & McCarren Sts
Reno, NV 89502
Phone: 775-827-8450
Fax: 775-826-0560

Old Town Mall
4001 S Virginia St
Reno, NV 89502
Phone: 775-823-9666
Fax: 775-823-4699

Park Lane Mall
Plumb Ln & Virginia St
Reno, NV 89502
www.shopparklanemall.com
Phone: 775-825-7878
Fax: 775-825-4375

Shopper's Square Mall
277 E Plumb Ln
Reno, NV 89502
Phone: 775-323-0430
Fax: 775-323-6824

Silver City Mall
406 Fairview Dr
Carson City, NV 89701
Phone: 775-883-3500

Town Center Mall
100 N Sierra St
Reno, NV 89501
Phone: 775-333-2828
Fax: 775-333-2828

Virginia Street Antique Mall
1251 S Virginia St
Reno, NV 89502
E-mail: jose@consumers1st.com
Phone: 775-324-4141
Fax: 775-324-7469

Media

Newspapers and Magazines

Daily Sparks Tribune*
1002 C St
Sparks, NV 89431
Phone: 775-358-8061
Fax: 775-359-3837
TF: 800-669-1338

Nevada Appeal Carson City Edition*
PO Box 2288
Carson City, NV 89702
tahoe.com/appeal
Phone: 775-882-2111
Fax: 775-887-2420
TF: 800-221-8013

Nevada Magazine
401 N Carson St
Carson City, NV 89701
E-mail: nevmag@aol.com
www.nevadamagazine.com
Phone: 775-687-5416
Fax: 775-687-6159
TF: 800-495-3281

Reno Gazette Journal*
PO Box 22000
Reno, NV 89520
www.rgj.com
Phone: 775-788-6200
Fax: 775-788-6458
TF: 800-648-5048

Reno Gazette Journal Carson City Edition*
311 N Carson St
Carson City, NV 89701
Phone: 775-885-5560
Fax: 775-885-5565

**Indicates major daily newspapers*

Television

KAME-TV Ch 21 (UPN)
4920 Brookside Ct
Reno, NV 89502
Phone: 775-856-2121
Fax: 775-856-5794

KNPB-TV Ch 5 (PBS)
1670 N Virginia St
Reno, NV 89503
www.knpb.org
Phone: 775-784-4555
Fax: 775-784-1438

KOLO-TV Ch 8 (ABC)
PO Box 10000
Reno, NV 89510
E-mail: admin@kolotv.com
www.kolotv.com
Phone: 775-858-8888
Fax: 775-858-8877

KREN-TV Ch 27 (WB)
940 Matley Ln Suite 15
Reno, NV 89502
Phone: 775-333-2727
Fax: 775-327-6827

KRNV-TV Ch 4 (NBC)
1790 Vassar St
Reno, NV 89502
E-mail: comments@krnv.com
www.krnv.com
Phone: 775-322-4444
Fax: 775-785-1206

KRXI-TV Ch 11 (Fox)
4920 Brookside Ct
Reno, NV 89502
Phone: 775-856-1100
Fax: 775-856-2100

KTVN-TV Ch 2 (CBS)
4925 Energy Way
Reno, NV 89502
E-mail: ktvn@ktvn.com
www.ktvn.com
Phone: 775-858-2222
Fax: 775-861-4298

Radio

KCBN-AM 1230 kHz (Nost)
300 E 2nd St 14th Fl
Reno, NV 89501
Phone: 775-829-1964
Fax: 775-825-3183
TF: 800-896-1669

KDOT-FM 104.5 MHz (Rock)
2900 Sutro St
Reno, NV 89512
www.kdot.com
Phone: 775-329-9261
Fax: 775-323-1450

KNIS-FM 91.3 MHz (Rel)
6363 Hwy 50 E
Carson City, NV 89701
Phone: 775-883-5647
Fax: 775-883-5704
TF: 800-541-5647

KODS-FM 103.7 MHz (Oldies)
300 E 2nd St 14th Fl
Reno, NV 89509
Phone: 775-829-1964
Fax: 775-825-3183

KOZZ-FM 105.7 MHz (CR)
2900 Sutro St
Reno, NV 89512
Phone: 775-329-9261
Fax: 775-323-1450

KPLY-AM 1270 kHz (Sports)
255 W Moana Ln Suite 208
Reno, NV 89509
Phone: 775-829-1964
Fax: 775-825-3183

KPTL-AM 1300 kHz (Oldies)
1960 Idaho St
Carson City, NV 89701
Phone: 775-884-8000
Fax: 775-882-3961

KRNO-FM 106.9 MHz (AC)
255 W Moana Ln Suite 208
Reno, NV 89509
Phone: 775-829-1964
Fax: 775-825-3183

KRZQ-FM 100.9 MHz (Alt)
300 E 2nd St
Reno, NV 89501
www.krzq.com
Phone: 775-333-0123
Fax: 775-333-0101

KTHX-FM 100.1 MHz (AAA)
300 E 3nd St 14th Fl
Reno, NV 89501
Phone: 775-333-0123
Fax: 775-333-0101

KUNR-FM 88.7 MHz (NPR)
University of Nevada MS-294
Reno, NV 89557
E-mail: kunr@unr.edu
www.kunr.org/
Phone: 775-784-1867
Fax: 775-784-1381

KWNZ-FM 97.3 MHz (CHR)
300 E 2nd St 14th Fl
Reno, NV 89501
www.kwnz.com
Phone: 775-829-1964
Fax: 775-333-0110

KZZF-FM 102.9 MHz (Oldies)
1960 Idaho
Carson City, NV 89701
Phone: 775-884-8000
Fax: 775-882-3961

Attractions

Since the opening of its first major casinos in 1935, gaming has become a favorite pastime at the many casinos of present-day Reno. "The Biggest Little Town in the World" sits between the slopes of the Sierra and the low eastern hills. Sierra trails provide hikers with a view of mountain forests, meadows, and scenic waterfalls. Southwest of Reno is Lake Tahoe, the largest alpine lake in North America. The Lake lies half in Nevada and half in California, and its size and amazing clarity make it ideal for all types of water sports. During the winter months, the Tahoe area is filled with visitors to its world-class alpine resorts. Reno is also home to more than 70 city parks, which offer a variety of outdoor recreational opportunities.

Animal Ark Wildlife Sanctuary & Nature Center
1265 Deerlodge Rd
Reno, NV 89506
Phone: 775-969-3111

Bowers Mansion
4005 Old Hwy 395
Washoe Valley, NV 89704
Phone: 775-849-0201

Brewery Arts Center
449 W King St
Carson City, NV 89703
E-mail: bac@powernet.net
www.breweryarts.org
Phone: 775-883-1976
Fax: 775-883-1922

Carson City Historical District
Carson City, NV
Phone: 775-687-7410

Carson City Symphony Orchestra
PO Box 2001
Carson City, NV 89702
Phone: 775-883-4154
Fax: 775-883-4371

Carson Hot Springs
1500 Hot Springs Rd
Carson City, NV 89706
Phone: 775-885-8844
Fax: 775-887-0617

Carson Valley Museum & Cultural Center
1477 Hwy 395
Gardnerville, NV 89410
Phone: 775-782-2555

Children's Museum of Northern Nevada
813 N Carson St
Carson City, NV 89701
www.cmnn.org
Phone: 775-884-2226
Fax: 775-884-2179

Fleischmann Planetarium The Space Place
University of Nevada
Reno, NV 89557
www.scs.unr.edu/planet/
Phone: 775-784-4811
Fax: 775-784-4822

Gothic North Theater
3697-A Kings Row
Reno, NV 89503
E-mail: info@gothic-north.org
www.gothic-north.org/
Phone: 775-329-7529

Historic Virginia City
Virginia City, NV
Phone: 775-847-0311
Fax: 775-847-0311

Lake Tahoe Nevada State Park
2005 Hwy 28
Incline Village, NV 89450
Phone: 775-831-0494
Fax: 775-831-2514

May Wilbur D Great Basin Adventure Park
1502 Washington St
Reno, NV 89503
Phone: 775-785-4153

National Automobile Museum
10 Lake St S
Reno, NV 89501
Phone: 775-333-9300
Fax: 775-333-9309

National Bowling Stadium
300 N Center St
Reno, NV 89501
bowl.renolaketahoe.com/main.html
Phone: 775-334-2600
Fax: 775-334-2606
TF: 800-304-2695

Nevada Gambling Museum
50 S 'C' St
Virginia City, NV 89440
Phone: 775-847-9022

Nevada Historical Society Museum
1650 N Virginia St
Reno, NV 89503
dmla.clan.lib.nv.us/docs/museums/reno/his-soc.htm
Phone: 775-688-1190
Fax: 775-688-2917

Nevada Museum of Art
160 W Liberty St
Reno, NV 89501
www.nevadaart.org
Phone: 775-329-3333
Fax: 775-329-1541

Nevada Opera Assn
PO Box 3256
Reno, NV 89505
Phone: 775-786-4046
Fax: 775-786-4063
TF: 800-992-2072

Nevada State Capitol
101 N Carson St
Carson City, NV 89701
Phone: 775-687-4811

Nevada State Library & Archives
100 N Stewart St
Carson City, NV 89701
dmla.clan.lib.nv.us/docs/nsla
Phone: 775-684-3360
Fax: 775-684-3330

Nevada State Museum
600 N Carson St
Carson City, NV 89701
dmla.clan.lib.nv.us/docs/museums/cc/carson.htm
Phone: 775-687-4810
Fax: 775-687-4168

Nevada State Railroad Museum
2180 S Carson St
Carson City, NV 89701
www.nsrm-friends.org
Phone: 775 687 6953
Fax: 775-687-8294

Ponderosa Ranch
100 Ponderosa Ranch Rd
Incline Village, NV 89451
www.ponderosaranch.com
Phone: 775-831-0691
Fax: 775-831-0113

Reno Municipal Band
PO Box 1900
Reno, NV 89502
www.sierrasource.com/RenoMunicipalBand/
Phone: 775-789-2878

Reno Philharmonic
300 S Wells Ave Suite 5
Reno, NV 89502
www.renophilharmonic.com
Phone: 775-323-6393
Fax: 775-323-6711

Roberts House Museum
1207 N Carson St
Carson City, NV 89701
Phone: 775-887-2174
Fax: 775-882-3559

Sierra Safari Zoo
10200 N Virginia St
Reno, NV 89506
Phone: 775-677-1101
Fax: 775-677-7874

Stewart Indian School Museum
5366 Snyder Ave
Carson City, NV 89701
Phone: 775-882-6929
Fax: 775-882-6929

Truckee River Walk
1st & Arlington Sts
Reno, NV 89501
Phone: 775-334-2262

Victorian Square
15th St & Pyramid Way
Sparks, NV 89431
Phone: 775-353-2291

Warren Engine Co No 1 Fire Museum
777 S Stewart St
Carson City, NV 89701
Phone: 775-887-2210
Fax: 775-887-2209

Washoe Lake State Recreation Area
4855 E Lake Blvd
Carson City, NV 89704
Phone: 775-687-4319
Fax: 775-684-8053

Way It Was Museum
113 N 'C' St & Sutton Ave
Virginia City, NV 89440
Phone: 775-847-0766

Western Nevada Musical Theater
2201 W College Pkwy Western Nevada Community College
Carson City, NV 89703
www.wncc.nevada.edu/asde/theater1.html
Phone: 775-887-3115
Fax: 775-887-3154

Wilbur D May Museum & Arboretum/ Botanical Gardens
1502 Washington St
Reno, NV 89503
Phone: 775-785-5961
Fax: 775-785-4707

Wild Island
250 Wild Island Ct
Sparks, NV 89434
www.wildisland.com
Phone: 775-331-9453
Fax: 775-359-5942

Sports Teams & Facilities

Nevada Zephyrs (soccer)
1331 E Plumb Ln Wooster High School Stadium
Reno, NV 89502
Phone: 775-826-7487
Fax: 775-826-1508

Annual Events

A Taste of Downtown (late June) .775-883-7654
Beer Tasting & Auction (early November) .775-883-1976
Best in the West Rib Cook-off (late August-early September) .775-356-3300
Big Easy (mid-July) .775-332-3333
Carson City IRPA Rodeo (early July) .775-577-9427
Carson City Mint/Nevada State Museum Coin Show (mid-September) .775-687-6953
Carson City Rendezvous (early June) .775-687-7410
Carson Valley Days (early June) .775-782-8144
Carson Valley Street Celebration (mid-September) .775-782-8144
Celebrate the River (early June) .775-827-7600
Celtic New Year Celebration (mid-October) .775-323-3138
Christmas on the Comstock (December) .775-847-0311
Christmas Tree Lighting (early December) .775-882-1565
Cinco de Mayo Chili Cook Off (early May) .775-847-0311
Comstock Historic Preservation Week (mid-May) .775-847-0311
Cowboy Jubilee & Poetry (early March) .775-883-1532
Eagle Valley Muzzleloaders Spring Rendevous (late April) .775-887-1221
Far West Regional Wheelchair Tennis Championship (mid-June) .775-852-7077
Farmers Market (June-August) .775-687-7410
Father's Day Pow Wow/Arts & Crafts Show (mid-June) .775-882-6929
Festival of Trees (early-late December) .775-827-7600
Great Italian Festival (mid-October) .775-786-5700
Great Reno Balloon Race (early September) .775-826-1181
High Desert Jazz Festival (mid-October) .775-883-1976
Hometown Farmers Market (mid-June-late August) .775-353-2291
Hot August Nights (early August) .775-356-1956
July 4th Celebration Week (late June-early July) .775-687-4680
Kit Carson Rendezvous & Wagon Train (mid-June) .775-884-3633
Kit Carson Trail Ghost Walk (late October) .775-687-7410
Kit Carson Trail Historic Home Tour (mid-June) .775-687-7410
Kit Carson Trail Walk (late May-late October) .775-687-7410
La Ka L'el Be Pow Wow (late October) .775-265-4191
Lake Tahoe Marathon (early October) .530-544-7095
Lake Tahoe Shakespeare Festival (late July-late August) .800-747-4697
Mother Earth Awakening Pow Wow (mid-March) .775-882-6929
Multi-Cultural Festival (mid-April) .775-887-3060
National Championship Air Races (mid-September) .775-972-6663
National Senior Pro Rodeo Finals (early-mid-November) .775-323-8842
Nevada Day Celebration (late October) .775-882-2600
Nevada Day Parade (October 31) .800-367-7366
Nevada State Fair (late August) .775-688-5767
Nevada State Railroad Museum's Transportation Fair (early July) .775-687-6953
Outdoor Movie Film Festival (July-August) .775-687-6953
Pony Express Re-ride (mid-June) .775-882-1283
Pops Party Concert (mid-June) .775-882-1565
Reno Basque Festival (late July) .775-329-1476
Reno Rodeo (mid-June) .775-329-3877
Reno Summer Arts Festival (July) .775-329-1324
Robert's House Antique Sale (May-early October) .775-882-1805
Rsvp Spring Fun Fair (late April-early May) .775-687-4680
Run What You Brung Classic Car Show (late June) .775-882-0829
Shakespeare at Sand Harbor (August) .775-831-0494
Silver & Snowflake Festival of Lights (November) .775-882-1565
Silver Dollar Car Classic (late July-early August) .775-687-7410
Silver State Marathon (late August) .775-849-0419
Skyfire (July 4) .775-332-3333
Sparks Hometown Christmas (early December) .775-353-2291
Stewart Indian School Museum Arts & Crafts Festival & Pow Wow (mid-June) .775-882-6929
Street Vibrations (late September) .775-329-7469
Uptown Downtown Artown Festival (July) .775-334-2536
Victorian Christmas Home Tour (mid-December) .775-882-1805
Virginia City Camel Races (mid-September) .775-847-0311
Virginia City Rodeo (late July) .775-847-0311
Wa She Shudeh Pow Wow (late July) .775-265-4191
Winter Wine & All That Jazz (mid-January) .775-687-7410

Richmond, Virginia

***County:* Independent City**

RICHMOND is located in south central Virginia on the James River. Major cities within 100 miles include Charlottesville, Fredericksburg, Norfolk, and Williamsburg, Virginia; and Washington, DC.

Area (Land) .... 60.1 sq mi
Area (Water)............................... 2.5 sq mi
Elevation.................................... 150 ft
Latitude ....37-55-36 N
Longitude............................... 77-46-06 W
Time Zone ....EST
Area Code...................................... 804

Climate

Richmond has a continental climate with mild winters and warm summers. Winter daytime high temperatures average around 50 degrees and lows average around 30. The average annual snowfall is just over 14 inches. Summer days are very warm, with average high temperatures in the mid-to-upper 80s, but evenings cool down into the 60s. Summer is the rainy season in Richmond, with July and August being the wettest months of the year.

Average Temperatures & Precipitation

Temperatures

	Jan	Feb	Mar	Apr	May	Jun	Jul	Aug	Sep	Oct	Nov	Dec
High	46	49	60	70	78	85	88	87	81	71	61	50
Low	26	28	36	45	54	63	68	66	59	47	38	30

Precipitation

	Jan	Feb	Mar	Apr	May	Jun	Jul	Aug	Sep	Oct	Nov	Dec
Inches	3.2	3.2	3.6	3.0	3.8	3.6	5.0	4.4	3.3	3.5	3.2	3.3

History

Originally inhabited by tribes of the Powhatan Confederacy, the Richmond area was discovered in 1607 by English Captain Christopher Newport. During the 1630s, the first permanent white settlement was established at the falls of the James River, and in 1644 Fort Charles was built to protect the new settlement from Indian attacks. In the years that followed, the area grew quickly as a major inland trading post. The town of Richmond, named for Richmond-upon-Thames, England, was founded in 1737 by Colonel William Byrd II and was incorporated as a city in 1742. Patrick Henry's famous "Give me liberty or give me death" speech, given at Richmond's Saint John's Church in 1775, was one of many key events of the American Revolution that took place in the city. During the early 1780s, Richmond became the state capital of Virginia.

Richmond played a key role in the Civil War as the capital of the Confederate States of America under the leadership of Jefferson Davis. In 1865, however, much of Richmond was evacuated and burned by Confederate forces, and the city was eventually occupied by General Ulysses S. Grant and his Union troops. In the years that followed the Civil War, Richmond was quickly rebuilt with the aid of northern capital. During the early 20th century, Richmond grew and prospered as a major inland trade center and one of the country's largest producers of tobacco.

Today, Richmond is the financial, commercial, and manufacturing center of the state of Virginia, with more than 25 major U.S. companies headquartered in the area. Home to more than 194,000 people, Richmond is Virginia's fourth largest city.

Population

1990 Census 202,798
1998 Estimate.............................194,173
% Change ....-4.3
2005 Projection 1,003,000*

Racial/Ethnic Breakdown
White.................................... 43.4%
Black 55.3%
Other 1.3%
Hispanic Origin (may be of any race) 0.9%

Age Breakdown
Under 5 years.............................. 6.9%
5 to 17.................................. 13.8%
18 to 20.................................. 5.6%
21 to 24.................................. 7.8%
25 to 34................................. 19.2%
35 to 44................................. 14.3%
45 to 54.................................. 8.6%
55 to 64.................................. 8.5%
65 to 74.................................. 8.3%
75+ years 7.0%
Median Age.................................33.2

Gender Breakdown
Male..................................... 45.8%
Female.................................. 54.2%

** Information given is for the Richmond-Petersburg Metropolitan Statistical Area (MSA), which includes the City of Richmond, as well as Charles City, Chesterfield, Dunwiddie, Goochland, Hanover, Henrico, New Kent, Powhatan, and Prince George counties.*

Government

Type of Government: Council-Manager

Richmond City Attorney
900 E Broad St Rm 300
Richmond, VA 23219
Phone: 804-646-7940
Fax: 804-646-6653

Richmond City Clerk
900 E Broad St Rm 200
Richmond, VA 23219
Phone: 804-764-6795
Fax: 804-646-7736

Richmond City Council
900 E Broad St Suite 200
Richmond, VA 23219
Phone: 804-646-7955
Fax: 804-646-7736

Richmond City Hall
900 E Broad St
Richmond, VA 23219
Phone: 804-780-7000

Richmond City Manager
900 E Broad Rm 201
Richmond, VA 23219
Phone: 804-646-7970
Fax: 804-646-7987

Richmond Economic Development Office
900 E Broad St Rm 305
Richmond, VA 23219
Phone: 804-780-5633
Fax: 804-780-6793

Richmond Finance Dept
900 E Broad St Rm 1003
Richmond, VA 23219
Phone: 804-646-5829
Fax: 804-646-6388

Richmond Fire Dept
501 N 9th St Rm 131
Richmond, VA 23219
Phone: 804-646-6663
Fax: 804-646-6671

Richmond Human Resources & Employee Relations Dept
900 E Broad St 9th Fl
Richmond, VA 23219
Phone: 804-646-5900
Fax: 804-646-6856

Richmond Mayor
900 E Broad St Suite 201
Richmond, VA 23219
Phone: 804-780-7977
Fax: 804-698-3027

Richmond Parks Recreation & Community Facilities Dept
900 E Broad St 4th Fl
Richmond, VA 23219
Phone: 804-646-5717
Fax: 804-646-7712

Richmond Police Dept
501 N 9th St
Richmond, VA 23219
Phone: 804-646-6700
Fax: 804-646-3974

Richmond Public Library
101 E Franklin St
Richmond, VA 23219
Phone: 804-646-4256
Fax: 804-646-7685

Richmond Public Utilities Dept
600 E Broad St Rm 831
Richmond, VA 23219
Phone: 804-646-5200
Fax: 804-646-2870

Richmond Public Works Dept
600 E Broad St 7th Fl
Richmond, VA 23219
Phone: 804-646-6430
Fax: 804-646-6629

Richmond Treasurer
900 E Broad St Rm 107
Richmond, VA 23219
Phone: 804-646-6474
Fax: 804-646-3904

Important Phone Numbers

AAA........804-285-8912
American Express Travel........804-740-2030
Driver's License/Vehicle Registration Information...804-367-0538
Emergency........911
Medical Referral........804-643-6631
Poison Control Center........804-828-9123
Richmond Assn of Realtors........804-358-5358
Richmond Real Estate Tax Information........804-646-5700
Richmond Tax Information........804-646-5700
Travelers Aid........804-643-0279
Virginia Dept of Taxation........804-367-8031
Voter Registration Information........804-780-5950
Weather........804-348-9382

Information Sources

Better Business Bureau Serving Central Virginia
701 E Franklin St Suite 712
Richmond, VA 23219
www.richmond.bbb.org
Phone: 804-648-0016
Fax: 804-648-3115

Greater Richmond Chamber of Commerce
201 E Franklin St
Richmond, VA 23219
www.grcc.com
Phone: 804-648-1234
Fax: 804-780-0344

Metropolitan Richmond Convention & Visitors Bureau
550 E Marshall St
Richmond, VA 23219
richmondva.org
Phone: 804-782-2777
Fax: 804-780-2577
TF: 800-370-9004

Richmond (Independent City)
900 E Broad St Rm 201
Richmond, VA 23219
www.ci.richmond.va.us
Phone: 804-780-7970
Fax: 804-646-7987

Richmond Center
400 E Marshall St
Richmond, VA 23219
www.richmondcenter.com
Phone: 804-783-7300
Fax: 804-225-0508
TF: 800-370-9004

Online Resources

4Richmond.com
www.4richmond.com

About.com Guide to Richmond
richmond.about.com/local/southeastus/richmond

Anthill City Guide Richmond
www.anthill.com/city.asp?city=richmondva

Area Guide Richmond
richmond.areaguides.net

City Knowledge Richmond
www.cityknowledge.com/va_richmond.htm

CitySearch Richmond
richmond.citysearch.com

DigitalCity Richmond
home.digitalcity.com/richmond

Essential Guide to Richmond
www.ego.net/us/va/ric

Excite.com Richmond City Guide
www.excite.com/travel/countries/united_states/virginia/richmond

Guest Guide Online
www.guestguideonline.com

Guide to Historic Richmond
freenet.vcu.edu/tourism/histrich/histrich.html

InRichmond.com
www.inrichmond.com

Insiders' Guide to Richmond
www.insiders.com/richmond-va/

Metro-Web Richmond
www.metro-web.com

Richmond Online
www.richmond-online.com/directory/

Style Weekly Online
www.styleweekly.com

Virtual Richmond
virtual-richmond.com/

Area Communities

Incorporated communities in the Richmond area with populations greater than 15,000 include:

Colonial Heights
PO Box 3401
Colonial Heights, VA 23834
Phone: 804-520-9265
Fax: 804-520-9338

Hopewell
300 N Main St
Hopewell, VA 23860
Phone: 804-541-2243
Fax: 804-541-2248

Petersburg
135 N Union St
Petersburg, VA 23803
Phone: 804-733-2323
Fax: 804-732-9212

Economy

Richmond is considered the commercial, financial, and manufacturing center of Virginia. Eight Fortune 500 companies, including CSX, Reynolds Metals, and Richfood Holdings are headquartered in Richmond. The three largest employment sectors in the Richmond metropolitan area are services, public administration, and retail trade. In addition to the major employers listed below, state and federal government rank number one and number five respectively, employing nearly 42,000 area residents in various departments. In Employment Review Magazine's 2000 poll, Greater Richmond was ranked as one of the top 20 best places to live and work in America.

Unemployment Rate	2.1%*
Per Capita Income	$28,635*
Median Family Income	$57,400*

** Information given is for the Richmond-Petersburg Metropolitan Statistical Area (MSA), which includes the City of Richmond, as well as Charles City, Chesterfield, Dunwiddie, Goochland, Hanover, Henrico, New Kent, Powhatan, and Prince George counties.*

Principal Industries & Number of Wage Earners

Richmond-Petersburg MSA* - 3rd Quarter 1999

Agriculture	3,745
Construction	34,557
Finance, Insurance, & Real Estate	48,178
Manufacturing	60,338
Mining	865
Retail Trade	96,280
Services	138,832
Transportation & Communications	27,270
Wholesale Trade	30,847

** Information given is for the Richmond-Petersburg Metropolitan Statistical Area (MSA), which includes the City of Richmond, as well as Charles City, Chesterfield, Dunwiddie, Goochland, Hanover, Henrico, New Kent, Powhatan, and Prince George counties.*

Major Employers

Cadmus Communications Corp
6620 W Broad St Suite 240
Richmond, VA 23230
E-mail: sales@cadmus.com
www.cadmus.com
Phone: 804-287-5680
Fax: 804-287-6267
TF: 800-476-2973

Capital One Bank
11013 W Broad St
Glen Allen, VA 23060
www.capitalone.com
Phone: 804-967-1000
Fax: 804-967-1220
TF: 800-955-7070

Circuit City Stores Inc
9950 Mayland Dr
Richmond, VA 23233
Phone: 804-527-4000
Fax: 804-967-2924
TF: 800-251-2665

Columbia/HCA Healthcare Corp
9100 Arboretum Pkwy Suite 140
Richmond, VA 23236
Phone: 804-327-7600
Fax: 804-330-4039

Defense Supply Center Richmond
8000 Jefferson Davis Hwy
Richmond, VA 23297
www.dscr.dla.mil/
Phone: 804-279-3861
Fax: 804-279-3575

Dominion Resources Inc
120 Tredegar St
Richmond, VA 23219
E-mail: dominion_resources@domres.com
www.domres.com
Phone: 800-552-4034
Fax: 804-819-2208

DuPont Advanced Fibers Systems
5401 Jefferson Davis Hwy PO Box 27001
Richmond, VA 23234
Phone: 804-383-2000

Heilig-Meyers Co
12560 W Creek Pkwy
Richmond, VA 23238
www.heiligmeyers.com
Phone: 804-784-7300
Fax: 804-784-7912

Honeywell Inc
PO Box 761
Hopewell, VA 23860
www.honeywell.com/careers
Phone: 804-541-5000
Fax: 804-541-5108

Medical College of Virginia Hospitals
Virginia Commonwealth University
PO Box 980510
Richmond, VA 23298
www.mcvh.org
Phone: 804-828-4682
Fax: 804-828-0170

Philip Morris USA Phone: 804-274-2000
PO Box 26603
Richmond, VA 23261
www.philipmorrisusa.com/careers

Richmond City Hall Phone: 804-780-7000
900 E Broad St
Richmond, VA 23219
www.ci.richmond.va.us

Trigon Blue Cross & Blue Shield Phone: 804-354-7000
2015 Staples Mill Rd Fax: 804-354-3835
Richmond, VA 23279 TF: 800-451-1527
E-mail: service@trigon.com
www.trigon.com/About/ss_bcbs2.htm

Ukrop's Super Markets Inc Phone: 804-379-7300
600 Southlake Blvd Fax: 804-794-7557
Richmond, VA 23236 TF: 800-868-2270
E-mail: ukrops@mindspring.com
www.ukrops.com

Virginia Commonwealth University Phone: 804-828-0100
907 Floyd Ave Fax: 804-828-1899
Richmond, VA 23284 TF: 800-841-3638
E-mail: vcuinfo@vcu.edu
www.vcu.edu

Quality of Living Indicators

Total Crime Index....................................15,564
(rates per 100,000 inhabitants)

Violent Crime
Murder/manslaughter........................... 72
Forcible rape 111
Robbery....................................1,035
Aggravated assault...........................1,026

Property Crime
Burglary 2,880
Larceny theft 8,339
Motor vehicle theft 2,101

Cost of Living Index..................................105.9
(national average = 100)

Median Home Price.................................$128,500

Education

Public Schools

Richmond City Public Schools Phone: 804-780-7700
301 N 9th St Fax: 804-780-4122
Richmond, VA 23219

Number of Schools
Elementary.................................. 32
Middle 10
High.. 9

Student/Teacher Ratio
All Grades 15.9:1

Private Schools

Number of Schools (all grades)..................... 58

Colleges & Universities

Bryant & Stratton Career College Richmond Phone: 804-745-2444
8141 Hull St Rd Fax: 804-745-6884
Richmond, VA 23235
www.bryantstratton.edu/main/campusdesc/rich.htm

J Sargeant Reynolds Community College Phone: 804-371-3000
PO Box 85622 Fax: 804-371-3650
Richmond, VA 23285
www.jsr.cc.va.us

Randolph-Macon College Phone: 804-798-8372
PO Box 5005 Fax: 804-752-4707
Ashland, VA 23005
www.rmc.edu

University of Richmond Phone: 804-289-8000
Richmond, VA 23173 Fax: 804-287-6003
www.urich.edu TF: 800-700-1662

Virginia Commonwealth University Phone: 804-828-0100
907 Floyd Ave Fax: 804-828-1899
Richmond, VA 23284 TF: 800-841-3638
E-mail: vcuinfo@vcu.edu
www.vcu.edu

Virginia State University Phone: 804-524-5000
1 Haydens Dr Fax: 804-524-5055
Petersburg, VA 23806 TF: 800-871-7611
E-mail: vsuadmin@vsu.edu
www.vsu.edu/

Virginia Union University Phone: 804-257-5600
1500 N Lombardy St Fax: 804-257-5818
Richmond, VA 23220 TF: 800-368-3227
www.vuu.edu

Hospitals

Bon Secours Saint Mary's Hospital Phone: 804-285-2011
5801 Bremo Rd Fax: 804-673-2230
Richmond, VA 23226

Bon Secours Stuart Circle Phone: 804-358-7051
413 Stuart Circle Fax: 804-354-1286
Richmond, VA 23220

Capitol Medical Center Phone: 804-775-4100
701 W Grace St Fax: 804-775-2557
Richmond, VA 23220

Children's Medical Center Phone: 804-828-9602
PO Box 980646 Fax: 804-828-6455
Richmond, VA 23298 TF: 800-828-1120

HCA Chippenham Medical Center Phone: 804-320-3911
7101 Jahnke Rd Fax: 804-323-8049
Richmond, VA 23225

HealthSouth Medical Center Phone: 804-747-5600
7700 E Parham Rd Fax: 804-527-5840
Richmond, VA 23294
www.healthsouth-richmond.com

Henrico Doctor's Hospital
1602 Skipwith Rd
Richmond, VA 23229
Phone: 804-289-4500
Fax: 804-287-4329

Hunter Holmes McGuire Veterans Affairs Medical Center
1201 Broad Rock Blvd
Richmond, VA 23249
Phone: 804-675-5000
Fax: 804-675-5539
TF: 800-784-8381

Johnston-Willis Hospital
1401 Johnston Willis Dr
Richmond, VA 23235
Phone: 804-330-2000
Fax: 804-330-2158

Medical College of Virginia Hospitals Virginia Commonwealth University
PO Box 980510
Richmond, VA 23298
www.mcvh.org
Phone: 804-828-4682
Fax: 804-828-0170

Memorial Regional Medical Center
8260 Atlee Rd
Mechanicsville, VA 23116
Phone: 804-764-6000
Fax: 804-764-6945

Retreat Hospital
2621 Grove Ave
Richmond, VA 23220
Phone: 804-254-5100
Fax: 804-254-5246

Richmond Community Hospital
1500 N 28th St
Richmond, VA 23223
Phone: 804-225-1700
Fax: 804-649-3311

Southside Regional Medical Center
801 S Adams St
Petersburg, VA 23803
Phone: 804-862-5000
Fax: 804-862-5948

Transportation

Airport(s)

Richmond International Airport (RIC)
5 miles E of downtown (approx 15 minutes) 804-226-3052

Mass Transit

Greater Richmond Transit
$1.25 Base fare 804-358-4782

Rail/Bus

Amtrak Station
7519 Staples Mill Rd
Richmond, VA 23228
Phone: 804-553-2903
TF: 800-872-7245

Greyhound Bus Station
2910 North Blvd
Richmond, VA 23230
Phone: 804-254-5910
TF: 800-231-2222

Utilities

Electricity
Virginia Power 804-771-3000
www.vapower.com

Gas
Richmond Dept of Public Utilities 804-644-3000
www.ci.richmond.va.us/dpu/index.htm

Water
Richmond Dept of Public Utilities 804-644-3000
www.ci.richmond.va.us/dpu/index.htm

Garbage Collection/Recycling
Richmond Trash Collection/Recycling Coordinator 804-646-0999

Telecommunications

Telephone
Verizon Communications 804-954-6222
www.verizon.com

Cable Television
AT & T Cable Services 804-266-1900

Internet Service Providers (ISPs)
i2020 Div Electron Systems of Richmond 804-649-1800
www.i2020.net
New Quest Communications Inc 804-452-2638
www.new-quest.net
Techcom Inc 804-861-9866
www.techcom.net

Banks

SunTrust Bank
PO Box 26665
Richmond, VA 23261
Phone: 804-782-5000
Fax: 804-782-5566

F & M Bank
9401 W Broad St
Richmond, VA 23294
Phone: 804-346-8080
Fax: 804-346-8723

First Union National Bank
800 E Main St
Richmond, VA 23219
Phone: 804-771-7008
Fax: 804-698-5472
TF: 800-275-3862

First Virginia Bank Colonial
700 E Main St
Richmond, VA 23219
Phone: 804-697-5200
Fax: 804-697-5261
TF: 800-382-4115

NationsBank
111 E Main St
Richmond, VA 23219
Phone: 804-788-2251
Fax: 804-788-3688

Wachovia Bank NA
1021 E Cary St
Richmond, VA 23219
Phone: 804-697-6710
Fax: 804-697-6717

Shopping

17th Street Market
17th & Cary Sts Shockoe Slip area
Richmond, VA 23219

6th Street Marketplace
550 E Broad St
Richmond, VA 23219
Phone: 804-648-6600
Fax: 804-788-0454

Antique Village
10203 Chamberlayne Rd
Mechanicsville, VA 23116
Phone: 804-746-8914

Carytown
Cary & Boulevard Sts
Richmond, VA 23220

Chesterfield Towne Center
11500 Midlothian Tpke
Richmond, VA 23235
Phone: 804-794-4660
Fax: 804-379-7661

Cloverleaf Mall
7201 Midlothian Tpke
Richmond, VA 23225
Phone: 804-276-8650
Fax: 804-276-7965

Fairfield Commons
4869 Nine Mile Rd
Richmond, VA 23223
Phone: 804-222-4167
Fax: 804-226-2510

Regency Square Mall
1420 Parham Rd
Richmond, VA 23229
Phone: 804-740-7467
Fax: 804-741-4763

Shockoe Slip
E Cary St
Richmond, VA 23219

Sycamore Square Shopping Village
Midlothian Tpke & Sycamore Square Dr
Midlothian, VA 23113
Phone: 804-320-7600
Fax: 804-330-8924

Media

Newspapers and Magazines

Richmond Times-Dispatch*
333 E Franklin St
Richmond, VA 23219
www.timesdispatch.com
Phone: 804-649-6000
Fax: 804-775-8059

Style Weekly
1118 W Main St
Richmond, VA 23220
E-mail: comments@myrichmond.com
www.myrichmond.com/styleweekly
Phone: 804-358-0825
Fax: 804-355-9089

Virginia Business Magazine
411 E Franklin St Suite 105
Richmond, VA 23219
virginiabusiness.com
Phone: 804-649-6999
Fax: 804-649-6311

**Indicates major daily newspapers*

Television

WCVE-TV Ch 23 (PBS)
23 Sesame St
Richmond, VA 23235
www.wcve.org/TV23-Frame1.HTM
Phone: 804-320-1301
Fax: 804-320-8729

WRIC-TV Ch 8 (ABC)
301 Arboretum Pl
Richmond, VA 23236
www.wric.com
Phone: 804-330-8888
Fax: 804-330-8883

WRLH-TV Ch 35 (Fox)
1925 Westmoreland St
Richmond, VA 23230
E-mail: fox35@fox35.com
www.fox35.com
Phone: 804-358-3535
Fax: 804-358-1495

WTVR-TV Ch 6 (CBS)
3301 W Broad St
Richmond, VA 23230
www.newschannel6.com
Phone: 804-254-3600
Fax: 804-254-3697

WUPV-TV Ch 65 (UPN)
3914 Wistar Rd
Richmond, VA 23228
Phone: 804-672-6565
Fax: 804-672-6571

WWBT-TV Ch 12 (NBC)
5710 Midlothian Tpke
Richmond, VA 23225
www.nbc12.com
Phone: 804-230-1212
Fax: 804-230-2793

Radio

WBBT-FM 107.3 MHz (Oldies)
300 Arboretum Pl Suite 595
Richmond, VA 23236
Phone: 804-327-9902
Fax: 804-327-9911

WCDX-FM 92.1 MHz (Urban)
2809 Emerywood Pkwy Suite 300
Richmond, VA 23294
www.power92jamz.com
Phone: 804-672-9299
Fax: 804-672-9314

WCVE-FM 88.9 MHz (NPR)
23 Sesame St
Richmond, VA 23235
E-mail: pr-radio@wcve.org
www.wcve.org/88-Frame1.HTM
Phone: 804-320-1301
Fax: 804-320-8729

WFTH-AM 1590 kHz (Rel)
227 E Belt Blvd
Richmond, VA 23224
Phone: 804-233-0765
Fax: 804-233-3725

WGCV-AM 1240 kHz (Rel)
4301 W Hundred Rd
Chester, VA 23831
Phone: 804-717-2000
Fax: 804-717-2009

WJRV-FM 105.7 MHz (Ctry)
2809 Emerywood Pkwy Suite 300
Richmond, VA 23294
Phone: 804-672-9299
Fax: 804-672-9314

WKHK-FM 95.3 MHz (Ctry)
812 Moorefield Park Dr Suite 300
Richmond, VA 23236
www.k95country.com
Phone: 804-330-5700
Fax: 804-330-4079

WKJS-FM 104.7 MHz (Urban)
2809 Emerywood Pkwy Suite 300
Richmond, VA 23294
Phone: 804-672-9299
Fax: 804-672-9314

WKLR-FM 96.5 MHz (CR)
812 Moorefield Park Dr Suite 300
Richmond, VA 23236
www.965theplanet.com
Phone: 804-330-7123
Fax: 804-330-4079

WLEE-AM 990 kHz (Sports)
306 W Broad St
Richmond, VA 23220
www.wlee990.com
Phone: 804-643-0990
Fax: 804-643-4990

WMXB-FM 103.7 MHz (AC)
812 Moorefield Park Dr Suite 300
Richmond, VA 23236
www.richmondsb103.com
Phone: 804-560-1037
Fax: 804-330-4079

WPLZ-FM 99.3 MHz (Oldies)
2809 Emerywood Pkwy Suite 300
Richmond, VA 23294
Phone: 804-672-9299
Fax: 804-672-9314

WRCL-FM 106.5 MHz (Oldies)
812 Moorefield Park Dr Suite 300
Richmond, VA 23236
Phone: 804-330-5700
Fax: 804-330-4079

WREJ-AM 1540 kHz (Rel)
6001 Wilkinson Rd
Richmond, VA 23227
Phone: 804-264-1047
Fax: 804-264-1245

WRNL-AM 910 kHz (Sports)
200 N 22nd St
Richmond, VA 23223
E-mail: sports@wrnl.com
www.wrnl.com
Phone: 804-780-3400
Fax: 804-780-3427

WRVA-AM 1140 kHz (N/T)
200 N 22nd St
Richmond, VA 23223
www.wrva.com
Phone: 804-780-3400
Fax: 804-780-3427

WRVQ-FM 94.5 MHz (CHR)
3245 Basie Rd
Richmond, VA 23228
E-mail: qmail@wrvq94.com
www.wrvq94.com
Phone: 804-576-3200
Fax: 804-576-3222

WRXL-FM 102.1 MHz (Rock)
3245 Basie Rd
Richmond, VA 23228
www.wrxl.com
Phone: 804-756-6400
Fax: 804-756-6444

WTVR-AM 1380 kHz (Nost)
3314 Cutshaw Ave
Richmond, VA 23230
Phone: 804-355-3217
Fax: 804-355-8682

WTVR-FM 98.1 MHz (AC)
3314 Cutshaw Ave
Richmond, VA 23230
E-mail: comments@lite98.com
www.lite98.com
Phone: 804-355-3217
Fax: 804-355-8682

WXGI-AM 950 kHz (Ctry)
701 German School Rd
Richmond, VA 23225
www.wxgi.com
Phone: 804-233-7666
Fax: 804-233-7681

Attractions

Thomas Jefferson designed the State Capitol Building in Richmond, which was built in 1785, and it was here that Aaron Burr was tried for treason, the Articles of Secession were ratified, Robert E. Lee became commander of the Virginia Army, and the Confederate Congress held its meetings. Patrick Henry's "Give me liberty..." speech was given in Richmond's Church Hill Historic Area, which is also the site of the Edgar Allen Poe Museum. Other historic sites in Richmond include the home of former Supreme Court Justice John Marshall and the Museum of the Confederacy.

Agecroft Hall
4305 Sulgrave Rd
Richmond, VA 23221
E-mail: agecroft@aol.com
www.agecrofthall.com
Phone: 804-353-4241
Fax: 804-353-2151

American Historical Foundation Museum
1142 W Grace St
Richmond, VA 23220
Phone: 804-353-1812
Fax: 804-359-4895
TF: 800-368-8080

Anderson Gallery
Virginia Commonwealth University 907 1/2 W Franklin St
Richmond, VA 23284
Phone: 804-828-1522
Fax: 804-828-8585

Annabel Lee
4400 E Main St Intermediate Terminal
Richmond, VA 23223
www.annabellee.com
Phone: 804-644-5700
Fax: 804-644-5760
TF: 800-752-7093

Appomattox Court House National Historical Park
PO Box 218
Appomattox, VA 24522
www.nps.gov/apco/
Phone: 804-352-8987
Fax: 804-352-8330

Barksdale Theatre
1601 Willow Lawn Dr Suite 301E
Richmond, VA 23230
E-mail: barksdalev@aol.com
Phone: 804-282-2620
Fax: 804-288-6470

Beth Ahabah Museum & Archives
1109 W Franklin St
Richmond, VA 23220
Phone: 804-353-2668
Fax: 804-358-3451

Black History Museum & Cultural Center of Virginia
00 Clay St
Richmond, VA 23219
members.spree.com/education/bhmv
Phone: 804-780-9093
Fax: 804-780-9107

Capitol Square
9th & Grace Sts
Richmond, VA 23219
Phone: 804-698-1788

Carpenter Center for the Performing Arts
600 E Grace St
Richmond, VA 23219
www.chp2001.com/carpentercenter/index.html
Phone: 804-225-9000
Fax: 804-649-7402

Chesterfield Museum
10201 Iron Bridge Rd
Chesterfield, VA 23832
Phone: 804-777-9663
Fax: 804-777-9643

Children's Museum of Richmond
2626 W Broad St
Richmond, VA 23220
Phone: 804-474-7000
Fax: 804-474-7099
TF: 877-295-2667

Church Hill Historic District
E Broad & E Main Sts
Richmond, VA 23223

City Hall Observation Deck
900 E Broad St
Richmond, VA 23219
Phone: 804-646-5990
Fax: 804-646-4902

Edgar Allan Poe Museum
1914-16 E Main St
Richmond, VA 23223
E-mail: peomuseum@erols.com
www.poemuseum.org/
Phone: 804-648-5523
Fax: 804-648-8729
TF: 888-213-2763

Ethyl IMAX Dome & Planetarium
2500 W Broad St
Richmond, VA 23220
www.smv.org/ethyl/index.html
Phone: 804-367-6552
Fax: 804-367-9348
TF: 800-659-1727

Fan The & Monument Ave
Monument Ave Belvidere St & The Blvd
Richmond, VA

Federal Reserve Bank of Richmond
701 E Byrd St
Richmond, VA 23219
www.rich.frb.org
Phone: 804-697-8000
Fax: 804-697-8490

Fredericksburg & Spotsylvania National Military Park
120 Chatham Ln
Fredericksburg, VA 22405
www.nps.gov/frsp/
Phone: 540-371-0802
Fax: 540-371-1907

Ginter Lewis Botanical Garden
1800 Lakeside Ave
Richmond, VA 23228
Phone: 804-262-9887
Fax: 804-262-9934

Governor's Mansion
Capitol Sq
Richmond, VA 23219
Phone: 804-371-2642

Hollywood Cemetery
Albemarle & Cherry Sts
Richmond, VA 23220
Phone: 804-648-8501
Fax: 804-644-7345

Landmark Theater
6 N Laurel St
Richmond, VA 23220
Phone: 804-646-4213
Fax: 804-646-6101

Maggie L Walker National Historic Site
600 N 2nd St
Richmond, VA 23219
www.nps.gov/malw/
Phone: 804-771-2017
Fax: 804-771-2226

Marshall John House
818 E Marshall St
Richmond, VA 23219
Phone: 804-648-7998

Maymont
1700 Hampton St
Richmond, VA 23220
www.maymont.org
Phone: 804-358-7166
Fax: 804-358-9994

Meadow Farm Museum
3400 Mountain Rd General Sheppard Crump Memorial Pk
Glen Allen, VA 23060
E-mail: henrec@co.henrico.va.us
www.co.henrico.va.us/rec/kmfarm.htm
Phone: 804-501-5520
Fax: 804-501-5284

Museum of the Confederacy
1201 E Clay St
Richmond, VA 23219
E-mail: info@moc.org
www.moc.org
Phone: 804-649-1861
Fax: 804-644-7150

Old Dominion Railway Museum
102 Hull St
Richmond, VA 23224
Phone: 804-233-6237

Paramount's Kings Dominion
16000 Theme Pkwy
Doswell, VA 23047
www.kingsdominion.com
Phone: 804-876-5000
Fax: 804-876-5864

Petersburg National Battlefield
1539 Hickory Hill Rd
Petersburg, VA 23803
www.nps.gov/pete/
Phone: 804-732-3531
Fax: 804-732-0835

Pocahontas State Park
10301 State Park Rd 4m S of US 10 & VA 655
Chesterfield, VA 23838
Phone: 804-796-4255
Fax: 804-796-4004
TF: 800-933-7275

Richmond Ballet
614 N Lombardy St
Richmond, VA 23220
Phone: 804-359-0906
Fax: 804-355-4640

Richmond National Battlefield Park
3215 E Broad St
Richmond, VA 23223
www.nps.gov/rich/
Phone: 804-226-1981
Fax: 804-771-8522

Richmond Philharmonic
922 Park Ave VCU Performing Arts Ctr
Richmond, VA 23284
www.bznet.com/philharmonic/
Phone: 804-673-4001
Fax: 804-673-4010

Richmond Symphony
6th & Grace Sts
Richmond, VA 23220
www.richmondsymphony.com
Phone: 804-788-1212
Fax: 804-788-1541

Saint John's Church
2401 E Broad St
Richmond, VA 23223
Phone: 804-648-5015

Science Museum of Virginia
2500 W Broad St
Richmond, VA 23220
www.smv.org
Phone: 804-367-6552
Fax: 804-367-9348
TF: 800-659-1727

Sherwood Forest Plantation
14501 John Tyler Memorial Hwy
Charles City, VA 23030
E-mail: ktyler1@aol.com
www.sherwoodforest.org
Phone: 804-829-5377
Fax: 804-829-2947

Shockoe Bottom Arts Center
2001 E Grace St
Richmond, VA 23223
Phone: 804-643-7959

Theatre IV
114 W Broad St
Richmond, VA 23220
www.theatreiv.org
Phone: 804-344-8040
Fax: 804-643-2671

TheatreVirginia
2800 Grove Ave
Richmond, VA 23221
E-mail: tva@erols.com
www.theatreva.com
Phone: 804-353-6161
Fax: 804-353-8799
TF: 877-353-6161

Three Lakes Nature Center & Aquarium
400 Sausiluta Dr
Richmond, VA 23227
Phone: 804-261-8230
Fax: 804-266-6938

Tuckahoe Plantation
12601 River Rd
Richmond, VA 23233
Phone: 804-784-5736
Fax: 804-784-5736

Valentine Museum
1015 E Clay St
Richmond, VA 23219
www.valentinemuseum.com/
Phone: 804-649-0711
Fax: 804-643-3510

Virginia Aviation Museum
5701 Huntsman Rd Richmond International Airport
Sandston, VA 23250
Phone: 804-236-3622

Virginia Fire & Police Museum
200 W Marshall St
Richmond, VA 23220
E-mail: trobinso@worldnet.att.net
Phone: 804-644-1849
Fax: 804-644-1850

Virginia Historical Society
428 N Boulevard
Richmond, VA 23220
www.vahistorical.org
Phone: 804-358-4901
Fax: 804-355-2399

Virginia House
4301 Sulgrave Rd
Richmond, VA 23221
Phone: 804-353-4251
Fax: 804-354-8247

Virginia Museum of Fine Arts
2800 Grove Ave
Richmond, VA 23221
www.vmfa.state.va.us
Phone: 804-340-1400
Fax: 804-340-1548

Virginia Opera
600 E Grace St Carpenter Center for the Performing Arts
Richmond, VA 23219
www.vaopera.org
Phone: 804-644-8168
Fax: 804-644-0415

Virginia State Capitol
9th & Grace Sts
Richmond, VA 23219
Phone: 804-698-1788

Wilton House Museum
215 S Wilton Rd
Richmond, VA 23226
wiltonhousemuseum.org
Phone: 804-282-5936
Fax: 804-288-9805
TF: 877-994-5866

Sports Teams & Facilities

Richmond Braves (baseball)
3001 North Blvd The Diamond
Richmond, VA 23230
E-mail: rbraves@i2020.net
www.rbraves.com
Phone: 804-359-4444
Fax: 804-359-0731

Richmond Coliseum
601 E Leigh St
Richmond, VA 23219
www.richmondcoliseum.org
Phone: 804-780-4970
Fax: 804-780-4606

Richmond International Raceway
602 E Laburnum Ave
Richmond, VA 23222
www.rir.com
Phone: 804-345-7223
Fax: 804-321-3833

Richmond Kickers (soccer)
McCloy & Douglas Dale Sts University of Richmond Stadium
Richmond, VA 23220
E-mail: rkickrs@aol.com
www.richmondkickers.com/
Phone: 804-644-5425
Fax: 804-359-5037

Richmond Renegades (hockey)
601 E Leigh St Richmond Coliseum
Richmond, VA 23219
www.renegades.com/
Phone: 804-643-7865
Fax: 804-649-0651

Southside Speedway
12800 Genito Rd
Midlothian, VA 23113
E-mail: racing@southsidespeedway.com
www.southsidespeedway.com
Phone: 804-763-3567

Annual Events

2nd Street Festival (early October) 804-643-2826
Agribusiness Food Festival (early August)..........804-228-3200
Arts in the Park (early May) 804-353-8198
Azalea Festival Parade (mid-April).................804-233-2093
Camptown Races (early May) 804-752-6678
Capital City Kwanzaa Festival (late December) 804-782-2777
Crestar Richmond Marathon (mid-November).......804-285-9495
Dogwood Dell Festival of the Arts (mid-June-mid-August).........................804-780-6091
Easter on Parade (late April)......................804-643-2826
Festival 1893 (mid-October)......................804-358-7166
Gardenfest of Lights (early-late December) 804-782-2777
Great Southern Weapons Fair (late November)......804-228-3200
Harvest Festival at Meadow Farm (mid-October) 804-501-5523
Historic Garden Week (mid-late April) 804-644-7776
James River Parade of Lights (November)..........804-748-1567
James River Wine Festival (early May) 804-359-4645
Old World Plant Sale (mid-April)..................804-353-4251
Rainbow of Arts (September) 804-748-1130
Second Street Festival (early October) 804-782-2777
State Fair of Virginia (late September-early October)..................804-228-3200
Strawberry Hill Races (early-mid-April) 804-228-3200
The Big Gig (mid-July)...........................804-643-2826
Ykrop's Target Family Jubilee (early June) 804-782-2777

Rochester, New York

***County:* Monroe**

ROCHESTER is located in western New York State along the southern shore of Lake Ontario. Major cities within 100 miles include Buffalo and Syracuse, New York and Toronto, Ontario, Canada.

Area (Land) .... 35.8 sq mi
Area (Water)................................ 1.3 sq mi
Elevation...................................... 515 ft
Latitude ....43-15-47 N
Longitude................................ 77-61-58 W
Time Zone .... EST
Area Code.. 716

Climate

Rochester's climate is strongly influenced by its proximity to Lake Ontario. Winters are cold, with average high temperatures in the low to mid-30s and lows in the upper teens. The average annual snowfall is just over 88 inches—nearly four times the national average. Summers are mild, as the heat is moderated by the lake, with average daytime highs in the upper 70s and lows in the upper 50s. August is the wettest month in Rochester, and January and February are the driest.

Average Temperatures & Precipitation

Temperatures

	Jan	Feb	Mar	Apr	May	Jun	Jul	Aug	Sep	Oct	Nov	Dec
High	31	33	43	56	68	76	81	78	72	61	48	36
Low	16	17	26	36	46	54	60	58	52	42	33	22

Precipitation

	Jan	Feb	Mar	Apr	May	Jun	Jul	Aug	Sep	Oct	Nov	Dec
Inches	2.1	2.1	2.3	2.6	2.7	3.0	2.7	3.4	3.0	2.4	2.9	2.7

History

Originally inhabited by the Seneca people, "Rochesterville," as Rochester was known, was founded in 1811. Although many European settlers at that time considered the town a malarial swamp, a few entrepreneurs, including Colonel Nathaniel Rochester for whom the city was named, decided to capitalize on Rochesterville's prime location along the banks of Lake Ontario, the Genesee River, and the Irondequoit Bay, which provided shipping access to the Great Lakes region. Completion of the Erie Canal in 1825 further developed the city's potential to become a major distribution center. Trade and industry, primarily flour milling, horticulture (Rochester has been called both the "Flour City" and the "Flower City"), and garment manufacturing, flourished in Rochester during the remainder of the 19th Century. The economic opportunities generated by new industry drew large numbers of European immigrants to the city, including Germans, Poles, Italians, and Jews. Rochester's diverse ethnic heritage, which includes Hispanic, African American, and Asian, as well as European culture, is evident today in the city's many ethnic neighborhoods, shops, and restaurants.

Several important figures in American history have called Rochester home throughout the years, including Lewis Henry Morgan, who is known for his contributions to the discipline of anthropology, and astronomer Lewis Swift, who discovered several comets. Rochester's two most famous residents were Frederick Douglass, the abolitionist who published his newspaper, The North Star, in the city; and Susan B. Anthony, a pioneer in the women's rights movement who is best known for her role in earning women the right to vote. Susan B. Anthony's Rochester home, now a museum, is a major historical attraction in the city.

In 1888, Rochester became the birthplace of amateur photography as George Eastman manufactured the first Kodak camera and opened a factory in the city. Today, Eastman Kodak is the area's largest employer and Rochester is known worldwide as a center for imaging. The Haloid Corporation (which came to be known as Xerox) was also founded in the city. Although periods of urban strife have had adverse affects on Rochester's population in recent decades, the 1990s have been good years for the city, and continued growth is expected. Rochester today has a strong economy and a relatively low unemployment rate. With a population of more than 216,000 people, Rochester is the third largest city in the state.

Population

1990 Census 230,356
1998 Estimate..............................216,887
% Change .... -5.8
2005 Projection 1,149,200*

Racial/Ethnic Breakdown
White.................................... 61.4%
Black 31.7%
Other...................................... 6.9%
Hispanic Origin (may be of any race) 8.7%

Age Breakdown
Under 6 years............................ 11.0%
6 to 14.................................. 11.6%
15 to 19.................................. 6.6%
20 to 21.................................. 3.8%
22 to 29................................. 17.6%
30 to 39................................. 17.4%
40 to 49................................. 10.2%
50 to 59.................................. 6.5%
60+ years 15.3%
Median Age................................. 29.7

Gender Breakdown
Male...................................... 47.2%

Female................................52.8%

** Information given is for the Rochester Metropolitan Statistical Area (MSA), which includes Genesee, Livingston, Monroe, Ontario, Orleans, and Wayne counties.*

Government

Type of Government: Mayor-Council

Central Library of Rochester & Monroe County
115 South Ave
Rochester, NY 14604
Phone: 716-428-8100
Fax: 716-428-8353

Rochester City Clerk
30 Church St Rm 300A
Rochester, NY 14614
Phone: 716-428-7431
Fax: 716-428-6347

Rochester City Council
30 Church St Rm 301A
Rochester, NY 14614
Phone: 716-428-7538
Fax: 716-428-6347

Rochester City Hall
30 Church St
Rochester, NY 14614
Phone: 716-428-7000
Fax: 716-428-6347

Rochester Economic Development Dept
30 Church St Rm 5A
Rochester, NY 14614
Phone: 716-428-6808
Fax: 716-428-6042

Rochester Fire Dept
150 S Plymouth Ave Rm 300
Rochester, NY 14614
Phone: 716-428-6739
Fax: 716-428-6785

Rochester Human Resource Management Bureau
30 Church St Rm 103A
Rochester, NY 14614
Phone: 716-428-7115
Fax: 716-428-6902

Rochester Mayor
30 Church St Rm 307A
Rochester, NY 14614
Phone: 716-428-7045
Fax: 716-428-6059

Rochester Parks & Recreation Bureau
400 Dewey Ave
Rochester, NY 14613
Phone: 716-428-6770
Fax: 716-428-6021

Rochester Planning Bureau
30 Church St Rm 010A
Rochester, NY 14614
Phone: 716-428-6953
Fax: 716-428-6864

Rochester Police Dept
150 S Plymouth Ave
Rochester, NY 14614
Phone: 716-428-6720
Fax: 716-428-6696

Rochester Treasury Dept
30 Church St Rm 111A
Rochester, NY 14614
Phone: 716-428-6705
Fax: 716-428-6774

Rochester Water Dept
10 Felix St
Rochester, NY 14608
Phone: 716-428-7500
Fax: 716-428-6353

Important Phone Numbers

AAA..716-461-4660
Driver's License/Vehicle Registration Information ...518-473-5595
Emergency 911
Events Line.....................................716-546-6810
Fair Business Council............................716-546-6776
Greater Rochester Assn of Realtors 716-292-5000
HotelDocs 800-468-3537
New York State Tax Information 800-225-5829
Poison Control Center 716-275-3232
Rochester Tax Accounting Office 716-428-6940
Time/Temp 716-974-1616
Voter Registration Information....................716-428-4550
Weather.......................................716-334-0013

Information Sources

Better Business Bureau Serving Western New York & the Capital District
741 Delaware Ave
Buffalo, NY 14209
www.buffalo.bbb.org
Phone: 716-881-5222
Fax: 716-883-5349

Greater Rochester Visitors Assn
126 Andrews St
Rochester, NY 14604
www.visitrochester.com
Phone: 716-546-3070
Fax: 716-232-4822
TF: 800-677-7282

International Business Council of Rochester
55 Saint Paul St
Rochester, NY 14604
www.rnychamber.com
Phone: 716-454-2220
Fax: 716-263-3679

Monroe County
39 W Main St Rm 101
Rochester, NY 14614
www.co.monroe.ny.us
Phone: 716-428-5151
Fax: 716-428-5447

Rochester Riverside Convention Center
123 E Main St
Rochester, NY 14604
www.rrcc.com
Phone: 716-232-7200
Fax: 716-232-1510

Online Resources

4Rochester.com
www.4rochester.com

@Rochester WWW Guide to Rochester
www.roch.com/sites

About.com Guide to Rochester
rochester.about.com/local/midlanticus/rochester

Anthill City Guide Rochester
www.anthill.com/city.asp?city=rochester

Big Guide
www.thebigguide.com/

City Knowledge Rochester
www.cityknowledge.com/ny_rochester.htm

DigitalCity Rochester
home.digitalcity.com/rochester

FreeTime Magazine
www.freetimemag.com

Gay Rochester Online
www.gayrochester.com/

Genesee Gateway
www.ggw.org/section

Guide to Rochester New York
www.nuwebny.com/rochest.htm

HotelGuide Rochester
hotelguide.net/rochester

Rochester City Net
www.excite.com/travel/countries/united_states/new_york/rochester

Area Communities

Communities in the Rochester area with populations greater than 10,000 include:

Brighton
2300 Elmwood Ave
Rochester, NY 14618
Phone: 716-473-8800
Fax: 716-473-8115

Gates
1605 Buffalo Rd
Gates, NY 14624
Phone: 716-247-6100
Fax: 716-247-0017

Greece
2505 W Ridge Rd
Rochester, NY 14626
Phone: 716-723-2364
Fax: 716-225-1915

Henrietta
475 Clakins Rd
Henrietta, NY 14467
Phone: 716-359-7040
Fax: 716-334-9667

Irondequoit
1280 Titus Ave
Rochester, NY 14617
Phone: 716-467-8840
Fax: 716-467-2862

Ogden
269 Ogden Center Rd
Spencerport, NY 14559
Phone: 716-352-2127
Fax: 716-352-4590

Penfield
3100 Atlantic Ave
Penfield, NY 14526
Phone: 716-340-8625
Fax: 716-340-8667

Perinton
1350 Turk Hill Rd
Fairport, NY 14450
Phone: 716-223-0770
Fax: 716-223-3629

Pittsford
11 S Main St
Pittsford, NY 14534
Phone: 716-248-6210
Fax: 716-248-6247

Sweden
PO Box 366
Brockport, NY 14420
Phone: 716-637-2144
Fax: 716-637-7389

Webster
1000 Ridge Rd
Webster, NY 14580
Phone: 716-872-1000
Fax: 716-872-1352

Economy

Known as the "World's Image Centre," Rochester is a world leader in imaging technology and in the field of optics. Eastman-Kodak, Xerox, and Bausch & Lomb were all founded in the city, and all remain among the area's top employers. More than 100,000 Rochester area residents are employed by imaging firms—some 34,000 by Eastman-Kodak alone, making the company the area's largest employer. Retail trade, education, and local government are also important components of the city's economic base.

Unemployment Rate	4.1%*
Per Capita Income	$26,170*
Median Family Income	$43,625**

** Information given is for the Rochester Metropolitan Statistical Area (MSA), which includes Monroe, Orleans, Ontario, Livingston, Genesee, and Wayne counties.*
*** Information given is for Monroe County.*

Principal Industries & Number of Wage Earners

Rochester MSA* - 2000

Construction	17,600
Finance, Insurance, & Real Estate	20,800
Government	86,000
Manufacturing	115,100
Retail Trade	93,200
Services	172,300
Transportation & Public Utilities	18,500
Wholesale Trade	23,900

** Information give is for the Rochester Metropolitan Statistical Area (MSA), which includes Monroe, Ontario, Orleans, Livingston, Genesee, and Wayne counties.*

Major Employers

Bausch & Lomb Inc
1 Bausch & Lomb Pl
Rochester, NY 14604
www.bausch.com
Phone: 716-338-6021
Fax: 716-338-6007
TF: 800-344-8815

Blue Cross & Blue Shield of the Rochester Area
165 Court St
Rochester, NY 14647
www.bcbsra.com
Phone: 716-454-1700
Fax: 716-238-4400
TF: 800-847-1200

Eastman Kodak Co
343 State St
Rochester, NY 14650
www.kodak.com
Phone: 716-724-4000
Fax: 716-724-0663
TF: 800-242-2424

Frontier Corp
180 S Clinton Ave
Rochester, NY 14646
E-mail: info@frontiercorp.com
www.frontiercorp.com
Phone: 716-777-1000
Fax: 716-325-7639
TF: 800-836-0342

Monroe County
39 W Main St Rm 101
Rochester, NY 14614
E-mail: mcplan@servtech.com
www.co.monroe.ny.us
Phone: 716-428-5151
Fax: 716-428-5447

Paychex Inc
911 Panorama Trail S
Rochester, NY 14625
www.paychex.com
Phone: 716-385-6666
Fax: 716-383-3449
TF: 800-828-4411

Rochester City Hall
30 Church St
Rochester, NY 14614
www.ci.rochester.ny.us
Phone: 716-428-7000
Fax: 716-428-6347

Rochester General Hospital
1425 Portland Ave
Rochester, NY 14621
www.viahealth.org/rgh
Phone: 716-338-4000
Fax: 716-922-4757

Rochester Institute of Technology
1 Lomb Memorial Dr
Rochester, NY 14623
E-mail: admissions@rit.edu
www.rit.edu
Phone: 716-475-2411
Fax: 716-475-7170

Strong Memorial Hospital
601 Elmwood Ave University of Rochester Medical Ctr
Rochester, NY 14642
www.urmc.rochester.edu/URMC
Phone: 716-275-2100
Fax: 716-244-8483

Unity Health System Saint Mary's Hospital
89 Genesee St
Rochester, NY 14611
www.unityhealth.org
Phone: 716-464-3000
Fax: 716-464-0044

University of Rochester
Rochester, NY 14627
E-mail: admit@macmail.cc.rochester.edu
www.rochester.edu
Phone: 716-275-2121
Fax: 716-756-0165

Wegmans Food Markets Inc
PO Box 844
Rochester, NY 14603
www.wegmans.com
Phone: 716-328-2550
Fax: 716-464-4626
TF: 800-934-6267

Xerox Corp
100 Clinton Ave S
Rochester, NY 14644
www.xerox.com
Phone: 716-423-5090

Quality of Living Indicators

Total Crime Index....................................16,101
(rates per 100,000 inhabitants)

Violent Crime
Murder/manslaughter............................ 28
Forcible rape 117
Robbery....................................... 818
Aggravated assault............................ 560

Property Crime
Burglary 3,010
Larceny theft 9,521
Motor vehicle theft 2,047

Cost of Living Index..................................109.0
(national average = 100)

Median Home Price..................................$87,700

Education

Public Schools

Rochester City School District
131 W Broad St
Rochester, NY 14614
www.rochester.k12.ny.us
Phone: 716-262-8100
Fax: 716-262-5151

Number of Schools
Elementary.................................. 40
Middle 9
High.. 8

Student/Teacher Ratio
All Grades 14.3:1

Private Schools

Number of Schools (all grades).................... 80+

Colleges & Universities

Bryant & Stratton Career College Henrietta
1225 Jefferson Rd
Rochester, NY 14623
www.bryantstratton.edu/main/campusdesc/Henrietta.htm
Phone: 716-292-5627
Fax: 716-292-6015

Bryant & Stratton Career College Rochester
150 Bellwood Dr
Rochester, NY 14606
Phone: 716-720-0660
Fax: 716-720-9226

Nazareth College of Rochester
4245 East Ave
Rochester, NY 14618
www.naz.edu
Phone: 716-586-2525
Fax: 716-389-2826
TF: 800-462-3944

Roberts Wesleyan College
2301 Westside Dr
Rochester, NY 14624
E-mail: admissions@roberts.edu
www.roberts.edu
Phone: 716-594-6000
Fax: 716-594-6371
TF: 800-777-4792

Rochester Institute of Technology
1 Lomb Memorial Dr
Rochester, NY 14623
E-mail: admissions@rit.edu
www.rit.edu
Phone: 716-475-2411
Fax: 716-475-7170

Saint John Fisher College
3690 East Ave
Rochester, NY 14618
E-mail: admissions@sjfc.edu
www.sjfc.edu
Phone: 716-385-8000
Fax: 716-385-8129
TF: 800-444-4640

State University of New York Brockport
350 New Campus Dr
Brockport, NY 14420
www.brockport.edu
Phone: 716-395-2211
Fax: 716-395-5452
TF: 800-382-8447

State University of New York Geneseo
1 College Cir
Geneseo, NY 14454
www.geneseo.edu
Phone: 716-245-5211
Fax: 716-245-5550

State University of New York Monroe Community College
1000 E Henrietta Rd
Rochester, NY 14623
www.monroecc.edu
Phone: 716-292-2000
Fax: 716-427-2749

Talmudical Institution of Upstate New York
769 Park Ave
Rochester, NY 14607
Phone: 716-473-2810
Fax: 716-442-0417

University of Rochester
Rochester, NY 14627
E-mail: admit@macmail.cc.rochester.edu
www.rochester.edu
Phone: 716-275-2121
Fax: 716-756-0165

Hospitals

Genesee Hospital
224 Alexander St
Rochester, NY 14607
Phone: 716-263-6000
Fax: 716-922-7620

Highland Hospital of Rochester
1000 South Ave
Rochester, NY 14620
Phone: 716-473-2200
Fax: 716-341-8221

Park Ridge Hospital
1555 Long Pond Rd
Rochester, NY 14626
www.unityhealth.org
Phone: 716-723-7000
Fax: 716-723-7187

Rochester General Hospital
1425 Portland Ave
Rochester, NY 14621
www.viahealth.org/rgh
Phone: 716-338-4000
Fax: 716-922-4757

Strong Memorial Hospital
601 Elmwood Ave University of Rochester Medical Ctr
Rochester, NY 14642
www.urmc.rochester.edu/URMC
Phone: 716-275-2100
Fax: 716-244-8483

Unity Health System Saint Mary's Hospital
89 Genesee St
Rochester, NY 14611
www.unityhealth.org
Phone: 716-464-3000
Fax: 716-464-0044

Transportation

Airport(s)

Greater Rochester International Airport (ROC)
4 miles SW of downtown (approx 15 minutes) 716-464-6000

Mass Transit

EZ Rider Entertainment Shuttle
Free 716-426-3520
Regional Transit Service (RTS)
$1.25 Base fare. 716-288-1700

Rail/Bus

Greyhound/Trailways Bus Station
187 Midtown Plaza
Rochester, NY 14604
Phone: 716-232-5121
TF: 800-231-2222

Utilities

Electricity
Rochester Gas & Electric Corp 716-546-1111
www.rge.com

Gas
Rochester Gas & Electric Corp 716-546-1111
www.rge.com

Water
Rochester Water Bureau 716-428-5990

Garbage Collection/Recycling
Rochester Dept of Environmental Services. 716-428-5990

Telecommunications

Telephone
Rochester Telephone 716-777-1200

Cable Television
Time Warner Cable. 716-756-5000
www.timewarner.com

Internet Service Providers (ISPs)
E-Znet Inc 716-262-2485
www.eznet.net
Frontier Corp. 716-777-1000
www.frontiercorp.com
mPower Communications Corp 716-218-6550
www.mpowercom.com
NetAccess Inc 716-756-5500
www.netacc.net
Netsville Inc. 716-232-5670
www.netsville.com
Rochester Free-Net. 716-594-5414
www.ggw.org
Rochester Public Access Inc.. 716-756-4500
www.rpa.net
Verio New York 716-263-3360
home.verio.net/local/frontpage.cfm?AirportCode=ROC

Banks

Charter One Bank
40 Franklin St
Rochester, NY 14604
Phone: 716-258-3032
Fax: 716-232-2029
TF: 800-458-1190

Chase Manhattan Bank
2900 Dewey Ave
Rochester, NY 14616
Phone: 716-935-9935

Fleet National Bank
1 East Ave
Rochester, NY 14638
Phone: 716-546-9100
Fax: 716-546-9207
TF: 800-841-4000

Key Bank NA
3420 Monroe Ave
Rochester, NY 14618
Phone: 716-381-7956
Fax: 716-381-4626
TF: 800-539-2968

Lyndon Guaranty Bank
3670 Mt Read Blvd
Rochester, NY 14616
Phone: 716-663-8930
Fax: 716-663-4089

M & T Bank
35 State St
Rochester, NY 14614
Phone: 716-546-3300
Fax: 716-258-1655

Upstate Bank
400 Andrews St Suite 210
Rochester, NY 14604
Phone: 716-454-3450
Fax: 716-454-3624

Shopping

Eastview Mall
672 E View Mall
Victor, NY 14564
Phone: 716-223-3693
Fax: 716-425-1809

Irondequoit Mall
285 Irondequoit Mall Dr
Rochester, NY 14622
Phone: 716-266-4000
Fax: 716-467-0189

Mall at Greece Ridge Center
271 Greece Ridge Ctr Dr
Rochester, NY 14626
Phone: 716-225-1140
Fax: 716-227-2525

Marketplace Mall
1 Miracle Mile Dr
Rochester, NY 14623
Phone: 716-424-6220
Fax: 716-427-2745

Midtown Plaza
211 Midtown Plaza
Rochester, NY 14604
Phone: 716-530-2000
Fax: 716-325-2576

Northfield Common
50 State St
Pittsford, NY 14534
Phone: 716-586-4322

Park Avenue Shopping District
Park Ave-betw Alexander St & Culver Rd
Rochester, NY 14607
Phone: 716-234-1909

Rochester Public Market
280 N Union St
Rochester, NY 14609
Phone: 716-428-6907

Village Gate Square
274 N Goodman St
Rochester, NY 14607
Phone: 716-442-9168

Village of Pittsford
21 N Main St
Pittsford, NY 14534
Phone: 716-586-4332
Fax: 716-586-4597

Media

Newspapers and Magazines

City Newspaper
250 N Goodman St
Rochester, NY 14607
E-mail: info@rochester-citynews.com
Phone: 716-244-3329
Fax: 716-244-1126

Daily Record*
PO Box 30006
Rochester, NY 14603
www.nydailyrecord.com
Phone: 716-232-6920
Fax: 716-232-2740

Democrat & Chronicle*
55 Exchange Blvd
Rochester, NY 14614
www.rochesterdandc.com
Phone: 716-232-7100
Fax: 716-258-2237
TF: 800-473-5274

Rochester Business Journal
55 Saint Paul St
Rochester, NY 14604
www.rbj.net
Phone: 716-546-8303
Fax: 716-546-3398

Suburban News
PO Box 106
Spencerport, NY 14559
www.westsidenewsinc.com
Phone: 716-352-3411
Fax: 716-352-4811

**Indicates major daily newspapers*

Television

WHEC-TV Ch 10 (NBC)
191 East Ave
Rochester, NY 14604
www.10nbc.com
Phone: 716-546-5670
Fax: 716-546-5688

WOKR-TV Ch 13 (ABC)
PO Box 20555
Rochester, NY 14602
www.rochestertoday.com
Phone: 716-334-8700
Fax: 716-334-8719

WROC-TV Ch 8 (CBS)
201 Humboldt St
Rochester, NY 14610
E-mail: wroc@frontiernet.net
www.wroctv.com
Phone: 716-288-8400
Fax: 716-288-1505

WUHF-TV Ch 31 (Fox)
360 East Ave
Rochester, NY 14604
www.foxnewsfirst.com
Phone: 716-232-3700
Fax: 716-546-4774

WXXI-TV Ch 21 (PBS)
PO Box 30021
Rochester, NY 14601
E-mail: responses@wxxi.pbs.org
www.wxxi.org
Phone: 716-325-7500
Fax: 716-258-0338

Radio

WBBF-FM 98.9 MHz (Oldies)
500 B Forman Bldg Suite 500
Rochester, NY 14604
Phone: 716-423-2900
Fax: 716-423-2947

WBEE-FM 92.5 MHz (Ctry)
500 B Forman Bldg
Rochester, NY 14604
www.wbee.com
Phone: 716-423-2900
Fax: 716-423-2947

WCMF-FM 96.5 MHz (Rock)
1700 HSBC Plaza
Rochester, NY 14604
www.96wcmf.com
Phone: 716-399-5700
Fax: 716-399-5750

WDKX-FM 103.9 MHz (Urban)
683 E Main St
Rochester, NY 14605
E-mail: wdkx@wdkx.com
www.wdkx.com
Phone: 716-262-2050
Fax: 716-262-2626

WEZO-AM 950 kHz (Nost)
500 B Forman Bldg Suite 500
Rochester, NY 14604
Phone: 716-423-2900
Fax: 716-423-2947

WHAM-AM 1180 kHz (N/T)
207 Midtown Plaza
Rochester, NY 14604
E-mail: wham@eznet.net
www.wham1180.com
Phone: 716-454-4884
Fax: 716-454-5081

WHTK-AM 1280 kHz (Sports)
207 Midtown Plaza
Rochester, NY 14604
Phone: 716-454-3942
Fax: 716-454-5081

WJZR-FM 105.9 MHz (Urban)
1237 E Main St
Rochester, NY 14609
Phone: 716-288-5020
Fax: 716-288-5165

WKGS-FM 106.7 MHz (CHR)
207 Midtown Plaza
Rochester, NY 14604
Phone: 716-454-3942
Fax: 716-454-5081

WMAX-FM 107.3 MHz (AAA)
207 Midtown Plaza
Rochester, NY 14604
Phone: 716-232-8870
Fax: 716-262-2334

WNVE-FM 95.1 MHz (Alt)
207 Midtown Plaza
Rochester, NY 14604
Phone: 716-246-0440
Fax: 716-454-5081

WPXY-FM 97.9 MHz (CHR)
1700 HSBC Plaza
Rochester, NY 14604
Phone: 716-262-2720
Fax: 716-399-5750

WQRV-FM 93.3 MHz (CR)
500 B Forman Bldg Midtown Plaza
Rochester, NY 14604
Phone: 716-423-2900
Fax: 716-423-2947

WRMM-FM 101.3 MHz (AC)
1700 Marine Midland Plaza Suite 300
Rochester, NY 14604
E-mail: marketing@warm1013.com
www.warm1013.com
Phone: 716-399-5700
Fax: 716-399-5750
TF: 800-840-1013

WRUR-FM 88.5 MHz (Misc)
PO Box 277356
Rochester, NY 14627
Phone: 716-275-6400

WVOR-FM 100.5 MHz (AC)
207 Midtown Plaza
Rochester, NY 14604
E-mail: wvorradio@aol.com
Phone: 716-454-3942
Fax: 716-454-5081

WXXI-AM 1370 kHz (NPR)
280 State St
Rochester, NY 14614
E-mail: response@wxxi.pbs.org
www.wxxi.org/
Phone: 716-325-7500
Fax: 716-258-0339

WXXI-FM 91.5 MHz (NPR)
PO Box30021
Rochester, NY 14603
E-mail: responses@wxxi.pbs.org
www.wxxi.org
Phone: 716-258-0340
Fax: 716-258-0339

WZNE-FM 94.1 MHz (Alt)
1700 HSBC Plaza Suite 300
Rochester, NY 14604
E-mail: thezone@lsweb.com
www.thezone941.com
Phone: 716-399-5700
Fax: 716-399-5750

Attractions

Rochester is corporate home of the Eastman-Kodak Company, and the former residence of the company's founder, George Eastman, houses the International Museum of Photography, the world's largest museum of photographic art and technology. Historical attractions in Rochester include the Susan B. Anthony House, a National Historic Landmark that is now a museum celebrating the accomplishments of the famous suffragist; and Mount Hope Cemetery, where Anthony, abolitionist Frederick Douglass, and founding father Colonel Nathanial Rochester were laid to rest. South of Rochester is Consensus Lake, part of the Finger Lakes region. The area extends to Otisco Lake, near Syracuse, and has waterfalls and gorges, as well as vineyards and various local wineries.

Brown's Race Historic District
60 Brown's Race
Rochester, NY 14614
Phone: 716-325-2030
Fax: 716-325-2414

Campbell-Whittlesey House
123 S Fitzhugh St
Rochester, NY 14608
Phone: 716-546-7028

Center at High Falls
60 Brown's Race
Rochester, NY 14614
Phone: 716-325-2030
Fax: 716-325-2414

Dryden Theatre at George Eastman House
900 East Ave
Rochester, NY 14607
www.eastman.org
Phone: 716-271-4090
Fax: 716-271-3970

Eastman Theatre
26 Gibbs St
Rochester, NY 14604
www.rochester.edu/eastman
Phone: 716-274-1110
Fax: 716-274-1088

Fagan Garth Dance
50 Chestnut St
Rochester, NY 14604
www.loopside.com/fagan
Phone: 716-454-3260
Fax: 716-454-6191

Genesee Brewing Co Inc
445 Saint Paul St
Rochester, NY 14605
Phone: 716-546-1030
Fax: 716-546-5011

Genesee Lighthouse at Charlotte
70 Lighthouse St
Rochester, NY 14612
Phone: 716-621-6179

Geva Theatre
75 Woodbury Blvd
Rochester, NY 14607
www.gevatheatre.org/
Phone: 716-232-1363
Fax: 716-232-4031

Hamlin Beach State Park
1 Camp Rd
Hamlin, NY 14464
Phone: 716-964-2462
Fax: 716-964-7821

International Museum of Photography at George Eastman House
900 East Ave
Rochester, NY 14607
E-mail: comments@geh.org
www.eastman.org/
Phone: 716-271-3361
Fax: 716-271-3970

Memorial Art Gallery of the University of Rochester
500 University Ave
Rochester, NY 14607
E-mail: maginfo@mag.rochester.edu
www.rochester.edu/mag/
Phone: 716-473-7720
Fax: 716-473-6266

Nazareth College Arts Center
4245 East Ave
Rochester, NY 14618
Phone: 716-389-2175
Fax: 716-389-2182

NTID Performing Arts
52 Lomb Memorial Dr
Rochester, NY 14623
Phone: 716-475-6400
Fax: 716-475-6787

Opera Theatre of Rochester
100 East Ave
Rochester, NY 14604
www.ggw.org/otr/
Phone: 716-235-7760
Fax: 716-232-5353

Park Avenue Shopping District
Park Ave-betw Alexander St & Culver Rd
Rochester, NY 14607
Phone: 716-234-1909

Pyramid Arts Center
PO Box 30330
Rochester, NY 14603
www.pyramidarts.org
Phone: 716-461-2222
Fax: 716-461-2223

Rochester Broadway Theatre League
100 East Ave
Rochester, NY 14604
Phone: 716-222-5000
Fax: 716-325-6742

Rochester Historical Society
485 East Ave
Rochester, NY 14607
Phone: 716-271-2705

Rochester Museum & Science Center
657 East Ave
Rochester, NY 14607
www.rmsc.org
Phone: 716-271-4320
Fax: 716-271-5935

Rochester Philharmonic Orchestra
25 Gibbs St Eastman Theatre
Rochester, NY 14605
E-mail: webnotes@rpo.org
www.rpo.org/
Phone: 716-222-5000

Seabreeze Park
4600 Culver Rd
Rochester, NY 14622
www.carousel.org/Seabreeze.html
Phone: 716-323-1900
Fax: 716-323-2225

Seneca Park Zoo
2222 Saint Paul St
Rochester, NY 14621
www.senecazoo.com
Phone: 716-266-6846
Fax: 716-342-1477

Sonnenberg Gardens
151 Charlotte St
Canandaigua, NY 14424
www.sonnenberg.org/
Phone: 716-394-4922
Fax: 716-394-2192

Stone-Tolan House
2370 East Ave
Rochester, NY 14610
Phone: 716-442-4606
Fax: 716-546-4788

Strasenburgh Planetarium
657 East Ave Rochester Museum & Science Ctr
Rochester, NY 14607
www.rmsc.org/html/planet/planet.html
Phone: 716-271-4320
Fax: 716-271-5935

Strong Museum
1 Manhattan Sq
Rochester, NY 14607
E-mail: strandd@vivanet.com
www.strongmuseum.org
Phone: 716-263-2700
Fax: 716-263-2493

Susan B Anthony House
17 Madison St
Rochester, NY 14608
www.susanbanthonyhouse.org/
Phone: 716-235-6124
Fax: 716-235-6212

Vietnam Veteran's Memorial
1440 South Ave
Rochester, NY 14620
Phone: 716-256-4950

Village of Pittsford
21 N Main St
Pittsford, NY 14534
Phone: 716-586-4332
Fax: 716-586-4597

Woodside Mansion
485 East Ave
Rochester, NY 14607
Phone: 716-271-2705

Sports Teams & Facilities

Rochester Americans (hockey)
100 Exchange St Rochester Community War Memorial Auditorium
Rochester, NY 14614
www.amerks.com
Phone: 716-454-5335
Fax: 716-454-3954

Rochester Knighthawks (lacrosse)
100 Exchange St Rochester Community War Memorial Auditorium
Rochester, NY 14614
Phone: 716-454-5335
Fax: 716-454-3954

Rochester Raging Rhinos (soccer)
333 N Plymouth Ave Frontier Field
Rochester, NY 14608
E-mail: info@rhinossoccer.com
www.rhinossoccer.com
Phone: 716-454-5425
Fax: 716-454-5453

Rochester Ravens
Library Rd Fauver Stadium
Rochester, NY 14620
Phone: 716-461-4813
Fax: 716-442-9527

Rochester Red Wings (baseball)
333 N Plymouth Ave Frontier Field
Rochester, NY 14608
E-mail: redwings@frontiernet.net
www.redwingsbaseball.com
Phone: 716-454-1001
Fax: 716-454-1056

Annual Events

Celebrate Your Roots at the Market (early October) 716-428-6907
Clothesline Art Festival (mid-September) 716-473-7720
Corn Hill Arts Festival (mid-July) 716-262-3142
Dickens Old Fashioned Christmas Festival (mid-November-late December) 716-392-3456
Festival of Lights (mid-November-early January) 716-394-4922
Flower City Market Days (mid-May-mid-June) 716-428-6907
Ghost Walk (mid-late October) 716-546-7029
Hilton Apple Fest (early October) 716-392-7773
Historic Hill Cumorah Pageant (early & mid-July) 315-597-6808
Lilac Festival (late May) 716-546-3070
Maplewood Rose Festival (mid-June) 716-428-6690
Monroe County Fair (early August) 716-334-4000
Park Avenue Festival (late July-early August) 716-428-6690
Rochester Air Show (late August) 716-256-4960
Rochester HarborFest (late June) 716-865-3320
Rochester International LPGA Tournament (early-mid-June) 716-427-7040
Rochester River Romance (early October) 716-428-6690
Time Warner MusicFest (mid-July) 716-428-6690
Yuletide in the Country (early-mid-December) 716-538-6822

Sacramento, California

***County:* Sacramento**

SACRAMENTO is located at the confluence of the Sacramento and American Rivers in Central California's Sacramento Valley, which is bordered by the Sierra Nevada Mountains to the east and the Coast Range to the west. Major cities within 100 miles include San Francisco, Oakland, Santa Rosa, and Stockton, California.

Area (Land) .... 96.3 sq mi
Area (Water)............................... 2.2 sq mi
Elevation....................................... 25 ft
Latitude ....38-58-17 N
Longitude............................... 121-49-33 W
Time Zone .... PST
Area Code....................................... 916

Climate

Sheltered from extreme weather patterns by mountain ranges both east and west of the city, Sacramento has a mild climate with abundant sunshine. Winter days are generally mild, with average high temperatures ranging from the low 50s to near 60 degrees, while evenings cool down to near 40 degrees. Snowfall is rare in Sacramento, averaging only one-tenth of an inch annually. Summer days feature high temperatures averaging near 90 degrees, but low humidity makes the heat more bearable; evening temperatures cool down significantly, averaging in the mid-50s. January is the wettest month of the year in Sacramento; the summer months of June, July, and August are the driest.

Average Temperatures & Precipitation

Temperatures

	Jan	Feb	Mar	Apr	May	Jun	Jul	Aug	Sep	Oct	Nov	Dec
High	53	60	64	71	80	88	93	92	87	78	63	53
Low	38	41	43	46	50	55	58	58	56	50	43	38

Precipitation

	Jan	Feb	Mar	Apr	May	Jun	Jul	Aug	Sep	Oct	Nov	Dec
Inches	3.7	2.9	2.6	1.2	0.3	0.1	0.1	0.1	0.4	1.1	2.7	2.5

History

The region known today as the Sacramento Valley was inhabited by Native Americans as early as 900 B.C., many of whom became victims of disease and settler hostility when the Spanish (and, later, pioneers from the eastern part of the country) began arriving in the 18th Century. During the early 1800s, the Spanish named the river that flowed through the valley the Sacramento (Spanish for "holy sacrament"). The city that today takes its name from the Sacramento River began when Swiss-American Captain John A. Sutter received a land grant from the Mexican government and founded the colony of New Helvetia in 1839. Sutter also constructed a fort, completed in 1844, that became an important trading post. Gold was discovered in the area in 1848, and the notorious California Gold Rush had begun. Shortly thereafter, the town of Sacramento City was established. Although it endured three devastating floods as well as a fire in its first few years of existence, the city's location at the gateway to Gold Rush country helped it to grow and prosper. In addition to mining, other industries that became important to Sacramento's economy include farming, fishing, and trade. In 1854, Sacramento was chosen as the capital city for the newly admitted State of California.

During the 1860s, Sacramento was chosen as the western terminus of the first transcontinetal railroad. Immigrants from China began arriving in Sacramento to work on the railroad's construction, which was completed in 1869. The arrival of the railroad, along with improvements in farming and flood control, led to further development in the Sacramento area. By the turn of the century, Sacramento County was home to nearly 46,000 people.

The military was an important factor in Sacramento's growth during the 20th Century. Mather Field was established nearby during World War I, and McClellan Air Base opened in 1939. During World War II, McClellan Air Base became Sacramento County's largest employer, drawing people from all over the United States who came to serve their country. The expanding population resulted in a boost to the area's overall economy—Sacramento County prospered during the 1940s, growing to more than 277,000 by decade's end. The city began to grow as an inland port during the 1960s, with the completion of a 42-mile deepwater channel to San Francisco Bay.

Despite recent and pending base closures (Mather Field closed in 1993 and McClellan Air Force Base is scheduled to close in 2001), Sacramento continues to thrive as an important regional commercial, manufacturing, and transportation center. Home to more than 404,000 people, Sacramento is the largest city in central California and the sixth largest in the entire state. Continued growth is anticipated in the Sacramento region in the coming years—Sacramento County's population is expected to exceed 1.4 million by the year 2010.

Population

1990 Census 369,365
1998 Estimate..............................404,168
% Change 9.4
2010 Projection 1,431,500*

Racial/Ethnic Breakdown

White.....................................60.1%
Black 15.3%
Other.....................................24.6%
Hispanic Origin (may be of any race) 16.2%

Age Breakdown

Under 5 years 8.2%
5 to 17 .... 18.0%
18 to 20 .... 4.2%
21 to 24 .... 6.3%
25 to 34 .... 19.3%
35 to 44 .... 15.6%
45 to 54 .... 8.9%
55 to 64 .... 7.4%
65 to 74 .... 6.9%
75+ years 5.2%
Median Age 31.8

Gender Breakdown

Male 48.4%
Female 51.6%

* *Information given is for Sacramento County.*

Government

Type of Government: Mayor-Council

Sacramento City Attorney
980 9th St 10th Fl
Sacramento, CA 95814
Phone: 916-264-5346
Fax: 916-264-7455

Sacramento City Clerk
915 'I' St Suite 304
Sacramento, CA 95814
Phone: 916-264-5427
Fax: 916-264-7672

Sacramento City Council
915 'I' St Suite 205
Sacramento, CA 95814
Phone: 916-264-5407
Fax: 916-264-7680

Sacramento City Hall
915 'I' St
Sacramento, CA 95814
Phone: 916-264-5427
Fax: 916-264-7672

Sacramento City Manager
915 'I' St Rm 101
Sacramento, CA 95814
Phone: 916-264-5704
Fax: 916-264-7618

Sacramento City Treasurer
926 J St Suite 300
Sacramento, CA 95814
Phone: 916-264-5168
Fax: 916-448-3139

Sacramento Downtown Dept
1030 15th St Suite 250
Sacramento, CA 95814
Phone: 916-264-8109
Fax: 916-264-8161

Sacramento Fire Dept
1231 'I' St Suite 401
Sacramento, CA 95814
Phone: 916-264-5266
Fax: 916-264-7079

Sacramento Mayor
915 'I' St Rm 205
Sacramento, CA 95814
Phone: 916-264-5300
Fax: 916-264-7680

Sacramento Neighborhoods Planning & Development Services Dept
1231 'I' St Suite 300
Sacramento, CA 95814
Phone: 916-264-5571
Fax: 916-264-5328

Sacramento Personnel Services Div
921 10th St Rm 100
Sacramento, CA 95814
Phone: 916-264-5726
Fax: 916-264-7326

Sacramento Police Dept
900 8th St
Sacramento, CA 95814
Phone: 916-264-5121
Fax: 916-448-4620

Sacramento Public Library
828 'I' St
Sacramento, CA 95814
Phone: 916-264-2770
Fax: 916-264-2755

Sacramento Public Works Dept
915 'I' St Suite 200
Sacramento, CA 95814
Phone: 916-264-7100
Fax: 916-264-5573

Sacramento Utilities Dept
1395 35th Ave
Sacramento, CA 95822
Phone: 916-264-1400
Fax: 916-264-1497

Important Phone Numbers

AAA 916-331-7610
American Express Travel 916-441-1526
California State Franchise Tax Board 916-845-4300
Driver's License/Vehicle Registration Information ... 916-657-6555
Emergency 911
HotelDocs 800-468-3537
Poison Control Center 800-876-4766
Road Conditions 800-427-7623
Sacramento Assn of Realtors 916-922-7711
Sacramento County Assessor 916-874-5231
Sacramento County Tax Collector 916-874-7913
Time 530-767-2676
Voter Registration Information 916-875-6451
Weather 916-646-2000

Information Sources

Better Business Bureau Serving North Central California
400 'S' St
Sacramento, CA 95814
www.sacramento.bbb.org
Phone: 916-443-6843
Fax: 916-443-0376

Downtown Sacramento Partnership Inc
900 J St 2nd Fl
Sacramento, CA 95814
www.downtownsac.org
Phone: 916-442-8575
Fax: 916-442-2053

Sacramento Area Commerce & Trade Organization
980 9th St Suite 1730
Sacramento, CA 95814
www.sactoedc.org
Phone: 916-441-2144
Fax: 916-441-2312

Sacramento Convention & Visitors Bureau
1303 J St Suite 600
Sacramento, CA 95814
www.sacramentocvb.org
Phone: 916-264-7777
Fax: 916-264-7788
TF: 800-292-2334

Sacramento Convention Center
1400 J St
Sacramento, CA 95814
www.sacto.org/cvsd/convctr/
Phone: 916-264-5291
Fax: 916-264-7687

Sacramento County
700 H St Rm 7650
Sacramento, CA 95814
www.co.sacramento.ca.us
Phone: 916-874-5833
Fax: 916-874-5885

Sacramento Metro Chamber of Commerce
917 7th St
Sacramento, CA 95814
www.metrochamber.org
Phone: 916-552-6800
Fax: 916-443-2672

Online Resources

4Sacramento.com
www.4sacramento.com

About.com Guide to Sacramento
sacramento.about.com/local/caus/sacramento

Access Sacramento
www.sacramento.org

Anthill City Guide Sacramento
www.anthill.com/city.asp?city=sacramento

Area Guide Sacramento
sacramento.areaguides.net

City Knowledge Sacramento
www.cityknowledge.com/ca_sacramento.htm

CitySearch Sacramento
sacramento.citysearch.com

DigitalCity Sacramento
home.digitalcity.com/sacramento

Excite.com Sacramento City Guide
www.excite.com/travel/countries/united_states/california/sacramento

InSacramento.com
www.insacramento.com

Lodging.com Sacramento California
www.lodging.com/auto/guides/sacramento-area-ca.html

Sacramento Art Scene Online
sacarts.com/

Sacramento City Information
www.pageweavers.com/sacvisitors.html

Sacramento Fun
www.sactofun.com/

Sacramento Sites
www.worldofweb.com/sacsite.html

Sacramento Valley Online
www.tourvision.com/

Sacramento Web World
www.sacweb.com/sac_world/

Sacramento's InfoVillage
infovillage.com

Sacramento.TheLinks.com
sacramento.thelinks.com/

SactoFUN.com
www.sactofun.com

SacTown
www.sactown.com

Area Communities

Incorporated communities in Greater Sacramento (including Sacramento, El Dorado, Placer, and Yolo counties) with populations greater than 10,000 include:

Davis
23 Russell Blvd
Davis, CA 95616
Phone: 530-757-5602
Fax: 530-753-1224

Folsom
50 Natoma St
Folsom, CA 95630
Phone: 916-355-7200
Fax: 916-355-7328

Galt
380 Civic Dr
Galt, CA 95632
Phone: 209-745-2961
Fax: 209-745-9794

Rocklin
3970 Rocklin Rd
Rocklin, CA 95677
Phone: 916-632-4000
Fax: 916-624-8018

Roseville
2005 Hilltop Cir
Roseville, CA 95747
Phone: 916-774-5325
Fax: 916-773-7348

West Sacramento
2101 Stone Blvd
West Sacramento, CA 95691
Phone: 916-373-5800
Fax: 916-372-8765

Woodland
300 1st St
Woodland, CA 95695
Phone: 530-661-5800
Fax: 530-661-5813

Economy

Greater Sacramento's diverse economic base ranges from almond growing to computer chip manufacturing. As California's state capital and the seat of Sacramento County, government plays a primary role in Sacramento's economy, employing more than 210,000 people at the federal, state, and local levels in Sacramento County alone. The State of California is the region's largest employer, providing jobs for more than 70,000 area residents (more people than the next ten largest employers combined). Services is the next largest employment sector in Sacramento County, with health care being the primary industry. Biotechnology and data processing, along with electronics, are the fastest-growing industries in Greater Sacramento.

Unemployment Rate 3.9%*
Per Capita Income $24,969*
Median Family Income $51,900**

** Information given is for Sacramento County.*
*** Information given is for the Sacramento Metropolitan Statistical Area (MSA), which includes the City of Davis, the City of Roseville, the City of Sacramento, the City of Woodland, El Dorado County, Placer County, Sacramento County, and Yolo County.*

Principal Industries & Number of Wage Earners

Sacramento County - 1999

Agriculture 20,000
Construction 48,300
Finance, Insurance, & Real Estate 53,700
Government 213,900

Manufacturing 56,500
Mining 500
Retail Trade.......... 137,000
Services 212,500
Transportation & Public Utilities 34,400
Wholesale Trade.......... 35,100

Major Employers

A Teichert & Son Inc
PO Box 15002
Sacramento, CA 95851
www.teichert.com
Phone: 916-484-3011
Fax: 916-484-6506

Blue Diamond Growers
1802 C St
Sacramento, CA 95814
www.bluediamond.com
Phone: 916-442-0771
Fax: 916-446-8620
TF: 888-285-1351

Hewlett-Packard Co
8000 Foothills Blvd
Roseville, CA 95747
www.hp.com
Phone: 916-786-8000
Fax: 916-785-6180

Intel Corp
1900 Prairie City Rd
Folsom, CA 95630
www.intel.com
Phone: 916-356-8080
Fax: 916-356-5427

Level One Communications Inc
9750 Goethe Rd
Sacramento, CA 95827
www.level1.com
Phone: 916-855-5000
Fax: 916-854-1101

Mercy Healthcare Corp
10540 White Rock Rd
Rancho Cordova, CA 95670
www.mercysacramento.org
Phone: 916-851-2000
Fax: 916-851-2727

NEC Computers Inc
15 Business Pkwy
Sacramento, CA 95826
www.nec-computers.com
Phone: 916-388-0101
Fax: 916-388-6459

Pride Industries
1 Sierragate Plaza Suite A200
Roseville, CA 95678
Phone: 916-783-5266
Fax: 800-888-0447

Raley's
PO Box 15618
Sacramento, CA 95852
E-mail: feedback@raleys.com
www.raleys.com
Phone: 916-373-3333
Fax: 916-371-1323
TF: 800-925-9989

Sacramento City Hall
915 'I' St
Sacramento, CA 95814
E-mail: city@sacto.org
www.sacto.org
Phone: 916-264-5427
Fax: 916-264-7672

Sacramento County
700 H St Rm 7650
Sacramento, CA 95814
www.co.sacramento.ca.us
Phone: 916-874-5833
Fax: 916-874-5885

Sacramento Unified School District
520 Capitol Mall
Sacramento, CA 95814
www.scusd.edu
Phone: 916-264-4300
Fax: 916-264-4496

Sutter Health
PO Box 160727
Sacramento, CA 95816
www.sutterhealth.org
Phone: 916-733-8800
Fax: 916-554-6500

University of California Davis
1 Shields Ave
Davis, CA 95616
E-mail: newsservice@ucdavis.edu
www.ucdavis.edu
Phone: 530-752-1011
Fax: 530-752-2553

Quality of Living Indicators

Total Crime Index.......... 31,620
(rates per 100,000 inhabitants)

Violent Crime
Murder/manslaughter.......... 31
Forcible rape 141
Robbery.......... 1,689
Aggravated assault.......... 1,515

Property Crime
Burglary 6,505
Larceny theft 15,733
Motor vehicle theft 6,006

Cost of Living Index.......... 106.6
(national average = 100)

Median Home Price.......... $133,800

Education

Public Schools

Sacramento Unified School District
520 Capitol Mall
Sacramento, CA 95814
www.scusd.edu
Phone: 916-264-4300
Fax: 916-264-4496

Number of Schools
Elementary.......... 59
Middle 11
High.......... 8

Student/Teacher Ratio
All Grades 22.5:1

Private Schools

Number of Schools (all grades).......... 100+

Colleges & Universities

American River College
4700 College Oak Dr
Sacramento, CA 95841
www.arc.losrios.cc.ca.us/
Phone: 916-484-8011
Fax: 916-484-8674

California State University Sacramento
6000 J St
Sacramento, CA 95819
www.csus.edu
Phone: 916-278-6011
Fax: 916-278-5603

Cosumnes River College
8401 Center Pkwy
Sacramento, CA 95823
wserver.crc.losrios.cc.ca.us
Phone: 916-688-7410
Fax: 916-688-7467

D-Q University
PO Box 409
Davis, CA 95617
Phone: 530-758-0470
Fax: 530-758-4891

Heald Business College Rancho Cordova
2910 Prospect Park Dr
Rancho Cordova, CA 95670
Phone: 916-638-1616
Fax: 916-853-8282
TF: 800-499-4333

ITT Technical Institute
10863 Gold Center Dr
Rancho Cordova, CA 95670
www.itt-tech.edu
Phone: 916-851-3900
Fax: 916-851-9225
TF: 800-488-8466

National Center of Continuing Education
114 N Sunrise Ave Suite 5B
Roseville, CA 95661
E-mail: ncce@worldnet.att.net
www.nursece.com
Phone: 916-786-4626
Fax: 916-786-4603
TF: 800-824-1254

Sacramento City College
3835 Freeport Blvd
Sacramento, CA 95822
www.scc.losrios.cc.ca.us/
Phone: 916-558-2111
Fax: 916-558-2190

Sierra Community College
5000 Rocklin Rd
Rocklin, CA 95677
www.sierra.cc.ca.us
Phone: 916-624-3333
Fax: 916-781-0455

Trinity Life Bible College
5225 Hillsdale Blvd
Sacramento, CA 95842
Phone: 916-348-4689
Fax: 916-334-2315

Hospitals

Kaiser Permanente Medical Center
2025 Morse Ave
Sacramento, CA 95825
Phone: 916-973-5000
Fax: 916-973-5717

Kaiser Permanente Medical Center
6600 Bruceville Rd
Sacramento, CA 95823
Phone: 916-688-2000
Fax: 916-688-2978
TF: 800-464-4000

Mercy General Hospital
4001 J St
Sacramento, CA 95819
www.mercysacramento.org/general.html
Phone: 916-453-4545
Fax: 916-453-4295

Mercy San Juan Hospital
6501 Coyle Ave
Carmichael, CA 95608
Phone: 916-537-5000
Fax: 916-537-5427

Methodist Hospital
7500 Hospital Dr
Sacramento, CA 95823
Phone: 916-423-3000
Fax: 916-423-5954

Roseville Medical Center
1 Medical Plaza
Roseville, CA 95661
Phone: 916-781-1000
Fax: 916-781-1624

Sutter General Hospital
2801 L St
Sacramento, CA 95816
Phone: 916-454-2222
Fax: 916-733-8894

Sutter Memorial Hospital
5151 F St
Sacramento, CA 95819
Phone: 916-454-3333
Fax: 916-733-8135

University of California Davis Medical Center
2315 Stockton Blvd
Sacramento, CA 95817
www.ucdmc.ucdavis.edu
Phone: 916-734-3096
Fax: 916-734-8080

Woodland Memorial Hospital
1325 Cottonwood St
Woodland, CA 95695
Phone: 530-662-3961
Fax: 530-666-4363

Transportation

Airport(s)

Sacramento Metropolitan Airport (SMF)
12 miles NW of downtown (approx 20 minutes) . . . 916-929-5411

Mass Transit

Regional Transit
$1.25 Base fare . . . 916-321-2877
River Otter Taxi Co
$5 Base fare . . . 916-448-4333

Rail/Bus

Amtrak Station
401 'I' St
Sacramento, CA 95814
Phone: 916-444-7094
TF: 800-872-7245

Greyhound Bus Station
715 L St
Sacramento, CA 95814
Phone: 916-444-7270
TF: 800-231-2222

Utilities

Electricity
Sacramento Municipal Utility District . . . 888-742-7683
www.smud.org

Gas
Pacific Gas & Electric Co . . . 800-743-5000
www.pge.com

Water
Sacramento Water Sewer & Storm Drain . . . 916-264-5371

Garbage Collection/Recycling
Sacramento Garbage Collection . . . 916-264-5454

Telecommunications

Telephone
Pacific Bell . . . 800-310-2355
www.pacbell.com

Cable Television
Cable America Corp . . . 916-364-0500
Comcast Cable . . . 916-927-3300
Sacramento County Cable TV Commission . . . 916-874-6661
Wireless Broadcasting . . . 916-928-2500

Internet Service Providers (ISPs)
Arden Computers Inc . . . 916-489-2000
www.ardennet.com
CalWeb Internet Services Inc . . . 916-641-9320
www.calweb.com
Coastal Web Online . . . 916-552-7922
www.cwo.com

Davis Community Network.....................530-750-0101
dcn.davis.ca.us
mother.com Inc...............................530-757-8070
www.mother.com
Quiknet Information Services Inc...............916-782-9700
www.quiknet.com
Verio Sacramento.............................916-856-1530
home.verio.net/local/frontpage.cfm?AirportCode=SMF

Banks

Bank of America National Trust & Savings Assn Phone: 916-373-6920
555 Capitol Mall
Sacramento, CA 95814

Bank of the West Phone: 916-483-7800
2581 Fair Oaks Blvd
Sacramento, CA 95825

California Bank & Trust Phone: 916-443-5761
1331 Broadway
Sacramento, CA 95818

California Federal Bank FSB Phone: 800-843-2265
5618 Freeport Blvd Fax: 916-395-6346
Sacramento, CA 95822

River City Bank Phone: 916-920-2265
2485 Natomas Park Dr Fax: 916-567-2784
Sacramento, CA 95833
www.rcbank.com

Sacramento Commercial Bank Phone: 916-443-4700
525 J St Fax: 916-443-8076
Sacramento, CA 95814
E-mail: scbinfo@scbusa.com
www.scbusa.com

Sanwa Bank California Phone: 916-441-7730
601 J St Fax: 916-446-7862
Sacramento, CA 95814

Union Bank Phone: 916-321-3164
700 L St Fax: 916-442-2176
Sacramento, CA 95814

US Bank NA Phone: 916-552-1800
980 9th St Fax: 916-556-5525
Sacramento, CA 95814 TF: 800-872-2657

Washington Mutual Bank FA Phone: 916-326-4500
930 K St Fax: 916-326-4563
Sacramento, CA 95814 TF: 800-788-7000

Wells Fargo Bank NA Phone: 916-440-4331
400 Capitol Mall Fax: 916-489-9376
Sacramento, CA 95814

Shopping

Antique Plaza Phone: 916-852-8517
11395 Folsom Blvd Fax: 916-852-8746
Rancho Cordova, CA 95742
www.antiqueplazaonline.com

Arden Fair Mall Phone: 916-920-1167
1689 Arden Way Fax: 916-920-8652
Sacramento, CA 95815
E-mail: ardenfair@hotmail.com
www.ardenfair.com/

Country Club Plaza Phone: 916-481-6716
2401 Butano Dr Fax: 916-481-5350
Sacramento, CA 95825
E-mail: ccpmall@aol.com

Florin Mall Phone: 916-421-0881
6117 Florin Rd Fax: 916-422-1534
Sacramento, CA 95823
E-mail: info@florinmall.com
www.florinmall.com

Folsom Premium Outlets Phone: 916-985-0313
13000 Folsom Blvd Fax: 916-985-0830
Folsom, CA 95630
www.premiumoutlets.com/location/folsom/fols.html

Macy's Phone: 916-444-3333
414 K St Downtown Plaza Mall
Sacramento, CA 95814

Old Sacramento Public Market Phone: 916-442-7644
1101 2nd St Fax: 916-264-8465
Sacramento, CA 95814
E-mail: oldsac@sacto.org
www.oldsacramento.com/public_market.htmlx

Pavilions Phone: 916-925-4463
563 Pavilions Ln
Sacramento, CA 95825

Sacramento's Antique Row Phone: 916-739-1757
855 57th St
Sacramento, CA 95819

Sunrise Mall Phone: 916-961-7150
6041 Sunrise Mall Fax: 916-961-7326
Citrus Heights, CA 95610
www.sunrise-mall.com

Town & Country Village Phone: 916-383-3333
7750 College Town Dr Suite 350 Fax: 916-383-3974
Sacramento, CA 95826

Westfield Shoppingtown Downtown Plaza Phone: 916-442-4000
547 L St Fax: 916-442-3117
Sacramento, CA 95814

Media

Newspapers and Magazines

Sacramento Bee* Phone: 916-321-1000
PO Box 15779 Fax: 916-321-1109
Sacramento, CA 95852 TF: 800-876-8700
www.sacbee.com

Sacramento Business Journal Phone: 916-447-7661
1401 21st St Suite 200 Fax: 916-444-7779
Sacramento, CA 95814
www.amcity.com/sacramento/

Sacramento Magazine
4471 D St
Sacramento, CA 95819
www.sacmag.com
Phone: 916-452-6200
Fax: 916-452-6061

Sacramento News & Review
1015 20th St
Sacramento, CA 95814
E-mail: sacramento@newsreview.com
www.newsreview.com/sacto
Phone: 916-498-1234
Fax: 916-498-7910

**Indicates major daily newspapers*

Television

KCRA-TV Ch 3 (NBC)
3 Television Cir
Sacramento, CA 95814
www.kcra.com
Phone: 916-446-3333
Fax: 916-441-4050

KMAX-TV Ch 31 (UPN)
500 Media Pl
Sacramento, CA 95815
www.paramountstations.com/KMAX
Phone: 916-925-3100
Fax: 916-921-3050

KNSO-TV Ch 51 (WB)
142 N 9th St Suite 8
Modesto, CA 95350
Phone: 209-529-5100
Fax: 209-575-4547

KOVR-TV Ch 13 (CBS)
2713 KOVR Dr
West Sacramento, CA 95605
www.kovr.com
Phone: 916-374-1313
Fax: 916-374-1304

KQCA-TV Ch 58 (WB)
58 Television Cir
Sacramento, CA 95814
Phone: 916-447-5858
Fax: 916-441-4050

KTXL-TV Ch 40 (Fox)
4655 Fruitridge Rd
Sacramento, CA 95820
Phone: 916-454-4422
Fax: 916-739-0559

KUVS-TV Ch 19 (Uni)
1710 Arden Way
Sacramento, CA 95815
www.univision.net/stations/kuvs.htm
Phone: 916-927-1900
Fax: 916-614-1906

KVIE-TV Ch 6 (PBS)
2595 Capitol Oaks Dr
Sacramento, CA 95833
E-mail: member@kvie.org
www.kvie.org
Phone: 916-929-5843
Fax: 916-929-7367

KXTV-TV Ch 10 (ABC)
400 Broadway
Sacramento, CA 95818
E-mail: kxtv10@kxtv10.com
www.kxtv10.com
Phone: 916-441-2345
Fax: 916-447-6107

Radio

KBMB-FM 103.5 MHz (CHR)
1017 Front St
Sacramento, CA 95814
www.kbmb.com
Phone: 916-440-9500
Fax: 916-444-6641

KCTC-AM 1320 kHz (Nost)
5345 Madison Ave
Sacramento, CA 95841
Phone: 916-334-7777
Fax: 916-334-1092
TF: 800-896-1669

KDND-FM 107.9 MHz (CHR)
5345 Madison Ave
Sacramento, CA 95841
www.endonline.com
Phone: 916-334-7777
Fax: 916-334-1092

KFBK-AM 1530 kHz (N/T)
1440 Ethan Way Suite 200
Sacramento, CA 95825
www.kfbk.com
Phone: 916-929-5325
Fax: 916-921-5555

KFIA-AM 710 kHz (Rel)
1425 River Park Dr Suite 520
Sacramento, CA 95815
E-mail: talk@kfia.com
www.kfia.com
Phone: 916-924-0710
Fax: 916-924-1587

KGBY-FM 92.5 MHz (AC)
1440 Ethan Way Suite 200
Sacramento, CA 95825
E-mail: webpage@y92.com
www.y92.com
Phone: 916-929-5325
Fax: 916-925-9292

KHTK-AM 1140 kHz (Sports)
5244 Madison Ave
Sacramento, CA 95841
www.khtk.com
Phone: 916-338-9200
Fax: 916-338-9159
TF: 800-920-1140

KHYL-FM 101.1 MHz (Oldies)
1440 Ethan Way Suite 200
Sacramento, CA 95825
Phone: 916-929-5325

KHZZ-FM 104.3 MHz (Oldies)
298 Commerce Cir
Sacramento, CA 95815
Phone: 916-641-1043
Fax: 916-641-1078

KNCI-FM 105.1 MHz (Ctry)
5244 Madison Ave
Sacramento, CA 95841
www.kncifm.com
Phone: 916-338-9200
Fax: 916-338-9208

KQPT-FM 100.5 MHz (Oldies)
280 Commerce Cir
Sacramento, CA 95815
www.radiozone.com
Phone: 916-635-1005
Fax: 916-923-6825

KRAK-AM 1470 kHz (Ctry)
5244 Madison Ave
Sacramento, CA 95841
www.krakam.com
Phone: 916-338-9200
Fax: 916-338-9202

KRXQ-FM 98.5 MHz (Rock)
5345 Madison Ave
Sacramento, CA 95841
www.krxq98rock.com
Phone: 916-334-7777
Fax: 916-339-4292

KSEG-FM 96.9 MHz (CR)
5345 Madison Ave
Sacramento, CA 95841
www.eagle969.com
Phone: 916-334-9690
Fax: 916-339-4280

KSFM-FM 102.5 MHz (CHR)
1750 Howe Ave Suite 500
Sacramento, CA 95825
www.ksfm.com
Phone: 916-920-1025
Fax: 916-929-5341

KSSJ-FM 94.7 MHz (CR)
5345 Madison Ave
Sacramento, CA 95841
E-mail: comments@kssj.com
www.kssj.com
Phone: 916-334-7777
Fax: 916-339-4290

KSTE-AM 650 kHz (N/T)
1440 Ethan Way Suite 200
Sacramento, CA 95825
E-mail: talk650kst@aol.com
www.talk650kste.com
Phone: 916-929-5325
Fax: 916-921-5555

KTKZ-AM 1380 kHz (N/T)
1425 River Park Dr Suite 520
Sacramento, CA 95815
www.ktkz.com
Phone: 916-924-9422
Fax: 916-924-1587

KWOD-FM 106.5 MHz (Alt)
801 K St 27th Fl
Sacramento, CA 95814
www.kwod.com
Phone: 916-448-5000
Fax: 916-448-1655

KXJZ-FM 88.9 MHz (NPR)
3416 American River Dr Suite B
Sacramento, CA 95864
E-mail: npr@csus.edu
www.csus.edu/npr
Phone: 916-480-5900
Fax: 916-487-3348
TF: 877-480-5900

KXOA-FM 93.7 MHz (AC)
5244 Madison Ave
Sacramento, CA 95841
www.arrow937.com
Phone: 916-338-9200
Fax: 916-338-9202

KXPR-FM 90.9 MHz (NPR)
3416 American River Dr Suite B
Sacramento, CA 95864
E-mail: npr@csus.edu
www.csus.edu/npr
Phone: 916-480-5900
Fax: 916-487-3348
TF: 877-480-5900

KYMX-FM 96.1 MHz (AC)
280 Commerce Cir
Sacramento, CA 95815
www.kymx.com
Phone: 916-923-6800
Fax: 916-923-9696

KZSA-FM 92.1 MHz (Span)
1436 Auburn Blvd
Sacramento, CA 95815
Phone: 916-646-4000
Fax: 916-646-1688

KZZO-FM 100.5 MHz (AAA)
280 Commerce Cir
Sacramento, CA 95815
www.thezone.com
Phone: 916-923-6800
Fax: 916-923-9696

Attractions

In the heart of Sacramento, the original fort built by the city's founder, Captain John Sutter, has been restored and transformed into Sutter's Fort State Historic Park, which depicts 19th Century life in the valley before the California Gold Rush. Sacramento's history as the gateway to Gold Rush country is displayed at the Old Sacramento Historic District, located on the banks of the Sacramento River. The district's shops and restaurants have been restored to their 1800s appearance, and old-time paddlewheelers grace the waterfront.

Artists' Collaborative Gallery
1007 2nd St
Sacramento, CA 95814
www.gogh.com/acg
Phone: 916-444-3764

B Street Theatre
2711 B St
Sacramento, CA 95816
Phone: 916-443-5300
Fax: 916-443-0874

Best of Broadway
4010 El Camino Ave Hiriam Johnson High School
Sacramento, CA 95821
www.bestofbroadway.org
Phone: 916-974-6280
Fax: 916-974-6281

Big Four Building
111 'I' St
Sacramento, CA 95814
Phone: 916-445-6645
Fax: 916-327-5655

California Exposition & State Fair
1600 Exposition Blvd
Sacramento, CA 95815
www.calexpo.org
Phone: 916-263-3247
Fax: 916-263-3304

California Military Museum
1119 2nd St
Sacramento, CA 95814
www.militarymuseum.org
Phone: 916-442-2883
Fax: 916-442-7532

California Peace Officers Memorial
10th St & Capitol Mall
Sacramento, CA 95814
Phone: 530-676-3315

California State Archives
1020 'O' St
Sacramento, CA 95814
www.ss.ca.gov/archives/archives.htm
Phone: 916-653-7715
Fax: 916-653-7134

California State Capitol
10th & L Sts
Sacramento, CA 95814
Phone: 916-324-0333
Fax: 916-445-3628

California State Indian Musuem
2618 K St
Sacramento, CA 95816
Phone: 916-324-7405
Fax: 916-322-5231

California State Railroad Museum
111 'I' St
Sacramento, CA 95814
E-mail: csrmf@csrmf.org
www.csrmf.org
Phone: 916-445-6645
Fax: 916-327-5655

Camellia Symphony Orchestra
PO Box 19786
Sacramento, CA 95819
Phone: 916-929-6655
Fax: 916-929-4292

Cathedral of the Blessed Sacrament
1017 11th St
Sacramento, CA 95814
Phone: 916-444-3070
Fax: 916-443-2749

Crest Theatre
1013 K St
Sacramento, CA 95814
E-mail: info@thecrest.com
www.thecrest.com
Phone: 916-442-7378
Fax: 916-442-5939

Crocker Art Museum
216 'O' St
Sacramento, CA 95814
www.crockerartmuseum.org
Phone: 916-264-5423
Fax: 916-264-7372

Del Paso Park
3565 Auburn Blvd
Sacramento, CA 95814
www.cityofsacramento.org/parks/arden.htm
Phone: 916-264-5200

Del Paso Regional Park
I-80 & Auburn St
Sacramento, CA 95820
Phone: 916-566-6581

di Rosa Preserve
5200 Carneros Hwy
Napa, CA 94559
Phone: 707-226-5991
Fax: 707-255-8934

Discover California Wine Tasting Room
114 J St
Sacramento, CA 95814
E-mail: info@discovercal.com
www.discovercal.com
Phone: 916-443-8275
Fax: 916-443-8285

Discovery Museum History Center
101 'I' St
Sacramento, CA 95814
www.thediscovery.org
Phone: 916-264-7057
Fax: 916-264-5100

Discovery Museum Science & Space Center
3615 Auburn Blvd
Sacramento, CA 95821
www.thediscovery.org
Phone: 916-575-3941
Fax: 916-575-3925

Fairytale Town
3901 Land Park Dr
Sacramento, CA 95822
Phone: 916-264-5233

Governor's Mansion
1520 H St
Sacramento, CA 95814
Phone: 916-324-0539

Governor's Mansion State Historic Park
1526 H St
Sacramento, CA 95814
Phone: 916-324-7405
Fax: 916-447-9318

Historic City Cemetery
1000 Broadway
Sacramento, CA 95818
Phone: 916-264-5621
Fax: 916-554-7508

Lassen Volcanic National Park
PO Box 100
Mineral, CA 96063
www.nps.gov/lavo/
Phone: 530-595-4444
Fax: 530-595-3262

McClellan Aviation Museum
3204 Palm Ave
Sacramento, CA 95652
Phone: 916-643-3192
Fax: 916-643-0389

Napa Valley Wine Train
1275 McKinstry St
Napa, CA 94559
www.winetrain.com
Phone: 707-253-2111
Fax: 707-253-9264
TF: 800-427-4124

Nimbus Fish Hatcheries
2001 Nimbus Rd
Rancho Cordova, CA 95670
Phone: 916-358-2820

Old Chinatown-Sacramento "Yee Fow"
Chinatown Mall-betw 3rd & 5th Sts
Sacramento, CA 95814
Phone: 916-448-6465
Fax: 916-448-8969

Old Sacramento Historic District
1111 2nd St Suite 300
Sacramento, CA 95814
E-mail: oldsac@sacto.org
www.oldsacramento.com
Phone: 916-264-7031
Fax: 916-264-7286

Old Sacramento Public Market
1101 2nd St
Sacramento, CA 95814
E-mail: oldsac@sacto.org
www.oldsacramento.com/public_market.htmlx
Phone: 916-442-7644
Fax: 916-264-8465

Old Sacramento Schoolhouse
Front & L Sts
Sacramento, CA 95814
Phone: 916-483-8818
Fax: 916-972-7041

Port of Sacramento
3251 Beacon Blvd Suite 210
West Sacramento, CA 95691
www.portofsacramento.com
Phone: 916-371-8000
Fax: 916-372-4802
TF: 888-258-7969

Roseville Telephone Museum
106 Vernon St
Roseville, CA 95678
Phone: 916-786-1621
Fax: 916-786-7170

Sacramento Ballet
1631 K St
Sacramento, CA 95814
www.sacballet.org
Phone: 916-552-5800
Fax: 916-552-5815

Sacramento Community Center Theater
14th & L Sts
Sacramento, CA 95814
Phone: 916-264-5181
Fax: 916-264-7317

Sacramento Opera Assn
3811 J St
Sacramento, CA 95816
E-mail: sacopera@pacbell.net
www.sacopera.org
Phone: 916-737-1000
Fax: 916-737-1032

Sacramento Philharmonic Orchestra
900 Howe Ave
Sacramento, CA 95825
Phone: 916-922-9200

Sacramento Theatre Co
1419 H St
Sacramento, CA 95814
www.sactheatre.org
Phone: 916-443-6722
Fax: 916-446-4066

Sacramento Traditional Jazz Society
2787 Del Monte St
West Sacramento, CA 95691
E-mail: stjs@earthlink.net
www.sacjazz.com
Phone: 916-372-5277
Fax: 916-372-3479

Sacramento Zoo
3930 W Land Park Dr
Sacramento, CA 95822
www.saczoo.com
Phone: 916-264-5166
Fax: 916-264-5887

Six Flags Marine World
2001 Marine World Pkwy
Vallejo, CA 94589
www.sixflags.com/marineworld
Phone: 707-644-4000
Fax: 707-644-0241

Sutter's Fort State Historic Park
2701 L St
Sacramento, CA 95816
cal-parks.ca.gov/DISTRICTS/goldrush/sfshp.htm
Phone: 916-324-0539

Towe Ford Museum of Automotive History
2200 Front St
Sacramento, CA 95818
www.classicar.com/museums/toweford/toweford.htm
Phone: 916-442-6802
Fax: 916-442-2646

Travels Through Time Science Fiction Museum
1017 Front St Suite B
Old Sacramento, CA 95814
Phone: 916-444-2320
Fax: 916-444-2320

Waterworld USA Phone: 916-924-3747
1600 Exposition Blvd Fax: 916-924-1314
Sacramento, CA 95815
www.sixflags.com/wwsacramento/index.cfm

Wells Fargo History Museum Phone: 916-440-4161
400 Capitol Mall Wells Fargo Ctr Fax: 916-498-0302
Sacramento, CA 95814

William Land Park Phone: 916-264-5200
Sutterville Rd & S Land Pk Dr
Sacramento, CA 95814

Yeaw Effie Nature Center Ansel Hoffman Park Phone: 916-489-4918
6700 Tarshes Dr Fax: 916-489-4983
Carmichael, CA 95609

Sports Teams & Facilities

ARCO Arena Phone: 916-928-0000
1 Sports Pkwy Fax: 916-928-0727
Sacramento, CA 95834
www.arcoarena.com

California Exposition & State Fair Phone: 916-263-3279
1600 Exposition Blvd Fax: 916-263-3198
Sacramento, CA 95815
www.racingfairs.org/lr-calex.html

Sacramento Kings Phone: 916-928-6900
1 Sports Pkwy ARCO Arena Fax: 916-928-0727
Sacramento, CA 95834
www.nba.com/kings

Sacramento Knights (soccer) Phone: 916-928-3650
1 Sports Pkwy ARCO Arena Fax: 916-928-6919
Sacramento, CA 95834
www.sacknights.com

Sacramento Monarchs (basketball) Phone: 916-928-3641
1 Sports Pkwy ARCO Arena Fax: 916-928-8109
Sacramento, CA 95834
www.wnba.com/monarchs

Sacramento River Rats (hockey) Phone: 916-263-3049
1600 Exposition Blvd CalExpo
Sacramento, CA 95852

Annual Events

Austrian Winterfest (mid-February)................916-635-4468
Autorama (early February)........................503-236-0632
Bockbierfest (early April).........................916-442-7360
California International Marathon (early December).............................916-983-4622
California State Fair (mid-August-early September) 916-263-3093
Chalk it Up to Sacramento! (late April) 916-484-5710
Chinese New Year Celebration (late February) 916-777-5880
Christmas Craft Faire (early December)............916-985-7452
Christmas Memories Celebration (December).......916-323-3047
Cinco de Mayo Celebrations (early May)............916-263-3021
Crawdad Festival (mid-June)......................916-777-5880
Downtown Concert Series (early May-late August).........................916-442-8575
Elk Grove Western Festival (early May) 916-685-3911
Fair Oaks Fiesta (early May)......................916-967-2903
Fair Oaks Renaissance Tudor Fayre (late June).....916-966-1036
Fall Collectors' Faire (mid-September).............916-558-3912
Festa Italiana (mid-August).......................916-482-5900
Festival de la Familia (late April).................916-326-5521
Festival of Cinema (late October)..................916-442-5189
Festival of the Arts (mid-April) 916-278-6156
Folsom Championship Rodeo (early July) 916-985-2698
Friday Night Concerts (early May-mid-July) 916-442-8575
Gift & Gourmet Show (mid-November) 916-483-9173
Greek Food Festival (early September).............916-443-2033
Highland Scottish Games (late April) 916-557-0764
International Railfair (early-mid-November) 916-991-4343
Japanese Cultural Bazaar (early August)............916-446-0121
LPGA Longs Drugs Challenge (late March-early April) 916-434-2224
Mardi Gras Parade (early February)................916-443-6223
Market at Summerfest (May-mid-August) 916-442-8575
Martin Luther King Community Celebration (mid-January)................................916-395-1895
Meadowview Jazz Festival (late June) 916-264-7337
Memorial Day Parade (late May)...................916-366-3987
Native American Arts & Crafts Show (late November)..............................916-324-0971
Oktoberfest (early October).......................916-442-7360
Old Sacramento Oktoberfest (early October)........916-558-3912
Pacific Coast Rowing Championship (mid-May).....916-985-7239
Pacific Rim Street Fest (mid-May) 916-264-7031
Pioneer Traders' & Crafts Faire (late April) 916-445-4422
Pony Express Reride (mid-June) 916-264-7031
Renaissance Faire & Tournament (mid-October)....916-355-7285
Sacramento Boat Show (mid-March) 916-263-3218
Sacramento Camellia Show (early March) 916-264-5181
Sacramento County Fair (early May)...............916-263-2975
Sacramento Heritage Festival (early June)..........916-481-2583
Sacramento Home & Garden Show (early March) 916-924-9934
Sacramento International Festival of Cinema (mid-late September) 916-442-7378
Sacramento Jazz Jubilee (late May)................916-372-5277
Sacramento Shakespeare Festival (July)............916-558-2228
Sacramento Sports Boat & RV Show (mid-February)...............................916-452-6403
Saint Patrick's Day Parade (mid-March) 916-264-7031
Saint Patrick's Day Weekend (mid-March)..........916-558-3912
Santa Parade (late November).....................916-443-6223
Shakespeare Lite! (mid-June-mid-July).............916-442-8575
Spring Collectors' Fair (mid-April) 916-264-7031
Spring Italian Music Festival (late May)............916-482-5900
Strauss Festival (late July) 916-685-3911
Sutter Street Antique Market (mid-April & mid-September)..................916-985-7452
Sutter Street Arts & Crafts Fair (early May)........916-985-2698
US National Handcar Races (early September)......916-445-1018
US Pro Water Ski & Pro Wake Board Tournament (late June)..................................800-334-6541
Water Festival (early June) 916-985-2698
Waterfront Art Fest (early May)...................916-442-7644
Wednesday Farmers' Market (May-November).......916-442-8575

Saint Louis, Missouri

***County:* Independent City**

SAINT LOUIS is located on the Mississippi River just south of its confluence with the Missouri River in eastern Missouri. Major cities within 100 miles include Columbia and Cape Girardeau, Missouri; and Carbondale and Springfield, Illinois.

Area (Land)	61.9 sq mi
Area (Water)	4.2 sq mi
Elevation	470 ft
Latitude	38-62-72 N
Longitude	90-19-78 W
Time Zone	CST
Area Code	314

Climate

Saint Louis has a continental climate with four distinct seasons. Winters are generally cold, with average high temperatures in the upper 30s to low 40s and average lows in the low to mid-20s. The average annual snowfall in Saint Louis is just under 20 inches. Summers are very warm and humid, with average high temperatures in the mid- to upper 80s and average lows in the upper 60s. May is the wettest month of the year in Saint Louis; January is the driest.

Average Temperatures & Precipitation

Temperatures

	Jan	Feb	Mar	Apr	May	Jun	Jul	Aug	Sep	Oct	Nov	Dec
High	38	43	55	67	76	85	89	87	80	69	55	42
Low	21	25	36	46	56	66	70	68	61	48	38	26

Precipitation

	Jan	Feb	Mar	Apr	May	Jun	Jul	Aug	Sep	Oct	Nov	Dec
Inches	1.8	2.1	3.6	3.5	4.0	3.7	3.9	2.9	3.1	2.7	3.3	3.0

History

Although the Saint Louis area had been inhabited by the Hopewell tribe (also known as "Mound Builders") as early as 500 B.C., the first permanent white settlement was not established in the area until the mid-18th Century. In 1763, a French fur trader named Pierre Laclede Liguest chose the area just south of the confluence of the Mississippi and Missouri Rivers as the site for a trading post. The following year, a village was established there and named Saint Louis in honor Louis XVI of France. From the time of its founding until just after the turn of the century, control of Saint Louis shifted between France and Spain, although the population remained predominantly French. In 1803, Saint Louis became part of the United States with the signing of the Louisiana Purchase, and formal ceremonies confirming the transaction were held in the city following year. The year 1804 also marked the beginning of westward expansion, as Lewis and Clark set off on their famous expedition from Saint Louis, earning the city the nickname "Gateway to the West."

Saint Louis prospered during the 19th century as a fur trading center and as an outfitting post for pioneers heading west. During the 1800s, Saint Louis also developed into a major transportation center—first for steamboat traffic and later as a railroad hub. In 1820, Missouri was admitted to the Union as a slave state under the Missouri Compromise; three years later, Saint Louis was incorporated as a city. The notorious Dred Scott Case, which resulted in a ruling that deemed slaves non-citizens, was held in Saint Louis during the 1840s and '50s. The 1850s also brought a wave of new German and Irish immigrants to Saint Louis, who arrived in the city seeking economic opportunities via the newly constructed railroad. Sympathies of Saint Louis' citizens were divided during the Civil War, but the city remained under Union control throughout the war, serving as a major supply base for some one million soldiers. In the years following the Civil War, Saint Louis continued to grow and prosper, becoming a leading manufacturing center.

In 1904, Saint Louis hosted both the Olympic Games and the World's Fair (also known as the Louisiana Purchase Exhibition), which drew more than 20 million visitors to the city during its six-month run. Saint Louis also gained importance as a major contributor to the growing aviation industry during the 20th Century as the site of the first international air meet (1910), the support behind Charles Lindbergh's nonstop transatlantic flight in the "Spirit of St. Louis" (1927), and the birthplace of McDonnell Douglas (1939), one of the country's leading aviation companies. Saint Louis continued to thrive as a manufacturing center during the war years, but the city's economy and population began to decline after 1950 as residents began moving out of the city and into the suburbs. Construction of Saint Louis' most famous landmark, the Gateway Arch, and Busch Stadium—home of the Saint Louis Cardinals—during the 1960s, as well as a series of major redevelopment projects that began in the 1970s, have contributed to the city's revival.

Today, Saint Louis is a vital manufacturing and transportation center, ranking as one of the nation's busiest inland ports. Although much of the ten-county, two-state (Missouri and Illinois) Saint Louis metropolitan area's population lives outside of the city itself, Saint Louis is Missouri's second-largest city, with a population of more than 339,000.

Population

1990 Census	396,685
1998 Estimate	339,316
% Change	-14.5

Racial/Ethnic Breakdown

White	50.9%
Black	47.5%
Other	1.6%
Hispanic Origin (may be of any race)	1.3%

Age Breakdown
Under 5 years . . . 7.9%
5 to 17 . . . 17.3%
18 to 20 . . . 4.3%
21 to 24 . . . 6.1%
25 to 34 . . . 18.3%
35 to 44 . . . 12.8%
45 to 54 . . . 8.0%
55 to 64 . . . 8.5%
65 to 74 . . . 8.4%
75+ years . . . 8.2%
Median Age . . . 32.8

Gender Breakdown
Male . . . 45.5%
Female . . . 54.5%

Government

Type of Government: Mayor-Board of Aldermen

Saint Louis Board of Aldermen
1200 Market St Rm 230
Saint Louis, MO 63103
Phone: 314-622-3287
Fax: 314-622-4273

Saint Louis City Counselor
1200 Market St Rm 314
Saint Louis, MO 63103
Phone: 314-622-3361
Fax: 314-622-4956

Saint Louis City Hall
1200 Market St
Saint Louis, MO 63103
Phone: 314-622-4000

Saint Louis Community Development Administration
1015 Locust St Suite 1200
Saint Louis, MO 63101
Phone: 314-622-3400
Fax: 314-622-3413

Saint Louis Fire Dept
1421 N Jefferson Ave
Saint Louis, MO 63106
Phone: 314-289-1953
Fax: 314-534-4371

Saint Louis Human Services Dept
634 N Grand Blvd 7th Fl
Saint Louis, MO 63103
Phone: 314-658-1168
Fax: 314-658-1149

Saint Louis Mayor
1200 Market St Rm 200
Saint Louis, MO 63103
Phone: 314-622-3201
Fax: 314-622-4955

Saint Louis Medical Examiner
1300 Clark Ave
Saint Louis, MO 63103
Phone: 314-622-4971
Fax: 314-622-4933

Saint Louis Parks Recreation & Forestry Dept
5600 Clayton Ave
Saint Louis, MO 63110
Phone: 314-289-5310
Fax: 314-535-3901

Saint Louis Personnel Dept
1200 Market St Rm 100
Saint Louis, MO 63103
Phone: 314-622-4308
Fax: 314-622-4293

Saint Louis Police Dept
1200 Clark St
Saint Louis, MO 63103
Phone: 314-444-5624
Fax: 314-444-5958

Saint Louis Public Library
1301 Olive St
Saint Louis, MO 63103
Phone: 314-241-2288
Fax: 314-539-0393

Saint Louis Public Utilities Dept
1640 S Kingshighway
Saint Louis, MO 63110
Phone: 314-664-8330
Fax: 314-664-6786

Saint Louis Streets Dept
1900 Hampton Ave
Saint Louis, MO 63139
Phone: 314-647-3111
Fax: 314-768-2888

Saint Louis Treasurer
1200 Market St Rm 220
Saint Louis, MO 63103
Phone: 314-622-4700
Fax: 314-622-3782

Important Phone Numbers

AAA . . . 314-576-7373
American Express Travel . . . 314-241-6400
Dental Referral . . . 314-965-5960
Disabled Accessibility Information . . . 314-622-3686
Driver's License Information . . . 573-751-4600
Emergency . . . 911
HotelDocs . . . 800-468-3537
Missouri State Dept of Revenue Taxpayer Services Office . . . 314-301-1660
Poison Control Center . . . 314-772-5200
Saint Louis Board of Realtors . . . 314-576-0033
Saint Louis City Collector of Revenue Earnings Tax Information . . . 314-622-3291
Saint Louis City Collector of Revenue Property Tax Information . . . 314-622-4108
Special Events . . . 314-421-2100
Time/Temp . . . 314-321-2522
Travelers Aid Society . . . 314-241-5820
Vehicle Registration Information . . . 573-751-4509
Voter Registration Information . . . 314-622-4201
Weather . . . 314-321-2222

Information Sources

Better Business Bureau Serving Eastern Missouri & Southern Illinois
12 Sunnen Dr Suite 121
Saint Louis, MO 63143
www.stlouis.bbb.org
Phone: 314-645-3300
Fax: 314-645-2666

Cervantes Convention Center at America's Center
701 Convention Plaza
Saint Louis, MO 63101
Phone: 314-342-5036
Fax: 314-342-5040

Regional Commerce & Growth Assn
1 Metropolitan Sq Suite 1300
Saint Louis, MO 63102
www.stlrcga.org
Phone: 314-231-5555
Fax: 314-444-1122
TF: 800-444-7653

Saint Louis Convention & Visitors Commission
1 Metropolitan Sq Suite 1100
Saint Louis, MO 63102
www.st-louis-cvc.com
Phone: 314-421-1023
Fax: 314-421-0039
TF: 800-325-7962

Saint Louis County
41 S Central Ave
Clayton, MO 63105
www.co.st-louis.mo.us
Phone: 314-615-5432
Fax: 314-615-7890

Online Resources

4SaintLouis.com
www.4stlouis.com

About.com Guide to Saint Louis
stlouis.about.com/local/midwestus/stlouis

Access America Saint Louis
www.accessamer.com/stlouis/

Area Guide Saint Louis
stlouis.areaguides.net

Boulevards Saint Louis
www.stlouis.com

City Knowledge Saint Louis
www.cityknowledge.com/mo_stlouis.htm

Cityhits Saint Louis
www.cityhits.com/index.shtml

CitySearch Saint Louis
stlouis.citysearch.com

DigitalCity St Louis
home.digitalcity.com/stlouis

Excite.com Saint Louis City Guide
www.excite.com/travel/countries/united_states/missouri/st_louis

Gay Saint Louis
www.gaystlouis.com/

Hill The
www.thehill-stl.com

MetroVille Saint Louis
stlouis.metroville.com

Riverfront Times
www.rftstl.com

Rough Guide Travel Saint Louis
travel.roughguides.com/content/972/

Saint Louis Community Information Network
stlouis.missouri.org/

Saint Louis Front Page
www.mooredesign.com/

StLouis.TheLinks.com
stlouis.thelinks.com/

Area Communities

Communities with populations greater than 10,000 in Greater Saint Louis (including Saint Louis, Franklin, Jefferson, and Saint Charles counties in Missouri; and Madison, Monroe, and Saint Clair counties in Illinois) include:

Alton
101 E 3rd St
Alton, IL 62002
Phone: 618-463-3522
Fax: 618-463-0972

Arnold
2101 Jeffco Blvd
Arnold, MO 63010
Phone: 636-296-2100
Fax: 636-282-2392

Ballwin
14811 Manchester Rd
Ballwin, MO 63011
Phone: 636-227-8580
Fax: 636-207-2320

Bellefontaine Neighbors
9641 Bellefontaine Rd
Bellefontaine Neighbors, MO 63137
Phone: 314-867-0076
Fax: 314-867-1790

Belleville
101 S Illinois St
Belleville, IL 62220
Phone: 618-233-6810
Fax: 618-233-6779

Bridgeton
11955 Natural Bridge Rd
Bridgeton, MO 63044
Phone: 314-739-7500
Fax: 314-739-5402

Chesterfield
16052 Swingley Ridge Rd
Chesterfield, MO 63017
Phone: 636-537-4000
Fax: 636-537-4798

Clayton
10 N Bemiston Ave
Clayton, MO 63105
Phone: 314-727-8100

Collinsville
125 S Center St
Collinsville, IL 62234
Phone: 618-344-5252
Fax: 618-346-1662

Crestwood
1 Detjen Dr
Saint Louis, MO 63126
Phone: 314-966-4700

Creve Coeur
300 N New Ballas Rd
Saint Louis, MO 63141
Phone: 314-432-6000
Fax: 314-872-2539

Edwardsville
118 Hillsboro Ave
Edwardsville, IL 62025
Phone: 618-692-7500
Fax: 618-692-7558

Fairview Heights
10025 Bunkum Rd
Fairview Heights, IL 62208
Phone: 618-489-2080
Fax: 618-489-2099

Ferguson
110 Church St
Saint Louis, MO 63135
Phone: 314-521-7721
Fax: 314-524-5173

Florissant
955 Rue St Francois
Florissant, MO 63031
Phone: 314-921-5700
Fax: 314-921-7111

Glen Carbon
151 N Main St
Glen Carbon, IL 62034
Phone: 618-288-1200
Fax: 618-288-1645

Hazelwood
415 Elm Grove Ln
Hazelwood, MO 63042
Phone: 314-839-3700
Fax: 314-839-0249

Kirkwood
139 S Kirkwood Rd
Kirkwood, MO 63122
Phone: 314-822-5802
Fax: 314-822-5863

Maryland Heights
212 Millwell Dr
Maryland Heights, MO 63043
Phone: 314-291-6550
Fax: 314-291-7457

O'Fallon (IL)
255 S Lincoln Ave
O'Fallon, IL 62269
Phone: 618-624-4500
Fax: 618-624-4508

O'Fallon (MO)
100 N Main St
O'Fallon, MO 63366
Phone: 636-240-2000
Fax: 636-978-4144

Saint Charles
200 N 2nd St
Saint Charles, MO 63301
Phone: 636-949-3282
Fax: 636-949-3286

University City
6801 Delmar Blvd
Saint Louis, MO 63130
Phone: 314-862-6767
Fax: 314-863-9146

Washington
405 Jefferson St
Washington, MO 63090
Phone: 636-390-1005
Fax: 636-239-8945

Webster Groves
4 E Lockwood Ave
Saint Louis, MO 63119
Phone: 314-963-5300
Fax: 314-963-7561

Economy

One of the busiest inland ports in the United States, Saint Louis has long been a leading transportation and manufacturing center. It is also the corporate home of some of the nation's top companies, including Anheuser-Busch, May Department Stores, McDonnell Douglas, Monsanto, and Ralston Purina. Although transportation and manufacturing remain important to Saint Louis' economy, services is currently the area's largest employment sector, with health care representing approximately one-third of the service positions in the city.

Unemployment Rate 4.1%*
Per Capita Income.......................... $29,089*
Median Family Income...................... $52,000*

** Information given is for the Saint Louis Missouri/Illinois Metropolitan Statistical Area (MSA), which includes the City of Saint Charles, City of Saint Louis, City of Sullivan, Franklin County, Jefferson County, Saint Charles County, and Saint Louis County, in Missouri; and the City of Alton, City of Granite, Clinton County, Jersey County, Madison County, Monroe County, and Saint Clair County, in Illinois.*

Principal Industries & Number of Wage Earners

City of Saint Louis - 4th Quarter 1999

Industry	Wage Earners
Agricultural Services, Forestry, & Fishing	371
Construction	7,530
Finance, Insurance, & Real Estate	21,060
Government	41,202
Manufacturing	36,122
Retail Trade	27,059
Services	82,104
Transportation & Public Utilities	21,163
Wholesale Trade	14,170

Major Employers

AG Edwards & Sons Inc
1 N Jefferson Ave
Saint Louis, MO 63103
www.agedwards.com
Phone: 314-955-3000
Fax: 314-955-4536

Anheuser-Busch Cos Inc
1 Busch Pl
Saint Louis, MO 63118
www.anheuser-busch.com
Phone: 314-577-2000
Fax: 314-577-2900
TF: 800-342-5283

Barnes-Jewish Hospital
216 S Kings Hwy
Saint Louis, MO 63110
www.bjc.org/bjh.html
Phone: 314-362-5000
Fax: 314-362-8877

Christian Hospital Northeast
11133 Dunn Rd
Saint Louis, MO 63136
Phone: 314-355-2300
Fax: 314-653-4153

Clark USA Inc
8182 Maryland Ave
Clayton, MO 63105
www.clarkusa.com
Phone: 314-854-9696
Fax: 314-854-1580
TF: 800-746-4322

DaimlerChrysler Corp Assembly Div
1001 N Highway Dr
Fenton, MO 63026
www.daimlerchrysler.com
Phone: 636-349-4026
Fax: 636-349-4034

Emerson Electric Co
8000 W Florissant Ave
Saint Louis, MO 63136
www.emersonelectric.com
Phone: 314-553-2000
Fax: 314-553-3527

May Department Stores Co
611 Olive St
Saint Louis, MO 63101
www.mayco.com
Phone: 314-342-6300
Fax: 314-342-3064

Memorial Hospital
4500 Memorial Dr
Belleville, IL 62226
Phone: 618-233-7750
Fax: 618-257-5658

Monsanto Co
800 N Lindbergh Blvd
Saint Louis, MO 63167
www.monsanto.com
Phone: 314-694-1000
Fax: 314-694-8506

Ralston Purina Co
Checkerboard Sq
Saint Louis, MO 63164
E-mail: oteam@ralston.com
www.ralston.com
Phone: 314-982-1000
Fax: 314-982-2917

Saint John's Mercy Medical Center
615 S New Ballas Rd
Saint Louis, MO 63141
Phone: 314-569-6000
Fax: 314-995-4222
TF: 800-876-3729

Saint Louis City Hall
1200 Market St
Saint Louis, MO 63103
stlouis.missouri.org
Phone: 314-622-4000

Saint Louis Public Schools
911 Locust St
Saint Louis, MO 63101
Phone: 314-231-3720
Fax: 314-231-3858

Saint Louis University
221 N Grand Blvd
Saint Louis, MO 63103
E-mail: admitme@sluvca.slu.edu
www.slu.edu
Phone: 314-977-2222
Fax: 314-977-2298

Schnuck Markets Inc
11420 Lackland Rd
Saint Louis, MO 63146
www.schnucks.com
Phone: 314-994-9900
Fax: 314-994-4465
TF: 800-264-4400

Trans World Airlines Inc
515 N 6th St 1 City Ctr
Saint Louis, MO 63101
www.twa.com
Phone: 314-589-3000
Fax: 314-589-3129
TF: 800-221-2000

Washington University
1 Brookings Dr
Saint Louis, MO 63130
www.wustl.edu
Phone: 314-935-5000
Fax: 314-935-4290
TF: 800-638-0700

Quality of Living Indicators

Total Crime Index....................................47,711
(rates per 100,000 inhabitants)

Violent Crime
Murder/manslaughter.......................... 130
Forcible rape 144
Robbery...................................2,792
Aggravated assault...........................4,545

Property Crime
Burglary 7,856
Larceny theft 25,599
Motor vehicle theft 6,645

Cost of Living Index....................................97.7
(national average = 100)

Median Home Price.................................$102,900

Education

Public Schools

Saint Louis Public Schools
911 Locust St
Saint Louis, MO 63101
Phone: 314-231-3720
Fax: 314-231-3858

Number of Schools
Elementary................................. 67
Middle 22
High....................................... 11

Student/Teacher Ratio
All Grades 14.4:1

Private Schools

Number of Schools (all grades).................. 156+

Colleges & Universities

Deaconess College of Nursing
6150 Oakland Ave
Saint Louis, MO 63139
E-mail: info@tenethealth.com
www.tenethealth.com/deaconessnursing
Phone: 314-768-3044
Fax: 314-768-5673

Fontbonne College
6800 Wydown Blvd
Saint Louis, MO 63105
www.fontbonne.edu
Phone: 314-862-3456
Fax: 314-889-1451

Harris-Stowe State College
3026 Laclede Ave
Saint Louis, MO 63103
www.hssc.edu
Phone: 314-340-3366
Fax: 314-340-3555

Lindenwood University
209 S Kingshighway
Saint Charles, MO 63301
www.lindenwood.edu
Phone: 636-949-2000
Fax: 636-949-4949

Maryville University of Saint Louis
13550 Conway Rd
Saint Louis, MO 63141
E-mail: admissions@maryville.edu
www.maryvillestl.edu
Phone: 314-529-9300
Fax: 314-529-9927
TF: 800-627-9855

Missouri Baptist College
1 College Park Dr
Saint Louis, MO 63141
www.mobap.edu
Phone: 314-434-1115
Fax: 314-434-7596
TF: 888-484-1115

Saint Louis Christian College
1360 Grandview Dr
Florissant, MO 63033
www.slcc4ministry.edu
Phone: 314-837-6777
Fax: 314-837-8291

Saint Louis College of Pharmacy
4588 Parkview Pl
Saint Louis, MO 63110
www.stlcop.edu
Phone: 314-367-8700
Fax: 314-367-2784

Saint Louis Community College
300 S Broadway
Saint Louis, MO 63102
E-mail: info@ccm.stlcc.cc.mo.us
www.stlcc.cc.mo.us
Phone: 314-539-5000
Fax: 314-539-5170

Saint Louis Community College Florissant Valley
3400 Pershall Rd
Ferguson, MO 63135
www.stlcc.cc.mo.us/fv/
Phone: 314-595-4200
Fax: 314-595-2224

Saint Louis Community College Forest Park
5600 Oakland Ave
Saint Louis, MO 63110
www.stlcc.cc.mo.us/fp/
Phone: 314-644-9100
Fax: 314-644-9752

Saint Louis Community College Meramec
11333 Big Bend Blvd
Kirkwood, MO 63122
www.stlcc.cc.mo.us/mcdocs/
Phone: 314-984-7500
Fax: 314-984-7051

Saint Louis Symphony Community Music School
560 Trinity Ave
Saint Louis, MO 63130
Phone: 314-863-3033
Fax: 314-286-4421

Saint Louis University
221 N Grand Blvd
Saint Louis, MO 63103
E-mail: admitme@sluvca.slu.edu
www.slu.edu
Phone: 314-977-2222
Fax: 314-977-2298

University of Missouri Saint Louis
8001 Natural Bridge Rd
Saint Louis, MO 63121
www.umsl.edu
Phone: 314-516-5000
Fax: 314-516-5310

Washington University
1 Brookings Dr
Saint Louis, MO 63130
www.wustl.edu
Phone: 314-935-5000
Fax: 314-935-4290
TF: 800-638-0700

Webster University
470 E Lockwood Ave
Saint Louis, MO 63119
www.webster.edu
Phone: 314-968-6900
Fax: 314-968-7115

Hospitals

Alexian Brothers Hospital
3933 S Broadway
Saint Louis, MO 63118
Phone: 314-865-3333
Fax: 314-865-7934

Alton Memorial Hospital
1 Memorial Dr
Alton, IL 62002
www.bjc.org/amh.html
Phone: 618-463-7311
Fax: 618-463-7850

Barnes Saint Peters Hospital
10 Hospital Dr
Saint Peters, MO 63376
Phone: 636-447-6600
Fax: 636-916-9414

Barnes-Jewish Hospital
216 S Kings Hwy
Saint Louis, MO 63110
www.bjc.org/bjh.html
Phone: 314-362-5000
Fax: 314-362-8877

Bethesda General Hospital
3655 Vista Ave
Saint Louis, MO 63110
Phone: 314-772-9200
Fax: 314-772-1819

Christian Hospital Northeast
11133 Dunn Rd
Saint Louis, MO 63136
Phone: 314-355-2300
Fax: 314-653-4153

DePaul Health Center
12303 De Paul Dr
Bridgeton, MO 63044
Phone: 314-344-6000
Fax: 314-344-6840

Doctors Hospital Wentzville
500 Medical Dr
Wentzville, MO 63285
Phone: 636-327-1000
Fax: 636-327-5413

Forest Park Hospital
6150 Oakland Ave
Saint Louis, MO 63139
www.forestparkhospital.com/ForestPark
Phone: 314-768-3000
Fax: 314-768-3136

Jefferson Memorial Hospital
PO Box 350
Crystal City, MO 63019
Phone: 636-933-1000
Fax: 636-933-1119

Lafayette Grand Hospital
3545 Lafayette Ave
Saint Louis, MO 63104
Phone: 314-865-6500

Memorial Hospital
4500 Memorial Dr
Belleville, IL 62226
Phone: 618-233-7750
Fax: 618-257-5658

Missouri Baptist Medical Center
3015 N Ballas Rd
Saint Louis, MO 63131
www.bjc.org/mbmc.html
Phone: 314-996-5000
Fax: 314-996-5373

Saint Anthony's Health Center
PO Box 340
Alton, IL 62002
Phone: 618-465-2571
Fax: 618-465-4569

Saint Anthony's Medical Center
10010 Kennerly Rd
Saint Louis, MO 63128
Phone: 314-525-1000
Fax: 314-525-4605

Saint Elizabeth's Hospital
211 S 3rd St
Belleville, IL 62222
www.apci.net/~ste
Phone: 618-234-2120
Fax: 618-234-4391

Saint John's Mercy Medical Center
615 S New Ballas Rd
Saint Louis, MO 63141
Phone: 314-569-6000
Fax: 314-995-4222
TF: 800-876-3729

Saint Joseph Health Center
300 1st Capitol Dr
Saint Charles, MO 63301
Phone: 636-947-5000
Fax: 636-947-5611

Saint Louis Children's Hospital
1 Children's Pl
Saint Louis, MO 63110
www.ihc.com/primary
Phone: 314-454-6000
Fax: 314-454-2101
TF: 800-678-5437

Saint Louis ConnectCare
5535 Delmar Blvd
Saint Louis, MO 63112
Phone: 314-361-2273
Fax: 314-879-6488

Saint Louis University Hospital
PO Box 15250
Saint Louis, MO 63110
www.slucare.edu
Phone: 314-577-8000
Fax: 314-268-5109
TF: 800-268-5880

Saint Luke's Hospital
232 S Woods Mill Rd
Chesterfield, MO 63017
Phone: 314-434-1500
Fax: 314-205-6865

Saint Mary's Health Center
6420 Clayton Rd
Richmond Heights, MO 63117
Phone: 314-768-8000
Fax: 314-768-8829
TF: 800-284-2854

Shriners Hospitals for Children Saint Louis Unit
2001 S Lindbergh Blvd
Saint Louis, MO 63131
www.shrinershq.org/Hospitals/Directory/stlouis.html
Phone: 314-432-3600
Fax: 314-432-2930
TF: 800-237-5055

SouthPointe Hospital
2639 Miami St
Saint Louis, MO 63118
www.tenethealth.com/Lutheran
Phone: 314-268-6000
Fax: 314-268-6156

SSM Cardinal Glennon Children's Hospital
1465 S Grand Blvd
Saint Louis, MO 63104
www.cardinalglennon.com
Phone: 314-577-5600
Fax: 314-268-6468

SSM Saint Joseph Hospital of Kirkwood
525 Couch Ave
Kirkwood, MO 63122
www.stjosephkirkwood.com/internet/home/stjokirk.nsf
Phone: 314-966-1500
Fax: 314-822-6302

Veterans Affairs Medical Center Phone: 314-487-0400
915 N Grand Blvd Fax: 314-289-7648
Saint Louis, MO 63106

Transportation

Airport(s)

Lambert Saint Louis International Airport (STL)
17 miles NW of downtown (approx 30 minutes) . . .314-426-8000

Mass Transit

Bi-State Transit System
$1.25 Base fare. 314-231-2345
MetroLink
$1.25 Base fare. 314-231-2345

Rail/Bus

Amtrak Station Phone: 314-331-3300
550 S 16th St TF: 800-872-7245
Saint Louis, MO 63103

Greyhound Bus Station Phone: 314-231-4485
1450 N 13th St TF: 800-231-2222
Saint Louis, MO 63106

Utilities

Electricity
AmerenUE 314-621-3222
www.ameren.com/about/au_amue.htm

Gas
Laclede Gas Co. 314-342-0500
www.lacledegas.com

Water
Saint Louis City Water Div 314-771-2255
Saint Louis County Water Co 314-991-0333

Garbage Collection/Recycling
Saint Louis City Refuse Div .314-353-8877

Telecommunications

Telephone
Southwestern Bell Telephone. 314-572-8811
www.swbell.com

Cable Television
AT & T Cable Services. 314-524-6880
www.cable.att.com
Cable America Corp 314-291-1970
Charter Communications. 636-207-7011

Internet Service Providers (ISPs)
ANET Access US. 314-997-4146
www.anet-stl.com
Applied Personal Computing Inc. 618-632-7282
www.apci.net
Brick Network 314-645-5550
www.brick.net
Charter Pipeline. 800-211-4450
www.chartercom.com/products/charter_pipeline
ezl dot com inc 618-659-3206
www.ezl.com
Internet 1st Inc. 888-881-4800
www.i1.net
Marz Online 314-231-8200
www.marz.com
Primary Network Internet Inc 314-995-5755
www.primary.net
Saint Louis Community Information Network. . . .314-622-3400
stlouis.missouri.org
Saint Louis Internet Connections LLC (iCON) . . .314-241-4266
www.icon-stl.net

Banks

Allegiant Bank Phone: 314-692-8200
2122 Kratky Rd Fax: 314-692-8500
Saint Louis, MO 63114 TF: 800-646-3624
www.allegiantbank.com

Bank of America NA Phone: 888-279-3121
800 Market St Fax: 314-466-5050
Saint Louis, MO 63101

Commerce Bank NA Phone: 314-726-2255
8000 Forsyth Blvd Fax: 314-746-8738
Clayton, MO 63105 TF: 800-746-8704

Equality Savings Bank Phone: 314-352-3333
4131 S Grand Blvd Fax: 314-352-7768
Saint Louis, MO 63118

First Bank Phone: 314-579-1600
1 First Missouri Ctr Fax: 314-434-2230
Saint Louis, MO 63141

Heartland Savings Bank FSB Phone: 314-512-8800
312 N 6th St Fax: 314-621-4789
Saint Louis, MO 63101 TF: 800-557-2781

Jefferson Bank & Trust Co Phone: 314-621-0100
2301 Market St Fax: 314-621-1267
Saint Louis, MO 63103 TF: 800-737-0018
E-mail: info@jeffersonbank-stl.com
www.jeffersonbank-stl.com

Jefferson Heritage Bank Phone: 314-773-3350
3353 California
Saint Louis, MO 63118

Mercantile Bank of Saint Louis NA Phone: 314-966-2530
721 Locust St
Saint Louis, MO 63101

Pulaski Bank FSB Phone: 314-878-2210
12300 Olive Blvd Fax: 314-878-0712
Saint Louis, MO 63141

South Side National Bank in Saint Louis Phone: 314-776-7000
3606 Gravois Ave Fax: 314-776-2332
Saint Louis, MO 63116

Southern Commercial Bank Phone: 314-481-6800
5515 S Grand Blvd Fax: 314-481-0173
Saint Louis, MO 63111
www.southerncommercial.net

Southwest Bank of Saint Louis Phone: 314-776-5200
2301 S Kingshighway Blvd Fax: 314-776-2146
Saint Louis, MO 63110

UMB of Saint Louis NA
2 S Broadway
Saint Louis, MO 63102
Phone: 314-621-1000
Fax: 314-621-8492

Union Planters Bank NA
3803 S Broadway
Saint Louis, MO 63118
Phone: 314-615-2300
Fax: 314-615-2394

Shopping

Cherokee Street Antique Row
2125 Cherokee St
Saint Louis, MO 63118
Phone: 314-773-8810

Chesterfield Mall
291 Chesterfield Mall
Chesterfield, MO 63017
Phone: 636-532-0777
Fax: 636-532-9728
E-mail: chesterfieldmall@rejacobsgroup.com
www.shopyourmall.com/mall_welcome.asp?map=yes&mall_select=675

Crestwood Plaza
164 Crestwood Plaza
Saint Louis, MO 63126
Phone: 314-962-2395
Fax: 314-962-2384
www.crestwood.shoppingtown.com

Dillard's
601 Washington Ave
Saint Louis, MO 63101
Phone: 314-231-5080

Famous-Barr
601 Olive St
Saint Louis, MO 63101
Phone: 314-444-3111
TF: 800-528-2345
www.mayco.com/fb/index.jsp

Grand South Grand
311 S Grand Blvd
Saint Louis, MO 63118
Phone: 314-773-7733
Fax: 314-773-1942

Jamestown Mall
Old Jamestown Rd & Lindbergh Blvd
Florissant, MO 63034
Phone: 314-355-3500
Fax: 314-355-8785
E-mail: jamestownmall@rejacobsgroup.com
www.shopyourmall.com/mall_welcome.asp?map=yes&mall_select=670

Laclede's Landing
801 N 2nd St
Saint Louis, MO 63102
Phone: 314-241-5875
Fax: 314-241-5862
E-mail: llanding@brick.net
www.lacledelanding-stlouis.com

Northwest Plaza
650-A Northwest Plaza
Saint Louis, MO 63074
Phone: 314-298-0071
Fax: 314-298-3481
TF: 800-264-7841
northwestplaza.shoppingtown.com

Plaza Frontenac
1701 S Lindbergh Blvd
Frontenac, MO 63131
Phone: 314-432-0604

Saint Louis Centre
515 N 6th St
Saint Louis, MO 63101
Phone: 314-231-5522
Fax: 314-231-4837

Saint Louis Galleria
1155 St Louis Galleria
Saint Louis, MO 63117
Phone: 314-863-6633
Fax: 314-863-8665
E-mail: info@saintlouisgalleria.com
www.saintlouisgalleria.com

Saint Louis Union Station
1820 Market St
Saint Louis, MO 63103
Phone: 314-421-6655
Fax: 314-421-3314

Saks Fifth Avenue
1 Plaza Frontenac
Frontenac, MO 63131
Phone: 314-567-9200

Media

Newspapers and Magazines

Belleville Journal
219 N Illinois St
Belleville, IL 62220
Phone: 618-277-7000
Fax: 618-277-7018

Chesterfield Journal
1714 Deer Tracks Trail
Saint Louis, MO 63131
Phone: 314-821-2462
Fax: 314-821-0843

Citizen Journal
1714 Deer Tracks Trail
Saint Louis, MO 63131
Phone: 314-821-2462
Fax: 314-821-0843

Collinsville Journal
113 E Clay St
Collinsville, IL 62234
Phone: 618-344-0264
Fax: 618-344-3611

Community News
5748 Helen Ave
Saint Louis, MO 63136
Phone: 314-261-5555
Fax: 314-261-2776

County Star Journal East
7751 N Lindbergh Rd
Hazelwood, MO 63042
Phone: 314-972-1111
Fax: 314-831-7643

East Saint Louis Journal
219 N Illinois St
Belleville, IL 62220
Phone: 618-277-7000
Fax: 618-281-7693

Jefferson County Journal
3500 Jeffco Blvd Suite 110
Arnold, MO 63010
Phone: 636-464-5883
Fax: 636-464-5824

North County East Journal
7751 N Lindbergh Blvd
Hazelwood, MO 63042
Phone: 314-972-1111
Fax: 314-831-7643

North County Journal West
7751 N Lindbergh Blvd
Hazelwood, MO 63042
Phone: 314-972-1111
Fax: 314-831-7643

North Side Journal
7751 N Lindberg Blvd
Hazelwood, MO 63042
Phone: 314-972-1111
Fax: 314-831-7643

Oakville/Mehlville Journal
4210 Chippewa St
Saint Louis, MO 63116
Phone: 314-664-2700
Fax: 314-664-8533

Press Journal
1714 Deer Tracks Trail
Saint Louis, MO 63131
Phone: 314-821-2462
Fax: 314-821-0843

Riverfront Times
6358 Delmar Blvd Suite 200
Saint Louis, MO 63130
Phone: 314-615-6666
Fax: 314-615-6655
www.rftstl.com

Saint Charles Journal
1529 Old Hwy 94-S Suite 108
Saint Charles, MO 63303
Phone: 636-724-1111
Fax: 636-946-0086

Saint Louis Business Journal
1 Metropolitan Sq Suite 2170
Saint Louis, MO 63102
www.amcity.com/stlouis
Phone: 314-421-6200
Fax: 314-621-5031

Saint Louis Post-Dispatch*
900 N Tucker Blvd
Saint Louis, MO 63101
E-mail: vtipton@stlnet.com
www.stlnet.com
Phone: 314-340-8000
Fax: 314-340-3050
TF: 800-365-0820

Saint Peters Journal
1529 Old Hwy 94-S Suite 108
Saint Charles, MO 63303
Phone: 636-724-1111
Fax: 636-946-0086

South City Journal
4210 Chippewa St
Saint Louis, MO 63116
Phone: 314-664-2700
Fax: 314-664-8533

South County Journal
4210 Chippewa St
Saint Louis, MO 63116
Phone: 314-664-2700
Fax: 314-664-8533

South Side Journal
4210 Chippewa St
Saint Louis, MO 63116
Phone: 314-664-2700
Fax: 314-664-8533

South West City Journal
4210 Chippewa St
Saint Louis, MO 63116
Phone: 314-664-2700
Fax: 314-664-8533

Southwest County Journal
4210 Chippewa St
Saint Louis, MO 63116
Phone: 314-664-2700
Fax: 314-664-8533

Washington Missourian
PO Box 336
Washington, MO 63090
Phone: 636-239-7701
Fax: 636-239-0915

Webster-Kirkwood Journal
1714 Deer Tracks Trail
Saint Louis, MO 63131
Phone: 314-821-2462
Fax: 314-821-0843

West County Journal
1714 Deer Tracks Trail
Saint Louis, MO 63131
Phone: 314-821-2462
Fax: 314-821-0843

Where Saint Louis
1750 S Brentwood Blvd Suite 511
Saint Louis, MO 63144
E-mail: info@wheremags.com
Phone: 314-968-4940
Fax: 314-968-0813

**Indicates major daily newspapers*

Television

KDNL-TV Ch 30 (ABC)
1215 Cole St
Saint Louis, MO 63106
Phone: 314-436-3030
Fax: 314-259-5569

KETC-TV Ch 9 (PBS)
3655 Olive St
Saint Louis, MO 63108
E-mail: letters@ketc.pbs.org
www.ketc.org
Phone: 314-725-2460
Fax: 314-512-9005

KMOV-TV Ch 4 (CBS)
1 S Memorial Dr
Saint Louis, MO 63102
www.kmov.com
Phone: 314-621-4444
Fax: 314-621-4775

KNLC-TV Ch 24 (Ind)
1411 Locust St
Saint Louis, MO 63103
www.hereshelpnet.org
Phone: 314-436-2424
Fax: 314-436-2434

KPLR-TV Ch 11 (WB)
4935 Lindell Blvd
Saint Louis, MO 63108
www.kplr.com
Phone: 314-367-7211
Fax: 314-454-6430

KSDK-TV Ch 5 (NBC)
1000 Market St
Saint Louis, MO 63101
Phone: 314-421-5055
Fax: 314-444-5164

KTVI-TV Ch 2 (Fox)
5915 Berthold Ave
Saint Louis, MO 63110
Phone: 314-647-2222
Fax: 314-647-8960

Radio

KATZ-AM 1600 kHz (Rel)
10155 Corporate Square Dr
Saint Louis, MO 63132
Phone: 314-692-5108
Fax: 314-692-5134

KATZ-FM 100.3 MHz (Urban)
10155 Corporate Square Dr
Saint Louis, MO 63132
www.kiss100-3.com
Phone: 314-692-5108
Fax: 314-692-5131

KDHX-FM 88.1 MHz (NPR)
3504 Magnolia St
Saint Louis, MO 63118
www.kdhxfm88.org
Phone: 314-664-3955
Fax: 314-664-1020

KEZK-AM 590 kHz (AC)
3100 Market St
Saint Louis, MO 63103
Phone: 314-531-0000
Fax: 314-969-7638

KEZK-FM 102.5 MHz (AC)
3100 Market St
Saint Louis, MO 63103
www.kezk.com
Phone: 314-531-0000
Fax: 314-969-7638

KFNS-AM 590 kHz (Sports)
8045 Big Bend Blvd
Saint Louis, MO 63119
E-mail: kfns@kfns.com
www.kfns.com
Phone: 314-962-0590
Fax: 314-962-7576

KFNS-FM 100.7 MHz (Sports)
8045 Big Bend Blvd
Saint Louis, MO 63119
E-mail: kfns@kfns.com
www.kfns.com
Phone: 314-962-0590
Fax: 314-962-7576

KFUO-FM 99.1 MHz (Clas)
85 Founders Ln
Clayton, MO 63105
www.classic99.com
Phone: 314-725-3030
Fax: 314-725-3801
TF: 800-844-0524

KIHT-FM 96.3 MHz (B/EZ)
8081 Manchester Rd
Saint Louis, MO 63144
www.k-hits.com
Phone: 314-781-9600
Fax: 314-781-3298

KLOU-FM 103.3 MHz (Oldies)
1910 Pine St Suite 225
Saint Louis, MO 63103
www.klou.com
Phone: 314-533-1033
Fax: 314-533-2103

KMJM-FM 104.9 MHz (Urban)
10155 Corporate Square Dr
Saint Louis, MO 63132
E-mail: majic@majic105fm.com
www.majic105fm.com
Phone: 314-692-5108
Fax: 314-692-5127
TF: 888-426-9105

KMOX-AM 1120 kHz (N/T)
1 Memorial Dr
Saint Louis, MO 63102
E-mail: kmox@kmox.com
www.kmox.com
Phone: 314-621-2345
Fax: 314-444-3230

KPNT-FM 105.7 MHz (Alt)
1215 Cole St
Saint Louis, MO 63106
E-mail: webdude@kpnt.com
www.kpnt.com
Phone: 314-231-1057
Fax: 314-259-5598

KSD-FM 93.7 MHz (CR)
1910 Pine St
Saint Louis, MO 63103
E-mail: hey937ksd@ksd.com
www.ksd.com
Phone: 314-436-9370
Fax: 314-231-7625

KSHE-FM 94.7 MHz (Rock)
700 St Louis Union Stn Annex Suite 101
Saint Louis, MO 63103
www.kshe95.com
Phone: 314-621-0095
Fax: 314-621-3428

KSLZ-FM 107.7 MHz (CHR)
10155 Corporate Square Dr
Saint Louis, MO 63132
www.z1077.com
Phone: 314-969-1077
Fax: 314-969-3299
TF: 888-570-1077

KTRS-AM 550 kHz (N/T)
638 W Port Plaza
Saint Louis, MO 63146
www.ktrs.com
Phone: 314-453-5500
Fax: 314-453-9704

KWMU-FM 90.7 MHz (NPR)
8001 Natural Bridge Rd
Saint Louis, MO 63121
E-mail: kwmu@umsl.edu
www.kwmu.org
Phone: 314-516-5968
Fax: 314-516-6397

KXOK-FM 97.1 MHz (Rock)
1215 Cole St
Saint Louis, MO 63106
E-mail: amshow@primary.net
www.97.fm
Phone: 314-231-9710
Fax: 314-259-5789

KYKY-FM 98.1 MHz (AC)
3100 Market St
Saint Louis, MO 63103
www.y98.com
Phone: 314-531-9898
Fax: 314-531-9810

WESL-AM 1490 kHz (Urban)
149 S 8th St
East Saint Louis, IL 62201
Phone: 618-271-7687
Fax: 618-875-4315

WEW-AM 770 kHz (Nost)
2740 Hampton Ave
Saint Louis, MO 63139
E-mail: wewradio@aol.com
www.wewradio.com
Phone: 314-781-9397
Fax: 314-781-8545

WIL-FM 92.3 MHz (Ctry)
8081 Manchester Rd
Saint Louis, MO 63144
www.wil92.com
Phone: 314-781-9600
Fax: 314-781-3298

WKKX-FM 106.5 MHz (Ctry)
800 St Louis Union Stn The Power House
Saint Louis, MO 63103
Phone: 314-621-4106
Fax: 314-621-3000

WRTH-AM 1430 kHz (Nost)
8081 Manchester Rd
Saint Louis, MO 63144
www.wrth-am.com
Phone: 314-781-9600
Fax: 314-781-3298

WVRV-FM 101.1 MHz (AAA)
1215 Cole St
Saint Louis, MO 63106
www.wvrv.com
Phone: 314-231-3699
Fax: 314-259-5598

WXTM-FM 104.1 MHz (Rock)
800 Union Stn
Saint Louis, MO 63103
www.extremeradio1041.com
Phone: 314-621-0400
Fax: 314-621-3000
TF: 800-455-1041

Attractions

The eastern Saint Louis skyline is dominated by the Gateway Arch, designed by Eero Saarinen and opened in 1965 as a symbol of the city's historic role as Gateway to the West. The Arch rises some 630 feet above the Mississippi in the riverfront area of Saint Louis. Along the north edge of the riverfront is Laclede's Landing, a 19th century neighborhood complete with cobblestone streets and cast iron street lamps that now serves as an entertainment district. In downtown Saint Louis is Union Station. Once the busiest passenger rail terminal in the U.S., the train shed is now a festival marketplace with more than 100 shops, as well as a major hotel, restaurants, and clubs. Just south of downtown is the headquarters of Anheuser-Busch, the world's largest brewer. A tour of its facilities includes the stables of the Budweiser Clydesdales. The city's Forest Park, which has been named one of the top ten urban parks in the country, is the site of the Saint Louis Art Museum, History Museum, Science Center, and the Saint Louis Zoo, a world-class facility with more than 6,000 animals. The Missouri Botanical Garden in Saint Louis has the nation's largest authentic Japanese garden, as well as woodland and scented gardens and a Climatron greenhouse that is a geodesic dome. The New Cathedral of Saint Louis is a Romanesque-Byzantine structure containing the world's largest collection of mosaic art.

American Kennel Club Museum of the Dog
1721 S Mason Rd
Saint Louis, MO 63131
commerce.bizonthe.net/intro.asp?company=amerkennelclubmuseum
Phone: 314-821-3647
Fax: 314-821-7381

American Theatre
416 N 9th St
Saint Louis, MO 63101
Phone: 314-962-4000

Anheuser-Busch Brewery
1 Busch Pl
Saint Louis, MO 63118
www.budweisertours.com
Phone: 314-577-2626
Fax: 314-577-7715

Arch Odyssey Theatre
11 N 4th St Underground at Gateway Arch
Saint Louis, MO 63102
Phone: 314-982-1410
Fax: 314-982-1527
TF: 877-982-1410

Black Madonna Shrine Phone: 636-938-5361
St Joseph's Rd
Eureka, MO 63025

Black World History Wax Museum Phone: 314-241-7057
2505 St Louis Ave Fax: 314-241-7058
Saint Louis, MO 63106

Campbell House Museum Phone: 314-421-0325
1508 Locust St Fax: 314-421-0113
Saint Louis, MO 63103
E-mail: campbellhousemuseum@worldnet.att.net
stlouis.missouri.org/501c/chm

Carondelet Park Phone: 314-289-5320
Grand Dr & Loughborough Ave
Saint Louis, MO 63110

Casino Queen Phone: 618-874-5000
200 S Front St Fax: 618-874-5008
East Saint Louis, IL 62201 TF: 800-777-0777
E-mail: queen@casinoqueen.com
www.casinoqueen.com

Cathedral of Saint Louis (New Cathedral) Phone: 314-533-2824
4431 Lindell Blvd Fax: 314-533-2844
Saint Louis, MO 63108

Center of Contemporary Arts Phone: 314-725-6555
524 Trinity Ave Fax: 314-725-6222
Saint Louis, MO 63130
E-mail: coca@cocastl.org
www.cocastl.org

Chatillon-DeMenil Mansion Phone: 314-771-5828
3352 DeMenil Pl Fax: 314-771-3475
Saint Louis, MO 63118

City Museum Phone: 314-231-2489
701 N 15th St Fax: 314-231-1009
Saint Louis, MO 63103
www.citymuseum.org

Concordia Historical Institute Phone: 314-505-7900
801 DeMun Ave Fax: 314-505-7901
Saint Louis, MO 63105
chi.lcms.org

Craft Alliance Gallery Phone: 314-725-1177
6640 Delmar Blvd Fax: 314-725-2068
Saint Louis, MO 63130
E-mail: calliance@stlnet.com
www.craftalliance.org

Dance Saint Louis Phone: 314-534-5000
634 N Grand Blvd Suite 1102 Fax: 314-534-5001
Saint Louis, MO 63103
E-mail: dancestl@primary.net
www.dancestlouis.org

DeMenil Mansion & Museum Phone: 314-771-5828
3352 DeMenil Pl Fax: 314-771-3475
Saint Louis, MO 63118

Eugene Field House & Saint Louis Toy Museum Phone: 314-421-4689
634 S Broadway Fax: 314-421-4689
Saint Louis, MO 63102

Forest Park Phone: 314-535-0100
5600 Clayton Ave Fax: 314-535-3901
Saint Louis, MO 63110

Forum for Contemporary Art Phone: 314-535-4660
3540 Washington Ave Fax: 314-535-1226
Saint Louis, MO 63108

Fox Theatre Phone: 314-534-1678
527 N Grand Blvd Fax: 314-534-8702
Saint Louis, MO 63103
www.fabulousfox.com

Gateway Arch Phone: 877-982-1410
St Louis Riverfront
Saint Louis, MO

General Daniel Bissell House Phone: 314-868-0973
10225 Bellefontaine Rd Fax: 314-868-8435
Saint Louis, MO 63137

Golden Eagle River Museum Phone: 314-846-9073
Bee Tree Pk
Saint Louis, MO 63129

Grand Center Phone: 800-572-7776
634 N Grand Ave Fax: 314-533-3345
Saint Louis, MO 63103

Grand South Grand Phone: 314-773-7733
311 S Grand Blvd Fax: 314-773-1942
Saint Louis, MO 63118

Grant's Farm Phone: 314-843-1700
10501 Gravois Rd Fax: 314-525-0822
Saint Louis, MO 63123
www.grantsfarm.com

Historic Christopher Hawken House Phone: 314-968-1857
1155 S Rock Hill Rd
Saint Louis, MO 63119

Historic Hanley House Phone: 314-290-8501
7600 Westmoreland St
Saint Louis, MO 63105

Historic Samuel Cupples House Phone: 314-977-3575
3673 W Pine Blvd Fax: 314-977-3581
Saint Louis, MO 63108
www.slu.edu/the_arts/cupples

Holocaust Museum & Learning Center Phone: 314-432-0020
12 Millstone Campus Dr Fax: 314-432-1277
Saint Louis, MO 63146

International Bowling Museum & Hall of Fame Phone: 314-231-6340
111 Stadium Plaza Fax: 314-231-4054
Saint Louis, MO 63102 TF: 800-966-2695
www.bowlingmuseum.com

Jefferson Barracks Historic Park Phone: 314-544-5714
533 Grant Rd Fax: 314-638-5009
Saint Louis, MO 63125

Jefferson National Expansion Memorial & Gateway Arch Phone: 314-655-1600
11 N 4th St Fax: 314-655-1641
Saint Louis, MO 63102
www.nps.gov/jeff

Jewel Box
Forest Pk
Saint Louis, MO 63110
Phone: 314-531-0080

Joplin Scott House
2658 Delmar Blvd
Saint Louis, MO 63103
Phone: 314-340-5790
Fax: 314-340-5793

Laclede's Landing
801 N 2nd St
Saint Louis, MO 63102
E-mail: llanding@brick.net
www.lacledelanding-stlouis.com
Phone: 314-241-5875
Fax: 314-241-5862

Laumeier Sculpture Park & Museum
12580 Rott Rd
Saint Louis, MO 63127
www.laumeier.com
Phone: 314-821-1209
Fax: 314-821-1248

Magic House/Saint Louis Children's Museum
516 S Kirkwood Rd
Saint Louis, MO 63122
www.magichouse.com
Phone: 314-822-8900
Fax: 314-822-8930

Maryland Heights Family Aquatic Center
2344 McKelvey Rd
Maryland Heights, MO 63043
Phone: 314-291-6550
Fax: 314-434-6365

Meyers John B House
180 Dunn Rd
Saint Louis, MO 63031
Phone: 314-837-7661

Mid-America Aquacenter/Saint Louis Children's Aquarium
416 Hanley Industrial Ct
Brentwood, MO 63144
hometown.aol.com/lsaquaman/myhomepage/index.html
Phone: 314-647-9594
Fax: 314-647-7874

Missouri Botanical Garden
PO Box 299
Saint Louis, MO 63166
E-mail: rland@admin.mobot.org
www.mobot.org
Phone: 314-577-5100
Fax: 314-577-9597

Missouri Historical Society
PO Box 11940
Saint Louis, MO 63112
www.mohistory.org
Phone: 314-746-4599
Fax: 314-454-3162

Muny Musical Theater
Forest Pk
Saint Louis, MO 63112
www.muny.com
Phone: 314-361-1900
Fax: 314-361-0009

Museum of Black Inventors
7 S Newstead Ave
Saint Louis, MO 63108
Phone: 314-533-1333

Museum of Contemporary & Religious Art
221 N Grand Blvd Saint Louis University Campus
Saint Louis, MO 63103
www.slu.edu/the_arts
Phone: 314-977-7170
Fax: 314-977-2999

Museum of Transportation
3015 Barrett Station Rd
Saint Louis, MO 63122
www.thetrainmuseum.org
Phone: 314-965-7998
Fax: 314-965-0242

Museum of Western Jesuit Missions
700 Howdershell Rd
Florissant, MO 63031
Phone: 314-361-5122
Fax: 314-758-7182

National Great Rivers Museum
2 Lock & Dam Rd
Alton, IL 62002
www.mvs.usace.army.mil/Rivers/rvc.htm
Phone: 618-462-6979

Old Cathedral Museum
209 Walnut St
Saint Louis, MO 63102
Phone: 314-231-3250
Fax: 314-231-4280

OMNIMAX Theater
5050 Oakland Ave Saint Louis Science Ctr
Saint Louis, MO 63110
www.slsc.org/
Phone: 314-289-4400
Fax: 314-289-4420
TF: 800-456-7572

Opera Theatre of Saint Louis
PO Box 191910
Saint Louis, MO 63119
E-mail: info@opera-stl.org
www.opera-stl.org
Phone: 314-961-0171
Fax: 314-961-7463

Portfolio Gallery & Educational Center
3514 Delmar Blvd
Saint Louis, MO 63103
Phone: 314-533-3323
Fax: 314-531-3401

Powder Valley Conservation Nature Center
11715 Cragwold Rd
Saint Louis, MO 63122
Phone: 314-301-1500
Fax: 314-301-1501

Powell Symphony Hall
718 N Grand Blvd
Saint Louis, MO 63103
www.slso.org/new_site/facilities/psh.htm
Phone: 314-533-2500
Fax: 314-286-4142

Repertory Theatre of Saint Louis
130 Edgar Rd
Saint Louis, MO 63119
E-mail: mail@repstl.org
www.repstl.org
Phone: 314-968-4925

Saint Louis Art Museum
1 Fine Arts Dr
Saint Louis, MO 63110
E-mail: infotech@slam.org
www.slam.org
Phone: 314-721-0072
Fax: 314-721-6172

Saint Louis Ballet
10 Kimler Dr
Maryland Heights, MO 63043
Phone: 314-567-4299
Fax: 314-567-4299

Saint Louis Black Repertory Co
3610 Grandel Sq
Saint Louis, MO 63108
Phone: 314-534-3807
Fax: 314-533-3345

Saint Louis Car Museum
1575 Woodson Rd
Saint Louis, MO 63114
www.stlouiscarmuseum.com
Phone: 314-993-1330
Fax: 314-993-1540

Saint Louis Science Center
5050 Oakland Ave
Saint Louis, MO 63110
E-mail: slscweb@slsc.org
www.slsc.org
Phone: 314-289-4400
Fax: 314-289-4420
TF: 800-456-7572

Saint Louis Symphony Orchestra
718 N Grand Blvd
Saint Louis, MO 63103
www.slso.org
Phone: 314-533-2500
Fax: 314-286-4170

Saint Louis Union Station
1820 Market St
Saint Louis, MO 63103
Phone: 314-421-6655
Fax: 314-421-3314

Saint Louis Walk of Fame
6504 Delmar Blvd
Saint Louis, MO 63130
www.stlouiswalkoffame.org
Phone: 314-727-7827

Saint Louis Zoological Park
1 Government Dr
Saint Louis, MO 63110
www.stlzoo.org
Phone: 314-781-0900
Fax: 314-647-7969

Shaw Arboretum at Missouri Botanical Garden
Hwy 100 & I-44
Gray Summit, MO 63039
www.mobot.org/MOBOT/arboretum
Phone: 636-451-3512

Six Flags Saint Louis
I-44 & Allenton Rd
Eureka, MO 63025
www.sixflags.com/stlouis
Phone: 636-938-5300
Fax: 636-587-3617

Soldiers Memorial Military Museum
1315 Chestnut St
Saint Louis, MO 63103
Phone: 314-622-4550
Fax: 314-622-4237

Soulard Farmer's Market
7th & Lafayette Sts
Saint Louis, MO 63104
Phone: 314-622-4180
Fax: 314-622-4184

Ulysses S Grant National Historic Site
7400 Grant Rd
Saint Louis, MO 63123
www.nps.gov/ulsg/
Phone: 314-842-1867
Fax: 314-842-1659

Washington University Gallery of Art
1 Brookings Dr
Saint Louis, MO 63130
Phone: 314-935-5490

Westport Playhouse
600 Westport Plaza
Saint Louis, MO 63146
Phone: 314-878-3322

Worldways Children's Museum
West County Ctr
Saint Louis, MO 63131
Phone: 314-909-0497

Sports Teams & Facilities

Busch Memorial Stadium
250 Stadium Plaza
Saint Louis, MO 63102
www.stlcardinals.com/Busch.html
Phone: 314-241-3900
Fax: 314-425-0640

Fairmount Park
9301 Collinsville Rd
Collinsville, IL 62234
www.fairmountpark.com
Phone: 618-345-4300
Fax: 618-344-8218

Gateway International Raceway
700 Raceway Blvd
Madison, IL 62060
www.gatewayir.com
Phone: 618-482-2400
Fax: 618-482-3919

Kiel Center
1401 Clark Ave
Saint Louis, MO 63103
www.kiel.com
Phone: 314-622-5400
Fax: 314-622-5410

Saint Louis Ambush (soccer)
1401 Clark Ave Kiel Ctr
Saint Louis, MO 63105
Phone: 314-962-4625
Fax: 314-968-0862

Saint Louis Blues
1401 Clark Ave Kiel Ctr
Saint Louis, MO 63103
www.stlouisblues.com
Phone: 314-622-2583
Fax: 314-622-2582

Saint Louis Cardinals
250 Stadium Plaza Busch Memorial Stadium
Saint Louis, MO 63102
E-mail: cardsmail@icon-stl.net
www.stlcardinals.com
Phone: 314-421-3060
Fax: 314-425-0640

Saint Louis Rams
901 N Broadway Trans World Dome
Saint Louis, MO 63101
www.stlouisrams.com
Phone: 314-425-8830
Fax: 314-342-5399

Saint Louis Vipers (roller hockey)
1819 Clarkson Rd Suite 301
Chesterfield, MO 63017
www.stlouisvipers.com
Phone: 636-530-1967
Fax: 636-530-7777

Team Saint Louis
12525 Sportport Rd SportPort Complex
Maryland Heights, MO 63043
Phone: 636-938-9997
Fax: 636-938-7411

Trans World Dome at America's Center
701 Convention Plaza
Saint Louis, MO 63101
Phone: 314-342-5036
Fax: 314-342-5040

Annual Events

African Arts Festival (late May) 314-935-5645
American Indian Society Powwow (mid-September) 314-544-5714
An Art Affair (mid-June) 314-576-7100
Art & Soul (late May) 314-436-6500
Art Happening (early September) 314-889-0433
Best of Missouri Market (early October) 314-577-9500
Big Muddy Roots & Blues Music Festival (early September) 314-241-5875
Cinco de Mayo Festival (May 5) 314-837-6100
Circus Flora (early-mid-May) 314-531-6273
Darkness Haunted Theme Park (mid-September-early November) 314-241-3456
Elvis Birthday Celebration (early January) 314-727-0880
Fair Saint Louis (early July) 314-434-3434
Festival of the Trees (late November) 314-849-4440
Goldenrod Ragtime (early September) 636-946-2020
Grand Festival of Nations (mid-June) 314-773-7733
Grand South Grand House Tour (mid-April) 314-773-4844
Great Apple Jubilee (early September) 314-233-0513

Great Forest Park Balloon Race (mid-September) .314-993-2468
Great Saint Louis Golf Show (mid-January) .800-221-1280
Great Saint Louis Kite Festival (early May) .800-916-0092
Greater Saint Louis Auto Show (late January-early February) .314-342-5000
Greater Saint Louis Beer Festival (early October) .314-576-7100
Greek Festival (late August-early September) .314-361-6924
Greentree Festival (early-mid-September) .314-822-5855
Hispanic Fair (early August) .314-837-6100
Historic Shaw Art Fair (early October) .314-771-3101
Holiday Festival of Lights (mid-November-early January) .314-577-7049
Holiday Flower Show (November-December) .314-577-5141
International Folkfest (mid-October) .314-773-9090
Japanese Festival (early September) .314-577-5100
Jazz It Up on the Landing (late May) .314-241-5875
Juneteenth Heritage & Jazz Festival (mid-June) .314-367-0100
Kwanzaa Holiday Expo (mid-December) .314-367-3440
Labor Day Parade & Picnic (early September) .314-647-6336
Laclede's Landing Big Muddy Blues Festival (early September) .314-241-5875
Lafayette Square Victorian Art Festival (early June) .314-772-5724
Laumeier Contemporary Art Fair (early May) .314-821-1209
Lewis & Clark Rendezvous (mid-May) .636-946-7776
May Day Celebration (mid-late May) .314-531-0120
Memorial Day Festival (late May) .314-241-5875
Miller Music Blast (early July) .314-241-5875
Missouri Chili Cook-off (late September) .314-961-2828
Missouri Spring Festival of Art (early April) .314-889-0433
Missouri WineFest (mid-February) .314-576-7100
Moonlight Ramble (mid-August) .314-644-4660
Octoberfest (early-late October) .636-482-4419
PrideFest (late June) .314-772-8888
Saint Louis Antiques Show (mid-May) .314-968-7340
Saint Louis Art Fair (early September) .314-863-0278
Saint Louis Blues Heritage Festival (mid-August) .314-644-1551
Saint Louis Boat & Sports Show (mid-February) .314-567-0020
Saint Louis County Fair & Air Show (early September) .636-530-9386
Saint Louis Earth Day Community Festival (early June) .314-962-5838
Saint Louis International Beer Festival (mid-October) .314-436-2337
Saint Louis International Film Festival (early November) .314-454-0042
Saint Louis Microbeer Festival (late May) .314-436-2337
Saint Louis National Charity Horse Show (mid-late September) .636-458-7994
Saint Louis Storytelling Festival (early May) .314-516-6886
Saint Louis Strassenfest (early August) .314-849-6322
Saint Pat's Festival (mid-March) .314-241-5875
Saint Patrick's Day Celebration (mid-March) .314-421-6655
Saint Patrick's Day Parade & Run (mid-March) .314-421-1800
Santa's Magical Kingdom (mid-November-early January) .636-938-5925
Six Flags Music Festival (mid-May) .800-323-0974
Soulard Bastille Day Celebration (mid-July) .314-773-6767
Soulard Mardi Gras (early-mid-February) .314-773-6767
Spring Home & Garden Show (late February) .314-994-7700
Strawberry Days (mid-late May) .636-482-4419
Taste of the Nation Food Festival (mid-April) .314-863-5500
Taste of Westport Food Festival (mid-May) .314-576-7100
Tilles Fall Arts & Crafts Fair (mid-September) .314-638-2100
Tilles Spring Arts & Crafts Fair (mid-May) .636-391-0922
Valley of Flowers Festival (early May) .314-837-0033
Washington Avenue Street Festival (late May) .314-436-6500
Way of Lights Christmas Display (late November-early January) .314-241-3400
Wednesday Jazz Festivals (June-early July) .314-577-5100
Whitaker Jazz Festival (early June) .314-577-5100
Winter Wonderland (late November-early January) .314-615-7275
World War II Weekend (late April) .314-544-5714
Wurstfest (late March) .800-932-8687

Salem, Oregon

***County:* Marion, Polk**

SALEM is located in the heart of the Willamette Valley of west central Oregon. Major cities within 100 miles include Portland, Eugene, and Springfield, Oregon and Vancouver, Washington.

Area (Land) .... 36.9 sq mi
Area (Water) .... 4.5 sq mi
Elevation .... 154 ft
Latitude .... 44-98-46 N
Longitude .... 123-01-77 W
Time Zone .... PST
Area Code 503

Climate

Salem's climate is moderated by warm prevailing winds off of the Pacific Ocean, located 55 miles to the west of the city. Winter high temperatures average in the mid-40s to low 50s, with lows in the low 30s. Although winter is considered the wet season in Salem, most of the precipitation falls in the form of rain, rather than snow-the average annual snowfall total is just below six and a half inches. Summer days are warm, with average high temperatures ranging from the mid-70s to the low 80s, while evenings cool down to near 50 degrees. July and August are the driest months of the year in Salem.

Average Temperatures & Precipitation

Temperatures

	Jan	Feb	Mar	Apr	May	Jun	Jul	Aug	Sep	Oct	Nov	Dec
High	46	52	56	60	67	75	82	82	76	64	52	46
Low	33	34	36	38	42	48	51	51	47	41	38	34

Precipitation

	Jan	Feb	Mar	Apr	May	Jun	Jul	Aug	Sep	Oct	Nov	Dec
Inches	5.9	4.5	4.2	2.4	1.9	1.3	0.6	0.8	1.6	3.0	6.3	6.9

History

Originally called "Chemetka," an Indian word meaning "meeting or resting place," the city known today as Salem was first settled in 1840 by Methodist missionary Jason Lee and his followers. In 1842 the missionaries established the Oregon Institute as a school for the local Native Americans. The Oregon Institute would later become Willamette University, the first chartered university west of the Rocky Mountains. In 1844 a town site was laid out on Institute lands and the community's name was changed to Salem, an Anglican form of the Hebrew word "shalom," which means "peace."

In 1851Salem became the capital of the Oregon Territory and remained the capital (except for a brief period in 1855 when the capital was temporarily relocated to Corvallis) when Oregon became a state in 1859. Settlers were attracted to Salem because of its location in the fertile Willamette Valley, which offered opportunities for farming. The area was sometimes referred to as the "Eden at the end of the [Oregon] Trail." The arrival of the railroad in 1871 also helped to spark growth in the area. Salem enjoyed consistent growth throughout the remainder of the 1800s that continued throughout the 20th Century. Salem has earned two "All-American City" awards - one in 1960-61 and one in 1982-83.

Spanning two counties - Marion County, for which it serves as the county seat, and Polk County - the City of Salem is now home to more than 126,000 people. It remains the governmental center of the State of Oregon as well as the primary commercial center for the Willamette Valley.

Population

1990 Census 107,793
1998 Estimate 126,702
% Change 17.5
2005 Projection 144,931

Racial/Ethnic Breakdown
White 88.7%
Black 0.8%
Other 10.5%
Hispanic Origin (may be of any race) 7.5%

Age Breakdown
Under 18 years 25.5%
18 to 24 .... 9.2%
25 to 34 .... 15.5%
35 to 49 .... 23.6%
50+ years 26.2%
Median Age 33.4

Gender Breakdown
Male 49.7%
Female 50.3%

Government

Type of Government: Mayor-Council

Salem City Attorney
555 Liberty St SE Rm 205
Salem, OR 97301
Phone: 503-588-6003
Fax: 503-361-2202

Salem City Council
555 Liberty St SE Rm 220
Salem, OR 97301
Phone: 503-588-6255
Fax: 503-588-6354

Salem City Hall
555 Liberty St SE
Salem, OR 97301
Phone: 503-588-6161
Fax: 503-588-6354

Salem City Manager
555 Liberty St SE Rm 220
Salem, OR 97301
Phone: 503-588-6255
Fax: 503-588-6354

Salem City Recorder
555 Liberty St SE Rm 205
Salem, OR 97301
Phone: 503-588-6091
Fax: 503-588-6057

Salem Community Development Dept
555 Liberty St SE Rm 305
Salem, OR 97301
Phone: 503-588-6173
Fax: 503-588-6005

Salem Community Services Dept
555 Liberty St SE Rm 300
Salem, OR 97301
Phone: 503-688-6261
Fax: 503-315-2567

Salem Finance Dept
555 Liberty St SE Rm 230
Salem, OR 97301
Phone: 503-588-6114
Fax: 503-588-6251

Salem Fire Dept
370 Trade St SE
Salem, OR 97301
Phone: 503-588-6181
Fax: 503-588-6371

Salem Mayor
555 Liberty St SE Rm 220
Salem, OR 97301
Phone: 503-588-6159
Fax: 503-588-6354

Salem Personnel Dept
555 Liberty St SE Rm 225
Salem, OR 97301
Phone: 503-558-6162
Fax: 503-588-6170

Salem Police Dept
555 Liberty St SE Rm 130
Salem, OR 97301
Phone: 503-588-6080

Salem Public Library
585 Liberty St SE
Salem, OR 97309
Phone: 503-588-6060
Fax: 503-588-6055

Salem Public Works Dept
555 Liberty St SE Rm 325
Salem, OR 97301
Phone: 503-588-6211
Fax: 503-588-6025

Important Phone Numbers

AAA....503-581-1608
American Express Travel....503-378-0084
Driver's License/Vehicle Registration Information....503-945-5000
Emergency....911
Marion County Assessor....503-588-5144
Marion County Tax Collector....503-588-5215
Oregon Dept of Revenue....503-378-4988
Polk County Assessor....503-623-8391
Polk County Treasurer....503-623-9264
Salem Assn of Realtors....503-399-1500
Time....503-363-7600
Voter Registration Information (Marion County)....503-588-5041
Voter Registration Information (Polk County)....503-623-9217
Weather....503-363-4131

Information Sources

Better Business Bureau Serving Oregon & Western Washington
333 SW 5th Ave Suite 300
Portland, OR 97204
www.portland.bbb.org
Phone: 503-226-3981
Fax: 503-226-8200

Marion County
100 High St NE Rm 1331
Salem, OR 97301
www.open.org/~marion
Phone: 503-588-5225
Fax: 503-373-4408

Oregon State Fair & Expo Center
2330 17th St NE
Salem, OR 97303
Phone: 503-378-3247
Fax: 503-373-1788

Polk County
850 Main St
Dallas, OR 97338
Phone: 503-623-9217
Fax: 503-623-0717

Salem Area Chamber of Commerce
1110 Commercial St NE
Salem, OR 97301
www.salemchamber.org
Phone: 503-581-1466
Fax: 503-581-0972

Salem Convention & Visitors Assn
1313 Mill St SE
Salem, OR 97301
www.scva.org
Phone: 503-581-4325
Fax: 503-581-4540
TF: 800-874-7012

Salem Economic Development Corp
350 Commercial St NE
Salem, OR 97301
www.sedcor.org
Phone: 503-522-6225
Fax: 503-588-6240

Online Resources

Anthill City Guide Salem
www.anthill.com/city.asp?city=salem

City Knowledge Salem
www.cityknowledge.com/or_salem.htm

Excite.com Salem City Guide
www.excite.com/travel/countries/united_states/oregon/salem

Salem (OR) Home Page
www.open.org/~salem

Salem OnLine
www.oregonlink.com/

WWWelcome to Salem Oregon
www.el.com/To/Salem

Area Communities

Communities in the Salem Metropolitan Statistical Area (MSA), which includes Marion and Polk counties with populations greater than 10,000 include:

Dallas
PO Box 67
Dallas, OR 97338
Phone: 503-623-2338
Fax: 503-623-2339

Keizer
PO Box 21000
Keizer, OR 97307
Phone: 503-390-3700
Fax: 503-393-9437

Woodburn
270 Montgomery St
Woodburn, OR 97071
Phone: 503-982-5222
Fax: 503-972-5244

Economy

Salem has a diverse economic base that ranges from agriculture to high-technology manufacturing. Agriculture remains vital to the Salem area's economy, as it has since the city's early history. Products include fruit and vegetable crops, horticultural products, grass seed, nursery stock, livestock, and dairy products. Marion County leads the state in agricultural commodity sales-totals reached record highs of more than $437 million in 1997. The Salem MSA is also one of the leading food processing centers in the United States. Government is the largest employment sector in the Salem MSA, followed by services and retail trade. The State of Oregon is Salem's single largest employer, providing jobs for more than 15,000 area residents at various agencies. The Federal Government is also among the area's top 15 employers, employing more than 1,500.

Unemployment Rate 9.3%*
Per Capita Income..........................$20,927*
Median Family Income......................$42,200*

** Information given is for the Salem Metropolitan Statistical Area (MSA), which includes Marion and Polk counties.*

Principal Industries & Number of Wage Earners

Salem MSA* - 1998

Construction 7,800
Finance, Insurance, Real Estate 6,800
Food Products 5,000
Government (Local, State, Federal and schools) 36,700
Lumber & Wood Products, including Manufactured Buildings... 4,000
Manufacturing (Less Food Products and Lumber & Wood Products)... 8,800
Miscellaneous 5,100
Services 31,100
Trade 27,900
Transportation, Communications, & Utilities............... 3,500

** Information given is for the Salem Metropolitan Statistical Area (MSA), which includes Marion and Polk counties.*

Major Employers

Chemeketa Community College
PO Box 14007
Salem, OR 97309
E-mail: postmaster@chemek.cc.or.us
www.chemek.cc.or.us
Phone: 503-399-5006
Fax: 503-399-3918

Fred Meyer Inc
3800 SE 22nd Ave
Portland, OR 97202
www.fredmeyer.com
Phone: 503-232-8844
TF: 800-858-9202

Marion County
100 High St NE Rm 1331
Salem, OR 97301
www.open.org/~marion
Phone: 503-588-5225
Fax: 503-373-4408

Mitsubishi Silicon America
1351 Tandem Ave NE
Salem, OR 97303
Phone: 503-371-0041
Fax: 503-361-3539

NORPAC Foods Inc
930 W Washington St
Stayton, OR 97383
www.norpac.com
Phone: 503-769-2101
Fax: 503-769-1274
TF: 800-733-9311

Roth's Foodliner Inc
4895 Indian School Rd NE
Salem, OR 97305
Phone: 503-393-7684
Fax: 503-393-4456

SAIF Corp
400 High St SE
Salem, OR 97312
www.saif.com
Phone: 503-373-8000
Fax: 503-373-8628

Salem City Hall
555 Liberty St SE
Salem, OR 97301
www.ci.salem.or.us
Phone: 503-588-6161
Fax: 503-588-6354

Salem Hospital
665 Winter St SE
Salem, OR 97301
E-mail: cr@salemhospital.org
www.salemhospital.org
Phone: 503-370-5200
Fax: 503-375-4846

Salem/Keizer School District
1309 Ferry St SE
Salem, OR 97301
www.salkeiz.k12.or.us
Phone: 503-399-3000
Fax: 503-378-7802

State Farm Insurance Co
4600 25th Ave NE
Salem, OR 97313
www.statefarm.com
Phone: 503-463-3000
Fax: 503-463-3100

Willamette University
900 State St
Salem, OR 97301
E-mail: undergrad-admission@willamette.edu
www.willamette.edu
Phone: 503-370-6303
Fax: 503-375-5363
TF: 877-542-2787

Quality of Living Indicators

Total Crime Index.. 9,631
(rates per 100,000 inhabitants)

Violent Crime
Murder/manslaughter............................ 2
Forcible rape 83
Robbery....................................... 144
Aggravated assault............................ 144

Property Crime
Burglary 1,293
Larceny theft 7,414
Motor vehicle theft 637

Cost of Living Index...................................... 108.8
(national average = 100)

Median Home Price..................................... $60,200

Education

Public Schools

Salem/Keizer School District
1309 Ferry St SE
Salem, OR 97301
www.salkeiz.k12.or.us
Phone: 503-399-3000
Fax: 503-378-7802

Number of Schools
Elementary.................................... 38

Middle 9
High 5

Student/Teacher Ratio
All Grades 27.0:1

Private Schools

Number of Schools (all grades) .... 10+

Colleges & Universities

Chemeketa Community College
PO Box 14007
Salem, OR 97309
E-mail: postmaster@chemek.cc.or.us
www.chemek.cc.or.us
Phone: 503-399-5006
Fax: 503-399-3918

Linfield College
900 S Baker St
McMinnville, OR 97128
www.linfield.edu
Phone: 503-434-2200
Fax: 503-434-2472
TF: 800-640-2287

Western Baptist College
5000 Deer Pk Dr SE
Salem, OR 97301
www.wbc.edu
Phone: 503-581-8600
Fax: 503-585-4316
TF: 800-845-3005

Western Oregon University
345 Monmouth Ave N
Monmouth, OR 97361
www.wosc.osshe.edu
Phone: 503-838-8000
Fax: 503-838-8067

Willamette University
900 State St
Salem, OR 97301
E-mail: undergrad-admission@willamette.edu
www.willamette.edu
Phone: 503-370-6303
Fax: 503-375-5363
TF: 877-542-2787

Hospitals

Salem Hospital
665 Winter St SE
Salem, OR 97301
www.salemhospital.org
Phone: 503-370-5200
Fax: 503-375-4846

Transportation

Airport(s)

Portland International Airport (PDX)
47 miles N of downtown Salem
(approx 75 minutes) 503-460-4234

Mass Transit

Cherriots Transit
$.75 Base fare 503-588-2877

Rail/Bus

Amtrak Station
500 13th St SE
Salem, OR 97301
Phone: 503-588-1551
TF: 800-872-7245

Greyhound Bus Station
450 Church St NE
Salem, OR 97301
Phone: 503-362-2428

Utilities

Electricity
Portland General Electric 503-399-7717
www.portlandgeneral.com
Salem Electric 503-362-3601
www.salemelectric.com

Gas
Northwest Natural Gas Co 503-585-6611
www.nwnatural.com

Water
Salem Water Service 503-588-6099

Garbage Collection/Recycling
Salem Garbage Service 503-390-4000

Telecommunications

Telephone
Qwest 800-244-1111
www.qwest.com

Cable Television
AT & T Cable Services 503-370-2770
www.cable.att.com

Internet Service Providers (ISPs)
Goldcom Internet Services 503-566-5796
www.goldcom.com
Network Connect Northwest Inc 503-363-4580
www.ncn.com
Oregon Public Information Network 503-588-6052
www.open.org
Quik Internet of The Capitol 503-485-7845
www.capitol.quik.com

Banks

Bank of Salem
1995 Commercial St SE
Salem, OR 97302
Phone: 503-585-5290
Fax: 503-585-7368

First Security Bank of Oregon
580 State St NE
Salem, OR 97301
Phone: 800-574-4200

Wells Fargo Bank
280 Liberty St NE
Salem, OR 97301
www.wellsfargo.com
Phone: 503-399-3541
Fax: 503-399-3584
TF: 800-869-3557

West Coast Bank
301 Church St NE
Salem, OR 97301
Phone: 503-399-2900
Fax: 503-399-2996

Shopping

Lancaster Mall
831 Lancaster Dr NE
Salem, OR 97301
Phone: 503-585-1338
Fax: 503-362-7297

Salem Centre
401 Center St NE Suite 172
Salem, OR 97301
Phone: 503-364-0495
Fax: 503-364-1284

Media

Newspapers and Magazines

Statesman Journal*
280 Church St NE
Salem, OR 97301
E-mail: online@statesmanjournal.com
www.statesmanjournal.com
Phone: 503-399-6611
Fax: 503-399-6706
TF: 800-452-2511

**Indicates major daily newspapers*

Television

KATU-TV Ch 2 (ABC)
2153 NE Sandy Blvd
Portland, OR 97232
local.katu.citysearch.com
Phone: 503-231-4222
Fax: 503-231-4263

KGW-TV Ch 8 (NBC)
1501 SW Jefferson St
Portland, OR 97201
www.kgw.com
Phone: 503-226-5000
Fax: 503-226-4448

KOIN-TV Ch 6 (CBS)
222 SW Columbia St
Portland, OR 97201
E-mail: koin06a@prodigy.com
www.koin.com
Phone: 503-464-0600
Fax: 503-464-0717

KOPB-TV Ch 10 (PBS)
7140 SW Macadam Ave
Portland, OR 97219
E-mail: kopb@opb.org
www.opb.org/
Phone: 503-244-9900
Fax: 503-293-1919

KPDX-TV Ch 49 (Fox)
910 NE ML King Jr Blvd
Portland, OR 97232
www.kpdx.com
Phone: 503-239-4949
Fax: 503-239-6184

Radio

KBZY-AM 1490 kHz (AC)
PO Box 14900
Salem, OR 97309
E-mail: kzby@cyberis.net
www.kbzy.com
Phone: 503-362-1490
Fax: 503-362-6545

KCCS-AM 1220 kHz (Rel)
1850 45th Ave NE
Salem, OR 97305
www.kccs.org
Phone: 503-364-1000
Fax: 503-364-1022
TF: 800-794-1220

KWBY-AM 940 kHz (Span)
PO Box 158
Woodburn, OR 97071
www.radio-fiesta.com
Phone: 503-981-9400
Fax: 503-981-3561

KYKN-AM 1430 kHz (N/T)
PO Box 1430
Salem, OR 97308
www.kykn.com
Phone: 503-390-3014
Fax: 503-390-3728

Attractions

Salem is one of the cities that occupy the hills of Oregon's wine country. Salem area wineries feature a variety of special events, plus tasting and tours for visitors. Salem and its neighboring towns are also known for beautiful iris gardens, including Cooley's and Schreiner's Iris Gardens. Twenty-six miles east of Salem is Silver Falls State Park, with ten spectacular waterfalls that range in height from 27 to 178 feet and are accessible to hikers. Each July, Salem hosts Oregon's largest juried art fair, the Salem Art Fair & Festival. The festival celebrated its 50th anniversary in the summer of 2000.

Brunk House
5705 Salem-Dallas Hwy NW
Salem, OR 97304
Phone: 503-371-8586

Bush Barn Art Center
600 Mission St SE
Salem, OR 97302
Phone: 503-581-2228

Bush House Museum
600 Mission St SE
Salem, OR 97302
www.oregonlink.com/bush_house
Phone: 503-363-4714

Champoeg State Park
8239 Champoeg Rd NE
Saint Paul, OR 97137
Phone: 503-678-1251

Chemeketa Community College Planetarium
4000 Lancaster Dr NE
Salem, OR 97305
Phone: 503-399-5161

Cooley's Gardens
11553 Silverton Rd NE
Silverton, OR 97381
E-mail: cooleyiris@aol.com
www.cooleysgardens.com
Phone: 503-873-5463
Fax: 503-873-5812

Deepwood Estate
1116 Mission St SE
Salem, OR 97302
www.oregonlink.com/deepwood
Phone: 503-363-1825

Enchanted Forest
8462 Enchanted Way SE
Turner, OR 97392
www.enchantedforest.com
Phone: 503-371-4242

Fort Clatsop National Memorial
Rt 3 Box 604-FC
Astoria, OR 97103
www.nps.gov/focl
Phone: 503-861-2471
Fax: 503-861-2585

Gilbert House Children's Museum
116 Marion St NE
Salem, OR 97301
E-mail: explore@teleport.com
www.acgilbert.org
Phone: 503-371-3631
Fax: 503-316-3485

Historic Downtown Salem
350 Commercial St NE
Salem, OR 97301
Phone: 503-371-4000

Historic Elsinore Theatre
170 High St SE
Salem, OR 97301
E-mail: stage@wvi.com
www.wvi.com/~stage
Phone: 503-375-3574
Fax: 503-375-0284

Honeywood Winery
1350 Hines St SE
Salem, OR 97302
Phone: 503-362-4111

Marion County Historical Society Museum
260 12th St SE
Salem, OR 97301
Phone: 503-364-2128
Fax: 503-391-5356

Mission Mill Museum
1313 Mill St SE
Salem, OR 97301
Phone: 503-585-7012
Fax: 503-588-9902

Mount Angel Abbey
1 Abbey Dr
Mount Angel, OR 97373
Phone: 503-845-3066

Oregon Coast Aquarium
2820 SE Ferry Slip Rd
Newport, OR 97365
E-mail: akh@aquarium.org
www.aquarium.org
Phone: 541-867-3474
Fax: 541-867-6846

Oregon State Capitol
900 Court St
Salem, OR 97310
Phone: 503-986-1388
Fax: 503-986-1131

Paul Jensen Arctic Museum
590 W Church St
Monmouth, OR 97361
E-mail: macem@wou.edu/wou/offices.html
Phone: 503-838-8468
Fax: 503-838-8289

Pentacle Theater
324 52nd Ave NW
Salem, OR 97304
www.oregonlink.com/pentacle_theater/index.html
Phone: 503-364-7121
Fax: 503-362-6393

Redhawk Winery
2995 Michigan City Ave NW
Salem, OR 97304
Phone: 503-362-1596
Fax: 503-589-9189

Saint Innocent Winery
1360 Tandem Ave NE
Salem, OR 97303
www.stinnocentwine.com
Phone: 503-378-1526
Fax: 503-378-1041

Salem Chamber Orchestra
Smith Auditorium Willamette University
Salem, OR 97308
Phone: 503-375-5483

Schreiner's Iris Gardens
3625 Quinaby Rd NE
Salem, OR 97303
www.oregonlink.com/iris/index.html
Phone: 503-393-3232
Fax: 503-393-5590

Silver Falls State Park
20024 Silver Falls Hwy SE
Sublimity, OR 97385
Phone: 503-873-8681

Thrill-Ville USA
8372 Enchanted Way SE
Turner, OR 97392
Phone: 503-363-4095

Western Antique Powerland
3995 Brooklake Rd NE
Salem, OR 97303
Phone: 503-393-2424

Willamette Mission State Park
10991 Wheatland Rd NE
Gervais, OR 97026
Phone: 503-393-1172
Fax: 503-393-8863

Willamette Valley Vineyards
8800 Enchanted Way SE
Turner, OR 97392
E-mail: information@wvv.com
www.wvv.com
Phone: 503-588-9463
Fax: 503-588-8894
TF: 800-344-9463

Witness Tree Vineyard
7111 Spring Valley Rd NW
West Salem, OR 97304
www.witnesstreevineyard.com
Phone: 503-585-7874

Woolen Mill Museum
1313 Mill St SE
Salem, OR 97301
Phone: 503-585-7012
Fax: 503-588-9902

Sports Teams & Facilities

Cascade Surge (soccer)
Mission & Winter Sts McCulloch Stadium
Salem, OR 97308
E-mail: surgerks@open.org
www.cascadesurge.com
Phone: 503-362-7308
Fax: 503-371-3639

Salem-Keizer Volcanoes (baseball)
6700 Field of Dreams Way Volcanoes Stadium
Keizer, OR 97307
E-mail: probasebal@aol.com
www.volcanoesbaseball.com
Phone: 503-390-2225
Fax: 503-390-2227

Willamette Valley Firebirds (soccer)
175 SW Twin Oaks Cir
Corvallis, OR 97333
Phone: 541-757-0776
Fax: 541-753-4187

Annual Events

Bite of Salem (late July) 503-581-4325
Celebrate Oregon Wine & Food Festival (mid-February) 503-581-0540
Civil War Reenactment (early July) 503-393-1172
Destruction Derby & Fireworks (early July) 503-581-4325
Festival of Lights Parade (mid-December) 800-874-7012
Holidays at the Capitol (December) 503-581-4325
Keizer Iris Festival (early May) 503-393-9111
Marion County Fair (early-mid-July) 503-581-1466
Oregon AG Fest (late April) 503-581-4325
Oregon State Fair (late August-early September) 503-378-3247
Quilt Show & Hand Weavers Sale (early October) 503-581-4325
Salem Art Fair & Festival (mid-July) 503-581-2228
Salem Belly Dance Festival (early August) 503-378-7875
Salem Collectors' Market (September-June) 503-393-1261
Salem Music on the Green (August) 503-581-4325
Salem Rodeo Days (mid-May) 503-371-6040
Sheep to Shawl (mid-June) 503-581-4325
Summer in the City Festival (late July) 503-581-4325
West Salem Waterfront Parade (late July) 503-581-4325

Salt Lake City, Utah

***County:* Salt Lake**

SALT LAKE City is located in a mountain valley, bordered by the Wasatch Mountains and the Oquirrh Mountains in north central Utah. Major cities within 100 miles include Ogden, Provo, and Logan, Utah.

Area (Land)	109.0 sq mi
Area (Water)	1.3 sq mi
Elevation	4,266 ft
Latitude	40-76-08 N
Longitude	111-89-03 W
Time Zone	MST
Area Code	801

Climate

Salt Lake City's climate is modified by the surrounding mountains and has four distinct seasons. Winters are cold, with average high temperatures in the upper 30s and low 40s and average lows in the low 20s. Annual snowfall totals average 58 inches. Summer days are hot, with average high temperatures near 90 degrees, while evenings cool down into the upper 50s and low 60s. April is the wettest month in Salt Lake City; July is the driest.

Average Temperatures & Precipitation

Temperatures

	Jan	Feb	Mar	Apr	May	Jun	Jul	Aug	Sep	Oct	Nov	Dec
High	36	44	52	61	72	83	92	89	79	66	51	38
Low	19	25	31	38	46	55	64	62	51	40	31	22

Precipitation

	Jan	Feb	Mar	Apr	May	Jun	Jul	Aug	Sep	Oct	Nov	Dec
Inches	1.1	1.2	1.9	2.1	1.8	0.9	0.8	0.9	1.3	1.4	1.3	1.4

History

Great Salt Lake City was founded in July 1847 by Brigham Young and his Mormon followers, who had set out in search of a place where they could practice their religion free of persecution, and Salt Lake City is known today as the "Mormon Capital of the World." The new city was laid out in a grid pattern that radiated from Temple Square, which remains the center of modern-day Salt Lake City. The city was a major trading post during the Gold Rush, as many pioneers passed through the area en route to California. In 1868, Great Salt Lake City dropped the "Great" from its name. The following year, the Golden Spike was driven at nearby Promontory Summit, opening Salt Lake City up to rail travel from the east and the west. The pioneers who settled in the city in the years that followed were drawn largely by the area's booming mining industry.

In 1892, after nearly 40 years of construction, the Mormon Temple was completed in Temple Square, and it remains Salt Lake City's most prominent landmark. Four years after the temple was completed, Utah became a state and Salt Lake City was chosen as its capital. New construction and the implementation of an electric trolley system aided the development of the city in the early 1900s—over the course of the first three decades of the 20th Century, the city's population tripled. Like most U.S. cities, Salt Lake City experienced difficult economic times during the Great Depression, but the city recovered during World War II as new military installations were built nearby, creating jobs and drawing thousands of newcomers to the area.

Today, with a population of more than 174,000, Salt Lake City continues to prosper as a center for technology. In the year 2002, Salt Lake City will become the largest city ever to host the Olympic Winter Games.

Population

1990 Census	159,925
1998 Estimate	174,348
% Change	9.0
2010 Projection	190,346

Racial/Ethnic Breakdown

White	87.0%
Black	1.7%
Other	11.3%
Hispanic Origin (may be of any race)	9.7%

Age Breakdown

Under 5 years	8.3%
5 to 14	15.4%
15 to 19	6.3%
20 to 24	9.6%
25 to 44	33.5%
45 to 64	14.3%
65+ years	14.5%
Median Age	31

Gender Breakdown

Male	49.3%
Female	50.7%

Government

Type of Government: Mayor-Council

Salt Lake City City Attorney
451 S State St Rm 505
Salt Lake City, UT 84111
Phone: 801-535-7788
Fax: 801-535-7640

Salt Lake City City Council
451 S State St Suite 304
Salt Lake City, UT 84111
Phone: 801-535-7600
Fax: 801-535-7651

Salt Lake City City Hall Phone: 801-535-7600
451 S State St Fax: 801-535-7651
Salt Lake City, UT 84111

Salt Lake City City Recorder Phone: 801-535-7671
451 S State St Rm 415 Fax: 801-535-7681
Salt Lake City, UT 84111

Salt Lake City Community & Economic Development Office Phone: 801-535-7777
451 S State St Rm 404 Fax: 801-535-6005
Salt Lake City, UT 84111

Salt Lake City Fire Dept Phone: 801-799-4103
315 E 200 South Fax: 801-799-3038
Salt Lake City, UT 84111

Salt Lake City Human Resources Office Phone: 801-535-7900
451 S Sate St Rm 115 Fax: 801-535-6614
Salt Lake City, UT 84111

Salt Lake City Mayor Phone: 801-535-7704
451 S State St Rm 306 Fax: 801-535-6331
Salt Lake City, UT 84111

Salt Lake City Parks Div Phone: 801-972-7800
1965 W 500 South Fax: 801-972-7847
Salt Lake City, UT 84104

Salt Lake City Police Dept Phone: 801-799-3800
315 E 200 South Fax: 801-799-3640
Salt Lake City, UT 84111

Salt Lake City Public Library Phone: 801-524-8200
209 E 500 South Fax: 801-524-8297
Salt Lake City, UT 84111

Salt Lake City Public Utilities Dept Phone: 801-483-6770
1530 SW Temple Fax: 801-483-6818
Salt Lake City, UT 84115

Salt Lake City Transportation Div Phone: 801-535-7112
333 S 200 East Suite 201 Fax: 801-535-6019
Salt Lake City, UT 84111

Salt Lake City Treasurer Phone: 801-535-7946
451 S State St Rm 228 Fax: 801-535-6082
Salt Lake City, UT 84111

Important Phone Numbers

AAA........801-364-5615
American Express Travel........801-328-9733
Driver's License Information........801-965-4437
Emergency........911
Medical Referral........801-355-7477
Poison Control Center........801-581-2151
Road Conditions........801-964-6000
Salt Lake Board of Realtors........801-486-4465
Salt Lake County Assessors Office........801-468-3050
Salt Lake County Treasurer........801-468-3404
Time/Temp........801-467-8463
Travelers Aid........801-359-4142
Utah State Tax Commission........801-297-2200
Vehicle Registration Information........801-297-7780
Voter Registration Information........801-468-3427
Weather........801-975-4499

Information Sources

Better Business Bureau Serving Utah Phone: 801-892-6009
5673 S Redwood Rd Fax: 801-892-6002
Salt Lake City, UT 84123
www.saltlakecity.bbb.org

Chamber Ogden/Weber Phone: 801-621-8300
2393 Washington Blvd Fax: 801-392-7609
Ogden, UT 84401 TF: 888-621-8306
www.chamberogdenweber.org

Eccles David Conference Center Phone: 801-395-3200
2415 Washington Blvd Fax: 801-395-3201
Ogden, UT 84401 TF: 800-237-2690
www.oecenter.com/dec.htm

Golden Spike Arena Events Center Phone: 801-399-8544
1000 N 1200 West Fax: 801-392-1995
Ogden, UT 84404 TF: 800-442-7362

Ogden City Hall Phone: 801-629-8150
2484 Washington Blvd Fax: 801-629-8154
Ogden, UT 84401
www.ogdencity.com

Ogden Community Development Dept Phone: 801-629-8901
2484 Washington Blvd Fax: 801-629-8902
Ogden, UT 84401
www.ogdencity.com/commdev

Ogden Mayor Phone: 801-629-8100
2484 Washington Blvd Suite 300 Fax: 801-629-8154
Ogden, UT 84401
www.ogdencity.com/admin/mayor/mayorpg.stm

Ogden/Weber Convention & Visitors Bureau Phone: 801-627-8288
2501 Wall Ave Union Stn Fax: 801-399-0783
Ogden, UT 84401 TF: 800-255-8824
www.ogdencvb.org/

Salt Lake City Area Chamber of Commerce Phone: 801-364-3631
175 E 400 South Suite 600 Fax: 801-328-5098
Salt Lake City, UT 84111
www.slachamber.com

Salt Lake Convention & Visitors Bureau Phone: 801-521-2822
90 S West Temple Fax: 801-534-4927
Salt Lake City, UT 84101
www.visitsaltlake.com

Salt Lake County Phone: 801-468-3000
2001 S State St Suite S2200 Fax: 801-468-3440
Salt Lake City, UT 84190
www.co.slc.ut.us

Salt Palace Convention Center Phone: 801-534-4777
100 S West Temple Fax: 801-534-6383
Salt Lake City, UT 84101 TF: 877-547-4656
www.saltpalace.com

Weber County Phone: 801-399-8610
2380 Washington Blvd Suite 350 Fax: 801-399-8314
Ogden, UT 84401
www.co.weber.ut.us

Weber County Library
2464 Jefferson Ave
Ogden, UT 84401
www.weberpl.lib.ut.us
Phone: 801-337-2617
Fax: 801-337-2615

Online Resources

4SaltLakeCity.com
www.4saltlakecity.com

About.com Guide to Salt Lake City
saltlakecity.about.com/local/mountainus/saltlakecity

Anthill City Guide Salt Lake City
www.anthill.com/city.asp?city=saltlake

Area Guide Salt Lake City
saltlakecity.areaguides.net

City Knowledge Ogden
www.cityknowledge.com/ut_ogden.htm

City Knowledge Salt Lake City
www.cityknowledge.com/ut_salt_lake_city.htm

CitySearch Salt Lake City
utah.citysearch.com

DigitalCity Salt Lake City
home.digitalcity.com/saltlakecity

Downtown Alliance
www.downtownslc.org/

Excite.com Ogden City Guide
www.excite.com/travel/countries/united_states/utah/ogden

Excite.com Salt Lake City City Guide
www.excite.com/travel/countries/united_states/utah/salt_lake_city

Insiders' Guide to Salt Lake City
www.insiders.com/saltlake/index.htm

Lodging.com Salt Lake City Utah
www.lodging.com/auto/guides/salt_lake_city-area-ut.html

Ogden Page
www.ogden-ut.com

Rough Guide Travel Salt Lake City
travel.roughguides.com/content/1268/

Area Communities

Communities in the Salt Lake City area with populations greater than 20,000 include:

Bountiful
790 S 100 East
Bountiful, UT 84010
Phone: 801-298-6146
Fax: 801-298-3171

Clearfield
55 S State St
Clearfield, UT 84015
Phone: 801-525-2700
Fax: 801-525-2868

Draper
12441 S 900 East
Draper, UT 84020
Phone: 801-576-6500
Fax: 801-576-6511

Layton
437 Wasatch Dr
Layton, UT 84041
Phone: 801-546-8500
Fax: 801-546-8577

Midvale
655 W Center St
Midvale, UT 84047
Phone: 801-567-7200
Fax: 801-567-0518

Murray
PO Box 57520
Murray, UT 84157
Phone: 801-264-2660
Fax: 801-264-2618

Ogden
2484 Washington Blvd
Ogden, UT 84401
Phone: 801-629-8150
Fax: 801-629-8154

Riverton
12765 S 1400 West
RIverton, UT 84065
Phone: 801-254-0704
Fax: 801-254-1810

Roy
5051 S 1900 West
Roy, UT 84067
Phone: 801-774-1000
Fax: 801-774-1030

Sandy
10000 Centennial Pkwy
Sandy, UT 84070
Phone: 801-568-7100
Fax: 801-568-7169

South Jordan
11175 S Redwood Rd
South Jordan, UT 84095
Phone: 801-254-3742
Fax: 801-254-3393

West Jordan
8000 S Redwood Rd
West Jordan, UT 84088
Phone: 801-569-5000
Fax: 801-565-8978

West Valley City
3600 S Constitution Blvd
West Valley City, UT 84119
Phone: 801-966-3600
Fax: 801-966-8455

Economy

The Salt Lake City area has one of the largest concentrations of biotechnology, high-techology, and software firms in the United States. Education and health care are also vital parts of Salt Lake City's economy—five of the area's top 15 employers are education or health care-related, including the county's largest employer, Intermountain Health Care. Services is currently the largest employment sector in Salt Lake County, followed by trade and government. The State of Utah is the county's second-largest employer, providing jobs for some 17,000 area residents, and the Internal Revenue Service also ranks among the top ten, employing 6,000 people in the Salt Lake City area.

Unemployment Rate	3.4%*
Per Capita Income	$24,300*
Median Family Income	$29,697

** Information given is for Salt Lake County.*

Principal Industries & Number of Wage Earners

Salt Lake County - 1998

Construction	32,809
Finance, Insurance, & Real Estate	38,893
Government	74,906
Manufacturing	57,955

Mining 2,715
Services 145,128
Trade 125,754
Transportation, Communications, & Utilities 41,339

Major Employers

Brigham Young University
D-238 ASB
Provo, UT 84602
E-mail: admissions@byu.edu
www.byu.edu
Phone: 801-378-1211
Fax: 801-378-2320

Convergys
860 W Levoy Dr
Salt Lake City, UT 84123
www.convergys.com
Phone: 801-715-8000
Fax: 801-579-2588

Davis County School District
45 E State St
Farmington, UT 84025
www.davis.k12.ut.us
Phone: 801-402-5261
Fax: 801-444-5354

Delta Air Lines
3842 W 1200 North
Salt Lake City, UT 84122
www.delta-air.com
Phone: 801-579-3507
Fax: 801-579-3526

England CR & Sons Inc
4701 W 2100 South
Salt Lake City, UT 84120
www.crengland.com
Phone: 801-972-2712
Fax: 801-974-3342
TF: 800-453-8826

Granite School District
340 E 3545 South
Salt Lake City, UT 84115
www.granite.k12.ut.us
Phone: 801-263-6100
Fax: 801-263-6128

Hill Air Force Base
Hill AFB, UT 84056
www.hill.af.mil
Phone: 801-777-1110
Fax: 801-777-3721

Intermountain Health Care Inc
36 S State St 22nd Fl
Salt Lake City, UT 84111
www.ihc.com
Phone: 801-442-2000
Fax: 801-442-3327

Jordan School District
9361 S 300 East
Sandy, UT 84070
Phone: 801-567-8100
Fax: 801-567-8056

PacifiCorp-Utah Power
1407 W North Temple St
Salt Lake City, UT 84116
Phone: 801-220-2000

Smith's Food & Drug Centers Inc
1550 S Redwood Rd
Salt Lake City, UT 84104
www.smithsfoodanddrug.com
Phone: 801-974-1400
Fax: 801-974-1310

University of Utah
201 S 1460 E
Salt Lake City, UT 84112
www.utah.edu
Phone: 801-581-7200
Fax: 801-581-7880
TF: 800-868-5618

Wal-Mart District Office
10425 State St
Sandy, UT 84070
Phone: 801-553-0603
Fax: 801-553-0706

Zions Co-op Mercantile Institution (ZCMI)
2200 S 900 West
Salt Lake City, UT 84137
www.mayco.com/zc/index.jsp
Phone: 801-579-6000
Fax: 801-579-6257
TF: 800-869-9971

Quality of Living Indicators

Total Crime Index 18,269
(rates per 100,000 inhabitants)

Violent Crime
Murder/manslaughter 16
Forcible rape 147
Robbery 485
Aggravated assault 610

Property Crime
Burglary 2,244
Larceny theft 12,922
Motor vehicle theft 1,845

Cost of Living Index 103.0
(national average = 100)

Median Home Price $137,900

Education

Public Schools

Salt Lake School District
440 E 100 South
Salt Lake City, UT 84111
www.slc.k12.ut.us
Phone: 801-578-8599
Fax: 801-578-8248

Number of Schools
Elementary 29
Middle 5
High 3

Student/Teacher Ratio
All Grades 22.2:1

Private Schools

Number of Schools (all grades) .... 20+

Colleges & Universities

ITT Technical Institute
920 W Levoy Dr
Murray, UT 84123
www.itt-tech.edu
Phone: 801-263-3313
Fax: 801-263-3497
TF: 800-365-2136

Latter Day Saints Business College
411 E South Temple St
Salt Lake City, UT 84111
www.ldsbc.edu
Phone: 801-524-8100
Fax: 801-524-1900
TF: 800-999-5767

Salt Lake Community College
4600 S Redwood Rd
Salt Lake City, UT 84130
E-mail: herdsc@slcc.edu
www.slcc.edu
Phone: 801-957-4111
Fax: 801-957-4958

Stevens Henager College
2168 Washington Blvd
Ogden, UT 84401
www.stevenshenager.com
Phone: 801-394-7791
Fax: 801-393-1748
TF: 800-371-7791

University of Utah
201 S 1460 E
Salt Lake City, UT 84112
www.utah.edu
Phone: 801-581-7200
Fax: 801-581-7880
TF: 800-868-5618

Utah State University
1600 Old Main Hill
Logan, UT 84322
E-mail: hscr@cc.usu.edu
www.usu.edu
Phone: 435-797-1000
Fax: 435-797-4077

Weber State University
3750 Harrison Blvd
Ogden, UT 84408
www.weber.edu
Phone: 801-626-6000
Fax: 801-626-6747

Westminster College of Salt Lake City
1840 S 1300 East
Salt Lake City, UT 84105
E-mail: admispub@wcslc.edu
www.wcslc.edu
Phone: 801-484-7651
Fax: 801-484-3252
TF: 800-748-4753

Hospitals

Alta View Hospital
9660 S 1300 East
Sandy, UT 84094
www.ihc.com/altaview
Phone: 801-501-2600
Fax: 801-576-2789
TF: 800-491-6976

Cottonwood Hospital Medical Center
5770 S 300 East
Murray, UT 84107
Phone: 801-262-3461
Fax: 801-269-2272

Davis Hospital & Medical Center
1600 W Antelope Dr
Layton, UT 84041
Phone: 801-825-9561
Fax: 801-774-7045

Lakeview Hospital
630 E Medical Dr
Bountiful, UT 84010
www.lakeviewhospital.com
Phone: 801-292-6231
Fax: 801-299-2534

LDS Hospital
8th Ave & C St
Salt Lake City, UT 84143
Phone: 801-321-1100
Fax: 801-408-5133

McKay-Dee Hospital Center
3939 Harrison Blvd
Ogden, UT 84409
Phone: 801-627-2800
Fax: 801-625-2032

Ogden Regional Medical Center
5475 S 500 East
Ogden, UT 84405
www.ogdenregional.com
Phone: 801-479-2111
Fax: 801-479-2091

Pioneer Valley Hospital
3460 S Pioneer Pkwy
West Valley City, UT 84120
Phone: 801-964-3100
Fax: 801-964-3247

Primary Children's Medical Center
100 N Medical Dr
Salt Lake City, UT 84113
Phone: 801-588-2000
Fax: 801-588-2318

Saint Mark's Hospital
1200 E 3900 South
Salt Lake City, UT 84124
www.stmarkshospital.com
Phone: 801-268-7111
Fax: 801-270-3489

Salt Lake Regional Hospital
1050 E South Temple St
Salt Lake City, UT 84102
Phone: 801-350-4111
Fax: 801-350-4522

University of Utah Hospital & Clinics
50 N Medical Dr
Salt Lake City, UT 84132
www.med.utah.edu
Phone: 801-581-2121
Fax: 801-585-2224

Veterans Affairs Medical Center
500 S Foothill Dr
Salt Lake City, UT 84148
Phone: 801-582-1565
Fax: 801-584-2518

Transportation

Airport(s)

Salt Lake City International Airport (SLC)
7 miles W of downtown (approx 12 minutes) 801-575-2400

Mass Transit

UTA Trolley
$1 Base fare 801-287-4636
Utah Transit Authority
$1 Base fare 801-287-4636

Rail/Bus

Amtrak Station
340 South 600 W
Salt Lake City, UT 84101
Phone: 801-322-3510
TF: 800-872-7245

Greyhound Bus Station
160 W South Temple
Salt Lake City, UT 84101
Phone: 801-355-9581
TF: 800-231-2222

Utilities

Electricity
Utah Power....................................801-220-2000
www.pacificorp.com/paccomp/utahpower/

Gas
Questar Gas Co...............................801-324-5111
www.questargas.com

Water
Salt Lake City Water Dept......................801-483-6900

Garbage Collection/Recycling
Salt Lake City Sanitation Dept..................801-535-6970

Telecommunications

Telephone
Qwest.......................................801-237-5511
www.qwest.com

Cable Television
AT & T Cable Services.........................801-485-0500
www.cable.att.com

Internet Service Providers (ISPs)
ArosNet Inc 801-532-2767
www.aros.net
Internet Connect Inc 801-364-4059
www.inconnect.com
Konnections 801-621-8511
www.konnections.com

ReliaNET Internet Services 801-626-0238
www.relia.net
XMission 801-539-0852
www.xmission.com

Banks

Bank One Utah NA
185 S State St
Salt Lake City, UT 84111
Phone: 801-481-5014
Fax: 801-481-5009
TF: 800-877-0608

First Security Bank of Utah NA
1985 E 7000 South
Salt Lake City, UT 84121
Phone: 801-246-6600

KeyBank NA Salt Lake City District
50 S Main St Suite 132
Salt Lake City, UT 84144
Phone: 801-535-1000
Fax: 801-535-1129
TF: 800-658-5399

Zions First National Bank
1 S Main St
Salt Lake City, UT 84111
E-mail: info@zionsbank.com
www.zionsbank.com
Phone: 801-524-4711
Fax: 801-524-4914

Shopping

Cottonwood Mall
4835 S Highland Dr
Salt Lake City, UT 84117
Phone: 801-278-0416
Fax: 801-278-1575

Crossroads Plaza
50 S Main St
Salt Lake City, UT 84144
www.crossroadsplaza.com
Phone: 801-531-1799
Fax: 801-532-4345

Downtown Ogden
2404 Washington Blvd
Ogden, UT 84401
Phone: 801-394-6634
Fax: 801-394-6647

Factory Stores at Park City
6699 N Landmark Dr
Park City, UT 84098
Phone: 435-645-7078
Fax: 435-645-7098
TF: 888-746-7333

Foothill Village
1400 Foothill Dr Suite 46
Salt Lake City, UT 84108
Phone: 801-582-3646
Fax: 801-582-2803

Gardner Village
1100 W 7800 South
West Jordan, UT 84088
www.gardnervillage.com
Phone: 801-566-8903
Fax: 801-566-5390

Mormon Handicraft
36 S State St Suite 220
Salt Lake City, UT 84111
www.mormonhandicraft.com
Phone: 801-355-2141
Fax: 801-531-9337

Newgate Mall
36th St & Wall Ave
Ogden, UT 84405
Phone: 801-621-1161

Ogden City Mall
24th St & Washington Blvd
Ogden, UT 84401
Phone: 801-399-1314

Ogden's Historic 25th St
Wall & Grant Aves
Ogden, UT 84401

South Towne Center
10450 S State St
Sandy, UT 84070
www.southtownecenter.com
Phone: 801-572-1516
Fax: 801-571-3927

Trolley Square
367 Trolley Sq
Salt Lake City, UT 84102
Phone: 801-521-9877
Fax: 801-521-1777

Valley Fair Mall
3601 Constitution Blvd
Salt Lake City, UT 84119
Phone: 801-969-6211
Fax: 801-969-6233

ZCMI Center Mall
36 S State St
Salt Lake City, UT 84111
www.zcmicentermall.com
Phone: 801-321-8743
Fax: 801-321-8776

Media

Newspapers and Magazines

Deseret News*
PO Box 1257
Salt Lake City, UT 84110
E-mail: cservice@desnews.com
www.desnews.com
Phone: 801-237-2800
Fax: 801-237-2121

Enterprise
136 S Main St Suite 721
Salt Lake City, UT 84101
www.slenterprise.com
Phone: 801-533-0556
Fax: 801-533-0684

Salt Lake City Weekly
60 W 400 South
Salt Lake City, UT 84101
www.avenews.com/index_cw.html
Phone: 801-575-7003
Fax: 801-575-8011

Salt Lake Tribune*
143 S Main St
Salt Lake City, UT 84110
E-mail: the.editors@sltrib.com
www.sltrib.com
Phone: 801-237-2800
Fax: 801-257-8525

Standard-Examiner*
455 23rd St
Ogden, UT 84401
www.standard.net
Phone: 801-625-4200
Fax: 801-625-4508
TF: 800-234-5505

Utah Business
85 E Fort Union Blvd
Midvale, UT 84047
E-mail: bpittman@uy801.homestar.net
www.utahbusiness.com
Phone: 801-568-0114
Fax: 801-568-0812

Your Green Sheet
PO Box 571408
Murray, UT 84157
E-mail: info@murraygreensheet.com
www.murraygreensheet.com
Phone: 801-261-4670
Fax: 801-261-4801

**Indicates major daily newspapers*

Television

KJZZ-TV Ch 14 (UPN)
5181 Amelia Earhart Dr
Salt Lake City, UT 84116
www.kjzz.com
Phone: 801-537-1414
Fax: 801-238-6415

KSL-TV Ch 5 (NBC)
PO Box 1160
Salt Lake City, UT 84110
E-mail: eyewitness@ksl.com
www.ksl.com/TV/
Phone: 801-575-5555
Fax: 801-575-5560

KSTU-TV Ch 13 (Fox)
5020 W Amelia Earhart Dr
Salt Lake City, UT 84116
www.fox13.com
Phone: 801-532-1300
Fax: 801-537-5335

KTVX-TV Ch 4 (ABC)
1760 Fremont Dr
Salt Lake City, UT 84104
E-mail: news@4utah.com
www.4utah.com
Phone: 801-975-4444
Fax: 801-975-4442

KUED-TV Ch 7 (PBS)
101 Wasatch Dr
Salt Lake City, UT 84112
eddy.media.utah.edu
Phone: 801-581-7777
Fax: 801-585-5096

KUTV-TV Ch 2 (CBS)
2185 S 3600 West
West Valley City, UT 84119
www.kutv.com
Phone: 801-973-3000
Fax: 801-973-3349

KUWB-TV Ch 30 (WB)
6135 S Stratler Ave
Murray, UT 84107
Phone: 801-281-0330
Fax: 801-281-4503

Radio

KALL-AM 910 kHz (N/T)
2801 S Decker Lake Dr
West Valley City, UT 84119
www.kall910.com
Phone: 801-575-5255
Fax: 801-908-1499

KANN-AM 1120 kHz (Rel)
PO Box 3880
Ogden, UT 84409
Phone: 801-776-0249

KBEE-FM 98.7 MHz (AC)
434 Bearcat Dr
Salt Lake City, UT 84115
E-mail: pdirector@b987.com
www.b987.com
Phone: 801-485-6700
Fax: 801-487-5369

KBER-FM 101.1 MHz (Rock)
434 Bearcat Dr
Salt Lake City, UT 84115
www.kber.com
Phone: 801-485-6700
Fax: 801-487-5369

KBZN-FM 97.9 MHz (NAC)
257 E 200 South Suite 400
Salt Lake City, UT 84111
E-mail: breeze@kbzn.com
www.kbzn.com
Phone: 801-670-9079
Fax: 801-364-8068

KCPW-FM 88.3 MHz (NPR)
445 Marsac Ave
Park City, UT 84060
E-mail: kcpw@ditell.com
Phone: 435-649-9004
Fax: 435-645-9063

KCPX-FM 105.7 MHz (Oldies)
280 S 400 West
Salt Lake City, UT 84101
E-mail: mountain@xmission.com
Phone: 801-303-4100
Fax: 801-303-4112

KDYL-AM 1280 kHz (Nost)
57 W South Temple Suite 700
Salt Lake City, UT 84101
Phone: 801-524-2600
Fax: 801-521-9234

KENZ-FM 107.5 MHz (AAA)
434 Bearcat Dr
Salt Lake City, UT 84115
www.1075.com
Phone: 801-485-6700
Fax: 801-487-5369

KFAN-AM 1320 kHz (Sports)
434 Bearcat Dr
Salt Lake City, UT 84115
E-mail: info@1320kfan.com
www.1320kfan.com
Phone: 801-485-6700
Fax: 801-487-5369

KISN-FM 97.1 MHz (AC)
4001 S 700 East Suite 800
Salt Lake City, UT 84101
Phone: 801-303-4100
Fax: 801-303-4112

KKAT-FM 101.9 MHz (Ctry)
2801 S Decker Lake Dr
West Valley City, UT 84119
www.kkat.com
Phone: 801-908-1300
Fax: 801-908-1429

KLO-AM 1430 kHz (Nost)
4155 Harrison Blvd Suite 206
Ogden, UT 84403
Phone: 801-627-1430
Fax: 801-627-0317

KNRS-AM 570 kHz (Nost)
2801 S Decker Lake Dr
Salt Lake City, UT 84119
Phone: 801-908-1300
Fax: 801-908-1459

KODJ-FM 94.1 MHz (Oldies)
2801 S Decker Lake Dr
West Valley City, UT 84119
www.oldies941.com
Phone: 801-575-5255
Fax: 801-908-1499

KOSY-FM 106.5 (Nost)
280 S 400 West Suite 200
Salt Lake City, UT 84101
Phone: 801-303-4100
Fax: 801-303-4112

KPCW-FM 91.9 MHz (NPR)
445 Marsac Ave
Park City, UT 84060
Phone: 435-649-9004
Fax: 435-645-9063

KQMB-FM 102.7 MHz (AC)
57 W South Temple Suite 700
Salt Lake City, UT 84101
www.star1027.com
Phone: 801-524-2600
Fax: 801-521-9234

KRAR-FM 106.9 MHz (Rock)
4455 S 5500 West
Hooper, UT 84315
Phone: 801-731-9000
Fax: 801-731-9666

KRSP-FM 103.5 MHz (CR)
57 W South Temple Suite 700
Salt Lake City, UT 84101
www.arrow1035.com
Phone: 801-524-2600
Fax: 801-521-9234

KSFI-FM 100.3 MHz (AC)
57 W South Temple Suite 700
Salt Lake City, UT 84101
E-mail: info@fm100.com
www.fm100.com
Phone: 801-524-2600
Fax: 801-521-9234

KSL-AM 1160 kHz (N/T)
PO Box 1160
Salt Lake City, UT 84110
E-mail: talk@ksl.com
www.ksl.com/radio/
Phone: 801-575-7600
Fax: 801-575-7625

KSOP-AM 1370 kHz (Ctry)
1285 W 2320 South
Salt Lake City, UT 84119
Phone: 801-972-1043
Fax: 801-974-0868

KSOP-FM 104.3 MHz (Ctry)
PO Box 25548
Salt Lake City, UT 84125
E-mail: ksop@ksopcountry.com
www.ksopcountry.com
Phone: 801-972-1043
Fax: 801-974-0868

KSOS-AM 800 kHz (Oldies)
4455 S 5500 West
Hooper, UT 84315
E-mail: ksos@ksos.com
www.ksos.com
Phone: 801-731-9000
Fax: 425-795-5083

KTCE-FM 92.3 MHz (CHR)
2835 E 3300 S
Salt Lake City, UT 84109
Phone: 801-371-9000
Fax: 801-412-6098

KUBL-FM 93.3 MHz (Ctry)
434 Bearcat Dr
Salt Lake City, UT 84115
E-mail: bull@xmission.com
Phone: 801-485-6700
Fax: 801-487-5369

KUER-FM 90.1 MHz (NPR)
101 S Wasatch Dr Rm 210
Salt Lake City, UT 84112
E-mail: fm90@media.utah.edu
Phone: 801-581-6625

KURR-FM 99.5 MHz (Rock)
2801 S Decker Lake Dr
West Valley City, UT 84119
www.rock99.com
Phone: 801-908-1300
Fax: 801-908-1499

KUUU-FM 92.1 MHz (CHR)
2835 E 3300 S
Salt Lake City, UT 84109
Phone: 801-570-9200
Fax: 801-412-6041

KWCR-FM 88.1 MHz (CHR)
2188 University Cir
Ogden, UT 84408
Phone: 801-626-6450
Fax: 801-626-6935

KWLW-AM 700 kHz (Ctry)
2801 S Decker Lake Dr
Salt Lake City, UT 84119
Phone: 801-908-1300
Fax: 801-908-1389

KXRK-FM 96.3 MHz (Alt)
517 W South Temple Suite 700
Salt Lake City, UT 84101
www.x96.com
Phone: 801-524-2600
Fax: 801-521-9234

KZHT-FM 94.9 MHz (CHR)
2801 S Decker Lake Dr
Salt Lake City, UT 84119
www.949zht.com
Phone: 801-908-1300
Fax: 801-908-1449

Attractions

Temple Square serves not only as the center of Salt Lake City, but also as the world center for the Mormon religion. The Mormon Tabernacle, home of the world-famous Mormon Tabernacle Choir; the beautiful Temple; and the world headquarters of the Church of Jesus Christ of Latter-day Saints, the LDS Church Office Building (with observation decks that provide spectacular views of the mountains and the valley) are all located in the Square. At Pioneer Trail State Park, located at the mouth of Emigration Canyon where Mormon pioneers first entered the valley, is the Old Deseret Pioneer Village, a living museum that depicts pioneer life in the area. Recreational attractions in Salt Lake City include the Raging Waters water theme park and the Utah Fun Dome, an indoor entertainment mall that includes miniature golf, skating, a 3-D theater, and a motion simulator. Of the many ski resorts in the Salt Lake City area, six are located in Wasatch-Cache National Forest. Among these is Snowbird in the Wasatch Mountains, with a 3,100-foot drop and a 125-passenger tram that provides mountaintop views of the area. Park City, located 29 miles east of Salt Lake City, is home to the U.S. Ski Team. (Park City is considered Utah's best ski destination and only bona fide resort town.) West of downtown Salt Lake City is the Great Salt Lake, the largest lake west of the Mississippi and the second saltiest body of water in the world (after the Dead Sea).

Ogden is just 35 miles north of Salt Lake City, in Weber County, with the Wasatch Mountains to the east of the city and the Great Salt Lake to the west. In addition to three ski resorts—Powder Mountain, Snowbasin, and Nordic Valley—Ogden has excellent areas for snowmobiling, tubing, and cross-country skiing. Most waters in the area are open year-round for fishing, and good trout fishing is available right in downtown Ogden. The fall color route up Ogden Canyon to Monte Cristo Park is considered one of the finest displays in Utah.

Abravanel Maurice Hall
123 W South Temple
Salt Lake City, UT 84101
Phone: 801-533-6407
Fax: 801-533-4268

Aperture Gallery
307 W 200 South Suite 1004
Salt Lake City, UT 84101
www.tssphoto.com/art.html
Phone: 801-363-9700
Fax: 801-363-9707
TF: 800-777-2076

Ballet West
50 W 200 South
Salt Lake City, UT 84101
www.balletwest.org/
Phone: 801-323-6901
Fax: 801-359-3504

Bear River Migratory Bird Refuge
Forest St 16 miles W of Brigham City
Brigham City, UT 84302
Phone: 435-723-5887

Beehive House
67 E South Temple St
Salt Lake City, UT 84111
Phone: 801-240-2671

Browning Firearms Museum
2501 Wall Ave Union Stn
Ogden, UT 84401
www.ogden-ut.com/attractions/UnionStation02.html
Phone: 801-393-9882
Fax: 801-629-8555

Browning-Kimball Car Collection
25th St & Wall Ave Union Stn
Ogden, UT 84401
Phone: 801-629-8444

Capitol Theatre
50 W 200 S
Salt Lake City, UT 84101
Phone: 801-323-6800
Fax: 801-538-2272
TF: 888-451-2787

Cathedral Church of St Mark
231 E 100 South
Salt Lake City, UT 84111
Phone: 801-322-3400
Fax: 801-322-3410

Catholic Cathedral of the Madeleine
331 E South Temple St
Salt Lake City, UT 84111
Phone: 801-328-8941
Fax: 801-364-6504

Chase Home Museum of Utah Folk Art Phone: 801-533-5760
1150 S 600 East
Salt Lake City, UT 84105
www.arts.utah.org/programs/fochase.html

Children's Museum of Utah Phone: 801-328-3383
840 N 300 West Fax: 801-328-3384
Salt Lake City, UT 84103
www.childmuseum.org

Collett Art Gallery Phone: 801-626-6420
2001 University Cir Weber State University Fax: 801-626-6976
Ogden, UT 84408

Daughters of the Utah Pioneers Museum Phone: 801-393-4460
2148 Grant Ave
Ogden, UT 84401

Delta Center Phone: 801-325-2000
301 W South Temple St Fax: 801-325-2578
Salt Lake City, UT 84101
www.deltacenter.com

Downtown Ogden Phone: 801-394-6634
2404 Washington Blvd Fax: 801-394-6647
Ogden, UT 84401

Eccles Community Art Center Phone: 801-392-6935
2580 Jefferson Ave Fax: 801-392-5295
Ogden, UT 84401

Eccles George S Dinosaur Park Phone: 801-393-3466
1544 E Park Blvd Fax: 801-399-0895
Ogden, UT 84401
E-mail: dinosaurpark@ci.ogden.ut.us
dinosaurpark.org

Eccles Spencer S & Hope F Railroad Center Phone: 801-629-8444
25th St & Wall Ave Union Stn
Ogden, UT 84401

Family History Library Phone: 801-240-2331
35 N West Temple St Fax: 801-240-1584
Salt Lake City, UT 84150
E-mail: fhl@ldschurch.org

Foothill Village Phone: 801-582-3646
1400 Foothill Dr Suite 46 Fax: 801-582-2803
Salt Lake City, UT 84108

Fort Buenaventura State Park/Historic Site Phone: 801-621-4808
2450 A Ave Fax: 801-392-2431
Ogden, UT 84401

Fort Douglas Military Museum Phone: 801-581-1710
32 Potter St Fort Douglas Fax: 801-581-1710
Salt Lake City, UT 84113

Gallivan Utah Center Plaza Phone: 801-532-0459
239 S Main St Fax: 801-521-8329
Salt Lake City, UT 84111

Goblin Valley State Park Phone: 435-564-3633
450 S Green River Blvd Fax: 435-564-3223
Green River, UT 84525 TF: 800-322-3770

Golden Spike National Historic Site Phone: 435-471-2209
PO Box 897 Fax: 435-471-2341
Brigham City, UT 84302
www.nps.gov/gosp/

Governor's Mansion Phone: 801-538-1005
603 E South Temple Fax: 801-538-1970
Salt Lake City, UT 84102

Great Salt Lake Phone: 801-250-1822
Exit 104 off I-80
Salt Lake City, UT 84404

Hale Centre Theater Phone: 801-984-9000
3333 S Decker Lake Dr Fax: 801-984-9009
West Valley City, UT 84119
E-mail: feedback@halecentretheatre.com
www.halecentretheatre.com/

Hansen Planetarium Phone: 801-538-2104
15 S State St Fax: 801-531-4948
Salt Lake City, UT 84111
www.utah.edu/Planetarium/

Hill Aerospace Museum Phone: 801-777-6818
7961 Wardleigh Rd Bldg 1955
Hill AFB, UT 84056
www.hill.af.mil/

Hogle Zoological Gardens Phone: 801-582-1631
2600 E Sunnyside Ave Fax: 801-584-1770
Salt Lake City, UT 84108
www.hoglezoo.org

Holy Trinity Greek Orthodox Church Phone: 801-328-9681
279 S 300 West Fax: 801-328-9688
Salt Lake City, UT 84101

International Peace Garden Phone: 801-972-7800
1000 S 900 West Jordan Park Fax: 801-972-7847
Salt Lake City, UT 84104

Lagoon & Pioneer Village Phone: 801-451-8000
375 N Hwy 91 Fax: 801-451-8015
Farmington, UT 84025 TF: 800-748-5246
E-mail: info@lagoonpark.com
www.lagoonpark.com

Latter Day Saints Church Office Building Observation Deck Phone: 801-240-3789
50 E North Temple St
Salt Lake City, UT 84150

Layton/Ott Planetarium Phone: 801-626-6855
Weber State University Lind Lecture Hall 2nd Fl
Ogden, UT 84408
www.physics.weber.edu

Liberty Park Phone: 801-972-7800
600 E 1000 South Fax: 801-972-7847
Salt Lake City, UT 84105

Lorin Farr Park Phone: 801-629-8284
Canyon Rd & Gramercy Ave
Ogden, UT 84401

Millstream Car Museum Phone: 801-394-9425
1450 Washington Blvd Fax: 801-392-9145
Ogden, UT 84404

Mormon Tabernacle
Temple Sq
Salt Lake City, UT 84103
Phone: 801-240-3221
Fax: 801-240-2033

Museum of Church History & Art
45 N West Temple St
Salt Lake City, UT 84150
Phone: 801-240-3310
Fax: 801-240-5342

Museum of Natural History
Weber State University Lind Lecture Hall
Ogden, UT 84408
Phone: 801-626-6653

Natural Bridges National Monument
HC 60 Box 1
Lake Powell, UT 84533
E-mail: nabr_interpretation@nps.gov
www.nps.gov/nabr/
Phone: 435-692-1234
Fax: 435-692-1111

Natural History Museum
2501 Wall Ave Union Stn
Ogden, UT 84401
Phone: 801-629-8444

Nordic Valley Ski Resort
3567 Nordic Valley Way
Eden, UT 84310
Phone: 801-392-0900

Off Broadway Theatre
272 S Main St
Salt Lake City, UT 84101
Phone: 801-355-4628
Fax: 801-355-4641

Ogden Canyon
SR 39
Ogden, UT 84404
Phone: 801-627-8288

Ogden Eccles Conference Center
2415 Washington Blvd
Ogden, UT 84401
www.oecenter.com
Phone: 801-395-3200
Fax: 801-395-3201
TF: 800-337-2690

Ogden Nature Center
966 W 12th St
Ogden, UT 84404
www.ogdennaturecenter.org
Phone: 801-621-7595
Fax: 801-621-1867

Ogden Symphony Ballet
2415 Washington Blvd Ogden Egyptian Theatre
Ogden, UT 84401
www.symphonyballet.org
Phone: 801-399-9214
Fax: 801-612-0757

Old Deseret Village
2601 Sunnyside Ave
Salt Lake City, UT 84108
Phone: 801-582-1847

Phillips Gallery
444 E 200 South
Salt Lake City, UT 84111
www.phillips-gallery.com
Phone: 801-364-8284
Fax: 801-364-8293

Pioneer Memorial Museum
300 N Main St
Salt Lake City, UT 84103
Phone: 801-538-1050
Fax: 801-538-1119

Powder Mountain Ski Resort
PO Box 450
Eden, UT 84310
Phone: 801-745-3772
Fax: 801-745-3619

Powell Myra Gallery
2501 Wall Ave Union Stn
Ogden, UT 84401
Phone: 801-629-8444

Raging Waters
1700 S 1200 West
Salt Lake City, UT 84104
Phone: 801-972-3300
Fax: 801-974-9686
TF: 800-333-3333

Red Butte Gardens & Arboretum
300 Wakara Way University of Utah
Salt Lake City, UT 84108
Phone: 801-581-4747
Fax: 801-585-6491

Repertory Dance Theatre
138 W 300 South
Salt Lake City, UT 84101
www.xmission.com/~rdt
Phone: 801-534-1000
Fax: 801-534-1110

Rio Grande Depot
300 S Rio Grande St
Salt Lake City, UT 84101
Phone: 801-533-3500

Ririe-Woodbury Dance Co
50 W 200 South
Salt Lake City, UT 84101
E-mail: dance@ririewoodbury.com
www.ririewoodbury.com
Phone: 801-323-6801
Fax: 801-359-3504

Rockport State Park
9040 N Hwy 302
Peoa, UT 84061
Phone: 435-336-2241
Fax: 435-336-2248
TF: 800-322-3770

Roy Historical Museum
5550 S 1700 West
Roy, UT 84067
Phone: 801-776-3626

Saint Joseph's Catholic Church
514 24th St
Ogden, UT 84401
Phone: 801-399-5627
Fax: 801-399-5918

Salt Lake Art Center
20 S West Temple
Salt Lake City, UT 84101
Phone: 801-328-4201
Fax: 801-322-4323

Salt Lake Community College Grand Theatre
1575 S State St
Salt Lake City, UT 84115
Phone: 801-957-3322
Fax: 801-957-3300

Salt Lake County Center for the Arts
50 W 200 S
Salt Lake City, UT 84101
Phone: 801-323-6800
Fax: 801-538-2272

Salt Lake Opera Theatre
48 W Broadway Suite 405 N
Salt Lake City, UT 84101
Phone: 801-328-2065

Shooting Star Saloon
7350 E 200 South
Huntsville, UT 84317
Phone: 801-745-2002

Smith Joseph Memorial Building
15 E South Temple St
Salt Lake City, UT 84111
Phone: 801-240-1266

Snowbasin Ski Resort
Hwy 226 17 miles E of Ogden
Huntsville, UT 84317
Phone: 801-399-1135

Social Hall Heritage Museum
55 S State St
Salt Lake City, UT 84103
Phone: 801-321-8745
Fax: 801-321-8776

Temple Square
50 E North Temple St
Salt Lake City, UT 84150
Phone: 801-240-2534
Fax: 801-240-1471
TF: 800-453-3860

Terrace Plaza Playhouse
99 E 4700 South
Ogden, UT 84405
Phone: 801-393-0070

This is the Place Heritage Park
2601 Sunnyside Ave
Salt Lake City, UT 84108
Phone: 801-582-1847

Timpanogos Cave National Monument
RR 3 Box 200
American Fork, UT 84003
www.nps.gov/tica/
Phone: 801-756-5239
Fax: 801-756-5661

Tivoli Gallery
255 S State St
Salt Lake City, UT 84111
Phone: 801-521-6288

Tracy Aviary
589 E 1300 South
Salt Lake City, UT 84105
E-mail: aviary@xmission.com
www.tracyaviary.org
Phone: 801-596-8500
Fax: 801-596-7325

Treehouse Children's Museum
24th St & Washington Blvd Ogden City Mall
Ogden, UT 84401
E-mail: treehouse@relia.net
www.relia.net/~treehouse/
Phone: 801-394-9663
Fax: 801-393-6820

Trolley Square
367 Trolley Sq
Salt Lake City, UT 84102
Phone: 801-521-9877
Fax: 801-521-1777

Two-Bit Street Trolley
2501 Wall Ave
Ogden, UT 84401
Phone: 800-255-8824
Fax: 801-399-0783

Union Station
2501 Wall Ave
Ogden, UT 84401
www.ogden-ut.com/attractions/UnionStation.html
Phone: 801-629-8444

Utah Fun Dome
4998 S 360 West
Murray, UT 84123
Phone: 801-263-8769
Fax: 801-265-3869

Utah Museum of Fine Arts
1530 E 370 S University of Utah
Salt Lake City, UT 84112
www.utah.edu/umfa/
Phone: 801-581-7332
Fax: 801-585-5198

Utah Museum of Natural History
1390 E Presidents Cir University of Utah
Salt Lake City, UT 84112
raven.umnh.utah.edu/
Phone: 801-581-6928
Fax: 801-585-3684

Utah Musical Theatre
1902 University Cir Weber State University
Ogden, UT 84408
Phone: 801-626-8500
Fax: 801-626-6811

Utah Opera Co
50 W 200 South
Salt Lake City, UT 84101
www.utahopera.org
Phone: 801-736-6868
Fax: 801-736-6815

Utah State Capitol
350 N Main St
Salt Lake City, UT 84114
Phone: 801-538-3000

Utah State Railroad Museum
2501 Wall Ave Union Stn
Ogden, UT 84401
Phone: 801-629-8444
Fax: 801-629-8555

Utah Symphony Orchestra
123 W South Temple St
Salt Lake City, UT 84101
E-mail: utsymph@aros.net
www.utahsymphony.org
Phone: 801-533-5626
Fax: 801-521-6634

Wall Enos A Mansion
411 E South Temple Latter Day Saints Business College
Salt Lake City, UT 84111
Phone: 801-524-8100
Fax: 801-524-1900
TF: 800-999-5767

Wasatch Brewery
1763 S 300 West
Salt Lake City, UT 84115
Phone: 801-466-8855
Fax: 801-484-6665

Wasatch-Cache National Forest
125 S State St
Salt Lake City, UT 84138
Phone: 801-524-3900
Fax: 801-524-3172

Wattis-Dumke Model Railroad Museum
2501 Wall Ave Union Stn
Ogden, UT 84401
Phone: 801-629-8446
Fax: 801-629-8555

Wheeler Historic Farm
6351 S 900 East
Salt Lake City, UT 84121
Phone: 801-264-2241
Fax: 801-264-2213

Willard Bay State Park
650 N 900 West
Willard, UT 84340
Phone: 435-734-9494
Fax: 435-734-2659
TF: 800-322-3770

Sports Teams & Facilities

Ogden Raptors (baseball)
2330 Lincoln Ave Lindquist Field
Ogden, UT 84401
www.ogden-raptors.com
Phone: 801-393-2400

Salt Lake Buzz (baseball)
13th S & West Temple St Franklin Quest Field
Salt Lake City, UT 84115
www.buzzbase.com
Phone: 801-485-3800
Fax: 801-485-6818

Utah Grizzlies (hockey)
3200 S Decker Lake Dr
Salt Lake City, UT 84119
www.utahgrizz.com
Phone: 801-988-8000
Fax: 801-988-7000

Utah Jazz
301 W South Temple St Delta Center
Salt Lake City, UT 84101
www.nba.com/jazz
Phone: 801-355-3865
TF: 800-358-7328

Utah Starzz (basketball)
301 W South Temple Delta Ctr
Salt Lake City, UT 84101
www.utahstarzz.com
Phone: 801-325-7827
Fax: 801-325-2516

Annual Events

A Taste of Ogden (early June) 801-394-6634
Bison Roundup (late October) 801-773-2941
Brewers Fest (mid-September)....................801-532-0459
Candlelight Christmas (mid-December) 801-582-7353
Christmas Lights at Temple Square
(late November-late December)..................801-240-1000
Christmas Village (December).....................801-629-8284
Cinco de Mayo (early May)........................801-359-9316
Days of '47 Celebration (mid-late July) 801-521-2822
Days of '47 Pioneer Parade (late July).............801-521-2822
Days of '47 World Championship Rodeo
(mid-late July) 801-521-2822
Deseret News Marathon (late July) 801-468-2560
Dickens Festival
(late November-early December) 801-538-8440
Festival of Lights (December).....................801-264-2241
Festival of the American West
(late July-early August).........................800-225-3378
Festival of Trees (early December) 801-588-3677
First Night New Years Eve Celebration
(December 31) 801-359-5118
First Night Ogden (December 31) 801-394-6634
Gem & Mineral Show (mid-March)................801-629-8444
Golden Spike Railroader's Festival
(early August).................................435-471-2209
Hispanic Dance (early September).................801-534-4777
Home & Garden Show (early-mid-March) 801-534-4777
Jazz Concert (early April).........................801-626-8500
Living Traditions Festival (mid-May) 801-596-5000
Madeleine Festival of Arts & Humanities
(late May) 801-560-9846
Memorial Day & Spring Celebration (late May) 801-582-7353
Mormon Miracle Pageant (mid-late June)...........435-835-3000
Nouveau Beaujolais Festival (late November) 435-645-6640
Ogden Christmas Parade (late November) 801-629-8242
Ogden Greek Festival (late September).............801-399-2231
Ogden Heritage Street Festival (mid-July)..........801-629-8242
Ogden Pioneer Days Rodeo & Celebration (July)....801-629-8214
Peach Days (early September) 435-723-3931
Scottish Celebration & Blessing of the Clans
(late October)................................801-363-3889
Snowbird's Winterfest (early December) 801-742-2222
Solstice Celebration (mid-June) 801-621-7595
Storytelling Festival (mid-November) 801-626-8500
Sundance Institute Film Festival (late January).....801-328-3456
US Freestyle Championships (early March).........801-742-2222
Utah Arts Festival (late June).....................801-322-2428
Utah Auto Show (late January)....................801-534-4777
Utah Boat & Fishing Show (mid-February).........801-534-4777
Utah State Fair (mid-September)..................801-538-8440
Weber County Fair (late July-August) 801-399-8711
Wildwoods Bash (mid-September).................801-621-7595

San Antonio, Texas

***County:* Bexar**

SAN ANTONIO is located at the edge of the Gulf Coastal Plains in south central Texas approximately 140 miles north of the Gulf of Mexico. The only major city within 100 miles is Austin, Texas.

Area (Land) .... 333.0 sq mi
Area (Water)................................ 4.5 sq mi
Elevation...................................... 701 ft
Latitude ....29-46-41 N
Longitude................................ 98-52-57 W
Time Zone ....CST
Area Code....................................... 210

Climate

San Antonio has a modified subtropical climate, with mild winters and hot summers. Winter high temperatures average in the low to mid-60s and lows average around 40 degrees. Snowfall is rare in San Antonio. Summer high temperatures average in the low to mid-90s and lows in the low to mid-70s. May is the wettest month of the year in San Antonio, while March and December are the driest.

Average Temperatures & Precipitation

Temperatures

	Jan	Feb	Mar	Apr	May	Jun	Jul	Aug	Sep	Oct	Nov	Dec
High	61	66	74	80	85	92	95	95	89	82	72	64
Low	38	41	50	58	66	73	75	75	69	59	49	41

Precipitation

	Jan	Feb	Mar	Apr	May	Jun	Jul	Aug	Sep	Oct	Nov	Dec
Inches	1.7	1.8	1.5	2.5	4.2	3.8	2.2	2.5	3.4	3.2	2.6	1.5

History

The area known today as San Antonio was inhabited by Native Americans of the Coahuilecan tribe as early as 100 A.D., and the first permanent European settlement was not established in the area until the late 17th Century. In 1691, a group of Spanish missionaries arrived in the region and founded the Mission San Francisco de los Tejas. Arriving on a saint's day, the missionaries named the area "San Antonio" in honor of Saint Anthony of Padua, who was commemorated by the holy day. Over the course of the next four decades, five other missions were established in San Antonio, including the mission of San Antonio de Valero, which is commonly known as "The Alamo." All six missions remain open to the public, and four of them still serve as Catholic parishes.

San Antonio was incorporated as a city in 1803. During the early 1800s, San Antonio served as an important military garrison, first for the Spanish and later for the Mexican army. Settlers led by Stephen F. Austin (who later became known as the "Father of Texas") began arriving in the area during the 1820s. In December 1835, during the Texas Revolution, San Antonio was captured by the Texans. For 12 days in 1836, volunteers at the Alamo in San Antonio fought against the forces of Mexican General Santa Anna. The 13th day the siege ended with 189 dead and a victory for the Mexican forces. This defeat inspired citizens to "Remember the Alamo" and eventually win Texas independence.

After the arrival of the railroad in 1877, San Antonio developed rapidly as a major distribution center along the cattle trail that ran from south Texas to Kansas. About that time, Fort Sam Houston—the first of a number of U.S. military installations to be established in the San Antonio area—was opened. In 1910, Aeroplane No. 1, the nation's first military aircraft, flew over Fort Sam Houston, earning the base a place in military aviation history. San Antonio continued to grow and prosper during the two World Wars as four more Air Force Bases (Kelly, Brooks, Lackland, and Randolph) were established near San Antonio, drawing military personnel from around the country, creating thousands of civilian positions, and boosting the area's overall economy. The five military installations are among San Antonio's 15 largest employers today.

Rich in history and culture, San Antonio remains an important regional center for commerce. Home to more than 1.1 million people, San Antonio is the second largest city in Texas and the eighth largest in the United States.

Population

1990 Census 935,393
1998 Estimate.......................... 1,114,130
% Change 14.0
2005 Projection 1,637,000*

Racial/Ethnic Breakdown

White.................................... 72.3%
Black 7.0%
Other.................................... 20.7%
Hispanic Origin (may be of any race) 55.6%

Age Breakdown

Under 5 years.............................. 8.5%
5 to 17.................................. 20.6%
18 to 20.................................. 5.2%
21 to 24.................................. 6.7%
25 to 34................................. 18.0%
35 to 44................................. 14.0%
45 to 54.................................. 8.9%
55 to 64.................................. 7.6%
65 to 74.................................. 6.3%
75+ years 4.2%
Median Age................................29.8

Gender Breakdown
Male 48.2%
Female 51.8%

** Information given is for the San Antonio Metropolitan Statistical Area (MSA), which includes Bexar, Comal, Guadelupe, and Wilson counties.*

Government

Type of Government: Council-Manager

San Antonio City Attorney
PO Box 839966
San Antonio, TX 78283
Phone: 210-207-8940
Fax: 210-207-4004

San Antonio City Clerk
PO Box 839966
San Antonio, TX 78283
Phone: 210-207-7253
Fax: 210-207-7032

San Antonio City Council
PO Box 839966
San Antonio, TX 78283
Phone: 210-207-7040
Fax: 210-207-7027

San Antonio City Hall
100 Military Plaza 2nd Fl
San Antonio, TX 78205
Phone: 210-207-7040
Fax: 210-207-7027

San Antonio City Manager
PO Box 839966
San Antonio, TX 78283
Phone: 210-207-7080
Fax: 210-207-4217

San Antonio Economic Development Dept
PO Box 839966
San Antonio, TX 78283
Phone: 210-207-8080
Fax: 210-207-8151

San Antonio Finance Dept
PO Box 839966
San Antonio, TX 78283
Phone: 210-207-8620
Fax: 210-207-4072

San Antonio Fire Dept
115 Auditorium Cir
San Antonio, TX 78205
Phone: 210-207-8400
Fax: 210-207-8542

San Antonio Human Resources Dept
111 Plaza de Armas
San Antonio, TX 78207
Phone: 210-207-8108
Fax: 210-207-4026

San Antonio Mayor
PO Box 839966
San Antonio, TX 78283
Phone: 210-207-7060
Fax: 210-207-4077

San Antonio Parks & Recreation Dept
950 E Hildebrand
San Antonio, TX 78212
Phone: 210-207-3000
Fax: 210-207-3045

San Antonio Planning Dept
PO Box 839966
San Antonio, TX 78283
Phone: 210-207-7873
Fax: 210-207-7897

San Antonio Police Dept
214 W Nueva St
San Antonio, TX 78207
Phone: 210-207-7360
Fax: 210-207-4377

San Antonio Public Library
600 Soledad St
San Antonio, TX 78205
Phone: 210-207-2500
Fax: 210-207-2603

San Antonio Public Works Dept
PO Box 839966
San Antonio, TX 78283
Phone: 210-207-8020
Fax: 210-207-4406

Important Phone Numbers

AAA 210-736-4691
American Express Travel 210-828-4809
Bexar County Tax Office 210-335-2251
Dental Referral 210-699-9529
Driver's License/Vehicle Registration Information . . . 210-615-5830
Emergency 911
Highway Conditions 800-452-9292
HotelDocs 800-468-3537
Medical Referral 210-734-6691
Poison Control Center 800-764-7661
San Antonio Board of Realtors 210-593-1200
San Antonio Property Tax Information System 210-207-8680
Texas Comptroller of Public Accounts 800-252-5555
Time/Temp 210-226-3232
Voter Registration Information 210-335-6625
Weather 210-225-0404

Information Sources

Alamodome
100 Montana St
San Antonio, TX 78203
www.alamodome.com
Phone: 210-207-3663
Fax: 210-207-3646
TF: 800-884-3663

Better Business Bureau Serving the South Central Area
1800 NE Loop 410 Suite 400
San Antonio, TX 78217
www.sanantonio.bbb.org
Phone: 210-828-9441
Fax: 210-828-3101

Bexar County
100 Dolorosa St
San Antonio, TX 78205
www.co.bexar.tx.us
Phone: 210-335-2011
Fax: 210-335-2926

Greater San Antonio Chamber of Commerce
602 E Commerce St
San Antonio, TX 78205
www.sachamber.org
Phone: 210-229-2100
Fax: 210-229-1600

Henry B Gonzalez Convention Center
200 E Market St
San Antonio, TX 78205
www.ci.sat.tx.us/convfac/
Phone: 210-207-8500
Fax: 210-223-1495

San Antonio Convention & Visitors Bureau
203 S Saint Marys St
San Antonio, TX 78205
www.sanantoniocvb.com
Phone: 210-207-6700
Fax: 210-207-6782
TF: 800-447-3372

Online Resources

4SanAntonio.com
www.4sanantonio.com

About.com Guide to San Antonio
sanantonio.about.com/local/southwestus/sanantonio

Alamo City Guide
www.alamocity.com

Anthill City Guide San Antonio
www.anthill.com/city.asp?city=sanantonio

Area Guide San Antonio
sanantonio.areaguides.net

Arrive @ San Antonio
www.arrive-at.com/sanantonio/

Boulevards San Antonio
www.sanantonio.com

Cain's San Antonio Page
www.cains.com/sa

City Knowledge San Antonio
www.cityknowledge.com/tx_sanantonio.htm

CitySearch San Antonio
sanantonio.citysearch.com

DigitalCity San Antonio
home.digitalcity.com/sanantonio

Everything San Antonio
www.esanantonio.com/

Excite.com San Antonio City Guide
www.excite.com/travel/countries/united_states/texas/san_antonio

Heart of San Antonio
heartofsanantonio.com

HotelGuide San Antonio
hotelguide.net/san_antonio

Lodging.com San Antonio Texas
www.lodging.com/auto/guides/san_antonio-area-tx.html

No Place But Texas
www.noplacebuttexas.com

Open World City Guides San Antonio
www.worldexecutive.com/cityguides/san_antonio/

San Antonio Food & Leisure
food-leisure.com

San Antonio Marketplace
samarketplace.com

SanAntonio.TheLinks.com
sanantonio.thelinks.com/

South Texas Outdoor Recreation Pages
wildtexas.com/

Virtual City San Antonio
www.txdirect.net/vcity-sa

Virtual Voyages San Antonio
www.virtualvoyages.com/usa/tx/san_anto/san_anto.sht

Area Communities

Communities in the four-county (Bexar, Comal, Guadelupe, & Wilson) San Antonio metropolitan area with populations greater than 5,000 include:

Alamo Heights
6116 Broadway St
Alamo Heights, TX 78209
Phone: 210-822-3331
Fax: 210-822-8197

Converse
405 S Seguin Rd
Converse, TX 78109
Phone: 210-658-5356
Fax: 210-659-0964

Floresville
1120 D St
Floresville, TX 78114
Phone: 830-393-3105
Fax: 830-393-2056

Kirby
112 Bauman St
Kirby, TX 78219
Phone: 210-661-3198
Fax: 210-661-4525

Leon Valley
6400 El Verde Rd
Leon Valley, TX 78238
Phone: 210-684-1391
Fax: 210-684-6988

Live Oak
8001 Shin Oak Dr
Live Oak, TX 78233
Phone: 210-653-9140
Fax: 210-653-2766

New Braunfels
424 S Castell Ave
New Braunfels, TX 78130
Phone: 830-608-2100
Fax: 830-608-2109

Schertz
PO Drawer I
Schertz, TX 78154
Phone: 210-658-3510
Fax: 210-659-3204

Seguin
205 N River St
Seguin, TX 78155
Phone: 830-379-3212
Fax: 830-401-2499

Universal City
PO Box 3008
Universal City, TX 78148
Phone: 210-659-0333
Fax: 210-659-7062

Windcrest
8601 Midcrown Dr
Windcrest, TX 78239
Phone: 210-655-0022
Fax: 210-655-8776

Economy

The U.S. Military has played a vital role in San Antonio's economy for much of the 20th Century, and five military installations are ranked among the area's 15 largest employers—Kelly Air Force Base, Fort Sam Houston, and Lackland Air Force Base are ranked numbers one, two, and three respectively. Although the Military is important to the area's economy, the government sector is, in fact, the third largest. Services is currently the largest and fastest-growing employment sector in the San Antonio metropolitan area, with health care and business services the leading industries. An important regional commercial center, trade (retail and wholesale) is San Antonio's second largest employment sector.

Unemployment Rate 3.4%*

Per Capita Income......................... $23,800*
Median Family Income..................... $41,900*

** Information given is for the San Antonio Metropolitan Statistical Area (MSA), which includes Bexar, Comal, Guadelupe, and Wilson counties.*

Principal Industries & Number of Wage Earners

San Antonio MSA* - June 2000

Construction.. 39,100
Finance, Insurance, & Real Estate....................... 51,900
Government.. 129,400
Manufacturing.. 55,000
Mining.. 2,000
Retail Trade.. 143,200
Services.. 230,100
Transportation & Public Utilities....................... 34,900
Wholesale Trade....................................... 32,100

** Information given is for the San Antonio Metropolitan Statistical Area (MSA), which includes Bexar, Comal, Guadelupe, and Wilson counties.*

Major Employers

Bexar County
100 Dolorosa St
San Antonio, TX 78205
www.co.bexar.tx.us
Phone: 210-335-2011
Fax: 210-335-2926

Brooks Air Force Base
Brooks AFB, TX 78235
www.brooks.af.mil
Phone: 210-536-1110
Fax: 210-536-3235

Fort Sam Houston
Fort Sam Houston, TX 78234
Phone: 210-221-1211
Fax: 210-221-1198

Frost National Bank
100 W Houston St
San Antonio, TX 78205
E-mail: frostbank@frostbank.com
www.frostbank.com
Phone: 210-220-4011
Fax: 210-220-4673
TF: 800-562-6732

H-E-B Grocery Co
646 S Main Ave
San Antonio, TX 78204
E-mail: inbasket@heb.com
www.hebgrocery.com
Phone: 210-938-8000
Fax: 210-938-8530

HB Zachry Co
PO Box 240130
San Antonio, TX 78224
E-mail: info@zachry.com
www.zachry.com
Phone: 210-475-8000
Fax: 210-475-8060

Lackland Air Force Base
Lackland AFB, TX 78236
E-mail: publicaf@lackland.af.mil
www.lackland.af.mil
Phone: 210-671-1110
Fax: 210-671-2022

Methodist Healthcare System
7550 W IH-10 Suite 1000
San Antonio, TX 78229
mhshealth.com
Phone: 210-377-1647
Fax: 210-349-0053

North East Independent School District
8961 Tesoro Dr
San Antonio, TX 78217
www.northeast.isd.tenet.edu
Phone: 210-804-7000
Fax: 210-804-7056

Northside Independent School District
5900 Evers Rd
San Antonio, TX 78238
www.nisd.net
Phone: 210-706-8500
Fax: 210-706-8627

Randolph Air Force Base
Randolph AFB, TX 78150
www.randolph.af.mil
Phone: 210-652-1110
Fax: 210-652-5412

San Antonio City Hall
100 Military Plaza 2nd Fl
San Antonio, TX 78205
www.ci.sat.tx.us
Phone: 210-207-7040
Fax: 210-207-7027

San Antonio Independent School District
141 Lavaca St
San Antonio, TX 78210
www.saisd.net
Phone: 210-299-5500
Fax: 210-299-5600

SBC Communications Inc
175 E Houston St
San Antonio, TX 78205
www.sbc.com
Phone: 210-821-4105
Fax: 210-351-2274
TF: 888-875-6388

Taco Cabana Inc
8918 Tesoro Dr Suite 200
San Antonio, TX 78217
Phone: 210-804-0990
Fax: 210-804-2425
TF: 800-842-0556

Ultramar Diamond Shamrock Corp
PO Box 696000
San Antonio, TX 78269
www.udscorp.com
Phone: 210-592-2000
Fax: 210-592-2031
TF: 800-333-3377

United Services Automobile Assn
9800 Fredericksburg Rd
San Antonio, TX 78288
/www.usaa.com
Phone: 210-498-2211
Fax: 210-498-9940
TF: 800-531-8222

University of Texas Health Science Center at San Antonio
7703 Floyd Curl Dr
San Antonio, TX 78229
www.uthscsa.edu
Phone: 210-567-2570
Fax: 210-567-6811

Valero Energy Corp
PO Box 500
San Antonio, TX 78292
www.valero.com
Phone: 210-370-2000
Fax: 210-370-2778
TF: 800-531-7911

West Teleservices Outbound
10931 Laureate Dr Suite 7140
San Antonio, TX 78249
E-mail: sales@west.com
Phone: 210-690-6900
Fax: 210-690-6963
TF: 800-521-6000

Quality of Living Indicators

Total Crime Index.................................. 76,777
(rates per 100,000 inhabitants)

Violent Crime
Murder/manslaughter........................... 96
Forcible rape................................ 599
Robbery...................................... 1,674
Aggravated assault........................... 3,971

Property Crime
Burglary..................................... 10,944

Larceny theft 53,898
Motor vehicle theft 5,595

Cost of Living Index.....................................90.9
(national average = 100)

Median Home Price...................................$91,800

Education

Public Schools

San Antonio Independent School District
Phone: 210-299-5500
Fax: 210-299-5600
141 Lavaca St
San Antonio, TX 78210
www.saisd.net

Number of Schools
Elementary 65
Middle 17
High... 8

Student/Teacher Ratio
All Grades 16.1:1

Private Schools

Number of Schools (all grades).................... 78+

Colleges & Universities

Alamo Community College District
Phone: 210-220-1500
Fax: 210-220-1584
811 W Houston St
San Antonio, TX 78207
www.accd.edu

ITT Technical Institute
Phone: 210-694-4612
Fax: 210-694-4651
TF: 800-880-0570
5700 Northwest Pkwy
San Antonio, TX 78249
www.itt-tech.edu

Our Lady of the Lake University
Phone: 210-434-6711
Fax: 210-431-4036
TF: 800-436-6558
411 SW 24th St
San Antonio, TX 78207
E-mail: hamid@lake.ollusa.edu
www.ollusa.edu

Palo Alto College
Phone: 210-921-5000
Fax: 210-921-5310
1400 W Villaret Blvd
San Antonio, TX 78224
E-mail: pacinfo@accd.edu
accd.edu/pac/pacmain/pachp.htm

Saint Mary's University
Phone: 210-436-3327
Fax: 210-431-6742
1 Camino Santa Maria St
San Antonio, TX 78228
www.stmarytx.edu

Saint Philip's College
Phone: 210-531-3200
Fax: 210-531-3235
1801 ML King Dr
San Antonio, TX 78203
www.accd.edu/spc/

San Antonio College
Phone: 210-733-2000
Fax: 210-733-2579
1300 San Pedro Ave
San Antonio, TX 78212
www.accd.edu/sac/

Texas Lutheran University
Phone: 830-372-8000
Fax: 830-372-8096
1000 W Court St
Seguin, TX 78155
E-mail: admissions@txlutheran.edu
www.txlutheran.edu

Trinity University
Phone: 210-999-7011
Fax: 210-999-8164
TF: 800-874-6489
715 Stadium Dr
San Antonio, TX 78212
E-mail: admissions@trinity.edu
www.trinity.edu

University of Texas San Antonio
Phone: 210-458-4011
Fax: 210-458-4571
6900 North Loop 1604 W
San Antonio, TX 78249
www.utsa.edu

University of the Incarnate Word
Phone: 210-829-6000
Fax: 210-829-3921
4301 Broadway St
San Antonio, TX 78209
www.uiw.edu

Hospitals

Audie L Murphy Memorial Veterans Hospital
Phone: 210-617-5300
Fax: 210-949-3296
7400 Merton Minter Blvd
San Antonio, TX 78284

Baptist Medical Center
Phone: 210-297-7000
Fax: 210-297-0701
111 Dallas St
San Antonio, TX 78205

Christus Santa Rosa Children's Hospital
Phone: 210-704-2011
Fax: 210-704-3010
518 W Houston
San Antonio, TX 78207
www.santarosahealth.org/9SRchildrenhospital.html

Christus Santa Rosa Health Care
Phone: 210-704-2011
Fax: 210-704-3010
519 W Houston
San Antonio, TX 78207
www.santarosahealth.org

Christus Santa Rosa Health Center Northwest
Phone: 210-705-6300
Fax: 210-705-6170
2827 Babcock Rd
San Antonio, TX 78229

Methodist Specialty & Transplant Hospital
Phone: 210-575-8110
Fax: 210-575-8303
8026 Floyd Curl Dr
San Antonio, TX 78229
www.mhshealth.com/facilities/sacomm/index.html

Metropolitan Methodist Hospital
Phone: 210-208-2200
Fax: 210-208-2657
1310 McCullough Ave
San Antonio, TX 78212
www.mhshealth.com/facilities/metro

Nix Health Care System
Phone: 210-271-1800
Fax: 210-271-2023
414 Navarro St
San Antonio, TX 78205

Northeast Baptist Hospital
Phone: 210-297-2000
Fax: 210-297-2610
8811 Village Dr
San Antonio, TX 78217

Northeast Methodist Hospital
12412 Judson Rd
San Antonio, TX 78233
www.mhshealth.com/facilities/nemeth
Phone: 210-650-4949
Fax: 210-637-2062

Saint Luke's Baptist Hospital
7930 Floyd Curl Dr
San Antonio, TX 78229
Phone: 210-297-5000
Fax: 210-297-0501

Southeast Baptist Hospital
4214 E Southcross Blvd
San Antonio, TX 78222
Phone: 210-297-3000
Fax: 210-297-0300

Southwest General Hospital
7400 Barlite Blvd
San Antonio, TX 78224
Phone: 210-921-2000
Fax: 210-921-3508

Southwest Texas Methodist Hospital
7700 Floyd Curl Dr
San Antonio, TX 78229
www.mhshealth.com/facilities/methodist/index.html
Phone: 210-575-4000
Fax: 210-575-4950

University Health System
4502 Medical Dr
San Antonio, TX 78229
Phone: 210-358-4000
Fax: 210-358-4090

Transportation

Airport(s)

San Antonio International Airport (SAT)
8 miles N of downtown (approx 20 minutes)......210-207-3411

Mass Transit

VIA Metropolitan Transit
$.75 Base fare................................210-362-2020
VIA Streetcar
$.50 Base fare................................210-362-2020

Rail/Bus

Amtrak Station
350 Hoefgen St
San Antonio, TX 78205
Phone: 210-223-3226
TF: 800-872-7245

Greyhound/Trailways Bus Station
500 N Saint Mary's St
San Antonio, TX 78205
Phone: 210-270-5824
TF: 800-231-2222

Utilities

Electricity
San Antonio City Public Service 210-353-2222
www.citypublicservice.com

Gas
San Antonio City Public Service 210-353-2222
www.citypublicservice.com

Water
San Antonio Water System.....................210-704-7297

Garbage Collection/Recycling
San Antonio Solid Waste Div..................210-522-8831

Telecommunications

Telephone
Southwestern Bell.............................210-360-2000
www.swbell.com

Cable Television
Omnivision.................................888-904-8860

Internet Service Providers (ISPs)
Compuvision Network Services LLC.............830-608-0808
www.compuvision.net
DCCI Internet Services.........................210-731-6611
www.dcci.com
Internet Direct Inc............................210-308-9800
www.txdirect.net
South Texas Internet Connections Inc 210-477-7842
www.stic.net
Texas Networking Inc 210-357-9202
www.texas.net

Banks

Bank of America NA
3500 San Pedro Ave
San Antonio, TX 78212
Phone: 210-828-7988
Fax: 210-826-4854
TF: 800-247-6263

Bank One Texas NA
154 E Commerce St
San Antonio, TX 78205
Phone: 210-271-8200

Broadway National Bank
1177 NE Loop 410
San Antonio, TX 78217
Phone: 210-283-6500
Fax: 210-283-6527

Chase Bank of Texas NA
1020 NE Loop 410
San Antonio, TX 78209
Phone: 210-829-6100
Fax: 210-829-6199

Citizens State Bank
1300 W Hildebrand Ave
San Antonio, TX 78201
Phone: 210-785-2300
Fax: 210-785-2301
TF: 800-870-2472

Compass Bank
12590 Bandera Rd
San Antonio, TX 78023
Phone: 210-695-4000

Frost National Bank
100 W Houston St
San Antonio, TX 78205
E-mail: frostbank@frostbank.com
www.frostbank.com
Phone: 210-220-4011
Fax: 210-220-4673
TF: 800-562-6732

Guaranty Federal Bank FSB
1100 NE Loop 410 1st Fl
San Antonio, TX 78209
Phone: 210-829-3779
Fax: 210-804-0851

International Bank of Commerce
2201 NW Military Hwy
San Antonio, TX 78213
Phone: 210-366-0617
Fax: 210-349-9310

Jefferson State Bank
2900 Fredericksburg Rd
San Antonio, TX 78201
E-mail: mail@jeffersonstatebank.com
www.jeffersonstatebank.com
Phone: 210-734-4311
Fax: 210-731-4652

Norwest Bank Texas NA
40 NE Loop 410
San Antonio, TX 78216
Phone: 210-856-5000
Fax: 210-856-5038
TF: 800-224-7334

Security National Bank of San Antonio
100 St Cloud Rd
San Antonio, TX 78228
www.snbsa.com
Phone: 210-734-7361
Fax: 210-734-2011

USAA FSB
10750 McDermott Fwy
San Antonio, TX 78230
Phone: 210-498-2265
Fax: 800-531-5717
TF: 800-531-2265

Wells Fargo Bank
8700 Crownhill Rd
San Antonio, TX 78209
Phone: 210-841-7800

Shopping

Crossroads of San Antonio
4522 Fredericksburg Rd
San Antonio, TX 78201
Phone: 210-735-9137
Fax: 210-732-5205

Ingram Park Mall
6301 NW Loop 410
San Antonio, TX 78238
Phone: 210-523-1228
Fax: 210-681-4614

La Villita
418 Villita St
San Antonio, TX 78205
hotx.com/sa/lavillita
Phone: 210-207-8610
Fax: 210-207-4390

Market Square/El Mercado
514 W Commerce St
San Antonio, TX 78207
Phone: 210-207-8600

North Star Mall
2000 North Star Mall
San Antonio, TX 78216
Phone: 210-342-2325
Fax: 210-342-7023

Rivercenter Mall
849 E Commerce St
San Antonio, TX 78205
Phone: 210-225-0000
Fax: 210-224-7294

Sunset Station
1174 E Commerce St
San Antonio, TX 78205
www.sunset-station.com
Phone: 210-223-6153

Windsor Park Mall
7900 IH-35 N
San Antonio, TX 78218
Phone: 210-654-9084
Fax: 210-654-4850

Media

Newspapers and Magazines

North San Antonio Recorder-Times
17400 Judson Rd
San Antonio, TX 78247
www.primetimenewspapers.com/recorder/northsid.htm
Phone: 210-453-3300
Fax: 210-828-3787

San Antonio Business Journal
70 NE Loop 410 Suite 350
San Antonio, TX 78216
www.amcity.com/sanantonio
Phone: 210-341-3202
Fax: 210-341-3031

San Antonio Current
1500 N Saint Mary's St
San Antonio, TX 78215
E-mail: sacurrent@aol.com
www.sacurrent.com
Phone: 210-227-0044
Fax: 210-227-7755

San Antonio Express-News*
Ave 'E' & 3rd St
San Antonio, TX 78205
www.expressnews.com
Phone: 210-225-7411
Fax: 210-250-3105
TF: 800-555-1551

**Indicates major daily newspapers*

Television

KABB-TV Ch 29 (Fox)
4335 NW Loop 410
San Antonio, TX 78229
E-mail: kabbtv@kabb.com
www.kabb.com
Phone: 210-366-1129
Fax: 210-377-4758

KENS-TV Ch 5 (CBS)
5400 Fredericksburg Rd
San Antonio, TX 78229
Phone: 210-366-5000
Fax: 210-377-0740

KLRN-TV Ch 9 (PBS)
501 Broadway St
San Antonio, TX 78215
www.klrn.org
Phone: 210-270-9000
Fax: 210-270-9078

KMOL-TV Ch 4 (NBC)
1031 Navarro St
San Antonio, TX 78205
E-mail: kmol@kmol.com
www.kmol.com
Phone: 210-226-4444
Fax: 210-224-9898

KRRT-TV Ch 35 (WB)
4335 NW Loop 410
San Antonio, TX 78229
E-mail: krrt@krrt.com
www.krrt.com
Phone: 210-366-1129
Fax: 210-442-6333

KSAT-TV Ch 12 (ABC)
1408 N Saint Mary's St
San Antonio, TX 78215
Phone: 210-351-1200
Fax: 210-351-1310

KVDA-TV Ch 60 (Tele)
6234 San Pedro Ave
San Antonio, TX 78216
www.kvda.com
Phone: 210-340-8860
Fax: 210-341-2051

KWEX-TV Ch 41 (Uni)
411 E Durango Blvd
San Antonio, TX 78204
www.univision.net/stations/kwex.htm
Phone: 210-227-4141
Fax: 210-226-0131

Radio

KAJA-FM 97.3 MHz (Ctry)
6222 NW IH-10
San Antonio, TX 78201
www.kj97.com
Phone: 210-736-9700
Fax: 210-735-8811

KCJZ-FM 106.7 MHz (Oldies)
8122 Datapoint Dr Suite 500
San Antonio, TX 78229
www.kcjz.com
Phone: 210-615-5400
Fax: 210-615-5300

KCOR-AM 1350 kHz (Span)
1777 NE Loop 410 Suite 400
San Antonio, TX 78217
Phone: 210-829-1075
Fax: 210-804-7820

KCYY-FM 100.3 MHz (Ctry)
8122 Datapoint Dr Suite 500
San Antonio, TX 78229
www.y100fm.com
Phone: 210-615-5400
Fax: 210-615-5300

KISS-FM 99.5 MHz (Rock)
8930 Four Winds Dr Suite 500
San Antonio, TX 78239
www.kissrocks.com
Phone: 210-646-0105
Fax: 210-871-6116

KKYX-AM 680 kHz (Ctry)
8122 Datapoint Dr Suite 500
San Antonio, TX 78229
www.kkyx.com
Phone: 210-615-5400
Fax: 210-615-5300

KLEY-FM 94.1 MHz (Span)
7800 I-10 W Suite 330
San Antonio, TX 78230
Phone: 210-340-1234
Fax: 210-340-1775

KLUP-AM 930 kHz (Nost)
8930 Four Winds Dr Suite 500
San Antonio, TX 78239
www.klup.com
Phone: 210-646-0105
Fax: 210-871-6116

KONO-AM 860 kHz (Oldies)
7800 I-10 W Suite 330
San Antonio, TX 78230
www.kono.com
Phone: 210-340-0800
Fax: 210-340-3118

KONO-FM 101.1 MHz (Oldies)
8122 Datapoint Dr Suite 500
San Antonio, TX 78229
www.kono101.com
Phone: 210-615-5400
Fax: 210-615-5300

KQXT-FM 101.9 MHz (AC)
6222 NW IH-10
San Antonio, TX 78201
www.kq102.com
Phone: 210-736-9700
Fax: 210-736-9776

KROM-FM 92.9 MHz (Span)
1777 NE Loop 410 Suite 400
San Antonio, TX 78217
E-mail: radiosales@estereolatino.com
www.929estereolatino.com
Phone: 210-829-1075
Fax: 210-804-7820

KSAH-AM 720 MHz (Span)
1777 NE Loop 410 Suite 803
San Antonio, TX 78217
Phone: 210-820-3503
Fax: 210-820-3428

KSJL-AM 810 kHz (Urban)
6222 NW IH-10
San Antonio, TX 78217
E-mail: sales@ksjl.com
www.ksjl.com
Phone: 210-736-9700
Fax: 210-735-8811

KSJL-FM 92.5 MHz (Urban)
6222 NW IH-10
San Antonio, TX 78201
E-mail: jockbox@ksjl.com
www.ksjl.com
Phone: 210-736-9700
Fax: 210-735-8811

KSMG-FM 105.3 MHz (AC)
8930 Four Winds Dr Suite 500
San Antonio, TX 78239
www.magic105.com
Phone: 210-646-0105
Fax: 210-871-6116

KSTX-FM 89.1 MHz (NPR)
8401 Datapoint Dr Suite 800
San Antonio, TX 78229
E-mail: kstx@tpr.org
www.tpr.org
Phone: 210-614-8977
Fax: 210-614-8983

KTFM-FM 102.7 MHz (CHR)
4050 Eisenhauer Rd
San Antonio, TX 78218
E-mail: janitor@ktfm.com
www.ktfm.com
Phone: 210-599-5500
Fax: 210-599-5588

KTSA-AM 550 kHz (N/T)
4050 Eisenhauer Rd
San Antonio, TX 78218
www.ktsa.com
Phone: 210-599-5500
Fax: 210-599-5588

KXTN-AM 1310 kHz (Span)
1777 NE Loop 410 Suite 400
San Antonio, TX 78217
www.kxtn.com
Phone: 210-829-1075
Fax: 210-804-7820

KXTN-FM 107.5 MHz (Span)
1777 NE Loop 410 Suite 400
San Antonio, TX 78217
www.kxtn.com
Phone: 210-829-1075
Fax: 210-804-7820

KXXM-FM 96.1 MHz (CHR)
6222 NW IH-10
San Antonio, TX 78201
E-mail: mixsales@mix961.com
www.mix961.com
Phone: 210-736-9700
Fax: 210-736-9778
TF: 800-373-9700

KZEP-FM 104.5 MHz (CR)
427 E 9th St
San Antonio, TX 78215
www.kzep.com
Phone: 210-226-6444
Fax: 210-225-5736

WOAI-AM 1200 kHz (N/T)
6222 NW IH-10
San Antonio, TX 78201
E-mail: woai@texas.net
www.woai.com
Phone: 210-736-9700
Fax: 210-735-8811

Attractions

The 2.6-mile Texas Star Trail in San Antonio features some 80 historic sites and landmarks, including the Alamo. Near the Texas Star Trail, too, is San Antonio's River Walk. Built a full story below street level, River Walk's restaurants, hotels, and bars sit on scenic stone pathways on both banks of the San Antonio River. River Walk's nightly celebration, Fiesta Noche del Rio, features dancers, trumpets, and flamenco guitarists. Southeast of River Walk, not far from the Alamo, is HemisFair Park, the onetime site of a world exposition and still home to the Tower of the Americas, a 750-foot structure that was once the symbol of Hemisfair, and the Institute of Texan Cultures. South of downtown San Antonio, the Mission Trail connects four of the beautiful stone missions built along the San Antonio River.

Alamo The
300 Alamo Plaza
San Antonio, TX 78205
E-mail: curator@swbell.net
www.thealamo.org
Phone: 210-225-1391
Fax: 210-229-1343

Arneson River Theatre
418 Villita St La Villita
San Antonio, TX 78205
Phone: 210-207-8610
Fax: 210-207-4390

Blue Star Arts Complex
116 Blue Star
San Antonio, TX 78204
Phone: 210-227-6960
Fax: 210-229-9412

Brackenridge Park
950 E Hildebrand Ave
San Antonio, TX 78212
Phone: 210-207-3000
Fax: 210-207-3045

Carver Community Cultural Center
226 N Hackberry
San Antonio, TX 78202
Phone: 210-207-7211
Fax: 210-207-4412

Cascade Caverns Park
226 Cascade Caverns Rd
Boerne, TX 78015
Phone: 830-755-8080

Cockrell Lila Theatre
200 E Market St
San Antonio, TX 78205
www.ci.sat.tx.us/convfac/lila.htm
Phone: 210-207-8500
Fax: 210-223-1495

Cowboy Museum & Gallery
209 Alamo Plaza
San Antonio, TX 78205
E-mail: cowboymuseum@earthlink.net
Phone: 210-229-1257
Fax: 210-223-3711

Emilie & Albert Friedrich Park
21480 Milsa St
San Antonio, TX 78283
Phone: 210-207-8480

Fort Sam Houston Museum & National Historic Landmark
1210 Stanley Rd
Fort Sam Houston, TX 78234
Phone: 210-221-1886
Fax: 210-221-1311

Guadalupe Cultural Arts Center
1300 Guadalupe St
San Antonio, TX 78207
E-mail: guadarts@aol.com
www.guadalupeculturalarts.org
Phone: 210-271-3151
Fax: 210-271-3480

Guenther House
205 E Guenther
San Antonio, TX 78204
www.guentherhouse.com
Phone: 210-227-1061
TF: 800-235-8186

Hertzberg Circus Museum
210 Market St
San Antonio, TX 78205
Phone: 210-207-7810

Institute of Texan Cultures
801 S Bowie HemisFair Pk
San Antonio, TX 78205
www.texancultures.utsa.edu
Phone: 210-458-2300
Fax: 210-458-2205

Japanese Tea Gardens
3800 N Saint Mary's St
San Antonio, TX 78212
Phone: 210-821-3120

Jose Antonio Navarro State Historic Site
228 S Laredo St
San Antonio, TX 78207
Phone: 210-226-4801

Josephine Theatre
339 W Josephine St
San Antonio, TX 78212
Phone: 210-734-4646
Fax: 210-734-0077

Kiddie Park
3015 Broadway
San Antonio, TX 78209
www.carousel.net/org/kiddie_park.html
Phone: 210-824-4351

King William Historic District
1032 S Alamo St
San Antonio, TX 78210
Phone: 210-227-8786
Fax: 210-227-8030

La Villita
418 Villita St
San Antonio, TX 78205
hotx.com/sa/lavillita
Phone: 210-207-8610
Fax: 210-207-4390

Lone Star Brewing Co Inc
600 Lone Star Blvd
San Antonio, TX 78204
Phone: 210-226-8301
Fax: 210-270-9430

Lonestar Buckhorn Museum
318 E Houston St
San Antonio, TX 78205
www.buckhornmuseum.com/
Phone: 210-247-4000
Fax: 210-247-4020

Majestic Theatre
208 E Houston St
San Antonio, TX 78205
www.themajestic.com/theatre.htm
Phone: 210-226-5700
Fax: 210-226-3377

Marion Koogler McNay Art Museum
6000 N New Braunfels Ave
San Antonio, TX 78209
www.mcnayart.org
Phone: 210-824-5368
Fax: 210-824-0218

Market Square/El Mercado
514 W Commerce St
San Antonio, TX 78207
Phone: 210-207-8600

Mission San Jose
701 E Pyron Ave
San Antonio, TX 78214
Phone: 210-922-0543

Natural Bridge Caverns
26495 Natural Bridge Caverns Rd
San Antonio, TX 78266
E-mail: nabrcavern@aol.com
www.naturalbridgetexas.com/caverns
Phone: 210-651-6101
Fax: 210-651-6144

Natural Bridge Wildlife Ranch
26515 Natural Bridge Caverns Rd
San Antonio, TX 78266
E-mail: nbwrinf@gvtc.com
www.nbwildliferanchtx.com
Phone: 830-438-7400
Fax: 830-438-3494

Nelson A Rockefeller Center for Latin American Art
200 W Jones Ave
San Antonio, TX 78215
Phone: 210-978-8100
Fax: 210-978-8134

Pabst Brewing Co
312 Pearl Pkwy
San Antonio, TX 78215
www.pabst.com
Phone: 210-226-0231
Fax: 210-226-2512

Pioneer Old Trail Drivers & Former Texas Rangers Museum
3805 Broadway St
San Antonio, TX 78209
Phone: 210-822-9011
Fax: 210-666-5607

Plaza Wax Museum
301 Alamo Plaza
San Antonio, TX 78205
www.plazatheatreofwax.com
Phone: 210-224-9299
Fax: 210-224-1516

Ripley's Believe It or Not! Museum
301 Alamo Plaza
San Antonio, TX 78205
E-mail: gmptow@aol.com
www.ripleys.com/sanantonio.htm
Phone: 210-224-9299
Fax: 210-224-1516

River Walk
Downtown San Antonio
San Antonio, TX 78205
Phone: 210-207-8480

Rivercenter IMAX
849 E Commerce St Rivercenter Mall 2nd Fl
San Antonio, TX 78205
E-mail: imax@imax-sa.com
www.imax-sa.com
Phone: 210-225-4629
Fax: 800-354-4629

San Antonio Botanical Gardens
555 Funston Pl
San Antonio, TX 78209
www.sabot.org
Phone: 210-207-3250
Fax: 210-207-3274

San Antonio Children's Museum
305 E Houston St
San Antonio, TX 78205
www.sakids.org
Phone: 210-212-4453
Fax: 210-242-1313

San Antonio Missions National Historical Park
2202 Roosevelt Ave
San Antonio, TX 78210
www.nps.gov/saan/
Phone: 210-534-8833
Fax: 210-534-1106

San Antonio Museum of Art
200 W Jones Ave
San Antonio, TX 78215
www.samuseum.org
Phone: 210-978-8100
Fax: 210-978-8134

San Antonio Symphony Orchestra
222 E Houston Majestic Bldg Suite 200
San Antonio, TX 78205
E-mail: sasympho@swbell.net
www.sasymphony.org/
Phone: 210-554-1000
Fax: 210-554-1008

San Antonio Zoological Gardens & Aquarium
3903 N Saint Mary's St
San Antonio, TX 78212
E-mail: sazoo@sazoo-aq.org
www.sazoo-aq.org
Phone: 210-734-7184
Fax: 210-734-7291

San Pedro Playhouse
San Pedro Pk & Ashby Cir
San Antonio, TX 78212
E-mail: sanpedplay@aol.com
www.members.tripod.com/san_pedro_playhouse
Phone: 210-733-7258
Fax: 210-734-2651

Sea World of Texas
10500 Sea World Dr
San Antonio, TX 78251
www.seaworld.com/seaworld/sw_texas/swtframe.html
Phone: 210-523-3000
Fax: 210-523-3199
TF: 800-722-2762

Six Flags Fiesta Texas
17000 IH-10 W
San Antonio, TX 78257
www.sixflags.com/sanantonio
Phone: 210-697-5000
Fax: 210-697-5415
TF: 800-473-4378

Spanish Governor's Palace
105 Military Plaza
San Antonio, TX 78205
Phone: 210-224-0601

Splashtown
3600 I-35 N
San Antonio, TX 78219
www.splashtownsa.com
Phone: 210-227-1100
Fax: 210-225-7946

Steves Homestead
509 King William St
San Antonio, TX 78204
E-mail: conservation@saconservation.org
www.saconservation.org/prop6.html
Phone: 210-225-5924

Sunset Station
1174 E Commerce St
San Antonio, TX 78205
www.sunset-station.com
Phone: 210-223-6153

Texas Transportation Museum
11731 Wetmore Rd McAllister Pk
San Antonio, TX 78247
Phone: 210-490-3554

Tower of the Americas
600 HemisFair Pkwy
San Antonio, TX 78205
Phone: 210-207-8615

Witte Museum
3801 Broadway St
San Antonio, TX 78209
www.wittemuseum.org
Phone: 210-357-1900
Fax: 210-357-1882

WW McAllister Park
13102 Jones-Maltsberger Rd
San Antonio, TX 78283
Phone: 210-207-8480

Sports Teams & Facilities

Alamodome
100 Montana St
San Antonio, TX 78203
www.alamodome.com
Phone: 210-207-3663
Fax: 210-207-3646
TF: 800-884-3663

Freeman Coliseum
3201 E Houston St
San Antonio, TX 78219
www.freeman-coliseum.com
Phone: 210-226-1177
Fax: 210-226-5081

San Antonio Iguanas (hockey)
3201 E Houston St Freeman Coliseum
Houston, TX 78219
www.sa-iguanas.com
Phone: 210-227-4449
Fax: 210-821-4592

San Antonio Missions (baseball)
Hwy 90 & Callaghan Rd Nelson Wolff Stadium
San Antonio, TX 78227
www.samissions.com
Phone: 210-675-7275
Fax: 210-670-0001

San Antonio Speedway
PO Box 1269
Helotes, TX 78023
Phone: 210-628-1499
Fax: 210-695-3034

San Antonio Spurs
100 Montana St Alamodome
San Antonio, TX 78203
www.nba.com/spurs
Phone: 210-554-7787
Fax: 210-554-7701

Annual Events

Alamo Bowl (December 30)........................210-226-2695
Alamo Irish Festival (mid-March).................210-344-4317
Artesanos del Pueblo (mid-November).............210-922-3218
Asi se baile (early-mid-June).......................210-822-2453
Celebrate San Antonio (December 31).............210-207-8480
Cinco de Mayo (early May)........................210-207-8600
Clogger's Showcase (early May)...................210-492-8700
Diez y Seis Parade & Festival (mid-September).....210-223-3151
Festival de Animales (late April)..................210-734-7184
Festival of the Armed Forces Air Show (late May)...................................210-207-6700
Fiesta Arts Fair (late April).......................210-224-1848
Fiesta De Las Luminarias (early-mid-December)....210-227-4262
Fiesta del Mercado (late April)....................210-207-8600
Fiesta Gartenfest (late April)......................210-222-1521
Fiesta Mariachi Festival (late April)................210-227-4262
Fiesta San Antonio (late April)....................210-227-5191
Fiestas Patrias (mid-September)..................210-207-8600
Floating Christmas Pageant (early-mid-December)..........................210-225-0000
Freedom Fest (early July)........................210-207-8600
Halloween/Dia de Los Muertos (late October).......210-207-8600
International Accordion Festival (late September-early October)..................210-207-6961
International Theatre Festival at San Antonio (late October)................................210-227-0123
Jazz Alive (late September).......................210-207-8480
Juneteenth Festival (mid-June)...................210-533-4383
Latino Laugh Festival (early June).................800-447-3372
Lighting Ceremony (late November-late December)...................................210-227-4262
Lowrider Custom Car & Truck Festival (early April)..................................210-432-1896
Martin Luther King Jr March & Rally (mid-January)................................210-207-7235
Miller Lite Mud Festival (mid-January).............210-227-4262
Mission San Jose Spring Festival (late April).......210-922-0543
National Sporting Clays Championship (mid-September).............................210-688-3371
Oktoberfest San Antonio (early-mid-October).......210-222-1521
Out at the Movies Gay & Lesbian Film Festival (late September).............................210-228-0201
Remembering the Alamo Living History Weekend (early March)...............................210-650-3343
Return of the Chili Queens (late May).............210-207-8600
Rhythm on the River (mid-late August)............210-227-4262
River Walk Arts & Crafts Fair (early December)....210-229-2104
Riverwalk Holiday Festival (early-mid-December)....210-227-4262
Riverwalk Holiday Parade (late November)..........210-227-4262
Saint Patrick's Day Celebration (March 17).........210-225-0000
Saint Patrick's River Dyeing (mid-March)..........210-497-8435
Saint Patrick's Street Parade (mid-March).........210-497-8435
San Antonio CineFestival (early June).............210-271-3151
San Antonio Conjunto Shootout (mid-July)........210-246-9626
San Antonio House Beautiful Show (late September-early October)..................800-527-7469
San Antonio Marathon (mid-November)............210-826-1888
San Antonio Stock Show & Rodeo (early-mid-February)..........................210-225-5851
Spring Renaissance Faire (April-June).............210-225-0731
Starving Artists Show (early April)................210-226-3593
Taste of New Orleans (mid-April).................210-637-8328
Tejano Conjunto Festival (mid-May)...............210-271-3151
Tejano Music Awards (early March)................210-222-8862
Texas Country Music Event (mid-September).......210-227-4262
Texas Folklife Festival (early June)................210-458-2300
Viva Botanica (early April)........................210-207-3255
Westin Texas Open at La Cantera (late September).............................210-341-0823
Wurstfest (mid-November).......................800-221-4369
Zoo Boo (late October)...........................210-734-7184

San Diego, California

***County:* San Diego**

SAN DIEGO is located on the southwest Pacific Coast of California. Major cities within 100 miles include Santa Ana and San Bernardino, California and Tijuana, Mexico.

Area (Land) .... 324.0 sq mi
Area (Water)............................... 47.9 sq mi
Elevation....................................... 42 ft
Latitude ....32-71-92 N
Longitude.............................. 117-16-21 W
Time Zone ....PST
Area Code....................................... 619

Climate

San Diego has a mild climate that is influenced by the city's proximity to the Pacific Ocean. Winters are mild with abundant sunshine. Winter high temperatures average in the mid-60s and low temperatures average near 50 degrees. The seabreeze moderates San Diego's summer temperatures—daytime highs average in the mid-70s, and evenings cool down into the mid-60s. January and March are the wettest months in San Diego, each averaging just under two inches of rain; July is the driest, with no significant precipitation at all on average.

Average Temperatures & Precipitation

Temperatures

	Jan	Feb	Mar	Apr	May	Jun	Jul	Aug	Sep	Oct	Nov	Dec
High	66	67	66	68	69	72	76	78	77	75	70	66
Low	49	51	53	56	60	62	66	67	66	61	54	49

Precipitation

	Jan	Feb	Mar	Apr	May	Jun	Jul	Aug	Sep	Oct	Nov	Dec
Inches	1.8	1.5	1.8	0.8	0.2	0.1	0.0	0.1	0.2	0.4	1.5	1.6

History

San Diego's harbor was first visited in 1542 by Portuguese explorer Juan Rodriguez Cabrillo. Six decades later, Spanish navigator Sabasitan Vizcaino explored the area, naming the bay San Diego, presumably in honor of San Diego de Alcala (Saint Didacus). Settlement in the San Diego area did not begin until 1769, when Spanish missionaries led by Father Junipero Serra established the first presidio and the first mission (Mission San Diego de Alcala) in California. The settlement developed slowly, shifting from Spanish to Mexican rule. In 1846, the United States gained control of the area from Mexico.

The arrival of the Santa Fe Railroad in the mid-1880s stimulated growth in San Diego, providing a link to the rest of the nation. The city's location in a rich agricultural region, coupled with its excellent harbor and rail access, helped it to grow into a major industrial and commercial center. The establishment of U.S. military installations during the 20th Century (including Naval Air Station North Island, Naval Station San Diego, Naval Submarine Base San Diego, Marine Corps base Camp Joseph H. Pendleton, Marine Corps Recruit Depot, and Marine Corp Air Station) further accelerated San Diego's growth. The area now has one of the largest military complexes in the entire world—which will expand even further with the relocation of the U.S. Space and Warfare Systems Command (SPAWAR) from Virginia to San Diego in 1997.

Today San Diego is an important commercial, manufacturing, and agricultural trade center as well as a major regional transportation center for the southwestern United States and northwestern Mexico. With a population of more than 1.2 million, San Diego is the second largest city in the state.

Population

1990 Census 1,110,623
1998 Estimate............................ 1,220,666
% Change 9.9
2005 Projection 3,223,500*

Racial/Ethnic Breakdown

White................................... 67.1%
Black 9.4%
Other................................... 23.5%
Hispanic Origin (may be of any race) 20.7%

Age Breakdown

Under 5 years............................. 7.3%
5 to 17.................................. 15.8%
18 to 20.................................. 6.1%
21 to 24.................................. 8.6%
25 to 34................................. 21.1%
35 to 44................................. 15.3%
45 to 54.................................. 8.7%
55 to 64.................................. 6.9%
65 to 74.................................. 6.1%
75+ years 4.1%
Median Age................................30.5

Gender Breakdown

Male..................................... 51.0%
Female................................... 49.0%

* *Information given is for San Diego County.*

Government

Type of Government: Mayor-Council

San Diego City Attorney
1200 3rd Ave Suite 1100
San Diego, CA 92101
Phone: 619-533-5800
Fax: 619-533-5856

San Diego City Clerk
202 C St
San Diego, CA 92101
Phone: 619-533-4000
Fax: 619-533-4045

San Diego City Council
202 C St 10th Fl
San Diego, CA 92101
Phone: 619-236-6440
Fax: 619-236-6529

San Diego City Hall
202 C St
San Diego, CA 92101
Phone: 619-236-5555

San Diego City Manager
202 C St 9th Fl
San Diego, CA 92101
Phone: 619-236-6363
Fax: 619-236-6067

San Diego Fire & Life Safety Services Dept
1010 2nd Ave 4th Fl
San Diego, CA 92101
Phone: 619-533-4300
Fax: 619-544-9351

San Diego Mayor
202 C St 11th Fl
San Diego, CA 92101
Phone: 619-236-6330
Fax: 619-236-7228

San Diego Parks & Recreation Dept
202 C St
San Diego, CA 92101
Phone: 619-236-6643
Fax: 619-236-6219

San Diego Personnel Dept
1200 3rd Ave Suite 300
San Diego, CA 92101
Phone: 619-236-6400
Fax: 619-236-6615

San Diego Planning & Development Review Dept
1222 1st Ave
San Diego, CA 92101
Phone: 619-236-6250
Fax: 619-236-7092

San Diego Police Dept
1401 Broadway
San Diego, CA 92101
Phone: 619-531-2000
Fax: 619-531-2530

San Diego Public Library
820 'E' St
San Diego, CA 92101
Phone: 619-236-5800
Fax: 619-236-5878

San Diego Transportation Dept
202 C St
San Diego, CA 92101
Phone: 619-236-6110
Fax: 619-525-8273

San Diego Treasurer
1222 1st Ave 2nd Fl
San Diego, CA 92101
Phone: 619-236-6196
Fax: 619-236-7134

San Diego Water Dept
202 C St 9th Fl
San Diego, CA 92101
Phone: 619-236-6750

Important Phone Numbers

AAA 619-233-1000
American Express Travel 619-297-8101
California State Franchise Tax Board 916-845-4300
Driver's License/Vehicle Registration Information 858-565-6691
Emergency 911
HotelDocs 800-468-3537
Medical Referral 800-827-4277
Poison Control Center 800-876-4766
San Diego Assn of Realtors 858-715-8000
San Diego County Tax Collector 619-236-3121
San Diego Treasurer 619-533-3171
Time 760-853-1212
Travelers Aid 619-231-7361
TravelMed 800-878-3627
Voter Registration Information 858-694-3400
Weather 858-289-1212

Information Sources

Better Business Bureau Serving San Diego & Imperial Counties
5050 Murphy Canyon Rd Suite 110
San Diego, CA 92123
www.sandiego.bbb.org
Phone: 858-496-2131
Fax: 858-496-2141

Chula Vista Chamber of Commerce
233 4th Ave
Chula Vista, CA 91910
www.chulavistachamber.org
Phone: 619-420-6602
Fax: 619-420-1269

Chula Vista City Hall
276 4th Ave
Chula Vista, CA 91910
www.ci.chula-vista.ca.us
Phone: 619-691-5044
Fax: 619-476-5939

Chula Vista Community Development Dept
276 4th Ave
Chula Vista, CA 91910
www.ci.chula-vista.ca.us/comdev.htm
Phone: 619-691-5047
Fax: 619-476-5310

Chula Vista Mayor
276 4th Ave
Chula Vista, CA 91910
www.ci.chula-vista.ca.us/govmain.htm#mayor
Phone: 619-691-5044
Fax: 619-476-5379

Chula Vista Public Library
365 F St
Chula Vista, CA 91910
www.infopeople.org/chulavista/library
Phone: 619-691-5069
Fax: 619-427-4246

San Diego Convention & Visitors Bureau
401 B St Suite 1400
San Diego, CA 92101
www.sandiego.org
Phone: 619-232-3101
Fax: 619-696-9371

San Diego Convention Center
111 W Harbor Dr
San Diego, CA 92101
www.sdccc.org
Phone: 619-525-5000
Fax: 619-525-5005

San Diego County
1600 Pacific Hwy
San Diego, CA 92101
www.co.san-diego.ca.us
Phone: 619-531-5507
Fax: 619-557-4056

San Diego Regional Chamber of Commerce
402 W Broadway Suite 1000
San Diego, CA 92101
sdchamber.org
Phone: 619-232-0124
Fax: 619-234-0571

Online Resources

4SanDiego.com
www.4sandiego.com

About San Diego
www.thewebstation.com/OgardTravel/SanDiego/

About.com Guide to San Diego
sandiego.about.com/local/caus/sandiego/

Accessible San Diego
www.accessandiego.com

All San Diego Travel Guide
www.sandiego.cc/sandiego/

Anthill City Guide San Diego
www.anthill.com/city.asp?city=sandiego

Area Guide San Diego
sandiego.areaguides.net

Boulevards San Diego
www.boulevards.com/cities/sandiego.html

Chula Vista California
chula-vista.com

ChulaVista.com
www.chulavista.com

City Knowledge San Diego
www.cityknowledge.com/ca_sandiego.htm

CitySearch San Diego
sandiego.citysearch.com

CuisineNet San Diego
www.menusonline.com/cities/san_diego/locmain.shtml

DesertUSA Guide to San Diego
www.desertusa.com/Cities/ca/sandiego.html

DigitalCity San Diego
home.digitalcity.com/sandiego

Discovering San Diego
www.discoversd.com/

Excite.com Chula Vista City Guide
www.excite.com/travel/countries/united_states/california/chula_vista

Excite.com San Diego City Guide
www.excite.com/travel/countries/united_states/california/san_diego

Gaslamp411.com
www.gaslamp411.com

Go San Diego
www.gosandiego.com

Go There San Diego
www.gothere.com

HomePort San Diego
www.homeport-sd.com/

Hometown Free-Press San Diego
emporium.turnpike.net/~walk/hometown/sandiego.htm

HotelGuide San Diego
hotelguide.net/san_diego

Insiders' Guide to San Diego
www.insiders.com/sandiego/

Lodging.com San Diego California
www.lodging.com/auto/guides/san_diego-area-ca.html

Niteoutsandiego.com
www.niteoutsandiego.com

Rough Guide Travel San Diego
travel.roughguides.com/content/1290/

San Diego 411
www.sandiego411.com

San Diego Black Pages
www.webcom.com/cjcook/SDBP/

San Diego California
san-diego-california.com

San Diego Golf Guide
san-diego-golf.com

San Diego Guide
www.sandiegan.com/

San Diego Historic Tours of America
www.historictours.com/sandiego/index.htm

San Diego Insider.com
www.sandiegoinsider.com

San Diego Online
www.sandiego-online.com/

San Diego Source
www.sddt.com/

San Diego Waterfront
www.sdwaterfront.com/

Sandiego.com
www.sandiego.com/

SanDiego.TheLinks.com
sandiego.thelinks.com/

Search San Diego
searchsd.com/index.html

ShowMEsandiego.com
www.showmesandiego.com/showmesd/index.shtml

Sights of San Diego
www.sightsofsandiego.com

Surf & Sun Beach Vacation Guide to San Diego
www.surf-sun.com/ca-san-diego-main.htm

Tour San Diego
www.toursandiego.com

Virtual Voyages San Diego
www.virtualvoyages.com/usa/ca/s_d/sd.sht

Web San Diego
www.websandiego.com/

Zoom-San Diego Arts & Entertainment
w3.thegroup.net/~zoom/

Area Communities

Incorporated communities in San Diego County with populations greater than 10,000 include:

Carlsbad
1200 Carlsbad Village Dr
Carlsbad, CA 92008
Phone: 760-434-2820
Fax: 760-720-9461

Chula Vista
276 4th Ave
Chula Vista, CA 91910
Phone: 619-691-5044
Fax: 619-476-5939

Coronado
1825 Strand Way
Coronado, CA 92118
Phone: 619-522-7300
Fax: 619-437-0371

El Cajon
200 E Main St
El Cajon, CA 92020
Phone: 619-441-1776
Fax: 619-441-1537

Encinitas
505 S Vulcan Ave
Encinitas, CA 92024
Phone: 760-633-2601
Fax: 760-633-2627

Escondido
201 N Broadway
Escondido, CA 92025
Phone: 760-741-4631
Fax: 760-432-4578

Imperial Beach
825 Imperial Beach Blvd
Imperial Beach, CA 91932
Phone: 619-423-8300
Fax: 619-429-9770

Lemon Grove
3232 Main St
Lemon Grove, CA 91945
Phone: 619-464-6934
Fax: 619-460-3716

National City
1243 National City Blvd
National City, CA 91950
Phone: 619-336-4200
Fax: 619-336-4376

Oceanside
300 N Coast Hwy
Oceanside, CA 92054
Phone: 760-966-4410
Fax: 760-966-8724

Poway
PO Box 789
Poway, CA 92074
Phone: 858-748-6600
Fax: 858-748-1455

San Marcos
1 Civic Center Dr
San Marcos, CA 92069
Phone: 760-744-1050
Fax: 760-744-7543

Santee
10601 Magnolia Ave
Santee, CA 92071
Phone: 619-258-4100
Fax: 619-562-1046

Solana Beach
635 S California Hwy 101
Solana Beach, CA 92075
Phone: 858-755-2998
Fax: 858-792-6513

Vista
600 Eucalyptus Ave
Vista, CA 92084
Phone: 760-726-1340
Fax: 760-639-6126

Economy

San Diego has a diverse economic base that ranges from nursery and flower crop production to national defense. From the Military to education, government plays a vital role in San Diego County's economy—more than half of the county's ten largest employers (including the State of California and the U.S. Government) are government-related. Services is the largest employment sector in San Diego County, with business services and health care being major industries. San Diego is considered one of the most desirable vacation destinations in the country and the tourism industry contributes more than three billion dollars to the region's economy annually. The manufacturing sector is another major contributor to San Diego's economy, with electronic equipment and industrial machinery the area's primary products. Located on one of the busiest international borders in the world, San Diego County's economy is also fueled by international trade.

Unemployment Rate 3.5%
Per Capita Income $26,500*
Median Family Income $45,000*

** Information given is for San Diego County.*

Principal Industries & Number of Wage Earners

San Diego County - February 2000

Industry	Wage Earners
Agriculture & Mining	11,000
Construction	67,700
Finance, Insurance, & Real Estate	68,400
Government	205,700
Manufacturing	129,800
Retail Trade	206,200
Services	382,200
Transportation, Communications, & Utilities	52,700
Wholesale Trade	50,900

Major Employers

Grossmont Union High School District
1100 Murray Dr
El Cajon, CA 92020
Phone: 619-644-8000
Fax: 619-465-1349

Kaiser Permanente Medical Care Program
4647 Zion Ave
San Diego, CA 92120
Phone: 619-528-5000

National Steel & Shipbuilding Co
PO Box 85278
San Diego, CA 92186
www.nassco.com
Phone: 619-544-3400
Fax: 619-544-3541

Pacific Bell
140 New Montgomery St
San Francisco, CA 94105
www.pacbell.com
Phone: 415-542-9000
Fax: 415-543-7079
TF: 800-303-3000

Qualcomm Inc
5775 Morehouse Dr
San Diego, CA 92121
www.qualcomm.com
Phone: 858-587-1121
Fax: 858-658-2100
TF: 800-349-4188

San Diego City Hall Phone: 619-236-5555
202 C St
San Diego, CA 92101
www.sannet.gov

San Diego Community College District Phone: 619-584-6500
3375 Camino del Rio S Fax: 619-584-6913
San Diego, CA 92108
www.sdccd.cc.ca.us

San Diego County Phone: 619-531-5507
1600 Pacific Hwy Fax: 619-557-4056
San Diego, CA 92101
www.co.san-diego.ca.us

San Diego Gas & Electric Co Phone: 619-696-2000
101 Ash St Fax: 858-654-1755
San Diego, CA 92101 TF: 800-411-7343
www.sdge.com

San Diego Police Dept Phone: 619-531-2000
1401 Broadway Fax: 619-531-2530
San Diego, CA 92101
www.sannet.gov/police

San Diego State University Phone: 619-594-5000
5500 Campanile Dr Fax: 619-594-4902
San Diego, CA 92182
www.sdsu.edu

San Diego Transit Corp Phone: 619-238-0100
100 16th St Fax: 619-696-8159
San Diego, CA 92101
www.sandag.cog.ca.us/sdmts/sdt.htm

San Diego Unified School District Phone: 619-725-8000
4100 Normal St Fax: 619-725-8001
San Diego, CA 92103
E-mail: communications@mail.sandi.net
www.sandi.net

Science Applications International Corp Phone: 858-546-6000
10260 Campus Point Dr Fax: 858-535-7589
San Diego, CA 92121
www.saic.com

Scripps Institutions of Medicine & Science Phone: 858-678-7000
4275 Campus Pointe Ct Fax: 619-687-6558
San Diego, CA 92121

Sempra Energy Corp Phone: 619-696-2000
101 Ash St Fax: 619-696-9202
San Diego, CA 92101
www.sempra.com

University of California San Diego Phone: 858-534-2230
9500 Gilman Dr Fax: 858-534-8206
La Jolla, CA 92093
E-mail: admissionsinfo@ucsd.edu
www.ucsd.edu

US Government Phone: 619-557-6165
880 Front St Suite 4218
San Diego, CA 92188

US Postal Service San Diego Div Phone: 858-674-0430
11251 Rancho Carmel Dr Fax: 858-674-0039
San Diego, CA 92199
new.usps.com

Quality of Living Indicators

Total Crime Index....................54,421
(rates per 100,000 inhabitants)

Violent Crime
Murder/manslaughter.......... 42
Forcible rape.......... 371
Robbery..........2,121
Aggravated assault..........6,210

Property Crime
Burglary..........7,349
Larceny theft..........28,388
Motor vehicle theft..........9,940

Cost of Living Index..........126.6
(national average = 100)

Median Home Price..........$231,600

Education

Public Schools

San Diego Unified School District Phone: 619-725-8000
4100 Normal St Fax: 619-725-8001
San Diego, CA 92103
E-mail: communications@mail.sandi.net
www.sandi.net

Number of Schools
Elementary.......... 116
Middle.......... 23
High.......... 16

Student/Teacher Ratio
All Grades.......... 23.1:1

Private Schools

Number of Schools (all grades).......... 100+

Colleges & Universities

California Pacific University Phone: 858-695-3292
9683 Tierra Grande St Rm 100 TF: 800-458-9667
San Diego, CA 92126
www.cpu.edu/

Cuyamaca College Phone: 619-670-1980
900 Rancho San Diego Pkwy Fax: 619-660-4399
El Cajon, CA 92019
michele.gcccd.cc.ca.us/cuyamaca

Design Institute of San Diego Phone: 858-566-1200
8555 Commerce Ave Fax: 858-566-2711
San Diego, CA 92121
E-mail: disdadm@msn.com
www.disd.edu

Grossmont-Cuyamaca Community College District Phone: 619-644-7690
8800 Grossmont College Dr Fax: 619-644-7933
El Cajon, CA 92020
www.gcccd.cc.ca.us/

ITT Technical Institute
9680 Granite Ridge Dr
San Diego, CA 92123
www.itt-tech.edu
Phone: 858-571-8500
Fax: 858-571-1277

Kelsey-Jenney College
201 'A' St
San Diego, CA 92101
E-mail: info@kelsey-jenney.com
www.kelsey-jenney.com
Phone: 619-233-7418
Fax: 619-615-1664

MiraCosta College
1 Barnard Dr
Oceanside, CA 92056
E-mail: bhall@mcc.miracosta.cc.ca.us
www.miracosta.cc.ca.us
Phone: 760-757-2121
Fax: 760-795-6626
TF: 888-201-8480

National University
11255 N Torrey Pines Rd
La Jolla, CA 92037
E-mail: mss@nunic.nu.edu
www.nu.edu
Phone: 858-642-8000
Fax: 858-642-8709
TF: 800-628-8648

National University
660 Bay Blvd
Chula Vista, CA 91910
www.nu.edu
Phone: 619-563-7415
Fax: 619-563-7414

Palomar College
1140 W Mission Rd
San Marcos, CA 92069
www.palomar.edu
Phone: 760-744-1150
Fax: 760-744-2932

Point Loma Nazarene University
3900 Lomaland Dr
San Diego, CA 92106
www.ptloma.edu
Phone: 619-849-2200
Fax: 619-849-2601

San Diego City College
1313 12th Ave
San Diego, CA 92101
www.city.sdccd.cc.ca.us/
Phone: 619-230-2400
Fax: 619-230-2135

San Diego Mesa College
7250 Mesa College Dr
San Diego, CA 92111
intergate.sdmesa.sdccd.cc.ca.us
Phone: 858-627-2600
Fax: 858-627-2960

San Diego Miramar College
10440 Black Mountain Rd
San Diego, CA 92126
intergate.miramar.sdccd.cc.ca.us
Phone: 858-536-7844
Fax: 858-693-1899

San Diego State University
5500 Campanile Dr
San Diego, CA 92182
www.sdsu.edu
Phone: 619-594-5000
Fax: 619-594-4902

Southern California Bible College
2075 E Madison Ave
El Cajon, CA 92019
www.scbcs.edu
Phone: 619-442-9841
Fax: 619-442-4510
TF: 800-554-7222

Southwestern College
900 Otay Lakes Rd
Chula Vista, CA 91910
swc.cc.ca.us
Phone: 619-421-6700
Fax: 619-482-6489

United States International University
10455 Pomerado Rd
San Diego, CA 92131
www.usiu.edu
Phone: 858-271-4300
Fax: 858-635-4739

University of California San Diego
9500 Gilman Dr
La Jolla, CA 92093
E-mail: admissionsinfo@ucsd.edu
www.ucsd.edu
Phone: 858-534-2230
Fax: 858-534-8206

University of San Diego
5998 Alcala Pk
San Diego, CA 92110
www.acusd.edu
Phone: 619-260-4600
Fax: 619-260-6836

Hospitals

Alvarado Hospital Medical Center
6655 Alvarado Rd
San Diego, CA 92120
www.tenethealth.com/Alvarado
Phone: 619-287-3270
Fax: 619-229-7020

Children's Hospital & Health Center
3020 Children's Way
San Diego, CA 92123
www.chsd.org
Phone: 858-576-1700
Fax: 858-495-4934

Green Hospital of Scripps Clinic
10666 N Torrey Pines Rd
La Jolla, CA 92037
www.scrippshealth.org/hospitals/green.html
Phone: 858-455-9100
Fax: 858-554-8986

Grossmont Hospital
PO Box 158
La Mesa, CA 91944
Phone: 619-465-0711
Fax: 619-461-7191

Kaiser Permanente Medical Center
4647 Zion Ave
San Diego, CA 92120
Phone: 619-528-5000
Fax: 619-528-5317

Mission Bay Memorial Hospital
3030 Bunker Hill St
San Diego, CA 92109
www.columbia.net/faciliti/ca/mission.html
Phone: 858-274-7721
Fax: 858-483-0655

Naval Medical Center
34800 Bob Wilson Dr
San Diego, CA 92134
159.71.170.20/index.html
Phone: 619-532-6400
Fax: 619-532-7755

Palomar Medical Center
555 E Valley Pkwy
Escondido, CA 92025
www.pphs.org/Palomar.htm
Phone: 760-739-3000
Fax: 760-739-3772

Paradise Valley Hospital
2400 E 4th St
National City, CA 91950
www.paradisevalleyhospital.org
Phone: 619-470-4321
Fax: 619-470-4209

Pomerado Hospital
15615 Pomerado Rd
Poway, CA 92064
www.pphs.org/hospitals/pomerado.htm
Phone: 858-485-6511
Fax: 858-613-4764

Scripps Memorial Hospital-Chula Vista
435 H St
Chula Vista, CA 91910
www.scrippshealth.org/hospitals/chula.html
Phone: 619-691-7000
Fax: 619-691-7522

Scripps Memorial Hospital-Encinitas
PO Box 230817
Encinitas, CA 92023
www.scrippshealth.org/hospitals/encinitas.html
Phone: 760-753-6501
Fax: 760-633-6594

Scripps Memorial Hospital-La Jolla
9888 Genesee Ave
La Jolla, CA 92037
www.scrippshealth.org/hospitals/lajolla.html
Phone: 858-457-4123
Fax: 858-626-6122

Scripps Mercy Hospital
4077 5th Ave
San Diego, CA 92103
www.scrippshealth.org/hospitals/mercy.html
Phone: 619-294-8111
Fax: 619-260-7397

Sharp Cabrillo Hospital
3475 Kenyon St
San Diego, CA 92110
Phone: 619-221-3400
Fax: 619-221-3704

Sharp Chula Vista Medical Center
751 Medical Center Ct
Chula Vista, CA 91911
Phone: 619-482-5800
Fax: 619-482-3604

Sharp Coronado Hospital & HealthCare Center
250 Prospect Pl
Coronado, CA 92118
Phone: 619-435-6251
Fax: 619-522-3782

Sharp Memorial Hospital
7901 Frost St
San Diego, CA 92123
Phone: 858-541-3400
Fax: 858-541-3714

Tri-City Medical Center
4002 Vista Way
Oceanside, CA 92056
www.tricitymed.org
Phone: 760-724-8411
Fax: 760-724-1010

University of California San Diego Medical Center
200 W Arbor Dr
San Diego, CA 92103
health.ucsd.edu
Phone: 619-543-6222
Fax: 619-543-7277

Veterans Affairs Medical Center
3350 La Jolla Village Dr
San Diego, CA 92161
Phone: 858-552-8585
Fax: 858-552-7509

Transportation

Airport(s)

San Diego International Airport - Lindbergh Field (SAN)
3 miles NW of downtown (approx 10 minutes) 619-231-2100

Mass Transit

San Diego Transit
$2 Base fare 619-233-3004
San Diego Trolley
$.75 Base fare 619-595-4949
San Diego-Coronado Ferry
$2 Base fare 619-234-4111

Rail/Bus

Greyhound Bus Station
120 W Broadway
San Diego, CA 92101
Phone: 619-239-8082
TF: 800-231-2222

San Diego Amtrak Station
1050 Kettner Blvd
San Diego, CA 92101
Phone: 619-239-9021
TF: 800-872-7245

Utilities

Electricity
San Diego Gas & Electric Co 619-696-2000
www.sdge.com

Gas
San Diego Gas & Electric Co 619-696-2000
www.sdge.com

Water
San Diego City Water Utilities 619-533-5290

Garbage Collection/Recycling
San Diego County Recycling Hotline 858-467-0103
San Diego Environmental Services Refuse Collection Dept 858-492-5060

Telecommunications

Telephone
Pacific Bell 714-339-5888
www.pacbell.com
Qwest 800-244-1111
www.qwest.com

Cable Television
Cox Communications 619-262-1122
www.cox.com
Daniels Cablevision 760-931-7000
Time Warner Cable 858-695-3220
www.timewarnersandiego.com

Internet Service Providers (ISPs)
American Digital Network Inc 858-576-4272
www.adnc.com
Ashton Communications Corp 956-984-4000
www.acnet.net
AT & T CERFnet 858-455-3900
www.cerf.net
CONNECTnet 858-450-0254
www.connectnet.com
CTS Network Services 858-637-3637
www.cts.com
Electriciti 619-540-8060
www.electriciti.com
MillenniaNet 858-279-6638
www.millennianet.com
Sandiego.com 619-220-8601
www.thegroup.net
Simply Internet 858-565-7873
www.simplyweb.net
Verio San Diego 858-535-5200
home.verio.net/local/frontpage.cfm?AirportCode=SAN
WANet Internet Services Div Software Design Assoc Inc 858-679-5900
www.wanet.net
zNET Internet Services 858-713-0700
www.znet.com

Banks

Bank of America NA
8949 Clairemont Mesa Blvd
San Diego, CA 92123
Phone: 858-452-8400

California Bank & Trust Phone: 858-677-2990
4320 La Jolla Village Dr Suite 100 Fax: 858-622-4829
San Diego, CA 92122

First National Bank Phone: 619-233-5588
401 W 'A' St Fax: 619-235-1268
San Diego, CA 92101

General Bank Phone: 858-277-2030
4688 Convoy St Fax: 858-277-3339
San Diego, CA 92111

Neighborhood National Bank Phone: 619-544-1642
303 A St Suite 409 Fax: 619-544-1644
San Diego, CA 92101

Peninsula Bank of San Diego Phone: 619-226-5431
1331 Rosecrans St Fax: 619-226-5481
San Diego, CA 92106
E-mail: info@mysandiegobank.com
www.mysandiegobank.com

San Diego National Bank Phone: 619-231-4989
1420 Kettner Blvd Fax: 619-233-7017
San Diego, CA 92101 TF: 888-724-7362
E-mail: kgregg@sdnb.com
www.sdnb.com

Union Bank of California NA Phone: 619-230-4666
1201 5th Ave
San Diego, CA 92101

Washington Mutual Bank Phone: 619-584-1840
4201 El Cajon Blvd Fax: 619-280-6685
San Diego, CA 92105

Wells Fargo Bank NA Phone: 619-702-6949
401 B St Fax: 619-702-6955
San Diego, CA 92101 TF: 800-869-3557

Shopping

Adams Avenue Phone: 619-282-7329
Adams Ave-betw Kensington & Normal Heights
San Diego, CA 92116
www.gothere.com/AdamsAve/

Bazaar del Mundo Inc Phone: 619-296-3161
2754 Calhoun St Fax: 619-296-3113
San Diego, CA 92110
E-mail: customerservice@bazaardelmundo.com
www.bazaardelmundo.com

Chula Vista Center Phone: 619-422-7500
555 Broadway Fax: 619-476-0455
Chula Vista, CA 91910

College Grove Marketplace Phone: 619-660-1000
Hwy 94 & College Ave Fax: 619-660-0706
San Diego, CA 92115

Fashion Valley Mall Phone: 619-688-9113
7007 Friars Rd Fax: 619-294-8291
San Diego, CA 92108

Ferry Landing Marketplace Phone: 619-435-8895
1201 1st St Suite K-6
Coronado, CA 92118

Grossmont Center Phone: 619-465-2900
5500 Grossmont Center Dr
La Mesa, CA 91942

Hazard Center Phone: 619-497-2674
7676 Hazard Center Dr Suite 500 Fax: 619-543-9785
San Diego, CA 92108

Horton Plaza Phone: 619-238-1596
324 Horton Plaza Fax: 619-239-4021
San Diego, CA 92101
E-mail: mstephens@westfieldamerica.com
www.hortonplaza.com

Macy's Phone: 619-299-9811
275 Fashion Valley Rd
San Diego, CA 92108

Mission Valley Center Phone: 619-296-6375
1640 Camino del Rio N Suite 1290 Fax: 619-692-0555
San Diego, CA 92108

Neiman Marcus Phone: 619-692-9100
7027 Friars Rd Fax: 619-298-8457
San Diego, CA 92108 TF: 888-888-4757
www.neimanmarcus.com

Old Town Esplanade Phone: 619-291-5700
2461 San Diego Ave Fax: 619-291-0715
San Diego, CA 92110

Plaza Bonita Phone: 619-267-2850
3030 Plaza Bonita Rd Fax: 619-472-5652
National City, CA 91950
www.plazabonita.shoppingtown.com

Robinsons-May Phone: 619-297-2511
1702 Camino del Rio N
San Diego, CA 92108

San Diego Factory Outlet Center Phone: 619-690-2999
4498 Camino De La Plaza
San Ysidro, CA 92173

Seaport Village Phone: 619-235-6569
849 W Harbor Dr Suite D Fax: 619-696-0025
San Diego, CA 92101
www.spvillage.com

Terra Nova Center Phone: 619-425-7990
374 E 'H' St Suite 1708
Chula Vista, CA 91910

University Towne Centre Phone: 858-546-8858
4545 La Jolla Village Dr Fax: 858-552-9065
San Diego, CA 92122
www.shoputc.com

Media

Newspapers and Magazines

Carlsbad Sun Phone: 760-510-2720
334 Via Vera Cruz Suite 200 Fax: 760-510-2724
San Marcos, CA 92069

San Diego Business Journal
4909 Murphy Canyon Rd Suite 200
San Diego, CA 92123
E-mail: sdbj@sdbj.com
www.sdbj.com
Phone: 858-277-6359
Fax: 858-277-2149

San Diego Daily Transcript*
PO Box 85469
San Diego, CA 92186
E-mail: editor@sddt.com
www.sddt.com
Phone: 619-232-4381
Fax: 619-236-8126
TF: 800-697-6397

San Diego Magazine
PO Box 85409
San Diego, CA 92186
www.sandiego-online.com
Phone: 619-230-9292
Fax: 619-230-0490

San Diego Reader
1703 India St
San Diego, CA 92101
E-mail: hrosen@sdreader.com
www.sdreader.com
Phone: 619-235-3000
Fax: 619-231-0489

San Diego Union-Tribune*
PO Box 120191
San Diego, CA 92112
E-mail: letters@uniontrib.com
www.uniontrib.com
Phone: 619-299-3131
Fax: 619-293-1896
TF: 800-244-6397

San Diego Weekly News
7670 Opportunity Rd Suite 100
San Diego, CA 92111
Phone: 858-565-9135
Fax: 858-565-4182

Star-News
279 3rd Ave
Chula Vista, CA 91910
Phone: 619-427-3000
Fax: 619-426-6346

**Indicates major daily newspapers*

Television

KFMB-TV Ch 8 (CBS)
7677 Engineer Rd
San Diego, CA 92111
E-mail: news8@kfmb.com
www.kfmb.com
Phone: 858-571-8888
Fax: 858-560-0627

KGTV-TV Ch 10 (ABC)
PO Box 85347
San Diego, CA 92186
www.sandiegoinsider.com/partners/kgtv
Phone: 619-237-1010
Fax: 619-527-0369

KNSD-TV Ch 7/39 (NBC)
8330 Engineer Rd
San Diego, CA 92111
E-mail: hinczsd@tvsknsd.nbc.com
www.nbc739.com
Phone: 858-279-3939
Fax: 858-279-1076

KPBS-TV Ch 15 (PBS)
5200 Campanile Dr
San Diego, CA 92182
E-mail: letters@kpbs.org
www.kpbs.org
Phone: 619-594-1515
Fax: 619-265-6417

KSWB-TV Ch 69 (WB)
7191 Engineer Rd
San Diego, CA 92111
www.kswbtv.com
Phone: 858-492-9269
Fax: 858-573-6600

KUSI-TV Ch 51 (Ind)
PO Box 719051
San Diego, CA 92171
Phone: 858-571-5151
Fax: 858-571-4852

XETV-TV Ch 6 (Fox)
8253 Ronson Rd
San Diego, CA 92111
www.fox6.com
Phone: 858-279-6666
Fax: 858-268-9388

Radio

KBZT-FM 94.9 MHz (Oldies)
1615 Murray Canyon Rd Suite 710
San Diego, CA 92108
E-mail: oldies949info@oldies949.com
www.oldies949.com
Phone: 858-452-9595
Fax: 619-543-1353

KFMB-AM 760 kHz (N/T)
PO Box 85888
San Diego, CA 92186
www.760kfmb.com
Phone: 858-292-7600
Fax: 858-279-7676

KFMB-FM 100.7 MHz (AC)
PO Box 85888
San Diego, CA 92186
www.histar.com
Phone: 858-292-7600
Fax: 858-279-3380

KFSD-FM 92.1 MHz (Clas)
550 Laguna Dr
Carlsbad, CA 92008
Phone: 760-729-5946
Fax: 760-434-2367
TF: 888-592-5277

KGB-FM 101.5 MHz (CR)
5745 Kearny Villa Rd Suite M
San Diego, CA 92123
www.101kgb.com
Phone: 858-565-6006
Fax: 858-277-1015
TF: 800-570-1015

KHTS-FM 93.3 MHz (CHR)
4891 Pacific Hwy
San Diego, CA 92110
www.channel933.com
Phone: 619-291-9191
Fax: 619-291-3299

KIFM-FM 98.1 MHz (NAC)
1615 Murray Canyon Rd Suite 710
San Diego, CA 92108
E-mail: connect@kifm.com
www.kifm.com
Phone: 619-297-3698
Fax: 858-587-4628

KIOZ-FM 105.3 MHz (Rock)
5745 Kearny Villa Rd Suite M
San Diego, CA 92123
www.kioz.com
Phone: 858-565-6006
Fax: 858-560-0742

KJQY-FM 94.1 MHz (Oldies)
5745 Kearny Villa Rd Suite M
San Diego, CA 92123
www.softoldies.com
Phone: 858-565-6006
Fax: 858-279-9553

KLNV-FM 106.5 MHz (Span)
600 W Broadway Suite 2150
San Diego, CA 92101
www.lanueva1065.com
Phone: 619-235-0600
Fax: 619-744-4300

KLQV-FM 102.9 MHz (Span)
600 W Broadway Suite 2150
San Diego, CA 92101
www.klove1029.com
Phone: 619-235-0600
Fax: 619-744-4300

KMSX-FM 95.7 MHz (AC)
5745 Kearny Villa Rd Suite M
San Diego, CA 92101
www.mix957.com
Phone: 858-565-6006
Fax: 858-279-9553

KOGO-AM 600 kHz (N/T)
5050 Murphy Canyon Rd
San Diego, CA 92123
www.kogo.com
Phone: 858-278-1130
Fax: 619-285-4364

KPBS-FM 89.5 MHz (NPR)
5200 Campanile Dr San Diego State University
San Diego, CA 92182
E-mail: letters@kpbs.org
www.kpbs.org
Phone: 619-594-8100
Fax: 619-265-6478

KPLN-FM 103.7 MHz (CR)
8033 Linda Vista Rd
San Diego, CA 92111
www.planetfm.com
Phone: 858-560-1037
Fax: 858-571-0326

KPOP-AM 1360 kHz (Nost)
5050 Murphy Canyon Rd
San Diego, CA 92123
Phone: 858-278-1130
Fax: 619-285-4372

KSDO-AM 1130 kHz (N/T)
5050 Murphy Canyon Rd
San Diego, CA 92123
www.ksdoradio.com
Phone: 858-278-1130
Fax: 858-715-3303

KSON-AM 1240 kHz (Misc)
1615 Murray Canyon Rd Suite 710
San Diego, CA 92108
Phone: 619-291-9797
Fax: 619-543-1353

KSON-FM 97.3 MHz (Ctry)
1615 Murray Canyon Rd Suite 710
San Diego, CA 92108
www.kson.com
Phone: 619-291-9797
Fax: 619-543-1353

KSPA-AM 1450 kHz (Nost)
550 Laguna Dr
Carlsbad, CA 92008
Phone: 760-729-5946
Fax: 760-434-2367

KXST-FM 102.1 MHz (AAA)
5015 Shoreham Pl Suite 102
San Diego, CA 92122
www.sets102.com
Phone: 858-578-0102
Fax: 858-320-7024

KYXY-FM 96.5 MHz (AC)
8033 Linda Vista Rd
San Diego, CA 92111
www.kyxy.com
Phone: 858-571-7600
Fax: 858-571-0326

XEMO-AM 860 kHz (Span)
5030 Camino de la Siesta Suite 103
San Diego, CA 92108
Phone: 619-497-0600
Fax: 619-497-1019

XHCR-FM 99.3 MHz (Ctry)
1690 Frontage Rd
Chula Vista, CA 91911
www.hotcountry.com
Phone: 619-575-9090
Fax: 619-423-1818

XHRM-FM 92.5 MHz (Oldies)
2434 Southport Way Suite A
National City, CA 91950
www.magic92five.com
Phone: 619-336-4900
Fax: 619-336-4925

XHTZ-FM 90.3 MHz (CHR)
1960 Frontage Rd
Chula Vista, CA 91911
E-mail: tj@z90.com
www.z90.com
Phone: 619-575-9090
Fax: 619-423-1818

XLTN-FM 104.5 MHz (Span)
1690 Frontage Rd
Chula Vista, CA 91911
Phone: 619-575-9090
Fax: 619-423-1818

XTRA-AM 690 kHz (Sports)
4891 Pacific Hwy
San Diego, CA 92110
www.xtrasports690.com
Phone: 619-291-9191
Fax: 619-291-5622

XTRA-FM 91.1 MHz (Rock)
4891 Pacific Hwy
San Diego, CA 92110
E-mail: loud91x@91x.com
www.91x.com
Phone: 619-291-9191
Fax: 619-291-3299

Attractions

The world-famous San Diego Zoo, a 100-acre tropical garden with 3,900 animal inhabitants, is located in Balboa Park, which is also home to a number of museums and the California Tower. The Tower is a prime example of the park's Spanish-Moorish architecture. Sea World is located at another prominent San Diego park, Mission Bay, which has 27 miles of beaches and facilities for boating, fishing, skiing, swimming, and public recreation. Between the winter months of December and February, the gray whales migrate south along the San Diego Coast on their way to Baja, and the Cabrillo National Monument observatory on the tip of Point Loma is an excellent vantage point from which to view them.

Anza-Borrego Desert State Park
200 Palm Canyon Dr
Borrego Springs, CA 92004
E-mail: feedback@desertusa.com
www.anzaborrego.statepark.org
Phone: 760-767-5311
Fax: 760-767-3427
TF: 800-444-7275

ARCO Olympic Training Center
2800 Olympic Pkwy
Chula Vista, CA 91915
Phone: 619-656-1500
Fax: 619-482-6200

Balboa Park
1549 El Prado
San Diego, CA 92101
Phone: 619-239-0512
Fax: 619-235-3065

Barona Casino
1000 Wildcat Canyon Rd
Lakeside, CA 92040
www.barona.com
Phone: 619-443-2300
Fax: 619-443-2856

Bazaar del Mundo Inc
2754 Calhoun St
San Diego, CA 92110
E-mail: customerservice@bazaardelmundo.com
www.bazaardelmundo.com
Phone: 619-296-3161
Fax: 619-296-3113

Belmont Park
3146 Mission Blvd
San Diego, CA 92109
Phone: 619-491-2988
Fax: 858-488-6658

Bernardo Winery
13330 Paseo del Verano Norte
San Diego, CA 92128
Phone: 858-487-1866
Fax: 858-673-5376

Birch Aquarium at Scripps
2300 Expedition Way
La Jolla, CA 92037
aquarium.ucsd.edu
Phone: 858-534-3474
Fax: 858-534-6692

Bonita Historical Museum
4035 Bonita Rd
Bonita, CA 91902
www.sandiegoinsider.com/community/groups/bonita
Phone: 619-267-5141
Fax: 619-267-5141

Cabrillo National Monument
1800 Cabrillo Memorial Dr
San Diego, CA 92106
www.nps.gov/cabr/
Phone: 619-557-5450
Fax: 619-557-5469

California Ballet Co
8276 Ronson Rd
San Diego, CA 92111
www.californiaballet.org
Phone: 858-560-5676
Fax: 858-560-0072

California Center for the Arts
340 N Escondido Blvd
Escondido, CA 92025
www.artcenter.org
Phone: 760-839-4138
Fax: 760-739-0205
TF: 800-988-4253

Children's Museum of San Diego
200 W Island Ave
San Diego, CA 92101
Phone: 619-233-8792
Fax: 619-233-8796

Chula Vista Heritage Museum
360 3rd Ave
Chula Vista, CA 91910
Phone: 619-476-5373

Chula Vista Nature Center
1000 Gunpowder Point Dr
Chula Vista, CA 91910
Phone: 619-409-5900
Fax: 619-409-5910

Cuyamaca Rancho State Park
12551 Hwy 79
Descanso, CA 92016
www.cuyamaca.statepark.org
Phone: 760-765-0755
Fax: 760-765-3021

Fern Street Circus
2323 Broadway Suite 108
San Diego, CA 92102
Phone: 619-235-9756
Fax: 619-231-7910

Firehouse Museum
1572 Columbia St
San Diego, CA 92101
www.globalinfo.com/noncomm/firehouse/Firehouse.HTML
Phone: 619-232-3473

Flower Fields at Carlsbad Ranch
5600 Avenida Encinas
Carlsbad, CA 92008
E-mail: info@theflowerfields.com
www.theflowerfields.com
Phone: 760-930-9123
Fax: 760-431-9020

Gaslamp Quarter
614 5th Ave Suite E
San Diego, CA 92101
www.gaslamp.com/
Phone: 619-233-5227
Fax: 619-233-4693

Granger Music Hall
1615 E 4th St
National City, CA 91950
Phone: 619-477-3451

Heritage-Americas Museum
2952 Jamacha Rd
El Cajon, CA 92019
Phone: 619-670-5194

Japanese Friendship Garden of San Diego
2215 Pan American Way E
San Diego, CA 92101
www.niwa.org
Phone: 619-232-2721
Fax: 619-232-0917

Junipero Serra Museum
2727 Presidio Dr
San Diego, CA 92103
Phone: 619-297-3258
Fax: 619-297-3281

La Jolla Playhouse
2910 La Jolla Village Dr
La Jolla, CA 92037
E-mail: ljplayhouse@ucsd.edu
www.lajollaplayhouse.com
Phone: 858-550-1010
Fax: 858-550-1075

Los Penasquitos Canyon Preserve
Mercy Rd-W Black Mountain Rd
San Diego, CA 92105
Phone: 858-538-8131

Mingei International Museum of Folk Art
1439 El Prado
Balboa Park, CA 92101
E-mail: mingei@mingei.org
www.mingei.org
Phone: 619-239-0003
Fax: 619-239-0605

Mission Basilica San Diego de Alcala
10818 San Diego Mission Rd
San Diego, CA 92108
Phone: 619-283-7319
Fax: 619-283-7762

Mission Bay Park
8 West to W Mission Bay Dr
San Diego, CA 92109
Phone: 619-221-8901

Mission Trails Regional Park
1 Father Junipero Serra Trail
San Diego, CA 92119
Phone: 619-685-1350

Museum of Contemporary Art
1001 Kettner Blvd
San Diego, CA 92101
www.mcasandiego.org
Phone: 619-234-1001
Fax: 619-234-1070

Museum of History & Art
1100 Orange Ave
Coronado, CA 92118
Phone: 619-435-7242
Fax: 619-435-8504

Museum of Photographic Arts
1649 El Prado
San Diego, CA 92101
E-mail: info@mopa.org
www.mopa.org/
Phone: 619-238-7559
Fax: 619-238-8777

Museum of San Diego History
1649 El Prado Balboa Pk
San Diego, CA 92101
edweb.sdsu.edu/sdhs
Phone: 619-232-6203
Fax: 619-232-6297

Old Globe Theatre/Simon Edison Centre for the Performing Arts
Balboa Pk
San Diego, CA 92112
oldglobe.org
Phone: 619-239-2255
Fax: 619-231-1037

Old Town State Historic Park
4002 Wallace St
San Diego, CA 92110
Phone: 619-220-5422
Fax: 619-220-5421

Old Town Trolley Tours Phone: 619-298-8687
2115 Kurtz St
San Diego, CA 92110
E-mail: scampbell@historictours.com
www.historictours.com/sandiego/trolley.htm

Orfila Vineyards & Winery Phone: 760-738-6500
13455 San Pasqual Rd Fax: 760-745-3773
Escondido, CA 92025
www.orfila.com

Reuben H Fleet Science Center Phone: 619-238-1233
1875 El Prado Fax: 619-685-5771
San Diego, CA 92101
www.rhfleet.org

San Diego Aerospace Museum Phone: 619-234-8291
2001 Pan American Plaza Balboa Pk Fax: 619-233-4526
San Diego, CA 92101
www.aerospacemuseum.org

San Diego Aircraft Carrier Museum Phone: 619-702-7700
1355 N Harbor Dr Fax: 619-238-1200
San Diego, CA 92101
E-mail: magic@midway.org
www.midway.org

San Diego Automotive Museum Phone: 619-231-2886
2080 Pan American Plaza Balboa Pk Fax: 619-231-9869
San Diego, CA 92101
www.sdautomuseum.org

San Diego Civic Light Opera Phone: 619-544-7827
2005 Pan American Plaza Starlight Bowl Fax: 619-544-0496
San Diego, CA 92101

San Diego Family Fun Center Phone: 858-560-7342
6999 Clairemont Mesa Blvd Fax: 858-560-5347
San Diego, CA 92111

San Diego Hall of Champions Sports Museum Phone: 619-234-2544
2131 Pan American Plaza Balboa Pk Fax: 619-234-4543
San Diego, CA 92101

San Diego Maritime Museum Phone: 619-234-9153
1306 N Harbor Dr Fax: 619-234-8345
San Diego, CA 92101
E-mail: info@sdmaritime.com
www.sdmaritime.com

San Diego Model Railroad Museum Phone: 619-696-0199
1649 El Prado Balboa Pk Fax: 619-696-0239
San Diego, CA 92101
www.sdmodelrailroadm.com/

San Diego Museum of Art Phone: 619-232-7931
1450 El Prado Balboa Pk Fax: 619-232-9367
San Diego, CA 92101
www.sdmart.com/

San Diego Museum of Man Phone: 619-239-2001
1350 El Prado Balboa Pk Fax: 619-239-2749
San Diego, CA 92101
E-mail: contact@museumofman.org
www.museumofman.org

San Diego Natural History Museum Phone: 619-232-3821
1788 El Prado Fax: 619-232-0248
San Diego, CA 92101
www.sdnhm.org

San Diego Opera Assn Phone: 619-232-7636
1200 3rd Ave 18th Fl Fax: 619-231-6915
San Diego, CA 92101
E-mail: facts@sdopera.com
www.sdopera.com

San Diego Railroad Museum Phone: 619-595-3030
1050 Kettner Blvd Fax: 619-595-3034
San Diego, CA 92101 TF: 888-228-9246
E-mail: wolfgang@train.sdrm.org
www.sdrm.org/

San Diego Repertory Theatre Phone: 619-231-3586
79 Horton Plaza Fax: 619-235-0939
San Diego, CA 92101
E-mail: marketing@sandiegorep.com
www.sandiegorep.com

San Diego Wild Animal Park Phone: 760-747-8702
15500 San Pasqual Valley Rd Fax: 760-746-7081
Escondido, CA 92027
www.sandiegozoo.org/wap

San Diego Zoo Phone: 619-231-1515
2920 Zoo Dr Fax: 619-231-0249
San Diego, CA 92101
www.sandiegozoo.org

San Luis Rey Mission Phone: 760-757-3651
4050 Mission Ave Fax: 760-757-4613
Oceanside, CA 92057
E-mail: mission@slctnet.com
sanluisrey.org

Sea World of California Phone: 619-226-3901
500 Sea World Dr Fax: 619-226-3996
San Diego, CA 92109
www.seaworld.com/seaworld/sw_california/swcframe.html

Seaport Village Phone: 619-235-6569
849 W Harbor Dr Suite D Fax: 619-696-0025
San Diego, CA 92101
www.spvillage.com

Spreckels Theatre Phone: 619-235-9500
121 Broadway Fax: 619-235-4654
San Diego, CA 92101

Theatre in Old Town Phone: 619-688-2494
4040 Twiggs St Fax: 619-688-0960
San Diego, CA 92110
E-mail: admin@theatreinoldtown.com
www.theatreinoldtown.com

Timken Museum of Art Phone: 619-239-5548
1500 El Prado Balboa Pk Fax: 619-233-6629
San Diego, CA 92101
gort.ucsd.edu/sj/timken

Torrey Pines State Reserve Phone: 858-755-2063
N Torrey Pines Rd Fax: 858-509-0981
San Diego, CA 92037
www.torreypines.com

Villa Montezuma Museum & Jesse Shepard House Phone: 619-239-2211
1925 K St
San Diego, CA 92102

Wells Fargo History Museum Phone: 619-238-3929
2733 San Diego Ave Fax: 619-298-8209
San Diego, CA 92110
wellsfargo.com/about/museum/info/

Whale Watching Phone: 619-222-1144
2803 Emerson St H & M Landing Fax: 619-222-0784
San Diego, CA 92106
E-mail: hmmail@hmlanding.com
www.hmlanding.com/nature.htm

Whaley House Museum Phone: 619-298-2482
2482 San Diego Ave
San Diego, CA 92110

White George & Anna Gunn Marston House Phone: 619-298-3142
3525 7th Ave Fax: 619-232-6297
San Diego, CA 92103

Sports Teams & Facilities

Del Mar Thoroughbred Club Phone: 858-755-1141
PO Box 700 Fax: 858-792-1477
Del Mar, CA 92014
www.dmtc.com

Qualcomm Stadium Phone: 619-641-3100
9449 Friars Rd Fax: 619-283-0460
San Diego, CA 92108
www.qualcomm.com/stadium

San Diego Chargers Phone: 619-280-2121
9449 Friars Rd Qualcomm Stadium Fax: 619-280-5107
San Diego, CA 92108
www.chargers.com

San Diego Flash (soccer) Phone: 858-581-2120
7250 Mesa College Dr Douglas Stadium Fax: 858-581-9419
San Diego, CA 92111
E-mail: sdflash@aol.com
www.sdflash.com

San Diego Gulls (hockey) Phone: 619-224-4625
3500 Sports Arena Blvd San Diego Sports Arena Fax: 619-224-3010
San Diego, CA 92110
www.sandiegoarena.com/gulls/gulls.htm

San Diego Padres Phone: 619-881-6500
9449 Friars Rd Qualcomm Stadium Fax: 619-497-5339
San Diego, CA 92108
E-mail: comments@padres.com
www.padres.com/

San Diego Sports Arena Phone: 619-225-9813
3500 Sports Arena Blvd Fax: 619-224-3010
San Diego, CA 92110
www.sandiegoarena.com

San Jose Municipal Stadium Phone: 408-297-1435
588 E Alma Ave Fax: 408-297-1453
San Jose, CA 95112
www.sjgiants.com/stadium_info.html

Annual Events

Adams Avenue Street Fair (late September) 619-282-7329
Art Alive (early May)............................619-232-7931
Arturo Barrios Invitational 10K/5K (late October)................................858-450-6510
Bonitafest (late September)......................619-472-8520
Borrego Springs Desert Festival (late October) 760-767-5555
Cabrillo Festival (late September) 619-557-5450
California American Indian Days Celebration (late September) 619-281-5964
Christmas on the Prado (early December)..........619-239-0512
Cinco de Mayo Celebration (early May).............619-422-1982
Concerts in the Park (early June-mid-August) 619-585-5627
Coronado Independence Day Celebration (July 4)....619-437-8788
Culligan Holiday Bowl (late December) 619-283-5808
Del Mar Fair (mid-June-early July) 858-755-1161
Del Mar National Horse Show (mid-April-early May) 858-792-4288
Downtown Third Avenue Lemon Festival (early August)................................619-422-1982
Fabulous Forties (mid-November).................619-691-5071
Fall Village Faire (early November)................760-434-8887
Fiesta Cinco de Mayo (early May)..................619-236-1212
First Night San Diego (December 31)..............619-280-5838
Harbor Avenues of the Arts (early July)...........760-416-2186
Harbor Day & Tall Ship Festival (mid-September) 619-426-2882
Harvest Festival (mid-October)....................619-615-4100
Holiday Bowl (late December).....................619-283-5808
Hot Air Balloon Classic (July 4)...................858-481-6800
International Summer Organ Festival (mid-June-late August)........................619-702-8138
La Jolla Festival of the Arts & Food Faire (mid-June) 619-236-1212
Lakeside Western Days & Rodeo (mid-April)........619-236-1212
Lemon Festival (early August) 619-422-1982
Mainly Mozart Festival (late May-early June)........619-239-0100
MCAS Miramar Air Show (mid-October) 619-236-1212
Nations of San Diego International Dance Festival (mid-January)...............................619-239-9255
Ocean Beach Kite Festival (early March) 619-236-1212
Oceanside Harbor Days (mid-September)...........760-722-1534
Pacific Beach Block Party & Street Faire (mid-May) 619-641-5823
Pacific Islander Festival (early July) 619-699-8797
Poinsettia Festival (mid-November)................760-943-1950
Poway Street Fair (November) 858-748-0022
Ramona Rodeo (mid-late May) 619-236-1212
Rancho Bernardo Fall Art & Wine Festival (early October)..............................858-487-1767
Rosarito-Ensenada 50 Mile Fun Bicycle Ride (late September) 619-583-3001
San Diego American Indian Cultural Days (late May) 619-281-5964
San Diego Blues Festival (mid-June) 619-283-9576
San Diego Boat Show (early January)..............858-274-9924
San Diego Crew Classic (early March) 619-236-1212
San Diego Dixieland Jazz Festival (late November) 619-297-5277
San Diego Harbor Parade of Lights (mid-late December)...........................619-232-3101

San Diego International Film Festival (February-May) 858-534-0497
San Diego International Triathlon (late June) 619-236-1212
San Diego Marathon (late January) 858-792-2900
San Diego New Year Celebration (February) 619-234-4447
San Diego Polo Matches (mid-June-mid-October) 858-481-9217
San Diego Street Scene (early-mid-September) 619-557-8490
Score Baja 1000 Race (early November) 619-236-1212
Soap Box Derby (mid-September) 619-427-9157
Starlight Yule Parade (early December) 619-422-1982
Taste of the Arts (mid-April) 619-585-5627
US Open Sandcastle Competition (late July) 619-424-6663
Vista Holiday Parade (early December) 760-726-1122
World Championship Over-the-Line Tournament (early-mid-July) 619-236-1212
World Series of Powerboats Racing (mid-September) 619-236-1212

San Francisco, California

County: **San Francisco**

SAN FRANCISCO is located along the northern California coast between the Pacific Ocean and the San Francisco Bay. Major cities within 100 miles include Oakland, San Jose, Stockton, Modesto, and Sacramento, California.

Area (Land) .... 46.7 sq mi
Area (Water).............................. 185.2 sq mi
Elevation.................................... 63 ft
Latitude ....37-77-50 N
Longitude.............................. 122-41-83 W
Time Zone ....PST
Area Code.................................... 415

Climate

San Francisco has a temperate marine climate. Winters are mild, with highs in the mid- to upper 50s and lows in the low to mid-40s. Summer days are also mild, with highs in the low 70s, while evenings cool down into the low to mid-50s. Fog is a common occurrence during the summer months. Winter is the rainy season in San Francisco, while summer is the driest.

Average Temperatures & Precipitation

Temperatures

	Jan	Feb	Mar	Apr	May	Jun	Jul	Aug	Sep	Oct	Nov	Dec
High	56	59	61	64	67	70	72	72	74	70	62	56
Low	42	45	46	47	50	53	54	55	55	52	47	43

Precipitation

	Jan	Feb	Mar	Apr	May	Jun	Jul	Aug	Sep	Oct	Nov	Dec
Inches	4.4	3.2	3.1	1.4	0.2	0.1	0.0	0.1	0.2	1.2	2.9	3.1

History

The San Francisco Bay area was not discovered by Europeans until 1769, when Spanish conquistador Gaspar de Portola came upon the bay during an overland expedition from Mexico. The area was first colonized in 1776 as the Presidio of San Francisco and the Mission Dolores, built by Father Junipero Serra. Over the course of the next 50 years the area was under Spanish and Mexican rule until 1846 when the United States gained control of California during the Mexican-American War.

In 1849, gold was discovered in Northern California, sparking the famous Gold Rush that would bring thousands of miners to the Bay area in search of fortune. The Gold Rush also brought numerous other types of economic opportunities to San Francisco—new industries were created to supply the miners (Levi Strauss was established during this time to manufacture blue jeans for the miners), and banks began popping up all around the city to finance their ventures. San Francisco's population exploded as a result, soaring from 800 residents in 1848 to 35,000 in 1852. San Francisco prospered through the remainder of the 1800s and during the early years of the 20th Century, but in 1906 earthquakes devastated the Bay area. Seven hundred people lost their lives and some 28,000 buildings were destroyed as a result of the San Francisco earthquake and the fires that it sparked. The city quickly rebuilt itself, however, and over the course of the past 90 years it has become a major U.S. center for finance and commerce.

San Francisco's cultural diversity is evident in its many ethnic neighborhoods, including Chinatown, Japantown, the Italian North Beach area, and the Hispanic Mission District. Home to nearly three-quarters of a million people, San Francisco is California's fourth largest city and the 12th largest city in the United States.

Population

1990 Census 723,959
1998 Estimate.............................745,774
% Change 3.0
2020 Projection 844,948

Racial/Ethnic Breakdown
White.................................. 53.6%
Black 10.9%
Other.................................. 35.5%
Hispanic Origin (may be of any race) 13.9%

Age Breakdown
Under 5 years.............................. 4.9%
5 to 17.................................. 11.2%
18 to 20.................................. 3.5%
21 to 24.................................. 6.8%
25 to 34.................................. 21.9%
35 to 44.................................. 17.9%
45 to 54.................................. 10.3%
55 to 64.................................. 8.8%
65 to 74.................................. 7.9%
75+ years 6.6%
Median Age................................35.8

Gender Breakdown
Male.................................. 50.1%
Female.................................. 49.9%

Government

Type of Government: Mayor-Board of Supervisors

San Francisco Board of Supervisors
City Hall 1 Dr Carlton B Goodlett Pl Rm 244
San Francisco, CA 94102
Phone: 415-554-5184
Fax: 415-554-4951

San Francisco City Administrator Phone: 415-554-4852
City Hall 1 Dr Carlton B Goodlett Pl Fax: 415-554-4849
Rm 352
San Francisco, CA 94102

San Francisco City Attorney Phone: 415-554-4700
City Hall 1 Dr Carlton B Goodlett Pl Fax: 415-554-4745
Rm 234
San Francisco, CA 94102

San Francisco City Hall Phone: 415-554-4000
1 Dr Carleton B Goodlett Pl Fax: 415-554-6160
San Francisco, CA 94102

San Francisco County Clerk Phone: 415-554-4955
City Hall 1 Dr Carlton B Goodlett Pl Fax: 415-252-3283
Rm 168
San Francisco, CA 94102

San Francisco Fire Dept Phone: 415-861-8000
698 2nd St Fax: 415-558-3323
San Francisco, CA 94107

San Francisco Human Resources Dept Phone: 415-557-4990
44 Gough St Fax: 415-557-4910
San Francisco, CA 94103

San Francisco Mayor Phone: 415-554-6141
1 Dr Carlton B Goodlett Pl City Hall Rm 200 Fax: 415-554-6160
San Francisco, CA 94102

San Francisco Planning Dept Phone: 415-558-6414
1660 Mission St 5th Fl Fax: 415-558-6409
San Francisco, CA 94103

San Francisco Police Dept Phone: 415-553-1667
850 Bryant St Hall of Justice Rm 505 Fax: 415-553-1669
San Francisco, CA 94103

San Francisco Public Library Phone: 415-557-4400
100 Larkin St Fax: 415-557-4239
San Francisco, CA 94102

San Francisco Public Utilities Commission Phone: 415-554-3155
1155 Market St 4th Fl Fax: 415-554-3161
San Francisco, CA 94103

San Francisco Public Works Dept Phone: 415-554-6920
City Hall 1 Dr Carlton B Goodlett Pl Fax: 415-554-6944
Rm 348
San Francisco, CA 94102

San Francisco Recreation & Park Dept Phone: 415-831-2700
Golden Gate Park 501 Stanyon St Fax: 415-221-8034
McLaren Lodge
San Francisco, CA 94117

San Francisco Treasurer & Tax Collector Phone: 415-554-4478
City Hall 1 Dr Carlton B Goodlett Pl Fax: 415-554-4672
Rm 140
San Francisco, CA 94102

Important Phone Numbers

AAA 415-565-2012
American Express Travel 415-908-3500
California State Franchise Tax Board. 916-845-4300
Driver's License/Vehicle Registration Information . . . 415-557-1179
Emergency 911
Events Line. 415-391-2001
HotelDocs 800-468-3537
Medical Referral. 415-561-0850
Poison Control Center 800-876-4766
San Francisco Assn of Realtors. 415-431-8500
San Francisco County Assessor's Office. 415-554-5596
San Francisco Treasurer/Tax Collector 415-554-4481
Time. 415-767-8900
Voter Registration Information. 415-554-4375
Weather 831-656-1725

Information Sources

Alameda County Phone: 510-272-6984
1221 Oak St Fax: 510-272-3784
Oakland, CA 94612
www.co.alameda.ca.us

Better Business Bureau Serving Oakland/San Francisco Area & Northwest Coastal California Phone: 510-238-1000
510 16th St Suite 550 Fax: 510-238-1018
Oakland, CA 94612
www.oakland.bbb.org

Fremont Chamber of Commerce Phone: 510-795-2244
39488 Stevenson Pl Suite 100 Fax: 510-795-2240
Fremont, CA 94539
www.fremontbusiness.com

Fremont City Hall Phone: 510-494-4800
39100 Liberty St Fax: 510-494-4257
Fremont, CA 94538
www.ci.fremont.ca.us

Fremont Economic Development Office Phone: 510-494-4800
PO Box 5006 Fax: 510-494-4257
Fremont, CA 94537

Fremont Main Library Phone: 510-745-1400
2400 Stevenson Blvd Fax: 510-793-2987
Fremont, CA 94538
www.aclibrary.org/branches/frm.html

Fremont Mayor Phone: 510-494-4811
PO Box 5006 Fax: 510-494-4257
Fremont, CA 94537

Moscone Center Phone: 415-974-4000
747 Howard St Fax: 415-974-4073
San Francisco, CA 94103
www.moscone.com

Oakland City Hall Phone: 510-238-3301
1 Frank H Ogawa Plaza 3rd Fl Fax: 510-238-2223
Oakland, CA 94612
www.oaklandnet.com

Oakland Community & Economic Development Agency Phone: 510-238-3015
250 Frank H Ogawa Plaza 3rd Fl Fax: 510-238-3691
Oakland, CA 94612
www.oaklandnet.com/government/ceda/ceda.html

Oakland Convention & Visitors Bureau
550 10th St
Oakland, CA 94607
Phone: 510-839-9000
Fax: 510-839-5924

Oakland Convention Center
550 10th St
Oakland, CA 94607
Phone: 510-451-4000
TF: 800-262-5526

Oakland Mayor
1 Frank H Ogawa Plaza 3rd Fl
Oakland, CA 94612
www.oaklandnet.com/government/government2.html
Phone: 510-238-3141
Fax: 510-238-4731

Oakland Metropolitan Chamber of Commerce
475 14th St
Oakland, CA 94612
www.oaklandchamber.com
Phone: 510-874-4800
Fax: 510-839-8817

Oakland Public Library
125 14th St
Oakland, CA 94612
www.oaklandlibrary.org
Phone: 510-238-3134

San Francisco Chamber of Commerce
465 California St Suite 900
San Francisco, CA 94104
www.sfchamber.com
Phone: 415-392-4520
Fax: 415-392-0485

San Francisco Civic Auditorium
99 Grove St
San Francisco, CA 94102
Phone: 415-974-4000
Fax: 415-974-4084

San Francisco Convention & Visitors Bureau
201 3rd St Suite 900
San Francisco, CA 94103
www.sfvisitor.org
Phone: 415-974-6900
Fax: 415-227-2602

San Francisco County
1 Dr Carleton B Goodlett Pl
San Francisco, CA 94102
www.ci.sf.ca.us
Phone: 415-554-4950

San Francisco Partnership
303 Sacramento St 2nd Fl
San Francisco, CA 94111
www.sfp.org
Phone: 415-364-1799
Fax: 415-982-6733
TF: 888-737-4249

Online Resources

4Oakland.com
www.4oakland.com

4SanFrancisco.com
www.4sanfrancisco.com

ABAG Online
www.abag.ca.gov

Access America San Francisco
www.accessamer.com/sanfrancisco/

Annual Guide for the Arts
www.guide4arts.com/sf/

Anthill City Guide Oakland
www.anthill.com/city.asp?city=oakland

Anthill City Guide San Francisco
www.anthill.com/city.asp?city=sanfrancisco

Area Guide Oakland
oakland.areaguides.net

Area Guide San Francisco
sanfrancisco.areaguides.net

Back in San Francisco
www.backinsf.com/

Bay Area Art Source
www.foggy.com/indexf.html

Bay Area eGuide
www.sfgate.com/eguide/

Bay Area Restaurant Guide
dine.com/barg

BayArea.com
www.bayarea.com

BayInsider.com
www.bayinsider.com/

Boulevards Oakland
www.oakland.com

Boulevards San Francisco
www.sanfrancisco.com

Bradmans.com San Francisco
www.bradmans.com/scripts/display_city.cgi?city=242

City Insights San Francisco
cityinsights.com/sanfran.htm

City Knowledge Oakland
www.cityknowledge.com/ca_oakland.htm

City Knowledge San Francisco
www.cityknowledge.com/ca_sanfrancisco.htm

Cityguide Online
www.ctguide.com/

CitySearch San Francisco
bayarea.citysearch.com

CityTravelGuide.com San Francisco
www.citytravelguide.com/san-francisco.htm

CuisineNet San Francisco
www.cuisinenet.com/restaurant/san_francisco/index.shtml

DigitalCity San Francisco
home.digitalcity.com/sanfrancisco

East Bay Online
www.sftoday.com/eastbay.htm

Essential Guide to San Francisco
www.ego.net/us/ca/sf/index.htm

Excite.com Fremont City Guide
www.excite.com/travel/countries/united_states/california/fremont

Excite.com Oakland City Guide
www.excite.com/travel/countries/united_states/california/oakland

Excite.com San Francisco City Guide
www.excite.com/travel/countries/united_states/california/san_francisco

Fabulous Oakland
www.sirius.com/~asta/oakland.html

Fine Art Museums of San Francisco
www.famsf.org/

Fog City Online
userwww.sfsu.edu/~ped/fogcity.htm

Gayot's Guide Restaurant Search San Francisco
www.perrier.com/restaurants/gayot.asp?area=SFC

HotelGuide San Francisco
sanfrancisco.hotelguide.net

Lodging.com San Francisco California
www.lodging.com/auto/guides/san_francisco-area-ca.html

OaklandCA.com
www.oaklandca.com

Open World City Guides San Francisco
www.worldexecutive.com/cityguides/san_francisco/

Q San Francisco Guide
www.qsanfrancisco.com/qsf/guide/

Rough Guide Travel San Francisco
travel.roughguides.com/content/3697/

San Francisco Bay Area CityWomen
www.citywomen.com/sfwomen.htm

San Francisco Bay Area Index
www.sfbayarea.com/index/

San Francisco Bay Guardian
www.sfbayguardian.com

San Francisco Bay Resource Home Page
www.sftoday.com/sfbay.htm

San Francisco California
san-francisco-california.com

San Francisco Graphic City Guide
www.futurecast.com/gcg/sanfran.htm

San Francisco Guide
www.sfguide.com/

San Francisco Home Page
www.wco.com/~chldress/sfhome/

San Francisco Insider
www.theinsider.com/sf

San Francisco Online
www.sfousa.com/

San Francisco Station
www.sfstation.com/

San Francisco.com
sanfrancisco.com

San FranZiskGo
www.transaction.net/sanfran/events/

SanFrancisco.TheLinks.com
sanfrancisco.thelinks.com/

Savvy Diner Guide to San Francisco Restaurants
www.savvydiner.com/sanfrancisco/

SFMission.com
www.sfmission.com

Surf & Sun Beach Vacation Guide to San Francisco
www.surf-sun.com/ca-san-francisco-main.htm

Time Out San Francisco
www.timeout.com/sanfrancisco/

Tourists Guide to San Francisco
www.hooked.net/users/manx/

Ultimate Resource for San Francisco
www.transaction.net/sanfran/ult/index.html

Union Street in San Francisco
www.unionstreet.com

Virtual Voyages San Francisco
www.virtualvoyages.com/usa/ca/s_f/sf.sht

Web Castro
www.webcastro.com/

WeekendEvents.com San Francisco
www.weekendevents.com/sanfrancisco/sanfran.html

World's Online Guide to Castro Street San Francisco
www.castroonline.com

Yahoo! San Francisco
sfbay.yahoo.com

Z San Francisco
www.zpub.com/sf/

Area Communities

Communities in the San Francisco Bay area, encompassing Alameda, Contra Costa, Napa, Solano, Marin, San Mateo, and Sonoma counties (Communities in Santa Clara County are included in the San Jose profile) with populations greater than 50,000 include:

Antioch
3rd & H St
Antioch, CA 94509
Phone: 925-779-7000
Fax: 925-779-7003

Berkeley
1900 Addison St
Berkeley, CA 94704
Phone: 510-644-6480
Fax: 510-644-8801

Concord
1950 Parkside Dr
Concord, CA 94519
Phone: 925-671-3000
Fax: 925-798-0636

Daly City
333 90th St
Daly City, CA 94015
Phone: 650-991-8000
Fax: 650-991-8228

Fairfield
1000 Webster St
Fairfield, CA 94533
Phone: 707-428-7551
Fax: 707-428-7631

Fremont
39100 Liberty St
Fremont, CA 94538
Phone: 510-494-4800
Fax: 510-494-4257

Hayward
777 B St
Hayward, CA 94545
Phone: 510-583-4400
Fax: 510-583-3636

Livermore
1052 S Livermore Ave
Livermore, CA 94550
Phone: 925-373-5140
Fax: 925-373-5135

Napa
955 School St
Napa, CA 94559
Phone: 707-257-9500
Fax: 707-257-9534

Oakland
1 Frank H Ogawa Plaza 3rd Fl
Oakland, CA 94612
Phone: 510-238-3301
Fax: 510-238-2223

Petaluma
11 English St
Petaluma, CA 94952
Phone: 707-778-4360
Fax: 707-778-4420

Pittsburg
PO Box 1518
Pittsburg, CA 94565
Phone: 925-252-4850
Fax: 925-252-4851

Redwood City
1017 Middlefield Rd
Redwood City, CA 94063
Phone: 650-780-7000
Fax: 650-780-7225

Richmond
2600 Barrett Ave
Richmond, CA 94804
Phone: 510-620-6513
Fax: 510-620-6542

San Leandro
835 E 14th St
San Leandro, CA 94577
Phone: 510-577-3351
Fax: 510-577-3340

San Mateo
330 W 20th Ave
San Mateo, CA 94403
Phone: 650-522-7000
Fax: 650-522-7001

San Rafael
PO Box 151560
San Rafael, CA 94915
Phone: 415-485-3070
Fax: 415-459-2242

Santa Rosa
100 Santa Rosa Ave
Santa Rosa, CA 95404
Phone: 707-543-3010
Fax: 707-543-3030

South San Francisco
400 Grand Ave
South San Francisco, CA 94080
Phone: 650-877-8500
Fax: 650-829-6609

Union City
34009 Alvarado Niles Rd
Union City, CA 94587
Phone: 510-471-3232
Fax: 510-475-7318

Vacaville
650 Merchant St
Vacaville, CA 95688
Phone: 707-449-5100
Fax: 707-449-5149

Vallejo
555 Santa Clara St
Vallejo, CA 94590
Phone: 707-648-4527
Fax: 707-648-4426

Walnut Creek
1666 N Main St
Walnut Creek, CA 94596
Phone: 925-943-5800
Fax: 925-256-3595

Economy

The San Francisco Bay area is a major center for finance, commerce, and technology. Financial companies that have their corporate headquarters in San Francisco include BankAmerica and Transamerica Corp. The world-famous "Silicon Valley," located just outside of San Francisco, is home to such high-technology giants as Hewlett-Packard, Apple Computer, and Lockheed Martin Space Systems Company, all of which are major employers. Government is also a major Bay area employer, providing more than 100,000 jobs at the federal, state, and local levels and in the military. The U.S. Federal Government is the area's largest employer, providing more than 25,000 jobs for area residents.

Unemployment Rate 2.3%
Per Capita Income.........................$41,128*
Median Family Income.....................$46,574

** Information given in for the San Francisco Metropolitan Statistical Area (MSA) which includes the City and County of San Francisco, Marin County, and San Mateo County.*

Principal Industries & Number of Wage Earners

San Francisco PMSA* - June 2000

Industry	Wage Earners
Construction	46,200
Farm	3,700
Finance, Insurance, & Real Estate	106,700
Government	136,500
Manufacturing	74,800
Mining	400
Retail Trade	178,900
Services	398,800
Transportation & Public Utilities	83,700
Wholesale Trade	46,900

** Information given in for the San Francisco Primary Metropolitan Statistical Area (PMSA), which includes Marin, San Francisco, and San Mateo counties.*

Major Employers

Alameda County
1221 Oak St
Oakland, CA 94612
E-mail: dpd@co.alameda.ca.us
www.co.alameda.ca.us
Phone: 510-272-6984
Fax: 510-272-3784

Apple Computer Inc
1 Infinite Loop
Cupertino, CA 95014
www.apple.com
Phone: 408-996-1010
Fax: 408-996-0275
TF: 800-767-2775

Bechtel Group Inc
PO Box 193965
San Francisco, CA 94119
www.bechtel.com
Phone: 415-768-1234
Fax: 415-768-9038

Chevron Corp
575 Market St
San Francisco, CA 94105
E-mail: chevweb@chevron.com
www.chevron.com
Phone: 415-894-7700
Fax: 415-894-0583

Contra Costa County
651 Pine St 11th Fl
Martinez, CA 94553
www.co.contra-costa.ca.us
Phone: 925-335-1080
Fax: 925-335-1098

Crowley Maritime Corp
155 Grand Ave
Oakland, CA 94612
www.crowley.com
Phone: 510-251-7500
Fax: 510-251-7625

Del Monte Foods Co
1 Market Plaza Stuart Street Towers
San Francisco, CA 94105
www.delmonte.com
Phone: 415-247-3000
Fax: 415-247-3565
TF: 800-543-3090

Dillingham Construction Corp
5960 Inglewood Dr
Pleasanton, CA 94588
E-mail: mktgsvcs@dillinghamconstruction.com
www.dillinghamconstruction.com
Phone: 925-463-3300
Fax: 925-463-1571

Gap Inc
1 Harrison St
San Francisco, CA 94105
E-mail: custserv@gap.com
www.gapinc.com
Phone: 650-952-4400
Fax: 650-874-7803
TF: 800-333-7899

Hewlett-Packard Co
3000 Hanover St
Palo Alto, CA 94304
www.hp.com
Phone: 650-857-1501
Fax: 650-857-5518
TF: 800-322-4772

Intel Corp
2200 Mission College Blvd
Santa Clara, CA 95052
www.intel.com
Phone: 408-765-8080
Fax: 408-765-1402
TF: 800-628-8686

Knowledge Universe Inc
3351 El Camino Real Suite 200
Menlo Park, CA 94027
E-mail: info@knowledgeu.com
www.knowledgeu.com
Phone: 650-549-3200
Fax: 650-549-3222

Lockheed Martin Space Systems Co
Missiles & Space Operations
1111 Lockheed Martin Way
Sunnyvale, CA 94089
lmms.external.lmco.com
Phone: 408-742-4321
Fax: 408-743-2239

Pacific Gas & Electric Co
PO Box 770000
San Francisco, CA 94177
www.pge.com
Phone: 415-973-7000
Fax: 415-543-0841
TF: 800-367-7731

Safeway Inc
5918 Stoneridge Mall Rd
Pleasanton, CA 94588
www.safeway.com
Phone: 925-467-3000
Fax: 925-467-3603

San Francisco City Hall
1 Dr Carleton B Goodlett Pl
San Francisco, CA 94102
www.ci.sf.ca.us
Phone: 415-554-4000
Fax: 415-554-6160

San Francisco County
1 Dr Carleton B Goodlett Pl
San Francisco, CA 94102
www.ci.sf.ca.us
Phone: 415-554-4950

Santa Clara County
70 W Hedding St
San Jose, CA 95110
claraweb.co.santa-clara.ca.us
Phone: 408-299-2424
Fax: 408-293-5649

Stanford University
Stanford, CA 94305
www.stanford.edu
Phone: 650-723-2300
Fax: 650-723-6050

Sun Microsystems Inc
901 San Antonio Rd
Palo Alto, CA 94303
www.sun.com
Phone: 650-960-1300
Fax: 650-786-3530
TF: 800-786-7638

Transamerica Corp
600 Montgomery St
San Francisco, CA 94111
www.transamerica.com
Phone: 415-983-4000
Fax: 415-983-4400

United Airlines
San Francisco International Airport
San Francisco, CA 94128
www.united.com
Phone: 800-241-6522

University of California San Francisco
500 Parnassus Ave
San Francisco, CA 94143
www.ucsf.edu
Phone: 415-476-9000
Fax: 415-476-9690

Wells Fargo & Co
420 Montgomery St 12th Fl
San Francisco, CA 94104
wellsfargo.com
Phone: 800-411-4932
Fax: 415-397-2987

Wilbur-Ellis Co
345 California St 27th Fl
San Francisco, CA 94104
www.wilburellis.com
Phone: 415-772-4000
Fax: 415-772-4011

Quality of Living Indicators

Total Crime Index....................................46,139
(rates per 100,000 inhabitants)

Violent Crime
Murder/manslaughter.......................... 58
Forcible rape 244
Robbery....................................3,927
Aggravated assault..........................3,108

Property Crime
Burglary 6,706
Larceny theft 25,349
Motor vehicle theft 6,747

Cost of Living Index....................................184.0
(national average = 100)

Median Home Price.................................$365,300

Education

Public Schools

San Francisco Board of Education
555 Franklin St
San Francisco, CA 94102
Phone: 415-241-6427
Fax: 415-241-6429

Number of Schools
Elementary 76
Middle 17
High 21

Student/Teacher Ratio
All Grades 20.1:1

Private Schools

Number of Schools (all grades) .... 200+

Colleges & Universities

Academy of Art College
79 New Montgomery St
San Francisco, CA 94105
www.academyart.edu
Phone: 415-274-2200
Fax: 415-263-4130
TF: 800-544-2787

Armstrong University
1608 Webster St
Oakland, CA 94612
www.armstrong-u.edu
Phone: 510-835-7900
Fax: 510-835-8935

Art Institutes International San Francisco
1170 Market St
San Francisco, CA 94102
www.aii.edu
Phone: 888-493-3261
Fax: 415-863-6344

California College of Arts & Crafts
5212 Broadway
Oakland, CA 94618
Phone: 510-653-8118
Fax: 510-594-3601
TF: 800-447-1278

California Culinary Academy Inc
625 Polk St
San Francisco, CA 94102
www.baychef.com
Phone: 415-771-3536
Fax: 415-771-2194
TF: 800-229-2433

California Maritime Academy
200 Maritime Academy Dr
Vallejo, CA 94590
E-mail: info@prop.csum.edu
www.csum.edu
Phone: 707-654-1000
Fax: 707-654-1336
TF: 800-561-1945

California State University Hayward
25800 Carlos Bee Blvd
Hayward, CA 94542
www.csuhayward.edu
Phone: 510-885-3000
Fax: 510-885-3816

Canada College
4200 Farm Hill Blvd
Redwood City, CA 94061
www.smcccd.cc.ca.us/smcccd/canada/canada.html
Phone: 650-364-1212
Fax: 650-306-3133

Chabot College
25555 Hesperian Blvd
Hayward, CA 94545
www.clpccd.cc.ca.us/cc/
Phone: 510-786-6600
Fax: 510-723-7510

City College of San Francisco
50 Phelan Ave
San Francisco, CA 94112
www.ccsf.cc.ca.us
Phone: 415-239-3000
Fax: 415-239-3936

College of Alameda
555 Atlantic Ave
Alameda, CA 94501
E-mail: pio341@peralta.cc.ca.us
www.peralta.cc.ca.us/coa/coa.htm
Phone: 510-522-7221
Fax: 510-769-6019

College of Marin
835 College Ave
Kentfield, CA 94904
E-mail: pio330@ccc-infonet.edu
www.marin.cc.ca.us
Phone: 415-457-8811
Fax: 415-460-0773

College of Marin Indian Valley Campus
1800 Ignacio Blvd
Novato, CA 94949
Phone: 415-883-2211
Fax: 415-485-0135

College of San Mateo
1700 W Hillsdale Blvd
San Mateo, CA 94402
www.smcccd.cc.ca.us/smcccd/csm/
Phone: 650-574-6161
Fax: 650-574-6506

Contra Costa College
2600 Mission Bell Dr
San Pablo, CA 94806
www.contracosta.cc.ca.us
Phone: 510-235-7800
Fax: 510-236-6768

Contra Costa Community College District
500 Court St
Martinez, CA 94553
www.collegesofcc.cc.ca.us
Phone: 925-229-1000
Fax: 925-370-6517

Devry Institute of Technology
6600 Dumbarton Cir
Fremont, CA 94555
E-mail: eharrell@ifn.net
www.fre.devry.edu
Phone: 510-574-1200
Fax: 510-742-0866
TF: 888-201-9941

Diablo Valley College
321 Golf Club Rd
Pleasant Hill, CA 94523
www.dvc.edu
Phone: 925-685-1230
Fax: 925-609-8085

Fashion Institute of Design & Merchandising San Francisco
55 Stockton St
San Francisco, CA 94108
www.fidm.com
Phone: 415-433-6691
Fax: 415-296-7299
TF: 800-422-3436

Golden Gate University
536 Mission St
San Francisco, CA 94105
www.ggu.edu
Phone: 415-442-7000
Fax: 415-442-7807
TF: 800-448-4968

Heald Business College Concord
2150 John Glenn Dr Suite 100
Concord, CA 94520
www.heald.edu/CampusInfo/CampusInfo.asp?campus=ccb
Phone: 925-827-1300
Fax: 925-827-1486
TF: 800-274-7704

Heald Business College Hayward
24301 Southland Dr Suite 500
Hayward, CA 94545
Phone: 510-784-7000
Fax: 510-783-3287
TF: 800-666-9609

Heald Business College San Francisco
350 Mission St
San Francisco, CA 94105
www.heald.edu
Phone: 415-808-3000
Fax: 415-808-3005
TF: 800-999-5455

Heald Institute of Technology
2860 Howe Rd
Martinez, CA 94553
Phone: 925-228-9000
Fax: 925-229-3792
TF: 800-937-7723

Heald Institute of Technology
350 Mission St
San Francisco, CA 94105
www.heald.edu
Phone: 415-441-5555
Fax: 415-808-3005
TF: 800-727-5445

Holy Names College
3500 Mountain Blvd
Oakland, CA 94619
www.hnc.edu
Phone: 510-436-1000
Fax: 510-436-1199

Laney College
900 Fallon St
Oakland, CA 94607
laney.peralta.cc.ca.us
Phone: 510-834-5740
Fax: 510-466-7394

Lincoln University
281 Masonic Ave
San Francisco, CA 94118
www.lincolnuca.edu
Phone: 415-221-1212
Fax: 415-387-9730

Los Medanos College
2700 E Leland Rd
Pittsburg, CA 94565
www.losmedanos.net
Phone: 925-439-2181
Fax: 925-427-1599

Merritt College
12500 Campus Dr
Oakland, CA 94619
www.merritt.edu
Phone: 510-531-4911
Fax: 510-436-2405

Mills College
5000 MacArthur Blvd
Oakland, CA 94613
E-mail: admission@mills.edu
www.mills.edu
Phone: 510-430-2255
Fax: 510-430-3298
TF: 800-876-4557

Napa Valley College
2277 Napa-Vallejo Hwy
Napa, CA 94558
nvc.cc.ca.us/nvc
Phone: 707-253-3000
Fax: 707-253-3064
TF: 800-826-1077

New College of California
50 Fell St
San Francisco, CA 94102
www.newcollege.edu/
Phone: 415-626-1694
Fax: 415-241-9525
TF: 800-335-6262

Ohlone College
43600 Mission Blvd
Fremont, CA 94539
www.ohlone.cc.ca.us
Phone: 510-659-6000
Fax: 510-659-5003

Patten College
2433 Coolidge Ave
Oakland, CA 94601
www.patten.edu
Phone: 510-533-8300
Fax: 510-534-4344

Peralta Community College District (System)
333 E 8th St
Oakland, CA 94606
www.peralta.cc.ca.us
Phone: 510-466-7200
Fax: 510-466-7394

Queen of the Holy Rosary College
43326 Mission Blvd
Fremont, CA 94539
Phone: 510-657-2468
Fax: 510-657-1734

Samuel Merritt College
370 Hawthorne Ave
Oakland, CA 94609
E-mail: information@samuelmerritt.edu
www.samuelmerritt.edu
Phone: 510-869-6511
Fax: 510-869-6525
TF: 800-607-6377

San Francisco Art Institute
800 Chestnut St
San Francisco, CA 94133
E-mail: sfainfo@cdmweb.sfai.edu
www.sfai.edu
Phone: 415-771-7020
Fax: 415-749-4592
TF: 800-345-7324

San Francisco College of Mortuary Science
1598 Dolores St
San Francisco, CA 94110
www.sfcms.org
Phone: 415-567-0674
Fax: 415-824-1390

San Francisco Conservatory of Music
1201 Ortega St
San Francisco, CA 94122
E-mail: cin@sfcm.edu
www.sfcm.edu
Phone: 415-564-8086
Fax: 415-759-3499

San Francisco State University
1600 Holloway Ave
San Francisco, CA 94132
E-mail: ugadmit@sfsu.edu
www.sfsu.edu
Phone: 415-338-1111
Fax: 415-338-3880

Sequoia Electronics Academy
1201 Brewster Ave
Redwood City, CA 94062
Phone: 650-365-6367
Fax: 650-367-7593

Shiloh Bible College
3295 School St
Oakland, CA 94602
Phone: 510-261-1907
Fax: 510-261-2002

Skyline College
3300 College Dr
San Bruno, CA 94066
www.smcccd.cc.ca.us/smcccd/skyline/skyline.html
Phone: 650-355-7000
Fax: 650-738-4338

Solano Community College
4000 Suisun Valley Rd
Suisun City, CA 94585
www.solano.cc.ca.us
Phone: 707-864-7000
Fax: 707-864-7175

Stanford University
Stanford, CA 94305
www.stanford.edu
Phone: 650-723-2300
Fax: 650-723-6050

University of California Berkeley
Berkeley, CA 94720
www.berkeley.edu
Phone: 510-642-6000
Fax: 510-643-5499

University of California San Francisco
500 Parnassus Ave
San Francisco, CA 94143
www.ucsf.edu
Phone: 415-476-9000
Fax: 415-476-9690

University of San Francisco
2130 Fulton St
San Francisco, CA 94117
www.usfca.edu
Phone: 415-422-6886
Fax: 415-422-2217
TF: 800-225-5873

Vista Community College
2020 Milvia St 3rd Fl
Berkeley, CA 94704
E-mail: scoopfoggy@aol.com
www.peralta.cc.ca.us/vista/vista.htm
Phone: 510-841-8431
Fax: 510-841-7333

Hospitals

Alameda County Medical Center-Highland Campus
1411 E 31st St
Oakland, CA 94602
Phone: 510-437-4800
Fax: 510-437-5005

Alta Bates Medical Center
2450 Ashby Ave
Berkeley, CA 94705
www.altabates.com
Phone: 510-540-4444
Fax: 510-548-4972

California Pacific Medical Center Davies Campus
Castro & Duboce Sts
San Francisco, CA 94114
www.cpmc.org
Phone: 415-565-6000
Fax: 415-565-6523

California Pacific Medical Center Pacific Campus
2333 Buchanan St
San Francisco, CA 94115
www.cpmc.org
Phone: 415-563-4321
Fax: 415-885-8633

Children's Hospital-Oakland
747 52nd St
Oakland, CA 94609
www.kron.com/kidsfirst
Phone: 510-428-3000
Fax: 510-654-8474
TF: 800-400-7337

Contra Costa Medical Center
2500 Alhambra Ave
Martinez, CA 94553
Phone: 925-370-5000
Fax: 925-370-5138

John Muir Medical Center
1601 Ygnacio Valley Rd
Walnut Creek, CA 94598
Phone: 925-939-3000
Fax: 925-947-3265

Kaiser Permanente Hospital
99 Montecillo Rd
San Rafael, CA 94903
Phone: 415-444-2000
Fax: 415-444-2492
TF: 800-464-4000

Kaiser Permanente Medical Center
27400 Hesperian Blvd
Hayward, CA 94545
Phone: 510-784-4000
Fax: 510-784-4228

Kaiser Permanente Medical Center
2425 Geary Blvd
San Francisco, CA 94115
Phone: 415-202-2000
Fax: 415-202-2572

Kaiser Permanente Medical Center
280 W MacArthur Blvd
Oakland, CA 94611
Phone: 510-596-1000
Fax: 510-596-7371

Kaiser Permanente Medical Center
1150 Veterans Blvd
Redwood City, CA 94063
Phone: 650-299-2000
Fax: 650-299-2421
TF: 800-464-4000

Kaiser Permanente Medical Center
1425 S Main St
Walnut Creek, CA 94596
Phone: 925-295-4000
Fax: 925-295-5186

Laurel Grove Hospital
19933 Lake Chabot Rd
Castro Valley, CA 94546
Phone: 510-727-2755
Fax: 510-727-2778

Marin General Hospital
PO Box 8010
San Rafael, CA 94912
Phone: 415-925-7000
Fax: 415-925-7933

Queen of the Valley Hospital
1000 Trancas St
Napa, CA 94558
Phone: 707-252-4411
Fax: 707-257-4032

Saint Francis Memorial Hospital
900 Hyde St
San Francisco, CA 94109
Phone: 415-353-6000
Fax: 415-353-6203

Saint Luke's Hospital
3555 Cesar Chavez St
San Francisco, CA 94110
Phone: 415-647-8600
Fax: 415-583-6314

Saint Mary's Medical Center
450 Stanyan St
San Francisco, CA 94117
www.chwbay.org/stmarys
Phone: 415-668-1000
Fax: 415-750-5708

Saint Rose Hospital
27200 Calaroga Ave
Hayward, CA 94545
Phone: 510-264-4000
Fax: 510-887-7421

San Francisco General Hospital Medical Center
1001 Potrero Ave
San Francisco, CA 94110
Phone: 415-206-8000
Fax: 415-206-8441

San Mateo County General Hospital
222 W 39th Ave
San Mateo, CA 94403
Phone: 650-573-2222
Fax: 650-573-2693

Santa Rosa Memorial Hospital
PO Box 522
Santa Rosa, CA 95402
Phone: 707-546-3210
Fax: 707-522-1531

Sequoia Hospital
170 Alameda Ave
Redwood City, CA 94062
www.chwbay.org/sequoia
Phone: 650-369-5811
Fax: 650-780-0532

Seton Medical Center
1900 Sullivan Ave
Daly City, CA 94015
www.chwbay.org/seton
Phone: 650-992-4000
Fax: 650-991-6817

Summit Medical Center
350 Hawthorne Ave
Oakland, CA 94609
www.summitmed.com
Phone: 510-655-4000
Fax: 510-869-6760

Sutter Medical Center of Santa Rosa
3325 Chanate Rd
Santa Rosa, CA 95404
Phone: 707-576-4000
Fax: 707-576-4318

Sutter Solano Medical Center
300 Hospital Dr
Vallejo, CA 94589
Phone: 707-554-4444
Fax: 707-648-3227

UCSF Medical Center
505 Parnassus Ave
San Francisco, CA 94143
Phone: 415-476-1000
Fax: 415-353-2765

Veterans Affairs Medical Center
4150 Clement St
San Francisco, CA 94121
www.sf.med.va.gov
Phone: 415-221-4810
Fax: 415-750-2177

Washington Hospital Phone: 510-797-1111
2000 Mowry Ave Fax: 510-791-3496
Fremont, CA 94538
www.whhs.com

Transportation

Airport(s)

San Francisco International Airport (SFO)
14 miles S of downtown (approx 25 minutes) 650-761-0800

Mass Transit

Bay Area Rapid Transit (BART)
$1.10 Base fare. 650-992-2278
Municipal Railway (MUNI Bus/Streetcar)
$1 Base fare 415-673-6864

Rail/Bus

Amtrak Station Phone: 415-546-4479
31 Embarcadero & Market TF: 800-872-7245
San Francisco, CA 94111

Greyhound Bus Station Phone: 415-495-1569
425 Mission St Transbay Stn TF: 800-231-2222
San Francisco, CA 94105

Utilities

Electricity
Pacific Gas & Electric Co 800-743-5000
www.pge.com

Gas
Pacific Gas & Electric Co 800-743-5000
www.pge.com

Water
San Francisco Water Dept. 415-923-2400

Garbage Collection/Recycling
Golden Gate Disposal Co. 415-626-4000
San Francisco Recycling Program. 415-554-3400
Sunset Scavenger Co 415-330-1300

Telecommunications

Telephone
Pacific Bell. 800-310-2355
www.pacbell.com

Cable Television
AT & T Cable Services. 415-863-9600
www.cable.att.com

Internet Service Providers (ISPs)
CASTLES Information Network 707-422-7311
www.castles.com
Direct Network Access Ltd 510-649-6110
www.dnai.com
DSP.Net 510-522-8516
www.dsp.com
emf.net 510-704-2929
www.emf.net
HoloNet. 510-704-0160
www.holonet.net
Institute for Global Communications (IGC) 415-561-6100
www.igc.org
ISP Networks. 415-778-5100
www.isp.net
LineX Communications 415-455-1650
linex.com
LMi.net 510-843-6389
www.lanminds.com
NapaNet. 707-257-2826
www.napanet.net
NetEase Inc 707-569-5000
www.neteze.com
NetTech Group Inc The. 650-655-2435
www.tngi.com
Nevada Bell Internet Services. 888-724-7253
public.nvbell.net
NOVO Corp. 415-646-7000
www.novocorp.com
Pacific Bell Internet Services. 888-724-7253
www.pacbell.net
QuakeNet Technoloogies 650-655-7100
www.quake.net
Sine Wave Solutions LLC 510-970-7448
www.sinewave.com
SoftNet Systems Inc 415-365-2500
www.softnet.com
SONIC.Net 707-522-1000
www.sonic.net
Value Net Internetwork Services Inc 925-943-5769
www.value.net
Verio San Francisco 415-836-7400
home.verio.net/local/frontpage.cfm?AirportCode=SFO
Zocalo 510-540-8000
www.zocalo.net

Banks

Bank of America NT & SA Phone: 888-279-3264
555 California St Fax: 415-241-5080
San Francisco, CA 94104

Bank of Canton of California Phone: 415-362-4100
555 Montgomery St Fax: 415-989-0103
San Francisco, CA 94111 TF: 800-874-0297
E-mail: bankaton@bankcanton.com
www.bankcanton.com

Bank of San Francisco Phone: 415-781-7810
550 Montgomery St Fax: 415-781-0536
San Francisco, CA 94111 TF: 800-338-3965

Bank of the Orient Phone: 415-338-0668
233 Sansome St Fax: 415-398-8949
San Francisco, CA 94104

Bank of the West Phone: 415-765-4886
295 Bush St Fax: 415-781-3217
San Francisco, CA 94104 TF: 800-488-2265

California Federal Bank FSB Phone: 415-904-1100
135 Main St Fax: 415-904-0379
San Francisco, CA 94105 TF: 800-843-2265
www.calfed.com

Citibank FSB Phone: 415-981-3180
260 California St Fax: 415-291-0796
San Francisco, CA 94111

First Republic Bank Phone: 415-392-1400
101 Pine St Fax: 415-391-8060
San Francisco, CA 94111

Pacific Bank NA Phone: 415-576-2700
351 California St 3rd Fl Fax: 415-362-4549
San Francisco, CA 94104
E-mail: info@pacificbank.com
www.pacificbank.com

Redwood Bank Phone: 415-788-3700
735 Montgomery St Fax: 415-391-9090
San Francisco, CA 94111

Sanwa Bank California Phone: 415-597-5189
444 Market St Fax: 415-597-5494
San Francisco, CA 94111
www.sanwa-bank-ca.com

Sterling Bank & Trust FSB Phone: 415-658-2888
600 Montgomery St 40th Fl
San Francisco, CA 94111

Union Bank of California NA Phone: 415-765-3434
400 California St 1st Fl Fax: 415-705-7088
San Francisco, CA 94104

United Commercial Bank Phone: 415-928-0700
711 Van Ness Ave Fax: 415-771-7121
San Francisco, CA 94102
E-mail: info@unitedcb.com
www.unitedcb.com

Washington Mutual Bank FA Phone: 415-749-6535
1500 Polk St Fax: 415-749-6542
San Francisco, CA 94109

Wells Fargo Bank NA Phone: 415-396-3053
420 Montgomery St Fax: 415-975-7195
San Francisco, CA 94104
www.wellsfargo.com

Shopping

Anchorage Shopping Center Phone: 415-775-6000
2800 Leavenworth St Fax: 415-441-4209
San Francisco, CA 94133

Bayfair Mall Phone: 510-357-6000
248 Bay Fair Mall Fax: 510-276-5928
San Leandro, CA 94578

Cannery The Phone: 415-771-3112
2801 Leavenworth St Fax: 415-771-2424
San Francisco, CA 94133
www.thecannery.com

Crocker Galleria Phone: 415-393-1505
50 Post St Fax: 415-392-5429
San Francisco, CA 94104
E-mail: info@shopatgalleria.com
www.shopatgalleria.com

Eastmont Mall Phone: 510-632-1131
7200 Bancroft Ave Fax: 510-636-1727
Oakland, CA 94605

Embarcardero Center Phone: 415-772-0500
Market & Drum Sts 4 Embarcardero Ctr Fax: 415-982-1780
Suite 2600
San Francisco, CA 94111

Foothill Square Shopping Center Phone: 510-562-9500
10700 MacArthur Blvd
Oakland, CA 94605

Fremont Hub Phone: 510-792-1720
39261 Fremont Hub Fax: 510-792-2785
Fremont, CA 94538

Ghirardelli Square Phone: 415-775-5500
900 N Point St Suite 100 Fax: 415-775-0912
San Francisco, CA 94109
E-mail: ghsqmail@aol.com
www.ghirardellisq.com

Hillsdale Shopping Center Phone: 650-345-8222
60 Hillsdale Mall Fax: 650-573-5457
San Mateo, CA 94403

Hilltop Mall Phone: 510-223-6900
2200 Hilltop Mall Rd Fax: 510-223-1453
Richmond, CA 94806

Jack London Village Phone: 510-893-7956
30 Jack London Sq Fax: 510-893-0319
Oakland, CA 94607
www.jacklondonvillage.com

Neiman Marcus Phone: 415-362-3900
150 Stockton St Fax: 415-291-9616
San Francisco, CA 94108
www.neimanmarcus.com

Newpark Mall Phone: 510-794-5522
2086 Newpark Mall Fax: 510-796-7968
Newark, CA 94560

Nordstrom Phone: 415-243-8500
865 Market St Fax: 415-977-5089
San Francisco, CA 94103

Oakland City Center
14th St-betw Clay St & Broadway
Oakland, CA 94612
www.oaklandcitycenter.com

Rincon Center Phone: 415-777-4100
101 Spear St Suite 222 Fax: 415-777-1104
San Francisco, CA 94105

Saks Fifth Avenue Phone: 415-986-4300
384 Post St
San Francisco, CA 94108

San Francisco Shopping Center Phone: 415-512-6776
865 Market St Box A Fax: 415-512-6770
San Francisco, CA 94103
www.sanfranciscoshopping.com

Southland Mall Phone: 510-782-5050
1 Southland Mall Fax: 510-887-9619
Hayward, CA 94545

Stoneridge Mall Phone: 925-463-2778
1 Stoneridge Mall Fax: 925-463-1467
Pleasanton, CA 94588

Stonestown Galleria
3251 20th Ave
San Francisco, CA 94132
E-mail: info@stonestowngalleria.com
www.stonestowngalleria.com
Phone: 415-759-2623
Fax: 415-564-0148

Sunvalley Mall
1 Sunvalley Mall
Concord, CA 94520
Phone: 925-825-0400
Fax: 925-825-1392

Tanforan Park Shopping Center
301 Tanforan Pk
San Bruno, CA 94066
Phone: 650-873-2000
Fax: 650-873-4210

Trans Pacific Centre
1000 Broadway
Oakland, CA 94607
Phone: 510-839-7651

Media

Newspapers and Magazines

Argus The*
PO Box 28884
Oakland, CA 94604
www.newschoice.com/WebNews/Index/AngArFpg2i.asp
Phone: 510-661-2600
Fax: 510-353-7029
TF: 800-595-9595

Bay Area Press
PO Box 10151
Oakland, CA 94610
Phone: 510-428-2000

East Bay Express
931 Ashby Ave
Berkeley, CA 94710
E-mail: ebxpress@aol.com
Phone: 510-540-7400
Fax: 510-540-7700

Independent The
PO Box 1198
Livermore, CA 94551
E-mail: editmail@compuserve.com
www.independentnews.com
Phone: 925-447-8700
Fax: 925-447-0212

Montclarion The
5707 Redwood Rd Suite 10
Oakland, CA 94619
Phone: 510-339-8777
Fax: 510-339-4066

Nob Hill Gazette
5 3rd St Hearst Bldg Suite 222
San Francisco, CA 94103
E-mail: nobhillnews@nobhillgazette.com
www.nobhillgazette.com
Phone: 415-227-0190
Fax: 415-974-5103

Oakland Tribune*
PO Box 28884
Oakland, CA 94604
www.newschoice.com/newspapers/alameda/tribune
Phone: 510-208-6300
Fax: 510-208-6477
TF: 800-595-9595

San Francisco
243 Vallejo St
San Francisco, CA 94111
E-mail: letters@sanfran.com
www.sanfran.com
Phone: 415-398-2800
Fax: 415-398-6777

San Francisco Bay Guardian
520 Hampshire St
San Francisco, CA 94110
E-mail: guardian@sfbg.com
www.sfbayguardian.com
Phone: 415-255-3100
Fax: 415-255-8955

San Francisco Business Times Magazine
275 Battery St Suite 940
San Francisco, CA 94111
www.amcity.com/sanfrancisco
Phone: 415-989-2522
Fax: 415-398-2494

San Francisco Chronicle*
901 Mission St
San Francisco, CA 94103
E-mail: chronletters@sfgate.com
www.sfgate.com/chronicle
Phone: 415-777-7100
Fax: 415-896-1107

San Francisco Examiner*
110 5th St
San Francisco, CA 94103
E-mail: letters@examiner.com
www.examiner.com
Phone: 415-777-2424
Fax: 415-777-2525

San Francisco Independent
1201 Evans Ave
San Francisco, CA 94124
Phone: 415-826-1100
Fax: 415-826-5371

SF Weekly
185 Berry St Suite 3800
San Francisco, CA 94107
E-mail: letters@sfweekly.com
www.sfweekly.com
Phone: 415-541-0700
Fax: 415-541-9096

Sonoma County Independent
540 Mendocino Ave
Santa Rosa, CA 95401
www.metroactive.com/sonoma
Phone: 707-527-1200
Fax: 707-527-1288

Where San Francisco Magazine
74 New Montgomery St Suite 320
San Francisco, CA 94105
E-mail: wherenews@aol.com
www.wheremags.com/SanFrancisco.html
Phone: 415-546-6101
Fax: 415-546-6108

**Indicates major daily newspapers*

Television

KBHK-TV Ch 44 (UPN)
650 California St 7th Fl
San Francisco, CA 94108
E-mail: list@upn44.com
www.upn44.com
Phone: 415-249-4444
Fax: 415-397-2841

KBWB-TV Ch 20 (WB)
2500 Marin St
San Francisco, CA 94124
www.wb20.com
Phone: 415-821-2020
Fax: 415-641-1163

KCNS-TV Ch 38 (Ind)
1550 Bryant St Suite 748
San Francisco, CA 94103
Phone: 415-863-3800
Fax: 415-863-3998

KDTV-TV Ch 14 (Uni)
50 Freemont St 41st Fl
San Francisco, CA 94105
www.univision.net/stations/kdtv.htm
Phone: 415-641-1400
Fax: 415-538-8053

KFTY-TV Ch 50 (Ind)
533 Mendocino Ave
Santa Rosa, CA 95401
www.newschannel50.com
Phone: 707-526-5050
Fax: 707-526-7429

KFWU-TV Ch 8 (Ind)
303-B N Main St
Fort Bragg, CA 95437
Phone: 707-964-8888
Fax: 707-964-8150

KGO-TV Ch 7 (ABC)
900 Front St
San Francisco, CA 94111
Phone: 415-954-7777
Fax: 415-956-6402

KICU-TV Ch 36 (Ind)
2102 Commerce Dr
San Jose, CA 95131
www.kicu.com
Phone: 408-953-3636
Fax: 408-953-3630

KKPX-TV Ch 65 (Ind)
660 Price Ave Suite B
Redwood City, CA 94063
Phone: 650-369-6565
Fax: 650-369-4969

KNTV-TV Ch 11 (ABC)
645 Park Ave
San Jose, CA 95110
www.kntv.com
Phone: 408-286-1111
Fax: 408-286-1530

KPIX-TV Ch 5 (CBS)
855 Battery St
San Francisco, CA 94111
E-mail: tvprog@kpix.com
www.kpix.com
Phone: 415-362-5550
Fax: 415-765-8916

KQED-TV Ch 9 (PBS)
2601 Mariposa St
San Francisco, CA 94110
E-mail: tv@kqed.org
www.kqed.org/tv
Phone: 415-864-2000
Fax: 415-553-2241

KRON-TV Ch 4 (NBC)
1001 Van Ness Ave
San Francisco, CA 94109
www.kron.com
Phone: 415-441-4444
Fax: 415-561-8136

KSTS-TV Ch 48 (Tele)
2349 Bering Dr
San Jose, CA 95131
Phone: 408-435-8848
Fax: 408-433-5921

KTEH-TV Ch 54 (PBS)
1585 Schallenberger Rd
San Jose, CA 95130
www.kteh.org/
Phone: 408-795-5400
Fax: 408-995-5446

KTNC-TV Ch 42 (Ind)
5101 Port Chicago Hwy
Concord, CA 94520
Phone: 925-686-4242
Fax: 925-825-4242

KTSF-TV Ch 26 (Ind)
100 Valley Dr
Brisbane, CA 94005
E-mail: ktsf26@ktsf.com
www.ktsf.com
Phone: 415-468-2626
Fax: 415-467-7559

KTVU-TV Ch 2 (Fox)
2 Jack London Sq
Oakland, CA 94607
E-mail: ktvu@team.insider.com
www.bayinsider.com/partners/ktvu/index.html
Phone: 510-834-1212
Fax: 510-272-9957

Radio

KABL-AM 960 kHz (Nost)
340 Townsend St Suite 5101
San Francisco, CA 94107
E-mail: 960kabl@960kabl.com
www.960kabl.com
Phone: 415-977-0960
Fax: 415-278-0960

KALW-FM 91.7 MHz (NPR)
500 Mansell St
San Francisco, CA 94134
E-mail: kalwradio@aol.com
www.sfusd.k12.ca.us/programs/kalw/kalw.htm
Phone: 415-841-4121
Fax: 415-841-4125

KBAY-FM 94.5 MHz (AC)
190 Park Center Plaza Suite 200
San Jose, CA 95113
www.kbay.com
Phone: 408-287-5775
Fax: 408-293-3341

KBLX-FM 102.9 MHz (NAC)
55 Hawthorne St Suite 900
San Francisco, CA 94105
E-mail: info@kblxfm.com
www.kblxfm.com
Phone: 415-284-1029
Fax: 415-764-4959

KBRG-FM 100.3 MHz (Span)
655 Campbell Technology Pkwy Suite 200
Campbell, CA 95008
Phone: 408-540-5600
Fax: 408-540-5587

KCBS-AM 740 kHz (N/T)
1 Embarcadero Ctr 32nd Fl
San Francisco, CA 94111
E-mail: kcbs@kpix.com
www.kcbs.com
Phone: 415-765-4000
Fax: 415-765-4080

KCSM-FM 91.1 MHz (NPR)
1700 Hillsdale Blvd
San Mateo, CA 94402
www.kcsm.org
Phone: 650-574-6427
Fax: 650-574-6675

KDFC-FM 102.1 MHz (Clas)
455 Market St Suite 2300
San Francisco, CA 94105
www.kdfc.com
Phone: 415-764-1021
Fax: 650-777-2291

KFAX-AM 1100 kHz (N/T)
PO Box 8125
Fremont, CA 94537
www.kfax.com
Phone: 510-713-1100
Fax: 510-505-1448

KFFG-FM 97.7 MHz (AAA)
55 Hawthorne St Suite 1100
San Francisco, CA 94105
www.kfog.com
Phone: 415-543-1045
Fax: 415-995-6867

KFOG-FM 104.5 MHz (AAA)
55 Hawthorne St Suite 1100
San Francisco, CA 94105
E-mail: tweak@a.crl.com
www.kfog.com
Phone: 415-543-1045
Fax: 415-995-6867
TF: 800-367-8261

KFRC-AM 610 kHz (Oldies)
500 Washington St 2nd Fl
San Francisco, CA 94111
www.kfrc.com
Phone: 415-391-9970
Fax: 415-951-2329

KFRC-FM 99.7 MHz (Oldies)
500 Washington St 2nd Fl
San Francisco, CA 94111
www.kfrc.com
Phone: 415-391-9970
Fax: 415-951-2329

KGO-AM 810 kHz (N/T)
900 Front St
San Francisco, CA 94111
www.kgoam810.com
Phone: 415-954-7777
Fax: 415-362-5827

KIOI-AM 910 kHz (AC)
340 Townsend St Suite 5101
San Francisco, CA 94107
Phone: 415-538-1013
Fax: 415-538-1000
TF: 800-800-1013

KIOI-FM 101.3 MHz (AC)
340 Townsend St Suite 5101
San Francisco, CA 94107
www.k101radio.com
Phone: 415-977-0960
Fax: 415-278-0960
TF: 800-800-1013

KIQI-AM 1010 kHz (Span)
2601 Mission St
San Francisco, CA 94110
Phone: 415-695-1010
Fax: 415-695-1023

KISQ-FM 98.1 MHz (AC)
750 Battery St Suite 200
San Francisco, CA 94111
E-mail: kiss981@aol.com
www.981kissfm.com
Phone: 415-788-5225
Fax: 415-981-2930

KITS-FM 105.3 MHz (Alt)
730 Harrison St Suite 300
San Francisco, CA 94107
E-mail: live105@live105.com
www.live105.com
Phone: 415-512-1053
Fax: 415-777-0608

KKSF-FM 103.7 MHz (NAC)
340 Townsend St
San Francisco, CA 94107
E-mail: comments@kksf.com
www.kksf.com
Phone: 415-975-5555
Fax: 415-975-5573

KLLC-FM 97.3 MHz (AC)
1 Embarcadero Ctr 32nd Fl
San Francisco, CA 94111
www.radioalice.com
Phone: 415-765-4000
Fax: 415-765-4084

KMEL-FM 106.1 MHz (Urban)
340 Townsend St
San Francisco, CA 94107
www.106kmel.com
Phone: 415-538-1061
Fax: 415-538-1060

KMKY-AM 1310 kHz (Misc)
384 Embarcadero W 3rd Fl
Oakland, CA 94607
Phone: 510-251-1400
Fax: 510-251-2110

KNBR-AM 680 kHz (Sports)
55 Hawthorne St Suite 1100
San Francisco, CA 94105
www.knbr.com
Phone: 415-995-6800
Fax: 415-995-6867

KOHL-FM 89.3 MHz (CHR)
43600 Mission Blvd
Fremont, CA 94539
Phone: 510-659-6221
Fax: 510-659-6001

KOIT-AM 1260 kHz (AC)
455 Market St Suite 2300
San Francisco, CA 94105
Phone: 415-777-0965
Fax: 415-896-0965

KOIT-FM 96.5 MHz (AC)
2125 Hamilton Ave Suite 2300
San Francisco, CA 94105
www.koit.com
Phone: 415-777-0965
Fax: 415-896-0965

KQED-FM 88.5 MHz (NPR)
2601 Mariposa St
San Francisco, CA 94110
E-mail: sponsor@kqed.org
www.kqed.org
Phone: 415-553-2129
Fax: 415-553-2118

KSAN-FM 107.7 MHz (CR)
55 Hawthorne St Suite 1100
San Francisco, CA 94105
E-mail: ksanradio@aol.com
www.ksan.com
Phone: 415-981-5726
Fax: 415-995-6867
TF: 888-300-5726

KSFO-AM 560 kHz (N/T)
900 Front St
San Francisco, CA 94111
www.ksfo560.com
Phone: 415-954-7449
Fax: 415-658-5401

KSOL-FM 98.9 MHz (Span)
55 Green St Suite 200
San Francisco, CA 94111
www.ksol.com
Phone: 415-733-5765
Fax: 415-733-5766

KUFX-FM 98.5 MHz (CR)
1420 Koll Cir Suite A
San Jose, CA 95112
Phone: 408-452-7900
Fax: 408-452-8030

KYCY-FM 93.3 MHz (Ctry)
500 Washington St Suite 450
San Francisco, CA 94111
www.radioy93.com
Phone: 415-391-9330
Fax: 415-951-2325

KYLD-FM 94.9 MHz (CHR)
340 Townsend St Suite 4949
San Francisco, CA 94107
www.wild949.com
Phone: 415-356-0949
Fax: 415-267-0949

KZOL-FM 99.1 MHz (Span)
55 Green St Suite 200
San Francisco, CA 94111
www.ksol.com
Phone: 415-989-5765
Fax: 415-733-5766
TF: 800-880-5765

KZQZ-FM 95.7 MHz (CHR)
400 2nd St 3rd Fl
San Francisco, CA 94107
E-mail: zpromotions@kzqz.com
www.z957.com
Phone: 415-957-0957
Fax: 415-356-8394

Attractions

The "City by the Bay" is well-known for its cable cars, the Golden Gate Bridge, and Lombard Street, which is called the "crookedest street in the world." The area known as The Embarcadero is home to other familiar names like Fisherman's Wharf, The Cannery, and Ghirardelli Square, all known for their shopping and dining venues. San Francisco's 1,000-acre Golden Gate Park offers not only natural beauty but also a myriad of recreational opportunities, special events such as San Francisco A la Carte A la Park, and festivals throughout the year. The park is also the site of numerous attractions such as the Asian Art Museum, the California Academy of Sciences, the M.H. de Young Memorial Museum, the Strybing Arboretum and Botanical Gardens, and the Japanese Tea Garden. San Francisco's distinctive neighborhoods include Chinatown, the site of the huge Chinese New Year parade; Haight-Ashbury, a quaint Victorian sector and former mecca of 60s counterculture; and Nob Hill, which provides the best view of the San Francisco Bay. On the Bay is one of San Francisco's most popular attractions, the infamous Alcatraz, which draws more than 1.1 million visitors annually.

Located just across the bay from San Francisco, Oakland has the fourth busiest port in the U.S. Directly on the waterfront are the shops and restaurants of historic Jack London Square; and next to the convention center are the 16 Victorian homes of Preservation Park.

Acres of Orchids
914 S Claremont St
San Mateo, CA 94402
Phone: 650-373-3900
Fax: 650-373-3913

Alcatraz Island
Pier 41
San Francisco, CA 94133
www.blueandgoldfleet.com
Phone: 415-705-5555
Fax: 415-433-5402

Alexander F Morrison Planetarium
California Academy of Sciences-Golden Gate Pk
San Francisco, CA 94118
E-mail: planetarium@calacademy.org
www.calacademy.org/planetarium/
Phone: 415-221-5100
Fax: 415-750-7346

Alice Art Center
1428 Alice St
Oakland, CA 94612
Phone: 510-238-7221
Fax: 510-238-7225

American Conservatory Theater
30 Grant Ave 6th Fl
San Francisco, CA 94108
www.act-sfbay.org
Phone: 415-834-3200
Fax: 415-834-3360

Anchor Brewing Co
1705 Mariposa St
San Francisco, CA 94107
Phone: 415-863-8350
Fax: 415-552-7094

Ansel Adams Center for Photography
250 4th St
San Francisco, CA 94103
E-mail: click@photoarts.com
www.friendsofphotography.org
Phone: 415-495-7000
Fax: 415-495-8517

Ardenwood Historic Farm
34600 Ardenwood Blvd
Fremont, CA 94555
www.stanford.edu/~wellis/ardenwd
Phone: 510-796-0663

Asian Art Museum of San Francisco
Golden Gate Pk
San Francisco, CA 94118
E-mail: info@asianart.org
www.asianart.org
Phone: 415-379-8800
Fax: 415-668-8928

Bay Area Discovery Museum-Fort Baker
557 McReynolds Rd
Sausalito, CA 94965
E-mail: info@badm.org
www.badm.org
Phone: 415-487-4398
Fax: 415-332-9671

Berkeley Art Museum & Pacific Film Archive
2625 Durant Ave
Berkeley, CA 94720
www.uampfa.berkeley.edu
Phone: 510-642-0808
Fax: 510-642-4889

Best of Broadway
1182 Market St Suite 320
San Francisco, CA 94102
www.bestofbroadway-sf.com
Phone: 415-551-2050
Fax: 415-551-2045

California Academy of Sciences
Golden Gate Pk
San Francisco, CA 94118
www.calacademy.org/
Phone: 415-750-7145
Fax: 415-750-7346

California Palace of the Legion of Honor Museum
34th Ave & Clement St
San Francisco, CA 94121
www.thinker.org/legion
Phone: 415-750-3600

Camron-Stanford House
1418 Lakeside Dr
Oakland, CA 94612
Phone: 510-444-1876
Fax: 510-874-7803

Cannery The
2801 Leavenworth St
San Francisco, CA 94133
www.thecannery.com
Phone: 415-771-3112
Fax: 415-771-2424

Cartoon Art Museum
814 Mission St
San Francisco, CA 94103
E-mail: toonart@wenet.net
www.cartoonart.org
Phone: 415-227-8666
Fax: 415-243-8666

Center for African & African-American Art & Culture
762 Fulton St
San Francisco, CA 94102
www.caaac.org/2.0/
Phone: 415-928-8546
Fax: 415-928-8549

Center for the Arts at Yerba Buena Gardens
701 Mission St
San Francisco, CA 94103
E-mail: yerbabuena@aol.com
www.yerbabuenaarts.org
Phone: 415-978-2700
Fax: 415-978-9635

Chabot Observatory & Science Center
10000 Skyline Blvd
Oakland, CA 94619
www.cosc.org
Phone: 510-530-3480
Fax: 510-530-3499

Children's Fairyland Theme Park
699 Bellevue Ave
Oakland, CA 94610
www.fairyland.org
Phone: 510-452-2259

Chinatown (San Francisco)
667 Grant Ave
San Francisco, CA 94108
www.sfchinatown.com
Phone: 415-982-6306
Fax: 415-982-6306

Chinatown (Oakland)
Broadway & Alice Sts & 7th to 13th Sts
Oakland, CA 94607
Phone: 510-893-8979
Fax: 510-893-8988

Chinese Historical Society of America
644 Broadway
San Francisco, CA 94133
www.chsa.org
Phone: 415-391-1188
Fax: 415-391-1150

Classical Philharmonic
210 Post St Suite 2
San Francisco, CA 94108
E-mail: cponca@aol.com
Phone: 415-989-6873
Fax: 415-477-8669

Cliff House/Ocean Beach
1090 Point Lobos Ave
San Francisco, CA 94121
Phone: 415-386-1170

Coit Tower
1 Telegraph Hill Blvd
San Francisco, CA 94133
Phone: 415-362-0808
Fax: 415-434-1234

Crown Point Press
20 Hawthorne St
San Francisco, CA 94105
E-mail: gallery@crownpoint.com
www.crownpoint.com
Phone: 415-974-6273
Fax: 415-495-4220

Dunsmuir House & Gardens
2960 Peralta Oaks Ct
Oakland, CA 94605
Phone: 510-562-0328
Fax: 510-562-8294

Ebony Museum
30 Jack London Sq Suite 208
Oakland, CA 94607
Phone: 510-763-0745

Eugene O'Neill National Historic Site
PO Box 280
Danville, CA 94526
www.nps.gov/euon
Phone: 925-838-0249
Fax: 925-838-9471

EXIT Theatre
156 Eddy St
San Francisco, CA 94102
E-mail: mail@sffringe.org
www.sffringe.org
Phone: 415-931-1094
Fax: 415-931-2699

Exploratorium
3601 Lyon St
San Francisco, CA 94123
www.exploratorium.edu
Phone: 415-563-7337
Fax: 415-561-0307

Fisherman's Wharf
1873 Market St
San Francisco, CA 94103
Phone: 415-626-7070
Fax: 415-626-4651

Fort Mason Center
Buchanan St & Marina Blvd
San Francisco, CA 94123
E-mail: contact@fortmason.org
www.fortmason.org
Phone: 415-441-3400
Fax: 415-441-3405

Fort Point National Historic Site
PO Box 29333
Presidio of San Francisco, CA 94129
www.nps.gov/fopo/
Phone: 415-556-1693
Fax: 415-556-8474

Fremont Symphony Orchestra
43600 Mission Blvd Ohlone College
Smith Ctr for the Performing Arts
Fremont, CA 94539
E-mail: acutter@aol.com
www.infolane.com/fmt-symph/
Phone: 510-794-1652
Fax: 510-794-1658

Ghirardelli Square
900 N Point St Suite 100
San Francisco, CA 94109
E-mail: ghsqmail@aol.com
www.ghirardellisq.com
Phone: 415-775-5500
Fax: 415-775-0912

Golden Gate Bridge
PO Box 9000
Presidio Station, CA 94129
www.goldengate.org
Phone: 415-257-4563

Golden Gate National Recreation Area
Fort Mason Bldg 201
San Francisco, CA 94123
www.nps.gov/goga/
Phone: 415-556-0560
Fax: 415-561-4234

Golden Gate Park
501 Stanyan St
San Francisco, CA 94117
www.ci.sf.ca.us/recpark/
Phone: 415-831-2700
Fax: 415-668-3330

Goode Joe Performance Group
3221 22nd St
San Francisco, CA 94110
E-mail: joegoode@dnai.com
www.joegoode.org
Phone: 415-648-4848
Fax: 415-648-5401

Haas-Lilienthal House
2007 Franklin St
San Francisco, CA 94109
www.sfheritage.org/haashouse.html
Phone: 415-441-3004
Fax: 415-441-3015

Jack London Square
Broadway & Embarcadero
Oakland, CA 94607
www.jacklondonsquare.com
Phone: 510-814-6000
Fax: 510-208-5569

Japanese Tea Garden
Golden Gate Pk
San Francisco, CA 94117
Phone: 415-831-2700
Fax: 415-668-3330

Japantown
San Francisco, CA
Phone: 415-395-9353

Jenkins Margaret Dance Co
3973-A 25th St
San Francisco, CA 94114
E-mail: mjdcinc@aol.com
Phone: 415-826-8399
Fax: 415-826-8392

Jewish Museum San Francisco
121 Steuart St
San Francisco, CA 94105
www.jewishmuseumsf.org
Phone: 415-591-8800
Fax: 415-591-8815

Joaquin Miller Park
3590 Sanborn Dr
Oakland, CA 94602
Phone: 510-238-6888

John McLaren Park
University & Wayland Sts
San Francisco, CA 94117
Phone: 415-831-2700

Judah L Magnes Museum
2911 Russell St
Berkeley, CA 94705
www.jfed.org/magnes/magnes.htm
Phone: 510-849-2710
Fax: 510-849-3673

Lake Merced
1 Harding Rd
San Francisco, CA 94132
Phone: 415-681-3310

Lake Merritt Boating Center
568 Bellevue Ave
Oakland, CA 94610
Phone: 510-444-3807
Fax: 510-238-7199

Lakeside Park
1520 Lakeside Dr
Oakland, CA 94610
Phone: 510-238-3208

Lincoln Park
34th Ave & Clement St
San Francisco, CA 94121
Phone: 415-831-2700

LINES Contemporary Ballet
50 Oak St 4th Fl
San Francisco, CA 94102
Phone: 415-863-3040
Fax: 415-863-1180

Marines Memorial Theatre
609 Sutter St Suite 200
San Francisco, CA 94102
www.marinesmemorialtheatre.com
Phone: 415-441-7444
Fax: 415-776-9674

Merritt Museum of Anthropology
12500 Campus Dr
Oakland, CA 94619
Phone: 510-531-4911
Fax: 510-436-2405

METREON Sony Entertainment Center
101 4th St
San Francisco, CA 94103
E-mail: communityrelations@metreon.com
www.metreon.com
Phone: 415-369-6000
Fax: 415-537-3455
TF: 888-807-9426

Mexican Museum
Fort Mason Ctr Bldg D
San Francisco, CA 94123
www.folkart.com/~latitude/museums/m_mexsf.htm
Phone: 415-202-9700
Fax: 415-441-7683

MH de Young Memorial Museum
75 Tea Garden Dr Golden Gate Pk
San Francisco, CA 94118
www.thinker.org/deyoung
Phone: 415-750-3600
Fax: 415-750-7692

Mission Dolores
3321 16th St
San Francisco, CA 94114
Phone: 415-621-8204
Fax: 415-621-2294

Mission San Jose
43300 Mission Blvd
Fremont, CA 94539
Phone: 510-657-1797
Fax: 510-651-8332

Morcom Amphitheatre of Roses
700 Jean St
Oakland, CA 94610
Phone: 510-597-5039

Muir Woods National Monument
Mill Valley, CA 94941
www.nps.gov/muwo/
Phone: 415-388-2596
Fax: 415-389-6957

Museo Italo-Americano
Fort Mason Ctr Bldg C
San Francisco, CA 94123
Phone: 415-673-2200
Fax: 415-673-2292

Museum of Children's Art
538 9th St
Oakland, CA 94607
www.mocha.org
Phone: 510-465-8770
Fax: 510-465-0772

Museum of Craft & Folk Art
Fort Mason Ctr Bldg A
San Francisco, CA 94123
www.sfcraftandfolk.org
Phone: 415-775-0990
Fax: 415-775-1861

Museum of Local History
190 Anza St
Fremont, CA 94539
Phone: 510-623-7907

Museum of the City of San Francisco
2801 Leavenworth St The Cannery 3rd Fl
San Francisco, CA 94133
www.sfmuseum.org
Phone: 415-928-0289
Fax: 415-928-6243

Napa Valley Wine Train
1275 McKinstry St
Napa, CA 94559
www.winetrain.com
Phone: 707-253-2111
Fax: 707-253-9264
TF: 800-427-4124

Niles Canyon Railway Museum
5550 Niles Canyon Rd
Sunol, CA 94586
ncry.org
Phone: 925-862-9063

Niles Depot
36997 Mission Blvd
Fremont, CA 94536
Phone: 510-797-4449

Niles Main St Assoc
37501 B Niles Blvd
Fremont, CA 94536
www.niles.org
Phone: 510-742-9868
Fax: 510-742-8525

Oakland Asian Cultural Center
388 9th St Suite 290
Oakland, CA 94607
www.asianculture.org
Phone: 510-208-6080
Fax: 510-208-6084

Oakland Ballet
1428 Alice St
Oakland, CA 94612
E-mail: oakballet@aol.com
www.oaklandballet.org
Phone: 510-452-9288
Fax: 510-452-9557

Oakland Chamber Orchestra
100 Redwood Rd
Oakland, CA 94619
Phone: 510-533-6145
Fax: 510-533-7670

Oakland East Bay Symphony
2025 Broadway Oakland Paramount Theater
Oakland, CA 94612
E-mail: admin@oebs.org
www.oebs.org
Phone: 510-444-0801
Fax: 510-444-0863

Oakland Lyric Opera
PO Box 20709
Oakland, CA 94612
E-mail: oaklandlyricopera@juno.com
Phone: 510-836-6772
Fax: 510-836-6774

Oakland Museum of California
1000 Oak St
Oakland, CA 94607
www.museumca.org
Phone: 510-238-2200
Fax: 510-238-2258
TF: 888-625-6873

Oakland Museum Sculpture Court
1111 Broadway City Center
Oakland, CA 94607
Phone: 510-238-3401
Fax: 510-238-2258

Oakland Youth Orchestra
1428 Alice St Suite 202M
Oakland, CA 94612
www.best.com/~coles/oyo/oyo.shtml
Phone: 510-832-7710

Oakland Zoo
9777 Golf Links Rd
Oakland, CA 94605
www.oaklandzoo.org
Phone: 510-632-9525
Fax: 510-635-5719

Palace of Fine Arts
3301 Lyon St
San Francisco, CA 94123
Phone: 415-567-6642
Fax: 415-567-4062

Paramount Theatre
2025 Broadway
Oakland, CA 94612
Phone: 510-465-6400
Fax: 510-893-5098

Paramount's Great America
PO Box 1776
Santa Clara, CA 95052
www.pgathrills.com
Phone: 408-988-1776
Fax: 408-986-5855

Pardee Home Museum
672 11th St
Oakland, CA 94607
www.pardeehome.org
Phone: 510-444-2187
Fax: 510-444-7120

Philharmonia Baroque Orchestra
180 Redwood St Suite 200
San Francisco, CA 94105
E-mail: info@philharmonia.org
www.philharmonia.org
Phone: 415-252-1288
Fax: 415-252-1488

Pier 39
Beach & Embarcadero Sts
San Francisco, CA 94119
E-mail: info@pier39.com
www.pier39.com
Phone: 415-981-7437
Fax: 415-981-8808
TF: 800-325-7437

Point Reyes National Seashore
Point Reyes, CA 94956
www.nps.gov/pore/
Phone: 415-663-8522

Port of Oakland Oakland Board of Port Commissioners
530 Water St
Oakland, CA 94607
www.portofoakland.com
Phone: 510-272-1100
Fax: 510-839-5104

Preservation Park
13th St & ML King Jr Way
Oakland, CA 94607
Phone: 510-874-7580

Randall Museum
199 Museum Way
San Francisco, CA 94114
www.wco.com/~dale/randall.html
Phone: 415-554-9604
Fax: 415-554-9609

Ripley's Believe It or Not! Museum
175 Jefferson St
San Francisco, CA 94133
E-mail: sanfran@ripleys.com
www.ripleysf.com
Phone: 415-771-6188
Fax: 415-771-1246

Rotary Nature Center
552 Bellevue Ave
Oakland, CA 94610
Phone: 510-238-3739

Safari West
3115 Porter Creek Rd
Santa Rosa, CA 95404
E-mail: langcos@wco.com
www.wco.com/~langcos
Phone: 707-579-2551
Fax: 707-579-8777

San Francisco Ballet Assn
455 Franklin St
San Francisco, CA 94102
E-mail: sfbmktg@sfballet.org
www.sfballet.org
Phone: 415-861-5600
Fax: 415-861-2684

San Francisco Fire Department Museum
655 Presidio Ave
San Francisco, CA 94115
Phone: 415-558-3546

San Francisco Maritime National Historical Park
Fort Mason Bldg E Rm 265
San Francisco, CA 94123
www.nps.gov/safr
Phone: 415-556-1659
Fax: 415-556-1624

San Francisco Museum of Modern Art
151 3rd St
San Francisco, CA 94103
www.sfmoma.org
Phone: 415-357-4000
Fax: 415-357-4037

San Francisco Opera Assn
301 Van Ness Ave
San Francisco, CA 94102
E-mail: editor@www.sfopera.com
www.sfopera.com
Phone: 415-861-4008
Fax: 415-621-7508

San Francisco Performing Arts Library & Museum
401 Van Ness Ave 4th Fl
San Francisco, CA 94102
E-mail: info@sfpalm.org
www.sfpalm.org
Phone: 415-255-4800
Fax: 415-255-1913

San Francisco Symphony
201 Van Ness Ave Davies Symphony Hall
San Francisco, CA 94102
E-mail: messages@sfsymphony.org
www.sfsymphony.org
Phone: 415-552-8000
Fax: 415-431-6857

San Francisco War Memorial & Performing Arts Center
401 Van Ness Ave Suite 110
San Francisco, CA 94102
Phone: 415-621-6600
Fax: 415-621-5091

San Francisco Zoological Gardens
1 Zoo Rd
San Francisco, CA 94132
www.sfzoo.com
Phone: 415-753-7080
Fax: 415-681-2039

Sausalito Information
780 Bridgeway
Sausalito, CA 94965
Phone: 415-332-0505

Savage Jazz Dance Co
530 E 8th St Suite 202
Oakland, CA 94606
members.xoom.com/savagejazz
Phone: 415-865-0213

Six Flags Marine World
2001 Marine World Pkwy
Vallejo, CA 94589
www.sixflags.com/marineworld
Phone: 707-644-4000
Fax: 707-644-0241

SS Jeremiah O'Brien
Fort Mason Ctr Bldg A
San Francisco, CA 94123
www.crl.com/~wefald/obrien.html
Phone: 415-441-3101
Fax: 415-441-3712

Steinhart Aquarium
California Academy of Sciences Golden Gate Pk
San Francisco, CA 94118
www.calacademy.org/aquarium/
Phone: 415-750-7247
Fax: 415-750-7269

Strybing Arboretum & Botanical Gardens
9th Ave & Lincoln Way
San Francisco, CA 94122
www.strybing.org
Phone: 415-753-7089
Fax: 415-661-7427

Sunday Music in the Courtyard
30 Jack London Sq
Oakland, CA 94607
Phone: 510-893-7956

Underwater World Aquarium
Pier 39
San Francisco, CA 94133
www.underwaterworld.com/
Phone: 415-623-5300
Fax: 415-623-5324
TF: 800-623-5300

USS Pampanito
Pier 45
San Francisco, CA 94133
E-mail: info@maritime.org
www.maritime.org/pamphome.shtml
Phone: 415-775-1943
Fax: 415-441-0365

USS Potomac
540 Water St Jack London Sq
Oakland, CA 94604
E-mail: usspotomac@aol.com
Phone: 510-271-8093
Fax: 510-839-4729

Wax Museum at Fisherman's Wharf
145 Jefferson St
San Francisco, CA 94133
E-mail: sales@waxmuseum.com
www.waxmuseum.com
Phone: 415-885-4834
Fax: 415-771-9248

Wells Fargo History Museum
420 Montgomery St
San Francisco, CA 94163
Phone: 415-396-2619
Fax: 415-391-8644

Western Aerospace Museum
Oakland International Airport North Field 8260 Boeing St Bldg 621
Oakland, CA 94614
www.crl.com/~michaelp/wam.html
Phone: 510-638-7100
Fax: 510-638-6530

Sports Teams & Facilities

3Com Park at Candlestick Point
Jamestown Ave & Harney Way
San Francisco, CA 94124
www.3com.com/3compark
Phone: 415-467-1994
Fax: 415-467-3049

Golden State Warriors
66th Ave & Hegenberger Rd Oakland Coliseum Arena
Oakland, CA 94621
www.nba.com/warriors
Phone: 510-762-2277

Network Assoc Coliseum
7000 Coliseum Way
Oakland, CA 94621
E-mail: skoss@netcom.com
Phone: 510-569-2121
Fax: 510-569-4246

Oakland Athletics
7000 Coliseum Way Network Assoc Coliseum
Oakland, CA 94621
E-mail: info@oaklandathletics.com
www.oaklandathletics.com
Phone: 510-638-0500

Oakland Raiders
7000 Coliseum Way Network Assoc Coliseum
Oakland, CA 94621
www.raiders.com
Phone: 510-569-2121
Fax: 510-569-4246

San Francisco 49ers
Jamestown & Harney 3Com Pk at Candlestick Pt
San Francisco, CA 94124
www.sf49ers.com
Phone: 415-468-2249
Fax: 415-467-9259

San Francisco Bay Seals (soccer)
25800 Carlos Bee Blvd Pioneer Stadium
Hayward, CA 94542
E-mail: seals@bayareaseals.com
www.bayareaseals.com
Phone: 510-881-7392
Fax: 510-881-7397

San Francisco Giants
24 Willie Mays Plaza Pacific Bell Pk
San Francisco, CA 94102
www.sfgiants.com
Phone: 415-468-3700

Annual Events

Arts of the Pacific Asian Show (mid-February) 310-455-2886
Black Cowboys Parade & Heritage Festival (early October) 510-238-7275
Boo in the Zoo (late October) 510-632-9525
Bouquets to Art (mid-late March) 415-750-3504
California International Dragon Boat Festival (late August) 510-452-4272
Carijama Oakland Carnival (late May) 510-535-2450
Carnaval (late May) 415-826-1401
Charlie Chaplin Days (early June) 510-742-9868
Cherry Blossom Festival (mid-April) 415-563-2313
Chinatown StreetFest (late August) 510-893-8979
Chinese New Year Celebration (late January) 415-974-6900
Christmas at Dunsmuir (December) 510-615-5555
Cinco de Mayo (early May) 510-869-3933
Cinco de Mayo Celebrations (early May) 415-826-1401
Contemporary Crafts Market (mid-March & early November) 415-995-4925
Dickens Holiday Fair (mid-December) 510-893-7956
Essence Music Festival (early July) 415-249-4625
Ethnic Dance Festival (mid-late June) 415-974-6900
Festival of Greece (mid-May) 510-531-3400
Festival of the Arts (late July) 510-795-2244
Festival of the Culinary Arts (mid-September) 800-229-2433
Fleet Week (mid-October) 415-705-5500
Folsom Street Festival (late September) 415-974-6900
Fourth of July Waterfront Festival (July 4) 415-777-7120
Fremont Family Carnival (mid-May) 510-494-4858
Ghirardelli Square Chocolate Festival (early-mid-September) 415-775-5500
Great Halloween & Pumpkin Festival (mid-October) 415-249-4625
Halloween on the Square (late October) 510-814-6000
Home & Garden Show (early May) 800-222-9351
International Asian-American Film Festival (early-mid-March) 415-863-0814
Italian Fiesta (mid-September) 510-814-6000
Juneteenth Celebration (mid-June) 510-632-9525
Las Americas (mid-September) 415-705-5500
Lighted Yacht Parade & Santa Parade (early December) 510-627-1640
Macy's Flower Show (mid-late April) 415-393-3724
Midsummer Mozart Festival (late July-mid-August) 415-954-0850
Mission Days (mid-June) 510-657-1797

Newark's Music at the Grove Summer Concert Series (early July-mid-August) 510-745-1124
Nihonmachi Street Fair (early August). 415-771-9861
Niles Antique Faire (late August). 510-742-9868
Niles Holiday Open House & Tree Lighting Ceremony (late November-late December). 510-742-9868
Niles Wildflower & Art Festival (early May) 510-742-9868
North Beach Festival (mid-June) 415-989-6426
Norway Day Festival (early May) 925-676-4708
Oakland Fourth of July Celebration (July 4) 510-814-6000
Oakland Jazzthere Festival (late July). 510-553-1293
Oakland Tree Lighting Ceremony (late November) 510-814-6000
Pacific Orchid Exposition (late February) 415-546-9608
Pacific Power Expo (early May) 510-452-6262
Pacific Sail Expo (late April). 800-817-7245
Potomac Public Cruise (mid-March-early November). 510-627-1215
Saint Patrick's Day Parade (mid-March) 415-661-2700
San Francisco Blues Festival (mid-September) 415-979-5588
San Francisco Examiner Bay to Breakers (mid-May) 415-777-7770
San Francisco Fall Antiques Show (late October) 415-546-6661
San Francisco Fringe Theater Festival (early-mid-September) 415-673-3847
San Francisco Garden Show (mid-March) 800-829-9751
San Francisco International Film Festival (late April-early May) 415-931-3456
San Francisco International Lesbian & Gay Film Festival (mid-late June) 415-703-8663
San Francisco Jazz Festival (late October-early November) 415-398-5655
San Francisco Jewish Film Festival (late July-early August). 415-621-0556
San Francisco Shakespeare Festival (July-early October). 415-422-2222
Scottish Highland Games (early July). 510-615-5555
Silver Star Pow Wow & Indian Market (mid-June) 415-554-0525
Sports & Boat Show (mid-January). 415-469-6065
Spring Boat Show (mid-April) .510-452-6262
Stern Grove Midsummer Music Festival (mid-June-mid-August). 415-252-6252
Stitches Fair & Market (late March) 800-237-7099
Street Performers Festival (early June) 415-705-5500
Summer Evening Concerts (mid-July-late August) 510-791-4340
Summer Jazz Series at Embracadero Center (mid-August-late September). 800-733-6318
Traditional Music & Dance Festival (mid-May). 415-771-3112
ZooLights at the Oakland Zoo (late November-early January) 510-632-9525
À la Carte à la Park (late August-early September). 415-383-9378

San Jose, California

***County:* Santa Clara**

SAN JOSE is located in northern California at the southern end of San Francisco Bay. Major cities within 100 miles include San Francisco, Oakland, Fremont, Monterey, Stockton, and Modesto, California.

Area (Land)	171.3 sq mi
Area (Water)	3.3 sq mi
Elevation	87 ft
Latitude	37-33-53 N
Longitude	121-89-39 W
Time Zone	PST
Area Code	408

Climate

San Jose has a temperate climate that features mild temperatures much of the year. Winter high temperatures average near 60 degrees, with lows in the low 40s. Summer days are warm, with highs near 80, while evenings cool down into the upper 50s. Winter is the rainy season in San Jose, with January being the wettest month, while summers tend to be dry. The city also averages 300 sunny days annually.

Average Temperatures & Precipitation

Temperatures

	Jan	Feb	Mar	Apr	May	Jun	Jul	Aug	Sep	Oct	Nov	Dec
High	58	63	65	70	75	80	82	82	81	75	64	58
Low	41	44	45	47	51	55	57	57	56	52	46	41

Precipitation

	Jan	Feb	Mar	Apr	May	Jun	Jul	Aug	Sep	Oct	Nov	Dec
Inches	2.8	2.2	2.6	1.2	0.3	0.1	0.1	0.1	0.2	0.9	2.1	2.0

History

Founded by Spaniards in November 1777 as the "Pueblo de San Jose de Guadelupe," San Jose was originally an agricultural supply center for the Presidios of San Francisco and Monterey. Incorporated in 1850, the city served as the first capital of the State of California from 1849 until 1851, when the capital was moved to Vallejo. San Jose's rich agricultural base fueled the city's early economy, earning San Jose the nickname the "Garden City." Agriculture remained important well into the 20th Century, as food processing and agricultural equipment manufacturing became important industries in San Jose.

The high-technology industry that San Jose is famous for today actually began during the early part of the century, as scientists and scholars at nearby Stanford University made technological advances that eventually led to the invention of the integrated circuit, semiconductors, and computers. These pioneers in high-technology encouraged their students to open companies in the area after graduation. The rapid development of "Silicon Valley" during the 1960s and 70s has led to a population explosion—San Jose's population soared from 95,000 in 1950 to nearly 860,000 in 1998, making the city the third largest in California and the 11th largest in the United States. Today, San Jose is considered the capital of Silicon Valley. The area encompasses a large portion of Santa Clara County, as well as parts of San Mateo and Alameda counties, and is home to more than 4,000 high technology companies, including such leaders as Hewlett-Packard, Apple Computer, and Lockheed.

Population

1990 Census	782,224
1998 Estimate	861,284
% Change	10.4
2005 Projection	1,876,700*

Racial/Ethnic Breakdown

White	63.0%
Black	4.7%
Other	32.3%
Hispanic Origin (may be of any race)	26.6%

Age Breakdown

18 to 24 years	10.5%
25 to 34	19.3%
35 to 49	24.1%
50+ years	18.7%
Median Age	31.3

Gender Breakdown

Male	50.7%
Female	49.3%

* *Information given is for Santa Clara County.*

Government

Type of Government: Mayor-City Council

San Jose City Clerk
801 N 1st St Rm 116
San Jose, CA 95110
Phone: 408-277-4424
Fax: 408-277-3285

San Jose City Council
801 N 1st St Rm 600
San Jose, CA 95110
Phone: 408-277-4241
Fax: 408-277-3868

San Jose City Hall
801 N 1st St
San Jose, CA 95110
Phone: 408-277-5722
Fax: 408-277-3131

San Jose City Manager
801 N 1st St Rm 436
San Jose, CA 95110
Phone: 408-277-5777
Fax: 408-277-3131

San Jose Economic Development Office
50 W San Fernando Suite 900
San Jose, CA 95113
Phone: 408-277-5880
Fax: 408-277-3615

San Jose Finance Dept
801 N 1st St Rm 110
San Jose, CA 95110
Phone: 408-277-4288
Fax: 408-277-5405

San Jose Fire Dept
4 N 2nd St Suite 1100
San Jose, CA 95113
Phone: 408-277-4444
Fax: 408-277-3259

San Jose Human Resources Dept
801 N 1st St Rm 207
San Jose, CA 95110
Phone: 408-277-4205
Fax: 408-277-3134

San Jose Mayor
801 N 1st St Rm 600
San Jose, CA 95110
Phone: 408-277-4237
Fax: 408-277-3868

San Jose Municipal Water System
3025 Tuers Rd
San Jose, CA 95121
Phone: 408-277-4218
Fax: 408-277-4954

San Jose Parks Recreation & Neighborhood Services Dept
4 N 2nd St Suite 600
San Jose, CA 95113
Phone: 408-277-4661
Fax: 408-277-3155

San Jose Planning Div
801 N 1st St Rm 400
San Jose, CA 95110
Phone: 408-277-4576
Fax: 408-277-3250

San Jose Police Dept
201 W Mission St
San Jose, CA 95110
Phone: 408-277-4214
Fax: 408-277-5771

San Jose Public Library
180 W San Carlos St
San Jose, CA 95113
Phone: 408-277-4822
Fax: 408-277-3187

San Jose Public Works Dept
801 N 1st St Rm 320
San Jose, CA 95110
Phone: 408-277-4333
Fax: 408-277-3156

Important Phone Numbers

AAA....408-985-9300
American Express Travel....408-244-1015
California State Franchise Tax Board....916-845-4300
Dental Referral....800-917-6453
Driver's License/Vehicle Registration Information....408-341-1350
Emergency....911
HotelDocs....800-468-3537
Medical Referral....408-866-4098
Road Conditions....800-427-7623
San Jose.Phone....408-295-2265
Santa Clara County Assn of Realtors....408-445-8595
Santa Clara County Tax Assessor....408-299-3227
Santa Clara County Tax Collector....408-299-2241
Time....831-767-8900
Voter Registration Information....408-299-8302
Weather....831-656-1725

Information Sources

Better Business Bureau Serving the Santa Clara Valley
2100 Forest Ave Suite 110
San Jose, CA 95128
www.sanjose.bbb.org
Phone: 408-278-7400
Fax: 408-278-7444

San Jose Convention & Visitors Bureau
333 W San Carlos St Suite 100
San Jose, CA 95110
www.sanjose.org
Phone: 408-977-0900
Fax: 408-977-0901
TF: 888-726-5673

San Jose McEnery Convention Center
150 W San Carlos St
San Jose, CA 95113
www.sjcc.com/sjmcc
Phone: 408-277-3900
Fax: 408-277-3535
TF: 800-533-2345

San Jose Silicon Valley Chamber of Commerce
310 S 1st St
San Jose, CA 95113
www.sjchamber.com
Phone: 408-291-5250
Fax: 408-286-5019

Santa Clara County
70 W Hedding St
San Jose, CA 95110
claraweb.co.santa-clara.ca.us
Phone: 408-299-2424
Fax: 408-293-5649

Online Resources

4SanJose.com
www.4sanjose.com

About.com Guide to Silicon Valley
siliconvalley.about.com/citiestowns/caus/siliconvalley/mbody.htm

Anthill City Guide San Jose
www.anthill.com/city.asp?city=sanjose

Area Guide San Jose
sanjose.areaguides.net

BayArea.com
www.bayarea.com

Boulevards San Jose
www.sanjose.com

City Knowledge San Jose
www.cityknowledge.com/ca_sanjose.htm

CitySearch San Jose
sanjose.citysearch.com

Excite.com San Jose City Guide
www.excite.com/travel/countries/united_states/california/san_jose

MetroActive Publishing Inc
www.metroactive.com

San Jose California
san-jose-california.com

San Jose Living
www.sjliving.com/

Savvy Diner Guide to San Jose Restaurants
www.savvydiner.com/sanjose/

Area Communities

Other communities in Santa Clara County with populations greater than 5,000 include:

Campbell — Phone: 408-866-2125, Fax: 408-374-6889
70 N 1st St
Campbell, CA 95008

Cupertino — Phone: 408-777-3200, Fax: 408-777-3333
10300 Torre Ave
Cupertino, CA 95014

Gilroy — Phone: 408-848-0420, Fax: 408-842-2409
7351 Rosanna St
Gilroy, CA 95020

Los Altos — Phone: 650-948-1491, Fax: 650-941-7419
1 N San Antonio Rd
Los Altos, CA 94022

Los Gatos — Phone: 408-354-6832, Fax: 408-354-8431
PO Box 949
Los Gatos, CA 95031

Milpitas — Phone: 408-586-3002, Fax: 408-586-3056
455 E Calaveras Blvd
Milpitas, CA 95035

Morgan Hill — Phone: 408-779-7259, Fax: 408-779-3117
17555 Peak Ave
Morgan Hill, CA 95037

Mountain View — Phone: 650-903-6300, Fax: 650-903-6039
500 Castro St
Mountain View, CA 94041

Palo Alto — Phone: 650-329-2311, Fax: 650-328-3631
250 Hamilton Ave
Palo Alto, CA 94301

Santa Clara — Phone: 408-984-3250, Fax: 408-241-6771
1500 Warburton Ave
Santa Clara, CA 95050

Saratoga — Phone: 408-868-1200, Fax: 408-868-1280
13777 Fruitvale Ave
Saratoga, CA 95070

Sunnyvale — Phone: 408-730-7500, Fax: 408-730-7699
456 W Olive Ave
Sunnyvale, CA 94086

Economy

The "Capital of Silicon Valley," San Jose is the nucleus of the nation's leading center for technology. San Jose/Silicon Valley and the San Francisco Bay area ranked at the top of Fortune's 1995 list of "Best Cities for Business." The San Jose Metropolitan Area is now home to over 11,400 high-tech companies employing over 250,000 people. Fortune 500 companies that call Santa Clara County home include Hewlett-Packard, Intel, Apple Computer, and Sun Microsystems. Business services and retail trade are also important to San Jose's economy—the metro area ranked first in California for retail sales per household in 1994.

Unemployment Rate 2.7%*
Per Capita Income $40,828
Median Family Income $50,281

** Information given is for Santa Clara County.*

Principal Industries & Number of Wage Earners

San Jose MSA (Santa Clara County) - June 2000

Industry	Wage Earners
Construction	50,100
Farm	5,100
Finance, Insurance, & Real Estate	33,300
Government	97,000
Manufacturing	245,500
Mining	100
Retail Trade	137,000
Services	344,200
Transportation & Public Utilities	29,400
Wholesale Trade	56,600

Major Employers

Adobe Systems Inc — Phone: 408-536-6000, Fax: 408-537-6000, TF: 800-833-6687
345 Park Ave
San Jose, CA 95110
E-mail: info@adobe.com
www.adobe.com

Apple Computer Inc — Phone: 408-996-1010, Fax: 408-996-0275, TF: 800-767-2775
1 Infinite Loop
Cupertino, CA 95014
www.apple.com

Applied Materials Inc — Phone: 408-727-5555, Fax: 408-986-7940
3050 Bowers Ave
Santa Clara, CA 95054
www.appliedmaterials.com

Cisco Systems Inc — Phone: 408-526-4000, Fax: 408-526-4100, TF: 800-553-6387
170 W Tasman Dr
San Jose, CA 95134
www.cisco.com

Hewlett-Packard Co — Phone: 650-857-1501, Fax: 650-857-5518, TF: 800-322-4772
3000 Hanover St
Palo Alto, CA 94304
www.hp.com

Intel Corp — Phone: 408-765-8080, Fax: 408-765-1402, TF: 800-628-8686
2200 Mission College Blvd
Santa Clara, CA 95052
www.intel.com

Kaiser Permanente Medical Center — Phone: 408-236-6400, Fax: 408-236-4408
900 Kiely Blvd
Santa Clara, CA 95051
www.kaisersantaclara.org

Lockheed Martin Space Systems Co
Missiles & Space Operations — Phone: 408-742-4321, Fax: 408-743-2239
1111 Lockheed Martin Way
Sunnyvale, CA 94089
lmms.external.lmco.com

National Semiconductor Corp — Phone: 408-721-5000, Fax: 408-732-4880
2900 Semiconductor Dr
Santa Clara, CA 95051
www.national.com

San Jose City Hall
801 N 1st St
San Jose, CA 95110
www.ci.san-jose.ca.us
Phone: 408-277-5722
Fax: 408-277-3131

San Jose State University
1 Washington Sq
San Jose, CA 95199
www.sjsu.edu
Phone: 408-924-1000
Fax: 408-924-2050

San Jose Unified School District
855 Lenzen Ave MC 82
San Jose, CA 95126
www.sjusd.k12.ca.us
Phone: 408-535-6000
Fax: 408-535-2362

Santa Clara County
70 W Hedding St
San Jose, CA 95110
claraweb.co.santa-clara.ca.us
Phone: 408-299-2424
Fax: 408-293-5649

Santa Clara Valley Health & Hospital System
751 S Bascom Ave
San Jose, CA 95128
Phone: 408-885-5000
Fax: 408-885-6459

Silicon Graphics Inc
1600 Amphitheatre Pkwy
Mountain View, CA 94043
E-mail: ir@corp.sgi.com
www.sgi.com
Phone: 650-960-1980
Fax: 650-933-0316

Stanford University
Stanford, CA 94305
www.stanford.edu
Phone: 650-723-2300
Fax: 650-723-6050

Stanford University Hospital
300 Pasteur Dr
Stanford, CA 94305
www-med.stanford.edu/shs
Phone: 650-723-2300
Fax: 650-723-8163

Sun Microsystems Inc
901 San Antonio Rd
Palo Alto, CA 94303
www.sun.com
Phone: 650-960-1300
Fax: 650-786-3530
TF: 800-786-7638

Xilinx Inc
2100 Logic Dr
San Jose, CA 95124
www.xilinx.com
Phone: 408-559-7778
Fax: 408-559-7114
TF: 800-494-5469

Quality of Living Indicators

Total Crime Index....................................30,382
(rates per 100,000 inhabitants)

Violent Crime
Murder/manslaughter........................... 29
Forcible rape 357
Robbery....................................... 901
Aggravated assault...........................3,868

Property Crime
Burglary 4,129
Larceny theft 17,925
Motor vehicle theft 3,173

Cost of Living Index....................................176.0
(national average = 100)

Median Home Price.................................$404,800

Education

Public Schools

San Jose Unified School District
855 Lenzen Ave MC 82
San Jose, CA 95126
www.sjusd.k12.ca.us
Phone: 408-535-6000
Fax: 408-535-2362

Number of Schools
Elementary 29
Middle 7
High.. 7

Student/Teacher Ratio
All Grades 24.5:1

Private Schools

Number of Schools (all grades) .... 67+

Colleges & Universities

Cogswell Polytechnical College
1175 Bordeaux Dr
Sunnyvale, CA 94089
E-mail: info@gateway.cogswell.edu
www.cogswell.edu
Phone: 408-541-0100
Fax: 408-747-0764
TF: 800-264-7955

DeAnza College
21250 Stevens Creek Blvd
Cupertino, CA 95014
E-mail: deanzainfo@fhda.edu
www.deanza.fhda.edu
Phone: 408-864-8419
Fax: 408-864-8329

Evergreen Valley College
3095 Yerba Buena Rd
San Jose, CA 95135
E-mail: evcinfo@unix.sjeccd.cc.ca.us
www.evc.edu
Phone: 408-274-7900
Fax: 408-223-9351

Foothill College
12345 El Monte Rd
Los Altos Hills, CA 94022
www.foothill.fhda.edu
Phone: 650-949-7777
Fax: 650-949-7048

Heald Institute of Technology
341-A Great Mall Pkwy
Milpitas, CA 95035
www.heald.edu
Phone: 408-934-4900
Fax: 408-934-7777
TF: 800-967-7576

Mission College
3000 Mission College Blvd
Santa Clara, CA 95054
www.wvmccd.cc.ca.us/mc/
Phone: 408-988-2200
Fax: 408-980-8980

National Hispanic University
14271 Story Rd
San Jose, CA 95127
E-mail: info@nhu.edu
www.nhu.edu
Phone: 408-254-6900
Fax: 408-254-1369

San Jose Christian College
790 S 12th St
San Jose, CA 95112
E-mail: sjcc1939@aol.com
www.sjchristiancol.edu
Phone: 408-293-9058
Fax: 408-293-7352
TF: 800-355-7522

San Jose City College
2100 Moorpark Ave
San Jose, CA 95128
www.sjcc.cc.ca.us
Phone: 408-298-2181
Fax: 408-298-1935

San Jose State University
1 Washington Sq
San Jose, CA 95199
www.sjsu.edu
Phone: 408-924-1000
Fax: 408-924-2050

Santa Clara University
500 El Camino Real
Santa Clara, CA 95053
E-mail: ugadmissions@scu.edu
www.scu.edu
Phone: 408-554-4764
Fax: 408-554-5255

Hospitals

Community Hospital of Los Gatos
815 Pollard Rd
Los Gatos, CA 95032
www.tenethealth.com/LosGatos
Phone: 408-378-6131
Fax: 408-866-3898

Good Samaritan Hospital
2425 Samaritan Dr
San Jose, CA 95124
www.goodsamsj.org
Phone: 408-559-2011
Fax: 408-559-2661

O'Connor Hospital
2105 Forest Ave
San Jose, CA 95128
www.chwbay.org/oconnor
Phone: 408-947-2500
Fax: 408-947-2710

Regional Medical Center of San Jose
225 N Jackson Ave
San Jose, CA 95116
Phone: 408-259-5000
Fax: 408-729-2884

Santa Clara Valley Medical Center
751 S Bascom Ave
San Jose, CA 95128
www.scvmed.org
Phone: 408-885-5000
Fax: 408-885-6610

Santa Teresa Community Hospital
250 Hospital Pkwy
San Jose, CA 95119
Phone: 408-972-7000
Fax: 408-972-6445
TF: 800-967-4677

Stanford University Hospital
300 Pasteur Dr
Stanford, CA 94305
www-med.stanford.edu/shs
Phone: 650-723-2300
Fax: 650-723-8163

Transportation

Airport(s)

San Jose International Airport (SJC)
3 miles NW of downtown (approx 15 minutes) 408-501-7600

Mass Transit

VTA
$1.10 Base fare 408-321-2300
VTA Light Rail
$1.10 Base fare 408-321-2300

Rail/Bus

Greyhound Bus Station
70 S Almaden Ave
San Jose, CA 95113
Phone: 408-295-4151
TF: 800-231-2222

San Jose Amtrak Station
65 Cahill St
San Jose, CA 95110
Phone: 408-287-7462
TF: 800-872-7245

Utilities

Electricity
Pacific Gas & Electric Co 800-743-5000
www.pge.com

Gas
Pacific Gas & Electric Co 800-743-5000
www.pge.com

Water
San Jose Water Co 408-279-7900

Garbage Collection/Recycling
Waste Management 408-982-0100

Telecommunications

Telephone
Pacific Bell 800-310-2355
www.pacbell.com

Cable Television
AT & T Cable Services 408-452-3355
www.cable.att.com
Coast Cablevision Inc 408-436-2930

Internet Service Providers (ISPs)
A-Link Network Services Inc 408-720-6161
www.alink.net
a2i communications 408-293-9706
www.rahul.net
Ablecom 408-280-1000
www.ablecom.net
APlatform 650-941-2647
www.aplatform.com
Bay Area Internet Solutions .408-545-0500
www.bayarea.net
INOW 408-946-6895
www.inow.com
Internet MainStreet 408-795-1441
www.mainstreet.net
ISP Channel 650-237-1400
www.ispchannel.com
IT Design USA Inc 408-342-0435
www.itdesign.com
KudoNet On-Line Services 408-738-1201
www.kudonet.com
Meernet LLC 650-618-1482
www.meer.net
NetGate Communications 408-565-9601
www.netgate.net
Silicon Valley Public Access Link (SV-PAL) 408-448-3071
www.svpal.org
Telocity Inc 408-863-6600
www.telocity.com
Verio Mountain View 650-964-2378
home.verio.net/local/frontpage.cfm?AirportCode=MNT

VPNet Technologies Inc. 408-404-1400
www.vpnet.com
WombatNet 650-462-8800
www.wombat.net

Banks

Bank of America NA
32 S 3rd St
San Jose, CA 95113
Phone: 408-277-7208
Fax: 408-277-7905

Bank of Santa Clara
2779 Aborn Rd
San Jose, CA 95121
Phone: 408-249-5900
Fax: 408-987-9555

Bank of the West
50 W San Fernando St
San Jose, CA 95113
Phone: 408-947-5005
Fax: 408-295-0494
TF: 800-488-2265

California Federal Bank FSB
883 Blossom Hill Rd
San Jose, CA 95123
Phone: 800-843-2265
Fax: 408-226-2639

Comerica Bank-California
55 W Santa Clara St
San Jose, CA 95113
Phone: 408-556-5000
Fax: 408-271-4074

Heritage Bank of Commerce
150 Almaden Blvd
San Jose, CA 95113
Phone: 408-947-6900

San Jose National Bank
1 N Market St
San Jose, CA 95113
E-mail: the.bank@sjnb.com
www.sjnb.com
Phone: 408-947-7562
Fax: 408-947-7049

Sanwa Bank of California
220 Almaden Blvd
San Jose, CA 95113
Phone: 408-998-0800
Fax: 408-971-1290

Union Bank of California NA
99 Almaden Blvd
San Jose, CA 95113
Phone: 408-279-7700
Fax: 408-292-3981

Washington Mutual Bank
5393 Almaden Expy
San Jose, CA 95118
Phone: 408-445-4200
Fax: 408-448-5329

Wells Fargo Bank NA
360 N Capitol Ave
San Jose, CA 95133
Phone: 408-998-3694

Shopping

Almaden Plaza Shopping Center
5353 Almaden Expy Suite 49
San Jose, CA 95118
Phone: 408-264-3766

Antique Row
W San Carlos St
San Jose, CA 95126
Phone: 408-947-8711

Eastridge Mall
2200 Tully Rd
San Jose, CA 95122
Phone: 408-238-3600
Fax: 408-274-9684

Great Mall of the Bay Area
447 Great Mall Dr
Milpitas, CA 95035
www.greatmallbayarea.com
Phone: 408-956-2033
Fax: 408-945-4027
TF: 800-625-5229

Macy's
2801 Stevens Creek Blvd
Santa Clara, CA 95050
Phone: 408-248-3333

Oakridge Mall
925-A Blossom Hill Rd
San Jose, CA 95123
Phone: 408-578-2910
Fax: 408-578-1148

Pavilion The
150 S 1st St
San Jose, CA 95113
Phone: 408-286-2076
Fax: 408-286-6899

San Jose Flea Market
1590 Berryessa Rd
San Jose, CA 95133
www.sjfm.com
Phone: 408-453-1110
Fax: 408-437-9011

Santa Teresa Shopping Center
870 Blossom Hill Rd
San Jose, CA 95123
Phone: 408-226-8933

Stanford Shopping Center
180 El Camino Real
Palo Alto, CA 94304
www.stanfordshop.com
Phone: 650-617-8585
Fax: 650-617-8227
TF: 800-772-9332

Vallco Fashion Park
10123 N Wolfe Rd
Cupertino, CA 95014
E-mail: vallcofashionpark@rejacobsgroup.com
www.shopyourmall.com/mall_welcome.asp?map=yes&mall_select=681
Phone: 408-255-5660
Fax: 408-725-0370

Valley Fair Shopping Center
2855 Stevens Creek Blvd Suite 2178
Santa Clara, CA 95050
Phone: 408-248-4451
Fax: 408-248-8614

Westgate Mall
1600 Saratoga Ave
San Jose, CA 95129
Phone: 408-379-9350
Fax: 408-379-4890

Willow Glen-Lincoln Avenue Shopping District
1275 Lincoln Ave Suite 3A
San Jose, CA 95125
Phone: 408-298-2100
Fax: 408-280-1104

Media

Newspapers and Magazines

Business Journal of San Jose
96 N 3rd St Suite 100
San Jose, CA 95112
www.bizjournals.com/sanjose
Phone: 408-295-3800
Fax: 408-295-5028

Cupertino Courier
20465 Silverado Ave
Cupertino, CA 95014
E-mail: courier@sjmetro.com
www.metroactive.com/papers/cupertino.courier
Phone: 408-255-7500
Fax: 408-252-3381

Los Altos Town Crier
138 Main St
Los Altos, CA 94022
E-mail: towncrier@losaltosonline.com
www.losaltosonline.com/latc.html
Phone: 650-948-4489
Fax: 650-948-6647

Los Gatos Weekly-Times
245 Almendra Ave
Los Gatos, CA 95030
www.metroactive.com/papers/los.gatos.weekly-times
Phone: 408-354-3110
Fax: 408-354-3917

Milpitas Post
59 Maryland Ave
Milpitas, CA 95035
www.milpitaspost.net
Phone: 408-262-2454
Fax: 408-263-9710

Palo Alto Weekly
703 High St
Palo Alto, CA 94301
E-mail: letters@paweekly.com
www.paweekly.com
Phone: 650-326-8210
Fax: 650-326-3928

San Jose City Times
550 S 1st St
San Jose, CA 95113
E-mail: metro@sjmetro.com
metroactive.com/metro
Phone: 408-298-8000
Fax: 408-298-0602

San Jose Mercury News*
750 Ridder Park Dr
San Jose, CA 95190
E-mail: websales@sjmercury.com
www.mercurycenter.com
Phone: 408-920-5000
Fax: 408-288-8060
TF: 800-818-6397

Sunnyvale Sun
160-B S Murphy Ave
Sunnyvale, CA 94087
www.metroactive.com/papers/sunnyvale.sun
Phone: 408-255-7500
Fax: 408-252-3381

Willow Glen Resident
550 S 1st St
San Jose, CA 95113
www.metroactive.com/papers/willow.glen.resident
Phone: 408-298-8000
Fax: 408-298-0602

**Indicates major daily newspapers*

Television

KNTV-TV Ch 11 (ABC)
645 Park Ave
San Jose, CA 95110
www.kntv.com
Phone: 408-286-1111
Fax: 408-286-1530

KPIX-TV Ch 5 (CBS)
855 Battery St
San Francisco, CA 94111
E-mail: tvprog@kpix.com
www.kpix.com
Phone: 415-362-5550
Fax: 415-765-8916

KRON-TV Ch 4 (NBC)
1001 Van Ness Ave
San Francisco, CA 94109
www.kron.com
Phone: 415-441-4444
Fax: 415-561-8136

KTEH-TV Ch 54 (PBS)
1585 Schallenberger Rd
San Jose, CA 95130
www.kteh.org/
Phone: 408-795-5400
Fax: 408-995-5446

KTVU-TV Ch 2 (Fox)
2 Jack London Sq
Oakland, CA 94607
E-mail: ktvu@team.insider.com
www.bayinsider.com/partners/ktvu/index.html
Phone: 510-834-1212
Fax: 510-272-9957

Radio

KARA-FM 105.7 MHz (AC)
750 Story Rd
San Jose, CA 95122
www.kara.com
Phone: 408-293-8030
Fax: 408-995-0823

KBAY-FM 94.5 MHz (AC)
190 Park Center Plaza Suite 200
San Jose, CA 95113
www.kbay.com
Phone: 408-287-5775
Fax: 408-293-3341

KCNL-FM 104.9 MHz (Alt)
1420 Koll Cir Suite A
San Jose, CA 95112
E-mail: feedback@channel1049.com
www.channel1049.com
Phone: 408-453-1049

KEZR-FM 106.5 MHz (AC)
190 Park Center Plaza Suite 200
San Jose, CA 95113
www.kezr.com
Phone: 408-287-5775
Fax: 408-293-3341

KFFG-FM 97.7 MHz (AAA)
55 Hawthorne St Suite 1100
San Francisco, CA 94105
www.kfog.com
Phone: 415-543-1045
Fax: 415-995-6867

KGO-AM 810 kHz (N/T)
900 Front St
San Francisco, CA 94111
www.kgoam810.com
Phone: 415-954-7777
Fax: 415-362-5827

KLOK-AM 1170 kHz (Span)
2905 S King Rd
San Jose, CA 95122
Phone: 408-274-1170
Fax: 408-274-1818

KRTY-FM 95.3 MHz (Ctry)
750 Story Rd
San Jose, CA 95122
www.krty.com
Phone: 408-293-8030
Fax: 408-995-0823

KSJO-FM 92.3 MHz (Rock)
1420 Koll Cir Suite A
San Jose, CA 95112
www.ksjo.com
Phone: 408-453-5400
Fax: 408-452-1330

KUSP-FM 88.9 MHz (NPR)
203 8th Ave
Santa Cruz, CA 95062
E-mail: kusp@cruzio.com
www4.cruzio.com/cruzio/404.html
Phone: 831-476-2800
Fax: 831-476-2802

Attractions

The Plaza de Cesar Chavez, with its tree-lined walkways, is the centerpiece of downtown San Jose. In the plaza area one can visit the Children's Discovery Museum, the largest children's museum on the West Coast, or the Tech Museum of Innovation, which showcases Silicon Valley technology. New attractions that are part of San Jose's downtown Renaissance include a 20-mile long state-of-the-art Light Rail system, the $140 million San Jose McEnery Convention Center, and the San Jose Arena, home of the NHL's San Jose Sharks. Just 30 minutes from San Jose is Santa Cruz, home of the Santa Cruz Beach Boardwalk, California's only remaining seaside amusement park. The city of Monterey, site of the Cannery Row area immortalized by John Steinbeck, is just 70 minutes from San Jose. On the Row is Monterey Bay Aquarium, considered one of the finest aquariums in the nation.

Ainsley House/Campbell Historical Museum
300 Grant St
Campbell, CA 95008
web.nvcom.com/chm
Phone: 408-866-2119
Fax: 408-379-6349

Almaden Lake Park
Almaden Expy & Coleman Ave
San Jose, CA 95120
www.sanjoseparks.org/alp/index.html
Phone: 408-277-5130
Fax: 408-997-2035

Alum Rock Park
16240 Alum Rock Ave
San Jose, CA 95127
E-mail: park_ranger@rocketmail.com
www.sanjoseparks.org/arp/index.html
Phone: 408-259-5477

American Museum of Quilts & Textiles
110 Paseo de San Antonio
San Jose, CA 95112
www.sjquiltmuseum.org/
Phone: 408-971-0323
Fax: 408-971-7226

American Musical Theatre of San Jose
1717 Technology Dr
San Jose, CA 95110
E-mail: info@amtsj.org
www.amtsj.org
Phone: 408-453-7108
Fax: 408-453-7123

Cannery Row
765 Wave St
Monterey, CA 93940
Phone: 831-649-6695
Fax: 831-373-4812

Cathedral Basilica of Saint Joseph
80 S Market St
San Jose, CA 95113
www.stjosephcathedral.org
Phone: 408-283-8100
Fax: 408-283-8110

Center for Beethoven Studies & Museum
San Jose State University Library Ira F Brilliant Ctr for Beethoven Studies
San Jose, CA 95192
www.sjsu.edu/depts/beethoven
Phone: 408-924-4590
Fax: 408-924-4715

Center for the Performing Arts
255 Almaden Blvd
San Jose, CA 95110
www.sjcc.com/cftpa
Phone: 408-277-3900
Fax: 408-277-3535

Children's Discovery Museum
180 Woz Way
San Jose, CA 95110
E-mail: will@cdm.org
www.cdm.org
Phone: 408-298-5437
Fax: 408-298-6826

Chinese Cultural Garden
2145 McKee Rd
San Jose, CA 95116
Phone: 408-251-3323
Fax: 408-251-2865

City Lights Theatre Co
529 S 2nd St
San Jose, CA 95112
E-mail: citylights@cltc.org
www.cltc.org
Phone: 408-295-4200
Fax: 408-295-8318

Fallon House
175 W Saint John St
San Jose, CA 95110
Phone: 408-993-8182
Fax: 408-993-8184

Happy Hollow Park & Zoo
1300 Senter Rd Kelley Pk
San Jose, CA 95112
E-mail: zoovet@netgate.net
www.acoates.com/happyhollow/happyhollow.html
Phone: 408-295-8383
Fax: 408-277-4470

History San Jose
1650 Senter Rd
San Jose, CA 95112
www.historysanjose.org
Phone: 408-287-2290
Fax: 408-287-2291

Intel Museum
2200 Mission College Blvd
Santa Clara, CA 95052
www.intel.com/intel/intelis/museum/
Phone: 408-765-0503
Fax: 408-765-1217

J Lohr Winery
1000 Lenzen Ave
San Jose, CA 95126
Phone: 408-288-5057
Fax: 408-993-2276

Japanese Friendship Garden
1300 Senter Rd Kelley Pk
San Jose, CA 95112
Phone: 408-295-8383
Fax: 408-277-4470

Japanese-American Museum
535 N 5th St
San Jose, CA 95112
www.jarc-m.org
Phone: 408-294-3138
Fax: 408-294-1657

Kelley Park
1300 Senter Rd
San Jose, CA 95112
www.ci.san-jose.ca.us/cae/parks/kp/
Phone: 408-277-4191
Fax: 408-277-3270

Lake Cunningham Regional Park
2305 S White Rd
San Jose, CA 95148
www.sanjoseparks.org/lcp
Phone: 408-277-4319

Lick Observatory
Mt Hamilton Rd
San Jose, CA 95140
www.ucolick.org
Phone: 408-274-5061

Mirassou Vineyards
3000 Aborn Rd
San Jose, CA 95135
E-mail: sales@mirassou.com
www.mirassou.com
Phone: 408-274-4000
Fax: 408-270-5881
TF: 888-647-2776

Monterey Bay Aquarium
886 Cannery Row
Monterey, CA 93940
www.mbayaq.org
Phone: 831-648-4800
Fax: 831-648-4810
TF: 800-555-3656

Monterey Museum of Art
559 Pacific St
Monterey, CA 93940
E-mail: mtry_art@mbay.net
www.montereyart.org
Phone: 831-372-5477
Fax: 831-372-5680

Montgomery Theater
San Carlos & Market Sts
San Jose, CA 95110
www.sjcc.com/montgomery_theater/index.html
Phone: 408-277-3900
Fax: 408-277-3535

Municipal Rose Garden
Naglee & Dana Aves
San Jose, CA 95126
Phone: 408-277-4191
Fax: 408-277-5422

Opera San Jose
2149 Paragon Dr
San Jose, CA 95131
operasj.org
Phone: 408-437-4450
Fax: 408-437-4455

Overfelt Gardens
2145 McKee Rd
San Jose, CA 95116
www.sanjoseparks.org/og
Phone: 408-251-3323
Fax: 408-251-2865

Paramount's Great America
PO Box 1776
Santa Clara, CA 95052
www.pgathrills.com
Phone: 408-988-1776
Fax: 408-986-5855

Peralta Adobe
175 W Saint John St
San Jose, CA 95110
www.historysanjose.org/plan-pf.html
Phone: 408-993-8182
Fax: 408-993-8184

Pinnacles National Monument
5000 Hwy 146
Paicines, CA 95043
www.nps.gov/pinn/
Phone: 831-389-4485
Fax: 831-389-4489

Prusch Farm Park
647 S King Rd
San Jose, CA 95116
www.sanjoseparks.org/pfp/index.html
Phone: 408-277-4567
Fax: 408-277-3820

Raging Waters Aquatic Theme Park
2333 S White Rd
San Jose, CA 95148
www.rwsplash.com
Phone: 408-270-8000
Fax: 408-270-2022

Rosicrucian Egyptian Museum
1342 Naglee Ave Rosicrucian Pk
San Jose, CA 95191
www.rcegyptmus.org
Phone: 408-947-3636
Fax: 408-947-3638

San Jose Center for the Performing Arts
255 Almaden Ave
San Jose, CA 95110
www.sjcc.com/cftpa/index.html
Phone: 408-277-5277
Fax: 408-277-3535
TF: 800-533-2345

San Jose Children's Musical Theatre
1401 N Parkmoor Ave
San Jose, CA 95126
E-mail: sjcmt@sjcmt.com
www.sjcmt.com
Phone: 408-288-5437
Fax: 408-288-6241

San Jose Cleveland Ballet
40 N 1st St 2nd Fl
San Jose, CA 95113
Phone: 408-288-2820
Fax: 408-993-9570

San Jose Flea Market
1590 Berryessa Rd
San Jose, CA 95133
www.sjfm.com
Phone: 408-453-1110
Fax: 408-437-9011

San Jose Museum of Art
110 S Market St
San Jose, CA 95113
E-mail: info@sjmusart.org
www.sjmusart.org
Phone: 408-271-6840
Fax: 408-294-2977

San Jose Repertory Theatre
101 Paseo de San Antonio
San Jose, CA 95113
E-mail: the_rep@vval.com
www.sjrep.com
Phone: 408-291-2266
Fax: 408-367-7237

San Jose Stage Co
490 S 1st St
San Jose, CA 95113
E-mail: rfirst@garlic.com
www.sanjose-stage.com
Phone: 408-283-7142
Fax: 408-283-7146

San Jose Symphony Orchestra
495 Almaden Blvd
San Jose, CA 95110
www.sanjosesymphony.org
Phone: 408-287-7383
Fax: 408-286-6391

Santa Cruz Beach Boardwalk
400 Beach St
Santa Cruz, CA 95060
www.beachboardwalk.com
Phone: 831-423-5590
Fax: 831-460-3335

Six Flags Marine World
2001 Marine World Pkwy
Vallejo, CA 94589
www.sixflags.com/marineworld
Phone: 707-644-4000
Fax: 707-644-0241

Tech Museum of Innovation
201 S Market St
San Jose, CA 95113
www.thetech.org
Phone: 408-294-8324
Fax: 408-279-7167

Winchester Mystery House
525 S Winchester Blvd
San Jose, CA 95128
www.winchestermysteryhouse.com
Phone: 408-247-2000
Fax: 408-247-2090

Youth Science Institute
296 Garden Hill Dr
Los Gatos, CA 95030
E-mail: info@ysi-org
www.ysi-ca.org
Phone: 408-356-4945
Fax: 408-358-3683

Sports Teams & Facilities

Bay Meadows Race Course
2600 S Delaware St
San Mateo, CA 94402
www.baymeadows.com
Phone: 650-574-7223
Fax: 650-573-4677

San Jose Arena
525 W Santa Clara St
San Jose, CA 95113
www.sj-arena.com
Phone: 408-287-7070
Fax: 408-999-5797
TF: 800-366-4423

San Jose Clash (soccer)
3550 Stevens Creek Suite 200
San Jose, CA 95117
www.sjearthquakes.com
Phone: 408-241-9922
Fax: 408-554-8886

San Jose Giants (baseball)
588 E Alma Ave Municipal Stadium
San Jose, CA 95112
E-mail: giantssj@aol.com
www.sjgiants.com
Phone: 408-297-1435
Fax: 408-297-1453

San Jose Municipal Stadium
588 E Alma Ave
San Jose, CA 95112
www.sjgiants.com/stadium_info.html
Phone: 408-297-1435
Fax: 408-297-1453

San Jose SaberCats (football)
600 E Brokaw Rd
San Jose, CA 95112
E-mail: sales@sanjosesabercats.com
www.sanjosesabercats.com
Phone: 408-573-5577
Fax: 408-573-5588

San Jose Sharks
525 W Santa Clara St San Jose Arena
San Jose, CA 95113
www.sj-sharks.com
Phone: 408-287-9200
Fax: 408-999-5707

Spartan Stadium
1257 S 10th St
San Jose, CA 95112
Phone: 408-924-1850
Fax: 408-924-1911

Annual Events

Almaden Art & Wine Festival (late September) 408-268-1133
Arts & Crafts & Music Festival
(late March & mid-May) 408-842-9316
Chinese Summer Festival (mid-July) 408-287-2290
Cinco de Mayo Festival (early May) 408-288-9471
CineQuest-San Jose Film Festival
(late February-early March) 408-995-5033
Clam Chowder Cook-Off (early February) 831-423-5590
Earth Day Celebration (late April) 408-295-8383
Fiestas Patrias (early May) 408-258-0663
Gay Pride Parade & Festival (mid-June)...........408-278-5563
Gold Rush Festival (late May).....................408-287-2290
Great Salsa Taste-Off (early May) 831-420-5273
Harvest Festival (late August-December) 800-321-1213
Hoi Tet Festival (mid-February)...................408-295-9210
Irish Week Celebration (mid-March) 408-279-6002
Italian American Cultural Festival
(early October)...............................408-293-7122
Japantown Certified Farmers' Market Sundays
(late April-late July)...........................408-298-4303
Juneteenth Festival (mid-June) 408-292-3157
Los Posadas (mid-December) 408-467-9890
Mariachi Conference & Festival (mid-July) 408-928-5500
Metro Fountain Blues Festival (early May) 408-924-6262
Mountain Winery Summer Series
(June-September).............................408-741-0763
Obon Festival (mid-July) 408-293-9292
Oktoberfest (mid-October).......................408-453-1110
San Jose America Festival (early July) 408-298-6861
San Jose Historical Museum Walking Tours
(May-October)................................408-287-2290
San Jose Holiday Parade (December) 408-995-6635
San Jose International Auto Show (January) 408-277-3900
San Jose Jazz Festival (mid-August)...............408-288-7557
San Pedro Square Brew Ha Ha (early October) 408-279-1775
Santa Clara County Fair (late July-early August) 408-494-3247
Santa Cruz Christmas Craft & Gift Festival
(late November)..............................831-423-5590
SoFa Street Fair (mid-September).................408-295-2265
Spring Wine Growers Festival (late April) 408-842-9316
Strawberry Festival (early June)..................408-379-3790
Wine & Arts Prune Festival (late May).............408-378-6252

Savannah, Georgia

***County:* Chatham**

SAVANNAH is located at the mouth of the Savannah River in southeastern Georgia. Major cities within 100 miles include Brunswick, Tybee Island, and St. Simons Island, Georgia, and Hilton Head, South Carolina.

Area (Land) .... 62.6 sq mi
Area (Water).... 3.3 sq mi
Elevation.... 42 ft
Latitude ....32-08-33 N
Longitude.... 81-10-00 W
Time Zone ....EST
Area Code.... 912

Climate

Savannah has a subtropical climate which features hot summers and mild winters. High temperatures during the winter months average in the low 60s, while evenings cool down to near 40 degrees. Temperatures occasionally dip below freezing in Savannah, but snowfall is rare, averaging less than a half-inch annually. Summer daytime high temperatures average around 90 degrees, with lows near 70. Summer is also the rainy season in Savannah, with August being the wettest month. November is the driest month of the year.

Average Temperatures & Precipitation

Temperatures

	Jan	Feb	Mar	Apr	May	Jun	Jul	Aug	Sep	Oct	Nov	Dec
High	60	62	70	78	84	89	91	90	85	78	70	62
Low	38	41	48	55	63	69	72	72	68	57	48	41

Precipitation

	Jan	Feb	Mar	Apr	May	Jun	Jul	Aug	Sep	Oct	Nov	Dec
Inches	3.6	3.2	3.8	3.0	4.1	5.7	6.4	7.5	4.5	2.4	2.2	3.0

History

Georgia's oldest city, Savannah is considered by many to be one of the most beautiful cities in the U.S. It was founded in 1733 by General James Oglethorpe as the first capital of the new colony of Georgia. Oglethorpe created Savannah's unique city plan featuring 24 public squares that servedas miniature parks for social gatherings. The parks (which still exist today, with azaleas, camellias, fountains, and monuments) were surrounded by churches, businesses, and residences, and each had its own distinct style and charm. The Port of Savannah opened in 1744 and the city began to grow as an important port of commerce, shipping goods to Europe. Savannah served as the capital of Georgia until 1786 and was incorporated as a city in 1789.

In 1793, Eli Whitney invented the cotton gin at Mulberry Grove, a Savannah area plantation. This invention helped to fuel Savannah's thriving cotton industry during the 19th Century, bringing great wealth to the city. Savannah was one of the few major southern cities spared during the Civil War. The city served as a supply point for the confederacy until it was captured by Union troops in December 1864. Instead of setting the city ablaze at the time of its capture, General Sherman was so captivated by Savannah's beauty that he instead presented the city as a Christmas gift to President Abraham Lincoln.

During the early to mid-1900s people began relocating from the downtown area of Savannah into the suburbs. Many of the city's historic homes were broken into apartments, and several historic landmarks were demolished during this period. In order to retain and restore Savannah's historic charm, local citizens formed the Historic Savannah Foundation during the 1950s. For the remainder of the 20th Century the city underwent a myriad of renovation and restoration projects, including the River Street Urban Renewal Project, which resulted in a new, bustling business and entertainment district along the city's riverfront.

The seat of Chatham County, Savannah, with a population exceeding 131,000, is currently Georgia's fourth largest city. A majority of the 24 original squares laid out in General Oglethorpe's city plan remain in Savannah today, and the city's historic charm has made it one of the leading tourist destinations in the state and in the region.

Population

1990 Census 137,812
1998 Estimate....131,674
% Change .... -4.5
2002 Projection 236,872*

Racial/Ethnic Breakdown

White.... 46.8%
Black 51.3%
Other.... 1.9%
Hispanic Origin (may be of any race) 1.4%

Age Breakdown

Under 5 years.... 8.2%
5 to 17.... 18.6%
18 to 20.... 5.1%
21 to 24.... 6.8%
25 to 34.... 17.3%
35 to 44.... 13.2%
45 to 54.... 8.9%
55 to 64.... 8.2%
65 to 74.... 8.1%
75+ years 5.7%
Median Age....31.4

Gender Breakdown
Male 47.1%
Female.................................. 52.9%

** Information given is for Chatham County.*

Government

Type of Government: Council-Manager

Chatham-Effingham-Liberty Regional Library
2002 Bull St
Savannah, GA 31401
Phone: 912-652-3600
Fax: 912-652-3638

Savannah City Attorney
PO Box 8996
Savannah, GA 31412
Phone: 912-232-2137
Fax: 912-238-9810

Savannah City Council
PO Box 1027
Savannah, GA 31402
Phone: 912-651-6441
Fax: 912-651-4260

Savannah City Hall
2 E Bay St
Savannah, GA 31402
Phone: 912-651-6790
Fax: 912-651-6408

Savannah City Manager
PO Box 1027
Savannah, GA 31402
Phone: 912-651-6415
Fax: 912-238-0872

Savannah Finance Dept
PO Box 1027
Savannah, GA 31402
Phone: 912-651-6440
Fax: 912-651-6432

Savannah Fire & Emergency Services Bureau
121 E Oglethorpe Ave
Savannah, GA 31401
Phone: 912-651-6758
Fax: 912-651-6757

Savannah Human Resources Dept
132 E Broughton St 5th Fl
Savannah, GA 31412
Phone: 912-651-6484
Fax: 912-651-6706

Savannah Leisure Services Bureau
PO Box 1027
Savannah, GA 31402
Phone: 912-351-3837
Fax: 912-351-3848

Savannah Mayor
PO Box 1027
Savannah, GA 31402
Phone: 912-651-6444
Fax: 912-651-6805

Savannah Police Dept
PO Box 8032
Savannah, GA 31412
Phone: 912-651-6664
Fax: 912-651-3645

Savannah Public Development Bureau
6 E Bay St
Savannah, GA 31402
Phone: 912-651-6521
Fax: 912-651-6525

Savannah Sanitation Bureau
PO Box 1027
Savannah, GA 31402
Phone: 912-651-6580
Fax: 912-651-6497

Savannah Water & Sewer Bureau
PO Box 1027
Savannah, GA 31402
Phone: 912-651-4241
Fax: 912-651-3681

Important Phone Numbers

Artsline 912-236-7284
Chatham County Tax Assessor 912-652-7271
Driver's License Information...................... 404-657-9300
Emergency 911
Georgia Dept of Revenue 912-356-2140
Medical Referral................................. 912-350-9355
Poison Control Center 800-282-5846
Savannah Board of Realtors....................... 912-354-1513
Time/Temp 912-369-1234
Travelers Aid.................................... 912-651-5310
Vehicle Registration Information 912-652-6800
Voter Registration Information.................... 912-652-7440
Weather.. 912-964-1700

Information Sources

Better Business Bureau Serving Southeast Georgia & Southeast South Carolina
6606 Abercorn St Suite 108C
Savannah, GA 31405
www.savannah.bbb.org
Phone: 912-354-7521
Fax: 912-354-5068

Chatham County
PO Box 8161
Savannah, GA 31412
www.co.chatham.ga.us/chatham/chatham.htm
Phone: 912-652-7175
Fax: 912-652-7874

Savannah Area Chamber of Commerce
101 E Bay St
Savannah, GA 31401
Phone: 912-644-6400
Fax: 912-644-6499
TF: 800-444-2427

Savannah Area Convention & Visitors Bureau
101 E Bay St
Savannah, GA 31401
www.savcvb.com
Phone: 912-644-6401
Fax: 912-644-6499
TF: 800-444-2427

Savannah Civic Center
Liberty & Montgomery Sts
Savannah, GA 31402
www.savannahcivic.com
Phone: 912-651-6550
Fax: 912-651-6552

Online Resources

About.com Guide to Savannah
savannah.about.com/citiestowns/southeastus/savannah

Anthill City Guide Savannah
www.anthill.com/city.asp?city=savannah

Area Guide Savannah
savannah.areaguides.net

Best Read Guide Savannah
bestreadguide.com/savannah

City Knowledge Savannah
www.cityknowledge.com/ga_savannah.htm

Creative Loafing Online Savannah
www.cln.com/savannah/newsstand/current/

Excite.com Savannah City Guide
www.excite.com/travel/countries/united_states/georgia/savannah/

Insiders' Guide to Savannah
www.insiders.com/savannah

Lodging.com Savannah Georgia
www.lodging.com/auto/guides/savannah-area-ga.html

Savannah Online
savannah-online.com

Savannah.com
www.savannahgeorgia.com

Area Communities

Communities in the Savannah area (Chatham and Bryan counties) with populations greater than 5,000 include:

Garden City — Phone: 912-966-7777, Fax: 912-966-7792
100 Main St
Garden City, GA 31408

Pooler — Phone: 912-748-7261, Fax: 912-748-0157
100 SW Hwy 80
Pooler, GA 31322

Richmond Hill — Phone: 912-756-3345, Fax: 912-756-3368
PO Box 250
Richmond Hill, GA 31324

Economy

Savannah has a diverse economic base that ranges from aircraft manufacturing to tourism. Services is currently Savannah's largest employment sector, followed by retail trade and manufacturing. A wide variety of products are manufactured in Savannah, including ships, food products, chemicals, paper products, and steel. Gulfstream Aerospace Corp., a jet aircraft manufacturer, is the area's single largest employer. Georgia State Government and the U.S. Army Corps of Engineers are also among Savannah's largest employers, providing jobs for more than 4,500 area residents collectively. Tourism is currently the fastest-growing sector of Savannah's economy - the city hosts more than five million visitors annually. In 1997 alone, tourism generated more than $860 million in revenue and created jobs for more than 23,000 area residents.

Unemployment Rate 4.7%*
Per Capita Income $24,320*
Median Family Income $27,076

** Information given is for Chatham County.*

Principal Industries & Number of Wage Earners

Chatham County - 1998

Industry	Wage Earners
Agricultural Services, Forestry &, Fishing	682
Construction	7,074
Finance, Insurance, & Real Estate	4,051
Manufacturing	15,744
Mining	7
Public Administration	7,410
Retail Trade	26,040
Services	44,263
Transportation, Communications, & Utilities	8,975
Wholesale Trade	4,898

Major Employers

Candler Hospital — Phone: 912-354-9211, Fax: 912-692-6350
5353 Reynolds St
Savannah, GA 31405

Chatham County — Phone: 912-652-7175, Fax: 912-652-7874
PO Box 8161
Savannah, GA 31412
www.co.chatham.ga.us/chatham/chatham.htm

Chatham County Board of Education — Phone: 912-201-5600, Fax: 912-201-7667
208 Bull St
Savannah, GA 31410
www.savannah.chatham.k12.ga.us

Fort James Corp — Phone: 912-826-5216, Fax: 912-826-4762
PO Box 828
Rincon, GA 31326
www.fortjames.com

Fort Stewart/Hunter Army Airfield — Phone: 912-767-1411
Fort Stewart, GA 31314
www.stewart.army.mil

Great Dane Trailers Inc — Phone: 912-644-2100, Fax: 912-644-2166
602 E Lathrop Ave
Savannah, GA 31415
E-mail: general_sales@greatdanetrailers.com
www.greatdanetrailers.com

Gulfstream Aerospace Corp — Phone: 912-965-3000, Fax: 912-965-3775
PO Box 2206
Savannah, GA 31402
E-mail: info@gulfaero.com
www.gulfstream.com

Kroger Co — Phone: 770-496-7400, Fax: 770-496-5376
2175 Parklake Dr NE
Atlanta, GA 30345
www.kroger.com

Memorial Health University Medical Center — Phone: 912-350-8000, Fax: 912-350-7073
4700 Waters Ave
Savannah, GA 31404
www.memorialhealth.com

Saint Joseph's Hospital — Phone: 912-925-4100, Fax: 912-692-5580
11705 Mercy Blvd
Savannah, GA 31419

Savannah City Hall — Phone: 912-651-6790, Fax: 912-651-6408
2 E Bay St
Savannah, GA 31402
www.ci.savannah.ga.us

Savannah Foods & Industries Inc — Phone: 912-234-1261, Fax: 912-651-5173
PO Box 339
Savannah, GA 31402
www.savfoods.com

Quality of Living Indicators

Total Crime Index 11,383
(rates per 100,000 inhabitants)

Violent Crime
Murder/manslaughter 40

Forcible rape 66
Robbery.................................... 660
Aggravated assault............................ 518

Property Crime
Burglary 1,968
Larceny theft 6,915
Motor vehicle theft...........................1,216

Cost of Living Index.....................................88.0
(national average = 100)

Median Home Price...................................$54,000

Education

Public Schools

Savannah-Chatham County Public Schools Phone: 912-201-5600
208 Bull St Fax: 912-201-7667
Savannah, GA 31410
www.savannah.chatham.k12.ga.us

Number of Schools
Elementary.................................. 29
Middle 8
High... 7

Student/Teacher Ratio
All Grades 15.0:1

Private Schools

Number of Schools (all grades).................... 20+

Colleges & Universities

Armstrong Atlantic State University Phone: 912-927-5275
11935 Abercorn St Fax: 912-921-5462
Savannah, GA 31419 TF: 800-633-2349
www.armstrong.edu

Savannah College of Art & Design Phone: 912-238-2483
342 Bull St Fax: 912-525-5983
Savannah, GA 31401
E-mail: admin@scad.edu
www.scad.edu

Savannah State University Phone: 912-356-2186
3219 College St Fax: 912-356-2253
Savannah, GA 31404 TF: 800-788-4803
www.savstate.edu

South College Phone: 912-691-6000
709 Mall Blvd Fax: 912-691-6070
Savannah, GA 31406
www.southcollege.edu

Hospitals

Candler Hospital Phone: 912-354-9211
5353 Reynolds St Fax: 912-692-6350
Savannah, GA 31405

Memorial Health University Medical Center Phone: 912-350-8000
4700 Waters Ave Fax: 912-350-7073
Savannah, GA 31404
www.memorialhealth.com

Saint Joseph's Hospital Phone: 912-925-4100
11705 Mercy Blvd Fax: 912-692-5580
Savannah, GA 31419

Transportation

Airport(s)

Savannah International Airport (SAV)
8 miles NW of downtown (approx 20 minutes) 912-964-0514

Mass Transit

Chatham Area Transit Authority
$.75 Base fare.................................912-236-2111

Rail/Bus

Amtrak Station Phone: 912-234-2611
2611 Seaboard Coastline Dr TF: 800-872-7245
Savannah, GA 31401

Greyhound Bus Station Phone: 800-231-2222
610 W Oglethorpe Ave
Savannah, GA 31401

Utilities

Electricity
Savannah Electric Co..........................800-437-3890
www.southernco.com/site/savannah/

Gas
Atlanta Gas Light Co 800-427-5463
www.aglc.com

Water
Savannah Water Services.......................912-651-6460

Garbage Collection/Recycling
Savannah Sanitation Bureau....................912-651-6579

Telecommunications

Telephone
BellSouth 800-356-3094
www.bellsouth.com

Cable Television
Jones Communications 912-354-7531

Internet Service Providers (ISPs)
Systems Connect Inc...........................912-356-9920
www.sysconn.com
Web Savannah 912-525-2599
www.websavannah.com

Banks

AmeriBank NA Phone: 912-921-7100
7393 Hodgson Memorial Dr Fax: 912-921-1661
Savannah, GA 31406
www.ameribank.net

Carver State Bank Phone: 912-233-9971
701 ML King Blvd Fax: 912-232-8666
Savannah, GA 31401

Coastal Bank Phone: 912-235-4400
27 Bull St Fax: 912-233-2433
Savannah, GA 31401

First Union National Bank
20 Bank St
Savannah, GA 31404
Phone: 912-651-5916
Fax: 912-651-5983
TF: 800-733-4008

Savannah Bank NA
25 Bull St
Savannah, GA 31401
Phone: 912-651-8200
Fax: 912-232-3733

SunTrust Bank
33 Bull St
Savannah, GA 31401
Phone: 912-944-1000
Fax: 912-944-1168
TF: 800-688-7878

Wachovia Bank NA
5354 Reynolds St
Savannah, GA 31405
Phone: 912-353-1010
Fax: 912-353-1016
TF: 800-922-4684

Shopping

City Market
219 W Bryan St
Savannah, GA 31401
www.savannahgeorgia.com/citymarket
Phone: 912-232-4903
Fax: 912-232-2142

Historic Railroad Shops
601 W Harris St
Savannah, GA 31401
E-mail: hrs@gnet.net
Phone: 912-651-6823
Fax: 912-651-3691

Oglethorpe Mall
7804 Abercorn St
Savannah, GA 31406
www.omall.com
Phone: 912-354-7038
Fax: 912-352-3365

River Street Historic District
River St-betw ML King Blvd & President St
Savannah, GA 31401
Phone: 912-234-0295
Fax: 912-234-4904

Savannah Festival Factory Stores
11 Gateway Blvd S
Savannah, GA 31419
Phone: 912-925-3089
Fax: 912-925-3163

Savannah Mall
14045 Abercorn St
Savannah, GA 31419
Phone: 912-927-7467
Fax: 912-927-0018

Twelve Oaks Shopping Center
5500 Abercorn St
Savannah, GA 31405
Phone: 912-355-1311
Fax: 912-355-1168

Media

Newspapers and Magazines

Savannah Morning News*
111 W Bay St
Savannah, GA 31401
www.savannahnow.com
Phone: 912-236-9511
Fax: 912-234-6522

**Indicates major daily newspapers*

Television

WJCL-TV Ch 22 (ABC)
10001 Abercorn Ext
Savannah, GA 31406
Phone: 912-925-0022
Fax: 912-921-2235

WSAV-TV Ch 3 (NBC)
1430 E Victory Dr
Savannah, GA 31404
E-mail: wsav@ix.netcom.com
www.wsav.com
Phone: 912-651-0300
Fax: 912-651-0304

WTGS-TV Ch 28 (Fox)
10001 Abercorn St
Savannah, GA 31420
Phone: 912-925-2287
Fax: 912-921-2235

WTOC-TV Ch 11 (CBS)
PO Box 8086
Savannah, GA 31412
E-mail: wtoctv@sava.gulfnet.com
www.wtoctv.com
Phone: 912-234-1111
Fax: 912-232-4945

WVAN-TV Ch 9 (PBS)
86 Vandiver St
Pembroke, GA 31321
Phone: 912-653-4996
Fax: 912-653-5537

Radio

WAEV-FM 97.3 MHz (AC)
24 W Henry St
Savannah, GA 31401
E-mail: mix97@wce.com
Phone: 912-232-0097
Fax: 912-232-6144

WCHY-FM 94.1 MHz (Ctry)
245 Alfred St
Savannah, GA 31408
Phone: 912-964-7794
Fax: 912-964-9414

WEAS-FM 93.1 MHz (Urban)
214 Television Cir
Savannah, GA 31406
www.e93.com
Phone: 912-961-9000
Fax: 912-961-7070

WGCO-FM 103.1 MHz (CHR)
401 Mall Blvd Suite 101D
Savannah, GA 31406
Phone: 912-351-9830
Fax: 912-352-4821

WGCO-FM 98.3 MHz (Oldies)
401 Mall Blvd Suite 101D
Savannah, GA 31406
Phone: 912-351-9830
Fax: 912-352-4821

WJCL-FM 96.5 MHz (Ctry)
214 Television Cir
Savannah, GA 31406
E-mail: promo@kix96.com
www.kix96.com
Phone: 912-921-0965
Fax: 912-961-7070

WMCD-FM 100.1 MHz (AC)
PO Box 958
Statesboro, GA 30459
Phone: 912-764-5446
Fax: 912-764-8827

WRHQ-FM 105.3 MHz (Rock)
1102 E 52nd St
Savannah, GA 31404
E-mail: wrhq1053@aol.com
www.wrhq.com
Phone: 912-234-1053
Fax: 912-354-6600

WSVH-FM 91.1 MHz (NPR)
12 Ocean Science Cir
Savannah, GA 31411
www.wsvh.org
Phone: 912-598-3300
Fax: 912-598-3306
TF: 800-673-7332

WWNS-AM 1240 kHz (N/T)
PO Box 958
Statesboro, GA 30459
Phone: 912-764-5446
Fax: 912-764-8827

Attractions

Situated at the confluence of the Savannah River and the Atlantic Ocean, Savannah is considered by many to be one of the nation's most beautiful cities. Its Historic District is the country's largest historic urban landmark, with more than two thousand architecturally and historically significant buildings and more than 20 public squares featuring azaleas, camellias, fountains, and monuments. Many of the historic homes in this area are private residences, but others are occupied by businesses, shops, or restaurants. Some of the houses now serve as museums, including the home that was the birthplace of Girl Scouts founder Juliette Gordon Low. Each March the city hosts a four-day event that includes a walking tour of private residences, churches, museums, and gardens in the Historic District. Thirty minutes from Savannah is Tybee Island, with white sand beaches and resort facilities that draw visitors for day trips as well as vacations. Georgia's oldest (1736) and tallest (154 ft.) lighthouse is located on the island. Fort Pulaski National Monument, which commemorates the site of an 1862 Civil War battle, is also located in the area. During the summer of 1996 Savannah hosted Olympic yachting and beach volleyball events.

Atlantic Star Casino Cruise
1 Old Hwy 80 Lazaretto Creek Marina
Savannah, GA 31328
Phone: 912-786-7827
Fax: 912-786-7828

Beach Institute African American Cultural Center
502 E Harris St
Savannah, GA 31401
Phone: 912-234-8000
Fax: 912-234-8001

Chatham County Garden Center & Botanical Gardens
1388 Eisenhower Dr
Savannah, GA 31405
Phone: 912-355-3883

City Lights Theatre Co
125 E Broughton St
Savannah, GA 31401
Phone: 912-234-9860

City Market
219 W Bryan St
Savannah, GA 31401
www.savannahgeorgia.com/citymarket
Phone: 912-232-4903
Fax: 912-232-2142

City Market Art Center
219 W Bryan St Suite 202
Savannah, GA 31401
Phone: 912-234-2327
Fax: 912-232-2142

Davenport House Museum
324 E State St
Savannah, GA 31401
Phone: 912-236-8097
Fax: 912-233-7938

First African Baptist Church
23 Montgomery St Franklin Sq
Savannah, GA 31401
Phone: 912-233-6597
Fax: 912-234-7950

Fort Frederica National Monument
Rt 9 Box 286-C
Saint Simons Island, GA 31522
E-mail: fofr_superintendent@nps.gov
www.nps.gov/fofr/
Phone: 912-638-3639
Fax: 912-638-3639

Fort Pulaski National Monument
US Hwy 80 E
Savannah, GA 31410
www.nps.gov/fopu/
Phone: 912-786-5787
Fax: 912-786-6023

Hamilton-Turner House & Museum
330 Abercorn St
Savannah, GA 31401
Phone: 912-233-4800
Fax: 912-233-9800

Historic Railroad Shops
601 W Harris St
Savannah, GA 31401
E-mail: hrs@gnet.net
Phone: 912-651-6823
Fax: 912-651-3691

Juliette Gordon Low National Girl Scout Center
10 E Oglethorpe Ave
Savannah, GA 31401
Phone: 912-233-4501
Fax: 912-233-4659

King-Tisdale Cottage Black History Museum
502 E Harris St
Savannah, GA 31401
Phone: 912-234-8000
Fax: 912-234-8001

Low Andrew House
329 Abercorn St
Savannah, GA 31401
Phone: 912-233-6854
Fax: 912-233-1828

Mighty Eighth Airforce Heritage Museum
175 Bourne Ave
Pooler, GA 31322
E-mail: mighty8cur@aol.com
www.mighty8thmuseum.com
Phone: 912-748-8888
Fax: 912-748-0209

Oatland Island Education Center
711 Sandtown Rd
Savannah, GA 31410
Phone: 912-898-3980
Fax: 912-898-3983

Old Fort Jackson
1 Old Fort Jackson Rd
Savannah, GA 31404
E-mail: ofs@g-net.net
www.chsgeorgia.org/site/ftjack/right.htm
Phone: 912-232-3945
Fax: 912-236-5126

Old Town Trolley Tours
234 ML King Blvd
Savannah, GA 31401
E-mail: savott@historictours.com
www.historictours.com/savannah/trolley.htm
Phone: 912-233-0083

Owens-Thomas House
124 Abercorn St
Savannah, GA 31401
E-mail: olivia alison@worldnet.att.net
Phone: 912-233-9743
Fax: 912-233-0102

Ralph Mark Gilbert Civil Rights Museum
460 ML King Jr Blvd
Savannah, GA 31401
Phone: 912-231-8900
Fax: 912-234-2577

River Street Historic District
River St-betw ML King Blvd & President St
Savannah, GA 31401
Phone: 912-234-0295
Fax: 912-234-4904

Savannah History Museum
303 ML King Jr Blvd
Savannah, GA 31401
www.chsgeorgia.org
Phone: 912-238-1779
Fax: 912-651-6827

Savannah National Wildlife Refuge
1000 Business Center Dr Suite 10
Savannah, GA 31405
E-mail: r4rw_ga.scr@fws.gov
Phone: 912-652-4415
Fax: 912-652-4385

Savannah River Queen & Georgia Queen Riverboats
9 E River St
Savannah, GA 31412
E-mail: sales@savannah-riverboat.com
www.savannah-riverboat.com
Phone: 912-232-6404
Fax: 912-234-7881
TF: 800-786-6404

Savannah Symphony Orchestra
225 Abercorn St
Savannah, GA 31401
E-mail: feedback@savannahsymphony.org
www.savannahsymphony.org
Phone: 912-236-9536
Fax: 912-234-1450

Savannah Theatre Co
222 Bull St
Savanah, GA 31401
E-mail: stc@savtheatre.org
www.savtheatre.org
Phone: 912-233-7764

Ships of the Sea Maritime Museum
41 ML King Blvd
Savannah, GA 31401
E-mail: info@shipsofthesea.org
www.shipsofthesea.org
Phone: 912-232-1511
Fax: 912-234-7363

Telfair Museum of Art
121 Barnard St
Savannah, GA 31401
www.telfair.org
Phone: 912-232-1177
Fax: 912-232-6954

Tybee Island
Tybee Island, GA 31328
www.tybeeisland.com
Phone: 912-786-5444

Tybee Island Lighthouse & Museum
30 Meddin Dr
Tybee Island, GA 31328
www.tybeeisland.com/tourinfo/museum/timuseum.htm
Phone: 912-786-5801
Fax: 912-786-6538

Tybee Marine Science Foundation
1510 Strand 14th St Parking Lot 10
Tybee Island, GA 31328
www.tybeeisland.com/tourinfo/tybeemsc/tybeemsc.htm
Phone: 912-786-5917
Fax: 912-786-5917

University of Georgia Aquarium
30 Ocean Science Cir
Savannah, GA 31411
Phone: 912-598-2496
Fax: 912-598-2302

Wormsloe Historic Site
7601 Skidaway Rd
Savannah, GA 31406
Phone: 912-353-3023
Fax: 912-353-3023

Sports Teams & Facilities

Grayson Stadium
1401 E Victory Dr
Savannah, GA 31414
Phone: 912-351-9150
Fax: 912-352-9722

King Martin Luther Jr Arena
Liberty & Montgomery St
Savannah, GA 31401
www.savannahcivic.com/arena.htm
Phone: 912-651-6550
Fax: 912-651-6552

Oglethorpe Speedway
267 Raymond Rd
Pooler, GA 31322
Phone: 912-964-8200
Fax: 912-964-9501

Savannah Sand Gnats (baseball)
1401 E Victory Dr Grayson Stadium
Savannah, GA 31414
Phone: 912-351-9150
Fax: 912-352-9722

Annual Events

4th of July Celebration (July 4) 912-234-0295
Arts-on-the-River Weekend (mid-May) 912-651-6417
Christmas on the River (early December) 912-234-0295
Georgia Heritage Celebration (early February) 912-651-2128
Hidden Gardens (mid-late April).................. 912-238-0248
Holiday Tour of Homes (mid-December) 912-231-1494
Jazz Festival (late September) 912-232-2222
New Years Eve at City Market (December 31)....... 912-232-4903
Nogs Tour of Hidden Gardens (mid-April).......... 912-644-6401
Oktoberfest on the River (early October)........... 912-234-0295
Saint Patrick's Day Celebration on the River (mid-March) 912-234-0295
Savannah Greek Festival (mid-October) 912-236-8256
Savannah Irish Festival (mid-February)............ 912-927-0331
Savannah Jazz Festival (late September) 912-232-2222
Savannah Maritime Festival (late August) 912-238-4434
Savannah Onstage International Arts Festival (early March) 912-236-5745
Savannah Tour of Homes & Gardens (late March) 912-234-8054
Scottish Games & Highland Gathering (mid-May) 912-644-6401
Seafood Festival (early May)....................... 912-234-0295
Siege & Reduction Weekend (mid-April) 912-786-5787
Southern Home Show (early March).............. 912-354-6193
Spring Fling (mid-April) 912-232-4903
Telfair Art Fair (early-mid-October) 912-232-1177

Scranton, Pennsylvania

***County:* Lackawanna**

SCRANTON is located in a valley where the Pocono and Endless Mountains meet along the banks of the Lackawanna River in northeastern Pennsylvania. Major cities within 100 miles include Allentown, Bethlehem, and Reading, Pennsylvania.

Area (Land)	25.2 sq mi
Area (Water)	0.2 sq mi
Elevation	754 ft
Latitude	41-40-89 N
Longitude	75-66-28 W
Time Zone	EST
Area Code	570

Climate

Scranton's climate has four distinct seasons. Winters are cold with frequent snowfall, an average of 50 inches per year. Summers are generally mild, with daytime high temperatures in the lower 80s and nighttime lows near 60 degrees. June and July are the wettest months in Scranton, while January and February are the driest.

Average Temperatures & Precipitation

Temperatures

	Jan	Feb	Mar	Apr	May	Jun	Jul	Aug	Sep	Oct	Nov	Dec
High	32	35	46	58	69	78	82	80	72	61	49	37
Low	18	19	28	38	48	57	62	60	53	42	34	23

Precipitation

	Jan	Feb	Mar	Apr	May	Jun	Jul	Aug	Sep	Oct	Nov	Dec
Inches	2.1	2.2	2.6	3.0	3.7	4.0	3.8	3.3	3.3	2.8	3.1	2.5

History

Originally settled in 1771, Scranton began to grow in 1840 when George W. Scranton, after whom the city is named, built the first anthracite-fueled blast furnace in the area. Scranton quickly became a major center for iron production, primarily iron rails for the growing railroad industry, which previously had to be imported from England. It is estimated that one in six rails in the United States was forged in Scranton. Over the course of the next six decades, Scranton's prosperous iron and steel industries drew large numbers of people to the city. At the turn of the century, these industries died off as all of the iron ore in the area had been utilized and steel production moved closer to Lake Erie. Anthracite mining fueled Scranton's economy until World War I, when new sources of fuel were developed and the demand for coal diminished. During the 1950s the city developed a successful plan for urban revitalization, which helped to diversify the city's economy and attract new industries to the area.

Population

1990 Census	81,805
1998 Estimate	74,683
% Change	-8.7

Racial/Ethnic Breakdown

White	97.2%
Black	1.6%
Other	1.2%
Hispanic Origin (may be of any race)	0.7%

Age Breakdown

Under 5 years	6.0%
5 to 17	14.9%
18 to 20	5.7%
21 to 24	6.2%
25 to 34	14.4%
35 to 44	12.2%
45 to 54	8.7%
55 to 64	10.0%
65 to 74	11.8%
75+ years	10.1%
Median Age	37.2

Gender Breakdown

Male	45.8%
Female	54.2%

Government

Type of Government: Mayor-Council

Scranton City Clerk
340 N Washington Ave
Scranton, PA 18503
Phone: 570-348-4113
Fax: 570-348-4207

Scranton City Council
340 N Washington Ave
Scranton, PA 18503
Phone: 570-348-4113
Fax: 570-348-4207

Scranton City Hall
340 N Washington Ave
Scranton, PA 18503
Phone: 570-348-4113
Fax: 570-348-4207

Scranton City Solicitor
340 N Washington Ave
Scranton, PA 18503
Phone: 570-348-4105
Fax: 570-348-4253

Scranton Economic & Community Development Dept
340 N Washington Ave
Scranton, PA 18503
Phone: 570-348-4216
Fax: 570-348-4123

Scranton Fire Dept
340 N Washington Ave
Scranton, PA 18503
Phone: 570-348-4132
Fax: 570-348-4119

Scranton Mayor
340 N Washington Ave
Scranton, PA 18503
Phone: 570-348-4100
Fax: 570-348-4251

Scranton Parks & Recreation Dept
982 Providence Rd
Scranton, PA 18508
Phone: 570-348-4186
Fax: 570-348-0270

Scranton Personnel Dept
340 N Washington Ave
Scranton, PA 18503
Phone: 570-348-4246
Fax: 570-348-4294

Scranton Police Dept
340 N Washington Ave
Scranton, PA 18503
Phone: 570-348-4130
Fax: 570-348-4228

Scranton Public Library
500 Vine St
Scranton, PA 18509
Phone: 570-348-3000
Fax: 570-348-3020

Scranton Public Works Dept
800 Providence Rd
Scranton, PA 18508
Phone: 570-348-4174
Fax: 570-348-0197

Scranton Treasurer
340 N Washington Ave
Scranton, PA 18503
Phone: 570-348-4107
Fax: 570-348-4199

Important Phone Numbers

AAA....................570-348-2511
Dental Referral....................570-344-9080
Driver's License/Vehicle Registration Information ...800-932-4600
Emergency 911
Lackawanna Collector of Taxes....................570-963-6756
Medical Referral....................570-344-3616
Pennsylvania Auditor General....................570-963-4528
Poison Control Center 800-521-6110
Scranton Board of Realtors 570-587-1757
Voter Registration Information....................570-963-6737

Information Sources

Better Business Bureau Serving Northeastern & Central Pennsylvania
PO Box 993
Scranton, PA 18501
www.nepa.bbb.org
Phone: 570-342-9129
Fax: 570-342-1282

Greater Scranton Chamber of Commerce
222 Mulberry St
Scranton, PA 18503
www.scrantonchamber.com
Phone: 570-342-7711
Fax: 570-347-6262

Lackawanna County
200 N Washington Ave
Scranton, PA 18503
Phone: 570-963-6723

Scranton Cultural Center
420 N Washington Ave
Scranton, PA 18503
Phone: 570-346-7369
Fax: 570-346-7365
TF: 800-669-8966

Online Resources

City Knowledge Scranton
www.cityknowledge.com/pa_scranton.htm

Excite.com Scranton City Guide
www.excite.com/travel/countries/united_states/pennsylvania/scranton

Scranton Tourist Fun Guide
www.microserve.net/~magicusa/index.html#funguide

Scranton: A Step Back in Time
www.microserve.net/~magicusa/scranton.html

Area Communities

Communities in the Scranton area with populations greater than 10,000 include:

Dunmore
400 S Blakely St
Dunmore, PA 18512
Phone: 570-344-4590
Fax: 570-343-8107

Kingston
500 Wyoming Ave
Kingston, PA 18704
Phone: 570-288-4576
Fax: 570-288-9493

Plains
126 N Main St
Plains, PA 18705
Phone: 570-829-3439
Fax: 570-829-0710

Wilkes-Barre
40 E Market St
Wilkes-Barre, PA 18711
Phone: 570-826-8259
Fax: 570-821-1197

Economy

Although Scranton's economy was based primarily on manufacturing in the city's early years, services is Lackawanna County's largest employment sector today. Health care is a major industry in the area, with three hospitals among the county's top 15 employers. In addition to the employers listed below, the U.S. Government and Pennsylvania State Government are among Lackawanna County's top 10, ranking number one and number nine respectively.

Unemployment Rate 4.8%*
Per Capita Income....................$24,572*
Median Family Income....................$28,431

** Information given is for Lackawanna County.*

Principal Industries & Number of Wage Earners

Lackawanna County - 1998

Agriculture 259
Construction....................3,016
Finance, Insurance, & Real Estate 5,602
Manufacturing 18,226
Mining.................... 91
Retail Trade....................18,976
Services 35,425
Transportation & Utilities 5,317
Wholesale Trade....................4,692

Major Employers

Allied Services Foundation
PO Box 1103
Scranton, PA 18501
www.allied-services.org
Phone: 570-348-1405
Fax: 570-348-1294

Community Medical Center
1822 Mulberry St
Scranton, PA 18510
Phone: 570-969-8000
Fax: 570-969-8951

Harcourt Learning Direct
925 Oak St
Scranton, PA 18515
www.harcourt-learning.com
Phone: 570-342-7701
Fax: 570-343-3620
TF: 800-233-0259

JC Penney Co Inc
80 Viewmont Mall
Scranton, PA 18508
www.jcpenney.net/company/career
Phone: 570-346-8401
Fax: 570-342-6388

Lackawanna County
200 N Washington Ave
Scranton, PA 18503
Phone: 570-963-6723

Mercy Hospital of Scranton
746 Jefferson Ave
Scranton, PA 18501
www.mhs-nepa.com/facilities/scranton.html
Phone: 570-348-7100
Fax: 570-348-7639

Metropolitan Life Insurance Co
1028 Morgan Hwy
Clarks Summit, PA 18411
www.metlife.com
Phone: 570-587-5161
Fax: 570-587-6352

Moses Taylor Hospital
700 Quincy Ave
Scranton, PA 18510
www.mth.org
Phone: 570-340-2100
Fax: 570-969-2039

Scranton School District
425 N Washington Ave
Scranton, PA 18503
www.scrsd.org/ssd/
Phone: 570-348-3400
Fax: 570-348-3563

Thomson Consumer Electronics Inc
North American Tube Div
1002 New Holland Ave
Lancaster, PA 17601
www.thomson-ato.com
Phone: 717-295-6100
Fax: 717-295-2804
TF: 800-338-0376

University of Scranton
Linden & Monroe Aves St Thomas Hall 3rd Fl
Scranton, PA 18510
E-mail: admissions@scranton.edu
www.scranton.edu
Phone: 570-941-7400
Fax: 570-941-6369

Wal-Mart
900 Commerce Blvd
Dickson City, PA 19519
www.walmartstores.com
Phone: 570-383-2354
Fax: 570-383-8634

WEA Mfg
1400 E Lackawanna Ave
Olyphant, PA 18448
Phone: 570-383-2471
Fax: 570-383-6722

Quality of Living Indicators

Cost of Living Index 98.5
(national average = 100)

Average Home Price $87,500

Education

Public Schools

Scranton School District
425 N Washington Ave
Scranton, PA 18503
www.scrsd.org/ssd/
Phone: 570-348-3400
Fax: 570-348-3563

Number of Schools
Elementary 13
Middle 3
High 2

Student/Teacher Ratio
All Grades 16.5:1

Private Schools

Number of Schools (all grades) .... 10+

Colleges & Universities

College Misericordia
301 Lake St
Dallas, PA 18612
E-mail: admiss@miseri.edu
www.miseri.edu
Phone: 570-674-6400
Fax: 570-675-2441
TF: 800-852-7675

Harcourt Learning Direct
925 Oak St
Scranton, PA 18515
www.harcourt-learning.com
Phone: 570-342-7701
Fax: 570-343-3620
TF: 800-233-0259

Johnson Technical Institute
3427 N Main Ave
Scranton, PA 18508
E-mail: johntech@jti.org
www.jti.org
Phone: 570-342-6404
Fax: 570-348-2181
TF: 800-293-9675

Keystone College
1 College Green
La Plume, PA 18440
www.keystone.edu
Phone: 570-945-5141
Fax: 570-945-7916
TF: 800-824-2764

King's College
133 N River St
Wilkes-Barre, PA 18711
www.kings.edu
Phone: 570-208-5900
Fax: 570-208-9049
TF: 800-955-5777

Lackawanna Junior College
501 Vine St
Scranton, PA 18509
members.aol.com/grifflew/ljc
Phone: 570-961-7810
Fax: 570-961-7843
TF: 877-346-3552

Marywood University
2300 Adams Ave
Scranton, PA 18509
www.marywood.edu
Phone: 570-348-6211
Fax: 570-961-4763

Pennsylvania State University Worthington Scranton
120 Ridge View Dr
Dunmore, PA 18512
www.sn.psu.edu
Phone: 570-963-2500
Fax: 570-963-2535

University of Scranton
Linden & Monroe Aves St Thomas Hall 3rd Fl
Scranton, PA 18510
E-mail: admissions@scranton.edu
www.scranton.edu
Phone: 570-941-7400
Fax: 570-941-6369

Wilkes University
PO Box 111
Wilkes-Barre, PA 18766
www.wilkes.edu
Phone: 570-824-4651
Fax: 570-408-4904
TF: 800-945-5378

Hospitals

Community Medical Center
1822 Mulberry St
Scranton, PA 18510
Phone: 570-969-8000
Fax: 570-969-8951

Marian Community Hospital
100 Lincoln Ave
Carbondale, PA 18407
Phone: 570-282-2100
Fax: 570-282-7177

Mercy Hospital of Scranton
746 Jefferson Ave
Scranton, PA 18501
www.mhs-nepa.com/facilities/scranton.html
Phone: 570-348-7100
Fax: 570-348-7639

Moses Taylor Hospital
700 Quincy Ave
Scranton, PA 18510
www.mth.org
Phone: 570-340-2100
Fax: 570-969-2039

Transportation

Airport(s)

Wilkes-Barre/Scranton International Airport (AVP)
7 miles SW of downtown (approx 20 minutes) 570-346-0672

Mass Transit

COLTS
$1.25 Base fare 570-346-2061

Rail/Bus

Martz/Trailways Bus Station
23 Lackawanna Ave
Scranton, PA 18503
Phone: 570-346-7113

Utilities

Electricity
PPL Utilities 800-342-5775
www.pplweb.com

Gas
PG Energy 570-961-8771
www.pgenergy.com

Water
Pennsylvania American Water Co 570-825-7100

Garbage Collection/Recycling
Scranton Public Works Dept 570-348-4180

Telecommunications

Telephone
Verizon Communications 717-299-8401
www.verizon.com

Cable Television
Adelphia Communications 570-451-4300

Internet Service Providers (ISPs)
epix Internet Services Inc 800-374-9669
www.epix.net
POWER! Net 570-321-0333
www.pcspower.net
Socantel Network 570-937-4114
www.socantel.net

Banks

Mellon Bank
400 Spruce St
Scranton, PA 18503
Phone: 570-343-9691
Fax: 570-344-5267
TF: 800-245-4920

Penn Security Bank & Trust Co
150 N Washington Ave
Scranton, PA 18503
Phone: 570-346-7741
Fax: 570-961-3768
TF: 800-327-0394

Pioneer American Bank NA
611 Luzerne St
West Scranton, PA 18504
Phone: 570-343-5915
Fax: 570-343-2710

Shopping

Carriage Barn
1550 Fairview Rd
Clarks Summit, PA 18411
E-mail: cbarnant@epix.net
www.carriagebarnantiques.com
Phone: 570-587-5405
Fax: 570-586-0712

Mall at Steamtown
300 The Mall at Steamtown
Scranton, PA 18503
Phone: 570-343-3400
Fax: 570-941-8623

Scranton Marketplace
710 Capouse Ave
Scranton, PA 18509
Phone: 570-346-8777

Viewmont Mall
Rt 6 & Scranton-Carbondale Hwy
Scranton, PA 18508
www.crownam.com/viewpage.htm
Phone: 570-346-9165
Fax: 570-346-6832

Media

Newspapers and Magazines

Scranton Times-Tribune*
149 Penn Ave
Scranton, PA 18503
E-mail: newsroom@scrantontimes.com
www.scrantontimes.com
Phone: 570-348-9100
Fax: 570-348-9135
TF: 800-228-4637

Times Tribune*
PO Box 3311
Scranton, PA 18505
www.scrantontimes.com
Phone: 570-348-9100
Fax: 570-348-9135

Weekender The Phone: 570-831-7320
90 E Market St Fax: 570-831-7375
Wilkes-Barre, PA 18703
E-mail: weekendr@microserve.net
www.theweekender.com

**Indicates major daily newspapers*

Television

WBRE-TV Ch 28 (NBC) Phone: 570-823-2828
62 S Franklin St Fax: 570-829-0440
Wilkes-Barre, PA 18701
E-mail: wbre@brigadoon.com
www.wbre.com

WILF-TV Ch 53 (Fox) Phone: 570-347-9653
916 Oak St Fax: 570-347-3141
Scranton, PA 18508

WNEP-TV Ch 16 (ABC) Phone: 570-346-7474
16 Montage Mountain Rd Fax: 570-347-0359
Moosic, PA 18507
E-mail: wneptv@aol.com
www.wnep.com

WSWB-TV Ch 56 (WB) Phone: 570-347-9653
916 Oak St Fax: 570-347-3141
Scranton, PA 18508

WVIA-TV Ch 44 (PBS) Phone: 570-344-1244
70 Old Boston Rd Fax: 570-655-1180
Pittston, PA 18640
www.wvia.org/tv/tv.html

WYOU-TV Ch 22 (CBS) Phone: 570-961-2222
419 Lackawanna Ave Fax: 570-344-4484
Scranton, PA 18503
www.wyou.com

Radio

WEJL-AM 630 kHz (Nost) Phone: 570-346-6555
149 Penn Ave Fax: 570-346-6038
Scranton, PA 18503

WEZX-FM 106.9 MHz (CR) Phone: 570-346-6555
149 Penn Ave Fax: 570-346-6038
Scranton, PA 18503
www.rock107.com

WEZX-FM 106.9 MHz (Rock) Phone: 570-961-1842
149 Penn Ave Fax: 570-346-6038
Scranton, PA 18503

WHLM-FM 106.5 MHz (AC) Phone: 570-784-5500
246 W Main St Fax: 570-784-1004
Bloomsburg, PA 17815
E-mail: mix106@whlm.com
www.whlm.com

WICK-AM 1400 kHz (Oldies) Phone: 570-344-1221
1049 N Sekol Rd Fax: 570-344-0996
Scranton, PA 18504
wick-am.com

WKRZ-FM 98.5 MHz (CHR) Phone: 570-883-9850
305 Hwy 315 Fax: 570-883-9851
Pittston, PA 18640
E-mail: feedback@wkrz.com
www.wkrz.com

WVMW-FM 91.5 MHz (Alt) Phone: 570-348-6202
2300 Adams Ave Marywood College Fax: 570-961-4769
Scranton, PA 18509

WWDL-FM 104.9 MHz (AC) Phone: 570-344-1221
1049 N Sekol Rd Fax: 570-344-0996
Scranton, PA 18504
E-mail: comments@wwdl.com
www.wwdl.com

Attractions

Scranton's industrial heritage is exhibited at three area attractions: the Steamtown National Historic Site, a collection of authentic locomotives and cars located in downtown Scranton; the Lackawanna Coal Mine Tour, which takes visitors to a restored mine 300 feet underground; and the Pennsylvania Anthracite Heritage Museum (one of four anthracite museums in the area), which explores the history of the people who settled and worked in the anthracite region. The Steamtown National Historic Site also features steam-powered rail excursions through the countryside.

Anthracite People Phone: 570-963-4804
c/o Pennsylvania Anthracite Heritage Fax: 570-963-4194
Museum Bald Mountain Rd RR #1
Scranton, PA 18504

Ballet Theatre of Scranton Phone: 570-347-0208
310 Penn Ave Fax: 570-961-0815
Scranton, PA 18503

Broadway Theatre of Northeast Pennsylvania Phone: 570-342-7784
108 N Washington Ave Suite 802
Scranton, PA 18501

Claws 'n' Paws Wild Animal Park Phone: 570-698-6154
Rt 590 Fax: 570-698-2957
Lake Ariel, PA 18436
www.microserve.net/~magicusa/clawspaws.html

Everhart Museum Phone: 570-346-7186
1901 Mulberry St Fax: 570-346-0652
Scranton, PA 18510
www.northeastweb.com/everhart

Holocaust Museum & Resource Center Phone: 570-961-2300
601 Jefferson Ave Fax: 570-346-6147
Scranton, PA 18510
E-mail: jaytov@mail.microserve.net
www.ncx.com/wwi/hmrc/

Houdini Museum Phone: 570-342-5555
1433 N Main Ave
Scranton, PA 18508
www.houdini.org

Lackawanna County Coal Mine Phone: 570-963-6463
Bald Mountain Rd Fax: 570-963-6701
Scranton, PA 18504

Lahey Family Fun Park Phone: 570-586-5699
500 Morgan Hwy Fax: 570-586-7109
Clarks Summit, PA 18411

Montage Mountain Ski Area
1000 Montage Mountain Rd
Scranton, PA 18505
E-mail: montage@sunlink.net
www.skimontage.com
Phone: 570-969-7669
Fax: 570-963-6621
TF: 800-468-7669

Music Box Dinner Playhouse
196 Hughes St
Swoyersville, PA 18704
members.aol.com/oreoking/musicbox.htm
Phone: 570-283-2195

Northeastern Pennsylvania Philharmonic
957 Broadcast Ctr
Avoca, PA 18641
www.nepaphil.org
Phone: 570-457-8301
Fax: 570-457-5901
TF: 800-836-3413

Pennsylvania Anthracite Heritage Museum
RR1 Bald Mountain Rd
Scranton, PA 18504
Phone: 570-963-4804
Fax: 570-963-4194

Pioneer Tunnel Coal Mine
19th & Oak Sts
Ashland, PA 17921
www.pioneertunnel.com
Phone: 570-875-3850
Fax: 570-875-3301

Providence Playhouse
1256 Providence Rd
Scranton, PA 18508
Phone: 570-342-9707

Saint Ann's Monastery
1230 Saint Ann St
Scranton, PA 18504
Phone: 570-347-5691
Fax: 570-347-9387

Scranton Cultural Center
420 N Washington Ave
Scranton, PA 18503
Phone: 570-346-7369
Fax: 570-346-7365
TF: 800-669-8966

Scranton Iron Furnace
159 Cedar Ave
Scranton, PA 18505
Phone: 570-963-3208

Scranton Public Theatre
PO Box 1451
Scranton, PA 18501
Phone: 570-344-3656

Slocum Hollow Family Fun Park
3200 N Main Ave
Scranton, PA 18508
Phone: 570-346-4386

Steamtown National Historic Site
150 S Washington Ave
Scranton, PA 18503
www.nps.gov/stea/
Phone: 570-340-5200
Fax: 570-340-5265

Upper Delaware Scenic & Recreational River
RR 2 Box 2428 River Rd
Beach Lake, PA 18405
E-mail: upde_interpretation@nps.gov
www.nps.gov/upde
Phone: 570-685-4871
Fax: 570-685-4874

Sports Teams & Facilities

Pocono Downs
1280 Hwy 315
Wilkes-Barre, PA 18702
Phone: 570-825-6681
Fax: 570-823-9407

Scranton/Wilkes-Barre Red Barons (baseball)
Lackawanna Stadium
Scranton, PA 18505
Phone: 570-963-6556
Fax: 570-963-6564

Annual Events

Armed Forces Airshow (mid-June) 570-824-1879
Artisan's Marketplace (late November) 570-586-8191
Carbondale Pioneer Days (late August).............570-282-7393
Jazz Fest at Cherry Blossom Time (late April)......570-208-4292
La Festa Italiana (early September)................800-229-3526
Moscow Country Fair (mid-August)................570-842-7252
Pennsylvania National Arts & Crafts Show (mid-March) 717-796-0531
Saint Patrick's Day Parade (mid-March) 570-348-3412
Wings Over Montage (early September) 570-969-7669

Seattle, Washington

***County:* King**

SEATTLE is located between Puget Sound and Lake Washington in northwestern Washington State. Major cities within 100 miles include Tacoma, Olympia, and Bellingham, Washington; and Victoria, British Columbia, Canada.

Area (Land) .... 83.9 sq mi
Area (Water)............................... 58.7 sq mi
Elevation...................................... 125 ft
Latitude ....47-60-64 N
Longitude.............................. 122-33-08 W
Time Zone .... PST
Area Code....................................... 206

Climate

Seattle's climate is influenced by the city's proximity to the Pacific Ocean as well as its location west of the Cascade Mountains. Winters are wet, but temperatures remain fairly mild, with average highs ranging from the mid-40s to low 50s and lows in the mid- to upper 30s. The average annual snowfall in Seattle is 15 inches. Summers are pleasant, with average daytime high temperatures in the low 70s and evening lows cooling down into the mid-50s. January is the wettest month of the year in Seattle, while July is the driest.

Average Temperatures & Precipitation

Temperatures

	Jan	Feb	Mar	Apr	May	Jun	Jul	Aug	Sep	Oct	Nov	Dec
High	46	51	54	58	64	70	74	74	69	60	52	46
Low	36	38	40	43	48	54	57	57	53	47	41	37

Precipitation

	Jan	Feb	Mar	Apr	May	Jun	Jul	Aug	Sep	Oct	Nov	Dec
Inches	5.4	4.0	3.8	2.6	2.0	1.8	0.9	1.3	2.0	3.3	5.5	6.0

History

Originally inhabited by Native Americans of the Duwamish, Suquamish, and Snohomish tribes, the Seattle area's first white settlement was established in 1851 at Alki Point. The settlement was moved the following year to the site of present-day downtown Seattle, and the community was named for Suquamish Chief Sealth (pronounced See-yat). In 1853, the first sawmill was built in Seattle, marking the beginning of the city's prosperous lumber industry.

Incorporated as a city in 1869, Seattle's early development was relatively slow until the arrival of the transcontinental railroad in nearby Tacoma in 1883. In the years that followed, Seattle's population jumped from just over 3,500 in 1880 to more than 42,800 a decade later. In 1893, Seattle itself became the western terminus of the Great Northern Pacific railroad and the city became an important distribution center for the area's rich timber and agricultural resources. During the 1890s, Seattle also flourished as an outfitting point for the Klondike Gold Rush. In 1909, Seattle hosted the Alaska-Yukon-Pacific Exposition, which drew more than 3.7 million visitors. By 1910, the city's population exceeded 237,000.

Trade became increasingly important to Seattle's economy during the early 1900s. The Port of Seattle was established in 1911 and, three years later, the opening of the Panama Canal further expanded Seattle's access to the rest of the world. Wartime industries such as shipbuilding and aerospace manufacturing sustained Seattle's economy for much of first half of the 20th Century, and by the 1950s Seattle's population had grown to nearly 575,000. In the years that followed World War II, Seattle-based Boeing Co. continued to pioneer advances in the aviation industry, including the invention of the first commercial jet plane, the Boeing 707. By the 1990s, the Port of Seattle had become the fourth-largest container port in the United States.

Although the city's population declined after the 1950s as residents began moving into the suburbs, Seattle is presently the largest city in Washington State today. Now home to more than 536,000 people, recent population figures reflect a new wave of growth in the city, and this trend is expected to continue into the 21st Century.

Population

1990 Census 516,259
1998 Estimate.............................536,978
% Change 4.0
2005 Projection 2,490,855*

Racial/Ethnic Breakdown

White.....................................75.3%
Black.....................................10.1%
Other.....................................14.6%
Hispanic Origin (may be of any race).........3.6%

Age Breakdown

Under 5 years..............................5.7%
5 to 17...................................10.8%
18 to 20...................................4.5%
21 to 24...................................7.6%
25 to 34..................................21.7%
35 to 44..................................18.1%
45 to 54...................................9.2%
55 to 64...................................7.4%
65 to 74...................................8.1%
75+ years 7.1%
Median Age................................34.9

Gender Breakdown
Male.................................... 48.8%
Female.................................. 51.2%

** Information given is for the Seattle-Bellevue-Everett Metropolitan Statistical Area (MSA), which includes the City of Bellevue, the City of Everett, the City of Seattle, Island County, King County, and Snohomish County.*

Government

Type of Government: Mayor-Council

Seattle City Clerk
600 4th Ave Rm 104
Seattle, WA 98104
Phone: 206-684-8344
Fax: 206-386-9025

Seattle City Council
600 4th Ave Rm 1100
Seattle, WA 98104
Phone: 206-684-8888
Fax: 206-684-8587

Seattle City Hall
600 4th Ave
Seattle, WA 98104
Phone: 206-386-1234
Fax: 206-684-5529

Seattle City Light
700 5th Ave Suite 3300
Seattle, WA 98104
Phone: 206-625-3000

Seattle Economic Development Office
600 4th Ave Rm 205
Seattle, WA 98104
Phone: 206-684-8090
Fax: 206-684-0379

Seattle Finance Div
600 4th Ave Rm 103
Seattle, WA 98104
Phone: 206-684-5212
Fax: 206-684-8625

Seattle Fire Dept
301 2nd Ave S
Seattle, WA 98104
Phone: 206-386-1401
Fax: 206-386-1412

Seattle Law Dept
600 4th Ave 10th Fl
Seattle, WA 98104
Phone: 206-684-8200
Fax: 206-684-8284

Seattle Mayor
600 4th Ave 12th Fl
Seattle, WA 98104
Phone: 206-684-4000
Fax: 206-684-5360

Seattle Parks & Recreation Dept
100 Dexter Ave N
Seattle, WA 98109
Phone: 206-684-7075
Fax: 206-233-7023

Seattle Personnel Div
710 2nd Ave 12th Fl
Seattle, WA 98104
Phone: 206-684-7664
Fax: 206-684-4157

Seattle Police Dept
610 3rd Ave
Seattle, WA 98104
Phone: 206-684-5577
Fax: 206-684-5525

Seattle Public Library
1000 4th Ave
Seattle, WA 98104
Phone: 206-386-4100
Fax: 206-386-4119

Seattle Public Utilities Dept
710 2nd Ave 10th Fl
Seattle, WA 98104
Phone: 206-684-5851
Fax: 206-684-4631

Seattle Strategic Planning Office
600 4th Ave Rm 300
Seattle, WA 98104
Phone: 206-684-8080
Fax: 206-233-0085

Seattle Transportation (SEATRAN)
600 4th Ave Municipal Bldg Rm 400
Seattle, WA 98104
Phone: 206-684-5087
Fax: 206-684-5063

Important Phone Numbers

AAA..206-448-5353
American Express Travel 206-441-8622
Driver's License Information.....................206-368-7262
Emergency 911
HotelDocs 800-468-3537
King County Office of Financial Management
Personal Property Tax Information 206-296-4290
King County Office of Financial Management Real
Property Tax Information.......................206-296-3850
Medical Referral.................................206-622-9933
Poison Control Center 206-526-2121
Seattle-King County Assn of Realtors 425-820-3277
Time/Temp 206-361-8463
Travelers Aid....................................206-461-3888
Vehicle Registration Information 206-296-4000
Voter Registration Information....................206-296-1608
Washington State Dept of Revenue 800-647-7706
Weather..206-464-2000

Information Sources

Better Business Bureau Serving Oregon & Western Washington
4800 S 188th St Suite 222
SeaTac, WA 98188
www.seatac.bbb.org
Phone: 206-431-2222
Fax: 206-431-2211

Greater Seattle Chamber of Commerce
1301 5th Ave Suite 2400
Seattle, WA 98101
www.seattlechamber.com
Phone: 206-389-7200
Fax: 206-389-7288

King County
516 3rd Ave Rm 400
Seattle, WA 98104
www.metrokc.gov
Phone: 206-296-4040
Fax: 206-296-0194

Seattle Community Network
PO Box 85539
Seattle, WA 98145
www.scn.org
Phone: 206-365-4528
Fax: 206-362-1495

Seattle-King County Convention & Visitors Bureau
520 Pike St Suite 1300
Seattle, WA 98101
www.seeseattle.org/home/skccvb.htm
Phone: 206-461-5840
Fax: 206-461-5855
TF: 800-535-7071

Washington State Convention & Trade Center
800 Convention Pl
Seattle, WA 98101
www.wsctc.com
Phone: 206-694-5000
Fax: 206-694-5399

Online Resources

4Seattle.com
www.4seattle.com

About.com Guide to Seattle/Tacoma
seattle.about.com/local/pacnwus/seattle

All Seattle
www.allcitynet.com/seattle

Anthill City Guide Seattle
www.anthill.com/city.asp?city=seattle

Area Guide Seattle
seattle.areaguides.net

Art Guide Northwest
www.artguidenw.com

Boulevards Seattle
www.seattle.com

Bradmans.com Seattle
www.bradmans.com/scripts/display_city.cgi?city=243

City Knowledge Seattle
www.cityknowledge.com/wa_seattle.htm

Cityhits Seattle
www.cityhits.com/seattle/

CitySearch Seattle
seattle.citysearch.com

CuisineNet Seattle
www.cuisinenet.com/restaurant/seattle/index.shtml

DigitalCity Seattle
www.digitalcity.com/seattle

Excite.com Seattle City Guide
www.excite.com/travel/countries/united_states/washington/seattle

Greater Seattle InfoGuide
www.seattleinfoguide.com/

Lodging.com Seattle Washington
www.lodging.com/auto/guides/seattle-area-wa.html

Rough Guide Travel Seattle
travel.roughguides.com/content/4604/

Savvy Diner Guide to Seattle Restaurants
www.savvydiner.com/seattle/

Seattle
sensemedia.net/seattle

Seattle CityWomen
www.citywomen.com/seatwomen.htm

Seattle Home Page
www.seattle.net/SeattleHome.html

Seattle Web
www.seattleweb.com/

Seattle.Bizhost.com
seattle.bizhost.com/

Seattle.TheLinks.com
seattle.thelinks.com/

SeattleSquare.com
www.seattlesquare.com/

Virtual Voyages Seattle
www.virtualvoyages.com/usa/wa/seattle/seattle.sht

Yahoo! Seattle
seattle.yahoo.com

Area Communities

Incorporated communities in the Greater Seattle area—including King, Kitsap, Island, and Snohomish counties (Pierce County is covered in the chapter on Tacoma)—with populations greater than 15,000 include:

Auburn
25 W Main St
Auburn, WA 98001
Phone: 253-931-3000
Fax: 253-288-3132

Bainbridge Island
280 Madison Ave N
Bainbridge Island, WA 98110
Phone: 206-842-7633
Fax: 206-842-5741

Bellevue
11511 Main St
Bellevue, WA 98004
Phone: 425-452-6810
Fax: 425-452-5241

Bothell
18305 101st Ave NE
Bothell, WA 98011
Phone: 425-486-3256
Fax: 425-487-1204

Bremerton
239 4th St
Bremerton, WA 98337
Phone: 360-478-5290
Fax: 360-478-5200

Burien
415 SW 150th St
Burien, WA 98166
Phone: 206-241-4647
Fax: 206-248-5539

Des Moines
21630 11th Ave S
Des Moines, WA 98198
Phone: 206-878-4595
Fax: 206-870-6540

Edmonds
121 5th Ave N
Edmonds, WA 98020
Phone: 425-775-2525
Fax: 425-771-0266

Everett
2930 Wetmore Ave
Everett, WA 98201
Phone: 425-259-8700
Fax: 425-257-8741

Federal Way
33530 1st Way S
Federal Way, WA 98003
Phone: 253-661-4000
Fax: 253-661-4075

Kent
220 4th Ave S
Kent, WA 98032
Phone: 253-859-3300
Fax: 253-856-6700

Kirkland
123 5th ave
Kirkland, WA 98033
Phone: 425-828-1100
Fax: 425-828-1290

Lynnwood
PO Box 5008
Lynnwood, WA 98046
Phone: 425-775-1971
Fax: 425-771-6144

Marysville
4822 Grove St
Marysville, WA 98270
Phone: 360-651-5000
Fax: 360-651-5033

Mercer Island
9611 SE 36th St
Mercer Island, WA 98040
Phone: 206-236-5300
Fax: 206-236-3651

Mountlake Terrace
23204 58th Ave W
Mountlake Terrace, WA 98043
Phone: 425-776-1161
Fax: 425-778-6421

Mukilteo
4480 Chennault Beach Rd
Mukilteo, WA 98275
Phone: 425-355-4141
Fax: 425-347-4544

Redmond
15670 NE 85th St
Redmond, WA 98052
Phone: 425-556-2900
Fax: 425-556-2198

Renton
1055 S Grady Way
Renton, WA 98055
Phone: 425-235-2500
Fax: 425-235-2513

SeaTac
17900 International Blvd Suite 401
SeaTac, WA 98188
Phone: 206-241-9100
Fax: 206-241-3999

Shoreline
17544 Midvale Ave N
Shoreline, WA 98133
Phone: 206-546-1700
Fax: 206-546-2200

Economy

Seattle's diverse economic base ranges from timber product manufacturing to cancer research. Major U.S. companies headquartered in Greater Seattle include Boeing, Microsoft, Seafirst Bank, Alaska Airlines, Nordstrom, and The Bon Marche. Services is the largest employment sector in King County, with health care, tourism, and business services the area's leading service-related industries. Home to the fourth largest port in the United States, trade also remains important to Seattle's economy—the Port of Seattle has moved more than one million containers annually over the past decade. Manufacturing remains strong in Seattle as well, with production of transportation equipment (including aircraft, trucks, and construction machinery) accounting for half of King County's total manufacturing jobs. Seattle has also become one of the leading centers for high technology in the United States—Greater Seattle has the nation's highest concentration of software companies per capita, and biotechnology is currently one of the region's fastest-growing industries.

Unemployment Rate 2.9%*
Per Capita Income.......................... $36,854*
Median Family Income..................... $62,600*

** Information given is for the Seattle-Bellevue-Everett Metropolitan Statistical Area (MSA), which includes the City of Bellevue, the City of Everett, the City of Seattle, Island County, King County, and Snohomish County.*

Principal Industries & Number of Wage Earners

King County - 1998

Industry	Wage Earners
Agriculture, Fishing, Forestry, & Hunting	2,727
Construction	55,844
Finance & Insurance	50,094
Manufacturing	140,129
Mining	558
Retail Trade	99,494
Services	326,468
Transportation & Warehousing	43,481
Wholesale Trade	64,885

Major Employers

Alaska Airlines Inc
PO Box 68900
Seattle, WA 98168
www.alaskaair.com
Phone: 206-433-3200
Fax: 206-433-3366
TF: 800-426-0333

Albertson's Inc
11000 NE 33rd Pl Suite 102
Bellevue, WA 98004
Phone: 425-897-1700
Fax: 425-822-2698

Baugh Enterprises Inc
PO Box 14135
Seattle, WA 98144
www.baughent.com
Phone: 206-726-8000
Fax: 206-328-9235

Boeing Co
PO Box 3707
Seattle, WA 98124
www.boeing.com
Phone: 206-655-1131
Fax: 206-655-3987

Bon Marche Inc
1601 3rd Ave
Seattle, WA 98181
www.federated-fds.com/divisions/bon1.html
Phone: 206-506-6000
Fax: 206-506-7722
TF: 800-552-7288

Costco Wholesale Corp
999 Lake Dr
Issaquah, WA 98027
www.costco.com
Phone: 425-313-8100
Fax: 425-313-8221

Fred Meyer Inc
3800 SE 22nd Ave
Portland, OR 97202
www.fredmeyer.com
Phone: 503-232-8844
TF: 800-858-9202

Group Health Cooperative
521 Wall St
Seattle, WA 98121
E-mail: info@ghc.org
www.ghc.org
Phone: 206-448-5643
Fax: 206-448-2361
TF: 888-901-4636

King County
516 3rd Ave Rm 400
Seattle, WA 98104
www.metrokc.gov
Phone: 206-296-4040
Fax: 206-296-0194

Lanoga Corp
17946 NE 65th St
Redmond, WA 98052
E-mail: info@lanogacorp.com
www.lanoga.com
Phone: 425-883-4125
Fax: 425-882-2959

Microsoft Corp
1 Microsoft Way
Redmond, WA 98052
www.microsoft.com
Phone: 425-882-8080
Fax: 425-936-7329
TF: 800-426-9400

Nordstrom Inc
1617 6th Ave Suite 500
Seattle, WA 98101
www.nordstrom.com
Phone: 206-628-2111
Fax: 206-628-1795

PACCAR Inc
777 106th Ave NE
Bellevue, WA 98004
www.paccar.com
Phone: 425-455-7400
Fax: 425-468-8206

Port of Seattle
PO Box 1209
Seattle, WA 98111
E-mail: comments@portseattle.org
www.portseattle.org
Phone: 206-728-3265
Fax: 206-728-3280

Puget Sound Energy Inc
PO Box 97034
Bellevue, WA 98009
www.psechoice.com
Phone: 425-454-6363
Fax: 425-462-3521

Seattle City Hall
600 4th Ave
Seattle, WA 98104
www.ci.seattle.wa.us
Phone: 206-386-1234
Fax: 206-684-5529

Sisters of Providence Health System
520 Pike Tower Suite 2500
Seattle, WA 98101
Phone: 206-464-3355
Fax: 206-464-3038

Swedish Medical Center
747 Broadway
Seattle, WA 98122
www.swedish.org
Phone: 206-386-6000
Fax: 206-386-2277

University of Washington
Seattle, WA 98195
E-mail: help@cac.washington.edu
www.washington.edu
Phone: 206-543-2100
Fax: 206-685-3655

Weyerhaeuser Co
33663 Weyerhaeuser Way S
Tacoma, WA 98003
www.weyerhaeuser.com
Phone: 253-924-2345

Quality of Living Indicators

Total Crime Index.................................49,760
(rates per 100,000 inhabitants)

Violent Crime
Murder/manslaughter........................... 45
Forcible rape 188
Robbery....................................1,642
Aggravated assault.........................2,291

Property Crime
Burglary 6,469
Larceny theft 30,485
Motor vehicle theft........................8,640

Cost of Living Index.................................118.7
(national average = 100)

Median Home Price.................................$183,700

Education

Public Schools

Seattle School District No 1
815 4th Ave N
Seattle, WA 98109
www.seattleschools.org
Phone: 206-298-7000
Fax: 206-298-7375

Number of Schools
Elementary.................................. 67
Middle 10
High....................................... 11

Student/Teacher Ratio
Grades K-3 .... 26.0:1
Grades 4-6................................ 28.0:1
Grades 7-12 .... 32.0:1

Private Schools

Number of Schools (all grades).................. 100+

Colleges & Universities

Antioch University
2326 6th Ave
Seattle, WA 98121
www.seattleantioch.edu
Phone: 206-441-5352
Fax: 206-441-3307

Art Institute of Seattle
2323 Elliott Ave
Seattle, WA 98121
E-mail: admissions@ais.edu
www.ais.edu
Phone: 206-448-0900
Fax: 206-448-2501
TF: 800-275-2471

Bellevue Community College
3000 Landerholm Cir SE House 2
Bellevue, WA 98007
www.bcc.ctc.edu
Phone: 425-641-2222
Fax: 425-603-4065

City University of Bellevue
335 116th Ave SE
Bellevue, WA 98004
www.cityu.edu
Phone: 425-637-1010
Fax: 425-450-4611
TF: 800-426-5596

Cornish College of the Arts
710 E Roy St
Seattle, WA 98102
E-mail: adm@cornish.edu
www.cornish.edu
Phone: 206-323-1400
Fax: 206-720-1011
TF: 800-726-2787

Edmonds Community College
20000 68th Ave W
Lynnwood, WA 98036
www.edcc.edu
Phone: 425-640-1500
Fax: 425-640-1159

Everett Community College
801 Wetmore Ave
Everett, WA 98201
www.evcc.ctc.edu
Phone: 425-388-9100
Fax: 425-388-9129

Green River Community College
12401 SE 320th St
Auburn, WA 98092
E-mail: jramsey@grcc.ctc.edu
www.greenriver.ctc.edu
Phone: 253-833-9111
Fax: 253-288-3454

Henry Cogswell College
2802 Wetmore Ave Suite 100
Everett, WA 98201
www.henrycogswell.edu
Phone: 425-258-3351
Fax: 425-257-0405

ITT Technical Institute
12720 Gateway Dr Suite 100
Seattle, WA 98168
www.itt-tech.edu
Phone: 206-244-3300
Fax: 206-246-7635
TF: 800-422-2029

North Seattle Community College
9600 College Way N
Seattle, WA 98103
E-mail: nsccinfo@nsccgate.sccd.ctc.edu
nsccux.sccd.ctc.edu/
Phone: 206-527-3600
Fax: 206-527-3635

Northwest College of the Assemblies of God
5520 108th Ave NE
Kirkland, WA 98033
E-mail: admissions@ncag.edu
www.nwcollege.edu
Phone: 425-822-8266
Fax: 425-827-0148
TF: 800-669-3781

Puget Sound Christian College
410 4th Ave N
Edmonds, WA 98020
members.aa.net/~bluvase/psccHome.html
Phone: 425-775-8686
Fax: 425-775-8688

Seattle Bible College
2363 NW 80th St
Seattle, WA 98117
E-mail: seattle_bc@msn.com
Phone: 206-784-1888
Fax: 206-784-2187

Seattle Central Community College
1701 Broadway
Seattle, WA 98122
seattlecentral.org
Phone: 206-587-3800
Fax: 206-344-4390

Seattle Community College District VI
1500 Harvard Ave
Seattle, WA 98122
seaccd.sccd.ctc.edu
Phone: 206-587-4155
Fax: 206-587-3883

Seattle Pacific University
3307 3rd Ave W
Seattle, WA 98119
www.spu.edu
Phone: 206-281-2000
Fax: 206-281-2669

Seattle University
900 Broadway
Seattle, WA 98122
www.seattleu.edu
Phone: 206-296-6000
Fax: 206-296-5656

Shoreline Community College
16101 Greenwood Ave N
Shoreline, WA 98133
oscar.ctc.edu/shoreline
Phone: 206-546-4101
Fax: 206-546-5835

South Seattle Community College
6000 16th Ave SW
Seattle, WA 98106
www.sccd.ctc.edu/south
Phone: 206-764-5300
Fax: 206-764-7947

University of Washington
Seattle, WA 98195
E-mail: help@cac.washington.edu
www.washington.edu
Phone: 206-543-2100
Fax: 206-685-3655

Western Washington University
516 High St
Bellingham, WA 98225
www.wwu.edu
Phone: 360-650-3000
Fax: 360-650-7369

Hospitals

Auburn Regional Medical Center
202 N Division St Plaza 1
Auburn, WA 98001
www.armcuhs.com
Phone: 253-833-7711
Fax: 253-939-2376

Children's Hospital & Regional Medical Center
PO Box 5371
Seattle, WA 98105
www.chmc.org
Phone: 206-526-2000
Fax: 206-527-3879

Eastside Hospital
2700 152nd Ave NE
Redmond, WA 98052
Phone: 425-883-5151
Fax: 425-883-5638

Evergreen Hospital Medical Center
12040 NE 128th St
Kirkland, WA 98034
www.evergreenhealthnet.org
Phone: 425-899-1000
Fax: 425-899-2713

Group Health Cooperative Central Hospital
201 16th Ave E
Seattle, WA 98112
Phone: 206-326-3000
Fax: 206-326-3436

Harborview Medical Center
325 9th Ave
Seattle, WA 98104
www.washington.edu/medical/hmc
Phone: 206-223-3000
Fax: 206-731-8699

Harrison Memorial Hospital
2520 Cherry Ave
Bremerton, WA 98310
www.harrisonhospital.org
Phone: 360-377-3911
Fax: 360-792-6527

Highline Community Hospital
16251 Sylvester Rd SW
Burien, WA 98166
www.hchnet.org
Phone: 206-244-9970
Fax: 206-246-5862

Northwest Hospital
1550 N 115th St
Seattle, WA 98133
www.nwhospital.org
Phone: 206-368-1700
Fax: 206-368-1291

Overlake Hospital Medical Center
1035 116th Ave NE
Bellevue, WA 98004
www.overlakehospital.org
Phone: 425-688-5000
Fax: 425-688-5650

Providence Everett Medical Center
1321 Colby Ave
Everett, WA 98201
www.providence.org/everett/pgmc.htm
Phone: 425-261-2000
Fax: 425-261-4051

Providence Pacific Clinic
916 Pacific Ave
Everett, WA 98201
Phone: 425-258-7123
Fax: 425-261-4051

Providence Seattle Medical Center
500 17th Ave
Seattle, WA 98122
www.providence.org/pugetsound
Phone: 206-320-2000
Fax: 206-320-3152

Saint Francis Hospital
34515 9th Ave S
Federal Way, WA 98003
www.fhshealth.org/stfrancis.html
Phone: 253-838-9700
Fax: 253-952-7988

Stevens Memorial Hospital
21601 76th Ave W
Edmonds, WA 98026
www.stevenshealthcare.org/Hospital.cfm
Phone: 425-640-4000
Fax: 425-640-4010

Swedish Medical Center
747 Broadway
Seattle, WA 98122
www.swedish.org
Phone: 206-386-6000
Fax: 206-386-2277

Swedish Medical Center/Bullard
5300 Tallman Ave NW
Seattle, WA 98107
www.swedish.org
Phone: 206-782-2700
Fax: 206-781-6155

University of Washington Medical Center Seattle
1959 NE Pacific St
Seattle, WA 98195
www.washington.edu/medical
Phone: 206-548-3300
Fax: 206-598-6965

Valley Medical Center
400 S 43rd St
Renton, WA 98055
www.valleymed.org
Phone: 425-228-3450
Fax: 425-656-4207
TF: 800-540-1814

Veterans Affairs Puget Sound Medical Center
1660 S Columbian Way
Seattle, WA 98108
Phone: 206-762-1010
Fax: 206-764-2224

Virginia Mason Medical Center
925 Seneca St
Seattle, WA 98111
www.vmmc.org
Phone: 206-624-1144
Fax: 206-583-6523

Transportation

Airport(s)

Seattle-Tacoma International Airport (SEA)
10 miles S of downtown (approx 20 minutes) 206-431-4444

Mass Transit

Metropolitan Transit
$1.25 Base fare 206-553-3000
Washington State Ferry System
fare varies with destination 206-464-6400

Rail/Bus

Greyhound Bus Station
811 Stewart St
Seattle, WA 98101
Phone: 206-628-5526
TF: 800-231-2222

King Street Amtrak Station
303 S Jackson St
Seattle, WA 98104
Phone: 206-382-4125
TF: 800-872-7245

Utilities

Electricity
Puget Sound Energy 206-464-1999
www.psechoice.com
Seattle City Light 206-625-3000
www.ci.seattle.wa.us/light

Gas
Puget Sound Energy 206-464-1999
www.psechoice.com

Water
Seattle Water Service 206-684-5900

Garbage Collection/Recycling
Seattle Public Utilities Solid Waste Div 206-684-7600

Telecommunications

Telephone
Qwest 800-244-1111
www.qwest.com

Cable Television
AT & T Cable Services 206-433-3434
Millennium Digital Media 425-865-0052

Internet Service Providers (ISPs)
2alpha 425-746-4140
www.2alpha.com
Alternate Access Inc 206-777-8888
www.aa.net
Blarg! Online Services Inc 425-401-9821
www.blarg.com
Computer System Enhancements 206-812-1020
www.cse-net.com
Eskimo North Inc 206-361-1161
www.eskimo.com
International Web Broadcasting Corp 425-290-1800
www.iwbc.net
Isomedia.com 425-869-5411
www.isomedia.com
Jet City Online 206-281-1774
www.jetcity.com
Northwest Link 425-451-1151
www.nwlink.com
Seanet Corp 206-343-7828
www.seanet.com
Seattle Community Network .206-365-4528
www.scn.org
ServNet Internet Services 206-789-4155
www.serv.net
Verio Bellevue 425-649-7400
home.verio.net/local/frontpage.cfm?AirportCode=SEA
VISUAL Internet Services Group 253-946-9426
www.oz.net/~visual
WinStar Northwest Nexus Inc 425-455-3505
www.nwnexus.com
WOLFE Internet Access Inc .206-463-9399
www.wolfe.net

Banks

Bank of America NA
701 5th Ave
Seattle, WA 98104
Phone: 206-358-3000
Fax: 206-358-6091
TF: 888-885-2242

Commerce Bank of Washington NA
601 Union St Suite 3600
Seattle, WA 98101
www.tcbwa.com
Phone: 206-292-3900
Fax: 206-625-9457

Continental Savings Bank
1314 6th Ave
Seattle, WA 98101
www.continentalsavings.com
Phone: 206-621-0100
Fax: 206-389-4458

KeyBank NA Seattle District
815 2nd Ave
Seattle, WA 98104
Phone: 206-447-5730
Fax: 206-447-5760
TF: 800-539-8189

Sterling Savings Bank
5512 22nd Ave NW
Seattle, WA 98107
Phone: 206-789-5755
Fax: 206-789-7511

US Bank NA
1420 5th Ave
Seattle, WA 98101
Phone: 206-344-3690
Fax: 206-344-4555

Washington Federal Savings & Loan Assn
425 Pike St
Seattle, WA 98101
Phone: 206-624-793
Fax: 206-624-233
TF: 800-324-937

Washington Mutual Bank
1201 3rd Ave
Seattle, WA 98101
www.wamu.com
Phone: 206-461-20
Fax: 206-554-27
TF: 800-756-80

Wells Fargo Bank NA
8517 35th Ave NE
Seattle, WA 98115
Phone: 206-523-77
Fax: 206-524-77

Shopping

Antiques at Pikes Place
92 Stewart St
Seattle, WA 98101
Phone: 206-441-9
Fax: 206-448-9

Bay Pavilion
1301 Alaskan Way
Seattle, WA 98101
Phone: 206-623-
Fax: 206-343-

Bellevue Square
302 Bellevue Sq
Bellevue, WA 98004
Phone: 425-454
Fax: 425-455

Bon Marche Inc
1601 3rd Ave
Seattle, WA 98181
www.federated-fds.com/divisions/bon1.html
Phone: 206-50
Fax: 206-50
TF: 800-55

City Centre
1420 5th Ave
Seattle, WA 98101
Phone: 206-65
Fax: 206-62

Downtown Seattle Assn
500 Union St
Seattle, WA 98101
Phone: 206-4

Nordstrom Inc
1617 6th Ave Suite 500
Seattle, WA 98101
www.nordstrom.com
Phone: 206-
Fax: 206-

Northgate Mall
555 Northgate Mall
Seattle, WA 98125
Phone: 206-362-4777
Fax: 206-361-8760

Pacific Place
600 Pine St
Seattle, WA 98101
Phone: 206-405-2655

Pike Place Market
1st Ave & Pike St
Seattle, WA 98101
E-mail: information@pikeplacemarket.org
www.pikeplacemarket.org
Phone: 206-682-7453
Fax: 206-625-0646

Pike Place Merchants Assn
93 Pike St Suite 312
Seattle, WA 98101
www.seattlespublicmarket.com
Phone: 206-587-0351

Pioneer Square Antique Mall
602 1st Ave
Seattle, WA 98104
Phone: 206-624-1164

Prime Outlets at Burlington
448 Fashion Way
Burlington, WA 98233
Phone: 360-757-3549

Rainier Square
4th & 5th Aves-betw Union & University Sts
Seattle, WA 98101
Phone: 206-623-0340

SeaTac Mall
1928 S SeaTac Mall
Federal Way, WA 98003
E-mail: info@seatacmall.com
www.seatacmall.com
Phone: 253-839-6151
Fax: 253-946-1413

Southcenter Mall
633 Southcenter Mall
Seattle, WA 98188
www.shopyourmall.com/mall_welcome.asp?map=yes&mall_select=650
Phone: 206-246-7400
Fax: 206-244-8607

Supermall of the Great Northwest
1101 SuperMall Way
Auburn, WA 98001
www.supermall.com
Phone: 253-833-9500
Fax: 253-833-9006
TF: 800-729-8258

University Village
2673 NE University Village Suite 7
Seattle, WA 98105
Phone: 206-523-0622
Fax: 206-525-3859

Westlake Center
400 Pine St
Seattle, WA 98101
Phone: 206-467-3044
Fax: 206-467-1603

Media

Newspapers and Magazines

Beacon Hill News/South District Journal
2314 3rd Ave
Seattle, WA 98121
Phone: 206-461-1300
Fax: 206-461-1289

Capitol Hill Times
2314 3rd Ave
Seattle, WA 98121
www.seamedia.com
Phone: 206-461-1300
Fax: 206-461-1289

Enterprise The
PO Box 977
Lynnwood, WA 98046
Phone: 425-775-7521
Fax: 425-774-8622

Globe The
PO Box 145
Marysville, WA 98270
Phone: 360-659-1300
Fax: 360-658-0350

Kirkland Courier
733 7th Ave Suite 204
Kirkland, WA 98033
E-mail: editor@kirklandcourier.com
Phone: 425-822-9166
Fax: 425-827-7716

Northshore Citizen
PO Box 647
Bothell, WA 98041
Phone: 425-486-1231
Fax: 425-483-3286

Puget Sound Business Journal
720 3rd Ave Suite 800
Seattle, WA 98104
E-mail: seattle@amcity.com.
www.amcity.com/seattle
Phone: 206-583-0701
Fax: 206-447-8510

Seattle Post-Intelligencer*
101 Elliott Ave W
Seattle, WA 98119
www.seattle-pi.com
Phone: 206-448-8000
Fax: 206-448-8166

Seattle Times*
PO Box 70
Seattle, WA 98111
E-mail: opinion@seatimes.com
www.seattletimes.com
Phone: 206-464-2111
Fax: 206-464-2261

Seattle Weekly
1008 Western Ave Suite 300
Seattle, WA 98104
E-mail: info@seattleweekly.com
www.seattleweekly.com
Phone: 206-623-0500
Fax: 206-467-4338

Stranger The
1535 11th Ave 3rd Fl
Seattle, WA 98122
E-mail: postmaster@thestranger.com
www.thestranger.com
Phone: 206-323-7101
Fax: 206-325-4865

West Seattle Herald
3500 SW Alaska St
Seattle, WA 98126
E-mail: wsherald@wolfenet.com
www.westseattleherald.com
Phone: 206-932-0300
Fax: 206-937-1223

Where Seattle Magazine
113 1st Ave N
Seattle, WA 98109
E-mail: wheresea@aol.com
Phone: 206-378-1300
Fax: 206-378-0023

**Indicates major daily newspapers*

Television

KCPQ-TV Ch 13 (Fox)
1813 Westlake Ave N
Seattle, WA 98109
E-mail: reception@kcpq.com
www.kcpq.com
Phone: 206-674-1313
Fax: 206-674-1777

KCTS-TV Ch 9 (PBS)
401 Mercer St
Seattle, WA 98109
E-mail: viewer@kcts.org
www.kcts.org
Phone: 206-728-6463
Fax: 206-443-6691

KING-TV Ch 5 (NBC)
333 Dexter Ave N
Seattle, WA 98109
E-mail: kingtv@king5.com
www.king5.com
Phone: 206-448-5555
Fax: 206-448-4525

(IRO-TV Ch 7 (CBS)
807 3rd Ave
eattle, WA 98121
-mail: kironews7@kiro-tv.com
ww.kirotv.com
Phone: 206-728-7777
Fax: 206-441-4840

)MO-TV Ch 4 (ABC)
0 4th Ave N
ttle, WA 98109
w.komotv.com
Phone: 206-443-4000
Fax: 206-443-3422

NG-TV Ch 16 (Ind)
Dexter Ave N
tle, WA 98109
.kongtv.com
Phone: 206-448-3166
Fax: 206-448-4525

V-TV Ch 11 (UPN)
ox 11411
na, WA 98411
l: kstw98d@prodigy.com
aramountstations.com/KSTW
Phone: 253-572-5789
Fax: 253-272-7581

-TV Ch 22 (WB)
xter Ave N
WA 98109
vbtv.com
Phone: 206-282-2202
Fax: 206-281-0207

V Ch 12 (Ind)
s St
m, WA 98225
rley.com/broadcast/tv/kvostv12.html
Phone: 360-671-1212
Fax: 360-647-0824
TF: 800-488-5867

Ch 33 (PAX)
rnational Blvd Suite 513
A 98188
et/KWPX
Phone: 206-439-0333
Fax: 206-246-5940

Radio

210 kHz (Oldies)
e Ave E
98102
m
Phone: 206-343-9700
Fax: 206-623-7677

K .3 MHz (Oldies)
1 Ave E
S 102
E tionbox@kbsg.com
w
Phone: 206-343-9700
Fax: 206-623-7677

K .3 MHz (Rel)
1 Ave N
S 33
w com
Phone: 206-546-7350
Fax: 206-546-7372

KING-FM 98.1 MHz (Clas)
333 Dexter Ave N Suite 400
Seattle, WA 98109
www.king.org
Phone: 206-448-3981
Fax: 206-448-0928

KIRO-AM 710 kHz (N/T)
1820 Eastlake Ave E
Seattle, WA 98102
www.kiro710.com
Phone: 206-726-7000
Fax: 206-726-5446

KIRO-FM 100.7 MHz (N/T)
1820 Eastlake Ave E
Seattle, WA 98102
www.1007thebuzz.com
Phone: 206-726-7000
Fax: 206-726-5446

KISW-FM 99.9 MHz (CR)
1100 Olive Way Suite 1650
Seattle, WA 98101
www.kisw.com
Phone: 206-285-7625
Fax: 206-215-9355

KIXI-AM 880 kHz (Nost)
3650 131st Ave SE Suite 550
Bellevue, WA 98006
E-mail: am880kixi@aol.com
www.kixi.com
Phone: 425-653-9462
Fax: 425-653-9464

KJR-AM 950 kHz (Sports)
190 Queen Anne Ave N Suite 100
Seattle, WA 98109
www.sportsradio950.com
Phone: 206-285-2295
Fax: 206-286-2376

KJR-FM 95.7 MHz (Oldies)
190 Queen Anne Ave N Suite 100
Seattle, WA 98109
www.kjrfm.com
Phone: 206-285-2295
Fax: 206-286-2376

KLSY-FM 92.5 MHz (AC)
3650 131st Ave SE Suite 550
Bellevue, WA 98006
www.klsyradio.com
Phone: 425-454-1540
Fax: 425-455-8849

KMIH-FM 104.5 MHz (CHR)
9100 SE 42nd St
Mercer Island, WA 98040
www.x104.fm
Phone: 206-236-3296
Fax: 206-236-3342

KMPS-FM 94.1 MHz (Ctry)
1000 Dexter Ave N Suite 100
Seattle, WA 98109
www.kmps.com
Phone: 206-805-0941
Fax: 206-805-0907

KMTT-FM 103.7 MHz (AAA)
1100 Olive Way Suite 1650
Seattle, WA 98101
E-mail: mountain@kmtt.com
www.kmtt.com
Phone: 206-233-1037
Fax: 206-233-8979

KNDD-FM 107.7 MHz (Alt)
1100 Olive Way Suite 1550
Seattle, WA 98101
www.kndd.com
Phone: 206-622-3251
Fax: 206-682-8349

KNWX-AM 770 kHz (N/T)
1820 Eastlake Ave E
Seattle, WA 98102
Phone: 206-726-7000
Fax: 206-726-5446

KOMO-AM 1000 kHz (N/T)
1809 7th Ave Suite 200
Seattle, WA 98101
E-mail: comments@komoradio.com
www.komo-am.com
Phone: 206-223-5700
Fax: 206-516-3110

KPLZ-FM 101.5 MHz (AC)
1809 7th Ave Suite 200
Seattle, WA 98101
www.kplz.com
Phone: 206-223-5703
Fax: 206-292-1015

KQBZ-FM 100.7 MHz (N/T)
1820 E Lake Ave E
Seattle, WA 98102
www.kqbz.com
Phone: 206-726-7000
Fax: 206-726-5446

KRPM-AM 1090 kHz (CHR)
1000 Dexter Ave N Suite 100
Seattle, WA 98109
Phone: 206-805-1061
Fax: 206-805-0922

KRWM-FM 106.9 MHz (AC)
3650 131st Ave SE Suite 550
Bellevue, WA 98006
www.warm1069.com
Phone: 425-373-5545
Fax: 425-373-5507

KUBE-FM 93.3 MHz (CHR)
190 Queen Anne Ave N Suite 100
Seattle, WA 98109
www.kube93.com
Phone: 206-285-2295
Fax: 206-286-2376

KUOW-FM 94.9 MHz (NPR)
4518 University Way NE Suite 310
Seattle, WA 98105
E-mail: kuow@u.washington.edu
www.kuow.washington.edu/kuow.html
Phone: 206-543-2710
Fax: 206-543-2720

KVI-AM 570 kHz (N/T)
1809 7th Ave Suite 200
Seattle, WA 98101
www.570kvi.com
Phone: 206-223-5700
Fax: 206-516-3194

KWJZ-FM 98.9 MHz (NAC)
3650 131st Ave SE Suite 550
Bellevue, WA 98006
E-mail: jazz@connectexpress.com
www.kwjz.com
Phone: 425-373-5536
Fax: 425-373-5548

KYPT-FM 96.5 MHz (Ctry)
1000 Dexter Ave N Suite 100
Seattle, WA 98109
Phone: 206-805-0965
Fax: 206-805-0932

KZOK-FM 102.5 MHz (CR)
1000 Dexter Ave N
Seattle, WA 98109
E-mail: comments@kzok.com
www.kzok.com
Phone: 206-805-0965
Fax: 206-805-0932

Attractions

Surrounded by the Cascade and Olympic mountain ranges, Puget Sound, and Lake Washington, Seattle offers spectacular views and a variety of attractions for residents and visitors alike. Seattle Center, one of the city's main attractions, is an urban park with outdoor stages and the Pacific Science Center. The Seattle Center is also the site of the Seattle Arts Festival, Bumbershoot, which is ranked among the top festivals nationwide. The Space Needle towers above Seattle Center and is visible from almost any part of the downtown area.

Underground tours of Pioneer Square, the birthplace of Seattle, lead below the streets and provide a glimpse of Seattle prior to the great fire of 1889. The Kingdome and Klondike Gold Rush National Historic Park are also located in Pioneer Square. Seattle's Pike Place Market, one of the last remaining farmer's markets in the country, is situated along the waterfront of Elliott Bay.

5th Avenue Theater
1308 5th Ave
Seattle, WA 98101
www.5thavenuetheatre.org
Phone: 206-625-0235
Fax: 206-292-9610

A Contemporary Theatre
700 Union St
Seattle, WA 98101
Phone: 206-292-7660
Fax: 206-292-7670

Bay Pavilion
1301 Alaskan Way
Seattle, WA 98101
Phone: 206-623-8600
Fax: 206-343-9173

Bellevue Art Museum
301 Bellevue Sq
Bellevue, WA 98004
E-mail: bam@bellevueart.org
www.bellevueart.org
Phone: 425-454-3322
Fax: 425-637-1799

Burke Museum of Natural History & Culture
NE 45th St & 17th Ave NE University of Washington
Seattle, WA 98195
E-mail: recept@u.washington.edu
www.washington.edu/burkemuseum
Phone: 206-543-7907
Fax: 206-685-3039

Center for Wooden Boats
1010 Valley St
Seattle, WA 98109
Phone: 206-382-2628
Fax: 206-382-2699

Charles & Emma Frye Art Museum
704 Terry Ave
Seattle, WA 98104
E-mail: fryeart@aol.com
fryeart.org
Phone: 206-622-9250
Fax: 206-223-1707

Children's Museum
305 Harrison St
Seattle, WA 98109
E-mail: tcm@thechildrensmuseum.org
www.thechildrensmuseum.org
Phone: 206-441-1768
Fax: 206-448-0910

Chittenden Hiram M Locks
3015 NW 54th St
Seattle, WA 98107
Phone: 206-783-7001
Fax: 206-782-3192

Civic Light Opera
34th Ave NE & 110th St Jane Addams Theatre
Seattle, WA 98125
E-mail: info@clo-online.org
www.clo-online.org
Phone: 206-363-2809
Fax: 206-363-0702

Dash Point State Park
5700 SW Dash Point Rd
Federal Way, WA 98023
Phone: 253-661-4955
Fax: 253-838-2777
TF: 800-452-5687

Daybreak Star Arts Center
PO Box 99100
Seattle, WA 98119
Phone: 206-285-4425
Fax: 206-282-3640

Discovery Park
3801 W Government Way
Seattle, WA 98199
Phone: 206-386-4236
Fax: 206-684-0195

Downtown Seattle Assn
500 Union St
Seattle, WA 98101
Phone: 206-461-5840

Experience Music Project
219 4th Ave N Seattle Space Needle
Seattle, WA 98109
Phone: 206-770-2700

Fireworks Fine Crafts Gallery
210 1st Ave S
Seattle, WA 98104
www.fireworksgallery.net
Phone: 206-682-8707
Fax: 206-467-6366
TF: 800-505-8882

Fun Forest Amusement Park
305 Harrison St
Seattle, WA 98109
www.funforest.com
Phone: 206-728-1585
Fax: 206-441-9897

Green Lake Park
7201 East Green Lake Dr N
Seattle, WA 98109
cityofseattle.net/parks/parkspaces/greenlak.htm
Phone: 206-684-0780
Fax: 206-684-0881

Henry Art Gallery
University of Washington Box 351410
Seattle, WA 98195
E-mail: hartg@u.washington.edu
www.henryart.org
Phone: 206-543-2281
Fax: 206-685-3123

Herbfarm The
32804 Issaquah Fall City Rd
Fall City, WA 98024
E-mail: HerbOrder@aol.com
www.theherbfarm.com
Phone: 206-784-2222
Fax: 206-789-2279

IMAX Theater
200 2nd Ave N
Seattle, WA 98109
www.pacsci.org/public/imax/theater
Phone: 206-443-2001

Imaxdome Theatre
Pier 59 Waterfront Pk
Seattle, WA 98101
Phone: 206-622-1868

Intiman Theatre
201 Mercer St Seattle Ctr
Seattle, WA 98109
Phone: 206-269-1900
Fax: 206-269-1928

Klondike Gold Rush National Historical Park Seattle Unit
117 S Main St
Seattle, WA 98104
E-mail: klse_ranger_activities@nps.gov
www.nps.gov/klgo
Phone: 206-553-7220
Fax: 206-553-0614

Lake Chelan National Recreation Area
2105 SR-20
Sedro Woolley, WA 98284
www.nps.gov/lach/
Phone: 360-856-5700
Fax: 360-856-1934

Museum of Flight
9404 East Marginal Way S
Seattle, WA 98108
www.museumofflight.org
Phone: 206-764-5700
Fax: 206-764-5707

Museum of History & Industry
2700 24th Ave E
Seattle, WA 98112
www.historymuse-nw.org
Phone: 206-324-1125
Fax: 206-324-1346

Nordic Heritage Museum
3014 NW 67th St
Seattle, WA 98117
E-mail: nordic@intelistep.com
www.nordicmuseum.com
Phone: 206-789-5707
Fax: 206-789-3271

North Cascades National Park
2105 SR-20
Sedro Woolley, WA 98284
E-mail: noca_interpretation@nps.gov
www.nps.gov/noca
Phone: 360-856-5700
Fax: 360-856-1934

Northwest Railway Museum
38625 SE King St
Snoqualmie, WA 98065
E-mail: visitorservices@trainmuseum.org
www.trainmuseum.org
Phone: 425-888-0373
Fax: 425-888-9311

Northwest Trek Wildlife Park
11610 Trek Dr E
Eatonville, WA 98328
www.nwtrek.org
Phone: 360-832-6117
Fax: 360-832-6118

Ocheami Afrikan Dance Co
PO Box 31635
Seattle, WA 98103
Phone: 206-329-8876

Olympic National Park
600 E Park Ave
Port Angeles, WA 98362
www.nps.gov/olym/
Phone: 360-452-4501
Fax: 360-452-0335

Pacific Northwest Ballet
301 Mercer St
Seattle, WA 98109
www.pnb.org
Phone: 206-441-9411
Fax: 206-441-2440

Pacific Science Center
200 2nd Ave N
Seattle, WA 98109
www.pacsci.org
Phone: 206-443-2001
Fax: 206-443-3631

Paramount Theatre
911 Pine St
Seattle, WA 98101
www.theparamount.com/main.html
Phone: 206-467-5510
Fax: 206-682-4837
TF: 800-562-8820

Pike Place Market
1st Ave & Pike St
Seattle, WA 98101
E-mail: information@pikeplacemarket.org
www.pikeplacemarket.org
Phone: 206-682-7453
Fax: 206-625-0646

Pioneer Square
PO Box 4333
Seattle, WA 98104
E-mail: psbia@pioneersquare.org
Phone: 206-622-6235
Fax: 206-667-9739

Pyramid Breweries Inc
91 S Royal Brougham Way
Seattle, WA 98134
www.pyramidbrew.com
Phone: 206-682-8322
Fax: 206-682-8420

Redhook Ale Brewery & Trolleyman Pub
3400 Phinney Ave N
Seattle, WA 98103
www.redhook.com/
Phone: 206-548-8000
Fax: 206-548-1305

Ross Lake National Recreation Area
2105 SR-20
Sedro Woolley, WA 98284
www.nps.gov/rola/
Phone: 360-856-5700
Fax: 360-856-1934

Seattle Aquarium
1483 Alaskan Way Waterfront Pk Pier 59
Seattle, WA 98101
www.seattleaquarium.org
Phone: 206-386-4300
Fax: 206-386-4328

Seattle Art Museum
100 University St
Seattle, WA 98101
www.seattleartmuseum.org
Phone: 206-625-8900
Fax: 206-654-3135

Seattle Asian Art Museum
1400 E Prospect St Volunteer Pk
Seattle, WA 98112
www.seattleartmuseum.org
Phone: 206-654-3206
Fax: 206-654-3191

Seattle Center
305 Harrison St
Seattle, WA 98109
www.seattlecenter.com
Phone: 206-684-7200
Fax: 206-684-7342

Seattle IMAX Dome Theatre
Pier 59 Waterfront Pk
Seattle, WA 98101
E-mail: info@seattleimaxdome.com
www.seattleimaxdome.com
Phone: 206-622-1869
Fax: 206-622-5837

Seattle Opera
PO Box 9248
Seattle, WA 98109
E-mail: webfeedback@seattleopera.org
www.seattleopera.org
Phone: 206-389-7600
Fax: 206-389-7651

Seattle Repertory Theatre
155 Mercer St
Seattle, WA 98109
www.seattlerep.org
Phone: 206-443-2210
Fax: 206-443-2379

Seattle Symphony Orchestra
200 University St Benaroya Hall
Seattle, WA 98109
www.seattlesymphony.org
Phone: 206-215-4747

Seattle Youth Symphony Orchestra
11065 5th Ave NE
Seattle, WA 98125
www.syso.org
Phone: 206-362-2300
Fax: 206-361-9254

Seward Park
5898 Lake Washington Blvd S
Seattle, WA 98109
Phone: 206-684-4075

Space Needle
219 4th Ave N
Seattle, WA 98109
E-mail: reservation@spaceneedle.com
spaceneedle.com
Phone: 206-443-9700
Fax: 206-441-7415

Thomas Burke Memorial Washington State Museum
University of Washington
Seattle, WA 98195
www.washington.edu/burkemuseum
Phone: 206-543-5590
Fax: 206-685-3039

Tillicum Village
2200 6th Ave Suite 804
Seattle, WA 98121
E-mail: mail@tillicumvillage.com
www.tillicumvillage.com
Phone: 206-443-1244
Fax: 206-443-4723
TF: 800-426-1205

Unexpected Productions
1428 Post Alley Market Theater
Seattle, WA 98101
E-mail: unexprod@aol.com
www.unexpectedproductions.org
Phone: 206-587-2414
Fax: 206-587-2413

Westlake Center
400 Pine St
Seattle, WA 98101
Phone: 206-467-3044
Fax: 206-467-1603

Wing Luke Asian Museum
407 7th Ave S
Seattle, WA 98104
www.wingluke.org
Phone: 206-623-5124
Fax: 206-623-4559

Woodland Park Zoological Gardens
5500 Phinney Ave N
Seattle, WA 98103
www.zoo.org
Phone: 206-684-4800
Fax: 206-684-4854

Sports Teams & Facilities

Emerald Downs
2300 Emerald Downs Dr
Auburn, WA 98001
E-mail: lauram@emdowns.com
www.emdowns.com
Phone: 253-288-7000
Fax: 253-288-7710
TF: 888-931-8400

Key Arena
305 Harrison St Seattle Ctr
Seattle, WA 98109
Phone: 206-684-7202
Fax: 206-684-7343

Safeco Field
1250 1st Ave
Seattle, WA 98134
www.safeco.com/safecofield/default.asp
Phone: 206-346-4000
Fax: 206-346-4300

Seattle Bigfoot
6303 NE 181st St Suite 201
Seattle, WA 98155
E-mail: billhur@johnlscott.com
Phone: 206-522-5626
Fax: 206-522-1446

Seattle International Raceway
31001 144th Ave SE
Kent, WA 98042
Phone: 253-631-1550
Fax: 253-630-0888

Seattle Mariners
1250 1st Ave Safeco Field
Seattle, WA 98134
www.mariners.org
Phone: 206-346-4000
Fax: 206-346-4300

Seattle SeaDogs (soccer)
1900 Queen Anne Ave N
Seattle, WA 98109
Phone: 206-281-5800
Fax: 206-281-5839

Seattle Seahawks
11220 NE 53rd St
Kirkland, WA 98033
www.seahawks.com
Phone: 425-827-9777
Fax: 425-827-9008

Seattle Sounders (soccer)
401 5th Ave N Seattle Memorial Stadium
Renton, WA 98109
www.seattlesounders.com
Phone: 206-622-3415
Fax: 425-643-3515
TF: 800-796-5425

Seattle SuperSonics
305 Harrison St Key Arena
Seattle, WA 98109
www.nba.com/sonics
Phone: 206-281-5800

Seattle Thunderbirds (hockey)
Key Arena Seattle Ctr
Seattle, WA 98109
www.seattleinsider.com/sports/hockey/seattle-thunderbirds.html
Phone: 425-869-7825
Fax: 425-497-0812

Annual Events

AT & T New Year's at the Needle (December 31)....206-443-2100
AT & T Summer Nights at the Pier (late June-late August)....206-281-8111
Bite of Seattle (late July)....206-232-2982
Bubble Festival (mid-August)....206-443-2001
Bumbershoot Festival (early September)....206-684-7200
Cherry Blossom & Japanese Cultural Festival (late April)....206-684-7200
Chinese New Year's Celebration (January)....206-382-1197
Cinco de Mayo Celebration (early May)....206-706-7776
Coffee Fest Seattle (early October)....206-232-2982
Eatonville Arts Festival (late July-early August)....360-832-4000
Family Fourth at Lake Union (July 4)....206-281-8111
Festival Sundiata (mid-February)....206-684-7200
Fiesta Patrias (mid-September)....206-706-7776
Fish & Fireworks on the 4th (July 4)....206-386-4320
Fourth of Jul-Ivars at the Waterfront (July 4)....206-587-6500
Hmong New Year's Celebration (early November)....206-684-7284
Holiday Parade of Boats Cruise (December)....206-674-3500
Imagination Celebration (early April)....206-684-7200
Indian Powwow (late July)....206-285-4425
Martin Luther King Celebration (mid-January)....206-684-7200
Northwest Flower & Garden Show (early February)....800-229-6311
Northwest Folklife Festival (late May)....206-684-7300
Pike Place Market Festival (late May)....206-587-0351
Pioneer Square Fire Festival (early June)....206-622-6235
Salmon Days Festival (early October)....425-392-0661
Seafair Summer Festival (early July-early August)....206-728-0123
Seattle Fringe Festival (mid-March)....206-526-1959
Seattle International Boat Show (mid-January)....206-634-0911
Seattle International Film Festival (mid-May-early June)....206-464-5830
Seattle Marathon (late November)....206-729-3660
University District Street Fair (mid-May)....800-535-7071
WCF Oktoberfest (mid-September)....425-888-7275
West Seattle Street Festival & Dance (mid-July)....206-935-9966
Winterfest (late November-early January)....206-684-7200

Shreveport, Louisiana

***County:* Caddo Parish**

SHREVEPORT is located in northwest Louisiana along the banks of the Red River. Major cities within 100 miles include Bossier City, Ruston, and Monroe, Louisiana; Texarkana and Tyler, Texas; and El Dorado, Arkansas.

Area (Land) .... 97.1 sq mi
Area (Water) .... 14.5 sq mi
Elevation .... 204 ft
Latitude .... 32-50-52 N
Longitude .... 93-74-85 W
Time Zone .... CST
Area Code 318

Climate

Shreveport's climate is characterized by high humidity for much of the year. Winters are mild, with average high temperatures in the upper 50s and low 60s and lows in the mid-30s. Snowfall is rare, with average annual totals just under two inches. Summer days are hot, with highs averaging in the low 90s, while evenings cool down to near 70 degrees. May is the wettest month in Shreveport, while September is the driest.

Average Temperatures & Precipitation

Temperatures

	Jan	Feb	Mar	Apr	May	Jun	Jul	Aug	Sep	Oct	Nov	Dec
High	55	61	69	77	83	90	93	93	87	79	68	59
Low	35	38	46	54	62	69	72	71	66	54	45	37

Precipitation

	Jan	Feb	Mar	Apr	May	Jun	Jul	Aug	Sep	Oct	Nov	Dec
Inches	3.9	3.9	3.6	3.8	5.1	4.3	3.7	2.4	3.1	3.7	4.5	4.1

History

The present-day city of Shreveport was originally the site of a massive logjam called the "Great Raft" in the Red River. In 1833, Captain Henry Miller Shreve, after whom the city was named, cleared the jam and founded the city of Shreveport. Two years later, the Shreve Town Company was formed to capitalize on the fertile land and abundant natural resources in the area, and pioneers were drawn by the economic opportunities created by Shreveport's rich agricultural base. The city's cotton and lumber industries prospered throughout the 19th Century. Petroleum and natural gas were discovered in the Shreveport area in the early 1900s, and the industry created by these discoveries sustained the city's economy throughout the 20th Century. The establishment of Barksdale Air Force Base in neighboring Bossier Parish in 1933 also helped to fuel the economy, drawing thousands of new residents to the area. The base remains Shreveport-Bossier's leading employer, and Bossier City is considered one of the fastest growing areas in the state of Louisiana.

Separated only by the Red River, Shreveport and Bossier City comprise the largest metro area in North Louisiana. Shreveport-Bossier is the trade and cultural center of a 200-mile radius extending into Arkansas, Louisiana, and Texas (known as the Ark-La-Tex). The seat of Caddo Parish, Shreveport is home to more than 188,000 people.

Population

1990 Census 198,525
1998 Estimate 188,319
% Change .... -5.1
2005 Projection 249,760*

Racial/Ethnic Breakdown
White 54.3%
Black 44.8%
Other 0.9%
Hispanic Origin (may be of any race) 1.1%

Age Breakdown
Under 5 years 8.0%
5 to 17 .... 20.4%
18 to 20 .... 4.4%
21 to 24 .... 5.5%
25 to 34 .... 15.8%
35 to 44 .... 14.2%
45 to 54 .... 9.4%
55 to 64 .... 8.7%
65 to 74 .... 7.6%
75+ years 6.1%
Median Age 32.5

Gender Breakdown
Male 46.1%
Female 53.9%

* *Information given is for Caddo Parish.*

Government

Type of Government: Mayor-Council

Shreve Memorial Library
424 Texas St
Shreveport, LA 71101
Phone: 318-226-5897
Fax: 318-226-4780

Shreveport City Attorney
PO Box 31109
Shreveport, LA 71130
Phone: 318-673-5200
Fax: 318-673-5230

Shreveport City Council
PO Box 31109
Shreveport, LA 71130
Phone: 318-673-5262
Fax: 318-673-5270

Shreveport City Hall
1234 Texas Ave
Shreveport, LA 71101
Phone: 318-673-2489
Fax: 318-673-5055

Shreveport Community Development Dept
1237 Murphy St
Shreveport, LA 71101
Phone: 318-673-7500
Fax: 318-673-7512

Shreveport Finance Dept
PO Box 31109
Shreveport, LA 71130
Phone: 318-673-5400

Shreveport Fire Dept
801 Crockett St
Shreveport, LA 71101
Phone: 318-673-6650
Fax: 318-673-6656

Shreveport Mayor
PO Box 31109
Shreveport, LA 71130
Phone: 318-673-5050
Fax: 318-673-5085

Shreveport Metropolitan Planning Commission
PO Box 31109
Shreveport, LA 71130
Phone: 318-673-6480
Fax: 318-673-6475

Shreveport Personnel Dept
PO Box 31109
Shreveport, LA 71130
Phone: 318-673-5150
Fax: 318-673-5161

Shreveport Police Dept
PO Drawer P
Shreveport, LA 71161
Phone: 318-673-6900
Fax: 318-673-6914

Shreveport Public Assembly & Recreation Dept
400 Clyde Fant Pkwy
Shreveport, LA 71101
Phone: 318-673-7727
Fax: 318-673-5105

Shreveport Public Works Office
1731 Kings Hwy
Shreveport, LA 71103
Phone: 318-673-6300
Fax: 318-673-6320

Shreveport Transit Authority (SporTran)
PO Box 7314
Shreveport, LA 71137
Phone: 318-673-7400
Fax: 318-673-7424

Shreveport Water & Sewerage Office
PO Box 31109
Shreveport, LA 71130
Phone: 318-673-7660
Fax: 318-673-7663

Important Phone Numbers

AAA 800-222-4357
Caddo Parish Tax Assessor 318-226-6702
Caddo-Shreveport Sales & Use Tax Commission 318-865-3312
Driver's License/Vehicle Registration Information 318-676-7523
Emergency 911
Events Line 318-226-9227
HotelDocs 800-468-3537
Louisiana State Revenue & Taxation Dept 318-676-7500
Poison Control Center 800-256-9822
Shreveport-Bossier Board of Realtors 318-797-0054
Time/Temp 318-425-0211
Voter Registration Information 318-226-6891
Weather 318-635-7575

Information Sources

Better Business Bureau Serving Ark-La-Tex
3612 Youree Dr
Shreveport, LA 71105
www.shreveport.bbb.org
Phone: 318-868-5146
Fax: 318-861-6426
TF: 800-372-4222

Bossier Chamber of Commerce
710 Benton Rd
Bossier City, LA 71111
www.bossierchamber.com
Phone: 318-746-0252
Fax: 318-746-0357

Bossier Civic Center
620 Benton Rd
Bossier City, LA 71111
Phone: 318-741-8900
Fax: 318-741-8910
TF: 800-522-4842

Caddo Parish
505 Travis St 8th Fl
Shreveport, LA 71101
www.caddo.org
Phone: 318-226-6900
Fax: 318-429-7630

Greater Shreveport Chamber of Commerce
400 Edwards St
Shreveport, LA 71101
www.shreveportchamber.org
Phone: 318-677-2500
Fax: 318-677-2541

Shreveport-Bossier Convention & Tourist Bureau
629 Spring St
Shreveport, LA 71101
www.shreveport-bossier.org/
Phone: 318-222-9391
Fax: 318-222-0056
TF: 800-551-8682

Shreveport-Bossier Visitor Center
100 John Wesley Blvd
Bossier City, LA 71112
Phone: 318-226-8884
Fax: 318-429-0647

Online Resources

About.com Guide to Shreveport
shreveport.about.com/citiestowns/southeastus/shreveport

Area Guide Shreveport
shreveport.areaguides.net

City Knowledge Shreveport
www.cityknowledge.com/la_shreveport.htm

Excite.com Shreveport City Guide
www.excite.com/travel/countries/united_states/louisiana/shreveport

Shreveport-Bossier Online
www.shreveport.com

Shreveport/Bossier Page
www.shreveport.net

Area Communities

Communities in the Shreveport-Bossier metro area (Caddo and Bossier parishes) with populations greater than 1,000 include:

Benton
PO Box 336
Benton, LA 71006
Phone: 318-965-2781
Fax: 318-965-2577

Blanchard
110 Main St
Blanchard, LA 71009
Phone: 318-929-2928
Fax: 318-929-2447

Bossier City
PO Box 5337
Bossier City, LA 71171
Phone: 318-741-8500
Fax: 318-741-8809

Greenwood
9381 Greenwood Rd
Greenwood, LA 71033
Phone: 318-938-7261
Fax: 318-938-1512

Haughton
118 W McKinley Ave
Haughton, LA 71037
Phone: 318-949-9401
Fax: 318-949-2609

Oil City
202 Allen
Oil City, LA 71061
Phone: 318-995-6681
Fax: 318-995-6633

Plain Dealing
205 W Palmetto Ave
Plain Dealing, LA 71064
Phone: 318-326-4234
Fax: 318-326-7022

Vivian
112 W Alabama St
Vivian, LA 71082
Phone: 318-375-3856
Fax: 318-375-5919

Economy

Government is an integral part of Shreveport-Bossier's economy—seven of the top 15 area employers (including the top five) are government-related. Barksdale Air Force Base, one of the nation's largest air bases, is the largest employer, providing jobs for more than 8,750 area civilians and military personnel. Services, retail trade, and manufacturing are also among the top employment sectors in Shreveport-Bossier, and several major U.S. corporations, including General Motors, General Electric, and AT & T, have operations in the area. The petroleum and natural gas industry that fueled Shreveport's economy for much of the 20th Century continues to play a role, but the area's economy has diversified significantly and other industries, including tourism, have gained dominance.

Unemployment Rate 4.6%*
Per Capita Income.......................... $22,858*
Median Family Income...................... $37,900*

** Information given is for the Shreveport Metropolitan Statistical Area (MSA), which includes the City of Shreveport as well as Caddo and Bossier parishes.*

Principal Industries & Number of Wage Earners

Shreveport-Bossier City MSA* - 1999

Industry	Wage Earners
Construction	9,100
Finance, Insurance, & Real Estate	6,400
Government	32,800
Manufacturing	19,000
Mining	2,100
Retail Trade	30,100
Services	54,300
Transportation, Communications, & Public Utilities	8,200
Wholesale Trade	8,800

** Information given is for the Shreveport-Bossier City Metropolitan Statistical Area (MSA), which includes Caddo, Bossier, and Webster parishes.*

Major Employers

Barksdale Air Force Base
Barksdale AFB, LA 71110
www.barksdale.af.mil
Phone: 318-456-3065
Fax: 318-456-5986

Bossier Parish School Board
PO Box 2000
Benton, LA 71006
Phone: 318-549-5000
Fax: 318-549-5044

Caddo Parish School Board
PO Box 32000
Shreveport, LA 71130
www.shreveport.net/edu/cadobrd.html
Phone: 318-636-0210
Fax: 318-631-5241

Christus Schumpert Health System
1 St Mary Pl
Shreveport, LA 71101
www.schumpert.org/employment.html
Phone: 318-681-4500
Fax: 318-681-4232

General Motors Corp
7600 General Motors Blvd
Shreveport, LA 71129
www.gm.com/careers
Phone: 318-683-9000
Fax: 318-456-9466

Harrah's Casino Shreveport
PO Box 1114
Shreveport, LA 71163
Phone: 318-424-7777
Fax: 318-424-5650
TF: 800-427-7247

Health Plus of Louisiana
2708 Greenwood Rd
Shreveport, LA 71103
Phone: 318-632-4590
Fax: 318-632-4463

Horseshoe Casino & Hotel
711 Horseshoe Blvd
Bossier City, LA 71111
www.horseshoecasinos.com
Phone: 318-742-0711
Fax: 318-741-7728

Isle of Capri Casino
711 Isle of Capri Blvd
Bossier City, LA 71111
www.isleofcapricasino.com
Phone: 318-678-7777
Fax: 318-226-1782
TF: 800-843-4753

Libbey Glass Inc
4302 Jewella Ave
Shreveport, LA 71109
www.libbey.com/Libbey/html.nsf/pages/LibbeyGlassSite
Phone: 318-636-0051
Fax: 318-636-5514

Louisiana State University Medical Center
1541 Kings Hwy
Shreveport, LA 71130
www.lsumc.edu
Phone: 318-675-5000
Fax: 318-675-7065

Lucent Technologies (AT & T)
PO Box 31111
Shreveport, LA 71130
www.lucent.com
Phone: 318-682-6000

Shreveport City Hall
1234 Texas Ave
Shreveport, LA 71101
www.ci.shreveport.la.us
Phone: 318-673-2489
Fax: 318-673-5055

State of Louisiana
1201 Capitol Access Rd
Baton Rouge, LA 70802
www.state.la.us/state/jobs.htm
Phone: 225-342-8285
Fax: 225-342-8058

US Postal Service
2400 Texas Ave
Shreveport, LA 71102
new.usps.com
Phone: 800-275-8777
Fax: 318-677-2339

Quality of Living Indicators

Total Crime Index....................................18,510
(rates per 100,000 inhabitants)

Violent Crime
Murder/manslaughter........................... 34
Forcible rape 128
Robbery...................................... 558
Aggravated assault...........................1,458

Property Crime
Burglary 3,863
Larceny theft 11,371
Motor vehicle theft 1,098

Cost of Living Index.................................92.7
(national average = 100)

Median Home Price..................................$83,200

Education

Public Schools

Caddo Parish School Board
PO Box 32000
Shreveport, LA 71130
www.shreveport.net/edu/cadobrd.html
Phone: 318-636-0210
Fax: 318-631-5241

Number of Schools
Elementary................................. 42
Middle 12
High.. 12

Student/Teacher Ratio
All Grades 16.7:1

Private Schools

Number of Schools (all grades).................... 21

Colleges & Universities

Bossier Parish Community College
2719 Airline Dr N
Bossier City, LA 71111
www.bpcc.cc.la.us
Phone: 318-746-9851
Fax: 318-742-8664

Centenary College
2911 Centenary Blvd
Shreveport, LA 71104
E-mail: postmaster@beta.centenary.edu
alpha.centenary.edu
Phone: 318-869-5011
Fax: 318-869-5026
TF: 800-234-4448

East Texas Baptist University
1209 N Grove St
Marshall, TX 75670
www.etbu.edu
Phone: 903-935-7963
Fax: 903-938-1705

Louisiana State University Shreveport Campus
1 University Pl
Shreveport, LA 71115
www.lsus.edu
Phone: 318-797-5000
Fax: 318-798-4138

Wiley College
711 Wiley Ave
Marshall, TX 75670
Phone: 903-927-3300
Fax: 903-938-8100
TF: 800-658-6889

Hospitals

Bossier Medical Center
2105 Airline Dr
Bossier City, LA 71111
www.bossiermed.org
Phone: 318-741-6000
Fax: 318-741-6585

Christus Schumpert Medical Center
1 St Mary Pl
Shreveport, LA 71120
Phone: 318-681-4500
Fax: 318-681-4465

Higland Hospital
1453 E Bert Kouns Industrial Loop
Shreveport, LA 71105
www.highlandhospital.com
Phone: 318-798-4300
Fax: 318-798-4375

Louisiana State University Medical Center
1541 Kings Hwy
Shreveport, LA 71130
www.lsumc.edu
Phone: 318-675-5000
Fax: 318-675-7065

Overton Brooks Veterans Affairs Medical Center
510 E Stoner Ave
Shreveport, LA 71101
Phone: 318-221-8411
Fax: 318-424-6156
TF: 800-863-7441

Shriners Hospitals for Children Shreveport Unit
3100 Samford Ave
Shreveport, LA 71103
www.shrinershq.org/Hospitals/Directry/shreveport.html
Phone: 318-222-5704
Fax: 318-424-7610

Willis Knighton Medical Center
2600 Greenwood Rd
Shreveport, LA 71103
Phone: 318-632-4600
Fax: 318-632-8630

Transportation

Airport(s)

Shreveport Regional Airport (SHV)
5 miles SW of downtown (approx 15 minutes) 318-673-5370

Mass Transit

SporTran City Transit
$.90 Base fare.................................318-221-7433

Rail/Bus

Greyhound Bus Station
2225 Beckett St
Bossier City, LA 71111
Phone: 318-746-7511
TF: 800-231-2222

Greyhound Bus Station
408 Fannin St
Shreveport, LA 71101
Phone: 318-221-4205

Utilities

Electricity
Southwestern Electric Power Co................318-868-1300
www.csw.com

Gas
Reliant Energy Inc Arkla Div 318-227-2555

Water
Shreveport Water Dept 318-673-5510

Garbage Collection/Recycling
Shreveport Green (Recycling) 318-868-6222
Shreveport Sanitation Dept 318-673-6300

Telecommunications

Telephone
BellSouth 800-832-0679
www.bellsouth.com

Cable Television
Cox Communications 318-746-2109
www.cox.com
Time Warner Cable 318-631-3060
www.twarner.com

Internet Service Providers (ISPs)
ShreveNet Inc 318-222-2638
www.shreve.net

Banks

Bank One Louisiana NA
400 Texas St
Shreveport, LA 71101
Phone: 318-226-2345
Fax: 318-226-2191

Citizens National Bank of Bossier City
9237 Mansfield Rd
Shreveport, LA 71118
Phone: 318-688-2265
Fax: 318-687-4420

City Bank & Trust of Shreveport
6025 Line Ave
Shreveport, LA 71106
www.citybt.com
Phone: 318-865-6555
Fax: 318-865-6582

Community Bank of Louisiana
9201 Walker Rd
Shreveport, LA 71118
Phone: 318-688-6833
Fax: 318-688-9522

Deposit Guaranty National Bank
333 Texas St
Shreveport, LA 71101
www.dgb.com
Phone: 318-429-1000
Fax: 318-429-1117
TF: 800-748-8501

First Louisiana Bank
1350 E 70th Ave
Shreveport, LA 71105
Phone: 318-798-5700
Fax: 318-797-6225

Hibernia National Bank
333 Travis St
Shreveport, LA 71101
Phone: 318-221-5406
Fax: 318-675-5109

Minden Bank & Trust Co
6205 Hearne Ave
Shreveport, LA 71108
Phone: 318-429-6060
Fax: 318-631-2735

Regions Bank
3100 N Market St
Shreveport, LA 71107
Phone: 318-674-1100

Tri-State Bank & Trust
4321 Youree Dr
Shreveport, LA 71105
Phone: 318-861-6184
Fax: 318-861-9046

Shopping

Libbey Glass Factory Outlet
4302 Jewella Ave
Shreveport, LA 71109
Phone: 318-621-0265
Fax: 318-621-0351

Mall Saint Vincent
1133 St Vincent Ave Suite 200
Shreveport, LA 71104
Phone: 318-227-9880
Fax: 318-424-0454

Pierre Bossier Mall
2950 E Texas St
Bossier City, LA 71111
Phone: 318-747-5700
Fax: 318-742-4739

Pierremont Mall
4801 Line Ave
Shreveport, LA 71106
Phone: 318-222-3119
Fax: 318-222-0566

South Park Mall
8924 Jewella Ave
Shreveport, LA 71118
Phone: 318-686-7627
Fax: 318-688-5744

Media

Newspapers and Magazines

Bossier Press Tribune
PO Box 6267
Bossier City, LA 71171
Phone: 318-747-7900
Fax: 318-747-5298

Times*
PO Box 30222
Shreveport, LA 71130
www.nwlouisiana.com
Phone: 318-459-3200
Fax: 318-459-3301
TF: 800-551-8892

**Indicates major daily newspapers*

Television

KLTS-TV Ch 24 (PBS)
72733 Perkins Rd
Baton Rouge, LA 70810
Phone: 225-767-5660
Fax: 225-767-4299

KMSS-TV Ch 33 (Fox)
3519 Jewella Ave
Shreveport, LA 71109
E-mail: kmss@kmsstv.com
www.kmssfox33.com
Phone: 318-631-5677
Fax: 318-631-4195

KSHV-TV Ch 45 (Ind)
3519 Jewella Ave
Shreveport, LA 71109
Phone: 318-631-4545
Fax: 318-631-4195

KSLA-TV Ch 12 (CBS)
1812 Fairfield Ave
Shreveport, LA 71101
www.ksla.com
Phone: 318-222-1212
Fax: 318-677-6703

KTAL-TV Ch 6 (NBC)
3150 N Market St
Shreveport, LA 71107
www.ktal.com
Phone: 318-425-2422
Fax: 318-425-2488

KTBS-TV Ch 3 (ABC)
312 E Kings Hwy
Shreveport, LA 71104
E-mail: ktbsnews@ktbs.com
www.ktbs.com
Phone: 318-861-5800
Fax: 318-862-9434

Radio

KDAQ-FM 89.9 MHz (NPR) Phone: 318-797-5150
1 University Pl Fax: 318-797-5153
Shreveport, LA 71115
E-mail: kdaq@aol.com
www.npr.org/members/KDAQ

KEEL-AM 710 kHz (N/T) Phone: 318-688-1130
6341 Westport Ave Fax: 318-687-8574
Shreveport, LA 71129

KITT-FM 93.7 MHz (Ctry) Phone: 318-688-1130
6341 Westport Ave Fax: 318-687-8574
Shreveport, LA 71129
www.catcountry937.com

KLKL-FM 92.1 MHz (Oldies) Phone: 318-222-3122
1300 Grimmett Dr Fax: 318-459-1493
Shreveport, LA 71107

KRMD-AM 1340 kHz (Sports) Phone: 318-865-5173
3109 Alexander Ave Fax: 318-865-3657
Shreveport, LA 71104

KRMD-FM 101.1 MHz (Ctry) Phone: 318-865-5173
3109 Alexander Ave Fax: 318-631-4195
Shreveport, LA 71104
www.krmd.com

KTAL-FM 98.1 MHz (CR) Phone: 318-425-2422
3150 N Market St Fax: 318-425-2486
Shreveport, LA 71107

KTUX-FM 98.9 MHz (Rock) Phone: 318-688-1130
6341 Westport Ave Fax: 318-687-8574
Shreveport, LA 71129
E-mail: ktux@broadcast.com
www.rebelrocker99x.com

KWKH-AM 1130 kHz (Ctry) Phone: 318-688-1130
6341 Westport Ave Fax: 318-687-8574
Shreveport, LA 71129
www.kwkh.com

Attractions

Shreveport's American Rose Center, which is the headquarters of the American Rose Society, has the largest rose garden in North America, featuring over 20,000 roses in more than 60 individual gardens on display. The RW Norton Art Gallery, also located in Shreveport, houses the Southwest's largest permanent collection of works by Frederic Remington and Charles M. Russell. The laser and neon-adorned Texas Street Bridge spans the Red River, connecting Shreveport with Bossier City, which is home to one of the nation's top thoroughbred racetracks, Louisiana Downs. Riverboat gambling is popular entertainment in both cities, and riverboat casinos include Harrah's and the Horseshoe Riverboat.

Ark-La-Tex Antique & Classic Vehicle Museum Phone: 318-222-0227
601 Spring St Fax: 318-222-5042
Shreveport, LA 71101
www.softdisk.com/comp/classic/

Barnwell Garden & Art Center Phone: 318-673-7703
601 Clyde Fant Pkwy Fax: 318-673-7707
Shreveport, LA 71101

East Bank Theatre Phone: 318-741-8310
630 Barksdale Blvd Fax: 318-741-8312
Bossier City, LA 71111

Eighth Air Force Museum Phone: 318-456-3067
Barksdale Air Force Base Fax: 318-456-5558
Bossier City, LA 71110

Gardens of the American Rose Center Phone: 318-938-5402
8877 Jefferson-Paige Rd
West Shreveport, LA 71119

Harrah's Casino Shreveport Phone: 318-424-7777
PO Box 1114 Fax: 318-424-5650
Shreveport, LA 71163 TF: 800-427-7247

Horseshoe Riverboat Casino Phone: 318-742-0711
7111 Horseshoe Blvd Fax: 318-742-1541
Bossier City, LA 71171 TF: 800-895-0711
www.horseshoecasinos.com/

Isle of Capri Casino Phone: 318-678-7777
711 Isle of Capri Blvd Fax: 318-226-1782
Bossier City, LA 71111 TF: 800-843-4753
www.isleofcapricasino.com

Louisiana State Exhibit Museum Phone: 318-632-2020
3015 Greenwood Rd Fax: 318-632-2056
Shreveport, LA 71109

Meadows Museum of Art of Centenary College Phone: 318-869-5169
2911 Centenary Blvd Fax: 318-869-5730
Shreveport, LA 71104

Olde Covered Bridge Garden Phone: 318-635-6296
6905 Greenwood Rd Fax: 318-635-0020
Shreveport, LA 71119

Pioneer Heritage Center Phone: 318-797-5332
1 University Pl Louisiana State University Fax: 318-797-5395
Shreveport, LA 71115

Poverty Point National Monument Phone: 318-926-5492
6859 Hwy 577 Fax: 318-926-5366
Pioneer, LA 71266
www.nps.gov/popo

RW Norton Art Gallery Phone: 318-865-4201
4747 Creswell Ave Fax: 318-869-0435
Shreveport, LA 71106
E-mail: norton@softdisk.com
www.softdisk.com/comp/norton

Sci-Port Discovery Center Phone: 318-424-3466
Lake St & Clyde Fant Pkwy
Shreveport, LA 71101
www.sciport.org

Shreveport Civic Theatre Phone: 318-673-5100
400 Clyde Fant Pkwy Fax: 318-673-5105
Shreveport, LA 71101

Shreveport Entertainment District Phone: 318-222-9391
Downtown Shreveport Riverfront
Shreveport, LA 71101

Shreveport Little Theatre
812 Maragret Pl
Shreveport, LA 71101
www.sltheatre.org
Phone: 318-424-4439
Fax: 318-424-4440

Shreveport Metropolitan Ballet
600 Clyde Fant Pkwy Civic Theatre
Shreveport, LA 71101
Phone: 318-865-8242

Shreveport Opera
212 Texas St Suite 101
Shreveport, LA 71101
Phone: 318-227-9503
Fax: 318-227-9518

Shreveport Regional Arts Council
800 Snow St
Shreveport, LA 71101
Phone: 318-673-6500
Fax: 318-673-6515

Shreveport Symphony
600 Clyde Fant Pkwy Civic Theatre
Shreveport, LA 71101
Phone: 318-227-8863
Fax: 318-222-7490

SPAR Planetarium
2820 Pershing Blvd
Shreveport, LA 71109
Phone: 318-673-7827

Sports Museum of Champions
700 Clyde Fant Pkwy
Shreveport, LA 71101
Phone: 318-221-0712
Fax: 318-221-7366

Spring Street Museum
525 Spring St
Shreveport, LA 71101
Phone: 318-424-0964
Fax: 318-424-0964

Strand Theatre
619 Louisiana Ave
Shreveport, LA 71101
www.thestrandtheatre.com
Phone: 318-226-1481
Fax: 318-424-5434
TF: 800-313-6373

Texas Street Bridge
Shreveport, LA
Phone: 318-222-9391

Theatre of Performing Arts
4005 Lakeshore Dr
Shreveport, LA 71109
Phone: 318-525-0740
Fax: 318-525-0720

Touchstone Wildlife & Art Museum
3386 Hwy 80 E
Haughton, LA 71037
Phone: 318-949-2323

Walter B Jacobs Memorial Nature Park
8012 Blanchard-Furrh Rd
Shreveport, LA 71107
Phone: 318-929-2806
Fax: 318-929-3718

Water Town USA
7670 W 70th St
Shreveport, LA 71129
Phone: 318-938-5473
Fax: 318-938-1183

Sports Teams & Facilities

Boothill Speedway
I-20 W to Exit 3
West Shreveport, LA 71102
Phone: 318-938-5373

Hirsch Coliseum
3207 Pershing Blvd
Shreveport, LA 71109
Phone: 318-635-1361
Fax: 318-631-4909

Independence Stadium
3301 Pershing Blvd
Shreveport, LA 71109
Phone: 318-673-7758
Fax: 318-673-7786

Louisiana Downs
8000 E Texas St
Bossier City, LA 71111
www.ladowns.com
Phone: 318-742-5555
Fax: 318-741-2615
TF: 800-648-0712

Shreveport Captains (baseball)
2901 Pershing Blvd Fairgrounds Field
Shreveport, LA 71109
E-mail: shvcaps@iamerica.net
www.shreveportcaptains.com
Phone: 318-636-5555
Fax: 318-636-5555

Shreveport Mudbugs (hockey)
3701 Hudson St 2nd Fl
Shreveport, LA 71109
E-mail: info@mudbugshockey.com
www.mudbugshockey.com
Phone: 318-636-2847
Fax: 318-636-2280

Annual Events

Artbreak (early May) 318-673-6500
Champion Lake Pro Classic (mid-June) 318-222-7442
Christmas in Roseland
(late November-early January) 318-938-5402
December on the Red
(late November-late December)..................318-222-9391
Downtown Neon Saturday Nights
(June-September)..............................318-673-6500
First Bloom Festival (late April) 318-938-5402
Fourth of July Celebration (July 4) 318-459-3515
Holiday in Dixie (early-mid-April) 318-865-5555
Jazz & Gumbo Music Festival (mid-May)...........318-226-4552
Let the Good Times Roll Festival (mid-June) 318-222-7403
Louisiana State Fair
(late October-early November) 318-635-1361
Mardi Gras in the Ark-La-Tex
(late February-early March)......................318-746-0252
Mudbug Madness (late May) 318-222-7403
Pioneer Days (late September) 318-938-7289
Rackets Over the Red
(late November-late December)..................318-222-7403
Red River Rally (early October) 318-222-9391
Red River Revel (early October)...................318-424-4000
Redbud Festival (mid-March) 318-226-8884
Sanford Independence Bowl (late December) 318-221-0712
Shreveport Open Golf Tournament (mid-April) 318-798-6463

Sioux Falls, South Dakota

***County:* Minnehaha**

SIOUX FALLS is located in southeastern South Dakota. The only major city within 100 miles is Sioux City, Iowa.

Area (Land)	43.3 sq mi
Area (Water)	0 sq mi
Elevation	1,442 ft
Latitude	43-55-00 N
Longitude	96-70-00 W
Time Zone	CST
Area Code	605

Climate

Sioux Falls' climate features four distinct seasons. Winters are cold, with average high temperatures in the 20s and lows in the single digits. More than three feet of snow falls during an average Sioux Falls winter. Summer days are warm, with high temperatures in the 80s, but evenings cool down dramatically into the high 50s or low 60s. June is the wettest month of the year, while January is the driest.

Average Temperatures & Precipitation

Temperatures

	Jan	Feb	Mar	Apr	May	Jun	Jul	Aug	Sep	Oct	Nov	Dec
High	24	30	42	59	71	81	86	83	73	61	43	28
Low	3	10	23	35	46	56	62	59	49	36	23	9

Precipitation

	Jan	Feb	Mar	Apr	May	Jun	Jul	Aug	Sep	Oct	Nov	Dec
Inches	0.5	0.6	1.6	2.5	3.0	3.4	2.7	2.9	3.0	1.8	1.1	0.7

History

Sioux Falls was founded in November 1856 by the Western Townsite Company, a Dubuque, Iowa investor group, and named for the triple waterfalls of Big Sioux River, but the city was abandoned in 1862 due to Lakota Indian uprisings. Three years later Fort Dakota was established in the area, and by 1870 settlers returned to reclaim and rebuild the town. Sioux Falls had become the largest city in the Dakotas by 1873, with 573 residents.

Sioux Falls grew quickly as an agricultural center. The city is home to the largest stockyards in the world. Although agribusiness remains the city's leading industry, many new businesses have been attracted to Sioux Falls in recent years, due to South Dakota's beneficial tax structure (there are no state or local personal income taxes, business inventory taxes, or corporate income taxes). In 1992, Sioux Falls was named the "Best Place to Live in America" by Money Magazine, and from 1993-1996 the city ranked among the top 50 on the list. The seat of Minnehaha County, Sioux Falls today is home to more than 116,000 people and remains the largest city in the state of South Dakota.

Population

1990 Census	100,836
1998 Estimate	116,762
% Change	15.8

Racial/Ethnic Breakdown

White	96.8%
Black	0.7%
Other	2.5%
Hispanic Origin (may be of any race)	0.6%

Age Breakdown

Under 5 years	7.9%
5 to 17	17.9%
18 to 20	4.7%
21 to 24	6.8%
25 to 34	19.8%
35 to 44	14.8%
45 to 54	8.7%
55 to 64	7.7%
65 to 74	6.5%
75+ years	5.2%
Median Age	31.3

Gender Breakdown

Male	47.6%
Female	52.4%

Government

Type of Government: Mayor-Council

Sioux Falls City Attorney
224 W 9th St
Sioux Falls, SD 57104
Phone: 605-367-4281
Fax: 605-367-7330

Sioux Falls City Clerk
224 W 9th St
Sioux Falls, SD 57104
Phone: 605-367-7094
Fax: 605-367-7801

Sioux Falls City Council
224 W 9th St
Sioux Falls, SD 57104
Phone: 605-367-7188
Fax: 605-367-8815

Sioux Falls City Hall
224 W 9th St
Sioux Falls, SD 57104
Phone: 605-367-7200
Fax: 605-367-8490

Sioux Falls Community Development Dept
224 W 9th St
Sioux Falls, SD 57104
Phone: 605-367-7125
Fax: 605-367-8798

Sioux Falls Finance Dept
224 W 9th St
Sioux Falls, SD 57104
Phone: 605-367-7093
Fax: 605-367-7700

Sioux Falls Fire Dept
2820 S Minnesota Ave
Sioux Falls, SD 57105
Phone: 605-367-7152
Fax: 605-367-7861

Sioux Falls Human Resources/Risk Management Dept
224 W 9th St
Sioux Falls, SD 57104
Phone: 605-367-7112
Fax: 605-367-7865

Sioux Falls Mayor
224 W 9th St
Sioux Falls, SD 57104
Phone: 605-367-7200
Fax: 605-367-8490

Sioux Falls Parks & Recreation Dept
600 E 7th St
Sioux Falls, SD 57103
Phone: 605-367-7060
Fax: 605-367-4326

Sioux Falls Planning & Building Services Dept
224 W 9th St
Sioux Falls, SD 57104
Phone: 605-367-7130
Fax: 605-367-7801

Sioux Falls Police Dept
500 N Minnesota Ave
Sioux Falls, SD 57104
Phone: 605-367-7259
Fax: 605-367-7316

Sioux Falls Water Div
1201 N Western Ave
Sioux Falls, SD 57104
Phone: 605-367-7031
Fax: 605-367-7341

Siouxland Libraries
201 N Main Ave
Sioux Falls, SD 57104
Phone: 605-367-7081
Fax: 605-367-4312

Important Phone Numbers

AAA 605-336-3690
Driver's License Information 800-952-3696
Emergency 911
Minnehaha County Real Estate/Mobile Home Tax Information 605-367-4214
Minnehaha Treasurer's Office 605-367-4214
Poison Control Center 800-352-2222
Sioux Falls Board of Realtors 605-334-4752
South Dakota Dept of Revenue 605-773-5131
Time/Temp 605-361-5050
Vehicle Registration Information 605-367-4216
Voter Registration Information 605-367-4220
Weather 605-330-4444

Information Sources

Minnehaha County
415 N Dakota Ave
Sioux Falls, SD 57104
Phone: 605-367-4206
Fax: 605-367-8314

Sioux Falls Area Chamber of Commerce
200 N Phillips Ave Suite 102
Sioux Falls, SD 57104
www.siouxfalls.org
Phone: 605-336-1620
Fax: 605-336-6499

Sioux Falls Arena
1201 West Ave N
Sioux Falls, SD 57104
Phone: 605-367-7288
Fax: 605-338-1463

Sioux Falls Convention & Visitors Bureau
200 N Phillips Ave Suite 102
Sioux Falls, SD 57104
www.siouxfalls.org/
Phone: 605-336-1620
Fax: 605-336-6499
TF: 800-333-2072

Sioux Falls Development Foundation Inc
200 N Phillips Ave Suite 101
Sioux Falls, SD 57104
Phone: 605-339-0103
Fax: 605-339-0055
TF: 800-658-3373

Siouxland Libraries
201 N Main Ave
Sioux Falls, SD 57104
www.siouxland.lib.sd.us
Phone: 605-367-7081
Fax: 605-367-4312

Online Resources

Area Guide Sioux Falls
siouxfalls.areaguides.net

Excite.com Sioux Falls City Guide
www.excite.com/travel/countries/united_states/south_dakota/sioux_falls

Area Communities

Communities in Minnehaha County with populations greater than 1,000 include:

Brandon
304 S Main Ave
Brandon, SD 57005
Phone: 605-582-6515

Dell Rapids
PO Box 10
Dell Rapids, SD 57022
Phone: 605-428-3595
Fax: 605-428-5969

Hartford
125 N Main Ave
Hartford, SD 57033
Phone: 605-528-3427
Fax: 605-528-3320

Economy

Sioux Falls has been a major center for agriculture for more than a century, and more than 80,000 Sioux Falls area residents are employed by agriculture-related businesses. The city is also becoming one of the largest centers for health care in the region. Health care-related employment doubled in Minnehaha County from 1980 to 1993, and four of Sioux Falls top 15 employers are in the health care field. The area's top employer, Sioux Valley Hospital, provides jobs for more than 4,500 people.

Sioux Falls' favorable tax structure, low operating costs, and relatively low cost of living have attracted numerous new businesses of all types to the city in recent years.

Unemployment Rate 1.2%*
Per Capita Income $23,547*
Median Family Income $53,200*

** Information given is for the Sioux Falls Metropolitan Statistical Area (MSA), which includes the City of Sioux Falls and Minnehaha County.*

Principal Industries & Number of Wage Earners

Sioux Falls MSA* - June 2000

Construction & Mining	5,900
Finance, Insurance, & Real Estate	14,200
Government	11,000
Manufacturing	13,700
Services	34,900
Trade	28,700
Transporation & Public Utilities	6,400

* *Information given is for the Sioux Falls Metropolitan Statistical Area (MSA), which includes Lincoln and Minnehaha counties.*

Major Employers

Associates Commerce Solutions
4 Parkway N
Deerfield, IL 60015
www.associatescommerce.com
Phone: 847-597-3000
Fax: 847-597-3266

Avera McKennan Hospital
800 E 21st St
Sioux Falls, SD 57105
www.mckennan.org
Phone: 605-322-8000
Fax: 605-322-7822

Citibank (South Dakota) NA
701 E 60th St N
Sioux Falls, SD 57117
Phone: 605-331-2626
Fax: 605-331-1185
TF: 800-843-0777

Good Samaritan Society
4800 W 57th St
Sioux Falls, SD 57117
www.good-sam.com/
Phone: 605-362-3100
Fax: 605-362-3240

Hutchinson Technology Inc
2301 E 60th St N
Sioux Falls, SD 57104
Phone: 605-367-9445
Fax: 605-978-2210

Hy-Vee Food Stores
1601 S Sycamore Ave
Sioux Falls, SD 57110
www.hy-vee.com/stripemploy.html
Phone: 605-334-4570
Fax: 605-334-4570

Midwest Coast Transport
PO Box 5233
Sioux Falls, SD 57117
Phone: 605-339-8400
Fax: 605-339-8457
TF: 800-843-6699

Morrell John & Co
PO Box 5266
Sioux Falls, SD 57117
www.johnmorrell.com
Phone: 605-338-8200
Fax: 605-330-3162

Norwest Bank South Dakota NA
101 N Phillips Ave
Sioux Falls, SD 57101
Phone: 605-575-7300
Fax: 605-575-4984
TF: 800-321-4141

Richard L Roudebush Veterans Affairs Medical Center
PO Box 5046
Sioux Falls, SD 57117
Phone: 605-336-3230
Fax: 605-333-6878

Sioux Falls City Hall
224 W 9th St
Sioux Falls, SD 57104
www.sioux-falls.org
Phone: 605-367-7200
Fax: 605-367-8490

Sioux Falls School District
201 E 38th St
Sioux Falls, SD 57105
Phone: 605-367-7900
Fax: 605-367-4637

Sioux Valley Hospital
1100 S Euclid Ave
Sioux Falls, SD 57117
E-mail: info@siouxvalley.org
www.siouxvalley.org
Phone: 605-333-1000
Fax: 605-333-7201

Sunshine Food Markets Inc
1300 W Elkhorn St
Sioux Falls, SD 57104
Phone: 605-336-2505
Fax: 605-336-1762

Quality of Living Indicators

Total Crime Index 4,378
(rates per 100,000 inhabitants)

Violent Crime

Murder/manslaughter	5
Forcible rape	75
Robbery	43
Aggravated assault	242

Property Crime

Burglary	620
Larceny theft	3,173
Motor vehicle theft	220

Cost of Living Index 96.1
(national average = 100)

Median Home Price $90,200

Education

Public Schools

Sioux Falls School District
201 E 38th St
Sioux Falls, SD 57105
Phone: 605-367-7900
Fax: 605-367-4637

Number of Schools

Elementary	24
Middle	5
High	3

Student/Teacher Ratio

All Grades 18.5:1

Private Schools

Number of Schools (all grades) 28

Colleges & Universities

Augustana College
2001 S Summit Ave
Sioux Falls, SD 57197
E-mail: info@inst.augie.edu
www.augie.edu
Phone: 605-274-0770
Fax: 605-274-5518
TF: 800-727-2844

Kilian Community College
224 N Phillips Ave
Sioux Falls, SD 57104
kcc.cc.sd.us
Phone: 605-336-1711
Fax: 605-336-2606
TF: 800-888-1147

National American University Sioux Falls Campus
2801 S Kiwanis Ave Suite 100
Sioux Falls, SD 57105
www.nationalcollege.edu/campusfalls.html
Phone: 605-334-5430
Fax: 605-334-1575
TF: 800-388-5430

University of Sioux Falls
1101 W 22nd St
Sioux Falls, SD 57105
www.thecoo.edu
Phone: 605-331-5000
Fax: 605-331-6615
TF: 800-888-1047

Hospitals

Avera McKennan Hospital
800 E 21st St
Sioux Falls, SD 57105
www.mckennan.org
Phone: 605-322-8000
Fax: 605 322-7822

Richard L Roudebush Veterans Affairs Medical Center
PO Box 5046
Sioux Falls, SD 57117
Phone: 605-336-3230
Fax: 605-333-6878

Sioux Valley Hospital
1100 S Euclid Ave
Sioux Falls, SD 57117
www.siouxvalley.org
Phone: 605-333-1000
Fax: 605-333-7201

Transportation

Airport(s)

Sioux Falls Regional Airport (FSD)
3 miles NW of downtown (approx 10 minutes) 605-336-0762

Mass Transit

Sioux Falls Transit
$1 Base fare 605-367-7183

Rail/Bus

Greyhound Bus Station
301 N Dakota Ave
Sioux Falls, SD 57104
Phone: 605-336-0885
TF: 800-231-2222

Utilities

Electricity
Northern States Power Co. 605-339-8200
www.nspco.com
Sioux Falls Municipal Light & Power 605-367-7006

Gas
MidAmerican Energy Co 888-427-5632
www.midamericanenergy.com

Water
Sioux Falls Water Dept 605-367-7031

Garbage Collection/Recycling
Waste Management 605-338-6611

Telecommunications

Telephone
Qwest 800-244-1111
www.qwest.com

Cable Television
Midcontinent Communications 605-339-3339

Internet Service Providers (ISPs)
Cybernex Inc 605-371-4440
www.sd.cybernex.net
Dakota Internet Services Inc 605-331-2050
www.dakota.net

Banks

BankFirst
2600 W 49th St
Sioux Falls, SD 57105
E-mail: customer.service@bankfirstcorp.com
www.bankfirstcorp.com
Phone: 605-361-2111
Fax: 605-361-2690

Citibank NA
701 E 60th St N
Sioux Falls, SD 57117
Phone: 605-331-2626
Fax: 605-331-1185
TF: 800-843-0777

CorTrust Bank
1801 S Marion Rd
Sioux Falls, SD 57106
Phone: 605-361-8356
Fax: 605-361-9237

Dacotah Bank
1707 S Marion Rd
Sioux Falls, SD 57106
Phone: 605-361-5636
Fax: 605-362-1331

F & M Bank
1901 41st St
Sioux Falls, SD 57105
Phone: 605-334-2548
Fax: 605-339-8862

First National Bank of Sioux Falls
PO Box 5186
Sioux Falls, SD 57117
Phone: 605-335-5100
Fax: 605-335-5191

First Premier Bank
601 S Minnesota Ave
Sioux Falls, SD 57104
www.firstpremierbank.com
Phone: 605-357-3000
Fax: 605-357-3185

First Savings Bank
2301 E 10th St
Sioux Falls, SD 57103
Phone: 605-373-9840
Fax: 605-373-9731

Founders Trust National Bank
418 S Minnesota Ave
Sioux Falls, SD 57104
www.founderstrust.com
Phone: 605-333-9828
Fax: 605-333-9843

Home Federal Savings Bank
PO Box 85307
Sioux Falls, SD 57118
www.homefederal.com
Phone: 605-338-7255
Fax: 605-334-0788

Home Federal Savings Bank
225 S Main Ave
Sioux Falls, SD 57104
Phone: 605-333-7620
Fax: 605-333-7621

Norwest Bank South Dakota NA
101 N Phillips Ave
Sioux Falls, SD 57101
Phone: 605-575-7300
Fax: 605-575-4984
TF: 800-321-4141

US Bank NA
141 N Main Ave
Sioux Falls, SD 57104
Phone: 605-339-8941
TF: 800-872-2657

Wells Fargo Bank
3201 N 4th Ave
Sioux Falls, SD 57104
Phone: 605-336-3933

Shopping

Empire Mall
4001 W 41st St
Sioux Falls, SD 57106
Phone: 605-361-3300
Fax: 605-361-5411

Main Street Sioux Falls
230 S Phillips Ave Suite 110
Sioux Falls, SD 57104
Phone: 605-338-4009
Fax: 605-338-8816

Western Mall
2101 W 41st St
Sioux Falls, SD 57105
E-mail: www.western.mall@ideasign.com
Phone: 605-336-6920
Fax: 605-336-5651

Media

Newspapers and Magazines

Argus Leader*
200 S Minnesota Ave
Sioux Falls, SD 57104
www.argusleader.com
Phone: 605-331-2200
Fax: 605-331-2294

**Indicates major daily newspapers*

Television

KDLT-TV Ch 46 (NBC)
3600 S Westport Ave
Sioux Falls, SD 57106
www.kdlt.com
Phone: 605-361-5555
Fax: 605-361-3982

KELO-TV Ch 11 (CBS)
501 S Phillips Ave
Sioux Falls, SD 57104
E-mail: kelotv@dakotaconnect.com
www.kelotv.com
Phone: 605-336-1100
Fax: 605-336-0202

KSFY-TV Ch 13 (ABC)
300 N Dakota Ave Suite 100
Sioux Falls, SD 57104
E-mail: ksfy@ksfy.com
www.ksfy.com
Phone: 605-336-1300
Fax: 605-336-7936

KTTW-TV Ch 17 (Fox)
2817 W 11th St
Sioux Falls, SD 57104
Phone: 605-338-0017
Fax: 605-338-7173

KUSD-TV Ch 2 (PBS)
Dakota & Cherry Sts Telecom Bldg
Vermillion, SD 57069
www.sdpb.org
Phone: 605-677-5861
Fax: 605-677-5010
TF: 800-456-0766

Radio

KBHE-FM 89.3 MHz (NPR)
PO Box 5000
Vermillion, SD 57069
www.sdpb.org
Phone: 605-677-5861
Fax: 605-677-5010

KCSD-FM 90.9 MHz (NPR)
1101 W 22nd St
Sioux Falls, SD 57105
Phone: 605-331-6690
Fax: 605-331-6692

KELO-AM 1320 kHz (Oldies)
500 S Phillips Ave
Sioux Falls, SD 57104
E-mail: keloam@mmi.net
www.keloam.com
Phone: 605-331-5350
Fax: 605-336-0415
TF: 800-529-5356

KELO-FM 92.5 MHz (AC)
500 S Phillips Ave
Sioux Falls, SD 57104
E-mail: kelofm@mmi.net
www.kelofm.com
Phone: 605-331-5350
Fax: 605-336-0415
TF: 800-529-5356

KESD-FM 88.3 MHz (NPR)
PO Box 5000
Vermillion, SD 57069
www.sdpb.org
Phone: 605-677-5861
Fax: 605-677-5010

KKLS-FM 104.7 MHz (CHR)
3205 S Meadow Ave
Sioux Falls, SD 57106
Phone: 605-361-6550
Fax: 605-361-5410

KNWC-AM 1270 kHz (Rel)
26908 S Tallgrass Ave
Sioux Falls, SD 57108
E-mail: knwc@knwc.org
www.knwc.org
Phone: 605-339-1270
Fax: 605-339-1271
TF: 888-569-5692

KRSD-FM 88.1 MHz (Clas)
Augustana College Box 737
Sioux Falls, SD 57197
Phone: 605-335-6666
Fax: 605-335-1259
TF: 800-228-7123

KSFS-AM 1520 kHz (Sports)
305 W 14th St
Sioux Falls, SD 57104
E-mail: thezone@dakotaconnect.com
www.ksfs.com
Phone: 605-335-8800
Fax: 605-335-8428

KSOO-AM 1140 kHz (N/T)
2600 S Spring Ave
Sioux Falls, SD 57105
www.ksoo.com
Phone: 605-339-1140
Fax: 605-339-2735

KTSD-FM 91.1 MHz (NPR)
PO Box 5000
Vermillion, SD 57069
www.sdpb.org
Phone: 605-677-5861
Fax: 605-677-5010

KTWB-FM 101.9 MHz (Ctry)
500 S Phillips Ave
Sioux Falls, SD 57104
www.ktwb.com
Phone: 605-331-5350
Fax: 605-336-0415

KXRB-AM 1000 kHz (Ctry)
3205 S Meadow Ave
Sioux Falls, SD 57106
www.kxrb.com
Phone: 605-361-6550
Fax: 605-361-5410

Attractions

Downtown Sioux Falls is home to the Great Plains Zoo and Delbridge Museum of Natural History, and replicas of Michelangelo's David and Moses are among the city's many public sculptures. The Falls of the Big Sioux River, the natural wonder for which the City of Sioux Falls was named, can be observed from three separate viewing areas. Ten miles northeast of downtown is the Earth Resources Observation System (EROS) Data Center, a program of the U.S. Department of the Interior. EROS houses millions of frames of satellite and aircraft photographs of the earth.

Buffalo Ridge Old West Ghost Town
I-90 5 miles W of Sioux Falls
Sioux Falls, SD 57115
Phone: 605-528-3931

Catfish Bay
5500 N Show Pl
Sioux Falls, SD 57104
Phone: 605-339-0911

Center for Western Studies
29th St & S Summit Ave Augustana College
Sioux Falls, SD 57197
inst.augie.edu/CWS
Phone: 605-274-4007
Fax: 605-274-4999
TF: 800-727-2844

Delbridge Museum of Natural History
805 S Kiwanis Ave
Sioux Falls, SD 57104
Phone: 605-367-7003
Fax: 605-367-8340

Falls Park
McClellan St & 3rd Ave
Sioux Falls, SD 57109
Phone: 605-367-7060

Great Plains Zoo
805 S Kiwanis Ave
Sioux Falls, SD 57104
Phone: 605-367-7059
Fax: 605-367-8340

Main Street Sioux Falls
230 S Phillips Ave Suite 110
Sioux Falls, SD 57104
Phone: 605-338-4009
Fax: 605-338-8816

Multi-Cultural Center of Sioux Falls
515 N Main Ave
Sioux Falls, SD 57104
Phone: 605-367-7400
Fax: 605-367-7404

Northern Plains Tribal Arts Gallery
1000 N West Ave Suite 230
Sioux Falls, SD 57104
Phone: 605-334-4060
Fax: 605-334-8415
TF: 800-658-4797

Old Courthouse Museum
200 W 6th St
Sioux Falls, SD 57104
Phone: 605-367-4210
Fax: 605-367-6004

Palisades State Park
25495 485th Ave
Garretson, SD 57030
Phone: 605-594-3824

Pettigrew Home & Museum
131 N Duluth Ave
Sioux Falls, SD 57104
Phone: 605-367-7097
Fax: 605-331-0467

Rehfeld's Galleries
210 S Phillips Ave
Sioux Falls, SD 57104
Phone: 605-336-9737
Fax: 605-336-2631

Sioux Empire Medical Museum
1100 S Euclid Ave
Sioux Falls, SD 57117
Phone: 605-333-6397
Fax: 605-333-1577

South Dakota Symphony Orchestra
Washington Pavilion of Arts & Science
Sioux Falls, SD 57104
Phone: 605-335-7933
Fax: 605-335-1958

Statue of Moses
30th St & Grange Ave
Sioux Falls, SD 57105
Phone: 605-336-5417

Thunder Road Family Fun Park
201 N Kiwanis Ave
Sioux Falls, SD 57104
E-mail: wtsthunder@aol.com
www.feelthethunder.com/siouxfalls.htm
Phone: 605-334-4181
Fax: 605-978-1831
TF: 888-943-7623

USGS AEROS Data Center
Mundt Federal Bldg
Sioux Falls, SD 57198
E-mail: edcweb@edcwww.cr.usgs.gov
edcwww.cr.usgs.gov
Phone: 605-594-6511
Fax: 605-594-6589
TF: 800-252-4547

USS South Dakota Battleship Memorial
12th St & Kiwanis Ave
Sioux Falls, SD 57102
Phone: 605-367-7060

Washington Pavilion of Arts & Science
301 S Main Ave
Sioux Falls, SD 57104
www.washingtonpavilion.org
Phone: 605-367-7397
Fax: 605-731-2402
TF: 877-927-4728

Wild Water West
26767 466th Ave
Sioux Falls, SD 57106
Phone: 605-339-2837
Fax: 605-361-3173

Sports Teams & Facilities

Huset's Speedway
Hwy 11
Brandon, SD 57005
www.husets-speedway.com
Phone: 605-582-3536
Fax: 605-582-6082

Sioux Falls Arena
1201 West Ave N
Sioux Falls, SD 57104
Phone: 605-367-7288
Fax: 605-338-1463

Sioux Falls Canaries (baseball)
West Ave N Sioux Falls Stadium
Sioux Falls, SD 57104
canaries.iw.net
Phone: 605-333-0179
Fax: 605-333-0139

Sioux Falls Skyforce (basketball)
1201 West Ave N Sioux Falls Arena
Sioux Falls, SD 57102
E-mail: skyforce@iw.net
skyforce.iw.net
Phone: 605-332-0605
Fax: 605-332-2305

Annual Events

Almost Forgotten Crafts (late April) 605-367-4210
Artists of the Plains Art Show & Sale (mid-February) 605-336-4007
Augustana Jazz Festival (early March) 605-336-4049
Festival of Choirs (early April) 605-367-7957
Northern Plains Tribal Art Show & Market (late September) 605-334-4060
Northern Prairie Storytelling Festival (early June) 605-331-6622
Sidewalk Arts Festival (early September) 605-336-1167
Sioux Empire Fair (early-mid-August) 605-367-7178
Sioux Empire Farm Show (late January) 605-373-2016
University of Sioux Falls Cougar Days (late September-early October) 605-331-5000
Viking Days (early October) 605-274-5521
Winter Fest (late January) 605-338-4009

Spokane, Washington

County: **Spokane**

SPOKANE is located at the falls of the Spokane River in east central Washington State, less than 20 miles from the Idaho border. Major cities within 100 miles include Coeur d'Alene and Lewiston, Idaho.

Area (Land) .... 55.9 sq mi
Area (Water)............................... 0.7 sq mi
Elevation....................................1,898 ft
Latitude ....47-66-56 N
Longitude.............................. 117-43-35 W
Time Zone ....PST
Area Code....................................... 509

Climate

Spokane's climate features four distinct seasons. Winters are cold and wet, with average high temperatures ranging from the low 30s to low 40s and average low temperatures in the 20s. The average annual snowfall in Spokane is just over 50 inches. Summer days are warm and dry, with average high temperatures ranging from the mid-70s to the low 80s, while evenings cool down dramatically into low 50s. December is the wettest month of the year in Spokane; July, August, and September are the driest.

Average Temperatures & Precipitation

Temperatures

	Jan	Feb	Mar	Apr	May	Jun	Jul	Aug	Sep	Oct	Nov	Dec
High	33	41	48	57	66	75	83	83	72	59	41	34
Low	21	26	30	35	42	49	54	54	46	36	29	22

Precipitation

	Jan	Feb	Mar	Apr	May	Jun	Jul	Aug	Sep	Oct	Nov	Dec
Inches	2.0	1.5	1.5	1.2	1.4	1.3	0.7	0.7	0.7	1.0	2.2	2.4

History

Spokane was named for the region's early Native American inhabitants—the name itself means "Children of the Sun." White settlers began arriving in the Spokane area in the 1860s, but the first permanent white settlement was not established until the early 1870s, when James N. Glover built a house and a sawmill powered by the Spokane Falls. The City of Spokane Falls (shortened to Spokane nine years later) was incorporated in 1881. The newly incorporated city was the only point where railroads could cross the Rockies and reach the Columbia Basin, and this factor, and, later, the gold fields of Idaho, contributed to the city's growth. In 1889, much of Spokane was destroyed by a fire, but the city was quickly rebuilt.

Today, Spokane is a major commercial, transportation, manufacturing, and cultural hub for the Inland Northwest, which includes parts of Washington, Idaho, Montana, and Oregon, as well as two Canadian provinces, British Columbia and Alberta. With a population of more than 184,000, Spokane is Washington's second largest city.

Population

1990 Census 177,165
1998 Estimate...............................184,058
% Change 3.9

Racial/Ethnic Breakdown
White......................................93.3%
Black 0.2%
Other 6.5%
Hispanic Origin (may be of any race) 2.1%

Age Breakdown
Under 5 years...............................7.5%
5 to 17....................................16.9%
18 to 20....................................4.7%
21 to 24....................................6.3%
25 to 34...................................17.5%
35 to 44...................................14.6%
45 to 54....................................8.5%
55 to 64....................................7.8%
65 to 74....................................8.5%
75+ years 7.7%
Median Age.................................33.4

Gender Breakdown
Male......................................47.7%
Female....................................52.3%

Government

Type of Government: Strong Mayor

Spokane City Clerk
808 W Spokane Falls Blvd
Spokane, WA 99201
Phone: 509-625-6350
Fax: 509-625-6217

Spokane City Council
808 W Spokane Falls Blvd
Spokane, WA 99201
Phone: 509-625-6255
Fax: 509-625-6217

Spokane City Hall
808 W Spokane Falls Blvd
Spokane, WA 99201
Phone: 509-625-6250
Fax: 509-625-6217

Spokane City Manager
808 W Spokane Falls Blvd
Spokane, WA 99201
Phone: 509-625-6262
Fax: 509-625-6217

Spokane Community Development Dept
808 W Spokane Falls Blvd
Spokane, WA 99201
Phone: 509-625-6325
Fax: 509-625-6315

Spokane Finance Dept
808 W Spokane Falls Blvd
Spokane, WA 99201
Phone: 509-625-6040
Fax: 509-625-6939

Spokane Fire Dept
44 W Riverside Ave
Spokane, WA 99201
Phone: 509-625-7080
Fax: 509-625-7039

Spokane Human Resources Dept
808 W Spokane Blvd 4th Fl
Spokane, WA 99201
Phone: 509-626-6363
Fax: 509-625-6379

Spokane Legal Dept
808 W Spokane Falls Blvd 5th Fl
Spokane, WA 99201
Phone: 509-625-6225
Fax: 509-625-6277

Spokane Mayor
808 W Spokane Falls Blvd
Spokane, WA 99201
Phone: 509-625-6250
Fax: 509-625-6217

Spokane Parks & Recreation Dept
808 W Spokane Falls Blvd
Spokane, WA 99201
Phone: 509-625-6200
Fax: 509-625-6205

Spokane Police Dept
1100 W Mallon Ave
Spokane, WA 99260
Phone: 509-625-4050
Fax: 509-625-4066

Spokane Public Library
906 W Main Ave
Spokane, WA 99201
Phone: 509-444-5336
Fax: 509-444-5366

Spokane Treasurer
808 W Spokane Falls Blvd
Spokane, WA 99201
Phone: 509-625-6030
Fax: 509-625-6990

Spokane Water & Hydroelectric Services
914 E North Foothills Dr
Spokane, WA 99207
Phone: 509-625-7800
Fax: 509-625-7816

Spokane Youth Dept
808 W Spokane Falls Blvd 6th Fl
Spokane, WA 99201
Phone: 509-625-6440
Fax: 509-625-6777

Important Phone Numbers

AAA....509-358-6900
Driver's License Information....509-482-3883
Emergency.... 911
HotelDocs....800-468-3537
Poison Control Center....206-526-2121
Spokane Assn of Realtors....509-326-9222
Spokane County Assessor's Office....509-477-5793
Spokane Taxes & Licenses Dept....509-625-6070
Time....509-458-8800
Vehicle Registration Information....509-477-2222
Voter Registration Information....509-477-2320
Washington State Dept of Revenue....800-647-7706
Weather....509-244-6395

Information Sources

Better Business Bureau Serving the Inland Northwest
508 W 6th Ave Suite 401
Spokane, WA 99204
www.spokane.bbb.org
Phone: 509-455-4200
Fax: 509-838-1079

Spokane Area Chamber of Commerce
PO Box 2147
Spokane, WA 99210
www.spokane.org/chamber/
Phone: 509-624-1393
Fax: 509-747-0077

Spokane Center
W 334 Spokane Falls Blvd
Spokane, WA 99201
www.spokane-areacvb.org/spokanecenter
Phone: 509-353-6500
Fax: 509-353-6511

Spokane Convention & Visitors Bureau
801 W Riverside Ave Suite 301
Spokane, WA 99201
www.spokane-areacvb.org
Phone: 509-624-1341
Fax: 509-623-1297
TF: 800-248-3230

Spokane County
1116 W Broadway Ave
Spokane, WA 99260
www.spokanecounty.org/
Phone: 509-477-2265
Fax: 509-477-2274

Spokane Economic Development Council
801 W Riverside Suite 302
Spokane, WA 99201
www.spokaneedc.org
Phone: 509-624-9285
Fax: 509-624-3759
TF: 800-776-5263

Online Resources

About.com Guide to Spokane
spokane.about.com/citiestowns/pacnwus/spokane

Anthill City Guide Spokane
www.anthill.com/city.asp?city=spokane

City Knowledge Spokane
www.cityknowledge.com/wa_spokane.htm

Excite.com Spokane City Guide
www.excite.com/travel/countries/united_states/washington/spokane

Spokane.net
www.spokane.net

Area Communities

Communities in Spokane County with populations greater than 1,000 include:

Airway Heights
PO Box 969
Airway Heights, WA 99001
Phone: 509-244-5578
Fax: 509-244-3413

Cheney
609 2nd St
Cheney, WA 99004
Phone: 509-235-7201
Fax: 509-235-7206

Deer Park
PO Box F
Deer Park, WA 99006
Phone: 509-276-8802
Fax: 509-276-5764

Medical Lake
PO Box 369
Medical Lake, WA 99022
Phone: 509-565-5000
Fax: 509-565-5008

Millwood
9103 E Frederick Ave
Spokane, WA 99206
Phone: 509-924-0960
Fax: 509-927-2867

Economy

Spokane is considered the primary economic hub of the Inland Northwest. For more than a century, Spokane has been an important transportation and distribution center in the Pacific Northwest, and trade continues to play a major role the area's economy—Spokane is presently the largest railroad center west of Omaha. A leading regional center for medicine as well, health care is currently Spokane's largest aggregate sector employer, providing jobs for nearly 20,000 area residents. Federal, state, and local government, although ranked the third largest sector based upon total number of employees, is a major contributor to Spokane's economy. Seven of Spokane County's top ten employers are government-related, including the county's largest employer, Fairchild Air Force Base, which is one of several military installations in the area (all four branches of the armed forces are represented in Spokane County).

Unemployment Rate 5.2%*
Per Capita Income.......................... $23,592*
Median Family Income...................... $28,778

** Information given is for Spokane County.*

Principal Industries & Number of Wage Earners

Spokane County - 1998

Agriculture, Forestry, & Fishing.......................... 1,481
Construction.. 9,681
Finance, Insurance, & Real Estate....................... 10,540
Government 28,607
Manufacturing 22,305
Mining 237
Retail Trade.. 34,268
Services 52,109
Transportation, Communications, & Utilities............... 7,091
Wholesale Trade...................................... 11,359

Major Employers

Agilent Technologies
24001 E Mission
Liberty Lake, WA 99019
www.agilent.com
Phone: 509-921-4001
Fax: 509-921-4300

Bank of America Credit Card Services
PO Box 2462
Spokane, WA 99210
Phone: 509-353-1258
Fax: 509-353-6103

Columbia Lighting Inc
PO Box 2787
Spokane, WA 99220
www.columbia-ltg.com
Phone: 509-924-7000
Fax: 509-921-7564

Dakotah Direct Inc
N 214 Wall St Suite 600
Spokane, WA 99201
www.dakotahdirect.com
Phone: 509-624-2401
Fax: 509-624-1505

Empire Health Consolidated Services
PO Box 248
Spokane, WA 99210
Phone: 509-473-7960
Fax: 509-473-7286

Fairchild Air Force Base
Fairchild AFB, WA 99011
www.fairchild.af.mil
Phone: 509-247-1212
Fax: 509-247-2120

Kaiser Aluminum & Chemical Corp
PO Box 15108
Spokane, WA 99215
Phone: 509-924-1500
Fax: 509-927-6309

Sacred Heart Medical Center
101 W 8th Ave
Spokane, WA 99204
www.shmc.org
Phone: 509-455-3131
Fax: 509-474-4496

Spokane City Hall
808 W Spokane Falls Blvd
Spokane, WA 99201
www.spokanecity.org
Phone: 509-625-6250
Fax: 509-625-6217

Spokane County
1116 W Broadway Ave
Spokane, WA 99260
www.spokanecounty.org/
Phone: 509-477-2265
Fax: 509-477-2274

Spokane School District #81
200 N Bernard
Spokane, WA 99201
www.sd81.k12.wa.us
Phone: 509-354-7265
Fax: 509-354-5963

State of Washington
600 S Franklin
Olympia, WA 98504
www.wa.gov/dop
Phone: 360-664-1960
Fax: 360-664-0499

Telect Inc
2111 N Molter Rd
Liberty Lake, WA 99019
E-mail: getinfo@telect.com
www.telect.com
Phone: 509-926-6000
Fax: 509-927-0852
TF: 800-551-4567

US Postal Service
2718 E 57th Ave
Spokane, WA 99223
new.usps.com
Phone: 509-626-6896

Quality of Living Indicators

Total Crime Index.................................... 14,976
(rates per 100,000 inhabitants)

Violent Crime
Murder/manslaughter............................ 6
Forcible rape 82
Robbery.. 364
Aggravated assault............................. 920

Property Crime
Burglary 3,152
Larceny theft 9,484
Motor vehicle theft 968

Cost of Living Index................................. 104.0
(national average = 100)

Median Home Price................................... $106,800

Education

Public Schools

Spokane School District #81
200 N Bernard
Spokane, WA 99201
www.sd81.k12.wa.us
Phone: 509-354-7265
Fax: 509-354-5963

Number of Schools
Elementary 35
Middle 6
High.. 5
Special 4

Student/Teacher Ratio
All Grades 19.9:1

Private Schools

Number of Schools (all grades) .... 30+

Colleges & Universities

Eastern Washington University
526 5th St MS 148
Cheney, WA 99004
E-mail: admissions@ewu.edu
www.ewu.edu
Phone: 509-359-6200
Fax: 509-359-6692
TF: 888-740-1914

Gonzaga University
E 502 Boone Ave
Spokane, WA 99258
www.gonzaga.edu
Phone: 509-328-4220
Fax: 509-323-5780
TF: 800-986-9585

ITT Technical Institute
N 1050 Argonne Rd
Spokane, WA 99212
www.itt-tech.edu
Phone: 509-926-2900
Fax: 509-926-2908
TF: 800-777-8324

Spokane Community College
1810 N Greene St
Spokane, WA 99217
E-mail: sccinfo@scc.spokane.cc.wa.us
www.scc.spokane.cc.wa.us
Phone: 509-533-7000
Fax: 509-533-8839
TF: 800-248-5644

Spokane Falls Community College
3410 W Fort George Wright Dr
Spokane, WA 99224
www.sfcc.spokane.cc.wa.us
Phone: 509-533-3500
Fax: 509-533-3237

Washington State University Spokane
601 W 1st Ave
Spokane, WA 99201
E-mail: brazier@wsu.edu
www.spokane.wsu.edu
Phone: 509-358-7500
Fax: 509-358-7505

Whitworth College
300 W Hawthorne Rd
Spokane, WA 99251
whitworth.edu
Phone: 509-777-1000
Fax: 509-777-3758
TF: 800-533-4668

Hospitals

Deaconess Medical Center Spokane
800 W 5th St
Spokane, WA 99204
www.deaconess-spokane.org
Phone: 509-458-5800
Fax: 509-473-7286

Holy Family Hospital
5633 N Lidgerwood St
Spokane, WA 99207
www.holy-family.org
Phone: 509-482-0111
Fax: 509-482-2481

Sacred Heart Medical Center
101 W 8th Ave
Spokane, WA 99204
www.shmc.org
Phone: 509-455-3131
Fax: 509-474-4496

Valley Hospital & Medical Center
12606 E Mission Ave
Spokane, WA 99216
Phone: 509-924-6650
Fax: 509-892-5653

Veterans Affairs Medical Center
4815 N Assembly St
Spokane, WA 99205
Phone: 509-328-4521
Fax: 509-434-7119

Transportation

Airport(s)

Spokane International Airport (GEG)
6 miles SW of downtown (approx 15 minutes) 509-624-3218

Mass Transit

Spokane Transit Authority
$.75 Base fare................................509-328-7433

Rail/Bus

Spokane Amtrak Station
W 221 1st Ave
Spokane, WA 99204
Phone: 509-624-5144

Trailways Bus Station
W 221 1st Ave
Spokane, WA 99201
Phone: 509-838-5262

Utilities

Electricity
Inland Power & Light Co Inc..................509-747-7151
www.inlandpower.com

Gas
Avista Corp.................................509-495-4817
www.avistacorp.com

Water
Spokane Utility Dept 509-625-6000

Garbage Collection/Recycling
Recycle Hotline 509-747-0242
Spokane Utility Dept 509-625-6000

Telecommunications

Telephone
Qwest.......................................800-244-1111
www.qwest.com

Cable Television
AT & T Cable Services.......................509-484-4900
www.cable.att.com

Internet Service Providers (ISPs)
Future Link 509-323-2880
www.thefuture.net
Internet On-Ramp Inc........................509-624-7267
www.ior.com
Verio Spokane 509-624-6798
home.verio.net/local/frontpage.cfm?AirportCode=GEG

Banks

Inland Northwest Bank
421 W Riverside Ave Suite 113
Spokane, WA 99201
Phone: 509-456-8888
Fax: 509-623-1787

Seattle-First National Bank
601 W Riverside Ave
Spokane, WA 99210
Phone: 509-353-1445
Fax: 509-353-1455

US Bank of Washington NA
428 W Riverside Ave
Spokane, WA 99201
Phone: 509-353-5025
Fax: 509-353-5032
TF: 800-872-2657

Washington Trust Bank
717 W Sprague Ave Suite 920
Spokane, WA 99204
Phone: 509-353-4122
Fax: 509-353-6962

Wells Fargo Bank
524 W Riverside Ave
Spokane, WA 99201
www.wellsfargo.com
Phone: 509-455-5773
Fax: 509-455-5718
TF: 800-869-3557

Shopping

Crescent Court
700 W Main Ave
Spokane, WA 99201
www.rosewood-hotels.com/crescent.htm
Phone: 509-459-6111
Fax: 509-325-7324

Flour Mill
621 W Mallon Ave
Spokane, WA 99201
Phone: 509-459-6100
Fax: 509-325-7324

Monroe Street Bridge Antique Market
604 N Monroe St
Spokane, WA 99201
Phone: 509-327-6398
Fax: 509-325-9545

Northtown Mall
4750 N Division St
Spokane, WA 99207
Phone: 509-482-0178
Fax: 509-483-0360

RiverPark Square
221 N Wall St Suite 212
Spokane, WA 99201
Phone: 509-838-7970
Fax: 509-623-1715

Shadle Shopping Center
2501 W Wellesley Ave
Spokane, WA 99205
Phone: 509-838-8500
Fax: 509-838-3099

Spokane Antique Mall
12 W Sprague
Spokane, WA 99204
Phone: 509-747-1466

Spokane Market Place
Ruby St & Desmet Ave
Spokane, WA 99207
Phone: 509-456-0100

University City Mall
Sprague Ave & University Rd
Spokane, WA 99206
Phone: 509-927-0470

Media

Newspapers and Magazines

Journal of Business
112 E 1st Ave
Spokane, WA 99202
E-mail: journal@spokanejournal.com
www.spokanejournal.com
Phone: 509-456-5257
Fax: 509-456-0624

Pacific Northwest Inlander
1003 E Trent Suite 110
Spokane, WA 99202
E-mail: inlander@iea.com
Phone: 509-325-0634
Fax: 509-325-0638

Spokesman Review*
PO Box 2160
Spokane, WA 99201
E-mail: editor@spokesman.com
www.spokane.net
Phone: 509-459-5000
Fax: 509-459-5482
TF: 800-338-8801

**Indicates major daily newspapers*

Television

KAYU-TV Ch 28 (Fox)
PO Box 30028
Spokane, WA 99223
Phone: 509-448-2828
Fax: 509-448-3815

KHQ-TV Ch 6 (NBC)
PO Box 8088
Spokane, WA 99203
www.msnbc.com/local/KHQ/default.asp
Phone: 509-448-6000
Fax: 509-448-4644

KREM-TV Ch 2 (CBS)
4103 S Regal St
Spokane, WA 99223
www.krem.com
Phone: 509-448-2000
Fax: 509-448-6397

KSKN-TV Ch 22 (UPN)
PO Box 8037
Spokane, WA 99203
Phone: 509-742-3563
Fax: 509-443-9100

KSPS-TV Ch 7 (PBS)
3911 S Regal St
Spokane, WA 99223
www.ksps.org/
Phone: 509-353-5777
Fax: 509-354-7757

KXLY-TV Ch 4 (ABC)
500 W Boone Ave
Spokane, WA 99201
E-mail: kxly@iea.com
www.kxly.com
Phone: 509-324-4000
Fax: 509-327-3932

Radio

KAEP-FM 105.7 MHz (Alt)
PO Box 30013
Spokane, WA 99223
www.1057thepeak.com
Phone: 509-448-1000
Fax: 509-448-7015

KAQQ-AM 590 kHz (Nost)
300 E 3rd Ave
Spokane, WA 99202
www.q59.com
Phone: 509-459-9800
Fax: 509-459-9850

KDRK-FM 93.7 MHz (Ctry)
PO Box 30013
Spokane, WA 99223
www.catcountry94.com
Phone: 509-448-1000
Fax: 509-448-7015

KEYF-FM 101.1 MHz (Oldies)
S 6019 Crestline St
Spokane, WA 99223
www.oldies1011.com
Phone: 509-441-3322
Fax: 509-448-6523

KGA-AM 1510 kHz (N/T)
PO Box 30013
Spokane, WA 99223
E-mail: 1510kga@iea.com
www.1510kga.com
Phone: 509-448-1000
Fax: 509-448-7015

KISC-FM 98.1 MHz (AC)
300 E 3rd Ave
Spokane, WA 99202
www.98kiss.com
Phone: 509-459-9800
Fax: 509-459-9850

KKZX-FM 98.9 MHz (CR)
5106 S Palouse Hwy
Spokane, WA 99223
www.kkzx.com
Phone: 509-448-9900
Fax: 509-448-4043

KPBX-FM 91.1 MHz (NPR)
N 2319 Monroe St
Spokane, WA 99205
E-mail: kpbx@kpbx.org
www.kpbx.org
Phone: 509-328-5729
Fax: 509-328-5764

KXLY-AM 920 kHz (N/T)
500 W Boone Ave
Spokane, WA 99201
www.kxly920.com
Phone: 509-328-6292
Fax: 509-325-0676

Attractions

Riverfront Park is a premier attraction in Spokane that includes the Flour Mill, a unique complex of restaurants, boutiques, and galleries, as well as views of Spokane Falls and the Spokane River. The newest attraction in Spokane is the Spokane River Centennial Trail, which begins at the confluence of the Spokane and Little Spokane rivers and ends at the Washington-Idaho border. The Trail also connects with the Idaho Centennial Trail. Mount Spokane State Park is known for its skiing both on Mount Kit Carson and on Mount Spokane. Three states and two Canadian provinces are visible from the top of Mount Spokane: Washington, Idaho, Montana, Alberta, and British Columbia.

Arbor Crest Winery
4705 N Fruit Hill Rd
Spokane, WA 99217
Phone: 509-927-9894
Fax: 509-927-0574

Bing Crosby Memorabilia Room at Gonzaga University
502 E Boone Ave
Spokane, WA 99258
Phone: 509-328-4220
Fax: 509-324-5718

Carr's One of a Kind in the World Museum
5225 N Freya St
Spokane, WA 99207
Phone: 509-489-8859
Fax: 509-489-8859
TF: 800-350-6469

Cat Tales Endangered Species Conservation Park
17020 N Newport Hwy
Mead, WA 99021
www.cattales.org
Phone: 509-238-4126

Caterina Winery
905 N Washington
Spokane, WA 99201
Phone: 509-328-5069
Fax: 509-325-7324

Chase Gallery
808 W Spokane Falls Blvd
Spokane, WA 99201
Phone: 509-625-6050
Fax: 509-625-6777

Children's Museum of Spokane
110 N Post St
Spokane, WA 99201
E-mail: cmspokane@aol.com
www.vpds.wsu.edu/cmos/
Phone: 509-624-5437
Fax: 509-624-6453

Corbin Art Center
507 W 7th Ave
Spokane, WA 99204
Phone: 509-625-6677
Fax: 509-458-2234

Douglas Gallery
120 N Wall
Spokane, WA 99201
Phone: 509-624-4179
Fax: 509-624-4170

Fairchild Air Force Base Heritage Museum
100 E Bong St
Fairchild AFB, WA 99011
Phone: 509-247-2100
Fax: 509-247-4110

Finch John A Arboretum
809 N Washington City Pk Maintenance
Spokane, WA 99201
Phone: 509-625-6655

Interplayers Ensemble
S 174 Howard
Spokane, WA 99201
www.interplayers.com
Phone: 509-455-7529
Fax: 509-624-5902

Jundt Art Museum
202 E Cataldo Ave Gonzaga University
Spokane, WA 99258
Phone: 509-328-4220
Fax: 509-323-5525

Knipprath Cellars
5634 E Commerce Ave
Spokane, WA 99212
Phone: 509-534-5121
Fax: 509-534-5148

Lake Roosevelt National Recreation Area
1008 Crest Dr
Coulee Dam, WA 99116
www.nps.gov/laro
Phone: 509-633-9441
Fax: 509-633-9332

Latah Creek Wine Cellars
13030 E Indiana
Spokane, WA 99216
www.latahcreek.com
Phone: 509-926-0164
Fax: 509-926-0710
TF: 800-528-2427

Manito Park
S Grand & 18th St
Spokane, WA 99203
Phone: 509-625-6622
Fax: 509-625-6958

Metropolitan Performing Arts Center
901 W Sprague Ave
Spokane, WA 99201
www.metmtg.com/themet
Phone: 509-835-2638
Fax: 509-227-7778

Mount Spokane State Park
N 26107 Mt Spokane Dr
Mead, WA 99201
Phone: 509-238-4258

Resort at Mount Spokane
24817 N Mount Spokane Park Dr
Spokane, WA 99021
Phone: 509-238-9114
Fax: 509-238-4243

Riverfront Park
507 Howard St
Spokane, WA 99201
Phone: 509-625-6600
Fax: 509-625-6630

Riverfront Park IMAX Theatre
507 N Howard St
Spokane, WA 99201
Phone: 509-625-6746
Fax: 509-625-6630

Saint John's Cathedral
127 E 12th Ave
Spokane, WA 99202
Phone: 509-838-4277

Spokane Civic Theatre
1020 N Howard St
Spokane, WA 99205
www.spokanecivictheatre.com
Phone: 509-325-1413
Fax: 509-325-9287
TF: 800-446-9576

Spokane Market Place
Ruby St & Desmet Ave
Spokane, WA 99207
Phone: 509-456-0100

Spokane Symphony
334 W Spokane Falls Blvd Spokane Opera House
Spokane, WA 99201
www.spokanesymphony.org
Phone: 509-624-1200
Fax: 509-326-3921

Turnbull National Wildlife Refuge
26010 S Smith Rd
Cheney, WA 99004
Phone: 509-235-4723
Fax: 509-235-4703

Uptown Opera
901 W Sprague Ave Metropolitan Performing Arts Ctr
Spokane, WA 99204
www.spokaneopera.com
Phone: 509-533-1150

Valley Repertory Theatre
12212 1/2 E Sprague Ave
Spokane, WA 99206
Phone: 509-927-6878

Worden Winery
7217 W Westbow St
Spokane, WA 99224
E-mail: wordenwines@aol.com
Phone: 509-455-7835
Fax: 509-838-4723

Sports Teams & Facilities

Playfair Race Course
Altamont & Main
Spokane, WA 99202
Phone: 509-534-0505
Fax: 509-534-0101

Spokane Arena
720 Mallon Ave W
Spokane, WA 99201
www.spokanearena.com
Phone: 509-324-7000
Fax: 509-324-7050

Spokane Chiefs (hockey)
701 W Mallon Ave Spokane Veterans Memorial Arena
Spokane, WA 99201
E-mail: spokanechiefs@worldnet.att.net
www.spokanechiefs.com/
Phone: 509-328-0450

Spokane Indians (baseball)
I-90 Interstate Fairgrounds
Spokane, WA 99202
Phone: 509-535-2922
Fax: 509-534-5368

Spokane Raceway Park
N 101 Hayford Rd
Spokane, WA 99224
Phone: 509-244-3663
Fax: 509-244-2472

Spokane Shadow
W 4918 Everett Joe Albi Stadium
Spokane, WA 99205
E-mail: robbinsjb@aol.com
www.spokaneshadow.com
Phone: 509-326-4625
Fax: 509-326-0636

Annual Events

AHRA World Finals Drag Racing (late July) 509-244-3663
ArtFest (early June) 509-456-3931
Arts & Crafts Christmas Show & Sale (mid-November). 509-924-0588
Bloomsday Race (early May) 509-838-1579
Bloomsday Trade Show (early May). 509-838-1579
Cathedral & the Arts Music Series (October-March). 509-838-4277
Cherry Pickers Trot & Pit Spit (mid-July). 509-238-6970
Christmas Arts & Crafts Sale (mid-November). 509-924-0588
Christmas Candlelight Concert (mid-December). 800-325-7328
Christmas Tree Elegance (late November-early December) 509-326-3136
Green Bluff Apple Festival (late September-late October) 509-238-4709
Homefest (mid-October). 509-838-8755
Mozart on a Summer's Eve (late July) 509-326-4942
Northwest Bach Festival (mid-February) 509-326-4942
Pig-Out in the Park (early September) 509-921-2205
Saint Patrick's Day Parade (mid-March) 509-747-3230
Shrine Circus (late March) 509-624-1341
Spokane Hoop Fest (late June). 509-747-3230
Spokane Interstate Fair (early-mid-September) 509-747-3230
Spokane Lilac Festival (mid-May) 509-747-3230

Springfield, Illinois

***County:* Sangamon**

SPRINGFIELD is located on the Sangamon River in central Illinois. Major cities within 100 miles include Peoria, Illinois and Saint Louis, Missouri.

Area (Land) .... 42.5 sq mi
Area (Water)............................... 6.3 sq mi
Elevation.................................... 600 ft
Latitude ....39-80-17 N
Longitude................................. 89-64-36 W
Time Zone ....CST
Area Code...................................... 217

Climate

Springfield's climate features four distinct seasons. Winters are cold, with average high temperatures in the mid-30s and lows in the upper teens to low 20s. The average annual snowfall in Springfield is 24.5 inches. Summer days are warm, with average highs in the mid-80s, while lows cool down into the mid-60s. April is the wettest month of the year in Springfield, while January is the driest.

Average Temperatures & Precipitation

Temperatures

	Jan	Feb	Mar	Apr	May	Jun	Jul	Aug	Sep	Oct	Nov	Dec
High	33	37	50	64	75	84	87	84	79	67	52	37
Low	16	20	32	43	52	62	66	63	56	44	34	22

Precipitation

	Jan	Feb	Mar	Apr	May	Jun	Jul	Aug	Sep	Oct	Nov	Dec
Inches	1.5	1.8	3.2	3.7	3.6	3.4	3.5	3.3	3.3	2.6	2.5	2.7

History

The community of Springfield, named for nearby Spring Creek, was founded in 1818. Sangamon County was established in 1821, and four years later, in 1825, Springfield was chosen as the county seat. During its early years the community developed primarily as a shipping and coal mining center. In 1837 Springfield became the state capital of Illinois. That year the town's most famous resident arrived: Abraham Lincoln lived in Springfield and practiced law there until he was elected to the United States presidency in 1861. Springfield was incorporated as a city in 1840, and by the 1850s it was home to more than 4,500 people.

Over the years, in addition to being the governmental center for the State of Illinois, Springfield has become a thriving center for commerce, industry, and finance. The city has also become a popular tourist destination for American History enthusiasts due to its many attractions dedicated to the life of Abraham Lincoln. Today, with a population of more than 117,000, Springfield is Illinois' fourth largest city as well as one of the fastest growing cities in the state.

Population

1990 Census 105,412
1998 Estimate.............................117,098
% Change 11.1

Racial/Ethnic Breakdown

White.................................... 85.6%
Black 13.0%
Other..................................... 1.4%
Hispanic Origin (may be of any race) 0.8%

Age Breakdown

Under 5 years.............................. 7.4%
5 to 17.................................. 16.9%
18 to 20.................................. 3.6%
21 to 24.................................. 5.8%
25 to 34................................. 18.1%
35 to 44................................. 15.4%
45 to 54.................................. 9.4%
55 to 64.................................. 8.5%
65 to 74.................................. 7.8%
75+ years 7.1%
Median Age.................................34.0

Gender Breakdown

Male..................................... 46.0%
Female................................... 54.0%

Government

Type of Government: Mayor-Aldermen

Lincoln Library
326 S 7th St
Springfield, IL 62701
Phone: 217-753-4900
Fax: 217-753-5329

Springfield Building & Zoning Dept
Municipal Ctr W Rm 304
Springfield, IL 62701
Phone: 217-789-2171
Fax: 217-789-2048

Springfield City Attorney
Municipal Ctr W Rm 100
Springfield, IL 62701
Phone: 217-789-2393
Fax: 217-789-2397

Springfield City Clerk
300 S 7th St Rm 106
Springfield, IL 62701
Phone: 217-789-2216
Fax: 217-789-2144

Springfield City Council
Municipal Ctr W Rm 305
Springfield, IL 62701
Phone: 217-789-2151
Fax: 217-789-2153

Springfield City Hall
300 S 7th St
Springfield, IL 62701
Phone: 217-789-2000

Springfield City Treasurer
Municipal Ctr W Rm 104
Springfield, IL 62701
Phone: 217-789-2224
Fax: 217-789-2297

Springfield City Water Light & Power
800 E Monroe St
Springfield, IL 62757
Phone: 217-789-2060
Fax: 217-789-2136

Springfield Economic Development Office
231 S 6th St
Springfield, IL 62701
Phone: 217-789-2377
Fax: 217-789-2380

Springfield Human Resources Dept
300 S 7th St Rm 201
Springfield, IL 62702
Phone: 217-789-2446
Fax: 217-789-2118

Springfield Mayor
800 E Monroe St Suite 300
Springfield, IL 62701
Phone: 217-789-2200
Fax: 217-789-2109

Springfield Police Dept
800 E Monroe St
Springfield, IL 62701
Phone: 217-788-8322
Fax: 217-788-8310

Springfield Public Works Dept
300 S 7th St
Springfield, IL 62701
Phone: 217-789-2255
Fax: 217-789-2366

Springfield Recreation Dept
1415 N Grand Ave E
Springfield, IL 62702
Phone: 217-789-2284
Fax: 217-789-2119

Important Phone Numbers

AAA 217-787-0741
American Express Travel 217-523-2525
Capitol Township Assessor 217-753-6725
Driver's License Information 217-782-4850
Emergency 911
HotelDocs 800-468-3537
Illinois Dept of Revenue 800-732-8866
Sangamon County Supervisor of Assessments 217-753-6805
Sangamon County Treasurer 217-753-6800
Springfield Assn of Realtors 217-698-7000
Time/Temp 217-747-1212
Vehicle Registration Information 800-252-8980
Voter Registration Information 217-753-6740
Weather 217-753-3000

Information Sources

Better Business Bureau Serving Central Illinois
3024 W Lake Ave Suite 200
Peoria, IL 61615
www.peoria.bbb.org
Phone: 309-688-3741
Fax: 309-681-7290
TF: 800-500-3780

Central Illinois Tourism Development Office
700 E Adams St
Springfield, IL 62701
Phone: 217-525-7980
Fax: 217-525-8004

Greater Springfield Chamber of Commerce
3 S Old State Capitol Plaza
Springfield, IL 62701
www.gscc.org
Phone: 217-525-1173
Fax: 217-525-8768

Prairie Capital Convention Center
1 Convention Ctr Plaza
Springfield, IL 62701
www.springfield-pccc.com
Phone: 217-788-8800
Fax: 217-788-0811

Sangamon County
200 S 9th St
Springfield, IL 62701
www.co.sangamon.il.us
Phone: 217-753-6706
Fax: 217-753-6672

Springfield Convention & Visitors Bureau
109 N 7th St
Springfield, IL 62701
www.springfield.il.us/visit/
Phone: 217-789-2360
Fax: 217-544-8711
TF: 800-545-7300

Online Resources

About.com Guide to Springfield
springfieldil.about.com/citiestowns/midwestus/springfieldil

Anthill City Guide Springfield
www.anthill.com/city.asp?city=springfield

Area Guide Springfield
springfieldil.areaguides.net

City Knowledge Springfield
www.cityknowledge.com/il_springfield.htm

Online Springfield
www.online-springfield.com

Springfield City Net
www.excite.com/travel/countries/united_states/illinois/springfield

Springfield Concert Web
www.springfieldmusic.com

Springfield-Illinois.com
www.springfield-illinois.com

Area Communities

Communities in Sangamon County with populations greater than 2,000 include:

Auburn
324 W Jefferson St
Auburn, IL 62615
Phone: 217-438-6151
Fax: 217-483-6614

Chatham
116 E Mulberry St
Chatham, IL 62629
Phone: 217-483-2451
Fax: 217-483-3574

Pawnee
PO Box 560
Pawnee, IL 62558
Phone: 217-625-2951
Fax: 217-625-7729

Riverton
1200 E Riverton Rd
Riverton, IL 62561
Phone: 217-629-9122
Fax: 217-629-9132

Rochester
1 Community Dr
Rochester, IL 62563
Phone: 217-498-7192
Fax: 217-498-9425

Sherman
401 St Johns Dr
Sherman, IL 62684
Phone: 217-496-2621
Fax: 217-496-3420

Economy

Government is Sangamon County's second largest employment sector, and Illinois State Government is its single largest employer, providing jobs for 21,600 local residents. In recent years the services sector has surpassed government as the county's largest employment sector, and healthcare is currently the dominant service industry (four of the county's ten largest employers are healthcare-related). The insurance industry also plays an important role in the area's economy-several major U.S. insurance companies are headquartered in Springfield.

Unemployment Rate 4.9%
Per Capita Income.........................$27,351*
Median Family Income.....................$36,516

** Information given is for Sangamon County.*

Principal Industries & Number of Wage Earners

Springfield MSA* - 1998

Finance, Insurance, & Real Estate 7,900
Government 34,000
Manufacturing 4,700
Mining/Construction....................................4,600
Retail Trade...18,600
Services 34,700
Transportation, Communications, & Public Utilities 4,800
Wholesale Trade.......................................4,800

** Information given is for the Springfield Metropolitan Statistical Area (MSA), which includes Sangamon and Menard counties.*

Major Employers

Ameritech
555 E Cook St Fl 1E
Springfield, IL 62721
www.ameritech.com
Phone: 800-624-8291

Blue Cross-Blue Shield of Illinois
2151 W White Oaks Dr
Springfield, IL 62704
Phone: 217-698-5100
Fax: 217-698-5220

Egizii Electric Inc
700 N MacArthur Blvd
Springfield, IL 62702
Phone: 217-528-4001
Fax: 217-528-1677

Horace Mann Insurance Co
1 Horace Mann Plaza
Springfield, IL 62715
E-mail: hmadmin@horacemann.com
www.horacemann.com
Phone: 217-789-2500
Fax: 217-788-5161
TF: 800-999-1030

Illinois National Guard
1301 N MacArthur Blvd
Springfield, IL 62702
www.il-arng.ngb.army.mil
Phone: 217-761-3739
Fax: 217-761-3538

Lincoln Land Community College
5250 Shepherd Rd
Springfield, IL 62794
www.llcc.cc.il.us
Phone: 217-786-2200
Fax: 217-786-2492

McGraw Enterprises Inc
1999 Wabash Ave
Springfield, IL 62704
Phone: 217-698-9103
Fax: 217-698-9105

Memorial Medical Center
701 N 1st St
Springfield, IL 62781
www.mhsil.com
Phone: 217-788-3000
Fax: 217-788-5591

Saint John's Hospital
800 E Carpenter St
Springfield, IL 62769
www.st-johns.org
Phone: 217-544-6464
Fax: 217-525-5601

Southern Illinois University School of Medicine
913 N Rutledge St
Springfield, IL 62702
www.slumed.edu
Phone: 217-524-0223
Fax: 217-524-1058

Springfield City Hall
300 S 7th St
Springfield, IL 62701
www.springfield.il.us
Phone: 217-789-2000

Springfield Clinic
1025 E 7th St
Springfield, IL 62703
www.springfieldclinic.com
Phone: 217-528-7541
Fax: 217-528-2842

Springfield Public School District #186
1900 W Monroe
Springfield, IL 62704
www.springfield.k12.il.us
Phone: 217-525-3000
Fax: 217-525-3005

Quality of Living Indicators

Total Crime Index....................................... na
(rates per 100,000 inhabitants)

Violent Crime
Murder/manslaughter........................... 10
Forcible rape .... na
Robbery..................................... 242
Aggravated assault............................ 835

Property Crime
Burglary 1,793
Larceny theft 4,954
Motor vehicle theft 373

Cost of Living Index....................................97.2
(national average = 100)

Median Home Price................................$86,100

Education

Public Schools

Springfield Public School District #186
1900 W Monroe
Springfield, IL 62704
www.springfield.k12.il.us
Phone: 217-525-3000
Fax: 217-525-3005

Number of Schools
Elementary 29
Middle 3
High 3

Student/Teacher Ratio
All Grades 18.1:1

Private Schools

Number of Schools (all grades) .... 20+

Colleges & Universities

Lincoln Land Community College
5250 Shepherd Rd
Springfield, IL 62794
www.llcc.cc.il.us
Phone: 217-786-2200
Fax: 217-786-2492

Robert Morris College Springfield Campus
3101 Montvale Dr
Springfield, IL 62704
www.rmcil.edu
Phone: 217-793-2500
Fax: 217-793-4210

Springfield College Illinois
1500 N 5th St
Springfield, IL 62702
www.sci.edu
Phone: 217-525-1420
Fax: 217-789-1698
TF: 800-635-7289

University of Illinois Springfield
Springfield, IL 62794
www.uis.edu
Phone: 217-206-6174
Fax: 217-786-7280
TF: 800-252-8533

Hospitals

Doctors Hospital
5230 S 6th St
Springfield, IL 60794
Phone: 217-529-7151
Fax: 217-529-9472

Memorial Medical Center
701 N 1st St
Springfield, IL 62781
www.mhsil.com
Phone: 217-788-3000
Fax: 217-788-5591

Saint John's Hospital
800 E Carpenter St
Springfield, IL 62769
www.st-johns.org
Phone: 217-544-6464
Fax: 217-525-5601

Transportation

Airport(s)

Capital Airport (SPI)
3 miles NW of downtown (approx 10 minutes) 217-788-1063

Mass Transit

Springfield Mass Transit
$.75 Base fare................................217-522-5531

Rail/Bus

Amtrak Station
3rd & Washington Sts
Springfield, IL 62701
Phone: 217-753-2013
TF: 800-872-7245

Greyhound Bus Station
2351 S Dirksen Pkwy
Springfield, IL 62704
Phone: 217-544-8466
TF: 800-231-2222

Utilities

Electricity
City Water Light & Power (CWLP)..............217-789-2030
www.cwlp.com

Gas
CILCO 888-672-5252
www.cilco.com

Water
City Water Light & Power (CWLP)..............217-789-2030
www.cwlp.com

Garbage Collection/Recycling
Capitol Waste Systems Inc 217-522-7797
Chatham Disposal..............................217-529-5361
Crenshaw Disposal Service 217-522-9317
Lasley Disposal Co 217-544-9024

Telecommunications

Telephone
Ameritech.....................................800-244-4444
www.ameritech.com

Cable Television
AT & T Cable Services..........................217-788-5656
www.cable.att.com

Internet Service Providers (ISPs)
FGInet Inc 217-544-2775
www.fgi.net

Banks

Athens State Bank
Rt 29 Andrew Rd
Springfield, IL 62707
Phone: 217-487-7766
Fax: 217-487-1148

Bank of Springfield
2600 Adlai Stevenson Dr
Springfield, IL 62703
www.bankofspringfield.com
Phone: 217-529-5555
Fax: 217-529-5080

Bank One Illinois NA
E Old State Capitol Plaza
Springfield, IL 62701
Phone: 217-525-9600
Fax: 217-525-2756
TF: 800-528-2870

Capital Community Bank
2950 S 6th St
Springfield, IL 62703
Phone: 217-544-2950
Fax: 217-544-3999

Carrollton Bank
Chatham Sqare Ctr
Springfield, IL 62791
Phone: 217-793-8696
Fax: 217-793-9503

First Bank
2201 Wabash Ave
Springfield, IL 62704
Phone: 217-546-5161
Fax: 217-546-9164

Illini Bank
120 S Chatham Rd
Springfield, IL 62704
Phone: 217-787-1651
Fax: 217-787-9718

Illinois National Bank
322 E Capitol
Springfield, IL 62701
Phone: 217-747-5500

Independent Bankers' Bank
3085 Stevenson Dr Suite 200
Springfield, IL 62703
Phone: 217-585-0734
Fax: 217-585-0396

Marine Bank
3050 W Wabash Ave
Springfield, IL 62704
Phone: 217-726-0600
Fax: 217-726-0619

Mercantile Bank of Illinois
205 S 5th St
Springfield, IL 62701
Phone: 217-753-7530
Fax: 217-753-7432

National City Bank of Michigan/Illinois
1 Old Capitol Plaza N
Springfield, IL 62794
Phone: 217-753-7100
Fax: 217-753-6267

Prairie State Bank & Trust
1361 Toronto Rd
Springfield, IL 62707
Phone: 217-786-2509
Fax: 217-786-2512

Security Bank
510 E Monroe St
Springfield, IL 62701
E-mail: security@securitybk.com
www.securitybk.com
Phone: 217-544-8471
Fax: 217-544-4398

Town & Country Bank of Springfield
1925 S MacArthur Blvd
Springfield, IL 62704
Phone: 217-787-3100
Fax: 217-787-7736

Union Planters Bank NA
1825 S 6th St
Springfield, IL 62703
Phone: 217-788-6400
Fax: 217-544-8389

Williamsville State Bank & Trust
2205 W Wabash Ave Suite 203-B
Springfield, IL 62704
Phone: 217-698-6355
Fax: 217-698-6356

Shopping

Capital City Shopping Center
3095 S Dirksen Pkwy
Springfield, IL 62703
Phone: 217-529-3581
Fax: 217-529-3594

Fairhills Mall
1911 W Monroe St
Springfield, IL 62704
Phone: 217-787-9636
Fax: 314-972-0006
TF: 888-790-4177

Town & Country Shopping Center
2403 S MacArthur Blvd
Springfield, IL 62704
Phone: 217-698-7511
Fax: 217-698-7540

White Oaks Mall
2501 W Wabash Ave
Springfield, IL 62704
Phone: 217-787-8560
Fax: 217-787-8579

Media

Newspapers and Magazines

State Journal-Register*
PO Box 219
Springfield, IL 62705
E-mail: sjr@sj-r.com
www.sj-r.com
Phone: 217-788-1300
Fax: 217-788-1551
TF: 800-397-6397

**Indicates major daily newspapers*

Television

WAND-TV Ch 17 (ABC)
904 South Side Dr
Decatur, IL 62521
E-mail: wandtv@aol.com
www.wandtv.com
Phone: 217-424-2500
Fax: 217-424-2583

WCIA-TV Ch 3 (CBS)
509 S Neil St
Champaign, IL 61820
www.wcia.com
Phone: 217-356-8333
Fax: 217-373-3663

WICS-TV Ch 20 (NBC)
2680 E Cook St
Springfield, IL 62703
E-mail: news20@fgi.net
www.fgi.net/news20/
Phone: 217-753-5620
Fax: 217-753-5681

WRSP-TV Ch 55 (Fox)
3003 Old Rochester Rd
Springfield, IL 62703
www.wrsptv.com
Phone: 217-523-8855
Fax: 217-523-4410

WSEC-TV Ch 14 (PBS)
PO Box 6248
Springfield, IL 62708
E-mail: viewer@wmec.pbs.org
www.convocom.org
Phone: 217-206-6647
Fax: 217-206-7267

Radio

WCVS-FM 96.7 MHz (CR)
3055 S 4th St
Springfield, IL 62703
E-mail: wcvs@fgi.net
www.fgi.net/wcvs
Phone: 217-544-9855
Fax: 217-528-5348

WDBR-FM 103.7 MHz (CHR)
3501 E Sangamon Ave
Springfield, IL 62707
www.wdbr.com
Phone: 217-753-5400
Fax: 217-753-7902

WFMB-AM 1450 kHz (Sports)
3055 S 4th St
Springfield, IL 62703
E-mail: wfmbam@fgi.net
www.fgi.net/wfmbam
Phone: 217-544-9855
Fax: 217-528-5348

WFMB-FM 104.5 MHz (Ctry)
3055 S 4th St
Springfield, IL 62703
www.fgi.net/wfmbfm
Phone: 217-544-9855
Fax: 217-528-5348

WNNS-FM 98.7 MHz (AC) Phone: 217-629-7077
PO Box 460 Fax: 217-629-7952
Springfield, IL 62705
www.wnns.com

WQLZ-FM 92.7 MHz (Rock) Phone: 217-629-7077
PO Box 460 Fax: 217-629-7952
Springfield, IL 62705
www.wqlz.com

WQQL-FM 101.9 MHz (Oldies) Phone: 217-753-5400
3501 E Sangamon Ave Fax: 217-753-7902
Springfield, IL 62707

WTAX-AM 1240 kHz (N/T) Phone: 217-753-5400
3501 E Sangamon Ave Fax: 217-753-7902
Springfield, IL 62707

WUIS-FM 91.9 MHz (NPR) Phone: 217-206-6516
University of Illinois Bldg L-130 PO Box 19243 Fax: 217-206-6527
Springfield, IL 62794
E-mail: wuis@uis.edu
www.uis.edu/~wuis/wuis2.htm

WYMG-FM 100.5 MHz (CR) Phone: 217-753-5400
3501 E Sangamon Ave Fax: 217-753-7902
Springfield, IL 62707
www.wymg.com

WYXY-FM 93.9 MHz (Ctry) Phone: 217-753-5400
3501 E Sangamon Ave Fax: 217-753-7902
Springfield, IL 62707

Attractions

With what may be the highest concentration of sites in America devoted to Abraham Lincoln, Springfield, Illinois provides a complete look at the life of the nation's 16th president. The home of the Lincoln family and the Lincoln-Herndon Law Offices are both located in the city. In addition, one can see the Lincoln Tomb and the Lincoln Depot, which even includes his ledger. At the five miles of wooded trails known as Lincoln Memorial Gardens, Maple Syrup Time is a featured event. Twenty miles northwest of Springfield is the reconstructed historic village of New Salem where Lincoln spent six years studying law and working various jobs. The Great American People Show, a group created to "pursue a passion for Lincoln," performs at New Salem, focusing both on Lincoln's life as well as other historical subjects.

Adams Wildlife Sanctuary Phone: 217-544-5781
2315 E Clear Lake Ave
Springfield, IL 62703
www.springfield.il.us/TOURISM/visitor/default3.htm

Adventure Village Inc Phone: 217-528-9207
Sangamon Ave & Peoria Rd
Springfield, IL 62702

Camp Butler National Cemetery Phone: 217-492-4070
5063 Camp Butler Rd Fax: 217-492-4072
Springfield, IL 62707

Dana-Thomas House Phone: 217-782-6776
301 E Lawrence Ave Fax: 217-788-9450
Springfield, IL 62703
www.online-springfield.com/sites/dth.html

Daughters of the Union Veterans of the Civil War Museum Phone: 217-544-0616
503 S Walnut St
Springfield, IL 62704

Edward's Place Phone: 217-523-2631
700 N 4th St Fax: 217-523-3866
Springfield, IL 62702

Executive Mansion Phone: 217-782-6450
410 E Jackson St Fax: 217-782-2771
Springfield, IL 62701
www.state.il.us/gov/mansion2

Grand Army of the Republic Memorial Museum Phone: 217-522-4373
629 S 7th St
Springfield, IL 62703

Illinois State Capitol Phone: 217-782-2099
2nd St & E Capitol Ave
Springfield, IL 62701

Illinois State Military Museum Phone: 217-761-3910
1301 N MacArthur Blvd Camp Lincoln Bldg 41 Fax: 217-761-3709
Springfield, IL 62702

Illinois State Museum Phone: 217-782-7386
Spring & Edwards Sts Fax: 217-782-1254
Springfield, IL 62706
www.museum.state.il.us

Illinois Vietnam Veterans Memorial Phone: 217-782-2717
Oak Ridge Cemetery
Springfield, IL 62702

Knight's Action Park & Caribbean Water Adventure Phone: 217-546-8881
1700 Recreation Dr Fax: 217-546-8995
Springfield, IL 62707 TF: 800-421-4386
E-mail: knightsap@aol.com
www.knightsactionpark.com

Lawrence Memorial Library Phone: 217-525-3144
101 E Laurel St Fax: 217-525-3090
Springfield, IL 62704

Lincoln Depot Phone: 217-544-8695
10th & Monroe Sts
Springfield, IL 62703

Lincoln Home National Historic Site Phone: 217-492-4241
413 S 8th St Fax: 217-492-4673
Springfield, IL 62701
www.nps.gov/liho/

Lincoln Memorial Garden Phone: 217-529-1111
2301 E Lake Dr Fax: 217-529-0134
Springfield, IL 62707
E-mail: lmg2301@lnw.net

Lincoln Tomb Phone: 217-782-2717
Oak Ridge Cemetery 1500 Monument Ave Fax: 217-524-3738
Springfield, IL 62702

Lincoln's New Salem Phone: 217-632-4000
Rt 1 Box 244A Fax: 217-632-4010
Petersburg, IL 62675

Old State Capitol Phone: 217-785-7961
Old State Capitol Mall
Springfield, IL 62701

Parks Telephone Museum Phone: 217-789-5303
529 S 7th St
Springfield, IL 62721

Robinson Henson Zoo Phone: 217-753-6217
1100 E Lake Dr Fax: 217-529-8748
Springfield, IL 62707
www.hensonrobinsonzoo.org

Springfield Ballet Co Phone: 217-544-1967
2820 S MacArthur Blvd Fax: 217-544-1968
Springfield, IL 62704

Springfield Children's Museum Phone: 217-789-0679
619 E Washington St Fax: 217-789-0682
Springfield, IL 62701

Springfield Muni Opera Phone: 217-793-6864
815 E Lake Dr
Springfield, IL 62705
E-mail: TheMuni@TheMuni.org
www.themuni.org

Springfield Theatre Centre Phone: 217-523-0878
101 E Lawrence Ave
Springfield, IL 62704

Thomas Rees Memorial Carillon Phone: 217-544-1751
Washington Pk
Springfield, IL 62704
E-mail: info@carillon-rees.org
www.carillon-rees.org

Washington Park Botanical Gardens Phone: 217-753-6228
Fayette & Chatham Rds Fax: 217-546-0257
Springfield, IL 62704

Sports Teams & Facilities

Springfield Capitals (baseball) Phone: 217-525-5500
1351 North Grant Ave E Lanphier Stadium Fax: 217-525-5508
Springfield, IL 62702
www.springfieldcapitals.com

Annual Events

Bluegrass Festival (early September) 217-632-4000
Capital City Farm Show (mid-January).............217-498-9404
Central Illinois Blues Fest (early September).......217-546-8881
Christmas Walk (early December) 217-544-1723
Chrysanthemum Festival (mid-late November)......217-753-6228
Dana-Thomas House Christmas
(mid-late December)..........................217-782-6776
Edwards Place Fine Crafts Fair (late September)....217-523-2631
Ethnic Festival (early September) 217-529-8189
Festival of Trees (mid-November) 217-788-3293
First Night Springfield (December 31)............800-545-7300
Harvest Feast at New Salem (early November)......217-632-4000
Holiday Lights at the Zoo (mid-late December) 217-753-6217
Holiday Market (mid-late November)...............217-529-1111
Illinois State Fair (mid-August)..................800-545-7300
Indian Summer Festival (mid-October) 217-529-1111
International Carillon Festival (early July)..........217-753-6219
International Ethnic Festival (early September).....217-529-8189
Keepsake Country Craft Show
(late January & mid-July) 217-787-8560
Maple Syrup Time (late February).................217-529-1111
Motorcycle Show & Swap Meet (late February) 217-788-8800
Old Capitol Art Fair (late May)....................800-545-7300
Springfield Air Rendezvous (mid-September).......800-545-7300
Springfield All Sports Show (late February) 217-629-7077
Springfield Scottish Highland Games & Celtic
Festival (mid-May) 217-546-5802
Summer Festival (mid-July).......................217-632-4000
Theatre in the Park (mid-June-late August).........217-632-4000
Traditional Music Festival (early September) 217-632-4000

Springfield, Massachusetts

County: **Hampden**

SPRINGFIELD is located in the Pioneer Valley in the south central portion of western Massachusetts, along the banks of the Connecticut River. Major cities within 100 miles include Worcester and Boston, Massachusetts; Albany, New York; and Bridgeport, Hartford, and New Haven, Connecticut.

Area (Land)	32.1 sq mi
Area (Water)	1.1 sq mi
Elevation	70 ft
Latitude	42-10-14 N
Longitude	72-59-03 W
Time Zone	EST
Area Code	413

Climate

Springfield has a moderate climate, with cold winters and warm summers. Winter high temperatures average in the mid-to upper 30s, with lows around 20 degrees. Summer days are warm, with average high temperatures in the low to mid-80s, while evenings cool down into the low 60s and upper 50s. Precipitation is fairly evenly distributed throughout the year.

Average Temperatures & Precipitation

Temperatures

	Jan	Feb	Mar	Apr	May	Jun	Jul	Aug	Sep	Oct	Nov	Dec
High	36	39	48	61	72	81	85	84	76	65	53	39
Low	18	20	29	38	48	57	63	61	53	43	35	23

Precipitation

	Jan	Feb	Mar	Apr	May	Jun	Jul	Aug	Sep	Oct	Nov	Dec
Inches	3.2	3.0	3.5	3.9	4.1	4.1	3.6	3.5	3.5	3.6	4.1	3.8

History

Springfield, Massachusetts, the "Crossroads of New England," was the first English settlement in the Pioneer Valley. Founded by Puritan William Pynchon in 1636, the city of Springfield was named in 1640 after the town in England that bears the same name. It is also sometimes referred to as the "Rifle City" due to its history as a center for manufacturing and storing weapons—in 1777, an arms depot was established in the city and two years later, Springfield became the home of the first federal armory. The Springfield Armory (now a National Historic Site) was founded by George Washington in 1779 and brought artisans and new types of manufacturing to Springfield. The Armory also became the subject of a poem by Henry Wadsworth Longfellow entitled "The Arsenal at Springfield." Weapons invented in Springfield include the U.S. musket (1795) and the Garand Rifle (1937), and the city is presently the corporate home of U.S. weapons manufacturer Smith & Wesson.

Over the course of the last two centuries, several other inventions have come out of Springfield, earning the city yet another nickname, "City of Firsts." Some of the most notable include the first railroad sleeping car in the United States, built by George Pullman in 1850; the first gasoline-powered automobile, the Duryea (1892); and the first gasoline-powered motorcycle, the Indian Motorcycle (1901). Springfield is also known as the birthplace of basketball, invented by James Naismith in 1891, and today is home to the Basketball Hall of Fame.

The third largest city in the Commonwealth of Massachusetts, Springfield today is home to more than 148,000 people.

Population

1990 Census	156,983
1998 Estimate	148,144
% Change	-5.6

Racial/Ethnic Breakdown

White	68.6%
Black	19.2%
Other	12.2%
Hispanic Origin (may be of any race)	16.9%

Age Breakdown

Under 5 years	8.5%
5 to 9	7.6%
10 to 14	6.7%
15 to 19	7.7%
20 to 24	9.0%
25 to 44	31.0%
45 to 54	7.9%
55 to 64	7.8%
65 to 74	7.8%
75+ years	5.9%
Median Age	30.6

Gender Breakdown

Male	47.1%
Female	52.9%

Government

Type of Government: Mayor-Council

Springfield Chief Financial Officer
36 Court St
Springfield, MA 01103
Phone: 413-787-6147
Fax: 413-787-6182

Springfield City Attorney
36 Court St
Springfield, MA 01103
Phone: 413-787-6085
Fax: 413-787-6173

Springfield City Clerk Phone: 413-787-6094
36 Court St Fax: 413-787-6502
Springfield, MA 01103

Springfield City Council Phone: 413-787-6170
36 Court St Fax: 413-787-6833
Springfield, MA 01103

Springfield City Hall Phone: 413-787-6000
36 Court St Fax: 413-787-6010
Springfield, MA 01103

Springfield City Library Phone: 413-739-3871
220 State St Fax: 413-263-6817
Springfield, MA 01103

Springfield Community Development Dept Phone: 413-787-6050
36 Court St Fax: 413-787-6027
Springfield, MA 01103

Springfield Fire Dept Phone: 413-787-6411
605 Worthington St Fax: 413-787-6432
Springfield, MA 01105

Springfield Mayor Phone: 413-787-6100
36 Court St Fax: 413-787-6104
Springfield, MA 01103

Springfield Personnel Dept Phone: 413-787-6055
36 Court St Rm 018
Springfield, MA 01103

Springfield Planning Dept Phone: 413-787-6020
36 Court St Fax: 413-787-6524
Springfield, MA 01103

Springfield Police Dept Phone: 413-787-6313
130 Pearl St Fax: 413-787-6805
Springfield, MA 01105

Springfield Public Parks & Recreation Dept Phone: 413-787-6440
200 Trafton Rd
Springfield, MA 01108

Springfield Public Works Dept Phone: 413-787-6224
1600 E Columbus Ave Fax: 413-787-6212
Springfield, MA 01103

Springfield Water & Sewer Commission Phone: 413-787-6256
PO Box 995 Fax: 413-787-6269
Springfield, MA 01101

Important Phone Numbers

AAA....413-785-1381
Driver's License/Vehicle Registration Information ...617-351-4500
Emergency 911
Hampden County Registrar of Deeds....413-748-8622
HotelDocs 800-468-3537
Massachusetts Dept of Revenue....617-887-6367
Poison Control Center 800-682-9211
Springfield Assessor's Dept 413-787-6160
Springfield Board of Realtors....413-785-1328
Voter Registration Information....413-787-6190
Weather....413-499-2627

Information Sources

Better Business Bureau Serving Western Massachusetts Phone: 413-734-3114
293 Bridge St Suite 320 Fax: 413-734-2006
Springfield, MA 01103
www.springfield-ma.bbb.org

Economic Development Council of Western Massachusetts Phone: 413-593-6421
255 Padgette St Suite 1 Fax: 413-593-5126
Chicopee, MA 01022 TF: 888-593-6421
www.ecdev-wma.com

Greater Springfield Chamber of Commerce Phone: 413-787-1555
1441 Main St Fax: 413-731-8530
Springfield, MA 01103
www.gschamber.org

Greater Springfield Convention & Visitors Bureau Phone: 413-787-1548
1441 Main St Fax: 413-781-4607
Springfield, MA 01103 TF: 800-723-1548
www.valleyvisitor.com

Hampden County Phone: 413-748-8600
50 State St Fax: 413-737-1611
Springfield, MA 01103

Springfield Civic Center Phone: 413-787-6600
1277 Main St Fax: 413-787-6645
Springfield, MA 01103 TF: 800-639-8602
www.civic-center.com

Online Resources

4Springfield.com
www.4springfield.com

Area Guide Springfield
springfieldma.areaguides.net

DigitalCity Springfield
www.digitalcity.com/springfield

Mass Live
www.masslive.com

Springfield Advocate
springfieldadvocate.com

Springfield City Guide
www.ci.springfield.ma.us/visitors.htm

Springfield City Net
www.excite.com/travel/countries/united_states/massachusetts/springfield

Area Communities

Springfield area communities with populations greater than 10,000 include:

Agawam Phone: 413-786-0400
36 Main St Fax: 413-786-9927
Agawam, MA 01001

Amherst
4 Boltwood Ave
Amherst, MA 01002
Phone: 413-256-4004
Fax: 413-256-4006

Belchertown
PO Box 607
Belchertown, MA 01007
Phone: 413-323-0400
Fax: 413-323-0411

Chicopee
17 Springfield St
Chicopee, MA 01013
Phone: 413-594-4711
Fax: 413-594-2160

East Longmeadow
60 Center Sq
East Longmeadow, MA 01028
Phone: 413-525-5400
Fax: 413-525-1025

Easthampton
43 Main St
Easthampton, MA 01027
Phone: 413-529-1460
Fax: 413-529-1488

Greenfield
14 Court Sq
Greenfield, MA 01301
Phone: 413-772-1560
Fax: 413-772-2238

Holyoke
536 Dwight St
Holyoke, MA 01040
Phone: 413-534-2166
Fax: 413-534-2322

Longmeadow
20 Williams St
Longmeadow, MA 01106
Phone: 413-565-4110

Ludlow
488 Chapin St
Ludlow, MA 01056
Phone: 413-583-5610
Fax: 413-583-5603

Northampton
210 Main St
Northampton, MA 01060
Phone: 413-586-6950
Fax: 413-586-1264

Palmer
4417 Main St Suite 10
Palmer, MA 01069
Phone: 413-283-2608
Fax: 413-283-2637

South Hadley
116 Main St
South Hadley, MA 01075
Phone: 413-538-5023
Fax: 413-538-7565

West Springfield
26 Central St
West Springfield, MA 01089
Phone: 413-263-3012

Westfield
59 Court St
Westfield, MA 01085
Phone: 413-572-6200
Fax: 413-572-6274

Wilbraham
240 Springfield St
Wilbraham, MA 01095
Phone: 413-596-8111
Fax: 413-596-2830

Economy

Springfield has a diverse economic base that ranges from healthcare to the manufacturing of board games. Major U.S. companies headquartered in the area include MassMutual Life Insurance Company, Smith & Wesson, and Milton Bradley. The services sector employs the greatest number of people in Springfield, and healthcare being the primary industry. Government—at the federal, state, and local levels—also plays a vital role in the area's economy, employing approximately 15 percent of Springfield's workforce.

Unemployment Rate 5.0%
Per Capita Income..........................$26,441*
Median Family Income......................$30,824

** Information given is for Hampden County.*

Principal Industries & Number of Wage Earners

City of Springfield - 1998

Agriculture, Forestry, & Fishing........................... 248
Construction..1,561
Finance, Insurance, & Real Estate........................7,207
Manufacturing 8,350
Services 29,037
Trade 14,533
Transportation, Communications, & Public Utilities 4,191

Major Employers

Baystate Medical Center
759 Chestnut St
Springfield, MA 01199
www.baystatehealth.com/1025/2052
Phone: 413-784-0000
Fax: 413-794-8274

Big Y Foods Inc
PO Box 7840
Springfield, MA 01102
E-mail: bigycust@aol.com
www.bigy.com
Phone: 413-784-0600
Fax: 413-732-8475
TF: 800-828-2688

Friendly Ice Cream Corp
1855 Boston Rd
Wilbraham, MA 01095
www.friendly.com
Phone: 413-543-2400
Fax: 413-543-3966

Holyoke Hospital
575 Beech St
Holyoke, MA 01040
www.holyokehealth.com
Phone: 413-534-2500
Fax: 413-534-2633

Massachusetts Mutual Life Insurance Co
1295 State St
Springfield, MA 01111
E-mail: info@massmutual.com
www.massmutual.com
Phone: 413-788-8411
Fax: 413-744-6005
TF: 800-272-2216

Mercy Hospital
271 Carew St
Springfield, MA 01104
Phone: 413-748-9000
Fax: 413-748-7078

Milton Bradley Co Div Hasbro Game Group
443 Shaker Rd
East Longmeadow, MA 01028
Phone: 413-525-6411
Fax: 413-525-1767

Smith & Wesson Corp
PO Box 2208
Springfield, MA 01102
E-mail: qa@smith-wesson.com
www.smith-wesson.com
Phone: 413-781-8300
Fax: 413-747-3217
TF: 800-331-0852

Smith College
7 College Ln
Northampton, MA 01063
www.smith.edu
Phone: 413-584-2700
Fax: 413-585-2527

Springfield City Hall
36 Court St
Springfield, MA 01103
www.ci.springfield.ma.us
Phone: 413-787-6000
Fax: 413-787-6010

Springfield Public Schools
PO Box 1410
Springfield, MA 01102
www.sps.springfield.ma.us
Phone: 413-787-7087
Fax: 413-787-7211

University of Massachusetts
Amherst, MA 01003
E-mail: beaubien@admin.umass.edu
www.umass.edu
Phone: 413-545-0111
Fax: 413-545-0483

US Postal Service
1883 Main St
Springfield, MA 01101
new.usps.com
Phone: 413-731-0528
Fax: 413-731-0304

Quality of Living Indicators

Total Crime Index....................................11,923
(rates per 100,000 inhabitants)

Violent Crime
Murder/manslaughter............................ 7
Forcible rape 127
Robbery..................................... 490
Aggravated assault...........................2,246

Property Crime
Burglary 3,044
Larceny theft 4,560
Motor vehicle theft 1,449

Cost of Living Index...................................118.3
(national average = 100)

Median Home Price.................................$111,700

Education

Public Schools

Springfield Public Schools
PO Box 1410
Springfield, MA 01102
www.sps.springfield.ma.us
Phone: 413-787-7087
Fax: 413-787-7211

Number of Schools
Elementary................................. 28
Middle 5
High.. 9
K-8... 3

Student/Teacher Ratio
All Grades 16.9:1

Private Schools

Number of Schools (all grades).................... 19+

Colleges & Universities

American International College
1000 State St
Springfield, MA 01109
www.aic.edu
Phone: 413-737-7000
Fax: 413-737-2803
TF: 800-242-3142

Amherst College
100 Bolt Wood Ave
Amherst, MA 01002
E-mail: admissio@unix.amherst.edu
www.amherst.edu
Phone: 413-542-2000
Fax: 413-542-2040

Bay Path College
588 Longmeadow St
Longmeadow, MA 01106
www.baypath.edu
Phone: 413-567-0621
Fax: 413-565-1103
TF: 800-782-7284

Elms College
291 Springfield St
Chicopee, MA 01013
www.elms.edu
Phone: 413-592-3189
Fax: 413-594-2781
TF: 800-255-3567

Holyoke Community College
303 Homestead Ave
Holyoke, MA 01040
www.hcc.mass.edu
Phone: 413-538-7000
Fax: 413-552-2192

Mount Holyoke College
50 College St
South Hadley, MA 01075
E-mail: admissions@mtholyoke.edu
www.mtholyoke.edu
Phone: 413-538-2000
Fax: 413-538-2409

Smith College
7 College Ln
Northampton, MA 01063
www.smith.edu
Phone: 413-584-2700
Fax: 413-585-2527

Springfield College
263 Alden St
Springfield, MA 01109
E-mail: admissions@spfldcol.edu
www.spfldcol.edu
Phone: 413-748-3000
Fax: 413-748-3694
TF: 800-343-1257

Springfield Technical Community College
1 Armory Sq
Springfield, MA 01101
www.stcc.mass.edu
Phone: 413-781-7822
Fax: 413-746-0344

University of Massachusetts
Amherst, MA 01003
E-mail: beaubien@admin.umass.edu
www.umass.edu
Phone: 413-545-0111
Fax: 413-545-0483

Western New England College
1215 Wilbraham Rd
Springfield, MA 01119
www.wnec.edu
Phone: 413-782-3111
Fax: 413-782-1777
TF: 800-325-1122

Hospitals

Baystate Medical Center
759 Chestnut St
Springfield, MA 01199
www.baystatehealth.com/1025/2052
Phone: 413-784-0000
Fax: 413-794-8274

Cooley Dickinson Hospital
30 Locust St
Northampton, MA 01060
www.cooley-dickinson.org
Phone: 413-582-2000
Fax: 413-586-9333

Franklin Medical Center
164 High St
Greenfield, MA 01301
Phone: 413-772-0211
Fax: 413-773-2100

Holyoke Hospital
575 Beech St
Holyoke, MA 01040
www.holyokehealth.com
Phone: 413-534-2500
Fax: 413-534-2633

Mercy Hospital
271 Carew St
Springfield, MA 01104
Phone: 413-748-9000
Fax: 413-748-7078

Transportation

Airport(s)

Bradley International Airport (BDL)
18 miles S of downtown Springfield
(approx 40 minutes) 860-292-2000

Mass Transit

Pioneer Valley Transit Authority
$.75 Base fare 413-781-7882

Rail/Bus

Amtrak Station
66 Lyman St Union Station
Springfield, MA 01103
Phone: 413-785-4230

Peter Pan Bus Station
1776 Main St
Springfield, MA 01102
Phone: 413-781-2900

Utilities

Electricity
Western Massachusetts Electric 413-746-0122
www.wmeco.com

Gas
Bay State Gas Co. 413-584-1088
baystategas.com

Water
Springfield Water Dept 413-787-6206

Garbage Collection/Recycling
Springfield Board of Public Works 413-787-6260

Telecommunications

Telephone
Verizon Communications 413-733-1776
www.verizon.com

Cable Television
AT & T Cable Services 413-731-8062

Internet Service Providers (ISPs)
Crocker Communications Inc 413-585-1250
www.crocker.com
fc.com Inc. 413-733-7333
www.fc.com
the spa! 413-539-9818
www.the-spa.com

Banks

Bank of Western Massachusetts
29 State St
Springfield, MA 01103
E-mail: info@bankwmass.com
www.bankwmass.com
Phone: 413-781-2265
Fax: 413-736-8626
TF: 800-331-5003

BankBoston NA
1350 Main St
Springfield, MA 01103
Phone: 413-787-0000

Charter One Bank FSB
20 Island Pond Rd
Springfield, MA 01108
Phone: 413-781-3330
Fax: 413-781-8927

Fleet National Bank
106 Island Pond Rd
Springfield, MA 01118
Phone: 800-841-4000
Fax: 413-787-8588

Hampden Savings Bank
19 Harrison Ave
Springfield, MA 01103
www.hampdensavings.com
Phone: 413-736-1812
Fax: 413-746-1018

Peoples Savings Bank
314 High St
Holyoke, MA 01040
Phone: 413-538-9500
Fax: 413-536-4072
TF: 800-342-9100

United Co-Operative Bank
95 Elm St
West Springfield, MA 01089
www.bankatunited.com
Phone: 413-787-1700
Fax: 413-788-5599

Westfield Savings Bank
1341 Main St
Springfield, MA 01103
Phone: 413-737-7225
Fax: 413-827-7501

Woronoco Savings Bank
800 Boston Rd
Springfield, MA 01119
Phone: 413-783-2011
Fax: 413-783-2057

Shopping

Holyoke Mall at Ingleside
50 Holyoke St
Holyoke, MA 01041
www.holyokemall.com
Phone: 413-536-1440
Fax: 413-536-5740

Shops at Baystate West
1500 Main St
Springfield, MA 01115
Phone: 413-733-2171

Media

Newspapers and Magazines

Sunday Republican
1860 Main St
Springfield, MA 01101
Phone: 413-788-1000
Fax: 413-788-1301

Union News*
1860 Main St
Springfield, MA 01101
E-mail: unews-letters@union-news.com
www.masslive.com/unionnews/index.html
Phone: 413-788-1000
Fax: 413-788-1301

**Indicates major daily newspapers*

Television

WFSB-TV Ch 3 (CBS)
3 Constitution Plaza
Hartford, CT 06103
www.wfsb.com
Phone: 860-728-3333
Fax: 860-728-0263

WGBY-TV Ch 57 (PBS)
44 Hampden St
Springfield, MA 01103
E-mail: wgby_feedback@wgbh.org
www.wgby.org/
Phone: 413-781-2801
Fax: 413-731-5093

WGGB-TV Ch 40 (ABC)
1300 Liberty St
Springfield, MA 01104
www.wggb.com
Phone: 413-733-4040
Fax: 413-781-1363

WTIC-TV Ch 61 (Fox)
1 Corporate Ctr
Hartford, CT 06103
www.fox61.com
Phone: 860-527-6161
Fax: 860-293-0178

WWLP-TV Ch 22 (NBC)
PO Box 2210
Springfield, MA 01102
E-mail: news@wwlp.com
www.wwlp.com
Phone: 413-786-2200
Fax: 413-786-7144

Radio

WACE-AM 730 kHz (Rel)
326 Chicopee St
Chicopee, MA 01013
Phone: 413-594-6654

WACM-AM 1490 kHz (Span)
34 Sylvan St
West Springfield, MA 01089
Phone: 413-781-5200
Fax: 413-734-2240

WAQY-FM 102.1 MHz (CR)
45 Fisher Ave
East Longmeadow, MA 01028
www.rock102.com
Phone: 413-525-4141
Fax: 413-525-4334

WFCR-FM 88.5 MHz (NPR)
PO Box 33630 Hampshire House
Amherst, MA 01003
E-mail: radio@wfcr.org
www.wfcr.org
Phone: 413-545-0100
Fax: 413-545-2546

WHMP-FM 99.3 MHz (Rock)
15 Hampton Ave
Northampton, MA 01060
www.993.com
Phone: 413-586-7400
Fax: 413-585-0927

WHYN-AM 560 kHz (N/T)
1331 Main St 5th Fl
Springfield, MA 01103
www.whynam560.com
Phone: 413-781-1011
Fax: 413-734-4434

WHYN-FM 93.1 MHz (AC)
1331 Main St 5th Fl
Springfield, MA 01103
www.whyn.com
Phone: 413-781-1011
Fax: 413-734-4434

WMAS-AM 1450 kHz (Nost)
101 West St
Springfield, MA 01104
E-mail: wmas@947wmas.com
www.947wmas.com
Phone: 413-737-1414
Fax: 413-737-1488

WMAS-FM 94.7 MHz (AC)
101 West St
Springfield, MA 01104
E-mail: wmas@947wmas.com
www.947wmas.com
Phone: 413-737-1414
Fax: 413-737-1488

WNNZ-AM 640 kHz (N/T)
1500 Main St
Springfield, MA 01115
E-mail: talk@wnnz.com
www.wnnz.com
Phone: 413-736-6400
Fax: 413-858-1958

WPKX-FM 97.9 MHz (Ctry)
1 Monarch Pl Suite 220
Springfield, MA 01144
E-mail: kix979@kix979.com
www.kix979.com
Phone: 413-732-5353
Fax: 413-732-7851
TF: 800-345-9759

WRNX-FM 100.9 MHz (AAA)
98 Lower Westfield Rd 3rd Fl
Holyoke, MA 01040
Phone: 413-536-1105
Fax: 413-536-1153

WSCB-FM 89.9 MHz (Misc)
263 Alden St
Springfield, MA 01109
Phone: 413-748-3131
Fax: 413-748-3712

WSPR-AM 1270 kHz (Span)
195 High St
Holyoke, MA 01040
Phone: 413-536-7229
Fax: 413-534-5542

WTCC-FM 90.7 MHz (Span)
1 Armory Sq
Springfield, MA 01105
Phone: 413-781-6628
Fax: 413-781-3747

Attractions

Historical attractions in Springfield include the Springfield Armory, a National Historic Site famous for its extensive weapons collection. Sometimes referred to as the "City of Homes," Springfield is also known for its many historic neighborhoods. Among these are the McKnight District, which includes nearly 900 late-19th Century Victorian homes, making it the largest collection of wood structures in New England from that time period. The city's main cultural resources are located in the area known as the Quadrangle. Among these are Springfield's Museum of Fine Arts, Central Library, and Science Museum. The National Memorial Basketball Hall of Fame in Springfield features interactive exhibits and memorabilia commemorating all facets of the game.

Bellamy Homestead
91-93 Church St
Chicopee, MA 01020
Phone: 413-594-6496

Chicopee Memorial State Park
570 Burnett Rd
Chicopee Falls, MA 01020
Phone: 413-594-9416

Children's Museum at Holyoke Inc
444 Dwight St
Holyoke, MA 01040
Phone: 413-536-7048
Fax: 413-533-2999

Connecticut Valley Historical Museum
194 State St
Springfield, MA 01103
www.quadrangle.org/CVHM.htm
Phone: 413-263-6800
Fax: 413-263-6898

George Walter Vincent Smith Art Museum
220 State St
Springfield, MA 01103
www.quadrangle.org/GWVS.htm
Phone: 413-263-6800

Historic Deerfield Inc
PO Box 321
Deerfield, MA 01342
Phone: 413-774-5581
Fax: 413-773-7415

Indian Motocycle Museum & Hall of Fame
33 Hendee St
Springfield, MA 01139
www.sidecar.com/indian/
Phone: 413-737-2624

Jasper Rand Art Museum
6 Elm St
Westfield, MA 01085
Phone: 413-568-7833
Fax: 413-568-7833

Lake Lorraine State Park
44 Lake Dr
Springfield, MA 01151
www.state.ma.us/dem/parks/llor.htm
Phone: 413-543-6628

Museum of Fine Arts
220 State St
Springfield, MA 01103
www.quadrangle.org/MFA.htm
Phone: 413-263-6800
Fax: 413-263-6889
TF: 800-625-7738

Naismith Memorial Basketball Hall of Fame
1150 W Columbus Ave
Springfield, MA 01101
E-mail: info@hoophall.com
www.hoophall.com
Phone: 413-781-6500
Fax: 413-781-1939
TF: 800-446-6752

New England Peace Pagoda
100 Cave Hill Rd
Leverett, MA 01054
Phone: 413-367-2202
Fax: 413-367-9369

Quadrangle The-Springfield Library & Museum Assn
220 State St
Springfield, MA 01103
www.quadrangle.org
Phone: 413-263-6800
Fax: 413-263-6807

Robinson State Park
North St
Agawam, MA 01030
www.state.ma.us/dem/parks/robn.htm
Phone: 413-786-2877

Six Flags New England
623 Main St
Agawam, MA 01001
www.sixflags.com/newengland
Phone: 413-786-9300
Fax: 413-786-4682
TF: 800-370-7488

Springfield Armory National Historic Site
1 Armory Sq
Springfield, MA 01105
E-mail: SPAR_INTERPRETATION@NPS.GOV
www.nps.gov/spar/
Phone: 413-734-6477
Fax: 413-747-8062

Springfield Library & Museums
220 State St
Springfield, MA 01103
www.spfldlibmus.org
Phone: 413-263-6800
Fax: 413-263-6807

Springfield Symphony Hall
1 Columbus Ctr
Springfield, MA 01103
www.symphonyhall.com
Phone: 413-788-7646
Fax: 413-737-9991

Springfield Symphony Orchestra
Court St Symphony Hall
Springfield, MA 01103
Phone: 413-733-2291

Stagewest
1 Columbus Ctr
Springfield, MA 01103
Phone: 413-781-2340

Storrowtown Village Museum
1305 Memorial Ave
West Springfield, MA 01089
Phone: 413-787-0136
Fax: 413-787-0127

Titanic Museum
208 Main St
Indian Orchard, MA 01151
www.titanic1.org/muss.html
Phone: 413-543-4770

Volleyball Hall of Fame
Heritage State Pk 444 Dwight St
Holyoke, MA 01040
E-mail: info@volleyhall.org
www.volleyhall.org
Phone: 413-536-0926
Fax: 413-539-6673

Westover Air Reserve Base
100 Lloyd St Suite 103
WestoverAir Reserve Base, MA 01022
www.afres.af.mil/units/439AW/Default.htm
Phone: 413-557-1110

Wistariahurst Museum
238 Cabot St
Holyoke, MA 01040
Phone: 413-534-2216
Fax: 413-534-2344

Zoo in Forest Park
Rt 83
Springfield, MA 01138
www.the-spa.com/zoo/
Phone: 413-733-2251

Sports Teams & Facilities

Southwick Motorcross
46 Powder Mill Rd
Southwick, MA 01077
Phone: 413-569-6801

Springfield Falcons (hockey)
1277 Main St Springfield Civic Ctr
Springfield, MA 01103
Phone: 413-787-6600

Springfield Sirens (soccer)
Bay St Fred Berte Stadium
Springfield, MA 01108
E-mail: spfldsiren@aol.com
www.springfieldsirens.com
Phone: 413-783-9158
Fax: 413-783-9158

Western Massachusetts Pioneers (soccer)
Winsor St Lusitano Stadium
Ludlow, MA 01056
E-mail: wmpioneers@aol.com
Phone: 413-583-4814
Fax: 413-583-8192

Annual Events

ACC Craft Fair (mid-June)........................413-737-2443
Antique-A-Rama (January)........................413-737-2443
Bright Nights at Forest Park (November-January)...413-733-3800
Columbus Day Parade (early October) 413-732-7449
Glendi Festival (early September) 413-737-1496

Holiday Gala (early December) .413-263-6800
Holyoke Saint Patrick's Parade (mid-March). 413-536-1646
Old Sturbridge Agricultural Fair (early October) 508-347-3362
Parade of the Big Balloons (late November) 413-733-3800
Peachbasket Festival & Hall of Fame Tip-Off Classic (late November). 413-781-6500
Peter Pan Taste of Springfield (mid-June). 413-733-3800
Puerto Rican Cultural Festival (late July) 413-737-7450
Star Spangled Springfield (July 4). 413-733-3800
The Big E-New England Great State Fair (September) 413-737-2443
Westfest (May) 413-568-2904

Springfield, Missouri

***County:* Greene**

SPRINGFIELD is located on the Ozark Mountain Plateau in southwestern Missouri. Major cities within 100 miles include Branson, Joplin, and Carthage, Missouri.

Area (Land) .... 67.9 sq mi
Area (Water)............................... 0.6 sq mi
Elevation...................................1,316 ft
Latitude ....37-21-53 N
Longitude............................... 93-29-81 W
Time Zone .... CST
Area Code....................................... 417

Climate

Springfield's climate features four distinct seasons. Winter days are cool, with average high temperatures in the low to mid-40s, with evening lows dipping into the low to mid-20s. The average annual snowfall in Springfield is 17 inches. Summer days are warm, with average highs ranging from the mid-80s to 90 degrees, with evenings cooling down into the mid-60s. June is the wettest month in Springfield, while January is the driest.

Average Temperatures & Precipitation

Temperatures

	Jan	Feb	Mar	Apr	May	Jun	Jul	Aug	Sep	Oct	Nov	Dec
High	42	46	57	68	76	84	90	89	80	70	57	45
Low	20	25	34	44	53	62	67	65	58	46	36	25

Precipitation

	Jan	Feb	Mar	Apr	May	Jun	Jul	Aug	Sep	Oct	Nov	Dec
Inches	1.8	2.1	3.9	4.2	4.4	5.1	2.9	3.5	4.6	3.6	3.8	3.2

History

Springfield was founded by Tennessee resident John Polk Campbell in 1829 at the site of a natural spring. By the time Campbell returned to the site the following year with his family, other pioneers had begun to settle the area. In 1833 Greene County, named for Revolutionary War General Nathanael Greene, was organized, and at the time it encompassed the entire southwest corner of Missouri. The following year a post office was established and the new community was first called "Springfield." It was chosen as the county seat of Greene County, and three years later, in 1838, was incorporated as a city. In 1858, Springfield became a regular stop along the Butterfield Overland Mail, a weekly stagecoach that ran from Tipton, Missouri to San Francisco, California, which contributed to growth in the area.

Due to Missouri's strategic location along both the Missouri and Mississippi Rivers, control of the state was a critical issue during the Civil War. Many battles were waged in Missouri, and several were fought in the Springfield area, including the Battle of Wilson's Creek, the first major battle west of the Mississippi. Although the Confederate army won the battle, their failure to pursue the retreating Union troops ultimately resulted in Missouri remaining under Union control throughout the war. Wilson's Creek National Park, located eight miles southwest of Springfield, commemorates this Civil War battle and is one of the area's leading tourist attractions.

After the war, in 1865, Springfield's town square became the site of the nation's first "Wild West" shoot-out between Wild Bill Hickock and Dave Tutt, who was killed in the incident. In 1870 the Atlantic-Pacific railroad arrived in Springfield, and the city rapidly became a major center for shipping agricultural commodities and equipment to other parts of the U.S. Later in that decade Springfield was dubbed "Queen City of the Ozarks" by a local newspaper. By the 1890s Springfield's population had tripled, and today, more than a century later, Springfield remains a leading U.S. center for agribusiness. It is currently home to more than 142,000 people and is Missouri's third largest city and the second fastest-growing city in the state.

Population

1990 Census 140,494
1998 Estimate..............................142,898
% Change 1.7

Racial/Ethnic Breakdown

White.................................... 95.7%
Black 2.5%
Other...................................... 1.8%
Hispanic Origin (may be of any race) 1.0%

Age Breakdown

Under 5 years.............................. 6.2%
5 to 17.................................. 14.4%
18 to 20................................... 8.8%
21 to 24................................... 9.1%
25 to 34................................. 16.5%
35 to 44................................. 12.9%
45 to 54................................... 8.8%
55 to 64................................... 8.2%
65 to 74................................... 8.0%
75+ years 7.2%
Median Age.................................31.8

Gender Breakdown

Male..................................... 47.3%
Female................................... 52.7%

Government

Type of Government: Council-Manager

Springfield Building Development Services Dept
840 Boonville Ave 1st Fl
Springfield, MO 65802
Phone: 417-864-1056
Fax: 417-864-1057

Springfield City Clerk
840 Boonville Ave
Springfield, MO 65802
Phone: 417-864-1651
Fax: 417-864-1649

Springfield City Council
840 Boonville Ave
Springfield, MO 65802
Phone: 417-864-1651
Fax: 417-864-1649

Springfield City Hall
840 Boonville Ave
Springfield, MO 65802
Phone: 417-864-1000
Fax: 417-864-1649

Springfield City Manager
840 Boonville Ave
Springfield, MO 65801
Phone: 417-864-1001
Fax: 417-864-1912

Springfield Finance Dept
PO Box 8368
Springfield, MO 65801
Phone: 417-864-1625
Fax: 417-864-1880

Springfield Fire Dept
830 Boonville Ave
Springfield, MO 65802
Phone: 417-864-1500
Fax: 417-864-1505

Springfield Human Resources Dept
840 Boonville Ave Rm 324
Springfield, MO 65802
Phone: 417-864-1607
Fax: 417-864-1186

Springfield Law Dept
840 Boonville Ave
Springfield, MO 65802
Phone: 417-864-1645
Fax: 417-864-1551

Springfield Mayor
840 Boonville Ave
Springfield, MO 65802
Phone: 417-864-1651
Fax: 417-864-1649

Springfield Parks Dept
1923 N Weller Ave
Springfield, MO 65803
Phone: 417-864-1049
Fax: 417-837-5811

Springfield Planning & Development Dept
840 Boonville Ave
Springfield, MO 65802
Phone: 417-864-1031
Fax: 417-864-1030

Springfield Police Dept
321 E Chestnut Expy
Springfield, MO 65802
Phone: 417-864-1782
Fax: 417-864-2052

Springfield Public Works Dept
840 Boonville Ave
Springfield, MO 65802
Phone: 417-864-1902
Fax: 417-864-1929

Springfield-Greene County Library
397 E Central St
Springfield, MO 65802
Phone: 417-874-8150
Fax: 417-874-8151

Important Phone Numbers

AAA....417-882-8040
American Express Travel....417-866-0477
Dental Referral....417-882-4117
Driver's License/Vehicle Registration Information....417-895-6552
Emergency....911
Greater Springfield Board of Realtors....417-883-1226
Greene County Assessor....417-868-4101
Medical Referral....417-887-1017
Missouri Dept of Revenue....417-895-6474
Poison Control Center....800-366-8888
Time/Temp....417-831-7700
Voter Registration Information....417-868-4055
Weather....417-866-1010

Information Sources

Better Business Bureau Serving Southwest Missouri
205 Park Central E Suite 509
Springfield, MO 65806
www.springfield-mo.bbb.org
Phone: 417-862-4222
Fax: 417-869-5544

Greene County
940 N Boonville Ave
Springfield, MO 65802
Phone: 417-868-4055
Fax: 417-868-4170

Springfield Area Chamber of Commerce
202 S John Q Hammons Pkwy
Springfield, MO 65801
www.spfld-mo-chamber.com
Phone: 417-862-5567
Fax: 417-862-1611

Springfield Missouri Convention & Visitors Bureau
3315 E Battlefield Rd
Springfield, MO 65804
www.springfieldmo.org
Phone: 417-881-5300
Fax: 417-881-2231
TF: 800-678-8767

Online Resources

About.com Guide to Springfield/Branson
springfieldmo.about.com/citiestowns/midwestus/springfieldmo

Anthill City Guide Springfield
www.anthill.com/city.asp?city=springfieldmo

Area Guide Springfield
springfieldmo.areaguides.net

Branson Connection
www.bransonconnection.com

ORION-Ozarks Regional Information Online Network
www.orion.org/

Springfield City Net
www.excite.com/travel/countries/united_states/missouri/springfield

Springfield Community Profile
springfield.missouri.org

Area Communities

Communities in Greene County with populations greater than 1,000 include:

Ash Grove
101 Calhoun Ave
Ash Grove, MO 65604
Phone: 417-751-2333
Fax: 417-751-3438

Battlefield
5434 S Tower Dr
Battlefield, MO 65619
Phone: 417-883-5840
Fax: 417-883-8189

Republic
213 N Main St
Republic, MO 65738
Phone: 417-732-6065
Fax: 417-732-2913

Strafford
PO Box 66
Strafford, MO 65757
Phone: 417-736-2154
Fax: 417-736-2390

Willard
PO Box 187
Willard, MO 65781
Phone: 417-742-3033
Fax: 417-742-3080

Economy

Springfield has healthy, diverse economy. Major U.S. corporations with a presence in the Springfield area include General Electric, 3M, Kraft Foods, and WorldCom Inc. Agribusiness, ranging from farming to agricultural equipment manufacturing, remains important to the area's economy, as it has for more than a century. Healthcare is also one of Springfield's leading industries - the area's two largest employers are healthcare-related. Services is currently the leading employment sector in the Springfield MSA, followed by retail trade and government. The State of Missouri also ranks among the area's ten largest employers, providing jobs for 2,000 area residents.

Unemployment Rate 2.3%*
Per Capita Income.......................... $18,139*
Median Family Income...................... $27,705

* *Information given is for Greene County.*

Principal Industries & Number of Wage Earners

Springfield MSA* - 1999

Finance 7,733
Government 20,642
Manufacturing 23,858
Mining & Construction.............................. 7,408
Retail Trade.. 34,000
Services 49,950
Transportation & Utilities 11,625
Wholesale Trade.................................... 12,275

* *Information given is for the Springfield Metropolitan Statistical Area (MSA), which includes Christian, Greene, and Webster counties.*

Major Employers

Aaron's Automotive Products Inc
2600 N Westgate Ave
Springfield, MO 65803
Phone: 417-831-5257
Fax: 417-831-0795

Assemblies of God
1445 N Boonville Ave
Springfield, MO 65802
E-mail: opr@ag.org
www.ag.org
Phone: 417-862-2781
Fax: 417-862-5554
TF: 800-641-4310

Associated Wholesale Grocers Inc
3201 E Division St
Springfield, MO 65802
www.awginc.com/careers
Phone: 417-875-4000
Fax: 417-875-4087

Bass Pro Shops
2500 E Kearney St
Springfield, MO 65898
www.basspro.com
Phone: 417-873-5000
Fax: 417-865-9812

City Utilities
301 E Central St
Springfield, MO 65802
Phone: 417-831-8311
Fax: 417-831-8406

Cox Health Systems
1423 N Jefferson Ave
Springfield, MO 65802
www.coxnet.org
Phone: 417-269-3000
Fax: 417-269-3104

Kraft Foods Inc
PO Box 3440
Springfield, MO 65804
www.kraftfoods.com/careers
Phone: 417-881-2701

O'Reilly Automotive Inc
233 S Patterson Ave
Springfield, MO 65802
www.oreillyauto.com
Phone: 417-862-3333
Fax: 417-874-7163

Saint John's Health System
1235 E Cherokee St
Springfield, MO 65804
Phone: 417-885-2000
Fax: 417-888-7799

Southwest Missouri State University
901 S National Ave
Springfield, MO 65804
E-mail: smsuinfo@vma.smsu.edu
www.smsu.edu
Phone: 417-836-5000
Fax: 417-836-6334
TF: 800-492-7900

Springfield City Hall
840 Boonville Ave
Springfield, MO 65802
E-mail: city@ci.springfield.mo.us
springfield.missouri.org/gov
Phone: 417-864-1000
Fax: 417-864-1649

Springfield Public Schools
940 N Jefferson
Springfield, MO 65802
E-mail: spsr12@pop.orion.org
sps.k12.mo.us
Phone: 417-864-3800
Fax: 417-864-3806

Tracker Marine Corp
2500 E Kearney
Springfield, MO 65803
www.tracker-marine.com
Phone: 417-873-5900
Fax: 417-873-5068

Willow Brook Foods Inc
405 N Jefferson Ave
Springfield, MO 65806
Phone: 417-862-3612
Fax: 417-837-4725

WorldCom Consumer Markets
1720 E Primrose St
Springfield, MO 65804
www.wcom.com
Phone: 417-268-2000
Fax: 417-268-2333

Quality of Living Indicators

Total Crime Index.................................. 11,499
(rates per 100,000 inhabitants)

Violent Crime
Murder 4
Forcible rape 65
Robbery.. 124
Aggravated assault............................. 359

Property Crime
Burglary 1,832
Larceny theft 8,402
Motor vehicle theft 737

Cost of Living Index....................................91.6
(national average = 100)

Median Home Price..................................$85,800

Education

Public Schools

Springfield Public Schools
940 N Jefferson
Springfield, MO 65802
E-mail: spsr12@pop.orion.org
sps.k12.mo.us
Phone: 417-864-3800
Fax: 417-864-3806

Number of Schools
Elementary.................................. 38
Middle 9
High.. 5

Student/Teacher Ratio
Elementary............................... 16.4:1
Middle 15.6:1
High.................................... 18.0:1

Private Schools

Number of Schools (all grades).................... 15+

Colleges & Universities

Baptist Bible College
628 E Kearney St
Springfield, MO 65803
E-mail: bbc@ncsi.net
www.seebbc.edu
Phone: 417-268-6060
Fax: 417-268-6694
TF: 800-228-5754

Central Bible College
3000 N Grant Ave
Springfield, MO 65803
www.cbcag.edu
Phone: 417-833-2551
Fax: 417-833-5141
TF: 800-831-4222

Drury College
900 N Benton Ave
Springfield, MO 65802
www.drury.edu
Phone: 417-873-7879
Fax: 417-873-7529
TF: 800-922-2274

Evangel University
1111 N Glenstone Ave
Springfield, MO 65802
www.evangel.edu
Phone: 417-865-2811
Fax: 417-865-9599
TF: 800-382-6435

Global University
1211 S Glenstone
Springfield, MO 65804
Phone: 417-862-9533
Fax: 417-862-0863
TF: 800-443-1083

Southwest Baptist University
1600 University Ave
Bolivar, MO 65613
E-mail: admitme@SBUniv.edu
www.sbuniv.edu
Phone: 417-326-5281
Fax: 417-328-1514
TF: 800-526-5859

Southwest Missouri State University
901 S National Ave
Springfield, MO 65804
E-mail: smsuinfo@vma.smsu.edu
www.smsu.edu
Phone: 417-836-5000
Fax: 417-836-6334
TF: 800-492-7900

Springfield College
1010 W Sunshine
Springfield, MO 65807
E-mail: ccenter@cci.edu
Phone: 417-864-7220
Fax: 417-864-5697
TF: 888-741-4271

Hospitals

Saint John's Regional Health Center
1235 E Cherokee St
Springfield, MO 65804
www.stjohns.net
Phone: 417-885-2000
Fax: 417-885-2288

Transportation

Airport(s)

Springfield-Branson Regional Airport (SGF)
8 miles NW of downtown (approx 20 minutes)....417-869-0300

Mass Transit

City Bus Service
$.75 Base fare................................417-831-8782

Rail/Bus

Greyhound/Trailways Bus Station
2425 E Kearney St
Springfield, MO 65803
Phone: 417-869-2975
TF: 800-231-2222

Utilities

Electricity
City Utilities.................................417-831-8300
www.cityutil.com

Gas
City Utilities.................................417-831-8300
www.cityutil.com

Water
City Utilities.................................417-831-8300
www.cityutil.com

Garbage Collection/Recycling
BFI/American Disposal........................417-865-1717
Springfield Recycling Hot Line.................417-864-1904
Waste Management............................417-831-5320

Telecommunications

Telephone
Southwestern Bell Telephone Co................800-246-4999
www.swbell.com

Cable Television
AT & T Cable Services.........................417-875-5500
www.cable.att.com

Internet Service Providers (ISPs)
Active Internet Corp..........................417-883-7993
www.axs.net
E-Guys.....................................417-862-9444
www.e-guys.com
ORION-Ozarks Regional Information Online Network...................................417-874-8120
www.orion.org/
Panther Creek Information Services............417-869-5718
www.pcis.net

United States Internet Presence Providers Inc. . . . 417-831-4828
www.usipp.com

Banks

Empire Bank Phone: 417-881-3100
1800 S Glenstone Fax: 417-882-9675
Springfield, MO 65804 TF: 888-231-4637

Great Southern Bank FSB Phone: 417-887-4400
1451 E Battlefield Rd Fax: 417-888-4533
Springfield, MO 65804 TF: 800-749-7113

Mercantile Bank of Saint Louis Phone: 417-868-4400
417 Saint Louis St Fax: 417-868-4408
Springfield, MO 65806

Metropolitan National Bank Phone: 417-862-2022
600 S Glenstone Ave Fax: 417-862-6318
Springfield, MO 65802

UMB Bank Phone: 417-887-5855
1150 E Battlefield St Fax: 417-887-1808
Springfield, MO 65807

Shopping

Apple Jack's Country Store & Craftmen's Mall Phone: 417-581-3899
1996 Evangel St
Ozark, MO 65721

Bass Country Antique Mall Phone: 417-869-8255
1832 S Campbell Ave Fax: 417-864-8209
Springfield, MO 65807

Battlefield Mall Phone: 417-883-7777
2825 S Glenstone Ave Fax: 417-883-2641
Springfield, MO 65804
www.shopsimon.com/smt/servlet/SMTMall?mid=174&pn=ENTRY&rs=0

Chesterfield Village Phone: 417-881-5293
Kansas Expy & James River Fwy Fax: 417-862-4573
Springfield, MO 65807

Class Act Flea Market Phone: 417-862-1370
224 E Commercial St
Springfield, MO 65803

Grand Village The Phone: 417-336-7280
2800 W 76 Country Music Blvd Fax: 417-336-7293
Branson, MO 65616 TF: 800-952-6626
www.gvshops.com

Ozark Antique Mall Phone: 417-581-5233
200 S 20th St Fax: 417-581-0325
Ozark, MO 65721

PFI Western Store Phone: 417-889-2668
2816 S Ingram Mill Rd Fax: 417-889-7204
Springfield, MO 65804 TF: 800-222-4734
E-mail: info@pfiwestern.com
www.pfiwestern.com

Traders Market Shopping Gallery Phone: 417-889-1145
1845 E Sunshine Fax: 417-882-0261
Springfield, MO 65804

Media

Newspapers and Magazines

Springfield Business Journal Phone: 417-831-3238
313 Park Central W Fax: 417-831-5478
Springfield, MO 65806
www.sbj.net

Springfield News Leader* Phone: 417-836-1100
PO Box 798 Fax: 417-837-1381
Springfield, MO 65801 TF: 800-695-2005
www.ozarksgateway.com/nl.htm

**Indicates major daily newspapers*

Television

KDEB-TV Ch 27 (Fox) Phone: 417-862-2727
2650 E Division St Fax: 417-831-4209
Springfield, MO 65803
www.fox27.com

KOLR-TV Ch 10 (CBS) Phone: 417-862-1010
2650 E Division St Fax: 417-862-6439
Springfield, MO 65803
www.kolr10.com

KOZK-TV Ch 21 (PBS) Phone: 417-865-2100
821 Washington Ave Fax: 417-863-1599
Springfield, MO 65802

KSPR-TV Ch 33 (ABC) Phone: 417-831-1333
1359 Saint Louis St Fax: 417-831-4125
Springfield, MO 65802 TF: 800-220-8222
E-mail: admin@kspr33.com
www.kspr33.com

KYTV-TV Ch 3 (NBC) Phone: 417-268-3000
PO Box 3500 Fax: 417-268-3100
Springfield, MO 65808
E-mail: ky3news@ky3.com
www.ky3.com

Radio

KADI-FM 99.5 MHz (Rel) Phone: 417-831-0995
1601 W Sunshine St Suite P Fax: 417-831-4026
Springfield, MO 65807
www.kadi.com

KGBX-FM 105.9 MHz (AC) Phone: 417-890-5555
1856 S Glenstone Ave Fax: 417-890-5050
Springfield, MO 65804
www.kgbx.com

KGMY-AM 1400 kHz (Sports) Phone: 417-890-5555
1856 S Glenstone Ave Fax: 417-890-5050
Springfield, MO 65804
www.mycountry.com

KLFJ-AM 1550 kHz (Misc) Phone: 417-831-1550
610 W College St Fax: 417-831-1231
Springfield, MO 65804

KSMU-FM 91.1 MHz (NPR) Phone: 417-836-5878
Southwest Missouri State University 901 S National Ave Fax: 417-836-5889
Springfield, MO 65804
E-mail: ksmu@netfocus.net
www.ksmu.org

KTOZ-AM 1060 kHz (Misc) Phone: 417-832-1060
610 W College St Fax: 417-864-4111
Springfield, MO 65804

KTOZ-FM 95.5 MHz (AC) Phone: 417-890-5555
1856 S Glenstone Ave Fax: 417-890-5050
Springfield, MO 65804

KTXR-FM 101.3 MHz (B/EZ) Phone: 417-862-3751
3000 E Chestnut Expy Fax: 417-869-7675
Springfield, MO 65802
E-mail: ktxrfm@ktxrfm.com
www.ktxrfm.com

KWTO-AM 560 kHz (N/T) Phone: 417-862-5600
3000 E Chestnut Expy Fax: 417-869-7675
Springfield, MO 65802

KXUS-FM 97.3 MHz (CR) Phone: 417-890-5555
1856 S Glenstone Ave Fax: 417-890-5050
Springfield, MO 65804
www.us97.com

Attractions

Located in the tablelands of the Ozark Mountain Plateau, Springfield, Missouri is within 90 minutes of many Missouri waterways and their abundant stock of crappie, rainbow trout, bluegill, and other fish. The Bass Pro Shops Outdoor World of Springfield is a premier attraction, with mounted wild game, a 30-foot waterfall, indoor boat showroom and firing range, and a 140,000-gallon aquarium. To the east of the city one can visit the home of the "Little House" series author, Laura Ingalls Wilder. Branson, Missouri, which has earned a reputation as the new Country Music Show Capital, lies south of Springfield. Mel Tillis, Glen Campbell, Roy Clark, and other country music celebrities perform at their own theaters in Branson.

76 Music Hall Phone: 417-335-2484
1945 W 76 Country Music Blvd Fax: 417-334-1647
Branson, MO 65616

Air & Military Museum Phone: 417-864-7997
2305 E Kearney St
Springfield, MO 65803

Bass Pro Shops Phone: 417-873-5000
2500 E Kearney St Fax: 417-865-9812
Springfield, MO 65898
www.basspro.com

Branson Scenic Railway Phone: 417-334-6110
206 E Main St Fax: 417-336-3909
Branson, MO 65616 TF: 800-287-2462

Children's Choirs of Southwest Missouri Phone: 417-885-7880
1926 S Glenstone
Springfield, MO 65804

Crystal Cave Phone: 417-833-9599
7225 N Crystal Cave Ln
Springfield, MO 65803

Dickerson Park Zoo Phone: 417-833-1570
3043 N Fort Fax: 417-833-4459
Springfield, MO 65803
www.dickersonparkzoo.org

Discovery Center of Springfield Phone: 417-862-9910
438 Saint Louis St Fax: 417-862-6898
Springfield, MO 65806

Dixie Stampede Dinner Attraction Phone: 417-336-3000
1525 W Hwy 76 Fax: 417-339-4350
Branson, MO 65616 TF: 800-520-5544
www.branson.com/branson/dixie/default.html

Exotic Animal Paradise Phone: 417-859-2016
124 Jungle Dr I-44 Fax: 417-859-4902
Strafford, MO 65757

Fantastic Caverns Phone: 417-833-2010
4872 N Farm Rd 125 Fax: 417-833-2042
Springfield, MO 65803
www.fantastic-caverns.com

Fellows Lake Phone: 417-831-8403
N FM 189 & FM 66
Springfield, MO 65803

Frisco Railroad Museum Inc Phone: 417-866-7573
543 E Commercial St
Springfield, MO 65803
www.frisco.org/frisco/frisco.html

George Washington Carver National Monument Phone: 417-325-4151
5646 Carver Rd Fax: 417-325-4231
Diamond, MO 64840
www.nps.gov/gwca/

Grand Palace The Phone: 417-336-1220
2700 W 76 Country Music Blvd Fax: 417-337-5170
Branson, MO 65616 TF: 800-884-4536
www.thegrandpalace.com/main.htm

Gray/Campbell Farmstead Phone: 417-862-6293
2400 S Scenic Fax: 417-862-6293
Springfield, MO 65807

Hammons Juanita K Hall for the Performing Arts Phone: 417-836-6776
525 Don Q Hammons Pkwy Fax: 417-836-6891
Springfield, MO 65804
www.hammonshall.smsu.edu

History Museum Phone: 417-864-1976
830 Boonville Ave 3rd Fl Fax: 417-864-2019
Springfield, MO 65802
www.historymuseumsgc.org

Missouri Sports Hall of Fame Phone: 417-889-3100
3861 E Stan Musial Dr Fax: 417-889-2761
Springfield, MO 65809 TF: 800-498-5678
mosportshalloffame.com

Ozark National Scenic Riverways Phone: 573-323-4236
PO Box 490 Fax: 573-323-4140
Van Buren, MO 63965
www.nps.gov/ozar/

Ozarks Discovery IMAX Theater
3562 Shepherd of the Hills Expy
Branson, MO 65616
members.aol.com/OzarksIMAX/index1.html
Phone: 417-335-3533
Fax: 417-336-5348
TF: 800-419-4832

Polynesian Princess
1358 Long Creek Rd
Branson, MO 65739
www.branson.com/branson/princess/princess.htm
Phone: 417-337-8366
Fax: 417-339-2941
TF: 800-653-6288

Precious Moments Chapel
4321 Chapel Rd
Carthage, MO 64836
E-mail: information@preciousmoments.com
www.preciousmoments.com
Phone: 417-359-3010
Fax: 417-359-2905
TF: 800-543-7975

Ride The Ducks
2320 W Hwy 76
Branson, MO 65616
Phone: 417-334-3825
Fax: 417-334-5382

Shepherd of the Hills Outdoor Theatre
5586 W Hwy 76
Branson, MO 65616
www.branson.com/branson/shepherd/shepherd.htm
Phone: 417-334-4191
Fax: 417-334-4617
TF: 800-653-6288

Showboat Branson Belle
4800 State Hwy 165
Branson, MO 65616
E-mail: tickets@silverdollarcity.com
www.silverdollarcity.com/showboat
Phone: 417-336-7171
Fax: 417-336-7410
TF: 800-227-8587

Silver Dollar City
399 Indian Point Rd
Branson, MO 65616
www.silverdollarcity.com
Phone: 417-336-7100
Fax: 417-338-8008
TF: 888-455-1383

Snow Bluff Ski & Fun Area
Hwy 13
Brighton, MO 65617
Phone: 417-376-2201

Springfield Art Museum
1111 E Brookside Dr
Springfield, MO 65807
E-mail: city@ci.springfield.mo.us
Phone: 417-837-5700
Fax: 417-837-5704

Springfield Ballet
311 E Walnut St
Springfield, MO 65806
Phone: 417-862-1343
Fax: 417-864-6577

Springfield Conservation Nature Center
4600 S Chrisman Ave
Springfield, MO 65804
Phone: 417-888-4237

Springfield Little Theatre
311 E Walnut St
Springfield, MO 65806
E-mail: slt@landerstheatre.org
www.landerstheatre.org
Phone: 417-869-1334
Fax: 417-869-4047

Springfield National Cemetery
1702 E Seminole St
Springfield, MO 65804
Phone: 417-881-9499

Springfield Regional Opera
311 E Walnut St
Springfield, MO 65806
Phone: 417-863-1960
Fax: 417-863-7416

Springfield Symphony Orchestra
1536 E Division
Springfield, MO 65803
www.orion.org/~symphony
Phone: 417-864-6683
Fax: 417-864-8967

Stafford Jim Theatre
3440 Hwy 76
Branson, MO 65616
www.jimstafford.com
Phone: 417-335-8080
Fax: 417-335-2643
TF: 800-677-8533

Stained Glass Theatre
1700 N Benton Ave
Springfield, MO 65803
Phone: 417-869-9018
Fax: 417-869-2574

Stone Hill Winery
601 State Hwy 165
Branson, MO 65616
E-mail: branson-info@stonehillwinery.com
www.stonehillwinery.com
Phone: 417-334-1897
Fax: 417-334-1942
TF: 888-926-9463

White Water
3505 W Hwy 76
Branson, MO 65616
www.silverdollarcity.com/whitewater/WWHome.htm
Phone: 417-334-7488
Fax: 417-334-7421

Wilder Laura Ingalls-Rose Wilder Lane Museum & Home
3068 Hwy A
Mansfield, MO 65704
Phone: 417-924-3626
Fax: 417-924-8580

Wilson's Creek National Battlefield
6424 W Farm Rd 182
Republic, MO 65738
www.nps.gov/wicr/
Phone: 417-732-2662
Fax: 417-732-1167

Annual Events

1860 Lifestyle Exposition (mid-September) 417-862-6293
Artsfest (early May)..............................417-869-8380
Buy.com Ozarks Open (mid-August)...............417-887-3400
Fall Hunting Classic (mid-August) 417-873-5111
Firefall (early July) 417-864-1049
First Night Springfield (December 31)............417-869-8380
Frisco Days (early June) 417-864-7015
Hall of Fame All-Star Game (early July)............417-889-3100
Halloween Spooktacular (late October).............417-833-1570
Ozark Empire Fair (late July-early August) 417-833-2660
Ozark Mountain Christmas Festival of Lights (early November-late December) 417-881-5300
Sheep & Wool Days (early June) 417-881-1659
SMSU Summer Tent Theater (late June-early August)........................417-836-5979
Watercolor USA (early June-early August)..........417-837-5700

Stockton, California

County: San Joaquin

STOCKTON is located in the San Joaquin Valley in north central California. Other major cities with 100 miles include Sacramento, Oakland, San Francisco, and San Jose, California.

Area (Land)	52.6 sq mi
Area (Water)	0.9 sq mi
Elevation	13 ft
Latitude	37-58-11 N
Longitude	121-18-24 W
Time Zone	PST
Area Code	209

Climate

Stockton's climate is moderated by sea breezes that enter the valley through gaps in the Coast Range. Summer days are hot and dry, with temperatures averaging around 90 degrees, but the sea breezes cool evening temperatures down to the mid-50s. Winters are generally mild, with high temperatures in the mid- to upper 50s, while nighttime temperatures often dip below freezing. The majority of the precipitation in Stockton falls between November and March.

Average Temperatures & Precipitation

Temperatures

	Jan	Feb	Mar	Apr	May	Jun	Jul	Aug	Sep	Oct	Nov	Dec
High	54	61	66	73	81	87	92	91	87	78	64	54
Low	36	39	42	45	49	54	56	56	53	47	41	36

Precipitation

	Jan	Feb	Mar	Apr	May	Jun	Jul	Aug	Sep	Oct	Nov	Dec
Inches	2.9	2.4	2.4	1.2	0.3	0.1	0.1	0.1	0.4	0.9	2.3	2.4

History

Stockton was founded in 1848 and brought to life during the Gold Rush, as miners traveled through the area from San Francisco to the mines of the Mother Lode. Eventually, the mines ran dry and the miners returned to the Stockton area, turning their efforts to farming in the fertile San Joaquin Valley. Stockton has been a major agricultural center since the 1870s, and successful farming has drawn large numbers of people to the area over the years. Stockton's waterways and access to major highways have helped to make the city one of California's fastest developing warehousing and distribution centers as well.

World War II brought about another period of rapid population growth in Stockton, when the city became a shipbuilding center for the Pacific Theater of Operation. In addition, Stockton Air Force Base was a training site for U.S. Air Force Flyers and the Port of Stockton was used as an Army Supply Base. Today, the Greater Stockton area is home to over a half-million people, 240,000 of whom live in the city of Stockton.

Population

1990 Census	210,943
1998 Estimate	240,143
% Change	13.8
2010 Projection	304,105

Racial/Ethnic Breakdown

White	57.5%
Black	9.6%
Other	33.2%
Hispanic Origin (may be of any race)	25.0%

Age Breakdown

Under 5 years	9.6%
5 to 17	22.2%
18 to 20	4.9%
21 to 24	6.3%
25 to 34	16.5%
35 to 44	14.5%
45 to 54	8.7%
55 to 64	6.8%
65 to 74	6.0%
75+ years	4.5%
Median Age	29.3

Gender Breakdown

Male	49.5%
Female	50.5%

Government

Type of Government: Council-Manager

Stockton City Attorney
425 N El Dorado St
Stockton, CA 95202
Phone: 209-937-8333
Fax: 209-937-8898

Stockton City Clerk
425 N El Dorado St
Stockton, CA 95202
Phone: 209-937-8459
Fax: 209-937-8447

Stockton City Council
425 N El Dorado St
Stockton, CA 95202
Phone: 209-937-8244
Fax: 209-937-8568

Stockton City Hall
425 N El Dorado St
Stockton, CA 95202
Phone: 209-937-8057
Fax: 209-937-8447

Stockton City Manager Phone: 209-937-8212
425 N El Dorado St Fax: 209-937-7149
Stockton, CA 95202

Stockton Community Development Dept Phone: 209-937-8444
425 N El Dorado St Fax: 209-937-8893
Stockton, CA 95202

Stockton Emergency Services Office Phone: 209-464-4650
425 N El Dorado St Fax: 209-937-8836
Stockton, CA 95202

Stockton Finance Dept Phone: 209-937-8460
425 N El Dorado St Fax: 209-937-8844
Stockton, CA 95202

Stockton Fire Dept Phone: 209-937-8801
425 N El Dorado St Fax: 209-937-8836
Stockton, CA 95202

Stockton Housing & Redevelopment Dept Phone: 209-937-8538
305 N El Dorado St Suite 200 Fax: 209-937-8822
Stockton, CA 95202

Stockton Mayor Phone: 209-937-8244
425 N El Dorado St Fax: 209-937-8568
Stockton, CA 95202

Stockton Municipal Utilities Dept Phone: 209-937-8750
2500 Navy Dr Fax: 209-937-8708
Stockton, CA 95206

Stockton Parks & Recreation Dept Phone: 209-937-8206
6 E Lindsay St Fax: 209-937-8260
Stockton, CA 95202

Stockton Planning Div Phone: 209-937-8266
345 N El Dorado St Fax: 209-937-8893
Stockton, CA 95202

Stockton Police Dept Phone: 209-937-8377
22 E Market St Fax: 209-937-8601
Stockton, CA 95202

Stockton Public Works Dept Phone: 209-937-8411
425 N El Dorado St Rm 317 Fax: 209-937-8277
Stockton, CA 95202

Stockton Treasury Div Phone: 209-937-8313
425 N El Dorado St Fax: 209-937-7184
Stockton, CA 95202

Stockton-San Joaquin County Public Library Phone: 209-937-8415
605 N El Dorado St
Stockton, CA 95202

Important Phone Numbers

AAA....209-952-4110
American Express Travel....209-952-6606
California State Franchise Tax Board....916-845-4300
Central Valley Assn of Realtors....209-858-1700
Dental Referral....800-422-8338
Driver's License/Vehicle Registration Information....209-948-7687
Emergency.... 911
Medical Referral....209-952-5299
Poison Control Center....800-876-4766
San Joaquin County Tax Collector....209-468-2133
Voter Registration Information....209-468-2885
Weather....209-982-1793

Information Sources

Better Business Bureau Serving the Mid Counties Phone: 209-948-4880
11 S San Joaquin St Suite 803 Fax: 209-465-6302
Stockton, CA 95202
www.stockton.bbb.org

Greater Stockton Chamber of Commerce Phone: 209-547-2770
445 W Weber Ave Suite 220 Fax: 209-466-5271
Stockton, CA 95203
www.stocktonchamber.org

San Joaquin County Phone: 209-468-2362
24 S Hunter St Rm 304
Stockton, CA 95202
www.co.san-joaquin.ca.us

Stockton Economic Development Div Phone: 209-937-8530
425 N El Dorado St Fax: 209-937-8904
Stockton, CA 95202
www.ci.stockton.ca.us/Econdev/pages/Edhome.thm

Stockton Memorial Civic Auditorium Phone: 209-941-8223
525 N Center St Fax: 209-941-8262
Stockton, CA 95202

Stockton/San Joaquin Convention & Visitors Bureau Phone: 209-943-1987
46 W Fremont St Fax: 209-943-6235
Stockton, CA 95202 TF: 800-350-1987
www.ssjcvb.org

Online Resources

4Stockton.com
www.4stockton.com

Anthill City Guide Stockton
www.anthill.com/city.asp?city=stockton

Excite.com Stockton City Guide
www.excite.com/travel/countries/united_states/california/stockton

StocktoNet
www.stocktonet.com/

Virtual Stockton.com
www.virtualstockton.com/

Area Communities

Communities in the Stockton/San Joaquin area with populations greater than 5,000 include:

Escalon Phone: 209-838-3556
PO Box 248 Fax: 209-838-8045
Escalon, CA 95320

Lathrop Phone: 209-858-2860
16775 Howland Rd Suite 1 Fax: 209-858-5259
Lathrop, CA 95330

Lodi
221 W Pine St
Lodi, CA 95240
Phone: 209-333-6700
Fax: 209-333-6807

Manteca
1001 W Center St
Manteca, CA 95337
Phone: 209-239-8400
Fax: 209-825-2333

Ripon
259 N Wilma Ave
Ripon, CA 95366
Phone: 209-599-2108
Fax: 209-599-2685

Tracy
325 E 10th St
Tracy, CA 95376
Phone: 209-831-4100
Fax: 209-831-4110

Economy

Agriculture continues to play a major role in Stockton's economy—four of the area's 15 major employers are agriculture-related. Government employs more than 32,000 Stockton area residents at the state and local levels. Health care is also an important industry, with Stockton hospitals employing more than 6,500 people.

Unemployment Rate 8.3%**
Per Capita Income $20,812**
Median Family Income $44,300*

** Information given is for San Joaquin County.*
*** Information given is for the Stockton-Lodi Metropolitan Statistical Area (MSA), which includes the City of Lodi, the City of Stockton, and San Joaquin County.*

Principal Industries & Number of Wage Earners

San Joaquin County - June 2000

Industry	Wage Earners
Construction	11,100
Farm	30,100
Finance, Insurance, & Real Estate	8,900
Government	36,000
Manufacturing	23,500
Mining	100
Retail Trade	33,600
Services	46,100
Transportation & Public Utilities	13,100
Wholesale Trade	9,900

Major Employers

California Cedar Products Co
400 Fresno Ave
Stockton, CA 95203
Phone: 209-944-5800
Fax: 209-944-9072

California Transportation Dept
1120 'N' St
Sacramento, CA 95814
www.dot.ca.gov
Phone: 916-654-5266
Fax: 916-654-6608

Dameron Hospital
525 W Acacia St
Stockton, CA 95203
Phone: 209-944-5550
Fax: 209-461-3108

Del Monte Foods Co
1 Market Plaza Stuart Street Towers
San Francisco, CA 94105
www.delmonte.com
Phone: 415-247-3000
Fax: 415-247-3565
TF: 800-543-3090

Diamond Walnut Growers Inc
PO Box 1727
Stockton, CA 95201
www.diamondwalnut.com
Phone: 209-467-6000
Fax: 209-467-6257

Pacific Bell
140 New Montgomery St
San Francisco, CA 94105
www.pacbell.com
Phone: 415-542-9000
Fax: 415-543-7079
TF: 800-303-3000

Pacific Gas & Electric Co
PO Box 770000
San Francisco, CA 94177
www.pge.com
Phone: 415-973-7000
Fax: 415-543-0841
TF: 800-367-7731

Saint Joseph's Health System
1800 N California St
Stockton, CA 95204
Phone: 209-943-2000
Fax: 209-461-5399

San Joaquin County
24 S Hunter St Rm 304
Stockton, CA 95202
www.co.san-joaquin.ca.us
Phone: 209-468-2362

San Joaquin Delta College
5151 Pacific Ave
Stockton, CA 95207
E-mail: questions@sjfcc.cc.ca.us
www.sjdccd.cc.ca.us
Phone: 209-954-5151
Fax: 209-954-5600

San Joaquin General Hospital
PO Box 1020
Stockton, CA 95201
Phone: 209-468-6000
Fax: 209-468-6136

Stockton City Hall
425 N El Dorado St
Stockton, CA 95202
www.ci.stockton.ca.us
Phone: 209-937-8057
Fax: 209-937-8447

Stockton Unified School District
701 N Madison St
Stockton, CA 95202
www.stockton.k12.ca.us
Phone: 209-953-4822
Fax: 209-953-4827

Tri Valley Growers
12667 Alcosta Blvd Suite 500
San Ramon, CA 94583
www.trivalleygrowers.com
Phone: 925-327-6400
Fax: 925-327-6977
TF: 800-227-6746

University of the Pacific
3601 Pacific Ave
Stockton, CA 95211
www.uop.edu
Phone: 209-946-2011
Fax: 209-946-2413
TF: 800-959-2867

Washington Mutual Bank
400 E Main St
Stockton, CA 95290
www.washingtonmutual.com
Phone: 209-460-2888
Fax: 209-460-2531
TF: 800-788-7000

Quality of Living Indicators

Total Crime Index 17,526
(rates per 100,000 inhabitants)

Violent Crime
Murder/manslaughter 27
Forcible rape 116

Robbery....................................1,011
Aggravated assault...........................1,553

Property Crime
Burglary...................................3,180
Larceny theft...............................9,669
Motor vehicle theft..........................1,970

Cost of Living Index....................................121.0
(national average = 100)

Median Home Price.................................$155,600

Education

Public Schools

Stockton Unified School District Phone: 209-953-4822
701 N Madison St Fax: 209-953-4827
Stockton, CA 95202
www.stockton.k12.ca.us

Number of Schools
Elementary.................................. 30
Middle...................................... 4
High.. 4

Student/Teacher Ratio
All Grades............................... 24.1:1

Private Schools

Number of Schools (all grades).................... 28+

Colleges & Universities

California State University Stanislaus Stockton Center Phone: 209-467-5300
612 E Magnolia St Fax: 209-467-5333
Stockton, CA 95202
www.csustan.edu

San Joaquin Delta College Phone: 209-954-5151
5151 Pacific Ave Fax: 209-954-5600
Stockton, CA 95207
E-mail: questions@sjfcc.cc.ca.us
www.sjdccd.cc.ca.us

University of the Pacific Phone: 209-946-2011
3601 Pacific Ave Fax: 209-946-2413
Stockton, CA 95211 TF: 800-959-2867
www.uop.edu

Hospitals

Dameron Hospital Phone: 209-944-5550
525 W Acacia St Fax: 209-461-3108
Stockton, CA 95203

Saint Joseph's Medical Center Phone: 209-943-2000
1800 N California St Fax: 209-461-3300
Stockton, CA 95204
www.sjrhs.org

San Joaquin General Hospital Phone: 209-468-6000
PO Box 1020 Fax: 209-468-6136
Stockton, CA 95201

Transportation

Airport(s)

Sacramento Metropolitan Airport (SMF)
62 miles N of downtown Stockton
(approx 75 minutes)...........................916-929-5411

Mass Transit

SMART Bus
$1.15 Base fare...............................209-943-1111

Rail/Bus

Amtrak Station Phone: 800-872-7245
735 S San Joaquin St
Stockton, CA 95203

Greyhound Bus Station Phone: 209-466-1521
121 S Center St TF: 800-231-2222
Stockton, CA 95202

Utilities

Electricity
Pacific Gas & Electric Co......................800-743-5000
www.pge.com

Gas
Pacific Gas & Electric Co......................800-743-5000
www.pge.com

Water
Stockton Municipal Utilities Dept...............209-937-8750
www.ci.stockton.ca.us/mud

Garbage Collection/Recycling
Stockton Scavenger..........................209-946-5711
Sunrise Sanitation...........................209-466-3604

Telecommunications

Telephone
Pacific Bell...................................800-310-2355
www.pacbell.com

Cable Television
AT & T Cable Services.........................209-473-4955

Internet Service Providers (ISPs)
Community Wide Web of Stockton Inc..........209-473-5950
cwws.net
InReach Internet Communications..............800-446-7322
www.inreach.com

Banks

Bank of Agriculture & Commerce Phone: 209-473-6800
2021 W March Ln Fax: 209-472-1619
Stockton, CA 95207

Bank of America Phone: 209-546-0230
503 W Benjamin Holt Dr Fax: 209-944-5007
Stockton, CA 95207

Bank of Stockton
PO Box 1110
Stockton, CA 95201
Phone: 209-464-8781
Fax: 209-465-5483
TF: 800-399-2265

Bank of the West
4932 Pacific Ave
Stockton, CA 95204
Phone: 209-957-2301
Fax: 209-957-2434

Pacific State Bank
1889 W March Ln
Stockton, CA 95207
Phone: 209-943-7400

Sanwa Bank California
4733-C Quail Lakes Dr
Stockton, CA 95207
Phone: 209-956-8960
Fax: 209-956-9077

Stockton Savings Bank
501 W Weber Ave
Stockton, CA 95203
Phone: 209-948-1675
Fax: 209-547-7773

Union Safe Deposit Bank
317 E Main St
Stockton, CA 95202
Phone: 209-946-5011

Shopping

Lincoln Center
Pacific Ave & Benjamin Holt St
Stockton, CA 95207
www.shoplincolncenter.com
Phone: 209-477-4868

Marketplace The
306 E Main St
Stockton, CA 95202
Phone: 209-943-5222
Fax: 209-943-0240

Sherwood Mall
5308 Pacific Ave
Stockton, CA 95207
Phone: 209-952-6277
Fax: 209-952-6282

Tracy Outlet Center
1005 E Pescadero Ave
Tracy, CA 95376
Phone: 209-833-1895
Fax: 209-833-1894

Weberstown Mall
4950 Pacific Ave
Stockton, CA 95207
Phone: 209-477-0245
Fax: 209-952-4671

Media

Television

KCRA-TV Ch 3 (NBC)
3 Television Cir
Sacramento, CA 95814
www.kcra.com
Phone: 916-446-3333
Fax: 916-441-4050

KMAX-TV Ch 31 (UPN)
500 Media Pl
Sacramento, CA 95815
www.paramountstations.com/KMAX
Phone: 916-925-3100
Fax: 916-921-3050

KOVR-TV Ch 13 (CBS)
2713 KOVR Dr
West Sacramento, CA 95605
www.kovr.com
Phone: 916-374-1313
Fax: 916-374-1304

KTXL-TV Ch 40 (Fox)
4655 Fruitridge Rd
Sacramento, CA 95820
Phone: 916-454-4422
Fax: 916-739-0559

KVIE-TV Ch 6 (PBS)
2595 Capitol Oaks Dr
Sacramento, CA 95833
E-mail: member@kvie.org
www.kvie.org
Phone: 916-929-5843
Fax: 916-929-7367

KXTV-TV Ch 10 (ABC)
400 Broadway
Sacramento, CA 95818
E-mail: kxtv10@kxtv10.com
www.kxtv10.com
Phone: 916-441-2345
Fax: 916-447-6107

Radio

KCJH-FM 90.1 MHz (Rel)
9019 West Ln
Stockton, CA 95210
Phone: 209-477-3690
Fax: 209-477-2762

KCVR-AM 1570 kHz (Span)
6820 Pacific Ave Suite 3A
Stockton, CA 95207
Phone: 209-474-0154
Fax: 209-474-0316

KJAX-AM 1280 kHz (N/T)
3600 Sisk Rd Suite 2B
Modesto, CA 95356
Phone: 209-545-5585
Fax: 209-545-5587

KJOY-FM 99.3 MHz (AC)
6820 Pacific Ave Suite 2
Stockton, CA 95207
Phone: 209-476-1230
Fax: 209-957-1833

KQOD-FM 100.1 MHz (Oldies)
306 E Main St
Stockton, CA 95202
www.greatoldies.com
Phone: 209-462-5367
Fax: 209-462-7959

KSTN-AM 1420 kHz (Oldies)
2171 Ralph Ave
Stockton, CA 95206
www.kstn.net
Phone: 209-948-5786

KSTN-FM 107.3 MHz (Span)
2171 Ralph Ave
Stockton, CA 95206
www.kstn.net/fm.htm
Phone: 209-948-5786

KUOP-FM 91.3 MHz (NPR)
3601 Pacific Ave
Stockton, CA 95211
E-mail: kuop@uop.edu
www.kuop.org
Phone: 209-946-2582
Fax: 209-946-2494
TF: 800-800-5867

KWIN-FM 97.7 MHz (NAC)
6820 Pacific Ave Suite 2
Stockton, CA 95207
www.kwin.com
Phone: 209-476-1230
Fax: 209-957-1833

KWNN-FM 98.3 MHz (CHR)
6820 Pacific Ave Suite 2
Stockton, CA 95207
Phone: 209-476-1230
Fax: 209-957-1833

Attractions

Micke Grove Park, located in nearby Lodi, is a popular entertainment spot in the Stockton area. A variety of attractions, including the San Joaquin Historical Society & Museum, which features agricultural exhibits that detail the history of the area, and a zoo are located within the park. Each June, Stockton hosts the San Joaquin County Fair, which features carnival rides, entertainers, exhibits, and horse racing at Winners Gaming and Sports Emporium. The Stockton Fairgrounds are also the site of the annual Stockton Ag Expo, a major agricultural trade show that includes seminars and displays from hundreds of exhibitors.

Ballet San Joaquin Phone: 209-477-4141
PO Box 70151
Stockton, CA 95267
www.stocktonet.com/community/arts/balletsj/

Children's Museum of Stockton Phone: 209-465-4386
402 W Weber Ave Fax: 209-465-4394
Stockton, CA 95203
E-mail: children@sonnet.com
www.sonnet.com/usr/children/

Clever Planetarium at Delta College Phone: 209-954-5051
5151 Pacific Ave
Stockton, CA 95207
www.sjdccd.cc.ca.us/Planetarium/index.html

Delicato Vineyards Phone: 209-824-3600
12001 S Hwy 99 Fax: 209-824-3400
Manteca, CA 95336
E-mail: wine@delicato.com
www.delicato.com

Delta Drama Music Dance & the Arts Phone: 209-954-5110
5151 Pacific Ave Fax: 209-954-5600
Stockton, CA 95207

Haggin Museum Phone: 209-462-4116
1201 N Pershing Ave
Stockton, CA 95203

John Muir National Historic Site Phone: 925-228-8860
4202 Alhambra Ave Fax: 925-228-8192
Martinez, CA 94553
www.nps.gov/jomu/

Micke Grove Park & Zoo Phone: 209-953-8840
11793 N Micke Grove Rd Fax: 209-331-7271
Lodi, CA 95240
www.mgzoo.com

Oak Ridge Vineyards Phone: 209-369-4758
6100 E Hwy 12 Fax: 209-369-0202
Lodi, CA 95240
www.oakridgevineyards.com

Oakwood Lake Resort Phone: 209-239-2500
874 E Woodard Ave Fax: 209-239-2060
Manteca, CA 95337 TF: 800-626-5253

Phillips Farms Phone: 209-368-7384
4580 W Hwy 12 Fax: 209-368-5801
Lodi, CA 95242

Pixie Woods Children's Fairyland Phone: 209-937-8220
Monte Diablo & Lewis Park Ave
Stockton, CA 95203

San Joaquin County Historical Society & Museum Phone: 209-331-2055
11793 N Micke Grove Rd Fax: 209-331-2057
Lodi, CA 95240
www.sanjoaquinhistory.org

Stockton Chorale Phone: 209-466-0540
PO Box 7711
Stockton, CA 95267
www.stocktonet.com/groups/chorale/index.html

Stockton Civic Theatre Phone: 209-473-2400
2312 Rose Marie Ln Fax: 209-473-1502
Stockton, CA 95207
www.californiamall.com/sct

Stockton Opera Phone: 209-946-2474
3601 Pacific Ave Fax: 209-946-2800
Stockton, CA 95211

Stockton Symphony Phone: 209-951-0196
5151 Pacific Ave Delta College Atherton Auditorium Fax: 209-951-1050
Stockton, CA 95207
E-mail: a-music@inreach.com
www.stocktonsymphony.org

University of the Pacific Drama & Dance Phone: 209-946-2116
3601 Pacific Ave
Stockton, CA 95211

UOP Conservatory of Music Phone: 209-946-2415
3601 Pacific Ave Fax: 209-946-2770
Stockton, CA 95211

Sports Teams & Facilities

Mudville Nine (baseball) Phone: 209-644-1900
Alpine & Sutter Sts Billy Hebert Field Fax: 209-644-1922
Stockton, CA 95204

Winners Gaming & Sports Emporium Phone: 209-466-3589
1658 S Airport Way Fax: 209-466-5141
Stockton, CA 95206

Annual Events

All-American WaterFest (July 4) 209-943-1987
Big Dog Poker Run (early September) 209-369-1041
California Dry Bean Festival (early August)......... 209-835-2131
Cherry Blossom Festival (mid-April)............... 209-953-8800
Eberhardt Bob Memorial Pro-Am Heart Invitational (late July) 209-477-2683
Festa Italiana (early June)........................ 209-368-3077
Lockeford Street Fairs (mid-April)................. 209-727-3142
Lodi Grape Festival & Harvest Fair (mid-September) 209-369-2771
Lodi Spring Wine Show (late March) 209-369-2771
Lodi Street Faires (early May & early October)...... 209-367-7840
San Joaquin County Fair (mid-late June)........... 209-466-5041
Stockton Ag Expo (late January) 209-547-2960
Stockton Asparagus Festival (late April)............ 209-943-1987
Stockton Hot & Cool Jazz Festival (late June) 888-474-7407
Stockton Obon Festival (late July)................ 209-466-6701
Wine on the Waterfront (early September).......... 209-464-7644
Wine Stroll (late September)....................... 209-464-5246
Wine Tasting Event (May)........................ 209-466-0331

Syracuse, New York

***County:* Onondaga**

SYRACUSE is located in central New York State. Major cities within 100 miles include Rochester and Binghamton, New York.

Area (Land) .... 25.1 sq mi
Area (Water) .... 0.6 sq mi
Elevation .... 406 ft
Latitude .... 43-02-27 N
Longitude .... 76-08-38 W
Time Zone .... EST
Area Code 315

Climate

Syracuse has a continental climate that features long, cold winters and mild summers. Winter high temperatures average in the low to mid-30s, and lows average from the mid-teens to around 20 degrees. Frequent heavy snowfall is common in Syracuse, with annual totals averaging 112 inches. Summer days are warm, with highs in the upper 70s and low 80s, while evenings cool down dramatically into the mid- to upper 50s. June, July, and September are the wettest months in Syracuse, while February is the driest.

Average Temperatures & Precipitation

Temperatures

	Jan	Feb	Mar	Apr	May	Jun	Jul	Aug	Sep	Oct	Nov	Dec
High	31	33	43	56	68	77	82	79	72	60	48	35
Low	14	15	25	36	46	54	59	58	51	41	33	21

Precipitation

	Jan	Feb	Mar	Apr	May	Jun	Jul	Aug	Sep	Oct	Nov	Dec
Inches	2.3	2.2	2.8	3.3	3.3	3.8	3.8	3.5	3.8	3.2	3.7	3.2

History

The area that is now Syracuse was once the capital of the Five Nations of the Iroquois. The first Europeans settled there in the mid-1650's. Among this group was Jesuit Father Simon Le Moyne, who first discovered the area's salt springs in 1654. This early settlement was abandoned in 1658 due to conflicts with the Iroquois. More than a century later, in the 1780s, a community called "Webster's Landing" was established, and the area became a major center for salt mining. In 1820, the name of the community was changed to Syracuse (after the city in Sicily), and in 1825 Syracuse was incorporated as a village. That same year, the Erie Canal, which ran through Syracuse, was completed and the village grew quickly as a major port. In 1847, the Village of Syracuse and its neighboring city, Salina, combined to form the City of Syracuse, and the city charter was approved by the New York State legislature.

The salt industry was the mainstay of Syracuse's economy for much of the 19th Century, but in the years following the Civil War, other industries developed in the area as well. Syracuse University was established in 1870, and higher education became an important part of the city's economy. During the latter part of the 19th Century, Syracuse also became a center for culture and the arts—Syracuse is presently home to more than 40 museums and the third-largest opera company in New York State. Throughout the 20th Century, various types of manufacturing, including transportation equipment, furniture, and pharmaceuticals, have created economic opportunities that aided the city's development.

Today, Syracuse is home to 152,000 people, and its location, along with its air and ground transportation network, have made it a major distribution center in the Northeastern United States. Syracuse also remains one of New York State's leading educational, cultural, and industrial centers.

Population

1990 Census 163,860
1998 Estimate 152,215
% Change .... -7.1

Racial/Ethnic Breakdown

White 75.0%
Black 20.3%
Other 5.7%
Hispanic Origin (may be of any race) 2.9%

Age Breakdown

Under 5 years 7.8%
5 to 17 .... 14.8%
18 to 20 .... 8.5%
21 to 24 .... 9.2%
25 to 34 .... 18.3%
35 to 44 .... 12.2%
45 to 54 .... 7.3%
55 to 64 .... 7.1%
65 to 74 .... 7.6%
75+ years 7.3%
Median Age 30.0

Gender Breakdown

Male 46.6%
Female 53.4%

Government

Type of Government: Mayor-Common Council

Syracuse City Administrator
233 E Washington St
Syracuse, NY 13202

Phone: 315-448-8005
Fax: 315-448-8067

Syracuse City Attorney
233 E Washington St Rm 300
Syracuse, NY 13202
Phone: 315-448-8400
Fax: 315-448-8381

Syracuse City Clerk
233 E Washington St Rm 231
Syracuse, NY 13202
Phone: 315-448-8216
Fax: 315-448-8489

Syracuse City Hall
203 City Hall
Syracuse, NY 13202
Phone: 315-448-8005
Fax: 315-448-8067

Syracuse Common Council
233 E Washington St Rm 314
Syracuse, NY 13202
Phone: 315-448-8466
Fax: 315-448-8423

Syracuse Community & Economic Development Dept
233 E Washington St Rm 219
Syracuse, NY 13202
Phone: 315-448-8100
Fax: 315-448-8036

Syracuse Finance Dept
233 E Washington St Rm 122
Syracuse, NY 13202
Phone: 315-448-8350
Fax: 315-471-6024

Syracuse Fire Dept
511 S State St
Syracuse, NY 13202
Phone: 315-473-5525
Fax: 315-422-7766

Syracuse Mayor
203 City Hall
Syracuse, NY 13202
Phone: 315-448-8005
Fax: 315-448-8067

Syracuse Parks Recreation & Youth Programs Dept
412 Spencer St
Syracuse, NY 13204
Phone: 315-473-4330
Fax: 315-428-8513

Syracuse Personnel Dept
201 E Washington St Rm 172
Syracuse, NY 13202
Phone: 315-448-8780
Fax: 315-448-8761

Syracuse Police Dept
511 S State St
Syracuse, NY 13202
Phone: 315-442-5250
Fax: 315-442-5198

Syracuse Public Works Dept
1200 Canal St Ext
Syracuse, NY 13210
Phone: 315-448-2489
Fax: 315-448-8531

Syracuse Treasurer
233 E Washington St Rm 122
Syracuse, NY 13202
Phone: 315-448-8310
Fax: 315-471-6024

Syracuse Water Dept
101 N Beech St
Syracuse, NY 13210
Phone: 315-473-2609
Fax: 315-473-2608

Syracuse Zoning Administration
201 E Washington St Rm 212
Syracuse, NY 13202
Phone: 315-448-8640
Fax: 315-448-8621

Important Phone Numbers

AAA 315-451-1115
American Express Travel 315-474-3393
Driver's License/Vehicle Registration Information 315-336-6790
Emergency 911
Greater Syracuse Assn of Realtors 315-472-3371
Medical Referral 315-424-8118
New York State Dept of Taxation & Finance 800-225-5829
Poison Control Center 315-476-4766
Syracuse Assessment Dept 315-448-8280
Time/Temp 315-474-8481
Voter Registration Information 315-435-3312
Weather 315-786-9969

Information Sources

Greater Syracuse Chamber of Commerce
572 S Salina St
Syracuse, NY 13202
chamber.cny.com
Phone: 315-470-1800
Fax: 315-471-8545

Oncenter Complex
800 S State St
Syracuse, NY 13202
www.oncenter.org
Phone: 315-435-8000
Fax: 315-435-8112

Onondaga County
401 Montgomery St
Syracuse, NY 13202
www.co.onondaga.ny.us
Phone: 315-435-2226
Fax: 315-435-3455

Syracuse Convention & Visitors Bureau
572 S Salina St
Syracuse, NY 13202
www.syracusecvb.org
Phone: 315-470-1910
Fax: 315-471-8545
TF: 800-234-4797

Online Resources

4Syracuse.com
www.4syracuse.com

About.com Guide to Syracuse
syracuse.about.com/local/midlanticus/syracuse

Anthill City Guide Syracuse
www.anthill.com/city.asp?city=syracuse

Area Guide Syracuse
syracuse.areaguides.net

City Knowledge Syracuse
www.cityknowledge.com/ny_syracuse.htm

DigitalCity Syracuse
www.digitalcity.com/syracuse

Excite.com Syracuse City Guide
www.excite.com/travel/countries/united_states/new_york/syracuse

NuWeb Guide to Syracuse
nuwebny.com/syracuse.htm

Sybercuse.com
www.sybercuse.com

Syracuse Area Business Directory
www.cny.com/Business/direct.html

Syracuse New Times
newtimes.rway.com

Area Communities

Communities in Onandaga County with populations greater than 5,000 include:

Baldwinsville
16 W Genesee St
Baldwinsville, NY 13027
Phone: 315-635-3521
Fax: 315-635-7868

Solvay
1100 Woods Rd
Solvay, NY 13209
Phone: 315-468-1679
Fax: 315-468-1473

Economy

With its central location and excellent transportation network, Syracuse has been an important distribution, manufacturing, and trade center for nearly a century. Major U.S. manufacturers with a presence in Syracuse include Carrier Corp. and Bristol-Myers Squibb. Education also still plays a vital role in the city's economy, but its economic base has diversified in recent years. The Syracuse metro area's largest employment sector is currently services, with the health care industry an important part of this sector—four of the area's top employers are health care-related. High-technology manufacturing is another industry that is rapidly expanding in Syracuse—Lockheed Martin, one of the nation's top high-tech companies, employs some 1,800 people at its local facility.

Unemployment Rate 4.3%*
Per Capita Income..........................$22,253*
Median Family Income......................$45,400*

** Information given is for the Syracuse Metropolitan Statistical Area (MSA), which includes Cayuga, Madison, Onondaga, and Oswego counties.*

Principal Industries & Number of Wage Earners

Syracuse MSA* - 1999

Industry	Wage Earners
Construction & Mining	14,100
Finance, Insurance & Real Estate	18,200
Government	60,400
Manufacturing	51,000
Retail Trade	59,200
Services	104,900
Transportation & Public Utilities	20,500
Wholesale Trade	20,100

** Information given is for rhe Syracuse Metropolitan Statistical Area (MSA), which includes Cayuga, Madison, Onondaga, and Oswego counties.*

Major Employers

Carrier Corp Carrier Transicold Div
Carrier Pkwy Bldge TR-20
Syracuse, NY 13221
E-mail: carrier.transicold@carrier.utc.com
www.carrier.transicold.com/carrier/ctdwwwop.nsf
Phone: 315-432-6000
Fax: 315-432-6207

Community-General Hospital of Greater Syracuse
4900 Broad Rd
Syracuse, NY 13215
www.cgh.org
Phone: 315-492-5011
Fax: 315-492-5329

Cooper Industries Inc Crouse-Hinds Div
PO Box 4999
Syracuse, NY 13221
www.crouse-hinds.com
Phone: 315-477-5531
Fax: 315-477-5717

Crouse Hospital
736 Irving Ave
Syracuse, NY 13210
www.crouse.org
Phone: 315-470-7111
Fax: 315-470-2851

Lockheed Martin Naval Electronics & Surveillance Systems Syracuse
PO Box 4840
Syracuse, NY 13221
www.lmco.com/orss
Phone: 315-456-0123
Fax: 315-456-0678

New Venture Gear Inc New Process Gear Div
6600 New Venture Gear Dr
East Syracuse, NY 13057
Phone: 315-432-4000
Fax: 315-432-4451

Niagara Mohawk Power Corp
300 Erie Blvd W
Syracuse, NY 13202
E-mail: customermail@nimo.com
www.nimo.com
Phone: 315-474-1511
Fax: 315-460-1429
TF: 800-932-0301

Saint Joseph's Hospital Health Center
301 Prospect Ave
Syracuse, NY 13203
www.sjhsyr.org
Phone: 315-448-5111
Fax: 315-448-5682
TF: 888-785-6371

State University of New York Upstate Medical University
155 Elizabeth Blackwell St
Syracuse, NY 13210
www.hscsyr.edu
Phone: 315-464-4570
Fax: 315-464-8867

Syracuse University
Syracuse, NY 13244
www.syr.edu
Phone: 315-443-1870
Fax: 315-443-4226

United Parcel Service
PO Box 4909
East Syracuse, NY 13057
www.upsjobs.com
Phone: 800-742-5877

Wegmans Food Markets Inc
PO Box 844
Rochester, NY 14603
www.wegmans.com
Phone: 716-328-2550
Fax: 716-464-4626
TF: 800-934-6267

Welch Allyn Inc
4341 State Street Rd
Skaneateles Falls, NY 13153
E-mail: info@mail.welchallyn.com
www.welchallyn.com
Phone: 315-685-4100
Fax: 315-685-4091
TF: 800-535-6663

Quality of Living Indicators

Total Crime Index....................................8,868
(rates per 100,000 inhabitants)

Violent Crime

Murder/manslaughter	9
Forcible rape	47
Robbery	483
Aggravated assault	900

Property Crime

Burglary	2,016
Larceny theft	4,663
Motor vehicle theft	750

Cost of Living Index....................................106.8
(national average = 100)

Median Home Price...................................$82,100

Education

Public Schools

Syracuse City School District Phone: 315-435-4499
725 Harrison St Fax: 315-435-4023
Syracuse, NY 13210
www.scsd.k12.ny.us

Number of Schools
Elementary.................................. 21
Middle 7
High... 4

Student/Teacher Ratio
All Grades 14.0:1

Private Schools

Number of Schools (all grades)..................... 37

Colleges & Universities

Bryant & Stratton Business Institute Syracuse Phone: 315-472-6603
953 James St Fax: 315-474-4383
Syracuse, NY 13203
www.bryantstratton.com/main/campusdesc/syr.htm

Cazenovia College Phone: 315-655-7000
22 Sullivan St Fax: 315-655-4143
Cazenovia, NY 13035 TF: 800-654-3210
www.cazcollege.edu

Le Moyne College Phone: 315-445-4100
1419 Salt Springs Rd Fax: 315-445-4540
Syracuse, NY 13214 TF: 800-333-4733
www.lemoyne.edu

State University of New York College of Environmental Science & Forestry Phone: 315-470-6500
1 Forestry Dr Fax: 315-470-6933
Syracuse, NY 13210
E-mail: esfweb@mailbox.syr.edu
www.esf.edu

State University of New York College of Environmental Science & Forestry-Ranger School Phone: 315-470-6600
1 Forestry Dr 106 Bray Hall Fax: 315-470-6933
Syracuse, NY 13210 TF: 800-777-7373
E-mail: esfweb@mailbox.syr.edu
www.esf.edu

State University of New York Onondaga Community College Phone: 315-469-7741
4941 Onondaga Rd Fax: 315-492-9208
Syracuse, NY 13215
www.sunyocc.edu

State University of New York Upstate Medical University Phone: 315-464-4570
155 Elizabeth Blackwell St Fax: 315-464-8867
Syracuse, NY 13210
www.hscsyr.edu

Syracuse University Phone: 315-443-1870
Syracuse, NY 13244 Fax: 315-443-4226
www.syr.edu

Hospitals

Community-General Hospital of Greater Syracuse Phone: 315-492-5011
4900 Broad Rd Fax: 315-492-5329
Syracuse, NY 13215
www.cgh.org

Crouse Hospital Phone: 315-470-7111
736 Irving Ave Fax: 315-470-2851
Syracuse, NY 13210
www.crouse.org

Saint Joseph's Hospital Health Center Phone: 315-448-5111
301 Prospect Ave Fax: 315-448-5682
Syracuse, NY 13203 TF: 888-785-6371
www.sjhsyr.org

University Hospital SUNY Health Center at Syracuse Phone: 315-464-5540
750 E Adams St Fax: 315-464-7101
Syracuse, NY 13210

Veterans Affairs Medical Center Phone: 315-476-7461
800 Irving Ave Fax: 315-477-4547
Syracuse, NY 13210 TF: 800-221-2883

Transportation

Airport(s)

Syracuse Hancock International Airport (SYR)
7 miles N of downtown (approx 15 minutes)......315-454-4330

Mass Transit

Centro Bus
$1 Base fare 315-442-3400
OnTrack Railroad
$1.50 Base fare...............................800-367-8724

Rail/Bus

Amtrak Station Phone: 315-477-1152
131 P & C Pkwy Suite 2 TF: 800-872-7245
Syracuse, NY 13208

Greyhound Bus Station Phone: 315-472-4421
130 P & C Pkwy TF: 800-231-2222
Syracuse, NY 13210

Utilities

Electricity
Niagara Mohawk Power Corp 800-932-0301
www.nimo.com

Gas
Niagara Mohawk Power Corp 800-932-0301
www.nimo.com

Water
Syracuse Water Dept 315-448-8238

Garbage Collection/Recycling
Operation Separation Hotline 315-453-2870
Syracuse Trash Pickup 315-448-2489

Telecommunications

Telephone
Verizon Communications 800-722-2300
www.verizon.com

Cable Television
Time Warner Cable 315-437-1401
www.twcny.com

Internet Service Providers (ISPs)
A-Znet.com! Inc 315-234-8966
www.a-znet.com
ATS Internet 315-454-0357
www.atsny.com
Borg Internet Services Inc 315-793-0036
www.borg.com
NetSite Systems Inc 315-446-5555
www.netsitesys.com

Banks

Chase Manhattan Bank
One Lincoln Ctr
Syracuse, NY 13202
Phone: 800-935-9935

Fleet Bank of New York
One Clinton Sq
Syracuse, NY 13221
Phone: 315-426-4100
Fax: 315-426-4207
TF: 800-844-4000

HSBC Bank USA
360 S Warren St
Syracuse, NY 13202
Phone: 315-424-3215
Fax: 315-424-2074

M & T Bank
101 S Salina St
Syracuse, NY 13202
Phone: 315-424-4582
Fax: 315-424-4441

Shopping

Armory Square
247 W Fayette St
Syracuse, NY 13202
Phone: 315-472-5510
Fax: 315-457-5659

Carousel Center
9090 Carousel Center Dr
Syracuse, NY 13290
www.carouselcenter.com
Phone: 315-466-7000
Fax: 315-466-5405

Fayetteville Mall
5351 N Burdick St
Fayetteville, NY 13066
Phone: 315-637-5163
Fax: 315-637-1336

Galleries of Syracuse The
441 S Salina St
Syracuse, NY 13202
Phone: 315-475-5351
Fax: 315-475-4263

Marshall Square Mall
720 University Ave
Syracuse, NY 13210
Phone: 315-422-3234

ShoppingTown Mall
3649 Erie Blvd E
Dewitt, NY 13214
Phone: 315-446-9160
Fax: 315-445-8742

Media

Newspapers and Magazines

Business Records
208 N Townsend St
Syracuse, NY 13203
Phone: 315-472-6911
Fax: 315-422-0040

Central New York Business Journal
231 Walton St
Syracuse, NY 13202
cnybusinessjournal.com/businessjournal/index.html
Phone: 315-472-3104
Fax: 315-478-8166

Herald-Journal*
PO Box 4915
Syracuse, NY 13221
www.syracuse.com
Phone: 315-470-0011
Fax: 315-470-3019
TF: 800-765-4569

Post-Standard*
PO Box 4915
Syracuse, NY 13221
E-mail: linhorst@syracuse.com
www.syracuse.com
Phone: 315-470-0011
Fax: 315-470-3081
TF: 800-765-4569

Syracuse New Times
1415 W Genesee St
Syracuse, NY 13204
E-mail: snt@syracusenewtimes.com
newtimes.rway.com
Phone: 315-422-7011
Fax: 315-422-1721

**Indicates major daily newspapers*

Television

WCNY-TV Ch 24 (PBS)
PO Box 2400
Syracuse, NY 13220
E-mail: wcny_online@wcny.pbs.org
www.wcny.org/tv
Phone: 315-453-2424
Fax: 315-451-8824

WIXT-TV Ch 9 (ABC)
5904 Bridge St
East Syracuse, NY 13057
E-mail: wixt@digitalsherpas.com
www.wixt.com
Phone: 315-446-9999
Fax: 315-446-9283

WNYS-TV Ch 43 (UPN)
1000 James St
Syracuse, NY 13203
Phone: 315-472-6800
Fax: 315-471-8889

WSTM-TV Ch 3 (NBC)
1030 James St
Syracuse, NY 13203
E-mail: wstm@aol.com
Phone: 315-474-5000
Fax: 315-474-5122

WSYT-TV Ch 68 (Fox)
1000 James St
Syracuse, NY 13203
www.fox68wsyt.com
Phone: 315-472-6800
Fax: 315-471-8889

WTVH-TV Ch 5 (CBS)
980 James St
Syracuse, NY 13203
www.wtvh.com
Phone: 315-425-5555
Fax: 315-425-0129

Radio

WAER-FM 88.3 MHz (NPR)
215 University Pl
Syracuse, NY 13244
E-mail: waerfm88@mailbox.syr.edu
web.syr.edu/~waerfm88/
Phone: 315-443-4021
Fax: 315-443-2148
TF: 888-918-3688

WAQX-FM 95.7 MHz (Rock)
1064 James St
Syracuse, NY 13203
www.waqx.com/
Phone: 315-472-0200
Fax: 315-472-1146

WBBS-FM 104.7 MHz (Ctry)
500 Plum St Suite 100
Syracuse, NY 13204
E-mail: b1047@sybercuse.com
www.sybercuse.com/b1047
Phone: 315-448-1047
Fax: 315-474-7879

WCNY-FM 91.3 MHz (NPR)
PO Box 2400
Syracuse, NY 13220
E-mail: wcny_online@wcny.pbs.org
www.wcny.org/classicfm
Phone: 315-453-2424
Fax: 315-451-8824
TF: 800-451-9269

WHEN-AM 620 kHz (Sports)
500 Plum St Suite 100
Syracuse, NY 13204
E-mail: info@sportsmonster.com
www.sybercuse.com/sportsmonster
Phone: 315-472-9797
Fax: 315-472-2323

WJPZ-FM 89.1 MHz (CHR)
316 Waverly Ave
Syracuse, NY 13210
www.z89.com
Phone: 315-443-4689
Fax: 315-443-4379

WMHR-FM 102.9 MHz (Rel)
4044 Makyes Rd
Syracuse, NY 13215
Phone: 315-469-5051
Fax: 315-469-4066

WNTQ-FM 93.1 MHz (CHR)
1064 James St
Syracuse, NY 13203
E-mail: hits93q@aol.com
www.93q.com
Phone: 315-472-0200
Fax: 315-478-5625

WSYR-AM 570 kHz (N/T)
500 Plum St
Syracuse, NY 13204
E-mail: info@wsyr.com
www.sybercuse.com/wsyr
Phone: 315-472-9797
Fax: 315-472-2323

WYYY-FM 94.5 MHz (AC)
500 Plum St
Syracuse, NY 13204
E-mail: y94fm@emi.com
www.sybercuse.com/y94fm
Phone: 315-472-9797
Fax: 315-478-6455

Attractions

More than 40 museums and galleries are located in Syracuse, including the Everson Museum of Art, designed by I.M. Pei. The city's Landmark Theatre, a movie palace built in 1928 featuring ornate Indo-Persian decorations, is listed on the National Register of Historic Places. Syracuse hosts a number of special events throughout the year, including the Great New York State Fair, the longest running state fair in the country, which runs for 12 days and attracts more than 860,000 visitors to Syracuse each summer.

Bristol Omnitheater
500 S Franklin St Museum of Science & Technology
Syracuse, NY 13202
www.most.org/omni_frame.html
Phone: 315-425-9068
Fax: 315-425-9072

Burnet Park Zoo
1 Conservation Pl
Syracuse, NY 13204
Phone: 315-435-8511
Fax: 315-435-8517

Central New York Regional Farmers & Flea Market
2100 Park St
Syracuse, NY 13208
Phone: 315-422-8647
Fax: 315-422-6897

Erie Canal Museum
318 Erie Blvd E
Syracuse, NY 13202
www.syracuse.com/eriecanal
Phone: 315-471-0593
Fax: 315-471-7220

Everson Museum of Art
401 Harrison St
Syracuse, NY 13202
www.everson.org
Phone: 315-474-6064
Fax: 315-474-6943

Fort Stanwix National Monument
112 E Park St
Rome, NY 13440
www.nps.gov/fost/
Phone: 315-336-2090
Fax: 315-339-3966

International Boxing Hall of Fame Museum
1 Hall of Fame Dr
Canastota, NY 13032
www.ibhof.com
Phone: 315-697-7095
Fax: 315-697-5356

Landmark Theatre
362 S Salina St
Syracuse, NY 13202
Phone: 315-475-7980
Fax: 315-475-7993

Mulroy John H Civic Center
421 Montgomery St
Syracuse, NY 13202
www.oncenter.org
Phone: 315-435-8000
Fax: 315-435-8272

Museum of Automobile History
321 N Clinton St
Syracuse, NY 13202
E-mail: info@autolit.com
www.autolit.com/Museum/index.htm
Phone: 315-478-2277
Fax: 315-432-8256

Museum of Science & Technology
500 S Franklin St
Syracuse, NY 13202
www.most.org
Phone: 315-425-9068
Fax: 315-425-9072

Onondaga Park
412 Spencer St
Syracuse, NY 13204
Phone: 315-473-4330
Fax: 315-428-8513

Sainte Marie among the Iroquois Living History Museum
1 Onondaga Lake Pkwy
Liverpool, NY 13088
Phone: 315 453-6767
Fax: 315-453-6762

Salt City Center for the Performing Arts
601 S Crouse Ave
Syracuse, NY 13210
Phone: 315-474-1122
Fax: 315-478-5912

Syracuse Opera
411 Montgomery St Suite 60
Syracuse, NY 13202
Phone: 315-475-5915
Fax: 315-475-6319

Syracuse Stage
820 E Genesee St
Syracuse, NY 13210
web.syr.edu/~syrstage
Phone: 315-443-3275
Fax: 315-443-1408

Syracuse Symphony Orchestra
411 Montgomery St John H Mulroy Civic Ctr
Syracuse, NY 13202
Phone: 315-424-8200
Fax: 315-424-1131
TF: 800-724-3810

Women's Rights National Historical Park
136 Fall St
Seneca Falls, NY 13148
www.nps.gov/wori/
Phone: 315-568-2991
Fax: 315-568-2141

Sports Teams & Facilities

Syracuse Crunch (hockey)
800 S State St Onondaga County War Memorial
Syracuse, NY 13202
www.syracusecrunch.com
Phone: 315-473-4444
Fax: 315-473-4449

Syracuse SkyChiefs (baseball)
1 Tex Simone Dr P & C Stadium
Syracuse, NY 13208
E-mail: baseball@skychiefs.com
skychiefs.com/skychiefs
Phone: 315-474-7833
Fax: 315-474-2658

Annual Events

Arabian Horse Championship (mid-July) 315-487-7711
Autumn in New York Horse Show (late September-early October) 315-487-7711
Downtown Farmer's Market (mid-June-October) 315-422-8284
Empire Appaloosa Show (early August) 315-487-7711
Festival of Centuries (late July) 315-453-6767
Golden Harvest Festival (early September) 315-638-2519
Great American Antiquefest (mid-July) 315-451-7275
Great New York State Fair (late August-early September) 315-487-7711
Holiday Festival of Trees (early December) 315-474-6064
Hot Air Balloon Festival (mid-June) 315-451-7275
International Auto Show Expo (mid-March) 315-487-7711
Lights on the Lake (late November-early January) 315-451-7275
New York Morgan Horse Show (mid-September) 315-487-7711
New York State Rhythm & Blues Fest (mid-July) ... 315-470-1910
Oktoberfest (mid-September) 315-451-7275
Pops in the Park (July) 315-473-4330
Saint Patrick's Day Parade (mid-March) 315-448-8044
Summerfame (mid-July) 315-963-4249
Syracuse Arts and Crafts Festival (mid-July) 315-422-8284
Syracuse International Horse Show (late June) 315-487-7711
Syracuse Jazz Fest (late June) 315-422-8284
Taste of Syracuse (early July) 315-484-1123
Thornden Rose Festival (mid-June) 315-473-4330
Winterfest (mid-February) 315-470-1900
Zoo Boo (late October) 315-435-8511

Tacoma, Washington

***County:* Pierce**

TACOMA is located along Commencement Bay at the southern end of Puget Sound in western Washington State. Major cities within 100 miles include Seattle and Olympia, Washington.

Area (Land) .... 48.0 sq mi
Area (Water).............................. 12.5 sq mi
Elevation.................................... 250 ft
Latitude ....47-25-31 N
Longitude.............................. 122-44-31 W
Time Zone ....PST
Area Code..................................... 253

Climate

Tacoma's temperate climate is moderated by its proximity to the ocean and the mountains. Winters are wet but fairly mild, with average high temperatures in the mid- to upper 40s and lows in the mid- to upper 30s. The average annual snowfall in Tacoma is 14.3 inches. Summers are pleasant, with daytime high temperatures averaging in the low to mid-70s; evenings cool down into the mid-50s. Most precipitation falls in Tacoma between October and April, with December being the wettest month—July is the driest.

Average Temperatures & Precipitation

Temperatures

	Jan	Feb	Mar	Apr	May	Jun	Jul	Aug	Sep	Oct	Nov	Dec
High	45	50	53	57	64	70	75	75	69	60	51	45
Low	35	37	39	41	46	52	55	56	52	46	40	36

Precipitation

	Jan	Feb	Mar	Apr	May	Jun	Jul	Aug	Sep	Oct	Nov	Dec
Inches	5.4	4.0	3.5	2.3	1.7	1.5	0.8	1.1	1.9	3.2	5.8	5.9

History

The Tacoma area was originally inhabited by Native Americans of the Puyallup and Nisqually Tribes. The city's name was derived from the white man's interpretation ("Tahoma") of the name "Tacobet," a Native American phrase meaning "Mother of Waters" that the natives had given to the massive mountain that rose above the valley where the present city lies. The mountain itself was renamed Mount Rainier by Captain George Vancouver, who explored the area in 1792. The first European settlement was founded in the Tacoma area with the establishment of a fur trading post, known as Fort Nisqually, in 1833. Early settlers utilized the natural resources of the land, and the lumber industry thrived, thus aiding the development of the city of Tacoma.

In 1873, Tacoma was selected as the western terminus of the Northern Pacific Railroad, and it became known as Washington's "City of Destiny." While the completion of the railroad in 1883 provided access to other parts of the country, Tacoma's location on Puget Sound's Commencement Bay made the city accessible to the rest of the world, making it an ideal distribution center. In the years that followed, Tacoma experienced phenomenal growth. The city's population soared from approximately 5,000 at the time of its incorporation in 1884 to 50,000 by 1892. However, the Panic of 1893 resulted in a dramatic drop in Tacoma's population, as nearly 13,000 residents left the area that year.

The 20th Century brought new growth to Tacoma, beginning in 1900 with the establishment of the Weyerhaeuser Timber Company. In 1918, three years after the opening of the Panama Canal, Commencement Bay was named as an official U.S. Port of Entry, and the Port of Tacoma has since become the sixth largest container port on the continent. The development of military bases, including Camp Lewis (now Fort Lewis) during World War I and McChord Air Force Base in 1938, also helped to fuel Tacoma's economy. Tacoma is now one of the country's major trade centers, earning it the title "Gateway to the Pacific Rim," with a current population of more than 179,000.

Population

1990 Census 176,664
1998 Estimate.............................179,814
% Change 1.8
2002 Projection 736,071*

Racial/Ethnic Breakdown

White.................................. 78.1%
Black 11.4%
Other.................................. 10.5%
Hispanic Origin (may be of any race) 3.8%

Age Breakdown

Under 5 years............................. 8.3%
5 to 17................................. 17.8%
18 to 20................................. 4.7%
21 to 24................................. 6.5%
25 to 34................................. 18.7%
35 to 44................................. 14.4%
45 to 54................................. 8.6%
55 to 64................................. 7.4%
65 to 74................................. 7.2%
75+ years 6.5%
Median Age...............................31.8

Gender Breakdown

Male.................................. 48.3%
Female................................. 51.7%

* *Information given is for Pierce County.*

Government

Type of Government: Council-Manager

Tacoma City Clerk Phone: 253-591-5171
747 Market St Rm 220 Fax: 253-591-5300
Tacoma, WA 98402

Tacoma City Council Phone: 253-591-5100
747 Market St Suite 1200 Fax: 253-591-5123
Tacoma, WA 98402

Tacoma City Hall Phone: 253-591-5000
747 Market St Fax: 253-591-5300
Tacoma, WA 98402

Tacoma City Manager Phone: 253-591-5130
747 Market St Suite 1200 Fax: 253-591-5123
Tacoma, WA 98402

Tacoma Economic Development Dept Phone: 253-591-5206
747 Market St Suite 900 Fax: 253-591-5232
Tacoma, WA 98402

Tacoma Finance Dept Phone: 253-591-5800
747 Market St Suite 132 Fax: 253-591-5757
Tacoma, WA 98402

Tacoma Fire Dept Phone: 253-591-5737
901 Fawcett Ave Fax: 253-591-5746
Tacoma, WA 98402

Tacoma Human Resources Dept Phone: 253-591-5400
747 Market St Rm 1336 Fax: 253-591-5793
Tacoma, WA 98402

Tacoma Legal Dept Phone: 253-591-5885
747 Market St Rm 1120
Tacoma, WA 98402

Tacoma Mayor Phone: 253-591-5100
747 Market St Suite 1200 Fax: 253-591-5123
Tacoma, WA 98402

Tacoma Metropolitan Parks District Phone: 253-305-1000
4702 S 19th St Fax: 253-305-1005
Tacoma, WA 98405

Tacoma Police Dept Phone: 253-591-5900
930 Tacoma Ave S Fax: 253-591-5949
Tacoma, WA 98402

Tacoma Public Library Phone: 253-591-5666
1102 Tacoma Ave S Fax: 253-591-5606
Tacoma, WA 98402

Tacoma Public Utilities Phone: 253-502-8000
3628 S 35th St Fax: 253-502-8762
Tacoma, WA 98409

Tacoma Public Works Dept Phone: 253-591-5525
747 Market St Suite 420
Tacoma, WA 98402

Important Phone Numbers

AAA 206-448-5353
American Express Travel 206-441-8622
Driver's License Information 253-593-2990
Emergency 911
Medical Referral 206-622-9933
Pierce County Assessor-Treasurer Information Line. . . 253-798-6111
Poison Control Center 800-732-6985
Tacoma-Pierce County Assn of Realtors 253-473-0232
Time/Temp 206-361-8463
Vehicle Registration Information 253-798-3649
Voter Registration Information 253-798-7430
Washington State Revenue Dept. 360-786-6100
Weather 206-464-2000

Information Sources

Better Business Bureau Serving Oregon & Western Washington Phone: 206-431-2222
4800 S 188th St Suite 222 Fax: 206-431-2211
SeaTac, WA 98188
www.seatac.bbb.org

Pierce County Phone: 253-798-3495
930 Tacoma Ave S Fax: 253-798-3428
Tacoma, WA 98402
www.co.pierce.wa.us

Tacoma Convention Center Phone: 253-572-3200
1320 Broadway Plaza Fax: 253-591-4105
Tacoma, WA 98402

Tacoma Dome Arena & Exhibition Hall Phone: 253-272-3663
2727 E D St Fax: 253-593-7620
Tacoma, WA 98421
www.ci.tacoma.wa.us/tdome

Tacoma-Pierce County Chamber of Commerce Phone: 253-627-2175
950 Pacific Ave Suite 300 Fax: 253-597-7305
Tacoma, WA 98402
www.tpchamber.org

Tacoma-Pierce County Visitor & Convention Bureau Phone: 253-627-2836
1001 Pacific Ave Suite 400 Fax: 253-627-8783
Tacoma, WA 98402 TF: 800-272-2662
www.tpctourism.org

Online Resources

About.com Guide to Seattle/Tacoma
seattle.about.com/local/pacnwus/seattle

All Tacoma
www.alltacoma.com

Anthill City Guide Tacoma
www.anthill.com/city.asp?city=tacoma

Area Guide Tacoma
tacoma.areaguides.net

City Knowledge Tacoma
www.cityknowledge.com/wa_tacoma.htm

Dining Northwest Tacoma
www.diningnw.com/cgi-bin/city.pl

Excite.com Tacoma City Guide
www.excite.com/travel/countries/united_states/washington/tacoma

Table in Seattle Dining Guide
www.atable.com

Tacoma Net
www.tacoma.net/

VisitTacoma.com
www.visittacoma.com

Area Communities

Incorporated communities in Pierce County with populations greater than 10,000 include:

Edgewood
2221 Meridian E
Edgewood, WA 98371
Phone: 253-952-3299
Fax: 253-952-3537

Lakewood
10510 Gravelly Lake Dr SW Siote 206
Lakewood, WA 98499
Phone: 253-589-2489
Fax: 253-589-3774

Puyallup
218 W Pioneer
Puyallup, WA 98371
Phone: 253-841-4321
Fax: 253-841-5484

University Place
3715 Bridgeport Way W
University Place, WA 98466
Phone: 253-566-5656
Fax: 253-566-5658

Economy

Tacoma has a diverse economic base that ranges from berry production to national defense. Services is the largest employment sector in Tacoma-Pierce County, with health care being the leading industry—one-third of the top 15 employers are healthcare-related. Government also plays a primary role in Tacoma's economy, with 9 of the top 15 employers being government-related, at the federal, state, and local levels. The U.S. Military alone provides jobs for more than 30,000 Tacoma area residents. Industries that were vital to Tacoma's early economy, including international trade and wood and paper manufacturing, remain important. High-technology is also a growing industry in the Tacoma area.

Unemployment Rate 4.6%*
Per Capita Income.......................... $22,511*
Median Family Income...................... $44,800

** Information given is for Pierce County.*

Principal Industries & Number of Wage Earners

Pierce County - 1998

Industry	Wage Earners
Agriculture, Forestry, & Fishing	2,987
Construction	12,533
Finance, Insurance, & Real Estate	12,336
Government	46,306
Manufacturing	25,016
Mining	166
Retail Trade	45,276
Services	63,757
Transportation & Public Utilities	8,336
Wholesale Trade	11,551

Major Employers

Bethel School District #403
516 176th St E
Spanaway, WA 98387
www.bethel.wednet.edu
Phone: 253-539-6000
Fax: 253-539-6158

Boeing Co
PO Box 3707
Seattle, WA 98124
www.boeing.com
Phone: 206-655-1131
Fax: 206-655-3987

Clover Park School District 400
10903 Gravelly Lake Dr SW
Lakewood, WA 98499
Phone: 253-589-7400
Fax: 253-589-7440

Fort Lewis
Fort Lewis, WA 98433
www.lewis.army.mil
Phone: 253-967-0146
Fax: 253-967-0613

Franciscan Health System
1717 S J St
Tacoma, WA 98405
Phone: 253-591-6958
Fax: 253-591-6941

Good Samaritan Hospital
PO Box 1247
Puyallup, WA 98371
Phone: 253-848-6661
Fax: 253-845-5966

Madigan Army Medical Center
9040 Jackson Ave
Tacoma, WA 98431
Phone: 253-968-1110
Fax: 253-968-1633

McChord Air Force Base
McChord AFB, WA 98438
www.mcchord.af.mil
Phone: 253-984-2621
Fax: 253-984-5824

MultiCare Health System
PO Box 5299
Tacoma, WA 98415
E-mail: information@multicare.com
www.multicare.com
Phone: 253-552-1251
Fax: 253-552-1180

Pierce County
930 Tacoma Ave S
Tacoma, WA 98402
www.co.pierce.wa.us
Phone: 253-798-3495
Fax: 253-798-3428

Puyallup School District
PO Box 370
Puyallup, WA 98371
www.puyallup.k12.wa.us
Phone: 253-841-1301
Fax: 253-841-8650

Puyallup Tribe
2002 E 28th St
Tacoma, WA 98404
Phone: 253-597-6200
Fax: 253-573-7929

Safeway Stores Inc
1121 124th Ave NE
Bellevue, WA 98005
Phone: 425-455-6444
Fax: 425-637-2253

Tacoma City Hall
747 Market St
Tacoma, WA 98402
E-mail: webmgr@ci.tacoma.wa.us
www.ci.tacoma.wa.us
Phone: 253-591-5000
Fax: 253-591-5300

Tacoma School District #10
PO Box 1357
Tacoma, WA 98401
www.tacoma.k12.wa.us
Phone: 253-571-1000
Fax: 253-571-1453

Western State Hospital
9601 Steilacoom Blvd SW
Tacoma, WA 98498
Phone: 253-582-8900
Fax: 253-756-2879

Quality of Living Indicators

Total Crime Index.....................................17,377
(rates per 100,000 inhabitants)

Violent Crime
Murder/manslaughter............................ 8
Forcible rape 155
Robbery..................................... 687
Aggravated assault............................1,503

Property Crime
Burglary 2,923
Larceny theft 9,433
Motor vehicle theft 2,668

Cost of Living Index..................................104.2
(national average = 100)

Average Home Price $131,655

Education

Public Schools

Tacoma School District #10
PO Box 1357
Tacoma, WA 98401
www.tacoma.k12.wa.us
Phone: 253-571-1000
Fax: 253-571-1453

Number of Schools
Elementary................................. 37
Middle 10
High.. 6

Student/Teacher Ratio
All Grades 19.4:1

Private Schools

Number of Schools (all grades).................... 25+

Colleges & Universities

Pacific Lutheran University
12180 Park Ave S
Tacoma, WA 98447
www.plu.edu
Phone: 253-531-6900
Fax: 253-536-5136

Pierce College
9401 Farwest Dr SW
Lakewood, WA 98498
E-mail: info@pierce.ctc.edu
www.pierce.ctc.edu
Phone: 253-964-6500
Fax: 253-964-6427

Tacoma Community College
6501 S 19th St
Tacoma, WA 98466
www.tacoma.ctc.edu
Phone: 253-566-5000
Fax: 253-566-6011

University of Puget Sound
1500 N Warner St
Tacoma, WA 98416
www.ups.edu
Phone: 253-879-3100
Fax: 253-879-3500
TF: 800-396-7191

University of Washington Tacoma
1900 Commerce St
Tacoma, WA 98402
www-uwt.u.washington.edu
Phone: 253-692-4400
Fax: 253-692-4414
TF: 800-736-7750

Hospitals

Good Samaritan Hospital
PO Box 1247
Puyallup, WA 98371
Phone: 253-848-6661
Fax: 253-845-5966

Madigan Army Medical Center
9040 Jackson Ave
Tacoma, WA 98431
Phone: 253-968-1110
Fax: 253-968-1633

Mary Bridge Children's Hospital & Health Center
315 MLK Way
Tacoma, WA 98405
www.multicare.com/marybridge/index.html
Phone: 253-552-1400
Fax: 253-552-1247

Puget Sound Hospital
215 S 36th St
Tacoma, WA 98404
Phone: 253-474-0561
Fax: 253-756-2450

Saint Joseph Medical Center
1717 S 'J' St
Tacoma, WA 98405
Phone: 253-627-4101
Fax: 253-591-6609

Tacoma General Hospital
PO Box 5299
Tacoma, WA 98405
Phone: 253-552-1000
Fax: 253-552-1180

Veterans Affairs Puget Sound Health Care Systems American Lake Div
9600 Veterans Dr SW
Tacoma, WA 98493
Phone: 253-582-8440
Fax: 253-589-4074

Western State Hospital
9601 Steilacoom Blvd SW
Tacoma, WA 98498
Phone: 253-582-8900
Fax: 253-756-2879

Transportation

Airport(s)

Seattle-Tacoma International Airport (SEA)
18 miles NE of downtown Tacoma
(approx 30 minutes) 206-431-4444

Mass Transit

Pierce County Transit
$1 Base fare 253-581-8000

Rail/Bus

Greyhound Bus Station
811 Stewart St
Seattle, WA 98101
Phone: 206-628-5526
TF: 800-231-2222

King Street Amtrak Station
303 S Jackson St
Seattle, WA 98104
Phone: 206-382-4125
TF: 800-872-7245

Utilities

Electricity
Tacoma Public Utilities........................253-502-8000
www.ci.tacoma.wa.us/TPU

Gas
Puget Sound Energy 425-454-2000
www.psechoice.com

Water
Tacoma Public Utilities 253-502-8000
www.ci.tacoma.wa.us/TPU

Garbage Collection/Recycling
Tacoma Recycling 253-565-5955
Tacoma Solid Waste Div 253-591-5544

Telecommunications

Telephone
Qwest 800-244-1111
www.qwest.com

Cable Television
AT & T Cable Services 253-383-4311
www.cable.att.com

Internet Service Providers (ISPs)
Worldstar Internet Technologies 253-566-6800
www.worldstar.net

Banks

Columbia Bank
1102 Broadway Plaza
Tacoma, WA 98402
Phone: 253-305-1900
Fax: 253-272-7103

Heritage Bank
5448 S Tacoma Way
Tacoma, WA 98409
Phone: 253-472-3333
Fax: 253-472-7573

KeyBank NA Tacoma District
1119 Pacific Ave
Tacoma, WA 98411
Phone: 253-305-7750
Fax: 253-305-7951
TF: 800-539-8189

US Bank of Washington NA
6723 S 19th St
Tacoma, WA 98466
Phone: 253-566-3990
Fax: 253-566-3993
TF: 800-872-2657

Washington Mutual Bank
6916 19th St W
Tacoma, WA 98466
Phone: 253-305-5390
Fax: 253-305-5396
TF: 800-756-8000

Westside Community Bank
4922 Bridgeport Way W
Tacoma, WA 98467
Phone: 253-565-9737
Fax: 253-565-9705

Shopping

Freighthouse Square
25th & E 'D' Sts
Tacoma, WA 98421
Phone: 253-305-0678
Fax: 253-627-0270

Lakewood Mall
10509 Gravelly Lake Dr SW Suite 700
Lakewood, WA 98499
Phone: 253-984-6100
Fax: 253-584-7476

South Hill Mall
3500 S Meridian
Puyallup, WA 98373
www.southhill-mall.com
Phone: 253-840-2828
Fax: 253-848-6836

Tacoma Mall
4502 S Steele St
Tacoma, WA 98409
Phone: 253-475-4565
Fax: 253-472-3413

Media

Newspapers and Magazines

Business Examiner
1517 S Fawcett Ave Suite 350
Tacoma, WA 98402
www.businessexaminer.com
Phone: 253-404-0891
Fax: 253-404-0892
TF: 800-540-8322

News Tribune*
1950 S State St
Tacoma, WA 98405
www.tribnet.com
Phone: 253-597-8511
Fax: 253-597-8274

**Indicates major daily newspapers*

Television

KBTC-TV Ch 28 (PBS)
1101 S Yakima Ave
Tacoma, WA 98405
Phone: 253-596-1528
Fax: 253-596-1623

KCPQ-TV Ch 13 (Fox)
1813 Westlake Ave N
Seattle, WA 98109
E-mail: reception@kcpq.com
www.kcpq.com
Phone: 206-674-1313
Fax: 206-674-1777

KCTS-TV Ch 9 (PBS)
401 Mercer St
Seattle, WA 98109
E-mail: viewer@kcts.org
www.kcts.org
Phone: 206-728-6463
Fax: 206-443-6691

KING-TV Ch 5 (NBC)
333 Dexter Ave N
Seattle, WA 98109
E-mail: kingtv@king5.com
www.king5.com
Phone: 206-448-5555
Fax: 206-448-4525

KIRO-TV Ch 7 (CBS)
2807 3rd Ave
Seattle, WA 98121
E-mail: kironews7@kiro-tv.com
www.kirotv.com
Phone: 206-728-7777
Fax: 206-441-4840

KOMO-TV Ch 4 (ABC)
100 4th Ave N
Seattle, WA 98109
www.komotv.com
Phone: 206-443-4000
Fax: 206-443-3422

KSTW-TV Ch 11 (UPN)
PO Box 11411
Tacoma, WA 98411
E-mail: kstw98d@prodigy.com
www.paramountstations.com/KSTW
Phone: 253-572-5789
Fax: 253-272-7581

KTWB-TV Ch 22 (WB)
945 Dexter Ave N
Seattle, WA 98109
www.ktwbtv.com
Phone: 206-282-2202
Fax: 206-281-0207

KVOS-TV Ch 12 (Ind)
1151 Ellis St
Bellingham, WA 98225
www.ackerley.com/broadcast/tv/kvostv12.html
Phone: 360-671-1212
Fax: 360-647-0824
TF: 800-488-5867

KWPX-TV Ch 33 (PAX)
18000 International Blvd Suite 513
SeaTac, WA 98188
www.pax.net/KWPX
Phone: 206-439-0333
Fax: 206-246-5940

Radio

KBSG-AM 1210 kHz (Oldies)
1280 Eastlake Ave E
Seattle, WA 98102
www.kbsg.com
Phone: 206-343-9700
Fax: 206-623-7677

KBSG-FM 97.3 MHz (Oldies)
1820 Eastlake Ave E
Seattle, WA 98102
E-mail: suggestionbox@kbsg.com
www.kbsg.com
Phone: 206-343-9700
Fax: 206-623-7677

KFNK-FM 104.9 MHz (Alt)
4301 S Pine St Suite 444
Tacoma, WA 98409
E-mail: whatithink@funkymonkey1049.fm
www.funkymonkey1049.fm
Phone: 253-671-0195
Fax: 253-671-2484

KHHO-AM 850 kHz (N/T)
950 Pacific Ave Suite 1200
Tacoma, WA 98402
Phone: 253-383-8850
Fax: 253-572-7850

KING-FM 98.1 MHz (Clas)
333 Dexter Ave N Suite 400
Seattle, WA 98109
www.king.org
Phone: 206-448-3981
Fax: 206-448-0928

KIRO-AM 710 kHz (N/T)
1820 Eastlake Ave E
Seattle, WA 98102
www.kiro710.com
Phone: 206-726-7000
Fax: 206-726-5446

KISW-FM 99.9 MHz (CR)
1100 Olive Way Suite 1650
Seattle, WA 98101
www.kisw.com
Phone: 206-285-7625
Fax: 206-215-9355

KIXI-AM 880 kHz (Nost)
3650 131st Ave SE Suite 550
Bellevue, WA 98006
E-mail: am880kixi@aol.com
www.kixi.com
Phone: 425-653-9462
Fax: 425-653-9464

KLSY-FM 92.5 MHz (AC)
3650 131st Ave SE Suite 550
Bellevue, WA 98006
www.klsyradio.com
Phone: 425-454-1540
Fax: 425-455-8849

KMPS-FM 94.1 MHz (Ctry)
1000 Dexter Ave N Suite 100
Seattle, WA 98109
www.kmps.com
Phone: 206-805-0941
Fax: 206-805-0907

KNDD-FM 107.7 MHz (Alt)
1100 Olive Way Suite 1550
Seattle, WA 98101
www.kndd.com
Phone: 206-622-3251
Fax: 206-682-8349

KOMO-AM 1000 kHz (N/T)
1809 7th Ave Suite 200
Seattle, WA 98101
E-mail: comments@komoradio.com
www.komo-am.com
Phone: 206-223-5700
Fax: 206-516-3110

KPLU-FM 88.5 MHz (NPR)
Pacific Lutheran University
Tacoma, WA 98447
E-mail: kplu@plu.edu
www.kplu.org
Phone: 253-535-7758
Fax: 253-535-8332
TF: 800-677-5758

KPLZ-FM 101.5 MHz (AC)
1809 7th Ave Suite 200
Seattle, WA 98101
www.kplz.com
Phone: 206-223-5703
Fax: 206-292-1015

KUBE-FM 93.3 MHz (CHR)
190 Queen Anne Ave N Suite 100
Seattle, WA 98109
www.kube93.com
Phone: 206-285-2295
Fax: 206-286-2376

KWJZ-FM 98.9 MHz (NAC)
3650 131st Ave SE Suite 550
Bellevue, WA 98006
E-mail: jazz@connectexpress.com
www.kwjz.com
Phone: 425-373-5536
Fax: 425-373-5548

Attractions

Point Defiance Park in Tacoma is 700 forested acres of a peninsula and bluff that juts into Puget Sound and includes a zoo and aquarium. The world's largest wood-domed structure, Tacoma Dome Arena and Exhibition Center, is the site of concerts, conventions, trade shows, and other events. Mount Rainier, located 74 miles southeast of Tacoma, can be seen from almost any vantage point in the city.

Art Concepts on Broadway
924 Broadway Plaza
Tacoma, WA 98402
Phone: 253-272-2202
Fax: 253-272-0899
TF: 800-758-7459

Broadway Center for the Performing Arts
901 Broadway
Tacoma, WA 98402
www.broadwaycenter.org
Phone: 253-591-5890
Fax: 253-591-2013

Camp 6 Logging Exhibit Museum
5400 N Pearl St Point Defiance Pk
Tacoma, WA 98407
www.angelady.com/index.html/C01
Phone: 253-752-0047

Children's Museum of Tacoma
936 Broadway
Tacoma, WA 98402
E-mail: cmtstaff@shl.uswest.net
www.ohwy.com/wa/c/childrmt.htm
Phone: 253-627-6031
Fax: 253-627-2436

Commencement Bay Maritime Center
705 Dock St
Tacoma, WA 98402
E-mail: west1943@earthlink.net
home.earthlink.net/~west1943
Phone: 253-272-2750

DuPont Historical Museum
207 Barksdale
Dupont, WA 98327
www.ohwy.com/wa/d/duponthm.htm
Phone: 253-964-8121

Emerald Queen Casino
2102 Alexander Ave
Tacoma, WA 98421
www.emeraldqueen.com
Phone: 253-594-7777
Fax: 253-272-6725
TF: 888-831-7655

Enchanted Parks Inc
36201 Enchanted Pkwy S
Federal Way, WA 98003
E-mail: info@wildwaves.com
www.wildwaves.com
Phone: 253-661-8000
Fax: 253-661-8065

Ezra Meeker Historical Society/Meeker Mansion
312 Spring St
Puyallup, WA 98371
www.meekermansion.org
Phone: 253-848-1770

Fort Lewis Military Museum
Fort Lewis Bldg 4320
Fort Lewis, WA 98433
Phone: 253-967-7206
Fax: 253-967-0837

Fort Nisqually Historic Site
5400 N Pearl St Point Defiance Pk
Tacoma, WA 98407
E-mail: FortNisqually@tacomaparks.com
www.fortnisqually.org
Phone: 253-591-5339
Fax: 253-759-6184

Karpeles Manuscript Library Museum
407 S G St
Tacoma, WA 98405
E-mail: kmuseumtaz@aol.com
www.rain.org/~karpeles/taq.html
Phone: 253-383-2575
Fax: 253-572-6044

Lakewold Gardens
12317 Gravelly Lake Dr SW
Lakewood, WA 98499
E-mail: info@lakewold.org
www.lakewold.org
Phone: 253-584-4106
Fax: 253-584-3021
TF: 888-858-4106

McCord Air Museum
McChord Air Force Base A & 18th Sts
Tacoma, WA 98438
Phone: 253-984-2485
Fax: 253-984-5113

Mount Rainier National Park
Tahoma Woods Star Route
Ashford, WA 98304
www.nps.gov/mora/
Phone: 360-569-2211
Fax: 360-569-2170

Northwest Trek Wildlife Park
11610 Trek Dr E
Eatonville, WA 98328
www.nwtrek.org
Phone: 360-832-6117
Fax: 360-832-6118

Old Town District
N 30th & McCarver Sts
Tacoma, WA 98403
Phone: 253-627-8215

Pacific Rim Bonsai Collection
33663 Weyerhaeuser Way S
Federal Way, WA 98003
E-mail: contactus@wdni.com
www.weyerhaeuser.com/bonsai/
Phone: 253-924-3153
Fax: 253-924-3837
TF: 800-525-5440

Pantages Theater
901 Broadway
Tacoma, WA 98402
Phone: 253-591-5890
Fax: 253-591-2013

Point Defiance Park
5400 N Pearl St
Tacoma, WA 98407
Phone: 253-305-1000
Fax: 253-305-1005

Point Defiance Zoo & Aquarium
5400 N Pearl St
Tacoma, WA 98407
www.pdza.org
Phone: 253-591-5337
Fax: 253-591-5448

Port of Tacoma
PO Box 1837
Tacoma, WA 98401
www.portoftacoma.com
Phone: 253-383-5841
Fax: 253-593-4534

Puget Sound Music Society
825 Center St
Tacoma, WA 98409
Phone: 253-588-1408
Fax: 253-383-1709

Random Modern Gallery
1102 Court D
Tacoma, WA 98402
E-mail: m2ic@halcyon.com
www.m2ic.com
Phone: 253-383-5659
Fax: 253-383-6051

Rialto Theater
9th St-betw Market & Broadway
Tacoma, WA 98402
Phone: 253-591-5890
Fax: 253-591-2013

Ruston Way Waterfront
3427 Ruston Way
Tacoma, WA 98402
Phone: 253-627-2836

Seymour WW Botanical Conservatory
316 S 'G' St Wright Pk
Tacoma, WA 98405
Phone: 253-591-5330

Shanaman Sports Museum of Tacoma
2727 E D St Tacoma Dome
Tacoma, WA 98421
E-mail: jnw@juno.com
www.tacomasports.com/museum.htm
Phone: 253-272-3663

Sprinker Recreation Center
14824 S 'C' St
Tacoma, WA 98444
Phone: 253-798-4000
Fax: 253-798-4024

Steilacoom Historical Museum
112 Main St
Steilacoom, WA 98388
www.ohwy.com/wa/s/steilahm.htm
Phone: 253-584-4133

Steilacoom Tribal Cultural Museum
1515 Lafayette St
Steilacoom, WA 98388
www.ohwy.com/wa/t/tribaccm.htm
Phone: 253-584-6308
Fax: 253-584-0224

Tacoma Actors Guild
915 Broadway 6th Fl
Tacoma, WA 98401
Phone: 253-272-2145
Fax: 253-272-3358

Tacoma Art Museum
1123 Pacific Ave
Tacoma, WA 98402
E-mail: info@tamart.org
www.tamart.org/
Phone: 253-272-4258
Fax: 253-627-1898

Tacoma Dome Arena & Exhibition Hall
2727 E D St
Tacoma, WA 98421
www.ci.tacoma.wa.us/tdome
Phone: 253-272-3663
Fax: 253-593-7620

Tacoma Little Theatre
210 N 'I' St
Tacoma, WA 98403
E-mail: tlt@nwrain.com
webforce.nwrain.com/tlthome/
Phone: 253-272-2281
Fax: 253-272-3972

Tacoma Master Chorale Phone: 253-565-6867
7116 6th Ave Tacoma Musical Playhouse
Tacoma, WA 98406

Tacoma Musical Playhouse Phone: 253-565-6867
7116 6th Ave Fax: 253-564-7863
Tacoma, WA 98406
www.tmp.org

Tacoma Nature Center Phone: 253-591-6439
1919 S Tyler Fax: 253-593-4152
Tacoma, WA 98405
E-mail: tnc@tacomaparks.com
www.tacomaparks.com

Tacoma Philharmonic Phone: 253-591-5894
901 Broadway Pantages Theater Fax: 253-591-0537
Tacoma, WA 98402

Tacoma Symphony Phone: 253-272-7264
727 Commerce St Suite 210 Fax: 253-272-1676
Tacoma, WA 98402 TF: 888-274-1376

Tacoma's Landmark Convention Center & Temple Theatre Phone: 253-272-2042
47 Saint Helens Ave Fax: 253-272-3793
Tacoma, WA 98402

Union Station Phone: 253-572-9310
1123 Pacific Ave
Tacoma, WA 98402

Washington State History Museum Phone: 253-272-3500
1911 Pacific Ave Fax: 253-272-9518
Tacoma, WA 98402 TF: 888-238-4373
E-mail: slile@wshs.wa.gov
www.wshs.org/text/mus_hist.htm

Sports Teams & Facilities

Cheney Stadium Phone: 253-752-7707
2502 S Tyler St Fax: 253-752-7135
Tacoma, WA 98405
E-mail: tacomapcl@aol.com

Emerald Downs Phone: 253-288-7000
2300 Emerald Downs Dr Fax: 253-288-7710
Auburn, WA 98001 TF: 888-931-8400
E-mail: lauram@emdowns.com
www.emdowns.com

Tacoma Rainiers (baseball) Phone: 253-752-7707
2502 S Tyler St Cheney Stadium Fax: 253-752-7135
Tacoma, WA 98405
www.rainiers.com

Tacoma Sabercats (hockey) Phone: 253-627-2673
1111 Fawcett Ave Suite 204 Fax: 253-573-1009
Tacoma, WA 98402
E-mail: colarusso@w-link.com
www.sabercats.com

Annual Events

Art a La Carte (early July) .253-627-2836
Candlelight Tour of Fort Nisqually (early October) .253-591-5339
Civil War Encampment & Battle Demonstration (late May) .800-260-5997
Daffodil Festival Grand Floral Parade (mid-April) .253-627-6176
Ethnic Fest (late July) .253-798-7590
Fantasylights (late November-early January) .253-798-4176
Festival of Trees (early December) .253-552-1368
First Night Tacoma (December 31) .253-798-7205
Floral Daffodil Marine Regatta (mid-April) .253-752-3555
Fort Nisqually Brigade Encampment (early August) .253-591-5339
Freedom Fair (early July) .253-761-9433
Gig Harbor Peninsula on Parade (early June) .253-851-6865
Holiday Parade & Tree Lighting (early December) .253-627-2175
Isia Spring Fever Skating Competition (mid-April) .253-798-4000
Jesus of Nazareth Drama (July-August) .253-475-6454
Junior Daffodil Parade (mid-April) .253-756-9020
Mardi Gras at Freighthouse Square (early February) .253-305-0678
Maritime Fest (mid-September) .253-383-2429
Meeker Days Hoedown & Blue Grass Festival (mid-June) .253-840-2631
Norwegian Heritage Festival (mid-May) .206-242-5289
Pierce County Fair (mid-August) .253-847-4754
Puyallup Spring Fair (mid-April) .253-841-5045
Queen Victoria's Birthday Celebration (late May) .253-591-5339
Scandinavian Days Festival (early October) .253-845-5446
Seafirst Freedom Fair & Fireworks Spectacular (July 4) .253-761-9433
Sprint PCS Taste of Tacoma (early July) .206-232-2982
Tacoma Farmers Market (June-September) .253-272-7077
Tacoma Old Town Blues Festival (mid-July) .253-627-1290
Tacoma Rail Fan Days (late April-early May) .253-627-2836
Tacoma Third Thursday Artwalk (early January-late December) .253-591-5341
Wednesday Night Concerts in the Park (early July-late August) .253-581-1076
Western Washington Fair (early September) .253-841-5045
WIAA Spring Fest (late May) .425-746-7102
Wintergrass Bluegrass Festival (late February) .253-926-4164
Zoolights (late December-early January) .253-591-5337

Tallahassee, Florida

County: **Leon**

TALLAHASSEE is located in the "panhandle" of northern Florida. Major cities within 200 miles include Pensacola and Jacksonville, Florida; Valdosta, Georgia; and Dothan, Alabama.

Area (Land) .... 63.3 sq mi
Area (Water)............................... 1.1 sq mi
Elevation...................................... 188 ft
Latitude ....30-42-90 N
Longitude............................... 84-26-33 W
Time Zone ....EST
Area Code...................................... 850

Climate

Tallahassee has a mild climate that features four seasons. The area's subtropical summers are hot and humid, with average high temperatures in the low 90s and lows near 70 degrees. Summer is also the rainy season in Tallahassee, with July being the wettest month. Winters are cool, with average highs in the mid-60s and lows near 40. Temperatures occasionally dip below freezing in Tallahassee, but snowfall is rare, occurring once every three or four years on average.

Average Temperatures & Precipitation

Temperatures

	Jan	Feb	Mar	Apr	May	Jun	Jul	Aug	Sep	Oct	Nov	Dec
High	63	66	74	80	86	91	91	91	89	82	73	66
Low	38	40	47	52	61	69	71	71	68	56	46	40

Precipitation

	Jan	Feb	Mar	Apr	May	Jun	Jul	Aug	Sep	Oct	Nov	Dec
Inches	4.8	5.6	6.2	3.7	4.8	6.9	8.8	7.5	5.6	2.9	3.9	5.0

History

The first Europeans arrived in the area known today as Tallahassee in 1528 on an expedition led by Panfilo de Narvaez. The following year the Spanish explorer Hernando de Soto and his men celebrated the first Christmas in the New World as they wintered in the area. In 1633 a mission chain was established from Saint Augustine to Tallahassee by Spanish missionaries. The native Apalachee Indians, who had inhabited northern Florida as early as 500 A.D., remained in the region until the early 1700s, when warfare and disease brought about by contact with Spaniards virtually destroyed the population. The remaining Apalachees fled the area, leading to the city's present name—Tallahassee is an Appalachee word meaning "old fields" or "abandoned fields."

During the 1700s, Creek Indians and other tribes who came to be known collectively as "Seminoles" (a name meaning "runaways") began arriving in the area. The Seminoles were eventually forced out by General Andrew Jackson in 1818. The following year, the United States gained possession of Florida from Spain and in 1822 the Territory of Florida was created. Florida's two major cities, Pensacola and Saint Augustine, competed for the designation of State Capital, but the territorial legislature established Leon County midway between the two cities in 1824 and named Tallahassee the county seat as well as the state capital. A log cabin served as Florida's first capitol building and Tallahassee was incorporated as a city in 1825.

During Tallahassee's early years, the city grew not only as a governmental center but also as an agricultural center. Many plantations were established in the area during the 19th Century, with cotton, corn, and sweet potatoes the primary crops. In 1834, the construction of the Tallahassee-St. Marks railroad, which is reported to be among the nation's oldest, also helped spur growth in the area. In 1845, Florida became the nation's 27th state. In 1851 the Seminary West of the Suwannee was established in Tallahassee; the seminary would later become the Florida State College for Women and, eventually, Florida State University (FSU). During the Civil War, Tallahassee made history by becoming the only Confederate capital east of the Mississippi River that was not captured by the Union.

Home to two of Florida's 10 state universities, FSU and Florida A&M University, as well as Tallahassee Community College, the state capital continues to grow and thrive not only as a political center, but also as a major center for education. Today, with a population exceeding 136,000, Tallahassee is Florida's eighth largest city as well as the fifth fastest-growing city in the state.

Population

1990 Census 124,773
1998 Estimate.............................136,628
% Change 9.5
2010 Projection 170,900

Racial/Ethnic Breakdown

White.................................... 68.2%
Black 29.1%
Other..................................... 2.7%
Hispanic Origin (may be of any race) 3.0%

Age Breakdown

Under 5 years.............................. 5.5%
5 to 17.................................. 13.5%
18 to 20................................. 12.9%
21 to 24................................. 13.9%
25 to 34................................. 17.9%
35 to 44................................. 13.7%
45 to 54.................................. 7.8%
55 to 64.................................. 5.9%
65 to 74.................................. 5.2%
75+ years 3.6%
Median Age................................27.1

Gender Breakdown
Male 47.6%
Female 52.4%

Government

Type of Government: Commission-Manager

Tallahassee City Attorney
300 S Adams St
Tallahassee, FL 32301
Phone: 850-891-8554
Fax: 850-891-8973

Tallahassee City Commission
300 S Adams St
Tallahassee, FL 32301
Phone: 850-891-8181
Fax: 850-891-8542

Tallahassee City Hall
300 S Adams St
Tallahassee, FL 32301
Phone: 850-891-0010
Fax: 850-891-8540

Tallahassee City Manager
300 S Adams St
Tallahassee, FL 32301
Phone: 850-891-8200
Fax: 850-891-8669

Tallahassee City Treasurer-Clerk
300 S Adams St
Tallahassee, FL 32301
Phone: 850-891-8130
Fax: 850-891-8210

Tallahassee Economic Development Dept
300 S Adams St
Tallahassee, FL 32301
Phone: 850-891-8625
Fax: 850-891-8886

Tallahassee Fire Dept
327 N Adams St
Tallahassee, FL 32301
Phone: 850-891-6600
Fax: 850-891-6606

Tallahassee Human Resources Dept
300 S Adams St
Tallahassee, FL 32301
Phone: 850-891-8214
Fax: 850-891-8067

Tallahassee Mayor
300 S Adams St
Tallahassee, FL 32301
Phone: 850-891-8181
Fax: 850-891-8542

Tallahassee Parks & Recreation Dept
912 Myers Park Dr
Tallahassee, FL 32301
Phone: 850-891-3824
Fax: 850-891-3850

Tallahassee Planning Dept
300 S Adams St
Tallahassee, FL 32301
Phone: 850-891-8600
Fax: 850-891-8734

Tallahassee Police Dept
234 E 7th Ave
Tallahassee, FL 32303
Phone: 850-891-4341
Fax: 850-891-4242

Tallahassee Public Works Dept
300 S Adams St
Tallahassee, FL 32301
Phone: 850-891-8197
Fax: 850-891-8733

Tallahassee TalTran (Transit System)
555 Appleyard Dr
Tallahassee, FL 32303
Phone: 850-891-5200
Fax: 850-891-5385

Tallahassee Water Utilities
300 S Adams St Box B-26
Tallahassee, FL 32301
Phone: 850-891-6129
Fax: 850-891-6170

Important Phone Numbers

AAA 850-878-6000
American Express Travel 850-224-6464
Driver's License Information 850-487-4303
Emergency 911
Florida Dept of Revenue Taxpayer Services 850-488-6800
HotelDocs 800-468-3537
Leon County Property Appraiser 850-488-6102
Leon County Tax Collector 850-488-4381
Poison Control Center 800-282-3171
Tallahassee Board of Realtors 850-224-7713
Time/Temp 850-584-3333
Vehicle Registration Information 850-488-7856
Voter Registration Information 850-488-1350
Weather 850-422-1212

Information Sources

Leon County
301 S Monroe St
Tallahassee, FL 32301
www.co.leon.fl.us
Phone: 850-488-4710
Fax: 850-414-5700

Tallahassee Area Convention & Visitors Bureau
106 E Jefferson St
Tallahassee, FL 32301
www.co.leon.fl.us/visitors/index.htm
Phone: 850-413-9200
Fax: 850-487-4621
TF: 800-628-2866

Tallahassee Area Visitor Information Center
401 S Monroe St New Capitol Bldg
Tallahassee, FL 32301
Phone: 850-413-9200
Fax: 850-487-4621
TF: 800-628-2866

Tallahassee Chamber of Commerce
100 N Duval St
Tallahassee, FL 32301
www.talchamber.com/
Phone: 850-224-8116
Fax: 850-561-3860

Tallahassee-Leon County Civic Center
505 W Pensacola St
Tallahassee, FL 32301
www.tlccc.org
Phone: 850-487-1691
Fax: 850-222-6947
TF: 800-322-3602

Online Resources

4Tallahassee.com
www.4tallahassee.com

About.com Guide to Tallahassee
tallahassee.about.com/citiestowns/southeastus/tallahassee

Anthill City Guide Tallahassee
www.anthill.com/city.asp?city=tallahassee

Area Guide Tallahassee
tallahassee.areaguides.net

City Knowledge Tallahassee
www.cityknowledge.com/fl_tallahassee.htm

Excite.com Tallahassee City Guide
www.excite.com/travel/countries/united_states/florida/tallahassee

InTallahassee.com
www.intallahassee.com

Tallahassee Freenet
www.freenet.scri.fsu.edu/

Tallahassee Online
www.tallahasseeonline.com/tlh/index.html

Tastebuds! Internet Guide to Tallahassee Food & Drink
www.tastebuds.com

Area Communities

Tallahassee is the only incorporated city in Leon County. Communities in the Tallahassee Metropolitan Statistical Area (which includes Gadsden County) with populations greater than 10,000 include:

Chattahoochee
22 Jefferson St
Chattahoochee, FL 32324
Phone: 850-663-4046
Fax: 850-663-2456

Gretna
PO Drawer 220
Gretna, FL 32332
Phone: 850-856-5257
Fax: 850-856-9454

Havana
PO Box 1068
Havana, FL 32333
Phone: 850-539-6493

Midway
PO Box 438
Midway, FL 32343
Phone: 850-574-2355
Fax: 850-574-0633

Quincy
404 W Jefferson St
Quincy, FL 32351
Phone: 850-627-7681
Fax: 850-875-3733

Economy

Government dominates Tallahassee's economic base. Approximately 40% of Leon County's workforce is government-employed at the federal, state and local levels. The State of Florida is the area's single largest employer, providing jobs for more than 22,000 people. Since the early 1990s, the chamber of commerce and local economic development corporations have been striving to attract new businesses and industries to the Capital Region to diversify the area's economic base. Services and retail trade are currently the Tallahassee area's second and third largest employment sectors.

Unemployment Rate 3.0%*
Per Capita Income.......................... $26,453*
Median Family Income...................... $54,000*

** Information given is for Leon County.*

Principal Industries & Number of Wage Earners

Tallahassee MSA* - 1998

Construction	6,000
Finance, Insurance, & Real Estate	6,300
Government	58,600
Manufacturing	4,900
Retail Trade	26,400
Services & Miscellaneous	41,700
Transportation & Public Utilities	4,100
Wholesale Trade	4,300

** Information given is for the Tallahassee Metropolitan Statistical Area (MSA), which includes Leon and Gadsden counties.*

Major Employers

Florida A & M University
Tallahassee, FL 32307
www.famu.edu
Phone: 850-599-3000
Fax: 850-599-3069

Florida State University
600 W College Ave
Tallahassee, FL 32306
E-mail: admissions@mailer.fsu.edu
www.fsu.edu
Phone: 850-644-2525
Fax: 850-644-0170

Leon County
301 S Monroe St
Tallahassee, FL 32301
www.co.leon.fl.us
Phone: 850-488-4710
Fax: 850-414-5700

Leon County Schools
2757 W Pensacola St
Tallahassee, FL 32310
www.leon.k12.fl.us
Phone: 850-487-7100
Fax: 850-487-7141

Leon County Sheriff's Office
PO Box 727
Tallahassee, FL 32302
lcso.leonfl.org
Phone: 850-922-3300
Fax: 850-922-3337

McDonald's
1201 Hays St
Tallahassee, FL 32301
www.mcdonalds.com/corporate/careers
Phone: 850-222-2359
Fax: 850-222-4717

McKenzie Tank Lines Inc
PO Box 1200
Tallahassee, FL 32302
www.mckenzietank.com
Phone: 850-576-1221
Fax: 850-574-2351
TF: 800-828-6495

Publix Super Markets
1940-79 N Monroe St
Tallahassee, FL 32303
www.publix.com/ap_employment_information.htm
Phone: 850-385-5121
Fax: 850-385-4891

Tallahassee City Hall
300 S Adams St
Tallahassee, FL 32301
www.state.fl.us/citytlh
Phone: 850-891-0010
Fax: 850-891-8540

Tallahassee Community College
444 Appleyard Dr
Tallahassee, FL 32304
E-mail: enroll@mail.tallahassee.cc.fl.us
www.tallahassee.cc.fl.us
Phone: 850-488-9200
Fax: 850-921-0653

Tallahassee Community Hospital
2626 Capital Medical Blvd
Tallahassee, FL 32308
www.ctch.com
Phone: 850-656-5000
Fax: 850-656-5198

Tallahassee Memorial Hospital
1300 Miccosukee Rd
Tallahassee, FL 32308
www.tmh.org
Phone: 850-681-1155
Fax: 850-841-6000

Tallahassee US Post Office
2800 S Adams St
Tallahassee, FL 32301
Phone: 850-216-4248
Fax: 850-942-6307

Tallahassee-Leon County Civic Center
505 W Pensacola St
Tallahassee, FL 32301
www.tlccc.org
Phone: 850-487-1691
Fax: 850-222-6947
TF: 800-322-3602

Wal-Mart
3535 Apalachee Pkwy
Tallahassee, FL 32311
www.walmartstores.com
Phone: 850-878-9868
Fax: 850-878-4935

Quality of Living Indicators

Total Crime Index....................................12,905
(rates per 100,000 inhabitants)

Violent Crime
Murder/manslaughter............................ 5
Forcible rape 142
Robbery...................................... 469
Aggravated assault............................1,336

Property Crime
Burglary 2,222
Larceny theft 7,808
Motor vehicle theft 923

Cost of Living Index....................................96.2
(national average = 100)

Median Home Price.................................$117,800

Education

Public Schools

Leon County Schools
2757 W Pensacola St
Tallahassee, FL 32310
www.leon.k12.fl.us
Phone: 850-487-7100
Fax: 850-487-7141

Number of Schools
Elementary................................. 23
Middle 10
High.. 4

Student/Teacher Ratio
All Grades 16.9:1

Private Schools

Number of Schools (all grades).................... 17+

Colleges & Universities

Florida A & M University
Tallahassee, FL 32307
www.famu.edu
Phone: 850-599-3000
Fax: 850-599-3069

Florida State University
600 W College Ave
Tallahassee, FL 32306
E-mail: admissions@mailer.fsu.edu
www.fsu.edu
Phone: 850-644-2525
Fax: 850-644-0170

Tallahassee Community College
444 Appleyard Dr
Tallahassee, FL 32304
E-mail: enroll@mail.tallahassee.cc.fl.us
www.tallahassee.cc.fl.us
Phone: 850-488-9200
Fax: 850-921-0653

Hospitals

Tallahassee Community Hospital
2626 Capital Medical Blvd
Tallahassee, FL 32308
www.ctch.com
Phone: 850-656-5000
Fax: 850-656-5198

Tallahassee Memorial Hospital
1300 Miccosukee Rd
Tallahassee, FL 32308
www.tmh.org
Phone: 850-681-1155
Fax: 850-841-6000

Transportation

Airport(s)

Tallahassee Regional Airport (TLH)
8 miles SW of downtown (approx 15 minutes) 850-891-7800

Mass Transit

Old Town Trolley
Free 850-413-9200
Taltran
$.75 Base fare.................................850-891-5200

Rail/Bus

Amtrak Station
918 1/2 Railroad Ave
Tallahassee, FL 32310
Phone: 850-224-2779

Greyhound/Trailways Bus Station
112 W Tennessee St
Tallahassee, FL 32301
Phone: 850-222-4240

Utilities

Electricity
City of Tallahassee Utilities 805-891-8120

Gas
City of Tallahassee Utilities 805-891-8120

Water
City of Tallahassee Utilities 805-891-8120

Garbage Collection/Recycling
City of Tallahassee Utilities 805-891-8120

Telecommunications

Telephone
Sprint 800-339-1811
www.sprint.com

Cable Television
Comcast Cable...............................850-574-4000

Internet Service Providers (ISPs)
Florida Digital Turnpike 850-222-5200
www.fdt.net
Tallahassee Free-Net 850-921-0822
www.freenet.tlh.fl.us
Vistech Communications Inc 850-942-0388
www.vistech.net

Banks

Amsouth Bank
201 S Monroe St
Tallahassee, FL 32301
Phone: 850-222-3727
Fax: 850-222-5545

Capital City Bank
2111 N Monroe St
Tallahassee, FL 32303
Phone: 850-671-0300
Fax: 850-878-9135

First Bank of Tallahassee
1997 Capital Cir NE
Tallahassee, FL 32308
Phone: 850-668-4034
Fax: 850-385-7427

NationsBank
315 S Calhoun St
Tallahassee, FL 32301
Phone: 850-561-1876
Fax: 850-561-1740
TF: 800-299-2265

SunTrust Bank
3522 Thomasville Rd
Tallahassee, FL 32308
Phone: 850-298-5111
Fax: 850-298-5094

Wakulla Bank
2101 Capital Cir NE
Tallahassee, FL 32308
Phone: 850-386-2222
Fax: 850-385-8231

Shopping

Downtown Tallahassee
106 E Jefferson St
Tallahassee, FL 32301
Phone: 850-413-9200
Fax: 850-487-4621

Governor's Square
1500 Apalachee Pkwy
Tallahassee, FL 32301
Phone: 850-671-4636
Fax: 850-942-0136

Parkway Center
Apalachee Pkwy & Magnolia Dr
Tallahassee, FL 32301

Pedler's Furniture Hospital
1114 Carriage Rd
Tallahassee, FL 32312
Phone: 850-580-2552

Tallahassee Mall
2415 N Monroe St
Tallahassee, FL 32303
Phone: 850-385-7145
Fax: 850-383-1155

Village Commons
1400 Village Square Blvd
Tallahassee, FL 32312

Media

Newspapers and Magazines

Tallahassee Democrat*
277 N Magnolia Dr
Tallahassee, FL 32301
E-mail: letters@freenet.fsu.edu
www.tdo.com
Phone: 850-599-2100
Fax: 850-599-2295
TF: 800-777-2154

Tallahassee Magazine
1932 Miccosukee Rd
Tallahassee, FL 32308
Phone: 850-878-0554
Fax: 850-656-1871

**Indicates major daily newspapers*

Television

WCTV-TV Ch 6 (CBS)
County Rd 12
Tallahassee, FL 32312
www.wctv6.com
Phone: 850-893-6666
Fax: 850-668-3851

WFSU-TV Ch 11 (PBS)
1600 Red Barber Plaza
Tallahassee, FL 32310
E-mail: wfsu-tv@mailer.fsu.edu
www.fsu.edu/~wfsu_tv/
Phone: 850-487-3170
Fax: 850-487-3093

WTLH-TV Ch 49 (Fox)
950 Commerce Blvd
Midway, FL 32343
E-mail: fox49@fox49.com
www.fox49.com
Phone: 850-576-4990
Fax: 850-576-0200

WTWC-TV Ch 40 (NBC)
8440 Deerlake Rd
Tallahassee, FL 32312
Phone: 850-893-4140
Fax: 850-893-6974

WTXL-TV Ch 27 (ABC)
7927 Thomasville Rd
Tallahassee, FL 32312
www.wtxl.com
Phone: 850-893-3127
Fax: 850-668-1460

Radio

WAIB-FM 103.1 MHz (Ctry)
PO Box 13909
Tallahassee, FL 32317
www.waib103.com
Phone: 850-386-8004
Fax: 850-422-1897

WBZE-FM 98.9 MHz (AC)
109B Ridgeland Rd
Tallahassee, FL 32312
www.989breeze.com
Phone: 850-385-0989
Fax: 850-224-8329

WCVC-AM 1330 kHz (Rel)
117 1/2 Henderson Rd
Tallahassee, FL 32312
E-mail: wcvc@webtv.net
www.mercies.com/wcvc
Phone: 850-386-7133
Fax: 850-386-2138

WFSQ-FM 91.5 MHz (Clas)
1600 Red Barber Plaza
Tallahassee, FL 32310
E-mail: wfsqfm@freenet.tlh.fl.us
www.fsu.edu/~wfsu_fm/915.html
Phone: 850-487-3086
Fax: 850-487-3293

WFSU-FM 88.9 MHz (NPR)
1600 Red Barber Plaza
Tallahassee, FL 32310
E-mail: wfsufm@freenet.tlh.fl.us
www.fsu.edu/~wfsu_fm/
Phone: 850-487-3086
Fax: 850-487-3093

WHBX-FM 96.1 MHz (Urban)
109-B Ridgeland Rd
Tallahassee, FL 32312
Phone: 850-385-1156
Fax: 850-224-8329

WNLS-AM 1270 kHz (Sports)
325 John Knox Rd Bldg G-200
Tallahassee, FL 32303
www.wnls.com
Phone: 850-386-6143
Fax: 850-383-0748

WOKL-FM 100.7 MHz (Oldies)
325 John Knox Rd Suite G
Tallahassee, FL 32303
www.wokl.com
Phone: 850-422-3107
Fax: 850-383-0747

WTNT-FM 94.9 MHz (Ctry)
325 John Knox Rd Bldg E-200
Tallahassee, FL 32303
www.wtntfm.com
Phone: 850-386-6143
Fax: 850-385-8789

WXSR-FM 101.5 MHz (Alt)
325 John Knox Rd Suite G
Tallahassee, FL 32303
www.x1015.com
Phone: 850-422-3107
Fax: 850-514-4440
TF: 877-422-3107

Attractions

The State Capitol Building in Tallahassee houses an art gallery, and its observation deck provides a panoramic view of the city. The adjacent Historic Old Capitol has been restored to its 1902 appearance, with red-striped awnings and a stained-glass dome. The two major educational institutions in Tallahassee are Florida State University, home of "Seminole" athletics, and Florida A&M University. The Black Archive Research Center and Museum at Florida A&M has an extensive collection of African-American artifacts. Fifteen miles south of Tallahassee, Wakulla Springs State Park's glass-bottom boat and riverboat cruises provide visitors with the opportunity to see alligators, exotic birds, turtles, and various other native animals.

Alfred B Maclay State Gardens
3540 Thomasville Rd
Tallahassee, FL 32308
Phone: 850-487-4556
Fax: 850-487-8808

Apalachicola National Forest
1773 Crawfordville Hwy
Crawfordville, FL 32327
www.r8web.com/florida/forests/apalachicola.htm
Phone: 850-926-3561
Fax: 850-926-1904

Birdsong Nature Center
2106 Meridian Rd
Thomasville, GA 31792
Phone: 229-377-4408
Fax: 229-377-4408

Black Archives Research Center & Museum
Florida A & M University 103 Howard Hall
Tallahassee, FL 32307
Phone: 850-599-3020
Fax: 850-561-2604

Brokaw-McDougall House
329 N Meridian St
Tallahassee, FL 32301
Phone: 850-891-3900
Fax: 850-891-3902

Columns The
100 N Duval St
Tallahassee, FL 32301
Phone: 850-224-8116

Downtown Tallahassee
106 E Jefferson St
Tallahassee, FL 32301
Phone: 850-413-9200
Fax: 850-487-4621

First Presbyterian Church
110 N Adams St
Tallahassee, FL 32301
Phone: 850-222-4504
Fax: 850-222-2215

Florida State University Museum of Fine Arts
W Tennessee & Copeland Sts Fine Arts Bldg
Tallahassee, FL 32306
Phone: 850-644-6836
Fax: 850-644-7229

Florida State University School of Theatre
Copeland & Call Sts
Tallahassee, FL 32306
Phone: 850-644-6500
Fax: 850-644-7420

Forest Capital State Museum
204 Forest Park Dr
Perry, FL 32347
Phone: 850-584-3227
Fax: 850-584-3488

Goodwood Plantation
1600 Miccosukee Rd
Tallahassee, FL 32308
Phone: 850-877-4202
Fax: 850-877-3090

Governor's Mansion
700 N Adams St
Tallahassee, FL 32303
Phone: 850-488-4661
Fax: 850-922-6110

Knott House Museum
301 E Park Ave
Tallahassee, FL 32301
Phone: 850-922-2459
Fax: 850-413-7261

Lake Jackson Mounds State Archaeological Site
3600 Indian Mounds Rd
Tallahassee, FL 32303
Phone: 850-562-0042

Lake Talquin State Forest Riverbluff Picnic Site
Hwy 20 & Jack Vause Landing Rd
Tallahassee, FL 32301
Phone: 850-922-6007

LeMoyne Art Foundation
125 N Gadsden St
Tallahassee, FL 32301
www.webvista.com/lemoyne/
Phone: 850-222-8800
Fax: 850-224-2714

Museum of Art Tallahassee
350 S Duval St
Tallahassee, FL 32301
Phone: 850-513-0700
Fax: 850-513-0143

Museum of Florida History
500 S Bronough St RA Gray Bldg
Tallahassee, FL 32399
www.dos.state.fl.us/dhr/museum
Phone: 850-488-1484
Fax: 850-921-2503

Natural Bridge Battlefield State Historic Site
1022 Desoto Park Dr
Tallahassee, FL 32301
Phone: 850-922-6007

Odyssey Science Center
350 S Duval St
Tallahassee, FL 32301
E-mail: edennis@odysseysciencecenter.org
odysseysciencecenter.org
Phone: 850-513-0700
Fax: 850-513-0143

Old Capitol
400 S Monroe St
Tallahassee, FL 32399
Phone: 850-487-1902
Fax: 850-921-2540

Pebble Hill Plantation
Hwy 319
Thomasville, GA 31792
E-mail: php@rose.net
www.pebblehill.com/html/home.htm
Phone: 229-226-2344
Fax: 229-226-0780

Saint Marks Historic Railroad State Trail
1022 Desoto Pk Dr
Tallahassee, FL 32301
Phone: 850-922-6007
Fax: 850-488-0366

San Luis Archaeological & Historic Site
2020 W Mission Rd
Tallahassee, FL 32304
Phone: 850-487-3711

Tallahassee Antique Car Museum
3550 Mahan Dr
Tallahassee, FL 32308
Phone: 850-942-0137
Fax: 850-942-5134

Tallahassee Ballet Co
PO Box 772
Tallahassee, FL 32302
www.freenet.tlh.fl.us/Tallahassee_Ballet
Phone: 850-222-1287

Tallahassee Little Theatre
1861 Thomasville Rd
Tallahassee, FL 32303
www.freenet.tlh.fl.us/TLT/
Phone: 850-224-4597
Fax: 850-224-4464

Tallahassee Museum of History & Natural Science
3945 Museum Dr
Tallahassee, FL 32310
E-mail: kcarr@freenet.tlh.fl.us
www.tallahasseemuseum.org
Phone: 850-576-1636
Fax: 850-574-8243

Tallahassee Symphony
Ruby Diamond Auditorium Florida State University Campus
Tallahassee, FL 32301
www.tsolive.org
Phone: 850-224-0461
Fax: 850-222-9092

Wakulla Springs State Park
550 Wakulla Park Dr
Wakulla Springs, FL 32305
Phone: 850-922-3633
Fax: 850-222-0451

Young Actors Theatre
609 Glenview Dr
Tallahassee, FL 32303
Phone: 850-386-6602
Fax: 850-422-2084

Sports Teams & Facilities

Tallahassee Scorpions (soccer)
133 N Monroe St
Tallahassee, FL 32301
Phone: 850-224-7700
Fax: 850-224-6300

Tallahassee Tiger Sharks (hockey)
505 W Pensacola St Civic Ctr
Tallahassee, FL 32301
www.tigersharkshockey.com
Phone: 850-224-7700

Annual Events

Annual Farm Day (early December) 850-413-9200
Caribbean Carnival (mid-August) 850-878-2198
Celebrate America (July 4).........................850-891-3866
Halloween Howl (late October)....................850-575-8684
Havana Music Fest (early March)..................850-539-8114
Hernando Desoto Winter Encampment (early January) 850-922-6007
Humanatee Festival (mid-May)....................850-922-6007
Jazz & Blues Festival (mid-March) 850-576-1636
Knott House Candlelight Tour (early December) 850-922-2459
Market Days (early December) 850-575-8684
Native American Heritage Festival (September) 850-576-8684
Natural Bridge Battle Reenactment (March) 850-925-6216
North Florida Fair (early November)...............850-878-3247
Rose Festival (late April) 800-704-2350
Southern Shakespeare Festival (early May).........850-513-3087
Spring Farm Days (April) 850-575-8684
Springtime Tallahassee (late March-early April).....850-224-5012
Summer Swamp Stomp (mid-July) 850-575-8684
Tallahassee Marathon (mid-January)..............850-893-9739
Watermelon Festival (late June)....................850-997-5552
Winter Festival (early December)..................850-413-9200
Zoobilee (early October)..........................850-575-8684

Tampa, Florida

County: **Hillsborough**

TAMPA is located on the east side of Tampa Bay along the central Gulf Coast of Florida. Major cities within 100 miles of the metro area include Saint Petersburg, Clearwater, Fort Myers, Lakeland, and Orlando, Florida.

Area (Land) .... 108.7 sq mi
Area (Water)............................... 58.6 sq mi
Elevation.. 48 ft
Latitude ....27-94-72 N
Longitude................................ 82-45-86 W
Time Zone ....EST
Area Code....................................... 813

Climate

Tampa has a subtropical climate with high humidity, abundant sunshine, and mild temperatures nearly year-round. Temperatures occasionally drop below 50 degrees and climb above 90 degrees, but the average winter temperature is 62.5 degrees and the average summer temperature is 81.4 degrees. Summer is the rainy season in the Tampa Bay area, with afternoon and evening thunderstorms an almost daily occurrence.

Average Temperatures & Precipitation

Temperatures

	Jan	Feb	Mar	Apr	May	Jun	Jul	Aug	Sep	Oct	Nov	Dec
High	70	71	77	82	87	90	90	90	89	84	78	72
Low	50	52	57	61	68	73	75	75	73	65	57	52

Precipitation

	Jan	Feb	Mar	Apr	May	Jun	Jul	Aug	Sep	Oct	Nov	Dec
Inches	2.0	3.1	3.0	1.2	3.1	5.5	6.6	7.6	6.0	2.0	1.8	2.2

History

The Tampa Bay area was originally settled before the 1500's by the Calusa Indians as an Indian fishing village. Due to the abundance of driftwood that the Indians used for firewood, the area was given the name "Tampa," which was derived from a Native American phrase meaning "sticks of fire." One of Tampa's earliest visitors was the famous explorer and Governor of Cuba, Hernando de Soto, who came to the area in 1539 on a quest for gold. Over the next 300 years, the area was gradually settled by farmers and escaped slaves. A military outpost was established by George Mercer Brooke in 1823, and Tampa was incorporated as a city in 1855 with a population of 800.

In the late 19th century, Tampa earned the title "Cigar Capital of the World" after Don Vicente Martinez Ybor, a Cuban exile, moved his cigar manufacturing business from Key West to the Tampa Bay area. The success of Ybor's business influenced other Cubans and Spaniards to open cigar factories, drawing large numbers of Cuban, Spanish, Italian, and German immigrants to the Tampa community known as Ybor City, which has been designated as a historic landmark district in Florida.

Transportation has played a significant role in Tampa's history. In the 1880s, Henry B. Plant built a railroad to the area and started a steamship line that ran from Tampa to Key West to Havana, spurring another economic boom that drew more settlers to the area. Plant also built the Tampa Bay Hotel, which later became the University of Tampa. The Tampa Bay area was also the site of the world's first scheduled airline flight, completed by Tony Jannus in 1914, who flew from Saint Petersburg to Tampa.

Population

1990 Census 280,015
1998 Estimate..............................289,156
% Change 3.3
2005 Projection 2,483,500*

Racial/Ethnic Breakdown

White.................................. 70.9%
Black 25.0%
Other.................................... 4.1%
Hispanic Origin (may be of any race) 15.0%

Age Breakdown

Under 5 years.............................. 7.5%
5 to 17.................................. 15.6%
18 to 20.................................. 4.8%
21 to 24.................................. 6.4%
25 to 34................................. 18.9%
35 to 44................................. 14.1%
45 to 54.................................. 9.4%
55 to 64.................................. 8.8%
65 to 74.................................. 8.3%
75+ years 6.3%
Median Age................................33.3

Gender Breakdown

Male.................................... 48.0%
Female.................................. 52.0%

** Information given is for the the Tampa Metropolitan Statistical Area (MSA), which includes the City of Tampa, the City of Saint Petersburg, and the City of Clearwater as well as Hernando County, Hillsborough County, Pasco County, and Pinellas County.*

Government

Type of Government: Mayor-Council

Tampa Business & Community Services Dept
306 E Jackson St Suite 2N
Tampa, FL 33602
Phone: 813-274-8091
Fax: 813-274-7410

Tampa City Clerk
315 E Kennedy Blvd
Tampa, FL 33602
Phone: 813-223-8396
Fax: 813-274-8306

Tampa City Council
315 E Kennedy Blvd 3rd Fl
Tampa, FL 33602
Phone: 813-274-8131
Fax: 813-274-7076

Tampa City Hall
306 E Jackson St
Tampa, FL 33602
Phone: 813-223-8211

Tampa Fire Dept
808 Zack St
Tampa, FL 33602
Phone: 813-274-7011
Fax: 813-274-7026

Tampa Legal Dept
315 E Kennedy Blvd 5th Fl
Tampa, FL 33602
Phone: 813-274-8996
Fax: 813-274-8809

Tampa Mayor
306 E Jackson St
Tampa, FL 33602
Phone: 813-274-8251
Fax: 813-274-7050

Tampa Parks Dept
7525 North Blvd
Tampa, FL 33604
Phone: 813-931-2121
Fax: 813-931-2120

Tampa Personnel Div
315 E Kennedy Blvd
Tampa, FL 33602
Phone: 813-274-8911
Fax: 813-274-8913

Tampa Planning & Management Dept
306 E Jackson St 8th Fl E
Tampa, FL 33602
Phone: 813-274-8401
Fax: 813-274-7327

Tampa Police Dept
411 N Franklin St
Tampa, FL 33602
Phone: 813-276-3201
Fax: 813-276-3776

Tampa Public Works Dept
306 E Jackson St 4th Fl N
Tampa, FL 33602
Phone: 813-274-8721
Fax: 813-274-8080

Tampa Recreation Dept
1420 N Tampa St
Tampa, FL 33602
Phone: 813-274-8615
Fax: 813-274-7429

Tampa Transportation Div
306 E Jackson St 4th Fl E
Tampa, FL 33602
Phone: 813-274-8333
Fax: 813-274-8901

Tampa Water Dept
306 E Jackson St
Tampa, FL 33602
Phone: 813-274-8663
Fax: 813-274-7435

Tampa-Hillsborough County Public Library System
900 N Ashley Dr
Tampa, FL 33602
Phone: 813-273-3652
Fax: 813-273-3707

Important Phone Numbers

AAA 813-289-5000
American Express Travel 813-273-0310
Dental Referral 800-511-8663
Driver's License Information 813-871-7658
Emergency 911
Florida Dept of Revenue 813-744-6325
Greater Tampa Assn of Realtors 813-879-7010
Hillsborough County Tax Collector 813-307-6500
HotelDocs 800-468-3537
Medical Referral 813-254-3484
Poison Control Center 813-253-4444
Travelers Aid 813-273-5936
Vehicle Registration Information 813-307-6500
Voter Registration Information 813-272-5850
Weather 813-645-2506

Information Sources

Better Business Bureau Serving West Florida
PO Box 7950
Clearwater, FL 33758
www.clearwater.bbb.org
Phone: 727-535-5522
Fax: 727-539-6301

Greater Tampa Chamber of Commerce
401 E Jackson St Suite 2100
Tampa, FL 33602
www.tampachamber.com
Phone: 813-228-7777
Fax: 813-223-7899
TF: 800-298-2672

Hillsborough County
601 E Kennedy Blvd
Tampa, FL 33602
www.hillsboroughcounty.org
Phone: 813-272-5900
Fax: 813-212-6718

Pinellas County
315 Court St
Clearwater, FL 33756
www.co.pinellas.fl.us
Phone: 727-464-3000
Fax: 727-464-4070

Saint Petersburg Area Chamber of Commerce
100 2nd Ave N Suite 150
Saint Petersburg, FL 33701
www.stpete.com
Phone: 727-821-4069
Fax: 727-895-6326

Saint Petersburg City Hall
175 5th St N
Saint Petersburg, FL 33701
www.stpete.org/cityhall.htm
Phone: 727-893-7111
Fax: 727-892-5365

Saint Petersburg Economic Development Dept
1 4th St N 9th Fl
Saint Petersburg, FL 33701
www.stpete.org/business.htm
Phone: 727-893-7100
Fax: 727-892-5465

Saint Petersburg Mayor
PO Box 2842
Saint Petersburg, FL 33731
www.stpete.org/mayor.htm
Phone: 727-893-7201
Fax: 727-892-5365

Saint Petersburg Public Library
3745 9th Ave N
Saint Petersburg, FL 33713
www.stpete.org/library.htm
Phone: 727-893-7724
Fax: 727-892-5432

Saint Petersburg/Clearwater Area Convention & Visitors Bureau
14450 46th St N Suite 108
Clearwater, FL 33762
www.stpete-clearwater.com
Phone: 727-464-7200
Fax: 727-464-7222
TF: 800-345-6710

Suncoast Free-Net Phone: 813-273-3711
900 N Ashley Dr Tampa-Hillborough County Public Library
Tampa, FL 33602
scfn.thpl.lib.fl.us

Tampa Convention Center Phone: 813-274-8511
333 S Franklin St Fax: 813-274-7430
Tampa, FL 33602 TF: 800-426-5630

Tampa/Hillsborough Convention & Visitors Assn Phone: 813-223-1111
400 N Tampa St Suite 1010 Fax: 813-229-6616
Tampa, FL 33602 TF: 800-826-8358
www.thcva.com

Online Resources

4Tampa.com
www.4tampa.com

About.com Guide to Tampa Bay
tampa.about.com/local/southeastus/tampa

Access America Tampa
www.accessamer.com/tampa/

Area Guide Saint Petersburg
saintpetersburg.areaguides.net

Area Guide Tampa
tampa.areaguides.net

City Knowledge Saint Petersburg
www.cityknowledge.com/fl_stpetersburg.htm

City Knowledge Tampa
www.cityknowledge.com/fl_tampa.htm

Cityhits Tampa
www.cityhits.com/tampa/

CitySearch Tampa/Saint Petersburg
tampabay.citysearch.com

DigitalCity Tampa Bay
home.digitalcity.com/tampabay

Essential Guide to Tampa Bay
www.ego.net/us/fl/tampa

Excite.com Saint Petersburg City Guide
www.excite.com/travel/countries/united_states/florida/st_petersburg

Excite.com Tampa City Guide
www.excite.com/travel/countries/united_states/florida/tampa

Go Tampa Bay
www.gotampabay.com

Hotel Guide Tampa/Saint Petersburg
hotelguide.net/tampa

Insiders' Guide to Tampa Bay
www.insiders.com/tampa/

Lodging.com Saint Petersburg Florida
www.lodging.com/auto/guides/st_petersburg-area-fl.html

Lodging.com Tampa Florida
www.lodging.com/auto/guides/tampa-area-fl.html

Saint Petersburg Home Page
www.stpete.org

Surf & Sun Beach Vacation Guide to Saint Petersburg
www.surf-sun.com/fl-st-petersburg-main.htm

Surf & Sun Beach Vacation Guide to Tampa Bay
www.surf-sun.com/fl-tampa-bay-main.htm

Tampa Bay Online Network
www.tampabayonline.net/home.htm

Tampa CityLink
www.usacitylink.com/citylink/tampa

Tampa Guide
www.tampaguide.com/

Tampa.TheLinks.com
tampa.thelinks.com/

WebCoast-Tampa Bay's Online Information Magazine
webcoast.tampa.fl.us/

Area Communities

Prominent unincorporated communities in Hillsborough County include Apollo Beach, Brandon, Carrollwood, and Sun City Center. Incorporated communities in the Tampa Bay area (Hillsborough and Pinellas counties) with populations greater than 10,000 include:

Clearwater Phone: 727-462-6900
PO Box 4748 Fax: 727-462-4052
Clearwater, FL 33758

Dunedin Phone: 727-733-4151
PO Box 1348 Fax: 727-738-1871
Dunedin, FL 34697

Largo Phone: 727-587-6700
201 Highland Ave Fax: 727-587-6703
Largo, FL 33770

Pinellas Park Phone: 727-541-0700
5141 78th Ave Fax: 727-544-7448
Pinellas Park, FL 33781

Plant City Phone: 813-757-9144
302 W Reynolds St Fax: 813-757-9154
Plant City, FL 33566

Safety Harbor Phone: 727-724-1555
750 Main St Fax: 727-724-1566
Safety Harbor, FL 34695

Saint Petersburg Phone: 727-893-7111
175 5th St N Fax: 727-892-5365
Saint Petersburg, FL 33701

Tarpon Springs Phone: 727-938-3711
324 E Pine St Fax: 727-942-5621
Tarpon Springs, FL 34689

Temple Terrace Phone: 813-989-7100
11250 N 56th St Fax: 813-989-7185
Temple Terrace, FL 33687

Economy

Hillsborough County is Florida's second largest employment market. Major industries range from agriculture (the area is the country's largest producer of tropical fish) to high technology and biomedicine. Hillsborough County serves as regional and national headquarters for several banks such as NationsBank, Citicorp, and Chase Manhattan, and insurance companies like Beneficial, USF & G, Metlife, and USAA. In addition to the major employers listed below, the State of Florida is also among the top 15.

Unemployment Rate 4.3%*
Per Capita Income.......................... $26,740
Median Family Income...................... $45,600*

** Information given is for the the Tampa Metropolitan Statistical Area (MSA), which includes the City of Tampa, the City of Saint Petersburg, and the City of Clearwater as well as Hernando County, Hillsborough County, Pasco County, and Pinellas County.*

Principal Industries & Number of Wage Earners

Hillsborough County - 1998

Agricultural Services, Forestry, & Fishing 11,708
Construction.. 26,669
Finance, Insurance, & Real Estate 45,150
Manufacturing 37,498
Retail Trade.. 89,692
Services 207,583
Transportation, Communications, & Public Utilities....... 30,292
Wholesale Trade....................................... 35,341

Major Employers

Hillsborough County
601 E Kennedy Blvd
Tampa, FL 33602
www.hillsboroughcounty.org
Phone: 813-272-5900
Fax: 813-212-6718

Hillsborough County School System
901 E Kennedy Blvd
Tampa, FL 33602
www.sdhc.k12.fl.us
Phone: 813-272-4000
Fax: 813-272-4073

James A Haley Veterans Hospital
13000 Bruce B Downs Blvd
Tampa, FL 33612
Phone: 813-972-2000
Fax: 813-978-5928

Kash n' Karry Food Stores Inc
6401-A Harney Rd
Tampa, FL 33610
www.kashnkarry.com
Phone: 813-620-1139
Fax: 813-626-9550

MacDill Air Force Base
2909 Nighthawk Suite 4
MacDill AFB, FL 33621
www.macdill.af.mil
Phone: 813-828-1110
Fax: 813-830-2215

Publix Super Markets Inc
PO Box 407
Lakeland, FL 33802
www.publix.com
Phone: 863-688-1188
Fax: 863-284-5571

Saint Joseph's Hospital
3001 W Dr ML King Blvd
Tampa, FL 33607
Phone: 813-870-4000
Fax: 813-870-4813

Tampa City Hall
306 E Jackson St
Tampa, FL 33602
www.ci.tampa.fl.us
Phone: 813-223-8211

Tampa General Hospital
Davis Islands
Tampa, FL 33606
www.tgh.org
Phone: 813-251-7551
Fax: 813-253-4017

Tampa International Airport
PO Box 22287
Tampa, FL 33622
www.tampaairport.com/
Phone: 813-870-8700
Fax: 813-875-6670

Tribune Co
202 S Parker St
Tampa, FL 33606
Phone: 813-259-7711
Fax: 813-259-7676

University of South Florida Tampa Campus
4202 E Fowler Ave
Tampa, FL 33620
E-mail: www@usf.edu
www.usf.edu
Phone: 813-974-2011
Fax: 813-974-9689

US Postal Service Tampa Div
5201 W Spruce St
Tampa, FL 33630
new.usps.com
Phone: 800-275-8777

Verizon Communications
201 N Franklin St
Tampa, FL 33602
www.verizon.com
Phone: 813-483-2212
Fax: 813-223-4866

Quality of Living Indicators

Total Crime Index.................................. 35,960
(rates per 100,000 inhabitants)

Violent Crime
Murder/manslaughter.......................... 40
Forcible rape 266
Robbery..................................... 2,464
Aggravated assault........................... 4,773

Property Crime
Burglary 5,720
Larceny theft 17,622
Motor vehicle theft 5,075

Cost of Living Index................................ 95.8
(national average = 100)

Median Home Price.................................. $94,000

Education

Public Schools

Hillsborough County School System
901 E Kennedy Blvd
Tampa, FL 33602
www.sdhc.k12.fl.us
Phone: 813-272-4000
Fax: 813-272-4073

Number of Schools
Elementary 105

Middle 32
High.. 16

Student/Teacher Ratio
All Grades 16.9:1

Private Schools

Number of Schools (all grades) .... 100+

Colleges & Universities

Eckerd College
4200 54th Ave S
Saint Petersburg, FL 33711
E-mail: admissions@eckerd.edu
www.eckerd.edu
Phone: 727-867-1166
Fax: 727-866-3359
TF: 800-456-9009

Florida College
119 N Glen Arven Ave
Temple Terrace, FL 33617
www.flcoll.edu
Phone: 813-988-5131
Fax: 813-899-6772
TF: 800-326-7655

Hillsborough Community College Dale Mabry Campus
PO Box 30030
Tampa, FL 33630
www.hcc.cc.fl.us
Phone: 813-253-7000
Fax: 813-253-7400

International Academy of Design
5225 Memorial Hwy
Tampa, FL 33634
www.academy.edu
Phone: 813-881-0007
Fax: 813-881-0008
TF: 800-222-3369

ITT Technical Institute
4809 Memorial Hwy
Tampa, FL 33634
www.itt-tech.edu
Phone: 813-885-2244
Fax: 813-888-6078
TF: 800-825-2831

Saint Petersburg Junior College
6605 5th Ave N
Saint Petersburg, FL 33710
www.spjc.cc.fl.us
Phone: 727-341-3239
Fax: 727-341-4792

Tampa Technical Institute
2410 E Bush Blvd
Tampa, FL 33612
Phone: 813-935-5700
Fax: 813-935-7415
TF: 800-992-4850

University of South Florida Tampa Campus
4202 E Fowler Ave
Tampa, FL 33620
E-mail: www@usf.edu
www.usf.edu
Phone: 813-974-2011
Fax: 813-974-9689

University of Tampa
401 W Kennedy Blvd
Tampa, FL 33606
www.utampa.edu
Phone: 813-253-3333
Fax: 813-258-7398
TF: 800-733-4773

Hospitals

All Children's Hospital
801 6th St S
Saint Petersburg, FL 33701
www.allkids.org
Phone: 727-898-7451
Fax: 727-892-8500
TF: 800-456-4543

Bayfront Medical Center
701 6th St S
Saint Petersburg, FL 33701
www.bayfront.org
Phone: 727-823-1234
Fax: 727-893-6970

Edward White Hospital
2323 9th Ave N
Saint Petersburg, FL 33713
Phone: 727-323-1111
Fax: 727-328-6135

James A Haley Veterans Hospital
13000 Bruce B Downs Blvd
Tampa, FL 33612
Phone: 813-972-2000
Fax: 813-978-5928

Mease Hospital Dunedin
601 Main St
Dunedin, FL 34698
www.mpmhealth.com/abou2.B.stm
Phone: 727-733-1111
Fax: 727-734-6977

Memorial Hospital of Tampa
2901 Swann Ave
Tampa, FL 33609
Phone: 813-873-6400
Fax: 813-873-6472

Morton Plant Hospital
300 Pinellas St
Clearwater, FL 33756
www.mpmhealth.com
Phone: 727-462-7000
Fax: 727-461-8860

Northside Hospital & Heart Institute
6000 49th St N
Saint Petersburg, FL 33709
Phone: 727-521-4411
Fax: 727-521-5114

Palms of Pasadena Hospital
1501 Pasadena Ave S
Saint Petersburg, FL 33707
www.tenethealth.com/PalmsPasadena
Phone: 727-381-1000
Fax: 727-341-7690

Saint Anthony's Hospital
1200 7th Ave N
Saint Petersburg, FL 33705
Phone: 727-825-1000
Fax: 727-825-1327
TF: 800-285-7568

Saint Joseph's Hospital
3001 W Dr ML King Blvd
Tampa, FL 33607
Phone: 813-870-4000
Fax: 813-870-4813

Saint Petersburg General Hospital
6500 38th Ave N
Saint Petersburg, FL 33710
www.stpetegeneralhospital.com
Phone: 727-384-1414
Fax: 727-341-4889

Shriners Hospitals for Children Tampa Unit
12502 N Pine Dr
Tampa, FL 33612
www.shrinershq.org/Hospitals/Directry/tampa.html
Phone: 813-972-2250
Fax: 813-978-9442
TF: 888-665-5437

South Florida Baptist Hospital
301 N Alexander St
Plant City, FL 33566
Phone: 813-757-1200
Fax: 813-757-8301

Sun Coast Hospital
2025 Indian Rocks Rd
Largo, FL 33774
Phone: 727-581-9474
Fax: 727-587-7604

Tampa General Hospital
Davis Islands
Tampa, FL 33606
www.tgh.org
Phone: 813-251-7551
Fax: 813-253-4017

Town & Country Hospital Phone: 813-885-6666
6001 Webb Rd Fax: 813-887-5112
Tampa, FL 33615

University Community Hospital Phone: 813-971-6000
3100 E Fletcher Ave Fax: 813-979-7313
Tampa, FL 33613

University Community Hospital Carrollwood Phone: 813-932-2222
7171 N Dale Mabry Hwy Fax: 813-558-8049
Tampa, FL 33614

Transportation

Airport(s)

Tampa International Airport (TPA)
4 miles W of downtown (approx 10 minutes) 813-870-8700

Mass Transit

HARTline
$1.15 Base fare................................813-254-4278

Rail/Bus

Amtrak Station Phone: 813-221-7602
601 Nebraska Ave TF: 800-872-7245
Tampa, FL 33602

Greyhound Bus Station Phone: 813-229-2174
610 E Polk St TF: 800-231-2222
Tampa, FL 33602

Utilities

Electricity
Tampa Electric Co 813-223-0800
www.teco.net/TampaElectric.html

Gas
Peoples Gas 813-272-1501
www.peoplesgas.com

Water
Tampa Water Dept 813-274-8663
www.ci.tampa.fl.us/dept_Water

Garbage Collection/Recycling
Tampa Garbage Collection......................813-348-1111
Tampa Recycling Services......................813-878-1144

Telecommunications

Telephone
Verizon Communications.......................800-828-7280
www.verizon.com

Cable Television
Time Warner Cable............................813-684-6400
www.twtampabay.com

Internet Service Providers (ISPs)
All World Network Inc.........................813-988-7772
www.allworld.com
Intelligence Network Online Inc (IntNet) 727-442-0114
www.intnet.net
Intermedia Communications Inc................813-829-0011
www.intermedia.com
Suncoast Free-Net 813-273-3711
scfn.thpl.lib.fl.us
Verio West Florida 727-812-8857
home.verio.net/local/frontpage.cfm?AirportCode=TPA

Banks

AmSouth Bank Phone: 813-226-1100
100 N Tampa St Fax: 813-226-1101
Tampa, FL 33602 TF: 800-267-6884

Bank of America Phone: 800-299-2265
101 E Kennedy Blvd Fax: 813-225-8528
Tampa, FL 33602

Bank of Tampa Phone: 813-872-1200
4400 N Armenia Ave Fax: 813-875-5092
Tampa, FL 33603

Central Bank of Tampa Phone: 813-253-3302
2307 W Kennedy Blvd Fax: 813-253-8826
Tampa, FL 33609
www.centralbank-tampa.com

Colonial Bank Phone: 813-626-5884
410 Ware Blvd Fax: 813-628-0491
Tampa, FL 33619

First Union National Bank Phone: 813-276-6000
100 S Ashley St Fax: 813-276-6515
Tampa, FL 33602

SunTrust Bank of Tampa Bay Phone: 813-224-2121
401 E Jackson St Fax: 813-224-2497
Tampa, FL 33602

Shopping

Bayside Market
5501 Gulf Blvd
Saint Pete Beach, FL 33706

Brandon Town Center Phone: 813-661-6255
459 Brandon Town Center Fax: 813-661-5261
Brandon, FL 33511
www.brandontowncenter.com

Countryside Mall Phone: 727-796-1079
27001 US 19 N Fax: 727-791-8470
Clearwater, FL 33761

Dillard's Phone: 727-344-4611
6901 22nd Ave N Fax: 727-341-6101
Saint Petersburg, FL 33710

John's Pass Village & Boardwalk Phone: 727-360-6957
501 150th Ave Fax: 727-391-4259
Madeira Beach, FL 33708 TF: 800-755-0677

Old Hyde Park Village Phone: 813-251-3500
748 S Village Cir Fax: 813-251-4158
Tampa, FL 33606

ParkSide Mall Phone: 727-527-7241
7200 US 19 N Fax: 727-527-8340
Pinellas Park, FL 33781

Pier The
800 2nd Ave NE
Saint Petersburg, FL 33701
www.stpete-pier.com
Phone: 727-821-6164

Seminole Mall
113th St & Park Blvd
Seminole, FL 33772
Phone: 727-392-8174
Fax: 727-392-3205

Tampa Bay Center
3302 W Dr ML King Blvd
Tampa, FL 33607
www.tampabaycenter.com
Phone: 813-879-6070
Fax: 813-871-5146

Tyrone Square
6901 22nd Ave N
Saint Petersburg, FL 33710
Phone: 727-345-0126
Fax: 727-345-5699

University Mall
2200 E Fowler Ave
Tampa, FL 33612
Phone: 813-971-3465
Fax: 813-971-0923

West Shore Plaza
250 West Shore Plaza
Tampa, FL 33609
www.westshoreplaza.com
Phone: 813-286-0790
Fax: 813-286-1250

Ybor Square
1901 N 13th St
Tampa, FL 33605
E-mail: yborsquare@earthlink.net
Phone: 813-247-4497
Fax: 813-248-8938

Media

Newspapers and Magazines

Business Journal of Tampa Bay
4350 W Cypress St Suite 400
Tampa, FL 33607
www.bizjournals.com/tampabay
Phone: 813-873-8225
Fax: 813-876-1827

Carrollwood News
5501 W Waters Ave Suite 404
Tampa, FL 33634
Phone: 813-249-5603
Fax: 813-249-5316

Community Connections
3210 E 7th Ave
Tampa, FL 33605
Phone: 813-248-3921
Fax: 813-247-5357

Saint Petersburg Times*
PO Box 1121
Saint Petersburg, FL 33731
E-mail: letters@sptimes.com
www.sptimes.com
Phone: 727-893-8111
Fax: 727-893-8675
TF: 800-333-7505

Seminole Beacon
10621 117th Dr N
Largo, FL 33773
Phone: 727-397-5563
Fax: 727-397-5900

Tampa Tribune*
202 S Parker St
Tampa, FL 33606
E-mail: tribletters@tampatrib.com
www.tampatrib.com
Phone: 813-259-7711
Fax: 813-259-7676
TF: 800-282-5588

Town 'n Country News
5501 W Waters Ave Suite 404
Tampa, FL 33634
Phone: 813-249-5603
Fax: 813-249-5316

Weekly Planet
1310 E 9th Ave
Tampa, FL 33605
www.weeklyplanet.com
Phone: 813-248-8888
Fax: 813-248-4600

**Indicates major daily newspapers*

Television

WBHS-TV Ch 50 (Ind)
12425 28th St N Suite 301
Saint Petersburg, FL 33716
Phone: 727-573-5550
Fax: 727-571-1931

WCLF-TV Ch 22 (Ind)
6922 142nd Ave N
Largo, FL 33771
Phone: 727-535-5622

WEDU-TV Ch 3 (PBS)
1300 N Blvd
Tampa, FL 33607
E-mail: outreach@wedu.pbs.org
www.wedu.org
Phone: 813-254-9338
Fax: 813-253-0826

WFLA-TV Ch 8 (NBC)
905 E Jackson St
Tampa, FL 33602
www.wfla.com
Phone: 813-228-8888
Fax: 813-225-2770

WFTS-TV Ch 28 (ABC)
4045 N Himes Ave
Tampa, FL 33607
E-mail: 28feedback@wfts.com
www.wfts.com
Phone: 813-354-2800
Fax: 813-870-2828

WMOR-TV Ch 32 (Ind)
7201 E Hillsborough Ave
Tampa, FL 33610
www.moretv32.com
Phone: 813-626-3232
Fax: 813-626-1961

WTOG-TV Ch 44 (UPN)
365 105th Terr NE
Saint Petersburg, FL 33716
Phone: 727-576-4444
Fax: 727-576-6155

WTSP-TV Ch 10 (CBS)
11450 Gandy Blvd N
Saint Petersburg, FL 33702
E-mail: news@channel10.com
www.wtsp.com
Phone: 727-577-1010
Fax: 727-576-6924

WTTA-TV Ch 38 (WB)
5510 W Gray St Suite 38
Tampa, FL 33609
Phone: 813-289-3838
Fax: 813-289-0000

WTVT-TV Ch 13 (Fox)
3213 W Kennedy Blvd
Tampa, FL 33609
E-mail: 13@wtvt.com
www.wtvt.com
Phone: 813-876-1313
Fax: 813-871-3135

WUSF-TV Ch 16 (PBS)
4202 Fowler Ave
Tampa, FL 33620
www.wusftv.usf.edu
Phone: 813-974-4000
Fax: 813-974-4806
TF: 800-654-3703

WXPX-TV Ch 66 (PAX)
11300 4th St N Suite 180
Saint Petersburg, FL 33716
www.pax.net/WXPX
Phone: 727-578-0066
Fax: 727-570-8206

Radio

WBBY-FM 107.3 MHz (AC)
877 Executive Ctr Dr W Suite 300
Saint Petersburg, FL 33706
www.coast1073.com
Phone: 813-229-8650
Fax: 727-576-8098

WDAE-AM 1250 kHz (Sports)
4002 Gandy Blvd
Tampa, FL 33611
www.620wdae.com
Phone: 813-839-9393
Fax: 813-831-6397

WDUV-FM 103.5 MHz (B/EZ)
4002-A Gandy Blvd
Tampa, FL 33611
Phone: 813-839-9393
Fax: 813-837-0300
TF: 800-932-6100

WFJO-FM 101.5 MHz (Oldies)
877 Executive Center Dr W Suite 300
Saint Petersburg, FL 33702
Phone: 727-576-1073
Fax: 727-577-1970

WFLA-AM 970 kHz (N/T)
4002-A Gandy Blvd
Tampa, FL 33611
E-mail: wfla97b@prodigy.com
www.970wfla.com
Phone: 813-839-9393
Fax: 813-831-3299

WFLZ-FM 93.3 MHz (CHR)
4002-A Gandy Blvd
Tampa, FL 33611
E-mail: bj933flz@aol.com
www.933flz.com
Phone: 813-839-9393
Fax: 813-831-3299

WGUL-AM 860 kHz (Nost)
35048 US Hwy 19 The Fountains
Palm Harbor, FL 34684
Phone: 727-849-2285
Fax: 727-781-4375

WGUL-FM 96.1 MHz (Nost)
35048 US Hwy 19 N The Fountains
Palm Harbor, FL 34684
Phone: 727-849-2285
Fax: 727-781-4375

WHPT-FM 102.5 MHz (CR)
11300 4th St N Suite 318
Saint Petersburg, FL 33716
Phone: 727-577-7131
Fax: 727-578-2477

WLLD-FM 98.7 MHz (CHR)
9721 Executive Ctr Dr Suite 200
Saint Petersburg, FL 33702
Phone: 727-568-0941
Fax: 727-579-9111

WMNF-FM 88.5 MHz (NPR)
1210 E ML King Blvd
Tampa, FL 33603
E-mail: wmnf@wmnf.org
www.wmnf.org
Phone: 813-238-8001
Fax: 813-238-1802

WMTX-FM 100.7 MHz (AC)
4002-A Gandy Blvd
Tampa, FL 33611
www.mixmeansvariety.com
Phone: 727-446-9352
Fax: 813-832-6235

WQYK-AM 1010 kHz (N/T)
5510 W Gray St Suite 130
Tampa, FL 33609
Phone: 813-287-0995
Fax: 813-636-0995

WQYK-FM 99.5 MHz (Ctry)
5510 W Gray St Suite 130
Tampa, FL 33609
www.wqyk.com
Phone: 813-287-0995
Fax: 813-636-0995

WRBQ-AM 1380 kHz (Urban)
5510 W Gray St Suite 130
Tampa, FL 33609
Phone: 813-287-1047
Fax: 813-289-2851

WRBQ-FM 104.7 MHz (Ctry)
5510 W Gray St Suite 130
Tampa, FL 33609
E-mail: qalm19b@prodigy.com
www.wrbq.com
Phone: 813-287-1047
Fax: 813-289-2851

WSJT-FM 94.1 MHz (NAC)
9721 Executive Center Dr N Suite 200
Saint Petersburg, FL 33702
www.wsjt.com
Phone: 727-579-1925
Fax: 727-579-8888

WSSR-FM 95.7 MHz (AC)
4002 Gandy Blvd
Tampa, FL 33611
Phone: 813-839-9393
Fax: 813-831-6397

WSUN-AM 620 kHz (Oldies)
11300 4th St N Suite 318
Saint Petersburg, FL 33716
Phone: 727-577-7131
Fax: 727-578-2477

WSUN-FM 97.1 MHz (Oldies)
11300 4th St N Suite 318
Saint Petersburg, FL 33716
Phone: 727-577-7131
Fax: 727-578-2477

WTBT-FM 103.5 MHz (CR)
13577 Feather Sound Dr Suite 550
Clearwater, FL 33762
thunder1035.com
Phone: 727-572-9808
Fax: 727-573-5515

WTMP-AM 1150 kHz (Urban)
5207 Washington Blvd
Tampa, FL 33619
E-mail: wtmpjams@gte.net
www.wtmp-am1150.com
Phone: 813-620-1300
Fax: 813-628-0713

WUSF-FM 89.7 MHz (NPR)
4202 E Fowler Ave WRB 219
Tampa, FL 33620
www.wusf.usf.edu
Phone: 813-974-4890
Fax: 813-974-5016

WWRM-FM 94.9 MHz (AC)
877 Executive Center Dr W Suite 300
Saint Petersburg, FL 33702
www.warm949.com
Phone: 727-576-1073
Fax: 727-576-8098

WXTB-FM 97.9 MHz (Rock)
13577 Feather Sound Dr Suite 550
Clearwater, FL 33762
www.98rock.com
Phone: 727-572-9808
Fax: 727-572-0935

WYUU-FM 92.5 MHz (Oldies)
PO Box 42925
Saint Petersburg, FL 33702
Phone: 727-579-1925
Fax: 727-579-8888

WZTM-AM 820 kHz (Span)
1915 N Dale Mabry Hwy Suite 200
Tampa, FL 33607
E-mail: wztm@broadcast.com
Phone: 813-871-1819
Fax: 813-871-1155

Attractions

Ybor City, located east of downtown Tampa, reflects the city's ethnic heritage and history as the "Cigar Capital of the World" in its 110 blocks of historic buildings. The area also features ethnic shops, restaurants, art studios and festivals. On Tampa's waterfront the

Florida Aquarium, a glass-domed structure with 4,350 specimens of fish, marine animals, and plants, is one of the largest aquariums in the world. The African-themed Busch Gardens, home of the Kumba, the largest and fastest steel roller coaster in the Southeast, is also located in Tampa. Tampa's neighboring city, Saint Petersburg, features a collection of beaches, parks, and yacht basins bordered on three sides by bays and the Gulf of Mexico. Saint Petersburg's resort-occupied islands on the Gulf of Mexico form the Saint Pete Beach area. One of the city's best known resorts is the Don CeSar, which was the vacation spot for F. Scott Fitzgerald in the 1920s and 30s.

Adventure Island
4500 Bougainvillea Ave
Tampa, FL 33617
www.adventureisland.com/waterparks/adventureisland/frame.html
Phone: 813-987-5600
Fax: 813-987-5654

American Stage
211 3rd St S
Saint Petersburg, FL 33701
Phone: 727-822-8814
Fax: 727-823-7529

Bayfront Center/Mahaffey Theater
400 1st St S
Saint Petersburg, FL 33701
Phone: 727-892-5798
Fax: 727-892-5858
TF: 800-874-9015

Bayside Market
5501 Gulf Blvd
Saint Pete Beach, FL 33706

Big Top Flea Market
9250 E Fowler Ave
Thonotosassa, FL 33592
Phone: 813-986-4004
Fax: 813-986-6296

Bobby's Indian Village
5221 N Orient Rd
Tampa, FL 33610
Phone: 813-620-3077
Fax: 813-620-1767

Boyd Hill Nature Park
1101 Country Club Way S
Saint Petersburg, FL 33705
Phone: 727-893-7326
Fax: 727-893-7720

Busch Gardens
3605 Bougainvillea Ave
Tampa, FL 33674
www.buschgardens.com/buschgardens/bg_tampa/frame.html
Phone: 813-987-5082
Fax: 813-987-5374

Caladesi Island State Park
3 Causeway Blvd
Dunedin, FL 34698
Phone: 727-469-5918

Celebration Station Entertainment Complex
10230 Palm River Rd
Tampa, FL 33619
www.celebrationstation.com
Phone: 813-661-4557
Fax: 813-661-2023

De Soto National Memorial
75th St NW
Bradenton, FL 34209
www.nps.gov/deso/
Phone: 941-792-0458
Fax: 941-792-5094

Europa SeaKruz
150 B Johns Pass Boardwalk
Madeira Beach, FL 33708
Phone: 727-393-5110
Fax: 727-392-5715
TF: 800-688-7529

Falk Theatre
428 W Kennedy Blvd
Tampa, FL 33606
Phone: 813-253-6238
Fax: 813-258-7211

Florida Aquarium
701 Channelside Dr
Tampa, FL 33602
www2.sptimes.com/Aquarium/Default.html
Phone: 813-273-4000
Fax: 813-224-9583
TF: 800-353-4741

Florida Holocaust Museum
55 5th St S
Saint Petersburg, FL 33701
www.flholocaustmuseum.org
Phone: 727-820-0100
Fax: 727-821-8435

Florida International Museum
100 2nd St N
Saint Petersburg, FL 33701
www.floridamuseum.org/
Phone: 727-821-1448
Fax: 727-898-0248
TF: 800-777-9882

Florida Orchestra
101 S Hoover Blvd Suite 100
Tampa, FL 33609
E-mail: florida_orchestra@juno.com
www.fl-orchestra.org
Phone: 813-286-1170
Fax: 813-286-2316
TF: 800-662-7286

Fort DeSoto Park
3500 Pinellas Bayway S
Tierra Verde, FL 33715
Phone: 727-866-2484
Fax: 727-866-2485

Great Explorations-The Hands on Museum
1120 4th St S
Saint Petersburg, FL 33701
Phone: 727-821-8885
Fax: 727-823-7287

Gulf Beaches Historical Museum
115 10th Ave
Saint Pete Beach, FL 33706
Phone: 727-360-2491
Fax: 727-363-6704

Henry B Plant Museum
401 W Kennedy Blvd
Tampa, FL 33606
www.plantmuseum.com
Phone: 813-254-1891
Fax: 813-258-7272

John & Mable Ringling Museum of Art
5401 Bay Shore Rd
Sarasota, FL 34243
E-mail: ringling@concentric.net
www.ringling.org
Phone: 941-359-5700
Fax: 941-359-5745

John's Pass Village & Boardwalk
501 150th Ave
Madeira Beach, FL 33708
Phone: 727-360-6957
Fax: 727-391-4259
TF: 800-755-0677

Kid City Children's Museum of Tampa
7550 North Blvd
Tampa, FL 33604
Phone: 813-935-8441
Fax: 813-915-0063

Lettuce Lake Park
6920 E Fletcher Ave
Tampa, FL 33637
Phone: 813-987-6204

Lowry Park Zoo
7530 North Blvd
Tampa, FL 33604
www.the-solution.com/zoo
Phone: 813-935-8552
Fax: 813-935-9486

Lyric Opera Assn
1183-D 85 Terr N
Saint Petersburg, FL 33702
Phone: 727-578-1657

MOSIMAX-IMAX Dome Theater
4801 E Fowler Ave
Tampa, FL 33617
E-mail: tjcouch@mosi.org
www.mosi.org/imax/imaxoff.html
Phone: 813-987-6300
Fax: 813-987-6310
TF: 877-987-4629

Museum of Fine Arts
255 Beach Dr NE
Saint Petersburg, FL 33701
www.fine-arts.org
Phone: 727-896-2667
Fax: 727-894-4638

Museum of Science & Industry
4801 E Fowler Ave
Tampa, FL 33617
www.mosi.org
Phone: 813-987-6300
Fax: 813-987-6310
TF: 800-995-6674

Old Hyde Park Village
748 S Village Cir
Tampa, FL 33606
Phone: 813-251-3500
Fax: 813-251-4158

Pier Aquarium
800 2nd Ave NE
Saint Petersburg, FL 33701
Phone: 727-895-7437
Fax: 727-821-6451

Pier The
800 2nd Ave NE
Saint Petersburg, FL 33701
www.stpete-pier.com
Phone: 727-821-6164

Saint Petersburg Museum of History
335 2nd Ave NE
Saint Petersburg, FL 33701
E-mail: spmh@ij.net
www.ij.net/spmh
Phone: 727-894-1052
Fax: 727-823-7276

Salvador Dali Museum
1000 3rd St S
Saint Petersburg, FL 33701
www.salvadordalimuseum.org
Phone: 727-823-3767
Fax: 727-894-6068
TF: 800-442-3254

Sawgrass Lake Park
7400 25th St N
Saint Petersburg, FL 33702
Phone: 727-217-7256
Fax: 727-217-7258

Seminole Indian Casino
5223 N Orient Rd
Tampa, FL 33610
Phone: 813-621-1302
Fax: 813-623-6862
TF: 800-282-7016

Shuffleboard Hall of Fame
559 Mirror Lake Dr N
Saint Petersburg, FL 33701
Phone: 727-822-2083

Suncoast Seabird Sanctuary
18328 Gulf Blvd
Indian Shores, FL 33785
webcoast.com/Seabird
Phone: 727-391-6211
Fax: 727-399-2923

Sunken Gardens
1825 4th St N
Saint Petersburg, FL 33701
Phone: 727-551-3100

Tampa Bay History Center
225 S Franklin St
Tampa, FL 33602
www2.sptimes.com/Holocaust_museum/default.html
Phone: 813-228-0097
Fax: 813-223-7021

Tampa Bay Performing Arts Center
1010 N WC MacInnes Pl
Tampa, FL 33602
E-mail: thecenter@tampacenter.com
www.tampacenter.com
Phone: 813-222-1000
Fax: 813-222-1057
TF: 800-955-1045

Tampa Museum of Art
600 N Ashley Dr
Tampa, FL 33602
E-mail: museum@ci.tampa.fl.us
www.ci.tampa.fl.us/museum
Phone: 813-274-8130
Fax: 813-274-8732

Tampa Theater
711 N Franklin St
Tampa, FL 33602
www.tampabayonline.com/tour/tpatheat.htm
Phone: 813-274-8286
Fax: 813-274-8978

USF Contemporary Art Museum
4202 E Fowler Ave Bldg CAM101
Tampa, FL 33620
www.arts.usf.edu/museum/
Phone: 813-974-2849
Fax: 813-974-5130

War Veterans' Memorial Park
9600 Bay Pines Blvd
Saint Petersburg, FL 33708
Phone: 727-549-6165

Wild Life on Easy Street
12802 Easy St
Tampa, FL 33625
Phone: 813-920-4130
Fax: 813-920-5924

Ybor City
2 miles E of downtown
Tampa, FL 33605

Ybor City State Museum
1818 9th Ave
Tampa, FL 33605
E-mail: info@ybormuseum.org
www.ybormuseum.org
Phone: 813-247-6323
Fax: 813-242-4010

Ybor Market
1632 E 7th Ave
Tampa, FL 33605
Phone: 813-231-2720
Fax: 813-237-6874

Sports Teams & Facilities

Bayfront Center Arena
400 1st St S
Saint Petersburg, FL 33701
www.stpete.org/bayarena.htm
Phone: 727-892-5798
Fax: 727-892-5858
TF: 800-874-9015

Bradenton Academics (soccer)
6000 53rd Ave W Soccer Academy
Bradenton, FL 34210
Phone: 941-758-4760
Fax: 941-753-2747

Clearwater Phillies (baseball)
800 Phillies Dr
Clearwater, FL 33755
www.clearwaterphillies.com
Phone: 727-441-8638
Fax: 727-447-3924

Derby Lane Greyhound Racing
10490 Gandy Blvd N
Saint Petersburg, FL 33702
www.derbylane.com
Phone: 727-576-1361
Fax: 727-579-4362

Expo Hall
4800 US Hwy 301 N
Tampa, FL 33610
Phone: 813-621-7821
Fax: 813-740-3505

Ice Palace
401 Channelside Dr
Tampa, FL 33602
www.tampabaylightning.com/guide.html
Phone: 813-223-6100
Fax: 813-223-0095

New York Yankees Spring Training (baseball)
1 Steinbrenner Dr Legends Field
Tampa, FL 33614
E-mail: yankees@yankees.com
www.yankees.com
Phone: 813-875-7753
Fax: 813-673-3199

Raymond James Stadium
4201 N Dale Mabry Hwy
Tampa, FL 33607
www.raymondjames.com/stadium
Phone: 813-350-6500
Fax: 813-673-4312

Saint Petersburg Devil Rays (baseball)
180 2nd Ave SE Al Lang Stadium
Saint Petersburg, FL 33701
www.stpetedevilrays.com
Phone: 727-822-3384
Fax: 727-825-3294

Tampa Bay Buccaneers
4201 N Dale Mabry Hwy Raymond James Stadium
Tampa, FL 33607
Phone: 813-673-4300

Tampa Bay Devil Rays
1 Tropicana Dr
Saint Petersburg, FL 33705
www.devilray.com/
Phone: 727-825-3137
Fax: 727-825-3111

Tampa Bay Downs Inc
PO Box 2007
Oldsmar, FL 34677
Phone: 813-855-4401
Fax: 813-854-3539
TF: 800-200-4434

Tampa Bay FireStix (softball)
5802 E Fowler Ave Suite 6
Tampa, FL 33617
E-mail: info@firestix.com
www.firestix.com
Phone: 813-980-3278
Fax: 813-980-3277

Tampa Bay Lightning
401 Channelside Dr Ice Palace
Tampa, FL 33602
Phone: 813-229-8800
Fax: 813-229-3350

Tampa Bay Mutiny (soccer)
4042 N Himes Ave
Tampa, FL 33607
E-mail: mlsmutiny@aol.com
www.tampabaymutiny.com
Phone: 813-288-0096
Fax: 813-353-3837

Tampa Bay Storm (football)
401 Channelside Dr
Tampa, FL 33602
tampastorm.com
Phone: 813-276-7300
Fax: 813-276-7301

Tampa Greyhound Track
8300 N Nebraska Ave
Tampa, FL 33604
Phone: 813-932-4313
Fax: 813-932-5048

Tampa Yankees (baseball)
1 Steinbrenner Dr Legends Field
Tampa, FL 33614
www.yankees.com
Phone: 813-879-2244
Fax: 813-673-3199

Tropicana Field
1 Tropicana Dr
Saint Petersburg, FL 33705
www.devilray.com/home.html
Phone: 727-825-3120
Fax: 727-825-3204
TF: 800-522-2801

Annual Events

4th of July Celebration (July 4) 727-821-6164
All Makes Auto Swap Meet (early February) 419-478-5292
American Stage in the Park (early April-mid-May) 727-822-8814
Brandon Balloon Classic (late April)...............813-689-1221
Celebrate America (early July) 727-562-4800
Country Folk Art Show (early January & mid-October)..................800-345-3247
Festival of States (late March-early April) 727-898-3654
Fiesta Day (mid-February)........................813-248-3712
First Night Saint Petersburg (December 31)........727-823-8906
Florida State Fair (mid-February) 813-621-7821
Florida Strawberry Festival (early March) 813-752-9194
Freedom Fest (early July) 813-223-1111
Gasparilla Distance Classic late February)..........813-229-7866
Gasparilla Festival of the Arts (early March)........813-876-1747
Gasparilla Pirate Fest (late January)...............813-223-1111
Greek Festival (early September)..................419-243-9189
GTE Classic (mid-February).......................813-265-4653
Guavaweeen (late October)........................813-248-3712
Hillsborough County Fair (late October-early November) 813-223-1111
Holiday Lighted Boat Parade (early December)......727-893-7329
Holiday Show of Fine Arts & Crafts (mid-November-late December) 727-822-7872
Illuminated Night Parade (mid-February) 813-248-3712
International Folk Fair (mid-March)...............727-551-3365
July 4th Celebration (July 4)......................727-893-7441
Largo Folk Festival (late January).................727-582-2123
Mainsail Arts Festival (mid-April) 727-892-5885
Mid-Winter Regatta (late February)................727-822-3873
Old Hyde Park Village Art Festival (early October & early February)................813-251-3500
Old Hyde Park Village Live Music Series (May-October)................................813-251-3500
Outback Bowl (January 1)........................813-874-2695
Pinellas County Fair (late March-early April) 727-541-6941
President's Cup Regatta (early March).............813-253-6241
Renaissance Festival (early March-mid-April).......727-586-5423
Ribfest (mid-November)..........................727-896-2727
Ruskin Seafood & Arts Festival (early November).............................813-645-3808
Sail Expo Saint Petersburg (early November).......727-464-7200
Saint Petersburg Fall Boat Show (mid-November)...............................727-892-5767
Saint Petersburg-Isla Mujeras Regatta (late April)...................................727-822-3873
Santa Parade (early December)....................727-893-7734
Snowfest (early December) 727-892-5874
Spring Boat Show (March) 727-892-5767
Sun 'n Fun EAA Fly-In (mid-April) 863-644-2431
Super Bowl XXXV (late January) 813-350-6500
Tampa Recreation's International Festival (mid-November)..............................813-931-2106
Taste of Florida (early October)...................813-259-7376
Taste of Pinellas (late May-early June).............727-892-4193
Thistle Mid-Winter Sailboat Races (early March)....727-822-3873
Winter Equestrian Festival (late January-early April) 813-623-5801

Toledo, Ohio

***County:* Lucas**

TOLEDO is located in northwestern Ohio where the Maumee River flows into Lake Erie. Major cities within 100 miles include Cleveland, Ohio and Detroit, Michigan.

Area (Land) .... 80.6 sq mi
Area (Water)............................... 3.5 sq mi
Elevation.................................... 587 ft
Latitude ....41-66-39 N
Longitude............................... 83-55-53 W
Time Zone ....EST
Area Code....................................... 419

Climate

Toledo has a moderate climate that is influenced by Lake Erie. Winters are cold, with high temperatures averaging in the low to mid-30s and lows averaging between the mid-teens and low 20s. The average annual snowfall total for Toledo is 37 inches. Summer days are warm, with high temperatures in the low 80s, while evenings cool down into the low 60s to high 50s. Humidity is generally high in Toledo. June is the wettest month, while February is the driest.

Average Temperatures & Precipitation

Temperatures

	Jan	Feb	Mar	Apr	May	Jun	Jul	Aug	Sep	Oct	Nov	Dec
High	30	33	46	59	71	80	83	81	74	62	62	35
Low	15	17	27	36	47	56	61	58	52	40	32	21

Precipitation

	Jan	Feb	Mar	Apr	May	Jun	Jul	Aug	Sep	Oct	Nov	Dec
Inches	1.8	1.7	2.7	3.0	2.9	3.8	3.3	3.3	2.9	2.0	2.8	2.9

History

Although the Toledo area was the site of a French trading post as early as 1680 and the home of Fort Industry from 1794 to 1808, the first permanent settlement was not established in the area until after the War of 1812. The city of Toledo was formed in 1833 with the consolidation of two neighboring villages, Port Lawrence and Vistula, and the new city was named for Toledo, Spain. Two years later, in 1835, Ohio and Michigan fought for control of the city during the Toledo War. Before any blood could be shed, President Andrew Jackson granted the city to Ohio—Michigan gained the Upper Peninsula as a compromise.

Toledo's location at the mouth of the Maumee River on Lake Erie, as well as the completion of the railroad in 1836 and the Wabash and Erie and the Miami and Erie Canals during the 1840s, enabled the city to develop quickly as a distribution center. During the latter part of the 19th Century, after gas and petroleum were discovered in the area, industry flourished in Toledo. The glassmaking industry for which the city is famous began in 1888, and several of the area's largest employers still represent this industry today. In 1959, the completion of the Saint Lawrence Seaway opened the door to international trade for Toledo. Today, with a population of more than 312,000, Toledo is one of the nation's leading inland ports for foreign trade and one of the top soft-coal-shipping ports in the world.

Population

1990 Census 332,943
1998 Estimate..............................312,174
% Change .... -6.2
2005 Projection 313,959

Racial/Ethnic Breakdown

White.................................... 77.0%
Black 29.7%
Other 3.3%
Hispanic Origin (may be of any race) 4.0%

Age Breakdown

Under 18 years............................ 26.5%
18 to 24.................................. 10.8%
25 to 34.................................. 16.1%
35 to 49.................................. 20.0%
50+ years 26.6%
Median Age.................................32.9

Gender Breakdown

Male...................................... 47.4%
Female.................................... 52.6%

Government

Type of Government: Mayor-Council

Toledo City Council
1 Government Ctr Suite 2120
Toledo, OH 43604
Phone: 419-245-1050
Fax: 419-245-1072

Toledo City Hall
1 Government Ctr
Toledo, OH 43604
Phone: 419-245-1001

Toledo Clerk of Council
1 Government Ctr Rm 2140
Toledo, OH 43604
Phone: 419-245-1060
Fax: 419-245-1072

Toledo Economic Development Div
1 Government Ctr Suite 1850
Toledo, OH 43604
Phone: 419-245-1286
Fax: 419-936-3672

Toledo Finance Dept
1 Government Ctr Suite 2070
Toledo, OH 43604
Phone: 419-245-1648
Fax: 419-245-1863

Toledo Fire & Rescue Operations Dept
545 N Huron St
Toledo, OH 43604
Phone: 419-245-1125
Fax: 419-245-1296

Toledo Human Resources Dept
1 Government Ctr
Toledo, OH 43604
Phone: 419-245-1500
Fax: 419-245-1511

Toledo Law Dept
1 Government Ctr Suite 2250
Toledo, OH 43604
Phone: 419-245-1020
Fax: 419-245-1090

Toledo Mayor
1 Government Ctr Suite 2200
Toledo, OH 43604
Phone: 419-245-1001
Fax: 419-245-1370

Toledo Parks Recreation & Forestry Dept
26 Main St
Toledo, OH 43605
Phone: 419-936-2875
Fax: 419-936-2878

Toledo Planning Commission
1 Government Ctr Suite 1620
Toledo, OH 43604
Phone: 419-245-1200
Fax: 419-936-3730

Toledo Police Dept
525 N Erie St
Toledo, OH 43624
Phone: 419-245-3200
Fax: 419-936-2308

Toledo Public Service Dept
420 Madison Ave Suite 100
Toledo, OH 43604
Phone: 419-245-1314
Fax: 419-936-7299

Toledo Public Utilities Dept
420 Madison Ave Suite 400
Toledo, OH 43604
Phone: 419-245-1844
Fax: 419-245-1853

Toledo-Lucas County Public Library
325 N Michigan St
Toledo, OH 43624
Phone: 419-259-5200
Fax: 419-255-1334

Important Phone Numbers

AAA....419-843-1212
American Express Travel....419-244-3322
Dental Referral....419-474-8611
Driver's License Information....419-885-0201
Emergency....911
Events Line....419-241-1111
Lucas County Auditor....419-213-4420
Medical Referral....419-251-1000
Ohio Dept of Taxation....419-245-2885
Poison Control Center....419-383-3897
Time/Temp....419-936-1212
Toledo Board of Realtors....419-535-3222
Toledo City Auditor....419-213-4420
Vehicle Registration Information....419-255-8247
Voter Registration Information....419-213-4001
Weather....419-936-1212

Information Sources

Better Business Bureau Serving Northwest Ohio & Southeast Michigan
3103 Executive Pkwy Suite 200
Toledo, OH 43606
www.toledobbb.org
Phone: 419-531-3116
Fax: 419-578-6001

Greater Toledo Convention & Visitors Bureau
401 Jefferson Ave
Toledo, OH 43604
www.toledocvb.com/
Phone: 419-321-6404
Fax: 419-255-7731
TF: 800-243-4667

Lucas County
1 Government Ctr Suite 800
Toledo, OH 43604
www.co.lucas.oh.us
Phone: 419-213-4500
Fax: 419-213-4532

Regional Growth Partnership
300 Madison Ave Suite 270
Toledo, OH 43604
www.rgp.org
Phone: 419-252-2700
Fax: 419-252-2724
TF: 800-815-6744

SeaGate Convention Centre
401 Jefferson Ave
Toledo, OH 43604
www.toledo-seagate.com
Phone: 419-255-3300
Fax: 419-255-7731
TF: 800-243-4667

Toledo Area Chamber of Commerce
300 Madison Ave Suite 200
Toledo, OH 43604
www.toledochamber.com
Phone: 419-243-8191
Fax: 419-241-8302

Online Resources

About.com Guide to Toledo
toledo.about.com/local/midwestus/toledo

Area Guide Toledo
toledo.areaguides.net

City Knowledge Toledo
www.cityknowledge.com/oh_toledo.htm

Excite.com Toledo City Guide
www.excite.com/travel/countries/united_states/ohio/toledo

Northwest Ohio Sites Online
nwohio.sitesonline.com

Toledo Home Page
www.toledolink.com/~matgerke/toledo/toledo.html

Toledo.com
www.toledo.com

ToledoGuide
www.toledoguide.com

Area Communities

Toledo area communities with populations greater than 5,000 include:

Bowling Green
304 N Church St
Bowling Green, OH 43402
Phone: 419-354-6204
Fax: 419-352-1262

Maumee
400 Conant St
Maumee, OH 43537
Phone: 419-897-7101
Fax: 419-897-7104

Northwood
6000 Wales Rd
Northwood, OH 43619
Phone: 419-693-9320
Fax: 419-693-6705

Oregon
5330 Seaman St
Oregon, OH 43616
Phone: 419-698-7028

Perrysburg
201 W Indiana Ave
Perrysburg, OH 43551
Phone: 419-872-8010
Fax: 419-872-8019

Rossford
133 Osborne St
Rossford, OH 43460
Phone: 419-661-4272
Fax: 419-661-4279

Sylvania
4927 N Holland Sylvania Rd
Sylvania, OH 43560
Phone: 419-882-0031
Fax: 419-885-8311

Economy

In addition to glass manufacturing, Toledo is also known for automotive manufacturing. All three major American auto makers have a presence in the metro area, and Chrysler's Jeep Assembly Division is the area's largest employer, providing jobs for more than 5,000 people. The services sector accounts for the largest number of jobs in the Toledo metro area, with health care being the leading industry. Educational institutions are also important part of Toledo's economy, providing jobs for thousands of area residents—four of Lucas County's top 15 employers are education-related.

Unemployment Rate 6.4%
Per Capita Income.......................... $24,630*
Median Family Income...................... $30,980

** Information given is for Lucas County.*

Principal Industries & Number of Wage Earners

Lucas County - 1998

Agriculture 1,578
Construction... 11,735
Finance, Insurance, & Real Estate 9,318
Government 26,887
Manufacturing 36,627
Mining 120
Services 75,706
Trade 62,613
Transportation & Public Utilities 11,099

Major Employers

BAX Global Inc
1 Air Cargo Pkwy E
Swanton, OH 43558
Phone: 419-867-9911
Fax: 419-867-0792

DaimlerChrysler Corp Toledo Assembly Div
4000 Stickney Ave
Toledo, OH 43612
career.daimlerchrysler.com
Phone: 419-727-2800
Fax: 419-727-2804

Dana Corp
PO Box 1000
Toledo, OH 43697
www.dana.com
Phone: 419-535-4500
Fax: 419-535-4643

General Motors Corp Powertrain Div
1455 W Alexis Rd
Toledo, OH 43612
www.gm.com/careers
Phone: 419-470-5000
Fax: 419-470-6456

Libbey Inc
300 Madison Ave
Toledo, OH 43604
www.libbey.com
Phone: 419-325-2100
Fax: 419-325-2369
TF: 888-794-8469

Medical College of Ohio Hospital
3000 Arlington Ave
Toledo, OH 43614
www.mco.edu
Phone: 419-383-4000
Fax: 419-383-3850

Meijer Inc
2929 Walker Ave NW
Grand Rapids, MI 49544
www.meijer.com
Phone: 616-453-6711
Fax: 616-791-2572

Owens Corning
1 Owens Corning Pkwy
Toledo, OH 43659
www.owenscorning.com
Phone: 419-248-8000
Fax: 419-248-5772

Owens-Illinois Inc
1 SeaGate
Toledo, OH 43666
www.o-i.com
Phone: 419-247-5000
Fax: 419-247-2839

Seaway Food Town Inc
1020 Ford St
Maumee, OH 43537
www.seawayfoodtown.com
Phone: 419-893-9401
Fax: 419-891-4214
TF: 800-221-8816

Sylvania Board of Education
6850 Monroe St
Sylvania, OH 43560
www.sylvania.k12.oh.us
Phone: 419-885-7901
Fax: 419-885-7048

The Andersons Inc
480 W Dussel Dr
Maumee, OH 43537
www.andersonsinc.com
Phone: 419-893-5050
Fax: 419-891-6655
TF: 800-537-3370

Toledo Public School District
420 E Manhattan Blvd
Toledo, OH 43608
www.tps.org
Phone: 419-729-8200
Fax: 419-729-8425

University of Toledo
2801 W Bancroft St
Toledo, OH 43606
www.utoledo.edu
Phone: 419-530-2072
Fax: 419-530-1490
TF: 800-586-5336

Quality of Living Indicators

Total Crime Index...................................... 23,229
(rates per 100,000 inhabitants)

Violent Crime
Murder/manslaughter........................... 16
Forcible rape 155
Robbery....................................... 910
Aggravated assault........................... 1,078

Property Crime
Burglary 4,721
Larceny theft 13,571
Motor vehicle theft 2,778

Cost of Living Index....................101.7
(national average = 100)

Median Home Price....................$98,100

Education

Public Schools

Toledo Public School District
420 E Manhattan Blvd
Toledo, OH 43608
www.tps.org
Phone: 419-729-8200
Fax: 419-729-8425

Number of Schools
Elementary.................... 47
Junior High.................... 8
High.................... 9

Student/Teacher Ratio
All Grades.................... 20.4:1

Private Schools

Number of Schools (all grades).................... 45+

Colleges & Universities

Bowling Green State University
Bowling Green, OH 43403
E-mail: admissions@bgnet.bgsu.edu
www.bgsu.edu
Phone: 419-372-2531
Fax: 419-372-6955

Davis College
4747 Monroe St
Toledo, OH 43623
E-mail: admissions@daviscollege.com
www.daviscollege.com
Phone: 419-473-2700
Fax: 419-473-2472
TF: 800-477-7021

Lourdes College
6832 Convent Blvd
Sylvania, OH 43560
E-mail: srutkows@lourdes.edu
www.lourdes.edu
Phone: 419-885-3211
Fax: 419-882-3987
TF: 800-878-3210

Owens Community College Toledo
30335 Oregon Rd
Toledo, OH 43699
www.owens.cc.oh.us
Phone: 419-666-0580
Fax: 419-661-7734
TF: 800-466-9367

University of Toledo
2801 W Bancroft St
Toledo, OH 43606
www.utoledo.edu
Phone: 419-530-2072
Fax: 419-530-1490
TF: 800-586-5336

Hospitals

Flower Hospital
5200 Harroun Rd
Sylvania, OH 43560
www.promedica.org/Hosp/flower.asp
Phone: 419-824-1444
Fax: 419-824-1199

Medical College of Ohio Hospital
3000 Arlington Ave
Toledo, OH 43614
www.mco.edu
Phone: 419-383-4000
Fax: 419-383-3850

Riverside Mercy Hospital
1600 N Superior St
Toledo, OH 43604
www.mercyweb.org/Ref_Desk/facilities/facilities_riverside.html
Phone: 419-729-6000
Fax: 419-729-6647

Saint Luke's Hospital
5901 Monclova Rd
Maumee, OH 43537
Phone: 419-893-5911
Fax: 419-891-8037

Saint Vincent Mercy Medical Center
2213 Cherry St
Toledo, OH 43608
www.mercyweb.org/Ref_Desk/facilities/facilities_stvincent.html
Phone: 419-321-3232
Fax: 419-251-3977
TF: 800-837-4664

Toledo Hospital & Toledo Children's Hospital
2142 N Cove Blvd
Toledo, OH 43606
www.promedica.org/hosp/tth.asp
Phone: 419-471-4218
Fax: 419-479-6901

Transportation

Airport(s)

Toledo Express Airport (TOL)
20 miles SW of downtown (approx 35 minutes)...419-865-2351

Mass Transit

TARTA
$.85 Base fare....................419-243-7433

Rail/Bus

Central Union Amtrak Station
412 Emerald Ave
Toledo, OH 43602
Phone: 419-246-0159

Greyhound/Trailways Bus Station
811 Jefferson Ave
Toledo, OH 43624
Phone: 419-248-4665
TF: 800-231-2222

Utilities

Electricity
Toledo Edison....................800-447-3333
www.firstenergycorp.com

Gas
Columbia Gas of Ohio....................419-248-5151
www.columbiagasohio.com

Water
Toledo Water Dept....................419-245-1800

Garbage Collection/Recycling
Toledo Sanitary District....................419-726-7891

Telecommunications

Telephone
Ameritech....................800-660-1000
www.ameritech.com

Cable Television
Buckeye Cable Systems 419-724-9800

Internet Service Providers (ISPs)
GlassCity Internet Inc 419-382-6800
www.glasscity.net
Wood County Free-Net 419-354-2727
www.wcnet.org

Banks

Charter One Bank FSB
337 N Huron St
Toledo, OH 43604
Phone: 419-259-5000
Fax: 419-259-5003
TF: 800-458-1190

Comerica Bank Midwest
3450 W Central Ave Suite 230
Toledo, OH 43606
Phone: 419-531-5566
Fax: 419-531-5256

Fifth Third Bank of Northwestern Ohio NA
606 Madison Ave
Toledo, OH 43604
Phone: 419-259-7890
Fax: 419-259-7624
TF: 800-972-3030

Huntington Bank
300 Madison Ave Suite 900
Toledo, OH 43604
Phone: 419-321-1098
Fax: 419-321-1053

Mid Am Bank
519 Madison Ave
Toledo, OH 43604
www.midam-bank.com
Phone: 419-249-3300
Fax: 419-249-3375

National City Bank
405 Madison Ave
Toledo, OH 43604
Phone: 419-259-7700
Fax: 419-259-7744
TF: 800-331-8275

Standard Federal Bank
300 Madison Ave Suite 100
Toledo, OH 43604
Phone: 419-249-1081
Fax: 419-249-1079
TF: 800-643-9600

Shopping

Crafts Mall
27072 Carronade Dr
Perrysburg, OH 43551
Phone: 419-874-8049

Franklin Park Mall
5001 Monroe St
Toledo, OH 43623
Phone: 419-473-3317
Fax: 419-473-0199

North Towne Square Mall
343 New Towne Square Dr
Toledo, OH 43612
Phone: 419-476-1771
Fax: 419-476-6633

Peddler's Alley
205 Farnsworth Rd
Waterville, OH 43566
Phone: 419-878-7910

Southwyck Shopping Center
2040 S Reynolds Rd
Toledo, OH 43614
Phone: 419-865-7161
Fax: 419-865-9503

Toledo Farmers Market
525 Market St
Toledo, OH 43602
E-mail: info@toledofarmersmarket.org
www.toledofarmersmarket.org/
Phone: 419-255-6765
Fax: 419-255-6765

Woodville Mall
3725 Williston Rd
Northwood, OH 43619
Phone: 419-693-0581
Fax: 419-693-9795

Media

Newspapers and Magazines

Blade*
541 N Superior St
Toledo, OH 43660
www.toledoblade.com
Phone: 419-724-6000
Fax: 419-724-6191
TF: 800-232-7253

Toledo Business Journal
27 Broadway St
Toledo, OH 43602
www.toledobiz.com
Phone: 419-244-8200
Fax: 419-244-5773

West Toledo Herald
PO Box 8830
Toledo, OH 43623
Phone: 419-885-9222
Fax: 419-885-0764

**Indicates major daily newspapers*

Television

WGTE-TV Ch 30 (PBS)
PO Box 30
Toledo, OH 43697
www.wgte.org/TV30.html
Phone: 419-243-3091
Fax: 419-243-9711

WLMB-TV Ch 40 (Ind)
26693 Eckel Rd PO Box 908
Perrysburg, OH 43552
Phone: 419-874-8862
Fax: 419-874-8867

WNWO-TV Ch 24 (NBC)
300 S Byrne Rd
Toledo, OH 43615
www.nbc24.com
Phone: 419-535-0024
Fax: 419-535-0202

WTOL-TV Ch 11 (CBS)
PO Box 1111
Toledo, OH 43699
E-mail: toledo11@aol.com
www.wtol.com
Phone: 419-248-1111
Fax: 419-244-7104

WTVG-TV Ch 13 (ABC)
4247 Dorr St
Toledo, OH 43607
Phone: 419-531-1313
Fax: 419-534-3898

WUPW-TV Ch 36 (Fox)
4 Sea Gate
Toledo, OH 43604
www.wupw.com
Phone: 419-244-3600
Fax: 419-244-8842

Radio

WBUZ-FM 106.5 MHz (Rock)
9900 Airport Hwy
Monclova, OH 43542
E-mail: wbuz@primenet.com
www.wbuz.com
Phone: 419-868-1065
Fax: 419-867-3700

WCWA-AM 1230 kHz (Nost)
124 N Summit St Suite 400
Toledo, OH 43604
E-mail: wcwa@wcwa.com
www.wcwa.com
Phone: 419-244-8321
Fax: 419-244-2483

WDMN-AM 1520 kHz (Rel)
1510 S Reynolds Rd
Maumee, OH 43537
Phone: 419-725-9366
Fax: 419-725-2600

WGTE-FM 91.3 MHz (NPR)
PO Box 30
Toledo, OH 43697
www.wgte.org/FM91.html
Phone: 419-243-3091
Fax: 419-243-9711

WIMX-FM 95.7 MHz (Urban)
5425 Southwick Blvd
Toledo, OH 43614
www.wimx.com
Phone: 419-868-7914
Fax: 419-868-8765

WIOT-FM 104.7 MHz (Rock)
124 N Summit St Suite 400
Toledo, OH 43604
E-mail: wiot@bright.net
www.wiot.com
Phone: 419-244-8321
Fax: 419-244-2483

WJUC-FM 107.3 MHz (Urban)
130 E Airport Hwy
Swanton, OH 43558
Phone: 419-826-9582
Fax: 419-826-9558

WKKO-FM 99.9 MHz (Ctry)
3225 Arlington Ave
Toledo, OH 43614
Phone: 419-385-2507
Fax: 419-385-2902

WLQR-AM 1470 kHz (Sports)
2965 Pickle Rd
Oregon, OH 43616
Phone: 419-691-1470
Fax: 419-691-0396

WMTR-FM 96.1 MHz (CHR)
303 1/2 N Defiance St
Archbold, OH 43502
Phone: 419-445-9050
Fax: 419-445-3531

WRQN-FM 93.5 MHz (Oldies)
3225 Arlington Ave
Toledo, OH 43614
Phone: 419-385-2507
Fax: 419-385-2902

WRVF-FM 101.5 MHz (AC)
125 S Superior St
Toledo, OH 43602
www.1015theriver.com
Phone: 419-244-8321
Fax: 419-242-2846

WSPD-AM 1370 kHz (N/T)
125 S Superior St
Toledo, OH 43602
www.wspd.com
Phone: 419-244-8321
Fax: 419-242-2846

WTOD-AM 1560 kHz (Ctry)
3225 Arlington Ave
Toledo, OH 43614
Phone: 419-385-2507
Fax: 419-385-2902

WTWR-FM 98.3 MHz (CHR)
14930 LaPlaisance Rd Suite 113
Monroe, MI 48161
www.tower98.com
Phone: 734-242-6600
Fax: 734-242-6599

WVKS-FM 92.5 MHz (AC)
125 S Superior St
Toledo, OH 43602
E-mail: bigdog@925kissfm.com
www.925kissfm.com
Phone: 419-244-8321
Fax: 419-244-7631

WWWM-FM 105.5 MHz (AC)
2965 Pickle Rd
Oregon, OH 43616
www.star1055.com
Phone: 419-691-1470
Fax: 419-691-0396

WXKR-FM 94.5 MHz (CR)
2965 Pickle Rd
Oregon, OH 43616
www.wxkr.com
Phone: 419-691-1470
Fax: 419-691-0396

Attractions

Toledo's riverfront area is a popular site for festivals and concerts, and the SS Willis B. Boyer Maritime Museum, a restored freighter representing the city's port heritage, is berthed along these shores. The Toledo/Maumee Trolley Tour passes historical sites of the area, including Wolcott House, which overlooks the Maumee River and serves as the centerpiece of six historical buildings depicting life in the 1800s. Toledo's Historic Old West End is lined with late Victorian houses and is considered one of the nation's richest collections of this architectural style.

Arawana Belle
Main & Cherry Sts
Maumee, OH 43537
Phone: 419-691-7447

Arawanna II
1321 Chantilly Dr
Maumee, OH 43537
Phone: 419-255-6200

Around the Bend Players
624 Woodville Rd
Toledo, OH 43605
E-mail: tomh@aroundthebendplayers.com
www.aroundthebendplayers.com
Phone: 419-691-3946
Fax: 419-698-8915

Cassandra Ballet of Toledo
3157 W Sylvania Ave
Toledo, OH 43613
Phone: 419-475-0458

COSI Center of Science & Industry
1 Discovery Way
Toledo, OH 43604
www.cosi.org
Phone: 419-244-2674
Fax: 419-255-2674

Erie Street Market/Toledo Warehouse District
237 S Erie St
Toledo, OH 43697
Phone: 419-255-7100

Fort Meigs State Memorial
29100 W River Rd
Perrysburg, OH 43552
Phone: 419-874-4121
TF: 800-686-1545

Historic Old West End
Toledo, OH 43620
Phone: 419-321-6404
TF: 800-243-4667

Maumee Bay State Park
1400 State Park Rd
Oregon, OH 43618
Phone: 419-836-7758
Fax: 419-836-8711

Murphy's Lighthouses Inc
2017 W Sylvania Ave
Toledo, OH 43613
Phone: 419-244-6444
Fax: 419-244-6444
TF: 800-288-0563

Oak Openings Preserve Metropark
4139 Girdham Rd
Swanton, OH 43558
Phone: 419-826-6463

Ohio Theatre The
3114 Lagrange St
Toledo, OH 43608
Phone: 419-241-6785
Fax: 419-241-2151

Pearson Metropark
4600 Starr Ave
Oregon, OH 43616
Phone: 419-535-3050
Fax: 419-535-3053

Queen of the Most Holy Rosary Cathedral
2535 Collingwood Blvd
Toledo, OH 43610
Phone: 419-244-9575
Fax: 419-242-1901

Ritter Planetarium/Brooks Observatory
University of Toledo
Toledo, OH 43606
www.rpbo.utoledo.edu
Phone: 419-530-2650
Fax: 419-530-5167

Sandpiper Canal Boat
Jefferson St & Maumee River
Toledo, OH 43606
Phone: 419-537-1212
Fax: 419-535-5520

Sauder Farm & Craft Village
22611 SR 2
Archbold, OH 43502
www.saudervillage.com
Phone: 419-446-2541
Fax: 419-445-5251
TF: 800-590-5755

Schedel Arboretum & Gardens
19255 Portage River Rd
Elmore, OH 43416
E-mail: schedelgardens@glasscity.net
www.schedel-gardens.org
Phone: 419-862-3182
Fax: 419-862-1909

Secor Metropark
10001 W Central Ave
Berkey, OH 43504
Phone: 419-535-3050

SS Willis B Boyer Maritime Museum
26 Main St International Pk
Toledo, OH 43605
Phone: 419-936-3070

Stranahan Theater
4645 Heather Downs Blvd
Toledo, OH 43614
Phone: 419-381-8851
Fax: 419-381-9525

Swan Creek Preserve Metropark
4659 Airport Hwy
Toledo, OH 43615
Phone: 419-535-3050

Toledo Ballet Assn
4645 Heather Downs Blvd Stranahan Theatre
Toledo, OH 43614
Phone: 419-471-0049
Fax: 419-471-9005

Toledo Botanical Garden
5403 Elmer Dr
Toledo, OH 43615
Phone: 419-936-2986
Fax: 419-936-2987

Toledo Firefighters Museum
918 Sylvania Ave
Toledo, OH 43612
Phone: 419-478-3473
Fax: 419-936-3293

Toledo Jazz Society
406 Adams St
Toledo, OH 43604
Phone: 419-241-5299
Fax: 419-241-4777

Toledo Museum of Art
2445 Monroe St
Toledo, OH 43620
www.toledomuseum.com
Phone: 419-255-8000
Fax: 419-255-5638
TF: 800-644-6862

Toledo Opera
406 Adams St
Toledo, OH 43604
www.toledo-opera.com
Phone: 419-255-7464
Fax: 419-255-6344

Toledo Repertory Theatre
16 10th St
Toledo, OH 43624
Phone: 419-243-7335
Fax: 419-243-0454

Toledo Symphony Orchestra
2 Maritime Plaza
Toledo, OH 43604
E-mail: tolsymorch@aol.com
www.toledosymphony.com
Phone: 419-241-1272
Fax: 419-321-6890
TF: 800-348-1253

Toledo Zoological Gardens & Museum of Science
2700 Broadway
Toledo, OH 43609
E-mail: iwd@iwebd.com
www.toledozoo.org
Phone: 419-385-5721
Fax: 419-389-8670

Village Players
2740 Upton Ave
Toledo, OH 43606
Phone: 419-472-6817

Wildwood Preserve Metropark
5100 W Central Ave Toledo Metroparks
Toledo, OH 43515
Phone: 419-535-3050

Wolcott House Museum
1031 River Rd
Maumee, OH 43537
Phone: 419-893-9602
Fax: 419-893-3108

Sports Teams & Facilities

Toledo Mud Hens (baseball)
2901 Key St Ned Skeldon Stadium
Maumee, OH 43537
E-mail: mudhens@mudhens.com
www.mudhens.com/
Phone: 419-893-9483
Fax: 419-893-5847

Toledo Raceway Park
5700 Telegraph Rd
Toledo, OH 43612
Phone: 419-476-7751
Fax: 419-476-7979

Toledo Speedway
5639 Benore Rd
Toledo, OH 43612
Phone: 419-727-1100
Fax: 419-727-3300

Toledo Sports Arena & Exhibit Hall
1 Main St
Toledo, OH 43605
Phone: 419-698-4545
Fax: 419-693-3299

Toledo Storm (hockey)
1 Main St Toledo Sports Arena
Toledo, OH 43605
E-mail: gostorm999@aol.com
www.thestorm.com/
Phone: 419-691-0200
Fax: 419-698-8998

Annual Events

Art on the Mall (mid-July)........................419-530-2586
Crosby Festival of the Arts (late June)............419-936-2986
First Night Toledo (December 31).................419-241-3777

German-American Festival (late August) 419-321-6404
Homespun Holidays (early-mid-December) 419-535-3050
House & Home Show (mid-February)............. 419-255-3300
Irish Festival (mid-July).......................... 419-321-6404
Jamie Farr LPGA Tournament
(late June-early July)........................... 419-882-7153
Kroger Freedom Celebration (early July) 419-243-8024
Lagrange Street Polish Festival (early July) 419-255-8406
Lights Before Christmas
(mid-November-late December) 419-385-5721
Lucas County Fair (late July) 419-893-2127
Northwest Ohio Rib-Off (early August) 419-242-9587
Old West End Historic Festival Home Tours
(early June)................................... 419-243-1100
Old West End Spring Festival (early June) 419-321-6404
Rallies by the River (June-July) 419-243-8024
RiverFest (early September) 419-243-8024
Rock Rhythm n' Blues (late May) 419-243-8024
Rod & Custom Auto-Rama (early March) 419-474-1006
Sunshine Bazaar & Quilt Auction (mid-October).... 419-865-0251
Toledo Area Artists Exhibition
(early July-early August)........................ 419-255-8000
Warren-Sherman Festival
(late July-early August)......................... 419-242-6479

Topeka, Kansas

County: **Shawnee**

TOPEKA is located in northeastern Kansas near the geographic center of the United States. Major cities within 100 miles include Kansas City, Kansas and Kansas City, Missouri.

Area (Land)	55.2 sq mi
Area (Water)	1.0 sq mi
Elevation	1,000 ft
Latitude	39-04-83 N
Longitude	95-67-78 W
Time Zone	CST
Area Code	913

Climate

Topeka's climate features four distinct seasons. Winters are cold, with average high temperatures in the upper 30s to low 40s and lows in the upper teens to low 20s. The average annual snowfall in Topeka is 21 inches. Summer days are very warm, with average highs in the mid- to upper 80s, while evening low temperatures drop into the mid-60s. May and June are the wettest months in Topeka; January and February are the driest.

Average Temperatures & Precipitation

Temperatures

	Jan	Feb	Mar	Apr	May	Jun	Jul	Aug	Sep	Oct	Nov	Dec
High	37	43	55	67	76	84	89	88	80	69	54	41
Low	16	22	32	43	53	63	68	65	56	44	32	21

Precipitation

	Jan	Feb	Mar	Apr	May	Jun	Jul	Aug	Sep	Oct	Nov	Dec
Inches	1.0	1.0	2.5	3.1	4.5	5.5	3.6	3.9	3.8	3.1	1.9	1.4

History

The Topeka area was originally inhabited by Native Americans of the Kanza (Kansas) tribe. The first permanent settlement in the area was established by the French-Canadian Pappan brothers who started a ferry service across the Kansas (Kaw) River in 1842. During the 1850s, Topeka was the site of frequent feuds between pro-slavery settlers and abolitionists, and the town itself was founded in 1854 when a group of abolitionists met at the crossroads of the Oregon Trail and the Santa Fe Trail. At that meeting, an agreement was drawn up that became the basis of the Topeka Association, an organization that played a significant role in the town's early development. One of the anti-slavery founders, Cyrus K. Holliday, became Topeka's first mayor when the town was incorporated three years later. In 1861, Topeka was chosen as the permanent state capital of Kansas.

In its early years, Topeka developed as a processing and distribution center for the area's agricultural products, which included wheat and cattle. The arrival of the railroad in the 1860s contributed significantly to the city's growth as Topeka became a division center for the Atchison, Topeka, and Santa Fe Railroad, which remains one of the area's leading employers today. In the 1940s and 1950s, government-related jobs (including the military) and manufacturing gained importance in Topeka. Several major U.S. manufacturers, including Goodyear Tire and Rubber and Hallmark Cards, established operations in the area during this period. Topeka today, with more than 118,000 residents, is the fourth largest city in the State of Kansas.

Population

1990 Census	119,883
1998 Estimate	118,977
% Change	-0.8

Racial/Ethnic Breakdown

White	84.7%
Black	10.6%
Other	4.7%
Hispanic Origin (may be of any race)	5.8%

Age Breakdown

Under 5 years	7.4%
5 to 17	17.2%
18 to 20	3.9%
21 to 24	6.1%
25 to 34	18.0%
35 to 44	14.4%
45 to 54	9.1%
55 to 64	9.2%
65 to 74	8.0%
75+ years	6.7%
Median Age	33.6

Gender Breakdown

Male	47.6%
Female	52.4%

Government

Type of Government: Strong Mayor-Council-Administrator

Topeka & Shawnee County Public Library
1515 SW 10th Ave
Topeka, KS 66604
Phone: 785-233-2040
Fax: 785-233-2055

Topeka Chief Administrative Officer
215 SE 7th St Rm 355
Topeka, KS 66603
Phone: 785-368-3725
Fax: 785-368-3909

Topeka City Attorney
215 SE 7th St Rm 353
Topeka, KS 66603
Phone: 785-368-3883
Fax: 785-368-3901

Topeka City Council
215 SE 7th St Rm 255
Topeka, KS 66603
Phone: 785-368-3710
Fax: 785-368-3958

Topeka City Hall
215 SE 7th St
Topeka, KS 66603
Phone: 785-368-3754
Fax: 785-368-3966

Topeka Fire Dept
324 SE Jefferson St
Topeka, KS 66607
Phone: 785-368-4000
Fax: 785-368-4030

Topeka Housing & Neighborhood Development Dept
2010 SE California
Topeka, KS 66605
Phone: 785-368-3711
Fax: 785-368-2546

Topeka Human Resources Dept
215 SE 7th St Rm 170
Topeka, KS 66603
Phone: 785-368-3867
Fax: 785-368-3605

Topeka Mayor
215 SE 7th St Rm 352
Topeka, KS 66603
Phone: 785-368-3895
Fax: 785-368-3850

Topeka Parks & Recreation Dept
215 SE 7th St Rm 259
Topeka, KS 66603
Phone: 785-295-3838
Fax: 785-368-3980

Topeka Police Dept
320 S Kansas Ave Suite 100
Topeka, KS 66603
Phone: 785-368-9551
Fax: 785-368-9458

Topeka Public Works Dept
515 S Kansas Ave
Topeka, KS 66603
Phone: 785-295-3801
Fax: 785-368-3806

Topeka Treasurer
215 SE 7th St Rm 358
Topeka, KS 66603
Phone: 785-368-3770
Fax: 785-368-3975

Topeka/Shawnee County Development Corp
515 S Kansas St Suite 405
Topeka, KS 66603
Phone: 785-368-3728
Fax: 785-368-2546

Important Phone Numbers

AAA....785-233-0222
Ask-A-Nurse....785-295-8333
Driver's License Information....785-266-7380
Emergency....911
HotelDocs....800-468-3537
Kansas Income Tax Dept....785-296-3051
Poison Control Center....800-332-6633
Shawnee County Treasurer....785-233-8200
Time/Temp....785-271-7575
Topeka Board of Realtors....785-267-3215
Vehicle Registration Information....785-233-8200
Voter Registration Information....785-266-0285
Weather....785-271-7575

Information Sources

Better Business Bureau Serving Northeast Kansas
501 SE Jefferson St Suite 24
Topeka, KS 66607
www.topeka.bbb.org
Phone: 785-232-0454
Fax: 785-232-9677

Greater Topeka Chamber of Commerce
120 SE 6th St Suite 110
Topeka, KS 66603
www.topekachamber.org
Phone: 785-234-2644
Fax: 785-234-8656

Kansas Expocentre
1 Expocentre Dr
Topeka, KS 66612
www.ksexpo.com
Phone: 785-235-1986
Fax: 785-235-2967

Shawnee County
200 SE 7th St
Topeka, KS 66603
Phone: 785-233-8200
Fax: 785-291-4912

Topeka Civic Theatre
3028 SW 8th Ave
Topeka, KS 66606
www.topekacivictheatre.com
Phone: 785-357-5211
Fax: 785-357-0719

Topeka Convention & Visitors Bureau
1275 SW Topeka Blvd
Topeka, KS 66612
www.topekacvb.org/
Phone: 785-234-1030
Fax: 785-234-8282
TF: 800-235-1030

Online Resources

Anthill City Guide Topeka
www.anthill.com/city.asp?city=topeka

Area Guide Topeka
topeka.areaguides.net

City Knowledge Topeka
www.cityknowledge.com/ks_topeka.htm

Excite.com Topeka City Guide
www.excite.com/travel/countries/united_states/kansas/topeka

Area Communities

Incorporated cities in Shawnee County with populations greater than 1,000 include:

Rossville
438 Main St
Rossville, KS 66533
Phone: 785-584-6155
Fax: 785-584-6667

Silver Lake
PO Box 92
Silver Lake, KS 66539
Phone: 785-582-4280
Fax: 785-582-4195

Economy

Topeka has a diverse economic base that includes agriculture, tire manufacturing, and health care. Services is the leading employment sector in Shawnee County, and health care is Topeka's leading service-related industry, employing more than 10,000 area residents. Government is the county's second largest employment sector—the State of Kansas alone employs more than 9,400 Topeka area residents, and the United States Government employs nearly 3,000 in various agencies.

Unemployment Rate....4.9%*
Per Capita Income....$25,508*
Median Family Income....$51,200*

** Information given is for Shawnee County.*

Principal Industries & Number of Wage Earners

Topeka MSA (Shawnee County) - 1998

Industry	Wage Earners
Agriculture	357
Construction	4,521
Finance, Insurance, & Real Estate	6,786
Government	21,944
Manufacturing	9,797
Mining	87
Retail Trade	18,278
Services	27,925
Transportation & Public Utilities	4,022
Wholesale Trade	3,662

Major Employers

Blue Cross & Blue Shield of Kansas
1133 SW Topeka Blvd
Topeka, KS 66629
E-mail: csc@bcbsks.com
www.bcbsks.com
Phone: 785-291-7000
Fax: 785-291-8465
TF: 800-432-0216

Burlington Northern & Santa Fe Railway
1001 NE Atchison St
Topeka, KS 66616
www.bnsf.com
Phone: 785-435-5616

Colmery-O'Neil Veterans Affairs Medical Center
2200 SW Gage Blvd
Topeka, KS 66622
Phone: 785-350-3111
Fax: 785-350-4309

Jostens School Products Group
4000 SE Adams St
Topeka, KS 66609
www.jostens.com/yearbook
Phone: 785-266-3300
Fax: 785-266-9424
TF: 800-262-9725

Menninger
PO Box 829
Topeka, KS 66601
Phone: 785-350-5000

Payless ShoeSource Inc
3231 SE 6th St
Topeka, KS 66607
www.payless.com
Phone: 785-233-5171
Fax: 785-295-6233
TF: 800-444-7463

Saint Francis Hospital & Medical Center
1700 SW 7th St
Topeka, KS 66606
E-mail: cr@stfrancistopeka.org
www.stfrancistopeka.org
Phone: 785-295-8000
Fax: 785-295-5584
TF: 800-444-2954

Stormont-Vail Regional Health Center
1500 SW 10th St
Topeka, KS 66604
www.stormontvail.org
Phone: 785-354-6000
Fax: 785-354-5346
TF: 800-432-2951

Topeka City Hall
215 SE 7th St
Topeka, KS 66603
www.topeka.org
Phone: 785-368-3754
Fax: 785-368-3966

Topeka School District (USD 501)
624 SW 24th
Topeka, KS 66611
www.topeka.k12.ks.us
Phone: 785-575-6100
Fax: 785-575-6161

Washburn University
1700 SW College Ave
Topeka, KS 66621
E-mail: zzdpadm@washburn.edu
www.washburn.edu
Phone: 785-231-1010
Fax: 785-231-1089
TF: 800-332-0291

Western Resources Inc
PO Box 889
Topeka, KS 66601
E-mail: corpcom@wstnres.com
www.wstnres.com
Phone: 785-575-6300
Fax: 785-575-6399
TF: 800-794-4780

Quality of Living Indicators

Total Crime Index 15,500
(rates per 100,000 inhabitants)

Violent Crime

Murder/manslaughter	16
Forcible rape	100
Robbery	415
Aggravated assault	1,008

Property Crime

Burglary	2,954
Larceny theft	10,189
Motor vehicle theft	818

Cost of Living Index 99.5
(national average = 100)

Median Home Price $80,200

Education

Public Schools

Topeka School District (USD 501)
624 SW 24th
Topeka, KS 66611
www.topeka.k12.ks.us
Phone: 785-575-6100
Fax: 785-575-6161

Number of Schools

Elementary	26
Middle	6
High	3

Student/Teacher Ratio

All Grades 16.3:1

Private Schools

Number of Schools (all grades) 28

Colleges & Universities

University of Kansas
Lawrence, KS 66045
www.ukans.edu
Phone: 785-864-2700
Fax: 785-864-5006
TF: 888-686-7323

Washburn University
1700 SW College Ave
Topeka, KS 66621
E-mail: zzdpadm@washburn.edu
www.washburn.edu
Phone: 785-231-1010
Fax: 785-231-1089
TF: 800-332-0291

Hospitals

Colmery-O'Neil Veterans Affairs Medical Center
2200 SW Gage Blvd
Topeka, KS 66622
Phone: 785-350-3111
Fax: 785-350-4309

Saint Francis Hospital & Medical Center
1700 SW 7th St
Topeka, KS 66606
www.stfrancistopeka.org
Phone: 785-295-8000
Fax: 785-295-5584
TF: 800-444-2954

Stormont-Vail Regional Health Center
1500 SW 10th St
Topeka, KS 66604
www.stormontvail.org
Phone: 785-354-6000
Fax: 785-354-5346
TF: 800-432-2951

Transportation

Airport(s)

Forbes Field (FOE)
6 miles S of downtown (approx 15-20 minutes) . . . 785-862-2362
Kansas City International Airport (MCI)
72 miles NE of downtown Topeka (approx 90 minutes) . . . 816-243-5237

Mass Transit

Topeka Metropolitan Transit Authority
$.80 Base fare . . . 785-233-2011

Rail/Bus

Amtrak Station
SE 5th & Holliday Sts
Topeka, KS 66607
Phone: 800-872-7245

Greyhound Bus Station
200 SE 3rd St
Topeka, KS 66603
Phone: 785-233-2301
TF: 800-231-2222

Utilities

Electricity
KPL . . . 800-537-0746

Gas
Kansas Gas Service . . . 800-537-0746
www.kgas.com

Water
Topeka Water Dept . . . 785-295-3818

Garbage Collection/Recycling
Shawnee County Refuse Dept . . . 785-233-4774
Topeka Waste Systems . . . 785-233-2811

Telecommunications

Telephone
Southwestern Bell Telephone Co . . . 800-246-4999
www.swbell.com

Cable Television
Cox Communications . . . 785-368-1080
www.cox.com

Internet Service Providers (ISPs)
ChronicleNetWorks . . . 800-480-7050
www.chroniclenetworks.com

Banks

Bank of America
534 S Kansas Ave
Topeka, KS 66603
Phone: 785-295-3400
Fax: 785-295-3426
TF: 800-444-2410

Capitol City Bank
3710 S Topeka Blvd
Topeka, KS 66609
www.capcitybank.com
Phone: 785-266-4575
Fax: 785-266-7680
TF: 800-431-7522

Central National Bank
800 SE Quincy St
Topeka, KS 66612
Phone: 785-234-2265
Fax: 785-234-9660

Commerce Bank & Trust Co
3035 S Topeka Blvd
Topeka, KS 66611
www.cbtks.com
Phone: 785-267-0123
Fax: 785-267-8473

Community National Bank
5431 SW 29th St
Topeka, KS 66614
E-mail: cnbtopeka@cnbtopeka.com
www.cnbtopeka.com
Phone: 785-271-6696
Fax: 785-271-6623

Fidelity State Bank & Trust Co
600 S Kansas Ave
Topeka, KS 66603
E-mail: fidelity@smartnet.net
Phone: 785-233-3465
Fax: 785-233-7571

Kaw Valley State Bank & Trust Co
1110 N Kansas Ave
Topeka, KS 66608
Phone: 785-232-6062
Fax: 785-232-6513

Mercantile Bank
800 SW Jackson St
Topeka, KS 66612
Phone: 785-291-1000
Fax: 785-291-1244

Shopping

Topeka Antique Mall
5247 SW 28th Ct
Topeka, KS 66614
Phone: 785-273-2969

Wal-Mart Supercenter
1501 SW Wanamaker Rd
Topeka, KS 66604
Phone: 785-271-6444

West Ridge Mall
1801 SW Wanamaker Rd
Topeka, KS 66604
Phone: 785-272-5119
Fax: 785-272-1483

White Lakes Mall
3600 S Topeka Blvd
Topeka, KS 66611
Phone: 785-266-4548

Media

Newspapers and Magazines

Topeka Capital-Journal*
616 SE Jefferson St
Topeka, KS 66607
E-mail: letters@cjnetworks.com
www.cjonline.com
Phone: 785-295-1111
Fax: 785-295-1230
TF: 800-777-7171

**Indicates major daily newspapers*

Television

KSNT-TV Ch 27 (NBC)
6835 NW Hwy 24
Topeka, KS 66618
E-mail: 27news@ksnt.com
www.ksnt.com
Phone: 785-582-4000
Fax: 785-582-5283

KTKA-TV Ch 49 (ABC)
PO Box 4949
Topeka, KS 66601
E-mail: 49email@newssource49.com
www.newssource49.com
Phone: 785-273-4949
Fax: 785-273-7811

KTWU-TV Ch 11 (PBS)
1700 College Ave
Topeka, KS 66621
ktwu.wuacc.edu
Phone: 785-231-1111
Fax: 785-231-1112

WIBW-TV Ch 13 (CBS)
PO Box 119
Topeka, KS 66601
E-mail: wibwtv@wibw.com
www.wibw.com
Phone: 785-272-3456
Fax: 785-272-0117

Radio

KANU-FM 91.5 MHz (NPR)
Broadcasting Hall University of Kansas
Lawrence, KS 66045
www.ukans.edu/~kanu-fm
Phone: 785-864-4530
Fax: 785-864-5278

KDVV-FM 100.3 MHz (CR)
5315 SW 7th St
Topeka, KS 66606
Phone: 785-272-2122
Fax: 785-272-6219

KJTY-FM 88.1 MHz (Rel)
1005 SW 10th St
Topeka, KS 66604
E-mail: joy88@cjnetworks.com
www.joy88.org
Phone: 785-357-8888
Fax: 785-357-0100
TF: 888-569-5589

KMAJ-AM 1440 kHz (N/T)
5315 SW 7th St
Topeka, KS 66606
www.kmaj.com
Phone: 785-272-2122
Fax: 785-272-6219

KMAJ-FM 107.7 MHz (AC)
5315 SW 7th St
Topeka, KS 66606
www.kmaj.com
Phone: 785-272-2122
Fax: 785-272-6219

KTPK-FM 106.9 MHz (Ctry)
2121 SW Chelsea Dr
Topeka, KS 66614
www.twister1069.com
Phone: 785-273-1069
Fax: 785-273-0123

WIBW-AM 580 kHz (N/T)
5600 SW 6th St
Topeka, KS 66606
Phone: 785-272-3456
Fax: 785-272-3536

WIBW-FM 97.3 MHz (Ctry)
5600 SW 6th St
Topeka, KS 66606
www.97country.com
Phone: 785-272-3456
Fax: 785-272-3536

Attractions

Topeka's 160-acre Gage Park encompasses a variety of attractions. Located within its boundaries are the Topeka Zoological Park, which includes a tropical rain forest among its numerous exhibits; the Helen Hocker Theater; the Renish Rose Garden, which features more than 400 varieties of roses that bloom from May through October, as well as a variety of annuals; and the restored Victorian carousel built by the Herschell-Spellman Company in 1908—one of only 200 such carousels that remain intact today. The Mulvane Art Museum, located at Washburn University in Topeka, features international print and American art, Kansas art, and mountain-plains art. The museum extends onto the campus grounds with sculptures by Mountain-Plains Region artists. Between Topeka and Lawrence is Big Springs, a former rest stop for Oregon Trail emigrants. Visitors to Serenata Farms in Big Springs can participate in different Historic Oregon Trail expeditions.

Brown Versus Board of Education National Historic Site
424 South Kansas Ave Suite 220
Topeka, KS 66603
www.nps.gov/brvb/
Phone: 785-354-4273
Fax: 785-354-7213

Carousel in the Park
Gage Pk
Topeka, KS 66606
Phone: 785-273-1191
Fax: 785-228-6065

Cedar Crest Governor's Mansion
1 SW Cedar Crest Dr
Topeka, KS 66606
Phone: 785-296-3636
Fax: 785-272-9024

Combat Air Museum
Hanger 602 J St Forbes Field
Topeka, KS 66619
www.cjnetworks.com/~superbatics
Phone: 785-862-3303
Fax: 785-862-3304

Gage Park
635 SW Gage Blvd
Topeka, KS 66606
Phone: 785-368-3700

Gallery of Fine Arts
1515 SW 10th St
Topeka, KS 66604
Phone: 785-233-2040
Fax: 785-233-2055

Harrah's Prairie Band Casino & Bingo Hall
Hwy 75 & 150th Rd
Mayetta, KS 66509
Phone: 785-966-7777
Fax: 785-966-7640

Hocker Helen Theater
700 SW Zoo Pkwy Gage Pk
Topeka, KS 66606
Phone: 785-273-1191
Fax: 785-228-6065

Kansas Museum of History Phone: 785-272-8681
6425 SW 6th St Fax: 785-272-8682
Topeka, KS 66615
www.kshs.org/places/museum.htm

Kansas National Guard Museum Phone: 785-862-1020
6700 S Topeka Blvd Forbes Field Bldg 301 Fax: 785-862-1066
Topeka, KS 66619

Kansas State Capitol Phone: 785-296-3966
10th & Jackson St
Topeka, KS 66612

Lake Shawnee Phone: 785-267-1156
3137 SE 29th St Fax: 785-266-0308
Topeka, KS 66605

Menninger Museum Phone: 785-350-5000
5800 SW 6th Ave Fax: 785-273-9150
Topeka, KS 66606

Mulvane Art Museum Phone: 785-231-1010
1700 SW College Ave Washburn University Fax: 785-234-2703
Topeka, KS 66621

Perry State Park Phone: 785-246-3449
5441 W Lake Rd Fax: 785-246-0224
Ozawkie, KS 66070

Phoenix Gallery Phone: 785-272-3999
2900 Oakley Ave Brookwood Shopping Ctr
Topeka, KS 66614

Reinisch Rose Garden Phone: 785-272-6150
6th & Gage Blvd Gage Pk
Topeka, KS 66606

Serenata Farms Phone: 785-887-6660
1895 E 56 Rd Big Springs
Lecompton, KS 66050

Topeka Performing Arts Center Phone: 785-297-9000
214 SE 8th Ave Fax: 785-234-2307
Topeka, KS 66603
www.tpactix.org

Topeka Symphony Phone: 785-232-2032
727 S Campus Ave Fax: 785-232-6204
Topeka, KS 66603
E-mail: tso@topekasymphony.org
www.topekasymphony.org

Topeka Zoological Park Phone: 785-272-5821
635 SW Gage Blvd Fax: 785-272-2539
Topeka, KS 66606
www.topeka.org/activity/zoo.htm

Ward Meade Park Phone: 785-295-3888
124 N Fillmore St
Topeka, KS 66606
E-mail: wardmead@ksnews.com
www.topeka.org/activity/wmeade.htm

Sports Teams & Facilities

Heartland Park Topeka Phone: 785-862-4781
1805 SW 71st St Fax: 785-862-2016
Topeka, KS 66619 TF: 800-437-2237
www.hpt.com

Landon Arena Phone: 785-235-1986
Kansas Expocentre 1 Expocentre Dr Fax: 785-235-2967
Topeka, KS 66612

Annual Events

Apple Festival (early October)....................785-295-3888
Cider Days (late September)......................785-235-1986
Combat Air Museum & Pancake Feed & Fall Fling
(late April)..................................785-862-3303
Fall Parade of Homes (early-mid-October)..........785-273-1260
Festival of Beers (early October).................785-862-3303
Festival of Trees (early December)................785-233-2566
Fiesta Mexicana (mid-July)........................785-232-5088
Gem & Mineral Show (mid-October)..................785-235-1986
Holiday Happenings (early December)...............785-368-3888
Huff N' Puff Balloon Rally (mid-September)........785-234-1030
Kansas River Valley Art Fair (late July)..........785-295-3888
KBHA Quarter Horse Show (late July)...............785-235-1986
KSHSAA Rodeo (mid-June)...........................785-235-1986
Miracle on Kansas Avenue Parade
(late November)..............................785-234-9336
Mountain Plains Art Fair (early June).............785-231-1010
NHRA Parts America Nationals
(late September-early October)...............800-437-2237
Sunflower Music Festival (June)...................785-231-1010
Topeka Boat & Outdoor Show (late January).........785-235-1986
Topeka Farm Show (early January)..................785-235-1986
Topeka Railroad Days
(late August-early September)................785-232-5533

Trenton, New Jersey

***County:* Mercer**

TRENTON is located along the Delaware River in west central New Jersey. Major cities within 100 miles include Atlantic City, Jersey City, and Newark, New Jersey; Philadelphia, Pennsylvania; Dover, Delaware; and New York, New York.

Area (Land) . . . . 7.7 sq mi
Area (Water) . . . . 0.5 sq mi
Elevation . . . . 54 ft
Latitude . . . . 40-21-69 N
Longitude . . . . 74-74-33 W
Time Zone . . . . EST
Area Code 609

Climate

Trenton has cold winters and warm summers, although periods of extreme heat and cold are brief, moderated by the city's proximity to the Atlantic Ocean. Winter high temperatures average in the upper 30s to low 40s, with lows in the mid 20s and an average annual snowfall total of 23.4 inches. Summer days are very warm, with highs averaging in the mid-80s, while evenings cool down into the mid-60s. Precipitation is fairly evenly distributed throughout the year. July is typically the wettest month, while October is the driest.

Average Temperatures & Precipitation

Temperatures

	Jan	Feb	Mar	Apr	May	Jun	Jul	Aug	Sep	Oct	Nov	Dec
High	38	41	52	63	73	82	86	85	78	66	55	43
Low	23	25	33	42	53	62	67	66	59	46	38	28

Precipitation

	Jan	Feb	Mar	Apr	May	Jun	Jul	Aug	Sep	Oct	Nov	Dec
Inches	3.2	2.8	3.5	3.6	3.8	3.7	4.3	3.8	3.4	2.6	3.3	3.4

History

English Quakers established the first permanent European settlement in the Trenton area in 1679. In 1714, Philadelphia merchant William Trent purchased a section of land along the Delaware River where a new community was laid out and, in 1721, the town was named Trenton after its founder. In 1746, Princeton University, which would later become one of the nation's highest ranked "Ivy League" schools, was established in nearby Princeton. Three decades later, on Christmas Day evening in 1776, Trenton became the site of one of the most important battles in the Revolutionary War. General George Washington and his troops crossed the Delaware River and surprised the British troops who were celebrating the holiday. The battle that ensued resulted in a major victory for the Americans. On two separate occasions (in 1784 and 1799) Trenton briefly served as the temporary capital of the United States, and the city was chosen as the capital of New Jersey in 1790. Two years later, in 1792, Trenton was incorporated as a city.

Trenton grew quickly as an industrial center. The city's pottery industry helped to fuel Trenton's early economy, and by the mid-19th century iron and steel had become primary products. In 1845, the Trenton Iron Company was established, and three years later the Roebling wire works was established in Trenton to manufacture steel cable for engineer John A. Roebling's suspension bridges. By 1925, Trenton was the country's leading pottery producer and ranked among the top 10 U.S. cities for rubber, wire and cable, and iron and steel production.

The capital of New Jersey and the seat of Mercer County, Trenton remains an important center for government, industry, commerce, and education.

Population

1990 Census 88,675
1998 Estimate 84,494
% Change . . . . -4.7

Racial/Ethnic Breakdown
White 49.3%
Black 42.2%
Other 8.5%
Hispanic Origin (may be of any race) 14.1%

Age Breakdown
Under 5 years 8.4%
5 to 17 . . . . 18.2%
18 to 20 . . . . 4.6%
21 to 24 . . . . 6.6%
25 to 34 . . . . 19.1%
35 to 44 . . . . 13.9%
45 to 54 . . . . 8.6%
55 to 64 . . . . 7.9%
65 to 74 . . . . 7.5%
75+ years 5.2%
Median Age 31.4

Gender Breakdown
Male 48.5%
Female 51.5%

Government

Type of Government: Mayor-Council

Trenton City Attorney
319 E State St
Trenton, NJ 08608
Phone: 609-989-3011
Fax: 609-989-4242

Trenton City Clerk
319 E State St
Trenton, NJ 08608
Phone: 609-989-3185
Fax: 609-989-3190

Trenton City Council
319 E State St
Trenton, NJ 08608
Phone: 609-989-3185
Fax: 609-989-3190

Trenton City Hall
319 E State St
Trenton, NJ 08608
Phone: 609-989-3185
Fax: 609-989-3190

Trenton Finance Dept
319 E State St
Trenton, NJ 08608
Phone: 609-989-3041
Fax: 609-989-4248

Trenton Fire Dept
244 Perry St
Trenton, NJ 08618
Phone: 609-989-4038
Fax: 609-989-4280

Trenton Mayor
319 E State St
Trenton, NJ 06808
Phone: 609-989-3030
Fax: 609-989-3939

Trenton Personnel Office
319 E State St
Trenton, NJ 08608
Phone: 609-989-3120
Fax: 609-989-4250

Trenton Police Dept
225 N Clinton Ave
Trenton, NJ 08609
Phone: 609-989-4055
Fax: 609-989-4270

Trenton Public Library
120 Academy St
Trenton, NJ 08608
Phone: 609-392-7188
Fax: 609-396-7655

Trenton Public Works Dept
319 E State St
Trenton, NJ 08608
Phone: 609-989-3151
Fax: 609-989-4287

Trenton Recreation Natural Resources & Culture Dept
319 E State St
Trenton, NJ 08608
Phone: 609-989-3843
Fax: 609-989-4290

Important Phone Numbers

AAA 609-419-1704
Driver's License/Vehicle Registration Information 609-292-6500
Emergency 911
HotelDocs 800-468-3537
Mercer County Board of Realtors 609-392-3666
New Jersey Tax Hotline 609-588-2200
Poison Control Center 800-764-7661
Travelers Aid of New Jersey 973-623-5052
Trenton Tax Collector 609-989-3070
Voter Registration Information 609-989-6750
Weather 609-261-6600

Information Sources

Better Business Bureau Serving Central New Jersey
1700 Whitehorse-Hamilton Sq Rd
Suite D-5
Trenton, NJ 08690
www.trenton.bbb.org
Phone: 609-588-0808
Fax: 609-588-0546

Mercer County
PO Box 8068
Trenton, NJ 08650
www.prodworks.com/trenton/mercer.htm
Phone: 609-989-6470
Fax: 609-989-1111

Mercer County Chamber of Commerce
214 W State St
Trenton, NJ 08608
www.mercerchamber.org
Phone: 609-393-4143
Fax: 609-393-1032

Trenton Convention & Visitors Bureau
Lafayette & Barrack Sts
Trenton, NJ 08608
Phone: 609-777-1770
Fax: 609-292-3771

Trenton Downtown Assn
23 E State St
Trenton, NJ 08608
www.trentonnj.com/downtown/default.htm
Phone: 609-393-8998
Fax: 609-396-4329

Online Resources

Area Guide Trenton
trenton.areaguides.net

City Knowledge Trenton
www.cityknowledge.com/nj_trenton.htm

Excite.com Trenton City Guide
www.excite.com/travel/countries/united_states/new_jersey/trenton

Trenton Home Page
www.prodworks.com/trenton

Area Communities

Communities in Mercer County with populations greater than 10,000 include:

East Windsor
16 Lanning Blvd
East Windsor, NJ 08520
Phone: 609-443-4000
Fax: 609-443-8303

Ewing
2 Municipal Dr
Ewing, NJ 08628
Phone: 609-883-2900
Fax: 609-771-0480

Hamilton
2090 Greenwood Ave
Hamilton, NJ 08650
Phone: 609-890-3500
Fax: 609-890-3632

Hopewell Township
201 Washington Crossing-Pennington Rd
Titusville, NJ 08560
Phone: 609-737-0605
Fax: 609-737-1022

Lawrence
2207 Lawrenceville Rd
Lawrenceville, NJ 08648
Phone: 609-844-7000
Fax: 609-895-1668

Princeton Borough
PO Box 390
Princeton, NJ 08542
Phone: 609-924-3118
Fax: 609-924-9714

Princeton Township
369 Witherspoon St
Princeton, NJ 08540
Phone: 609-924-5176
Fax: 609-497-9101

West Windsor
PO Box 38
Princeton Junction, NJ 08550
Phone: 609-799-2400
Fax: 609-799-2044

Economy

Although Trenton is still known for manufacturing steel cables, the area's economic base has diversified significantly in recent years. New industries such as research and development are rapidly gaining importance in Mercer County. The services sector employs the greatest number of people in the county, with health care playing a principal role—four of the top 15 employers are hospitals. As the state capital and county seat, government is also a major employment sector in Trenton, employing more than 51,000 area residents. Higher education is also important to Mercer County's economy—Princeton University, one of the nation's leading educational institutions, is the county's largest employer, providing more than 4,800 jobs.

Unemployment Rate 8.8%
Per Capita Income.......................... $37,551*
Median Family Income...................... $65,000*

** Information given is for Mercer County.*

Principal Industries & Number of Wage Earners

Trenton Labor Market Area (Mercer County) - 1999

Construction & Mining.................................. 4,800
Finance, Insurance, & Real Estate 11,200
Government 51,500
Manufacturing 16,400
Retail Trade.. 26,800
Services 75,400
Transportation & Public Utilities 7,300
Wholesale Trade...................................... 6,800

Major Employers

American Cyanamid Co Phone: 609-799-0400
PO Box 400 Fax: 609-275-3502
Princeton, NJ 08543
www.cyanamid.com

American Reinsurance Co Phone: 609-243-4200
555 College Rd E Fax: 609-243-4257
Princeton, NJ 08543 TF: 800-255-5676

Bristol-Myers Squibb Co Worldwide Medicines Group Phone: 609-252-4000
Rt 206 & Provinceline Rd
Princeton, NJ 08540
www.bms.com/aboutbms/ourbus/pharma.html

Capital Health System at Mercer Phone: 609-394-4000
PO Box 1658 Fax: 609-394-4032
Trenton, NJ 08618

Covance Inc Phone: 609-452-8550
210 Carnegie Ctr Fax: 609-452-9375
Princeton, NJ 08540 TF: 888-268-2623
E-mail: feedback@covance.com
www.covance.com

Educational Testing Service Phone: 609-921-9000
Rosedale Rd Fax: 609-734-5410
Princeton, NJ 08541
E-mail: etsinfo@ets.org
www.ets.org

Fuld Helene Medical Center Phone: 609-394-6000
750 Brunswick Ave Fax: 609-394-6687
Trenton, NJ 08638

General Motors Corp Delphi Systems Div Phone: 609-771-6200
1445 Parkway Ave Fax: 609-771-6580
Trenton, NJ 08650

Lockheed Martin Corp Phone: 609-490-3400
PO Box 800 Fax: 609-490-2868
Princeton, NJ 08543
lmpeople.external.lmco.com/careers

McGraw-Hill Inc Phone: 609-426-5000
PO Box 666 Fax: 609-426-5170
Hightstown, NJ 08520
www.mcgraw-hill.com/careeropps

Medical Center at Princeton Phone: 609-497-4000
253 Witherspoon St Fax: 609-497-4977
Princeton, NJ 08540
www.mcp.org

New Jersey Manufacturers Insurance Co Phone: 609-883-1300
301 Sullivan Way Fax: 609-882-3457
West Trenton, NJ 08628 TF: 800-232-6600
www.njm.com

Princeton University Phone: 609-258-3000
Princeton, NJ 08544 Fax: 609-258-5920
E-mail: q3436@pucc.princeton.edu
www.princeton.edu

Rider University Phone: 609-896-5000
2083 Lawrenceville Rd Fax: 609-895-5766
Lawrenceville, NJ 08648
www.rider.edu

Saint Francis Medical Center Phone: 609-599-5000
601 Hamilton Ave Fax: 609-599-6257
Trenton, NJ 08629
www.healthytimes.com/stfrancis.html

Sarnoff Corp Phone: 609-734-2000
201 Washington Rd Fax: 609-734-2221
Princeton, NJ 08540
www.sarnoff.com

Trenton City Hall Phone: 609-989-3185
319 E State St Fax: 609-989-3190
Trenton, NJ 08608
www.ci.trenton.nj.us

US Postal Service Phone: 609-799-1054
331 N Post Rd Fax: 609-799-3221
Princeton Junction, NJ 08550
new.usps.com

Quality of Living Indicators

Total Crime Index...................................... 5,960
(rates per 100,000 inhabitants)

Violent Crime
Murder/manslaughter........................... 15
Forcible rape 58
Robbery.. 535

Aggravated assault.............................. 522

Property Crime
Burglary 1,169
Larceny theft 2,657
Motor vehicle theft 1,004

Cost of Living Index..................................125.5
(national average = 100)

Median Home Price.................................$144,200

Education

Public Schools

Trenton Public School System
108 N Clinton Ave
Trenton, NJ 08609
www.trenton.k12.nj.us
Phone: 609-989-2400
Fax: 609-989-2860

Number of Schools
Elementary................................. 18
Middle 4
High....................................... 1

Student/Teacher Ratio
All Grades 15.6:1

Private Schools

Number of Schools (all grades).................... 35+

Colleges & Universities

College of New Jersey
Rt 31
Ewing, NJ 08628
www.trenton.edu
Phone: 609-771-1855
Fax: 609-637-5174

Mercer County Community College
PO Box B
Trenton, NJ 08690
www.mccc.edu
Phone: 609-586-4800
Fax: 609-586-6944

Princeton University
Princeton, NJ 08544
E-mail: q3436@pucc.princeton.edu
www.princeton.edu
Phone: 609-258-3000
Fax: 609-258-5920

Rider University
2083 Lawrenceville Rd
Lawrenceville, NJ 08648
www.rider.edu
Phone: 609-896-5000
Fax: 609-895-5766

Rider University Westminster Choir College
101 Walnut Ln
Princeton, NJ 08540
E-mail: wccinfo@rider.edu
westminster.rider.edu
Phone: 609-921-7100
Fax: 609-921-8829

Thomas Edison State College
101 W State St
Trenton, NJ 08608
E-mail: admissions@call.tesc.edu
www.tesc.edu
Phone: 609-984-1102
Fax: 609-984-8447

Hospitals

Capital Health System at Mercer
PO Box 1658
Trenton, NJ 08618
Phone: 609-394-4000
Fax: 609-394-4032

Fuld Helene Medical Center
750 Brunswick Ave
Trenton, NJ 08638
Phone: 609-394-6000
Fax: 609-394-6687

Medical Center at Princeton
253 Witherspoon St
Princeton, NJ 08540
www.mcp.org
Phone: 609-497-4000
Fax: 609-497-4977

RWJ University Hospital at Hamilton
1 Hamilton Health Pl
Hamilton, NJ 08690
Phone: 609-586-7900
Fax: 609-584-6429

Saint Francis Medical Center
601 Hamilton Ave
Trenton, NJ 08629
www.healthytimes.com/stfrancis.html
Phone: 609-599-5000
Fax: 609-599-6257

Transportation

Airport(s)

Philadelphia International Airport (PHL)
39 miles W of downtown Trenton
(approx 60 minutes) 215-937-6937

Mass Transit

NJ Transit
$1 Base fare 973-762-5100

Rail/Bus

Amtrak Station
72 S Clinton Ave
Trenton, NJ 08609
Phone: 800-872-7245

Utilities

Electricity
Public Service Electric & Gas Co 800-350-7734

Gas
Public Service Electric & Gas Co 800-350-7734

Water
Trenton Water Dept 609-989-3223

Garbage Collection/Recycling
Trenton Solid Waste Management Dept..........609-989-3175

Telecommunications

Telephone
Verizon Communications.......................800-755-1068
www.verizon.com

Cable Television

Cable Television Network of New Jersey 609-392-4360
Comcast Cablevision...........................609-394-3861
Comcast Digital Cable 609-737-9000
TKR Cable....................................609-586-7000

Internet Service Providers (ISPs)

Advanced Online Services Inc (AOSI) 609-514-0010
www.aosi.com
New Jersey Computer Connection...............609-896-2799
www.njcc.com
New Jersey Internet 973-697-3338
www.nji.com
RCN Corp 609-734-3700
www.rcn.com
Verio New Jersey..............................800-358-4437
home.verio.net/local/frontpage.cfm?AirportCode=EWI

Banks

First Union Bank
370 Scotch Rd
Pennington, NJ 08628
Phone: 609-771-5700
Fax: 609-530-7267

Fleet Bank
200 E State St
Trenton, NJ 08608
Phone: 609-421-2003
Fax: 609-396-9492

Sovereign Bank
33 W State St
Trenton, NJ 08608
Phone: 609-396-7502
Fax: 609-396-5170

Summit Bank
150 W State St
Trenton, NJ 08608
Phone: 609-695-1100
Fax: 609-695-2631

Shopping

Independence Mall
2465 South Broad St
Hamilton, NJ 08610
Phone: 609-888-1116

Palmer Square
47 Hulfish St
Princeton, NJ 08542
Phone: 609-921-2333
Fax: 609-921-3797
TF: 800-644-3489

Princeton Forrestal Village
US 1 & College Rd
Princeton, NJ 08540
Phone: 609-799-7400
Fax: 609-799-0245

Quaker Bridge Mall
150 Quaker Bridge Mall
Lawrenceville, NJ 08648
E-mail: info@quakerbridgemall.com
www.quakerbridgemall.com
Phone: 609-799-8177
Fax: 609-275-6523

Media

Newspapers and Magazines

Town Topics
PO Box 664
Princeton, NJ 08542
Phone: 609-924-2200

Trenton Times*
500 Perry St
Trenton, NJ 08618
www.nj.com
Phone: 609-396-3232
Fax: 609-394-2819

Trentonian*
600 Perry St
Trenton, NJ 08602
www.trentonian.com
Phone: 609-989-7800
Fax: 609-393-6072

**Indicates major daily newspapers*

Television

KYW-TV Ch 3 (CBS)
101 S Independence Mall E
Philadelphia, PA 19106
www.kyw.com
Phone: 215-238-4700
Fax: 215-238-4783
TF: 800-238-4700

WABC-TV Ch 7 (ABC)
7 Lincoln Sq
New York, NY 10023
abcnews.go.com/local/wabc
Phone: 212-456-7777
Fax: 212-456-2381

WCAU-TV Ch 10 (NBC)
10 Monument Rd
Bala Cynwyd, PA 19004
www.nbc10.com
Phone: 610-668-5510
Fax: 610-668-3700

WCBS-TV Ch 2 (CBS)
524 W 57th St
New York, NY 10019
www.cbs2ny.com
Phone: 212-975-4321
Fax: 212-975-9387

WNBC-TV Ch 4 (NBC)
30 Rockefeller Plaza
New York, NY 10112
E-mail: nbc4ny@nbc.com
www.newschannel4.com
Phone: 212-664-4444
Fax: 212-664-2994

WNJT-TV Ch 52 (PBS)
25 S Stockton St
Trenton, NJ 08611
Phone: 609-777-5000
Fax: 609-633-2927

WNYW-TV Ch 5 (Fox)
205 E 67th St
New York, NY 10021
Phone: 212-452-5555
Fax: 212-249-1182

WPVI-TV Ch 6 (ABC)
4100 City Line Ave
Philadelphia, PA 19131
abcnews.go.com/local/wpvi
Phone: 215-878-9700
Fax: 215-581-4530

WTXF-TV Ch 29 (Fox)
330 Market St
Philadelphia, PA 19106
www.foxphiladelphia.com
Phone: 215-925-2929
Fax: 215-925-2420

Radio

WBUD-AM 1260 kHz (N/T)
218 Ewingville Rd
Trenton, NJ 08638
Phone: 609-882-4600
Fax: 609-883-6684
TF: 800-876-9599

WKXW-FM 101.5 MHz (N/T)
PO Box 5698
Trenton, NJ 08638
E-mail: nj1015@nj1015.com
www.nj1015.com
Phone: 609-882-4600
Fax: 609-883-6684

WNJT-FM 88.1 MHz (NPR)
25 S Stockton St
Trenton, NJ 08608
Phone: 609-777-5036
Fax: 609-777-5400

WTSR-FM 91.3 MHz (Misc)
2000 Pennington Rd College of New Jersey
Ewing, NJ 08628
E-mail: wtsr@tcnj.edu
www.tcnj.edu/~wtsr
Phone: 609-771-3200
Fax: 609-637-5113

WTTM-AM 1680 kHz (Sports)
619 Alexander Rd 3rd Fl
Princeton, NJ 08540
Phone: 609-419-0300
Fax: 609-419-0143

WWFM-FM 89.1 MHz (Clas)
1200 Old Trenton Rd
Trenton, NJ 08690
www.wwfm.org
Phone: 609-587-8989
Fax: 609-586-4533

Attractions

The New Jersey State Capitol Complex in Trenton houses not only state government offices but also historical attractions, including the Old Barracks Museum where Washington's troops were quartered after crossing the Delaware and taking the city of Trenton in 1776. The Old Masonic Lodge at the Capitol Complex now houses Trenton's Convention and Visitors Bureau; and the War Memorial, past site of gubernatorial inaugurations and political gatherings, is now a concert hall and theater. Located at the Capitol Complex also are the State House, Museum, and Archives, which illustrate the history of New Jersey through architecture and exhibits; and the State House Annex and Library.

Artworks Gallery
19 Everett Alley
Trenton, NJ 08611
Phone: 609-394-9436
Fax: 609-394-9551

Contemporary Victorian Townhouse Museum
176 W State St
Trenton, NJ 08608
Phone: 609-392-9727

Greater Trenton Symphony
28 W State St Suite 202
Trenton, NJ 08608
Phone: 609-394-1338
Fax: 609-394-1394

John Abbott II House
2200 Kuser Rd
Trenton, NJ 08619
Phone: 609-585-1686

Mercer County Waterfront Park
1 Thunder Rd
Trenton, NJ 08611
Phone: 609-394-8326
Fax: 609-394-9666

Meredith Havens Fire Museum
244 Perry St
Trenton, NJ 08618
Phone: 609-989-4038
Fax: 609-989-4280

Mill Hill Playhouse
Front & Montgomery Sts
Trenton, NJ 08608
Phone: 609-989-3038

New Jersey State House
125 W State St
Trenton, NJ 08625
Phone: 609-633-2709

New Jersey State Museum
205 W State St
Trenton, NJ 08625
E-mail: feedback@sos.state.nj.us
www.state.nj.us/state/museum/musidx.html
Phone: 609-292-6300
Fax: 609-599-4098

Old Barracks Museum
Barrack St
Trenton, NJ 08608
E-mail: barracks@omni.voicenet.com
www.voicenet.com/~barracks/
Phone: 609-396-1776
Fax: 609-777-4000

Passage Theatre Co
Front & Montgomery Sts
Trenton, NJ 08608
Phone: 609-392-0766

Trent William House
15 Market St
Trenton, NJ 08611
Phone: 609-989-3027
Fax: 609-278-7890

Trenton Battle Monument
Trenton, NJ 08638
Phone: 609-737-0623

Trenton City Museum at Ellarslie Mansion
319 E State St
Trenton, NJ 08608
www.ellarslie.org
Phone: 609-989-3632
Fax: 609-989-3624

War Memorial Theatre
W Lafayette St
Trenton, NJ 08625
Phone: 609-984-8484
Fax: 609-777-0581

Sports Teams & Facilities

New Brunswick Brigade (soccer)
Joyce Kilmer Ave Memorial Stadium
New Brunswick, NJ 08901
Phone: 732-517-0278
Fax: 732-517-0278

New Brunswick Power (soccer)
Joyce Kilmer Ave Memorial Stadium
New Brunswick, NJ 08901
Phone: 732-517-0278
Fax: 732-517-0278

New Jersey Wildcats
Old Trenton Rd Mercer County Pk
Trenton, NJ 08690
Phone: 609-860-2995
Fax: 609-860-2995

Trenton Thunder (baseball)
1 Thunder Rd Waterfront Pk
Trenton, NJ 08611
www.trentonthunder.com
Phone: 609-394-8326
Fax: 609-394-9666

Annual Events

Crossing The (December 25)......................215-493-4076
First Union Classic The (early June)..............609-777-1770
Heritage Days (June) 609-777-1770
Super Science Weekend (January)................609-984-0676
Trenton Jazz Festival (late August)...............609-777-1770

Tucson, Arizona

County: **Pima**

TUCSON is located in south central Arizona, 65 miles north of the U.S.-Mexican border. Major cities within 100 miles include Phoenix, Arizona and Nogales, Mexico.

Area (Land) .... 156.3 sq mi
Area (Water)................................ 0.4 sq mi
Elevation....................................2,386 ft
Latitude ....32-22-17 N
Longitude............................... 110-92-58 W
Time Zone .... MST
Area Code....................................... 520

Climate

Tucson has a warm, dry climate. Summer days are hot with high temperatures averaging near 100 degrees, while evenings cool down dramatically into the low 70s. The average humidity during the spring and summer months is only 10%, but summertime afternoon thunderstorms are common, with July and August being the wettest months. Snowfall is very rare in Tucson, where winter high temperatures average in the low to mid-60s and lows average around 40 degrees.

Average Temperatures & Precipitation

Temperatures

	Jan	Feb	Mar	Apr	May	Jun	Jul	Aug	Sep	Oct	Nov	Dec
High	63	68	73	81	90	100	99	97	93	84	73	64
Low	39	41	45	50	58	68	74	72	68	57	46	40

Precipitation

	Jan	Feb	Mar	Apr	May	Jun	Jul	Aug	Sep	Oct	Nov	Dec
Inches	0.9	0.7	0.7	0.3	0.2	0.2	2.4	2.2	1.7	1.1	0.7	1.1

History

Originally settled by the Hohokam Indians as early as the first century A.D., then later by the Pima and Tohomo O'odham tribes, the Tucson area was once called "Stjukshon," a Native American phrase meaning "spring at the foot of the black mountain." The area was first visited by Europeans in the late 17th Century when Father Eusebio Francisco Kino, a missionary for the Spanish church, explored the area around 1690. The city of Tucson, as it came to be called, was founded in 1775 by Irishman Hugh O'Connor as the site for the Presidio of San Augustin. The presidio was often referred to as the "Old Pueblo," a nickname still used for Tucson today.

Tucson was under Spanish and Mexican rule until 1854, when it became a part of the United States Territory of Arizona with the Gadsden Purchase. The city served as the territorial capital from 1867 until 1877, the year it was incorporated. Tucson was a typical "Wild West" town during the mid-to-late 1800s, and gunfights were common occurrences. In 1880, the first railroad arrived in Tucson, and more white settlers came to the area. The intermingling of cultures remains evident in Tucson's architecture, where old pueblos still stand among modern skyscrapers, as well as in the city's population, where Yaqui and Papago are still spoken by some residents and Spanish is the first language of one in seven Tucsonians.

Arizona Territorial University, which later became the University of Arizona, was established in Tucson in 1891, and during World War II Davis Monthan Air Field became an important training base. Both the U of A and Davis Monthan remain among the Tucson metropolitan area's largest employers. Tucson today, with a population of more than 460,000 is Arizona's second largest city.

Population

1990 Census 408,754
1998 Estimate..............................460,466
% Change 10.8
2010 Projection 517,336

Racial/Ethnic Breakdown

White.................................... 74.6%
Black 42.5%
Other.................................... 17.1%
Hispanic Origin (may be of any race) 29.3%

Age Breakdown

Under 5 years.............................. 7.9%
5 to 17.................................. 16.7%
18 to 20.................................. 6.5%
21 to 24.................................. 8.0%
25 to 34................................. 18.9%
35 to 44................................. 13.7%
45 to 54.................................. 8.3%
55 to 64.................................. 7.5%
65 to 74.................................. 7.2%
75+ years 5.4%
Median Age.................................30.6

Gender Breakdown

Male..................................... 48.3%
Female................................... 51.7%

Government

Type of Government: Mayor-City Council

Tucson City Clerk
PO Box 27210
Tucson, AZ 85726
Phone: 520-791-4213
Fax: 520-791-4017

Tucson City Hall
PO Box 27210
Tucson, AZ 85726
Phone: 520-791-4204
Fax: 520-791-5198

Tucson City Manager
255 W Alameda St
Tucson, AZ 85701
Phone: 520-791-4204
Fax: 520-791-5198

Tucson Community Services Dept
310 N Commerce Park Loop
Tucson, AZ 85745
Phone: 520-791-4171
Fax: 520-791-4340

Tucson Development Services Dept
201 N Stone Ave 1st Fl
Tucson, AZ 85701
Phone: 520-791-5550
Fax: 520-791-4340

Tucson Economic Development Office
PO Box 27210
Tucson, AZ 85726
Phone: 520-791-5093
Fax: 520-791-5413

Tucson Finance Dept
PO Box 27210
Tucson, AZ 85726
Phone: 520-791-4893
Fax: 520-791-4941

Tucson Fire Dept
PO Box 27210
Tucson, AZ 85726
Phone: 520-791-4511
Fax: 520-791-3231

Tucson Human Resources Dept
PO Box 27210
Tucson, AZ 85726
Phone: 520-791-4241
Fax: 520-791-4236

Tucson Mayor
PO Box 27210
Tucson, AZ 85701
Phone: 520-791-4201
Fax: 520-791-5348

Tucson Parks & Recreation Dept
900 S Randolph Way
Tucson, AZ 85716
Phone: 520-791-4873
Fax: 520-791-4008

Tucson Planning Dept
PO Box 27210
Tucson, AZ 85726
Phone: 520-791-4505
Fax: 520-791-4130

Tucson Police Dept
270 S Stone Ave
Tucson, AZ 85701
Phone: 520-791-4441
Fax: 520-791-5491

Tucson Transportation Dept
PO Box 27210
Tucson, AZ 85726
Phone: 520-791-4372
Fax: 520-791-4608

Tucson Water Dept
310 W Alameda St
Tucson, AZ 85701
Phone: 520-791-2666
Fax: 520-791-3293

Tucson-Pima Public Library
101 N Stone Ave
Tucson, AZ 85701
Phone: 520-791-4393
Fax: 520-791-3213

Important Phone Numbers

AAA....520-296-7461
American Express Travel....520-795-8400
Arizona Revenue Dept Taxpayer Assistance Line....800-634-6494
Dental Referral....602-957-4777
Driver's License/Vehicle Registration Information....520-629-9808
Emergency....911
HotelDocs....800-468-3537
Medical Referral....520-694-8888
Pima County Assessor's Office....520-740-8630
Pima County Treasurer....520-740-8344
Poison Control Center....520-626-6016
Road Conditions....888-411-7623
Travelers Aid....520-622-8900
Tucson Board of Realtors....520-327-4218
Voter Registration Information....520-623-2649
Weather....520-881-3333

Information Sources

Better Business Bureau Serving the Tucson Area
3620 N 1st Ave Suite 136
Tucson, AZ 85719
www.tucson.bbb.org
Phone: 520-888-5353
Fax: 520-888-6262

Greater Tucson Economic Council
33 N Stone Ave Suite 800
Tucson, AZ 85701
www.futurewest.com
Phone: 520-882-6079
Fax: 520-622-6413

Metropolitan Tucson Convention & Visitors Bureau
130 S Scott Ave
Tucson, AZ 85701
www.visittucson.org
Phone: 520-624-1817
Fax: 520-884-7804
TF: 800-638-8350

Pima County
130 W Congress St 10th Fl
Tucson, AZ 85701
www.co.pima.az.us
Phone: 520-740-8661
Fax: 520-740-8171

Tucson Convention Center
260 S Church St
Tucson, AZ 85701
Phone: 520-791-4101
Fax: 520-791-5572

Tucson Metropolitan Chamber of Commerce
465 W St Mary's Rd
Tucson, AZ 85701
www.tucsonchamber.org
Phone: 520-792-2250
Fax: 520-882-5704

Online Resources

4Tucson.com
www.4tucson.com

About.com Guide to Tucson
tucson.about.com/citiestowns/southwestus/tucson

Anthill City Guide Tucson
www.anthill.com/city.asp?city=tucson

Area Guide Tucson
tucson.areaguides.net

Boulevards Tucson
www.boulevards.com/cities/tucson.html

City Knowledge Tucson
www.cityknowledge.com/az_tucson.htm

DesertUSA Guide to Tucson
www.desertusa.com/Cities/az/az_tucson.html

EMOL Tucson
www.opus1.com/emol/tucson/tucindex.html

Excite.com Tucson City Guide
www.excite.com/travel/countries/united_states/arizona/tucson

Insiders' Guide to Tucson
www.insiders.com/tucson/

InsideTucson.com
www.insidetucson.com

Internet Tucson
www.itucson.com

Lodging.com Tucson Arizona
www.lodging.com/auto/guides/tucson-area-az.html

Rough Guide Travel Tucson
travel.roughguides.com/content/1187/

Tucson CityWomen
www.citywomen.com/tcwomen.htm

Tucson Community Pages
www.tucsonet.com/tucsonet/

Tucson DesertNet
desert.net

Tucson Home Page
tucson.com/tucson

Tucson Online
www.pima.com

Tucson Territory
www.tucsonterritory.com/

Tucson Weekly Observer
bonzo.com/observer

Tucson's Community Web Project
tucson.com/project

Ultimate Arizona Vacation Guide
www.webcreationsetc.com/Azguide/Tucson/

Virtual Voyages Tucson
www.virtualvoyages.com/usa/az/tucson/tucson.sht

Area Communities

Tucson area communities with populations greater than 5,000 include:

Marana
13251 Lon Adams Rd
Marana, AZ 85653
Phone: 520-682-3401
Fax: 520-682-2654

Oro Valley
11000 N La Canada Dr
Oro Valley, AZ 85737
Phone: 520-229-4700
Fax: 520-297-0428

South Tucson
1601 S 6th Ave
South Tucson, AZ 85713
Phone: 520-792-2424
Fax: 520-628-9619

Economy

Government is one of the largest employment sectors in metropolitan Tucson, employing more than 71,000 residents at the federal, state, and local levels—Arizona State Government is the area's second largest employer, providing more than 9,500 jobs for area residents. High technology and scientific research are also major industries in the Tucson area, which is sometimes referred to as "Optics Valley." The city's large number of manufacturers of high-tech equipment includes more than 13 optics firms, 300 companies involved in software development, and more than 60 aerospace-related companies.

Unemployment Rate	4.5%
Per Capita Income	$21,607
Median Family Income	$31,410

Principal Industries & Number of Wage Earners

Pima County - 1999

Construction	22,000
Finance, Insurance, & Real Estate	13,400
Government	71,600
Manufacturing	30,500
Mining	2,100
Services	110,100
Trade	71,000
Transportation, Communications, & Public Utilities	13,600

Major Employers

American Airlines
3350 E Valencia Rd
Tucson, AZ 85706
www.aacareers.com
Phone: 520-294-9555

Amphitheater School District
701 W Wetmore Rd
Tucson, AZ 85705
www.amphi.com
Phone: 520-696-5000
Fax: 520-696-5064

Asarco Inc
1150 N 7th Ave
Tucson, AZ 85705
Phone: 520-798-7500
Fax: 520-798-7782

Carondelet Health Care Corp
1601 W St Mary's Rd
Tucson, AZ 85745
Phone: 520-622-5833
Fax: 520-740-6067

Circle K Co
7840 E Broadway Blvd Suite 201
Tucson, AZ 85710
www.circlek.com
Phone: 520-722-6434
Fax: 520-751-6999

Davis-Monthan Air Force Base
Davis-Monthan AFB, AZ 85707
www.dm.af.mil
Phone: 520-228-3204
Fax: 520-228-3328

HealthPartners of Southern Arizona
5301 E Grant Rd
Tucson, AZ 85712
Phone: 520-327-5461
Fax: 520-324-2443

Intuit
2800 E Commerce Center Pl
Tucson, AZ 85706
www.intuit.com/corporate/hr
Phone: 520-901-3000
Fax: 520-901-3083

Pima Community College
4905 E Broadway Blvd
Tucson, AZ 85709
E-mail: pimaInfo@pimacc.pima.edu
www.pima.edu/
Phone: 520-206-4500
Fax: 520-206-4790

Pima County
130 W Congress St 10th Fl
Tucson, AZ 85701
www.co.pima.az.us
Phone: 520-740-8661
Fax: 520-740-8171

Sunnyside School District
2238 E Ginter Rd
Tucson, AZ 85706
www.sunnysideud.k12.az.us
Phone: 520-741-2500
Fax: 520-545-2120

Tucson City Hall
PO Box 27210
Tucson, AZ 85726
E-mail: web@ci.tucson.az.us
www.ci.tucson.az.us
Phone: 520-791-4204
Fax: 520-791-5198

Tucson Medical Center
5301 E Grant Rd
Tucson, AZ 85712
www.tmcaz.com
Phone: 520-327-5461
Fax: 520-324-5277
TF: 800-526-5353

Tucson Unified School District No 1
1010 E 10th St
Tucson, AZ 85719
www.tusd.k12.az.us
Phone: 520-617-7233
Fax: 520-798-8683

University Medical Center
1501 N Campbell Ave
Tucson, AZ 85724
www.azumc.com
Phone: 520-694-0111
Fax: 520-694-4085

University of Arizona
Tucson, AZ 85721
E-mail: uainfo-team@listserv.arizona.edu
www.arizona.edu
Phone: 520-621-2211
Fax: 520-621-9799

Quality of Living Indicators

Total Crime Index....................45,296
(rates per 100,000 inhabitants)

Violent Crime
Murder/manslaughter.......... 45
Forcible rape 364
Robbery..........1,485
Aggravated assault..........2,940

Property Crime
Burglary 6,736
Larceny theft 28,022
Motor vehicle theft..........5,704

Cost of Living Index..........99.3
(national average = 100)

Median Home Price..........$117,700

Education

Public Schools

Pima County School Superintendent
130 W Congress St 4th Fl
Tucson, AZ 85701
Phone: 520-740-8451
Fax: 520-623-9308

Tucson Unified School District No 1
1010 E 10th St
Tucson, AZ 85719
www.tusd.k12.az.us
Phone: 520-617-7233
Fax: 520-798-8683

Number of Schools
Elementary.......... 76
Middle 21
High.......... 15

Student/Teacher Ratio
All Grades 21.3:1

Private Schools

Number of Schools (all grades).......... 31+

Colleges & Universities

Chaparral Career College
4585 E Speedway Blvd Suite 204
Tucson, AZ 85712
chap-col.edu
Phone: 520-327-6866
Fax: 520-325-0108

ITT Technical Institute
1840 E Benson Hwy
Tucson, AZ 85714
www.itt-tech.edu
Phone: 520-294-2944
Fax: 520-889-9528
TF: 800-950-2944

Pima Community College
4905 E Broadway Blvd
Tucson, AZ 85709
E-mail: pimaInfo@pimacc.pima.edu
www.pima.edu/
Phone: 520-206-4500
Fax: 520-206-4790

University of Arizona
Tucson, AZ 85721
E-mail: uainfo-team@listserv.arizona.edu
www.arizona.edu
Phone: 520-621-2211
Fax: 520-621-9799

Hospitals

Carondelet Saint Joseph's Hospital
350 N Wilmot Rd
Tucson, AZ 85711
Phone: 520-296-3211
Fax: 520-721-3921

Carondelet Saint Mary's Hospital
1601 W St Mary's Rd
Tucson, AZ 85745
Phone: 520-622-5833
Fax: 520-792-2962

El Dorado Hospital & Medical Center
1400 N Wilmot Rd
Tucson, AZ 85712
www.eldoradohospital.com
Phone: 520-886-6361
Fax: 520-885-1507

Kino Community Hospital
2800 E Ajo Way
Tucson, AZ 85713
Phone: 520-294-4471
Fax: 520-741-6766
TF: 800-388-5501

Northwest Medical Center
6200 N La Cholla Blvd
Tucson, AZ 85741
Phone: 520-742-9000
Fax: 520-469-8610

Southern Arizona Veterans Healthcare System
3601 S 6th Ave
Tucson, AZ 85723
Phone: 520-792-1450
Fax: 520-629-1811

Tucson Medical Center
5301 E Grant Rd
Tucson, AZ 85712
www.tmcaz.com
Phone: 520-327-5461
Fax: 520-324-5277
TF: 800-526-5353

University Medical Center
1501 N Campbell Ave
Tucson, AZ 85724
www.azumc.com
Phone: 520-694-0111
Fax: 520-694-4085

Transportation

Airport(s)

Tucson International Airport (TUS)
12 miles S of downtown (approx 15 minutes) 520-573-8000

Mass Transit

Old Pueblo Trolley
$1 Base fare 520-792-1802
Sun Tran
$.85 Base fare 520-792-9222

Rail/Bus

Amtrak Station
400 E Toole Ave
Tucson, AZ 85701
Phone: 520-623-4442

Greyhound Bus Station
2 S 4th Ave
Tucson, AZ 85701
Phone: 520-792-3475
TF: 800-231-2222

Utilities

Electricity
Tucson Electric Power Co 520-571-4000
www.tucsonelectric.com

Gas
Southwest Gas Corp 520-889-1888
www.swgas.com

Water
Tucson Water 520-791-2650

Garbage Collection/Recycling
RETHINK IT Recycling Information Line 520-791-5000
Tucson Trash Collection 520-791-3171

Telecommunications

Telephone
Qwest 602-630-5060
www.qwest.com

Cable Television
Comcast Digital Cable 520-744-1900
Cox Communications 520-648-0005
www.cox.com
People's Choice TV 520-750-9900
Western Cablevision 520-578-0382

Internet Service Providers (ISPs)
ACES Research Inc 520-322-6500
www.aces.com

Banks

Bank of America
33 N Stone Ave
Tucson, AZ 85701
Phone: 520-792-7818
Fax: 520-792-7994
TF: 800-944-0404

Compass Bank
120 N Stone Ave
Tucson, AZ 85701
Phone: 520-620-3270
Fax: 520-620-3244
TF: 800-822-5127

National Bank of Arizona
335 N Wilmot Rd
Tucson, AZ 85711
Phone: 520-571-1500
Fax: 520-513-0134

Wells Fargo Bank
1 S Church Ave
Tucson, AZ 85701
Phone: 520-620-3413
Fax: 520-620-3410

Shopping

Antique Mall
3130 E Grant Rd
Tucson, AZ 85716
Phone: 520-326-3070

Dillard's
4550 N Oracle Rd
Tucson, AZ 85705
Phone: 520-293-4550

El Con Mall
3601 E Broadway Blvd Suite 5B
Tucson, AZ 85716
Phone: 520-795-9958
Fax: 520-323-1856

Foothills Mall
7401 N La Cholla Blvd
Tucson, AZ 85741
Phone: 520-742-7191
Fax: 520-797-0936

Fourth Avenue Historic District
4th Ave
Tucson, AZ 85705
Phone: 520-624-5004
Fax: 520-624-5933

Indoor Swap Meet at Marketplace USA
3750 E Irvington Rd
Tucson, AZ 85714
Phone: 520-745-5000
Fax: 520-571-9163

Macys Park Mall
5850 E Broadway Blvd
Tucson, AZ 85711
Phone: 520-322-2100

Marketplace USA
3750 E Irvington Rd
Tucson, AZ 85714
Phone: 520-745-5000
Fax: 520-571-9163

Old Town Artisans
186 N Meyer Ave
Tucson, AZ 85701
Phone: 520-623-6024

Park Place
5870 E Broadway Blvd
Tucson, AZ 85711
www.park-mall.com
Phone: 520-747-7575
Fax: 520-571-7652

Plaza Palomino
2970 N Swan Rd
Tucson, AZ 85712
Phone: 520-795-1177
Fax: 520-795-7872

River Center
5605 E River Rd
Tucson, AZ 85715
Phone: 520-577-7272

Tucson Mall
4500 N Oracle Rd
Tucson, AZ 85705
Phone: 520-293-7330
Fax: 520-293-0543

Media

Newspapers and Magazines

Arizona Daily Star*
PO Box 26807
Tucson, AZ 85726
E-mail: wnett@azstarnet.com
www.azstarnet.com
Phone: 520-573-4220
Fax: 520-573-4107

Tucson Citizen*
PO Box 26767
Tucson, AZ 85726
E-mail: citizen@tucsoncitizen.com
www.tucsoncitizen.com
Phone: 520-573-4560
Fax: 520-573-4569

Tucson Lifestyle Magazine
7000 E Tanque Verde Rd Suite 11
Tucson, AZ 85715
Phone: 520-721-2929
Fax: 520-721-8665

Tucson Weekly
PO Box 2429
Tucson, AZ 85702
E-mail: tucsonweekly@desert.net
www.tucsonweekly.com
Phone: 520-792-3630
Fax: 520-792-2096

**Indicates major daily newspapers*

Television

KGUN-TV Ch 9 (ABC)
7280 E Rosewood St
Tucson, AZ 85710
www.kgun9.com
Phone: 520-722-5486
Fax: 520-733-7050

KHRR-TV Ch 40 (Tele)
2919 E Broadway Blvd
Tucson, AZ 85716
Phone: 520-322-6888
Fax: 520-881-7926

KMSB-TV Ch 11 (Fox)
1855 N 6th Ave
Tucson, AZ 85705
Phone: 520-770-1123
Fax: 520-629-7185

KOLD-TV Ch 13 (CBS)
7831 N Business Park Dr
Tucson, AZ 85743
E-mail: admin@kold-tv.com
www.kold-tv.com
Phone: 520-744-1313
Fax: 520-744-5235

KTTU-TV Ch 18 (UPN)
1855 N 6th Ave
Tucson, AZ 85705
Phone: 520-624-0180
Fax: 520-629-7185

KUAT-TV Ch 6 (PBS)
University of Arizona PO Box 210067
Tucson, AZ 85721
w3.arizona.edu/~kuat/tv/index.html
Phone: 520-621-5828
Fax: 520-621-4122

KUVE-TV Ch 52 (Uni)
2301 N Forbes Blvd Suite 108
Tucson, AZ 85745
www.univision.net/stations/kuve.htm
Phone: 520-622-0984
Fax: 520-620-0046

KVOA-TV Ch 4 (NBC)
PO Box 5188
Tucson, AZ 85703
www.kvoa.com
Phone: 520-792-2270
Fax: 520-620-1309

Radio

KCEE-AM 790 kHz (Oldies)
PO Box 5886
Tucson, AZ 85703
Phone: 520-623-7556
Fax: 520-792-1019

KCUB-AM 1290 kHz (Ctry)
575 W Roger Rd
Tucson, AZ 85705
Phone: 520-887-1000
Fax: 520-887-6397

KFFN-AM 1490 kHz (Sports)
3438 N Country Club Rd
Tucson, AZ 85716
E-mail: thefan@theriver.com
www.theriver.com/thefan
Phone: 520-795-1490
Fax: 520-327-2260

KIIM-FM 99.5 MHz (Ctry)
575 W Roger Rd
Tucson, AZ 85705
www.kiimfm.com
Phone: 520-887-1000
Fax: 520-887-6397

KKLD-FM 94.9 MHz (AC)
3438 N Country Club Rd
Tucson, AZ 85716
E-mail: mixfm@theriver.com
www.theriver.com/mixfm
Phone: 520-795-1490
Fax: 520-327-2260

KLPX-FM 96.1 MHz (Rock)
1920 W Copper Dr
Tucson, AZ 85745
Phone: 520-622-6711
Fax: 520-624-3226

KNST-AM 940 kHz (N/T)
4400 E Broadway Blvd Suite 200
Tucson, AZ 85711
Phone: 520-323-9400
Fax: 520-327-9384

KRQQ-FM 93.7 MHz (CHR)
4400 E Broadway Blvd Suite 200
Tucson, AZ 85711
Phone: 520-323-9400
Fax: 520-327-9384

KTKT-AM 990 kHz (N/T)
1920 W Copper Pl
Tucson, AZ 85745
www.ktkt.com
Phone: 520-622-6711
Fax: 520-624-3226

KUAT-AM 1550 kHz (NPR)
PO Box 210067
Tucson, AZ 85721
E-mail: radio@kuat.arizona.edu
w3.arizona.edu/~kuat/radio/index.html
Phone: 520-621-7548
Fax: 520-621-3360

KUAZ-FM 89.1 MHz (NPR)
PO Box 210067
Tucson, AZ 85721
E-mail: kuat@arizona.edu
Phone: 520-621-7548
Fax: 520-621-9105

KWFM-FM 92.9 MHz (Oldies)
3202 N Oracle Rd
Tucson, AZ 85705
E-mail: cool-fm@theriver.com
www.theriver.com/cool-fm/
Phone: 520-623-7556
Fax: 520-628-2122

Attractions

The Arizona-Sonora Desert Museum in Tucson features more than 300 species of live animals and some 1,300 species of plants indigenous to the Sonoran Desert. The Sonoran Desert is the only place in the world where saguaro cactus grow, and the largest concentration of this cactus is found at Saguaro National Park just outside

Tucson (both east and west of the city). Saguaro-rib ceilings are featured in two rooms of Old Town Artisans, an artisans' marketplace in downtown Tucson. The downtown area is known as the Tucson Arts District due to the city's efforts to use arts as a unifying force for the area. Fine artwork can also be seen at the San Xavier del Bac Mission, located southwest of the city on the Tohono O'odham Indian Reservation; the Mission has been called the "Sistine Chapel of North America." Kitt Peak National Observatory, which houses the world's largest collection of astronomical telescopes, is also located just outside Tucson; and the Santa Catalina Mountains are only a 30-minute drive from the city. Other area attractions include Biosphere 2, a 3.15-acre closed system with seven ecosystems; Coronado National Forest; and the town of Tombstone, featuring the infamous OK Corral and Boot Hill cemetery.

390th Memorial Museum Phone: 520-574-0287
6000 E Valencia Rd Fax: 520-574-3030
Tucson, AZ 85706
www.390th.org

Arizona Historical Society Phone: 520-628-5774
949 E 2nd St Fax: 520-629-8966
Tucson, AZ 85719
www.tempe.gov/ahs

Arizona Opera Co Phone: 520-293-4336
3501 N Mountain Ave Fax: 520-293-5097
Tucson, AZ 85719
www.azopera.com

Arizona State Museum Phone: 520-621-6302
1013 E University Blvd University of Arizona Fax: 520-621-2976
Tucson, AZ 85721
www.statemuseum.arizona.edu

Arizona Theatre Co Phone: 520-884-8210
40 E 14th St Brady Court Fax: 520-628-9129
Tucson, AZ 85701

Arizona-Sonora Desert Museum Phone: 520-883-1380
2021 N Kinney Rd Fax: 520-883-2500
Tucson, AZ 85743
www.desertmuseum.org

Biosphere 2 Phone: 520-896-6200
32540 S Biosphere Rd Fax: 520-896-6471
Oracle, AZ 85623
www.bio2.edu

Breakers Water Park Phone: 520-682-2530
8555 W Tangerine Rd Fax: 520-682-2247
Marana, AZ 85705

Casino of the Sun Phone: 520-883-1700
7406 S Camino de Oeste Fax: 520-883-0983
Tucson, AZ 85746 TF: 800-344-9435

Center for Creative Photography Phone: 520-621-7968
1030 N Olive Rd Bldg 103 University of Arizona Fax: 520-621-9444
Tucson, AZ 85721
E-mail: oncenter@ccp.arizona.edu
dizzy.library.arizona.edu/branches/ccp

Chiricahua National Monument Phone: 520-824-3560
HCR 2 Box 6500 Fax: 520-824-3421
Willcox, AZ 85643
www.nps.gov/chir/

Civic Orchestra of Tucson Phone: 520-791-9246
PO Box 42764
Tucson, AZ 85733

Cocoraque Ranch Cattle Drives Phone: 520-682-8594
6255 N Diamond Hills Ln
Tucson, AZ 85743

Colossal Cave Mountain Park Phone: 520-647-7275
16711 E Colossal Cave Rd Fax: 520-647-3299
Vail, AZ 85641
E-mail: info@colossalcave.com
www.colossalcave.com

Coronado National Forest Phone: 520-749-8700
5700 N Sabino Canyon Rd Fax: 520-670-4719
Tucson, AZ 85750
www.fs.fed.us/r3/coronado

Coronado National Memorial Phone: 520-366-5515
4101 E Montezuma Canyon Rd Fax: 520-366-5707
Hereford, AZ 85615
www.nps.gov/coro/

DeGrazia Art Museum Phone: 520-299-9191
6300 N Swan Rd Fax: 520-299-1381
Tucson, AZ 85718 TF: 800-545-2185

Desert Diamond Casino Phone: 520-294-7777
7350 S Old Nogales Hwy Fax: 520-295-2771
Tucson, AZ 85706

Flandrau Science Center & Planetarium Phone: 520-621-4515
University of Arizona 1601 University Blvd Fax: 520-621-8451
Tucson, AZ 85721
www.flandrau.org

Fort Bowie National Historic Site Phone: 520-847-2500
PO Box 158 Fax: 520-847-2221
Bowie, AZ 85605
www.nps.gov/fobo

Fort Huachuca Museum Phone: 520-533-5736
Fort Huachuca Army Post Fax: 520-533-5736
Sierra Vista, AZ 85636

Fort Lowell Museum Phone: 520-885-3832
2900 N Craycroft Rd
Tucson, AZ 85712

Fourth Avenue Historic District Phone: 520-624-5004
4th Ave Fax: 520-624-5933
Tucson, AZ 85705

Franklin Museum Phone: 520-326-8038
3420 N Vine St
Tucson, AZ 85719

Funtasticks Family Fun Park Phone: 520-888-5739
221 E Wetmore Rd
Tucson, AZ 85705

Gateway Ice Center Phone: 520-290-8800
7333 E Rosewood St Fax: 520-290-2326
Tucson, AZ 85710

Gene C Reid Regional Park Phone: 520-791-4873
900 S Randolph Way City of Tucson Parks & Recreation Dept Fax: 520-791-4008
Tucson, AZ 85716

Golf N' Stuff Family Fun Center
6503 E Tanque Verde Rd
Tucson, AZ 85715
Phone: 520-296-2366
Fax: 520-296-0229

International Wildlife Museum
4800 W Gates Pass Rd
Tucson, AZ 85745
www.arizonaguide.com/iwm/
Phone: 520-629-0100
Fax: 520-622-1205

Invisible Theatre
1400 N 1st Ave
Tucson, AZ 85719
Phone: 520-882-9721
Fax: 520-884-5410

John F Kennedy Regional Park
3700 S Mission Rd
Tucson, AZ 85706
Phone: 520-791-4873

Justin's Water World
3551 San Joaquin Rd
Tucson, AZ 85735
Phone: 520-883-8340
Fax: 520-578-0823

Kitt Peak National Observatory
950 N Cherry Ave
Tucson, AZ 85719
E-mail: kpno@noao.edu
www.noao.edu/kpno/kpno.html
Phone: 520-318-8600
Fax: 520-318-8724

OK Corral
308 Allen St
Tombstone, AZ 85638
E-mail: okcorral@ok-corral.com
www.ok-corral.com
Phone: 520-457-3456

Old Pueblo Archaeology Center
1000 E Fort Lowell Rd
Tucson, AZ 85717
Phone: 520-798-1201
Fax: 520-798-1966

Old Town Artisans
186 N Meyer Ave
Tucson, AZ 85701
Phone: 520-623-6024

Old Tucson Studios
201 S Kinney Rd
Tucson, AZ 85735
www.emol.org/emol/tucson/oldtucson/otindex.html
Phone: 520-883-0100
Fax: 520-578-1269

Organ Pipe Cactus National Monument
RR 1 Box 100
Ajo, AZ 85321
www.nps.gov/orpi/
Phone: 520-387-6849
Fax: 520-387-7144

Picture Rocks Miniature Horse Ranch
6611 N Taylor Ln
Tucson, AZ 85743
Phone: 520-682-8009
Fax: 520-616-7022

Pima Air & Space Museum
6000 E Valencia Rd
Tucson, AZ 85706
E-mail: pimaair@azstarnet.com
www.pimaair.org/
Phone: 520-574-0462
Fax: 520-574-9238

Red Rock State Park
4050 Lower Red Rock Loop Rd
Sedona, AZ 86336
www.pr.state.az.us/parkhtml/redrock.html
Phone: 520-282-6907
Fax: 520-282-5972

Reid Park Zoo
1100 S Randolph Way
Tucson, AZ 85716
Phone: 520-791-3204
Fax: 520-791-5378

Rialto The
318 E Congress St
Tucson, AZ 85701
Phone: 520-740-0126

RW Webb Winery/Dark Mountain Brewery
13605 E Benson Hwy
Vail, AZ 85641
Phone: 520-762-5777
Fax: 520-762-5898

Sabino Canyon
5900 N Sabino Canyon Rd
Tucson, AZ 85750
mmm.arizonaguide.com/sabino.canyon.tours
Phone: 520-749-2327
Fax: 520-749-9679

Saguaro National Park
3693 S Old Spanish Trail
Tucson, AZ 85730
www.nps.gov/sagu/
Phone: 520-733-5100
Fax: 520-733-5183

San Xavier Del Bac Mission
1950 W San Xavier Rd
Tucson, AZ 85746
Phone: 520-294-2624

Scottish Rite Cathedral
160 S Scott Ave
Tucson, AZ 85701
Phone: 520-622-8364
Fax: 520-622-8660

Sosa-Carrillo-Fremont House Museum
151 S Granada Ave
Tucson, AZ 85701
Phone: 520-622-0956
Fax: 520-628-5695

Temple of Music & Art
330 S Scott Ave
Tucson, AZ 85701
Phone: 520-884-8210
Fax: 520-628-9129

Tohono Chul Park
7366 N Paseo del Norte
Tucson, AZ 85704
mmm.arizonaguide.com/tohonochul
Phone: 520-575-8468
Fax: 520-797-1213

Triple C Chuckwagon Suppers
8900 W Bopp Rd
Tucson, AZ 85735
E-mail: camps4@earthlink.net
www.ccc-chuckwagon.com
Phone: 520-883-2333
Fax: 520-883-0360
TF: 800-446-1798

Tucson Arts District
downtown
Tucson, AZ 85702
E-mail: artdist@azstarnet.com
tucson.com/TAD/TADHome.HTML
Phone: 520-624-9977
Fax: 520-624-4994

Tucson Botanical Gardens
2150 N Alvernon Way
Tucson, AZ 85712
Phone: 520-326-9255
Fax: 520-324-0166

Tucson Children's Museum
200 S 6th Ave
Tucson, AZ 85701
www.azstarnet.com/~tuchimu/
Phone: 520-884-7511
Fax: 520-792-0639

Tucson Mountain Park
Ajo Way & Kinney Rd
Tucson, AZ 85713
Phone: 520-740-2690

Tucson Museum of Art & Historic Block
140 N Main Ave
Tucson, AZ 85701
www.azstarnet.com/~tmaedu/
Phone: 520-624-2333
Fax: 520-624-7202

Tucson Symphony Orchestra Phone: 520-882-8585
2175 N 6th Ave
Tucson, AZ 85705
E-mail: info@tucsym.org
www.tucsym.org

Tumacacori National Historical Park Phone: 520-398-2341
1891 E Frontage Rd Fax: 520-398-9271
Tumacacori, AZ 85640
www.nps.gov/tuma

UApresents Phone: 520-621-3341
1020 E University Blvd
Tucson, AZ 85721
E-mail: presents@u.arizona.edu
uapresents.arizona.edu

University of Arizona Museum of Art Phone: 520-621-7567
Park Ave & Speedway Blvd University of Arizona Fax: 520-621-8770
Tucson, AZ 85721
artmuseum.arizona.edu/art.html

Valley of the Moon Park Phone: 520-323-1331
2544 E Allen Rd
Tucson, AZ 85716

Yozeum The Phone: 520-322-0100
2900 N Country Club Fax: 520-325-1614
Tucson, AZ 85716
www.playmaxx.com

Sports Teams & Facilities

Arizona Diamondbacks Spring Training (baseball) Phone: 520-434-1400
Tucson Electric Park 2500 E Ajo Way
Tucson, AZ 85713

Arizona Stadium Phone: 520-621-4622
1 National Championship Dr Fax: 520-621-9690
Tucson, AZ 85721

Chicago White Sox Spring Training (baseball) Phone: 520-434-1111
Tucson Electric Park 2500 E Ajo Way
Tucson, AZ 85713

Colorado Rockies Spring Training (baseball) Phone: 520-327-9467
3400 E Camino Campestre Hi Corbett Field Fax: 520-327-5910
Tucson, AZ 85716 TF: 800-388-7625

Hi Corbett Field Phone: 520-327-9700
3400 E Camino Campestre Fax: 520-327-2370
Tucson, AZ 85716

Tucson Greyhound Park Phone: 520-884-7576
2601 S 3rd Ave Fax: 520-624-9389
Tucson, AZ 85713
www.tucdogtrak.com

Tucson Raceway Park Phone: 520-762-9200
PO Box 18759 Fax: 520-762-5053
Tucson, AZ 85731
www.tucsonracewaypark.com

Tucson Sidewinders (baseball) Phone: 520-434-1021
2500 E Ajo Way Tucson Electrical Pk Fax: 520-889-9477
Tucson, AZ 85713
www.tucsonsidewinders.com

Annual Events

4th Avenue Street Fair (late March & early December) .520-624-5004
Balloon Glo (early December) .520-621-9034
Big Boys Toy Show (early April) .520-762-3247
Cinco de Mayo (early May) .520-791-4873
Cochise Cowboy Poetry & Music Gathering (early February) .520-459-3868
Desert Thunder Pro Rodeo (late October) .520-721-1621
El Tour de Tucson (late November) .520-745-2033
Fall Festival (mid-October) .520-394-0060
Fall Home & Garden Show (mid-October) .520-795-3025
Fiesta de los Chiles (late October) .520-326-9255
Holiday Craft Market (late November) .520-624-2333
Independence Day (July 4) .520-791-4860
Indian America (early January) .520-622-4900
International Mariachi Conference (late April) .520-884-9920
Juneteenth Festival (mid-June) .520-791-4355
La Fiesta de los Vaqueros Rodeo (late February) .520-624-1817
Luminaria Nights (early December) .520-326-9255
Music Under the Stars (mid-May-mid-June) .520-791-4873
Norteno Music Festival (late August) .520-622-2801
Pima County Fair (mid-April) .520-762-9100
Shakespeare in the Park (late June) .520-791-4079
Spring Fling (early April) .520-621-5610
Spring Home & Patio Show (early April) .520-795-3025
Square & Round Dance & Clogging Festival (mid-January) .520-885-5032
Summerset Suite (June-July) .520-743-3399
Touchstone Energy Tucson Open (early-mid-January) .800-882-7660
Tucson Gem & Mineral Show (mid-February) .520-322-5773
Tucson Heritage Experience Festival (early October) .520-621-3701
Tucson Marathon (early December) .520-320-0667
Tucson Rodeo (late February) .520-741-2233
Vigilante Days (early August) .800-457-3423
Western Music Festival (mid-November) .520-743-9794
Wildflower Festival (early April) .520-742-6455
Wyatt Earp Days (late May) .800-457-3423

Tulsa, Oklahoma

***County:* Tulsa**

TULSA is located along the Arkansas River in northeastern Oklahoma. Major cities within 100 miles include Oklahoma City, Oklahoma and Joplin, Missouri.

Area (Land) .... 172.6 sq mi
Area (Water)................................ 4.2 sq mi
Elevation...................................... 750 ft
Latitude ....36-15-39 N
Longitude............................... 95-99-25 W
Time Zone ....CST
Area Code.. 918

Climate

Tulsa's climate features four distinct seasons that are influenced by cooler air flowing south from the Great Plains and Canada and warm, moist air flowing northward from the Gulf of Mexico. Winters are generally mild, although short periods of cold and snowy weather are not uncommon. Winter high temperatures average in the upper 40s, with lows in the upper 20s. The average annual snowfall in Tulsa is 5.4 inches. Summer days are hot, with high temperatures averaging in the low 90s, while evenings cool down into the low 70s. May is the wettest month in Tulsa, while January is the driest.

Average Temperatures & Precipitation

Temperatures

	Jan	Feb	Mar	Apr	May	Jun	Jul	Aug	Sep	Oct	Nov	Dec
High	45	51	62	73	80	88	94	93	84	74	60	49
Low	25	30	39	50	59	68	73	71	63	51	40	29

Precipitation

	Jan	Feb	Mar	Apr	May	Jun	Jul	Aug	Sep	Oct	Nov	Dec
Inches	1.5	2.0	3.5	3.7	5.6	4.4	3.1	3.1	4.7	3.7	3.1	2.2

History

The Tulsa area was originally settled by members of the Creek Nation who had traveled to Oklahoma along the infamous Trail of Tears. The first permanent settlement in the area was established in 1836 and was originally called Tullahassee or Tulsi, a Creek word meaning "old town." The name of the town was officially changed to Tulsey Town when the first post office was established in the area, and eventually shortened to Tulsa, as the city is known today. The city was located on Indian Territory until its incorporation at the turn of the century and Tulsa today has one of the largest concentrations of American Indians in the United States.

In its early days, Tulsa was a popular resting place for cattlemen traveling from Texas to the slaughterhouses in Kansas City and Chicago. White settlement in Tulsa began with the arrival of the Frisco Railroad in 1882. Improvements in transportation access and the oil boom of the early 1900s brought a myriad of economic opportunities to Tulsa, and the city and surrounding area grew quickly as a center for oil production. At the time of Tulsa's incorporation in 1898, the city was home to 200 people, but over the course of the next 22 years Tulsa's population skyrocketed to 72,000. The city was considered the "Oil Capital of the World" from the 1920s until World War II, when many companies began concentrating their efforts offshore. Tulsa, however, continued to grow during the 1940s as many aircraft companies were established in the area to supply the war effort. The aviation industry continues to play a major role in Tulsa's economy today.

Tulsa is currently home to nearly 381,000 people. With a diverse economy and low cost of living, the city's growth is expected to continue into the 21st Century, exceeding 400,000 by the year 2004.

Population

1990 Census 367,302
1998 Estimate..............................381,393
% Change 3.8
2004 Projection 409,360

Racial/Ethnic Breakdown

White.................................... 76.9%
Black 15.3%
Other..................................... 7.8%
Hispanic Origin (may be of any race) 3.0%

Age Breakdown

Under 5 years.............................. 8.6%
6 to 13.................................. 11.1%
14 to 17................................... 5.0%
18 to 24................................... 9.6%
25 to 34.................................. 15.9%
35 to 44.................................. 16.1%
45 to 54.................................. 11.7%
55 to 64................................... 8.5%
65 to 74................................... 7.7%
75 to 84................................... 4.3%
85+ years 1.4%
Median Age.................................34.9

Gender Breakdown

Male..................................... 47.9%
Female................................... 52.1%

Government

Type of Government: Mayor-Council

Tulsa City Attorney
200 Civic Ctr Rm 316
Tulsa, OK 74103
Phone: 918-596-7717
Fax: 918-596-9700

Tulsa City Clerk Phone: 918-596-7513
200 Civic Ctr Rm 903 Fax: 918-699-3183
Tulsa, OK 74103

Tulsa City Council Phone: 918-596-1990
200 Civic Ctr Suite 200 Fax: 918-596-1964
Tulsa, OK 74103

Tulsa City Hall Phone: 918-596-2100
200 Civic Ctr
Tulsa, OK 74103

Tulsa City-County Library Phone: 918-596-7977
400 Civic Ctr Fax: 918-596-7990
Tulsa, OK 74103

Tulsa Economic Development Corp Phone: 918-585-8332
907 S Detroit Suite 1001 Fax: 918-585-2473
Tulsa, OK 74120

Tulsa Finance Dept Phone: 918-596-7522
200 Civic Ctr 10th Fl Fax: 918-596-7224
Tulsa, OK 74103

Tulsa Fire Dept Phone: 918-596-9441
411 S Frankfort Ave Fax: 918-596-9383
Tulsa, OK 74120

Tulsa Human Resources Dept Phone: 918-596-7427
200 Civic Ctr Rm 105 Fax: 918-596-2327
Tulsa, OK 74103

Tulsa Mayor Phone: 918-596-7411
200 Civic Ctr Fax: 918-596-9010
Tulsa, OK 74103

Tulsa Parks & Recreation Dept Phone: 918-596-7275
707 S Houston St Suite 200 Fax: 918-596-7249
Tulsa, OK 74127

Tulsa Police Dept Phone: 918-596-9378
600 Civic Ctr Fax: 918-596-9330
Tulsa, OK 74103

Tulsa Public Works Dept Phone: 918-596-9608
200 Civic Ctr Rm 512 Fax: 918-596-7397
Tulsa, OK 74103

Tulsa Urban Development Dept Phone: 918-596-2600
110 S Hartford St Suite 200 Fax: 918-596-2608
Tulsa, OK 74120

Tulsa Water Supply Systems Phone: 918-596-9598
707 S Houston Ave Rm 401 Fax: 918-596-1516
Tulsa, OK 74127

Important Phone Numbers

AAA....................918-748-1000
American Express Travel....................918-743-8856
Dental Referral....................918-451-1017
Driver's License Information....................918-299-2601
Emergency.................... 911
Greater Tulsa Assn of Realtors....................918-663-7500
Oklahoma Income Tax Div....................918-581-2761
Poison Control Center....................800-764-7661
Time/Temp....................918-477-1000
Tulsa County Assessor....................918-596-5139
Vehicle Registration Information....................918-299-2120
Voter Registration Information....................918-596-5780
Weather....................918-743-3311

Information Sources

Better Business Bureau Serving Eastern Oklahoma Phone: 918-492-1266
6711 S Yale Ave Suite 230 Fax: 918-492-1276
Tulsa, OK 74136
www.tulsabbb.org

Metropolitan Tulsa Chamber of Commerce Phone: 918-585-1201
616 S Boston Ave Suite 100 Fax: 918-585-8016
Tulsa, OK 74119
www.tulsachamber.com

Tulsa Convention & Visitors Bureau Phone: 918-585-1201
616 S Boston Ave Suite 100 Fax: 918-592-6244
Tulsa, OK 74119 TF: 800-558-3311
www.tulsachamber.com/cvb.htm

Tulsa Convention Center Phone: 918-596-7177
100 Civic Ctr Fax: 918-596-7155
Tulsa, OK 74103 TF: 800-678-7177
www.tulsaconvention.com

Tulsa County Phone: 918-596-5000
500 S Denver Ave Fax: 918-596-5215
Tulsa, OK 74103

Online Resources

4Tulsa.com
www.4tulsa.com

About.com Guide to Tulsa
tulsa.about.com/citiestowns/southwestus/tulsa

Access Tulsa
www.accesstulsa.com

Anthill City Guide Tulsa
www.anthill.com/city.asp?city=tulsa

Area Guide Tulsa
tulsa.areaguides.net

Art Access
www.webtek.com/arts/

Best of Tulsa
www.bestoftulsa.com

City Knowledge Tulsa
www.cityknowledge.com/ok_tulsa.htm

Excite.com Tulsa City Guide
www.excite.com/travel/countries/united_states/oklahoma/tulsa

Tulsa InSite
www.tulsainsite.com

Tulsa Web
www.tulsaweb.com/

Tulsa.Com
www.tulsa.com

Urban Tulsa
www.bestoftulsa.com/urbantulsa

Area Communities

Tulsa area communities with populations greater than 10,000 include:

Bartlesville
401 S Johnstone
Bartlesville, OK 74005
Phone: 918-337-5242
Fax: 918-337-5261

Bixby
116 W Needles Ave
Bixby, OK 74008
Phone: 918-366-4430
Fax: 918-366-6373

Broken Arrow
PO Box 610
Broken Arrow, OK 74013
Phone: 918-251-5311
Fax: 918-251-6642

Claremore
104 S Muskogee Ave
Claremore, OK 74017
Phone: 918-341-8842
Fax: 918-341-7705

Okmulgee
111 E 4th St
Okmulgee, OK 74447
Phone: 918-756-4060
Fax: 918-758-1122

Owasso
PO Box 180
Owasso, OK 74055
Phone: 918-272-2251
Fax: 918-272-4999

Sand Springs
PO Box 338
Sand Springs, OK 74063
Phone: 918-246-2501
Fax: 918-245-7101

Sapulpa
PO Box 1130
Sapulpa, OK 74067
Phone: 918-224-3040

Economy

Tulsa's economic base has diversified significantly since the city's days as the "Oil Capital of the World." Although the petroleum industry still contributes to Tulsa's economy and several major oil companies, including Citgo, Amoco, and Occidental, have operations in the city, other industries have gained prominence in the area's economy. The healthcare industry has become the single largest employment sector in Tulsa today. The aviation industry also contributes significantly to the city's economy, employing more than 30,000 local residents in manufacturing and service positions. Major aircraft and aerospace companies with operations in Tulsa include American Airlines and Boeing.

Unemployment Rate 3.1%**
Per Capita Income.......................... $25,927*
Median Family Income...................... $32,619

** Information given is for the Tulsa Metropolitan Statistical Area (MSA), which includes Tulsa, Creek, Osage, Rogers, and Wagoner counties.*
*** Information given is for Tulsa County.*

Principal Industries & Number of Wage Earners

Tulsa MSA* - March 2000

Industry	Wage Earners
Construction	18,600
Finance, Insurance, & Real Estate	22,300
Government	43,700
Manufacturing	55,000
Mining	7,100
Retail Trade	69,100
Services	125,000
Transportation & Public Utilities	32,400
Wholesale Trade	21,700

** Information given is for the Tulsa Metropolitan Statistical Area (MSA), which includes Tulsa, Creek, Osage, Rogers, and Wagoner counties.*

Major Employers

American Airlines
3800 N Mingo Rd
Tulsa, OK 74116
www.aacareers.com
Phone: 918-292-2110

Avis Rent A Car
4500 S 129th East Ave
Tulsa, OK 74134
www.avis.com/company/employment
Phone: 918-624-4000
Fax: 918-621-4800

Bank of Oklahoma NA
PO Box 2300
Tulsa, OK 74192
www.bankofoklahoma.com
Phone: 918-588-6000
Fax: 918-588-6962
TF: 800-234-6181

CITGO Petroleum Corp
6100 S Yale Ave
Tulsa, OK 74136
www.citgo.com
Phone: 918-495-4000
Fax: 918-495-4511
TF: 800-756-2484

First Data Corp
4500 S 129th East Ave
Tulsa, OK 74134
www.firstdatacorp.com
Phone: 918-641-4002
Fax: 918-641-4302

Hillcrest Medical Center
1120 S Utica Ave
Tulsa, OK 74104
www.hillcrest.com
Phone: 918-579-1000
Fax: 918-579-5011

Saint Francis Hospital
6161 S Yale Ave
Tulsa, OK 74136
www.saintfrancis.com
Phone: 918-494-2200
Fax: 918-494-1775
TF: 800-888-9599

Saint John Medical Center
1923 S Utica Ave
Tulsa, OK 74104
www.sjmc.org
Phone: 918-744-2345
Fax: 918-744-2570

Tulsa City Hall
200 Civic Ctr
Tulsa, OK 74103
www.ci.tulsa.ok.us
Phone: 918-596-2100

Tulsa City School District
3027 S New Haven Ave
Tulsa, OK 74114
www.tulsaschools.org
Phone: 918-745-6800
Fax: 918-746-6874

Tulsa County
500 S Denver Ave
Tulsa, OK 74103
Phone: 918-596-5000
Fax: 918-596-5215

Tulsa Regional Medical Center
744 W 9th St
Tulsa, OK 74127
Phone: 918-587-2561
Fax: 918-599-1750

Williams
1 Williams Ctr
Tulsa, OK 74172
www.williams.com
Phone: 918-573-2000
Fax: 918-573-2296
TF: 800-945-5426

WorldCom Inc
PO Box 21348
Tulsa, OK 74121
www.wcom.com
Phone: 918-590-3210
Fax: 918-590-1167

Quality of Living Indicators

Total Crime Index 28,303
(rates per 100,000 inhabitants)

Violent Crime
Murder/manslaughter 41
Forcible rape 235
Robbery 887
Aggravated assault 3,284

Property Crime
Burglary 6,558
Larceny theft 14,070
Motor vehicle theft 3,228

Cost of Living Index 94.2
(national average = 100)

Median Home Price $92,800

Education

Public Schools

Tulsa City School District
3027 S New Haven Ave
Tulsa, OK 74114
www.tulsaschools.org
Phone: 918-745-6800
Fax: 918-746-6874

Number of Schools
Elementary 56
Middle 15
High 9

Student/Teacher Ratio
Elementary 16.0:1
Middle 15.0:1
High 16.0:1

Private Schools

Number of Schools (all grades) 35

Colleges & Universities

Oral Roberts University
7777 S Lewis Ave
Tulsa, OK 74171
www.oru.edu
Phone: 918-495-6161
Fax: 918-495-6222
TF: 800-678-8876

Rogers State University
1701 W Will Rogers Blvd
Claremore, OK 74017
E-mail: info@rsu.edu
www.rsu.edu
Phone: 918-341-7510
Fax: 918-343-7546
TF: 800-256-7511

Spartan School of Aeronautics
PO Box 582833
Tulsa, OK 74158
E-mail: spartan@mail.webtek.com
www.spartan.edu
Phone: 918-836-6886
Fax: 918-831-5287
TF: 800-331-1204

Tulsa Community College Metro Campus
909 S Boston Ave
Tulsa, OK 74119
www.tulsa.cc.ok.us
Phone: 918-595-7000
Fax: 918-595-7347

University of Tulsa
600 S College Ave
Tulsa, OK 74104
E-mail: admission@utulsa.edu
www.utulsa.edu
Phone: 918-631-2000
Fax: 918-631-5033
TF: 800-331-3050

Hospitals

Children's Medical Center
5300 E Skelly Dr
Tulsa, OK 74153
Phone: 918-664-6600
Fax: 918-628-6306

Hillcrest Doctors' Hospital
2323 S Harvard Ave
Tulsa, OK 74114
Phone: 918-744-4000
Fax: 918-746-3309

Hillcrest Medical Center
1120 S Utica Ave
Tulsa, OK 74104
www.hillcrest.com
Phone: 918-579-1000
Fax: 918-579-5011

Saint Francis Hospital
6161 S Yale Ave
Tulsa, OK 74136
www.saintfrancis.com
Phone: 918-494-2200
Fax: 918-494-1775
TF: 800-888-9599

Saint John Medical Center
1923 S Utica Ave
Tulsa, OK 74104
www.sjmc.org
Phone: 918-744-2345
Fax: 918-744-2570

Tulsa Regional Medical Center
744 W 9th St
Tulsa, OK 74127
Phone: 918-587-2561
Fax: 918-599-1750

Transportation

Airport(s)

Tulsa International Airport (TUL)
9 miles NE of downtown (approx 10 minutes) 918-838-5000

Mass Transit

Metropolitan Tulsa Transit Authority
$.75 Base fare 918-585-1195

Rail/Bus

Greyhound/Trailways Bus Station
317 S Detroit Ave
Tulsa, OK 74120
Phone: 918-584-4428
TF: 800-231-2222

Utilities

Electricity
Public Service Co of Oklahoma 918-586-0400

Gas
Oklahoma Natural Gas Co 918-834-8000
www.ong.com

Water
Tulsa Water Dept 918-596-9511

Garbage Collection/Recycling
Tulsa Refuse Dept 918-596-9511

Telecommunications

Telephone
Southwestern Bell Telephone Co 800-640-8911
www.swbell.com

Cable Television
Cox Communications 918-459-3500
www.cox.com

Internet Service Providers (ISPs)
Galaxy Star Systems 918-835-3655
www.galstar.com
Internet Connection 918-742-3510
www.cottagesoft.com

Banks

Bank of America
515 S Boulder Ave
Tulsa, OK 74103
Phone: 888-279-3247

Bank of Oklahoma NA
PO Box 2300
Tulsa, OK 74192
www.bankofoklahoma.com
Phone: 918-588-6000
Fax: 918-588-6962
TF: 800-234-6181

Bank One Oklahoma NA
PO Box 1
Tulsa, OK 74102
Phone: 918-586-1000
Fax: 918-586-5957
TF: 800-695-0955

F & M Bank & Trust Co
1330 S Harvard
Tulsa, OK 74112
Phone: 918-744-1330
Fax: 918-743-1134

Local America Bank
2118 S Yale Ave
Tulsa, OK 74114
Phone: 918-744-0770

Peoples State Bank
445 S Lewis Ave
Tulsa, OK 74114
Phone: 918-583-9800

Stillwater National Bank
2547 E 21st St
Tulsa, OK 74114
Phone: 918-523-3750

Valley National Bank
2020 E 21st St
Tulsa, OK 74114
Phone: 918-495-1700

Shopping

Brookside
4606 E 67th St
Tulsa, OK 74135
www.shopbrookside.com
Phone: 918-591-8760

Cherry Street District
Cherry St-betw Peoria & Harvard Sts
Tulsa, OK 74120
www.cherryst.com
Phone: 918-587-2566
Fax: 918-584-4092

Eastland Mall
14002 E 21st St
Tulsa, OK 74134
Phone: 918-438-3400
Fax: 918-437-6130
TF: 800-654-3024

Farm The
5321 S Sheridan Rd Suite 27
Tulsa, OK 74145
www.farmshoppingcenter.com
Phone: 918-622-3860
Fax: 918-622-4675

Tulsa Promenade
4107 S Yale Ave
Tulsa, OK 74135
Phone: 918-627-9224
Fax: 918-663-9385

Utica Square
1579 E 21st St
Tulsa, OK 74114
www.uticasquare.com
Phone: 918-742-5531
Fax: 918-747-0766

Woodland Hills Mall
7021 S Memorial Dr
Tulsa, OK 74133
www.woodlandhillsmall.com
Phone: 918-250-1449
Fax: 918-250-9084

Media

Newspapers and Magazines

Tulsa World*
315 S Boulder Ave
Tulsa, OK 74103
E-mail: tulsaworld@fax.webtek.com
www.tulsaworld.com
Phone: 918-583-2161
Fax: 918-581-8353
TF: 800-897-3557

Urban Tulsa
2318 E Admiral Blvd
Tulsa, OK 74110
E-mail: urbantul@urbantulsa.com
www.urbantulsa.com
Phone: 918-592-5550
Fax: 918-592-5970

**Indicates major daily newspapers*

Television

KETA-TV Ch 13 (PBS)
7403 N Kelley St
Oklahoma City, OK 73111
www.oeta.onenet.net
Phone: 405-848-8501
Fax: 405-841-9216

KJRH-TV Ch 2 (NBC)
3701 S Peoria Ave
Tulsa, OK 74105
www.teamtulsa.com
Phone: 918-743-2222
Fax: 918-748-1436

KOKI-TV Ch 23 (Fox)
5416 S Yale Suite 500
Tulsa, OK 74135
E-mail: fox23@fox23.com
www.fox23.com
Phone: 918-491-0023
Fax: 918-491-6650

KOTV-TV Ch 6 (CBS)
PO Box 6
Tulsa, OK 74101
www.kotv.com/
Phone: 918-582-6666
Fax: 918-581-8616

KTFO-TV Ch 41 (UPN)
5416 S Yale Ave Suite 500
Tulsa, OK 74135
E-mail: upn41@upn41.com
www.upn41.com
Phone: 918-491-0023
Fax: 918-866-6393

KTUL-TV Ch 8 (ABC)
PO Box 8
Tulsa, OK 74101
E-mail: ktulgmo@ad.com
www.ktul.com
Phone: 918-445-8888
Fax: 918-445-9316

KWHB-TV Ch 47 (Ind)
8835 S Memorial Dr
Tulsa, OK 74133
www.kwhb.com
Phone: 918-254-4701
Fax: 918-254-5614

Radio

KAKC-AM 1300 kHz (N/T)
5801 E 41st St Suite 900
Tulsa, OK 74135
Phone: 918-664-2810
Fax: 918-665-0555

KBEZ-FM 92.9 MHz (AC)
7030 S Yale Ave Suite 711
Tulsa, OK 74136
Phone: 918-496-9336
Fax: 918-495-1850

KCFO-AM 970 kHz (Rel)
3737 S 37th West Ave
Tulsa, OK 74107
Phone: 918-445-1186
Fax: 918-446-7508

KMOD-FM 97.5 MHz (Rock)
5801 E 41st St Suite 900
Tulsa, OK 74135
www.kmod.com
Phone: 918-664-2810
Fax: 918-665-0555

KMYZ-FM 104.5 MHz (Alt)
5810 E Skelly Dr Suite 801
Tulsa, OK 74135
E-mail: edgetulsa@aol.com
www.edgeline.com
Phone: 918-665-3131
Fax: 918-663-6622

KRAV-FM 96.5 MHz (AC)
7136 S Yale Ave Suite 500
Tulsa, OK 74136
Phone: 918-491-9696
Fax: 918-493-5385

KRMG-AM 740 kHz (N/T)
7136 S Yale Ave
Tulsa, OK 74136
Phone: 918-493-7400
Fax: 918-493-5321

KTFX-FM 102.3 MHz (Ctry)
8107 E Admiral Pl
Tulsa, OK 74115
Phone: 918-836-5512

KVOO-AM 1170 kHz (Ctry)
4590 E 29th St
Tulsa, OK 74114
E-mail: info@kvoo.com
www.kvoo.com
Phone: 918-743-7814
Fax: 918-743-7613

KVOO-FM 98.5 MHz (Ctry)
4590 E 29th St
Tulsa, OK 74114
E-mail: info@kvoo.com
www.kvoo.com
Phone: 918-743-7814
Fax: 918-743-7613

KWEN-FM 95.5 MHz (Ctry)
7136 S Yale Ave Suite 500
Tulsa, OK 74136
Phone: 918-493-7400
Fax: 918-493-2376

KWGS-FM 89.5 MHz (NPR)
600 S College Ave
Tulsa, OK 74104
E-mail: fm89@kwgs.org
www.kwgs.org
Phone: 918-631-2577
Fax: 918-631-3695
TF: 888-594-5947

Attractions

Tulsa was built by wealthy oil barons, and its early history is interpreted at the Gilcrease Museum, founded by oilman Thomas Gilcrease. Tulsa was also the terminus of the infamous Trail of Tears of the 1830s. Today, the city has the second highest American Indian population in the country, and the annual Inter-Tribal Indian Club of Tulsa Pow Wow of Champions involves more than 35 tribes. Nearby Tahlequah is home to the Cherokee Nation and includes the Cherokee Heritage Center and the Cherokee National Museum. Other Tulsa area attractions include the Will Rogers Home, Birthplace, and Memorial; Grand Lake O' the Cherokees recreation area; and the Woolaroc Museum and Nature Preserve.

Arkansas River Historical Society
5350 Cimarron Rd
Catoosa, OK 74015
Phone: 918-266-2291
Fax: 918-266-7678

Cherokee Heritage Center & National Museum
Willis Rd PO Box 515
Tahlequah, OK 74464
www.leftmoon.com/cnhs
Phone: 918-456-6007
Fax: 918-456-6165
TF: 888-999-6007

Creek Nation Tulsa Bingo
81st St & Riverside Dr
Tulsa, OK 74132
E-mail: info@tulsabingo.com
www.tulsabingo.com
Phone: 918-299-8510
Fax: 918-299-0345

Davis JM Arms & Historical Museum
333 N Lynn Riggs Blvd
Claremore, OK 74017
E-mail: silver@tulsawalk.com
www.state.ok.us/~jmdavis/
Phone: 918-341-5707
Fax: 918-341-5771

Elsing Museum
8555 S Lewis Ave
Tulsa, OK 74136
Phone: 918-298-3628

Hogue Alexander Gallery of Art
University of Tulsa Phillips Hall
Tulsa, OK 74104
Phone: 918-631-2202
Fax: 918-631-3423

Mohawk Park
5701 E 36th St N
Tulsa, OK 74115
Phone: 918-596-7275

Oklahoma Jazz Hall of Fame
322 N Greenwood Ave
Tulsa, OK 74120
E-mail: info@okjazz.com
www.okjazz.com
Phone: 918-596-1001
Fax: 918-596-1005

Philbrook Museum of Art
2727 S Rockford Rd
Tulsa, OK 74114
www.philbrook.org
Phone: 918-749-7941
Fax: 918-743-4230
TF: 800-324-7941

River Parks
717 S Houston Ave
Tulsa, OK 74127
Phone: 918-596-2001
Fax: 918-596-2004

Theatre Tulsa
207 N Main St Performing Arts Ctr
Tulsa, OK 74103
E-mail: theatretul@aol.com
www.theatretulsa.org
Phone: 918-587-8402
Fax: 918-592-0848

Thomas Gilcrease Institute of American History & Art
1400 Gilcrease Museum Rd
Tulsa, OK 74127
www.gilcrease.org
Phone: 918-596-2700
Fax: 918-596-2770

Tulsa Ballet Theatre
4512 S Peoria Ave
Tulsa, OK 74105
E-mail: tulsaballet@fax.webtek.com
www.webtek.com/tulsaballet/
Phone: 918-749-6030
Fax: 918-749-0532

Tulsa Garden Center
2435 S Peoria Ave
Tulsa, OK 74114
Phone: 918-746-5125
Fax: 918-746-5128

Tulsa Opera
101 E 3rd St Tulsa Performing Arts Ctr
Tulsa, OK 74103
www.tulsapac.com
Phone: 918-596-7111
Fax: 918-596-7144
TF: 800-364-7111

Tulsa Performing Arts Center
110 E 2nd St
Tulsa, OK 74103
E-mail: tulsapac@earthlink.net
www.tulsapac.com
Phone: 918-596-7122
Fax: 918-596-7144
TF: 800-364-7122

Tulsa Philharmonic Orchestra
101 E 3rd St Tulsa Performing Arts Ctr
Tulsa, OK 74103
E-mail: tulsaphil@mail.webtek.com
www.webtek.com/tulsaphil/
Phone: 918-747-7445
Fax: 918-747-7496

Tulsa Zoo
5701 E 36th St North
Tulsa, OK 74115
www.tulsazoo.com
Phone: 918-669-6600
Fax: 918-669-6260

Will Rogers Memorial
1720 W Will Rogers Blvd
Claremore, OK 74017
E-mail: wrinfo@willrogers.org
www.willrogers.org
Phone: 918-341-0719
Fax: 918-343-8119
TF: 800-324-9455

Woolaroc Museum & Nature Preserve
Hwy 123
Bartlesville, OK 74003
www.woolaroc.org/
Phone: 918-336-0307
Fax: 918-336-0084

Sports Teams & Facilities

Fair Meadows at Tulsa
PO Box 4735
Tulsa, OK 74159
E-mail: racing@fairmeadows.com
www.fairmeadows.com
Phone: 918-743-7223
Fax: 918-743-8053

Tulsa Drillers (baseball)
4802 E 15th St Drillers Stadium
Tulsa, OK 74112
Phone: 918-744-5901
Fax: 918-747-3267

Tulsa Ice Oilers (hockey)
100 Civic Ctr Tulsa Convention Ctr
Tulsa, OK 74133
www.tulsaoilers.com
Phone: 918-632-7825
Fax: 918-632-0006

Tulsa Roughnecks (soccer)
12150 E 11th St
Broken Arrow, OK 74012
E-mail: ammskt@aol.com
Phone: 918-838-9901
Fax: 918-838-8071

Tulsa Speedway
4424 E 66th St North
Tulsa, OK 74117
E-mail: tulsaspeedway@tulspeedway.com
www.tulspeedway.com
Phone: 918-425-7551
Fax: 918-425-0646

Annual Events

Akdar Shrine Circus (late February-early March) 918-587-6658
Bok Williams Jazz on Greenwood (early August & mid-August) 918-584-3378
Chili Bowl Midget Nationals (early January) 918-838-3777
Chili Cookoff & Bluegrass Festival (early-mid-September) 918-583-2617
Christmas Parade of Lights (early December) 918-583-2617
Gatesway International Balloon Festival (late July-early August) 918-251-2676
Greater Tulsa Antiques Show (mid-March) 918-682-7420
Greater Tulsa Home & Garden Show (mid-March) 918-663-5820
International Auto Show (mid-March) 918-742-2626
Juneteenth on Greenwood Heritage Festival (mid-June) 918-582-1741
Longhorn Rodeo (late January) 918-596-7177
Mayfest (mid-May) 918-582-6435
National Rod & Custom Car Show (late February) 918-257-8073
Oklahoma Scottish Games & Gathering (mid-September) 918-560-0228
Oktoberfest (mid-October) 918-596-2001
Pow Wow of Champions (mid-August) 918-744-1113
Reggaefest/World Peace Festival (late June) 918-596-2001
Tulsa Boat Sport & Travel Show (January) 918-744-1113
Tulsa Boom River Celebration & Great American Duck Drop (July 4) 918-596-2001
Tulsa Championship Rodeo (early May) 918-744-1113
Tulsa Charity Horse Show (late April) 918-742-5556
Tulsa County Free Fair (early August) 918-746-3709
Tulsa Easter Pageant (early April) 918-596-5990
Tulsa Morgan Horse Extravaganza (early August) 918-744-1113
Tulsa Nationals Wrestling Tournament (mid-January) 918-366-4411
Tulsa State Fair (late September-early October) 918-744-1113
Tulsa Women's Show (early February) 800-225-4342
TulsaFest (late June) 918-595-7776
Zoolightful (December) 918-560-0228

Washington, District of Columbia

County: **Independent City**

WASHINGTON, DC is located at the confluence of the Potomac and Anacostia Rivers bordering northeastern Virginia and southwestern Maryland. Major cities within 100 miles include Arlington, Alexandria, and Richmond, Virginia; and Baltimore and Annapolis, Maryland.

Area (Land) .... 61.0 sq mi
Area (Water) .... 7.0 sq mi
Elevation .... 420 ft
Latitude .... 38-89-29 N
Longitude .... 77-03-65 W
Time Zone .... EST
Area Code 202

Climate

Winters in Washington, DC are generally mild, with average high temperatures in the low to mid-40s and lows in the low to mid-20s. The average annual snowfall is just above 17 inches. Summers are warm and humid, with average high temperatures in the mid 80s; evening lows average in the low 60s. May is the wettest month in the Capital, while January is the driest.

Average Temperatures & Precipitation

Temperatures

	Jan	Feb	Mar	Apr	May	Jun	Jul	Aug	Sep	Oct	Nov	Dec
High	40	44	55	65	74	83	87	86	79	68	57	45
Low	21	23	32	40	50	59	64	63	55	42	34	26

Precipitation

	Jan	Feb	Mar	Apr	May	Jun	Jul	Aug	Sep	Oct	Nov	Dec
Inches	2.7	2.8	3.2	3.1	4.0	3.9	3.5	3.9	3.4	3.2	3.3	3.2

History

The United States Constitution, ratified in 1788, included a clause giving Congress the authority to establish a District that would become the seat of the U.S. government. The site for the new capital was chosen by President George Washington in 1790 on an area of land along the Potomac River that had been ceded by Maryland and Virginia. The new capital was called the City of Washington in the territory of Columbia; the name eventually became Washington, District of Columbia or Washington, DC. Construction on the U.S. Capitol began in 1793, and seven years later Congress moved from Philadelphia to Washington. The Georgetown area of the city was considered a separate town within the District for nearly 20 years, until it was merged with Washington in 1895. (Alexandria, Virginia was originally part of the District of Columbia, but was returned to Virginia in 1847.)

The District of Columbia's local government structure has undergone a number of changes since its establishment in the early 19th Century. The current Mayor-Council form of government has been in place only since 1974. Although the District is not a state, a bill for the admission of the State of New Columbia has been under congressional consideration since 1983. If statehood is granted, the District of Columbia will remain intact as the nation's capital, consisting of the White House, the U.S. Capitol, the Supreme Court, and the National Mall and its adjacent federal monuments and government buildings; the remainder of the District will become the State of New Columbia.

As the nation's capital, Washington, DC is the governmental center of the United States. Home to the Smithsonian Institution, the National Gallery, and the Kennedy Center for the Performing Arts, as well as several top universities (including Georgetown, Howard, and George Washington Universities), the District is also among the nation's leading cultural and educational centers. The Capital and surrounding area feature hundreds of attractions commemorating events and leading figures in American history.

Of the more than 560,000 people now living in Washington, DC, more than 200,000 are employed by the U.S. Federal Government.

Population

1990 Census 606,900
1998 Estimate 523,124
% Change .... -13.8
2010 Projection 560,300

Racial/Ethnic Breakdown
White 29.6%
Black 65.8%
Other 4.6%
Hispanic Origin (may be of any race) 5.4%

Age Breakdown
Under 5 years 6.9%
5 to 17 .... 13.0%
18 to 24 .... 11.1%
25 to 44 .... 39.3%
45 to 64 .... 19.4%
65+ years 13.2%
Median Age 34.2

Gender Breakdown
Male 46.6%
Female 53.4%

Government

Type of Government: Mayor-Council

Washington DC Chief Financial Officer
441 4th St NW Suite 1150N
Washington, DC 20001
Phone: 202-727-2476
Fax: 202-737-5258

Washington DC City Hall Phone: 202-724-8000
441 4th St NW
Washington, DC 20001

Washington DC Council Phone: 202-724-8000
441 4th St NW Fax: 202-347-3070
Washington, DC 20001

Washington DC Economic Development Dept Phone: 202-727-6365
441 4th St NW Rm 1140 N Fax: 202-727-6703
Washington, DC 20001

Washington DC Fire & Emergency Medical Services Dept Phone: 202-673-3320
1923 Vermont Ave NW Fax: 202-462-0807
Washington, DC 20001

Washington DC Health Dept Phone: 202-442-5999
825 N Captiol St NE Suite 440 Fax: 202-442-4788
Washington, DC 20002

Washington DC Mayor Phone: 202-727-2980
441 4th St NW Fax: 202-727-0505
Washington, DC 20001

Washington DC Medical Examiner Phone: 202-698-9000
1910 Massachusetts Ave SE Bldg 27 Fax: 202-698-9100
Washington, DC 20003

Washington DC Metropolitan Police Dept Phone: 202-727-4218
300 Indiana Ave NW Municipal Ctr Fax: 202-727-9524
Washington, DC 20001

Washington DC Parks & Recreation Dept Phone: 202-673-7665
3149 16th St NW Fax: 202-673-2087
Washington, DC 20010

Washington DC Personnel Office Phone: 202-442-9600
441 4th St NW Suite 300S Fax: 202-727-6827
Washington, DC 20001

Washington DC Planning Office Phone: 202-442-7600
801 N Capitol St NE 4th Fl Fax: 202-442-7637
Washington, DC 20002

Washington DC Public Library Phone: 202-727-1101
901 G St NW Rm 400 Fax: 202-727-1129
Washington, DC 20001

Washington DC Public School System Phone: 202-442-4222
825 N Capitol St NE 9th Fl Fax: 202-442-5026
Washington, DC 20002

Washington DC Public Works Dept Phone: 202-939-8000
2000 14th St NW Frank Reeves Ctr Fax: 202-939-8191
Washington, DC 20009

Washington DC Washington Area Metropolitan Transit Authority Phone: 202-962-1234
600 5th St NW Fax: 202-962-2045
Washington, DC 20001

Washington DC Water & Sewer Authority Phone: 202-787-2000
5000 Overlook Ave SW Fax: 202-787-2333
Washington, DC 20032

Important Phone Numbers

AAA .202-331-3000
American Express Travel .202-457-1300
Dental Referral .202-547-7613
Dial-a-Museum .202-357-2020
Driver's License/Vehicle Registration Information .202-727-5000
Emergency 911
Greater Capital Area Assn of Realtors .202-789-8889
Medical Referral .202-877-3627
Poison Control Center .202-625-3333
Time .202-844-1111
Travelers Aid .301-773-6361
Voter Registration Information .202-727-2525
Washington DC Office of Tax & Revenue .202-727-4829
Weather .202-936-1212

Information Sources

Alexandria (Independent City) Phone: 703-838-4000
301 King St Suite 2300 Fax: 703-838-6433
Alexandria, VA 22314
ci.alexandria.va.us

Alexandria Chamber of Commerce Phone: 703-549-1000
801 N Fairfax St Suite 402 Fax: 703-739-3805
Alexandria, VA 22314
www.alexchamber.com

Alexandria City Hall Phone: 703-838-4000
301 King St Fax: 703-838-6433
Alexandria, VA 22314
ci.alexandria.va.us

Alexandria Convention & Visitors Bureau Phone: 703-838-4200
221 King St Fax: 703-838-4683
Alexandria, VA 22314 TF: 800-388-9119
www.funside.com

Alexandria Economic Development Partnership Inc Phone: 703-739-3820
1055 N Fairfax St Suite 204 Fax: 703-739-1384
Alexandria, VA 22314
ci.alexandria.va.us/aedp

Alexandria Library Phone: 703-838-4555
717 Queen St Fax: 703-838-4524
Alexandria, VA 22314
www.alexandria.lib.va.us

Alexandria Mayor Phone: 703-838-4500
301 King St City Hall Fax: 703-838-6433
Alexandria, VA 22314
ci.alexandria.va.us/amacc/amacc.htm

Arlington Chamber of Commerce Phone: 703-525-2400
2009 N 14th St Suite 111 Fax: 703-522-5273
Arlington, VA 22201
www.arlingtonchamber.com

Arlington Convention & Visitors Service Phone: 703-228-3000
735 S 18th St Fax: 800-677-6267
Arlington, VA 22202
www.co.arlington.va.us/acvs

Arlington County
2100 Clarendon Blvd 1 Courthouse Plaza Suite 302
Arlington, VA 22201
www.co.arlington.va.us
Phone: 703-228-3120
Fax: 703-228-3295

Arlington County Public Library
1015 N Quincy St
Arlington, VA 22201
www.co.arlington.va.us/lib
Phone: 703-228-5990
Fax: 703-228-7720

Arlington Economic Development Dept
2100 Clarendon Blvd Rm 709
Arlington, VA 22201
www.co.arlington.va.us/ded/ded.htm
Phone: 703-228-0808
Fax: 703-228-3574

Arlington Visitors Center
735 S 18th St
Arlington, VA 22202
Phone: 703-228-5720
Fax: 703-892-9469
TF: 800-677-6267

Better Business Bureau Serving Metropolitan Washington
1411 K St NW 10th Fl
Washington, DC 20005
www.dc.bbb.org
Phone: 202-393-8000
Fax: 202-393-1198

DC Committee to Promote Washington
1212 New York Ave NW Suite 200
Washington, DC 20005
Phone: 202-724-5644
Fax: 202-724-2445

District of Columbia Chamber of Commerce
1301 Pennsylvania Ave NW Suite 309
Washington, DC 20004
www.dcchamber.org
Phone: 202-347-7201
Fax: 202-638-6764

Washington Convention Center
900 9th St NW
Washington, DC 20001
www.dcconvention.com
Phone: 202-789-1600
Fax: 202-789-8365
TF: 800-368-9000

Washington DC Convention & Visitors Assn
1212 New York Ave NW Suite 600
Washington, DC 20005
www.washington.org
Phone: 202-789-7000
Fax: 202-789-7037

WETA/CapAccess
2775 S Quincy St
Arlington, VA 22206
www.capaccess.org
Phone: 703-998-2430
Fax: 703-824-7350

Online Resources

123 Washington D.C.
www.123washingtondc.com

1999 Guide to Washington D.C.
www.district-of-columbia.com

4Alexandria.com
www.4alexandria.com

4WashingtonDC.com
www.4washingtondc.com

About.com Guide to Washington DC
dc.about.com/local/midlanticus/dc

ALEX Electronic Alexandria Community
www.alex.org

Alexandria City Guide
alexandriacity.com

Annual Guide for the Arts
www.guide4arts.com/dc/

Anthill City Guide Alexandria
www.anthill.com/city.asp?city=alexandriawood

Anthill City Guide Washington DC
www.anthill.com/city.asp?city=washingtondc

Area Guide Alexandria
alexandriava.areaguides.net

Area Guide Arlington
arlingtonva.areaguides.net

Area Guide Washington DC
washington.areaguides.net

Arlington City Net
www.excite.com/travel/countries/united_states/virginia/arlington

ArtWOW
www.cais.com/koan/artwow.html

Bradmans.com Washington DC
www.bradmans.com/scripts/display_city.cgi?city=244

City Knowledge Washington DC
www.cityknowledge.com/dc.htm

CityTravelGuide.com Washington DC
www.citytravelguide.com/washington-dc.htm

Columbia Heights
innercity.org/columbiaheights

CuisineNet Washington DC
www.cuisinenet.com/restaurant/washington/index.shtml

DC.TheLinks.com
dc.thelinks.com

DigitalCity Washington
home.digitalcity.com/washington

District The
www.thedistrict.com

Excite.com Alexandria City Guide
www.excite.com/travel/countries/united_states/virginia/alexandria

Excite.com Washington DC City Guide
www.excite.com/travel/countries/united_states/district_of_columbia/washington/

Fiesta Page
www.fiesta.com

Gayot's Guide Restaurant Search Washington DC
www.perrier.com/restaurants/gayot.asp?area=WDC

Guide to Washington DC
www.physics.georgetown.edu/Wash.html

I-95 Exit Information Guide Northern Virginia
www.usastar.com/i95/cityguide/nova.htm

I-95 Exit Information Guide Washington DC
www.usastar.com/i95/cityguide/washdc.htm

Insiders' Guide to Washington DC
www.insiders.com/washington-dc/

Lodging.com Alexandria Virginia
www.lodging.com/auto/guides/alexandria-va.html

Lycos Regional - Washington DC
dir.lycos.com/Regional/North_America/United_States/Washington,_DC

Online City Guide to Alexandria
www.olcg.com/va/alexandria/index.html

Open World City Guides Washington DC
www.worldexecutive.com/cityguides/washington/

PlacesToStay Alexandria
pts.placestostay.com/destination/usa/virginia/alexandria/dest.asp

Rough Guide Travel Washington DC
travel.roughguides.com/content/552/

Time Out Washington DC
www.timeout.com/washingtondc/

Washington City Paper
www.washingtoncitypaper.com

Washington DC City Pages
www.dcpages.com/

Washington DC CityWomen
www.citywomen.com/dcwomen.htm

Washington DC Historic Tours of America
www.historictours.com/washington/index.htm

Washington DC Homepage
www.dchomepage.net

Washington Web
www.washweb.net

Yahoo! DC
dc.yahoo.com

Area Communities

Beltsville, Bethesda, Potomac, and Silver Spring, Maryland and Mount Vernon and Reston, Virginia are among the largest unincorporated communities in the Washington, DC area. Arlington (County), Virginia is another prominent area community. Incorporated cities and towns in the Washington metropolitan area with populations greater than 10,000 include:

Alexandria Phone: 703-838-4000
301 King St Fax: 703-838-6433
Alexandria, VA 22314

College Park Phone: 301-864-8666
4500 Knox Rd Fax: 301-699-8029
College Park, MD 20740

Fairfax Phone: 703-385-7800
10455 Armstrong St Fax: 703-385-7811
Fairfax, VA 22030

Falls Church Phone: 703-248-5004
300 Park Ave Fax: 703-248-5146
Falls Church, VA 22046

Frederick Phone: 301-694-1380
101 N Court St Fax: 301-662-4819
Frederick, MD 21701

Gaithersburg Phone: 301-258-6300
31 S Summit Ave Fax: 301-948-6149
Gaithersburg, MD 20877

Herndon Phone: 703-787-7368
730 Elden St Fax: 703-787-7325
Herndon, VA 20170

Hyattsville Phone: 301-985-5009
4310 Gallatin St Fax: 301-985-5007
Hyattsville, MD 20781

Manassas Phone: 703-257-8200
PO Box 560 Fax: 703-335-0042
Manassas, VA 20108

Rockville Phone: 301-309-3000
111 Maryland Ave Fax: 301-762-7153
Rockville, MD 20850

Takoma Park Phone: 301-270-1700
7500 Maple Ave Fax: 301-270-8794
Takoma Park, MD 20912

Vienna Phone: 703-255-6300
127 Center St S Fax: 703-255-5722
Vienna, VA 22180

Economy

Services is the largest employment sector in Washington DC, employing more than 275,000 area residents. However, the government sector is a close second providing jobs for more than 222,000 people, more than 80 percent of whom work for the U.S. Federal Government. Although government dominates Washington's economy, the following list of top business and institutional employers in the District of Columbia reflects the diversity of industry that exists in the nation's capital.

Unemployment Rate 5.7%
Per Capita Income.......................... $29,383
Median Family Income...................... $52,187

Principal Industries & Number of Wage Earners

District of Columbia - 1999

Construction	9,000
Finance, Insurance, & Real Estate	31,300
Government	222,700
Manufacturing	12,000
Mining	100
Retail Trade	42,100
Services	275,800
Transportation, Communications, & Public Utilities	17,400
Wholesale Trade	5,600

Major Employers

AARP
601 'E' St NW
Washington, DC 20049
E-mail: member@aarp.org
www.aarp.org
Phone: 202-434-2277
Fax: 202-434-2525
TF: 800-424-3410

American Building Maintenance Inc
113 Clermont Ave
Alexandria, VA 22304
Phone: 703-461-7501
Fax: 703-461-3750

American University
4400 Massachusetts Ave NW
Washington, DC 20016
www.american.edu
Phone: 202-885-1000
Fax: 202-885-6014

Bureau of National Affairs Inc
1231 25th St NW
Washington, DC 20037
www.bna.com
Phone: 202-452-4200
Fax: 202-452-4610
TF: 800-372-1033

Children's National Medical Center
111 Michigan Ave NW
Washington, DC 20010
www.cnmc.org
Phone: 202-884-5000
Fax: 202-884-5561
TF: 800-787-0080

Danaher Corp
1250 24th St NW Suite 800
Washington, DC 20037
www.danaher.com
Phone: 202-828-0850
Fax: 202-828-0860

Fannie Mae
3900 Wisconsin Ave NW
Washington, DC 20016
www.fanniemae.com
Phone: 202-752-7000
Fax: 202-752-5980
TF: 800-732-6643

George Washington University
2121 'I' St NW
Washington, DC 20052
gwis.circ.gwu.edu
Phone: 202-994-1000
Fax: 202-994-0325
TF: 800-447-3765

George Washington University Hospital
901 23rd St NW
Washington, DC 20037
E-mail: hsaaep@mail.gwumc.edu
www.gwhospital.com
Phone: 202-715-4000
Fax: 202-715-4402

Georgetown University
37th & 'O' Sts NW
Washington, DC 20057
www.georgetown.edu
Phone: 202-687-3600
Fax: 202-687-5084

Georgetown University Medical Center
3800 Reservoir Rd NW
Washington, DC 20007
gumc.georgetown.edu
Phone: 202-687-5055
Fax: 202-784-2875

Greater Southeast Community Hospital
1310 Southern Ave SE
Washington, DC 20032
www.greatersoutheast.baweb.com
Phone: 202-574-6000
Fax: 202-574-7188

Howard University
2400 6th St NW
Washington, DC 20059
www.howard.edu
Phone: 202-806-6100
Fax: 202-806-4466

Howard University Hospital
2041 Georgia Ave NW
Washington, DC 20060
www.huhosp.org
Phone: 202-865-6100
Fax: 202-745-3731

Hyatt Regency
400 New Jersey Ave NW
Washington, DC 20001
E-mail: pr@hyattdc.com
www.hyatt.com/usa/washington/hotels/hotel_wasrw.html
Phone: 202-737-1234
Fax: 202-737-5773
TF: 800-233-1234

INTELSAT
3400 International Dr NW
Washington, DC 20008
www.intelsat.com
Phone: 202-944-6800
Fax: 202-944-7898

Marriott International Inc
10400 Fernwood Rd
Bethesda, MD 20817
www.marriott.com
Phone: 301-380-3000
Fax: 301-380-7752
TF: 800-228-9290

Potomac Electric Power Co
1900 Pennsylvania Ave NW
Washington, DC 20068
E-mail: communications@pepco.com
www.pepco.com
Phone: 202-872-2000
Fax: 202-331-4824

Riggs National Corp
1503 Pennsylvania Ave
Washington, DC 20006
Phone: 301-887-6000
Fax: 202-835-8522

ULLICO Inc
111 Massachusetts Ave NW
Washington, DC 20001
www.ullico.com
Phone: 202-682-0900
Fax: 202-682-4911
TF: 800-431-5425

US Office Products Co
1025 Thomas Jefferson St NW Suite 600E
Washington, DC 20007
www.usop.com
Phone: 202-339-6700
Fax: 202-339-6744
TF: 800-330-6347

Washington Hospital Center
110 Irving St NW
Washington, DC 20010
www.whcenter.org
Phone: 202-877-7000
Fax: 202-877-7826

Washington Post
1150 15th St NW
Washington, DC 20071
www.washingtonpost.com
Phone: 202-334-6000
Fax: 202-334-7502

Quality of Living Indicators

Total Crime Index....................46,171
(rates per 100,000 inhabitants)

Violent Crime
Murder/manslaughter.................... 260
Forcible rape.................... 190
Robbery....................3,606
Aggravated assault....................4,932

Property Crime
Burglary 6,361
Larceny theft 24,321
Motor vehicle theft 6,501

Cost of Living Index 120.3
(national average = 100)

Median Home Price $176,500

Education

Public Schools

Washington DC Public School System
825 N Capitol St NE 9th Fl
Washington, DC 20002
www.k12.dc.us
Phone: 202-442-4222
Fax: 202-442-5026

Number of Schools
Elementary 110
Middle 23
High 23

Student/Teacher Ratio
All Grades 17.3:1

Private Schools

Number of Schools (all grades) .... 90+

Colleges & Universities

American University
4400 Massachusetts Ave NW
Washington, DC 20016
www.american.edu
Phone: 202-885-1000
Fax: 202-885-6014

Capitol College
11301 Springfield Rd
Laurel, MD 20708
E-mail: ccinfo@capitol-college.edu
www.capitol-college.edu
Phone: 301-369-2800
Fax: 301-953-3876
TF: 800-950-1992

Catholic University of America
620 Michigan Ave NE
Washington, DC 20064
www.cua.edu
Phone: 202-319-5000
Fax: 202-319-6533
TF: 800-673-2772

Columbia Union College
7600 Flower Ave
Takoma Park, MD 20912
www.cuc.edu
Phone: 301-891-4000
Fax: 301-891-4167
TF: 800-835-4212

Corcoran School of Art
500 17th St NW
Washington, DC 20006
www.corcoran.edu/csa
Phone: 202-639-1800
Fax: 202-639-1802

Florida Institute of Technology
4875 Eisenhower Ave Suite 200
Alexandria, VA 22304
www.segs.fit.edu
Phone: 703-751-1060
Fax: 703-751-4592

Gallaudet University
800 Florida Ave NE
Washington, DC 20002
www.gallaudet.edu
Phone: 202-651-5000
Fax: 202-651-6107

George Mason University
4400 University Dr MSN 3A4
Fairfax, VA 22030
E-mail: admissions@admissions.gmu.edu
www.gmu.edu
Phone: 703-993-1000
Fax: 703-993-2392

George Washington University
2121 'I' St NW
Washington, DC 20052
gwis.circ.gwu.edu
Phone: 202-994-1000
Fax: 202-994-0325
TF: 800-447-3765

George Washington University Mount Vernon College
2100 Foxhall Rd NW
Washington, DC 20007
E-mail: gwadm@www.gwu.edu
www.gwu.edu
Phone: 202-625-0400
Fax: 202-625-4688
TF: 800-682-4636

Georgetown University
37th & 'O' Sts NW
Washington, DC 20057
www.georgetown.edu
Phone: 202-687-3600
Fax: 202-687-5084

Howard University
2400 6th St NW
Washington, DC 20059
www.howard.edu
Phone: 202-806-6100
Fax: 202-806-4466

Maryland College of Art & Design
10500 Georgia Ave
Silver Spring, MD 20902
www.mcadmd.org
Phone: 301-649-4454
Fax: 301-649-2940

Marymount University
2807 N Glebe Rd
Arlington, VA 22207
E-mail: admissions@marymount.edu
www.marymount.edu
Phone: 703-522-5600
Fax: 703-522-0349
TF: 800-548-7638

Montgomery College Rockville Campus
51 Mannakee St
Rockville, MD 20850
E-mail: arrweb@mc.cc.md.us
www.montgomerycollege.com
Phone: 301-279-5000
Fax: 301-279-5037

Montgomery College Takoma Park Campus
7600 Takoma Ave
Takoma Park, MD 20912
Phone: 301-650-1501
Fax: 301-650-1497

Northern Virginia Community College Alexandria Campus
3001 N Beauregard St
Alexandria, VA 22311
www.nv.cc.va.us/alexandria/
Phone: 703-845-6200
Fax: 703-845-6046

Oblate College
391 Michigan Ave NE
Washington, DC 20017
Phone: 202-529-5244
Fax: 202-636-9444

Southeastern University
501 'I' St SW
Washington, DC 20024
E-mail: compctr@admin.seu.edu
www.seu.edu
Phone: 202-488-8162
Fax: 202-488-8093

Strayer University
1025 15th St NW
Washington, DC 20005
www.strayer.edu
Phone: 202-408-2400
Fax: 202-289-1831
TF: 888-478-7293

Strayer University Alexandria Campus
2730 Eisenhower Ave
Alexandria, VA 22314
www.strayer.edu
Phone: 703-329-9100
Fax: 703-329-9602

Strayer University Arlington Campus
3045 Columbia Pike
Arlington, VA 22204
www.strayer.edu
Phone: 703-892-5100
Fax: 703-769-2677
TF: 888-478-7293

Trinity College
125 Michigan Ave NE
Washington, DC 20017
www.trinitydc.edu
Phone: 202-884-9000
Fax: 202-884-9229
TF: 800-492-6882

University of Maryland College Park
College Park, MD 20742
E-mail: inform-editor@umail.umd.edu
inform.umd.edu
Phone: 301-405-1000
Fax: 301-314-9693
TF: 800-422-5867

University of the District of Columbia
4200 Connecticut Ave NW
Washington, DC 20008
www.udc.edu
Phone: 202-274-5000
Fax: 202-274-6073

Washington Bible College/Capital Bible Seminary
6511 Princess Garden Pkwy
Lanham, MD 20706
E-mail: info@bible.edu
www.bible.edu
Phone: 301-552-1400
Fax: 301-552-2775
TF: 800-787-0256

Hospitals

Alexandria Hospital
4320 Seminary Rd
Alexandria, VA 22304
Phone: 703-504-3000
Fax: 703-504-3700

Arlington Hospital
1701 N George Mason Dr
Arlington, VA 22205
www.arlhosp.org
Phone: 703-558-5000
Fax: 703-558-6553

Children's National Medical Center
111 Michigan Ave NW
Washington, DC 20010
www.cnmc.org
Phone: 202-884-5000
Fax: 202-884-5561
TF: 800-787-0080

District of Columbia General Hospital
19th St & Massachusetts Ave SE
Washington, DC 20003
Phone: 202-675-5000
Fax: 202-675-5650

George Washington University Hospital
901 23rd St NW
Washington, DC 20037
www.gwhospital.com
Phone: 202-715-4000
Fax: 202-715-4402

Georgetown University Medical Center
3800 Reservoir Rd NW
Washington, DC 20007
gumc.georgetown.edu
Phone: 202-687-5055
Fax: 202-784-2875

Greater Southeast Community Hospital
1310 Southern Ave SE
Washington, DC 20032
www.greatersoutheast.baweb.com
Phone: 202-574-6000
Fax: 202-574-7188

Howard University Hospital
2041 Georgia Ave NW
Washington, DC 20060
www.huhosp.org
Phone: 202-865-6100
Fax: 202-745-3731

Inova Mount Vernon Hospital
2501 Parker's Ln
Alexandria, VA 22306
www.inova.org/mvh
Phone: 703-664-7000
Fax: 703-664-7004

Northern Virginia Community Hospital
601 S Carlin Springs Rd
Arlington, VA 22204
Phone: 703-671-1200
Fax: 703-578-2281

Providence Hospital
1150 Varnum St NE
Washington, DC 20017
Phone: 202-269-7000
Fax: 202-269-7160

Sibley Memorial Hospital
5255 Loughboro Rd NW
Washington, DC 20016
www.sibley.org
Phone: 202-537-4000
Fax: 202-243-2246

Veterans Affairs Medical Center
50 Irving St NW
Washington, DC 20422
Phone: 202-745-8000
Fax: 202-745-8530
TF: 888-553-0242

Washington Hospital Center
110 Irving St NW
Washington, DC 20010
www.whcenter.org
Phone: 202-877-7000
Fax: 202-877-7826

Transportation

Airport(s)

Ronald Reagan Washington National Airport (DCA)
4 miles S of downtown (approx 20 minutes) 703-417-8000
Washington Dulles International Airport (IAD)
31 miles W of downtown (approx 35 minutes) 703-572-2730

Mass Transit

Metrorail/Metrobus
$1.10 Base fare. 202-637-7000

Rail/Bus

Amtrak Auto Train
8006 Lorton Rd
Lorton, VA 22079
Phone: 703-690-3615
TF: 800-872-7245

Amtrak Station
50 Massachusetts Ave NE Union Station
Washington, DC 20002
Phone: 202-484-7540
TF: 800-872-7245

Greyhound Bus Station
1005 NE 1st St
Washington, DC 20002
Phone: 202-289-5154
TF: 800-231-2222

Utilities

Electricity
PEPCO 202-833-7500
www.pepco.com

Gas
Washington Gas Co. 703-750-1000
www.washgas.com

Water
Washington DC Water Dept 202-354-3600

Garbage Collection/Recycling
Washington DC Solid Waste Collection Dept 202-645-4301

Telecommunications

Telephone
Verizon Communications 202-346-1000
www.verizon.com

Cable Television
District Cablevision 202-635-5100

Internet Service Providers (ISPs)
ALEX Electronic Alexandria Community 703-836-3729
www.alex.org
CapuNet LLC 301-881-4900
www.capu.net
Cyber Realm Inc 301-947-0100
www.cyberrealm.net
Cyber Services Inc 703-749-9590
www.cs.net
Digital Gateway Systems Inc 703-749-2884
web.dgsys.com
digitalNATION Communications Inc 703-642-2800
www.dn.net
LaserNet LLC 703-591-4232
www.laser.net
PatriotNet 703-277-7737
www.patriot.net/patriotnet
SprintLink 703-904-2000
www.sprintlink.net
Verio Virginia 703-749-7955
home.verio.net/local/frontpage.cfm?AirportCode=RFK
Xecunet LLC 301-682-9972
www.xecu.net

Banks

Bank of America
888 17th St NW
Washington, DC 20006
Phone: 202-624-4400
Fax: 202-624-5678

Citibank FSB
1775 Pennsylvania Ave NW
Washington, DC 20006
Phone: 202-828-7640
Fax: 202-828-5913

First Union National Bank
740 15th St NW
Washington, DC 20005
Phone: 202-637-7652
Fax: 202-637-7689

Riggs Bank NA
800 17th St NW
Washington, DC 20006
Phone: 202-835-5240
Fax: 202-835-5270
TF: 800-368-5800

SunTrust Bank
1445 New York Ave NW
Washington, DC 20005
Phone: 202-879-6000
TF: 800-273-7827

Shopping

Ballston Common
4238 Wilson Blvd
Arlington, VA 22203
www.ballston-common.com
Phone: 703-243-8088
Fax: 703-525-4247

Chevy Chase Pavilion
5335 Wisconsin Ave NW
Washington, DC 20015
Phone: 202-686-5335
Fax: 202-686-5334

Christmas Attic Inc
125 S Union St
Alexandria, VA 22314
www.christmasattic.com
Phone: 703-548-2829
Fax: 703-684-7064
TF: 800-881-0084

City Place Mall
8661 Colesville Rd
Silver Spring, MD 20910
Phone: 301-589-1091
Fax: 301-589-0581

Fair Oaks Shopping Center
11750 Fair Oaks
Fairfax, VA 22033
Phone: 703-359-8300
Fax: 703-273-0547

Fashion Centre at Pentagon City
1100 S Hayes St
Arlington, VA 22202
Phone: 703-415-2400
Fax: 703-415-2175

Georgetown Park
3222 M St NW Suite 140
Washington, DC 20007
Phone: 202-342-8190
Fax: 202-342-1458

Hecht's
1201 G St NW
Washington, DC 20005
Phone: 202-628-6661
Fax: 202-628-0783

House in the Country
107 N Fairfax St
Alexandria, VA 22314
E-mail: hc@christmasattic.com
207.32.92.57
Phone: 703-548-4267
Fax: 703-548-1008
TF: 800-771-8427

Landmark Mall
5801 Duke St
Alexandria, VA 22314
Phone: 703-941-2582
Fax: 703-941-2590

Mazza Gallerie
5300 Wisconsin Ave NW
Washington, DC 20015
Phone: 202-966-6114
Fax: 202-362-0471

Montgomery Mall
7101 Democracy Blvd
Bethesda, MD 20817
Phone: 301-469-6000
Fax: 301-469-7612

Pavilion at the Old Post Office
1100 Pennsylvania Ave NW
Washington, DC 20004
Phone: 202-289-4224
Fax: 202-898-0653

Potomac Mills
2700 Potomac Mills Cir Suite 307
Prince William, VA 22192
www.millscorp.com/potomac
Phone: 703-643-1855
Fax: 703-643-1054

Shops at National Place
1331 Pennsylvania Ave NW Suite 900
Washington, DC 20004
Phone: 202-662-1204
Fax: 202-662-1212

Strawbridge's
685 N Glebe Rd
Arlington, VA 22203
www.mayco.com/sc/index.jsp
Phone: 703-558-1200
Fax: 703-524-2985

Thieves Market Antiques Mall
8101 Richmond Hwy
Alexandria, VA 22309
E-mail: tmantiques@thievesmarketantiques.com
www.thievesmarketantiques.com
Phone: 703-360-4200
Fax: 703-360-5002

Tysons Corner Center
1961 Chain Bridge Rd Suite 105
McLean, VA 22102
www.shoptysons.com
Phone: 703-893-9400
TF: 888-289-7667

Tysons Galleria
2001 International Dr
McLean, VA 22102
Phone: 703-827-7700
Fax: 703-827-0976

Union Station
50 Massachusetts Ave NE
Washington, DC 20002
Phone: 202-371-9441

Village At Shirlington
2700 S Quincy St
Arlington, VA 22206
Phone: 703-379-0007
Fax: 703-671-7420

White Flint Mall
11301 Rockville Pike
North Bethesda, MD 20895
Phone: 301-468-5777
Fax: 301-816-9231

Media

Newspapers and Magazines

Alexandria Gazette Packet
1610 King St
Alexandria, VA 22314
Phone: 703-838-0302
Fax: 703-549-9655

Alexandria Journal*
6408 Edsall Rd
Alexandria, VA 22312
www.jrnl.com
Phone: 703-560-4000
Fax: 703-846-8366
TF: 800-531-1223

Arlington Connection
1600 Scotts Crossing Rd
McLean, VA 22102
Phone: 703-821-5050
Fax: 703-917-0991

Arlington Journal*
6408 Edsall Rd
Alexandria, VA 22312
E-mail: exp@aol.com
www.jrnl.com
Phone: 703-560-4000
Fax: 703-846-8366

Fairfax Times
1760 Reston Pkwy Suite 411
Fairfax, VA 22090
www.fairfaxtimes.com
Phone: 703-437-5400
Fax: 703-437-6019

Gaithersburg Gazette
1200 Quince Orchard Blvd
Gaithersburg, MD 20878
E-mail: editor@gazette.net
www.gazette.net
Phone: 301-948-3120
Fax: 301-670-7183

Historic Alexandria Quarterly
PO Box 178
Alexandria, VA 22313
ci.alexandria.va.us/oha/oha-main/oha-quarterly.html
Phone: 703-838-4554
Fax: 703-838-6451

Richmond Times-Dispatch Alexandria Bureau
108 S Columbus St Suite 201
Alexandria, VA 22314
Phone: 703-548-8758
Fax: 703-548-9036

Washington Business Journal
1555 Wilson Blvd Suite 400
Arlington, VA 22209
www.amcity.com/washington
Phone: 703-875-2200
Fax: 703-875-2231

Washington City Paper
2390 Champlain St NW
Washington, DC 20009
E-mail: mail@washcp.com
www.washingtoncitypaper.com
Phone: 202-332-2100
Fax: 202-332-8500

Washington Post*
1150 15th St NW
Washington, DC 20071
www.washingtonpost.com
Phone: 202-334-6000
Fax: 202-334-7502

Washington Post Alexandria/Arlington Bureau
526 King St Suite 515
Alexandria, VA 22314
Phone: 703-518-3000
Fax: 703-518-3001

Washington Times*
3600 New York Ave NE
Washington, DC 20002
www.americasnewspaper.com
Phone: 202-636-3000
Fax: 202-269-3419

Washingtonian Magazine
1828 L St NW Suite 200
Washington, DC 20036
www.washingtonian.com
Phone: 202-296-3600
TF: 877-532-6083

**Indicates major daily newspapers*

Television

WBDC-TV Ch 50 (WB)
2121 Wisconsin Ave NW Suite 350
Washington, DC 20007
Phone: 202-965-5050
Fax: 202-965-0050

WDCA-TV Ch 20 (UPN)
5202 River Rd
Bethesda, MD 20816
E-mail: programming@upn20email.com
www.paramountstations.com/WDCA
Phone: 301-986-9322
Fax: 301-654-3517

WETA-TV Ch 26 (PBS)
3620 S 27th St
Arlington, VA 22206
E-mail: info@weta.com
www.weta.org
Phone: 703-998-2600
Fax: 703-998-3401

WHUT-TV Ch 32 (PBS)
2222 4th St NW
Washington, DC 20059
Phone: 202-806-3200
Fax: 202-806-3300

WJLA-TV Ch 7 (ABC)
3007 Tilden St NW
Washington, DC 20008
www.abc7dc.com
Phone: 202-364-7777
Fax: 202-364-7734

WPXW-TV Ch 66 (PAX)
6199 Old Arrington Ln
Fairfax Station, VA 22039
Phone: 703-503-7966
Fax: 703-503-1225

WRC-TV Ch 4 (NBC)
4001 Nebraska Ave NW
Washington, DC 20016
www.nbc4dc.com
Phone: 202-885-4000
Fax: 202-885-4104

WTMW-TV Ch 14 (Ind)
3565 Lee Hwy
Arlington, VA 22207
Phone: 703-528-0051
Fax: 703-528-2956

WTTG-TV Ch 5 (Fox)
5151 Wisconsin Ave NW
Washington, DC 20016
Phone: 202-244-5151
Fax: 202-244-1745
TF: 800-988-4885

WUSA-TV Ch 9 (CBS)
4100 Wisconsin Ave NW
Washington, DC 20016
E-mail: 9news@wusatv.com
www.wusatv9.com
Phone: 202-895-5999
Fax: 202-966-7948

Radio

WABS-AM 780 kHz (Rel)
5545 Lee Hwy
Arlington, VA 22207
Phone: 703-534-2000
Fax: 703-534-3330

WAMU-FM 88.5 MHz (NPR)
American University
Washington, DC 20016
E-mail: feedback@wamu.org
www.wamu.org
Phone: 202-885-1200
Fax: 202-885-1269

WARW-FM 94.7 MHz (CR)
5912 Hubbard Dr
Rockville, MD 20852
www.classicrock947.com
Phone: 301-984-6000
Fax: 301-468-2490

WASH-FM 97.1 MHz (AC)
1801 Rockville Pike
Rockville, MD 20852
www.washfm.com
Phone: 301-984-9710
Fax: 301-255-4344

WAVA-FM 105.1 MHz (Rel)
1901 N Moore St Suite 200
Arlington, VA 22209
www.wava.com
Phone: 703-807-2266
Fax: 703-807-2248

WBIG-FM 100.3 MHz (Oldies)
1801 Rockville Pike 6th Fl
Rockville, MD 20852
www.oldies100.com
Phone: 301-468-1800
Fax: 301-770-0236

WBIS-AM 1190 kHz (N/T)
1081 Bay Ridge Rd
Annapolis, MD 21403
www.wbis1190.com
Phone: 410-269-0700
Fax: 410-269-0692

WCTN-AM 950 kHz (Rel)
7825 Tuckerman Ln Suite 211
Potomac, MD 20854
E-mail: wctn@wctn.net
www.wctn.net
Phone: 301-299-7026
Fax: 301-299-5301

WETA-FM 90.9 MHz (NPR)
2775 S Quincy St
Arlington, VA 22206
E-mail: radio@weta.com
www.weta.org/weta/fm
Phone: 703-998-2790
Fax: 703-824-7288

WFAX-AM 1220 kHz (Rel)
161-B Hillwood Ave
Falls Church, VA 22046
E-mail: wfax@erols.com
www.wfaxam.com
Phone: 703-532-1220
Fax: 703-533-7572

WFSI-FM 107.9 MHz (Rel)
918 Chesapeake Ave
Annapolis, MD 21403
www.wfsiradio.com
Phone: 410-268-6200

WGMS-FM 103.5 MHz (Clas)
3400 Idaho Ave NW
Washington, DC 20016
www.wgms.com
Phone: 202-895-5000
Fax: 202-895-4168

WGTS-FM 91.9 MHz (Rel)
7600 Flower Ave
Takoma Park, MD 20912
E-mail: wgts@wgts.org
www.wgts.org
Phone: 301-891-4200
Fax: 301-270-9191

WHFS-FM 99.1 MHz (Alt)
4200 Parliament Pl Suite 300
Lanham, MD 20706
www.whfs.com
Phone: 301-306-0991
Fax: 301-731-0431

WHUR-FM 96.3 MHz (Urban)
529 Bryant St NW
Washington, DC 20059
Phone: 202-806-3500
Fax: 202-806-3522

WILC-AM 900 kHz (Span)
PO Box 42
Laurel, MD 20725
Phone: 301-419-2122
Fax: 301-419-2409

WJFK-AM 1300 kHz (N/T)
1 W Pennsylvania Ave Suite 850
Baltimore, MD 21204
www.1300wjfk.com
Phone: 410-823-1570
Fax: 410-821-5482

WJFK-FM 106.7 MHz (N/T)
10800 Main St
Fairfax, VA 22030
Phone: 703-691-1900
Fax: 703-352-0111

WJMO-FM 99.5 MHz (Oldies)
1801 Rockville Pike 6th Fl
Rockville, MD 20852
E-mail: wgay995@aol.com
Phone: 301-468-9429
Fax: 301-770-3541

WJZW-FM 105.9 MHz (NAC)
4400 Jenifer St NW
Washington, DC 20015
Phone: 202-895-2300
Fax: 202-686-3064

WKYS-FM 93.9 MHz (Urban)
5900 Princess Garden Pkwy Suite 800
Lanham, MD 20706
Phone: 301-306-1111
Fax: 301-306-9609

WMAL-AM 630 kHz (N/T)
4400 Jenifer St NW
Washington, DC 20015
www.wmal.com
Phone: 202-686-3100
Fax: 202-686-3061

WMET-AM 1150 kHz (N/T)
8945 N Westland Dr Suite 302
Gaithersburg, MD 20877
Phone: 301-921-0093

WMMJ-FM 102.3 MHz (Urban)
5900 Princess Garden Pkwy Suite 800
Lanham, MD 20706
Phone: 301-306-1111
Fax: 301-306-9609

WMZQ-FM 98.7 MHz (Ctry)
1801 Rockville Pike 6th Fl
Rockville, MD 20852
www.wmzqfm.com
Phone: 301-231-8231
Fax: 301-984-4895

WNAV-AM 1430 kHz (AC)
PO Box 829
Annapolis, MD 21404
www.wnav.com
Phone: 410-263-1430
Fax: 410-268-5360

WOL-AM 1450 kHz (N/T)
5900 Princess Garden Pkwy
Lanham, MD 20706
Phone: 301-306-1111
Fax: 301-306-9609

WPGC-FM 95.5 MHz (CHR) Phone: 301-441-3500
6301 Ivy Ln Suite 800 Fax: 301-345-9505
Greenbelt, MD 20770

WRQX-FM 107.3 MHz (AC) Phone: 202-686-3100
4400 Jenifer St NW Fax: 202-686-3091
Washington, DC 20015
www.mix1073fm.com

WTEM-AM 980 kHz (Sports) Phone: 301-231-7798
11300 Rockville Pike Suite 707 Fax: 301-881-8030
Rockville, MD 20852
E-mail: tcastle@erols.com
www.wtem.com

WTOP-AM 1500 kHz (N/T) Phone: 202-895-5000
3400 Idaho Ave NW Fax: 202-895-5140
Washington, DC 20016

WTOP-FM 107.7 MHz (N/T) Phone: 202-895-5000
3400 Idaho Ave NW Fax: 202-895-5140
Washington, DC 20016

WWDC-FM 101.1 MHz (Rock) Phone: 301-587-7100
8750 Brookville Rd Fax: 301-565-3329
Silver Spring, MD 20910
www.dc101.com

WWRC-AM 570 kHz (N/T) Phone: 301-587-4900
8750 Brookville Rd Fax: 301-587-8086
Silver Spring, MD 20910

WWVZ-FM 103.9 MHz (CHR) Phone: 301-662-2148
6633 Mt Philip Rd Fax: 301-663-0636
Frederick, MD 21703

WWZZ-FM 104.1 MHz (CHR) Phone: 703-522-1041
2000 15th St N Suite 200 Fax: 703-526-0250
Arlington, VA 22201
www.thez.com

WYCB-AM 1340 kHz (Rel) Phone: 301-306-1111
5900 Princess Garden Pkwy Suite 800 Fax: 301-306-9609
Lanham, MD 20706

Attractions

The U.S. Capitol Building, which has been the seat of Congress for almost 200 years, is open to the public, and visitors can observe the U.S. government at work. On Capitol Hill also are the Library of Congress and the U.S. Supreme Court, both of which also are open to the public. Beginning at the Capitol and continuing on to the Potomac River is a grassy area called The Mall. Located here are museums and art galleries of the Smithsonian Institution, as well as the Washington Monument. The White House, which offers free tours daily, is just north of the Washington Monument, and to the south, on the Tidal Basin, is the Jefferson Memorial. The Lincoln Memorial sits at the west end of The Mall, and close by this area is the Vietnam Veterans Memorial ("The Wall"). Arlington National Cemetery, site of the Tomb of the Unknowns and John F. Kennedy's final resting place, is located on the other side of the Potomac River. Other attractions in the Capitol area include the National Archives; the Bureau of Engraving and Printing, where new money is printed and old money is destroyed; the U.S. Holocaust Memorial Museum; Ford's Theatre, where President Lincoln was assassinated; and the National Cathedral. Mount Vernon, the home of George Washington, is in nearby Alexandria, Virginia.

African-American Civil War Memorial Phone: 202-667-2667
10th & U Sts NW Fax: 202-667-6771
Washington, DC 20001
E-mail: afroamcivilwar@yahoo.com
www.afroamcivilwar.org

Alexandria African-American Heritage Park Phone: 703-838-4356
Holland Ln betw Duke St & Eisenhower Ave
Alexandria, VA 22314
ci.alexandria.va.us/oha/bhrc/bh-heritage-park.html

Alexandria Archaeology Museum Phone: 703-838-4399
105 N Union St Rm 327 Fax: 703-838-6491
Alexandria, VA 22314
E-mail: archaeology@ci.alexandria.va.us
ci.alexandria.va.us/oha/archaeology

Alexandria Ballet Phone: 703-548-0035
201 Prince St Athenaeum Fax: 703-768-7471
Alexandria, VA 22314

Alexandria Chorale Society Phone: 703-548-4734
101 Callahan Dr George Washington National Memorial Auditorium
Alexandria, VA 22314

Alexandria Harmonizers Phone: 703-836-0969
PO Box 11274
Alexandria, VA 22312
www.harmonizers.org

Alexandria National Cemetery Phone: 703-690-2217
1450 Wilkes St
Alexandria, VA 22314

Alexandria Seaport Foundation's Seaport Center Phone: 703-549-7078
Alexandria Waterfront
Alexandria, VA 22314
E-mail: asfhqs@aol.com
www.capaccess.org/snt/alexsea/

Alexandria Symphony Orchestra Phone: 703-845-8005
PO Box 11835 Fax: 703-845-8007
Alexandria, VA 22312
E-mail: nseeger@alexsym.org
www.alexsym.org

American Horticultural Society at River Farm Phone: 703-768-5700
7931 E Boulevard Dr TF: 800-777-7931
Alexandria, VA 22308
www.ahs.org/nonmembers/riverfarm.htm

American Sportscasters Assn Hall of Fame & Museum Phone: 202-628-3200
601 F St NW Fax: 202-661-5172
Washington, DC 20004

Anacostia Museum (Smithsonian Institution) Phone: 202-357-1300
1901 Fort Pl SE Fax: 202-287-3183
Washington, DC 20560

Archives of American Art Phone: 202-314-3900
901 D St SW Suite 704 Fax: 202-314-3987
Washington, DC 20560
www.si.edu/artarchives

Arena Stage
1101 6th St SW
Washington, DC 20024
E-mail: info@arenastage.org
www.arenastage.org
Phone: 202-488-3300
Fax: 202-488-4056

Arlington Arts Center
3550 Wilson Blvd
Arlington, VA 22201
E-mail: artscenter@erols.com
Phone: 703-524-1494
Fax: 703-527-4050

Arlington Historical Museum
1805 S Arlington Ridge Rd
Arlington, VA 22202
Phone: 703-892-4204

Arlington House-Robert E Lee Memorial
George Washington Memorial Pkwy
Turkey Run Pk
McLean, VA 22101
www.nps.gov/arho/
Phone: 703-557-0613
Fax: 703-235-9063

Arlington National Cemetery
Arlington Cemetery
Arlington, VA 22211
E-mail: manit@fmmc.army.mil
www.arlingtoncemetery.org
Phone: 703-697-2131
Fax: 703-614-6339

Arlington Symphony
4238 Wilson Blvd Suite 3064
Arlington, VA 22203
Phone: 703-528-1817
Fax: 703-528-1911

Arthur M Sackler Gallery (Smithsonian Institution)
1050 Independence Ave SW
Washington, DC 20560
www.si.edu/asia
Phone: 202-357-4880
Fax: 202-357-4911

Arts & Industries Building
900 Jefferson Dr SW
Washington, DC 20560
www.si.edu/ai
Phone: 202-357-2700

Arts Afire Glass Gallery
112 N Royal St
Alexandria, VA 22314
E-mail: artsafire@bellatlantic.net
www.artsafire.com
Phone: 703-838-9785
Fax: 703-838-9787

B'nai B'rith Klutznick National Jewish Museum
1640 Rhode Island Ave NW
Washington, DC 20036
Phone: 202-857-6583
Fax: 202-857-1099

Birchmere Music Hall
3701 Mt Vernon Ave
Alexandria, VA 22305
E-mail: birch@birchmere.com
www.birchmere.com
Phone: 703-549-7500

Black History Resource Center
638 N Alfred St
Alexandria, VA 22314
E-mail: black.history@ci.alexandria.va. us
ci.alexandria.va.us/oha/bhrc
Phone: 703-838-4356
Fax: 703-706-3999

Bon Air Park
850 N Lexington St
Arlington, VA 22205
Phone: 703-228-4747

Bureau of Engraving & Printing
14th & C Sts SW
Washington, DC 20228
Phone: 202-874-2485
Fax: 202-874-3177

Cameron Run Regional Park
4001 Eisenhower Ave
Alexandria, VA 22314
www.nvrpa.org/cameron.html
Phone: 703-960-0767

Capital Children's Museum
800 3rd St NE
Washington, DC 20002
www.ccm.org/
Phone: 202-675-4120
Fax: 202-675-4140

Carlyle House Museum & Historic Park
121 N Fairfax St
Alexandria, VA 22314
Phone: 703-549-2997
Fax: 703-549-5738

Chesapeake & Ohio Canal National Historical Park
PO Box 4
Sharpsburg, MD 21782
E-mail: choh_chief_ranger@nps.gov
www.nps.gov/choh/
Phone: 301-739-4200
Fax: 301-739-5275

Chevy Chase Pavilion
5335 Wisconsin Ave NW
Washington, DC 20015
Phone: 202-686-5335
Fax: 202-686-5334

Chinquapin Park
3210 King St
Alexandria, VA 22314
Phone: 703-838-4343

Christ Church
118 N Washington St
Alexandria, VA 22314
Phone: 703-549-1450
Fax: 703-683-2677

Clark Street Playhouse
601 S Clark St
Arlington, VA 22202
Phone: 703-418-4808

Confederate Statue Appomattox
Prince & S Washington Sts
Alexandria, VA 22314

Congressional Cemetery
1801 'E' St SE
Washington, DC 20003
Phone: 202-543-0539

Constitution Gardens
900 Ohio Dr SW Survey Lodge
Washington, DC 20024
www.nps.gov/coga
Phone: 202-426-6841
Fax: 202-426-1844

Corcoran Gallery of Art
500 17th St NW
Washington, DC 20006
E-mail: admofc@corcoran.org
www.corcoran.org
Phone: 202-639-1700
Fax: 202-639-1768

Dandy Restaurant Cruise Ship
0 Prince St
Alexandria, VA 22314
E-mail: dandy1@erols.com
www.dandydinnerboat.com
Phone: 703-683-6076

DAR Museum
1776 D St NW
Washington, DC 20006
www.dar.org/museum/index.html
Phone: 202-879-3241
Fax: 202-628-0820

Decatur House Museum Phone: 202-842-0920
748 Jackson Pl NW Fax: 202-842-0030
Washington, DC 20006
E-mail: decatur-house@nthp.org

Discovery Creek Children's Museum of Washington DC Phone: 202-364-3111
5125 MacArthur Blvd NW Suite 10 Fax: 202-364-3114
Washington, DC 20016
E-mail: discovery_creek@capaccess.org
www.discoverycreek.org

Discovery Theater Phone: 202-357-1500
900 Jefferson Dr SW Fax: 202-357-2588
Washington, DC 20560

Drug Enforcement Administration Museum & Visitors Center Phone: 202-307-3463
700 Army Navy Dr
Arlington, VA 22202

Dumbarton House Phone: 202-337-2288
2715 Q St NW Fax: 202-337-0348
Washington, DC 20007

Dumbarton Oaks Research Library & Collection Phone: 202-339-6400
1703 32nd St NW Fax: 202-339-6419
Washington, DC 20007
www.doaks.org

Ellipse Arts Center Phone: 703-228-7710
4350 N Fairfax Dr Fax: 703-516-4468
Arlington, VA 22203
E-mail: ellipse@erols.com

Farmer's Market Phone: 800-388-9119
301 King St Market Sq
Alexandria, VA 22314

Folger Shakespeare Library Phone: 202-544-4600
201 East Capitol St SE Fax: 202-544-4623
Washington, DC 20003

Ford's Theatre National Historic Site Phone: 202-426-6924
511 10th St NW Fax: 202-426-1845
Washington, DC 20004
E-mail: ford's_theatre@nps.gov
www.nps.gov/foth

Fort Ward Museum & Historic Site Phone: 703-838-4848
4301 W Braddock Rd Fax: 703-671-7350
Alexandria, VA 22304
E-mail: fort.ward@ci.alexandria.va.us
ci.alexandria.va.us/oha/fortward

Fort Washington Park Phone: 301-763-4600
13551 Fort Washington Rd Fax: 301-763-1389
Fort Washington, MD 20744
www.nps.gov/fowa/

Franciscan Monastery Phone: 202-526-6800
1400 Quincy St NE Fax: 202-529-9889
Washington, DC 20017

Frank Lloyd Wright's Pope-Leighey House Phone: 703-780-3264
9000 Richmond Hwy Woodlawn Plantation Fax: 703-780-8509
Alexandria, VA 22309

Franklin Delano Roosevelt Memorial Phone: 202-619-7222
900 Ohio Dr SW
Washington, DC 20024

Freer Gallery of Art (Smithsonian Institution) Phone: 202-357-4880
1050 Independence Ave Fax: 202-633-9105
Washington, DC 20560
www.si.edu/asia/

Friendship Fire House Museum Phone: 703-838-3891
107 S Alfred St
Alexandria, VA 22314
E-mail: friendship@ci.alexandria.va.us
ci.alexandria.va.us/oha/friendship

Gadsby's Tavern Museum Phone: 703-838-4242
134 N Royal St Fax: 703-838-4270
Alexandria, VA 22314
E-mail: gadsbys.tavern@ci.alexandria.va.us
ci.alexandria.va.us/oha/gadsby

Geographica Phone: 202-857-7588
17th & M Sts NW
Washington, DC 20036

George Mason Center for the Arts Phone: 703-993-8888
George Mason University
Fairfax, VA 22030

George Washington Birthplace National Monument Phone: 804-224-1732
RR 1 Box 717 Fax: 804-224-2142
Washington's Birthplace, VA 22443
www.nps.gov/gewa/

George Washington Carver Nature Trail Phone: 202-357-1300
1901 Fort Pl SE Anacostia Museum Fax: 202-287-3183
Washington, DC 20020

George Washington Masonic National Memorial Phone: 703-683-2007
101 Callahan Dr Fax: 703-519-9270
Alexandria, VA 22301
www.gwmemorial.org

George Washington Memorial Parkway Phone: 703-285-2598
Turkey Run Pk Fax: 703-285-2398
McLean, VA 22101
www.nps.gov/gwmp/

George Washington's Mount Vernon Estate & Gardens Phone: 703-780-2000
George Washington Memorial Pkwy Fax: 703-799-8698
Mount Vernon, VA 22121
www.mountvernon.org

Georgetown Historic District Phone: 202-789-7000
Wisconsin Ave-betw 29th & 37th Sts
Washington, DC 20007

Grey House Potters Phone: 703-522-7738
5509 Wilson Blvd
Arlington, VA 22205

Gulf Branch Nature Center Phone: 703-228-3403
3608 N Military Rd Fax: 703-228-4401
Arlington, VA 22207

Gunston Hall Plantation
10709 Gunston Rd
Mason Neck, VA 22079
E-mail: historic@gunstonhall.org
gunstonhall.org
Phone: 703-550-9220
Fax: 703-550-9480

Hillwood Museum & Gardens
4155 Linnean Ave NW
Washington, DC 20008
Phone: 202-686-8500
Fax: 202-966-7846

Hirshhorn Museum & Sculpture Garden (Smithsonian Institution)
Independence Ave & 7th St SW
Washington, DC 20560
www.si.edu/hirshhorn/
Phone: 202-357-3091
Fax: 202-786-2682

Jefferson Memorial
1600 Basin Dr
Washington, DC 20242
www.nps.gov/thje
Phone: 202-426-6841
Fax: 202-426-1844

Jewish Historical Society of Greater Washington
701 3rd St NW
Washington, DC 20001
Phone: 202-789-0900
Fax: 202-789-0485

John F Kennedy Center for the Performing Arts
2700 F St NW
Washington, DC 20566
E-mail: comments@kennedy-center.org
kennedy-center.org
Phone: 202-416-8000
Fax: 202-416-8205
TF: 800-444-1324

Jones Point Park
100 Jones Point Dr
Alexandria, VA 22314
Phone: 703-838-4343

Kenilworth Aquatic Gardens
Anacostia Ave & Douglas St NE
Washington, DC 20019
Phone: 202-426-6905
Fax: 202-426-5991

Kennedy Center Opera House Orchestra
John F Kennedy Center for the Performing Arts
Washington, DC 20566
Phone: 202-416-8215
Fax: 202-416-8105

Korean War Veterans Memorial
c/o National Capital Parks - Central 900 Ohio Dr SW
Washington, DC 20242
www.nps.gov/kwvm/home.htm
Phone: 202-426-6841
Fax: 202-426-1835

Kreeger Museum
2401 Foxhall Rd NW
Washington, DC 20007
www.kreegermuseum.com
Phone: 202-338-3552
Fax: 202-337-3051

Langley IMAX Theater
6th St & Independence Ave SW
Washington, DC 20560
www.nasm.edu/nasm/IMAX/langley.html
Phone: 202-357-1675
Fax: 202-357-3726

Lee-Fendall House Museum
614 Oronoco St
Alexandria, VA 22314
Phone: 703-548-1789

Library of Congress
101 Independence Ave SE
Washington, DC 20540
www.loc.gov
Phone: 202-707-5000
Fax: 202-707-9199

Lillian & Albert Small Jewish Museum
701 3rd St NW
Washington, DC 20001
www.jewishculture.org/jewishmuseums/small.htm
Phone: 202-789-0900
Fax: 202-789-0485

Lincoln Memorial
900 Ohio Dr SW National Capitol Park Central
Washington, DC 20024
www.nps.gov/linc/
Phone: 202-426-6841
Fax: 202-426-1844

Lincoln Theatre
1215 U St NW
Washington, DC 20009
Phone: 202-328-9177
Fax: 202-328-9245

Little Theatre of Alexandria
600 Wolfe St
Alexandria, VA 22314
Phone: 703-683-5778
Fax: 703-683-1378

Lloyd House
220 N Washington St
Alexandria, VA 22314
Phone: 703-838-4577

Long Branch Nature Center
625 S Carlin Springs Rd
Arlington, VA 22204
Phone: 703-228-6535
Fax: 703-845-2654

Lyceum History Museum
201 S Washington St
Alexandria, VA 22314
E-mail: lyceum@ci.alexandria.va.us
ci.alexandria.va.us/oha/lyceum
Phone: 703-838-4994
Fax: 703-838-4997

Lyndon Baines Johnson Memorial Grove on the Potomac
George Washington Memorial Pkwy Turkey Run Pk
McLean, VA 22101
www.nps.gov/lyba/
Phone: 703-285-2598
Fax: 703-285-2398

Manassas National Battlefield Park
6511 Sudley Rd
Manassas, VA 20109
www.nps.gov/mana/
Phone: 703-361-1339
Fax: 703-754-1107

Marine Corps Memorial
Rt 50 & George Washington Memorial Pkwy
Arlington, VA 22211
Phone: 703-289-2510
Fax: 703-289-2598

Mary McLeod Bethune Council House National Historic Site
1318 Vermont Ave NW
Washington, DC 20005
www.nps.gov/mamc/
Phone: 202-673-2402
Fax: 202-673-2414

MetroStage
PO Box 329
Alexandria, VA 22313
Phone: 703-548-9044
Fax: 703-548-9089

Mount Vernon Chamber Orchestra Assn
201 S Washington St Lyceum
Alexandria, VA 22314
Phone: 703-799-8229
Fax: 703-360-7391

Mount Vernon Forest Trail
Alexandria, VA 22314
Phone: 703-780-2000

Mount Vernon Ladies' Assn of the Union
PO Box 110
Mount Vernon, VA 22121
www.mountvernon.org
Phone: 703-780-2000
Fax: 703-799-8698

National Air & Space Museum Smithsonian Institution
Independence Ave & 6th St SW
Washington, DC 20560
E-mail: vportway@www.nasm.edu
www.nasm.edu
Phone: 202-357-2700
Fax: 202-357-2426

National Aquarium
14th & Constitution Ave NW
Washington, DC 20230
E-mail: aqua@doc.gov
Phone: 202-482-2826
Fax: 202-482-4946

National Archives & Records Administration
8601 Adelphi Rd
College Park, MD 20740
E-mail: inquire@nara.gov
www.nara.gov
Phone: 301-713-7360
Fax: 301-713-6169

National Building Museum
401 F St NW
Washington, DC 20001
www.nbm.org
Phone: 202-272-2448
Fax: 202-272-2564

National Capital Region (NCR)
1100 Ohio Dr SW
Washington, DC 20242
Phone: 202-619-7222
Fax: 202-619-7302

National Cathedral
Massachusetts & Wisconsin Aves NW
Washington, DC 20016
Phone: 202-537-6200
Fax: 202-537-5661

National Firearms Museum
11250 Waples Mill Rd
Fairfax, VA 22030
www.nrahq.org/shooting/museum
Phone: 703-267-1600
Fax: 703-267-3913

National Gallery of Art
6th St & Constitution Ave NW
Washington, DC 20565
www.nga.gov
Phone: 202-737-4215
Fax: 202-842-2356

National Garden to Commemorate Congress's Bicentennial
245 1st St SW
Washington, DC 20024
www.nationalgarden.org
Phone: 202-226-4083
Fax: 202-225-7910

National Geographic Society
1145 17th St NW
Washington, DC 20036
E-mail: askngs@nationalgeographic.com
www.nationalgeographic.com
Phone: 202-857-7000
Fax: 202-775-6141
TF: 800-647-5463

National Geographic Society Explorer's Hall
1145 17th St NW
Washington, DC 20036
www.nationalgeographic.com/explorer
Phone: 202-857-7589
Fax: 202-857-5530

National Law Enforcement Officers Memorial
605 'E' St NW
Washington, DC 20004
Phone: 202-737-3400
Fax: 202-737-3405

National Mall
900 Ohio Dr SW
Washington, DC 20024
www.nps.gov/nama
Phone: 202-426-6841
Fax: 202-426-1844

National Museum of African Art (Smithsonian Institution)
950 Independence Ave SW
Washington, DC 20560
www.si.edu/organiza/museums/africart/start.htm
Phone: 202-357-4600
Fax: 202-357-4879

National Museum of American History (Smithsonian Institution)
14th St & Constitution Ave NW
Washington, DC 20560
americanhistory.si.edu
Phone: 202-357-2700
Fax: 202-633-8053

National Museum of Health & Medicine
6825 16th St NW
Washington, DC 20306
natmedmuse.afip.org
Phone: 202-782-2200
Fax: 202-782-3573

National Museum of Natural History (Smithsonian Institution)
10th St & Constitution Ave NW
Washington, DC 20560
www.mnh.si.edu/nmnhweb.html
Phone: 202-357-2664
Fax: 202-357-4779

National Museum of Women in the Arts
1250 New York Ave NW
Washington, DC 20005
www.nmwa.org
Phone: 202-783-5000
Fax: 202-393-3245
TF: 800-222-7270

National Portrait Gallery (Smithsonian Institution)
F & 8th Sts NW
Washington, DC 20560
www.npg.si.edu
Phone: 202-357-1915
Fax: 202-633-9188

National Postal Museum (Smithsonian Institution)
2 Massachusetts Ave NE
Washington, DC 20560
Phone: 202-633-9360
Fax: 202-633-9393

National Shrine of Immaculate Conception
4th St & Michigan Ave NE
Washington, DC 20017
Phone: 202-526-8300
Fax: 202-526-8313

National Symphony Orchestra
JFK Ctr for the Performing Arts New Hampshire Ave & F St NW
Washington, DC 20566
kennedy-center.org/stage/nso
Phone: 202-416-8100
Fax: 202-416-8105
TF: 800-444-1324

National Theatre
1321 'E' St NW
Washington, DC 20004
www.nationaltheatre.org
Phone: 202-628-6161
Fax: 202-638-4830
TF: 800-447-7400

National Zoological Park
3001 Connecticut Ave NW
Washington, DC 20008
www.si.edu/natzoo
Phone: 202-673-4717
Fax: 202-673-4900

Navy Historical Center
M St SE Washington Navy Yard
Washington, DC 20003
www.history.navy.mil
Phone: 202-433-4882
Fax: 202-433-8200

Netherlands Carillon Phone: 703-289-2500
Turkey Run Park
Arlington, VA 22101

Newseum Phone: 703-284-3544
1101 Wilson Blvd Fax: 703-284-3777
Arlington, VA 22209 TF: 888-639-7386
www.newseum.org

Oceans of Wildlife Fine Art Gallery Phone: 703-739-3202
201 King St
Alexandria, VA 22314
www.alexandriacity.com/art/wyland.htm

Octagon The Museum Phone: 202-638-3221
1799 New York Ave NW Fax: 202-879-7764
Washington, DC 20006
www.aafpages.org/octabout.htm

Old Guard Museum Phone: 703-696-6670
Sheridan Ave Fort Myer Bldg 249 Fax: 703-696-4256
Arlington, VA 22211

Old Presbyterian Meeting House Phone: 703-549-6670
321 S Fairfax St
Alexandria, VA 22314

Old Stone House Phone: 202-426-6851
3051 M St NW Fax: 202-426-0215
Washington, DC 20007

Old Town Trolley Tours Phone: 202-832-9800
2640 Reed St NE Fax: 202-832-9040
Washington, DC 20018
E-mail: wdcott@historictours.com
www.historictours.com/Washington/dctrolley.htm

Old Warsaw Galleries Phone: 703-548-9188
319 Cameron St
Alexandria, VA 22314

Opera Theatre of Northern Virginia Phone: 703-528-1433
125 S Old Glebe Rd Thomas Jefferson Theatre Fax: 703-812-5039
Arlington, VA 22205

Oronoco Bay Park Phone: 703-838-4343
Pendleton & Madison Sts
Alexandria, VA 22314

Pavilion at the Old Post Office Phone: 202-289-4224
1100 Pennsylvania Ave NW Fax: 202-898-0653
Washington, DC 20004

Pennsylvania Avenue National Historic Site Phone: 202-426-6841
National Mall Parks 900 Ohio Dr SW Fax: 202-426-1835
Washington, DC 20024
www.nps.gov/paav

Pentagon The Phone: 703-695-1776
Arlington, VA 20301
www.defenselink.mil/pubs/pentagon

Phillips Collection Phone: 202-387-2151
1600 21st St NW Fax: 202-387-2436
Washington, DC 20009
www.phillipscollection.org

Piscataway Park Phone: 301-763-4600
13551 Fort Washington Rd Fax: 301-763-1389
Fort Washington, MD 20744
www.nps.gov/pisc/

Potomac Heritage National Scenic Trail Phone: 202-619-7025
National Mall 1100 Ohio Dr SW Fax: 202-401-0017
Washington, DC 20242
www.nps.gov/pohe

Potomac Heritage National Scenic Trail Phone: 703-838-4200
Alexandria, VA 22314

Potomac Overlook Regional Park Phone: 703-528-5406
2845 N Marcey Rd Fax: 703-528-0750
Arlington, VA 22207

Prince Royal Gallery Phone: 703-548-5151
204 S Royal St
Alexandria, VA 22314
E-mail: princeroyal@look.net
look.net/princeroyal

Prince William Forest Park Phone: 703-221-7181
18100 Park Headquarters Rd Fax: 703-221-4322
Triangle, VA 22172
www.nps.gov/prwi/

Renwick Gallery of the National Museum of American Art (Smithsonian Institution) Phone: 202-357-2531
Pennsylvania Ave & 17th St NW Fax: 202-786-2810
Washington, DC 20006
nmaa-ryder.si.edu/collections/renwick/main.html

Richmond National Battlefield Park Phone: 804-226-1981
3215 E Broad St Fax: 804-771-8522
Richmond, VA 23223
www.nps.gov/rich/

Rock Creek Park Phone: 202-282-1063
3545 Williamsburg Ln NW Fax: 202-282-7612
Washington, DC 20008
www.nps.gov/rocr

Saint Matthew's Cathedral Phone: 202-347-3215
1725 Rhode Island Ave NW Fax: 202-347-7184
Washington, DC 20036

Shakespeare Theatre Phone: 202-547-1122
450 7th St NW Fax: 202-638-3869
Washington, DC 20004
www.shakespearedc.org

Shenandoah National Park Phone: 540-999-2243
3655 US Hwy 211E Fax: 540-999-3679
Luray, VA 22835
www.nps.gov/shen/

Signature Theatre Phone: 703-820-9771
3806 S Four Mile Run Dr Fax: 703-820-7790
Arlington, VA 22206
sig-online.org

Stabler-Leadbeater Apothecary Museum Phone: 703-836-3713
107 S Fairfax St
Alexandria, VA 22314
www.apothecary.org

Sully Plantation
3601 Sully Rd
Chantilly, VA 20151
E-mail: fcpaweb@co.fairfax.va.us
www.co.fairfax.va.us/parks
Phone: 703-437-1794
Fax: 703-787-3314

Textile Museum
2320 'S' St NW
Washington, DC 20008
www.textilemuseum.org
Phone: 202-667-0441
Fax: 202-483-0994

Theodore Roosevelt Island
George Washington Pkwy Turkey Run Pk
McLean, VA 22101
www.nps.gov/this/
Phone: 703-289-2530
Fax: 703-289-2598

Thomas Jefferson Memorial & Tidal Basin
900 Ohio Dr SW National Capital Region Mall Operations
Washington, DC 20024
E-mail: national_mall@nps.gov
www.nps.gov/thje/
Phone: 202-426-6841
Fax: 202-426-1844

Thomas Jefferson Theatre
125 S Old Glebe Rd
Arlington, VA 22204
Phone: 703-228-5900
Fax: 703-979-3744

Torpedo Factory Art Center
105 N Union St
Alexandria, VA 22314
www.torpedofactory.org
Phone: 703-838-4565
Fax: 703-549-6877

Tudor Place
1644 31st St NW
Washington, DC 20007
E-mail: ctuggle@tudorplace.org
www.tudorplace.org
Phone: 202-965-0400
Fax: 202-965-0164

US Air Force Band Strolling Strings
201 McChord St Bolling Air Force Base
Washington, DC 20332
www.bolling.af.mil/band
Phone: 202-767-4224
Fax: 202-767-0686

US Botanic Garden
245 1st St SW
Washington, DC 20024
Phone: 202-225-8333
Fax: 202-225-1561

US Capitol
1st St & Independence Ave
Washington, DC 20510
E-mail: feedback@aoc.gov
www.aoc.gov
Phone: 202-225-6827

US Holocaust Memorial Museum
100 Raoul Wallenburg Pl SW
Washington, DC 20024
E-mail: membership@ushmm.org
www.ushmm.org
Phone: 202-488-0400
Fax: 202-488-2690

US Marine Corps Memorial-Iwo Jima
Rt 50 & Arlington National Cemetery
Arlington, VA 22211
Phone: 703-352-5900

US National Arboretum
3501 New York Ave NE
Washington, DC 20002
www.ars-grin.gov/na
Phone: 202-245-2726
Fax: 202-245-4575

US Navy Memorial & Naval Heritage Center
701 Pennsylvania Ave NW Suite 123
Washington, DC 20004
www.history.navy.mil
Phone: 202-737-2300
Fax: 202-737-2308
TF: 800-821-8892

US Supreme Court
1st St & Maryland Ave NE
Washington, DC 20543
www.supremecourtus.gov
Phone: 202-479-3030

Vietnam Veterans Memorial
Corner Constitution Ave NW & Henry Bacon Dr National Capitol Park Central
Washington, DC 20020
thewall-usa.com
Phone: 202-634-1568

Vietnam Women's Memorial
21st & Constitution Ave NW & Henry Bacon Dr
Washington, DC 20024
Phone: 202-426-6841

Warner Theatre
1299 Pennsylvania Ave NW
Washington, DC 20004
www.warnertheatre.com
Phone: 202-783-4000
Fax: 202-783-0204

Washington Ballet
3515 Wisconsin Ave NW
Washington, DC 20016
www.washingtonballet.org
Phone: 202-362-3606
Fax: 202-362-1311

Washington Design Center
300 D St SW Suite 630
Washington, DC 20024
www.sonaco.com/cityguide/sightstosee/970.htm
Phone: 202-554-5053
Fax: 202-488-3711

Washington Dolls' House & Toy Museum
5236 44th St NW
Washington, DC 20015
Phone: 202-244-0024
Fax: 202-237-1659

Washington Monument
15th & Independence Ave NW
Washington, DC 20024
E-mail: national_mall@nps.gov
www.nps.gov/wamo/
Phone: 202-426-6841
Fax: 202-426-1844

Washington National Cathedral
Wisconsin & Massachusetts Aves NW
Washington, DC 20016
www.cathedral.org/cathedral
Phone: 202-537-6200
Fax: 202-364-6600

Washington Opera
2600 Virginia Ave NW Suite 104
Washington, DC 20037
E-mail: mail@dc-opera.org
www.dc-opera.org
Phone: 202-295-2420
Fax: 202-295-2479
TF: 800-876-7372

West End Dinner Theatre
4615 Duke St
Alexandria, VA 22304
E-mail: wedt@wedt.com
www.wedt.com
Phone: 703-370-2500

White House
1600 Pennsylvania Ave NW
Washington, DC 20500
www.nps.gov/whho
Phone: 202-208-1631
Fax: 202-208-1643

White House Visitors Center Phone: 202-456-7041
Pennsylvania Ave
Washington, DC 20500
www.whitehouse.gov/WH/Tours/visitors_center.html

Wolf Trap Farm Park for the Performing Arts Phone: 703-255-1868
1624-A Trap Rd
Vienna, VA 22182
www.nps.gov/wotr/

Women in Military Service for America Memorial Phone: 800-472-5883
Arlington National Cemetery Fax: 703-931-4208
Arlington, VA 22211 TF: 800-222-2294
E-mail: wimsa@aol.com
www.womensmemorial.org

Woodlawn Plantation Phone: 703-780-4000
9000 Richmond Hwy Fax: 703-780-8509
Alexandria, VA 22309

Woodrow Wilson House Museum Phone: 202-387-4062
2340 'S' St NW Fax: 202-483-1466
Washington, DC 20008
www.nthp.org/main/sites/wilsonhouse.htm

Woolly Mammoth Theatre Co Phone: 202-393-3939
1401 Church St NW Fax: 202-667-0904
Washington, DC 20005

Sports Teams & Facilities

Kennedy Robert F Memorial Stadium Phone: 202-547-9077
2400 E Capitol St Fax: 202-547-7460
Washington, DC 20003
www.dcsec.dcgov.org

MCI Center Phone: 202-628-3200
601 F St NW Fax: 202-661-5083
Washington, DC 20004
www.mcicenter.com

Northern Virginia Majestics Phone: 703-680-6562
3001 Old Bridge Rd Fax: 703-590-6202
Woodbridge, VA 22192
E-mail: nvmajestics@aol.com

Northern Virginia Royals Phone: 703-492-9944
PO Box 1447 Fax: 703-492-9944
Centerville, VA 20120

Rosecroft Raceway Phone: 301-567-4000
6336 Rosecroft Dr Fax: 301-567-9267
Fort Washington, MD 20744
www.rosecroft.com

Washington Capitals Phone: 202-266-2200
601 F St NW MCI Ctr Fax: 202-266-2210
Washington, DC 20004
E-mail: feedback@washingtoncaps.com
www.washingtoncaps.com

Washington DC United (soccer) Phone: 703-478-6600
13832 Redskin Dr Fax: 703-736-9451
Herndon, VA 20171
E-mail: info@dcunited.com
www.dcunited.com

Washington Mystics (basketball) Phone: 202-628-3200
601 F St NW MCI Ctr Fax: 202-661-5122
Washington, DC 20004
www.wnba.com/mystics/index.html

Washington Redskins Phone: 301-276-6050
Redskins Rd FedEx Field Fax: 301-276-6001
Landover, MD 20785
www.redskins.com

Washington Wizards Phone: 202-628-3200
601 F St NW MCI Ctr TF: 800-551-7328
Washington, DC 20004
www.nba.com/wizards

Annual Events

18th Century Grand Ball (mid-April) 703-838-4242
18th Century Masquerade Ball (October)...........703-838-4242
African-American Festival (late July) 703-838-4844
Alexandria Arts Safari (early October) 800-388-9119
Alexandria Holiday Tree Lighting Ceremony (late November).............................800-388-9119
Alexandria Red Cross Waterfront Festival (mid-June) 703-549-8300
An 1800s Christmas (late November-late December)..................703-780-4000
Annual Needlework Exhibition (March) 703-780-4000
Annual Tour of Historic Alexandria Homes (late September) 800-388-9119
Antiques in Alexandria (mid-March)...............703-549-5922
Arlington County Fair (mid-August)...............703-920-4556
Arlington Farmers Market (mid-April-mid-December)......................703-228-6400
Braddock Day (early April).......................703-549-2997
Campagna Center's Scottish Christmas Walk Weekend (early December).............................703-549-0111
Candlelight Tours & Concerts (December) 703-437-1794
Candlelight Vigil (mid-May).......................202-737-3400
Capitol Jazz Festival (early June)..................301-218-0404
Carlyle Housewarming (early August)..............703-549-2997
Chinese New Year Parade (mid-February) 202-357-2700
Christmas at Arlington (December)................703-557-0613
Christmas in Camp Open House (mid-December)..............................703-838-4848
Christmas on 'S' Street (December)...............202-387-4062
Civil War Reunion Day (mid-June) 703-838-4848
Civil War Symposium (mid-May).................703-838-4848
Crafts Fair (mid-September)......................703-780-2000
Crossroads Village Antique Car Show (late July) 810-736-7100
Crystal City Water Park (late May-late August)......703-413-0789
DC Spring Antiques Fair (early March) 301-924-5002
DC Winter Antiques Fair (early December).........301-924-5002
Dulles International Antiques Show & Sale (mid-April) 703-802-0066
Earth Day (mid-May) 703-838-4844
Fairfax Fair (early June) 703-324-3247
Fall Harvest Family Days (late October)............703-780-2000
Festival of American Folklife (late June-early July)..........................202-357-2700
First Night Alexandria (December 31) 800-388-9119
Founder's Day Water Lily Festival (late July) 202-426-6905
Friendship Fire House Festival (early August) 703-838-4399

Gadsby's Tavern Museum 18th Century Fair (late June) .703-838-4242
Garden Fair & Plant Sale (late April) .202-544-8733
General & Mrs Lee's Wedding Anniversary (June 30) .703-557-0613
George Washington Birthday Celebration Weekend (mid-February) .703-549-7662
George Washington Birthday Night Ball (February) .703-838-4242
George Washington Celebration Parade (mid-February) .703-549-7662
Goodwill Embassy Tour (early May) .202-636-4225
Harambee Carnival (early March) .301-530-3697
Hard Times Chili Cook-Off (late September) .800-388-9119
Herndon Festival (early June) .703-435-6868
Historic Alexandria Antiques Show & Sale (mid-November) .800-388-9119
Historic Alexandria Candlelight Tours (mid-December) .703-838-4242
Historic Alexandria Hauntings Family-Friendly Trick or Treat (late October) .703-838-4242
Historic Garden Tour of Alexandria (mid-late April) .804-644-7776
History Walking Tours (April-October) .703-838-4200
Holiday Concert: Bethesdoy Chamber Singers (early December) .202-785-2040
Independence Day Celebration (July 4) .703-780-2000
Independence Day Parade (July 4) .202-619-7222
International Children's Festival (mid-September) .703-642-0862
Irish Festival (early August) .703-838-4844
Italian Festival (early September) .703-838-4844
Joy To The World Holiday/Grand Illumination (early December) .703-528-3527
Juneteenth Commemoration (mid-late June) .703-838-4356
Labor Day Jazz Celebration (early September) .703-435-6868
Lee Birthday Celebrations (mid-January) .703-838-4200
Light Up Rosslyn (late November-late February) .703-522-6628
Marine Corps Marathon (mid-October) .202-789-7000
Marine Corps Sunset Parades (late May-mid-August) .202-433-4173
Martin Luther King Jr Birthday Observance (mid-January) .202-619-7222
Memorial Day Ceremonies at Arlington National Cemetery (late May) .202-685-2892
Memorial Day Jazz Festival (late May) .703-838-4844
Mount Vernon by Candlelight Weekends (late November-mid-December) .703-780-2000
Mount Vernon's Wine Tasting & Sunset Tour (mid-May) .703-799-8604
National Cherry Blossom Festival (late March-early April) .202-728-1137
National Cherry Blossom Parade (early April) .202-728-1137
National Christmas Tree Lighting/Pageant of Peace (December) .202-619-7222
Northern Virginia Christmas Market (mid-November) .757-486-0220
Rosslyn Jazz Festival (early September) .703-522-6628
Saint Patrick's Day Celebration & Parade (early March) .703-549-4535
Saint Patrick's Day Parade (mid-March) .301-879-1717
Saint Patricks Day Celebration (March 17) .703-557-0613
Scottish Heritage Festival (late September) .703-838-4844
Smithsonian Kite Festival (late March) .202-357-3030
Smithsonian's Craft Show (late April) .202-357-2700
Taste of Arlington (mid-May) .703-486-0626
Taste of DC (early October) .202-724-4093
Tavern Day (early August) .703-838-4242
Theodore Roosevelt's Birthday Celebration (late October) .703-289-2553
USA & Alexandria Birthday Celebration (early-mid-July) .703-838-4343
Veterans Day Ceremonies (November 11) .202-619-7222
Virginia Scottish Games & Festival (late July) .703-912-1943
Washington Boat Show (mid-February) .202-789-1600
Washington Flower & Garden Show (early March) .202-789-1600
Washington International Filmfest (early-mid-April) .202-724-5613
Washington International Flower & Garden Show (early March) .703-823-7960
Washington National Cathedral Flower Mart (early May) .202-537-6200
Washington Theatre Festival (mid-July-mid-August) .202-462-1073
White House Christmas Tours (late December) .202-456-7041
White House Easter Egg Roll (mid-April) .202-456-2200
White House Spring Garden Tours (mid-April) .202-456-2200
Wolf Trap Summer Season (late May-mid-September) .703-255-1868

West Palm Beach, Florida

County: **Palm Beach**

WEST PALM BEACH is located in southeastern Florida. Major cities within 100 miles include Fort Lauderdale, Fort Pierce, and Miami, Florida.

Area (Land) .... 49.3 sq mi
Area (Water) .... 3.0 sq mi
Elevation .... 21 ft
Latitude .... 26-44-51 N
Longitude .... 80-07-34 W
Time Zone .... EST
Area Code 561

Climate

West Palm Beach has a subtropical climate that is greatly influenced by its proximity to the Atlantic Ocean. Sea breezes moderate temperatures during the winter and summer. Winters are mild, with average high temperatures in the mid-70s and lows in the mid- to upper 50s. Summer days are very warm, with average highs in the upper 80s, while evenings typically cool down only into the low to mid-70s. May through October is the rainy season in West Palm Beach, with September being the wettest month. December is the driest month of the year in West Palm Beach.

Average Temperatures & Precipitation

Temperatures

	Jan	Feb	Mar	Apr	May	Jun	Jul	Aug	Sep	Oct	Nov	Dec
High	75	76	79	82	86	88	90	90	89	85	80	76
Low	56	57	61	65	70	73	75	75	75	71	65	59

Precipitation

	Jan	Feb	Mar	Apr	May	Jun	Jul	Aug	Sep	Oct	Nov	Dec
Inches	2.8	2.7	3.7	2.9	6.1	8.1	6.1	6.0	8.5	6.6	4.7	2.5

History

West Palm Beach was founded in 1893 when Henry Flagler brought his East Coast Railway to the area. Flagler was also instrumental in developing the island of Palm Beach, bordered by the Atlantic Ocean on the east and Lake Worth on the west, as an exclusive upscale resort town. West Palm Beach, located across Lake Worth, was developed as the commercial counterpart to Palm Beach, and many of the laborers and craftsman who worked on Flagler's Palm Beach mansions and hotels lived in West Palm Beach. In 1894, the town of West Palm Beach was incorporated as a city, and 14 years later it was chosen as the county seat of the newly formed Palm Beach County. In 1910, West Palm Beach was home to 1,700 people.

West Palm Beach grew rapidly during the Florida land boom of the early 1920s, quadrupling its population to over 30,000 over a seven year period. The opening of the West Palm Beach Canal and the arrival of the Seaboard Air Line Railway during the mid-20s also aided the city's economy by providing distribution routes for the area's plentiful sugar, citrus, and vegetable crops. However, the latter part of what began as a prosperous decade for West Palm Beach brought difficult times—two devastating hurricanes struck the area within a two-year period and land speculators abandoned the area, causing property values to drop sharply.

The years following World War II brought new development to West Palm Beach. Veterans began moving to Florida, and the West Palm Beach metropolitan area was the fourth fastest growing in the United States during the 1950s. Palm Beach County is a leading agricultural and commercial center and with over 4 million tourists visiting each year, the county is a leading tourist destination as well. West Palm Beach today is home to more than 76,000 people, and the population of Palm Beach County is expected to exceed one million by the year 2005.

Population

1990 Census 67,643
1998 Estimate 76,308
% Change 12.6
2005 Projection 1,168,000*

Racial/Ethnic Breakdown

White 63.4%
Black 32.6%
Other 4.0%
Hispanic Origin (may be of any race) 14.2%

Age Breakdown

Under 5 years 6.9%
5 to 17 .... 14.0%
18 to 20 .... 4.1%
21 to 24 .... 5.9%
25 to 34 .... 19.0%
35 to 44 .... 13.9%
45 to 54 .... 9.2%
55 to 64 .... 8.8%
65 to 74 .... 9.2%
75+ years 9.0%
Median Age 35.1

Gender Breakdown

Male 47.8%
Female 52.2%

** Information given is for Palm Beach County.*

Government

Type of Government: Mayor-City Commission

West Palm Beach City Administrator
PO Box 3366
West Palm Beach, FL 33402
Phone: 561-659-8024
Fax: 561-659-8066

West Palm Beach City Attorney
PO Box 3366
West Palm Beach, FL 33402
Phone: 561-659-8017
Fax: 561-659-8053

West Palm Beach City Clerk
PO Box 3366
West Palm Beach, FL 33402
Phone: 561-659-8020
Fax: 561-653-2657

West Palm Beach City Commission
PO Box 3366
West Palm Beach, FL 33402
Phone: 561-659-8099
Fax: 561-659-8066

West Palm Beach City Hall
200 2nd St
West Palm Beach, FL 33401
Phone: 561-659-8000
Fax: 561-659-8039

West Palm Beach Engineering Services Div
1000 45th St Suite 15
West Palm Beach, FL 33407
Phone: 561-659-8040
Fax: 561-659-8039

West Palm Beach Finance Dept
PO Box 3366
West Palm Beach, FL 33402
Phone: 561-659-8050
Fax: 561-659-8073

West Palm Beach Fire Dept
500 N Dixie Hwy
West Palm Beach, FL 33401
Phone: 561-835-2900
Fax: 561-659-8089

West Palm Beach Housing & Community Development Dept
PO Box 3366
West Palm Beach, FL 33402
Phone: 561-835-7300
Fax: 561-835-7348

West Palm Beach Human Resources Dept
1000 45th St Suite 12
West Palm Beach, FL 33407
Phone: 561-659-8028
Fax: 561-659-8072

West Palm Beach Library
100 Clematis St
West Palm Beach, FL 33401
Phone: 561-659-8010
Fax: 561-835-7020

West Palm Beach Mayor
PO Box 3366
West Palm Beach, FL 33402
Phone: 561-659-8025
Fax: 561-659-8066

West Palm Beach Planning & Zoning Dept
200 2nd St
West Palm Beach, FL 33402
Phone: 561-659-8031
Fax: 561-653-2605

West Palm Beach Police Dept
600 Banyan Blvd
West Palm Beach, FL 33401
Phone: 561-653-3400
Fax: 561-653-3529

West Palm Beach Public Works Dept
PO Box 3366
West Palm Beach, FL 33402
Phone: 561-659-8048

West Palm Beach Recreation Dept
1100 Southern Blvd
West Palm Beach, FL 33405
Phone: 561-835-7025
Fax: 561-835-7033

West Palm Beach Utilities Dept
1000 45th St Suite 15
West Palm Beach, FL 33407
Phone: 561-659-8085
Fax: 561-659-8039

Important Phone Numbers

AAA....800-926-4222
Artsline....800-882-2787
Driver's License Information....561-681-6333
Emergency....911
Florida Revenue Dept Taxpayers Service....561-640-2800
HotelDocs....800-468-3537
Medical Referral....800-466-3726
Palm Beach County Tax Collector....561-355-2622
Poison Control Center....800-282-3171
Realtors Assn of the Palm Beaches....561-688-9294
Time/Temp....561-832-3801
Vehicle Registration Information....561-355-2622
Voter Registration Information....561-355-2650
West Palm Beach Tax Collector....561-355-2264

Information Sources

Better Business Bureau Serving the Palm Beach Area
580 Village Blvd Suite 340
West Palm Beach, FL 33409
www.westpalm.bbb.org
Phone: 561-686-2200
Fax: 561-686-2775

Chamber of Commerce of the Palm Beaches
401 N Flagler Dr
West Palm Beach, FL 33401
palmbeaches.com
Phone: 561-833-3711
Fax: 561-833-5582

Palm Beach County
PO Box 1989
West Palm Beach, FL 33401
www.co.palm-beach.fl.us
Phone: 561-355-2030
Fax: 561-355-3990

Palm Beach County Convention & Visitors Bureau
1555 Palm Beach Lakes Blvd Suite 204
West Palm Beach, FL 33401
www.palmbeachfl.com
Phone: 561-471-3995
Fax: 561-471-3990

Online Resources

About.com Guide to West Palm Beach
westpalmbeach.about.com/local/southeastus/westpalmbeach

Anthill City Guide West Palm Beach
www.anthill.com/city.asp?city=westpalmbeach

Area Guide West Palm Beach
westpalmbeach.areaguides.net

Boca Raton
bocaraton.com

City Knowledge West Palm Beach
www.cityknowledge.com/fl_west_palm_beach.htm

Come to the Sun Guide to South Florida
www.cometothesun.com

DigitalCity South Florida
home.digitalcity.com/southflorida

DiningGuide Palm Beaches
diningguide.net/palm_beaches

HotelGuide Palm Beaches
hotelguide.net/palm_beaches

Insiders' Guide to Boca Raton & the Palm Beaches
www.insiders.com/boca

InSouthFlorida.com
www.insouthflorida.com

Lodging.com Palm Beaches Florida
www.lodging.com/auto/guides/palm_beaches-area-fl.html

MetroGuide Palm Beaches
metroguide.net/palm_beaches

Palm Beach Interactive
www.gopbi.com

West Palm Beach Florida
westpalmbeach.com

West Palm Beach Gay & Lesbian Guide
www.southfloridafun.com/westpalmbeach/index.shtml

Area Communities

Palm Beach County communities with populations greater than 10,000 include:

Belle Glade
110 SW Ave 'E'
Belle Glade, FL 33430
Phone: 561-996-0100
Fax: 561-992-2215

Boca Raton
201 W Palmetto Park Rd
Boca Raton, FL 33432
Phone: 561-393-7700
Fax: 561-393-7704

Boynton Beach
100 E Boynton Beach Blvd
Boynton Beach, FL 33425
Phone: 561-375-6000
Fax: 561-375-6090

Delray Beach
100 NW 1st Ave
Delray Beach, FL 33444
Phone: 561-243-7000
Fax: 561-243-3774

Greenacres
5985 10th Ave N
Greenacres, FL 33463
Phone: 561-642-2000
Fax: 561-642-2037

Jupiter
210 Military Trail
Jupiter, FL 33458
Phone: 561-746-5134
Fax: 561-575-9730

Lake Worth
7 N Dixie Hwy
Lake Worth, FL 33460
Phone: 561-586-1600
Fax: 561-586-1798

North Palm Beach
501 US Hwy 1
North Palm Beach, FL 33408
Phone: 561-841-3355
Fax: 561-881-7469

Palm Beach Gardens
10500 N Military Trail
Palm Beach Gardens, FL 33410
Phone: 561-799-4100
Fax: 561-799-4111

Riviera Beach
600 W Blue Heron Blvd
Riviera Beach, FL 33404
Phone: 561-845-4000
Fax: 561-863-3236

Royal Palm Beach
1050 Royal Palm Beach Blvd
Royal Palm Beach, FL 33411
Phone: 561-790-5100
Fax: 561-790-5174

Wellington
14000 Greenbriar Blvd
Wellington, FL 33414
Phone: 561-791-4000
Fax: 561-791-4045

Economy

The West Palm Beach economy ranges from agriculture to aerospace manufacturing. Major corporations that have their corporate headquarters or divisions in Palm Beach County include W.R. Grace, Pratt & Whitney, IBM, Motorola, and Scott Paper. Agriculture is Palm Beach County's leading industry—nearly 11 percent of the nation's sugar is produced in the western part of the county. Palm Beach is the largest agricultural county in Florida and the fifth largest in the entire country. Hosting more than four million visitors annually, tourism is vital to Palm Beach County's economy, and more than 52,000 area residents are employed in tourism-related positions.

Unemployment Rate 4.9%**
Per Capita Income.......................... $40,044**
Median Family Income...................... $55,600*

** Information given is for Palm Beach County.*
*** Information given is for the West Palm Beach-Boca Raton-Delray Beach Metropolitan Statistical Area (MSA), which includes the City of Boca Raton, the City of Delray Beach, the City of West Palm Beach, and Palm Beach County.*

Principal Industries & Number of Wage Earners

Palm Beach County - 1998

Industry	Wage Earners
Agricultural Services, Forestry, & Fishing	18,635
Construction	26,156
Finance, Insurance, & Real Estate	31,753
Manufacturing	30,641
Mining	14
Retail Trade	91,388
Services	156,750
Transportation, Communications, & Public Utilities	15,692
Wholesale Trade	21,821

Major Employers

Bethesda Memorial Hospital
2815 S Seacrest Blvd
Boynton Beach, FL 33435
www.bethesdaweb.com
Phone: 561-737-7733
Fax: 561-735-7057

Boca Raton Community Hospital
800 Meadows Rd
Boca Raton, FL 33486
www.brch.com
Phone: 561-395-7100
Fax: 561-750-4715

Boca Raton Resort & Club
501 E Camino Real
Boca Raton, FL 33431
E-mail: reservations@bocaresort.com
www.bocaresort.com
Phone: 561-447-3000
Fax: 561-447-3183
TF: 800-327-0101

Florida Power & Light Co
6001 Village Blvd
West Palm Beach, FL 33407
www.fpl.com
Phone: 561-697-8000
Fax: 561-640-2197

IBM Corp
1555 Palm Beach Lakes Blvd
West Palm Beach, FL 33401
www-1.ibm.com/employment
Phone: 561-684-6000

Motorola Inc MIMS
3301 Quantum Blvd
Boynton Beach, FL 33426
motorolacareers.com
Phone: 561-739-2000
Fax: 561-739-8255

Office Depot Inc
2200 Old Germantown Rd
Delray Beach, FL 33445
www.officedepot.com
Phone: 561-278-4800
Fax: 561-265-4406
TF: 800-937-3600

Palm Beach County
PO Box 1989
West Palm Beach, FL 33401
www.co.palm-beach.fl.us
Phone: 561-355-2030
Fax: 561-355-3990

Palm Beach County School District
3364 Forest Hill Blvd
West Palm Beach, FL 33406
www.palmbeach.k12.fl.us
Phone: 561-434-8000
Fax: 561-434-8899

Palm Beach Newspapers Inc
PO Box 24700
West Palm Beach, FL 33416
www.gopbi.com
Phone: 561-820-4100
Fax: 561-820-4407

Pratt & Whitney Government Engines & Space Propulsion Div
PO Box 109600
West Palm Beach, FL 33410
www.pratt-whitney.com/engines
Phone: 561-796-2000
Fax: 561-796-5876
TF: 800-327-3246

Saint Mary's Medical Center
901 45th St
West Palm Beach, FL 33407
www.ihswpb.com/MCMaryMain.html
Phone: 561-844-6300
Fax: 561-881-2907

Quality of Living Indicators

Total Crime Index....................................12,803
(rates per 100,000 inhabitants)

Violent Crime
Murder/manslaughter........................... 20
Forcible rape 65
Robbery...................................... 721
Aggravated assault............................ 764

Property Crime
Burglary 2,094
Larceny theft 7,197
Motor vehicle theft..........................1,942

Cost of Living Index...................................103.8
(national average = 100)

Median Home Price................................$131,000

Education

Public Schools

Palm Beach County School District
3364 Forest Hill Blvd
West Palm Beach, FL 33406
www.palmbeach.k12.fl.us
Phone: 561-434-8000
Fax: 561-434-8899

Number of Schools
Elementary.................................. 83
Middle 24
High.. 18

Student/Teacher Ratio
All Grades 17.2:1

Private Schools

Number of Schools (all grades).................... 35+

Colleges & Universities

Barry University
701 N Congress Ave
Boynton Beach, FL 33426
Phone: 561-364-8220
Fax: 561-364-8113

Florida Atlantic University
777 Glades Rd
Boca Raton, FL 33431
E-mail: barton@fau.edu
www.fau.edu
Phone: 561-297-3000
Fax: 561-297-2758
TF: 800-299-4328

Institute of Career Education
1750 45th St
West Palm Beach, FL 33407
www.vocedu.com
Phone: 561-881-0220
Fax: 561-881-3831

Lynn University
3601 N Military Trail
Boca Raton, FL 33431
E-mail: admission@lynn.edu
www.lynn.edu
Phone: 561-994-0770
Fax: 561-241-3552
TF: 800-544-8035

New England Institute of Technology
1126 53rd Ct
West Palm Beach, FL 33407
Phone: 561-842-8324
Fax: 561-842-9503
TF: 800-826-9986

Northwood University Florida Campus
2600 N Military Trail
West Palm Beach, FL 33409
E-mail: info@northwood.edu
www.northwood.edu
Phone: 561-478-5510
Fax: 561-640-3328
TF: 800-458-8325

Palm Beach Atlantic College
PO Box 24708
West Palm Beach, FL 33416
E-mail: admit@pbac.edu
www.pbac.edu
Phone: 561-803-2000
Fax: 561-803-2155
TF: 888-468-6722

Palm Beach Community College Central Campus
4200 Congress Ave
Lake Worth, FL 33461
E-mail: dill s@popmail.firn.edu
www.pbcc.cc.fl.us
Phone: 561-439-8000
Fax: 561-439-8255

South College
1760 N Congress Ave
West Palm Beach, FL 33409
www.southcollege.edu
Phone: 561-697-9200
Fax: 561-697-9944

Hospitals

Bethesda Memorial Hospital
2815 S Seacrest Blvd
Boynton Beach, FL 33435
www.bethesdaweb.com
Phone: 561-737-7733
Fax: 561-735-7057

Boca Raton Community Hospital
800 Meadows Rd
Boca Raton, FL 33486
www.brch.com
Phone: 561-395-7100
Fax: 561-750-4715

Delray Medical Center
5352 Linton Blvd
Delray Beach, FL 33484
www.tenethealth.com/Delray
Phone: 561-498-4440
Fax: 561-495-3103

Good Samaritan Medical Center
1309 N Flagler Dr
West Palm Beach, FL 33401
www.ihswpb.com/MCGoodSamMain.html
Phone: 561-655-5511
Fax: 561-650-6127

JFK Medical Center
5301 Congress Ave
Atlantis, FL 33462
Phone: 561-965-7300
Fax: 561-642-3623

Jupiter Medical Center
1210 S Old Dixie Hwy
Jupiter, FL 33458
www.jupitermed.com
Phone: 561-747-2234
Fax: 561-744-4493

Palm Beach Gardens Medical Center
3360 Burns Rd
Palm Beach Gardens, FL 33410
www.tenethealth.com/PalmBeachGardens
Phone: 561-622-1411
Fax: 561-694-7160

Saint Mary's Medical Center
901 45th St
West Palm Beach, FL 33407
www.ihswpb.com/MCMaryMain.html
Phone: 561-844-6300
Fax: 561-881-2907

Veterans Affairs Medical Center
7305 N Military Trail
West Palm Beach, FL 33410
Phone: 561-882-8262
Fax: 561-882-6707
TF: 800-972-8262

West Boca Medical Center
21644 State Rd 7
Boca Raton, FL 33428
www.tenethealth.com/WestBoca
Phone: 561-488-8000
Fax: 561-883-7020

Transportation

Airport(s)

Palm Beach International Airport (PBI)
3 miles W of downtown (approx 10 minutes) 561-471-7412

Mass Transit

Palm Tran Bus Service
$1 Base fare 561-233-4287
Tri-Rail
fare varies with destination 800-874-7245

Rail/Bus

Amtrak
201 S Tamarind Ave
West Palm Beach, FL 33401
Phone: 561-832-6169
TF: 800-872-7245

Greyhound Bus Station
205 S Tamarind Ave
West Palm Beach, FL 33401
Phone: 561-833-8534
TF: 800-231-2222

Utilities

Electricity
Florida Power & Light Co 561-697-8000
www.fpl.com

Gas
Florida Public Utilities 561-278-2636
www.fpuc.com

Water
Palm Beach County Water Utilities 561-740-4600

Garbage Collection/Recycling
Palm Beach County Solid Waste Authority 561-697-2700

Telecommunications

Telephone
BellSouth Telecommunications Inc 800-753-0710
www.bellsouth.com

Cable Television
Adelphia Cable 561-627-3600
Comcast Cable 561-478-5866

Internet Service Providers (ISPs)
Atlantic Internet 561-362-6777
www.aibusiness.net
US Internet Technologies Inc 561-964-9841
www.us-it.net
Verio South Florida 561-615-0001
home.verio.net/local/frontpage.cfm?AirportCode=PBI

Banks

Colonial Bank
2000 Palm Beach Lakes Blvd
West Palm Beach, FL 33409
Phone: 561-683-1600
Fax: 561-683-2597

Community Savings FA
971 Village Blvd
West Palm Beach, FL 33409
Phone: 561-478-9100
Fax: 561-478-9488
TF: 800-992-1273

Fidelity Federal Bank & Trust
218 Datura St
West Palm Beach, FL 33401
www.fidfed.com
Phone: 561-659-9900
Fax: 561-659-9968

First Union National Bank
303 Banyan Blvd
West Palm Beach, FL 33401
Phone: 561-838-5364
Fax: 561-838-4918

Mackinac Savings Bank FSB
2901-A N Military Trail
West Palm Beach, FL 33409
Phone: 561-686-2352
Fax: 561-638-2616

NationsBank NA
2881 N Military Trail
West Palm Beach, FL 33409
Phone: 561-683-6000
Fax: 561-683-8225

Republic Security Bank Phone: 561-655-8511
450 S Australian Ave Fax: 561-650-2431
West Palm Beach, FL 33401
www.republicsecuritybank.com

Sterling Bank FSB Phone: 561-968-1000
1661 Congress Ave Fax: 561-968-1220
West Palm Beach, FL 33406

SunTrust Bank South Florida NA Phone: 561-655-4481
422 Belvedere Rd Fax: 561-832-3359
West Palm Beach, FL 33405

Union Planters Bank Phone: 877-848-2265
6080 Okeechobee Blvd Fax: 561-478-4590
West Palm Beach, FL 33417

Washington Mutual Bank Phone: 561-478-9101
2959 N Military Trail Crosstown Plaza Fax: 561-478-4162
West Palm Beach, FL 33409 TF: 800-782-8875

Shopping

Atlantic Avenue Phone: 561-278-0424
downtown-betw Swinton Ave & A1A Fax: 561-278-0555
Delray Beach, FL 33483

Boynton Beach Mall Phone: 561-736-7900
801 N Congress Ave Fax: 561-736-7907
Boynton Beach, FL 33426

Dr Flea's Flea Market Phone: 561-965-1500
1200 S Congress Ave Fax: 561-965-0433
West Palm Beach, FL 33406

Gardens of the Palm Beaches Phone: 561-622-2115
3101 PGA Blvd Fax: 561-694-9380
Palm Beach Gardens, FL 33410

Mizner Park Phone: 561-362-0606
407 Plaza Real Fax: 561-750-8825
Boca Raton, FL 33432

Palm Beach Mall Phone: 561-683-9186
1801 Palm Beach Lakes Blvd Fax: 561-683-9266
West Palm Beach, FL 33401

Town Center at Boca Raton Phone: 561-368-6000
6000 Glades Rd Fax: 561-338-0891
Boca Raton, FL 33431

Uptown Downtown Flea Market & Outlet Mall Phone: 561-684-5700
5700 Okeechobee Blvd Fax: 561-697-3734
West Palm Beach, FL 33417

Media

Newspapers and Magazines

Boca Thursday Phone: 954-698-6397
601 Fairway Dr Fax: 954-429-1207
Deerfield Beach, FL 33441

Boynton Beach Times Phone: 954-698-6397
PO Box 1189 Fax: 954-429-1207
Deerfield Beach, FL 33441

Delray Beach Times Phone: 954-698-6397
PO Box 1189 Fax: 954-429-1207
Deerfield Beach, FL 33441

Lake Worth Herald & Coastal Observer Phone: 561-585-9387
PO Box 191 Fax: 561-585-5434
Lake Worth, FL 33460

Palm Beach Daily Business Review Phone: 561-820-2060
330 Clematis St Suite 114 Fax: 561-820-2077
West Palm Beach, FL 33401

Palm Beach Illustrated Phone: 561-659-0210
1000 N Dixie Hwy Suite C Fax: 561-659-1736
West Palm Beach, FL 33401

Palm Beach Post* Phone: 561-820-4100
PO Box 24700 Fax: 561-820-4407
West Palm Beach, FL 33416
E-mail: letters@pbpost.com
www.pbpost.com

South Florida Business Journal Phone: 954-359-2100
4000 Hollywood Blvd Suite 695 South Fax: 954-359-2135
Hollywood, FL 33021
www.amcity.com/southflorida

Town Crier Phone: 561-793-7606
12788 W Forest Hill Blvd Suite 1003 Fax: 561-793-6090
Wellington, FL 33414
E-mail: thecrier@magg.net
www.thecrier.com

Wellington/Royal Palm Beach Forum Phone: 561-791-7790
11320 Fortune Cir Suite G-32 Fax: 561-791-7593
Wellington, FL 33414

West Boca Times Phone: 954-698-6397
601 Fairway Dr Fax: 954-429-1207
Deerfield Beach, FL 33441
E-mail: gukley@gate.net

**Indicates major daily newspapers*

Television

WFGC-TV Ch 61 (Ind) Phone: 561-642-3361
2406 S Congress Ave Suite 1900 Fax: 561-967-5961
West Palm Beach, FL 33406

WFLX-TV Ch 29 (Fox) Phone: 561-845-2929
4119 W Blue Heron Blvd Fax: 561-863-1238
West Palm Beach, FL 33404

WPEC-TV Ch 12 (CBS) Phone: 561-844-1212
1100 Fairfield Dr Fax: 561-881-0731
West Palm Beach, FL 33407 TF: 800-930-9732
www.gopbi.com/partners/news12

WPTV-TV Ch 5 (NBC) Phone: 561-655-5455
622 N Flagler Dr Fax: 561-653-5719
West Palm Beach, FL 33401
E-mail: wptv@magg.net
www.wptv.com

WPXP-TV Ch 67 (PAX) Phone: 561-686-6767
500 Australian Ave S Suite 510 Fax: 561-682-3475
West Palm Beach, FL 33401 TF: 800-646-7296
www.pax.net/WPXP

WTVX-TV Ch 34 (UPN)
4411 Beacon Cir Majestic Plaza Suite 5
West Palm Beach, FL 33407
Phone: 561-841-3434
Fax: 561-848-9150

Radio

WAYF-FM 88.1 MHz (AC)
800 Northpointe Pkwy Suite 881
West Palm Beach, FL 33407
www.wayfm.com
Phone: 561-881-1929
Fax: 561-840-1929

WBZT-AM 1290 kHz (N/T)
3071 Continental Dr
West Palm Beach, FL 33407
www.1290wbzt.com
Phone: 561-616-6600
Fax: 561-881-8553

WDBF-AM 1420 kHz (Nost)
2710 W Atlantic Ave
Delray Beach, FL 33445
Phone: 561-278-1420
Fax: 561-278-1898

WEAT-FM 104.3 MHz (AC)
701 Northpoint Pkwy Suite 500
West Palm Beach, FL 33407
E-mail: veras@veras.com
www.sunny1043.com
Phone: 561-686-9505
Fax: 561-689-4043

WIRK-FM 107.9 MHz (Ctry)
701 Northpoint Pkwy Suite 500
West Palm Beach, FL 33407
E-mail: wirk@quinncom.net
www.wirk.com
Phone: 561-686-9505
Fax: 561-686-0157

WJBW-FM 99.5 MHz (Nost)
2710 W Atlantic Ave
Delray Beach, FL 33445
www.wjbw.com
Phone: 561-278-1420
Fax: 561-278-1898

WJNA-AM 1230 kHz (Nost)
2406 S Congress Ave
West Palm Beach, FL 33409
Phone: 561-432-5100
Fax: 561-432-5111

WJNO-AM 1040 kHz (N/T)
3071 Continental Dr
West Palm Beach, FL 33407
Phone: 561-616-6600
Fax: 561-616-6677

WKGR-FM 98.7 MHz (CR)
3071 Continental Dr
West Palm Beach, FL 33407
www.gater.com
Phone: 561-616-6600
Fax: 561-881-8880

WLDI-FM 95.5 MHz (CHR)
3071 Continental Dr
West Palm Beach, FL 33407
E-mail: wild955@aol.com
www.wild955.com
Phone: 561-616-6600
Fax: 561-616-6677

WLVJ-AM 640 kHz (Rel)
1601 Belvedere Rd Suite 204E
West Palm Beach, FL 33406
Phone: 561-688-9585
Fax: 561-688-9601

WMBX-FM 102.3 MHz (AC)
901 Northpoint Pkwy Suite 400
West Palm Beach, FL 33407
www.mix1023.com
Phone: 561-616-4600
Fax: 561-684-6311

WOLL-FM 105.5 MHz (Oldies)
3071 Continental Dr
West Palm Beach, FL 33407
Phone: 561-616-6600
Fax: 561-616-6677

WPBZ-FM 103.1 MHz (Alt)
901 Northpoint Pkwy Suite 501
West Palm Beach, FL 33407
E-mail: buzz103@quinncom.net
www.buzz103.com
Phone: 561-616-4600
Fax: 561-688-0209

WRLX-FM 92.1 MHz (AC)
2406 S Congress Ave
West Palm Beach, FL 33406
Phone: 561-432-5100
Fax: 561-432-5111

WRMF-FM 97.9 MHz (AC)
2406 S Congress Ave
West Palm Beach, FL 33406
www.gopbi.com/partners/wrmf
Phone: 561-432-5100
Fax: 561-432-5111

WSWN-AM 900 kHz (Urban)
2001 SR 715
Belle Glade, FL 33430
Phone: 561-996-2063
Fax: 561-996-1852

WWLV-FM 94.3 MHz (Nost)
3071 Continental Dr
West Palm Beach, FL 33407
Phone: 561-616-6600
Fax: 561-881-8880

WXEL-TV Ch 42 (PBS)
PO Box 6607
West Palm Beach, FL 33405
E-mail: comments@wxel.org
www.wxel.org
Phone: 561-737-8000
Fax: 561-369-3067

WZZR-FM 92.7 MHz (N/T)
PO Box 0093
Port Saint Lucie, FL 34985
E-mail: lovedocs@wzzr.com
www.wzzr.com
Phone: 561-335-9300
Fax: 561-335-3291

Attractions

Located in the heart of downtown West Palm Beach and marking the entrance to the city is the newly constructed Raymond F. Kravis Center for the Performing Arts, which offers both concerts and Broadway productions. A number of regional performing groups, including the Palm Beach Opera, Palm Beach Pops, and the Florida Philharmonic Orchestra, make their home at the Kravis Center. West Palm Beach is also home to the Norton Gallery of Art; the Palm Beach Zoo at Dreher Park a 22-acre tropical zoological garden with 128 species and more than 500 animals; the Palm Beach Kennel Club, a greyhound track established in 1932; and the South Florida Science Museum.

Armory Art Center
1703 Lake Ave
West Palm Beach, FL 33401
www.armoryart.org
Phone: 561-832-1776
Fax: 561-832-0191

Atlantic Avenue
downtown-betw Swinton Ave & A1A
Delray Beach, FL 33483
Phone: 561-278-0424
Fax: 561-278-0555

Ballet Florida
500 Fern St
West Palm Beach, FL 33401
E-mail: georgepb@ix.netcom.com
www.balletflorida.com
Phone: 561-659-1212
Fax: 561-659-2222
TF: 800-540-0172

Boca Pops
100 NE 1st Ave
Boca Raton, FL 33432
www.bocapops.org
Phone: 561-393-7677
Fax: 561-393-7364
TF: 888-876-7677

Boca Raton Museum of Art
801 W Palmetto Park Rd
Boca Raton, FL 33486
E-mail: bocart@gate.net
www.bocamuseum.org
Phone: 561-392-2500
Fax: 561-391-6410

Caldwell Theatre Co
7873 N Federal Hwy
Boca Raton, FL 33487
www.caldwelltheatre.com
Phone: 561-241-7380
Fax: 561-997-6917

Callery-Judge Grove
4001 Seminole-Pratt Whitney Rd
Loxahatchee, FL 33470
Phone: 561-793-1676
Fax: 561-790-5466
TF: 800-967-2643

Cason Cottage Museum
5 NE 1st St
Delray Beach, FL 33444
www.delraybeachhistoricalsociety.org/casoncottage.html
Phone: 561-243-0223
Fax: 561-265-3764

Children's Museum
498 Crawford Blvd
Boca Raton, FL 33432
Phone: 561-368-6875
Fax: 561-395-7764

Dickinson Jonathan State Park
16450 SE Federal Hwy
Hobe Sound, FL 33455
Phone: 561-546-2771
Fax: 561-744-7604

Florida History Center & Museum
805 N US 1 Burt Reynolds Park
Jupiter, FL 33477
Phone: 561-747-6639
Fax: 561-575-3292

Florida Philharmonic Orchestra
701 Okeechobee Blvd Raymond Kravis Center for the Performing Arts
West Palm Beach, FL 33401
Phone: 561-655-7228
Fax: 561-655-7287
TF: 800-226-1812

Gaines Park
1501 N Australian Ave
West Palm Beach, FL 33401
Phone: 561-835-7090

Gumbo Limbo Nature Center
1801 N Ocean Blvd
Boca Raton, FL 33432
E-mail: gumbolimb@aol.com
www.fau.edu/gumbo/gumbo.htm
Phone: 561-338-1473
Fax: 561-338-1483

Henry Morrison Flagler Museum
1 Whitehall Way
Palm Beach, FL 33480
E-mail: flagler@flagler.org
www.flagler.org
Phone: 561-655-2833
Fax: 561-655-2826

Hibel Museum of Art
701 Lake Ave
Lake Worth, FL 33460
www.hibel.com
Phone: 561-833-6870

International Museum of Cartoon Art
201 Plaza Real Mizner Pk
Boca Raton, FL 33432
E-mail: correspondence@cartoon.org
www.cartoon.org
Phone: 561-391-2200
Fax: 561-391-2721

Knollwood Groves & Hallapatee Indian Village
8053 Lawrence Rd
Boynton Beach, FL 33436
www.knollwoodgroves.com
Phone: 561-734-4800
Fax: 561-737-6700
TF: 800-222-9696

Kravis Raymond F Center for the Performing Arts
701 Okeechobee Blvd
West Palm Beach, FL 33401
E-mail: kravis@kravis.org
www.kravis.org
Phone: 561-832-7469
Fax: 561-835-0738
TF: 800-572-8471

Lawrence E Will Museum
530 S Main St
Belle Glade, FL 33430
Phone: 561-996-3453
Fax: 561-996-2304

Lion Country Safari
2003 Lion Country Safari Rd
Loxahatchee, FL 33470
www.lioncountrysafari.com
Phone: 561-793-1084
Fax: 561-793-9603

Loxahatchee National Wildlife Refuge
10216 Lee Rd
Boynton Beach, FL 33437
Phone: 561-734-8303
Fax: 561-369-7190

Marine Life Center
14200 US Hwy 1 Loggerhead Pk
Juno Beach, FL 33408
www.marinelife.org
Phone: 561-627-8280
Fax: 561-627-8305

Morikami Museum & Japanese Gardens
4000 Morikami Pk Rd
Delray Beach, FL 33446
E-mail: morikami@co.palm-beach.fl.us
www.morikami.org
Phone: 561-495-0233
Fax: 561-499-2557

Mounts Botanical Gardens
531 N Military Trail
West Palm Beach, FL 33415
E-mail: jeterjm@gate.net
www.mounts.org
Phone: 561-233-1700
Fax: 561-233-1782

Northwood University Art Gallery
2600 N Military Trail
West Palm Beach, FL 33409
Phone: 561-478-5555
Fax: 561-640-3328

Norton Ann Sculpture Gardens
253 Barcelona Rd
West Palm Beach, FL 33401
Phone: 561-832-5328
Fax: 561-835-9305

Norton Museum of Art
1451 S Olive Ave
West Palm Beach, FL 33401
E-mail: museum@norton.org
www.norton.org/
Phone: 561-832-5194
Fax: 561-659-4689

Okeeheelee Park
7715 Forest Hill Blvd
West Palm Beach, FL 33413
Phone: 561-964-4420
Fax: 561-233-1406

Old School Square Cultural Arts Center
51 N Swinton Ave
Delray Beach, FL 33444
www.oldschool.org
Phone: 561-243-7922
Fax: 561-243-7018

Palm Beach Opera
415 S Olive Ave
West Palm Beach, FL 33401
E-mail: pbopera@pbopera.org
www.pbopera.org
Phone: 561-833-7888
Fax: 561-833-8294

Palm Beach Photographic Centre
55 NE 2nd Ave
Delray Beach, FL 33444
E-mail: pbphoto@workshop.org
www.workshop.org
Phone: 561-276-9797
Fax: 561-276-1932

Palm Beach Pops
701 Okeechobee Blvd Raymond Kravis Center for the Performing Arts
West Palm Beach, FL 33401
Phone: 561-832-7469
Fax: 561-832-9686
TF: 800-448-2472

Palm Beach Zoo at Dreher Park
1301 Summit Blvd
West Palm Beach, FL 33405
E-mail: pbzoo@palmbeachzoo.org
www.palmbeachzoo.org
Phone: 561-533-0887
Fax: 561-585-6085

Pine Jog Environmental Education Center
6301 Summit Blvd
West Palm Beach, FL 33415
E-mail: pinejog@aol.com
Phone: 561-686-6600
Fax: 561-687-4968

Rapids Water Park
6566 N Military Trail
West Palm Beach, FL 33407
www.rapidswaterpark.com
Phone: 561-848-6272
Fax: 561-848-2822

Royal Poinciana Playhouse
70 Royal Poinciana Plaza
Palm Beach, FL 33480
Phone: 561-659-3310
Fax: 561-659-7141

Society of the Four Arts
2 Four Arts Plaza
Palm Beach, FL 33480
Phone: 561-655-7226
Fax: 561-655-7233

South Florida Science Museum
4801 Dreher Trail N
West Palm Beach, FL 33405
www.sfsm.org
Phone: 561-832-1988
Fax: 561-833-0551

Spanish River Park
3001 N Ocean Blvd
Boca Raton, FL 33431
Phone: 561-393-7815

Sports Immortals Museum
6830 N Federal Hwy
Boca Raton, FL 33487
www.sportsimmortals.com
Phone: 561-997-2575
Fax: 561-997-6949

Sports Teams & Facilities

Florida Bobcats (football)
1 Panther Pkwy National Car Rental Ctr
Sunrise, FL 33323
www.floridabobcats.com
Phone: 954-577-9009
Fax: 954-577-9008

Jupiter Hammerheads (baseball)
Roger Dean Stadium 4751 Main St
Jupiter, FL 33458
Phone: 561-775-1818
Fax: 561-691-6886

Moroso Motor Sports Park
17047 Beeline Hwy
Palm Beach Gardens, FL 33410
Phone: 561-622-1400
Fax: 561-626-2053

Palm Beach Kennel Club
1111 N Congress Ave
West Palm Beach, FL 33409
www.pbkennelclub.com
Phone: 561-683-2222
Fax: 561-683-4361

Palm Beach Polo
11199 Polo Club Rd
West Palm Beach, FL 33414
Phone: 561-793-1113
Fax: 561-798-7345

Palm Beach Polo & Country Club
11199 Polo Club Rd
Wellington, FL 33414
E-mail: info@pbpolo.com
www.pbpolo.com
Phone: 561-798-7000
Fax: 561-798-7330

Royal Palm Polo Sports Club
18000 Jog Rd
Boca Raton, FL 33496
Phone: 561-734-7656
Fax: 561-994-2553

Annual Events

$25,000 Arthur J Rooney Sr-Saint Patrick's Invitational (mid-March) 561-683-2222
$25,000 Bob Balfe/Molyneux Cup Puppy Stakes (late April) 561-683-2222
$25,000 Fall Futurity (late October) 561-683-2222
$25,000 He's My Man Royal Palm Classic (late January) 561-683-2222
$25,000 James W Paul 3/8th Mile Derby (late February) 561-683-2222
$25,000 Palm Beach Invitational (late March) 561-683-2222
All Florida Exhibit (late May-mid-July) 561-392-2500
All Ford Show (early October) 561-622-1400
Antiques Show & Sale (mid-February) 561-243-0223
Artigras (mid-February) 561-694-2300
Boca Festival Days (August) 561-395-4433
Boca Raton Outdoor Art Festival (late February) 561-392-2500
Bon Festival (mid-August) 561-495-0233
Boynton Beach's GALA (late March) 561-742-6221
Challenge Cup Polo Tournament (early-late January) 561-793-1440
Chris Evert Pro-Celebrity Tennis Classic (early December) 561-394-2400
Delray Affair (mid-April) 561-278-0424
Downtown Delray Craft Festival (late February-early March) 954-472-3755
Festival of Trees (December) 561-243-7356
Fiesta of Arts (early February) 561-393-7806
Fine Arts Festival (late November) 561-746-3101
Florida Winter Equestrian Festival (January-March) 561-793-5867
FOTOFusion (late January) 561-276-9797
Fourth on Flagler (July 4) 561-659-8007
Gold Cup of the Americas (early-mid-March) 561-793-1440
Harvest Fest (mid-November) 561-278-0424
Hatsume Fair (late February) 561-495-0233
Holiday Street Parade (early December) 561-393-7827
Indian River Pow Wow (late February) 561-978-4500
Jet Car Nationals (late April) 561-622-1400
Moroso Chrysler Classic Show (mid-September) 561-622-1400
Oktoberfest (mid-late October) 561-967-6464
Old-time Street Celebration (early February) 561-393-7806
Oshogatsu Japanese New Year Celebration (early January) 561-495-0233
Palm Beach Boat Show (late March) 800-940-7642
Palm Beach International Art & Antiques Fair (late January-early February) 561-220-2690

Palm Beach International Food & Wine Festival
(late February-early March) .561-220-2690
Palm Beach Seafood Festival (early February) .561-832-6397
Palm Beach Tropical Flower Show
(late February) .561-655-5522
PGA Seniors' Championship (mid-April) .561-624-8400
Pioneer Days Festival (late May) .561-793-0333
Seafare (October) .561-747-6639
South Florida Fair (mid-January-early February) .561-793-0333
Spring Fling (mid-April) .561-393-7827
Sterling Cup Polo Tournament
(late January-mid-February) .561-793-1440
SunFest of Palm Beach County
(late April-early May) .561-659-5980
Tropical Fruit Festival (late June) .561-833-0506
US Croquet National Championship
(mid-October) .561-753-9141
US Open Polo Championship
(mid-March-mid-April) .561-793-1440
West Palm Beach Italian Festival (early April) .561-832-6397
Wine & All That Jazz (late July) .561-395-4433
Winter Fantasy on the Waterway
(early December) .561-395-4433
Winter Festival (late February) .561-451-4485

Wichita, Kansas

***County:* Sedgwick**

WICHITA is located in south central Kansas at the confluence of the Arkansas and Little Arkansas rivers. Major cities within 100 miles include Abilene and Salina, Kansas.

Area (Land) .... 115.1 sq mi
Area (Water)................................ 2.2 sq mi
Elevation....................................1,035 ft
Latitude ....37-69-22 N
Longitude............................... 97-33-72 W
Time Zone ....CST
Area Code....................................... 316

Climate

Wichita has four distinct seasons, including an especially long autumn, and an average of 225 sunny days annually. Winter days are generally mild, with average high temperatures in the 40s, while evening low temperatures drop to around 20 degrees. The average annual snowfall in Wichita is 15 inches. Summer days are hot, with average highs in the low 90s, and evenings are pleasant, with average low temperatures near 70 degrees. June is the wettest month in Wichita, while January is the driest.

Average Temperatures & Precipitation

Temperatures

	Jan	Feb	Mar	Apr	May	Jun	Jul	Aug	Sep	Oct	Nov	Dec
High	40	46	57	68	77	87	93	91	81	71	55	43
Low	19	24	34	45	54	65	70	68	59	47	34	23

Precipitation

	Jan	Feb	Mar	Apr	May	Jun	Jul	Aug	Sep	Oct	Nov	Dec
Inches	0.8	1.0	2.4	2.4	3.8	4.3	3.1	3.0	3.5	2.2	1.6	1.2

History

Originally inhabited by Native Americans of the Wichita Tribe, the Wichita area was founded as a trading post at the confluence of the Arkansas and Little Arkansas Rivers by James West in 1865. White settlement began in the area three years later, and Wichita was chosen as the seat of Sedgwick County and incorporated as a city in 1871. During its early years, the town flourished as a popular stop along the Chisholm Trail, which ran from Texas to the market in nearby Abliene, where cattlemen would spend their earnings on their return from the long cattle drives. From 1876 through the first few decades of the 20th Century, with the help of new railroad lines that provided access to the rest of the country, Wichita grew quickly as a manufacturing and agricultural marketing center—by 1910, the city was home to 50,000 people. The discovery of oil in the surrounding area also helped fuel Wichita's economy during the early 1900s.

During World War I the aviation industry that would sustain Wichita through much of the 20th Century was established. Clyde Cessna, whose company remains a world leader in general aviation manufacturing, built the first Cessna airplane in the city. In the years that followed, several other aircraft manufacturers established operations in Wichita, including the Wichita Airplane Company, Boeing, Beech Aircraft (now Raytheon Aircraft Company), and (later) Learjet Inc. Despite the economic setbacks that struck the city during the Great Depression, Wichita's aircraft industry managed to bounce back. During World War II, the aircraft industry drew thousands of people seeking economic opportunities to Wichita, many of whom established residence there once the war ended.

The "Air Capital of the World," Wichita today is home to more than 329,000 people, making it the largest city in Kansas. Although Wichita's economy has diversified significantly in the past two decades, the aviation industry continues to play a vital role—the area's top three employers are aircraft and aerospace manufacturers.

Population

1990 Census 304,017
1998 Estimate.............................329,211
% Change 8.3
2004 Projection 573,769*

Racial/Ethnic Breakdown

White.................................. 82.3%
Black 11.3%
Other.................................... 6.4%
Hispanic Origin (may be of any race) 5.0%

Age Breakdown

Under 5 years............................ 8.6%
5 to 17................................. 17.9%
18 to 20.................................. 4.1%
21 to 24.................................. 6.4%
25 to 34................................ 19.4%
35 to 44................................ 14.5%
45 to 54.................................. 8.7%
55 to 64.................................. 8.1%
65 to 74.................................. 7.2%
75+ years 5.2%
Median Age................................31.7

Gender Breakdown

Male.................................... 48.6%
Female.................................. 51.4%

** Information given is for the Wichita Metropolitan Statistical Area (MSA), which includes Sedgwick, Butler, and Harvey counties.*

Government

Type of Government: Council-Manager

Wichita City Attorney
455 N Main St 13th Fl
Wichita, KS 67202
Phone: 316-268-4681
Fax: 316-268-4335

Wichita City Clerk
455 N Main St 13th Fl
Wichita, KS 67202
Phone: 316-268-4529
Fax: 316-268-4519

Wichita City Council
455 N Main St 1st Fl
Wichita, KS 67202
Phone: 316-268-4331
Fax: 316-268-4333

Wichita City Hall
455 N Main St
Wichita, KS 67202
Phone: 316-268-4331
Fax: 316-268-4567

Wichita City Manager
455 N Main St City Hall 13th Fl
Wichita, KS 67202
Phone: 316-268-4351
Fax: 316-268-4519

Wichita Economic Development Office
455 N Main St City Hall 12th Fl
Wichita, KS 67202
Phone: 316-268-4502
Fax: 316-268-4656

Wichita Finance Dept
455 N Main St 12th Fl
Wichita, KS 67202
Phone: 316-268-4434
Fax: 316-268-4656

Wichita Fire Dept
455 N Main St 11th Fl
Wichita, KS 67202
Phone: 316-268-4241
Fax: 316-268-4409

Wichita Housing Services Dept
307 Riverview St
Wichita, KS 67203
Phone: 316-268-4683
Fax: 316-337-9103

Wichita Mayor
455 N Main St 1st Fl
Wichita, KS 67202
Phone: 316-268-4331
Fax: 316-268-4333

Wichita Metro Transit Authority
777 E Waterman St
Wichita, KS 67202
Phone: 316-265-1450
Fax: 316-337-9287

Wichita Metropolitan Area Planning Dept
455 N Main St 10th Fl
Wichita, KS 67202
Phone: 316-268-4421
Fax: 316-268-4390

Wichita Parks & Recreation Dept
455 N Main St 11th Fl
Wichita, KS 67202
Phone: 316-268-4398
Fax: 316-337-9095

Wichita Personnel Dept
455 N Main St 2nd Fl
Wichita, KS 67202
Phone: 316-268-4531
Fax: 316-268-4286

Wichita Police Dept
455 N Main St 4th Fl
Wichita, KS 67202
Phone: 316-268-4158
Fax: 316-337-9030

Wichita Public Library
223 S Main St
Wichita, KS 67202
Phone: 316-261-8500
Fax: 316-262-4540

Wichita Public Works Dept
455 N Main St 8th Fl
Wichita, KS 67202
Phone: 316-268-4422
Fax: 316-337-9027

Wichita Water & Sewer Dept
455 N Main St 8th Fl
Wichita, KS 67202
Phone: 316-268-4515
Fax: 316-268-4514

Important Phone Numbers

AAA 316-685-5241
American Express Travel 316-686-7375
Driver's License Information 316-942-0723
Emergency 911
Fun Fone Events Recording 316-262-7474
HotelDocs 800-468-3537
Kansas Dept of Revenue 785-296-3963
Poison Control Center 316-688-2277
Sedgwick County Controller 316-383-7591
Sedgwick County Treasurer 316-383-7707
Time/Temp 316-436-1200
Vehicle Registration Information 316-383-7331
Voter Registration Information 316-383-7410
Weather 316-681-1371
Wichita Area Assn of Realtors 316-263-3167

Information Sources

Better Business Bureau Serving Kansas (Except the Northeast)
328 Laura St
Wichita, KS 67211
www.wichita.bbb.org
Phone: 316-263-3146
Fax: 316-263-3063

Century II Convention & Cultural Center
225 W Douglas Ave
Wichita, KS 67202
Phone: 316-264-9121
Fax: 316-268-9268

Sedgwick County
525 N Main St Rm 211
Wichita, KS 67203
www.southwind.net/sedgwick/
Phone: 316-383-7666
Fax: 316-383-7961

Wichita Area Chamber of Commerce
350 W Douglas Ave
Wichita, KS 67202
www.wichitakansas.org
Phone: 316-265-7771
Fax: 316-265-7502

Wichita Convention & Visitors Bureau
100 S Main St Suite 100
Wichita, KS 67202
www.wichita-cvb.org
Phone: 316-265-2800
Fax: 316-265-0162
TF: 800-288-9424

Online Resources

4Wichita.com
www.4wichita.com

About.com Guide to Wichita
wichita.about.com/local/midwestus/wichita

Anthill City Guide Wichita
www.anthill.com/city.asp?city=wichita

Area Guide Wichita
wichita.areaguides.net

City Knowledge Wichita
www.cityknowledge.com/ks_wichita.htm

Excite.com Wichita City Guide
www.excite.com/travel/countries/united_states/kansas/wichita

Wichita CityLink
www.usacitylink.com/citylink/wichita/

Wichita Kansas Cyberguide
www2.southwind.net/~vic/Wichita/index.html

Wichita.TheLinks.com
wichita.thelinks.com/

Area Communities

Communities located in the Wichita metropolitan area with populations greater than 5,000 include:

Andover
909 N Andover Rd
Andover, KS 67002
Phone: 316-733-1303
Fax: 316-733-4634

Augusta
PO Box 489
Augusta, KS 67010
Phone: 316-775-4510
Fax: 316-775-4566

Bel Aire
4551 N Auburn St
Wichita, KS 67220
Phone: 316-744-2451
Fax: 316-744-3739

Derby
611 Mulberry Rd
Derby, KS 67037
Phone: 316-788-1519
Fax: 316-788-6067

El Dorado
220 E 1st Ave
El Dorado, KS 67042
Phone: 316-321-9100
Fax: 316-321-6282

Haysville
PO Box 404
Haysville, KS 67060
Phone: 316-524-3243
Fax: 316-524-6764

Mulvane
211 N 2nd Ave
Mulvane, KS 67110
Phone: 316-777-1143
Fax: 316-777-4081

Newton
201 E 6th St
Newton, KS 67114
Phone: 316-284-6001
Fax: 316-284-6090

Park City
6110 N Hydraulic St
Park City, KS 67219
Phone: 316-744-2026
Fax: 316-744-3865

Economy

Some 40,000 Wichita area residents are employed in the aircraft and aerospace manufacturing industry. Boeing is the area's largest employer, and the company's Wichita facility is the largest single-site aerospace manufacturing center in the world, producing part of every Boeing jetliner manufactured. The health care industry has also become a major contributor to Wichita's economy in recent years, providing jobs for more than 25,000 people in the metro area. Two of Greater Wichita's largest employers—Via Christi Health System and Columbia Wesley Medical Center—oversee the operation of more than five individual health care facilities in the metro area. Nearly half of Wichita's top 15 employers are government-related, including the State of Kansas and the U.S. Government, which are numbers four and six, respectively.

Unemployment Rate 3.7%
Per Capita Income.......................... $26,821*
Median Family Income...................... $34,610

** Information given is for Sedgwick County.*

Principal Industries & Number of Wage Earners

Sedgwick County - 1998

Industry	Wage Earners
Agriculture	1,246
Construction	12,712
Finance, Insurance, & Real Estate	9,145
Government	25,792
Manufacturing	68,052
Mining	1,112
Retail Trade	42,101
Services	62,295
Transportation & Public Utilities	9,804
Wholesale Trade	14,999

Major Employers

Boeing Commercial Airplane Group Wichita Div
PO Box 7730
Wichita, KS 67277
Phone: 316-526-2121
Fax: 316-523-2823

Cessna Aircraft Co
1 Cessna Blvd
Wichita, KS 67215
www.cessna.textron.com
Phone: 316-517-6000
Fax: 316-517-7250

Dillon Food Stores
2700 E 4th Ave
Hutchinson, KS 67501
Phone: 316-665-5511
Fax: 316-669-3167

Koch Industries Inc
4111 E 37th St N
Wichita, KS 67220
www.kochind.com
Phone: 316-828-5500
Fax: 316-828-5913

Learjet Inc
1 Learjet Way
Wichita, KS 67209
www.learjet.com
Phone: 316-946-2000
Fax: 316-946-2163
TF: 800-289-5327

McConnell Air Force Base
McConnell AFB, KS 67221
www.mcconnell.af.mil
Phone: 316-652-6100
Fax: 316-652-3148

Raytheon Aircraft Co
PO Box 85
Wichita, KS 67201
E-mail: raytheonaircraft@raytheon.com
www.raytheon.com/rac
Phone: 316-676-7111
Fax: 316-676-5687

Sedgwick County
525 N Main St Rm 211
Wichita, KS 67203
www.southwind.net/sedgwick/
Phone: 316-383-7666
Fax: 316-383-7961

Via Christi Health System
3600 E Harry St
Wichita, KS 67218
www.via-christi.org
Phone: 316-685-1111
Fax: 316-689-4731

Wesley Medical Center
550 N Hillside Ave
Wichita, KS 67214
www.wesleymc.com
Phone: 316-688-2000
Fax: 316-688-7410
TF: 800-362-0288

Wichita City Hall
455 N Main St
Wichita, KS 67202
www.ci.wichita.ks.us
Phone: 316-268-4331
Fax: 316-268-4567

Wichita State University
1845 N Fairmount St
Wichita, KS 67260
www.twsu.edu
Phone: 316-978-3456
Fax: 316-978-3174
TF: 800-362-2594

Wichita Unified School District 259
201 N Water St
Wichita, KS 67202
E-mail: info@usd259.com
www.usd259.com
Phone: 316-973-4553
Fax: 316-973-4595

Quality of Living Indicators

Total Crime Index....................................20,977
(rates per 100,000 inhabitants)

Violent Crime
Murder/manslaughter........................... 27
Forcible rape 169
Robbery...................................... 700
Aggravated assault...........................1,031

Property Crime
Burglary 3,990
Larceny theft 13,388
Motor vehicle theft 1,672

Cost of Living Index....................................96.2
(national average = 100)

Median Home Price..................................$91,500

Education

Public Schools

Wichita Unified School District 259
201 N Water St
Wichita, KS 67202
E-mail: info@usd259.com
www.usd259.com
Phone: 316-973-4553
Fax: 316-973-4595

Number of Schools
Elementary................................. 55
Middle 16
High.. 11

Student/Teacher Ratio
All Grades 16.3:1

Private Schools

Number of Schools (all grades).................... 35+

Colleges & Universities

Friends University
2100 University St
Wichita, KS 67213
www.friends.edu
Phone: 316-295-5000
Fax: 316-295-5701
TF: 800-794-6945

Newman University
3100 McCormick Ave
Wichita, KS 67213
www.newmanu.edu
Phone: 316-942-4291
Fax: 316-942-4483
TF: 877-639-6268

Wichita Area Technical College
301 S Grove St
Wichita, KS 67211
Phone: 316-973-8400
Fax: 316-973-8489

Wichita State University
1845 N Fairmount St
Wichita, KS 67260
www.twsu.edu
Phone: 316-978-3456
Fax: 316-978-3174
TF: 800-362-2594

Hospitals

Veterans Affairs Medical Center
5500 E Kellogg St
Wichita, KS 67218
Phone: 316-685-2221
Fax: 316-651-3666
TF: 888-878-6881

Via Christi Regional Medical Center
929 N Saint Francis St
Wichita, KS 67214
www.via-christi.org/vcrmcweb.nsf/home
Phone: 316-268-5000
Fax: 316-291-7971
TF: 800-362-0070

Wesley Medical Center
550 N Hillside Ave
Wichita, KS 67214
www.wesleymc.com
Phone: 316-688-2000
Fax: 316-688-7410
TF: 800-362-0288

Transportation

Airport(s)

Midcontinent Airport (ICT)
6 miles SW of downtown (approx 12 minutes) 316-946-4700

Mass Transit

Wichita Transit
$1 Base fare 316-265-7221

Rail/Bus

Greyhound/Trailways Bus Station
312 S Broadway
Wichita, KS 67202
Phone: 316-265-7711

Utilities

Electricity
Kansas Gas & Electric.........................316-383-8600
www.wstnres.com

Gas
Kansas Gas & Electric.........................316-383-8600
www.wstnres.com

Water
Wichita Water Dept .316-265-1300

Garbage Collection/Recycling
SS Express Sanitation Service LLC .316-522-9133
Waste Management of Wichita .316-721-4510

Telecommunications

Telephone
Southwestern Bell Telephone Co .800-246-4999
www.swbell.com

Cable Television
Cox Communications .316-262-0661
www.cox.com

Internet Service Providers (ISPs)
SouthWind Internet Access Inc .316-263-7963
www.southwind.net
Veracom.net .316-263-9955
www.veracom.net

Banks

Bank of America
100 N Broadway St
Wichita, KS 67202
Phone: 316-261-4251
Fax: 316-261-2241
TF: 888-279-3121

Commerce Bank
150 N Main St
Wichita, KS 67202
Phone: 316-261-4700
Fax: 316-261-4747
TF: 800-866-9095

Emprise Bank
PO Box 2970
Wichita, KS 67201
Phone: 316-383-4400
Fax: 316-383-4399
TF: 800-201-7118

Intrust Bank NA
105 N Main St
Wichita, KS 67202
E-mail: intrust@intrustbank.com
www.intrustbank.com
Phone: 316-383-1111
Fax: 316-383-5805

Southwest National Bank of Wichita
400 E Douglas Ave
Wichita, KS 67202
Phone: 316-291-5303
Fax: 316-291-5274
TF: 800-747-5303

Shopping

Clifton Square
3700 E Douglas Ave Suite 12
Wichita, KS 67208
Phone: 316-686-2177
Fax: 316-686-2266

Delano Township Square
915 W Douglas Ave
Wichita, KS 67213
Phone: 316-263-2323
Fax: 316-263-3255

Eastgate Plaza Shopping Center
8235 E Kellogg St
Wichita, KS 67207
Phone: 316-682-6787

Old Town District
Douglas St-betw Washington & 2nd Sts
Wichita, KS 67202
Phone: 316-265-2800

Town West Square
4600 W Kellogg St
Wichita, KS 67209
Phone: 316-945-9374
Fax: 316-945-8617

Towne East Square
7700 E Kellogg St
Wichita, KS 67207
Phone: 316-686-3341
Fax: 316-684-0740

Wichita Mall
4165 E Harry
Wichita, KS 67218
Phone: 316-686-9072

Media

Newspapers and Magazines

Wichita Business Journal
110 S Main St Suite 200
Wichita, KS 67202
www.amcity.com/wichita
Phone: 316-267-6406
Fax: 316-267-8570

Wichita Eagle*
PO Box 820
Wichita, KS 67201
E-mail: eaglenws@aol.com
www.wichitaeagle.com/
Phone: 316-268-6000
Fax: 316-268-6627

**Indicates major daily newspapers*

Television

KAKE-TV Ch 10 (ABC)
1500 N West St
Wichita, KS 67203
www.kake.com
Phone: 316-943-4221
Fax: 316-943-5374

KPTS-TV Ch 8 (PBS)
PO Box 288
Wichita, KS 67201
E-mail: tv8@kpts.org
Phone: 316-838-3090
Fax: 316-838-8586

KSAS-TV Ch 24 (Fox)
316 N West St
Wichita, KS 67203
E-mail: foxfeedback@foxkansas.com
www.ksasfox24.com
Phone: 316-942-2424
Fax: 316-292-1195

KSNW-TV Ch 3 (NBC)
833 N Main St
Wichita, KS 67203
E-mail: ksnw@aol.com
www.ksnw.com
Phone: 316-265-3333
Fax: 316-292-1195

KWCH-TV Ch 12 (CBS)
2815 E 37th St North
Wichita, KS 67219
E-mail: news@kwch.com
www.kwch.com/
Phone: 316-838-1212
Fax: 316-831-6193
TF: 888-512-6397

Radio

KANR-FM 92.7 MHz (N/T)
746 N Maize Rd Suite 300
Wichita, KS 67212
Phone: 316-721-6161
Fax: 316-721-9191

KEYN-FM 103.7 MHz (Oldies)
2120 N Woodlawn St Suite 352
Wichita, KS 67208
www.keyn.com
Phone: 316-685-2121
Fax: 316-685-1287

KFDI-FM 101.3 MHz (Ctry)
4200 N Old Lawrence Rd
Wichita, KS 67219
E-mail: spike@kfdi.com
www.kfdi.com
Phone: 316-838-9141
Fax: 316-838-3607

KFH-AM 1330 kHz (N/T)
2120 N Woodlawn St Suite 352
Wichita, KS 67208
www.1330kfh.com
Phone: 316-685-2121
Fax: 316-685-3314

KHCC-FM 90.1 MHz (NPR)
815 N Walnut St Suite 300
Hutchinson, KS 67501
www.radioks.org
Phone: 316-662-6646

KICT-FM 95.1 MHz (Rock)
734 N Maize Rd
Wichita, KS 67212
E-mail: staff@t95.com
www.t95.com
Phone: 316-722-5600
Fax: 316-722-0722

KKRD-FM 107.3 MHz (CHR)
2402 E 37th St N
Wichita, KS 67219
E-mail: kkrd@southwind.net
www.1073kkrd.com
Phone: 316-832-9600
Fax: 316-832-0112

KMUW-FM 89.1 MHz (NPR)
3317 E 17th St
Wichita, KS 67208
E-mail: kmuw@twsu.edu
www.kmuw.org
Phone: 316-978-6789
Fax: 316-978-3946

KNSS-AM 1240 kHz (N/T)
2402 E 37th St N
Wichita, KS 67219
www.1240knss.com
Phone: 316-832-9600
Fax: 316-832-9688

KQAM-AM 1480 kHz (Sports)
2120 N Woodlawn St Suite 352
Wichita, KS 67208
E-mail: kqam@southwind.net
www.kqam.com
Phone: 316-685-2121
Fax: 316-685-3314

KRBB-FM 97.9 MHz (AC)
2402 E 37th St North
Wichita, KS 67219
www.b98fm.com/home/home.html
Phone: 316-832-9600
Fax: 316-832-0443

KRZZ-FM 96.3 MHz (CR)
2402 E 37th St North
Wichita, KS 67219
www.krzz.com
Phone: 316-832-9600
Fax: 316-832-0112

KTLI-FM 99.1 MHz (Rel)
125 N Market St Suite 1900
Wichita, KS 67202
E-mail: ktli@light99.com
www.light99.com
Phone: 316-303-9999
Fax: 316-303-9900

KWSJ-FM 105.3 MHz (Jazz)
2120 N Woodlawn St Suite 352
Wichita, KS 67208
www.kwsj.com
Phone: 316-685-2121
Fax: 316-685-3314

KZSN-FM 102.1 MHz (Ctry)
2120 N Woodlawn Suite 352
Wichita, KS 67208
www.kzsn.com
Phone: 316-685-2121
Fax: 316-685-1287

Attractions

In the mid-1800s, James R. Mead established the trading post from which the city of Wichita grew as a cowtown on the Chisholm Trail. A pictorial display of this trail, made famous by Jesse Chisholm (Mead's assistant), is located at the Wichita-Sedgwick County Historical Museum. Life in Wichita between 1865-1880 is illustrated in the open-air exhibit areas of the Old Cowtown Museum, which includes in its complex Wichita's first jail, six historic houses, and a working blacksmith shop. The sculptures of native artist Gina Salerno, created from the trunks of dead and dying trees, can be seen in Wichita's parks and recreation areas; more than 40 of these creations are scattered throughout the city. On the fringe of downtown Wichita is Botanica, the Wichita Gardens. Among its exhibits are a Shakespeare garden, a terrace garden with cascading pools, and formal gardens with native plants.

Allen-Lambe House Museum & Study Center
255 N Roosevelt St
Wichita, KS 67208
E-mail: allenlam@southwind.net
www2.southwind.net/~allenlam/
Phone: 316-687-1027
Fax: 316-687-2991

Barnacle Bill's Fanta Sea Water Park
3330 N Woodlawn
Wichita, KS 67220
Phone: 316-682-8656
Fax: 316-682-7557

Botanica The Wichita Gardens
701 Amidon St
Wichita, KS 67203
E-mail: botanica@southwind.net
www.botanica.org
Phone: 316-264-0448
Fax: 316-264-0587

Cabaret Old Town
412 1/2 E Douglas Ave
Wichita, KS 67202
Phone: 316-265-4400

Cheney State Park & Wildlife Area
16000 NE 50th St
Cheney, KS 67025
Phone: 316-542-3664

Coleman Factory Outlet Store & Museum
235 N Saint Francis St
Wichita, KS 67202
www.coleman.com
Phone: 316-264-0836
Fax: 316-264-6526
TF: 800-835-3278

Crown Uptown Professional Dinner Theatre
3207 E Douglas St
Wichita, KS 67214
www.crownuptown.com
Phone: 316-681-1566
Fax: 316-681-1925

Eberly Farm
13111 W 21st St North
Wichita, KS 67235
Phone: 316-722-3580
Fax: 316-722-3591

Exploration Place
300 N McLean Blvd
Wichita, KS 67203
www.exploration.org
Phone: 316-263-3373
Fax: 316-263-4545

Fort Larned National Historic Site
Rt 3
Larned, KS 67550
www.nps.gov/fols/
Phone: 316-285-6911
Fax: 316-285-3571

Great Plains Nature Center
6232 East 29th St N
Wichita, KS 67220
www.gpnc.org
Phone: 316-683-5499
Fax: 316-688-9555

Great Plains Transportation Museum Phone: 316-263-0944
700 E Douglas St
Wichita, KS 67202

Ice Sports Wichita Phone: 316-337-9199
505 W Maple St Fax: 316-337-9155
Wichita, KS 67213
E-mail: wichita@icesports.com
www.icesports.com/Wichita/right.html

Indian Center Museum Phone: 316-262-5221
650 N Seneca St Fax: 316-262-4216
Wichita, KS 67203
E-mail: icm@southwind.net
www.theindiancenter.com

Joyland Amusement Park Phone: 316-684-0179
2801 S Hillside St Fax: 316-684-1478
Wichita, KS 67216

Kansas African American Museum Phone: 316-262-7651
601 N Water St
Wichita, KS 67203

Kansas Aviation Museum Phone: 316-683-9242
3350 S George Washington Blvd Fax: 316-683-0573
Wichita, KS 67210
E-mail: craner@ccnet.com
www.saranap.com/kam.html

Kansas Wildlife Exhibit Phone: 316-683-5499
Nims & Murdock Sts Central Riverside Pk Fax: 316-688-9555
Wichita, KS 67202
www.gpnc.org/kansas.htm

Keeper of the Plains Statue Phone: 316-262-5221
650 N Seneca St Fax: 316-262-4216
Wichita, KS 67203

Lake Afton Public Observatory Phone: 316-794-8995
1845 Fairmount Fax: 316-978-3350
Wichita, KS 67260
E-mail: facsme@wsuhub.uc.twsu.edu
www.twsu.edu/~obswww

Lowell D Holmes Museum of Anthropology Phone: 316-978-3195
108 Neff Hall Wichita State University
Wichita, KS 67260
www.twsu.edu/~ldhmawww/

Metropolitan Ballet Phone: 316-687-5880
Century II Concert Hall
Wichita, KS 67202

Mosley Street Melodrama Phone: 316-263-0222
234 N Mosley St Oldtown Fax: 316-263-7999
Wichita, KS 67202
E-mail: administrator@internet-schminternet.com
www.mosleystreet.com

Music Theatre of Wichita Phone: 316-265-3107
225 W Douglas Century II Concert Hall Fax: 316-265-8708
Wichita, KS 67202

Old Cowtown Museum Phone: 316-264-0671
1871 Sim Park Dr Fax: 316-264-2937
Wichita, KS 67203
E-mail: cowtown@southwind.net
www.old-cowtown.org

Old Town District Phone: 316-265-2800
Douglas St-betw Washington & 2nd Sts
Wichita, KS 67202

Omnisphere & Science Center Phone: 316-337-9178
220 S Main St
Wichita, KS 67202
www.ci.wichita.ks.us/arts/omnisphere/omnisphere.asp

Sedgwick County Park Phone: 316-943-0192
6501 West 21st St N Fax: 316-942-3127
Wichita, KS 67212

Sedgwick County Zoo Phone: 316-942-2213
5555 Zoo Blvd Fax: 316-942-3781
Wichita, KS 67212
E-mail: director@scz.org
www.scz.org

Society of Decorative Painters Museum Phone: 316-269-9300
393 N McLean Blvd Fax: 316-269-9191
Wichita, KS 67203

Ulrich Edwin A Museum of Art Phone: 316-978-3664
1845 Fairmount St Wichita State University Fax: 316-978-3898
Wichita, KS 67208
E-mail: ulrichma@twsuvm.uc.twsu.edu
www.twsu.edu/~ulrich

Watson Park Phone: 316-529-9940
3055 S Lawrence Rd
Wichita, KS 67217

Wichita Art Museum Phone: 316-268-4921
619 Stackman Dr Fax: 316-268-4980
Wichita, KS 67203
E-mail: wam@feist.com
www.feist.com/~wam/

Wichita Center for the Arts Phone: 316-634-2787
9112 E Central Fax: 316-634-0593
Wichita, KS 67206
E-mail: wca@southwind.net
www.wcfta.com

Wichita Community Theatre Phone: 316-686-1282
258 N Fountain
Wichita, KS 67208

Wichita Farm & Art Market Phone: 316-262-3555
835 E 1st St North
Wichita, KS 37202

Wichita Symphony Orchestra Phone: 316-267-7658
225 W Douglas Suite 207 Fax: 316-267-1937
Wichita, KS 67202
E-mail: symphony@louverture.com
www.wso.org

Wichita-Sedgewick County Historical Museum Phone: 316-265-9314
204 S Main St Fax: 316-265-9319
Wichita, KS 67202
www.wscribe.com/history

Sports Teams & Facilities

81 Speedway
7700 N Broadway
Wichita, KS 67219
Phone: 316-755-1781
Fax: 316-744-1881

Lawrence Dumont Stadium
300 S Sycamore St
Wichita, KS 67213
www.wichitawranglers.com/ldstdm.html
Phone: 316-267-3372
Fax: 316-267-3382
TF: 800-677-4824

Wichita Greyhound Park
1500 East 77th St N
Valley Center, KS 67147
www.wgpi.com
Phone: 316-755-4000
Fax: 316-755-2405
TF: 800-872-2894

Wichita International Raceway
61st St N & Ridge Rd
Wichita, KS 67204
Phone: 316-755-3474

Wichita Thunder (hockey)
1229 East 85th St N Kansas Coliseum
Valley Center, KS 67147
www.wichitathunder.com/
Phone: 316-264-4625
Fax: 316-264-3037

Wichita Wings (soccer)
1229 East 85th St N Kansas Coliseum
Wichita, KS 67147
www.wichita-wings.com/
Phone: 316-262-3545
Fax: 316-263-8531

Wichita Wranglers (baseball)
300 S Sycamore St Lawrence-Dumont Stadium
Wichita, KS 67213
www.wichitawranglers.com
Phone: 316-267-3372
Fax: 316-267-3382

Annual Events

An Old Fashioned Christmas (early December) 316-264-0671
Asian Festival (late October).......................316-689-8729
Celebrate (early July) 316-943-4221
Cinco De Mayo Festival (early May)................800-288-9424
Equi-Fest of Kansas (late February) 316-755-1243
Fall Festival Arts & Crafts Show (late September) 316-773-9300
Holiday Wreath Festival (mid-November)...........316-264-3386
Holidays at the Wichita Art Museum (early December) 316-268-4921
Kansas Day Celebration (late January) 316-265-3933
Mexican Independence Weekend (mid-September) 316-265-2800
Mid-America All-Indian Center Pow Wow (late July) 316-262-5221
Midian Shrine Circus (mid-March) 316-264-7551
Midwest Winefest (late April) 316-838-7707
Multicultural Street Fair (mid-May) 316-267-2817
National BMX Tournament (mid-February).........316-755-1243
Old Sedgwick County Fair (early October)..........316-264-0671
Park City Bluegrass Festival (early May) 316-744-2026
Polkatennial (early May)...........................316-722-4201
Prairie Port Festival (late July)....................316-321-3150
Saint Patrick's Day Parade (mid-March) 316-946-1322
Sand Creek Folklife Festival (late April)...........316-283-7925
Sheplers Wrangler Pro Rodeo Classic (mid-February)...............................316-755-1243
Tulip Festival (mid-April) 316-264-0448
US Hot Rod Thunder Nationals (mid-January)......316-755-1243
Wichita Black Arts Festival (early September) 316-337-9222
Wichita Home Show (early February) 316-265-4226
Wichita Indian Art Market & Exhibition (mid-April) 316-262-5221
Wichita Jazz Festival (late April) 316-773-4333
Wichita Lawn Flower & Garden Show (early March) 316-721-8740
Wichita River Festival (early-mid-May).............316-267-2817

Wilmington, Delaware

County: **New Castle**

WILMINGTON is located in northeastern Delaware. Major cities within 100 miles include Dover, Delaware; Philadelphia, Pennsylvania; Trenton, New Jersey; Baltimore, Maryland; and Washington, DC.

Area (Land)	10.8 sq mi
Area (Water)	6.2 sq mi
Elevation	100 ft
Latitude	39-74-58 N
Longitude	75-54-69 W
Time Zone	EST
Area Code	302

Climate

Temperatures in Wilmington are moderated by the city's proximity to the Atlantic Ocean—periods of extreme cold or hot weather are usually very brief. Winters are generally cold, with average high temperatures around 40 degrees and lows in the mid-20s. The average annual snowfall in Wilmington is just under 21 inches. Summer days are warm, with average highs in the mid-80s, while evenings cool down into the mid-60s. Precipitation is fairly evenly distributed throughout the year—July tends to be the wettest month, while February and October are the driest.

Average Temperatures & Precipitation

Temperatures

	Jan	Feb	Mar	Apr	May	Jun	Jul	Aug	Sep	Oct	Nov	Dec
High	39	42	52	63	73	81	86	84	78	67	56	44
Low	22	25	33	42	52	62	67	66	58	46	37	28

Precipitation

	Jan	Feb	Mar	Apr	May	Jun	Jul	Aug	Sep	Oct	Nov	Dec
Inches	3.0	2.9	3.4	3.4	3.8	3.6	4.2	3.4	3.4	2.9	3.3	3.5

History

Delaware's largest city, Wilmington was originally the site of the first Swedish colony in the United States. Christinahamn, as the colony was originally named, served as the capital of New Sweden from its founding in 1638 until 1643, and again in 1654. Over the course of the next decade control of the area switched from Swedish to Dutch to English rule. In 1682 William Penn took possession of the area and a half-century later the Quakers had a settlement platted that they named Willingtown (after the area's first developer, Thomas Willing). In 1739, Willingtown officially became a borough and was renamed Wilmington (after the Earl of Wilmington, Spencer Compton).

By the time Wilmington was incorporated as a city in 1832, the area had already become a center for business and industry. In 1802 E.I. du Pont de Nemours established a powder mill on Brandywine Creek (the powder mill stands today as a museum), which led to the development of E.I. du Pont de Nemours & Company (du Pont), one of the leading chemical manufacturers in the world today. The completion of the Philadelphia, Wilmington, and Baltimore Railroad in 1837 further accelerated Wilmington's industrial growth, and by 1860, Wilmington was home to more than 21,000 people. During the Civil War, Wilmington's existing industries expanded and new industries were established as the city became a leading producer of ships, gunpowder, and other war necessities. The new industries created economic opportunities that drew thousands of new residents to the area in the years that followed. During the late 1800s Wilmington also developed an elaborate park system, and the city today features more than 550 acres of parkland that provide numerous recreational opportunities.

By 1920 Wilmington's population exceeded 110,000, and its economy flourished through both World Wars. Although the mid-1900s saw a movement of many of Wilmington's residents out of the city and into the surrounding suburbs, the city's prosperous business climate has remained intact. Wilmington is not only the financial and corporate center of Delaware, it is also known as the "Corporate Capital of the World," with more than half of the Fortune 500 companies headquartered there. The city's many business incentives, including a favorable tax structure (Delaware has no sales tax) and prime location, continue to attract business of all types to the city each year.

Population

1990 Census	71,529
1998 Estimate	71,678
% Change	0.2

Racial/Ethnic Breakdown

White	42.1%
Black	52.3%
Other	5.6%
Hispanic Origin (may be of any race)	7.1%

Age Breakdown

Under 5 years	7.3%
5 to 17	17.6%
18 to 20	4.1%
21 to 24	6.1%
25 to 34	19.1%
35 to 44	14.3%
45 to 54	9.0%
55 to 64	7.8%
65 to 74	8.0%
75+ years	6.7%
Median Age	32.7

Gender Breakdown
Male.......46.5%
Female.......53.5%

Government

Type of Government: Council-Mayor

Wilmington City Clerk
800 N French St
Wilmington, DE 19801
Phone: 302-571-4180
Fax: 302-571-4071

Wilmington City Council
800 N French St
Wilmington, DE 19801
Phone: 302-571-4180
Fax: 302-571-4071

Wilmington City Hall
800 N French St
Wilmington, DE 19801
Phone: 302-571-4180
Fax: 302-571-4071

Wilmington City Solicitor
800 N French St
Wilmington, DE 19801
Phone: 302-571-4200
Fax: 302-571-4565

Wilmington Finance Dept
800 N French St
Wilmington, DE 19801
Phone: 302-571-4300
Fax: 302-571-4283

Wilmington Fire Dept
300 N Walnut St
Wilmington, DE 19801
Phone: 302-571-4581
Fax: 302-573-5768

Wilmington Mayor
800 N French St
Wilmington, DE 19801
Phone: 302-571-4100
Fax: 302-571-4102

Wilmington Parks & Recreation Dept
22 S Heald St
Wilmington, DE 19801
Phone: 302-571-4250
Fax: 302-573-5790

Wilmington Personnel Dept
800 N French St 4th Fl
Wilmington, DE 19801
Phone: 302-571-4280
Fax: 302-571-4298

Wilmington Planning & Community Development Dept
800 N French St 7th Fl
Wilmington, DE 19801
Phone: 302-571-4130
Fax: 302-571-4119

Wilmington Police Dept
300 N Walnut St
Wilmington, DE 19801
Phone: 302-571-4404
Fax: 302-573-5768

Wilmington Public Library
10th & Market Sts
Wilmington, DE 19801
Phone: 302-571-7400
Fax: 302-654-9132

Wilmington Public Works Dept
800 N French St
Wilmington, DE 19801
Phone: 302-571-4220
Fax: 302-571-4579

Wilmington Real Estate & Housing Dept
800 N French St 7th Fl
Wilmington, DE 19801
Phone: 302-571-4057
Fax: 302-573-5588

Important Phone Numbers

AAA.......302-368-7700
Delaware Revenue Div.......302-577-3300
Driver's License/Vehicle Registration Information . . .302-434-3200
Emergency....... 911
Medical Referral.......302-428-4100
New Castle County Board of Realtors.......302-762-4800
New Castle County Tax Billing.......302-323-2600
Poison Control Center.......800-722-7112
Time/Temp.......302-475-8463
Travelers Aid.......302-656-1696
Voter Registration Information.......302-577-3464
Weather.......302-429-9000
Wilmington City Auditor.......302-571-4345
Wilmington Finance Dept Earned Income Tax Div. . .302-571-4300

Information Sources

Better Business Bureau Serving Delaware
1010 Concord Ave Suite 101
Wilmington, DE 19802
www.wilmington.bbb.org
Phone: 302-594-9200
Fax: 302-594-1052

Delaware State Chamber of Commerce
PO Box 671
Wilmington, DE 19899
www.dscc.com
Phone: 302-655-7221
Fax: 302-654-0691

Greater Wilmington Convention & Visitors Bureau
100 W 10th St Suite 20
Wilmington, DE 19801
www.wilmcvb.org
Phone: 302-652-4088
Fax: 302-652-4726
TF: 800-422-1181

New Castle County
87 Reads Way New Castle Corporate Commons
Newcastle, DE 19720
www.co.new-castle.de.us
Phone: 302-571-7500
Fax: 302-571-7857

Online Resources

Area Guide Wilmington
wilmingtonde.areaguides.net

I-95 Exit Information Guide Wilmington
www.usastar.com/i95/cityguide/wilmingtondelaware.htm

Wilmington.com
www.wilmington.com

Area Communities

Communities in New Castle County with populations greater than 1,000 include:

Delaware City
407 Clinton St
Delaware City, DE 19706
Phone: 302-834-4573
Fax: 302-832-5545

Elsmere
11 Poplar Ave
Wilmington, DE 19805
Phone: 302-998-2215
Fax: 302-998-9920

Middletown
216 N Broad St
Middletown, DE 19709
Phone: 302-378-1827
Fax: 302-378-1167

New Castle
220 Delaware St
New Castle, DE 19720
Phone: 302-322-9802
Fax: 302-322-9814

Newark
220 Elkton Rd
Newark, DE 19711
Phone: 302-366-7070
Fax: 302-366-7067

Newport
226 N James St
Wilmington, DE 19804
Phone: 302-994-6403
Fax: 302-996-0214

Economy

Wilmington is the corporate home of hundreds of U.S. companies and has an economic base that ranges from steel manufacturing to banking. Wilmington is considered the financial center of Delaware, and recently passed legislation has provided incentives for banks and other financial institutions (both U.S.-based and international) to relocate to Wilmington. New Castle County's fastest growing employment sectors include finance, insurance, and real estate. Government also plays a major role in Wilmington's economy—federal, state, and local government are all among New Castle County's top 10 employers, with Delaware State Government being the largest single employer in the county.

Unemployment Rate 3.9%
Per Capita Income.......................... $32,295*
Median Family Income...................... $26,389

** Information given is for New Castle County.*

Principal Industries & Number of Wage Earners

New Castle County - 1997

Industry	Wage Earners
Agricultural Services, Forestry, & Fishing	1,513
Construction	14,507
Finance, Insurance, & Real Estate	45,727
Manufacturing	43,408
Mining	46
Retail Trade	45,989
Services	82,780
Transportation & Public Utilities	11,968
Wholesale Trade	13,644

Major Employers

AstraZeneca LP
1800 Concord Pike
Wilmington, DE 19850
www.astrazeneca-us.com
Phone: 302-886-3000
Fax: 302-886-2972
TF: 800-456-3669

Christiana Care Health System
501 W 14th St
Wilmington, DE 19801
E-mail: healthcare@christianacare.org
www.christianacare.org
Phone: 302-428-2203
Fax: 302-428-2564

Christina School District
83 E Main St
Newark, DE 19711
Phone: 302-454-2000
Fax: 302-454-5380

Conectiv
800 King St PO Box 231
Wilmington, DE 19899
www.conectiv.com
Phone: 302-224-6200
TF: 800-266-3284

DaimlerChrysler Corp
550 S College Ave
Newark, DE 19713
www.daimlerchrysler.com
Phone: 302-453-5117
Fax: 302-453-5534

Dean Witter Discover & Co
919 Market St Suite 300
Wilmington, DE 19801
www.msdw.com
Phone: 302-657-2000
Fax: 302-657-2049

Delaware Technical & Community College Stanton Campus
400 Stanton-Christiana Rd
Newark, DE 19713
E-mail: info@dtcc.edu
www.dtcc.edu/stanton-wilmington
Phone: 302-454-3900
Fax: 302-368-6620

DuPont EI de Nemours & Co Inc
1007 Market St
Wilmington, DE 19898
E-mail: info@dupont.com
www.dupont.com
Phone: 302-774-1000
Fax: 302-774-7321
TF: 800-441-7515

General Motors Corp
801 Boxwood Rd
Wilmington, DE 19899
www.gm.com/careers
Phone: 302-428-7000
Fax: 302-428-7927

Gore WL & Assoc Inc
551 Papermill Rd
Newark, DE 19714
www.wlgore.com
Phone: 302-738-4880
Fax: 302-738-7710

Hercules Inc
1313 N Market St Hercules Plaza
Wilmington, DE 19894
www.herc.com
Phone: 302-594-5000
Fax: 302-594-5400
TF: 800-441-7600

MBNA America Bank NA
Wilmington, DE 19884
www.mbnainternational.com
Phone: 302-453-9930
Fax: 302-456-8541
TF: 800-441-7048

New Castle County
87 Reads Way New Castle Corporate Commons
Newcastle, DE 19720
www.co.new-castle.de.us
Phone: 302-571-7500
Fax: 302-571-7857

Red Clay Consolidated School District
1400 N Washington St
Wilmington, DE 19801
www.dataservice.org/redclay
Phone: 302-651-2600
Fax: 302-651-2615

University of Delaware
51 E Main St
Newark, DE 19716
www.udel.edu
Phone: 302-831-2000
Fax: 302-831-6788

Wilmington City Hall
800 N French St
Wilmington, DE 19801
www.ci.wilmington.de.us
Phone: 302-571-4180
Fax: 302-571-4071

Wilmington Trust Co
1100 N Market St
Wilmington, DE 19890
E-mail: info@wilmingtontrust.com
www.wilmingtontrust.com
Phone: 302-651-1000
Fax: 302-651-8937
TF: 800-441-7120

Quality of Living Indicators

Cost of Living Index 128.0
(national average = 100)

Median Home Price $120,600

Education

Public Schools

Red Clay Consolidated School District
1400 N Washington St
Wilmington, DE 19801
www.dataservice.org/redclay
Phone: 302-651-2600
Fax: 302-651-2615

Number of Schools
Elementary 13
Middle 6
High 4

Student/Teacher Ratio

Private Schools

Number of Schools (all grades) .... 58+

Colleges & Universities

Delaware Technical & Community College Stanton Campus
400 Stanton-Christiana Rd
Newark, DE 19713
E-mail: info@dtcc.edu
www.dtcc.edu/stanton-wilmington
Phone: 302-454-3900
Fax: 302-368-6620

Goldey Beacom College
4701 Limestone Rd
Wilmington, DE 19808
E-mail: gbc@goldey.gbc.edu
goldey.gbc.edu
Phone: 302-998-8814
Fax: 302-996-5408
TF: 800-833-4877

University of Delaware
51 E Main St
Newark, DE 19716
www.udel.edu
Phone: 302-831-2000
Fax: 302-831-6788

Wilmington College
320 N DuPont Hwy
New Castle, DE 19720
www.wilmcoll.edu
Phone: 302-328-9401
Fax: 302-328-5902
TF: 877-967-5464

Hospitals

DuPont Hospital for Children
1600 Rockland Rd
Wilmington, DE 19803
www.kidshealth.org/ai
Phone: 302-651-4000
Fax: 302-651-4055

Saint Francis Hospital
PO Box 2500
Wilmington, DE 19805
Phone: 302-421-4800
Fax: 302-421-4832

Veterans Affairs Medical Center
1601 Kirkwood Hwy
Wilmington, DE 19805
Phone: 302-994-2511
Fax: 302-633-5516
TF: 800-450-8262

Transportation

Airport(s)

Philadelphia International Airport (PHL)
20 miles NE of downtown Wilmington
(approx 45 minutes) 215-937-6937

Mass Transit

Dart
$1.15 Base fare 302-658-8960

Rail/Bus

Greyhound Bus Station
101 N French St
Wilmington, DE 19801
Phone: 302-655-6111
TF: 800-231-2222

Wilmington Amtrak Station
ML King Jr Blvd & French St
Wilmington, DE 19801
Phone: 302-429-6523

Utilities

Electricity
Delmarva Power & Light Co 302-454-0300
cpd.conectiv.com

Gas
Delmarva Power & Light Co 302-454-0300
cpd.conectiv.com

Water
Wilmington Water Dept 302-571-4220

Garbage Collection/Recycling
Wilmington Dept of Sanitation 302-571-4216

Telecommunications

Telephone
Verizon Communications 302-761-6000
www.verizon.com

Cable Television
Comcast Cable 302-656-3370

Internet Service Providers (ISPs)
DCANet (Consult Dynamics) 302-654-1019
www.dca.net
DiamondNet 302-427-2400
www.diamondnet.org

Banks

First Union National Bank
920 N King St Rodney Sq
Wilmington, DE 19801
Phone: 302-888-7500
Fax: 302-888-7513

First USA
300 N King St
Wilmington, DE 19801
www.firstusa.com
Phone: 302-594-8600
Fax: 302-594-8625
TF: 800-756-5800

Mellon Bank Delaware NA
10th & Market Sts
Wilmington, DE 19801
Phone: 302-421-2228
Fax: 302-992-7705
TF: 800-323-7105

PNC Bank
222 Delaware Ave
Wilmington, DE 19801
Phone: 302-429-7130
Fax: 302-429-2818

Wilmington Trust Co
1100 N Market St
Wilmington, DE 19890
E-mail: info@wilmingtontrust.com
www.wilmingtontrust.com
Phone: 302-651-1000
Fax: 302-651-8937
TF: 800-441-7120

Shopping

Christiana Mall
715 Christiana Mall
Newark, DE 19702
Phone: 302-731-9815
Fax: 215-893-0891

Concord Mall
4737 Concord Pike
Wilmington, DE 19803
Phone: 302-478-9271
Fax: 302-479-8313

Olde Ridge Village Shoppes
Ridge Rd & US Rt 202
Chadds Ford, PA 19317
Phone: 610-558-0466

Perryville Outlet Center
68 Heather Ln Suite 46
Perryville, MD 21903
Phone: 410-378-9399
Fax: 410-378-3298

Prices Corner Shopping Center
3202 Kirkwood Hwy
Wilmington, DE 19808
Phone: 302-999-9758

Media

Newspapers and Magazines

Dialog The
1925 Delaware Ave
Wilmington, DE 19806
E-mail: thedialog@aol.com
Phone: 302-573-3109
Fax: 302-573-2397

New Castle Business Ledger
153 E Chestnut Hill Rd Suite 104
Newark, DE 19713
E-mail: ledger@dca.net
www.ncbl.com/
Phone: 302-737-0923
Fax: 302-737-9019

News Journal*
950 W Basin Rd
New Castle, DE 19720
www.delawareonline.com
Phone: 302-324-2617
Fax: 302-324-5518

**Indicates major daily newspapers*

Television

KYW-TV Ch 3 (CBS)
101 S Independence Mall E
Philadelphia, PA 19106
www.kyw.com
Phone: 215-238-4700
Fax: 215-238-4783
TF: 800-238-4700

WCAU-TV Ch 10 (NBC)
10 Monument Rd
Bala Cynwyd, PA 19004
www.nbc10.com
Phone: 610-668-5510
Fax: 610-668-3700

WPVI-TV Ch 6 (ABC)
4100 City Line Ave
Philadelphia, PA 19131
abcnews.go.com/local/wpvi
Phone: 215-878-9700
Fax: 215-581-4530

WTXF-TV Ch 29 (Fox)
330 Market St
Philadelphia, PA 19106
www.foxphiladelphia.com
Phone: 215-925-2929
Fax: 215-925-2420

Radio

WDEL-AM 1150 kHz (N/T)
PO Box 7492
Wilmington, DE 19803
E-mail: wdel@dpnet.net
www.wdel.com
Phone: 302-478-2700
Fax: 302-478-0100

WILM-AM 1450 kHz (N/T)
1215 French St
Wilmington, DE 19801
www.wilm.com
Phone: 302-656-9800
Fax: 302-655-1450

WJBR-FM 99.5 MHz (A/C)
3001 Philadelphia Pike
Claymont, DE 19703
www.wjbr.com
Phone: 302-791-4110
Fax: 302-791-9669

WMPH-FM 91.7 MHz (Misc)
5201 Washington St Ext
Wilmington, DE 19809
E-mail: radio@wmph.org
www.wmph.org
Phone: 302-762-7199
Fax: 302-762-7042

WSTW-FM 93.7 MHz (CHR)
2727 Shipley Rd
Wilmington, DE 19810
E-mail: wstw@delaware.com
www.wstw.com
Phone: 302-478-2700
Fax: 302-478-0100

Attractions

Brandywine River Museum
Rt 1 & Rt 100
Chadds Ford, PA 19317
E-mail: bmuse1@aol.com
www.brandywinemuseum.org
Phone: 610-388-2700
Fax: 610-388-1197

Brandywine Zoo
1001 North Park Dr
Wilmington, DE 19801
Phone: 302-571-7747

Chadds John House
RR 100
Chadds Ford, PA 19317
E-mail: cfhs@voicenet.com
www.voicenet.com/~cfhs
Phone: 610-388-7376
Fax: 610-388-7480

Chaddsford Winery
632 Baltimore Pike
Chadds Ford, PA 19317
E-mail: cfwine@chaddsford.com
www.chaddsford.com
Phone: 610-388-6221
Fax: 610-388-0360

Christina Cultural Arts Center
705 Market St
Wilmington, DE 19801
Phone: 302-652-0101
Fax: 302-652-7480

Delaware Art Museum
2301 Kentmere Pkwy
Wilmington, DE 19806
E-mail: orangfan@aol.com
www.delart.mus.de.us
Phone: 302-571-9590
Fax: 302-571-0220

Delaware Center for the Contemporary Arts
103 E 16th St
Wilmington, DE 19801
E-mail: dcca@dca.net
www.thedcca.org
Phone: 302-656-6466
Fax: 302-656-6944

Delaware History Museum
504 Market St
Wilmington, DE 19801
www.hsd.org/dhm.htm
Phone: 302-656-0637
Fax: 302-655-7844

Delaware Museum of Natural History
4840 Kenneth Pike
Wilmington, DE 19807
www.delmnh.org
Phone: 302-658-9111
Fax: 302-658-2610

Delaware Symphony Orchestra
1200 N DuPont Hwy Delaware State University
Dover, DE 19901
E-mail: info@desymphony.org
www.desymphony.org
Phone: 302-652-5577
Fax: 302-657-5692

Delaware Theatre Co
200 Water St
Wilmington, DE 19801
Phone: 302-594-1100
Fax: 302-594-1107

Delaware Toy & Miniature Museum
Rt 141
Wilmington, DE 19807
E-mail: toys@thomes.net
www.thomes.net/toys
Phone: 302-427-8697
Fax: 302-427-8654

First USA Riverfront Art Center
800 S Madison St
Wilmington, DE 19801
Phone: 302-777-1600
Fax: 302-655-7844
TF: 888-395-0005

Fort Delaware State Park
45 Clinton St
Delaware City, DE 19706
Phone: 302-834-7941

George Read II House & Garden
42 The Strand
New Castle, DE 19720
www.hsd.org/read.htm
Phone: 302-322-8411

Grand Opera House
818 N Market St
Wilmington, DE 19801
E-mail: grandinfo@grandoperahouse.org
grandoperahouse.org
Phone: 302-658-7897
Fax: 302-652-5346
TF: 800-374-7263

Hagley Museum & Library
298 Buck Rd
Wilmington, DE 19807
www.hagley.lib.de.us
Phone: 302-658-2400
Fax: 302-658-0568

Heart Education Center
1096 Old Churchmans Rd
Newark, DE 19713
Phone: 302-633-0200
Fax: 302-633-3964

Henry Francis Winterthur DuPont Museum
Rt 52
Winterthur, DE 19735
E-mail: llock@udel.edu
www.winterthur.org
Phone: 302-888-4600
Fax: 302-888-4880
TF: 800-448-3883

Historic Houses of Odessa
2 Main St
Odessa, DE 19730
Phone: 302-378-4069

Historical Society of Delaware
505 Market St
Wilmington, DE 19801
E-mail: hsd@dca.net
www.hsd.org/
Phone: 302-655-7161
Fax: 302-655-7844

Immanuel Episcopal Church
2nd & Harmony Sts On the Green
New Castle, DE 19720
Phone: 302-328-2413
Fax: 302-328-6636

Kalmar Nyckel Shipyard & Museum
1124 E 7th St
Wilmington, DE 19801
www.kalnyc.org
Phone: 302-429-7447
Fax: 302-429-0350

Lincoln Room of the University of Delaware
2600 Pennsylvania Ave
Wilmington, DE 19806
Phone: 302-573-4468

Longwood Gardens
1001 Longwood Rd
Kennett Square, PA 19348
www.longwoodgardens.com
Phone: 610-388-1000
Fax: 610-388-2183
TF: 800-737-5500

Nemours Mansion & Gardens
1600 Rockland Rd
Wilmington, DE 19803
www.kidshealth.org/nf/mansion/index.html
Phone: 302-651-6912
Fax: 302-651-6933

New Castle Presbyterian Church
25 E 2nd St
New Castle, DE 19720
Phone: 302-328-3279
Fax: 302-328-5670

Old Court House
211 Delaware St
New Castle, DE 19720
Phone: 302-323-4453
Fax: 302-323-5319

Old Swedes Church & Hendrickson House Museum
606 Church St
Wilmington, DE 19801
www.oldswedes.org
Phone: 302-652-5629
Fax: 302-652-8615

Old Town Hall
512 Market St Mall
Wilmington, DE 19801
www.hsd.org/oth.htm
Phone: 302-655-7161
Fax: 302-655-7844

OperaDelaware
824 N Market St Suite 200
Wilmington, DE 19801
E-mail: opinfo@operadel.org
www.operadel.org
Phone: 302-658-8063
Fax: 302-658-4991

Phillips Mushroom Place Museum
909 E Baltimore Pike
Kennett Square, PA 19348
www.phillipsmushroomplace.com
Phone: 610-388-6082
Fax: 610-388-3985

Playhouse Theatre
10th & Market Sts DuPont Bldg
Wilmington, DE 19801
E-mail: tickets.playhouse@usa.dupont.com
www.playhousetheatre.com
Phone: 302-656-4401
Fax: 302-594-1437
TF: 800-338-0881

Quaker Hill Historic Preservation Foundation
521 West St
Wilmington, DE 19801
Phone: 302-658-4200
Fax: 302-658-9075

Rockwood Museum
610 Shipley Rd
Wilmington, DE 19809
E-mail: info@rockwood.org
Phone: 302-761-4340

Sewell C Biggs Museum of American Art
PO Box 711
Dover, DE 19903
www.biggsmuseum.org
Phone: 302-674-2111
Fax: 302-674-5133

University of Delaware Center for Black Culture
192 S College Ave
Newark, DE 19716
Phone: 302-831-2991
Fax: 302-831-4097

Wilmington & Western Railroad
PO Box 5787
Wilmington, DE 19808
E-mail: schedule@wwrr.com
www.wwrr.com
Phone: 302-998-1930
Fax: 302-998-7408

Wilmington Drama League Community Theatre
10 W Lea Blvd
Wilmington, DE 19802
Phone: 302-764-1172
Fax: 302-764-7904

Sports Teams & Facilities

Delaware Genies (soccer)
301 McKennan's Church Rd Randy White Alumni Stadium
New Castle, DE 19808
Phone: 302-326-1930
Fax: 302-326-1932

Delaware Park
777 Delaware Pk Blvd
Wilmington, DE 19804
www.delpark.com
Phone: 302-994-2521
Fax: 302-993-2355

Delaware Wizards (soccer)
301 McKennan's Church Rd Randy White Alumni Stadium
Wilmington, DE 19808
Phone: 302-326-1930
Fax: 302-326-1932

Wilmington Blue Rocks (baseball)
801 S Madison St
Wilmington, DE 19801
E-mail: info@bluerocks.com
www.bluerocks.com
Phone: 302-888-2015
Fax: 302-888-2032

Annual Events

A Christmas Display (mid-November-early January) 610-388-6741
A Day in Old New Castle (mid-late May) 302-322-8411
African Festival (early-mid-July) 302-657-2108
Christmas 1895-An Engagement at Rockwood (late November-early January) 302-761-4340
Chrysanthemum Festival (early-late November)..... 610-388-1000
Civil War Reenactment (late May) 305-655-5704
Clifford Brown Jazz Festival (early June)........... 302-571-4205
Cool Blues & Micro Brew (early-mid-August)....... 302-571-4100
DuPont Riverfest (late September) 302-658-1870
Festival of Fountains (May) 610-388-1000
First Night Wilmington (December 31) 302-658-9327
Garrison Days (mid-August) 302-834-7941
Greek Festival (early June) 302-654-4447
Hagley's Craft Fair (mid-October) 302-658-2400
Hagley's Storybook Garden Party (late April) 302-658-2400
Ice Cream Festival (mid-July)..................... 302-761-4340
Jazz Fest (early September) 610-388-6221
Rehoboth Jazz Festival (mid-October) 800-296-8742
Saint Anthony's Italian Festival (mid-June) 302-421-3790
Saint Patrick's Day Parade (March)................ 302-652-2970
Saint Patrick's Day Tea (mid-March) 302-761-4340
Taste of Wilmington Festival (late September)...... 302-888-2929
Wilmington Flower Market (early May)............. 302-995-5699
Wilmington Garden Day (early May) 302-428-6172
Yuletide at Winterthur (mid-November-early January) 800-448-3883

Winston-Salem, North Carolina

***County:* Forsyth**

WINSTON-SALEM is located in the Piedmont Triad region of central North Carolina. Major cities within 100 miles include Greensboro, High Point, Raleigh/Durham, Chapel Hill, and Charlotte, North Carolina.

Area (Land) .... 71.1 sq mi
Area (Water)............................... 0.6 sq mi
Elevation.................................... 912 ft
Latitude ....36-09-97 N
Longitude.............................. 80-24-44 W
Time Zone ....EST
Area Code...................................... 336

Climate

Winston-Salem's climate is moderated by the Brushy Mountains and the Blue Ridge Mountains that lie to the west of the city and protect the area from extreme cold. Winters are generally mild, with high temperatures averaging near 50 degrees and average lows in the high 20s and low 30s. The average annual snowfall in Winston-Salem is nine inches. Summer days are very warm, with average high temperatures in the mid-80s, while evenings cool down into the mid-60s. Precipitation is fairly evenly distributed throughout the year in Winston-Salem—July tends to be the wettest month, while April is the driest.

Average Temperatures & Precipitation

Temperatures

	Jan	Feb	Mar	Apr	May	Jun	Jul	Aug	Sep	Oct	Nov	Dec
High	47	51	60	70	77	84	87	86	80	70	61	51
Low	27	29	37	46	55	63	67	66	60	47	39	31

Precipitation

	Jan	Feb	Mar	Apr	May	Jun	Jul	Aug	Sep	Oct	Nov	Dec
Inches	3.2	3.3	3.7	2.8	4.0	3.8	4.5	3.9	3.5	3.5	3.0	3.4

History

The first Europeans to settle in the area known today as Winston-Salem were Moravians who migrated south from Pennsylvania in the mid-18th Century. In 1766 the settlers founded the town of Salem (a name derived from "shalom," the Hebrew word for peace). Trades, crafts, and manufacturing flourished in Salem, due in large part to the strong work ethic of its Moravian residents. Salem was also an important educational center—Salem College, founded by the early settlers, was among the first colleges for women in the country. Present-day Winston-Salem is home to several institutions of higher education, including Wake Forest University.

During the 1800s other settlers came to the Piedmont region in search of economic opportunities. Forsyth County was established in 1849 and a new town called Winston was founded to serve as the new county seat. The tobacco and cotton industries prospered in Winston, and the new town became a leading commercial and industrial hub following the arrival of the railroad in 1853.

In 1913, the towns of Salem and Winston merged to form the city of Winston-Salem. The following year R.J. Reynolds Tobacco Company introduced Camel brand cigarettes, which proved to be a best seller for the company and consequently a major boost for Winston-Salem's economy. The tobacco industry continues to play a vital role in the city's economy—RJR Nabisco, which now owns the R.J. Reynolds Tobacco Company, remains Greater Winston-Salem's largest employer. Home to more than 164,000 people, Winston-Salem today is North Carolina's fourth largest city.

Population

1990 Census 150,958
1998 Estimate.............................164,316
% Change 1.2
2010 Projection 319,890*

Racial/Ethnic Breakdown

White.................................... 56.5%
Black 37.3%
Other..................................... 6.2%
Hispanic Origin (may be of any race) 0.9%

Age Breakdown

Under 5 years............................. 6.7%
5 to 17.................................. 15.0%
18 to 20.................................. 5.9%
21 to 24.................................. 7.3%
25 to 34................................. 18.2%
35 to 44................................. 14.3%
45 to 54.................................. 9.6%
55 to 64.................................. 9.0%
65 to 74.................................. 7.9%
75+ years 6.2%
Median Age.................................33.3

Gender Breakdown

Male..................................... 43.6%
Female................................... 56.4%

** Information given is for Forsyth County.*

Government

Type of Government: Council-Manager

Winston-Salem Board of Aldermen
PO Box 2511
Winston-Salem, NC 27102

Phone: 336-727-2189
Fax: 336-727-2880

Winston-Salem City Attorney
PO Box 2511
Winston-Salem, NC 27102
Phone: 336-727-2056
Fax: 336-727-2880

Winston-Salem City Hall
101 N Main St
Winston-Salem, NC 27101
Phone: 336-727-2123
Fax: 336-748-3060

Winston-Salem City Manager
PO Box 2511
Winston-Salem, NC 27102
Phone: 336-727-2123
Fax: 336-748-3060

Winston-Salem Economic Development Dept
101 N Main St Rm 122
Winston-Salem, NC 27102
Phone: 336-727-2741
Fax: 336-727-2880

Winston-Salem Finance Dept
PO Box 2511
Winston-Salem, NC 27102
Phone: 336-727-2608
Fax: 336-727-2566

Winston-Salem Fire Dept
725 N Cherry St
Winston-Salem, NC 27102
Phone: 336-773-7900
Fax: 336-773-7974

Winston-Salem Human Resources Dept
101 N Main St 1st Fl
Winston-Salem, NC 27102
Phone: 336-727-2895
Fax: 336-748-3053

Winston-Salem Mayor
PO Box 2511
Winston-Salem, NC 27102
Phone: 336-727-2058
Fax: 336-748-3241

Winston-Salem Planning Board
PO Box 2511
Winston-Salem, NC 27102
Phone: 336-727-2087
Fax: 336-748-3163

Winston-Salem Police Dept
PO Box 2511
Winston-Salem, NC 27102
Phone: 336-773-7760
Fax: 336-773-7996

Winston-Salem Public Works Dept
PO Box 2511
Winston-Salem, NC 27102
Phone: 336-727-2545
Fax: 336-727-2361

Winston-Salem Recreation & Parks Dept
836 Oak St Suite 200
Winston-Salem, NC 27101
Phone: 336-727-2227
Fax: 336-727-2066

Winston-Salem Transit Authority
1060 N Trade St
Winston-Salem, NC 27102
Phone: 336-727-2000
Fax: 336-727-8104

Important Phone Numbers

AAA.......................................336-774-1200
Driver's License Information.....................336-761-2259
Emergency 911
Forsyth County Tax Assessor......................336-727-2655
Medical Referral.................................336-716-2255
North Carolina Dept of Revenue...................336-761-2314
Poison Control Center 800-848-6946
Vehicle Registration Information 336-725-2796
Voter Registration Information....................336-727-2162
Western Piedmont Assn of Realtors................336-768-5560

Information Sources

Benton Convention Center
301 W 5th St
Winston-Salem, NC 27102
Phone: 336-727-2976
Fax: 336-727-2879

Better Business Bureau Serving Northwest North Carolina
500 W 5th St Suite 202
Winston-Salem, NC 27101
www.winstonsalem.bbb.org
Phone: 336-725-8348
Fax: 336-777-3727

Forsyth County
PO Box 20099
Winston-Salem, NC 27120
www.co.forsyth.nc.us
Phone: 336-761-2250
Fax: 336-761-2018

Greater Winston-Salem Chamber of Commerce
601 W 4th St
Winston-Salem, NC 27101
www.winstonsalem.com
Phone: 336-725-2361
Fax: 336-721-2209

Winston-Salem Convention & Visitors Bureau
601 W 4th St
Winston-Salem, NC 27101
www.wscvb.com
Phone: 336-728-4200
Fax: 336-728-4220
TF: 800-331-7018

Online Resources

Anthill City Guide Winston-Salem
www.anthill.com/city.asp?city=winstonsalem

Area Guide Winston-Salem
winston.areaguides.net

City Knowledge Winston-Salem
www.cityknowledge.com/nc_winstonsalem.htm

CityTravelers.com Guide to Winston-Salem
www.citytravelers.com/winstonsalem.htm

Excite.com Winston-Salem City Guide
www.excite.com/travel/countries/united_states/north_carolina/winston-salem

Welcome to Winston-Salem
www.webpress.net/ncnetworks/ws-intr.html

Area Communities

Communities in Forsyth County with populations greater than 5,000 include:

Clemmons
PO Box 1710
Clemmons, NC 27012
Phone: 336-766-7511
Fax: 336-766-7536

Kernersville
134 E Mountain St
Kernersville, NC 27284
Phone: 336-996-3121
Fax: 336-996-4822

Lewisville
PO Box 547
Lewisville, NC 27023
Phone: 336-945-5558
Fax: 336-945-5531

Economy

Manufacturing, primarily tobacco and textile industries, plays a vital role in Winston-Salem's economy—R.J. Reynolds Tobacco Company and Sara Lee (whose textile manufacturing divisions in Winston-Salem include Champion athletic apparel and WonderBra lingerie) are among Winston-Salem's top five employers. In recent years, however, services has surpassed manufacturing as the largest employment sector in Forsyth County. Health care is the leading service-related industry, providing jobs for more than 10 percent of the Winston-Salem area's total workforce.

Unemployment Rate 2.3%*
Per Capita Income $31,304*
Median Family Income $43,900*

** Information given is for Forsyth County.*

Principal Industries & Number of Wage Earners

Greensboro/Winston-Salem/High Point MSA* - 1999

Construction & Mining 34,800
Finance, Insurance, & Real Estate 35,300
Government 71,800
Manufacturing 158,600
Retail Trade 113,000
Services 180,100
Transportation & Public Utilities 35,000
Wholesale Trade 35,400

** Information given is for the Greensboro/Winston-Salem/High Point Metropolitan Statistical Area (MSA), which includes Alamance, Davidson, Davie, Forsyth, Guilford, Randolph, Stokes, and Yadkin counties.*

Major Employers

AMP Inc
3700 Reidsville Rd
Winston-Salem, NC 27052
www.amp.com
Phone: 336-720-9222
Fax: 336-727-5621

BB & T Corp
200 W 2nd St
Winston-Salem, NC 27101
E-mail: feedback@bbandt.com
www.bbandt.com
Phone: 336-733-2000
Fax: 336-733-2009

Forsyth County
PO Box 20099
Winston-Salem, NC 27120
www.co.forsyth.nc.us
Phone: 336-761-2250
Fax: 336-761-2018

Integon Corp
500 W 5th St
Winston-Salem, NC 27152
E-mail: marketing@integon.com
www.integon.com
Phone: 336-770-2000
Fax: 336-770-2122
TF: 877-468-3466

Novant Health Inc
3333 Silas Creek Pkwy
Winston-Salem, NC 27103
www.novanthealth.org
Phone: 336-718-5475
Fax: 336-718-9863

RJ Reynolds Tobacco Co
PO Box 2959
Winston-Salem, NC 27102
www.rjrt.com
Phone: 336-741-5000
Fax: 336-741-4238

Sara Lee Corp
470 W Hanes Mill Rd
Winston-Salem, NC 27102
www.saralee.com/careers
Phone: 336-519-4400
Fax: 336-519-7160

US Airways Inc
2345 Crystal Dr Crystal Pk 4
Arlington, VA 22227
www.usairways.com
Phone: 703-872-7000
Fax: 703-294-5097
TF: 800-428-4322

Wachovia Bank NA
100 N Main St
Winston-Salem, NC 27150
www.wachovia.com/careers
Phone: 336-770-5000
Fax: 336-732-2191

Wake Forest University
1834 Wake Forest Rd
Winston-Salem, NC 27106
www.wfu.edu
Phone: 336-759-5000
Fax: 336-758-6074

Wake Forest University Baptist Medical Center
Medical Center Blvd
Winston-Salem, NC 27157
www.wfubmc.edu
Phone: 336-716-2011
Fax: 336-716-2067

Winston-Salem City Hall
101 N Main St
Winston-Salem, NC 27101
www.ci.winston-salem.nc.us
Phone: 336-727-2123
Fax: 336-748-3060

Winston-Salem State University
601 ML King Jr Dr
Winston-Salem, NC 27110
www.wssu.edu
Phone: 336-750-2000
Fax: 336-750-2079
TF: 800-257-4052

Winston-Salem/Forsyth County Schools
PO Box 2513
Winston-Salem, NC 27102
wsfcs.k12.nc.us
Phone: 336-727-2816
Fax: 336-727-2008

Quality of Living Indicators

Total Crime Index 16,899
(rates per 100,000 inhabitants)

Violent Crime
Murder/manslaughter 17
Forcible rape 110
Robbery 626
Aggravated assault 1,339

Property Crime
Burglary 3,653
Larceny theft 10,017
Motor vehicle theft 1,137

Cost of Living Index 97.9
(national average = 100)

Median Home Price $124,800

Education

Public Schools

Winston-Salem/Forsyth County Schools
PO Box 2513
Winston-Salem, NC 27102
wsfcs.k12.nc.us
Phone: 336-727-2816
Fax: 336-727-2008

Number of Schools
Elementary 37
Middle 14
High 8
Special 6

Student/Teacher Ratio
All Grades 15.0:1

Private Schools

Number of Schools (all grades) .... 20+

Colleges & Universities

Forsyth Technical Community College
2100 Silas Creek Pkwy
Winston-Salem, NC 27103
www.forsyth.tec.nc.us
Phone: 336-723-0371
Fax: 336-761-2399

High Point University
833 Montlieu Ave
High Point, NC 27262
acme.highpoint.edu
Phone: 336-841-9000
Fax: 336-841-4599

North Carolina School of the Arts
1533 S Main St
Winston-Salem, NC 27127
www.ncarts.edu
Phone: 336-770-3399
Fax: 336-770-3366

Piedmont Baptist College
716 Franklin St
Winston-Salem, NC 27101
E-mail: help@pbc.edu
www.pbc.edu
Phone: 336-725-8344
Fax: 336-725-5522

Salem College
PO Box 10548
Winston-Salem, NC 27108
E-mail: admissions@salem.edu
www.salem.edu
Phone: 336-721-2600
Fax: 336-721-2832

Wake Forest University
1834 Wake Forest Rd
Winston-Salem, NC 27106
www.wfu.edu
Phone: 336-759-5000
Fax: 336-758-6074

Winston-Salem State University
601 ML King Jr Dr
Winston-Salem, NC 27110
www.wssu.edu
Phone: 336-750-2000
Fax: 336-750-2079
TF: 800-257-4052

Hospitals

Forsyth Medical Center
3333 Silas Creek Pkwy
Winston-Salem, NC 27103
www.forsythmedicalcenter.org
Phone: 336-718-5000
Fax: 336-718-9258

Wake Forest University Baptist Medical Center
Medical Center Blvd
Winston-Salem, NC 27157
www.wfubmc.edu
Phone: 336-716-2011
Fax: 336-716-2067

Transportation

Airport(s)

Piedmont Triad International Airport (GSO)
27 miles E of downtown Winston-Salem
(approx 25 minutes) 336-665-5600

Smith Reynolds Airport (INT)
2 1/2 miles NE of downtown
(approx 5 minutes) 336-767-6361

Mass Transit

Winston-Salem Transit Authority
$1 Base fare 336-727-2000

Rail/Bus

Greyhound/Trailways Bus Station
250 Greyhound Ct
Winston-Salem, NC 27102
Phone: 336-724-1429
TF: 800-231-2222

Utilities

Electricity
Duke Power Co 336-727-4300
www.dukepower.com

Gas
Piedmont Natural Gas Co 336-761-8101
www.piedmontng.com

Water
Winston-Salem Water Dept 336-727-2355

Garbage Collection/Recycling
Waste Management of the Piedmont 336-723-2784
Winston-Salem Sanitation Dept 336-727-2638

Telecommunications

Telephone
BellSouth 800-767-2355
www.bellsouth.com

Cable Television
Time Warner Cable 336-785-3390
www.timewarner.com

Internet Service Providers (ISPs)
NetUnlimited Inc 336-722-8300
www.netunlimited.com
Red Barn Data Center Internet Services 336-774-1600
www.rbdc.com

Banks

BB & T Bank
110 Straford Rd
Winston-Salem, NC 27104
Phone: 336-773-1100
Fax: 336-773-0114

Central Carolina Bank & Trust Co
2804 Fairlawn Dr
Winston-Salem, NC 27106
Phone: 336-659-2840
Fax: 336-659-2843

Centura Bank
2150 Country Club Rd
Winston-Salem, NC 27113
Phone: 336-631-5600
Fax: 336-631-5603

First Union National Bank
3375 Robinhood Rd
Winston-Salem, NC 27106
Phone: 336-761-3850
Fax: 336-726-0934

Old North State Bank
161 S Stratford Rd
Winston-Salem, NC 27103
Phone: 336-631-3900
Fax: 336-631-3922

Salem Trust Bank
2140 Country Club Rd
Winston-Salem, NC 27104
Phone: 336-777-1400
Fax: 336-723-9102

Wachovia Bank NA
100 N Main St
Winston-Salem, NC 27150
www.wachovia.com/careers
Phone: 336-770-5000
Fax: 336-732-2191

Shopping

Hanes Mall
3320 Silas Creek Pkwy
Winston-Salem, NC 27103
E-mail: hanesmall@rejacobsgroup.com
www.shopyourmall.com/mall_welcome.asp?map=yes&mall_select=685
Phone: 336-765-8323

Marketplace Mall
2101 Peters Creek Pkwy
Winston-Salem, NC 27127
Phone: 336-724-1451
Fax: 336-722-7780

Reynolda Village
114 Reynolda Village Suite F
Winston-Salem, NC 27106
Phone: 336-758-5584

Stratford Oaks Mini Mall
514 S Stratford Rd
Winston-Salem, NC 27103
Phone: 336-725-1821
Fax: 336-725-6918

Media

Newspapers and Magazines

Winston-Salem Journal*
418 N Marshall St
Winston-Salem, NC 27101
w-s-journal.com
Phone: 336-727-7211
Fax: 336-727-4071

**Indicates major daily newspapers*

Television

WFMY-TV Ch 2 (CBS)
1615 Phillips Ave
Greensboro, NC 27405
E-mail: fmy2@aol.com
www.wfmy.com
Phone: 336-379-9369
Fax: 336-273-9433

WGHP-TV Ch 8 (Fox)
PO Box HP-8
High Point, NC 27261
www.fox8wghp.com
Phone: 336-841-8888
Fax: 336-841-5169

WGPX-TV Ch 16 (PAX)
1114 N Old Henry Blvd
Greensboro, NC 27405
www.paxtv.com/WGPX
Phone: 336-272-9227
Fax: 336-272-9298

WUNL-TV Ch 26 (PBS)
PO Box 14900
Research Triangle Park, NC 27709
Phone: 919-549-7000
Fax: 919-549-7201

WXII-TV Ch 12 (NBC)
700 Coliseum Dr
Winston-Salem, NC 27116
E-mail: newschannel12@wxii.com
www.wxii.com
Phone: 336-721-9944
Fax: 336-721-0856

WXLV-TV Ch 45 (ABC)
3500 Myer Lee Dr
Winston-Salem, NC 27101
www.wxlv.com
Phone: 336-722-4545
Fax: 336-631-9205

Radio

WAAA-AM 980 kHz (Urban)
4950 Indiana Ave
Winston-Salem, NC 27106
Phone: 336-767-0430
Fax: 336-767-0433

WBFJ-AM 1550 kHz (Rel)
1249 Trade St
Winston-Salem, NC 27101
E-mail: wbfj@netunlimited.net
www.wbfj.org
Phone: 336-721-1560
Fax: 336-777-1032

WFDD-FM 88.5 MHz (NPR)
56 Wake Forest Rd
Winston-Salem, NC 27109
E-mail: wfdd@wfu.edu
Phone: 336-758-8850
Fax: 336-758-5193

WHSL-FM 100.3 MHz (Ctry)
PO Box 5897
High Point, NC 27262
Phone: 336-727-0995
Fax: 336-887-0104

WMAG-FM 99.5 MHz (AC)
PO Box 5897
High Point, NC 27262
www.wmagradio.com
Phone: 336-727-0995
Fax: 336-887-0104

WMQX-FM 93.1 MHz (Oldies)
7819 National Service Rd Suite 401
Greensboro, NC 27409
Phone: 336-605-5200
Fax: 336-605-5221

WSJS-AM 600 kHz (N/T)
PO Box 3018
Winston-Salem, NC 27102
www.wsjs.com
Phone: 336-727-8826
Fax: 336-777-3910

WTOB-AM 1380 kHz (N/T)
4405 Providence Ln
Winston-Salem, NC 27106
E-mail: wtob@wtob.com
www.wtob.com
Phone: 336-759-0363
Fax: 336-759-0366

WTQR-FM 104.1 MHz (Ctry)
PO Box 3018
Winston-Salem, NC 27102
www.wtqr.com
Phone: 336-727-8826
Fax: 336-777-3929

WXRA-FM 94.5 MHz (Rock)
PO Box 3018
Winston-Salem, NC 27102
www.wxra945.com
Phone: 336-727-8826
Fax: 336-777-3929

Attractions

Historical sites in Winston-Salem include the restored German Moravian town of Old Salem from which present-day Winston-Salem evolved, which stands today as a living museum where costumed interpreters re-enact period life and exhibits are displayed in ten buildings. The city is also home to the modern SciWorks: The Science Center and Environmental Park of Forsyth County, which features dozens of interactive science exhibits, a planetarium, an outdoor amphitheater, nature trails, and more. The former country estate of tobacco magnate R.J. Reynolds and his wife, Katharine, is now the

Reynolda House Museum of American Art, which features paintings and sculptures by noted American artists, and hosts a variety of creative events, including book discussions and dramatic readings. Tanglewood Park in nearby Clemmons has two top-rated golf courses, plus horseback riding, tennis, camping, and swimming.

Delta Fine Arts Center
1511 E 3rd St
Winston-Salem, NC 27101
Phone: 336-722-2625
Fax: 336-722-9449

Diggs Gallery
Winston-Salem State University
Winston-Salem, NC 27101
Phone: 336-750-2458

Historic Bethabara Park
2147 Bethabara Rd
Winston-Salem, NC 27106
Phone: 336-924-8191
Fax: 336-924-0535

Lawrence Joel Veterans Memorial Coliseum
2825 University Pkwy
Winston-Salem, NC 27105
www.ljvm.com
Phone: 336-725-5635
Fax: 336-727-2922

Museum of Anthropology
PO Box 7267 Reynolds Stn
Winston-Salem, NC 27109
E-mail: moa@wfu.edu
www.wfu.edu/MOA
Phone: 336-758-5282
Fax: 336-758-5116

Museum of Early Southern Decorative Arts
924 S Main St
Winston-Salem, NC 27108
store.yahoo.com/oldsalemonline
Phone: 336-721-7360
Fax: 336-721-7367
TF: 800-441-5305

North Carolina Black Repertory Co
610 Coliseum Dr
Winston-Salem, NC 27106
Phone: 336-723-2266
Fax: 336-723-2223

Old Salem
600 S Main St
Winston-Salem, NC 27101
www.oldsalem.org
Phone: 336-721-7300
Fax: 336-721-7335
TF: 800-441-5305

Piedmont Chamber Singers
845 W 5th St
Winston-Salem, NC 27101
Phone: 336-722-4022

Piedmont Craftsmen
1204 Reynolda Rd
Winston-Salem, NC 27104
E-mail: pci@bellsouth.net
www.piedmontcraftsmen.org
Phone: 336-725-1516
Fax: 336-722-6038

Piedmont Opera Theatre
405 W 4th St Stephens Ctr
Winston-Salem, NC 27101
E-mail: piedop@nr.infi.net
www.piedmontopera.org
Phone: 336-725-7101
Fax: 336-725-7131

Reynolda House Museum of American Art
2250 Reynolda Rd
Winston-Salem, NC 27106
www.ols.net/users/rh
Phone: 336-725-5325
Fax: 336-721-0991

RJ Reynolds Tobacco Co
PO Box 2959
Winston-Salem, NC 27102
www.rjrt.com
Phone: 336-741-5000
Fax: 336-741-4238

Sawtooth Center for Visual Arts
226 N Marshall St
Winston-Salem, NC 27101
www.sawtooth.org
Phone: 336-723-7395
Fax: 336-773-0132

Sciworks Science Center & Environmental Park of Forsyth County
400 Hanes-Mill Rd
Winston-Salem, NC 27105
E-mail: info@sciworks.org
www.sciworks.org
Phone: 336-767-6730
Fax: 336-661-1777

Southeastern Center for Contemporary Art
750 Marguerite Dr
Winston-Salem, NC 27106
Phone: 336-725-1904
Fax: 336-722-6059

Stevens Center
405 W 4th St
Winston-Salem, NC 27101
Phone: 336-723-6320
Fax: 336-722-7240

Tanglewood Park
4061 Clemmons Rd
Clemmons, NC 27012
www.tanglewoodpark.org
Phone: 336-778-6300
Fax: 336-778-6304

Tanglewood Park Golf Course
4601 Clemmons Rd
Clemmons, NC 27012
Phone: 336-778-6320
Fax: 336-766-8991

Vintage Theatre
7 Vintage Ave
Winston-Salem, NC 27127
Phone: 336-750-0000

Wake Forest University Fine Arts Gallery
Scales Fine Arts Center Bldg Wake Forest University
Winston-Salem, NC 27106
Phone: 336-758-5000

Westbend Vineyards
5394 Williams Rd
Lewisville, NC 27023
Phone: 336-945-5032
Fax: 336-945-5294
TF: 877-901-5032

Winston-Salem Piedmont Triad Symphony
610 Coliseum Dr
Winston-Salem, NC 27106
www.wssymphony.org
Phone: 336-725-1035
Fax: 336-725-3924

Sports Teams & Facilities

Carolina Dynamo (soccer)
2920 School Pk Rd High Point Athletic Complex
High Point, NC 27265
E-mail: colleenk@northstate.net
www.carolinadynamo.com
Phone: 336-869-1022
Fax: 336-869-1190

Lawrence Joel Veterans Memorial Coliseum
2825 University Pkwy
Winston-Salem, NC 27105
www.ljvm.com
Phone: 336-725-5635
Fax: 336-727-2922

Piedmont Spark (soccer)
2920 School Park Rd High Point
Athletic Complex
High Point, NC 27265
Phone: 336-869-1022
Fax: 336-869-1190

Winston-Salem Warthogs (baseball)
401 Deacon Blvd Ernie Shore Field
Winston-Salem, NC 27105
E-mail: warthogs@warthogs.com
www.warthogs.com
Phone: 336-759-2233
Fax: 336-759-2042

Annual Events

Candle Tea Christmas Festival (early December) 336-722-6171
Carolina Craftsmen Labor Day Classic
(mid-September) 336-274-5550
Christmas Parade (late November) 336-777-3796
Crosby Celebrity Golf Tournament
(late May-early June). 336-721-2246
Dixie Classic Fair (early October) 336-727-2236
Fiddle & Bow Festival (September). 336-727-1038
First Night Piedmont (December 31) 336-722-0066
Greek Festival (mid-May). 336-765-7145
Music at Sunset (late June). 336-725-1035
National Black Theater Festival (early August) 336-723-2266
Old Salem Christmas (mid-December) 800-441-5305
Piedmont Crafts Fair (mid-November) 336-725-1516
Salem Christmas (late December) 336-721-7300
Tanglewood Festival of Lights
(mid-November-mid-January) 336-778-6300
Vantage Championship Seniors Golf Tournament
(early September) 336-721-2246
Winston-Salem Crafts Guild Craft Show
(mid-November). 252-727-2976

Worcester, Massachusetts

***County:* Worcester**

WORCESTER is located in central Massachusetts. Major cities within 100 miles include Boston and Springfield, Massachusetts; Manchester and Portsmouth, New Hampshire; and Hartford, Connecticut.

Area (Land) .... 37.6 sq mi
Area (Water) .... 1.0 sq mi
Elevation .... 480 ft
Latitude .... 42-25-74 N
Longitude .... 71-79-79 W
Time Zone .... EST
Area Code 508

Climate

Worcester has a continental climate with four distinct seasons. Winters are cold, with an average January temperature of 22.8 degrees and an average annual snowfall of 67.6 inches—more than three times the national average. Summers are mild and pleasant, with daytime high temperatures in the upper 70s and nighttime lows around 60 degrees. Precipitation is fairly evenly distributed throughout the year in Worcester.

Average Temperatures & Precipitation

Temperatures

	Jan	Feb	Mar	Apr	May	Jun	Jul	Aug	Sep	Oct	Nov	Dec
High	31	33	42	54	66	75	79	77	70	60	47	35
Low	15	17	25	35	45	54	60	59	51	41	31	20

Precipitation

	Jan	Feb	Mar	Apr	May	Jun	Jul	Aug	Sep	Oct	Nov	Dec
Inches	3.7	3.5	4.0	3.9	4.3	3.9	3.9	3.8	4.0	4.3	4.5	4.1

History

The Heart of the Commonwealth, the area surrounding Worcester along Lake Quinsigamond was first settled in 1713. Located 40 miles from Boston, en route to the west, Worcester grew quickly, became a town in 1722, and was later incorporated as a city in 1848. A major transportation center, the city was connected to Boston, New York, and other points West via the Boston Turnpike; and the Blackstone Canal provided access to Providence, Rhode Island and, ultimately, the world via the Atlantic Ocean. Worcester's location made it an ideal place for industry. In the early days, steel fabrication, abrasives, machine tooling, printing, and envelope manufacturing were major industries. (The first Valentine card was printed in Worcester.) Science has been the main focus of Worcester's industry in the 20th century—the nation's first experiments in rockets were conducted in the city and biotechnology is a major enterprise in Worcester's present economy.

Today, the county seat of Worcester County is home to more than 166,000 people, making it the second largest city in Massachusetts. Recently completed redevelopment projects in Worcester include a new state-of-the-art convention center and a multi-million dollar "medical city," creating additional business and employment opportunities for area residents.

Population

1990 Census 169,759
1998 Estimate 166,535
% Change .... -1.9
2010 Projection 176,753

Racial/Ethnic Breakdown

White 87.1%
Black 4.5%
Other 8.4%
Hispanic Origin (may be of any race) 9.6%

Age Breakdown

Under 5 years 7.3%
5 to 17 .... 14.9%
18 to 20 .... 7.1%
21 to 24 .... 7.8%
25 to 34 .... 18.5%
35 to 44 .... 12.3%
45 to 54 .... 8.0%
55 to 64 .... 8.0%
65 to 74 .... 8.6%
75+ years 7.5%
Median Age 31.8

Gender Breakdown

Male 47.6%
Female 52.4%

Government

Type of Government: Council-Manager

Worcester City Clerk
455 Main St Rm 206
Worcester, MA 01608
Phone: 508-799-1121
Fax: 508-799-1194

Worcester City Council
455 Main St Rm 112
Worcester, MA 01608
Phone: 508-799-1049
Fax: 508-799-1015

Worcester City Hall
455 Main St
Worcester, MA 01608
Phone: 508-799-1000
Fax: 508-799-1208

Worcester City Manager
455 Main St Rm 309
Worcester, MA 01608
Phone: 508-799-1175
Fax: 508-799-1208

Worcester Fire Dept
141 Grove St
Worcester, MA 01605
Phone: 508-799-1816
Fax: 508-799-1819

Worcester Human Resources Dept
455 Main St Rm 109
Worcester, MA 01608
Phone: 508-799-1030
Fax: 508-799-1040

Worcester Law Dept
455 Main St Rm 301
Worcester, MA 01608
Phone: 508-799-1161
Fax: 508-799-1163

Worcester Mayor
455 Main St
Worcester, MA 01608
Phone: 508-799-1153
Fax: 508-799-1156

Worcester Parks Recreation & Cemetery Dept
125 Green Hill Pkwy
Worcester, MA 01605
Phone: 508-799-1190
Fax: 508-799-1293

Worcester Planning & Community Development Office
418 Main St
Worcester, MA 01608
Phone: 508-799-1400
Fax: 508-799-1406

Worcester Police Dept
9-11 Lincoln Sq
Worcester, MA 01608
Phone: 508-799-8611
Fax: 508-799-8680

Worcester Public Library
160 Fremont St
Worcester, MA 01603
Phone: 508-799-1655
Fax: 508-799-1652

Worcester Public Works Dept
20 E Worcester St
Worcester, MA 01604
Phone: 508-799-1430
Fax: 508-799-1448

Worcester Treasury Dept
455 Main St Rm 203
Worcester, MA 01608
Phone: 508-799-1075
Fax: 508-799-1097

Important Phone Numbers

AAA 508-853-7000
American Express Travel 508-755-4375
Dental Referral 508-753-5276
Driver's License/Vehicle Registration Information 617-351-4500
Emergency 911
Greater Worcester Board of Realtors 508-752-7290
Massachusetts Dept of Revenue 617-887-6367
Medical Referral 781-893-4610
Poison Control Center 800-682-9211
Voter Registration Information 617-635-4635
Weather 508-792-9600
Worcester Treasurer 508-799-1083

Information Sources

Better Business Bureau Serving Central New England & Northeast Connecticut
PO Box 16555
Worcester, MA 01601
www.worcester.bbb.org
Phone: 508-755-2548
Fax: 508-754-4158

Worcester Area Chamber of Commerce
33 Waldo St
Worcester, MA 01608
chamber.worcester.ma.us
Phone: 508-753-2924
Fax: 508-754-8560

Worcester County
2 Main St County Courthouse
Worcester, MA 01608
Phone: 508-798-7700
Fax: 508-798-7741

Worcester County Convention & Visitors Bureau
33 Waldo St
Worcester, MA 01608
www.worcester.org
Phone: 508-753-2920
Fax: 508-754-2703
TF: 800-231-7557

Worcester's Centrum Centre
50 Foster St
Worcester, MA 01608
www.centrumcentre.com
Phone: 508-755-6800
Fax: 508-929-0111

Online Resources

4Worcester.com
www.4worcester.com

About.com Guide to Worcester
worcester.about.com/citiestowns/newenglandus/worcester

Area Guide Worcester
worcester.areaguides.net

City Knowledge Worcester
www.cityknowledge.com/ma_worcester.htm

Excite.com Worcester City Guide
www.excite.com/travel/countries/united_states/massachusetts/worcester

Welcome to Worcester
www.worcester.ma.us

Worcester Web
speed.city-net.com/~lmann/ww/

Area Communities

Worcester County communities with populations greater than 10,000 include:

Athol
584 Main St
Athol, MA 01331
Phone: 978-249-4551
Fax: 978-249-4551

Auburn
102 Central St
Auburn, MA 01501
Phone: 508-832-7720
Fax: 508-832-6145

Charlton
37 Main St
Charlton, MA 01507
Phone: 508-248-5900
Fax: 508-248-2066

Clinton
242 Church St
Clinton, MA 01510
Phone: 978-365-4119
Fax: 978-365-4130

Fitchburg
718 Main St
Fitchburg, MA 01420
Phone: 978-345-9592
Fax: 978-345-9595

Gardner
95 Pleasant St
Gardner, MA 01440
Phone: 978-632-1900
Fax: 978-630-3778

Grafton
30 Providence Rd
Grafton, MA 01519
Phone: 508-839-5335
Fax: 508-839-4602

Harvard
13 Ayer Rd
Harvard, MA 01451
Phone: 978-456-4100
Fax: 978-456-4107

Holden
1196 Main St
Holden, MA 01520
Phone: 508-829-0265
Fax: 508-829-0252

Leicester
3 Washburn Sq
Leicester, MA 01524
Phone: 508-892-7000
Fax: 508-892-7070

Milford
52 Main St
Milford, MA 01757
Phone: 508-634-2303
Fax: 508-634-2324

Millbury
127 Elm St
Millbury, MA 01527
Phone: 508-865-9110
Fax: 508-865-8043

Northborough
63 Main St
Northborough, MA 01532
Phone: 508-393-5001
Fax: 508-393-6996

Northbridge
7 Main St
Whitinsville, MA 01588
Phone: 508-234-2001
Fax: 508-234-7640

Oxford
325 Main St
Oxford, MA 01540
Phone: 508-987-6032
Fax: 508-987-6048

Shrewsbury
100 Maple Ave
Shrewsbury, MA 01545
Phone: 508-841-8507
Fax: 508-842-0587

Southbridge
41 Elm St
Southbridge, MA 01550
Phone: 508-764-5405
Fax: 508-764-5425

Spencer
157 Main St
Spencer, MA 01562
Phone: 508-885-7500
Fax: 508-885-7528

Uxbridge
21 S Main St
Uxbridge, MA 01569
Phone: 508-278-8608
Fax: 508-278-8605

Webster
PO Box 249
Webster, MA 01570
Phone: 508-949-3800
Fax: 508-949-3888

Westborough
34 W Main St
Westborough, MA 01581
Phone: 508-366-3030
Fax: 508-366-3099

Economy

Several Fortune 500 companies are headquartered or have divisions in the Worcester area, including Allmerica Financial and Coca-Cola. The largest employment sectors in Worcester are services (primarily health care), trade, and government. Biotechnology is also a major industry in Worcester. The city is the site of the Massachusetts Biotechnology Research Park, which is home to a number of top companies in the field, including Alpha Beta Technology, BASF Bioresearch Corp., and Hybridon, Inc.

Unemployment Rate 3.7%
Per Capita Income.......................... $28,587*
Median Family Income...................... $36,261

** Information given is for Worcester County.*

Principal Industries & Number of Wage Earners

City of Worcester - 1998

Agricultural Services, Forestry, & Fishing 150
Construction.. 2,456
Finance, Insurance, & Real Estate 9,122
Government 17,505
Manufacturing 13,319
Services 37,069
Trade 17,926
Transportation, Communications, & Public Utilities 2,769

Major Employers

Allmerica Financial Corp
440 Lincoln St
Worcester, MA 01653
www.allmerica.com
Phone: 508-855-1000
Fax: 508-853-6332
TF: 800-533-7881

Data General Corp
4400 Computer Dr
Westborough, MA 01580
E-mail: feedback@dg.com
www.dg.com
Phone: 508-898-5000
Fax: 508-898-4686
TF: 800-344-3577

Fallon Community Health Plan Inc
10 Chestnut St
Worcester, MA 01608
www.fchp.org
Phone: 508-799-2100
Fax: 508-798-1272

Fleet Bank of Massachusetts
446 Main St
Worcester, MA 01608
Phone: 508-756-0922
Fax: 508-831-2507

Massachusetts Electric Co
25 Research Dr
Westborough, MA 01582
E-mail: masselectric@neesnet.com
www.masselectric.com
Phone: 508-389-2000
TF: 888-211-1111

National Grid USA
25 Research Dr
Westborough, MA 01582
www.nationalgrid.com/usa
Phone: 508-389-2000
Fax: 508-389-2028

Norton Co
1 New Bond St
Worcester, MA 01606
www.norton.sgna.com
Phone: 508-795-5000
Fax: 508-795-5741
TF: 800-543-4335

Price Chopper
29 Sunderland Rd
Worcester, MA 01604
www.pricechopper.com/careers
Phone: 508-752-7062
Fax: 508-792-3209

Saint Vincent Hospital
25 Winthrop St
Worcester, MA 01608
www.stvincenthospital.com
Phone: 508-798-1234
Fax: 508-798-1119

UMass Medical School
55 Lake Ave N
Worcester, MA 01655
www.ummed.edu
Phone: 508-856-0011
Fax: 508-856-1743

UMass Memorial Health Care
365 Plantation St 1 Biotech
Worcester, MA 01605
Phone: 508-793-6611
Fax: 508-334-8680

United Parcel Service
1045 University Dr
Norwood, MA 02062
www.upsjobs.com
Phone: 781-551-2581
Fax: 781-551-2550

Verizon Communications
15 Chester St
Worcester, MA 01609
www.verizon.com
Phone: 508-798-5830

Worcester City Hall
455 Main St
Worcester, MA 01608
www.ci.worcester.ma.us
Phone: 508-799-1000
Fax: 508-799-1208

Worcester Public Schools
20 Irving St
Worcester, MA 01609
www.wpsweb.com
Phone: 508-799-3115
Fax: 508-799-3666

Quality of Living Indicators

Total Crime Index 9,685
(rates per 100,000 inhabitants)

Violent Crime
Murder/manslaughter 8
Forcible rape 147
Robbery 339
Aggravated assault 1,229

Property Crime
Burglary 1,550
Larceny theft 5,249
Motor vehicle theft 1,163

Cost of Living Index 95.0
(national average = 100)

Median Home Price $138,700

Education

Public Schools

Worcester Public Schools
20 Irving St
Worcester, MA 01609
www.wpsweb.com
Phone: 508-799-3115
Fax: 508-799-3666

Number of Schools
Elementary 40
Middle 5
High 4

Student/Teacher Ratio
All Grades 16.6:1

Private Schools

Number of Schools (all grades) .... 19+

Colleges & Universities

Anna Maria College
50 Sunset Ln
Paxton, MA 01612
www.anna-maria.edu
Phone: 508-849-3300
Fax: 508-849-3362
TF: 800-344-4586

Assumption College
500 Salisbury St
Worcester, MA 01609
E-mail: amahoney@eve.assumption.edu
www.assumption.edu
Phone: 508-767-7000
Fax: 508-756-1780
TF: 888-882-7786

Becker College
61 Sever St
Worcester, MA 01609
Phone: 508-791-9241
Fax: 508-890-1500

Clark University
950 Main St
Worcester, MA 01610
E-mail: admissions@vax.clarku.edu
www.clarku.edu
Phone: 508-793-7711
Fax: 508-793-8821
TF: 800-462-5275

College of the Holy Cross
1 College St
Worcester, MA 01610
E-mail: admission@holycross.edu
www.holycross.edu
Phone: 508-793-2011
Fax: 508-793-3888
TF: 800-442-2421

Quinsigamond Community College
670 W Boylston St
Worcester, MA 01606
www.qcc.mass.edu
Phone: 508-853-2300
Fax: 508-852-6943

Worcester Polytechnic Institute
100 Institute Rd
Worcester, MA 01609
www.wpi.edu
Phone: 508-831-5000
Fax: 508-831-5875

Worcester State College
486 Chandler St
Worcester, MA 01602
www.worc.mass.edu
Phone: 508-793-8000
Fax: 508-929-8193

Hospitals

Clinton Hospital
201 Highland St
Clinton, MA 01510
Phone: 978-368-3000
Fax: 978-368-1360

Harrington Memorial Hospital
100 South St
Southbridge, MA 01550
www.harringtonhospital.org
Phone: 508-765-9771
Fax: 508-764-2464

Health Alliance Leominster Hospital
60 Hospital Rd
Leominster, MA 01453
www.healthalliance.com/lh_history.htm
Phone: 978-537-4811
Fax: 978-466-2730

Heywood Hospital
242 Green St
Gardner, MA 01440
www.heywood.org
Phone: 978-632-3420
Fax: 978-630-6595

Hubbard Regional Hospital
340 Thompson Rd
Webster, MA 01570
Phone: 508-943-2600
Fax: 508-949-1544

Marlborough Hospital
157 Union St
Marlborough, MA 01752
Phone: 508-485-1121
Fax: 508-485-9123

Memorial Health Care Hahnemann Campus
119 Belmont St
Worcester, MA 01605
Phone: 508-792-8000
Fax: 508-793-6006

MetroWest Medical Center
115 Lincoln St
Framingham, MA 01702
www.mwmc.com
Phone: 508-383-1000
Fax: 508-383-1166

Milford-Whitinsville Regional Hospital
14 Prospect St
Milford, MA 01757
www.mwrh.com
Phone: 508-473-1190
Fax: 508-473-7460

Saint Vincent Hospital
25 Winthrop St
Worcester, MA 01608
www.stvincenthospital.com
Phone: 508-798-1234
Fax: 508-798-1119

UMass Memorial Health Care Memorial Campus
119 Belmont St
Worcester, MA 01605
Phone: 508-793-6611
Fax: 508-334-0333

University of Massachusetts Medical Center
55 Lake Ave N
Worcester, MA 01655
www.ummed.edu
Phone: 508-856-0011
Fax: 508-856-1743

Worcester Memorial Hospital
119 Belmont St
Worcester, MA 01605
Phone: 508-793-6611
Fax: 508-334-5049

Transportation

Airport(s)

Worcester Regional Airport (ORH)
4 miles W of downtown (approx 15 minutes) 508-799-1741

Mass Transit

Worcester Regional Transit Authority
$1 Base fare 508-791-9782

Rail/Bus

Amtrak Station
45 Shrewsbury St
Worcester, MA 01604
Phone: 508-755-0356

Greyhound Bus Station
75 Madison St
Worcester, MA 01608
Phone: 508-754-3247
TF: 800-231-2222

Utilities

Electricity
Massachusetts Electric..........................888-211-1111
www.masselectric.com

Gas
Commonwealth Gas Co 508-481-7900
www.comgas.com

Water
Worcester Water Div...........................508-799-1485

Garbage Collection/Recycling
Worcester Sanitation Div.......................508-799-1495

Telecommunications

Telephone
Verizon Communications.......................508-798-5830
www.verizon.com

Cable Television
Charter Communications.......................508-853-1515

Internet Service Providers (ISPs)
Cyberonic Internet Communications Inc.........888-929-2372
www.1699.com
Orbit Data Systems Inc........................508-753-8776
www.os.com
Solutions Plus Inc 508-756-7600
www.splusnet.com

Banks

Bank of Boston
100 Front St
Worcester, MA 01608
Phone: 508-770-7000
Fax: 508-770-7784

Bay State Savings Bank
28-32 Franklin St
Worcester, MA 01608
Phone: 508-791-8161
Fax: 508-792-5217

Commerce Bank & Trust Co
386 Main St
Worcester, MA 01608
E-mail: branchadmin@bankatcommerce.com
www.bankatcommerce.com
Phone: 508-797-6800
Fax: 508-797-6834
TF: 800-698-2265

Family Bank
370 Main St
Worcester, MA 01608
Phone: 508-791-6271
Fax: 508-797-5062
TF: 800-322-3264

First Massachusetts Bank
295 Park Ave
Worcester, MA 01609
E-mail: firstmass@banknorth.com
firstmass.banknorth.com
Phone: 508-752-2584
Fax: 508-751-8090
TF: 800-390-6443

Flagship Bank & Trust Co
120 Front St
Worcester, MA 01608
Phone: 508-799-4321
Fax: 508-797-4628

Shopping

Auburn Mall
385 Southbridge St
Auburn, MA 01501
Phone: 508-832-3488
Fax: 508-832-6250

Greendale Mall
7 Neponset St
Worcester, MA 01606
Phone: 508-856-9400
Fax: 508-852-5294

Olde Shrewsbury Village
1000 Boston Tpke
Shrewsbury, MA 01545
Phone: 508-842-7467
Fax: 508-842-6100

Worcester Common Fashion Outlet
110 Front St
Worcester, MA 01608
Phone: 508-755-4381

Media

Newspapers and Magazines

Telegram & Gazette*
PO Box 15012
Worcester, MA 01615
E-mail: info@telegram.com
www.telegram.com
Phone: 508-793-9100
Fax: 508-793-9281
TF: 800-678-6680

Worcester Magazine
172 Shrewsbury St
Worcester, MA 01604
E-mail: editorial@worcestermag.com
www.worcestermag.com
Phone: 508-755-8004
Fax: 508-755-8860

Worcester Phoenix
108 Grove St Suite 18
Worcester, MA 01605
E-mail: worcester-feedback@phx.com
www.worcesterphoenix.com
Phone: 508-767-9777
Fax: 508-795-0439

**Indicates major daily newspapers*

Television

WBZ-TV Ch 4 (CBS)
1170 Soldiers Field Rd
Boston, MA 02134
www.wbz.com
Phone: 617-787-7000
Fax: 617-254-6383

WCVB-TV Ch 5 (ABC)
5 TV Pl
Needham, MA 02492
E-mail: wcvb@aol.com
www.wcvb.com
Phone: 781-449-0400
Fax: 781-449-6681

WFXT-TV Ch 25 (Fox)
25 Fox Dr
Dedham, MA 02026
Phone: 781-326-8825
Fax: 781-467-7213

WGBH-TV Ch 2 (PBS)
125 Western Ave
Boston, MA 02134
www.wgbh.org
Phone: 617-492-2777
Fax: 617-787-0714

WHDH-TV Ch 7 (NBC)
7 Bulfinch Pl
Boston, MA 02114
E-mail: stationmanagement@whdh.com
www.whdh.com
Phone: 617-725-0777
Fax: 617-723-6117

WJAR-TV Ch 10 (NBC)
23 Kenney Dr
Cranston, RI 02920
E-mail: mail.box10@nbc.com
www.nbc10wjar.com
Phone: 401-455-9100
Fax: 401-455-9140

WWLP-TV Ch 22 (NBC)
PO Box 2210
Springfield, MA 01102
E-mail: news@wwlp.com
www.wwlp.com
Phone: 413-786-2200
Fax: 413-786-7144

Radio

WAAF-FM 107.3 MHz (Rock)
200 Friberg Pkwy Suite 4000
Westborough, MA 01581
www.waaf.com
Phone: 508-836-9223
Fax: 508-366-0745

WCHC-FM 88.1 MHz (Alt)
1 College St College of the Holy Cross
Worcester, MA 01610
E-mail: wchcfm_bag@hotmail.com
carver.holycross.edu/studentorgs/wchc
Phone: 508-793-2474
Fax: 508-793-3643

WCUW-FM 91.3 MHz (Misc)
910 Main St
Worcester, MA 01610
E-mail: wcuw@splusnet.com
www.wcuw.com
Phone: 508-753-1012

WICN-FM 90.5 MHz (NPR)
6 Chatham St
Worcester, MA 01609
www.wicn.org
Phone: 508-752-0700
Fax: 508-752-7518

WKOX-AM 1200 kHz (Span)
100 Mount Wayte Ave
Framingham, MA 01702
Phone: 508-820-2400
Fax: 508-820-2458

WORC-AM 1310 kHz (N/T)
27 Douglas Rd
Webster, MA 01570
E-mail: worcradio@aol.com
www.worcradio.com
Phone: 508-799-0581
Fax: 508-943-0405

WSRS-FM 96.1 MHz (AC)
96 Stereo Ln
Paxton, MA 01612
E-mail: wsrsfm@aol.com
www.wsrs.com
Phone: 508-795-0580
Fax: 508-757-1779

WTAG-AM 580 kHz (N/T)
96 Stereo Ln
Paxton, MA 01612
www.wtag.com
Phone: 508-795-0580
Fax: 508-757-1779

WVNE-AM 760 kHz (Rel)
70 James St Suite 201
Worcester, MA 01603
E-mail: wvne@aol.com
www.lifechangingradio.com
Phone: 508-831-9863
Fax: 508-831-7964

WXLO-FM 104.5 MHz (AC)
250 Commercial St
Worcester, MA 01608
E-mail: wxlo@wxlo.com
www.wxlo.com
Phone: 508-752-1045
Fax: 508-793-0824

Attractions

Worcester is home to the American Antiquarian Society, a national research library that preserves the single largest collection of printed materials related to literature, history, and culture of the first 250 years of the United States; and the Higgins Armory Museum, which contains a sizable collection of medieval and Renaissance armor and weaponry in a Gothic castle setting. Worcester is also the site of the New England Science Center and the world-class art collection of the Worcester Art Museum. Outdoor attractions in Worcester include the Broad Meadow Brook WIldlife Sanctuary, the largest urban sanctuary in New England; and the New England Rowing Championships, a series of collegiate crew events held each May at Lake Quinsigamond.

American Antiquarian Society Phone: 508-755-5221
185 Salisbury St Fax: 508-753-3311
Worcester, MA 01609
E-mail: library@mwa.org
www.americanantiquarian.org

American Textile History Museum Phone: 978-441-0400
491 Dutton St Fax: 978-441-1412
Lowell, MA 01854
www.athm.org

ARTworks Gallery Phone: 508-755-7808
261 Park Ave Fax: 508-756-7684
Worcester, MA 01609

Broad Meadow Brook Wildlife Sanctuary Phone: 508-753-6087
414 Massasoit Rd Fax: 508-755-0148
Worcester, MA 01604

Cantor Iris & B Gerald Art Gallery Phone: 508-793-3356
1 College St Fax: 508-793-3030
Worcester, MA 01610
www.holycross.edu/departments/cantor/website/

Capen Hill Nature Sanctuary Phone: 508-248-5516
56 Capen Rd Fax: 508-248-5516
Charlton City, MA 01508
E-mail: capenhill@gis.net

Central Massachusetts Symphony Orchestra Phone: 508-754-1234
10 Tuckerman St Tuckerman Hall Fax: 508-754-5329
Worcester, MA 01609

EcoTarium Phone: 508-929-2700
222 Harrington Way Fax: 508-929-2701
Worcester, MA 01604
E-mail: info@ecotarium.org
www.ecotarium.org

Foothills Theater Phone: 508-754-3314
100 Front St Suite 137 Fax: 508-767-0676
Worcester, MA 01608

Hebert Candy Mansion Phone: 508-845-8051
575 Hartford Pike Fax: 508-842-3065
Shrewsbury, MA 01545

Hellenic Sports Hall of Fame Phone: 508-485-0736
180 Bolton St Fax: 508-481-7532
Marlborough, MA 01752

Higgins Armory Museum Phone: 508-853-6015
100 Barber Ave Fax: 508-852-7697
Worcester, MA 01606
E-mail: higgins@higgins.org
www.higgins.org

Mechanics Hall Phone: 508-752-5608
321 Main St Fax: 508-754-8442
Worcester, MA 01608
www.mechanicshall.org

Old Sturbridge Village Phone: 508-347-3362
1 Old Sturbridge Village Rd Fax: 508-347-0375
Sturbridge, MA 01566
www.osv.org

Olde Shrewsbury Village Phone: 508-842-7467
1000 Boston Tpke Fax: 508-842-6100
Shrewsbury, MA 01545

Opera Worcester Inc Phone: 508-752-8201
486 Chandler St Sullivan Auditorium Fax: 508-752-0766
Worcester, MA 01602

Quinsigamond State Park Phone: 508-755-6880
10 N Lake Ave
Worcester, MA 01605

Salisbury Lyric Opera Phone: 508-799-3848
11 Chamberlain Pkwy Fax: 508-799-3848
Worcester, MA 01602

Salisbury Mansion Phone: 508-753-8278
40 Highland St Fax: 508-753-9070
Worcester, MA 01609

Spooky World Phone: 978-838-0200
100 River Rd
Berlin, MA 01503

Tower Hill Botanical Gardens Phone: 508-869-6111
PO Box 598 Fax: 508-869-0314
Boylston, MA 01505
www.towerhillbg.org

Tuckerman Hall Phone: 508-754-1234
10 Tuckerman St Fax: 508-754-5329
Worcester, MA 01609

Willard House & Clock Museum Phone: 508-839-3500
11 Willard St Fax: 508-839-3599
North Grafton, MA 01536
www.nawcc.org/museum/willard/willard.htm

Worcester Art Museum Phone: 508-799-4406
55 Salisbury St Fax: 508-798-5646
Worcester, MA 01609
www.worcesterart.org

Worcester Center for Crafts Phone: 508-753-8183
25 Sagamore Rd Fax: 508-797-5626
Worcester, MA 01605
www.craftcenter.worcester.org

Worcester Forum Theatre Ensemble Phone: 508-799-9166
6 Chatham St Fax: 508-799-9558
Worcester, MA 01609

Worcester Historical Museum
30 Elm St
Worcester, MA 01609
E-mail: theworchistmu@aol.com
Phone: 508-753-8278
Fax: 508-753-9070

Sports Teams & Facilities

Boston Renegades (soccer)
175 Union Ave Bowditch Field
Framingham, MA 01702
Phone: 508-872-8998
Fax: 508-870-0884

Worcester IceCats (hockey)
50 Foster St The Centrum
Worcester, MA 01608
www.worcestericecats.com
Phone: 508-798-5400
Fax: 508-799-5267

Annual Events

A Celebration of Craftmanship (mid-August)........508-347-3362
AppleFest (October) 978-464-2300
Beginning of a New England Christmas The (early-mid-December)..........................508-347-3362
Brimfield Outdoor Antique Shows (early September) 800-628-8379
First Night Worcester (December 31).............508-799-1400
Harvest Festival (September) 978-779-5521
Longsjo Bike Race (early July)....................978-464-2300
LPGA Golf Tournament (early August).............508-865-4441
New England Rowing Championships (early May) 508-753-2920
New England Summer Nationals (early July) 508-987-3375
Spencer Fair (September) 508-753-2920
Taste of Massachusetts (August) 978-779-5521
Worcester Music Festival (September-May).........508-754-3231

Index of Cities & Counties